EIGHTEENTH-CENTURY
ENGLISH LITERATURE

EDITED BY

GEOFFREY TILLOTSON

Late of Birkbeck College, University of London

PAUL FUSSELL, Jr.

Rutgers University

MARSHALL WAINGROW

Claremont Graduate School

with the assistance of

BREWSTER ROGERSON

Kansas State University

EIGHTEENTH-CENTURY ENGLISH LITERATURE

Harcourt, Brace & World, Inc.

New York / Chicago / San Francisco / Atlanta

COPYRIGHTS AND ACKNOWLEDGMENTS

WILLIAM BLAKE. Letters from *The Letters of William Blake*, ed. Geoffrey Keynes (1956), by permission of Rupert Hart-Davis Ltd. Selections from *The Writings of William Blake*, ed. Geoffrey Keynes (3 vols., 1925), by permission of The Nonesuch Press Ltd.

JAMES BOSWELL. Selection from *Boswell on the Grand Tour: Germany and Switzerland, 1764*, ed. Frederick A. Pottle. Copyright 1928, 1953 by Yale University. Published by William Heinemann Ltd., London. Used with permission of McGraw-Hill Book Company.

ROBERT BURNS. Selection from *The Burns Chronicle* (1927): The Burns Federation, Kilmarnock.

JOHN DRYDEN. Selection from *Poems by John Dryden*, ed. James Kinsley (4 vols., 1958), by permission of The Clarendon Press, Oxford.

HENRY FIELDING. Selections from *The Covent-Garden Journal*, ed. G. E. Jensen (2 vols., 1915), by permission of Yale University Press.

THOMAS GRAY. Letters from *The Correspondence of Thomas Gray*, ed. Paget Toynbee and Leonard Whibley (3 vols., 1935), by permission of The Clarendon Press, Oxford.

SAMUEL JOHNSON. Letters from *The Letters of Samuel Johnson*, ed. R. W. Chapman (3 vols., 1952), by permission of The Clarendon Press, Oxford. Selection from *Diaries, Prayers, and Annals*, ed. E. L. McAdam, Jr. (1958), by permission of Yale University Press. Selection (in the headnote to William Collins) from *The Lives of the Poets*, ed. G. B. Hill (3 vols., 1905), by permission of The Clarendon Press, Oxford. Selections from *The Poems of Samuel Johnson*, ed. D. N. Smith and E. L. McAdam, Jr. (1941), by permission of The Clarendon Press, Oxford.

SAMUEL PEPYS. Selection from *The Diary of Samuel Pepys*, ed. H. B. Wheatley (10 vols., 1893–99), by permission of G. Bell & Sons Ltd.

ALEXANDER POPE. Pope's notes to all selections except *The New Dunciad* from the Twickenham edition of his works, ed. John Butt (1939–67), by permission of Yale University Press.

SAMUEL RICHARDSON. Letter (in the headnote to Richardson) from A. D. McKillop, *Early Masters of English Fiction* (1956): University Press of Kansas.

CHRISTOPHER SMART. Selection reprinted by permission of the publishers from *Jubilate Agno*, ed. W. H. Bond, Cambridge, Mass.: Harvard University Press, 1954, and by permission of Rupert Hart-Davis Ltd.

SIR RICHARD STEELE AND JOSEPH ADDISON. Selections from *The Spectator*, ed. D. F. Bond (5 vols., 1965), by permission of The Clarendon Press, Oxford.

JONATHAN SWIFT. Letter from *The Correspondence of Alexander Pope*, ed. George Sherburn (5 vols., 1956), by permission of The Clarendon Press, Oxford. Selections from *The Poems of Jonathan Swift*, ed. Harold Williams (3 vols., 1937, 1958), by permission of The Clarendon Press, Oxford. Selections from *The Prose Works of Jonathan Swift*, ed. Herbert Davis (13 vols., 1939–59), by permission of Basil Blackwell & Mott Ltd.

HORACE WALPOLE. Letters from *Horace Walpole's Correspondence*, ed. W. S. Lewis, Vols. I, II, X, XI, XVI, XVIII, XXIX, XX, XXXIII, copyright 1937, 1937, 1941, 1944, 1951, 1954, 1955, © 1960, © 1965, respectively, by Yale University Press. Letters from *The Letters of Horace Walpole*, ed. Mrs. Paget Toynbee (16 vols., 1904), and letter from *Supplement to the Letters of Horace Walpole*, ed. Paget Toynbee (1918–25), by permission of The Clarendon Press, Oxford.

A NOTE ON THE SPINE. The coat of arms reproduced on the spine of this book is that of the Worshipful Company of Stationers and Papermakers of London. This ancient City Company was originally a guild of stationers and craftsmen who made and dealt in parchment, paper, quill pens, and materials for binding books. In 1557, eighty-one years after printing was first introduced into England, the Stationers were granted a charter that gave them the monopoly of the "Art or Mystery of Printing." At the same time they received their coat of arms from the College of Heralds. For many years it was the custom to enter titles of books to be printed by members of the Company in the Stationers' Register, which is thus a record of the first printing of many famous works known to students of English literature.

A NOTE ON THE FACSIMILES. The fifteen facsimiles from *The Gentleman's Magazine* on pages 835–49 are reproduced by courtesy of the Princeton University Library.

ISBN: 0-15-520957-4

Library of Congress Catalog Card Number: 69-11483

PRINTED IN THE UNITED STATES OF AMERICA

Preface

Our aim in this anthology is to provide a larger and more prepossessing collection of eighteenth-century writings than has hitherto been available, and to provide them in trustworthy texts without modernization. Our selection has been made with an eye to literary merit, and in trying to determine what constitutes literary merit in the eighteenth century we have allowed the comic and the satiric ample room, while straitening the space customarily allotted to the sentimental. We have also tried to recognize the importance of works of theology, philosophy, criticism, polemic, practical advice, and travel. The reader will thus find here, in addition to the standard authors, selections from writers who have not been represented in anthologies of this kind: Thomas Sprat, John Locke, John Tillotson, Francis Atterbury, John Dennis, Joseph Butler, William Law, Samuel Richardson, and Tobias Smollett. We have begun the book with sufficient writing of the Restoration to imply the genealogy of eighteenth-century achievements, and we have concluded it with that part of Blake's work which strikes us as emanating from eighteenth-century thematic and stylistic concerns. Representing the drama posed a challenge to our criterion of literary merit. The four plays we have included illustrate the generic types of Restoration and eighteenth-century drama and the artistic predicament in which drama found itself: Dryden's *Marriage A-la-Mode* offers the advantage of exhibiting elements of the Restoration heroic play together with elements of Restoration comedy; Gay's *Beggar's Opera*, Fielding's *Tragedy of Tragedies*, and Sheridan's *The Critic*, in addition to presenting their own delights, serve to delineate by satiric implication the kind of tiresome contemporary plays that they so conspicuously are not. For reasons of space we have had to exclude prose fiction.

Most works have been given complete; the few that are not complete are represented by self-contained parts. Believing that it is not satisfactory to present anything but the whole of *Gulliver's Travels* and very substantial parts of Boswell's *Life of Johnson*, we have not offered a mere selection from either.

For those who may be curious about the look of eighteenth-century letterpress, we have included fifteen facsimile pages from *The Gentleman's Magazine*. And in the two miscellanies of poems, one for the first half of the century, one for the second, we have brought together a varied group of poems and presented them cheek by jowl in the way Jacob Tonson and Robert Dodsley presented them to contemporary readers in their popular collections.

In our introductions, headnotes, and footnotes we have tried not only to embody the most recent scholarship but also to respond to the most penetrating modern criticism—criticism that has found eighteenth-century English literature to be quite other than the place of rest and refreshment it was once thought to be. All we have done that is new we have done in a sincere effort to communicate our excitement about the best of eighteenth-century writing.

On the principle that successive printings of a text tend to adulterate it, we have generally chosen the first edition of each work (and, where discrepancies are known, the first state of the first edition) as our copy-text. Thus the authority for accidentals of spelling, capitalization, and punctuation rests on the edition that is presumably closest to the copy originally prepared by the author for the press. When a text has been revised in the author's lifetime, we have introduced into our copy-text the latest substantive revisions clearly ascertainable as the author's own. Where we have been fortunate enough to have a well-edited modern text, we have generally adopted its readings, even though it may not recognize first editions as the authority for accidentals.

Although our aim in general has been a precise transcription of the originals, four systematic departures from this practice seemed necessary: (1) palpable errors of the press have been silently corrected; but we have assumed that the eighteenth-century compositor tended to follow copy, and we have therefore usually imputed variations in spelling, as well as other anomalies, to authors rather than to printers and preserved them unchanged; (2) s has been substituted for long ſ; (3) the eighteenth-century convention of repeating quotation marks down the left margin has been discarded in favor of modern practice, and, where confusion might result, we have brought double and single quotation marks into conformity with modern American usage; and (4) decorative initial capitals have been standardized. With these exceptions, our texts reproduce the spelling, capitalization, italicization, and punctuation of the originals. When we have had to depart from these principles we have so indicated in the headnotes, which give the source of every text. Titles (as they appear at the head of the texts), date lines, salutations, and closings reproduce the spelling and punctuation of the originals, but capitalization and type styles have been normalized to establish a consistent style for display elements throughout the book. Titles at the head of texts are given in the form that appeared last in the author's lifetime. All titles not clearly the author's own, as well as all elements that did not appear as part of the original titles, are enclosed in brackets. Where a partial title is more familiar than the full one, we have used the partial title, but with ellipses to indicate omissions. The scrupulous reader should also be warned that occasionally the demands of the context have obliged us to render foreign expressions rather than to translate them literally.

It will be immediately apparent to scholars how deeply we are indebted to the standard works of scholarship and criticism. We cannot here acknowledge all our thefts; we can only express our grateful awareness of all here that is not our own. We owe much to the following library staffs: those of the British Museum, the Bodleian, and the University of London; Harvard, Yale, Princeton, Princeton Theological Seminary, Rutgers, Duke, the University of North Carolina, the University of Illinois, Hamilton College, and the Honnold Library of the Claremont Colleges; the New York and Boston Public Libraries; and the Henry E. Huntington and William Andrews Clark Memorial Libraries.

We wish to thank the many scholars and students who have been kind in donating their assistance and encouragement: Walter J. Bate, Michael Bliss, H. F. Brooks, D. D. Brown, Harry J. Carroll, M. L. Clarke, Leonore Ewert, the late DeLancey Ferguson, Albert B. Friedman, Arthur Friedman, Stephen Glass, Josiah Gould, Guido Guarino, Clayton M. Hall, Benjamin B. Hoover, B. Jenkins, Arthur Johnston, Carol Landon, Wilmarth S. Lewis, Nancy McNally, Samuel H. Monk, Robert E. Moore, Walter Moskalew, James Parsons, Charles Ryskamp, Benjamin Saltman, Donald S. Taylor, William B. Todd, Theodore Waldman, and Ralph M. Wardle. The Research Council of Rutgers University has provided generous and imaginative support, and its Associate Director, C. F. Main, has from the beginning given us the benefit of his interest and criticism. Finally we must thank Mrs. Dorothy Couchman, Mrs. Anneliese Smith, and Mrs. Catherine Tramz for cheerful and efficient secretarial help.

G. T.
P. F.
M. W.
B. R.

Contents

ix

JOHN LOCKE

JOHN TILLOTSON

FRANCIS ATTERBURY

Part Two ALL

THE AGE OF POPE

MATTHEW PRIOR

DANIEL DEFOE

BERNARD MANDEVILLE

ANTHONY ASHLEY COOPER, THIRD EARL OF SHAFTESBURY

SIR RICHARD STEELE *and* JOSEPH ADDISON

JONATHAN SWIFT

ALEXANDER POPE

JAMES THOMSON

HENRY FIELDING

SAMUEL RICHARDSON

Part Three   THOSE ✓'ED

❧❧❧❧❧❧❧❧❧❧❧❧❧❧❧❧❧❧❧❧❧❧❧❧

A MISCELLANY OF POEMS

✓SIR JOHN DENHAM

EDMUND WALLER

THOMAS D'URFEY

✓JOHN POMFRET

HYMNS AND DIVINE SONGS

Part Four ALL

FACSIMILES
FROM *THE GENTLEMAN'S MAGAZINE*

Part Five ALL

WRITERS
OF THE MID-CENTURY

WILLIAM COLLINS

JOSEPH *and* THOMAS WARTON

THOMAS GRAY

Part Six   ALL

THE AGE OF JOHNSON

JAMES BOSWELL

R 9/9/74

✓CHRISTOPHER SMART

HORACE WALPOLE, FOURTH EARL OF ORFORD

SIR JOSHUA REYNOLDS

RICHARD BRINSLEY SHERIDAN

THOMAS CHATTERTON

Part Seven NONE

✿✿✿✿✿✿✿✿✿✿✿✿✿✿✿✿✿✿✿✿✿✿

WRITERS
OF THE END
OF THE CENTURY

GEORGE CRABBE

ROBERT BURNS

WILLIAM BLAKE

Part Eight

A MISCELLANY OF POEMS

HYMNS AND DIVINE SONGS

General Introduction

The English eighteenth century has been given a number of names by people seeking to locate its essence. It has been called The Enlightenment, The Age of Reason, The Neoclassical Period, and The Augustan Age. But the more closely we attend to the actual writings, the more we perceive that the literature and thought of the period are too varied, surprising, and complex to contain themselves comfortably under any of these labels.

However applicable to Continental tendencies during the eighteenth century, "The Enlightenment" will not do as a term descriptive of the intellectual state of England, for the term connotes a degree of downright religious and social skepticism that we simply do not find in English writing. We must never forget that England got through the eighteenth century without a revolution and that the century fittingly ends with Edmund Burke's strenuous rejection of both the French Revolution and the Enlightenment philosophy that sustained it. A label like "The Age of Reason" likewise misrepresents the real state of things, for one of the main satiric targets of writers so central as Swift and Johnson is Cartesian reasoning as it interferes with an appropriate empirical response to the actual world. Swift's reasonable Modest Proposer, who calmly suggests that the poverty-stricken Irish solve their food problem by eating their children "stewed, roasted, baked, or boiled," proceeds on the same "reasonable"—that is, inhuman—premises as Soame Jenyns, whom Johnson excoriates for airily glossing over palpable human evils.

Again, the trouble with the term "Neoclassicism" is that, however much light it may shed on the methods of minor poetry, it fails us when we try to apply it to the really memorable achievements of the century. Works like Swift's *A Tale of a Tub* (1704) or Gay's *Beggar's Opera* (1728) or Boswell's *Life of Johnson* (1791) are *sui generis:* they owe less to Greek or Roman precedents than most Romantic works. If we are searching for neoclassicism, we will find more of it in Keats and Robert Bridges than in, say, Goldsmith.

Like "Neoclassical," the term "Augustan" has its limits too. It is true that in a way the imaginations of Dryden, Pope, Prior, and Gay are sometimes suffused with a light emanating from the Roman Augustan Age, when writers like Virgil and Horace transformed an inherited Greek tradition to give it a local habitation and a name. But the success of middle-class writers like Defoe and Richardson constitutes an embarrassment to any descriptive title for early eighteenth-century literature that emphasizes unduly its learned elegance, its intellectual respect for its audience, and its fondness for satire and wit. It is instructive too to keep in mind Samuel Johnson's identity as a vigorous opponent of neoclassicism. As an empiricist, he despised neoclassical pastoral and "the puerilities of obsolete mythology," and it was his skepticism that exposed the ultimate hollowness of the dogmatic critical talk about the neoclassical "unities" in the serious drama. Perhaps after all the best way to refer to this whole body of writing is to call it Eighteenth-Century English Literature. At least if we do so, we run little risk of forming a priori conceptions that are bound to interfere with a fresh and accurate reading of the works.

II

The eighteenth-century English mind was created by the reaction to the civil disorders of the seventeenth century. For decades the public peace had been violated by religious quarrels. Dryden in *Religio Laici* (1682) voices the new yearning for peace and quiet and suggests how it is to be achieved:

> after hearing what our Church can say,
> If still our Reason runs another way,
> That private Reason 'tis more Just to curb,
> Than by Disputes the publick Peace disturb.

Thus, for a century after the restoration of Charles II in 1660, the word *Puritan* was a term of contempt among the sophisticated, and the word *enthusiasm*, applied to either religion or politics, was a handy tool for reminding an audience of the grave dangers of innovation. As England recovered itself in 1660 and set its face toward a safer kind of society, the parliamentary system developed as a mechanism for compromising differences in a civilized way: the concept of the *via media* spread out from ethics to color politics and social theory. The way to understand the fear of early eighteenth-century writers for extreme changes of any kind is to remember the destruction and hatred that extremes had generated within living memory.

The reestablishment of society on a new common-sense basis after the civil wars had large reflections in literature and critical theory. The sense of "a new start" is everywhere. In his *Secular Masque* (1700), Dryden puts the seventeenth century behind him in these terms:

> All, all, of a piece throughout;
> Thy Chase had a Beast in View;
> Thy Wars brought nothing about;
> Thy Lovers were all untrue.
> 'Tis well an Old Age is out,
> And time to begin a New.

Alexander Pope indicates that a new age is going to require a new attention to precision, control, and "correctness" in poetry: "Late, very late, correctness grew our care, / When the tir'd nation breath'd from civil war." And in prose, the sense of a new start is going to require a new attention to the virtues of clarity and order.

Indeed, it was a time when there was a remarkable agreement about what constituted a good style in both poetry and prose. Style in both was to be a reflection of exactitude of perception and orderliness of arrangement. When in *The Mechanical Operation of the Spirit* (1704) Jonathan Swift burlesques a speaker whom he characterizes as a pedant, a comical materialist, and a loony, he has him write as much like Robert Burton and as little like Cicero as possible. The utopian stylistic ideal imputed by Swift to his Brobdingnagians reflects the general ambition of early eighteenth-century writers: "Their style is clear, masculine, and smooth, but not florid." And a man so different from Swift as Daniel Defoe, miles away in social class and education, agrees with him on style:

> If any man were to ask me what I should suppose to be a perfect style . . . I would answer, that in which a man speaking to five hundred people, of all common and various capacities, idiots or lunatics excepted, should be understood by them all, and in the same sense in which the speaker intended to be understood.

It was the same in poetry. Reprehended now were the flowers and conceits and the occasionally astonishing rhythms of the seventeenth century. These were labeled "false wit." What was wanted was "true wit": a comfortable degree of predictability and effects of economy, clarity, and vigor. As Pope says in the *Essay on Criticism* (1711):

> *Words* are like *Leaves;* and where they most abound,
> Much *Fruit* of *Sense* beneath is rarely found.
> *False Eloquence*, like the *Prismatic Glass*,
> Its gawdy Colours spreads on *ev'ry place;*
>
> · · ·
>
> But true *Expression*, like th' unchanging *Sun*,
> *Clears*, and *improves* whate'er it shines upon.

Such an ideal of style presupposes an audience whose mind is very much like the poet's own. This unquestioned presupposition is due in large part to the wide acceptance of the epistemology and psychology of Locke.

III

Everyone read John Locke's *Essay Concerning Humane Understanding* (1690), and those who could not read were somehow aware of what it said, just as in later times the influence of Marx, Darwin, and Freud has spread well beyond the small number of people who have actually read them. The validity of Lockean psychology was unquestioned by most writers of the eighteenth century. In his *Essay*, Locke had concluded that the experience of the senses is the sole avenue of knowledge and that new ideas are the result not of private "inspiration" but rather of new combinations and arrangement of public materials lodged in the memory. So plausible and stunning was Locke's picture of the uniform human mind that the whole literature of the eighteenth century can be said to constitute a series of enactments of its implications. Swift's disdain for the farcical Dissenters who claim inspiration and a special "inner light" is very like Burke's contempt, over eighty years later, for the French Revolutionists who imagine that they have been vouchsafed a special vision of society denied to their forefathers and most of their contemporaries. The wide commitment to Locke's findings about the mind tended to give the thought and the writing of the eighteenth century a notably skeptical and public cast. In the seventh of his *Discourses* (1776), Sir Joshua Reynolds reasoned:

> As the imagination is incapable of producing any thing originally of itself, and can only vary and combine those ideas with which it is furnished by means of the senses, there will be necessarily an agreement in the imaginations as in the senses of men. There being this agreement, it follows, that . . . we must regulate our affections of every kind by that of others. The well-disciplined mind acknowledges this authority, and submits its own opinion to the public voice.

After all, if the nature of man is, in essentials, uniform, and if ideas enter the mind only through external experience, then truth must be both simple and ultimately apparent to all. The general mind of the eighteenth century thus believes that what is real and important is what is public and "normal" rather than private and singular. What is true is what all men recognize as truth. And "all men" includes the dead majority as well as the living minority. As the minor critic Charles Gildon put it in 1718:

> Aristotle gives not his rules as legislators do their laws, without any other reason than his will. All that he advances is confirmed by reasons drawn from the common sentiments of mankind, so that men themselves become the rule and measure of what he lays down. . . . For good sense, and right reason [he means "true wit"], is of all countries and places; the same subjects which caused so many tears to be shed in the Roman theatre produce the same effect on ours; and those things that then gave distaste do the same now.

What is recognized as truth by one but denied by most is mere "opinion," and literature, which by its nature aspires to permanence, is not made of opinions.

One result of the preeminence of Lockean psychology was the prevalence of highly public and social kinds of literature. Satire flourishes while lyric all but disappears; confession is displaced by social observation. The eighteenth century is the great age of British oratory, biography, lexicography. The high value placed on common, general knowledge stimulated the production of numberless encyclopedias and compendia of learning. It was in 1768 that the first edition of the *Encyclopædia Britannica* appeared. The preeminence of public truth over private speculation helps make the eighteenth century the great age of anecdote and literary-social documentation, from Joseph Spence's *Anecdotes* (1820) of Pope to Hester Lynch Thrale's *Anecdotes* (1786) of Johnson. It is hard to imagine a Horace Walpole or a James Boswell functioning at any other time, for what is required for their kind of documentary and anecdotal obsession is a conviction that what happens in "society" is interesting and important and that a writer's main business is to erect some general portrait of human nature that will subsume individuality within a large paradigm of uniformity. When we contrast the great works of the early part of the century with those of the latter part, we perceive a special tendency in the later works toward the reportorial and the documentary. If *Gulliver's Travels* (1726) and *The Dunciad* (1728–43) appeal largely through symbolic means, creating fictive worlds and peopling them with cautionary moral grotesques, later works like Boswell's *Life of Johnson*, Gibbon's *History of the Decline and Fall of the Roman Empire* (1776–88), and Burke's *Reflections on the Revolution in France* (1790) succeed through their acute attention to the actual, the empirical, the historical. A similar fondness for the demonstrable and the practical is reflected in the popularity of works of travel, geography, and history. A record of library borrowings at Bristol during the 1770's suggests that the most popular books among the middle-class were not novels, plays, and poems, but rather books like Captain Cook's anthropological reports from the South Seas, David Hume's *History of England* (1754–62), and Oliver Goldsmith's *History of the Earth and of Animated Nature* (1774).

It seems likely, too, that the Lockean intellectual climate, with its emphasis on the validity of the publicly knowable, helps explain the conspicuous sociability of the age. Johnson voices an eighteenth-century commonplace when he asserts that "men are designed for the succour and comfort of each other." The reader making his first acquaintance with the writers of the period will be struck by such phenomena as Pope's sociability, Johnson's massive contempt for "unclubbable" men, Hume's and Reynolds's devotion to dinner parties, Gibbon's perpetual party-going in Switzerland, Walpole's elegant gossiping, and the prevalence of gambling—a quintessentially social pastime in the sense that one cannot do it alone. One significant legacy of the age is Edmond Hoyle's durable set of whist rules, which appeared in 1760. Those placed outside the borders of social life by excessive shyness or privacy of mind are generally described by the epithet "poor." Thus Johnson speaks of "poor Collins" and "poor Kit Smart." And Johnson never tires of repeating to Boswell the exhortation "Be not solitary!"

The contemporary sense of the social, as well as the general preference for benign and humanized scenery, is happily expressed by Richard Brinsley Sheridan's sister Elizabeth. She reports on the delights of Bath in the 1780's:

> The present Mall of Bath . . . I think the pleasantest I ever was in as one is literally walking in the fields with a most beautiful prospect all around at the same time that you meet all the company that is now here. There is something whimsical yet pleasing in seeing a number of well-dressed people walking in the same fields where cows and horses are grazing as quietly as if no such intruders came among them.

And even though the cult of rural retirement enticed many away from the city, the inspiration was less primitivistic than Horatian and Virgilian, with distinct overtones of social elegance. A typical country solitary is the genteel William Shenstone, who panted for the regular visits of fashionable people who came to admire his taste in gardening. The hermit in Johnson's *Rasselas* (1759), after enduring fifteen years of solitude, found himself the prey of "vanities of imagination" and concluded that "the life of a solitary man will be certainly miserable." He wisely decided to return to the city, "on which, as he approached it, he gazed with rapture."

The eighteenth-century poet and artist was conceived of as a member of society, not a special creature withdrawn from it. As Edgar Wind has said, "In the eighteenth century a lively exchange between the artist and his public was still taken for granted. Hogarth laughed at poets who lived in garrets and pursued their fancies; he ridiculed musicians enraged by the popular music of the streets. The true artist was in contact with his public." Unheard of as yet was the Romantic conception of the artist as a retired and sensitive soul, working only as he is moved by the spirit. As Wind has pointed out, in Hogarth's portraits of the artist, the sympathy is with the populace that intrudes and violates the artist's pretensions. But in the Romantic period, the drawings of Rowlandson, although they depict similar confrontations between artist and public, contrive to reverse Hogarth's sympathies: the viewer is now invited to sympathize with the artist as a sensitive and long-suffering servant of Higher Things.

The profundity of the contemporary commitment to the idea of society and its norms is suggested even by the image systems that appear repeatedly in the works of the major writers. Eminently social and public images of traveling, architecture, and organized military action and groupings of personified passions and ideas recur in poetry and prose alike. One favorite image is that of various kinds of clothing, used to symbolize the inherited social and institutional forms that redeem human life from the brutal and the primitive. As Pope puts it,

> Expression is the *Dress* of *Thought*, and still
> Appears more *decent* as more *suitable;*
> A vile Conceit in pompous Words exprest,
> Is like a Clown in regal Purple drest;
> For diff'rent *Styles* with diff'rent *Subjects* sort,
> As several Garbs with Country, Town, and Court.

Johnson perceives that "life . . . is barren enough surely with all her trappings." And he goes on: "Let us therefore be cautious how we strip her." Burke uses a similar figure in his impassioned commentary on the French Revolution:

> All the decent drapery of life is to be rudely torn off. All the superadded ideas, furnished from the wardrobe of a moral imagination, which the heart owns, and the understanding ratifies, as necessary to cover the defects of our naked, shivering nature, and to raise it to dignity in our own estimation, are to be exploded as a ridiculous, absurd, and antiquated fashion.

And even the minor poet Erasmus Darwin reveals a similar devotion to the pre-eminence of the inherited and the public when he writes, "The Muses are young ladies; we expect to see them dressed."

IV

Although the eighteenth century, with its prevailing public and social idea of what human beings should be, produced the heroic oratorios of Handel, the civilized paintings of Reynolds and Gainsborough, the serene Grecian urns of Josiah Wedgwood, and the elegant furniture of the Adam brothers, all was by no means civility and grace. As Lord David Cecil has said, "England in the eighteenth century was a robust, red-blooded, uproarious place . . . . How people ate and drank! . . . With what unflagging virile relish they swore, and begat bastards, and gambled and attended executions and proclaimed their belief in liberty and their contempt for the wretched frog-eaters on the other side of the Channel!" But even the uproariousness and the relish were often a thin veneer laid over a seething underworld of death, violence, filth, and insanity. If the age produced its Chesterfields and its Horace Walpoles, it produced also its Christopher Smarts and its Thomas Chattertons, not to mention the starving hordes of city prostitutes and abandoned children who make brief, furtive appearances in Boswell's *Life of Johnson* as well as in the poems of Blake. Crabbe's mad and sadistic Peter Grimes is as "characteristic" of the period as Fanny Burney's genteel Evelina.

Disease and violent death were the commonplaces of daily life, producing, as M. Dorothy George has pointed out, "that sense of instability, of liability to sudden ruin, which runs through so much eighteenth-century literature." Every mother could assume that half her children would die in infancy. Typical is the experience of Johnson's friend Mrs. Thrale, whose five living children were all that remained of twelve. The *Annual Register* for 1780 prints this typical bill of mortality:

Died under two years of age	6810
2 and 5	1713
5 and 10	598
10 and 20	602

If the London citizen could justify from the Prayer Book the fact of infant mortality, he was further reminded of the fragility of the human condition by the heads of traitors adorning Temple Bar and by the frequent public hangings of thieves and highwaymen, events attended by such harmless, upper-middle-class figures as James Boswell and George Selwyn. Some reformers, like the author of *Hanging Not Punishment Enough* (1701), advocated torture as a deterrent against crime. G. Olliffe, M.A., in *An Essay Humbly Offered for an Act to Prevent Capital Crimes* (1731), argued that breaking the criminal's body on the wheel would be an efficacious antidote against serious crime.

The London mob, notorious for its touchiness, was always ready to burst into violence. In the anti-Catholic riots of 1780 over 450 people were killed and wounded in the city, seventy-two houses were burned down, and the inmates of four prisons were released. The whole metropolis was in a state of terror for six days. Nor was violence at home only in London. Cockfighting and the baiting of bulls and bears by vicious dogs were standard rural pastimes, and no country fair was thought successful without considerable blood-letting among the bumpkins. In 1785 the traveler John Byng observed this announcement in the town of Yattendon, in Somersetshire:

> This is to give Notice, that Yattendon Revel will be kept as usual on Monday, the 11th of July instant, and . . . there will be given a Good Gold-laced Hat, of 27s. value, to be played for at Cudgels; the man who breaks most heads to have the prize; 2s. will be given to each man that positively breaks a head, for the first ten heads that are broke; and 1s. to the man that has his head broke . . . the blood to run an inch or be deemed no head.

Sometimes the British fondness for assaults took a more comical turn and produced scenes worthy of Smollett. *The Universal Chronicle* for July 2–9, 1759, reported:

> We hear from Coventry, that an Officer belonging to a recruiting party . . . endeavoured to enlist a Farrier [blacksmith], by taking him to a publick house, and offering to treat him with variety of liquors, in order to intoxicate him, which

the Farrier refused to accept, unless the Officer would agree to drink glass for glass with him in a private room by themselves; the Officer complied, and drank with the Farrier till he fell off his chair; upon which the Farrier took an instrument out of his pocket with which he drew several of the Officer's teeth, and then made clear off.

Drink was the avocation of all classes. The upper class consumed claret, port, and brandy; the sober middle class, strong beer; and the lower, cheap gin. One sign in a gin shop read: "Drunk for a penny, dead drunk for twopence, straw for nothing." In the *Middlesex Records* we read of a shoemaker who, in 1728, punished a fractious nine-year-old apprentice not only by whipping him with a great leather strap and a broomstick but by depriving him of his rightful copious allowance of ale and allowing him only water: the court determined that the apprentice had been unfairly used and ordered his indentures to be voided. After two years' experience as a London police magistrate Henry Fielding observed, "Gin is the principal sustenance . . . of more than a hundred thousand people in this metropolis. Many of these wretches there are, who swallow pints of this poison within the twenty-four hours; the dreadful effects of which I have the misfortune every day to see, and to smell too." Because sanitation was primitive and the London water supply untrustworthy, "it seemed almost a hygienic duty," as Derek Hudson remarks, "to drink wine and to take snuff." Although garbage and animal filth were apparent everywhere in London, more noisome stenches were associated with Edinburgh. There it was the householders' habit to empty their night vessels from their upper windows, warning the passers-by with the friendly shout "Gardy loo [Look out for the water]!"

It is within this context of violence, excess, and filth that we should contemplate Swift's cold fury at complacency, Samuel Johnson's fears of damnation, and William Blake's vision of England glorified. Renaissance England had been as dangerous and dirty, but the danger and dirt had seemed to most people the inevitable and unimprovable consequences of the Fall of Man. It was the unique affliction of people in the eighteenth century to labor under a consciousness both of the fallen estate of man and of his new obligations and opportunities to redeem his lot by institutional and humanitarian reform. The confusions engendered by these ultimately contradictory views of man's nature—the orthodox religious view and the modern secular view— perhaps help to explain the frequency of neurosis and outright insanity among serious people during this period. William Collins went hopelessly mad; Johnson himself, by his own troubled admission, was sometimes only dubiously sane; the unsuccessful suicide William Cowper trembled under a conviction that he was damned; Christopher Smart spent years in asylums. In addition, signs of instability appear in James Boswell's compulsive debauchery, in Thomas Gray's cloistered withdrawal from life, and in Chatterton's, Macpherson's, and the forger William Ireland's will to deceive. For a period sometimes called The Age of Reason, it was a time when the irrational and the self-destructive rose dangerously near the surface. We can assess the "reasonableness" of the age by noticing that Sir John Hawkins, writing his life of Johnson in the late 1780's, felt it necessary to assure his readers that Johnson's amateur chemical experiments were not undertaken, as they might assume, in an attempt to transmute lead into gold.

Just when it would seem to have been most needed, the Established Church appeared largely incapable of performing its customary consolatory functions. Although in the preceding century no one would have thought it extraordinary enough for comment, in his own time Johnson's traditional piety became conspicuous and famous. On the other hand, most people found the offices of the Church neither as plausible nor as necessary as they had seemed a century before. On his deathbed the Roman Catholic Alexander Pope had to be reminded that the ministrations of a priest might be appropriate, and James Boswell was not alone in thinking that all that a man needed was "a decent system of mild Christianity." Desire for a benign religion was evident, and the Church responded to the pressure by emphasizing the idea of divine mercy at the expense of the idea of divine justice: it was as if the Glorious Revolution of 1688 had supplied the Church with a model of a new kind of deity and a new kind of universe, a universe ruled, as A. R. Humphreys has said, "not by an autocrat but by a constitutional monarch."

The clergy was weakened not only by Deism and Latitudinarianism but also by absenteeism and poverty. Numerous rural divines held many small livings at once and delegated their duties to miserably paid curates while, like Laurence Sterne, they sought more sophisticated society in London. Traveling in the Midlands in 1789, John Byng wrote:

> About religion I have made some enquiry . . . and find it lodged in the hands of the Methodists; as the greater clergy do not attend their duty, and the lesser neglect it; . . . at most places the curates never attend regularly, or to any effect, or comfort, so no wonder that the people are gone over to Methodism.

Reminiscing in 1815, the Edinburgh publisher William Creech described the change in Scottish urban customs during a twenty-year period:

> In 1763 it was fashionable to go to church, and people were interested about religion. Sunday was strictly observed by all ranks as a day of devotion; and it was disgraceful to be seen on the streets during the time of public worship. . . .
> In 1783 attendance on church was greatly neglected, and particularly by the men. Sunday was by many made a day of relaxation; and young people were allowed to stroll about at all hours . . . . and evenings were frequently loose and riotous.

This sudden, rapid growth of open secularism after centuries of traditional public piety is the background against which many literary phenomena of the eighteenth century become fully significant. The Deistic warmth of Pope's *Essay on Man* (1733–34), the religious scrupulosity of Johnson, the passionate institutional conservatism of Burke, and the apocalyptic obsessions of Blake would all seem unlikely except in an age reeling from the sudden collapse of religious and humanistic institutions that shortly before had seemed not merely permanent but unassailable.

The popularity of satire, that literary act which is the century's trademark, seems to reflect the decline of the Church. Traditional Christianity and satire are alike in this, that each sees things in terms of corruption that must be reformed or redeemed. When operating as a satirist, a writer exposes his target as corrupt as a means of positing the mode of its redemption. The satirist's action is thus like the clergyman's, and when the clergyman's traditional duty falls into disuse, it easily passes to the writer. Thinking in the context of Fall and Redemption, Paradise Lost and Regained, and Corruption and Reformation is a constant intellectual and emotional pattern in a society that is or has been Christian. Even if the Church loses interest in this pattern, it is so traditional that it is going to be enacted somewhere, and in the eighteenth century it is taken over and enacted repeatedly by the satirists.

V

Just as we must know something of the unique intellectual, emotional, social, and theological backgrounds if we are to interpret eighteenth-century literature accurately and sensitively, we must also accustom ourselves to a different theory of literature from theories that have prevailed at other times. In approaching eighteenth-century poetry, we should be especially careful to reject most of the nineteenth- and twentieth-century stereotypes of what a poet is supposed to be. To read eighteenth-century poetry as if it were attempting autobiography or "self-expression" is to miss the whole point. Far from representing "the spontaneous overflow of powerful feelings," poetry in the eighteenth century was commonly thought of as a mode of rhetoric, defined as the art of persuasion by means of the selection and arrangement of a multitude of traditional techniques of argument. Its nearest sister art was public speaking, as George Campbell explained in *The Philosophy of Rhetoric* (1776):

> Poetry indeed is properly no other than a particular mode or form of certain branches of oratory . . . . The same medium—language—is made use of; the same general rules of composition in narration, description, argumentation, are observed; and the same tropes and figures, either for beautifying or invigorating the diction, are employed in both.

Thus a poem like, say, Goldsmith's *The Deserted Village* (1770) is designed primarily to exert a certain influence on the reader; it is not designed to admit us into the actual emotions and opinions of the author. While, as James Sutherland has said, the nineteenth- and twentieth-century poet may behave as if the whole world is his confessional, the eighteenth-century poet, like his Roman predecessors, takes a more traditional way: he conceives of his job as akin to that of the attorney at law who has a jury to convince and whose success depends on his subtle manipulation of a body of inherited arguments, "turns," illustrations, allusions, figures, and received phrases. The lawyer is not trying to be "original" or "creative" in the nineteenth-century sense; he is trying instead to win his case. And the achievement of neither the lawyer nor the eighteenth-century poet can be enjoyed without a knowledge of what he is trying to do. The emotional impact of the work on the educated reader—always to be distinguished from the "specialist"—is what the poet focuses on; he tends to reserve artistically irrelevant personal revelations for his closet, his intimate conversation, and his private correspondence. To say all this is to suggest that the eighteenth-century reader was more interested in the behavior of poems than in the behavior of poets. Indeed, the extravagant interest in the biographical particulars of the makers of poems is largely a development of the following centuries.

The eighteenth-century theory of poetry as a mode of oratory is a perfectly natural outgrowth of the education in the Latin classics that, until late in the century, was all but universal. It is perhaps significant that the only poets represented in this volume who did not undergo the traditional formal study of the Roman poets and rhetoricians are Chatterton, Burns, and Blake. Their susceptibility to the appeal of native ballad or song forms and styles is the result, in part, of their having access to no other tradition to imitate. All the others began by studying at school the works of the Roman rhetoricians and oratorical theorists, especially Quintilian and Cicero, and then proceeded to apply the devices of Roman argumentation and persuasive description as they wrote their own Latin school poems; only after this careful groundwork did they essay the composition of their own poems in English.

In addition to the irrelevant modern values of exuberant "creativity" and flamboyant self-revelation in poetry, there is another pitfall to be avoided by the modern reader of eighteenth-century poems. To most twentieth-century readers a poem is a poem, and we sense little important difference in kind between, for example, T. S. Eliot's *The Waste Land* and one of Ezra Pound's *Cantos*. But in the eighteenth century the line of distinction between the various poetic kinds was still clear and firm, just as it had been in Roman artistic theory. One began writing a poem with an awareness of what *kind* of poem one wanted to write and with a consciousness of the meter, diction, figures, and structure appropriate to that kind and to no other. One wrote, that is, not a "poem" but a song, a pastoral, an elegy, an ode, an epitaph, a satire, or an epigram. It is true that the hard-and-fast distinctions between the kinds—together with the magisterial ascendancy of Latin education—seemed to fade as the century drew to a close. And yet the conservative critic the Reverend Joseph Robertson, writing in 1799, still discriminates the poetic genres and suggests the traditional hierarchy, running from epic at the top, through stage tragedy and comedy, to pastoral, elegy, "lyric"—that is, Horatian and Pindaric odes—and, at the bottom, satire. And the best contemporary criticism of poetry brought to bear on a given poem only those criteria appropriate to its kind. Thus a song, for example, was not condemned because of its triviality, for triviality was considered the one indispensable characteristic of the genre. Every poem, that is, was not expected to be profound. All emotions and attitudes, not the momentous alone, had their place in poems; but all were not expected in every poem. In this theory of the distinctions between the poetic kinds there was ample room for the playful, the sardonic, the whimsical, and the comic, as well as for the noble, the sublime, and the beautiful. The result of this conception of the poetic kinds is a poetry of an astonishing variety, a poetry in which the comic especially finds a conspicuous place. Poetry had not yet been appropriated to the uses of the solemn and the beautiful alone.

In speculating about the distinctions between the kinds, contemporary critics frequently availed themselves of analogues drawn from the inorganic art of architecture. Dryden had said, "'Tis with a Poet, as with a Man who designs to build." And over a half-century later Johnson instinctively compares the playwright to the architect who plans fortresses, and he readily perceives a parallel between the epic poem and the palace. Besides suggesting the static quality and the unchanging psychological basis of the various poetic kinds, such architectural analogues imply that the whole body of poetry constitutes a sort of permanent city of art—almost, perhaps, a restored city of Rome—made up of groups of predominantly public buildings designed for different political, legal, religious, and social purposes. The very metaphor in which the poetic kinds are commonly discussed betokens both the urban and the urbane commitments of those who employ it.

One way in which the poet could exhibit his skill was by his initial selection of a poetic kind suited to his talents. Johnson is thus to be admired for writing no sonnets and composing instead theatrical prologues, satires, elegies, and songs. In the same way, Johnson as a critic had more respect for the genre of the Pindaric ode than his strictures on Gray's odes might suggest. His complaints in the *Life of Gray* (1781) are in part expressions of regret that the author of the *Elegy Written in a Country Church-Yard* (1751) ever so far forgot himself as to attempt the Pindaric ode, a poetic kind quite unsuited to his genius. Another way in which the poet could exhibit his mastery of his art was by attending carefully to the dictional requirements of his chosen poetic kind. One of the faults Johnson finds with the late seventeenth-century poet Abraham Cowley is that he seems occasionally unaware that each poetic kind requires a different level of idiom; Cowley, Johnson says, "makes no selection of words . . . . He has given not only the same numbers [i.e., meter], but the same diction, to the gentle Anacreon and the tempestuous Pindar."

From what has been said so far it is clear that the eighteenth-century reader was expected to be highly sensitive to the meaning of poetic styles. He was expected also to take pleasure in recognizing the way new poems worked certain significant changes on the traditional—and ultimately Roman or Greek—originals. Just as the pleasure offered by Pope's *Epistle to Augustus* (1737) depends largely on the reader's familiarity with Horace's original, so most of the delight offered in Gray's *Ode on the Death of a Favourite Cat* (1748) depends on the reader's knowledge of the conventions of the classical elegy. We can see the same kind of witty intercourse between the contemporary and the classical in the late eighteenth-century art of portrait painting as well. The painters Allan Ramsay the Younger and Sir Joshua Reynolds were fond of posing their sitters in such a way as to evoke memories of the original poses of the classical sculpture that most educated Englishmen had studied in Rome during their youthful Grand Tours. For example, when Ramsay painted a full-length portrait of Norman MacLeod, he carefully reversed the pose of the *Apollo Belvedere*. Reynolds did the same a few years later in a portrait of the Honorable Augustus Keppel. The viewer's recognition of the reversed pose of the classical statue added an extra dimension of delight; and besides flattering the sitter, the pose added historical meaning to the portrayal. Contemporary painting, like poetry, had its own hierarchy of genres. History painting, with its depiction of noble events from sacred or secular history, was at the top, as we should expect of a kind of painting so susceptible of vigorous ethical expression. Portraiture, devoted to "the human face divine," stood next. Landscape was third. Still life was regarded as the lowest serious kind. It is notable that the theory of painting a century later would tend to rank these kinds in the reverse order.

All this emphasis on rhetoric and the classical theory of the kinds might seem to promise only a barren mechanism and formality in the arts. But in the eighteenth century the British awareness of the classical dimension was kept loose and flexible by the eccentricity, "humorousness," and empiricism of the British character. During the eighteenth century nothing struck foreign observers more forcibly than the British flair for eccentricity. As Voltaire once wrote back to a friend, "Reason is free here and walks her own way, hippocondriaks especially are well come. No manner of living appears strange; we have men who walk six miles a day for their health, feed upon roots, never taste flesh, wear a coat in winter thinner than y^r ladies do in the hottest days." The British delight in variety, novelty, and eccentricity helped keep eighteenth-century aesthetic theory from freezing into a rigid set of a priori "rules" and mechanical habits. Nothing seems more characteristic of the inventive and whimsical use of classical literature by the eighteenth-century English than Allan Ramsay the Younger's setting and singing the twenty-third ode of Catullus to the tune of the popular song *Sally in Our Alley*. And the following account of a contemporary funeral, as reported in *The Gentleman's Magazine*, is instructive:

> The six gentlemen who followed [the coffin of Mr. John Underwood, of Cambridgeshire] to the grave sang the last stanza of the 20th Ode of the second book of Horace. No bell was tolled, no one invited but the six gentlemen, and no relation followed his corpse; the coffin was painted green, and he laid in it with all his clothes on. Under his head was placed Sanadon's Horace, at his feet Bentley's Milton; in his left hand a little edition of Horace . . . . After the ceremony was over, they went back to his house, where his sister had provided a cold supper; the cloth being taken away, the gentlemen sang the 31st Ode of the first book of Horace, drank a chearful glass, and went home about eight.

Safe in the hands of a nation of humorists like these, the classics were in no danger of exerting an excessively rigid or pompous influence on either life or literature.

VI

Pope died in 1744, Swift in 1745. With the disappearance of these two emblems of literary self-assurance, a shift seems to take place in the literature and the taste of the age. And there are political and economic reasons as well for considering the mid-1740's the beginning of a new orientation. It was in 1746 that the meager forces of Charles Edward Stuart, known to his admirers then and since as Bonnie Prince Charlie, were defeated at the Battle of Culloden. Heir of the exiled Roman Catholic James II and thus the Young Pretender to the British throne, Charles planned—or so many of his followers hoped—to oust the constitutional Protestant monarchy of the Hanovers and to restore a more conservative reign reflecting orthodox ideas of royal authority deriving from divine right. When Charles was driven from the Scottish moors in 1746, much else seemed to retire with him, including an ideal of extravagant chivalric heroism and a conception of society as a mysterious and fixed reflection of divine, hierarchic order. What was destroyed forever, as Janet Adam Smith has said, "was not just the Stuart succession but . . . a social order alien to the mercantile spirit." After 1746 mercantile and industrial and utilitarian goals—the targets of Swift's and Pope's vigorous humanistic satire—tend increasingly to set the tone of English society. After 1746 it was perhaps more clear than it had been in 1660 or even in 1689 that the old world had drawn to a close and that the modern era had begun.

Much of the literature of the remainder of the eighteenth century reflects a conservative longing for lost heroic values of the kind associated with the preceding century, and the elegiac motif is seldom absent. We can point not only to the work of Collins and Gray but to Samuel Johnson regretting Dr. Levet, Edward Gibbon recording the sad dissolution of the Roman empire and memorializing Julian the Apostate, and Edmund Burke mourning the death of European chivalry and remembering Marie Antoinette. The dark awareness of mutability and loss seems to be a primary constituent of the later eighteenth-century consciousness: both a bold peasantry and the splendors of antiquity are gone, and their loss can never be supplied.

As Oliver F. Sigworth has pointed out, "Except that the term had not been invented, a man of the 1740's might have spoken, just as we do today, of the 'fragmentation of modern life.'" One indication of the contemporary sense of fragmentation is a new uncertainty of taste. It is clear that new and divisive forces are at work. A good example is the situation in architecture and interior decoration, where we find that the common, prevailing style of the early part of the century, the Palladian, or neo-classic, is beginning to yield to a confused mixture of more exotic modes, chiefly the neo-Gothic and the "Chinese."

During the 1740's, encouraged by the publication of Batty Langley's *Gothic Architecture, Improved by Rules and Proportions* (1742), builders were experimenting with a revival of the style that would become famous a few years later with Horace Walpole's construction of his Gothic castle at Strawberry Hill. An example of the simultaneous multiplicity of styles that characterizes much mid-century architecture as well as literature is the country house built about 1762 by Lord Bangor in county Down, Northern Ireland. The front of the house has a Palladian façade with Ionic capitals atop chaste classical pillars. But the back of the same house has a Gothic façade, with ogee arches, pinnacles, and a battlemented parapet. Inside, the front three rooms are Palladian in decoration; the back three are Gothic. The literary equivalent of all this is something like James Thomson's *Castle of Indolence* (1748) or William Shenstone's *The Schoolmistress* (1737–48), poems that employ the "Gothic" Spenserian stanza in the service of witty or "Roman" attitudes.

This unfocused and superficial yearning for the exotic and the novel is apparent also in the Chinese style, whose beginnings likewise are to be found in the 1740's. Tea, porcelain, and goldfish became socially obligatory, and pagodas and "Chinese gardens" sprang up everywhere. Under the influence of the designer and furniture maker Thomas Chippendale, furniture, fireplaces, and bric-a-brac began to exhibit an "oriental" absence of symmetry, as if in reaction to a surfeit of Palladian harmony. One of the popular spectacles on the Thames during the 1750's was the Duke of Cumberland's "mandarin yacht," elaborately done in the Chinese style; and one of the many literary reflections of this fashion is Oliver Goldsmith's *Chinese Letters* of the early 1760's, later issued as *The Citizen of the World*.

The uneasy awareness of an increasing fragmentation of traditional tastes and attitudes is revealed also in a number of odd—many think unreadable—poems belonging to the 1740's. For example, both Edward Young's *Night Thoughts* (1742–45) and Robert Blair's *The Grave* (1743) conduct their traditional Christian arguments within disturbing new contexts of hopelessness and despair. The rapid acceleration during the 1740's of religious "enthusiasm"—of which the Wesleys' Methodist movement is the most conspicuous fruit—bespeaks something of the same apparent dissolution of the old certainties.

There is another index, and a more subtle one, of tentative shifts in taste during the decade 1740–1750. Up to this time those who had speculated about versification had assumed that the staple line of English poetry, the iambic pentameter, had to consist strictly of ten syllables, and that "extra" syllables in words had to be omitted for the sake of syllabic predictability and regularity. Thus, in a line like Pope's "The conquering force of unresisted steel," the word *conquering* would be reduced by the reader to a word of two syllables (con-kring) to keep the line within the ten-syllable limit, and the reader could assure himself that his alteration of the word was one of the specific beauties associated with poetry. It was in 1745 that some very different notions of the structure of the English poetic line were first advanced by the minor critic Samuel Say, who argued with passion that the natural prose accents of the words comprising a poetic line must provide the expressive rhythmical pattern, and, furthermore, that it is the rhythmical variety of a poetic line rather than its regularity which is the source of metrical delight. This was a revolutionary critical opinion, and it is significant that it belongs, like much else that suggests the end of one world and the beginning of another, to the mid-1740's.

But despite all this tentative exploration of the new, the decades following the 1740's retained much that was traditional. Indeed, the uneasy experimentation was confined largely to surfaces, while underneath, the literature and thought reveal a fundamentally old-fashioned bias. During the second part of the century as well as the first, it was generally assumed that the proper study of mankind—and the proper subject of literature—was man as a universal creature, essentially unaltered by the accidents of history, nationality, or geography. The unique quality of man, regarded as a creature distinct from the animals, was still assumed to be his moral sense, his capacity for conceiving of his behavior in ethical and ritualistic terms and for regulating it in accordance with large public imperatives. Regardless of his particular temporary disguise as technician or specialist, every man would be found to be, in his moral essence, the same. Thus Johnson's assertion that "we are perpetually moralists, but we are geometricians only by chance" echoes for the latter part of the century John Locke's assertion of 1690, "Our business here is not to know all things, but those which concern our conduct." Like the writing of the early part of the century, that of the later concerns itself largely with questions of universal moral choices, and although satire loses some of its vigor, it still serves as a primary weapon against innovators and others who willfully depart from a universal, normal, and thus "correct" human nature, the kind of human nature disclosed in classical literature and anatomized psychologically by Locke.

VII

Although the spirit of the Roman classics—especially Horace, Virgil, and Cicero—colored literature until the end of the century, another important influence on the habits of some late eighteenth-century writers was the revival of interest in the British medieval ballads, a revival nourished by the larger antiquarian movement of this age which was the first to cherish and collect "antiques." To Augustans like Pope and Gay, antiquaries were figures of fun and sitting targets for satire, for antiquaries struck them as amateur scholars who had chosen to abandon the study of the literature of classical antiquity in favor of the relics of a largely local, vernacular medieval past. In an age in which *Gothic* was still a synonym for *barbaric*, it was natural for classically oriented wits and humanists to sense dangers in the contemplation of medieval literature. In the first version of *The Dunciad* (1728), Pope enunciates the general early eighteenth-century attitude toward literary antiquarianism:

> But who is he, in closet close y-pent,
> Of sober face, with learned dust besprent?
> Right well mine eyes arede the myster wight,
> On parchment scraps y-fed, and Wormius hight.
> To future ages may thy dulness last,
> As thou preserv'st the dulness of the past!

In the same way, Gay, in his "Proeme" to *The Shepherd's Week* (1714) adopts a pseudo-Spenserian diction for his mock-antiquarian discourse on pastoral.

But a new interest in medieval ballads and folk song was developing even during Pope's lifetime. As early as 1711 Joseph Addison was recommending the classical simplicity of the ballad of *Chevy Chase* (*The Spectator*, Nos. 70 and 74) and the pathos of *The Two Children in the Wood* (*The Spectator*, No. 85). Addison argued shrewdly that the medieval British ballads manifested a classical—indeed, a Homeric—simplicity, in refreshing contrast to the "Gothic" crotchets and "false wit" of many seventeenth-century Metaphysical lyrics. "Nature" and the ballads were, he found, the same. Addison's interest in balladry was shared by the Oxford antiquary Thomas Hearne as well as by the Scottish poet Allan Ramsay, whose two anthologies, *The Evergreen* (1724) and *The Tea-Table Miscellany* (1723–37), kept a multitude of ballads before the reading public. The meters and many of the rhetorical conventions of the British hymn, as composed by the Wesleys, Toplady, and Cowper, owe much to the contemporary ballad revival.

The culmination of this enthusiasm over British balladry was the publication of a book that exerted a considerable force on the literature of the later eighteenth century. Thomas Percy's *Relics of Ancient English Poetry*, published in 1765, contained 176 poems and the important *Essay on the Ancient Minstrels of England*, in which Percy developed a conception of the poet as the kind of instinctual, passionate, and shaggy creature who was to make repeated appearances in later literature. Percy's researches into balladry and folk song foreshadowed Burns's antiquarian recovery of old Scottish songs; they influenced Chatterton's decision to produce pseudo-ballads like *Bristowe Tragedie* (1772); and they stimulated Blake to experiment with ballad stanzas and conventions in his notable early lyrics. The next generation was no less enthusiastic about ballads and pseudo-ballads: the author of *Monody on the Death of Chatterton* (1794) is better known for his balladic *Rime of the Ancient Mariner* (1798), and one of the first works of the young Walter Scott was the Percy-inspired *Minstrelsy of the Scottish Border* (1802–03).

The continuity between the literary antiquarianism of the later eighteenth century and the romantic medievalism of poets like Coleridge and the Keats of *The Eve of St.*

Agnes (1819) brings us, finally, to the question of the usefulness of the well-worn label "pre-Romantic," which has sometimes been applied to many of the literary phenomena of the latter part of the eighteenth century. Indeed, for many decades it has been assumed that one of the most interesting things about the literature of the second half of the century (Samuel Johnson excepted) lies in its preparatory motions toward the Romantic period. In the early years of the twentieth century, when the Romantic poets ranked as the restorers of true light to the realms of imagination, it was quite natural for readers to search backward into earlier literature for portents of their arrival and to value the later poetry of the eighteenth century chiefly in proportion to its foreshadowings of Romantic delights. For years the term "pre-Romantic" has been used with a sense of an implicit endorsement of the qualities it describes. But though we read the Romantic poets with appreciation today, we do not, perhaps, position them quite so high on Parnassus as our fathers did, and we no longer feel impelled to see earlier writers reflected in their light. Northrop Frye, who has devised the term "The Age of Sensibility" to describe the literary period from the death of Pope to the end of the eighteenth century, observes of the concept "pre-Romantic" that it "has the peculiar demerit of committing us to anachronism before we start, and imposing a false teleology on everything we study." He continues: "Not only did the 'pre-Romantics' not know that the Romantic movement was going to succeed them, but there has probably never been a case on record of a poet's having regarded a later poet's work as the fulfillment of his own." Thus, instead of considering the writers of the later eighteenth century engaged in "preparing"—even unconsciously—for something more splendid in the offing, we may find it more rewarding to see them occupying themselves with a series of quite self-sufficient enterprises—enterprises that require of us no false, unhistorical illumination of Romantic critical theory for their appreciation. The customary search for "Romantic" characteristics in the works of writers like Cowper, Collins, Gray, Smart, Chatterton, and Burns is a barren exercise; these poets deserve a more sophisticated reading than they have generally had from the twentieth century. A profitable new direction is indicated in Frye's suggestion of what these poets were doing: "In view of the fact that they did not know that the Romantic movement was to succeed them, it seems better to look at them rather as attempting to get English poetry back on Renaissance rails."

But even when we have learned to take the poetry of this period on its own terms instead of on Wordsworth's or Matthew Arnold's, we will probably not conclude that the unique literary achievement of the later eighteenth century is its output of poems. Nor can we say, despite the undoubted brilliance of the novels of Smollett and Sterne and the comedies of Goldsmith and Sheridan, that it is the fiction or the drama of the period that are its proudest productions. The latter part of the century is distinguished rather by its output of extraordinary intellectual and critical prose. Although we see a waxing and a waning of fashions like graveyard poems, ballad imitations, odes strutting on tiptoe, picaresque and sentimental and Shandyesque and Gothic novels, and both weeping and laughing comedies, the stream of great works of discursive prose is constant: there is hardly a year without its masterpiece. We have Hume's *Philosophical Essays Concerning Human Understanding* in 1748; Johnson's *Rambler* from 1750 to 1752; Hume's *History of England* from 1754 to 1762; William Robertson's

History of Scotland in 1759; Blackstone's *Commentaries on the Laws of England* from 1765 to 1769; the first of Reynolds's *Discourses* in 1769; Adam Smith's *The Wealth of Nations* in 1776; Gibbon's *History of the Decline and Fall of the Roman Empire* from 1776 to 1788; the histories of music by Sir John Hawkins and Charles Burney in 1776; Robertson's *History of America* in 1777; Hume's *Dialogues Concerning Natural Religion* in 1779; Johnson's *Lives of the Poets* from 1779 to 1781; Boswell's *Tour to the Hebrides* in 1785; Gilbert White's *Natural History of Selborne* in 1789; Burke's *Reflections on the Revolution in France* in 1790; and Boswell's *Life of Johnson* in 1791. Once we perceive how many of these works issue either from members of Samuel Johnson's Literary Club or from persons reached in one way or another by Johnson's influence, we are in a position to sense and value the major literary achievement of the age: the unremitting production of persisting masterpieces of the kind that the age, following Johnson's cue, delighted to call "manly," couched in a prose at once energetic and easy, devoted to exploring every dimension of social man's earthly station. Of metaphysics we have none, nor do we encounter speculations about man's prenatal or postmortal circumstances. It is rather the massive Johnsonian subject of the continuity and the dignity of the uniquely human—man's will, conscience, and yearning for order and peace—menaced as always by brutality, vanity, sloth, and stupidity, that provided the materials which the major writers of the later eighteenth century—like their predecessors in the Age of Pope—shaped into works of permanent usefulness and beauty.

Part One

SOME WRITERS OF THE RESTORATION

Thomas Sprat

1635–1713

Thomas Sprat was born at Beaminster in Dorset, the son of Thomas Sprat, a clergy-man who was probably curate of that parish. After a provincial schooling he was admitted in 1651 to Wadham College, Oxford, where he took a succession of degrees: Bachelor of Arts in 1654, Master of Arts in 1657, and Bachelor of Divinity and Doctor of Divinity in 1669. Though not a scientist himself, Sprat, a Fellow of the college, was an intimate of the group of scientists who in 1660 under the leadership of Dr. John Wilkins, the college warden, formed the nucleus of the Royal Society, and it is for his *History of the Royal Society* (1667) that Sprat is best remembered. He won his early reputation, however, as a poet (his main entry in the *Cambridge Bibliography of English Literature* is, significantly, under the "Minor Verse" of the Restoration and eighteenth century). In 1659 he published *To the Happy Memory of the Most Renowned Prince Oliver, Lord Protector*, and a number of poems followed, both satiric and Pindaric. The latter were in imitation of odes by his friend Abraham Cowley, whose works he brought out, together with a life, after Cowley's death in 1667. It was through Cowley's patron, the Duke of Buckingham, that Sprat received two of his early clerical appointments, Prebendary of Carlton-cum-Thurlby in 1660 and Rector of Uffington in 1669, both in the diocese of Lincoln. With Buckingham (and others) he was to compose in 1671 the famous satire on the heroic drama—and Dryden—*The Rehearsal*.

Sprat grew into a staunch High-Churchman and defender of the divine right theory of kingship. Charles II returned the compliment with a chaplaincy in 1676, and Sprat rapidly rose from Curate of St. Margaret's, Westminster, the same year to Canon of Windsor in 1681, Dean of Westminster in 1683, and Bishop of Rochester in 1684. The following year, presumably by royal command, Sprat turned his pen to an account of the Rye House Plot of 1683 against the monarch. With the accession of James II in 1685, Sprat lost no ground but was much embarrassed (and condemned) for his membership the next year in the new king's retaliatory Ecclesiastical Com-mission, which sought to punish a number of bishops for seditious libel. The evidence for Sprat's alleged timeserving, whether in this affair or for his stand during the Revolution of 1688, is not entirely conclusive. In the latter event, he opposed the declaration of a vacancy in the throne after James's flight, but he did come to comply with the accession of William and Mary. In 1692 he was falsely accused of partici-pating in a plot to restore James but was easily exonerated. His last years passed without notable incident, and he died in 1713. As Dean of Westminster, Sprat had arranged for extensive repairs of the abbey under the direction of his old friend Christopher Wren. It was there that he was laid to rest.

A facsimile reproduction of the first edition of *The History of the Royal Society* with critical notes and a searching introduction was published by J. I. Cope and H. W. Jones in 1958. There is no definitive biography of Sprat. The account by W. P. Courtney in the *Dictionary of National Biography* has been amplified and corrected by H. W. Jones in *Notes and Queries*, CXCVII (1952), 10–14 and 118–23. Jones, together with Adrian Whitworth, has also published a *Check List* (1952) of Sprat's writings. George Williamson's *The Senecan Amble: A Study in Prose Form from Bacon to Collier* (1951) contains a pertinent chapter, "Reform and the Royal Society."

THE HISTORY
OF THE ROYAL-SOCIETY . . .

✾

Of *The History of the Royal Society* (1667), Johnson wrote:

This is one of the few books which selection of sentiment and elegance of diction have been able to preserve, though written upon a subject flux and transitory. *The History of the Royal Society* is now read, not with the wish to know what they were then doing, but how their transactions are exhibited by Sprat.

If Johnson's view of the subject (as opposed to the style) seems depreciatory, that view in fact reflects a "modern" acceptance of science and its progressive character. But it was just because the science of Sprat's day was new—and in many quarters suspect—that the *History* needed to be written. Sprat's task was to justify the new science exactly on the ground where it was most commonly attacked—that is, its alleged fruitlessness. Placing his virtuosi squarely in the empirical Baconian tradition, Sprat argues the case for their inestimable superiority over their generalizing, dogmatizing, enthusiastic, and superstitious predecessors in natural philosophy. Above all, perhaps, it is the pacifying tendency of the new scientific method that distinguishes it from the old. According to Sprat, the pursuit of truth, properly conceived, should be an occasion not for bitter private disputation but for collaborative harmony. In this way science can even serve as the corrective to political and religious dissension. In the third part of the *History*

Sprat enumerates the failings in the English character, concluding:

The Fourth mischief by which the greatness of the *English* is suppress'd, is a want of union of *Interests*, and *Affections*. This is originally caus'd by a Natural reservedness, to which our Temper is inclin'd: but it has bin heighten'd by our *Civil differences*, and *Religious distractions*. For the sweetning of such dissentions, it is not best at first to meet, and convers about affairs of state, or spiritual controversies. For those did first occasion our *animosities*, and the more they are rubb'd, the rawer they will prove. But the most effectual remedy to be us'd is, first to assemble about some *calm*, and *indifferent* things, especially *Experiments*. In them there can be no cause of mutual *Exasperations*: In them they may agree, or dissent without faction, or fierceness: and so from induring each others *company*, they may rise to a bearing of each others *opinions;* from thence to an exchange of good *Offices;* from thence to real *Friendship:* Till at last by such a Gentle, and easy *Method*, our several *Interests* and *Sects* may come to suffer one another, with the same peaceableness as men of different *Trades* live one by another in the same *Street*.

Hand in hand with the program for a new science went a program for a reformed language. As the Royal Society rejected the scholastic in favor of the empirical method of inquiry, so did it reject the old Ciceronian rhetoric in favor of the plain style. Sprat's mentor Wilkins went so far as to write an *Essay Towards a Real Character and a Philosophical Language* (1668), in which he advocated a strictly scientific sign language. But Sprat recognized the need for a literary language as well, and his argument is that just as experimental science can be a spur to more harmonious social relations, so can it greatly enlarge the resources of the literary imagination and its modes of expression. The plain style of philosophical discourse has its analogue in a literary style that is thoroughly grounded in sensuous experience:

> The use of Experiments to this Purpose is evident, by the wonderful Advantage that my Lord *Bacon* receiv'd from them. This excellent Writer was abundantly recompenc'd for his noble Labours in that *Philosophy*, by a vast Treasure of admirable *Imaginations* which it afforded him, wherewith to express and adorn his Thoughts about other Matters. But I will not confine this *Observation* to one single *Author*, though he was one of the first and most artificial [i.e., artful] Managers of this way of Wit. I will venture to declare in general of the *English Tongue*, that as it contains a greater Stock of *natural* and *mechanical Discoveries*, so it is also more enrich'd with beautiful *Conceptions*, and inimitable *Similitudes*, gather'd from the *Arts* of Men's Hands and the *Works* of Nature, than ever any other *Language* could produce.

If Sprat himself is no Bacon, he is still a competent witness to his own claim for the serviceability to literature of a knowledge of the arts and sciences.

The text is that of the first edition, *The History of the Royal-Society of London, for the Improving of Natural Knowledge* (1667). The second and last edition published in Sprat's lifetime (1702), though called corrected, offers no corrections of consequence in the extracts printed here.

✿

[EPISTLE DEDICATORY]

TO THE KING.

SIR,
OF all the Kings of Europe, *Your Majesty was the first* who confirm'd this Noble Design of Experiments, *by Your own Example, and by a Public Establishment. An Enterprize equal to the most renoun'd Actions of the best Princes. For, to increase the Powers of all Mankind, and to free them from the bondage of Errors, is greater Glory than to enlarge Empire, or to put Chains on the necks of Conquer'd Nations.*

What Reverence all Antiquity had for the Authors of Natural Discoveries, is evident by the Diviner sort of Honor they conferr'd on them. Their Founders of Philosophical Opinions were only admir'd by their own Sects.

Their Valiant Men and Generals did seldome rise higher than to Demy-Gods and Heros. But the Gods they Worshipp'd with Temples and Altars, were those who instructed the World to Plow, *to* Sow, *to* Plant, *to* Spin, *to* build Houses, *and to find out New Countries. This Zeal indeed, by which they express'd their Gratitude to such Benefactors, degenerated into Superstition: yet has it taught us, That a higher degree of Reputation is due to* Discoverers, *than to the Teachers of* Speculative Doctrines, *nay even to* Conquerors *themselves.*

Nor has the True God himself omitted to shew his value of Vulgar[1] Arts. *In the whole History of the first Monarchs of the World, from* Adam *to* Noah, *there is no mention of their* Wars, *or their* Victories: *All that is Recorded is this, They liv'd so many years, and taught their Posterity to keep Sheep, to till the Ground, to plant Vineyards, to dwell in Tents, to build Cities, to play on the Harp and Organs, and to work in Brass and Iron. And if they deserv'd a Sacred Remembrance, for one Natural or Mechanical Invention, Your Majesty will certainly obtain Immortal Fame, for having establish'd a perpetual Succession of* Inventors.

I am | (*May it please Your Majesty*) | Your Majesties most humble, | and most obedient | *Subject,* and *Servant,*

THO. SPRAT.

FROM

THE FIRST PART

Sect. IX. *The Philosophy of the Schole-men.°*

But my other instance comes neerer home, and it is of the *Schole-men.* Whose works when I consider, it puts into my thoughts, how farre more importantly a good Method of thinking, and a right course of apprehending things, does contribute towards the attaining of perfection in true knowledge, then the strongest, and most vigorous wit in the World, can do without them. It cannot without injustice be deny'd, that they were men of extraordinary strength of mind: they had a great quickness of imagination, and subtilty of distinguishing: they very well understood the

---

THE HISTORY OF THE ROYAL SOCIETY: *Epistle Dedicatory.*
1. **Vulgar:** common. *The First Part.* **Schole-men:** scholastic teachers and writers of the Middle Ages, who specialized in logic, metaphysics, and theology.

consequence[1] of propositions: their natural endowments were excellent: their industry commendable: But they lighted on a wrong path at first, and wanted[2] matter to contrive:[3] and so, like the *Indians*, onely express'd a wonderful Artifice, in the ordering of the same Feathers into a thousand varities of Figures. I will not insist long on the Barbarousness of their style: though that too might justly be censur'd: for all the *antient Philosophers*, though they labor'd not to be full, and adorn'd in their Speech: yet they always strove to be easie, naturall, and unaffected. *Plato* was allow'd by all to be the chief Master of *speaking*, as well as of *thinking*. And even *Aristotle* himself, whom alone these men ador'd, however he has been since us'd by his *Commentators*, was so carefull about his words, that he was esteem'd one of the purest, and most polite Writers of his time. But the want of good Language, not being the *Schole-mens* worst defect, I shall pass it over: and rather stop a little, to examine the *matter* itself, and *order* in which they proceeded.

The *Subjects* about which they were most conversant, were either some of those *Arts*, which *Aristotle* had drawn into Method, or the more speculative parts of our *Divinity*. These they commonly handled after this fashion. They began with some generall Definitions of the things themselves, according to their universal Natures: Then divided them into their parts, and drew them out into severall propositions, which they layd down as Problems: these they controverted on both sides: and by many nicities of Arguments, and citations of Authorities, confuted their adversaries, and strengthned their own dictates. But though this Notional Warr had been carry'd on with farr more care, and calmness amongst them, then it was: yet was never able to do any great good towards the enlargement of knowledge: Because it rely'd on *generall Terms*, which had not much foundation in *Nature;* and also because they took no other course, but that of *disputing*.

That this insisting altogether on establish'd *Axioms*, is not the most usefull way, is not only cleer in such airy conceptions, which they manag'd: but also in those things, which lye before every mans observation, which belong to the life, and passions, and manners of men; which, one would think, might be sooner reduc'd into standing Rules. As for example: To make a prudent man in the affairs of State, It is not enough, to be well vers'd in all the conclusions, which all the *Politicians* in the World have devis'd, or to be expert in the Nature of Government, and Laws, Obedience, and Rebellion, Peace, and War: Nay rather a man that relyes altogether on such universal precepts, is almost certain to miscarry. But there must be a sagacity of judgement in particular things: a dexterity in discerning the advantages of occasions: a study of the humour,[4] and interest of the people he is to govern: The same is to be found in *Philosophy;* a thousand fine Argumentations, and Fabricks[5] in the mind, concerning the Nature of *Body*, *Quantity*, *Motion*, and the like, if they only hover a-loof,[6] and are not squar'd to particular matters, they may give an empty satisfaction, but no benefit, and rather serve to *swell*, then *fill* the Soul.

But besides this, the very way of *disputing* itself, and inferring one thing from another alone, is not at all proper for the spreading of knowledge. It serves admirably well indeed, in those Arts, where the connexion between the propositions is necessary, as in the *Mathematicks*, in which a long train of *Demonstrations*, may be truly collected, from the certainty of the first foundation: But in things of probability onely, it seldom or never happens, that after some little progress, the main subject is not left, and the contenders fall not into other matters, that are nothing to the purpose: For if but one link in the whole chain be loose, they wander farr away, and seldom, or never recover their first ground again. In brief, *disputing* is a very good instrument, to sharpen mens wits, and to make them versatil, and wary defenders of the Principles, which they already know: but it can never much augment the *solid substance* of *Science* itself: And me thinks compar'd to *Experimenting*, it is like *Exercise* to the Body in comparison of *Meat*: For running, walking, wrestling, shooting, and other such active sports, will keep men in health, and breath, and a vigorous temper: but it must be a supply of new food that must make them grow: so it is in this case; much contention, and strife of argument, will serve well to explain obscure things, and strengthen the weak, and give a good, sound, masculine colour,[7] to the whole masse of knowledge: But it must be a continued addition of observations, which must nourish, and increase, and give new Blood, and flesh, to the *Arts* themselves.

---

1. **consequence:** logical sequence. 2. **wanted:** lacked. 3. **contrive:** work upon, form.

4. **humour:** disposition. 5. **Fabricks:** constructions. 6. **a-loof:** at a distance. 7. **masculine colour:** strong character.

But this has been only hitherto spoken, against the *Method* of the *Schole-men* in General; on supposition, that they took the best course, that could be in that kind. I shall now come, to weigh that too. For it may easily be prov'd, that those very Theories, on which they built all their subtle webs, were not at all Collected, by a sufficient information from the things themselves. Which if it can be made out, I hope, it will be granted, that the force and vigour of their Wit did more hurt, then good: and onely serv'd to carry them the faster out of the right way, when they were once going. The *Peripateticks*[8] themselves do all grant, that the first rise of knowledge must be from the *Senses*, and from an induction[9] of their reports: Well then; how could the *Schole-men* be proper[10] for such a business, who were ty'd by their *Cloysterall life*, to such a strictness of hours,[11] and had seldom any larger prospects of *Nature*, then the Gardens of their *Monast'ries?* It is a common observation, that mens studies are various, according to the different courses of life, to which they apply themselves; or the tempers of the places, wherein they live. They who are bred up in *Commonwealths*, where the greatest affairs are manag'd by the violence of popular assemblies, and those govern'd by the most plausible speakers: busie themselves chiefly about *Eloquence;* they who follow a *Court*, especially intend the ornament of Language, and *Poetry*, and such more delicate Arts, which are usually there in most request: they who retire from humane things, and shut themselves up in a narrow compass, keeping company with a very few, and that too in a solemne way, addict themselves, for the most part, to some melancholy contemplations, or to *devotion*, and the thoughts of another world. That therefore which was fittest for the *Schole-mens* way of life, we will allow them. But what sorry kinds of Philosophy must they needs produce, when it was a part of their *Religion*, to separate themselves, as much as they could, from the converse[12] of mankind? when they were so farr from being able to discover the secrets of *Nature*, that they had scarce opportunity, to behold enough of its common works? If any shall be inclinable to follow the directions of such men in Natural things, rather then of those, who make it their employment: I shall believe, they will be irrational enough, to think, that a man may draw an exacter Description of *England*, who has never been here, then

the most industrious Mr. *Cambden*,[13] who had travell'd over every part of this Country, for that very purpose. Whoever shall soberly profess, to be willing to put their shoulders, under the burthen of so great an enterprise, as to represent to mankind, the whole Fabrick, the parts, the causes, the effects of Nature: ought to have their eyes in all parts, and to receive information from every quarter of the earth: they ought to have a constant universall intelligence:[14] all discoveries should be brought to them: the Treasuries of all former times should be laid open before them: the assistance of the present should be allow'd them: so farr are the narrow conceptions of a few private[15] Writers, in a dark Age, from being equall to so vast a design. There are indeed some operations of the mind, which may be best perform'd by the simple strength of mens own particular thoughts; such are invention, and judgement, and disposition: For in them a security from noise, leaves the Soul at more liberty, to bring forth, order, and fashion the heap of matter, which had been before supply'd to its use. But there are other works also, which require as much aid, and as many hands, as can be found. And such is this of observation: Which is the great Foundation of Knowledge: Some must gather, some must bring, some separate, some examine: and (to use a Similitude, which the present time of the year, and the ripe fields, that lye before my eyes, suggest to me) it is in *Philosophy*, as in *Husbandry*: Wherein we see, that a few hands will serve to measure out, and fill into sacks, that Corn, which requires very many more laborers, to sow, and reap, and bind, and bring it into the Barn.

But now it is time for me to dismiss this subtle generation of Writers: whom I would not have prosecuted so farr, but that they are still esteem'd by some men, the onely Masters of Reason. If they would be content, with any thing less then an Empire in Learning, we would grant them very much. We would permit them to be great, and profound Wits, as *Angelicall*, and *Seraphical*,[16] as they pleas'd: We would commend them, as we are wont to do *Chaucer*; we would confess, that they are admirable in comparison of the ignorance of their own Age: And, as

8. **The Peripateticks:** the school of Aristotle. 9. **an induction:** a bringing together. 10. **proper:** qualified. 11. **hours:** canonical hours. 12. **converse:** society.

13. **Mr. Cambden:** William Camden (1551–1623), author of *Britannia sive Florentissimorum Regnorum, Angliae, Scotiae, Hiberniae Chorographica Descriptio* (1586). 14. **intelligence:** system for securing and exchanging knowledge. 15. **private:** individual. 16. **Angelicall, and Seraphical:** according to J. I. Cope and H. W. Jones, a sneer at the expense of Aquinas, the "Angelical Doctor," and Bonaventura, the "Seraphical Doctor."

Sir *Philip Sidney* of him,[17] we would say of them; that it is to be wonder'd, how they could see so cleerly then, and we can see no cleerer now: But that they should still be set before us, as the great Oracles of all Wit, we can never allow. Suppose, that I should grant, that they are most usefull in the controversies of our *Church*, to defend us against the Heresies, and Schisms of our times: what will thence follow, but that they ought to be confin'd, within their own Bounds, and not be suffer'd to hinder the enlargement of the territories of other *Sciences?* Let them still prevail in the *Scholes*, and let them govern in disputations: But let them not over-spread all sorts of knowledge. That would be as ridiculous, as if, because we see, that Thorns, and Briers, by reason of their sharpness, are fit to stop a gap, and keep out wild Beasts; we should therefore think, they deserv'd to be planted all over every Field. And yet I should not doubt,[18] (if it were not somewhat improper to the present discourse) to prove, that even in *Divinity* itself, they are not so necessary, as they are reputed to be: and that all, or most of our Religious controversies, may be as well decided, by plain reason, and by considerations, which may be fetch'd from the *Religion of mankind*, the Nature of *Government*, and *humane Society*, and *Scripture* itself, as by the multitudes of Authorities, and subtleties of disputes, which have been heretofore in use.

FROM

THE SECOND PART

Sect. XI. *Their matter.*

Of the *extent* of the *matter*, about which they have been already conversant, and intend to be hereafter; there can be no better measure taken, than by giving a *general prospect* of all the objects of mens thoughts: which can be nothing else, but either *God*, or *Men*, or *Nature*.

As for the First, they meddle no otherwise with *Divine things*, than onely as the *Power*, and *Wisdom*,

and *Goodness* of the *Creator*, is display'd in the admirable order, and workman-ship of the Creatures. It cannot be deny'd, but it lies in the *Natural Philosophers* hands, best to advance that part of *Divinity:* which, though it fills not the mind, with such *tender*, and *powerful* contemplations, as that which shews us Man's *Redemption* by a *Mediator;* yet it is by no means to be pass'd by unregarded: but is an excellent ground to establish the other. This is *a Religion*, which is confirm'd, by the unanimous agreement of all sorts of Worships: and may serve in respect to *Christianity*, as *Solomon*'s Porch[1] to the *Temple;* into the one the *Heathens* themselvs did also enter; but into the other, onely God's *peculiar*[2] People.

In men, may be consider'd the *Faculties*,[3] and operations of their *Souls;*[4] The *constitution of their Bodies*, and the *works of their Hands*. Of these, the *first* they omit: both because the knowledg and direction of them have been before undertaken, by some *Arts*, on which they have no mind to intrench, as the *Politicks, Morality,* and *Oratory:* and also because the *Reason*, the *Understanding*, the *Tempers*, the *Will*, the *Passions* of Men, are so hard to be reduc'd to any certain observation of the *senses;* and afford so much room to the *observers* to falsifie or counterfeit: that if such discourses should be once entertain'd; they would be in danger of falling into *talking*, instead of *working*, which they carefully avoid. Such subjects therefore as these, they have hitherto kept out. But yet, when they shall have made more progress, in *material* things, they will be in a condition, of pronouncing more boldly on them too. For, though Man's *Soul*, and *Body* are not onely one *natural Engine* (as some have thought) of whose motions of all sorts, there may be as certain an accompt given, as of those of a Watch or Clock: yet by long studying of the *Spirits*, of the *Bloud*, of the *Nourishment*, of the parts, of the *Diseases*, of the *Advantages*, of the accidents which belong to *humane bodies* (all which will come within their Province) there may, without question, be very neer ghesses made, even at the more *exalted*, and *immediate* Actions of the *Soul;* and that too, without destroying its *Spiritual* and *Immortal* Being.

These two Subjects, *God*, and the *Soul*, being onely forborn:[5] In all the rest, they wander, at their pleasure: In the frame of *Mens bodies*, the ways for strong,

---

17. as . . . him: "*Chaucer* undoubtedly did excellently in his *Troilus* and *Creseid:* of whome trulie I knowe not whether to mervaile more, either that hee in that mistie time could see so clearly, or that wee in this cleare age, goe so stumblingly after him. Yet had hee great wants, fit to be forgiven in so reverent an Antiquitie" (*Defense of Poesy* [1595]). **18. doubt:** hesitate.

The Second Part. **1. Porch:** the entranceway to the temple. **2. peculiar:** special, chosen. **3. Faculties:** powers. **4. Souls:** minds. **5. being . . . forborn:** being the only ones avoided.

healthful, and long life: In the *Arts of Mens Hands*, those that either *necessity*, *convenience*, or *delight* have produc'd: In the *works of Nature*, their helps, their varieties, redundancies,[6] and defects: and in bringing all these to the *uses of humane Society*.

Sect. XX. *Their manner of Discourse.*

Thus they have directed, judg'd, conjectur'd upon, and improved *Experiments*. But lastly, in these, and all other businesses, that have come under their care; there is one thing more, about which the *Society* has been most sollicitous; and that is, the manner of their *Discourse*: which, unless they had been very watchful to keep in due temper, the whole spirit and vigour of their *Design*, had been soon eaten out, by the luxury and redundance of *speech*. The ill effects of this superfluity of talking, have already overwhelm'd most other *Arts* and *Professions;* insomuch, that when I consider the means of *happy living*, and the causes of their corruption, I can hardly forbear recanting what I said before;[7] and concluding, that *eloquence* ought to be banish'd out of all *civil Societies*, as a thing fatal to *Peace* and good *Manners*. To this opinion I should wholly incline; if I did not find, that it is a Weapon, which may be as easily procur'd by *bad* men, as *good*: and that, if these should onely[8] cast it away, and those retain it; the *naked Innocence* of vertue, would be upon all occasions expos'd to the *armed Malice* of the wicked.[9] This is the chief reason, that should now keep up the *Ornaments of speaking*, in any request: since they are so much degenerated from their original usefulness. They were at first, no doubt, an admirable Instrument in the hands of *Wise Men*: when they were onely employ'd to describe *Goodness*, *Honesty*, *Obedience;* in larger, fairer, and more moving Images: to represent *Truth*, cloth'd with Bodies; and to bring *Knowledg* back again to our very senses, from whence it was at first deriv'd to our understandings. But now they are generally chang'd to worse uses: They make the *Fancy* disgust[10] the best things, if they come sound, and unadorn'd: they are in open defiance against *Reason;* professing, not to hold much correspondence with that; but with its Slaves, *the Passions:* they give the mind a motion too changeable, and bewitching, to consist with

right practice. Who can behold, without indignation, how many mists and uncertainties, these specious *Tropes* and *Figures*[11] have brought on our Knowledg? How many rewards, which are due to more profitable, and difficult *Arts*, have been still snatch'd away by the easie vanity of *fine speaking*? For now I am warm'd with this just Anger, I cannot with-hold my self, from betraying the shallowness of all these seeming Mysteries; upon which, *we Writers*, and *Speakers*, look so bigg. And, in few words, I dare say: that of all the Studies of men, nothing may be sooner obtain'd, than this vicious abundance of *Phrase*, this trick of *Metaphors*, this volubility of *Tongue*, which makes so great a noise in the World. But I spend words in vain; for the evil is now so inveterate, that it is hard to know whom to *blame*, or where to begin to *reform*. We all value one another so much, upon this beautiful deceipt; and labour so long after it, in the years of our education: that we cannot but ever after think kinder of it, than it deserves. And indeed, in most other parts of Learning, I look on it to be a thing almost utterly desperate in its cure: and I think, it may be plac'd amongst those *general mischiefs;* such, as the *dissention* of Christian Princes, the *want of practice*[12] in Religion, and the like; which have been so long spoken against, that men are become insensible about them; every one shifting off the fault from himself to others; and so they are only made bare common places of complaint. It will suffice my present purpose, to point out, what has been done by the *Royal Society*, towards the correcting of its excesses in *Natural Philosophy;* to which it is, of all others, a most profest enemy.

They have therefore been most rigorous in putting in execution, the only Remedy, that can be found for this *extravagance:* and that has been, a constant Resolution, to reject all the amplifications, digressions, and swellings of style: to return back to the primitive purity, and shortness, when men deliver'd so many *things*, almost in an equal number of *words*. They have exacted from all their members, a close, naked, natural way of speaking; positive expressions; clear senses; a native easiness: bringing all things as near the Mathematical plainness, as they can: and preferring the language of Artizans, Countrymen, and Merchants, before that, of Wits, or Scholars.

And here, there is one thing, not to be pass'd by; which will render this establish'd custom of the

---

6. **redundancies:** superfluities. 7. **what . . . before:** in his proposal for an English academy, for the purpose of purifying the language (*The History of the Royal Society*, Part I, secs. xix–xx). 8. **these . . . onely:** these only should. 9. **the armed . . . wicked:** Cf. Eph. 6:16. 10. **disgust:** dislike.

11. **Tropes and Figures:** figures of speech. 12. **want of practice:** lack of observance.

Society, well nigh everlasting: and that is, the general constitution of the minds of the *English*. I have already often insisted on some of the prerogatives of *England;*[13] whereby it may justly lay claim, to be the Head of a *Philosophical league*, above all other Countries in *Europe:* I have urg'd its scituation, its present Genius, and the disposition of its Merchants; and many more such *arguments* to incourage us, still remain to be us'd: But of all others, this, which I am now alledging, is of the most weighty, and important consideration. If there can be a true character given of the *Universal Temper* of any Nation under Heaven: then certainly this must be ascrib'd to our Countrymen: that they have commonly an unaffected sincerity; that they love to deliver their minds with a sound simplicity; that they have the middle qualities, between the reserv'd subtle southern, and the rough unhewn Northern people: that they are not extreamly prone to speak: that they are more concern'd, what others will think of the strength, than of the fineness of what they say: and that an universal modesty possesses them. These Qualities are so conspicuous, and proper to our Soil; that we often hear them objected to us, by some of our neighbour Satyrists,[14] in more disgraceful expressions. For they are wont to revile the *English*, with a want of familiarity; with a melancholy dumpishness; with slowness, silence, and with the unrefin'd sullenness of their behaviour. But these are only the reproaches of partiality, or ignorance: for they ought rather to be commended for an honourable integrity; for a neglect of circumstances, and flourishes; for regarding things of *greater* moment, more than *less;* for a scorn to deceive as well as to be deceiv'd: which are all the best indowments, that can enter into a *Philosophical Mind*. So that even the position of our climate, the air, the influence of the heaven, the composition of the English blood; as well as the embraces of the Ocean, seem to joyn with the labours of the *Royal Society*, to render our Country, a Land of *Experimental knowledge*. And it is a good sign, that Nature will reveal more of its secrets to the English, than to others: because it has already furnish'd them with a Genius so well proportion'd, for the receiving, and retaining its mysteries.

And now, to come to a close of the second part of the *Narration:* The *Society* has reduc'd its principal observations, into one *common-stock;* and laid them up in publique *Registers*, to be nakedly[15] transmitted to the next Generation of Men; and so from them, to their Successors. And as their purpose was, to heap up a mixt Mass of *Experiments*, without digesting them into any perfect model: so to this end, they confin'd themselves to no order of subjects; and whatever they have recorded, they have done it, not as compleat Schemes of opinions, but as bare unfinish'd Histories.

In the order of their *Inquisitions*,[16] they have been so free; that they have sometimes committed themselves to be guided, according to the seasons of the year: sometimes, according to what any foreiner, or English Artificer,[17] being present, has suggested: sometimes, according to any extraordinary accident in the Nation, or any other casualty,[18] which was hapned in their way. By which roving, and unsettled course, there being seldome any reference of one matter to the next; they have prevented others, nay even their own hands, from corrupting,[19] or contracting the work: they have made the raising of *Rules*, and *Propositions*, to be a far more difficult *task*, than it would have been, if their *Registers* had been more *Methodical*. Nor ought this neglect of consequence, and order, to be only thought to proceed from their *carelessness;* but from a mature, and well grounded *præmeditation*. For it is certain, that a too sudden striving to reduce the *Sciences*, in their beginnings, into Method, and Shape, and Beauty; has very much retarded their increase. And it happens to the Invention of Arts, as to children in their younger years: in whose Bodies, the same *applications*,[20] that serve to make them strait, slender, and comely; are often found very mischievous, to their ease, their strength, and their growth.

By their fair, and equal, and submissive way of *Registring* nothing, but *Histories*, and *Relations;*[21] they have left room for others, that shall succeed, to *change*, to *augment*, to *approve*, to *contradict* them, at their discretion. By this, they have given *posterity* a far greater power of judging them; than ever they took over those, that went before them. By this, they have

13. of England: particularly in Part II, sec. xiii. **14. neighbour Satyrists:** notably, Samuel Sorbière, whose *Relation d'un voyage en Angleterre* (1664) had criticized the Royal Society among other English institutions. Sprat replied the following year with *Observations on M. de Sorbière's Voyage into England*.

15. nakedly: without organization. **16. Inquisitions:** inquiries, investigations. **17. Artificer:** practitioner of the arts or sciences, savant. **18. casualty:** chance occurrence. **19. corrupting:** in the sense of breaking the composition down into constituent parts. **20. applications:** of medicaments. **21. Relations:** accounts, reports.

made a firm *confederacy*, between their own *present labours*, and the Industry of *Future Ages*; which how beneficial it will prove hereafter, we cannot better ghesse, than by recollecting, what wonders it would in all likelyhood have produc'd e're this; if it had been begun in the Times of the *Greeks*, or *Romans*, or *Scholemen*; nay even in the very last resurrection of learning. What depth of *Nature*, could by this time have been hid from our view? What Faculty of the Soul would have been in the dark? What part of human infirmities, not provided against? if our Predecessors, a thousand, nay even a hundred, years ago, had begun to add by little, and little to the store: if they would have indeavour'd to be *Benefactors*, and not *Tyrants* over our Reasons; if they would have communicated to us, more of their *Works*, and less of their *Wit*.

This complaint, which I here take up, will appear the juster; if we consider, that the first *learned Times* of the *Antients*, and all those, that follow'd after them, down to this day, would have receiv'd no prejudice[22] at all; if their *Philosophers* had chiefly bestow'd their pains, in making *Histories of Nature*, and not in *forming of Sciences*: perhaps indeed the names of some particular men, who had the luck to compile those *Systemes*, and *Epitomes* which they gave us, would have been less glorious, than they are. Though that too may be doubted: and (if we may conclude any thing surely, upon a matter so changeable, as *Fame* is) we have reason enough to believe, that these later Ages would have honour'd *Plato*, *Aristotle*, *Zeno*, and *Epicurus*, as much, if not more, than now they do: if they had only set things in a way of[23] propagating Experiences down to us; and not impos'd their *imaginations* on us, as the only *Truths*. This may be well enough suppos'd; seeing it is common to all mankind, still to esteem dearer the memories of their *Friends*, than of those that pretend to be their *Masters*.

But this matter of *reputation*, was only the *private* concernment of five, or six. As for the Interest of those Times in general, I will venture to make good:[24] that in all effects of *true knowledge*, they might have been as happy, without those *Bodies of Arts*, as they were with them; *Logick*, and the *Mathematicks* only excepted. To instance in their *Physicks*: they were utterly useless, in respect of the good of mankind: they themselves did almost confess so much, by reserving all their *Natural*

Philosophy, for the retirements of their Wisemen. What help did it ever bring to the vulgar? What visible benefit to any City, or Country in the World? Their *Mechanicks*, and *Artificers*[25] (for whom the True *Natural Philosophy* should be principally intended) were so far from being assisted by those *abstruse Doctrines*; that perhaps scarce any one of those Professions, and Trades, has well understood *Aristotles Principles of Bodies*, from *his own* Time down to *ours*. Hence then we may conclude, that those *first Times*, wherein these *Arts* were made, had been nothing dammag'd; if, instead of raising so many *Speculative Opinions*, they had only minded the laying of a *solid ground-work*, for a vast Pile of *Experiments*, to be continually augmenting through all Ages.

And I will also add; that, if such a course had been at first set on foot, *Philosophy* would by this means have been kept closer to *material things*; and so, in probability, would not have undergone so many *Eclipses*, as it has done ever since. If we reckon from its first setting forth in the *East*; we shall find, that in so long a Tract of Time, there have not been above four, or five hundred years, at several intervals, wherein it has been in any request[26] in the World. And if we look back on all the alterations, and subversions of *States*, that have hapned in Civil Nations, these three thousand years: we may still behold, that the *Sciences of mens brains*, have been always subject to be far more injur'd by such vicissitudes, than the *Arts of their hands*. What cause can be assign'd for this? Why was Learning the first thing, that was constantly swept away, in all destructions of Empire, and forein inundations? Why could not that have weather'd out the storm, as well as most sorts of Manufactures: which, though they began as soon, or before the other, yet they have remain'd, through all such changes, unalter'd; except for the better? The Reason of this is evident. It is, because *Philosophy* had been spun out, to so fine a thread, that it could be known but only to those, who would throw away all their whole Lives upon it. It was made too subtile, for the *common*, and *gross* conceptions of men of business. It had before in a measure been banish'd, by the Philosophers themselves, out of the World; and shut up in the shades of their walks. And by this means, it was first look'd upon, as most *useless*; and so fit, soonest to be *neglected*. Whereas if at first it had been made to converse more with the senses, and to assist familiarly in all occasions

---

22. **prejudice:** unfavorable opinion. 23. **in . . . of:** with a view to. 24. **make good:** prove, demonstrate.

25. **Artificers:** here, inventors. 26. **request:** demand, vogue.

of *human life;* it would, no doubt, have been thought needful to be preserv'd, in the most *Active,* and *ignorant* Time. It would have escap'd the fury of the Barbarous people; as well as the Arts of *Ploughing, Gard'ning, Cookery, making Iron and Steel, Fishing, Sailing,* and many more such necessary handicrafts have done.

But it is too late to lament this error of the Antients; seeing it is not now to be repair'd. It is enough, that we gather from hence; that by bringing *Philosophy* down again to mens sight, and practice, from whence it was flown away so high: the *Royal Society* has put it into a condition of standing out, against the In-vasions of *Time,* or even *Barbarisme* it self: that by establishing it on a firmer foundation, than the *airy Notions* of men alone, upon all the *works of Nature;* by turning it into one of the *Arts* of *Life,* of which men may see there is daily need; they have provided, that it cannot hereafter be extinguish'd, at the loss of a Library, at the overthrowing of a Language, or at the death of some few *Philosophers:* but that men must lose their *eyes,* and *hands,* and must leave off desiring to make their *Lives* convenient, or pleasant; before they can be willing to *destroy* it.

John Wilmot, Second Earl of Rochester

1647–80

John Wilmot was born on April 1, 1647, at Ditchley in Oxfordshire, the only child of the Cavalier general Henry, Viscount Wilmot (later First Earl of Rochester), by Anne St. John, a member of a prominent Puritan family. He succeeded to the earldom at the age of eleven and before he was thirteen entered Wadham College, Oxford, where he was exposed to the most advanced scientific and philosophical thinking in the university. (It was here that the nucleus of the Royal Society was formed under the guidance of John Wilkins.) In February, 1661, the King, not forgetting his debt to his father, who in 1650 helped him escape after the Battle of Worcester, rewarded the son with a pension of five hundred pounds a year and arranged for his Grand Tour under the tutelage of Sir Andrew Balfour, a learned Scottish physician and virtuoso.

Toward the end of 1664 young Rochester returned to England and the life of a courtier. Charles II's court was one of the most glittering—and corrupt—in English history, and Rochester, the supposed model for Dorimant in Sir George Etherege's *The Man of Mode* (1676), is the nobleman whose popular image has been most completely identified with it. He quickly became the leader of a fashionable group known as "the merry gang," which included, besides Etherege, such poetical courtiers as John Sheffield, Earl of Mulgrave (afterward Duke of Buckingham), with whom he later fell out; Charles Sackville, Lord Buckhurst (afterward Earl of Dorset); Sir Charles Sedley; and Henry Savile, Rochester's closest friend. What made so young a man so eligible for this eminence is suggested by Bishop Burnet's description of him in his *Some Passages of the Life and Death of the Right Honorable John Earl of Rochester* (1680):

> He was a Graceful and well shaped Person, tall and well-made, if not a little too slender: He was exactly well bred, and what by a modest behaviour natural to him, what by a Civility become almost as natural, his Conversation was easie and obliging. He had a strange Vivacity of thought, and vigour of expression: His Wit had a subtilty and sublimity both, that were scarce imitable.

In 1665 Rochester met and, with the encouragement of the King, courted a much sought-after young heiress, Elizabeth Malet, but was rebuffed by both her and her family. Not uncharacteristically, the rejected suitor took the matter into his own hands and abducted the unwilling lady, but he was apprehended and imprisoned in the Tower. Soon released, he proceeded to redeem himself as a volunteer in the Navy, serving with valor in engagements against the Dutch in 1665 and 1666. That war over for Rochester, he renewed the siege of Miss Malet, and this time he won the lady, though still not her parents. They were married in January, 1667, and in July the earl added to his dignity by sitting in the House of Lords.

However, Rochester was not to distinguish himself either as a husband or as a statesman; it was perhaps in the art of satire only that, as Andrew Marvell said of him, he "had the right veine." Burnet, our best contemporary commentator, writes that

> he laid out his Wit very freely in *Libels* and *Satyrs* in which he had a peculiar Talent of mixing his Wit with his Malice, and fitting both with such apt words, that Men were tempted to be pleased with them: from thence his Composures [i.e., compositions] came to be easily known, for few had such a way of tempering these together as he had.

Although he occasionally displeased his victims—among them the Poet Laureate, John Dryden, and the King himself—Rochester, undaunted, continued to write his verses, which circulated freely about the court in manuscript (they were never intended for publication, though some got printed in broadsides). As a satirist Rochester seems to prefigure his great Augustan successors, in realism and energy if not in polish, and as a critic of the *haut monde* he perhaps has the advantage over them in having been born into this society.

As a prominent member of the Restoration court, Rochester naturally took an active interest in the theater, but his was more that of a patron than of a practitioner. He helped Dryden—to what extent is not known—with his *Marriage A-la-Mode* (1671), for which he received the Epistle Dedicatory, and was himself working on an adaptation of John Fletcher's tragedy *Valentinian* (1647) in his last years (it was, though unfinished, produced posthumously at Drury Lane in February, 1684). As a patron he advanced the careers of some minor playwrights, but perhaps his most notable contribution to the theater was his discovery of Elizabeth Barry, whom he turned into one of the great actresses of the age and of course his mistress as well.

A connection of a very different order is credited with saving Rochester from the errors of his ways at the end of his life. Late in 1679, while convalescing from a serious illness, he met Gilbert Burnet, formerly professor of divinity at Glasgow University and now a famous preacher in England, whose *History of the Reformation* (Vol. I) had just come out. Rochester and Burnet carried on a dialogue into the spring of 1680, examining the most difficult points in the Christian religion; the courtier found in the cleric a formidable antagonist to his skepticism. The force of Burnet's reasoning (from the base of latitudinarian Anglicanism) seemed to operate on Rochester's intellectual doubts and physical decline to prepare him for a spiritual conversion. It came, none the less genuinely for being traditionally late, in June, 1680, only a few weeks before his death, and appears to have been triggered by his hearing his mother's chaplain, Robert Parsons, read the passage prophetic of the sufferings of Christ in the Second Book of Isaiah.

We may let Bishop Burnet have the summary word, with all its ironic reverberations:

> Thus he lived and thus he died in the Three and Thirtieth Year of his Age. Nature had fitted him for great things, and his Knowledge and Observation qualify'd him to have been one of the most extraordinary Men, not only of this Nation, but of the Age he lived in: And I do verily believe, that if God had thought fit to have continued him longer in the World, he had been the Wonder and Delight of all that knew him.

The definitive edition of the works is D.M.Vieth's (1968). *Rochester's Poems on Several Occasions*, ed. James Thorpe (1950), is a facsimile of the Huntington Library copy of the edition that appeared in 1680 under the title *Poems on Several Occasions by the Right Honourable, the E. of R——*, with the false imprint "Antwerp." *Poems by John Wilmot, Second Earl of Rochester*, ed. V. de S. Pinto (1953), generally follows the edition brought out in 1691 by Jacob Tonson under the title *Poems, &c. on Several Occasions, by the Right Honourable John Late Earl of Rochester*. A full treatment of the textual problem is D. M. Vieth's *Attribution in Restoration Poetry: A Study of Rochester's Poems of 1680* (1963). Pinto's *Enthusiast in Wit* (1962) is the best biography.

[A] SATYR [AGAINST MANKIND]

❧

This, the most famous of Rochester's poems, appeared in a broadside in 1679, without the so-called epilogue (ll. 174 ff.).

The text reprinted here is that of the Huntington Library copy of the 1680 edition, with variants introduced from the broadside.

❧

WEre I (who to my cost already am
One of those strange prodigious° Creatures *Man*.)
A Spirit free, to choose for my own share,
What Case° of Flesh, and Blood, I pleas'd to weare,
I'd be a *Dog*, a *Monkey*, or a *Bear*.
Or any thing but that vain *Animal*,
Who is so proud of being rational.
The senses are too gross, and he'll contrive
A Sixth, to contradict the other Five;

And before certain instinct, will preferr   10
Reason, which Fifty times for one does err.
Reason, an *Ignis fatuus*,° in the *Mind*,
Which leaving light of *Nature*, sense behind;
Pathless and dang'rous wandring ways it takes,
Through errors Fenny-*Boggs*, and Thorny *Brakes*;
Whilst the misguided follower, climbs with pain,
Mountains of Whimseys, heap'd in his own Brain:
Stumbling from thought to thought, falls headlong
     down,
Into doubts boundless Sea, where like to drown,
Books bear him up awhile, and make him try,   20
To swim with Bladders° of *Philosophy*;
In hopes still t' oretake th' escaping light,
The *Vapour* dances in his dazling° sight,
Till spent, it leaves him to eternal Night.
Then Old Age, and experience, hand in hand,
Lead him to death, and make him understand,
After a search so painful, and so long,
That all his Life he has been in the wrong;
Hudled in dirt, the reas'ning *Engine*° lyes,
Who was so proud, so witty, and so wise.   30

12. Ignis fatuus: delusive guide. **21. Bladders:** floats. **23. dazling:** dazzled. **29. reas'ning Engine:** an image inspired by the growing mechanical view of the world—and of man himself.

A SATYR AGAINST MANKIND. **2. prodigious:** monstrous, unnatural. **4. Case:** condition.

Pride drew him in, as *Cheats*, their *Bubbles*° catch,
And made him venture, to be made a *Wretch*.
His wisdom did his happiness destroy,
Aiming to know what *World* he shou'd enjoy;
And *Wit*, was his vain frivolous pretence,
Of pleasing others, at his own expence.
For *Witts* are treated just like common *Whores*,
First they're enjoy'd, and then kickt out of *Doores*:
The pleasure past, a threatning doubt remains,
That frights th' enjoyer, with succeeding pains: 40
Women and *Men* of *Wit*, are dang'rous Tools,
And ever fatal to admiring *Fools*.
Pleasure allures, and when the *Fopps* escape,
'Tis not that they're belov'd, but fortunate,
And therefore what they fear, at heart they hate.
    But now methinks some formal Band,° and
        Beard,
Takes me to task, come on Sir I'm prepar'd.
    Then by your favour, any thing that's writ
Against this gibeing jingling knack call'd Wit,
Likes me° *abundantly, but you take care,*   50
Upon this point, not to be too severe.
Perhaps my Muse, were fitter for this part,
For I profess, I can be very smart
On Wit, which I abhor with all my heart:
I long to lash it in some sharp Essay,
But your grand indiscretion bids me stay,
And turns my Tide of Ink another way.
What rage ferments in your degen'rate mind,
To make you rail at Reason, and Mankind?
Blest glorious Man! to whom alone kind Heav'n,   60
An everlasting Soul *has freely giv'n;*
Whom his great Maker *took such care to make,*
That from himself he did the Image *take;*
And this fair frame, in shining Reason *drest,*
To dignifie his Nature, above Beast.
Reason, *by whose aspiring influence,*
We take a flight beyond material sense,
Dive into Mysteries, then soaring pierce,
The flaming limits of the Universe,
Search Heav'n and Hell, find out what's acted there,   70
And give the World true grounds of hope and fear.
    Hold mighty Man, I cry, all this we know,
From the Pathetique Pen of *Ingello;*°

From *Patricks Pilgrim,*° *Sibbs* Soliloquies,°
And 'tis this very reason I despise.
This supernatural gift, that makes a *Myte,*°
Think he's the Image of the Infinite:
Comparing his short life, void of all rest,
To the *Eternal,* and the ever blest.
This busie, puzling, stirrer up of doubt,   80
That frames deep *Mysteries*, then finds 'em out;
Filling with Frantick Crowds of thinking *Fools,*
Those Reverend° *Bedlams, Colledges,* and *Schools.*
Borne on whose Wings, each heavy *Sot* can pierce,
The limits of the boundless Universe.
So charming° Oyntments make an Old *Witch* flie,
And bear a Crippled Carcass through the Skie.
'Tis this exalted Pow'r, whose bus'ness lies,
In *Nonsense,* and impossibilities.
This made a Whimsical *Philosopher,*°   90
Before the spacious *World,* his *Tub* prefer,
And we have modern *Cloysterd Coxcombs,* who
Retire to think, cause they have naught to do.
But thoughts are giv'n for Actions government,
Where Action ceases, thoughts impertinent:
Our *Sphere* of Action, is lifes happiness,
And he who thinks Beyond, thinks like an *Ass.*
Thus, whilst against false reas'ning I inveigh,
Lown° right *Reason,* which I wou'd obey:
That *Reason* that distinguishes by sense,   100
And gives us *Rules,* of good, and ill from thence:
That bounds desires, with a reforming Will,
To keep 'em more in vigour, not to kill.
Your *Reason* hinders, mine helps t' enjoy,
Renewing Appetites, yours wou'd destroy.
My Reason is my *Friend,* yours is a *Cheat,*
Hunger calls out, my Reason bids me eat;
Perversly yours, your Appetite does mock,
This asks for Food, that answers what's a Clock?
This plain distinction Sir your doubt secures,°   110
'Tis not true Reason I despise but yours.
Thus I think Reason righted, but for *Man,*
I'le nere recant defend him if you can.

---

74. **Patricks Pilgrim:** Simon Patrick (1626–1707), Bishop of
Ely, wrote *The Parable of the Pilgrim* (1664), a forerunner of
Bunyan's *Pilgrim's Progress* (1678–84). **Sibbs Soliloquies:**
Richard Sibbes, or Sibbs, or Sibs, D.D. (1577–1635),
Puritan divine, was the author of numerous religious tracts.
76. **Myte:** a standard satiric view of man as a minute
insect. 83. **Reverend:** venerable. 86. **charming:** magical.
90. **Philosopher:** Diogenes the Cynic (c. 400–c. 325 B.C.),
who in carrying out his ascetic convictions is said to have
lived in a tub. 99. **own:** admit, acknowledge. 110. **secures:**
satisfies.

---

31. **Bubbles:** dupes. 46. **Band:** the Geneva band, a clerical
dress worn by parsons of the period. 50. **Likes me:** I like.
73. **Ingello:** Nathaniel Ingelo, D.D. (c. 1621–83), was the
author of a religious romance, *Bentivolio and Urania*
(1660).

For all his Pride, and his Philosophy,
'Tis evident, *Beasts* are in their degree,
As wise at least, and better far than he.
Those *Creatures* are the wisest who attain,
By surest means, the ends at which they aim.
If therefore *Jowler°* finds, and Kills his *Hares*,
Better than *Meres°* supplyes Committee Chairs; 120
Though one's a *States-man*, th' other but a *Hound*,
Jowler, in Justice, wou'd be wiser found.
You see how far *Mans* wisdom here extends,
Look next, if humane Nature makes amends;
Whose Principles, most gen'rous are, and just,
And to whose *Moralls*, you wou'd sooner trust.
Be judge you self, I'le bring it to the test,
Which is the basest *Creature Man*, or *Beast?*
Birds, feed on *Birds*, *Beasts*, on each other prey,
But Savage *Man* alone, does *Man*, betray: 130
Prest by necessity, they Kill for Food,
Man undoes *Man*, to do himself no good.
With Teeth, & Claws, by Nature arm'd they hunt,
Natures allowance, to supply their want.
But *Man*, with smiles, embraces, Friendships, praise,
Unhumanely his Fellows life betrays;
With voluntary pains, works his distress,
Not through necessity, but wantonness.
For hunger, or for Love, they fight, or tear,
Whilst wretched *Man* is still in Arms for fear. 140
For fear he armes, and is of Armes afraid,
By fear, to fear, successively betray'd.
Base fear, the source whence his best passions came,
His boasted Honor, and his dear bought Fame.
That lust of Pow'r, to which he's such a *Slave*,
And for the which alone he dares be brave:
To which his various Projects are design'd,
Which makes him gen'rous, affable, and kind.
For which he takes such pains to be thought wise,
And screws° his actions, in a forc'd disguise: 150
Leading a tedious life in Misery,
Under laborious, mean *Hypocrisie*.
Look to the bottom of his vast design,
Wherein *Mans* Wisdom, Pow'r, and Glory joyn;
The good he acts, the ill he does endure,
'Tis all for fear, to make himself secure.
Meerly for safety, after Fame we thirst,
For all Men wou'd be *Cowards* if they durst.
And honesty's against all common sense,
Men must be *Knaves*, 'tis in their own defence. 160

Mankind's dishonest; if you think it fair,
Amongst known *Cheats*, to play upon the square,
You'le be undone——
Nor can weak truth, your reputation save,
The *Knaves* will all agree to call you *Knave*.
Wrong'd shall he live, insulted o're, opprest,
Who dares be less a *Villain*, than the rest.
Thus Sir you see what humane Nature craves,
Most Men are *Cowards*, all Men shou'd be *Knaves:*
The diff'rence lyes (as far as I can see) 170
Not in the thing it self, but the degree;
And all the subject matter of debate,
Is only who's a *Knave*, of the first *Rate?*
    All this with indignation have I hurl'd,
At the pretending part of the proud World,
Who swolne with selfish vanity, devise,
False freedomes, holy Cheats, and formal Lyes
Over their fellow *Slaves* to tyrannize.
    But if in *Court*, so just a Man there be,
(In *Court*, a just Man, yet unknown to me.) 180
Who does his needful flattery direct,
Not to oppress, and ruine, but protect;
Since flattery, which way so ever laid,
Is still a Tax on that unhappy Trade.
If so upright a *States-Man*, you can find,
Whose passions bend to his unbyass'd Mind;
Who does his Arts, and *Pollicies* apply,
To raise his *Country*, not his *Family;*
Nor while his Pride, own'd° Avarice withstands,
Receives Aureal° Bribes, from *Friends* corrupted
     hands. 190
    Is there a *Church-Man* who on *God* relyes?
Whose Life, his Faith, and Doctrine Justifies?
Not one blown up, with vain Prelatique Pride,
Who for reproof of Sins, does *Man* deride:
Whose envious heart with his obstrep'rous sawcy°
     Eloquence,
Dares chide at *Kings*, and raile at Men of sense.
Who from his Pulpit, vents more peevish Lyes,
More bitter railings, scandals, Calumnies,
Than at a Gossipping,° are thrown about,
When the good *Wives* get drunk, and then fall
     out. 200
None of that sensual *Tribe*, whose Tallents lye,
In Avarice, *Pride*, *Sloth*, and *Gluttony*.

---

119. **Jowler:** a common name for a heavy-jawed dog.
120. **Meres:** Sir Thomas Meres (1635–1715), Member of Parliament for Lincoln. 150. **screws:** strains.

189. **own'd:** admitted, acknowledged. 190. **Aureal:** golden.
195. **sawcy:** insolent. 199. **Gossipping:** a social gathering of women, especially at lying-ins and christenings. The original meaning of *gossip* was "godparent."

Who hunt good Livings, but abhor good Lives,
Whose Lust exalted, to that height arrives,
They act Adultery with their own *Wives*.
And e're a score of Years compleated be,
Can from the lofty *Pulpit* proudly see,
Half a large *Parish*, their own *Progeny*.

    Nor doating B——° who wou'd be ador'd,
For domineering at the *Councel Board;*   210
A greater *Fop*, in business at Fourscore,
Fonder of serious *Toyes*, affected more,
Than the gay glitt'ring *Fool*, at Twenty proves,
With all his noise, his tawdrey *Cloths*, and *Loves*.

    But a meek humble *Man*, of modest sense,
Who Preaching peace, does practice continence;
Whose pious life's a proof he does believe,
Misterious truths, which no *Man* can conceive.
If upon *Earth* there dwell such *God-like Men*,
I'le here recant my *Paradox* to them.   220
Adore those *Shrines* of *Virtue*, *Homage* pay,
And with the *Rabble World*, their *Laws* obey.
If such there are, yet grant me this at least,
Man differs more from *Man*, than *Man* from *Beast*.

THE MAIM'D DEBAUCHEE

The meter of this poem appears to be a parody of that
in Sir William Davenant's romantic epic *Gondibert*
(1651).

    The text is that of the Huntington Library copy of
the 1680 edition, with variants from the 1691 edition.

AS some brave *Admiral*, in former *War*,
Depriv'd of force, but prest with° courage still;
Two *Rival-Fleets*, appearing from a far,
Crawles to the top of an adjacent *Hill*.

From whence (with thoughts full of concern) he views
The wise, and daring Conduct of the fight,
And each bold Action, to his *Mind* renews,
His present glory, and his past delight.

From his fierce *Eyes*, flashes of rage he throws,
As from black *Clouds*, when *Lightning* breaks away, 10

Transported, thinks himself amidst his *Foes*,
And absent, yet enjoys the Bloody *Day*.

So when my *Days* of impotence approach,
And I'm by *Pox*,° and *Wines* unlucky chance,
Drov'n from the pleasing *Billows* of debauch,
On the dull *Shore* of lazy temperance.

My pains at last some respite shall afford,
Whilst I behold the *Battails* you maintain,
When *Fleets* of *Glasses* Sail about the *Board*,°
From whose Broad-sides *Volleys* of *Wit* shall rain. 20

Nor shall the sight of *Honourable Scars*,
Which my too forward *Valour* did procure,
Frighten new Listed° *Souldiers* from the *Warrs*,
Past joys have more than paid what I endure.

Shou'd some brave *Youth* (worth being drunk) prove
    nice,°
And from his fair Inviter meanly shrink,
'Twou'd please the *Ghost* of my departed *Vice*,
If at my *Councel*, He repent and drink.

Or shou'd some cold complexion'd *Sot* forbid,
With his dull *Morals*, our *Nights* brisk *Alarmes*,° 30
I'll fire his Blood by telling what I did,
When I was strong, and able to bear Armes.

I'll tell of *Whores* Attacqu'd, their Lords at home,
Bawds Quarters beaten up, and *Fortress* won,
Windows demolisht, *Watches*° overcome,
And handsome ills, by my contrivance done.

Nor shall our *Love-fits Cloris*° be forgot,
When each the well-look'd *Link-Boy*,° strove t' enjoy
And the best Kiss, was the deciding *Lot*,
Whether the *Boy* us'd you, or I the *Boy*. 40

With Tales like these, I will such heat inspire,
As to important mischief shall incline.
I'll make them long some *Antient Church* to fire,
And fear no lewdness the're called to by *Wine*.

Thus *States-man-like*, I'll sawcily° impose,
And safe from danger *Valiantly* advise,
Shelter'd in impotence, urge you to blows,
And being good for nothing else, be wise.

---

209. **B——**: bishop. THE MAIM'D DEBAUCHEE. 2. **prest with**: impelled by.

14. **Pox**: syphilis. 19. **Board**: table. 23. **Listed**: enlisted.
25. **nice**: shy, reluctant. 30. **Alarmes**: calls to arms. 35.
Watches: guards. 37. **Cloris**: a stock female name in pastoral poetry. 38. **Link-Boy**: a boy who carried a torch ("link") to light the way of passengers along the street. 45. **sawcily**: insolently.

UPON NOTHING

☙❧

The text is that of the Huntington Library copy of the 1680 edition, but with the improved punctuation of the 1691 edition.

☙❧

NOthing thou *Elder Brother* ev'n to shade,°
Thou hadst a Being, e're the *World* was made,
And (well fixt) art alone of ending not afraid.

E're time, and place, were, time, and place, were not
When *Primitive Nothing*, something strait begot,
Then all proceeded from the great united—What?

Something, the gen'ral *Attribute* of all,
Sever'd from thee, it's sole *Original*,
Into thy boundless self, must undistinguish'd fall.

Yet something did thy mighty Pow'r command,   10
And from thy fruitful emptinesses hand,
Snatcht *Men*, *Beasts*, *Birds*, *Fire*, *Aire*, and *Land*.

Matter, the wicked'st *Off spring* of thy *Race*,
By forme assisted, flew from thy embrace,
And *Rebel Light* obscur'd thy reverend dusky Face.

With form, and *Matter*, time, and place, did join,
Body, thy *Foe*, with thee did *Leagues* combine,°
To spoil thy peaceful *Realm*, and ruin all thy *Line*.

But *Turn-Coat Time* assists the *Foe* in vain,
And brib'd by thee, assists thy short-liv'd *Reign*,   20
And to thy hungry *Womb* drives back thy *Slaves* again.

Tho *Mysteries* are barr'd from *Laich°-Eyes*,
And the Divine alone, with *Warrant* pryes,
Into thy *Bosome*, where thy truth in private lyes.

Yet this of thee, the wise may freely say,
Thou from the *Virtuous* nothing tak'st away,
And to be part of thee, the *Wicked* wisely pray.

Great *Negative*, how vainly wou'd the *Wise*,
Enquire, define, distinguish, teach, devise,
Didst thou not stand to point° their dull *Philosophies*. 30

Is, or is not, the Two great ends of *Fate*,
And true, or false, the Subject of debate,
That perfect, or destroy, the vast designs of *Fate*.

When they have rack'd the *Politicians* Breast,
Within thy *Bosome*, most securely rest,
And when reduc'd to thee, are least unsafe, & best.

But *Nothing*, why does something still permit,
That Sacred *Monarchs* shou'd at *Councel* sit,
With *Persons* highly thought, at best, for *Nothing* fit.

Whil'st weighty *Something* modestly abstains,   40
From *Princes Coffers*, and from *States-Mens* Brains,
And *Nothing* there, like stately *Nothing* reigns.

Nothing who dwellst with *Fools*, in grave disguise,
For whom they Reverend shapes, & forms devise.
Lawn-sleeves, & *Furrs*, & *Gowns*,° when they like thee
     look wise.

French Truth, *Dutch* Prowess, *British* Policy,
Hybernian Learning, *Scotch* Civility,
Spaniards dispatch, *Danes* Wit,° are mainly seen in
     thee.

The great *Mans* gratitude to his best *Friend*,
Kings Promises, *Whores* Vows, towards thee they
     bend,   50
Flow swiftly into thee, and in thee ever end.

UPON HIS DRINKING A BOWL

☙❧

This poem is said to be an imitation of Anacreon's eighteenth ode, but if so, it is so free as to defy comparison.

The text is that of the Huntington Library copy of the 1680 edition, with a variant in punctuation from the 1691 edition.

☙❧

UPON NOTHING. **1. shade:** darkness. **17. Leagues combine:** confederate. **22. Laich:** (laic) lay, laymen's. **30. point:** give point, or meaning, to.

45. Lawn-sleeves . . . Gowns: garments emblematic of high office; lawn sleeves represent bishops. **46–48. French . . . Wit:** All these national "virtues" are of course ironically meant to convey actual vices or deficiencies.

V*Ulcan* contrive me such a Cup,
    As *Nestor* us'd of old;°
Shew all thy skill to trim it up,
    Damask° it round with *Gold*.

Make it so large, that fill'd with *Sack*,
    Up to the swelling brim;
Vast Toasts, on the delicious *Lake*,
    Like *Ships* at *Sea* may swim.

Engrave not *Battail* on his Cheek,
    With *War* I've nought to do;   10
I'm none of those that took *Mastrich*,°
    Nor *Yarmouth Leager*° knew.

Let it no name of *Planets* tell,
    Fixt *Stars*, or *Constellations;*
For I am no Sir *Sydrophell*,°
    Nor none of his *Relations*.

But carve thereon a spreading *Vine*,
    Then add Two lovely *Boys;*
Their Limbs in Amorous folds intwine,
    The *Type* of future joys.   20

Cupid, and *Bacchus*, my *Saints* are,
    May drink, and Love, still reign,
With *Wine*, I wash away my cares,
    And then to *Cunt* again.

LOVE AND LIFE, A SONG

The text is that of the Huntington Library copy of the
1680 edition.

ALl my past Life is mine no more,
    The flying hours are gone;
Like transitory *Dreams* giv'n o're,°
    Whose *Images* are kept in store,
        By *Memory* alone.

UPON HIS DRINKING A BOWL. **1–2. a Cup . . . old:** See
Odyssey, III. 40 ff. **4. Damask:** weave with figured designs.
11. Mastrich: Maastricht, capital of the province of Limburg,
in Holland, was taken by the French, with English support,
in the summer of 1673. **12. Yarmouth Leager:** the camp
at Yarmouth, where troops under Prince Rupert waited in
July, 1673, for an invasion of Holland that never took place.
15. Sir Sydrophell: Sidrophel is the astrologer satirized in
Samuel Butler's *Hudibras* (1663–78). LOVE AND LIFE, A SONG.
3. giv'n o're: ended.

What ever is to come, is not,
    How can it then be mine?
The present *Moment*'s all my *Lot*,
And that as fast as it is got,
    Phillis, is wholly thine.   10

Then talk not of inconstancy,
    False *Hearts*, and broken *Vows*,
If I by *Miracle* can be,
This live-long *Minute*° true to thee,
    'Tis all that *Heav'n* allows.

SONG

The text is that of the Huntington Library copy of the
1680 edition, with variants in punctuation from the
1691 edition.

P*Hillis*, be gentler I advice,
    Make up for time mispent,
When *Beauty* on its *Death-Bed* lyes,
    'Tis high time to repent.

Such is the *Malice* of your *Fate*,
    That makes you old so soon,
Your pleasure ever comes too late,
    How early e're begun.

Think what a wretched thing is she,
    Whose *Stars* contrive in spight,   10
The *Morning* of her love shou'd be,
    Her fading *Beauties Night*.

Then if to make your ruin more,
    You'll peevishly be coy,
Dye with the scandal of a *Whore*,
    And never know the joy.

14. This . . . Minute: the whole length of this minute.

Samuel Pepys

1633–1703

Samuel Pepys was born February 23, 1633, in London, the son of a tailor who had prospered since coming to the city some twenty years before. He was educated at St. Paul's School in London and at Cambridge; he took his degree in 1654, afterward entering the employ of his cousin Edward Montagu, who was later rewarded for the considerable part he played in King Charles's restoration by being created Earl of Sandwich. Before becoming Montagu's factotum, Pepys met and married Elizabeth le Marchant de St. Michel, the daughter of a French Huguenot who had emigrated to England with Queen Henrietta Marie and had subsequently lost his place at court. She was only fifteen years old at the time and, though poor, pretty.

During the fifteen years of their marriage, Elizabeth was an object of pride and affection but also a source of irritation for her husband. He was sorely tried by her temper, her untidiness, her addiction to fashion, her unteachableness and indifference to what pleased him, and her inveterate quarreling with servants. She must have suffered her fair share though as the wife of a jealous and compulsively philandering husband. The *Diary* unfolds a procession of women in Pepys's life—servants, tradeswomen, actresses—who appear variously as objects of impromptu caresses, planned seductions, and more or less steady liaisons. Yet Pepys's fondness for Elizabeth appears to have been unimpaired by his countless infidelities.

Pepys worked as hard as he played, rising in the course of time from Clerk of the Acts on the Navy Board to Secretary of the Admiralty. The Navy Board had the responsibility of maintenance and supply, not military operations, and in the position of Clerk of the Acts, procured for him by Montagu, Pepys, with "no previous experience," had to master a most complicated operation. So well did he succeed that when the Navy Office was accused by Parliament of mishandling a million pounds, no one could make the defense but Pepys. The result was exoneration for the Navy Office and no little personal celebrity. Pepys's success however transcends this episode; his real achievement was to reduce the cost of naval maintenance and supply to a degree unknown before. While he did nothing to reform—and something to perpetuate—the standard operating procedure of accepting gifts from contractors, he at least forced their prices down to reasonable levels before spending the King's money, which was always in appallingly short supply. Dubbed by the Duke of Albemarle "the right hand of the Navy," Pepys well earned the accolade.

Though a conscientious public servant, Pepys was not one to neglect private pastimes. The *Diary* records hundreds of plays attended, many of them more than once. He was a voracious and wide-ranging reader. He knew a good deal about music, played several instruments, and composed a number of songs. Although not a scientist, he was elected to the Royal Society in 1665 and even served as its president from 1684 to 1686. He was especially taken with the society's medical experiments, such as blood transfusions, and with their new mechanical gadgets and scientific instruments. He himself owned and used microscopes and telescopes, though he characteristically shuddered at their cost.

Pepys's failing eyesight caused him to stop writing his diary (on May 31, 1669) and to seek a diversion from his work by touring Holland and France. The trip produced lasting benefits for Pepys, but in France his wife contracted a fatal illness. She died in London in November, 1669.

In 1673, when the Duke of York was forced under the Test Act to resign as Lord High Admiral, Pepys was appointed Secretary of the Admiralty and was put in virtual charge of that office by the King. Pepys's administrative skills were now applied on a wider front than management and supply, and with equal success. David Hume wrote in his *History of England* (1754–62) that "the administration of the admiralty under Pepys is still regarded as a model for order and economy." But his career was interrupted by the machinations surrounding the Popish Plot; in 1679 he was imprisoned on a fabricated charge of complicity and was not released until a year later, when the Attorney General dropped the proceedings. Until 1684, when Charles II restored Pepys to his office, the Navy was governed (badly, Pepys said) by a commission. Pepys continued in the office when the Duke of York, a long-time admirer of his talents, acceded to the throne in 1685. But James II's flight to France in 1688 signaled the end of Pepys's career in the Navy. He performed his official duties for the last time in February, 1689.

After his resignation, Pepys lived in retirement in his house in York Buildings, which he retained despite the efforts of the commissioners of the Navy to force his removal. In 1690 he was disturbed by a few days' imprisonment in the Gate House, Westminster, for "suspicion of being affected to King James." Otherwise, as he wrote, "I have nothing to do but read, walk, and prepare for all the chances attending this obliging world." He kept up his interest in the Royal Society, and his correspondence with Newton in his final years is the only written record of the great scientist's consideration of mathematical probability. He also kept up his literary interests, and in his copy of *Fables Ancient and Modern* there was later discovered a letter from "Mr. Dryden to S. P. upon his translating at his request Chaucer's Prologue to his Parson's Tale."

Pepys, who as the *Diary* shows was as attentive to his own accounts as to the Navy's, was able to maintain a high standard of living in retirement. Nevertheless, in 1701 he moved into the mansion of his former clerk and old friend, Will Hewer, in Clapham, where he died on May 26, 1703. Informed of the death of the man who "had ben for neere 40 years, so my particular Friend," John Evelyn, another famous diarist, wrote in his own diary: "This [day] dyed Mr. Sam: Pepys, a very worthy, Industrious, & curious person, none in England exceeding him in the Knowledge of the Navy . . . [He] was universaly beloved, Hospitable, Generous, Learned in many things, skill'd in Musick, a very great Cherisher of Learned men, of whom he had the Conversation."

The most nearly complete and standard edition is H. B. Wheatley's *The Diary of Samuel Pepys* (10 vols., 1893–99; often reprinted), which will be superseded by the forthcoming edition under the editorship of Robert Latham and William Matthews. The standard biography is Arthur Bryant's *Samuel Pepys* (3 vols., 1933–39); J. R. Tanner's *Mr. Pepys: An Introduction to the Diary Together with a Sketch of His Later Life* (1925) and J. H. Wilson's popular biography, *The Private Life of Mr. Pepys* (1959), may also be consulted. *The Letters of Samuel Pepys and His Family Circle* have been edited by H. T. Heath (1955). There are, finally, a number of specialized studies of Pepys, among them M. H. Nicolson's *Pepys' Diary and the New Science* (1965).

FROM

[THE DIARY OF SAMUEL PEPYS]

Although neither can be credited with inventing the diary as a literary form, Pepys and John Evelyn together are generally regarded as having brought it to fruition. The essence of diary writing involves a paradox: the writer presumes that recording the minute particularities of daily life is an important act, whereas relatively few of the happenings recorded can in and of themselves be considered momentous. What counts for most is the reflection of the mind of the diarist, and the less confined his field, the more appealing will the reflection be. As Johnson remarked to Boswell, "There is nothing, Sir, too little for so little a creature as man." "The great thing to be recorded," he advised him later, "is the state of your own mind; and you should write down every thing that you remember, for you cannot judge at first what is good or bad; and write immediately while the impression is fresh, for it will not be the same a week afterwards." If Pepys's *Diary* strikes us as much less introspective than Boswell's *Journal*, it is still, and inevitably, as much the mirror of a mind and the image of a distinctive personality as it is a portrait of an age.

In writing his diary Pepys utilized the system of shorthand described in Thomas Shelton's *Tachygraphy* (1638) along with a cipher apparently of his own invention. Interspersed with the shorthand are words in longhand, usually proper names, and a sprinkling of French, Spanish, Latin, and Greek and of English dialect words to render the bawdier passages. If facility was the prime motive behind his use of shorthand, the other devices clearly point to a concern for secrecy as well.

The diary, with the rest of Pepys's library, was inherited by his nephew John Jackson, who was to have the use of it during his lifetime. At his death in 1724 the library went, as Pepys had desired, to Magdalene College, Cambridge. There the diary remained untranslated until, prompted by the appearance of Evelyn's *Diary* in 1818, someone examined it and turned it over to John Smith, an undergraduate of St. John's College, for transcription. The result was a much abridged and thoroughly expurgated edition brought out under the superintendence of Richard Neville, Lord Braybrooke, in 1825 as *Memoirs of Samuel Pepys*. Responding to criticism of his editorial zeal, Lord Braybrooke restored some passages in a subsequent edition, and between 1875 and 1879 Mynors Bright brought out a new edition in six volumes containing about four-fifths of the original diary.

The first appearance of the *Diary* in 1825 excited considerable interest. In *The Edinburgh Review* in 1826 the critic Francis Jeffrey judged the author "possessed of the most indiscriminating, insatiable, and miscellaneous curiosity, that ever prompted the researches, or supplied the pen, of a daily chronicler." And in the same year Sir Walter Scott, commenting on the value of the *Diary* as an historical document, observed: "If quitting the broad path of history we seek for minute information concerning ancient manners and customs, the progress of arts and sciences, and the various branches of antiquity, we have never seen a mine so rich as the volumes before us."

The text is that of H. B. Wheatley's edition (10 vols., 1893–99).

March 26, 1660

This day it is two years since it pleased God that I was cut of the stone at Mrs. Turner's in Salisbury Court.[1] And did resolve while I live to keep it a

THE DIARY OF SAMUEL PEPYS. **I. I . . . Court:** Pepys had been successfully operated on for a kidney stone that had passed into his bladder. The operation was performed at the house of his cousin Jane Turner because his father's house, also in Salisbury Court, was too small.

festival, as I did the last year at my house, and for ever to have Mrs. Turner and her company with me. But now it pleases God that I am where I am[2] and so prevented to do it openly; only within my soul I can and do rejoice, and bless God, being at this time blessed be his holy name, in as good health as ever I was in my life. This morning I rose early, and went about making of an establishment[3] of the whole Fleet, and a list of all the ships, with the number of men and guns. About an hour after that, we had a meeting of the principal commanders and seamen, to proportion out the number of these things. After that to dinner, there being very many commanders on board. All the afternoon very many orders were made, till I was very weary. At night Mr. Sheply[4] and W. Howe[5] came and brought some bottles of wine and some things to eat in my cabin, where we were very merry, remembering the day of being cut for the stone. Captain Cuttance[6] came afterwards and sat drinking a bottle of wine till eleven, a kindness he do not usually do the greatest officer in the ship. After that to bed.

May 2, 1660

In the morning at a breakfast of radishes at the Purser's[7] cabin. After that to writing till dinner. At which time comes Dunne[8] from London, with letters that tell us the welcome news of the Parliament's votes yesterday, which will be remembered for the happiest May-day that hath been many a year to England.[9] The King's letter was read in the House, wherein he submits himself and all things to them, as to an Act of Oblivion[10] to all, unless they shall please to

except any, as to the confirming of the sales of the King's and Church lands,[11] if they see good. The House upon reading the letter, ordered £50,000 to be forthwith provided to send to His Majesty for his present supply; and a committee chosen to return an answer of thanks to His Majesty for his gracious letter; and that the letter be kept among the records of the Parliament; and in all this not so much as one No. So that Luke Robinson[12] himself stood up and made a recantation for what he done, and promises to be a loyal subject to his Prince for the time to come. The City of London have put out a Declaration, wherein they do disclaim their owing[13] any other government but that of a King, Lords, and Commons. Thanks was given by the House to Sir John Greenville,[14] one of the bedchamber to the King, who brought the letter, and they continued bare[15] all the time it was reading. Upon notice made from the Lords to the Commons, of their desire that the Commons would join with them in their vote for King, Lords, and Commons; the Commons did concur and voted that all books whatever that are out against the Government of King, Lords, and Commons, should be brought into the House and burned. Great joy all yesterday at London, and at night more bonfires than ever, and ringing of bells, and drinking of the King's health upon their knees in the streets, which methinks is a little too much. But every body seems to be very joyfull in the business, insomuch that our sea-commanders now begin to say so too, which a week ago they would not do. And our seamen, as many as had money or credit for drink, did do nothing else this evening. This day came Mr. North (Sir Dudley North's son)[16] on board, to spend a little time here, which my Lord[17] was a little troubled at, but he seems to be a fine gentleman, and at night did play his part[18] exceeding well at first

---

2. **where I am:** Pepys was now aboard the *Swiftsure* in his new capacity as secretary to Sir Edward Montagu (1625–72), Commander of the British Fleet. 3. **establishment:** accounting. 4. **Mr. Sheply:** Edward Shepley, steward of Montagu's country estate at Hinchingbroke, in Huntingdonshire. 5. **W. Howe:** William Howe, also in Montagu's service. 6. **Captain Cuttance:** Roger Cuttance, captain of Montagu's flagship, the *Naseby*. In 1665 he was knighted and promoted to Captain of the Fleet. 7. **the Purser:** The purser on board the *Naseby* was a Mr. Pierce. 8. **Dunne:** Thomas Dunne, or Donne, appears in the *Diary* most commonly as a messenger, but it is not clear whether he was a servant or a seaman. 9. **the happiest . . . England:** On May 1 the Declaration of Breda—Charles II's statement of policy in anticipation of his restoration—was carried to Parliament, read, and inserted in the record. 10. **Act of Oblivion:** A Bill of General Pardon, Indemnity, and Oblivion was introduced into the House of Commons on May 9. After much sharp debate it was at length sent to the Lords on July 11 and received Charles's assent on August 29.

11. **the sales . . . lands:** Many Crown and Church lands had been annexed by the Commonwealth government, and, although the King is here represented as willing to guarantee these transfers, they finally reverted to their former owners. 12. **Luke Robinson:** (1611–69), Member of Parliament for Scarborough and a loyal adherent of the Rump Parliament. 13. **owing:** owing allegiance to. 14. **Sir . . . Greenville:** Sir John Grenville (1628–1701). He was created Earl of Bath in 1661. 15. **bare:** bareheaded. 16. **Mr. . . . son:** Sir Dudley North (d. 1677), Fourth Baron North, had two sons: Charles (d. 1690), who succeeded to the baronage, and Francis (1637–85), who became a prominent lawyer and judge. Sir Dudley's wife, Anne, was Montagu's cousin. 17. **my Lord:** a courtesy title for Montagu; he did not become a peer until July 12. 18. **his part:** his musical part.

sight. After musique I went up to the Captain's Cabin with him and Lieutenant Ferrers,[19] who came hither to-day from London to bring this news to my Lord, and after a bottle of wine we all to bed.

May 23, 1660[20]

The Doctor[21] and I waked very merry, only my eye was very red and ill in the morning from yesterday's hurt.[22] In the morning came infinity of people on board from the King to go along with him. My Lord, Mr. Crew,[23] and others, go on shore to meet the King as he comes off from shore, where Sir R. Stayner[24] bringing His Majesty into the boat, I hear that His Majesty did with a great deal of affection kiss my Lord upon his first meeting. The King, with the two Dukes[25] and Queen of Bohemia,[26] Princess Royal,[27] and Prince of Orange,[28] came on board, where I in their coming in kissed the King's, Queen's, and Princess's hands, having done the other before. Infinite shooting off of the guns, and that in a disorder on purpose, which was better than if it had been otherwise. All day nothing but Lords and persons of honour on board, that we were exceeding full. Dined in a great deal of state, the Royall company by themselves in the coach,[29] which was a blessed sight to see. I dined with Dr. Clerke,[30] Dr. Quarterman,[31] and Mr. Darcy[32] in my cabin.

19. **Lieutenant Ferrers:** William Ferrers, Montagu's master of horse. 20. **May 23, 1660:** On May 14 the fleet had anchored off The Hague (at Scheveling), attending the arrival on board of Charles II and his court. 21. **The Doctor:** Dr. Timothy Clarke (d. 1672), one of the original Fellows of the Royal Society and subsequently physician to the King. He was sharing a cabin with Pepys. 22. **yesterday's hurt:** Pepys had, for the first time in his life, fired a salute with one of the ship's cannon, "but holding my head too much over the gun, I had almost spoiled my right eye" (*Diary*, May 22, 1660). 23. **Mr. Crew:** John Crew (1598–1679), a wealthy Presbyterian, was Montagu's father-in-law. He was created Baron Crew of Stene in 1661. 24. **Sir R. Stayner:** Sir Richard Stayner (d. 1662), Rear Admiral and captain of the *Swiftsure*. 25. **the two Dukes:** Charles's brothers: James, Duke of York (later James II), and Henry, Duke of Gloucester, who died of smallpox four months later. 26. **Queen of Bohemia:** Elizabeth (1596–1662), sister of Charles I. 27. **Princess Royal:** Charles II's sister, Mary, Princess of Orange. She too died of smallpox, on December 24 of this year. 28. **Prince of Orange:** the ten-year-old son of the widowed Princess of Orange; afterward William III. 29. **the coach:** a cabin near the stern of a man-of-war, usually occupied by the captain. 30. **Dr. Clerke:** Dr. Timothy Clarke. 31. **Dr. Quarterman:** William Quartermaine (1618–67), one of the King's physicians. 32. **Mr. Darcy:** Marmaduke Darcy (1614–87), Charles's companion during his exile.

This morning Mr. Lucy[33] came on board, to whom and his company of the King's Guard in another ship my Lord did give three dozen of bottles of wine. He made friends between Mr. Pierce and me. After dinner the King and Duke altered the name of some of the ships,[34] viz. the Nazeby into Charles; the Richard, James; the Speaker, Mary; the Dunbar (which was not in company with us), the Henry; Winsly, Happy Return; Wakefield, Richmond; Lambert, the Henrietta; Cheriton, the Speedwell; Bradford, the Success. That done, the Queen, Princess Royal, and Prince of Orange, took leave of the King, and the Duke of York went on board the London, and the Duke of Gloucester, the Swiftsure. Which done, we weighed anchor, and with a fresh gale and most happy weather we set sail for England. All the afternoon the King walked here and there, up and down (quite contrary to what I thought him to have been), very active and stirring. Upon the quarterdeck he fell into discourse of his escape from Worcester,[35] where it made me ready to weep to hear the stories that he told of his difficulties that he had passed through, as his travelling four days and three nights on foot, every step up to his knees in dirt, with nothing but a green coat and a pair of country breeches on, and a pair of country shoes that made him so sore all over his feet, that he could scarce stir. Yet he was forced to run away from a miller and other company, that took them for rogues. His sitting at table at one place, where the master of the house, that had not seen him in eight years, did know him, but kept it private; when at the same table there was one that had been of his own regiment at Worcester, could not know him, but made him drink the King's health, and said that the King was at least four fingers higher than he. At another place he was by some servants of the house made to drink, that they might know him not to be a Roundhead,[36] which they swore he was. In another place at his inn, the master of the house, as the King was standing with his hands upon the back of a chair

33. **Mr. Lucy:** not identified. 34. **altered . . . ships:** Many of the ships' names were displeasing to Royalist ears. Naseby, for instance, was the scene of a major defeat of the Royalists in 1645. 35. **his . . . Worcester:** Charles had been recognized in Scotland in 1650, and the following year he began his invasion southward. On September 3, 1651, his forces were completely routed at the Battle of Worcester. Thirty years after making his escape from the disaster, he dictated an account of it to Pepys. 36. **a Roundhead:** a Puritan or adherent of the Parliamentary cause, so called from their custom of wearing their hair close cut.

by the fire-side, kneeled down and kissed his hand, privately, saying, that he would not ask him who he was, but bid God bless him whither he was going.[37] Then the difficulty of getting a boat to get into France, where he was fain to plot with the master thereof to keep his design from the four men and a boy (which was all his ship's company), and so got to Fécamp in France.[38] At Rouen he looked so poorly, that the people went into the rooms before he went away to see whether he had not stole something or other. In the evening I went up to my Lord to write letters for England, which we sent away with word of our coming, by Mr. Edw. Pickering.[39] The King supped alone in the coach; after that I got a dish, and we four supped in my cabin, as at noon. About bed-time my Lord Bartlett[40] (who I had offered my service to before) sent for me to get him a bed, who with much ado I did get to bed to my Lord Middlesex[41] in the great cabin below, but I was cruelly troubled before I could dispose of him, and quit myself of him. So to my cabin again, where the company still was, and were talking more of the King's difficulties; as how he was fain to eat a piece of bread and cheese out of a poor boy's pocket; how, at a Catholique house, he was fain to lie in the priest's hole[42] a good while in the house for his privacy. After that our company broke up, and the Doctor and I to bed. We have all the Lords Commissioners[43] on board us, and many others. Under sail all night, and most glorious weather.

May 25, 1660

By the morning we were come close to the land, and every body made ready to get on shore. The King and the two Dukes did eat their breakfast before they went, and there being set some ship's diet before them, only to show them the manner of the ship's diet, they eat of nothing else but pease[44] and pork, and boiled beef. I had Mr. Darcy in my cabin and Dr. Clerke, who eat[45] with me, told me how the King had given £50 to Mr. Sheply for my Lord's servants, and £500 among the officers and common men of the ship. I spoke with the Duke of York about business,[46] who called me Pepys by name, and upon my desire did promise me his future favour.[47] Great expectation of the King's making some Knights, but there was none. About noon (though the brigantine[48] that Beale[49] made was there ready to carry him) yet he would go in my Lord's barge[50] with the two Dukes. Our captain steered, and my Lord went along bare with him. I went, and Mr. Mansell,[51] and one of the King's foot-men, with a dog that the King loved, (which [dirted] the boat, which made us laugh, and methink that a King and all that belong to him are but just as others are), in a boat by ourselves, and so got on shore when the King did, who was received by General Monk[52] with all imaginable love and respect at his entrance upon the land of Dover. Infinite the crowd of people and the horsemen, citizens, and noblemen of all sorts. The Mayor of the town came and gave him his white staff, the badge of his place, which the King did give him again.[53] The Mayor also presented him from the town a very rich Bible, which he took and said it was the thing beloved above all things in the world. A canopy was provided for him to stand under, which he did, and talked awhile with General Monk and others, and so into a stately coach there set for him, and so away through the town towards Canterbury, without making any stay at Dover. The shouting and joy expressed by all is past imagination. Seeing that my Lord did not stir out of his barge, I got into a boat,

---

37. In . . . going: This incident occurred on October 6 at the George Inn, located in Mere. **38. Fécamp in France:** where Charles landed on October 16 after six weeks of flight from Worcester. **39. Mr. Edw. Pickering:** the younger brother of Sir Gilbert Pickering (1613–68), who was Montagu's brother-in-law and an influential republican. **40. Lord Bartlett:** a mistake for Lord Berkeley. George Berkeley (1628–96), First Earl of Berkeley, had been sent with five other peers to congratulate the King officially in the name of the House of Lords. **41. Lord Middlesex:** Charles Sackville (1638–1706), Earl of Middlesex and Earl of Dorset. Sharing of beds was common in seventeenth-century England. **42. the priest's hole:** As Catholicism was pro-scribed, Catholic families often maintained secure hiding-places for priests. **43. Lords Commissioners:** who formed the Navy Board, which in Pepys's time was wholly con-cerned with the supply and maintenance of the Navy at sea. It was composed of seven members: a treasurer, a comptroller, a surveyor, a secretary or Clerk of the Acts (Pepys's office), and three extra commissioners.

44. pease: peas or, more likely, pea soup (pease porridge). **45. eat:** ate. **46. I . . . business:** The Duke of York was made Lord High Admiral on June 6, 1660. Pepys was told of the appointment on May 16. **47. future favour:** The Duke of York was of course heir to the throne, since Charles II had no legitimate offspring. **48. brigantine:** a small vessel used chiefly for landings. **49. Beale:** not identified. **50. barge:** the second boat of a man-of-war, used for landing the chief officers. **51. Mr. Mansell:** a "Reformado" (a vol-unteer serving without a commission, but with the rank of an officer) of the *Charles*. **52. General Monk:** George Monk, or Monck (1608–70), military and naval leader and one of the architects of the Restoration. He was created Duke of Albemarle in July. **53. again:** back.

and so into his barge, whither Mr. John Crew stepped, and spoke a word or two to my Lord, and so returned, we back to the ship, and going did see a man almost drowned that fell out of his boat into the sea, but with much ado was got out. My Lord almost transported with joy that he had done all this without any the least blur or obstruction in the world, that could give an offence to any, and with the great honour he thought it would be to him. Being overtook by the brigantine, my Lord and we went out of our barge into it, and so went on board with Sir. W. Batten,[54] and the Vice and Rear-Admirals.[55] At night my Lord supped and Mr. Thomas Crew[56] with Captain Stoakes,[57] I supped with the Captain, who told me what the King had given us. My Lord returned late and at his coming did give me order to cause the marke to be gilded, and a Crown and C.R.[58] to be made at the head of the coach table, where the King to-day with his own hand did mark his height, which accordingly I caused the painter to do, and is now done as is to be seen.

October 13, 1660

To my Lord's in the morning, where I met with Captain Cuttance, but my Lord not being up I went out to Charing Cross, to see Major-general Harrison[59] hanged, drawn, and quartered; which was done there, he looking as cheerful as any man could do in that condition. He was presently cut down, and his head and heart shown to the people, at which there was great shouts of joy. It is said, that he said that he was sure to come shortly at the right hand of Christ to judge them that now had judged him; and that his wife do expect his coming again. Thus it was my chance to see the King beheaded[60] at White Hall, and to see the first blood shed in revenge for the blood of the King at Charing Cross. From thence to my Lord's and took Captain Cuttance and Mr. Sheply to the Sun Tavern, and did give them some oysters. After that

I went by water home, where I was angry with my wife for her things lying about, and in my passion kicked the little fine basket, which I bought her in Holland, and broke it, which troubled me after I had done it. Within all the afternoon setting up shelves in my study. At night to bed.

November 3, 1661

(Lord's day). This day I stirred not out, but took physique,[61] and it did work very well, and all the day as I was at leisure I did read in Fuller's Holy Warr,[62] which I have of late bought, and did try to make a song in the praise of a liberall genius (as I take my own to be) to all studies and pleasures, but it not proving to my mind I did reject it and so proceeded not in it. At night my wife and I had a good supper by ourselves of a pullet hashed, which pleased me much to see my condition[63] come to allow ourselves a dish like that, and so at night to bed.

August 17, 1662

(Lord's day). Up very early, this being the last Sunday that the Presbyterians are to preach, unless they read the new Common Prayer and renounce the Covenant,[64] and so I had a mind to hear Dr. Bates's[65] farewell sermon, and walked thither, calling first at my brother's,[66] where I found that he is come home after being a week abroad with Dr. Pepys,[67] nobody knows where, nor I but by chance, that he was gone, which troubles me. So I called only at the door, but did not ask for him, but went to Madam Turner's to know whether she went to church, and to tell her that I

54. **Sir W. Batten:** Sir William Batten (d. 1667), Admiral and Surveyor to the Navy. **55. the Vice . . . Rear-Admirals:** John Lawson (d. 1665), captain of the *London*, and Sir Richard Stayner, of the *Swiftsure*. **56. Mr. . . . Crew:** (1623–97), son of John Crew. **57. Captain Stoakes:** Captain Jonathan Stoakes, or Stokes (d. 1664), captain of the *Royal James*. **58. C.R.:** Carolus Rex (King Charles). **59. Major-general Harrison:** Thomas Harrison (1606–60) had brought Charles I to Whitehall for trial and had signed the warrant for his execution. **60. see . . . beheaded:** on January 30, 1649, when Pepys was fifteen years old.

61. **physique:** generally, medicine; here, probably a cathartic. **62. Fuller's . . . Warr:** Thomas Fuller's *History of the Holy War*, first published in Cambridge in 1639. Pepys was a friend of the eminent antiquarian, who died on August 16 of this year. **63. condition:** financial condition. **64. the last . . . Covenant:** The Solemn League and Covenant (1643) had provided for the establishment of a Presbyterian state church. The Act of Uniformity, designed to remove Nonconformists from positions of influence, took effect on August 24, 1662; it kept from preferment about two thousand Presbyterian and Independent ministers who refused to accept completely the Book of Common Prayer. **65. Dr. Bates:** William Bates (1625–99), minister of St. Dunstan's, known as the "silver-tongued" divine. He was named Doctor of Divinity by royal mandate in 1661. **66. my brother's:** Thomas Pepys (1634–64), one year younger than Samuel, had taken over his father's tailor shop in Salisbury Court in August, 1661. **67. Dr. Pepys:** Thomas Pepys, M.D. (1621–65), Pepys's second cousin, the son of Pepys's great-uncle, Talbot Pepys.

would dine with her; and so walked to St. Dunstan's, where, it not being seven o'clock yet, the doors were not open; and so I went and walked an hour in the Temple-garden, reading my vows,[68] which it is a great content to me to see how I am a changed man in all respects for the better, since I took them, which the God of Heaven continue to me, and make me thankful for. At eight o'clock I went, and crowded in at a back door among others, the church being half-full almost before any doors were open publicly; which is the first time that I have done so these many years since I used to go with my father and mother, and so got into the gallery, beside the pulpit, and heard very well. His text was, "Now the God of Peace—;" the last Hebrews, and the 20th verse: he making a very good sermon, and very little reflections in it to any thing of the times. Besides the sermon, I was very well pleased with the sight of a fine lady that I have often seen walk in Graye's Inn Walks,[69] and it was my chance to meet her again at the door going out, and very pretty and sprightly she is, and I believe the same that my wife and I some years since did meet at Temple Bar gate and have sometimes spoke of. So to Madam Turner's, and dined with her. She had heard Parson Herring[70] take his leave; tho' he, by reading so much of the Common Prayer as he did, hath cast himself out of the good opinion of both sides.[71] After dinner to St. Dunstan's again; and the church quite crowded before I came, which was just at one o'clock; but I got into the gallery again, but stood in a crowd and did exceedingly sweat all the time. He pursued his text again very well; and only at the conclusion told us, after this manner: "I do believe that many of you do expect that I should say something to you in reference to the time, this being the last time that possibly I may appear here. You know it

is not my manner to speak any thing in the pulpit that is extraneous to my text and business; yet this I shall say, that it is not my opinion, fashion, or humour that keeps me from complying with what is required of us; but something which, after much prayer, discourse, and study yet remains unsatisfied, and commands me herein. Wherefore, if it is my unhappiness not to receive such an illuminacion as should direct me to do otherwise, I know no reason why men should not pardon me in this world, and am confident that God will pardon me for it in the next." And so he concluded. Parson Herring read a psalm and chapters before sermon; and one was the chapter in the Acts, where the story of Ananias and Sapphira is.[72] And after he had done, says he, "This is just the case of England at present. God he bids us to preach, and men bid us not to preach; and if we do, we are to be imprisoned and further punished. All that I can say to it is, that I beg your prayers, and the prayers of all good Christians, for us." This is all the exposition he made of the chapter in these very words, and no more. I was much pleased with Dr. Bates's manner of bringing in the Lord's Prayer after his own; thus, "In whose comprehensive words we sum up all our imperfect desires; saying, 'Our Father,'" &c. Church being done and it raining I took a hackney coach and so home, being all in a sweat and fearful of getting cold. To my study at my office, and thither came Mr. Moore[73] to me and walked till it was quite dark. Then I wrote a letter to my Lord Privy Seale as from my Lord for Mr.——— to be sworn directly by deputy to my Lord, he denying to swear him as deputy together with me.[74] So that I am now clear of it, and the profit is now come to be so little that I am not displeased at my getting off so well. He being gone I to my study and read, and so to eat a bit of bread and cheese and so to bed. I hear most of the Presbyters took their leaves to-day, and that the City is much dissatisfied with it. I pray God keep peace among us, and make the Bishops careful of bringing in good men in their rooms,[75] or else all will fly a-pieces; for bad ones will not [go] down with the City.

68. reading my vows: Pepys regularly made resolutions for a better and more productive life; the previous New Year's Eve he had taken "a solemn oath about abstaining from plays and wine." 69. Graye's Inn Walks: Gray's Inn was one of the four Inns of Court, the legal institutions of London. "The chief ornament belonging to this Inn, is its spacious garden, the benefit of which is enjoyed by the public, every body decently dressed being allowed the recreation of walking in it every day. This garden consists of gravel walks, between vistas of very lofty trees, of grass plots, agreeable slopes, and a long terras with a portico at each end" (London and Its Environs Described [1761]). 70. Parson Herring: John Herring (1610–88), minister of St. Bride's. Pepys had earlier called one of his efforts "a lazy poor sermon" (Diary, January 22, 1660). 71. of . . . sides: Presbyterians and Independents.

72. where . . . is: Acts 5:1–10. 73. Mr. Moore: Henry Moore, a lawyer and apparently a member of John Crew's household. He and Pepys were both appointed Clerks of the Privy Seal in 1660. 74. as . . . me: In his office of Clerk of the Privy Seal Pepys had been acting as deputy to Montagu. He now appears to be trying to secure that post for his friend Moore. The Lord Privy Seal at this time was John, Second Baron Robartes (1606–85). 75. rooms: places.

September 27, 1662

Up betimes[76] and among my workmen, and with great pleasure see the posts in the entry taken down beyond expectation, so that now the boy's room being laid into the entry do make my coming in very handsome, which was the only fault remaining almost in my house.[77] We sat all the morning, and in the afternoon I got many jobbs done to my mind, and my wife's chamber put into a good readiness against her coming,[78] which she did at night, for Will did, by my leave to go, meet her upon the road, and at night did bring me word she was come to my brother's, by my order. So I made myself ready and put things at home in order, and so went thither to her. Being come, I found her and her maid and dogg very well, and herself grown a little fatter than she was. I was very well pleased to see her, and after supper to bed, and had her company with great content and much mutual love, only I do perceive that there has been falling out between my mother and she, and a little between my father and she; but I hope all is well again, and I perceive she likes Brampton House and seat[79] better than ever I did myself, and tells me how my Lord hath drawn a plot of some alteracions to be made there, and hath brought it up, which I saw and like well. I perceive my Lord and Lady have been very kind to her, and Captn. Ferrers so kind that I perceive I have some jealousy of him, but I know what is the Captain's manner of carriage, and therefore it is nothing to me. She tells me of a Court[80] like to be in a little time, which troubles me, for I would not willingly go out of town.

October 24, 1662

After with great pleasure lying a great while talking and sporting in bed with my wife (for we have been for some years now, and at present more and more, a very happy couple, blessed be God), I got up and

to my office, and having done there some business, I by water, and then walked to Deptford[81] to discourse with Mr. Cowly and Davis[82] about my late conceptions about keeping books of the distinct works done in the yards, against which I find no objection but their ignorance and unwillingness to do anything of pains[83] and what is out of their ordinary dull road, but I like it well, and will proceed in it. So home and dined there with my wife upon a most excellent dish of tripes of my own directing, covered with mustard, as I have heretofore seen them done at my Lord Crew's,[84] of which I made a very great meal, and sent for a glass of wine for myself, and so to see Sir W. Pen,[85] who continues bed-rid in great pain, and hence to the Treasury to Sir J. Minnes[86] paying off of tickets,[87] and at night home, and in my study (after seeing Sir. W. Batten, who also continues ill) I fell to draw out my conceptions about books for the clerk that cheques in the yard to keep according to the distinct works there, which pleases me very well, and I am confident it will be of great use. At 9 at night home, and to supper, and to bed. This noon came to see me and sat with me a little after dinner Mr. Pierce, the chyrurgeon,[88] who tells me how ill things go at Court: that the King do show no countenance[89] to any that belong to the Queen;[90] nor, above all, to such English as she brought over with her, or hath here since, for fear they should tell her how he carries himself to Mrs. Palmer;[91] insomuch that though he has a promise, and is sure of being made her chyrurgeon, he is at a loss what to do in it, whether to take it or no, since the King's mind

76. **betimes:** early. 77. **the only . . . house:** Pepys was much preoccupied with improvements in his house in Seething Lane. The "boy's room" was the room of his servant Will Wayneman. 78. **her coming:** Pepys had sent his wife to stay with his parents in the country while the house was being remodeled. 79. **Brampton . . . seat:** Pepys had inherited his uncle Robert Pepys's house and estate at Brampton, in Herefordshire, and his parents had retired there in 1661. Montagu's estate at Hinchingbroke was about a mile from Brampton. 80. **a Court:** a judicial court. The reference here is to a session of the court in the country. Since his uncle's death Pepys had been involved in several lawsuits concerning his inheritance.

81. **Deptford:** The main navy yard was at Deptford, about four miles by land from London Bridge. 82. **Mr. . . . Davis:** Clerk of the Cheque and Storekeeper at Deptford respectively. 83. **of pains:** difficult. 84. **my . . . Crew:** John Crew. 85. **Sir W. Pen:** Sir William Penn (1621–70), father of the founder of Pennsylvania and one of the three extra commissioners of the Navy Board. 86. **Sir J. Minnes:** Sir John Minnes (1599–1671), Comptroller of the Navy. 87. **paying . . . tickets:** The Navy in its financial embarrassment resorted to payment in scrip, negotiable only in London. The evils of the ticket system reached a climax in the autumn of 1665, when the Navy Office was obliged to suspend payment. 88. **Mr. . . . chyrurgeon:** Dr. James Pierce, surgeon to the Duke of York. 89. **countenance:** approval, favor. 90. **the Queen:** Charles married Catherine of Braganza (1638–1705), daughter of King John IV of Portugal, on May 21 of this year. 91. **Mrs. Palmer:** Barbara Villiers (1641–1709), Lady Castlemaine, a famous beauty who became the King's mistress soon after the Restoration. Her husband, Roger Palmer (1634–1705), was created Earl of Castlemaine in 1661.

is so altered in favour to[92] all her dependants, whom she is fain to let go back into Portugall (though she brought them from their friends against their wills with promise of preferment), without doing any thing for them. But he tells me that her own physician did tell him within these three days that the Queen do know how the King orders things, and how he carries himself to my Lady Castlemaine and others, as well as any body; but though she hath spirit enough, yet seeing that she do no good by taking notice of it, for the present she forbears it in policy; of which I am very glad. But I pray God keep us in peace; for this, with other things, do give great discontent to all people.

December 25, 1662

(Christmas Day). Up pretty early, leaving my wife not well in bed, and with my boy walked, it being a most brave[93] cold and dry frosty morning, and had a pleasant walk to White Hall,[94] where I intended to have received the Communion with the family,[95] but I came a little too late. So I walked up into the house and spent my time looking over pictures, particularly the ships in King Henry the VIIIth's Voyage to Bullen;[96] marking the great difference between their build then and now. By and by down to the chappell again where Bishopp Morley[97] preached upon the song of the Angels, "Glory to God on high, on earth peace, and good will towards men." Methought he made but a poor sermon, but long, and reprehending the mistaken jollity of the Court for the true joy that shall and ought to be on these days, he particularized concerning their excess in plays and gaming, saying that he whose office it is to keep the gamesters in order and within bounds, serves but for a second rather in a duell, meaning the groom-porter.[98] Upon which it was worth observing how far they are come from taking the reprehensions of a bishopp seriously, that they all laugh in the chappell when he reflected on their

ill actions and courses. He did much press us to joy in these publique days of joy, and to hospitality. But one that stood by whispered in my ear that the Bishopp himself do not spend one groat to the poor himself. The sermon done, a good anthem followed, with vialls,[99] and then the King came down to receive the Sacrament. But I staid not, but calling my boy from my Lord's lodgings, and giving Sarah[100] some good advice, by my Lord's order, to be sober and look after the house, I walked home again with great pleasure and there dined by my wife's bed-side with great content, having a mess of brave plum-porridge[101] and a roasted pullet for dinner, and I sent for a mince-pie abroad, my wife not being well to make any herself yet. After dinner sat talking a good while with her, her [pain] being become less, and then to see Sir W. Pen a little, and so to my office, practising arith-metique[102] alone and making an end of last night's book with great content till eleven at night, and so home to supper and to bed.

December 26, 1662

Up, my wife to the making of Christmas pies all day, being now pretty well again, and I abroad to several places about some businesses, among others bought a bake-pan in Newgate Market, and sent it home, it cost me 16s. So to Dr. Williams,[103] but he is out of town, then to the Wardrobe.[104] Hither come Mr. Battersby;[105] and we falling into a discourse of a new book of drollery in verse called Hudebras,[106] I would needs go find it out, and met with it at the Temple: cost me 2s. 6d. But when I came to read it, it is so silly an abuse of the Presbyter Knight going to

99. vialls: viols, forerunners of the violin and viola; also, the Italian viola da gamba. 100. Sarah: Montagu's maid. 101. plum-porridge: the traditional Christmas plum pudding. 102. practising arithmetique: In his zeal to correct any corruption in the financial affairs of the Navy, Pepys set out to learn mathematics. It was not at all uncommon at this time for a man of Pepys's station to be ignorant of even simple arithmetic. 103. Dr. Williams: a friend of Pepys's who frequently treated his wife. 104. the Wardrobe: Among his many duties Montagu was Master of the Wardrobe, in charge of furniture and ceremonial dress for the royal family and government officials. As was commonly the case, a house went with the office and was known simply as The Wardrobe. 105. Mr. Battersby: a friend from whom Pepys had earlier borrowed one hundred pounds. 106. a new . . . Hudebras: The first edition of Samuel Butler's *Hudibras* (1663–78) is dated 1663, but books were often published in advance of the imprint date.

92. in . . . to: with respect to the favor he shows to. 93. brave: fine, splendid. 94. White Hall: Whitehall, in Westminster, the palace of English monarchs from Henry VIII to William III. 95. Communion . . . family: The royal family had its own chapel at Whitehall. 96. Bullen: Boulogne, which was taken by Henry VIII in 1554. The pictures are now at Hampton Court. 97. Bishopp Morley: George Morley, D.D. (1597–1684), Bishop of Winchester. Morley preached the coronation sermon in 1661. 98. groom-porter: an officer of the royal household in charge of gaming in the court.

the warrs that I am ashamed of it; and by and by meeting at Mr. Townsend's[107] at dinner, I sold it to him for 18*d*. Here we dined with many tradesmen that belong to the Wardrobe, but I was weary soon of their company, and broke up dinner as soon as I could, and away, with the greatest reluctancy and dispute (two or three times my reason stopping my sense[108] and I would go back again) within myself, to the Duke's house and saw "The Villaine,"[109] which I ought not to do without my wife, but that my time is now out that I did undertake it for.[110] But, Lord! to consider how my natural desire is to pleasure, which God be praised that he has given me the power by my late oaths to curb so well as I have done, and will do again after two or three plays more. Here I was better pleased with the play than I was at first, understanding the design better than I did. Here I saw Gosnell[111] and her sister at a distance, and could have found it in my heart to have accosted them, but thought not prudent. But I watched their going out and found that they came, she, her sister and another woman, alone, without any man, and did go over the fields a foot. I find that I have an inclination to have her come again, though it is most against my interest either of profit or content of mind, other than for their singing. Home on foot, in my way calling at Mr. Rawlinson's[112] and drinking only a cup of ale there. He tells me my uncle[113] has ended his purchase, which cost him £4,500, and how my uncle do express his trouble that he has with his wife's relations, but I understand his great intentions are for the Wights that hang upon him[114] and by whose advice this estate is bought. Thence home, and found my wife busy among her pies, but angry

for some saucy words that her mayde Jane[115] has given her, which I will not allow of, and therefore will give her warning to be gone. As also we are both displeased for some slight[116] words that Sarah,[117] now at Sir W. Pen's, hath spoke of us, but it is no matter. We shall endeavour to joyne the lion's skin to the fox's tail.[118] So to my office alone a while, and then home to my study and supper and bed. Being also vexed at my boy for his staying playing abroad when he is sent of errands, so that I have sent him to-night to see whether their country carrier[119] be in town or no, for I am resolved to keep him no more.

October 20, 1663

Up and to the office, where we sat; and at noon Sir G. Carteret,[120] Sir J. Minnes, and I to dinner to my Lord Mayor's,[121] being invited, where was the Farmers of the Customes,[122] my Lord Chancellor's[123] three sons, and other great and much company, and a very great noble dinner, as this Mayor is good for nothing else. No extraordinary discourse of anything, every man being intent upon his dinner, and myself willing to have drunk some wine to have warmed my belly, but I did for my oath's sake willingly refrain it, but am so well pleased and satisfied afterwards thereby, for it do keep me always in so good a frame of mind that I hope I shall not ever leave this practice. Thence home, and took my wife by coach to White Hall, and she set down at my Lord's lodgings, I to a Committee of Tangier,[124] and thence with her homeward, calling at several places by the way. Among others at Paul's Churchyard,[125] and while I was in Kirton's

107. Mr. Townsend: Montagu's deputy at the Wardrobe. **108. sense:** feelings, inclination. **109. The Villaine:** a tragedy by Thomas Porter (1636–80), which Pepys had seen when it was first acted on October 20 by the Duke's Company in Lincoln's Inn Fields, one of the two new theatrical companies established after the Restoration; the other was the King's Company at the Theatre Royal, Bridges Street, Drury Lane. **110. my . . . for:** The period covered by Pepys's vow had expired. **111. Gosnell:** Winifred Gosnell, an actress with the Duke's Company, had been briefly engaged as companion to Mrs. Pepys. Pepys was delighted with her, being especially taken by her singing. **112. Mr. Rawlinson:** Daniel Rawlinson kept the Mitre Tavern in Fenchurch Street. **113. my uncle:** apparently William Wight, the half brother of Pepys's father. A well-to-do fishmonger, he once proposed to Elizabeth Pepys that they have a child "between them," offering her five hundred pounds and promising to make the child his heir (*Diary*, May 11, 1664). **114. hang . . . him:** are his dependents.

115. mayde Jane: Jane Wayneman, sister to Pepys's boy, Will. **116. slight:** slighting. **117. Sarah:** not Montagu's servant, but a maid whom Pepys had recently discharged from his household. **118. joyne . . . tail:** join force and cunning. **119. their . . . carrier:** the carrier, or public conveyance, that would take Will and his sister back to the country. **120. Sir. G. Carteret:** Sir George Carteret (d. 1680), Treasurer of the Navy. **121. Lord Mayor:** Sir John Robinson (1625–80). **122. Farmers . . . Customes:** agents who paid a fixed sum for the right to collect duties in a given area. **123. Lord Chancellor:** Edward Hyde (1609–74), First Earl of Clarendon, was Lord Chancellor from the Restoration until 1667 (see n. 355). **124. Committee of Tangier:** In August, 1662, Pepys had been appointed to the commission set up to govern England's new possession, Tangier, acquired as part of Queen Catherine's dowry. **125. Paul's Churchyard:** "the area round St. Paul's cathedral, surrounded on the north and west chiefly by booksellers and toy-shops, and on the south side by the makers of chairs, screens and cabinets" (*London and Its Environs Described* [1761]).

shop,[126] a fellow came to offer kindness or force[127] to my wife in the coach, but she refusing, he went away, after the coachman had struck him, and he the coachman. So I being called, went thither, and the fellow coming out again of a shop, I did give him a good cuff or two on the chops, and seeing him not oppose me, I did give him another; at last found him drunk, of which I was glad, and so left him, and home, and so to my office awhile, and so home to supper and to bed. This evening, at my Lord's lodgings, Mrs. Sarah talking with my wife and I how the Queen do, and how the King tends her being so ill. She tells us that the Queen's sickness is the spotted fever;[128] that she was as full of the spots as a leopard: which is very strange that it should be no more known; but perhaps it is not so. And that the King do seem to take it much to heart, for that he hath wept before her; but, for all that, that he hath not missed one night since she was sick, of supping with my Lady Castlemaine; which I believe is true, for she[129] says that her husband hath dressed[130] the suppers every night; and I confess I saw him myself coming through the street dressing of a great supper to-night, which Sarah says is also for the King and her; which is a very strange thing.

November 3, 1663

Up and to the office, where busy all the morning, and at noon to the Coffee-house, and there heard a long and most passionate discourse between two doctors of physique, of which one was Dr. Allen,[131] whom I knew at Cambridge, and a couple of apothecarys; these maintaining chymistry against their Galenicall physique;[132] and the truth is, one of the apothecarys whom they charged[133] most, did speak very prettily, that is, his language and sense good, though perhaps he might not be so knowing a physician as to offer to contest with them. At last they

came to some cooler terms, and broke up. I home, and there Mr. Moore coming by my appointment dined with me, and after dinner came Mr. Goldsborough, and we discoursed about the business of his mother,[134] but could come to no agreement in it but parted dissatisfied. By and by comes Chapman, the periwigg-maker, and upon my liking it, without more ado I went up, and there he cut off my haire, which went a little to my heart at present to part with it; but, it being over, and my periwigg on, I paid him £3 for it; and away went he with my owne haire to make up another of, and I by and by, after I had caused all my mayds to look upon it; and they conclude it do become me; though Jane was mightily troubled for my parting of my own haire, and so was Besse, I went abroad to the Coffee-house, and coming back went to Sir W. Pen and there sat with him and Captain Cocke[135] till late at night, Cocke talking of some of the Roman history very well, he having a good memory. Sir W. Pen observed mightily,[136] and discoursed much upon my cutting off my haire, as he do of every thing that concerns me, but it is over, and so I perceive after a day or two it will be no great matter.

November 18, 1663

Up, and after being ready, and done a little business at the office, I and Mr. Hater[137] by water to Redriffe, and so walked to Deptford, where I have not been a very great while, and there paid off the Milford[138] in very good order, and all respect showed me in the office as much as there used to be to any of the rest or the whole board. That done at noon I took Captain Terne,[139] and there coming in by chance Captain Berkeley,[140] him also to dinner with me to the Globe. Captain Berkeley, who was lately come from Algier,[141]

---

126. **Kirton's shop:** Joseph Kirton's bookshop. 127. **kindness or force:** the "choice" of submitting to him by her own will or by force. 128. **the spotted fever:** a name loosely applied to a variety of fevers accompanied by spots on the skin. 129. **she:** Sarah. 130. **dressed:** prepared, ordered. 131. **Dr. Allen:** Thomas Allen, M.D. (d. 1684). 132. **Galenicall physique:** The dispute between Galenic and chemical medicine began in the sixteenth century and involved the method of treatment of disease (conceived as bodily imbalances); the school of Galen advocated herbal or vegetable remedies, while the other school (derived from Paracelsus) advocated treatment by chemicals. The official position of the Royal College of Physicians was "Galenicall." 133. **charged:** attacked.

134. **the business . . . mother:** Mrs. Goldsborough owed money to Pepys's uncle Robert, and the matter had dragged on for more than two years. 135. **Captain Cocke:** Captain George Cocke (d. 1679), a captain in the army of Charles I and the owner of a large tannery. He was elected to the Royal Society in 1666. 136. **mightily:** at great length. 137. **Mr. Hater:** Thomas Hayter, Pepys's clerk, who succeeded him as Clerk of the Acts in 1674 and in 1679 as Secretary of the Admiralty. 138. **the Milford:** the ship. 139. **Captain Terne:** Henry Terne, captain of both the *Milford* and the *Portsmouth*, was killed in battle against the Dutch in June, 1666. 140. **Captain Berkeley:** William Berkeley (1639–66), captain of the *Bristol*. Knighted in 1664, he too was killed in battle against the Dutch in June, 1666. 141. **lately . . . Algier:** Algiers was a center of piracy, and, despite a treaty negotiated in 1662, the English navy was still obliged to patrol the Straits of Gibraltar.

did give us a good account of the place, and how the Basha[142] there do live like a prisoner, being at the mercy of the soldiers and officers, so that there is nothing but a great confusion there. After dinner came Sir W. Batten, and I left him to pay off another ship, and I walked home again reading of a little book of new poems of Cowley's[143] given me by his brother.[144] Abraham do lie, it seems, very sicke still, but like to recover.[145] At my office till late, and then came Mr. Hollyard[146] so full of discourse and Latin that I think he hath got a cupp,[147] but I do not know; but full of talke he is in defence of Calvin and Luther. He begun this night the fomentation[148] to my wife, and I hope it will do well with her. He gone, I to the office again a little, and so to bed. This morning I sent Will with my great letter of reproof to my Lord Sandwich,[149] who did give it into his owne hand. I pray God give a blessing to it, but confess I am afeard what the consequence may be to me of good or bad, which is according to the ingenuity[150] that he do receive it with. However, I am satisfied that it will do him good, and that he needs it.

MY LORD,

I do verily hope that neither the manner nor matter of this advice will be condemned by your Lordship, when for my defence in the first I shall alledge my double attempt, since your return from Hinchinbroke, of doing it personally, in both of which your Lordship's occasions, no doubtfulnesse[151] of mine, prevented me, and that being now fearful of a sudden summons to Portsmouth, for the discharge of some ships there, I judge it very unbecoming the duty which every bit of bread I eat tells me I owe to your Lordship to expose the safety of your honour to the uncertainty of my return. For the matter, my Lord, it is such as could I in any measure think safe to conceal from, or

likely to be discovered[152] to you by any other hand, I should not have dared so far to owne[153] what from my heart I believe is false, as to make myself but the relater of other's discourse; but, sir, your Lordship's honour being such as I ought to value it to be, and finding both in city and court that discourses pass to your prejudice, too generally for mine or any man's controllings but your Lordship's, I shall, my Lord, without the least greatening or lessening the matter, do my duty in laying it shortly before you.

People of all conditions, my Lord, raise matter of wonder from your Lordship's so little appearance at Court: some concluding thence their disfavour[154] thereby, to which purpose I have had questions asked me, and endeavouring to put off such insinuations by asserting the contrary, they have replied, that your Lordship's living so beneath your quality, out of the way, and declining of Court attendance, hath been more than once discoursed about the King. Others, my Lord, when the chief ministers of State, and those most active of the Council[155] have been reckoned up, wherein your Lordship never used to want[156] an eminent place, have said, touching your Lordship, that now your turn was served, and the King had given you a good estate, you left him to stand or fall as he would, and, particularly in that of the Navy, have enlarged upon your letting fall all service there.

Another sort, and those the most, insist upon the bad report of the house wherein your Lordship, now observed in perfect health again, continues to sojourne, and by name have charged one of the daughters for a common courtizan,[157] alledging both places and persons where and with whom she hath been too well known, and how much her wantonnesse occasions, though unjustly, scandal to your Lordship, and that as well to gratifying of some enemies as to the wounding of more friends I am not able to tell.

Lastly, my Lord, I find a general coldness in all persons towards your Lordship, such as, from my first dependance on you, I never yet knew, wherein I shall not offer to interpose any thoughts or advice of mine, well knowing your Lordship needs not any. But with a most faithful assurance that no person or papers under Heaven is privy to what I

---

142. **the Basha:** (or pasha) the governor. 143. **a little . . . Cowley's:** Abraham Cowley's (1618–67) *Verses Lately Written upon Several Occasions* (1663). 144. **his brother:** Thomas Cowley (c. 1615–69), Clerk of the Cheque at Deptford. 145. **like to recover:** He did. His illness was described by Thomas Sprat as "a dangerous lingering fever." 146. **Mr. Hollyard:** Thomas Hollier, surgeon of St. Thomas' Hospital, the doctor who had cut Pepys for the stone (see n. 1) and was now treating Mrs. Pepys for an abscess. 147. **hath . . . cupp:** is drunk. 148. **fomentation:** application of hot compresses. 149. **Lord Sandwich:** Montagu, who was created Earl of Sandwich on July 12, 1660. 150. **ingenuity:** candor, openness. 151. **doubtfulnesse:** uncertainty.

152. **discovered:** revealed. 153. **owne:** make known. 154. **their disfavour:** the disfavor of the court towards Montagu. 155. **the Council:** the Privy Council. 156. **want:** lack. 157. **charged . . . courtizan:** During the previous spring Montagu had taken lodgings in Chelsea with a Mrs. Becke to convalesce from a serious illness. Mrs. Becke had an attractive daughter, Betty.

here write,[158] besides myself and this, which I shall be careful to have put into your owne hands, I rest confident of your Lordship's just construction of my dutifull intents[159] herein, and in all humility take leave, may it please your Lordship, | Your Lordship's most obedient Servant,

S. P.

The foregoing letter was sealed up, and enclosed in this that follows:—

MY LORD,

If this finds your Lordship either not alone, or not at leisure, I beg the suspending your opening of the enclosed till you shall have both, the matter very well bearing such a delay, and in all humility remain, may it please your Lordship, | Your Lordship's most obedient Servant,

S. P.

November 17, 1663.

My servant hath my directions to put this into your Lordship's owne hand, but not to stay for any answer.

November 22, 1663

(Lord's day). Up pretty early, and having last night bespoke[160] a coach, which failed me this morning, I walked as far as the Temple, and there took coach, and to my Lord's lodgings, whom I found ready to go to chappell; but I coming, he begun, with a very serious countenance, to tell me that he had received my late letter, wherein first he took notice of my care of him and his honour, and did give me thanks for that part of it where I say that from my heart I believe the contrary of what I do there relate to be the discourse of others; but since I intended it not a reproach, but matter of information, and for him to make a judgment of it for his practice, it was necessary for me to tell him the persons of whom I have gathered the several particulars which I there insist on. I would have made excuses in it; but, seeing him so earnest in it, I found myself forced to it, and so did tell him Mr. Pierce, the chyrurgeon, in that of[161] his Lordship's living being discoursed of at Court; a mayd servant[162]

that I kept, that lived at Chelsy school; and also Mr. Pickering,[163] about the report touching the young woman; and also Mr. Hunt,[164] in Axe Yard, near whom she lodged. I told him the whole city do discourse concerning his neglect of business; and so I many times asserting my dutifull intention in all this, and he owning his accepting of it as such. That that[165] troubled me most in particular is, that he did there assert the civility of the people of the house, and the young gentlewoman, for whose reproach he was sorry. His saying that he was resolved how to live, and that though he was taking a house, meaning to live in another manner, yet it was not to please any people, or to stop report, but to please himself, though this I do believe he might say that he might not seem to me to be so much wrought upon by what I have writ; and lastly, and most of all, when I spoke of the tenderness that I have used in declaring this to him, there being nobody privy to it, he told me that I must give him leave to except one.[166] I told him that possibly somebody might know of some thoughts of mine, I having borrowed some intelligence in this matter from them, but nobody could say they knew of the thing itself what I writ. This, I confess, however, do trouble me, for that he seemed to speak it as a quick retort, and it must sure be Will. Howe,[167] who did not see anything of what I writ, though I told him indeed that I would write; but in this, I think, there is no great hurt. I find him, though he cannot but owne his opinion of my good intentions, and so he did again and again profess it, that he is troubled in his mind at it; and I confess, I think I may have done myself an injury for his good, which, were it to do again, and that I believed he would take it no better, I think I should sit quietly without taking any notice of it, for I doubt[168] there is no medium between his taking it very well or very ill. I could not forbear weeping before him at the latter end, which, since, I am ashamed of, though I cannot see what he can take it to proceed from but my tenderness and good will to him. After this discourse was ended, he began to talk very cheerfully of other things, and I walked with him to White Hall,

158. **with . . . write:** In the preceding entry of the *Diary* Pepys reports that he brought Henry Moore to his office "and there I read to him the letter I have wrote to send to my Lord." 159. **dutifull intents:** Pepys's concern for Montagu's reputation was not wholly selfless, as his own position depended upon that of "my Lord." Furthermore, Montagu owed him seven hundred pounds. 160. **bespoke:** ordered. 161. **in . . . of:** with respect to. 162. **a mayd servant:** Mary Ashwell, who had been in the Pepys household from March 12 to August 25 of this year.

163. **Mr. Pickering:** Edward Pickering. 164. **Mr. Hunt:** an official in the Excise who was Pepys's neighbor when he resided in Axe Yard. 165. **That that:** that which, what. 166. **except one:** In the next entry Pepys writes that he is "satisfied that the one person whom he said he would take leave to except is not Mr. Moore" (see n. 158). 167. **Will. Howe:** It was Howe who first informed Pepys of Montagu's carryings-on (*Diary*, August 10, 1663). 168. **doubt:** suspect.

and we discoursed of the pictures in the gallery, which, it may be, he might do out of policy, that the boy might not see any strangeness in him; but I rather think that his mind was somewhat eased, and hope that he will be to me as he was before. But, however, I doubt not when he sees that I follow my business, and become an honour to him, and not to be like to need him, or to be a burden to him, and rather able to serve him than to need him, and if he do continue to follow business, and so come to his right witts again, I do not doubt but he will then consider my faithfulnesse to him, and esteem me as he ought. At chappell I had room in the Privy Seale pew[169] with other gentlemen, and there heard Dr. Killigrew[170] preach, but my mind was so, I know not whether troubled, or only full of thoughts of what had passed between my Lord and me that I could not mind it, nor can at this hour remember three words. The anthem was good after sermon, being the fifty-first psalme, made for five voices by one of Captain Cooke's boys,[171] a pretty boy. And they say there are four or five of them that can do as much. And here I first perceived that the King is a little musicall, and kept good time with his hand all along the anthem. Up into the gallery after sermon and there I met Creed.[172] We saluted one another and spoke but not one word of what had passed yesterday between us, but told me he was forced to such a place to dinner and so we parted. Here I met Mr. Povy,[173] who tells me how Tangier had like to have been betrayed, and that one of the King's officers is come, to whom 8,000 pieces of eight were offered for his part. Hence I to the King's

Head ordinary,[174] and there dined, good and much company, and a good dinner: most of their discourse was about hunting, in a dialect[175] I understand very little. Thence by coach to our own church,[176] and there my mind being yet unsettled I could mind nothing, and after sermon home and there told my wife what had passed, and thence to my office, where doing business only to keep my mind employed till late, and so home to supper, to prayers, and to bed.

August 7, 1664

(Lord's day). Lay long caressing my wife and talking, she telling me sad stories of the ill, improvident, disquiett, and sluttish manner that my father and mother and Pall[177] live in the country, which troubles me mightily, and I must seek to remedy it. So up and ready, and my wife also, and then down and I showed my wife, to her great admiration and joy, Mr. Gauden's present[178] of plate,[179] the two flaggons, which indeed are so noble that I hardly can think that they are yet mine. So blessing God for it, we down to dinner mighty pleasant, and so up after dinner for a while, and I then to White Hall, walked thither, having at home met with a letter of Captain Cooke's, with which he had sent a boy[180] for me to see, whom he did intend to recommend to me. I therefore went and there met and spoke with him. He gives me great hopes of the boy, which pleases me, and at Chappell I there met Mr. Blagrave,[181] who gives a report of the boy, and he showed me him, and I spoke to him, and the boy seems a good willing boy to come to me, and I hope will do well. I am to speak to Mr. Townsend to hasten his clothes for him, and then he is to come. So I walked homeward and met with Mr. Spong,[182] and he with me as far as the Old Exchange talking of many ingenuous[183] things, musique, and at last of glasses,[184] and I find him still the same ingenuous man that ever he was, and do among other fine things tell

169. **the Privy . . . pew:** Clerks of the Privy Seal were entitled to a place in the chapel at Whitehall. Although Pepys had resigned his clerkship more than a year before, he evidently still claimed his seat. 170. **Dr. Killigrew:** Henry Killigrew, D.D. (1631–1700), author of sermons, Latin verse, and plays; father of Anne Killigrew, celebrated in Dryden's famous ode (see later in Part One). 171. **Captain . . . boys:** Henry Cooke (1616–72), a captain in the Royalist forces during the Civil War, was a musician and Master of the Children at the Chapel Royal. Among his boys were John Blow, Pelham Humfrey (the "pretty boy"), and Henry Purcell. 172. **Creed:** John Creed, Montagu's secretary and Deputy Treasurer to the Fleet. He had sent Pepys a gift in return for help with his accounts, but Pepys, thinking the gift an insufficient recognition of his efforts, had returned it. Creed married Elizabeth Pickering, daughter of Sir Gilbert Pickering and Montagu's sister Elizabeth, in 1668. 173. **Mr. Povy:** Thomas Povy (1633–85), First Treasurer of Tangier, an office in which Pepys succeeded him in 1665. Povy sponsored Pepys's election to the Royal Society the same year.

174. **ordinary:** restaurant. 175. **dialect:** lingo. 176. **our own church:** St. Olave's Church, Hart Street. 177. **Pall:** Pepys's sister Pauline, at this time twenty-four. 178. **Mr. . . . present:** Dennis Gauden was Victualer of the Navy. Pepys's administrative position with the Navy Board made him a particular object of the generosity of suppliers to the Navy. The following year Gauden's present was cash—five hundred pounds. 179. **plate:** gold or (as in this instance) silver utensils. 180. **a boy:** Tom Edwards. 181. **Mr. Blagrave:** Thomas Blagrave (d. 1688), a Clerk of the Cheque and a member of the King's private orchestra. He had previously given Pepys music lessons. 182. **Mr. Spong:** an instrument maker. 183. **ingenuous:** ingenious. 184. **glasses:** magnifying glasses.

microscope — new science — induction

me that by his microscope of his owne making he do discover that the wings of a moth is made just as the feathers of the wing of a bird, and that most plainly and certainly. While we were talking came by several poor creatures carried by, by constables, for being at a conventicle.[185] They go like lambs, without any resistance. I would to God they would either conform, or be more wise, and not be catched! Thence parted with him, mightily pleased with his company, and away homeward, calling at Dan Rawlinson, and supped there with my uncle Wight, and then home and eat again for form sake with her,[186] and then to prayers and to bed.

September 9, 1664

Up, and to put things in order against[187] dinner. I out and bought several things, among others, a dozen of silver salts;[188] home, and to the office, where some of us met a little, and then home, and at noon comes my company, namely, Anthony and Will Joyce and their wives,[189] my aunt James newly come out of Wales, and my cozen Sarah Gyles. Her husband did not come, and by her I did understand afterwards, that it was because he was not yet able to pay me the 40s. she had borrowed a year ago of me. I was as merry as I could, giving them a good dinner; but W. Joyce did so talk, that he made every body else dumb, but only laugh at him. I forgot there was Mr. Harman and his wife, my aunt, a very good harmlesse woman. All their talke is of her and my two she-cozen Joyces and Will's little boy Will (who was also here to-day), down to Brampton to my father's next week, which will be trouble and charge to them, but however my father and mother desire to see them, and so let them. They eyed mightily my great cupboard of plate, I this day putting my two flaggons upon my table; and indeed it is a fine sight, and better than ever I did hope to see of my owne. Mercer[190] dined with us at table, this being her first dinner in my house. After dinner left them and to White Hall, where a small Tangier Committee, and so back again home, and there my wife and Mercer and Tom[191] and I sat till eleven at night, singing and fiddling, and a great

joy it is to see me master of so much pleasure in my house, that it is and will be still, I hope, a constant pleasure to me to be at home. The girle plays pretty well upon the harpsicon,[192] but only ordinary tunes, but hath a good hand; sings a little, but hath a good voyce and eare. My boy, a brave boy, sings finely, and is the most pleasant boy at present, while his ignorant[193] boy's tricks last, that ever I saw. So to supper, and with great pleasure to bed.

November 15, 1664

That I might not be too fine for the business I intend this day, I did leave off my fine new cloth suit lined with plush and put on my poor black suit, and after office done (where much business, but little done), I to the 'Change,[194] and thence Bagwell's wife[195] with much ado followed me through Moorfields to a blind[196] alehouse, and there I did caress her and eat and drink and many hard looks and sooth[197] the poor wretch did give me, and I think verily was troubled at what I did, but at last after many protestings by degrees I did arrive at what I would, with great pleasure, and then in the evening, it raining, walked into town to where she knew where she was, and then I took coach and to White Hall to a Committee of Tangier, where, and every where else, I thank God, I find myself growing in repute; and so home, and late, very late, at business, nobody minding it but myself, and so home to bed, weary and full of thoughts. Businesses grow high[198] between the Dutch and us on every side.

December 31, 1664

At the office all the morning, and after dinner there again, dispatched first my letters, and then to my accounts, not of the month but of the whole yeare also, and was at it till past twelve at night, it being bitter cold; but yet I was well satisfied with my worke, and, above all, to find myself, by the great blessing of God, worth £1,349, by which, as[199] I have spent very

185. conventicle: secret meeting of Nonconformists. 186. her: Mrs. Pepys. 187. against: in preparation for. 188. salts: saltcellars. 189. Anthony . . . wives: Anthony and Will Joyce, who were brothers, had married Kate and Mary Fenner, cousins of Pepys's. 190. Mercer: Mary Mercer, a companion to Mrs. Pepys. 191. Tom: Tom Edwards, Pepys's new servant.

192. harpsicon: harpsichord. 193. ignorant: in the sense of unsophisticated. 194. the 'Change: the Royal Exchange, the financial center of London and the place to get the latest news. 195. Bagwell's wife: Mrs. Bagwell had visited Pepys's office the year before, seeking a better job for her husband, a carpenter in the navy yard at Deptford. The *Diary* records several meetings with Mrs. Bagwell, with which may be associated the several known advancements for her husband. 196. blind: out-of-the-way. 197. hard . . . sooth: both stern and soft looks. 198. Businesses . . . high: affairs grow tense. 199. as: just as.

largely, so I have laid up above £500 this yeare above what I was worth this day twelvemonth. The Lord make me for ever thankful to his holy name for it! Thence home to eat a little and so to bed. Soon as ever the clock struck one, I kissed my wife in the kitchen by the fireside, wishing her a merry new yeare, observing that I believe I was the first proper wisher of it this year, for I did it as soon as ever the clock struck one.

So ends the old yeare, I bless God, with great joy to me, not only from my having made so good a yeare of profit, as having spent £420 and laid up £540 and upwards;[200] but I bless God I never have been in so good plight[201] as to my health in so very cold weather as this is, nor indeed in any hot weather, these ten years, as I am at this day, and have been these four or five months. But I am at a great losse to know whether it be my hare's foote,[202] or taking every morning of a pill of turpentine,[203] or my having left off the wearing of a gowne.[204] My family is, my wife, in good health, and happy with her; her woman Mercer, a pretty, modest, quiett mayde; her chamber-mayde Besse, her cook mayde Jane,[205] the little girl Susan, and my boy, which I have had about half a yeare, Tom Edwards, which I took from the King's chappell, and a pretty and loving quiett family I have as any man in England. My credit[206] in the world and my office grows daily, and I am in good esteeme with everybody, I think. My troubles of my uncle's estate pretty well over; but it comes to be but of little profit to us, my father being much supported by my purse. But great vexations remain upon my father and me from my brother Tom's death and ill condition,[207] both to our disgrace and discontent, though no great reason for either. Publique matters are all in a hurry about a Dutch warr.[208] Our preparations great; our provocations against them great; and, after all our

presumption, we are now afeard as much of them, as we lately contemned them. Every thing else in the State quiett, blessed be God! My Lord Sandwich at sea with the fleete at Portsmouth; sending some about to cruise for taking of ships, which we have done to a great number. This Christmas I judged it fit to look over all my papers and books; and to tear all that I found either boyish or not to be worth keeping, or fit to be seen, if it should please God to take me away suddenly. Among others, I found these two or three notes, which I thought fit to keep—

AGE OF MY GRANDFATHER'S CHILDREN.

Thomas,   1595.
Mary, March 16, 1597.
Edith, October 11, 1599.
John (my Father), January 14, 1601.
My father and mother married at Newington, in Surry. Octob. 15, 1626.

THEYR CHILDREN'S AGES.

Mary, July 24, 1627.   *mort.*
Paulina, Sept. 18, 1628.   *mort.*
Esther, March 27, 1630.   *mort.*
John, January 10, 1631.   *mort.*
Samuel, Febr. 23, 1632.
Thomas, June 18, 1634.   *mort.*
Sarah, August 25, 1635.   *mort.*
Jacob, May 1, 1637.   *mort.*
Robert, Nov. 18, 1638.   *mort.*
Paulina, Oct. 18, 1640.
John, Novemb. 26, 1641.   *mort.*[209]
December 31, 1664.

CHARMES.

I. FOR STENCHING OF BLOOD.

Sanguis mane in te,
Sicut Christus fuit in se;
Sanguis mane in tuâ venâ
Sicut Christus in suâ poenâ;
Sanguis mane fixus,
Sicut Christus quando fuit crucifixus.[210]

---

200. **and upwards:** and then some. 201. **plight:** condition. 202. **hare's foote:** "which is my preservative against wind, for I never had a fit of the collique since I wore it" (*Diary*, March 26, 1665). 203. **pill of turpentine:** "which keeps me always loose" (*Diary*, March 26, 1665). 204. **gowne:** night-shirt. 205. **cook . . . Jane:** Jane Birch (not to be confused with other maids named Jane in the Pepys household). She arrived on June 27, 1664, and married Tom Edwards in 1669. 206. **credit:** reputation. 207. **my . . . condition:** Thomas Pepys had died on March 15, leaving many debts and an illegitimate child by his maidservant. 208. **Dutch warr:** The trade rivalry of the English and Dutch had led to military confrontations in West Africa, the Straits of Gibraltar, and in English ports. War was formally declared by England on March 4, 1665.

209. **John . . . mort:** John actually died in 1677; his death must have been recorded at a later date. The dates given here are Old Style. 210. **Sanguis mane in te . . . crucifixus:**

Blood remain in you,
As Christ's was in himself;
Blood remain in your vein,
As Christ in his pain;
Blood remain fixed,
As Christ when he was crucified.

2. A THORNE.

Jesus, that was of a Virgin born,
Was pricked both with nail and thorn;
It neither wealed,[211] nor belled,[212] rankled,[213] nor
     boned;[214]
In the name of Jesus no more shall this.

          Or, thus:—

Christ was of a Virgin born,
And he was pricked with a thorn;
And it did neither bell, nor swell;
And I trust in Jesus this never will.

3. A CRAMP.

Cramp be thou faintless,
As our Lady was sinless,
When she bare Jesus.

4. A BURNING.

There came three Angells out of the East;
The one brought fire, the other brought frost—
Out fire; in frost.
In the name of the Father, and Son, and Holy Ghost.
                                             AMEN.

June 10, 1665

   Lay long in bed, and then up and at the office all the
morning. At noon dined at home, and then to the
office busy all the afternoon. In the evening home to
supper; and there, to my great trouble, hear that the
plague[215] is come into the City (though it hath these
three or four weeks since its beginning been wholly
out of the City); but where should it begin but in my
good friend and neighbour's, Dr. Burnett, in Fan-
church Street:[216] which in both points troubles me
mightily. To the office to finish my letters and then
home to bed, being troubled at the sicknesse, and my
head filled also with other business enough, and
particularly how to put my things and estate in order,
in case it should please God to call me away, which
God dispose of to his glory!

August 22, 1665

   Up, and after much pleasant talke and being importuned by my wife and her two mayds, which are both
good wenches, for me to buy a necklace of pearle for
her, and I promising to give her one of £60 in two
years at furthest, and in less if she pleases me in her
painting,[217] I went away and walked to Greenwich,
in my way seeing a coffin with a dead body therein,
dead of the plague, lying in an open close[218] belonging
to Coome farme, which was carried out last night,
and the parish have not appointed any body to bury
it; but only set a watch there day and night, that nobody should go thither or come thence, which is a
most cruel thing: this disease making us more cruel
to one another than if we are doggs. So to the King's
House,[219] and there met my Lord Bruncker[220] and Sir
J. Minnes, and to our lodgings again that are appointed
for us,[221] which do please me better to day than last
night, and are set a doing.[222] Thence I to Deptford,
where by appointment I find Mr. Andrews[223] come,
and to the Globe, where we dined together and did
much business as to our Plymouth gentlemen;[224] and
after a good dinner and good discourse, he being a
very good man, I think verily, we parted and I to the
King's yard, walked up and down, and by and by out
at the back gate, and there saw the Bagwell's wife's
mother and daughter, and went to them, and went in
to the daughter's house with the mother, and *faciebam
le cose que ego tenebam a mind to con elle*,[225] and
drinking and talking, by and by away, and so walked
to Redriffe, troubled to go through the little lane,

---

211. wealed: pustuled. **212. belled:** swelled up. **213.
rankled:** festered. **214. boned:** threw bone splinters. **215.
the plague:** The London Plague of 1665 took nearly seventy
thousand lives out of a population of about a half million.
There were forty-three deaths in May, six hundred in June,
and thirty thousand in the peak month of September. **216. in
my . . . Street:** Alexander Burnett, Pepys's physician, died
of the plague on August 25. Fenchurch Street was only two
blocks from Seething Lane, where Pepys lived.

217. her painting: Elizabeth was presently at work on "a
picture of our Saviour," which Pepys thought "mighty finely
done" (*Diary*, September 27, 1665). **218. open close:** farm-
yard. **219. the King's House:** Built by Humphrey, Duke of
Gloucester, in 1433, it was partially restored by Charles II
and William III. In 1694 it was converted into a hospital for
aged and disabled sailors. **220. Lord Bruncker:** William,
Viscount Brouncker (1620–84), a physician and mathematician and first president of the Royal Society. He had been
appointed Extra Commissioner of the Navy Board on
December 7, 1664. **221. that . . . us:** By August the plague
had greatly accelerated (Pepys noted the closing of two out
of three shops), and the Navy Board had petitioned that their
meetings be held outside the city, at Greenwich. **222. set a
doing:** at work. **223. Mr. Andrews:** John Andrews, steward
to John Crew. **224. Plymouth gentlemen:** Pepys had contracted with a Mr. Yeabsly, a Plymouth merchant, for the
victualing of the garrison at Tangier. Andrews appears to
have been involved in the deal, by which Pepys realized
three hundred pounds. **225. faciebam . . . elle:** I did the
thing I had a mind to with her.

where the plague is, but did and took water[226] and home, where all well; but Mr. Andrews not coming to even accounts, as I expected, with relation to something of my profit, I was vexed that I could not settle to business, but home to my viall,[227] though in the evening he did come to my satisfaction. So after supper (he being gone first) I to settle my journall and to bed.

May 5, 1666

At the office all the morning. After dinner upon a letter from the fleete from Sir W. Coventry[228] I did do a great deale of worke for the sending away of the victuallers that are in the river, &c., too much to remember. Till 10 at night busy about letters and other necessary matter of the office. About 11 I home, it being a fine moonshine and so my wife and Mercer come into the garden, and, my business being done, we sang till about twelve at night, with mighty pleasure to ourselves and neighbours, by their casements opening, and so home to supper and to bed.

September 2, 1666

(Lord's day). Some of our mayds sitting up late last night to get things ready against our feast to-day, Jane called us up about three in the morning, to tell us of a great fire[229] they saw in the City. So I rose and slipped on my night-gowne, and went to her window, and thought it to be on the backside of Marke-lane[230] at the farthest; but, being unused to such fires as followed, I thought it far enough off; and so went to bed again and to sleep. About seven rose again to dress myself, and there looked out at the window, and saw the fire not so much as it was and further off. So to my closett to set things to rights after yesterday's cleaning. By and by Jane comes and tells me that she hears that above 300 houses have been burned down to-night by the fire we saw, and that it is now burning down

all Fish-street,[231] by London Bridge. So I made myself ready presently,[232] and walked to the Tower, and there got up upon one of the high places, Sir J. Robinson's[233] little son going up with me; and there I did see the houses at that end of the bridge all on fire, and an infinite great fire on this and the other side the end of the bridge; which, among other people, did trouble me for poor little Michell[234] and our Sarah on the bridge. So down, with my heart full of trouble, to the Lieutenant of the Tower, who tells me that it begun this morning in the King's baker's house in Pudding-lane, and that it hath burned St. Magnus's Church and most part of Fish-street already. So I down to the water-side, and there got a boat and through bridge, and there saw a lamentable fire. Poor Michell's house, as far as the Old Swan,[235] already burned that way, and the fire running further, that in a very little time it got as far as the Steele-yard, while I was there. Everybody endeavouring to remove their goods, and flinging into the river or bringing them into lighters[236] that lay off; poor people staying in their houses as long as till the very fire touched them, and then running into boats, or clambering from one pair of stairs by the water-side to another. And among other things, the poor pigeons, I perceive, were loth to leave their houses, but hovered about the windows and balconys till they were, some of them burned, their wings, and fell down. Having staid, and in an hour's time seen the fire rage every way, and nobody to my sight, endeavouring to quench it, but to remove their goods, and leave all to the fire, and having seen it get as far as the Steele-yard, and the wind mighty high and driving it into the City; and every thing, after so long a drought, proving combustible, even the very stones of churches, and among other things the poor steeple by which pretty Mrs.

226. **took water:** took the water route. 227. **viall:** viol.
228. **Sir W. Coventry:** Sir William Coventry (1628–86), secretary to the Duke of York (Lord High Admiral), was appointed Extra Commissioner of the Navy Board in 1662.
229. **a great fire:** The Great Fire of 1666 started in the shop and house of the King's baker, Farynor, in Pudding Lane. The wind carried it down Thames Street, where highly combustible materials (tallow, oil, spirits, hemp, etc.) were located, and the fire promptly grew out of control. 230. **Marke-lane:** Mark Lane ran parallel to Pepys's street, Seething Lane.

231. **Fish-street:** Fish Street ran onto London Bridge, at the foot of which stood the church of St. Magnus the Martyr, where the two lines of fire (from Pudding Lane and Thames Street) converged. The fire consumed the church and started across the bridge. 232. **presently:** at once. 233. **Sir J. Robinson:** Sir John Robinson was now Lieutenant of the Tower. 234. **little Michell:** William, the son of Mr. and Mrs. Michell, booksellers of Westminster Hall. Young Michell had recently married Betty Howlett, whom Pepys "from a girl did use to call my second wife, and mighty pretty she is" (*Diary*, January 9, 1664). The couple were established in a brandy shop in Old Swan Lane, near London Bridge. It was destroyed in the fire but soon rebuilt. 235. **the Old Swan:** a famous old tavern in Thames Street. 236. **lighters:** barges.

———[237] lives, and whereof my old schoolfellow Elborough is parson,[238] taken fire in the very top, and there burned till it fell down: I to White Hall (with a gentleman with me who desired to go off from the Tower, to see the fire, in my boat); to White Hall, and there up to the King's closett[239] in the Chappell, where people come about me, and I did give them an account dismayed them all, and word was carried in to the King. So I was called for, and did tell the King and Duke of Yorke what I saw, and that unless his Majesty did command houses to be pulled down nothing could stop the fire. They seemed much troubled, and the King commanded me to go to my Lord Mayor[240] from him, and command him to spare no houses, but to pull down before the fire every way. The Duke of York bid me tell him that if he would have any more soldiers he shall; and so did my Lord Arlington[241] afterwards, as a great secret. Here meeting with Captain Cocke, I in his coach, which he lent me, and Creed with me to Paul's,[242] and there walked along Watlingstreet, as well as I could, every creature coming away loaden with goods to save, and here and there sicke people carried away in beds. Extraordinary good goods carried in carts and on backs. At last met my Lord Mayor in Canningstreet,[243] like a man spent, with a handkercher about his neck. To the King's message he cried, like a fainting woman, "Lord! what can I do? I am spent: people will not obey me. I have been pulling down houses; but the fire overtakes us faster than we can do it." That he needed no more soldiers; and that, for himself, he must go and refresh himself, having been up all night. So he left me, and I him, and walked home, seeing people all almost distracted, and no manner of means used to quench the fire. The houses, too, so very thick thereabouts, and full of matter for burning, as pitch and tarr, in Thames-street; and warehouses of oyle, and wines, and brandy, and other things. Here I saw Mr. Isaake Houblon,[244] the handsome man, prettily dressed and

dirty, at his door at Dowgate, receiving some of his brothers' things, whose houses were on fire; and, as he says, have been removed twice already; and he doubts[245] (as it soon proved) that they must be in a little time removed from his house also, which was a sad consideration. And to see the churches all filling with goods by people who themselves should have been quietly there at this time. By this time it was about twelve o'clock; and so home, and there find my guests, which was Mr. Wood[246] and his wife Barbary Sheldon, and also Mr. Moone:[247] she mighty fine, and her husband, for aught I see, a likely[248] man. But Mr. Moone's design and mine, which was to look over my closett[249] and please him with the sight thereof, which he hath long desired, was wholly disappointed; for we were in great trouble and disturbance at this fire, not knowing what to think of it. However, we had an extraordinary good dinner, and as merry as at this time we could be. While at dinner Mrs. Batelier[250] come to enquire after Mr. Woolfe and Stanes[251] (who, it seems, are related to them), whose houses in Fish-street are all burned, and they in a sad condition. She would not stay in the fright. Soon as dined, I and Moone away, and walked through the City, the streets full of nothing but people and horses and carts loaden with goods, ready to run over one another, and removing goods from one burned house to another. They now removing out of Canningstreete (which received goods in the morning) into Lumbard-streete,[252] and further; and among others I now saw my little goldsmith, Stokes,[253] receiving some friend's goods, whose house itself was burned the day after. We parted at Paul's; he home, and I to Paul's Wharf, where I had appointed a boat to attend me, and took in Mr. Carcasse[254] and his brother, whom I met in the streete, and carried them below and above

237. Mrs. ———: Mrs. Horsely, whom Mrs. Pepys called "the handsomest woman in England" (*Diary*, May 29, 1666). Pepys was taken by her beauty and sought her out, unsuccessfully, at church on August 5. **238. my . . . parson:** Thomas Elborough, B.A. and M.A., Cambridge. The church, St. Lawrence Poultney, was destroyed in the fire and not rebuilt. **239. closett:** private chamber. **240. Lord Mayor:** Sir Thomas Bludworth (d. 1682), a vintner. His daughter married Judge Jeffreys, notorious English jurist. **241. Lord Arlington:** Henry Bennet (1618–85), Baron (later Earl of) Arlington, Secretary of State. **242. Paul's:** St. Paul's Cathedral. **243. Canningstreet:** Cannon Street. **244. Mr. . . . Houblon:** The Houblons were a family of merchants.

245. doubts: suspects. **246. Mr. Wood:** the son of William Wood, a wealthy timber merchant and mast-maker. **247. Mr. Moone:** secretary to Lord Bellasis, Governor of Tangier. **248. likely:** seemingly capable. **249. my closett:** Pepys had converted one of the spare rooms in his house to a study, where he kept his books. **250. Mrs. Batelier:** Mary Batelier, who with her husband kept a haberdasher's shop in the Royal Exchange. Pepys called her "one of the finest women I ever saw in my life" (*Diary*, July 26, 1665). **251. Mr. . . . Stanes:** Stanes was a glazier; Wolfe's occupation is not in evidence. **252. Lumbard-streete:** The fire did not spread to Lombard Street until well into the second day. **253. Stokes:** Humphrey Stokes, goldsmith at the Black Horse in Lombard Street. **254. Mr. Carcasse:** James Carcasse, a clerk in the Ticket Office, where seamen's pay tickets were redeemed. He was dismissed from his post at Pepys's insistence in 1667.

bridge to and again[255] to see the fire, which was now got further, both below and above, and no likelihood of stopping it. Met with the King and Duke of York in their barge, and with them to Queenhithe,[256] and called Sir Richard Browne[257] to them. Their order was only to pull down houses apace, and so below bridge at the water-side; but little was or could be done, the fire coming upon them so fast. Good hopes there was of stopping it at the Three Cranes above, and at Buttolph's Wharf below bridge, if care be used; but the wind carries it into the City, so as we know not by the water-side what it do there. River full of lighters and boats taking in goods, and good goods swimming in the water, and only I observed that hardly one lighter or boat in three that had the goods of a house in, but there was a pair of Virginalls[258] in it. Having seen as much as I could now, I away to White Hall by appointment, and there walked to St. James's Parke, and there met my wife and Creed and Wood and his wife, and walked to my boat; and there upon the water again, and to the fire up and down, it still encreasing, and the wind great. So near the fire as we could for smoke; and all over the Thames, with one's face in the wind, you were almost burned with a shower of fire-drops. This is very true; so as houses were burned by these drops and flakes of fire, three or four, nay, five or six houses, one from another. When we could endure no more upon the water, we to a little ale-house on the Bankside, over against the Three Cranes, and there staid till it was dark almost, and saw the fire grow; and, as it grew darker, appeared more and more, and in corners and upon steeples, and between churches and houses, as far as we could see up the hill of the City, in a most horrid malicious bloody flame, not like the fine flame of an ordinary fire. Barbary and her husband away before us. We staid till, it being darkish, we saw the fire as only one entire arch of fire from this to the other side the bridge, and in a bow up the hill for an arch of above a mile long: it made me weep to see it. The churches, houses, and all on fire and flaming at once; and a horrid noise the flames made, and the cracking of houses at their ruine. So home with a sad heart, and there find every body discoursing and lamenting the fire; and poor Tom Hater come with some few of his goods saved

out of his house, which is burned upon Fish-streete Hill. I invited him to lie at my house, and did receive his goods, but was deceived in his lying there,[259] the newes coming every moment of the growth of the fire; so as we were forced to begin to pack up our owne goods, and prepare for their removal; and did by moonshine (it being brave[260] dry, and moonshine, and warm weather) carry much of my goods into the garden, and Mr. Hater and I did remove my money and iron chests into my cellar, as thinking that the safest place. And got my bags of gold into my office, ready to carry away, and my chief papers of accounts also there, and my tallys into a box by themselves. So great was our fear, as[261] Sir W. Batten hath carts come out of the country to fetch away his goods this night. We did put Mr. Hater, poor man, to bed a little; but he got but very little rest, so much noise being in my house, taking down of goods.

September 5, 1666

I lay down in the office again upon W. Hewer's[262] quilt, being mighty weary, and sore in my feet with going till I was hardly able to stand. About two in the morning my wife calls me up and tells me of new cryes of fire, it being come to Barkeing Church, which is the bottom of our lane. I up, and finding it so, resolved presently to take her away, and did, and took my gold, which was about £2,350, W. Hewer, and Jane,[263] down by Proundy's boat to Woolwich; but, Lord! what a sad sight it was by moone-light to see the whole City almost on fire, that you might see it plain at Woolwich, as if you were by it. There, when I come, I find the gates[264] shut, but no guard kept at all, which troubled me, because of discourse now begun, that there is plot in it, and that the French had done it. I got the gates open, and to Mr. Shelden's,[265] where I locked up my gold, and charged my wife and W. Hewer never to leave the room without one of

255. to and again: to and fro. 256. Queenhithe: a harbor in Thames Street. 257. Sir . . . Browne: (d. 1690), a leader of the Presbyterian party, returned to the service of the King and was made a baronet and Lord Mayor at the Restoration. 258. a pair . . . Virginalls: a harpsichord.

259. deceived . . . there: ill-advised in inviting him (because of the direction the fire took). 260. brave: exceedingly. 261. as: that. 262. W. Hewer: William Hewer (c. 1643–1715), Pepys's chief clerk and faithful friend. He became Treasurer for Tangier in 1686 and a temporary Commissioner of the Navy in 1688. Pepys named Hewer his executor, and, together with John Jackson, Pepys's nephew and principal heir, Hewer established the Pepysian Library at Magdalene College, Cambridge. 263. Jane: Pepys's cook. 264. the gates: of the navy yard. 265. Mr. Shelden: William Sheldon, Clerk of the Cheque, at whose house Pepys had lodged his wife during the plague the previous summer.

them in it, night or day. So back again, by the way seeing my goods well in the lighters at Deptford, and watched well by people. Home, and whereas I expected to have seen our house on fire, it being now about seven o'clock, it was not. But to the fyre, and there find greater hopes than I expected; for my confidence[266] of finding our Office on fire was such, that I durst not ask any body how it was with us, till I come and saw it not burned. But going to the fire, I find by the blowing up of houses, and the great helpe given by the workmen out of the King's yards,[267] sent up by Sir W. Pen, there is a good stop given to it, as well as at Marke-lane end as ours; it having only burned the dyall[268] of Barking Church, and part of the porch, and was there quenched. I up to the top of Barking steeple, and there saw the saddest sight of desolation that I ever saw; every where great fires, oyle-cellars, and brimstone, and other things burning. I became afeard to stay there long, and therefore down again as fast as I could, the fire being spread as far as I could see it; and to Sir W. Pen's, and there eat a piece of cold meat, having eaten nothing since Sunday,[269] but the remains of Sunday's dinner. Here I met with Mr. Young and Whistler;[270] and having removed all my things, and received good hopes that the fire at our end is stopped, they and I walked into the town, and find Fanchurch-streete, Gracious-streete,[271] and Lumbard-streete all in dust. The Exchange a sad sight, nothing standing there, of all the statues or pillars, but Sir Thomas Gresham's picture[272] in the corner. Walked into Moorefields (our feet ready to burn, walking through the towne among the hot coles), and find that full of people, and poor wretches carrying their goods there, and every body keeping his goods together by themselves (and a great blessing it is to them that it is fair weather for them to keep abroad[273] night and day); drank there, and paid twopence for a plain penny loaf. Thence homeward, having passed through Cheapside and Newgate Market, all burned, and seen Anthony Joyce's house in fire. And took up (which I keep by me) a piece of glasse of Mercers'

Chappell[274] in the streete, where much more was, so melted and buckled with the heat of the fire like parchment. I also did see a poor cat taken out of a hole in the chimney, joyning to the wall of the Exchange, with the hair all burned off the body, and yet alive. So home at night, and find there good hopes of saving our office; but great endeavours of watching all night, and having men ready; and so we lodged them in the office, and had drink and bread and cheese for them. And I lay down and slept a good night about midnight, though when I rose I heard that there had been a great alarme of French and Dutch being risen, which proved nothing. But it is a strange thing to see how long this time did look since Sunday, having been always full of variety of actions, and little sleep, that it looked like a week or more, and I had forgot almost the day of the week.

September 15, 1666

All the morning at the office, Harman[275] being come to my great satisfaction to put up my beds and hangings, so I am at rest, and followed my business all day. Dined with Sir W. Batten, mighty busy about this account,[276] and while my people were busy, wrote near thirty letters and orders with my owne hand. At it till eleven at night; and it is strange to see how clear my head was, being eased of all the matter of all these letters; whereas one would think that I should have been dazed. I never did observe so much of myself[277] in my life. In the evening there comes to me Captain Cocke, and walked a good while in the garden. He says he hath computed that the rents of houses lost by this fire in the City comes to £600,000 per annum; that this will make the Parliament more quiet than otherwise they would have been, and give the King a more ready supply; that the supply must be by excise, as it is in Holland; that the Parliament will see it necessary to carry on the warr; that the late storm hindered our beating the Dutch fleete, who were gone out only to satisfy the people, having no business to do but to avoid us; that the French, as late in the yeare as it is, are coming; that the Dutch are

266. **confidence**: expectation. 267. **yards**: dockyards. 268. **dyall**: clock. 269. **having . . . Sunday**: The night before Pepys had supped at the office "upon a shoulder of mutton from the cook's" (*Diary*, September 4, 1666)—evidently forgotten in the excitement. 270. **Mr. . . . Whistler**: flagmakers. 271. **Gracious-streete**: Gracechurch Street. 272. **Gresham's picture**: statue. Sir Thomas Gresham (1519–79), Queen Elizabeth's financial agent, founded the Royal Exchange. 273. **keep abroad**: stay outdoors.

274. **Mercers' Chappell**: Mercers' Hall and Chapel were both destroyed by the fire and later rebuilt by the Company (the first of the twelve great companies of London). 275. **Harman**: an upholster, married to Pepys's aunt. 276. **this account**: On the previous day Sir William Coventry had asked Pepys to assemble for Parliament an account of the Navy's expenditures in the war against the Dutch. 277. **observe . . . myself**: look after so much by myself.

really in bad condition, but that this unhappinesse of ours do give them heart; that there was a late difference between my Lord Arlington and Sir W. Coventry about neglect in the last to send away an express of the other's in time; that it come before the King, and the Duke of Yorke concerned himself in it; but this fire hath stopped it. The Dutch fleete is not gone home but rather to the North, and so dangerous to our Gottenburgh fleete.[278] That the Parliament is likely to fall foul upon[279] some persons; and, among others, on the Vice-chamberlaine,[280] though we both believe with little ground. That certainly never so great a loss as this was borne so well by citizens in the world; he believing that not one merchant upon the 'Change will break upon it.[281] That he do not apprehend there will be any disturbances in State upon it; for that all men are busy in looking after their owne business to save themselves. He gone, I to finish my letters, and home to bed; and find to my infinite joy many rooms clean; and myself and wife lie in our own chamber again. But much terrified in the nights now-a-days with dreams of fire, and falling down of houses.

November 14, 1666

Up, and by water to White Hall, and thence to Westminster, where I bought several things, as a hone, ribbon, gloves, books, and then took coach and to Knipp's[282] lodging, whom I find not ready to go home with me. So I away to do a little business, among others to call upon Mr. Osborne[283] for my Tangier warrant for the last quarter, and so to the Exchange for some things for my wife, and then to Knipp's again, and there staid reading of Waller's verses,[284] while she finished dressing, her husband[285] being by.

I had no other pastime. Her lodging very mean, and the condition she lives in; yet makes a shew without doors, God bless us! I carried him along with us into the City, and set him down in Bishopsgate Street, and then home with her. She tells me how Smith, of the Duke's house, hath killed a man[286] upon a quarrel in play;[287] which makes every body sorry, he being a good actor, and, they say, a good man, however this happens. The ladies of the Court do much bemoan him, she says. Here she and we alone at dinner to some good victuals, that we could not put off,[288] that was intended for the great dinner of my Lord Hinchingbroke's,[289] if he had come. After dinner I to teach her my new recitative of "It is decreed,"[290] of which she learnt a good part, and I do well like it and believe shall be well pleased when she hath it all, and that it will be found an agreeable thing. Then carried her home, and my wife and I intended to have seen my Lady Jemimah[291] at White Hall, but the Exchange Streete was so full of coaches, every body, as they say, going thither to make themselves fine against tomorrow night, that, after half an hour's stay, we could not do any [thing], only my wife to see her brother,[292] and I to go speak one word with Sir G. Carteret about office business, and talk of the general complexion of matters, which he looks upon, as I do, with horrour, and gives[293] us all for an undone people. That there is no such thing as a peace in hand, nor possibility of any without our begging it, they being as high, or higher, in their terms than ever, and tells me that, just now, my Lord Hollis[294] had been with him, and wept to think in what a condition we are fallen. He shewed me my Lord Sandwich's letter

278. The Dutch . . . fleete: A part of the English fleet had been dispatched to the Baltic for naval supplies. **279. fall . . . upon:** collide with (a nautical term). **280. the Vice-chamberlaine:** Sir George Carteret. He was summoned by Parliament to explain the conduct of the Navy Office. On October 2 Pepys himself appeared before the Committee of Navy Accounts and managed so well as to clear the way for a sizable appropriation. **281. break . . . it:** be ruined by it. **282. Knipp:** Mary Knep, or Knepp, actress and singer. Pepys met her the year before and described her as "pretty enough; but the most excellent, mad-humoured thing, and sings the noblest that ever I heard in my life" (*Diary*, December 6, 1665). **283. Mr. Osborne:** clerk to Gauden, the victualer. **284. Waller's verses:** poems by Edmund Waller (1606–87), first published in 1645. (See the selections from Waller in Part Three.) **285. her husband:** "an ill, melancholy, jealous-looking fellow" (*Diary*, December 8, 1665).

286. Smith . . . man: William Smith (d. 1695), a sometime barrister, was an actor in the Duke's Company, of which he became co-manager in 1676–77. He escaped punishment for the killing. **287. in play:** while gambling. **288. put off:** Pepys may mean "postpone eating." **289. Lord Hinchingbroke:** Montagu's eldest son, Edward (1648–88), First Viscount Hinchingbroke (later Second Earl of Sandwich). His connection with the Knepps is not known. **290. It is decreed:** one of four songs composed by Pepys, this one using words by Ben Jonson. **291. Lady Jemimah:** Montagu's eldest daughter, whose marriage the previous year to Philip Carteret, Sir George's eldest son, Pepys had managed. **292. her brother:** Balthazar "Balty" St. Michel. He held various naval offices, becoming Deputy Treasurer of the Fleet in 1667. **293. gives:** represents. **294. Lord Hollis:** Denzil Holles, or Hollis (1599–1680), First Baron Holles of Ifield, was Ambassador to Paris from 1663 to 1666.

to him, complaining of the lack of money,[295] which Sir G. Carteret is at a loss how in the world to get the King to supply him with, and wishes him, for that reason, here; for that he fears he will be brought to disgrace there, for want of supplies. He says the House[296] is yet in a bad humour; and desiring to know whence it is that the King stirs not, he says he minds it not, nor will be brought to it, and that his servants of[297] the House do, instead of making the Parliament better, rather play the rogue one with another, and will put all in fire. So that, upon the whole, we are in a wretched condition, and I went from him in full apprehensions of it. So took up my wife, her brother being yet very bad, and doubtful whether he will recover or no, and so to St. Ellen's,[298] and there sent my wife home, and myself to the Pope's Head, where all the Houblons were, and Dr. Croone,[299] and by and by to an exceeding pretty supper, excellent discourse of all sorts, and indeed are a set of the finest gentlemen that ever I met withal[300] in my life. Here Dr. Croone told me, that, at the meeting at Gresham College[301] to-night, which, it seems, they now have every Wednesday again, there was a pretty experiment of the blood of one dogg let out, till he died, into the body of another on one side, while all his own run out on the other side. The first died upon the place, and the other very well, and likely to do well. This did give occasion to many pretty wishes, as of the blood of a Quaker to be let into an Archbishop, and such like; but, as Dr. Croone says, may, if it takes, be of mighty use to man's health, for the amending of bad blood by borrowing from a better body. After supper, James Houblon and another brother took me aside and to talk of some businesses of their owne, where I am to serve them, and will, and then to talk of publique matters, and I do find that they and all merchants else do give over trade and the nation for lost, nothing being done with care or foresight, no convoys granted, nor any thing done to satisfaction; but do think that the Dutch and French will master us the next yeare, do what we can: and so do I, unless necessity makes the King to mind his business, which might yet save all. Here we sat talking till past one in the morning, and then home, where my people sat up for me, my wife and all, and so to bed.

November 15, 1666

This [morning] come Mr. Shepley (newly out of the country) to see me; after a little discourse with him, I to the office, where we sat all the morning, and at noon home, and there dined, Shepley with me, and after dinner I did pay him £70, which he had paid my father for my use in the country. He being gone, I took coach and to Mrs. Pierce's, where I find her as fine as possible, and himself[302] going to the ball at night at Court, it being the Queen's birth-day, and so I carried them in my coach, and having set them into the house, and gotten Mr. Pierce to undertake the carrying in my wife, I to Unthanke's,[303] where she appointed to be, and there told her, and back again about business to White Hall, while Pierce went and fetched her and carried her in. I, after I had met with Sir W. Coventry and given him some account of matters, I also to the ball, and with much ado got up to the loft,[304] where with much trouble I could see very well. Anon the house grew full, and the candles light, and the King and Queen and all the ladies set:[305] and it was, indeed, a glorious sight to see Mrs. Stewart[306] in black and white lace, and her head and shoulders dressed with dyamonds, and the like a great many great ladies more, only the Queen none; and the King in his rich vest of some rich silke and silver trimming, as the Duke of York and all the dancers were, some of cloth of silver, and others of other sorts, exceeding rich. Presently after the King was come in, he took the Queene, and about fourteen more couple there was, and begun the Bransles.[307] As many of the men as I can remember presently, were, the King,

295. lack of money: Pepys's account (*Diary*, October 10, 1666) shows the cost of the war thus far to have been £3,200,000, of which almost a million was still owing. **296. the House:** Parliament. **297. servants of:** representatives in. **298. St. Ellen's:** St. Helen's Church, which escaped the fire. **299. Dr. Croone:** William Croone (1633–84), physician and professor of rhetoric at Gresham College. **300. withal:** with. **301. Gresham College:** Sir Thomas Gresham provided in his will for the establishment of the college, to be supported by rents from the Royal Exchange. Dr. Croone describes a meeting of the Royal Society, which had made its home at the college since its founding in 1660.

302. himself: James Pierce, the purser aboard the *Swiftsure*. **303. Unthanke:** Mrs. Pepys's tailor. **304. loft:** gallery. **305. set:** sat. **306. Mrs. Stewart:** Frances Teresa Stewart (1647–1702) was reported to be the greatest beauty at Charles's court and, perhaps less justly, his mistress. She married Charles Stuart (1639–72), Fifth Duke of Richmond, the following year. **307. the Bransles:** (*branle*) a group dance of French origin, probably similar to the country dance called the brawl by Shakespeare and later dramatists.

Duke of York, Prince Rupert,[308] Duke of Monmouth,[309] Duke of Buckingham,[310] Lord Douglas,[311] Mr. Hamilton,[312] Colonell Russell,[313] Mr. Griffith,[314] Lord Ossory,[315] Lord Rochester;[316] and of the ladies, the Queene, Duchess of York,[317] Mrs. Stewart, Duchess of Monmouth,[318] Lady Essex Howard,[319] Mrs. Temple,[320] Swedes Embassadress,[321] Lady Arlington,[322] Lord George Barkeley's daughter,[323] and many others I remember not; but all most excellently dressed in rich petticoats and gowns, and dyamonds, and pearls. After the Bransles, then to a Corant,[324] and now and then a French dance; but that so rare that the Corants grew tiresome, that I wished it done. Only Mrs. Stewart danced mighty finely, and many French dances, specially one the King called the New Dance, which was very pretty; but upon the whole matter, the business of the dancing of itself was not extraordinary pleasing. But the clothes and sight of the persons was indeed very pleasing, and worth my coming, being never likely to see more gallantry[325] while I live, if I should come twenty times. About

twelve at night it broke up, and I to hire a coach with much difficulty, but Pierce had hired a chair for my wife, and so she being gone to his house, he and I, taking up Barker[326] at Unthanke's, to his house, whither his wife was come home a good while ago and gone to bed. So away home with my wife, between displeased with the dull dancing, and satisfied at the clothes and persons. My Lady Castlemayne, without whom all is nothing, being there, very rich, though not dancing. And so after supper, it being very cold, to bed.

December 31, 1666

Rising this day with a full design to mind nothing else but to make up my accounts for the year past, I did take money, and walk forth to several places in the towne as far as the New Exchange, to pay all my debts, it being still a very great frost and good walking. I staid at the Fleece Tavern in Covent Garden while my boy Tom went to W. Joyce's to pay what I owed for candles there.[327] Thence to the New Exchange to clear my wife's score, and so going back again I met Doll Lane (Mrs. Martin's sister), with another young woman of the Hall,[328] one Scott, and took them to the Half Moon Taverne and there drank some burnt wine with them, without more pleasure, and so away home by coach, and there to dinner, and then to my accounts, where in, at last, I find them clear and right; but, to my great discontent, do find that my gettings this year have been £573 less than my last: it being this year in all but £2,986; whereas, the last, I got £3,560. And then again my spendings this year have exceeded my spendings the last by £644: my whole spendings last year being but £509; whereas this year, it appears, I have spent £1,154, which is a sum not fit to be said that ever I should spend in one year, before I am master of a better estate than I am. Yet, blessed be God! and I pray God make me thankful for it, I do find myself worth in money, all good,[329] above £6,200; which is above £1,800 more than I was the last year. This, I trust in God, will make me thankfull

308. **Prince Rupert:** (1619–82), first cousin to the King; son of Charles I's sister, Elizabeth (1596–1662), Queen of Bohemia. He served with Pepys as a Commissioner for Tangier. 309. **Duke of Monmouth:** James Scott (1649–85), illegitimate son of Charles by Lucy Walters. (See Dryden's *Absalom and Achitophel* later in Part One.) 310. **Duke of Buckingham:** George Villiers (1628–86). 311. **Lord Douglas:** James Douglas (1646–1700), Second Marquis of Douglas. 312. **Mr. Hamilton:** not identified. 313. **Colonell Russell:** John Russell, third son of Francis, Fourth Earl of Bedford; a colonel in the King's Guards. 314. **Mr. Griffith:** not identified. 315. **Lord Ossory:** Thomas Butler (1634–80), Earl of Ossory, the eldest son of James, First Duke of Ormonde. 316. **Lord Rochester:** John Wilmot (1647–80), Second Earl of Rochester. He was at this time eighteen years old. (See the selections from Rochester earlier in Part One.) 317. **Duchess of York:** Anne Hyde (1637–71), the eldest daughter of Lord Clarendon. She married the Duke of York secretly in France in 1659 and publicly at the Restoration. 318. **Duchess of Monmouth:** Anne (1651–1732), *suo jure* Countess of Buccleuch. 319. **Lady . . . Howard:** only daughter of James Howard, Third Earl of Suffolk. She was married the following year to Edward Griffin (First Baron Griffin of Braybrooke, 1688). 320. **Mrs. Temple:** Anne Temple (d. 1718) became the second wife of Sir Charles Lyttelton, Governor of Jamaica. 321. **Swedes Embassadress:** There were two ambassadors from Sweden, Lord George Flemming and Lord Peter Julius Coyet. 322. **Lady Arlington:** Isabella de Nassau (1631–1718), wife of Lord Arlington. She was the sister of Lady Amelia de Nassau, the wife of Lord Ossory. 323. **Barkeley's daughter:** Lord Berkeley had seven daughters. 324. **Corant:** a fast, lively dance (cf. the Italian *coranta* and the French *courante*). 325. **gallantry:** splendor, magnificence.

326. **Barker:** Mrs. Barker had joined the household in October as Mrs. Pepys's new companion. 327. **what . . . there:** Will Joyce was in the tallow trade. 328. **Doll . . . Hall:** Westminster Hall housed the courts of Chancery and the King's Bench but also hundreds of booths of stationers, booksellers, milliners, etc. Betty Martin kept a haberdasher's shop there. Pepys enjoyed the favors of Mrs. Martin and her sister for many years. The Scott woman is not identified. 329. **all good:** none counterfeit.

for what I have, and carefull to make up by care next year what by my negligence and prodigality I have lost and spent this year. The doing of this, and entering of it fair,[330] with the sorting of all my expenses, to see how and in what points I have exceeded, did make it late work, till my eyes become very sore and ill, and then did give over, and supper, and to bed. Thus ends this year of publick wonder[331] and mischief to this nation, and, therefore, generally wished by all people to have an end. Myself and family well, having four mayds and one clerk, Tom, in my house, and my brother,[332] now with me, to spend time in order to[333] his preferment. Our healths all well, only my eyes with overworking them are sore as candlelight comes to them, and not else; publick matters in a most sad condition; seamen discouraged for want of pay, and are become not to be governed; nor, as matters are now, can any fleete go out next year. Our enemies, French and Dutch, great, and grow more by our poverty. The Parliament backward in raising, because jealous of the spending of the money; the City less and less likely to be built again, every body settling elsewhere, and nobody encouraged to trade. A sad, vicious, negligent Court, and all sober men there fearful of the ruin of the whole kingdom this next year; from which, good God deliver us! One thing I reckon remarkable in my owne condition is, that I am come to abound in good plate, so as at all entertainments to be served wholly with silver plates, having two dozen and a half.

April 16, 1667

Up, and to the office, where sat all the morning, at noon home to dinner, and thence in haste to carry my wife to see the new play[334] I saw yesterday, she not knowing it. But there, contrary to expectation, find "The Silent Woman."[335] However, in; and there Knipp come into the pit. I took her by me, and here we met with Mrs. Horsley, the pretty woman—an acquaintance of Mercer's, whose house is burnt. Knipp tells me the King was so angry at the liberty taken by

Lacy's part to abuse him to his face,[336] that he commanded they should act no more, till Moone[337] went and got leave for them to act again, but not this play.[338] The King mighty angry; and it was bitter indeed, but very true and witty. I never was more taken with a play than I am with this "Silent Woman," as old as it is, and as often as I have seen it. There is more wit in it than goes to ten new plays. Thence with my wife and Knipp to Mrs. Pierce's,[339] and saw her closet again, and liked her picture.[340] Thence took them all to the Cake-house, in Southampton Market-place, where Pierce told us the story how, in good earnest,[341] [the King] is offended with the Duke of Richmond's marrying, and Mrs. Stewart's sending the King his jewels again. As she tells it, it is the noblest romance and example of a brave lady that ever I read in my life. Pretty[342] to hear them talk of yesterday's play, and I durst not own to my wife to have seen it. Thence home and to W. Batten's, where we have made a bargain for the ending of some of the trouble about some of our prizes[343] for £1,400. So home to look on my new books that I have lately bought, and then to supper and to bed.

August 16, 1667

Up, and at the office all the morning, and so at noon to dinner, and after dinner my wife and I to the Duke's playhouse, where we saw the new play acted yesterday, "The Feign Innocence, or Sir Martin Marr-all;" a play made by my Lord Duke of Newcastle, but, as every body says, corrected by Dryden.[344]

---

330. fair: clearly. **331. wonder:** the "prodigy" of the fire. **332. my brother:** John Pepys (1641–77) had come down from Cambridge this fall with a master's degree and ordained. **333. in . . . to:** with a view to. **334. the new play:** Edward Howard's *The Change of Crowns*. It remained in manuscript until 1949 when it was edited by F. S. Boas. **335. The Silent Woman:** Ben Jonson's *Epicene, or the Silent Woman* (1609).

336. the King . . . face: Charles had also attended the play the night before and had seen John Lacy "act the country-gentleman come up to Court, who do abuse the Court with all imaginable wit and plainness about selling of places, and doing every thing for money" (*Diary*, April 15, 1667). **337. Moone:** Michael Mohun (c. 1620–84), "said to be the best actor in the world" (*Diary*, November 20, 1660). **338. not . . . play:** *The Change of Crowns* does not appear to have been acted again. **339. Mrs. Pierce:** the purser's wife. **340. her picture:** her portrait by John Hales (d. 1679). Pepys had seen "her new picture by Hales" on May 23, 1666, and did not like it. Nor did he like the one of her husband, also by Hales, which he saw on September 16, 1667. **341. in . . . earnest:** seriously. **342. Pretty:** pleasant. **343. prizes:** booty from captured Dutch ships, which Pepys and other members of the Navy Board had illegally appropriated. **344. a play . . . Dryden:** William Cavendish (1592–1676), Duke of Newcastle, furnished Dryden with what amounted to a bare translation of Molière's *L'Etourdi* (1665); hence the play is generally regarded as Dryden's.

It is the most entire piece of mirth, a complete farce from one end to the other, that certainly was ever writ. I never laughed so in all my life. I laughed till my head [ached] all the evening and night with the laughing; and at very good wit therein, not fooling. The house full, and in all things of mighty content to me. Thence to the New Exchange with my wife, where, at my bookseller's, I saw "The History of the Royall Society,"[345] which, I believe, is a fine book, and have bespoke one in quires.[346] So home, and I to the office a little, and so to my chamber, and read the history of 88 in Speede,[347] in order to my seeing the play thereof[348] acted to-morrow at the King's house. So to supper in some pain by the sudden change of the weather cold and my drinking of cold drink, which I must I fear begin to leave off, though I shall try it as long as I can without much pain. But I find myself to be full of wind, and my anus to be knit together[349] as it is always with cold. Every body wonders that we have no news from Bredah of the ratification of the peace;[350] and do suspect that there is some stop in it. So to bed.

November 29, 1667

Waked about seven o'clock this morning with a noise I supposed I heard, near our chamber, of knocking, which, by and by, increased: and I, more awake, could distinguish it better. I then waked my wife, and both of us wondered at it, and lay so a great while, while that increased, and at last heard it plainer, knocking, as if it were breaking down a window for people to get out; and then removing of stools and chairs; and plainly, by and by, going up and down our stairs. We lay, both of us, afeard; yet I would have

rose, but my wife would not let me. Besides, I could not do it without making noise; and we did both conclude that thieves were in the house, but wondered what our people did, whom we thought either killed, or afeard, as we were. Thus we lay till the clock struck eight, and high day. At last, I removed my gown and slippers safely[351] to the other side of the bed over my wife: and there safely rose, and put on my gown and breeches, and then, with a firebrand in my hand, safely opened the door, and saw nor heard any thing. Then (with fear, I confess) went to the maid's chamber-door, and all quiet and safe. Called Jane up, and went down safely, and opened my chamber door, where all well. Then more freely about, and to the kitchen, where the cook-maid up, and all safe. So up again, and when Jane come, and we demanded whether she heard no noise, she said, "yes, and was afeard," but rose with the other maid, and found nothing; but heard a noise in the great stack of chimneys that goes from Sir J. Minnes through our house;[352] and so we sent,[353] and their chimneys have been swept this morning, and the noise was that, and nothing else. It is one of the most extraordinary accidents in my life, and gives ground to think of Don Quixote's adventures how people may be surprised, and the more from an accident last night, that our young gibb-cat[354] did leap down our stairs from top to bottom, at two leaps, and frighted us, that we could not tell well whether it was the cat or a spirit, and do sometimes think this morning that the house might be haunted. Glad to have this so well over, and indeed really glad in my mind, for I was much afeard, I dressed myself and to the office both forenoon and afternoon, mighty hard putting papers and things in order to my extraordinary satisfaction, and consulting my clerks in many things, who are infinite helps to my memory and reasons of things, and so being weary, and my eyes akeing, having overwrought them to-day reading so much shorthand, I home and there to supper, it being late, and to bed. This morning Sir W. Pen and I did walk together a good while, and he tells me that the Houses are not likely to agree after

345. **The History . . . Society:** by Thomas Sprat (1635–1713), Bishop of Rochester; published this year. (See the selection from *The History of the Royal Society* earlier in Part One.) 346. **in quires:** unbound. Pepys had all his books uniformly bound. 347. **the history . . . Speede:** John Speed (1552–1629), historian and cartographer, published his *History of Great Britain* in 1611. The number 88 refers of course to the year of the defeat of the Spanish Armada by the English. 348. **the play thereof:** Thomas Heywood's *If You Know Not Me, You Know Nobody, or the Troubles of Queen Elizabeth* (1605). 349. **knit together:** contracted. 350. **the ratification . . . peace:** The ignominious Peace of Breda, ending the war with the Dutch, was signed on July 21. Both countries were moved to a settlement of their differences by the menacing incursions of France in the Spanish Netherlands.

351. **safely:** stealthily. 352. **through our house:** Pepys's "house" was actually but a section of a long, two-story brick building, within which the limits of each residence were ill-defined. Pepys had earlier quarreled with his neighbor Minnes over the ownership of a room and had quieted him only by an investigation which established his title to it. 353. **sent:** inquired. 354. **gibb-cat:** male cat.

their free conference yesterday,[355] and he fears what may follow.

February 27, 1668

All the morning at the office, and at noon home to dinner, and thence with my wife and Deb.[356] to the King's House, to see "The Virgin Martyr,"[357] the first time it hath been acted a great while: and it is mighty pleasant; not that the play is worth much, but it is finely acted by Becke Marshall.[358] But that which did please me beyond any thing in the whole world was the wind-musique when the angel comes down,[359] which is so sweet that it ravished me, and indeed, in a word, did wrap up my soul so that it made me really sick, just as I have formerly been when in love with my wife; that neither then, nor all the evening going home, and at home, I was able to think of any thing, but remained all night transported, so as I could not believe that ever any musick hath that real command over the soul of a man as this did upon me: and makes me resolve to practice wind-musique,[360] and to make my wife do the like.

March 4, 1668

Up betimes and with Sir W. Pen in his coach to White Hall, there to wait upon the Duke of York and the Commissioners of the Treasury, W. Coventry

and Sir John Duncombe,[361] who do declare that they cannot find the money we demand, and we that less than what we demand will not set out the fleet intended, and so broke up, with no other conclusion than that they would let us have what they could get and we would improve[362] that as well as we could. So God bless us, and prepare us against the consequences of these matters. Thence, it being a cold wet day, I home with Sir J. Minnes in his coach, and called by the way at my bookseller's and took home with me Kercher's Musurgia[363] very well bound, but I had no comfort to look upon them, but as soon as I come home fell to my work at the office, shutting the doors, that we, I and my clerks, might not be interrupted, and so, only with room for a little dinner, we very busy all the day till night that the officers met for me to give them the heads[364] of what I intended to say,[365] which I did with great discontent to see them all rely on me that have no reason at all to trouble myself about it, nor have any thanks from them for my labour, but contrarily Brouncker looked mighty dogged,[366] as thinking that I did not intend to do it so as to save him. This troubled me so much as, together with the shortness of the time and muchness of the business, did let me be at it till but about ten at night, and then quite weary, and dull, and vexed, I could go no further, but resolved to leave the rest to to-morrow morning, and so in full discontent and weariness did give over[367] and went home, with[out] supper vexed and sickish to bed, and there slept about three hours, but then waked, and never in so much trouble in all my life of mind, thinking of the task I have upon me, and upon what dissatisfactory grounds, and what the issue of it may be to me.

March 5, 1668

With these thoughts I lay troubling myself till six o'clock, restless, and at last getting my wife to talk to

355. the Houses . . . yesterday: The dispute was over the arraignment of Lord Clarendon, already dismissed from office as Lord Chancellor, for high treason. On November 12 the House of Lords refused the charge of impeachment on the grounds that no particular act was specified; the Commons thereupon passed a resolution on December 2 charging the Lords with obstructing justice. Clarendon had meanwhile, on November 29, fled to France; the Lords accepted his flight as a confession of guilt and proceeded to banish him from the country. 356. Deb.: Deborah Willet, Mrs. Pepys's new companion, joined the household on September 30, 1667, when she was described by Pepys as "very pretty, and so grave as I never saw a little thing in my life. Indeed I think her a little too good for my family, and so well carriaged as I hardly ever saw." Pepys was caught by his wife in a compromising position with the girl, and she departed on November 14, 1668. 357. The Virgin Martyr: a tragedy (1622) by Philip Massinger and Thomas Dekker. 358. Becke Marshall: Rebecca Marshall, a very popular actress with the King's Company, played the lead, Dorothea. 359. the wind-musique . . . down: at the end of the play. The angel is Dorothea. There is no musical direction in the printed play. 360. practice wind-musique: Pepys played the flageolet as well as the bass viol and took a considerable interest, both technical and theoretical, in musical sound.

361. Sir . . . Duncombe: (c. 1622–87), appointed Commissioner of the Treasury in 1667. 362. improve: make the most of. 363. Kercher's Musurgia: Athanasius Kircher's *Musurgia Universalia sive Ars Magna Consoni et Dissoni* (1650) "contains, among much rubbish, valuable matter on the nature of sound and the theory of composition" (Grove's *Dictionary of Music and Musicians*). Pepys had bought the book on February 22 for thirty-five shillings. 364. heads: main points. 365. what . . . say: Following the signing of the peace treaty with the Dutch, Parliament had appointed a Committee of Miscarriages to investigate suspected wartime abuses. On Pepys, who knew more about this matter than any other member of the Navy Board, fell the entire burden of defense. 366. dogged: surly. 367. give over: quit.

me to comfort me, which she at last did, and made me resolve to quit my hands of this Office, and endure the trouble of it no longer than till I can clear myself of it. So with great trouble, but yet with some ease, from this discourse with my wife, I up, and to my Office, whither come my clerks, and so I did huddle[368] the best I could some more notes for my discourse to-day, and by nine o'clock was ready, and did go down to the Old Swan, and there by boat, with T. H.[369] and W. H.[370] with me, to Westminster, where I found myself come time enough, and my brethren all ready. But I full of thoughts and trouble touching the issue of this day; and, to comfort myself, did go to the Dog[371] and drink half-a-pint of mulled sack,[372] and in the Hall[373] did drink a dram of brandy at Mrs. Hewlett's;[374] and with the warmth of this did find myself in better order as to courage, truly. So we all up to the lobby; and between eleven and twelve o'clock, were called in, with the mace[375] before us, into the House, where a mighty full House; and we stood at the bar,[376] namely, Brouncker, Sir J. Minnes, Sir T. Harvey,[377] and myself, W. Pen being in the House, as a Member.[378] I perceive the whole House was full, and full of expectation of our defence what it would be, and with great prejudice. After the Speaker[379] had told us the dissatisfaction of the House, and read the Report of the Committee, I began our defence most acceptably and smoothly, and continued at it without any hesitation or losse, but with full scope, and all my reason free about me, as if it had been at my own table, from that time till past three in the afternoon; and so ended, without any interruption from the Speaker; but we withdrew. And there all my Fellow-Officers, and all the world that was within hearing, did congratulate me, and cry up[380] my speech as the best thing they ever heard; and my Fellow-Officers overjoyed in it; we were called in again by and by to answer only one question, touching our paying tickets to ticket-mongers;[381] and so out; and we were in hopes to have had a vote this day in our favour, and so the generality of the House was; but my speech, being so long, many had gone out to dinner and come in again half drunk; and then there are two or three that are professed enemies to us and every body else; among others, Sir T. Littleton,[382] Sir Thomas Lee,[383] Mr. Wiles,[384] the coxcomb whom I saw heretofore at the cock-fighting, and a few others; I say, these did rise up and speak against the coming to a vote now, the House not being full, by reason of several being at dinner, but most because that the House was to attend the King this afternoon, about the business of religion, wherein they pray him to put in force all the laws against Nonconformists and Papists;[385] and this prevented it, so that they put it off to to-morrow come se'nnight.[386] However, it is plain we have got great ground;[387] and everybody says I have got the most honour that any could have had opportunity of getting; and so with our hearts mightily overjoyed at this success, we all to dinner to Lord Brouncker's—that is to say, myself, T. Harvey, and W. Pen, and there dined; and thence with Sir Anthony Morgan,[388] who is an acquaintance of Brouncker's, a very wise man, we after dinner to the King's house, and there saw part of "The Discontented Colonel,"[389] but could take no great pleasure in it, because of our coming in in the middle of it. After the play, home with W. Pen, and there to my wife, whom W. Hewer had told of my success, and she overjoyed, and I also as to my particular;[390] and, after talking awhile, I betimes to bed, having had no quiet rest a good while.

368. **huddle:** hastily work up. 369. **T. H.:** Thomas Hayter. 370. **W. H.:** William Hewer. 371. **the Dog:** a famous tavern in King Street, Westminster, frequented by Ben Jonson. 372. **mulled sack:** white wine, sweetened, spiced, thickened (with egg yolks), and heated. 373. **the Hall:** Westminster Hall. 374. **Mrs. Hewlett:** probably Mrs. Howlett, mother of Betty Michell. Pepys had visited, and drunk, with Mr. and Mrs. Howlett at their house on March 1. 375. **mace:** sergeant at arms. 376. **the bar:** the rail or barrier that marks off an area near the door of the House where nonmembers may assemble on business. 377. **Sir T. Harvey:** Sir Thomas Harvey had bought Lord Berkeley's place as an extra commissioner in 1665. 378. **as a Member:** for Weymouth. 379. **the Speaker:** Sir Edward Turnour (1617–76). He resigned in 1671 to become Chief Baron of the Exchequer. 380. **cry up:** proclaim.

381. **ticket-mongers:** The system of ticket payments (see n. 87) created a lively market for merchants, who, discounting the tickets as much as fifty percent, preyed on seamen who needed cash to live. 382. **Sir T. Littleton:** Sir Thomas Lyttelton (1624–81), Second Baron Lyttelton. 383. **Sir Thomas Lee:** (d. 1691). 384. **Mr. Wiles:** not identified. 385. **they . . . Papists:** The King was disposed to alleviate the oppressed condition of Protestant Nonconformists and Roman Catholics alike, but the High-Church party persisted in opposing all bills for toleration and demanded the enforcement of the Act of Uniformity (1662). 386. **se'nnight:** a week. 387. **got . . . ground:** made great progress. 388. **Sir . . . Morgan:** (1621–68), one of the original Fellows of the Royal Society. 389. **The Discontented Colonel:** *Bren(n)oralt, or the Discontented Colonel* (1639), by Sir John Suckling (1609–42). 390. **my particular:** my particular part in it.

March 6, 1668

Up betimes, and with Sir D. Gawden[391] to Sir W. Coventry's chamber: where the first word he said to me was, "Good-morrow, Mr. Pepys, that must be Speaker of the Parliament-house:" and did protest I had got honour for ever in Parliament. He said that his brother,[392] that sat by him, admires me; and another gentleman said that I could not get less than £1,000 a-year if I would put on a gown and plead at the Chancery-bar; but, what pleases me most, he tells me that the Sollicitor-Generall[393] did protest that he thought I spoke the best of any man in England. After several talks with him alone, touching his own businesses, he carried me to White Hall, and there parted; and I to the Duke of York's lodgings, and find him going to the Park, it being a very fine morning, and I after him; and, as soon as he saw me, he told me, with great satisfaction, that I had converted a great many yesterday, and did, with great praise of me, go on with the discourse with me. And, by and by, overtaking the King, the King and Duke of York come to me both; and he[394] said, "Mr. Pepys, I am very glad of your success yesterday;" and fell to talk of my well speaking; and many of the Lords there. My Lord Barkeley did cry me up for what they had heard of it; and others, Parliament-men there, about the King, did say that they never heard such a speech in their lives delivered in that manner. Progers,[395] of the Bedchamber, swore to me afterwards before Brouncker, in the afternoon, that he did tell the King that he thought I might teach the Sollicitor-Generall. Every body that saw me almost[396] come to me, as Joseph Williamson[397] and others, with such eulogys as cannot be expressed. From thence I went to Westminster Hall, where I met Mr. G. Montagu,[398] who come to me and kissed me, and told me that he had often heretofore kissed my hands, but now he would kiss my lips: protesting that I was another Cicero, and said, all the world said the same of me. Mr. Ashburnham,[399] and every creature I met there of the Parliament, or that knew anything of the Parliament's actings, did salute me with this honour: Mr. Godolphin;[400] Mr. Sands,[401] who swore he would go twenty mile, at any time, to hear the like again, and that he never saw so many sit four hours together to hear any man in his life, as there did to hear me; Mr. Chichly,[402] Sir John Duncomb, and everybody do say that the kingdom will ring of my abilities, and that I have done myself right for my whole life: and so Captain Cocke, and others of my friends, say that no man had ever such an opportunity of making his abilities known; and, that I may cite all at once, Mr. Lieutenant of the Tower[403] did tell me that Mr. Vaughan[404] did protest to him, and that, in his hearing it, said so to the Duke of Albemarle,[405] and afterwards to W. Coventry, that he had sat twenty-six years in Parliament and never heard such a speech there before: for which the Lord God make me thankful! and that I may make use of it not to pride and vain-glory, but that, now I have this esteem, I may do nothing that may lessen it! I spent the morning thus walking in the Hall, being complimented by everybody with admiration: and at noon stepped into the Legg[406] with Sir William Warren,[407] who was in the Hall, and there talked about a little of his business, and thence into the Hall a little more, and so with him by coach as far as the Temple almost, and there 'light,[408] to follow my Lord Brouncker's coach, which I spied, and so to Madam Williams's,[409] where I overtook him, and agreed upon meeting this afternoon, and so home to dinner, and after dinner with W. Pen, who come to my house to call me, to White Hall, to wait on the Duke of York, where he again and all the company magnified me, and several in the Gallery: among others, my Lord Gerard,[410] who never knew me before nor spoke to me, desires his being better

391. Sir D. Gawden: Dennis Gauden had been knighted the previous October. **392. his brother:** Henry Coventry (1619–85), Ambassador to Sweden in 1664 and 1671, later Secretary of State. **393. the Sollicitor-Generall:** Sir Heneage Finch (1621–82) became Attorney General in 1670 and Lord Chancellor in 1675; he was created Earl of Nottingham in 1682. **394. he:** the King. **395. Progers:** Edward Progers (1617–1714), Groom of the Bedchamber to Charles II. **396. Every . . . almost:** almost everybody that saw me. **397. Joseph Williamson:** (1634–1701), Keeper of the King's Library at Whitehall in 1661; knighted in 1672; president of the Royal Society from 1667 to 1680. **398. Mr. G. Montagu:** George Montagu (c. 1624–81), Montagu's cousin.

399. Mr. Ashburnham: Sir Denny Ashburnham (d. 1697). **400. Mr. Godolphin:** Sidney Godolphin (1645–1712), Queen Anne's Lord Treasurer. **401. Mr. Sands:** not identified. **402. Mr. Chichly:** Thomas Chicheley (1618–99), knighted in 1670. **403. Mr. . . . Tower:** Sir John Robinson. **404. Mr. Vaughan:** Sir John Vaughan (1603–74), appointed Chief Justice of the Common Pleas in 1668. **405. Duke of Albemarle:** General Monk. **406. the Legg:** a tavern in King Street. **407. Sir William Warren:** a shipbuilder. **408. 'light:** alighted. **409. Madam Williams:** Brouncker's mistress. **410. Lord Gerard:** Charles Gerard (d. 1694), First Baron Gerard of Brandon, Captain of the Guards.

acquainted with me; and [said] that, at table where he was, he never heard so much said of any man as of me, in his whole life. We waited on the Duke of York, and thence into the Gallery, where the House of Lords waited the King's coming out of the Park, which he did by and by; and there, in the Vane-room,[411] my Lord Keeper[412] delivered a message to the King, the Lords being about him, wherein the Barons of England, from many good arguments, very well expressed in the part he read out of, do demand precedence in England of all noblemen of either of the King's other two kingdoms,[413] be their title what it will; and did shew that they were in England reputed but as Commoners, and sat in the House of Commons, and at conferences with the Lords did stand bare. It was mighty worth my hearing: but the King did only say that he would consider of it, and so dismissed them. Thence Brouncker and I to the Committee of Miscarriages sitting in the Court of Wards, expecting with Sir D. Gawden to have been heard against Prince Rupert's complaints for want of victuals.[414] But the business of Holmes's charge against Sir Jer. Smith,[415] which is a most shameful scandalous thing for Flag officers to accuse one another of, and that this should be heard here before men that understand it not at all, and after it hath been examined and judged in before the King and Lord High Admirall and other able seamen to judge, it is very hard.[416] But this business did keep them all the afternoon, so we not heard but put off to another day. Thence, with the Lieutenant of the Tower, in his coach home; and there, with great pleasure, with my wife, talking and playing at cards a little—she, and I, and W. Hewer, and Deb., and so, after a little supper, I to bed.

March 12, 1668

Up, and to the office, where all the morning, at noon home, and after dinner with wife and Deb., carried them to Unthanke's, and I to Westminster Hall expecting our being with the Committee this afternoon about Victualling business, but once more waited in vain. So after a turn or two with Lord Brouncker, I took my wife up and left her at the 'Change while I to Gresham College, there to shew myself; and was there greeted by Dr. Wilkins,[417] Whistler,[418] and others, as the patron of the Navy Office, and one that got great fame by my late speech to the Parliament. Here I saw a great trial of the goodness[419] of a burning glass, made of a new figure,[420] not spherical (by one Smithys,[421] I think, they call him), that did burn a glove of my Lord Brouncker's from the heat of a very little fire, which a burning glass of the old form, or much bigger, could not do, which was mighty pretty. Here I heard Sir Robert Southwell[422] give an account of some things committed to him by the Society at his going to Portugall, which he did deliver in a mighty handsome manner. Thence went away home, and there at my office as long as my eyes would endure, and then home to supper, and to talk with Mr. Pelling,[423] who tells me what a fame I have in the City for my late performance; and upon the whole I bless God for it. I think I have, if I can keep it, done myself a great deal of repute. So by and by to bed.

May 2, 1668

Up, and at the office all the morning. At noon with Lord Brouncker in his coach as far as the Temple, and there 'light and to Hercules Pillars,[424] and there dined, and thence to the Duke of York's playhouse, at a little past twelve, to get a good place in the pit, against[425] the new play, and there setting a poor man to keep

411. **the Vane-room:** the King's drawing room, named from the fact that the main weathercock in the palace was situated above it. **412. Lord Keeper:** Sir Orlando Bridg(e)-man (1606–74). He presided at the trial of the regicides. **413. two kingdoms:** Scotland and Ireland. **414. Prince . . . victuals:** Prince Rupert had complained about the inefficiency of the victualing service in supplying the fleet during the Second Dutch War. **415. Holmes's . . . Smith:** Captain Robert Holmes (1622–92) had charged Sir Jeremy Smith (d. 1675) with cowardice and misbehavior in an engagement with the Dutch on July 26, 1666. In the ensuing controversy Smith was exonerated and Holmes, as a result of Smith's counteraccusations, was mildly chastised. As Pepys goes on to say, there was a court martial, but apparently it was unable to decide the question and referred it back to the King. **416. hard:** bad or, in the nautical sense, extreme.

417. **Dr. Wilkins:** John Wilkins, D.D. (1614–72), Bishop of Exeter and one of the original Fellows of the Royal Society. **418. Whistler:** Daniel Whistler, M.D. (d. 1684), professor of geometry at Gresham College from 1648 to 1657 and another of the original Fellows of the Royal Society. **419. goodness:** strength, power. **420. figure:** shape. **421. Smithys:** His name is given as Smethwick in Thomas Birch's *History of the Royal Society* (1756–57). **422. Sir . . . Southwell:** (1635–1702), Envoy Extraordinary to Portugal from 1665 to 1668. He became president of the Royal Society in 1690. **423. Mr. Pelling:** an apothecary. **424. Hercules Pillars:** a tavern in Fleet Street. **425. against:** for.

my place,[426] I out, and spent an hour at Martin's, my bookseller's, and so back again, where I find the house quite full. But I had my place, and by and by the King comes and the Duke of York; and then the play begins, called "The Sullen Lovers; or, The Impertinents,"[427] having many good humours in it, but the play tedious, and no design at all in it. But a little boy, for a farce,[428] do dance Polichinelli,[429] the best that every anything was done in the world, by all men's report: most pleased with that, beyond anything in the world, and much beyond all the play. Thence to the King's house to see Knepp, but the play done;[430] and so I took a hackney alone, and to the park,[431] and there spent the evening, and to the lodge, and drank new milk. And so home to the Office, ended my letters, and, to spare my eyes, home, and played on my pipes, and so to bed.

May 5, 1668

Up, and all the morning at the office. At noon home to dinner and Creed with me, and after dinner he and I to the Duke of York's playhouse; and there coming late, he and I up to the balcony-box, where we find my Lady Castlemayne and several great ladies; and there we sat with them, and I saw "The Impertinents" once more, now three times, and the three only days it hath been acted. And to see the folly how the house do this day cry up the play more than yesterday! and I for that reason like it, I find, the better, too; by Sir Positive At-all, I understand, is meant Sir Robert Howard.[432] My Lady pretty well pleased with it; but here I sat close to her fine woman, Willson, who indeed is very handsome, but, they say, with child by the King. I asked, and she told me this was the first time her Lady had seen it, I having a mind to say something to her. One thing of familiarity[433] I observed in my

Lady Castlemayne: she called to one of her women, another that sat by this,[434] for a little patch[435] off her face, and put it into her mouth and wetted it, and so clapped it upon her own by the side of her mouth, I suppose she feeling a pimple rising there. Thence with Creed to Westminster Hall, and there met with cozen Roger,[436] who tells me of the great conference this day between the Lords and Commons, about the business of the East India Company,[437] as being one of the weightiest conferences that hath been, and managed as weightily. I am heartily sorry I was not there, it being upon a mighty point of the privileges of the subjects of England, in regard to the authority of the House of Lords, and their[438] being condemned by them as the Supreme Court, which, we say, ought not to be, but by appeal from other Courts. And he tells me that the Commons had much the better of them, in reason and history there quoted, and believes the Lords will let it fall. Thence to walk in the Hall, and there hear that Mrs. Martin's child, my god-daughter,[439] is dead, and so by water to the Old Swan, and thence home, and there a little at Sir W. Pen's, and so to bed.

September 4, 1668

Up, and met at the Office all the morning; and at noon my wife, and Deb., and Mercer, and W. Hewer and I to the Fair,[440] and there, at the old house, did

426. setting . . . place: a common practice before the institution of reserved seats. 427. The Sullen . . . Impertinents: a new comedy by Thomas Shadwell (c. 1642–92). 428. for a farce: Various kinds of entertainment—dramatic, musical, choreographic, and mechanical (e.g., puppet shows) —preceded the performance of plays in this period. 429. Polichinelli: Punchinello, the prototype of Punch, a grotesque puppet buffoon. 430. done: was no longer being performed. The play was The Surprizal by Sir Robert Howard (see n. 432); Knepp played Emilia. Pepys had attended the performance the day before, and two previous ones as well. 431. the park: Hyde Park. 432. Sir . . . Howard: (1626–98), Dryden's brother-in-law and collaborator on The Indian Queen (1664); the Crites of the Essay of Dramatic Poesy, published this year. 433. of familiarity: unceremonious, natural.

434. this: Wilson. 435. patch: Fashionable ladies wore patches on their faces, either to heighten their complexions or to conceal blemishes. 436. cozen Roger: Roger Pepys (1617–88), a lawyer and Member of Parliament for Cambridge from 1660 to 1679. 437. the business . . . Company: A trader named Skinner had petitioned the House of Lords for redress of damages suffered at the hands of the East India Company. The House of Lords awarded Skinner heavy damages, but the company petitioned the House of Commons for protection, claiming that the Lords had no jurisdiction in such a complaint that was not first heard in the ordinary law courts. The Lords thereupon voted the company's petition a libel; the Commons in reply censured the Lords for acting in opposition to the rights of English subjects; and the Lords returned by declaring the Commons' vote of censure a breach of privilege. The dispute was put aside with the close of the Parliamentary session on May 9, and was finally "settled" in 1670 by the simple expedient of striking from the records all debate on the point. 438. their: the subjects'. 439. my god-daughter: born November 24, 1666. 440. the Fair: Bartholomew Fair, which opened on St. Bartholomew's Eve, August 23. After the Restoration the fair was extended from its traditional three days to fourteen; in 1708 it was reduced to three again.

eat a pig, and was pretty merry, but saw no sights, my wife having a mind to see the play "Bartholomew-Fayre,"[441] with puppets. Which we did, and it is an excellent play; the more I see it, the more I love the wit of it; only the business of abusing the Puritans begins to grow stale, and of no use, they being the people that, at last, will be found the wisest. And here Knepp come to us, and sat with us, and thence took coach in two coaches, and losing one another, my wife, and Knepp, and I to Hercules Pillars, and there supped, and I did take from her mouth the words and notes of her song of "the Larke," which pleases me mightily. And so set her at home, and away we home, where our company come home before us. This night Knepp tells us that there is a Spanish woman lately come over, that pretends to sing as well as Mrs. Knight;[442] both of which I must endeavour to hear. So, after supper, to bed.

September 19, 1668

Up, and to the office, where all the morning busy, and so dined with my people at home, and then to the King's playhouse, and there saw "The Silent Woman;" the best comedy, I think, that ever was wrote; and sitting by Shadwell the poet, he was big with admiration of it. Here was my Lord Brouncker and W. Pen and their ladies in the box, being grown mighty kind of a sudden; but, God knows, it will last but a little while, I dare swear. Knepp did her part[443] mighty well. And so home straight, and to work, and [? wrote] particularly to my cozen Roger, who, W. Hewer and my wife writes me,[444] do use them with mighty plenty and noble entertainment: so home to supper, and to bed. All the news now is, that Mr. Trevor is for certain now to be Secretary, in Morrice's place,[445] which the Duke of York did himself tell me yesterday; and also that Parliament is to be adjourned to the 1st of March,[446] which do please me well, hoping thereby to get my things in a little better order than I should have done; and the less attendances at that end of the town in winter. So home to supper and to bed.

January 23, 1669

Up, and again to look after the setting things right against dinner, which I did to very good content. So to the office, where all the morning till noon, when word brought me to the Board that my Lord Sandwich was come; so I presently rose, leaving the Board ready to rise,[447] and there[448] I found my Lord Sandwich, Peterborough,[449] and Sir Charles Harbord;[450] and presently after them comes my Lord Hinchingbroke, Mr. Sidney,[451] and Sir William Godolphin.[452] And after greeting them, and some time spent in talk, dinner was brought up, one dish after another, but a dish at a time, but all so good; but, above all things, the variety of wines, and excellent of their kind, I had for them, and all in so good order, that they were mightily pleased, and myself full of content at it: and indeed it was, of a dinner of about six or eight dishes, as noble as any man need to have, I think; at least, all was done in the noblest manner that ever I had any, and I have rarely seen in my life better anywhere else, even at the Court. After dinner, my Lords to cards, and the rest of us sitting about them and talking, and looking on my books and pictures, and my wife's drawings, which they commend mightily; and mighty merry all day long, with exceeding great content, and so till seven at night; and so took their leaves, it being dark and foul weather. Thus was this entertainment over, the best of its kind, and the fullest of honour and content to me, that ever I had in my life: and shall not easily have so good again. The truth is, I have some fear that I am more behind-hand[453] in the world for these last two years, since I have not, or for some time could not, look after my accounts, which do a little allay my pleasure. But I do trust in God I am pretty well yet, and resolve, in a very little time, to look into my accounts, and see how they stand. So to my wife's chamber, and there supped, and got her cut my hair and look[454] my shirt, for I have itched mightily these 6 or 7 days, and when all comes to all she finds that I am lousy, having found

441. Bartholomew-Fayre: Ben Jonson's comedy (1614); "with puppets" refers to the preliminary entertainment. **442. Mrs. Knight:** mistress of Charles II and a celebrated singer. **443. her part:** the title role. **444. my . . . me:** Mrs. Pepys had left on the fifteenth to visit Roger Pepys at Cambridge and see the Stourbridge Fair. **445. Mr. . . . place:** Sir John Trevor (d. 1673) replaced Sir William Morrice (1602–76) as Secretary of State. **446. 1st of March:** Parliament adjourned November 11, 1668, until March 1, 1669, on which date it was prorogued until the following October 19.

447. rise: adjourn, recess. **448. there:** at Pepys's house. **449. Peterborough:** Henry Mordaunt (c. 1624–97), Second Earl of Peterborough; member of the Tangier Commission and former Governor of Tangier in 1661–62. **450. Sir . . . Harbord:** (c. 1640–72), a navy officer and a protégé of Montagu's. **451. Mr. Sidney:** Montagu's second son, Sidney (d.1727). His son married the famous Lady Mary Wortley (1689–1762). (See the selection from Lady Mary Wortley Montagu in Part Three.) **452. Sir . . . Godolphin:** (d. 1696), Ambassador to Spain in 1671. **453. behind-hand:** financially set back. **454. look:** look over, examine.

in my head and body about twenty lice, little and great, which I wonder at, being more than I have had I believe these 20 years. I did think I might have got them from the little boy,[455] but they did presently look him, and found none. So how they come I know not, but presently did shift myself,[456] and so shall be rid of them, and cut my hair close to my head, and so with much content to bed.

May 24, 1669

To White Hall, and there all the morning, and thence home, and giving order for some business and setting my brother[457] to making a catalogue of my books, I back again to W. Hewer to White Hall, where I attended the Duke of York, and was by him led to [the King], who expressed great sense of my misfortune in my eyes, and concernment for their recovery; and accordingly signified, not only his assent to my desire therein, but commanded me to give them rest this summer, according to my late petition[458] to the Duke of York. W. Hewer and I dined alone at the Swan; and thence, having thus waited on the King, spent till four o'clock in St. James's Park, when I met my wife at Unthanke's, and so home.

May 31, 1669

Up very betimes, and so continued all the morning with W. Hewer, upon examining and stating my accounts, in order to the fitting myself to go abroad beyond sea, which the ill condition of my eyes, and my neglect for a year or two, hath kept me behind-hand in, and so as to render it very difficult now, and troublesome to my mind to do it; but I this day made a satisfactory entrance therein. Dined at home, and in the afternoon by water to White Hall, calling by the

way at Michell's, where I have not been many a day till just the other day, and now I met her mother there and knew her husband to be out of town. And here je did baiser elle, but had not opportunity para hazer[459] some with her as I would have offered if je had had it. And thence had another meeting with the Duke of York, at White Hall, on yesterday's work, and made a good advance: and so, being called by my wife, we to the Park, Mary Batelier, and a Dutch gentleman, a friend of hers, being with us. Thence to "The World's End," a drinking-house by the Park; and there merry, and so home late.

And thus ends all that I doubt[460] I shall ever be able to do with my own eyes in the keeping of my Journal, I being not able to do it any longer, having done now so long as to undo my eyes almost every time that I take a pen in my hand; and, therefore, whatever comes of it, I must forebear: and, therefore, resolve, from this time forward, to have it kept by my people[461] in long-hand, and must therefore be contented to set down no more than is fit for them and all the world to know; or, if there be any thing, which cannot be much, now my amours to Deb. are past,[462] and my eyes hindering me in almost all other pleasures, I must endeavour to keep a margin in my book open, to add, here and there, a note in short-hand with my own hand.

And so I betake myself to that course, which is almost as much as to see myself go into my grave: for which, and all the discomforts that will accompany my being blind,[463] the good God prepare me!

S. P.

455. little boy: possibly Pepys's servant Tom Edwards. **456. shift myself:** change clothes. **457. my brother:** John. **458. my . . . petition:** Increasingly troubled over his eyes, Pepys had requested a leave of absence to travel in Europe and rest.

459. para hazer: to do. **460. doubt:** suspect. **461. kept . . . people:** There are a variety of other journals by Pepys, covering short periods and usually concerned with particular matters. **462. my . . . past:** Pepys had finally been caught by his wife in an intimacy with Deb, who was discharged as Mrs. Pepys's price for her forgiveness. **463. my . . . blind:** Pepys did not go blind. He suffered from astigmatism and, as he grew older, far-sightedness. At this time only the latter affliction was correctable. He had to have the help of clerks in reading, but otherwise he was not seriously handicapped.

John Dryden

1631–1700

With John Dryden a new voice seems to enter English writing, or an old voice speaking virtually a new language. The language is substantially that of modern man. As T. S. Eliot has said, "It is hardly too much to say that Dryden found the English speechless, and he gave them speech." This new voice is that of the forum and the public speaker. Dryden's ideal was the image of the classical orator, and his writing, no matter how domesticated it may seem, resonates always with something of the gravity, the "manliness," and the magnificence of ancient Rome. Dryden has been called the first English man of letters: like a Roman *rhetor*, he was consciously a public professional, whether in his political and religious satires, his poems on public occasions, his plays, or his criticism. Even his lyrics are written to be overheard by multitudes.

He was born in Aldwinckle, Northamptonshire, the son of Erasmus Dryden and Mary Pickering, both of Puritan families soon to be allied with Parliament against the King. When he entered Westminster School as a King's Scholar around 1646, the school was under the regulation of a committee chosen by Parliament; but the rigorous classical education superintended by Dr. Richard Busby, famous for never having spoiled a child, was unaffected. In 1649, Dryden's first poem, *Upon the Death of Lord Hastings* (a schoolmate), was published in a commemorative volume entitled *Lachrymae Musarum*. If it is still read, it is read for the condescending amusement its decadent Metaphysical style affords. The next year he was elected to Trinity College, Francis Bacon's old college, which was at this time the center of the new science at Cambridge. He received his degree here in 1654. It is not surprising that he obtained no fellowship in the college, for he seems to have had no leanings toward scholarship: his curiosity was always wide-ranging and various rather than particular and constant. At any rate his studies supplied him with that fund of general knowledge he was later to say was indispensable for a poet and with a fondness and respect for those ancient authors he would later emulate.

Dryden then moved to London and is thought to have held a minor post in the Commonwealth government, obtained for him, no doubt, by his cousin, Sir Gilbert Pickering, a member of the Protector's Council. After Cromwell's death in 1658, Dryden wrote his first important poem, a funeral oration entitled *Heroic Stanzas to the Glorious Memory of Oliver* [Cromwell], which appeared the following year in a volume with poems on the same subject by Edmund Waller and Thomas Sprat.

Astraea Redux, written the next year to celebrate the restoration of Charles II, is remarkable because we hear in it the voice of the orator speaking with a new sureness and we meet for the first time that conscious parallel between England and Rome, Charles and Augustus, that Dryden elaborated throughout his career.

The change of loyalties these two poems suggest has occasioned witty insinuations of political trimming. Dismissing allegations of timeserving, Johnson said of Dryden's change to the Royalists at Charles's restoration, "The reproach of inconstancy was, on this occasion, shared with such numbers that it produced neither hatred nor disgrace; if he changed, he changed with the nation." Dryden's conversion to Rome, apparently accomplished in 1685, the same year as the Catholic James's accession to the throne, has been harder to explain. The coincidence is unlucky, for it obscures what was probably a long process of development in his thought, rather than a sudden reversal. His growing conservatism in politics and religion was the result of a growing skepticism about man's ability to answer ultimate questions for himself—a skepticism he shared with his age. Many men despaired of their own ability to know, and they sought assurance from an authority or tradition outside themselves. Dryden's conversions were both in the direction of this faith in authority. The fact that he did not revert to Protestantism after James was deposed, and thereby lost his court offices, lends credence to the principles behind his choices.

Dryden's genius matured late. In 1663, at the age of thirty-two, he had produced only a few poems. During that year, however, he married Lady Elizabeth Howard, and with her brother Sir Robert, with whom he had been friendly for several years, he collaborated on a heroic play, *The Indian Queen*, produced in 1664. In the same year he published *The Rival Ladies*, dedicated to the Earl of Orrery, himself a writer of heroic plays, to whom Dryden addressed his essay on dramatic rhyme. But if his dedication to writing was late, it was complete. For the next twenty years he was engaged in supplying plays for the newly chartered theaters, and he continued to employ himself writing until the end of his life.

We have it from Congreve that Dryden's hereditary income gave him "little more than a bare competency." In 1668 he succeeded William Davenant as Poet Laureate, a post that carried an annual stipend of one hundred pounds. His appointment was not confirmed until 1670, however, at which time he was also appointed Historiographer Royal and received an additional one hundred pounds. He continued in these two positions for almost twenty years until, as a Catholic, he was unable to take the oath of allegiance to William and Mary. The two stipends afforded him some security and, except for the last days of Charles's reign (when the Laureate received only half his stipend because of the King's desperate financial troubles), allowed him to pursue writing projects for other than gain.

Of Dryden's almost thirty plays none has held the stage. Indeed, very few have continued to be read for pleasure. His heroic plays were the most admired during his lifetime, for they had sensational plots, exotic settings, and noble heroes gorgeously torn between love and honor. The fact that love triumphed more often than honor did not diminish their appeal. These plays are satirized in *The Rehearsal* (1671), attributed to the Duke of Buckingham and several collaborators. In comedy Dryden was less successful and less at ease. His comedies, the best of which are *Marriage A-la-Mode* (1671) and *The Spanish Friar* (1681), have the exuberance and raillery we have come to relish in Restoration comedy, but little of the subtlety and verbal wit of the very best. His most famous play, *All for Love* (1678)—the only play, he declares, that he wrote for himself—is also his best. A tragedy on the subject of Antony and Cleopatra, its reputation has unfortunately suffered by comparison to Shakespeare's greater play on the same subject. Yet it has a grandeur of its own and within its own terms is almost faultless. Though it is seldom played, it may still be read with delight. His years of writing for the stage, "to which," he said, "my genius never much inclined me," strengthened his command of the couplet, exercised his public voice, and afforded occasions for some of his best critical writing. His career in the theater also brought him fame and the assurance of an audience for his serious non-dramatic poetry.

Dryden is clearly at his best in the nondramatic poems in which on important public occasions he uses his wide general learning and fertile invention to inform and instruct his readers. His detractors said that he was given to chopping logic in heroic verse. It is true, as Johnson says, that his power was "to reason in verse"; he appealed to the best in his audience—that is, their capacity for reason—and required of them that they appear better than they were, more dignified and more reasonable, for he thought with the rest of his age that man was not a reasonable animal but an animal capable of reason. He demanded as much of himself. The calling of the poet was an important one and the talents required not mean. He believed that "a man should have a reasonable, philosophical and in some measure mathematical head to be a complete and excellent poet; and besides this should have experience in all sorts of humors and manners of men; should be thoroughly skilled in conversation and should have a great knowledge of mankind in general." As early as 1666 in the Preface to *Annus Mirabilis*, a long historical poem celebrating England's victory over the Dutch fleet and the courage of the citizens of London during the Great Fire of London, Dryden speaks of the craft of the poet, using the terms of classical oratory. This preface, which contains a complete heroic aesthetic in small, makes it clear that Dryden is not thinking of rhetoric in the Renaissance sense of tropes and figures but as the whole creative process for poetry.

In 1678, when he was nearing fifty, he put his long rhetorical training to use in formal verse satire, the form that came most naturally to him and for which he is best remembered. His first satire, the brilliant *Mac Flecknoe*, written for private circulation, has a purely literary subject, but Dryden endows it with a kind of largeness and grandeur that transforms the rough, personal, and fantastic sort of satire of the Renaissance into a much more controlled and classical vehicle, the kind of writing by which "a man could be reasoned into truth." The year 1681 brought the occasion for his finest and most majestic satire, *Absalom and Achitophel*. No classical orator could have gone at his task with greater relish and invention than Dryden. The occasion was public; the actors, kings and princes; the subject, rebellion. The task of defending the King and discrediting his very popular Opposition demanded great tact. He succeeds by employing a biblical setting and a biblical story that parallel the contemporary events, thereby removing them from the frenzy of the moment, flattering both sides, and encouraging his audience to see the importance of the debate. Everyone was eager to decipher the code of the characters, and sales were brisk.

Dryden's two great religious poems, *Religio Laici* (1682) and *The Hind and the*

Panther (1687), are much more personal poems and may be regarded as "occasional" only in the sense that they are both responses to particular events (in the first instance, a translation of Father Simon's *Histoire critique du Vieux Testament* [1685], which cast a skeptical light on Scriptural authority and thus on the Protestant faith, and, in the second, his own conversion to Rome, which he is careful to defend in the poem). They are both intelligent and persuasive and display that "vigorous genius operating upon large materials" which Johnson so much admired in Dryden. One passage from *The Hind and the Panther* that Eliot praised as "an exact statement in verse," of great "nobility and elegance," with surprising "originality of versification and language," illustrates the deep feeling and conviction Dryden is capable of expressing:

> But, gracious God, how well dost thou provide
> For erring judgments an unerring guide!
> Thy throne is darkness in the abyss of light,
> A blaze of glory that forbids the sight.
> O teach me to believe Thee thus concealed,
> And search no farther than Thyself revealed;
> But her alone for my director take,
> Whom Thou hast promised never to forsake!
> My thoughtless youth was winged with vain desires;
> My manhood, long misled by wandering fires,
> Followed false lights; and when their glimpse was gone,
> My pride struck out new sparkles of her own.
> Such was I, such by nature still I am;
> Be Thine the glory, and be mine the shame!

With these poems Dryden's reputation was secure. Not only was he the most famous writer in England, but he had perfected a verse texture that was to remain a standard for the next hundred years. In what he called "the other harmony of prose" he developed a sparse and sinuous style, easy and natural. Anyone who reads his prefaces and critical essays today knows that he is reading the English of modern man: the syntax is plain and the words common and still in use. Dryden wrote a prose (Matthew Arnold said two hundred years later) "such as we would all gladly use if we only knew how."

But Dryden's prefaces and critical essays are interesting for another reason. Occasional in nature, witty, and frequently contradictory, they present nevertheless a unified theory of criticism—the first in English—based on a supple understanding of the rhetorical theory of his classical models. He reinterpreted and domesticated a whole literary tradition that had been largely misunderstood during the Renaissance. One of his finest pieces of literary criticism, *An Essay of Dramatic Poesy* (1668), is cast in the mode of a Ciceronian dialogue in which no speaker dominates, as Socrates does in the Platonic dialogues, but a nice balance is achieved between opposing voices. This fact is profoundly characteristic of Dryden's mind: it shows his delight in speculation, his inventiveness in argument, his ease in marshaling evidence. He is like a lawyer with powerful literary leanings. Dryden's last great work of criticism, his Preface to the *Fables* (1700), was written the year before he died. It shows the largeness of his mind and its continued vigor in his last years. The Preface reveals as always the working poet ruminating on his craft, and while it is less systematic than *An Essay of Dramatic Poesy*, it has a professional literary concern, the art of storytelling. He compares Homer and Virgil not on the basis of their elegant images or their "numbers," but on the basis of their design—and in this respect he gives Virgil second place. The real subject though is Chaucer, England's greatest teller of tales, and, in comparison with both Ovid and Boccaccio, Dryden confesses that the homely, English Chaucer pleases him best.

After 1689 Dryden was again forced to support himself by writing. Returning to the theater, he wrote five more plays. He translated Juvenal (1692), Persius (1692), and Virgil (1697) for the enterprising publisher Jacob Tonson; and he prepared his collection of "fables" from Homer, Chaucer, Ovid, and Boccaccio (*Fables Ancient and Modern*). In 1697 he produced a splendid ode, *Alexander's Feast*, for the annual concert held on St. Cecilia's Day, and in the last year of his life celebrated the coming of a new age in his *Secular Masque* (1700).

Of Dryden's personal and domestic life we know little since we have no contemporary biography. He complained often of penury. He seems to have been jealous of his fame (perhaps because he knew it to be the source of any future financial success he might have), and frequently, even in the years during which he enjoyed royal favor, he entered into battle with lesser writers who are now remembered only because of Dryden's satiric hits. We can surmise how bitter he found the irony of being succeeded as Poet Laureate by Shadwell. He is said to have been less brilliant in conversation than in writing, but a pleasant picture comes down to us of his advising young poets and entering into literary debate at Will's Coffee House, where he had a seat of honor both summer and winter.

Yet it is possible to get, as Johnson did, a vivid picture of the man from the works themselves. No one has given a better account of Dryden's genius than has Johnson. In his *Life of Pope*, he compares Dryden with his literary successor:

> Of genius, that power which constitutes a poet; that quality without which judgement is cold and knowledge is inert; that energy which collects, combines, amplifies, and animates; the superiority must, with some hesitation, be allowed to Dryden. . . . Dryden's performances were always hasty, either excited by some external occasion, or extorted by domestick necessity; he composed without consideration, and published without correction. What his mind could supply at call, or gather in one excursion, was all that he sought, and all that he gave. . . . If the flights of Dryden therefore are higher, Pope continues longer on the wing. If of Dryden's fire the blaze is brighter, of Pope's the heat is more regular and constant. Dryden often surpasses expectation, and Pope never falls below it. Dryden is read with frequent astonishment, and Pope with perpetual delight.

The standard bibliography of Dryden is Hugh Macdonald's *John Dryden: A Bibliography of Early Editions and of Drydeniana* (1939). The standard biography is C. E. Ward's *Life of John Dryden* (1961); Ward also edited *The Letters of John Dryden* (1942).

J. M. Osborn's *John Dryden: Some Biographical Facts and Problems* (rev. ed., 1965), a still valuable supplement, contains an excellent critical survey of Dryden's biographers. Editions of Dryden's works are plentiful. For the criticism, W. P. Ker's *Essays of John Dryden* (2 vols., 1900) is still useful, though it has been superseded to a large extent by George Watson's *John Dryden: Of Dramatic Poesy and Other Critical Essays* (2 vols., 1962). Similarly, for the poems, G. R. Noyes's *Poetical Works of John Dryden* (rev. ed., 1950) remains valuable for its full notes, though virtually superseded by James Kinsley's excellent *Poems of John Dryden* (4 vols., 1958). But all editions of Dryden seem doomed to the shadows by the California *Dryden*, of which three volumes are published (1956, 1962, 1966.) Montague Summers's *Dryden: The Dramatic Works* (6 vols., 1931–32) remains for now the standard edition of the plays. The numerous general and special critical studies include Mark Van Doren, *The Poetry of John Dryden* (1920, 1931, 1946); T. S. Eliot, *John Dryden: The Poet, the Dramatist, the Critic* (1932); L. I. Bredvold, *The Intellectual Milieu of John Dryden* (1934); William Frost, *Dryden and the Art of Translation* (1955); B. N. Schilling, *Dryden and the Conservative Myth* (1961); A. W. Hoffman, *John Dryden's Imagery* (1962); A. C. Kirsch, *Dryden's Heroic Drama* (1965); Alan Roper, *Dryden's Poetic Kingdoms* (1965); Earl Miner, *Dryden's Poetry* (1967); and Phillip Harth, *Contexts of Dryden's Thought* (1968). Finally, two useful compilations should be cited: S. H. Monk's *John Dryden: A List of Critical Studies Published from 1895 to 1948* (1950) and J. M. Aden's *The Critical Opinions of John Dryden: A Dictionary* (1963).

TO MY HONOR'D FRIEND, DR CHARLETON . . .

The title continues: *on His Learned and Useful Works; and More Particularly This of Stone-Heng, by Him Restored to the True Founders*. This is one of two commendatory poems—the other by Sir Robert Howard—published with *Chorea Gigantum, or, the Most Famous Antiquity of Great Britain, Vulgarly Called Stone-Heng, Standing on Salisbury Plain, Restored to the Danes; by Walter Charleton, Dr. in Physic, and Physician in Ordinary to His Majesty* (1663). The work was an answer to Inigo Jones's theory that Stonehenge was built by the Romans as a temple dedicated to the god Coelus; Charleton believed it to be the work of the Danes, "as a place wherein to elect and inaugurate their supreme Commander, King of England." Dryden's poem was probably composed in the middle months of 1662. In

November he was proposed by Charleton and elected to the Royal Society.

The text is that of the first printing, in *Chorea Gigantum*.

THE longest Tyranny that ever sway'd,
Was that wherein our Ancestors betray'd
Their free-born *Reason* to the *Stagirite*,°
And made his Torch their universal Light.
So *Truth*, while onely one suppli'd the State,
Grew scarce, and dear, and yet sophisticate.°
Until 'twas bought, like Emp'rique° Wares, or
    Charms,

TO MY HONOR'D FRIEND, DR. CHARLETON. **3. the Stagirite:** Aristotle, the authority of whose rationalist philosophy is attacked from the position of Baconian empiricism. **6. sophisticate:** artificial. **7. Emp'rique:** empiric, quack.

Hard words seal'd up with *Aristotle*'s *Armes*.
Columbus was the first that shook his *Throne*;
And found a *Temp'rate* in a *Torrid* Zone:°   10
The fevrish aire fann'd by a cooling breez,
The fruitful Vales set round with shady Trees;
And guiltless *Men*, who danc'd away their time,
Fresh as their *Groves*, and *Happy* as their *Clime*.°
Had we still paid that homage to a *Name*,
Which onely *God* and *Nature* justly claim;
The *Western* Seas had been our utmost bound,
Where *Poets* still might dream the *Sun* was drown'd:
And all the *Starrs*, that shine in *Southern* Skies,
Had been admir'd by none but *Salvage*° Eyes.   20
   Among th' *Assertors* of free Reason's claim,
Th' *English* are not the least in Worth, or Fame.
The World to *Bacon* does not onely owe
Its *present* Knowledge, but its *future* too.
Gilbert° shall live, till *Load-stones* cease to draw,
Or *British* Fleets the boundless Ocean awe.
And noble *Boyle*,° not less in *Nature* seen,
Than his great *Brother*° read in *States* and *Men*.
The *Circling* streams, once thought but pools, of blood
(Whether Life's fewel, or the Bodie's food)   30
From dark Oblivion *Harvey*'s name° shall save;
While *Ent*° keeps all the honour that he gave.
Nor are *You*, Learned Friend, the least renown'd;
Whose Fame, not circumscrib'd with *English* ground,
Flies like the nimble journeys of the Light;
And is, like that, unspent too in its flight.
What ever *Truths* have been, by *Art*, or *Chance*,
Redeem'd from *Error*, or from *Ignorance*,
Thin in their *Authors*, (like rich veins of Ore)
Your Works unite, and still discover more.   40
Such is the healing virtue of Your Pen,
To perfect Cures on *Books*, as well as *Men*.
Nor is This Work the least: You well may give
To *Men* new vigour, who make *Stones* to live.

Through You, the *DANES* (their short Dominion
   lost)
A longer Conquest than the *Saxons* boast.
STONE-HENG, once thought a *Temple*, You have found
A *Throne*, where Kings, our Earthly Gods, were
   Crown'd.
Where by their wondring Subjects They were seen,
Joy'd with their Stature, and their Princely meen.°   50
Our *Soveraign* here above the rest might stand;
And here be chose again to rule the Land.
   These Ruines sheltred once *His* Sacred Head,
Then when from *Wor'sters* fatal Field *He* fled;°
Watch'd by the Genius of this Royal place,
And mighty Visions of the Danish Race.
His *Refuge* then was for a *Temple* shown:
But, *He* Restor'd, 'tis now become a *Throne*.

[AH HOW SWEET IT IS TO LOVE]

This song comes from *Tyrannic Love*, Act IV, scene i, where it is sung by the spirit Damilcar to St. Catharine, the heroine of the play.
   The text is that of the first edition (1670).

AH how sweet it is to love,
Ah how gay is young desire!
And what pleasing pains we prove
When we first approach Loves fire!
   Pains of Love be sweeter far
   Than all other pleasures are.

Sighs which are from Lovers blown,
Do but gently heave the Heart:
Ev'n the tears they shed alone
Cure, like trickling Balm their smart.   10
   Lovers when they lose their breath,
   Bleed away in easie death.

9–10. Columbus . . . Zone: Aristotle had believed the torrid zone to be uninhabitable. **11–14. The fevrish . . . Clime:** a typical description of an earthly paradise. **20. Salvage:** savage. **25. Gilbert:** William Gilbert (1540–1603), physician to Queen Elizabeth and James I, made important discoveries in magnetism. **27. Boyle:** Robert Boyle (1627–91), the chemist; one of the founders of the Royal Society. **28. Brother:** Roger Boyle (1621–79), Earl of Orrery. Dryden alludes to his accomplishments in politics and drama. **31. Harvey's name:** William Harvey (1578–1657), who discovered the circulation of the blood. **32. Ent:** Sir George Ent (1604–89) defended Harvey's theory. He was an original member of the Royal Society and later was president of the College of Physicians.

50. meen: mien. **54. when . . . fled:** in 1651. Charleton, in his Dedication to *Chorea Gigantum* (1663), credits the King's account of his escape with the inspiration for his research into the origin of Stonehenge.

Love and Time with reverence use,
Treat 'em like a parting friend:
Nor the golden gifts refuse
Which in youth sincere they send:
  For each year their price is more,
  And they less simple than before.

Love, like Spring-tides full and high,
Swells in every youthful vein: 20
But each Tide does less supply,
Till they quite shrink in again:
  If a flow in Age appear,
  'Tis but rain, and runs not clear.

PREFACE
[TO *AN EVENING'S LOVE*]

❧

An Evening's Love was first performed in June, 1668, and first printed in 1671, when two editions appeared. The present text is that of the first of these editions, with some minor corrections.

❧

I Had thought, Reader, in this Preface to have written somewhat concerning the difference betwixt the Playes of our Age, and those of our Predecessors on the *English* Stage: to have shewn in what parts of Dramatick Poesie we were excell'd by *Ben. Johnson*, I mean, humour, and contrivance of Comedy; and in what we may justly claim precedence of *Shakespear* and *Fletcher*,[1] namely in Heroick Playes: but this design I have wav'd on second considerations; at least deferr'd it till I publish the Conquest of *Granada*, where the discourse will be more proper.[2] I had also prepar'd to treat of the improvement of our Language since *Fletcher's* and *Johnson's* dayes, and consequently of our refining the Courtship, Raillery, and Conversation of Playes: but as I am willing to decline that envy which I shou'd draw on my self from some old Opiniatre[3] judges of the Stage; so likewise I am prest

in time so much that I have not leisure, at present, to go thorough with it. Neither, indeed, do I value a reputation gain'd from Comedy so far as to concern my self about it any more than I needs must in my own defence: for I think it, in it's own nature, inferiour to all sorts of Dramatick writing. Low Comedy especially requires, on the Writers part, much of conversation[4] with the vulgar: and much of ill nature in the observation of their follies. But let all men please themselves according to their several tastes: that which is not pleasant to me may be to others who judge better: and, to prevent an accusation from my enemies, I am sometimes ready to imagine that my disgust of low Comedy proceeds not so much from my judgement as from my temper; which is the reason why I so seldom write it; and that when I succeed in it, (I mean so far as to please the Audience) yet I am nothing satisfi'd with what I have done;[5] but am often vex'd to hear the people laugh, and clap, as they perpetually do, where I intended 'em no jest; while they let pass the better things without taking notice of them. Yet even this confirms me in my opinion of slighting popular applause, and of contemning that approbation which those very people give, equally with me, to the Zany[6] of a Mountebank; or to the appearance of an Antick[7] on the Theatre, without wit on the Poets part, or any occasion of laughter from the Actor, besides the ridiculousness of his habit and his Grimaces.

But I have descended before I was aware, from Comedy to Farce; which consists principally of Grimaces. That I admire not any Comedy equally with Tragedy, is, perhaps, from the sullenness of my humor; but that I detest those Farces, which are now the most frequent entertainments of the Stage, I am sure I have reason on my side. Comedy consists, though of low persons, yet of natural actions, and characters; I mean such humours, adventures, and designes, as are to be found and met with in the world. Farce, on the other side, consists of forc'd humours, and unnatural events: Comedy presents us with the imperfections of humane nature. Farce entertains us with what is monstruous and chimerical: the one

---

PREFACE TO *An Evening's Love*. **1. Fletcher:** John Fletcher (1579–1625), English playwright known for the comedies he wrote alone and with other dramatists and especially for his collaboration on tragicomedies with Francis Beaumont (c. 1584–1616). **2. where . . . proper:** See *Defence of the Epilogue*, below. **3. Opiniatre:** opinionated.

4. conversation: intercourse. **5. yet . . . done:** a view contradicted by Johnson in his *Life of Dryden* (see Part Six): "Dryden was no rigid judge of his own pages; he seldom struggled after supreme excellence, but snatched in haste what was within his reach, and when he could content others was himself contented." **6. Zany:** clownish assistant. **7. Antick:** clown.

causes laughter in those who can judge of men and manners; by the lively representation of their folly or corruption; the other produces the same effect in those who can judge of neither, and that only by its extravagances. The first works on the judgment and fancy; the latter on the fancy only: There is more of satisfaction in the former kind of laughter, and in the latter more of scorn. But, how it happens that an impossible adventure should cause our mirth, I cannot so easily imagine. Something there may be in the oddness of it, because on the Stage it is the common effect of things unexpected to surprize us into a delight: and that is to be ascrib'd to the strange appetite, as I may call it, of the fancy; which, like that of a longing Woman,[8] often runs out into the most extravagant desires; and is better satisfi'd sometimes with Loam, or with the Rinds of Trees, than with the wholsome nourishments of life. In short, there is the same difference betwixt Farce and Comedy, as betwixt an Empirique[9] and a true Physitian: both of them may attain their ends; but what the one performs by hazard, the other does by skill. And as the Artist is often unsuccessful, while the Mountebank succeeds; so Farces more commonly take the people than Comedies. For to write unnatural things, is the most probable way of pleasing them, who understand not Nature. And a true Poet often misses of applause, because he cannot debase himself to write so ill as to please his Audience.

After all, it is to be acknowledg'd, that most of those Comedies, which have been lately written, have been ally'd too much to Farce: and this must of necessity fall out till we forbear the translation of *French Plays:* for their Poets wanting judgement to make, or to maintain true characters, strive to cover their defects with ridiculous Figures and Grimaces. While I say this I accuse my self as well as others: and this very play would rise up in judgement against me, if I would defend all things I have written to be natural: but I confess I have given too much to the people in it, and am asham'd for them as well as for my self, that I have pleas'd them at so cheap a rate: not that there is anything here which I would not defend to an ill-natur'd judge: (for I despise their censures, who I am sure wou'd write worse on the same subject:) but because I love to deal clearly and plainly, and to speak of my own faults with more criticism, then I would of another Poets. Yet I think

8. **a longing Woman:** a pregnant woman. 9. **Empirique:** empiric, quack.

it no vanity to say that this Comedy has as much of entertainment in it as many other which have bin lately written: and, if I find my own errors in it, I am able at the same time to arraign all my Contemporaries for greater. As I pretend not that I can write humour, so none of them can reasonably pretend to have written it as they ought. *Johnson* was the only man of all Ages and Nations who has perform'd it well; and that but in three or four of his Comedies: the rest are but a *Crambe bis cocta;*[10] the same humours a little vary'd and written worse: neither was it more allowable in him, than it is in our present Poets, to represent the follies of particular persons; of which many have accus'd him. *Parcere personis, dicere de vitiis*[11] is the rule of Plays. And *Horace* tells you that the old Comedy amongst the *Grecians* was silenc'd for the too great liberties of the Poets.

> ———— —*In vitium libertas excidit & vim*
> *Dignam lege regi: lex est accepta chorusque*
> *Turpiter obticuit, sublato jure nocendi.*[12]

Of which he gives you the reason in another place: where having given the precept

> *Neve immunda crepent, ignominiosaque dicta:*

He immediately subjoyns,

> *Offenduntur enim, quibus est equus, & pater, & res.*[13]

But *Ben. Johnson* is to be admir'd for many excellencies; and can be tax'd with fewer failings than any *English* Poet. I know I have been accus'd as an enemy of his writings;[14] but without any other reason than that I do not admire him blindly, and without looking into his imperfections. For why should he only be exempted from those frailties, from which *Homer* and *Virgil* are not free? Or why should there be any *ipse dixit* in our Poetry, any more than there is in our Philosophy? I admire and applaud him where

10. **Crambe bis cocta:** "warmed-over cabbage," i.e., an old story (Juvenal, *Satires*, III. vii. 154). 11. **Parcere . . . vitiis:** to spare individuals and speak [only] of vices. This is the rule of satire in general; cf. *Verses on the Death of Dr. Swift*, l. 460, in Part Two. 12. **In . . . nocendi:** "Its freedom sank into excess and an outrage deserving to be regulated by law. A law was enacted, and the chorus to its shame became mute, its right to defame being withdrawn" (*Ars Poetica*, ll. 282–84). 13. **Neve . . . res:** The Satyrs should beware of . . . "cracking their foul and scurrilous jokes. For some take offense—knights, freeborn, and substantial citizens" (*Ibid.*, ll. 247–48). 14. **I have . . . writings:** See the headnote to *Mac Flecknoe*, below.

I ought: those who do more do but value themselves in their admiration of him: and, by telling you they extoll *Ben. Johnson*'s way, would insinuate to you that they can practice it. For my part I declare that I want judgement to imitate him: and shou'd think it a great impudence in my self to attempt it. To make men appear pleasantly ridiculous on the Stage was, as I have said, his talent: and in this he needed not the acumen of wit, but that of judgement. For the characters and representations of folly are only the effects of observation; and observation is an effect of judgment. Some ingenious men, for whom I have a particular esteem, have thought I have much injur'd *Ben. Johnson* when I have not allow'd his wit to be extraordinary: but they confound the notion of what is witty with what is pleasant.[15] That *Ben. Johnson*'s Playes were pleasant he must want reason who denyes: But that pleasantness was not properly wit, or the sharpness of conceit; but the natural imitation of folly: which I confess to be excellent in it's kind, but not to be of that kind which they pretend. Yet if we will believe *Quintilian* in his Chapter *de Movendo risu*, he gives his opinion of both in these following words. *Stulta reprehendere facillimum est; nam per se sunt ridicula: & a derisu non procul abest risus: sed rem urbanam facit aliqua ex nobis adjectio.*[16]

And some perhaps wou'd be apt to say of *Johnson* as it was said of *Demosthenes; Non displicuisse illi jocos, sed non contigisse*,[17] I will not deny but that I approve most the mixt way of Comedy; that which is neither all wit, nor all humour, but the result of both. Neither so little of humour as *Fletcher* shews, nor so little of love and wit, as *Johnson*. Neither all cheat, with which the best Playes of the one are fill'd, nor all adventure, which is the common practice of the other. I would have the characters well chosen, and kept distant from interfaring with each other; which is more than *Fletcher* or *Shakespear* did: but I would have more of the *Urbana, venusta, salsa, faceta*[18] and the rest which

Quintilian reckons up as the ornaments of wit; and these are extremely wanting in *Ben. Johnson*. As for repartie in particular; as it is the very soul of conversation, so it is the greatest grace of Comedy, where it is proper to the Characters: there may be much of acuteness in a thing well said; but there is more in a quick reply: *sunt, enim, longe venustiora omnia in respondendo quam in provocando.*[19] Of one thing I am sure, that no man ever will decry wit, but he who despairs of it himself; and who has no other quarrel to it but that which the Fox had to the Grapes. Yet, as Mr. *Cowley*,[20] (who had a greater portion of it than any man I know) tells us in his *Character of Wit*, rather than all wit let there be none;[21] I think there's no folly so great in any Poet of our Age as the superfluity and wast of wit was in some of our predecessors: particularly we may say of *Fletcher* and of *Shakespear*, what was said of *Ovid*, *In omni ejus ingenio, facilius quod rejici, quam quod adjici potest, invenies.*[22] The contrary of which was true in *Virgil* and our incomparable *Johnson*.

Some enemies of Repartie have observ'd to us, that there is a great latitude in their Characters, which are made to speak it: And that it is easier to write wit than humour; because in the characters of humour, the Poet is confin'd to make the person speak what is only proper to it. Whereas all kind of wit is proper in the Character of a witty person. But, by their favour, there are as different characters in wit as in folly. Neither is all kind of wit proper in the mouth of every ingenious person. A witty Coward and a witty Brave must speak differently. *Falstaffe* and the *Lyar*, speak not like *Don John* in the *Chances*, and *Valentine* in *Wit without Money*.[23] And *Johnson*'s *Truwit* in the *Silent Woman*,[24] is a Character different from all of them. Yet it appears that this one Character of Wit was more difficult to the Author, than all his images of humour in the Play: For those he could describe

---

15. **pleasant:** amusing. 16. **Stulta . . . adjectio:** "It is easy to make fun of folly, for it is laughable in itself, and laughter is related to mockery; but by adding something of our own we make it witty" (*Institutio Oratoria*, VI. iii. 71; *& a derisu . . . risus* is something added of Dryden's own—at least it is not in Quintilian). 17. **Non . . . contigisse:** "that he lacked the power to make jokes, not that he disliked them" (*Ibid.*, l. 2). 18. **the Urbana . . . faceta:** The terms mentioned signify respectively, according to Quintilian, the language of the city and learning (as opposed to rusticity); grace and charm; spice or piquancy; and (not risibility but) polished elegance (*Ibid.*, ll. 17 ff.).

19. **sunt . . . provocando:** "for all wit is far more witty in a retort than in an attack" (*Ibid.*, l. 13). 20. **Mr. Cowley:** Abraham Cowley (1618–67), Metaphysical poet and essayist. 21. **rather . . . none:** "Jewels at nose, and lips but ill appear; / Rather than all things, Wit, let none be there" (*Ode: Of Wit*, ll. 35–36). 22. **In . . . invenies:** "In all the creations of his talent, you will more easily find something that can be abridged than amplified" (Quintilian, *Institutio Oratoria*, VI. iii. 5; for *potest, invenies* read *possit, invenient*). Quintilian was in fact talking about Cicero, not Ovid. 23. **Chances, Wit . . . Money:** two comedies by Fletcher. 24. **the Silent Woman:** *Epicene, or the Silent Woman* (1609).

and manage from his observation of men; this he has taken, at least a part of it, from books: witness the Speeches in the first Act, translated *verbatim* out of *Ovid de Arte Amandi*.[25] To omit what afterwards he borrowed from the sixth Satyre of *Juvenal* against Women.[26]

However, if I should grant, that there were a greater latitude in Characters of Wit, than in those of Humour; yet that latitude would be of small advantage to such Poets who have too narrow an imagination to write it. And to entertain an Audience perpetually with Humour, is to carry them from the conversation of Gentlemen, and treat them with the follies and extravagances of *Bedlam*.

I find I have launch'd out farther than I intended in the beginning of this Preface. And that in the heat of writing, I have touch'd at something, which I thought to have avoided. 'Tis time now to draw homeward: and to think rather of defending my self, than assaulting others. I have already acknowledg'd that this Play is far from perfect: but I do not think my self oblig'd to discover the imperfections of it to my Adversaries, any more than a guilty person is bound to accuse himself before his Judges. 'Tis charg'd upon me that I make debauch'd persons (such as they say my Astrologer and Gamester are) my Protagonists, or the chief persons of the *Drama*: and that I make them happy in the conclusion of my Play; against the Law of Comedy, which is to reward virtue and punish vice. I answer first, that I know no such law to have been constantly observ'd in Comedy, either by the Ancient or Modern Poets. *Choerea* is made happy in the *Eunuch*, after having deflour'd a Virgin: and *Terence* generally does the same through all his Plays, where you perpetually see, not only debauch'd young men enjoy their Mistresses, but even the Courtezans themselves rewarded and honour'd in the Catastrophe. The same may be observ'd in *Plautus* almost every where. *Ben. Johnson* himself, after whom I may be proud to erre, has given me more than once the example of it. That in the *Alchemist* is notorious, where *Face*, after having contriv'd and carried on the great cozenage[27]

of the Play, and continued in it without repentance to the last, is not only forgiven by his Master, but inrich'd by his consent, with the spoiles of those whom he had cheated. And, which is more, his Master himself, a grave man, and a Widower, is introduc'd taking his Man's counsel, debauching the Widow first, in hope to marry her afterward. In the *Silent Woman*, *Dauphine*, (who with the other two Gentlemen, is of the same Character with my *Celadon* in the *Maiden Queen*, and with *Wildblood* in this) professes himself in love with all the Collegiate Ladies: and they likewise are all of the same Character with each other, excepting only Madam *Otter*, who has something singular: yet this naughty *Dauphine* is crown'd in the end with the possession of his Uncles Estate, and with the hopes of enjoying all his Mistresses. And his friend Mr. *Truwit* (the best Character of a Gentleman which *Ben. Johnson* ever made) is not asham'd to pimp for him. As for *Beaumont*[28] and *Fletcher*, I need not alledge examples out of them; for that were to quote almost all their Comedies. But now it will be objected that I patronize vice by the authority of former Poets, and extenuate my own faults by recrimination. I answer that as I defend my self by their example; so that example I defend by reason, and by the end of all Dramatique Poesie. In the first place therefore give me leave to shew you their mistake who have accus'd me. They have not distinguish'd, as they ought, betwixt the rules of Tragedy and Comedy. In Tragedy, where the Actions and Persons are great, and the crimes horrid, the laws of justice are more strictly to be observ'd: and examples of punishment to be made to deterre mankind from the pursuit of vice. Faults of this kind have been rare amongst the Ancient Poets: for they have punish'd in *Oedipus*, and in his posterity, the sinne which he knew not he had committed. *Medea* is the only example I remember at present, who escapes from punishment after murder. Thus Tragedie fulfils one great part of its institution; which is by example to instruct. But in Comedy it is not so; for the chief end of it is divertisement and delight: and that so much, that it is disputed, I think, by *Heinsius*, before[29] *Horace* his Art of Poetry, whether instruction

---

25. the Speeches . . . Amandi: *Epicene, or the Silent Woman*, I. i. 105–09: *Ars Amatoria*, III. 135–40; *Epicene*, I. i. 114–26: *Ars Amatoria*, III. 217–18 and 225–34; *Epicene*, I. i. 128–32: *Ars Amatoria*, III. 243–46. The adaptations of Ovid are not, however, confined to the first act; see the edition of Jonson by C. H. Herford and Percy and Evelyn Simpson, X. 7 ff. **26. what . . . Women:** for True-Wit's portrait of the Collegiate Ladies in II. ii. **27. cozenage:** deception.

28. Beaumont: Francis Beaumont (*c.* 1584–1616), English dramatist known primarily for his collaboration with John Fletcher on a number of tragicomedies. **29. before:** before the tribunal of. But the Dutch classical scholar Heinsius (1580–1655) actually asserts what Dryden denies (*Comoedia enim delectat & docet*), in a note to line 270 of the *Art of Poetry* (1612 edition).

be any part of its employment. At least I am sure it can be but its secondary end: for the business of the Poet is to make you laugh: when he writes humour he makes folly ridiculous; when wit, he moves you, if not alwayes to laughter, yet to a pleasure that is more noble. And if he works a cure on folly, and the small imperfections in mankind, by exposing them to publick view, that cure is not perform'd by an immediate operation. For it works first on the ill nature of the Audience; they are mov'd to laugh by the representation of deformity; and the shame of that laughter, teaches us to amend what is ridiculous in our manners. This being, then, establish'd, that the first end of Comedie is delight, and instruction only the second; it may reasonably be inferr'd that Comedy is not so much oblig'd to the punishment of the faults which it represents, as Tragedy. For the persons in Comedy are of a lower quality, the action is little, and the faults and vices are but the sallies of youth, and the frailties of humane nature, and not premeditated crimes: such to which all men are obnoxious,[30] not such, as are attempted only by few, and those abandonn'd to all sense of vertue; such as move pity and commiseration; not detestation and horror; such in short as may be forgiven, not such as must of necessity be punish'd. But, lest any man should think that I write this to make libertinism amiable; or that I car'd not to debase the end and institution of Comedy, so I might thereby maintain my own errors, and those of better Poets; I must farther declare, both for them and for my self, that we make not vicious persons happy, but only as heaven makes sinners so: that is by reclaiming them first from vice. For so 'tis to be suppos'd they are, when they resolve to marry; for then enjoying what they desire in one, they cease to pursue the love of many. So *Chaerea* is made happy by *Terence*, in marrying her whom he had deflour'd: And so are *Wildblood* and the *Astrologer* in this Play.

There is another crime with which I am charg'd, at which I am yet much less concern'd, because it does not relate to my manners, as the former did, but only to my reputation as a Poet: A name of which I assure the Reader I am nothing proud; and therefore cannot be very solicitous to defend it. I am tax'd with stealing all my Playes, and that by some who should be the last men from whom I would steal any part of 'em. There is one answer which I will not make; but it has been

made for me by him to whose Grace and Patronage I owe all things.

Et spes & ratio studiorum, In Caesare *tantum.*[31]

And without whose command they shou'd no longer be troubl'd with any thing of mine, that he only desir'd that they who accus'd me of theft would always steal him Playes like mine. But though I have reason to be proud of this defence, yet I should wave it, because I have a worse opinion of my own Comedies than any of my Enemies can have. 'Tis true, that where ever I have lik'd any story in a Romance, Novel, or forreign Play, I have made no difficulty, nor ever shall, to take the foundation of it, to build it up, and to make it proper for the *English* Stage. And I will be so vain to say it has lost nothing in my hands: But it always cost me so much trouble to heighten it, for our Theatre (which is incomparably more curious in all the ornaments of Dramatick Poesie, than the *French* or *Spanish*) that when I had finish'd my Play, it was like the Hulk of *Sir Francis Drake*, so strangely alter'd, that there scarce remain'd any Plank of the Timber which first built it. To witness this I need go no farther than this Play: It was first *Spanish*, and call'd *El Astrologo fingido;* then made *French* by the younger *Corneille:* and is now translated into *English*, and in print, under the name of the *Feign'd Astrologer*.[32] What I have perform'd in this will best appear by comparing it with those: you will see that I have rejected some adventures which I judg'd were not divertising: that I have heightned those which I have chosen, and that I have added others which were neither in the *French* nor *Spanish*. And besides you will easily discover that the Walk of the *Astrologer* is the least considerable in my Play: for the design of it turns more on the parts of *Wildblood* and *Jacinta*, who are the chief persons in it. I have farther to add, that I seldome use the wit and language of any Romance, or Play which I undertake to alter: because my own invention (as bad as it is) can furnish me with nothing so dull as what is there. Those who have call'd *Virgil, Terence*, and *Tasso Plagiaries* (though they much injur'd them,) had yet a better colour for their

---

30. **obnoxious:** liable.

31. **Et . . . tantum:** "On Caesar alone depend the hopes and prospects of literary pursuits" (Juvenal, *Satires*, III. vii. 1). The patron is the Duke of Newcastle, to whom *An Evening's Love* is dedicated. 32. **It . . . Astrologer:** The Spanish play was by Calderón (1600–81), the French (*Le Feint Astrologue* [1651]) by Thomas Corneille (1625–1709), and the English (1668) anonymous.

accusation: For *Virgil* has evidently translated *Theocritus*, *Hesiod*, and *Homer*, in many places; besides what he has taken from *Ennius* in his own language. *Terence* was not only known to translate *Menander*, (which he avows also in his Prologues) but was said also to be help't in those Translations by *Scipio* the *African*, and *Laelius*. And *Tasso*, the most excellent of modern Poets, and whom I reverence next to *Virgil*, has taken both from *Homer* many admirable things which were left untouch'd by *Virgil*, and from *Virgil* himself where *Homer* cou'd not furnish him. Yet the bodies of *Virgil's* and *Tasso's* Poems were their own: and so are all the Ornaments of language and elocution in them. The same (if there were any thing commendable in this Play) I could say for it. But I will come nearer to our own Countrymen. Most of *Shakespear's* Playes, I mean the Stories of them, are to be found in the *Hecatommuthi*, or hundred Novels of *Cinthio*.[33] I have, my self, read in his *Italian*, that of *Romeo and Juliet*, the *Moor of Venice*, and many others of them. *Beaumont* and *Fletcher* had most of theirs from *Spanish Novels*: witness the *Chances*, the *Spanish Curate*, *Rule a Wife and have a Wife*, the *Little French Lawyer*, and so many others of them as compose the greatest part of their Volume in folio. *Ben. Johnson*, indeed, has design'd his Plots himself; but no man has borrow'd so much from the Ancients as he has done: And he did well in it, for he has thereby beautifi'd our language.

But these little Criticks do not well consider what is the work of a Poet, and what the Graces of a Poem: the Story is the least part of either: I mean the foundation of it, before it is modell'd by the art of him who writes it; who formes it with more care, by exposing only the beautiful parts of it to view, than a skilful Lapidary sets a Jewel. On this foundation of the Story the Characters are rais'd: and, since no Story can afford Characters enough for the variety of the *English* Stage, it follows that it is to be alter'd, and inlarg'd, with new persons, accidents, and designes, which will almost make it new. When this is done, the forming it into Acts, and Scenes, disposing of actions and passions into their proper places, and beautifying both with descriptions, similitudes, and propriety of language, is the principal employment of the Poet; as being the largest field of fancy, which is the principall quality

requir'd in him: For so much the word ποιητὴς implies. Judgement, indeed, is necessary in him; but 'tis fancy that gives the life touches, and the secret graces to it; especially in serious Plays, which depend not much on observation. For to write humour in Comedy (which is the theft of Poets from mankind) little of fancy is requir'd; the Poet observes only what is ridiculous, and pleasant folly, and by judging exactly what is so, he pleases in the representation of it.

But in general, the employment of a Poet, is like that of a curious[34] Gunsmith, or Watchmaker: the Iron or Silver is not his own; but they are the least part of that which gives the value: The price lyes wholly in the workmanship. And he who works dully on a Story, without moving laughter in a Comedy, or raising concernments in a serious Play, is no more to be accounted a good Poet, than a Gunsmith of the *Minories*[35] is to be compar'd with the best workman of the Town.

But I have said more of this than I intended; and more, perhaps, than I needed to have done: I shall but laugh at them hereafter, who accuse me with so little reason; and withall contemn their dulness, who, if they could ruine that little reputation I have got, and which I value not, yet would want both wit and learning to establish their own; or to be rememberd in after ages for any thing, but only that which makes them ridiculous in this.

[YOU CHARM'D ME NOT WITH THAT FAIR FACE]

This song is from *An Evening's Love*, Act II, where it is sung by the hero Wildblood to the heroine Jacintha. The text is that of the first edition (1671).

You charm'd me not with that fair face
    Though it was all divine:
To be anothers is the Grace,
    That makes me wish you mine.
The Gods and Fortune take their part
    Who like young Monarchs fight;

---

33. Most . . . Cinthio: Cinthio's work (1565) was the source of *Othello* and a partial source of *Two Gentlemen of Verona*, *Twelfth Night*, and *Measure for Measure*, but not of *Romeo and Juliet*.

34. curious: painstaking. **35. Minories:** a street near the Tower of London where armorers were established.

And boldly dare invade that heart
  Which is anothers right.
First mad with hope we undertake
  To pull up every barr;   10
But once possess'd, we faintly make
  A dull defensive warr.
Now every friend is turn'd a foe
  In hope to get our store:
And passion makes us Cowards grow,
  Which made us brave before.

EPILOGUE [TO THE SECOND PART OF *THE CONQUEST OF GRANADA*]

In his Preface to *An Evening's Love* (1671) Dryden promised a comparison of Restoration and Elizabethan drama, to be published with *The Conquest of Granada*. He fulfilled his promise with this Epilogue.
  The text is that of the first edition (1672).

THey, who have best succeeded on the Stage,
Have still conform'd their Genius to their Age.
Thus *Jonson* did Mechanique° humour show,
When men were dull, and conversation low.
Then, Comedy was faultless, but 'twas course:
Cobbs Tankard was a jest, and *Otter's* horse.°
And as their Comedy, their love was mean:
Except, by chance, in some one labour'd Scene,
Which must attone for an ill-written Play.
They rose; but at their height could seldome stay.   10
Fame then was cheap, and the first commer sped;
And they have kept it since, by being dead.
But were they now to write when Critiques weigh
Each Line, and ev'ry word, throughout a Play,
None of 'em, no not *Jonson*, in his height
Could pass, without allowing grains for weight.
Think it not envy that these truths are told,
Our Poet's not malicious, though he's bold.

'Tis not to brand 'em that their faults are shown,
But, by their errours, to excuse his own.   20
If Love and Honour° now are higher rais'd,
'Tis not the Poet, but the Age is prais'd.
Wit's now ariv'd to a more high degree;
Our native Language more refin'd and free.
Our Ladies and our men now speak more wit
In conversation, than those Poets writ.
Then, one of these is, consequently, true;
That what this Poet writes comes short of you,
And imitates you ill, (which most he fears)
Or else his writing is not worse than theirs.   30
Yet, though you judge, (as sure the Critiques will)
That some before him writ with greater skill,
In this one praise he has their fame surpast,
To please an Age more Gallant than the last.

DEFENCE OF THE EPILOGUE. OR, AN ESSAY ON THE DRAMATIQUE POETRY OF THE LAST AGE

The critical response to the "bold" Epilogue, as Dryden called it, prompted his *Defence*, which was affixed to the first three editions of the play.
  The text is that of the first edition (1672), with corrections.

THE promises of Authors, that they will write again, are in effect, a threatning of their Readers with some new impertinence, and they who perform not what they promise, will have their pardon on easy terms. 'Tis from this consideration that I could be glad to spare you the trouble which I am now giving you, of a *Postscript*,[1] if I were not oblig'd by many reasons to write somewhat concerning our present Playes, and those of our predecessors on the English stage. The truth is, I have so farr ingag'd my self in a bold *Epilogue* to this Play, wherein I have somewhat tax'd the former writing, that it was necessary for me either not to print it, or to show that I could defend it. Yet,

---

THE CONQUEST OF GRANADA: *Epilogue.* **3. Mechanique:** lower-class. **6. Cobbs . . . horse:** Cob, the water-bearer in *Every Man in His Humor* (1598); Otter, the amphibious captain in *Epicene* (1609), whose "humor" for gaming leads him to call his drinking cups his bull, his bear, and his horse.

21. Love and Honour: the twin themes of heroic drama. DEFENCE OF THE EPILOGUE. **1. Postscript:** a correction in the second edition (1673) of *Preface.*

I would so maintain my opinion of the present Age, as not to be wanting in my veneration for the past: I would ascribe to dead Authors their just praises, in those things wherein they have excell'd us: and in those wherein we contend with them for the preheminence, I would acknowledge our advantages to the Age, and claim no victory from our wit. This being what I have propos'd to my self, I hope I shall not be thought arrogant when I inquire into their Errors. For, we live in an Age, so Sceptical, that as it determines little, so it takes nothing from Antiquity on trust: and I profess to have no other ambition in this Essay, than that Poetry may not go backward, when all other Arts and Sciences are advancing. Whoever censures me for this inquiry, let him hear his Character from *Horace*:

> *Ingeniis non ille favet plauditque sepultis,*
> *Nostra sed impugnat; nos nostraque lividus odit.*[2]

He favours not dead wits, but hates the living.

It was upbraided to that excellent Poet that he was an enemy to the writings of his Predecessor *Lucilius*, because he had said, *Lucilium lutulentum fluere,*[3] that he ran muddy: and that he ought to have retrench'd from his Satyrs many unnecessary verses. But *Horace* makes *Lucilius* himself to justifie him from the imputation of Envy, by telling you that he would have done the same had he liv'd in an age which was more refin'd.

> *Si foret hoc nostrum, fato, delapsus in aevum,*
> *Detraheret sibi multa, recideret omne quod ultra*
> *Perfectum traheretur:*[4] &c.

And, both in the whole course of that Satyr, and in his most admirable Epistle to *Augustus*,[5] he makes it his business to prove that Antiquity alone is no plea for the excellency of a Poem: but, that one Age learning from another, the last (if we can suppose an equallity of wit in the writers,) has the advantage of knowing more, and better than the former: and this I think is the state of the question in dispute. It is therefore my part to make it clear, that the Language,

Wit, and Conversation of our Age are improv'd and refin'd above the last: and then it will not be difficult, to inferr, that our Playes have receiv'd some part of those advantages.

In the first place, therefore, it will be necessary to state, in general, what this refinement is of which we treat: and that I think will not be defin'd amiss: *An improvement of our Wit, Language, and Conversation: or, an alteration in them for the better.*

To begin with *Language*. That an Alteration is lately made in ours or since the Writers of the last Age (in which I comprehend *Shakespear, Fletcher*[6] and *Jonson*) is manifest. Any man who reads those excellent Poets, and compares their language with what is now written, will see it almost in every line. But, that this is an *Improvement* of the Language, or an alteration for the better, will not so easily be granted. For many are of a contrary opinion, that the English tongue was then in the height of its perfection; that, from *Jonsons* time to ours, it has been in a continual declination; like that of the *Romans* from the Age of *Virgil* to *Statius*, and so downward to *Claudian*: of which, not onely *Petronius*, but *Quintilian* himself so much complains, under the person of *Secundus*, in his famous Dialogue *de causis corruptae eloquentiae.*[7]

But, to shew that our Language is improv'd; and that those people have not a just value for the Age in which they live, let us consider in what the refinement of a language principally consists: that is, *either in rejecting such old words or phrases which are ill sounding, or improper, or in admitting new, which are more proper, more sounding and more significant.*

The Reader will easily take notice, that when I speak of rejecting improper words and phrases I mention not such as are Antiquated by custome onely: and, as I may say, without any fault of theirs: for in this case the refinement can be but accidental: that is when the words and phrases which are rejected happen to be improper. Neither would I be understood (when I speak of impropriety in Language) either wholly to accuse the last Age, or to excuse the present; and least of all my self. For all writers have their imperfections and failings: but I may safely conclude in the general, that our improprieties are less frequent, and less gross

---

2. Ingeniis . . . odit: "That [man] does not favor and applaud these buried geniuses, but assails ours, and in his envy hates us and what is ours" (*Epistles,* II. i. 88–89). **3. Lucilium . . . fluere:** (*At dixi fluere hunc lutulentum*) "But I said that he flows muddy" (*Satires,* I. x. 50). **4. Si . . . traheretur:** "If he had fallen by fate into this our age, he would remove much from his work, would prune off all that was prolonged beyond the limits of perfection" (*Ibid.,* ll. 68–70; for *detraheret* read *detereret*). **5. Epistle to Augustus:** *Epistles,* II. i.

6. Fletcher: John Fletcher (1579–1625), English playwright known for the comedies he wrote alone and with other dramatists and especially for his collaboration on tragi-comedies with Francis Beaumont (c. 1584–1616). **7. de . . . eloquentiae:** *Concerning the Causes of the Decline of Oratory* (*De Oratoribus*), now attributed to Tacitus.

than theirs. One Testimony of this is undeniable, that we are the first who have observ'd them: and, certainly, to observe errours is a great step to the correcting of them. But, malice and partiality set apart, let any man who understands English, read diligently the works of *Shakespear* and *Fletcher;* and I dare undertake that he will find, in every page either some *Solecism* of Speech, or some notorious flaw in Sence: and yet these men are reverenc'd when we are not forgiven. That their wit is great and many times their expressions noble, envy it self cannot deny.

———*Neque ego illis detrahere ausim*
Haerentem capiti, multa cum laude, coronam:[8]

but the times were ignorant in which they liv'd. Poetry was then, if not in its infancy among us, at least not arriv'd to its vigor and maturity: witness the lameness of their Plots: many of which, especially those which they writ first, (for even that Age refin'd it self in some measure,) were made up of some ridiculous, incoherent story, which, in one Play many times took up the business of an Age. I suppose I need not name *Pericles Prince* of *Tyre*, nor the Historical Plays of *Shakespear*. Besides many of the rest as the *Winters Tale, Love's labour lost, Measure for Measure*, which were either grounded on impossibilities, or at least, so meanly written, that the Comedy neither caus'd your mirth, nor the serious part your concernment. If I would expatiate on this Subject, I could easily demonstrate that our admir'd *Fletcher*, who writ after him, neither understood correct Plotting, nor that which they call *the Decorum of the Stage*. I would not search in his worst Playes for examples: he who will consider his *Philaster*, his *Humorous Lieutenant*, his *Faithful Shepheardess;* and many others which I could name, will find them much below the applause which is now given them. He will see *Philaster* wounding his Mistriss, and afterwards his Boy, to save himself: Not to mention the Clown who enters immediately, and not only has the advantage of the Combat against the Heroe, but diverts you from your serious concernment, with his ridiculous and absurd Raillery. In his *Humorous Lieutenant* you find his *Demetrius* and *Leoncius* staying in the midst of a routed Army to hear the cold mirth of the *Lieutenant:* and *Demetrius* afterwards appearing with a Pistol in

his hand, in the next Age to *Alexander* the Great. And for his *Shepheard*, he falls twice into the former indecency of wounding Women. But these absurdities, which those Poets committed, may more properly be call'd the Ages fault than theirs, for, besides the want of Education and Learning, (which was their particular unhappiness) they wanted the benefit of converse:[9] but of that, I shall speak hereafter, in a place more proper for it. Their Audiences knew no better: and therefore were satisfy'd with what they brought. Those who call theirs the *Golden Age of Poetry*, have only this reason for it, that they were then content with Acorns, before they knew the use of Bread: or that ἅλις δρυός[10] was become a Proverb. They had many who admir'd them, and few who blam'd them: and, certainly, a severe Critique is the greatest help to a good Wit: he does the Office of a Friend, while he designs that of an Enemy: and his malice keeps a Poet within those bounds, which the Luxuriancy of his Fancy would tempt him to overleap.

But it is not their Plots which I meant, principally to tax: I was speaking of their Sence and Language: and I dare almost challenge any man to show me a page together, which is correct in both. As for *Ben. Johnson*, I am loath to name him, because he is a most Judicious Writer; yet he very often falls into these errors. And I once more beg the Readers pardon, for accusing him or them. Only let him consider that I live in an age where my least faults are severely censur'd: and that I have no way left to extenuate my failings but my showing as great in those whom we admire.

Cædimus, inque vicem præbemus crura sagittis.[11]

And what correctness, after this, can be expected from *Shakespear* or from *Fletcher*, who wanted that Learning and care which *Johnson* had? I will therefore spare my own trouble of inquiring into their faults: who had they liv'd now, had doubtless written more correctly. I suppose it will be enough for me to affirm (as I think I safely may) that these and the like errors which I tax'd in the most correct of the last Age, are such, into which we doe not ordinarily fall.

9. converse: society. **10.** ἅλις δρυός: "enough of acorns" (quoted by Cicero, *Ad Atticum*, II. 19). **11. Cædimus . . . sagittis:** "We alternately strike and expose our own legs to the arrows" (Persius, *Satires*, iv. 42). At this point a long series of illustrations of bad writing from Jonson was omitted from the second and subsequent editions. We defer to Dryden's judgment in the present text. Another short omission occurs at the end of the paragraph.

8. Neque . . . coronam: "Nor would I dare to snatch from them the garland that clings to the head with much praise" (Horace, *Satires*, I. x. 48–49; for *illis* read *illi*).

As for the other part of refining, which consists in receiving new Words and Phrases, I shall not insist much on it. 'Tis obvious that we have admitted many: some of which we wanted, and, therefore our Language is the richer for them: as it would be by importation of Bullion: others are rather Ornamental than Necessary; yet by their admission, the Language is become more courtly: and our thoughts are better drest. These are to be found scatter'd in the Writers of our Age: and it is not my business to collect them. They who have lately written with most care, have, I believe, taken the Rule of *Horace* for their guide; that is, not to be too hasty in receiving of Words: but rather to stay till Custome has made them familiar to us,

Quem penes, arbitrium est, & jus & norma loquendi.[12]

For I cannot approve of their way of refining, who corrupt our *English* Idiom by mixing it too much with *French:* that is a Sophistication[13] of Language, not an improvement of it: a turning *English* into *French,* rather than a refining of *English* by *French.* We meet daily with those Fopps, who value themselves on their Travelling, and pretend they cannot express their meaning in *English,* because they would put off to us some *French* Phrase of the last Edition: without considering that, for ought they know, we have a better of our own; but these are not the men who are to refine us: their Talent is to prescribe Fashions, not Words: at best they are onely serviceable to a Writer, so as *Ennius* was to *Virgil.* He may *Aurum ex stercore colligere;*[14] for 'tis hard if, amongst many insignificant Phrases, there happen not something worth preserving: though they themselves, like *Indians,* know not the value of their own Commodity.

There is yet another way of improving Language, which Poets especially have practic'd in all Ages: that is by applying receiv'd words to a new Signification: and this I believe, is meant by *Horace,* in that Precept which is so variously constru'd by Expositors:

Dixeris Egregie, notum si callida verbum,
Reddiderit junctura novum.[15]

And, in this way, he himself had a particular happiness: using all the Tropes, and particularly Metaphors, with that grace which is observable in his Odes: where the Beauty of Expression is often greater than that of thought: as in that one example, amongst an infinite number of others; *Et vultus nimium lubricus aspici.*[16]

And therefore though he innovated little, he may justly be call'd a great Refiner of the *Roman* Tongue. This choice of words, and height'ning of their natural signification, was observ'd in him by the Writers of the following Ages: for *Petronius* says of him, *& Horatii curiosa felicitas.*[17] By this graffing,[18] as I may call it, on old words, has our Tongue been Beautified by the three fore mention'd Poets, *Shakespear, Fletcher* and *Johnson:* whose Excellencies I can never enough admire, and in this, they have been follow'd especially by Sir *John Suckling*[19] and Mr. *Waller,*[20] who refin'd upon them: neither have they, who now succeed them, been wanting in their endeavours to adorn our Mother Tongue: but it is not so lawful for me to praise my living Contemporaries, as to admire my dead Predecessors.

I should now speak of the Refinement of Wit: but I have been so large on the former Subject that I am forc'd to contract my self in this. I will therefore onely observe to you, that the wit of the last Age, was yet more incorrect than their language. *Shakespear,* who many times has written better than any Poet, in any Language, is yet so far from writing Wit always, or expressing that Wit according to the Dignity of the Subject, that he writes in many places below—the dullest Writer of ours, or of any precedent Age. Never did any Author precipitate himself from such heights of thought to so low expressions, as he often does. He is the very *Janus*[21] of Poets; he wears, almost every where two faces: and you have scarce begun to admire the one, e're you despise the other. Neither is the Luxuriance of *Fletcher,* (which his friends have tax'd in him,) a less fault than the carelessness of *Shakespear.* He does not well always, and, when he does, he is a true *Englishman;* he knows not when to

16. Et . . . aspici: "and her face too seductive to behold" (*Odes,* I. xix. 8). 17. & . . . felicitas: "and the assiduous felicity of Horace" (*Satyricon,* l. 118). 18. graffing: grafting. 19. Sir . . . Suckling: (1609–42), Cavalier poet. 20. Mr. Waller: Edmund Waller (1606–87). (See the selections from Waller in Part Three.) 21. Janus: the Roman deity who kept the gates of heaven, represented as having a face on both the front and back of his head; thus he was able to look to both past and future at the same time. Here, the image denotes simply an oscillating inconsistency.

12. Quem . . . loquendi: "in whose hands is decision, and right, and standard of speaking" (*Ars Poetica,* l. 72). 13. Sophistication: debasement. 14. Aurum . . . colligere: Pick up gold from the dung (proverbial). 15. Dixeris . . . novum: "You will have expressed yourself excellently, if a skillful setting will have rendered a well-known word new" (*Ars Poetica,* ll. 47–48).

give over. If he wakes in one Scene he commonly slumbers in another: And if he pleases you in the first three Acts, he is frequently so tir'd with his labor, that he goes heavily in the fourth and, sinks under his burden in the fifth.

For *Ben. Johnson,* the most judicious of Poets, he always writ properly; and as the Character requir'd: and I will not contest farther with my Friends who call that Wit. It being very certain, that even folly it self, well represented, is Wit in a larger signification: and that there is Fancy, as well as Judgement in it; though not so much or noble: because all Poetry being imitation, that of Folly is a lower exercise of Fancy, though perhaps as difficult as the other: for 'tis a kind of looking downward in the Poet; and representing that part of Mankind which is below him.

In these low Characters of Vice and Folly, lay the excellency of that inimitable Writer: who, when at any time, he aim'd at Wit, in the stricter sence, that is, Sharpness of Conceit, was forc'd either to borrow from the Ancients, as, to my knowledge he did very much from *Plautus:* or, when he trusted himself alone, often fell into meanness of expression. Nay, he was not free from the lowest and most groveling kind of Wit, which we call clenches;[22] of which, *Every Man in his Humour,* is infinitely full: and, which is worse, the wittiest persons in the *Drama* speak them. His other Comedies are not exempted from them: will you give me leave to name some few? *Asper,* in which Character he personates himself, (and he neither was, nor thought himself a fool.) exclaiming against the ignorant Judges of the Age, speaks thus:

> *How monstrous and detested is 't, to see*
> *A fellow, that has neither Art nor Brain,*
> *Sit like an* Aristarchus, *or Stark-Ass,*
> *Taking Mens Lines, with a* Tobacco Face,
> *In* Snuffe,[23] &c.

And presently after

I mar'le whose wit 'twas to put a Prologue in yond Sackbut's mouth? they might well think he would be out of Tune, and yet you'd play upon him too.[24] Will you have another of the same stamp?

O, I cannot abide these limbs of Sattin, *or rather* Satan.[25]

But, it may be you will object that this was *Asper, Macilente,* or, *Carlo Buffone:* you shall, therefore, hear him speak in his own person: and, that, in the two last

lines, or sting of an Epigram; 'tis Inscrib'd to *Fine Grand:* who, he says, was indebted to him for many things, which he reckons there: and concludes thus;

> *Forty things more,* dear Grand, *which you know true,*
> *For which, or pay me quickly, or I'le pay you.*[26]

This was then the mode of wit, the vice of the Age and not *Ben. Johnson's,* for you see, a little before him, that admirable wit, Sir *Philip Sidney,*[27] perpetually playing with his words. In his time, I believe, it ascended first into the Pulpit: where (if you will give me leave to clench too) it yet finds the benefit of its Clergy: for they are commonly the first corrupters of Eloquence, and the last reform'd from vicious Oratory: as a famous *Italian* has observ'd before me, in his Treatise of the Corruption of the *Italian Tongue;*[28] which he principally ascribes to Priests and preaching Friars.

But, to conclude with what brevity I can; I will only add this in the defence of our present Writers, that if they reach not some excellencies of *Ben. Johnson;* (which no Age, I am confident, ever shall) yet, at least, they are above that meanness of thought which I have tax'd, and which is frequent in him.

That the wit of this Age is much more Courtly, may easily be prov'd by viewing the Characters of Gentlemen which were written in the last. First, for *Jonson, Truewit* in the *Silent Woman,* was his Master-piece: and *Truewit* was a Scholar-like kind of man, a Gentleman with an allay of Pedantry: a man who seems mortifi'd to the world, by much reading. The best of his discourse, is drawn, not from the knowledge of the Town, but Books. and, in short, he would be a fine Gentleman, in an University. *Shakespear* show'd the best of his skill in his *Mercutio,* and he said himself, that he was forc'd to kill him in the third Act, to prevent being kill'd by him. But, for my part, I cannot find he was so dangerous a person: I see nothing in him but what was so exceeding harmless, that he might have liv'd to the end of the Play, and dy'd in his bed, without offence to any man.

Fletcher's Don John[29] is our onely Bug-bear: and yet, I may affirm, without suspition of flattery, that he now speaks better, and that his Character is maintain'd with much more vigour in the fourth and fifth Acts than

---

22. **clenches:** puns. 23. **How . . . Snuffe:** *Every Man out of His Humor,* Induction, ll. 177–81. 24. **I . . . too:** *Ibid.,* Prologue. 25. **O . . . Satan:** *Ibid.,* IV. iv.

26. **Forty . . . you:** *Epigrams,* lxxiii. 21–22. 27. **Sir . . . Sidney:** (1554–86), Elizabethan poet and scholar. 28. **Treatise . . . Tongue:** not identified. 29. **Don John:** in *The Chances* (1682).

it was by *Fletcher* in the three former. I have alwayes acknowledg'd the wit of our Predecessors, with all the veneration which becomes me, but, I am sure, their wit was not that of Gentlemen, there was ever somewhat that was ill-bred and Clownish in it: and which confest the conversation[30] of the Authors.

And this leads me to the last and greatest advantage of our writing, which proceeds from conversation. In the Age, wherein those Poets liv'd, there was less of gallantry than in ours; neither did they keep the best company of theirs. Their fortune has been much like that of *Epicurus*, in the retirement of his Gardens: to live almost unknown, and to be celebrated after their decease. I cannot find that any of them were conversant in Courts, except *Ben. Johnson*: and his *genius* lay not so much that way, as to make an improvement by it: greatness was not, then, so easy of access, nor conversation so free as now it is. I cannot, therefore, conceive it any insolence to affirm, that, by the knowledge, and pattern of their wit, who writ before us, and by the advantage of our own conversation, the discourse and Raillery of our *Comedies* excell what has been written by them. and this will be deny'd by none, but some few old fellows who value themselves on their acquaintance with the *Black-Friars*:[31] who, because they saw their Playes, would pretend a right to judge ours. The memory of these grave Gentlemen is their only Plea for being Wits. they can tell a story of *Ben. Jonson*, and perhaps have had fancy enough to give a supper in *Apollo*[32] that they might be call'd his Sons: and because they were drawn in to be laught at in those times, they think themselves now sufficiently intitled to laugh at ours. Learning I never saw in any of them, and wit no more than they could remember. In short, they were unlucky to have been bred in an unpolish'd Age, and more unlucky to live to a refin'd one. They have lasted beyond their own, and are cast behind ours: and not contented to have known little at the age of twenty, they boast of their ignorance at threescore.

Now, if any ask me, whence it is that our conversation is so much refin'd? I must freely, and without flattery, ascribe it to the Court: and, in it, particularly to the King; whose example gives a law to it. His own mis-fortunes and the Nations, afforded him an opportunity, which is rarely allow'd to Sovereign Princes,

I mean of travelling, and being conversant in the most polish'd Courts of *Europe;* and, thereby, of cultivating a Spirit, which was form'd by Nature, to receive the impressions of a gallant and generous education. At his return, he found a Nation lost as much in Barbarism as in Rebellion. and as the excellency of his Nature forgave the one, so the excellency of his manners reform'd the other: the desire of imitating so great a pattern, first waken'd the dull and heavy spirits of the *English*, from their natural reserv'dness: loosen'd them, from their stiff forms of conversation; and made them easy and plyant to each other in discourse. Thus, insensibly, our way of living became more free: and the fire of the English wit, which was before stifled under a constrain'd melancholy way of breeding, began first to display its force: by mixing the solidity of our Nation, with the air and gayety of our neighbours. This being granted to be true, it would be a wonder, if the Poets, whose work is imitation, should be the onely persons in three kingdoms, who should not receive advantage by it: or, if they should not more easily imitate the wit and conversation of the present age, than of the past.

Let us therefore admire the beauties and the heights of *Shakespear*, without falling after him into a carelessness and (as I may call it) a Lethargy of thought, for whole Scenes together. Let us imitate, as we are able, the quickness and easiness of *Fletcher*, without proposing him as a pattern to us, either in the redundancy[33] of his matter, or the incorrectness of his language. Let us admire his wit and sharpness of conceit; but, let us at the same time acknowledge that it was seldome so fix'd, and made proper to his characters, as that the same things might not be spoken by any person in the Play: let us applaud his Scenes of Love; but, let us confess that he understood not either greatness or perfect honour in the parts of any of his women. In fine, let us allow, that he had so much fancy, as when he pleas'd he could write wit: but that he wanted so much Judgment as seldome to have written humour; or describ'd a pleasant folly. Let us ascribe to *Jonson* the height and accuracy of Judgment, in the ordering of his Plots, his choice of characters, and maintaining what he had chosen, to the end: but let us not think him a perfect pattern of imitation; except it be in humour: for Love, which is the foundation of all *Comedies* in other Languages, is scarcely mention'd in any of his Playes: and for humour it self, the Poets

---

30. conversation: society. **31. Black-Friars:** the theater built by Burbage in 1596. **32. Apollo:** a room in the Devil Tavern, Temple Bar, frequented by Jonson and the "Tribe of Ben."

33. redundancy: superfluity, prolixity.

of this Age will be more wary than to imitate the meanness of his persons. Gentlemen will now be entertain'd with the follies of each other: and though they allow *Cob* and *Tib*[34] to speak properly, yet they are not much pleas'd with their Tankard or with their Raggs: And, surely, their conversation can be no jest to them on the *Theatre*, when they would avoid it in the street.

To conclude all, let us render to our Predecessors what is their due, without confineing our selves to a servile imitation of all they writ: and, without assuming to our selves the Title of better Poets, let us ascribe to the gallantry and civility of our age the advantage which we have above them; and to our knowledge of the customs and manners of it, the happiness we have to please beyond them.

MARRIAGE A-LA-MODE

Marriage A-la-Mode, Dryden's best-known comedy (or tragicomedy), was composed in the spring of 1671 and acted later that year with notable success. It did not, however, escape the burlesque shafts of *The Rehearsal* (first produced in December); Buckingham and his collaborators apparently found the serious plot worthy of specimens from Dryden's earlier heroic plays. The subsequent theatrical history of *Marriage A-la-Mode* suggests that for a time at least the comic plot was indeed distinctly favored: in 1707 a pastiche of comic episodes from this and another play of Dryden's, *Secret Love*, was put together by Colley Cibber under the title *Marriage A-La-Mode; or, the Comical Lovers*, and in 1756 a two-act version of Dryden's play was produced as *The Frenchified Lady Never in Paris*. Still, however vulnerable the highly conventional "tragic" action may be in itself, it should be studied for its effective interplay with the comic plot in the development of the old heroic theme of love versus honor.

The text is that of the first edition (1673), with one or two corrections (supported by the 1701 folio).

To the Right Honourable,
The EARL of ROCHESTER.°

MY LORD,

I Humbly Dedicate to Your Lordship that Poem, of which you were pleas'd to appear an early Patron, before it was Acted on the Stage. I may yet go farther, with your permission, and say, That it receiv'd amendment from your noble hands, e're it was fit to be presented. You may please likewise to remember, with how much favour to the Authour, and indulgence to the Play, you commended it to the view of His Majesty, then at *Windsor*,[1] and by His Approbation of it in Writing, made way for its kind reception on the *Theatre*. In this Dedication therefore, I may seem to imitate a Custom of the Ancients, who offer'd to their Gods the Firstlings of the Flock, which I think they call'd *Ver Sacrum*,[2] because they help'd 'em to increase. I am sure, if there be any thing in this Play, wherein I have rais'd my self beyond the ordinary lowness of my Comedies, I ought wholly to acknowledge it to the favour, of being admitted into your Lordship's Conversation. And not onely I, who pretend not to this way, but the best Comick Writers of our Age, will joyn with me to acknowledge, that they have copy'd the Gallantries of Courts, the Delicacy of Expression, and the Decencies of Behaviour, from your Lordship, with more success, then if they had taken their Models from the Court of *France*. But this, my Lord, will be no wonder to the world, which knows the excellencie of your Natural parts, and those

MARRIAGE A-LA-MODE. **To . . . Rochester:** Johnson may quite possibly have had this dedication—among other of Dryden's panegyrics—in mind when he wrote: "Of dramatick immorality, he did not want examples among his predecessors, or companions among his contemporaries; but in the meanness and servility of hyperbolical adulation I know not whether, since the days in which the Roman emperors were deified, he has ever been equalled. . . . When once he has undertaken the task of praise he no longer retains shame in himself, nor supposes it in his patron. . . . With his praises of others and of himself is always intermingled a strain of discontent and lamentation, a sullen growl of resentment, or a querulous murmur of distress." Ironically, within two years Dryden was to lose the patronage of Rochester and suffer a satiric attack at his hands (*The Allusion to the Tenth Satire of Horace*)—an eventuality Dryden seems almost to prophesy at the end of the dedication. (See the Rochester section earlier in Part One.) **1. at Windsor:** in June and July, 1671. **2. Ver Sacrum:** literally, sacred, or consecrated, spring.

you have acquir'd in a Noble Education. That which with more reason I admire, is, that being so absolute a Courtier, you have not forgot, either the ties of Friendship, or the practise of Generosity. In my little Experience of a Court (which I confess I desire not to improve) I have found in it much of Interest, and more of Detraction: Few men there have that assurance of a Friend, as not to be made ridiculous by him, when they are absent. There are a midling sort of Courtiers, who become happy by their want of wit; but they supply that want, by an excess of malice to those who have it. And there is no such persecution as that of fools: they can never be considerable enough to be talk'd of themselves; so that they are safe onely in their obscurity, and grow mischievous to witty men, by the great diligence of their envy, and by being always present to represent and aggravate their faults. In the mean time they are forc'd, when they endeavour to be pleasant, to live on the Offalls of their Wit, whom they decry; and either to quote it, (which they do unwillingly) or to pass it upon others for their own. These are the men who make it their business to chase Wit from the Knowledge of Princes, lest it should disgrace their ignorance. And this kind of malice your Lordship has not so much avoided, as surmounted. But if by the excellent temper of a Royal Master, always more ready to hear good than ill, if by his inclination to love you, if by your own merit and address, if by the charmes of your Conversation, the Grace of your Behaviour, your knowledge of Greatness and Habitude in Courts, you having been able to preserve your self with Honour in the midst of so dangerous a Course; yet at least the remembrance of those Hazards has inspir'd you with pity for other men, who being of an inferiour Wit and Quality to you, are yet Persecuted, for being that in Little, which your Lordship is in Great. For the quarrel of those people extends it self to any thing of sense; and if I may be so vain to own it amongst the rest of the Poets, has sometimes reach'd to the very borders of it, even to me. So that, if our general good fortune had not rais'd up your Lordship to defend us, I know not whether any thing had been more ridiculous in Court, than Writers. 'Tis to your Lordship's favour we generally owe our Protection and Patronage: And to the Nobleness of your Nature, which will not suffer the least shadow of your Wit to be contemn'd in other men. You have been often pleas'd not onely to excuse my imperfections, but to vindicate what was tolerable in my Writings from

their censures. And what I never can forget, you have not onely been careful of my Reputation, but of my Fortune. You have been Sollicitous to supply my neglect of my self; and to overcome the fatal Modesty of Poets, which submits them to perpetual wants, rather then to become importunate with those people, who have the liberality of Kings in their disposing; and who dishonouring the Bounty of their Master, suffer such to be in necessity, who endeavour at least to please him: and for those whose entertainment He has generously provided, if the Fruits of His Royal favour were not often stopp'd in other hands. But your Lordship has given me occasion, not to complain of Courts, whil'st you are there. I have found the effects of your Mediation in all my Concernments; and they were so much the more noble in you, because they were wholly voluntary. I became your Lordship's (if I may venture on the Similitude) as the world was made, without knowing him who made it; and brought onely a passive obedience to be your Creature. This Nobleness of yours I think my self the rather oblig'd to own, because otherwise it must have been lost to all remembrance: for you are endued with that excellent quality of a frank Nature, to forget the good which you have done.

But, my Lord, I ought to have consider'd, that you are as great a Judge, as you are a Patron; and that in praising you ill, I shall incurre a higher note of ingratitude, then that I thought to have avoided. I stand in need of all your accustom'd goodness for the Dedication of this Play: which though, perhaps, it be the best of my Comedies, is yet so faulty, that I should have fear'd you, for my Critick, if I had not with some policy given you the trouble of being my Protector. Wit seems to have lodg'd it self more Nobly in this Age, than in any of the former: and people of my mean condition, are onely Writers, because some of the Nobility, and your Lordship in the first place, are above the narrow praises which Poesie could give you. But let those who love to see themselves exceeded, encourage your Lordship in so dangerous a quality: for my own part, I must confess, that I have so much of self interest, as to be content with reading some Papers of your Verses, without desiring you should proceed to a Scene or Play: with the common prudence of those, who are worsted in a Duel, and declare they are satisfied when they are first wounded. Your Lordship has but another step to make, and from the Patron of Wit, you may become its Tyrant: and Oppress our little Reputations with more ease then you now protect them. But these my Lord, are designs, which I am sure you harbour not; any more then the *French King* is contriving the Conquest of the *Swissers*.[3] 'Tis a barren Triumph, which is not worth your pains, and wou'd onely rank him amongst your Slaves, who is already, | *My Lord,* | *Your Lordships* | Most obedient and most | faithful Servant,

JOHN DRYDEN.

PROLOGUE°

Lord, how reform'd and quiet we are grown,
Since all our Braves and all our Wits are gone:
Fop-corner° now is free from Civil War:
White-Wig and Vizard make no longer jar.
France, and the Fleet, have swept the Town so clear,
That we can Act in peace, and you can hear.
'Twas a sad sight, before they march'd from home,
To see our Warriours, in Red Wastecoats, come,
With hair tuck'd up, into our Tireing-room.°
But 'twas more sad to hear their last Adieu,   10
The Women sob'd, and swore they would be true;

And so they were, as long as e're they cou'd:
But powerful Guinnee° cannot be withstood,
And they were made of Play house flesh and bloud.
Fate did their Friends for double use ordain,
In Wars abroad, they grinning Honour° gain,
And Mistresses, for all that stay, maintain.
Now they are gone, 'tis dead Vacation here,
For neither Friends nor Enemies appear.
Poor pensive Punk° now peeps ere Plays begin,   20
Sees the bare Bench, and dares not venture in:
But manages her last Half-crown° with care,
And trudges to the Mall,° on foot, for Air.
Our City Friends so far will hardly come,
They can take up with Pleasures nearer home;
And see gay Shows, and gawdy Scenes elsewhere:°
For we presume they seldom come to hear.
But they have now ta'n up a glorious Trade,
And cutting Moorcraft,° struts in Masquerade.
There's all our hope, for we shall show to day,   30
A Masquing Ball, to recommend our Play:
Nay, to endear 'em more, and let 'em see,
We scorn to come behind in Courtesie,
We'll follow the new Mode which they begin,
And treat 'em with a Room, and Couch within:
For that's one way, how e're the Play fall short,
T' oblige the Town, the City, and the Court.

Persons Represented.

MEN.

			By
Polydamas, Usurper of *Sicily*			Mr. *Wintershall.*
Leonidas, the Rightful Prince, unknown			Mr. *Kynaston.*
Argaleon, Favourite to *Polydamas*			Mr. *Lydall.*
Hermogenes, Foster-father to *Leonidas*			Mr. *Cartwright.*
Eubulus, his Friend and Companion			Mr. *Watson.*
Rhodophil, Captain of the Guards			Mr. *Mohun.*
Palamede, a Courtier			Mr. *Hart.*

3. the Swissers: his Swiss guard. *Prologue.* The Prologue, spoken by Charles Hart, who played the part of Palamede, was first published in the *Covent Garden Drollery* in 1672. The present text is from the first edition of the play (1673). **3. Fop-corner:** a section of the pit where the fops congregated. **9. Tireing-room:** dressing room.

13. Guinnee: (guinea) money. **16. grinning Honour:** Falstaff's description of death in *1 Henry IV,* V. iii. 62–65. **20. Punk:** prostitute. **22. Half-crown:** the price a prostitute charged her client. **23. the Mall:** a fashionable promenade in St. James's Park. **24–26. Our . . . elsewhere:** The citizens were being drawn off by the new rival theater, the Duke's, in Dorset Garden, where more and more spectacle was being offered. **29. cutting Moorcraft:** swaggering Morecraft, a usurer turned gallant in Beaumont and Fletcher's *The Scornful Lady* (c. 1614).

WOMEN.

	By
Palmyra, Daughter to the Usurper	Mrs. Coxe.
Amalthea, Sister to Argaleon	Mrs. James.
Doralice, Wife to Rhodophil	Mrs. Marshall.
Melantha, an Affected Lady	Mrs. Bowtell.
Philotis, Woman to Melantha	Mrs. Reeve.
Belisa, Woman to Doralice	Mrs. Slade.
Artemis, a Court-Lady	Mrs. Uphill.

Scene, SICILIE.

ACT I

SCENE I.

Walks near the Court.

Enter Doralice *and* Beliza.

Dor. BEliza, bring the lute into this Arbor, the Walks are empty: I would try the Song the Princess *Amalthea* bad me learn.

[*They go in, and sing.*

1.

WHy should a foolish Marriage Vow,
   Which long ago was made,
Oblige us to each other now
   — When Passion is decay'd?
We lov'd, and we lov'd, as long as we cou'd,
   — Till our love was lov'd out in us both:
But our Marriage is dead, when the Pleasure is fled: 10
   'Twas Pleasure first made it an Oath.

2.

If I have Pleasures for a Friend,
   And farther love in store,
What wrong has he whose joys did end,
   And who cou'd give no more?
'Tis a madness that he
Should be jealous of me,
Or that I shou'd bar him of another:
For all we can gain,
Is to give our selves pain,   20
When neither can hinder the other.

Enter Palamede, *in Riding Habit, and hears the Song.*
Re-enter Doralice *and* Beliza.

Bel. Madam, a Stranger.

Dor. I did not think to have had witnesses of my bad singing.

Pala. If I have err'd, Madam, I hope you'l pardon the curiosity of a Stranger; for I may well call my self so, after five years absence from the Court: But you have freed me from one error.

Dor. What's that, I beseech you?   29

Pala. I thought good voices, and ill faces, had been inseparable; and that to be fair and sing well, had been onely the priviledge of Angels.

Dor. And how many more of these fine things can you say to me?

Pala. Very few, Madam, for if I should continue to see you some hours longer: You look so killingly, that I should be mute with wonder.   37

Dor. This will not give you the reputation of a Wit with me: you travelling Monsieurs live upon the stock you have got abroad, for the first day or two: to repeat with a good memory, and apply with a good grace, is all your wit. And, commonly, your Gullets are sew'd up, like Cormorants:° When you have regorg'd what you have taken in, you are the leanest things in Nature.

Pala. Then, Madam, I think you had best make that use of me; let me wait on you for two or three days together, and you shall hear all I have learnt of extraordinary, in other Countreys: And one thing which I never saw till I came home, that is, a Lady of a better voice, better face, and better wit, than any I have seen abroad. And, after this, if I should not declare my self most passionately in love with you, I should have less wit than yet you think I have.   54

Act I, scene i. **43. like Cormorants:** Cormorants, provided with a tourniquet around the lower part of the neck to keep them from swallowing, were used to catch fish.

Dor. A very plain, and pithy Declaration. I see, Sir, you have been travelling in *Spain* or *Italy*, or some of the hot Countreys, where men come to the point immediately. But are you sure these are not words of course? For I would not give my poor heart an occasion of complaint against me, that I engag'd it too rashly, and then could not bring it off.   61

Pala. Your heart may trust it self with me safely; I shall use it very civilly while it stays, and never turn it away, without fair warning to provide for it self.

Dor. First, then, I do receive your passion with as little consideration, on my part, as ever you gave it me, on yours. And now see what a miserable wretch you have made your self.

Pala. Who, I miserable? Thank you for that. Give me love enough, and life enough, and I defie *Fortune*.

Dor. Know then, thou man of vain imagination, know, to thy utter confusion, that I am vertuous.   72

Pala. Such another word, and I give up the ghost.

Dor. Then, to strike you quite dead, know, that I am marry'd too.

Pala. Art thou marry'd; O thou damnable vertuous Woman?

Dor. Yes, marry'd to a Gentleman; young, handsome, rich, valiant, and with all the good qualities that will make you despair, and hang your self.   80

Pala. Well, in spight of all that, I'll love you: *Fortune* has cut us out for one another; for I am to be marry'd within these three days. Marry'd past redemption, to a young, fair, rich, and vertuous Lady: And, it shall go hard, but I will love my Wife as little, as I perceive you do your Husband.

Dor. Remember I invade no propriety:° My servant° you are onely till you are marry'd.

Pala. In the mean time, you are to forget you have a Husband.   90

Dor. And you, that you are to have a Wife.

Bel. (*Aside to her Lady.*) O Madam, my Lord's just at the end of the Walks; and, if you make not haste, will discover you.

Dor. Some other time, new Servant, we'll talk further of the premises;° in the mean while, break not my first commandment, that is, not to follow me.

Pala. But where, then shall I find you again?

Dor. At Court. Yours for two days, Sir.

Pala. And nights, I beseech you, Madam.   100

[*Exit Doralice and Beliza.*

Pala. Well, I'll say that for thee, thou art a very dextrous Executioner; thou hast done my business at one stroke: Yet I must marry another—and yet I must love this; and if it lead me into some little inconveniencies, as jealousies, and duels, and death, and so forth; yet while sweet love is in the case, *Fortune* do thy worst, and avant° Mortality.

Enter Rodophil, who seems speaking to one within.

CAPT. OF GUARDS

Rho. Leave 'em with my Lieutenant, while I fetch new Orders from the King. How? *Palamede!*

[*Sees* Palamede.

Pala. Rhodophil!   110

Rho. Who thought to have seen you in *Sicily*?

Pala. Who thought to have found the Court so far from *Syracuse*?

Rho. The King best knows the reason of the progress.° But answer me, I beseech you, what brought you home from travel?

Pala. The commands of an old rich Father.

Rho. And the hopes of burying him?   118

Pala. Both together, as you see, have prevail'd on my good nature. In few words, My old man has already marry'd me; for he has agreed with another old man, as rich and as covetous as himself; the Articles are drawn, and I have given my consent, for fear of being dis-inherited; and yet know not what kind of woman I am to marry.

Rho. Sure your Father intends you some very ugly wife; and has a mind to keep you in ignorance, till you have shot the gulf.°   128

Pala. I know not that; but obey I will, and must.

Rho. Then, I cannot chuse but grieve for all the good Girls and Curtizans of *France* and *Italy*: They have lost the most kind-hearted, doting, prodigal, humble servant, in *Europe*.

Pala. All I could do in these three years, I stay'd behind you, was to comfort the poor Creatures, for the loss of you. But what's the reason that in all this time, a friend could never hear from you?

Rho. Alass, dear *Palamede*, I have had no joy to write, nor indeed to do any thing in the World to please me: The greatest misfortune imaginable is faln upon me.   141

Pala. Prithee, what's the matter?

Rho. In one word, I am marry'd; wretchedly

---

87. propriety: property, right of possession. **88. servant:** lover. **96. premises:** the aforementioned matters.

107. avant: (avaunt) Be off! Away! **115. progress:** royal journey. **128. shot the gulf:** To "shoot the gulf" is to accomplish an almost impossible task.

marry'd; and have been above these two years. Yes, faith, the Devil has had power over me, in spight of my Vows and Resolutions to the contrary.

Pala. I find you have sold your self for filthy lucre; she's old, or ill-condition'd.

Rho. No, none of these: I'm sure she's young; and, for her humor, she laughs, sings, and dances eternally; and, which is more, we never quarrel about it, for I do the same.   152

Pala. You're very fortunate indeed: Then the case is plain, she is not handsome.

Rho. A great beauty too, as people say.

Pala. As people say? Why, you should know that best your self.

Rho. Ask those, who have smelt to a strong perfume two years together, what's the scent.

Pala. But here are good qualities enough for one woman.   161

Rho. Ay, too many, *Palamede*, if I could put 'em into three or four women, I should be content.

Pala. O, now I have found it, you dislike her for no other reason, but because she's your wife.

Rho. And is not that enough? All that I know of her perfections now, is only by memory; I remember, indeed, that about two years ago I lov'd her passionately; but those golden days are gone, *Palamede:* Yet I lov'd her a whole half year, double the natural   170 term of any Mistress, and think in my conscience I could have held out another quarter; but then the World began to laugh at me, and a certain shame of being out of fashion, seiz'd me: At last, we arriv'd at that point, that there was nothing left in us to make us new to one another: yet still I set a good face upon the matter, and am infinite fond of her before company; but, when we are alone, we walk like Lions in a room, she one way, and I another: and we lie with our backs to each other so far distant, as if the fashion of great Beds was onely invented to keep Husband and Wife sufficiently asunder.   182

Pala. The truth is, your disease is very desperate; but, though you cannot be cur'd, you may be patch'd up a little; you must get you a Mistress, *Rhodophil:* that, indeed, is living upon Cordials;° but, as fast as one fails, you must supply it with another. You're like a Gamester, who has lost his estate; yet, in doing that, you have learn'd the advantages of Play, and can arrive to live upon 't.   190

Rho. Truth is, I have been thinking on 't, and have just resolv'd to take your counsel; and, faith, considering the damn'd disadvantages of a marry'd man, I have provided well enough, for a poor humble sinner, that is not ambitious of great matters.

Pala. What is she, for a Woman?

Rho. One of the Stars of *Syracuse*, I assure you: Young enough, fair enough, and, but, for one quality, Just such a woman as I would wish.   199

Pala. O Friend, this is not an age to be critical in Beauty: when we had good store of handsome women, and but few Chapmen,° you might have been more curious in your choice; but now the price is enhanc'd° upon us, and all Mankind set up for Mistresses, so that poor little creatures, without beauty, birth, or breeding, but onely impudence, go off at unreasonable rates: and a man, in these hard times, snaps at 'em, as he does at Broad-gold,° never examines the weight, but takes light, or heavy,° as he can get it.   210

Rho. But my Mistris has one fault that's almost unpardonable; for, being a Town-Lady, without any relation to the Court, yet she thinks her self undone, if she be not seen there three or four times a day, with the Princess *Amalthea*. And for the King, she haunts, and watches him so narrowly in a morning, that she prevents° even the Chymists who beset his Chamber, to turn their Mercury into his Gold.°

Pala. Yet, hitherto, me-thinks, you are no very unhappy man.   220

Rho. With all this, she's the greatest Gossip in Nature; for, besides the Court, she's the most eternal Visiter of the Town: and yet manages her time so well, that she seems ubiquitary.° For my part, I can compare her to nothing but the Sun; for, like him, she takes no rest, nor ever sets in one place, but to rise in another.

Pala. I confess she had need be handsome with these qualities.   229

Rho. No Lady can be so curious of a new Fashion, as she is of a new French-word; she's the very Mint

---

186. **Cordials:** stimulants.

202. **Chapmen:** customers. 204. **enhanc'd:** raised, inflated. 208. **Broad-gold:** or broadpiece, the twenty-shilling coin that was the predecessor of the guinea. 209. **light, or heavy:** The broadpieces were often mutilated. 217. **prevents:** arrives before. 218. **to . . . Gold:** perhaps rather than a direct allusion to Charles II's interest in alchemy, a submerged allusion to venereal disease, for which mercury was a specific. The joke would not of course apply to the king of the play. 224. **ubiquitary:** ubiquitous.

of the Nation; and as fast as any Bullion comes out of *France*, coins it immediately into our Language.

Pala. And her name is——

Rho. No naming; that's not like a Cavalier: Find her, if you can, by my description; and I am not so ill a painter, that I need write the name beneath the Picture.

Pala. Well, then, how far have you proceeded in your love?   240

Rho. 'Tis yet in the bud, and what fruit it may bear I cannot tell; for this insufferable humour, of haunting the Court, is so predominant, that she has hitherto broken all her assignations with me, for fear of missing her visits there.

Pal. That's the hardest part of your adventure: but, for ought I see, Fortune has us'd us both alike; I have a strange kind of Mistris too in Court, besides her I am to marry.   249

Rho. You have made haste to be in love then; for, if I am not mistaken, you are but this day arriv'd.

Pala. That's all one, I have seen the Lady already, who has charm'd me, seen her in these Walks, courted her, and receiv'd, for the first time, an answer that does not put me into despair.

To them, Argaleon, Amalthea, Artemis.

I'll tell you at more leisure my adventures. The Walks fill apace, I see. Stay, is not that the young Lord *Argaleon, the Kings Favourite*?

Rho. Yes, and as proud as ever, as ambitious, and as revengeful.   260

Pala. How keeps he the Kings favour with these qualities?

Rho. *Argaleon*'s father help'd him to the Crown: besides, he gilds over all his vices to the King, and, standing in the dark to him,° sees all his inclinations, interests and humours, which he so times and sooths, that, in effect, he reigns.

Pala. His sister *Amalthea*, who, I ghess, stands by him, seems not to be of his temper.

Rho. O, she's all goodness and generosity.   270

Arga. *Rhodophil*, the King expects you earnestly.

Rho. 'Tis done, my Lord, what he commanded: I onely waited his return from Hunting. Shall I attend your Lordship to him?

Arga. No; I go first another way.   [*Exit hastily.*

Pala. He seems in haste, and discompos'd.

Amal. [*To Rhod. after a short whisper.*] Your

265. standing . . . him: hidden from his view.

friend? then he must needs be of much merit.

Rho. When he has kis'd the King's hand, I know he'll beg the honour to kiss yours. Come, *Palamede.* [*Exeunt Rhodo. and Pala. bowing to Amal.*

Arte. Madam, you tell me most surprising news.

Amal. The fear of it, you see,   283
Has discompos'd my brother; but to me
All that can bring my Country good, is welcome.

Arte. It seems incredible, that this old King,
Whom all the world thought childless,
Should come to search the farthest parts of *Sicily*,
In hope to find an Heir.

Amal. To lessen your astonishment, I will   290
Unfold some private passages of State,
Of which you yet are ignorant: Know, first,
That this *Polydamas*, who Reigns, unjustly
Gain'd the Crown.

Arte. Somewhat of this I have confus'dly heard.

Amal. I'll tell you all in brief: *Theagenes*,
Our last great King,
Had, by his Queen, one onely Son, an Infant
Of three years old, call'd, after him, *Theagenes*;
The General, this *Polydamas*, then marri'd: 300
The publick Feasts for which were scarcely past,
When a Rebellion in the heart of *Sicily*
Call'd out the King to Arms.

Arte.   *Polydamas*
Had then a just excuse to stay behind.

Amal. His temper was too warlike to accept it:
He left his Bride, and the new joys of marriage,
And follow'd to the Feild. In short, they fought,
The Rebels were o'rcome; but in the Fight
The too bold King receiv'd a mortal wound.
When he perceiv'd his end approaching near,   310
He call'd the General, to whose care he left
His Widow Queen, and Orphan Son; then dy'd.

Arte. Then false *Polydamas* betray'd his trust?

Amal. He did; and with my father's help, for which
Heav'n pardon him, so gain'd the Soldiers hearts,
That in few days he was saluted King:
And when his crimes had impudence enough
To bear the eye of day,
He march'd his Army back to *Syracuse*.
But see how heav'n can punish wicked men   320
In granting their desires: the news was brought him
That day he was to enter it, that *Eubulus*,
Whom his dead Master had left Governour,
Was fled, and with him bore away the Queen,
And Royal Orphan; but, what more amaz'd him,
His wife, now big with child, and much detesting

Her husband's practices, had willingly
Accompani'd their flight.

    Arte.   How I admire her vertue!

    Amal.   What became
Of her, and them, since that, was never known;
Onely, some few days since, a famous Robber   331
Was taken with some Jewels of vast price,
Which, when they were delivered to the King,
He knew had been his Wife's; with these, a Letter,
Much torn, and sulli'd, but which yet he knew
To be her writing.

    Arte.   Sure from hence he learn'd
He had a Son.

    Amal.   It was not left so plain:
The Paper onely said, she dy'd in childbed:
But when it should have mention'd Son, or Daughter,
Just there it was torn off.

    Arte.   Madam, the King.   340

To them, Polydamas, Argaleon, *Guard, and Attendants.*

    Arga.   The Robber, though thrice Rack'd,
       confess'd no more,
But that he took those Jewels near this place.

    Poly.   But yet the circumstances strongly argue,
That those, for whom I search, are not far off.

    Arga.   I cannot easily believe it.

    Arte.   No,
You would not have it so.   [*aside.*

    Poly.   Those I employ'd, have, in the neighbouring
       Hamlet,
Amongst the Fishers Cabins, made discovery
Of some young persons, whose uncommon beauty,
And graceful carriage, make it seem suspicious   350
They are not what they seem: I therefore sent
The Captain of my Guards, this morning early,
With orders to secure and bring 'em to me.

       Enter Rhodophil *and* Palamede.

O here he is. Have you perform'd my will?

    Rho.   Sir, those whom you commanded me to
      bring,
Are waiting in the Walks.

    Poly.   Conduct 'em hither.

    Rho.   First, give me leave
To beg your notice of this Gentleman.

    Poly.   He seems to merit it. His name and quality?

    Rho.   *Palamede,* son to Lord *Cleodemus* of *Palermo,*
And new return'd from travel.

       [Palamede *approaches, and kneels to kiss the
             Kings hand.*

    Poly.   You're welcome.
I knew your father well, he was both brave   362
And honest; we two once were fellow-soldiers
In the last Civil Wars.

    Pala.   I bring the same unquestion'd honesty
And zeal to serve your Majesty; the courage
You were pleased to praise in him,
Your Royal prudence, and your Peoples love,
Will never give me leave to try° like him
In Civil Wars, I hope it may in Foreign.

    Poly.   Attend the Court, and it shall be my care
To find out some employment, worthy of you.   372
Go, *Rhodophil,* and bring in those without.

       [*Exeunt* Rho. & Pala.

Rhodophil *returns again immediately, and with him*
  Enter Hermogenes, Leonidas, *and* Palmyra.

Behold two miracles!
       [*Looking earnestly on* Leon. *and* Palmyra.
Of different sexes, but of equal form:
So matchless both, that my divided soul
Can scarcely ask the Gods a Son, or Daughter,
For fear of losing one. If from your hands,
You Powers, I shall this day receive a Daughter,
Argaleon, she is yours; but, if a Son,   380
Then *Amalthea's* love shall make him happy.

    Arga.   Grant, heav'n, this admirable Nymph may
      prove
That issue which he seeks.

    Amal.   *Venus Urania,*° if thou art a Goddess,
Grant that sweet Youth may prove the Prince of *Sicily.*

    Poly.   Tell me, old man, and tell me true, from
      whence   [*to* Her.
Had you that Youth and Maid?

    Her.   From whence you had
Your Scepter, Sir: I had 'em from the Gods.

    Poly.   The Gods then have not such another gift.
Say who their Parents were.

    Her.   My Wife, and I.

    Arga.   It is not likely, a Virgin of so excellent a
      beauty   391
Should come from such a Stock.

    Amal.   Much less, that such a Youth, so sweet, so
      graceful,
Should be produc'd from Peasants.

    Her.   Why, Nature is the same in Villages,

---

368. try: put (myself) to the test. **384. Venus Urania:**
daughter of Uranus and goddess of beauty and generation.

And much more fit to form a noble issue
Where it is least corrupted.
    Poly.   He talks, too like a man that knew the world
To have been long a Peasant. But the Rack
Will teach him other language. Hence with him.   400
             [As the Guards are carrying him away, his
                        Peruke falls off.
Sure I have seen that face before. *Hermogenes!*
'Tis he, 'tis he who fled away with *Eubulus,*
And with my dear *Eudoxia.*
    Her.   Yes, Sir, I am *Hermogenes.*
And if to have been loyal be a crime,
I stand prepar'd to suffer.
    Poly.   If thou would'st live, speak quickly,
What is become of my *Eudoxia?*
Where is the Queen and young *Theagenes?*
Where *Eubulus?* and which of these is mine?   410
            [Pointing to Leon. *and* Palm.
    Her.   *Eudoxia* is dead, so is the Queen.
The infant King her son, and *Eubulus.*
    Poly.   Traitor, 'tis false: produce 'em or——
    Her.   Once more
I tell you, they are dead; but leave° to threaten,
For you shall know no further.
    Poly.   Then prove indulgent to my hopes, and be
My friend for ever. Tell me, good *Hermogenes,*
Whose Son is that brave Youth?
    Her.   Sir, he is yours.
    Poly.   Fool that I am, thou see'st that so I wish it,
And so thou flatter'st me.
    Her.   By all that's holy.   420
    Poly.   Again. Thou canst not swear too deeply.
Yet hold, I will beleive thee:——yet I doubt.
    Her.   You need not, Sir.
    Arga.   Beleive him not; he sees you credulous,
And would impose his own base issue on you,
And fix it to your Crown.
    Amal.   Behold his goodly shape and feature, Sir,
Methinks he much resembles you.
    Arga.   I say, if you have any issue here,
I must be that fair creature;   430
By all my hopes I think so.
    Amal.   Yes, Brother, I believe you by your hopes,
For they are all for her.
    Poly.   Call the Youth nearer.
    Her.   *Leonidas,* the King would speak with you.
    Poly.   Come near, and be not dazled with the
    splendor,

And greatness of a Court.
    Leon.   I need not this incouragement.
I can fear nothing but the Gods.
And for this glory, after I have seen
The Canopy of State spread wide above   440
In the Abyss of Heaven, the Court of Stars,
The blushing Morning, and the rising Sun,
What greater can I see?
    Poly.   This speaks thee born a Prince, thou art thy
    self   *[Embracing him.*
That rising Sun, and shalt not see on earth,
A brighter then thy self.——All of you witness,
That for my son I here receive this Youth,
This brave, this——but I must not praise him further,
Because he now is mine.
    Leon.   I wonnot, Sir, believe   *[kneeling.*
That I am made your sport;   451
For I find nothing in my self, but what
Is much above a scorn;° I dare give credit
To whatsoe'r a King, like you, can tell me.
Either I am, or will deserve to be your Son.
    Arga.   I yet maintain it is impossible
This young man should be yours; for, if he were,
Why should *Hermogenes* so long conceal him
When he might gain so much by his discovery?
    Her.   I stay'd a while to make him worthy,
                      [To the King.
    Sir, of you.   460
But in that time I found
Somewhat within him, which so mov'd my love,
I never could resolve to part with him.
    Leon.   You ask too many questions, and are
                    [To Argaleon.
Too sawcy for a subject.
    Arga.   You rather over-act your part, and are
Too soon a Prince.
    Leon.   Too soon you'l find me one.
    Poly.   Enough, *Argaleon;*
I have declar'd him mine: and you, *Leonidas,*
Live well with him I love.   470
    Arga.   Sir, if he be your Son, I may have leave
To think your Queen had Twins: look on this Virgin;
Hermogenes would enviously deprive you
Of half your treasure.
    Her.   Sir, she is my daughter.
I could, perhaps, thus aided by this Lord,
Prefer her to be yours; but truth forbid
I should procure her greatness by a Lie.

----

414. leave: cease.

453. scorn: insult.

Poly. Come hither, beauteous Maid: are you not sorry
Your father will not let you pass for mine?

Palm. I am content to be what heav'n has made me.

Poly. Could you not wish your self a Princess then?

Palm. Not to be Sister to *Leonidas*. 482

Poly. Why, my sweet Maid?

Palm. Indeed I cannot tell;
But I could be content to be his Handmaid.

Arga. I wish I had not seen her.   [*Aside.*

Palm. I must weep for your good fortune;
                                   [*To* Leonidas.
Pray pardon me, indeed I cannot help it.

Leonidas, (alas, I had forgot,
Now I must call you Prince) but must I leave you?

Leon. I dare not speak to her; for if I should,
                                              [*Aside.*
I must weep too. 491

Poly. No, you shall live at Court, sweet Innocence,
And see him there. *Hermogenes,*
Though you intended not to make me happy,
Yet you shall be rewarded for th' event.
Come, my *Leonidas*, let's thank the Gods;
Thou for a Father, I for such a Son. [*Exeunt all but*

Leonidas *and Palmyra.*

Leon. My dear *Palmyra*, many eyes observe me,
And I have thoughts so tender, that I cannot
In publick speak 'em to you: some hours hence 500
I shall shake off these crowds of fawning Courtiers,
And then——   [*Exit* Leonidas.

Palm. Fly swift, you hours, you measure time for
      me in vain,
Till you bring back *Leonidas* again.
Be shorter now; and to redeem that wrong,
When he and I are met, be twice as long. [*Exit.*

ACT II

SCENE I

Melantha *and Philotis.*

Phil. Count *Rhodophil's* a fine Gentleman indeed,
Madam; and I think deserves your affection.

Mel. Let me die but he's a fine man; he sings, and
dances *en Francois,* and writes the *Billets doux* to a
miracle.°

Act II, scene i. **4–5. to a miracle:** marvelously well.

Phil. And those are no small tallents, to a Lady that
understands, and values the *French* ayr, as your
Ladyship does. 8

Mel. How charming is the *French* ayr! and what
an *etourdy bete*° is one of our untravel'd Islanders!
when he would make his Court to me, let me die, but
he is just *Æsop's Ass,*° that would imitate the courtly
French in his addresses; but, in stead of those, comes
pawing upon me, and doing all things so *mal a
droitly.* 15

Phil. 'Tis great pity *Rhodophil's* a married man,
that you may not have an honourable Intrigue with
him.

Mel. Intrigue, *Philotis!* that's an old phrase; I have
laid that word by: *Amour* sounds better. But thou art
heir to all my cast° words, as thou art to my old
Wardrobe. Oh Count *Rhodophil! Ah mon cher!* I
could live and die with him. 23

Enter Palamede *and a Servant.*

Ser. Sir, this is my Lady.

Pala. Then this is she that is to be Divine, and
Nymph, and Goddess, and with whom I am to be
desperately in love.
                    [*Bows to her, delivering a Letter.*
This letter, Madam, which I present you from your
father, has given me both the happy opportunity, and
the boldness, to kiss the fairest hands in *Sicily.* 30

Mel. Came you lately from *Palermo,* Sir?

Pala. But yesterday, Madam.

Mel. [*Reading the Letter*] *Daughter, receive the
bearer of this Letter, as a Gentleman whom I have chosen
to make you happy;* (O *Venus,* a new Servant sent me!
and let me die but he has the ayre of a gallant *homme*)
his father is the rich Lord Cleodemus, *our neighbour: I
suppose you'l find nothing disagreeable in his person or
converse;*° *both which he has improv'd by travel. The
Treaty is already concluded, and I shall be in Town within
these three days; so that you have nothing to do, but to
obey your careful Father.* 42

(*To* Pala.) Sir, my Father, for whom I have a blind
obedience, has commanded me to receive your
passionate addresses; but you must also give me leave
to avow, that I cannot merit 'em, from so accomplish'd
a Cavalier.

10. etourdy bete: (*bête étourdie*) harebrained fool. **12. Æsop's
Ass:** who, in imitating the dog's fawning upon his master,
was repulsed. **21. cast:** cast off. **39. converse:** conversation.

Pala. I want many things, Madam, to render me accomplish'd; and the first and greatest of 'em is your favour.   50

Mel. Let me die, *Philotis*, but this is extremely *French*; but yet Count *Rhodophil*——A Gentleman, Sir, that understands the *Grand mond* so well, who has hanted° the best conversations,° and who (in short) has voyag'd, may pretend to the good graces of any Lady.

Pala. (*Aside*) Hay day! *Grand mond! conversation! voyag'd! and good graces!* I find my Mistris is one of those that run mad in new *French* words.°   59

Mel. I suppose, Sir, you have made the *Tour* of *France;* and having seen all that's fine there, will make a considerable reformation in the rudeness of our Court: for, let me die, but an unfashion'd, untravel'd, meer *Sicilian*, is a *Bete;* and has nothing in the world of an *honete homme.*°

Pala. I must confess, Madam, that——

Mel. And what new *Minouets* have you brought over with you! their *Minouets* are to a miracle! and our *Sicilian Jigs* are so dull and sad to 'em!

Pala. For *Minouets*, Madam——   70

Mel. And what new Plays are there in vogue? and who danc'd best in the last Grand Ballet? Come, sweet Servant, you shall tell me all.

Pala. (*Aside*) Tell her all? why, she asks all, and will hear nothing——To answer in order, Madam, to your demands——

Mel. I am thinking what a happy couple we shall be! for you shall keep up your correspondence abroad, and every thing that's new writ, in *France*, and fine, I mean all that's delicate, and *bien tourné,*° we will have first.   81

Pala. But, Madam, our fortune——

Mel. I understand you, Sir; you'l leave that to me: for the mennage° of a family, I know it better then any Lady in *Sicily.*

---

54. **hanted:** (haunted) frequented. **conversations:** circles, companies. 59. **new . . . words:** As this passage shows, the development of English usage has obscured the identity of certain gallicisms, and it is not always easy to distinguish "new French words" (and idioms) from those that may have been well assimilated into English at this time. The systematic use of italics in the text would have been a service to posterity, but since we are denied that, we should be alert to Melantha's addiction to "the French ayr," even in such phrases below as "pay my devoirs" and "That imports not." 65. **honete homme:** (*honnête homme*) roughly, gentleman. 80. **bien tourné:** well-turned, well-expressed. 84. **mennage:** (*ménage*) domestic arrangements.

Pala. Alas, Madam, we——

Mel. Then, we will never make visits together, nor see a Play, but always apart; you shall be every day at the King's *Levé,*° and I at the Queen's;° and we will never meet, but in the Drawing-room.   90

Phil. Madam, the new Prince is just pass'd by the end of the Walk.

Mel. The new Prince, say'st thou? Adieu, dear Servant; I have not made my court to him these two long hours. O, 'tis the sweetest Prince! so obligeant, charmant, ravissant, that—Well, I'll make haste to kiss his hands; and then make half a score visits more, and be with you again in a twinkling.   98

[*Exit, running with* Philotis.

Pala. (*Solus*) Now heaven, of thy mercy, bless me from this tongue; it may keep the field against a whole Army of Lawyers, and that in their own language, *French Gibberish.*° 'Tis true, in the day-time, 'tis tolerable, when a man has field-room to run from it; but, to be shut up in a bed with her, like two Cocks in a pit; humanity cannot support it: I must kiss all night, in my own defence, and hold her down, like a Boy at cuffs,° nay, and give her the rising blow° every time she begins to speak.   108

Enter Rhodophil.

But here comes *Rhodophil*. 'Tis pretty odd that my Mistris should so much resemble his: the same News-monger, the same passionate lover of a Court, the same—But *Basta,*° since I must marry her, I'll say nothing, because he shall not laugh at my misfortune.

Rho. Well, *Palamede*, how go the affairs of love? You've seen your Mistris?

Pala. I have so.

Rho. And how, and how? has the old *Cupid*, your Father, chosen well for you? is he a good Woodman°?

Pala. She's much handsomer then I could have imagin'd: In short, I love her, and will marry her.

Rho. Then you are quite off from your other Mistris?   122

Pala. You are mistaken, I intend to love 'em both, as a reasonable man ought to do. For, since all women

---

89. **Levé:** (*levée*) levee, a morning audience held by a person of distinction before or upon rising from bed. **at the Queen's:** There is of course no queen in the play—until the very end. 102. **French Gibberish:** the mixture of English, Latin, and French that infected the English law. 107. **at cuffs:** fighting. **the rising blow:** uppercut; but clearly the sexual meaning is uppermost. 112. **Basta:** no matter; enough! 118. **Woodman:** hunter, marksman.

have their faults, and imperfections, 'tis fit that one of 'em should help out t' other.

Rho. This were a blessed Doctrine, indeed, if our Wives would hear it; but, they're their own enemies: if they would suffer us but now and then to make excursions, the benefit of our variety would be theirs; instead of one continu'd, lazy, tyr'd love, they would, in their turns, have twenty vigorous, fresh, and active loves.   133

Pala. And I would ask any of 'em, whether a poor narrow Brook, half dry the best part of the year, and running ever one way, be to be compar'd to a lusty Stream, that has Ebbs and Flows?

Rho. Ay; or is half so profitable for Navigation?

Enter Doralice, walking by, and reading.

Pala. Ods my life, *Rhodophil,* will you keep my counsel?   140

Rho. Yes: where's the secret?

Pala. There 'tis.   [*Showing* Doralice.
I may tell you, as my friend, *sub sigillo,*° &c. this is that very numerical° Lady, with whom I am in love.

Rho. By all that's vertuous, my Wife!   [*Aside.*

Pala. You look strangely: how do you like her? is she not very handsome?

Rho. Sure he abuses° me.   [*Aside.*
Why the devil do you ask my judgment?   [*To him.*

Pala. You are so dogged° now, you think no man's Mistris handsome, but your own. Come, you shall hear her talk too; she has wit, I assure you.   152

Rho. This is too much, *Palamede.*   [*Going back.*

Pala. Prethee do not hang back so:
    [*Pulling him forward.*
of an old try'd Lover, thou art the most bashful fellow!

Dor. Were you so near, and would not speak,
    [*Looking up.*
dear Husband?

Pala. Husband, quoth a! I have cut out a fine piece of work for my self.   [*Aside.*

Rho. Pray, Spouse, how long have you been acquainted with this Gentleman?   162

Dor. Who, I acquainted with this Stranger? To my best knowledge, I never saw him before.

Enter Melantha, at the other end.

Pala. Thanks, Fortune, thou hast help'd me.
    [*Aside.*

143. **sub sigillo:** literally, under the seal; confidentially.
144. **numerical:** identical. 148. **abuses:** deceives. 150.
dogged: doglike, faithful.

Rho. *Palamede,* this must not pass so: I must know your Mistris a little better.

Pala. It shall be your own fault else. Come, I'll introduce you.

Rho. Introduce me! where?   170

Pala. There. To my Mistris.
    [*Pointing to* Melantha, *who swiftly passes over
        the stage.*

Rho. Who? *Melantha!* O heavens, I did not see her.

Pala. But I did: I am an Eagle where I love; I have seen her this half hour.

Dor. (*Aside.*) I find he has wit, he has got off so readily; but it would anger me, if he should love *Melantha.*

Rho. (*Aside.*) Now I could e'en wish it were my Wife he lov'd: I find he's to be marri'd to my Mistris.

Pala. Shall I run after, and fetch her back again, to present you to her?   182

Rho. No, you need not; I have the honour to have some small acquaintance with her.

Pala. (*Aside.*) O *Jupiter!* what a blockhead was I not to find it out! My Wife that must be, is his Mistris. I did a little suspect it before; well, I must marry her, because she's handsome, and because I hate to be dis-inherited for a younger Brother, which I am sure I shall be if I disobey; and yet I must keep in with *Rhodophil,* because I love his Wife.   191

(*To* Rhodo.) I must desire you to make my excuse to your Lady, if I have been so unfortunate to cause any mistake; and, withall, to beg the honour of being known to her.

Rho. O, that's but reason. Hark you, Spouse, pray look upon this Gentleman as my friend; whom, to my knowledge, you have never seen before this hour.

Dor. I'm so obedient a Wife, Sir, that my Husbands commands shall ever be a Law to me.   201

*Enter Melantha again, hastily, and runs
to embrace Doralice.*

Mela. O, my dear, I was just going to pay my devoirs to you; I had not time this morning, for making my Court to the King, and our new Prince. Well never Nation was so happy, and all that, in a young Prince; and he's the kindest person in the World to me, let me die, if he is not.

Dor. He has been bred up far from Court, and therefore—

Mel. That imports not: Though he has not seen

the *Grand mond*, and all that, let me die but he has the air of the Court, most absolutely.   212

Pala.   But yet, Madam, he——

Mel.   O, Servant, you can testifie that I am in his good Graces. Well, I cannot stay long with you, because I have promis'd him this Afternoon to—— But hark you, my dear, I'll tell you a Secret.

                                             [*Whispers to* Doralice.

Rho.   The Devil's in me, that I must love this Woman.   [*Aside.*

Pala.   The Devil's in me, that I must marry this Woman.   [*Aside.*

Mel.   (*Raising her Voice.*) So the Prince and I—— But you must make a Secret of this, my dear, for I would not for the World your Husband should hear it, or my Tyrant, there, that must be.   225

Pala.   Well, fair impertinent, your whisper is not lost, we hear you.   [*Aside.*

Mel.   I'll tell you, my dear, the Prince took me by the hand, and press'd it *al a derobbée,*° because the King was near, made the *doux yeux* to° me, and, *in suitte,*° said a thousand Gallantries, or let me die, my dear.   232

Dor.   Then I am sure you——

Mel.   You are mistaken, my dear.

Dor.   What, before I speak?

Mel.   But I know your meaning; you think, my dear, that I assum'd something of *fierté*° into my Countenance, to *rebute*° him; but, quite contrary, I regarded him, I know not how to express it in our dull Sicilian Language, *d' un ayr enjouué;*° and said nothing but *ad autre,*° *ad autre*, and that it was all *grimace,*° and would not pass upon me.   242

                 Enter Artemis: Melantha *sees her, and*
                       runs away from Doralice.

To Artemis. My dear, I must beg your pardon, I was just making a *loose*° from *Doralice*, to pay my respects to you: Let me die, if I ever pass time so agreeably as in your company, and if I would leave it for any Lady's in *Sicily.*

Arte.   The Princess *Amalthea* is coming this way.

                 Enter Amalthea: Melantha *runs to her.*

Mel.   O dear Madam! I have been at your

Lodgings, in my new *Galeche,*° so often, to tell you of a new *Amour*, betwixt two persons whom you would little suspect for it; that, let me die, if one of my Coach-horses be not dead, and another quite tyr'd, and sunk under the *fatigue*.   254

Amal.   O, *Melantha*, I can tell you news, the Prince is coming this way.

Mel.   The Prince, O sweet Prince! He and I are to——and I forgot it.——Your pardon, sweet Madam, for my abruptness. Adieu, my dears. Servant, *Rodophil;* Servant, Servant, Servant All.   [*Exit running.*

Amal.   *Rodophil*, a word with you.   [*Whispers.*

Dor.   to *Pala.* Why do you not follow your Mistress, Sir?   263

Pala.   Follow her? Why, at this rate she'll be at the *Indies* within this half hour.

Dor.   However, if you can't follow her all day, you'll meet her at night, I hope?

Pala.   But can you, in charity, suffer me to be so mortify'd, without affording me some relief? If it be but to punish that *sign*° of a Husband there; that lazy matrimony, that dull insipid taste, who leaves such delicious fare at home, to dine abroad, on worse meat, and to pay dear for 't into the bargain.   273

Dor.   All this is in vain: Assure your self, I will never admit of any visit from you in private.

Pala.   That is to tell me, in other words, my condition is desperate.

Dor.   I think you in so ill a condition, that I am resolved to pray for you, this very evening, in the close Walk, behind the Terras; for that's a 280 private place, and there I am sure no body will disturb my devotions. And so, good-night, Sir. [*Exit.*

Pala.   This is the newest way of making an appoint- ment, I ever heard of: let women alone to contrive the means; I find we are but dunces to 'em. Well, I will not be so prophane a wretch as to interrupt her devotions; but to make 'em more effectual, I'll down upon my knees, and endeavour to joyn my own with 'em.   [*Exit.*

Amal.   (*to* Rhodophil) I know already they do not love each other; and that my Brother acts but a forc'd obedience to the Kings commands; so that, if a quarrel should arise betwixt the Prince and him, I were most miserable on both sides.   294

Rho.   There shall be nothing wanting in me, Madam, to prevent so sad a consequence.

---

229. al a derobbée: (*à la dérobée*) on the sly. **230. made . . . to:** made eyes at. **230–31. in suitte:** (*ensuite*) afterward. **237. fierté:** pride. **238. rebute:** repulse. **240. d' un ayr enjouué:** (*d'un air enjoué*) with a sprightly air. **241. ad autre:** (*à d'autres*) nonsense!; literally, (tell it) to others. **grimace:** affectation. **244. making a loose:** breaking away.

250. Galeche: calash, a light, low carriage with a removable hood. **270. sign:** semblance, pretense.

Enter the King, Leonidas; *the King*
whispers Amalthea.

(*To himself*) I begin to hate this *Palamede*, because he
is to marry my Mistris: yet break with him I dare not,
for fear of being quite excluded from her company.
'Tis a hard case when a man must go by his Rival to
his Mistris: but 'tis at worst but using him like a pair
of heavy Boots in a dirty journey; after I have
foul'd him all day, I'll throw him off at night.   [*Exit.*

Amal. (*to the King*) This honour is too great for
me to hope.   305

Poly.   You shall this hour have the assurance of it.
Leonidas, come hither; you have heard,
I doubt not, that the Father of this Princess
Was my most faithful friend, while I was yet
A private man; and when I did assume   310
This Crown, he serv'd me in that high attempt.
You see, then, to what gratitude obliges me;
Make your addresses to her.

Leon.   Sir, I am yet too young to be a Courtier;
I should too much betray my ignorance,
And want of breeding, to so fair a Lady.

Amal.   Your language speaks you not bred up in
     Desarts,
But in the softness of some *Asian* Court,
Where luxury and ease invent kind words,
To cozen° tender Virgins of their hearts.   320

Poly.   You need not doubt
But in what words soe're a Prince can offer
His Crown and Person, they will be receiv'd.
You know my pleasure, and you know your duty.

Leon.   Yes, Sir, I shall obey, in what I can.

Poly.   In what you can, *Leonidas*? Consider,
He's both your King, and Father, who commands you.
Besides, what is there hard in my injunction?

Leon.   'Tis hard to have my inclination forc'd.
I would not marry, Sir; and, when I do,   330
I hope you'll give me freedom in my choice.

Poly.   View well this Lady,
Whose mind as much transcends her beauteous face,
As that excels all others.

Amal.   My beauty, as it ne'r could merit love,
So neither can it beg: and, Sir, you may
Beleive that, what the King has offer'd you,
I should refuse, did I not value more
Your person then your Crown.

Leon.   Think it not pride,
Or my new fortunes swell me to contemn you;   340

Think less, that I want eyes to see your beauty;
And least of all think duty wanting in me
T' obey a father's will: but——

Poly.   But what, *Leonidas*?
For I must know your reason; and be sure
It be convincing too.

Leon.   Sir, ask the Stars,
Which have impos'd love on us, like a fate,
Why minds are bent to one, and fly another?
Ask why all beauties cannot move all hearts?
For though there may
Be made a rule for colour, or for feature;   350
There can be none for liking.

Poly.   *Leonidas*, you owe me more
Then to oppose your liking to my pleasure.

Leon.   I owe you all things, Sir; but something too
I owe my self.

Poly.   You shall dispute no more; I am King,
And I will be obey'd.

Leon.   You are a King, Sir; but you are no God;
Or if you were, you could not force my will.   359

Poly.   But you are just, you Gods; O you are just,
                                                        [*Aside.*
In punishing the crimes of my rebellion
With a rebellious Son!
Yet I can punish him, as you do me.
Leonidas, there is no jesting with
My will: I ne'r had done so much to gain
A Crown, but to be absolute in all things.

Amal.   O, Sir, be not so much a King, as to
Forget you are a Father: Soft indulgence
Becomes that name. Though Nature gives you pow'r,
To bind his duty, 'tis with silken Bonds: 370
Command him, then, as you command your self:
He is as much a part of you, as are
Your Appetite, and Will, and those you force not,
But gently bend, and make 'em pliant to your
     Reason.

Poly.   It may be I have us'd too rough a way:
Forgive me, my *Leonidas*; I know
I lie as open to the gusts of passion,
As the bare Shore to every beating Surge:
I will not force thee, now; but I intreat thee,
Absolve° a Father's vow, to this fair Virgin: 380
A vow, which hopes of having such a Son
First caus'd.

Leon.   Show not my disobedience by your pray'rs,
For I must still deny you, though I now
Appear more guilty to my self, than you:

---

320. cozen: defraud.

380. Absolve: discharge.

I have some reasons, which I cannot utter,
That force my disobedience; yet I mourn
To death, that the first thing you e'r injoyn'd me,
Should be that onely one command in Nature
Which I could not obey.   390
    Poly.   I did descend too much below my self
When I intreated him. Hence, to thy Desart,°
Thou'rt not my son, or art not fit to be.
    Amal.   Great Sir, I humbly beg you, make not me
                                              [*kneeling.*
The cause of your displeasure. I absolve
Your vow: far, far from me, be such designs;
So wretched a desire of being great,
By making him unhappy. You may see
Something so noble in the Prince his nature,
As grieves him more not to obey, then you   400
That you are not obey'd.
    Poly.   Then, for your sake,
I'll give him one day longer, to consider
Not to deny; for my resolves are firm
As Fate, that cannot change.
                              [*Exeunt King and* Amal.
    Leon.   And so are mine.
This beauteous Princess, charming as she is,
Could never make me happy: I must first
Be false to my *Palmyra*, and then wretched.
But, then, a Father's anger!
Suppose he should recede from his own vow,
He never would permit me to keep mine.   410
        Enter Palmyra; Argaleon *following her,*
                a little after.

See, she appears!
I'll think no more of any thing, but her.
Yet I have one hour good ere I am wretched.
But, Oh! *Argaleon* follows her! so night
Treads on the foot-steps of a Winter's Sun,
And stalks all black behind him.
    Palm.   O *Leonidas*,
(For I must call you still by that dear name)
Free me from this bad man.
    Leon.   I hope he dares not be injurious to you.
    Arga.   I rather was injurious to my self,   420
Then her.
    Leon.   That must be judg'd when I hear what you
    said.
    Arga.   I think you need not give your self that
    trouble:

392. **Desart**: desert.

It concern'd us alone.
    Leon.   You answer sawcily, and indirectly:
What interest can you pretend in her?
    Arga.   It may be, Sir, I made her some expressions
Which I would not repeat, because they were
Below my rank, to one of hers.
    Leon.   What did he say, *Palmyra?*   430
    Palm.   I'll tell you all: First, he began to look,
And then he sigh'd, and then he look'd again;
At last, he said my eyes wounded his heart:
And, after that, he talk'd of flames, and fires;
And such strange words, that I believ'd he conjur'd.
    Leon.   O my heart! Leave me, *Argaleon.*
    Arga.   Come, sweet *Palmyra*,
I will instruct you better in my meaning:
You see he would be private.
    Leon.   Go your self,
And leave her here.
    Arga.   Alas, she's ignorant,   440
And is not fit to entertain a Prince.
    Leon.   First learn what's fit for you; that's to obey.
    Arga.   I know my duty is to wait on you.
A great King's Son, like you, ought to forget
Such mean converse.°
    Leon.   What? a disputing Subject?
Hence; or my sword shall do me justice, on thee.
    Arga.   Yet I may find a time——   [*Going.*
    Leon.   What's that you mutter,
                                    [*going after him.*
To find a time?
    Arga.   To wait on you again——
(*Softly*) In the mean while I'll watch you.
                    [*Exit, and watches during the Scene.*
    Leon.   How precious are the hours of Love in
        Courts!   450
In Cottages, where Love has all the day,
Full, and at ease, he throws it half away.°
Time gives himself, and is not valu'd, there;
But sells, at mighty rates, each minute, here.
There, he is lazy, unemploy'd, and slow;
Here, he's more swift; and yet has more to do.
So many of his hours in publick move,

445. **converse**: society. 451–52. **In . . . away**: In the Epistle
Dedicatory to his first tragicomedy, *The Rival Ladies* (1664),
Dryden stated his belief that rhyme is most appropriately
used in the drama for scenes of argumentation and discourse
"on the result of which the doing or not doing of some
considerable action should depend." Another protracted
excursion into rhymed couplets occurs in a dialogue
between the same characters in IV. iv.

That few are left for privacy, and Love.

   Palm. The Sun, methinks, shines faint and dimly, here;
Light is not half so long, nor half so clear.   460
But, Oh! when every day was yours and mine,
How early up! what haste he made to shine!

   Leon. Such golden days no Prince must hope to see;
Whose ev'ry Subject is more bless'd then he.

   Palm. Do you remember, when their talks were done,
How all the Youth did to our Cottage run?
While winter-winds were whistling loud without,
Our chearful hearth was circled round about:
With strokes in ashes Maids their Lovers drew;°
And still you fell to me, and I to you.   470

   Leon. When Love did of my heart possession take,
I was so young, my soul was scarce awake:
I cannot tell when first I thought you fair;
But suck'd in Love, insensibly as Ayre.

   Palm. I know too well when first my love began,
When, at our Wake,° you for the Chaplet° ran:
Then I was made the Lady of the May,
And, with the Garland, at the Goal did stay:
Still, as you ran, I kept you full in view;
I hop'd, and wish'd, and ran, methought, for you. 480
As you cam near, I hastily did rise,
And stretch'd my arm out-right, that held the prize.
The custum was to kiss whom I should crown:
You kneel'd; and, in my lap, your head laid down.
I blush'd, and blush'd, and did the kiss delay:
At last, my Subjects forc'd me to obey;
But, when I gave the Crown, and then the kiss,
I scarce had breath to say, Take that—and this.

   Leon. I felt, the while, a pleasing kind of smart;
The kiss went, tingling, to my very heart.   490
When it was gone, the sense of it did stay;
The sweetness cling'd upon my lips all day,
Like drops of Honey, loath to fall away.

   Palm. Life, like a prodigal, gave all his store
To my first youth, and now can give no more.
You are a Prince; and, in that high degree,
No longer must converse° with humble me.

   Leon. 'Twas to my loss the Gods that title gave;
A Tyrant's Son is doubly born a Slave:

He gives a Crown; but, to prevent my life   500
From being happy, loads it with a Wife.

   Palm. Speak quickly; what have you resolv'd to do?

   Leon. To keep my faith inviolate to you.
He threatens me with exile, and with shame,
To lose my birth-right, and a Prince his name;
But there's a blessing which he did not mean,
To send me back to Love and You again.

   Palm. Why was not I a Princess for your sake?
But Heav'en no more such miracles can make:
And, since That cannot, This must never be;   510
You shall not lose a Crown for love of me.
Live happy, and a nobler choice pursue;
I shall complain of Fate; but not of you.

   Leon. Can you so easily without me live?
Or could you take the counsel which you give?
Were you a Princess would you not be true?

   Palm. I would; but cannot merit it from you.

   Leon. Did you not merit, as you do, my heart;
Love gives esteem; and then it gives desert.
But if I basely could forget my vow,   520
Poor helpless Innocence, what would you do?

   Palm. In Woods, and Plains, where first my love began,
There would I live, retir'd from faithless man:
I'd sit all day within some lonely shade,
Or that close Arbour which your hands have made:
I'd search the Groves, and ev'ry Tree, to find
Where you had carv'd our names upon the rind:
Your Hook, your Scrip,° all that was yours, I'd keep,
And lay 'em by me when I went to sleep.
Thus would I live: and Maidens, when I die,   530
Upon my Hearse white True-love-knots° should tie:
And thus my Tomb should be inscrib'd above,
Here the forsaken Virgin rests from love.

   Leon. Think not that time or fate shall e'r divide
Those hearts, which Love and mutual Vows have ty'd:
But we must part; farewell, my Love.

   Palm.   Till when?

   Leon. Till the next age of hours we meet agen.
Mean time——we may
When near each other we in publick stand,
Contrive to catch a look, or steal a hand: 540
Fancy will every touch, and glance improve:
And draw the most spirituous parts of Love.

---

469. **With . . . drew:** The identity of a lover was thought to be revealed by the chance formation of his initial in the ashes on the hearth. 476. **Wake:** festival. **Chaplet:** wreath of flowers. 497. **converse:** associate.

528. **Your . . . Scrip:** your shepherd's crook and wallet. 531. **True-love-knots:** an ornament in the form of double or intertwined loops, used as a symbol of true love.

Our souls sit close, and silently within;
And their own Web from their own Intrals spin.
And when eyes meet far off, our sense is such,
That, Spider-like, we feel the tender'st touch.

[Exeunt.

ACT III

SCENE I.

Enter Rhodophil, *meeting* Doralice *and* Artemis.
Rhodophil *and* Doralice *embrace.*

Rho.   My own dear heart!

Dor.   My own true love!   *[She starts back.*
I had forgot my self to be so kind; indeed I am very
angry with you, dear; you are come home an hour
after you appointed: If you had staid a minute longer,
I was just considering, whether I should stab, hang, or
drown myself.   *[Embracing him.*

Rho.   Nothing but the King's business could have
hinder'd me; and I was so vext, that I was just laying
down my Commission, rather then have fail'd   10
my Dear.   *[Kissing her hand.*

Arte.   Why, this is love as it should be, betwixt
Man and Wife: such another Couple would bring
Marriage into fashion again. But is it always thus
betwixt you?

Rho.   Always thus! this is nothing. I tell you there
is not such a pair of Turtles° in all *Sicily;* there is such
an eternal Cooing and kissing betwixt us, that indeed
it is scandalous before civil company.   19

Dor.   Well, if I had imagin'd, I should have been
this fond fool, I would never have marri'd the man I
lov'd: I marri'd to be happy; and have made my self
miserable, by over-loving. Nay, and now, my case is
desperate; for I have been marry'd above these two
years, and find my self every day worse and worse in
love: nothing but madness can be the end on 't.

Arte.   Doat on, to the extremity, and you are
happy.   28

Dor.   He deserves so infinitely much, that, the
truth is, there can be no doating° in the matter; but to
love well, I confess, is a work that pays it self: 'tis
telling° gold, and after taking it for ones pains.

Rho.   By that I should be a very covetous person;

for I am ever pulling out my money, and putting it
into my pocket again.

Dor.   O dear *Rhodophil!*

Rho.   O sweet *Doralice!*   *[Embracing each other.*

Arte.   (*Aside*) Nay, I am resolv'd, I'll never interrupt Lovers: I'll leave 'em as happy as I found 'em.

[Steals away.

Rho.   What, is she gone?   *[Looking up.*

Dor.   Yes; and without taking leave.   41

Rho.   Then there's enough for this time.

[Parting from her.

Dor.   Yes sure, the Scene's done, I take it.

*[They walk contrary ways on the stage; he, with his
hands in his pocket, whistling; she, singing a
dull melancholly Tune.*

Rho.   Pox o' your dull tune, a man can't think for
you.

Dor.   Pox o' your damn'd whistling; you can
neither be company to me your self, nor leave me to
the freedom of my own fancy.

Rho.   Well, thou art the most provoking Wife!

Dor.   Well, thou art the dullest Husband, thou art
never to be provok'd.   51

Rho.   I was never thought dull, till I marry'd thee;
and now thou hast made an old knife of me, thou hast
whetted me so long, till I have no edge left.

Dor.   I see you are in the Husbands fashion; you
reserve all your good humours for your Mistresses,
and keep your ill for your wives.

Rho.   Prethee leave me to my own cogitations; I
am thinking over all my sins, to find for which of them
it was I marry'd thee.   60

Dor.   Whatever your sin was, mine's the punishment.

Rho.   My comfort is, thou art not immortal; and
when that blessed, that divine day comes, of thy
departure, I'm resolv'd I'll make one Holy-day more
in the Almanack, for thy sake.

Dor.   Ay, you had need make a Holy-day for me,
for I am sure you have made me a Martyr.   68

Rho.   Then, setting my victorious foot upon thy
head, in the first hour of thy silence, (that is, the first
hour thou art dead, for I despair of it before) I will
swear by thy Ghost, an oath as terrible to me, as
Styx is to the Gods, never more to be in danger of the
Banes° of Matrimony.

Dor.   And I am resolv'd to marry the very same

Act III, scene i. **17. Turtles:** turtledoves. **30. doating:** loving
to excess. **32. telling:** counting.

74. Banes: an old form of *banns,* pronounced with a long
a. But the intended pun is obvious.

day thou dy'st, if it be but to show how little I'm concern'd for thee.   77

Rho. Prethee, *Doralice*, why do we quarrel thus a-days°? ha? this is but a kind of Heathenish life, and does not answer the ends of marriage. If I have err'd, propound what reasonable atonement may be made, before we sleep, and I shall not be refractory: but withall consider, I have been marry'd these three years, and be not too tyrannical.

Dor. What° should you talk of a peace abed, when you can give no security for performance of Articles?

Rho. Then, since we must live together, and both of us stand upon our terms, as to matter of dying first, let us make our selves as merry as we can with our misfortunes.   90

Why there's the devil on 't! if thou couldst make my enjoying thee but a little less easie, or a little more unlawful, thou shouldst see, what a Termagant Lover I would prove. I have taken such pains to enjoy thee, *Doralice*, that I have fanci'd thee all the fine women in the Town, to help me out. But now there's none left for me to think on, my imagination is quite jaded. Thou art a Wife, and thou wilt be a Wife, and I can make thee another no longer.   [*Exit* Rhodophil.

Dor. Well, since thou art a Husband, and   100 wilt be a Husband, I'll try if I can find out another! 'Tis a pretty time we Women have on 't, to be made Widows, while we are marry'd. Our Husbands think it reasonable to complain, that we are the same, and the same to them, when we have more reason to complain, that they are not the same to us. Because they cannot feed on one dish, therefore we must be starv'd. 'Tis enough that they have a sufficient Ordinary° provided, and a Table ready spread for 'em: if they cannot fall too and eat heartily, the fault is theirs; and 'tis pity, methinks, that the good creature should be lost, when many a poor sinner would be glad on 't.   112

Enter Melantha, and Artemis to her.

Mel. Dear, my dear, pity me; I am so chagrin to day, and have had the most signal affront at Court! I went this afternoon to do my devoir to Princess *Amalthea*, found her, convers'd with her, and help'd to make her court some half an hour; after which, she went to take the ayr, chose out two Ladies to go with her, that came in after me, and left me most barbarously behind her.   120

Arte. You are the less to be piti'd, *Melantha*, because you subject your self to these affronts, by coming perpetually to Court, where you have no business nor employment.

Mel. I declare, I had rather of the two, be *railly'd*,° nay, *mal traittée* at Court, then be Deifie'd in the Town: for, assuredly, nothing can be so *ridicule*, as a meer° Town-Lady.   128

Dor. Especially at Court. How I have seen 'em crowd and sweat in the Drawing-room, on a Holiday-night! for that's their time to swarm, and invade the Presence. O, how they catch at a bow, or any little salute from a Courtier, to make show of their acquaintance! and rather then be thought to be quite unknown, they court'sie to one another; but they take true pains to come near the Circle,° and press and peep upon the Princess, to write Letters into the Countrey how she was dress'd, while the Ladies that stand about make their court to her with abusing them.   140

Arte. These are sad truths, *Melantha;* and therefore I would e'en advise you to quit the Court, and live either wholly in the Town; or, if you like not that, in the Countrey.

Dor. In the Countrey! nay, that's to fall beneath the Town; for they live there upon our offals here: their entertainment of wit, is onely the remembrance of what they had when they were last in Town; they live this year upon the last years knowledge, as their Cattel do all night, by chewing the Cud of what they eat in the afternoon.   151

Mel. And they tell, for news, such unlikely stories; a letter from one of us is such a present to 'em, that the poor souls wait for the Carriers-day° with such devotion, that they cannot sleep the night before.

Arte. No more then I can, the night before I am to go a journey.

Dor. Or I, before I am to try on a new Gown.

Mel. A Song that's stale here, will be new there a twelve-moneth hence; and if a man of the Town by chance come amongst 'em, he's reverenced for teaching 'em the Tune.   162

---

125. railly'd: (*raillée*) rallied, ridiculed. **128. meer:** The meaning of *mere* has shifted from "nothing less than" to "nothing more than." The first sense better applies here: an absolute, a downright town lady. **136. the Circle:** the ring of fashionable people around the throne. **154. the Carriers-day:** In the country, letters were still delivered by the common carrier, in spite of the efforts of the Post Office to crack down. As postage was paid by the recipient, revenue was being lost.

79. a-days: daily. **85. What:** why. **108. Ordinary:** a regular daily meal.

Dor. A friend of mine,° who makes Songs some-times, came lately out of the West, and vow'd he was so put out of count'nance with a Song of his; for at the first Countrey-Gentleman's he visited, he saw three Tailors cross-leg'd upon the Table in the Hall, who were tearing out as loud as ever they could sing,

——*After the pangs of a desperate Lover, &c.*

and all that day he heard nothing else, but the Daughters of the house and the Maids, humming it over in every corner, and the Father whistling it.   172

Arte. Indeed I have observ'd of my self, that when I am out of Town but a fortnight, I am so humble, that I would receive a Letter from my Tailor or Mercer for a favour.

Mel. When I have been at grass° in the Summer, and am new come up again, methinks I'm to be turn'd into *ridicule* by all that see me; but when I have been once or twice at Court, I begin to value my self again, and to despise my Countrey-acquaintance.   181

Arte. There are places where all people may be ador'd, and we ought to know our selves so well as to chuse 'em.

Dor. That's very true; your little Courtiers wife, who speaks to the King but once a moneth, need but go to a Town-Lady; and there she may vapour,° and cry, *The King and I*, at every word. Your Town-Lady, who is laugh'd at in the Circle, takes her Coach into the City, and there she's call'd your Honour,   190 and has a Banquet from the Merchants Wife whom she laughs at for her kindness. And, as for my finical Cit,° she removes but to her Countrey-house, and there insults over the Countrey Gentlewoman that never comes up; who treats her with Frumity° and Custard, and opens her dear bottle of *Mirabilis*° beside, for a Jill-glass of it at parting.

Arte. At last, I see, we shall leave *Melantha* where we found her; for, by your description of the Town and Countrey, they are become more dreadful to her, then the Court, where she was affronted. But you forget we are to wait on the Princess *Amalthea.* Come, *Doralice.*   203

Dor. Farewell, *Melantha.*

Mel. Adieu, my dear.

Arte. You are out of charity with her, and therefore I shall not give your service.

Mel. Do not omit it, I beseech you; for I have such a tender for the Court, that I love it ev'n from the Drawing-room to the Lobby, and can never be *rebutée* by any usage. But, hark you, my Dears, one thing I had forgot of great concernment.   212

Dor. Quickly then, we are in haste.

Mel. Do not call it my service, that's too vulgar; but do my *baise mains*° to the Princess *Amalthea;* that is *Spirituelle!*

Dor. To do you service then, we will *prendre* the *Carrosse*° to Court, and do your *Baise mains* to the Princess *Amalthea,* in your phrase *Spirituellé.*   219

[*Exeunt* Artemis *and* Doralice.

Enter Philotis, *with a Paper in her hand.*

Mel. O, are you there, Minion? And, well, are not you a most precious damsel, to retard all my visits for want of language, when you know you are paid so well for furnishing me with new words for my daily conversation? Let me die, if I have not run the risque already, to speak like one of the vulgar; and if I have one phrase left in all my store that is not thrid-bare & *usé,* and fit for nothing but to be thrown to Peasants.

Phil. Indeed, Madam, I have been very diligent in my vocation; but you have so drain'd all the *French* Plays and Romances, that they are not able to supply you with words for your daily expences.   232

Mel. Drain'd? what a word's there! *Epuisée,* you sot you. Come, produce your morning's work.

Phil. 'Tis here, Madam.   [*Shows the paper.*

Mel. O, my *Venus!* fourteen or fifteen words to serve me a whole day! Let me die, at this rate I cannot last till night. Come, read your works: twenty to one half of 'em will not pass muster neither.

Phil. *Sottises.*°   240

Mel. *Sottises: bon.* That's an excellent word to begin withall: as for example; He, or she said a thousand *Sottises* to me. Proceed.

Phil. *Figure:* as what a figure of a man is there! *Naive,* and *Naiveté.*

Mel. *Naive!* as how?

Phil. Speaking of a thing that was naturally said; It

163. A friend . . . mine: Dryden. The song quoted is from *An Evening's Love* (1671). 177. at grass: put to pasture, rusticated. 187. vapour: brag. 193. finical Cit: *Cit* was a derogatory term for the middle-class dwellers (citizens) in London; *finical* means affectedly refined. 195. Frumity: (frumenty, furmety) a dish made of boiled and seasoned wheat. 196. Mirabilis: (*aqua mirabilis*) a cordial.

215. do . . . mains: pay my respects; literally, hand-kissing. 217-18. prendre the Carrosse: take the carriage. 240. Sottises: stupidities.

was so *naive:* or such an innocent piece of simplicity; 'twas such a *naiveté.* 249

Mel. Truce with your interpretations: make haste.

Phil. Foible, Chagrin, Grimace, Embarrasse, Double entendre, Equivoque,° Esclaircissement,° Suitté,° Beveue,° Facòn,° Panchant,° Coup d' etourdy,° and Ridicule.

Mel. Hold, hold; how did they begin?

Phil. They began at *Sottises,* and ended *en Ridicule.*

Mel. Now give me your Paper in my hand, and hold you my Glass, while I practise my postures for the day.

[*Melantha laughs in the Glass.*
How does that laugh become my face? 260

Phil. Sovereignly well, Madam.

Mel. *Sovereignly!* Let me die, that's not amiss. That word shall not be yours; I'll invent it, and bring it up my self: my new Point Gorget° shall be yours upon 't: not a word of the word, I charge you.

Phil. I am dumb, Madam.

Mel. That glance, how sutes it with my face?

[*Looking in the Glass again.*

Phil. 'Tis so *languissant.*

Mel. *Languissant!* that word shall be mine too, and my last *Indian-Gown°* thine for 't. That sigh? 270

[*Looks again.*

Phil. 'Twill make many a man sigh, Madam. 'Tis meer *Incendiary.*

Mel. Take my Guimp Petticoat° for that truth. If thou hast more of these phrases, let me die but I could give away all my Wardrobe, and go naked for 'em.

Phil. Go naked? then you would be a *Venus,* Madam. O *Jupiter!* what had I forgot? this Paper was given me by *Rhodophil's* Page. 279

Mel. (*Reading the Letter*) ——Beg the favour from you.——Gratifie my passion——so far——assignation——in the Grotto——behind the Terras——clock this evening——Well, for the *Billets doux* there's no man in *Sicily* must dispute with *Rhodophil;* they are so *French,* so *gallant,* and so *tendre,* that I cannot resist the

252. **Equivoque:** pun, ambiguity. **Esclaircissement:** (*éclaircissement*) explanation, understanding. **Suitté:** probably *suitte,* attendants. 253. **Beveue:** (*bévue*) blunder. **Facòn:** (*façon*) making, fashioning; manner, mode. **Panchant:** penchant. **Coup d' etourdy:** (*coup d'étourdie*) blunder. 264. **Point Gorget:** a needlepoint lace wimple. 270. **Indian-Gown:** a showy gown made in India. 273. **Guimp Petticoat:** a petticoat trimmed with gimp, a corded or wired material.

temptation of the assignation. Now go you away, *Philotis;* it imports me to practise what I shall say to my Servant when I meet him. 288

[*Exit Philotis.*
Rhodophil, you'll wonder at my assurance to meet you here; let me die, I am so out of breath with coming, that I can render you no reason of it. Then he will make this *repartee;* Madam, I have no reason to accuse you for that which is so great a favour to me. Then I reply, But why have you drawn me to this solitary place? let me die but I am apprehensive of some violence from you. Then, says he; Solitude, Madam, is most fit for Lovers; but by this fair hand——Nay, now I vow you're rude. Sir. O fie, fie, fie; I hope you'l be honourable?——You'd laugh at me if I should, Madam——What do you mean to throw me down thus? Ah me! ah, ah, ah. 301

Enter Polydamas, Leonidas, and Guards.

O *Venus!* the King and Court. Let me die but I fear they have found my *foible,* and will turn me into ridicule. [*Exit running.*

Leon. Sir, I beseech you.

Poly. Do not urge my patience.

Leon. I'll not deny But what your Spies inform'd you of, is true: I love the fair *Palmyra;* but I lov'd her Before I knew your title to my bloud.

Enter Palmyra, guarded.

See, here she comes; and looks, amid'st her Guards, Like a weak Dove under the Falcon's gripe. 311 O heav'n, I cannot bear it.

Poly. Maid, come hither. Have you presum'd so far, as to receive My Son's affection?

Palm. Alas, what shall I answer? to confess it Will raise a blush upon a Virgin's face; Yet I was ever taught 'twas base to lie.

Poly. You've been too bold, and you must love no more.

Palm. Indeed I must; I cannot help my love; I was so tender when I took the bent, 320 That now I grow that way.

Poly. He is a Prince: and you are meanly born.

Leon. Love either finds equality, or makes it: Like death, he knows no difference in degrees, But plains, and levels all.

Palm. Alas, I had not render'd up my heart, Had he not lov'd me first; but he prefer'd me

Above the Maidens of my age and rank;
Still shun'd their company, and still sought mine;
I was not won by gifts, yet still he gave;   330
And all his gifts, though small, yet spoke his love.
He pick'd the earliest Strawberries in Woods,
The cluster'd Filberds, and the purple Grapes:
He taught a prating Stare° to speak my name;
And when he found a Nest of Nightingales,
Or callow Linnets, he would show 'em me,
And let me take 'em out.
    Poly.   This is a little Mistris, meanly born,
Fit onely for a Prince his vacant hours,
And then, to laugh at her simplicity,   340
Not fix a passion there. Now hear my sentence.
    Leon.   Remember, ere you give it, 'tis pronounc'd
Against us both.
    Poly.   First, in her hand
There shall be plac'd a Player's painted Sceptre,
And, on her head, a gilded Pageant Crown;
Thus shall she go,
With all the Boys attending on her Triumph:
That done, be put alone into a Boat,
With bread and water onely for three days,   350
So on the Sea she shall be set adrift,
And who relieves her, dies.
    Palm.   I onely beg that you would execute
The last part first: let me be put to Sea;
The bread and water, for my three days life,
I give you back, I would not live so long;
But let me scape the shame.
    Leon.   Look to me, Piety;° and you, O Gods, look
    to my piety:
Keep me from saying that which misbecomes a son;
But let me die before I see this done.   360
    Poly.   If you for ever will abjure her sight,
I can be yet a father; she shall live.
    Leon.   Hear, O you Pow'rs, is this to be a father?
I see 'tis all my happiness and quiet
You aim at, Sir; and take 'em:
I will not save ev'n my *Palmyra's* life
At that ignoble price; but I'll die with her.
    Palm.   So had I done by you,
Had Fate made me a Princess: Death, methinks,
Is not a terrour now;   370
He is not fierce, or grim, but fawns, and sooths me,
And slides along, like *Cleopatra's* Aspick,
Off'ring his service to my troubled breast.

    Leon.   Begin what you have purpos'd when you
    please,
Lead her to scorn, your triumph shall be doubled.
As holy Priests
In pity go with dying malefactours,
So will I share her shame.
    Poly.   You shall not have your will so much; first
    part 'em,
Then execute your office.
    Leon.   No; I'll die   380
In her defence.   [*Draws his sword.*
    Palm.   Ah, hold, and pull not on
A curse, to make me worthy of my death:
Do not by lawless force oppose your Father,
Whom you have too much disobey'd for me.
    Leon.   Here, take it, Sir, and with it, pierce my
    heart:
      [*Presenting his sword to his father upon his knees.*
You have done more, in taking my *Palmyra.*
You are my Father, therefore I submit.
    Poly.   Keep him from any thing he may design
Against his life, whil'st the first fury lasts;
And now perform what I commanded you.   390
    Leon.   In vain; if sword and poison be deni'd me,
I'll hold my breath and die.
    Palm.   Farewell, my last° *Leonidas;* yet live,
I charge you live, till you believe me dead.
I cannot die in peace, if you die first.
If life's a blessing, you shall have it last.
    Poly.   Go on with her, and lead him after me.

    Enter Argaleon *hastily, with* Hermogenes.

    Arga.   I bring you, Sir, such news as must amaze
    you,
And such as will prevent you from an action
Which would have rendred all your life unhappy.   400
    Poly.   *Hermogenes,* you bend your knees in vain,
      [*Hermogenes kneels.*
My doom's already past.
    Her.   I kneel not for *Palmyra,* for I know
She will not need my pray'rs; but for my self:
With a feign'd tale I have abus'd your ears,
And therefore merit death; but since, unforc'd,
I first accuse my self, I hope your mercy.
    Poly.   Haste to explain your meaning.
    Her.   Then, in few words, *Palmyra* is your daughter.

---

334. Stare: starling. **358. Piety:** *Pietas,* in Roman mythology, the personification of piety and dutiful respect.

393. last: Answering Saintsbury, who followed Scott in printing *lost,* Montague Summers defends the reading of the text, adducing the rare sense "one and only."

Poly. How can I give belief to this Impostor?
He who has once abus'd me, often may. 411
I'll hear no more.

Arga. For your own sake, you must.

Her. A parent's love (for I confess my crime)
Mov'd me to say, *Leonidas* was yours;
But when I heard *Palmyra* was to die,
The fear of guiltless bloud so stung my conscience,
That I resolv'd, ev'n with my shame, to save
Your daughter's life. 418

Poly. But how can I be certain, but that interest,
Which mov'd you first to say your son was mine,
Does not now move you too, to save your daughter?

Her. You had but then my word; I bring you now
Authentick testimonies. Sir, in short,
[*Delivers on his knees a Jewel, and a Letter.*
If this will not convince you, let me suffer.

Poly. I know this Jewel well; 'twas once my
mothers, [*Looking first on the Jewel.*
Which, marrying, I presented to my wife.
And this, O this, is my *Eudocia's* hand.
This was the pledge of love given to Eudocia,
Who, dying, to her young Palmyra *leaves it:*
And this when you, my dearest Lord, receive, 430
Own here, and think on me, dying Eudocia.
Take it; 'tis well there is no more to read,
[*To* Argaleon.
My eyes grow full, and swim in their own light.
[*He embraces* Palmyra.

Palm. I fear, Sir, this is your intended Pageant.
You sport your self at poor *Palmyra's* cost;
But if you think to make me proud,
Indeed I cannot be so: I was born
With humble thoughts, and lowly, like my birth.
A real fortune could not make me haughty,
Much less a feign'd.

Poly. That was her mother's temper.
I have too much deserv'd thou shouldst suspect 441
That I am not thy father; but my love
Shall henceforth show I am. Behold my eyes,
And see a father there begin to flow:
This is not feign'd, *Palmyra.*

Palm. I doubt no longer, Sir; you are a King,
And cannot lie: falshood's a vice too base
To find a room in any Royal breast;
I know, in spight of my unworthiness,
I am your child; for when you would have kill'd me,
Methought I lov'd you then. 451

Arga. Sir, we forget the Prince *Leonidas,*
His greatness should not stand neglected thus.

Poly. Guards, you may now retire: Give him his
sword,
And leave him free.

Leon. Then the first use I make of liberty
Shall be, with your permission, mighty Sir,
To pay that reverence to which Nature binds me.
[*kneels to* Hermogenes.

Arga. Sure you forget your birth, thus to misplace
This act of your obedience; you should kneel 460
To nothing but to Heav'n, and to a King.

Leon. I never shall forget what Nature owes,
Nor be asham'd to pay it; though my father
Be not a King, I know him brave and honest,
And well deserving of a worthier son.

Poly. He bears it gallantly.

Leon. Why would you not instruct me, Sir, before
[*To* Herm.
Where I should place my duty?
From which, if ignorance have made me swerve,
I beg your pardon for an erring son. 470

Palm. I almost grieve I am a Princess, since
It makes him lose a Crown.

Leon. And next, to you, my King, thus low I kneel,
T' implore your mercy; if in that small time
I had the honour to be thought your son,
I pay'd not strict obedience to your will:
I thought, indeed, I should not be compell'd,
But thought it as your son; so what I took
In duty from you, I restor'd in courage;
Because your son should not be forc'd. 480

Poly. You have my pardon for it.

Leon. To you, fair Princess, I congratulate
Your birth; of which I ever thought you worthy:
And give me leave to add, that I am proud
The Gods have pick'd me out to be the man
By whose dejected fate yours is to rise;
Because no man could more desire your fortune,
Or franklier part with his to make you great.

Palm. I know the King, though you are not his
son,
Will still regard you as my Foster-brother, 490
And so conduct you downward from a Throne,
By slow degrees, so unperceiv'd and soft,
That it may seem no fall: or, if it be,
May Fortune lay a bed of down beneath you.

Poly. He shall be rank'd with my Nobility,
And kept from scorn by a large pension giv'n him.

Leon. You are all great and Royal in your gifts;
[*Bowing.*
But at the Donor's feet I lay 'em down:

Should I take riches from you, it would seem
As I did want a soul to bear that poverty   500
To which the Gods design'd my humble birth:
And should I take your Honours without merit,
It would appear, I wanted manly courage
To hope 'em, in your service, from my sword.
    Poly.   Still brave, and like your self.
The Court shall shine this night in its full splendor,
And celebrate this new discovery.
Argaleon, lead my daughter: as we go
I shall have time to give her my commands,
In which you are concern'd.   510
                    [*Exeunt all but* Leonidas.
    Leon.   Methinks I do not want
That huge long train of fawning followers,
That swept a furlong after me.
'Tis true, I am alone;
So was the Godhead ere he made the world,
And better serv'd Himself, then serv'd by Nature.
And yet I have a Soul
Above this humble fate. I could command,
Love to do good; give largely to true merit;
All that a King should do: But though these are not
My Province, I have Scene° enough within   521
To exercise my vertue.
All that a heart, so fix'd as mine, can move,
Is, that my niggard fortune starves my love.   [*Exit.*

COURTIER   SCENE II.   RHODO'S WIFE

Palamede *and* Doralice *meet: she with a Book in
her hand, seems to start at sight of him.*

    Dor.   'Tis a strange thing that no warning will
serve your turn; and that no retirement will secure me
from your impertinent addresses! Did not I tell you,
that I was to be private here at my devotions?
    Pala.   Yes; and you see I have observ'd my Cue
exactly: I am come to releive you from them. Come,
shut up, shut up your Book; the man's come who is to
supply all your necessities.
    Dor.   Then, it seems, you are so impudent to think
it was an assignation? this, I warrant, was your lewd
interpretation of my innocent meaning.   11
    Pala.   *Venus* forbid that I should harbour so un-
reasonable a thought of a fair young Lady, that you

should lead me hither into temptation. I confess I
might think indeed it was a kind of honourable
challenge, to meet privately without Seconds, and
decide the difference betwixt the two Sexes; but
heaven forgive me if I thought amiss.
    Dor.   You thought too, I'll lay my life on 't, that
you might as well make love to me, as my Husband
does to your Mistris.   21
    Pala.   I was so unreasonable to think so too.
    Dor.   And then you wickedly inferr'd, that there
was some justice in the revenge of it: or at least but
little injury; for a man to endeavour to enjoy that,
which he accounts a blessing, and which is not valu'd
as it ought by the dull possessour. Confess your
wickedness, did you not think so?
    Pala.   I confess I was thinking so, as fast as I could;
but you think so much before me, that you will let
me think nothing.   31
    Dor.   'Tis the very thing that I design'd: I have
forestall'd all your arguments, and left you without a
word more, to plead for mercy. If you have any thing
farther to offer, ere Sentence pass——Poor Animal,
I brought you hither onely for my diversion.
    Pala.   That you may have, if you'll make use of me
the right way; but I tell thee, woman, I am now past
talking.
    Dor.   But it may be, I came hither to hear what
fine things you could say for your self.   41
    Pala.   You would be very angry, to my knowledge,
if I should lose so much time to say many of 'em——
By this hand you would——
    Dor.   Fie, *Palamede,* I am a woman of honour.
    Pala.   I see you are; you have kept touch with your
assignation: and before we part, you shall find that I
am a man of honour——yet I have one scruple of
conscience——
    Dor.   I warrant you will not want° some naughty
argument or other to satisfie your self——I hope you
are afraid of betraying your friend?   52
    Pala.   Of betraying my friend! I am more afraid of
being betray'd by you to my friend. You women now
are got into the way of telling first your selves: a man
who has any care of his reputation will be loath to
trust it with you.
    Dor.   O you charge your faults upon our Sex:
you men are like Cocks, you never make love, but
you clap your wings, and crow when you have done.
    Pala.   Nay, rather you women are like Hens; you

---

521. Scene: emended to *seen* in successive quarto editions, but
scene in the sense of a place for action, room to play a part,
intelligibly carries out the contrast with *Province.*

Act III, scene ii. **50. want:** lack.

never lay, but you cackle an hour after, to discover°
your Nest——But I'll venture it for once.   63

Dor. To convince you that you are in the wrong,
I'll retire into the dark Grotto, to my devotion, and
make so little noise, that it shall be impossible for you
to find me.

Pala. But if I find you——

Dor. Ay, if you find me——But I'll put you to
search in more corners then you imagine.   70

> [*She runs in, and he after her.*

Enter Rhodophil *and* Melantha.

Mel. Let me die, but this solitude, and that Grotto
are scandalous; I'll go no further; besides, you have a
sweet Lady of your own.

Rho. But a sweet Mistris, now and then, makes my
sweet Lady so much more sweet.

Mel. I hope you will not force me?

Rho. But I will, if you desire it.

Pala. (*Within*) Where the devil are you, Madam?
S'death, I begin to be weary of this hide and seek: if
you stay a little longer, till the fit's over, I'll hide in my
turn, and put you to the finding me.   81

> [*He enters, and sees* Rhodophil *and* Melantha.

How! *Rhodophil* and my Mistris!

Mel. My servant to apprehend me! this is *Surprenant au dernier.*°

Rho. I must on; there's nothing but impudence
can help me out.

Pala. *Rhodophil,* How came you hither in so good
company?

Rho. As you see, *Palamede;* an effect of pure
friendship; I was not able to live without you.   90

Pala. But what makes my Mistris with you?

Rho. Why, I heard you were here alone, and could
not in civility but bring her to you.

Mel. You'll pardon the effects of a passion which
I may now avow for you, if it transported me beyond
the rules of *bien seance.*°

Pala. But who told you I was here? they that told
you that, may tell you more, for ought I know.

Rho. O, for that matter, we had intelligence.

Pala. But let me tell you, we came hither so very
privately, that you could not trace us.   101

Rho. Us? what us? you are alone.

Pala. Us! the devil's in me for mistaking: me, I
meant. Or us; that is, you are me, or I you, as we are
friends: that's us.

Dor. *Palamede, Palamede.*   [*Within.*

Rho. I should know that voice? who's within
there, that calls you?

Pala. Faith I can't imagine; I believe the place is
haunted.   110

Dor. *Palamede, Palamede,* All-cocks hidden.°

> [*Within.*

Pala. Lord, lord, what shall I do? Well, dear
friend, to let you see I scorn to be jealous, and that I
dare trust my Mistris with you, take her back, for I
would not willingly have her frighted, and I am
resolv'd to see who's there; I'll not be danted° with a
Bug-bear, that's certain: prethee dispute it not, it shall
be so; nay, do not put me to swear, but go quickly:
there's an effect of pure friendship for you now.

Enter Doralice, *and looks amaz'd, seeing them.*

Rho. *Doralice!* I am thunder-struck to see you
here.   121

Pala. So am I! quite thunder-struck. Was it you
that call'd me within? (I must be impudent.)

Rho. How came you hither, Spouse?

Pala. Ay, how came you hither? And, which is
more, how could you be here without my knowledge?

Dor. (*To her husband*) O, Gentleman, have I
caught you i' faith! have I broke forth in ambush
upon you! I thought my suspicions would prove true.

Rho. Suspicions! this is very fine, Spouse! Prethee
what suspicions?   131

Dor. O, you feign ignorance: why, of you and
Melantha; here have I staid these two hours, waiting
with all the rage of a passionate, loving wife, but
infinitely jealous, to take you two in the manner; for
hither I was certain you would come.

Rho. But you are mistaken, Spouse, in the occasion; for we came hither on purpose to find *Palamede,*
on intelligence he was gone before.   139

Pala. I'll be hang'd then if the same party who
gave you intelligence, I was here, did not tell your
wife you would come hither: now I smell malice on
't on both sides.

Dor. Was it so, think you? nay, then, I'll confess
my part of the malice too. As soon as ever I spi'd my
husband and *Melantha* come together, I had a strange
temptation to make him jealous in revenge; and that
made me call *Palamede, Palamede,* as though there
had been an Intrigue between us.

---

62. **discover:** reveal. **83–84. Surprenant au dernier:**
most astonishing. **96. bien seance:** (*bienséance*) propriety.

111. **All-cocks hidden:** (Cock's-Odin or cock's-hoddin) a
boys' game of hide-and-seek. **116. danted:** daunted.

Mel.   Nay, I avow, there was an apparence of an
Intrigue between us too.   151
Pala.   To see how things will come about!
Rho.   And was it onely thus, my dear *Doralice*?
                                                            [*Embraces.*
Dor.   And did I wrong none,° *Rhodophil*, with a
false suspicion?   [*Embracing him.*
Pala. (*Aside*) Now am I confident we had all four
the same design: 'tis a pretty odd kind of game this,
where each of us plays for double stakes: this is just
thrust and parry with the same motion; I am to get his
Wife, and yet to guard my own Mistris. But I am
vilely suspitious, that, while I conquer in the Right
Wing, I shall be routed in the Left: for both our
women will certainly betray their party, because they
are each of them for gaining of two, as well as we;
and I much fear,   165
If their necessities and ours were known,
They have more need of two, then we of one.
                                      [*Exeunt, embracing one another.*

ACT IV

SCENE I.°

Enter Leonidas, *musing,* Amalthea *following him.*

Amal.   Yonder he is, and I must speak, or die;
And yet 'tis death to speak; yet he must know
I have a passion for him, and may know it
With a less blush; because to offer it
To his low fortunes, shows I lov'd before,
His person, not his greatness.
Leon.   First scorn'd, and now commanded from the
      Court!
The King is good; but he is wrought to this
By proud *Argaleon*'s malice.
What more disgrace can Love and Fortune joyn   10
T' inflict upon one man? I cannot now
Behold my dear *Palmyra:* she, perhaps, too
Is grown asham'd of a mean ill-plac'd love.
Amal.   Assist me, *Venus*, for I tremble when
                                                                  [*Aside.*
I am to speak, but I must force my self.
Sir, I would crave but one short minute with you,
                                                                  [*To him.*
And some few words.

154. **none:** a corruption of *mine own.*

Leon.   The proud *Argaleon*'s sister!
                                                                  [*Aside.*
Amal.   Alas, it will not out; shame stops my mouth.
                                                                  [*Aside.*
Pardon my errour, Sir, I was mistaken,
And took you for another.   20
Leon.   In spight of all his guards, I'll see *Palmyra;*
                                                                  [*Aside.*
Though meanly born, I have a Kingly Soul yet.
Amal.   I stand upon a precipice, where fain
I would retire, but Love still thrusts me on:
Now I grow bolder, and will speak to him.
Sir, 'tis indeed to you that I would speak,   [*To him.*
And if——
Leon.   O, you are sent to scorn my fortunes;
Your Sex and Beauty are your priviledge;
But should your Brother——
Amal.   Now he looks angry, and I dare not speak.
I had some business with you, Sir,   31
But 'tis not worth your knowledge.
Leon.   Then 'twill be charity to let me mourn
My griefs alone, for I am much disorder'd.
Amal.   'Twill be more charity to mourn 'em with
      you:
Heav'n knows I pity you.
Leon.   Your pity, Madam,
Is generous, but 'tis unavailable.°
Amal.   You know not till 'tis tri'd.
Your sorrows are no secret; you have lost
A Crown, and Mistris.
Leon.   Are not these enough?   40
Hang two such weights on any other soul,
And see if it can bear 'em.
Amal.   More; you are banish'd, by my Brother's
      means,
And ne'r must hope again to see your Princess;
Except as Pris'ners view fair Walks and Streets,
And careless Passengers going by their grates,
To make 'em feel the want of liberty.
But, worse then all,
The King this morning has injoyn'd his Daughter
T' accept my Brother's love.
Leon.   Is this your pity?   50
You aggravate my griefs, and print 'em deeper
In new and heavier stamps.
Amal.   'Tis as Physicians show the desperate ill
T' indear° their Art, by mittigating pains
They cannot wholly cure: when you despair

Act IV, scene i. **37. unavailable:** unavailing. **54. indear:**
enhance the value of.

Of all you wish, some part of it, because
Unhop'd for, may be grateful;° and some other——
   Leon. What other?
   Amal. Some other may——
My shame has seiz'd me, and I can go   [*Aside.*
No farther——   61
   Leon. These often failing, sighs, and interruptions,
Make me imagine you have grief like mine:
Have you ne'r lov'd?
   Amal.   I? never: 'tis in vain;
I must despair in silence.   [*Aside.*
   Leon. You come as I suspected then, to mock,
At least observe my griefs: take it not ill
That I must leave you.   [*Is going.*
   Amal. You must not go with these unjust opinions.
Command my life, and fortunes; you are wise,   70
Think, and think well, what I can do to serve you.
   Leon. I have but one thing in my thoughts and
      wishes:
If by your means I can obtain the sight
Of my ador'd *Palmyra;* or, what's harder,
One minutes time, to tell her, I die hers.
               [*She starts back.*
I see I am not to expect it from you;
Nor could, indeed, with reason.
   Amal. Name any other thing: is *Amalthea*
So despicable, she can serve your wishes
In this alone?
   Leon.   If I should ask of heav'n,   80
I have no other suit.
   Amal. To show you, then, I can deny you nothing,
Though 'tis more hard to me then any other,
Yet I will do 't for you.
   Leon. Name quickly, name the means, speak my
      good Angel.
   Amal. Be not so much o'rjoy'd; for, if you are,
I'll rather dye then do 't. This night the Court
Will be in *Masquerade;*
You shall attend on me; in that disguise
You may both see and speak to her,   90
If you dare venture it.
   Leon. Yes, were a God her Guardian,
And bore in each hand thunder, I would venture.
   Amal. Farewell then; two hours hence I will
      expect you: [*Exit.*
My heart's so full, that I can stay no longer.
   Leon. Already it grows dusky; I'll prepare
With haste for my disguise. But who are these?

57. **grateful:** pleasing.

Enter Hermogenes *and* Eubulus.

   Her. 'Tis he; we need not fear to speak to him.
   Eub. *Leonidas.*
   Leon.   Sure I have known that voice.
   Her. You have some reason, Sir; 'tis *Eubulus,*
Who bred you with the Princess; and, departing,
Bequeath'd you to my care.   102
   Leon. My Foster,° Father! let my knees express
               [*Kneeling.*
My joys for your return!
   Eub. Rise, Sir, you must not kneel.
   Leon.   E'r since you left me,
I have been wandring in a maze of fate,
Led by false fires of a fantastick glory,
And the vain lustre of imagin'd Crowns,
But, ah! why would you leave me? or how could you
Absent your self so long?   110
   Eub. I'll give you a most just account of both:
And something more I have to tell you, which
I know must cause your wonder; but this place,
Though almost hid in darkness, is not safe.
Already I discern some coming towards us
              [*Torches appear.*
With lights, who may discover me. *Hermogenes,*
Your lodgings are hard° by, and much more private.
   Her. There you may freely speak.
   Leon.   Let us make haste;
For some affairs, and of no small importance,   119
Call me another way.   [*Exeunt.*

Enter Palamede *and* Rhodophil, *with Vizor Masques in
their hands, and Torches before 'em.*

   Pala. We shall have noble sport to night, *Rhodophil;* this Masquerading is a most glorious invention.
   Rho. I believe it was invented first by some
jealous Lover, to discover the haunts of his Jilting
Mistris; or, perhaps, by some distressed servant, to
gain an opportunity with a jealous man's wife.
   Pala. No, it must be the invention of a woman, it
has so much subtilty and love in it.
   Rho. I am sure 'tis extremely pleasant; for to go
unknown, is the next degree to going invisible. 130
   Pala. What with our antique° habits, and feign'd
voices, do you know me? and I know you? Methinks
we move and talk just like so many over-grown
Puppets.

103. **Foster:** an archaic word for *foster parent.* 117. **hard:** near.
131. **antique:** antic.

Rho. Masquerade is onely Vizor-masque° improv'd, a heightening of the same fashion.

Pala. No; Masquerade is Vizor-masque in debauch; and I like it the better for 't: for, with a Vizor-masque, we fool our selves into courtship, for the sake of an eye that glanc'd; or a hand that stole it self   140 out of the glove sometimes, to give us a sample of the skin: but in Masquerade there is nothing to be known, she's all *Terra incognita,* and the bold discoverer leaps ashoar, and takes his lot among the wild *Indians* and *Salvages,* without the vile consideration of safety to his person, or of beauty, or wholesomeness in his Mistris.

Enter Beliza.

Rho. *Beliza,* what make you here?   148
Bel. Sir, my Lady sent me after you, to let you know, she finds her self a little indispos'd, so that she cannot be at Court, but is retir'd to rest, in her own appartment, where she shall want° the happiness of your dear embraces to night.

Rho. A very fine phrase, *Beliza,* to let me know my wife desires to lie alone.

Pala. I doubt,° *Rhodophil,* you take the pains sometimes to instruct your wife's Woman in these elegancies.   158

Rho. Tell my dear Lady, that since I must be so unhappy as not to wait on her to night, I will lament bitterly for her absence. 'Tis true, I shall be at Court, but I will take no divertisement there; and when I return to my solitary bed, if I am so forgetful of my passion as to sleep, I will dream of her; and betwixt sleep and waking, put out my foot towards her side, for mid-night consolation; and not finding her, I will sigh, and imagine my self a most desolate widower.   167

Bel. I shall do your commands, Sir.   [*Exit.*
Rho. (*Aside*) She's sick as aptly for my purpose, as if she had contriv'd it so: well, if ever woman was a help-meet for man, my Spouse is so; for within this hour I receiv'd a Note from *Melantha,* that she would meet me this evening in Masquerade in Boys habit, to rejoyce with me before she entred into fetters; for I find she loves me better then *Palamede,* onely because he's to be her husband. There's something of antipathy in the word Marriage to the nature of love; marriage is the meer Ladle of affection, that cools it when 'tis never so fiercely boiling over.   179

Pala. Dear *Rhodophil,* I must needs beg your pardon; there is an occasion fall'n out which I had forgot: I cannot be at Court to night.

Rho. Dear *Palamede,* I am sorry we shall not have one course° together at the herd; but I find your Game lies single: good fortune to you with your Mistris.   [*Exit.*

Pala. He has wish'd me good fortune with his Wife: there's no sin in this then, there's fair leave° given. Well, I must go visit the sick; I cannot resist the temptations of my charity. O what a difference   190 will she find betwixt a dull resty° Husband, and a quick vigorous Lover! he sets out like a Carrier's Horse, plodding on, because he knows he must, with the Bells of Matrimony chiming so melancholly about his neck, in pain till he's at his journeys end, and dispairing to get thither, he is fain to fortifie imagination with the thoughts of another woman: I, take heat after heat, like a well-breath'd Courser, and——But hark, what noise is that? swords!   199

[*Clashing of swords within.*
Nay, then have with you.   [*Exit Palamede.*

Re-enter Palamede, *with* Rhodophil: *and* Doralice *in man's habit.*

Rho. Friend, your relief was very timely, otherwise I had been oppress'd.
Pala. What was the quarrel?
Rho. What I did, was in rescue of this Youth.
Pala. What cause could he give 'em?
Dor. The cause was nothing but only the common cause of fighting in Masquerades: they were drunk, and I was sober.
Rho. Have they not hurt you?   209
Dor. No; but I am exceeding ill, with the fright on 't.
Pala. Let's lead him to some place where he may refresh himself.
Rho. Do you conduct him then.
Pala. (*Aside*) How cross° this happens to my design of going to *Doralice!* for I am confident she was sick on purpose that I should visit her. Hark you, *Rhodophil,* could not you take care of the stripling? I am partly engag'd to night.   219
Rho. You know I have business: but come, Youth, if it must be so.
Dor. (*To* Rhodophil) No, good Sir, do not give

---

135. **Vizor-masque:** the "disguise" of courtesans. 152. **want:** lack. 156. **doubt:** suspect.

184. **course:** pursuit (of game). 188. **fair leave:** permission. 191. **resty:** sluggish. 215. **cross:** unfavorably.

your self that trouble; I shall be safer, and better
pleas'd with your friend here.

Rho.   Farewell then; once more I wish you a good
adventure.

Pala.   Damn this kindness! now must I be troubled
with this young Rogue, and miss my opportunity
with *Doralice.*   229

> [*Exit* Rhodophil *alone,* Palamede *with*
> Doralice.

SCENE II.

Enter Polydamas.

Argaleon counsel'd well to banish him,
He has, I know not what,
Of greatness in his looks, and of high fate,
That almost awes me; but I fear my Daughter,
Who hourly moves me for him, and I mark'd
She sigh'd when I but nam'd *Argaleon* to her.
But see, the Maskers: hence my cares, this night,
At least take truce, and find me on my pillow.

*Enter the Princess in Masquerade, with Ladies: at the
other end,* Argaleon *and Gentlemen in Masquerade:
then* Leonidas *leading* Amalthea.
*The King sits. A Dance.
After the Dance,*

Amal.   (*To* Leonidas) That's the Princess;
I saw the habit ere she put it on.   10

Leon.   I know her by a thousand other signs,
She cannot hide so much Divinity.
Disguis'd, and silent, yet some graceful motion
Breaks from her, and shines round her like a Glory.

> [*Goes to* Palmyra.

Amal.   Thus she reveals her self, and knows it not:
Like Love's Dark-lantern I direct his steps,
And yet he sees not that which gives him light.

Palm.   I know you; but, alas, *Leonidas,*

> [*To* Leonidas.

Why should you tempt this danger on your self?

Leon.   Madam, you know me not, if you believe
I would not hazard greater for your sake: 21
But you, I fear, are chang'd.

Palm.   No, I am still the same;
But there are many things became *Palmyra*
Which ill become the Princess.

Leon.   I ask nothing
Which Honour will not give you leave to grant:
One hours short audience, at my fathers house,
You cannot sure refuse me.

Palm. Perhaps I should, did I consult strict vertue;
But something must be given to Love and you.   30
When would you I should come?

Leon.   This evening, with the speediest opportunity.
I have a secret to discover to you,
Which will surprise, and please you.

Palm.   'Tis enough.
Go now; for we may be observ'd and known.
I trust your honour; give me not occasion
To blame my self, or you.

Leon.   You never shall repent your good opinion.

> [*Kisses her hand, and Exit.*

Arga.   I cannot be deceiv'd; that is the Princess:
One of her Maids betray'd the habit to me;   40
But who was he with whom she held discourse?
'Tis one she favours, for he kiss'd her hand.
Our shapes are like, our habits near the same:
She may mistake, and speak to me for him.
I am resolv'd, I'll satisfie my doubts,
Though to be more tormented.   [*Exit.*

SONG.

I.

WHil'st Alexis *lay prest*
In her Arms he lov'd best,
With his hands round her neck,
And his head on her breast,   50
He found the fierce pleasure too hasty to stay,
And his soul in the tempest just flying away.

2.

When Coelia *saw this,*
With a sigh, and a kiss,
She cry'd, Oh my dear, I am robb'd of my bliss;
'Tis unkind to your Love, and unfaithfully done,
To leave me behind you, and die all alone.

3.

The Youth, though in haste,
And breathing his last,
In pity dy'd slowly, while she dy'd more fast;   60
*Till at length she cry'd, Now, my dear, now let us
      go,*
Now die, my Alexis, *and I will die too.*

4.

Thus intranc'd they did lie,
Till Alexis *did try*
To recover new breath, that again he might die:
Then often they di'd; but the more they did so,
*The Nymph di'd more quick, and the Shepherd
      more slow.*

Another Dance. After it, Argaleon re-enters, and stands by the Princess.

Palm.   Leonidas, what means this quick return?

[*To Arga.*

Arga.   O heav'n! 'tis what I fear'd.
Palm.   Is ought of moment happen'd since you went?   70
Arga.   No, Madam, but I understood not fully Your last commands.
Palm.   And yet you answer'd to 'em. Retire; you are too indiscreet a Lover: I'll meet you where I promis'd.   [*Exit.*
Arga.   O my curst fortune! what have I discover'd?

[*Whispers to the King.*

Poly.   But are you certain you are not deceiv'd?
Arga.   Upon my life.
Poly.   Her honour is concern'd. Somewhat I'll do; but I am yet distracted, And know not where to fix. I wish'd a child, And Heav'n, in anger, granted my request.   80 So blind we are, our wishes are so vain, That what we most desire, proves most our pain.

[*Exeunt omnes.*

SCENE III.

An Eating-house. Bottles of Wine on the Table. Palamede; and Doralice in Man's habit.

Dor.   (*Aside*) Now cannot I find in my heart to discover my self, though I long he should know me.
Pala.   I tell thee, Boy, now I have seen thee safe, I must be gone: I have no leisure to throw away on thy raw conversation: I am a person that understand better things, I.   6
Dor.   Were I a woman, Oh how you'd admire me! cry up every word I said, and scrue your face into a submissive smile; as I have seen a dull Gallant act Wit, and counterfeit pleasantness, when he whispers to a great Person in a Play-house; smile, and look briskly, when the other answers, as if something of extraordinary had past betwixt 'em, when, heaven knows, there was nothing else but, What a clock does your Lordship think it is? and my Lord's *repertee* is, 'Tis almost Park-time:° or, at most, Shall we out of the Pit, and go behind the Scenes for an Act or two? And yet such fine things as these, would be wit in a Mistris's mouth.   19

Act IV, scene iii. **16. Park-time:** time for riding in the park.

Pala.   Ay, Boy; there's Dame Nature in the case: he who cannot find wit in a Mistris, deserves to find nothing else, Boy. But these are riddles to thee, child, and I have not leisure to instruct thee; I have affairs to dispatch, great affairs; I am a man of business.
Dor.   Come, you shall not go: you have no affairs but what you may dispatch here, to my knowledge.
Pala.   I find now, thou art a Boy of more understanding then I thought thee; a very lewd wicked Boy: o' my conscience thou wouldst debauch me, and hast some evil designs upon my person.   30
Dor.   You are mistaken, Sir; I would onely have you show me a more lawful reason why you would leave me, then I can why you should not, and I'll not stay you; for I am not so young, but I understand the necessities of flesh and bloud, and the pressing occasions of mankind, as well as you.
Pala.   A very forward and understanding Boy! Thou art in great danger of a Pages wit, to be brisk at 14, and dull at 20. But I'll give thee no further account; I must, and will go.   40
Dor.   My life on 't, your Mistris is not at home.
Pala.   This Imp will make me very angry. I tell thee, young Sir, she is at home; and at home for me; and, which is more, she is abed for me, and sick for me.
Dor.   For you onely?
Pala.   Ay, for me onely.
Dor.   But how do you know she's sick abed?
Pala.   She sent her Husband word so.
Dor.   And are you such a novice in Love, to believe a Wife's message to her Husband?   51
Pala.   Why, what the devil should be her meaning else?
Dor.   It may be, to go in Masquerade as well as you; to observe your haunts and keep you company without your knowledge.
Pala.   Nay, I'll trust her for that: she loves me too well, to disguise her self from me.
Dor.   If I were she, I would disguise on purpose to try your wit; and come to my servant like a Riddle, Read me, and take me.   61
Pala.   I could know her in any shape: my good Genius would prompt me to find out a handsome woman: there's something in her, that would attract me to her without my knowledge.
Dor.   Then you make a Load-stone of your Mistris?
Pala.   Yes, and I carry Steel about me, which has been so often touch'd, that it never fails to point to the North Pole.

Dor. Yet still my mind gives me,° that you have met her disguis'd to night, and have not known her.   72

Pala. This is the most pragmatical° conceited little fellow, he will needs understand my business better then my self. I tell thee, once more, thou dost not know my Mistris.

Dor. And I tell you, once more, that I know her better then you do.

Pala. The Boy's resolv'd to have the last word. I find I must go without reply.   [*Exit.*

Dor. Ah mischief, I have lost him with my fooling. Palamede, Palamede.   82

He returns. She plucks off her Peruke, and puts it on again when he knows her.

Pala. O Heavens! is it you, Madam?

Dor. Now, where was your good Genius, that would prompt you to find me out?

Pala. Why, you see I was not deceiv'd; you, your self, were my good Genius.

Dor. But where was the Steel, that knew the Loadstone, ha?

Pala. The truth is, Madam, the Steel has lost its vertue; and therefore, if you please, we'll new touch it.   92

Enter Rhodophil; *and* Melantha *in Boy's habit.* Rhodophil *sees* Palamede *kissing* Doralice's *hand.*

Rho. Palamede again! am I fall'n into your quarters? What? ingaging with a Boy? is all honourable?

Pala. O, very honourable on my side. I was just chastising this young Villain; he was running away, without paying his share of the reckoning.

Rho. Then I find I was deceiv'd in him.

Pala. Yes, you are deceiv'd in him: 'tis the archest rogue, if you did but know him.   100

Mel. Good Rhodophil, let us get off *al-a derobbée*, for fear I should be discover'd.

Rho. There's no retiring now; I warrant you for° discovery: now have I the oddest thought, to entertain you before your Servants face, and he never the wiser; 'twill be the prettiest juggling trick to cheat him when he looks upon us.

Mel. This is the strangest *caprice* in you.

Pala. (*To* Doralice) This *Rhodophil's* the unluckiest fellow to me! this is now the second time he has bar'd

the Dice° when we were just ready to have nick'd° him; but if ever I get the Box again——   112

Dor. Do you think he will not know me? Am I like my self?

Pala. No more then a Picture in the Hangings.°

Dor. Nay, then he can never discover me, now the wrong side of the Arras° is turn'd towards him.

Pala. At least, 'twill be some pleasure to me, to enjoy what freedom I can while he looks on; I will storm the Out-works of Matrimony even before his face.   121

Rho. What Wine have you there, *Palamede?*

Pala. Old *Chios*,° or the rogue's damn'd that drew it.

Rho. Come, to the most constant of Mistresses, that I believe is yours, *Palamede.*

Dor. Pray spare your Seconds;° for my part I am but a weak Brother.

Pala. Now, to the truest of Turtles; that is your Wife, *Rhodophil,* that lies sick at home in the bed of honour.   131

Rho. Now let's have one common health, and so have done.

Dor. Then, for once, I'll begin it. Here's to him that has the fairest Lady of *Sicily* in Masquerade to night.

Pala. This is such an obliging health, I'll kiss thee, dear Rogue, for thy invention.   [*Kisses her.*

Rho. He who has this Lady, is a happy man, without dispute.——I'm most concern'd in this, I am sure.   [*Aside.*

Pala. Was it not well found out, *Rhodophil?*   142

Mel. Ay, this was *bien trouvée*° indeed.

Dor. (*To* Melantha.) I suppose I shall do you a kindness to enquire if you have not been in *France,* Sir?

Mel. To do you service, Sir.

Dor. O, Monsieur, *vot valet bien humble.*°   [*Saluting her.*

Mel. *Votrè esclaue, Monsieur, de tout Mon Coeur.*°   [*Returning the salute.*

111. bar'd the Dice: nullified the throw. nick'd: To "nick" is to win at dice. 115. the Hangings: tapestries. 116–17. the wrong . . . Arras: Arrases, or wall tapestries, were sometimes hung at a distance from the wall, allowing for concealment. 123. Old Chios: (Chian) the wine of Chios, an island, now called Scio, in the Grecian archipelago. 127. your Seconds: those who are to second the toast. 143. bien trouvée: well said. 148. vot . . . humble: your most humble servant. 149. Votrè . . . Coeur: your slave (esclave), Sir, with all my heart.

70. gives me: gives me to understand. 73. pragmatical: officious. 103. warrant you for: guarantee you against.

Dor. I suppose, sweet Sir, you are the hope 150
and joy of some thriving Citizen, who has pinch'd
himself at home, to breed you abroad, where you have
learnt your Exercises, as it appears most aukwardly, and
are returned with the addition of a new-lac'd bosom
and a Clap, to your good old father, who looks at you
with his mouth,° while you spout *French* with your
Man Monsieur.°   157

Pala. Let me kiss thee again for that, dear Rogue.

Mel. And you, I imagine, are my young Master,
whom your Mother durst not trust upon salt water,
but left you to be your own Tutour at fourteen, to be
very brisk and *entreprenant,*° to endeavour to be
debauch'd ere you have learnt the knack on 't, to
value your self upon a Clap before you can get it,
and to make it the height of your ambition to get a
Player for your Mistris.

Rho. (*embracing Mel.*) O dear young Bully,° thou
hast tickled him with a *repertee* i' faith.

Mel. You are one of those that applaud our
Countrey Plays, where drums, and trumpets, and
bloud, and wounds are wit.   171

Rho. Again, my Boy? let me kiss thee most
abundantly.

Dor. You are an admirer of the dull *French* Poetry,
which is so thin, that it is the very Leaf-gold° of Wit,
the very Wafers and whip'd Cream of sense, for which
a man opens his mouth and gapes, to swallow nothing:
and to be an admirer of such profound dulness, one
must be endow'd with a great perfection of impudence
and ignorance.   180

Pala. Let me embrace thee most vehemently.

Mel. I'll sacrifice my life for *French* Poetry.

                                        [*Advancing.*

Dor. I'll die upon the spot for our Countrey Wit.

Rho. (*to Melantha.*) Hold, hold, young *Mars:*
Palamede, draw back your *Hero.*

Pala. 'Tis time; I shall be drawn in for a Second
else at the wrong weapon.°

Mel. O that I were a man for thy sake!

Dor. You'll be a man as soon as I shall.   189

Enter a Messenger to Rhodophil.

Mess. Sir, the King has instant business with you.

I saw the Guard drawn up by your Lieutenant
Before the Palace-gate, ready to march.

Rhod. 'Tis somewhat sodain; say that I am coming.

                                    [*Exit Messenger.*

Now, *Palamede,* what think you of this sport?
This is some suddain tumult: will you along?

Pala. Yes, yes, I will go; but the devil take me if
ever I was less in humour. Why, the pox, could they
not have staid their tumult till to morrow? then I had
done my business, and had been ready for 'em. Truth
is, I had a little transitory crime to have committed
first; and I am the worst man in the world at repenting, till a sin be throughly done: but what shall we do
with the two Boys?   203

Rho. Let them take a lodging in the house till the
business be over.

Dor. What, lie with a Boy? for my part, I own it,
I cannot endure to lie with a Boy.

Mel. Let me die, if I enter into a pair of sheets
with him that hates the *French.*

Dor. Pish, take no care for us, but leave us in the
streets; I warrant you, as late as it is, I'll find my
lodging as well as any drunken Bully of 'em all.   212

Rho. I'll fight in meer revenge, and wreak my
     passion   [*Aside.*
On all that spoil this hopeful assignation.

Pala. I'm sure we fight in a good quarrel:
Rogues may pretend Religion, and the Laws;
But a kind Mistris is the *Good old Cause.*°   [*Exeunt.*

SCENE IV.

Enter Palmyra, Eubulus, Hermogenes.

Palm. You tell me wonders; that *Leonidas*
Is Prince *Theagenes,* the late King's Son.

Eub. It seem'd as strange to him, as now to you,
Before I had convinc'd him; But, besides
His great resemblance to the King his Father,
The Queen his Mother lives, secur'd by me
In a Religious House; to whom each year
I brought the news of his increasing virtues.
My last long absence from you both, was caus'd
By wounds which, in my journey, I receiv'd,   10
When set upon by thieves; I lost those Jewels
And Letters, which your dying Mother left.

Her. The same he means, which, since, brought to
     the King,

---

156. with his mouth: agape. 157. Man Monsieur: French
servant. 162. entreprenant: adventurous. 167. Bully:
fellow; here, a term of endearment. 175. Leaf-gold: gold
leaf. 187. at . . . weapon: with a weapon I am not
expert in, i.e., in the wrong kind of encounter.

218. the Good . . . Cause: the slogan of the Puritan
rebels, repeated sardonically by their opponents.

Made him first know he had a Child alive:
'Twas then my care of Prince *Leonidas*
Caus'd me to say he was th' Usurpers Son;
Till, after forc'd by your apparent danger,
I made the true discovery of your birth,
And once more hid my Prince's.

              Enter Leonidas.

    Leon. *Hermogenes*, and *Eubulus*, retire;   20
Those of our party, whom I left without,
Expect your aid and counsel.   [*Exeunt ambo.*
    Palm. I should, *Leonidas*, congratulate
This happy change of your exalted fate;
    But, as my joy, so you my wonder move;
Your looks have more of Business, then of Love:
And your last words some great design did show.
    Leon. I frame not any to be hid from you.
You, in my love, all my designs may see;
But what have love and you design'd for me?   30
Fortune, once more, has set the ballance right:
First, equall'd us, in lowness; then, in height.
Both of us have so long, like Gamesters, thrown,
Till Fate comes round, and gives to each his own.
As Fate is equal, so may Love appear:
Tell me, at least, what I must hope, or fear.
    Palm. After so many proofs, how can you call
My love in doubt? Fear nothing; and hope, all.
Think what a Prince, with honour, may receive,
Or I may give without a Parents leave.   40
    Leon. You give, and then restrain the grace you
    show;
As ostentatious Priests, when Souls they wooe,
Promise their Heav'n to all, but grant to few.
But do for me, what I have dar'd for you.
I did no argument from duty bring:
Duty's a Name; and Love's a Real thing.
    Palm. Man's love may, like wild torrents, over-
    flow;
Woman's as deep, but in its banks must go.
My love is mine; and that I can impart;
But cannot give my person, with my heart.   50
    Leon. Your love is then no gift:
For when the person it does not convey,
'Tis to give Gold, and not to give the Key.
    Palm. Then ask my Father.
    Leon.   He detains my Throne:
Who holds back mine, will hardly give his own.
    Palm. What then remains?
    Leon.   That I must have recourse
To Arms; and take my Love and Crown, by force.

Hermogenes is forming the design;
And with him, all the brave and loyal joyn.
    Palm. And is it thus you court *Palmyra's* bed?   60
Can she the murd'rer of her Parent wed?
Desist from force: so much you well may give
To Love, and Me, to let my Father live.
    Leon. Each act of mine my love to you has shown;
But you, who tax my want of it, have none.
You bid me part with you, and let him live;
But they should nothing ask, who nothing give.
    Palm. I give what vertue and what duty can,
In vowing ne'r to wed another man.
    Leon. You will be forc'd to be *Argaleon's* wife. 70
    Palm. I'll keep my promise, though I lose my life.
    Leon. Then you lose Love, for which we both
    contend;
For Life is but the means, but Love's the end.
    Palm. Our Souls shall love hereafter.
    Leon.   I much fear,
That Soul which could deny the Body here,
To taste of love, would be a niggard there.
    Palm. Then 'tis past hope: our cruel fate, I see,
Will make a sad divorce 'twixt you and me.
For, if you force employ, by Heav'n I swear,   79
And all bless'd Beings,——
    Leon.   Your rash Oath forbear.
    Palm. I never——
    Leon.   Hold once more. But, yet, as he
Who scapes a dangerous leap, looks back to see;
So I desire, now I am past my fear,
To know what was that Oath you meant to swear.
    Palm. I meant that if you hazarded your life,
Or sought my Father's, ne'r to be your Wife.
    Leon. See now, *Palmyra*, how unkind you prove!
Could you, with so much ease, forswear my love?
    Palm. You force me with your ruinous design.
    Leon. Your Father's life is more your care, then
    Mine.   90
    Palm. You wrong me: 'tis not; though it ought to
    be;
You are my Care, heav'n knows, as well as he.
    Leon. If now the execution I delay,
My Honour, and my Subjects, I betray.
All is prepar'd for the just enterprize;
And the whole City will to morrow rise.
The Leaders of the party are within,
And *Eubulus* has sworn that he will bring,
To head their Arms, the person of their King.
    Palm. In telling this, you make me guilty too;   100
I therefore must discover what I know:

What Honour bids you do, Nature bids me prevent;
But kill me first, and then pursue your black intent.
  Leon. *Palmyra*, no; you shall not need to die;
Yet I'll not trust so strict a piety.
Within there.

              Enter Eubulus.

           Eubulus, a Guard prepare;
Here, I commit this pris'ner to your care.
      [*Kisses* Palmyra's *hand; then gives it to*
                          Eubulus.
  Palm. *Leonidas,* I never thought these bands
Could e'r be giv'n me by a Lover's hands.   109
  Leon. *Palmyra,* thus your Judge himself arraigns;
                        [*kneeling.*
He who impos'd these bonds, still wears your chains:
When you to Love or Duty false must be,
Or to your Father guilty, or to me,
These chains, alone, remain to set you free.
             [*Noise of swords clashing.*
  Poly. (*within*) Secure these, first; then search the
  inner room.
  Leon. From whence do these tumultous clamours
  come?

          Enter Hermogenes, *hastily.*

  Her. We are betray'd; and there remains alone
This comfort, that your person is not known.

  Enter the King, Argaleon, Rhodophil, Palamede,
    Guards; some like Citizens as prisoners.

  Poly. What mean these midnight-consultations
  here,
Where I, like an unsummon'd guest, appear?   120
  Leon. Sir——
  Arga.   There needs no excuse; 'tis understood;
You were all watching, for your Prince's good.
  Poly. My reverend City-friends, you are well met!
On what great work were your grave wisdoms set?
Which of my actions were you scanning here?
What *French* invasion have you found to fear?°
  Leon. They are my friends; and come, Sir, with
  intent
To take their leaves before my banishment.
  Poly. Your exile, in both sexes friends can find:

Act IV, scene iv. **123–26. My . . . fear:** an allusion to the City
of London's opposition to Charles II and the fear that he was
plotting, with the support of Louis XIV, to impose an
absolute government.

I see the Ladies, like the men, are kind.   130
                    [*Seeing* Palmyra.
  Palm. Alas, I came but——   [*kneeling.*
  Poly.   Adde not to your crime
A lie: I'll hear you speak some other time.
How? *Eubulus!* nor time, nor thy disguise,
Can keep thee, undiscover'd, from my eyes.
A Guard there; seize 'em all.
  Rho. Yield, Sir; what use of valour can be shown?
  Leon. One, and unarm'd, against a multitude!
O for a sword!
    [*He reaches at one of the Guards Halberds, and is*
                        seiz'd behind.
        I w' not lose my breath
In fruitless pray'rs; but beg a speedy death.
  Palm. O spare Leonidas, and punish me.   140
  Poly. Mean Girl, thou want'st an Advocate for
  thee.
Now the mysterious knot will be unty'd;
Whether the young King lives, or where he dy'd:
To morrows dawn shall the dark riddle clear;
Crown all my joys; and dissipate my fear.
                    [*Exeunt omnes.*

ACT V

SCENE I.

Palamede, Straton. Palamede *with a
Letter in his hand.*

  Pal. This evening, say'st thou? will they both be
here?
  Stra. Yes Sir; both my old Master, and your
Mistris's Father: the old Gentlemen ride hard this
journey; they say, it shall be the last time they will see
the Town; and both of 'em are so pleas'd with this
marriage, which they have concluded for you, that I
am afraid they will live some years longer to trouble
you, with the joy of it.   9
  Pal. But this is such an unreasonable thing, to
impose upon me to be marri'd to morrow; 'tis
hurrying a man to execution, without giving him
time to say his pray'rs.
  Stra. Yet, if I might advise you, Sir, you should
not delay it: for your younger Brother comes up with
'em, and is got already into their favours. He has
gain'd much upon my old Master, by finding fault
with Inn-keepers Bills, and by starving us, and our
Horses, to show his frugality; and he is very well with

your Mistris's Father, by giving him Receipts° for the Splene, Gout, and Scurvy, and other infirmities of old age.   22

Pal. I'll rout him, and his Countrey education: Pox on him, I remember him before I travell'd, he had nothing in him but meer Jocky;° us'd to talk loud, and make matches, and was all for the crack of the field:° sense and wit were as much banish'd from his discourse, as they are when the Court goes out of Town to a Horserace. Go now and provide your Master's Lodgings.   30

Stra. I go, Sir.   [*Exit.*

Pal. It vexes me to the heart, to leave all my designs with *Doralice* unfinish'd; to have flown her so often to a mark, and still to be bob'd at retrieve:° if I had but once enjoy'd her, though I could not have satisfi'd my stomach, with the feast, at least I should have relish'd my mouth a little; but now——

Enter Philotis.   WOMAN TO MELANTHA

Phil. Oh, Sir, you are happily met; I was coming to find you.

Pal. From your Lady, I hope.   40

Phil. Partly from her; but more especially from my self: she has just now receiv'd a Letter from her Father, with an absolute command to dispose her self to marry you to morrow.

Pal. And she takes it to the death?

Phil. Quite contrary: the Letter could never have come in a more lucky minute; for it found her in an ill humour with a Rival of yours, that shall be nameless, about the pronunciation of a *French* word.   49

Pal. Count *Rhodophil*; never disguise it, I know the *Amour*: but I hope you took the occasion to strike in for me?

Phil. It was my good fortune to do you some small service in it; for your sake I discommended him all over: cloaths, person, humour, behaviour, every thing; and to sum up all, told her, It was impossible to find a marri'd man that was otherwise; for they were all so mortifi'd at home with their wives ill humours, that they could never recover themselves to be company abroad.   60

Pal. Most divinely urg'd!

Phil. Then I took occasion to commend your

---

good qualifications: as, the sweetness of your humour, the comeliness of your person, your good Meene, your valour; but, above all, your liberality.

Pal. I vow to Gad I had like to have forgot that good quality in my self, if thou had'st not remember'd me on 't: here are five Pieces° for thee.   68

Phil. Lord, you have the softest hand, Sir! it would do a woman good to touch it: Count *Rhodophil*'s is not half so soft; for I remember I felt it once, when he gave me ten Pieces for my New-years gift.

Pal. O, I understand you, Madam; you shall find my hand as soft again as Count *Rhodophil*'s: there are twenty Pieces for you. The former was but a Retaining Fee; now I hope you'l plead for me.

Phil. Your own merits speak enough. Be sure onely to ply her with *French* words, and I'll warrant you'll do your business. Here are a list of her phrases for this day: use 'em to her upon all occasions, and foil her at her own weapon; for she's like one of the old *Amazons*, she'l never marry, except it be the man who has first conquer'd her.   83

Pal. I'll be sure to follow your advice: but you'll forget to further my design.

Phil. What, do you think I'll be ungrateful?—— But, however, if you distrust my memory, put some token on my finger to remember it by: that Diamond there would do admirably.

Pal. There 'tis; and I ask your pardon heartily for calling your memory into question: I assure you I'll trust it another time, without putting you to the trouble of another token.   COURT LADY   93

Enter Palmyra *and* Artemis.

Art. Madam, this way the prisoners are to pass; Here you may see *Leonidas.*

Palm. Then here I'll stay, and follow him to death.

Enter Melantha *hastily.*

Mela. O, here's her Highness!
Now is my time to introduce my self, and to make my court to her, in my new *French* phrases. Stay, let me read my catalogue——*suitte, figure, chagrin, naivete,* and let me die for the Parenthesis of all.   101

Pal. (*aside*) Do, persecute her; and I'll persecute thee as fast in thy own dialect.

Mel. Madam, the Princess! let me die, but this is a most horrid spectacle, to see a person who makes so

---

Act V, *scene* i. **20. Receipts:** recipes. **25. Jocky:** horsemanship. **26–27. the crack . . . field:** the star performers, the betting favorites. **34. to a mark . . . retrieve:** to have marked the prey and be cheated of it.

68. Pieces: guineas.

grand a figure in the Court, without the *Suitte* of a Princess, and entertaining your *Chagrin* all alone; (*Naivete* should have been there, but the disobedient word would not come in.)

Palm. What is she, *Artemis*? 110

Art. An impertinent Lady, Madam; very ambitious of being known to your Highness.

Pal. (*to Melantha*) Let me die, Madam, if I have not waited you here these two long hours, without so much as the *Suitte* of a single Servant to attend me; entertaining my self with my own *Chagrin*, till I had the honour to see your Ladiship, who are a person that makes so considerable a figure in the Court. 118

Mel. Truce with your *douceurs*,° good servant; you see I am addressing to the Princess; pray do not *embarrass* me——*embarrass* me! what a delicious French word do you make me lose upon you too!

(*To the Princess*) Your Highness, Madam, will please to pardon the *Beveue* which I made, in not sooner finding you out to be a Princess: but let me die if this *Eclaircissement* which is made this day of your quality, does not ravish me; and give me leave to tell you—— 128

Pal. But first give me leave to tell you, Madam, that I have so great a tender for your person, and such a *panchant* to do you service, that——

Mel. What, must I still be troubled with your *Sottises*? (There's another word lost, that I meant for the Princess, with a mischief to you) But your Highness, Madam——

Pal. But your Ladiship, Madam——

Enter Leonidas *guarded, and led over the Stage.*

Mel. Out upon him, how he looks, Madam! now he's found no Prince, he is the strangest figure of a man; how could I make that *Coup d' etourdy* to think him one? 140

Palm. Away, impertinent——My dear *Leonidas*!

Leon. My dear *Palmyra*!

Palm. Death shall never part us; My Destiny is yours. [*He is led off; she follows.*

Mel. Impertinent! Oh I am the most unfortunate person this day breathing: that the Princess should thus *rompre en visiere*,° without occasion. Let me die but I'll follow her to death, till I make my peace.

Pal. (*holding her*) And let me die, but I'll follow you to the Infernals till you pity me. 150

119. douceurs: sweet nothings. 147. rompre en visiere: quarrel openly (with me); literally, break through the visor.

Mel. (*turning towards him angrily*) Ay, 'tis long of you° that this *Malheur*° is fall'n upon me; your impertinence has put me out of the good graces of the Princess, and all that, which has ruin'd me and all that, and therefore let me die but I'll be reveng'd, and all that.

Pal. *Façon, façon,*° you must and you shall love me, and all that; for my old man is coming up, and all that; and I am *desesperé au dernier,*° and will not be disinherited, and all that. 160

Mel. How durst you interrupt me so *mal a propos*, when you knew I was addressing to the Princess?

Pal. But why would you address your self so much *a contretemps*° then?

Mel. Ah *mal peste*°!

Pal. Ah I' *enrage*°!

Phil. *Radoucissez vous, de grace, Madame; vous étes bien en colere pour peu de chose. Vous n' entendez pas la raillerie gallante.*° 169

Mel. *Ad' autres, ad' autres:* he mocks himself of me, he abuses me: ah me unfortunate! [*cries!*

Phil. You mistake him, Madam, he does but accomodate his phrase to your refin'd language. *Ah, qu' il est un Cavalier accomply!*° pursue your point, Sir—— [*To him.*

Pal. *Ah qu'il fait beau dans ces boccages;* [*Singing Ah que le ciel donne un beau jour!*° There I was with you, with a *minouét.*

Mel. Let me die now, but this singing is fine, and extremely *French* in him: [*Laughs.* But then, that he should use my own words, as it were in contempt of me, I cannot bear it. [*Crying.*

Pal. *Ces beaux sejours, ces doux ramages*—— 183 [*Singing.*

Mel. *Ces beaux Sejours, ces doux ramages,* [*Singing after him. Ces beaux sejours, nous invitent a l'amour!*° Let me die

151-52. 'tis . . . you: it is owing to you. 152. **Malheur:** calamity. 157. **façon, façon:** Nonsense! 159. **desesperé au dernier:** utterly desperate. 164. **a contretemps:** at the wrong moment. 165. **mal peste:** a plague on it! 166. **I' enrage:** I'm getting mad. 167–69. **Radoucissez . . . gallante:** Calm yourself, for pity's sake, madam. You're in a rage over very little. You don't understand gallant raillery. 173–74. **Ah . . . accomply:** Oh, what an accomplished cavalier he is! 176–77. **Ah qu'il . . . jour:** "Oh, how beautiful it is in the woods, / Oh, what a fair day heaven gives us!" The song is taken from Molière's *Le Bourgeois Gentilhomme* (1670), as is "Vois, ma Climène," which follows. 184–85. **Ces beaux Sejours . . . l'amour:** "These beautiful places, these sweet warblings, / These beautiful places invite us to love."

but he sings *en Cavalier*,° and so humours the
Cadence.   [*Laughing.*

Pal.   *Voy, ma Clymene, voy soubs ce chesne,*   188
                                            [*Singing again.*
S' entrebaiser ces oiseaux amoreux!° Let me die now,
but that was fine. Ah, now, for three or four brisk
Frenchmen, to be put into Masquing habits, and to sing
it on a Theatre, how witty it would be! and then to
dance helter skelter to a *Chanson a boire:*° *toute la
terre, toute la terre est a moy!*° what's matter though it
were made, and sung, two or three years ago in
Cabarets, how it would attract the admiration, especially of every one that's an *eveille*°!

Mel.   Well; I begin to have a tender for you; but
yet, upon condition, that——when we are marri'd,
you——   200
                                [*Pal. sings, while she speaks.*

Phil.   You must drown her voice: if she makes her
French conditions, you are a slave for ever.

Mel.   First, will you engage——that

Pal.   Fa, la, la, la, &c.   [*Louder.*

Mel.   Will you hear the conditions?

Pal.   No; I will hear no conditions! I am resolv'd
to win you *en Francois:* to be very aiery, with abundance of noise, and no sense: Fa, la, la, la, &c.   208

Mel.   Hold, hold: I am vanquish'd with your
gayeté d' esprit. I am yours, and will be yours, *sans
nulle reserve, ny condition:* and let me die, if I do not
think my self the happiest Nymph in *Sicily*——My
dear *French* Dear, stay but a *minuite,* till I *raccommode*
my self with the Princess; and then I am yours, *jusq'
a la mort.*

Allons donc——   [*Exeunt Mel. Philot.*

Pal. (*Solus, fanning himself with his hat*) I never
thought before that wooing was so laborious an
exercise; if she were worth a million, I have deserv'd
her; and now, me-thinks too, with taking all   220
this pains for her, I begin to like her. 'Tis so; I have
known many, who never car'd for Hare nor Partridge,
but those they caught themselves would eat heartily:
the pains, and the story a man tells of the taking of
'em, makes the meat go down more pleasantly.
Besides, last night I had a sweet dream of her, and,
Gad, she I have once dream'd of, I am stark mad till
I enjoy her, let her be never so ugly.

---

186. en Cavalier: in the style of a cavalier. **188–89. Voy . . .
amoreux:** "Look, my Climène, look under this oak, / How
these amorous birds kiss one another!" **193. Chanson a
boire:** drinking song. **193–94. toute . . . moy:** All the world,
all the world is mine! **197. an eveille:** wide-awake, bright.

Enter Doralice.

Dor.   Who's that you are so made to enjoy,
Palamede?   230

Pal.   You may easily imagine that, sweet *Doralice.*

Dor.   More easily then you think I can: I met just
now with a certain man, who came to you with
Letters, from a certain old Gentleman, yclipped° your
father; whereby I am given to understand, that to
morrow you are to take an Oath in the Church to be
grave henceforward, to go ill-dress'd and slovenly, to
get heirs for your estate, and to dandle 'em for your
diversion; and, in short, that Love and Courtship are
to be no more.   240

Pal.   Now have I so much shame to be thus
apprehended in the manner, that I can neither speak
nor look upon you; I have abundance of grace in me,
that I find: But if you have any spark of true friendship
in you, retire a little with me to the next room, that
has a couch or bed in 't, and bestow your charity upon
a poor dying man: a little comfort from a Mistris,
before a man is going to give himself in Marriage, is as
good as a lusty dose of Strong-water° to a dying
Malefactour; it takes away the sense of hell, and
hanging from him.   251

Dor.   No, good *Palamede,* I must not be so injurious
to your Bride: 'tis ill drawing from the Bank to day,
when all your ready money is payable to morrow.

Pal.   A Wife is onely to have the ripe fruit, that
falls of it self; but a wise man will always preserve a
shaking for a Mistris.

Dor.   But a Wife for the first quarter is a Mistris.

Pal.   But when the second comes.

Dor.   When it does come, you are so given to
variety, that you would make a Wife of me in another
quarter.   262

Pal.   No, never, except I were married to you:
marri'd people can never oblige one another; for all
they do is duty, and consequently there can be no
thanks: but love is more frank and generous then he is
honest; he's a liberal giver, but a cursed pay-master.°

Dor.   I declare I will have no Gallant; but, if I
would, he should never be a marri'd man; a marri'd
man is but a Mistris's half-servant, as a Clergy-man is
but the King's half-subject; for a man to come to me
that smells o' th' Wife! 's life, I wou'd as soon wear
her old Gown after her, as her Husband.   273

---

234. yclipped: called. **249. Strong-water:** alcoholic spirits.
267. pay-master: one who pays what is due.

Pal. Yet 'tis a kind of fashion to wear a Princess cast shoes, you see the Countrey Ladies buy 'em to be fine in them.   276

Dor. Yes, a Princess shoes may be worn after her, because they keep their fashion, by being so very little us'd; but generally a marri'd man is the creature of the world the most out of fashion; his behaviour is dumpish, his discourse his wife and family, his habit so much neglected, it looks as if that were marri'd too; his Hat is marri'd, his Perruke is marri'd, his Breeches are marri'd, and if we could look within his Breeches, we should find him marri'd there too.

Pal. Am I then to be discarded for ever? pray do but mark how terrible that word sounds; For ever! it has a very damn'd sound, *Doralice.*

Dor. Ay, for ever! it sounds as hellishly to me, as it can do to you, but there's no help for 't.   290

Pal. Yet if we had but once enjoy'd one another; but then once onely, is worse then not at all; it leaves a man with such a lingring after it.

Dor. For ought I know 'tis better that we have not; we might upon trial have lik'd each other less, as many a man and woman, that have lov'd as desperately as we, and yet when they came to possession, have sigh'd, and cri'd to themselves, Is this all?   298

Pal. That is onely, if the Servant were not found a man of this world; but if, upon trial, we had not lik'd each other, we had certainly left loving; and faith, that's the greater happiness of the two.

Dor. 'Tis better as 'tis; we have drawn off already as much of our Love as would run clear; after possessing, the rest is but jealousies, and disquiets, and quarrelling, and piecing.°

Pal. Nay, after one great quarrel, there's never any sound piecing; the love is apt to break in the same place again.   309

Dor. I declare I would never renew a love; that's like him who trims an old Coach for ten years together, he might buy a new one better cheap.°

Pal. Well, Madam, I am convinc'd, that 'tis best for us not to have enjoy'd; but Gad, the strongest reason is, because I cann't help it.

Dor. The onely way to keep us new to one another, is never to enjoy, as they keep grapes by hanging 'em upon a line, they must touch nothing if you would preserve 'em fresh.   319

Pal. But then they wither, and grow dry in the

very keeping; however I shall have a warmth for you, and an eagerness, every time I see you; and if I chance to out-live *Melantha*——

Dor. And if I chance to out-live *Rhodophil*——

Pal. Well, I'll cherish my body as much as I can upon that hope. 'Tis true, I would not directly murder the wife of my bosome; but to kill her civilly, by the way of kindness, I'll put° as fair as another man: I'll begin to morrow night, and be very wrathful with her, that's resolv'd on.   330

Dor. Well, Palamede, here's my hand, I'll venture to be your second Wife, for all your threatenings.

Pal. In the mean time I'll watch you hourly, as I would the ripeness of a Melon, and I hope you'll give me leave now and then to look on you, and to see if you are not ready to be cut yet.

Dor. No, no, that must not be, Palamede, for fear the Gardener should come and catch you taking up the glass.°   339

Enter Rhodophil.

Rho. (*Aside*) Billing so sweetly! now I am confirm'd in my suspicions; I must put an end to this, ere it go further.   [*Aside.*

(*To Doralice*) Cry you mercy, Spouse; I fear I have interrupted your recreations.

Dor. What recreations?

Rho. Nay, no excuses, good Spouse; I saw fair hand convey'd to lip, and prest, as though you had been squeezing soft wax together for an Indenture.° *Palamede,* you and I must clear this reckoning; why would you have seduc'd my wife?   350

Pal. Why would you have debauch'd my Mistris?

Rho. What do you think of that civil couple, that play'd at a Game call'd, *Hide and Seek,* last evening, in the Grotto?

Pal. What do you think of that innocent pair, who made it their pretence to seek for others, but came, indeed, to hide themselves there?

Rho. All things consider'd, I begin vehemently to suspect, that the young Gentleman I found in your company last night, was a certain youth of my acquaintance.   361

Pal. And I have an odd imagination, that you could never have suspected my small Gallant, if your little villanous *Frenchman* had not been a false Brother.

---

306. **piecing:** mending, making up. 312. **better cheap:** at a better bargain.

328. **put:** exert myself, thrust (as a weapon). 339. **the glass:** frame for plants. 348. **for an Indenture:** for sealing a contract.

Rho. Farther Arguments are needless; Draw off; I shall speak to you now by the way of *Bilbo.*°

[*Claps his hand to his sword.*

Pal. And I shall answer you by the way of Danger-field.° [*Claps his hand on his.*

Dor. Hold, hold; are not you two a couple of mad fighting fools, to cut one another's throats for nothing? 371

Pal. How for nothing? he courts the woman I must marry.

Rho. And he courts you whom I have marri'd.

Dor. But you can neither of you be jealous of what you love not.

Rho. Faith I am jealous, and that makes me partly suspect that I love you better then I thought.

Dor. Pish! a meer jealousie of honour. 379

Rho. Gad I am afraid there's something else in 't; for *Palamede* has wit, and if he loves you, there's something more in ye then I have found: some rich Mine, for ought I know, that I have not yet discover'd.

Pal. 'S life, what's this? here's an argument for me to love *Melantha;* for he has lov'd her, and he has wit too, and, for ought I know, there may be a Mine: but, if there be, I am resolv'd I'll dig for 't.

Dor. (*to Rhod.*) Then I have found my account° in raising your jealousie: O! 'tis the most delicate sharp sawce to a cloy'd stomach; it will give you a new edge, *Rhodophil.* 391

Rho. And a new point too, *Doralice,* if I could be sure thou art honest.°

Dor. If you are wise, believe me for your own sake: Love and Religion have but one thing to trust to; that's a good sound faith. Consider, if I have play'd false, you can never find it out by any experiment you can make upon me.

Rho. No? Why, suppose I had a delicate screw'd Gun,° if I left her clean, and found her foul, I should discover, to my cost, she had been shot in. 401

Dor. But if you left her clean, and found her onely rusty, you would discover, to your shame, she was onely so for want of shooting.

Pal. *Rhodophil,* you know me too well, to imagine I speak for fear; and therefore in consideration of our past friendship, I will tell you, and bind it by all things holy, that *Doralice* is innocent.

Rho. Friend, I will believe you, and vow the same

---

366. Bilbo: a sword made in Bilbao, Spain. **367–68. Dangerfield:** a conventional name for a ruffian. **388. found my account:** profited. **393. honest:** chaste. **399–400. screw'd Gun:** a gun with a grooved bore.

for your *Melantha;* but the devil on 't is, how we shall keep 'em so. 411

Pal. What dost think of a blessed community betwixt us four, for the solace of the women, and relief of the men? Methinks it would be a pleasant kind of life: Wife and Husband for the standing Dish,° and Mistris and Gallant for the Desert.

Rhod. But suppose the Wife and the Mistris should both long for the standing Dish, how should they be satisfi'd together? 419

Pal. In such a case they must draw lots: and yet that would not do neither; for they would both be wishing for the longest cut°?

Rho. Then I think, *Palamede,* we had as good make a firm League, not to invade each others propriety.°

Pal. Content, say I. From henceforth let all acts of hostility cease betwixt us; and that in the usual form of Treaties, as well by Sea as by Land, and in all Fresh waters. 428

Dor. I will adde but one *Proviso,* That who ever breaks the League, either by war abroad, or by neglect at home, both the Women shall revenge themselves, by the help of the other party.

Rho. That's but reasonable. Come away, *Doralice;* I have a great temptation to be sealing Articles in private.

Palam. Hast thou so? [*Claps him on the shoulder.* Fall on, *Machduff,* And curst be he that first cries, Hold, enough.

Enter Polydamas, Palmyra, Artemis, Argaleon: *after them,* Eubulus, *and* Hermogenes, *guarded.*

Palm. Sir, on my knees I beg you.

Pol. Away, I'll hear no more. 440

Palm. For my dead Mother's sake; you say you lov'd her, And tell me I resemble her. Thus she Had begg'd.

Pol. And thus had I deny'd her.

Palm. You must be merciful.

Arga. You must be constant.

Pol. Go, bear 'em to the torture; you have boasted You have a King to head you: I would know To whom I must resign.

Eub. This is our recompence For serving thy dead Queen.

Her. And education

---

416. standing Dish: the dish that is served each day or at each meal. **422. cut:** lot. **424. propriety:** property.

Of thy daughter.   449
    Arga. You are too modest, in not naming all
His obligations to you: why did you
Omit his Son, the Prince *Leonidas?*
    Pol.   That Imposture
I had forgot; their tortures shall be doubled.
    Her.   You please me, I shall die the sooner.
    Eub.   No; could I live an age, and still be rack'd,
I still would keep the secret.   [*As they are going off,*

            Enter Leonidas, *guarded.*

    Leon. Oh wither do you hurry innocence!
If you have any justice, spare their lives;
Or if I cannot make you just, at least   460
I'll teach you to more purpose to be cruel.
    Palm. Alas, what does he seek!
    Leon. Make me the object of your hate and
        vengeance!
Are these decrepid bodies worn to ruine,
Just ready, of themselves, to fall asunder,
And to let drop the soul,
Are these fit subjects for a Rack, and Tortures?
Where would you fasten any hold upon 'em?
Place pains on me; united fix 'em here;   469
I have both youth, and strength, and soul to bear 'em:
And if they merit death, then I much more;
Since 'tis for me they suffer.
    Her.   Heav'n forbid
We should redeem our pains, or worthless lives,
By our exposing yours.
    Eub.   Away with us: Farewell, Sir.
I onely suffer in my fears for you.
    Arga. So much concern'd for him? then my
                                    [*Aside.*
Suspicion's true.
        [*Whispers the King.*]
    Palm. Hear yet my last request, for poor *Leonidas;*
Or take my life with his.   480
    Arga. Rest satisfi'd; *Leonidas* is he.   [*To the King.*
    Pol.   I am amaz'd:° what must be done?
    Arga. Command his execution instantly;
Give him not leisure to discover° it;
He may corrupt the Soldiers.
    Pol.   Hence with that Traitour; bear him to his
        death:
Haste there, and see my will perform'd.
    Leon. Nay, then I'll die like him the Gods have
        made me.

482. amaz'd: alarmed. 484. discover: reveal.

Hold, Gentlemen; I am——   489
                          [*Argaleon stops his mouth.*
    Arga. Thou art a Traitor; 'tis not fit to hear thee.
    Leon. I say I am the——   [*Getting loose a little.*
    Arga. So; gag him, and lead him off.
                          [*Again stopping his mouth.*

        Leonidas, Hermogenes, Eubulus, *led off.*
        Polydamas and Argaleon *follow.*

    Palm. Duty and Love, by turns possess my soul,
And struggle for a fatal victory:
I will discover he's the King; Ah, no:
That will perhaps save him;
But then I am guilty of a father's ruine.
What shall I do, or not do? either way
I must destroy a Parent, or a Lover.
Break heart; for that's the least of ills to me,   500
And Death the onely cure.   [*Swoons.*
    Arte. Help, help the Princess.
    Rho.   Bear her gently hence, where she may
Have more succour.
                    [*She is born off,* Arte. *follows her.*
                    [*Shouts within, and clashing of swords.*
    Pal.   What noise is that?

                          SISTER TO ARGA
            Enter Amalthea, *running.*

    Amal. Oh, Gentlemen, if you have loyalty,
Or courage, show it now: *Leonidas*
Broke on the sudden from his Guards, and snatching
A sword from one, his back against the Scaffold,
Bravely defends himself; and own aloud   510
He is our long lost King, found for this moment;
But, if your valours help not, lost for ever.
Two of his Guards, mov'd by the sense of virtue,
Are turn'd for him, and there they stand at Bay
Against an host of foes.
    Rho.   Madam, no more;
We lose time: my command, or my example,
May move the Soldiers to the better cause.   518
You'll second me?   [*To Pal.*
    Pal.   Or die with you: no Subject e'r can meet
A nobler fate, then at his Sovereign's feet.   [*Exeunt.*
                    [*Clashing of swords within, and shouts.*

        Enter Leonidas, Rhodophil, Palamede, Eubulus,
            Hermogenes, *and their party, victorious.*
            Polydamas *and* Argaleon, *disarm'd.*

    Leon. That I survive the dangers of this day,

Next to the Gods, brave friends, be yours the honour.
And let Heav'n witness for me, that my joy
Is not more great for this my right restor'd,
Than 'tis, that I have power to recompence
Your Loyalty and Valour. Let mean Princes
Of abject souls, fear to reward great actions;
I mean to show,
That whatsoe'r subjects, like you, dare merit,
A King, like me, dares give——   530
   Rho.   You make us blush, we have deserv'd so
    little.
   Pal.   And yet instruct us how to merit more.
   Leon.   And as I would be just in my rewards,
So should I in my punishments; these two,
This the Usurper of my Crown, the other
Of my *Palmyra*'s love, deserve that death
Which both design'd for me.
   Pol.   And we expect it.
   Arga.   I have too long been happy to live wretched.
   Pol.   And I too long have govern'd, to desire
A life without an Empire.   540
   Leon.   You are *Palmyra*'s father; and as such,
Though not a King, shall have obedience paid
From him who is one. Father, in that name,
All injuries forgot, and duty own'd.   [*Embraces him.*
   Pol.   O, had I known you could have been this
    King,
Thus God-like, great and good, I should have wish'd
T' have been dethron'd before. 'Tis now I live,
And more then Reign; now all my joys flow pure,
Unmix'd with cares, and undisturb'd by conscience.

Enter Palmyra, Amalthea, Artemis, Doralice
and Melantha.

   Leon.   See, my *Palmyra* comes! the frighted bloud
Scarce yet recall'd to her pale cheeks,   551
Like the first streaks of light broke loose from dark-
   ness,
And dawning into blushes.——Sir, you said,
                    [*To* Polyda.
Your joys were full; Oh, would you make mine so!
I am but half-restor'd without this blessing.
   Pol.   The Gods, and my Palmyra, make you happy,
As you make me.   [*Gives her hand to* Leonidas.
   Palmy.   Now all my prayers are heard:
I may be dutiful, and yet may love.
Virtue, and patience, have at length unravell'd
The knots which Fortune ty'd.   560
   Mel.   Let me die, but I'll congratulate his Majesty:

how admirably well his Royalty becomes him!
Becomes! that is *luy sied,*° but our damn'd Language
expresses nothing.
   Pal.   How? does it become him already? 'twas but
just now you said, he was such a figure of a man.
   Mel.   True, my dear, when he was a private man
he was a figure; but since he is a King, methinks he
has assum'd another figure: he looks so grand,   569
and so August.   [*Going to the King.*
   Pal.   Stay, stay; I'll present you when it is more
convenient. I find I must get her a place at Court; and
when she is once there, she can be no longer ridiculous;
for she is young enough, and pretty enough, and fool
enough, and *French* enough, to bring up a fashion there
to be affected.
   Leon.   (*to* Rhodophil) Did she then lead you to this
brave attempt?
(*To* Amalthea) To you, fair *Amalthea,* what I am,
And what all these, from me, we joyntly owe: 580
First, therefore, to your great desert, we give
Your Brother's life; but keep him under guard,
Till our new power be setled. What more grace
He may receive, shall from his future carriage
Be given, as he deserves.
   Arga.   I neither now desire, nor will deserve it;
My loss is such as cannot be repair'd,
And to the wretched, life can be no mercy.
   Leon.   Then be a prisoner always: thy ill fate,
And pride will have it so: but since, in this, I cannot,
Instruct me, generous *Amalthea,* how   591
A King may serve you.
   Amal.   I have all I hope,
And all I now must wish; I see you happy.
Those hours I have to live, which Heav'n in pity
Will make but few, I vow to spend with Vestals:
The greatest part, in pray'rs for you; the rest
In mourning my unworthiness.
Press me not farther to explain my self;
'Twill not become me, and may cause your trouble.
   Leon.   Too well I understand her secret grief,
                        [*Aside.*
But dare not seem to know it.——Come my fairest,
                     [*To* Palmyra.
Beyond my Crown, I have one joy in store;
To give that Crown to her whom I adore.   603
                     [*Exeunt omnes.*

---

563. luy sied: becomes him.

EPILOGUE°

Thus have my Spouse and I inform'd the Nation,
And led you all the way to Reformation.
Not with dull Morals, gravely writ, like those,
Which men of easie Phlegme,° with care compose.
Your Poets of stiff words, and limber sense,
Born on the confines of indifference.
But by examples drawn, I dare to say,
From most of you, who hear, and see the Play.
There are more Rhodophils in this Theatre,
More Palamedes, and some few Wives, I fear.   10
But yet too far our Poet would not run,
Though 'twas well offer'd, there was nothing done.
He would not quite the Woman's frailty bare,
But stript 'em to the waste, and left 'em there.
And the men's faults are less severely shown,
For he considers that himself is one.
Some stabbing Wits, to bloudy Satyr bent,
Would treat both Sexes with less complement:
Would lay the Scene at home, of Husbands tell,
For Wenches, taking up their Wives i' th' Mell,   20
And a brisk bout which each of them did want,
Made by mistake of Mistris and Gallant.
Our modest Authour, thought it was enough
To cut you off a Sample of the stuff:
He spar'd my shame, which you, I'm sure, would not,
For you were all for driving on the Plot:
You sigh'd when I came in to break the sport,
And set your teeth when each design fell short.
To Wives, and Servants all good wishes lend,
But the poor Cuckold seldom finds a friend.   30
Since therefore Court and Town will take no pity,
I humbly cast my self upon the City.

PROLOGUE
[TO *AURENG-ZEBE*]

Aureng-Zebe was first performed at the Theatre Royal
in 1675; it was printed the following year. In the Dedication to the Earl of Mulgrave, Dryden writes:

I desire to be no longer the *Sysiphus* of the Stage;
to rowl up a Stone with endless Labour (which, to

Epilogue. This is spoken by Rhodophil. **4. men . . .
Phlegme:** cold, dull, sluggish men.

follow the Proverb, *Gathers no Moss*) and which is
perpetually falling down again; I never thought my
self very fit for an Employment, where many of my
Predecessors have excell'd me in all kinds; and
some of my Contemporaries, even in my own
partial Judgment, have outdone me in *Comedy*.

Dryden's interests had by this time shifted from the
drama to the epic poem.

The text is that of the first edition (1676).

❦

Our Author by experience finds it true,
'Tis much more hard to please himself than you:°
And out of no feign'd modesty, this day,
Damns his laborious Trifle of a Play:
Not that its worse than what before he writ,
But he has now another taste of Wit;
And to confess a truth, (though out of time)
Grows weary of his long-lov'd Mistris, Rhyme.°
Passion's too fierce to be in Fetters bound,
And Nature flies him like Enchanted Ground.   10
What Verse can do, he has perform'd in this,
Which he presumes the most correct of his:
But spite of all his pride a secret shame,
Invades his breast at *Shakespear's* sacred name:
Aw'd when he hears his Godlike *Romans* rage,
He, in a just despair, would quit the Stage.
And to an Age less polish'd, more unskill'd,
Does, with disdain the foremost Honours yield.
As with the greater Dead he dares not strive,
He wou'd not match his Verse with those who live: 20
Let him retire, betwixt two Ages cast,
The first of this, and hindmost of the last.
A losing Gamester, let him sneak away;
He bears no ready Money from the Play.°
The Fate which governs Poets, thought it fit,
He shou'd not raise his Fortunes by his Wit.
The Clergy thrive, and the litigious Bar;
Dull Heroes fatten with the spoils of War:
All Southern Vices, Heav'n be prais'd, are here;

PROLOGUE TO *Aureng-Zebe*. **2. 'Tis . . . you:** Cf. the Preface
to *An Evening's Love*, above, p. 80. **8. Grows . . . Rhyme:**
Aureng-Zebe (1676) was the last of Dryden's rhymed heroic
plays. Its rhymed couplets are freer than his earlier style
and approach blank verse in their movement. Dryden
had zealously defended the use of rhyme in his *Essay of
Dramatic Poesy* (1668). **24. He . . . Play:** Dryden was a
shareholder in the foundering Theatre Royal.

But Wit's a luxury you think too dear.   30
When you to cultivate the Plant are loath,
'Tis a shrewd sign 'twas never of your growth:
And Wit in Northern Climates will not blow,
Except, like *Orange-trees*, 'tis hous'd from Snow.
There needs no care to put a Play-house down,
'Tis the most desart place of all the Town.
We and our Neighbours,° to speak proudly, are
Like Monarchs, ruin'd with expensive War.
While, like wise *English*, unconcern'd, you sit,
And see us play the Tragedy of Wit.   40

[CAN LIFE BE A BLESSING]

❦

This song from *Troilus and Cressida*, Act III, scene ii, is sung to the sleeping lovers by musicians hired by Pandarus.
    The text is that of the first edition (1679).

❦

1

Can life be a blessing,
Or worth the possessing,
Can life be a blessing if love were away?
Ah no! though our love all night keep us waking,
And though he torment us with cares all the day,
Yet he sweetens he sweetens our pains in the taking,
There's an hour at the last, there's an hour to repay.

2

In every possessing,
The ravishing blessing,
In every possessing the fruit of our pain,
Poor lovers forget long ages of anguish,
Whate're they have suffer'd and done to obtain;
'Tis a pleasure, a pleasure to sigh and to languish,
When we hope, when we hope to be happy again.

37. Neighbours: the rival Duke's Company at Dorset Garden.

THE EPILOGUE SPOKEN TO THE KING AT THE OPENING THE PLAY-HOUSE AT OXFORD ON SATURDAY LAST. BEING MARCH THE NINETEENTH
1681

✿

This epilogue was written for a special performance of Charles Saunders's *Tamerlane the Great* (1681) before Members of Parliament assembled at Oxford against the threat of rebellion. Charles arrived on March 14, opened the Parliament on March 21, and dissolved it a week later.
    The text follows James Kinsley's transcription of the copy (1681) in the Christ Church Library, Oxford.

❦

As from a darkn'd Roome some Optick glass
Transmits the distant Species° as they pass;
The worlds large Landscape is from far descry'd,
And men contracted on the Paper glide;
Thus crowded *Oxford* represents Mankind,
And in these Walls *Great Brittain* seems Confin'd.
Oxford is now the publick *Theater;*
And you both Audience are, and Actors here.
The gazing World on the New Scene attend,
Admire the turns, and wish a prosp'rous end.   10
This Place the seat of Peace, the quiet Cell
Where Arts remov'd from noisy business dwell,
Shou'd calm your Wills, unite the jarring parts,
And with a kind Contagion seize your hearts:
Oh! may its Genius, like soft Musick move,
And tune you all to Concord and to Love.
Our Ark that has in Tempests long been tost,
Cou'd never land on so secure a Coast.
From hence you may look back on Civil Rage,
And view the ruines of the former Age.   20
Here a New World its glories may unfold,
And here be sav'd the remnants of the Old.
But while your daies on publick thoughts are bent
Past ills to heal, and future to prevent;

EPILOGUE SPOKEN TO THE KING. **2. Species:** reflected images.

Some vacant houres allow to your delight,
Mirth is the pleasing buisness of the Night,
The Kings Prerogative, the Peoples right.
Were all your houres to sullen cares confind,
The Body wou'd be Jaded by the Mind.
'Tis Wisdoms part betwixt extreams to Steer: 30
Be Gods in Senates, but be Mortals here.

ABSALOM
AND ACHITOPHEL

Absalom and Achitophel was written during the middle
months of 1681, when Whig opposition to Charles II,
though on the decline since the Popish Plot of 1678,
lingered on. In November, 1680, the Whig leader
Shaftesbury advocated in the Lords a bill to exclude
Charles's Catholic brother, James, Duke of York, from
succession. Shaftesbury's party favored the succession
of the King's illegitimate but Protestant son, the Duke
of Monmouth. When his exclusion bill failed to pass
the Lords, Shaftesbury appealed to Charles at the
Oxford Parliament in the spring of 1681 to legitimate
Monmouth. Shaftesbury was seized on July 2, 1681,
and charged with high treason. He was tried on
November 24, a week after the appearance of Dryden's
poem, which seems to have been written at the King's
request and published to serve the time. But Shaftesbury
was acquitted by a grand jury packed by Whig sheriffs.

Biblical parallels to contemporary politics had long
been exploited by poets and pamphleteers, and Dryden
had been many times anticipated in the application of
the David-Absalom-Achitophel story to the troubles of
Charles. But only his version has outlasted the political
occasion and overcome the distractions of the allegorical
translation.

Absalom and Achitophel was widely read and rapidly
ran into several editions. The present text is that of the
first edition (1681), with a good number of substantive
variants and a few corrections introduced from the
later editions.

IN pious times, e'r Priest-craft did begin,
Before *Polygamy* was made a sin;
When man, on many, multiply'd his kind,
E'r one to one was, cursedly, confind:
When Nature prompted, and no law deny'd
Promiscuous use of Concubine and Bride;

Then, *Israel's* Monarch,° after Heaven's own heart,
His vigorous warmth did, variously, impart
To Wives and Slaves: And, wide as his Command,
Scatter'd his Maker's Image through the Land.   10
Michal,° of Royal blood, the Crown did wear,
A Soyl ungratefull to the Tiller's care:
Not so the rest; for several Mothers bore
To Godlike *David*, several Sons before.
But since like slaves his bed they did ascend,
No True Succession could their seed attend.
Of all this Numerous Progeny was none
So Beautifull, so brave as *Absolon:*°
Whether, inspir'd by some diviner Lust,
His Father got him with a greater Gust;   20
Or that his Conscious destiny made way
By manly beauty to Imperiall sway.
Early in Foreign fields he won Renown,
With Kings and States ally'd to *Israel's* Crown:°
In Peace the thoughts of War he coud remove,
And seem'd as he were only born for love.
What e'r he did was done with so much ease,
In him alone, 'twas Natural to please.
His motions all accompanied with grace;
And *Paradise* was open'd in his face.   30
With secret Joy, indulgent *David* view'd
His Youthfull Image in his Son renew'd:
To all his wishes Nothing he deny'd,
And made the Charming *Annabel*° his Bride.
What faults he had (for who from faults is free?)
His Father coud not, or he woud not see.
Some warm excesses, which the Law forbore,
Were constru'd Youth that purg'd by boyling o'r:
And *Amnon's* Murther,° by a specious Name,
Was call'd a Just Revenge for injur'd Fame.   40
Thus Prais'd, and Lov'd, the Noble Youth remain'd,
While *David*, undisturb'd, in *Sion*° raign'd.
But Life can never be sincerely° blest:
Heaven punishes the bad, and proves° the best.
The *Jews*,° a Headstrong, Moody, Murmuring race,

ABSALOM AND ACHITOPHEL. **7. Israel's Monarch:** Charles
II. See I Sam. 13: 13–14. **11. Michal:** Princess Catherine
of Portugal, Charles's queen. See II Sam. 6: 23. **18.
Absolon:** James Scott (1649–85), Duke of Monmouth;
son of Charles II and Lucy Walter. **23–24. Early . . .
Crown:** Monmouth fought with the French against the
Dutch in 1672–73 and with the Dutch against the French in
1678. **34. Annabel:** Anne, Countess of Buccleuch. **39.
Amnon's Murther:** probably an allusion to the assault on
(but not murder of) Sir John Coventry by Monmouth's men
in December, 1670, for having aspersed the King. **42. Sion:**
London. **43. sincerely:** completely. **44. proves:** makes a
trial of. **45. The Jews:** the English.

As ever try'd th' extent and stretch of grace;
God's pamper'd people whom, debauch'd with ease,
No King could govern, nor no God could please;
(Gods they had tri'd of every shape and size
That God-smiths could produce, or Priests devise.) 50
These *Adam*-wits,° too fortunately free,
Began to dream they wanted° libertie;
And when no rule, no president° was found
Of men, by Laws less circumscrib'd and bound,
They led their wild desires to Woods and Caves,
And thought that all but Savages were Slaves.
They who when *Saul*° was dead, without a blow,
Made foolish *Ishbosheth*° the Crown forgo;
Who banisht *David* did from *Hebron*° bring,
And, with a Generall Shout, proclaim'd him King: 60
Those very *Jewes*, who, at their very best,
Their Humour more than Loyalty exprest,
Now wondred why, so long, they had obey'd
An Idoll Monarch which their hands had made:
Thought they might ruine him they could create;
Or melt him to that Golden Calf, a State.°
But these were randome bolts: No form'd Design,
Nor Interest made the Factious Croud to joyn:
The sober part of *Israel*, free from stain,
Well knew the value of a peacefull raign: 70
And, looking backward with a wise afright,
Saw Seames of wounds, dishonest° to the sight;
In contemplation of whose ugly Scars,
They Curst the memory of Civil Wars.
The moderate sort of Men, thus qualifi'd,
Inclin'd the Ballance to the better side:
And *David*'s mildness manag'd it so well,
The Bad found no occasion to Rebell.
But, when to Sin our byast Nature leans,
The carefull Devil is still at hand with means; 80
And providently Pimps for ill desires:
The Good old Cause° reviv'd, a Plot requires.
Plots, true or false, are necessary things,
To raise up Common-wealths, and ruin Kings.
    Th' inhabitants of old *Jerusalem*°
Were *Jebusites*:° the Town so call'd from them;

And their's the Native right—
But when the chosen people° grew more strong,
The rightfull cause at length became the wrong:
And every loss the men of *Jebus* bore, 90
They still were thought God's enemies the more.
Thus, worn and weaken'd, well or ill content,
Submit they must to *David*'s Government:
Impoverisht, and depriv'd of all Command,
Their Taxes doubled as they lost their Land,
And, what was harder yet to flesh and blood,
Their Gods disgrac'd, and burnt like common wood.
This set the Heathen Priesthood° in a flame;
For Priests of all Religions are the same:
Of whatsoe'r descent their Godhead be, 100
Stock, Stone, or other homely pedigree,
In his defence his Servants are as bold
As if he had been born of beaten gold.
The *Jewish Rabbins*° thô their Enemies,
In this conclude them honest men and wise:
For 'twas their duty, all the Learned think,
T' espouse his Cause by whom they eat and drink.
From hence began that Plot,° the Nation's Curse,
Bad in it self, but represented worse.
Rais'd in extremes, and in extremes decry'd; 110
With Oaths affirm'd, with dying Vows deny'd.
Not weigh'd, or winnow'd by the Multitude;
But swallow'd in the Mass, unchew'd and Crude.
Some Truth there was, but dash'd and brew'd with
    Lyes;
To please the Fools, and puzzle all the Wise.
Succeeding times did equal folly call,
Believing nothing, or believing all.
Th' *Egyptian*° Rites the *Jebusites* imbrac'd;
Where Gods were recommended by their Tast.°
Such savory Deities must needs be good, 120
As serv'd at once for Worship and for Food.
By force they could not Introduce these Gods;
For Ten to One, in former days was odds.
So Fraud was us'd, (the Sacrificers° trade,)
Fools are more hard to Conquer than Perswade.
Their busie Teachers mingled with the *Jews*;

---

51. Adam-wits: reasoning like Adam, i.e., falsely. **52. wanted:** lacked. **53. president:** precedent. **57. Saul:** Oliver Cromwell. **58. Ishbosheth:** Richard Cromwell. See II Sam. 3—4. **59. Hebron:** Scotland, where Charles was crowned on January 1, 1651, ten years before he became king of England. See II Sam. 5: 1–5. **66. State:** republic. **72. dishonest:** shameful. **82. The Good . . . Cause:** the slogan of the Puritan rebellion. Here it stands for the Commonwealth of 1649–53. **85. Jerusalem:** London. **86. Jebusites:** Roman Catholics. See Judg. 1:21 and 19:10.

88. the chosen people: the Protestants. **98. Heathen Priesthood:** Roman Catholic priests. **104. Jewish Rabbins:** Church of England priests. **108. that Plot:** the alleged Popish Plot of 1678, which, led by the Jesuits and supported by the French, was supposed to have aimed at the overthrow of the King, the Government, and the Protestant religion. **118. Egyptian:** French, i.e., Catholic. **119. by . . . Tast:** the doctrine of transubstantiation, which Dryden was later (as a Roman Catholic) to defend in *The Hind and the Panther* (1687). **124. Sacrificers:** priests'.

And rak'd, for Converts, even the Court and Stews:°
Which *Hebrew* Priests° the more unkindly took,
Because the Fleece accompanies the Flock.
Some thought they God's Anointed meant to Slay 130
By Guns, invented since full many a day:
Our Authour swears it not; but who can know
How far the Devil and *Jebusites* may go?
This Plot, which fail'd for want of common Sense,
Had yet a deep and dangerous Consequence:
For, as when raging Fevers boyl the Blood,
The standing Lake soon floats into a Flood;
And every hostile Humour, which before
Slept quiet in its Channels, bubbles o'r:
So, several Factions from this first Ferment, 140
Work up to Foam, and threat the Government.
Some by their Friends, more by themselves thought
   wise,
Oppos'd the Power, to which they could not rise.
Some had in Courts been Great, and thrown from
   thence,
Like Feinds, were harden'd in Impenitence.
Some by their Monarch's fatal mercy grown,
From Pardon'd Rebels, Kinsmen to the Throne;
Were rais'd in Power and publick Office high:
Strong Bands, if Bands ungratefull men could tye.
   Of these the false *Achitophel*° was first: 150
A Name to all succeeding Ages Curst.
For close Designs, and crooked Counsels fit;
Sagacious, Bold, and Turbulent of wit:
Restless, unfixt in Principles and Place;
In Power unpleas'd, impatient of Disgrace.
A fiery Soul, which working out its way, ⎫
Fretted° the Pigmy Body° to decay: ⎬
And o'r inform'd° the Tenement of Clay. ⎭
A daring Pilot in extremity;
Pleas'd with the Danger, when the Waves went
   high 160
He sought the Storms; but for a Calm unfit,
Would Steer too nigh the Sands, to boast his Wit.

Great Wits are sure to Madness near ally'd;
And thin Partitions do their Bounds divide:
Else, why should he, with Wealth and Honour blest,
Refuse his Age the needful hours of Rest?
Punish a Body which he coud not please;
Bankrupt of Life, yet Prodigal of Ease?
And all to leave, what with his Toyl he won,
To that unfeather'd, two Leg'd thing,° a Son: 170
Got, while his Soul did hudled° Notions try;
And born a shapeless Lump, like Anarchy.
In Friendship False, Implacable in Hate:
Resolv'd to Ruine or to Rule the State.
To Compass this the Triple Bond° he broke; ⎫
The Pillars of the publick Safety shook: ⎬
And fitted *Israel* for a Foreign Yoke.° ⎭
Then, seiz'd with Fear, yet still affecting Fame,
Usurp'd a Patriott's All-attoning Name.
So° easie still it proves in Factious Times, 180
With publick Zeal to cancel private Crimes:
How safe is Treason, and how sacred ill,
Where none can sin against the Peoples Will:
Where Crouds can wink; and no offence be known,
Since in anothers guilt they find their own.
Yet, Fame deserv'd, no Enemy can grudge;
The Statesman we abhor, but praise the Judge.°
In *Israels* Courts ne'r sat an *Abbethdin*°
With more discerning Eyes, or Hands more clean:
Unbrib'd, unsought, the Wretched to redress; 190
Swift of Dispatch, and easie of Access.
Oh, had he been content to serve the Crown,
With vertues only proper to the Gown;
Or, had the rankness of the Soyl been freed
From Cockle,° that opprest the Noble seed:
David, for him his tunefull Harp had strung,
And Heaven had wanted° one Immortal song.°

---

127. Stews: brothels. **128. Hebrew Priests:** Anglican clergymen. **150. Achitophel:** Anthony Ashley Cooper (1621–83), First Earl of Shaftesbury and Lord Chancellor from 1672 to 1673. He had served the Royalist party both in the Civil War and after the Restoration but joined the Opposition in 1673. "Achitophel" ("Ahitophel" in the Authorized Version) was used by the Puritans as an opprobrious designation for Charles I's ministers but was adopted by the Royalists for their own purposes. **157. Fretted:** eroded. The whole image is that of a turbulent river. **Pigmy Body:** Shaftesbury's body was crippled and dwarfed. **158. o'r inform'd:** overflowed.

170. unfeather'd . . . thing: the definition of man attributed to Plato. **171. hudled:** confused, disordered; perhaps concealed, hushed up. Dryden's allusion is obscure. **175. Triple Bond:** England's triple alliance with Holland and Sweden against France, formed in 1668. Four years later England was at war with Holland, supported by France. Charles had in the interim negotiated secret treaties with the French. **177. Foreign Yoke:** that of France. **180–91. So . . . Access:** added in the second edition (1681). **187. the Judge:** As Lord Chancellor, Shaftesbury was the presiding judge in the Court of Chancery. **188. an Abbethdin:** a justice of the Jewish civil court. **195. Cockle:** weeds. **197. wanted:** lacked. **one . . . song:** perhaps David's lament for Absalom in II Sam. 18:33, or Psalm 3, or Psalm 109. The last had been interpreted in the seventeenth century as a judgment on Absalom and Achitophel.

But wilde Ambition loves to slide, not stand;
And Fortunes Ice prefers to Vertues Land:
Achitophel, grown weary to possess   200
A lawfull Fame, and lazy Happiness;
Disdain'd the Golden fruit to gather free,
And lent the Croud his Arm to shake the Tree.
Now, manifest of° Crimes, contriv'd long since,
He stood at bold Defiance with his Prince:
Held up the Buckler of the Peoples Cause,
Against the Crown; and sculk'd behind the Laws.
The wish'd occasion of the Plot he takes,
Some Circumstances finds, but more he makes.
By buzzing Emissaries, fills the ears   210
Of listning Crowds, with Jealosies° and Fears
Of Arbitrary Counsels brought to light,
And proves the King himself a *Jebusite:*°
Weak Arguments! which yet he knew fulwell,
Were strong with People easie to Rebell.
For, govern'd by the *Moon*, the giddy *Jews*
Tread the same track when she the Prime° renews:
And once in twenty Years, their Scribes Record,
By natural Instinct they change their Lord.
Achitophel still wants a Chief, and none   220
Was found so fit as Warlike *Absolon:*
Not, that he wish'd his Greatness to create,
(For Politions neither love nor hate:)
But, for he knew, his Title not allow'd,
Would keep him still depending on the Crowd:
That Kingly power, thus ebbing out, might be
Drawn to the dregs of a Democracy.°
Him he attempts, with studied Arts to please,
And sheds his Venome, in such words as these.

    Auspicious Prince! at whose Nativity   230
Some Royal Planet rul'd the Southern sky;
Thy longing Countries Darling and Desire;
Their cloudy Pillar, and their guardian Fire:
Their second *Moses*, whose extended Wand
Divides the Seas, and shews the promis'd Land:
Whose dawning Day, in every distant age,
Has exercis'd the Sacred Prophets rage:
The Peoples Prayer, the glad Deviners Theam,
The Young-mens Vision, and the Old mens Dream°!
Thee, *Saviour*, Thee, the Nations Vows confess;   240
And, never satisfi'd with seeing, bless:

Swift, unbespoken° Pomps, thy steps proclaim,
And stammerring Babes are taught to lisp thy Name.
How long wilt thou the general Joy detain;
Starve, and defraud the People of thy Reign?
Content ingloriously to pass thy days
Like one of Vertues Fools that feeds on Praise;
Till thy fresh Glories, which now shine so bright,
Grow Stale and Tarnish with our daily sight.
Believe me, Royal Youth, thy Fruit must be,   250
Or° gather'd Ripe, or rot upon the Tree.
Heav'n, has to all allotted, soon or late,
Some lucky Revolution of their Fate:
Whose Motions, if we watch and guide with Skill,
(For humane Good depends on humane Will,)
Our Fortune rolls, as from a smooth Descent,
And, from the first Impression, takes the Bent:
But, if unseiz'd, she glides away like wind;
And leaves repenting Folly far behind.
Now, now she meets you, with a glorious prize,   260
And spreads her Locks before her as she flies.
Had thus Old *David*, from whose Loyns you spring,
Not dar'd, when Fortune call'd him, to be King,
At *Gath*° an Exile he might still remain,
And heavens Anointing Oyle had been in vain.
Let his successfull Youth your hopes engage,
But shun th' example of Declining Age:
Behold him setting in his Western Skies,
The Shadows lengthning as the Vapours rise.   269
He is not now, as when on *Jordan*'s Sand°   ⎫
The Joyfull People throng'd to see him Land,   ⎬
Cov'ring the *Beach*, and blackning all the *Strand*: ⎭
But, like the Prince of Angels from his height,
Comes tumbling downward with diminish'd light;
Betray'd by one poor Plot to publick Scorn,
(Our only blessing since his Curst Return:)
Those heaps of People which one Sheaf did bind,
Blown off and scatter'd by a puff of Wind.
What strength can he to your Designs oppose,
Naked of Friends, and round beset with Foes?   280
If *Pharaoh*'s° doubtfull Succour he shoud use,
A Foreign Aid woud more Incense the *Jews:*
Proud *Egypt* woud dissembled Friendship bring;
Foment the War, but not support the King:
Nor woud the Royal Party e'r unite
With *Pharaoh*'s Arms, t' assist the *Jebusite;*

---

204. **manifest of:** evidencing. 211. **Jealosies:** suspicions.
213. **the King . . . Jebusite:** Charles's Roman Catholic
sympathies were well known; on his deathbed he is supposed
to have professed the faith. 217. **the Prime:** the beginning
of her cycle. 227. **Democracy:** popular government. 239.
The Young-mens . . . Dream: an allusion to Joel 2:28.

242. **unbespoken:** not prearranged. 251. **Or:** either. 264.
Gath: Brussels, where Charles spent the last years of his
exile. See I Sam. 27:1–4. 270. **Jordan's Sand:** Dover Beach.
See II Sam. 19:9–15. 281. **Pharaoh:** Louis XIV.

Or if they shoud, their Interest soon woud break,
And with such odious Aid make *David* weak.
All sorts of men by my successfull Arts,
Abhorring Kings, estrange their alter'd Hearts   290
From *David*'s Rule: And 'tis the general Cry,
Religion, Common-wealth, and Liberty.
If you as Champion of the publique Good,
Add to their Arms a Chief of Royal Blood;
What may not *Israel* hope, and what Applause
Might such a General gain by such a Cause?
Not barren Praise alone, that Gaudy Flower,
Fair only to the sight, but solid Power:
And Nobler is a limited Command,
Giv'n by the Love of all your Native Land,   300
Than a Successive Title,° Long, and Dark,
Drawn from the Mouldy Rolls of *Noah*'s Ark.
    What cannot Praise effect in Mighty Minds,
When Flattery Sooths, and when Ambition Blinds!
Desire of Power, on Earth a Vitious Weed,
Yet, sprung from High, is of Cælestial Seed:
In God 'tis Glory: And when men Aspire,
'Tis but a Spark too much of Heavenly Fire.
Th' Ambitious Youth, too Covetous of Fame,
Too full of Angells Metal° in his Frame,   310
Unwarily was led from Vertues ways;
Made Drunk with Honour, and Debauch'd with
        Praise.
Half loath, and half consenting to the Ill,
(For Loyal Blood within him strugled still)
He thus reply'd—And what Pretence have I
To take up Arms for Publick Liberty?
My Father Governs with unquestion'd Right;
The Faiths Defender, and Mankinds Delight:
Good, Gracious, Just, observant of the Laws;
And Heav'n by Wonders has Espous'd his Cause.   320
Whom has he Wrong'd in all his Peaceful Reign?
Who sues for Justice to his Throne in Vain?
What Millions has he Pardon'd of his Foes,
Whom Just Revenge did to his Wrath expose?
Mild, Easy, Humble, Studious of our Good;
Enclin'd to Mercy, and averse from Blood.
If Mildness Ill with Stubborn *Israel* Suite,
His Crime is God's beloved Attribute.
What could he gain, his People to Betray,
Or change his Right, for Arbitrary Sway?   330

Let Haughty *Pharaoh* Curse with such a Reign,
His Fruitfull *Nile*, and Yoak a Servile Train.
If *David*'s Rule *Jerusalem* Displease,
The *Dog-star*° heats their Brains to this Disease.
Why then shoud I, Encouraging the Bad,
Turn Rebell, and run Popularly Mad?
Were he a Tyrant who, by Lawless Might,
Opprest the *Jews*, and Rais'd the *Jebusite*,
Well might I Mourn; but Natures Holy Bands
Woud Curb my Spirits, and Restrain my Hands: 340
The People might assert their Liberty;
But what was Right in them, were Crime in me.
His Favour leaves me nothing to require;
Prevents my Wishes, and outruns Desire.
What more can I expect while *David* lives,
All but his Kingly Diadem he gives;
And that: But there he Paus'd; then Sighing, said,
Is Justly Destin'd for a Worthier Head.
For when my Father from his Toyls shall Rest,
And late Augment the Number of the Blest: 350
His Lawfull Issue shall the Throne ascend,
Or the *Collateral* Line where that shall end.
His Brother,° though Opprest with Vulgar Spight,
Yet Dauntless and Secure of Native Right,
Of every Royal Vertue stands possest;
Still Dear to all the Bravest, and the Best.
His Courage Foes, his Friends his Truth Proclaim;
His Loyalty the King, the World his Fame.
His Mercy even th' Offending Crowd will find,
For sure he comes of a Forgiving Kind.   360
Why shoud I then Repine at Heavens Decree;
Which gives me no Pretence to Royalty?
Yet oh that Fate Propitiously Enclind,
Had rais'd my Birth, or had debas'd my Mind;
To my large Soul, not all her Treasure lent,
And then Betray'd it to a mean Descent.
I find, I find my mounting Spirits Bold,
And *David*'s Part disdains my Mothers Mold.
Why am I Scanted by a Niggard Birth,
My Soul Disclaims the Kindred of her Earth: 370
And made for Empire, Whispers me within;
Desire of Greatness is a Godlike Sin.
    Him Staggering so when Hells dire Agent found,
While fainting Vertue scarce maintain'd her Ground,

---

301. a **Successive Title:** a title by succession. 310. **Angells Metal:** the spirit (mettle) of ambition; with a pun on both *metal* and *angel* (coin). The phrase here means motivated by venality as well as the love of fame.

334. **Dog-star:** Sirius, which accompanies the midsummer sun, was thought to be the producer of great heat and was thus associated with "midsummer madness" or the "dog days." 353. **His Brother:** James (1633–1701), Duke of York; a Catholic, and therefore under suspicion.

He pours fresh Forces in, and thus Replies:
  Th' Eternal God Supreamly Good and Wise,
Imparts not these Prodigious Gifts in vain;
What Wonders are Reserv'd to bless your Reign?
Against your will your Arguments have shown,
Such Vertue's only given to guide a Throne.   380
Not that your Father's Mildness I contemn;
But Manly Force becomes the Diadem.
'Tis true, he grants the People all they crave;
And more perhaps than Subjects ought to have:
For Lavish grants suppose a Monarch tame,
And more his Goodness than his Wit proclaim.
But when shoud People strive their Bonds to break,
If not when Kings are Negligent or Weak?
Let him give on till he can give no more,
The Thrifty Sanhedrin° shall keep him poor: 390
And every Sheckle which he can receive,
Shall cost a Limb of his Prerogative.
To ply him with new Plots, shall be my care,
Or plunge him deep in some Expensive War;
Which when his Treasure can no more Supply,
He must, with the Remains of Kingship, buy.
His faithful Friends, our Jealousies and Fears,
Call *Jebusites;* and *Pharaoh's* Pentioners:
Whom, when our Fury from his Aid has torn,
He shall be Naked left to publick Scorn.   400
The next Successor,° whom I fear and hate,
My Arts have made Obnoxious to the State;
Turn'd all his Vertues to his Overthrow,
And gain'd our Elders to pronounce a Foe.
His Right, for Sums of necessary Gold,
Shall first be Pawn'd, and afterwards be Sold:
Till time shall Ever-wanting *David* draw,
To pass your doubtfull Title into Law:
If not; the People have a Right Supreme
To make their Kings; for Kings are made for
    them.   410
All Empire is no more than Pow'r in Trust,
Which when resum'd, can be no longer Just.
Succession, for the general Good design'd,
In its own wrong a Nation cannot bind:
If altering that, the People can relieve,
Better one Suffer, than a Nation grieve.
The *Jews* well know their power: e'r *Saul* they Chose,
God was their King, and God they durst Depose.°

Urge now your Piety, your Filial Name,
A Father's Right, and fear of future Fame;   420
The publick Good, that Universal Call,
To which even Heav'n Submitted, answers all.
Nor let his Love Enchant your generous Mind;
'Tis Natures trick to Propagate her Kind.
Our fond Begetters, who woud never dye,
Love but themselves in their Posterity.
Or let his Kindness by th' Effects be try'd,
Or let him lay his vain Pretence aside.
God said he lov'd your Father; coud he bring
A better Proof, than to Anoint him King?   430
It surely shew'd he lov'd the Shepherd well,
Who gave so fair a Flock as *Israel.*
Woud *David* have you thought his Darling Son?
What means he then, to Alienate° the Crown?
The name of Godly he may blush to bear:
'Tis after God's own heart° to Cheat his Heir.
He to his Brother gives Supreme Command;
To you a Legacy of Barren Land:
Perhaps th' old Harp, on which he thrums his Layes:
Or some dull *Hebrew* Ballad in your Praise.   440
Then the next Heir, a Prince, Severe and Wise,
Already looks on you with Jealous Eyes;
Sees through the thin Disguises of your Arts,
And markes your Progress in the Peoples Hearts.
Though now his mighty Soul its Grief contains;
He meditates Revenge who least Complains.
And like a Lyon, Slumbring in the way,
Or Sleep-dissembling, while he waits his Prey,
His fearless Foes within his Distance draws;
Constrains his Roaring, and Contracts his Paws; 450
Till at the last, his time for Fury found,
He shoots with suddain Vengeance from the Ground:
The Prostrate Vulgar,° passes o'r, and Spares;
But with a Lordly Rage, his Hunters teares.
Your Case no tame Expedients will afford;
Resolve on Death, or Conquest by the Sword,
Which for no less a Stake than Life, you Draw;
And Self-defence is Natures Eldest Law.
Leave the warm People no Considering time;
For then Rebellion may be thought a Crime.   460
Prevail your self of what Occasion gives,
But try your Title while your Father lives:
And that your Arms may have a fair Pretence,
Proclaim, you take them in the King's Defence:

---

390. **Sanhedrin:** the supreme council of the Jews; here, Parliament. 401. **Successor:** James. 417–18. e'r . . . **Depose:** Saul, the first king of Israel, replaced a government by judges; Cromwell, the Lord Protector, replaced the Commonwealth.

434. **Alienate:** convey the property title to another. 436. **after . . . heart:** David was "a man after [God's] own heart" (I Sam. 13:14). 453. **Vulgar:** common people.

Whose Sacred Life each minute woud Expose,
To Plots, from seeming Friends, and secret Foes.
And who can sound the depth of *David*'s Soul?
Perhaps his fear, his kindness may Controul.
He fears his Brother, though he loves his Son,
For plighted Vows too late to be undone. 470
If so, by Force he wishes to be gain'd,
Like womens Leachery, to seem Constrain'd:
Doubt not, but when he most affects the Frown,
Commit a pleasing Rape upon the Crown.
Secure his Person to secure your Cause;
They who possess the Prince, possess the Laws.

He said, And this Advice above the rest,
With *Absalom*'s Mild nature suited best;
Unblam'd of Life (Ambition set aside,)
Not stain'd with Cruelty, nor puft with Pride; 480
How happy had he been, if Destiny
Had higher plac'd his Birth, or not so high!
His Kingly Vertues might have claim'd a Throne,
And blest all other Countries but his own:
But charming Greatness, since so few refuse;
'Tis Juster to Lament him, than Accuse.
Strong were his hopes a Rival to remove,
With blandishments to gain the publick Love;
To Head the Faction while their Zeal was hot,
And Popularly prosecute the Plot. 490
To farther this, *Achitophel* Unites
The Malecontents of all the *Israelites;*
Whose differing Parties he could wisely Joyn,
For several Ends, to serve the same Design.
The Best, and of the Princes some were such,
Who thought the power of Monarchy too much:
Mistaken Men, and Patriots in their Hearts;
Not Wicked, but Seduc'd by Impious Arts.
By these the Springs of Property were bent,
And wound so high, they Crack'd the
    Government. 500
The next for Interest sought t' embroil the State,
To sell their Duty at a dearer rate;
And make their *Jewish* Markets of the Throne,
Pretending publick Good, to serve their own.
Others thought Kings an useless heavy Load,
Who Cost too much, and did too little Good.
These were for laying Honest *David* by,
On Principles of pure good Husbandry.
With them Joyn'd all th' Haranguers of the
    Throng,
That thought to get Preferment by the Tongue. 510
Who follow next, a double Danger bring,
Not only hating *David*, but the King,

The *Solymæan* Rout;° well Verst of old,
In Godly Faction, and in Treason bold;
Cowring and Quaking at a Conqueror's Sword,
But Lofty to a Lawfull Prince Restor'd;
Saw with Disdain an *Ethnick*° Plot begun,
And Scorn'd by *Jebusites* to be Out-done.
Hot *Levites*° Headed these; who pul'd before
From th' *Ark*, which in the Judges days they bore, 520
Resum'd their Cant, and with a Zealous Cry,
Pursu'd their old belov'd Theocracy.
Where Sanhedrin and Priest inslav'd the Nation,
And justifi'd their Spoils by Inspiration;
For who so fit for Reign as *Aaron*'s Race,°
If once Dominion they could found in Grace?
These led the Pack; tho not of surest scent,
Yet deepest mouth'd against the Government.
A numerous Host of dreaming Saints° succeed;
Of the true old Enthusiastick° breed: 530
'Gainst Form and Order they their Power employ;
Nothing to Build and all things to Destroy.
But far more numerous was the herd of such,
Who think too little, and who talk too much.
These, out of meer instinct, they knew not why,
Ador'd their fathers God, and Property:
And, by the same blind benefit of Fate,
The Devil and the Jebusite did hate:
Born to be sav'd, even in their own despight;
Because they could not help believing right. 540
Such were the tools; but a whole Hydra more
Remains, of sprouting heads too long, to score.
Some of their Chiefs were Princes of the Land:
In the first Rank of these did *Zimri*° stand:
A man so various, that he seem'd to be
Not one, but all Mankinds Epitome.

---

513. **Solymæan Rout:** London rabble. (Solyma stands
for Jerusalem.) 517. **Ethnick:** literally, of the Gentiles; here,
the Jebusites or Roman Catholics. 519. **Hot Levites:** the
Presbyterian clergy, which under the Commonwealth ("in
the Judges days") enjoyed the sanction of the state, then
lost their benefices ("pul'd before / From th' Ark")
under the reestablishment of the Anglican Church by the
Act of Conformity in 1662. 525. **Aaron's Race:** the
priesthood. See I Chron. 6:49. 529. **dreaming Saints:** the
Elect. 530. **Enthusiastick:** fanatic; literally, possessed by a
god. 544. **Zimri:** George Villiers (1628–87), Second Duke of
Buckingham, was a member of the Cabal ministry but was
impeached in 1674 and joined the Opposition. He was one of
the principal authors of *The Rehearsal* (performed in 1671),
which ridicules the heroic play and Dryden, portraying him
as Mr. Bayes. Buckingham is the lecherous murderer, Zimri,
of Num. 25:6–15 and the conspiratorial murderer, Zimri, of
I Kings 16:8–20 and II Kings 9:31.

Stiff in Opinions, always in the wrong;
Was every thing by starts, and nothing long:
But, in the course of one revolving Moon,
Was Chymist, Fidler, States-Man, and Buffoon: 550
Then all for Women, Painting, Rhiming, Drinking;
Besides ten thousand freaks that dy'd in thinking.
Blest Madman, who coud every hour employ,
With something New to wish, or to enjoy!
Rayling° and praising were his usual Theams;
And both (to shew his Judgment) in Extreams:
So over Violent, or over Civil,
That every man, with him, was God or Devil.
In squandring Wealth was his peculiar Art:
Nothing went unrewarded, but Desert.   560
Begger'd by Fools, whom still he found° too late:
He had his Jest, and they had his Estate.
He laught himself from Court, then sought Relief
By forming Parties, but coud ne're be Chief:
For, spight of him, the weight of Business fell
On *Absalom* and wise *Achitophel*:
Thus, wicked but in will, of means bereft,
He left not Faction, but of that was left.
    Titles and Names 'twere tedious to Reherse
Of Lords, below the Dignity of Verse.   570
Wits warriors Common-wealthsmen, were the best:
Kind Husbands and meer Nobles all the rest.
And, therefore in the name of Dulness, be
The well hung *Balaam*° and cold *Caleb*° free.
And Canting *Nadab*° let Oblivion damn,
Who made new porridge for the Paschal Lamb.
Let Friendships holy band some Names assure:
Some their own Worth, and some let Scorn secure.
Nor shall the Rascall Rabble here have Place,
Whom Kings no Titles gave, and God no Grace: 580
Not Bull-fac'd *Jonas*,° who could Statutes draw
To mean Rebellion, and make Treason Law.

555. **Rayling:** abusing. 561. **found:** found out. **574. The
well . . . Balaam:** probably Theophilus Hastings, Seventh
Earl of Huntingdon, who returned to the King's party in
1681 (the year *Absalom and Achitophel* appeared). See Num.
22—24. "Well hung" could mean verbally fluent or sexually
potent. **Caleb:** probably Arthur Capel, Earl of Essex. See
Num. 13—14. **575. Nadab:** William, Lord Howard of
Escrick, a dissenting preacher, who when confined in the
Tower was said to have taken the sacrament according to the
Book of Common Prayer (called porridge by Dissenters),
using a hot ale known as lamb's wool instead of wine. See
Lev. 10:1-2. **581. Jonas:** Sir William Jones, Attorney
General and prosecutor in the Popish Plot. He resigned in
1679 to join the Opposition and help write the exclusion
bill.

But he, tho bad, is follow'd by a worse,
The wretch, who Heavens Annointed dar'd to Curse.
Shimei,° whose Youth did early Promise bring
Of Zeal to God, and Hatred to his King;
Did wisely from Expensive Sins refrain,
And never broke the Sabbath, but for Gain:
Nor ever was he known an Oath to vent,
Or Curse unless against the Government.   590
Thus, heaping Wealth, by the most ready way
Among the Jews, which was to Cheat and Pray;
The City, to reward his pious Hate
Against his Master, chose him Magistrate:
His Hand a Vare° of Justice did uphold;
His Neck was loaded with a Chain of Gold.
During his Office, Treason was no Crime.
The Sons of *Belial*° had a glorious Time:
For *Shimei*, though not prodigal of pelf,
Yet lov'd his wicked Neighbour as himself: 600
When two or three were gather'd to declaim }
Against the Monarch of *Jerusalem*, }
Shimei was always in the midst of them. }
And, if they Curst the King when he was by,
Woud rather Curse, than break good Company.
If any durst his Factious Friends accuse,
He pact a Jury of dissenting Jews:
Whose fellow-feeling, in the godly Cause,
Would free the suffring Saint from Humane Laws.
For Laws are only made to Punish those,   610
Who serve the King, and to protect his Foes.
If any leisure time he had from Power,
(Because 'tis Sin to misimploy an hour;)
His business was, by Writing,° to Persuade,
That Kings were Useless, and a Clog to Trade:
And, that his noble Stile he might refine,
No *Rechabite* more shund the fumes of Wine.°
Chast were his Cellars, and his Shrieval Board°
The Grossness of a City Feast abhor'd:
His Cooks, with long disuse, their Trade forgot;   620
Cool was his Kitchen, tho his Brains were hot.

585. **Shimei:** Slingsby Bethel, inveterate republican and one
of the two Whig sheriffs of London, who packed juries to
thwart the prosecutions of the court party, notably Shaftesbury's. See II Sam. 16:5-14. 595. **Vare:** staff. 598. **Sons of
Belial:** wicked men in general, but rebels in particular. See
Deut. 13:13 and II Sam. 20:1-2. It has been suggested that
Dryden also exploits the familiar pun on Balliol College,
which was hospitable to the Whigs during the Oxford
Parliament in 1681. 614. **by Writing:** *The Interest of Princes
and States* (1680). **617. No . . . Wine:** The Jewish sect of
Rechabites vowed to abstain from wine drinking. See Jer.
35:14. 618. **Shrieval Board:** sheriff's dinner table.

Such frugal Vertue Malice may accuse,
But sure 'twas necessary to the Jews:
For Towns once burnt, such Magistrates require
As dare not tempt Gods Providence by fire.°
With Spiritual food he fed his Servants well,
But free from flesh, that made the Jews Rebel:
And *Moses*'s Laws he held in more account,
For forty days of Fasting in the Mount.

    To speak the rest, who better are forgot,   630
Would tyre a well breath'd Witness of the Plot:
Yet, *Corah*,° thou shalt from Oblivion pass;
Erect thy self thou Monumental Brass:
High as the Serpent of thy mettall made,°
While Nations stand secure beneath thy shade.
What tho his Birth were base, yet Comets rise
From Earthy Vapours ere they shine in Skies.
Prodigious Actions may as well be done
By Weavers issue, as by Princes Son.
This Arch-Attestor for the Publick Good,   640
By that one Deed Enobles all his Bloud.
Who ever ask'd the Witnesses high race,
Whose Oath with Martyrdom did *Stephen*° grace?
Ours was a *Levite*, and as times went then,
His Tribe were Godalmightys Gentlemen.
Sunk were his Eyes, his Voyce was harsh and loud,
Sure signs he neither Cholerick was, nor Proud:
His long Chin prov'd his Wit; his Saintlike Grace
A Church Vermilion, and a *Moses*'s Face;°
His Memory, miraculously great,   650
Could Plots, exceeding mans belief, repeat;
Which, therefore cannot be accounted Lies,
For humane Wit could never such devise.
Some future Truths are mingled in his Book;
But, where the witness faild, the Prophet Spoke:
Some things like Visionary flights appear;
The Spirit caught him up, the Lord knows where:
And gave him his *Rabinical* degree
Unknown to Foreign University.°
His Judgment yet his Memory did excel;   660

Which peic'd his wondrous Evidence so well:
And suited to the temper of the times;
Then groaning under Jebusitick Crimes.
Let *Israels* foes suspect his heav'nly call,
And rashly judge his Writ Apocryphal;
Our Laws for such affronts have forfeits made:
He takes his life, who takes away his trade.°
Were I my self in witness *Corahs* place,
The wretch who did me such a dire disgrace,
Should whet my memory, though once forgot,   670
To make him an Appendix of my Plot.
His Zeal to heav'n, made him his Prince despise,
And load his person with indignities:
But Zeal peculiar priviledg affords;
Indulging latitude to deeds and words.
And *Corah* might for *Agag*'s murther call,
In terms as course as *Samuel* us'd to *Saul*.°
What others in his Evidence did Joyn,
(The best that could be had for love or coyn,)
In *Corah*'s own predicament will fall: 680
For *witness* is a Common Name to all.

    Surrounded thus with Freinds of every sort,
Deluded *Absalom*, forsakes the Court:
Impatient of high hopes, urg'd with renown,
And Fir'd with near possession of a Crown,
Th' admiring Croud are dazled with surprize,
And on his goodly person feed their eyes:
His joy conceal'd, he sets himself to show;
On each side bowing popularly low:
His looks, his gestures, and his words he frames,   690
And with familiar ease repeats their Names.
Thus, form'd by Nature, furnish'd out with Arts,
He glides unfelt into their secret hearts:
Then with a kind compassionating look,
And sighs, bespeaking pity ere he spoak:
Few words he said; but easy those and fit:
More slow than Hybla drops,° and far more sweet.

    I mourn, my Countrymen, your lost Estate;
Tho far unable to prevent your fate:
Behold a Banisht man,° for your dear cause   700
Expos'd a prey to Arbitrary laws!

624–25. For . . . fire: an ironic suggestion that generous cooking ("fire") might provoke the jealous gods to make London the main dish (an allusion to the Great Fire of 1665). **632. Corah:** Titus Oates, the chief "Witness of the Plot." See Num. 16. **634. the Serpent . . . made:** Moses made a brass serpent to save the Jews in the wilderness. See Num. 21:6–9. **643. Stephen:** the first Christian martyr. See Acts 6:9–15. **649. a Moses's Face:** the ruddy complexion of a well-fed clergyman; the shining face of a Moses descended from Mount Sinai. Dryden ironically equates the two. **659. University:** The University of Salamanca denied Oates's claim to have taken a Doctor of Divinity degree there.

666–67. Our . . . trade: Dryden advances the ironic argument that in exposing Oates as a false witness, you take away his trade, which is his life, and you are therefore guilty of a capital crime. **676–77. And . . . Saul:** See I Sam. 15. Agag is probably Lord Stafford, accused by Oates and condemned to death in December, 1680. **697. Hybla drops:** honey (from Hybla, in Sicily). **700. a Banisht man:** Monmouth was banished in September, 1679, but returned uninvited from Holland in November.

Yet oh! that I alone cou'd be undone,
Cut off from Empire, and no more a Son!
Now all your Liberties a spoil are made; ⎫
Ægypt and Tyrus° intercept your Trade,   ⎬
And Jebusites your Sacred Rites invade.   ⎭
My Father, whom with reverence yet I name,
Charm'd into Ease, is careless of his Fame:
And, brib'd with petty summs of Forreign Gold,
Is grown in Bathsheba's° Embraces old: 710
Exalts his Enemies, his Freinds destroys:
And all his pow'r against himself employs.
He gives, and let him give my right away:
But why should he his own, and yours betray?
He only, he can make the Nation bleed,
And he alone from my revenge is freed.
Take then my tears (with that he wip'd his Eyes)
'Tis all the Aid my present power supplies:
No Court Informer can these Arms accuse,
These Arms may Sons against their Fathers use,   720
And, tis my wish, the next Successors Reign
May make no other Israelite complain.

    Youth, Beauty, Graceful Action, seldom fail:
But Common Interest always will prevail:
And pity never Ceases to be shown
To him, who makes the peoples wrongs his own.
The Croud, (that still believes their Kings oppress)
With lifted hands their young Messiah bless:
Who now begins his Progress° to ordain;
With Chariots, Horsemen, and a numerous train: 730
From East to West his Glories he displaies:
And, like the Sun, the promis'd land survays.
Fame runs before him, as the morning Star;
And shouts of Joy salute him from afar:
Each house receives him as a Guardian God;
And Consecrates the Place of his aboad:
But hospitable treats did most Commend
Wise Issachar,° his wealthy western friend.
This moving Court, that caught the peoples Eyes,
And seem'd but Pomp, did other ends disguise: 740
Achitophel had form'd it, with intent
To sound the depths, and fathom where it went:
The Peoples hearts, distinguish Friends from Foes;
And try their strength, before they came to blows:

Yet all was colour'd with a smooth pretence
Of specious love, and duty to their Prince.
Religion, and Redress of Grievances,
Two names, that always cheat and always please,
Are often urg'd; and good King David's life
Indanger'd by a Brother and a Wife.°   750
Thus, in a Pageant Show, a Plot is made;
And Peace it self is War in Masquerade.
Oh foolish Israel! never warn'd by ill,
Still the same baite, and circumvented still!
Did ever men forsake their present ease,
In midst of health Imagine a desease;
Take pains Contingent mischiefs to foresee,
Make Heirs for Monarks, and for God decree?
What shall we think! can People give away
Both for themselves and Sons, their Native sway? 760
Then they are left Defensless, to the Sword
Of each unbounded Arbitrary Lord:
And Laws are vain, by which we Right enjoy,
If Kings unquestiond can those laws destroy.
Yet, if the Crowd be Judge of fit and Just,
And Kings are onely Officers in trust,
Then this resuming° Cov'nant was declar'd
When Kings were made, or is for ever bard:
If those who gave the Scepter, coud not tye
By their own deed their own Posterity,   770
How then coud Adam bind his future Race?
How coud his forfeit on mankind take place?
Or how coud heavenly Justice damn us all,
Who nere consented to our Fathers fall?
Then Kings are slaves to those whom they Command,
And Tenants to their Peoples pleasure stand.
Add, that the Pow'r for Property allowd,°
Is mischeivously seated in the Crowd:
For who can be secure of private Right,
If Sovereign sway may be dissolv'd by might?   780
Nor is the Peoples Judgment always true:
The most may err as grosly as the few.
And faultless Kings run down, by Common Cry,
For Vice, Oppression, and for Tyranny.
What Standard is there in a fickle rout,°
Which, flowing to the mark, runs faster out°?
Nor only Crowds, but Sanhedrins may be
Infected with this publick Lunacy:

705. Ægypt and Tyrus: France and Holland. 710. Bath-sheba: the Duchess of Portsmouth, Louise-Renée de Kéroualle. 729. his Progress: Monmouth's journey through England, begun on July 26, 1680, to win popular support. 738. Wise Issachar: Thomas Thynne of Wiltshire. Wise is sarcastic. See Gen. 49:14-15.

750. a Brother . . . Wife: Both the Duke of York and Queen Catherine were accused of treason by Oates and his confederates. 767. resuming: revoked. 777. that . . . allowd: that the recognized possession of power. 785. rout: mob. 786. Which . . . out: which flows and ebbs like the tides.

And Share the madness of Rebellious times,
To Murther Monarchs for Imagin'd crimes.   790
If they may Give and Take when e'r they please,
Not Kings alone, (the Godheads Images,)
But Government it self at length must fall
To Natures state; where all have Right to all.
Yet, grant our Lords the People Kings can make,
What Prudent men a setled Throne woud shake?
For whatsoe'r their Sufferings were before,
That Change they Covet makes them suffer more.
All other Errors but disturb a State;
But Innovation is the Blow of Fate.   800
If ancient Fabricks nod, and threat to fall,
To Patch the Flaws, and Buttress up the Wall,
Thus far 'tis Duty; but here fix the Mark:
For all beyond it is to touch our Ark.°
To change Foundations, cast the Frame anew,
Is work for Rebels who base Ends pursue:
At once Divine and Humane Laws controul;
And mend the Parts by ruine of the Whole.
The Tampering World is subject to this Curse,
To Physick their Disease into a worse.   810
　　Now what Relief can Righteous *David* bring?
How Fatall 'tis to be too good a King!
Friends he has few, so high the Madness grows;
Who dare be such, must be the Peoples Foes:
Yet some there were, ev'n in the worst of days;
Some let me name, and Naming is to praise.
　　In this short File *Barzillai*° first appears;
Barzillai crown'd with Honour and with Years:
Long since, the rising Rebells he withstood
In Regions Waste, beyond the *Jordans* Flood: 820
Unfortunately Brave to buoy the State;
But sinking underneath his Masters Fate:
In Exile with his Godlike Prince he Mourn'd;
For him he Suffer'd, and with him Return'd.
The Court he practis'd, not the Courtier's art:
Large was his Wealth, but larger was his Heart:
Which, well the Noblest Objects knew to choose,
The Fighting Warriour, and Recording Muse.
His Bed coud once a Fruitfull Issue boast:
Now more than half a Father's Name is lost.°   830
His Eldest Hope,° with every Grace adorn'd,

By me (so Heav'n will have it) always Mourn'd,
And always honour'd, snatcht in Manhoods prime
By' unequal Fates, and Providences crime:
Yet not before the Goal of Honour won,
All parts fulfill'd of Subject and of Son;
Swift was the Race, but short the Time to run.
Oh Narrow Circle, but of Pow'r Divine,
Scanted in Space, but perfect in thy Line!
By Sea, by Land, thy Matchless Worth was
　　known;   840
Arms thy Delight, and War was all thy Own:
Thy force, Infus'd, the fainting *Tyrians* prop'd:
And Haughty *Pharaoh* found his Fortune stop'd.
Oh Ancient Honour, Oh Unconquer'd Hand,
Whom Foes unpunish'd never coud withstand!
But *Israel* was unworthy of thy Name:
Short is the date of all Immoderate Fame.
It looks as Heaven our Ruine had design'd,
And durst not trust thy Fortune and thy Mind.
Now, free from Earth, thy disencumbred Soul   850
Mounts up, and leaves behind the Clouds and Starry
　　Pole:
From thence thy kindred legions mayst thou bring
To aid the guardian Angel of thy King.
Here stop my Muse, here cease thy painfull flight;
No Pinions can pursue Immortal height:
Tell good *Barzillai* thou canst sing no more,
And tell thy Soul she should have fled before;
Or fled she with his life, and left this Verse
To hang on her departed Patron's Herse°?
Now take thy steepy flight from heaven, and see   860
If thou canst find on earth another *He*,
Another he would be too hard to find,
See then whom thou canst see not far behind.
Zadock the Priest,° whom, shunning Power and Place,
His lowly mind advanc'd to *David*'s Grace:
With him the *Sagan* of *Jerusalem*,°
Of hospitable Soul and noble Stem;
Him of the Western dome,° whose weighty sense
Flows in fit words and heavenly eloquence.
The Prophets Sons° by such example led,   870
To Learning and to Loyalty were bred:

---

804. **touch our Ark:** commit sacrilege. 817. **Barzillai:**
James Butler, Duke of Ormonde and Lord Lieutenant of
Ireland (see l. 820). See II Sam. 19:31–39. 830. **Now . . .
lost:** Six of his ten children were now dead. 831. **His . . .
Hope:** Thomas, Earl of Ossory, who died after a distinguished military career the year before Dryden's poem came
out. Thus the elegy.

859. **Herse:** (hearse) the structure over the bier which
carried ornaments and epitaphs written by friends. 864.
Zadock the Priest: William Sancroft, Archbishop of
Canterbury. See II Sam. 8:17. 866. **Sagan of Jerusalem:**
second-ranking priest; here, Henry Compton, Bishop of
London. 868. **Him . . . dome:** John Dolben, Dean of
Westminster; soon to become Archbishop of York. 870. **The
Prophets Sons:** the boys of Westminster School.

For *Colleges* on bounteous Kings depend,
And never Rebell was to Arts a friend.
To these succeed the Pillars of the Laws,
Who best cou'd plead and best can judge a Cause.
Next them a train of Loyal Peers ascend:
Sharp judging *Adriel*° the Muses friend,
Himself a Muse—In Sanhedrins debate
True to his Prince; but not a Slave of State.
Whom *David*'s love with Honours did adorn,   880
That from his disobedient Son were torn.°
Jotham° of piercing wit and pregnant thought,
Indew'd by nature, and by learning taught
To move Assemblies, who but onely try'd
The worse awhile, then chose the better side;
Nor chose alone, but turn'd the balance too;
So much the weight of one brave man can doe.
Hushai° the friend of *David* in distress,
In publick storms of manly stedfastness;
By foreign treaties he inform'd his Youth;   890
And join'd experience to his native truth.
His frugal care supply'd the wanting Throne,
Frugal for that, but bounteous of his own:
'Tis easy conduct when Exchequers flow,
But hard the task to manage well the low:
For Soveraign power is too deprest or high,
When Kings are forc'd to sell, or Crowds to buy.
Indulge one labour more my weary Muse,
For *Amiel*,° who can *Amiel*'s praise refuse?
Of ancient race by birth, but nobler yet   900
In his own worth, and without Title great:
The Sanhedrin long time as chief he rul'd,
Their Reason guided and their Passion coold;
So dexterous was he in the Crown's defence,
So form'd to speak a Loyal Nation's Sense,
That as their band was *Israel*'s Tribes in small,

So fit was he to represent them all.
Now rasher Charioteers the Seat ascend,
Whose loose Carriers his steady Skill commend:
They like th' unequal Ruler of the Day,°   910
Misguide the Seasons and mistake the Way;
While he withdrawn at their mad Labour smiles,
And safe enjoys the Sabbath of his Toyls.
    These were the chief, a small but faithful Band
Of Worthies, in the Breach who dar'd to stand,
And tempt th' united Fury of the Land.
With grief they view'd such powerful Engines bent,
To batter down the lawful Government.
A numerous Faction with pretended frights,
In Sanhedrins to plume° the Regal Rights.   920
The true Successour from the Court remov'd:
The Plot, by hireling Witnesses improv'd.
These Ills they saw, and as their Duty bound,
They shew'd the King the danger of the Wound:
That no Concessions from the Throne woud please,
But Lenitives fomented the Disease:
That *Absalom*, ambitious of the Crown,
Was made the Lure to draw the People down:
That false *Achitophel*'s pernitious Hate,
Had turn'd the Plot to Ruine Church and State: 930
The Councill violent, the Rabble worse
That *Shimei* taught *Jerusalem* to Curse.
    With all these loads of Injuries opprest,
And long revolving, in his carefull Breast,
Th' event of things; at last his patience tir'd,
Thus from his Royal Throne by Heav'n inspir'd,
The God-like *David* spoke:° with awfull fear
His Train their Maker in their Master hear.
    Thus long have I, by native mercy sway'd,
My wrongs dissembl'd, my revenge delay'd: 940
So willing to forgive th' Offending Age,
So much the Father did the King asswage.
But now so far my Clemency they slight,
Th' Offenders question my Forgiving Right.°
That one was made for many, they contend:
But 'tis to Rule, for that's a Monarch's End.

---

877. Adriel: John Sheffield (1648–1721), Third Earl of Mulgrave, author of *An Essay on Satire* (1680) and *An Essay on Poetry* (1682). He was Dryden's friend and patron. **880–81. Whom . . . torn:** In 1679 the offices of Governor of Hull and Lord Lieutenant of Yorkshire were transferred from Monmouth to Mulgrave. **882. Jotham:** George Savile (1633–95), Marquis (1682) of Halifax. See Judg. 9:1–21. Halifax had been associated with Shaftesbury and the Opposition from 1674 to 1679, but he had always opposed the exclusionist policy and succeeded in turning the balance against it in the House of Lords in 1680. **888. Hushai:** Laurence Hyde, Earl of Rochester (1682), First Lord of the Treasury from 1679 to 1685. He was another of Dryden's patrons. See II Sam. 16:16–19 and I Chron. 27:33. **899. Amiel:** Edward Seymour, Speaker of the House of Commons from 1673 to 1678.

910. Ruler . . . Day: Phaethon. **920. plume:** pluck. **937. The God-like . . . spoke:** David's speech is derived in part from Charles's speech before the Oxford Parliament on March 21, 1681, and more especially from a pamphlet published anonymously in June and attributed to Dryden himself, entitled *His Majesties Declaration Defended in a Letter to a Friend.* **944. Th' Offenders . . . Right:** The Commons questioned the right of the King in pardoning Lord Danby in March, 1679, and commuting the penalty against Lord Stafford in December, 1680.

They call my tenderness of Blood, my Fear:
Though Manly tempers can the longest bear.
Yet, since they will divert my Native course,
'Tis time to shew I am not Good by Force.   950
Those heap'd Affronts that haughty Subjects bring,
Are burthens for a Camel, not a King:
Kings are the publick Pillars of the State,
Born to sustain and prop the Nations weight:
If my Young *Samson* will pretend a Call
To shake the Column, let him share the Fall:
But oh that yet he woud repent and live!
How easie 'tis for Parents to forgive!
With how few Tears a Pardon might be won
From Nature, pleading for a Darling Son!°   960
Poor pitied Youth, by my Paternal care,
Rais'd up to all the Height his Frame coud bear:
Had God ordain'd his fate for Empire born,
He woud have given his Soul another turn:
Gull'd with a Patriots name, whose Modern sense
Is one that would by Law supplant his Prince:
The Peoples Brave,° the Politicians Tool;
Never was Patriot yet, but was a Fool.
Whence comes it that Religion and the Laws
Should more be *Absalom*'s than *David*'s Cause?   970
His old Instructor, e're he lost his Place,°
Was never thought indu'd with so much Grace.
Good Heav'ns, how Faction can a Patriot Paint!
My Rebel ever proves my Peoples Saint:
Would *They* impose an Heir upon the Throne?
Let Sanhedrins be taught to give their Own.°
A King's at least a part of Government,
And mine as requisite as their Consent:
Without my Leave a future King to choose,
Infers a Right the Present to Depose: 980
True, they Petition me t' approve their Choise,
But *Esau*'s Hands suite ill with *Jacob*'s Voice.°
My Pious Subjects for my Safety pray,
Which to Secure they take my Power away.
From Plots and Treasons Heaven preserve my years,
But Save me most from my Petitioners.
Unsatiate as the barren Womb or Grave;
God cannot Grant so much as they can Crave.
What then is left but with a Jealous Eye
To guard the Small remains of Royalty?   990

The Law shall still direct my peacefull Sway,
And the same Law teach Rebels to Obey:
Votes shall no more Establish'd Pow'r controul,
Such Votes as make a Part exceed the Whole:
No groundless Clamours shall my Friends remove,
Nor Crowds have power to Punish e're they Prove:
For Gods, and Godlike Kings their Care express,
Still to Defend their Servants in distress.   998
Oh that my Power to Saving were confin'd: ⎫
Why am I forc'd, like Heaven, against my mind, ⎬
To make Examples of another Kind? ⎭
Must I at length the Sword of Justice draw?
Oh curst Effects of necessary Law!
How ill my Fear they by my Mercy scan,°
Beware the Fury of a Patient Man.
Law they require, let Law then shew her Face;
They coud not be content to look on Grace,
Her hinder parts, but with a daring Eye
To tempt the terror of her Front, and Dye.°
By their own arts 'tis Righteously decreed,   1010
Those dire Artificers of Death shall bleed.
Against themselves their Witnesses will Swear,°
Till Viper-like their Mother Plot they tear:
And suck for Nutriment that bloody gore
Which was their Principle of Life before.
Their *Belial* with their *Belzebub* will fight;
Thus on my Foes, my Foes shall do me Right:
Nor doubt th' event:° for Factious crowds engage
In their first Onset, all their Brutal Rage;
Then, let 'em take an unresisted Course,   1020
Retire and Traverse, and Delude their Force:
But when they stand all Breathless, urge the fight,
And rise upon 'em with redoubled might:
For Lawfull Pow'r is still Superiour found,
When long driven back, at length it stands the ground.
    He said. Th' Almighty, nodding, gave Consent;
And Peals of Thunder shook the Firmament.
Henceforth a Series of new time began,
The mighty Years in long Procession ran:
Once more the God-like *David* was Restor'd,   1030
And willing Nations knew their Lawfull Lord.

957–60. But . . . Son: added to th e third edition (1681). **967. Brave:** bully. **971. His . . . Place:** Shaftesbury was dismissed as Lord President of the Council in October, 1679. **976. their Own:** what is theirs to give. **982. But . . . Voice:** See Gen. 27:22.

1004. scan: judge. **1006–09. Law they . . . Dye:** Law is likened to the face of God, which Moses was forbidden to see on penalty of death (see Ex. 33:20–23); mercy, then, is the "hinder parts," or the permitted view. **1012. Against . . . Swear:** This was actually engineered by the court party in 1681. **1018. event:** outcome.

MAC FLECKNOE

The immediate occasion for Dryden's lampoon on the dramatist Thomas Shadwell remains a matter for conjecture. From 1668 the two were engaged in critical controversy, but with no sign of personal animus. In the Preface to *The Sullen Lovers* (1668) Shadwell defended Ben Jonson against what he considered Dryden's insufficient appreciation in *An Essay of Dramatic Poesy* (1668) and incidentally made some jibes at the kind of heroic play Dryden was writing; Dryden made his counterattack in the Preface to *An Evening's Love* (1671). Perhaps Shadwell's praise of *The Rehearsal* (1671) in his Dedication to his *History of Timon of Athens* (1678) was interpreted by Dryden as a descent from mere literary controversy to personal insult. In any case, Dryden's lampoon was written in 1678—doubtless for private circulation. It was not published until 1682 and then in an unauthorized edition (with the following subtitle: "A Satyr upon the *True-Blew-Protestant* Poet, T. S. By the Author of *Absalom & Achitophel*"). Ten years later Dryden acknowledged his authorship in his *Discourse Concerning the Original and Progress of Satire.*

The text is from *Miscellany Poems* (1684).

ALL humane things are subject to decay,
And, when Fate summons, Monarchs must obey:
This *Fleckno*° found, who, like *Augustus*,° young
Was call'd to Empire, and had govern'd long:
In Prose and Verse, was own'd, without dispute
Through all the Realms of *Non-sense*, absolute.
This aged Prince now flourishing in Peace,
And blest with issue of a large increase,
Worn out with business, did at length debate
To settle the succession of the State: 10
And pond'ring which of all his Sons was fit
To Reign, and wage immortal War with Wit;
Cry'd, 'tis resolv'd; for Nature pleads that He
Should onely rule, who most resembles me:

MAC FLECKNOE. **3. Fleckno:** Richard Flecknoe, an Irish Catholic priest, appears to have been chosen by Dryden to father Shadwell because of his wide reputation as a poetaster. No clear-cut personal grievance on Dryden's part has been brought to light. **Augustus:** Octavius, later Augustus, Caesar (63 B.C.–A.D. 14), the first Roman emperor.

Sh—— alone my perfect image bears,
Mature in dullness from his tender years.
Sh—— alone, of all my Sons, is he
Who stands confirm'd in full stupidity.
The rest to some faint meaning make pretence,
But *Sh*—— never deviates into sense.   20
Some Beams of Wit on other souls may fall,
Strike through and make a lucid intervall;
But *Sh*——'s genuine night admits no ray,
His rising Fogs prevail upon the Day:
Besides his goodly Fabrick° fills the eye,
And seems design'd for thoughtless Majesty:
Thoughtless as Monarch Oakes, that shade the plain,
And, spread in solemn state, supinely reign.
Heywood and *Shirley*° were but Types of thee,
Thou last great Prophet of Tautology: 30
Even I, a dunce of more renown than they,
Was sent before but to prepare thy way;
And coursly clad in *Norwich* Drugget° came
To teach the Nations in thy greater name.
My warbling Lute, the Lute I whilom° strung
When to King *John* of *Portugal*° I sung,
Was but the prelude to that glorious day,
When thou on silver *Thames* did'st cut thy way,
With well tim'd Oars before the Royal Barge,
Swell'd with the Pride of thy Celestial charge;   40
And big with Hymn, Commander of an Host,
The like was ne'er in *Epsom* blankets tost.°
Methinks I see the new *Arion*° Sail,
The Lute still trembling underneath thy nail.
At thy well sharpned thumb from Shore to Shore
The Treble squeaks for fear, the Bases roar:
Echoes from *Pissing-Ally*,° *Sh*—— call,
And *Sh*—— they resound from *A*—— *Hall*.°
About thy boat the little Fishes throng,
As at the Morning Toast,° that Floats along.   50

25. Fabrick: body. The allusion is to Shadwell's corpulence. **29. Heywood and Shirley:** Thomas Heywood (*c.* 1570–1641) and James Shirley (1596–1666), Elizabethan dramatists neglected by Dryden's age. **33. Norwich Drugget:** coarse woolen. Shadwell was from Norfolk. Dryden here likens Flecknoe to John the Baptist as forerunner of Christ. **35. whilom:** formerly. **36. King . . . Portugal:** whom Flecknoe claimed as a patron. **42. in . . . tost:** which is what happens to Sir Samuel Hearty, the would-be wit of Shadwell's *The Virtuoso* (1676). **43. Arion:** a legendary Greek musician saved from drowning by music-loving dolphins. **47. Pissing-Ally:** There were two alleys so dubbed in Dryden's London: one in the City and one near the Thames. **48. A—— Hall:** The first edition gives the name "Aston," but the place has not been identified. **50. Toast:** waste.

Sometimes as Prince of thy Harmonious band
Thou weild'st thy Papers in thy threshing hand.
St. *Andre*'s feet° ne'er kept more equal time,
Not ev'n the feet of thy own *Psyche*'s rhime:
Though they in number as in sense excell;
So just, so like tautology they fell,
That, pale with envy, *Singleton*° forswore ⎫
The Lute and Sword which he in Triumph bore, ⎬
And vow'd he ne'er would act *Villerius*° more. ⎭
Here stopt the good old *Syre;* and wept for joy   60
In silent raptures of the hopefull boy.
All arguments, but most his Plays, perswade,
That for anointed dullness he was made.
    Close to the Walls which fair *Augusta*° bind,
(The fair *Augusta* much to fears° inclin'd)
An ancient fabrick, rais'd t' inform the sight,
There stood of yore, and *Barbican*° it hight:
A watch Tower once; but now, so Fate ordains,
Of all the Pile an empty name remains.
From its old Ruins Brothel-houses rise,   70
Scenes of lewd loves, and of polluted joys.
Where their vast Courts the Mother-Strumpets keep,
And, undisturb'd by Watch, in silence sleep.
Near these a Nursery° erects its head,
Where Queens are form'd, and future Hero's bred;
Where unfledg'd Actors learn to laugh and cry, ⎫
Where infant Punks° their tender Voices try, ⎬
And little *Maximins*° the Gods defy. ⎭
Great *Fletcher*° never treads in Buskins here,
Nor greater *Johnson*° dares in Socks appear.   80
But gentle *Simkin*° just reception finds
Amidst this Monument of vanisht minds:
Pure Clinches,° the suburbian Muse affords;
And *Panton*° waging harmless War with words.

Here *Fleckno*, as a place to Fame well known,
Ambitiously design'd his *Sh*——'s Throne.
For ancient *Decker*° propheci'd long since, ⎫
That in this Pile should Reign a mighty Prince, ⎬
Born for a scourge of Wit, and flayle of Sense: ⎭
To whom true dulness should some *Psyches* owe,   90
But Worlds of *Misers*° from his pen should flow;
Humorists and Hypocrites it should produce,
Whole *Raymond* families, and Tribes of *Bruce*.
    Now Empress *Fame* had publisht the renown,
Of *Sh*——'s Coronation through the Town.
Rows'd by report of Fame, the Nations meet,
From near *Bun-Hill*, and distant *Watling-street*.°
No *Persian* Carpets spread th' Imperial way,
But scatter'd Limbs of mangled Poets lay:
From dusty shops neglected Authors come,   100
Martyrs of Pies, and Reliques of the Bum.°
Much *Heywood*, *Shirly*, *Ogleby*° there lay,
But loads of *Sh*—— almost choakt the way.
Bilk't *Stationers*° for Yeomen stood prepar'd,
And *H*——° was Captain of the Guard.
The hoary Prince in Majesty appear'd,
High on a Throne of his own Labours rear'd.
At his right hand our young *Ascanius*° sat
Rome's other hope,° and pillar of the State.
His Brows thick fogs, instead of glories, grace,   110
And lambent dullness plaid arround his face.°
As *Hannibal* did to the Altars come,
Sworn by his *Syre* a mortal Foe to *Rome;*°
So *Sh*—— swore, nor should his Vow bee vain,
That he till Death true dullness would maintain;
And in his father's Right, and Realms defence,
Ne'er to have peace with Wit, nor truce with Sense.
The King himself the sacred Unction° made,

---

53. St. . . . feet: St. André was a French dancing master imported by the court. He was the choreographer for Shadwell's opera *Psyche* (1675). **57. Singleton:** John Singleton, a court musician. **59. Villerius:** a character in Sir William Davenant's opera *The Siege of Rhodes* (1656). **64. Augusta:** London. **65. fears:** aroused by the Popish Plot. **67. Barbican:** A barbican is the outer defense of a city. The Barbican of London stood in Aldersgate Street. **74. a Nursery:** a school for young actors; here, the one built by Lady Davenant in 1671. **77. Punks:** prostitutes. **78. little Maximins:** Maximin is the bombastic hero of Dryden's *Tyrannic Love* (1670). As the line indicates, Dryden was himself embarrassed by his creation. **79. Fletcher:** John Fletcher (1579–1625), noted for his tragedies ("Buskins"). **80. Johnson:** Ben Jonson (1573–1637), noted for his comedies ("Socks"). **81. Simkin:** simpleton, a theatrical character-type. **83. Clinches:** puns. **84. Panton:** apparently another farcical character like Simkin.

87. Decker: Thomas Dekker (*c.* 1572–*c.* 1632), the dramatist, ridiculed in Jonson's *The Poetaster* (1602). **91. Misers:** *The Miser* (1672), *The Humorists* (1671), and *The Hypocrite* (unpublished) were three plays by Shadwell. Raymond and Bruce are characters in *The Humorists* and *The Virtuoso* respectively. **97. From . . . Watling-street:** The difference between "near" and "distant" here is negligible—as is the sphere of Shadwell's influence. **101. Martyrs . . . Bum:** Their books remaindered to bakeries and privies. **102. Ogleby:** John Ogilby (1600–76), Scottish translator and printer. **104. Bilk't Stationers:** cheated booksellers. **105. H——:** Henry Herringman, publisher of both Shadwell and Dryden until 1678. **108. Ascanius:** the son of Aeneas. **109. Rome's . . . hope:** See *Aeneid*, XII. 168. **110–11. His . . . face:** See *Aeneid*, II. 680–84. **112–13. As . . . Rome:** See Livy, *Ab Urbe Condita*, XXI. 1. **118. the sacred Unction:** the sacramental oil with which the king was anointed at his coronation.

As King by Office, and as Priest by Trade:°
In his sinister hand, instead of Ball,°   120
He plac'd a mighty Mug of potent Ale;
Love's Kingdom° to his right he did convey,
At once his Sceptre and his rule of Sway;
Whose righteous Lore the Prince had practis'd young,
And from whose Loyns recorded *Psyche* sprung.
His Temples last with Poppies° were o'erspread,
That nodding seem'd to consecrate his head:
Just at that point of time, if Fame not lye,
On his left hand twelve reverend *Owls*° did fly.
So *Romulus*, 'tis sung,° by *Tyber's Brook*,   130
Presage of Sway from twice six Vultures took.
Th' admiring throng loud acclamations make,
And Omens of his future Empire take.
The *Syre* then shook the honours° of his head,
And from his brows damps of oblivion shed
Full on the filial dullness: long he stood,   ⎫
Repelling from his Breast the raging God;   ⎬
At length burst out in this prophetick mood: ⎭

   Heavens bless my Son, from *Ireland* let him reign
To farr *Barbadoes* on the Western main;°   140
Of his Dominion may no end be known,
And greater than his Father's be his Throne.
Beyond loves Kingdom let him stretch his Pen;
He paus'd, and all the people cry'd *Amen*.
Then thus, continu'd he, my Son advance
Still in new Impudence, new Ignorance.
Success let others teach, learn thou from me
Pangs without birth, and fruitless Industry.
Let *Virtuoso's* in five years be Writ;
Yet not one thought accuse thy toyl of wit.   150
Let gentle *George*° in triumph tread the Stage,
Make *Dorimant* betray, and *Loveit* rage;
Let *Cully*, *Cockwood*, *Fopling*,° charm the Pit,

And in their folly shew the Writers wit.
Yet still thy fools shall stand in thy defence,
And justifie their Author's want of sense.
Let 'em be all by thy own model made
Of dullness, and desire no foreign aid:
That they to future ages may be known,
Not Copies drawn, but Issue of thy own.   160
Nay let thy men of wit too be the same,
All full of thee, and differing but in name;
But let no alien *S—dl—y*° interpose
To lard with wit thy hungry *Epsom* prose.
And when false flowers of *Rhetorick* thou would'st
   cull,
Trust Nature, do not labour to be dull;
But write thy best, and top; and in each line,
Sir *Formal's*° oratory will be thine.
Sir *Formal*, though unsought, attends thy quill,
And does thy *Northern Dedications*° fill.   170
Not let false friends seduce thy mind to fame,
By arrogating *Johnson's*° Hostile name.
Let Father *Fleckno* fire thy mind with praise,
And Uncle *Ogleby* thy envy raise.
Thou art my blood, where *Johnson* has no part;
What share have we in Nature or in Art?
Where did his wit on learning fix a brand,
And rail at Arts he did not understand?
Where made he love in Prince *Nicander's*° vein,
Or swept the dust in *Psyche's* humble strain?   180
Where sold he Bargains,° Whip-stitch, kiss my Arse,
Promis'd a Play° and dwindled to a Farce?
When did his Muse from *Fletcher* scenes purloin,
As thou whole *Eth'ridg* dost transfuse to thine?
But so transfus'd as Oyl on Waters flow,
His always floats above, thine sinks below.
This is thy Province, this thy wondrous way,
New Humours to invent for each new Play:°
This is that boasted Byas of thy mind,
By which one way, to dullness, 'tis inclin'd.   190

119. **Priest by Trade:** a reference to Flecknoe's vocation.
120. **Ball:** At the coronation the king holds a globe, emblematic of the world, in his left hand and a scepter in his right.
122. **Love's Kingdom:** a play by Flecknoe (1664). 126. **Poppies:** traditionally regarded as soporific and also as sterilizing. In fact, Shadwell was an opium addict. 129. **reverend Owls:** Here Dryden exploits the vulgar error that owls are wise. 130. **'tis sung:** in Plutarch's life. 134. **honours:** decorations, ornaments; thus, hair. This and the following lines parody the classical situation of the anointing of the heir by the father (king or god). 139-40. **from . . . main:** a vast but uncultivated or worthless empire. 151. **gentle George:** Sir George Etherege (1634-91), one of the leading Restoration writers of comedy. 152-53. **Dorimant, Loveit, Cully, Cockwood, Fopling:** all characters in Etherege's plays.

163. **S—dl—y:** Sir Charles Sedley (c. 1639-1701), wit and playwright, wrote the Prologue to Shadwell's *Epsom-Wells* (1673) and, it was rumored, helped with the play itself. 168. **Sir Formal:** Sir Formal Trifle, a character in *The Virtuoso*. 170. **Northern Dedications:** dedications of his plays to the Duke and Duchess of Newcastle. 172. **Johnson:** Ben Jonson. (See the headnote to this selection.) 179. **Nicander:** a character in *Psyche*. 181. **sold he Bargains:** met an innocent question with a coarse answer, as in this line (echoing Sir Samuel Hearty in *The Virtuoso*). 182. **Promis'd a Play:** in the Dedication to *The Virtuoso*. 188. **New . . . Play:** Shadwell's boast in the *Virtuoso* Dedication.

Which makes thy writings lean on one side still,
And in all changes that way bends thy will.°
Nor let thy mountain belly make pretence
Of likeness;° thine's a tympany° of sense.
A Tun° of Man in thy Large bulk is writ,
But sure thou'rt but a Kilderkin° of wit.
Like mine thy gentle numbers feebly creep,
Thy Tragick Muse gives smiles, thy Comick sleep.
With whate'er gall thou sett'st thy self to write,
Thy inoffensive Satyrs never bite.   200
In thy fellonious heart, though Venom lies,
It does but touch thy *Irish* pen,° and dyes.
Thy Genius calls thee not to purchase fame
In keen Iambicks,° but mild Anagram:°
Leave writing Plays, and chuse for thy command
Some peacefull Province in Acrostick Land.
There thou maist wings display and Altars raise,
And torture one poor word Ten thousand ways.
Or if thou would'st thy diff'rent talents suit,
Set thy own Songs, and sing them to thy lute.   210
He said, but his last words were scarcely heard,
For *Bruce* and *Longvil* had a *Trap* prepar'd,
And down they sent the yet declaiming Bard.°
Sinking he left his Drugget robe behind,
Born upwards by A subterranean wind.
The Mantle fell to the young Prophet's part,°
With double portion of his Father's Art.

189–92. This . . . will: Dryden parodies lines from
Shadwell's Epilogue to *The Humorists:*

A Humor is the Byas of the Mind,
By which with violence 'tis one way inclin'd:
It makes our Actions lean on one side still,
And in all Changes that way bends the will.

194. likeness: to Jonson. **tympany:** a tumor or swelling.
195. Tun: a large wine cask. **196. Kilderkin:** a quarter of a
tun. **202. thy . . . pen:** In the Dedication to *The Tenth
Satire of Juvenal* (1687) Shadwell naively protested against
this appellation as being erroneous in fact. Dryden was of
course not only carrying out his fictional genealogy but also
exploiting the traditional English association of ideas of
barbarousness with Ireland. **204. Iambicks:** satire (from
Greek practice). **Anagram:** Anagrams, acrostics, picture
poems ("wings" and "altars") are all forms of "false wit,"
decried earlier by Cowley and later by Addison. **212–13. For
. . . Bard:** the trick played on Sir Formal Trifle in *The
Virtuoso.* **216. The Mantle . . . part:** an allusion to Elisha's
taking up the mantle of Elijah in II Kings 2:9–13.

RELIGIO LAICI
OR A LAYMANS FAITH.
A POEM

Ornari res ipsa negat; contenta doceri°

Although Dryden had long been concerned with
problems of religious belief, the immediate occasion of
Religio Laici, published in November, 1682, was the
appearance earlier that year of Henry Dickinson's
translation of Father Simon's *Histoire critique du Vieux
Testament.* Simon's work, in challenging the reliability
of the Hebrew Scriptures, shook the ground underneath
those reformed churches for whom the Bible alone
provided the canon of faith. In this poem Dryden
asserts the fideistic position against the rationalists, and
with characteristic conservatism he falls back on the
authority of the Church's traditional interpretations as
he recoils from the excesses of private guidance. Moving
in the direction of Roman Catholicism, Dryden was to
convert three years later.

The text is that of the first issue of the first edition
(1682), with variants from the second issue.

PREFACE

A Poem with so bold a Title, and a Name prefix'd,
from which the handling of so serious a Subject wou'd
not be expected, may reasonably oblige the Author,
to say somewhat in defence both of himself, and of his
undertaking. In the first place, if it be objected to me
that being a *Layman*, I ought not to have concern'd
my self with Speculations, which belong to the
Profession of *Divinity;* I cou'd Answer, that perhaps,
Laymen, with equal advantages of Parts and Knowledge, are not the most incompetent Judges of Sacred
things; But in the due sense of my own weakness and
want of Learning, I plead not this: I pretend not to
make my self a Judge of Faith, in others, but onely to
make a Confession of my own; I lay no unhallow'd
hand upon the Ark; but wait on it, with the Reverence
that becomes me at a distance: In the next place I will

RELIGIO LAICI. **Ornari . . . doceri:** "My very subject, content to be taught, spurns adornment" (Manilius, *Astronomica,*
III. 39).

ingenuously confess, that the helps I have us'd in this small Treatise, were many of them taken from the Works of our own Reverend Divines of the Church of *England;* so that the Weapons with which I Combat Irreligion, are already Consecrated; though I suppose they may be taken down as lawfully as the Sword of *Goliah* was by *David,*[1] when they are to be employed for the common Cause, against the Enemies of Piety. I intend not by this to intitle them to[2] any of my errours; which, yet, I hope are only those of Charity to Mankind; and such as my *own* Charity has caus'd me to commit, that of *others* may more easily excuse. Being naturally inclin'd to Scepticism in Philosophy, I have no reason to impose my Opinions, in a Subject which is above it: But whatever they are, I submit them with all reverence to my Mother Church, accounting them no further mine, than as they are Authoriz'd, or at least, uncondemn'd by her. And, indeed, to secure my self on this side, I have us'd the necessary Precaution, of showing this Paper before it was Publish'd to a judicious and learned Friend,[3] a Man indefatigably zealous in the service of the Church and State: and whose Writings, have highly deserv'd of both. He was pleas'd to approve the body of the Discourse, and I hope he is more my Friend, than to do it out of Complaisance: 'Tis true he had too good a tast to like it all; and amongst some other faults recommended to my second view, what I have written, perhaps too boldly on St. *Athanasius:* which he advised me wholy to omit. I am sensible enough that I had done more *prudently* to have follow'd his opinion: But then I could not have satisfied my self, that I had done honestly not to have written what was my own. It has always been my *thought,* that Heathens, who never did, nor without Miracle cou'd hear of the name of Christ were yet in a possibility of Salvation. Neither will it enter easily into my belief, that before the coming of our Saviour, the whole World, excepting only the Jewish Nation, shou'd lye under the inevitable necessity of everlasting Punishment, for want of that Revelation, which was confin'd to so small a spot of ground as that of *Palaestine.* Among the Sons of *Noah* we read of one onely who was accurs'd;[4] and if a blessing in the ripeness of time was

reserv'd for *Japhet,* (of whose Progeny we are,) it seems unaccountable to me, why so many Generations of the same Offspring, as preceeded our Saviour in the Flesh, shou'd be all involv'd in one common condemnation, and yet that their Posterity shou'd be Intitled to the hopes of Salvation: As if a Bill of Exclusion had passed only on the Fathers, which debar'd not the Sons from their Succession. Or that so many Ages had been *deliver'd over* to Hell, and so many *reserv'd* for Heaven, and that the Devil had the first choice, and God the next. Truly I am apt to think, that the revealed Religion which was taught by *Noah* to all his Sons, might continue for some Ages in the whole Posterity. That afterwards it was included wholly in the Family of *Sem* is manifest: but when the Progenies of *Cham* and *Japhet* swarm'd into Colonies, and those Colonies were subdivided into many others; in process of time their Descendants lost by little and little the Primitive and Purer Rites of Divine Worship, retaining onely the notion of one Deity; to which succeeding Generations added others: (for Men took their Degrees in those Ages from Conquerours to Gods.) Revelation being thus Eclipsed to almost all Mankind, the light of Nature as the next in Dignity was substituted; and that is it which St. *Paul* concludes to be the Rule of the Heathens;[5] and by which they are hereafter to be judg'd. If my supposition be true, then the consequence which I have assum'd in my Poem may be also true; namely, that Deism, or the Principles of Natural Worship, are onely the faint remnants or dying flames of reveal'd Religion in the Posterity of *Noah:* And that our Modern Philosophers, nay and some of our Philosophising Divines have too much exalted the faculties of our Souls, when they have maintain'd that by their force, mankind has been able to find out that there is one Supream Agent or Intellectual Being which we call God: that Praise and Prayer are his due Worship; and the rest of those deducements, which I am confident are the remote effects of Revelation, and unatainable by our Discourse, I mean as simply considerd, and without the benefit of Divine Illumination. So that we have not lifted up our selves to God, by the weak Pinions of our Reason, but he has been pleasd to descend to us: and what *Socrates* said of him, what *Plato* writ, and the rest of the Heathen Philosophers of several Nations, is all no more than the Twilight of Revelation, after the Sun of it was set in the Race of *Noah.* That there

Preface. **1. the Sword . . . David:** See I Sam. 21:9. **2. intitle . . . to:** attribute to them. **3. Friend:** John Tillotson (1630–94), Archbishop of Canterbury, who was at this time Dean of St. Paul's, has been suggested as the friend. (See the sermon by Tillotson later in Part One.) **4. Among . . . accurs'd:** See Gen. 9:24–27.

5. the Rule . . . Heathens: See Rom. 2:14–15.

is some thing above us, some Principle of *motion,* our Reason can apprehend, though it cannot discover what it is, by its own Vertue. And indeed 'tis very improbable, that we, who by the strength of our faculties cannot enter into the knowledg of any *Beeing,* not so much as of our *own,* should be able to find out by them, that Supream Nature, which we cannot otherwise define, than by saying it is Infinite; as if Infinite were definable, or Infinity a Subject for our narrow understanding. They who wou'd prove Religion by Reason, do but weaken the cause which they endeavour to support: 'tis to take away the Pillars from our Faith, and prop it onely with a twig: 'tis to design a Tower like that of *Babel,* which if it were possible (as it is not) to reach Heaven, would come to nothing by the confusion of the Workmen. For every man is Building a several way; impotently conceipted[6] of his own Model, and his own Materials: Reason is always striving, and always at a loss, and of necessity it must so come to pass, while 'tis exercis'd about that which is not its proper object. Let us be content at last, to know God, by his own Methods; at least so much of him, as he is pleas'd to reveal to us, in the sacred Scriptures; to apprehend them to be the word of God, is all our Reason has to do; for all beyond it is the work of Faith, which is the Seal of Heaven impress'd upon our humane understanding.

And now for what concerns the Holy Bishop *Athanasius,* the Preface of whose Creed[7] seems inconsistent with my opinion; which is, That Heathens may possibly be sav'd; in the first place I desire it may be consider'd that it is the Preface onely, not the Creed it self, which, (till I am better inform'd) is of too hard a digestion for my Charity. 'Tis not that I am ignorant how many several Texts of Scripture seemingly support that Cause; but neither am I ignorant how all those Texts may receive a kinder, and more mollified Interpretation. Every man who is read in Church History, knows *that* Belief was drawn up after a long contestation with *Arrius,*[8] concerning the Divinity of our Blessed Saviour, and his being one Substance with the Father; and that thus compild, it

was sent abroad among the Christian Churches, as a kind of Test, which whosoever took, was look'd on as an Orthodox Believer. 'Tis manifest from hence, that the Heathen part of the Empire was not concerned in it: for its business was not to distinguish betwixt Pagans and Christians, but betwixt Hereticks and true Believers. This, well consider'd, takes off the heavy weight of Censure, which I wou'd willingly avoid from so venerable a Man; for if this Proportion, *whosoever will be sav'd,* be restrained onely, to those to whom it was intended, and for whom it was compos'd, I mean the Christians; then the Anathema, reaches not the Heathens, who had never heard of Christ, and were nothing interessed in that dispute. After all, I am far from blaming even that Prefatory addition to the Creed, and as far from cavilling at the continuation of it in the Liturgy of the Church; where on the days appointed, 'tis publickly read: For I suppose there is the same reason for it now, in opposition to the Socinians,[9] as there was then against the Arrians; the one being a Heresy, which seems to have been refin'd out of the other; and with how much more plausibility of Reason it combats our Religion, with so much more caution to be avoided: and therefore the prudence of our Church is to be commended which has interpos'd her Authority for the recommendation of this Creed. Yet to such as are grounded in the true belief, those explanatory Creeds, the *Nicene*[10] and this of *Athanasius* might perhaps be spar'd: for what is supernatural, will always be a mystery in spight of Exposition: and for my own part the plain Apostles Creed, is most sutable to my weak understanding; as the simplest diet is the most easy of Digestion.

I have dwelt longer on this Subject than I intended; and longer than, perhaps, I ought; for having laid down, as my Foundation, that the Scripture is a Rule; that in all things needfull to Salvation, it is clear, sufficient, and ordain'd by God Almighty for that purpose, I have left my self no right to interpret obscure places, such as concern the possibility of eternal happiness to Heathens: because whatsoever is obscure is concluded not necessary to be known.

But, by asserting the Scripture to be the Canon of our Faith, I have unavoidably created to my self two

6. conceipted: conceived, designed. **7. the Preface . . . Creed:** "Whosoever will be saved, before all things it is necessary that he hold the Catholic [i.e., Christian] faith. Which faith except every one do keep whole and undefiled, without doubt he shall perish everlastingly." **8. Arrius:** The Greek churchman Arius denied the doctrine of the Trinity and held Christ to be a created being. His doctrine was condemned by the First Council of Nicaea in 325.

9. Socinians: a sect originating in sixteenth-century Italy that rejected the doctrine of the Trinity and the divinity of Christ but allowed Him to be a man of miraculous conception. **10. Nicene:** the confession of faith formulated and decreed by the First Council of Nicaea.

sorts of Enemies: The Papists indeed, more directly, because they have kept the Scripture from us, what they cou'd; and have reserv'd to themselves a right of Interpreting what they have deliver'd under the pretence of Infalibility: and the Fanaticks more collaterally, because they have assum'd what amounts to an Infalibility, in the private Spirit: and have detorted[11] those Texts of Scripture, which are not necessary to Salvation, to the damnable uses of Sedition, disturbance and destruction of the Civil Government. To begin with the Papists, and to speak freely, I think them the less dangerous (at least in appearance) to our present State; for not onely the Penal Laws are in Force against them, and their number is contemptible;[12] but also their Peerage and Commons are excluded from Parliaments, and consequently those Laws in no probability of being Repeal'd. A General and Uninterrupted Plot of their Clergy, ever since the Reformation, I suppose all Protestants believe. For 'tis not reasonable to think but that so many of their Orders, as were outed from their fat possessions, wou'd endeavour a reentrance against those whom they account Hereticks. As for the late design, Mr. *Colemans* Letters,[13] for ought I know are the best Evidence; and what they discover, without wyre-drawing[14] their Sence, or malicious Glosses, all Men of reason conclude credible. If there be any thing more than this requir'd of me, I must believe it as well as I am able, in spight of the Witnesses, and out of a decent conformity to the Votes of Parliament: For I suppose the Fanaticks will not allow the private Spirit in this Case: Here the Infallibility is at least in one part of the Government; and our understandings as well as our wills are represented. But to return to the Roman Catholicks, how can we be secure from the practice of Jesuited Papists in that Religion? For not two or three of that Order, as some of them would impose upon us, but almost the whole Body of them are of opinion, that their Infallible Master has a right over Kings, not onely in Spirituals but Temporals. Not to name *Mariana, Bellarmine, Emanuel Sa, Molina, Santarel, Simancha,*[15] and at the least twenty others of Foreign

Countries; we can produce of our own Nation, *Campian,* and *Doleman* or *Parsons,*[16] besides many are nam'd whom I have not read, who all of them attest this Doctrine, that the Pope can Depose and give away the Right of any Sovereign Prince, *si vel paulum deflexerit,* if he shall never so little Warpe:[17] but if he once comes to be Excommunicated, then the Bond of obedience is taken off from Subjects; and they may and ought to drive him like another *Nebuchadnezzar,*[18] *ex hominum Christianorum Dominatu,* from exercising Dominion over Christians: and to this they are bound by virtue of Divine Precept, and by all the tyes of Conscience under no less Penalty than Damnation. If they answer me (as a Learned Priest has lately Written,) that this Doctrine of the Jesuits is not *de fide,*[19] and that consequently they are not oblig'd by it, they must pardon me, if I think they have said nothing to the purpose; for 'tis a Maxim in their Church, where Points of Faith are not decided, and that Doctors are of contrary opinions, they may follow which part they please; but more safely the most receiv'd and most Authoriz'd. And their Champion *Bellarmine* has told the World, in his Apology,[20] that the King of *England* is a Vassal to the Pope, *ratione directi Dominii,* and that he holds in Villanage[21] of his Roman Landlord. Which is no new claim put in for *England.* Our Chronicles are his Authentique Witnesses, that, King *John* was depos'd by the same Plea, and *Philip Augustus* admitted Tenant. And which makes the more for *Bellarmine,* the French King was again ejected when our King submitted to the Church, and the Crown receiv'd under the sordid Condition of a Vassalage.

'Tis not sufficient for the more moderate and wellmeaning Papists, (of which I doubt not there are many) to produce the Evidences of their Loyalty to the late King, and to declare their Innocency in this Plot; I will grant their behaviour in the first, to have been as Loyal and as brave as they desire; and will be willing to hold them excus'd as to the second, (I mean when it comes to my turn, and after my betters; for 'tis a madness to be sober alone, while the Nation continues

---

11. **detorted:** twisted, perverted. 12. **contemptible:** inconsiderable. 13. **Mr. . . . Letters:** Edward Coleman, secretary to the Duchess of York, was executed in December, 1678, for conspiring, in correspondence with Louis XIV's Jesuit confessor, Père de la Chaise, to establish the Catholic faith in England. The letters were a lucky bit of evidence supporting Titus Oates's fabrication of a Popish Plot. 14. **wyredrawing:** straining. 15. **Mariana . . . Simancha:** Catholic writers of the sixteenth and seventeenth centuries.

16. **Campian . . . Parsons:** Edmund Campion (1540–81) and Robert Parsons (1546–1610) were English Jesuits who sought to reestablish Catholicism in England. Campion was executed in 1581; Parsons escaped to Rome, where he published under the name of Doleman. 17. **Warpe:** deviate from the straight path. 18. **Nebuchadnezzar:** See Dan. 4:28–33. 19. **de fide:** an article of faith. 20. **Apology:** *Apologia Roberti Bellarmini pro Responsione Sua ad Librum Jacobi Magnae Britanniae Regis* (1610). 21. **Villanage:** (villeinage) tenure by service rendered to the lord.

Drunk:) but that saying of their Father *Cres:*[22] is still running in my head, that they may be dispens'd with in their Obedience to an Heretick Prince, while the necessity of the times shall oblige them to it: (for that (as another of them tells us,) is onely the effect of Christian Prudence) but when once they shall get power to shake him off, an Heretick is no lawful King, and consequently to rise against him is no Rebellion. I should be glad therefore, that they wou'd follow the advice which was charitably given them by a Reverend Prelate of our Church; namely, that they would joyn in a publick Act of disowning and detesting those Jesuitick Principles; and subscribe to all Doctrines which deny the Popes Authority of Deposing Kings, and releasing Subjects from their Oath of Allegiance: to which I shou'd think they might easily be induc'd, if it be true that this present Pope[23] has condemn'd the Doctrine of King-killing (a Thesis of the Jesuites) amongst others *ex Cathedra* (as they call it) or in open consistory.

Leaving them, therefore, in so fair a way (if they please themselves) of satisfying all reasonable Men, of their sincerity and good meaning to the Government, I shall make bold to consider that other extream of our Religion, I mean the Fanaticks, or Schismaticks, of the English Church. Since the Bible has been Translated into our Tongue, they have us'd it so, as if their business was not to be sav'd but to be damnd by its Contents. If we consider onely them, better had it been for the English Nation, that it had still remain'd in the original Greek and Hebrew, or at least in the honest Latine of St. *Jerome*, than that several Texts in it, should have been prevaricated to the destruction of that Government, which put it into so ungrateful hands.

How many Heresies the first Translation of *Tyndal*[24] produced in few years, let my Lord *Herbert*'s History of *Henry* the Eighth[25] inform you; Insomuch that for the gross errours in it, and the great mischiefs it occasion'd, a Sentence pass'd on the first Edition of the Bible, too shamefull almost to be repeated. After the short Reign of *Edward* the Sixth (who had continued to carry on

the Reformation, on other principles than it was begun) every one knows that not onely the chief promoters of that work, but many others, whose Consciences wou'd not dispence with Popery, were forc'd, for fear of persecution, to change Climates: from whence returning at the beginning of Queen *Elizabeth*'s Reign, many of them who had been in *France*, and at *Geneva*, brought back the rigid opinions and imperious discipline of *Calvin*, to graffe[26] upon our Reformation. Which, though they cunningly conceal'd at first, (as well knowing how nauseously that Drug wou'd go down in a lawfull Monarchy, which was prescrib'd for a rebellious Commonwealth) yet they always kept it in reserve; and were never wanting to themselves either in Court or Parliament, when either they had any prospect of a numerous Party of Fanatique Members in the one, or the encouragement of any Favourite in the other, whose Covetousness was gaping at the Patrimony of the Church. They who will consult the Works of our venerable *Hooker*, or the account of his Life, or more particularly the Letter written to him on this Subject, by *George Cranmer*,[27] may see by what gradations they proceeded; from the dislike of Cap and Surplice, the very next step was Admonitions to the Parliament against the whole Government Ecclesiastical: then came out Volumes in English and Latin in defence of their Tenets: and immediately, practices were set on foot to erect their Discipline without Authority. Those not succeeding, Satyre and Rayling was the next: And *Martin Mar-Prelate*[28] (the *Marvel*[29] of those times) was the first Presbyterian Scribler, who sanctify'd Libels and Scurrility to the use of the Good Old Cause. Which was done (says my Authour) upon this account; that (their serious Treatises having been fully answered and refuted) they might compass by rayling what they had lost by reasoning; and when their Cause was sunk in Court and Parliament, they might at least hedge in a stake amongst the Rabble: for to their ignorance all things are Wit which are

---

22. Father Cres: Hugh Paulinus Serenus Cressy (c. 1605–74), an English Benedictine monk and chaplain to Queen Catherine. **23. this . . . Pope:** Innocent XI (1611–89). **24. the first . . . Tyndal:** William Tyndal, a Lutheran divine, was the first to translate the New Testament (with the Pentateuch) into English (1525). The work was condemned by Henry VIII, and Tyndal was executed. **25. Lord . . . Eighth:** Edward Herbert, Lord Herbert of Cherbury. his *History* appeared in 1649.

26. graffe: graft. **27. the Works . . . Cranmer:** The English theologian Richard Hooker (c. 1554–1600) published his *Of the Laws of Ecclesiastical Polity* in 1593. The life referred to is probably Izaak Walton's, which appeared in 1665. Cranmer's letter is included in both Hooker's work and Walton's life. **28. Martin Mar-Prelate:** the assumed name of the author, or authors, of a series of anti-Episcopal tracts (1588–90), chiefly engineered by John Penry, a Welsh clergyman, who was executed in 1593 for treason. **29. Marvel:** the poet Andrew Marvell (1621–78), who engaged in political pamphleteering for the Whigs.

abusive; but if Church and State were made the Theme, then the Doctoral Degree of Wit was to be taken at *Billingsgate:*[30] even the most Saintlike of the Party, though they durst not excuse this contempt and villifying of the Government, yet were pleas'd, and grin'd at it with a pious smile; and call'd it a judgment of God against the Hierarchy. Thus Sectaries, we may see, were born with teeth, foulmouth'd and scurrilous from their Infancy: and if Spiritual Pride, Venome, Violence, Contempt of Superiours and Slander had been the marks of Orthodox Belief; the Presbytery and the rest of our Schismaticks, which are their Spawn, were always the most visible Church in the Christian World.

'Tis true, the Government was too strong at that time for a Rebellion; but to shew what proficiency they had made in *Calvin*'s School, even *Then* their mouths water'd at it: for two of their gifted Brotherhood (*Hacket* and *Coppinger*)[31] as the Story tells us, got up into a Pease-Cart,[32] and harangued the People, to dispose them to an insurrection, and to establish their Discipline by force: so that however it comes about, that now they celebrate Queen *Elizabeth*'s Birth-night,[33] as that of their Saint and Patroness; yet then they were for doing the work of the Lord by Arms against her; and in all probability, they wanted but a Fanatique Lord Mayor and two Sheriffs of their Party to have compass'd it.

Our venerable *Hooker,* after many Admonitions which he had given them, toward the end of his Preface, breaks out into this Prophetick speech. *"There is in every one of these Considerations most just cause to fear, lest our hastiness to embrace a thing of so perilous Consequence* (meaning the Presbyterian Discipline) *should cause Postery*[34] *to feel those Evils, which as yet are more easy for us to prevent, than they would be for them to remedy."*

How fatally this *Cassandra* has foretold we know too well by sad experience: the Seeds were sown in the time of Queen *Elizabeth,* the bloudy Harvest ripened

in the Reign of King *Charles* the Martyr: and because all the Sheaves could not be carried off without shedding some of the loose Grains, another Crop is too like to follow; nay I fear 'tis unavoidable if the Conventiclers[35] be permitted still to scatter.

A man may be suffer'd to quote an Adversary to our Religion, when he speaks Truth: and 'tis the observation of *Meimbourg* in his History of Calvinism,[36] that where-ever that Discipline was planted and embrac'd, Rebellion, Civil War and Misery attended it. And how indeed should it happen otherwise? Reformation of Church and State has always been the ground of our Divisions in *England.* While we were Papists, our Holy Father rid us, by pretending authority out of the Scriptures to depose Princes,[37] when we shook off his Authority, the Sectaries furnish'd themselves with the same Weapons, and out of the same Magazine, the Bible. So that the Scriptures, which are in themselves the greatest security of Governours, as commanding express obedience to them, are now turn'd to their destruction; and never since the Reformation has there wanted a Text of their interpreting to authorize a Rebel. And 'tis to be noted by the way, that the Doctrines of King-killing and Deposing, which have been taken up onely by the worst Party of the Papists, the most frontless Flatterers of the Pope's Authority, have been espous'd, defended and are still maintain'd by the whole Body of Nonconformists and Republicans. 'Tis but dubbing themselves the People of God, which 'tis the interest of their Preachers to tell them they are, and their own interest to believe; and after that, they cannot dip into the Bible, but one Text or another will turn up for their purpose: If they are under Persecution (as they call it,) then that is a mark of their Election; if they flourish, then God works Miracles for their Deliverance, and the Saints are to possess the Earth.

They may think themselves to be too roughly handled in this Paper; but I who know best how far I could have gone on this Subject, must be bold to tell them they are spar'd: though at the same time I am not ignorant that they interpret the mildness of a Writer to them, as they do the mercy of the Government; in the one they think it Fear, and conclude it

---

30. Billingsgate: the seat of vituperative or foul language (from the fishmarket at Billingsgate). **31. Hacket and Coppinger:** William Hacket was a fanatic who proclaimed himself the Messiah; Edmund Coppinger one of his prophets. Hacket was executed July 28, 1591; Coppinger died in prison. **32. Pease-Cart:** Preaching from a market gardener's cart was a common practice. **33. Queen . . . Birth-night:** Dryden confuses the Queen's birthdate with the date of her accession (November 17, 1558). The latter was celebrated with an anti-Catholic demonstration and "pope-burning." **34. Postery:** posterity.

35. Conventiclers: Nonconformists. **36. Meimbourg . . . Calvinism:** Louis Maimbourg, *Histoire du Calvinisme* (1682). **37. Princes:** The first issue of the first edition contains at this point a parenthesis omitted in subsequent printings: "(a Doctrine which, though some Papists may reject, no Pope has hitherto deny'd, nor ever will,)."

Weakness in the other. The best way for them to confute me, is, as I before advis'd the Papists, to disclaim their Principles, and renounce their Practices. We shall all be glad to think them true Englishmen when they obey the King, and true Protestants when they conform to the Church Discipline.

It remains that I acquaint the Reader, that the Verses were written for an ingenious young Gentleman my Friend; upon his Translation of *The Critical History of the Old Testament*, compos'd by the learned Father *Simon:*[38] The Verses therefore are address'd to the Translatour of that Work, and the style of them is, what it ought to be, Epistolary.

If any one be so lamentable a Critique as to require the Smoothness, the Numbers and the Turn of Heroick Poetry in this Poem; I must tell him, that if he has not read *Horace*, I have studied him, and hope the style of his Epistles is not ill imitated here. The Expressions of a Poem, design'd purely for Instruction, ought to be Plain and Natural, and yet Majestick: for here the Poet is presum'd to be a kind of Law-giver, and those three qualities which I have nam'd are proper to the Legislative style. The Florid, Elevated and Figurative way is for the Passions; for Love and Hatred, Fear and Anger, are begotten in the Soul by shewing their Objects out of their true proportion; either greater than the Life, or less; but Instruction is to be given by shewing them what they naturally are. A Man is to be cheated into Passion, but to be reason'd into Truth.

DIM, as the borrow'd beams of Moon and Stars
To *lonely, weary, wandring* Travellers,
Is *Reason* to the Soul: And as on high,
Those rowling Fires *discover* but the Sky
Not light us *here;* So *Reason's* glimmering Ray
Was lent, not to *assure* our *doubtfull* way,
But *guide* us upward to a *better Day.*
And as those nightly Tapers disappear
When Day's bright Lord ascends our Hemisphere;
So pale grows *Reason* at *Religions* sight; 10
So *dyes,* and so *dissolves* in *Supernatural Light.*

Some few, whose Lamp shone brighter, have been led
From Cause to Cause, to *Natures* secret head;
And found that *one first principle* must be:
But *what,* or *who,* that UNIVERSAL HE;
Whether some *Soul* incompassing this Ball
Unmade, unmov'd; yet *making, moving All;*
Or various *Atom's,* interfering° Dance
Leapt into *Form,* (the Noble work of Chance;) 19
Or this great *All* was from *Eternity;*
Not ev'n the *Stagirite°* himself could see;
And *Epicurus Guess'd* as well as He:
As *blindly grop'd* they for a *future State;*
As *rashly Judg'd* of *Providence* and *Fate:*

Opinions of the several Sects of Philosophers concerning the Summum Bonum.

But least of all could their Endeavours find
What most concern'd the good of Humane kind:
For *Happiness* was never to be found;
But vanish'd from 'em, like Enchanted ground.
One thought *Content* the Good to be enjoy'd:
This, every little *Accident* destroy'd: 30
The *wiser Madmen* did for *Vertue* toyl:
A Thorny, or at best a barren Soil:
In *Pleasure* some their glutton Souls would steep;
But found their Line too short, the Well too deep;
And leaky Vessels which no *Bliss* cou'd keep.
Thus, *anxious Thoughts* in *endless Circles* roul,
Without a *Centre* where to fix the *Soul:*
In this wilde Maze their vain Endeavours end.
How can the *less* the *Greater* comprehend?
Or *finite Reason* reach *Infinity?* 40
For what cou'd *Fathom GOD* were *more* than *He.*

Systeme of Deisme.

The *Deist* thinks he stands on firmer ground;

---

38. **the Verses . . . Simon:** See the headnote to this selection.

18. **interfering:** colliding. 21. **Stagirite:** Aristotle.

Cries ἔυρεκα: the mighty Secret's found:
God is that *Spring* of *Good; Supreme*, and
    Best;
We, made to *serve*, and in that Service
    blest;
If so, some *Rules* of Worship must be
    given,
Distributed alike to all by Heaven:
Else *God* were *partial*, and to *some* deny'd
The Means his Justice shou'd for *all*
    provide.
This *general Worship* is to *PRAISE*, and
    PRAY: 50
One part to *borrow* Blessings, one to *pay:*
And when frail Nature slides into *Offence*,
The *Sacrifice* for *Crimes* is *Penitence*.
Yet, since th' Effects of Providence, we
    find
Are variously dispens'd to Humane kind;
That *Vice Triumphs*, and *Vertue suffers* here,
(A Brand that Sovereign Justice cannot
    bear;)
Our Reason prompts us to a *future* State:
The *last Appeal* from *Fortune*, and from
    Fate:
Where God's all-righteous ways will
    be declar'd;   60
The *Bad* meet *Punishment*, the *Good*,
    Reward.

*Of
Reveal'd
Religion.*
    Thus Man by his own strength to
        Heaven wou'd soar:
And wou'd not be Oblig'd to God for
    more.
Vain, wretched Creature, how art thou
    misled
To think thy Wit these God-like
    Notions bred!
These Truths are not the product of thy
    Mind,
But dropt from Heaven, and of a Nobler
    kind.
Reveal'd Religion first inform'd thy Sight,
And *Reason* saw not, till *Faith* sprung the
    Light.
Hence all thy *Natural Worship* takes
    the *Source:*   70
'Tis *Revelation* what thou thinkst
    Discourse.
Else, how com'st *Thou* to see these truths
    so clear,

Which so obscure to *Heathens* did appear?
Not *Plato* these, nor *Aristotle* found:
Socrates. Nor He whose Wisedom *Oracles*
    renown'd.°
Hast thou a Wit so deep, or so sublime,
Or canst thou lower dive, or higher climb?
Canst *Thou*, by *Reason*, more of *God-head*
    know
Than *Plutarch*, *Seneca*, or *Cicero?*
Those *Gyant Wits*, in happyer Ages
    born,   80
(When *Arms*, and *Arts* did *Greece* and
    Rome adorn)
Knew no such *Systeme:* no such *Piles* cou'd
    raise
Of *Natural Worship*, built on *Pray'r* and
    Praise,
To One sole GOD.
Nor did Remorse, to Expiate Sin,
    prescribe:
But slew their fellow Creatures for a
    Bribe:
The guiltless *Victim* groan'd for their
    Offence;
And *Cruelty*, and *Blood* was *Penitence*.
If *Sheep* and *Oxen* cou'd Attone for Men
Ah! at how cheap a rate the *Rich* might
    Sin!   90
And great Oppressours might Heavens
    Wrath beguile
By offering his own Creatures for a Spoil!
    Dar'st thou, poor Worm, offend
        Infinity?
And must the Terms of Peace be given by
    Thee?
Then *Thou* art *Justice* in the *last Appeal;*
Thy easie God instructs Thee to *rebell:*
And, like a King remote, and weak, must
    take
What Satisfaction *Thou* art pleas'd to
    make.
    But if there be a *Pow'r* too *Just*, and
        strong
To wink at *Crimes*, and bear unpunish'd
    Wrong;   100
Look humbly upward, see his Will disclose
The *Forfeit*° first, and then the *Fine* impose:

---

75. renown'd: made famous, celebrated. **102. Forfeit:**
crime, transgression.

A *Mulct*° *thy* Poverty cou'd never pay
Had not *Eternal Wisedom* found the way:
And with Cœlestial Wealth supply'd thy
    Store:
His Justice makes the *Fine*, *his Mercy* quits
    the *Score*.
See God descending in thy Humane Frame;
Th' *offended*, suff'ring in th' *Offenders*
    Name:
All thy Misdeeds to him imputed see,
And all his Righteousness devolv'd on
    thee.   110
    For granting we have Sin'd, and that
    th' offence
Of *Man*, is made against *Omnipotence*,
Some Price, that bears *proportion*, must be
    paid;
And *Infinite* with *Infinite* be weigh'd.
See then the *Deist lost: Remorse* for *Vice*,
Not paid, or *paid*, *inadequate* in price:
What farther means can *Reason* now
    direct,
Or what Relief from *humane Wit* expect?
That shews us *sick;* and sadly are we sure
Still to be *Sick*, till *Heav'n* reveal the
    Cure.   120
If then *Heaven's Will* must needs be
    understood,
(Which must, if we want *Cure*, and
    Heaven, be *Good*)
Let all Records of *Will reveal'd* be
    shown;
With *Scripture*, all in equal ballance
    thrown,
And *our one Sacred Book* will be *That*
    one.
    Proof needs not here, for whether we
    compare
That Impious, Idle, Superstitious Ware
Of *Rites*, *Lustrations*,° *Offerings*, (which
    before,
In various Ages, various Countries bore)
With *Christian Faith* and *Vertues*, we shall
    find   130
None answ'ring the great ends of humane
    kind
But *This one Rule of Life: That* shews us
    best

How *God* may be *appeas'd*, and *Mortals*
    blest.
Whether from length of *Time* its worth
    we draw,
The *World* is scarce more *Ancient* than the
    Law:
Heav'ns early Care prescrib'd for every
    Age;
First, in the *Soul*, and after, in the *Page*.
Or, whether more abstractedly we look,
Or on the *Writers*, or the *written Book*,
Whence, but from *Heav'n*, cou'd men
    unskill'd in Arts,   140
In several Ages born, in several parts,
Weave such *agreeing Truths?* or *how*, or
    why
Shou'd *all* conspire to cheat us with a *Lye?*
Unask'd their *Pains*, *ungratefull* their *Advice*,
Starving their *Gain*, and *Martyrdom* their
    Price.
    If on the Book it self we cast our view,
Concurrent Heathens prove the Story
    True:
The *Doctrine*, *Miracles;* which must
    convince,
For *Heav'n* in *Them* appeals to *humane*
    Sense:
For though they *prove* not, they *Confirm*
    the Cause,   150
When what is *Taught* agrees with *Natures*
    Laws.
    Then for the *Style; Majestick* and *Divine*,
It speaks no less than God in every *Line:*
Commanding words; whose *Force* is still the
    same
As the first *Fiat* that produc'd our Frame.
All Faiths *beside*,° or° did by *Arms* ascend;
Or *Sense* indulg'd has made *Mankind* their
    Friend:
This *onely* Doctrine does our *Lusts* oppose:
Unfed by Natures Soil, in which it grows;
Cross to our *Interests*, curbing Sense, and
    Sin;   160
Oppress'd without, and undermin'd
    within,
It thrives through pain; its own
    Tormentours tires;
And with a stubborn patience still aspires.

---

103. Mulct: fine. **128. Lustrations:** ceremonial purifications.   **156. Faiths beside:** other faiths. **or:** either.

To what can *Reason* such Effects assign
Transcending *Nature*, but to *Laws Divine?*
Which in that Sacred Volume are
    contain'd;
Sufficient, clear, and for that use ordain'd.

    But stay: the *Deist* here will urge anew,
No *Supernatural Worship* can be *True:*
Because a *general Law* is that alone   170
Which must to *all*, and every *where* be
    known:
A *Style* so large as not *this* Book can claim
Nor ought that bears *reveal'd* Religions
    Name.
'Tis said the sound of a *Messiah's Birth*
Is gone through all the habitable Earth:
But still that Text must be confin'd alone
To what was *Then* inhabited, and known:
And what Provision cou'd from *thence*
    accrue
To *Indian* Souls, and Worlds discover'd
    New?
In other parts it helps, that Ages past,   180
The Scriptures there were *known*, and were
    imbrac'd,
Till Sin spread once again the Shades of
    Night:
What's that to these who never *saw* the
    Light?

    Of all Objections this indeed is chief
To startle Reason, stagger frail Belief:
We grant, 'tis true, that Heav'n from
    humane Sense
Has hid the secret paths of *Providence:*
But *boundless Wisedom, boundless Mercy,*
    may
Find ev'n for those *be-wildred* Souls, a *way:*
If from his *Nature Foes* may Pity claim,   190
Much more may *Strangers* who ne'er heard
    his *Name.*
And though *no Name* be for *Salvation*
    known,
But that of his *Eternal Sons* alone;
Who knows how far transcending
    Goodness can
Extend the *Merits* of *that* Son to *Man?*
Who knows what *Reasons* may his *Mercy*
    lead;
Or *Ignorance invincible* may plead?
Not onely *Charity* bids hope the *best*,
But *more* the great Apostle has exprest:

That, if the Gentiles, (whom no Law
    inspir'd,)   200
By Nature did what was by *Law requir'd;*
They, who the written Rule had never known,
Were to themselves both Rule and Law alone:
To Natures plain indictment they shall plead;
And, by their Conscience, be condemn'd or
    freed.°
Most righteous Doom! because a *Rule*
    reveal'd
Is *none* to *Those*, from whom it was
    conceal'd.
Then those who follow'd *Reasons* Dictates
    right;
Liv'd up, and lifted high their *Natural*
    Light;
With *Socrates* may see their Maker's
    Face,   210
While Thousand *Rubrick-Martyrs*° want a
    place.
    Nor does it baulk my *Charity*, to find
Th' *Egyptian* Bishop° of another mind:
For, though his *Creed Eternal Truth*
    contains,
'Tis hard for *Man* to doom to *endless pains*
All who believ'd not all, his *Zeal* requir'd;
Unless he first cou'd prove he was
    inspir'd.
Then let us either think he meant to say
This Faith, where *publish'd*, was the onely
    way;
Or else conclude that, *Arius* to confute,   220
The good old Man, too eager in dispute,
Flew high; and as his *Christian* Fury rose
Damn'd all for *Hereticks* who durst *oppose.*

    Thus far my Charity this path has try'd;
(A much unskilfull, but well meaning
    guide:)
Yet what they are, ev'n these crude
    thoughts were bred
By reading that, which better thou hast
    read,
Thy Matchless Author's work: which
    thou, my Friend,
By well translating better dost commend:

200–205. if . . . freed: See Rom. 2:14–15. **211. Rubrick-Martyrs:** martyrs in the calendar of saints. **213. Egyptian Bishop:** Athanasius (*c.* 293–373). He was Bishop of Alexandria during the reign of Constantine.

Those youthfull hours which, of thy
    Equals most   230
In *Toys* have *squander'd*, or in *Vice* have
    lost,
Those hours hast thou to Nobler use
    employ'd;
And the severe Delights of Truth enjoy'd.
Witness this weighty Book, in which
    appears
The crabbed Toil of many thoughtfull
    years,
Spent by thy Authour, in the Sifting Care
Of *Rabbins* old Sophisticated Ware
From Gold Divine; which he who well
    can sort
May afterwards make *Algebra* a Sport.
A Treasure, which if *Country-Curates*
    buy,   240
They *Junius,* and *Tremellius*° may defy:
Save pains in various readings, and
    Translations;
And without *Hebrew* make most learn'd
    quotations.
A Work so full with various Learning
    fraught,
So nicely pondred, yet so strongly
    wrought,
As Natures height and Arts last hand
    requir'd:
As much as Man cou'd compass,
    uninspir'd.
Where we may see what *Errours* have been
    made
Both in the *Copiers* and *Translaters Trade:*
How *Jewish, Popish,* Interests have
    prevail'd,   250
And where *Infallibility* has *fail'd.*
    For some, who have his secret meaning
    ghes'd,
Have found our Authour not too *much* a
    Priest:
For *Fashion-sake* he seems to have recourse
To *Pope,* and *Councils,* and *Traditions*
    force:
But he that *old* Traditions cou'd subdue,
Cou'd not but find the weakness of the
    New:

If *Scripture,* though deriv'd from *heav'nly*
    birth,
Has been but carelesly preserv'd on
    Earth;
If *God's own People,* who of *God* before   260
Knew what we know, and had been
    promis'd more,
In fuller Terms, of Heaven's assisting Care,
And who did neither *Time,* nor *Study* spare
To keep this Book *untainted, unperplext;*
Let in gross *Errours* to corrupt the *Text:*
Omitted *paragraphs,* embroyl'd the *Sense;*
With vain *Traditions* stopt the gaping
    Fence,
Which every common hand pull'd up
    with ease:
What Safety from such *brushwood-helps*°
    as these?
If *written words* from time are not
    secur'd,   270
How can we think have *oral Sounds*
    endur'd?
Which *thus* transmitted, if *one* Mouth has
    fail'd,
Immortal Lyes on *Ages* are intail'd:
And that some such have been, is prov'd
    too plain;
If we consider *Interest, Church,* and *Gain.*

Of the In-   Oh but says one, *Tradition* set aside,
fallibility   Where can we hope for an *unerring Guid?*
of Tradition, For since th' *original* Scripture has been
in General.   lost,
All Copies *disagreeing, maim'd* the *most,*
Or *Christian Faith* can have no *certain*
    ground,   280
Or *Truth* in *Church Tradition* must be
    found.
    Such an *Omniscient* Church we wish
    indeed;
'Twere worth *Both Testaments,* and cast in
    the *Creed:*
But if *this Mother* be a *Guid* so sure,
As can all *doubts* resolve, all *truth* secure,
Then her *Infallibility,* as well
Where Copies are *corrupt,* or *lame,* can
    tell;
Restore *lost Canon* with as little pains,
As *truly explicate* what still *remains:*   289

241. Junius, and Tremellius: Calvinist divines of the
sixteenth century, who collaborated on a translation of
the Bible into Latin.

269. brushwood-helps: insubstantial assistance.

Which yet no *Council* dare *pretend* to
    doe;
Unless like *Esdras*,° they cou'd *write*
    it new:
Strange Confidence, still to *interpret*
    true,
Yet not be sure that all they have
    explain'd,
Is in the blest *Original* contain'd.
More Safe, and much more modest 'tis,
    to say
God wou'd not leave Mankind without a
    way:
And that the *Scriptures*, though not
    every where
Free from Corruption, or intire, or clear,
Are uncorrupt, sufficient, clear, intire,
In *all* things which our needfull *Faith*
    require.   300
If *others* in the same *Glass better* see
'Tis for *Themselves* they look, but not
    for *me:*
For MY Salvation must its Doom receive
Not from what *OTHERS*, but what *I*
    believe.

Objection in behalf of Tradition; urg'd by Father Simon.

      Must *all Tradition* then be set aside?
This to affirm were Ignorance, or Pride.
Are there not many points, some needfull
    sure
To saving Faith, that Scripture leaves
    obscure?
Which every Sect will wrest a several way
(For what *one* Sect Interprets, *all* Sects
    may:)   310
We hold, and say we prove from
    Scripture plain,
That *Christ* is GOD; the bold *Socin-
ian*
From the *same* Scripture urges he's but
    MAN.
Now what Appeal can end th' important
    Suit;
Both parts *talk* loudly, but the *Rule* is *mute?*
    Shall I speak plain, and in a Nation free
Assume an honest *Layman's Liberty?*
I think (according to my little Skill,
To my own Mother-Church submitting
    still)

That many have been sav'd, and many
    may,   320
Who never heard this Question brought
    in play.
Th' *unletter'd* Christian, who believes in
    gross,°
Plods on to *Heaven;* and ne'er is at a loss:
For the *Streight-gate*° wou'd be made
    streighter yet,
Were *none* admitted there but men of *Wit.*
The few, by Nature form'd, with Learning
    fraught,
Born to instruct, as others to be taught,
Must Study well the Sacred Page; and see
Which Doctrine, this, or that, does best
    agree
With the whole Tenour of the Work
    Divine: 330
And plainlyest points to Heaven's reveal'd
    Design:
Which Exposition flows from *genuine
Sense;*
And which is *forc'd* by *Wit* and *Eloquence.*
Not that Traditions parts are useless here:
When general, old, disinteress'd and clear:
That Ancient Fathers thus expound the
    Page,
Gives *Truth* the reverend Majesty of *Age:*
Confirms its force, by biding every *Test;*
For best *Authority's* next *Rules* are *best.*°
And still the nearer to the Spring we
    go   340
More limpid, more unsoyl'd the Waters
    flow.
Thus, *first Traditions* were a proof alone;
Cou'd we be *certain* such they *were*, so
    known:
But since some Flaws in long descent may
    be,
They make not *Truth* but *Probability.*
Even *Arius* and *Pelagius*° durst *provoke*°
To what the *Centuries preceding* spoke.

---

322. in gross: in general, on the whole. **324. the Streight-gate:** "Strait is the gate, and narrow is the way, which leadeth unto life, and few there be that find it" (Matt. 7:14). **339. For . . . best:** The oldest rules, or statements, of the oldest commentators are best, since they are nearest to the source. **346. Pelagius:** a British (or Irish) lay monk who around the turn of the fifth century went to Rome, where he propagated the heresy that man had the power to achieve salvation fundamentally by his own efforts. **provoke:** appeal.

291. Esdras: See II Esd. 14.

Such difference is there in an oft-told Tale:
But Truth by its own Sinews will prevail.
Tradition written therefore more
    commends   350
Authority, than what from *Voice* descends:
And this, as perfect as its kind can be,
Rouls down to us the Sacred History:
Which, from the *Universal Church receiv'd,*
Is *try'd,* and *after,* for its *self* believ'd.

The Second Objection.

    The partial *Papists* wou'd infer from
      hence
Their Church, in last resort, shou'd Judge
    the *Sense.*

Answer to the Objec-tion.

But first they wou'd assume, with
    wondrous Art,
Themselves to be the *whole,* who are but
    part
Of that vast Frame, the Church; yet grant
    they were   360
The handers down, can they from thence
    infer
A right t' interpret? or wou'd they alone
Who brought the Present, claim it for
    their own?
The *Book*'s a *Common Largess* to *Mankind;*
Not more for *them,* than *every* Man
    design'd:
The *welcome News* is in the *Letter* found;
The *Carrier*'s not Commission'd to
    expound.
It *speaks* it *Self,* and what it does contain,
In all things *needfull* to be *known,* is *plain.*
    In times o'ergrown with Rust and
      Ignorance,   370
A gainfull Trade their Clergy did advance:
When want of Learning kept the *Laymen*
    low,
And none but *Priests* were *Authoriz'd* to
    know:
When what small Knowledge was, in
    them did dwell;
And he a *God* who cou'd but *Reade* or
    Spell;
Then *Mother Church* did mightily prevail:
She parcel'd out the Bible by *retail:*
But still *expounded* what She *sold* or *gave;*
To keep it in *her Power* to *Damn* and *Save:*
Scripture was *scarce,* and as the Market
    went,   380
Poor *Laymen* took *Salvation* on *Content;*

As needy men take *Money,* good or bad:
God's Word they had not, but the *Priests*
    they had.
Yet, whate'er *false Conveyances*° they
    made,
The *Lawyer* still was *certain* to be paid.
In those dark times they learn'd their knack
    so well,
That by long use they grew *Infallible:*
At last, a knowing Age began t' enquire
If *they* the *Book,* or *That* did *them* inspire:
And, making narrower search they found,
    thô late,   390
That what they thought the *Priest*'s, was
    Their Estate:
Taught by the *Will produc'd* (the written
    Word)
How long they had been *cheated* on
    Record.°
Then, every man who saw the Title fair,
Claim'd a Child's part, and put in for a
    Share:
Consulted Soberly his private good;
And sav'd himself as cheap as e'er he cou'd.
'Tis true, my Friend, (and far be Flattery
    hence)
This good had full as bad a Consequence:
The Book thus put in every vulgar
    hand,   400
Which each presum'd he best cou'd
    understand,
The *Common Rule* was made the *common
    Prey;*
And at the mercy of the *Rabble* lay.
The tender Page with horney Fists was
    gaul'd;°
And he was gifted most that loudest
    baul'd:
The *Spirit* gave the *Doctoral Degree:*
And every member of a *Company*
Was of *his Trade,* and of the *Bible free.*
Plain *Truths* enough for needfull *use* they
    found;
But men wou'd still be itching to
    expound: 410

---

384. Conveyances: transfers of property. **393. on Record:** by documentary evidence or proof. **404. gaul'd:** (galled) chafed.

Each was ambitious of th' obscurest place,
No measure ta'n from *Knowledge*, all from
   GRACE.
Study and *Pains* were now no more their
   Care;
Texts were explain'd by *Fasting*, and by
   Prayer:
This was the Fruit the *private Spirit*
   brought;
Occasion'd by *great Zeal*, and *little Thought*.
While Crouds unlearn'd, with rude
   Devotion warm,
About the Sacred Viands buz and swarm,
The *Fly-blown Text* creates a *crawling
   Brood;*
And turns to *Maggots* what was meant for
   Food.   420
*A Thousand daily Sects rise up, and dye;
A Thousand more the perish'd Race supply:*
So all we make of Heavens discover'd Will
Is, not to have it, or to use it ill.
The Danger's much the same; on several
   Shelves
If *others* wreck *us*, or *we* wreck our *selves*.
   What then remains, but, waving each
      Extreme,
The Tides of Ignorance, and Pride to stem?
Neither so rich a Treasure to forgo;
Nor proudly seek beyond our pow'r to
   know: 430
Faith is not built on disquisitions vain;
The things we *must* believe, are *few*, and
   plain:
But since men *will* believe more than they
   need;
And every man will make *himself* a Creed:
In doubtfull questions 'tis the safest way
To learn what unsuspected° Ancients say:
For 'tis not likely *we* shou'd higher Soar
In search of Heav'n, than *all the Church
   before:*
Nor can we be deceiv'd, unless we see
The *Scripture*, and the *Fathers disagree.*   440
If after all, they stand suspected still,
(For no man's Faith depends upon his
   Will;)
'Tis some Relief, that points not clearly
   known,

436. **unsuspected:** beyond suspicion.

Without much hazard may be let alone:
And, after hearing what our Church can
   say,
If still our Reason runs another way,
That private Reason 'tis more Just to curb,
Than by Disputes the publick Peace
   disturb.
For points obscure are of small use to
   learn:
But *Common quiet is Mankind's concern.* 450
   Thus have I made my own Opinions
      clear:
Yet neither Praise expect, nor Censure
   fear:
And this unpolish'd, rugged Verse, I chose;
As fittest for Discourse, and nearest Prose:
For, while from *Sacred Truth* I do not
   swerve,
Tom Sternhold's,° or *Tom Shadwell's*°
   Rhimes will serve.

TO THE MEMORY
OF MR. OLDHAM

John Oldham (1653–83) earned a reputation with his *Satires upon the Jesuits,* published in 1679. Dryden's elegy was one of several collected in *The Works of Mr. John Oldham, Together with His Remains* (1684). The text is from that edition.

FArewel, too little and too lately known,
Whom I began to think and call my own;
For sure our Souls were near ally'd; and thine
Cast in the same Poetick mould with mine.
One common Note on either Lyre did strike,
And Knaves and Fools we both abhorr'd alike:
To the same Goal did both our Studies drive,
The last set out the soonest did arrive.

456. **Tom Sternhold:** Thomas Sternhold (d. 1549), with John Hopkins, rendered the Psalms into English verse. Their translations first appeared between 1549 and 1562. **Tom Shadwell:** Thomas Shadwell (c. 1642–92), playwright and poet. He is the subject of Dryden's satirical *Mac Flecknoe* (see above).

Thus *Nisus* fell upon the slippery place,
While his young Friend perform'd and won the Race.°
O early ripe! to thy abundant store   11
What could advancing Age have added more?
It might (what Nature never gives the young)
Have taught the numbers of thy native Tongue.
But Satyr needs not those, and Wit will shine
Through the harsh cadence of a rugged line.
A noble Error, and but seldom made,
When Poets are by too much force betray'd.   18
Thy generous fruits, though gather'd ere their prime
Still shew'd a quickness; and maturing time
But mellows what we write to the dull sweets of
        Rime.
Once more, hail and farewel; farewel thou young,
But ah too short, *Marcellus*° of our Tongue;
Thy Brows with Ivy, and with Laurels bound;
But Fate and gloomy Night encompass thee around.

TO THE PIOUS MEMORY
OF THE ACCOMPLISHT
YOUNG LADY MRS ANNE
KILLIGREW, EXCELLENT
IN THE TWO SISTER-ARTS
OF POESIE, AND PAINTING.
AN ODE

Anne Killigrew (1660–85) was the daughter of Dr.
Henry Killigrew, Almoner to the Duke of York and
Master of the Savoy Hospital, and the niece of Thomas
Killigrew, one of the owner-managers of the Theatre
Royal, for whom Dryden wrote most of his plays.
She died on June 16, 1685, of smallpox. *Poems by Mrs.
Anne Killigrew* was published late the same year (though
the title page bears the date 1686), prefixed by Dryden's
ode, which Johnson called "undoubtedly the noblest
ode that our language ever has produced."

    The text is that of the first printing (1686), with
variants introduced from the second printing of the ode
in the miscellany entitled *Examen Poeticum* (1693).

I.

Thou Youngest Virgin-Daughter of the Skies,
Made in the last Promotion of the Blest;
Whose Palmes, new pluckt from Paradise,
In spreading Branches more sublimely rise,
Rich with Immortal Green above the rest:
Whether, adopted to some Neighbouring Star,
Thou rol'st above us, in thy wand'ring Race,
    Or, in Procession fixt and regular,
    Mov'd with the Heavens Majestick Pace;
    Or, call'd to more Superiour Bliss,   10
Thou tread'st, with Seraphims, the vast Abyss.
What ever happy Region is thy place,
Cease thy Celestial Song a little space;
(Thou wilt have Time enough for Hymns Divine,
    Since Heav'ns Eternal Year is thine.)
Hear then a Mortal Muse thy Praise rehearse,°
    In no ignoble Verse;
But such as thy own voice did practise here,
When thy first Fruits of Poesie were giv'n;
To make thy self a welcome Inmate there: 20
    While yet a young Probationer,
        And Candidate of Heav'n.

II.

If by Traduction° came thy Mind,
    Our Wonder is the less to find
A Soul so charming from a Stock so good;
Thy Father° was transfus'd into thy Blood:
So wert thou born into the tuneful strain,
(An early, rich, and inexhausted Vain.)
    But if thy Præexisting Soul
    Was form'd, at first, with Myriads more,   30
It did through all the Mighty Poets roul,
    Who *Greek* or *Latine* Laurels wore.
And was that *Sappho* last, which once it was before.
    If so, then cease thy flight, O *Heav'n-born Mind!*
    Thou hast no Dross to purge from thy Rich Ore:
    Nor can thy Soul a fairer Mansion find,
    Than was the Beauteous Frame she left behind:
Return, to fill or mend the Quire,° of thy Celestial
        kind.

TO THE MEMORY OF MR. OLDHAM. **9–10. Thus . . . Race:**
See *Aeneid,* V. 328. **23. Marcellus:** the nephew of Augustus,
whose early death Virgil memorialized in the *Aeneid,* VI.
854–86.

TO THE PIOUS MEMORY OF MRS. ANNE KILLIGREW. **16. rehearse:**
recite. **23. Traduction:** genetic inheritance. **26. Thy Father:**
Henry Killigrew was the author of a tragedy, *The Conspiracy*
(1638), later revised and published as *Palantus and Eudora*
(1653). **38. Quire:** choir.

III.

May we presume to say, that at thy Birth,
New joy was sprung in Heav'n, as well as here on
    Earth.   40
For sure the Milder Planets did combine
On thy Auspicious Horoscope to shine,
And ev'n the most Malicious were in Trine.°
    Thy Brother-Angels at thy Birth
    Strung each his Lyre, and tun'd it high,
    That all the People of the Skie
Might know a Poetess was born on Earth.
        And then if ever, Mortal Ears
        Had heard the Musick of the Spheres!
        And if no clust'ring Swarm of Bees   50
On thy sweet Mouth distill'd their golden Dew,°
    'Twas that, such vulgar Miracles,
    Heav'n had not Leasure to renew:
For all the Blest Fraternity of Love
Solemniz'd there thy Birth, and kept thy Holyday
    above.

IV.

O Gracious God! How far have we
Prophan'd thy Heav'nly Gift of Poesy?
Made prostitute and profligate the Muse,
Debas'd to each obscene and impious use,
Whose Harmony was first ordain'd Above   60
For Tongues of Angels, and for Hymns of Love?
O wretched We! why were we hurry'd down
    This lubrique° and adult'rate age,
    (Nay added fat Pollutions of our own)
    T' increase the steaming Ordures of the Stage?
What can we say t' excuse our *Second Fall?*
Let this thy *Vestal*, Heav'n, attone for all!
Her *Arethusian* Stream° remains unsoil'd,
Unmixt with Forreign Filth, and undefil'd,
Her Wit was more than Man, her Innocence a
    Child!   70

V.

Art she had none, yet wanted none:
    For Nature did that Want supply,
    So rich in Treasures of her Own,
    She might our boasted Stores defy:
Such Noble Vigour did her Verse adorn,
That it seem'd borrow'd, where 'twas only born.
Her Morals too were in her Bosome bred
    By great Examples daily fed,
What in the best of Books, her Fathers Life, she read.
And to be read her self she need not fear,   80
Each Test, and ev'ry Light, her Muse will bear,
Though *Epictetus*° with his Lamp were there.
Ev'n Love (for Love sometimes her Muse exprest)
Was but a *Lambent-flame* which play'd about her
    Brest:
Light as the Vapours of a Morning Dream,
So cold herself, whilst she such Warmth exprest,
'Twas *Cupid* bathing in *Diana's* Stream.

VI.

Born to the Spacious Empire of the *Nine*,
One would have thought, she should have been
    content
To manage well that Mighty Government: 90
But what can young ambitious Souls confine?
    To the next Realm she stretcht her Sway,
    For *Painture*° neer adjoyning lay,
A plenteous Province, and alluring Prey.
A Chamber of Dependences° was fram'd,
(As Conquerors will never want Pretence,
    When arm'd, to justifie the Offence)
And the whole Fief,° in right of Poetry she claim'd.
    The Country open lay without Defence:
    For Poets frequent In-rodes there had made,   100
    And perfectly could represent
    The Shape, the Face, with ev'ry Lineament;
And all the large Demains° which the *Dumb-sister*°
    sway'd,
    All bow'd beneath her Government,
    Receiv'd in Triumph wheresoe're she went.
Her Pencil drew, what e're her Soul design'd,
And oft the happy Draught surpass'd the Image in her
    Mind.

---

43. **in Trine:** in astrology, 120 degrees distant from each other and therefore of benign influence. **50–51. And . . . Dew:** an allusion to the legend of the bees resting on the lips of the infant Plato in prophecy of his eloquence. **63. lubrique:** (lubricous) lewd, wanton. **68. Arethusian Stream:** Arethusa, a nymph of Elis, was rescued by the goddess Artemis from the pursuit of the river god Alpheus and was transformed into a fountain on the island of Ortygia, in Sicily. Alpheus nevertheless succeeded in mingling his waters with those of the fountain of Arethusa, whereas Anne Killigrew's "Stream remains unsoil'd."

82. **Epictetus:** apparently an error for Diogenes. **93. Painture:** the art of painting. **95. A Chamber . . . Dependences:** a subject province. **98. Fief:** territory. **103. Demains:** domains. **the Dumb-sister:** a personification of painting.

The *Sylvan* Scenes of Herds and Flocks,
And fruitful Plains and barren Rocks,
Of shallow Brooks that flow'd so clear,   110
The Bottom did the Top appear;
Of deeper too and ampler Flouds,
Which as in Mirrors, shew'd the Woods;
Of lofty Trees with Sacred Shades,
And Perspectives of pleasant Glades,
Where Nymphs of brightest Form appear,
And shaggy Satyrs standing neer,
Which them at once admire and fear.
The Ruines too of some Majestick Piece,
Boasting the Pow'r of ancient *Rome* or *Greece*,   120
Whose Statues, Freezes, Columns broken lie,
And though deface't, the Wonder of the Eie,
What Nature, Art, bold Fiction e're durst frame,
Her forming Hand gave Feature to the Name.
So strange a Concourse ne're was seen before,
But when the peopl'd Ark the whole Creation bore.

VII.

The Scene then chang'd, with bold Erected Look
Our Martial King° the sight with Reverence strook:
For not content t' express his Outward Part,
Her hand call'd out the Image of his Heart,   130
His Warlike Mind, his Soul devoid of Fear,
His High-designing Thoughts, were figur'd there,
As when, by Magick, Ghosts are made appear.
Our Phenix Queen° was portrai'd too so bright,
Beauty alone could Beauty take so right:
Her Dress, her Shape, her matchless Grace,
Were all observ'd, as well as heav'nly Face.
With such a Peerless Majesty she stands,
As in that Day she took the Crown from Sacred
    hands:
Before a Train of Heroins was seen,   140
In *Beauty* foremost, as in Rank, the Queen!
    Thus nothing to her *Genius* was deny'd,
But like a Ball of Fire the further thrown,
    Still with a greater Blaze she shone,
And her bright Soul broke out on ev'ry side.
What next she had design'd, Heaven only knows,
To such Immod'rate Growth her Conquest rose,
That Fate alone its Progress could oppose.

VIII.

Now all those Charmes, that blooming Grace,
The well-proportion'd Shape, and beauteous Face,   150
Shall never more be seen by Mortal Eyes;
In Earth the much lamented Virgin lies!
    Not Wit, nor Piety could Fate prevent;
    Nor was the cruel *Destiny* content
    To finish all the Murder at a Blow,
To sweep at once her Life, and Beauty too;
But, like a hardn'd Fellon, took a pride
    To work more Mischievously slow,
    And plunder'd first, and then destroy'd.
O double Sacriledge on things Divine,   160
To rob the Relique, and deface the Shrine!
    But thus *Orinda*° dy'd:
Heav'n, by the same Disease, did both translate,
As equal were their Souls, so equal was their Fate.

IX.

Mean time her Warlike Brother° on the Seas
His waving Streamers to the Winds displays,
And vows for his Return, with vain Devotion, pays.
    Ah, Generous Youth, that Wish forbear,
    The Winds too soon will waft thee here!
    Slack all thy Sailes, and fear to come,   170
Alas, thou know'st not, Thou art wreck'd at home!
No more shalt thou behold thy Sisters Face,
Thou hast already had her last Embrace.
But look aloft, and if thou ken'st from far,
Among the *Pleiad's* a New-kindl'd Star,
If any sparkles, than the rest, more bright,
'Tis she that shines in that propitious Light.

X.

When in mid-Aire, the Golden Trump shall sound,
    To raise the Nations under ground;
    When in the Valley of *Jehosaphat*,°   180
The Judging God shall close the Book of Fate;
    And there the last Assizes keep,
    For those who Wake, and those who Sleep;
    When ratling Bones together fly,
From the four Corners of the Skie,
When Sinews o're the Skeletons are spread,
Those cloath'd with Flesh, and Life inspires the Dead:

128. **Our . . . King**: James II. 134. **Our . . . Queen**: Queen Mary, crowned April 23, 1685.

162. **Orinda**: the name given to Katharine Philips (1631–64), another poetess who died of smallpox. Anne Killigrew was among those who praised her. 165. **her . . . Brother**: Henry Killigrew (d. 1712), a naval captain who was at this time in the Mediterranean. He later became an admiral. 180. **the Valley . . . Jehosaphat**: See Joel 3:2.

The Sacred Poets first shall hear the Sound,
 And formost from the Tomb shall bound:
For they are cover'd with the lightest Ground
And streight, with in-born Vigour, on the Wing, 191
Like mounting Larkes, to the New Morning sing.
There *Thou*, Sweet Saint, before the Quire shalt
  go,
As Harbinger of Heav'n, the Way to show,
The Way which thou so well hast learn'd below.

A SONG FOR ST. CECILIA'S DAY

❦

St. Cecilia, a Roman convert to Christianity martyred in the third century, is the patron saint of music. She is commemorated on November 22, and from 1683 public concerts were given on this day for which original compositions were commissioned. Dryden provided two odes—the present one in 1687 and *Alexander's Feast* in 1697. The music for the first presentation of this ode was composed by the court musician, Giovanni Baptista Draghi, but it is Handel's setting, written in 1739, that perfectly complements the poem.

 The text is that of the first edition (1687).

❦

FROM Harmony, from heav'nly Harmony
 This universal Frame began.
 When Nature underneath a heap
  Of jarring Atomes lay,°
 And cou'd not heave her Head,
The tuneful Voice was heard from high,
 Arise ye more than dead.
Then cold, and hot, and moist, and dry,
In order to their stations leap,
 And MUSICK's pow'r obey. 10
From Harmony, from heav'nly Harmony
 This universal Frame began:
 From Harmony to Harmony
Through all the compass of the Notes it ran,
The Diapason° closing full in Man.

II

What Passion cannot MUSICK raise and quell!
 When *Jubal*° struck the corded Shell,
 His list'ning Brethren stood around
 And wond'ring on their Faces fell
 To worship that Celestial Sound. 20
Less than a God they thought there cou'd not dwell
 Within the hollow of that Shell
 That spoke so sweetly and so well.
What Passion cannot MUSICK raise and quell!

III

 The TRUMPETS loud Clangor
  Excites us to Arms
 With shrill Notes of Anger
  And mortal Alarms.
 The double double double beat
  Of the thundring DRUM 30
Cryes, heark the Foes come;
Charge, Charge, 'tis too late to retreat.

IV

 The soft complaining FLUTE
 In dying Notes discovers
 The Woes of hopeless Lovers,
Whose Dirge is whisper'd by the warbling LUTE.

V

 Sharp VIOLINS proclaim
Their jealous Pangs, and Desperation,
Fury, frantick Indignation,
Depth of Pains, and height of Passion, 40
 For the fair, disdainful Dame.

VI

 But oh! what Art can teach
 What human Voice can reach
 The sacred ORGANS praise?
 Notes inspiring holy Love,
 Notes that wing their heav'nly ways
  To mend the Choires above.

VII

Orpheus° cou'd lead the savage race;
And Trees unrooted left their place;
 Sequacious of° the Lyre: 50

A SONG FOR ST. CECILIA'S DAY. **3–4. When . . . lay:** the Epicurean conception of warring atoms of the four elements: earth, fire, water, and air. **15. Diapason:** the combination of all the notes or parts of the harmony.

17. Jubal: "the father of all such as handle the harp and organ" (Gen. 4:21). **48–50. Orpheus . . . Lyre:** According to legend, Orpheus was able to charm trees and stones and tame wild beasts by his beautiful playing of the lyre. **50. Sequacious of:** following.

But bright *CECILIA* rais'd the wonder high'r;
When to her ORGAN, vocal Breath was giv'n
An Angel heard, and straight appear'd
    Mistaking Earth for Heaven.

Grand CHORUS

As from the pow'r of sacred Lays
    The Spheres began to move,
And sung the great Creator's praise
    To all the bless'd above;
So when the last and dreadful hour
This crumbling Pageant shall devour,   60
The TRUMPET *shall be heard on high,*
The Dead shall live, the Living die,°
And MUSICK *shall untune the Sky.*

TO MY DEAR FRIEND
MR. CONGREVE,
ON HIS COMEDY CALL'D
THE DOUBLE-DEALER

William Congreve appears to have entered Dryden's
life as one of his coadjutors in the translation of Juvenal
that Dryden was making in 1692. Congreve contributed
the translation of the eleventh satire as well as a poetic
tribute to Dryden that was prefixed to the translations
of Persius which appeared in the same volume. In
December of 1693 Congreve's comedy *The Double-
Dealer* was acted with considerable success. Dryden's
last play, *Love Triumphant*, was acted in the beginning
of the next year and failed. The juxtaposition of a rising
and a falling star provides the context for Dryden's
generous tribute to his young successor.

    The text is that of the first printing, in *The Double-
Dealer, a Comedy* (1694).

WELL then; the promis'd hour is come at last;
The present Age of Wit obscures the past:
Strong were our Syres; and as they Fought they Writ,
Conqu'ring with force of Arms, and dint of Wit;
Theirs was the Gyant Race, before the Flood;
And thus, when *Charles* Return'd, our Empire stood.

61–62. The Trumpet . . . die: an echo of I Cor. 15:52.

Like *Janus*° he the stubborn Soil manur'd,
With Rules of Husbandry the rankness cur'd:
Tam'd us to manners, when the Stage was rude;
And boistrous *English* Wit, with Art indu'd.°   10
Our Age was cultivated thus at length;
But what we gain'd in skill we lost in strength.
Our Builders were, with want of Genius, curst;
The second Temple° was not like the first:
Till You, the best *Vitruvius*,° come at length;
Our Beauties equal; but excel our strength.
Firm *Dorique* Pillars found Your solid Base:
The Fair *Corinthian* Crowns the higher Space;
Thus all below is Strength, and all above is Grace.
In easie Dialogue is *Fletcher*'s Praise:°   20
He mov'd the mind, but had not power to raise.
Great *Johnson*° did by strength of Judgment please:
Yet doubling *Fletcher*'s Force, he wants his Ease.
In differing Tallents both adorn'd their Age;
One for the Study, t' other for the Stage.
But both to *Congreve* justly shall submit,
One match'd in Judgment, both o'er-match'd in
    Wit.
In Him all Beauties of this Age we see;
Etherege his Courtship, *Southern*'s Purity;
The Satire, Wit, and Strength of Manly *Witcherly*.°
All this in blooming Youth you have Atchiev'd;   31
Nor° are your foil'd Contemporaries griev'd;
So much the sweetness of your manners move,
We cannot envy you because we Love.
Fabius might joy in *Scipio*, when he saw
A Beardless Consul made against the Law,
And joyn his Suffrage to the Votes of *Rome;*°
Though He with *Hannibal* was overcome.

TO MY DEAR FRIEND MR. CONGREVE. **7. Janus:** the Roman
deity credited with giving man the knowledge of agriculture and civil law. **10. indu'd:** invested. **14. The
second Temple:** built after the Exile. **15. Vitruvius:** Marcus
Vitruvius Pollio, Roman architect and engineer under
Augustus. **20. In . . . Praise:** Dryden had praised Fletcher
in *An Essay of Dramatic Poesy* (1668) for the perfection of his
repartee. **22. Johnson:** Ben Jonson. **29–30. Etherege,
Southern, Witcherly:** Sir George Etherege (1634–91),
Thomas Southerne (1660–1746), and William Wycherley
(1640–1716), Restoration dramatists. **32. Nor:** The text reads:
"Now." **35–37. Fabius . . . Rome:** Scipio was elected
consul in 205 B.C. after his victories in Spain. His proposal to
invade Africa, despite the presence of Hannibal in Italy, was
opposed in the Senate by Fabius, who was notorious for his
passive military tactics.

Thus old *Romano* bow'd to *Raphel*'s Fame;
And Scholar to the Youth he taught, became.° 40
    Oh that your Brows my Lawrel had sustain'd,
Well had I been Depos'd,° if You had reign'd!
The Father had descended for the Son;
For only You are lineal to the Throne.
Thus when the State one *Edward* did depose;
A Greater *Edward* in his room arose.°
But now, not I, but Poetry is curs'd;
For *Tom* the Second reigns like *Tom* the first.°
But let 'em not mistake my Patron's° part;
Nor call his Charity their own desert. 50
Yet this I Prophecy; Thou shalt be seen,
(Tho' with some short Parenthesis between:)
High on the Throne of Wit; and seated there,
Not mine (that's little) but thy Lawrel wear.
Thy first attempt° an early promise made;
That early promise this has more than paid.
So bold, yet so judiciously you dare,
That Your least Praise, is to be Regular.
Time, Place, and Action, may with pains be wrought,
But Genius must be born; and never can be taught. 60
This is Your Portion; this Your Native Store;
Heav'n that but once was Prodigal before,
To *Shakespeare* gave as much; she cou'd not give
    him more.
    Maintain Your Post: That's all the Fame You need;
For 'tis impossible you shou'd proceed.
Already I am worn with Cares and Age;
And just abandoning th' Ungrateful Stage:
Unprofitably kept at Heav'ns expence,
I live a Rent-charge° on his Providence:
But You, whom ev'ry Muse and Grace adorn, 70
Whom I foresee to better Fortune born,
Be kind to my Remains; and oh defend,
Against Your Judgment Your departed Friend!

39–40. Thus . . . became: Giulio Romano, Raphael's pupil, here seems to be confused with Pietro Vanucci, Raphael's teacher. **42. Depos'd:** as Poet Laureate and Historiographer Royal by Shadwell in 1688. Dryden as a Catholic could not take the oaths of office required under William and Mary. **45–46. Edward, Edward:** Edward II and Edward III. **48. Tom the Second . . . first:** In 1692 Thomas Rymer succeeded Shadwell as Historiographer Royal. (Nahum Tate succeeded as Poet Laureate.) **49. my Patron:** The Earl of Dorset dispensed these offices in his capacity as Lord Chamberlain. Dryden had dedicated his *Satires of Juvenal and Persius* to him in 1692. **55. Thy . . . attempt:** *The Old Bachelor* (1693). Dryden is said to have put the finishing touches on it. **69. Rent-charge:** a rent granted to someone other than the landlord.

Let not the Insulting Foe my Fame pursue;
But shade those Lawrels which descend to You:
And take for Tribute what these Lines express:
You merit more; nor cou'd my Love do less.

ALEXANDER'S FEAST; OR THE POWER OF MUSIQUE. AN ODE, IN HONOUR OF ST. CECILIA'S DAY

❧

Alexander's Feast was performed on November 22, 1697, with music (now lost) by Jeremiah Clarke. It was scored magnificently by Handel in 1736.
    The text is that of the first edition (1697).

❧

I.

'Twas at the Royal Feast, for *Persia* won°,
    By *Philip*'s Warlike Son:°
    Aloft in awful State
    The God-like Heroe sate
      On his Imperial Throne:
His valiant Peers were plac'd around;
Their Brows with Roses and with Myrtles bound.
(So shou'd Desert in Arms be Crown'd:)
The Lovely *Thais*° by his side,
Sate like a blooming *Eastern* Bride 10
In Flow'r of Youth and Beauty's Pride.
    Happy, happy, happy Pair!
    None but the Brave
    None but the Brave
    None but the Brave deserves the Fair.

CHORUS.

Happy, happy, happy Pair!
None but the Brave
None but the Brave
None but the Brave deserves the Fair.

II.

Timotheus° plac'd on high 20
    Amid the tuneful Quire,

ALEXANDER'S FEAST. **1. Persia won:** in 331 B.C. **2. Philip's . . . Son:** Alexander the Great (356–325 B.C.), son of Philip II of Macedonia. **9. Thais:** Thaïs, Alexander's Athenian mistress. **20. Timotheus:** Alexander's music master.

With flying Fingers touch'd the Lyre:
The trembling Notes ascend the Sky,
                    And Heav'nly Joys inspire.
The Song° began from *Jove;*
Who left his blissful Seats above,
(Such is the Pow'r of mighty Love.)
A Dragon's fiery Form bely'd the God:
Sublime on Radiant Spires° He rode,
    When He to fair *Olympia* press'd: 30
    And while He sought her snowy Breast:
Then, round her slender Waste he curl'd,
And stamp'd an Image of himself, a Sov'raign of the World.
The list'ning Crowd admire° the lofty Sound,
A present Deity, they shout around:
A present Deity the vaulted Roofs rebound.
    With ravish'd Ears
    The Monarch hears,
    Assumes the God,
    Affects to nod,   40
And seems to shake the Spheres.

CHORUS.

With ravish'd Ears
The Monarch hears,
Assumes the God,
Affects to Nod,
And seems to shake the Spheres.

III.

The Praise of *Bacchus* then, the sweet Musician sung;
    Of *Bacchus* ever Fair, and ever Young:
    The jolly God in Triumph comes;
    Sound the Trumpets; beat the Drums: 50
    Flush'd with a purple Grace°
    He shews his honest° Face,
Now give the Hautboys° breath; He comes, He comes.
    Bacchus ever Fair and Young,
    Drinking Joys did first ordain:
    Bacchus Blessings are a Treasure;
    Drinking is the Soldiers Pleasure;
        Rich the Treasure,
        Sweet the Pleasure;
        Sweet is Pleasure after Pain.   60

CHORUS.

Bacchus Blessings *are a Treasure,*
Drinking is the Soldier's Pleasure;
    Rich the Treasure,
    Sweet the Pleasure;
    Sweet is Pleasure after Pain.

IV.

Sooth'd with the Sound the King grew vain;
    Fought all his Battails o'er again;
And thrice He routed all his Foes; and thrice He slew the slain.
    The Master° saw the Madness rise;
    His glowing Cheeks, his ardent Eyes;   70
    And while He Heav'n and Earth defy'd,
    Chang'd his hand,° and check'd his Pride.
    He chose a Mournful Muse
    Soft Pity to infuse:
    He sung *Darius*° Great and Good,
        By too severe a Fate,
    Fallen, fallen, fallen, fallen,
        Fallen from his high Estate
                    And weltring in his Blood:
Deserted at his utmost Need,   80
By those his former Bounty fed:°
On the bare Earth expos'd He lyes,
With not a Friend to close his Eyes.

With down-cast Looks the joyless Victor sate,
    Revolveing in his alter'd Soul
    The various Turns of Chance below;
    And, now and then, a Sigh he stole;
    And Tears began to flow.

CHORUS.

Revolveing in his alter'd Soul
    The various Turns of Chance below;   90
    And, now and then, a Sigh he stole;
    And Tears began to flow.

V.

The Mighty Master smil'd to see
That Love was in the next Degree:
'Twas but a Kindred-Sound to move;
For Pity melts the Mind to Love.
    Softly sweet, in *Lydian*° Measures,
    Soon He sooth'd his Soul to Pleasures.

25–33. The Song . . . World: Alexander, like other heroes, was believed to be of divine origin, a notion supported by the claim of his mother, Olympias, that he was begot by a supernatural serpent. **29. Spires:** coils. **34. admire:** wonder at. **51. a purple Grace:** wine. **52. honest:** open, frank; possibly, comely. **53. Hautboys:** oboes.

69. The Master: Timotheus. **72. Chang'd his hand:** changed his tune. **75. Darius:** Darius III (*c.* 380–330 B.C.), the Persian emperor. **80–81. Deserted . . . fed:** Darius was slain by his own followers after being defeated by Alexander. **97. Lydian:** soft, plaintive; one of the four principal musical modes in ancient Greece.

War, he sung, is Toil and Trouble;
Honour but an empty Bubble.   100
  Never ending, still beginning,
Fighting still, and still destroying,
  If the World be worth thy Winning,
Think, O think, it worth Enjoying.
  Lovely *Thais* sits beside thee,
  Take the Good the Gods provide thee.

The Many° rend the Skies, with loud Applause;
So Love was Crown'd, but Musique won the Cause.
  The Prince, unable to conceal his Pain,
    Gaz'd on the Fair   110
      Who caus'd his Care,
    And sigh'd and look'd, sigh'd and look'd,
    Sigh'd and look'd, and sigh'd again:
At length, with Love and Wine at once oppress'd,
The vanquish'd Victor sunk upon her Breast.

CHORUS.

The Prince, unable to conceal his Pain,
  Gaz'd on the Fair
    Who caus'd his Care,
  And sigh'd and look'd, sigh'd and look'd,
  Sigh'd and look'd, and sigh'd again: 120
At length, with Love and Wine at once oppress'd,
The vanquish'd Victor sunk upon her Breast.

VI.

Now strike the Golden Lyre again:
A lowder yet, and yet a lowder Strain.
Break his Bands of Sleep asunder,
And rouze him, like a rattling Peal of Thunder.
    Hark, hark, the horrid Sound
      Has rais'd up his Head,
      As awak'd from the Dead,
      And amaz'd, he stares around.   130
Revenge,° Revenge, *Timotheus* cries,
    See the Furies arise!
    See the Snakes that they rear,
    How they hiss in their Hair,
And the Sparkles that flash from their Eyes!
    Behold a ghastly Band,
    Each a Torch in his Hand!
Those are *Grecian* Ghosts, that in Battail were slayn,
              And unbury'd remain
              Inglorious on the Plain.   140

Give the Vengeance due
  To the Valiant Crew.
Behold how they toss their Torches on high,
    How they point to the *Persian* Abodes,
And glitt'ring Temples of their Hostile Gods!
The Princes applaud, with a furious Joy;
And the King seyz'd a Flambeau, with Zeal to destroy;
    Thais led the Way,
    To light him to his Prey,
And, like another *Hellen*, fir'd another *Troy*.   150

CHORUS.

And the King seyz'd a Flambeau, with Zeal to destroy;
    Thais led the Way,
    To light him to his Prey,
And, like another Hellen, *fir'd another* Troy.

VII.

    Thus, long ago
  'Ere heaving Bellows learn'd to blow,
    While Organs yet were mute;
  Timotheus, to his breathing Flute,
        And sounding Lyre,
Cou'd swell the Soul to rage, or kindle soft
Desire.   160
  At last Divine *Cecilia* came,
  Inventress of the Vocal Frame;°
The sweet Enthusiast,° from her Sacred Store,
    Enlarg'd the former narrow Bounds,
    And added Length to solemn Sounds,
With Nature's Mother-Wit, and Arts unknown
before.
  Let old *Timotheus* yield the Prize,
    Or both divide the Crown;
  He rais'd a Mortal to the Skies;
  She drew an Angel down.°   170

Grand CHORUS.

At last, Divine Cecilia *came,*
Inventress of the Vocal Frame;
The sweet Enthusiast, from her Sacred Store,
  Enlarg'd the former narrow Bounds,
  And added Length to solemn Sounds,
With Nature's Mother-Wit, and Arts unknown before.
  Let old Timotheus *yield the Prize,*
    Or both divide the Crown;
  He rais'd a Mortal to the Skies;
  She drew an Angel down.   180

---

107. The Many: (meinie) retinue, company. **131. Revenge:**
Thaïs is supposed to have persuaded Alexander to set
fire to the palace of Persepolis in revenge for the burning of
Athens by the Persians 150 years earlier.

162. the Vocal Frame: the organ. **163. Enthusiast:** used in
the etymological sense of "one possessed by a god." **170.
She . . . down:** Cf. *A Song for St. Cecilia's Day*, above, l. 53.

PREFACE
[TO THE *FABLES* . . .]

Fables Ancient and Modern; Translated into Verse, from Homer, Ovid, Boccace and Chaucer: with Original Poems was Dryden's last major work. It was published in March, 1700, a short time before his death (May 1). The Preface gives us Dryden's last thoughts on the art of translation, which occupied so much of his varied literary career, and a considerable bonus in the form of a comparative evaluation of four great poets.

The text is that of the first edition (1700), with a few errors corrected.

'TIS with a Poet, as with a Man who designs to build, and is very exact, as he supposes, in casting up the Cost beforehand: But, generally speaking, he is mistaken in his Account, and reckons short of the Expence he first intended: He alters his Mind as the Work proceeds, and will have this or that Convenience more, of which he had not thought when he began. So has it hapned to me; I have built a House, where I intended but a Lodge: Yet with better Success than a certain Nobleman,[1] who beginning with a Dog-kennil, never liv'd to finish the Palace he had contriv'd.

From translating the First of *Homer*'s *Iliads*, (which I intended as an Essay[2] to the whole Work) I proceeded to the Translation of the Twelfth Book of *Ovid*'s *Metamorphoses*, because it contains, among other Things, the Causes, the Beginning, and Ending, of the *Trojan* War: Here I ought in reason to have stopp'd; but the Speeches of *Ajax* and *Ulysses* lying next in my way, I could not balk 'em. When I had compass'd them, I was so taken with the former Part of the Fifteenth Book, (which is the Master-piece of the whole *Metamorphoses*) that I enjoyn'd my self the pleasing Task of rendring it into *English*. And now I found, by the Number of my Verses, that they began to swell into a little Volume; which gave me an Occasion of looking backward on some Beauties of my Author,

in his former Books: There occur'd to me the Hunting of the Boar, *Cinyras* and *Myrrha*, the good-natur'd Story of *Baucis* and *Philemon*, with the rest, which I hope I have translated closely enough, and given them the same Turn of Verse, which they had in the Original; and this, I may say without vanity, is not the Talent of every Poet: He who has arriv'd the nearest to it, is the Ingenious and Learned *Sandys*,[3] the best Versifier of the former Age; if I may properly call it by that Name, which was the former Part of this concluding Century. For *Spencer* and *Fairfax*[4] both flourish'd in the Reign of Queen *Elizabeth*: Great Masters in our Language; and who saw much farther into the Beauties of our Numbers, than those who immediately followed them. *Milton* was the Poetical Son of *Spencer*, and Mr. *Waller*[5] of *Fairfax*; for we have our Lineal Descents and Clans, as well as other Families: *Spencer* more than once insinuates, that the Soul of *Chaucer* was transfus'd into his Body;[6] and that he was begotten by him Two hundred years after his Decease. *Milton* has acknowledged to me, that *Spencer* was his Original; and many besides my self have heard our famous *Waller* own, that he deriv'd the Harmony of his Numbers from the *Godfrey of Bulloign*, which was turn'd into *English* by Mr. *Fairfax*. But to return: Having done with *Ovid* for this time, it came into my mind, that our old *English* Poet *Chaucer* in many Things resembled him, and that with no disadvantage on the Side of the Modern Author, as I shall endeavour to prove when I compare them: And as I am, and always have been studious to promote the Honour of my Native Country, so I soon resolv'd to put their Merits to the Trial, by turning some of the *Canterbury* Tales into our Language, as it is now refin'd: For by this Means both the Poets being set in the same Light, and dress'd in the same *English* Habit, Story to be compar'd with Story, a certain Judgment may be made betwixt them, by the Reader, without obtruding my Opinion on him:

PREFACE TO THE *Fables*. **1. a certain Nobleman:** probably George Villiers (1628–87), *Second* Duke of Buckingham, a collaborator in *The Rehearsal* (1671) and the Zimri of *Absalom and Achitophel*, above, l. 544. **2. an Essay:** a trial run.

3. Sandys: George Sandys (1578–1644) published a translation of Ovid's *Metamorphoses* in 1626. **4. Spencer and Fairfax:** Edmund Spenser (c. 1552–99) and Edward Fairfax (d. 1635). Fairfax's translation of Tasso under the title *Godfrey of Bulloigne, or the Recovery of Jerusalem* was published in 1600. **5. Mr. Waller:** Edmund Waller (1606–87). (See the selections from Waller in Part Three.) **6. the Soul . . . Body:**

> through infusion sweete
> Of thine owne spirit, which doth in me surviue,
> I follow here the footing of the feete.
>
> (*Faerie Queene*, IV. ii. 34)

Or if I seem partial to my Country-man, and Predecessor in the Laurel, the Friends of Antiquity are not few: And besides many of the Learn'd, *Ovid* has almost all the *Beaux*, and the whole Fair Sex his declar'd Patrons.[7] Perhaps I have assum'd somewhat more to my self than they allow me; because I have adventur'd to sum up the Evidence: But the Readers are the Jury; and their Privilege remains entire to decide according to the Merits of the Cause: Or, if they please to bring it to another Hearing, before some other Court. In the mean time, to follow the Thrid[8] of my Discourse, (as Thoughts, according to Mr. *Hobbs*,[9] have always some Connexion) so from *Chaucer* I was led to think on *Boccace*,[10] who was not only his Contemporary, but also pursu'd the same Studies; wrote Novels in Prose, and many Works in Verse; particularly is said to have invented the Octave Rhyme,[11] or *Stanza* of Eight Lines, which ever since has been maintain'd by the Practice of all *Italian* Writers, who are, or at least assume the Title of *Heroick Poets:*[12] He and *Chaucer*, among other Things, had this in common, that they refin'd their Mother-Tongues; but with this difference, that *Dante* had begun to file their Language, at least in Verse, before the time of *Boccace*, who likewise receiv'd no little Help from his Master *Petrarch:* But the Reformation of their Prose was wholly owing to *Boccace* himself; who is yet the Standard of Purity in the *Italian* Tongue; though many of his Phrases are become obsolete, as in process of Time it must needs happen. *Chaucer* (as you have formerly been told by our learn'd Mr. *Rhymer*[13]) first adorn'd and amplified our barren Tongue from the *Provencall*, which was then the most polish'd of all the Modern Languages: But this Subject has been copiously treated by that great Critick, who deserves no little Commendation from us his Countrymen. For these Reasons of Time, and Resemblance of

Genius, in *Chaucer* and *Boccace*, I resolv'd to join them in my present Work; to which I have added some Original Papers of my own; which whether they are equal or inferiour to my other Poems, an Author is the most improper Judge; and therefore I leave them wholly to the Mercy of the Reader: I will hope the best, that they will not be condemn'd; but if they should, I have the Excuse of an old Gentleman, who mounting on Horseback before some Ladies, when I was present, got up somewhat heavily, but desir'd of the Fair Spectators, that they would count Fourscore and eight before they judg'd him. By the Mercy of God, I am already come within Twenty Years of his Number, a Cripple in my Limbs, but what Decays are in my Mind, the Reader must determine. I think my self as vigorous as ever in the Faculties of my Soul, excepting only my Memory, which is not impair'd to any great degree; and if I lose not more of it, I have no great reason to complain. What Judgment I had, increases rather than diminishes; and Thoughts, such as they are, come crowding in so fast upon me, that my only Difficulty is to chuse or to reject; to run them into Verse, or to give them the other Harmony of Prose. I have so long studied and practis'd both, that they are grown into a Habit, and become familiar to me. In short, though I may lawfully plead some part of the old Gentleman's Excuse; yet I will reserve it till I think I have greater need, and ask no Grains of Allowance for the Faults of this my present Work, but those which are given of course to Humane Frailty. I will not trouble my Reader with the shortness of Time in which I writ it; or the several Intervals of Sickness:[14] They who think too well of their own Performances, are apt to boast in their Prefaces how little Time their Works have cost them; and what other Business of more importance interfer'd: But the Reader will be as apt to ask the Question, Why they allow'd not a longer Time to make their Works more perfect? and why they had so despicable an Opinion of their Judges, as to thrust their indigested Stuff upon them, as if they deserv'd no better?

With this Account of my present Undertaking, I conclude the first Part of this Discourse: In the second Part, as at a second Sitting, though I alter not the Draught, I must touch the same Features over again, and change the Dead-colouring[15] of the Whole. In

7. **Patrons:** patrons of the *Ars Amoris.* 8. **Thrid:** thread. 9. **according . . . Hobbs:** in *Leviathan*, I. iii. 10. **Boccace:** Giovanni Boccaccio (1313–75). 11. **Octave Rhyme:** Boccaccio established (but did not invent) *ottava rima* as a narrative verse form in Italian. 12. **Heroick Poets:** such as Ariosto and Tasso. 13. **Mr. Rhymer:** Thomas Rymer (1641–1713), in *A Short View of Tragedy* (1693). It is hard to believe that there is not at least a grain of sarcasm in this praise of Rymer, whom Dryden had attacked in the Dedication to *Examen Poeticum* (1693) as among the venomous insects "who manifestly aim at the destruction of our Poetical Church and State. Who allow nothing to their Country-Men, either of this or of the former Age." Here Dryden is asking his countrymen to allow something to Rymer.

14. **Sickness:** Dryden suffered in his later years from gout, gravel, deafness, and erysipelas, or St. Anthony's fire. 15. **Dead-colouring:** the first, preparatory, layer of color.

general I will only say, that I have written nothing which savours of Immorality or Profaneness; at least, I am not conscious to my self of any such Intention. If there happen to be found an irreverent Expression, or a Thought too wanton, they are crept into my Verses through my Inadvertency: If the Searchers find any in the Cargo, let them be stav'd[16] or forfeited, like Counterbanded Goods; at least, let their Authors be answerable for them, as being but imported Merchandise, and not of my own Manufacture. On the other Side, I have endeavour'd to chuse such Fables, both Ancient and Modern, as contain in each of them some instructive Moral, which I could prove by Induction, but the Way is tedious; and they leap foremost into sight, without the Reader's Trouble of looking after them. I wish I could affirm with a safe Conscience, that I had taken the same Care in all my former Writings; for it must be own'd, that supposing Verses are never so beautiful or pleasing, yet if they contain any thing which shocks Religion, or Good Manners, they are at best, what *Horace* says of good Numbers without good Sense, *Versus inopes rerum, nugæque canoræ:*[17] Thus far, I hope, I am Right in Court, without renouncing to my other Right of Self-defence, where I have been wrongfully accus'd, and my Sense wire-drawn[18] into Blasphemy or Bawdry, as it has often been by a Religious Lawyer, in a late Pleading against the Stage;[19] in which he mixes Truth with Falshood, and has not forgotten the old Rule, of calumniating strongly, that something may remain.

I resume the Thrid of my Discourse with the first of my Translations, which was the First *Iliad* of *Homer*. If it shall please God to give me longer Life, and moderate Health, my Intentions are to translate the whole *Ilias;* provided still, that I meet with those Encouragements from the Publick, which may enable me to proceed in my Undertaking with some Chearfulness. And this I dare assure the World before-hand, that I have found by Trial, *Homer* a more pleasing Task than *Virgil*, (though I say not the Translation will be less laborious.) For the *Grecian* is more according to my Genius, than the *Latin* Poet. In the Works of the two Authors we may read their Manners, and natural Inclinations, which are wholly different. *Virgil* was of a quiet, sedate Temper; *Homer* was violent, impetuous,

and full of Fire. The chief Talent of *Virgil* was Propriety of Thoughts, and Ornament of Words: *Homer* was rapid in his Thoughts, and took all the Liberties both of Numbers, and of Expressions, which his Language, and the Age in which he liv'd allow'd him: *Homer*'s Invention was more copious, *Virgil*'s more confin'd: So that if *Homer* had not led the Way, it was not in *Virgil* to have begun Heroick Poetry: For, nothing can be more evident, than that the *Roman* Poem is but the Second Part of the *Ilias;* a Continuation of the same Story: And the Persons already form'd: The Manners of *Æneas*, are those of *Hector* superadded to those which *Homer* gave him. The Adventures of *Ulysses* in the *Odysseis*, are imitated in the first Six Books of *Virgil*'s *Æneis:* And though the Accidents are not the same, (which would have argu'd him of a servile, copying, and total Barrenness of Invention) yet the Seas were the same, in which both the *Heroes* wander'd; and *Dido* cannot be deny'd to be the Poetical Daughter of *Calypso*. The Six latter Books of *Virgil*'s Poem, are the Four and twenty *Iliads* contracted: A Quarrel occasion'd by a Lady, a Single Combate, Battels fought, and a Town besieg'd. I say not this in derogation to *Virgil*, neither do I contradict any thing which I have formerly said in his just Praise: For his *Episodes* are almost wholly of his own Invention; and the Form which he has given to the Telling, makes the Tale his own, even though the Original Story had been the same. But this proves, however, that *Homer* taught *Virgil* to design: And if Invention be the first Vertue of an Epick Poet, then the *Latin* Poem can only be allow'd the second Place. Mr. *Hobbs*, in the Preface to his own bald Translation of the *Ilias*,[20] (studying Poetry as he did Mathematicks, when it was too late) Mr. *Hobbs*, I say, begins the Praise of *Homer* where he should have ended it. He tells us, that the first Beauty[21] of an Epick Poem consists in Diction, that is, in the Choice of Words, and Harmony of Numbers: Now, the Words are the Colouring of the Work, which in the Order of Nature is last to be consider'd. The Design, the Disposition, the Manners, and the Thoughts, are all before it: Where any of those are wanting or imperfect, so much wants or is imperfect in the Imitation of Humane Life; which is in the very Definition of a Poem. Words indeed, like

---

16. stav'd: destroyed, as a cask is broken up. **17. Versus . . . canoræ:** "verses void of substance, and melodious trifles" (*Ars Poetica*, l. 322). **18. wire-drawn:** stretched. **19. by . . . Stage:** Jeremy Collier in *A Short View of the Immorality and Profaneness of the English Stage* (1698).

20. Translation . . . Ilias: Hobbes's translation of the *Iliad* (1676) and the *Odyssey* (1673–75) were published together in 1677. **21. the first Beauty:** in fact mentioned, but not ranked, first.

glaring Colours, are the first Beauties that arise, and strike the Sight; but if the Draught be false or lame, the Figures ill dispos'd, the Manners obscure or inconsistent, or the Thoughts unnatural, then the finest Colours are but Dawbing, and the Piece is a beautiful Monster at the best. Neither *Virgil* nor *Homer* were deficient in any of the former Beauties; but in this last, which is Expression, the *Roman* Poet is at least equal to the *Grecian*, as I have said elsewhere; supplying the Poverty of his Language, by his Musical Ear, and by his Diligence. But to return: Our two Great Poets, being so different in their Tempers, one Cholerick and Sanguin, the other Phlegmatick and Melancholick; that which makes them excel in their several Ways, is, that each of them has follow'd his own natural Inclination, as well in Forming the Design, as in the Execution of it. The very *Heroes* shew their Authors: *Achilles* is hot, impatient, revengeful, *Impiger, iracundus, inexorabilis, acer,*[22] &c. Æneas patient, considerate, careful of his People, and merciful to his Enemies; ever submissive to the Will of Heaven, *quo fata trahunt retrahuntque, sequamur.*[23] I could please my self with enlarging on this Subject, but am forc'd to defer it to a fitter Time. From all I have said, I will only draw this Inference, That the Action of *Homer* being more full of Vigour than that of *Virgil*, according to the Temper of the Writer, is of consequence more pleasing to the Reader. One warms you by Degrees; the other sets you on fire all at once, and never intermits his Heat. 'Tis the same Difference which *Longinus* makes[24] betwixt the Effects of Eloquence in *Demosthenes*, and *Tully*. One persuades; the other commands. You never cool while you read *Homer*, even not in the Second Book, (a graceful Flattery to his Countrymen;) but he hastens from the Ships, and concludes not that Book till he has made you an Amends by the violent playing of a new Machine. From thence he hurries on his Action with Variety of Events, and ends it in less Compass than Two Months. This Vehemence of his, I confess, is more suitable to my Temper: and therefore I have translated his First Book with greater Pleasure than any Part of *Virgil*: But it was not a Pleasure without Pains: The continual Agitations of the Spirits, must needs be a Weakning of any Constitution, especially in Age: and many Pauses are required for Refreshment betwixt the Heats; the *Iliad* of its self being a third part longer than all *Virgil*'s Works together.

This is what I thought needful in this Place to say of *Homer*. I proceed to *Ovid*, and *Chaucer;* considering the former only in relation to the latter. With *Ovid* ended the Golden Age of the *Roman* Tongue: From *Chaucer* the Purity of the *English* Tongue began. The Manners of the Poets were not unlike: Both of them were well-bred, well-natur'd, amorous, and Libertine, at least in their Writings, it may be also in their Lives. Their Studies were the same, Philosophy, and Philology.[25] Both of them were knowing in Astronomy, of which *Ovid*'s Books of the *Roman* Feasts, and *Chaucer*'s Treatise of the *Astrolabe*, are sufficient Witnesses. But *Chaucer* was likewise an Astrologer, as were *Virgil, Horace, Persius*, and *Manilius*. Both writ with wonderful Facility and Clearness; neither were great Inventors: For *Ovid* only copied the *Grecian* Fables; and most of *Chaucer*'s Stories were taken from his *Italian* Contemporaries, or their Predecessors: *Boccace* his *Decameron* was first publish'd; and from thence our *Englishman* has borrow'd many of his *Canterbury Tales:*[26] Yet that of *Palamon* and *Arcite* was written in all probability by some *Italian* Wit, in a former Age;[27] as I shall prove hereafter: The Tale of *Grizild* was the Invention of *Petrarch;* by him sent to *Boccace;* from whom it came to *Chaucer:*[28] *Troilus* and *Cressida* was also written by a *Lombard* Author;[29] but much amplified by our *English* Translatour, as well as beautified; the Genius of our Countrymen in general being rather to improve an Invention, than to invent themselves; as is evident not only in our Poetry, but in many of our Manufactures. I find I have anticipated already, and taken up from *Boccace* before I come to him: But there is so much less behind; and I am of the Temper of most Kings, *who love to be in Debt,*[30] are

---

22. Impiger . . . acer: "indefatigable, wrathful, inexorable, fierce" (Horace, *Ars Poetica*, l. 121). **23. quo . . . sequamur:** "Let us follow whither the Fates draw and recall us" (*Aeneid*, V. 709). **24. the same . . . makes:** in *On the Sublime*, XII. 4–5.

25. Philology: letters. **26. from . . . Tales:** The case for Chaucer's indebtedness to the *Decameron* (1471) has never been proved. **27. that . . . Age:** The source of Chaucer's *Knight's Tale*, the story of Palamon and Arcite, was in fact Boccaccio's *Teseida* (1475). **28. The Tale . . . Chaucer:** Petrarch had taken the story of Griselda from the *Decameron*, translated it into Latin, and sent it to Boccaccio. Chaucer's source is Petrarch's version, not Boccaccio's. **29. Troilus . . . Author:** Chaucer speaks of "myn auctor called Lollius" (*Troilus and Criseyde*, I. 394), but his actual source was Boccaccio's *Filostrato* (c. 1480). Dryden got his misinformation from Speght's edition of Chaucer (1598, reprinted in 1687). **30. the Temper . . . Debt:** William III was pouring money into the war against France.

all for present Money, no matter how they pay it afterwards: Besides, the Nature of a Preface is rambling; never wholly out of the Way, nor in it. This I have learn'd from the Practice of honest *Montaign*, and return at my pleasure to *Ovid* and *Chaucer*, of whom I have little more to say. Both of them built on the Inventions of other Men; yet since *Chaucer* had something of his own, as *The Wife of Baths Tale, The Cock and the Fox*,[31] which I have translated, and some others, I may justly give our Countryman the Precedence in that Part; since I can remember nothing of *Ovid* which was wholly his. Both of them understood the Manners; under which Name I comprehend the Passions, and, in a larger Sense, the Descriptions of Persons, and their very Habits: For an Example, I see *Baucis* and *Philemon* as perfectly before me, as if some ancient Painter had drawn them; and all the Pilgrims in the *Canterbury* Tales, their Humours, their Features, and the very Dress, as distinctly as if I had supp'd with them at the *Tabard* in *Southwark*: Yet even there too the Figures of *Chaucer* are much more lively, and set in a better Light: Which though I have not time to prove; yet I appeal to the Reader, and am sure he will clear me from Partiality. The Thoughts and Words remain to be consider'd, in the Comparison of the two Poets; and I have sav'd my self one half of that Labour, by owning that *Ovid* liv'd when the *Roman* Tongue was in its Meridian; *Chaucer*, in the Dawning of our Language: Therefore that Part of the Comparison stands not on an equal Foot, any more than the Diction of *Ennius*[32] and *Ovid;* or of *Chaucer*, and our present *English*. The Words are given up as a Post not to be defended in our Poet, because he wanted the Modern Art of Fortifying. The Thoughts remain to be consider'd: And they are to be measur'd only by their Propriety; that is, as they flow more or less naturally from the Persons describ'd, on such and such Occasions. The Vulgar Judges, which are Nine Parts in Ten of all Nations, who call Conceits and Jingles Wit, who see *Ovid* full of them, and *Chaucer* altogether without them, will think me little less than mad, for preferring the *Englishman* to the *Roman:* Yet, with their leave, I must presume to say, that the Things they admire are only glittering Trifles, and so far

from being Witty, that in a serious Poem they are nauseous, because they are unnatural. Wou'd any Man who is ready to die for Love, describe his Passion like *Narcissus?* Wou'd he think of *inopem me copia fecit*,[33] and a Dozen more of such Expressions, pour'd on the Neck of one another, and signifying all the same Thing? If this were Wit, was this a Time to be witty, when the poor Wretch was in the Agony of Death? This is just *John Littlewit* in *Bartholomew Fair*, who had a Conceit (as he tells you) left him in his Misery; a miserable Conceit.[34] On these Occasions the Poet shou'd endeavour to raise Pity: But instead of this, *Ovid* is tickling you to laugh. *Virgil* never made use of such Machines,[35] when he was moving you to commiserate the Death of *Dido:* He would not destroy what he was building. *Chaucer* makes *Arcite* violent in his Love, and unjust in the Pursuit of it: Yet when he came to die, he made him think more reasonably: He repents not of his Love, for that had alter'd his Character; but acknowledges the Injustice of his Proceedings, and resigns *Emilia* to *Palamon*. What would *Ovid* have done on this Occasion? He would certainly have made *Arcite* witty on his Death-bed. He had complain'd he was farther off from Possession, by being so near, and a thousand such Boyisms,[36] which *Chaucer* rejected as below the Dignity of the Subject. They who think otherwise, would by the same Reason prefer *Lucan* and *Ovid* to *Homer* and *Virgil*, and *Martial* to all Four of them. As for the Turn of Words, in which *Ovid* particularly excels all Poets; they are sometimes a Fault, and sometimes a Beauty, as they are us'd properly or improperly; but in strong Passions always to be shunn'd, because Passions are serious, and will admit no Playing. The *French* have a high Value for them; and I confess, they are often what they call Delicate, when they are introduc'd with Judgment; but *Chaucer* writ with more Simplicity, and follow'd Nature more closely, than to use them. I have thus far, to the best of my Knowledge, been an upright Judge betwixt the Parties in Competition, not medling with the Design nor the Disposition of it; because the Design was not their own; and in the disposing of it they were equal. It remains that I say somewhat of *Chaucer* in particular.

In the first place, As he is the Father of *English*

---

31. The Cock . . . Fox: *The Nun's Priest's Tale*. Neither tale can be considered a pure invention, although the actual source of the first is unknown and of the second doubtful. **32. Ennius:** Quintus Ennius (239–*c.* 169 B.C.), Latin poet.

33. inopem . . . fecit: "Plenty made me poor" (*Metamorphoses*, III. 466). **34. John . . . Conceit:** Ben Jonson, *Bartholomew Fair*, I. i. **35. Machines:** devices. **36. Boyisms:** puerilities.

Poetry, so I hold him in the same Degree of Veneration as the *Grecians* held *Homer*, or the *Romans Virgil:* He is a perpetual Fountain of good Sense; learn'd in all Sciences; and therefore speaks properly on all Subjects: As he knew what to say, so he knows also when to leave off; a Continence which is practis'd by few Writers, and scarcely by any of the Ancients, excepting *Virgil* and *Horace*. One of our late great Poets[37] is sunk in his Reputation, because he cou'd never forgive[38] any Conceit which came in his way; but swept like a Drag-net, great and small. There was plenty enough, but the Dishes were ill sorted; whole Pyramids of Sweet-meats, for Boys and Women; but little of solid Meat, for Men: All this proceeded not from any want of Knowledge, but of Judgment; neither did he want that in discerning the Beauties and Faults of other Poets; but only indulg'd himself in the Luxury of Writing; and perhaps knew it was a Fault, but hop'd the Reader would not find it. For this Reason, though he must always be thought a great Poet, he is no longer esteem'd a good Writer: And for Ten Impressions, which his Works have had in so many successive Years, yet at present a hundred Books are scarcely purchas'd once a Twelvemonth: For, as my last Lord *Rochester* said, though somewhat profanely, *Not being of God, he could not stand.*

Chaucer follow'd Nature every where; but was never so bold to go beyond her: And there is a great Difference of being *Poeta* and *nimis Poeta*,[39] if we may believe *Catullus*,[40] as much as betwixt a modest Behaviour and Affectation. The Verse of *Chaucer*, I confess, is not Harmonious to us; but 'tis like the Eloquence of one whom *Tacitus* commends, it was *auribus istius temporis accommodata:*[41] They who liv'd with him, and some time after him, thought it Musical; and it continues so even in our Judgment, if compar'd with the Numbers of *Lidgate* and *Gower* his Contemporaries: There is the rude Sweetness of a *Scotch* Tune in it, which is natural and pleasing, though not perfect. 'Tis true, I cannot go so far as he who publish'd the last Edition of him;[42] for he would make

us believe the Fault is in our Ears, and that there were really Ten Syllables in a Verse where we find but Nine: But this Opinion is not worth confuting; 'tis so gross and obvious an Errour, that common Sense (which is a Rule in every thing but Matters of Faith and Revelation) must convince the Reader, that Equality of Numbers in every Verse which we call *Heroick*,[43] was either not known, or not always practis'd in *Chaucer's* Age. It were an easie Matter to produce some thousands of his Verses, which are lame for want of half a Foot, and sometimes a whole one, and which no Pronunciation can make otherwise. We can only say, that he liv'd in the Infancy of our Poetry, and that nothing is brought to Perfection at the first. We must be Children before we grow Men. There was an *Ennius*, and in process of Time a *Lucilius*, and a *Lucretius*, before *Virgil* and *Horace;* even after *Chaucer* there was a *Spencer*, a *Harrington*, a *Fairfax*, before *Waller* and *Denham* were in being: And our Numbers were in their Nonage till these last appear'd. I need say little of his Parentage, Life, and Fortunes: They are to be found at large in all the Editions of his Works. He was employ'd abroad, and favour'd by *Edward* the Third, *Richard* the Second, and *Henry* the Fourth, and was Poet, as I suppose, to all Three of them. In *Richard's* Time, I doubt,[44] he was a little dipt in the Rebellion of the Commons;[45] and being Brother-in-Law to *John of Ghant*,[46] it was no wonder if he follow'd the Fortunes of that Family; and was well with *Henry* the Fourth[47] when he had depos'd his Predecessor. Neither is it to be admir'd,[48] that *Henry*, who was a wise as well as a valiant Prince, who claim'd by Succession, and was sensible that his Title was not sound, but was rightfully in *Mortimer*, who had married the Heir of *York;* it was not to be admir'd, I say, if that great Politician should be pleas'd to have the greatest Wit of those Times in his Interests, and to be the Trumpet of his Praises. *Augustus* had given him

---

37. **One . . . Poets:** Abraham Cowley (1618–67), Metaphysical poet and essayist. **38. forgive:** forego. **39. Poeta . . . Poeta:** "a poet" and "too much of a poet." **40. Catullus:** a mistake for Martial (*Epigrams*, III. 44). **41. auribus . . . accommodata:** "suited to the ears of that time" (Cicero, *De Oratore*, XXI. 2; for *istius temporis* read *iudicum*). **42. he . . . him:** Speght argued in a note to his second edition (1602) that "his verses, although in divers places they may seeme to us to stand of unequall measures: yet a

skillful Reader, that can scan them in their nature, shall find it otherwise." The skill in reading Chaucer was a late development, and the rule of sounding the final *e* has by itself rid us of countless metrical embarrassments. **43. every . . . Heroick:** iambic pentameter. **44. doubt:** suspect. **45. he . . . Commons:** a misapprehension taken from Speght, based on the ascription to Chaucer of Usk's *Testament of Love*, in which the speaker makes a confession to this effect. **46. Brother-in-Law . . . Ghant:** (Gaunt). The alleged relationship has never been verified. **47. well . . . Fourth:** who increased the annuity granted Chaucer by Richard II; Chaucer lived less than a year after the new reign began. **48. admir'd:** wondered at.

the Example, by the Advice of *Mæcenas*, who recommended *Virgil* and *Horace* to him; whose Praises help'd to make him Popular while he was alive, and after his Death have made him Precious to Posterity. As for the Religion of our Poet, he seems to have some little Byas towards the Opinions of *Wickliff*, after *John of Ghant* his Patron; somewhat of which appears in the Tale of *Piers Plowman:*[49] Yet I cannot blame him for inveighing so sharply against the Vices of the Clergy in his Age: Their Pride, their Ambition, their Pomp, their Avarice, their Worldly Interest, deserv'd the Lashes which he gave them, both in that, and in most of his *Canterbury Tales:* Neither has his Contemporary *Boccace*, spar'd them. Yet both those Poets liv'd in much esteem, with good and holy Men in Orders: For the Scandal which is given by particular Priests, reflects not on the Sacred Function. *Chaucer's Monk*, his *Chanon*,[50] and his *Fryar*, took[51] not from the Character of his *Good Parson*. A Satyrical Poet is the Check of the Laymen, on bad Priests. We are only to take care, that we involve not the Innocent with the Guilty in the same Condemnation. The Good cannot be too much honour'd, nor the Bad too coursly us'd: For the Corruption of the Best, becomes the Worst. When a Clergy-man is whipp'd, his Gown is first taken off, by which the Dignity of his Order is secur'd: If he be wrongfully accus'd, he has his Action of Slander; and 'tis at the Poet's Peril, if he transgress the Law. But they will tell us, that all kind of Satire, though never so well deserv'd by particular Priests, yet brings the whole Order into Contempt. Is then the Peerage of *England* any thing dishonour'd, when a Peer suffers for his Treason? If he be libell'd, or any way defam'd, he has his *Scandalum Magnatum*[52] to punish the Offendor. They who use this kind of Argument, seem to be conscious to themselves of somewhat which has deserv'd the Poet's Lash; and are less concern'd for their Publick Capacity, than for their Private: At least, there is Pride at the bottom of their Reasoning. If the Faults of Men in Orders are only to be judg'd among themselves, they are all in some sort Parties: For, since they say the Honour of their Order is concern'd in every Member of it, how can

we be sure, that they will be impartial Judges? How far I may be allow'd to speak my Opinion in this Case, I know not: But I am sure a Dispute of this Nature caus'd Mischief in abundance betwixt a King of *England* and an Archbishop of *Canterbury*;[53] one standing up for the Laws of his Land, and the other for the Honour (as he call'd it) of God's Church; which ended in the Murther of the Prelate, and in the whipping of his Majesty from Post to Pillar for his Penance. The Learn'd and Ingenious Dr. *Drake*[54] has sav'd me the Labour of inquiring into the Esteem and Reverence which the Priests have had of old; and I would rather extend than diminish any part of it: Yet I must needs say, that when a Priest provokes me without any Occasion given him, I have no Reason, unless it be the Charity of a *Christian*, to forgive him: *Prior læsit*[55] is Justification sufficient in the Civil Law. If I answer him in his own Language, Self-defence, I am sure, must be allow'd me; and if I carry it farther, even to a sharp Recrimination, somewhat may be indulg'd to Humane Frailty. Yet my Resentment has not wrought so far, but that I have follow'd *Chaucer* in his Character of a Holy Man,[56] and have enlarg'd on that Subject with some Pleasure, reserving to my self the Right, if I shall think fit hereafter, to describe another sort of Priests, such as are more easily to be found than the Good Parson; such as have given the last Blow to Christianity in this Age, by a Practice so contrary to their Doctrine. But this will keep cold till another time. In the mean while, I take up *Chaucer* where I left him. He must have been a Man of a most wonderful comprehensive Nature, because, as it has been truly observ'd of him, he has taken into the Compass of his *Canterbury Tales* the various Manners and Humours (as we now call them) of the whole *English* Nation, in his Age. Not a single Character has escap'd him. All his Pilgrims are severally distinguish'd from each other; and not only in their Inclinations, but in their very Phisiognomies and Persons. *Baptista Porta*[57] could not have describ'd their Natures better, than by the Marks which the Poet gives them. The Matter and Manner of their Tales, and of their Telling,

---

49. **in . . . Plowman:** *The Plowman's Tale*, included in Speght's edition, was later rejected from the Chaucer canon by Tyrwhitt (1775). Dryden seems to have confused the work with *Piers Plowman*, attributed to William Langland, which also attacks the clergy. **50. Chanon:** canon. **51. took:** detracted. **52. Scandalum Magnatum:** a law protecting those in high office from slander.

53. **a King . . . Canterbury:** Henry II and Thomas à Becket. **54. Dr. Drake:** James Drake (1667–1707), in his reply to Collier, *The Ancient and Modern Stages Surveyed* (1699). **55. Prior læsit:** self-defense; literally, "He hit me first." The quotation is from Terence's *The Eunuch*, l. 6. **56. in . . . Man:** in *The Canterbury Tales*, Prologue, ll. 477–528. **57. Baptista Porta:** Giovanni Battista della Porta (c. 1538–1615), author of *De Humana Physiognomia* (1586).

are so suited to their different Educations, Humours, and Callings, that each of them would be improper in any other Mouth. Even the grave and serious Characters are distinguish'd by their several sorts of Gravity: Their Discourses are such as belong to their Age, their Calling, and their Breeding; such as are becoming of them, and of them only. Some of his Persons are Vicious, and some Vertuous; some are unlearn'd, or (as *Chaucer* calls them) Lewd, and some are Learn'd. Even the Ribaldry of the Low Characters is different: The *Reeve*, the *Miller*, and the *Cook*, are several Men, and distinguish'd from each other, as much as the mincing Lady Prioress, and the broad-speaking gap-tooth'd Wife of *Bathe*. But enough of this: There is such a Variety of Game springing up before me, that I am distracted in my Choice, and know not which to follow. 'Tis sufficient to say according to the Proverb, that here is God's Plenty. We have our Fore-fathers and Great Grand-dames all before us, as they were in *Chaucer*'s Days; their general Characters are still remaining in Mankind, and even in *England*, though they are call'd by other Names than those of *Moncks*, and *Fryars*, and *Chanons*, and *Lady Abbesses*, and *Nuns:* For Mankind is ever the same, and nothing lost out of Nature, though every thing is alter'd. May I have leave to do my self the Justice, (since my Enemies will do me none, and are so far from granting me to be a good Poet, that they will not allow me so much as to be a Christian, or a Moral Man) may I have leave, I say, to inform my Reader, that I have confin'd my Choice to such Tales of *Chaucer*, as savour nothing of Immodesty. If I had desir'd more to please than to instruct, the *Reve*, the *Miller*, the *Shipman*, the *Merchant*, the *Sumner*, and above all, the *Wife of Bathe*, in the Prologue to her Tale, would have procur'd me as many Friends and Readers, as there are *Beaux* and Ladies of Pleasure in the Town. But I will no more offend against Good Manners: I am sensible as I ought to be of the Scandal I have given by my loose Writings; and make what Reparation I am able, by this Publick Acknowledgment. If any thing of this Nature, or of Profaneness, be crept into these Poems, I am so far from defending it, that I disown it. *Totum hoc indictum volo.*[58] *Chaucer* makes another manner of Apologie for his broad-speaking, and *Boccace* makes the like; but I will follow neither of them. Our Country-man, in the end of his Characters, before the *Canterbury Tales*, thus excuses

58. **Totum . . . volo:** I wish all that unsaid.

the Ribaldry, which is very gross, in many of his Novels.

> *But first, I pray you, of your courtesy,*
> *That ye ne arrete it nought my villany,*
> *Though that I plainly speak in this mattere*
> *To tellen you her words, and eke her chere:*
> *Ne though I speak her words properly,*
> *For this ye knowen as well as I,*
> *Who shall tellen a tale after a man*
> *He mote rehearse as nye, as ever He can:*
> *Everich word of it been in his charge,*
> *All speke he, never so rudely, ne large.*
> *Or else he mote tellen his tale untrue,*
> *Or feine things, or find words new:*
> *He may not spare, altho he were his brother,*
> *He mote as well say o word as another.*
> *Christ spake himself full broad in holy Writ,*
> *And well I wote no Villany is it.*
> *Eke* Plato *saith, who so can him rede,*
> *The words mote been Cousin to the dede.*[59]

Yet if a Man should have enquir'd of *Boccace* or of *Chaucer*, what need they had of introducing such Characters, where obscene Words were proper in their Mouths, but very undecent to be heard; I know not what Answer they could have made: For that Reason, such Tales shall be left untold by me. You have here a *Specimen* of *Chaucer*'s Language, which is so obsolete, that his Sense is scarce to be understood; and you have likewise more than one Example of his unequal Numbers, which were mention'd before. Yet many of his Verses consist of Ten Syllables, and the Words not much behind our present *English*: As for Example, these two Lines, in the Description of the Carpenter's Young Wife:

> *Wincing she was, as is a jolly Colt,*
> *Long as a Mast, and upright as a Bolt.*[60]

I have almost done with *Chaucer*, when I have answer'd some Objections relating to my present Work. I find some People are offended that I have turn'd these Tales into modern *English;* because they think them unworthy of my Pains, and look on *Chaucer* as a dry, old-fashion'd Wit, not worth receiving. I have often heard the late Earl of *Leicester*[61] say, that Mr. *Cowley* himself was of that opinion; who having read him over at my Lord's Request, declar'd he had no Taste of him. I dare not advance my

59. **But . . . dede:** Prologue, ll. 725–42. 60. **Wincing . . . Bolt:** The Miller's Tale, ll. 77–78. *Wincing* here means "skittish." 61. **Earl of Leicester:** Philip Sidney (1619–98), Third Earl of Leicester.

Opinion against the Judgment of so great an Author: But I think it fair, however, to leave the Decision to the Publick: Mr. *Cowley* was too modest to set up for a Dictatour; and being shock'd perhaps with his old Style, never examin'd into the depth of his good Sense. *Chaucer*, I confess, is a rough Diamond, and must first be polish'd e'er he shines. I deny not likewise, that living in our early Days of Poetry, he writes not always of a piece; but sometimes mingles trivial Things, with those of greater Moment. Sometimes also, though not often, he runs riot, like *Ovid*, and knows not when he has said enough. But there are more great Wits, beside *Chaucer*, whose Fault is their Excess of Conceits, and those ill sorted. An Author is not to write all he can, but only all he ought. Having observ'd this Redundancy in *Chaucer*, (as it is an easie Matter for a Man of ordinary Parts to find a Fault in one of greater) I have not ty'd my self to a Literal Translation; but have often omitted what I judg'd unnecessary, or not of Dignity enough to appear in the Company of better Thoughts. I have presum'd farther in some Places, and added somewhat of my own where I thought my Author was deficient, and had not given his Thoughts their true Lustre, for want of Words in the Beginning of our Language. And to this I was the more embolden'd, because (if I may be permitted to say it of my self) I found I had a Soul congenial to his, and that I had been conversant in the same Studies. Another Poet, in another Age, may take the same Liberty with my Writings; if at least they live long enough to deserve Correction. It was also necessary sometimes to restore the Sense of *Chaucer*, which was lost or mangled in the Errors of the Press: Let this Example suffice at present: in the Story of *Palamon* and *Arcite*, where the Temple of *Diana* is describ'd, you find these Verses, in all the Editions of our Author:

> There saw I Danè *turned unto a Tree,*
> I mean not the Goddess Diane,
> But Venus *Daughter, which that hight* Danè.

Which after a little Consideration I knew was to be reform'd into this Sense, that *Daphne* the Daughter of *Peneus* was turn'd into a Tree. I durst not make thus bold with *Ovid*, lest some future *Milbourn*[62] should arise, and say, I varied from my Author, because I understood him not.

62. Milbourn: Luke Milbourne (1649–1720), who wrote *Critical Notes on Dryden's Virgil* (1698), after an unsuccessful attempt of his own at translating the first book of the *Aeneid* (1687).

But there are other Judges who think I ought not to have translated *Chaucer* into *English*, out of a quite contrary Notion: They suppose there is a certain Veneration due to his old Language; and that it is little less than Profanation and Sacrilege to alter it. They are farther of opinion, that somewhat of his good Sense will suffer in this Transfusion, and much of the Beauty of his Thoughts will infallibly be lost, which appear with more Grace in their old Habit. Of this Opinion was that excellent Person, whom I mention'd, the late Earl of *Leicester*, who valu'd *Chaucer* as much as Mr. *Cowley* despis'd him. My Lord dissuaded me from this Attempt, (for I was thinking of it some Years before his Death) and his Authority prevail'd so far with me, as to defer my Undertaking while he liv'd, in deference to him: Yet my Reason was not convinc'd with what he urg'd against it. If the first End of a Writer be to be understood, then as his Language grows obsolete, his Thoughts must grow obscure, *multa renascentur quæ nunc cecidere; cadentque quæ nunc sunt in honore vocabula, si volet usus, quem penes arbitrium est & jus & norma loquendi.*[63] When an ancient Word for its Sound and Significancy deserves to be reviv'd, I have that reasonable Veneration for Antiquity, to restore it. All beyond this is Superstition. Words are not like Land-marks, so sacred as never to be remov'd: Customs are chang'd, and even Statutes are silently repeal'd, when the Reason ceases for which they were enacted. As for the other Part of the Argument, that his Thoughts will lose of their original Beauty, by the innovation of Words; in the first place, not only their Beauty, but their Being is lost, where they are no longer understood, which is the present Case. I grant, that something must be lost in all Transfusion, that is, in all Translations; but the Sense will remain, which would otherwise be lost, or at least be maim'd, when it is scarce intelligible; and that but to a few. How few are there who can read *Chaucer*, so as to understand him perfectly? And if imperfectly, then with less Profit, and no Pleasure. 'Tis not for the Use of some old *Saxon* Friends,[64] that I have taken these Pains with

63. multa . . . loquendi: "Many words shall revive, which now have fallen into disuse; and those which now are in esteem shall become obsolete; if usage shall wish it, in whose hands is the decision, and right, and standard of speaking" (Horace, *Ars Poetica*, ll. 70–72). **64. 'Tis . . . Friends:** Anglo-Saxon scholars were making notable contributions around this time: George Hickes's *Institutiones Grammaticae Anglo-Saxonicae* (1689), Edmund Gibson's edition of the *Anglo-Saxon Chronicle* (1692), and Edward Thwaite's edition of the *Heptateuch* (1698).

him: Let them neglect my Version, because they have no need of it. I made it for their sakes who understand Sense and Poetry, as well as they; when that Poetry and Sense is put into Words which they understand. I will go farther, and dare to add, that what Beauties I lose in some Places, I give to others which had them not originally: But in this I may be partial to my self; let the Reader judge, and I submit to his Decision. Yet I think I have just Occasion to complain of them, who because they understand *Chaucer*, would deprive the greater part of their Countrymen of the same Advantage, and hoord him up, as Misers do their Grandam Gold,[65] only to look on it themselves, and hinder others from making use of it. In sum, I seriously protest, that no Man ever had, or can have, a greater Veneration for *Chaucer*, than my self. I have translated some part of his Works, only that I might perpetuate his Memory, or at least refresh it, amongst my Countrymen. If I have alter'd him any where for the better, I must at the same time acknowledge, that I could have done nothing without him: *Facile est inventis addere*,[66] is no great Commendation; and I am not so vain to think I have deserv'd a greater. I will conclude what I have to say of him singly, with this one Remark: A Lady of my Acquaintance, who keeps a kind of Correspondence with some Authors of the Fair Sex in *France*, has been inform'd by them, that *Mademoiselle de Scudery*, who is as old as *Sibyl*, and inspir'd like her by the same God of Poetry, is at this time translating *Chaucer* into modern *French*. From which I gather, that he has been formerly translated into the old *Provencall*,[67] (for, how she should come to understand Old *English*, I know not.) But the Matter of Fact being true, it makes me think, that there is something in it like Fatality; that after certain Periods of Time, the Fame and Memory of Great Wits should be renew'd, as *Chaucer* is both in *France* and *England*. If this be wholly Chance, 'tis extraordinary; and I dare not call it more, for fear of being tax'd with Superstition.

Boccace comes last to be consider'd, who living in the same Age with *Chaucer*, had the same Genius, and follow'd the same Studies: Both writ Novels, and each of them cultivated his Mother-Tongue: But the greatest Resemblance of our two Modern Authors being in their familiar Style, and pleasing way of relating Comical Adventures, I may pass it over, because I have translated nothing from *Boccace* of that Nature. In the serious Part of Poetry, the Advantage is wholly on *Chaucer*'s Side; for though the *Englishman* has borrow'd many Tales from the *Italian*, yet it appears, that those of *Boccace* were not generally of his own making, but taken from Authors of former Ages, and by him only modell'd: So that what there was of Invention in either of them, may be judg'd equal. But *Chaucer* has refin'd on *Boccace*, and has mended the Stories which he has borrow'd, in his way of telling; though Prose allows more Liberty of Thought, and the Expression is more easie, when unconfin'd by Numbers. Our Countryman carries Weight, and yet wins the Race at disadvantage. I desire not the Reader should take my Word; and therefore I will set two of their Discourses on the same Subject, in the same Light, for every Man to judge betwixt them. I translated *Chaucer* first, and amongst the rest, pitch'd on the Wife of *Bath*'s Tale; not daring, as I have said, to adventure on her Prologue; because 'tis too licentious: There *Chaucer* introduces an old Woman of mean Parentage, whom a youthful Knight of Noble Blood was forc'd to marry, and consequently loath'd her: The Crone being in bed with him on the wedding Night, and finding his Aversion, endeavours to win his Affection by Reason, and speaks a good Word for her self, (as who could blame her?) in hope to mollifie the sullen Bridegroom. She takes her Topiques from the Benefits of Poverty, the Advantages of old Age and Ugliness, the Vanity of Youth, and the silly Pride of Ancestry and Titles without inherent Vertue, which is the true Nobility. When I had clos'd *Chaucer*, I return'd to *Ovid*, and translated some more of his Fables; and by this time had so far forgotten the Wife of *Bath*'s Tale, that when I took up *Boccace*, unawares I fell on the same Argument of preferring Virtue to Nobility of Blood, and Titles, in the Story of *Sigismonda;* which I had certainly avoided for the Resemblance of the two Discourses, if my Memory had not fail'd me. Let the Reader weigh them both; and if he thinks me partial to *Chaucer*, 'tis in him to right *Boccace*.

I prefer in our Countryman, far above all his other Stories, the Noble Poem of *Palamon* and *Arcite*, which is of the *Epique* kind, and perhaps not much inferiour to the *Ilias* or the *Æneis*: the Story is more pleasing than either of them, the Manners as perfect, the Diction

65. Grandam Gold: hoarded wealth. **66. Facile . . . addere:** It is easy to add to what has already been discovered. **67. that Mademoiselle . . . Provencall:** No translation of Chaucer by Mlle. de Scudéry is known, nor is there any extant version in medieval French.

as poetical, the Learning as deep and various; and the Disposition full as artful: only it includes a greater length of time; as taking up seven years at least; but *Aristotle* has left undecided the Duration of the Action; which yet is easily reduc'd into the Compass of a year, by a Narration of what preceded the Return of *Palamon* to *Athens.* I had thought for the Honour of our Nation, and more particularly for his, whose Laurel, tho' unworthy, I have worn after him, that this Story was of *English* Growth, and *Chaucer*'s own: But I was undeceiv'd by *Boccace;* for casually looking on the End of his seventh *Giornata,* I found *Dioneo* (under which name he shadows himself) and *Fiametta* (who represents his Mistress, the natural Daughter of *Robert* King of *Naples*) of whom these Words are spoken. *Dioneo e Fiametta gran pezza cantarono insieme d' Arcita, e di Palamone:*[68] by which it appears that this Story was written before the time of *Boccace;* but the Name of its Author being wholly lost, *Chaucer* is now become an Original; and I question not but the Poem has receiv'd many Beauties by passing through his Noble Hands. Besides this Tale, there is another of his own Invention, after the manner of the *Provencalls,* call'd *The Flower and the Leaf;*[69] with which I was so particularly pleas'd, both for the Invention and the Moral; that I cannot hinder my self from recommending it to the Reader.

As a Corollary to this Preface, in which I have done Justice to others, I owe somewhat to my self: not that I think it worth my time to enter the Lists with one M——,[70] or one B——,[71] but barely to take notice, that such Men there are who have written scurrilously against me without any Provocation. *M——,* who is in Orders, pretends amongst the rest this Quarrel to me, that I have fallen foul on Priesthood; If I have, I am only to ask Pardon of good Priests, and am afraid his part of the Reparation will come to little. Let him be satisfied that he shall not be able to force himself upon me for an Adversary. I contemn him too much to enter into Competition with him. His own Translations of *Virgil* have answer'd his Criticisms on mine. If (as they say, he has declar'd in Print) he prefers the Version of *Ogilby*[72] to mine, the World has made him the same Compliment: For 'tis agreed on all hands, that he writes even below *Ogilby:* That, you will say, is not easily to be done; but what cannot *M——* bring about? I am satisfy'd however, that while he and I live together, I shall not be thought the worst Poet of the Age. It looks as if I had desir'd him underhand to write so ill against me: But upon my honest Word I have not brib'd him to do me this Service, and am wholly guiltless of his Pamphlet. 'Tis true I should be glad, if I could persuade him to continue his good Offices, and write another Critique on any thing of mine: For I find by Experience he has a great Stroke with the Reader, when he condemns any of my Poems to make the World have a better Opinion of them. He has taken some Pains with my Poetry; but no body will be persuaded to take the same with his. If I had taken to the Church (as he affirms, but which was never in my Thoughts) I should have had more Sense, if not more Grace, than to have turn'd my self out of my Benefice by writing Libels on my Parishioners. But his Account of my Manners and my Principles, are of a Piece with his Cavils and his Poetry: And so I have done with him for ever.

As for the City Bard, or Knight Physician,[73] I hear his Quarrel to me is, that I was the Author of *Absalom and Achitophel,* which he thinks is a little hard on his Fanatique Patrons in *London.*

But I will deal the more civilly with his two Poems,[74] because nothing ill is to be spoken of the Dead: And therefore Peace be to the *Manes*[75] of his *Arthurs.* I will only say that it was not for this Noble Knight that I drew the Plan of an Epick Poem on King *Arthur* in my Preface to the Translation of *Juvenal.* The Guardian Angels of Kingdoms were Machines too ponderous for him to manage; and therefore he rejected them as *Dares* did the Whirl-bats of *Eryx* when they were thrown before him by *Entellus:*[76] Yet from that Preface he plainly took his Hint: For he began immediately upon the Story; though he had the Baseness not to acknowledge his Benefactor; but in stead of it, to traduce me in a Libel.

I shall say the less of Mr. *Collier,* because in many Things he has tax'd me justly; and I have pleaded

---

68. **Dioneo . . . Palamone:** "Dioneo and Fiametta sang together a long time of Arcita and Palamone" (*Decameron,* VII. x. Epilogue). 69. **The Flower . . . Leaf:** not by Chaucer. 70. **M——:** Milbourne. 71. **B——:** Sir Richard Blackmore (1654–1729), physician to William III and Anne, poetaster, and the *bête noire* of the Augustan wits. He had attacked Dryden in the Preface to his *Prince Arthur* (1695) and again in *A Satire Against Wit* (1700).

72. **Ogilby:** John Ogilby (1600–76), prolific translator of Latin and Greek poets and a printer. Dryden satirized him in *Mac Flecknoe,* above, l. 102. 73. **City . . . Physician:** Blackmore. 74. **two Poems:** *Prince Arthur* (1695) and *King Arthur* (1697). 75. **Manes:** shades. 76. **as . . . Entellus:** See *Aeneid,* V. 400.

Guilty to all Thoughts and Expressions of mine, which can be truly argu'd of Obscenity, Profaneness, or Immorality; and retract them. If he be my Enemy, let him triumph; if he be my Friend, as I have given him no Personal Occasion to be otherwise, he will be glad of my Repentance. It becomes me not to draw my Pen in the Defence of a bad Cause, when I have so often drawn it for a good one. Yet it were not difficult to prove, that in many Places he has perverted my Meaning by his Glosses; and interpreted my Words into Blasphemy and Baudry, of which they were not guilty. Besides that, he is too much given to Horse-play in his Raillery; and comes to Battel, like a Dictatour from the Plough. I will not say, *The Zeal of God's House has eaten him up;*[77] but I am sure it has devour'd some Part of his Good Manners and Civility. It might also be doubted, whether it were altogether Zeal, which prompted him to this rough manner of Proceeding; perhaps it became not one of his Function to rake into the Rubbish of Ancient and Modern Plays; a Divine might have employ'd his Pains to better purpose, than in the Nastiness of *Plautus* and *Aristophanes;* whose Examples, as they excuse not me, so it might be possibly suppos'd, that he read them not without some Pleasure. They who have written Commentaries on those Poets, or on *Horace, Juvenal,* and *Martial,* have explain'd some Vices, which without their Interpretation had been unknown to Modern Times. Neither has he judg'd impartially betwixt the former Age and us.

There is more Baudry in one Play of *Fletcher's,* call'd *The Custom of the Country,* than in all ours together. Yet this has been often acted on the Stage in my remembrance. Are the Times so much more reform'd now, than they were Five and twenty Years ago? If they are, I congratulate the Amendment of our Morals. But I am not to prejudice the Cause of my Fellow-Poets, though I abandon my own Defence: They have some of them answer'd for themselves, and neither they nor I can think Mr. *Collier* so formidable an Enemy, that we should shun him. He has lost Ground at the latter end of the Day, by pursuing his Point too far, like the Prince of *Condé* at the Battel of *Senneph:*[78] From Immoral Plays, to No Plays; *ab abusu ad usum, non valet consequentia.*[79] But being a

Party, I am not to erect my self into a Judge. As for the rest of those who have written against me, they are such Scoundrels, that they deserve not the least Notice to be taken of them. *B——* and *M——* are only distinguish'd from the Crowd, by being remember'd to their Infamy.

——*Demetri, Teque Tigelli*
Discipularum inter jubeo plorare cathedras.[80]

SECULAR MASQUE

The *Secular Masque,* together with a Prologue, Epilogue, and Song, was written as an afterpiece for a production of Fletcher's *The Pilgrim* (revised by Sir John Vanbrugh), probably first performed on April 29, 1700, just two days before Dryden's death. The production was a benefit for Dryden himself. *Secular* (from the Latin *saeculum,* an "age") refers to the turn of the previous century; the masque reviews the ages of English man from the accession of James I.

The text is that of the first printing, in *The Pilgrim* (1700), with a few errors corrected.

Enter Janus°

Janus.   CHRONOS,° *Chronos,* mend thy Pace,
           An hundred times the rowling Sun
           Around the Radiant Belt° has run
           In his revolving Race.
           Behold, behold, the Goal in sight,
           Spread thy Fans,° and wing thy flight.

Enter Chronos, *with a Scythe in his hand, and a great Globe on his Back, which he sets down at his entrance.*

Chronos.   Weary, weary of my weight,
           Let me, let me drop my Freight,
                And leave the World behind.
           I could not bear   10

80. **Demetri . . . cathedras:** "Demetrius, I bid you, and you, Tigellius, lament among the chairs of your lady pupils" (Horace, *Satires,* I. x. 90–91). SECULAR MASQUE. **Janus:** the Roman deity credited with giving man the knowledge of agriculture and civil law. Here the god, represented as having two faces, looks forward to the new century. **1. Chronos:** the god of time. **3. the Radiant Belt:** the zodiac. **6. Fans:** wings.

77. **The Zeal . . . up:** See Ps. 69:9 and John 2:17. **78. the Battel . . . Senneph:** (Senef) in Flanders, on August 11, 1674, against the Prince of Orange (now William III of England). **79. ab . . . consequentia:** Abuse is no argument against the use of a thing.

Another Year
The Load of Human-Kind.

Enter Momus° *Laughing.*

Momus.   Ha! ha! ha! Ha! ha! ha! well hast thou
      done,
      To lay down thy Pack,
      And lighten thy Back,
      The World was a Fool, e'er since it
        begun,
      And since neither *Janus,* nor *Chronos,*
        nor I,
      Can hinder the Crimes,
      Or mend the Bad Times,
      'Tis better to Laugh than to Cry.   20

Cho. of all 3.   *'Tis better to Laugh than to Cry.*
Janus.   Since *Momus* comes to laugh below,
      Old Time begin the Show,
      That he may see, in every Scene,
      What Changes in this Age have been,
Chronos.   Then Goddess of the Silver Bow begin.

Horns, or Hunting-Musique within.

Enter Diana.°

Diana.   With Horns and with Hounds I waken
      the Day,
      And hye to my Woodland walks
       away;
      I tuck up my Robe, and am buskin'd°
       soon,
      And tye to my Forehead a wexing°
       Moon.   30
      I course the fleet Stagg, unkennel the
       Fox,
      And chase the wild Goats or'e
       summets of Rocks,
      With shouting and hooting we pierce
       thro' the Sky;
      And Eccho turns Hunter, and doubles
       the Cry.
Cho. of all.   *With shouting and hooting, we pierce*
      through the Skie,
      And Eccho turns Hunter, and doubles the
      Cry.

Janus.   Then our Age was in it's Prime,
Chronos.   Free from Rage.
Diana.   ——— ———And free from Crime.
Momus.   A very Merry, Dancing, Drinking,
      Laughing, Quaffing, and unthinking
      Time.   40
Cho. of all.   *Then our Age was in it's Prime,*
      Free from Rage, and free from Crime,
      A very Merry, Dancing, Drinking,
      Laughing, Quaffing, and unthinking
      Time.

Dance of Diana's Attendants.

Enter Mars.°

Mars.   Inspire° the Vocal Brass, Inspire;
      The World is past its Infant Age:
        Arms and Honour,
        Arms and Honour,
      Set the Martial Mind on Fire,
      And kindle Manly Rage.   50
      Mars has lookt the Sky to Red;
      And Peace, the Lazy Good, is fled.
      Plenty, Peace, and Pleasure fly;
        The Sprightly Green
      In *Woodland*-Walks, no more is seen;
      The Sprightly Green, has drunk the
       Tyrian Dye.°
Cho. of all.   *Plenty, Peace, &c.*
Mars.   Sound the Trumpet, Beat the Drum,
      Through all the World around;
      Sound a Reveille, Sound, Sound,   60
      The Warrior God is come.
Cho. of all.   *Sound the Trumpet, &c.*
Momus.   Thy Sword within the Scabbard keep,
      And let Mankind agree;
      Better the World were fast asleep,
      Than kept awake by Thee.
      The Fools are only thinner,
        With all our Cost and Care;
      But neither side a winner,
        For Things are as they were.   70
Cho. of all.   *The Fools are only, &c.*

Enter Venus.°

Momus: the god of ridicule and censure. **Diana:** the goddess of the moon, personified as a huntress; here she represents England before the Civil War. **29. buskin'd:** booted. **30. wexing:** waxing.

Mars: the god of war; here he represents the next age—the age of the Civil War and the Commonwealth. **45. Inspire:** blow into. **56. the Tyrian Dye:** the color of blood. **Venus:** the goddess of love and beauty; here she represents the reigns of Charles II and James II.

Venus.	Calms appear, when Storms are past;
	Love will have his Hour at last:
	Nature is my kindly Care;
	Mars destroys, and I repair;
	Take me, take me, while you may,
	Venus comes not ev'ry Day.
Cho. of all.	*Take her, take her, &c.*
Chronos.	The World was then so light,
	I scarcely felt the Weight; 80
	Joy rul'd the Day, and Love the Night.
	But since the Queen of Pleasure left the
	Ground,
	I faint, I lag,
	And feebly drag
	The pond'rous Orb around.

Momus.	All, all, of a piece throughout;
Pointing	
to *Diana.* ⎫	Thy Chase had a Beast in View;
to *Mars.* ⎬	Thy Wars brought nothing about;
to *Venus.* ⎭	Thy Lovers were all untrue.
Janus.	'Tis well an Old Age is out, 90
Chro.	And time to begin a New.
Cho. of all.	*All, all, of a piece throughout;*
	Thy Chase had a Beast in View;
	Thy Wars brought nothing about;
	Thy Lovers were all untrue.
	'Tis well an Old Age is out,
	And time to begin a New.

Dance of Huntsmen, Nymphs, Warriours and
    Lovers.

John Locke

1632–1704

To most literate Englishmen in the half-century after his death, John Locke was one of the few thinkers who might without impudence be mentioned in the same breath with the great Sir Isaac Newton. For as Newton had won an unparalleled conquest for the human mind by showing that it was capable of grasping the very laws of nature, Locke had turned his eye upon the mind itself, and, appealing simply to the facts of every man's experience, had given a plain and persuasive account of the mechanism of human understanding. He had done much besides. In his *Two Treatises of Government* (1690) he had made what seemed to his countrymen a classic statement of the principles of civil liberty underlying the Revolution of 1688; he had impressed an age that was increasingly distrustful of mysteries and miracles by defending Christianity as the most *reasonable* of religions; he had written significantly on education and public finance; and everywhere he had displayed a practicality and sound judgment that recommended him to the ordinary man of sense. Though there were some, particularly among the clergy, who found his views unacceptable and dangerous, the sheer representativeness of his outlook gave him a dominant influence in British intellectual life. On the Continent, too, such men as Voltaire and Diderot revered him as a liberator of modern thought—the judicious, the wise, the philosophic Locke.

He had been slow to find his true calling. His father, an attorney in the little Somerset town of Pensford, saw to his early education at home and then sent him in 1646 to study under the famous Dr. Busby at Westminster School. Six years later, at the age of twenty, Locke went up to Christ Church College, Oxford, where it did not take him long to acquire a distaste for philosophy. In that day philosophy at Oxford was little more than a relic of medieval scholasticism, so engrossed in the art of winning arguments that it seemed to have no room for the problems of contemporary life. But for a young man who might want a career in the Church or a permanent place in his college there was no avoiding the traditional logic and metaphysics, and Locke prudently went ahead to take his degrees. In 1659 he began to tutor in Greek and philosophy at Christ Church. Meanwhile, he had found something more satisfying in the lectures of the medical faculty and in the scientific projects that Sir Robert Boyle and a new generation of experimentalists were encouraging at Oxford. In time his medical interests came to overshadow all the rest, and in 1666, when he was at last obliged to choose a profession, he set up amateur practice in Oxford.

In that same year chance brought him into attendance on Lord Ashley, a rising Whig politician who was later to become the First Earl of Shaftesbury—Dryden's false Achitophel. It was presumably through Ashley's influence that Locke's student-ship at Christ Church was made permanent in 1666. The appointment however did not require Locke to teach, and within a few months Ashley had installed him at Exeter House, his London home, as his personal physician. When Ashley's life was threatened in 1668 by "an imposthume in the breast," Locke performed the operation that saved him, and Ashley, who had already come to respect his judgment of people and policies, would not hear of his returning to regular practice. For the next fifteen years, except for one long sojourn in France for reasons of health, Locke divided his time between Oxford and London, mostly at his Lordship's call. It was he who found a wife for Ashley's unpromising son, and who later helped to educate the earl's favorite grandchild—the future third earl, author of the *Characteristicks* (1711). As Shaftesbury's trusted adviser he had unmatched opportunities to observe the actual conduct of civil and religious affairs, but in time his position became more dangerous than instructive. After 1679, as Shaftesbury threw himself single-mindedly into one intrigue after another to prevent the Roman Catholic Duke of York from succeeding to the throne, Locke found himself under constant suspicion of designs against the state. Few men were more discreet than he, and no one ever knew how far he was involved; but when Shaftesbury fled to Holland, and died there in 1683, Locke saw fit to make his own escape to the Continent. A few months later he was deprived of his studentship at Oxford by the express command of Charles II.

Though he had to go into hiding once or twice to avoid being captured by British agents, for the better part of the next five years he was able to live quietly in Holland under the friendly eye of William of Orange, devoting himself to philosophical studies. His reading of Descartes some years before had convinced him that it was possible, after all, to talk sense about the problems of philosophy, but his services to Shaftesbury and the trials of persistent asthma had left him little freedom for inquiries of his own. Now, however, he had the time to think out the implications of his views and to write as he pleased. In 1689, when the Revolution enabled him to return to England, he brought with him a remarkable cargo of manuscripts, and, declining the diplomatic posts that William would happily have offered him, settled down to preparing his work for the press. The next six years saw all his major writings into print: the first letter on toleration in 1689; the *Essay Concerning Humane Understanding* and the *Two Treatises of Government* in 1690; *Some Thoughts Concerning Education* in 1693; and the *Reasonableness of Christianity* in 1695. Of these, only the *Essay* and the treatise on education were at first printed under his own name, but the *Essay* alone was enough to turn him into a celebrity.

In 1691, finding that not even the pleasures of fame could inure his lungs to the coal smoke of London, he accepted an invitation from Sir Francis Masham and his wife to come to live at Oates, their country seat in Essex, and for the remaining thirteen years of his life he made his home there, enjoying the society of Lady Masham, long one of his closest friends, and writing as steadily as his health would allow. He did not lose touch with public affairs, but though he journeyed up to London periodically between 1696 and 1700 to serve as a commissioner for trade and published influential works on trade and coinage, he spent most of his time in revising his major books for new editions and in an unwelcome controversy with Bishop Stillingfleet, one of those divines who felt that Locke had opened a door to irreligion with his "new way of Ideas." After 1700 declining health forced him into complete retirement, and in the autumn of 1704 he died, at the age of seventy-two.

Since the three-volume *Works* of 1714, various collections of his writings have appeared, but there is no complete edition. The *Philosophical Works* were edited by J. A. St. John in 1843, and the *Educational Writings* by J. L. Axtell in 1968. The *Two Treatises of Government*, which are available in several reprints, were critically edited by Peter Laslett in 1960. Since 1894 the standard edition of the *Essay* has been that by A. C. Fraser (2 vols., reprinted 1959); the edition by John Yolton in Everyman's Library (2 vols., 1961) is a reprint of the posthumous fifth edition of 1706. Of the older biographies the best is that by H. R. Fox Bourne (2 vols., 1876), but Maurice Cranston's *John Locke: A Biography* (1957) is now the standard life. A good brief evaluation of Locke's place in the thought of his time is given by Basil Willey in *The Seventeenth-Century Background* (1953); a more detailed historical study is John Yolton's *John Locke and the Way of Ideas* (1956). Among the systematic accounts of his philosophy may be mentioned Samuel Alexander's *Locke* (1908), D. J. O'Connor's *John Locke* (1952), and especially R. I. Aaron's *John Locke* (2nd ed., 1955). On his political thought, see J. W. Gough's *Locke's Political Philosophy* (1950); on his literary influence, Kenneth MacLean's *John Locke and English Literature of the Eighteenth Century* (1936).

FROM

AN ESSAY CONCERNING HUMANE UNDERSTANDING

❦

To Voltaire, writing his *Letters Concerning the English Nation* in 1733, the whole history of philosophical speculation about the soul seemed little more than a dismal trail of errors—until the appearance of the *Essay Concerning Humane Understanding*. With that work, a sage had stepped forward at last to put an end to long ages of mere guesswork and superstition and, "in the same Manner as an excellent Anatomist explains the Springs of the human Body," had revealed for the first time the workings of the human soul. Step by step he had traced the natural history of the mind from birth to maturity, showing how it comes to be supplied with ideas and how it constructs the most complicated notions out of these simple materials. For Voltaire, as for many another reader from Addison to Laurence Sterne, the most impressive of Locke's achievements was his concrete new psychology, which swept away the chaos of theories about innate ideas, humors, and animal spirits that popular tradition had handed down; in such matters Locke's authority was, as the young Edmund Burke commented in 1756, "doubtless as great as that of any man can be." More than a century later, the philosopher John Stuart Mill, looking back on an era in which the *Essay* had prompted the best work of Berkeley and Hume and had helped to make British empiricism a major force in western philosophy, still saw Locke primarily as "the unquestioned founder of the analytic philosophy of mind"—or of what would now be known as epistemology, the study of the nature and grounds of *knowing*.

The whole fabric of Locke's theory of knowledge required more than four hundred pages to unfold, and it is not to be represented in a brief selection. But the first principles of his new empirical psychology—the rejection of innate ideas and the derivation of all the raw materials of knowledge from sensation or reflection—are sketched out in the famous opening chapter of Book II.

In Book IV Locke surveyed the grounds and degrees of knowledge; this study led him inevitably to the topic of faith. There could be no greater error, he felt, than to cry up faith in opposition to reason, as though the truths of religion were accessible only to those who had abandoned rationality. Faith, indeed, must sometimes lead the way, where our reason is able to give us nothing more than faint glimpses of the truth. But in a rational world true faith cannot possibly be *at odds* with reason, and any faith or opinion that affirms what the clear light of understanding obliges us to deny can be no more than a delusion. One sort of "faith" in particular seemed to Locke an insupportable abuse of reason, and when he revised the *Essay* for its fourth edition in 1700, he added an entirely new chapter exposing its follies. To him and his contemporaries, *enthusiasm* meant the kind of rapt individualism that characterized sects like the Ranters and Muggletonians and early Quakers, who believed (or professed to believe) that their religious convictions came to them by direct inspiration from God. With his indictment of this most extravagant species of "wrong assent" Locke rounded out the common-sense rationalism, developed earlier in the *Essay* and in the *Reasonableness of Christianity* (1695), that was to serve as one of the acknowledged foundations of eighteenth-century rational theology.

The text for the chapter from Book II, basically that of the first edition (1689, dated 1690), accepts the revisions made by Locke in the editions of 1694 and 1700. The text for the chapter from Book IV is that of the edition of 1700.

⬥

BOOK II. CHAP. I

Of Ideas in general, and their Original.

§.1. [Idea *is the Object of Thinking*.] Every Man being conscious to himself, That he thinks, and that which his Mind is employ'd about whilst thinking, being the *Ideas*,[1] that are there, 'tis past doubt, that Men have in their Minds several *Ideas*, such as are those expressed by the words, *Whiteness, Hardness, Sweetness, Thinking, Motion, Man, Elephant, Army, Drunkenness*, and others: It is in the first place then to be enquired, How he comes by them? I know it is a received[2] Doctrine, That Men have native *Ideas*, and original Characters

AN ESSAY CONCERNING HUMANE UNDERSTANDING: *Book II.*
1. Ideas: For Locke the term includes both sensory impressions and concepts—whatever is or can be an object of thought. Thus ideas make up the sum total of the specific contents of consciousness. **2. received:** commonly accepted.

stamped upon their Minds, in their very first being. This Opinion I have at large examined already; and, I suppose, what I have said in the fore-going Book,[3] will be much more easily admitted, when I have shewed, whence the Understanding may get all the *Ideas* it has, and by what ways and degrees they may come into the Mind; for which I shall appeal to every ones own Observation and Experience.

§.2. [*All* Ideas *come from Sensation or Reflection*.] Let us then suppose the Mind to be, as we say, white Paper,[4] void of all Characters, without any *Ideas;* How comes it to be furnished? Whence comes it by that vast store, which the busie and boundless Fancy of Man has painted on it, with an almost endless variety? Whence has it all the materials of Reason and Knowledge? To this I answer, in one word, From *Experience:* In that, all our Knowledge is founded; and from that it ultimately derives it self. Our Observation employ'd either about *external, sensible Objects;* or about the *internal Operations of our Minds,* perceived and reflected on by our selves, is that, which supplies our Understandings with all the materials of thinking. These two are the Fountains of Knowledge, from whence all the *Ideas* we have, or can naturally have, do spring.

§.3. [*The* Objects *of Sensation one Source of* Ideas.] First, *Our Senses*, conversant about particular, sensible Objects, do *convey into the Mind*, several distinct *Perceptions* of things, according to those various ways, wherein those Objects do affect them: And thus we come by those *Ideas*, we have of *Yellow, White, Heat, Cold, Soft, Hard, Bitter, Sweet*, and all those which we call sensible qualities, which when I say the senses convey into the mind, I mean, they from external objects convey into the mind what produces there those *Perceptions*. This great Source, of most of the *Ideas* we have, depending wholly upon our Senses, and derived by them to the Understanding, I call *SENSATION*.

§.4. [*The* Operations *of our Minds, the other Source of*

3. the fore-going Book: In Book I Locke argued that there were no grounds for believing any ideas or principles to be *innately* present in men's minds. A doctrine of innate ideas had been endorsed in one form or another by influential thinkers, including Descartes, and was regarded by many as a bulwark of Christian theology, but Locke had to refute this doctrine if he was to establish his own theory that all ideas are derived from experience. **4. white Paper:** Locke's equivalent for the ancient Stoic phrase *tabula rasa*. The Stoics taught that the mind at birth is a *tabula rasa*, a blank tablet, on which the first traces of knowledge are imprinted by sensory experience.

them.] Secondly, The other Fountain, from which Experience furnisheth the Understanding with *Ideas*, is the *Perception of the Operations of our own Minds* within us, as it is employ'd about the *Idea's* it has got; which Operations, when the Soul comes to reflect on, and consider, do furnish the Understanding with another sett of *Ideas*, which could not be had from things without; and such are, *Perception, Thinking, Doubting, Believing, Reasoning, Knowing, Willing,* and all the different actings of our own Minds; which we being conscious of, and observing in our selves, do from these receive into our Understandings, as distinct *Ideas*, as we do from Bodies affecting our Senses. This Source of *Ideas*, every Man has wholly in himself: And though it be not Sense, as having nothing to do with external Objects; yet it is very like it, and might properly enough be call'd internal Sense. But as I call the other *Sensation*, so I call this *REFLECTION*, the *Ideas* it affords being such only, as the Mind gets by reflecting on its own Operations within it self. By *REFLECTION* then, in the following part of this Discourse, I would be understood to mean, that notice which the Mind takes of its own Operations, and the manner of them, by reason whereof, there come to be *Ideas* of these Operations in the Understanding. These two, I say, *viz.* External, Material things, as the Objects of *SENSATION;* and the Operations of our own Minds within, as the Objects of *REFLECTION*, are, to me, the only Originals, from whence all our *Idea's* take their beginnings. The term *Operations* here, I use in a large sence, as comprehending not barely the Actions of the Mind about its *Ideas*, but some sort of Passions arising sometimes from them, such as is the satisfaction or uneasiness arising from any thought.

§.5. [*All our Ideas are of the one or the other of these.*] The Understanding seems to me, not to have the least glimmering of any *Ideas*, which it doth not receive from one of these two: *External Objects furnish the Mind with the Ideas of sensible qualities,* which are all those different perceptions they produce in us: And the *Mind furnishes the Understanding with Ideas of its own Operations*. These, when we have taken a full survey of them, and their several Modes, Combinations, and Relations, we shall find to contain all our whole stock of *Ideas*; and that we have nothing in our Minds, which did not come in, one of these two ways. Let any one examine his own Thoughts, and throughly search into his Understanding, and then let him tell me, Whether all the original *Ideas* he has there, are any

other than of the Objects of his *Senses*, or of the Operations of his Mind, considered as Objects of his *Reflection:* and how great a mass of Knowledge soever he imagines to be lodged there, he will, upon taking a strict view, see that he has not any *Idea* in his Mind, but what one of these two have imprinted; though, perhaps, with infinite variety compounded and enlarged, by the Understanding, as we shall see hereafter.[5]

§.6. [*Observable in Children.*] He that attentively considers the state of a *Child*, at his first coming into the World, will have little reason to think him stored with plenty of *Ideas*, that are to be the matter of his future Knowledge. 'Tis by degrees he comes to be furnished with them: And though the *Ideas* of obvious and familiar qualities, imprint themselves, before the Memory begins to keep a Register of Time and Order, yet 'tis often so late before some unusual qualities come in the way, that there are few Men that cannot recollect the beginning of their acquaintance with them: And if it were worth while, no doubt a Child might be so ordered,[6] as to have but a very few, even of the ordinary *Ideas*, till he were grown up to a Man. But all that are born into the World being surrounded with Bodies, that perpetually and diversly affect them, variety of *Idea's*, whether care be taken about it, or no, are imprinted on the Minds of Children. *Light*, and *Colours*, are busie and at hand every-where, when the Eye is but open; *Sounds*, and some *tangible Qualities*, fail not to sollicite their proper Senses, and force an entrance to the Mind; but yet, I think, it will be granted easily, That if a Child were kept in a place, where he never saw any other but Black and White, till he were a Man, he would have no more *Ideas* of Scarlet or Green, than he that from his Childhood never tasted an Oyster, or a Pine-Apple, has of those particular Relishes.

§.7. [*Men are differently furnished with these, according to the different Objects they converse with.*] Men then come to be furnished, with fewer or more simple *Ideas* from without, according as the *Objects*, they converse with afford greater or less variety; and from the Operation of their Minds within, according as they more or less *reflect* on them. For, though he that contemplates the Operations of his Mind, cannot but have plain and clear *Ideas* of them; yet unless he turn

5. hereafter: in the remainder of Book II, which surveys the mental operations by which the simple ideas given in experience are developed into complex ideas and abstractions.
6. ordered: regulated.

his Thoughts that way, and considers them *attentively*, he will no more have clear and distinct *Ideas* of all the *Operations of his Mind*, and all that may be observed therein, than he will have all the particular *Ideas* of any Landscape, or of the Parts and Motions of a Clock, who will not turn his Eyes to it, and with attention heed all the Parts of it. The Picture, or Clock may be so placed, that they may come in his way every Day; but yet he will have but a confused *Idea* of all the Parts they are made up of, till he *applies himself with attention*, to consider them each in particular.

§.8. [Ideas *of Reflexion later, because they need Attention.*] And hence we see the Reason, why 'tis pretty late before most Children get *Ideas* of the Operations of their own Minds; and some have not any very clear, or perfect *Ideas* of the greatest part of them all their Lives. Because, though they pass there continually; yet like floating Visions, they make not deep Impressions enough, to leave in the Mind clear distinct lasting *Ideas*, till the Understanding turns inwards upon its self, *reflects* on its own *Operations*, and makes them the Object of its own Contemplation. Children, when they come first into it, are surrounded with a world of new things, which, by a constant sollicitation of their senses, draw the mind constantly to them, forward to take notice of new, and apt to be delighted with the variety of changing objects. Thus the first Years are usually imploy'd and diverted in looking abroad, and acquainting themselves with what is to be found without; and so growing up in a constant attention to outward Sensations, seldom make any considerable Reflection on what passes within them, till they come to be of riper Years; and some scarce ever at all.

§.9. [*The Soul begins to have* Ideas, *when it begins to perceive.*] To ask, *at what time a Man has first any Ideas*, is to ask, when he begins to perceive, having *Ideas* and Perception being the same thing. I know it is an Opinion, that the Soul always thinks,[7] and that it has the actual Perception of *Ideas* in its self constantly, as long as it exists; and that actual thinking is as inseparable from the Soul, as actual Extension is from the Body; which if true, to enquire after the beginning of a Man's *Idea's*, is the same, as to enquire after the beginning of his Soul. For by this Account, Soul and its *Ideas*, as Body and its Extension, will begin to exist both at the same time.

§.10. [*The Soul thinks not always; for, this wants Proofs.*] But whether the Soul be supposed to exist antecedent to, or coeval with, or some time after the first Rudiments of Organisation, or the beginnings of Life in the Body, I leave to be disputed by those, who have better thought of that matter. I confess my self, to have one of those dull Souls, that doth not perceive it self always to contemplate *Ideas*,[8] nor can conceive it any more necessary for the *Soul always to think*, than for the Body always to move: the perception of *Idea's*, being (as I conceive) to the Soul, what motion is to the Body, not its Essence, but one of its Operations: And therefore, though thinking be supposed never so much the proper Action of the Soul; yet it is not necessary, to suppose, that it should be always thinking, always in Action. That, perhaps, is the Privilege of the infinite Author and Preserver of all things, *who never slumbers nor sleeps;* but is not competent to[9] any finite Being, at least not to the Soul of Man. We know certainly by Experience, that we sometimes think, and thence draw this infallible Consequence, That there is something in us, that has a Power to think: But whether that Substance perpetually thinks, or no, we can be no farther assured, than Experience informs us. For to say, that actual thinking is essential to the Soul, and inseparable from it, is, to beg what is in Question, and not to prove it by Reason; which is necessary to be done, if it be not a self-evident Proposition. But whether this, *That the Soul always thinks*, be a self-evident Proposition, that every Body assents to at first hearing, I appeal to Mankind. 'Tis doubted whether I thought all last night, or no; the Question being about a matter of fact, 'tis begging it, to bring, as a proof for it, an Hypothesis, which is the very thing in dispute: by which way one may prove any thing, and 'tis but supposing that all watches, whilst the balance beats, think, and 'tis sufficiently proved, and past doubt, that my watch thought all last night. But he, that would not deceive himself, ought to build his Hypothesis on matter of fact, and make it out by sensible experience, and not presume on matter of fact, because of his Hypothesis, that is, because he supposes

---

7. the Soul . . . thinks: Descartes and his followers held that consciousness is the essential property of the soul and thus that a man's soul "thinks" uninterruptedly throughout life.

8. those . . . Ideas: Said Voltaire, "With regard to my self, I shall boast that I have the Honour to be as stupid in this Particular as Mr. Locke." He was satisfied, as were most laymen, that Locke had "destroyed innate Ideas."
9. competent to: within the capacity of.

it to be so: which way of proving, amounts to this, That I must necessarily think all last night, because another supposes I always think, though I my self cannot perceive, that I always do so.

But Men in love with their Opinions, may not only suppose what is in question, but alledge wrong matter of fact. How else could any one make it an *inference* of mine, *that a thing is not, because we are not sensible of it in our sleep.* I do not say there is no Soul in a Man, because he is not sensible of it in his sleep; But I do say, he cannot think at any time waking or sleeping, without being sensible of it. Our being sensible of it is not necessary to any thing, but to our thoughts; and to them it is; and to them it will always be necessary, till we can think without being conscious of it.

§.11. [*It is not always conscious of it.*] I grant that the Soul in a waking Man is never without thought, because it is the condition of being awake: But whether sleeping without dreaming be not an Affection[10] of the whole Man, Mind as well as Body, may be worth a waking Man's Consideration; it being hard to conceive, that any thing should think, and not be conscious of it. If the *Soul* doth *think in a sleeping Man,* without being conscious of it, I ask, whether, during such thinking, it has any Pleasure or Pain, or be capable of Happiness or Misery? I am sure the Man is not, no more than the Bed or Earth he lies on. For to be happy or miserable without being conscious of it, seems to me utterly inconsistent and impossible. Or if it be possible, that the Soul can, whilst the Body is sleeping, have its Thinking, Enjoyments, and Concerns; its Pleasure or Pain apart, which the Man is not conscious of, nor partakes in, It is certain, that *Socrates* asleep, and *Socrates* awake, is not the same Person; but his Soul when he sleeps, and *Socrates* the Man consisting of Body and Soul when he is waking, are two Persons: Since waking *Socrates*, has no Knowledge of, or Concernment for that Happiness, or Misery of his Soul, which it enjoys alone by it self whilst he sleeps, without perceiving any thing of it, no more than he has for the Happiness, or Misery of a Man in the *Indies,* whom he knows not. For if we take wholly away all Consciousness of our Actions and Sensations, especially of Pleasure and Pain, and the concernment that accompanies it, it will be hard to know wherein to place personal Identity.

§.12. [*If a sleeping Man thinks without knowing it, the sleeping and waking Man are two Persons.*] The Soul,

during sound Sleep, thinks, say these Men. *Whilst it thinks* and perceives, it is capable certainly of those of Delight or Trouble, as well as any other Perceptions; and *it must necessarily be conscious of its own Perceptions.* But it has all this a-part: The sleeping Man, 'tis plain, is conscious of nothing of all this. Let us suppose then the Soul of *Castor*,[11] whilst he is sleeping, retired from his Body, which is no impossible Supposition for the Men I have here to do with, who so liberally allow Life, without a thinking Soul to all other Animals. These Men cannot then judge it impossible, or a contradiction, That the Body should live without the Soul; nor that the Soul should subsist and think, or have Perception, even Perception of Happiness or Misery, without the Body. Let us then, as I say, suppose the Soul of *Castor* separated, during his Sleep, from his Body, to think apart. Let us suppose too, that it chooses for its Scene of Thinking, the Body of another Man, *v.g. Pollux*, who is sleeping without a Soul: For if *Castor's* Soul, can think whilst *Castor* is asleep, what *Castor* is never conscious of, 'tis no matter what Place it chooses to think in. We have here then the Bodies of two Men with only one Soul between them, which we will suppose to sleep and wake by turns; and the Soul still[12] thinking in the waking Man, whereof the sleeping Man is never conscious, has never the least Perception. I ask then, Whether *Castor* and *Pollux*, thus, with only one Soul between them, which thinks and perceives in one, what the other is never conscious of, nor is concerned for, are not two as distinct Persons, as *Castor* and *Hercules;* or, as *Socrates*, and *Plato* were? And whether one of them might not be very happy, and the other very miserable? Just by the same Reason, they make the Soul and the Man two Persons, who make the Soul think apart, what the Man is not conscious of. For, I suppose, no body will make Identity of persons, to consist in the Soul's being united to the very same numerical particles of matter: For if that be necessary to Identity, 'twill be impossible, in that constant flux of the particles of our Bodies, that any Man should be the same person, two days, or two moments together.

§.13. [*Impossible to convince those that sleep without dreaming, that they think.*] Thus, methinks, every drousie nod shakes their Doctrine, who teach, That

---

10. **Affection:** state that affects.

11. **Castor:** in Greek mythology, the half brother and inseparable companion of Pollux, mentioned just below.
12. **still:** continuously.

the Soul is always thinking. Those, at least, who do at any time *sleep without dreaming*, can never be convinced, That their Thoughts are sometimes for four hours busie without their knowing of it; and if they are taken in the very act, waked in the middle of that sleeping contemplation, can give no manner of account of it.

§.14. [*That Men dream without remembring it, in vain urged.*] 'Twill perhaps be said, That the *Soul thinks*, even *in the soundest Sleep, but the Memory retains it not.* That the Soul in a sleeping Man should be this moment busie a thinking, and the next moment in a waking Man, not remember, nor be able to recollect one jot of all those Thoughts, is very hard to be conceived, and would need some better Proof than bare Assertion to make it be believed. For who can without any more ado, but being barely told so, imagine, That the greatest part of Men, do, during all their Lives, for several hours every Day, think of something, which if they were asked, even in the middle of these Thoughts, they could remember nothing at all of? Most Men, I think, pass a great part of their Sleep without dreaming. I once knew a Man, that was bred a Scholar, and had no bad Memory, who told me, he had never dream'd in his Life, till he had that Fever, he was then newly recovered of, which was about the Five or Six and Twentieth Year of his Age. I suppose the World affords more such Instances: At least every ones Acquaintance, will furnish him with Examples enough of such, as pass most of their Nights without dreaming.

§.15. [*Upon this Hypothesis, the Thoughts of a sleeping Man ought to be most rational.*] *To think often, and never to retain it so much as one moment, is a very useless sort of thinking:* and the Soul in such a state of thinking, does very little, if at all, excel that of a Looking-glass, which constantly receives variety of Images, or *Ideas*, but retains none; they disappear and vanish, and there remain no footsteps of them; the Looking-glass is never the better for such *Ideas*, nor the Soul for such Thoughts. Perhaps it will be said, that in a waking Man, the materials of the Body are employ'd, and made use of, in thinking; and that the memory of Thoughts, is retained by the impressions that are made on the Brain, and the traces there left after such thinking; but that in the *thinking of the Soul*, which is not perceived *in a sleeping Man*, there the Soul thinks apart, and *making no use of the Organs of the Body, leaves no impressions on it, and consequently no memory* of such Thoughts. Not to mention again the absurdity of two distinct Persons, which follows from this

Supposition, I answer farther, That whatever *Ideas* the Mind can receive, and contemplate without the help of the Body, it is reasonable to conclude, it can retain without the help of the Body too, or else the Soul, or any separate Spirit, will have but little advantage by thinking. If it has no memory of its own Thoughts; if it cannot lay them up for its use, and be able to recall them upon any occasion; if it cannot reflect upon what is past, and make use of its former Experiences, Reasonings, and Contemplations, to what purpose does it think? They who make the Soul a thinking Thing, at this rate will not make it a much more noble Being, than those do, whom they condemn for allowing it to be nothing but the subtilest parts of Matter.[13] Characters drawn on Dust, that the first breath of wind effaces; or Impressions made on a heap of Atoms, or animal Spirits, are altogether as useful, and render the Subject as noble, as the Thoughts of a Soul that perish in thinking; that once out of sight, are gone for ever, and leave no memory of themselves behind them. Nature never makes excellent things, for mean or no uses: and it is hardly to be conceived, that our infinitely wise Creator, should make so admirable a Faculty, as the power of Thinking, that Faculty which comes nearest the Excellency of his own incomprehensible Being, to be so idly and uselessly employ'd, at least $\frac{1}{4}$ part of its time here, as to think constantly, without remembring any of those Thoughts, without doing any good to its self or others, or being any way useful to any other part of the Creation. If we will examine it, we shall not find, I suppose, the motion of dull and sensless matter, any where in the Universe, made so little use of, and so wholly thrown away.

§.16. [*On this Hypothesis the Soul must have* Ideas *not derived from Sensation or Reflexion, of which there is no appearance.*] 'Tis true, we have sometimes instances of Perception, whilst we are *asleep*, and retain the memory of those *Thoughts:* but how *extravagant* and incoherent for the most part they are; how little conformable to the Perfection and Order of a rational Being, those who are acquainted with Dreams, need not be told. This I would willingly be satisfied in, Whether the Soul, when it thinks thus apart, and as it were separate from the Body, acts less rationally then[14]

13. nothing . . . Matter: This view was associated with Democritus (c. 460–c. 370 B.C.) and Epicurus (c. 340–c. 270 B.C.) among the Ancients; among modern materialists the most notorious was Thomas Hobbes (1588–1679). 14. then: than.

when conjointly with it, or no: If its separate Thoughts be less rational, then these Men must say, That the Soul owes the perfection of rational thinking to the Body: If it does not, 'tis a wonder that our Dreams should be, for the most part, so frivolous and irrational; and that the Soul should retain none of its more rational Soliloquies and Meditations.

§.17. [*If I think when I know it not, no body else can know it.*] Those who so confidently tell us, That the Soul always actually thinks, I would they would also tell us, what those *Ideas* are, that are in the Soul of a Child, before, or just at the union with the Body, before it hath received any by *Sensation.* The *Dreams* of sleeping Men, *are,* as I take it, all *made up of the waking Man's Ideas,* though, for the most part, oddly put together. 'Tis strange, if the Soul has *Ideas* of its own, that it derived not from *Sensation* or *Reflection,* (as it must have, if it thought before it received any impressions from the Body) that it should never, in its private thinking, (so private, that the Man himself perceives it not) retain any of them, the very moment it wakes out of them, and then make the Man glad with new discoveries. Who can find it reason, that the Soul should, in its retirement, during sleep, have so many hours thoughts, and yet never light on any of those *Ideas* it borrowed not from *Sensation* or *Reflection,* or at least preserve the memory of none, but such, which being occasioned from the Body, must needs be less natural to a Spirit? 'Tis strange, the Soul should never once in a Man's whole life, recal over any of its pure, native Thoughts, and those *Ideas* it had before it borrowed any thing from the Body; never bring into the waking Man's view, any other *Ideas,* but what have a tangue of the Cask,[15] and manifestly derive their Original from that union. If it always thinks, and so had *Ideas* before it was united, or before it received any from the Body, 'tis not to be supposed, but that during sleep, it recollects its native *Ideas,* and during that retirement from communicating with the Body, whilst it thinks by it self, the *Ideas* it is busied about, should be sometimes, at least, those more natural and congenial ones which it had in it self, underived from the Body, or its own operations about them, which since the waking Man never remembers, we must from this Hypothesis conclude, either that the Soul remembers something that the Man does not; or else that Memory belongs only to such *Ideas,* as are derived from the Body, or the Minds Operations about them.

§.18. [*How knows any one that the Soul always thinks? For if it be not a self-evident Proposition, it needs proof.*] I would be glad also to learn from these men, who so confidently pronounce, that the humane Soul, or, which is all one, that a man always thinks, how they come to know it; nay, *how they come to know that they themselves think, when they themselves do not perceive it.* This, I am afraid, is to be sure without proofs; and to know, without perceiving: 'Tis, I suspect, a confused Notion, taken up to serve an Hypothesis; and none of those clear Truths, that either their own Evidence forces us to admit, or common Experience makes it impudence to deny. For the most that can be said of it, is, That 'tis possible the Soul may always think, but not always retain it in memory: And, I say, it is as possible, that the Soul may not always think; and much more probable, that it should sometimes not think, than that it should often think, and that a long while together, and not be conscious of it self the next moment after, that it had thought.

§.19. [*That a Man should be busie in thinking, and yet not retain it the next moment, very improbable.*] To suppose the Soul to think, and the Man not perceive it, is, as has been said, to make two persons in one man: And if one considers well these mens way of speaking, one shall be led into a suspicion, that they do so. For they who tell us, that the Soul always thinks, do never, that I remember, say, That a man always thinks. Can the Soul think, and not the Man? Or a Man think, and not be conscious of it? This, perhaps, would be suspected of *Jargon*[16] in others. If they say, The man thinks always, but is not always conscious of it; they may as well say, His Body is extended, without having parts. For 'tis altogether as intelligible to say, that a body is extended without parts, as that any thing *thinks, without being conscious of it,* or perceiving, that it does so. They who talk thus, may, with as much reason, if it be necessary to their Hypothesis, say, That a Man is always hungry, but that he does not always feel it: Whereas hunger consists in that very sensation, as thinking consists in being conscious that one thinks. If they say, That a man is always conscious to himself of thinking; I ask, How they know it? Consciousness is the perception of what passes in a man's own mind. Can another man perceive, that I am conscious of any

---

15. **the Cask:** the body.

16. **suspected of Jargon:** mistrusted as unintelligible talk.

thing, when I perceive it not my self? No man's Knowledge here, can go beyond his Experience. Wake a Man out of a sound sleep, and ask him, What he was that moment thinking on. If he himself be conscious of nothing he then thought on, he must be a notable Diviner of Thoughts, that can assure him, that he was thinking: May he not with more reason assure him, he was not asleep? This is something beyond Philosophy; and it cannot be less than Revelation, that discovers[17] to another, Thoughts in my mind, when I can find none there my self: And they must needs have a penetrating sight, who can certainly see, that I think, when I cannot perceive it my self, and when I declare, That I do not; and yet can see, that Dogs or Elephants do not think, when they give all the demonstration of it imaginable, except only telling us, that they do so. This some may suspect to be a step beyond the *Rosecrucians*;[18] it seeming easier to make ones self invisible to others, than to make another's thoughts visible to me, which are not visible to himself. But 'tis but defining the Soul to be a substance, that always thinks, and the business is done. If such a definition be of any Authority, I know not what it can serve for, but to make many men suspect, That they have no Souls at all, since they find a good part of their Lives pass away without thinking. For no Definitions, that I know, no Suppositions of any Sect, are of force enough to destroy constant Experience; and, perhaps, 'tis the affectation of knowing beyond what we perceive, that makes so much useless dispute, and noise, in the World.

§.20. [*No Ideas but from Sensation or Reflection, evident, if we observe Children.*] I see no Reason therefore to believe, that the *Soul thinks before the Senses have furnished it with Ideas* to think on; and as those are increased, and retained; so it comes, by Exercise, to improve its Faculty of thinking in the several parts of it, as well as afterwards, by compounding those *Ideas*, and reflecting on its own Operations, it increases its Stock as well as Facility, in remembring, imagining, reasoning, and other modes of thinking.

§.21. He that will suffer himself, to be informed by Observation and Experience, and not make his own Hypothesis the Rule of Nature, will find few Signs of a Soul accustomed to much thinking in a new born Child, and much fewer of any Reasoning at all. And yet it is hard to imagine, that the rational Soul should think so much, and not reason at all. And he that will consider, that Infants, newly come into the World, spend the greatest part of their time in Sleep, and are seldom awake, but when either Hunger calls for the Teat, or some Pain, (the most importunate of all Sensations) or some other violent Impression on the Body, forces the mind to perceive, and attend to it, He, I say, who considers this, will, perhaps, find Reason to imagine, That *a Fœtus in the Mother's Womb, differs not much from the State of a Vegetable;* but passes the greatest part of its time without Perception or Thought, doing very little, but sleep in a Place, where it needs not seek for Food, and is surrounded with Liquor,[19] always equally soft, and near of the same Temper;[20] where the Eyes have no Light, and the Ears, so shut up, are not very susceptible of Sounds; and where there is little or no variety, or change of Objects to move the Senses.

§.22. Follow *a Child* from its Birth, and observe the alterations that time makes; and you shall find, as the mind by the Senses comes more and more to be furnished with *Ideas*, it comes to be more and more awake; thinks more, the more it has matter to think on. After some time, it begins to know the Objects, which being most familiar with it, have made lasting Impressions. Thus it comes, by degrees, to know the Persons it daily converses with, and distinguish them from Strangers; which are Instances and Effects of its coming to retain and distinguish the *Ideas* the Senses convey to it: And so we may observe, how the Mind, *by degrees*, improves in these, and *advances* to the Exercise of those other Faculties of *Enlarging, Compounding,* and *Abstracting* its *Ideas,* and of reasoning about them, and reflecting upon all these, of which, I shall have occasion to speak more hereafter.

§.23. If it shall be demanded then, *When a Man begins to have any Ideas?* I think, the true Answer is, When he first has any *Sensation.* For since there appear not to be any *Ideas* in the Mind, before the Senses have conveyed any in, I conceive that *Ideas* in the Understanding, are coeval with *Sensation;* which is such an Impression or Motion, made in some part of the Body, as produces some Perception in the Understanding.

---

17. **discovers:** discloses. 18. **Rosecrucians:** members of the Rosicrucian Order, a secret society dating from the early years of the seventeenth century, which claimed esoteric knowledge of the world of spirits; some Rosicrucians professed to know the secret of invisibility.

19. **Liquor:** liquid. 20. **Temper:** consistency, or condition.

§.24. [*The original of all our Knowledge.*] The *Impressions* then, that are made on our *Senses* by outward Objects, that are extrinsical to the Mind, and *its own Operations,* about the Impressions, *reflected* on by its self, as proper Objects to be contemplated by it, *are,* I conceive, *the Original of all Knowledge;* and the first Capacity of Humane Intellect, is, That the Mind is fitted to receive the Impressions made on it; either, through the *Senses,* by outward Objects; or by its own Operations, when it *reflects* on them. This is the first step a Man makes towards the Discovery of any thing, and the Ground-work, whereon to build all those Notions, which ever he shall have naturally in this World. All those sublime Thoughts, which towre above the Clouds, and reach as high as Heaven its self, take their Rise and Footing here: In all that great Extent wherein the mind wanders, in those remote Speculations, it may seem to be elevated with, it stirs not one jot beyond those *Ideas,* which *Sense* or *Reflection,* have offered for its Contemplation.

§.25. [*In the reception of simple* Ideas, *the Understanding is for the most part passive.*] In this Part, the *Understanding* is meerly *passive;* and whether or no, it will have these Beginnings, and as it were materials of Knowledge, is not in its own Power. For the Objects of our Senses, do, many of them, obtrude their particular *Ideas* upon our minds, whether we will or no: And the Operations of our minds, will not let us be without, at least some obscure Notions of them. No Man, can be wholly ignorant of what he does, when he thinks. These *simple Ideas,* when offered to the mind, *the Understanding can* no more refuse to have, nor alter, when they are imprinted, nor blot them out, and make new ones in it self, than a mirror can refuse, alter, or obliterate the Images or *Ideas,* which the Objects set before it do therein produce. As the Bodies that surround us, do diversly affect our Organs, the mind is forced to receive the Impressions; and cannot avoid the Perception of those *Ideas,* that are annexed to them.

BOOK IV. CHAP. XIX

Of Enthusiasm.

§.1. [*Love of Truth necessary.*] He that would seriously set upon the search of Truth, ought in the first Place to prepare his Mind with a Love of it. For he that Loves it not, will not take much Pains to get it; nor be much concerned when he misses it. There is no Body in the Commonwealth of Learning, who does not profess himself a lover of Truth: and there is not a rational Creature that would not take it amiss to be thought otherwise of. And yet for all this one may truly say, there are very few lovers of Truth for Truths sake, even amongst those, who perswade themselves that they are so. How a Man may know whether he be so in earnest is worth enquiry: And I think there is this one unerring mark of it, *viz.* The not entertaining any Proposition with greater assurance than the Proofs it is built upon will warrant. Whoever goes beyond this measure of Assent, 'tis plain receives not Truth in the Love of it; loves not Truth for Truths sake, but for some other bye end.[1] For the evidence that any Proposition is true (except such as are self-evident) lying only in the Proofs a Man has of it, whatsoever degrees of Assent he affords it beyond the degrees of that Evidence, 'tis plain all that surplusage of assurance is owing to some other Affection,[2] and not to the Love of Truth: It being as impossible, that the Love of Truth should carry my Assent above the Evidence, that there is to me, that it is true, As that the Love of Truth should make me assent to any Proposition, for the sake of that Evidence, which it has not, that it is true: which is in effect to Love it as a Truth, because it is possible or probable that it may not be true. In any Truth that gets not possession of our Minds by the irresistible Light of Self-evidence, or by the force of Demonstration,[3] the Arguments that gain it Assent, are the vouchers and gage of its Probability to us; and we can receive it for no other than such as they deliver it to our Understandings. Whatsoever Credit or Authority we give to any Proposition more than it receives from the Principles and Proofs it supports it self upon, is owing to our Inclinations that way, and is so far a Derogation from the Love of Truth as such: which as it can receive no Evidence from our Passions or Interests, so it should receive no Tincture from them.

Book IV. **1. bye end:** private or ulterior purpose. **2. Affection:** passion, emotional interest. **3. by the irresistible . . . Demonstration:** According to Locke, genuine knowledge comes only by way of immediate intuitive conviction (when something is self-evident) or logical demonstration (as in the proof of a geometrical theorem). Evidence that falls short of these two grounds of certainty may produce *opinion* of various degrees of probability, but it cannot produce knowledge.

§.2. [*A forwardness to dictate, from whence.*] The assuming an Authority of Dictating to others, and a forwardness to prescribe to their Opinions, is a constant concomitant of this bias and corruption of our Judgments. For how almost can it be otherwise, but that he should be ready to impose on others Belief, who has already imposed on his own? Who can reasonably expect Arguments and Conviction from him, in dealing with others, whose Understanding is not accustomed to them in his dealing with himself? Who does Violence to his own Faculties, Tyrannizes over his own Mind, and usurps the Prerogative that belongs to Truth alone, which is to command Assent by only its own Authority, *i.e.* by and in proportion to that Evidence which it carries with it.

§.3. [*Force of Enthusiasm.*] Upon this occasion I shall take the Liberty to consider a third Ground of Assent,[4] which with some Men has the same Authority, and is as confidently relied on as either *Faith* or *Reason*, I mean *Enthusiasm.* Which laying by Reason would set up Revelation without it. Whereby in effect it takes away both Reason and Revelation, and substitutes in the room of it, the ungrounded Fancies of a Man's own Brain, and assumes them for a Foundation both of Opinion and Conduct.

§.4. [*Reason and Revelation.*] *Reason* is natural *Revelation*, whereby the eternal Father of Light, and Fountain of all Knowledge communicates to Mankind that portion of Truth, which he has laid within the reach of their natural Faculties: *Revelation* is natural *Reason* enlarged by a new set of Discoveries communicated by GOD immediately, which *Reason* vouches the Truth of, by the Testimony and Proofs it gives, that they come from GOD. So that he that takes away *Reason*, to make way for *Revelation*, puts out the Light of both, and does much what[5] the same, as if he should perswade a Man to put out his Eyes the better to receive the remote Light of an invisible Star by a Telescope.

§.5. [*Rise of Enthusiasm.*] Immediate *Revelation* being a much easier way for Men to establish their Opinions, and regulate their Conduct, than the tedious and not always successful Labour of strict Reasoning, it is no wonder, that some have been very apt to pretend to Revelation, and to perswade themselves, that they are under the peculiar[6] guidance of Heaven in their Actions and Opinions, especially in those of them, which they cannot account for by the ordinary Methods of Knowledge, and Principles of Reason. Hence we see, that in all Ages, Men, in whom Melancholy[7] has mixed with Devotion, or whose conceit of themselves has raised them into an Opinion of a greater familiarity with GOD, and a nearer admittance to his Favour than is afforded to others, have often flatter'd themselves with a perswasion of an immediate intercourse with the Deity, and frequent communications from the divine Spirit. GOD I own cannot be denied to be able to enlighten the Understanding by a Ray darted into the Mind immediately from the Fountain of Light: This they understand he has promised to do, and who then has so good a title to expect it, as those who are his peculiar[8] People, chosen by him and depending on him?

§.6. [*Enthusiasm.*] Their Minds being thus prepared, whatever groundless Opinion comes to settle it self strongly upon their Fancies, is an Illumination from the Spirit of GOD, and presently of divine Authority: And whatsoever odd Action they find in themselves a strong Inclination to do, that impulse is concluded to be a call or direction from Heaven, and must be obeyed; 'tis a Commission from above, and they cannot err in executing it.

§.7. This I take to be properly Enthusiasm, which though founded neither on Reason, nor Divine Revelation, but rising from the Conceits[9] of a warmed or over-weening Brain, works yet, where it once gets footing, more powerfully on the Perswasions and Actions of Men, than either of those two, or both together: Men being most forwardly obedient to the impulses they receive from themselves; And the whole Man is sure to act most vigorously, where the whole Man is carried by a natural Motion. For strong conceit like a new Principle carries all easily with it, when got above common Sense, and freed from all restraint of Reason, and check of Reflection, it is heightened into a Divine Authority, in concurrence with our own Temper and Inclination.

§.8. [*Enthusiasm mistaken for seeing and feeling.*] Though the odd Opinions and extravagant Actions,

---

4. third . . . Assent: The first two, discussed in earlier chapters of Book IV, are *faith* and *reason.* **5. much what:** much.

6. peculiar: individual. **7. Melancholy:** a pathological condition of the mind that showed itself either in acute depression or (as here) a sluggish unwillingness to stir from one's own preconceptions. **8. peculiar:** own. **9. Conceits:** notions, fancies.

Enthusiasm has run Men into, were enough to warn them against this wrong Principle so apt to misguide them both in their Belief and Conduct: yet the Love of something extraordinary, the Ease and Glory it is to be inspired and be above the common and natural ways of Knowledge so flatters many Men's Laziness, Ignorance and Vanity, that when once they are got into this way of immediate *Revelation*, of Illumination without search, and of certainty without Proof, and without Examination, 'tis a hard matter to get them out of it. Reason is lost upon them, they are above it: they see the Light infused into their Understandings, and cannot be mistaken; 'tis clear and visible there; like the Light of bright Sunshine, shews it self, and needs no other Proof, but its own Evidence: they feel the Hand of GOD moving them within, and the impulses of the Spirit, and cannot be mistaken in what they feel. Thus they support themselves, and are sure Reason hath nothing to do with what they see and feel in themselves: what they have a sensible Experience of admits no doubt, needs no probation. Would he not be ridiculous who should require to have it proved to him, that the Light shines, and that he sees it? It is its own Proof, and can have no other. When the Spirit brings Light into our Minds, it dispels Darkness. We see it, as we do that of the Sun at Noon, and need not the twilight of Reason to shew it us. This Light from Heaven is strong, clear, and pure, carries its own Demonstration with it, and we may as rationally take a Glow-worme to assist us to discover the Sun, as to examine the celestial Ray by our dim Candle,[10] Reason.

§.9. This is the way of talking of these Men: they are sure, because they are sure: and their Perswasions are right, only because they are strong in them. For, when what they say is strip'd of the Metaphor of seeing and feeling, this is all it amounts to: and yet these Similes so impose on them, that they serve them for certainty in themselves, and demonstration to others.

§.10. [*Enthusiasm how to be discover'd.*] But to examine a little soberly this internal Light, and this feeling on which they build so much. These Men have, they say, clear Light, and they see; They have an awaken'd Sense, and they feel: This cannot, they

are sure, be disputed them. For when a Man says he sees or he feels, no Body can deny it him, that he does so. But here let me ask: This seeing is it the perception of the Truth of the Proposition, or of this, that it is a Revelation from GOD? This feeling is it a perception of an Inclination or Fancy to do something, or of the Spirit of GOD moving that Inclination? These are two very different Perceptions, and must be carefully distinguish'd, if we would not impose upon our selves. I may perceive the Truth of a Proposition, and yet not perceive, that it is an immediate Revelation from GOD. I may perceive the Truth of a Proposition in *Euclid*, without its being, or my perceiving it to be, a Revelation: Nay I may perceive I came not by this Knowledge in a natural way, and so may conclude it revealed, without perceiving that it is a Revelation from GOD. Because there be Spirits, which, without being divinely commissioned, may excite those *Ideas* in me, and lay them in such order before my Mind, that I may perceive their Connexion. So that the Knowledge of any Proposition coming into my Mind, I know not how, is not a Perception that it is from GOD. Much less is a strong Perswasion, that it is true, a Perception that it is from GOD, or so much as true. But however it be called light and seeing; I suppose, it is at most but Belief, and Assurance: and the Proposition taken for a Revelation is not such, as they know, to be true, but take to be true. For where a Proposition is known to be true, Revelation is needless: And it is hard to conceive how that can be a Revelation to any one of what he knows already. If therefore it be a Proposition which they are perswaded, but do not know, to be true, whatever they may call it, it is not seeing, but believing. For these are two ways, whereby Truth comes into the Mind, wholly distinct, so that one is not the other. What I see I know to be so by the Evidence of the thing it self: what I believe I take to be so upon the Testimony of another: But this Testimony I must know to be given, or else what ground have I of believing? I must see that it is GOD that reveals this to me, or else I see nothing. The question then here is, How do I know that GOD is the Revealer of this to me; that this Impression is made upon my Mind by his holy Spirit, and that therefore I ought to obey it? If I know not this, how great soever the Assurance is, that I am possess'd with, it is groundless; whatever Light I pretend to, it is but *Enthusiasm*. For whether the Proposition supposed to be revealed, be in it self evidently true, or visibly probable, or by the natural ways of Knowledge uncertain, the

---

10. dim Candle: In the *Reasonableness of Christianity* (1695) Locke himself speaks of the light of reason as "the Candle of the Lord." Proverbs 20:27 was a much-quoted text in his day.

Proposition that must be well grounded, and manifested to be true is this, that GOD is the Revealer of it, and that what I take to be a Revelation is certainly put into my Mind by him, and is not an Illusion drop'd in by some other Spirit, or raised by my own phancy. For if I mistake not, these Men receive it for true, because they presume GOD revealed it. Does it not then stand them upon,[11] to examine upon what Grounds they presume it to be a Revelation from GOD? or else all their Confidence is mere Presumption: and this Light, they are so dazled with, is nothing, but an *ignis fatuus*[12] that leads them continually round in this Circle. *It is a Revelation, because they firmly believe it,* and *they believe it, because it is a Revelation.*

§.11. [*Enthusiasm fails of Evidence, that the Proposition is from GOD.*] In all that is of Divine *Revelation* there is need of no other Proof but that it is an Inspiration from GOD: For he can neither deceive nor be deceived. But how shall it be known, that any Proposition in our Minds is a Truth infused by God; a Truth that is reveal'd to us by him, which he declares to us, and therefore we ought to believe? Here it is that *Enthusiasm* fails of the Evidence it pretends to. For Men thus possessed boast of a Light whereby they say, they are enlightened, and brought into the Knowledge of this or that Truth. But if they know it to be a Truth, they must know it to be so either by its own self-evidence to natural Reason; or by the rational Proofs that make it out to be so. If they see and know it to be a Truth, either of these two ways, they in vain suppose it to be a Revelation: For they know it to be true by the same way, that any other Man naturally may know, that it is so without the help of Revelation. For thus all the Truths of what kind soever, that Men uninspired are enlightened with, came into their Minds, and are established there. If they say they know it to be true, because it is a *Revelation* from GOD, the reason is good: but then it will be demanded, how they know it to be a Revelation from GOD. If they say by the Light it brings with it, which shines bright in their Minds, and they cannot resist, I beseech them to consider, whether this be any more, than what we have taken notice of already, *viz.* that it is a Revelation because they strongly believe it to be true. For all the Light they speak of is but a strong, though ungrounded

perswasion of their own Minds that it is a Truth. For rational Grounds from Proofs that it is a Truth they must acknowledge to have none, for then it is not received as a *Revelation*, but upon the ordinary Grounds, that other Truths are received: And if they believe it to be true, because it is a *Revelation*, and have no other reason for its being a *Revelation*, but because they are fully perswaded without any other reason that it is true, they believe it to be a Revelation only because they strongly believe it to be a Revelation, which is a very unsafe ground to proceed on, either in our Tenets, or Actions: And what readier way can there be to run our selves into the most extravagant Errors and Miscarriages than thus to set up phancy for our supreme and sole Guide, and to believe any Proposition to be true, any Action to be right, only because we believe it to be so? The strength of our Perswasions are no Evidence at all of their own rectitude: Crooked things may be as stiff and unflexible as streight: and Men may be as positive and peremptory in Error as in Truth. How come else the untractable Zealots in different and opposite Parties? For if the Light, which every one thinks he has in his Mind, which in this Case is nothing but the strength of his own Perswasion, be an Evidence that it is from GOD, contrary Opinions may have the same title to be inspirations; and GOD will be not only the Father of Lights, but of opposite and contradictory Lights, leading Men contrary ways; and contradictory Propositions will be divine Truths, if an ungrounded strength of Assurance be an Evidence, that any Proposition is a Divine Revelation.

§.12. [*Firmness of Perswasion no Proof that any Proposition is from GOD.*] This cannot be otherwise, whilst firmness of Perswasion is made the cause of Believing, and confidence of being in the Right, is made an Argument of Truth; St. *Paul* himself believed he did well, and that he had a call to it, when he persecuted the Christians, whom he confidently thought in the Wrong:[13] But yet it was he, and not they, who were mistaken. Good Men are Men still, liable to Mistakes, and are sometimes warmly engaged in Errors, which they take for divine Truths, shining in their Minds with the clearest Light.

§.13. [*Light in the Mind, what.*] Light, true Light in the Mind is, or can be nothing else but the Evidence of the Truth of any Proposition; and if it be not a self-evident Proposition, all the Light it has, or can have,

---

11. Does . . . upon: are they not under obligation. **12. ignis fatuus:** a false fire; hence, a misleading notion.

13. St. Paul . . . Wrong: See Acts 22:1–21.

is from the clearness and validity of those Proofs, upon which it is received. To talk of any other light in the Understanding is to put our selves in the dark, or in the power of the Prince of Darkness, and by our own consent, to give our selves up to Delusion to believe a Lie. For if strength of Perswasion be the Light, which must guide us; I ask how shall any one distinguish between the delusions of Satan, and the inspirations of the Holy Ghost? He can transform himself into an Angel of Light. And they who are led by this Son of the Morning[14] are as fully satisfied of the Illumination, *i.e.* are as strongly perswaded, that they are enlightend by the Spirit of God, as any one who is so: They acquiesce and rejoyce in it, are acted[15] by it: and no body can be more sure, nor more in the right (if their own strong belief may be judge) than they.

§.14. [*Revelation must be judged of by Reason.*] He therefore that will not give himself up to all the Extravagancies of Delusion and Error must bring this Guide of his *Light within* to the Tryal. God when he makes the Prophet does not unmake the Man. He leaves all his Faculties in their natural State, to enable him to judge of his Inspirations, whether they be of divine Original or no. When he illuminates the Mind with supernatural Light, he does not extinguish that which is natural. If he would have us assent to the Truth of any Proposition, he either evidences that Truth by the usual Methods of natural Reason, or else makes it known to be a Truth, which he would have us assent to, by his Authority, and convinces us that it is from him, by some Marks which Reason cannot be mistaken in. *Reason* must be our last Judge and Guide in every Thing. I do not mean, that we must consult Reason, and examine whether a Proposition revealed from God can be made out by natural Principles, and if it cannot, that then we may reject it: But consult it we must, and by it examine, whether it be a *Revelation* from God or no: And if *Reason* finds it to be revealed from GOD, *Reason* then declares for it, as much as for any other Truth, and makes it one of her Dictates. Every Conceit that throughly warms our Fancies must pass for an Inspiration, if there be nothing but the Strength of our Perswasions, whereby to judge of our Perswasions: If *Reason* must not examine their Truth by something extrinsical to the Perswasions themselves; Inspirations

and Delusions, Truth and Falshood will have the same Measure, and will not be possible to be distinguished.

§.15. [*Belief no Proof of Revelation.*] If this internal Light, or any Proposition which under that Title we take for inspired, be conformable to the Principles of Reason or to the Word of GOD,[16] which is attested Revelation, *Reason* warrants it, and we may safely receive it for true, and be guided by it in our Belief and Actions: If it receive no Testimony nor Evidence from either of these Rules, we cannot take it for a *Revelation*, or so much as for true, till we have some other Mark that it is a *Revelation*, besides our believing that it is so. Thus we see the holy Men of GOD, who had *Revelations* from GOD, had something else besides that internal Light of assurance in their own Minds, to testify to them, that it was from GOD. They were not left to their own Perswasions alone, that those Perswasions were from GOD; But had outward Signs to convince them of the Author of those Revelations. And when they were to convince others, they had a Power given them to justify the Truth of their Commission from Heaven; and by visible Signs to assert the divine Authority of the Message they were sent with. *Moses* saw the Bush burn without being consumed, and heard a Voice out of it.[17] This was something besides finding an impulse upon his Mind to go to *Pharaoh*, that he might bring his Brethren out of *Egypt:* and yet he thought not this enough to authorise him to go with that Message, till GOD by another Miracle, of his Rod turned into a Serpent,[18] had assured him of a Power to testify his Mission by the same Miracle repeated before them, whom he was sent to. *Gideon* was sent by an Angel to deliver *Israel* from the *Mideanites*, and yet he desired a Sign to convince him, that this Commission was from GOD.[19] These and several the like Instances to be found among the Prophets of old, are enough to shew, that they thought not an inward seeing or perswasion of their own Minds without any other Proof a sufficient Evidence, that it was from GOD, though the Scripture does not every where mention their demanding or having such Proofs.

§.15. In what I have said I am far from denying, that GOD can, or doth sometimes enlighten Mens Minds in the apprehending of certain Truths, or excite them

---

14. **Son . . . Morning:** Isa. 14:12. **15. acted:** prompted in their actions.

16. **Word of God:** the Bible. **17. Moses . . . it:** See Ex. 3:2–4. **18. his . . . Serpent:** See Ex. 4:2–9. **19. Gideon . . . God:** See Judg. 6:11–40.

to Good Actions by the immediate influence and assistance of the Holy Spirit, without any extraordinary Signs accompanying it. But in such Cases too we have Reason and the Scripture, unerring Rules to know whether it be from GOD or no. Where the Truth imbraced is consonant to the *Revelation* in the written word of GOD; or the Action conformable to the dictates of right *Reason* or Holy Writ, we may be assured that we run no risque in entertaining it as such, because though perhaps it be not an immediate Revelation from GOD, extraordinarily operating on our Minds, yet we are sure it is warranted by that Revelation which he has given us of Truth. But it is not the strength of our private perswasion within our selves, that can warrant it to be a Light or Motion from Heaven: Nothing can do that but the written Word of GOD without us, or that Standard of Reason which is common to us with all Men. Where Reason or Scripture is express[20] for any Opinion or Action, we may receive it as of divine Authority: But 'tis not the strength of our own Perswasions which can by it self give it that Stamp. The bent of our own Minds may favour it as much as we please; That may shew it to be a Fondling of our own, but will by no means prove it to be an Offspring of Heaven, and of divine Original.

20. express: clear and explicit.

John Tillotson

1630–1694

"I remember, when I was a boy, I used to read one Tillotson's sermons; and, I am sure, if a man practised half so much as in one of those sermons, he will go to heaven." So says the surgeon at The Dragon in Fielding's *Joseph Andrews* (1742). The subject of this humble tribute, John Tillotson, Archbishop of Canterbury, was perhaps the most popular preacher of his time. He was born in 1630 at Sowerby, Yorkshire, into a Puritan family and was educated at Clare Hall, Cambridge, at a time when the Cambridge Platonists were infusing moral philosophy and theology with rationalism. Ordained in 1660 or 1661, Tillotson assented to the Act of Uniformity in 1662, despite his Presbyterian leanings, and the next year was elected preacher to the Society of Lincoln's Inn. His great reputation as a preacher was made in the years following at St. Lawrence Jewry, where he held the Tuesday Lectureship and where his father-in-law, Dr. John Wilkins, was rector. Wilkins, a founder of the Royal Society, was no mean theologian himself and composed a number of treatises, as well as sermons, which Tillotson published after his death. One treatise, *On the Principles and Duties of Natural Religion* (1678), includes a preface by Tillotson that sets forth views very similar to those contained in the sermon by which we have chosen to represent him. In 1672 Tillotson was himself elected to the Royal Society and in the same year was appointed Dean of Canterbury.

Like many another Anglican clergyman, Tillotson found himself at the Revolution in an embarrassing if not compromising position. He had accepted, and even preached, the Laudian doctrine of passive obedience and nonresistance to the Crown; yet it was exceedingly tempting to support the overthrow of the Catholic James II in favor of the deliverers of the Established Church, William and Mary. Tillotson, in fact, took no active part in the Revolution, as much as he welcomed it. But his sympathies were known, and though he sought no personal aggrandizement, he was rewarded with the post of Dean of St. Paul's in November, 1689, and that of Archbishop of Canterbury, which he held from May, 1691, until his death in 1694.

Moderation is the keynote to the life and writings of Tillotson. In 1668 he had joined Wilkins and others in an attempt—foiled by the High-Church party in the Commons—to break down the barriers that were keeping Dissenters from returning to the fold of the Church of England. He was forever combating superstition (equated with Catholicism) on the one side and fanaticism (equated with the Protestant sectarians) on the other.

Are not the things, about which we differ, in their nature indifferent? that is, things about which there ought to be no difference among wise men? are they not at a great distance from the life and essence of religion, and rather good or bad as they tend to the peace and unity of the church, or are made use of to schism and faction, than necessary or evil in themselves?

John Beardmore, a pupil of Tillotson's at Clare Hall, remembered him as "a practical preacher." Of his sermons he wrote:

His discourses generally aim'd, either to excite in men an awful sense of God, and to enkindle devotion towards him, or to stir up to a holy, religious, and virtuous conversation [i.e., behavior in society] . . . . He seldom preach'd controversies; except those between us and the church of *Rome;* which indeed he did purposely, when he saw there was an absolute necessity for it . . . . And as for practical subjects, I believe there were few remarkable texts of Scripture, either of the Old or New Testament, or however few heads of practical divinity, but he handled them at one time or other in the course of his preaching. And for this reason some would call him a moral preacher, as a diminution to him, as if he preach'd moral virtue rather than grace: But this is but a calumny upon him. He did not indeed treat upon the inexplicable and ineffable operations of grace, as some have taken upon them to do, but with what good effect I cannot tell. . . . I remember a notion he told me now above 30 years ago, *viz.* that Christianity, as to the practical part of it, was nothing else but the religion of nature, or pure morality, save only praying and making all our addresses to God in the name, and through the mediation of our Saviour, and the use of the two sacraments of Baptism and the Lord's Supper; "and, *said he,* want of understanding and prac-tising according to this principle hath broken the peace of *Christendom,* and it can never be restored, till this principle and notion obtain again."

Tillotson's fame as a preacher owed perhaps as much to his style as to his thoughts. Bishop Burnet, who preached his funeral sermon, observed on that occasion:

No Man . . . knew better that Art of preserving the Majesty of things under a Simplicity of Words; tempering these so equally together, that neither did his Thoughts sink, nor his Stile swell: keeping always the due Mean between a low Flatness and the Dresses of false Rhetorick. Together with the Pomp of Words he did also cut off all Superfluities and needless Enlargements: He said what was just necessary to give clear Ideas of things, and no more: He laid aside all long and affected Periods: His Sentences were short and clear; and the whole Thread was of a piece, plain and distinct.

Burnet was not alone in praising Tillotson for this achievement of style. In his *English Pulpit Oratory from Andrewes to Tillotson* (1932), W. Fraser Mitchell puts it in a historical perspective:

Tillotson's style came to embody the earnestness of the Puritans with the rational element of the Cambridge Platonists in a form acceptable to the Anglicans of the period. Other men, both before and concurrently, it is true, played a part in the movement towards plainness—Latitudinarians, Royal Society preachers, men of individual genius like South and Barrow—but the fact remains that it was Tillotson who finally secured once and for all the triumph of the plain style in preaching, and was so largely instrumental in diffusing a taste for plainness and perspicuity in prose in general.

A number of Tillotson's sermons were printed separately and in small collections during his lifetime. After his death two rival editions appeared: a one-volume folio *Works*, containing fifty-four previously printed sermons and his *Rule of Faith*, was published in 1696 and a fourteen-volume octavo edition (each volume bearing a different title), containing two hundred sermons, appeared between 1695 and 1704. The latter, brought out by Tillotson's chaplain, Ralph Barker, is considered the more authoritative edition of the two, although a critical edition of Tillotson's works remains a scholarly desideratum. A life of Tillotson by Thomas Birch, including in an appendix the *Memorials* by John Beardmore, first appeared in Volume I of the 1752 edition of the *Works* (a combination of the two rival editions). Two hundred years intervened before another full treatment of Tillotson; this was by L. G. Locke in his *Tillotson: A Study in Seventeenth-Century Literature* (1954), Volume IV of *Anglistica*.

SERMON I

Of the great Duties of Natural Religion, with the Ways and Means of knowing them.

🐝

Tillotson, like many before and after him, attempted a reconciliation of natural and revealed religion. Divine revelation is given a twofold office: confirming and clarifying the light of nature and setting forth truths that are beyond, but not contrary to, reason. Still, since the pernicious differences among men tend to derive from revelation, or interpretations of revelation, Tillotson generally looked for "the life and essence of religion" in its moral rather than its doctrinal substance.

This sermon appears to have been first printed by Barker; our text is from Volume IV of *Several Discourses . . . by the most Reverend Dr. John Tillotson . . .* (2nd ed., 1700; copy at Yale), the earliest version we have been able to locate.

🐝

MICAH. 6. 6, 7, 8

Wherewith shall I come before the Lord, and bow my self before the high God? shall I come before him with burnt offerings, with Calves of a year old?

Will the Lord be pleased with thousands of Rams, or with ten thousands of Rivers of Oyl? shall I give my first born for my transgression, the fruit of my body for the sin of my soul?

He hath shewed thee, O man, what is good; and what doth the Lord require of thee, but to do justly, and to love mercy, and to walk humbly with thy God?

In the beginning of this Chapter, the Prophet tells the People of *Israel*, that *the Lord had a Controversie with them;* and that he might direct them how to take up this quarrel, he brings in one making this enquiry in the name of the People; *Wherewith shall I come before the Lord, and bow my self before the high God?* That is, by what kind of Worship or Devotion may I address my self to him in the most acceptable manner? by what means may I hope to appease his displeasure? To satisfie this enquiry, he first instanceth in the chief kinds of Sacrifices and Expiations that were in use among the *Jews* and *Heathens; Shall I come before him with burnt offerings?* the constant Sacrifice that was offered to God by way of acknowledgment of his Dominion over the Creatures; *with Calves of a year old?* which was the Sin-offering which the High-Priest offered for himself. Or Will he rather accept of those great and costly Sacrifices which were offered upon Solemn and Publick Occasions, such as that was which *Solomon* offered at the Dedication of the Temple[1]? *Will the Lord be pleased with thousands of Rams, or with ten thousands of Rivers of Oyl?* Or if none of these will do, shall I try to attone him after the manner of the *Heathen*, by the dearest thing in the World, the first-born of my Children? *Shall I give my first-born for my transgression, the fruit of my Body for the sin of my soul?* If God was to be appeased at all, surely they thought it must be by some of these ways, for beyond these they could imagine nothing of greater value and efficacy.

But the Prophet tells them that they were quite out of the way, in thinking to pacifie God upon these terms, that there are other things which are much better and more pleasing to him than any of these Sacrifices. For some of them were expressly forbidden by God, as *the offering up of our Children;* and for the rest, they were not good in themselves, but meerly by vertue of their Institution, and because they were commanded. But the things which he would recommend to them, are such as are good in their own nature, and required of us by God upon that account. *He hath shewed thee, O Man, what is good, and what doth the Lord require of thee, but to do justly, and to love mercy, and to walk humbly with thy God?*

So that in these words you have,

First, An Enquiry which is the best way to appease God when he is offended; *Wherewith shall I come before the Lord, and bow my self before the high God?*

Secondly, The way that Men are apt to take in this Case; and that is by some external piece of Religion and Devotion; such as Sacrifice was both among *Jews* and *Heathen. Shall I come before him with Burnt-offerings,* &c. By which questions the Prophet intimates that Men are very apt to pitch upon this course.

Thirdly, The course which God himself directs to, and which will effectually pacifie him. *He hath shewed thee, O Man, what is good; and what doth the Lord thy God require of thee,* &c.

The *First* being a meer question, there needs no more to be said of it; only that it is a question of great importance; What is the most effectual way to appease God when we have offended him? For who can bear his indignation, and who can stand before

him, when once he is angry? Let us consider then, in the

Second place, the way that Men are apt to take to pacifie God; and that is by some external piece of Religion and Devotion, such as were Sacrifices among the *Jews* and *Heathen. Shall I come before him with Burnt-offerings?* This is the way which Men are most apt to chuse. The *Jews,* you see, pitched upon the external parts of their Religion, those which were most pompous and solemn, the richest and most costly Sacrifices; so they might but keep their Sins, they were well enough content to offer up any thing else to God; they thought nothing too good for him, provided he would not oblige them to become better.

And thus it is among our selves, when we apprehend God is displeased with us, and his Judgments abroad in the Earth, we are content to do any thing, but *to learn righteousness;* we are willing to submit to any kind of external Devotion and Humiliation, to Fast, and Pray, to afflict our selves, and to cry mightily unto God; things some of them good in themselves, but the least part of that which God requires of us.

And as for the Church of *Rome,* in case of publick Judgments and Calamities, they are the most inquisitive[2] and (as they pretend) the most skilful People in the world to pacifie God; and they have a thousand solemn devices to this purpose. I do not wrong them, by representing them enquiring after this manner. "Shall I go before a *Crucifix,* and bow my self to it, as to *the high God?* And, because the Lord is *a great King,* and it is perhaps too much boldness and arrogancy to make immediate Addresses always to him; to which of the *Saints* or *Angels* shall I go to mediate for me, and intercede on my behalf? Will the Lord be pleased with thousands of *Pater-Nosters,* or with ten thousands of *Ave-Marys?* Shall the *Host* travel in procession, or my self undertake a tedious *Pilgrimage?* Or shall I list my self a Souldier for *the Holy War,* or for *the Extirpation of Hereticks?*[3] Shall I give half my Estate to a *Convent* for my Transgression, or chastise and punish my Body for the Sin of my Soul?" Thus Men deceive themselves, and will submit to all the extravagant Severities, that the Petulancy and Folly of Men can devise and

---

SERMON I. **1. which Solomon . . . Temple:** "And Solomon offered a sacrifice of peace-offerings, which he offered unto the Lord, two and twenty thousand oxen, and an hundred and twenty thousand sheep. So the king and all the children of Israel dedicated the house of the Lord" (I Kings 8:63).

2. inquisitive: in the sense of "given to inquiring how."
3. Or . . . Hereticks: Tillotson wrote elsewhere, "We [Anglicans] do not teach men to break faith with heretics or infidels; nor to destroy and extirpate those who differ from us, with fire and sword."

impose upon them. And indeed it is not to be imagined, when Men are once under the Power of Superstition, how ridiculous they may be, and yet think themselves religious; how prodigiously they may play the Fool, and yet believe they please God; what cruel and barbarous things they may do to themselves and others, and yet be *verily perswaded they do God good Service.*

And what is the Mystery of all this, but that Men are loath to do that without which, nothing else that we do is acceptable to God? They *hate to be reformed;* and for this Reason, they will be content to do any Thing, rather than be put to the Trouble of Mending themselves; every thing is easie in comparison of this Task, and God may have any Terms of them, so he will let them be quiet in their Sins, and excuse them from the real Virtues of a good Life. And this brings me to the

Third Thing, which I principally intended to speak to. The Course which God himself directs to, and which will effectually pacifie him. *He hath shewed thee, O Man, what is good; and what doth the Lord require of thee, but to do justly, and to love Mercy, and to walk humbly with thy God?* In the handling of which, I shall,

First, Consider those several Duties which God here requires of us, and upon the Performance of which he will be pacified towards us.

Secondly, By what Ways and Means God hath discovered these Duties to us, and the Goodness of them; *He hath shewed thee, O Man, what is good, &c.*

I. We will briefly consider the several Duties which God here requires of us, and upon the Performance of which he will be pacified towards us; *What doth the Lord require of thee, but to do Justly, and to love Mercy, and to walk humbly with thy God?*

It was usual among the *Jews* to reduce all the Duties of Religion to these three Heads, *Justice, Mercy,* and *Piety;* under the first two, comprehending the Duties which we owe to one another, and under the third the Duties which we owe to God.

1. *Justice.* And I was going to tell you what it is, but I considered that every Man knows it, as well as any Definition can explain it to him. I shall only put you in mind of some of the principal Instances of it, and the several Virtues comprehended under it. And,

First, Justice is concerned in the making of Laws; that they be such as are equal and reasonable, useful and beneficial, for the Honour of God and Religion, and for the publick good of Human Society; This is a great Trust, in the discharge of which, if Men be byassed by Favour or Interest, and drawn aside from the Consideration and Regard of the publick Good, it is a far greater Crime, and of worse Consequence, than any private Act of Injustice between Man and Man.

And then, Justice is also concerned in the due Execution of Laws; which are the Guard of Private Property, the Security of Publick Peace, and of Religion and Good Manners. And,

Lastly, In the Observance of Laws, and Obedience to them; which is a Debt that every Man owes to Humane Society.

But more especially Justice is concerned in the Observance of those Laws, whether of God or Man, which respect the Rights of Men, and their mutual Commerce and Intercourse with one another. That we use Honesty and Integrity in all our Dealings, in Opposition to Fraud and Deceit; Truth and Fidelity, in Opposition to Falshood and Breach of Trust; Equity and good Conscience, in Opposition to all kind of Oppression and Exaction.[4] These are the principal Branches, and Instances of this great and comprehensive Duty of Justice; the Violation whereof is so much the greater Sin, because this Virtue is the firmest Bond of Humane Society, upon the Observation whereof, the Peace and Happiness of Mankind does so much depend.

2. *Mercy,* which does not only signifie the inward Affection of Pity and Compassion towards those that are in Misery and Necessity, but the Effects of it, in the Actual Relief of those whose Condition calls for our Charitable Help and Assistance; By feeding the Hungry, and cloathing the Naked, and visiting the Sick, and vindicating the Oppressed, and comforting the afflicted, and ministring Ease and Relief to them if it be in our Power. And this is a very lovely Virtue, and argues more Goodness in Men than mere *Justice* doth. For *Justice* is a strict Debt; but *Mercy* is Favour and Kindness. And this perhaps may be the reason of the different Expressions in the Text, that when God barely commands us *to do justly,* he requires we should *love Mercy,* that is, take a particular Pleasure and Delight in the Exercise of this Virtue, which is so proper and agreeable to Mankind, that we commonly call it *Humanity,* giving it its Name from our very Nature. In short, it is so excellent a Virtue, that I should be very sorry that any Religion should be able to pretend to the Practice of it more than our own.

---

4. Exaction: arbitrary or exorbitant demand of money or services.

3. *Piety; To walk humbly with thy God. To walk humbly in the fear of the Lord;* so the *Chaldee* Paraphrase[5] renders these Words. And this Phrase may comprehend all those Acts of Religion which refer immediately to God; A firm Belief of his Being and Perfections; an awful Sense of him, as the dread Sovereign and righteous Judge of the World; a due Regard to his Service, and a reverent behaviour of our selves towards him in all Acts of Worship and Religion, in Opposition to Atheism and a Prophane Neglect and Contempt of God and Religion; a new and monstrous kind of Impiety! which of late Years hath broke in upon us, and got head among us, not only contrary to the Example of former Ages, but in Despight of the very Genius and Temper of the Nation, which is naturally devout and zealous in Religion.

Or else this Phrase of *walking humbly with God,* may refer more particularly to the Posture and Condition of the People of *Israel* at that time, who were fallen under the heavy Displeasure of God for their Sins. And then the Duty required is, that being sensible how highly God hath been offended by us, by the general Corruption and Viciousness of the Age, which like a Leprosie hath spread it self almost over the whole Body of the Nation, and by that open Lewdness and those insolent Impieties which are daily committed amongst us; I say, that being deeply sensible of this, we do with all Humility acknowledge our Sins to God, and repent of them, and implore his Mercy and Forgiveness, and resolve by his grace *to turn every one from the evil of our ways,*[6] and from *the wickedness that is in our hands;* which God grant we may every one do *this Day,*[7] according to the pious design and intention of it. And if we be sincere in this Resolution, *who can tell but God may turn and repent, and turn away his anger from us, that we perish not.*[8] Nay, we have great reason to believe, that he will be pacified towards us. So he hath declared, *Isa.* I. 16. *Wash ye, make you clean, put away the evil of your doings from before mine eyes, cease to do evil, learn to do well, seek judgment, relieve the oppressed, judge the fatherless, plead for the widow; come now and let us reason together, saith the Lord; though your* sins *be as scarlet, they shall be as white as snow, though they are red like crimson, they shall be as wooll.* But if we continue unreformed, God will say to us, as he does there[9] to the people of *Israel, To what purpose is the multitude of your Sacrifices unto me? your calling of Assemblies I cannot away with, it is iniquity, even the solemn meeting; and when ye spread forth your hands, I will hide mine eyes from you; when ye make many prayers, I will not hear.* To which, let me add that excellent Saying of the Son of *Syrach* to this purpose *Ecclesiastic.* 34. 25, 26. *He that washeth himself after the touching of a dead body, if he touch it again, what availeth his washing? So is it with a Man that fasteth for his Sins, and goeth again and doth the same things. Who will hear his Prayer, or what doth his humbling profit him?*

II. Let us consider by what ways and means God hath made known these Duties to us, and the goodness and the obligation of them. *He hath shewed thee, O Man, what is good; and what doth the Lord require of thee?* I shall mention *Five* ways whereby God hath discovered this to us.

1. By a kind of natural Instinct.
2. By natural Reason.
3. By the general vote and consent of Mankind.
4. By external Revelation.
5. By the inward Dictates and Motions of God's Spirit upon the Minds of Men.

First, By a kind of natural Instinct, by which I mean a secret Impression upon the Minds of Men, whereby they are naturally carried to approve some things as good and fit, and to dislike other things, as having a native evil and deformity in them. And this I call *a natural Instinct,* because it does not seem to proceed so much from the exercise of our Reason, as from a natural propension and inclination, like those Instincts which are in Brute Creatures, of natural affection and care towards their young ones. And that these Inclinations are precedent to all reason and discourse about them, evidently appears by this, that they do put forth themselves every whit as vigorously in young persons, as in those of riper Reason; in the rude and ignorant sort of People, as in those who are more polish'd and refin'd. For we see plainly that the young and ignorant have as strong impressions of Piety and Devotion, as true a sense of gratitude and justice and pity, as the wiser and more knowing part of Mankind. A plain indication, that the Reason of Mankind is

---

5. the Chaldee Paraphrase: the Targums, the translations or paraphrases of the Old Testament books in the Aramaic dialect. **6. turn . . . ways:** Cf. II Kings 17:13, II Chron. 7:14, Ezek. 33:11, and Zech. 1:4. **7. this Day:** [original note] *This Sermon was Preach'd upon occasion of a public Fast.* **8. who . . . not:** "Who can tell if God will turn and repent, and turn away from his fierce anger, that we perish not?" (Jon. 3:9).

9. there: a compilation from Isa. 1:11, 13, and 15.

prevented[10] by a kind of *natural instinct* and *anticipation* concerning the good or evil, the comeliness or deformity of these things. And though this do not equally extend to all the instances of our Duty, yet as to the great lines and essential parts of it, Mankind hardly need to consult any other Oracle, than the meer propensions and inclinations of their Nature; as, whether we ought to reverence the Divine Nature, to be grateful to those who have conferred benefits upon us, to speak the truth, to be faithful to our promise, to restore that which is committed to us in trust, to pity and relieve those that are in misery, and in all things to do to others as we would have them do to us. And this will further appear, if we consider these two things,

1. That Men are naturally innocent or guilty to themselves, according to what they do in these things. So the Apostle tells us, *Rom.* 2. 14, 15. *When the Gentiles which have not the Law, do by nature the things contained in the Law, these having not the Law, are a Law unto themselves, and do shew the effect of the Law written in their hearts, their Consciences also bearing witness, and their thoughts by turns* (that is, according as they do well or ill) *accusing or excusing them.*[11] There is a secret comfort in innocence, and a strange pleasure and satisfaction in being acquitted by our own Minds for what we do. But on the contrary, when we contradict these natural Dictates, what uneasiness do we find in our own Breasts? Nay even before the Fact is committed, our Conscience is strangely disquieted at the thoughts of it. When a Man does but design to do a bad thing, he is guilty to himself, as if he had committed it. Of this we have a considerable instance, in the first violence that was offered to Nature, *Gen.* 4. 6. *The Lord said unto Cain, why art thou wroth, and why is thy countenance fallen?* The very thought of that Wickedness which he did but then design, did disorder his Mind, and make a change in his very Countenance. Guilt is the natural Concomitant of heinous Crimes, which so soon as ever a Man commits, his Spirit receives a secret wound, which causeth a great deal of smart and anguish. For guilt is restless, and puts the Mind of Man into an unnatural working and

fermentation, never to be settled again but by Repentance. *The Wicked are like the troubled Sea when it cannot rest;*[12] which plainly shews that the Mind of Man hath a kind of *Natural sense* of Good and Evil; because when ever we offend against Nature, our Consciences are touched to the quick, and we receive a sting into our Soul, which shoots and pains us, when ever we reflect upon what we have done. I appeal to that witness which every Man carries in his breast, whether this be not true.

2. Men are naturally full of hopes and fears, according as they follow or go against these natural Dictates. A good Conscience is apt to fill Men with confidence and good hopes. It does not only give ease; but security to the Mind of Man, against the dread of Invisible Powers, and the fearful apprehensions of a future Judgment. Whereas guilt fills Men with dismal apprehensions of danger, and continual misgivings concerning their own safety. Thus it was with *Cain* after he had slain his Brother; *It shall come to pass that every one that findeth me shall slay me.*[13] Nay, when a Man hath done a secret fault, which none can accuse him of, yet then is he haunted with the terrors of his own Mind, and cannot be secure in his own apprehensions; which plainly shews that Men are conscious to themselves, when they do well, and when they do amiss; and that the same *Natural Instinct* which prompts Men to their Duty, fills them with good hopes when they have done it, and with secret fears and apprehensions of danger when they have done contrary to it.

Secondly, God shews Men what is good, by Natural Reason; and that *two* ways; By the convenience[14] of things to our Nature; and by their tendency to our Happiness and Interest.

First, Reason shews us the convenience of things to our Nature; and whatever is agreeable to the Primitive design and intention of Nature, that we call *good;* whatever is contrary thereto, we call *evil.* For Example, *to honour and love God.* It is natural to honour great power and perfection, and to love goodness wherever it is. So likewise, *gratitude* is natural, to acknowledge benefits received, and to be ready to requite them, and the contrary is monstrous, and universally abhorred; and there is no greater sign that any thing is contrary to Nature, than if it be detested by the whole kind.

---

10. **prevented:** preceded. 11. **When . . . them:** "For when the Gentiles, which have not the law, do by nature the things contained in the law, these, having not the law, are a law unto themselves: Which shew the work of the law written in their hearts, their conscience also bearing witness, and their thoughts the mean while accusing or else excusing one another."

12. **The Wicked . . . rest:** "But the wicked are like the troubled sea, when it cannot rest, whose waters cast up mire and dirt" (Isa. 57:20). 13. **It . . . me:** Gen. 4:14. 14. **convenience:** accord, fitness.

It is agreeable also to Nature to be *just*, and *to do to others, as we would have them do to us;* for this is to make our own natural inclinations and desires, the rule of our dealing with others; and *to be merciful;* for no Man that hath not devested himself of humanity, can be cruel and hard-hearted to others, without feeling a pain in himself.

Secondly, Reason shews us the Tendency of these Things to our Happiness and Interest. And indeed the notion of *good* and *evil* does commonly refer to the Consequences of things, and we call that *good*, which will bring some Benefit and Advantage to us, and that *evil* which is likely to produce some Mischief and Inconvenience; and by this rule Reason discovers to us that these Duties are *good*.

To begin with *Piety* towards God. Nothing can more evidently tend to our Interest, than to make him our Friend, upon whose Favour our Happiness depends. So likewise for *Gratitude;* it is a Virtue, to which if Nature did not prompt us, our interest would direct us; for every Man is ready to place Benefits there where he may hope for a thankful Return. *Temperance* does apparently conduce to our Health, which, next to a good Conscience, is the most pleasant and valuable thing in the World; whereas the intemperate Man is an open Enemy to himself, and continually making Assaults upon his own Life. *Mercy* and *Pity* are not more welcome to others, than they are delightful and beneficial to our selves; for we do not only gratifie our own Nature and Bowels,[15] by relieving those who are in misery, but we provoke Mankind by our Example to the like Tenderness, and do prudently bespeak the Commiseration of others towards us, when it shall be our Turn to stand in need of it. And if we be wise enough, our Reason will likewise direct us to be *just*, as the surest Art of thriving in this World; It gives a Man a Reputation, which is a powerful Advantage in all the Affairs of this World; It is the shortest and easiest way of dispatching Business, the plainest, and least entangled; and though it be not so *sudden* a way of growing rich, as Fraud and Oppression: yet it is much *surer* and more *lasting*, and not liable to those terrible Back-blows and after-reckonings, to which Estates got by Injustice are.

And natural Reason does not only shew us that these things are *good*, but that *the Lord requires them of us*, that is, that they have the Force and Obligation of

Laws. For there needs nothing more to make any thing a *Law*, than a sufficient declaration, that it is *the Will of God;* and this God hath sufficiently signified to Mankind by the very Frame of our Natures, and of those principles and faculties which he hath endued us withal; so that whenever we act contrary to these, we plainly disobey the Will of him that made us, and violate those Laws which he hath Enacted in our Natures, and written upon our Hearts.

And this is all the *Law* that the greatest part of Mankind were under, before the Revelation of the Gospel. From *Adam* to *Moses*, the World was almost solely governed by the *Natural Law;* which seems to be the meaning of that hard Text, *Rom.* 5. 13. *For until the Law Sin was in the World*, that is, before the *Law* of *Moses* was given, Men were capable of offending against some *other Law*, for otherwise Sin could not have been imputed to them, for *Sin is not imputed where there is no Law*. And then it follows; *Nevertheless Death reigned from Adam to Moses, even over them that had not sinned after the similitude of Adam's Transgression;* that is, during that space from *Adam* to *Moses* Men sinned against the *natural Law*, and were liable to Death upon that account, though they had not offended against an express Revelation from God, as *Adam* had done; for *that* the Apostle seems to mean, by *sinning after the Similitude of* Adam's *Transgression*.

Thirdly, God hath shewn us what is good by the general Vote and Consent of Mankind. Not that all Mankind do agree concerning Virtue and Vice; but that as to the greater Duties of *Piety, Justice, Mercy*, and the like, the Exceptions are but few in comparison, and not enough to infringe a general Consent. And of this I shall offer to you this threefold Evidence.

1. That these Virtues are generally praised and held in esteem by Mankind, and the contrary Vices generally reproved and evil spoken of. Now to praise any thing, is to give Testimony to the Goodness of it, and to censure any thing, is to declare that we believe it to be evil. And if we consult the History of all Ages, we shall find that the things which are generally praised in the Lives of Men, and recommended to the Imitation of Posterity are Piety and Devotion, Gratitude and Justice, Humanity and Charity; and that the contrary to these are marked with Ignominy and Reproach; the former are commended even in Enemies, and the latter are branded even by those who had a kindness for the Persons that were guilty of them. So constant hath Mankind always been in the Commendation of Virtue, and in the Censure of Vice.

---

15. Bowels: The bowels were considered the seat of the sympathetic emotions.

Nay we find not only those who are virtuous themselves, giving their Testimony and Applause to Virtue, but even those who are vicious; not out of love to Goodness, but from the Conviction of their own Minds, and from a secret Reverence they bear to the common Consent and Opinion of Mankind. And this is a great Testimony, because it is the Testimony of an Enemy extorted by the meer light and force of Truth.

And on the contrary; Nothing is more ordinary than for *Vice to reprove Sin*, and to hear Men condemn the like, or the same things in others, which they allow in themselves. And this is a clear Evidence, that Vice is generally condemned by Mankind, that many Men condemn it in themselves; and those who are so kind as to spare themselves, are very quick-sighted to spie a Fault in any body else, and will censure a bad Action done by another, with as much Freedom and Impartiality, as the most virtuous Man in the World.

And to this consent of Mankind about Virtue and Vice, the Scripture frequently appeals. As when it commands us *to provide things honest in the Sight of all Men;*[16] *and by well-doing to put to silence the Ignorance of foolish Men;*[17] intimating that there are some things so confessedly good, and owned to be such by so general a Vote of Mankind, that the worst of Men have not the Face to open their Mouths against them. And it is made the Character of a virtuous Action, if it be *lovely*, and *commendable*, and *of good report*. Philip. 4. 8. *Whatsoever things are lovely, whatsoever things are of good report, if there be any Virtue, if there be any praise, make account of these things;*[18] intimating to us, that Mankind do generally concur in the Praise and Commendation of what is virtuous.

2. Men do generally glory and stand upon their Innocency, when they do virtuously; but are ashamed, and out of Countenance, when they do the contrary. Now Glory and Shame are nothing else but an Appeal to the Judgment of others concerning the good or evil of our Actions. There are indeed some such Monsters as are impudent in their Impieties, but these are but few in comparison. Generally Mankind is

modest, the greatest part of those who do evil are apt to blush at their own Faults, and to confess them in their Countenance, which is an Acknowledgment that they are not only guilty to themselves that they have done amiss, but that they are apprehensive that others think so. For Guilt is a Passion respecting our selves, but Shame regards others. Now it is a sign of Shame, that Men love to conceal their Faults from others, and commit them secretly, in the dark and without Witnesses, and are afraid even of a Child or a Fool: Or if they be discovered in them, they are solicitous to excuse and extenuate them, and ready to lay the fault upon any body else, or to transfer their Guilt, or as much of it as they can, upon others. All which are certain Tokens, that Men are not only naturally guilty to themselves, when they commit a Fault; but that they are sensible also what Opinions others have of these things.

And on the contrary, Men are apt to stand upon their Justification, and to glory when they have done well. The Conscience of a Man's own Virtue and Integrity, lifts up his Head and gives him Confidence before others, because he is satisfied they have a good Opinion of his Actions. What a good Face does a Man naturally set upon a good Deed? And how does he sneak, when he hath done wickedly, being sensible that he is condemned by others, as well as by himself? No Man is afraid of being upbraided for having dealt honestly or kindly with others, nor does account it any Calumny or Reproach, to have it reported of him, that he is a sober and chast Man. No Man blusheth, when he meets a Man with whom he hath kept his Word, and discharged his Trust: but every Man is apt to do so, when he meets one with whom he has dealt dishonestly, or who knows some notorious Crime by him.

3. Vice is generally forbidden and punished by Humane Laws: but against the contrary Virtues there never was any Law. Some Vices are so manifestly evil in themselves, or so mischievous to Humane Society, that the Laws of most Nations have taken care to discountenance them by severe Penalties. Scarce any Nation was ever so barbarous, as not to maintain and vindicate the Honour of their Gods and Religion by publick Laws. Murder and Adultery, Rebellion and Sedition, Perjury and breach of Trust, Fraud and Oppression, are Vices severely prohibited by the Laws of most Nations. A clear Indication, what Opinion the generality of Mankind, and the Wisdom of Nations have always had of these things.

---

16. provide . . . Men: "Recompense to no man evil for evil. Provide things honest in the sight of all men" (Rom. 12:17). **17. and . . . Men:** "For so is the will of God, that with well doing ye may put to silence the ignorance of foolish men" (I Pet. 2:15). **18. Whatsoever . . . things:** "Finally, brethren, whatsoever things are true, whatsoever things are honest, whatsoever things are just, whatsoever things are pure, whatsoever things are lovely, whatsoever things are of good report; if there be any virtue, and if there be any praise, think on these things" (Phil. 4:8).

But now against the contrary Virtues there never was any Law. No Man was ever impeached for *living soberly, righteously, and godly in this present World*. A plain Acknowledgment, that Mankind always thought them good, and never were sensible of the Inconvenience of them; for had they been so, they would have provided against them by Laws. This St. *Paul* takes notice of[19] as a great Commendation of the Christian Virtues; *The fruit of the spirit is Love, Joy, Peace, Long-suffering, Gentleness, Kindness, Fidelity, Meekness, Temperance; against such there is no Law;* the greatest Evidence that could be given, that these things are unquestionably *good* in the Esteem of Mankind, *against such there is no Law*. As if he had said, turn over the Law of *Moses*, search those of *Athens*, and *Sparta*, and the *twelve Tables* of the *Romans*, and those innumerable Laws that have been added since; and you shall not in any of them find any of those Virtues that I have mentioned, condemned and forbidden. A clear Evidence that Mankind never took any exception against them, but are generally agreed about the Goodness of them.

Fourthly, God hath shewn us what is good by External Revelation. In former Ages of the World, God revealed his will to particular Persons in an extraordinary manner, and more especially to the Nation of the *Jews*, the rest of the World being in a great measure left to the conduct of natural Light. But in these later Ages he hath made a publick Revelation of his Will by his Son. And this as to the matter of our Duty, is the same in Substance with the Law of Nature; For our Saviour comprehends all under these two general Heads, *the love of God*, and *of our Neighbour*. The Apostle reduceth all to three, *Sobriety, Justice*, and *Piety; The grace of God that brings Salvation hath appeared to all men, teaching us that denying ungodliness and worldly lusts, we should live soberly, righteously, and godly in this present World*.[20] So that if we believe the Apostle, the Gospel teacheth us the very same things which Nature dictated to Men before; only it hath made a more perfect discovery of them. So that whatever was doubtful and obscure before, is now certain and plain; the Duties are still the same, only it offers us more powerful Arguments, and a greater Assistance to the performance of those Duties; so that we may now much better say, than the

Prophet could in his days, *He hath shewed thee, O Man, what is good; and what it is that the Lord requires of thee.*

Fifthly, and *lastly*, God shews us what is good by the motions of his Spirit upon the Minds of Men. This the Scripture assures us of, and good Men have experience more especially of it; though it be hard to give an account of it, and to say what motions are from the Spirit of God, and what from our own Minds; for, *as the wind blows where it listeth, and we hear the sound of it, but know not whence it comes, nor whither it goes;*[21] so are the Operations of the Spirit of God upon the Minds of Men, secret and imperceptible.

And thus I have done with the *three* things I propounded to speak to. All that now remains, is to make some *Inferences* from what hath been said, by way of Application.

First, Seeing God hath so abundantly provided that we should know our Duty, we are altogether inexcusable, if we do not do it. Because *he hath shewed thee, O Man, what is good, and what the Lord requires of thee;* therefore *thou art inexcusable, O Man, whosoever thou art*,[22] who livest in a contradiction to this light. God hath acquainted us with our Duty, by such ways as may most effectually both direct and engage us to the practice of it; we are prompted to it by a kind of natural Instinct, and strong Impressions upon our Minds of the difference of good and evil; we are led to the knowledge, and urged to the practice of it, by our Nature, and by our Reason, and by our Interest, and by that which is commonly very prevalent among Men, the general voice and consent of Mankind; and by the most powerful and governing passions in Humane Nature, by hope and by fear, and by shame; by the prospect of advantage, by the apprehension of danger, and by the sense of honour; and to take away all possible excuse of ignorance from us, by an express Revelation from God, the clearest and most perfect that ever was made to the World. So that when ever we do contrary to our Duty, in any of these great Instances, we offend against all these, and do in the highest degree fall under the heavy Sentence of our

19. St. . . . of: in Gal. 5:22–23; for *Kindness* read *goodness;* for *Fidelity* read *faith*. 20. The grace . . . World: Titus II:11–12.

21. the wind . . . goes: "The wind bloweth where it listeth, and thou hearest the sound thereof, but canst not tell whence it cometh, and whither it goeth: so is every one that is born of the Spirit" (John 3:8). 22. therefore . . . art: "Therefore thou art inexcusable, O man, whosoever thou art that judgest: for wherein thou judgest another, thou condemnest thyself; for thou that judgest doest the same things" (Rom. 2:1).

Saviour, *This is the Condemnation, that light is come into the World, and men loved darkness rather than light.*[23]

Secondly, You see hence what are the great Duties of Religion, which God mainly requires of us, and how reasonable they are; *Piety* towards God, and *Justice* and *Charity* towards Men; the knowledge whereof is planted in our Nature, and grows up with our Reason. And these are things which are unquestionably *good*, and against which we can have no exception; things that were never reproved, nor found fault with by Mankind, neither our Nature nor our Reason riseth up against them, or dictates any thing to the contrary. We have all the Obligation, and we have all the Encouragement to them, and are secure on all hands in the practice of them. In the doing of these things, there is no danger to us from the Laws of Men, no fear of displeasure from God, no offence or sting from our own Minds.

And these things which are so agreeable to our Nature, and our Reason, and our Interest, are the great things which our Religion requires of us, more valuable in themselves, and more acceptable to God than *whole Burnt-offerings and Sacrifices,* more than *thousands of Rams, and ten thousands of Rivers of Oyl;* more than if we offered to him *all the Beasts of the Forest, and the Cattle upon a thousand Hills.*[24] We are not to neglect any Institution of God; but above all, we are to secure the observance of those great Duties to which we are directed by our very Nature, and tyed by the surest and most sacred of all other Laws, those which God hath riveted in our Souls, and written upon our Hearts: And that Mankind might have no pretence left to excuse them from these, the Christian Religion hath set us free from those many positive and outward observances, that the *Jewish* Religion was incumbred withall; that we might be wholly intent upon these great Duties, and mind nothing in comparison of the real and Substantial Virtues of a good Life.

Thirdly, You see, in the last place, what is the best way to appease the displeasure of God towards a sinful Nation. God seems to have as great a Controversie with us, as he had with the People of *Israel,* and his wrath is of late years most visibly gone out against us; and proportionably to the full measure of our Sins, it hath been poured out upon us in full Vials. How have the Judgments of God followed us? And how close have they followed one another? What fearful Calamities have our eyes seen? enough to make the ears of every one that hears them to tingle. What terrible and hazardous Wars have we been engaged in? What a raging Pestilence[25] did God send among us, that swept away thousands, and ten thousands in our streets? What a dreadful and fatal Fire,[26] that was not to be checked and resisted in its course, 'till it had laid in Ashes one of the Greatest and Richest Cities in the World? What unseasonable Weather have we had of late? as if for the Wickedness of Men upon the Earth, the very *Ordinances of Heaven* were *changed,* and *Summer, and Winter, Seed-time, and Harvest,* had forgotten their *appointed Seasons.* And, which is more and sadder than all this, what dangerous attempts have been made upon our Religion, by the restless Adversaries of it?

And now surely, *after all this is come upon us for our sins,* it is time for us to look up to him that smites us, and to think of taking up this quarrel. 'Tis time to enquire as they do in the Text, *Wherewith shall we come before the Lord, and bow our selves before the high God?* And we are apt to take the same course they did, to endeavour to appease God by some external Devotion. We have now betaken our selves to Prayer and Fasting, and 'twas very fit, nay necessary we should do so; but let us not think this is all God expects from us. These are but the *Means* to a further *End,* to oblige us for the future to the practice of a good Life. The outward profession of Religion is not lost amongst us, there appears still in Men a great and commendable zeal for the Reformed Religion, and there hath been too much occasion for it; but that which God chiefly expects from us, is Reformed Lives. Piety and Virtue are in a great measure gone from among us, the Manners of Men are strangely corrupted, *the great and weighty things of the Law* are neglected, *Justice* and *Mercy, Temperance* and *Chastity, Truth* and *Fidelity,* so that we may take up *David's* Complaint, *Help Lord! for the Righteous man ceaseth, for the faithful fail from among the Children of Men.*[27]

And 'till the Nation be brought back to a sober sense of Religion, from an airy and phantastical Piety, to real and unaffected Devotion, and from a factious contention about things indifferent, to the serious practice of what is necessary; from our violent heats

---

23. **This . . . light:** John 3:19. **24. all . . . Hills:** "For every beast of the forest is mine, and the cattle upon a thousand hills" (Ps. 50:10).

25. **Pestilence:** the Great Plague in 1665–66. **26. Fire:** the Great Fire of London in 1666. **27. for . . . Men:** Ps. 12:1; for *Righteous* read *godly.*

and animosities, to a more peaceable temper, and by a mutual condescension on all sides, to a nearer and stronger union among our selves, 'till we recover in some measure, our ancient Virtue and Integrity of manners, we have reason to fear, that God will still have a Controversie with us, notwithstanding all our noise and zeal about Religion.

This is the true, this is the only course to appease the indignation of God, and to draw down his Favour and Blessing upon a poor distracted and gasping Nation. *He hath shewed thee, O man, what is good; and what doth the Lord require of thee, but to do justly, and to love mercy, and to walk humbly with thy God?*

I have but one word more, and that is to put you presently upon the practice of one of these Duties that I have been perswading you to, and that is *Mercy*, and *Alms to the Poor*. If what I have already said, have had its effect upon you, I need not use any other Arguments; if it have not, I have hardly the heart to use any. I shall only put you in mind again, that God values this above all our external Devotion, *he will have mercy rather than sacrifice;* that this is the way to find mercy with God, and to have our Prayers speed

in Heaven; and without this, all our Fasting and Humiliation signifies nothing. And to this purpose I will only read to you those plain and perswasive words of the Prophet, which do so fully declare unto us the whole Duty of this Day, and particularly urge us to this of Charity, *Isa.* 58. 5, 6, 7, 8, 9. *Is it such a Fast that I have chosen? a day for a Man to afflict his Soul? Is it to bow down his head as a bulrush, and to spread sackcloath and ashes under him? Wilt thou call this a Fast, and an acceptable Day unto the Lord? Is not this the Fast that I have chosen? to loose the bands of wickedness, to undoe the heavy burthens, and to let the oppressed go free, and that ye break every yoke? Is it not to deal thy bread to the hungry, and that thou bring the Poor that are cast out to thy house? when thou seest the Naked, that thou cover him, and that thou hide not thy self from thine own Flesh? Then shall thy light break forth as the Morning, and thy Salvation*[28] *shall spring forth speedily, and thy Righteousness shall go before thee, and the Glory of the Lord shall be thy reward. Then thou shalt call, and the Lord shall answer; thou shalt cry, and he shall say, here I am.*

28. thy Salvation: Read *thine health.*

Francis Atterbury

1663–1732

Francis Atterbury had a checkered career; he was a churchman—he became Bishop of Rochester in 1713—and a politician—his support for the Pretender led in 1722 to his imprisonment in the Tower and later to his banishment. Among Tory propagandists of the age of Anne, when he was at his zenith, not even his friend Swift outranked him. His claim on posterity, however, lies not in his polemical writings but in the quality of his literary criticism, exhibited at its best in his letters to Pope and in the Preface reprinted here. Few critics have been more sensitive to the importance of meter. Waller was outstanding as a metrist and an innovator in meter, and his achievement, which proved more helpful for Pope than did even Dryden's, Atterbury well understood.

H. C. Beeching's biography, *Francis Atterbury* (1909), can be fleshed out by turning to *The Correspondence of Alexander Pope*, ed. George Sherburn (5 vols., 1956). In the absence of a modern standard edition, one uses *The Miscellaneous Works of Francis Atterbury*, ed. J. Nichols (5 vols., 1789–98).

PREFACE
[TO *THE SECOND PART OF MR. WALLER'S POEMS...*]

Three years after Edmund Waller's death in 1687, the uncollected portions of his work—a play altered from Beaumont and Fletcher, a prose account of his trial for treason in 1643, and a small sheaf of occasional poems—appeared in print, with a commendatory preface that has always been ascribed, on good grounds, to Francis Atterbury. There was nothing of conspicuous merit in the new collection, but, as the Preface noted, the very name of Waller was enough to ensure that all who were genuinely interested in the estate of poetry would welcome the publication. For Waller was one of the acknowledged founders of modern poetry, a reformer to whom virtually every knowing craftsman was in debt. It was commonly held that, for various reasons including the unregulated condition of the language itself, even the greatest of older poets had written "incorrectly"—not only Chaucer, but Spenser and Shakespeare and indeed nearly every poet before the generation of Waller and Sir John Denham. Waller's special praise was that he had imposed upon himself the ideal of correctness and had learned to make the language flow evenly and sweetly in the measures of verse; his work, especially in the heroic couplet, provided such men as the young Dryden with an object-lesson in smooth, exact versification. Later it would be generally agreed that it was Dryden, not Waller, who brought the new poetry to its perfection. But Dr. Johnson, who saw Waller's limitations as a poet, still cautioned against denying him the credit that is due to one who refines and improves the resources of his art. For more than half a century the popular estimate of Waller's service to poetry differed little from Atterbury's in this essay.

The text is that of the first edition, *The Second Part of Mr. Waller's Poems. Containing, His Alteration of the Maids Tragedy, and Whatever of His Is Yet Unprinted: Together with Some Other Poems, Speeches, &c. That Were Printed Severally, and Never Put into the First Collection of His Poems* (1690). A few obvious misprints have been corrected.

✦

THE Reader need be told no more in commendation of these Poems, than that they are Mr. *Waller*'s: A Name that carries every thing in it, that's either Great or Graceful in Poetry. He was indeed the Parent of *English* Verse, and the first that shew'd us our Tongue had Beauty and Numbers in it. Our Language owes more to him than the *French* does to *Cardinal Richlieu*, and the whole Academy.[1] A Poet cannot think of him, without being in the same rapture *Lucretius* is in, when *Epicurus* comes in his way.[2]

Tu pater & rerum inventor, Tu patria nobis
Suppeditas præcepta: Tuisque ex Inclyte, chartis
Floriferis ut Apes in saltibus omnia libant,
Omnia Nos itidem depascimur aurea dicta:
Aurea, perpetua semper dignissima vita.[3]

PREFACE TO *The Second Part of Mr. Waller's Poems.* **1. Academy:** The Académie française, founded by Cardinal Richelieu in 1635, had standing authority to refine and regulate the French language. **2. the same . . . way:** The Roman poet Lucretius (*c.* 99–55 B.C.) avowedly based his philosophic poem *De Rerum Natura* on the teachings of the Greek thinker Epicurus (*c.* 340–*c.* 270 B.C.). **3. Tu pater . . . vita:**

Thou, *Parent* of *Philosophy*, hast shown
The way to Truth with Precepts of thine own.
For as from sweetest Flowers the labouring Bee
Extracts her *pretious* Juice; *Great Soul*, from thee
We all our *golden sentences* derive,
Golden, and fit *eternally* to live.
(*De Rerum Natura*, III. 9–13 [Creech translation])

The Tongue came into his hands, like a rough Diamond; he polish'd it first, and to that degree that all Artists since him have admired the Workmanship, without pretending to mend it. *Sucklyn* and *Carew*,[4] I must confess, wrote some few things smoothly enough, but as all they did in this kind was not very considerable, so 'twas a little later than the earliest pieces of Mr. *Waller*. He undoubtedly stands first in the List of Refiners, and for ought I know, last too; for I question whether in *Charles* the Second's Reign, *English* did not come to its full perfection; and whether it has not had its *Augustean Age*,[5] as well as the *Latin*. It seems to be already mix'd with Foreign Languages, as far as its purity will bear; and, as Chymists say of their *Menstruums*,[6] to be quite sated[7] with the Infusion. But Posterity will best judge of this—In the mean time, 'tis a surprizing Reflection, that between what *Spencer* wrote last, and *Waller* first, there should not be much above twenty years distance:[8] and yet the one's Language, like the Money of that time, is as currant now as ever; whilst the other's words are like old Coyns, one must go to an Antiquary to understand their true meaning and value. Such advances may a great Genius make, when it undertakes any thing in earnest!

Some Painters will hit the chief Lines, and master strokes of a Face so truly, that through all the differences of Age, the Picture shall still bear a Resemblance. This Art was Mr. *Waller*'s; he sought out, in this flowing Tongue of ours, what parts would last, and be of standing use and ornament; and this he did so successfully, that his Language is now as fresh as it was at first setting out. Were we to judge barely by the wording, we could not know what was wrote at twenty, and what at fourscore. He complains indeed of a Tyde of words[9] that comes in upon the *English* Poet, o'reflows whate're he builds: but this was less his case than any mans, that ever wrote; and the mischief on 't is, this very complaint will last long enough to confute it self. For though *English* be

4. Sucklyn and Carew: Sir John Suckling (1609–42) and Thomas Carew (1595–1639), Cavalier poets. **5. Augustean Age:** age of highest excellence. It was during the reign of Augustus Caesar (27 B.C.–A.D. 14) that classical Latin attained its zenith. **6. Menstruums:** solvents. **7. sated:** saturated. **8. between . . . distance:** The second part of Spenser's *Faerie Queene* appeared in 1596; Waller's first known poem was written in 1623. (See the selections from Waller in Part Three.) **9. He . . . words:** See Waller's *Of English Verse* in Part Three.

mouldring Stone, as he tells us there, yet he has certainly pick'd the best out of a bad Quarry.

We are no less beholding to him for the new turn of Verse, which he brought in, and the improvement he made in our Numbers. Before his time, men Rhym'd indeed, and that was all: as for the harmony of measure, and that dance of words, which good ears are so much pleas'd with, they knew nothing of it. Their *Poetry* then was made up almost entirely of monosyllables; which, when they come together in any cluster, are certainly the most harsh untunable things in the World. If any man doubts of this, let him read ten lines in *Donne*,[10] and he'll be quickly convinc'd. Besides, their Verses ran all into one another, and hung together, throughout a whole Copy, like the *hook't Attoms*,[11] that compose a Body in *Des Cartes*. There was no distinction of parts, no regular stops, nothing for the Ear to rest upon—But as soon as the Copy began, down it went, like a Larum,[12] incessantly; and the Reader was sure to be out of Breath, before he got to the end of it. So that really Verse in those days was but down-right Prose, tagg'd with Rhymes. Mr. *Waller* remov'd all these faults, brought in more Polysyllables, and smoother measures; bound up his thoughts better, and in a cadence more agreeable to the nature of the Verse he wrote in: So that where-ever the natural stops of that were, he contriv'd the little breakings of his sense so as to fall in with 'em. And for that reason, since the stress of our Verse lyes commonly upon the last Syllable, you'll hardly ever find him using a word of no force there. I would say if I were not afraid the Reader would think me too nice,[13] that he commonly closes with Verbs, in which we know the Life of Language consists.

Among other improvements, we may reckon that of *his Rhymes*. Which are always good, and very often the better for being *new*.[14] He had a fine Ear, and knew how quickly that Sense was cloy'd by the same round of chiming Words still returning upon it. 'Tis a decided Case by the great Master of Writing. *Quae*

sunt ampla & Pulchra, diu placere possunt; quae lepida & concinna, (amongst which Rhyme must, whether it will or no, take its place) *cito satietate afficiunt aurium sensum fastidiosissimum.*[15] This he understood very well, and therefore, to take off the danger of a Surfeit that way, strove to please by Variety, and new sounds. Had he carried this Observation (among others) as far as it would go, it must, methinks, have shown him the incurable fault of this jingling kind of Poetry, and have led his later judgment to blank Verse. But he continu'd an obstinate Lover of Rhyme to the very last: 'Twas a Mistress, that never appear'd unhand-some in his Eyes, and was courted by him long after *Sacharissa*[16] was forsaken. He had rais'd it, and brought it to that perfection we now enjoy it in: And the Poet's temper (which has always a little vanity in it) would not suffer him ever to slight a thing, he had taken so much pains to adorn. My Lord *Roscommon*[17] was more impartial: No man ever Rhym'd truer and evener than he; yet he is so just as to confess, that 'tis but a Trifle, and to wish the Tyrant dethron'd, and blank Verse set up in its room. There is a third person, the living Glory of our English Poetry,[18] who has disclaim'd the use of it upon the Stage, tho no man ever employ'd it there so happily as He. 'Twas the strength of his Genius that first brought it into credit in Plays; and 'tis the force of his Example that has thrown it out agen. In other kinds of writing it continues still; and will do so, till some excellent Spirit arises, that has leisure enough, and resolution to break the charm, and free us from the *troublesome bondage of Rhyming.*[19]

As Mr. *Milton* very well calls it, and has prov'd it as well, by what he has wrote in another way. But this is a thought for times at some distance; the present Age is a little too Warlike: It may perhaps furnish out matter for a good Poem in the next, but 'twill hardly

---

15. Quae . . . fastidiosissimum: "Thus the grand and beautiful can please at length, but the neat and graceful [i.e., rhyme] quickly satiate the hearing, the most fastidious of our senses" (Cicero, *Rhetorica ad Herennium*, IV. xxiii. 32). **16. Sacharissa:** the poetical name of Lady Dorothy Sidney, to whom Waller addressed several of his most gallant love poems. **17. Roscommon:** Wentworth Dillon, Earl of Roscommon; his *Essay on Translated Verse* (1684) contains the sentiment attributed to him here. **18. the living . . . Poetry:** John Dryden (1631–1700). After long advocacy of rhymed verse in serious drama, he turned to blank verse for his most ambitious effort, *All for Love* (1678). **19. the troublesome . . . Rhyming:** See the note "On the Verse" that Milton prefixed to the second edition of *Paradise Lost*.

---

10. Donne: John Donne (1573–1631). It is in such poems as his *Satires* that his versification is most rugged and "incor-rect." **11. hook't Attoms:** According to Descartes in his *Principles of Philosophy* (1644), the matter of which terrestrial objects are made consists of tiny particles that hang together by the jagged edges or "hooks" along their sides. **12. Larum:** alarm. **13. nice:** minutely particular. **14. Which . . . new:** Atterbury seems to have favored beginning a new sentence with a dependent clause. See below "As Mr. *Milton* . . . ."

encourage one now: Without Prophesying, a Man may easily know, what sort of Lawrels[20] are like to be in request?

Whilst I am talking of Verse, I find my self, I don't know how, betray'd into a great deal of Prose. I intended no more than to put the Reader in mind, what respect was due to any thing that fell from the Pen of Mr. *Waller*. I have heard his last Printed Copies, which are added in the several Editions of his Poems, very slightly spoken of; but certainly they don't deserve it. They do indeed discover themselves to be his last, and that's the worst we can say of 'em. He is there *Jam Senior: Sed cruda Deo viridisque Senectus.*[21] The same censure perhaps will be past on the pieces of this second part. I shall not so far engage for 'em, as to pretend they are all equal to whatever he wrote in the vigour of his Youth. Yet they are so much of a piece with the rest, that any Man will at first sight know 'em to be Mr. *Waller*'s. Some of 'em were wrote very early, but not put in former Collections, for reasons obvious enough,[22] but which are now ceas'd. The Play[23] was alter'd, to please the Court: 'Tis not to be doubted who sat for the two Brothers Characters.[24] 'Twas agreeable to the sweetness of Mr. *Waller*'s Temper, to soften the rigour of the Tragedy, as he expresses it; but whether it be so agreeable to the Nature of Tragedy it self, to make every thing come off easily, I leave to the Criticks. In the Prologue, and Epilogue, there are a few Verses that he has made use of upon another occasion. But the Reader may be pleased to allow that in him, that has been allowed so long in *Homer* and *Lucretius*. Exact Writers dress up their thoughts so very well always, that when they have need of the same sense, they can't put it into other words, but it must be to its prejudice. Care has been taken in this Book to get together every thing of Mr. *Waller*'s, that's not put into the former Collection;[25] so that between both, the Reader may make the set compleat.

It will perhaps be contended after all, that some of these ought not to have been Publish'd: And Mr. *Cowly*'s decision will be urg'd, that a neat Tomb of Marble is a better Monument, than a great Pile of Rubbish,[26] &c. It might be answer'd to this, that the Pictures and Poems of great Masters have been always valu'd, tho the last hand weren't put to 'em. And I believe none of those Gentlemen that will make the objection would refuse a Sketch of *Raphael*'s, or one of *Titian*'s draughts of the first sitting.

I might tell 'em too, what care has been taken by the Learned, to preserve the Fragments of the Ancient Greek and Latin Poets: There has been thought to be a Divinity in what they said, and therefore the least pieces of it have been kept up and reverenc'd, like Religious reliques. And I am sure, take away the *mille anni*,[27] and Impartial reasoning will tell us, there is as much due to the Memory of Mr. *Waller*, as to the most celebrated names of Antiquity.

But to wave the dispute now of what *ought* to have been done; I can assure the Reader, what *would* have been had this Edition been delay'd. The following Poems were got abroad, and in a great many hands: It were vain to expect that amongst so many admirers of Mr. *Waller*, they should not meet with one fond enough to Publish 'em. They might have staid indeed, till by frequent transcriptions they had been corrupted extreamly, and jumbled together with things of another kind: But then they would have found their way into the World. So 'twas thought a greater piece of kindness to the Author, to put 'em out; whilst they continue genuine and unmix'd; and such, as he himself, were he alive might own.

20. **Lawrels:** poetical merits. 21. **Jam . . . Senectus:** "aged now, but with the fresh and vigorous old age of a god" (*Aeneid*, VI. 304). 22. **reasons . . . enough:** reasons of political discretion. 23. **The Play:** an adaptation of Beaumont and Fletcher's *Maid's Tragedy* (c. 1611). 24. **who . . . Characters:** Two royal brothers in the play were flatteringly modeled after Charles II and James, Duke of York.

25. **the former Collection:** Waller's *Poems* (first authorized edition, 1664). 26. **Pile of Rubbish:** In the Preface to his *Poems* (1656), Abraham Cowley (1618–67) complained that various pieces he would have preferred to leave unpublished had been given out by well-meaning friends, who were thus providing him with the wrong kind of memorial. 27. **mille anni:** thousand years; Atterbury means here the advantage of being ancient. The phrase is from Juvenal's seventh satire, in which he mocks the sort of poet who "yields to Homer on no other score / Than that he lived a thousand years before."

Part Two

THE AGE
OF
POPE

Matthew Prior

1664–1721

When Johnson wrote that Matthew Prior was "one of those that have burst out from an obscure original to great eminence," he was alluding primarily to Prior's diplomatic career, not to the Prior we know as the first master of English familiar verse. The poet himself called himself "only a poet by accident," and devoted his life, including a considerable amount of his poetry, to the tactful cultivation of friends, patrons, and monarchs—a practice that led eventually, in 1712, to a position as Minister Plenipotentiary to the court of Louis XIV.

The son of a joiner, Prior was born in Westminster, Middlesex. His first patron, the Earl of Dorset, found him working for his uncle at the Rhenish Tavern, and, impressed by his skill in translating Horace, helped him return to Westminster School, which Prior had been forced to leave when his father died. In 1681 Prior was elected a King's Scholar at Westminster, and as such appeared destined for Christ Church, Oxford; but in order to be near his Westminster friends, and in spite of Lord Dorset's wishes, he went on to Cambridge. In 1687 he collaborated with one of these friends, Charles Montague, in composing *The Country Mouse and the City Mouse*, a parody of Dryden's *The Hind and the Panther*, published that year. Its success was followed by the political advancement of the well-born Montague, whereas the poor mouse, Prior, had to wait until 1690, when, through Dorset's influence, he was appointed secretary to the English ambassador at The Hague. During his seven years in that office he gained the confidence of William III, who called him *Secrétaire du Roi* and made him a Gentleman of the King's Bed Chamber.

In 1701, presented by Dorset with a pocket borough, Prior sat briefly in Parliament, where he concluded a gradual but clearly opportunistic shift from Whig to Tory by voting to impeach his friend Montague, now Lord Halifax, for a supposed part in the unpopular Partition Treaty affecting the Spanish Succession. Of the four lords impeached, only Portland had known of the treaty before it was signed, but Prior justified himself, perhaps disingenuously, on the grounds that the impeachment was a necessary political act to free the King of responsibility. As a result, Prior lost the friendship of Halifax, but found a new patron in the Tory Earl of Jersey.

Prior's diplomatic career was crowned by his brilliant service in the negotiations over commercial rights between England and France preceding the Peace of Utrecht of 1713. But when Queen Anne died in 1714, he was recalled by the Whigs to answer for his part in what was regarded as a compromising peace and was kept in custody for two years, all the while refusing to bear witness against Oxford or against Bolingbroke, a friend and patron, who had escaped to France and to the Pretender.

For most of his life Prior wrote occasional and casual verse. In 1707 the piratical publisher Curll brought out seventeen of Prior's previously printed poems under the conventional title *Poems on Several Occasions*. Prior, of course, repudiated the edition and went to work on his own collection of fifty-one poems, including nineteen previously unpublished, which appeared under the same title at the end of the following year (though dated 1709). After his political fall, Prior was reduced to the small income of his Cambridge fellowship, which he had prudently retained since 1688, and to mend his fortunes, his friends prepared a subscription edition, again under the same title, which was published in 1718. Swift, one of his good friends and an old companion in wit, took charge of distribution in Ireland and managed to get a hard-won seventy subscriptions at two guineas each. Included in the subscription edition were two long poems, *Alma*, a dialogue on the relation of body and mind written in Prior's adaptation of Hudibrastic verse, and *Solomon*, a sober philosophical treatment of that abiding theme, the Vanity of the World. In his last years Prior produced his best prose pieces, including his imaginary conversations between eminent men, *Dialogues of the Dead*, which were not published until 1907. Prior's own, self-acknowledged "last piece of vanity" was to leave five hundred pounds for a monument to himself, to be erected in Westminster Abbey, where he was buried near Spenser, a poet he had admired from his youth.

The poetry of Prior inspired one of Johnson's most agile critical balancing acts:

> If Prior's poetry be generally considered his praise will be that of correctness and industry, rather than of compass of comprehension or activity of fancy. . . . Prior is never low, nor very often sublime. . . . He has many vigorous but few happy lines; he has every thing by purchase, and nothing by gift . . . . His phrases are original, but they are sometimes harsh . . . . In his greater compositions there may be found more rigid stateliness than graceful dignity. . . . His numbers are such as mere diligence may attain; they seldom offend the ear, and seldom sooth it . . . . His verses always roll, but they seldom flow.

But another poet took exception, especially to the charge that Prior's verse was constrained rather than "easy," and it is probably Cowper's judgment, rather than Johnson's, that will stand:

> His reputation as an author who, with much labour indeed, but with admirable success, has embellished all his poems with the most charming ease, stood unshaken till Johnson thrust his head against it. . . . Every man conversant with verse-writing knows, and knows by painful experience, that the familiar style is of all styles the most difficult to succeed in. To make verse speak the language of prose, without being prosaic,—to marshal the words of it in such an order as they might naturally take in falling from the lips of an extemporary speaker, yet without meanness, harmoniously, elegantly, and without seeming to displace a syllable for the sake of the rhyme, is one of the most arduous tasks a poet can undertake. He that could accomplish this task was Prior; many have imitated his excellence in this particular, but the best copies have fallen far short of the original.

A good, concise bibliography of Prior is to be found in Bonamy Dobrée's *English Literature in the Earlier Eighteenth Century, 1700–1740* (1959). The standard biography is C. K. Eves's *Matthew Prior: Poet and Diplomatist* (1939). *The Literary Works of Matthew Prior*, ed. H. B. Wright and M. K. Spears (2 vols., 1959), is the definitive edition. We have, upon a comparison of our own, accepted the claim of these editors for the superior authority of the 1718 edition of Prior's poems (the last in his lifetime) over previous printings, even in the matter of accidentals, and have therefore followed them in choosing as copy-texts the reprintings of that edition. On the other hand, their further discrimination of superior and inferior *copies* of the 1718 edition has not, so far as our selection is concerned, proved compelling, and we have confidently transcribed from the copy in the William Andrews Clark Library.

AN ODE

The text is from *Poems on Several Occasions* (1718).

I.

WHILE blooming Youth, and gay Delight
   Sit on thy rosey Cheeks confest;°
Thou hast, my Dear, undoubted Right
   To triumph o'er this destin'd° Breast.
My Reason bends to what thy Eyes ordain;
For I was born to Love, and Thou to Reign.

II.

But would You meanly thus rely
   On Power, You know I must Obey?
Exert a Legal Tyranny,
   And do an Ill, because You may?   10
Still must I Thee, as Atheists Heav'n adore;
Not see thy Mercy, and yet dread thy Power?

III.

Take Heed, my Dear, Youth flies apace:
   As well as CUPID, TIME is blind:
Soon must those Glories of thy Face
   The Fate of vulgar° Beauty find:
The Thousand LOVES, that arm thy potent Eye,
Must drop their Quivers, flag their Wings, and die.

IV.

Then wilt Thou sigh, when in each Frown
   A hateful Wrinkle more appears;   20
And putting peevish Humours° on,
   Seems but the sad Effect of Years:
Kindness it self too weak a Charm will prove,
To raise the feeble Fires of aged Love.

V.

Forc'd Compliments, and formal Bows
   Will show Thee just above Neglect:
The Heat, with which thy Lover glows,
   Will settle into cold Respect:
A talking dull *Platonic* I shall turn;
Learn to be civil, when I cease to burn.   30

VI.

Then shun the Ill, and know, my Dear,
   Kindness and Constancy will prove
The only Pillars fit to bear
   So vast a Weight, as that of Love.
If Thou can'st wish to make My Flames endure;
Thine must be very fierce, and very pure.

VII.

Haste, CELIA, haste, while Youth invites;
   Obey kind CUPID's present Voice;
Fill ev'ry Sense with soft Delights,
   And give thy Soul a Loose to Joys: 40
Let Millions of repeated Blisses prove,
That Thou all Kindness art, and I all Love.

AN ODE. **2. confest:** manifest. **4. destin'd:** doomed. **16. vulgar:** common.

21. Humours: moods.

VIII.

Be Mine, and only Mine: take care
    Thy Looks, thy Thoughts, thy Dreams to guide
To Me alone; nor come so far,
    As liking any Youth beside:
What Men e'er court Thee, fly 'em, and believe,
They're Serpents all, and Thou the tempted EVE.

IX.

So shall I court thy dearest Truth;
    When Beauty ceases to engage: 50
So thinking on thy charming Youth,
    I'll love it o'er again in Age:
So TIME it self our Raptures shall improve;
While still We wake to Joy, and live to Love.

WRITTEN AT THE HAGUE,
IN THE YEAR 1696

The text is from *Miscellaneous Works of . . . Matthew Prior* (1740). The verses as they appear in manuscript (Wright and Spears, p. 158) are arranged in rhymed couplets rather than in quatrains. The title given here is that of the printed version; from a later printing the poem came to be known as *The Secretary*.

WHILE with labour assid'ous
    due pleasure I mix,
And in one day atone
    for the bus'ness of six,
In a little Dutch-chaise
    on a Saturday night,
On my left hand my HORACE,
    a NYMPH° on my right.
No Memoire° to compose,
    and no Post-Boy to move,°   10
That on Sunday may hinder
    the softness of love;
For her, neither visits,

nor parties of tea,
Nor the long-winded cant
    of a dull refugée.°
This night and the next
    shall be her's, shall be mine,
To good or ill fortune
    the third we resign: 20
Thus scorning the world,
    and superior to fate,
I drive on my car
    in processional state;
So with PHIA thro' Athens
    PYSISTRATUS rode,
Men thought her MINERVA,
    and him a new GOD.°
But why should I stories
    of Athens rehearse,   30
Where people knew love,
    and were partial to verse,
Since none can with justice
    my pleasures oppose,
In Holland half drowned
    in int'rest° and prose:
By Greece and past ages,
    what need I be try'd,
When the Hague and the present,
    are both on my side,   40
And is it enough,
    for the joys of the day;
To think what ANACREON,°
    or SAPPHO° would say.
When good VANDERGOES,°
    and his provident VROUGH,°
As they gaze on my triumph,
    do freely allow,
That search all the province,
    you'd find no man there is   50
So bless'd as the *Englishen Heer*
    SECRETARIS.°

---

16. **refugée:** Holland was a haven for religious and political refugees. **25–28. So . . . God:** According to Herodotus, the restoration of Pisistratus, tyrant of Athens, about 559 B.C., was accomplished by the hoax of passing off a beautiful woman as the goddess Athene, who proclaimed her wish that the exile be returned to power. **36. int'rest:** profit. **43. Anacreon:** Greek lyric poet (b. *c.* 570 B.C.). **44. Sappho:** poetess of Lesbos (b. *c.* 612 B.C.). **45. Vandergoes:** a common Dutch surname. **46. Vrough:** spouse. **51–52. the Englishen . . . Secretaris:** Prior, who was secretary to the English ambassador to The Hague from 1690 to 1697.

WRITTEN AT THE HAGUE, IN THE YEAR 1696. **8. a Nymph:** The manuscript reads "and [blank]." **9. Memoire:** a term in diplomacy meaning memorandum or report. **10. move:** bestir.

A FABLE

✿

The text is from *Poems on Affairs of State* (1703).

✿

IN *Æsop*'s Tales an honest Wretch we find,
Whose Years and Comforts equally declin'd;
He in two Wives had two domestick Ills,
For different Age they had, and different Wills;
One pluckt his black Hairs out, and one his grey,
The Man for Quietness did both obey,
Till all his Parish saw his Head quite bare,
And thought he wanted Brains as well as Hair.

The Moral.

The Parties, hen-peckt *W——m*, are thy Wives,
The Hairs they pluck are thy Prerogatives;°   10
Tories thy Person hate, the Whigs thy Power,
Tho much thou yieldest, still they tug for more,
Till this poor Man and thou alike are shown,
He without Hair, and thou without a Crown.

TO A CHILD OF QUALITY OF FIVE YEARS OLD, THE AUTHOR SUPPOS'D FORTY

✿

The child was Lady Mary Villiers, daughter of Edward Villiers, First Earl of Jersey. She was married in 1710 to Henry Thynne, widowed the same year, and was married again the next year to George Granville, Lord Lansdowne. She died in 1735.

The text is from *Poetical Miscellanies: The Fifth Part* (1704).

✿

LORDS, Knights, and Squires, the num'rous Band
    That wear the Fair Miss *Mary*'s Fetters,
Were summon'd, by her high Command,
    To show their Passion by their Letters.

My Pen amongst the rest I took,
    Least° those bright Eyes that cannot read
Shou'd dart their kindling Fires, and look
    The Pow'r they have to be obey'd.

Nor Quality, nor Reputation,
    Forbid me yet my Flame to tell,   10
Dear Five Years old befriends my Passion,
    And I may Write 'till she can Spell.

For while she makes her Silk-worms Beds
    With all the tender things I swear,
Whilst all the House my Passion reads,
    In Papers round her Baby's Hair.

She may receive and own my Flame,
    For tho' the strictest *Prudes* shou'd know it,
She'll pass for a most virtuous Dame,
    And I for an unhappy Poet.   20

Then too, alas, when she shall tear
    The Lines some younger Rival sends,
She'll give me leave to Write, I fear,
    And we shall still continue Friends.

For as our diff'rent Ages move,
    'Tis so ordain'd, wou'd Fate but mend it,
That I shall be past making Love,
    When she begins to comprehend it.

TO A LADY: SHE REFUSING TO CONTINUE A DISPUTE WITH ME, AND LEAVING ME IN THE ARGUMENT. AN ODE

✿

The lady was Elizabeth Singer (1674–1737), poetess and correspondent of Prior.

The text is from *Poems on Several Occasions* (1718).

✿

A FABLE. **10. Prerogatives:** the special rights of the sovereign, theoretically not subject to restriction.

TO A CHILD OF QUALITY OF FIVE YEARS OLD. **6. Least:** lest.

I.

SPARE, Gen'rous Victor, spare the Slave,
   Who did unequal War pursue;
That more than Triumph He might have,
   In being overcome by You.

II.

In the Dispute whate'er I said,
   My Heart was by my Tongue bely'd;
And in my Looks You might have read,
   How much I argu'd on your side.

III.

You, far from Danger as from Fear,
   Might have sustain'd an open Fight: 10
For seldom your Opinions err;
   Your Eyes are always in the right.

IV.

Why, fair One, would You not rely
   On Reason's Force with Beauty's join'd?
Cou'd I their Prevalence deny;
   I must at once be deaf and blind.

V.

Alas! not hoping to subdue,
   I only to the Fight aspir'd:
To keep the beauteous Foe in view
   Was all the Glory I desir'd.   20

VI.

But She, howe'er of Vict'ry sure,
   Contemns the Wreath too long delay'd;
And, arm'd with more immediate Pow'r,
   Calls cruel Silence to her Aid.

VII.

Deeper to wound, She shuns the Fight:
   She drops her Arms, to gain the Field:
Secures her Conquest by her Flight;
   And triumphs, when She seems to yield.

VIII.

So when the PARTHIAN turn'd his Steed,
   And from the Hostile Camp withdrew;   30
With cruel Skill the backward Reed°
   He sent; and as He fled, He slew.

TO A LADY. **31. Reed:** arrow. The ancient Parthians were
famous for the method of fighting described in this quatrain.

IN IMITATION
OF ANACREON

This is an imitation in the manner rather than in the
measure of the sixth-century B.C. Greek lyric poet
Anacreon, who founded a school of verse, known as
Anacreontic.
   The text is from *Poems on Several Occasions* (1718).

LET 'em Censure: what care I?
The Herd of Criticks I defie.
Let the Wretches know, I write
Regardless of their Grace, or Spight.
No, no: the Fair, the Gay, the Young
Govern the Numbers° of my Song.
All that They approve is sweet:
And All is Sense, that They repeat.

   Bid the warbling Nine° retire:
VENUS, String thy Servant's Lyre: 10
Love shall be my endless Theme:
Pleasure shall triumph over Fame:
And when these Maxims I decline,
APOLLO, may Thy Fate be Mine:
May I grasp at empty Praise;
And lose the Nymph, to gain the Bays.°

AN ODE

The text is from *Poems on Several Occasions* (1718).

IN IMITATION OF ANACREON. **6. Numbers:** lines, or metrics.
9. the warbling Nine: the Muses. **14–16. Apollo . . .
Bays:** The love-fearing Daphne, pursued by the love-struck
Apollo, prayed to her father, the river god Peneus, to be
saved and was transformed into a laurel (or bay) tree. The
tree's leaves were thereafter consecrated by Apollo and replaced the oak wreath as the victor's prize at the Apollonian
festival. Prior has obscured the analogy.

I.

THE Merchant, to secure his Treasure,
   Conveys° it in a borrow'd Name:
EUPHELIA serves to grace my Measure;°
   But CLOE is my real Flame.

II.

My softest Verse, my darling Lyre
   Upon EUPHELIA's Toylet° lay;
When CLOE noted her Desire,
   That I should sing, that I should play.

III.

My Lyre I tune, my Voice I raise;
   But with my Numbers° mix my Sighs: 10
And whilst I sing EUPHELIA's Praise,
   I fix my Soul on CLOE's Eyes.

IV.

Fair CLOE blush'd: EUPHELIA frown'd:
   I sung and gaz'd: I play'd and trembl'd:
And VENUS to the LOVES around
   Remark'd, how ill We all dissembl'd.

CUPID MISTAKEN

Prior's poem, inspired by a poem by the French poet
Gilles Durant (1554–1615), Sieur de la Bergerie, was set
to music and was frequently reprinted.
   The text is from *Poems on Several Occasions* (1718).

I.

AS after Noon, one Summer's Day,
   VENUS stood bathing in a River;
CUPID a-shooting went that Way,
   New strung his Bow, new fill'd his Quiver.

II.

With Skill He chose his sharpest Dart:
   With all his Might his Bow He drew:
Swift to His beauteous Parent's Heart
   The too well-guided Arrow flew.

AN ODE. **2. Conveys:** transfers by deed or legal process. **3.
grace my Measure:** (1) adorn my verse; (2) improve my
reputation. **6. Toylet:** the table on which toilet articles are
placed. **10. Numbers:** verses.

III.

I faint! I die! the Goddess cry'd:
   O cruel, could'st Thou find none other,   10
To wreck thy Spleen on? Parricide!
   Like NERO, Thou hast slain thy Mother.

IV.

Poor CUPID sobbing scarce could speak;
   Indeed, Mamma, I did not know Ye:
Alas! how easie my Mistake?
   I took You for your Likeness, CLOE.

A BETTER ANSWER

The last in a sequence of nine poems, *A Better Answer* is
preceded by *Cloe Jealous* and *Answer to Cloe Jealous, in
the Same Style. The Author Sick.*
   The text is from *Poems on Several Occasions* (1718).

I.

DEAR CLOE, how blubber'd is that pretty Face?
   Thy Cheek all on Fire, and Thy Hair all uncurl'd:
Pr'ythee quit this Caprice; and (as Old FALSTAF says)
   Let Us e'en talk a little like Folks of This World.°

II.

How can'st Thou presume, Thou hast leave to destroy
   The Beauties, which VENUS but lent to Thy
      keeping?
Those Looks were design'd to inspire Love and Joy:
   More ord'nary Eyes may serve People for weeping.

III.

To be vext at a Trifle or two that I writ,
   Your Judgment at once, and my Passion You
      wrong: 10
You take that for Fact, which will scarce be found
      Wit:
   Od's° Life! must One swear to the Truth of a Song?

A BETTER ANSWER. **4. Let . . . World:** a paraphrase of *II
Henry IV*, V. iii. 101. **12. Od's:** God's.

IV.

What I speak, my fair CLOE, and what I write, shews
    The Diff'rence there is betwixt Nature and Art:
I court others in Verse; but I love Thee in Prose:
    And They have my Whimsies; but Thou hast my
      Heart.

V.

The God of us Verse-men (You know Child) the
    SUN,°
    How after his Journeys He sets up his Rest:
If at Morning o'er Earth 'tis his Fancy to run;
    At Night he reclines on his THETIS's° Breast.   20

VI.

So when I am weary'd with wand'ring all Day;
    To Thee my Delight in the Evening I come:
No Matter what Beauties I saw in my Way:
    They were but my Visits; but Thou art my Home.°

VII.

Then finish, Dear CLOE, this Pastoral War;
    And let us like HORACE and LYDIA agree:°
For Thou art a Girl as much brighter than Her,
    As He was a Poet sublimer than Me.

ANOTHER

Another is the third in a series of unrelated epigrams.
Beginning with *Another* and ending with *Phyllis's Age*,
the poems in the present sequence are all, except for
On the Same, based on French sources.
    The text is from *Poems on Several Occasions* (1718).

YES, every Poet is a Fool:
    By Demonstration NED can show it:
Happy, cou'd NED's inverted Rule
    Prove every Fool to be a Poet.

17. The God . . . Sun: Apollo. **20. Thetis:** Thetis was
a goddess of the sea. **23–24. No . . . Home:** an echo of
A Midsummer Night's Dream, III. ii. 171–73. **26. like . . .
agree:** See Horace, *Odes*, III. ix.

WRITTEN IN AN OVID

The text is from *Poems on Several Occasions* (1718).

OVID is the surest Guide,
    You can name, to show the Way
To any Woman, Maid, or Bride,
    Who resolves to go astray.

A TRUE MAID

The text is from *Poems on Several Occasions* (1718).

NO, no; for my Virginity,
    When I lose that, says ROSE, I'll dye:
Behind the Elmes, last Night, cry'd DICK,
    ROSE, were You not extreamly Sick?

A REASONABLE AFFLICTION

The text is from *Poems on Several Occasions* (1718).

ON His Death-Bed poor LUBIN lies:
    His Spouse is in Despair:
With frequent Sobs, and mutual Cries,
    They Both express their Care.

A diff'rent Cause, says Parson SLY,
    The same Effect may give:
Poor LUBIN fears, that He shall Die;
    His Wife, that He may Live.

ON THE SAME

On the Same is the third in a series of poems on the subject of Helen and her eyebrows.
The text is from *Poems on Several Occasions* (1718).

HELEN was just slipt into Bed:
Her Eye-brows on the Toilet lay:
  Away the Kitten with them fled,
As Fees belonging to her Prey.°

For this Misfortune careless JANE,
Assure your self, was loudly rated:°
  And Madam getting up again,
With her own Hand the Mouse-Trap baited.

On little Things, as Sages write,
Depends our Human Joy, or Sorrow: 10
  If We don't catch a Mouse To-night,
Alas! no Eye-brows for To-morrow.

PHYLLIS'S AGE

The text is from *Poems on Several Occasions* (1718).

HOW old may PHYLLIS be, You ask,
  Whose Beauty thus all Hearts engages?
To Answer is no easie Task;
  For She has really two Ages.

Stiff in Brocard,° and pinch'd in Stays,
  Her Patches, Paint, and Jewels on;
All Day let Envy view her Face;
  And PHYLLIS is but Twenty-one.

Paint, Patches, Jewels laid aside,
  At Night Astronomers agree,   10
The Evening has the Day bely'd;
  And PHYLLIS is some Forty-three.

ON THE SAME. **4. Prey:** office of preying. **6. rated:** scolded.
PHYLLIS'S AGE. **5. Brocard:** brocade.

AN EPITAPH

The epigraph is from Seneca's tragedy *Thyestes:* "Let the mighty, if they will, walk the slippery heights of the court."
The text is from *Poems on Several Occasions* (1718).

Stet quicunque volet potens
Aulæ culmine lubrico, &c.
                    SENEC.

INTERR'D beneath this Marble Stone,
Lie Saunt'ring JACK, and Idle JOAN.
While rolling Threescore Years and One
Did round this Globe their Courses run;
If Human Things went Ill or Well;
If changing Empires rose or fell;
The Morning past, the Evening came,
And found this Couple still the same.
They Walk'd and Eat, good Folks: What then?
Why then They Walk'd and Eat again: 10
They soundly slept the Night away:
They did just Nothing all the Day:
And having bury'd Children Four,
Wou'd not take Pains to try for more.
Nor Sister either had, nor Brother:
They seem'd just Tally'd° for each other.

  Their Moral° and Oeconomy
Most perfectly They made agree:
Each Virtue kept it's proper Bound,
Nor Trespass'd on the other's Ground.   20
For Fame, nor Censure They regarded:
They neither Punish'd, nor Rewarded.
He car'd not what the Footmen did:
Her Maids She neither prais'd, nor chid:
So ev'ry Servant took his Course;
And bad at First, They all grew worse.
Slothful Disorder fill'd His Stable;
And sluttish Plenty deck'd Her Table.
Their Beer was strong; Their Wine was *Port;*
Their Meal was large; Their Grace was short.   30

AN EPITAPH. **16. Tally'd:** suited. **17. Moral:** morality.

They gave the Poor the Remnant-meat,
Just when it grew not fit to eat.

They paid the Church and Parish-Rate;
And took, but read not the Receit:
For which They claim'd their *Sunday*'s Due,
Of slumb'ring in an upper Pew.

No Man's Defects sought They to know;
So never made Themselves a Foe.
No Man's good Deeds did They commend;
So never rais'd Themselves a Friend.   40
Nor cherish'd They Relations poor:
That might decrease Their present Store:
Nor Barn nor House did they repair:
That might oblige Their future Heir.

They neither Added, nor Confounded:°
They neither Wanted,° nor Abounded.
Each *Christmas* They Accompts did clear;
And wound their Bottom° round the Year.
Nor Tear, nor Smile did They imploy
At News of Public Grief, or Joy.   50
When Bells were Rung, and Bonfires made;
If ask'd, They ne'er deny'd their Aid:
Their Jugg was to the Ringers carry'd;
Who ever either Dy'd, or Marry'd.
Their Billet° at the Fire was found;
Who ever was Depos'd, or Crown'd.

Nor Good, nor Bad, nor Fools, nor Wise;
They wou'd not learn, nor cou'd advise:
Without Love, Hatred, Joy, or Fear,
They led—a kind of—as it were: 60
Nor Wish'd, nor Car'd, nor Laugh'd, nor Cry'd:
And so They liv'd; and so They dy'd.

THE INCURABLE.
AN EPIGRAM

The text is from *Miscellaneous Works of . . . Matthew
Prior* (1740).

PHYLLIS you boast of perfect health in vain,
And laugh at those who of their ills complain:
That with a frequent fever CLOE burns,
And STELLA's plumpness into dropsy turns.
O! PHILLIS, while the patients are nineteen,
Little, alas! are their distempers° seen.
But Thou for all Thy seeming Health art ill,
Beyond thy lover's hopes, or BLACKMORE's° skill;
No lenitives can thy disease asswage,
I tell Thee, 'Tis incurable—'tis Age.   10

ON A PRETTY
MADWOMAN

The text is from *Miscellaneous Works of . . . Matthew
Prior* (1740).

I.
WHILE mad OPHELIA we lament,
    And Her distraction mourn,
Our grief's misplac'd, Our tears mispent,
Since what for Her condition's meant
    More justly fits Our Own.

II.
For if 'tis happiness to be,
    From all the turns of Fate,
From dubious joy, and sorrow free;
OPHELIA then is blest, and we
    Misunderstand Her state.   10

III.
The Fates may do whate'er they will,
    They can't disturb her mind,
Insensible of good, or ill,
OPHELIA is OPHELIA still,
    Be Fortune cross or kind.

IV.
Then make with reason no more noise,
    Since what should give relief,
The quiet of Our mind destroys,
Or° with a full spring-tide of joys,
    Or a dead-ebb of grief.   20

THE INCURABLE. **6. distempers:** ailments, diseases. **8. Blackmore:** Sir Richard Blackmore (1654–1729), physician and
poet; a favorite target of the Augustan wits. ON A PRETTY
MADWOMAN. **19. Or:** either.

45. Confounded: spent, wasted. **46. Wanted:** lacked. **48.
wound . . . Bottom:** literally, wound their thread up;
figuratively, put everything in order. **55. Billet:** firewood.

Daniel Defoe

1660–1731

Daniel Defoe was born plain Daniel Foe, son of a dissenting tallow chandler in the parish of St. Giles, Cripplegate, just outside the walls of London. As the son of a Dissenter, he could not look forward to Oxford or Cambridge, and it might have been expected that he would be apprenticed to a trade; but he was evidently a clever boy, and his father Henry Foe had ambitions for him. Intending him for the Presbyterian ministry, he sent him at the age of ten or eleven to a private school in Dorking, and thereafter to the notable dissenting academy kept by the Reverend Charles Morton at Newington Green, where he was tutored in an astonishing range of useful subjects from modern languages to astronomy. His was not a gentleman's education as that term was commonly understood—classical learning was never to be his strong suit—but under Morton he read substantially in modern history and civil law, geography and political economy, natural science and philosophy, and he learned to write the plain, free, and vigorous English that later seemed to come so effortlessly to him.

He was with Morton for the better part of five years and in 1679 was still ostensibly headed for the ministry. But sometime during the next two years he changed his mind and set up as a merchant instead, trading at first what was then called "hosiery." Enemy pamphleteers could sting him in later life by referring to him as a sock salesman, though in fact he was something more like a wholesaler's agent in haberdashery. With his quick eye for opportunity, he was soon dealing in a variety of other items—wine and brandy, wool, real estate, and the mixed cargoes of trading ships in which he had somehow acquired an interest. How he financed all this is unknown, but his father's credit must have been useful, and he was evidently willing to speculate far beyond his means. During the first stage of his career as a tradesman, he took time out to contract a good marriage in 1684 to Mary Tuffley, who brought him a dowry of thirty-seven hundred pounds, and then to plunge recklessly into Monmouth's Rebellion in 1685, on the losing side. There may have been more romantic fervor in the second of these ventures than in the first, for young Daniel Foe was a wholehearted Protestant and a Whig, firmly opposed to a Catholic king for England. His marriage, on the other hand, he seems to have arranged on sound commercial principles. Be that as it may, the rebellion failed but the marriage endured; Mary Foe bore her husband eight children and survived a turbulent and at times dangerous life with him for more than fifty years.

Obliged to lie low after his escapade with Monmouth, he spent much of the next year or two in traveling on the Continent and riding about England on commercial errands. But once he was back in London, he could not resist taking a part in the deepening public resistance to James II—this time not as a soldier but as a pamphleteer. In 1687 and 1688 he turned out anonymous pamphlets against the King's religious policies, and when the Revolution brought the Protestant William and Mary to the throne, he devoted an ambitious tract to the great deliverance that God had sent to England. For him it was indeed a Glorious Revolution, answering profoundly to his own convictions, and as for the new king, Dutchman or no, William became his one political hero.

Ironically, it was in William's own war with France from 1689 to 1697 that Daniel Foe met his first disaster. To his maze of trading ventures, which by now extended to diving bells and civet cats, he added the risky enterprise of insuring ships in wartime. But the lucrative possibilities of trade with France were now cut off, and as the war dragged on over many long months and ship after ship was sunk at sea, he was faced with terrifying losses. He turned and twisted desperately to save himself and to beat off creditors who were pursuing him with charges of fraud. At last there was no recourse; in 1692 he was declared bankrupt, for the huge sum of seventeen thousand pounds.

It was a lasting blow to his reputation, and to his pride, but with the driving energy that never failed him for long, he set out to pay his debts. He had already shown his value as a propagandist for William's policies, and now that he needed to rely on his pen for a livelihood, he was drawn more and more into the service of the court, first as a pamphleteer and later as an unofficial agent of the King. Around 1695, as if to point up the distinction of being confidentially employed by the Crown, he began to use the gentlemanly French *de* before his name, becoming Daniel Defoe instead of mere Mr. Foe. He launched forth into business again, establishing a tile factory on some land he owned in Essex, and he began, too, to write for himself. In 1697 he completed his first substantial book, *An Essay upon Projects*, filled with characteristically enterprising schemes for improving public institutions, manners, and trade. Four years later, with his business flourishing and a large share of his old debt paid off, he scored his first great success as a writer, with *The True-Born Englishman*, a long satirical poem in which he trounced all those loyal Britons who sneered at their king for being a foreigner. William was grateful; the public was edified; Defoe was in his boldest and most buoyant frame of mind. Then, within a year, William was dead, Anne's accession had virtually banished the Whigs from office, and Defoe brought the world about his ears with a single pamphlet.

In the uproar that followed his publication of *The Shortest-Way with the Dissenters* in 1702, he was treated with unusual severity. The public disgrace of the pillory was bitter enough, but perhaps even worse was the brutal indefiniteness of his detention in Newgate, during which his tileworks failed for want of proper management. He and his family were destitute once again. This experience taught him to draw upon his animal cunning whenever he was hard-pressed; it made him wily and treacherous. But Defoe lost none of his ability under such circumstances, and though the party leaders of the next two reigns knew well that duplicity was as easy for him as breathing, they sought him out and paid him to write for them. Robert Harley, who hired him first, had the advantage of his gratitude, for Harley saw to it that the Crown paid the fine releasing him from prison in 1703. For the remainder of Anne's reign, Defoe served the Tory ministry as paid pamphleteer and secret agent. He took part effectively in the negotiations that led to the union of England and Scotland in 1707, and during the nine years from 1704 to 1713 he edited single-handed the most notable of his journalistic projects, the famous *Review of the Affairs of France*, which commented three times a week on foreign and domestic affairs. When the accession of George I brought the Whigs into power in 1714, the very ministers who had most cause to regard Defoe as "a false, shuffling, prevaricating rascal"—the words are Addison's—hastened to get him into their pay and proceeded to set him up as editor of a series of nominally Tory journals, where he was in a position to undermine Tory arguments. It was a role that Defoe understood, for he had previously edited Whig journals in the interest of the Tories. By 1720 he even had the art of doing both at once; as for his own politics, he could say quite plausibly that his aim had always been to advocate the reasonable and moderate course, the true middle way between partisan extremes.

In his late fifties, Defoe might well have qualified as the ablest and most prolific of hack writers, with a few isolated works that came near to being literature but little prospect of a permanent reputation. But in 1719, at the age of fifty-nine, he suddenly struck the vein that was to make him famous. With no unusual expectations, he published what purported to be the true account of the strange, surprising adventures of one Robinson Crusoe, a mariner of York, written by himself. From the first, the book was popular—so popular that Defoe wasted no time in producing a sequel and then a third part. Realizing that his fictitious narrative, with its utterly convincing air of truth, had uncovered a market for "true histories" of other lives besides Crusoe's, he set about filling the demand. In the fictional memoirs that he poured out with astonishing energy in the next five years—among them, *Captain Singleton* in 1720, *Moll Flanders* and *Colonel Jacque* in 1722, and *The Fortunate Mistress* (*Roxana*) in 1724—he earned the position he occupies in virtually every history of prose fiction as the progenitor if not the actual founder of the English novel. But Defoe was not the man to be satisfied with fictitious people and events, even if they could be made to point a moral. He had been in the thick of public affairs too long to give up his chosen part as debater of issues and interpreter of the contemporary scene, and even as the narratives grew under his hand he continued to turn out other works, long and short, on the subjects that had always interested him: the *Tour thro' the Whole Island of Great Britain* (1724–26) and the first volume of his *Complete English Tradesman* (1725), plus a horde of lesser publications. Even this was not the end of his literary activity. He was still serving as editor of a periodical in 1730, a few months before his death, and bringing out pamphlets on inland trade and street robberies.

Despite his furious rate of publication and the success of his fictional narratives, Defoe was rarely able to do more than make ends meet financially, and in the last months of his life he was forced to go into hiding—as he had done more than once before—to avoid debtor's prison. He came back in secret to the very parish in London where he had been born, and on April 24, 1731, he died there—"of a lethargy," it said in a contemporary notice, though it seems a strange word to apply to Daniel Defoe.

Of the more than five hundred works catalogued in J. R. Moore's *Checklist of the Writings of Daniel Defoe* (1960), only a handful have been critically edited. The popular narratives are available in various reprints, the best of which belong to the Oxford English Novels Series, and in the Shakespeare Head edition of the *Novels and Selected Writings* (1927–28). A good selection of pamphlets and excerpts from longer works has been edited by J. T. Boulton under the title *Daniel Defoe* (1965). There is a facsimile edition of the *Review* by A. W. Secord (1938). Defoe's *Letters*, edited by G. H. Healey (1955), are of interest chiefly to students of his political service to Robert Harley. Of the biographies, the most balanced is James Sutherland's *Defoe* (2nd ed., 1950); also important are Paul Dottin's *Daniel Defoe et ses romans* (1924) and J. R. Moore's *Daniel Defoe: Citizen of the Modern World* (1958). In *Defoe and the Nature of Man*, M. E. Novak writes on ideological elements in Defoe's fiction. A. W. Secord's *Studies in the Narrative Method of Defoe* (1924) and G. A. Starr's *Defoe and Spiritual Auto-biography* (1965) are recommended, as are the chapters on Defoe in A. D. McKillop's *Early Masters of English Fiction* (1956) and Ian Watt's *Rise of the Novel* (1957).

THE SHORTEST-WAY WITH THE DISSENTERS: OR PROPOSALS FOR THE ESTABLISHMENT OF THE CHURCH

During the reign of William III, the various sects of Protestant Nonconformists were able to gain a measure of freedom from the drastic laws that had been enacted against them after the Restoration. Conservative Anglicans considered every attempt to soften the laws against Dissenters a deadly blow to the Church, but the King's insistence upon "toleration" made it difficult for them to fight for their views. Then in 1702, with her first speech from the throne, Queen Anne gave a sudden lift to the hopes of the High-Church party. While she promised to uphold the Toleration Act, by which Dissenters were guaranteed freedom from persecution, she added, "My own principles must always keep me entirely firm to the interests and religion of the Church of England." Within days, a new toughness was apparent in the dealings of High-Church Tories, and a bill to discontinue the practice of occasional conformity —the means by which Dissenters could qualify for public office—was introduced into Parliament. The bill quickly passed the Commons, and a tense struggle developed over it in the House of Lords. Sermons and fiercely worded pamphlets whipped up public sentiment

on both sides, and neither side seemed to have a clear advantage. Late in 1702, at the peak of the excitement, there appeared an anonymous pamphlet called *The Shortest-Way with the Dissenters*, proclaiming grimly that the hour for weakness was past, and the time had come to destroy the enemies of the true Church. It was evidently the work of a Tory High-Flyer poised for the kill. High-Churchmen quoted it with relish; the Dissenters were understandably alarmed. Then it was rumored that the pamphlet was a hoax, a deliberate plan to discredit the High-Churchmen by carrying their arguments to a bloodthirsty extreme, and that the real author was Daniel Defoe. Both factions were outraged. The pamphlet was ordered burned by the public hangman, and a warrant was issued for Defoe's arrest. Four months later he was thrown into Newgate, and in July, 1703, he was tried and found guilty of seditious libel. For a variety of reasons, some having little enough to do with the *Shortest-Way*, he was harshly punished— condemned to stand three times in the pillory and detained indefinitely in Newgate because he could not pay the heavy fine that would have gained his release. His exposure in the pillory, however, turned un-expectedly into a triumph, for the crowds that might have humiliated him took his part instead, cheering him and decking the pillory with flowers. Meanwhile, the *Shortest-Way* continued to find readers, and even while he was in personal danger he allowed it to be reprinted in two separate collections of his writings. It was good for sales, of course, but it was also good in itself, and though he had misjudged the power of its irony in the first place, he had too high an opinion of it to want it to be buried. Its ultimate effect on the dispute over occasional conformity was probably small, but the controversial bill was defeated in the House of Lords in December, 1703.

The text is based on the first edition (1702) but incorporates the verbal changes in the collected editions of 1703, 1705, and 1710.

🔱

SIR *Roger L'Estrange*[1] tells us a Story in his Collection of Fables, of the Cock and the Horses. The Cock was gotten to Roost in the Stable, among the Horses, and there being no Racks, or other Conveniencies for him, it seems, he was forc'd to roost upon the Ground; the Horses jostling about for room, and putting the Cock in danger of his Life, he gives them this grave Advice; *Pray Gentlefolks let us stand still, for fear we should tread upon one another.*

THERE are some People in the World, who now they are *unpearcht*, and reduc'd to an Equality with other People, and under strong and very just Apprehensions of being further treated as they deserve, begin with *Æsop*'s-Cock, to Preach up Peace and Union, and the Christian Duties of Moderation, forgetting, that when they had the Power in their Hands, those Graces were Strangers in their Gates.

It is now near Fourteen Years,[2] that the Glory and Peace of the purest and most flourishing Church in the World has been Ecclips'd, Buffetted, and Disturb'd, by a sort of Men, who God in his Providence has suffer'd to insult over her, and bring her down; these have been the Days of her Humiliation and Tribulation: She has born with an invincible Patience the Reproach of the Wicked, and God has at last heard her Prayers, and deliver'd her from the Oppression of the Stranger.

And now they find their Day is over, their Power gone, and the Throne of this Nation possest by a Royal, *English*, True, and ever Constant Member of, and Friend to the Church of *England*. Now they find that they are in danger of the Church of *England*'s just Resentments; now they cry out *Peace, Union, Forbearance*, and *Charity*, as if the Church had not too long

harbour'd her Enemies under her Wing, and nourish'd the viperous Brood, till they hiss and fly in the Face of the Mother that cherish'd them.

No Gentlemen, the Time of Mercy is past, your *Day of Grace is over;* you shou'd have practis'd Peace, and Moderation, and Charity, if you expected any your selves.

We have heard none of this Lesson for Fourteen Years past: We have been huff'd and bully'd with your Act of Tolleration;[3] you have told us that you are the *Church establish'd by Law*, as well as others; have set up your Canting-Synagogues at our Church-Doors, and the Church and her Members have been loaded with Reproaches, with Oaths, Associations, Abjurations, and what not; where has been the Mercy, the Forbearance, the Charity you have shewn to *tender Consciences of the Church* of *England*, that cou'd not take Oaths *as fast as you made 'em;* that having sworn Allegiance to their lawful and rightful King, cou'd not dispence with that Oath, *their King being still alive,*[4] and swear to your new *Hodge-podge of a Dutch-Government.* These have been turn'd out of their Livings, and they and their Families left to starve; their Estates double Tax'd, to carry on a War[5] they had *no Hand in,* and you *got nothing by:* What Account can you give of the Multitudes you have forc'd to comply, against their Consciences, with your new *sophistical Politicks*, who like new Converts in *France,*[6] Sin because they can't Starve. And now the Tables are turn'd upon you, you *must not be Persecuted, 'tis not a Christian Spirit.*

You have *Butcher'd* one King, *Depos'd* another King, and made a *mock King* of a Third;[7] and yet you cou'd have the Face to expect to be employ'd and trusted

3. **Act of Tolleration:** an Act exempting Protestant Dissenters from the harsher persecuting acts of the two preceding reigns. Though it did not secure religious equality for the Dissenters, it recognized dissent as legal. 4. **their . . . alive:** At the accession of William and Mary some four hundred Anglican clergymen had refused to take the oaths of supremacy and allegiance on the ground that their oaths to the banished James II were still in effect; these "nonjurors" were turned out of their livings and subjected to civil discipline, to the bitter indignation of the High-Church party. 5. **War:** William's first war against Louis XIV of France, from 1689 to 1697. 6. **new . . . France:** Louis XIV's persecution of the Huguenots was so intense as to lead to mass "conversions" among those who could not flee the country. 7. **Butcher'd . . . Third:** Charles I, executed in 1642; James II, deposed in 1688; William III, bound by the principles of the Revolution to accept an increased measure of Parliamentary government.

THE SHORTEST-WAY WITH THE DISSENTERS. **1. Sir . . . L'Estrange:** (1616–1704), Tory journalist and savage pamphleteer against the Dissenters. His *Fables* (1692), drawn from Aesop and other writers, were widely popular. **2. Fourteen Years:** since the Revolution of 1688 and the passage of the Toleration Act.

by the Fourth; any body that did not know the Temper of your Party, wou'd stand amaz'd at the Impudence, as well as Folly, to think of it.

Your Management of your *Dutch Monarch*, whom you reduc'd to a meer *King of Cl——s*,[8] is enough to give any future Princes such an Idea of your Principles, as to warn them sufficiently from coming into your Clutches; and God be thank'd, the Queen is out of your Hands, knows you, and will have a care of you.

There is no doubt but the supreme Authority of a Nation has in it self a Power, *and a Right to that Power*, to execute the Laws upon any Part of that Nation it governs. The execution of the known Laws of the Land, and that with but a gentle Hand neither, was all that the phanatical Party[9] of this Land have ever call'd Persecution; this they have magnified to a height, that the Sufferings of the *Hugonots* in *France* were not to be compar'd with—Now to execute the known Laws of a Nation upon those who transgress them, after voluntarily consenting to the making those Laws, can never be call'd Persecution, but Justice. But Justice is always Violence to the Party offending, for every Man is Innocent in his own Eyes. The first execution of the Laws against Dissenters in *England*, was in the Days of King *James* the First; and what did it amount to, truly, the worst they suffer'd, was at their own request, to let them go to *New-England*, and erect a new Collony, and give them great Privileges, Grants, and suitable Powers, keep them under Protection, and defend them against all Invaders, and receive no Taxes or Revenue from them. This was the cruelty of the Church of *England*, fatal Lenity! 'Twas the ruin of that excellent Prince, King *Charles* the First. Had King *James* sent all the Puritans in *England* away to the *West-Indies*, we had been a national unmix'd Church; the Church of *England* had been kept undivided and entire.

To requite the Lenity of the Father, they take up Arms against the Son; Conquer, Pursue, Take, Imprison, and at last put to Death the anointed of God, and Destroy the very Being and Nature of Government, setting up a sordid Impostor,[10] who had neither Title to Govern, nor Understanding to Manage, but supplied that want with Power, bloody and desperate Councils and Craft, without Conscience.

Had not King *James* the First witheld the full execution of the Laws; had he given them strict

Justice, he had clear'd the Nation of them, and the Consequences had been plain; his *Son had never been murther'd by them*, nor the Monarchy overwhelm'd; 'twas *too much Mercy* shewn them, was the ruin of his Posterity, and the ruin of the Nation's Peace. One would think the Dissenters should not have the Face to believe that we are to be wheedl'd and canted into Peace and Toleration, when they know that they have once requited us with a civil War, and once with an intollerable and unrighteous Persecution for our former Civillity.

Nay, to encourage us to be Easy with them, 'tis apparent, that they never had the Upper-hand of the Church, but they treated her with all the Severity, with all the Reproach and Contempt as was possible: What Peace, and what Mercy did they shew the Loyal Gentry of the Church of *England* in the time of their Triumphant Common-wealth? How did they put all the Gentry of *England* to ransom, whether they were actually in Arms for the King or not, making People compound for their Estates, and starve their Families? How did they treat the Clergy of the Church of *England*, sequester'd[11] the Ministers, devour'd the Patrimony of the Church, and divided the Spoil, by sharing the Church-Lands among their Soldiers, and turning her Clergy out to starve; just such Measure as they have meted, shou'd be measur'd them again.

Charity and Love is the known Doctrine of the Church of *England*, and 'tis plain she has put it in practice towards the Dissenters, even beyond what they ought, till she has been wanting to her self, and in effect, unkind to her own Sons; particularly, in the too much Lenity of King *James* the First, mentioned before, had he so rooted the Puritans from the Face of the Land, which he had an opportunity early to have done, they had not had the Power to vex the Church, as since they have done.

IN the Days of King *Charles* the Second, how did the Church reward their bloody Doings with Lenity and Mercy, *except the barbarous Regicides*[12] *of the pretended Court of Justice;* not a Soul suffer'd for all the Blood in an unnatural War: King *Charles* came in all Mercy and Love, cherish'd them, preferr'd them, employ'd them, witheld the rigour of the Law, and

---

8. Cl——s: probably *Clouts*—worthless rags. 9. phanatical Party: the Dissenters. 10. Impostor: Oliver Cromwell.

11. sequester'd: deprived them of their livings. 12. Regicides: those responsible for the execution of Charles I. At the Restoration, Parliament excluded thirteen regicide judges from the general pardon of the Act of Indemnity; they were hanged, drawn, and quartered.

oftentimes, even against the Advice of his Parliament, gave them liberty of Conscience; and how did they requite him with the villainous Contrivance to Depose and Murther him and his Successor at the *Rye-Plot*.[13]

KING *James*, as if Mercy was the inherent Quality of the Family, began his Reign with unusual Favour to them: Nor could their joining with the Duke of *Monmouth*[14] against him, move him to do himself Justice upon them; but that mistaken Prince thought to win them by Gentleness and Love, proclaim'd an universal Liberty[15] to them, and rather discountenanc'd the Church of England than them; how they requited him all the World knows.

THE late Reign is too fresh in the Memory of all the World to need a Comment; how under Pretence of joining with the Church in redressing some Grievances, they pusht things to that extremity, in conjunction with some mistaken Gentlemen, as to Depose the late King, as if the Grievance of the Nation cou'd not have been redress'd but by the absolute ruin of the Prince: Here's an Instance of their Temper, their Peace, and Charity. To what height they carried themselves during the Reign of a King of their own; how they crope into all Places of Trust and Profit; how they insinuated into the Favour of the King, and were at first preferr'd to the highest Places in the Nation; how they engrost the Ministry, and *above all, how pitifully they Manag'd*, is too plain to need any Remarks.

BUT particularly, their Mercy and Charity, the Spirit of Union, they tell us so much of, has been remarkable in *Scotland*, if any Man wou'd see the Spirit of a Dissenter, let him look into *Scotland;* there they made entire Conquest of the Church, trampled down the sacred Orders, and suppret the Episcopal Government, with an absolute, and as they suppose, irretrievable Victory, tho', 'tis possible, *they may find*

themselves mistaken: Now 'twou'd be a very proper Question to ask their *Impudent Advocate, the Observator*,[16] Pray how much Mercy and Favour did the Members of the Episcopal Church find in *Scotland*, from the *Scotch* Presbyterian-Government; and I shall undertake for the Church of *England*, that the Dissenters shall still receive as much here, tho' they deserve but little.

In a small Treatise of the Sufferings of the Episcopal Clergy in *Scotland*, 'twill appear, what Usage they met with, how they not only lost their Livings, but in several Places, were plunder'd and abus'd in their Persons; the Ministers that cou'd not conform, turn'd out, with numerous Families, and no Maintenance, and hardly Charity enough left to relieve them with a bit of Bread; and the Cruelties of the Party[17] are innumerable, and not to be attempted in this short Piece.

And now to prevent the distant Cloud which they perceiv'd to hang over their Heads from *England;* with a true Presbyterian Policy, they put in for *a union of Nations*,[18] that *England* might unite their Church with the Kirk of *Scotland*, and their Presbyterian Members sit in our House of Commons, and their Assembly of *Scotch* canting Long-Cloaks in our Convocation;[19] what might have been, if our Phanatick, Whiggish-States-men had continu'd, God only knows; but we hope we are out of fear of that now.

'Tis alledg'd by some of the Faction, and they began to Bully us with it; that if we won't unite with them, they will not settle the Crown[20] with us again, but when her Majesty dies, will chuse a King for themselves.

If they won't, we must make them, and 'tis not the first time we have let them know that we are able: The Crowns of these Kingdoms have not so far disowned the right of Succession, but they may retrieve it again, and if *Scotland* thinks to come off from a Successive to an Elective State of Government, *England* has not promised not to assist the right Heir, and put them into possession, without any regard to their ridiculous Settlements.

13. **the Rye-Plot:** an unsuccessful plot, then attributed to the Whigs, to assassinate Charles II and his brother at Rye House in 1683. 14. **Duke of Monmouth:** illegitimate son of Charles II whose claim to the throne was supported by the Whigs against that of James II. In 1685 he led an abortive rebellion against James. (See Dryden's *Absalom and Achitophel* in Part One.) 15. **universal Liberty:** James's Declaration of Indulgence in 1687 eased religious restrictions upon Nonconformists, both Catholic and Protestant. Defoe himself condemned James's act as an abuse of the royal prerogative.

16. **the Observator:** the most prominent Whig periodical of the moment, edited from 1702 to 1707 by John Tutchin. 17. **the Party:** the Dissenters; here, the Scottish Presbyterians. 18. **union of Nations:** political union of England and Scotland; it was under negotiation in 1702 and accomplished in 1707. 19. **Convocation:** the ruling representative assembly of the Church of England. 20. **settle the Crown:** agree upon a single sovereign for both nations.

THESE are the Gentlemen, these their ways of treating the Church, both at home and abroad. Now let us examine the Reasons they pretend to give why we shou'd be favourable to them, why we should continue and tollerate them among us.

First, THEY are very Numerous, they say, they are a great Part of the Nation, and we cannot suppress them.

To this may be answer'd 1. THEY are not so Numerous as the Protestants in *France,* and yet the *French* King effectually clear'd the Nation of them[21] at once, and we don't find he misses them at home.

But I am not of the Opinion they are so Numerous as is pretended; their Party is more Numerous than their Persons, and those mistaken People of the Church, who are misled and deluded by their wheedling Artifices, to join with them, make their Party the greater; but those will open their Eyes, when the Government shall set heartily about the work, and come off from them, as some Annimals, which they say, always desert a House when 'tis likely to fall.

2dly. The more Numerous, the more Dangerous, and therefore the more need to suppress them; and God has suffer'd us to bear them as Goads in our sides, for not utterly extinguishing them long ago.

3dly. If we are to allow them, only because we cannot suppress them, then it ought to be tryed whether we can or no; and I am of Opinion 'tis easy to be done, and cou'd prescribe Ways and Means, if it were proper, but I doubt not the Government will find effectual Methods for the rooting the Contagion from the Face of this Land.

ANOTHER Argument they use, which is this, That 'tis a time of War, and we have need to unite against the common Enemy.[22]

WE answer, this common Enemy had been no Enemy, if they had not made him so; he was quiet, in peace, and no way disturb'd, or encroach'd upon us, and we know no reason we had to quarrel with him.

But further, We make no question but we are able to deal with this common Enemy without their help; but why must we unite with them because of the Enemy? Will they go over to the Enemy, if we do not prevent it by a union with them?—We are very well contented they shou'd; and make no question, we shall be ready to deal with them and the common Enemy too, and better without them than with them.

Besides, if we have a common Enemy, there is the more need to be secure against our private Enemies; if there is one common Enemy, we have the less need to have an Enemy in our Bowels.

'Twas a great Argument some People used against suppressing the Old-Money,[23] that 'twas a time of War, and 'twas too great a Risque for the Nation to run, if we shou'd not master it we shou'd be undone; and yet the Sequel prov'd the Hazard was not so great, but it might be mastered; and the Success was answerable. The suppressing the Dissenters is not a harder Work, nor a Work of less necessity to the Publick; we can never enjoy a settled uninterrupted Union and Tranquility in this Nation, till the Spirit of Whiggisme, Faction, and Schism is melted down like the Old-Money.

To talk of the Difficulty, is to Frighten our selves with Chimaeras and Notions of a Powerful Party, which are indeed a Party without Power; Difficulties often appear greater at a distance, than when they are search'd into with Judgment, and distinguish'd from the Vapours and Shadows that attend them.

We are not to be frightned with it; this Age is wiser than that, by all our own Experience, *and their's too;* King *Charles* the First, had early supprest this Party, if he had took more deliberate Measures. In short, 'tis not worth arguing, to talk of their Arms, their *Monmouths,* and *Shaftsburys,* and *Argiles*[24] are gone, their *Dutch-Sanctuary* is at an end, Heaven has made way for their Destruction, and if we do not close with the Divine occasion, we are to blame our selves, and may remember that we had once an opportunity to serve the Church of *England,* by extirpating her implacable Enemies, and having let slip the Minute that Heaven presented, may experimentally Complain, *Post est Occasio Calva.*[25]

Here are some popular Objections in the way.

---

21. clear'd . . . them: Most of the Huguenots who were not imprisoned, forcibly converted, or massacred left the country and settled elsewhere, many of them in England. **22. common Enemy:** Louis XIV.

23. Old-Money: In 1696 William and his financial advisers boldly retired the old, clipped silver coinage and introduced a sound new one—at a cost of more than a million pounds. **24. Argiles:** The Ninth Earl of Argyle led an armed revolt against James II in 1685, but failed. Shaftesbury was the Whig leader who supported both Argyle and Monmouth. **25. Post . . . Calva:** Opportunity is bald behind (and so must be seized by the forelock).

As first, THE Queen has promis'd them, to continue them in their tollerated Liberty; and has told us she will be a religious Observer of her Word.

WHAT her Majesty will do we cannot help, but what, as the Head of the Church, she ought to do, is another Case: Her Majesty has promised to Protect and Defend the Church of *England*, and if she cannot effectually do that without the Destruction of the Dissenters, she must of course dispence with one Promise to comply with another. But to answer *this Cavil more effectually:* Her Majesty did never promise to maintain the Tolleration, to the Destruction of the Church; but it is upon supposition that it may be compatible with the well being and safety of the Church, which she had declar'd she would take especial Care of: Now if these two Interests clash, 'tis plain her Majesties Intentions are to Uphold, Protect, Defend, and Establish the Church, and this we conceive is impossible.

Perhaps it may be said, THAT the Church is in no immediate danger from the Dissenters, and therefore 'tis time enough: But this is a weak Answer.

For first, IF a Danger be real, the Distance of it is no Argument against, but rather a Spur to quicken us to prevention, lest it be too late hereafter.

And 2dly, Here is the Opportunity, and the only one perhaps that ever the Church had to secure her self, and destroy her Enemies.

The Representatives of the Nation have now an Opportunity, the Time is come which all good Men ha' wish'd for, that the Gentlemen of *England* may serve the Church of *England;* now they are protected and encouraged by a Church of *England* Queen.

What will ye do for your Sister in the Day that she shall be spoken for.[26]

If ever you will establish the best Christian Church in the World.

If ever you will suppress the Spirit of Enthusiasm.[27]

If ever you will free the Nation from the viperous Brood that have so long suck'd the Blood of their Mother.

If ever you will leave your Posterity free from Faction and Rebellion, this is the time.

This is the time to pull up this heretical Weed of Sedition, that has so long disturb'd the Peace of our Church, and poisoned the good Corn.

BUT, says another Hot and Cold Objector, this is renewing Fire and Faggot, reviving the Act *De Heret. Comburendo:*[28] This will be Cruelty in its Nature, and Barbarous to all the World.

I answer, 'TIS Cruelty to kill a Snake or a Toad in cold Blood, but the Poyson of their Nature makes it a Charity to our Neighbours, to destroy those Creatures, not for any personal Injury receiv'd, but for prevention; not for the Evil they have done, but for the Evil they may do.

Serpents, Toads, Vipers, &c. are noxious to the Body, and poison the sensative Life; these poyson the Soul, corrupt our Posterity, ensnare our Children, destroy the Vitals of our Happyness, our future Felicity, and contaminate the whole Mass.

Shall any Law be given to such wild Creatures? Some Beasts are for Sport, and the Huntsmen give them advantages of Ground, but some are knockt on the Head by all possible ways of Violence and Surprize.

I do not prescribe Fire and Fagot; but as *Scipio* said of *Carthage, Delenda est Carthago,*[29] they are to be rooted out of this Nation, if ever we will live in Peace, serve God, or enjoy our Own; as for the Manner, I leave it to those Hands who have a Right to execute God's Justice on the Nation's and the Church's Enemies.

BUT if we must be frighted from this Justice, under the specious Pretences, and odious Sense of Cruelty, nothing will be effected: 'Twill be more Barbarous to our own Children, and dear Posterity, when they shall reproach their Fathers, as we do ours, and tell us, "You had an Opportunity to root out this cursed Race from the World, under the Favour and Protection of a True *English* Queen; and out of your foolish Pity you spar'd them, because, forsooth, you would not be Cruel, and now our Church is supprest and persecuted, our Religion trampl'd under Foot, our Estates plundred, our Persons imprisoned and dragg'd to Jails, Gibbets, and Scaffolds; your sparing this *Amalakite* Race[30] is our Destruction, your Mercy to them proves Cruelty to your poor Posterity."

28. De . . . Comburendo: Of the Burning of Heretics. This grim statute, dating from 1401, had been revoked by Parliament in 1677. **29. Delenda est Carthago:** Carthage must be destroyed—a constant theme in Cato's (not Scipio's) speeches on Roman commerce. **30. Amalakite Race:** the race of Amalek (Deut. 25:17), enemies of the chosen people.

26. What . . . for: See Song of Sol. 8:8. **27. Enthusiasm:** the illusion that one's beliefs and impulses are directly inspired by God. (See Locke's chapter on enthusiasm in Part One.)

HOW just will such Reflections be, when our Posterity shall fall under the merciless Clutches of this uncharitable Generation, when our Church shall be swallow'd up in Schism, Faction, Enthusiasme, and Confusion; when our Government shall be devolv'd upon Foreigners, and our Monarchy dwindled into a Republick.

'Twou'd be more rational for us, if we must spare this Generation, to summon our own to a general Massacre, and as we have brought them into the World Free, send them out so, and not betray them to Destruction by our supine negligence, and then cry *it is Mercy*.

Moses was a merciful meek Man, and yet with what Fury did he run thro' the Camp, and cut the Throats of Three and thirty thousand of his dear *Israelites*, that were fallen into Idolatry;[31] what was the reason? 'twas Mercy to the rest, to make these Examples, to prevent the Destruction of the whole Army.

How many Millions of future Souls we save from Infection and Delusion, if the present Race of poison'd Spirits were purg'd from the Face of the Land.

'TIS vain to trifle in this matter, the light foolish handling of them by Mulcts, Fines, &c. 'tis their Glory and their Advantage; if the Gallows instead of the Counter,[32] and the Gallies instead of the Fines, were the Reward of going to a Conventicle,[33] to preach or hear, there wou'd not be so many Sufferers, the Spirit of Martyrdom is over; they that will go to Church to be chosen Sheriffs and Mayors, would go to forty Churches rather than be Hang'd.

If one severe Law were made, and punctually executed, that who ever was found at a Conventicle, shou'd be Banished the Nation, and the Preacher be Hang'd, we shou'd soon see an end of the Tale, they wou'd all come to Church; and one Age wou'd make us all One again.

TO talk of 5 *s.* a Month for not coming to the Sacrament, and 1 *s. per* Week for not coming to Church, this is such a way of converting People as never was known, this is selling them a Liberty to transgress for so much Money: If it be not a Crime, why don't we give them full Licence? And if it be, no Price ought to compound for the committing it,

for that is selling a Liberty to People to sin against God and the Government.

If it be a Crime of the highest Consequence, both against the Peace and Welfare of the Nation, the Glory of God, the Good of the Church, and the Happyness of the Soul, let us rank it among capital Offences, and let it receive a Punishment in proportion to it.

We Hang Men for Trifles, and Banish them for things not worth naming, but an Offence against God and the Church, against the Welfare of the World, and the Dignity of Religion, shall be bought off for 5 *s.* this is such a shame to a Christian Government, that 'tis with regret I transmit it to Posterity.

IF Men sin against God, affront his Ordinances, rebell against his Church, and disobey the Precepts of their Superiors, let them suffer as such capital Crimes deserve, so will Religion flourish, and this divided Nation be once again united.

And yet the Title of Barbarous and Cruel will soon be taken off from this Law too. I am not supposing that all the Dissenters in *England* shou'd be Hang'd or Banish'd, but as in cases of Rebellions and Insurrections, if a few of the Ring-leaders suffer, the Multitude are dismist, so a few obstinate People being made Examples there's no doubt but the Severity of the Law would find a stop in the Compliance of the Multitude.

To make the reasonableness of this matter out of question, and more unanswerably plain, let us examine for what it is that this Nation is divided into Parties and Factions, and let us see how they can justify a Separation, or we of the Church of *England* can justify our bearing the Insults and Inconveniencies of the Party.

ONE of their leading Pastors, and a Man of as much Learning as most among them, in his Answer to a Pamphlet,[34] entituled, *An Enquiry into the occasional Conformity*, hath these Words, P. 27 *Do the Religion of the Church and the Meeting-houses make two Religions? Wherein do they differ? The Substance of the same Religion is common to them both; and the Modes and Accidents are the things in which only they differ.* P. 28 *Thirty nine Articles are given us for the summary of our Religion,*

---

31. with . . . Idolatry: See Ex. 32:7–28. **32. Counter:** debtor's prison. **33. Conventicle:** secret or illegal gathering for religious worship.

34. Pamphlet: The *Enquiry* (1698) was Defoe's own work. The answer was by John Howe, a prominent Presbyterian divine.

Thirty six contain the Substance of it, wherein we agree; Three the additional Appendices, about which we have some differences.

Now, if as by their own acknowledgment, the Church of *England* is a true Church, and the Difference between them is only a few *Modes and Accidents*, Why shou'd we expect that they will suffer Gallows and Gallies, corporeal Punishment and Banishment for these Trifles; there is no question but they will be wiser; even their own Principles won't bear them out in it, they will certainly comply with the Laws, and with Reason, and tho' at the first, Severity may seem hard, the next Age will feel nothing of it; the Contagion will be rooted out; the Disease being cur'd, there will be no need of the Operation, but if they should venture to transgress, and fall into the Pit, all the World must condemn their Obstinacy, as being without Ground from their own Principles.

Thus the Pretence of Cruelty will be taken off, and the Party actually suppress, and the Disquiets they have so often brought upon the Nation, prevented.

THEIR Numbers, and their Wealth, makes them Haughty, and that is so far from being an Argument to perswade us to forbear them, that 'tis a Warning to us, without any more delay, to reconcile them to the Unity of the Church, or remove them from us.

AT present, Heaven be prais'd, they are not so Formidable as they have been, and 'tis our own fault if ever we suffer them to be so; Providence, and the Church of *England*, seems to join in this particular, that now the Destroyers of the Nations Peace may be overturn'd, and to this end the present Opportunity seems to be put into our Hands.

To this end her present Majesty seems reserv'd to enjoy the Crown, that the Ecclesiastick as well as Civil Rights of the Nation may be restor'd by her Hand.

To this end the Face of Affairs have receiv'd such a Turn in the process of a few Months, as never has been before; the leading Men of the Nation, the universal Cry of the People, the unanimous Request of the Clergy, agree in this, that the Deliverance of our Church is at hand.

For this end has Providence given us such a Parliament, such a Convocation, such a Gentry, and such a Queen as we never had before.

AND what may be the Consequences of a Neglect of such Opportunities? The Succession of the Crown has but a dark Prospect, another *Dutch* Turn[35] may make the Hopes of it ridiculous, and the Practice impossible: Be the House of our future Princes never so well inclin'd, they will be Foreigners; and many Years will be spent in suiting the Genius of Strangers to this Crown, and the Interests of the Nation; and how many Ages it may be before the *English* Throne be fill'd with so much Zeal and Candour,[36] so much Tenderness, and hearty Affection to the Church, as we see it now cover'd with, who can imagine.

'Tis high time then for the Friends of the Church of *England*, to think of Building up, and Establishing her, in such a manner, that she may be no more Invaded by Foreigners, nor Divided by Factions, Schisms, and Error.

IF this cou'd be done by gentle and easy Methods, I shou'd be glad, but the Wound is coroded, the Vitals begin to mortifie, and nothing but Amputation of Members can compleat the Cure; all the ways of Tenderness and Compassion, all perswasive Arguments have been made use of in vain.

THE Humour of the Dissenters has so encreas'd among the People, that they hold the Church in Defiance, and the House of God is an Abomination among them: Nay, they have brought up their Posterity in such pre-possest Aversions to our Holy Religion, that the ignorant Mob think we are all Idolaters, and Worshippers of *Baal;* and account it a Sin to come within the Walls of our Churches.

The primitive Christians were not more shie of a Heathen-Temple, or of Meat offer'd to Idols, nor the *Jews* of Swine's-Flesh, than some of our Dissenters are of the Church, and the Divine Service solemnized therein.

THIS Obstinacy must be rooted out with the Profession of it, while the Generation are left at liberty daily to affront God Almighty, and Dishonour his Holy Worship, we are wanting in our Duty to God, and our Mother the Church of *England*.

How can we answer it to God, to the Church, and to our Posterity, to leave them entangled with Fanaticisme, Error, and Obstinacy, in the Bowels of the Nation; to leave them an Enemy in their Streets, that in time may involve them in the same Crimes,

35. Dutch Turn: Under the Act of Settlement of 1701, the succession would pass to the German House of Hanover if Anne should leave no heir. **36. Candour:** good will, fairness of mind.

and endanger the utter Extirpation of Religion in the Nation.

WHAT's the Difference betwixt this, and being subjected to the Power of the Church of *Rome*, from whence we have reform'd? If one be an extreme on one Hand, and one on another, 'tis equally destructive to the Truth, to have Errors settled among us, let them be of what Nature they will.

Both are Enemies of our Church, and of our Peace, and why shou'd it not be as criminal to admit an Enthusiast as a Jesuit? Why shou'd the *Papist* with his Seven Sacraments be worse than the *Quaker* with no Sacraments at all? Why shou'd Religious-houses be more intollerable than Meeting-houses—*Alas the Church of England!* What with Popery on one Hand, and Schismaticks on the other; how has she been Crucify'd between two Thieves.

Now *let us Crucifie the Thieves.* Let her Foundations be establish'd upon the Destruction of her Enemies: The Doors of Mercy being always open to the returning Part of the deluded People: Let the Obstinate be rul'd with the Rod of Iron.

Let all true Sons of so Holy and Oppressed a Mother, exasperated by her Afflictions, harden their Hearts against those who have oppress'd her.

And may God Almighty put it into the Hearts of all the
    Friends of Truth, to lift up a Standard against Pride
    and Antichrist, that the Posterity of the Sons of Error
    may be rooted out from the Face of this Land for
    ever—.

FROM

A JOURNAL
OF THE PLAGUE YEAR

In the summer of 1720, Londoners were alarmed by news of a violent outbreak of bubonic plague in and around Marseilles. Although the government moved quickly to cut off trade with the infected ports, London watched apprehensively as the dread disease hung on through the winter and flared up again in the warm months of 1721. Defoe was then busy with articles and pamphlets on economic questions, and probably with *Moll Flanders* as well; but, spurred on by the popular excitement, and perhaps by the government's need to defend the costly embargo on Mediterranean shipping

from the attacks of an irate merchant class, he made plans for dealing with the plague in his own way. Early in 1722, within a span of five weeks, he brought out not one but two considerable books on the subject—an instructive treatise called *Due Preparations for the Plague, as Well for Soul as Body* and his famous *Journal of the Plague Year.* The *Journal* purported to be the "observations or memorials" of one H. F., a sober, unassuming tradesman of London, who had seen with his own eyes the horrors of the worst visitation in living memory, the Great Plague of 1665. So authentic is the impression of eyewitness reporting that it comes almost as a shock to remember how old Defoe himself was in 1665. Some of what he describes, however, he could perhaps have seen, and the London of his early youth must still have been full of grim relics of that terrible year. His uncle Henry Foe is said to have stayed in the city throughout the plague, and he might well have told the boy memorable stories of those times; he may even have been the model for H. F., the saddler. Much of what Defoe put into the *Journal,* however, he got from books—from the bills of mortality and other public records and from medical and devotional volumes in his own well-stocked library. (For these, see Watson Nicholson's *Historical Sources of Defoe's Journal of the Plague Year* [1919].) But here, as so often in Defoe, it is impossible to separate what he had seen for himself from what he borrowed or invented, or to disentangle fiction from fact. Events, rumors, vital statistics, anecdotes, and local details, whatever their source, all take on an equal appearance of fact under the impress of his powerful realistic imagination. He is not telling the literal history of the plague but reenacting it in the experience of an ordinary man and letting that man vouch for the facts himself. The *Journal* is one of Defoe's characteristic "honest cheats," and by common consent one of his best—true and untrue, sometimes at odds with the literal evidence, but massively convincing.

Given here are the opening passage, three selections from the body of the book, and the concluding pages—about one fifth of the whole. The text is that of the first edition (1722).

IT was about the Beginning of *September* 1664, that I, among the Rest of my Neighbours, heard in ordinary Discourse, that the Plague was return'd again in *Holland;* for it had been very violent there, and particularly at *Amsterdam* and *Roterdam,* in the Year 1663. whither *they say,* it was brought, some said from *Italy,* others from the *Levant*[1] among some Goods,

---

A JOURNAL OF THE PLAGUE YEAR. **I. Levant:** the Orient.

which were brought home by their[2] Turkey Fleet; others said it was brought from *Candia;*[3] others from *Cyprus.* It matter'd not, from whence it come; but all agreed, it was come into *Holland* again.

We had no such thing as printed News Papers[4] in those Days, to spread Rumours and Reports of Things; and to improve them by the Invention of Men, as I have liv'd to see practis'd since. But such things as these were gather'd from the Letters of Merchants, and others, who corresponded abroad, and from them was handed about by Word of Mouth only; so that things did not spread instantly over the whole Nation, as they do now. But it seems that the Government had a true Account of it, and several Counsels were held about Ways to prevent its coming over; but all was kept very private. Hence it was, that this Rumour died off again, and People began to forget it, as a thing we were very little concern'd in, and that we hoped was not true; till the latter End of *November,* or the Beginning of *December* 1664, when two Men, said to be French-men, died of the Plague in *Long Acre,*[5] or rather at the upper End of *Drury-Lane.* The Family they were in, endeavour'd to conceal it as much as possible; but as it had gotten some Vent in the Discourse of the Neighbourhood, the Secretaries of State[6] gat Knowledge of it. And concerning themselves to inquire about it, in order to be certain of the Truth, two Physicians and a Surgeon were order'd to go to the House, and make Inspection. This they did; and finding evident Tokens of the Sickness upon both the Bodies that were dead, they gave their Opinions publickly, that they died of the Plague: Whereupon it was given in to the Parish Clerk, and he also return'd them to the Hall;[7] and it was printed in the weekly Bill of Mortality in the usual manner, thus,

> Plague   2.   *Parishes infected*   1.

The People shew'd a great Concern at this, and began to be allarm'd all over the Town, and the more, because in the last Week in *December* 1664, another Man died in the same House, and of the same Distemper: And then we were easy again for about six Weeks, when none having died with any Marks of Infection, it was said, the Distemper was gone; but after that, I think it was about the 12th of *February,* another died in another House, but in the same Parish, and in the same manner.

This turn'd the Peoples Eyes pretty much towards that End of the Town; and the weekly Bills shewing an Encrease of Burials in St. *Giles's* Parish more than usual, it began to be suspected, that the Plague was among the People at that End of the Town; and that many had died of it, tho' they had taken Care to keep it as much from the Knowlege of the Publick, as possible: This possess'd the Heads of the People very much, and few car'd to go thro' *Drury-Lane,* or the other Streets suspected, unless they had extraordinary Business, that obliged them to it.

This Encrease of the Bills stood thus; the usual Number of Burials in a Week, in the Parishes of St. *Giles's* in the Fields, and St. *Andrew's* Holborn were from 12 to 17 or 19 each, few more or less; but from the Time that the Plague first began in St. *Giles's* Parish, it was observ'd, that the ordinary Burials encreased in Number considerably. *For Example,*

From *Dec.* 27th to *Jan.*	3.	St. *Giles's*	16
		St. *Andrew's*	17
Jan. 3. to	10.	St. *Giles's*	12
		St. *Andrew's*	25
Jan. 10. to	17.	St. *Giles's*	18
		St. *Andrew's*	18
Jan. 17. to	24.	St. *Giles's*	23
		St. *Andrew's*	16
Jan. 24. to	31.	St. *Giles's*	24
		St. *Andrew's*	15
Jan. 30. to *Feb.*	7.	St. *Giles's*	21
		St. *Andrew's*	23
Feb. 7. to	14.	St. *Giles's*	24

whereof one of the Plague.

The like Encrease of the Bills was observ'd in the Parishes of St. *Brides,* adjoining on one Side of *Holborn* Parish, and in the Parish of St. *James Clarkenwell,* adjoining on the other Side of *Holborn;* in both which Parishes, the usual Numbers that died weekly, were from 4 to 6 or 8, whereas at that time they were increas'd, as follows.

---

2. **their:** the Dutch. 3. **Candia:** Crete. 4. **no . . . Papers:** There were two weekly papers in 1665, but both were under government control, and they contained little domestic news. 5. **Long Acre:** a street in the parish of St. Giles-in-the-Fields. 6. **Secretaries of State:** two government ministers whose authority included domestic as well as foreign affairs. 7. **the Hall:** Guildhall, the City Hall.

From *Dec.* 20. to *Dec.*   27.   St. *Brides* ———— 0.
                                    St. *James* ———— 8

Dec. 27. to *Jan.*   3.   St. *Brides* ———— 6
                              St. *James* ———— 9

Jan.   3. to ———— 10.   St. *Brides* ———— 11
                              St. *James* ———— 7

Jan.   10. to ———— 17.   St. *Brides* ———— 12
                              St. *James* ———— 9

Jan.   17. to ———— 24.   St. *Brides* ———— 9
                              St. *James* ———— 15

Jan.   24. to ———— 31.   St. *Brides* ———— 8
                              St. *James* ———— 12

Jan.   31. to *Feb.*   7.   St. *Brides* ———— 13
                                 St. *James* ———— 5

Feb.   7. to ———— 14.   St. *Brides* ———— 12
                              St. *James* ———— 6

Besides this, it was observ'd with great Uneasiness by the People, that the weekly Bills in general encreas'd very much during these Weeks, altho' it was at a Time of the Year, when usually the Bills are very moderate.

The usual Number of Burials within the Bills of Mortality for a Week, was from about 240 or there-abouts, to 300. The last was esteem'd a pretty high Bill; but after this we found the Bills successively encreasing, as follows.

		Buried	Increased
Dec. the 20. to the 27th,	Buried	291.	————
	27. to the 3 *Jan.*	349.	58
January	3. to the 10.	394.	45
	10. to the 17.	415.	21
	17. to the 24.	474.	59

This last Bill was really frightful, being a higher Number than had been known to have been buried in one Week, since the preceeding Visitation of 1656.

However, all this went off again, and the Weather proving cold, and the Frost which began in *December*, still continuing very severe, even till near the End of *February*, attended with sharp tho' moderate Winds, the Bills decreas'd again, and the City grew healthy, and every body began to look upon the Danger as good as over; only that still the Burials in St. *Giles*'s continu'd high: From the Beginning of *April* especially they stood at 25 each Week, till the Week from the 18th to the 25th, when there was buried in St. *Giles*'s Parish 30, whereof two of the Plague, and 8 of the Spotted-Feaver,[8] which was look'd upon as

8. **Spotted-Feaver:** typhus.

the same thing; likewise the Number that died of the Spotted-Feaver in the whole increased, being 8 the Week before, and 12 the Week abovenamed.

This alarm'd us all again, and terrible Apprehensions were among the People, especially the Weather being now chang'd and growing warm, and the Summer being at Hand: However, the next Week there seem'd to be some Hopes again, the Bills were low, the Number of the Dead in all was but 388, there was none of the Plague, and but four of the Spotted-Feaver.

But the following Week it return'd again, and the Distemper was spread into two or three other Parishes (*viz.*) St. *Andrew's-Holborn*, St. *Clement's-Danes*, and to the great Affliction of the City,[9] one died within the Walls, in the Parish of St. *Mary-Wool-Church*, that is to say, in *Bearbinder-lane* near the *Stocks-market;* in all there was nine of the Plague, and six of the Spotted-Feaver. It was however upon Inquiry found, that this *French-man* who died in *Bearbinder-lane*, was one who having liv'd in *Long-Acre*, near the infected Houses, had removed for fear of the Distemper, not knowing that he was already infected.

This was the beginning of *May*, yet the Weather was temperate, variable and cool enough, and People had still some Hopes: That which encourag'd them was, that the City was healthy, the whole 97 Parishes buried but 54, and we began to hope, that as it was chiefly among the People at that End of the Town, it might go no farther; and the rather, because the next Week which was from the 9th of *May* to the 16th there died but three, of which not one within the whole City or Liberties,[10] and St. *Andrew*'s buried but 15, which was very low: 'Tis true, St. *Giles*'s buried two and thirty, but still as there was but one of the Plague, People began to be easy, the whole Bill also was very low, for the Week before, the Bill was but 347, and the Week above-mentioned but 343: We continued in these Hopes for a few Days, but it was but for a few; for the People were no more to be deceived thus; they searcht the Houses, and found that the Plague was really spread every way, and that many died of it every Day: So that now all our

9. **the City:** London proper, i.e., the part enclosed by the medieval walls. Although Defoe sometimes speaks of the whole metropolis as "the City," more often he uses the term in the narrower sense. 10. **Liberties:** the populous areas just outside the City walls; not part of the City, but under the jurisdiction of its authorities.

Extenuations abated, and it was no more to be concealed, nay it quickly appeared that the Infection had spread it self beyond all Hopes of Abatement; that in the Parish of St. *Giles's*, it was gotten into several Streets, and several Families lay all sick together; And accordingly in the Weekly Bill for the next Week, the thing began to shew it self; there was indeed but 14 set down of the Plague, but this was all Knavery and Collusion, for in St. *Giles's* Parish they buried 40 in all, whereof it was certain most of them died of the Plague, though they were set down of other Distempers; and though the Number of all the Burials were not increased above 32, and the whole Bill being but 385, yet there was 14 of the Spotted-Feaver, as well as 14 of the Plague; and we took it for granted upon the whole, that there was 50 died that Week of the Plague.

The next Bill was from the 23d of *May* to the 30th, when the Number of the Plague was 17: But the Burials in St. *Giles's* were 53, a frightful Number! of whom they set down but 9 of the Plague: But on an Examination more strictly by the Justices of the Peace, and at the Lord Mayor's Request, it was found there were 20 more, who were really dead of the Plague in that Parish, but had been set down of the Spotted-Feaver or other Distempers, besides others concealed.

But those were trifling Things to what followed immediately after; for now the Weather set in hot, and from the first Week in *June*, the Infection spread in a dreadful Manner, and the Bills rise high, the Articles of the Feaver, Spotted-Feaver, and Teeth, began to swell: For all that could conceal their Distempers, did it to prevent their Neighbours shunning and refusing to converse with them; and also to prevent Authority shutting up their Houses, which though it was not yet practised, yet was threatned, and People were extremely terrify'd at the Thoughts of it.

The Second Week in *June*, the Parish of St. *Giles's*, where still the Weight of the Infection lay, buried 120, whereof though the Bills said but 68 of the Plague; every Body said there had been 100 at least, calculating it from the usual Number of Funerals in that Parish as above.

Till this Week the City continued free, there having never any died except that one *Frenchman*, who I mention'd before, within the whole 97 Parishes. Now there died four within the City, one in *Wood-street*, one in *Fenchurch street*, and two in *Crooked-lane*: *Southwark* was entirely free, having not one yet died on that Side of the Water.

I liv'd without *Aldgate*[11] about mid-way between *Aldgate Church* and *White-Chappel-Bars*, on the left Hand or North-side of the Street; and as the Distemper had not reach'd to that Side of the City, our Neighbourhood continued very easy: But at the other End of the Town, their Consternation was very great; and the richer sort of People, especially the Nobility and Gentry, from the West-part of the City throng'd out of Town, with their Families and Servants in an unusual Manner; and this was more particularly seen in *White-Chapel;* that is to say, the Broad-street where I liv'd: Indeed nothing was to be seen but Waggons and Carts, with Goods, Women, Servants, Children, &c. Coaches fill'd with People of the better Sort, and Horsemen attending them, and all hurrying away; then empty Waggons, and Carts appear'd and Spare-horses with Servants, who it was apparent were returning or sent from the Countries to fetch more People: Besides innumerable Numbers of Men on Horseback, some alone, others with Servants, and generally speaking, all loaded with Baggage and fitted out for travelling, as any one might perceive by their Appearance.

This was a very terrible and melancholy Thing to see, and as it was a Sight which I cou'd not but look on from Morning to Night; for indeed there was nothing else of Moment to be seen, it filled me with very serious Thoughts of the Misery that was coming upon the City, and the unhappy Condition of those that would be left in it.

This Hurry of the People was such for some Weeks, that there was no getting at the Lord-Mayor's Door without exceeding Difficulty; there was such pressing and crouding there to get passes and Certificates of Health, for such as travelled abroad; for without these, there was no being admitted to pass thro' the Towns upon the Road, or to lodge in any Inn: Now as there had none died in the City for all this time, My Lord Mayor gave Certificates of Health without any Difficulty to all those who liv'd in the 97 Parishes, and to those within the Liberties too for a while.

This Hurry, I say, continued some Weeks, that is to say, all the Month of *May* and *June*, and the more because it was rumour'd that an order of the Government was to be issued out, to place Turn-pikes and Barriers on the Road, to prevent Peoples travelling; and that the Towns on the Road, would not suffer

---

11. without Aldgate: outside Aldgate, a gate in the eastern side of the City walls.

People from *London* to pass, for fear of bringing the Infection along with them, though neither of these Rumours had any Foundation, but in the Imagination; especially at first.

I now began to consider seriously with my Self, concerning my own Case, and how I should dispose of my self; that is to say, whether I should resolve to stay in *London*, or shut up my House and flee, as many of my Neighbours did. I have set this particular down so fully, because I know not but it may be of Moment to those who come after me, if they come to be brought to the same Distress, and to the same Manner of making their Choice and therefore I desire this Account may pass with them, rather for a Direction to themselves to act by, than a History of my actings, seeing it may not be of one Farthing value to them to note what became of me.

I had two important things before me; the one was the carrying on my Business and Shop; which was considerable, and in which was embark'd all my Effects in the World; and the other was the Preservation of my Life in so dismal a Calamity, as I saw apparently was coming upon the whole City; and which however great it was, my Fears perhaps as well as other Peoples, represented to be much greater than it could be.

The first Consideration was of great Moment to me; my Trade was *a Sadler*, and as my Dealings were chiefly not by a Shop or Chance Trade, but among the Merchants, trading to the *English* Colonies in *America*, so my effects lay very much in the hands of such: I was a single Man 'tis true, but I had a Family of Servants, who I kept at my Business, had a House, Shop, and Ware-houses fill'd with Goods; and in short, to leave them all as things in such a Case must be left, that is to say, without any Overseer or Person fit to be trusted with them, had been to hazard the Loss not only of my Trade, but of my Goods, and indeed of all I had in the World.

I had an Elder Brother at the same Time in *London*, and not many Years before come over from *Portugal;* and advising with him, his Answer was in three words the same that was given in another Case quite different, *(viz.) Master save thy self.*[12] In a Word, he was for my retiring into the Country, as he resolv'd to do himself with his Family; telling me, what he had it seems, heard abroad, that the best Preparation for the Plague was to run away from it. As to my Argument of losing my Trade, my Goods, or Debts, he quite confuted me: He told me the same thing, which I argued for my staying, *(viz) That I would trust God with my Safety and Health,* was the strongest Repulse to my Pretentions of losing my Trade and my Goods; for, says he, is it not as reasonable that you should trust God with the Chance or Risque of losing your Trade, as that you should stay in so imminent a Point of Danger, and trust him with your Life?

I could not argue that I was in any Strait, as to a Place where to go, having several Friends and Relations in *Northamptonshire,* whence our Family first came from; and particularly, I had an only Sister in *Lincolnshire,* very willing to receive and entertain me.

My Brother, who had already sent his Wife and two Children into *Bedfordshire,* and resolv'd to follow them, press'd my going very earnestly; and I had once resolv'd to comply with his Desires, but at that time could get no Horse: For tho' it is true, all the People did not go out of the City of *London;* yet I may venture to say, that in a manner all the Horses did; for there was hardly a Horse to be bought or hired in the whole City for some Weeks. Once I resolv'd to travel on Foot with one Servant; and, as many did, lie at no Inn, but carry a Soldiers Tent with us, and so lie in the Fields, the Weather being very warm, and no Danger from taking cold: I say, as many did, because several did so at last, especially those who had been in the Armies in the War[13] which had not been many Years past; and I must needs say, that speaking of second Causes,[14] had most of the people that travelled, done so, the Plague had not been carried into so many Country-Towns and Houses, as it was, to the great Damage, and indeed to the Ruin of abundance of People.

But then my Servant who I had intended to take down with me, deceiv'd me; and being frighted at the Encrease of the Distemper, and not knowing when I should go, he took other Measures, and left me, so I was put off for that Time; and one way or other, I always found that to appoint to go away was always cross'd by some Accident or other, so as to disappoint[15] and put it off again; and this brings in a Story which otherwise might be thought a needless Digression, *(viz,)* about these Disappointments being from Heaven.

12. **Master . . . self:** See Matt. 27:40.

13. **the War:** the Civil War of 1642–49. 14. **second Causes:** immediate rather than ultimate causes; the *first* or ultimate cause would be God's will. 15. **disappoint:** dis-appoint, defeat the intention.

I mention this Story also as the best Method I can advise any Person to take in such a Case, especially, if he be one that makes Conscience of his Duty, and would be directed what to do in it, namely, that he should keep his Eye upon the particular Providences which occur at that Time, and look upon them complexly, as they regard one another, and as altogether[16] regard the Question before him, and then I think, he may safely take them for Intimations from Heaven of what is his unquestion'd Duty to do in such a Case; I mean as to going away from, or staying in the Place where we dwell, when visited with an infectious Distemper.

It came very warmly into my Mind, one Morning, as I was musing on this particular thing, that as nothing attended us without the Direction or Permission of Divine Power, so these Disappointments must have something in them extraordinary; and I ought to consider whether it did not evidently point out, or intimate to me, that it was the Will of Heaven I should not go. It immediately follow'd in my Thoughts, that if it really was from God, that I should stay, he was able effectually to preserve me in the midst of all the Death and Danger that would surround me; and that if I attempted to secure my self by fleeing from my Habitation, and acted contrary to these Intimations, which I believed to be Divine, it was a kind of flying from God, and that he could cause his Justice to overtake me when and where he thought fit.

These thoughts quite turn'd my Resolutions again, and when I came to discourse with my Brother again I told him, that I enclin'd to stay and take my Lot in that Station in which God had plac'd me, and that it seem'd to be made more especially my Duty, on the Account of what I have said.

My Brother, tho' a very Religious Man himself, laught at all I had suggested about its being an Intimation from Heaven, and told me several Stories of such fool-hardy People, as he call'd them, as I was; that I ought indeed to submit to it as a Work of Heaven, if I had been any way disabled by Distempers or Diseases, and that then not being able to go, I ought to acquiesce in the Direction of him, who having been my Maker, had an undisputed Right of Soveraignity in disposing of me; and that then there had been no Difficulty to determine which was the Call of his Providence, and which was not: But that I

should take it as an Intimation from Heaven, that I should not go out of Town, only because I could not hire a Horse to go, or my Fellow was run away that was to attend me, was ridiculous, since at the same Time I had my Health and Limbs, and other Servants, and might, with Ease, travel a Day or two on foot, and having a good Certificate of being in perfect Health, might either hire a Horse, or take Post on the Road, as I thought fit.

Then he proceeded to tell me of the mischeivous Consequences which attended the Presumption of the *Turks* and *Mahometans* in *Asia* and in other Places, where he had been (for my Brother being a Merchant, was a few Years before, as I have already observ'd, returned from abroad, coming last from *Lisbon*) and how presuming upon their profess'd predestinating Notions, and of every Man's End being predetermin'd and unalterably before-hand decreed, they would go unconcern'd into infected Places, and converse with infected Persons, by which Means they died at the Rate of Ten or Fifteen Thousand a-Week, whereas the *Europeans*, or Christian Merchants, who kept themselves retired and reserv'd, generally escap'd the Contagion.

Upon these Arguments my Brother chang'd my Resolutions again, and I began to resolve to go, and accordingly made all things ready; for in short, the Infection increased round me, and the Bills were risen to almost 700 a-Week, and my Brother told me, he would venture to stay no longer. I desir'd him to let me consider of it but till the next Day, and I would resolve; and as I had already prepar'd every thing as well as I could, as to my Business, and who to entrust my Affairs with, I had little to do but to resolve.

I went Home that Evening greatly oppress'd in my Mind, irresolute, and not knowing what to do; I had set the Evening wholly apart to consider seriously about it, and was all alone; for already People had, as it were by a general Consent, taken up the Custom of not going out of Doors after Sun-set, the Reasons I shall have Occasion to say more of by-and-by.

In the Retirement of this Evening I endeavoured to resolve first, what was my Duty to do, and I stated the Arguments with which my Brother had press'd me to go into the Country, and I set against them the strong Impressions which I had on my Mind for staying; the visible Call I seem'd to have from the particular Circumstance of my Calling, and the Care due from me for the Preservation of my Effects, which were, as I might say, my Estate; also the

16. **altogether:** all together.

Intimations which I thought I had from Heaven, that to me signify'd a kind of Direction to venture, and it occurr'd to me, that if I had what I might call a Direction to stay, I ought to suppose it contain'd a Promise of being preserved, if I obey'd.

This lay close to me, and my Mind seemed more and more encouraged to stay than ever, and supported with a secret Satisfaction, that I should be kept: Add to this that turning over the Bible, which lay before me, and while my Thoughts were more than ordinarily serious upon the Question, I cry'd out, WELL, *I know not what to do, Lord direct me!* and the like; and [at] that Juncture I happen'd to stop turning over the Book at the 91st *Psalm*, and casting my Eye on the second Verse, I read on to the 7th Verse exclusive: and after that, included the 10th, as follows. *I will say of the Lord, He is my refuge, and my foretress, my God, in him will I trust. Surely he shall deliver thee from the snare of the fowler, and from the noisom pestilence. He shall cover thee with his feathers, and under his wings shalt thou trust: his truth shall be thy shield and buckler. Thou shalt not be afraid for the terror by night, nor for the arrow that flieth by day: Nor for the pestilence that walketh in darkness: nor for the destruction that wasteth at noon-day. A thousand shall fall at thy side, and ten thousand at thy right hand: but it shall not come nigh thee. Only with thine eyes shalt thou behold and see the reward of the wicked. Because thou hast made the Lord which is my refuge, even the most High, thy habitation: There shall no evil befal thee, neither shall any plague come nigh thy dwelling,* &c.

I scarce need tell the Reader, that from that Moment I resolv'd that I would stay in the Town, and casting my self entirely upon the Goodness and Protection of the Almighty, would not seek any other Shelter whatever; and that as my Times were in his Hands, he was as able to keep me in a Time of the Infection as in a Time of Health; and if He did not think fit to deliver me, still I was in his Hands, and it was meet he should do with me as should seem good to him.

With this Resolution I went to Bed; and I was farther confirm'd in it the next Day, by the Woman being taken ill with whom I had intended to entrust my House and all my Affairs: But I had a farther Obligation laid on me on the same Side; for the next Day I found my self very much out of Order also; so that if I would have gone away, I could not, and I continued ill three or four Days, and this intirely determin'd my Stay; so I took my leave of my Brother, who went away to *Darking* in *Surry*, and

afterwards fetch'd a Round farther into *Buckinghamshire*, or *Bedfordshire*, to a Retreat he had found out there for his Family.

It was a very ill Time to be sick in, for if any one complain'd, it was immediately said he had the Plague; and tho' I had indeed no Symptoms of that Distemper, yet being very ill, both in my Head and in my Stomach, I was not without Apprehension, that I really was infected; but in about three Days I grew better, the third Night I rested well, sweated a little, and was much refresh'd; the Apprehensions of its being the Infection went also quite away with my Illness, and I went about my Business as usual.

These Things however put off all my Thoughts of going into the Country; and my Brother also being gone, I had no more Debate either with him, or with my self, on that Subject.

It was now mid-*July*, and the Plague which had chiefly rag'd at the other End of the Town, and as I said before, in the Parishes of St. *Giles*'s, St. *Andrews Holbourn*, and towards *Westminster*, began now to come *Eastward* towards the Part where I liv'd. It was to be observ'd indeed, that it did not come strait on towards us; for the City, that is to say within the Walls, was indifferently healthy still; nor was it got then very much over the Water into *Southwark*; for tho' there died that Week 1268 of all Distempers, whereof it might be suppos'd above 900 died of the Plague; yet there was but 28 in the whole City, within the Walls; and but 19 in *Southwark*, *Lambeth* Parish included; whereas in the Parishes of St. *Giles*, and St. *Martins in the Fields* alone, there died 421.

But we perceiv'd the Infection kept chiefly in the out-Parishes, which being very populous, and fuller also of Poor, the Distemper found more to prey upon than in the City, as I shall observe afterward; we perceiv'd I say, the Distemper to draw our Way; (*viz.*) by the Parishes of *Clerken-Well*, *Cripplegate*, *Shoreditch*, and *Bishopsgate*; which last two Parishes joining to *Aldgate*, *White-Chapel*, and *Stepney*, the Infection came at length to spread its utmost Rage and violence in those Parts, even when it abated, at the *Western* Parishes where it began.

It was very strange to observe, that in this particular Week, from the 4th to the 11th of *July*, when, as I have observ'd, there died near 400 of the Plague in the two Parishes of St. *Martin*'s, and St. *Giles in the Fields* only, there died in the Parish of *Aldgate* but four, in the Parish of *White-Chapel* three, in the Parish of *Stepney* but one.

Likewise in the next week, from the 11th of *July* to the 18th, when the Week's Bill was 1761, yet there died no more of the Plague, on the whole *Southwark* Side of the Water than sixteen.

But this Face of things soon changed, and it began to thicken in *Cripplegate* Parish especially, and in *Clerken-Well;* so, that by the second Week in *August, Cripplegate* Parish alone, buried eight hundred eighty six, and *Clerken-Well* 155; of the first eight hundred and fifty, might well be reckoned to die of the Plague; and of the last, the Bill it self said, 145 were of the Plague.

During the Month of *July,* and while, as I have observ'd, our Part of the Town seem'd to be spar'd, in Comparison of the *West* part, I went ordinarily about the Streets, as my Business requir'd, and particularly went generally, once in a Day, or in two Days, into the City, to my Brother's House, which he had given me charge of, and to see if it was safe: And having the Key in my Pocket, I used to go into the House, and over most of the Rooms, to see that all was well; for tho' it be something wonderful to tell, that any should have Hearts so hardned, in the midst of such a Calamity, as to rob and steal; yet certain it is, that all Sorts of Villanies, and even Levities and Debaucheries were then practis'd in the Town, as openly as ever, I will not say quite as frequently, because the Numbers of People were many ways lessen'd.

But the City it self began now to be visited too, I mean within the Walls; but the Number of People there were indeed extreamly lessen'd by so great a Multitude having been gone into the Country; and even all this Month of *July* they continu'd to flee, tho' not in such Multitudes as formerly. In *August* indeed, they fled in such a manner, that I began to think, there would be really none but Magistrates and Servants left in the City.

As they fled now out of the City, so I should observe, that the Court removed early, (*viz.*) in the Month of *June,* and went to *Oxford,* where it pleas'd God to preserve them; and the Distemper did not, *as I heard of,* so much as touch them; for which I cannot say, that I ever saw they shew'd any great Token of Thankfulness, and hardly any thing of Reformation, tho' they did not want being told that their crying Vices might, without Breach of Charity, be said to have gone far, in bringing that terrible Judgment upon the whole Nation.

The Face of *London* was now indeed strangely

alter'd, I mean the whole Mass of Buildings, City, Liberties, Suburbs, *Westminster, Southwark,* and altogether; for as to the particular Part called the City, or within the Walls, that was not yet much infected; but in the whole, the Face of Things, I say, was much alter'd; Sorrow and Sadness sat upon every Face; and tho' some Part were not yet over-whelm'd, yet all look'd deeply concern'd; and as we saw it apparently coming on, so every one look'd on himself, and his Family, as in the utmost Danger: were it possible to represent those Times exactly to those that did not see them, and give the Reader due Ideas of the Horror that every where presented it self, it must make just Impressions upon their Minds, and fill them with Surprize. *London* might well be said to be all in Tears; the Mourners did not go about the Streets[17] indeed, for no Body put on black, or made a formal Dress of Mourning for their nearest Friends; but the Voice of Mourning was truly heard in the Streets; the shriecks of Women and Children at the Windows, and Doors of their Houses, where their dearest Relations were, perhaps dying, or just dead, were so frequent to be heard, as we passed the Streets, that it was enough to pierce the stoutest Heart in the World, to hear them. Tears and Lamentations were seen almost in every House, especially in the first Part of the Visitation; for towards the latter End, Mens Hearts were hardned, and Death was so always before their Eyes, that they did not so much concern themselves for the Loss of their Friends, expecting, that themselves should be summoned the next Hour.

Business led me out sometimes to the other End of the Town, even when the Sickness was chiefly there; and as the thing was new to me, as well as to every Body else, it was a most surprising thing, to see those Streets, which were usually so thronged, now grown desolate, and so few People to be seen in them, that if I had been a Stranger, and at a Loss for my Way, I might sometimes have gone the Length of a whole Street, I mean of the by-Streets, and see no Body to direct me, except Watchmen, set at the Doors of such Houses as were shut up; of which I shall speak presently.

One Day, being at that Part of the Town, on some special Business, Curiosity led me to observe things more than usually; and indeed I walk'd a great Way where I had no Business; I went up *Holbourn,* and there the Street was full of People; but they walk'd

17. **Mourners . . . Streets:** See Eccles. 12:5.

in the middle of the great Street, neither on one Side or other, because, as I suppose, they would not mingle with any Body that came out of Houses, or meet with Smells and Scents from Houses that might be infected.

The Inns-of-Court[18] were all shut up; nor were very many of the Lawyers in the Temple, or *Lincolns-Inn*, or *Greyes-Inn*, to be seen there. Every Body was at peace, there was no Occasion for Lawyers; besides, it being in the Time of the Vacation too, they were generally gone into the Country. Whole Rows of Houses in some Places, were shut close up; the Inhabitants all fled, and only a Watchman or two left.

When I speak of Rows of Houses being shut up, I do not mean shut up by the Magistrates; but that great Numbers of Persons followed the Court, by the Necessity of their Employments, and other Dependencies: and as others retir'd, really frighted with the Distemper, it was a mere desolating of some of the Streets: But the Fright was not yet near so great in the City, abstractly so called; and particularly because, tho' they were at first in a most inexpressible Consternation, yet as I have observ'd, that the Distemper intermitted often at first; so they were as it were, allarm'd, and unallarm'd again, and this several times, till it began to be familiar to them; and that even, when it appear'd violent, yet seeing it did not presently spread into the City, or the *East* and *South* Parts, the People began to take Courage, and to be, as I may say, a little hardned: It is true, a vast many People fled, as I have observ'd, yet they were chiefly from the *West* End of the Town; and from that we call the Heart of the City, that is to say, among the wealthiest of the People; and such People as were unincumbred with Trades and Business: But of the rest, the Generality stay'd, and seem'd to abide the worst: So that in the Place we call the Liberties, and in the Suburbs, in *Southwark*, and in the *East* Part, such as *Wapping*, *Ratclif*, *Stepney*, *Rotherhith*, and the like, the People generally stay'd, except here and there a few wealthy Families, who, as above, did not depend upon their Business.

It must not be forgot here, that the City and Suburbs were prodigiously full of People, at the time of this Visitation, I mean, at the time that it began; for tho' I have liv'd to see a farther Encrease, and

mighty Throngs of People settling in *London*, more than ever, yet we had always a Notion, that the Numbers of People, which the Wars being over, the Armies disbanded, and the Royal Family and the Monarchy being restor'd, had flock'd to *London*, to settle into Business; or to depend upon, and attend the Court for Rewards of Services, Preferments, *and the like*, was such, that the Town was computed to have in it above a hundred thousand people more than ever it held before; nay, some took upon them to say, it had twice as many, because all the ruin'd Families of the royal Party, flock'd hither: All the old Soldiers set up Trades here, and abundance of Families settled here; again, the Court brought with them a great Flux of Pride, and new Fashions; All People were grown gay and luxurious; and the Joy of the Restoration had brought a vast many families to *London*.

I often thought, that as *Jerusalem* was besieg'd[19] by the *Romans*, when the *Jews* were assembled together, to celebrate the Passover, by which means, an incredible Number of People were surpriz'd there, who would otherwise have been in other Countries: So the Plague entred *London*, when an incredible Increase of People had happened occasionally, by the particular Circumstances above-nam'd: As this Conflux of the People, to a youthful and gay Court, made a great Trade in the City, especially in every thing that belong'd to Fashion and Finery; So it drew by Consequence, a great Number of Work-men, Manufacturers, and the like, being mostly poor People, who depended upon their Labour. And I remember in particular, that in a Representation to my Lord Mayor, of the Condition of the Poor, it was estimated, that, there were no less than an Hundred Thousand Ribband Weavers in and about the City; the chiefest Number of whom, lived then in the Parishes of *Shoreditch*, *Stepney*, *White-chapel*, and *Bishopsgate*; that namely, about *Spittle-fields*;[20] that is to say, as *Spittle-fields* was then; for it was not so large as now, by one fifth Part.

By this however, the Number of People in the whole may be judg'd of; and indeed, I often wondred, that after the prodigious Numbers of People that went away at first, there was yet so great a Multitude left, as it appear'd there was.

But I must go back again to the Beginning of this Surprizing Time, while the Fears of the People were

---

18. Inns-of-Court: the buildings occupied by the four law societies—Gray's Inn, the Inner Temple, the Middle Temple, and Lincoln's Inn.

19. besieg'd: in 66–65 B.C. **20. Spittle-fields:** Spitalfields, then a relatively open area east of Whitechapel.

young, they were encreas'd strangely by several odd Accidents, which put altogether, it was realy a wonder the whole Body of the People did not rise as one Man, and abandon their Dwellings, leaving the Place as a Space of Ground designed by Heaven for an Akeldama,[21] doom'd to be destroy'd from the Face of the Earth; and that all that would be found in it, would perish with it. I shall Name but a few of these Things; but sure they were so many, and so many Wizards and cunning People propagating them, that I have often wonder'd there was any, (Women especially,) left behind.

In the first Place, a blazing Star or Comet appear'd for several Months before the Plague, as there did the Year after another, a little before the Fire; the old Women, and the Phlegmatic Hypocondriac Part of the other Sex, who I could almost call old Women too, remark'd (especially afterward tho' not, till both those Judgments were over,) that those two Comets pass'd directly over the City, and that so very near the Houses, that it was plain, they imported something peculiar to the City alone; that the Comet before the Pestilence, was of a faint, dull, languid Colour, and its Motion very heavy, solemn and slow: But that the Comet before the Fire, was bright and sparkling, or as others said, flaming, and its Motion swift and furious; and that accordingly, One foretold a heavy Judgment, slow but severe, terrible and frightful, as was the Plague; But the other foretold a Stroak, sudden, swift, and fiery as the Conflagration; nay, so particular some People were, that as they look'd upon that Comet preceding the Fire, they fancied that they not only saw it pass swiftly and fiercely, and cou'd perceive the Motion with their Eye, but even they heard it; that it made a rushing mighty Noise, fierce and terrible, tho' at a distance, and but just perceivable.

I saw both these Stars; and I must confess, had so much of the common Notion of such Things in my Head, that I was apt to look upon them, as the Fore-runners and Warnings of Gods Judgments; and especially when after the Plague had followed the first, I yet saw another of the like kind; I could not but say, God had not yet sufficiently scourg'd the City.

But I cou'd not at the same Time carry these Things to the height that others did, knowing too, that natural Causes are assign'd by the Astronomers for such Things; and that their Motions, and even their Revolutions are calculated, or pretended to be calculated; so that they cannot be so perfectly call'd the Fore-runners or Fore-tellers, much less the procurers of such Events, as Pestilence, War, Fire, and the like.

But let my Thoughts, and the Thoughts of the Philosophers be, or have been what they will, these Things had a more then ordinary Influence upon the Minds of the common People, and they had almost universal melancholly Apprehensions of some dreadful Calamity and Judgment coming upon the City; and this principally from the Sight of this Comet, and the little Allarm that was given in December, by two People dying at St. Giles's, as above.

The Apprehensions of the People, were likewise strangely encreas'd by the Error of the Times; in which, I think, the People, from what Principle I cannot imagine, were more adicted to Prophesies, and Astrological Conjurations, Dreams, and old Wives Tales, than ever they were before or since: Whether this unhappy Temper was originally raised by the Follies of some People who got Money by it; that is to say, by printing Predictions, and Prognostications I know not; but certain it is, Books frighted them terribly; such as Lilly's Almanack, Gadbury's Astrological Predictions; Poor Robin's Almanack and the like; also several pretended religious Books; one entituled, Come out of her my People, least you be partaker of her Plagues;[22] another call'd, Fair Warning; another, Britains Remembrancer, and many such; all, or most Part of which, foretold directly or covertly the Ruin of the City: Nay, some were so Enthusiastically bold, as to run about the Streets, with their Oral Predictions, pretending they were sent to preach to the City; and One in particular, who, like Jonah to Nenevah,[23] cry'd in the Streets, yet forty Days, and LONDON shall be destroy'd. I will not be positive, whether he said yet forty Days, or yet a few Days. Another run about Naked, except a pair of Drawers about his Waste, crying Day and Night; like a man that Josephus[24] mentions, who cry'd, woe to Jerusalem! a little before the Destruction of that City: So this poor naked Creature[25] cry'd, O! the Great, and the Dreadful God! and said no more, but repeated those Words continually, with a Voice and Countenance full of horror, a swift Pace, and no

21. **Akeldama:** Aceldama, the field of blood (Acts 1:19).

22. **Come . . . Plagues:** See Rev. 18:4. 23. **like . . . Nenevah:** See Jon. 3:4. 24. **Josephus:** Flavius Josephus (A.D. 37–c. 100), Jewish historian, writer of a famous account of the Roman conquest of Jerusalem. 25. **this . . . Creature:** identified in another passage as Solomon Eagle, a Quaker.

Body cou'd ever find him to stop, or rest, or take any Sustenance, at least, that ever I cou'd hear of. I met this poor Creature several Times in the Streets, and would have spoke to him, but he would not enter into Speech with me, or any one else; but held on his dismal Cries continually.

These Things terrified the People to the last Degree; and especially when two or three Times, as I have mentioned already, they found one or two in the Bills, dead of the Plague at St. *Giles*.

. . .

I went all the first Part of the Time freely about the Streets, tho' not so freely as to run my self into apparent Danger, except when they dug the great Pit in the Church-Yard of our Parish of *Algate;* a terrible Pit it was, and I could not resist my Curiosity to go and see it; as near as I may judge, it was about 40 Foot in Length, and about 15 or 16 Foot broad; and at the Time I first looked at it, about nine Foot deep; but it was said, they dug it near 20 Foot deep afterwards, in one Part of it, till they could go no deeper for the Water: for they had it seems, dug several large Pits before this, for tho' the Plague was long a-coming to our Parish, yet when it did come, there was no Parish in or about *London*, where it raged with such Violence as in the two Parishes of *Algate* and *White-Chapel*.

I say they had dug several Pits in another Ground, when the Distemper began to spread in our Parish, and especially when the Dead-Carts began to go about, which was not in our Parish, till the beginning of *August*. Into these Pits they had put perhaps 50 or 60 Bodies each, then they made larger Holes, wherein they buried all that the Cart brought in a Week, which by the middle, to the End of *August*, came to, from 200 to 400 a Week; and they could not well dig them larger, because of the Order of the Magistrates, confining them to leave no Bodies within six Foot of the Surface; and the Water coming on, at about 17 or 18 Foot, they could not well, I say, put more in one Pit; but now at the Beginning of *September*, the Plague raging in a dreadful Manner, and the Number of Burials in our Parish increasing to more than was ever buried in any Parish about *London*, of no larger Extent, they ordered this dreadful Gulph to be dug; for such it was rather than a Pit.

They had supposed this Pit would have supply'd them for a Month or more, when they dug it, and some blam'd the Church Wardens for suffering such a frightful Thing, telling them they were making Preparations to bury the whole Parish, and the like; but Time made it appear, the Church-Wardens knew the Condition of the Parish better than they did; for the Pit being finished the 4th of *September*, I think, they began to bury in it the 6th, and by the 20th, which was just two Weeks, they had thrown into it 1114 Bodies, when they were obliged to fill it up, the Bodies being then come to lie within six Foot of the Surface: I doubt not but there may be some antient Persons alive in the Parish, who can justify the Fact of this, and are able to shew even in what Part of the Church-Yard, the Pit lay better than I can; the Mark of it also was many Years to be seen in the Church-Yard on the Surface lying in Length, Parallel with the Passage which goes by the West Wall of the Church Yard, out of *Houndsditch*, and turns East again into *White-Chappel*, coming out near the Three Nuns Inn.

It was about the 10th of *September*, that my Curiosity led, or rather drove me to go and see this Pit again, when there had been near 400 People buried in it; and I was not content to see it in the Day-time, as I had done before; for then there would have been nothing to have been seen but the loose Earth; for all the Bodies that were thrown in, were immediately covered with Earth, by those they call'd the Buryers, which at other Times were call'd Bearers; but I resolv'd to go in the Night and see some of them thrown in.

There was a strict Order to prevent People coming to those Pits, and that was only to prevent Infection: But after some Time, that Order was more necessary, for People that were Infected and near their End, and dilirious also, would run to those Pits wrapt in Blankets, or Rugs, and throw themselves in, and as they said, bury themselves: I cannot say, that the Officers suffered any willingly to lie there; but I have heard, that in a great Pit in *Finsbury*, in the Parish of *Cripplegate*, it lying open then to the Fields; for it was not then wall'd about, [some] came and threw themselves in, and expired there, before they threw any Earth upon them; and that when they came to bury others, and found them there, they were quite dead, tho' not cold.

This may serve a little to describe the dreadful Condition of that Day, tho' it is impossible to say any Thing that is able to give a true Idea of it to those who did not see it, other than this; that it was indeed *very, very, very* dreadful, and such as no Tongue can express.

I got Admittance into the Church-Yard by being

acquainted with the Sexton, who attended, who, tho' he did not refuse me at all, yet earnestly perswaded me not to go; telling me very seriously, for he was a good religious and sensible Man, that it was indeed, their Business and Duty to venture, and to run all Hazards; and that in it they might hope to be preserv'd; but that I had no apparent Call to it, but my own Curiosity, which he said, he believ'd I would not pretend, was sufficient to justify my running that Hazard. I told him I had been press'd in my Mind to go, and that perhaps it might be an Instructing Sight, that might not be without its Uses. Nay, says the good Man, if you will venture upon that Score, 'Name of God go in; for depend upon it, 'twill be a Sermon to you, it may be, the best that ever you heard in your Life. 'Tis a speaking Sight, says he, and has a Voice with it, and a loud one, to call us all to Repentance; and with that he opened the Door and said, Go, if you will.

His Discourse had shock'd my Resolution a little, and I stood wavering for a good while; but just at that Interval I saw two Links[26] come over from the End of the *Minories*,[27] and heard the Bellman,[28] and then appear'd a Dead-Cart, *as they call'd it*, coming over the Streets so I could no longer resist my desire of seeing it, and went in: There was no Body, as I could perceive at first, in the Church-Yard, or going into it, but the Buryers, and the Fellow that drove the Cart, or rather led the Horse and Cart, but when they came up, to the Pit, they saw a Man go to and again, mufled up in a brown Cloak, and making Motions with his Hands, under his Cloak, as if he was in a great Agony; and the Buryers immediately gathered about him, supposing he was one of those poor dilirious, or desperate Creatures, that used to pretend, as I have said, to bury themselves; he said nothing as he walk'd about, but two or three times groaned very deeply, and loud, and sighed as he would break his Heart.

When the Buryers came up to him they soon found he was neither a Person infected and desperate, as I have observed above, or a Person distempered in Mind, but one oppress'd with a dreadful Weight of Grief indeed, having his Wife and several of his Children, all in the Cart, that was just come in with him, and he followed in an Agony and excess of Sorrow. He mourned heartily, as it was easy to see, but with a kind of Masculine Grief, that could not give it self Vent by Tears; and calmly desiring the Buriers to let him alone, said he would only see the Bodies thrown in, and go away, so they left importuning him; but no sooner was the Cart turned round, and the Bodies shot into the Pit promiscuously, which was a Surprize to him, for he at least expected they would have been decently laid in, tho' indeed he was afterwards convinced that was impracticable; I say, no sooner did he see the Sight, but he cry'd out aloud unable to contain himself; I could not hear what he said, but he went backward two or three Steps, and fell down in a Swoon: the Buryers ran to him and took him up, and in a little While he came to himself, and they led him away to the *Pye-Tavern* over-against the End of *Houndsditch*, where, it seems, the Man was known, and where they took care of him. He look'd into the Pit again, as he went away, but the Buryers had covered the Bodies so immediately with throwing in Earth, that tho' there was Light enough, for there were Lanthorns and Candles in them, plac'd all Night round the Sides of the Pit, upon the Heaps of Earth, seven or eight, or perhaps more, yet nothing could be seen.

This was a mournful Scene indeed, and affected me almost as much as the rest; but the other was awful, and full of Terror, the Cart had in it sixteen or seventeen Bodies, some were wrapt up in Linen Sheets, some in Rugs, some little other than naked, or so loose, that what Covering they had, fell from them, in the shooting out of the Cart, and they fell quite naked among the rest; but the Matter was not much to them, or the Indecency much to any one else, seeing they were all dead, and were to be huddled together into the common Grave of Mankind, as we may call it, for here was no Difference made, but Poor and Rich went together; there was no other way of Burials, neither was it possible there should, for Coffins were not to be had for the prodigious Numbers that fell in such a Calamity as this.

. . .

It was now the Beginning of *August*, and the Plague grew very violent and terrible in the Place where I liv'd, and Dr. *Heath*[29] coming to visit me, and finding

---

26. **Links:** torches. 27. **Minories:** a street running northward from the Tower of London into Whitechapel. 28. **Bellman:** the man who went ahead of the dead-cart, ringing a bell and crying "Bring out your dead."

29. **Dr. Heath:** a friendly physician, mentioned several times in the *Journal* and perhaps modeled after Dr. Nathaniel Hodges, whose *Loimologia* (1667) was one of Defoe's sources for medical information about the Plague.

that I ventured so often out in the Streets, earnestly perswaded me to lock my self up and my Family,[30] and not to suffer any of us to go out of Doors; to keep all our Windows fast, Shutters and Curtains close, and never to open them; but first, to make a very strong Smoke in the Room, where the Window, or Door was to be opened, with Rozen and Pitch, Brimstone, or Gunpowder, and the like; and we did this for some Time; But as I had not laid in a Store of Provision for such a retreat, it was impossible that we could keep within Doors entirely; however, I attempted, tho' it was so very late, to do something towards it; and first, as I had Convenience both for Brewing and Baking, I went and bought two Sacks of Meal, and for several Weeks, having an Oven, we baked all our own Bread; also I bought Malt, and brew'd as much Beer as all the Casks I had would hold, and which seem'd enough to serve my House for five or six Weeks; also I laid in a Quantity of Salt-butter and *Cheshire* Cheese; but I had no Flesh-meat, and the Plague raged so violently among the Butchers, and Slaughter-Houses, on the other Side of our Street, where they are known to dwell in great Numbers, that it was not advisable, so much as to go over the Street among them.

And here I must observe again, that this Necessity of going out of our Houses to buy Provisions, was in a great Measure the Ruin of the whole City, for the People catch'd the Distemper, on those Occasions, one of another, and even the Provisions themselves were often tainted, at least I have great Reason to believe so; and therefore I cannot say with Satisfaction what I know is repeated with great Assurance, that the Market People, and such as brought Provisions, to Town, were never infected: I am certain, the Butchers of *White-Chapel* where the greatest Part of the Flesh-meat was killed, were dreadfully visited, and that at last to such a Degree, that few of their Shops were kept open, and those that remain'd of them, kill'd their Meat at *Mile-End,*[31] and that way, and brought it to Market upon Horses.

However, the poor People cou'd not lay up Provisions, and there was a necessity, that they must go to Market to buy, and others to send Servants or their Children; and as this was a Necessity which renew'd it self daily; it brought abundance of unsound People to the Markets, and a great many that went thither Sound, brought Death Home with them.

It is true, People us'd all possible Precaution, when any one bought a Joint of Meat in the Market, they would not take it of the Butchers Hand, but take it off the Hooks themselves. On the other Hand, the Butcher would not touch the Money, but have it put into a Pot full of Vinegar which he kept for that purpose. The Buyer carry'd always small Money to make up any odd Sum, that they might take no Change. They carry'd Bottles for Scents, and Perfumes in their Hands, and all the Means that could be us'd, were us'd: But then the Poor cou'd not do even these things, and they went at all Hazards.

Innumerable dismal Stories we heard every Day on this very Account: Sometimes a Man or Woman dropt down Dead in the very Markets; for many People that had the Plague upon them, knew nothing of it; till the inward Gangreen had affected their Vitals and they dy'd in a few Moments; this caus'd, that many died frequently in that Manner in the Streets suddainly, without any warning: Others perhaps had Time to go to the next Bulk or Stall;[32] or to any Door, Porch, and just sit down and die, as I have said before.

These Objects were so frequent in the Streets, that when the Plague came to be very raging, on one Side, there was scarce any passing by the Streets, but that several dead Bodies would be lying here and there upon the Ground; on the other hand it is observable, that tho' at first, the People would stop as they went along, and call to the Neighbours to come out on such an Occasion; yet, afterward, no Notice was taken of them; but that, if at any Time we found a Corps lying, go cross the Way, and not come near it; or if in a narrow Lane or Passage, go back again, and seek some other Way to go on the Business we were upon; and in those Cases, the Corps was always left, till the Officers had notice, to come and take them away; or till Night, when the Bearers attending the Dead-Cart would take them up, and carry them away: Nor did those undaunted Creatures, who performed these Offices, fail to search their Pockets, and sometimes strip off their Cloths, if they were well drest, as sometimes they were, and carry off what they could get.

But to return to the Markets; the Butchers took that Care, that if any Person dy'd in the Market, they

---

30. Family: Besides himself, it consisted of an elderly house-keeper, a maidservant, and two apprentices. **31. Mile-End:** a district on the eastern outskirts of London.

32. Bulk or Stall: bench or booth in front of a shop.

had the Officers always at Hand, to take them up upon Hand-barrows, and carry them to the next Church-Yard; and this was so frequent that such were not entred in the weekly Bill, found Dead in the Streets or Fields, as is the Case now; but they went into the general Articles of the great Distemper.

But now the Fury of the Distemper encreased to such a Degree, that even the Markets were but very thinly furnished with Provisions, or frequented with Buyers, compair'd to what they were before; and the Lord-Mayor caused the Country-People who brought Provisions, to be stop'd in the Streets leading into the Town, and to sit down there with their Goods, where they sold what they brought, and went immediately away; and this Encourag'd the Country People greatly to do so, for they sold their Provisions at the very Entrances into the Town, and even in the Fields; as particularly in the Fields beyond *White-Chappel*, in *Spittle fields*. Note, *Those Streets now called* Spittle-Fields, *were then indeed open Fields:* Also in St. *George's-fields* in *Southwark*, in *Bun-Hill* Fields, and in a great Field, call'd *Wood's-Close* near *Islington;* thither the Lord-Mayor, Aldermen, and Magistrates, sent their Officers and Servants to buy for their Families, themselves keeping within Doors as much as possible; and the like did many other People; and after this Method was taken, the Country People came with great chearfulness, and brought Provisions of all Sorts, and very seldom got any harm; which I suppose, added also to that Report of their being Miraculously preserv'd.

As for my little Family, having thus as I have said, laid in a Store of Bread, Butter, Cheese, and Beer, I took my Friend and Physician's Advice, and lock'd my self up, and my Family, and resolv'd to suffer the hardship of Living a few Months without Flesh-Meat, rather than to purchase it at the hazard of our Lives.

But tho' I confin'd my Family, I could not prevail upon my unsatisfy'd Curiosity to stay within entirely my self; and tho' I generally came frighted and terrified Home, yet I cou'd not restrain; only that indeed, I did not do it so frequently as at first.

I had some little Obligations indeed upon me, to go to my Brothers House, which was in *Coleman's-street* Parish, and which he had left to my Care, and I went at first every Day, but afterwards only once, or twice a Week.

In these Walks I had many dismal Scenes before my Eyes, as particularly of Persons falling dead in the Streets, terrible Shrieks and Skreekings of Women,

who in their Agonies would throw open their Chamber Windows, and cry out in a dismal Surprising Manner; it is impossible to describe the Variety of Postures, in which the Passions of the Poor People would Express themselves.

Passing thro' *Token-House-Yard*, in *Lothbury*, of a sudden a Casement violently opened just over my Head, and a Woman gave three frightful Skreetches, and then cry'd *Oh! Death, Death, Death!* in a most inimitable Tone, and which struck me with Horror and a Chilness, in my very Blood. There was no Body to be seen in the whole Street, neither did any other Window open; for People had no Curiosity now in any Case; nor could any Body help one another; so I went on to pass into *Bell-Alley*.

Just in *Bell-Alley*, on the right Hand of the Passage, there was a more terrible Cry than that, tho' it was not so directed out at the Window, but the whole Family was in a terrible Fright, and I could hear Women and Children run skreaming about the Rooms like distracted, when a Garret Window opened, and some body from a Window on the other Side the Alley, call'd and ask'd, *What is the Matter?* upon which, from the first Window it was answered, *O Lord, my Old Master has hang'd himself!* The other ask'd again, *Is he quite dead?* and the first answer'd, *Ay, ay, quite dead; quite dead and cold!* This Person was a Merchant, and a Deputy Alderman and very rich. I care not to mention the Name, tho' I knew his Name too, but that would be an Hardship to the Family, which is now flourishing again.

But, this is but one; it is scarce credible what dreadful Cases happened in particular Families every Day; People in the Rage of the Distemper, or in the Torment of their Swellings, which was indeed intollerable, running out of their own Government, raving and distracted, and oftentimes laying violent Hands upon themselves, throwing themselves out at their Windows, shooting themselves, *&c.* Mothers murthering their own Children, in their Lunacy, some dying of meer Grief as a Passion, some of meer Fright and Surprize, without any Infection at all; others frighted into Idiotism, and foolish Distractions, some into dispair and Lunacy; others into mellancholy Madness.

The Pain of the Swelling was in particular very violent, and to some intollerable; the Physicians and Surgeons may be said to have tortured many poor Creatures, even to Death. The Swellings in some grew hard, and they apply'd violent drawing Plasters, or

Pultices, to break them; and if these did not do, they cut and scarified them in a terrible Manner: In some, those Swellings were made hard, partly by the Force of the Distemper, and partly by their being too violently drawn, and were so hard, that no Instrument could cut them, and then they burnt them with Causticks, so that many died raving mad with the Torment; and some in the very Operation. In these Distresses, some for want of Help to hold them down in their Beds, or to look to them, laid Hands upon themselves, as above. Some broke out into the Streets, perhaps naked, and would run directly down to the River, if they were not stopt by the Watchmen, or other Officers, and plunge themselves into the Water, wherever they found it.

It often pierc'd my very Soul to hear the Groans and Crys of those who were thus tormented, but of the Two, this was counted the most promising Particular in the whole Infection; for, if these Swellings could be brought to a Head, and to break and run, or as the Surgeons call it, to digest, the Patient generally recover'd; whereas those, who like the Gentlewoman's Daughter,[33] were struck with Death at the Beginning, and had the Tokens[34] come out upon them, often went about indifferent easy, till a little before they died, and some till the Moment they dropt down, as in Appoplexies and Epelepsies, is often the case; such would be taken suddenly very sick, and would run to a Bench or Bulk, or any convenient Place that offer'd it self, or to their own Houses, if possible, *as I mentioned before*, and there sit down, grow faint and die. This kind of dying was much the same, as it was with those who die of common Mortifications, who die swooning, and as it were, go away in a Dream; such as died thus, had very little Notice of their being infected at all, till the Gangreen was spread thro' their whole Body; nor could Physicians themselves, know certainly how it was with them, till they opened[35] their Breasts, or other Parts of their Body, and saw the Tokens.

We had at this Time a great many frightful Stories told us of Nurses and Watchmen, who looked after the dying People, *that is to say*, hir'd Nurses, who attended infected People, using them barbarously, starving them, or by other wicked Means, hastening their End, *that is to say*, murthering of them: And Watchmen being set to guard Houses that were shut up, when there has been but one person left, and perhaps, that one lying sick, that they have broke in and murthered that Body, and immediately thrown them out into the Dead-Cart! and so they have gone scarce cold to the Grave.

I cannot say, but that some such Murthers were committed, and I think two were sent to Prison for it, but died before they could be try'd; and I have heard that three others, at several Times, were excused for Murthers of that kind; but I must say I believe nothing of its being so common a Crime, as some have since been pleas'd to say, nor did it seem to be so rational, where the People were brought so low as not to be able to help themselves, for such seldom recovered, and there was no Temptation to commit a Murder, at least, none equal to the Fact where they were sure Persons would die in so short a Time; and could not live.

That there were a great many Robberies and wicked Practises committed even in this dreadful Time I do not deny; the Power of Avarice was so strong in some, that they would run any Hazard to steal and to plunder, and particularly in Houses where all the Families, or Inhabitants have been dead, and carried out, they would break in at all Hazards, and without Regard to the Danger of Infection, take even the Cloths off, of the dead Bodies, and the Bed-cloaths from others where they lay dead.

This, *I suppose*, must be the Case of a Family in *Houndsditch*, where a Man and his Daughter, *the rest of the Family being, as I suppose, carried away before by the Dead-Cart*, were found stark naked, one in one Chamber, and one in another, lying Dead on the Floor; and the Cloths of the Beds, from whence, 'tis supposed they were roll'd off by Thieves, stoln, and carried quite away.

It is indeed to be observ'd, that the Women were in all this Calamity, the most rash, fearless, and desperate Creatures; and as there were vast Numbers that went about as Nurses, to tend those that were sick, they committed a great many petty Thieveries in the Houses where they were employed; and some of them were publickly whipt for it, when perhaps, they ought rather to have been hanged for Examples; for Numbers of Houses were robbed on these Occasions, till at length, the Parish Officers were sent to recommend Nurses to the Sick, and always took an Account who it was they sent, so as that they might call them to

33. the Gentlewoman's Daughter: a girl who died of the plague less than two hours after the tokens of it were discovered on her body. **34. Tokens:** spots of various color and size appearing anywhere on the body but most often on the breast, back, or thighs. **35. opened:** uncovered.

account, if the House had been abused where they were placed.

But these Robberies extended chiefly to Wearing-Cloths, Linen, and what Rings, or Money they could come at, when the Person dyed who was under their Care, but not to a general Plunder of the Houses; and I could give an Account of one of these Nurses, who several Years after, being on her Death-bed, confest with the utmost Horror, the Robberies she had committed at the Time of her being a Nurse, and by which she had enriched her self to a great Degree: But as for murthers, I do not find that there was ever any Proof of the Facts, in the manner, as it has been reported, *except as above*.

They did tell me indeed of a Nurse in one place, that laid a wet Cloth upon the Face of a dying Patient, who she tended, and so put an End to his Life, who was Just expiring before: And another that smother'd a young Woman she was looking to, when she was in a fainting fit, and would have come to her self: Some that kill'd them by giving them one Thing, some another, and some starved them by giving them nothing at all: But these Stories had two Marks of Suspicion that always attended them, which caused me always to slight them, and to look on them as meer Stories, that People continually frighted one another with. (1.) That wherever it was that we heard it, they always placed the Scene at the farther End of the Town, opposite, or most remote from where you were to hear it: If you heard it in *White-Chapel*, it had happened at St. *Giles's*, or at *Westminster*, or *Holborn*, or that End of the Town; if you heard of it at that End of the Town, then it was done in *White-Chapel*, or the *Minories*, or about *Cripplegate* Parish: If you heard of it in the City, why, then it had happened in *Southwark;* and if you heard of it in *Southwark*, then it was done in the City, and the like.

In the next Place, of what Part soever you heard the Story, the Particulars were always the same, especially that of laying a wet double Clout[36] on a dying Man's Face, and that of smothering a young Gentlewoman; so that it was apparent, at least to my Judgment, that there was more of Tale than of Truth in those Things.

However, I cannot say, but it had some Effect upon the People, and particularly that, *as I said before*, they grew more cautious who they took into their Houses, and who they trusted their Lives with; and had them always recommended, if they could; and where they could not find such, for they were not very plenty, they applied to the Parish Officers.

But here again, the Misery of that Time lay upon the Poor, who being infected, had neither Food or Physick; neither Physician or Appothecary to assist them, or Nurse to attend them: Many of those died calling for help, and even for Sustenance out at their Windows, in a most miserable and deplorable manner; but it must be added, that when ever the Cases of such Persons or Families, were represented to my Lord-Mayor, they always were reliev'd.

It is true, in some Houses where the People were not very poor; yet, where they had sent perhaps their Wives and Children away; and if they had any Servants, they had been dismist; *I say it is true, that* to save the Expences, many such as these shut themselves in, and not having Help, dy'd alone.

A Neighbour and Acquaintance of mine, having some Money owing to him from a Shopkeeper in *White-Cross street*, or there abouts, sent his Apprentice, a youth about 18 Years of Age, to endeavour to get the Money: He came to the Door, and finding it shut, knockt pretty hard, and as he thought, heard some Body answer within, but was not sure, So he waited, and after some stay knockt again, and then a third Time, when he heard some Body coming down Stairs.

At length the Man of the House came to the Door; he had on his Breeches or Drawers, and a yellow Flannel Wastcoat; no Stockings, a pair of Slipt-Shoes,[37] a white Cap on his head; and as the young Man said, Death in his Face.

When he open'd the Door, says he, *what do you disturb me thus for?* the Boy, tho' a little surpriz'd, reply'd, *I come from such a one, and my Master sent me for the Money, which he says you know of: Very well Child*, returns the living Ghost, *call as you go by at* Cripplegate *Church, and bid them ring the Bell*, and with those Words, shut the Door again, and went up again and Dy'd, The same Day; nay, perhaps the same Hour. This, the young Man told me himself, and I have Reason to believe it. This was while the Plague was not come to a Height: I think it was in *June;* Towards the latter End of the Month, it must be before the Dead Carts came about, and while they used the Ceremony of Ringing the Bell for the Dead, which was over for certain, in that Parish at least, before the Month of *July;* for by the 25th of *July*, there died 550

---

36. **Clout:** cloth.

37. **Slipt-Shoes:** slippers.

and upward in a Week, and then they cou'd no more bury in Form,[38] Rich or Poor.

. . .

I could dwell a great while upon the Calamities of this dreadful time, and go on to describe the Objects that appear'd among us every Day, the dreadful Extravagancies which the Distraction of sick People drove them into; how the Streets began now to be fuller of frightful Objects, and Families to be made even a Terror to themselves: But after I have told you, as I have above, that One Man being tyed in his Bed, and finding no other Way to deliver himself, set the Bed on fire with his Candle, which unhappily stood within his reach, and Burnt himself in his Bed. And how another, by the insufferable Torment he bore, daunced and sung naked in the Streets, not knowing one Extasie from another, I say, after I have mention'd these Things, What can be added more? What can be said to represent the Misery of these Times, more lively to the Reader, or to give him a more perfect Idea of a complicated Distress?

I must acknowledge that this time was Terrible, that I was sometimes at the End of all my Resolutions, and that I had not the Courage that I had at the Beginning. As the Extremity brought other People abroad, it drove me Home, and except, having made my Voyage down to *Blackwall* and *Greenwich*, as I have related, which was an Excursion, I kept afterwards very much within Doors, as I had for about a Fortnight before; I have said already, that I repented several times that I had ventur'd to stay in Town, and had not gone away with my Brother, and his Family, but it was too late for that now; and after I had retreated and stay'd within Doors a good while, before my Impatience led me Abroad, then they call'd me, as I have said, to an ugly and dangerous Office,[39] which brought me out again; but as that was expir'd, while the hight of the Distemper lasted, I retir'd again, and continued close ten or twelve Days more. During which many dismal Spectacles represented themselves in my View, out of my own Windows, and in our own Street, as that particularly from *Harrow-Alley*, of the poor outrageous Creature which danced and sung in his Agony, and many others there were: Scarse a Day or Night pass'd over, but some

dismal Thing or other happened at the End of that *Harrow-Alley*, which was a Place full of poor People, most of them belonging to the Butchers, or to Employments depending upon the Butchery.

Sometimes Heaps and Throngs of People would burst out of that Alley, most of them Women, making a dreadful Clamour, mixt or Compounded of Skreetches, Cryings and Calling one another, that we could not conceive what to make of it; almost all the dead Part of the Night the dead Cart stood at the End of that Alley, for if it went in it could not well turn again, and could go in but a little Way. There, I say, it stood to receive dead Bodys, and as the Church-Yard was but a little Way off, if it went away full it would soon be back again: It is impossible to describe the most horrible Cries and Noise the poor People would make at their bringing the dead Bodies of their Children and Friends out to the Cart, and by the Number one would have thought, there had been none left behind, or that there were People enough for a small City liveing in those Places: Several times they cryed Murther, sometimes Fire; but it was esie to perceive it was all Distraction, and the Complaints of Distress'd and distemper'd People.

I believe it was every where thus at that time, for the Plague rag'd for six or seven Weeks beyond all that I have express'd; and came even to such a height, that in the Extremity, they began to break into that excellent Order, of which I have spoken so much, in behalf of the Magistrates, namely, that no dead Bodies were seen in the Streets or Burials in the Day-time, for there was a Necessity, in this Extremity, to bear with its being otherwise, for a little while.

One thing I cannot omit here, and indeed I thought it was extraordinary, at least, it seemed a remarkable Hand of Divine Justice, (*viz.*) That all the Predictors, Astrologers, Fortune-tellers, and what they call'd cunning-Men, Conjurers, and the like; calculators of Nativities, and dreamers of Dreams, and such People, were gone and vanish'd, not one of them was to be found: I am, verily, perswaded that a great Number of them fell in the heat of the Calamity, having ventured to stay upon the Prospect of getting great Estates; and indeed their Gain was but too great for a time through the Madness and Folly of the People; but now they were silent, many of them went to their long Home, not able to foretel their own Fate, or to calculate their own Nativities; some have been critical[40]

38. **in Form:** decently. 39. **an ugly . . . Office:** The examiner of infected houses had the duty of deciding whether the surviving inmates should be shut up inside them.

40. **critical:** confident of their own accuracy.

enough to say, that every one of them dy'd; I dare not affirm that; but this I must own, that I never heard of one of them that ever appear'd after the Calamity was over.

But to return to my particular Observations, during this dreadful part of the Visitation; I am now come, as I have said, to the Month of *September*, which was the most dreadful of its kind, I believe, that ever *London* saw; for, by all the Accounts which I have seen of the preceding Visitations which have been in *London*, nothing has been like it; the Number in the Weekly Bill amounting to almost 40,000 from the 22d of *August*, to the 26th of *September*, being but five Weeks, the particulars of the Bills are as follows, (*viz.*)

From *August* the 22d to the 29th	7496
To the 7th of *September* ————	8252
To the 12th ———— ————	7690
To the 19th ———— ————	8297
To the 26th ———— ————	6460
	38195

This was a prodigious Number of itself, but if I should add the Reasons which I have to believe that this Account was deficient, and how deficient it was, you would with me, make no Scruple to believe that there died above ten Thousand a Week for all those Weeks, one Week with another, and a proportion for several Weeks both before and after: The Confusion among the People, especially within the City at that time, was inexpressible; the Terror was so great at last, that the Courage of the People appointed to carry away the Dead, began to fail them; nay, several of them died altho' they had the Distemper before, and were recover'd; and some of them drop'd down when they have been carrying the Bodies even at the Pitside, and just ready to throw them in; and this Confusion was greater in the City, because they had flatter'd themselves with Hopes of escaping: And thought the bitterness of Death was past: One Cart they told us, going up *Shoreditch*, was forsaken of the Drivers, or being left to one Man to drive, he died in the Street, and the Horses going on, overthrew the Cart, and left the Bodies, some thrown out here, some there, in a dismal manner; Another Cart was it seems found in the great Pit in *Finsbury* Fields, the Driver being Dead, or having been gone and abandon'd it, and the Horses running too near it, the Cart fell in and drew the Horses in also: It was

suggested that the Driver was thrown in with it, and that the Cart fell upon him, by Reason his Whip was seen to be in the Pit among the Bodies; but that, I suppose, cou'd not be certain.

In our Parish of *Aldgate*, the dead-Carts were several times, as I have heard, found standing at the Church-yard Gate, full of dead Bodies, but neither Bell man or Driver, or any one else with it; neither in these, or many other Cases, did they know what Bodies they had in their Cart, for sometimes they were let down with Ropes out of Balconies and out of Windows; and sometimes the Bearers brought them to the Cart, sometimes other People; nor, *as the Men themselves said*, did they trouble themselves to keep any Account of the Numbers.

.   .   .

I would be glad, if I could close the Account of this melancholy Year with some particular Examples historically; I mean of the Thankfulness to God our Preserver for our being delivered from this dreadful Calamity; certainly the Circumstances of the Deliverance, as well as the terrible Enemy we were delivered from, call'd upon the whole Nation for it; the Circumstances of the Deliverance were indeed very remarkable, as I have in part mention'd already, and particularly the dreadful Condition, which we were all in, when we were, to the Surprize of the whole Town, made joyful with the Hope of a Stop of the Infection.

Nothing, but the immediate Finger of God, nothing, but omnipotent Power could have done it; the Contagion despised all Medicine, Death rag'd in every Corner; and had it gone on as it did then, a few Weeks more would have clear'd the Town of all, and every thing that had a Soul: Men every where began to despair, every Heart fail'd them for Fear, People were made desperate thro' the Anguish of their Souls, and the Terrors of Death sat in the very Faces and Countenances of the People.

In that very Moment, when we might very well say, Vain was the Help of Man;[41] I say in that very Moment it pleased God, with a most agreeable Surprize, to cause the Fury of it to abate, even of it self, and the Malignity declining, as I have said, tho' infinite Numbers were sick, yet fewer died; and the very first Week's Bill decreased 1843, a vast Number indeed!

41. Vain . . . Man: See Ps. 60:11.

It is impossible to express the Change that appear'd in the very Countenances of the People, that *Thursday Morning*,[42] when the Weekly Bill came out; it might have been perceived in their Countenances, that a secret Surprize and Smile of Joy sat on every Bodies Face; they shook one another by the Hands in the Streets, who would hardly go on the same Side of the way with one another before; where the Streets were not too broad, they would open their Windows and call from one House to another, and ask'd how they did, and if they had heard the good News, that the Plague was abated; Some would return when they said good News, and ask, *What good News?* and when they answered, that the Plague was abated, and the Bills decreased almost 2000, they would cry out, *God be praised;* and would weep aloud for Joy, telling them they had heard nothing of it; and such was the Joy of the People that it was as it were Life to them from the Grave. I could almost set down as many extravagant things done in the Excess of their Joy, as of their Grief; but that would be to lessen the Value of it.

I must confess my self to have been very much dejected just before this happen'd; for the prodigious Number that were taken sick the Week or two before, besides those that died, was such, and the Lamentations were so great every where, that a Man must have seemed to have acted even against his Reason, if he had so much as expected to escape; and as there was hardly a House, but mine, in all my Neighbourhood, but what was infected; so had it gone on, it would not have been long, that there would have been any more Neighbours to be infected; indeed it is hardly credible, what dreadful Havock the last three Weeks had made, for if I might believe the Person, whose Calculations I always found very well grounded, there were not less than 30000 People dead, and near 100 thousand fallen sick in the three Weeks I speak of; for the Number that sickened was surprising, indeed it was astonishing, and those whose Courage upheld them all the time before, sunk under it now.

In the Middle of their Distress, when the Condition of the City of *London* was so truly calamitous, just then it pleased God, as it were, by his immediate Hand to disarm this Enemy; the Poyson was taken out of the Sting, it was wonderful, even the Physicians themselves were surprized at it; wherever they visited, they found their Patients better, either they had sweated kindly, or the Tumours were broke, or the Carbuncles went down, and the Inflammations round them chang'd Colour, or the Fever was gone, or the violent Head-ach was asswag'd, or some good Symptom was in the Case; so that in a few Days, every Body was recovering, whole Families that were infected and down, that had Ministers praying with them, and expected Death every Hour, were revived and healed, and none died at all out of them.

Nor was this by any new Medicine found out, or new Method of Cure discovered, or by any Experience in the Operation, which the Physicians or Surgeons had attain'd to; but it was evidently from the secret invisible Hand of him, that had at first sent this Disease as a Judgment upon us; and let the Atheistic part of Mankind call my Saying this what they please, it is no Enthusiasm; it was acknowledg'd at that time by all Mankind; the Disease was enervated and its Malignity spent, and let it proceed from whencesoever it will, let the Philosophers search for Reasons in Nature to account for it by, and labour as much as they will to lessen the Debt they owe to their Maker; those Physicians, who had the least Share of Religion in them, were oblig'd to acknowledge that it was all supernatural, that it was extraordinary, and that no Account could be given of it.

If I should say, that this is a visible Summons to us all to Thankfulness, especially we that were under the Terror of its Increase, perhaps it may be thought by some, after the Sense[43] of the thing was over, an officious canting of religious things, preaching a Sermon instead of writing a History, making my self a Teacher instead of giving my Observations of things; and this restrains me very much from going on here, as I might otherwise do: But if ten Leapers[44] were healed, and but one return'd to give Thanks, I desire to be as that one, and to be thankful for my self.

Nor will I deny, but there were Abundance of People who to all Appearance were very thankful at that time; for their Mouths were stop'd, even the Mouths of those, whose Hearts were not extraordinary long affected with it: But the Impression was so strong at that time, that it could not be resisted, no not by the worst of the People.

It was a common thing to meet People in the Street, that were Strangers, and that we knew nothing at all of, expressing their Surprize. Going one Day thro' *Aldgate,* and a pretty many People being passing and

---

42. that . . . Morning: in mid-October, 1665.

43. Sense: actual experience. 44. Leapers: lepers. See Luke 17:12–19.

repassing, there comes a Man out of the End of the *Minories*, and looking a little up the Street and down, he throws his Hands abroad, *Lord, what an Alteration is here!* Why, last Week I came along here, and hardly any Body was to be seen; another Man, I heard him, adds to his words, 'tis all wonderful, 'tis all a Dream: Blessed be God, says a third Man, and let us give Thanks to him, for 'tis all his own doing: Human Help and human Skill was at an End. These were all Strangers to one another: But such Salutations as these were frequent in the Street every Day; and in Spight of a loose Behaviour, the very common People went along the Streets, giving God Thanks for their Deliverance.

It was now, as I said before, the People had cast off all Apprehensions, and that too fast; indeed we were no more afraid now to pass by a Man with a white Cap upon his Head, or with a Cloth wrapt round his Neck, or with his Leg limping, occasion'd by the Sores in his Groyn, all which were frightful to the last Degree, but the Week before; but now the Street was full of them, and these poor recovering Creatures, give them their Due, appear'd very sensible of their unexpected Deliverance; and I should wrong them very much, if I should not acknowledge, that I believe many of them were really thankful; but I must own, that for the Generality of the People it might too justly be said of them, as was said of the Children of *Israel*,[45] after their being delivered from the Host of *Pharaoh*, when they passed the *Red-Sea*, and look'd back, and saw the *Egyptians* overwhelmed in the Water, *viz.* That *they sang his Praise, but they soon forgot his Works.*

I can go no farther here, I should be counted censorious, and perhaps unjust, if I should enter into the unpleasant Work of reflecting, whatever Cause there was for it, upon the Unthankfulness and Return of all manner of Wickedness among us, which I was so much an Eye-Witness of my self; I shall conclude the Account of this calamitous Year therefore with a coarse but sincere Stanza of my own, which I plac'd at the End of my ordinary Memorandums, the same Year they were written:

> *A dreadful Plague in* London *was,*
> *In the Year Sixty Five,*
> *Which swept an Hundred Thousand Souls*
> *Away; yet I alive!*

H. F.

45. as . . . Israel: See Ex. 14.

FROM

A TOUR THRO' THE WHOLE ISLAND OF GREAT BRITAIN . . .

In 1724, at the age of sixty-four, Defoe published anonymously the first volume of one of his most ambitious projects, no less than a one-man survey of "the present State of Things" in England, Scotland, and Wales. By the end of 1726 he had completed, in three volumes, this *Tour thro' the Whole Island of Great Britain, Divided* [to quote from the original title page] *into Circuits or Journies. Giving a Particular and Diverting Account of Whatever is Curious and Worth Observation: Particularly Fitted for the Reading of Such as Desire to Travel over the Island.* It was a task for which he was uniquely equipped both by temperament and by experience. Whatever he might think of the shortcomings of his fellow countrymen, he was himself a trueborn Englishman, proud of the wealth, vigor, and diversity of the British nation and eager to promote the spirit of enterprise that seemed to be constantly changing the face of the terrain and improving the condition of life. He knew the country as few men did in his time. For four decades he had been traveling up and down the land on commercial and political business until there were few corners of it that he had not seen—and his was no ordinary memory. But recollections, however vivid, would hardly suffice for an account of the present state of things, and Defoe took unusual pains to bring his matter up to date. More than once during the composition of the *Tour* he posted off to a region he had not seen in years to check on some item of trade or topography or local custom that he wanted to include. Other details he lifted without ceremony from previous authors, on his lifelong principle of using whatever came to hand. The *Tour* is one of the most personal of his books; in it he could do what he pleased, and it shows the natural bent of his interests. Unfailingly he looks first for the sources of wealth and commercial activity. He probes everywhere into local trade and its relation to the sustaining economy of London; he surveys the quantity and quality of crops and manufactures, the means of transport by land and water, the manners and employments of the people, the public buildings and great houses that ornament the landscape, and the forms of local government. Antiquities, too, he mentions in their place, but with a respectful attention that cannot disguise his preference for what is new and still abuilding. And when he finds a locality that has nothing in it to interest him, he does not hesitate to say so. The result is not an objective guidebook so much as a leisurely panoramic view of provincial Britain. The *Tour* was successful from the first and after Defoe's death was several times revised by other writers, including Samuel Richardson. In its original form it is a document of unmatched importance to social and economic historians of the early eighteenth century. In the classic *English Social History* (1944) of G. M. Trevelyan, the very age itself figures as "Defoe's England," and it is principally the *Tour* that justifies the phrase.

The text is that of the first edition (1724).

※

LETTER II

. . . From a little beyond *Hastings* to *Bourn*, we ride upon the Sands in a strait Line for Eighteen Miles, all upon the Coast of *Sussex*, passing by *Pemsey*, or *Pevensey* Haven, and the Mouth of the River, which cometh from *Battle*, without so much as knowing that there was a River, the Tide being out, and all the Water of the ordinary Chanel of the River sinking away in the Sands: This is that famous Strand where *William* the *Norman*[1] landed with his whole Army; and near to which, namely, at the Town of *Battle* abovenamed, which is about Nine Miles off, he Fought that Memorable Fight[2] with *Harold*, then King of *England*; in which the fate of this Nation was determined, and where Victory gave the Crown to the Conqueror and his Race, of the particulars of all which, our Histories are full; this Town of *Battle* is remarkable for little now, but for making the finest Gun-Powder, and the best perhaps in *Europe*. Near this Town of *Battle*, they show us a Hill with a Beacon upon it, which since the Beacon was set up, indeed has been call'd Beacon Hill, as is usual in such cases; but was before that call'd *Standard-Hill*, being the place where *William* the Conqueror set up his Great Standard of Defiance, the Day before the great Battle with *Harold* and the English.

From the beginning of *Rumney Marsh*, that is to say, at *Sandgate*, or *Sandfoot* Castle near *Hith*,[3] to this Place, the Country is a rich Fertile Soil, full of feeding Grounds, and where an infinite number of large Sheep are fed every Year, and sent up to *London* Market; these *Rumney Marsh* Sheep, are counted rather larger than the *Leicester-shire* and *Lincolnshire* Sheep, of which so much is said elsewhere.

Besides the vast quantity of Sheep as above, abundance of large Bullocks are fed in this part of the Country; and especially those they call Stall'd Oxen, that is, House fed, and kept within the Farmers Sheds or Yards, all the latter Season,[4] where they are fed for the Winter Market. This I noted, because these Oxen are generally the largest Beef in *England*.

From hence it was that, turning North, and traversing the deep, dirty, but rich Part of these two Counties, I had the curiosity to see the great Foundaries, or Iron-Works, which are in this County,[5] and where they are carry'd on at such a prodigious Expence of Wood, that even in a Country almost all over-run with Timber, they begin to complain of the consuming it for those Furnaces, and leaving the next Age to want Timber for building their Navies: I must own, however, that I found that Complaint perfectly groundless, the Three Counties of *Kent*, *Sussex*, and *Hampshire*, (all which lye contiguous to one another) being one inexhaustible Store-House of Timber never to be destroy'd, but by a general Conflagration, and able at this time to supply Timber to rebuild all the Royal Navies in Europe, if they were all to be destroy'd, and set about the building them together.

After I had fatigued my self in passing this deep and heavy part of the Country, I thought it would not be Foreign to my design, if I refresh'd my self with a view of *Tunbridge-Wells*, which were not then above Twelve Miles out of my way.

When I came to the Wells, which were Five Miles nearer to me than the Town, supposing me then at *Battle* to the Southward of them; I found a great deal of good Company there, and that which was more particular, was, that it happen'd to be at the time when his Royal Highness the Prince of *Wales*[6] was there with abundance of the Nobility, and Gentry of the Country, who to Honour the Prince's coming, or

A TOUR THRO' THE WHOLE ISLAND OF GREAT BRITAIN: *Letter II*.
1. William the Norman: William the Conqueror (1027–87). **2. Memorable Fight:** the Battle of Hastings, fought October 14, 1066, the decisive battle of the Norman Conquest.

3. Hith: Hythe, one of the Cinque Ports, some thirty-five miles up the coast from Hastings. **4. latter Season:** the last stages of readying them for sale. **5. this County:** Kent. **6. Prince of Wales:** George Augustus, later (1727) King George II.

satisfy their own Curiosity, throng'd to that Place; so that at first I found it very difficult to get a Lodging.

The Prince appear'd upon the Walks, went into the Raffling Shops,[7] and to every publick Place, saw every thing, and let every body see him, and went away, with the Duke of *Dorset*, and other of his Attendance for *Portsmouth;* so in Two or Three Days, things return'd all to their Antient Chanel, and *Tunbridge* was just what it used to be.

The Ladies that appear here, are indeed the glory of the Place; the coming to the Wells to drink the Water is a meer matter of custom; some drink, more do not, and few drink Physically:[8] But Company and Diversion is in short the main business of the Place; and those People who have nothing to do any where else, seem to be the only People who have any thing to do at *Tunbridge*.

After the Appearance is over at the Wells, (where the Ladies are all undress'd[9]) and at the Chapel, the Company go home; and as if it was another Species of People, or a Collection from another Place, you are surpriz'd to see the Walks covered with Ladies compleatly dress'd and gay to profusion; where rich Cloths, Jewels, and Beauty not to be set out by (but infinitely above) Ornament, dazzles the Eyes from one end of the Range to the other.

Here you have all the Liberty of Conversation in the World, and any thing that looks like a Gentleman, has an address[10] agreeable, and behaves with decency and good Manners, may single out whom he pleases, that does not appear engag'd, and may talk, rally, be merry, and say any decent thing to them; but all this makes no Acquaintance, nor is it taken so, or understood to mean so; if a Gentleman desires to be more intimate, and enter into any Acquaintance particular, he must do it by proper application, not by the ordinary meeting on the Walks, for the Ladies will ask no Gentleman there, to go off of the Walk, or invite any one to their Lodgings, except it be a sort of Ladies of whom I am not now speaking.

As for Gaming, Sharping, Intrieguing; as also Fops, Fools, Beaus, and the like, *Tunbridge* is as full of these, as can be desired, and it takes off much of the Diversion of those Persons of Honour and Virtue, who go there to be innocently recreated: However a Man of Character, and good behaviour cannot be there any time,

but he may single out such Company as may be suitable to him, and with whom he may be as merry as Heart can wish.

The Air here is excellent good, the Country Healthful, and the Provisions of all sorts very reasonable: Particularly, they are supply'd with excellent Fish, and that of almost all sorts, from *Rye*, and other Towns on the Sea-Coast; and I saw a Turbut of near 20 l. weight sold there for 3 s.: In the Season of Mackarel, they have them here from *Hastings*, within three Hours of their being taken out of the Sea, and the difference which that makes in their goodness, I need not mention.

They have likewise here abundance of Wild-Fowl, of the best sorts; such as Pheasant, Partridge, Woodcock, Snipe, Quails, also Duck, Mallard, Teal, &c. particularly they have from the *South-Downs*, the Bird call'd *a Wheatear*, or *as we may call them*, the English *Ortolans*, the most delicious Taste for a Creature of one Mouthful, *for 'tis little more*, that can be imagin'd; but these are very dear at *Tunbridge*, they are much Cheaper at *Seaford*, *Lewis*, and that side of the Country.

In a word, *Tunbridge* wants nothing that can add to the Felicities of Life, or that can make a Man or Woman compleatly happy, always provided they have Money; for without Money a Man is no-body at *Tunbridge*, any more than at any other Place; and when any Man finds his Pockets low, he has nothing left to think of, but to be gone, for he will have no Diversion in staying there any longer.

And yet *Tunbridge* also is a Place in which a Lady *however Virtuous*, yet for want of good Conduct may as soon Shipwreck her Character as in any part of *England;* and where, when she has once injur'd her Reputation, 'tis as hard to restore it; nay, some say no Lady ever recover'd her Character at *Tunbridge*, if she first wounded it there: But this is to be added too, that a Lady very seldom suffers that way at *Tunbridge*, without some apparent Folly of her own; for that they do not seem so apt to make havock of one another's Reputation here, by Tattle and Slander, as I think they do in some other Places in the World; particularly at *Epsome*, *Hampstead*,[11] and such like Places; which I take to be, because the Company who frequent *Tunbridge*, seem to be a Degree or two above the

---

7. **Raffling Shops:** gambling houses. 8. **Physically:** for medical reasons. 9. **undress'd:** in ordinary, informal dress. 10. **address:** bearing, manner of addressing others.

11. **Epsome, Hampstead:** watering places near London that had been fashionable in Queen Anne's day but were now full of doubtful company.

Society of those other Places, and therefore are not so very apt, either to meddle with other Peoples Affairs, or to Censure if they do; both which are the Properties of that more Gossiping Part of the World.

In this I shall be much misunderstood, if it is thought I mean the Ladies only, for I must own I look just the other way; and if I may be allow'd to use my own Sex so Coursly, it is really among them that the Ladies Characters first, and oftnest receive unjust Wounds; and I must confess the Malice, the Reflections, the Busy Meddling, the Censuring, the Tatling from Place to Place, and the making havock of the Characters of Innocent Women, is found among the Men Gossips more than among their own Sex, and at the *Coffee-Houses* more than at the *Tea-Table;* then among the Women themselves, what is to be found of it there, is more among the Chamber-Maids, than among their Mistresses; slander is a meaness below Persons of Honour and Quality, and to do injustice to the Ladies, especially, is a Degree below those who have any share of Breeding and Sense: On this account you may observe, 'tis more practis'd among the Citizens than among the Gentry, and in Country Towns and Villages, more than in the City, and so on, till you come to the meer *Canail,*[12] the Common Mobb of the Street, and there, no Reputation, no Character can shine without having Dirt thrown upon it every Day: *But this is a digression.*

I left *Tunbridge,* for the same Reason that I give, why others should leave it, when they are in my Condition; namely, that I found my Money almost gone; and tho' I had Bills of Credit to supply my self in the Course of my intended Journey; yet I had none there: so I came away, or as they call it there, I retir'd; and came to *Lewes,* through the deepest, dirtiest, but many ways the Richest, and most Profitable Country in all that Part of *England.*

*   *   *

12. **Canail:** (*canaille*) rabble, riffraff.

Bernard Mandeville

❧❧❧❧❧❧❧❧❧❧❧❧❧❧❧❧❧❧❧❧❧❧❧

1670–1733

Born in 1670 into a prominent Dutch family, Bernard Mandeville was baptized on November 20 at Rotterdam. He attended the Erasmus School there, before entering the University of Leyden in October, 1685, in order to study medicine. In 1691 he received his degree of Doctor of Medicine and set up practice as a specialist in nervous disorders; he thereby became the fourth Mandeville in as many generations to enter the medical profession.

During the 1690's Mandeville visited London—"to learn the Language," he says— and remained there for the rest of his life. He married an Englishwoman, and the couple had at least two children. In England, Mandeville continued his medical practice; *A Treatise of the Hypochondriac and Hysteric Passions*, brought out in 1711, reportedly won the admiration of Johnson. As a practitioner, however, Mandeville appears to have had only moderate success. But he certainly learned the language.

The Grumbling Hive: or, Knaves Turn'd Honest was first published as a pamphlet in 1705. It reappeared in 1714 with an elaborate commentary—the whole entitled *The Fable of the Bees: or, Private Vices, Publick Benefits*—which consisted of twenty prose "remarks" on the poem and the essay reprinted here, *An Enquiry into the Origin of Moral Virtue*. The next edition of the work, in 1723, contained expanded "remarks" and two new essays, *An Essay on Charity and Charity-Schools* and *A Search into the Nature of Society*. Provocative as Mandeville's thesis was, his book did not draw fire till now (perhaps the attack on the charity schools did it). His critics, among the more notable of whom were William Law, John Dennis, and Bishop Berkeley, apparently saw in Mandeville's writing an example of private vice without the compensatory public benefit. The Grand Jury of Middlesex officially declared *The Fable of the Bees* a public nuisance. Undeterred, Mandeville went ahead with a continuation, which consisted of a preface and six dialogues, and published it as Part II in 1729.

If Mandeville was an offense to most of his contemporaries, he is something of a puzzle to us. The question for modern critics seems to be, not How shall we answer his argument?, but How are we to understand it? Some critics have argued that Mandeville, a libertine, was actually satirizing the moral position he assumes in the Preface; others that Mandeville, a Christian moralist, aimed to expose the delusive attractions of the world. Mandeville himself complained of being misunderstood and implied that the right answer to the second question would have forestalled the first. In the Preface to the first edition of *The Fable* he denies that *The Grumbling Hive* is a

"Satyr upon Virtue and Morality, and the whole wrote for the Encouragement of Vice." Rather, its purpose is "to shew the Impossibility of enjoying all the most elegant Comforts of Life that are to be met with in an industrious, wealthy and powerful Nation, and at the same time be bless'd with all the Virtue and Innocence that can be wish'd for in a Golden Age." From these words we might easily assume that Mandeville intends to moralize. But later he suggests that his book might teach those who enjoy material comforts to submit more cheerfully to the inevitable "Inconveniences" (moral improprieties) that make them possible. Is he then, contrary to the purpose he sets forth in the Preface, encouraging vice? Or is his aim perhaps neither to moralize nor to corrupt? People are notorious, he says, for their incapacity "to be made better by any thing that could be said to them." "Better" in this context practically assures us that we are being worked over by a studious ironist. Indeed, Mandeville is not easy to pin down. At times he seems bent only on attacking the hypocrisies and complacencies of those who, professing to love virtue, thrive on the vicious foundations of civilized society; at other times he seems more concerned with the vices and the alleged benefits themselves.

F. B. Kaye, Mandeville's chief interpreter, has described his method as that of juxtaposing "the utilitarian principles by which the world is inevitably controlled and the demands of rigoristic ethics, and showing their irreconcilability." According to Kaye, the effect of the juxtaposition is to reduce to absurdity the rigoristic point of view, the idea that the source of moral action is complete selflessness. The fact that Mandeville himself never openly denied this impracticable point of view does not mean that he really believed in the rigorist doctrine; it only means that he found it convenient to pretend that he did.

Mandeville seems to be anticipating the ethics of utilitarianism by asking us to accept any form of behavior that contributes to the general good. A complete utilitarian however would call all such forms good; Mandeville does not—he calls them vices. Conversely, those forms of behavior that not only do not appear to serve the general good but seem actually subversive of it are to the utilitarian vices; to Mandeville virtues.

Mandeville is far from being a systematic moral philosopher however, and he does not avoid some common traps of logic. Taking the position that has come to be called psychological egoism, he refers all public achievements back to forms of behavior that are self-regarding if not downright self-indulgent. At the same time he refers morality itself back to the same starting point. Whether a person seeks to win fame or to shun blame, it is pride that causes him to act. Pride motivates all so-called moral acts. Logically, of course, Mandeville thus destroys the rigorist position, which defines virtue as goodness free of self-regard and anything short of this as vice. Now Mandeville cannot distinguish virtue from vice at all, and his famous paradox collapses. Here is at least one reason why, as Kaye noted, he does not flatly deny the rigorist position even though he has reduced it to absurdity.

But Mandeville is not a logician, he is a rhetorician; he is not a philosopher, he is a satirist. And if the effectiveness of satire depends less upon the absolute clarity and perfect consistency of the satirist's views than upon his skill in calling into question the absolute clarity and perfect consistency of those of his audience, then Mandeville is an effective satirist. At its most forcible, his argument makes us regard with equal seriousness both sides of his paradox (culture *and* its discontents) without reducing either to absurdity, and without enabling us to effect the easy reconciliation of material and moral values which *The Fable of the Bees* is at bottom mocking.

The standard edition of *The Fable of the Bees* is by F. B. Kaye (2 vols., 1924; reprinted 1957). There is a recent abridgment by Irwin Primer (1962).

FROM

THE FABLE OF THE BEES: OR, PRIVATE VICES, PUBLICK BENEFITS

❀

The texts for *The Grumbling Hive* and *An Enquiry into the Origin of Moral Virtue* are those of the first editions, 1705 and 1714 respectively. We have incorporated a few revisions from subsequent editions in Mandeville's lifetime.

❀

THE GRUMBLING HIVE: OR, KNAVES TURN'D HONEST

A Spacious Hive well stock'd with Bees,
That lived in Luxury and Ease;
And yet as fam'd for Laws and Arms,
As yielding large and early Swarms;
Was counted the great Nursery
Of Sciences and Industry.
No Bees had better Government,
More Fickleness, or less Content.
They were not Slaves to Tyranny,
Nor ruled by wild Democracy;   10
But Kings, that could not wrong, because
Their Power was circumscrib'd by Laws.

    These Insects lived like Men, and all
Our Actions they perform'd in small:
They did whatever's done in Town,
And what belongs to Sword, or Gown:°
Tho' th' Artful Works, by nimble Slight;°
Of minute Limbs, 'scaped Human Sight

Yet we've no Engines, Labourers,
Ships, Castles, Arms, Artificers,   20
Craft, Science, Shop, or Instrument;
But they had an Equivalent:
Which, since their Language is unknown,
Must be call'd, as we do our own.
As grant, that among other Things
They wanted° Dice, yet they had Kings;
And those had Guards; from whence we may
Justly conclude, they had some Play;°
Unless a Regiment be shewn
Of Soldiers, that make use of none.   30

    Vast Numbers thronged the fruitful Hive;
Yet those vast Numbers made 'em thrive;
Millions endeavouring to supply
Each other's Lust° and Vanity;
Whilst other Millions were employ'd,
To see their Handy-works destroy'd;°
They furnish'd half the Universe;
Yet had more Work than Labourers.
Some with vast Stocks, and little Pains
Jump'd into Business of great Gains;   40
And some were damn'd to Sythes and Spades,
And all those hard laborious Trades;
Where willing Wretches daily sweat,
And wear out Strength and Limbs to eat:
Whilst others follow'd Mysteries,°
To which few Folks bind Prentices;
That want° no Stock, but that of Brass,°
And may set up without a Cross;°
As Sharpers, Parasites, Pimps, Players,
Pick-Pockets, Coiners, Quacks, Sooth-Sayers,   50

THE FABLE OF THE BEES: *The Grumbling Hive*. **16. Sword, or Gown:** the military or legal professions. **17. Slight:** sleight.

26. wanted: lacked. **28. Play:** gambling. **34. Lust:** desire. **36. destroy'd:** consumed. **45. Mysteries:** trades. **47. want:** require. **Brass:** (1) the metal; (2) shamelessness. **48. without a Cross:** without money. The figure of a cross was stamped on some coins, and the name came to be applied to coins generally.

And all those, that, in Enmity
With down-right Working, cunningly
Convert to their own Use the Labour
Of their good-natur'd heedless Neighbour.
These were called Knaves; but, bar° the Name,
The grave Industrious were the Same.
All Trades and Places knew some Cheat,
No Calling was without Deceit.

    The Lawyers, of whose Art the Basis
Was raising Feuds and splitting Cases,°   60
Opposed all Registers,° that Cheats
Might make more Work with dipt° Estates;
As were 't° unlawful, that one's own,
Without a Law-Suit, should be known.
They kept off Hearings wilfully,
To finger the refreshing Fee;°
And to defend a wicked Cause,
Examin'd and survey'd the Laws;
As Burglars Shops and Houses do;
To find out where they'd best break through.   70

    Physicians valued Fame and Wealth
Above the drooping Patient's Health,
Or their own Skill: The greatest Part
Study'd, instead of Rules of Art,
Grave pensive Looks, and dull Behaviour;
To gain th' Apothecary's Favour,
The Praise of Mid-wives, Priests and all,
That served at Birth, or Funeral;
To bear with th' ever-talking Tribe,°
And hear my Lady's Aunt prescribe;   80
With formal Smile, and kind How d 'ye,
To fawn on all the Family;
And, which of all the greatest Curse is,
T' endure th' Impertinence of Nurses.

    Among the many Priests of *Jove*,
Hir'd to draw Blessings from Above,
Some few were learn'd and eloquent,
But Thousands hot° and ignorant:

Yet all past Muster, that could hide
Their Sloth, Lust, Avarice and Pride;   90
For which they were as famed, as Taylors
For Cabbage;° or for Brandy, Sailors:
Some meagre look'd, and meanly clad
Would mystically pray for Bread,
Meaning by that an ample Store,
Yet lit'rally receiv'd no more;
And, whilst these holy Drudges starv'd,
The lazy Ones, for which they serv'd,
Indulg'd their Ease, with all the Graces
Of Health and Plenty in their Faces.   100

    The Soldiers, that were forced to fight,
If they survived, got Honour by 't;
Tho' some, that shunn'd the bloody Fray,
Had Limbs shot off, that ran away:
Some valiant Gen'rals fought the Foe;
Others took Bribes to let them go:
Some ventur'd always, where 'twas warm;
Lost now a Leg, and then an Arm;
Till quite disabled, and put by,
They lived on half their Salary;   110
Whilst others never came in Play,
And staid at Home for Double Pay.°

    Their Kings were serv'd; but Knavishly
Cheated by their own Ministry;
Many, that for their Welfare slaved,
Robbing the very Crown they saved:
Pensions were small, and they lived high,
Yet boasted of their Honesty.
Calling, whene'er they strain'd their Right,
The slipp'ry Trick a Perquisite;°   120
And, when Folks understood their Cant,
They chang'd that for Emolument;
Unwilling to be short, or plain,
In any thing concerning Gain:
For there was not a Bee, but would
Get more, I won't say, than he should;
But than he dared to let them know,
That pay'd for 't; as your Gamesters do,
That, tho' at fair Play, ne'er will own
Before the Losers what they've won.   130

---

55. bar: except for. **60. splitting Cases:** To split a case was to bring an action for a part rather than the whole of the cause of the action. Francis Grose's *Classical Dictionary of the Vulgar Tongue* (3rd ed., 1796), ed. Eric Partridge (1963), gives "split cause" as a slang term for a lawyer. **61. Registers:** the records of legal documents affecting landed property. **62. dipt:** mortgaged. **63. As were 't:** as though it were. **66. refreshing Fee:** The first edition reads: "retaining," which makes sense; but as a "refresher" was an extra fee paid to counsel in cases which were prolonged, we do not hesitate to adopt the reading of later editions. **79. th' ever-talking Tribe:** old women. **88. hot:** fervent, enthusiastic.

92. Cabbage: pieces of cloth left over from the cutting, appropriated by the tailors. **110–12. They . . . Pay:** Disabled officers received half pay while those who did not fight at all remained on full pay. **120. Perquisite:** side income incidental to a profession or office.

But who can all their Frauds repeat!
The very Stuff, which in the Street
They sold for Dirt t' enrich the Ground,
Was often by the Buyers found
Sophisticated° with a Quarter
Of Good-for-nothing, Stones and Mortar;
Tho' Flail° had little Cause to mutter,
Who sold the other Salt for Butter.

Justice her self, famed for fair Dealing,
By Blindness had not lost her Feeling;   140
Her Left Hand, which the Scales should hold,
Had often dropt 'em, bribed with Gold;
And, tho' she seem'd impartial,
Where Punishment was corporal,
Pretended to a reg'lar Course,
In Murther, and all Crimes of Force;
Tho' some, first Pillory'd for Cheating,
Were hang'd in Hemp of their own beating;
Yet, it was thought, the Sword she bore
Check'd but the Desp'rate and the Poor;   150
That, urged by mere Necessity,
Were tied up to the wretched Tree°
For Crimes, which not deserv'd that Fate,
But to secure the Rich, and Great.

Thus every Part was full of Vice,
Yet the whole Mass a Paradice;
Flatter'd in Peace, and fear'd in Wars
They were th' Esteem of Foreigners,
And lavish of their Wealth and Lives,
The Ballance° of all other Hives.   160
Such were the Blessings of that State;
Their Crimes conspired to make 'em Great;
And Vertue, who from Politicks
Had learn'd a Thousand cunning Tricks,
Was, by their happy Influence,
Made Friends with Vice: And ever since
The Worst of all the Multitude
Did something for the common Good.

This was the State's Craft, that maintain'd
The Whole, of which each Part complain'd: 170
This, as in Musick Harmony,
Made Jarrings in the Main agree;
Parties directly opposite
Assist each oth'r, as 'twere for Spight;

135. **Sophisticated:** adulterated. 137. **Flail:** from the saying "to be threshed with your own flail." 152. **the wretched
Tree:** the gallows. Cf. l. 234. 160. **The Ballance:** the
equal.

And Temp'rance with Sobriety
Serve Drunkenness and Gluttony.

The Root of evil Avarice,
That damn'd ill-natur'd baneful Vice,
Was Slave to Prodigality,
That Noble Sin; whilst Luxury   180
Employ'd a Million of the Poor,
And odious Pride a Million more.
Envy it self, and Vanity
Were Ministers of Industry;
Their darling Folly, Fickleness
In Diet, Furniture, and Dress,
That strange ridic'lous Vice, was made
The very Wheel, that turn'd the Trade.
Their Laws and Cloaths were equally
Objects of Mutability;   190
For, what was well done for a Time,
In half a Year became a Crime;
Yet whilst they alter'd thus their Laws,
Still finding and correcting Flaws,
They mended by Inconstancy
Faults, which no Prudence could foresee.

Thus Vice nursed Ingenuity,
Which join'd with Time, and Industry
Had carry'd Life's Conveniencies,
It's real Pleasures, Comforts, Ease,   200
To such a Height, the very Poor   ⎫
Lived better than the Rich before; ⎬
And nothing could be added more: ⎭

How vain is Mortal Happiness!
Had they but known the Bounds of Bliss;
And, that Perfection here below
Is more, than Gods can well bestow,
The grumbling Brutes had been content
With Ministers and Government.
But they, at every ill Success,   210
Like Creatures lost without Redress,
Cursed Politicians, Armies, Fleets;
Whilst every one cry'd, Damn the Cheats,
And would, tho' Conscious of his own,
In Others barb'rously bear none.

One, that had got a Princely Store,
By cheating Master, King, and Poor,
Dared cry aloud; The Land must sink
For all it's Fraud; And whom d'ye think
The Sermonizing Rascal chid?   220
A Glover that sold Lamb for Kid.

The least Thing was not done amiss,
Or cross'd the Publick Business;
But all the Rogues cry'd brazenly,
Good Gods, had we but Honesty!
Merc'ry smiled at th' Impudence;
And Others call'd it want of Sence,
Always to rail at what they loved:
But *Jove*, with Indignation moved,
At last in Anger swore, he'd rid   230
The bawling Hive of Fraud, and did.
The very Moment it departs,
And Honesty fills all their Hearts;
There shews 'em, like th' Instructive Tree,°
Those Crimes, which they're ashamed to see;
Which now in Silence they confess,
By Blushing at their Uglyness;
Like Children, that would hide their Faults,
And by their Colour own their Thoughts;
Imag'ning, when they're look'd upon,   240
That Others see, what they have done.

    But, Oh ye Gods! What Consternation,
How vast and sudden was th' Alteration!
In half an Hour, the Nation round,
Meat fell a Penny in the Pound.
The Mask Hypocrisie's flung down,
From the great Statesman to the Clown;°
And some, in borrow'd Looks well known,
Appear'd like Strangers in their own.
The Bar was silent from that Day;   250
For now the willing Debtors pay,
Ev'n what's by Creditors forgot;
Who quitted them,° that had it not.
Those, that were in the Wrong, stood mute,
And dropt the patch'd° vexatious Suit.
On which, since nothing less can thrive,
Than Lawyers in an honest Hive,
All, except those, that got enough,
With Ink-horns by their Sides troop'd off.

    Justice hang'd some, set others free;   260
And, after Goal-delivery,°
Her Presence be'ng no more requir'd,
With all her Train, and Pomp retir'd.
First march'd some Smiths, with Locks and Grates,
Fetters, and Doors with Iron-Plates;

Next Goalers, Turnkeys, and Assistants:
Before the Goddess, at some distance,
Her chief and faithful Minister
Squire Catch,° and Laws great Finisher,
Bore not th' imaginary Sword,°   270
But his own Tools, an Ax and Cord:
Then on a Cloud the Hood-wink'd° fair
Justice her self was push'd by Air:
About her Chariot, and behind,
Were Sergeants, Bums° of every kind,
Tip-staffs,° and all those Officers,
That squeeze a Living out of Tears.

    Tho' Physick° lived, whilst Folks were ill,
None would prescribe, but Bees of Skill;
Which, through the Hive dispers'd so wide,   280
That none of 'em had need to ride,
Waved vain Disputes; and strove to free
The Patients of their Misery;
Left° Drugs in cheating Countries grown,
And used the Product of their own,
Knowing the Gods sent no Disease
To Nations without Remedies.

    Their Clergy rouz'd from Laziness,
Laid not their Charge on Journey-Bees;°
But serv'd themselves, exempt from Vice,   290
The Gods with Pray'r and Sacrifice;
All those, that were unfit, or knew,
Their Service might be spared, withdrew:
Nor was there Business for so many,
(If th' Honest stand in need of any.)
Few only with the High-Priest staid,
To whom the rest Obedience paid:
Himself, employ'd in holy Cares,
Resign'd to others State-Affairs:
He chased no Starv'ling from his Door,   300
Nor pinch'd the Wages of the Poor;

But at his House the Hungry's fed,
The Hireling finds unmeasur'd Bread,
The needy Trav'ler Board and Bed.

Among the King's great Ministers,
And all th' inferiour Officers
The Change was great; for frugally
They now lived on their Salary.
That a poor Bee should Ten times come,
To ask his Due, a trifling Sum,   310
And by some well-hir'd Clerk be made,
To give a Crown, or ne'er be paid;
Would now be call'd a down-right Cheat,
Tho' formerly a Perquisite.
All Places; managed first by Three,
Who watch'd each other's Knavery,
And often for a Fellow-feeling,
Promoted one another's Stealing;
Are happily supply'd by one;
By which some Thousands more are gone.   320

No Honour now could be content,
To live, and owe for what was spent.
Liv'ries in Brokers Shops are hung,
They part with Coaches for a Song;
Sell stately Horses by whole Sets;
And Country-Houses to pay Debts.

Vain Cost is shunn'd as much as Fraud;
They have no Forces kept Abroad;
Laugh at th' Esteem of Foreigners,
And empty Glory got by Wars;   330
They fight but for their Country's Sake,
When Right or Liberty's at Stake.

Now mind the glorious Hive, and see,
How Honesty and Trade agree:
The Shew is gone, it thins apace;
And looks with quite another Face,
For 'twas not only that they went,
By whom vast Sums were Yearly spent;
But Multitudes, that lived on them,
Were daily forc'd to do the Same.   340
In vain to other Trades they'd fly;
All were o'er-stock'd accordingly.

The Price of Land, and Houses falls;
Mirac'lous Palaces, whose Walls,
Like those of *Thebes*, were raised by Play,°

Are to be lett; whilst the once gay,
Well-seated Houshold Gods would be
More pleased t' expire in Flames, than see
The mean Inscription on the Door
Smile at the lofty Ones they bore.°   350
The Building Trade is quite destroy'd,
Artificers are not employ'd;
No Limner° for his Art is famed;
Stone-cutters, Carvers are not named.

Those, that remain'd, grown temp'rate, strive,
Not how to spend; but how to live;
And, when they paid their Tavern Score,
Resolv'd to enter it no more:
No Vintners Jilt° in all the Hive
Could wear now Cloth of Gold and thrive;   360
Nor *Torcol*° such vast Sums advance,
For *Burgundy* and *Ortelans;*°
The Courtier's gone, that with his Miss
Supp'd at his House on *Christmass* Peas;°
Spending as much in Two Hours stay,
As keeps a Troop of Horse a Day.

The haughty *Chloe*, to live Great,
Had made her Husband rob the State:
But now she sells her Furniture,
Which th' *Indies* had been ransack'd for;   370
Contracts th' expensive Bill of Fare,
And wears her strong Suit a whole Year:
The slight and fickle Age is past;
And Cloaths, as well as Fashions last.
Weavers that join'd rich Silk with Plate,°
And all the Trades subordinate,
Are gone. Still Peace and Plenty reign,
And every Thing is cheap, tho' plain:
Kind Nature, free from Gard'ners Force,
Allows all Fruits in her own Course;   380
But Rarities cannot be had,
Where Pains to get 'em are not paid.

344–45. whose . . . Play: The wall of Thebes was according to legend raised by the magical music of Amphion's lyre. Mandeville, playing on *Play*, attributes the building of palaces to gambling, or commercial speculation.

346–50. whilst . . . bore: The images of the Lares and Penates, the household gods of Roman antiquity, traditionally occupied the central room of the house. "The mean Inscription" is the name of the new (and lower-class) occupant of the house. 353. Limner: artist; especially a portrait painter. 359. Jilt: mistress. 361. Torcol: a character in Edward Ravenscroft's comedy *The English Lawyer* (1678). 362. Ortelans: garden buntings, considered a delicacy. 364. Christmass Peas: probably peas artificially forced to provide an out-of-season delicacy for those people rich enough to afford them. 375. Plate: silver (or gold) plate.

As Pride and Luxury decrease,
So by degrees they leave the Seas.
Not Merchants now; but Companies
Remove whole Manufacturies.
All Arts and Crafts neglected lie;
Content the Bane of Industry,
Makes 'em admire their homely Store,
And neither seek, nor covet more.   390

So few in the vast Hive remain;
The Hundredth part they can't maintain
Against th' Insults of numerous Foes;
Whom yet they valiantly oppose:
Till some well-fenced Retreat is found;
And here they die, or stand their Ground.
No Hireling in their Armies known;
But bravely fighting for their own,
Their Courage and Integrity
At last were crown'd with Victory.   400
They triumph'd not without their Cost;
For many Thousand Bees were lost.
Hard'ned with Toils, and Exercise
They counted Ease it self a Vice;
Which so improved their Temperance;
That, to avoid Extravagance,
They flew into a hollow Tree,
Blest with Content and Honesty.

The MORAL.

THen leave Complaints: Fools only strive
To make a Great an honest Hive.   410
T' enjoy the World's Conveniencies,
Be famed in War, yet live in Ease
Without great Vices, is a vain
Eutopia seated in the Brain.
Fraud, Luxury, and Pride must live;
Whilst we the Benefits receive.
Hunger's a dreadful Plague, no doubt,
Yet who digests or thrives without?
Do we not owe the Growth of Wine
To the dry, crooked, shabby Vine?   420
Which, whilst its Shutes neglected stood,
Choak'd other Plants, and ran to Wood;
But blest us with its Noble Fruit;
As soon as it was tied, and cut:
So Vice is beneficial found,
When it's by Justice lopt, and bound;
Nay, where the People would be great,
As necessary to the State,
As Hunger is to make 'em eat.

Bare Vertue can't make Nations live   430
In Splendour; they, that would revive
A Golden Age, must be as free,
For Acorns, as for Honesty.°

AN ENQUIRY
INTO THE ORIGIN
OF MORAL VIRTUE

THE INTRODUCTION.

*One of the greatest Reasons why so few People under-
stand themselves, is, that most Writers are always teaching
Men what they should be, and hardly ever trouble their
heads with telling them what they really are. As for my
part, without any Compliment to the Courteous Reader,
or my self, I believe Man (besides Skin, Flesh, Bones, &c.
that are obvious to the Eye) to be a Compound of various
Passions, that all of them, as they are provoked and come
uppermost, govern him by turns, whether he will or no. To
shew, that these Qualifications, which we all pretend to be
asham'd of, are the great support of a flourishing Society,
has been the subject of the foregoing Poem. But there being
some Passages in it seemingly Paradoxical, I have in the
Preface promised some explanatory Remarks on it; which,
to render more useful, I have thought fit to enquire, how
Man no better qualify'd, might yet by his own Imperfections
be taught to distinguish between Virtue and Vice: And here
I must desire the Reader once for all to take notice, that
when I say Men, I mean neither Jews nor Christians;
but meer Man, in the State of Nature and Ignorance of the
true Deity.*

ALL untaught Animals are only Sollicitous of
pleasing themselves, and naturally follow the bent of
their own Inclinations, without considering the good
or harm that from their being pleased will accrue to
others. This is the Reason, that in the wild State of
Nature those Creatures are fittest to live peaceably
together in great Numbers, that discover[1] the least
of Understanding, and have the fewest Appetites to
gratify, and consequently no Species of Animals is,
without the Curb of Government, less capable of
agreeing long together in Multitudes than that of

431–33. they . . . Honesty: Mandeville cites as an example
to England the noble life of the Arcadians with their humble
fare of acorns. *An Enquiry into the Origin of Moral Virtue.* **1.**
discover: reveal, show.

Man; yet such are his Qualities, whether good or bad, I shall not determine, that no Creature besides himself can ever be made sociable: But being an extraordinary selfish and headstrong as well as cunning Animal, however he may be subdued by superior Strength, it is impossible by force alone to make him tractable, and receive the Improvements he is capable of.

The chief Thing therefore, which Lawgivers and other Wise Men, that have laboured for the Establishment of Society, have endeavour'd, has been to make the People they were to govern, believe, that it was more beneficial for every body to conquer than indulge his Appetites, and much better to mind the Publick than what seem'd his private Interest. As this has always been a very difficult Task, so no Wit or Eloquence has been left untried to compass² it; and the Moralists and Philosophers of all Ages employ'd their utmost Skill to prove the truth of so useful an Assertion. But whether Mankind would have ever believ'd it or not, it is not likely that any body could have perswaded them to disapprove of their natural Inclinations, or prefer the good of others to their own, if at the same time he had not shew'd them an Equivalent to be enjoy'd as a Reward for the Violence, which by so doing they of necessity must commit upon themselves. Those that have undertaken to civilise Mankind, were not ignorant of this; but being unable to give so many real Rewards as would satisfy all Persons for every individual Action, they were forc'd to contrive an imaginary one, that as a general Equivalent for the trouble of Self-denial should serve on all occasions, and without costing any thing either to themselves or others, be yet a most acceptable Recompence to the Receivers.

They thoroughly examin'd all the Strength and Frailties of our Nature, and observing that none were either so savage as not to be charm'd with Praise, or so despicable as patiently to bear Contempt, justly concluded, that Flattery must be the most powerful Argument that cou'd be used to Human Creatures. Making use of this bewitching Engine,³ they extoll'd the Excellency of our Nature above other Animals, and setting forth with unbounded Praises the Wonders of our Sagacity and vastness of Understanding, bestow'd a thousand Encomiums on the Rationality of our Souls, by the help of which we were capable of performing the most noble Atchievements. Having by this artful way of Flattery insinuated themselves into the Hearts of Men, they began to instruct them in the Notions of Honour and Shame; representing the one as the worst of all Evils, and the other as the highest good to which Mortals could aspire: Which being done, they laid before them how unbecoming it was the Dignity of such sublime Creatures to be sollicitous about gratifying those Appetites, which they had in common with Brutes, and at the same time unmindful of those higher qualities that gave them the preeminence over all visible Beings. They indeed confess'd, that those impulses of Nature were very pressing; that it was troublesome to resist, and very difficult wholly to subdue them: But this they only used as an Argument to demonstrate, how glorious the Conquest of them was on the one hand, and how scandalous on the other not to attempt it.

To introduce moreover an Emulation amongst Men, they divided the whole Species in two Classes, vastly differing from one another: The one consisted of abject, low minded People, that always hunting after immediate Enjoyment, were wholly incapable of Self-denial, and without regard to the good of others, had no higher Aim than their private Advantage; such as being enslaved by Voluptuousness, yielded without Resistance to every gross desire, and made no use of their Rational Faculties but to heighten their Sensual Pleasures. These vile grov'ling Wretches, they said, were the Dross of their kind, and having only the Shape of Men, differ'd from Brutes in nothing but their outward Figure. But the other Class was made up of lofty high-spirited Creatures, that free from sordid Selfishness, esteem'd the Improvements of the Mind to be their fairest Possessions; and setting a true value upon themselves, took no delight but in imbellishing that Part in which their Excellency consisted; such as despising whatever they had in common with irrational Creatures, opposed by the help of Reason their most violent Inclinations; and making a continual War with themselves to promote the Peace of others, aim'd at no less than the Publick Welfare and the Conquest of their own Passions.

*Fortior est qui se quam qui fortissima Vincit
Maenia⁴* ——— ——— ——— ———

These they call'd the true Representatives of their sublime Species, exceeding in worth the first Class by

2. **compass:** accomplish. 3. **Engine:** contrivance, snare.

4. **Fortior . . . Maenia:** "He who conquers himself is stronger than he who conquers the strongest cities" (Prov. 16:32).

more degrees, than that it self was superior to the Beasts of the Field.[5]

As in all Animals that are not too imperfect to discover[6] Pride, we find, that the finest and such as are the most beautiful and valuable of their kind, have generally the greatest Share of it; so in Man, the most perfect of Animals, it is so inseparable from his very Essence (how cunningly soever some may learn to hide or disguise it) that without it the Compound he is made of would want[7] one of the chiefest Ingredients: Which, if we consider, it is hardly to be doubted but Lessons and Remonstrances, so skillfully adapted to the good Opinion Man has of himself, as those I have mentioned, must, if scatter'd amongst a Multitude, not only gain the assent of most of them, as to the Speculative part, but likewise induce several, especially the fiercest, most resolute, and best among them, to endure a thousand Inconveniencies, and undergo as many hardships, that they may have the pleasure of counting themselves Men of the second Class, and consequently appropriating to themselves all the Excellencies they have heard of it.

From what has been said we ought to expect in the first place, that the Heroes who took such extraordinary Pains to master some of their natural Appetites, and preferr'd the good of others to any visible Interest of their own, would not recede an Inch from the fine Notions they had receiv'd concerning the Dignity of Rational Creatures; and having ever the Authority of the Government on their side, with all imaginable Vigour assert the Esteem that was due to those of the second Class, as well as their superiority over the rest of their kind. In the second, that those who wanted a sufficient Stock of either Pride or Resolution, to buoy them up in mortifying of what was dearest to them, follow'd the sensual dictates of Nature, would yet be asham'd of confessing themselves to be those despicable Wretches that belong'd to the inferior Class, and were generally reckon'd to be so little remov'd from Brutes; and that therefore in their own Defence they would say, as others did, and hiding their own Imperfections as well as they could, cry up[8] Self-denial and Publick-spiritedness as much as any: For it is highly probable, that some of them, convinced by the real Proofs of Fortitude and Self-Conquest they had seen, would admire in others

what they found wanting in themselves; others be afraid of the Resolution and Prowess of those of the second Class, and that all of them were kept in awe by the Power of their Rulers, wherefore it is reasonable to think, that none of them (whatever they thought in themselves) would dare openly contradict, what by every body else was thought Criminal to doubt of.

This was (or at least might have been) the manner after which Savage Man was broke;[9] from whence it is evident, that the first Rudiments of Morality, broach'd by skilfull Politicians, to render Men useful to each other as well as tractable, were chiefly contriv'd; that the Ambitious might reap the more Benefit from, and govern vast Numbers of them with the greater Ease and Security. This Foundation of Politicks being once laid, it is impossible that Man should long remain uncivilis'd: For even those who only strove to gratify their Appetites, being continually cross'd by others of the same Stamp, could not but observe, that whenever they check'd their Inclinations, or but follow'd them with more Circumspection, they avoided a world of Troubles, and often escap'd many of the Calamities that generally attended the too eager pursuit after Pleasure.

First, they receiv'd, as well as others, the benefit of those Actions that were done for the good of the whole Society, and consequently could not forbear wishing well to those of the superior Class that perform'd them. Secondly, the more intent they were in seeking their own Advantage, without Regard to others, the more they were hourly convinced, that none stood so much in their way as those that were most like themselves.

It being the Interest then of the very worst of them, more than any, to preach up Publick-spiritedness, that they might reap the Fruits of the Labour and Self-denial of others, and at the same time indulge their own Appetites with less disturbance, they agreed with the rest, to call every thing, which, without Regard to the Publick, Man should commit to gratify any of his Appetites, VICE; if in that Action there could be observ'd the least prospect, that it might either be injurious to any of the Society, or ever render himself less serviceable to others: And to give the Name of VIRTUE to every Performance, by which Man, contrary to the impulse of Nature, should endeavour the Benefit of others, or the Conquest of his own Passions, out of a Rational Ambition of being good.

5. superior . . . Field: Cf. the conclusion of Rochester's *A Satyr Against Mankind* earlier in Part One. 6. discover: reveal, show. Mandeville plays on the word *imperfect*. 7. want: lack. 8. cry up: praise.

9. broke: (broken) tamed.

It shall be objected, that no Society was ever any ways civilis'd before the major part had agreed upon some Worship or other of an over ruling Power, and consequently that the Notions of Good and Evil, and the Distinction between *Virtue* and *Vice*, were never the Contrivance of Politicians, but the pure effect of Religion. Before I answer this Objection, I must repeat what I have said already, that in this *Enquiry into the Origin of Moral Virtue* I speak neither of *Jews* or *Christians*, but Man in his State of Nature and Ignorance of the true Deity; and then I affirm, that the Idolatrous Superstitions of all other Nations, and the pitiful Notions they had of the Supreme Being were incapable of exciting Man to Virtue, and good for nothing but to awe and amuse a rude and unthinking Multitude. It is evident from History, that in all considerable Societies, how stupid or ridiculous soever Peoples received Notions have been, as to the Deities they worship'd, Human Nature has ever exerted itself in all its branches, and that there is no Earthly Wisdom or Moral Virtue, but at one time or other Men have excell'd in it in all Monarchies and Commonwealths, that for Riches and Power have been any ways remarkable.

The *Ægyptians* not satisfy'd with having Deify'd all the ugly Monsters they could think on, were so silly as to adore the Onions of their own sowing; yet at the same time their Country was the most famous Nursery of Arts and Sciences in the World, and themselves more eminently skill'd in the deepest Mysteries of Nature than any Nation has been since.

No States or Kingdoms under Heaven have yielded more or greater Paterns in all sorts of Moral Virtues than the *Greek* and *Roman* Empires, more especially the latter; and yet how loose, absurd, and ridiculous were their Sentiments as to Sacred Matters: For without reflecting on the extravagant Number of their Deities, if we only consider the infamous Stories they father'd upon them, it is not to be denied but that their Religion, far from teaching Men the Conquest of their Passions, and the way to Virtue, seem'd rather contriv'd to justify their Appetites, and encourage their Vices. But if we would know what made 'em excel in Fortitude, Courage and Magnanimity, we must cast our Eyes on the Pomp of their Triumphs, the Magnificence of their Monuments and Arches, their Trophies, Statues, and Inscriptions; the variety of their Military Crowns, their Honours decreed to the Dead, Publick Encomiums on the Living, and other imaginary Rewards they bestow'd on Men of Merit; and we shall find, that what carried so many of them to the utmost Pitch of Self-denial, was nothing but their Policy in making use of the most effectual Means that human Pride could be flatter'd with.

It is visible then that it was not any Heathen Religion or other Idolatrous Superstition, that first put Man upon crossing his Appetites and subduing his dearest Inclinations, but the skilful Management of wary Politicians; and the nearer we search into human Nature, the more we shall be convinc'd, that the Moral Virtues are the Political Offspring which Flattery begot upon Pride.

There is no Man of what Capacity or Penetration soever, that is wholly Proof against the witchcraft of Flattery, if artfully perform'd, and suited to his Abilities. Children and Fools will swallow Personal Praise, but those that are more cunning, must be manag'd with greater Circumspection; and the more general the Flattery is, the less it is suspected by those it is levell'd at. What you say in Commendation of a whole Town is receiv'd with Pleasure by all the Inhabitants: Speak in Commendation of Letters in general, and every Man of Learning will think himself in particular obliged to you. You may safely praise the Employment a Man is of, or the Country he was born in; because you give him an opportunity of screening the Joy he feels upon his own account, under the Esteem which he pretends to have for others.

It is common among cunning Men, that understand the Power which Flattery has upon Pride, when they are afraid they shall be impos'd upon to enlarge, tho' much against their Conscience, upon the Honour, fair Dealing and Integrity of the Family, Country, or sometimes the Profession of him they suspect; because they know that Men often will change their Resolution, and act against their Inclination, that they may have the Pleasure of continuing to appear in the Opinion of some what they are conscious not to be in reality. Thus Sagacious Moralists draw Men like Angels, in hopes that the Pride at least of some will put 'em upon copying after the beautiful Originals which they are represented to be.

When the Incomparable Sir *Richard Steele*, in the usual Elegance of his easy Style, dwells on the Praises of his sublime Species, and with all the Embellishments of Rhetorick, sets forth the Excellency of Human Nature, it is impossible not to be charm'd with his happy Turns of Thought, and the Politeness of his Expressions. But tho' I have been often moved by the Force of his Eloquence, and ready to swallow the ingenious Sophistry with Pleasure, yet I could never be so serious but reflecting on his artful Encomiums, I thought on the Tricks made use of by the Women that would teach Children to be mannerly. When an awkward Girl before she can either Speak or Go,[10] begins after many entreaties to make the first rude Essays of[11] Curt'sying: The Nurse falls in an extasy of Praise; *There's a delicate Curt'sy! O fine Miss! There's a pretty Lady! Mama! Miss can make a better Curt'sy than her Sister* Molly! The same is eccho'd over by the Maids, whilst Mama almost hugs the Child to pieces; only Miss *Molly*, who being four Years older, knows how to make a very handsome Curt'sy, wonders at the Perverseness of their Judgment, and swelling with Indignation, is ready to cry at the Injustice that is done her, till being whisper'd in the Ear that it is only to please the Baby, and that she is a Woman; she grows Proud at being let into the Secret, and rejoicing at the Superiority of her Understanding, repeats what has been said with large Additions, and insults[12] over the weakness of her Sister, whom all this while she fancies to be the only Bubble[13] among them. These extravagant Praises would by any one, above the Capacity of an Infant, be call'd fulsome Flatteries, and, if you will, abominable Lies; yet Experience teaches us, that by the help of such gross Encomiums, young Misses will be brought to make pretty Curt'sies, and behave themselves womanly much sooner, and with less trouble, than they would without them. 'Tis the same with Boys, whom they'll strive to perswade, that all fine Gentlemen do as they are bid, and that none but Beggar Boys are rude, or dirty their Cloaths; nay, as soon as the wild Brat with his untaught Fist begins to fumble for his Hat, the Mother, to make him pull it off, tells him before he is two Years old, that he is a Man; and if he repeats that Action when she desires him, he's presently a Captain, a Lord Mayor, a King, or something higher if she can think of it, till egg'd on by the force of Praise, the little Urchin endeavours to imitate Man as well as he can, and strains all his Faculties to appear what his shallow Noddle imagines he is believ'd to be.

The meanest Wretch puts an inestimable value upon himself, and the highest wish of the Ambitious Man is to have all the World, as to that particular, of his Opinion: So that the most insatiable Thirst after Fame that ever Heroe was inspired with, was never more than an ungovernable Greediness to engross the Esteem and Admiration of others in future Ages as well as his own; and (what Mortification soever this Truth might be to the second Thoughts of an *Alexander* or a *Caesar*) the great Recompence in view, for which the most exalted Minds have with so much Alacrity, sacrifis'd their Quiet, Health, sensual Pleasures, and every inch of themselves, has never been any thing else but the Breath of Man, the Aerial Coyn of Praise. Who can forbear laughing when he thinks on all the great Men that have been so serious on the Subject of that *Macedonian* Madman, his capacious Soul, that mighty Heart, in one Corner of which, according to *Lorenzo Gratian*, the World was so commodiously Lodged, that in the whole there was room for Six more? Who can forbear Laughing, I say, when he compares the fine things that have been said of *Alexander*, with the End he proposed to himself from his vast Exploits, to be proved from his own Mouth; when the vast Pains he took to pass the *Hydaspes* forced him to cry out? *Oh ye* Athenians, *could you believe what Dangers I expose my self to, to be praised by you!*[14] To define then the Reward of Glory in the amplest manner, the most that can be said of it, is, that it consists in a superlative Felicity which a Man, who is conscious of having perform'd a noble Action, enjoys in Self love, whilst he is thinking on the Applause he expects of others.

But here I shall be told, that besides the noisy Toils of War and publick Bustle of the Ambitious, there are noble and generous Actions that are perform'd in Silence; that Virtue being its own Reward, those who are really Good have a satisfaction in their Consciousness of being so, which is all the Recompence they expect from the most worthy Performances; that among the Heathens there have been Men, who when they did good to others, were so far from coveting Thanks and Applause, that they took all imaginable Care to be for ever conceal'd from those on whom they bestow'd their Benefits, and consequently that Pride has no hand in spurring Man on to the highest pitch of Self-denial.

In Answer to this I say, that it is impossible to judge of a Man's Performance, unless we are thoroughly acquainted with the Principle and Motive from which

---

10. **Go:** walk. 11. **Essays of:** attempts at. 12. **insults:** exults, triumphs. 13. **Bubble:** dupe.

14. **Oh . . . you:** Mandeville borrows this passage from the article on Alexander in Bayle's *Dictionary* (1697–1706).

he acts. Pity, tho' it is the most gentle and the least mischievous of all our Passions, is yet as much a Frailty of our Nature, as Anger, Pride, or Fear. The weakest Minds have generally the greatest Share of it, for which Reason none are more Compassionate than Women and Children. It must be own'd, that of all our Weaknesses it is the most amiable, and bears the greatest Resemblance to Virtue; nay, without a considerable mixture of it the Society could hardly subsist: But as it is an impulse of Nature, that consults neither the publick Interest nor our own Reason, it may produce Evil as well as Good. It has help'd to destroy the Honour of Virgins, and corrupted the Integrity of Judges, and whoever acts from it as a Principle, what good soever he may bring to the Society, has nothing to boast of but that he has indulged a Passion that has happened to be beneficial to the Publick. There is no Merit in saving an Innocent Babe ready to drop into the Fire: The Action is neither good nor bad, and what Benefit soever the Infant received, we only obliged our selves; for to have seen it fall, and not strove to hinder it, would have caused a Pain which Self-preservation compell'd us to prevent: Nor has a rich Prodigal, that happens to be of a commiserating Temper, and loves to gratify his Passions, greater Virtue to boast of when he relieves an Object of Compassion with what to himself is a trifle.

But such Men as without complying with any weakness of their own, can part from what they value themselves, and from no other Motive but their Love to Goodness, perform a worthy Action in Silence: Such Men, I confess, have acquir'd more refin'd Notions of Virtue than those I have hitherto spoke of; yet even in these (with which the World has yet never swarm'd) we may discover no small Symptoms of Pride, and the humblest Man alive must confess, that the Reward of a Virtuous Action, which is the Satisfaction that ensues upon it, consists in a certain Pleasure he procures to himself by Contemplating on his own Worth: Which Pleasure, together with the occasion of it, are as certain Signs of Pride, as looking pale and trembling at any imminent Danger, are the Symptoms of Fear.

If the too scrupulous Reader should at first View condemn these Notions concerning the Origin of Moral Virtue, and think them perhaps offensive to Christianity, I hope he'll forbear his Censures, when he shall consider, that nothing can render the unsearchable depth of the Divine Wisdom more conspicuous than that *Man*, whom Providence had designed for Society, should not only by his own Frailties and Imperfections be led into the Road to Temporal Happiness, but likewise receive, from a seeming Necessity of Natural Causes, a Tincture of that Knowledge, in which he was afterwards to be made perfect by the True Religion, to his Eternal Welfare.

Anthony Ashley Cooper,
Third Earl of Shaftesbury

❧❧❧❧❧❧❧❧❧❧❧❧❧❧❧❧❧❧❧❧❧❧❧❧

1671–1713

Anthony Ashley Cooper, Third Earl of Shaftesbury, nowadays scarcely earns a mention by historians of philosophy, but he was much read in England and Europe during the eighteenth century. His grandfather was the Whig politician after whom Dryden created his Achitophel. Since his father was a feeble man, Cooper was placed in his grandfather's charge. The philosopher John Locke, whom he described as his "friend and foster-father," directed his education. After learning Greek and Latin, he attended first a private school, then Winchester, which he left in 1686 for his Grand Tour—three years' travel in Germany, Italy, and France. Back in England he spent five years in private study before entering Parliament in 1695. He prepared a maiden speech in support of a bill to allow counsel to prisoners on trial for treason; abashed before the House, he forgot his words but saved himself by felicitously comparing his difficulty with the plight of a man pleading for his life without assistance. In failing health from the strain of Parliamentary work, he gave up his seat in 1698 and retired for a year to Holland, where he became acquainted with the philosophers Le Clerc and Bayle. In his absence John Toland surreptitiously published his *Inquiry Concerning Virtue*.

Cooper returned to England in 1699 and soon after succeeded to the earldom. At first he busied himself with family affairs; then in 1701 he was urgently called to the House of Lords to support the Whigs in the controversy over the partition treaties. He responded by working hard for King William and the war party. But the following year, on the accession of Anne, he again retired to private life, retrenched his expenses, and spent another year in Holland. In the year 1708 he published his *Letter Concerning Enthusiasm*, prompted by the arrival in England of the "French prophets," a group of displaced religious enthusiasts. In 1709 he married, remaining "as happy a man now as ever," and his heir was born on February 9, 1711.

All this time Shaftesbury's health was declining, and after publishing his *Characteristicks of Men, Manners, Opinions, Times*—which included, besides the two treatises already mentioned, his *Sensus Communis: An Essay on the Freedom of Wit and Humour* (1709), his *Moralists* (1709), his *Soliloquy, or Advice to an Author* (1710), and some miscellaneous reflections—he left England for Italy. The short remainder of his life he spent at Naples, devoting himself to writing. He died on February 15, 1713, "with perfect cheerfulness and . . . sweetness of temper."

Shaftesbury's writings were popular mainly because of their concern with the prime question of the century, how to live. They sought to "refine our Spirits, improve our Understandings, [and] mend our Manners." To the question how to live Shaftesbury no doubt felt that his own life held the key. First, he had had the comfortable advantages of high birth and wealth and had been schooled in a gentlemanly code of conduct, much polished over the generations. Further, his position had provided the opportunity to become a connoisseur of the arts and to participate in public affairs. His world was marred only by his failing health, but even that could not disturb the genteel tranquility that his philosophical writings recommended to others. "To *philosophize*," he said, "in a just Signification, is but To carry *Good-Breeding* a step higher."

Writing a half-century later than Thomas Hobbes, Shaftesbury is, philosophically, directly opposed to him. For Hobbes, man, who exists in a state of nature, is motivated solely by self-interest and is basically at war with society. He agrees to live in peace with his fellows under governmental authority only to protect himself from others and to provide himself with the most secure opportunities for the satisfaction of his own ambitions. Shaftesbury asserted the opposite: man is altruistic and, though he has a natural love for himself, he has "*natural Affections*" for other men. He wrote:

> 'Tis impossible to suppose a mere sensible Creature originally so ill-constituted, and unnatural, as that from the moment he comes to be try'd by sensible Objects, he shou'd have no one good Passion towards his Kind, no Foundation either of Pity, Love, Kindness, or social Affection. 'Tis full as impossible to conceive, that a rational Creature coming first to be try'd by rational Objects, and receiving into his Mind the Images or Representations of Justice, Generosity, Gratitude, or other Virtue, shou'd have no *Liking* of these, or *Dislike* of their Contrarys.

According to Shaftesbury the moral standards by which conduct is regulated are discovered by intuition and so are not to be formulated through rational argument. But though his standards are absolute and therefore beyond proof by argument, he attempted to show that they were consistent with the nature of things as he conceived it.

In the *Inquiry Concerning Virtue* he sketched out his view of the universe. He began by acknowledging with Hobbes "that every Creature has a private Good and Interest of his own; which Nature has compel'd him to seek." But this man was not the ferocious and solitary individualist Hobbes envisioned, "who had neither Mate nor Fellow of any kind; nothing of his own Likeness, towards which he stood well-affected or inclin'd; nor any thing without, or beyond himself, for which he had the least Passion or Concern." For Shaftesbury man was inseparably linked to his fellows. This bond among men reflected for Shaftesbury the interdependence of all beings and all objects, the "SYSTEM *of all Things, and a Universal Nature.*"

Shaftesbury believed too in the absolute validity of goodness and wisdom and held that these are the attributes of God. He naturally concluded that of systems possible such a God could only have formed the best and that whatever is must be right, although it may be uncomfortable. Pope's words in his *Essay on Man* (1733–34), "All

Discord, Harmony, not understood; / All partial Evil, universal Good," reveal his debt to Shaftesbury. If, then, all things are working together for good, it is clear that good for any species and any individual lies in participation in the joint labor:

> To deserve the name of *Good* or *Virtuous*, a Creature must have all his Inclinations and Affections, his Dispositions of Mind and Temper, sutable, and agreeing with the Good of his *Kind*, or of that *System* in which he is included, and of which he constitutes a PART. To stand thus well affected, and to have one's Affections *right* and *intire*, not only in respect of one's self, but of Society and the Publick: This is *Rectitude*, *Integrity*, or VIRTUE.

Man's great advantage over all other species is his ability to reflect on his actions. Shaftesbury writes:

> In a Creature capable of forming general Notions of Things, not only the outward Beings which offer themselves to the Sense, are the Objects of the Affection; but the very *Actions* themselves, and the *Affections* of Pity, Kindness, Gratitude, and their Contrarys, being brought into the Mind by Reflection, become Objects. So that, by means of this reflected Sense there arises another kind of Affection towards those very Affections themselves, which have been already felt, and are now become the Subject of a new Liking or Dislike.

The capacity for liking or disliking these moral abstracts, for discriminating between them, is what Shaftesbury calls the moral sense. Shaftesbury did not believe that our moral reflection takes the form of analysis and calculation, but that

> the Case is the same in the *mental* or *moral* Subjects, as in the ordinary *Bodys*, or common Subjects of *Sense*. The Shapes, Motions, Colours, and Proportions of these latter being presented to our Eye; there necessarily results a Beauty or Deformity, according to the different Measure, Arrangement and Disposition of their several Parts. So in *Behaviour* and *Actions*, when presented to our Understanding, there must be found, of necessity, an apparent Difference according to the Regularity or Irregularity of the Subjects.

Moral, like aesthetic, discrimination works intuitively. The good is beautiful; hence, moral judgment is an exercise of taste. And as our aesthetic taste may be improved, so may our moral taste; a person may, as Pope was to argue in *An Essay on Criticism* (1711), become an expert in one as in the other:

> The TASTE of Beauty, and the *Relish* of what is decent, just, and amiable, perfects the *Character* of the GENTLEMAN, and the PHILOSOPHER. And the Study of such a TASTE or *Relish* will, as we suppose, be ever the great Employment and Concern of him, who covets as well to be *wise* and *good*, as *agreeable* and *polite*.

Shaftesbury offered a welcome alternative to Hobbes, who it was widely thought was an atheist. At the same time, part of his popularity was due to his being, while no atheist, not much of a Christian either. He was thoroughly "enlightened" in suggesting that man should not look for guidance to any authority—including the

Church—but should look for himself into his own nature. Shaftesbury would not accept the claims of revealed religion without question, but believed that there is "something previous to Revelation, some antecedent Demonstration of Reason" by which we may gain a knowledge of the Deity. We must frame for ourselves a "Notion of what is *morally excellent*" and "trust to . . . Reason which tells us, that nothing beside *what is so*, can have place in *the* DEITY."

For the religious insight of the Jews Shaftesbury had no great respect, and he was no less antagonistic to the Calvinist doctrine of the corruption of man than to the Hobbesian conception of man in the state of nature. Gloomy fanaticism and atheism he found alike vicious. He wrote, "Nothing beside ill Humour . . . can bring a Man to think seriously that the World is govern'd by any devilish or malicious Power . . . I very much question whether any thing, besides ill Humour, can be the Cause of Atheism." The man of good humor, knowing that "all things are kindly and well dispos'd," will turn aside from such moroseness with a smile. In his *Letter Concerning Enthusiasm*, Shaftesbury blandly announced that fanaticism was best countered by wit and ridicule, for nothing would so surely explode its pretensions. True religion, good-humored religion, would always be impervious to ridicule. Shaftesbury's opponents oversimplified his idea into the proposition "Ridicule is a test of truth," but Shaftesbury was not so categorical. He felt bound to point out, for example, that the free use of wit and humor he advocated was "only . . . the Liberty of *the Club*, and . . . that sort of Freedom which is taken amongst *Gentlemen* and *Friends*, who know one another perfectly well." This recommendation that wit and humor should be applied to religion started a debate that continued through the century.

If belief in God has an important place in the good life as Shaftesbury saw it, it is because that belief is appropriate to our nature. In the *Inquiry Concerning Virtue* he discusses the relation between virtue and religious belief, concluding that theism can lead to virtue:

> For where the Theistical Belief is intire and perfect, there must be a steddy Opinion of the Superintendency of a Supreme Being, a Witness and Spectator of human Life, and conscious of whatsoever is felt or acted in the Universe: So that in the perfectest Recess, or deepest Solitude, there must be *One* still presum'd remaining with us; whose Presence singly must be of more moment than that of the most August Assembly on Earth.

But Shaftesbury insists over and over again that we love virtue for its own sake, however influential the inner presence of God. The argument of Pascal's "wager"— we had better believe in God because if He turns out to exist we shall have assured our salvation, and if not we shall be none the worse—Shaftesbury repudiates as he repudiates the idea of a reward in the next life, proffered as an incentive to virtue by many religious systems:

> If the Love of doing Good, be not, of it-self, a *good* and *right* Inclination; I know not how there can possibly be such a thing as *Goodness* or *Virtue*. If the Inclination be *right*; 'tis a perverting of it, to apply it solely to *the Reward*, and make us conceive such Wonders of the Grace and Favour which is to attend Virtue; when there is so little shewn of the intrinsick Worth or Value of the Thing it-self.

Here we reach the basis of Shaftesbury's philosophy—the belief in "the *eternal Measures*, and immutable independent Nature of *Worth* and VIRTUE" and the belief in our capacity as human beings to recognize Worth and Virtue within us. Possessing them, we have the moral sense, a "*natural* and *just* Sense of Right and Wrong."

The best editions are J. M. Robertson's (2 vols., 1900) and Benjamin Rand's (1914). For criticism, see R. L. Brett's *The Third Earl of Shaftesbury: A Study in Eighteenth-Century Literary Theory* (1951). C. A. Moore's "Shaftesbury and the Ethical Poets in England," in *Backgrounds of English Literature, 1700–1760* (1953), is illuminating.

SENSUS COMMUNIS:°
AN ESSAY ON THE FREEDOM
OF WIT AND HUMOUR . . .

❧

The text is that of the first edition, *Sensus Communis: An Essay on the Freedom of Wit and Humour. In a Letter to a Friend* (1709). The essay was incorporated into the *Characteristicks* in 1711 and revised along with the rest in 1714. The two issues of 1711 and the revised edition of 1714 are included in the collation, as is the marked copy of 1711 (now in the British Museum) which Shaftesbury used in preparing the 1714 edition. Substantive changes authorized by 1711 and the corrected 1711 copy have been admitted into the text, which also adopts those few readings where 1714 did not follow Shaftesbury's manuscript corrections. Occasionally an accidental has also been adopted from the manuscript corrections in deference to an explicit indication by Shaftesbury.

❧

SENSUS COMMUNIS: *Part III*. **Sensus Communis:** common sense; *common* means "held in common by all or most of mankind." In any given matter the common sense is the impression spontaneously arrived at by most normal observers. Shaftesbury holds that certain moral sentiments receive an almost universal sanction from such observers; from this idea of moral consensus it is only a step to his famous contention that men have an innate moral sense.

PART III

SECT. III.

YOU have heard it (my Friend!)[1] as a common Saying, that *Interest governs the World*. But, I believes whoever looks narrowly into the Affairs of it, will find, that *Passion, Humour, Caprice, Zeal, Faction*, and a thousand other Springs, which are counter to *Self-Interest*, have as considerable a part in the Movements of this Machine. There are more Wheels and Counter-Poises in this Engine than are easily imagin'd. 'Tis of too complex a kind, to fall under one simple View, or be explain'd thus briefly in a word or two. The Studiers of this *Mechanism* must have a very partial Eye, to overlook all other Motions besides those of the lowest and narrowest Compass. 'Tis hard, that in the Plan or Description of this Clock-work, no Wheel or Ballance shou'd be allow'd on the side of the better and more enlarg'd Affections; that nothing shou'd be understood to be done in *Kindness* or *Generosity;* nothing in *pure good Nature* or *Friendship*, or thro any *social* or *natural Affection* of any kind; when, perhaps, the main Springs of this Machine will be found to be either these very *natural Affections* themselves, or a compound kind deriv'd from them, and retaining more than one half of their Nature.

But here (my Friend!) you must not expect that I shou'd draw you up a formal *Scheme*[2] of the Passions,

---

1. my Friend: an unnamed young gentleman, brought up chiefly at court. Cf. the beginning of section iv and of sections i and ii in Part IV. **2. Scheme:** system.

or pretend to shew you their *Genealogy* and *Relation;* how they are interwoven with one another, or interfere with our Happiness and Interest. 'Twou'd be out of the Genius[3] and Compass of such a letter as this, to frame a just *Plan* or *Model;* by which you might, with an accurate View, observe what Proportion the *friendly* and *natural Affections* seem to bear in this Order of Architecture.

Modern Projectors, I know, wou'd willingly rid their Hands of these *natural* Materials; and wou'd fain build after a more uniform way. They wou'd new frame the Human Heart; and have a mighty Fancy to reduce all its Motions, Ballances and Weights, to that one Principle and Foundation of a cool and deliberate *Selfishness*.[4] Men, it seems, are unwilling to think they can be so outwitted, and impos'd on by Nature, as to be made to serve her Purposes, rather than their own. They are asham'd to be drawn thus out of *themselves*, and forc'd from what they esteem their *true Interest*.

There has been in all times a sort of narrow-minded Philosophers, who have thought to set this Difference to rights, by conquering *Nature* in themselves. A Primitive Father and Founder[5] among these, saw well this Power of *Nature*, and understood it so far, that he earnestly exhorted his Followers neither to beget Children, nor serve their Country. There was no dealing with Nature, it seems, while these alluring Objects stood in the way. *Relations, Friends, Countrymen, Laws, Politick Constitutions, the Beauty of Order and Government,* and *the Interest of Society and Mankind,* were Objects which, he well saw, wou'd *naturally* raise a stronger Affection than any which was grounded upon the narrow bottom of mere Self. His Advice, therefore, not to marry, nor engage at all in the Publick, was wise, and sutable to his Design. There was no way to be truly a Disciple of this Philosophy, but to leave Family, Friends, Country, and Society, *to cleave to it.*—And, in good earnest, who wou'd not, if it were *Happiness* to do so?—The Philosopher, however, was *kind*, in telling us his Thought. 'Twas a Token of his *Fatherly Love* of Mankind.

*Tu Pater, & rerum Inventor! Tu Patria nobis
Suppeditas præcepta!*[6]

But the Revivers of this Philosophy in latter Days, appear to be of a lower Genius. They seem to have understood less of this force of Nature, and thought to alter *the Thing*, by shifting *a Name.* They wou'd so explain all the social Passions, and natural Affections, as to denominate 'em *of the selfish kind.* Thus Civility, Hospitality, Humanity towards Strangers or People in Distress, is only *a more deliberate Selfishness.* An honest Heart is only *a more cunning one:* and Honesty and good Nature, *a more deliberate,* or *better regulated Self-Love.* The *Love* of Kindred, Children and Posterity, is purely *Love of Self,* and of *one's own immediate Blood:* As if, by this Reckoning, all Mankind were not included; *All* being of *one Blood,* and join'd by Inter-Marriages and Alliances; as they have been transplanted in Colonys, and mix'd one with another. And thus *Love of one's Country,* and *Love of Mankind,* must also be *Self-Love. Magnanimity* and *Courage,* no doubt, are Modifications of this universal *Self-Love!* For *Courage* (says our modern Philosopher[7]) is *constant Anger.* And *all Men* (says a witty Poet[8]) *wou'd be Cowards if they durst.*

That the Poet, and the Philosopher both, were *Cowards,*[9] may be yielded perhaps without Dispute. They may have spoken the best of their Knowledg. But for *true Courage,* it has so little to do with *Anger;* that there lies always the strongest Suspicion against it, where this Passion is highest. The *true* Courage is the *cool* and *calm.* The bravest of Men have the least of a brutal bullying Insolence; and in the very time of Danger are found the most serene, pleasant, and free. Rage, we know, can make a Coward forget himself and fight. But what is done in *Fury,* or *Anger,* can never be plac'd to the Account of *Courage.* Were it otherwise, Womankind might claim to be the *stoutest* Sex: For their Hatred and Anger have ever been allow'd the strongest and most lasting.

Other Authors[10] there have been of a yet inferiour Kind: a sort of Distributers and petty Retailers of this Wit; who have run Changes, and Divisions,[11] without end, upon this Article of *Self-Love.* You have the very

3. **Genius:** character. 4. **Selfishness:** The principal target here is the egoistic ethics of Thomas Hobbes. (Cf. the selections from Butler and Mandeville also in Part Two.) 5. **A Primitive . . . Founder:** the Greek philosopher Epicurus (c. 341–270 B.C.). 6. **Tu . . . præcepta:** "Father, and discoverer of things, you sustain us with fatherly guidance" (Lucretius' tribute to Epicurus, *De Rerum Natura,* III. 9–10).

7. **modern Philosopher:** Hobbes in *Leviathan,* I. vi. 8. **a witty Poet:** Lord Rochester. See his *Satyr Against Mankind,* l. 158, in Part One. 9. **the Poet . . . Cowards:** Hobbes made no secret of his own timorousness; Rochester's fame in this particular rested on a charge (since discredited) that he refused to fight when challenged to a duel. 10. **Other Authors:** In a footnote Shaftesbury cites La Rochefoucauld, whose *Maximes* (1665) were celebrated for their relentless probing into the selfishness of human motives. 11. **Changes, and Divisions:** variations (both terms from music).

same Thought spun out a hundred Ways, and drawn into Motto's, and Devises,[12] to set forth this Riddle; That "act as disinterestedly or generously as you please, *Self* still is at the bottom, and nothing else." Now if these Gentlemen, who delight so much in the Play of Words, but are cautious how they grapple closely with Definitions, wou'd tell us only what *Self-Interest* was, and determine[13] *Happiness*, and *Good*, there wou'd be an End of this Enigmatical Wit. For in this we shou'd all agree, that Happiness was to be pursu'd, and in fact was always sought after: but whether found in *following Nature*, and giving way to *common* Affection; or in suppressing it, and turning every Passion towards *private* Advantage, a narrow *Self*-End, or the Preservation of *mere Life*; this wou'd be the matter in Debate between us. The Question wou'd not be, "Who *lov'd* himself; or Who *not*": but "Who lov'd and serv'd himself the *rightest*, and after *the* truest manner."

'Tis the height of Wisdom, no doubt, to be rightly *selfish*. And to value Life, as far as Life is good, belongs as much to Courage as to Discretion. But a wretched Life is no wise Man's Wish. To be without *Honesty*,[14] is, in effect, to be without *natural Affection* or *Sociableness* of any kind. And a Life without *natural Affection, Friendship*, or *Sociableness*, wou'd be found a wretched one, were it to be try'd. 'Tis as these Feelings and Affections are intrinsically valuable and worthy, that *Self-Interest* is to be rated and esteem'd. A Man is by nothing so much *himself*, as by his *Temper*, and *the Character of his Passions and Affections*. If he loses what is manly and worthy in these, he is as much lost to himself as when he loses his Memory and Understanding. The least step into Villany or Baseness, changes the Character and Value of a Life. He who wou'd preserve Life at any rate, must abuse *himself* more than any-one can abuse him. And if Life be not a dear Thing indeed, he who has refus'd to live a Villain, and has prefer'd Death to a base Action, has been a Gainer by the Bargain.

SECT. IV.

'Tis well for you (my Friend!) that in your Education you have had little to do with the *Philosophy*, or *Philosophers* of our Days. A good Poet, and an honest Historian, may afford Learning enough for *a Gentleman*. And such a one, whilst he reads these Authors as his Diversion, will have a truer relish of their sense, and understand 'em better, than a *Pedant*, with all his Labours, and the Assistance of his Volumes of Commentators. I am sensible, that of old 'twas the Custom to send the Youth of highest Quality to *Philosophers* to be form'd. 'Twas in their Schools, in their Company and by their Precepts and Example, that the illustrious Pupils were inur'd to Hardship, and exercis'd in the severest Courses of Temperance and Self-denial. By such an early Discipline, they were fitted for the Command of others; to maintain their Country's Honour in War, rule wisely in the State, and fight against Luxury and Corruption in times of Prosperity and Peace. If any of these Arts are comprehended in *University-Learning*, 'tis well. But as some Universitys in the World are now model'd, they seem not so very effectual to these Purposes, nor so fortunate in preparing for a right Practice of the World, or a just Knowledg of Men and Things. Had you been thorow-pac'd[15] in the *Ethicks* or *Politicks* of the Schools, I shou'd never have thought of writing a word to you upon *common Sense*, or *the Love of Mankind*. I shou'd not have cited the Poet's *Dulce & Decorum*.[16] Nor, if I had made a Character[17] for you, as he for his noble Friend, shou'd I have crown'd it with his

Non ille pro caris Amicis
Aut Patria timidus perire.[18]

Our Philosophy now-a-days runs after the manner of that able Sophister,[19] who said, "*Skin for Skin: All that a Man has, will he give for his Life*." 'Tis Orthodox Divinity, as well as sound Philosophy, with some Men, to rate *Life* by the Number and Exquisiteness of *the pleasing Sensations*. These they constantly set in opposition to *dry Virtue* and *Honesty*. And upon this foot, they think it proper to call all Men Fools, who wou'd hazard *a Life*, or part with any of these *pleasing*

---

12. **Devises:** either emblems or contrivances. 13. **determine:** literally, settle the boundaries of. 14. **Honesty:** virtue. Though he occasionally uses the word to mean little more than truthfulness or good faith, Shaftesbury often expects it to carry overtones of the French conception of the *honnête homme*—naturalness, good sense, and fairness of mind.

15. **thorow-pac'd:** fully indoctrinated. 16. **Dulce & Decorum:** "sweet and fitting" (Horace, *Odes*, III. ii. 13). Speaking earlier of certain ancient examples of disinterested virtue, Shaftesbury wrote, "Whoever wished to do good, DULCE ET DECORUM EST was his sole Reason. 'Twas *Inviting* and *Becoming*. 'Twas *Good* and *Honest*. And that this is still a good Reason, and according to *Common Sense*, I will endeavour to satisfy you." 17. **Character:** character sketch. 18. **Non . . . perire:** "He is not afraid to die for his dear friends or his fatherland!" (Horace, *Odes*, IV. ix. 51-52). 19. **Sophister:** namely, Satan. See Job 2:4.

Sensations; except on the Condition of being repaid in the same Coin, and with good Interest into the Bargain. Thus, it seems, we are to learn Virtue by Usury; and inhance the Value of *Life,* and of the *Pleasures of Sense,* in order to be wise, and to *live well.*

But you, my Friend, are stubborn in this Point: and instead of being brought to think mournfully of Death, or to repine at the Loss of what you may sometimes hazard by your Honesty, you can laugh at such Maxims as these; and divert your self with the improv'd Selfishness, and Philosophical Cowardice of these fashionable Moralists. You will not be taught to value *Life,* at their rate, or degrade HONESTY as they do, who make it only *a Name.* You are persuaded there is something more in the Thing than *Fashion* or *Applause;* that WORTH and MERIT are substantial, and no way variable by *Fancy* or *Will;* and that HONOUR is as much it self, when acting *by it self,* and *unseen,* as when *seen,* and applauded by all the World.

Shou'd One, who had the Countenance of a Gentleman, ask me, "Why I wou'd avoid being *nasty,* when no body was present." In the first place I shou'd be fully satisfy'd that he himself was a very nasty Gentleman who cou'd ask this Question; and that it wou'd be a hard matter for me to make him ever conceive what *true Cleanliness* was. However, I might, notwithstanding this, be contented to give him a slight Answer, and say, "'Twas because I had a Nose." Shou'd he trouble me further, and ask again, "What if I had a Cold? Or what if naturally I had no such nice²⁰ Smell?" I might answer perhaps, "That I car'd as little to see my self *nasty,* as that others shou'd see me in that condition." But what if it were *in the Dark?* Why even then, tho I had neither Nose, nor Eyes, my Sense of the Matter wou'd be still the same; my Nature wou'd rise at the Thought of what was sordid: or if it did not; I shou'd have a wretched Nature indeed, and *hate my self* for a Beast. *Honour my self* I never cou'd; whilst I had no better a sense of what, in reality, I ow'd my self, and what became me, as *a human Creature.*

Much in the same manner have I heard it ask'd, *Why shou'd a Man be honest in the Dark?* What a Man must be to ask this Question, I won't say. But for Those who have no better a Reason for being *honest* than the Fear of *a Gibbet* or *a Jail;* I shou'd not, I confess, much covet their Company, or Acquaintance. And if any Guardian of mine who had kept his Trust,

and given me back my Estate when I came of Age, had been discover'd to have acted thus, thro *Fear* only of what might happen to him; I shou'd for my own part, undoubtedly, continue civil and respectful to him: but for my Opinion of his Worth, it wou'd be such as the PYTHIAN God²¹ had of his Votary, who *devoutly fear'd* him, and *therefore* restor'd to a Friend what had been deposited in his Hands.

> *Reddidit ergo* metu, *non moribus; & tamen omnem*
> *Vocem adyti dignam templo, veramque probavit,*
> *Extinctus tota pariter cum prole domoque.*²²

I know very well that many Services to the Publick are done merely for the sake of *a Gratuity;* and that *Informers* in particular, are to be taken care of, and sometimes made *Pensioners of State.* But I must beg pardon for the particular Thoughts I may have of these Gentlemens Merit; and shall never bestow my Esteem on any other than the *voluntary* Discoverers of Villany, and *hearty* Prosecutors of their Country's Interest. And in this respect, I know nothing greater or nobler than the undertaking and managing some important Accusation; by which some high Criminal of State, or some form'd Body of Conspirators against the Publick, may be arraign'd and brought to Punishment, thro the honest Zeal and publick Affection of a private Man.

I know too, that the mere Vulgar of Mankind often stand in need of such a rectifying Object as *the Gallows* before their Eyes. Yet I have no belief, that any Man of a liberal Education, or common Honesty, ever needed to have recourse to this Idea in his Mind, the better to restrain him from playing the Knave. And if A SAINT had no other Virtue than what was rais'd in him by the same Objects of Reward and Punishment, in a more distant State; I know not whose Love or Esteem he might gain besides: but for my own part, I shou'd never think him worthy of mine.

> *Nec furtum feci, nec fugi, si mihi dicat*
> *Servus: Habes pretium, loris non ureris, aio.*
> *Non hominem occidi: Non pasces in cruce corvos.*
> *Sum Bonus & Frugi: Renuit, negat atque Sabellus.*²³

20. nice: sensitive.

21. Pythian God: Apollo. **22. Reddidit . . . domoque:** "So he gave it back—but out of fear, not virtue; and even so, he proved the oracle true and worthy to be the god's voice, for he and all his house perished" (Juvenal, *Satires,* V. xiii. 202–05). **23. Nec . . . Sabellus:** "If my slave were to say to me, 'I never stole or ran away,' I should answer, 'You have your reward, you are not flogged.' 'I never killed anyone!'—'you won't hang on a cross to feed crows.' 'I am good and honest!'—my friend Sabellus shakes his head and can't agree" (Horace, *Epistles,* I. xvi. 46–49).

FROM

PART IV

SECT. I.

BY this time (my Friend!) you may possibly, I hope, be satisfy'd, that as I am in earnest in defending *Raillery*, so I can be sober too in the Use of it. 'Tis in reality a serious Study, to learn to temper and regulate that *Humour* which Nature has given us, as a more lenitive Remedy against Vice, and a kind of Specifick against Superstition and Melancholy Delusion. There is a great difference between seeking how to raise a Laugh from every thing; and seeking, in every thing, what justly may be laugh'd at. For nothing is ridiculous, except what is deform'd: Nor is any thing proof against *Raillery*, except what is handsom and just. And therefore 'tis the hardest thing in the World, to deny *Fair* HONESTY the use of this Weapon, which can never bear an Edge against herself, and bears against every thing contrary.

If the very *Italian Buffoons*[1] were to give us the Rule in these Cases, we shou'd learn by them, that in their lowest and most scurrilous way of Wit, there was nothing so successfully to be play'd upon, as the Passions of Cowardice and Avarice. One may defy the World to turn real *Bravery* or *Generosity* into Ridicule. A Glutton, or mere Sensualist, is as ridiculous as the other two Characters. Nor can an unaffected *Temperance* be made the Subject of Contempt to any besides the grossest and most contemptible of Mankind. Now these *three* Ingredients make up a virtuous Character: as *the contrary three* a vicious one. How therefore can we possibly make a Jest of Honesty? —To laugh *both* ways, is nonsensical. And if the Ridicule lie against *Sottishness, Avarice,* and *Cowardice;* you see the Consequence. A Man must be soundly ridiculous, who, with all the Wit imaginable, wou'd go about to ridicule Wisdom, or laugh at Honesty, or Good Manners.

A Man of thorow *Good-Breeding,* whatever else he be, is incapable of doing a rude or brutal Action. He never *deliberates* in this case, or considers of the Matter by prudential Rules of Self-Interest and Advantage. He acts from his Nature, in a manner necessarily, and without Reflection: and if he did not, it were impossible for him to answer his Character, or be found

that truly well-bred Man, on every occasion. 'Tis the same with the *Honest Man.* He can't deliberate in the Case of a plain Villany. *A Plum*[2] is no Temptation to him. He likes and loves himself too well, to change Hearts with one of those corrupt Miscreants, who amongst 'em, gave that name to a round Sum of Mony gain'd by Rapine and Plunder of the Commonwealth. He who wou'd enjoy *a Freedom of Mind,* and be truly *Possessor of himself,* must be above the Thought of stooping to what is villanous or base. He on the other side, who has a Heart to stoop, must necessarily quit the Thought of *Manliness, Resolution, Friendship, Merit,* and *a Character with himself and others:* But to affect these Enjoyments and Advantages, together with the Privileges of a licentious Principle; to pretend to enjoy Society, and *a free Mind,* in company with *a knavish Heart,* is as ridiculous as the way of Children, who eat their Cake, and afterwards cry for it. When Men begin to *deliberate* about Dishonesty, and finding it go less against their Stomach, ask slily, "Why they shou'd stick at a good Piece of Knavery for a good Sum?" They shou'd be told, as Children, that *They can't eat their Cake, and have it.*

When Men, indeed, are become *accomplish'd Knaves,* they are past *crying for their Cake.* They know Themselves, and are *known* by Mankind. 'Tis not These who are so much envy'd or admir'd. The *moderate* Kind are the more taking with us. Yet had we Sense, we shou'd consider 'tis in reality the *thorow profligate Knave,* the very *compleat unnatural Villain* alone, who can any way bid for Happiness with the *Honest Man.* True Interest is wholly on *one* side, or *the other.* All between is Inconsistency, Irresolution, Remorse, Vexation, and an Ague-Fit:[3] from hot to cold; from one Passion to another quite contrary; a perpetual Discord of Life; and an alternate Disquiet and Self-Dislike. The only Rest or Repose must be thro *one,* determin'd, considerate Resolution: which when once taken, must be courageously kept; and the Passions and Affections brought under Obedience to it; the Temper steel'd and harden'd to the Mind; the Disposition to the Judgment. Both must agree; else all must be Disturbance and Confusion. So that to think with one's self, in good earnest, "Why may not one do this *little* Villany, or commit this *one* Treachery, and but for *once;*" is the most ridiculous Imagination in the world, and contrary to COMMON SENSE. For a

---

Part IV. **1. Buffoons:** actors in the farcical roles of the commedia dell'arte.

2. Plum: (or plumb) a fortune of £100,000. **3. Ague-Fit:** alternating chills and fever.

common honest Man, whilst left to himself, and undisturb'd by Philosophy and subtle Reasonings about his Interest, gives no other Answer to the Thought of Villany, than that *he can't possibly find in his heart* to set about it, or conquer the natural Aversion he has to it. And this is *natural*, and *just*.

The Truth is; as Notions stand now in the World, with respect to Morals; Honesty is like to gain little by Philosophy, or deep Speculations of any kind. In the main, 'tis best to stick to *Common Sense*, and go no further. Mens first Thoughts, in this matter, are generally better than their second: their natural Notions better than those refin'd by Study, or Consultations with Casuists.[4] According to common Speech, as well as common Sense, *Honesty is the best Policy:* But according to refin'd Sense, the only *well-advis'd* Persons, as to this World, are *errant[5] Knaves;* and they alone are thought to serve themselves, who serve their Passions, and indulge their loosest Appetites and Desires.—Such, it seems, are *the Wise*, and such *the Wisdom of this World!*

An ordinary Man talking of a vile Action, in a way of *Common Sense*, says naturally and heartily, "He wou'd not be guilty of such a thing for the whole World." But *speculative Men* find great Modifications in the Case; many ways of Evasion; many Remedys; many Alleviations. A good Gift *rightly* apply'd; a *right* Method of suing out a Pardon; good Alms-Houses, and Charitable Foundations erected for *right* Worshippers; and a good Zeal shewn for the *right* Belief, may sufficiently atone for *one wrong Practice;* especially when it is such as raises a Man to a considerable power (as they say) of *doing Good*, and serving *the true Cause*.

Many a good Estate, many a high Station has been gain'd upon such a Bottom as this. Some *Crowns* too may have been purchas'd on these terms: and some great *Emperors* (if I mistake not) there have been of old, who were much assisted by these or the like Principles; and in return were not ingrateful to the Cause and Party which had assisted 'em. The Forgers of such Morals have been amply endow'd: and the World has paid roundly for its Philosophy; since the original plain Principles of Humanity, and the simple honest Precepts of *Peace* and *mutual Love*, have, by a sort of spiritual Chymists, been so sublimated,[6] as to become the highest Corrosives; and passing thro their Limbecks,[7] have yielded the strongest Spirit of *mutual Hatred* and *malignant Persecution*.

SECT. II.

But our Humours (my Friend) incline us not to melancholy Reflections. Let the *solemn* Reprovers of Vice proceed in the manner most sutable to their Genius, and Character. I am ready to congratulate with 'em on the Success of their Labours, in that authoritative way which is allow'd 'em. I know not in the mean while, why others may not be allow'd to *ridicule* Folly, and recommend Wisdom and Virtue (if possibly they can) in a way of Pleasantry and Mirth. I know not why Poets, or such as write chiefly for the Entertainment of themselves and others, may not be allow'd this Privilege. And if it be the Complaint of our *standing Reformers*, that they are not heard so well by *the Gentlemen of Fashion;* if they exclaim against those airy Wits who fly to *Ridicule* as a Protection, and make successful Sallys from that Quarter; why shou'd it be deny'd one, who is but *a Volunteer* in this Cause, to engage the Adversary on his own Terms, and expose himself willingly to such Attacks, on the single Condition only of being allow'd *fair Play* in the same kind?

By *Gentlemen of Fashion*, I understand those to whom a natural good Genius, or the Force of good Education, has given a *Sense* of what is *naturally graceful* and *becoming*. Some by mere Nature, others by Art and Practice, are Masters of an Ear in Musick, an Eye in Painting, a Fancy in the ordinary things of Ornament and Grace, a Judgment in Proportions of all kinds, and a general good Taste in most of those Subjects which make the Amusement and Delight of the ingenious[8] People of the World. Let such Gentlemen as these be as extravagant as they please, or as irregular in their Morals; they must at the same time discover their Inconsistency, live at variance with themselves, and in contradiction to that Principle, on which they ground their highest Pleasure and Entertainment.

Of all other Beautys which *Virtuosos*[9] pursue, *Poets* celebrate, *Musicians* sing, and *Architects* or *Artists*, of whatever kind, describe or form; the most delightful, the most engaging and pathetick,[10] is that which is

---

4. **Casuists:** persons who argue moral questions by concentrating not on principles but on the subtleties of individual cases. 5. **errant:** arrant. 6. **sublimated:** refined.

7. **Limbecks:** alembics, vessels used in distilling. 8. **ingenious:** intelligent, acute. 9. **Virtuosos:** connoisseurs, persons skilled, as Dr. Johnson puts it, "in antique or natural curiosities." 10. **pathetick:** capable of arousing one's emotions.

drawn from real *Life* and from the *Passions*. Nothing affects the Heart like that which is purely *from it self,* and *of its own nature; such as the Beauty of Sentiments; the Grace of Actions; the Turn of Characters,* and *the Proportions and Features of a human Mind.* This Lesson of Philosophy, even a Romance, a Poem, or a Play may teach us; whilst the fabulous Author[11] leads us with such Pleasure thro the Labyrinth of the Affections, and interests us, whether we will or no, in the Passions of his Heros and Heroines:

> —*Angit,*
> *Irritat, mulcet, falsis terroribus implet,*
> *Ut Magus.*[12]

Let Poets, or the Men of Harmony, deny, if they can, this Force of *Nature*, or withstand this *moral Magick*. They, for their parts, carry a double Portion of this Charm about 'em. For in the first place, the very Passion which inspires 'em, is it self *the Love of Numbers,*[13] *Decency,*[14] and *Proportion;* and this too, not in a narrow sense, or after a *selfish* way (for Who of them composes for *himself?*) but in a friendly social View; for the Pleasure and Good of others; even down to Posterity, and future Ages. And in the next place, 'tis evident in these Performers, that their chief Theme, and Subject, that which raises their Genius the most, and by which they so effectually move others, is purely *Manners*, and the *moral Part*. For this is the Effect, and this the Beauty of their Art; "in vocal Measures of Syllables, and Sounds, to express the Harmony and Numbers of an inward kind; and represent the Beautys of a human Soul, by proper Foils, and Contrarietys, which serve as Graces in this Limning,[15] and render this Musick of the Passions more powerful and enchanting."

The Admirers of Beauty in the Fair Sex, wou'd laugh, perhaps, to hear of a *moral Part* in their Amours. Yet, what a stir is made about *a Heart!* What curious Search of *Sentiments,* and *tender Thoughts!* What Praises of *a Humour,* a *Sense,* a je-ne-scai-quoy[16] *of Wit,* and all those *Graces of a Mind* which these Virtuoso-Lovers delight to celebrate! Let them settle this Matter among themselves; and regulate, as they think fit, the Proportions which these different Beautys hold one to another: They must allow still, there is a Beauty of the Mind; and such as is essential in the Case. Why else is the very *Air of Foolishness* enough to cloy a Lover, at first sight? Why does an *Idiot-Look* and *Manner* destroy the Effect of all those outward Charms, and rob the *Fair-One* of her Power; tho regularly arm'd, in all the Exactness of Feature and Complexion? We may imagine what we please of a substantial solid Part of Beauty: but were the Subject to be well criticiz'd, we shou'd find, perhaps, that what we most admir'd, even in the Turn of *outward* Features, was only a mysterious Expression, and a kind of shadow of something *inward* in the Temper: and that when we were struck with a *Majestick* Air, a *sprightly Look,* an *Amazon bold* Grace, or a contrary *soft* and *gentle* one; 'twas chiefly the Fancy of these Characters or Qualitys which wrought on us: our Imagination being busied in forming beauteous Shapes and Images of this rational kind, which entertain'd the Mind, and held it in Admiration; whilst other Passions of a lower Species were employ'd another way. The preliminary Addresses, the Declarations, the Explanations, Confidences, Clearings; the Dependence on something mutual, something felt by way of Return; the *Spes animi credula mutui:*[17] all these become necessary Ingredients in the Affair of Love, and are authentically establish'd by the Men of Elegance and Art in this way of Passion.

Nor can the Men of cooler Passions, and more deliberate Pursuits, withstand the force of Beauty, in other Subjects. Every-one is a *Virtuoso,* of a higher or lower degree: Every-one pursues a GRACE, and courts a VENUS of one kind or another. The *Venustum,*[18] the *Honestum,* the *Decorum* of Things, will force its way. They who refuse to give it Scope in the nobler Subjects of a rational and moral kind, will find its Prevalency elsewhere, in an inferiour Order of Things. They who overlook the *main* Springs of Action, and despise the Thought of Numbers and Proportion in *a Life at large,* will in the mean *Particulars* of it, be no less taken up, and engag'd; as either in the Study of common Arts, or in the Care and Culture of mere *mechanick* Beautys. The Models of Houses, Buildings,

---

11. **fabulous Author:** author who deals in fictitious rather than actual events and persons. 12. **Angit . . . Magus:** "distresses, inflames, soothes, fills [our hearts] with illusory terrors, like a magician" (Horace, *Epistles,* II. i. 211–13). 13. **Numbers:** harmonious versification. 14. **Decency:** fitness. 15. **Limning:** painting. (The quotation marks setting off this passage appear to be used merely for emphasis.) 16. **je-ne-scai-quoy:** an "I know not what," a quality so subtle that it cannot be identified.

17. **Spes . . . mutui:** "credulous hope of mutual joy" (Horace, *Odes,* IV. i. 30). 18. **Venustum:** the beautiful. Shaftesbury's own equivalent for this trio of terms is just below: fair, noble, handsome.

and their accompanying Ornaments; the Plans of Gardens and their Compartments; the ordering of Walks, Plantations,[19] Avenues; and a thousand other Symmetrys, will succeed in the room of that happier and higher Symmetry and Order of a Mind. The *Species* of *Fair, Noble, Handsome*, will discover it self on a thousand Occasions, and in a thousand Subjects. The *Specter* still will haunt us, in some Shape or other: and when driven from our cool Thoughts, and frighted from *the Closet*,[20] will meet us even *at Court*, and fill our Heads with Dreams of Grandure, Titles, Honours, and a false Magnificence and Beauty; to which we are ready to sacrifice our highest Pleasure and Ease; and for the sake of which, we become the merest Drudges, and most abject Slaves.

The Men of Pleasure, who seem the greatest Contemners of this Philosophical Beauty, are forc'd often to confess her Charms. They can as heartily as others commend *Honesty;* and are as much struck with the Beauty of a *generous Part*. They admire the Thing it self; tho not the Means. And, if possible, they wou'd so order it, as to make Probity and Luxury agree. But the Rules of Harmony will not permit it. The Dissonancys are too strong. However, the Attempts of this kind are not unpleasant to observe. For tho some of the Voluptuous are found sordid Pleaders for Baseness and Corruption of every sort: yet others, more generous, endeavour to keep Measures with Honesty; and understanding Pleasure better, are for bringing it under some Rule. They condemn *this* manner: they praise *the other*. "So far was *right:* but further, *wrong.* Such a Case was allowable: but such a one, not to be admitted." They introduce a *Justice,* and an *Order* in their Pleasures. They wou'd bring *Reason* to be of their Party, account in some manner for their Lives, and form themselves to some kind of Consonancy, and Agreement: Or shou'd they find this impracticable on certain Terms, they wou'd chuse to sacrifice their other Pleasures to those which arise from a generous Behaviour, a Regularity of Conduct, and a Consistency of Life and Manners:

Et veræ Numerosque Modosque ediscere vitæ.[21]

Other Occasions will put us upon this Thought: but chiefly a strong View of *Merit*, in a *generous* Character, oppos'd to some detestably *vile one.* Hence

it is that among Poets, the *Satirists* seldom fail in doing Justice to VIRTUE. Nor are any of the nobler Poets false to this Cause. Even modern Wits, whose Turn is all towards Gallantry and Pleasure, when bare-fac'd *Villany* stands in their way, and brings the contrary Species in view, can sing in passionate Strains the Praises of plain *Honesty.*

When we are highly Friends with the World, successful with the Fair, and prosperous in the possession of other Beautys; we may perchance, as is usual, despise this sober Mistress. But when we see, in the issue,[22] what *Riot* and *Excess* naturally produce in the World; when we find that by *Luxury's* means, and for the service of vile Interests, Knaves are advanc'd above us, and the vilest of Men prefer'd before the honestest; we then behold VIRTUE in a new Light, and by the assistance of such a Foil, can discern the Beauty of *Honesty,* and the reality of those Charms, which before we understood not to be either natural, or powerful.

SECT. III.

And thus, after all, the most natural Beauty in the World is *Honesty,* and *Moral Truth.* For all *Beauty is* TRUTH. *True* Features make the Beauty of a Face; and true Proportions the Beauty of Architecture; as *true* Measures that of Harmony and Musick. In Poetry, which is all Fable, *Truth* still is the Perfection. And whoever is Scholar enough to read the ancient Philosopher,[23] or his modern Copists,[24] upon the nature of a Dramatick and Epick Poem, will easily understand this account of *Truth.*

A Painter, if he has any Genius, understands the *Truth* and Unity of Design; and knows he is even then unnatural, when he follows Nature too close, and strictly copys *Life.* For his Art allows him not to bring *All* Nature into his Piece, but *a Part* only. However, his Piece, if it be beautiful, and carrys *Truth,* must be *a Whole,* by it self, compleat, independent, and withal as *great* and comprehensive as he can make it. So that Particulars, on this occasion, must yield to the general Design; and all Things be subservient to that which is principal: in order to form a certain *Easiness of Sight;* a simple, clear, and *united*

---

19. **Plantations:** plantings of trees. 20. **Closet:** small private room. 21. **Et . . . vitæ:** "to learn well the rhythms and measures of a true life" (Horace, *Epistles*, II. ii. 144).

22. **issue:** outcome. 23. **the ancient Philosopher:** Aristotle. In Chapters vii and xxiii of the *Poetics* he relates the beauty of a plot to the unity and order of the parts of which it is composed. 24. **Copists:** imitators, followers; in particular, Le Bossu, writer of a treatise on epic poetry (1675).

View, which wou'd be broken and disturb'd by the Expression of any thing peculiar, or distinct.[25]

Now the Variety of Nature is such as to distinguish every thing she forms, by a *peculiar* original Character; which, if strictly observ'd, will make the Subject appear unlike to any thing extant in the World besides. But this Effect the good Poet and Painter seek industriously to prevent. They hate *Minuteness*,[26] and are afraid of *Singularity;* which wou'd make their Images, or Characters, appear capricious and fantastical. The mere Face-Painter,[27] indeed, has little in common with the Poet; but, like the mere Historian,[28] copys what he sees, and minutely traces every Feature, and odd Mark. 'Tis otherwise with the Men of Invention and Design. 'Tis from the *many* Objects of Nature, and not from *a particular-one*, that those Genius's form the Idea of their Work. Thus the best Artists are said to have been indefatigable in studying the best Statues: as esteeming them a better Rule, than the perfectest Human Bodys cou'd afford. And thus some considerable Wits have recommended the best Poems;[29] as preferable to the best of Historys; and better teaching the *Truth* of Characters, and Nature of Mankind.

Nor can this Criticism be thought high-strain'd. Tho Few confine themselves to these Rules; Few are insensible of 'em. Whatever Quarter we may give to our vitious Poets, or other Composers of irregular and short-liv'd Works; we know very well that the standing[30] Pieces of good Artists must be form'd after a more uniform way. Every just Work of theirs comes under those natural Rules of Proportion, and *Truth*. The Creature of their Brain must be like one of Nature's Formation. It must have a Body and Parts proportionable: or the very Vulgar will not fail to criticize the Work, when *it has neither Head nor Tail*. For so *common Sense* (according to just Philosophy) judges of those Works which want the Justness of *a Whole*, and shew their Author, however curious and exact in Particulars, to be in the main a very Bungler:

Infœlix operis summa, *quia ponere* Totum
Nescit.[31]

Such is Poetical, and such (if I may so call it) *Graphical*, or *Plastick*[32] Truth. Narrative, or *Historical Truth*, must needs be highly estimable; especially when we consider how Mankind, who are become so deeply interested in the Subject, have suffer'd by the want of Clearness in it. 'Tis it self a part of *Moral Truth*. To be a Judg in *one*, requires a Judgment in *the other*. The Morals, the Character, and Genius of an Author, must be thorowly consider'd: And the Historian or Relater of Things important to Mankind, must, whoever he be, approve himself many ways to us; both in respect of his Judgment, Candour, and Disinterestedness; e'er we are bound to take any thing on his Authority. And as for *critical Truth;* or the Judgment and Determination of what Commentators, Translators, Paraphrasts, Grammarians, and others have, on this occasion, deliver'd to us; in the midst of such Variety of Stile, such different Readings, such Interpolations, and Corruptions in the Originals; such Mistakes of Copists, Transcribers, Editors, and a hundred such Accidents, to which antient Books are subject; it becomes, upon the whole, *a Matter of nice Speculation:* considering, withal, that the Reader, tho an able Linguist, must be supported by so many other Helps from Chronology, Natural Philosophy, Geography, and other Sciences.

And thus many previous *Truths* are to be examin'd, and understood, in order to judg rightly of *Historical Truth*, and of the past Actions and Circumstances of Mankind, as deliver'd to us by antient Authors of different Nations, Ages, Times, and different in their Characters and Interests. Some *Moral* and *Philosophical Truths* there are withal so evident in themselves, that 'twou'd be easier to imagine half Mankind to have run mad, and join'd precisely in one and the same Species of Folly, than to admit any thing as *Truth*, which shou'd be advanc'd against such *natural Knowledg, fundamental Reason*, and *common Sense.*

This I have mention'd the rather, because some modern Zealots appear to have no better knowledg of TRUTH, nor better manner of judging it, than by *counting Noses.* By this Rule, if they can poll an indifferent Number out of a *Mob;* if they can produce a

---

25. peculiar, or distinct: distinguished from the rest by an undue amount of individualizing detail. **26. They . . . Minuteness:** See in Part Six Johnson's *Rasselas*, Ch. x, on numbering the streaks of the tulip. **27. Face-Painter:** portrait painter. **28. Historian:** compiler of records of events. The conception of the historian as a creative interpreter of the past developed later. **29. some . . . Poems:** most prominently, Aristotle in Chapter ix of the *Poetics*. **30. standing:** established.

31. Infælix . . . Nescit: "unhappy in the final result of his work, because he does not know how to represent a whole" (Horace, *Ars Poetica*, ll. 34–35). **32. Plastick:** as in painting and sculpture.

Set of *Lancashire* Noddles, remote provincial Head-Pieces, or visionary Assemblers, to attest a Story of *a Witch upon a Broom-Stick*, and *a Flight in the Air;* they triumph in the solid Proof of their new Prodigy, and cry, *Magna est Veritas & prævalebit!*[33]

Religion, no doubt, is much indebted to these Men of Prodigy; who, in such a discerning Age, wou'd set her on the foot of popular Tradition; and venture her on the same bottom with Parish-Tales, and Gossiping Storys of *Imps, Goblins,* and *Demoniacal Pranks,* invented to fright Children, or make Practice for common Exorcists, and *Cunning-Men.*[34] For by that Name, you know, Country People are us'd to call those Dealers in Mystery, who are thought to conjure *in an honest way,* and foil the Devil at his own Weapon.

But now (my Friend!) I can perceive 'tis time to put an End to these Reflections; lest by endeavouring to expound things any further, I shou'd be drawn from my way of *Humour,* to harangue profoundly on these Subjects. But shou'd you find I had moraliz'd in any tolerable manner, according to *common Sense,* and without *Canting;* I cou'd be satisfy'd with my Performance, such as it is, without fearing what Disturbance I might possibly give to some formal

Censors of the Age; whose Discourses and Writings are of another strain. I have taken the Liberty, you see, to *laugh,* upon some Occasions: And if I have either laugh'd wrong, or been impertinently serious; I can be content to be *laugh'd at,* in my Turn. If contrariwise I am rail'd at, I can *laugh* still, as before; and with fresh Advantage to my Cause. For tho, in reality, there cou'd be nothing less a laughing Matter, than the provok'd Rage, Ill-Will, and Fury of certain zealous Gentlemen, were they arm'd as lately they have been known; yet as the Magistrate has since taken care to pare their Talons, there is nothing very terrible in their Encounter. On the contrary, there is something comical in the Case. It brings to one's mind the Fancy of those Grotesque Figures, and Dragon-Faces, which are seen often in the Frontispiece,[35] and on the Corner Stones of old Buildings. They seem plac'd there, as the *Defenders* and *Supporters* of the Edifice; but with all their Grimace, are as harmless to People without, as they are useless to the Building within. Great Efforts of Anger to little purpose, serve for Pleasantry and Farce. Exceeding *Fierceness,* with perfect *Inability* and *Impotence,* makes the highest Ridicule.

I am, Dear Friend, | Affectionately Yours, *&c.*

---

33. Magna . . . prævalebit: "Truth is great, and shall prevail"—Shaftesbury's reading of I Esd. 4:41. **34. Cunning-Men:** according to Dr. Johnson, men who profess "to tell fortunes or teach how to recover stolen goods."

35. Frontispiece: ornamented front.

Sir Richard Steele   1672–1729

Joseph Addison   1672–1719

Richard Steele was born in Dublin on March 12, 1672, early orphaned, and brought up by his aunt, Lady Mildmay, and her husband, Henry Gascoigne, secretary to Lord Ormond, Lord Lieutenant of Ireland. He was sent to school at Dublin Castle and then to the Charterhouse in London, where he met and became friends with Joseph Addison. Addison left for Oxford in 1687, and Steele followed him two years later.

At Merton College Steele became a vigorous supporter of the Whig party and entered on a lifelong commitment to politics. He never attained ministerial office, as Addison did, but he occupied a variety of positions in the government and served in Parliament from 1713 to 1714 and again from 1715 to 1722. In 1714 he was expelled from the House of Commons because of the warmth with which he expressed his opinions in print, and it was this same predilection that eventually alienated Addison, whose character he aspersed in a pamphlet debate with him over the Peerage Bill in 1719.

Steele had left Oxford to join Ormond's Horse Guards in 1692. He served on the Continent for two years, then returned to England to launch his literary career with the publication in 1694 of *The Procession*, a poem occasioned by the death of Queen Mary. The work was dedicated to Lord Cutts, who rewarded the author with a commission in his Coldstream Guards, a station that served as an entrée into fashionable London society. In 1700 Steele joined the wits in their *Commendatory Verses*, an ironic offering to Sir Richard Blackmore in return for his *Satire Against Wit*, published that year. Steele, who had resented Blackmore's mention of Addison, was singled out for a reply in Blackmore's *Discommendatory Verses* (1700).

There was as much of the moralist as of the wit in Steele, and that side found its purest expression in a devotional manual, *The Christian Hero* (1701), which he is said to have composed during long nights of guard duty in the Tower. This attempt at religious edification appears to have been coolly received by the general public and positively resented by his fellow officers. Perhaps to make amends, Steele turned to comedy and produced, with varying but better success, three plays in close succession, *The Funeral* (1702), *The Lying Lover* (1703), and *The Tender Husband* (1705).

By now Steele was separated from the Army and was giving his full attention to politics and his career as a writer. In 1706 he became Gentleman-Usher to Prince George, and the next year he was rewarded for his services to the Whigs with the editorship of *The Gazette*, the official journal of the government. He held this post only until 1710 when he was ousted with a turn of the political wheel. Between 1709 and 1712 Steele was occupied with the publication of *The Tatler* and *The Spectator*, the two periodicals on which Steele and Addison collaborated to make their fame. Their partnership dissolved in 1712; Steele stepped up his political activities and at the same time began a number of new periodicals, notably *The Guardian*, but none of them approached the success of the earlier ones. When the Whigs were returned to power following the death of Queen Anne in 1714, Steele, although he was knighted the year after, was disappointed of a prominent place in the new government. He resented offers of lesser posts but found some solace in obtaining a license as patentee of the Drury Lane Theatre. Yet even that reward was to involve him in years of political and legal strife.

Steele's last success was once again as a playwright. *The Conscious Lovers*, produced on November 18, 1722, had an extraordinary run of eighteen performances and won critical acclaim as well. It is, indeed, perhaps the best sentimental comedy (so-called) of the age; unlike most of them, it works imaginatively through the moral problems posed by a restrictive social view of love and marriage. With this play Steele's literary career was virtually over. The next year he suffered an incapacitating stroke and remained an invalid at Carmarthen in Wales, where he died on September 1, 1729.

Joseph Addison was born on May 1, 1672, the son of the rector of Milston, in Wiltshire. After only a year at the Charterhouse, he proceeded to Queen's College, Oxford, and then to Magdalen (where a long, wooded walk beside a stream has come to be known as Addison's Walk). At Magdalen he received a bachelor's degree in 1691 and a master's degree two years later.

In June, 1693, Addison's first published work, *To Mr. Dryden*, appeared in the collection *Examen Poeticum*, edited by Dryden himself. The next year four of his poems were included in Tonson's *Miscellany*, and Addison was beginning to cut a literary figure. But as with Steele his ambitions were primarily political. One of the four poems from the *Miscellany* was *An Account of the Greatest English Poets*, in which Charles Montague (later Lord Halifax), an important Whig but minor poet, was given a place; a year later, in 1695, Addison courted another powerful Whig when he dedicated his *Poem to His Majesty* to Lord Somers. A clear sign of favor was not to come, however, until 1699, when he received a grant to travel on the Continent in order to prepare himself for the diplomatic service. The Grand Tour bore immediate fruit in a verse *Letter from Italy*, which Johnson found to be "more correct, with less appearance of labour, and more elegant, with less ambition of ornament, than any other of his poems."

When Addison returned to England in 1703 he found the Whigs out of power and himself with no prospects, until he was approached by Halifax and others about commemorating the Battle of Blenheim in verse. A draft of the poem won from Lord Treasurer Godolphin an appointment as Commissioner of Appeal in Excise, and *The Campaign* was published in December, 1705, with immediate success. Jacob Tonson rushed in to capitalize on Addison's celebrity and brought out his *Remarks on Several Parts of Italy* with dispatch.

The next year, 1706, Addison tried his hand at writing an English opera, *Rosamond*. It failed, but the publication of the text in 1707 won a poetical tribute from Thomas

Tickell, then an undergraduate at Addison's own college, Queen's, and later his companion, secretary, executor, and editor. Addison continued to involve himself in politics: he was elected to Parliament in 1707 and appointed secretary to the new Lord Lieutenant of Ireland, Lord Wharton, in 1709; in 1710 he started up *The Whig Examiner* to rebut the Tory *Examiner*, conducted by Swift.

It was while Addison was in Dublin that he first saw *The Tatler*, and it was not long before he was himself contributing to the popular new periodical that was being edited by his old friend Steele. Addison's essays begin with Number 18 and total forty-two in all; in the last number, published on January 2, 1711, he is handsomely though anonymously acknowledged as the author of the best of the papers. Two months later, *The Spectator*, jointly planned and conducted by Addison and Steele, started its even more spectacular career. Published as a daily, it ran to 555 numbers and had an average circulation of three to four thousand but reached many times that number of readers. Swift wrote to Stella that all Grub Street had given up its other endeavors in order to imitate *The Spectator*.

On December 6, 1712, *The Spectator* made its last appearance, probably because Addison felt himself growing stale. In 1713 he returned to the theater with what Johnson calls "unquestionably the noblest production of Addison's genius," *Cato: A Tragedy*. The play had the unusually long run of a month (in part owing to the popular interpretation of it as an allegory in favor of the Whigs) and drew high praise from such estimable critics as Bishop Berkeley, Edward Young, and Pope (who wrote the Prologue).

Addison's political star was to rise higher than Steele's when the Whigs, for whom they both labored, took over after the Queen's death in 1714. No doubt Addison's moderation had much to do with his being chosen to conduct a new periodical, *The Freeholder* (December, 1715–June, 1716), which sought to iron out party differences in support of administration policies. In 1717 he was appointed Secretary of State under Lord Sunderland, and the next year he retired on a large pension.

But his last years were marred by failing health and broken friendships. Politics had earlier estranged him from Swift, and the same was to happen with Steele. The falling out with Pope after 1713, on the other hand, resulted from literary rivalries involving members of Addison's "little Senate." (Pope later detailed his criticism of Addison in *An Epistle to Dr. Arbuthnot* [1735].) Addison died on June 17, 1719, attended by the devoted Tickell. According to Edward Young, Addison summoned his stepson, Lord Warwick, to his bedside, so that he might see "in what peace a Christian can die."

The standard edition of *The Tatler* is still that of G. A. Aitken (4 vols., 1899); *The Spectator* happily is now available in a definitive modern edition by D. F. Bond (5 vols., 1965). Aitken also wrote a *Life of Richard Steele* (2 vols., 1889); more recent biographies are Willard Connely's *Sir Richard Steele* (1934) and Calhoun Winton's *Captain Steele: The Early Career of Richard Steele* (1964). *The Correspondence of Richard Steele* was edited by Rae Blanchard (1941). For Addison the standard biography is Peter Smithers's *The Life of Joseph Addison* (2nd ed., 1968). Walter Graham edited *The Letters of Joseph Addison* (1954). For a comprehensive survey of the genre to which *The Tatler* and *The Spectator* belong, Graham's *English Literary Periodicals* (1930) may be consulted.

FROM

THE TATLER

By *Isaac Bickerstaff* Esq;

Quicquid agunt Homines nostri Farrago Libelli.°

※

On April 12, 1709, the first *Tatler* appeared. As editor of *The Gazette*, Steele had access to prime sources of news; he also took advantage of the fact that *The Gazette* was published on non-Post-days to scoop the official periodical by letting the news of *The Tatler* reach the country first. Yet the news can account for only a small part of the great success of the paper. Indeed it is difficult to account for it with any certainty at all. There had been a long and lively tradition of periodical essay writing in England, and there are few if any components of *The Tatler* that were completely new. But Steele's distinctive style and tone seem to have made all the difference. John Gay, in his review of the periodicals of the time entitled *The Present State of Wit* (1711), may exaggerate both the originality and the influence of *The Tatler*, but it is interesting to see how it struck a sensitive contemporary:

To give you my own thoughts of this Gentleman's Writings, I shall in the first place observe, that there is this noble difference between him and all the rest of our Polite and Gallant Authors: The latter have endeavour'd to please the Age by falling in with them, and incouraging them in their fashionable Vices, and false notions of things. It would have been a jest, sometime since, for a Man to have asserted, that any thing Witty could be said in praise of a Marry'd State, or that Devotion and Virtue were any way necessary to the Character of a fine Gentleman. Bickerstaff ventur'd to tell the Town, that they were a parcel of Fops, Fools, and vain Cocquets; but in such a manner, as even pleased them, and made them more than half enclin'd to believe that he spoke Truth. . . .

'Tis incredible to conceive the effect his Writings have had on the Town; How many Thousand follies they have either quite banish'd, or given a very great check to; how much Countenance they

have added to Vertue and Religion; how many People they have render'd happy, by shewing them it was their own fault if they were not so; and lastly, how intirely they have convinc'd our Fops, and Young Fellows, of the value and advantages of Learning. . . .

Lastly, His Writings have set all our Wits and Men of Letters upon a new way of Thinking, of which they had little or no Notion before; and tho' we cannot yet say that any of them have come up to the Beauties of the Original, I think we may venture to affirm, that every one of them Writes and Thinks much more justly than they did some time since.

The complicated printing history of *The Tatler* (described in detail by W. B. Todd in *Studies in Bibliography*, XV [1962]) compels us to settle for a drastically simplified model of what a definitive text should be. Our text is that of the original separate folio issues, with variants supplied from the collected octavo edition, entitled *The Lucubrations of Isaac Bickerstaff Esq.* (4 vols., 1710–11).

※

NUMB. 1

Tuesday, April 12. 1709.

THO' *the other Papers which are publish'd for the Use of the good People of* England *have certainly very wholesom Effects, and are laudable in their particular Kinds, they do not seem to come up to the main Design of such Narrations, which, I humbly presume, should be principally intended for the Use of Politick Persons, who are so publick-spirited as to neglect their own Affairs to look into Transactions of State. Now these Gentlemen, for the most Part, being Persons of strong Zeal and weak Intellects, It is both a Charitable and Necessary Work to offer something, whereby such worthy and well-affected[1] Members of the Commonwealth may be instructed, after their Reading,[2] what to think: Which shall be the End and Purpose of this my Paper, wherein I shall from Time to Time Report and Consider all Matters of what Kind soever that shall occur to Me, and publish such my Advices[3] and Reflections every Tuesday, Thursday, and Saturday, in the Week, for the Convenience of the Post.[4] I resolve also to have something which may be of Entertainment to the Fair Sex,*

THE TATLER. **Quicquid . . . Libelli:** a compression of Juvenal, *Satires*, I. i. 85–86: "Quidquid agunt homines, votum timor via voluptas / gaudia discursus, nostri farrago libelli est" ("Whatever men do—their longings, their fears, their angers, their pleasures, their delights, their comings and goings—these form the medley of my little book.").

Number 1. **1. well-affected:** well-disposed. **2. after . . . Reading:** in a manner befitting their knowledge. **3. Advices:** news. **4. for . . . Post:** The post left London on these days for other parts of the country.

in Honour of whom I have invented the Title of this Paper. I therefore earnestly desire all Persons, without Distinction, to take it in for the present Gratis, and hereafter at the Price of one Penny, forbidding all Hawkers to take more for it at their Peril. And I desire all Persons to consider, that I am at a very great Charge[5] for proper Materials for this Work, as well as that before I resolv'd upon it, I had settled a Correspondence in all Parts of the Known and Knowing World; and forasmuch as this Globe is not trodden upon by mere Drudges of Business only, but that Men of Spirit and Genius are justly to be esteem'd as considerable Agents in it, we shall not upon a Dearth of News present you with musty Foreign Edicts, or dull Proclamations, but shall divide our Relation of the Passages which occur in Action or Discourse throughout this Town, as well as elswhere, under such Dates of Places as may prepare you for the Matter you are to expect, in the following Manner:

All Accounts of Gallantry, Pleasure, and Entertainment, shall be under the Article of White's Chocolate-house;[6] Poetry, under that of Will's Coffee-house;[7] Learning, under the Title of Græcian;[8] Foreign and Domestick News, you will have from St. James's Coffee-house;[9] and what else I have to offer on any other Subject, shall be dated from my own Apartment.

I once more desire my Reader to consider, That as I cannot keep an Ingenious[10] Man to go daily to Will's, under Twopence each Day merely for his Charges; to White's, under Sixpence; nor to the Græcian, without allowing him some Plain Spanish,[11] to be as able as others at the Learned Table; and that a good Observer cannot speak with even Kidney[12] at St. James's without clean Linnen. I say, these Considerations will, I hope, make all

Persons willing to comply with my Humble Request (when my Gratis Stock is exhausted) of a Penny a Piece; especially since they are of some Proper Amusement, and that it is impossible for me to want[13] Means to entertain 'em, having, besides the Helps of my own Parts,[14] the Power of Divination, and that I can, by casting a Figure,[15] tell you all that will happen before it comes to pass.

But this last Faculty I shall use very sparingly, and speak but of few Things 'till they are pass'd, for fear of divulging Matters which may offend our Superiors.

White's Chocolate-house, April 7. GALLANTRY, PLEASURE, ENTERTAINMENT
THE deplorable Condition of a very pretty Gentleman, who walks here at the Hours when Men of Quality first appear, is what is very much lamented. His History is, That on the 9th of September, 1705. being in his One and twentieth Year, he was washing his Teeth at a Tavern Window in Pall-Mall, when a fine Equipage pass'd by, and in it a young Lady who look'd up at him; away goes the Coach, and the young Gentleman pull'd off his Night-Cap, and instead of rubbing his Gums, as he ought to do, out of[16] the Window 'till about Four a Clock sits him down, and spoke not a Word 'till Twelve at Night; after which, he began to enquire, If any Body knew the Lady . . . The Company ask'd, What Lady? But he said no more, 'till they broke up at Six in the Morning. All the ensuing Winter he went from Church to Church every Sunday, and from Play-house to Play-house every Night in the Week, but could never find the Original of the Picture which dwelt in his Bosom. In a Word, his Attention to any Thing, but his Passion, was utterly gone. He has lost all the Money he ever play'd for, and been confuted in every Argument he has enter'd upon since the Moment he first saw her. He is of a Noble Family, has naturally a very good Air, is of a frank, honest Temper: But this Passion has so extreamly maul'd him, that his Features are set and uniform'd,[17] and his whole Visage is deaden'd by a long Absence of Thought. He never appears in any Alacrity,[18] but when rais'd by Wine; at which Time he is sure to come hither, and throw away a great deal of Wit on Fellows, who have no Sense further than just to observe, That our poor Lover has most Understanding when he's Drunk, and is least in his Senses when he's Sober.

---

5. **Charge:** expense. 6. **White's Chocolate-house:** Founded in 1693 in St. James's Street, White's became a favorite rendezvous of men of fashion, especially those with gaming instincts. In The Rake's Progress, which appeared in 1735, Hogarth depicts gamblers at play in a room in White's, oblivious of the fire (in 1733) that is destroying it. After the fire, White's was moved next to the St. James's Coffee House, where it remained as a chocolate house until 1755 when it became a private club. 7. **Will's Coffee-house:** Established by William Urwin in Bow Street, Covent Garden, soon after the Restoration, Will's was the home of the wits, over whom Dryden presided until his death in 1700. Although Will's continued to flourish thereafter, it met stiff competition in Button's, established by Addison in 1712–13. 8. **Græcian:** in Devereux Court, Strand. Named evidently after its founder, one Constantine, a Greek, it was frequented by members of the Royal Society. 9. **St. . . . Coffee-house:** Established in 1705 by John Elliott, it appears to have been a favorite haunt of Whig politicians. 10. **Ingenious:** able, talented. 11. **Plain Spanish:** ready money. 12. **Kidney:** disposition.

13. **want:** lack. 14. **Parts:** talents. 15. **casting a Figure:** making a horoscope. 16. **out of:** at. 17. **uniform'd:** unanimated. 18. **Alacrity:** liveliness.

The Reader is desir'd to take Notice of the Article from this Place from Time to Time, for I design to be very exact in the Progress this unhappy Gentleman makes, which may be of great Instruction to all who actually are, or who ever shall be, in Love.

Will's Coffee-house, April 8. POETRY

On Thursday last was acted, for the Benefit of Mr. *Betterton*, the Celebrated Comedy, call'd *Love for Love*. Those excellent Players, Mrs. *Barry*, Mrs. *Bracegirdle*, and Mr. *Dogget*, tho' not at present concern'd in the House, acted on that Occasion.[19] There has not been known so great a Concourse of Persons of Distinction as at that Time; the Stage it self was cover'd with Gentlemen and Ladies, and when the Curtain was drawn, it discovered even there a very splendid Audience. This unusual Encouragement, which was given to a Play for the Advantage of so Great an Actor, gives an undeniable Instance, That the True Relish for Manly Entertainments and Rational Pleasures is not wholly lost. All the Parts were acted to Perfection; the Actors were careful of their Carriage, and no one was guilty of the Affectation to insert Witticisms of his own, but a due Respect was had to the Audience, for encouraging this accomplish'd Player. It is not now doubted but Plays will revive, and take their usual Place in the Opinion of Persons of Wit and Merit, notwithstanding their late Apostacy in Favour of Dress and Sound.[20] This Place[21] is very much alter'd since Mr. *Dryden* frequented it; where you us'd to see *Songs*, *Epigrams*, and *Satyrs*, in the Hands of every Man you met, you have now only a Pack of Cards; and instead of the Cavils about the Turn of the Expression, the Elegance of the Style, and the like, the Learned now dispute only about the Truth of the Game. But however, the Company is alter'd, all have shewn a great Respect for Mr. *Betterton*. And the very Gaming Part of this House

have been so much touch'd with a Sense of the Uncertainty of Humane Affairs, (which alter with themselves every Moment) that in this Gentleman, they pitied *Mark Anthony* of *Rome*, *Hamlett* of *Denmark*, *Mithridates* of *Pontus*, *Theodosius* of *Greece*,[22] and *Henry* the Eighth of *England*. It is well known, he has been in the Condition of each of those illustrious Personages for several Hours together, and behav'd himself in those high Stations, in all the Changes of the Scene, with suitable Dignity. For these Reasons, we intend to repeat this Favour to him on a proper Occasion, lest he who can instruct us so well in personating Feigned Sorrows, should be lost to us by suffering under Real Ones. The Town is at present in very great Expectation of seeing a Comedy now in Rehearsal, which is the 25th Production of my Honour'd Friend Mr. *Thomas D'Urfey*;[23] who, besides his great Abilities in the Dramatick, has a peculiar Talent in the Lyrick Way of Writing, and that with a Manner wholly new and unknown to the Antient *Greeks* and *Romans*, wherein he is but faintly imitated in the Translations of the Modern *Italian* Opera's.

St. James's Coffee-house, April 11. FOREIGN & DOMESTIC NEWS

Letters from the *Hague*[24] of the 16th say, That Major General *Cadogan*[25] was gone to *Brussels*, with Orders to disperse proper Instructions for assembling the whole Force of the Allies in *Flanders* in the Beginning of the next Month. The late Offers concerning Peace, were made in the Style of Persons who think themselves upon equal Terms: But the Allies have so just a Sense of their present Advantages, that they will not admit of a Treaty, except *France* offers what

---

19. Those . . . Occasion: Congreve's play was first performed in 1695 at the new theater in Lincoln's Inn Fields by the new company managed by Thomas Betterton (c. 1635–1710). Elizabeth Barry (1658–1713) and Anne Bracegirdle (c. 1663–1748) played Mrs. Frail and Angelica respectively; both came out of retirement to play the same roles in the benefit performance on April 7, 1709, at Drury Lane. Betterton played Valentine and Thomas Doggett (d. 1721), about this time a manager of the theater in the Haymarket, played Ben in both performances. **20. Dress and Sound:** the spectacular elements of theatrical production, which threatened to overwhelm the dramatic. Cf. *The Spectator*, below, No. 42. **21. This Place:** Will's.

22. Mithridates . . . Greece: *Mithridates, King of Pontus* and *Theodosius; or, the Force of Love*, both by Nathaniel Lee (c. 1653–92). **23. a Comedy . . . D'Urfey:** *The Modern Prophets; or, New Wit for a Husband* by Thomas D'Urfey (1653–1723) opened at Drury Lane on May 3, 1709. (See the selection from D'Urfey in Part Three.) **24. the Hague:** Troops began assembling at The Hague in the spring of 1709. The Duke of Marlborough, commander of the Allied forces against the French, was raising a large army while at the same time engaged in seeking a peace. The intentions of the French were uncertain. Marlborough had learned from an intercepted letter of February 7 that they projected a large offensive in Flanders in April, aimed at recapturing the fortress at Lille, which the English had taken in December, 1708. On the other hand, the French were faced with a famine and economic collapse and had sought a separate peace with the Dutch. **25. Major . . . Cadogan:** William (1675–1726), First Earl of Cadogan, Marlborough's right-hand man.

is more suitable to her present Condition. At the same Time we make Preparations, as if we were alarm'd by a greater Force than that which we are carrying into the Field. Thus this Point seems now to be argued Sword in Hand. This was what a Great General[26] alluded to, when being ask'd the Names of those who were to be Plenipotentiaries for the ensuing Peace; answer'd, with a serious Air, *There are about an Hundred thousand of us.* Mr. *Kidney,*[27] who has the Ear of the greatest Politicians that come hither, tells me, There is a Mail come in to Day with Letters, dated *Hague, April* 19. *N. S.* which say, a Design of bringing Part of our Troops into the Field at the latter End of this Month, is now alter'd to a Resolution of marching towards the Camp about the 20th of the next. Prince *Eugene*[28] was then return'd thither from *Amsterdam.* He sets out from *Brussels* on *Tuesday:* The Greater Number of the General Officers at the *Hague,* have Orders to go at the same Time. The Squadron at *Dunkirk* consists of seven Vessels. There happen'd t'other Day, in the Road of *Scheveling,* an Engagement between a Privateer of *Zealand* and one of *Dunkirk.* The *Dunkirker,* carrying 33 Pieces of Cannon, was taken and brought into the *Texel.* It is said, the Courier of Monsieur *Rouille*[29] is return'd to him from the Court of *France.* Monsieur *Vendosme*[30] being reinstated in the Favour of the Dutchess of *Burgundy,* is to command in *Flanders.*

Mr. *Kidney* added, that there were Letters of the 17th from *Ghent,* which give an Account, that the Enemy had form'd a Design to surprise two Battalions of the Allies which lay at *Alost;* but those Battalions receiv'd Advice of their March, and retir'd to *Dendermond.* Lieutenant General *Wood*[31] appear'd on this Occasion at the Head of 5000 Foot and 1000 Horse, upon which the Enemy withdrew without making any further Attempt.

26. **a Great General:** Marlborough. 27. **Mr. Kidney:** a waiter at the St. James's Coffee House. He is described in the Advertisement to *The Spectator,* No. 24, as the former "Keeper of the Book-Debts of the outlying Customers, and Observer of those who go off without paying." 28. **Prince Eugene:** François de Savoie (1663–1736), Prince Eugène, the commander of the forces of the Empire. 29. **Monsieur Rouille:** Pierre Rouille, Louis XIV's emissary on the peace mission to the Dutch. 30. **Monsieur Vendosme:** Louis Joseph (1654–1712), Duc de Vendôme, a French general. Disgusted at the conduct of the Duke of Burgundy at the Battle of Oudenarde, he had retired from the war. 31. **Lieutenant . . . Wood:** Cornelius Wood (d. 1712) distinguished himself as a cavalry leader under Marlborough.

From my own Apartment.

I am sorry I am oblig'd to trouble the Publick with so much Discourse upon a Matter which I at the very first mentioned as a Trifle, *viz.* the Death of Mr. *Partridge,*[32] under whose Name there is an *Almanack* come out for the Year 1709. In one Page of which it is asserted by the said *John Partridge,* That he is still living, and not only so, but that he was also living some Time before, and even at the Instant when I writ of his Death. I have in another Place, and in a Paper by it self, sufficiently convinc'd this Man that he is dead, and if he has any Shame, I don't doubt but that by this Time he owns it to all his Acquaintance: For tho' the Legs and Arms, and whole Body of that Man may still appear and perform their animal Functions; yet since, as I have elsewhere observ'd, his Art is gone, the Man is gone. I am, as I said, concern'd, that this little Matter should make so much Noise; but since I am engag'd, I take my self oblig'd in Honour to go on in my Lucubrations, and by the Help of these Arts of which I am Master, as well as my Skill in Astrological Speculations, I shall, as I see Occasion, proceed to confute other dead Men, who pretend to be in Being, that they are actually deceased. I therefore give all Men fair Warning to mend their Manners, for I shall from Time to Time print Bills of Mortality; and I beg the Pardon of all such who shall be nam'd therein, if they who are good for Nothing shall find themselves in the Number of the Deceas'd.

Advertisement.

A Vindication of *Isaac Bickerstaff* Esq; against what is objected to Him by Mr. *Partridge,* in his Almanack for the present Year 1709. By the said *Isaac Bickerstaff* Esq; *London:* Printed in the Year 1709.

NUMB. 163

Idem Inficeto est inficetior Rure
Simul Poemata attigit; neque idem unquam
Æqué est beatus, ac Poema cum scribit:
Tam gaudet in se, tamque se ipse miratur.

32. **Mr. Partridge:** John Partridge, an astrologer, medical quack, and almanac maker. (See the headnote to the selection from Swift's *Bickerstaff Papers* later in Part Two.)

Nimirum idem omnes fallimur; neque est quisquam
Quem non in aliqua re videre Suffenum
Possis.[1]———Catul. de Suffeno.

From Saturday April 22. to Tuesday April 25. 1710.

Will's Coffee-house, April 24.

I Yesterday came hither about Two Hours before the Company generally make their Appearance, with a Design to read over all the News-Papers; but upon my sitting down, I was accosted by *Ned Softly*, who saw me from a Corner in the other End of the Room, where I found he had been writing something. Mr. *Bickerstaff*, says he, I observe by a late Paper of yours,[2] that you and I are just of a[3] Humour; for you must know, of all Impertinencies, there is nothing which I so much hate as News. I never read a *Gazette*[4] in my Life; and never trouble my Head about our Armies, whether they win or lose, or in what Part of the World they lie encamped. Without giving me Time to reply, he drew a Paper of Verses out of his Pocket, telling me, That he had something which would entertain me more agreeably, and that he would desire my Judgment upon every Line, for that we had Time enough before us till the Company came in.

Ned Softly is a very pretty Poet, and a great Admirer of easy Lines.[5] *Waller* is his Favourite: And as that admirable Writer has the best and worst Verses of any among our great *English* Poets, *Ned Softly* has got all the bad Ones without Book, which he repeats upon Occasion, to show his Reading, and garnish his Conversation. *Ned* is indeed a true *English* Reader, incapable of relishing the great and masterly Strokes of this Art; but wonderfully pleased with the little *Gothick*[6] Ornaments of Epigrammatical Conceits, Turns, Points,[7] and Quibbles, which are so frequent in the most admired of our *English* Poets, and practised by those who want[8] Genius and Strength to represent, after the Manner of the Ancients, Simplicity in its natural Beauty and Perfection.

Finding my self unavoidably engaged in such a Conversation, I was resolved to turn my Pain into a Pleasure, and to divert my self as well as I could with so very odd a Fellow. You must understand, says *Ned*, that the Sonnet I am going to read to you was written upon a Lady, who showed me some Verses of her own making, and is perhaps the best Poet of our Age. But you shall hear it. Upon which he begun to read as follows:

> To Mira *on her incomparable Poems.*
>
> 1.
>
> *When dress'd in Lawrel Wreaths you shine,*
> *And tune your soft melodious Notes,*
> *You seem a Sister of the Nine,*
> *Or,* Phœbus *self in Petticoats.*
>
> 2.
>
> *I fancy, when your Song you sing,*
> *(Your Song you sing with so much Art)*
> *Your Pen was pluck'd from Cupid's Wing;*
> *For ah! it wounds me like his Dart.*

Why, says I, this is a little Nosegay of Conceits, a very Lump of Salt:[9] Every Verse hath something in it that piques;[10] and then the Dart in the last Line is certainly as pretty a Sting in the Tail of an Epigram (for so I think your Criticks call it) as ever entered into the Thought of a Poet. Dear Mr. *Bickerstaff*, says he, shaking me by the Hand, every Body knows you to be a Judge of these Things; and to tell you truly, I read over *Roscommon*'s Translation of *Horace*'s *Art of Poetry*[11] Three several[12] Times, before I sat down to write the Sonnet which I have shown you. But you shall hear it again, and pray observe every Line of it, for not one of them shall pass without your Approbation.

> *When dress'd in Lawrel Wreaths you shine.*

That is, says he, when you have your Garland on; when you are writing Verses. To which I replied, I know your Meaning: A Metaphor! The same, said he, and went on.

> *And tune your soft melodious Notes.*

Number 163. 1. Idem . . . Possis: "That same man is more of a clod than your cloddish country bumpkin when he decides to tackle poetry. And yet no one is happier than he when he is writing a poem. He is so taken with himself and so overwhelmed by himself. Everyone falls too readily into the same trap. In some way or other you can find a Suffenus in everyone" (Catullus, *Carmina*, xxii. 14–20; for *Inficeto* and *inficetior* read *infaceto* and *infacetior*). 2. Paper of yours: Number 160. 3. just of a: of the same. 4. Gazette: the official journal of the government. 5. easy Lines: verses that give the effect of having been written without labor. 6. Gothick: barbaric. Cf. *The Spectator*, below, No. 70. 7. Turns, Points: turns of phrase, turns of thought. 8. want: lack.

9. Lump of Salt: something pungent. 10. piques: stimulates. 11. Roscommon's . . . Poetry: The Earl of Roscommon's translation, in blank verse, was first published in 1680. A new edition came out in 1709. 12. several: different.

Pray observe the Gliding of that Verse; there is scarce a Consonant in it: I took Care to make it run upon Liquids. Give me your Opinion of it. Truly, said I, I think it as good as the former. I am very glad to hear you say so, says he; but mind the next.

You seem a Sister of the Nine.

That is, says he, you seem a Sister of the Muses; for if you look into ancient Authors, you will find it was their Opinion, that there were Nine of them. I remember it very well, said I; but pray proceed.

Or Phœbus self in Petticoats.

Phœbus, says he, was the God of Poetry. These little Instances, Mr. *Bickerstaff,* show a Gentleman's Reading. Then to take off from the Air of Learning, which *Phœbus* and the Muses have given to this First Stanza, you may observe, how it falls all of a sudden into the Familiar; *in Petticoats!*

Or Phœbus self in Petticoats.

Let us now, says I, enter upon the Second Stanza. I find the First Line is still a Continuation of the Metaphor.

I fancy, when your Song you sing.

It is very right, says he; but pray observe the Turn of Words in those Two Lines. I was a whole Hour in adjusting of them, and have still a Doubt upon me, Whether in the Second Line it should be, *Your Song you sing;* or, *You sing your Song?* You shall hear them both.

I fancy, when your Song you sing,
(Your Song you sing with so much Art.)

OR,

I fancy, when your Song you sing,
You sing your Song with so much Art.

Truly, said I, the Turn is so natural either Way, that you have made me almost giddy with it. Dear Sir, said he, grasping me by the Hand, you have a great deal of Patience; but pray what do you think of the next Verse;

Your Pen was pluck'd from Cupid's Wing.

Think! says I, I think you have made *Cupid* look like a little Goose. That was my Meaning, says he: I think the Ridicule is well enough hit off. But we now come to the last, which sums up the whole Matter:

For Ah! it wounds me like his Dart.

Pray how do you like that *Ah!* Doth it not make a pretty Figure in that Place? *Ah!* It looks as if I felt the Dart, and cried out at being pricked with it.

For Ah! it wounds me like his Dart.

My Friend *Dick Easy,* continued he, assured me, he would rather have written that *Ah!* than to have been the Author of the *Æneid.* He indeed objected, that I made *Mira's* Pen like a Quill in one of the Lines, and like a Dart in the other. But as to that—Oh! as to that, says I, it is but supposing *Cupid* to be like a Porcupine, and his Quills and Darts will be the same thing. He was going to embrace me for the Hint; but half a Dozen Criticks coming into the Room, whose Faces he did not like, he conveyed the Sonnet into his Pocket, and whispered me in the Ear, he would show it me again as soon as his Man had written it over fair.

NUMB. 169

O Rus! Quando ego te aspiciam, quandoque licebit
Nunc veterum Libris, nunc Somno, & inertibus Horis,
Ducere sollicitæ Jucunda Oblivia Vitæ?[1]

HOR.

From Saturday May 6. to Tuesday May 9. 1710.

From my own Apartment, May 8. WHATEVER ELSE
THE Summer Season now approaching, several of our Family have invited me to pass away a Month or Two in the Country, and indeed nothing could be more agreeable to me than such a Recess, did I not consider that I am by Two Quarts a worse Companion than when I was last among my Relations: And I am admonished by some of our Club, who have lately visited *Staffordshire,* that they drink at a greater Rate than they did at that Time. As every Soil does not produce every Fruit or Tree, so every Vice is not the Growth of every Kind of Life; and I have, ever since I could think, been astonished, that Drinking should be the Vice of the Country. If it were possible to add to all our Senses, as we do to that of Sight, by Perspectives,[2] we should methinks more particularly

Number 169. **1.** *O . . . Vitæ:* "Oh countryside! When shall I see you? When shall I be allowed to forget life's worries and divide my time pleasantly among old familiar books, naps, and times when I just do nothing?" (Horace, *Satires,* II. vi. 60–62). **2. Perspectives:** lenses, spectacles.

labour to improve them in the Midst of the Variety of beauteous Objects which Nature has produced to entertain us in the Country; and do we in that Place destroy the Use of what Organs we have? As for my Part, I cannot but lament the Destruction that has been made of the Wild Beasts of the Field, when I see large Tracts of Earth possessed by Men who take no Advantage of their being rational, but lead meer[3] Animal Lives, making it their whole Endeavour to kill in themselves all they have above Beasts; to wit, the Use of Reason, and Tast of Society. It is frequently boasted in the Writings of Orators and Poets, That it is to Eloquence and Poesy we owe that we are drawn out of Woods and Solitudes into Towns and Cities, and from a wild and savage Being become acquainted with the Laws of Humanity and Civility. If we are obliged to these Arts for so great Service, I could wish they were employed to give us a Second Turn; that as they have brought us to dwell in Society (a Blessing which no other Creatures know) so they would perswade us, now they have settled us, to lay out all our Thoughts in surpassing each other in those Faculties in which only we excel other Creatures. But it is at present so far otherwise, that the Contention seems to be, who shall be most eminent in Performances wherein Beasts enjoy greater Abilities than we have. I'll undertake,[4] were the Butler and Swinherd, at any true Esquire's[5] in *Great Britain*, to keep and compare Accounts of what Wash[6] is drank up in so many Hours in the Parlour and the Pigsty, it would appear, the Gentleman of the House gives much more to his Friends than his Hogs.

This, with many other Evils, arises from the Error in Men's Judgments, and not making true Distinctions between Persons and Things. It is usually thought, That a few Sheets of Parchment, made before a Male and Female of wealthy Houses come together, give the Heirs and Descendants of that Marriage Possession of Lands and Tenements; but the Truth is, there is no Man who can be said to be Proprietor of an Estate, but he who knows how to enjoy it. Nay, it shall never be allowed, that the Land is not a Waste, when the Matter[7] is uncultivated. Therefore, to avoid Confusion, it is to be noted, that a Peasant with a great Estate is but an Incumbent,[8] and that he must be a Gentleman to be a Landlord. A Landlord enjoys what he has with

his Heart, an Incumbent with his Stomach. Gluttony, Drunkenness, and Riot, are the Entertainments of an Incumbent; Benevolence, Civility, Social and Human Virtues, the Accomplishments of a Landlord. Who, that has any Passion for his native Country, does not think it worse than conquered, when so large Divisions of it are in the Hands of Salvages, that know no Use of Property but to be Tyrants; or Liberty, but to be unmannerly. A Gentleman in a Country Life enjoys Paradise with a Temper fit for it; a Clown[9] is cursed in it with all the cutting[10] and unruly Passions Man could be tormented with when he was expelled from it.

There is no Character more deservedly esteemed than that of a Country Gentleman, who understands the Station in which Heaven and Nature have plac'd him. He is Father to his Tenants, and Patron to his Neighbours, and is more superior to those of lower Fortune by his Benevolence than his Possessions. He justly divides his Time between Solitude and Company, so as to use the one for the other. His Life is spent in the good Offices of an Advocate, a Referee, a Companion, a Mediator, and a Friend. His Council and Knowledge are a Guard to the Simplicity and Innocence of those of lower Talents, and the Entertainment and Happiness of those of equal. When a Man in a Country Life has this Turn,[11] as it is to be hoped Thousands have, he lives in a more happy Condition than any is described in the Pastoral Descriptions of Poets, or the vain-glorious Solitudes recorded by Philosophers.

To a Thinking Man it would seem prodigious,[12] that the very Situation in a Country Life does not incline Men to a Scorn of the mean Gratifications some take in it. To stand by a Stream naturally lulls the Mind into Composure and Reverence; to walk in Shades diversifies that Pleasure; and a bright Sunshine makes a Man consider all Nature in Gladness, and himself the happiest Being in it, as he is the most conscious of her Gifts and Enjoyments. It would be the most impertinent Piece of Pedantry imaginable to form our Pleasures by Imitation of others. I will not therefore mention *Scipio* and *Lælius*,[13] who are generally produced on this Subject as Authorities for the

---

3. meer: utterly. **4. I'll undertake:** I venture to say. **5. Esquire:** country squire. **6. Wash:** any inferior beverage. **7. the Matter:** the substance, i.e., the soil. **8. Incumbent:** holder, occupant.

9. a Clown: a rustic. **10. cutting:** acutely wounding. **11. Turn:** bent, disposition. **12. prodigious:** unnatural, monstrous. **13. Scipio and Lælius:** Scipio Africanus Major (236–184 B.C.), the Roman general who gave up his eminence for the private life, and his fellow soldier and friend Laelius (fl. 210–160 B.C.).

Charms of a Rural Life. He that does not feel the Force of agreeable Views and Situations in his own Mind, will hardly arrive at the Satisfactions they bring from the Reflexions of others. However, they who have a Tast that Way, are more particularly inflamed with Desire when they see others in the Enjoyment of it, especially when Men carry into the Country a Knowledge of the World as well as of Nature. The Leisure of such Persons is endear'd[14] and refin'd by Reflexion upon Cares and Inquietudes. The Absence of past Labours doubles present Pleasures, which is still augmented, if the Person in Solitude has the Happiness of being addicted to Letters.[15] My Cousin *Frank Bickerstaff* gives me a very good Notion of this sort of Felicity in the following Letter.

SIR,

I Write this to communicate to you the Happiness I have in the Neighbourhood[16] and Conversation of the noble Lord whose Health you enquired after in your last. I have bought that little Hovel which borders upon his Royalty;[17] but am so far from being oppressed by his Greatness, that I who know no Envy, and he who is above Pride, mutually recommend our selves to each other by the Difference of our Fortunes. He esteems me for being so well pleased with a little, and I admire him for enjoying so handsomely a great deal. He has not the little Tast of observing the Colour of a Tulip, or the Edging of a Leaf of Box,[18] but rejoices in open Views, the Regularity of this Plantation, and the Wildness of another, as well as the Fall[19] of a River, the Rising of a Promontory, and all other Objects fit to entertain a Mind like his, that has been long versed in great and publick Amusements. The Make of the Soul is as much seen in Leisure as in Business. He has long lived in Courts, and been admired in Assemblies, so that he has added to Experience a most charming Eloquence; by which he communicates to me the Idea's of my own Mind upon the Objects we meet with, so agreeably, that with his Company in the Fields, I at once enjoy the Country, and a Landskip[20] of it. He is now altering the Course of Canals and Rivulets, in which he has an Eye to his Neighbour's Satisfaction, as well as his own. He often makes me Presents by turning the Water into my Grounds, and sends me Fish by their own Streams. To avoid my Thanks,

he makes Nature the Instrument of his Bounty, and does all good Offices so much with the Air of a Companion, that his Frankness[21] hides his own Condescension, as well as my Gratitude. Leave the World[22] to it self, and come see us, | *Your affectionate Cousin,*

FRANCIS BICKERSTAFF.

NUMB. 217

Atq; Deos atq; Astra vocat crudelia Mater.[1]

From Saturday August 26. to Tuesday August 29. 1710.

From my own Apartment, August 28.

AS I was passing by a Neighbour's House this Morning, I overheard the Wife of the Family speaking Things to her Husband which gave me much Disturbance, and put me in mind of a Character which I wonder I have so long omitted, and that is, an outragious Species of the Fair Sex which is distinguished by the Term Scolds. The Generality of Women are by Nature loquacious: Therefore meer Volubility of Speech is not to be imputed to[2] them, but should be considered with Pleasure when it is used to express such Passions as tend to sweeten or adorn Conversation: But when, thro' Rage, Females are vehement in their Eloquence, nothing in the World has so ill an Effect upon the Features; for by the Force of it, I have seen the most Amiable become the most Deformed; and she that appeared one of the Graces, immediately turned into one of the Furies. I humbly conceive, the great Cause of this Evil may proceed from a false Notion the Ladies have of what we call a Modest Woman. They have too narrow a Conception of this lovely Character, and believe they have not at all forfeited their Pretensions to it, provided they have no Imputations on their Chastity. But alas! the young Fellows know they pick out better Women in the Side-Boxes,[3] than many of those who pass upon the World and themselves for Modest.

Modesty never rages, never murmurs, never pouts: When it is ill treated, it pines, it beseeches, it languishes. The Neighbour I mention is one of your

---

14. **endear'd**: enhanced. 15. **Letters**: literature. 16. **Neighbourhood**: company. 17. **Royalty**: domain. 18. **Box**: an evergreen tree or shrub, found in ornamental gardens. 19. **Fall**: waterfall. 20. **Landskip**: (landscape) description.

21. **Frankness**: open, unreserved manner. 22. **the World**: the world of affairs. *Number 217.* 1. **Atq . . . Mater**: from Virgil's *Eclogues*, where Daphnis's mother, lamenting his death, "cried out against the cruelty of both gods and stars" (v. 23). 2. **imputed to**: in the sense of an accusation; cf. *Imputations* toward the end of this paragraph. 3. **the Side-Boxes**: of the theaters. The presumption is that women who frequent the theaters are immodest.

common modest Women, that is to say, those as are ordinarily reckoned such. Her Husband knows every Pain in Life with her but Jealousy. Now because she is clear[4] in this Particular, the Man can't say his Soul's his own, but she cries, No modest Woman is respected now a Day. What adds to the Comedy in this Case is, that it is very ordinary with this Sort of Women to talk in the Language of Distress: They will complain of the forlorn Wretchedness of their Condition, and then the poor helpless Creatures shall throw the next Thing they can lay their Hands on at the Person who offends them. Our Neighbour was only saying to his Wife, She went[5] a little too fine, when she immediately pulled his Periwig off, and stamping it under her Feet, wrung her Hands, and said, Never modest Woman was so used! These Ladies of irresistible Modesty are those who make Virtue unamiable; not that they can be said to be virtuous, but as[6] they live without Scandal; and being under the common Denomination of being such, Men fear to meet their Faults in those who are as agreeable as they are innocent.

I take the Bully among Men, and the Scold among Women, to draw the Foundation of their Actions from the same Defect in the Mind. A Bully thinks Honour consists wholly in being brave, and therefore has Regard to no one[7] Rule of Life, if he preserves himself from the Accusation of Cowardize. The froward[8] Woman knows Chastity to be the first Merit in a Woman; and therefore, since no one can call her one ugly Name, she calls all Mankind all the rest.

These Ladies, where their Companions are so imprudent as to take their Speeches for any other than Exercises of their own Lungs, and their Husbands Patience, gain by the Force of being resisted, and flame with open Fury, which is no Way to be opposed but by being neglected:[9] Tho' at the same Time Human Frailty makes it very hard to relish the Philosophy of contemning even frivolous Reproach. There is a very pretty Instance of this Infirmity in the Man of the best Sense that ever was, no less a Person than *Adam* himself. According to *Milton's* Description of the First Couple, as soon as they had fallen, and the turbulent Passions of Anger, Hatred, and Jealousy,

first enter'd their Breasts, *Adam* grew moody, and talked to his Wife, as you may find it in the 359th Page, and 9th Book, of *Paradise Lost*, in the *Octavo* Edition,[10] which, out of Heroicks,[11] and put into Domestick Stile, would run thus:

"Madam, If my Advices had been of any Authority with you when that strange Desire of Gadding possessed you this Morning, we had still been happy: But your cursed Vanity and Opinion of your own Conduct, which is certainly very wavering when it seeks Occasions of being proved,[12] has ruined both your self, and me who trusted you."

Eve had no Fan in her Hand to ruffle, or Tucker to pull down, but with a reproachful Air she answered,

"Sir, Do you impute that to my Desire of Gadding, which might have happened to your self with all your Wisdom and Gravity? The Serpent spoke so excellently, and with so good a Grace, that—Besides, What Harm had I ever done him, that he should design me any? Was I to have been always at your Side, I might as well have continued there, and been but your Rib still: But if I was so weak a Creature as you thought me, Why did you not interpose your sage Authority more absolutely? You denied me going as faintly, as you say I resisted the Serpent. Had not you been too easie, neither you or I had now transgressed."

Adam replied, "Why, *Eve*, hast thou the Impudence to upbraid me as the Cause of thy Transgression for my Indulgence to thee? Thus it will ever be with him who trusts too much to Woman: At the same Time that she refuses to be governed, if she suffers by her Obstinacy, she will accuse the Man that shall leave her to her self."

> Thus they in mutual Accusation spent
> The fruitless Hours, but neither self condemning:
> And of their vain Contest appear'd no End.

This to the Modern will appear but a very faint Piece of Conjugal Enmity; but you are to consider, that they were but just begun to be angry, and they wanted[13] new Words for expressing their new Passions. But her accusing him of letting her go, and telling him how good a Speaker, and how fine a

---

4. **clear:** innocent. 5. **went:** dressed. 6. **but as:** but only as. 7. **no one:** not a single. 8. **froward:** (forward) perverse, refractory. 9. **no . . . neglected:** The only, or best, way to oppose them is to ignore them.

10. **Octavo Edition:** the seventh (1705) or the eighth (1707), both published by Jacob Tonson. 11. **Heroicks:** heroic verse (iambic pentameter). 12. **wavering . . . proved:** unsure of itself if it needs to seek occasions of being tested. 13. **wanted:** lacked.

Gentleman the Devil was, we must reckon, allowing for the Improvements of Time, that she gave him the same Provocation as if she had called him Cuckold. The passionate and familiar Terms with which the same Case, repeated daily for so many Thousand Years, has furnished the present Generation, were not then in Use; but the Foundation of Debate has ever been the same, a Contention about their Merit and Wisdom. Our general[14] Mother was a Beauty, and hearing there was another now in the World, could not forbear (as *Adam* tells her) showing her self, though to the Devil, by whom the same Vanity made her liable to be betrayed.

I cannot, with all the Help of Science and Astrology, find any other Remedy for this Evil, but what was the Medicine in this first Quarrel; which was, as appeared in the next Book,[15] that they were convinced of their being both weak, but one weaker than the other.

If it were possible that the Beauteous could but rage a little before a Glass, and see their pretty Countenances grow wild, it is not to be doubted but it would have a very good Effect; but that would require Temper:[16] For Lady *Firebrand*, upon observing her Features swell when her Maid vexed her the other Day, stamped her Dressing-Glass under her Feet. In this Case, when one of this Temper is moved, she is like a Witch in an Operation, and makes all Things turn round with her. The very Fabrick[17] is in a Vertigo when she begins to charm. In an Instant, whatever was the Occasion that moved her Blood, she has such intolerable Servants, *Betty* is so aukward, *Tom* can't carry a Message, and her Husband has so little Respect for her, that she, poor Woman, is weary of this Life, and was born to be unhappy.

Desunt Multa.[18]

Advertisement.

The Season now coming on in which the Town will begin to fill, Mr. Bickerstaff gives Notice, That from the First of October next, he will be much wittier than he has hitherto been.

---

14. **general:** common. 15. **the next Book:** X. 914–65.
16. **Temper:** a good temper, equanimity. 17. **Fabrick:**
building. 18. **Desunt Multa:** Many things are wanting.

NUMB. 263

—Minimâ contentos Nocte Britannos.[1]
Juv. Sat. 2.

From Tuesday December 12. to Thursday December 14. 1710.

From my own Apartment, December 13.
AN old Friend of mine being lately come to Town, I went to see him on *Tuesday* last about Eight a Clock in the Evening, with a Design to sit with him an Hour or two, and talk over old Stories; but upon enquiring after him, his Servant told me he was just gone to Bed. The next Morning, as soon as I was up and dressed, and had dispatched a little Business, I came again to my Friend's House about Eleven a Clock, with a Design to renew my Visit; but upon asking for him, his Servant told me he was just sat down to Dinner. In short, I found that my old-fashioned Friend religiously adhered to the Example of his Fore-fathers, and observed the same Hours that had been kept in the Family ever since the Conquest.

It is very plain that the Night was much longer formerly in this Island than it is at present. By the Night, I mean that Portion of Time which Nature has thrown into Darkness, and which the Wisdom of Mankind had formerly dedicated to Rest and Silence. This used to begin at Eight a Clock in the Evening, and conclude at Six in the Morning. The Curfeu, or Eight a Clock Bell, was the Signal throughout the Nation for putting out their Candles and going to Bed.

Our Grandmothers, tho' they were wont to sit up the last in the Family, were all of them fast asleep at the same Hours that their Daughters are busy at Crimp and Basset.[2] Modern Statesmen are concerting Schemes, and engaged in the Depth of Politicks, at the Time when their Fore-Fathers were laid down quietly to Rest, and had nothing in their Heads but Dreams. As we have thus thrown Business and Pleasure into the Hours of Rest, and by that Means made the natural Night but half as long as it should be, we are forced to piece it out with a great Part of the Morning; so that near Two thirds of the Nation lie fast asleep for several Hours in broad Day-light. This

---

Number 263. **1. Minimâ . . . Britannos:** "the Britons happy with their short nights" (Juvenal, *Satires*, I. ii. 161). **2. Crimp and Basset:** a card game.

Irregularity is grown so very fashionable at present, that there is scarce a Lady of Quality in *Great Britain* that ever saw the Sun rise. And if the Humour encreases in Proportion to what it has done of late Years, it is not impossible but our Children may hear the Bell-Man[3] going about the Streets at Nine a Clock in the Morning, and the Watch making their Rounds till Eleven. This unaccountable Disposition in Mankind to continue awake in the Night, and sleep in Sunshine, has made me enquire, Whether the same Change of Inclination has happened to any other Animals? For this Reason I desired a Friend of mine in the Country to let me know, Whether the Lark rises as early as he did formerly? And whether the Cock begins to crow at his usual Hour? My Friend has answered me, That his Poultry are as regular as ever, and that all the Birds and the Beasts of his Neighbourhood keep the same Hours that they have observed in the Memory of Man; and the same which, in all Probability, they have kept for these Five Thousand Years.

If you would see the Innovations that have been made among us in this Particular, you may only look into the Hours of Colleges, where they still dine at Elevan, and sup at Six, which were doubtless the Hours of the whole Nation at the Time when those Places were founded. But at present the Courts of Justice are scarce opened in *Westminster-Hall*[4] at the Time when *William Rufus* used to go to Dinner in it. All Business is driven forward: The Land-Marks of our Fathers (if I may so call them) are removed, and planted further up into the Day; insomuch that I am afraid our Clergy will be obliged (if they expect full Congregations) not to look any more upon Ten a Clock in the Morning as a Canonical Hour.[5] In my own Memory the Dinner has crept by Degrees from Twelve a Clock to Three, and where it will fix no Body knows.

I have sometimes thought to draw up a Memorial[6] in the Behalf of Supper against Dinner, setting forth, That the said Dinner has made several Encroachments upon the said Supper, and entered very far upon his Frontiers; That he has banished him out of several Families, and in all has driven him from his Head

Quarters, and forced him to make his Retreat into the Hours of Midnight; and in short, That he is now in Danger of being entirely confounded and lost in a Breakfast. Those who have read *Lucian*, and seen the Complaints of the Letter *T.* against *S.*[7] upon Account of many Injuries and Usurpations of the same Nature, will not, I believe, think such a Memorial forced and unnatural. If Dinner has been thus postponed, (or if you please) kept back from Time to Time, you may be sure that it has been in Compliance with the other Business of the Day, and that Supper has still observed a proportionable Distance. There is a venerable Proverb, which we have all of us heard in our Infancy, of *putting the Children to Bed, and laying the Goose to the Fire*. This was one of the Jocular Sayings of our Forefathers, but may be properly used in the Literal Sense at present. Who would not wonder at this perverted Relish of those who are reckoned the most polite Part of Mankind, that prefer Sea Coals[8] and Candles to the Sun, and exchange so many chearful Morning Hours for the Pleasures of Midnight Revels and Debauches? If a Man was only to consult his Health, he would chuse to live his whole Time (if possible) in Day-light, and to retire out of the World into Silence and Sleep while the raw Damps and unwholesome Vapours fly abroad without a Sun to disperse, moderate, or controul them. For my own Part, I value an Hour in the Morning as much as common Libertines do an Hour at Midnight. When I find my self awakened into Being, and perceive my Life renewed within me, and at the same Time see the whole Face of Nature recovered out of the dark uncomfortable State in which it lay for several Hours, my Heart overflows with such secret Sentiments of Joy and Gratitude as are a Kind of implicit Praise to the great Author of Nature. The Mind in these early Seasons of the Day is so refreshed in all its Faculties, and born up with such new Supplies of Animal Spirits, that she finds her self in a State of Youth, especially when she is entertained with the Breath of Flowers, the Melody of Birds, the Dews that hang upon the Plants, and all

---

3. the Bell-Man: the town crier. **4. Westminster-Hall:** Westminster Hall, the legal center of England, was originally built in the reign of William Rufus (*c.* 1056–1100) as an annex to the royal palace at Westminster. **5. Canonical Hour:** an hour appointed for prayer. **6. Memorial:** memorandum, petition.

7. Complaints . . . S.: *Judicium Vocalium* (*The Consonants at Law*), which, according to his editor, A. M. Harmon, is probably not Lucian's work, is a mock lament for certain corruptions of the Attic dialect, especially the replacement of the double *s* by the double *t*. **8. Sea Coals:** so called because they were carried by sea from the collieries. In *The Spectator*, No. 530, Will Honeycomb uses sea coals as a symbol of the vicious artifices of town life ("Sin and Sea-Coal").

those other Sweets of Nature that are peculiar to the Morning.

It is impossible for a Man to have this Relish of Being, this exquisite Tast of Life, who does not come into the World before it is in all its Noise and Hurry; who loses the Rising of the Sun, the still Hours of the Day, and immediately upon his first getting up plunges himself into the ordinary Cares or Follies of the World.

I shall conclude this Paper with *Milton's* inimitable Description of *Adams's* awakening *Eve* in Paradise, which indeed would have been a Place as little delightful as a barren Heath or Desart to those who slept in it. The Fondness[9] of the Posture in which *Adam* is represented, and the Softness of his Whisper, are Passages in this Divine Poem that are above all Commendation, and rather to be admired than praised.

> *Now Morn her Rosie Steps in th' Eastern Clime*
> *Advancing, sow'd the Earth with Orient Pearl,*
> *When Adam wak'd, so custom'd; for his Sleep*
> *Was Airy-light from pure Digestion bred,*
> *And temperate Vapours bland, which th' only Sound*
> *Of Leaves and fuming Rills, Aurora's Fan*
> *Lightly dispers'd, and the shrill Matin Song*
> *Of Birds on ev'ry Bough; so much the more*
> *His wonder was to find unwaken'd Eve,*
> *With Tresses discompos'd, and glowing Cheek,*
> *As through unquiet Rest: He on his Side*
> *Leaning half rais'd, with Looks of Cordial Love*
> *Hung over her enamour'd, and beheld*
> *Beauty, which whether waking or asleep,*
> *Shot forth peculiar Graces. Then with Voice*
> *Mild, as when Zephyrus on Flora breaths,*
> *Her hand soft touching, whisper'd thus, Awake,*
> *My fairest, my espous'd, my latest found,*
> *Heaven's last best Gift, my ever new Delight,*
> *Awake, the Morning shines, and the fresh Field*
> *Calls us; we lose the Prime, to mark how spring*
> *Our tended Plants, how blows the Citron Grove,*
> *What drops the Myrrhe, and what the Balmy Reed,*
> *How Nature paints her Colours, how the Bee*
> *Sits on the Bloom extracting liquid Sweet.*
> *Such Whisp'ring wak'd her, but with startled Eye*
> *On Adam, whom embracing, thus she spake:*
> *O Sole! in whom my Thoughts find all Repose,*
> *My Glory, my Perfection, glad I see*
> *Thy Face, and Morn return'd.*[10]—

9. **Fondness:** tenderness. 10. **Now . . . return'd:** *Paradise Lost,* V. 1–30.

NUMB. 271

From Saturday December 30. to Tuesday January 2. 1710.

THE Printer having informed me, that there are as many of these Papers printed as will make Four Volumes, I am now come to the End of my Ambition in this Matter, and have nothing further to say to the World under the Character of *Isaac Bickerstaff*. This Work has indeed for some Time been disagreeable to me, and the Purpose of it wholly lost by my being so long understood as the Author. I never designed in it to give any Man any secret Wound by my Concealment, but spoke in the Character of an old Man, a Philosopher, an Humorist, an Astrologer, and a Censor, to allure my Reader with the Variety of my Subjects, and insinuate, if I could, the Weight of Reason with the Agreeableness of Wit. The general Purpose of the Whole has been to recommend Truth, Innocence, Honour, and Virtue, as the chief Ornaments of Life; but I considered, that Severity of Manners was absolutely necessary to him who would censure others; and for that Reason, and that only, chose to talk in a Mask. I shall not carry my Humility so far as to call my self a vicious Man, but at the same Time must confess, my Life is at best but pardonable: And with no greater Character than this, a Man would make but an indifferent Progress in attacking prevailing and fashionable Vices, which Mr. *Bickerstaff* has done with a Freedom of Spirit that would have lost both its Beauty and Efficacy, had it been pretended to by Mr. *Steele*.

As to the Work it self, the Acceptance it has met with is the best Proof of its Value; but I should err against that Candour which an honest Man should always carry about him, if I did not own, that the most approved Pieces in it were written by others, and those which have been most excepted against by my self. The Hand that has assisted me[1] in those noble Discourses upon the Immortality of the Soul, the glorious Prospects of another Life, and the most sublime Idea's of Religion and Virtue, is a Person who is too fondly my Friend ever to own them: But I should little deserve to be his, if I usurped the Glory of them. I must acknowledge at the same Time, that I think the finest Strokes of Wit and Humour in all Mr. *Bickerstaff's* Lucubrations are those for which he is also beholden to him.[2]

Number 271. 1. **The Hand . . . me:** Addison. 2. **the finest . . . him:** Of the present selection, Number 163 is ascribed to Addison (by Aitken).

As for the Satyrical Parts of these Writings, those against the Gentlemen who profess Gaming are the most licentious; but the main of them I take to come from losing Gamesters as Invectives against the Fortunate, for in very many of them I was very little else but the Transcriber. If any have been more particularly marked at, such Persons may impute it to their own Behaviour (before they were touched upon) in publickly speaking their Resentment against the Author, and professing they would support any Man who should insult him. When I mention this Subject, I hope, Major-General *Davenport*, Brigadier *Bisset*, and my Lord *Forbes*,[3] will accept of my Thanks for their frequent good Offices, in professing their Readiness to partake any Danger that should befal me in so just an Undertaking, as the Endeavour to banish Fraud and Couzenage[4] from the Presence and Conversation of Gentlemen.

But what I find is the least excusable Part of all this Work, is, that I have in some Places in it touched upon Matters which concern both the Church and State. All I shall say for this is, that the Points I alluded to are such as concerned every Christian and Freeholder[5] in *England;* and I could not be cold enough to conceal my Opinion on Subjects which related to either of those Characters. But Politicks apart. I must confess, it has been a most exquisite Pleasure to me to frame Characters of Domestick Life, and put those Parts of it which are least observed into an agreeable View, to enquire into the Seeds of Vanity and Affectation, to lay before my Readers the Emptiness of Ambition: In a Word, to trace human Life through all its Mazes and Recesses, and show much shorter Methods than Men ordinarily practise, to be happy, agreeable and great.

But to enquire into Men's Faults and Weaknesses has something in it so unwelcome, that I have often seen People in Pain to act before me, whose Modesty only make them think themselves liable to Censure. This, and a Thousand other nameless Things, have made it an irksome Task to me to personate Mr. *Bickerstaff* any longer; and I believe it does not often happen, that the Reader is delighted where the Author is displeased.

All I can now do for the further Gratification of the Town, is to give them a faithful Index and Explication of Passages and Allusions, and sometimes of Persons,[6] intended in the several scattered Parts of the Work. At the same Time the succeeding Volumes shall discover which of the whole have been written by me, and which by others, and by whom, as far as I am able, or permitted.

Thus I have voluntarily done what I think all Authors should do when called upon. I have published my Name to my Writings, and given my self up to the Mercy of the Town (as *Shakespeare* expresses it) with all my Imperfections on my Head.[7] The indulgent Readers, | *Most Obliged*, | *Most Obedient*, | *Humble Servant,*

RICHARD STEELE.

FROM

THE SPECTATOR

The last *Tatler* was published on January 2, 1711, the first *Spectator* on March 1 of the same year. The new periodical, the first to be published daily, was to depart from its predecessor in abandoning the news and eschewing politics in favor of topics of more general and permanent interest. The change in names is itself suggestive of the change in conception, the more detached and reflective character of Addison emerging as the dominant one in the new collaboration. When the Spectator says, "I shall endeavour to enliven Morality with Wit, and to temper Wit with Morality" (Number 10), he is simply carrying on the work of Mr. Bickerstaff; but a new note is sounded in the same number when he adds: "It was said of *Socrates*, that he brought Philosophy down from Heaven, to inhabit among Men; and I shall be ambitious to have it said of me, that I have brought Philosophy out of Closets and Libraries, Schools and Colleges, to dwell in Clubs and Assemblies, at Tea-Tables, and in Coffee-Houses."

Of the original series of 555 *Spectators*, which ran to December 6, 1712, Addison and Steele wrote about ninety per cent, although many of Steele's numbers consisted simply of letters contributed by readers. (In the present selection all but Number 193 are by Addison.) A second series, begun in the summer of 1714 and ending in December, was issued thrice weekly by Addison without Steele, though with the considerable assistance of Thomas Tickell and Eustace Budgell.

3. **Davenport, Bisset, Forbes:** Major General Sherrington Davenport (d. 1719), Brigadier Andrew Bisset (d. 1742), and George (d. 1765), Lord Forbes, an officer in both the Navy and the Horse Guards. 4. **Couzenage:** (cozenage) deception. 5. **Freeholder:** property owner.

6. **give . . . Persons:** This laudable plan was not executed. 7. **with . . . Head:** *Hamlet*, I. v. 79.

Most of the critical papers in *The Spectator* (nearly sixty of them) are by Addison, and as they are the ones that are likely to engage the attention of the student of literature most closely, it is perhaps proper to introduce them with a historical reminder from Dr. Johnson:

Addison is now to be considered as a critick; a name which the present generation is scarcely willing to allow him. His criticism is condemned as tentative or experimental rather than scientifick, and he is considered as deciding by taste rather than by principles.

It is not uncommon for those who have grown wise by the labour of others to add a little of their own, and overlook their masters. Addison is now despised by some who perhaps would never have seen his defects, but by the lights which he afforded them. That he always wrote as he would think it necessary to write now cannot be affirmed; his instructions were such as the character of his readers made proper. That general knowledge which now circulates in common talk was in his time rarely to be found. Men not professing learning were not ashamed of ignorance; and in the female world any acquaintance with books was distinguished only to be censured. His purpose was to infuse literary curiosity by gentle and unsuspected conveyance into the gay, the idle, and the wealthy; he therefore presented knowledge in the most alluring form, not lofty and austere, but accessible and familiar. When he shewed them their defects, he shewed them likewise that they might be easily supplied. His attempt succeeded; enquiry was awakened, and comprehension expanded. An emulation of intellectual elegance was excited, and from his time to our own life has been gradually exalted, and conversation purified and enlarged.

The text is that of the edition by D. F. Bond (5 vols., 1965), which follows the same textual principles as those adopted for this anthology.

NO. 12

Wednesday, March 14, 1711

> *. . . Veteres avias tibi de pulmone revello.*[1]
>   PER.

THE SPECTATOR: *Number 12.* **1. Veteres . . . revello:** "I pluck the old wives' notions from your breast" (Persius, *Satires*, v. 92).

AT my coming to *London*, it was some time before I could settle my self in a House to my likeing. I was forced to quit my first Lodgings, by reason of an officious Land-lady, that would be asking me every Morning how I had slept. I then fell into an honest Family, and lived very happily for above a Week; when my Land-lord, who was a jolly good-natur'd Man, took it into his Head that I wanted Company, and therefore would frequently come into my Chamber to keep me from being alone. This I bore for Two or Three Days; but telling me one Day that he was afraid I was melancholy, I thought it was high time for me to be gone, and accordingly took new Lodgings that very Night. About a Week after, I found my jolly Land-lord, who, as I said before was an honest hearty Man, had put me into an Advertisement of the *Daily Courant*, in the following Words. *Whereas a melancholy Man left his Lodgings on* Thursday *last in the Afternoon, and was afterwards seen going towards* Islington; *If any one can give Notice of him to* R.B. *Fishmonger in the* Strand, *he shall be very well rewarded for his Pains.* As I am the best Man in the World to keep my own Counsel, and my Land-lord the Fishmonger not knowing my Name, this Accident of my Life was never discovered[2] to this very Day.

I am now settled with a Widow-woman, who has a great many Children, and complies with my Humour in every thing. I do not remember that we have exchang'd a Word together these Five Years; my Coffee comes into my Chamber every Morning without asking for it; if I want[3] Fire I point to my Chimney, if Water to my Bason: Upon which my Land-lady nodds, as much as to say she takes my Meaning, and immediately obeys my Signals. She has likewise model'd[4] her Family so well, that when her little Boy offers to pull me by the Coat or prattle in my Face, his eldest Sister immediately calls him off and bids him not disturb the Gentleman. At my first entering into the Family, I was troubled with the Civility of their rising up to me every time I came into the Room; but my Land-lady observing that upon these Occasions I always cried pish and went out again, has forbidden any such Ceremony to be used in the House; so that at present I walk into the Kitchin or Parlour without being taken notice of, or giving any Interruption to the Business or Discourse of the Family. The Maid will ask her Mistress (tho' I am

2. discovered: disclosed. **3. want:** need. **4. model'd:** trained.

by[5]) whether the Gentleman is ready to go to Dinner, as the Mistress (who is indeed an excellent Housewife) scolds at the Servants as heartily before my Face as behind my Back. In short, I move up and down the House and enter into all Companies, with the same Liberty as a Cat or any other domestick Animal, and am as little suspected of telling any thing that I hear or see.

I remember last Winter there were several young Girls of the Neighbourhood sitting about the Fire with my Land-lady's Daughters, and telling Stories of Spirits and Apparitions. Upon my opening the Door the young Women broke off their Discourse, but my Land-lady's Daughters telling them that it was no Body but the Gentleman (for that is the Name which I go by in the Neighbourhood as well as in the Family) they went on without minding me. I seated my self by the Candle that stood on a Table at one End of the Room; and pretending to read a Book that I took out of my Pocket, heard several dreadful Stories of Ghosts as pale as Ashes that had stood at the Feet of a Bed, or walked over a Church-yard by Moon-light: And of others that had been conjured into the *Red-Sea*, for disturbing People's Rest, and drawing their Curtains at Midnight; with many other old Womens Fables of the like Nature. As one Spirit raised another, I observed that at the End of every Story the whole Company closed their Ranks and crouded about the Fire: I took Notice in particular of a little Boy, who was so attentive to every Story, that I am mistaken if he ventures to go to bed by himself this Twelvemonth. Indeed they talked so long, that the Imaginations of the whole Assembly were manifestly crazed, and I am sure will be the worse for it as long as they live. I heard one of the Girls, that had looked upon me over her Shoulder, asking the Company how long I had been in the Room, and whether I did not look paler than I used to do. This put me under some Apprehensions that I should be forced to explain my self if I did not retire; for which Reason I took the Candle in my Hand, and went up into my Chamber, not without wondering at this unaccountable Weakness in reasonable Creatures, that they should love to astonish and terrify one another. Were I a Father, I should take a particular Care to preserve my Children from these little Horrours of Imagination, which they are apt to contract when they are young, and are not able to shake off when they are in Years. I have known a

Soldier that has enter'd a Breach,[6] affrighted at his own Shadow; and look pale upon a little scratching at his Door, who the Day before had march'd up against a Battery of Cannon. There are Instances of Persons, who have been terrify'd, even to Distraction, at the Figure of a Tree or the shaking of a Bull-rush.[7] The Truth of it is, I look upon a sound Imagination as the greatest Blessing of Life, next to a clear Judgment and a good Conscience. In the mean Time, since there are very few whose Minds are not more or less subject to these dreadful Thoughts and Apprehensions, we ought to arm our selves against them by the Dictates of Reason and Religion, *to pull the old Woman out of our Hearts* (as *Persius* expresses it in the Motto of my Paper,) and extinguish those impertinent[8] Notions which we imbibed at a Time that we were not able to judge of their Absurdity. Or if we believe, as many wise and good Men have done, that there are such Phantoms and Apparitions as those I have been speaking of, let us endeavour to establish to our selves an Interest in him who holds the Reins of the whole Creation in his Hand, and moderates them after such a Manner, that it is impossible for one Being to break loose upon another without his Knowledge and Permission.

For my own Part, I am apt to join in Opinion with those who believe that all the Regions of Nature swarm with Spirits; and that we have Multitudes of Spectators on all our Actions, when we think our selves most alone: But instead of terrifying my self with such a Notion, I am wonderfully pleased to think that I am always engaged with such an innumerable Society in searching out the Wonders of the Creation, and joining in the same Consort of Praise and Adoration.

Milton has finely described this mixed Communion of Men and Spirits in Paradise;[9] and had doubtless his Eye upon a Verse in old *Hesiod*,[10] which is almost Word for Word the same with his third Line in the following Passage.

. . . Nor think, though Men were none,
That Heav'n would want Spectators, God want Praise:
Millions of spiritual Creatures walk the Earth
Unseen, both when we wake and when we sleep;

6. a Breach: a gap in a fortification. **7. Bull-rush:** The bulrush because of its apparent towering strength and actual fragility came to serve as a metaphor for a delusive danger. **8. impertinent:** silly, absurd. **9. in Paradise:** *Paradise Lost,* IV. 675–88. **10. a Verse . . . Hesiod:** *Works and Days,* ll. 251–52.

5. by: standing by, there

All these with ceaseless Praise his Works behold
Both Day and Night. How often from the Steep
Of ecchoing Hill or Thicket, have we heard
Celestial Voices to the midnight Air,
Sole, or responsive each to others Note,
Singing their great Creator: Oft in Bands,
While they keep Watch, or nightly Rounding walk,
With heav'nly Touch of instrumental Sounds,
In full harmonick Number join'd, their Songs
Divide the Night, and lift our Thoughts to Heaven.

NO. 42

Wednesday, April 18, 1711

Garganum mugire putes nemus aut mare Thuscum,
Tanto cum strepitu ludi spectantur, & artes,
Divitiæque peregrinæ; quibus oblitus actor
Cum stetit in Scena, concurrit dextera lævæ.
Dixit adhuc aliquid? Nil sane. Quid placet ergo?
Lana Tarentino violas imitata veneno.[1]

HOR.

ARISTOTLE has observ'd, that ordinary Writers in Tragedy endeavour to raise Terrour and Pity in their Audience, not by proper Sentiments and Expressions, but by the Dresses and Decorations of the Stage.[2] There is something of this Kind very ridiculous in the *English* Theatre. When the Author has a Mind to terrify us, it thunders; when he would make us melancholy, the Stage is darken'd. But among all our tragick Artifices, I am the most offended at those which are made use of to inspire us with magnificent Ideas of the Persons that speak. The ordinary Method of making an Heroe, is to clap a huge Plume of Feathers upon his Head, which rises so very high, that there is often a greater Length from his Chin to the Top of his Head, than to the Sole of his Foot. One would believe, that we thought a great Man and

a tall Man the same thing. This very much embarrasses the Actor, who is forced to hold his Neck extremely stiff and steady all the while he speaks; and notwithstanding any Anxieties which he pretends for his Mistress, his Country, or his Friends, one may see by his Action, that his greatest Care and Concern is to keep the Plume of Feathers from falling off his Head. For my own Part, when I see a Man uttering his Complaints under such a Mountain of Feathers, I am apt to look upon him rather as an unfortunate Lunatick, than a distress'd Heroe. As these superfluous Ornaments upon the Head make a great Man, a Princess generally receives her Grandeur from those additional Incumbrances that fall into her Tail: I mean the broad sweeping Train that follows her in all her Motions, and finds constant Employment for a Boy who stands behind her to open and spread it to Advantage. I do not know how others are affected at this Sight, but, I must confess, my Eyes are wholly taken up with the Page's Part; and as for the Queen, I am not so attentive to any thing she speaks, as to the right adjusting of her Train, lest it should chance to trip up her Heels, or incommode her, as she walks to and fro upon the Stage. It is, in my Opinion, a very odd Spectacle, to see a Queen venting her Passion in a disordered Motion, and a little Boy taking Care all the while that they do not ruffle the Tail of her Gown. The Parts that the two Persons act on the Stage at the same Time, are very different: The Princess is afraid lest she should incur the Displeasure of the King her Father, or lose the Heroe her Lover, whilst her Attendant is only concern'd lest she should entangle her Feet in her Petticoat.

We are told, that an ancient tragick Poet,[3] to move the Pity of his Audience for his exiled Kings and distressed Heroes, used to make the Actors represent them in Dresses and Cloaths that were threadbare and decay'd. This Artifice for moving Pity, seems as ill contriv'd, as that we have been speaking of to inspire us with a great Idea of the Persons introduc'd upon the Stage. In short, I would have our Conceptions rais'd by the Dignity of Thought and Sublimity of Expression, rather than by a Train of Robes or a Plume of Feathers.

Another mechanical Method of making great Men, and adding Dignity to Kings and Queens, is to accompany them with Halberts and Battle-axes.

Number 42. **1. Garganum . . . veneno:** "You would think the Garganian forest and the Tuscan sea were roaring when the people with so much commotion watch the shows, with their tricks and imported adornments. The actor, up to his ears in these things, comes on stage. Immediate applause. 'Has he said anything yet?' 'Not a thing.' 'Then what's everybody applauding for?' 'That material looks just like Tarentine violet' " (Horace, *Epistles*, II. i. 202–07). **2. ordinary . . . Stage:** "Fear and pity sometimes result from what is seen on the stage and are sometimes aroused by the actual arrangement of the incidents, which is preferable and the mark of a better poet" (*Poetics*, xiv. 1–3 [Loeb translation]).

3. an ancient . . . Poet: Euripides, according to Aeschylus, in Aristophanes' *The Frogs*, ll. 1063–64.

Two or three Shifters of Scenes, with the two Candle-Snuffers, make up a compleat Body of Guards upon the *English* Stage; and by the Addition of a few Porters dress'd in red Coats, can represent above a dozen Legions. I have sometimes seen a Couple of Armies drawn up together upon the Stage, when the Poet has been dispos'd to do Honour to his Generals. It is impossible for the Reader's Imagination to multiply twenty Men into such prodigious Multitudes, or to fancy that two or three hundred thousand Soldiers are fighting in a Room of forty or fifty Yards in Compass. Incidents of such Nature should be told, not represented.

> . . . *Non tamen intus*
> *Digna geri promes in scenam: multaque tolles*
> *Ex oculis, quæ mox narret facundia præsens.*[4]
> HOR.

> *Yet there are things improper for a Scene,*
> *Which Men of Judgment only will relate.*
> L. ROSCOM.[5]

I should therefore, in this Particular, recommend to my Countrymen the Example of the *French* Stage, where the Kings and Queens always appear unattended, and leave their Guards behind the Scenes. I should likewise be glad if we imitated the *French* in banishing from our Stage the Noise of Drums, Trumpets, and Huzzas; which is sometimes so very great, that when there is a Battle in the *Hay-Market* Theatre, one may hear it as far as *Charing-Cross.*

I have here only touched upon those Particulars which are made use of to raise and aggrandize the Persons of a Tragedy; and shall shew in another Paper the several Expedients which are practiced by Authors of a vulgar Genius[6] to move Terrour, Pity, or Admiration, in their Hearers.

The Taylor and the Painter often contribute to the Success of a Tragedy more than the Poet. Scenes affect ordinary Minds as much as Speeches; and our Actors are very sensible, that a well-dress'd Play has sometimes brought them as full Audiences, as a well-written one. The *Italians* have a very good Phrase to express this Art of imposing upon the Spectators by Appearances: They call it the *Fourberia della Scena,* *The Knavery or trickish Part of the Drama.* But however

the Show and Outside of the Tragedy may work upon the Vulgar,[7] the more understanding Part of the Audience immediately see through it and despise it.

A good Poet will give the Reader a more lively Idea of an Army or a Battle in a Description, than if he actually saw them drawn up in Squadrons and Batallions, or engaged in the Confusion of a Fight. Our Minds should be open'd to great Conceptions and inflamed with glorious Sentiments by what the Actor speaks, more than by what he appears. Can all the Trappings or Equipage of a King or Hero, give *Brutus* half that Pomp and Majesty which he receives from a few Lines in *Shakespear?*

NO. 58

Monday, May 7, 1711

> *Ut pictura poesis erit . . .*[1]
> HOR.

NOTHING is so much admired and so little understood as Wit. No Author that I know of has written professedly upon it; and as for those who make any Mention of it, they only treat on the Subject as it has accidentally fallen in their Way, and that too in little short Reflections, or in general declamatory Flourishes, without entering into the Bottom of the Matter. I hope therefore I shall perform an acceptable Work to my Countrymen if I treat at large upon this Subject; which I shall endeavour to do in a Manner suitable to it, that I may not incur the Censure which a famous Critick[2] bestows upon one who had written a Treatise upon *the Sublime* in a low groveling Stile. I intend to lay aside a whole Week for this Undertaking, that the Scheme of my Thoughts may not be broken and interrupted; and I dare promise my self, if my Readers will give me a Week's Attention, that this great City will be very much changed for the better by next *Saturday* Night. I shall endeavour to make what I say intelligible to ordinary Capacities; but if my Readers

---

4. **Non . . . præsens:** Horace, *Ars Poetica,* ll. 182–84. 5. **L. Roscom:** The Earl of Roscommon's blank-verse translation of *Ars Poetica* first appeared in 1680. A new edition came out in 1709. 6. **vulgar Genius:** ordinary ability.

7. **the Vulgar:** common people. *Number 58.* 1. **Ut . . . erit:** "A poem will be like a picture" (Horace, *Ars Poetica,* l. 361). 2. **a famous Critick:** Longinus (220–73), at the beginning of the treatise formerly attributed to him, entitled *On the Sublime,* now thought to have been written during the first half of the first century A.D. The opponent was Caecilius.

meet with any Paper that in some Parts of it may be a little out of their Reach, I would not have them discouraged, for they may assure themselves the next shall be much clearer.

As the great and only End of these my Speculations is to banish Vice and Ignorance out of the Territories of *Great Britain*, I shall endeavour as much as possible to establish among us a Taste of polite Writing. It is with this View that I have endeavoured to set my Readers right in several Points relating to Operas and Tragedies; and shall from Time to Time impart my Notions of Comedy, as I think they may tend to its Refinement and Perfection. I find by my Bookseller that these Papers of Criticism, with that upon Humour, have met with a more kind Reception than indeed I could have hoped for from such Subjects; for which Reason I shall enter upon my present Undertaking with greater Chearfulness.

In this and one or two following Papers I shall trace out the History of false Wit, and distinguish the several Kinds of it as they have prevailed in different Ages of the World. This I think the more necessary at present, because I observed there were Attempts on foot last Winter to revive some of those antiquated Modes of Wit that have been long exploded out of the Commonwealth of Letters. There were several Satyrs and Panegyricks handed about in Acrostick, by which Means some of the most arrant undisputed Blockheads about the Town began to entertain ambitious Thoughts, and to set up for polite Authors. I shall therefore describe at length those many Arts of false Wit, in which a Writer does not shew himself a Man of a beautiful Genius, but of great Industry.

The first Species of false Wit which I have met with is very venerable for its Antiquity, and has produced several Pieces which have lived very near as long as the *Iliad* it self: I mean those short Poems printed among the minor *Greek* Poets, which resemble the Figure of an Egg, a Pair of Wings, an Ax, a Shepherd's Pipe, and an Altar.

As for the first, it is a little oval Poem, and may not improperly be called a Scholar's Egg. I would endeavour to hatch it, or, in more intelligible Language, to translate it into *English*, did not I find the Interpretation of it very difficult; for the Author seems to have been more intent upon the Figure of his Poem, than upon the Sense of it.

The Pair of Wings consist of twelve Verses, or rather Feathers, every Verse decreasing gradually in its Measure according to its Situation in the Wing.

The Subject of it (as in the rest of the Poems which follow) bears some remote Affinity with the Figure, for it describes a God of Love, who is always painted with Wings.

The Ax methinks would have been a good Figure for a Lampoon, had the Edge of it consisted of the most satyrical Parts of the Work; but as it is in the Original, I take it to have been nothing else but the Posy[3] of an Ax which was consecrated to *Minerva*, and was thought to have been the same that *Epeus*[4] made use of in the building of the *Trojan* Horse; which is a Hint I shall leave to the Consideration of the Criticks. I am apt to think that the Posy was written originally upon the Ax, like those which our modern Cutlers inscribe upon their Knives; and that therefore the Posy still remains in its ancient Shape, though the Ax it self is lost.

The Shepherd's Pipe may be said to be full of Musick, for it is composed of nine different Kinds of Verses, which by their several Lengths resemble the nine Stops of the old musical Instrument, that is likewise the Subject of the Poem.

The Altar is inscribed with the Epitaph of *Troilus* the Son of *Hecuba*; which, by the Way, makes me believe, that these false Pieces of Wit are much more ancient than the Authors to whom they are generally ascribed; at least I will never be perswaded, that so fine a Writer as *Theocritus* could have been the Author of any such simple Works.

It was impossible for a Man to succeed in these Performances who was not a kind of Painter, or at least a Designer: He was first of all to draw the Outline of the Subject which he intended to write upon, and afterwards conform the Description to the Figure of his Subject. The Poetry was to contract or dilate itself according to the Mould in which it was cast. In a Word, the Verses were to be cramped or extended to the Dimensions of the Frame that was prepared for them; and to undergo the Fate of those Persons whom the Tyrant *Procrustes* used to lodge in his Iron Bed; if they were too short he stretched them on a Rack, and if they were too long chopped off a Part of their Legs, till they fitted the Couch which he had prepared for them.

Mr. *Dryden* hints at this obsolete kind of Wit in one of the following Verses, in his *Mac Flecno;* which an *English* Reader cannot understand, who does not

---

3. **the Posy:** a poetic inscription. 4. **Epeus:** See *Aeneid*, II. 264.

know that there are those little Poems abovementioned in the Shape of Wings and Altars.

> . . . *Chuse for thy Command*
> *Some peaceful Province in Acrostick Land;*
> *There may'st thou* Wings *display and* Altars *raise,*
> *And torture one poor Word a thousand Ways.*[5]

This Fashion of false Wit was revived by several Poets of the last Age, and in particular may be met with among Mr. *Herbert's* Poems;[6] and if I am not mistaken, in the Translation of *Du Bartas.*[7] I do not remember any other Kind of Work among the Moderns which more resembles the Performances I have mentioned, than that famous Picture of King *Charles* the First, which has the whole Book of *Psalms* written in the Lines of the Face and the Hair of the Head. When I was last at *Oxford* I perused one of the Whiskers; and was reading the other, but could not go so far in it as I would have done, by reason of the Impatience of my Friends and Fellow-Travellers, who all of them pressed to see such a Piece of Curiosity. I have since heard, that there is now an eminent Writing-Master in Town, who has transcribed all the *Old Testament* in a full-bottom'd Perriwig; and if the Fashion should introduce the thick Kind of Wigs which were in Vogue some few Years ago, he promises to add two or three supernumerary Locks that shall contain all the *Apocrypha.* He designed this Wig originally for King *William,* having disposed of the two Books of *Kings* in the two Forks of the Foretop;[8] but that glorious Monarch dying before the Wig was finished, there is a Space left in it for the Face of any one that has a mind to purchase it.

But to return to our ancient Poems in Picture, I would humbly propose, for the Benefit of our modern Smatterers in Poetry, that they would imitate their Brethren among the Ancients in those ingenious Devices. I have communicated this Thought to a young Poetical Lover of my Acquaintance, who intends to present his Mistress with a Copy of Verses made in the Shape of her Fan; and if he tells me true, has already finished the three first Sticks of it. He has likewise promised me to get the Measure of his Mistress's Marriage-Finger, with a Design to make a Posie in the Fashion of a Ring which shall exactly fit it. It is so very easy to enlarge upon a good Hint, that I do not question but my ingenious Readers will apply what I have said to many other Particulars; and that we shall see the Town filled in a very little Time with Poetical Tippets,[9] Handkerchiefs, Snuff-Boxes, and the like Female Ornaments. I shall therefore conclude with a Word of Advice to those admirable *English* Authors who call themselves Pindarick Writers,[10] that they would apply themselves to this Kind of Wit without Loss of Time, as being provided better than any other Poets with Verses of all Sizes and Dimensions.

NO. 61

Thursday, May 10, 1711

> *Non equidem hoc studeo, bullatis ut mihi nugis*
> *Pagina turgescat, dare pondus idonea fumo.*[1]
> PERS.

THERE is no kind of false Wit which has been so recommended by the Practice of all Ages, as that which consists in a Jingle of Words, and is comprehended under the general Name of *Punning.* It is indeed impossible to kill a Weed, which the Soil has a natural Disposition to produce. The Seeds of Punning are in the Minds of all Men, and tho' they may be subdued by Reason, Reflection and good Sense, they will be very apt to shoot up in the greatest Genius, that is not broken[2] and cultivated by the Rules of Art. Imitation is natural to us, and when it does not raise the Mind to Poetry, Painting, Musick, or other more noble Arts, it often breaks out in Punns and Quibbles.[3]

Aristotle, in the Eleventh Chapter of his Book of Rhetorick,[4] describes two or three kinds of Punns, which he calls Paragrams,[5] among the Beauties of

---

5. Chuse . . . Ways: ll. 205–08. **6. Mr. . . . Poems:** In *The Temple* (1633) by George Herbert (1593–1633) there is one poem entitled *The Altar* and another called *Easter Wings.* **7. the Translation . . . Bartas:** Du Bartas's *Divine Weeks and Works,* translated by Joshua Sylvester (1605). Addison's reference is to the preliminary matter, especially Sylvester's Dedication to the King, a poem printed in successive pages in the design of a pillar. **8. Foretop:** forelock.

9. Tippets: hood-, cape-, or scarflike garments. **10. Pindarick Writers:** See *The Spectator,* below, No. 160. *Number 61.* **1. Non . . . fumo:** "No indeed, I am not interested in swelling my pages with windy nothings by way of giving substance to mist" (Persius, *Satires,* v. 19–20). **2. broken:** tamed. **3. Quibbles:** word play. **4. in . . . Rhetorick:** III. xi. 6–8. **5. Paragrams:** A paragram is a play on words that results from altering a letter or group of letters in a word.

good Writing, and produces Instances of them out of some of the greatest Authors in the *Greek* Tongue. *Cicero* has sprinkled several of his Works with Punns, and in his Book where he lays down the Rules of Oratory, quotes abundance of Sayings as Pieces of Wit, which also upon Examination prove arrant Punns.[6] But the Age in which *the Punn* chiefly flourished, was the Reign of King *James* the First. That learned Monarch was himself a tolerable Punnster, and made very few Bishops or Privy-Counsellors that had not some time or other signalized themselves by a Clinch,[7] or a *Conundrum*.[8] It was therefore in this Age that the Punn appeared with Pomp and Dignity. It had before been admitted into merry[9] Speeches and ludicrous Compositions, but was now delivered with great Gravity from the Pulpit, or pronounced in the most solemn manner at the Council-Table. The greatest Authors, in their most serious Works, made frequent use of Punns. The Sermons of Bishop *Andrews*,[10] and the Tragedies of *Shakespear*, are full of them. The Sinner was punned into Repentance by the former, as in the Latter nothing is more usual than to see a Hero weeping and quibbling for a dozen Lines together.[11]

I must add to these great Authorities, which seem to have given a kind of Sanction to this Piece of false Wit, that all the Writers of Rhetorick have treated of Punning with very great Respect, and divided the several kinds of it into hard Names, that are reckoned among the Figures of Speech, and recommended as Ornaments in Discourse. I remember a Country School-master of my Acquaintance told me once, that he had been in Company with a Gentleman whom he looked upon to be the greatest *Paragrammatist* among the Moderns. Upon Enquiry, I found my learned Friend had dined that Day with Mr. *Swan*, the famous Punnster;[12] and desiring him to give me some Account of Mr. *Swan's* Conversation, he told me that he generally talked in the *Paranomasia*,[13] that he sometimes gave into the *Plocè*,[14] but that

in his humble Opinion he shined most in the *Antanaclasis*.[15]

I must not here omit, that a famous University[16] of this Land was formerly very much Infested with Punns; but whether or no this might not arise from the Fens and Marshes in which it was situated, and which are now drain'd, I must leave to the Determination of more skilful Naturalists.

After this short History of Punning, one would wonder how it should be so entirely banish'd out of the Learned World, as it is at present, especially since it had found a Place in the Writings of the most ancient Polite Authors. To account for this, we must consider, that the first Race of Authors, who were the great Heroes in Writing, were destitute of all Rules and Arts of Criticism; and for that Reason, though they excel later Writers in Greatness of Genius, they fall short of them in Accuracy and Correctness. The Moderns cannot reach their Beauties, but can avoid their Imperfections. When the World was furnish'd with these Authors of the first Eminence, there grew up another Set of Writers, who gained themselves a Reputation by the Remarks which they made on the Works of those who preceded them. It was one of the Employments of these Secondary Authors, to distinguish the several kinds of Wit by Terms of Art, and to consider them as more or less perfect, according as they were founded in Truth. It is no wonder therefore, that even such Authors as *Isocrates*, *Plato* and *Cicero*, should have such little Blemishes as are not to be met with in Authors of a much inferior Character, who have written since those several Blemishes were discover'd. I do not find that there was a proper Separation made between Punns and true Wit by any of the ancient Authors, except *Quintilian* and *Longinus*. But when this Distinction was once settled, it was very natural for all Men of Sense to agree in it. As for the Revival of this false Wit, it happen'd about the time of the Revival of Letters, but as soon as it was once detected, it immediately vanish'd and disappear'd. At the same time there is no Question, but as it has sunk in one Age and rose in another, it will again recover it self in some distant Period of Time, as Pedantry and Ignorance shall prevail upon Wit and Sense. And, to speak the Truth, I do very much

---

6. in . . . Punns: *De Oratore*, ii. 61–63. 7. Clinch: (or clench) a play on words, a pun. 8. Conundrum: pun (an obsolete meaning). 9. merry: facetious. 10. Bishop Andrews: Lancelot Andrewes (1555–1626), Bishop of Winchester. 11. nothing . . . together: Cf. Johnson's Preface to Shakespeare in Part Six. 12. famous Punnster: not further identified. 13. Paranomasia: (paronomasia) a rhetorical term for the pun. Johnson in his *Dictionary* defines it as "a rhetorical figure, in which, by the change of a letter or syllable, several things are alluded to." 14. Plocè: the repetition of a word for emphasis or to express a particular meaning.

15. Antanaclasis: The *OED* quotes Johnson's *Dictionary*: "a figure in rhetorick, when the same word is repeated in a different, if not in a contrary signification; as, *In thy youth learn some craft, that in old age thou mayst get thy living without craft*." 16. University: Cambridge.

apprehend, by some of the last Winter's Productions, which had their Sets of Admirers, that our Posterity will in a few Years degenerate into a Race of Punnsters: At least, a Man may be very excusable for any Apprehensions of this kind, that has seen *Acrosticks* handed about the Town with great Secresie and Applause; to which I must also add a little *Epigram* called the *Witches Prayer*, that fell into Verse when it was read either backward or forward,[17] excepting only, that it Cursed one way and Blessed the other. When one sees there are actually such Pains-takers among our *British* Wits, who can tell what it may end in? If we must Lash one another, let it be with the manly Strokes of Wit and Satyr; for I am of the old Philosopher's Opinion, That if I must suffer from one or the other, I would rather it should be from the Paw of a Lion, than the Hoof of an Ass.[18] I do not speak this out of any Spirit of Party. There is a most crying Dulness on both sides. I have seen Tory *Acrosticks* and Whig *Anagrams*, and do not quarrel with either of them, because they are *Whigs* or *Tories*, but because they are *Anagrams* and *Acrosticks*.

But to return to Punning. Having pursued the History of a Punn, from its Original to its Downfal, I shall here define it to be a Conceit arising from the use of two Words that agree in the Sound, but differ in the Sense. The only way therefore to try a Piece of Wit is to translate it into a different Language, if it bears the Test you may pronounce it true; but if it vanishes in the Experiment, you may conclude it to have been a Punn. In short, one may say of a Punn as the Country-man described his Nightingale, that it is *vox & præterea nihil*, a Sound, and nothing but a Sound.[19] On the contrary, one may represent true Wit by the Description which *Aristinetus* makes of a fine Woman, When she is *dress'd* she is Beautiful, when she is *undress'd* she is Beautiful:[20] Or, as *Mercerus*[21] has translated it more Emphatically, *Induitur, formosa est: Exuitur, ipsa forma est.*

17. fell . . . forward: the way witches were supposed to recite their prayers. 18. of the old . . . Ass: apparently an adaptation of Aesop's fable (Number 14 in Sir Roger L'Estrange's edition), in which the old lion himself regards the beating by an ass as the utmost indignity he suffered. 19. vox . . . Sound: "A man plucked a nightingale and finding almost no meat, said, 'It's all voice ye are, and nought else'" (Plutarch, *Moralia*, 233A [15] [Loeb translation]). 20. the Description . . . Beautiful: from the first letter of the first book of Aristenetus' stories dealing with famous erotic themes of classical antiquity. 21. Mercerus: Josias Mercier brought out the first edition of Aristenetus in Paris in 1595.

NO. 62

Friday, May 11, 1711

Scribendi recte Sapere est & principium & fons.[1]
                                        HOR.

MR. *LOCK* has an admirable Reflection upon the Difference of Wit and Judgment, whereby he endeavours to shew the Reason why they are not always the Talents of the Same Person. His Words are as follow: *And hence, perhaps, may be given some Reason of that common Observation, That Men who have a great deal of Wit and prompt Memories, have not always the clearest Judgment, or deepest Reason. For Wit lying most in the Assemblage of Ideas, and putting those together with Quickness and Variety, wherein can be found any Resemblance or Congruity thereby to make up pleasant Pictures and agreeable Visions in the Fancy; Judgment, on the contrary, lies quite on the other Side, In separating carefully one from another, Ideas wherein can be found the least Difference, thereby to avoid being misled by Similitude and by Affinity to take one thing for another. This is a Way of proceeding quite contrary to Metaphor and Allusion; wherein, for the most Part, lies that Entertainment and Pleasantry of Wit which strikes so lively on the Fancy, and is therefore so acceptable to all People.*[2]

This is, I think, the best and most philosophical Account that I have ever met with of Wit, which generally, tho' not always, consists in such a Resemblance and Congruity of Ideas as this Author mentions. I shall only add to it, by way of Explanation, That every Resemblance of Ideas is not that which we call Wit, unless it be such an one that gives *Delight* and *Surprize* to the Reader: These two Properties seem essential to Wit, more particularly the last of them. In order therefore that the Resemblance in the Ideas be Wit, it is necessary that the Ideas should not lie too near one another in the Nature of things; for where the Likeness is obvious, it gives no Surprize. To compare one Man's Singing to that of another, or to represent the Whiteness of any Object by that of Milk and Snow, or the Variety of its Colours by those of the Rainbow, cannot be called Wit, unless, besides this obvious Resemblance, there be some further Congruity discovered in the two Ideas that is capable

Number 62. 1. **Scribendi . . . fons:** "Good writing springs first and foremost from wisdom" (Horace, *Ars Poetica*, l. 309). 2. **And . . . People:** *An Essay Concerning Humane Understanding*, II. xi. 2.

of giving the Reader some Surprize. Thus when a Poet tells us, the Bosom of his Mistress is as white as Snow, there is no Wit in the Comparison; but when he adds, with a Sigh, that it is as cold too, it then grows into Wit.[3] Every Reader's Memory may supply him with innumerable Instances of the same Nature. For this Reason, the Similitudes[4] in Heroick Poets, who endeavour rather to fill the Mind with great Conceptions, than to divert it with such as are new and surprizing, have seldom any thing in them that can be called Wit. Mr. *Lock's* Account of Wit, with this short Explanation, comprehends most of the Species of Wit, as Metaphors, Similitudes, Allegories, Ænigmas,[5] Mottos, Parables, Fables, Dreams, Visions, dramatick Writings, Burlesque, and all the Methods of Allusion: As there are many other Pieces of Wit (how remote soever they may appear at first Sight from the foregoing Description) which upon Examination will be found to agree with it.

As *true Wit* generally consists in this Resemblance and Congruity of Ideas, *false Wit* chiefly consists in the Resemblance and Congruity sometimes of single Letters, as in Anagrams, Chronograms,[6] Lipograms,[7] and Acrosticks: Sometimes of Syllables, as in Ecchos[8] and Doggerel Rhymes: Sometimes of Words, as in Punns and Quibbles; and sometimes of whole Sentences or Poems, cast into the Figures of *Eggs*, *Axes*, or *Altars:* Nay some carry the Notion of Wit so far, as to ascribe it even to external Mimickry; and to look upon a Man as an ingenious Person, that can resemble the Tone, Posture, or Face of another.

As *true Wit* consists in the Resemblance of Ideas, and *false Wit* in the Resemblance of Words, according to the foregoing Instances; there is another kind of Wit which consists partly in the Resemblance of Ideas, and partly in the Resemblance of Words; which for Distinction Sake I shall call *mixt Wit*. This Kind of Wit is that which abounds in *Cowley*, more than in any Author that ever wrote. Mr. *Waller* has likewise a great deal of it. Mr. *Dryden* is very sparing in it. *Milton* had a Genius much above it. *Spencer* is in the same Class with *Milton*. The *Italians*, even in their Epic Poetry, are full of it. Monsieur *Boileau*, who formed himself upon the ancient Poets, has every where rejected it with Scorn. If we look after mixt Wit among the *Greek* Writers, we shall find it no where but in the Epigrammatists. There are indeed some Strokes of it in the little Poem ascribed to *Musæus*,[9] which by that, as well as many other Marks, betrays it self to be a modern Composition. If we look into the *Latin* Writers, we find none of this mixt Wit in *Virgil*, *Lucretius*, or *Catullus;* very little in *Horace*, but a great deal of it in *Ovid*, and scarce any thing else in *Martial*.

Out of the innumerable Branches of mixt Wit,[10] I shall chuse one Instance which may be met with in all the Writers of this Class. The Passion of Love in its Nature has been thought to resemble Fire; for which Reason the Words Fire and Flame are made use of to signify Love. The witty Poets therefore have taken an Advantage from the doubtful[11] Meaning of the Word Fire, to make an infinite Number of Witticisms. *Cowley* observing the cold Regard of his Mistress's Eyes, and at the same Time their Power of producing Love in him, considers them as Burning-Glasses made of Ice; and finding himself able to live in the greatest Extremities of Love, concludes the Torrid Zone to be habitable. When his Mistress has read his Letter written in Juice of Lemmon by holding it to the Fire, he desires her to read it over a second time by Love's Flames. When she weeps, he wishes it were inward Heat that distilled those Drops from the Limbeck.[12] When she is absent he is beyond eighty, that is, thirty Degrees nearer the Pole than when she is with him. His ambitious Love is a Fire that naturally mounts upwards, his happy Love is the Beams of Heaven, and his unhappy Love Flames of Hell. When it does not let him sleep, it is a Flame that sends up no Smoak; when it is opposed by Counsel and Advice, it is a Fire that rages the more by the Wind's blowing upon

---

3. when . . Wit: D. F. Bond quotes the following couplet from a poem by an obscure contemporary poet, John Ayloffe: "Her Breast is like a Heap of solid Snow, / Boasting its Colour, and its coldness too." **4. Similitudes:** similes. **5. Ænigmas:** An enigma is a short description, made from purposely obscure metaphors, that depends for its meaning on the ingenuity of the reader or listener. **6. Chronograms:** A chronogram is a phrase, sentence, or inscription, in which certain numeral letters, often distinguished by size, express by their total numerical value a date or epoch. The example given in the *OED* is: "LorD haVe MerCIe Vpon Vs" (the total is 1666). **7. Lipograms:** A lipogram is a composition that omits any words containing a certain letter or letters. **8. Ecchos:** An echo is a poetic device that involves the repetition in one line of the concluding syllables of the preceding line, thus supplying an answer to its question or some other sense of continuity.

9. Musæus: Musaeus Grammaticus, Greek poet, believed to have lived during the late fifth century A.D. **10. mixt Wit:** The following examples of "mixt wit" are all contained in the collection of poems published by Cowley in 1647 as *The Mistress*. **11. doubtful:** ambiguous. **12. Limbeck:** alembic.

it. Upon the dying of a Tree in which he had cut his Loves, he observes that his written Flames had burnt up and withered the Tree. When he resolves to give over his Passion, he tells us that one burnt like him for ever dreads the Fire. His Heart is an *Ætna*, that instead of *Vulcan*'s Shop encloses *Cupid*'s Forge in it. His endeavouring to drown his Love in Wine, is throwing Oil upon the Fire. He would insinuate to his Mistress, that the Fire of Love, like that of the Sun (which produces so many living Creatures) should not only warm but beget. Love in another Place cooks Pleasure at his Fire. Sometimes the Poet's Heart is frozen in every Breast, and sometimes scorched in every Eye. Sometimes he is drowned in Tears, and burnt in Love, like a Ship set on fire in the Middle of the Sea.

The Reader may observe in every one of these Instances, that the Poet mixes the Qualities of Fire with those of Love; and in the same Sentence speaking of it both as a Passion and as real Fire, surprizes the Reader with those seeming Resemblances or Contradictions that make up all the Wit in this kind of Writing. Mixt Wit therefore is a Composition of Punn and true Wit, and is more or less perfect as the Resemblance lies in the Ideas or in the Words: Its Foundations are laid partly in Falsehood and partly in Truth: Reason puts in her Claim for one Half of it, and Extravagance for the other. The only Province therefore for this kind of Wit, is Epigram, or those little occasional Poems that in their own Nature are nothing else but a Tissue of Epigrams. I cannot conclude this Head[13] of *mixt Wit*, without owning that the admirable Poet out of whom I have taken the Examples of it, had as much true Wit as any Author that ever writ; and indeed all other Talents of an extraordinary Genius.

It may be expected, since I am upon this Subject, that I should take Notice of Mr. *Dryden*'s Definition of Wit; which, with all the Deference that is due to the Judgement of so great a Man, is not so properly a Definition of Wit, as of good Writing in general. Wit, as he defines it, is "a Propriety of Words and Thoughts adapted to the Subject."[14] If this be a true Definition of Wit, I am apt to think that *Euclid* was the greatest Wit that ever set Pen to Paper: It is

certain there never was a greater Propriety of Words and Thoughts adapted to the Subject, than what that Author has made use of in his Elements. I shall only appeal to my Reader, if this Definition agrees with any Notion he has of Wit: If it be a true one, I am sure Mr. *Dryden* was not only a better Poet, but a greater Wit than Mr. *Cowley*, and *Virgil* a much more facetious[15] Man than either *Ovid* or *Martial*.

Bouhours, whom I look upon to be the most penetrating of all the *French* Criticks, has taken Pains to shew, That it is impossible for any Thought to be beautiful which is not just, and has not its Foundation in the Nature of things: That the Basis of all Wit is Truth; and that no Thought can be valuable, of which good Sense is not the Ground-work.[16] *Boileau* has endeavoured to inculcate the same Notion in several Parts of his Writings, both in Prose and Verse.[17] This is that natural Way of writing, that beautiful Simplicity, which we so much admire in the Compositions of the Ancients; and which no Body deviates from, but those who want Strength of Genius to make a Thought shine in its own natural Beauties. Poets who want[18] this Strength of Genius to give that majestick Simplicity to Nature, which we so much admire in the Works of the Ancients, are forced to hunt after foreign Ornaments, and not to let any Piece of Wit of what Kind soever escape them. I look upon these Writers as *Goths*[19] in Poetry, who, like those in Architecture, not being able to come up to the beautiful Simplicity of the old *Greeks* and *Romans*, have endeavoured to supply its Place with all the Extravagancies of an irregular Fancy. Mr. *Dryden* makes a very handsome Observation on *Ovid*'s writing a Letter from *Dido* to *Æneas* in the following Words:[20] "*Ovid* (says he, speaking of *Virgil*'s Fiction of *Dido* and *Æneas*) takes it up after him, even in the

---

13. **Head:** topic. 14. **a Propriety . . . Subject:** "a propriety of thoughts and words; or, in other terms, thoughts and words elegantly adapted to the subject" (The Author's Apology, prefixed to *The State of Innocence* [1667]).

15. **facetious:** witty, humorous. 16. **That it . . . Groundwork:** Dominique Bouhours (1628–1702), in the First Dialogue from *La Manière de bien penser dans les ouvrages d'esprit* (1687). The work was translated into English in 1705 "by a person of quality" under the title *The Art of Criticism*. 17. **Boileau . . . Verse:** For example: "What is a new or brilliant or extraordinary thought? It is not, as the ignorant suppose, a thought that nobody has ever had before, or might even have been expected to have. On the contrary, it is a thought which must have occurred to everyone, and which someone is the first to have conceived of putting into words. A witty remark is a witty remark only in that it says a thing that everyone thinks, and says it in a lively, acute, and refreshing way" (Preface to the 1701 edition of Boileau's *Works*). 18. **want:** lack. 19. **Goths:** barbarians. 20. **the following Words:** in "The Dedication of the Aeneis."

same Age, and makes an ancient Heroine of *Virgil's* new-created *Dido;* dictates a Letter for her just before her Death to the ungrateful Fugitive; and, very unluckily for himself, is for measuring a Sword with a Man so much superior in Force to him, on the same Subject. I think I may be Judge of this, because I have translated both. The famous Author of the Art of Love has nothing of his own; he borrows all from a greater Master in his own Profession, and, which is worse, improves nothing which he finds: Nature fails him, and being forced to his old Shift, he has Recourse to Witticism. This passes indeed with his soft[21] Admirers, and gives him the Preference to *Virgil* in their Esteem."

Were not I supported by so great an Authority as that of Mr. *Dryden,* I should not venture to observe, That the Taste of most of our *English* Poets, as well as Readers, is extremely *Gothick.* He quotes Monsieur *Segrais*[22] for a threefold Distinction of the Readers of Poetry: In the first of which he comprehends the Rabble of Readers, whom he does not treat as such with regard to their Quality, but to their Numbers and the Coarseness of their Taste. His Words are as follow:[23] "*Segrais* has distinguished the Readers of Poetry, according to their Capacity of judging, into three Classes. (He might have said the same of Writers too if he had pleased.) In the lowest Form he places those whom he calls *Les Petits Esprits,* such things as are our upper-Gallery Audience in a Play-house; who like nothing but the Husk and Rind of Wit, prefer a Quibble, a Conceit, an Epigram, before solid Sense and elegant Expression: These are Mob-Readers. If *Virgil* and *Martial* stood for Parliament-Men, we know already who would carry it. But though they make the greatest Appearance in the Field, and cry the loudest, the best on 't[24] is they are but a Sort of *French* Huguenots, or *Dutch* Boors,[25] brought over in Herds, but not naturalized; who have not Lands of two Pounds *per Annum* in *Parnassus,* and therefore are not privileg'd to poll. Their Authors are of the same Level, fit to represent them on a Mountebank's Stage, or to be Masters of the Ceremonies in a Bear-Garden: Yet these are they who have the most Admirers. But it often happens, to their Mortification, that as their Readers improve their Stock of Sense, (as they may by

reading better Books, and by Conversation with Men of Judgement) they soon forsake them."

I must not dismiss this Subject without observing, that as Mr. *Lock* in the Passage above-mentioned has discovered the most fruitful Source of Wit, so there is another of a quite contrary Nature to it, which does likewise branch it self out into several Kinds. For not only the *Resemblance* but the *Opposition* of Ideas does very often produce Wit; as I cou'd shew in several little Points, Turns, and Antitheses, that I may possibly enlarge upon in some future Speculation.

NO. 70

Monday, May 21, 1711

Interdum vulgus rectum videt.[1]

HOR.

WHEN I travelled, I took a particular Delight in hearing the Songs and Fables that are come from Father to Son, and are most in vogue among the common People of the Countries through which I passed; for it is impossible that any thing should be universally tasted and approved by a Multitude, tho' they are only the Rabble of a Nation, which hath not in it some peculiar Aptness to please and gratify the Mind of Man. Human Nature is the same in all reasonable Creatures; and whatever falls in[2] with it, will meet with Admirers amongst Readers of all Qualities and Conditions. *Moliere,* as we are told by Monsieur *Boileau,*[3] used to read all his Comedies to an old Woman who was his House-keeper, as she sat with him at her Work[4] by the Chimney-Corner; and could foretell the Success of his Play in the Theatre, from the Reception it met at his Fire-Side: For he tells us the Audience always followed the old Woman, and never failed to laugh in the same Place.

I know nothing which more shews the essential and inherent Perfection of Simplicity of Thought, above that which I call the Gothick Manner in Writing, than this, that the first pleases all Kinds of Palates, and the latter only such as have formed to themselves a wrong artificial Taste upon little fanciful Authors and Writers of Epigram. *Homer, Virgil,* or

---

21. **soft:** lenient; perhaps, impressionable. 22. **Segrais:** Jean Regnault de Segrais's translation of Virgil appeared between 1668 and 1681. 23. **as follow:** again from "The Dedication of the Aeneis." 24. **the best on 't:** the best that can be said of them. 25. **Boors:** (Boers) peasants.

Number 70. **1. Interdum . . . videt:** "Sometimes the people see things right" (Horace, *Epistles,* II. i. 63). **2. falls in:** accords, conforms. **3. by . . . Boileau:** in *Critical Reflections on Longinus* (*Works* [1711–12], ii. 89). **4. Work:** needlework.

Milton, so far as the Language of their Poems is understood, will please a Reader of plain common Sense, who would neither relish nor comprehend an Epigram of *Martial* or a Poem of *Cowley:* So, on the contrary, an ordinary Song or Ballad that is the Delight of the common People, cannot fail to please all such Readers as are not unqualified for the Entertainment by their Affectation or Ignorance; and the Reason is plain, because the same Paintings of Nature which recommend it to the most ordinary Reader, will appear beautiful to the most refined.

The old Song of *Chevy Chase* is the favourite Ballad of the common People of *England;* and *Ben. Johnson* used to say he had rather have been the Author of it than of all his Works. Sir *Philip Sidney* in his Discourse of Poetry[5] speaks of it in the following Words; *I never heard the old Song of* Piercy *and* Douglas, *that I found not my Heart more moved than with a Trumpet; and yet is sung by some blind Crowder[6] with no rougher Voice than rude Stile; which being so evil apparelled in the Dust and Cobweb of that uncivil Age, what would it work trimmed in the gorgeous Eloquence of* Pindar? For my own Part, I am so professed an Admirer of this antiquated Song, that I shall give my Reader a Critick[7] upon it, without any further Apology for so doing.

The greatest modern Criticks have laid it down as a Rule, That an heroick Poem should be founded upon some important Precept of Morality, adapted to the Constitution of the Country in which the Poet writes. *Homer* and *Virgil* have formed their Plans in this View. As *Greece* was a Collection of many Governments, who suffered very much among themselves, and gave the *Persian* Emperour, who was their common Enemy, many Advantages over them by their mutual Jealousies and Animosities, *Homer*, in order to establish among them an Union, which was so necessary for their Safety, grounds his Poem upon the Discords of the several *Grecian* Princes who were engaged in a Confederacy against an *Asiatick* Prince, and the several Advantages which the Enemy gained by such their Discords. At the Time the Poem we are now treating of was written, the Dissentions of the Barons, who were then so many petty Princes, ran very high, whether they quarrell'd among themselves or with their Neighbours, and produced unspeakable Calamities to the Country: The Poet, to deter Men from

such unnatural Contentions, describes a bloody Battle and dreadful Scene of Death, occasioned by the mutual Feuds which reigned in the Families of an *English* and *Scotch* Nobleman. That he design'd this for the Instruction of his Poem, we may learn from his four last Lines, in which, after the Example of the modern Tragedians, he draws from it a Precept for the Benefit of his Readers.

> *God save the King and bless the Land*
> *In Plenty, Joy, and Peace;*
> *And grant henceforth that foul Debate*
> *'Twixt Noblemen may cease.*

The next Point observed by the greatest Heroic Poets, hath been to celebrate Persons and Actions which do Honour to their Country: Thus *Virgil*'s Hero was the Founder of *Rome, Homer*'s a Prince of *Greece;* and for this Reason *Valerius Flaccus* and *Statius*, who were both *Romans*, might be justly derided for having chosen the Expedition of the *Golden Fleece* and *the Wars of Thebes*, for the Subjects of their Epic Writings.[8]

The Poet before us, has not only found out an Hero in his own Country, but raises the Reputation of it by several beautiful Incidents. The *English* are the first who take the Field, and the last who quit it. The *English* bring only Fifteen hundred to the Battle, the *Scotch* Two thousand. The *English* keep the Field with Fifty three: The *Scotch* retire with Fifty five: All the rest on each Side being slain in Battle. But the most remarkable Circumstance of this Kind, is the different Manner in which the *Scotch* and *English* Kings receive the News of this Fight, and of the great Mens Deaths who commanded in it.

> *This News was brought to* Edinburgh,
> *Where* Scotland'*s King did reign,*
> *That brave Earl* Douglas *suddenly*
> *Was with an Arrow slain.*
>
> *O heavy News, King* James *did say,*
> Scotland *can Witness be,*
> *I have not any Captain more*
> *Of such Account as he.*
>
> *Like Tydings to King* Henry *came*
> *Within as short a Space,*
> *That* Piercy *of* Northumberland
> *Was slain in* Chevy-Chace.

---

5. **Discourse of Poetry:** *An Apology for Poetry* (1595). 6. **Crowder:** fiddler. 7. **Critick:** critique.

8. **Epic Writings:** the unfinished *Argonautica* of Valerius Flaccus (d. 92 or 93 A.D.) and the *Thebaid* of Statius (c. 45–96 A.D.).

Now God be with him, said our King,
  Sith 'twill no better be,
I trust I have within my Realm
  Five hundred as good as he.

Yet shall not Scot nor Scotland say
  But I will Vengeance take,
And be revenged on them all
  For brave Lord Piercy's Sake.

This Vow full well the King perform'd
  After on Humble-down,
In one Day Fifty Knights were slain
  With Lords of great Renown.

And of the rest of small Account
  Did many Thousands dye, &c.

At the same Time that our Poet shews a laudable Partiality to his Country-men, he represents the *Scots* after a Manner not unbecoming so bold and brave a People.

  Earl Douglas on a milk-white Steed,
    Most like a Baron bold,
  Rode foremost of the Company
    Whose Armour shone like Gold.

His Sentiments and Actions are every Way suitable to an Hero. One of us two, says he, must dye: I am an Earl as well as your self, so that you can have no Pretence for refusing the Combat: However, says he, 'tis Pity, and indeed would be a Sin, that so many innocent Men should perish for our Sakes; rather let you and I end our Quarrel in single Fight.

  E'er thus I will out-braved be,
    One of us two shall dye;
  I know thee well, an Earl thou art,
    Lord Piercy, so am I.

  But trust me, Piercy, Pity it were,
    And great Offence, to kill
  Any of these our harmless Men,
    For they have done no Ill.

  Let thou and I the Battle try,
    And set our Men aside;
  Accurst be he, Lord Piercy said,
    By whom this is deny'd.

When these brave Men had distinguished themselves in the Battle and in single Combat with each other, in the Midst of a generous Parly, full of heroic Sentiments, the *Scotch* Earl falls; and with his dying Words encourages his Men to revenge his Death, representing

to them, as the most bitter Circumstance of it, that his Rival saw him fall.

  With that there came an Arrow keen
    Out of an English bow,
  Which struck Earl Douglas to the Heart
    A deep and deadly Blow.

  Who never spoke more Words than these,
    Fight on my merry Men all;
  For why, my Life is at an End,
    Lord Piercy sees my Fall.

Merry Men, in the Language of those Times, is no more than a chearful Word for Companions and Fellow-Soldiers. A Passage in the Eleventh Book of *Virgil's Æneids* is very much to be admired, where *Camilla* in her last Agonies, instead of weeping over the Wound she had received, as one might have expected from a Warriour of her Sex, considers only (like the Hero of whom we are now speaking) how the Battle should be continued after her Death.

  Tum sic exspirans, &c.[9]

  A gathering Mist o'erclouds her chearful Eyes;
  And from her Cheeks the rosie Colour flies.
  Then, turns to her, whom, of her Female Train,
  She trusted most, and thus she speaks with Pain.
  Acca, 'tis past! He swims before my Sight,
  Inexorable Death; and claims his Right.
  Bear my last Words to Turnus, fly with Speed,
  And bid him timely to my Charge succeed:
  Repel the Trojans, and the Town relieve:
  Farewel. . . .

Turnus did not die in so heroic a Manner; tho' our Poet seems to have had his Eye upon *Turnus's* Speech in the last Verse

  Lord Piercy sees my Fall.
    . . . Vicisti, & victum tendere palmas
  Ausonii videre . . . .[10]

Earl *Piercy's* Lamentation over his Enemy is generous, beautiful, and passionate; I must only caution the Reader not to let the Simplicity of the Stile, which one may well pardon in so old a Poet, prejudice him against the Greatness of the Thought.

---

9. Tum . . . &c.: *Aeneid,* XI. 820 ff. Addison gives Dryden's translation (XI. 1193–1202). **10. Vicisti . . . videre:** "You are the victor, and the Ausonians have seen me—the vanquished—stretch forth my hands" (*Ibid.,* XII. 936–37).

Then leaving Life Earl Piercy *took*
  The dead Man by the Hand,
And said Earl Douglas for thy Life
  Would I had lost my Land.

O Christ! my very Heart doth bleed
  With Sorrow for thy Sake;
For sure a more renowned Knight
  Mischance did never take.

That beautiful Line *Taking the dead Man by the Hand,*
will put the Reader in Mind of *Æneas*'s Behaviour
towards *Lausus,* whom he himself had slain as he came
to the Rescue of his aged Father.

At vero ut vultum vidit morientis, & ora,
Ora modis Anchisiades, pallentia miris:
Ingemuit, miserans graviter, dextramque tetendit,[11] &c.

The pious Prince beheld young Lausus *dead;*
He griev'd, he wept; then grasp'd his Hand, and said,
Poor hapless Youth! What Praises can be paid
To Worth so great . . . !

I shall take another Opportunity to consider the
other Parts of this old Song.

NO. 105

Saturday, June 30, 1711

> . . . *Id arbitror*
> *Adprime in vita esse utile, ne quid nimis.*[1]
> TER. ANDR.

MY Friend, WILL. HONEYCOMB, values himself very
much upon what he calls the Knowledge of Mankind,
which has cost him many Disasters in his Youth; for
WILL. reckons every Misfortune that he has met with
among the Women, and every Rencounter[2] among
the Men, as Parts of his Education, and fancies he
should never have been the Man he is, had not he
broke Windows, knocked down Constables, disturbed
honest People with his Midnight Serenades, and beat
up a Lewd Woman's Quarters, when he was a young
Fellow. The engaging in Adventures of this nature
WILL. calls the studying of Mankind, and terms this
Knowledge of the Town the Knowledge of the

World. WILL. ingenuously confesses that for half his
Life his Head ached every Morning with reading of
Men over-night, and at present Comforts himself
under certain Pains which he endures from time to
time, that without them he could not have been
acquainted with the Gallantries of the Age. This
WILL. looks upon as the Learning of a Gentleman,
and regards all other kinds of Science as the Accomplishments of one whom he calls a Scholar, a Bookish
Man, or a Philosopher.

For these Reasons WILL. shines in mixt Company,
where he has the Discretion not to go out of his
Depth, and has often a certain way of making his real
Ignorance appear a seeming one. Our Club however
has frequently caught him tripping, at which times
they never spare him. For as WILL. often insults us
with the Knowledge of the Town, we sometimes
take our Revenge upon him by our Knowledge of
Books.

He was last Week producing two or three Letters
which he writ in his Youth to a Coquet Lady. The
Raillery of them was natural, and well enough for a
meer Man of the Town; but, very unluckily, several
of the Words were wrong spelt. WILL. laught this off
at first as well as he could, but finding himself pushed
on all sides, and especially by the *Templar,*[3] he told
us, with a little Passion, that he never liked Pedantry
in Spelling, and that he spelt like a Gentleman, and
not like a Scholar: Upon this WILL. had Recourse to
his old Topick of showing the narrow Spiritedness,
the Pride and Ignorance of Pedants; which he carried
so far, that upon my retiring to my Lodgings, I could
not forbear throwing together such Reflections as
occurred to me upon that Subject.

A Man who has been brought up among Books,
and is able to talk of nothing else, is a very indifferent[4]
Companion, and what we call a Pedant. But, methinks, we should enlarge the Title, and give it every
one that does not know how to think out of his
Profession, and particular way of Life.

What is a greater Pedant than a meer Man of the
Town? Barr him the Play-houses, a Catalogue of the
reigning Beauties, and an Account of a few fashionable
Distempers that have befallen him, and you strike
him Dumb. How many a pretty Gentleman's Knowledge lies all within the Verge of the Court? He will

---

11. **At . . . tetendit:** *Ibid.,* X. 821–23. The translation appears
to be a reworking of Dryden's (X. 1165–70), if it is not someone else's entirely. *Number 105.* **1. Id . . . nimis:** "This,
I would judge, is especially useful in life: nothing in excess"
(Terence, *Andria,* ll. 60–61). **2. Rencounter:** skirmish, duel.

3. **Templar:** a member of the Inner or Middle Temple,
two of London's Inns of Court. **4. very indifferent:** rather
poor.

tell you the Names of the Principal Favourites, repeat the shrewd Sayings of a Man of Quality, whisper an Intrigue that is not yet blown upon by common Fame;[5] or, if the Sphere of his Observations is a little larger than ordinary, will perhaps enter into all the Incidents, Turns and Revolutions in a Game of Ombre.[6] When he has gone thus far he has shown you the whole Circle of his Accomplishments, his Parts[7] are drained, and he is disabled from any further Conversation. What are these but rank Pedants? and yet these are the Men who value themselves most on their Exemption from the Pedantry of Colleges.

I might here mention the Military Pedant, who always talks in a Camp, and is storming Towns, making Lodgments,[8] and fighting Battels from one end of the Year to the other. Every thing he speaks smells of Gunpowder; if you take away his Artillery from him, he has not a Word to say for himself. I might likewise mention the Law Pedant, that is perpetually putting Cases, repeating the Transactions of *Westminster-Hall*,[9] wrangling with you upon the most indifferent Circumstances of Life, and not to be convinced of the Distance of a Place, or of the most trivial Point in Conversation, but by dint of Argument. The State-Pedant is wrapt up in News, and lost in Politicks. If you mention either of the Kings of *Spain* or *Poland*, he talks very notably, but if you go out of the *Gazette*[10] you drop him. In short, a meer Courtier, a meer Soldier, a meer Scholar, a meer any thing, is an insipid Pedantick Character, and equally ridiculous.

Of all the Species of Pedants, which I have mentioned, the Book-Pedant is much the most supportable; he has at least an exercised Understanding, and a Head which is full though confused, so that a Man who converses with him may often receive from him hints of things that are worth knowing, and what he may possibly turn to his own Advantage, tho' they are of little use to the Owner. The worst kind of Pedants among Learned Men are such as are naturally endued[11] with a very small Share of common Sense, and have read a great number of Books without Taste or Distinction.

The Truth of it is, Learning, like Travelling, and all

other Methods of Improvement, as it finishes[12] good Sense, so it makes a silly Man ten thousand times more insufferable, by supplying variety of Matter to his Impertinence,[13] and giving him an Opportunity of abounding in Absurdities.

Shallow Pedants cry up[14] one another much more than Men of solid and useful Learning. To read the Titles they give an Editor, of Collator of a Manuscript, you would take him for the Glory of the Common Wealth of Letters, and the Wonder of his Age; when perhaps upon Examination you find that he has only Rectify'd a *Greek* Particle, or laid out a whole Sentence in proper Comma's.

They are obliged indeed to be thus lavish of their Praises, that they may keep one another in Countenance;[15] and it is no wonder if a great deal of Knowledge, which is not capable of making a Man Wise, has a natural Tendency to make him Vain and Arrogant.

NO. 159

Saturday, September 1, 1711

. . . *Omnem quæ nunc obducta tuenti*
Mortales hebetat visus tibi, & humida circum
Caligat, nubem eripiam. . . .[1]

VIRG.

WHEN I was at *Grand Cairo* I picked up several Oriental Manuscripts, which I have still by me. Among others I met with one entituled, *The Visions of Mirzah*,[2] which I have read over with great Pleasure. I intend to give it to the Publick when I have no other Entertainment for them; and shall begin with the first Vision,[3] which I have translated Word for Word as follows.

"ON the fifth Day of the Moon, which according to the Custom of my Fore-fathers I always keep holy, after having washed my self and offered up my

---

5. **blown . . . Fame:** made stale by common gossip. 6. **Game of Ombre:** See Pope, *The Rape of the Lock*, iii. 27 ff., later in Part Two. 7. **Parts:** talents. 8. **making Lodgments:** gaining footholds. 9. **Westminster-Hall:** the legal headquarters of England. 10. **the Gazette:** the official journal of the government. 11. **endued:** endowed.

12. **finishes:** completes, perfects. 13. **Impertinence:** folly. 14. **cry up:** advertise, puff. 15. **in Countenance:** from being abashed or discouraged. *Number 159.* 1. **Omnem . . . eripiam:**

. . . while I dissolve
The Mists and Films that mortal Eyes involve:
Purge from your sight the Dross. . . .
(*Aeneid*, II. 604–06 [Dryden's translation, II. 819–21])

2. **Mirzah:** the title given to a royal Persian prince. 3. **the first Vision:** the only one to be published.

Morning Devotions, I ascended the high Hills of *Bagdat*, in order to pass the rest of the Day in Meditation and Prayer. As I was here airing my self on the Tops of the Mountains, I fell into a profound Contemplation on the Vanity of humane Life; and passing from one Thought to another, Surely, said I, Man is but a Shadow and Life a Dream. Whilst I was thus musing, I cast my Eyes towards the Summit of a Rock that was not far from me, where I discovered one in the Habit of a Shepherd, with a little Musical Instrument in his Hand. As I looked upon him he applied it to his Lips, and began to play upon it. The Sound of it was exceeding sweet, and wrought into a Variety of Tunes that were inexpressibly melodious, and altogether different from any thing I had ever heard. They put me in mind of those heavenly Airs that are played to the departed Souls of good Men upon their first Arrival in Paradise, to wear out the Impressions of their last Agonies, and qualify them for the Pleasures of that happy Place. My Heart melted away in secret Raptures.

"I had been often told that the Rock before me was the Haunt of a Genius; and that several had been entertained with Musick who had passed by it, but never heard that the Musician had before made himself visible. When he had raised my Thoughts, by those transporting Airs which he played, to taste the Pleasures of his Conversation, as I looked upon him like one astonished, he beckoned to me, and by the waving of his Hand directed me to approach the Place where he sat. I drew near with that Reverence which is due to a superior Nature; and as my Heart was entirely subdued by the captivating Strains I had heard, I fell down at his Feet and wept. The Genius smiled upon me with a Look of Compassion and Affability that familiarized him to my Imagination, and at once dispelled all the Fears and Apprehensions with which I approached him. He lifted me from the Ground, and taking me by the Hand, *Mirzah*, said he, I have heard thee in thy Soliloquies, follow me.

"He then led me to the highest Pinnacle of the Rock, and placing me on the Top of it, Cast thy Eyes Eastward, said he, and tell me what thou seest. I see, said I, a huge Valley and a prodigious Tide of Water rolling through it. The Valley that thou seest, said he, is the Vale of Misery, and the Tide of Water that thou seest is Part of the great Tide of Eternity. What is the Reason, said I, that the Tide I see rises out of a thick Mist at one End, and again loses it self in a thick Mist at the other? What thou seest, said he, is

that Portion of Eternity which is called Time, measured out by the Sun, and reaching from the Beginning of the World to its Consummation. Examine now, said he, this Sea that is thus bounded with Darkness at both Ends, and tell me what thou discoverest in it. I see a Bridge, said I, standing in the Midst of the Tide. The Bridge thou seest, said he, is humane Life; consider it attentively. Upon a more leisurely Survey of it, I found that it consisted of threescore and ten entire[4] Arches, with several broken Arches, which added to those that were entire made up the Number about an hundred. As I was counting the Arches, the Genius told me, that this Bridge consisted at first of a thousand Arches; but that a great Flood swept away the rest, and left the Bridge in the ruinous Condition I now beheld it. But tell me further, said he, what thou discoverest on it. I see Multitudes of People passing over it, said I, and a black Cloud hanging on each End of it. As I looked more attentively, I saw several of the Passengers dropping thro' the Bridge, into the great Tide that flowed underneath it; and upon further Examination, perceived there were innumerable Trap-doors that lay concealed in the Bridge, which the Passengers no sooner trod upon, but they fell through them into the Tide and immediately disappeared. These hidden Pit-falls were set very thick at the Entrance of the Bridge, so that Throngs of People no sooner broke through the Cloud, but many of them fell into them. They grew thinner towards the Middle, but multiplied and lay closer together towards the End of the Arches that were entire.

"There were indeed some Persons, but their Number was very small, that continued a kind of hobbling March on the broken Arches, but fell through one after another, being quite tired and spent with so long a Walk.

"I passed some Time in the Contemplation of this wonderful Structure, and the great Variety of Objects which it presented. My Heart was filled with a deep Melancholy to see several dropping unexpectedly in the Midst of Mirth and Jollity, and catching at every thing that stood by them to save themselves. Some were looking up towards the Heavens in a thoughtful Posture, and in the Midst of a Speculation stumbled and fell out of Sight. Multitudes were very busy in the Pursuit of Bubbles that glittered in their Eyes and danced before them, but often when they thought

4. **entire**: intact.

themselves within the Reach of them their Footing failed, and down they sunk. In this Confusion of Objects, I observed some with Scymetars in their Hands, and others with Urinals,[5] who ran to and fro upon the Bridge, thrusting several Persons on Trapdoors which did not seem to lie in their Way, and which they might have escaped had they not been thus forced upon them.

"The Genius seeing me indulge my self in this melancholy Prospect, told me I had dwelt long enough upon it: Take thine Eyes off the Bridge, said he, and tell me if thou yet seest any thing thou dost not comprehend. Upon looking up, What mean, said I, those great Flights of Birds that are perpetually hovering about the Bridge, and settling upon it from Time to Time? I see Vultures, Harpyes, Ravens, Cormorants, and among many other feathered Creatures several little winged Boys, that perch in great Numbers upon the middle Arches. These, said the Genius, are Envy, Avarice, Superstition, Despair, Love, with the like Cares and Passions that infest humane Life.

"I here fetched a deep Sigh, Alass, said I, Man was made in vain! How is he given away to Misery and Mortality! tortured in Life, and swallowed up in Death! The Genius being moved with Compassion towards me, bid me quit so uncomfortable a Prospect: Look no more, said he, on Man in the first Stage of his Existence, in his setting out for Eternity; but cast thine Eye on that thick Mist into which the Tide bears the several Generations of Mortals that fall into it. I directed my Sight as I was ordered, and (whether or no the good Genius strengthned it with any supernatural Force, or dissipated Part of the Mist that was before too thick for the Eye to penetrate) I saw the Valley opening at the further End, and spreading forth into an immense Ocean, that had a huge Rock of Adamant running through the Midst of it, and dividing it into two equal Parts. The Clouds still rested on one Half of it, insomuch that I could discover nothing in it; but the other appeared to me a vast Ocean planted with innumerable Islands, that were covered with Fruits and Flowers, and interwoven with a thousand little shining Seas that ran among them. I could see Persons dressed in glorious Habits, with Garlands upon their Heads, passing among the Trees, lying down by the Sides of Fountains, or resting on Beds of Flowers; and could hear a confused[6] Harmony of singing Birds, falling Waters, humane Voices, and musical Instruments. Gladness grew in me upon the Discovery of so delightful a Scene. I wished for the Wings of an Eagle, that I might fly away to those happy Seats; but the Genius told me there was no Passage to them, except through the Gates of Death that I saw opening every Moment upon the Bridge. The Islands, said he, that lie so fresh and green before thee, and with which the whole Face of the Ocean appears spotted as far as thou canst see, are more in Number than the Sands on the Sea-shore; there are Myriads of Islands behind those which thou here discoverest, reaching further than thine Eye or even thine Imagination can extend it self. These are the Mansions of good Men after Death, who according to the Degree and Kinds of Virtue in which they excelled, are distributed among these several Islands, which abound with Pleasures of different Kinds and Degrees, suitable to the Relishes and Perfections of those who are settled in them; every Island is a Paradise accommodated to its respective Inhabitants. Are not these, O *Mirzah*, Habitations worth contending for? Does Life appear miserable, that gives thee Opportunities of earning such a Reward? Is Death to be feared, that will convey thee to so happy an Existence? Think not Man was made in vain, who has such an Eternity reserved for him. I gazed with inexpressible Pleasure on these happy Islands. At length said I, shew me now, I beseech thee, the Secrets that lie hid under those dark Clouds which cover the Ocean on the other Side of the Rock of Adamant. The Genius making me no Answer, I turned about to address my self to him a second time, but I found that he had left me; I then turned again to the Vision which I had been so long contemplating, but instead of the rolling Tide, the arched Bridge, and the happy Islands, I saw nothing but the long hollow Valley of *Bagdat*, with Oxen, Sheep, and Camels, grazing upon the Sides of it."

The End of the first Vision of Mirzah.

---

5. Scymetars, Urinals: weapons of aggression (swords and chamberpots) of soldiers and physicians respectively.

6. confused: mixed, blended (*not* disorderly, discordant).

NO. 160

Monday, September 3, 1711

> . . . *Cui mens divinior, atque os*
> *Magna sonaturum, des nominis hujus honorem.*[1]
>
> HOR.

THERE is no Character more frequently given to a Writer, than that of being a Genius. I have heard many a little Sonneteer called a *fine Genius*. There is not an Heroick Scribler in the Nation, that has not his Admirers who think him a *great Genius;* and as for your Smatterers in Tragedy, there is scarce a Man among them who is not cried up by one or other for a *prodigious Genius.*

My Design in this Paper is to consider what is properly a great Genius, and to throw some Thoughts together on so uncommon a Subject.

Among great Genius's, those few draw the Admiration of all the World upon them, and stand up as the Prodigies of Mankind, who by the meer Strength of natural Parts, and without any Assistance of Art or Learning, have produced Works that were the Delight of their own Times and the Wonder of Posterity. There appears something nobly wild and extravagant in these great natural Genius's, that is infinitely more beautiful than all the Turn and Polishing of what the *French* call a *Bel Esprit*, by which they would express a Genius refined by Conversation, Reflection, and the Reading of the most polite Authors. The greatest Genius which runs through the Arts and Sciences, takes a kind of Tincture from them, and falls unavoidably into Imitation.

Many of these great natural Genius's that were never disciplined and broken[2] by Rules of Art, are to be found among the Ancients, and in particular among those of the more Eastern Parts of the World. *Homer* has innumerable Flights that *Virgil* was not able to reach, and in the Old Testament we find several Passages more elevated and sublime than any in *Homer*. At the same Time that we allow a greater and more daring Genius to the Ancients, we must own that the greatest of them very much failed in, or, if you will, that they were much above the Nicety and Correctness of the Moderns. In their Similitudes

and Allusions,[3] provided there was a Likeness, they did not much trouble themselves about the Decency of the Comparison: Thus *Solomon* resembles[4] the Nose of his Beloved to the Tower of *Libanon* which looketh toward *Damascus;*[5] as the Coming of a Thief in the Night is a Similitude of the same Kind in the New Testament.[6] It would be endless to make Collections of this Nature: *Homer* illustrates one of his Heroes encompassed with the Enemy, by an Ass in a Field of Corn that has his Sides belaboured by all the Boys of the Village without stirring a Foot for it;[7] and another of them tossing to and fro in his Bed, and burning with Resentment, to a Piece of Flesh broiled on the Coals.[8] This particular Failure in the Ancients, opens a large Field of Raillery to the little Wits, who can laugh at an Indecency but not relish the Sublime in these Sorts of Writings. The present Emperor of *Persia*, conformable to this Eastern way of Thinking, amidst a great many pompous Titles, denominates himself the Sun of Glory and the *Nutmeg of Delight*. In short, to cut off all Cavilling against the Ancients, and particularly those of the warmer Climates, who had most Heat and Life in their Imaginations, we are to consider that the Rule of observing what the *French* call the *Bienseance*[9] in an Allusion, has been found out of latter Years and in the colder Regions of the World; where we would make some Amends for our want of Force and Spirit, by a scrupulous Nicety and Exactness in our Compositions. Our Countryman *Shakespear* was a remarkable Instance of this first kind of great Genius's.

I cannot quit this Head[10] without observing that *Pindar* was a great Genius of the first Class, who was hurried on by a natural Fire and Impetuosity to vast Conceptions of things, and noble Sallies of Imagination. At the same Time, can any thing be more ridiculous than for Men of a sober and moderate Fancy to imitate this Poet's Way of Writing in those monstrous Compositions which go among us under the Name of Pindaricks? When I see People copying Works, which, as *Horace* has represented them,[11] are singular in their Kind and inimitable; when I see Men

---

3. **Similitudes and Allusions:** similes and metaphors. 4. **resembles:** likens. 5. **the Tower . . . Damascus:** Song of Sol. 7:4. 6. **a Similitude . . . Testament:** a simile for the coming of the day of the Lord in I Thess. 5:2 and II Pet. 3:10. 7. **one . . . it:** See *Iliad*, XI. 558 ff. 8. **another . . . Coals:** See *Odyssey*, XX. 25 ff. 9. **Bienseance:** decorum, propriety. 10. **Head:** topic, division of the subject. 11. **as . . . them:** in *Odes*, IV. ii. 1–4.

Number 160. 1. **Cui . . . honorem:** "You should grant the honor of this name [poet] to one who is inspired and can utter great things" (Horace, *Satires*, I. iv. 43–44). 2. **broken:** tamed.

following Irregularities by Rule, and by the little Tricks of Art straining after the most unbounded Flights of Nature, I cannot but apply to them that Passage in *Terence*.

> . . . *incerta hæc si tu postules*
> *Ratione certa facere, nihilo plus agas,*
> *Quàm si des operam, ut cum ratione insanias.*[12]

In short a modern pindarick Writer compared with *Pindar*, is like a Sister among the *Camisars*[13] compared with *Virgil's* Sybil:[14] There is the Distortion, Grimace, and outward Figure, but nothing of that divine Impulse which raises the Mind above it self, and makes the Sounds more than humane.

There is another kind of Great Genius's which I shall place in a second Class, not as I think them inferior to the first, but only for distinction's sake as they are of a different kind. This second Class of great Genius's are those that have formed themselves by Rules, and submitted the Greatness of their natural Talents to the Corrections and Restraints of Art. Such among the *Greeks* were *Plato* and *Aristotle*, among the *Romans Virgil* and *Tully*, among the *English Milton* and Sir *Francis Bacon*.

The Genius in both these Classes of Authors may be equally great, but shews itself after a different Manner. In the first it is like a rich Soil in a happy Climate, that produces a whole Wilderness of noble Plants rising in a thousand beautiful Landskips without any certain Order or Regularity. In the other it is the same rich Soil under the same happy Climate, that has been laid out in Walks and Parterres, and cut into Shape and Beauty by the Skill of the Gardener.

The great Danger in these latter kind of Genius's, is, least[15] they cramp their own Abilities too much by Imitation, and form themselves altogether upon Models, without giving the full Play to their own natural Parts. An Imitation of the best Authors, is not to compare with a good Original; and I believe we may observe that very few Writers make an extraordinary Figure in the World, who have not something in their Way of thinking or expressing themselves that is peculiar to them and entirely their own.

It is odd to consider what great Genius's are sometimes thrown away upon Trifles.

I once saw a Shepherd, says a famous *Italian* Author, who used to divert himself in his Solitudes with tossing up Eggs and catching them again without breaking them: In which he had arrived to so great a Degree of Perfection, that he would keep up four at a Time for several Minutes together playing in the Air, and falling into his Hand by Turns. I think, says the Author, I never saw a greater Severity than in this Man's Face; for by his wonderful Perseverance and Application, he had contracted the Seriousness and Gravity of a Privy-Counsellour; and I could not but reflect with my self, that the same Assiduity and Attention had they been rightly applied, might have made him a greater Mathematician than *Archimedes*.

NO. 193

Thursday, October 11, 1711

> . . . *Ingentem foribus domus alta superbis*
> *Mane salutantum totis vomit ædibus undam.*[1]
>
> VIRG.

WHEN we look round us, and behold the strange variety of Faces and Persons which fill the Streets with Business and Hurry, it is no unpleasant Amusement to make Guesses at their different Pursuits, and judge by their Countenances what it is that so anxiously engages their present Attention. Of all this busie Crowd there are none who would give a Man inclined to such Enquiries better Diversion for his Thoughts, than those whom we call good Courtiers, and such as are assiduous at the Levées[2] of Great Men. These Worthies are got into an habit of being Servile with an Air, and enjoy a certain Vanity in being known for understanding how the World passes. In the pleasure of this they can rise early, go abroad sleek and well dressed, with no other Hope or Purpose but to make a Bow to a Man in Court Favour, and be thought, by some insignificant Smile of his, not a little engaged in his Interests and Fortunes. It is wondrous that a Man can get over the Natural Existence and Possession of

---

12. **incerta . . . insanias:** "If you tried to turn these uncertainties into certainties by a system of reasoning, you'd do no more good than if you set yourself to be mad on a system" (*The Eunuch*, ll. 61–63 [Loeb translation]). 13. **the Camisars:** (or Camisards) a French Calvinist sect of the Cevennes, known in England as the French Prophets. 14. **Virgil's Sybil:** See *Aeneid*, VI. 42 ff. 15. **least:** lest.

Number 193. 1. **Ingentem . . . undam:** "No Palace, with a lofty Gate, he wants, / T' admit the Tydes of early Visitants" (Virgil, *Georgics*, II. 461–62 [Dryden's translation, II. 643–44]). 2. **Levées:** A levee is a morning audience held by a person of distinction before or upon rising from bed.

his own Mind so far, as to take delight either in paying or receiving such cold and repeated Civilities. But what maintains the Humour[3] is, that outward Show is what most Men pursue, rather than real Happiness. Thus both the Idol and Idolater equally impose upon themselves in pleasing their Imaginations this way. But as there are very many of her Majesty's good Subjects who are extreamly uneasie at their own Seats in the Country, where all from the Skies to the Center of the Earth is their own, and have a mighty longing to shine in Courts, or be Partners in the Power of the World; I say, for the benefit of these, and others who hanker after being in the Whisper[4] with great Men, and vexing their Neighbours with the Changes they would be capable of making in the appearance at a Country Sessions, it would not methinks be amiss to give an Account of that Market for Preferment, a great Man's Levée.

For ought I know, this Commerce between the Mighty and their Slaves, very justly represented, might do so much good as to incline the Great to regard Business rather than Ostentation; and make the Little know the use of their Time too well, to spend it in vain Applications and Addresses.

The famous Doctor in *Moorfields*, who gained so much Reputation for his Horary[5] Predictions, is said to have had in his Parlour different Ropes to little Bells, which hung in the Room above Stairs, where the Doctor thought fit to be oraculous. If a Girl had been deceived by her Lover one Bell was pulled; and if a Peasant had lost a Cow the Servant rung another. This Method was kept in respect to all other Passions and Concerns, and the skilful Waiter below sifted[6] the Enquirer, and gave the Doctor Notice accordingly. The Levée of a great Man is laid after the same manner, and twenty Whispers, false Alarms, and private Intimations pass backward and forward, from the Porter, the Valet, and the Patron himself, before the gaping Crew who are to pay their Court are gathered together; when the Scene is ready, the Doors fly open and discover his Lordship.

There are several ways of making this first Appearance: You may be either half dressed, and washing your self, which is, indeed, the most stately; but this way of opening is peculiar to Military Men, in whom there is something graceful in exposing themselves naked; but the Politicians, or Civil Officers, have usually affected to be more reserved, and preserve a certain Chastity of Deportment. Whether it be Hieroglyphical,[7] or not, this Difference in the Military and Civil List, I will not say, but have ever understood the Fact to be, that the close[8] Minister is buttoned up, and the brave Officer open-breasted on these Occasions.

However that is, I humbly conceive the business of a Levée is to receive the Acknowledgements of a Multitude, that a Man is Wise, Bounteous, Valiant, and Powerful. When the first shot of Eyes are made, it is wonderful to observe how much Submission[9] the Patron's Modesty can bear, and how much Servitude the Client's Spirit can descend to. In the vast multiplicity of Business, and the Crowd about him, my Lord's Parts[10] are usually so great, that, to the Astonishment of the whole Assembly, he has something to say to every Man there, and that so suitable to his Capacity, as any Man may judge that it is not without Talents that Men can arrive at great Employments. I have known a great Man ask a Flag-Officer, which way was the Wind, a Commander of Horse the present Price of Oats, and a Stock-Jobber[11] at what Discount such a Fund was, with as much ease as if he had been bred to each of those several ways of Life. Now this is extreamly obliging; for at the same time that the Patron informs himself of Matters, he gives the Person of whom he enquires an opportunity to exert himself. What adds to the Pomp of those Interviews is, that it is performed with the greatest Silence and Order imaginable. The Patron is usually in the midst of the Room, and some humble Person gives him a Whisper, which his Lordship answers aloud, *It is well. Yes, I am of your Opinion. Pray inform your self further, you may be sure of my Part in it.* This happy Man is dismissed, and my Lord can turn himself to a Business of a quite different Nature, and off-hand give as good an Answer as any great Man is obliged to. For the chief Point is to keep in Generals; and if there be any thing offered that's Particular, to be in haste.

But we are now in the height of the Affair, and my Lord's Creatures have all had their Whispers round to keep up the Farce of the thing, and the Dumb Show is become more general. He casts his Eye to that Corner, and there to Mr. such a one; to the other, *and when did you come to Town?* and perhaps just

---

3. **Humour:** caprice. 4. **in the Whisper:** intimate. 5. **Horary:** hourly. 6. **sifted:** examined closely.

7. **Hieroglyphical:** symbolic. 8. **close:** reserved. 9. **Submission:** deference, homage. 10. **Parts:** abilities. 11. **Stock-Jobber:** stockbroker, speculator.

before he nods to another, and enters with him, *but, Sir, I am glad I see you, now I think of it.* Each of those are happy for the next four and twenty Hours; and those who bow in Ranks undistinguished, and by Dozens at a time, think they have very good Prospects if they may hope to arrive at such Notices half a Year hence.

The Satyrist says there is seldom common Sense in high Fortune;[12] and one would think, to behold a Levée, that the Great were not only infatuated with their Station, but also that they believed all below were seized too, else how is it possible they could think of imposing upon themselves and others in such a degree, as to set up a Levée for any thing but a direct Farce? But such is the Weakness of our Nature, that when Men are a little exalted in their Condition, they immediately conceive they have additional Senses, and their Capacities enlarged not only above other Men, but above human Comprehension it self. Thus it is ordinary to see a great Man attend one listning, bow to one at a distance, and call to a third at the same instant. A Girl in new Ribbons is not more taken with her self, nor does she betray more apparent Coquettries, than even a Wise Man in such a Circumstance of Courtship. I do not know any thing that I ever thought so very distasteful as the Affectation which is recorded of *Cæsar*, to wit, that he would dictate to three several[13] Writers at the same time. This was an Ambition below the Greatness and Candour of his Mind. He indeed (if any Man had Pretensions to greater Faculties than any other Mortal) was the Person; but such a way of acting is Childish, and Inconsistent with the manner of our Being. And it appears from the very nature of things that there cannot be any thing effectually dispatched in the Distraction of a Publick Levée, but the whole seems to be a Conspiracy of a Sett of Servile Slaves, to give up their own Liberty to take away their Patron's Understanding.

NO. 291

Saturday, February 2, 1712

> . . . *Ubi plura nitent in carmine, non ego paucis*
> *Offendar maculis, quas aut Incuria fudit,*
> *Aut Humana parum cavit Natura.* . . .[1]
>
> HOR.

I HAVE now consider'd *Milton's Paradise Lost* under those four great Heads of the Fable, the Characters, the Sentiments, and the Language;[2] and have shewn that he excels, in general, under each of these Heads. I hope that I have made several Discoveries which may appear new, even to those who are versed in Critical Learning. Were I indeed to chuse my Readers, by whose Judgment I would stand or fall, they should not be such as are acquainted only with the *French* and *Italian* Criticks, but also with the Ancient and Modern who have written in either of the learned Languages. Above all, I would have them well versed in the *Greek* and *Latin* Poets, without which a Man very often fancies that he understands a Critick, when in reality he does not comprehend his Meaning.

It is in Criticism, as in all other Sciences and Speculations; one who brings with him any implicit[3] Notions and Observations which he has made in his reading of the Poets, will find his own Reflections methodized and explained, and perhaps several little Hints that had passed in his Mind, perfected and improved in the Works of a good Critick; whereas one who has not these previous Lights, is very often an utter Stranger to what he reads, and apt to put a wrong Interpretation upon it.

Nor is it sufficient, that a Man who sets up for a Judge in Criticism, should have perused the Authors above-mentioned, unless he has also a clear and Logical Head. Without this Talent he is perpetually puzzled and perplexed amidst his own Blunders, mistakes the Sense of those he would confute, or if he chances to think right, does not know how to convey his Thoughts to another with Clearness and Perspicuity. *Aristotle*, who was the best Critick, was also

---

12. **there . . . Fortune:** *Rarus enim ferme sensus communis in illa / fortuna* (Juvenal, *Satires*, III. viii. 73–74). Steele mistranslates (or misremembers) *sensus communis*, meaning common human sympathy or fellow feeling, as common sense. 13. **several:** different.

Number 291. **1. Ubi . . . Natura:** "If most of the poetry is polished, I will not be annoyed by the few slips which either negligence has sprinkled here and there, or which human nature has been careless about" (Horace, *Ars Poetica*, ll. 351–53). **2. those . . . Language:** Numbers 267, 273, 279, and 285. Thirteen more papers on *Paradise Lost* followed on successive Saturdays. **3. implicit:** vague, unformulated.

one of the best Logicians that ever appeared in the World.

Mr. *Lock*'s Essay on Human Understanding would be thought a very odd Book for a Man to make himself Master of, who would get a Reputation by Critical Writings; though at the same time it is very certain, that an Author who has not learn'd the Art of distinguishing between Words and Things, and of ranging his Thoughts, and setting them in proper Lights, whatever Notions he may have, will lose himself in Confusion and Obscurity. I might further observe, that there is not a *Greek* or *Latin* Critick who has not shewn, even in the stile of his Criticisms, that he was a Master of all the Elegance and Delicacy of his Native Tongue.

The truth of it is, there is nothing more absurd, than for a Man to set up for a Critick, without a good Insight into all the Parts of Learning; whereas many of those who have endeavoured to signalize themselves by Works of this Nature among our *English* Writers, are not only defective in the above-mentioned Particulars, but plainly discover[4] by the Phrases which they make use of, and by their confused way of thinking, that they are not acquainted with the most common and ordinary Systems of Arts and Sciences. A few general Rules extracted out of the *French* Authors, with a certain Cant of Words,[5] has sometimes set up an Illiterate heavy Writer for a most judicious and formidable Critick.

One great Mark, by which you may discover a Critick who has neither Taste nor Learning, is this, that he seldom ventures to praise any Passage in an Author which has not been before received and applauded by the Publick, and that his Criticism turns wholly upon little Faults and Errors. This part of a Critick is so very easie to succeed in, that we find every ordinary Reader, upon the publishing of a new Poem, has Wit and Ill-nature enough to turn several Passages of it into Ridicule, and very often in the right Place. This Mr. *Dryden* has very agreeably remarked in those two celebrated Lines,

> *Errors, like Straws, upon the Surface flow;*
> *He who would search for Pearls must dive below.*[6]

A true Critick ought to dwell rather upon Excellencies than Imperfections, to discover the concealed Beauties of a Writer, and communicate to the World such things as are worth their Observation. The most exquisite Words and finest Strokes of an Author are those which very often appear the most doubtful[7] and exceptionable, to a Man who wants[8] a Relish for polite Learning; and they are these, which a sower undistinguishing Critick generally attacks with the greatest Violence. *Tully* observes, that it is very easie to brand or fix a Mark upon what he calls *Verbum ardens*, or, as it may be rendered into *English*, *a glowing bold Expression*, and to turn it into Ridicule by a cold ill-natured Criticism.[9] A little Wit is equally capable of exposing a Beauty, and of aggravating a Fault; and though such a Treatment of an Author naturally produces Indignation in the Mind of an understanding Reader, it has however its effect among the generality of those whose Hands it falls into, the Rabble of Mankind being very apt to think that every thing which is laughed at with any mixture of Wit, is ridiculous in it self.

Such a Mirth[10] as this, is always unseasonable in a Critick, as it rather prejudices the Reader than convinces him, and is capable of making a Beauty, as well as a Blemish, the Subject of Derision. A Man, who cannot write with Wit on a proper Subject, is dull and stupid, but one who shews it in an improper place, is as impertinent and absurd. Besides, a Man who has the Gift of Ridicule is apt to find Fault with any thing that gives him an Opportunity of exerting his beloved Talent, and very often censures a Passage, not because there is any Fault in it, but because he can be merry[11] upon it. Such kinds of Pleasantry are very unfair and disingenuous in Works of Criticism, in which the greatest Masters, both Ancient and Modern, have always appeared with a serious and instructive Air.

As I intend in my next Paper to shew the Defects in *Milton*'s *Paradise Lost*, I thought fit to premise these few Particulars, to the End that the Reader may know I enter upon it, as on a very ungrateful[12] Work, and that I shall just point at the Imperfections, without endeavouring to enflame them with Ridicule. I must also observe with *Longinus*,[13] that the Productions of a great Genius, with many Lapses and Inadvertencies, are infinitely preferable to the Works of an inferior

---

4. **discover:** reveal. 5. **Cant of Words:** mechanical phrasing, jargon. 6. **Errors . . . below:** *All for Love*, Prologue, ll. 25–26.

7. **doubtful:** obscure. 8. **wants:** lacks. 9. **it is . . . Criticism:** See Cicero, *De Oratore*, viii. 27. 10. **a Mirth:** jocularity, ridicule. 11. **merry:** facetious. 12. **ungrateful:** unpleasant. 13. **with Longinus:** in *On the Sublime*, Ch. xxxiii.

kind of Author, which are scrupulously exact and conformable to all the Rules of correct Writing.

I shall conclude my Paper with a Story out of *Boccalini*,[14] which sufficiently shews us the Opinion that Judicious Author entertained of the sort of Criticks I have been here mentioning. A famous Critick, says he, having gathered together all the Faults of an Eminent Poet, made a Present of them to *Apollo*, who received them very graciously, and resolved to make the Author a suitable Return for the Trouble he had been at in collecting them. In order to this, he set before him a Sack of Wheat, as it had been just threshed out of the Sheaf. He then bid him pick out the Chaff from among the Corn, and lay it aside by it self. The Critick applied himself to the Task with great Industry and Pleasure, and after having made the due Separation, was presented by *Apollo* with the Chaff for his Pains.

NO. 317

Tuesday, March 4, 1712

. . . *fruges consumere nati.*[1]

HOR.

AUGUSTUS, a few Moments before his Death, asked his Friends who stood about him, if they thought he had acted his Part well; and upon receiving such an Answer as was due to his extraordinary Merit, *Let me then*, says he, *go off the Stage with your Applause;*[2] using the Expression with which the *Roman* Actors made their *Exit* at the Conclusion of a Dramatick Piece. I could wish that Men, while they are in Health, wou'd consider well the Nature of the Part they are engaged in, and what Figure it will make in the Minds of those they leave behind them: whether it was worth coming into the World for, whether it be suitable to a reasonable Being, in short, whether it appears Graceful[3] in this Life, or will turn to Advantage in the next. Let the Sycophant, or Buffoon, the Satyrist, or the Good Companion, consider with himself, when his Body shall be laid in the Grave, and his Soul pass into another State of Existence, how much it will redound to his Praise to have it said of him, that no

Man in *England* Eat better, that he had an admirable Talent at turning his Friends into Ridicule, that no body out-did him at an Ill-natured Jest, or that he never went to Bed before he had dispatched his third Bottle. These are, however, very common Funeral Orations, and Elogiums[4] on deceased Persons who have acted among Mankind with some Figure and Reputation.

But if we look into the Bulk of our Species, they are such as are not likely to be remember'd a Moment after their Disappearance. They leave behind them no Traces of their Existence, but are forgotten as tho' they had never been. They are neither wanted by the Poor, regretted by the Rich, nor celebrated by the Learned. They are neither miss'd in the Common-wealth, nor lamented by private Persons. Their Actions are of no Significancy to Mankind, and might have been performed by Creatures of much less Dignity, than those who are distinguished by the Faculty of Reason. An eminent *French* Author speaks somewhere to the following Purpose:[5] I have often seen from my Chamber-window two noble Creatures, both of them of an erect Countenance, and endow'd with Reason. These two intellectual Beings are employ'd from Morning to Night, in rubbing two smooth Stones one upon another; that is, as the Vulgar phrase it, in polishing Marble.

My Friend, Sir ANDREW FREEPORT, as we were sitting in the Club last Night, gave us an Account of a sober Citizen,[6] who died a few Days since. This honest Man being of greater Consequence in his own Thoughts, than in the Eye of the World, had for some Years past kept a Journal of his Life. Sir ANDREW shewed us one Week of it. Since the Occurrences set down in it mark out such a Road of Action, as that I have been speaking of, I shall present my Reader with a faithful Copy of it; after having first informed him, that the Deceased Person had in his Youth been bred to Trade, but finding himself not so well turned for Business, he had for several Years last past lived altogether upon a moderate Annuity.

---

14. a Story . . . Boccalini: Traiano Boccalini (1556–1613), *Advices from Parnassus in Two Centuries* (trans. 1706), pp. 184–85. *Number 317.* **1. fruges . . . nati:** "born only to consume the fruits of the earth" (Horace, *Epistles*, I. ii. 27). **2. Let . . . Applause:** Suetonius, *Lives of the Caesars*, II. xcix. 1. **3. Graceful:** pleasing, becoming.

4. Elogiums: epitaphs. **5. An eminent . . . Purpose:** D. F. Bond cites a passage in La Bruyère's *Caractères* (1688), the point of which however is to distinguish triviality from utter uselessness. **6. a sober Citizen:** Bond quotes John Nichols, who brought out an edition of *The Spectator* in 1788–89: "It is said that this journal was a banter on a member of a congregation of Independents. A Mr. Nesbit —who is referred to in Dunton's 'Life and Errors'—was the minister of this congregation, and was constantly consulted on every subject by the journalist."

MONDAY, *Eight a Clock*. I put on my Cloaths and walked into the Parlour.

Nine a Clock, ditto. Tied my Knee-strings, and washed my Hands.

Hours Ten, Eleven and Twelve. Smoaked three Pipes of *Virginia*. Read the *Supplement*[7] and *Daily Courant*. Things go ill in the North. Mr. *Nisby's* Opinion thereupon.

One a Clock in the Afternoon. Chid *Ralph* for mislaying my Tobacco-Box.

Two a Clock. Sat down to Dinner. *Mem.*[8] Too many Plumbs, and no Sewet.

From Three to Four. Took my Afternoon's Nap.

From Four to Six. Walked into the Fields. Wind, S.S.E.

From Six to Ten. At the Club. Mr. *Nisby's* Opinion about the Peace.[9]

Ten a Clock. Went to Bed, slept sound.

TUESDAY, BEING HOLLIDAY, *Eight a Clock*. Rose as usual.

Nine a Clock. Washed Hands and Face, shaved, put on my double soaled Shoes.

Ten, Eleven, Twelve. Took a Walk to *Islington*.

One. Took a Pot of Mother *Cob's* Mild.

Between Two and Three. Returned, dined on a Knuckle of Veal and Bacon. *Mem.* Sprouts wanting.

Three. Nap as usual.

From Four to Six. Coffee-house. Read the News. A Dish of Twist.[10] Grand Vizier strangled.[11]

From Six to Ten. At the Club. Mr. *Nisby's* Account of the great Turk.

Ten. Dream of the Grand Vizier. Broken Sleep.

WEDNESDAY, *Eight a Clock*. Tongue of my Shooe Buckle broke. Hands but not Face.

Nine. Paid off the Butchers Bill. *Mem.* To be allowed[12] for the last Leg of Mutton.

Ten, Eleven. At the Coffee-house. More Work in the North. Stranger in a black Wigg asked me how Stocks went.

From Twelve to One. Walked in the Fields. Wind to the South.

From One to Two. Smoaked a Pipe and a half.

Two. Dined as usual. Stomach good.

Three. Nap broke by the falling of a Pewter Dish. *Mem.* Cookmaid in Love, and grown careless.

From Four to Six. At the Coffee-house. Advice[13] from *Smyrna*, that the Grand Vizier was first of all strangled, and afterwards beheaded.

Six a Clock in the Evening. Was half an Hour in the Club before any Body else came. Mr. *Nisby* of Opinion, that the Grand Vizier was not strangled the Sixth Instant.

Ten at Night. Went to Bed. Slept without waking till Nine next Morning.

THURSDAY, *Nine a Clock*. Staid within till Two a Clock for Sir *Timothy*. Who did not bring me my Annuity according to his Promise.

Two in the Afternoon. Sate down to Dinner. Loss of Appetite. Small Beer sowr. Beef overcorn'd.

Three. Could not take my Nap.

Four and Five. Gave *Ralph* a Box on the Ear. Turn'd off my Cookmaid. Sent a Message to Sir *Timothy*. *Mem.* I did not go to the Club to Night. Went to Bed at Nine a Clock.

FRIDAY. Pass'd the Morning in Meditation upon Sir *Timothy*, who was with me a Quarter before Twelve.

Twelve a Clock. Bought a new Head to my Cane, and a Tongue to my Buckle. Drank a Glass of Purl[14] to recover Appetite.

Two and Three. Dined, and Slept well.

From Four to Six. Went to the Coffee-house. Met Mr. *Nisby* there. Smoaked several Pipes. Mr. *Nisby* of opinion that laced Coffee[15] is bad for the Head.

Six a Clock. At the Club as Steward. Sat late.

Twelve a Clock. Went to Bed, dreamt that I drank Small-beer with the Grand Vizier.

SATURDAY. Waked at Eleven, walked in the Fields, Wind N.E.

Twelve. Caught in a Shower.

One in the Afternoon. Returned home, and dried my self.

---

7. the Supplement: a supplement to the Tory *Post Boy*. It appeared three times a week from 1708 to 1712. **8. Mem.:** memorandum. **9. the Peace:** Negotiations for terminating the War of the Spanish Succession were concluded with the so-called Peace of Utrecht in 1713. **10. Twist:** a drink made by mixing two others, often liquors: tea and coffee, gin and brandy. **11. Grand . . . strangled:** Mehemet Bashaw, deposed as Grand Vizier, was reported by the *Post Boy*, April 29, 1712, beheaded at Mytilene (Lesbos). **12. allowed:** credited.

13. Advice: news. **14. Purl:** formerly, an infusion of bitter herbs, often wormwood, in ale or beer. The word now means a mixture of hot beer with gin and sometimes ginger and sugar. The drink is taken as a morning pick-up. **15. laced Coffee:** coffee with spirits or sugar; here, doubtless the former.

Two. Mr. *Nisby* dined with me. First Course Marrow-bones, Second Ox Cheek, with a Bottle of *Brooks* and *Hellier.*[16]

Three a Clock. Overslept my self.

Six. Went to the Club. Like to have faln into a Gutter. Grand Vizier certainly Dead.

&c.

I question not, but the Reader will be surprized to find the above-mentioned Journalist taking so much care of a Life that was filled with such inconsiderable Actions, and received so very small Improvements; and yet, if we look into the Behaviour of many whom we daily converse with, we shall find that most of their Hours are taken up in those three Important Articles of Eating, Drinking and Sleeping. I do not suppose that a Man loses his Time, who is not engaged in Publick Affairs, or in an Illustrious Course of Action. On the contrary, I believe our Hours may very often be more profitably laid out in such Transactions as make no Figure in the World, than in such as are apt to draw upon them the Attention of Mankind. One may become wiser and better by several Methods of Employing ones self in Secrecy and Silence, and do what is laudable without Noise or Ostentation. I would, however, recommend to every one of my Readers, the keeping a Journal of their Lives for one Week, and setting down punctually their whole Series of Employments during that Space of Time. This kind of Self-Examination would give them a true State of themselves, and incline them to consider seriously what they are about. One Day would rectifie the Omissions of another, and make a Man weigh all those indifferent[17] Actions, which, though they are·easily forgotten, must certainly be accounted for.

NO. 409

Thursday, June 19, 1712

. . . *Musæo contingere cuncta lepore.*[1]

LUCR.

GRATIAN very often recommends *the fine Taste*, as the utmost Perfection of an accomplished Man.[2] As this Word arises very often in Conversation, I shall endeavour to give some Account of it, and to lay down Rules how we may know whether we are possessed of it, and how we may acquire that fine Taste of Writing, which is so much talked of among the Polite World.

Most Languages make use of this Metaphor, to express that Faculty of the Mind, which distinguishes all the most concealed Faults and nicest Perfections in Writing. We may be sure this Metaphor would not have been so general in all Tongues, had there not been a very great Conformity between that Mental Taste, which is the Subject of this Paper, and that Sensitive[3] Taste which gives us a Relish of every different Flavour that affects the Palate. Accordingly we find, there are as many Degrees of Refinement in the intellectual Faculty, as in the Sense, which is marked out by this common Denomination.

I knew a Person who possessed the one in so great a Perfection, that after having tasted ten different Kinds of Tea, he would distinguish, without seeing the Colour of it, the particular Sort which was offered him; and not only so, but any two sorts of them that were mixt together in an equal Proportion; nay, he has carried the Experiment so far, as upon tasting the Composition of three different sorts, to name the Parcels from whence the three several Ingredients were taken. A Man of a fine Taste in Writing will discern, after the same manner, not only the general Beauties and Imperfections of an Author, but discover the several Ways of thinking and expressing himself, which diversify him from all other Authors, with the several Foreign Infusions of Thought and Language, and the particular Authors from whom they were borrowed.

After having thus far explained what is generally meant by a fine Taste in Writing, and shown the Propriety of the Metaphor which is used on this Occasion, I think I may define it to be *that Faculty of the Soul, which discerns the Beauties of an Author with Pleasure, and the Imperfections with Dislike.* If a Man would know whether he is possessed of this Faculty, I would have him read over the celebrated Works of Antiquity, which have stood the Test of so many different Ages and Countries; or those Works among the Moderns, which have the Sanction of the Politer Part of our Contemporaries. If upon the Perusal of such Writings he does not find himself delighted in an

---

16. Brooks and Hellier: wine merchants. **17. indifferent:** unimportant. *Number 409.* **1. Musæo . . . lepore:** "to grace each subject with wit" (Lucretius, *De Rerum Natura,* I. 934; for *contingere* read *contingens.* **2. an accomplished Man:** Baltasar Gracián (1601–58), author of *Arte de Ingenio* (1642).

3. Sensitive: sensory.

extraordinary manner, or, if upon reading the admired Passages in such Authors, he finds a Coldness and Indifference in his Thoughts, he ought to conclude, not (as is too usual among tasteless Readers) that the Author wants those Perfections which have been admired in him, but that he himself wants the Faculty of discovering them.

He should, in the second place, be very careful to observe, whether he tastes the distinguishing Perfections, or, if I may be allowed to call them so, the Specifick Qualities of the Author whom he peruses; whether he is particularly pleased with *Livy* for his manner of telling a Story, with *Sallust* for his entering into those internal Principles of Action which arise from the Characters and Manners of the Persons he describes, or with *Tacitus* for his displaying those outward[4] Motives of Safety and Interest, which give birth to the whole Series of Transactions which he relates.

He may likewise consider, how differently he is affected by the same Thought, which presents it self in a great Writer, from what he is when he finds it delivered by a Person of an ordinary Genius. For there is as much difference in apprehending a Thought cloathed in *Cicero*'s Language, and that of a common Author, as in seeing an Object by the Light of a Taper, or by the Light of the Sun.

It is very difficult to lay down Rules for the acquirement of such a Taste as that I am here speaking of. The Faculty must in some degree be born with us, and it very often happens, that those who have other Qualities in Perfection are wholly void of this. One of the most eminent Mathematicians of the Age has assured me, that the greatest Pleasure he took in reading *Virgil*, was in examining *Æneas* his[5] Voyage by the Map; as I question not but many a Modern Compiler of History would be delighted with little more in that Divine Author, than in the bare matters of Fact.

But notwithstanding this Faculty must in some measure be born with us, there are several Methods for Cultivating and Improving it, and without which it will be very uncertain, and of little use to the Person that possesses it. The most natural Method for this Purpose is to be conversant among the Writings of the most Polite Authors. A Man who has any Relish for fine Writing, either discovers new Beauties, or receives stronger Impressions from the Masterly Stroaks of a great Author every time he peruses him: Besides that he naturally wears himself into[6] the same manner of Speaking and Thinking.

Conversation with Men of a Polite Genius is another Method for improving our Natural Taste. It is impossible for a Man of the greatest Parts to consider any thing in its whole Extent, and in all its variety of Lights. Every Man, besides those general Observations which are to be made upon an Author, forms several Reflections that are peculiar to his own manner of Thinking; so that Conversation will naturally furnish us with Hints which we did not attend to, and make us enjoy other Mens Parts and Reflections as well as our own. This is the best Reason I can give for the Observation which several have made, that Men of great Genius in the same way of Writing seldom rise up singly, but at certain Periods of Time appear together, and in a Body; as they did at *Rome* in the Reign of *Augustus*, and in *Greece* about the Age of *Socrates*. I cannot think that *Corneille*, *Racine*, *Moliere*, *Boileau*, *la Fontaine*, *Bruyere*, *Bossu*, or the *Daciers*, would have written so well as they have done, had they not been Friends and Contemporaries.

It is likewise necessary for a Man who would form to himself a finished Taste of good Writing, to be well versed in the Works of the best *Criticks* both Ancient and Modern. I must confess that I could wish there were Authors of this kind, who, beside the Mechanical Rules which a Man of very little Taste may discourse upon, would enter into the very Spirit and Soul of fine Writing, and shew us the several Sources of that Pleasure which rises in the Mind upon the Perusal of a noble Work. Thus altho' in Poetry it be absolutely necessary that the Unities of Time, Place and Action, with other Points of the same Nature should be thoroughly explained and understood; there is still something more essential, to the Art, something that elevates and astonishes the Fancy, and gives a Greatness of Mind to the Reader, which few of the Criticks besides *Longinus* have consider'd.[7]

Our general Taste in *England* is for Epigram, turns of Wit, and forced Conceits, which have no manner of Influence,[8] either for the bettering or enlarging the Mind of him who reads them, and have been carefully avoided by the greatest Writers, both among the

---

4. **outward:** external, physical, as opposed to spiritual. **5. Æneas his:** Aeneas'.

6. **wears . . . into:** gradually becomes disposed to. **7. few . . . consider'd:** But see the selection from John Dennis later in Part Two. **8. no . . . Influence:** no influence whatever.

Ancients and Moderns. I have endeavoured in several of my Speculations to banish this *Gothic* Taste which has taken Possession among us. I entertained the Town for a Week together with an Essay upon Wit,[9] in which I endeavoured to detect several of those false kinds which have been admir'd in the different Ages of the World; and at the same time to shew wherein the nature of true Wit consists. I afterwards gave[10] an Instance of the great force which lies in a natural Simplicity of Thought to affect the Mind of the Reader, from such Vulgar Pieces as have little else besides this single Qualification to recommend them. I have likewise examined the Works of the greatest Poet which our Nation or perhaps any other has produced, and particularized most of those rational and manly Beauties which give a value to that Divine Work.[11] I shall next *Saturday* enter upon an Essay *on the Pleasures of the Imagination*, which though it shall consider that Subject at large,[12] will perhaps suggest to the Reader what it is that gives a Beauty to many Passages of the finest Writers both in Prose and Verse. As an Undertaking of this nature is entirely new, I question not but it will be receiv'd with Candour.[13]

NO. 411

Saturday, June 21, 1712

Avia Pieridum peragro loca, nullius ante
Trita solo; juvat integros accedere fonteis;
Atque haurire: . . . .[1]

LUCR.

OUR Sight is the most perfect and most delightful of all our Senses. It fills the Mind with the largest Variety of Ideas [,] converses[2] with its Objects at the greatest Distance, and continues the longest in Action without being tired or satiated with its proper Enjoyments. The Sense of Feeling can indeed give us a Notion of Extention, Shape, and all other Ideas that enter at the Eye, except Colours; but at the same time it is very much streightned and confined in its Operations, to the number, bulk, and distance of its particular Objects. Our Sight seems designed to supply all these Defects, and may be considered as a more delicate and diffusive kind of Touch, that spreads it self over an infinite Multitude of Bodies, comprehends the largest Figures, and brings into our reach some of the most remote Parts of the Universe.

It is this Sense which furnishes the Imagination with its Ideas; so that by the Pleasures of the Imagination or Fancy (which I shall use promiscuously[3]) I here mean such as arise from visible Objects, either when we have them actually in our view, or when we call up their Ideas into our Minds by Paintings, Statues, Descriptions, or any the like Occasion. We cannot indeed have a single Image in the Fancy that did not make its first Entrance through the Sight; but we have the Power of retaining, altering and compounding those Images, which we have once received, into all the varieties of Picture and Vision that are most agreeable to the Imagination; for by this Faculty a Man in a Dungeon is capable of entertaining himself with Scenes and Landskips more beautiful than any that can be found in the whole Compass of Nature.

There are few Words in the *English* Language which are employed in a more loose and uncircumscribed Sense than those of the *Fancy* and the *Imagination*. I therefore thought it necessary to fix and determine the Notion of these two Words,[4] as I intend to make use of them in the Thread of my following Speculations, that the Reader may conceive rightly what is the Subject which I proceed upon. I must therefore desire him to remember, that by the Pleasures of the Imagination, I mean only such Pleasures as arise originally from Sight, and that I divide these Pleasures into two kinds: My Design being first of all to Discourse of those Primary Pleasures of the Imagination, which entirely proceed from such Objects as are before our Eyes; and in the next place to speak of those Secondary Pleasures of the Imagination which flow from the Ideas of visible Objects, when the Objects are not actually before the Eye, but are called up into our Memories, or form'd into agreeable Visions of Things that are either Absent or Fictitious.

The Pleasures of the Imagination, taken in their full Extent, are not so gross as those of Sense, nor so refined as those of the Understanding. The last are,

---

9. an Essay . . . Wit: Numbers 58–63. **10. afterwards gave:** in Numbers 70, 74, and 85 (all on ballads). **11. Divine Work:** Numbers 267 ff. treat *Paradise Lost.* **12. at large:** in a general way. **13. with Candour:** kindly, with an open mind. *Number 411.* **1. Avia . . . haurire:** "I wander over the tracts of the Pierides never before traveled and am pleased to be the first to drink at virgin springs" (Lucretius, *De Rerum Natura,* I. 926–28). **2. converses:** engages.

3. promiscuously: without distinction. **4. to . . . Words:** As D. F. Bond's notes to this number indicate, the ideas set forth here were rather better established than Addison would seem to allow.

indeed, more preferable, because they are founded on some new Knowledge or Improvement in the Mind of Man; yet it must be confest, that those of the Imagination are as great and as transporting as the other. A beautiful Prospect delights the Soul, as much as a Demonstration;[5] and a Description in *Homer* has charmed more Readers than a Chapter in *Aristotle*. Besides, the Pleasures of the Imagination have this Advantage, above those of the Understanding, that they are more obvious, and more easie to be acquired. It is but opening the Eye, and the Scene enters. The Colours paint themselves on the Fancy, with very little Attention of Thought or Application of Mind in the Beholder. We are struck, we know not how, with the Symmetry of any thing we see, and immediately assent to the Beauty of an Object, without enquiring into the particular Causes and Occasions of it.

A Man of a Polite Imagination, is let into a great many Pleasures that the Vulgar[6] are not capable of receiving. He can converse[7] with a Picture, and find an agreeable Companion in a Statue. He meets with a secret Refreshment in a Description, and often feels a greater Satisfaction in the Prospect of Fields and Meadows, than another does in the Possession. It gives him, indeed, a kind of Property in every thing he sees, and makes the most rude uncultivated Parts of Nature administer to his Pleasures: So that he looks upon the World, as it were, in another Light, and discovers in it a Multitude of Charms, that conceal themselves from the generality of Mankind.

There are, indeed, but very few who know how to be idle and innocent,[8] or have a Relish of any Pleasures that are not Criminal; every Diversion they take is at the Expence of some one Virtue or another, and their very first Step out of Business is into Vice or Folly. A Man should endeavour, therefore, to make the Sphere of his innocent Pleasures as wide as possible, that he may retire into them with Safety, and find in them such a Satisfaction as a wise Man would not blush to take. Of this Nature are those of the Imagination, which do not require such a Bent of Thought as is necessary to our more serious Employments, nor, at the same time, suffer the Mind to sink into that Negligence and Remissness, which are apt to accompany our more sensual Delights, but, like a gentle Exercise to the Faculties, awaken them from Sloth and Idleness,

without putting them upon any Labour or Difficulty.

We might here add, that the Pleasures of the Fancy are more conducive to Health, than those of the Understanding, which are worked out by Dint of Thinking, and attended with too violent a Labour of the Brain. Delightful Scenes, whether in Nature, Painting, or Poetry, have a kindly Influence on the Body, as well as the Mind, and not only serve to clear and brighten the Imagination, but are able to disperse Grief and Melancholly, and to set the Animal Spirits in pleasing and agreeable Motions. For this reason Sir *Francis Bacon*, in his Essay upon Health,[9] has not thought it improper to prescribe to his Reader a Poem or a Prospect, where he particularly dissuades him from knotty and subtile Disquisitions, and advises him to pursue Studies, that fill the Mind with splendid and illustrious[10] Objects, as Histories, Fables, and Contemplations of Nature.

I have in this Paper, by way of Introduction, settled the Notion of those Pleasures of the Imagination, which are the Subject of my present Undertaking, and endeavoured, by several Considerations, to recommend to my Reader the Pursuit of those Pleasures. I shall, in my next Paper, examine the several Sources from whence these Pleasures are derived.

NO. 412

Monday, June 23, 1712

. . . Divisum sic breve fiet Opus.[1]
MART.

I SHALL first consider those Pleasures of the Imagination, which arise from the actual View and Survey of outward Objects: And these, I think, all proceed from the Sight of what is *Great, Uncommon*, or *Beautiful*. There may, indeed, be something so terrible or offensive, that the Horrour or Loathsomness of an Object may over-bear[2] the Pleasure which results from its *Greatness, Novelty*, or *Beauty;* but still there will be such a Mixture of Delight in the very Disgust it gives us, as any of these three Qualifications are most conspicuous and prevailing.

---

5. **Demonstration:** logical or empirical proof. 6. **the Vulgar:** ordinary people. 7. **converse:** commune. 8. **idle and innocent:** i.e., at the same time.

9. **Essay . . . Health:** Number 30. 10. **illustrious:** clear, evident. *Number 412.* 1. **Divisum . . . Opus:** "The work thus divided will become brief" (Martial, *Epigrams*, IV. lxxxii. 8). 2. **over-bear:** outweigh.

By *Greatness*, I do not only mean the Bulk of any single Object, but the Largeness of a whole View, considered as one entire Piece. Such are the Prospects of an open Champian[3] Country, a vast uncultivated Desart, of huge Heaps of Mountains, high Rocks and Precipices, or a wide Expanse of Waters, where we are not struck with the Novelty or Beauty of the Sight, but with that rude kind of Magnificence which appears in many of these stupendous Works of Nature. Our Imagination loves to be filled with an Object, or to graspe at any thing that is too big for its Capacity. We are flung into a pleasing Astonishment at such un-bounded Views, and feel a delightful Stillness and Amazement in the Soul at the Apprehension of them. The Mind of Man naturally hates every thing that looks like a Restraint upon it, and is apt to fancy it self under a sort of Confinement, when the Sight is pent up in a narrow Compass, and shortned on every side by the Neighbourhood of Walls or Mountains. On the contrary, a spacious Horison is an Image of Liberty, where the eye has Room to range abroad, to expatiate at large on the Immensity of its Views, and to lose it self amidst the Variety of Objects that offer themselves to its Observation. Such wide and undetermined[4] Prospects are as pleasing to the Fancy, as the Speculations of Eternity or Infinitude are to the Understanding. But if there be a Beauty or Uncom-monness joyned with this Grandeur, as in a troubled Ocean, a Heaven adorned with Stars and Meteors, or a spacious Landskip cut out into Rivers, Woods, Rocks, and Meadows, the Pleasure still[5] grows upon us, as it arises from more than a single Principle.

Every thing that is *new* or *uncommon* raises a Pleasure in the Imagination, because it fills the Soul with an agreeable Surprise, gratifies its Curiosity, and gives it an Idea of which it was not before possest. We are, indeed, so often conversant with one Sett of Objects, and tired out with so many repeated Shows of the same Things, that whatever is *new* or *uncommon* contributes a little to vary Human Life, and to divert our Minds, for a while, with the Strangeness of its Appearance: It serves us for a kind of Refreshment, and takes off from that Satiety we are apt to complain of in our usual and ordinary Entertainments. It is this that bestows Charms on a Monster, and makes even the Imperfections of Nature please us. It is this that recommends Variety, where the Mind is every Instant called off to something new, and the Attention not suffered to dwell too long, and waste it self on any particular Object. It is this, likewise, that improves what is great or beautiful, and makes it afford the Mind a double Entertainment. Groves, Fields, and Meadows, are at any Season of the Year pleasant to look upon, but never so much as in the opening of the Spring, when they are all new and fresh, with their first Gloss upon them, and not yet too much accus-tomed and familiar to the Eye. For this reason there is nothing that more enlivens a Prospect than Rivers, Jetteaus,[6] or Falls of Water, where the Scene is per-petually shifting, and entertaining the Sight every Moment with something that is new. We are quickly tired with looking upon Hills and Valleys, where every thing continues fixt and settled in the same Place and Posture, but find our Thoughts a little agitated and relieved at the sight of such Objects as are ever in Motion, and sliding away from beneath the Eye of the Beholder.

But there is nothing that makes its way more directly to the Soul than *Beauty*, which immediately diffuses a secret Satisfaction and Complacency[7] thro' the Imagination, and gives a Finishing to any thing that is Great or Uncommon. The very first Discovery of it strikes the Mind with an inward Joy, and spreads a Chearfulness and Delight through all its Faculties. There is not perhaps any real Beauty or Deformity more in one piece of Matter than another, because we might have been so made, that whatsoever now appears loathsom to us, might have shewn it self agreeable; but we find by Experience, that there are several Modifications of Matter which the Mind, without any previous Consideration, pronounces at first sight Beautiful or Deformed. Thus we see that every different Species of sensible Creatures has its different Notions of Beauty, and that each of them is most affected with the Beauties of its own kind. This is no where more remarkable than in Birds of the same Shape and Proportion, where we often see the Male determined in his Courtship by the single Grain or Tincture of a Feather, and never discovering any Charms but in the Colour of its Species.

Scit thalamo servare fidem, sanctasque veretur
Connubii leges, non illum in pectore candor
Sollicitat niveus; neque pravum accendit amorem
Splendida Lanugo, vel honesta in vertice crista,

---

3. **Champian:** (champaign) flat and open. 4. **undeter-mined:** open, unlimited. 5. **still:** more and more.

6. **Jetteaus:** (or jettos, from *jets d'eau*) ornamental jets of water. 7. **Complacency:** pleasure, delight.

Purpureusve nitor pennarum; ast agmina latè
Fœminea explorat cautus, maculasque requirit
Cognatas, paribusque interlita corpora guttis:
Ni faceret, pictis sylvam circum undique monstris
Confusam aspiceres vulgò, partusque biformes,
Et genus ambiguum, & Veneris monumenta nefandæ.
　Hinc merula in nigro se oblectat nigra marito,
Hinc socium lasciva petit Philomela canorum,
Agnoscitque pares sonitus, hinc Noctua tetram
Caniciem alarum, & Glaucos miratur ocellos.
Nempe sibi semper constat, crescitque quotannis
Lucida progenies, castos confessa parentes;
Dum virides inter saltus lucosque sonoros
Vere novo exultat, plumasque decora Juventus
Explicat ad solem, patriisque coloribus ardet.[8]

There is a second kind of *Beauty* that we find in the several Products of Art and Nature, which does not work in the Imagination with that Warmth and Violence as the Beauty that appears in our proper[9] Species, but is apt however to raise in us a secret Delight, and a kind of Fondness for the Places or Objects in which we discover it. This consists either in the Gaiety or Variety of Colours, in the Symmetry and Proportion of Parts, in the Arrangement and Disposition of Bodies, or in a just Mixture and Concurrence of all together. Among these several kinds of Beauty the Eye takes most Delight in Colours. We no where meet with a more glorious or pleasing Show in Nature, than what appears in the Heavens at the rising and setting of the Sun, which is wholly made up

---

8. Scit . . . ardet: These verses—by Addison—are translated in the 1744 duodecimo edition as follows:

　The feather'd Husband, to his Partner true,
　Preserves connubial Rites inviolate.
　With cold Indifference every Charm he sees,
　The milky Whiteness of the stately Neck,
　The shining Down, proud Crest, and purple Wings:
　But cautious with a searching Eye explores
　The female Tribes, his proper Mate to find,
　With kindred Colours mark'd: Did he not so,
　The Grove with painted Monsters wou'd abound,
　Th' ambiguous Product of unnatural Love.
　The Black-bird hence selects her sooty Spouse;
　The Nightingale her musical Compeer,
　Lur'd by the well-known Voice: the Bird of Night,
　Smit with his dusky Wings, and greenish Eyes,
　Wo[o]s his dun Paramour. The beauteous Race
　Speak the chaste Loves of their Progenitors;
　When, by the Spring invited, they exult
　In Woods and Fields, and to the Sun unfold
　Their Plumes, that with paternal Colours glow.

9. proper: own.

of those different Stains[10] of Light that shew themselves in Clouds of a different Situation. For this Reason we find the Poets, who are always addressing themselves to the Imagination, borrowing more of their Epithets from Colours than from any other Topic.

As the Fancy delights in every thing that is Great, Strange, or Beautiful, and is still more pleased the more it finds of these Perfections in the same Object, so is it capable of receiving a new Satisfaction by the Assistance of another Sense. Thus any continued Sound, as the Musick of Birds, or a Fall of Water, awakens every moment the Mind of the Beholder, and makes him more attentive to the several Beauties of the Place that lie before him. Thus if there arises a Fragrancy of Smells or Perfumes, they heighten the Pleasures of the Imagination, and make even the Colours and Verdure of the Landskip appear more agreeable; for the Ideas of both Senses recommend each other, and are pleasanter together than when they enter the Mind separately: As the different Colours of a Picture, when they are well disposed, set off one another, and receive an additional Beauty from the Advantage of their Situation.

NO. 413

Tuesday, June 24, 1712

　. . . *Causa latet, vis est notissima* . . . .[1]
　　　　　　　　　　　　　　　OVID.

THOUGH in Yesterday's Paper we considered how every thing that is *Great, New,* or *Beautiful,* is apt to affect the Imagination with Pleasure, we must own that it is impossible for us to assign the necessary Cause of this Pleasure, because we know neither the Nature of an Idea, nor the Substance of a Human Soul, which might help us to discover the Conformity or Disagreeableness[2] of the one to the other; and therefore, for want of such a Light, all that we can do in Speculations of this kind, is to reflect on those Operations of the Soul that are most agreeable, and to range, under their proper Heads, what is pleasing or displeasing to the Mind, without being able to trace out the several

---

10. Stains: natural spots or patches of color different from the color of the background. *Number 413.* **1. Causa . . . notissima:** "The cause is secret, but the effect is known" (Ovid, *Metamorphoses,* IV. 287). **2. Disagreeableness:** disagreement.

necessary and efficient Causes[3] from whence the Pleasure or Displeasure arises.

Final Causes[4] lye more bare and open to our Observation, as there are often a great Variety that belong to the same Effect; and these, tho' they are not altogether so satisfactory, are generally more useful than the other, as they give us greater Occasion of admiring the Goodness and Wisdom of the first Contriver.

One of the Final Causes of our Delight, in any thing that is *great*, may be this. The Supreme Author of our Being has so formed the Soul of Man, that nothing but himself can be its last, adequate, and proper Happiness. Because, therefore, a great Part of our Happiness must arise from the Contemplation of his Being, that he might give our Souls a just Relish of such a Contemplation, he has made them naturally delight in the Apprehension of what is Great or Unlimited. Our Admiration,[5] which is a very pleasing Motion of the Mind, immediately rises at the Consideration of any Object that takes up a great deal of room in the Fancy, and, by consequence, will improve into the highest pitch of Astonishment and Devotion when we contemplate his Nature, that is neither circumscribed by Time nor Place, nor to be comprehended by the largest Capacity of a Created Being.

He has annexed a secret Pleasure to the Idea of any thing that is *new* or *uncommon*, that he might encourage us in the Pursuit after Knowledge, and engage us to search into the Wonders of his Creation; for every new Idea brings such a Pleasure along with it, as rewards any Pains we have taken in its Acquisition, and consequently serves as a Motive to put us upon fresh Discoveries.

He has made everything that is *beautiful in our own Species* pleasant, that all Creatures might be tempted to multiply their Kind, and fill the World, with Inhabitants; for 'tis very remarkable that whereever Nature is crost in the Production of a Monster (the Result of any unnatural Mixture) the Breed is incapable of propagating its Likeness, and of founding a new Order of Creatures; so that unless all Animals were allured by the Beauty of their own Species, Generation would be at an end, and the Earth unpeopled.

In the last place, he has made every thing that is beautiful in all other Objects pleasant, or rather has made so many Objects appear beautiful, that he might render the whole Creation more gay and delightful. He has given almost every thing about us the Power of raising an agreeable Idea in the Imagination: So that it is impossible for us to behold his Works with Coldness or Indifference, and to survey so many Beauties without a secret Satisfaction and Complacency.[6] Things would make but a poor Appearance to the Eye, if we saw them only in their proper[7] Figures and Motions: And what Reason can we assign for their exciting in us many of those Ideas which are different from any thing that exists in the Objects themselves, (for such are Light and Colours) were it not to add Supernumerary[8] Ornaments to the Universe, and make it more agreeable to the Imagination? We are every where entertained with pleasing Shows and Apparitions, we discover imaginary Glories in the Heavens, and in the Earth, and see some of this Visionary Beauty poured out upon the whole Creation; but what a rough unsightly Sketch of Nature should we be entertained with, did all her Colouring disappear, and the several Distinctions of Light and Shade vanish? In short, our Souls are at present delightfully lost and bewildered in a pleasing Delusion, and we walk about like the Enchanted Hero of a Romance, who sees beautiful Castles, Woods and Meadows; and at the same time hears the warbling of Birds, and the purling of Streams; but upon the finishing of some secret Spell, the fantastick Scene breaks up, and the disconsolate Knight finds himself on a barren Heath, or in a solitary Desart. It is not improbable that something like this may be the State of the Soul after its first Separation, in respect of the Images it will receive from Matter; tho' indeed the Ideas of Colours are so pleasing and beautiful in the Imagination, that it is possible the Soul will not be deprived of them, but perhaps find them excited by some other Occasional Cause, as they are at present by the different Impressions of the subtle Matter on the Organ of Sight.

I have here supposed that my Reader is acquainted with that great Modern Discovery, which is at present universally acknowledged by all the Enquirers into Natural Philosophy: Namely, that Light and Colours, as apprehended by the Imagination, are only Ideas in

---

3. **efficient Causes:** An efficient cause is the immediate cause of a particular result. 4. **Final Causes:** A final cause is equivalent to Aristotle's fourth cause: the end or purpose of an action. 5. **Admiration:** sense of wonder.

6. **Complacency:** pleasure, delight. 7. **proper:** own. 8. **Supernumerary:** additional.

the Mind, and not Qualities that have any Existence in Matter. As this is a Truth which has been proved incontestably by many Modern Philosophers, and is indeed one of the finest Speculations in that Science, if the *English* Reader would see the Notion explained at large, he may find it in the Eighth Chapter of the Second Book of Mr. *Lock*'s Essay on Human Understanding.

NO. 414

Wednesday, June 25, 1712

> . . . *Alterius sic*
> *Altera poscit opem res & conjurat amicè.*[1]
>
> Hor.

IF we consider the Works of *Nature* and *Art*, as they are qualified to entertain the Imagination, we shall find the last very defective, in Comparison of the former; for though they may sometimes appear as Beautiful or Strange, they can have nothing in them of that Vastness and Immensity, which afford so great an Entertainment to the Mind of the Beholder. The one may be as Polite and Delicate as the other, but can never shew her self so August and Magnificent in the Design. There is something more bold and masterly in the rough careless Strokes of Nature, than in the nice Touches and Embellishments of Art. The Beauties of the most stately Garden or Palace lie in a narrow Compass, the Imagination immediately runs them over, and requires something else to gratifie her; but, in the wide Fields of Nature, the Sight wanders up and down without Confinement, and is fed with an infinite variety of Images, without any certain Stint[2] or Number. For this Reason we always find the Poet in love with a Country-Life, where Nature appears in the greatest Perfection, and furnishes out all those Scenes that are most apt to delight the Imagination.

> *Scriptorum chorus omnis amat nemus & fugit Urbes.*[3]
>
> Hor.

> *Hic Secura quies, & nescia fallere vita,*
> *Dives opum variarum; hic latis otia fundis,*
> *Speluncæ, vivique lacus, hic frigida Tempe,*
> *Mugitusque boum, mollesque sub arbore somni.*[4]
>
> Vir.

But tho' there are several of these wild Scenes, that are more delightful than any artificial Shows; yet we find the Works of Nature still more pleasant, the more they resemble those of Art: For in this case our Pleasure arises from a double Principle; from the Agreeableness of the Objects to the Eye, and from their Similitude to other Objects: We are pleased as well with comparing their Beauties, as with surveying them, and can represent them to our Minds, either as Copies or Originals. Hence it is that we take Delight in a Prospect which is well laid out, and diversified with Fields and Meadows, Woods and Rivers, in those accidental Landskips of Trees, Clouds and Cities, that are sometimes found in the Veins of Marble, in the curious Fret-work of Rocks and Grottos, and, in a Word, in any thing that hath such a Variety or Regularity as may seem the Effect of Design, in what we call the Works of Chance.

If the Products of Nature rise in Value, according as they more or less resemble those of Art, we may be sure that artificial Works receive a greater Advantage from their Resemblance of such as are natural; because here the Similitude is not only pleasant, but the Pattern more perfect. The prettiest Landskip I ever saw, was one drawn on the Walls of a dark Room, which stood opposite on one side to a navigable River, and on the other to a Park. The Experiment is very common in Opticks. Here you might discover the Waves and Fluctuations of the Water in strong and proper Colours, with the Picture of a Ship entering at one end, and sailing by Degrees through the whole Piece. On another there appeared the Green Shadows of Trees, waving to and fro with the Wind, and Herds of Deer among them in Miniature, leaping about upon

---

Number 414. **1. Alterius . . . amicè:** "so much does the one require the assistance of the other, and so amicably do they conspire" (Horace, *Ars Poetica*, ll. 410–11). **2. Stint:** limited amount. **3. Scriptorum . . . Urbes:** "The whole choir of poets love the grove and avoid cities" (Horace, *Epistles*, II. ii. 77).

4. Hic . . . somni:

> Unvex'd with Quarrels, undisturb'd with Noise,
> The Country King his peaceful Realm enjoys:
> Cool Grots, and living Lakes, the Flow'ry Pride
> Of Meads, and Streams that thro' the Valley glide;
> And shady Groves that easie Sleep invite,
> And after toilsome Days, a soft repose at Night.

(Virgil, *Georgics*, II. 467–70 [Dryden's translation, II. 659–64])

the Wall.[5] I must confess, the Novelty of such a sight may be one occasion of its Pleasantness to the Imagination, but certainly the chief Reason is its near Resemblance to Nature, as it does not only, like other Pictures, give the Colour and Figure, but the Motion of the Things it represents.

We have before observed, that there is generally in Nature something more Grand and August, than what we meet with in the Curiosities of Art. When, therefore, we see this imitated in any measure, it gives us a nobler and more exalted kind of Pleasure than what we receive from the nicer[6] and more accurate Productions of Art. On this Account our *English* Gardens are not so entertaining to the Fancy as those in *France* and *Italy*, where we see a large Extent of Ground covered over with an agreeable mixture of Garden and Forest, which represent every where an artificial Rudeness, much more charming than that Neatness and Elegancy which we meet with in those of our own Country. It might, indeed, be of ill Consequence to the Publick, as well as unprofitable to private Persons, to alienate[7] so much Ground from Pasturage, and the Plow, in many Parts of a Country that is so well peopled, and cultivated to a far greater Advantage. But why may not a whole Estate be thrown into a kind of Garden by frequent Plantations, that may turn as much to the Profit, as the Pleasure of the Owner? A Marsh overgrown with Willows, or a Mountain shaded with Oaks, are not only more beautiful, but more beneficial, than when they lie bare and unadorned. Fields of Corn[8] make a pleasant Prospect, and if the Walks were a little taken care of that lie between them, if the natural Embroidery of the Meadows were helpt and improved by some small Additions of Art, and the several Rows of Hedges set off by Trees and Flowers, that the Soil was capable of

receiving, a Man might make a pretty Landskip of his own Possessions.

Writers, who have given us an Account of *China*, tell us, the Inhabitants of that Country laugh at the Plantations of our *Europeans*, which are laid out by the Rule and Line; because, they say, any one may place Trees in equal Rows and uniform Figures. They chuse rather to shew a Genius in Works of this Nature, and therefore always conceal the Art by which they direct themselves. They have a Word, it seems, in their Language, by which they express the particular Beauty of a Plantation that thus strikes the Imagination at first Sight, without discovering what it is that has so agreeable an Effect.[9] Our *British* Gardeners, on the contrary, instead of humouring Nature, love to deviate from it as much as possible. Our Trees rise in Cones, Globes, and Pyramids. We see the Marks of the Scissars upon every Plant and Bush. I do not know whether I am singular in my Opinion, but, for my own part, I would rather look upon a Tree in all its Luxuriancy and Diffusion of Boughs and Branches, than when it is thus cut and trimmed into a Mathematical Figure; and cannot but fancy that an Orchard in Flower looks infinitely more delightful, than all the little Labyrinths of the most finished Parterre.[10] But as our great Modellers of Gardens have their Magazines[11] of Plants to dispose of, it is very natural for them to tear up all the Beautiful Plantations of Fruit Trees, and contrive a Plan that may most turn to their own Profit, in taking off[12] their Evergreens, and the like Moveable Plants, with which their Shops are plentifully stocked.

NO. 415

Thursday, June 26, 1712

Adde tot egregias urbes, operumque laborem:[1]
VIRG.

HAVING already shewn how the Fancy is affected by the Works of Nature, and afterwards considered in general both the Works of Nature and of Art, how

---

5. The prettiest . . . Wall: D. F. Bond quotes Hugh Blair's *Lectures on Rhetoric and Belles Lettres* (1783): "The scene, which I am inclined to think Mr. Addison here refers to, is Greenwich Park, with the prospect of the Thames, as seen by a Camera Obscura, which is placed in a small room in the upper story of the Observatory; where I remember to have seen, many years ago, the whole scene here described, corresponding so much to Mr. Addison's account of it in this passage, that, at the time, it recalled it to my memory. As the Observatory stands in the middle of the Park, it overlooks, from one side, both the river and the park; and the objects afterwards mentioned, the ships, the trees, and the deer, are presented in one view, without needing any assistance from opposite walls." **6. nicer:** more precise, delicate. **7. alienate:** transfer. **8. Corn:** grain.

9. They have . . . Effect: D. F. Bond cites as Addison's source Sir William Temple's essay *Upon the Gardens of Epicurus; or, of Gardening, in the Year 1685* from his *Works* (1720). **10. Parterre:** a level, ornamental arrangement of flower beds. **11. Magazines:** stocks, storehouses. **12. taking off:** disposing of. *Number 415.* **1. Adde . . . laborem:** "Next add our Cities of Illustrious Name, / Their costly Labour and stupend'ous Frame" (Virgil, *Georgics*, II. 155 [Dryden's translation, II. 213–14]).

they mutually assist and compleat each other, in forming such Scenes and Prospects as are most apt to delight the Mind of the Beholder, I shall in this Paper throw together some Reflections on that Particular Art, which has a more immediate Tendency, than any other, to produce those primary Pleasures of the Imagination, which have hitherto been the Subject of this Discourse. The Art I mean is that of Architecture, which I shall consider only with regard to the Light in which the foregoing Speculations have placed it, without entring into those Rules and Maxims which the great Masters of Architecture have laid down, and explained at large in numberless Treatises upon that Subject.

Greatness, in the Works of Architecture, may be considered as relating to the Bulk and Body of the Structure, or to the *Manner* in which it is built. As for the first, we find the Antients, especially among the Eastern Nations of the World, infinitely superior to the Moderns.

Not to mention the Tower of *Babel*, of which an old Author says, there were the Foundations to be seen in his time, which looked like a Spacious Mountain; what could be more noble than the Walls of *Babylon*, its hanging Gardens, and its Temple to *Jupiter Belus*,[2] that rose a Mile high by Eight several Stories, each Story a Furlong in Height, and on the Top of which was the *Babylonian* Observatory? I might here, likewise, take Notice of the huge Rock that was cut into the Figure of *Semiramis*,[3] with the smaller Rocks that lay by it in the Shape of Tributary Kings; the Prodigious Basin, or artificial Lake, which took in the whole *Euphrates*, till such time as a new Canal was formed for its Reception, with the several Trenches through which that River was conveyed. I know there are Persons who look upon some of these Wonders of Art as Fabulous, but I cannot find any Grounds for such a Suspicion, unless it be that we have no such Works among us at present. There were indeed many greater Advantages for Building in those Times, and in that Part of the World, than have been met with ever since. The Earth was extreamly fruitful, Men lived generally on Pasturage, which requires a much smaller number of Hands than Agriculture: There were few Trades to employ the busie Part of Mankind, and fewer Arts and Sciences to give Work to Men of Speculative Tempers; and what is more than all the rest, the Prince was absolute; so that when he went to War, he put himself at the Head of a whole People: As we find *Semiramis* leading her three Millions to the Field, and yet overpower'd by the Number of her Enemies. 'Tis no wonder, therefore, when she was at Peace, and turned her Thoughts on Building, that she could accomplish so great Works, with such a prodigious Multitude of Labourers: Besides that, in her Climate, there was small Interruption of Frosts and Winters, which make the Northern Workmen lie half the Year Idle. I might mention too, among the Benefits of the Climate, what Historians say of the Earth, that it sweated out a Bitumen[4] or natural kind of Mortar, which is doubtless the same with that mentioned in Holy Writ, as contributing to the Structure of *Babel*. *Slime they used instead of Mortar.*[5]

In *Egypt* we still see their Pyramids, which answer to the Descriptions that have been made of them; and I question not but a Traveller might find out some Remains of the Labyrinth that covered a whole Province, and had a hundred Temples disposed among its several Quarters and Divisions.

The Wall of *China* is one of these Eastern Pieces of Magnificence, which makes a Figure even in the Map of the World, altho' an Account of it would have been thought Fabulous, were not the Wall it self still extant.

We are obliged to Devotion for the noblest Buildings, that have adorned the several Countries of the World. It is this which has set Men at work on Temples and Publick Places of Worship, not only that they might, by the Magnificence of the Building, invite the Deity to reside within it, but that such stupendous Works might, at the same time, open the Mind to vast Conceptions, and fit it to converse with the Divinity of the Place. For every thing that is Majestick, imprints an Awfullness and Reverence on the Mind of the Beholder, and strikes in[6] with the Natural Greatness of the Soul.

In the Second place we are to consider *Greatness of Manner* in Architecture, which has such force upon the Imagination, that a small Building, where *it*

2. **Jupiter Belus:** Belus, the name of an ancient oriental king, was used as a divine title (as "Zeus Belus" in Herodotus, I. clxxxi. 2). 3. **Semiramis:** the legendary ruler of Assyria and builder of Babylon; the historical personage behind the legend was Sammuramat, wife of the Assyrian king Shamshi-Adad V and regent from 810 to 805 B.C. during the minority of her son, Adad-Nirari III.

4. **Bitumen:** a mineral found in Palestine and Babylon, used in ancient times as mortar. 5. **Slime . . . Mortar:** See Gen. 11:3. 6. **strikes in:** fits in, agrees.

appears, shall give the Mind nobler Ideas than one of twenty times the Bulk, where the Manner is ordinary or little. Thus, perhaps, a Man would have been more astonished with the Majestick Air that appeared in one of *Lysippus's* Statues of *Alexander*, tho' no bigger than the Life, than he might have been with Mount *Athos*, had it been cut into the Figure of the Heroe, according to the Proposal of *Phidias*,[7] with a River in one Hand, and a City in the other.

Let any one reflect on the Disposition of Mind he finds in himself, at his first Entrance into the *Pantheon* at *Rome*, and how his Imagination is filled with something Great and Amazing; and, at the same time, consider how little, in proportion, he is affected with the Inside of a *Gothick* Cathedral, tho' it be five times larger than the other; which can arise from nothing else, but the Greatness of the Manner in the one, and the Meanness in the other.

I have seen an Observation upon this Subject in a *French* Author, which very much pleased me. It is in Monsieur *Freart's* Parallel of the Ancient and Modern Architecture.[8] I shall give it the Reader with the same Terms of Art which he has made use of. *I am observing* (says he) *a thing which, in my Opinion, is very curious, whence it proceeds, that in the same quantity of Superficies,[9] the one* Manner *seems great and magnificent, and the other poor and trifling; the Reason is fine and uncommon. I say then, that to introduce into Architecture this Grandeur of Manner, we ought so to proceed, that the Division of the Principal Members of the Order[10] may consist but of few Parts, that they be all great and of a bold and ample Relievo,[11] and Swelling; and that the Eye, beholding nothing little and mean, the Imagination may be more vigorously touched and affected with the Work that stands before it. For Example; In a Cornice, if the Gola or Cymatium[12] of the Corona, the Coping,[13] the Modillions[14] or Dentelli,[15] make a noble Show by their graceful*

Projections, *if we see none of that ordinary Confusion which is the Result of those little Cavities, Quarter Rounds[16] of the Astragal,[17] and I know not how many other intermingled Particulars, which produce no effect in great and massy Works, and which very unprofitably take up Place to the prejudice of the Principal Member, it is most certain that this Manner will appear Solemn and Great; as on the contrary, that will have but a poor and mean Effect, where there is a Redundancy of those smaller Ornaments, which divide and scatter the Angles of the Sight into such a Multitude of Rays, so pressed together that the whole will appear but a Confusion.*

Among all the Figures in Architecture, there are none that have a greater Air than the Concave and the Convex; and we find in all the Ancient and Modern Architecture, as well in the remote Parts of *China*, as in Countries nearer home, that round Pillars and Vaulted Roofs make a great part of those Buildings which are designed for Pomp and Magnificence. The Reason I take to be, because in these Figures we generally see more of the Body, than in those of other Kinds. There are, indeed, Figures of Bodies, where the Eye may take in two Thirds of the Surface; but as in such Bodies the Sight must split upon several Angles, it does not take in one uniform Idea, but several Ideas of the same kind. Look upon the Outside of a Dome, your Eye half surrounds it; look up into the Inside, and at one Glance you have all the Prospect of it; the entire Concavity falls into your Eye at once, the Sight being as the Center that collects and gathers into it the Lines of the whole Circumference: In a Square Pillar, the Sight often takes in but a Fourth part of the Surface, and, in a Square Concave, must move up and down to the different Sides, before it is Master of all the inward Surface. For this Reason, the Fancy is infinitely more struck with the view of the open Air, and Skies, that passes through an Arch, than what comes through a Square, or any other Figure. The Figure of the Rainbow does not contribute less to its Magnificence, than the Colours to its Beauty, as it is very Poetically described by the Son of *Sirach: Look upon the Rainbow, and praise him that made it; very beautiful it is in its Brightness; it encompasses the Heavens with a Glorious Circle, and the Hands of the most High have bended it.*[18]

---

7. Phidias: an error for Stasicrates (Plutarch's *Life of Alexander*, par. lxxii). **8. in . . . Architecture:** in Chapter ii of Roland Fréart's *Parallèle de l'architecture antique et de la moderne* (1650). The work was translated by John Evelyn in 1664. **9. Superficies:** surface area, extent. **10. the Order:** an architectural system or assemblage, as for example the five orders of classical architecture. **11. Relievo:** relief. **12. Gola or Cymatium:** A cyma (or cymatium) or gola (or gula) is a cornice molding that has the outline of a concave and a convex line. **13. Coping:** the uppermost section of a wall; it usually has a sloping top to throw off water. **14. Modillions:** projecting decorative brackets placed under the corona of the cornice of an entablature. **15. Dentelli:** (dentils) small rectangular blocks that lie in a row like teeth under the corona of the cornice.

16. Quarter Rounds: convex moldings with the outline of quarter circles. **17. Astragal:** a small convex molding, or semicircular section, with the outline of half to three quarters of a circle. It is used at the top or bottom of columns and to separate the parts of the architrave in ornamental entablatures. **18. Look . . . it:** Eccles. 43:11–12.

Having thus spoken of that Greatness which affects the Mind in Architecture, I might next shew the Pleasure that arises in the Imagination from what appears new and beautiful in this Art; but as every Beholder has naturally a greater Taste of these two Perfections in every Building which offers it self to his View, than of that which I have hitherto considered, I shall not trouble my Reader with any Reflections upon it. It is sufficient for my present purpose, to observe, that there is nothing in this whole Art which pleases the Imagination, but as it is Great, Uncommon, or Beautiful.

NO. 416

Friday, June 27, 1712

Quatenûs hoc simile est oculis, quod mente videmus.[1]
LUCR.

I AT first divided the Pleasures of the Imagination, into such as arise from Objects that are actually before our Eyes, or that once entered in at our Eyes, and are afterwards called up into the Mind, either barely by its own Operations, or on occasion of something without us, as Statues or Descriptions. We have already considered the first Division, and shall therefore enter on the other, which, for Distinction sake, I have call'd the Secondary Pleasures of the Imagination. When I say the Ideas we receive from Statues, Descriptions, or such like Occasions, are the same that were once actually in our View, it must not be understood that we had once seen the very Place, Action, or Person which are carved or described. It is sufficient, that we have seen Places, Persons, or Actions, in general, which bear a Resemblance, or at least some remote Analogy with what we find represented. Since it is in the Power of the Imagination, when it is once Stocked with particular Ideas, to enlarge, compound, and vary them at her own Pleasure.

Among the different Kinds of Representation, *Statuary* is the most natural, and shews us something *likest* the Object that is represented. To make use of a common Instance, let one who is born Blind take an Image in his Hands, and trace out with his Fingers the different Furrows and Impressions of the Chissel, and he will easily conceive how the Shape of a Man, or Beast, may be represented by it; but should he draw his Hand over a *Picture*, where all is smooth and uniform, he would never be able to imagine how the several Prominencies and Depressions of a Human Body could be shewn on a plain Piece of Canvas, that has in it no Unevenness or Irregularity. *Description* runs yet further from the things it represents than Painting; for a Picture bears a real Resemblance to its Original, which Letters and Syllables are wholly void of. Colours speak all Languages, but Words are understood only by such a[2] People or Nation. For this reason, tho Mens Necessities quickly put them on finding out Speech, Writing is probably of a later Invention than Painting; particularly we are told, that in *America* when the *Spaniards* first arrived there, Expresses were sent to the Emperor of *Mexico* in Paint, and the News of his Country delineated by the Strokes of a Pencil, which was a more natural way than that of Writing, tho' at the same time much more imperfect, because it is impossible to draw the little Connexions of Speech, or to give the Picture of a Conjunction or an Adverb. It would be yet more strange, to represent visible Objects by Sounds that have no Ideas annexed to them, and to make something like Description in *Musick*. Yet it is certain, there may be confused, imperfect Notions of this Nature raised in the Imagination by an Artificial[3] Composition of Notes; and we find that great Masters in the Art are able, sometimes, to set their Hearers in the heat and hurry of a Battel, to overcast their Minds with melancholy Scenes and Apprehensions of Deaths and Funerals, or to lull them into pleasing Dreams of Groves and Elisiums.

In all these Instances, this Secondary Pleasure of the Imagination proceeds from that Action of the Mind, which compares the Ideas arising from the Original Objects, with the Ideas we receive from the Statue, Picture, Description, or Sound that represents them. It is impossible for us to give the necessary Reason, why this Operation of the Mind is attended with so much Pleasure, as I have before observed on the same Occasion;[4] but we find a great variety of Entertainments derived from this single Principle: For it is this that not only gives us a relish of Statuary, Painting and Description, but makes us delight in all the Actions and Arts of Mimickry. It is this that makes the several

---

Number 416. **1. Quatenûs . . . videmus:** "because what we see with the mind is like what we see with the eye" (Lucretius, *De Rerum Natura*, IV. 750 [altered]).

2. such a: a certain (i.e., each people understands only its own language). **3. Artificial:** artful, skillful. **4. before . . . Occasion:** in *The Spectator*, above , No. 413.

kinds of Wit pleasant, which consists, as I have formerly shown, in the Affinity of Ideas: And we may add, it is this also that raises the little Satisfaction we sometimes find in the different sorts of false Wit; whether it consist in the Affinity of Letters, as in Anagram, Acrostick; or of Syllables, as in Doggerel Rhimes, Ecchos; or of Words, as in Puns, Quibbles; or of a whole Sentence or Poem, to Wings, and Altars. The *final Cause*, probably, of annexing Pleasure to this Operation of the Mind, was to quicken and encourage us in our Searches after Truth, since the distinguishing one thing from another, and the right discerning betwixt our Ideas, depends wholly upon our comparing them together, and observing the Congruity or Disagreement that appears among the several Works of Nature.

But I shall here confine my self to those Pleasures of the Imagination, which proceed from Ideas raised by *Words*, because most of the Observations that agree with Descriptions, are equally Applicable to Painting and Statuary.

Words, when well chosen, have so great a Force in them, that a Description often gives us more lively Ideas than the Sight of Things themselves. The Reader finds a Scene drawn in stronger Colours, and painted more to the Life in his Imagination, by the help of Words, than by an actual Survey of the Scene which they describe. In this Case the Poet seems to get the better of Nature; he takes, indeed, the Landskip after her,[5] but gives it more vigorous Touches, heightens its Beauty, and so enlivens the whole Piece, that the Images, which flow from the Objects themselves, appear weak and faint, in Comparison of those that come from the Expressions. The Reason, probably, may be, because in the Survey of any Object we have only so much of it painted on the Imagination, as comes in at the Eye; but in its Description, the Poet gives us as free a View of it as he pleases, and discovers to us several Parts, that either we did not attend to, or that lay out of our Sight when we first beheld it. As we look on any Object, our Idea of it is, perhaps, made up of two or three simple Ideas; but when the Poet represents it, he may either give us a more complex Idea of it, or only raise in us such Ideas as are most apt to affect the Imagination.

It may be here worth our while to Examine, how it comes to pass that several Readers, who are all acquainted with the same Language, and know the Meaning of the Words they read, should nevertheless have a different Relish of the same Descriptions. We find one transported with a Passage, which another runs over with Coldness and Indifference, or finding the Representation extremely natural, where another can perceive nothing of Likeness and Conformity. This different Taste must proceed, either from the *Perfection of Imagination* in one more than in another, or from the *different Ideas* that several Readers affix to the same Words. For, to have a true Relish, and form a right Judgment of a Description, a Man should be born with a good Imagination, and must have well weighed the Force and Energy that lie in the several Words of a Language, so as to be able to distinguish which are most significant and expressive of their proper Ideas, and what additional Strength and Beauty they are capable of receiving from Conjunction with others. The Fancy must be warm, to retain the Print of those Images it hath received from outward Objects; and the Judgment discerning, to know what Expressions are most proper to cloath and adorn them to the best Advantage. A Man who is deficient in either of these Respects, tho' he may receive the general Notion of a Description, can never see distinctly all its particular Beauties: As a Person, with a weak Sight, may have the confused Prospect of a Place that lies before him, without entering into its several Parts, or discerning the variety of its Colours in their full Glory and Perfection.

NO. 417

Saturday, June 28, 1712

> *Quem tu Melpomene semel*
> *Nascentem placido lumine videris,*
> *   Illum non labor Istmius*
> *Clarabit pugilem, non equus impiger, &c.*
> *Sed quæ Tibur aquæ fertile perfluunt,*
> *   Et Spissæ nemorum comæ*
> *Fingent Æolio carmine nobilem.*[1]
>
>   HOR.

Number 417. **1. Quem . . . nobilem:** "Him, O Melpomene, whom at his birth you have once viewed with a benign aspect, the Isthmian contest shall not render eminent as a wrestler; the swift horse shall not [draw him triumphant in a Grecian car] . . . but such waters as flow through the fertile Tibur, and the dense leaves of the groves, shall make him distinguished for the Aeolian verse" (Horace, *Odes*, IV. iii. 1–4, 10–12).

---

5. after her: after her manner, in her likeness.

WE may observe, that any single Circumstance of what we have formerly seen often raises up a whole Scene of Imagery, and awakens numberless Ideas that before slept in the Imagination; such a particular Smell or Colour is able to fill the Mind, on a sudden, with the Picture of the Fields or Gardens where we first met with it, and to bring up into View all the Variety of Images that once attended it. Our Imagination takes the Hint, and leads us unexpectedly into Cities or Theatres, Plains or Meadows. We may further observe, when the Fancy thus reflects on the Scenes that have past in it formerly, those, which were at first pleasant to behold, appear more so upon Reflection, and that the Memory heightens the Delightfulness of the Original. A *Cartesian* would account for both these Instances in the following Manner.

The Sett of Ideas, which we received from such a Prospect or Garden, having entered the Mind at the same time, have a Sett of Traces belonging to them in the Brain, bordering very near upon one another; when, therefore, any one of these Ideas arises in the Imagination, and consequently dispatches a flow of Animal Spirits to its proper Trace, these Spirits, in the violence of their Motion, run not only into the Trace, to which they were more particularly directed, but into several of those that lie about it: By this means they awaken other Ideas of the same Sett, which immediately determine a new Dispatch of Spirits, that in the same manner open other Neighbouring Traces, till at last the whole Sett of them is blown up, and the whole Prospect or Garden flourishes in the Imagination. But because the Pleasure we received from these Places far surmounted, and overcame the little Disagreeableness we found in them, for this Reason there was at first a wider Passage worn in the Pleasure Traces, and, on the contrary, so narrow a one in those which belonged to the disagreeable Ideas, that they were quickly stopt up, and rendered incapable of receiving any Animal Spirits, and consequently of exciting any unpleasant Ideas in the Memory.

It would be in vain to enquire, whether the Power of Imagining Things strongly proceeds from any greater Perfection in the Soul, or from any nicer Texture in the Brain of one Man than of another. But this is certain, that a noble Writer should be born with this Faculty in its full Strength and Vigour, so as to be able to receive lively Ideas from outward Objects, to retain them long, and to range them together, upon occasion, in such Figures and Representations as are most likely to hit the Fancy of the Reader. A Poet should take as much Pains in forming his Imagination, as a Philosopher in cultivating his Understanding. He must gain a due Relish of the Works of Nature, and be throughly conversant in the various Scenary of a Country Life.

When he is stored with Country Images, if he would go beyond Pastoral, and the lower kinds of Poetry, he ought to acquaint himself with the Pomp and Magnificence of Courts. He should be very well versed in every thing that is noble and stately in the Productions of Art, whether it appear in Painting or Statuary, in the great Works of Architecture which are in their present Glory, or in the Ruins of those which flourished in former Ages.

Such Advantages as these help to open a Man's Thoughts, and to enlarge his Imagination, and will therefore have their Influence on all Kinds of Writing, if the Author knows how to make right use of them. And among those of the learned Languages who excell in this Talent, the most perfect in their several Kinds, are perhaps *Homer*, *Virgil*, and *Ovid*. The first strikes the Imagination wonderfully with what is Great, the second with what is Beautiful, and the last with what is Strange. Reading the *Iliad* is like travelling through a Country uninhabited, where the Fancy is entertained with a thousand Savage Prospects of vast Desarts, wide uncultivated Marshes, huge Forests, mis-shapen Rocks and Precipices. On the contrary, the *Æneid* is like a well-ordered Garden, where it is impossible to find out any Part unadorned, or to cast our Eyes upon a single Spot, that does not produce some beautiful Plant or Flower. But when we are in the *Metamorphosis*, we are walking on enchanted Ground, and see nothing but Scenes of Magick lying round us.

Homer is in his Province, when he is describing a Battel or a Multitude, a Heroe or a God. *Virgil* is never better pleas'd, than when he is in his *Elysium*, or copying out an entertaining Picture. *Homer*'s Epithets generally mark out what is Great, *Virgil*'s what is Agreeable. Nothing can be more Magnificent than the Figure *Jupiter* makes in the First *Iliad*, nor more Charming than that of *Venus* in the First *Æneid*.

’Η, καὶ κυανέῃσιν ἐπ’ ὀφρύσι νεῦσε Κρονίων·
’Αμβρόσιαι δ’ ἄρα χαῖται ἐπερρώσαντο ἄνακτος,
Κρατὸς ἀπ’ ’Αθανάτοιο· μέγαν δ’ ἐλέλιξεν
"Ολυμπον.[2]

2. ’Η. . . "Ολυμπον: "The son of Chronos spake, and bowed his dark brow in assent, and the ambrosial locks waved from the king's immortal head; and he made great Olympus to quake" (*Iliad*, I. 528-30 [Loeb translation]).

Dixit, & avertens roseâ cervice refulsit:
Ambrosiæque comæ divinum vertice odorem
Spiravere: Pedes vestis defluxit ad imos:
Et vera incessu patuit Dea . . .[3]

Homer's Persons are most of them God-like and Terrible: *Virgil* has scarce admitted any into his Poem, who are not beautiful, and has taken particular Care to make his Heroe so.

. . . lumenque juventæ
Purpureum, & lætos oculis afflavit honores.[4]

In a Word, *Homer* fills his Readers with Sublime *Ideas*, and, I believe, has raised the Imagination of all the good Poets that have come after him. I shall only instance *Horace*, who immediately takes Fire at the first Hint of any Passage in the *Iliad* or *Odyssee*, and always rises above himself, when he has *Homer* in his View. *Virgil* has drawn together, into his *Æneid*, all the pleasing Scenes his Subject is capable of admitting, and in his *Georgics* has given us a Collection of the most delightful Landskips that can be made out of Fields and Woods, Herds of Cattle, and Swarms of Bees.

Ovid, in his *Metamorphosis*, has shewn us how the Imagination may be affected by what is Strange. He describes a Miracle in every Story, and always gives us the Sight of some new Creature at the end of it. His Art consists chiefly in well-timing his Description, before the first Shape is quite worn off, and the new one perfectly finish'd; so that he every where entertains us with something we never saw before, and shews Monster after Monster, to the end of the *Metamorphosis*.

If I were to name a Poet that is a perfect Master in all these Arts of working on the Imagination, I think *Milton* may pass for one: And if his *Paradise Lost* falls short of the *Æneid* or *Iliad* in this respect, it proceeds rather from the Fault of the Language in which it is written, than from any Defect of Genius in the Author.

3. Dixit . . . Dea:

> Thus having said, she turn'd, and made appear
> Her Neck refulgent, and dishevel'd Hair;
> Which flowing from her Shoulders, reach'd the Ground,
> And widely spread Ambrosial Scents around:
> In length of Train descends her sweeping Gown,
> And by her graceful Walk, the Queen of Love is known.
>   (*Aeneid*, I. 402–05 [Dryden's translation, I. 556–61])

4. lumenque . . . honores: "And giv'n his rowling Eyes a sparkling grace; / And breath'd a youthful vigour on his Face" (*Ibid.*, ll. 590–91; for *afflavit* read *adflarat* [828–29]).

So Divine a Poem in *English*, is like a stately Palace built of Brick, where one may see Architecture in as great a Perfection as in one of Marble, tho' the Materials are of a coarser Nature. But to consider it only as it regards our present Subject: What can be conceiv'd greater than the Battel of Angels, the Majesty of Messiah, the Stature and Behaviour of Satan and his Peers? What more beautiful than *Pandæmonium*, Paradise, Heaven, Angels, *Adam* and *Eve?* What more strange, than the Creation of the World, the several Metamorphoses of the fallen Angels, and the surprising Adventures their Leader meets with in his Search after Paradise? No other Subject could have furnished a Poet with Scenes so proper to strike the Imagination, as no other Poet could have painted those Scenes in more strong and lively Colours.

NO. 418

Monday, June 30, 1712

. . . ferat & rubus asper amomum.[1]
                                    VIRG.

THE Pleasures of these Secondary Views of the Imagination, are of a wider and more universal Nature than those it has, when joined with Sight; for not only what is Great, Strange or Beautiful, but any Thing that is Disagreeable when look'd upon, pleases us in an apt Description. Here, therefore, we must enquire after a new Principle of Pleasure, which is nothing else but the Action of the Mind, which *compares* the Ideas that arise from Words, with the Ideas that arise from the Objects themselves; and why this Operation of the Mind is attended with so much Pleasure, we have before considered. For this Reason therefore, the Description of a Dung-hill is pleasing to the Imagination, if the Image be represented to our Minds by suitable Expressions; tho', perhaps, this may be more properly called the Pleasure of the Understanding than of the Fancy, because we are not so much delighted with the Image that is contained in the Description, as with the Aptness of the Description to excite the Image.

Number 418. **1. ferat . . . amomum:** "and the rough bramble bear spices" (Virgil, *Eclogues*, III. 89 [Loeb translation]).

But if the Description of what is Little, Common or Deformed, be acceptable to the Imagination, the Description of what is Great, Surprising or Beautiful, is much more so; because here we are not only delighted with *comparing* the Representation with the Original, but are highly pleased with the Original it self. Most Readers, I believe, are more charmed with *Milton's* Description of Paradise, than of Hell; they are both, perhaps, equally perfect in their Kind, but in the one the Brimstone and Sulphur are not so refreshing to the Imagination, as the Beds of Flowers, and the Wilderness of Sweets in the other.

There is yet another Circumstance which recommends a Description more than all the rest, and that is, if it represents to us such Objects as are apt to raise a secret Ferment in the Mind of the Reader, and to work, with Violence, upon his Passions. For, in this Case, we are at once warmed and enlightned, so that the Pleasure becomes more Universal, and is several ways qualified to entertain us. Thus, in Painting, it is pleasant to look on the Picture of any Face, where the Resemblance is hit, but the Pleasure encreases, if it be the Picture of a Face that is beautiful, and is still greater, if the Beauty be softned with an Air of Melancholly or Sorrow. The two leading Passions which the more serious Parts of Poetry endeavour to stir up in us, are Terror and Pity. And here, by the way, one would wonder how it comes to pass, that such Passions as are very unpleasant at all other times, are very agreeable when excited by proper Descriptions. It is not strange, that we should take Delight in such Passages as are apt to produce Hope, Joy, Admiration, Love, or the like Emotions in us, because they never rise in the Mind without an inward Pleasure which attends them. But how comes it to pass, that we should take delight in being terrified or dejected by a Description, when we find so much Uneasiness in the Fear or Grief which we receive from any other Occasion?

If we consider, therefore, the Nature of this Pleasure, we shall find that it does not arise so properly from the Description of what is Terrible, as from the Reflection we make on our selves at the time of reading it. When we look on such hideous Objects, we are not a little pleased to think we are in no Danger of them. We consider them at the same time, as Dreadful and Harmless; so that the more frightful Appearance they make, the greater is the Pleasure we receive from the Sense of our own Safety. In short, we look upon the Terrors of a Description, with the same Curiosity and Satisfaction that we survey a dead Monster.

> . . . *Informe cadaver*
> *Protrahitur, nequeunt expleri corda tuendo*
> *Terribiles oculos: vultum, villosaque setis*
> *Pectora semiferi, atque extinctos faucibus ignes.*[2]
> VIRG.

It is for the same Reason that we are delighted with the reflecting upon Dangers that are past, or in looking on a Precipice at a distance, which would fill us with a different kind of Horrour, if we saw it hanging over our Heads.

In the like manner, when we read of Torments, Wounds, Deaths, and the like dismal Accidents, our Pleasure does not flow so properly from the Grief which such melancholly Descriptions give us, as from the secret Comparison which we make between our selves and the Person who suffers. Such Representations teach us to set a just Value upon our own Condition, and make us prize our good Fortune which exempts us from the like Calamities. This is, however, such a kind of Pleasure as we are not capable of receiving, when we see a Person actually lying under the Tortures that we meet with in a Description; because, in this Case, the Object presses too close upon our Senses, and bears so hard upon us, that it does not give us time or leisure to reflect on our selves. Our Thoughts are so intent upon the Miseries of the Sufferer, that we cannot turn them upon our own Happiness. Whereas, on the contrary, we consider the Misfortunes we read in History or Poetry, either as past, or as fictitious, so that the Reflection upon our selves rises in us insensibly, and over-bears the Sorrow we conceive for the Sufferings of the Afflicted.

But because the Mind of Man requires something more perfect in Matter, than what it finds there, and can never meet with any Sight in Nature which sufficiently answers its highest Ideas of Pleasantness; or, in other Words, because the Imagination can fancy to it self Things more Great, Strange, or Beautiful, than the Eye ever saw, and is still sensible of some Defect in what it has seen; on this account it is the part of a Poet to humour the Imagination in its own Notions, by mending and perfecting Nature where he describes a Reality, and by adding greater Beauties than are put together in Nature, where he describes a Fiction.

2. **Informe . . . ignes:**

The wond'ring Neighbourhood, with glad surprize,
Behold his shagged Breast, his Gyant Size,
His Mouth that flames no more, and his extinguish'd Eyes.
(*Aeneid*, VIII. 264–67 [Dryden's translation, VIII. 352–54])

He is not obliged to attend her in the slow Advances which she makes from one Season to another, or to observe her Conduct, in the successive Production of Plants and Flowers. He may draw into his Description all the Beauties of the Spring and Autumn, and make the whole Year contribute something to render it the more agreeable. His Rose-trees, Wood-bines, and Jessamines, may flower together, and his Beds be covered at the same time with Lillies, Violets, and Amaranths. His Soil is not restrained to any particular Sett of Plants, but is proper either for Oaks or Mirtles, and adapts it self to the Products of every Climate. Oranges may grow wild in it; Myrrh may be met with in every Hedge, and if he thinks it proper to have a Grove of Spices, he can quickly command Sun enough to raise it. If all this will not furnish out an agreeable Scene, he can make several new Species of Flowers, with richer Scents and higher Colours, than any that grow in the Gardens of Nature. His Consorts of Birds may be as full and harmonious, and his Woods as thick and gloomy as he pleases. He is at no more Expence in a long Vista, than a short one, and can as easily throw his Cascades from a Precipice of half a Mile high, as from one of twenty Yards. He has his choice of the Winds, and can turn the Course of his Rivers in all the variety of *Meanders*, that are most delightful to the Reader's Imagination. In a word, he has the modelling of Nature in his own Hands, and may give her what Charms he pleases, provided he does not reform her too much, and run into Absurdities, by endeavouring to excell.

NO. 419

Tuesday, July 1, 1712

. . . mentis gratissimus Error.[1]
HOR.

THERE is a kind of Writing, wherein the Poet quite loses sight of Nature, and entertains his Reader's Imagination with the Characters and Actions of such Persons as have many of them no Existence, but what he bestows on them. Such are Fairies, Witches, Magicians, Demons, and departed Spirits. This Mr. *Dryden* calls *the Fairie way of Writing*,[2] which is, indeed, more difficult than any other that depends on the

Poet's Fancy, because he has no Pattern to follow in it, and must work altogether out of his own Invention.

There is a very odd turn of Thought required for this sort of Writing, and it is impossible for a Poet to succeed in it, who has not a particular Cast of Fancy, and an Imagination naturally fruitful and superstitious. Besides this, he ought to be very well versed in Legends and Fables, antiquated Romances, and the Traditions of Nurses and old Women, that he may fall in with our natural Prejudices, and humour those Notions which we have imbibed in our Infancy. For, otherwise, he will be apt to make his Fairies talk like People of his own Species, and not like other Setts of Beings, who converse with different Objects, and think in a different manner from that of Mankind;

> *Sylvis deducti caveant, me Judice, Fauni*
> *Ne velut innati triviis ac pæne forenses*
> *Aut nimium teneris juvenentur versibus . . .*[3]
> HOR.

I do not say with Mr. *Bays* in the *Rehearsal*, that Spirits must not be confined to speak Sense,[4] but it is certain their Sense ought to be a little discoloured, that it may seem particular,[5] and proper to the Person and the Condition of the Speaker.

These Descriptions raise a pleasing kind of Horrour in the Mind of the Reader, and amuse[6] his Imagination with the Strangeness and Novelty of the Persons who are represented in them. They bring up into our Memory the Stories we have heard in our Child-hood, and favour those secret Terrours and Apprehensions to which the Mind of Man is naturally subject. We are pleased with surveying the different Habits and Behaviours of Foreign Countries, how much more must we be delighted and surprised when we are led, as it were, into a new Creation, and see the Persons and Manners of another Species? Men of cold Fancies, and Philosophical Dispositions, object to this kind of Poetry, that it has not Probability enough to affect the Imagination. But to this it may be answered, that we

---

Number 419. **1. mentis . . . Error:** "a most pleasant delusion" (Horace, *Epistles*, II. ii. 140). **2. This . . . Writing:** in the Dedication of *King Arthur* (1691).

3. **Sylvis . . . versibus:** "In my judgment the Fauns that are brought out of the woods should not be too sportive with their tender strains, as if they were educated in the city, and almost at the bar . . ." (Horace, *Ars Poetica*, ll. 244–46). **4. Spirits . . . Sense:** "Did you ever hear any people in clouds speak plain? They must be all for flight of fancy, at its full range, without the least check or control upon it. When once you tie up spirits and people in clouds to speak plain, you spoil all" (Buckingham and others, *The Rehearsal*, V. i). **5. particular:** individual. **6. amuse:** arrest.

are sure, in general, there are many Intellectual Beings in the World besides our selves, and several Species of Spirits, who are subject to different Laws and Oeconomies from those of Mankind;[7] when we see, therefore, any of these represented naturally, we cannot look upon the Representation as altogether impossible; nay, many are prepossest with such false Opinions, as dispose them to believe these particular Delusions; at least, we have all heard so many pleasing Relations in favour of them, that we do not care for seeing through the Falshood, and willingly give our selves up to so agreeable an Imposture.

The Ancients have not much of this Poetry among them, for, indeed, almost the whole Substance of it owes its Original to the Darkness and Superstition of later Ages, when pious Frauds were made use of to amuse[8] Mankind, and frighten them into a Sense of their Duty. Our Forefathers looked upon Nature with more Reverence and Horrour, before the World was enlightened by Learning and Philosophy, and loved to astonish themselves with the Apprehensions of Witchcraft, Prodigies, Charms and Enchantments. There was not a Village in *England* that had not a Ghost in it, the Churchyards were all haunted, every large Common had a Circle of Fairies belonging to it, and there was scarce a Shepherd to be met with who had not seen a Spirit.

Among all the Poets of this Kind our *English* are much the best, by what I have yet seen, whether it be that we abound with more Stories of this Nature, or that the Genius of our Country is fitter for this sort of Poetry. For the *English* are naturally Fanciful, and very often disposed by that Gloominess and Melancholly of Temper, which is so frequent in our Nation, to many wild Notions and Visions, to which others are not so liable.

Among the *English*, *Shakespear* has incomparably excelled all others. That noble Extravagance of Fancy, which he had in so great Perfection, throughly qualified him to touch this weak superstitious Part of his Reader's Imagination; and made him capable of succeeding, where he had nothing to support him besides the Strength of his own Genius. There is something so wild and yet so solemn in the Speeches of his Ghosts, Fairies, Witches, and the like Imaginary Persons, that we cannot forbear thinking them natural, tho' we have no Rule by which to judge of them, and

must confess, if there are such Beings in the World, it looks highly probable they should talk and act as he has represented them.

There is another sort of Imaginary Beings, that we sometimes meet with among the Poets, when the Author represents any Passion, Appetite, Virtue or Vice, under a visible Shape, and makes it a Person or an Actor in his Poem. Of this Nature are the Descriptions of Hunger and Envy in *Ovid*,[9] of Fame in *Virgil*,[10] and of Sin and Death in *Milton*.[11] We find a whole Creation of the like shadowy Persons in *Spencer*, who had an admirable Talent in Representations of this kind. I have discoursed of these Emblematical Persons in former Papers, and shall therefore only mention them in this Place. Thus we see how many ways Poetry addresses it self to the Imagination, as it has not only the whole Circle of Nature for its Province, but makes new Worlds of its own, shews us Persons who are not to be found in Being, and represents even the Faculties of the Soul, with her several Virtues and Vices, in a sensible[12] Shape and Character.

I shall, in my two following Papers, consider in general, how other kinds of Writing are qualified to please the Imagination, with which I intend to conclude this Essay.

NO. 420

Wednesday, July 2, 1712

. . . *Quocunque volunt mentem Auditoris agunto.*[1]
Hor.

AS the Writers in Poetry and Fiction borrow their several Materials from outward Objects, and join them together at their own Pleasure, there are others who are obliged to follow Nature more closely, and to take entire Scenes out of her. Such are Historians, natural Philosophers, Travellers, Geographers, and, in a Word, all who describe visible Objects of a real Existence.

It is the most agreeable Talent of an Historian, to

---

7. there . . . Mankind: Cf. *The Spectator*, above, No. 12.
8. amuse: beguile, deceive.

9. Hunger . . . Ovid: *Metamorphoses*, II. 768 ff. and VIII. 799 ff. **10. Fame in Virgil:** *Aeneid*, IV. 173 ff. **11. Sin . . . Milton:** In Number 357 Addison praises such "beautiful extended Allegories" as those of Sin and Death in Book X of *Paradise Lost* but criticizes their use in an heroic poem "as principal Actors" on the ground that they weaken the credibility of the action. **12. sensible:** sensuously embodied. *Number 420.* **1. Quocunque . . . agunto:** "and carry away the soul of the auditor wheresoever they please" (Horace, *Ars Poetica*, l. 100; for *volunt mentem* read *volent animum*).

be able to draw up his Armies and fight his Battels in proper Expressions, to set before our Eyes the Divisions, Cabals, and Jealousies of Great Men, and to lead us Step by Step into the several Actions and Events of his History. We love to see the Subject unfolding it self by just Degrees, and breaking upon us insensibly,[2] that so we may be kept in a pleasing Suspence, and have Time given us to raise our Expectations, and to side with one of the Parties concerned in the Relation. I confess this shews more the Art than the Veracity of the Historian, but I am only to speak of him as he is qualified to please the Imagination. And in this respect *Livy* has, perhaps, excelled all who ever went before him, or have written since his Time. He describes every thing in so lively a manner, that his whole History is an admirable Picture, and touches on such proper Circumstances in every Story, that his Reader becomes a kind of Spectator, and feels in himself all the variety of Passions, which are correspondent to the several Parts of the Relation.

But among this Sett of Writers, there are none who more gratifie and enlarge the Imagination, than the Authors of the new Philosophy,[3] whether we consider their Theories of the Earth or Heavens, the Discoveries they have made by Glasses,[4] or any other of their Contemplations on Nature. We are not a little pleased to find every green Leaf swarm with Millions of Animals, that at their largest Growth are not visible to the naked Eye. There is something very engaging to the Fancy, as well as to our Reason, in the Treatises of Metals, Minerals, Plants and Meteors. But when we survey the whole Earth at once, and the several Planets that lie within its Neighbourhood, we are filled with a pleasing Astonishment, to see so many Worlds hanging one above another, and sliding round their Axles[5] in such an amazing Pomp and Solemnity. If, after this, we contemplate those wide Fields of *Ether*, that reach in height as far as from *Saturn* to the fixt Stars, and run abroad almost to an Infinitude, our Imagination finds its Capacity filled with so immense a Prospect, and puts it self upon the Stretch to comprehend it. But if we yet rise higher, and consider the fixt Stars as so many vast Oceans of Flame, that are each of them attended with a different Sett of Planets, and still discover new Firmaments and new Lights, that are sunk farther in those unfathomable Depths of *Ether*, so

as not to be seen by the strongest of our Telescopes, we are lost in such a Labyrinth of Suns and Worlds, and confounded with the Immensity and Magnificence of Nature.

Nothing is more pleasant to the Fancy, than to enlarge it self, by Degrees, in its Contemplation of the various Proportions which its several Objects bear to each other, when it compares the Body of Man to the Bulk of the whole Earth, the Earth to the Circle it describes round the Sun, that Circle to the Sphere of the fixt Stars, the Sphere of the fixt Stars to the Circuit of the whole Creation, the whole Creation it self to the Infinite Space that is every where diffused about it; or when the Imagination works downward, and considers the Bulk of a Human Body, in respect of an Animal, a hundred times less than a Mite, the particular Limbs of such an Animal, the different Springs which actuate the Limbs, the Spirits which set these Springs a going, and the proportionable Minuteness of these several Parts, before they have arrived at their full Growth and Perfection. But if, after all this, we take the least Particle of these Animal Spirits, and consider its Capacity of being wrought into a World, that shall contain within those narrow Dimensions a Heaven and Earth, Stars and Planets, and every different Species of living Creatures, in the same Analogy and Proportion they bear to each other in our own Universe; such a Speculation, by reason of its Nicety, appears ridiculous to those who have not turned their Thoughts that way, tho', at the same time, it is founded on no less than the Evidence of a Demonstration.[6] Nay, we might yet carry it farther, and discover in the smallest Particle of this little World, a new inexhausted Fund of Matter, capable of being spun out into another Universe.

I have dwelt the longer on this Subject, because I think it may shew us the proper Limits, as well as the Defectiveness, of our Imagination; how it is confined to a very small Quantity of Space, and immediately stopt in its Operations, when it endeavours to take in any thing that is very great, or very little. Let a Man try to conceive the different Bulk of an Animal, which is twenty, from another which is a hundred times less than a Mite, or to compare, in his Thoughts, a length of a thousand Diameters of the Earth, with that of a Million, and he will quickly find that he has no different Measures in his Mind, adjusted to such extraordinary Degrees of Grandeur or Minuteness.

---

2. insensibly: imperceptibly. **3. Philosophy:** science. **4. Glasses:** telescopes and microscopes. **5. Axles:** *Axle* is the old word for *axis.*

6. Demonstration: practical proof.

The Understanding, indeed, opens an infinite Space on every side of us, but the Imagination, after a few faint Efforts, is immediately at a stand, and finds her self swallowed up in the Immensity of the Void that surrounds it: Our Reason can pursue a Particle of Matter through an infinite variety of Divisions, but the Fancy soon loses sight of it, and feels in it self a kind of Chasm, that wants to be filled with Matter of a more sensible Bulk.[7] We can neither widen nor contract the Faculty to the Dimensions of either Extreme: The Object is too big for our Capacity, when we would comprehend the Circumference of a World, and dwindles into nothing, when we endeavour after the Idea of an Atome.

It is possible this Defect of Imagination may not be in the Soul it self, but as it acts in Conjunction with the Body. Perhaps there may not be room in the Brain for such a variety of Impressions, or the Animal Spirits may be incapable of figuring[8] them in such a manner, as is necessary to excite so very large or very minute Ideas. However it be, we may well suppose that Beings of a higher Nature very much excell us in this respect, as it is probable the Soul of Man will be infinitely more perfect hereafter[9] in this Faculty, as well as in all the rest; insomuch that, perhaps, the Imagination will be able to keep Pace with the Understanding, and to form in it self distinct Ideas of all the different Modes and Quantities of Space.

NO. 421

Thursday, July 3, 1712

Ignotis errare locis, ignota videre
Flumina gaudebat; studio minuente laborem.[1]

Ov.

THE Pleasures of the Imagination are not wholly confined to such particular Authors as are conversant in material Objects, but are often to be met with among the Polite Masters of Morality, Criticism, and other Speculations abstracted from Matter; who, though they do not directly treat of the visible Parts of Nature, often draw from them their Similitudes, Metaphors, and Allegories. By these Allusions a Truth in the Understanding is as it were reflected by the Imagination; we are able to see something like Colour and Shape in a Notion, and to discover a Scheme of Thoughts traced out upon Matter. And here the Mind receives a great deal of Satisfaction, and has two of its Faculties gratified at the same time, while the Fancy is busy in copying after the Understanding, and transcribing Ideas out of the Intellectual World into the Material.

The Great Art of a Writer shews it self in the Choice of pleasing Allusions, which are generally to be taken from the *great* or *beautiful* Works of Art or Nature; for though whatever is New or Uncommon is apt to delight the Imagination, the chief Design of an Allusion being to illustrate and explain the Passages of an Author, it should be always borrowed from what is more known and common, than the Passages which are to be explained.

Allegories, when well chosen, are like so many Tracks of Light in a Discourse, that make every thing about them clear and beautiful. A noble Metaphor, when it is placed to an Advantage, casts a kind of Glory round it, and darts a Lustre through a whole Sentence: These different Kinds of Allusion are but so many different Manners of Similitude, and, that they may please the Imagination, the Likeness ought to be very exact, or very agreeable, as we love to see a Picture where the Resemblance is just, or the Posture and Air graceful. But we often find eminent Writers very faulty in this respect; great Scholars are apt to fetch their Comparisons and Allusions from the Sciences in which they are most conversant, so that a Man may see the Compass of their Learning in a Treatise on the most indifferent[2] Subject. I have read a Discourse upon Love, which none but a profound Chymist could understand, and have heard many a Sermon that should only have been preached before a Congregation of *Cartesians*. On the contrary, your Men of Business usually have recourse to such Instances as are too mean and familiar. They are for drawing the Reader into a Game of Chess or Tennis, or for leading him from Shop to Shop, in the Cant of particular Trades and Employments. It is certain, there may be found an infinite Variety of very agreeable Allusions in both these kinds, but, for the generality, the most entertaining ones lie in the Works of Nature, which are Obvious to all Capacities, and more delightful than what is to be found in Arts and Sciences.

---

7. **sensible Bulk:** sensuous embodiment. 8. **figuring:** picturing. 9. **hereafter:** i.e., in the Hereafter. *Number 421.* 1. **Ignotis . . . laborem:** "delighting to wander in unknown lands and to see strange rivers, his eagerness making light of toil" (Ovid, *Metamorphoses*, IV. 294–95 [Loeb translation]).

2. **indifferent:** inconsequential.

It is this Talent of affecting the Imagination, that gives an Embellishment to good Sense, and makes one Man's Compositions more agreeable than another's. It setts off all Writings in general, but is the very Life and highest Perfection of Poetry. Where it shines in an Eminent Degree, it has preserved several Poems for many Ages, that have nothing else to recommend them; and where all the other Beauties are present, the Work appears dry and insipid, if this single one be wanting. It has something in it like Creation; It bestows a kind of Existence, and draws up to the Reader's View, several Objects which are not to be found in Being. It makes Additions to Nature, and gives a greater variety to God's Works. In a word, it is able to beautifie and adorn the most illustrious Scenes in the Universe, or to fill the Mind with more glorious Shows and Apparitions, than can be found in any Part of it.

We have now discovered[3] the several Originals of those Pleasures that gratifie the Fancy; and here, perhaps, it would not be very difficult to cast under their proper Heads those contrary Objects, which are apt to fill it with Distaste and Terrour; for the Imagination is as liable to Pain as Pleasure. When the Brain is hurt by any Accident, or the Mind disordered by Dreams or Sickness, the Fancy is over-run with wild dismal Ideas, and terrified with a thousand hideous Monsters of its own framing.

> *Eumenidum veluti demens videt Agmina Pentheus,*
> *Et solem geminum, & duplices se ostendere Thebas.*
> *Aut Agamemnonius scenis agitatus Orestes,*
> *Armatam facibus matrem & serpentibus atris*
> *Cum videt, ultricesque sedent in limine Diræ.*[4]
>   VIR.

There is not a Sight in Nature so mortifying as that of a Distracted Person, when his Imagination is troubled, and his whole Soul disordered and confused. *Babylon* in Ruins is not so melancholly a Spectacle. But to quit so disagreeable a Subject, I shall only

consider, by way of Conclusion, what an infinite Advantage this Faculty gives an Almighty Being over the Soul of Man, and how great a measure of Happiness or Misery we are capable of receiving from the Imagination only.

We have already seen the Influence that one Man has over the Fancy of another, and with what Ease he conveys into it a Variety of Imagery; how great a Power then may we suppose lodged in him, who knows all the ways of affecting the Imagination, who can infuse what Ideas he pleases, and fill those Ideas with Terrour and Delight to what Degree he thinks fit? He can excite Images in the Mind, without the help of Words, and make Scenes rise up before us and seem present to the Eye, without the Assistance of Bodies or Exterior Objects. He can transport the Imagination with such beautiful and glorious Visions, as cannot possibly enter into our present Conceptions, or haunt it with such ghastly Spectres and Apparitions, as would make us hope for Annihilation, and think Existence no better than a Curse. In short, he can so exquisitely ravish or torture the Soul through this single Faculty, as might suffice to make up the whole Heaven or Hell of any finite Being.

This Essay on the Pleasures of the Imagination having been published in separate Papers, I shall conclude it with a Table of the principal Contents in each Paper.

The CONTENTS.

---

3. discovered: disclosed. **4. Eumenidum . . . Diræ:**

Like *Pentheus*, when distracted with his Fear,
He saw two Suns, and double *Thebes* appear:
Or mad *Orestes*, when his Mother's Ghost
Full in his Face, infernal Torches tost;
And shook her snaky locks: He shuns the sight,
Flies o're the Stage, surpris'd with mortal fright;
The Furies guard the Door; and intercept his flight.
(*Aeneid*, IV. 469–73; for *videt* read *fugit* [Dryden's translation,
                                        IV. 681–87])

PAPER III.

Why the Necessary Cause *of our being pleased with what is* Great, New *or* Beautiful, *unknown. Why the* Final Cause *more known and more useful. The Final Cause of our being pleased with what is* Great. *The Final Cause of our being pleased with what is* New. *The Final Cause of our being pleased with what is* Beautiful *in our own* Species. *The Final Cause of our being pleased with what is* Beautiful *in general.*

PAPER IV.

The Works of Nature *more pleasant to the Imagination than those of Art. The Works of Nature still more pleasant, the more they* resemble *those of Art. The Works of Art more pleasant, the more they* resemble *those of Nature. Our* English Plantations *and* Gardens *considered in the foregoing Light.*

PAPER V.

Of Architecture *as it affects the Imagination.* Greatness *in Architecture relates either to the* Bulk *or to the* Manner. *Greatness of Bulk in the* Ancient Oriental Buildings. *The ancient Accounts of these Buildings confirmed, 1. From the Advantages, for raising such Works, in the first Ages of the World and in the Eastern Climates: 2. From several of them which are still* Extant. *Instances how* Greatness *of* Manner *affects the Imagination. A* French Author's *Observation on this Subject. Why Concave and Convex Figures give a Greatness of Manner to Works of Architecture. Every thing that pleases the Imagination in Architecture is either* Great, Beautiful *or* New.

PAPER VI.

The Secondary Pleasures *of the Imagination. The several Sources of these Pleasures (Statuary, Painting, Description and Musick) compared together. The* Final Cause *of our receiving Pleasure from these several Sources. Of Descriptions in Particular. The Power of* Words *over the Imagination. Why one Reader more pleased with Descriptions than another.*

PAPER VII.

How a whole Sett of Ideas Hang *together, &c: A Natural Cause assigned for it. How to perfect the Imagination of a Writer. Who among the* Ancient Poets *had this*

Faculty in its greatest Perfection. Homer *excelled in Imagining what is* Great; Virgil *in Imagining what is* Beautiful; Ovid *in Imagining what is* New. *Our own Country-man* Milton, *very perfect in all three respects.*

PAPER VIII.

Why any thing that is unpleasant *to behold, pleases the Imagination when well Described. Why the Imagination receives a more Exquisite Pleasure from the Description of what is* Great, New, *or* Beautiful. *This Pleasure still heightened, if what is described raises* Passion *in the Mind. Disagreeable* Passions *pleasing when raised by apt Descriptions. Why* Terrour *and Grief are pleasing to the Mind, when excited by Descriptions. A particular Advantage the Writers in Poetry and Fiction have to please the Imagination. What Liberties are allowed them.*

PAPER IX.

Of that kind of Poetry which Mr. Dryden *calls the* Fairy-way of Writing. *How a Poet should be Qualified for it. The Pleasures of the Imagination that arise from it. In this respect, why the* Moderns *excell the* Ancients. *Why the* English *excell the* Moderns. *Who the Best among the* English. *Of* Emblematical[5] *Persons.*

PAPER X.

What Authors please the Imagination who have nothing *to do with Fiction. How* History *pleases the Imagination. How the* Authors of the New Philosophy *please the Imagination. The Bounds and Defects of the Imagination. Whether these Defects are* Essential *to the Imagination.*

PAPER XI.

How those please the Imagination who treat of Subjects abstracted *from Matter, by Allusions taken from it. What Allusions most pleasing to the Imagination. Great Writers how Faulty in this respect. Of the Art of Imagining in General. The Imagination capable of Pain as well as Pleasure. In what Degree the Imagination is capable either of Pain or Pleasure.*

5. Emblematical: allegorical.

Jonathan Swift

1667–1745

Jonathan Swift was born in Dublin on November 30, 1667, seven months after the death of his father, who had settled in Ireland at the time of the Restoration. His paternal grandfather, the Reverend Thomas Swift, was an Anglican who had suffered under the Puritans, while his maternal grandfather, the Reverend James Ericke, was a Puritan who had suffered under the Anglicans. Swift was to take the paternal line in working out his intellectual and spiritual salvation, and although what *he* suffered cannot be called persecution, it was perhaps something worse: a profound sense of alienation from his world, which his powerful imagination only succeeded in confirming.

Always a kind of displaced person—an Englishman by blood living among Irishmen, an Anglican by choice surrounded by Roman Catholics or, in his own diocese, Presbyterians—Swift made an ominous start in life when he was snatched from his cradle by a loving but misguided nurse, who carried him to Whitehaven, where he remained separated from his mother for three years. From the age of six, Swift (now restored to Dublin) attended the grammar school in Kilkenny, while his mother went to live with her sister in Leicester. Around this time he appears to have become the ward of his uncles. In 1682 he entered Trinity College, Dublin, where, according to his autobiography (a fragment written in the third person), "by the ill treatment of his nearest relations, he was so discouraged and sunk in his spirits, that he too much neglected some parts of his academic studyes." The narrative goes on to belittle his scholastic achievement and the worth of the *speciali gratia* degree he took, but he seems to have exaggerated the deficiency of the one and the stigma of the other. As one might have expected of him, he did best in language and literature and worst in philosophy and formal rhetoric.

In 1689, when the ousted King James was advancing toward Dublin to establish a base of operations for the recovery of the throne, the authorities of Trinity College permitted a general evacuation. Swift, who by this time had nearly satisfied the residence requirement for the master's degree, left to join his mother in Leicester. As a result of his family's connections, Swift's life now took a decisive turn. Sir William Temple, son of the benefactor of Swift's family in Ireland, invited him to Moor Park, near Farnham in Surrey, to serve as his secretary. Residing at Moor Park for ten years off and on, Swift was to acquire an education in humane letters, a knowledge of court affairs, a hope—never realized—for preferment in England,

and a woman to love. The woman was Esther Johnson; known as Stella, she was but an eight-year-old girl at the time of Swift's arrival at Moor Park. The daughter of Temple's housekeeper (the evidence for the claim—then and now—that she was also Temple's daughter is unconvincing), she seems to have enjoyed a privileged status in the household, perhaps because Temple's own daughter had died a few years before. The household was large, consisting of Temple and his distinguished wife, Dorothy Osborne; his sister Martha, Lady Giffard; Lady Temple's poor cousin Rebecca Dingley; and Temple's widowed daughter-in-law, her mother, and her children. Irregular as it may have been, it was the closest thing to a family that Swift was ever to enjoy. Later, after Temple's death, he settled Stella and Mrs. Dingley in Ireland, and to the end of Stella's life he found no lasting home away from hers.

Swift's original appointment as Temple's secretary was probably intended by both parties as a temporary expedient. In 1690 Swift followed King William to Ireland on his expedition to wrest the country from the clutches of King James. Evidently he was hopeful of securing, through Temple's court connections, a place under the new regime. Nothing materialized, however, but his pindaric *Ode to the King. On His Irish Expedition* (1691), a poem that, in the panegyric vein, is typical of Swift's earliest verse. In December, 1691, Swift was back at Moor Park, and it was not long before the balance of dependency shifted to him. So it may be inferred at least from the fact that Temple did little or nothing to foster an independent career for his literary aide, who, thrown upon his own resources, entered Oxford and took a master's degree in July, 1692, as a step toward ordination. Swift nevertheless remained at Moor Park for over two more years before leaving in October, 1694, to become deacon, and several months later priest, in Dublin. Although Temple was "extreme angry" at Swift's departure, he yielded to his humble appeal for the letter of recommendation that proved necessary for his ordination. In February, Swift became Prebendary of Kilroot in the Cathedral of Connor, a situation that left practically everything to be desired. The parishes were isolated, the churches in disrepair, and—what must have been worst of all to him—the parishioners were mostly Presbyterians of Scottish descent. He lasted a year and a few months, and though he did not resign the prebend until 1698, he returned to Moor Park around June of 1696.

If Kilroot was a professional disappointment, it was matched by a personal trauma. Swift fell in love—with Jane "Varina" Waring, the daughter of the Archdeacon of Dromore—and while he eventually got over her, he never got over *it*. Varina met Swift's passion with hesitation; her reaction prompted a remarkable love letter, or rather lecture on April 29, 1696, containing a marriage proposal which if hortatory was at least possible to accept. It was refused, and four years later, on May 4, 1700, Swift wrote another equally remarkable letter in response to her renewal of negotiations, this time laying down terms that were calculated only to affront. The man of feeling had given way to the satirist; Swift was never again to commit himself unguardedly to the expression of passionate love.

Back at Moor Park as Temple's secretary, Swift was engaged primarily in preparing Temple's papers for publication. Fortunately these editorial labors left time for the exercise of his original genius. The brilliant satire on the corruptions in religion and learning, *A Tale of a Tub*, probably first conceived at Kilroot, was brought to completion during these years and was published in 1704 in a volume that also contained

The Battle of the Books, Swift's mock-epic advocacy of Temple's side in the controversy over the Ancients and the Moderns, and *The Mechanical Operation of the Spirit,* Swift's concise statement of what the *Tale* was all about.

Temple died in January, 1699, leaving Swift a legacy of one hundred pounds and a career still to find. Accepting a post as chaplain to the Earl of Berkeley, who was bound for Ireland as a Lord Justice, Swift was again to be disappointed of his hopes. The deanery of Derry was vacant, he wanted it, it was given to another, and he had to settle for the vicarship of Laracor and a prebend of St. Patrick's. But a new and brighter prospect appeared on the horizon, and it came ironically with the fall of the Whigs to whom he had looked for preferment. In 1701 the triumphant Tory government, in the fashion of the times, sought to dispose of its predecessors (and always potential successors), Somers, Orford, and Halifax, by impeachment proceedings. Swift rushed to their defense with an allegorical *Discourse of the Contests and Dissensions Between the Nobles and Commons in Athens and Rome,* a work that marks the beginning of his career as a political polemicist.

Essentially Swift was a moderate in his politics, and he sought to mediate between the extreme factions of both parties. He adhered to the Revolutionary Settlement and subscribed to the doctrine of Parliamentary authority in determining the succession of the monarchy, in contrast to the doctrine of the divine right of kings. On the other hand, as a High-Churchman, he believed in the right of the state to require adherence to the established religion as a condition for holding political office, and thus he was an inveterate opponent of occasional conformity, a practice that opened the door to Dissenters. Since the Whigs seemed to be the general protectors of the (Protestant) succession at the same time they sought to broaden the base of their power by admitting the dissenting element, and since the Tories seemed to be the protectors of the Church of England at the same time many of them were at least ideologically committed to the succession of the Stuart line, even though it took a Catholic turn with James, Swift was not unperplexed in his allegiance. At any rate, with the death of King William in March, 1702, Swift came to England in anticipation of a return of the Whigs to power, but though he had ingratiated himself with his *Discourse,* no preferment was forthcoming. In the winter of 1703 he was again in London, arranging for the publication of *A Tale of a Tub* and becoming acquainted with Prior, Addison, Steele, and Vanbrugh. For the next few years he remained in Ireland, where if solace was to be found, it was doubtless in the company of Stella chiefly.

In November, 1707, Swift was commissioned by Archbishop King to solicit the Queen's Bounty for a remission of the First Fruits for the Church of Ireland. The mission failed, as did Swift's hope for the chaplaincy to the new Lord Lieutenant of Ireland, the Whig leader Lord Wharton, who rapidly rose to the top of Swift's list of knaves. He remained in London, nevertheless, for a year and a half, strengthening his reputation as a wit (especially by the *Bickerstaff Papers*) and confirming his friendship with the Whig circle of writers (especially by helping Steele launch *The Tatler*). At the same time, however, he was producing four tracts on religion—*Sentiments of a Church of England Man, Abolishing Christianity, A Project for the Advancement of Religion,* and *A Letter Concerning the Sacramental Test*—which, while ostensibly neutral politically, in one way or another managed to locate the threats to religion and morality in Whig policies.

Swift was now psychologically ready for the political change that was about to take place. In the summer of 1710, the Whigs fell, and the Tories under the leadership of Harley and St. John took over the reins of government. Swift, who had been back in Ireland for a year, was again sent to apply for the remission of the First Fruits, and this time he succeeded. The Tories did not make the same mistake as the Whigs: they promptly adopted Swift and put him to work as their chief propagandist. In October he assumed the editorship of their journal, *The Examiner*, with the assignment of justifying the change in ministry, of preparing the public for the peace that the Tory party was working (and secretly negotiating) for, and of allaying fears that the Tories would bring back the Pretender and popery. He continued to write for *The Examiner* until June, 1711, and in November of that year he capped these efforts with a pamphlet, *The Conduct of the Allies*, which sought to expose the mercenary motives of the war party. Other pamphlets designed to serve the cause of the Tory ministry followed in 1712, two of them—*A Letter to the October Club* and *A Letter to a Whig Lord*—aimed at winning adherents to the Harleian (and Swiftian) policy of moderation. During the last months of this year Swift started writing *The History of the Last Session of Parliament and of the Peace of Utrecht*, which the ministry neglected to promote in time for its own use; it was not published until after Swift's death, and then under the better-known title *The History of the Four Last Years of the Queen*.

For his services to the Tory administration Swift no doubt expected the fulfillment of his old ambition—preferment in England. But apparently his powerful friends were not powerful enough to overcome the resentment of the Queen, which was said to have originated with the publication of *A Tale of a Tub* (widely regarded as scandalous, since it came from the pen of a clergyman), or the antipathy of the Queen's favorite, the Duchess of Somerset, who never forgave Swift for publishing that part of Temple's *Memoirs* which reflected on the character of her uncle, Lord Essex. Instead, he was to receive, through the gift of the Duke of Ormond, the deanery of St. Patrick's in Dublin, a post of considerable prestige, though Swift could not "feel joy at passing my days in Ireland." The Queen died on August 1, 1714, Whig power became entrenched, and Swift's chances for preferment in England were doomed.

The period from September, 1710, when Swift went to England on his second mission for the Church of Ireland, to June, 1713, when he returned to Dublin to be installed as Dean of St. Patrick's, is intimately recorded in the famous *Journal to Stella* (actually letters written to both Esther Johnson and Rebecca Dingley). But another woman had entered Swift's life during his previous stay in England between 1707 and 1709, and by this time the relationship had become serious. Esther "Vanessa" Vanhomrigh, of Dutch extraction, was born in Ireland but moved to London with her mother and other family after her father's death. Swift was a frequent visitor at their house, where, as with Stella, he adopted the role of intimate mentor. Unhappily, as their letters show, Vanessa's admiration turned to passion, which succeeded only in stiffening Swift's reserve. The comedy Swift makes of the affair in his *Cadenus to Vanessa* (apparently composed for her eyes alone) could not have been wholly appreciated. As Ricardo Quintana observes, "It is tragically clear that Vanessa was unable to accept the rôle created for her: there is little to indicate that Stella ever wanted to change hers."

Resigned to permanent exile in Ireland, Swift began in 1720 to engage himself more vigorously in Irish causes, though the character of Irish patriot was not one he relished. As he later wrote to Pope, "What I do is owing to perfect rage and resentment, and the mortifying sight of slavery, folly, and baseness about me, among which I am forced to live." His task was the exasperating one of rousing a people to look after its own interests, and Swift undertook it sometimes in the implicitly hopeful voice of the straightforward expositor of abuses and remedies and sometimes in the implicitly desperate voice of the ironic endorser of the *status quo*. The causes he took up and shouldered throughout the remainder of his productive life were mainly the improvement of Irish agriculture and manufacture and the encouragement of home consumption, the protection of the currency against the threats of devaluation from English coinages, the protection of the rights of the clergy, and the care of the poor. The most famous—and best—specimens of his nationalistic essays are *The Drapier's Letters* (1724–25) and *A Modest Proposal* (1729), but the condition of Ireland must have been a primary inspiration for his monumental satire on intellectual, moral, and spiritual subservience, *Gulliver's Travels*, which Swift started to write between 1720 and 1721 and published in 1726. The passage from the letter to Pope, quoted above, might well have come from the pen of Gulliver returned from his travels.

In April, 1727, Swift returned to England to assist Pope in the preparation of their joint *Miscellanies*, which appeared in three installments: 1727, 1728, and 1732. The illness he had suffered from his early years at Moor Park, an affliction of the inner ear causing dizziness and deafness (Ménière's disease, or labyrinthine vertigo), grew worse and sent him back to Dublin in September. In January Stella died. Swift, now in his sixties, continued to occupy himself with Irish affairs and such private pastimes as his *Complete Collection of Genteel Conversation* (1738) and *Directions to Servants* (1745). He also produced in these years a considerable body of verse in a wide range of tone and significance; the most resonant are perhaps the *Verses on the Death of Dr. Swift* (1731) and *On Poetry: A Rapsody* (1733). In 1734 he was busy overseeing, while affecting to disown, the edition of his collected works that George Faulkner was printing in Dublin. It ran to eight volumes by 1742. In January, 1735, he arranged for a grant of land in Oxmantown Green to establish the site for an insane asylum (later named St. Patrick's Hospital) he had already provided for in his will. As his spokesman says at the end of *Verses on the Death of Dr. Swift*:

> "HE gave the little Wealth he had,
> To build a House for Fools and Mad:
> And shew'd by one satyric Touch,
> No Nation wanted it so much."

In August, 1742, after a period of gradual decline, he was himself declared insane. He died on October 19, 1745, and was buried in St. Patrick's Cathedral, near Stella.

For the publication of his *Tale of a Tub* Swift composed two dedications, one to Lord Somers and the other to "His Royal Highness, Prince Posterity." The latter proved the more munificent patron, and Swift's achievements have been rewarded by both a constant reading public and the devotion of scholars. In our own time especially—

Swift's preference for the Ancients over the Moderns notwithstanding—the preferments have been handsomely given. Sir Harold Williams's edition of the *Poems* (3 vols., 1937, 1958) and the *Journal to Stella* (2 vols., 1948), Herbert Davis's edition of the *Prose Works* (13 vols., 1939–59), and Williams's edition of the *Correspondence* (5 vols., 1963–65) are imposing works of textual and editorial scholarship. In addition there have been numerous important biographical and critical studies, of which only a selection can be given here (we omit particularly those studies, however important, that concentrate on individual works): Ricardo Quintana, *The Mind and Art of Jonathan Swift* (1936, 1953); Herbert Davis, *The Satire of Jonathan Swift* (1947); J. M. Bullitt, *Jonathan Swift and the Anatomy of Satire* (1953); Martin Price, *Swift's Rhetorical Art* (1953); W. B. Ewald, Jr., *The Masks of Jonathan Swift* (1954); L. A. Landa, *Swift and the Church of Ireland* (1954); J. M. Murry, *Jonathan Swift, a Critical Biography* (1954); Irvin Ehrenpreis, *The Personality of Jonathan Swift* (1958) and *Swift: The Man, His Works, and the Age* (3 vols., Vol. I, 1962, Vol. II, 1968); and E. W. Rosenheim, *Swift and the Satirist's Art* (1963). The standard bibliography is now A. H. Scouten's revision of H. Teerink's *A Bibliography of the Writings of Jonathan Swift* (1963). Useful guides to Swift scholarship are L. A. Landa and J. E. Tobin's *Jonathan Swift: A List of Critical Studies Published from 1845 to 1945* (1945) and J. J. Stathis's *A Bibliography of Swift Studies, 1945–1965* (1967).

VERSES WROTE IN A LADY'S IVORY TABLE-BOOK°

Anno. 1698.

The text is that of the first printing, in *Miscellanies in Prose and Verse* (1711). The poem is dated 1706 in Faulkner's edition of Swift's *Works* (1735).

PERUSE my Leaves thro' ev'ry Part,
And think thou seest my owners Heart,
Scrawl'd o'er with Trifles thus, and quite
As hard, as senseless, and as light:
Expos'd to every Coxcomb's Eyes,
But hid with Caution from the Wise.

Here you may read (*Dear Charming Saint*)
Beneath (*A new Receit° for Paint°*)
Here in Beau-spelling (*tru tel deth*)
There in her own (*far an el breth*) 10
Here (*lovely Nymph pronounce my doom*)
There (*A safe way to use Perfume*)
Here, a Page fill'd with Billet Doux;
On t' other side (*laid out° for Shoes*)
(*Madam, I dye without your Grace*)
(Item, *for half a Yard of Lace*.)
Who that had Wit would place it here,
For every peeping Fop to Jear.°
To think that your Brains Issue is
Expos'd to th' Excrement of his,° 20
In power of Spittle and a Clout°
When e're he please to blot it out;
And then to heighten the Disgrace
Clap his own Nonsense in the place.
Whoe're expects to hold his part°
In such a Book and such a Heart,

8. **Receit:** recipe. **Paint:** cosmetics. 14. **laid out:** spent. 18. **Jear:** jeer. 19–20. **To . . . his:** This couplet was omitted in succeeding editions. *Excrement* here means "excretion"; specifically, the "Spittle" of the next line. 21. **Clout:** cloth. 25. **hold his part:** hold his own.

VERSES WROTE IN A LADY'S IVORY TABLE-BOOK. **Table-Book:** memorandum book.

If he be Wealthy and a Fool
Is in all Points the fittest Tool,
Of whom it may be justly said,
He's a Gold Pencil tipt with Lead.   30

A DESCRIPTION
OF THE MORNING

❦

The text is that of the first printing, in *The Tatler*, No. 9
(April 30, 1709), with variants incorporated from
Faulkner's edition of Swift's *Works* (1735).

❦

Now hardly° here and there a Hackney-Coach°
Appearing, show'd the Ruddy Morn's Approach.
Now *Betty*° from her Master's Bed had flown,
And softly stole to discompose her own.
The Slipshod 'Prentice from his Master's Dore,
Had par'd° the Dirt, and sprinkled round the Floor.
Now *Moll* had whirl'd her Mop with dext'rous Airs,
Prepar'd to scrub the Entry and the Stairs.
The Youth with Broomy Stumps began to trace   9
The Kennel Edge, where Wheels had worn the Place.°
The Smallcoal-Man° was heard with Cadence deep,
Till drown'd in shriller Notes of Chimney-sweep.
Duns° at his Lordship's Gate began to meet,
And Brickdust° *Moll* had scream'd through half the
      Street.
The Turn-key now his Flock returning sees,
Duly let out a'Nights to steal for Fees.°
The watchful Bayliffs take their silent Stands;°
And School-boys lag with Satchels in their Hands.°

A DESCRIPTION OF THE MORNING. **1. hardly:** violently. **Hackney-Coach:** a hired four-wheeled coach, drawn by two
horses and seating six. **3. Betty:** a stock name for a maidservant. **6. par'd:** sliced off (as turf) or perhaps, simply, reduced.
9–10. The Youth . . . Place: [Swift's note] *To find old Nails.*
[Such scavengers of the gutter were called kennel-rakers.] **11.
Smallcoal-Man:** a vendor of small pieces of coal or charcoal.
13. Duns: creditors, bill collectors. **14. Brickdust:** powdered
brick, used for cleaning knives. **15–16. The Turn-key . . .
Fees:** The jailer lets his prisoners out at night to steal so that
they can pay the fees he exacts for their comforts. **17.
Stands:** stations. **18. And . . . Hands:** Cf. Jacques'
second "age of man" in *As You Like It*, II. vii. 145–47:

> Then the whining schoolboy, with his satchel
> And shining morning face, creeping like snail
> Unwillingly to school.

A DESCRIPTION
OF A CITY SHOWER

❦

The text is that of the first printing, in *The Tatler*, No.
238 (October 17, 1710), with variants from Faulkner's
edition of Swift's *Works* (1735). When the issue of *The
Tatler* appeared, Swift wrote in the *Journal to Stella*,
"This day came out the *Tatler* made up wholly of my
Shower, and a preface to it. They say 'tis the best thing
I ever writ, and I think so too." Ten days later, Rowe
and Prior "both fell commending my *Shower* beyond
any thing that has been written of the kind: there never
was such a Shower since Danaë's, &c."

❦

Careful Observers may fortel the Hour,
(By sure Prognosticks) when to dread a Shower:
While Rain depends,° the pensive Cat gives o'er
Her Frolicks, and pursues her Tail no more.
Returning Home at Night, you'll find the Sink°
Strike your offended Sense with double Stink;
If you be wise, then go not far to dine,
You'll spend in Coach-Hire more than save in Wine.
A coming Shower your shooting Corns° presage,
Old Aches° throb, your hollow Tooth will rage.   10
Sauntring in Coffee-house is *Dulman* seen,
He damns the Climate, and complains of Spleen.°

Mean while the *South*° rising with dabbled Wings,
A sable Cloud athwart the Welkin° flings,
That swill'd more Liquor than it could contain,
And, like a Drunkard, gives it up again.
Brisk *Susan* whips her Linen from the Rope,°
While the first drizz'ling Shower is born aslope:°
Such is that sprinkling which some careless Quean°
Flirts° on you from her Mop, but not so clean: 20
You fly, invoke the Gods, then turning, stop
To rail; she singing, still whirls on her Mop.

A DESCRIPTION OF A CITY SHOWER. **3. depends:** is impending
5. Sink: sewer. **9. your . . . Corns:** the shooting pains in
your corns. **10. Aches:** pronounced "aitches." **12. Spleen:**
melancholy. **13. the South:** the south wind. **14. Welkin:** sky.
See Gay, *The Shepherd's Week*, "Monday," note to l. 3, later
in Part Two. **17. whips . . . Rope:** gathers her laundry
quickly from the clothesline. **18. is . . . aslope:** falls
slantingly. **19. Quean:** wench. **20. Flirts:** To "flirt" is to
propel with a jerk.

Nor yet the Dust had shun'd th' unequal Strife,
But, aided by the Wind, fought still for Life;
And wafted with its Foe, by violent Gust,
'Twas doubtful which was Rain, and which was
    Dust.°
Ah! Where must needy Poet seek for Aid,
When Dust and Rain at once his Coat invade;
Sole Coat, where Dust cemented by the Rain,
Erects the Nap, and leaves a cloudy Stain.   30

   Now in contiguous° Drops the Flood comes down,
Threat'ning with Deluge this *Devoted°* Town:
To Shops in Crowds the daggled° Females fly,
Pretend to cheapen° Goods, but nothing buy.
The Templer° spruce, while every Spout's a-broach,°
Stays till 'tis fair, yet seems to call a Coach:
The tuck'd-up Sempstress walks with hasty Strides,
While Streams run down her oil'd° Umbrella's Sides.
Here various Kinds, by various Fortunes led,
Commence Acquaintance underneath a Shed,   40
Triumphant Tories, and desponding Whigs,°
Forget their Feuds, and join to save their Wigs:
Box'd in a Chair° the Beau impatient sits,
While Spouts run clatt'ring o'er the Roof by Fits,
And ever and anon with frightful Din
The Leather° sounds, he trembles from within.
So when *Troy* Chair-men bore the Wooden Steed,
Pregnant with *Greeks*, impatient to be freed,
(Those Bully *Greeks*, who, as the Moderns do,
Instead of paying Chair-men, run them thro'°)   50
Laoco'n struck the Outside with his Spear,°
And each imprison'd Hero quak'd for Fear.

   Now from all Parts the swelling Kennels flow,
And bear their Trophies with them as they go:
Filths of all Hues and Odors seem to tell
What Streets they sail'd from, by the Sight and Smell.
They, as each Torrent drives, with rapid Force

From *Smithfield°* or *St. 'Pulchre's°* shape their Course,
And in huge Confluent° join'd at *Snow-Hill°* Ridge,
Fall from the *Conduit* prone° to *Holborn-Bridge.°*   60
Sweepings from Butchers Stalls, Dung, Guts and
    Blood,
Drown'd Puppies, stinking Sprats, all drench'd in
    Mud,
Dead Cats and Turnep-Tops come tumbling
    down the Flood.°

CADENUS AND VANESSA

The text is from *Miscellanies. The Last Volume* (1727),
with Swift's own corrections from his copy of the
Miscellanies, variants from Faulkner's edition of Swift's
Works (1735), and Swift's corrections from his copy of
Faulkner's edition.

The date of composition of the poem has been
debated. Swift himself assigned it to 1713 in the *Miscellanies*,
and other references of his would fix it about that
time or a little earlier. He was not installed as Dean of
St. Patrick's until June, 1713 (*Cadenus* is an anagram for
Decanus); if the poem was written before, the title would
have to be regarded as proleptic. It is also possible, of
course, that the name was introduced in a later revision.
In any case, the purpose of the poem is plain: to deal
with the rising passion of Esther "Vanessa" Vanhomrigh.

THE *Shepherds* and the *Nymphs* were seen
Pleading before the *Cyprian* Queen.°
The Council° for the Fair began,
Accusing that false Creature, *Man*.

26. 'Twas . . . Dust: [Swift's note] *'Twas doubtful which
was Sea, and which was Sky. Garth Disp.* [Read *'Tis, is, and
is* (*The Dispensary*, V. 176).] 31. contiguous: one upon
another. 32. Devoted: doomed. 33. daggled: splashed with
mud. 34. cheapen: bargain for. 35. Templer: member of
the Inner or Middle Temple, the law schools and legal
societies of London. Spout's a-broach: drainpipe is pouring
out water; literally, vented. 38. oil'd: made of oiled silk. 41.
Triumphant . . . Whigs: [Swift's note] *N.B. This was the
first Year of the Earl of* OXFORD's *Ministry.* [The Tory ministry
led by Oxford and Bolingbroke was formed just about the
time Swift's poem was published.] 43. Chair: sedan chair. 46.
Leather: the leather roof. 50. run . . . thro': i.e., with their
swords. 51. Laoco'n . . . Spear: See *Aeneid*, II. 50–53.

58. Smithfield: the market place for cattle, sheep, and
horses. St. 'Pulchre's: St. Sepulchre's Church, on
the north side of the top of Snow Hill. 59. Confluent:
united flow. Snow Hill: extended from the upper
end of the Little Old Bailey to Holborn Bridge. 60.
prone: downward. Holborn-Bridge: which spanned
Fleet ditch. 61–63. Sweepings . . . Flood: [Swift's note]
*These three last lines were intended against that licentious Manner
of modern Poets, in making three Rhimes together, which they call
Triplets; and the last of the three, was two or some Times more
Syllables longer, called an* Alexandrian. *These Triplets and
Alexandrians were brought in by* DRYDEN, *and other Poets in
the Reign of* CHARLES II. *They were the mere Effect of Haste,
Idleness, and Want of Money; and have been wholely avoided by
the best Poets, since these Verses were written.* CADENUS AND
VANESSA. 2. the Cyprian Queen: Aphrodite (Venus). 3.
Council: counsel.

The Brief with weighty Crimes was charg'd,
On which the Pleader much enlarg'd;
That *Cupid* now has lost his Art,
Or blunts the Point of ev'ry Dart;
His Altar now no longer smokes,
His Mother's Aid no Youth invokes: 10
This tempts Free-thinkers to refine,°
And bring in doubt their Pow'r divine;
Now Love is dwindled to Intrigue,
And Marriage grown a Money-League.°
Which Crimes aforesaid (with her Leave)
Were (as he humbly did conceive)
Against our Sov'reign Lady's Peace,
Against the Statutes in that Case,
Against her Dignity and Crown:
Then pray'd an Answer, and sat down.   20

The *Nymphs* with Scorn beheld their Foes:
When the Defendant's Council rose,
And, what no Lawyer ever lack'd,
With Impudence° own'd all the Fact.°
But, what the gentlest Heart would vex,
Laid all the Fault on t' other Sex.
That modern Love is no such Thing
As what those antient Poets sing;
A Fire celestial, chaste, refin'd,
Conceiv'd and kindled in the Mind,   30
Which having found an equal Flame,
Unites, and both become the same,
In different Breasts together burn,
Together both to Ashes turn.
But Women now feel no such Fire,
And only know the gross Desire;
Their Passions move in lower Spheres,
Where-e'er Caprice or Folly steers.
A Dog, a Parrot, or an Ape,
Or some worse Brute in human Shape,   40
Engross the Fancies of the Fair,
The few soft Moments they can spare,
From Visits to receive and pay,
From Scandal, Politicks, and Play,
From Fans, and Flounces, and Brocades,
From Equipage° and Park-Parades,°
From all the thousand Female Toys,
From every Trifle that employs

The out or inside of their Heads,
Between their Toylets and their Beds.   50

In a dull Stream, which moving slow
You hardly see the Current flow,
If a small Breeze obstructs the Course,
It whirls about for Want of Force,
And in its narrow Circle gathers
Nothing but Chaff, and Straws, and Feathers:
The Current of a Female Mind
Stops thus, and turns with ev'ry Wind;
Thus whirling round, together draws
Fools, Fops, and Rakes, for Chaff and Straws. 60
Hence we conclude, no Women's Hearts
Are won by Virtue, Wit, and Parts;°
Nor are the Men of Sense to blame,
For Breasts incapable of Flame;
The Fault must on the *Nymphs* be plac'd,
Grown so corrupted in their Taste.

The Pleader having spoke his best,
Had Witness ready to attest,
Who fairly could on Oath depose,°
When Questions on the Fact arose,   70
That ev'ry Article was true;
Nor further those Deponents knew:°
Therefore he humbly would insist,
The Bill might be with Costs dismist.°

The Cause° appear'd of so much Weight,
That *Venus*, from her Judgment-Seat,
Desir'd them not to talk so loud,
Else she must interpose a Cloud:
For if the Heav'nly Folk should know
These Pleadings in the Courts below,   80
That Mortals here disdain to love;
She ne'er could shew her Face above.
For Gods, their Betters, are too wise
To value that which Men despise.
And then, said she, my Son and I
Must strole in Air 'twixt Land and Sky;
Or else, shut out from Heaven and Earth,
Fly to the Sea, my Place of Birth;°
There live with daggl'd *Mermaids* pent,
And keep on Fish perpetual *Lent*.   90

---

11. **refine:** make subtle arguments. 14. **League:** compact, alliance. 24. **Impudence:** shamelessness. **the Fact:** the crime as charged. 46. **Equipage:** carriages, horses, and attendant servants. **Park-Parades:** assemblies of riders and promenaders in the park.

62. **Parts:** abilities, talents. 69. **depose:** testify. 72. **Nor . . . knew:** Nor did those witnesses know anything to the contrary. 74. **The Bill . . . dismist:** The bill of indictment ought to be dismissed and only the court costs paid. 75. **Cause:** case. 88. **my . . . Birth:** According to one legend, Aphrodite was generated from sea foam containing the genitals of Uranus, which Cronus had cut off and cast away.

But since the Case appear'd so nice,°
She thought it best to take Advice.
The *Muses*, by their King's° Permission,
Tho' Foes to Love, attend the Session,
And on the Right Hand took their Places
In Order; on the Left, the *Graces:*
To whom she might her Doubts propose
On all Emergencies that rose.
The *Muses* oft were seen to frown;
The *Graces* half asham'd look'd down;   100
And 'twas observ'd, there were but few ⎫
Of either Sex, among the Crew,
Whom she or her Assessors° knew. ⎭
The Goddess soon began to see
Things were not ripe for a Decree,
And said she must consult her Books,
The *Lovers Fleta's,*° *Bractons,*° *Cokes.*°
First to a dapper Clerk she beckon'd,
To turn to *Ovid*, Book the Second;°
She then referr'd them to a Place   110
In *Virgil* (*vide Dido*'s Case:°)
As for *Tibullus*'s Reports,°
They never pass'd for Law in Courts;
For *Cowley*'s Briefs, and Pleas of *Waller*,
Still their Authority was smaller.

    There was on both Sides much to say:
She'd hear the Cause another Day,
And so she did, and then a Third,
She heard it—there she kept her Word;
But with Rejoinders and Replies,   120
Long Bills,° and Answers, stuff'd with Lies,
Demur,° Imparlance,° and Essoign,°

The Parties ne'er could Issue join:°
For Sixteen Years the Cause was spun,
And then stood where it first begun.

    Now, gentle *Clio*,° sing or say,
What *Venus* meant by this Delay.
The Goddess much perplex'd in Mind,
To see her Empire thus declin'd,
When first this grand Debate arose   130
Above her Wisdom to compose,°
Conceiv'd a Project in her Head,
To work her Ends; which if it sped,°
Wou'd shew the Merits of the Cause,
Far better than consulting Laws.

    In a glad Hour *Lucina*'s° Aid
Produc'd on Earth a wond'rous Maid,
On whom the Queen of Love was bent
To try a new Experiment:
She threw her Law-books on the Shelf,   140
And thus debated with herself.

    Since Men alledge they ne'er can find
Those Beauties in a Female Mind,
Which raise a Flame that will endure
For ever, uncorrupt and pure;
If 'tis with Reason they complain,
This Infant shall restore my Reign.
I'll search where ev'ry Virtue dwells,
From Courts inclusive, down to Cells,°
What Preachers talk, or Sages write,   150
These I will gather and unite,
And represent them to Mankind
Collected in that Infant's Mind.

    This said, she plucks in Heav'ns high Bow'rs
A Sprig of *Amaranthine*° Flow'rs,
In Nectar thrice infuses Bays,°
Three times refin'd in *Titan*'s Rays:°
Then call the *Graces* to her Aid,
And sprinkles thrice the new-born Maid.
From whence the tender Skin assumes   160
A Sweetness above all Perfumes;
From whence a Cleanliness remains,

---

91. nice: delicate. **93. their King:** Apollo. **103. Assessors:** judicial advisers. **107. Fleta:** *Fleta*, a Latin commentary on English law (*c.* 1290), was edited by John Selden in 1647. **Bractons:** Henry de Bracton (d. 1268) was the author of *De Legibus et Consuetudinibus Angliae*, published by Tottel in 1569. **Cokes:** Sir Edward Coke (1552–1634), the eminent English jurist and author of the *Institutes of the Laws of England* (1628 ff.). **109. Ovid . . . Second:** of *Ars Amatoria*, in which the lover is advised how to hold the affections of his mistress. **111. Dido's Case:** in the fourth book of the *Aeneid*. **112. Tibullus's Reports:** the love poems of the Roman poet Tibullus (*c.* 54–19 B.C.), which are marked by complaints to fickle mistresses. The "Briefs" and "Pleas" of line 114 carry out Swift's conceit. **121. Bills:** written statements of the case. **122. Demur:** (or demurrer) a plea that questions the legality of the claim without denying the facts of the case. **Imparlance:** an extension of time for the purpose (real or alleged) of negotiating an amicable settlement. **Essoign:** (or essoin) an excuse for not appearing in court at the appointed time.

123. Issue join: agree upon the point to be disputed. **126. Clio:** Muse of epic poetry and history. **131. compose:** settle. **133. sped:** prospered. **136. Lucina:** in Roman mythology the goddess who presides over childbirth. **149. From . . . Cells:** including every place, from courts to cells, i.e., even the humblest dwellings. **155. Amaranthine:** everlasting, fadeless. **156. Bays:** bay leaves. **157. Titan's Rays:** Titan (Helios) was the sun god.

Incapable of outward Stains;
From whence that Decency of Mind,
So lovely in the Female Kind,
Where not one careless Thought intrudes,
Less modest than the Speech of Prudes;
Where never Blush was call'd in Aid,
That spurious Virtue in a Maid,
A Virtue but at second-hand;   170
They blush because they understand.

    The *Graces* next wou'd act their Part,
And shew'd but little of their Art;
Their Work was half already done,
The Child with native Beauty shone,
The outward Form no Help requir'd:
Each breathing on her thrice, inspir'd
That gentle, soft, engaging Air,
Which in old Times adorn'd the Fair;
And said, "*Vanessa* be the Name,   180
By which thou shalt be known to Fame:
Vanessa, by the Gods enroll'd:
Her Name on Earth—shall not be told."

    But still the Work was not compleat,
When *Venus* thought on a Deceit:
Drawn by her Doves, away she flies,
And finds out *Pallas*° in the Skies:
Dear *Pallas*, I have been this Morn
To see a lovely Infant born:
A Boy in yonder Isle below,   190
So like my own, without his Bow,
By Beauty cou'd your Heart be won,
You'd swear it is *Apollo*'s Son;
But it shall ne'er be said, a Child
So hopeful, has by me been spoil'd;
I have enough besides to spare,
And give him wholly to your Care.

    Wisdom's above suspecting Wiles:
The Queen of Learning gravely smiles,
Down from *Olympus* comes with Joy,   200
Mistakes *Vanessa* for a Boy;
Then sows within her tender Mind
Seeds long unknown to Womankind,
For manly Bosoms chiefly fit,
The Seeds of Knowledge, Judgment, Wit.
Her Soul was suddenly endu'd°
With Justice, Truth and Fortitude;

With Honour, which no Breath can Stain,
Which Malice must attack in vain;
With open Heart and bounteous Hand: 210
But *Pallas* here was at a Stand;
She knew in our degen'rate Days
Bare Virtue could not live on Praise,
That Meat must be with Money bought;
She therefore, upon second Thought,
Infus'd, yet as it were by Stealth,
Some small Regard for State° and Wealth:
Of which, as she grew up, there stay'd
A Tincture in the prudent Maid:
She manag'd her Estate with Care,   220
Yet lik'd three Footmen to her Chair.
But lest he shou'd neglect his Studies
Like a young Heir, the thrifty Goddess
(For fear young Master shou'd be spoil'd,)
Wou'd use him like a younger Child;
And, after long computing, found
'Twou'd come to just Five Thousand Pound.°

    The Queen of Love was pleas'd, and proud,
To see *Vanessa* thus endow'd;
She doubted not but such a Dame   230
Thro' ev'ry Breast wou'd dart a Flame;
That ev'ry rich and lordly Swain
With Pride wou'd drag about her Chain;°
That Scholars wou'd forsake their Books
To study bright *Vanessa*'s Looks:
As she advanc'd, that Womankind
Wou'd by her Model form their Mind,
And all their Conduct wou'd be try'd
By her, as an unerring Guide.
Offending Daughters oft wou'd hear   240
Vanessa's Praise rung in their Ear:
Miss *Betty*, when she does a Fault,
Lets fall her Knife, or spills the Salt,
Will thus be by her Mother chid,
" 'Tis what *Vanessa* never did."
Thus by the Nymphs and Swains ador'd,
My Pow'r shall be again restor'd,
And happy Lovers bless my Reign—
So *Venus* hop'd, but hop'd in vain.

    For when in time the *Martial Maid*°   250
Found out the Trick that *Venus* play'd,

---

187. **Pallas:** Pallas Athene, the goddess of wisdom. 206.
endu'd: endowed.

217. **State:** property, possessions. 222–27. **But . . . Pound:**
Younger sons, destined to a lesser inheritance, were trained
to some occupation that would augment their income. 233.
drag . . . Chain: submit to his attachment to her. 250. **the**
Martial Maid: Pallas Athene.

She shakes her Helm, she knits her Brows,
And fir'd with Indignation vows,
To-morrow, ere the setting Sun,
She'd all undo, that she had done.

But in the Poets we may find,
A wholesome Law, Time out of mind,
Had been confirm'd by Fate's Decree;
That Gods, of whatso'er Degree,
Resume° not what themselves have giv'n,   260
Or any Brother-God in Heav'n:
Which keeps the Peace among the Gods,
Or they must always be at Odds.
And *Pallas*, if she broke the Laws,
Must yield her Foe the stronger Cause;
A Shame to one so much ador'd
For Wisdom, at *Jove*'s Council-Board.
Besides, she fear'd the Queen of Love
Wou'd meet with better Friends above.
And tho' she must with Grief reflect,   270
To see a Mortal Virgin deck'd
With Graces, hitherto unknown
To Female Breasts, except her own;
Yet she wou'd act as best became
A Goddess of unspotted Fame:
She knew, by Augury Divine,
Venus wou'd fail in her Design:
She study'd well the Point, and found
Her Foe's Conclusions were not sound,
From Premisses erroneous brought,   280
And therefore the Deductions nought,
And must have contrary Effects
To what her treach'rous Foe expects.

In proper Season *Pallas* meets
The Queen of Love, whom thus she greets,
(For Gods, we are by *Homer* told,
Can in Celestial Language scold)
Perfidious Goddess! but in vain
You form'd this Project in your Brain,
A Project for thy Talents fit,   290
With much Deceit and little Wit;
Thou hast, as thou shalt quickly see,
Deceiv'd thy self, instead of me;
For how can Heav'nly Wisdom prove
An Instrument to earthly Love?
Know'st thou not yet that Men commence
Thy Votaries, for Want of Sense?

Nor shall *Vanessa* be the Theme
To manage thy abortive Scheme;
She'll prove the greatest of thy Foes: 300
And yet I scorn to interpose,
By using neither Skill, nor Force,
Leave all Things to their Nat'ral Course.

The Goddess thus pronounc'd her Doom:
When, lo! *Vanessa* in her Bloom,
Advanc'd like *Atalanta*'s Star,°
But rarely seen, and seen from far:
In a new World with Caution stept,
Watch'd all the Company she kept,
Well knowing from the Books she read   310
What dangerous Paths young Virgins tread;
Wou'd seldom at the Park appear,
Nor saw the Play-House twice a Year;
Yet not incurious, was inclin'd
To know the Converse° of Mankind.

First issu'd from Perfumers Shops
A Croud of fashionable Fops;
They ask'd her, how she lik'd the Play,
Then told the Tattle of the Day,
A Duel fought last Night at Two,   320
About a Lady—You know who;
Mention'd a new *Italian*,° come
Either from *Muscovy*° or *Rome;*
Gave Hints of who and who's together;
Then fell to talking of the Weather:
Last Night was so extremely fine,
The Ladies walk'd till after Nine.
Then in soft Voice and Speech absurd,
With Nonsense ev'ry second Word,
With Fustian from exploded° Plays,   330
They celebrate her Beauty's Praise,
Run o'er their Cant of stupid Lies,
And tell° the Murders of her Eyes.

With silent Scorn *Vanessa* sat,
Scarce list'ning to their idle Chat;

260. **Resume:** take back.

306. **Atalanta's Star:** The best-known accounts of the Atalanta myth say nothing of her being turned into a star. She was a virgin huntress and an unbeatable foot racer, losing her only race, through a trick, to Melanion (Hippomenes), who took her in marriage as his prize. Both were later turned into lions for profaning a temple with their love-making. 315. **Converse:** society. 322. **a new Italian:** a new opera singer. 323. **Muscovy:** Russia. 330. **exploded:** hissed off the stage; from the etymological sense: to drive out by clapping. 333. **tell:** count.

Further than sometimes by a Frown,
When they grew pert, to pull them down.
At last she spitefully was bent
To try their Wisdom's full Extent;
And said, she valu'd nothing less   340
Than Titles, Figure, Shape, and Dress;
That, Merit should be chiefly plac'd
In Judgment, Knowledge, Wit, and Taste;
And these, she offer'd to dispute,
Alone distinguish'd Man from Brute:
That, present Times have no Pretence
To Virtue, in the Noblest Sense,
By *Greeks* and *Romans* understood,
To perish for our Country's Good.
She nam'd the antient Heroes round,   350
Explain'd for what they were renown'd;
Then spoke with Censure, or Applause,
Of foreign Customs, Rites, and Laws;
Thro' Nature, and thro' Art she rang'd,
And gracefully her Subject chang'd:
In vain: her Hearers had no Share
In all she spoke, except to stare.
Their Judgment was upon the Whole,
—That Lady is the dullest Soul—
Then tipt their Forehead in a Jeer,   360
As who should say—she wants it here;°
She may be handsome, young and rich,
But none will burn her for a Witch.°

A Party next of glitt'ring Dames,
From round the Purlieus of *St. James*,°
Came early, out of pure Good-will,
To see the Girl in Deshabille.°
Their Clamour 'lighting from their Chairs,
Grew louder, all the Way up Stairs;
At Entrance loudest, where they found   370
The Room with Volumes litter'd round
Vanessa held *Montaigne*, and read,
Whilst Mrs. *Susan*° comb'd her Head:
They call'd for Tea and Chocolate,
And fell into their usual Chat,
Discoursing with important Face,
On Ribbons, Fans, and Gloves and Lace;

Shew'd Patterns just from *India* brought,
And gravely ask'd her what she thought,
Whether the Red or Green were best,   380
And what they cost? *Vanessa* guess'd,
As came into her Fancy first,
Nam'd half the Rates,° and lik'd the worst.
To Scandal next—What aukward Thing
Was that, last *Sunday* in the Ring°?
—I'm sorry *Mopsa* breaks° so fast;
I said her Face would never last.
Corinna with that youthful Air,
Is thirty, and a Bit to spare.
Her Fondness for a certain Earl   390
Began, when I was but a Girl.
Phyllis, who but a Month ago
Was marry'd to the *Tunbridge* Beau,
I saw coquetting t' other Night
In publick with that odious Knight.

They railly'd° next *Vanessa*'s Dress;
That Gown was made for Old Queen *Bess.*
Dear Madam, Let me set your Head:°
Don't you intend to put on Red°?
A Pettycoat without a Hoop!   400
Sure, you are not asham'd to stoop;
With handsome Garters at your Knees,
No matter what a Fellow sees.

Fill'd with Disdain, with Rage inflam'd,
Both of her self and Sex° asham'd,
The Nymph stood silent out of spight,
Nor wou'd vouchsafe° to set them right.
Away the fair Detractors went,
And gave, by turns, their Censures Vent.
She's not so handsome, in my Eyes: 410
For Wit, I wonder where it lies.
She's fair and clean, and that's the most;
But why proclaim her for a Toast?
A Baby Face, no Life, nor Airs,
But what she learnt at Country Fairs;
Scarce knows what Diff'rence is between
Rich *Flanders* Lace, and Colberteen.°

360–61. Then . . . here: Then touched their foreheads lightly, with a grimace, as if to say, She lacks sense. 363. But . . . Witch: She would hardly be credited with unusual mental powers. 365. St. James: St. James's Palace. 367. in Deshabille: (dishabille) informally dressed. 373. Mrs. Susan: like "Betty," a stock name for a maidservant. The title "Mrs." was not restricted to married women.

383. Rates: prices. 385. the Ring: the riding course in Hyde Park. 386. breaks: a reference to ruptures in the skin, or a general deterioration of the complexion. The names of the ladies in this passage are taken from pastoral romance. 396. railly'd: ridiculed. 398. set . . . Head: adjust your hair. 399. Red: rouge. 405. Sex: her sex. 407. vouchsafe: deign, condescend. 417. Colberteen: (or colbertine) a coarse, lacelike fabric, named after the French minister Colbert.

I'll undertake my little *Nancy*
In *Flounces* has a better Fancy.°
With all her Wit, I wou'd not ask   420
Her Judgment, how to buy a Mask.°
We begg'd her but to patch° her Face,
She never hit one proper Place;
Which every Girl at five Years old
Can do as soon as she is told.
I own, that out-of-fashion Stuff
Becomes the *Creature* well enough.
The Girl might pass, if we cou'd get her
To know the World a little better.
(*To know the World!* a modern Phrase,   430
For Visits, Ombre,° Balls and Plays.)

    Thus, to the World's perpetual Shame,
The *Queen of Beauty* lost her Aim.
Too late with Grief she understood,
Pallas had done more Harm than Good;
For great Examples are but vain,
Where Ignorance begets Disdain.
Both Sexes, arm'd with Guilt and Spite,
Against *Vanessa's* Pow'r unite;
To copy her, few Nymphs aspir'd;   440
Her Virtues fewer Swains admir'd:
So Stars beyond a certain Height
Give Mortals neither Heat nor Light.

    Yet some of either Sex, endow'd
With Gifts superior to the Crowd,
With Virtue, Knowledge, Taste and Wit,
She condescended to admit:
With pleasing Arts she could reduce
Mens Talents to their proper Use;
And with Address° each Genius held   450
To that wherein it most excell'd;
Thus making others Wisdom known,
Cou'd please them, and improve her own.
A modest Youth said something new,
She plac'd it in the strongest View.°
All humble Worth she strove to raise;
Would not be prais'd, yet lov'd to praise.

The Learned met with free Approach,°
Although they came not in a Coach.
Some Clergy too she wou'd allow,   460
Nor quarrell'd at their aukward Bow.
But this was for *Cadenus'* sake;
A Gownman° of a diff'rent Make.
Whom *Pallas*, once *Vanessa's* Tutor,
Had fix'd on for her Coadjutor.°

    But *Cupid*, full of Mischief, longs
To vindicate his Mother's Wrongs.
On *Pallas* all Attempts are vain;
One way he knows to give her Pain:
Vows, on *Vanessa's* Heart to take   470
Due Vengeance, for her Patron's sake.
Those early Seeds by *Venus* sown,
In spight of *Pallas*, now were grown;
And *Cupid* hop'd they wou'd improve
By Time, and ripen into Love.
The Boy made use of all his Craft,
In vain discharging many a Shaft,
Pointed at Col'nels, Lords, and Beaux;
Cadenus warded off the Blows:
For placing still° some Book betwixt,   480
The Darts were in the Cover fix'd,
Or often blunted and recoil'd,
On *Plutarch's* Morals° struck, were spoil'd.

    The Queen of Wisdom cou'd foresee,
But not prevent the Fates Decree;
And human Caution tries in vain
To break that Adamantine Chain.
Vanessa, tho' by *Pallas* taught,
By *Love* invulnerable thought,
Searching in Books for Wisdom's Aid,   490
Was, in the very Search, betray'd.

    Cupid, tho' all his Darts were lost,
Yet still resolv'd to spare no Cost;
He could not answer to° his Fame
The Triumphs of that stubborn Dame,
A Nymph so hard to be subdu'd,
Who neither was Coquette nor Prude.
I find, said he, she wants a Doctor,
Both to adore her and instruct her;

---

419. **Fancy:** taste. 421. **Mask:** Masks were worn by ladies at balls, masquerades, and other entertainments. 422. **patch:** Patches of black silk were used by fashionable ladies to cover blemishes or simply to provide a striking contrast for the complexion. 431. **Ombre:** a card game, prominent in *The Rape of the Lock* (see iii. 27 ff., later in Part Two). 450. **Address:** adroitness. 455. **the strongest View:** the best light.

458. **free Approach:** easy access. 463. **Gownman:** clergyman. 465. **Coadjutor:** helper, assistant. 480. **still:** always. 483. **Plutarch's Morals:** the *Moralia*, essays and dialogues on miscellaneous subjects. 494. **answer to:** reconcile.

I'll give her what she most admires,   500
Among those venerable Sires.
Cadenus is a Subject fit,
Grown old in Politicks and Wit;
Caress'd by Ministers of State,
Of half Mankind the Dread and Hate.
Whate'er Vexations Love attend,
She need no Rivals apprehend.
Her Sex, with universal Voice,
Must laugh at her capricious Choice.

  Cadenus many things had writ;   510
Vanessa much esteem'd his Wit,
And call'd for his Poetick Works;°
Mean time the Boy in secret lurks,
And while the Book was in her Hand,
The Urchin from his private Stand°
Took Aim, and shot with all his Strength
A Dart of such prodigious Length,
It pierc'd the feeble Volume thro',
And deep transfix'd her Bosom too.
Some Lines, more moving than the rest,   520
Stuck to the Point that pierc'd her Breast;
And, born directly to her Heart,
With Pains unknown° increas'd the Smart.

  Vanessa, not in Years a Score,
Dreams of a Gown of forty-four;°
Imaginary Charms can find,
In Eyes with Reading almost blind;
Cadenus now no more appears
Declin'd in Health, advanc'd in Years.
She fancies Musick in his Tongue,   530
Nor further looks, but thinks him young.
What Mariner is not afraid,
To venture in a Ship decay'd?
What Planter will attempt to yoke
A Sapling with a falling Oak?
As Years increase, she brighter shines,
Cadenus with each Day declines,
And he must fall a Prey to Time,
While she continues in her Prime.°

Cadenus, common Forms apart,°   540
In every Scene had kept his Heart;
Had sigh'd and languish'd, vow'd, and writ,
For Pastime, or to shew his Wit;
But Time, and Books, and State Affairs
Had spoil'd his fashionable Airs;
He now cou'd praise, esteem, approve,
But understood not what was Love.
His Conduct might have made him styl'd
A Father, and the Nymph his Child.
That innocent Delight he took   550
To see the Virgin mind her Book,
Was but the Master's secret Joy
In School to hear the finest Boy.
Her Knowledge with her Fancy grew;
She hourly press'd for something new;
Ideas came into her Mind
So fast, his Lessons lagg'd behind:
She reason'd, without plodding long,
Nor ever gave her Judgment wrong.
But now a sudden Change was wrought,   560
She minds no longer what he taught.°
Cadenus was amaz'd to find
Such Marks of a distracted Mind;
For tho' she seem'd to listen more
To all he spoke, than e'er before;
He found her Thoughts would absent range,
Yet guess'd not whence could spring the Change.
And first he modestly conjectures
His Pupil might be tir'd with Lectures;
Which help'd to mortify his Pride,   570
Yet gave him not the Heart to chide;
But in a mild dejected Strain,
At last he ventur'd to complain:
Said, she shou'd be no longer teiz'd;°
Might have her Freedom when she pleas'd:
Was now convinc'd he acted wrong,
To hide her from the World so long;

---

512. **Poetick Works:** perhaps the *Miscellanies in Prose and Verse* (1711). 515. **private Stand:** hidden position. 523. **unknown:** hitherto unknown. 524–25. **Vanessa . . . forty-four:** Swift was not always accurate in his figures. Vanessa was born in 1687 or 1688; she was therefore past twenty when Swift, who was born in 1667, was forty-four. Furthermore, Swift was forty-six at the time he became Dean of St. Patrick's. 539. **Prime:** At this point Swift suppressed the two following lines, which appear in the several unauthorized editions of 1726: "STRANGE, that a Nymph by *Pallas* nurst, / In Love should make Advances first."

540. **common . . . apart:** though he kept to the common forms (of expressing sentiment). 561. **taught:** The 1726 editions continue:

> She wish'd her Tutor were her Lover;
> Resolv'd she would her Flame discover:
> And when *CADENUS* would expound
> Some Notion subtil or [and] profound,
> The Nymph would gently press his Hand,
> As if she seem'd to understand;
> Or dext'rously dissembling [dissemble] Chance,
> Would Sigh, and steal a secret Glance.

574. **teiz'd:** annoyed, vexed.

And in dull Studies to engage
One of her tender Sex and Age.
That ev'ry Nymph with Envy own'd,   580
How she might shine in the *Grand-Monde*,
And ev'ry Shepherd was undone
To see her cloister'd like a Nun.
This was a visionary Scheme,
He wak'd, and found it but a Dream;
A Project far above his Skill,
For Nature must be Nature still.
If he were bolder than became
A Scholar to a Courtly Dame,
She might excuse a Man of Letters;   590
Thus Tutors often treat their Betters.
And since his Talk offensive grew,
He came to take his last Adieu.

   Vanessa, fill'd with just Disdain,
Wou'd still her Dignity maintain,
Instructed from her early Years
To scorn the Art of Female Tears.

   Had he employ'd his Time so long,
To teach her what was Right and Wrong,
Yet cou'd such Notions entertain,   600
That all his Lectures were in vain?
She own'd the wand'ring of her Thoughts,
But he must answer for her Faults.
She well remember'd to her Cost,
That all his Lessons were not lost.
Two Maxims she could still produce,
And sad Experience taught their Use:
That Virtue, pleas'd by being shown,
Knows nothing which it dare not own;
Can make us without Fear disclose   610
Our inmost Secrets to our Foes:
That common Forms were not design'd
Directors to a noble Mind.
Now, said the Nymph, to let you see
My Actions with your Rules agree,
That I can vulgar Forms despise,
And have no Secrets to disguise.°
I knew by what you said and writ,
How dang'rous Things were Men of Wit,
You caution'd me against their Charms,   620
But never gave me equal Arms:
Your Lessons found the weakest Part,
Aim'd at the Head, but reach'd the Heart.

Cadenus felt within him rise
Shame, Disappointment, Guilt, Surprize.
He knew not how to reconcile
Such Language, with her usual Style:
And yet her Words were so exprest,
He cou'd not hope she spoke in Jest.
His Thoughts had wholly been confin'd   630
To form and cultivate her Mind.
He hardly knew, 'till he was told,
Whether the Nymph were Young or Old;
Had met her in a publick Place,
Without distinguishing her Face.
Much less could his declining Age
Vanessa's earliest Thoughts engage.
And if her Youth Indifference met,
His Person must Contempt beget.
Or grant her Passion be sincere,   640
How shall his Innocence be clear?
Appearances were all so strong,
The World must think him in the Wrong;
Wou'd say, He made a treach'rous Use
Of Wit, to flatter and seduce:
The Town wou'd swear he had betray'd,
By Magick Spells, the harmless Maid;
And ev'ry Beau wou'd have his Jokes,
That Scholars were like other Folks:
That when Platonick Flights are over,   650
The Tutor turns a mortal Lover.
So tender of the Young and Fair?
It shew'd a true Paternal Care—
Five thousand Guineas in her Purse?
The Doctor might have fancy'd° worse.—

   Hardly° at length he Silence broke,
And faulter'd ev'ry Word he spoke;
Interpreting her Complaisance,
Just as a Man *sans Consequence.*°
She rally'd well, he always knew,   660
Her Manner now was something new;
And what she spoke was in an Air,
As serious as a Tragick Play'r.
But those who aim at Ridicule
Shou'd fix upon some certain Rule,
Which fairly° hints they are in jest,
Else he must alter his Protest:
For, let a Man be ne'er so wise,
He may be caught with sober Lies;

---

617. disguise: The 1726 editions continue: "I'll fully prove
your Maxims true, / By owning here [thus] my Love for [to]
you."

655. fancy'd: given his heart to someone. **656. Hardly:** with
difficulty. **659. Just . . . Consequence:** as if he were a
person of no importance (to her). **666. fairly:** plainly.

A Science which he never taught,   670
And, to be free,° was dearly bought:
For, take it in its proper Light,
'Tis just what Coxcombs call, *a Bite*.°

    But not to dwell on Things minute,
Vanessa finish'd the Dispute,
Brought weighty Arguments to prove
That Reason was her Guide in Love.
She thought he had himself describ'd,
His Doctrines when she first imbib'd;°
What he had planted, now was grown;   680
His Virtues she might call her own;
As he approves, as he dislikes,
Love or Contempt, her Fancy strikes.
Self-Love, in Nature rooted fast,
Attends us first, and leaves us last:
Why she likes him, admire° not at her,
She loves herself, and that's the Matter.
How was her Tutor wont to praise
The Genius's of ancient Days!
(Those Authors he so oft had nam'd   690
For Learning, Wit, and Wisdom fam'd;)
Was struck with Love, Esteem, and Awe,
For Persons whom he never saw.
Suppose *Cadenus* flourish'd then,
He must adore such God-like Men.
If one short Volume cou'd comprise
All that was witty, learn'd, and wise,
How wou'd it be esteem'd, and read,
Altho' the Writer long were dead?
If such an Author were alive,   700
How all wou'd for his Friendship strive;
And come in Crowds to see his Face:
And this she takes to be her Case.
Cadenus answer'd every End,
The Book, the Author, and the Friend.
The utmost her Desires will reach,
Is but to learn what he can teach;
His Converse° is a System, fit
Alone to fill up all her Wit;
While ev'ry Passion of her Mind   710
In him is center'd and confin'd.

    Love can with Speech inspire a Mute,
And taught *Vanessa* to dispute.

This Topick, never touch'd before,
Display'd her Eloquence the more:
Her Knowledge, with such Pains acquir'd,
By this new Passion grew inspir'd.
Thro' this she made all Objects pass,
Which gave a Tincture o'er the Mass:
As Rivers, tho' they bend and twine,   720
Still to the Sea their Course incline;
Or, as Philosophers, who find
Some fav'rite System to their Mind,
In ev'ry Point to make it fit,
Will force all Nature to submit.

    Cadenus, who cou'd ne'er suspect
His Lessons wou'd have such Effect,
Or be so artfully apply'd,
Insensibly came on her Side;°
It was an unforeseen Event,   730
Things took a Turn he never meant.
Whoe'er excels in what we prize,
Appears a Hero to our Eyes;
Each Girl when pleas'd with what is taught,
Will have the Teacher in her Thought.
When Miss delights in her Spinnet,
A Fidler may a Fortune get;
A Blockhead with melodious Voice
In Boarding-Schools can have his Choice;
And oft' the Dancing-Master's Art   740
Climbs from the Toe to touch the Heart.
In Learning let a Nymph delight,
The Pedant gets a Mistress by 't.
Cadenus, to his Grief and Shame,
Cou'd scarce oppose *Vanessa*'s Flame;
And tho' her Arguments were strong,
At least, cou'd hardly wish them wrong.
Howe'er it came, he cou'd not tell,
But, sure, she never talk'd so well.
His Pride began to interpose,   750
Preferr'd before a Crowd of Beaux,
So bright a Nymph to come unsought,
Such Wonder by his Merit wrought;
'Tis Merit must with her prevail,
He never knew her Judgment fail.
She noted all she ever read,
And had a most discerning Head.

    'Tis an old Maxim in the Schools,
That Flattery's the Food of Fools;

Yet now and then your Men of Wit 760
Will condescend to take a Bit.°

So when *Cadenus* could not hide,
He chose to justify his Pride;
Constr'ing° the Passion she had shown,
Much to her Praise, more to his Own.
Nature in him had Merit plac'd,
In her, a most judicious Taste.
Love, hitherto a transient Guest,
Ne'er held Possession of his Breast;
So, long attending at the Gate, 770
Disdain'd to enter in so late.
Love, why do we one Passion call?
When 'tis a Compound of them all;
Where hot and cold, where sharp and sweet,
In all their Equipages meet;
Where Pleasures mix'd with Pains appear,
Sorrow with Joy, and Hope with Fear.
Wherein his Dignity and Age
Forbid *Cadenus* to engage.
But Friendship in its greatest Height, 780
A constant, rational Delight,
On Virtue's Basis fix'd to last,
When Love's Allurements long are past;
Which gently warms, but cannot burn;
He gladly offers in return:
His Want of Passion will redeem,
With Gratitude, Respect, Esteem:
With that Devotion we bestow,
When Goddesses appear below.

While thus *Cadenus* entertains 790
Vanessa in exalted Strains,
The Nymph in sober Words intreats
A Truce with all sublime Conceits.°
For why such Raptures, Flights, and Fancies,
To her, who durst not read Romances;
In lofty Style to make Replies,
Which he had taught her to despise.
But when her Tutor will affect
Devotion, Duty, and Respect,
He fairly abdicates his Throne, 800
The Government is now her own:
He has a Forfeiture incurr'd,
She vows to take him at his Word,
And hopes he will not think it strange
If both shou'd now their Stations change.

The Nymph will have her Turn, to be
The Tutor; and the Pupil, he:
Tho' she already can discern,
Her Scholar is not apt° to learn;
Or wants Capacity to reach 810
The Science she designs to teach:
Wherein his Genius was below
The Skill of ev'ry common Beau;
Who, tho' he cannot spell, is wise
Enough to read a Lady's Eyes;
And will each accidental Glance
Interpret for a kind Advance.

But what Success *Vanessa* met,
Is to the World a Secret yet:
Whether the Nymph, to please her Swain, 820
Talks in a high Romantick Strain;
Or whether he at last descends
To act° with less Seraphick Ends;
Or, to compound° the Business, whether
They temper Love and Books together;
Must never to Mankind be told,
Nor shall the conscious° Muse unfold.

Mean time the mournful *Queen of Love*
Led but a weary Life above.
She ventures now to leave the Skies, 830
Grown by *Vanessa*'s Conduct wise.
For tho' by one perverse Event
Pallas had cross'd her first Intent,
Tho' her Design was not obtain'd,
Yet had she much Experience gain'd;
And, by the Project vainly try'd,
Cou'd better now the *Cause* decide.

She gave due Notice, that both Parties,
Coram Regina prox' die Martis,°
Should at their Peril without fail 840
Come and appear, and save their Bail.
All met, and Silence thrice proclaim'd,
One Lawyer to each Side was nam'd.
The Judge discover'd° in her Face
Resentments for her late Disgrace;
And, full of Anger, Shame, and Grief,
Directed them to mind their Brief;
Nor spend their Time to shew their Reading;

---

761. **Bit:** bite. 764. **Constr'ing:** construing. 793. **Conceits:** affectations of thought and style.

809. **apt:** ready, equipped. 823. **act:** *like* and *love* in other editions. 824. **compound:** compose, settle. 827. **conscious:** knowing. 839. **Coram . . . Martis:** The translation "*Before the Queen on Tuesday next*" is given in other editions. 844. **discover'd:** revealed.

She'd have a summary° Proceeding.
She gather'd, under ev'ry Head,   850
The Sum of what each Lawyer said;
Gave her own Reasons last; and then
Decreed the Cause against the *Men.*

But, in a weighty Case like this,
To shew she did not judge amiss,
Which evil Tongues might else° report,
She made a Speech in open Court;
Wherein she grievously complains,
"How she was cheated by the Swains:
On whose Petition (humbly shewing   860
That Women were not worth the wooing,
And that unless the Sex would mend,
The Race of Lovers soon must end:)
She was at Lord knows what Expence,
To form a Nymph of Wit and Sense;
A Model for her Sex design'd,
Who never cou'd one Lover find.
She saw her Favour was misplac'd;
The *Fellows* had a wretched Taste;
She needs must tell them to their Face,   870
They were a stupid, senseless Race:
And were she to begin agen,
She'd study to reform the *Men;*
Or add some Grains of Folly more
To *Women* than they had before,
To put them on an equal Foot;
And this, or nothing else, wou'd do 't.
This might their mutual Fancy strike,
Since ev'ry Being loves its *Like.*

"But now, repenting what was done,   880
She left all Business to her Son:
She puts the World in his Possession,
And let him use it at Discretion."

The Cry'r was order'd to dismiss
The Court, who made his last *O yes!*°
The Goddess wou'd no longer wait;
But rising from her Chair of State,
Left all below at Six and Sev'n,
Harness'd her Doves, and flew to Heav'n.

THE PROGRESS
OF BEAUTY

Written A D: 1719

❧

The text is that of Stella's transcript, printed in *The Poems of Jonathan Swift*, ed. Harold Williams (3 vols., 1937, 1958), with variants incorporated from *Miscellanies. The Last Volume* (1727). The stanzas beginning at lines 17, 37, 73, and 113 are found only in Stella's transcript.

❧

When first Diana° leaves her Bed
Vapors and Steams her Looks disgrace,
A frouzy dirty colour'd red
Sits on her cloudy wrinckled Face.

But by degrees when mounted high
Her artificiall Face appears
Down from her Window in the Sky,
Her Spots are gone, her Visage clears.

'Twixt earthly Femals and the Moon
All Parallells exactly run;   10
If Celia should appear too soon
Alas, the Nymph would be undone.

To see her from her Pillow rise
All reeking in a cloudy Steam,
Crackt Lips, foul Teeth, and gummy Eyes,
Poor Strephon, how would he blaspheme!

The Soot or Powder which was wont
To make her Hair look black as Jet,
Falls from her Tresses on her Front
A mingled Mass of Dirt and Sweat.   20

Three Colours, Black, and Red, and White,
So gracefull in their proper Place,
Remove them to a diff'rent Light
They form a frightfull hideous Face,

---

849. **summary:** shortened. 856. **else:** otherwise. 885. **O yes:** (oyez, oyes) Hear ye!

THE PROGRESS OF BEAUTY. 1. **Diana:** the goddess of the moon; here, the moon itself.

For instance; when the Lilly slipps
Into the Precincts of the Rose,
And takes Possession of the Lips,
Leaving the Purple° to the Nose.

So Celia went entire° to bed,
All her Complexions safe and sound,　　　　30
But when she rose, White, Black, and Red,
Though still in Sight, had chang'd their
　　Ground.°

The Black, which would not be confin'd
A more inferior Station seeks
Leaving the fiery red behind,
And mingles in her muddy Cheeks.

The Paint by Perspiration cracks,
And falls in Rivulets of Sweat,
On either Side you see the Tracks,
While at her Chin the Conflu'ents° met.　　40

A Skillfull Houswife thus her Thumb
With Spittle while she spins, anoints,
And thus the brown Meanders° come
In trickling Streams betwixt her Joynts.

But Celia can with ease reduce
By help of Pencil, Paint and Brush
Each Colour to it's Place and Use,
And teach her Cheeks again to blush.

She knows her Early self no more,
But fill'd with Admiration, stands,　　　　50
As Other Painters oft adore
The Workmanship of their own Hands.

Thus after four important Hours
Celia's the Wonder of her Sex;
Say, which among the Heav'nly Pow'rs
Could cause such marvellous Effects.

Venus, indulgent to her Kind
Gave Women all their Hearts could wish
When first she taught them where to find
White Lead,° and Lusitanian Dish.°　　　　60

Love with White lead cements his Wings,
White lead was sent us to repair
Two brightest, brittlest earthly Things
A Lady's Face, and China ware.

She ventures now to lift the Sash,
The Window is her proper Sphear;
Ah Lovely Nymph be not too rash,
Nor let the Beaux approach too near.

Take Pattern by your Sister Star,
Delude at once and Bless our Sight,　　　　70
When you are seen, be seen from far,
And chiefly chuse to shine by Night.

In the Pell-Mell° when passing by,
Keep up the Glasses° of your Chair,
Then each transported Fop will cry,
G—d d—m me Jack, she's wondrous fair.

But, Art no longer can prevayl
When the Materialls all are gone,
The best Mechanick° Hand must fayl
Where Nothing's left to work upon.　　　　80

Matter, as wise Logicians say,
Cannot without a Form subsist,
And Form, say I, as well as They,
Must fayl if Matter bring no Grist.°

And this is fair Diana's Case
For, all Astrologers maintain
Each Night a Bit drops off her Face
When Mortals say she's in her Wain.°

While Partridge° wisely shews the Cause
Efficient of the Moon's Decay,　　　　　90
That Cancer with his pois'nous Claws
Attacks her in the milky Way:

But Gadbury° in Art profound
From her pale Cheeks pretends to show
That Swain Endymion° is not sound,
Or else, that Mercury's her Foe.

---

28. the Purple: the red (purple designates various shades of red or blood-color). **29. entire:** intact. **32. Ground:** the painting surface or first coating. **40. Conflu'ents:** joining streams. **43. Meanders:** windings. **60. White Lead:** used as a pigment. **Lusitanian Dish:** a term we have been unable to find elsewhere, but in all likelihood it derives from "Brazil," which originally signified a species of redwood tree and later the red dyestuff that was extracted from it. ("Lusitania" is the Latin name for Portugal.)

73. the Pell-Mell: "Pallmall, a very handsome street, inhabited by several persons of the first quality, extending from the end of the Haymarket to St. James's palace" (*London and Its Environs Described* [1761]). **74. Glasses:** windows. **79. Mechanick:** craftsman's. **84. Grist:** the stuff to be formed or shaped. **88. Wain:** wane. **89. Partridge:** John Partridge, an astrologer, medical quack, and almanac maker. See the headnote to *The Bickerstaff Papers*, below. **93. Gadbury:** John Gadbury (1627–1704), a rival astrologer and suspected Popish plotter whom Partridge attacked in print. **95. Endymion:** the mythical lover of the moon goddess.

But, let the Cause be what it will,
In half a Month she looks so thin
That Flamstead° can with all his Skill
See but her Forehead and her Chin.   100

Yet as she wasts, she grows discreet,
Till Midnight never shows her Head;
So rotting Celia stroles the Street
When sober Folks are all a-bed.

For sure if this be Luna's Fate,
Poor Celia, but of mortall Race
In vain expects a longer Date
To the Materialls of Her Face.

When Mercury her Tresses mows
To think of Black-head Combs is vain,   110
No Painting can restore a Nose,
Nor will her Teeth return again.

Two Balls of Glass may serve for Eyes,
White Lead can plaister up a Cleft,°
But these alas, are poor Supplyes
If neither Cheeks, nor Lips be left.

Ye Pow'rs who over Love preside,
Since mortal Beautyes drop° so soon,
If you would have us well supply'd,
Send us new Nymphs with each new Moon.   120

THE PROGRESS
OF POETRY

❧

The text is that of the first printing, in *Miscellanies. The
Last Volume* (1727).

❧

THE Farmer's Goose, who in the Stubble,
Has fed without Restraint, or Trouble;
Grown fat with Corn° and Sitting still,
Can scarce get o'er the Barn-Door Sill:

And hardly° waddles forth, to cool
Her Belly in the neighb'ring Pool:
Nor loudly cackles at the Door;
For Cackling shews the Goose is poor.

But when she must be turn'd to graze,
And round the barren Common° strays,   10
Hard Exercise, and harder Fare
Soon make my Dame grow lank and spare:
Her Body light, she tries her Wings,
And scorns the Ground, and upward springs,
While all the Parish, as she flies,
Hear Sounds harmonious from the Skies.

Such is the Poet, fresh in Pay,
(The third Night's Profits of his Play;)°
His Morning-Draughts° 'till Noon can swill,
Among his Brethren of the Quill: 20
With good Roast Beef his Belly full,
Grown lazy, foggy, fat, and dull:
Deep sunk in Plenty, and Delight,
What Poet e'er could take his Flight?
Or stuff'd with Phlegm up to the Throat,°
What Poet e'er could sing a Note?
Nor *Pegasus* could bear the Load,
Along the high celestial Road;
The Steed, oppress'd, would break his Girth,°
To raise the Lumber° from the Earth.   30

But, view him in another Scene,
When all his Drink is *Hippocrene*,°
His Money spent, his Patrons fail,
His Credit out° for Cheese and Ale;
His Two-Year's Coat so smooth and bare,
Through ev'ry Thread it lets in Air;
With hungry Meals his Body pin'd,
His Guts and Belly full of Wind;
And, like a Jockey for a Race,
His Flesh brought down to Flying-Case:°   40
Now his exalted Spirit loaths
Incumbrances of Food and Cloaths;

---

99. Flamstead: John Flamsteed (1646–1719), Astronomer
Royal. **114. a Cleft:** a crack in the skin, a chap. **118. drop:**
die. THE PROGRESS OF POETRY. **3. Corn:** grain.

5. hardly: with difficulty. **10. Common:** unenclosed wasteland. **18. The third . . . Play:** Playwrights were paid the
receipts (above the house charges) from the third night's performance, and sometimes also from the sixth and ninth, of the
initial run. **19. Morning-Draughts:** beverages drunk in the
morning before breakfast. **25. stuff'd . . . Throat:**
phlegmatic, sluggish (from luxurious living). **29. Girth:** the
belt or band that secures the pack. **30. Lumber:** superfluous
fat. **32. Hippocrene:** the sacred fountain of the Muses on
Mount Helicon; hence, poetic inspiration. **34. out:** used up.
40. Flying-Case: racing condition.

And up he rises like a Vapour,
Supported high on Wings of Paper;
He singing flies, and flying sings,
While from below all *Grub-street* rings.

A SATIRICAL ELEGY
ON THE DEATH OF
A LATE FAMOUS GENERAL

The object of this satire (more witty than just) is the Duke of Marlborough, who died on June 16, 1722. Swift had previously lampooned him in his poem *The Fable of Midas*, published February 14, 1712; in January of the next year he noted in the *Journal to Stella* that

> the Duke pretended to think me his greatest Enemy, & got People to tell me so, and very mildly to let me know how gladly he would have me softned towrds him. I bid a Lady of his Acquaintance & mine let him know, that I had hindred many a bitter thing against him, not for his own sake, but because I thought it looked base; and I desired every thing should be left him except Power.

The text is that of the first printing, in *The Gentleman's Magazine*, XXXIV, 244 (May, 1764).

HIS Grace! impossible! what dead!
Of old age too, and in his bed!
And could that mighty warrior fall,
And so inglorious after all!
Well, since he's gone, no matter how,
The last loud trump must wake him now;
And, trust me, as the noise grows stronger,
He'll wish to sleep a little longer.
And could he be indeed so old
As by the news-papers we're told!   10
Threescore,° I think, is pretty high,
'Twas time in conscience he should die:
This world he cumber'd long enough,
He burnt his candle to a snuff,
And that's the reason some folks think,
He left behind *so great a stink*.

ON THE DEATH OF A LATE FAMOUS GENERAL. **11. Threescore:** Marlborough was actually seventy-two at his death.

Behold his funeral appears,
Nor widows sighs, nor orphans tears,
Wont at such time each heart to pierce,
Attend the progress of his herse.   20
But what of that, his friends may say,
He had those honours in his day;
True to his profit and his pride,
He made them weep before he dy'd.

Come hither, all ye empty things
Ye bubbles rais'd by breath of kings,
Who float upon the tide of state,
Come hither, and behold your fate:
Let pride be taught by this rebuke,
How very mean a thing's a D—ke;   30
From all his ill-got honours flung,
Turn'd to that dirt, from whence he sprung.

ADVICE
TO THE GRUB-STREET
VERSE-WRITERS

Written in the Year 1726

The text is that of the first printing, in Faulkner's edition of Swift's *Works* (1735).

YE Poets ragged and forlorn,
    Down from your Garrets haste,
Ye Rhimers, dead as soon as born,
    Not yet consign'd to Paste;°

I KNOW a Trick to make you thrive;
    O, 'tis a quaint Device:
Your still-born Poems shall revive,
    And scorn to wrap up Spice.

GET all your Verses printed fair,
    Then, let them well be dry'd;   10
And, *Curl*° must have a special Care
    To leave the Margin wide.

ADVICE TO THE GRUB-STREET VERSE-WRITERS. **4. Paste:** pasteboard. **11. Curl:** Edmund Curll (1675-1747), the most notorious of English piratical publishers.

LEND these to Paper-sparing *Pope;*
 And, when he sits to write,
No Letter with an *Envelope*
 Could give him more Delight.°

WHEN *Pope* has fill'd the Margins round,
 Why, then recal your Loan;
Sell them to *Curl* for Fifty Pound,
 And swear they are your own. 20

STELLA'S BIRTH-DAY

March 13. 172$\frac{6}{7}$

❧

Her last—Stella died on January 28, 1728.
 The text is that of the first printing, in *Miscellanies.
The Last Volume* (1727); one variant has been incorpo-
rated from Faulkner's edition of Swift's *Works* (1735).

❧

THIS Day, whate'er the Fates decree,
Shall still be kept with Joy by me:
This Day then, let us not be told,
That you are sick, and I grown old,
Nor think on our approaching Ills,
And talk of Spectacles and Pills;
To morrow will be Time enough
To hear such mortifying Stuff.
Yet, since from Reason may be brought
A better and more pleasing Thought, 10
Which can in spite of all Decays,
Support a few remaining Days:
From not the gravest of Divines,
Accept for once some serious Lines.

 Although we now can form no more
Long Schemes of Life, as heretofore;
Yet you, while Time is running fast,
Can look with Joy on what is past.

 Were future Happiness and Pain,
A mere Contrivance of the Brain, 20
As Atheists argue, to entice,
And fit their Proselytes for Vice;

(The only Comfort they propose,
To have Companions in their Woes.)
Grant this the Case, yet sure 'tis hard,
That Virtue, stil'd° its own Reward,
And by all Sages understood
To be the chief of human Good,
Should acting, die, nor leave behind
Some lasting Pleasure in the Mind, 30
Which by Remembrance will assuage,
Grief, Sickness, Poverty, and Age;
And strongly shoot a radiant Dart,
To shine through Life's declining Part.

 Say, *Stella,* feel you no Content,
Reflecting on a Life well spent?
Your skilful Hand employ'd to save
Despairing Wretches from the Grave;
And then supporting with your Store,
Those whom you dragg'd from Death before: 40
(So Providence on Mortals waits,
Preserving what it first creates)
Your gen'rous Boldness to defend
An innocent and absent Friend;
That Courage which can make you just,
To Merit humbled in the Dust:
The Detestation you express
For Vice in all its glitt'ring Dress:
That Patience under tort'ring Pain,
Where stubborn Stoicks would complain. 50

 Shall these like empty Shadows pass,
Or Forms reflected from a Glass?
Or mere Chimæra's in the Mind,
That fly and leave no Marks behind?
Does not the Body thrive and grow
By Food of twenty Years ago?
And, had it not been still supply'd,
It must a thousand Times have dy'd.
Then, who with Reason can maintain,
That no Effects of Food remain? 60
And, is not Virtue in Mankind
The Nutriment that feeds the Mind?
Upheld by each good Action past,
And still continued by the last:
Then, who with Reason can pretend,
That all Effects of Virtue end?

 Believe me *Stella,* when you show
That true Contempt for Things below,

13–16. **Lend . . . Delight:** Pope was given to writing his
compositions on scraps of paper and letters he had received.
A cover to a letter gave him a relatively free hand.

STELLA'S BIRTH-DAY. **26. stil'd:** styled.

Nor prize your Life for other Ends
Than merely to oblige your Friends;   70
Your former Actions claim their Part,
And join to fortify your Heart.
For Virtue in her daily Race,
Like *Janus*, bears a double Face;°
Looks back with Joy where she has gone,
And therefore goes with Courage on.
She at your sickly Couch will wait,
And guide you to a better State.

O then, whatever Heav'n intends,
Take Pity on your pitying Friends;   80
Nor let your Ills affect your Mind,
To fancy they can be unkind.
Me, surely me, you ought to spare,
Who gladly would your Suff'rings share;
Or give my Scrap of Life to you,
And think it far beneath your Due;
You, to whose Care so oft I owe,
That I'm alive to tell you so.

DIRECTIONS
FOR A BIRTH-DAY SONG

Oct: 30. 1729

This poem is addressed to Matthew Pilkington, a poor
Irish parson and poetaster, whom Swift befriended and
later disowned. He was the husband of the more famous
Laetitia Pilkington, whose *Memoirs* (1748) contain much
Swiftiana. The butt of the satire is Laurence Eusden,
appointed Poet Laureate in 1718, whose office it was to
supply the annual New Year and birthday odes. In the
competition for royal favor, other poets commonly
made their unofficial offerings, and Pilkington's was
printed in his *Poems on Several Occasions*, which appeared
first in Dublin in 1730, then a year later in London.
The London edition, according to the title page, was
"revised by the Reverend Dr. Swift."

The text is that of the manuscript copy by Charles
Ford, as printed in *The Poems of Jonathan Swift*, ed.
Harold Williams (3 vols., 1937, 1958), with one
exception noted below.

74. **Like . . . Face:** Janus, the Roman god of doorways and
of the rising and setting of the sun, was represented as having
two faces, one looking to the east and the other to the west.

To form a just and finish'd piece,
Take twenty Gods of Rome or Greece,
Whose Godships are in chief request,
And fit your present Subject best.
And should it be your Hero's case
To have both male & female Race,
Your bus'ness must be to provide
A score of Goddesses beside.
Some call their Monarchs Sons of Saturn,
For which they bring a modern Pattern,   10
Because they might have heard of one
Who often long'd to eat his Son:°
But this I think will not go down,
For here the Father kept his Crown.
Why then appoint him Son of Jove,
Who met his Mother in a grove;
To this we freely shall consent,
Well knowing what the Poets meant:
And in their Sense, 'twixt me and you,
It may be literally true.°   20
Next, as the Laws of Song require,
He must be greater than his Sire:
For Jove, as every School-boy knows,
Was able Saturn to depose;
And sure no Christian Poet breathing
Should be more scrup'lous than a Heathen.
Or if to Blasphemy it tends,
That's but a trifle among Friends.
Your Hero now another Mars is,
Makes mighty Armys turn their Arses.   30
Behold his glitt'ring Faulchion° mow
Whole Squadrons with a single blow:
While Victory, with Wings outspread,
Flyes like an Eagle or'e his head;
His milk-white Steed upon it's haunches,
Or pawing into dead mens paunches.
As Overton° has drawn his Sire
Still seen o'r'e many an Alehouse fire.
Then from his Arm hoarse thunder rolls
As loud as fifty mustard bowls;°   40
For thunder still his arm supplyes,
And lightning always in his Eyes:

DIRECTIONS FOR A BIRTH-DAY SONG. 11–12. **one . . . Son:**
George I and the Prince of Wales. 20. **literally true:** George
II's mother, Sophia Dorothea, was accused of an extramarital
affair and confined in a German castle until her death in 1726.
31. **Faulchion:** (falchion) broadsword. 37. **Overton:** Henry
Overton, print-seller and publisher of mezzotint portraits.
40. **mustard bowls:** A mustard bowl is a wooden bowl in
which mustard seed was pounded. The term is used to refer
to the instrument that produces stage thunder.

They both are cheap enough in Conscience,°
And serve to eccho ratling Nonsense;
The rumbling words march fierce along,
Made trebly dreadfull in your Song.

Sweet Poet, hir'd for birth-day Rimes,
To sing of Wars choose peaceful times.
What tho for fifteen years and more
Janus hath lock'd his Temple-door°?   50
Tho not a Coffee-house we read in
Hath mention'd arms on this side Sweden;°
Nor London Journals, nor the Post-men,
Tho fond of warlike Lyes as most men;
Thou still with Battles stuff thy head full
For must a Hero not be dreadfull?

Dismissing Mars, it next must follow
Your Conqu'rer is become Apollo:
That he's Apollo, is as plain, as
That Robin Walpole is Mecaenas:°   60
But that he struts, and that he squints,
You'd know him by Apollo's Prints°
Old Phœbus is but half as bright,
For yours can shine both day and night,
The first perhaps may once an Age
Inspire you with poetick Rage;
Your Phœbus royal, every day
Not only can inspire, but pay.

Then make this new Apollo sit
Sole Patron, Judge, and God of Wit.   70
"How from his Altitude he stoops,
To raise up Virtue when she droops,
On Learning how his Bounty flows,
And with what Justice he bestows.
Fair Isis,° and ye Banks of Cam,°
Be witness if I tell a Flam:°
What Prodigys in Arts we drain
From both your Streams in George's Reign!
As from the flowry Bed of Nile—"
But here's enough to shew your Style.   80
Broad Innuendos, such as this,
If well apply'd, can hardly miss:

For when you bring your Song in print,
He'll get it read,° and take the hint,
(It must be read before 'tis warbled
The paper gilt, & Cover marbled)
And will be so much more your Debter
Because he never knew a letter.
And as he hears his Wit and Sence,
To which he never made pretence,   90
Set out in Hyperbolick Strains,
A Guinea shall reward your pains.
For Patrons never pay so well,
As when they scarce have learn'd to spell.

Next call him Neptune with his Trident,
He rules the Sea, you see him ride in 't;
And if provok'd, he soundly ferks° his
Rebellious Waves with rods like Xerxes.°
He would have seiz'd the Spanish Plate,
Had not the Fleet gone out too late,   100
And in their very Ports besiege,
But that he would not disoblige,
And made the Rascals pay him dearly
For those affronts they give him yearly.

'Tis not deny'd that when we write,
Our Ink is black, our Paper white;
And when we scrawl our Paper o'r'e,
We blacken what was white before.
I think this Practice only fit
For dealers in Satyrick Wit: 110
But you some white-lead ink must get,
And write on paper black as Jet:
Your Int'rest lyes to learn the knack
Of whitening what before was black.

Thus your Encomiums, to be strong,
Must be apply'd directly wrong:
A Tyrant for his Mercy praise,
And crown a Royal Dunce with Bays:
A squinting Monkey load with charms;
And paint a Coward fierce in arms.   120
Is he to Avarice inclin'd?
Extol him for his generous mind:
And when we starve for want of Corn,
Come out with Amalthea's Horn.°
For all experience this evinces

---

43. in Conscience: in truth. **50. Janus . . . Temple-door:** The doors of the temple of Janus in the Roman Forum were left open in time of war and kept shut in time of peace. **52. Sweden:** The bellicosity of Sweden during this era was notorious. **60. Mecaenas:** a generous patron of the arts (after the patron of Horace and Virgil). **61-2. But . . . Prints:** The manuscript gives an alternative for this couplet: "But that he squints, and that he struts, / You'd know him by Apollo's Cuts." **75. Isis:** the local name for the upper Thames. **Cam:** the river from which Cambridge derives it name. **76. a Flam:** an idle story, a fabrication.

84. He'll . . . read: a jibe at George II's illiteracy. **97. ferks:** (or firks) beats, lashes. **98. like Xerxes:** Xerxes, King of Persia (485–465 B.C.), in wrath ordered that the Hellespont be scourged when a storm destroyed the bridge his forces had made. **124. Amalthea's Horn:** Amalthea, a nurse of Zeus, sometimes appeared in the form of a she-goat, whose horns flowed with nectar and ambrosia.

The only art of pleasing Princes;°
For Princes love you should descant
On Virtues which they know they want.

    One Compliment I had forgot,
But Songsters must omit it not.   130
(I freely grant the Thought is old)
Why then, your Hero must be told,
In him such Virtues lye inherent,
To qualify him God's Vicegerent,°
That with no° Title to inherit,
He must have been a King by Merit.
Yet be the Fancy old or new,
'Tis partly false, and partly true,
And take it right, it means no more
Than George and William claim'd before.°   140

    Should some obscure inferior fellow
As Julius,° or the Youth of Pella,°
When all your list of Gods is out,
Presume to shew his mortal snout,
And as a Deity intrude,
Because he had the world subdu'd:
Oh! let him not debase your Thoughts,
Or name him, but to tell his Faults.

    Of Gods I only quote the best,
But you may hook in° all the rest.   150
    Now Birth-day Bard, with joy proceed
To praise your Empress, and her Breed.
First, of the first. To vouch° your Lyes
Bring all the Females of the Skyes:
The Graces and their Mistress Venus
Must venture down to entertain us.
With bended knees when they adore her
What Dowdys they appear before her!
Nor shall we think you talk at random,
For Venus might be her great Grandam.   160
Six thousand years hath liv'd the Goddess,
Your Heroine hardly fifty odd° is.

Besides you Songsters oft have shewn,
That she hath Graces of her own:
Three Graces° by Lucina° brought her,
Just three; and every Grace a Daughter.
Here many a King his heart and Crown
Shall at their snowy feet lay down:
In Royal Robes they come by dozens
To court their English German Cousins,   170
Besides a pair of princely Babyes,°
That five years hence will both be Hebes.°

    Now see her seated on her Throne
With genuin lustre all her own.
Poor Cynthia° never shone so bright,
Her Splendor is but borrow'd light;
And only with her Brother linkt
Can shine, without him is extinct.
But Carolina shines the clearer
With neither Spouse nor Brother near her,°   180
And darts her Beams or'e both our Isles,
Tho George is gone a thousand miles.
Thus Berecynthia° takes her place,
Attended by her heavenly Race,
And sees a Son in every God
Unaw'd by Jove's all-shaking Nod.

    Now sings his little Highness Freddy,°
Who struts like any King already.
With so much beauty, shew me any maid
That could refuse this charming Ganymede,°   190
Where Majesty with Sweetness vyes,
And like his Father early wise.
Then cut him out a world of work,
To conquer Spain, and quell the Turk.
Foretell his Empire crown'd with Bays,
And golden Times, and Halcyon days,
But swear his Line shall rule the Nation
For ever—till the Conflagration.°

125–26. For . . . Princes: This couplet does not appear in our copy text. It is included in another contemporary manuscript version and in the first printing in Swift's *Works*, ed. Deane Swift (1765). As the omission has every appearance of a scribal error, caused by the repetition of the initial word, *For*, we have restored it to the present text. 134. Vicegerent: deputy, representative. 135. with no: if there were no. 139–40. no . . . before: Both William III and George I came to the English throne by a succession that was indirect and legislated by Parliament, rather than by title or divine right. 142. Julius: Julius Caesar. the Youth . . . Pella: Alexander the Great (356–323 B.C.), born at Pella, in Macedonia. 150. hook in: round up, drag in. 153. vouch: attest, verify. 162. hardly . . . odd: Queen Caroline was forty-six.

165. Three Graces: Anne (b. 1709), Amelia (b. 1711), and Caroline Elizabeth (b. 1713). Lucina: in Roman mythology, the goddess who presides over childbirth. 171. a pair . . . Babyes: Mary (b. 1723) and Louisa (b. 1724). 172. Hebes: Hebe was the daughter of Zeus and Hera and handmaiden of the gods. 175. Cynthia: another name for Diana, the moon goddess. 179–80. But . . . her: Queen Caroline was regent during the King's absence in Hanover in 1729, and several times thereafter. 183. Berecynthia: (Berecyntia) another name for Cybele, a Phrygian goddess. 187. Freddy: Frederick (1707–51), Prince of Wales. He did not succeed his father, but his son did—as George III. 190. Ganymede: (Ganymedes) Zeus' cup-bearer; a prototype of childish prettiness and charm. 198. the Conflagration: the end of the world.

But now it comes into my mind,
We left a little Duke° behind;   200
A Cupid in his face and size,
And only wants to want his eyes.°
Make some provision for the Yonker,°
Find him a Kingdom out to conquer;
Prepare a Fleet to waft him o'r'e,
Make Gulliver his Commodore,
Into whose pocket valiant Willy put,
Will soon subdue the Realm of Lilliput.
  A skilfull Critick justly blames
Hard, tough, cramp,° gutt'rall, harsh, stiff Names.
The Sense can ne're be too jejune,   211
But smooth your words to fit the tune,
Hanover may do well enough;
But George, and Brunswick° are too rough.
Hesse Darmstedt° makes too rough a sound,
And Guelph° the strongest ear will wound.
In vain are all attempts from Germany
To find out proper words for Harmony:
And yet I must except the Rhine,
Because it clinks to° Caroline.   220
Hail Queen of Britain, Queen of Rhymes,
Be sung ten hundred thousand times.
Too happy were the Poets Crew,
If their own happyness they knew.
Three Syllables did never meet
So soft, so sliding, and so sweet.
Nine other tuneful words like that
Would prove ev'n Homer's Numbers° flat.
Behold three beauteous Vowels stand
With Bridegroom liquids° hand in hand,   230
In Concord here for ever fixt,
No jarring consonant betwixt.

May Caroline continue long,
For ever fair and young—in Song.
What tho the royal Carcase must
Squeez'd in a Coffin turn to dust;
Those Elements her name compose,
Like Atoms are exempt from blows.°
  Tho Caroline may fill your gaps
Yet still you must consult the Maps,   240
Find Rivers with harmonious names,
Sabrina,° Medway, and the Thames.
Britannia long will wear like Steel
But Albion's° cliffs are out at heel,
And Patience can endure no more
To hear the Belgick Lyon° roar.
Give up the phrase of haughty Gaul,
But proud Iberia soundly maul,
Restore the Ships by Philip° taken,
And make him crouch to save his bacon.°   250
  Nassau,° who got the name of glorious
Because he never was victorious,
A hanger on has always been,
For old acquaintance bring him in.
  To Walpole you might lend a Line,
But much I fear he's in decline;
And if you chance to come too late
When he goes out, you share his fate,
And bear the new Successor's frown;
Or whom you once sung up, sing down.   260
  Reject with scorn that stupid Notion
To praise your Hero for Devotion:
Nor entertain a thought so odd,
That Princes should believe in God:
But follow the securest rule,
And turn it all to ridicule,
'Tis grown the choicest Wit at Court,
And gives the Maids of Honor Sport.
For since they talk'd with Doctor Clark,°
They now can venture in the dark.   270

200. a little Duke: William Augustus (b. 1721), second son of the Prince of Wales and Princess Caroline, was created Duke of Cumberland in July of this year. It was for this child that Gay wrote his *Fables* in 1727 (see later in Part Two). 202. wants . . . eyes: needs to be blind (to resemble Cupid completely). 203. Yonker: young nobleman; originally a Dutch or German word and therefore peculiarly apt for this Hanoverian descendant. 210. cramp: difficult to pronounce. 214. Brunswick: The German House of Brunswick was divided in 1546 into the elder branch, Brunswick-Wolfenbüttel, which later became simply the House of Brunswick, and the younger branch, Brunswick-Lüneburg, which became the House of Hanover. 215. Hesse Darmstedt: the younger branch of the House of Hesse, founded in 1567. 216. Guelph: (or Welf) the European dynastic family, which by 1180 retained only Brunswick and Lüneburg and which became the Duchy of Brunswick in 1235. 220. clinks to: rhymes with. 228. Numbers: measures, rhythms. 230. liquids: *r* and *l*.

238. Like . . . blows: Atom-smashing was of course as yet undreamed of. 242. Sabrina: the Latin name of the Severn. 244. Albion: the poetic name for England. 246. the Belgick Lyon: apparently a reference to the Netherlands' determined effort to keep themselves from being overrun by France. 249. Philip: Philip V of Spain. 250. to . . . bacon: to save his skin. 251. Nassau: William III was Prince of Orange-Nassau, in the Dutch cadet line of the princely Nassau family of Europe. 269. Doctor Clark: Samuel Clarke (1675–1729), a controversial Latitudinarian divine with a scientific bent, was an intimate of the Princess of Wales, with whom he, joined by other philosophers, held weekly discussions. He died in May of the present year.

That sound Divine the Truth has spoke all
And pawn'd° his word Hell is not local.°
This will not give them half the trouble
Of Bargains sold,° or meanings double.

    Supposing now your Song is done,
To Minheer Hendel° next you run,
Who artfully will pare and prune
Your words to some Italian Tune.
Then print it in the largest letter,
With Capitals, the more the better.   280

    Present it boldly on your knee,
And take a Guinea for your Fee.

VERSES ON THE DEATH OF DR. S[WIFT], D.S.P.D.° OCCASIONED BY READING A MAXIM IN ROCHEFOUCAULT

This poem was composed in 1731 and was first published by Charles Bathurst in a cut version in 1739, under the supervision of Dr. William King, Principal of St. Mary Hall, Oxford, and Pope. But Swift proceeded the same year to have the poem printed entire by Faulkner in Dublin. Faulkner left many blanks in the texts and the notes; we give here the version reconstructed by Sir Harold Williams in *The Poems of Jonathan Swift* (3 vols., 1937, 1958) from contemporary manuscript additions to

272. pawn'd: pledged. **is not local:** is not an actual place. **274. Bargains sold:** "to sell a bargain; a species of wit, much in vogue about the latter end of the reign of Queen Anne, and frequently alluded to by Dean Swift, who says the maids of honour often amused themselves with it. It consisted in the seller naming his or her hinder parts, in answer to the question. What? which the buyer was artfully led to ask. As a specimen, take the following instance: A lady would come into a room full of company, apparently in a fright, crying out, It is white, and follows me! On any of the company asking, What? she sold him the bargain, by saying, Mine a——e" (Francis Grose, *A Classical Dictionary of the Vulgar Tongue* [3rd ed., 1796], ed. Eric Partridge [1963]). **276. Minheer Hendel:** George Frideric Handel (1685-1759), who had been Kapellmeister to George, Elector of Hanover, turned his second visit to England into a permanent residence when his patron succeeded to the English throne in 1714. **VERSES ON THE DEATH OF DR. SWIFT. D.S.P.D.:** Dean of St. Patrick's, Dublin.

copies of Faulkner (Williams retrieved one note from a copy of Bathurst). Occasionally quotation marks have been adjusted or added in order to clarify passages of dialogue.

AS *Rochefoucault* his Maxims drew
From Nature, I believe 'em true:
They argue no corrupted Mind
In him; the Fault is in Mankind.

    THIS Maxim more than all the rest
Is thought too base for human Breast;
"In all Distresses of our Friends
We first consult our private Ends,
While Nature kindly bent to ease us,
Points out some Circumstance to please us."   10

    IF this perhaps your Patience move
Let Reason and Experience prove.

    WE all behold with envious Eyes,
Our *Equal* rais'd above our *Size;*
Who wou'd not at a crowded Show,
Stand high himself, keep others low?
I love my Friend as well as you,
But would not have him stop my View;
Then let him have the higher Post;
I ask but for an Inch° at most.   20

    IF in a Battle you should find,
One, whom you love of all Mankind,
Had some heroick Action done,
A Champion kill'd, or Trophy won;
Rather than thus be over-topt,
Would you not wish his Lawrels cropt?

    DEAR honest *Ned* is in the Gout,
Lies rackt with Pain, and you without:°
How patiently you hear him groan!
How glad the Case is not your own!   30

    WHAT Poet would not grieve to see,
His Brethren write as well as he?
But rather than they should excel,
He'd wish his Rivals all in Hell.

    HER End when Emulation misses,
She turns to Envy, Stings and Hisses:
The strongest Friendship yields to Pride,
Unless the Odds be on our Side.

20. an Inch: an inch still higher. **28. without:** outside (his room).

VAIN human Kind! Fantastick Race!
Thy various Follies, who can trace?   40
Self-love, Ambition, Envy, Pride,
Their Empire in our Hearts divide:
Give others Riches, Power, and Station,
'Tis all on me an Usurpation.
I have no Title to aspire;
Yet, when you sink, I seem the higher.
In POPE, I cannot read a Line,
But with a Sigh, I wish it mine:
When he can in one Couplet fix
More Sense than I can do in Six: 50
It gives me such a jealous Fit,
I cry, Pox take him, and his Wit.

WHY must I be outdone by GAY,
In my own hum'rous biting Way?

ARBUTHNOT° is no more my Friend,
Who dares to Irony pretend;
Which I was born to introduce,
Refin'd it first, and shew'd its Use.

ST. JOHN, as well as PULTNEY° knows,
That I had some repute for Prose;   60
And till they drove me out of Date,
Could maul a Minister of State:
If they have mortify'd my Pride,
And made me throw my Pen aside;
If with such Talents Heav'n hath blest 'em
Have I not Reason to detest 'em?

To all my Foes, dear Fortune, send
Thy Gifts, but never to my Friend:
I tamely can endure the first,
But, this with Envy makes me burst.   70

THUS much may serve by way of Proem,°
Proceed we therefore to our Poem.

THE Time is not remote, when I
Must by the Course of Nature dye:
When I foresee my special Friends,
Will try to find their private Ends:
Tho' it is hardly° understood,
Which way my Death can do them good;

Yet, thus methinks, I hear 'em speak;
"See, how the Dean begins to break:°   80
Poor Gentleman, he droops apace,°
You plainly find it in his Face:
That old Vertigo in his Head,
Will never leave him, till he's dead:
Besides, his Memory decays,
He recollects not what he says;
He cannot call his Friends to Mind;
Forgets the Place where last he din'd:
Plyes you with Stories o'er and o'er,
He told them fifty Times before.   90
How does he fancy we can sit,
To hear his out-of-fashion'd Wit?
But he takes up with younger Fokes,
Who for his Wine will bear his Jokes:
Faith, he must make his Stories shorter,
Or change his Comrades once a Quarter:
In half the Time, he talks them round;°
There must another Sett be found.

"FOR Poetry, he's past his Prime,
And takes an Hour to find a Rhime: 100
His Fire is out, his Wit decay'd,
His Fancy sunk, his Muse a Jade.
I'd have him throw away his Pen;
But there's no talking to some Men."

AND, then their Tenderness appears,
By adding largely to my Years:
"He's older than he would be reckon'd,
And well remembers Charles the Second."°

"HE hardly° drinks a Pint of Wine;
And that, I doubt,° is no good Sign.   110
His Stomach too begins to fail:
Last Year we thought him strong and hale;
But now, he's quite another Thing;
I wish he may hold out till Spring."

THEN hug themselves, and reason thus;
"It is not yet so bad with us."

IN such a Case they talk in Tropes,°
And, by their Fears express their Hopes:
Some great Misfortune to portend,
No Enemy can match a Friend;   120

---

55. Arbuthnot: John Arbuthnot (1667–1735), Queen Anne's physician. Arbuthnot was also a writer and a friend of Swift and Pope. (See Pope's *Epistle to Dr. Arbuthnot* later in Part Two.) **59. St. John, Pultney:** See Swift's notes to lines 194 and 196. **71. Proem:** preface, introduction. **77. hardly:** with difficulty.

80. break: fail in health. **81. apace:** quickly. **97. talks . . . round:** exhausts his stories and has to start over. **107–08. He's . . . Second:** Charles II died in 1685, when Swift was eighteen years old. **109. hardly:** with difficulty. **110. doubt:** suspect. **117. in Tropes:** figuratively.

With all the Kindness they profess,
The Merit of a lucky Guess,
(When daily Howd'y's° come of Course,°
And Servants answer; *Worse and Worse*)
Wou'd please 'em better than to tell,
That, GOD be prais'd, the Dean is well.
Then he who prophecy'd the best,
Approves° his Foresight to the rest:
"You know, I always fear'd the worst,
And often told you so at first:"   130
He'd rather chuse that I should dye,
Than his Prediction prove a Lye.
Not one foretels I shall recover;
But, all agree, to give me over.°

YET shou'd some Neighbour feel a Pain,
Just in the Parts, where I complain;
How many a Message would he send?
What hearty Prayers that I should mend?
Enquire what Regimen I kept;
What gave me Ease, and how I slept?   140
And more lament, when I was dead,
Than all the Sniv'llers round my Bed.

MY good Companions, never fear,
For though you may mistake a Year;
Though your Prognosticks run too fast,
They must be verify'd at last.

BEHOLD the fatal Day arrive!
"How is the Dean?" "He's just alive."
Now the departing Pray'r is read:
"He hardly breathes." "The Dean is dead."   150
Before the Passing-Bell° begun,
The News thro' half the Town has run.
"O, may we all for Death prepare!"
"What has he left? And who's his Heir?"
"I know no more than what the News is,
'Tis all bequeath'd to publick Uses."
"To publick Use! A perfect Whim!
What had the Publick done for him!"
"Meer Envy, Avarice, and Pride!
He gave it all:—But first he dy'd."   160
"And had the Dean, in all the Nation,
No worthy Friend, no poor Relation?
So ready to do Strangers good,
Forgetting his own Flesh and Blood?"

Now Grub-Street Wits are all employ'd;
With Elegies, the Town is cloy'd:
Some Paragraph in ev'ry Paper,
To *curse* the *Dean*, or *bless* the *Drapier*.°

THE Doctors tender of their Fame,
Wisely on me lay all the Blame: 170
"We must confess his Case was nice;°
But he would never take Advice:
Had he been rul'd, for ought appears,
He might have liv'd these Twenty Years:
For when we open'd him we found,
That all his vital Parts were sound."

FROM *Dublin* soon to *London* spread,
'Tis told at Court, the Dean is dead.°

KIND Lady *Suffolk*° in the Spleen,°
Runs laughing up to tell the Queen.   180
The Queen, so Gracious, Mild, and Good,
Cries, "Is he gone? 'Tis time he shou'd.
He's dead you say; why let him rot;
I'm glad the Medals were forgot.°

168. the Drapier: [Swift's note] *The Author imagines, that the Scriblers of the prevailing Party, which he always opposed, will libel him after his Death; but that others will remember him with Gratitude, who consider the Service he had done to* Ireland, *under the Name of M. B. Drapier, by utterly defeating the destructive Project of* Wood's *Half-pence, in five Letters to the People of* Ireland, *at that Time read universally, and convincing every Reader.* [See the first of *The Drapier's Letters*, below.] **171. nice:** delicate. **178. the Dean . . . dead:** [Swift's note] *The Dean supposeth himself to dye in* Ireland. [He did.] **179. Lady Suffolk:** [Swift's note] Mrs. Howard, *afterwards Countess of* Suffolk, *then of the Bed-chamber to the Queen, professed much Friendship for the Dean. The Queen then Princess, sent a dozen times to the Dean (then in* London) *with her Command to attend her; which at last he did, by Advice of all his Friends. She often sent for him afterwards, and always treated him very Graciously. He taxed her with a Present worth Ten Pounds, which she promised before he should return to* Ireland, *but on his taking Leave, the Medals were not ready.* **in the Spleen:** in low spirits. **184. the Medals . . . forgot:** [Swift's note] *The Medals were to be sent to the Dean in four Months, but she forgot them, or thought them too dear. The Dean, being in* Ireland, *sent Mrs. Howard a Piece of* Indian *Plad made in that Kingdom: which the Queen seeing took from her, and wore it herself, and sent to the Dean for as much as would cloath herself and Children, desiring he would send the Charge of it. He did the former. It cost thirty-five Pounds, but he said he would have nothing except the Medals. He was the Summer following in* England, *was treated as usual, and she being then Queen, the Dean was promised a Settlement in* England, *but returned as he went, and, instead of Favour or Medals, hath been ever since under her Majesty's Displeasure.*

123. Howd'y's: How is he? **of Course:** automatically.
128. Approves: commends. **134. over:** up. **151. the Passing-Bell:** the death knell.

I promis'd them, I own;° but when?
I only was the Princess then;
But now as Consort of the King,
You know 'tis quite a different Thing."

    Now, *Chartres*° at Sir *Robert's* Levee,°
Tells, with a Sneer, the Tidings heavy: 190
"Why, is he dead without his Shoes°?"
(Cries *Bob*)° "I'm sorry for the News;
Oh, were the Wretch but living still,
And in his Place my good Friend *Will;*°
Or, had a Mitre on his Head°
Provided *Bolingbroke*° were dead."

    Now *Curl* his Shop from Rubbish drains;
Three genuine Tomes of *Swift's* Remains.°

And then to make them pass the glibber,°
Revis'd by *Tibbalds, Moore, and Cibber.*°   200
He'll treat me as he does my Betters.
Publish my Will, my Life, my Letters.°
Revive the Libels born to dye;
Which POPE must bear, as well as I.

    Here shift the Scene, to represent
How those I love, my Death lament.
Poor POPE will grieve a Month; and GAY
A Week; and ARBUTHNOTT a Day.

    ST. JOHN himself will scarce forbear,
To bite his Pen, and drop a Tear.   210
The rest will give a Shrug and cry,
I'm sorry; but we all must dye.
Indifference clad in Wisdom's Guise,
All Fortitude of Mind supplies:
For how can stony Bowels melt,
In those who never Pity felt;
When *We* are lash'd, *They* kiss the Rod;°
Resigning to the Will of God.

    THE Fools, my Juniors by a Year,
Are tortur'd with Suspence and Fear.   220
Who wisely° thought my Age a Screen,
When Death approach'd, to stand between:
The Screen remov'd, their Hearts are trembling,
They mourn for me without dissembling.

    MY female Friends, whose tender Hearts
Have better learn'd to act their Parts.
Receive the News in *doleful Dumps,*
"The Dean is dead, (*and what is Trumps?*)"
"Then Lord have Mercy on his Soul.
(Ladies I'll venture for the *Vole.*°)"   230

185. own: confess. 189. Chartres: [Swift's note] *Chartres is a most infamous, vile Scoundrel, grown from a Foot-Boy, or worse, to a prodigious Fortune both in England and Scotland: He had a Way of insinuating himself into all Ministers under every Change, either as Pimp, Flatterer, or Informer. He was Tryed at Seventy for a Rape, and came off by sacrificing a great Part of his Fortune (he is since dead, but this Poem still preserves the Scene and Time it was writ in.)* [Francis Charteris was convicted of rape (and pardoned) in 1730, when he was about fifty-five years old.] Levee: a morning audience held by a person of distinction before or upon rising from bed. 191. without his Shoes: To die in one's shoes meant to meet death violently, especially by hanging. 192. Cries Bob: [Swift's note] *Sir Robert Walpole, Chief Minister of State, treated the Dean in 1726, with great Distinction, invited him to Dinner at Chelsea, with the Dean's Friends chosen on Purpose; appointed an Hour to talk with him of* Ireland, *to which Kingdom and* People *the Dean found him no great Friend; for he defended* Wood's *Project of Half-pence, &c. The Dean would see him no more; and upon his next Year's return to* England, *Sir Robert on an accidental Meeting, only made a civil Compliment, and never invited him again.* 194. Will: [Swift's note] *Mr. William Pultney, from being Mr. Walpole's intimate Friend, detesting his Administration, opposed his Measures, and joined with my Lord Bolingbroke, to represent his Conduct in an excellent Paper, called the* Craftsman, *which is still continued.* [See l. 274 and note.] 195. had a . . . Head: was a bishop. 196. Bolingbroke: [Swift's note] *Henry St. John, Lord Viscount* Bolingbroke, *Secretary of State to Queen Anne of blessed Memory. He is reckoned the most Universal Genius in* Europe; *Walpole dreading his Abilities, treated him most injuriously, working with King George, who forgot his Promise of restoring the said Lord, upon the restless Importunity of* Walpole. 197–98. Now . . . Remains: [Swift's note] *Curl hath been the most infamous Bookseller of any Age or Country: His Character in Part may be found in Mr.* POPE'S Dunciad. *He published three Volumes all charged on the Dean, who never writ three Pages of them: He hath used many of the Dean's Friends in almost as vile a Manner.*

199. pass the glibber: more saleable. 200. Tibbalds . . . Cibber: [Swift's note] *Three stupid Verse Writers in* London, *the last to the Shame of the Court, and the highest Disgrace to Wit and Learning, was made Laureat.* Moore, *commonly called* Jemmy Moore, *Son of Arthur Moore, whose Father was Jaylor of Monaghan in Ireland. See the Character of* Jemmy Moore, *and* Tibbalds, Theobald *in the Dunciad* [see later in Part Two]. 201–02. He'll . . . Letters: [Swift's note] *Curl is notoriously infamous for publishing the Lives, Letters, and last Wills and Testaments of the Nobility and Ministers of State, as well as of all the Rogues, who are hanged at* Tyburn. *He hath been in Custody of the House of Lords for publishing or forging the Letters of many Peers; which made the Lords enter a Resolution in their Journal Book, that no Life or Writings of any Lord should be published without the Consent of the next Heir at Law, or Licence from their House.* 217. kiss the Rod: submit to chastisement. 221. wisely: ironic, of course; cf. l. 213. 230. the Vole: all the tricks.

"Six Deans they say must bear the Pall.
(I wish I knew what *King* to call.)"
"Madam, your Husband will attend
The Funeral of so good a Friend."
"No Madam, 'tis a shocking Sight,
And he's engag'd To-morrow Night!
My Lady *Club* wou'd take it ill,
If he shou'd fail her at *Quadrill*.°
He lov'd the Dean. (*I lead a Heart*.)
But dearest Friends, they say, must part.   240
His Time was come, he ran his Race;
We hope he's in a better Place."

WHY do we grieve that Friends should dye?
No Loss more easy to supply.
One Year is past; a different Scene;
No further mention of the Dean;
Who now, alas, no more is mist,
Than if he never did exist.
Where's now this Fav'rite of *Apollo*?
Departed; *and his Works must follow*:   250
Must undergo the common Fate;
His Kind of Wit is out of Date.
Some Country Squire to *Lintot*° goes,
Enquires for SWIFT in Verse and Prose:
Says *Lintot*, "I have heard the Name:
He dy'd a Year ago." "The same."
He searcheth all his Shop in vain;
"Sir you may find them in *Duck-lane*:°
I sent them with a Load of Books,
Last *Monday* to the Pastry-cooks.°   260
To fancy they cou'd live a Year!
I find you're but a Stranger here.
The Dean was famous in his Time;
He had a Kind of Knack at Rhyme:
His way of Writing now is past;
The Town hath got a better Taste:
I keep no antiquated Stuff;
But, spick and span I have enough.
Pray, do but give me leave to shew 'em;

Here's *Colley Cibber*'s Birth-day Poem.°   270
This Ode you never yet have seen,
By *Stephen Duck*,° upon the Queen.
Then, here's a Letter finely penn'd
Against the *Craftsman*° and his Friend;
It clearly shews that all Reflection
On Ministers, is disaffection.
Next, here's Sir *Robert*'s Vindication,°
And Mr. *Henly*'s° last Oration:
The Hawkers have not got 'em yet,
Your Honour please to buy a Set?   280

"HERE'S *Wolston*'s Tracts,° the twelfth Edition;
'Tis read by ev'ry Politician:
The Country Members,° when in Town,
To all their Boroughs send them down:
You never met a Thing so smart;
The Courtiers have them all by Heart:
Those Maids of Honour (who can read)
Are taught to use them for their Creed.
The Rev'rend Author's good Intention,
Hath been rewarded with a Pension: 290
He doth an Honour to his Gown,
By bravely running *Priest-craft* down:

---

238. **Quadrill:** (quadrille) a four-handed card game that replaced ombre as the popular pastime. 253. **Lintot:** [Swift's note] Bernard Lintot, *a Bookseller* in London. *Vide Mr. Pope's Dunciad.* [See *The Dunciad*, I. 28 and note, later in Part Two. Lintot (1675–1736) published works of many Augustan writers, including Pope, Gay, and Steele. Gay's *On a Miscellany of Poems* (see later in Part Two), which he first published in 1712, was dedicated to him.] 258. **Duck-lane:** [Swift's note] *A Place* in London *where old Books are sold.* 259–60. **a Load . . . Pastry-cooks:** for use as wrappers.

270. **Colley . . . Poem:** Cibber (1671–1757) was appointed Poet Laureate in 1730. 272. **Stephen Duck:** (1705–56), the rustic poet patronized by Queen Caroline. Swift lampooned him in *On Stephen Duck, the Thresher, and Favorite Poet, A Quibbling Epigram* (1730, the year Duck's *Poems on Several Subjects* came out). (See the selection from Duck in Part Three.) 274. **the Craftsman:** the official organ of the Opposition to Walpole, launched in December, 1726. 277. **Sir Robert's Vindication:** [Swift's note] Walpole *hires a Set of Party Scriblers, who do nothing else but write in his Defence.* 278. **Mr. Henly:** [Swift's note] Henly *is a Clergyman who wanting both Merit and Luck to get Preferment, or even to keep his Curacy in the Established Church, formed a new Conventicle, which he calls an Oratory. There, at set Times, he delivereth strange Speeches compiled by himself and his Associates, who share the Profit with him: Every Hearer pays a Shilling each Day for Admittance. He is an absolute Dunce, but generally reputed crazy.* 281. **Wolston's Tracts:** [Swift's note] Wolston *was a Clergyman, but for want of Bread, hath in several Treatises, in the most blasphemous Manner, attempted to turn Our Saviour and his Miracles into Ridicule. He is much caressed by many great Courtiers, and by all the Infidels, and his Books read generally by the Court Ladies.* [But Swift confuses Thomas Woolston (1670–1733), Deist theological writer who was convicted of blasphemy, and William Woollaston (1660–1724), moral philosopher and author of *Religion of Nature Delineated* (1722, 1724).] 283. **Country Members:** Members of Parliament from the country.

He shews, as sure as GOD's in *Gloc'ster*,°
That *Jesus* was a Grand Impostor:
That all his Miracles were Cheats,
Perform'd as Juglers do their Feats:
The Church had never such a Writer:
A Shame, he hath not got a Mitre!"

SUPPOSE me dead; and then suppose
A Club assembled at the *Rose;*°   300
Where from Discourse of this and that,
I grow the Subject of their Chat:
And, while they toss my Name about,
With Favour some, and some without;
One quite indiff'rent° in the Cause,
My Character impartial draws:

"THE DEAN, if we believe Report,
Was never ill receiv'd at Court:
As for his Works in Verse and Prose,
I own my self no Judge of those: 310
Nor, can I tell what Criticks thought 'em;
But, this I know, all People bought 'em;
As with a moral View design'd
To cure the Vices of Mankind:
His Vein, ironically grave,
Expos'd the Fool, and lash'd the Knave:
To steal a Hint was never known,
But what he writ was all his own.

"HE never thought an Honour done him,
Because a Duke was proud to own him: 320
Would rather slip aside, and chuse
To talk with Wits in dirty Shoes:
Despis'd the Fools with Stars and Garters,°
So often seen caressing *Chartres:*°
He never courted Men in Station,
Nor Persons had in Admiration;°
Of no Man's Greatness was afraid,
Because he sought for no Man's Aid.
Though trusted long in great Affairs,
He gave himself no haughty Airs: 330
Without regarding private Ends,
Spent all his Credit for his Friends:

And only chose the Wise and Good;
No Flatt'rers; no Allies in Blood;°
But succour'd Virtue in Distress,
And seldom fail'd of good Success;
As Numbers in their Hearts must own,
Who, but for him, had been unknown.

"WITH Princes kept a due Decorum,
But never stood in Awe before 'em: 340
He follow'd *David's* Lesson just,°
In Princes never put thy Trust.
And, would you make him truly sower;
Provoke him with *a slave in Power:*
The *Irish* Senate, if you nam'd,
With what Impatience he declaim'd!
Fair LIBERTY was all his Cry;
For her he stood prepar'd to die;
For her he boldly stood alone;
For her he oft expos'd his own.   350
Two Kingdoms, just as Faction led,
Had set a Price upon his Head;
But, not a Traytor cou'd be found,
To sell him for Six Hundred Pound.°

"HAD he but spar'd his Tongue and Pen,
He might have rose like other Men:
But, Power was never in his Thought;
And, Wealth he valu'd not a Groat:
Ingratitude he often found,
And pity'd those who meant the Wound: 360
But, kept the Tenor° of his Mind,
To merit well of human Kind:
Nor made a Sacrifice of those
Who still° were true, to please his Foes.
He labour'd many a fruitless Hour
To reconcile his Friends in Power;

293. God's in Gloc'ster: an old proverb deriving from the prevalence of monks in Gloucestershire. **300. the Rose:** the Rose Tavern, in Covent Garden. **305. indiff'rent:** disinterested. **323. Stars and Garters:** insignia of the orders of knighthood. **324. Chartres:** [Swift's note] *See the Notes before on Chartres.* [See l. 189 and note.] **326. had in Admiration:** held in awe.

334. Allies in Blood: relatives. **341. just:** exactly. **351-54. Two . . . Pound:** [Swift's note] *In the Year* 1713, *the late Queen was prevailed with by an Address of the House of Lords in* England, *to publish a Proclamation, promising Three Hundred Pounds to whatever Person would discover the Author of a Pamphlet called,* The Publick Spirit of the Whiggs; *and in Ireland, in the Year* 1724, *my Lord* Carteret *at his first coming into the Government, was prevailed on to issue a Proclamation for promising the like Reward of Three Hundred Pounds, to any Person who could discover the Author of a Pamphlet called,* The Drapier's Fourth Letter, &c. *writ against that destructive Project of coining Half-pence for* Ireland; *but in neither Kingdoms was the Dean discovered.* **361. Tenor:** habit. **364. still:** always.

Saw Mischief by a Faction brewing,
While they pursu'd each others Ruin.
But, finding vain was all his Care,
He left the Court in meer° Despair.°   370

"AND, oh! how short are human Schemes!
Here ended all our golden Dreams.
What ST. JOHN's Skill in State Affairs,
What ORMOND's Valour,° OXFORD's Cares,
To save their sinking Country lent,
Was all destroy'd in one Event.
Too soon that precious Life was ended,°
On which alone, our Weal depended.
When up a dangerous Faction starts,
With Wrath and Vengeance in their Hearts:°   380
By solemn League and Cov'nant bound,°
To ruin, slaughter, and confound;
To turn Religion to a Fable,
And make the Government a Babel:°

Pervert the Law, disgrace the Gown,
Corrupt the Senate, Rob the Crown;
To sacrifice old England's Glory,
And make her infamous in Story.
When such a Tempest shook the Land,
How could unguarded Virtue stand?   390

"WITH Horror, Grief, Despair the Dean
Beheld the dire destructive Scene:
His Friends in Exile, or the Tower,
Himself within the Frown of Power;
Pursu'd by base envenom'd Pens,°
Far to the Land of Slaves and Fens;°
A servile Race in Folly nurs'd,
Who truckle most, when treated worst.

By° Innocence and Resolution,
He bore continual Persecution;   400
While Numbers to Preferment rose;
Whose Merits were, to be his Foes.
When, ev'n his own familiar° Friends
Intent upon their private Ends;
Like Renegadoes now he feels,
Against him lifting up their Heels.°

"THE Dean did by his Pen defeat
An infamous destructive Cheat.°
Taught Fools their Int'rest how to know;
And gave them Arms to ward the Blow.   410
Envy hath own'd it was his doing,
To save that helpless Land from Ruin,
While they who at the Steerage stood,
And reapt the Profit, sought his Blood.

"To save them from their evil Fate,
In him was held a Crime of State.

365–70. He . . . Despair: [Swift's note] *Queen* ANNE's *Ministry fell to Variance from the first Year after their Ministry began: Harcourt the Chancellor, and Lord Bolingbroke the Secretary, were discontented with the Treasurer Oxford, for his too much Mildness to the Whig Party; this Quarrel grew higher every Day till the Queen's Death: The Dean, who was the only Person that endeavoured to reconcile them, found it impossible; and thereupon retired to the Country about ten Weeks before that fatal Event: Upon which he returned to his Deanry in Dublin, where for many Years he was worryed by the new People in Power, and had Hundreds of Libels writ against him in England.* **370. meer:** utter. **374. Ormond's Valour:** James Butler (1665–1745), Second Duke of Ormonde, was Lord Lieutenant of Ireland between 1703 and 1707 and successor to Marlborough as commander in chief of the allied forces in 1712; he helped to bring about the dishonorable peace advocated by the Tories. He followed Bolingbroke into exile in 1715 and took part in the ill-fated Jacobite attempt of that year. **377. Too . . . ended:** [Swift's note] *In the Height of the Quarrel between the Ministers, the Queen died.* **379–80. When . . . Hearts:** [Swift's note] *Upon Queen* ANNE's *Death the Whig Faction was restored to Power, which they exercised with the utmost Rage and Revenge; impeached and banished the Chief Leaders of the Church Party, and stripped all their Adherents of what Employments they had, after which England was never known to make so mean a Figure in* Europe. *The greatest Preferments in the Church in both Kingdoms were given to the most ignorant Men, Fanaticks were publickly caressed,* Ireland *utterly ruined and enslaved, only great Ministers heaping up Millions, and so Affairs continue until this present third Day of May, 1732, and are likely to go on in the same Manner.* **381. By . . . bound:** an allusion to the establishment in 1643 of Scottish Presbyterianism as the price of supporting the Puritan Revolution. As a loyal Anglican, Swift was unsympathetic to any resistance to episcopacy. **384. a Babel:** a confused assemblage.

394–95. Himself . . . Pens: [Swift's note] *Upon the Queen's Death, the Dean returned to live in Dublin, at his Deanry-House: Numberless Libels were writ against him in* England, *as a Jacobite; he was insulted in the Street, and at Nights was forced to be attended by his Servants armed.* **396. the Land . . . Fens:** [Swift's note] *The Land of Slaves and Fens,* is Ireland. **399. By:** because of (his). **403. familiar:** intimate. **406. Against . . . Heels:** them kicking him. **408. An infamous . . . Cheat:** [Swift's note] *One* Wood, *a Hardware-man from* England, *had a Patent for coining Copper Half-pence in* Ireland, *to the Sum of* 108,000l. *which in the Consequence, must leave that Kingdom without Gold or Silver (See Drapier's Letters.).*

A wicked Monster on the Bench,
Whose Fury Blood could never quench;°
As vile and profligate a Villain,
As modern *Scroggs*, or old *Tressilian;*°   420
Who long all Justice had discarded,
Nor fear'd he GOD, nor Man regarded;
Vow'd on the Dean his Rage to vent,
And make him of his Zeal repent;
But Heav'n his Innocence defends,
The grateful People stand his Friends:
Not Strains of Law, nor Judges Frown,
Nor Topicks° brought to please the Crown,
Nor Witness hir'd, nor Jury pick'd,
Prevail to bring him in convict.   430

"IN Exile° with a steady Heart,
He spent his Life's declining Part;
Where, Folly, Pride, and Faction sway,
Remote from ST. JOHN, POPE, and GAY.

"HIS Friendship there to few confin'd,
Were always of the midling Kind:°
No Fools of Rank, a mungril Breed,
Who fain would pass for Lords indeed:

Where Titles give no Right or Power,
And Peerage is a wither'd Flower,°   440
He would have held it a Disgrace,
If such a Wretch had known his Face.
On Rural Squires, that Kingdom's Bane,
He vented oft his Wrath in vain:
Biennial Squires,° to Market brought;
Who sell their Souls and Votes for Naught;
The Nation stript go joyful back,
To rob the Church, their Tenants rack,°
Go Snacks° with Thieves and Rapparees,°
And, keep the Peace, to pick up Fees: 450
In every Jobb to have a Share,
A Jayl or Barrack° to repair;
And turn the Tax for publick Roads
Commodious to° their own Abodes.

"PERHAPS I may allow, the Dean
Had too much Satyr in his Vein;
And seem'd determin'd not to starve it,
Because no Age could more deserve it.
Yet, Malice never was his Aim;
He lash'd the Vice but spar'd the Name.   460
No Individual could resent,
Where Thousands equally were meant.
His Satyr points at no Defect,
But what all Mortals may correct;
For he abhorr'd that senseless Tribe,
Who call it Humour when they jibe:
He spar'd a Hump or crooked Nose,
Whose Owners set not up for Beaux.
True genuine Dulness mov'd his Pity,
Unless it offer'd to be witty.   470
Those, who their Ignorance confess'd,
He ne'er offended with a Jest;

417–18. A wicked . . . quench: [Swift's note] *One Whitshed was then Chief Justice: He had some Years before prosecuted a Printer for a Pamphlet writ by the Dean, to perswade the People of Ireland to wear their own Manufactures. Whitshed sent the Jury down eleven Times, and kept them nine Hours, until they were forced to bring in a special Verdict. He sat as Judge afterwards on the Tryal of the Printer of the Drapier's Fourth Letter; but the Jury, against all he could say or swear, threw out the Bill: All the Kingdom took the Drapier's Part, except the Courtiers, or those who expected Places. The Drapier was celebrated in many Poems and Pamphlets: His Sign was set up in most Streets of Dublin (where many of them still continue) and in several Country Towns.* **420. Scroggs, Tressilian:** [Swift's note] *Scroggs was Chief Justice under King Charles the Second: His Judgment always varied in State Tryals, according to Directions from Court. Tressilian was a wicked Judge, hanged above three hundred Years ago.* [Sir William Scroggs (c. 1623–83), appointed Lord Chief Justice in 1678, was impeached in 1680. Sir Robert Tresilian, Chief Justice of the King's Bench, was impeached for treason in 1387 and hanged the next year.] **428. Topicks:** arguments. **431. In Exile:** [Swift's note] *In Ireland, which he had Reason to call a Place of Exile; to which Country nothing could have driven him, but the Queen's Death, who had determined to fix him in England, in Spight of the Dutchess of Somerset, &c.* **435–36. His . . . Kind:** [Swift's note] *In Ireland the Dean was not acquainted with one single Lord Spiritual or Temporal. He only conversed with private Gentlemen of the Clergy or Laity, and but a small Number of either.*

439–40. Where . . . Flower: [Swift's note] *The Peers of Ireland lost a great Part of their Jurisdiction by one single Act, and tamely submitted to this infamous Mark of Slavery without the least Resentment, or Remonstrance.* **445. Biennial Squires:** [Swift's note] *The Parliament (as they call it) in Ireland meet but once in two Years; and, after giving five Times more than they can afford, return Home to reimburse themselves by all Country Jobs and Oppressions, of which some few only are here mentioned.* **448. their . . . rack:** raise their rent. **449. Go Snacks:** divide the loot. **Rapparees:** [Swift's note] *The Highway-Men in Ireland are, since the late Wars there, usually called Rapparees, which was a Name given to those Irish Soldiers who in small Parties used, at that Time, to plunder the Protestants.* **452. Barrack:** [Swift's note] *The Army in Ireland is lodged in Barracks, the building and repairing whereof, and other Charges, have cost a prodigious Sum to that unhappy Kingdom.* **454. Commodious to:** to the advantage of.

But laugh'd to hear an Idiot quote,
A Verse from *Horace*, learn'd by Rote.

"HE knew an hundred pleasant Stories,
With all the Turns of *Whigs* and *Tories:*
Was chearful to his dying Day,
And Friends would let him have his Way.

"HE gave the little Wealth he had,
To build a House for Fools and Mad: 480
And shew'd by one satyric Touch,
No Nation wanted it so much:
That Kingdom° he hath left his Debtor,
I wish it soon may have a Better."

THE DAY OF JUDGEMENT

✥

This poem is referred to in a letter from Lord Chesterfield to Voltaire (printed in *Letters to His Son* [1774]).
The passage—in French—may be translated thus:

A propos of these [sectarian] follies, I send you
herewith a piece on them by the brilliant Dr.
Swift, which I believe will not displease you. It was
never printed—you will easily divine the reason—
but it is authentic. I have the original written in his
own hand. His Jupiter, on the day of judgment,
treats them a little like you treat them, and as they
deserve.

The text of the poem was contributed to *The St.
James's Chronicle* for April 9-12, 1774, by a pseudony-
mous person who had just been reading Chesterfield's
Letters and was moved to supply the omission of the
verses there. The fourth edition of the *Letters* (October
29, 1774) included the poem, but from a version printed
in *The Monthly Review* (July, 1774) purporting to correct
that in *The St. James's Chronicle*. As the authority of *The
Monthly Review* text is not evident, we follow the first
printing.

✥

WITH a Whirl of Thought oppress'd,
I sink from Reverie to Rest.
An horrid Vision seiz'd my Head,
I saw the Graves give up their Dead.
Jove, arm'd with Terrors, burst the Skies,
And Thunder roars, and Light'ning flies!
Amaz'd, confus'd, its Fate unknown,
The World stands trembling at his Throne.
While each pale Sinner hangs his Head,
Jove, nodding, shook the Heav'ns, and said,   10
"Offending Race of Human Kind,
By Nature, Reason, Learning, blind;
You who thro' Frailty step'd aside,
And you who never fell—*thro' Pride;*
You who in different Sects have shamm'd,
And come to see each other damn'd;
(So some Folks told you, but they knew
No more of Jove's Designs than you)
The World's mad Business now is o'er,
And I resent these Pranks no more.   20
I to such Blockheads set my Wit!
I damn such Fools!—Go, go, you're bit."°

THE BEASTS CONFESSION
TO THE PRIEST,
ON OBSERVING HOW
MOST MEN MISTAKE
THEIR OWN TALENTS

Written in the Year 1732

✥

The text is that of the first edition, printed by Faulkner
in 1738.

✥

THE PREFACE

I *HAVE been long of Opinion, that there is not a more
general and greater Mistake, or of worse Consequences
through the Commerce of Mankind, than the wrong
Judgments they are apt to entertain of their own Talents:*

---

483. That Kingdom: [Swift's note] *Meaning* Ireland, *where
he now lives, and probably may dye.*

THE DAY OF JUDGEMENT. **22. bit:** deceived, taken in.

I knew a stuttering Alderman in London, *a great Frequenter of Coffee-Houses; who, when a fresh News-Paper
was brought in, constantly seized it first, and read it aloud
to his Brother Citizens; but in a Manner, as little intelligible
to the Standers-by as to himself. How many Pretenders to
Learning expose themselves by chusing to discourse on
those very Parts of Science wherewith they are least
acquainted? It is the same Case in every other Qualification. By the Multitude of those who deal in Rhimes from
Half a Sheet to Twenty, which come out every Minute,
there must be at least five hundred Poets in the City and
Suburbs of* London; *half as many Coffee-House Orators,
exclusive of the Clergy; forty thousand Politicians; and
four thousand five hundred profound Scholars: Not to
mention the Wits, the Railliers, the Smart Fellows, and
Criticks; all as illiterate and impudent as a Suburb Whore.
What are we to think of the fine dressed Sparks, proud of
their own Personal Deformities, which appear the more
hideous by the* Contrast *of wearing Scarlet and Gold,
with what they call Toupees*[1] *on their Heads, and all the
Frippery of a modern Beau, to make a Figure before
Women; some of them with Hump-Backs, others hardly
five Foot high, and every Feature of their Faces distorted;
I have seen many of these insipid Pretenders entering into
Conversation with Persons of Learning, constantly making
the grossest Blunders in every Sentence, without conveying
one single Idea fit for a rational Creature to spend a
Thought on; perpetually confounding all Chronology and
Geography even of present Times. I compute, that* London
*hath eleven native Fools of the Beau and Puppy-Kind, for
one among us in* Dublin; *besides two thirds of ours
transplanted thither, who are now naturalized; whereby
that overgrown Capital exceeds ours in the Article of
Dunces by forty to one; and what is more to our further
Mortification, there is not one distinguished Fool of* Irish
*Birth or Education, who makes any Noise in that famous
Metropolis, unless the* London *Prints be very partial or
defective; whereas* London *is seldom without a Dozen of
their own educating, who engross the Vogue for half a
Winter together, and are never heard of more, but give
Place to a new Sett. This hath been the constant Progress
for at least thirty Years past, only allowing for the Change
of Breed and Fashion.*

THE BEASTS CONFESSION: *Preface.* 1. Toupees: [Swift's note]
Wigs with long black Tails, worn for some Years past.
November 1738.

ADVERTISEMENT

*The following Poem is grounded upon the universal
Folly in Mankind of mistaking their Talents; by which
the Author doth a great Honour to his own Species,
almost equalling them with certain Brutes; wherein,
indeed, he is too partial, as he freely confesseth: And yet
he hath gone as low as he well could, by specifying four
Animals; the Wolf, the Ass, the Swine and the Ape; all
equally mischievous, except the last, who outdoes them
in the Article of Cunning: So great is the Pride of
Man.*

WHEN Beasts could speak, (the Learned say
They still can do so every Day)
It seems, they had Religion then,
As much as now we find in Men.
It happen'd when a Plague broke out,
(Which therefore made them more devout)
The King of Brutes (to make it plain,
Of Quadrupeds I only mean)
By Proclamation gave Command,
That ev'ry Subject in the Land   10
Should to the Priest confess their Sins;
And, thus the pious Wolf begins:

GOOD Father, I must own with Shame,
That, often I have been to blame:
I must confess, on *Friday* last,
Wretch that I was, I broke my Fast:
But, I defy the basest Tongue
To prove I did my Neighbour wrong;
Or ever went to seek my Food
By Rapine, Theft, or Thirst of Blood.   20

THE Ass approaching next, confess'd,
That in his Heart he lov'd a Jest:
A Wag he was, he needs must own,
And could not let a Dunce alone:
Sometimes his Friend he would not spare,
And might perhaps be too severe:
But yet, the worst that could be said,
He was a *Wit* both born and bred;
And if it be a Sin or Shame,
Nature alone must bear the Blame: 30
One Fault he hath, is sorry for 't,
His Ears are half a Foot too short;
Which could he to the Standard bring,
He'd shew his Face before the K——:

Then, for his Voice, there's none disputes
That he's the Nightingal of Brutes.

THE Swine with contrite Heart allow'd,
His Shape and Beauty made him proud:
In Dyet was perhaps too nice,°
But Gluttony was ne'er his Vice: 40
In ev'ry Turn of Life content,
And meekly took what Fortune sent:
Inquire through all the Parish round
A better Neighbour ne'er was found:
His Vigilance might some displease;
'Tis true, he hated Sloth like Pease.°

THE Mimick Ape began his Chatter,
How evil Tongues his Life bespatter:
Much of the cens'ring° World complain'd,
Who said, his Gravity was feign'd: 50
Indeed, the Strictness of his Morals
Engag'd him in a hundred Quarrels:
He saw, and he was griev'd to see 't,
His Zeal was sometimes indiscreet:
He found, his Virtues too severe
For our corrupted Times to bear;
Yet, such a lewd licentious Age
Might well excuse a Stoick's Rage.

THE Goat advanc'd with decent Pace;
And, first excus'd his youthful Face;   60
Forgiveness begg'd, that he appear'd
('Twas Nature's Fault) without a Beard.
'Tis true, he was not much inclin'd
To Fondness for the Female Kind;
Not, as his Enemies object,
From Chance, or natural Defect;
Not by his frigid Constitution;
But, through a pious Resolution;
For, he had made a holy Vow
Of Chastity, as Monks do now;   70
Which he resolv'd to keep for ever hence,
As strictly too; as doth his Reverence.°

APPLY the Tale, and you shall find
How just it suits with human Kind.
Some Faults we own: But, can you guess?
Why?—Virtues carry'd to Excess;
Wherewith our Vanity endows us,
Though neither Foe nor Friend allows us.°

THE Lawyer swears, you may rely on 't,
He never squeez'd a needy Clyent: 80
And, this he makes his constant Rule;
For which his Brethren call him Fool:
His Conscience always was so nice,
He freely gave the Poor Advice;
By which he lost, he may affirm,
A hundred Fees last *Easter* Term.°
While others of the learned Robe
Would break the Patience of a *Job*,
No Pleader at the Bar could match
His Diligence and quick Dispatch;   90
Ne'er kept a Cause,° he well may boast,
Above a Term or two at most.

THE cringing Knave who seeks a Place
Without Success; thus tells his Case:
Why should he longer mince the Matter?
He fail'd, because he could not flatter:
He had not learn'd to turn his Coat,
Nor for a Party give his Vote:
His Crime he quickly understood;
Too zealous for the Nation's Good: 100
He found, the Ministers resent it,
Yet could not for his Heart° repent it.

THE Chaplain vows, he cannot fawn,
Though it would raise him to the Lawn:°
He pass'd his Hours among his Books;
You find it in his meagre Looks:
He might, if he were worldly-wise,
Preferment get, and spare his Eyes:
But own'd, he had a stubborn Spirit
That made him trust alone in Merit: 110
Would rise by Merit to Promotion;
Alass! a meer Chymerick Notion.

THE Doctor, if you will believe him,
Confess'd a Sin, and God forgive him:
Call'd up at Mid-night, ran to save
A blind old Beggar from the Grave:
But, see how *Satan* spreads his Snares;
He quite forgot to say his Pray'rs.
He cannot help it for his Heart
Sometimes to act the Parson's Part: 120

---

39. **nice:** particular, fastidious. 46. **Pease:** peas. 49. **cens'ring:** censuring. 72. **his Reverence** [Swift's note] *The Priest his Confessor.* 78. **allows us:** credits us (with them).

86. **Easter Term:** The law courts, like the universities, divided their sessions into terms. 91. **kept a Cause:** held back a case. 102. **for his Heart:** to save his life. 104. **the Lawn:** a bishopric. Sleeves made of a fine linen known as lawn were an emblem of this office.

Quotes from the Bible many a Sentence
That moves his Patients to Repentance:
And, when his Med'cines do no good,
Supports their Minds with heav'nly Food.
At which, however well intended,
He hears the Clergy are offended;
And grown so bold behind his Back
To call him Hypocrite and Quack.
In his own Church he keeps a Seat;
Says Grace before, and after Meat;   130
And calls, without affecting Airs,
His Houshold twice a Day to Pray'rs.
He shuns Apothecary's Shops;
And hates to cram the Sick with Slops:
He scorns to make his Art a Trade;
Nor bribes my Lady's fav'rite Maid.
Old Nurse-keepers° would never hire
To recommend him to the Squire;
Which others, whom he will not name,
Have often practis'd to their Shame.   140

THE Statesman tells you with a *Sneer*,
His Fault is to be too *Sincere;*
And, having no sinister Ends,
Is apt to disoblige his Friends.
The Nation's Good, his Master's° Glory,
Without Regard to *Whig* or *Tory*,
Were all the Schemes he had in View;
Yet he was seconded by few:
Though some had spread a thousand Lyes;
'Twas *He* defeated the EXCISE.°   150
'Twas known, tho' he had born° Aspersion;
That, *Standing Troops* were his Aversion:°
His Practice was, in ev'ry Station
To serve the King, and please the Nation.
Though hard to find in ev'ry Case
The fittest Man to fill a Place:
His Promises he ne'er forgot,
But took Memorials° on the Spot:
His Enemies, for want of Charity,
Said, he affected Popularity: 160
'Tis true, the People understood,
That all he did was for their Good;

Their kind Affections he has try'd;°
No Love is lost on either Side.
He came to Court with Fortune clear,
Which now he runs out° every Year;
Must, at the Rate that he goes on,
Inevitably be undone.
Oh! if his Majesty would please
To give him but a Writ of Ease,°   170
Would grant him Licence to retire,
As it hath long been his Desire,
By fair Accounts it would be found
He's poorer by ten thousand Pound.
He owns, and hopes it is no Sin,
He ne'er was partial to his Kin;
He thought it base for Men in Stations,
To crowd the Court with their Relations:
His Country was his dearest Mother,
And ev'ry virtuous Man his Brother: 180
Through Modesty, or aukward Shame,
(For which he owns himself to blame)
He found the wisest Men he could,
Without Respect to Friends, or Blood;
Nor ever acts on private Views,
When he hath Liberty to chuse.

THE Sharper swore he hated Play,°
Except to pass an Hour away:
And, well he might; for to his Cost,
By want of Skill, he always lost: 190
He heard, there was a Club of Cheats
Who had contriv'd a thousand Feats;
Could change the Stock,° or cog a Dye,°
And thus deceive the sharpest Eye:
No Wonder how his Fortune sunk,
His Brothers fleece him when he's drunk.

I OWN, the Moral not exact;
Besides, the Tale is false in Fact;
And, so absurd, that could I raise up
From Fields *Elyzian*, fabling *Esop;*   200
I would accuse him to his Face
For libelling the *Four-foot* Race.
Creatures of ev'ry Kind but ours
Well comprehend their nat'ral Powers;

---

137. **Nurse-keepers:** sick-nurses. **145. his Master's:** ambiguously the King's or God's. **150. the Excise:** Walpole's excise bill, introduced in 1733 to prevent smuggling, met with so much opposition that it was abandoned, **151. born:** borne. **152. Standing . . . Aversion:** From the time of the Peace of Ryswick in September, 1697, it was popular in England to oppose a standing army. **158. Memorials:** notes, memoranda.

163. **try'd:** tested; with the ironic suggestion of abusive treatment. Similarly, in the next line, Swift uses the ironic phrase "No love is lost" with mock innocence. **166. runs out:** exhausts. **170. Writ of Ease:** a written statement of discharge from employment. **187. Play:** gambling. **193. the Stock:** the undealt part of a deck of cards. **cog a Dye:** conceal or manipulate dice.

While We, whom *Reason* ought to sway,
Mistake our Talents ev'ry Day:°
The Ass was never known so stupid
To act the Part of *Tray*, or *Cupid;*
Nor leaps upon his Master's Lap,
There to be stroak'd and fed with Pap;   210
As *Esop* would the World perswade;°
He better understands his Trade:
Nor comes whene'er his Lady whistles;
But, carries Loads, and feeds on Thistles;
Our Author's Meaning, I presume, is
A Creature *bipes et implumis;*°
Wherein the Moralist design'd
A Compliment on Human-Kind:
For, here he owns, that now and then
Beasts may *degen'rate* into Men.°   220

ON POETRY: A RAPSODY

A rhapsody is a disconnected or miscellaneous composition marked by an effusive, extravagant style.
Swift's self-mockery is really a pointer to the *object* of
his satire.

The poem was first published in Dublin (it was
reprinted in London) as a folio pamphlet on December
31, 1733; we take our text from this edition, incorporating variants from Faulkner's edition of Swift's *Works*
(1735). Additional passages, preserved by Lord Orrery
and Sir Walter Scott, which were suppressed apparently
in fear of political reprisal, are reproduced in the
footnotes.

ALL Human Race wou'd fain be *Wits*,
And Millions miss, for one that hits.
Young's universal Passion, *Pride*,°
Was never known to spread so wide.
Say *Britain*, cou'd you ever boast,—
Three *Poets* in an Age at most?
Our chilling Climate hardly bears
A *Sprig* of Bays° in Fifty Years:
While ev'ry Fool his Claim alledges,
As if it grew in common Hedges.   10
What Reason can there be assign'd
For this Perverseness in the Mind?
Brutes find out where their Talents lie:
A *Bear* will not attempt to fly:
A founder'd° *Horse* will oft debate,
Before he tries a five-barr'd Gate:°
A *Dog* by Instinct turns aside,
Who sees the Ditch too deep and wide.
But *Man* we find the only Creature,
Who, led by *Folly*, combats *Nature;*   20
Who, when *she* loudly cries, *Forbear*,
With Obstinacy fixes there;
And, where his *Genius* least inclines,
Absurdly bends his whole Designs.

Not *Empire* to the Rising-Sun,
By Valour, Conduct, Fortune won;
Nor highest *Wisdom* in Debates
For framing Laws to govern States;
Nor Skill in Sciences profound,
So large to grasp the Circle round;°   30
Such heavenly Influence require,
As how to strike the *Muses Lyre.*

Not Beggar's Brat, on Bulk° begot;
Not Bastard of a Pedlar *Scot;*
Not Boy brought up to cleaning Shoes,
The Spawn of *Bridewell*,° or the Stews;°
Not Infants dropt, the spurious Pledges
Of *Gipsies* littering° under Hedges,

203–06. **Creatures . . . Day:** Cf. Rochester's *A Satyr
Against Mankind* in Part One. 211. **As . . . perswade:** in his
fable *The Ass and the Little Dog.* Swift's criticism of Aesop is
of course ironic: the method of both was to reveal human
nature through the fanciful depictions of animal nature,
whether the latter are made to appear "natural" or not. 216.
bipes et implumis: [Swift's note] *A Definition of Man, disapproved by all Logicians. Homo est Animal bipes, implume,
erecto vultu.* 220. **Beasts . . . Men:** [Swift's note] *Vide
Gulliver in his Account of the* Houyhnhnms.

ON POETRY. **3. Young's . . . Pride:** a collection of satires
by Edward Young (1683–1765) called *The Universal Passion*
(see Part Three), published 1725–28. The first four prompted
Swift's short poem *On Reading Dr. Young's Satires, Called the
Universal Passion.* (See also the selection from Young in Part
Five.) **8. A Sprig . . . Bays:** symbol of poetic genius.
15. founder'd: lame. **16. five-barr'd Gate:** high fence or
hurdle. **30. the Circle round:** the whole world. **33. Bulk:**
a projection on the front of a shop for the displaying of
wares. **36. Bridewell:** a poorhouse and prison. **the Stews:**
the brothel quarters. **38. littering:** (1) making their beds;
(2) procreating.

Are so disqualified by Fate
To rise in *Church*, or *Law*, or *State*,   40
As he, whom *Phebus*° in his Ire
Hath *blasted* with poetick Fire.

What hope of Custom° in the *Fair*,
While not a Soul demands your Ware?
Where you have nothing to produce
For private Life, or publick Use?
Court, *City*, *Country* want you not;
You cannot bribe, betray, or plot.
For Poets, Law makes no Provision:
The Wealthy have you in Derision.   50
Of State-Affairs you cannot smatter,°
Are awkward when you try to flatter.
Your Portion,° taking *Britain* round,°
Was just one annual Hundred Pound.°
Now not so much as in Remainder°
Since *Cibber* brought in an Attainder;°
For ever fixt by Right Divine,
(A Monarch's Right) on *Grubstreet* Line.
Poor starv'ling Bard, how small thy Gains!
How unproportion'd to thy Pains!   60

And here a *Simile* comes Pat° in:
Tho' *Chickens* take a Month to fatten,
The Guests in less than half an Hour
Will more than half a Score devour.
So, after toiling twenty Days,
To earn a Stock of Pence and Praise,
Thy Labours, grown the Critick's Prey,
Are swallow'd o'er a Dish of Tea;
Gone, to be never heard of more,
Gone, where the *Chickens* went before.   70

How shall a new Attempter learn
Of diff'rent Spirits to discern,
And how distinguish, which is which,
The Poet's Vein, or scribling Itch°?
Then hear an old experienc'd Sinner
Instructing thus a young Beginner.

Consult yourself, and if you find
A powerful Impulse urge your Mind,
Impartial judge within your Breast
What Subject you can manage best;   80
Whether your Genius most inclines
To Satire, Praise, or hum'rous Lines;
To Elegies in mournful Tone,
Or Prologue sent from Hand unknown.
Then rising with *Aurora*'s Light,°
The Muse invok'd, sit down to write;
Blot out, correct, insert, refine,
Enlarge, diminish, interline;
Be mindful, when Invention fails,
To scratch your Head, and bite your Nails.   90

Your Poem finish'd, next your Care
Is needful, to transcribe it fair.
In modern Wit all printed Trash, is
Set off with num'rous *Breaks*——and *Dashes*—

To Statesmen wou'd you give a Wipe,°
You print it in *Italick Type*.
When Letters are in vulgar° Shapes,
'Tis ten to one the Wit escapes;
But when in *Capitals* exprest,
The dullest Reader smoaks° a Jest: 100
Or else perhaps he may invent
A better than the Poet meant,
As learned Commentators view
In *Homer* more than *Homer* knew.

Your Poem in its modish Dress,
Correctly fitted for the Press,
Convey by Penny-Post to *Lintot*,°
But let no Friend alive look into 't.
If *Lintot* thinks 'twill quit° the Cost,
You need not fear your Labour lost: 110
And, how agreeably surpriz'd
Are you to see it advertiz'd!
The Hawker shews you one in Print,
As fresh as Farthings from the Mint:
The Product of your Toil and Sweating;
A Bastard of your own begetting.

Be sure at *Will*'s° the following Day,
Lie Snug, to hear what Criticks say.

---

41. Phebus: Apollo. **43. Custom:** selling. **51. smatter:** talk superficially. **53. Portion:** share, allotment. **round:** all around, inclusively. **54. Hundred Pound:** [Swift's note] Paid to the Poet Laureat, which Place was given to one *Cibber*, a Player. **55. in Remainder:** the residual interest of an estate, predetermined by the original conveyance. **56. an Attainder:** an act declaring the forfeiture of the estate and civil rights of a criminal condemned to death. **61. Pat:** aptly. **74. scribling Itch:** Juvenal's *scribendi cacoethes* (*Satires*, III. vii. 52).

85. with . . . Light: at dawn. **95. a Wipe:** a jibe. **97. vulgar:** common, ordinary. **100. smoaks:** notices, catches on to. **107. Lintot:** Bernard Lintot (1675–1736), a London bookseller and publisher. He published many works of the Augustan writers. **109. quit:** offset. **117. Will's:** the famous coffee house in Covent Garden where the wits congregated.

And if you find the general Vogue°
Pronounces you a stupid Rogue; 120
Damns all your Thoughts as low and little,
Sit still, and swallow down your Spittle.
Be silent as a Politician,
For talking may beget Suspicion:
Or praise the Judgment of the Town,
And help yourself to run it down.
Give up your fond paternal Pride,
Nor argue on the weaker Side;
For Poems read without a Name
We justly praise, or justly blame: 130
And Criticks have no partial Views,
Except they know whom they abuse.
And since you ne'er provok'd their Spight,
Depend upon 't their Judgment 's right:
But if you blab, you are undone;
Consider what a Risk you run.
You lose your Credit all at once;
The Town will mark you for a Dunce:
The vilest Doggrel *Grubstreet* sends,
Will pass for yours with Foes and Friends. 140
And you must bear the whole Disgrace,
'Till some fresh Blockhead takes your Place.

Your Secret kept, your Poem sunk,
And sent in Quires to line a Trunk;°
If still you be dispos'd to rhime,
Go try your Hand a second Time.
Again you fail, yet Safe 's the Word,°
Take Courage, and attempt a Third.
But first with Care imploy your Thoughts,
Where Criticks mark'd your former Faults. 150
The trivial Turns, the borrow'd Wit,
The *Similes* that nothing fit;
The *Cant* which ev'ry Fool repeats,
Town-Jests, and Coffee-house Conceits;
Descriptions tedious, flat and dry,
And introduc'd the Lord knows why;
Or where we find your Fury set
Against the harmless Alphabet;
On A's and B's your Malice vent,
While Readers wonder whom you meant. 160
A publick, or a private *Robber;*
A *Statesman,* or a South-Sea *Jobber.*°
A *Prelate* who no God believes;

A ———,° or Den of Thieves.°
A Pick-purse at the Bar, or Bench;
A Duchess, or a Suburb-Wench.°
Or oft when Epithets you link,
In gaping Lines to fill a Chink;°
Like stepping Stones to save a Stride,
In Streets where Kennels° are too wide: 170
Or like a Heel-piece to support
A Cripple with one Foot too short:
Or like a Bridge that joins a Marish°
To Moorlands of a diff'rent Parish.
So have I seen ill-coupled° Hounds,
Drag diff'rent Ways in miry Grounds.
So Geographers in *Afric*-Maps
With Savage-Pictures fill their Gaps;
And o'er unhabitable Downs
Place Elephants for want of Towns. 180

But tho' you miss your third Essay,°
You need not throw your Pen away.
Lay now aside all Thoughts of Fame,
To spring more profitable Game.
From Party-Merit seek Support;
The vilest Verse thrives best at Court.°
A Pamphlet in Sir *Bob*'s Defence
Will never fail to bring in Pence;
Nor be concern'd about the Sale,
He pays his Workmen on the Nail.° 190

164. ———: "Parliament." **Thieves:** canceled lines: "A House of Peers, or Gaming Crew, / A griping [i.e., grasping] Monarch, or a Jew." **166. Suburb-Wench:** prostitute (from the suburbs of London where the rabble dwelt). **168. In . . . Chink:** in lines conspicuous as mere fillers. **170. Kennels:** gutters. **173. Marish:** marsh. **175. ill-coupled:** not securely teamed. **181. Essay:** attempt. **186. Court:** canceled lines:

> And may you ever have the luck
> To rhyme almost as ill as Duck;
> And, though you never learn'd to scan verse,
> Come out with some lampoon on D'Anvers.

Stephen Duck was a rustic poet patronized by Queen Caroline. (See the selection from Duck in Part Three.) "Caleb D'Anvers" was the general pseudonym used by the editor of, and contributors to, *The Craftsman,* the official organ of the Opposition to Walpole. **190. on the Nail:** on the spot, without delay. Canceled lines:

> Display the blessings of the Nation,
> And praise the whole Administration,
> Extoll yͤ Bench of Bishops round,
> Who at them rail bid God Confound:
> To Bishop-Haters answer thus
> (The only Logick us'd by Us)
> What tho' they don't believe in Christ
> Deny them Protestants—thou ly'st.

119. Vogue: current opinion or belief. **144. to . . . Trunk:** Paper or linen was used to line traveling cases. **147. Safe . . . Word:** a Scottish proverb, derived from the watchword of soldiers spoken when a great danger had passed. **162. Jobber:** broker.

A Prince the Moment he is crown'd,
Inherits ev'ry Virtue round,°
As Emblems of the sov'reign Pow'r,
Like other Bawbles of the Tow'r.°
Is gen'rous, valiant, just and wise,
And so continues 'till he dies.
His humble *Senate* this professes,
In all their *Speeches, Votes, Addresses.*
But once you fix him in a Tomb,
His Virtues fade, his Vices bloom;   200
And each Perfection wrong imputed
Is fully at his Death confuted.
The Loads of Poems in his Praise,
Ascending make one Funeral-Blaze.°
As soon as you can hear his Knell,
This God on Earth turns *Devil* in Hell.
And, lo, his Ministers of State,
Transform'd to Imps,° his Levee wait.
Where, in the Scenes of endless Woe,
They ply their former Arts below.   210
And as they sail in *Charon's* Boat,
Contrive to bribe the Judge's Vote.
To *Cerberus* they give a Sop,
His triple-barking Mouth to stop:
Or in the Iv'ry Gate of Dreams,
Project * * * and * * * * * * *:°
Or hire their Party-Pamphleteers,
To set *Elysium* by the Ears.°

  Then *Poet,* if you mean to thrive,
Employ your Muse on Kings alive;   220
With Prudence gath'ring up a Cluster
Of all the Virtues you can muster:
Which form'd into a Garland sweet,
Lay humbly at your Monarch's Feet;
Who, as the Odours reach his Throne,
Will smile, and think 'em all his own:
For *Law* and *Gospel* both determine
All Virtues lodge in royal Ermine.
(I mean the Oracles of Both,
Who shall depose it upon Oath.)   230

Your Garland in the following Reign,
Change but the Names, will do again.

  But if you think this Trade too base,
(Which seldom is the Dunce's Case)
Put on the Critick's Brow, and sit
At *Wills* the puny Judge of Wit.
A Nod, a Shrug, a scornful Smile,
With Caution us'd, may serve a-while.
Proceed no further in your Part,
Before you learn the Terms of Art: 240
(For you can never be too far gone,
In all our modern Criticks Jargon.)
Then talk with more authentick Face,
Of *Unities, in Time and Place.*
Get Scraps of *Horace* from your Friends,
And have them at your Fingers Ends.
Learn *Aristotle's* Rules by Rote,
And at all Hazards boldly quote:
Judicious *Rymer*° oft review:
Wise *Dennis,*° and profound *Bossu.*°   250
Read all the *Prefaces* of *Dryden,*
For these our Criticks much confide in,
(Tho' meerly writ at first for filling
To raise the Volume's Price, a Shilling.)

  A forward Critick often dupes us
With sham Quotations *Peri Hupsous:*°
And if we have not read *Longinus,*
Will magisterially out-shine us.
Then, lest with *Greek* he over-run ye,
Procure the Book for Love or Money,   260
Translated from *Boileau's* Translation,°
And quote *Quotation* on *Quotation.*

  At *Wills* you hear a Poem read,
Where *Battus*° from the Table-head,

---

192. **round:** either (1) in considerable quantity or (2) finished to perfection. 194. **Bawbles . . . Tow'r:** a reference to the museum pieces housed in the Tower of London, e.g., the spoils of the defeated Spanish Armada. 204. **Funeral-Blaze:** canceled lines: "His panegyrics then are ceased, / He grows a tyrant, dunce, or beast." 208. **Imps:** children of the devil, evil spirits. 216. * * * . . . * * *: Excise and South-Sea Schemes (as the use of letters, along with dashes and asterisks, in other editions indicates). 218. **by the Ears:** at variance.

249. **Judicious Rymer:** Thomas Rymer (1641–1713), English critic. 250. **Wise Dennis:** John Dennis (1657–1735), English playwright and critic. (See the selection from Dennis later in Part Two.) **profound Bossu:** René Le Bossu (1631–89), author of *Traité du poème épique* (1675). 256. **Peri Hupsous:** [Swift's note] A famous Treatise of *Longinus.* [It is better known now by its translated title, *On the Sublime.* The treatise is now thought to have been written in the first half of the first century A.D.—at least 150 years before Longinus was born.] 261. **Boileau's Translation:** [Swift's note] By Mr. *Welsted.* [Leonard Welsted (1688–1747) published his translation of Longinus's works in 1712; Boileau's had appeared in 1694.] 264. **Battus:** *Battos* is Greek for *stammerer.* The word was used as the name for a Greek king who had difficulty in speaking; here it means a critic who cannot even speak properly.

Reclining on his Elbow-chair,
Gives Judgment with decisive Air.
To him the Tribe of circling Wits,
As to an Oracle submits.
He gives Directions to the Town,
To cry it up, or run it down.   270
(Like *Courtiers*, when they send a Note,
Instructing *Members* how to Vote.)
He sets the Stamp of Bad and Good,
Tho' not a Word be understood.
Your Lesson learnt, you'll be secure
To get the Name of *Connoisseur*.
And when your Merits once are known,
Procure Disciples of your own.

    For Poets (you can never want° 'em,
Spread thro' *Augusta Trinobantum°*)   280
Computing by their Pecks of Coals,°
Amount to just Nine thousand Souls.
These o'er their proper Districts govern,
Of Wit and Humour, Judges sov'reign.
In ev'ry Street a City-bard
Rules, like an Alderman his Ward.
His indisputed Rights extend
Thro' all the Lane, from End to End.
The Neighbours round admire his *Shrewdness*,
For Songs of *Loyalty* and *Lewdness*.   290
Out-done by none in Rhyming well,
Altho' he never learnt to spell.

    Two bordering Wits contend for Glory;
And one is *Whig*, and one is *Tory*.
And this, for Epicks claims the Bays,
And that, for Elegiack Lays.
Some famed for Numbers soft and smooth,
By Lovers spoke in *Punch*'s Booth.°
And some as justly Fame extols
For lofty Lines in *Smithfield* Drols.°   300

Bavius in *Wapping* gains Renown,
And *Mævius* reigns o'er *Kentish-Town*:°
Tigellius° plac'd in *Phœbus*' Car,
From *Ludgate* shines to *Temple-bar*.°
Harmonious *Cibber* entertains
The Court with annual Birth-day Strains;
Whence *Gay* was banish'd in Disgrace,°
Where *Pope* will never show his Face;
Where *Y——°* must torture his Invention,
To flatter *Knaves*, or lose his *Pension*.   310

    But these are not a thousandth Part
Of Jobbers in the Poets Art,
Attending each his proper Station,
And all in due Subordination;
Thro' ev'ry Alley to be found,
In Garrets high, or under Ground:
And when they join their *Pericranies*,°
Out skips a *Book of Miscellanies*.
Hobbes clearly proves that ev'ry Creature
Lives in a State of War by Nature.   320
The Greater for the Smaller watch,
But meddle seldom with their Match.
A Whale of moderate Size will draw
A Shole of Herrings down his Maw.
A Fox with Geese his Belly crams;
A Wolf destroys a thousand Lambs.
But search among the rhiming Race,
The Brave are worried by the Base.
If, on *Parnassus*' Top you sit,
You rarely bite, are always bit: 330
Each Poet of inferior Size
On you shall rail and criticize;
And strive to tear you Limb from Limb,
While others do as much for him.

---

279. want: be without. **280. Augusta Trinobantum:**
The Trinobantes (or Trinovantes) were an ancient people
of southeastern Britain; they sided with Julius Caesar
against the Belgic settlers from Gaul. **281. Pecks of Coals:**
Like Pope in *The Dunciad* (see later in Part Two) Swift jeers
at the poets who cannot afford to buy coal—expensive
because it had to be brought to the southeast by boat from
county Durham—except in small quantities. Swift felt, as did
Dr. Johnson, that bad poets ought to be doing something
else for a living. **298. in Punch's Booth:** in Punch and
Judy shows. **300. Smithfield Drols:** farces or puppet
shows.

301–02. Bavius . . . Kentish-Town: Bavius and
Maevius were ancient Roman poets, mentioned by Virgil
in *Eclogues*, iii. 90. Wapping and Kentish Town were
hamlets near London and are now part of London. **303.
Tigellius:** Tigellius Hermogenes was a favored singer of
Julius Caesar, Cleopatra, and Octavian; he is mentioned in
Horace's *Satires*, I. ii. 3 and I. iii. 4. **304. Ludgate, Temple-
bar:** Ludgate was one of the four ancient gates of the City of
London; it was made into a prison in 1373 and razed in 1760.
Temple Bar was another gateway, at the end of Fleet Street.
307. Whence . . . Disgrace: apparently a reference to the
prohibition of *Polly;* see the headnote to *The Beggar's Opera*
later in Part Two. **309. Y——:** Edward Young, whose
poem *The Installment* was addressed to Walpole and won
him a pension. **317. Pericranies:** from *pericranium;* the
meaning here is "brains" or "wits."

The Vermin only teaze and pinch
Their Foes superior by an Inch.
So, Nat'ralists observe, a Flea
Hath smaller Fleas that on him prey,
And these have smaller yet to bite 'em,
And so proceed *ad infinitum:*   340
Thus ev'ry Poet in his Kind,
Is bit by him that comes behind;
Who, tho' too little to be seen,
Can teaze, and gall, and give the Spleen;°
Call Dunces, Fools, and Sons of Whores,
Lay *Grubstreet* at each others Doors:
Extol the *Greek* and *Roman* Masters,
And curse our modern Poetasters.
Complain, as many an ancient Bard did,
How Genius is no more rewarded;   350
How wrong a Taste prevails among us;
How much our Ancestors out-sung us;
Can personate° an awkward Scorn
For those who are not Poets born:
And all their Brother Dunces lash,
Who crowd the Press with hourly Trash.

O, *Grubstreet!* how do I bemoan thee,
Whose graceless Children scorn to own thee!
Their filial Piety forgot,
Deny their Country like a SCOT:°   360
Tho' by their Idiom and Grimace
They soon betray their native Place:
Yet *thou* hast greater Cause to be
Asham'd of them, than they of thee.
Degenerate from their ancient Brood,
Since first the Court allow'd them Food.

Remains a Difficulty still,
To purchase Fame by writing ill:
From *Flecknoe*° down to *Howard*'s° Time,
How few have reach'd the *low Sublime*°?   370
For when our high-born *Howard* dy'd,
Blackmore° alone his Place supply'd:
And least° a Chasm should intervene,
When Death had finish'd *Blackmore*'s Reign,
The *leaden Crown* devolv'd to thee,
Great Poet of the *Hollow-Tree*.°
But, oh, how unsecure thy Throne!
Ten thousand Bards thy Right disown:
They plot to turn in factious Zeal,
Duncenia to a Common-weal;°   380
And with rebellious Arms pretend
An equal Priv'lege to *descend.*

In Bulk there are not more Degrees,
From *Elephants* to *Mites* in Cheese,
Than what a curious° Eye may trace
In Creatures of the rhiming Race.
From bad to worse, and worse they fall,
But, who can reach to Worst of all?
For, tho' in Nature Depth and Height
Are equally held infinite,   390
In Poetry the Height we know;
'Tis only infinite below.
For Instance: When you rashly think,
No Rhymer can like *Welsted* sink.°
His Merits ballanc'd you shall find,
The *Laureat*° leaves him far behind.

---

344. give the Spleen: make melancholy and hypochondriac. **353. personate:** put on, assume. **360. like a Scot:** "Mr. Davies mentioned my name, and respectfully introduced me to him. I was much agitated; and recollecting his prejudice against the Scotch, of which I had heard much, I said to Davies, 'Don't tell where I come from.' —'From Scotland,' cried Davies, roguishly. 'Mr. Johnson, (said I) I do indeed come from Scotland, but I cannot help it.' I am willing to flatter myself that I meant this as light pleasantry to sooth and conciliate him, and not as an humiliating abasement at the expence of my country. But however that might be, this speech was somewhat unlucky; for with that quickness of wit for which he was so remarkable, he seized the expression 'come from Scotland,' which I used in the sense of being of that country; and, as if I had said that I had come away from it, or left it, retorted, 'That, Sir, I find, is what a very great many of your countrymen cannot help'" (Boswell's *Life of Johnson*).

369. Flecknoe: See Dryden's *Mac Flecknoe* in Part One. **Howard:** either Sir Robert Howard (Dryden's collaborator) or his brother Edward. **370. the low Sublime:** See Pope's *Peri Bathous* later in Part Two. **372. Blackmore:** Sir Richard Blackmore (1654–1729), physician and poet; a favorite target of the Augustan wits. **373. least:** lest. **376. Hollow-Tree:** [Swift's note] Lord G——. [William Luckyn Grimston (1683–1756), Baron Dunboyne and Viscount Grimston in the Irish peerage, published his play *The Lawyer's Fortune, or Love in a Hollow Tree* in 1705.] **380. Duncenia . . . Common-weal:** a monarchy to a republic. **385. curious:** careful. **394. No . . . sink:** [Swift's note] *Vide* The Treatise on the *Profound*, and Mr. *Pope's Dunciad*. **396. The Laureat:** "That *Feilding*" in the first and some other editions. In Faulkner's edition (1735) appears the note: "*In the* London *Edition, instead of* Laureat, *was maliciously inserted Mr.* Fielding, *for whose ingenious Writings the supposed Author hath manifested a great Esteem.*" The "Laureat" meant is Cibber.

Concannen,° more aspiring Bard,
Climbs downwards, deeper, by a Yard:
Smart JEMMY MOOR° with Vigor drops,
The Rest pursue as thick as Hops: 400
With Heads to Points° the Gulph they enter,
Linkt perpendicular to the Centre:
And as their Heels elated rise,
Their Heads attempt the nether Skies.

O, what Indignity and Shame
To prostitute the Muse's Name,
By flatt'ring ———° whom Heaven design'd
The Plague and Scourges of Mankind.
Bred up in Ignorance and Sloth,
And ev'ry Vice that nurses both.°   410

Fair *Britain* in thy Monarch blest,
Whose Virtues bear the strictest Test;
Whom never *Faction* cou'd bespatter,
Nor *Minister,* nor *Poet* flatter.
What Justice in rewarding Merit?
What Magnanimity of Spirit?°
What Lineaments divine we trace
Thro' all his Figure, Mien and Face;

Tho' Peace with Olive bind his Hands,
Confest the conqu'ring Hero stands.   420
Hydaspes, Indus, and the *Ganges,*°
Dread from his Hand impending Changes.
From him the *Tartar,* and *Chinese,*
Short by the Knees° intreat for Peace.
The *Consort*° of his Throne and Bed,
A perfect Goddess born and bred.
Appointed sov'reign Judge to sit
On Learning, Eloquence and Wit.
Our eldest Hope, divine *Iülus,*°
(Late, very late, O, may he rule us.)   430
What early Manhood has he shown,
Before his downy Beard was grown!
Then think, what Wonders will be done
By going on as he begun;
An Heir for *Britain* to secure
As long as Sun and Moon endure.

The Remnant of the royal Blood,
Comes pouring on me like a Flood.
Bright Goddesses, in Number five;°
Duke *William,*° sweetest Prince alive.   440

Now sing the *Minister of State,*°
Who shines alone, without a Mate.
Observe with what majestick Port
This *Atlas* stands to prop the Court:
Intent the Publick Debts to pay,
Like prudent *Fabius*° by *Delay.*
Thou great Vicegerent of the King,
Thy Praises ev'ry Muse shall sing.
In all Affairs thou sole Director,
Of Wit and Learning chief Protector;   450
Tho' small the Time thou has to spare,
The Church is thy peculiar Care.
Of pious Prelates what a Stock
You chuse to rule the Sable-flock.

397. Concannen: Matthew Concanen (1701–49), political hack and poetaster. He was an antagonist of Pope's and a late-comer to *The Dunciad* (II. 299), to which Swift here alludes. **399. Jemmy Moor:** See *Verses on the Death of Dr. Swift,* above, l. 200 and note. **401. to Points:** upright. **407. ———:** "kings." **410. both:** canceled lines: "Perhaps you say Augustus shines / Immortal made in Virgil's Lines, / And Horace brought yᵉ tunefull Choir / To sing his Virtues on yᵉ Lyre, / Without reproach of flattery true / Because their Praises were his due / For in those Ages Kings we find, / Were Animals of human kind, / But now go search all Europe round / Among yᵉ savage Monsters crown'd / With Vice polluting every Throne / I mean all Kings except our own, / In vain you make yᵉ strictest View / To find a King in all yᵉ Crew, / With whom a Footman out of Place / Wou'd not conceive a high disgrace / A burning Shame, a crying Sin / To take, his mornings Cup of Gin. / Thus all are destin'd to obey / Some Beast of Burthen or of Prey / Tis sung Prometheus forming Man / Thro' all the brutal Species ran, / Each proper Quality to find / Adapted to a human Mind, / A mingled Mass of Good & Bad, / The worst & best that could be had / Then from a Clay of Mixture base / He shap'd a King to rule yᵉ Race / Endow'd with Gifts from every Brute / That best yᵉ regal Nature suit, / Thus think on Kings, yᵉ Name denotes / Hogs, Asses, Wolves, Baboons, & Goats / To represent in figure just / Sloth, Folly, Rapine, Mischeif, Lust / O! were they all but Nebuchadnazzars / What Herds of Kings would turn to Grazers." **416. Spirit:** canceled lines: "How well his publick Thrift is shewn? / All coffers full except his own."

421. Hydaspes . . . Ganges: the three great rivers of India; "Hydaspes" is the ancient name of the Jhelum. **424. Short . . . Knees:** on bended knee. **425. The Consort:** Queen Caroline. **429. divine Iülus:** Frederick Louis, Prince of Wales. Iulus was the son of Aeneas. Cf. *Directions for a Birth-Day Song,* above, ll. 187 ff. **439. Number five:** Cf. *Directions,* ll. 165 ff. **440. Duke William:** Cf. *Directions,* ll. 200 ff. **441. Minister of State:** Sir Robert Walpole (1676–1745). **446. prudent Fabius:** [Swift's note] *Unus Homo nobis Cunctando* restituit rem. [The quotation is from Ennius (239–c. 169 B.C.), and may be translated: "One man by delay saved the state." The man was Quintus Fabius Maximus, who "saved the state" by avoiding battle with Hannibal.]

You raise the Honour of the Peerage,
Proud to attend you at the Steerage.°
You dignify the noble Race,
Content yourself with humbler Place.
Now Learning, Valour, Virtue, Sense,
To Titles give the sole Pretence.°   460
St. George beheld thee with Delight,
Vouchsafe to be an azure Knight,
When on thy Breast and Sides *Herculean*,
He fixt the *Star* and *String Cerulean*.°

    Say, Poet, in what other Nation,
Shone ever such a Constellation.
Attend ye *Popes*, and *Youngs*, and *Gays*,
And tune your Harps, and strow° your Bays.
Your Panegyricks here provide,
You cannot err on Flatt'ry's Side.°   470
Above the Stars exalt your Stile,
You still are low ten thousand Mile.
On *Lewis*° all his Bards bestow'd,
Of Incense many a thousand Load;
But *Europe* mortify'd his Pride,
And swore the fawning Rascals ly'd:
Yet what the World refus'd to *Lewis*,
Apply'd to ———° exactly true is:
Exactly true! Invidious° Poet!
'Tis fifty thousand Times below it.   480

    Translate me now some Lines, if you can,
From *Virgil*, *Martial*, *Ovid*, *Lucan;*
They could all Pow'r in Heaven divide,
And do no Wrong to either Side:
They teach you how to split a Hair,
Give ———° and *Jove* an equal Share.°
Yet, why should we be lac'd so straight;
I'll give my ＊ ＊ ＊ ＊ ＊° Butter-weight.°
And Reason good; for many a Year
———° never intermeddl'd here: 490

Nor, tho' his Priests be duly paid,
Did ever we *desire* his Aid:
We now can better do without him,
Since *Woolston*° gave us Arms to rout him.
＊ ＊ ＊ ＊ ＊ *Cætera desiderantur*° ＊ ＊ ＊ ＊ ＊

A CHARACTER, PANEGYRIC, AND DESCRIPTION OF THE LEGION CLUB

Written in the Year, 1736

In this poem, as in others he wrote during this period, Swift employs his satire in the cause of the clergy against the landowners who were attempting to deprive them of their traditional tithes.

    The text is from Volume XI (1763) of Faulkner's edition of Swift's *Works*, where the poem is introduced with a note asserting that it was "carefully printed from the Author's Manuscript; whereas all other Editions whatever, are spurious and incorrect, as they were stolen, mangled, and interpolated." One variant ("fearless" in line 20) is incorporated from the first edition (1736).

AS I strole the City,° oft I
Spy a Building° large and lofty,
Not a Bow-shot from the College,°
Half the Globe from Sense and Knowledge.
By the prudent Architect°
Plac'd against the Church° direct;
Making good my Grandame's Jest,
Near the Church—you know the rest.°

    TELL us what this Pile contains?
Many a Head that holds no Brains.   10

---

456. Steerage: apparently in the sense of "ship of state." **460. Pretence:** claim to merit. **461–64. St. . . . Cerulean:** Walpole received the Order of Knight of the Garter (of which St. George is the patron) in 1726. **468. strow:** (strew) scatter. **473. Lewis:** Louis XIV. **478. ———:** "George." **479. Invidious:** grudging. **486. ———:** "George." **equal Share:** [Swift's note] *Divisum Imperium cum* Jove Caesar *habet.* [The quotation has not been identified. Translated it means: "Caesar has divided the empire with Jupiter."] **488. ＊ ＊ ＊ ＊ ＊:** "monarch." **Butter-weight:** eighteen or more ounces to the pound; in other words, good measure. **490. ———:** "Christ"; supplied from Orrery's copy of the first edition; Faulkner printed "Jove."

494. Woolston: Thomas Woolston. See *Verses on the Death of Dr. Swift,* above, l. 281 and note. **495. Cætera desiderantur:** The rest is wanting. THE LEGION CLUB. **1. the City:** Dublin. **2. a Building:** the new Irish Parliament House, begun in 1728. **3. the College:** Trinity College. **5. the prudent Architect:** Sir Edward Lovet Pearce (d. 1733), Surveyor General of Ireland. **6. the Church:** St. Andrew's Church. **8. the rest:** "The nearer the Church the farther from God."

These Demoniacs° let me dub
With the Name of *Legion Club*.°
Such Assemblies you might swear,
Meet when Butchers bait a Bear;
Such a Noise, and such haranguing,
When a Brother Thief is hanging.
Such a Rout, and such a Rabble
Run to hear Jackpudding° gabble,
Such a Croud their Ordure throws
On a fearless Villain's Nose.   20

COULD I from the Building's Top
Hear the rattling Thunder drop,
While the Devil upon the Roof,
If the Devil be Thunder Proof,
Should, with Poker fiery red,
Crack the Stones, and melt the Lead;
Drive them down on every Skull,
While the Den of Thieves is full;
Quite destroy that Harpies Nest,
How might then our Isle be blest;   30
For Divines allow, that God
Sometimes makes the Devil his Rod:
And the Gospel will inform us,
He can punish Sins enormous.

YET should *Swift* endow the Schools
For his Lunatics and Fools,°
With a Rood° or two of Land,
I allow the Pile may stand.
You perhaps will ask me, why so?
But it is with this Proviso,   40
Since the House is like to last,
Let a royal Grant be pass'd,
That the Club have Right to dwell,
Each within his proper Cell;
With a Passage left to creep in,
And a Hole above for peeping.

LET them, when they once get in
Sell the Nation for a Pin;
While they sit a picking Straws
Let them rave of making Laws;   50
While they never hold their Tongue,
Let them dabble in their Dung;

Let them form a grand Committee,
How to plague and starve the City;
Let them stare, and storm, and frown,
When they see a Clergy-Gown;
Let them, ere they crack a Louse,
Call for th' Orders° of the House;
Let them with their gosling Quills,
Scribble senseless Heads of Bills;   60
We may, while they strain their Throats,
Wipe our A——s with their V——s.

LET Sir *T——*,° that rampant Ass,
Stuff his Guts with Flax and Grass:°
But before the Priest he fleeces,
Tear the Bible all to Pieces.
At the Parsons, *Tom*, Halloo, Boy,°
Worthy Offspring of a Shoeboy,°
Footman, Traytor, vile Seducer,
Perjur'd Rebel, brib'd Accuser;   70
Lay thy paltry Privilege° aside,
Sprung from Papists and a Regicide;
Fall a working like a Mole,
Raise the Dirt about your Hole.

COME, assist me, Muse obedient,
Let us try some new Expedient;
Shift the Scene for half an Hour,
Time and Place are in thy Power.
Thither, gentle Muse, conduct me,
I shall ask, and you instruct me.   80

SEE the Muse unbars the Gate,
Hark, the Monkeys, how they prate!

ALL ye Gods,° who rule the Soul,
Styx, through Hell whose Waters roll!
Let me be allow'd to tell
What I heard in yonder Hell.

58. th' Orders: the prescribed mode of proceeding. **63. Sir T——:** Sir Thomas Prendergast (d. 1760), Second Baronet; the subject of Swift's poem *Noisy Tom*. **64. Flax and Grass:** a reference to the tithes claimed by the clergy which the Irish Parliament was engaged in legislating away. **67. Halloo, Boy:** a cry to incite dogs to the chase. **68. a Shoeboy:** Sir Thomas Prendergast (*c.* 1660–1709), an ardent Roman Catholic and Jacobite who took part in a conspiracy to assassinate William III in 1696, turned informer, and was substantially rewarded. He died from wounds received at the Battle of Malplaquet. **71. paltry Privilege:** Members of Parliament were accorded certain privileges, notably immunity from arrest in civil matters. Cf. l. 116. **83. All ye Gods:** Parallels between the following lines and the *Aeneid* (VI. 264 ff.) are cited in Faulkner's edition and reprinted in Williams's.

11. Demoniacs: persons possessed by a demon or evil spirits. **12. Legion Club:** Swift's reference here is to Mark 5:9: "My name is Legion: for we are many." **18. Jackpudding:** a clown or mountebank's assistant. **35–36. Yet . . . Fools:** Cf. *Verses on the Death of Dr. Swift*, above, ll. 479–80. **37. a Rood:** thirty and one fourth square yards; rood, rod, perch, and pole are various terms for the same measurement.

NEAR the Door an Entrance gapes,
Crouded round with antic Shapes;
Poverty, and *Grief*, and *Care*,
Causeless *Joy*, and true *Despair*;   90
Discord periwigg'd with Snakes,
See the dreadful Strides she takes.

BY this odious Crew beset,
I began to rage and fret
And resolv'd to break their Pates,
Ere we enter'd at the Gates;
Had not *Clio* in the Nick,
Whisper'd me, let down your Stick;
What, said I, is this the Mad-House?
These, she answered, are but Shadows,   100
Phantoms bodiless and vain,
Empty Visions of the Brain.

IN the Porch *Briareus* stands,
Shews a Bribe in all his Hands:
Briareus the Secretary,
But we Mortals call him *Carey*.°
When the Rogues their Country fleece,
They may hope for Pence a Piece.

CLIO, who had been so wise
To put on a Fool's Disguise,   110
To bespeak some Approbation,
And be thought a near Relation;
When she saw three hundred Brutes,
All involv'd in wild Disputes;
Roaring till their Lungs were spent,
P—l—ge of P—l—m—nt,
Now a new Misfortune feels,
Dreading to be laid by th' Heels,
Never durst a Muse before
Enter that Infernal Door;   120
Clio stifled with the Smell,
Into Spleen and Vapours fell;
By the *Stygian* Steams that flew,
From the dire infectious Crew.
Not the Stench of Lake *Avernus*,
Could have more offended her Nose;
Had she flown but o'er the Top,
She would feel her Pinions drop,
And by Exhalations dire,
Though a Goddess, must expire.   130
In a Fright she crept away,
Bravely I resolv'd to stay.

WHEN I saw the Keeper frown,
Tipping him with half a Crown;
Now, said I, we are alone,
Name your Heroes one by one.

WHO is that Hell-featur'd Brawler,
Is it Satan? No, 'tis *W*——°
In what Figure can a Bard dress,
Jack, the Grandson of Sir *Hardress*°?   140
Honest Keeper, drive him further,
In his Looks are Hell and Murther;
See the scowling Visage drop,
Just as when he murther'd *T*——°

KEEPER, shew me where to fix
On the Puppy Pair of *Dicks*;
By their lanthorn Jaws and Leathern,
You might swear they both are Brethren:
Dick Fitz-Baker,° *Dick* the Player,°
Old Acquaintance are you there?   150
Dear Companions hug and kiss,
Tost *old Glorious*° in your Piss.
Tie them, Keeper, in a Tether,
Let them stare and stink together;
Both are apt to be unruly,
Lash them daily, lash them duly,
Though 'tis hopeless to reclaim them,
Scorpion Rods° perhaps may tame them.

KEEPER, yon old Dotard smoke,°
Sweetly snoring in his Cloak.   160
Who is he? 'Tis hum-drum *W*——,°
Half encompass'd by his Kin.

138. W——: Lieutenant Colonel John Waller of Castletown in county Limerick; Member of Parliament for Doneraile. **140. Sir Hardress:** Sir Hardress Waller (*c.* 1604–*c.* 1666), one of the judges who condemned Charles I, had settled in Ireland around 1630. He was imprisoned at the Restoration. **144. T——:** The Reverend Roger Throp, rector of Kilcorman, county Limerick, died in January, 1736, after being persecuted by Waller, his patron. **149. Dick Fitz-Baker:** Richard Tighe, Privy Councillor and Member of Parliament. He is the "Timothy" of Swift's poem *Mad Mullinix and Timothy*. "Fitz-Baker" alludes to Tighe's descent from a supplier of Cromwell's armies. **Dick the Player:** Richard Bettesworth, sergeant at law and Member of Parliament. He is lampooned in Swift's *On the Words—Brother Protestants, and Fellow Christians.* "Player" alludes to his histrionic manner. **152. old Glorious:** William III. **158. Scorpion Rods:** the term for whips specially made to inflict dire pain. **159. smoke:** notice, observe. **161. W——:** The Wynne family was represented by three Members of Parliament at this time: two Owens for the county and borough of Sligo and one John for the borough of Castlebar.

106. Carey: Walter Carey was secretary to the Duke of Dorset when the Duke was Lord Lieutenant of Ireland.

There observe the Tribe of *B——m*,°
For he never fails to bring 'em;
While he sleeps the whole Debate,
They submissive round him wait;
Yet would gladly see the Hunks
In his Grave, and search his Trunks.
See they gently twitch his Coat,
Just to yawn, and give his Vote;   170
Always firm in his Vocation,
For the Court against the Nation.

THESE are *A——s, Jack* and *Bob*,°
First in every wicked Jobb,
Son and Brother to a queer,
Brainsick Brute, they call a Peer,°
We must give them better Quarter,
For their Ancestor° trod Mortar;
And at *Hoath*° to boast his Fame,
On a Chimney cut his Name.   180

THERE sit *C——s, D——*, and *H——*,°
How they swagger from their Garrison.
Such a Triplet could you tell
Where to find on this Side Hell?
H——, and *D——*, and *C——*,
Souse them in their own Excrements.
Every Mischief in their Hearts,
If they fail 'tis Want of Parts.

BLESS us, *Morgan*°! Art thou there, Man?
Bless mine Eyes! Art thou the Chairman?   190

Chairman to yon damn'd Committee,
Yet I look on thee with Pity.
Dreadful Sight! What, learned *Morgan*,
Metamorphos'd to a Gorgon!
For thy horrid Looks, I own,
Half convert me to a Stone.
Hast thou been so long at School,
Now to turn a factious Tool!
Alma Mater° was thy Mother,
Every young Divine thy Brother.   200
Thou a disobedient Varlet,
Treat thy Mother like a Harlot?
Thou, ungrateful to thy Teachers,
Who are all grown reverend Preachers!
Morgan! Would it not surprise one?
Turn thy Nourishment to Poison!
When you walk among your Books,
They reproach you with their Looks;
Bind them fast, or from the Shelves
They'll come down to right themselves;   210
Homer, Plutarch, Virgil, Flaccus,°
All in Arms prepare to back us:
Soon repent, or put to Slaughter
Every *Greek* and *Roman* Author.
While you in your Faction's Phrase
Send the Clergy all to graze;
And to make your Project pass,
Leave them not a Blade of Grass.

How I want° thee, humourous *Hogart*°!
Thou, I hear, a pleasant Rogue art;   220
Were but you and I acquainted,
Every Monster should be painted,
You should try your graving° Tools
On this odious Group of Fools;
Draw the Beasts as I describe 'em,
Form their Features, while I gibe 'em;
Draw them like, for I assure you,
You will need no *Car'catura*.°
Draw them so that we may trace
All the Soul in every Face.   230
Keeper, I must now retire,
You have done what I desire:

163. Tribe of **B——m:** Sir John Bingham was Member of Parliament for county Mayo and his brother Henry for the borough of Castlebar. **173. These . . . Bob:** John Allen, Member of Parliament for the borough of Carysfort, and his uncle Robert Allen, for the county of Wicklow. **176. Brainsick . . . Peer:** Joshua, Second Viscount Allen. He had attacked Swift in 1730 as an enemy of the Government. **178. their Ancestor:** John Allen, Lord Allen's great-grandfather, an architect. **179. Hoath:** Howth Castle in county Dublin (where a portrait of Swift as The Drapier is hung). **181. C——s . . . H——:** (1) either Henry or Nathaniel Clements, Members of Parliament for the boroughs of Cavan and Duleck respectively; (2) Michael O'Brien Dilkes, Member of Parliament for the borough of Castle-martyr; and (3) William Harrison, Member of Parliament for the borough of Bannow. **189. Morgan:** Dr. Marcus Antonius Morgan, Member of Parliament for the borough of Athy. He was chairman of the committee that reported to the Commons in favor of the petition of the graziers for relief from the tithe of agistment, whereby they had to allow the parson's cattle to feed in their pastures. Swift, supporting the clergy, of course opposed the petition.

199. **Alma Mater:** bounteous mother, a designation for several goddesses in Roman antiquity; applied to colleges and universities in the sense of "fostering mother." **211. Flaccus:** Horace. **219. want:** need. **humourous Hogart:** the artist William Hogarth (1697–1764); "humorous" in the sense that he depicted the "humors" or tempers of his society. **223. graving:** engraving. **228. Car'catura:** caricature, exaggeration.

But I feel my Spirits spent,
With the Noise, the Sight, the Scent.

PRAY be patient, you shall find
Half the best are still behind;
You have hardly seen a Score,
I can shew two hundred more.
Keeper, I have seen enough,
Taking then a Pinch of Snuff;   240
I concluded, looking round 'em,
May their God, the Devil confound 'em.

WHEN I COME TO BE OLD

1699

These "resolutions" must have been written not long
after the death of Swift's patron, Sir William Temple.
While a number of them seem to betray reservations
about his character and manners, Swift's admiration for
Temple was deep and lasting.

The text is transcribed from the reproduction of
Swift's manuscript in Volume I of *The Prose Works of
Jonathan Swift*, ed. Herbert Davis (1939).

Not to marry a young Woman.
Not to keep young Company unless they reely desire
it.
Not to be peevish or morose, or suspicious.
Not to scorn present Ways, or Wits, or Fashions, or
Men, or War, &c.
Not to be fond of Children, or let them come near me
hardly.°
Not to tell the same Story over & over to the same
People.
Not to be covetous.
Not to neglect decency, or cleenlyness, for fear of
falling into Nastyness.
Not to be over severe with young People, but give
Allowances for their youthfull follyes, and
Weeknesses.

Not to be influenced by, or give ear to knavish tatling
Servants, or others.   10
Not to be too free of advise nor trouble any but those
that desire it.
To desire some good Friends to inform me wch of
these Resolutions I break, or neglect, & wherein;
and reform accordingly.
Not to talk much, nor of my self.
Not to boast of my former beauty, or strength, or
favor with Ladyes, &c.
Not to hearken to Flatteryes, nor conceive I can be
beloved by a young woman. et eos qui hereditatem
captant odisse ac vitare.°
Not to be positive or opiniatre.°
Not to sett up for observing all these Rules; for fear I
should observe none.

A MEDITATION
UPON A BROOM-STICK . . .

The title continues: *According to the Style and Manner
of the Honourable Robert Boyle's Meditations. Written in
the Year 1703.* This little parody of Boyle's *Occasional
Reflections upon Several Subjects* (1664) catches Swift in
the characteristic act of employing the witty conceit
to expose human nature.

The text is that of the first edition (1710), with
variants incorporated from Faulkner's edition of Swift's
Works (1735).

THIS single Stick, which you now behold Ingloriously lying in that neglected Corner, I once knew
in a Flourishing State in A Forest, it was full of Sap,
full of Leaves, and full of Boughs; but now, in vain
does the busie Art of Man pretend to Vye with
Nature, by tying that wither'd Bundle of Twigs to its
sapless Trunk; It is now at best but the Reverse of
what it was, a Tree turn'd upside down, the Branches
on the Earth, and the Root in the Air; It is now
handled by every Dirty Wench, condemn'd to do her
Drudgery, and by a Capricious kind of Fate, destin'd
to make other Things Clean, and be Nasty it self:

WHEN I COME TO BE OLD. **5. or . . . hardly:** deleted in the
manuscript.

15. et . . . vitare: and to loathe and shun those who hunt
legacies—a pet aversion of the Roman satirists. **16. opiniatre:**
opinionated.

At Length, worn to the Stumps in the Service of the Maids, It is either thrown out of Doors, or condemn'd to its last use of kindling a Fire. When I beheld this, I sigh'd, and said within my self, SURELY MORTAL MAN IS A BROOM-STICK; Nature sent him into the World Strong and Lusty, in a Thriving Condition, wearing his own Hair on his Head, the proper Branches of this Reasoning Vegetable, till the Axe of Intemperance has lopt off his Green Boughs, and left him a wither'd Trunk: He then flies to Art, and puts on a Perriwig, valuing himself upon an Unnatural Bundle of Hairs, all cover'd with Powder that never grew on his Head; but now should this our *Broom-Stick* pretend to enter the Scene, proud of those *Birchen* Spoils it never bore, and all cover'd with Dust, tho' the Sweepings of the Finest Lady's Chamber, we should be apt to Ridicule and Despise its Vanity, Partial Judges that we are! of Our own Excellencies, and other Men's Defaults.[1]

But a *Broom-stick*, perhaps you'll say, is an Emblem of a Tree standing on its Head; and pray what is Man, but a Topsy-turvy Creature, his Animal Faculties perpetually mounted on his Rational; His Head where his Heels should be; groveling on the Earth, and yet with all his Faults, he sets up to be an universal Reformer and Corrector of Abuses, a Remover of Grievances, rakes into every Slut's Corner[2] of Nature, bringing hidden Corruptions to the Light, and raises a mighty Dust where there was none before, sharing deeply all the while, in the very same Pollutions he pretends to sweep away: His last Days are spent in Slavery to Women, and generally the least deserving; 'till worn to the Stumps, like his Brother *Bezom*,[3] he's either kickt out of Doors, or made use of to kindle Flames, for others to warm Themselves by.

FROM

THE BICKERSTAFF PAPERS

Swift's *nom de guerre* on this occasion is thought to have been taken from the sign of a locksmith; it was soon to be used, less aptly, by Steele for *The Tatler*. Swift's victim was John Partridge (born John Hewson), a successful astrologer, medical quack, and almanac maker, who had been much under attack and many

A MEDITATION UPON A BROOM-STICK. **1. Defaults:** defects. **2. Slut's Corner:** a corner left unclean. **3. Bezom:** (besom) broom.

times parodied before Swift delivered his *coup de grâce*. Partridge had repeatedly challenged rival astrologers in the art of drawing nativities and making predictions, especially of the death of individuals. Swift's response to the challenge was *Predictions for the Year 1708*, published before the end of January, which out-Partridged Partridge in its predictions and in the process casually foretold *his* death. A number of wits proceeded to join in the fun; Swift himself followed through with *The Accomplishment of the First of Mr. Bickerstaff's Predictions* (1708) and *A Vindication of Isaac Bickerstaff Esq.* (1709).

Swift chose Partridge as his target as much for his abuse of the Church of England as for his charlatanism. But Swift could hardly have hoped for so direct a hit: at his "death" Partridge's name was struck from the rolls of the Company of Stationers, and he thereby lost his right to publish his almanac.

PREDICTIONS FOR THE YEAR 1708 . . .

The first-edition title continues: *Wherein the Month and Day of the Month Are Set Down, the Persons Named, and the great Actions and Events of next Year particularly related, as they will come to pass. Written to Prevent the People of England from Being Further Impos'd on by Vulgar Almanack-Makers. By Isaac Bickerstaff Esq;*

The text is that of the first edition (1708), with variants incorporated from Faulkner's edition of Swift's *Works* (1735).

HAVING long considered the gross Abuse of Astrology in this Kingdom, upon debating the Matter with my self, I could not possibly lay the Fault upon the Art, but upon those gross Impostors who set up to be the Artists. I know several learned Men have contended that the whole is a Cheat; that it is absurd and ridiculous to imagine, the Stars can have any Influence at all upon humane Actions, Thoughts or Inclinations: And whoever hath not bent his Studies that Way, may be excused for thinking so, when he sees in how wretched a manner this noble Art is treated by a few mean illiterate Traders between us and the Stars; who import a yearly Stock of Nonsense, Lies, Folly and

Impertinence, which they offer to the World as genuine from the Planets, although they descend from no greater a Height than their own Brains.

DECEPTION

I intend in a short Time to publish a large and rational Defence of this Art, and therefore shall say no more in its Justification at present, than that it hath been in all Ages defended by many learned Men, and among the rest by *Socrates* himself, whom I look upon as undoubtedly the wisest of uninspired Mortals: To which if we add, that those who have condemned this Art, although otherwise Learned, having been such as either did not apply their Studies this Way, or at least did not succeed in their Applications: Their Testimony will not be of much weight to its Disadvantage, since they are liable to the common Objection of condemning what they did not understand.

WILL DEFEND ASTROLOGY LATER —

HE HAS NOT CONDEMNED IT

Nor am I at all offended, or think it an Injury to the Art, when I see the common Dealers in it, the *Students in Astrology*, the *Philomaths*,[1] and the rest of that Tribe, treated by wise Men with the utmost Scorn and Contempt; but I rather wonder, when I observe Gentlemen in the Country, rich enough to serve the Nation in Parliament, poring in *Partridge*'s Almanack, to find out the Events of the Year at Home and Abroad; not daring to propose a Hunting Match, until *Gadbury*[2] or he hath fixt the Weather.

ACTION OF THESE PEOPLE IS CONTRARY TO WHAT HE EXPECTS

I will allow either of the Two I have mention'd, or any other of the Fraternity, to be not only Astrologers, but Conjurers too, if I do not produce an hundred Instances in all their Almanacks, to convince any reasonable Man, that they do not so much as understand Grammar and Syntax; that they are not able to spell any Word out of the usual Road, nor even in their Prefaces to write common Sense or intelligible *English*. Then for their Observations and Predictions, they are such as will equally suit any Age or Country in the World. *This Month a certain great Person will be threatned with Death or Sickness*. This the News Paper will tell them, for there we find at the End of the Year, that no Month passes without the Death of some Person of Note; and it would be hard if it should be otherwise, when there are at least Two thousand Persons of Note in this Kingdom, many of them old, and the Almanack-maker has the liberty of chusing

the sickliest Season of the Year where he may fix his Prediction. Again; *This Month an eminent Clergyman will be preferr'd;* of which there may be some Hundreds, half of them with one Foot in the Grave. Then, *Such a Planet in such a House shews great Machinations, Plots and Conspiracies, that may in time be brought to Light:* After which, if we hear of any Discovery, the Astrologer gets the Honour, if not, his Prediction still stands good. And at last, *God preserve King* William *from all his open and secret Enemies. Amen.* When, if the King should happen to have died, the Astrologer plainly foretold it; otherwise it passeth but for the pious Ejaculation of a Loyal Subject: Although it unluckily happened in some of their Almanacks, that poor King *William* was pray'd for many Months after he was dead, because it fell out that he died about the beginning of the Year.

To mention no more of their impertinent Predictions; What have we to do with their Advertisements about *Pills and Drinks for the Venereal Disease,* or their mutual Quarrels in Verse and Prose of *Whig* and *Tory,* wherewith the Stars have little to do.

Having long observed and lamented these, and a hundred other Abuses of this Art, too tedious to repeat, I resolved to proceed in a new Way, which I doubt not will be to the general Satisfaction of the Kingdom: I can this Year produce but a Specimen of what I design for the future: having employ'd most part of my Time in adjusting and correcting the Calculations I made for some Years past, because I would offer nothing to the World of which I am not as fully satisfied, as that I am now alive. For these two last Years I have not failed in above one or two Particulars, and those of no very great Moment. I exactly foretold the Miscarriage at *Toulon,*[3] with all its Particulars; and the loss of Admiral *Shovell,*[4] although I was mistaken as to the Day, placing that Accident about thirty six Hours sooner than it happen'd; but upon reviewing my Schemes, I quickly found the Cause of that Error. I likewise foretold the Battle at *Almanza*[5] to the very Day and Hour, with

---

THE BICKERSTAFF PAPERS: *Predictions for the Year 1708.* **1. Philomaths:** lovers of learning; a term often applied to astrologers and prognosticators. **2. Gadbury:** John Gadbury (1627–1704), a rival astrologer and suspected Popish plotter whom Partridge attacked in print.

3. the Miscarriage . . . Toulon: The siege of Toulon, in which the Allies were repulsed, took place in the summer of 1707. **4. Admiral Shovell:** Sir Cloudesley Shovell (1650–1707), Commander of the Fleet, was shipwrecked in the Scilly Islands on his return from Toulon. He was discovered and allowed to perish by a woman who coveted his emerald ring. **5. Almanza:** the scene in April, 1707, of the French victory, led by the Duke of Berwick, over the English, Spanish, and Portuguese, under the Earl of Galway.

the Loss on both Sides, and the Consequences thereof. All which I shewed to some Friends many Months before they happened. That is, I gave them Papers sealed up, to open at such a Time, after which they were at liberty to read them; and there they found my Predictions true in every Article, except one or two very minute.

As for the few following Predictions I now offer the World, I forbore to publish them till I had perused the several Almanacks for the Year we are now entred upon. I found them all in the usual Strain, and I beg the Reader will compare their Manner with mine: And here I make bold to tell the World, that I lay the whole Credit of my Art upon the Truth of these Predictions; And I will be content, that *Partridge*, and the rest of his Clan, may hoot me for a Cheat and Impostor if I fail in any single Particular of Moment. I believe, any Man who reads this Paper will look upon me to be at least a Person of as much Honesty and Understanding, as a common Maker of Almanacks. I do not lurk in the Dark; I am not wholly unknown in the World; I have set my Name at length, to be a Mark of Infamy to Mankind if they shall find I deceive them.

In one Point I must desire to be forgiven, that I talk more sparingly of Home Affairs; As it would be Imprudence to discover[6] Secrets of State, so it might be dangerous to my Person, but in smaller Matters, and such as are not of publick Consequence, I shall be very free; and the Truth of my Conjectures will as much appear from these as the other. As for the most signal Events abroad in *France*, *Flanders*, *Italy* and *Spain*, I shall make no Scruple to Predict them in plain Terms: Some of them are of Importance, and I hope I shall seldom mistake the Day they will happen; therefore I think good to inform the Reader, that I all along make use of the *Old Style* observ'd in *England*,[7] which I desire he will compare with that of the News-Papers, at the time they relate the Actions I mention.

I must add one Word more; I know it hath been the Opinion of several learned Persons, who think well enough of the true Art of Astrology, That the Stars do only *incline*, and not *force*, the Actions or Wills of Men: And therefore, however I may proceed by right

Rules, yet I cannot in Prudence so confidently assure that the Events will follow exactly as I predict them.

I hope I have maturely consider'd this Objection, which in some Cases is of no little Weight: For Example; A Man may by the Influence of an over-ruling Planet be disposed or inclined to Lust, Rage, or Avarice, and yet by the force of Reason overcome that evil Influence; and this was the Case of *Socrates*: But the great Events of the World usually depending upon Numbers of Men, it cannot be expected they should all unite to cross their Inclinations, from pursuing a general Design, wherein they unanimously agree. Besides, the Influence of the Stars reacheth to many Actions and Events, which are not any way in the Power of Reason; as Sickness, Death, and what we commonly call Accidents, with many more, needless to repeat.

But now it is time to proceed to my Predictions, which I have begun to calculate from the time that the *Sun* enters into *Aries*. And this I take to be properly the Beginning of the natural Year.[8] I persue them to the Time that he enters *Libra*, or somewhat more, which is the busy Period of the Year. The Remainder I have not yet adjusted, upon Account of several Impediments needless here to mention: Besides, I must remind the Reader again, that this is but a Specimen of what I design in succeeding Years to treat more at large, if I may have Liberty and Encouragement.

My first Prediction is but a Trifle, yet I will mention it, to shew how ignorant those Sottish Pretenders to Astrology are in their own Concerns: It relates to *Partridge* the Almanack-maker; I have consulted the Star of his Nativity by my own Rules, and find he will infallibly dye upon the 29th of *March* next, about Eleven at night, of a raging Feaver; therefore I advise him to consider of it, and settle his Affairs in time.

The Month of *APRIL* will be observable for the Death of many great Persons. On the 4th, will dye the *Cardinal de Noailles*, *Archbishop of Paris:*[9] On the 11th, the young Prince of *Asturias*, Son to the Duke of *Anjou:*[10] On the 14th, a great *Peer* of this Realm will dye at his Country House: On the 19th, an old

---

6. **discover:** disclose. 7. **the Old . . . England:** The Gregorian calendar in use on the Continent was not adopted in England until 1752. "Old Style" ran eleven days behind "New Style."

8. **natural Year:** The vernal equinox was set at March 21 in the fourth century A.D. Old Style years usually began on March 25. 9. **Cardinal . . . Paris:** Louis Antoine de Noailles (1651–1729). 10. **Prince . . . Anjou:** Louis, son of the Duke of Anjou, who was Philip V of Spain, held the title of Prince of Asturias as heir to the throne. Philip abdicated in 1724 in favor of his son but resumed the crown when Louis died soon after.

Layman of great Fame for Learning: And on the 23rd, an eminent Goldsmith in *Lombard Street*.[11] I could mention others, both at home and abroad, if I did not consider such Events of very little use or Instruction to the Reader, or to the World.

As to Publick Affairs: On the 7th of this Month, there will be an Insurrection in *Dauphiné*,[12] occasion'd by the Oppressions of the People, which will not be quieted in some Months.

On the 15th, will be a violent Storm on the South-East Coast of *France*, which will destroy many of their Ships, and some in the very Harbour.

The 19th, will be famous for the Revolt of a whole Province or Kingdom, excepting one City, by which the Affairs of a certain Prince in the Alliance will take a better Face.

MAY, against common Conjectures, will be no very busy Month in *Europe*, but very signal for the Death of the *Dauphin*,[13] which will happen on the 7th, after a short Fit of Sickness, and grievous Torments with the Strangury.[14] He dies less lamented by the Court, than the Kingdom.

On the 9th, a *Mareschal* of *France* will break his Leg by a Fall from his Horse. I have not been able to discover whether he will then dye or not.

On the 11th, will begin a most important Siege, which the Eyes of all *Europe* will be upon: I cannot be more Particular, for in relating Affairs that so nearly concern the *Confederates*, and consequently this Kingdom, I am forc'd to confine my self, for several Reasons very obvious to the Reader.

On the 15th, News will arrive of a very *Surprizing Event;* than which nothing could be more unexpected.

On the 19th, three noble Ladies of this Kingdom will, against all Expectation, prove with Child, to the great Joy of their Husbands.

On the 23d, a famous Buffoon of the Play-house will dye a ridiculous Death suitable to his Vocation.

JUNE. This Month will be distinguish'd at home by the utter dispersing of those ridiculous deluded Enthusiasts, commonly call'd the *Prophets;*[15] occasion'd chiefly by seeing the Time come when many of their Prophesies were to be fulfill'd, and then finding themselves deceiv'd by contrary Events. It is indeed to be admir'd how any Deceiver can be so weak to foretel Things near at hand, when a very few Months must of necessity discover the Imposture to all the World; in this Point less prudent than common Almanack-makers, who are so wise to wander in generals, talk dubiously, and leave to the Reader the Business of interpreting.

On the 1st of this Month, a *French* General will be kill'd by a random Shot of a Cannon Ball.

On the 6th, a Fire will break out in the Suburbs of *Paris,* which will destroy above a thousand Houses; and seems to be the foreboding of what will happen, to the Surprise of all *Europe,* about the End of the following Month.

On the 10th, a great Battle will be fought, which will begin at Four of the Clock in the Afternoon, and last till nine at Night with great Obstinacy, but no very decisive Event. I shall not name the Place, for the Reasons aforesaid; but the Commanders on each Left Wing will be kill'd. —I see Bonfires, and hear the Noise of Guns, for a Victory.

On the 14th, there will be a false Report of the *French* King's Death.

On the 20th, Cardinal *Portocarero*[16] will dye of a Dissentery, with great Suspicion of Poison; but the Report of his Intention to revolt to King *Charles,*[17] will prove false.

JULY. The 6th of this Month, a *certain General* will, by a Glorious Action, recover the Reputation he lost by former Misfortunes.

On the 12th, a *Great Commander* will dye a Prisoner in the Hands of his Enemies.

On the 14th, a shameful Discovery will be made, of a *French* Jesuit giving Poison to a great Foreign General, and when he is put to the Torture, will make wonderful Discoveries.

---

11. Lombard Street: "Lombard street was anciently, as well as at present, inhabited by bankers, the first of whom were Italians chiefly from Lombardy, whence the word Lombards became anciently applied to all bankers, and this street retained the name of Lombards or Bankers street" (*London and Its Environs Described* [1761]). **12. in Dauphiné:** on the southern front. **13. the Dauphin:** Louis of France (1661–1711), son of Louis XIV and Marie-Thérèse. **14. the Strangury:** an ailment causing slow and painful emission of urine.

15. the Prophets: the French Prophets, a refugee Protestant sect in England. **16. Cardinal Portocarero:** Luis Manuel Fernandez de Portocarrero (1635–1709), one of the rulers of Spain under Philip V, whom he was in large part responsible for placing on the throne. He fell from power in 1703 and for a time switched his allegiance to the Empire and its candidate, the Archduke Charles. **17. King Charles:** The Archduke Charles (1685–1740), son of Emperor Leopold I, was the unsuccessful candidate of the Grand Alliance for the Spanish throne. He became Holy Roman Emperor in 1711.

In short, this will prove a Month of great Action, if I might have Liberty to relate the Particulars.

At home, the Death of an old famous Senator will happen on the 15th at his Country House, worn with Age and Diseases.

But that which will make this Month memorable to all Posterity, is the Death of the *French* King *Lewis* the Fourteenth, after a Weeks Sickness at *Marli*,[18] which will happen on the 29th, about six a Clock in the Evening. It seems to be an Effect of the Gout in his Stomach, follow'd by a Flux.[19] And in three Days after Monsieur *Chamillard*[20] will follow his Master, dying suddenly of an Apoplexy.

In this Month likewise an *Ambassador* will dye in *London*, but I cannot assign the Day.

AUGUST. The Affairs of *France* will seem to suffer no Change for a while under the Duke of *Burgundy's*[21] Administration; but the Genius that animated the whole Machine being gone, will be the Cause of mighty Turns and Revolutions in the following Year. The new King makes yet little Change either in the Army or the Ministry, but the Libels against his Grandfather that fly about his very Court, give him uneasiness.

I see an Express[22] in mighty haste, with Joy and Wonder in his Looks, arriving by the break of Day on the 26th of this Month, having travel'd in three Days a prodigious Journey by Land and Sea. In the Evening I hear Bells and Guns, and see the Blazing of a Thousand Bonfires.

A Young Admiral of noble Birth does likewise this Month gain immortal Honour by a great Atchievement.

The Affairs of *Poland* are this Month entirely settl'd: *Augustus* resigns his Pretensions, which he had again taken up for some time: *Stanislaus* is peaceably posses'd of the Throne:[23] and the King of *Sweden* declares for the Emperor.

I cannot omit one particular Accident here at home,

that near the End of this Month much Mischief will be done at *Bartholomew* Fair[24] by the Fall of a Booth.

SEPTEMBER. This Month begins with a very surprising Fit of Frosty Weather, which will last near twelve Days.

The Pope[25] having long languish'd last Month, the Swellings in his Legs breaking, and the Flesh Mortifying, will dye on the 11th Instant, and in three Week's time, after a mighty Contest, be succeeded by a Cardinal of the *Imperial* Faction, but Native of *Tuscany*, who is now about Sixty-One Years old.

The *French* Army Acts now wholly on the Defensive, strongly fortified in their Trenches; and the young *French* King sends Overtures for a Treaty of Peace, by the Duke of *Mantua*;[26] which, because it is a matter of State that concerns us here at home, I shall speak no further of it.

I shall add but one Prediction more, and that in Mystical Terms, which shall be included in a Verse out of *Virgil*.

> *Alter erit jam Tethys, & altera quæ vehat Argo*
> *Dilectos Heroas.*[27]

Upon the 25th Day of this Month, the fulfilling of this Prediction will be manifest to every Body.

This is the furthest I have proceeded in my Calculations for the present Year. I do not pretend, that these are all the great Events which will happen in this Period, but that those I have set down will infallibly come to pass. It may perhaps still be objected, why I have not spoke more particularly of Affairs at home, or of the Success of our Armies abroad, which I might and could very largely have done; but those in Power have wisely discourag'd Men from meddling in Publick Concerns, and I was resolv'd by no Means to give the least Offence. This I will venture to say, That it will be a Glorious Campaign for the *Allies*, wherein the *English* Forces, both by Sea and Land, will have their full Share of Honour; That Her Majesty Queen ANNE will continue in Health and Prosperity; And, That no ill Accident will arrive to any in the Chief Ministry.

---

18. Marli: Louis XIV's chateau near Versailles. **19. a Flux:** a dysentery. **20. Monsieur Chamillard:** Michel de Chamillard, or Chamillart (1651–1721), resigned as Minister of Finance in 1708 and as Minister of War in 1709. **21. Duke of Burgundy:** Louis (1682–1712), Duc de Bourgogne, son of the Dauphin and father of Louis XV. **22. an Express:** an express messenger. **23. Stanislaus . . . Throne:** In 1706 Augustus II (1670–1733), King of Poland and Elector of Saxony, by the terms of the Treaty of Altranstadt gave up the Polish crown to Stanislaus I; he got it back after the defeat of Charles XII of Sweden by the Russians at Poltava in 1709.

24. Bartholomew Fair: which took place on August 24. **25. The Pope:** Clement XI (1649–1721). **26. Duke of Mantua:** The dukedom of Mantua was ruled by the Italian princely family of Gonzaga; its last representative, Carlo Ferdinando di Gonzaga, died on July 5 of this year, whereupon the duchy was annexed by Austria. **27. Alter . . . Heroas:** *Alter erit tum Tiphys, et altera quæ vehat Argo / delectos heroas* ["A second Tiphys shall then arise, and a second Argo to carry chosen heroes"] (*Eclogues*, iv. 34–35).

As to the particular Events I have mention'd, the Readers may judge by the fulfilling of them, whether I am of the Level with common Astrologers; who, with an old paultry Cant, and a few Pot-hooks[28] for Planets to amuse the Vulgar, have, in my Opinion, too long been suffer'd to abuse the World: But an honest Physitian ought not to be despis'd, because there are such Things as Mountebanks. I hope I have some share of Reputation, which I would not willingly forfeit for a Frolick or Humour; And I believe no Gentleman, who reads this Paper, will look upon it to be of the same Cast or Mould with the common Scribbles that are every Day hawk'd about. My Fortune hath plac'd me above the little Regard of writing for a few Pence, which I neither value nor want: Therefore let not wise Men too hastily condemn this Essay, intended for a good Design to cultivate and improve an ancient Art, long in Disgrace by having fallen into mean unskilful Hands. A little Time will determine, whether I have deceiv'd others, or my self; and I think it is no very unreasonable Request, that Men would please to suspend their Judgments till then. I was once of the Opinion with those who despise all Predictions from the Stars, till in the Year 1686, a Man of Quality shew'd me written in his *Album*, That the most learned Astronomer Captain *Hally*[29] assur'd him, He would never believe any thing of the Stars influence, if there were not a great Revolution in *England* in the Year 1688. Since that Time I began to have other Thoughts, and after eighteen Years diligent Study and Application, I think I have no Reason to repent of my Pains. I shall detain the Reader no longer than to let him know, that the Account I design to give of next Years Events, shall take in the principal Affairs that happen in *Europe;* and if I be denied the Liberty of offering it to my own Country, I shall appeal to the Learn'd World, by publishing it in *Latin*, and giving order to have it printed in *Holland*.[30]

---

28. Pot-hooks: scrawls, unintelligible characters. **29. Captain Hally:** Edmund, or Edmond, Halley (1656–1742). He held a captain's commission in the Navy while pursuing his astronomical researches. **30. printed in Holland:** The Netherlands was notorious in the eighteenth century for lax printing and publishing standards.

THE ACCOMPLISHMENT OF THE FIRST OF MR. BICKERSTAFF'S PREDICTIONS . . .

❧

The first-edition title continues: *Being an Account of the Death of Mr. Partrige, the Almanack-Maker, upon the 29th Instant. In a Letter to a Person of Honour.* The Accomplishment was published on March 30, the day following the "death."

The text is that of the first edition (1708), with variants incorporated from Faulkner's edition of Swift's *Works* (1735).

❧

MY LORD,

IN Obedience to your Lordship's Commands, as well as to satisfie my own Curiosity, I have for some Days past enquired constantly after *Partrige*, the Almanack-maker, of whom it was foretold in Mr. *Bickerstaff*'s Predictions, publish'd about a Month ago, that he should die the 29th Instant about Eleven at Night, of a Raging Fever. I had some sort of Knowledge of him when I was employ'd in the Revenue, because he used every Year to present me with his Almanack, as he did other Gentlemen, upon the Score of some little Gratuity we gave him: I saw him accidentally once or twice about ten Days before he died, and observed he began very much to Droop and Languish, although I hear his Friends did not seem to apprehend him in any Danger. About Two or Three Days ago he grew Ill, was confin'd first to his Chamber, and in a few Hours after to his Bed, where Dr. *Case* and Mrs. *Kirleus*[1] were sent for to Visit and to Prescribe to him. Upon this Intelligence I sent thrice every Day one Servant or other to enquire after his Health; and yesterday, about Four in the Afternoon, Word was brought me that he was past Hopes; upon which I prevailed with my self to go and see him, partly out of Commiseration, and, I confess, partly out of

---

Accomplishment of the First Prediction. **1. Dr. . . . . Kirleus:** [Swift's note] *Two famous Quacks at that Time in* London.

Curiosity. He knew me very well, seem'd surprized at my Condescention, and made me Complements upon it as well as he could in the Condition he was. The People about him said he had been for some Time delirious; but when I saw him he had his Understanding as well as ever I knew, and spoke Strong and Hearty, without any seeming Uneasiness or Constraint. After I had told him I was sorry to see him in those Melancholy Circumstances, and said some other Civilities, suitable to the Occasion, I desired him to tell me freely and ingenuously[2] whether the Predictions Mr. *Bickerstaff* had publish'd relating to his Death had not too much affected and work'd on his Imagination. He confess'd he had often had it in his Head, but never with much Apprehension till about a Fortnight before; since which Time it had the perpetual Possession of his Mind and Thoughts, and he did verily believe was the true Natural Cause of his present Distemper: For, said he, I am thoroughly perswaded, and I think I have very good Reasons, that Mr. *Bickerstaff* spoke altogether by Guess, and knew no more what will happen this Year than I did my self. I told him his Discourse surprized me, and I would be glad he were in a State of Health to be able to tell me what Reason he had to be convinced of Mr. *Bickerstaff*'s Ignorance. He reply'd, I am a Poor Ignorant Fellow, Bred to a Mean Trade,[3] yet I have Sense enough to know that all Pretences of foretelling by Astrology are Deceits, for this manifest Reason, because the Wise and Learned, who can only judge whether there be any Truth in this Science, do all unanimously agree to laugh at and despise it; and none but the Poor, Ignorant, Vulgar, give it any Credit, and that only upon the Word of such silly Wretches as I and my Fellows, who can hardly Write or Read. I then ask'd him why he had not Calculated his own Nativity, to see whether it agreed with *Bickerstaff*'s Predictions? At which he shook his Head, and said, O! Sir, this is no Time for Jesting, but for Repenting those Fooleries, as I do now from the very Bottom of my Heart. By what I can gather from you, said I, the Observations and Predictions you printed with your Almanacks were meer[4] Impositions upon the People. He reply'd, If it were otherwise I should have the less to answer for. We have a Common Form for all those Things; as to foretelling the Weather, we never meddle with

that, but leave it to the Printer, who takes it out of any Old Almanack as he thinks fit; the rest was my own Invention, to make my Almanack Sell, having a Wife to Maintain, and no other Way to get my Bread, for mending Old Shoes is a Poor Livelihood: And (added he, sighing,) I wish I may not have done more Mischief by my Physick[5] than my Astrology, although I had some good Receits[6] from my Grandmother, and my own Compositions were such as I thought could at least do no Hurt.

I had some other Discourse with him, which now I cannot call to mind; and I fear I have already tired your Lordship. I shall only add One Circumstance, that on his Death-bed he declar'd himself a Nonconformist, and had a Fanatick Preacher to be his Spiritual Guide. After Half an Hour's Conversation I took my Leave, being almost stifled by the Closeness of the Room. I imagined he could not hold out long, and therefore withdrew to a little Coffee-house hard by, leaving a Servant at the House with Orders to come immediately, and tell me as near as he could the Minute when *Partrige* should expire, which was not above Two Hours after; when looking upon my Watch, I found it to be above Five Minutes after Seven; by which it is clear that Mr. *Bickerstaff* was mistaken almost Four Hours in his Calculation. In the other Circumstances he was exact enough; but whether he has not been the Cause of this Poor Man's Death, as well as the Predictor, may be very reasonably disputed. However, it must be confess'd the Matter is odd enough, whether we should endeavour to account for it by Chance, or the Effect of Imagination: For my own Part, although I believe no Man hath less Faith in these Matters, yet I shall wait with some Impatience, and not without Expectation, the fulfilling of Mr. *Bickerstaff*'s Second Prediction, That the Cardinal *de Noailles* is to die upon the 4th of *April;* and if that should be verified as exactly as this of Poor *Partrige*, I must own I should be wholly surprized, and at a loss, and should infallibly expect the Accomplishment of all the rest.

---

2. **ingenuously:** straightforwardly, honestly. 3. **a Mean Trade:** Partridge was a cobbler before taking up astrology. 4. **meer:** utter.

5. **Physick:** practice of medicine. 6. **Receits:** recipes; here, prescriptions.

A VINDICATION OF ISAAC BICKERSTAFF ESQ; . . .

✥

The first-edition title continues: *Against What Is Objected to Him by Mr. Partridge, in His Almanack for the Present Year 1709. By the Said Isaac Bickerstaff Esq;*

The text is that of the first edition (1709), with variants incorporated from Faulkner's edition of Swift's *Works* (1735).

✥

MR. *Partridge* hath been lately pleased to treat me after a very rough Manner in *that which is called*, His Almanack for the present Year:[1] Such Usage is very undecent from *one Gentleman to another*, and does not at all contribute to the Discovery of Truth, which ought to be the great End in all Disputes of the *Learned*. To call a Man *Fool* and *Villain*, and *impudent Fellow*, only for differing from him in a Point meerly Speculative, is in my humble Opinion a very improper Style for a Person of *his Education*. I appeal to the *Learned World*, whether in my last Year's Predictions, I gave him the least Provocation for such unworthy Treatment. Philosophers have differed in all Ages, but the discreetest among them have always differed as became Philosophers. Scurrility and Passion, in a Controversy among *Scholars*, is just so much of nothing to the purpose; and at best, a tacit Confession of a weak Cause: My Concern is not so much for my own Reputation, as that of the *Republick of Letters*, which Mr. *Partridge* hath endeavoured to wound

through my Sides.[2] If Men of publick Spirit must be superciliously treated for their ingenuous[3] Attempts, how will true useful Knowledge be ever advanced? I wish Mr. *Partridge* knew the Thoughts which *Foreign Universities* have conceived of his ungenerous Proceedings with me; but I am too tender of his Reputation to publish them to the World. That Spirit of Envy and Pride, which blasts so many rising Genius's in our Nation, is yet unknown among *Professors* abroad; The Necessity of justifying my self, will excuse my Vanity, when I tell the Reader, that I have near an hundred *honorary* Letters[4] from several Parts of *Europe*, (some as far as *Muscovy*[5]) in Praise of my Performance. Besides several others which, as I have been credibly informed, were open'd in the Post Office, and never sent me. It is true, the *Inquisition* in *Portugal* was pleased to burn my Predictions, and condemn the Author and Readers of them;[6] but I hope at the same time, it will be considered in how deplorable a State *Learning* lies at present in that Kingdom: And with the profoundest Veneration for *Crown'd Heads*, I will presume to add, That it a little concerned *his Majesty* of *Portugal*,[7] to interpose his Authority in behalf of a *Scholar* and a *Gentleman*, the Subject of a Nation with which he is now in so strict an Alliance. But the other Kingdoms and States of *Europe* have treated me with more Candor and Generosity. If I had Leave to print the *Latin* Letters transmitted to me from Foreign Parts, they would fill a Volume, and be a full Defence against all that Mr. *Partridge*, or his Accomplices of the *Portugal Inquisition*, will be ever able to Object; who, by the Way, are the only Enemies my Predictions have ever met with at Home or Abroad. But I hope I know better what is due to the Honour of a *learned Correspondence*, in so tender a Point. Yet some of those illustrious Persons will perhaps excuse me for transcribing a Passage or two[8] in my own Vindication. The most Learned Monsieur *Leibnits* thus addresseth to me his Third

---

A Vindication of Isaac Bickerstaff Esq. **1. Mr. . . . Year:** "You may remember there was a Paper publish'd predicting my Death on the 29th of *March* at Night, 1708. and after the day was past, the same Villain told the World I was dead, and how I died; and that he was with me at the time of my death. I thank God, by whose Mercy I have my Being, that I am still alive, and (excepting my Age) as well as ever I was in my Life; as I was also at that 29th of *March*. And that Paper was said to be done by one *Bickerstaffe*, Esq; but that was a Sham-Name; it was done by an *Impudent Lying Fellow*. But his Prediction did not prove true: What will he say to excuse that? For the Fool had consider'd the *Star of my Nativity*, as he said. Why the truth is, he will be hard put to it to find a *Salvo* for his Honor. It was a bold Touch, and he did not know but it might prove true" (*Merlinus Liberatus* [1709]).

2. through my Sides: by attacking me. **3. ingenuous:** honest, straightforward. **4. honorary Letters:** letters conferring honor. **5. Muscovy:** Russia. **6. the Inquisition . . . them:** [Swift's note] *This is Fact, as the Author was assured by Sir Paul Methuen, then Ambassador to that Crown.* **7. his . . . Portugal:** John V, who reigned from 1706 to 1750. **8. a Passage . . . two:** [Swift's note] *The Quotations here inserted, are in Imitation of Dr. Bentley, in some Part of the famous Controversy between him and* Charles Boyle, *Esq; afterwards Earl of* Orrery. [The controversy—over the relative merits of the Ancients and the Moderns—is the subject of Swift's *Battle of the Books* (1704).]

Letter: *Illustrissimo Bickerstaffio Astrologiæ instauratori,*[9] &c. Monsieur *le Clerc* quoting my Predictions in a Treatise he published last Year, is pleased to say, *Itâ nuperime Bickerstaffius magnum illud Angliæ sidus.*[10] Another great Professor writing of me, has these Words: *Bickerstaffius, nobilis Anglus, Astrologorum hujusce Seculi facilè Princeps.*[11] Signior *Magliabecchi,* the *Great Duke*'s famous Library-Keeper,[12] spends almost his whole Letter in Compliments and Praises. It is true, the renowned *Professor* of Astronomy at *Utrecht,*[13] seems to differ from me in one Article; but it is after the modest manner that becomes a Philosopher; as, *Pace tanti viri dixerim:*[14] And, *Page* 55. he seems to lay the Error upon the Printer, (as indeed it ought) and says, *Vel forsan error Typographi, cum alioquin Bickerstaffius vir doctissimus,*[15] &c.

If Mr. *Partridge* had followed these Examples in the Controversy between us, he might have spared me the Trouble of justifying my self in so publick a Manner. I believe few Men are readier to own their Errors than I, or more thankful to those who will please to inform him of them. But it seems, this Gentleman, instead of encouraging the Progress of his own Art, is pleased to look upon all Attempts of that Kind as an Invasion of his Province. He has been indeed so wise, to make no Objection against the Truth of my Predictions, except in one single Point, relating to himself: And to demonstrate how much Men are blinded by their own Partiality, I do solemnly assure the Reader, that he is the only Person from whom I ever heard that Objection offer'd; which Consideration alone, I think will take off all its Weight.

With my utmost Endeavours, I have not been able to trace above Two Objections ever made against the Truth of my last Year's Prophecies: The First is of a *French* Man, who was pleased to publish to the World,

That *the Cardinal* de Noailles *was still alive, notwithstanding the pretended Prophecy of Monsieur* Biquerstaffe: But how far a *Frenchman,* a *Papist,* and an *Enemy,* is to be believed in his own Cause, against an *English Protestant,* who is *true to the Government,* I shall leave to the candid and impartial Reader.

The other Objection is the unhappy Occasion of this Discourse, and relates to an Article in my Predictions, which foretold the Death of Mr. *Partridge* to happen on *March* 29. 1708. This he is pleased to contradict absolutely in the Almanack he hath publish'd for the present Year, and in that ungentlemanly Manner, (pardon the Expression) as I have above related. In that Work, he very roundly asserts, That he *is not only now alive, but was likewise alive upon that very 29th* of March, *when I had foretold he should die.* This is the Subject of the present Controversie between us; which I design to handle with all Brevity, Perspicuity and Calmness: In this Dispute, I am sensible, the Eyes not only of *England,* but of all *Europe,* will be upon us: And the *Learned* in every Country will, I doubt not, take Part on that Side where they find most Appearance of Reason and Truth.

Without entring into Criticisms of *Chronology* about the Hour of his Death, I shall only prove, that Mr. *Partridge* is not alive. And my First Argument is thus: Above a Thousand Gentlemen having bought his Almanack for this Year, meerly to find what he said against me; at every Line they read, they would lift up their Eyes, and cry out, betwixt Rage and Laughter, *They were sure no Man* alive *ever writ such damn'd Stuff as this.* Neither did I ever hear that Opinion disputed. So that Mr. *Partridge* lies under a *Dilemma,* either of disowning his Almanack, or allowing himself to be, *No Man* alive. But now,[16] if an *uninformed* Carcass walks still about, and is pleased to call it self *Partridge,* Mr. *Bickerstaff* does not think himself any way answerable for that. Neither had the said Carcass any Right to beat the poor Boy, who happen'd to pass by it in the Street, crying, *A full and true Account of Dr.* Partridge's *Death,*[17] &c.

Secondly, Mr. *Partridge* pretends to tell Fortunes,

9. **Illustrissimo . . . instauratori:** to Bickerstaff, that most distinguished restorer of astrology. 10. **Itâ . . . sidus:** so most recently Bickerstaff, that great star of England. Jean Le Clerc, or Leclerc (1657–1736), was a Swiss Protestant theologian who championed Arminianism. 11. **Bickerstaffius . . . Princeps:** Bickerstaff, a noble Englishman, and easily the leading astrologer in this our era. 12. **Library-Keeper:** Antonio Magliabechi, or Magliabecchi (1633–1714), was a Florentine scholar and librarian to Cosimo III (1642–1723), Grand Duke of Tuscany. 13. **Professor . . . Utrecht:** There was no astronomy professorship at the University of Utrecht until 1732. Behind Swift's apparently fictitious reference stands the general reputation of the Dutch for achievements in this field. 14. **Pace . . . dixerim:** Let me say it, with all due respect to such a great man. 15. **Vel . . . doctissimus:** Or perhaps this is a typographical error, since in all other respects Bickerstaff is a most learned man.

16. **But now:** At this point the first edition reads: "Secondly, Death is defined by all Philosophers, a Separation of the Soul and Body. Now it is certain, that the poor Woman who has best Reason to know, has gone about for some time to every Alley in the Neighbourhood, and swore to the Gossips, that *Her Husband had neither Life nor Soul in him.* Therefore . . . ." In the revision, the arguments were renumbered in conformity with the deletion. 17. **A full . . . Death:** Swift's *Accomplishment.*

[handwritten at bottom:]
1. NO MAN ALIVE EVER WRIT SUCH DAMN'D STUFF
2. CONVERSES W/ THE DEVIL TO TELL FORTUNES ACC'DING TO THE CHURCH
3. ALIVE NOW AS WELL AS ON THE 29TH OF MARCH
4. WOULD NOT BEGIN W/ A FALSEHOOD

and recover stolen Goods; which all the Parish says he must do by conversing with the Devil, and other evil Spirits: And no wise Man will ever allow he could converse personally with either, till after he was dead.

Thirdly, I will plainly prove him to be dead, out of his own Almanack for this Year, and from the very Passage which he produceth to make us think him alive. He there says, *He is not only now alive, but was also alive upon that very 29th of* March, *which* I *foretold he should die on:* By this, he declares his Opinion, That a Man may be alive *now*, who was not alive a Twelve-month ago. And indeed, there lies the Sophistry of his Argument. He dares not assert he was alive ever since the 29th of *March*, but that he *is now alive, and was so on that day:* I grant the latter; for he did not die till night, as appears by the printed Account of his Death, in a *Letter to a Lord;*[18] and whether he be since revived, I leave the World to judge. This indeed is perfect cavilling, and I am ashamed to dwell any longer upon it.

Fourthly, I will appeal to Mr. *Partridge* himself, whether it be probable I could have been so indiscreet, to begin my Predictions with the *only* Falshood that ever was pretended[19] to be in them; and this is an Affair at Home, where I had so many Opportunities to be exact; and must have given such Advantages against me to a Person of Mr. *Partridge's* Wit and Learning, who, if he could possibly have rais'd one single Objection more against the Truth of my Prophecies, would hardly have spared me.

And here I must take Occasion to reprove the above-mentioned Writer of the Relation of Mr. *Partridge's* Death, in a *Letter to a Lord;* who was pleased to tax me with a Mistake of *four whole Hours* in my Calculation of that Event. I must confess, this Censure pronounced with an Air of Certainty, in a Matter that so nearly concerned me, and by a *grave judicious Author*, moved me not a little. But although I was at that Time out of Town, yet several of my Friends, whose Curiosity had led them to be exactly informed, (for as to my own Part, having no Doubt at all in the Matter, I never once thought of it) assured me I computed to something under half an Hour; which (I speak my private Opinion) is an Error of no very great Magnitude, that Men should raise Clamour about it. I shall only say, it would not be amiss, if that Author would henceforth be more tender of other Men's Reputation as well as his own. It is well there

were no more Mistakes of that kind; if there had, I presume he would have told me of them with as little Ceremony.

There is one Objection against Mr. *Partridge's* Death, which I have sometimes met with, although indeed very slightly offered; That he still continues to write Almanacks. But this is no more than what is common to all of that Profession; *Gadbury, Poor Robin, Dove, Wing*,[20] and several others, do yearly publish their Almanacks, although several of them have been dead since before the *Revolution*. Now the Natural Reason of this, I take to be, That whereas it is the Priviledge of other Authors, *to live after their Deaths;* Almanack-makers are alone excluded, because their Dissertations treating only upon the Minutes as they pass, become useless as those go off. In Consideration of which, *Time*, whose *Registers* they are, gives them a Lease in Reversion,[21] to continue their Works after their Death.[22]

I should not have given the Publick, or my self, the Trouble of this Vindication, if my Name had not been made use of by several Persons, to whom I never lent it; one of which, a few days ago, was pleased to father on me a new Set of Predictions.[23] But I think these are Things too Serious to be trifled with. It grieved me to the Heart, when I saw my Labours, which had cost me so much Thought and Watching, bawl'd about by common Hawkers, which I only intended for the weighty Consideration of the gravest Persons. This prejudiced the World so much at first, that several of my Friends had the Assurance to ask me, Whether I were in Jest? To which I only answered coldly, *That the Event would shew.* But it is the Talent of our Age and Nation, to turn Things of the greatest Importance

---

20. Gadbury . . . Wing: John Gadbury (1627–1704), an astrologer and rival of Partridge. Robin published his almanac after the Restoration; Dove and Wing both put theirs out during the first half of the seventeenth century. **21. a Lease . . . Reversion:** Such a lease, granting the right of succeeding to something at some future time, would be contingent upon the expiration of a previous grant or upon the death of the leaseholder. Swift plays with the notion that almanac makers, not being able to "succeed" in life, are compensated by being allowed to "succeed" themselves in death. **22. Death:** The first edition continues: "Or, perhaps a Name can *make* an Almanack, as well as it can *sell* one. And to strengthen this Conjecture, I have heard the Booksellers affirm, That they have desired Mr *Partridge* to spare himself further Trouble, and only lend them his Name, which could make Almanacks much better than himself." **23. a new . . . Predictions:** *A Continuation of the Predictions for the Remaining Part of the Year 1708. From the Month of September, till the Month of March, . . . By Isaac Bickerstaff, Esq.*

---

18. Letter . . . Lord: again, *The Accomplishment.* **19. pretended:** alleged.

into Ridicule. When the End of the Year had *verified all my Predictions*, out comes Mr. *Partridge*'s Almanack, disputing the Point of his Death; so that I am employed, like the General, who was forced to kill his Enemies twice over, whom a *Necromancer* had raised to Life. If Mr. *Partridge* hath practiced the same Experiment upon himself, and be again alive, long may he continue so; but that doth not in the least contradict my Veracity: For I think I have clearly proved, by *invincible Demonstration*, that he died at farthest within half an Hour of the Time I foretold; and not four Hours sooner, as the above-mentioned Author, in his Letter to a Lord, hath maliciously suggested, with Design to blast my Credit, by charging me with so gross a Mistake.

FROM

THE TATLER

In 1709, as the new periodical *The Tatler* was getting under way, Swift seems to have furnished his (then) friend Steele with a number of suggestions. He contributed in addition the present article and the two poems *A Description of the Morning* and *A Description of a City Shower*.

The text is that of the first (uncollected) edition, with variants incorporated from Faulkner's edition of Swift's *Works* (1735).

NO. 230

From my own Apartment, September 27.[1]
THE following Letter hath laid before me many great and manifest Evils in the World of Letters which I had overlooked; but they open to me a very busy Scene, and it will require no small Care and Application to amend Errors which are become so universal. The Affectation of Politeness is exposed in this Epistle with a great deal of Wit and Discernment; so that whatever Discourses I may fall into hereafter upon the Subjects the Writer treats of, I shall at present lay the Matter before the World without the least Alteration from the Words of my Correspondent.

THE TATLER: *Number 230.* **1. September** 27: The paper was published September 28, 1710.

To Isaac Bickerstaff Esq;

SIR,

THere are some Abuses among us of great Consequence, the Reformation of which is properly your Province; although as far as I have been conversant in your Papers, you have not yet considered them. These are the deplorable Ignorance that for some Years hath reigned among our *English* Writers, the great Depravity of our Tast, and the continual Corruption of our Style. I say nothing here of those who handle particular Sciences, Divinity, Law, Physick, and the like; I mean the Traders in History and Politicks, and the *Belles Lettres;* together with those by whom Books are not Translated, but (as the common Expressions are) *Done out of French, Latin,* or other Language, and *Made English.* I cannot but observe to you, that until of late Years, a *Grubstreet* Book was always bound in Sheep-skin, with suitable Print and Paper, the Price never above a Shilling, and taken off[2] wholly by common Tradesmen or Country Pedlars; but now they appear in all Sizes and Shapes, and in all Places: They are handed about from Lap-fulls in every Coffee-house to Persons of Quality; are shewn in *Westminster-Hall*[3] and the Court of Requests.[4] You may see them gilt and in Royal Paper[5] of Five or Six Hundred Pages, and rated accordingly. I would engage to furnish you with a Catalogue of *English* Books published within the Compass of Seven Years past, which at the first Hand would cost you a Hundred Pounds, wherein you shall not be able to find Ten Lines together of common Grammar or common Sense.

These Two Evils, Ignorance and Want of Tast, have produced a Third; I mean the continual Corruption of our *English* Tongue,[6] which, without some timely

2. **taken off**: bought up. 3. **Westminster-Hall:** the Court of Justice. 4. **the Court . . . Requests:** a small-claims court. 5. **Royal Paper:** paper for printing, measuring twenty-five by twenty inches. 6. **the continual . . . Tongue:** In 1712 Swift published *A Proposal for Correcting, Improving and Ascertaining the English Tongue*, in which he carries on the campaign of the Royal Society, Roscommon, Dryden, and Defoe (among others) to establish some authority for controlling the development of the English language. In his *Life of Swift* Dr. Johnson said the work was "written without much knowledge of the general nature of language, and without any accurate enquiry into the history of other tongues. The certainty and stability which, contrary to all experience, he thinks attainable, he proposes to secure by instituting an academy; the decrees of which every man would have been willing, and many would have been proud to disobey, and which, being renewed by successive elections, would in a short time have differed from itself."

Remedy, will suffer more by the false Refinements of Twenty Years past, than it hath been improved in the foregoing Hundred. And this is what I design chiefly to enlarge upon, leaving the former Evils to your Animadversion.

But instead of giving you a List of the late Refinements crept into our Language, I here send you the Copy of a Letter I received some Time ago from a most accomplished Person in this Way of Writing; upon which I shall make some Remarks. It is in these Terms:

Sir,

I *cou'dn't* get the Things you sent for all *about Town* —I *thôt* to *ha'* come down my self, and then *I'd h' brôt 'um;* but I *ha'n't don't,* and I believe I *can't do 't,* that's *Pozz—Tom* begins to *gi'mself* Airs, because *he's* going with the *Plenipo's*[7]—'Tis said, the *French* King will *bamboozl' us agen,* which *causes many Speculations.* The *Jacks*[8] and others of that *Kidney* are very *uppish,* and *alert upon 't,* as you may see by their *Phizz's—Will Hazzard* has got the *Hipps,*[9] having lost *to the Tune of* Five Hundr'd Pound, *thô* he understands Play[10] very well, *no body better.* He has promis't me upon *Rep,* to leave off Play; but you know 'tis a Weakness *he's* too apt to *give into, thô* he has as much Wit as any Man, *no body more.* He has lain *incog* ever since—The *Mobb's*[11] very quiet with us now—I believe you *thôt* I *banter'd* you in my last like a *Country Put*[12]—I *sha'n't* leave Town this Month, &c.

This Letter is in every Point an admirable Pattern of the present polite Way of Writing, nor is it of less Authority for being an Epistle. You may gather every Flower of it, with a Thousand more of equal Sweetness, from the Books, Pamphlets, and single Papers, offered us every Day in the Coffee-houses: And these are the Beauties introduced to supply the Want of Wit, Sense, Humour, and Learning, which formerly were looked upon as Qualifications for a Writer. If a Man of Wit, who died Forty Years ago, were to rise from the Grave on Purpose,[13] How would he be able to read this Letter? And after he had got through that Difficulty, How would he be able to understand it? The first Thing that strikes your Eye, is the *Breaks* at the End of almost every Sentence, of which I know not the Use, only that it is a Refinement, and very

frequently practised. Then you will observe the Abbreviations and Elisions, by which Consonants of most obdurate Sound are joined together, without one softening Vowel to intervene; and all this only to make one Syllable of Two, directly contrary to the Example of the *Greeks* and *Romans,* altogether of the *Gothick* Strain,[14] and a natural Tendency towards relapsing into Barbarity, which delights in Monosyllables, and uniting of Mute Consonants, as it is observable in all the Northern Languages. And this is still more visible in the next Refinement, which consists in pronouncing the first Syllable in a Word that hath many, and dismissing the rest; such as *Phizz, Hipps, Mobb, Pozz, Rep,* and many more, when we are already overloaded with Monosyllables, which are the Disgrace of our Language. Thus we cram one Syllable, and cut off the rest, as the Owl fattened her Mice after she had bit off their Legs, to prevent them from running away; and if ours be the same Reason for maiming of Words, it will certainly answer the End, for I am sure no other Nation will desire to borrow them. Some Words are hitherto but fairly[15] split, and therefore only in their Way to Perfection; as *Incog,* and *Plenipo's:* But in a short Time it is to be hoped, they will be further dock'd to *Inc,* and *Plen.* This Reflection has made me of late Years very impatient for a Peace, which I believe would save the Lives of many brave Words, as well as Men. The War hath introduced abundance of Polysyllables, which will never be able to live many more Campagnes. *Speculations, Operations, Preliminaries, Ambassadors, Pallisadoes,*[16] *Communication, Circumvallation,*[17] *Battalions,* as numerous as they are, if they attack us too frequently in our Coffee-houses, we shall certainly put them to Flight, and cut off the Rear.

The Third Refinement observable in the Letter I send you, consists in the Choice of certain Words invented by some *pretty Fellows,* such as *Banter,*[18] *Bamboozle, Country Put,* and *Kidney,*[19] as it is there applied, some of which are now struggling for the Vogue, and others are in Possession of it. I have done

---

7. **Plenipo's:** plenipotentiaries. 8. **Jacks:** Jacobites. 9. **Hipps:** hypochondria or spleen. 10. **Play:** gambling. 11. **Mobb:** mob; from *mobile vulgus.* 12. **Country Put:** bumpkin, lout. 13. **on Purpose:** with the purpose of reading this letter.

14. **of the Gothick Strain:** barbaric. 15. **fairly:** moderately, tolerably. 16. **Pallisadoes:** fortifications resembling palisades. 17. **Circumvallation:** a trench or rampart around a besieged place, or the process of making one. 18. **Banter:** In Johnson's *Dictionary, banter* is called "a barbarous word, without etymology, unless it be derived from *badiner,* Fr." 19. **Kidney:** temperament, disposition; class, kind. Johnson observes that the word is found "in ludicrous language"—he means sportive, not low. The usage is old and apparently not disreputable.

my utmost for some Years past to stop the Progress of *Mobb* and *Banter*, but have been plainly born down by Numbers, and betrayed by those who promised to assist me.

In the last Place, you are to take Notice of certain choice Phrases scattered through the Letter, some of them tolerable enough, till they were worn to Rags by servile Imitators. You might easily find them, although they were not in a different Print, and therefore I need not disturb them.

These are the false Refinements in our Style which you ought to correct: First, by Arguments and fair Means; but if those fail, I think you are to make Use of your Authority as Censor, and by an Annual *Index Expurgatorius*[20] expunge all Words and Phrases that are offensive to good Sense, and condemn those barbarous Mutilations of Vowels and Syllables. In this last Point, the usual Pretence is, That they spell as they speak: A noble Standard for Language! To depend upon the Caprice of every Coxcomb, who because Words are the Cloathing of our Thoughts, cuts them out and shapes them as he pleases, and changes them oftener than his Dress. I believe all reasonable People would be content that such Refiners were more sparing of their Words, and liberal in their Syllables. On this Head, I should be glad you would bestow some Advice upon several young Readers in our Churches, who coming up from the University full fraught with Admiration of our Town Politeness, will needs correct the Style of their Prayer Books. In reading the Absolution, they are very careful to say *pardons* and *absolves;*[21] and in the Prayer for the Royal Family, it must be *endue 'um, enrich 'um, prosper 'um,* and *bring 'um.*[22] Then in their Sermons they use all the modern Terms of Art,[23] *Sham,*[24] *Banter, Mob, Bubble,*[25] *Bully, Cutting,*[26] *Shuffling,*[27] and *Palming;*[28] all which,

and many more of the like Stamp, as I have heard them often in the Pulpit from such young Sophisters,[29] so I have read them in some of *those Sermons that have made a great Noise of late*. The Design, it seems, is to avoid the dreadful Imputation of Pedantry; to shew us, that they know the Town, understand Men and Manners, and have not been poring upon old unfashionable Books in the University.

I should be glad to see you the Instrument of introducing into our Style that Simplicity which is the best and truest Ornament of most Things in human Life, which the politer Ages always aimed at in their Building and Dress, (*Simplex Munditiis*)[30] as well as their Productions of Wit. It is manifest, that all new affected Modes of Speech, whether borrowed from the Court, the Town, or the Theatre, are the first perishing Parts in any Language; and as I could prove by many Hundred Instances, have been so in ours. The Writings of *Hooker*,[31] who was a Country Clergyman, and of *Parsons* the Jesuit,[32] both in the Reign of Queen *Elizabeth*, are in a Style that, with very few Allowances, would not offend any present Reader; much more clear and intelligible than those of Sir *H. Wotton*,[33] Sir *Robert Naunton*,[34] *Osborn*,[35]

---

20. Index Expurgatorius: in imitation of the Roman Catholic *Index librorum prohibitorum*. **21. pardons and absolves:** rather than *pardoneth* and *absolveth*. **22. endue . . . 'um:** "Endue them with thy holy Spirit; enrich them with thy heavenly grace; prosper them with all happiness; and bring them to thine everlasting kingdom, through Jesus Christ our Lord. Amen" (Book of Common Prayer). Swift is of course writhing over the *'ums*. **23. Art:** learning. **24. Sham:** trick, cheat (both verb and noun); "a low word" (Johnson's *Dictionary*). **25. Bubble:** a cheat, the person cheated, to cheat; "a cant word" (Johnson's *Dictionary*). **26. Cutting:** perhaps "swaggering" (*OED*). But other possible meanings are suggested by Francis Grose's *A Classical Dictionary of the Vulgar Tongue* (3rd ed., 1796), ed. Eric Partridge (1963), under *cut:* "drunk. A little cut over the head; slightly intoxicated. To cut; to leave a person or

company." This last meaning has been revived in contemporary slang: "to cut out" and "to cut a class." **27. Shuffling:** shifty actions; an old usage deriving from the practices of cardsharps. **28. Palming:** tricking, cheating; from the practice in gambling of concealing a card, dice, etc. **29. Sophisters:** undergraduates above the rank of freshman. The exact year or years varies with the university; thus, at Cambridge, a student in his second or third year; at Swift's own Trinity College, Dublin, third or fourth year. **30. Simplex Munditiis:** "simple in its elegance" (Horace, *Odes*, I. v. 1). **31. Hooker:** Richard Hooker (c. 1554–1600), author of *The Laws of Ecclesiastical Polity* (1594, 1597). The philosophical Hooker became a country clergyman by choice. **32. Parsons the Jesuit:** Robert Parsons, or Persons (1546–1610), was a convert to Roman Catholicism whose missionary work and writings were dedicated to bringing England back into the Roman Church. **33. Sir H. Wotton:** Sir Henry Wotton (1568–1639), an agent of the Earl of Essex, was a diplomat, Provost of Eton College, and a dabbler in poetry and science. A collection of his works, *Reliquiae Wottonianae*, was brought out in 1651, with a prefatory elegy by Abraham Cowley and a memoir by Izaak Walton. **34. Sir . . . Naunton:** Sir Robert Naunton (1563–1635) also got his start serving the Earl of Essex; he was later patronized by George Villiers, Duke of Buckingham. His *Fragmenta Regalia*, an account of the chief courtiers during Queen Elizabeth's reign, was posthumously published in 1641. **35. Osborn:** Francis Osborne (1593–1659) was the author of the widely read *Advice to a Son* (1656, 1658) and the gossipy *Traditional Memoirs of the Reigns of Queen Elizabeth and King James I* (1658).

Daniel the Historian,[36] and several others who writ later; but being Men of the Court, and affecting the Phrases then in Fashion, they are often either not to be understood, or appear perfectly ridiculous.

What Remedies are to be applied to these Evils, I have not Room to consider, having, I fear, already taken up most of your Paper. Besides, I think it is our Office only to represent Abuses, and yours to redress them. I am, with great Respect,

SIR, Your, &c.

AN ARGUMENT
[AGAINST] THE ABOLISHING
OF CHRISTIANITY
IN ENGLAND . . .

Written in the Year, 1708.

Although Swift was still on the side of the Whigs at this time, his famous ironical tract was directed at them and at all those who favored the repeal of the Test Act (1673), which was designed to strengthen the Anglican establishment by requiring at least a show of allegiance (occasional conformity) as a condition of political office-holding. But while Swift, in this light, may be regarded as only one of many partisan propagandists, the essay transcends its immediate context and takes its place among Swift's most enduring, because most universally relevant, satires.

The text is that of the first printing, in *Miscellanies in Prose and Verse* (1711), where the title reads: *An Argument to Prove That the Abolishing of Christianity in England, May as Things Now Stand, Be Attended with Some Inconveniencies, and Perhaps Not Produce Those Many Good Effects Proposed Thereby.* We have incorporated the variants and italics (partly or wholly Swift's) in Faulkner's edition of Swift's *Works* (1735).

I AM very sensible what a Weakness and Presumption it is, to reason against the general Humor and Disposition of the World. I remember it was with great Justice, and a due regard to the Freedom both of the Publick and the Press, forbidden upon severe Penalties to Write, or Discourse, or lay Wagers against the *Union,*[1] even before it was confirmed by Parliament, because that was look'd upon as a Design, to oppose the Current of the People, which besides the Folly of it, is a manifest Breach of the Fundamental Law that makes this Majority of Opinion the Voice of God. In like manner, and for the very same Reasons, it may perhaps be neither safe nor prudent to argue against the abolishing of Christianity: at a Juncture when all Parties appear so unanimously determined upon the Point, as we cannot but allow from their Actions, their Discourses, and their Writings. However, I know not how, whether from the Affectation of Singularity, or the Perverseness of Human Nature, but so it unhappily falls out, that I cannot be entirely of this Opinion. Nay, although I were sure, an Order were issued out for my immediate Prosecution by the Attorney General, I should still confess that in the present Posture of our Affairs at home or abroad, I do not yet see the absolute Necessity of extirpating the Christian Religion from among us.

THIS perhaps may appear too great a Paradox even for our wise and paradoxical Age to endure; therefore I shall handle it with all Tenderness, and with the utmost Deference to that great and profound Majority which is of another Sentiment.

AND yet the Curious may please to observe, how much the Genius of a Nation is liable to alter in half an Age. I have heard it affirmed for certain by some very old People, that the contrary Opinion was even in their Memories as much in Vogue as the other is now; And, that a Project for the abolishing Christianity would then have appeared as singular, and been thought as absurd, as it would be at this time to write or discourse in it's Defence.

THEREFORE I freely own that all Appearances are against me. The System of the Gospel after the Fate of other Systems is generally antiquated and exploded; and the Mass or Body of the common People, among whom it seems to have had it's latest Credit, are now grown as much ashamed of it as their Betters. Opinions like Fashions always descending

---

36. Daniel the Historian: Samuel Daniel (1562–1619), better known as a poet than as a historian. His poetical *Civil Wars* appeared in eight books between 1595 and 1609; his prose *History of England* in two parts, 1612 and 1617.

AN ARGUMENT AGAINST THE ABOLISHING OF CHRISTIANITY. **1. the Union:** of England and Scotland in 1707.

from those of Quality to the middle sort, and thence to the Vulgar, where at length they are dropt and vanish.

BUT here I would not be mistaken, and must therefore be so bold as to borrow a Distinction from the Writers on the other side, when they make a Difference between Nominal and Real *Trinitarians.*[2] I hope no Reader imagines me so weak to stand up in the Defence of *real* Christianity, such as used in Primitive Times (if we may believe the Authors of those Ages) to have an Influence upon Mens Belief and Actions: To offer at the restoring of That would indeed be a wild Project; It would be to dig up Foundations, to destroy at one Blow *all* the Wit, and *half* the Learning of the Kingdom; to break the entire Frame and Constitution of Things, to ruin Trade, extinguish Arts and Sciences with the Professors of them; In short, to turn our Courts, Exchanges, and shops into Deserts; and would be full as absurd as the Proposal of *Horace,*[3] where he advises the *Romans* all in a Body to leave their City, and seek a new Seat in some remote Part of the World, by way of Cure for the Corruption of their Manners.

THEREFORE I think this Caution was in it self altogether unnecessary (which I have inserted only to prevent all Possibility of Caviling) since every candid Reader will easily understand my Discourse to be intended only in Defence of *nominal* Christianity, the other having been for some time wholly laid aside by general Consent, as utterly inconsistent with our present Schemes of Wealth and Power.

BUT why we should therefore cast off the Name and Title of Christians, although the general Opinion and Resolution be so violent for it, I confess I cannot (with submission)[4] apprehend the Consequence necessary. However, since the Undertakers[5] propose such wonderful Advantages to the Nation by this Project, and advance many plausible Objections against the System of Christianity, I shall briefly consider the Strength of both, fairly allow them their greatest Weight, and offer such Answers as I think most reasonable. After which I will beg leave to shew what Inconveniencies may possibly happen by such an Innovation, in the present Posture of our Affairs.

First, ONE great Advantage proposed by the abolishing of Christianity is, That it would very much

enlarge and establish Liberty of Conscience, that great Bulwark of our Nation, and of the *Protestant* Religion, which is still too much limited by *Priest-craft,*[6] notwithstanding all the good Intentions of the Legislature, as we have lately found by a severe Instance. For it is confidently reported, that two Young Gentlemen of great Hopes, bright Wit, and profound Judgment, who upon a thorough Examination of Causes and Effects, and by the meer Force of natural Abilities, without the least Tincture of Learning, having made a Discovery, that there was no God, and generously communicating their Thoughts for the good of the Publick; were some time ago by an unparalleled Severity, and upon I know not what *obsolete* Law, broke[7] only for *Blasphemy.* And as it hath been wisely observed, if Persecution once begins no Man alive knows how far it may reach, or where it will end.

IN answer to all which, with deference to wiser Judgments, I think this rather shews the Necessity of a *nominal* Religion among us. Great Wits love to be free with the highest Objects, and if they cannot be allowed a *God* to revile or renounce; they will *speak Evil of Dignities,*[8] abuse the Government, and reflect upon the Ministry,[9] which I am sure few will deny to be of much more pernicious Consequence, according to the saying of *Tiberius, Deorum Offensa Diis curae.*[10] As to the particular Fact related, I think it is not fair to argue from one Instance, perhaps another cannot be produced, yet (to the Comfort of all those who may be apprehensive of Persecution) Blasphemy we know is freely spoke a Million of times in every Coffee-House and Tavern, or wherever else *good Company* meet. It must be allowed indeed that to Break an *English Free-born* Officer only for Blasphemy, was, to speak the gentlest of such an Action, a very high strain of absolute Power. Little can be said in Excuse for the General; Perhaps he was afraid it might give Offence to the Allies, among whom, for ought I know, it may be the Custom of the Country to believe a God. But if he argued, as some have done, upon a mistaken Principle, that an Officer who is guilty of speaking Blasphemy, may sometime or other proceed so far as to raise a Mutiny, the Consequence is by no means to be admitted; For, surely, the

---

2. **Trinitarians:** See *On the Trinity,* below. 3. **the Proposal . . . Horace:** in Epode xvi. 4. **with submission:** respectfully. 5. **Undertakers:** promoters.

6. **Priest-craft:** the Anglican clergy. 7. **broke:** cashiered. 8. **speak . . . Dignities:** See II Pet. 2:10. 9. **the Ministry:** the Cabinet. 10. **Deorum . . . curae:** *Deorum iniurias dis curae* ["Injuries done the gods are the concern of the gods"] (Tacitus, *Annals,* I. 73).

Commander of an *English* Army is like to be but ill obey'd, whose Soldiers fear and reverence him as little as they do a Deity.

IT is further objected against the Gospel System, that it obliges Men to the Belief of Things too difficult for free Thinkers,[11] and such who have shaken off the Prejudices that usually cling to a confin'd Education. To which I answer, that Men should be cautious how they raise Objections which reflect upon the Wisdom of the Nation. Is not every body freely allowed to believe whatever he pleaseth, and to publish his Belief to the World whenever he thinks fit, especially if it serve to strengthen the Party which is in the Right. Would any indifferent Foreiner, who should read the Trumpery lately written by *Asgil*,[12] *Tindall*,[13] *Toland*,[14] *Coward*,[15] and Forty more, imagine the Gospel to be our Rule of Faith, and confirmed by Parliaments. Does any Man either Believe, or say he believes, or desire to have it thought that he says he Believes one Syllable of the Matter, and is any Man worse received upon that Score, or does he find his want of *Nominal* Faith a disadvantage to him in the Pursuit of any Civil or Military Employment? What if there be an old dormant Statute or two[16] against him, are they not now obsolete, to a degree, that *Empson* and *Dudley*[17] themselves if they were now alive, would find it impossible to put them in Execution?

IT is likewise urged, that there are by Computation in this Kingdom above Ten Thousand Parsons, whose Revenues added to those of my Lords the Bishops, would suffice to maintain at least Two Hundred Young Gentlemen of Wit and Pleasure, and Free-thinking Enemies to Priest-Craft, narrow Principles, Pedantry, and Prejudices, who might be an Ornament to the Court and Town: And then, again, so great a Number of able (bodied) Divines might be a Recruit to our Fleet and Armies. This indeed appears to be a Consideration of some Weight: But then on the other side, several Things deserve to be considered likewise: As, First, Whether it may not be thought necessary that in certain Tracts of Country, like what we call Parishes, there should be *one* Man at least, of Abilities to Read and Write. Then it seems a wrong Computation, that the Revenues of the Church throughout this Island would be large enough to maintain Two Hundred Young Gentlemen, or even half that Number, after the present refined way of Living, that is, to allow each of them such a Rent,[18] as in the modern Form of Speech, would make them *easy*.[19] But still there is in this Project a greater Mischief behind; And we ought to beware of the Woman's Folly, who killed the Hen that every Morning laid her a Golden Egg. For, pray what would become of the Race of Men in the next Age, if we had nothing to trust to besides the Scrophulous consumptive Productions furnished by our Men of Wit and Pleasure, when having squandred away their Vigor, Health and Estates, they are forced by some disagreeable Marriage to piece up their broken Fortunes, and entail Rottenness[20] and Politeness on their Posterity. Now, here are Ten Thousand Persons reduced by the wise Regulations of *Henry* the Eighth,[21] to the necessity of a low Dyet, and moderate Exercise, who are the only great Restorers of our Breed, without which the Nation would in an Age or two become but one great Hospital.

11. free Thinkers: meaning, primarily, the Deists. **12. Asgil:** John Asgill (1659–1738), author of *An Argument Proving That According to the Covenant of Eternal Life Revealed in the Scriptures, Man May Be Translated from Hence into That Eternal Life Without Passing Through Death* (1700), a legalistic argument claiming that Christ paid the death penalty for all Christians, rendering them exempt. The book was ordered burned and Asgill expelled from the House of Commons in 1707. **13. Tindall:** Matthew Tindal (1657–1733), brought up as an Anglican, was for a time a Catholic and then turned Low-Churchman and Deist. In 1706 he published the sensational *Rights of the Christian Church Asserted Against the Romish and All Other Priests Who Claim an Independent Power over It.* The controversy it provoked culminated in Tindal's Deistic treatise *Christianity as Old as the Creation, or the Gospel a Republication of the Religion of Nature* (1730). **14. Toland:** John Toland (1670–1722) is said to have launched the Deist-Orthodox controversy with his *Christianity Not Mysterious* in 1696. He thereafter published numerous political and religious pamphlets. **15. Coward:** William Coward (*c.* 1657–1725), a physician, published a number of works attacking the notion of the spirituality and immortality of the soul as an entity separate from the body, affirming rather the immortality of the whole man at the Resurrection. Though not exactly a Deist, his rationalistic arguments made him appear an ally. **16. Statute or two:** The Corporation Act (1661) and the Test Act (1673) both required officeholders to be communicants in the Anglican Church.

17. Empson and Dudley: Sir Richard Empson, or Emson (d. 1510), and Edmund Dudley (*c.* 1462–1510), agents of Henry VII, were charged by contemporary historians with exacting taxes and fines from enemies of the Crown by resorting to obsolete laws and other underhand practices. Both were executed soon after Henry VIII succeeded to the throne. **18. a Rent:** an income. **19. easy:** comfortable, well off. **20. Rottenness:** physical unsoundness, corruption. **21. the wise . . . Eighth:** a reference to his appropriation of the revenues of the Church.

ANOTHER Advantage proposed by the Abolishing of Christianity, is the clear Gain of one Day in Seven, which is now entirely lost, and consequently the Kingdom one Seventh less considerable in Trade, Business, and Pleasure; beside the Loss to the Publick of so many Stately Structures now in the Hands of the Clergy, which might be converted into Theatres, Exchanges,[22] Market-houses, common Dormitories,[23] and other Publick Edifices.

I hope I shall be forgiven a hard Word if I call this a perfect Cavil. I readily own there hath been an old Custom time out of mind, for People to assemble in the Churches every *Sunday*, and that shops are still frequently shut, in order as it is conceived, to preserve the Memory of that antient Practice, but how this can prove a hindrance to Business or Pleasure, is hard to imagine. What if the Men of Pleasure are forced one Day in the Week to Game at Home instead of the *Chocolate-House*.[24] Are not the *Taverns* and *Coffee-Houses* open? Can there be a more convenient Season[25] for taking a Dose of Physick[26]? Are fewer Claps got upon *Sundays* than other Days? Is not that the chief Day for Traders to Sum up the Accounts of the Week, and for Lawyers to prepare their Briefs? But I would fain know how it can be pretended that the Churches are misapplied.[27] Where are more Appointments and Rendevouzes of Gallantry? Where more Care to appear in the foremost Box with greater Advantage of Dress? Where more Meetings for Business? Where more Bargains driven of all sorts? And where so many Conveniences or Incitements to Sleep?

THERE is one Advantage greater than any of the foregoing, proposed by the Abolishing of Christianity, that it will utterly extinguish Parties among us, by removing those Factious[28] Distinctions of High and Low Church, of *Whig* and *Tory*, *Presbyterian* and *Church of England*, which are now so many grievous Clogs upon Publick Proceedings, and dispose Men to prefer the gratifying themselves or depressing their Adversaries, before the most important Interest of the State.

I confess, if it were certain that so great an Advantage would redound to the Nation by this Expedient, I would submit and be silent: But, will any Man say that if the Words, *Whoring, Drinking, Cheating, Lying, Stealing*, were by Act of Parliament ejected out of the *English* Tongue and Dictionaries; We should all Awake next Morning Chast and Temperate, Honest and Just, and Lovers of Truth. Is this a fair[29] Consequence? Or if the Physicians would forbid us to pronounce the Words *Pox, Gout, Rhumatism* and *Stone*, would that Expedient serve like so many *Talismans* to destroy the Diseases themselves. Are Party and Faction rooted in Mens Hearts no deeper than Phrases borrowed from Religion, or founded upon no firmer Principles? And is our Language so poor that we cannot find other Terms to express them? Are Envy, Pride, Avarice and Ambition such ill Nomenclators,[30] that they cannot furnish Appellations for their Owners? Will not *Heydukes*[31] and *Mamalukes*,[32] *Mandarins*[33] and *Patshaws*,[34] or any other Words formed at Pleasure, serve to distinguish those who are in the Ministry from others who *would be in it if they could?* What, for instance, is easier than to vary the Form of Speech, and instead of the Word, Church, make it a Question in Politicks, Whether the Monument[35] be in Danger? Because Religion was nearest at hand to furnish a few convenient Phrases, is our Invention so barren, we can find no other? Suppose for Argument sake, that the *Tories* favoured *Margarita*, the *Whigs*, Mrs. *Tofts*, and the *Trimmers Valentini*,[36]

---

29. fair: likely. **30. Nomenclators:** A nomenclator in Roman antiquity was a person whose job it was to identify for his employer the people with whom he came in contact, e.g., in office-seeking. The term came to mean anyone who names or classifies objects. **31. Heydukes:** (Hey ducks) in Hungary, the name for an elite infantry; in Poland, the name for the liveried attendants of the nobility. **32. Mamalukes:** (mamelukes) the military organization, originally composed of Caucasian slaves, that ruled Egypt for several centuries. **33. Mandarins:** the administrative rulers of China. **34. Patshaws:** (padishahs, padshahs) a Persian title, equivalent to "Great King" or "Emperor," applied to both Asian and European monarchs. **35. the Monument:** Christopher Wren's memorial to the Great Fire of 1666. **36. Margarita, Mrs. Tofts, Valentini:** [Swift's note] Italian *Singers then in* Vogue. [Francesca Margherita de l'Epine (d. 1746), known as Margarita or the Tawny Tuscan, married, in 1718, Dr. Pepusch, the German composer and orchestrator of *The Beggar's Opera* (see later in Part Two). Katherine Tofts (c. 1680–1756), an English singer of Italian and English opera, retired in 1709 after a brilliant career. Valentini, a male soprano or *castrato*, would of course be the choice of the "Trimmers."]

---

22. Exchanges: places for the transaction of business. **23. common Dormitories:** lodging houses. **24. Chocolate-House:** A number of the more fashionable chocolate and coffee houses, notably White's in St. James's Street, were notorious gambling centers. **25. Season:** time. **26. Physick:** literally, medicine; figuratively, drink. **27. misapplied:** misused. **28. Factious:** factional.

would not *Margaritians, Toftians* and *Valentinians* be very tolerable Marks of Distinction? The *Prasini* and *Veneti*,[37] two most virulent Factions in *Italy*, began (if I remember right) by a Distinction of Colors in Ribbans, which we might do with as Good a Grace about the Dignity of the *Blew* and the *Green*,[38] and would serve as properly to divide the Court, the Parliament, and the Kingdom between them, as any Terms of Art whatsoever, borrowed from Religion. Therefore I think there is little Force in this Objection against Christianity, or Prospect of so great an Advantage as is proposed in the abolishing of it.

IT is again objected as a very absurd ridiculous Custom, that a Set of Men should be suffered, much less employed and hired, to bawl[39] one Day in Seven against the Lawfulness of those Methods most in use towards the Pursuit of Greatness, Riches and Pleasure, which are the constant Practice of all Men alive on the other Six. But this Objection is I think, a little unworthy so refined an Age as ours. Let us argue this Matter calmly; I appeal to the Breast of any polite Free Thinker, whether in the Pursuit of gratifying a predominant Passion, he hath not always felt a wonderful Incitement, by reflecting it was a Thing forbidden; And therefore we see, in order to cultivate this Taste, the Wisdom of the Nation hath taken special Care, that the Ladies should be furnished with Prohibited Silks, and the Men with Prohibited Wine;[40] And indeed it were to be wisht, that some other Prohibitions were promoted, in order to improve the Pleasures of the Town, which for want of such Expedients begin already, as I am told, to flag and grow languid, giving way daily to cruel Inroads from the Spleen.

IT is likewise proposed as a great Advantage to the Publick, that if we once discard the System of the Gospel, all Religion will of course be banished for ever, and consequently along with it, those grievous Prejudices of Education, which under the Names of Virtue, Conscience, Honor, Justice, and the like, are so apt to disturb the Peace of human Minds, and the Notions whereof are so hard to be eradicated by Right

Reason or Free Thinking, sometimes during the whole Course of our Lives.

HERE first I observe how difficult it is to get rid of a Phrase which the World is once grown fond of, although the occasion that first produced it, be entirely taken away. For several Years past, if a Man had but an ill-favoured Nose, the deep Thinkers of the Age would some way or other contrive to impute the Cause to the Prejudice of his Education. From this Fountain are said to be derived all our foolish Notions of Justice, Piety, Love of our Country, all our Opinions of God or a Future State, Heaven, Hell and the like: And there might formerly perhaps have been some Pretence for this Charge. But so effectual Care hath been since taken to remove those Prejudices, by an entire Change in the Methods of Education, that (with Honour I mention it to our Polite Innovators) the Young Gentlemen who are now on the Scene, seem to have not the least Tincture left of those Infusions, or String of those Weeds,[41] and by consequence the Reason for abolishing Nominal Christianity upon that Pretext, is wholly ceast.

FOR the rest, it may perhaps admit a Controversy, whether the banishing all Notions of Religion whatsoever, would be convenient for the Vulgar.[42] Not that I am in the least of Opinion with those who hold Religion to have been the Invention of Politicians, to keep the lower Part of the World in Awe by the fear of Invisible Powers; unless Mankind were then very different from what it is now: For I look upon the Mass or Body of our People here in *England*, to be as Free Thinkers, that is to say, as Stanch Unbelievers, as any of the highest Rank. But I conceive some scattered Notions about a Superior Power to be of singular Use for the Common People, as furnishing excellent Materials to keep Children quiet when they grow peevish, and providing Topicks of Amusement in a tedious Winter Night.

LASTLY, It is proposed as a singular Advantage, that the abolishing of Christianity will very much contribute to the uniting of *Protestants*, by enlarging the Terms of Communion so as to take in all sorts of *Dissenters*, who are now shut out of the Pale upon Account of a few Ceremonies which all Sides confess to be Things indifferent:[43] That this alone will effectually answer the great Ends of a Scheme for

---

37. **Prasini and Veneti:** rivals in the Roman chariot races and antagonists in the civil war under Justinian. 38. **Blew . . . Green:** Ribbons of these colors were the insignia of the Order of the Garter and of the Thistle. In *Gulliver's Travels* (1726) Swift satirizes the timeserving for which, as he saw it, they were rewards. 39. **to bawl:** to shout at the top of one's voice. 40. **Prohibited Silks, Prohibited Wine:** contraband during the war with France.

41. **String . . . Weeds:** thread of those garments (of education). 42. **the Vulgar:** the common people. 43. **indifferent:** immaterial, unimportant.

Comprehension,[44] by opening a large noble Gate, at which all Bodies may enter; whereas the chaffering[45] with *Dissenters*, and dodging about this or the other Ceremony, is but like opening a few Wickets,[46] and leaving them at jar,[47] by which no more than one can get in at a time, and that, not without stooping, and sideling, and squeezing his Body.

TO all this I answer; that there is one darling Inclination of Mankind, which usually affects to be a Retainer[48] to Religion, though she be neither it's Parent, it's Godmother, or it's Friend; I mean the Spirit of Opposition, that lived long before Christianity, and can easily subsist without it. Let us for instance, examine wherein the Opposition of Sectaries among us consists, we shall find Christianity to have no share in it at all. Does the Gospel any where prescribe a starcht squeezed Countenance, a Stiff formal Gate, a singularity of Manners and Habit, or any affected Modes of Speech[49] different from the reasonable Part of Mankind. Yet, if Christianity did not lend it's name, to stand in the Gap, and to employ or divert these Humors, they must of necessity be spent in Contraventions to the Laws of the Land, and Disturbance of the Publick Peace. There is a Portion of Enthusiasm[50] assigned to every Nation, which if it hath not proper Objects to work on, will burst out and set all in a Flame. If the Quiet of a State can be bought by only flinging Men a few Ceremonies to devour, it is a Purchase no Wise Man would refuse. Let the Mastiffs amuse themselves about a Sheepskin stufft with Hay, provided it will keep them from Worrying the Flock. The Institution of Convents abroad, seems in one Point a strain of great Wisdom, there being few Irregularities in human Passions, that may not have recourse to vent themselves in some of those Orders, which are so many Retreats for the Speculative, the Melancholy, the Proud, the Silent, the Politick and the Morose, to spend themselves, and evaporate the Noxious Particles; for each of whom we in this Island are forced to provide a several Sect of Religion, to keep them Quiet; and whenever Christianity shall be abolished, the Legislature must find some other Expedient to employ and entertain them. For what imports it how large a Gate you open, if

there will be always left a Number who place a Pride and a Merit in refusing to enter?

HAVING thus consider'd the most important Objections against Christianity, and the chief Advantages proposed by the Abolishing thereof; I shall now with equal Deference and Submission to wiser Judgments as before, proceed to mention a few Inconveniencies that may happen, if the Gospel should be repealed; which perhaps the Projectors may not have sufficiently considered.

AND first, I am very sensible how much the Gentlemen of Wit and Pleasure are apt to murmur, and be choqued[51] at the sight of so many daggled-tail[52] Parsons, who happen to fall in their way, and offend their Eyes; but at the same Time these wise Reformers do not consider what an Advantage and Felicity it is, for great Wits to be always provided with Objects of Scorn and Contempt, in order to exercise and improve their Talents, and divert their Spleen from falling on each other or on themselves, especially when all this may be done without the least imaginable *Danger to their Persons.*

AND to urge another Argument of a parallel Nature. If Christianity were once abolished, how could the Free Thinkers, the Strong Reasoners, and the Men of profound Learning, be able to find another Subject so calculated in all Points whereon to display their Abilities. What wonderful Productions of Wit should we be deprived of, from those whose Genius by continual Practice hath been wholly turn'd upon Railery and Invectives against Religion, and would therefore never be able to shine or distinguish themselves upon any other Subject. We are daily complaining of the great decline of Wit among us, and would we take away the greatest, perhaps the only Topick we have left? Who would ever have suspected *Asgil* for a Wit, or *Toland* for a Philosopher, if the inexhaustible Stock of Christianity had not been at hand to provide them with Materials. What other Subject through all Art or Nature could have produced *Tindall* for a profound Author, or furnished him with Readers. It is the wise Choice of the Subject that alone adorns and distinguishes the Writer. For, had a Hundred such Pens as these been employed on the side of Religion, they would have immediately sunk into Silence and Oblivion.

---

44. Comprehension: a Protestant union. **45. chaffering:** dealing, bargaining. **46. Wickets:** small doors or gates. **47. at jar:** (ajar) partly open. **48. Retainer:** servant. **49. a starcht . . . Speech:** Swift is describing certain Puritan sects. **50. Enthusiasm:** religious zeal.

51. choqued: shocked (cf. French *choquer*, "to knock about"). **52. daggled-tail:** with the skirts of their garments dirtied from trailing on the ground; in general, slovenly.

NOR do I think it wholly groundless, or my Fears altogether imaginary, that the Abolishing of Christianity may perhaps bring the Church in Danger, or at least put the Senate[53] to the Trouble of another Securing Vote. I desire I may not be mistaken; I am far from presuming to affirm or think that the Church is in Danger at present, or as Things now stand, but we know not how soon it may be so when the Christian Religion is repealed. As plausible as this Project seems, there may a dangerous Design lurk under it; Nothing can be more notorious, than that the *Atheists, Deists, Socinians,*[54] *Anti-Trinitarians,* and other Subdivisions of Free Thinkers, are Persons of little Zeal for the present Ecclesiastical Establishment: Their declared Opinion is for repealing the Sacramental Test, they are very indifferent with regard to Ceremonies, nor do they hold the *Jus Divinum*[55] of Episcopacy. Therefore this may be intended as one Politick step towards altering the Constitution of the Church Established, and setting up *Presbytery* in the stead, which I leave to be further considered by those at the Helm.

IN the last Place, I think nothing can be more plain, than that by this Expedient, we shall run into the Evil we chiefly pretend to avoid; and that the Abolishment of the *Christian* Religion, will be the readiest Course we can take to introduce Popery. And I am the more inclined to this Opinion, because we know it hath been the constant Practice of the *Jesuits* to send over Emissaries, with Instructions to personate themselves Members of the several prevailing Sects amongst us. So it is recorded, that they have at sundry Times appeared in the Guise *of Presbyterians, Anabaptists, Independents* and *Quakers,* according as any of these were most in Credit; So, since the Fashion hath been taken up of exploding Religion, the *Popish* Missionaries have not been wanting to mix with the Free-Thinkers; among whom, *Toland* the great Oracle of the *Anti-Christians* is an *Irish* Priest, the Son of an *Irish* Priest;[56] and the most learned and ingenious Author[57] of a Book called the *Rights of the Christian*

Church, was in a proper Juncture reconciled to the *Romish* Faith, whose true Son, as appears by a hundred Passages in his Treatise he still continues. Perhaps I could add some others to the Number; but the Fact is beyond Dispute, and the Reasoning they proceed by is right: For supposing Christianity to be extinguished, the People will never be at Ease till they find out some other Method of Worship; which will as infallibly produce Superstition, as this will end in *Popery*.

AND therefore, if notwithstanding all I have said, it shall still be thought necessary to have a Bill brought in for repealing Christianity; I would humbly offer an Amendment; that instead of the Word, Christianity, may be put Religion in general, which I conceive will much better answer all the good Ends proposed by the Projectors of it. For, as long as we leave in being, a God and his Providence, with all the necessary Consequences which curious and inquisitive Men will be apt to draw from such Premises, we do not strike at the Root of the Evil, though we should ever so effectually annihilate the present Scheme of the Gospel; For, of what use is Freedom of Thought, if it will not produce Freedom of Action, which is the sole End, how remote soever in Appearance, of all Objections against Christianity; And therefore, the Free-Thinkers consider it as a sort of Edifice, wherein all the Parts have such a mutual Dependence on each other, that if you happen to pull out one single Nail, the whole Fabrick must fall to the Ground. This was happily exprest by him who had heard of a Text brought for proof of the Trinity, which in an antient Manuscript was differently read; He thereupon immediately took the Hint, and by a sudden Deduction of a long *Sorites,*[58] most Logically concluded; Why, if it be as you say, I may safely Whore and Drink on, and defy the Parson. From which, and many the like Instances easy to be produced, I think nothing can be more manifest, than that the Quarrel is not against any particular Points of hard digestion in the Christian System, but against Religion in general, which by laying Restraints on human Nature, is supposed the great Enemy to the Freedom of Thought and Action.

UPON the whole, if it shall still be thought for the Benefit of Church and State, that Christianity be abolished; I conceive however, it may be more convenient to defer the Execution to a Time of Peace,

---

53. the Senate: Parliament. **54. Socinians:** followers of the Italian Socinus (1539–1604), who denied, among other orthodox tenets of Christianity, the Trinity and the divinity of Christ. **55. Jus Divinum:** divinely sanctioned authority. Swift himself was not entirely easy in holding this view. **56. Toland . . . Priest:** In 1708, the year Swift wrote the present piece, the Irish Franciscan College at Prague cleared Toland of the suspicion of illegitimacy. Although Toland was brought up a Catholic, he became a Protestant before he was sixteen. **57. Author:** Matthew Tindal.

58. Sorites: a chain of reasoning in which the predicate of one proposition forms the subject of the next.

and not venture in this Conjuncture to disoblige our Allies, who as it falls out, are all Christians, and many of them, by the Prejudices of their Education, so bigotted, as to place a sort of Pride in the Appellation. If upon being rejected by them, we are to trust to an Alliance with the *Turk*, we shall find our selves much deceived: For, as he is too remote, and generally engaged in War with the *Persian* Emperor, so his People would be more Scandalized at our Infidelity, than our Christian Neighbours. Because, the *Turks* are not only strict observers of Religious Worship; but what is worse, believe a God, which is more than is required of us even while we preserve the Name of Christians.

TO conclude, Whatever some may think of the great Advantages to Trade by this favourite Scheme, I do very much apprehend, that in Six Months time after the Act is past for the Extirpation of the Gospel, the Bank, and *East-India* Stock, may fall at least One *per Cent*. And since that is Fifty times more than ever the Wisdom of our Age thought fit to venture for the *Preservation* of Christianity, there is no Reason we should be at so great a Loss meerly for the sake of *destroying* it.

ON THE TRINITY

Swift does not appear to have placed a high value on his sermons—only twelve (including one doubtfully his) were printed. Unlike his other writings, they are neither distinguished nor distinguishable from the products of most of his contemporaries. Perhaps the simple require-ment of explaining and edifying was enough to hamper his genius for imaginative exploration. In any case, such a sermon as *On the Trinity* has the virtue of showing us the sentiments, straightforwardly expressed, of the orthodox and conservative Anglican clergyman who stood behind the madcap satirist. *On the Trinity* is an answer, of which there were many in Swift's day and before, to Deistic and other rationalist criticisms of the Christian mysteries.

The text is that of the first printing, in *Three Sermons* (1744).

I Epist. Gen. of St. JOHN V. 7.

For there are Three that bear Record in Heaven,
the Father, the Word, and the Holy Ghost;
and these Three are One.

THIS Day[1] being set apart to acknowledge our Belief in the Eternal TRINITY, I thought it might be proper to employ my present Discourse entirely upon that Subject; and I hope to handle it in such a Manner, that the most Ignorant among you may return home better informed of your Duty in this great Point, than probably you are at present.

It must be confessed, that by the Weakness and Indiscretion of busy (or at best, of well-meaning) People, as well as by the Malice of those who are Enemies to all Revealed Religion, and are not content to possess their own Infidelity in Silence, without communicating it to the Disturbance of Mankind; I say, by these Means, it must be confessed, that the Doctrine of the Trinity hath suffered very much, and made Christianity suffer along with it. For these two Things must be granted: First, That Men of wicked Lives would be very glad there were no Truth in Christianity at all; and secondly, If they can pick out any one single Article in the Christian Religion which appears not agreeable to their own corrupted Reason, or to the Arguments of those bad People, who follow the Trade of seducing others, they presently conclude that the Truth of the whole Gospel must sink along with that one Article; which is just as wise, as if a Man should say, because he dislikes one Law of his Country, he will therefore observe no Law at all; and yet, that one Law may be very reasonable in itself, altho' he does not allow it, or does not know the Reason of the Lawgivers.

Thus it hath happened with the great Doctrine of the Trinity; which Word is indeed not in Scripture, but was a Term of Art invented in the earlier Times to express the Doctrine by a single Word, for the sake of Brevity and Convenience. The Doctrine then, as delivered in Holy Scripture, tho' not exactly in the same Words, is very short, and amounts only to this, That the Father, the Son, and the Holy Ghost, are each of them God, and yet that there is but One God. For, as to the Word *Person*, when we say there are three

ON THE TRINITY. **I. This Day:** Trinity Sunday, the eighth Sunday after Easter. The year the sermon was preached is not known.

Persons; and as to those other Explanations in the *Athanasian* Creed this Day read to you (whether compiled by *Athanasius* or no)[2] they were taken up three hundred Years after Christ, to expound this Doctrine; and I will tell you upon what Occasion. About that time there sprang up a Heresy of a People called *Arrians*, from one *Arrius*[3] the Leader of them. These denied our Saviour to be God, although they allowed all the rest of the Gospel (wherein they were more sincere than their Followers among us.) Thus the Christian World was divided into two Parts, till at length, by the Zeal and Courage of Saint *Athanasius*, the *Arrians* were condemned in a General Council,[4] and a Creed formed upon the true Faith, as Saint *Athanasius* hath settled it. This Creed is now read at certain times in our Churches, which although it is useful for Edification to those who understand it, yet since it contains some nice and philosophical Points which few People can comprehend, the Bulk of Mankind is obliged to believe no more than the Scripture-Doctrine, as I have deliver'd it. Because that Creed was intended only as an Answer to the *Arrians* in their own Way, who were very subtle Disputers.

But this Heresy having revived in the World about an hundred Years ago, and continued ever since; not out of a Zeal to Truth, but to give a Loose to Wickedness, by throwing off all Religion; several Divines, in order to answer the Cavils of those Adversaries to Truth and Morality, began to find out farther Explanations of this Doctrine of the Trinity, by Rules of Philosophy; which have multiplied Controversies to such a Degree, as to beget Scruples that have perplexed the Minds of many sober Christians, who otherwise could never have entertained them.

I must therefore be so bold to affirm, that the Method taken by many of those learned Men to defend the Doctrine of the Trinity, hath been founded upon a Mistake.

It must be allowed, that every Man is bound to follow the Rules and Directions of that Measure of Reason which God hath given him; and indeed he cannot do otherwise if he will be sincere, or act like a Man. For Instance: If I should be commanded by an Angel from Heaven to believe it is Midnight at Noon-day; yet I could not believe him. So if I were directly told in Scripture, that *Three* are *One*, and *One* is *Three*, I could not conceive or believe it in the natural common Sense of that Expression, but must suppose that something dark or mystical was meant, which it pleased God to conceal from me and from all the World. Thus in the Text, *There are Three that bear Record*, &c. Am I capable of knowing and defining what Union and what Distinction there may be in the Divine Nature? which possibly may be hid from the Angels themselves. Again, I see it plainly declared in Scripture that there is but one God; and yet I find our Saviour claiming the Prerogative of God in knowing Men's Thoughts; in saying *He and his Father are one;*[5] and, *before Abraham was, I am.*[6] I read, that the Disciples worshipped him: That *Thomas* said to him, *My Lord and my God.*[7] And Saint *John*, Chap. 1st, *In the Beginning was the Word, and the Word was with God, and the Word was God.* I read likewise that the Holy Ghost bestowed the Gift of Tongues, and the Power of working Miracles,[8] which,[9] if rightly considered, is as great a Miracle as any, that a Number of illiterate Men should of a sudden be qualified to speak all the Languages then known in the World, such as could be done by the Inspiration of God alone. From these several Texts it is plain that God commands us to believe there is an Union and there is a Distinction; but what that Union, or what that Distinction is, all Mankind are equally ignorant, and must continue so, at least till the Day of Judgment, without some new Revelation.

But because I cannot conceive the Nature of this Union and Distinction in the Divine Nature, am I therefore to reject them as absurd and impossible, as I would if any one told me that three Men are one, and one Man is three? We are told, that a Man and his Wife are one Flesh;[10] this I can comprehend the Meaning of; yet, literally taken, it is a thing impossible. But the Apostle tells us, *We see but in part, and we know but in part;*[11] and yet we would comprehend all the secret Ways and Workings of God.

Therefore I shall again repeat the Doctrine of the Trinity, as it is positively affirmed in Scripture: That

2. whether . . . no: The so-called Athanasian Creed, long attributed to Athanasius (295–373), the Christian Bishop of Alexandria, was not formulated until the sixth century. **3. Arrius:** Arius (d. 336), a Greek Christian priest at Alexandria, propounded the so-called Arian heresy, which held that God is supreme and unknowable and that Christ is a subordinate deity not coeternal with God. **4. General Council:** the Council of Nicaea held in 325.

5. He . . . one: See John 10:30. **6. before . . . am:** John 8:58. **7. My . . . God:** John 20:28. **8. the Holy . . . Miracles:** See Acts 2:1–21 and Mark 16:17–18. **9. which:** the "gift of tongues." **10. Man . . . Flesh:** See Gen. 2:24 and Eph. 5:31. **11. We . . . part:** not a quotation, but a paraphrase of the famous verse in I Cor. See n. 18.

God is there expressed in three different Names, as Father, as Son, and as Holy Ghost; that each of these is God, and that there is but one God. But this Union and Distinction are a Mystery utterly unknown to Mankind.

This is enough for any good Christian to believe on this great Article, without ever inquiring any farther. And this can be contrary to no Man's Reason, although the Knowledge of it is hid from him.

But there is another Difficulty of great Importance among those who quarrel with the Doctrine of the Trinity, as well as with several other Articles of Christianity; which is, that our Religion abounds in Mysteries, and these they are so bold to revile as Cant, Imposture, and Priest-craft. It is impossible for us to determine for what Reasons God thought fit to communicate some Things to us in part, and leave some part a Mystery. But so it is in Fact, and so the Holy Scriptures tell us in several Places. For instance: The Resurrection and Change of our Bodies are called Mysteries by Saint *Paul;*[12] our Saviour's Incarnation is another: The Kingdom of God is called a Mystery by our Saviour, to be only known to his Disciples;[13] so is Faith and the Word of God by Saint *Paul:*[14] I omit many others. So that to declare against all Mysteries without Distinction or Exception, is to declare against the whole Tenor of the New Testament.

There are two Conditions that may bring a Mystery under Suspicion. First, When it is not taught and commanded in Holy Writ; or, secondly, When the Mystery turns to the Advantage of those who preach it to others. Now, as to the first, it can never be said, that we preach Mysteries without Warrant from Holy Scripture, although I confess this of the Trinity may have sometimes been explained by human Invention, which might perhaps better have been spared. As to the second; it will not be possible to charge the Protestant Priesthood with proposing any temporal Advantage to themselves by broaching or multiplying, or preaching of Mysteries. Does this Mystery of the Trinity, for Instance, and the Descent of the Holy Ghost, bring the least Profit or Power to the Preachers? No; it is as great a Mystery to themselves as it is to the meanest of their Hearers; and may be rather a Cause of Humiliation, by putting their Understanding in that Point upon a Level with the most ignorant of their

Flock. It is true indeed, the *Roman* Church hath very much enriched herself by trading in Mysteries, for which they have not the least Authority from Scripture, and were fitted only to advance their own temporal Wealth and Grandeur; such as *Transubstantiation, Worshipping of Images, Indulgences* for Sins, *Purgatory,* and *Masses* for the *Dead;* with many more: But it is the perpetual Talent of those who have Ill-Will to our Church, or a Contempt for all Religion, taken up by the Wickedness of their Lives, to charge us with the Errors and Corruptions of Popery, which all Protestants have thrown off near two hundred Years: Whereas those Mysteries held by us have no Prospect of Power, Pomp, or Wealth, but have been ever maintained by the universal Body of true Believers from the Days of the Apostles, and will be so to the Resurrection; neither will the Gates of Hell prevail against them.

It may be thought perhaps a strange thing, that God should require us to believe Mysteries, while the Reason or Manner of what we are to believe is above our Comprehension, and wholly concealed from us: neither doth it appear at first sight, that the believing or not believing them doth concern either the Glory of God, or contribute to the Goodness or Wickedness of our Lives. But this is a great and dangerous Mistake. We see what a mighty Weight is laid upon Faith, both in the Old and New Testament. In the former we read how the Faith of *Abraham* is praised, who could believe that God would raise from him a great Nation, at the very same time that he was commanded to sacrifice his only Son,[15] and despaired of any other Issue. And this was to him a great Mystery. Our Saviour is perpetually preaching Faith to his Disciples, or reproaching them with the Want of it; and Saint *Paul* produceth numerous Examples of the Wonders done by Faith. And all this is highly reasonable; for, Faith is an entire Dependence upon the Truth, the Power, the Justice, and the Mercy of God; which Dependence will certainly incline us to obey him in all things. So that the great Excellency of Faith consists in the Consequence it hath upon our Actions: As, if we depend upon the Truth and Wisdom of a Man, we shall certainly be more disposed to follow his Advice. Therefore, let no Man think that he can lead as good a moral Life without Faith, as with it; for this Reason, Because he who has no Faith, cannot, by the Strength of his own Reason or Endeavours, so easily resist

---

12. The Resurrection . . . Paul: See I Cor. 15:51. **13. The Kingdom . . . Disciples:** See I Cor. 4:1. **14. by . . . Paul:** See Rom. 16:25–26.

15. commanded . . . Son: See Gen. 22.

Temptations, as the other who depends upon God's Assistance in the overcoming his Frailties, and is sure to be rewarded for ever in Heaven for his Victory over them. *Faith*, says the Apostle, *is the Evidence of Things not seen:*[16] He means, that Faith is a Virtue by which any thing commanded us by God to believe, appears evident and certain to us, although we do not see, nor can conceive it; because, by Faith we entirely depend upon the Truth and Power of God.

It is an old and true Distinction, that Things may be above our Reason without being contrary to it. Of this Kind are the Power, the Nature, and the universal Presence of God, with innumerable other Points. How little do those who quarrel with Mysteries, know of the commonest Actions of Nature? The Growth of an Animal, of a Plant, or of the smallest Seed, is a Mystery to the wisest among Men. If an ignorant Person were told that a Load-stone would draw Iron at a Distance, he might say it was a Thing contrary to his Reason, and could not believe before he saw it with his Eyes.

The Manner whereby the Soul and Body are united, and how they are distinguished, is wholly unaccountable to us. We see but one Part, and yet we know we consist of two; and this is a Mystery we cannot comprehend, any more than that of the Trinity.

From what hath been said, it is manifest, that God did never command us to believe, nor his Ministers to preach, any Doctrine which is contrary to the Reason he hath pleased to endow us with; but for his own wise Ends has thought fit to conceal from us the Nature of the Thing he commands; thereby to try our Faith and Obedience, and encrease our Dependence upon him.

It is highly probable, that if God should please to reveal unto us this great Mystery of the Trinity, or some other Mysteries in our Holy Religion, we should not be able to understand them, unless he would at the same time think fit to bestow on us some new Powers or Faculties of the Mind, which we want[17] at present, and are reserved till the Day of Resurrection to Life eternal. *For now,* as the Apostle says, *we see through a Glass darkly, but then Face to Face.*[18]

Thus, we see, the Matter is brought to this Issue; we must either believe what God directly commands us in Holy Scripture, or we must wholly reject the Scripture, and the Christian Religion which we pretend to profess: But this, I hope, is too desperate a Step for any of us to make.

I have already observed, that those who preach up the Belief of the Trinity, or of any other Mystery, cannot propose any Temporal Advantage to themselves by so doing. But this is not the Case of those who oppose these Doctrines. Do *they* lead better moral Lives than a good Christian? Are *they* more just in their Dealings? more chaste, or temperate, or charitable? Nothing at all of this; but on the contrary, their Intent is to overthrow all Religion, that they may gratify their Vices without any Reproach from the World, or their own Conscience; and are zealous to bring over as many others as they can to their own Opinions; because it is some kind of imaginary Comfort to have a Multitude on their Side.

There is no Miracle mention'd in Holy Writ, which, if it were strictly examined, is not as much contrary to common Reason, and as much a Mystery as this Doctrine of the Trinity; and therefore we may with equal Justice deny the Truth of them all. For Instance: It is against the Laws of Nature, that a Human Body should be able to walk upon the Water, as Saint *Peter* is recorded to have done;[19] or that a dead Carcase should be raised from the Grave after three Days, when it began to corrupt; which those who understand Anatomy will pronounce to be impossible by the common Rules of Nature and Reason. Yet these Miracles, and many others, are positively affirmed in the Gospel; and these we must believe, or give up our Holy Religion to Atheists and Infidels.

I shall now make a few Inferences and Observations from what hath been said.

First, It would be well if People would not lay so much Weight on their own Reason in Matters of Religion, as to think every thing impossible and absurd which they cannot conceive. How often do we contradict the right Rules of Reason in the whole Course of our Lives? *Reason* itself is true and just, but the *Reason* of every particular Man is weak and wavering, perpetually sway'd and turn'd by his Interests, his Passions, and his Vices. Let any Man but consider, when he hath a Controversy with another, though his Cause be ever so unjust, though the whole World be against him, how blinded he is by the Love of himself, to believe that Right is Wrong, and Wrong is Right, when it makes for his own Advantage.

---

16. Faith . . . seen: Heb. 11:1. **17. want:** lack. **18. For . . . Face:** I Cor. 13:12.

19. as . . . done: See Matt. 14:28–29.

Where is then the right Use of his Reason which he so much boasts of, and which he would blasphemously set up to controul the Commands of the Almighty?

Secondly. When Men are tempted to deny the Mysteries of Religion, let them examine and search into their own Hearts, whether they have not some favourite Sin which is of their Party in this Dispute, and which is equally contrary to other Commands of God in the Gospel. For, why do Men love Darkness rather than Light? The Scripture tells us, *Because their Deeds are evil;*[20] and there can be no other Reason assigned. Therefore when Men are curious and inquisitive to discover some weak Sides in Christianity, and inclined to favour every thing that is offered to its Disadvantage, it is plain they wish it were not true, and those Wishes can proceed from nothing but an evil Conscience; because, if there be Truth in our Religion, their Condition must be miserable.

And therefore, *Thirdly,* Men should consider, that raising Difficulties concerning the Mysteries in Religion, cannot make them more wise, learned, or virtuous; better Neighbours, or Friends, or more serviceable to their Country; but, whatever they pretend, will destroy their inward Peace of Mind, by perpetual Doubts and Fears arising in their Breasts. And, God forbid we should ever see the Times so bad, when dangerous Opinions in Religion will be a Means to get Favour and Preferment; altho' even in such a Case it would be an ill Traffick,[21] to gain the World, and lose our own Souls. So that upon the whole it will be impossible to find any real Use towards a virtuous or happy Life, by denying the Mysteries of the Gospel.

Fourthly. Those strong Unbelievers, who expect that all Mysteries should be squared and fitted to their own Reason, might have somewhat to say for themselves, if they could satisfy the general Reason of Mankind in their other Opinions; but herein they are miserably defective, absurd, and ridiculous; they strain at a Gnat, and swallow a Camel;[22] they can believe that the World was made by Chance; that God doth not concern himself with Things below, will neither punish Vice, nor reward Virtue; that Religion was invented by cunning Men to keep the World in Awe; with many other Opinions equally false and detestable, against the common Light of Nature as well as Reason; against the universal Sentiments of all civilized Nations, and offensive to the Ears even of a sober Heathen.

Lastly. Since the World abounds with pestilent Books particularly written against this Doctrine of the Trinity; it is fit to inform you, that the Authors of them proceed wholly upon a Mistake: They would shew how impossible it is that *Three* can be One, and *One* can be Three; whereas the Scripture saith no such Thing, at least in that Manner they would make it: But only that there is some kind of Unity and Distinction in the Divine Nature, which Mankind cannot possibly comprehend: Thus the whole Doctrine is short and plain, and in itself uncapable of any Controversy; since God himself hath pronounced the Fact, but wholly concealed the Manner. And therefore many Divines who thought fit to answer those wicked Books, have been mistaken too, by answering Fools in their Folly; and endeavouring to explain a Mystery which God intended to keep secret from us. And as I would exhort all Men to avoid reading those wicked Books written against this Doctrine, as dangerous and pernicious; so I think they may omit the Answers, as unnecessary. This I confess will probably affect but few or none among the Generality of our Congregations, who do not much trouble themselves with Books, at least of this kind. However, many who do not read themselves, are seduced by others that do; and thus become Unbelievers upon Trust and at second Hand; and this is too frequent a Case: For which Reason I have endeavoured to put this Doctrine upon a short and sure Foot, levelled to the meanest Understanding; by which we may, as the Apostle directs, be ready always to give an Answer to every Man that asketh us a Reason of the Hope that is in us, with Meekness and Fear.[23]

And thus I have done with my Subject, which probably I should not have chosen, if I had not been invited to it by the Occasion of this Season, appointed on purpose to celebrate the Mysteries of the Trinity, and the Descent of the Holy Ghost, wherein we pray to be kept stedfast in this Faith; and what this Faith

---

20. Because . . . evil: See John 3:19. **21. Traffick:** trade, bargain. **22. strain. . . Camel:** Matt. 23:24.

23. be . . . Fear: The allusion appears to be to Col. 4:3–6: "Withal praying also for us, that God would open unto us a door of utterance, to speak the mystery of Christ, for which I am also in bonds: That I may make it manifest, as I ought to speak. Walk in wisdom toward them that are without, redeeming the time. Let your speech be always with grace, seasoned with salt, that ye may know how ye ought to answer every man."

is I have shewn you in the plainest Manner I could. For upon the whole, it is no more than this: God commands us, by our Dependence upon his Truth and his holy Word, to believe a Fact that we do not understand. And this is no more than what we do every Day in the Works of Nature, upon the Credit of Men of Learning. Without Faith we can do no Works acceptable to God; for if they proceed from any other Principle, they will not advance our Salvation; and this Faith, as I have explained it, we may acquire without giving up our Senses, or contradicting our Reason. May God of his infinite Mercy inspire us with true Faith in every Article and Mystery of our Holy Religion, so as to dispose us to do what is pleasing in his sight; and this we pray through Jesus Christ, to whom, with the Father and the Holy Ghost, the mysterious incomprehensible One GOD, be all Honour and Glory now and for evermore. *Amen*.

A LETTER
FROM A LAY-PATRON
TO A GENTLEMAN,
DESIGNING
FOR HOLY ORDERS

This work was reprinted under the following title, by which it is better known: *A Letter to a Young Gentleman, Lately Enter'd into Holy Orders. By a Person of Quality.* But "Lay-Patron" has the merit of suggesting immediately Swift's point of view, that of a Doctor of Humane Letters rather than a Doctor of Divinity. As Herbert Davis remarks, Swift here "takes occasion to declare his conviction, which never changed, that learning and civilization are the best allies of religion."

The text is that of the rare copy of the first edition (Dublin, 1720) in the Cashel Diocesan Library, county Tipperary. A few variants have been introduced from Faulkner's edition of Swift's *Works* (1735).

Dated January the 9th. 1719–20.

SIR,

ALthough it were against my Knowledge or Advice that you entred into Holy Orders, under the present Dispositions of Mankind towards the *Church*, yet since it is now supposed too late to recede (at least according to the general Practice and Opinion) I cannot forbear offering my Thoughts to you upon this new Condition of Life you are engaged in.

I could heartily wish that the Circumstances of your Fortune, had enabled you to have continued some Years longer in the University; at least, 'till you were ten Years standing; to have lay'd in a competent stock of human Learning, and some Knowledge in Divinity before you attempted to appear in the World. For I cannot but lament the common Course which at least Nine in Ten of those who enter into the Ministry are obliged to run. When they have taken a Degree, and are consequently grown a Burden to their Friends, who now think themselves fully discharged, they get into Orders as soon as they can; (upon which I shall make no Remarks) first sollicite a Readership, and if they be very fortunate arrive in time to a Curacy here in Town, or else are sent to be Assistants in the Country, where they probably continue several Years (many of them their whole Lives) with thirty or forty Pounds a Year for their Support, untill some Bishop who happens to be not overstocked with Relations, or attached to Favourites, or is content to supply his Diocess without Colonies from *England*, bestows them some inconsiderable Benefice, when it is odds they are already encumbred with a numerous Family. I would be glad to know what Intervals of Life such Persons can possibly set apart for Improvement of their Minds; or which way they could be furnisht with Books, the Library they brought with them from their College being usually not the most numerous, or judiciously chosen. If such Gentlemen arrive to be great Scholars, it must I think be either by means supernatural, or by a method altogether out of any Road yet known to the Learned. But I conceive the Fact directly otherwise, and that many of them lose the greatest Part of the small Pittance they received at the University.

I take it for granted, that you intend to pursue the beaten Track, and are already desirous to be seen in a Pulpit, only I hope you will think it proper to pass your Quarentine among some of the Desolate Churches five Miles round this Town, where you may at least Learn to *Read* and to *Speak* before you venture to expose your Parts in a City Congregation; not that these are better Judges, but because, if a Man must needs expose his Folly, it is more safe and discreet to do so, before few Witnesses and in a scattered Neighbourhood. And you will do well if you can prevail upon some intimate and judicious Friend to be your constant Hearer, and allow him with the utmost

Freedom to give you notice of whatever he shall find amiss either in your Voice or Gesture; for want of which early warning, many Clergymen continue defective and sometimes ridiculous to the end of their Lives, neither is it rare to observe among excellent and learned Divines, a certain ungratious manner, or an unhappy Tone of Voice, which they never have been able to shake off.

I could likewise have been glad if you had applied your self a little more to the study of the English Language, than I fear you have done; the neglect whereof is one of the most general Defects among the Scholars of this Kingdom, who seem to have not the least Conception of a Style, but run on in a flat kind of Phraseology, often mingled with barbarous Terms and Expressions, peculiar to the Nation: Neither do I perceive that any Person, either finds or acknowledges his wants upon this Head, or in the least desires to have them supplyed. Proper Words in proper Places, makes the true Definition of a Style. But this would require too ample a Disquisition to be now dwelt on: However, I shall venture to name one or two Faults, which are easy to be remedied with a very small Portion of Abilities.

The first is the frequent use of obscure Terms, which by the Women are called *Hard Words*, and by the better sort of Vulgar,[1] *Fine Language*. Than which I do not know a more universal, inexcusable, and unnecessary Mistake among the Clergy of all Distinctions, but especially the younger Practitioners. I have been curious enough to take a List of several hundred Words in a Sermon of a new Beginner, which not one of his Hearers among a hundred could possibly understand, neither can I easily call to mind any Clergyman of my own Acquaintance who is wholly exempt from this Error, although many of them agree with me in the dislike of the Thing. But I am apt to put my self in the place of the Vulgar, and think many Words difficult or obscure, which the Preacher will not allow to be so, because those words are obvious to Scholars. I believe the method observed by the famous Lord *Falkland*[2] in some of his Writings would not be an ill one for young Divines, I was assured by an old Person of Quality who knew him well, that when he doubted whether a Word were perfectly intelligible or no, he used to consult one of his Lady's Chamber-maids (not the Waiting-woman, because it was possible she might be conversant in Romances) and by her Judgment was guided whether to receive or reject it. And if that great Person thought such a Caution necessary in Treatises offered to the learned World, it will be sure at least as proper in Sermons, where the meanest Hearer is supposed to be concerned, and where very often a Lady's Chamber-maid may be allowed to equal half the Congregation, both as to Quality and Understanding. But I know not how it comes to pass, that Professors in most Arts and Sciences, are generally the worst qualified to explain their meanings to those who are not of their Tribe: A Common Farmer shall make you understand in three Words, *that his Foot is out of Joynt, or his Collarbone broken* wherein a *Surgeon*, after a hundred Terms of Art, if you are not a Scholar, shall leave you to seek;[3] It is frequently the same Case in Law, Physick, and even many of the meaner Arts.

And upon this Account it is, that among *hard Words*, I number likewise those which are peculiar to Divinity as it is a Science, because I have observed several Clergymen otherwise little fond of obscure Terms, yet in their Sermons very liberal of those which they find in Ecclesiastical Writers, as if it were our Duty to understand them; which I am sure it is not. And I defy the greatest Divine to produce any Law either of God or Man which obliges me to comprehend the meaning of *Omniscience, Omnipresence, Ubiquity, Attribute, Beatifick Vision*, with a thousand others so frequent in Pulpits, any more than that of *Excentrick, Idiosyncracy, Entity*, and the like. I believe I may venture to insist further, that many Terms used in holy Writ, particularly by St. *Paul*, might with more discretion be changed into plainer Speech, except when they are introduced as part of a Quotation.

I am the more earnest in this Matter, because it is a general Complaint, and the justest in the World. For a Divine has nothing to say to the wisest Congregation of any Parish in this Kingdom, which he may not express in a manner to be understood by the meanest among them. And this Assertion must be true, or else God requires from us more than we are able to perform. However, not to contend whether a Logician might possibly put a Case that would serve for an Exception, I will appeal to any Man of Letters, whether at least nineteen in twenty of those perplexing Words might not be changed into easy ones, such as naturally

LETTER TO A GENTLEMAN. **1. Vulgar:** common people. **2. Lord Falkland:** Lucius Cary (*c.* 1610–43), Second Viscount Falkland, politician, poet, and theological writer.

3. to seek: searching, inquiring.

first occur to ordinary Men, and probably did so at first to those very Gentlemen who are so fond of the former.

We are often reproved by Divines from the Pulpits, on Account of our Ignorance in Things Sacred, and perhaps with Justice enough. However, it is not very reasonable for them to expect, that *common Men* should understand Expressions which are never made use of in *common Life*. No Gentleman thinks it safe or prudent to send a Servant with a Message, without repeating it more than once, and endeavouring to put it into Terms brought down to the Capacity of the Bearer: Yet after all this Care, it is frequent for Servants to mistake, and sometimes occasion Misunderstandings between Friends. Although the common Domesticks, in some Gentlemen's Families, may have more Opportunities of improving their Minds than the ordinary sort of Tradesmen.

It is usual for Clergymen who are taxed with this learned Defect, to quote Dr. *Tillotson*,[4] and other famous Divines in their Defence; without considering the Difference between elaborate discourses upon important Occasions, delivered to Princes or Parliaments, written with a View of being made publick, and a plain Sermon intended for the middle or lower size of People. Neither do they seem to remember the many Alterations, Additions and Expungings made by Great Authors in those Treatises which they prepare for the Publick. Besides, that excellent Prelate abovementioned, was known to Preach after a much more popular Manner in the City Congregations; And if in those parts of his Works he be any where too obscure for the understandings of many who may be supposed to have been his Hearers, it ought to be numbred among his Omissions.

The fear of being thought Pedants hath been of pernicious Consequence to young Divines. This hath wholly taken many of them off from their severer Studies in the University, which they have exchanged for Plays, Poems, and Pamphlets, in order to qualify them for Tea-Tables and Coffee-Houses. This they usually call *Polite Conversation; knowing the World;* and *Reading Men instead of Books.* These Accomplishments when applied in the Pulpit, appear by a quaint, terse,[5] florid Style, rounded into Periods and Cadencies, commonly without either Propriety or Meaning. I have listen'd with my utmost Attention for half an

hour to an Orator of this Species, without being able to understand, much less to carry away one single Sentence out of a whole Sermon. Others, to shew that their Studies have not been confined to Sciences, or Antient Authors, will talk in the Style of a gaming-Ordinary,[6] and *White-Fryars*,[7] where I suppose the Hearers can be little edified by the Terms of *Palming, Shuffling, Biting, Bamboozling*,[8] and the like, if they have not been sometimes conversant among Pickpockets and sharpers. And truly, as they say, a Man is known by his Company, so it should seem, that a Man's Company may be known by his manner of expressing himself, either in publick Assemblies, or private Conversation.

It would be endless to run over the several Defects of Style among us; I shall therefore say nothing of the *Mean* and the *Paultry* (which are usually attended by the *Fustian*) much less of the *Slovenly* or *Indecent*.[9] Two Things I will just warn you against; The first is the frequency of flat unnecessary Epithets, and the other is the folly of using old Thread-bare Phrases, which will often make you go out of your Way to find and apply them, are nauseous to rational Hearers, and will seldom express your meaning as well as your own natural Words.

Although as I have already observed, our English Tongue be too little cultivated in this Kingdom; yet the Faults are nine in ten owing to Affectation, and not to the want of Understanding. When a Man's Thoughts are clear, the properest Words will generally offer themselves first, and his own Judgment will direct him in what Order to place them, so as they may be best understood. Where Men err against this Method, it is usually on purpose; and to shew their Learning, their Oratory, their Politeness, or their Knowledge of the World. In short, that Simplicity without which no human performance can arrive to any great Perfection, is no where more eminently useful than in this.

---

4. **Dr. Tillotson:** John Tillotson (1630–94), Archbishop of Canterbury. (See the selection from Tillotson in Part One.) 5. **terse:** polished, refined.

6. **gaming-Ordinary:** gambling house. 7. **White-Fryars:** "a number of lanes, alleys, and passages extending from the west side of Water lane to the Temple, and from Fleet street to the Thames. It took its name from the White Friars, or Carmelites, who had their house in this place next to Fleet street . . . . In the year 1608, the inhabitants obtained several liberties, privileges and exemptions by a charter granted them by King James I. and this rendered the place an asylum for insolvent debtors, cheats, and gamesters . . . ." (*London and Its Environs Described* [1761]). 8. **Palming . . . Bamboozling:** all terms for cheating. 9. **Indecent:** tasteless, indelicate.

I have been considering that part of Oratory which relates to the moving of the Passions: This I observe is in esteem and practice among some Church Divines, as well as among all the Preachers and Hearers of the Fanatick or Enthusiastick Strain. I will here deliver to you (perhaps with more Freedom than Prudence) my Opinion upon the Point.

The two great Orators of *Greece* and *Rome*, *Demosthenes* and *Cicero*, although each of them a Leader (or as the *Greeks* called it a *Demagogue*) in a popular State; yet seem to differ in their practice upon this Branch of their Art; the former who had to deal with a People of much more Politeness, Learning and Wit, laid the greatest Weight of his Oratory, upon the Strength of his Arguments offered to their Understanding and Reason: Whereas *Tully*[10] considered the Dispositions of a fiercer, more Ignorant, and less Mercurial Nation, by dwelling almost entirely on the pathetick[11] part.

But the principal Thing to be remembred is, that the constant Design of both these Orators in all their Speeches was to drive some one particular Point, either the Condemnation or Acquittal of an accused Person, a Persuasive to War, the enforcing of a Law, and the like; which was determined upon the Spot, according as the Oratory on either Side prevailed. And here it was often found of absolute necessity to enflame or cool the Passions of the Audience, especially at *Rome* where *Tully* Spoke, and with whose Writings young Divines (I mean those among them who read old Authors) are more conversant than with those of *Demosthenes*, who by many Degrees excelled the other at least as an Orator. But I do not see how this Talent of moving the Passions can be of any great Use towards directing Christian Men in the Conduct of their Lives, at least in these Northern Climates, where I am confident, the strongest Eloquence of that kind will leave few Impressions upon any of our Spirits deep enough to last till the next Morning; or rather to the next Meal.

But what hath chiefly put me out of Conceit[12] with this moving Manner of preaching, is the frequent Disappointment it meets with. I know a Gentleman, who made it a Rule in Reading, to skip over all Sentences where he spy'd a Note of Admiration[13] at the End. I believe those Preachers who abound in *Epiphonema's*,[14] if they could look about them, would find one part of their Congregation out of Countenance, and the other asleep, except perhaps an old Female Beggar or two in the Isles,[15] who (if they be sincere) may probably groan at the Sound.

Nor is it a wonder that this expedient should so often miscarry, which requires so much Art and Genius to arrive at any perfection in it, as every Man will find, much sooner than learn by consulting *Cicero* himself.

I therefore entreat you to make use of this Faculty (if you be ever so unfortunate as to think you have it) as seldom, and with as much Caution as you can, else I may probably have Occasion to say of you as a great Person said of another upon this very Subject. A Lady askt him coming out of Church, whether it were not a very moving Discourse? *Yes,* said he, *I was extreamly sorry, for the Man is my Friend.*

If in Company you offer something for a Jest, and no-body seconds you in your own Laughter, or seems to relish what you said, you may condemn their Taste if you please, and appeal to better Judgments; but in the mean time, it must be agreed you make a very indifferent[16] Figure; and it is at least equally ridiculous to be disappointed in endeavouring to make other Folks grieve, as to make them laugh.

A plain convincing Reason may possibly Operate upon the Mind both of a Learned and Ignorant Hearer as long as they live, and will Edify a thousand times more than the Art of wetting the Handkerchiefs of a whole Congregation, if you were sure to attain it.

If your Arguments be strong, in God's Name offer them in as moving a Manner as the Nature of the Subject will properly admit, wherein Reason and good Advice will be your safest Guides; but beware of letting the pathetick part swallow up the Rational; For I suppose *Philosophers* have long agreed, that passion should never prevail over Reason.

As I take it, the two principal Branches of preaching, are first to tell the People what is their Duty, and then to convince them that it is so. The Topicks for both these, we know are brought from *Scripture* and *Reason*. Upon the former, I wish it were oftner practiced to instruct the Hearers in the Limits, Extent, and Compass of every Duty, which requires a good deal of Skill and Judgment: The other Branch, is I think not so difficult. But what I would offer upon both, is

---

10. **Tully:** Cicero. 11. **pathetick:** emotional. 12. **put . . . Conceit:** made me dissatisfied. 13. **Note of Admiration:** exclamation point.

14. **Epiphonema's:** striking exclamations or reflections at the conclusion of works or passages. 15. **Isles:** aisles. 16. **indifferent:** bad.

this; that it seems to be in the power of a reasonable Clergyman, if he will be at the pains, to make the most ignorant Man comprehend what is his Duty, and to convince him by Arguments drawn to the Level of his Understanding, that he ought to perform it.

But I must remember that my Design in this *Paper* was not so much to instruct you in your Business either as a Clergyman or a Preacher, as to warn you against some Mistakes which are obvious to the generality of Mankind as well as to me; and we who are Hearers, may be allowed to have some Opportunities in the Quality of being Standers by. Only perhaps I may now again Transgress by desiring you to express the Heads of your Divisions in as few and clear Words as you possibly can, otherwise, I and many thousand others will never be able to retain them, nor consequently to carry away a Syllable of the Sermon.

I shall now mention a particular wherein your whole Body will be certainly against me, and the Laity almost to a Man on my Side. However it came about, I cannot get over the prejudice of taking some little offence at the Clergy for perpetually reading their Sermons; perhaps my frequent hearing of Foreigners, who never make use of Notes, may have added to my Disgust. And I cannot but think, that whatever is read, differs as much from what is repeated without Book, as a Copy doth from an Original. At the same time, I am highly sensible what an extream Difficulty it would be upon you to alter this Method, and that, in such a Case, your Sermons would be much less valuable than they are, for want of time to improve and correct them. I would therefore gladly come to a Compromise with you in this Matter. I knew a Clergyman of some Distinction, who appeared to deliver his Sermon, without looking into his Notes, which when I complimented him upon, he assured me he could not repeat Six Lines; but his Method was to write the whole Sermon in a large plain Hand, with all the Forms of Margin, Paragraph, marked Page, and the like; then on *Sunday* Morning, he took care to run it over five or six times, which he could do in an Hour; and when he deliver'd it, by pretending to turn his Face from one side to the other, he would (in his own Expression) pick up the Lines, and cheat his People by making them believe he had it all by Heart. He farther added, that whenever he happened by neglect to omit any of these Circumstances, the Vogue of the *Parish* was, *Our Doctor gave us but an indifferent Sermon to Day.* Now among us, many Clergymen act so directly contrary to this Method, that from a Habit of saving *Time* and *Paper* which they acquired at the University, they write in so diminutive a Manner, with such frequent Blots and Interlineations, that they are hardly able to go on without perpetual Hesitations or extemporary Expletives: And I desire to know what can be more inexcusable, than to see a Divine, and a Scholar, at a loss in reading his own Compositions, which it is supposed he has been preparing with much *Pains* and *Thought* for the Instruction of his People. The want of a little more Care in this Article, is the Cause of much ungraceful Behaviour. You will observe some Clergymen with their Heads held down from the beginning to the end, within an Inch of the Cushion, to read what is hardly legible; which besides the untoward manner, hinders them from making the best Advantage of their Voice: Others again have a Trick of popping up and down every Moment from their *Paper* to the Audience, like an idle School-boy on a Repetition-day.[17]

Let me entreat you therefore to add one half Crown a Year to the Article of *Paper;* to transcribe your Sermons in as large and plain a Manner as you can, and either make no Interlineations, or change the whole Leaf; for we your Hearers would rather you should be less correct than perpetually stammering, which I take to be one of the worst *Solecisms*[18] in *Rhetorick:* And lastly read your Sermons once or twice for a few Days before you preach it: To which you will probably answer some Years hence, *That it was but just finished when the last Bell rang to Church;* and I shall readily believe, but not excuse you.

I cannot forbear warning you in the most earnest manner against endeavouring at Wit in your Sermons, because by the strictest Computation, it is very near a Million to one that you have none; and because too many of your Calling have consequently made themselves everlastingly ridiculous by attempting it. I remember several young Men in this Town, who could never leave the *Pulpit* under half a dozen *Conceits;* and this Faculty adhered to those Gentlemen a longer or shorter time exactly in proportion to their several Degrees of Dullness: Accordingly, I am told that some of them retain it to this Day. I heartily wish the Brood were at an End.

Before you enter into the common unsufferable Cant of taking all Occasions to disparage the Heathen

---

17. Repetition-day: day for reciting. **18. Solecisms:** improprieties, incongruities.

Philosophers, I hope you will differ from some of your Brethren, by first enquiring what those *Philosophers* can say for themselves. The System of Morality to be gathered out of the Writings or Sayings of those ancient Sages, falls undoubtedly very short of that delivered in the Gospel, and wants besides, the divine Sanction which our Saviour gave to His. Whatever is further related by the Evangelists, contains chiefly, Matters of Fact, and consequently of Faith, such as the Birth of Christ, His being the Messiah, His Miracles, His Death, Resurrection, and Ascension. None of which can properly come under the Apellation of human Wisdom, being intended only to make us Wise unto Salvation. And therefore in this Point, nothing can be justly laid to the Charge of the Philosophers further than that they were ignorant of certain Facts which happened long after their Death. But I am deceived, if a better Comment could be any where collected, upon the Moral Part of the Gospel, than from the Writings of those excellent Men; Even that Divine Precept of loving our Enemies, is at large insisted on by *Plato*, who puts it as I remember into the Mouth of *Socrates*.[19] And as to the Reproach of Heathenism, I doubt[20] they had less of it than the corrupted *Jews* in whose Time they lived. For it is a gross piece of Ignorance among us to conceive, that in those Polite and learned Ages, even Persons of any tolerable Education, much less the wisest Philosophers did acknowledge or worship any more than one Almighty Power under several Denominations, to whom they allowed all those Attributes we ascribe to the Divinity: And as I take it, human Comprehension reacheth no further: Neither did our Saviour think it necessary to explain to us the Nature of God, because as I suppose it would be impossible without bestowing on us other Faculties than we possess at present. But the true Misery of the Heathen World, appears to be what I before mentioned, the want of a Divine Sanction, without which the Dictates of the Philosophers failed in the Point of Authority, and consequently the Bulk of Mankind lay indeed under a great Load of Ignorance even in the Article of Morality, but the Philosophers themselves did not. Take the Matter in this Light, and it will afford Field enough for a Divine to enlarge on, by shewing the Advantages which the Christian World has over the Heathen, and the absolute Necessity of Divine Revelation, to make the Knowledge of the true God, and the Practice of Virtue more universal in the World.

I am not ignorant how much I differ in this Opinion from some ancient Fathers in the Church, who arguing against the Heathens, made it a principal Topick to decry their Philosophy as much as they could: Which I hope is not altogether our present Case. Besides it is to be considered, that those Fathers lived in the Decline of *Literature;* and in my Judgment (who should be unwilling to give the least offence) appear to be rather most excellent, Holy Persons, than of transcendent Genius and Learning. Their genuine Writings, (for many of them have extremely suffered by spurious Additions) are of admirable use for confirming the Truth of ancient Doctrines and Discipline, by showing the State and Practice of the primitive Church. But among such of them as have fallen in my Way, I do not remember any whose Manner of arguing or exhorting I could heartily recommend to the Imitation of a young Divine when he is to speak from the Pulpit. Perhaps I judge too hastily; there being several of them in whose Writings I have made very little Progress, and in others none at all. For I perused only such as were recommended to me, at a Time when I had more Leisure and a better Disposition to read, than have since fallen to my Share.

To return then to the Heathen Philosophers, I hope you will not only give them Quarter, but make their Works a considerable Part of your Study: To these I will venture to add the principal Orators and Historians, and perhaps a few of the Poets: By the reading of which, you will soon discover your Mind and thoughts to be enlarged, your Imagination extended and refined, your Judgment directed, your Admiration[21] lessened, and your Fortitude encreased: All which Advantages must needs be of excellent Use to a Divine, whose Duty it is to preach and practice the Contempt of human Things.

I would say something concerning Quotations, wherein I think you cannot be too sparing, except from Scripture, and the primitive Writers of the Church. As to the former, when you offer a Text as a Proof or an Illustration, we your Hearers expect to be fairly used, and sometimes think we have Reason to complain, especially of You younger Divines, which makes us fear that some of you conceive you have no more to do than to turn over a Concordance, and there having found the principal Word, introduce as

---

19. that . . . **Socrates:** not in so many words; but cf. *Republic* 335 and *Crito* 49^{d-e}. **20. doubt:** suspect.

21. **Admiration:** wonder, astonishment.

much of the Verse as will serve your Turn, although in reality it makes nothing for you. I do not altogether disapprove the Manner of interweaving Texts of Scripture through the Style of your Sermon, wherein however, I have sometimes observed great Instances of Indiscretion and Impropriety, against which I therefore venture to give you a Caution.

As to Quotations from ancient Fathers, I think they are best brought in to confirm some Opinion controverted by those who differ from us: In other Cases we give you full Power to adopt the Sentence for your own rather than tell us, *As St. Austin excellently observes.* But to mention modern Writers by Name, or use the Phrase of *a Late excellent Prelate of our Church,* and the like, is altogether intolerable, and for what Reason I know not, makes every rational Hearer ashamed. Of no better a Stamp is your *Heathen Philosopher* and *famous Poet,* and *Roman Historian,* at least in common Congregations, who will rather believe you on your own Word than on that of *Plato* or *Homer.*

I have lived to see Greek and Latin almost entirely driven out of the Pulpit, for which I am heartily glad. The frequent Use of the Latter was certainly a Remnant of Popery which never admitted Scripture in the Vulgar Language, And I wonder,[22] that Practice was never accordingly objected to us by the Fanaticks.

The Mention of Quotations puts me in mind of common-Place-Books, which have been long in use by industrious young Divines, and I hear do still continue so; I know they are very beneficial to Lawyers and Physicians, because they are collections of Facts or Cases, whereupon a great Part of their several Faculties depend; Of these I have seen several, but never yet any written by a Clergyman; Only from what I am informed, they generally are Extracts of Theological and Moral Sentences drawn from Ecclesiastical and other Authors, reduced under proper Heads, usually begun, and perhaps finished while the Collectors were young in the Church, as being intended for Materials or Nurseries to stock future Sermons. You will observe the wise Editors of ancient Authors, when they meet a Sentence worthy of being distinguished, take special Care to have the first Word printed in Capital Letters, that you may not overlook it. Such for Example as *the Inconstancy of Fortune, the Goodness of Peace, the Excellency of Wisdom, the Certainty of Death, That Prosperity makes Men insolent, and*

Adversity humble; and the like eternal Truths, which every Plowman knows well enough, although he never heard of *Aristotle* or *Plato.* If Theological Common-place Books be no better filled, I think they had better be laid aside, and I could wish that Men of tolerable Intellectuals would trust to their own natural Reason, improved by a general Conversation with Books, to enlarge on Points which they are supposed already to understand. If a rational Man reads an excellent Author with just Application, he shall find himself extreamly improved, and perhaps insensibly led to imitate that Author's Perfections, although in a little Time he should not remember one Word in the Book, nor even the Subject it handled; For Books give the same Turn to our Thoughts and way of Reasoning, that good and ill Company do to our Behaviour and Conversation; without either loading our Memories, or making us even sensible of the Change. And particularly I have observed in Preaching, that no Men succeed better than those who trust entirely to the Stock or Fund of their own Reason, advanced indeed, but not overlaid by Commerce with Books: Whoever only reads in order to transcribe wise and shining Remarks, without entring into the Genius and Spirit of the Author, as it is probable he will make no very judicious Extract, so he will be apt to trust to that Collection in all his Compositions, and be misled out of the regular way of thinking, in order to introduce those Materials which he hath been at the pains to gather: And the product of all this will be found a manifest incoherent piece of Patch-work.

Some Gentlemen abounding in their University Erudition, are apt to fill their Sermons with Philosophical Terms and Notions of the Metaphysical or abstracted kind, which generally have one Advantage, to be equally understood by the Wise, the Vulgar and the Preacher himself. I have been better entertained, and more informed by a Chapter in the *Pilgrims Progress* than by a long Discourse upon the *Will* and the *Intellect,* and *simple* or *complex Idea's.* Others again, are fond of dilating on *Matter* and *Motion,* talk of the *Fortuitous Concourse of Atoms,* of *Theories,* and *Phænomena;* directly against the Advice of St. *Paul,*[23] who yet appears to have been conversant enough in those kinds of Studies.

I do not find that you are any where directed in the Canons or Articles, to attempt explaining the Mysteries of the Christian Religion. And indeed since

22. I wonder: I am surprised (that).

23. against . . . Paul: Cf. I Cor. 1:19 ff. and 3:18 ff.

Providence intended there should be Mysteries, I do not see how it can be agreeable to *Piety*, *Orthodoxy* or good *Sense*, to go about such a Work. For, to me there seems to be a manifest Dilemma in the Case: If you explain them, they are Mysteries no longer; if you fail, you have Laboured to no purpose. What I should think most reasonable and safe for you to do upon this Occasion, is upon Solemn Days, to deliver the Doctrine as the Church holds it, and confirm it by Scripture. For my part, having considered the Matter impartially, I can see no great Reason which those Gentlemen you call the *Free-Thinkers* can have for their Clamour against Religious Mysteries; since it is plain, they were not invented by the Clergy, to whom they bring no Profit, nor acquire any Honour. For every Clergyman is ready either to tell us the utmost he knows, or to confess that he doth not understand them; Neither is it strange that there should be Mysteries in Divinity as well as in the commonest Operations of Nature.[24]

And here I am at a Loss what to say upon the frequent Custom of preaching against *Atheism*, *Deism*, *Free-Thinking*, and the like, as young Divines are particularly fond of doing, especially when they exercise their Talent in Churches frequented by People of Quality, which as it is but an ill Compliment to the Audience; so I am under some doubt whether it answers the End. Because Persons under those Imputations are generally no great Frequenters of Churches, and so the Congregation is but little edifyed for the sake of three or four Fools who are past Grace. Neither do I think it any part of *Prudence* to perplex the Minds of well-disposed People with Doubts which probably would never have otherwise come into their Heads. But I am of Opinion, and dare be positive in it, that not one in a hundred of those who pretend to be *Free-Thinkers*, are really so in their Hearts. For there is one Observation which I never knew to fail, and I desire you will examine it in the Course of your Life, that no Gentleman of a liberal Education, and regular in his Morals, did ever profess himself a *Free-Thinker*: Where then are these kind of People to be found? Amongst the worst part of the Soldiery made up of Pages, younger Brothers of obscure Families, and others of desperate Fortunes; or else among idle Town Fops; and now and then a drunken 'Squire of the Country. Therefore nothing can be plainer, than that

Ignorance and Vice are two Ingredients absolutely necessary in the Composition of those you generally call *Free-Thinkers*, who in propriety of Speech *are no Thinkers at all*. And since I am in the Way of it; pray consider one Thing farther: As young as you are, you cannot but have already observed, what a violent Run[25] there is among too many weak people against University Education. Be firmly assured, That the whole Cry is made up by those who were either never sent to a College; or through their Irregularities and Stupidity never made the least Improvement while they were there. I have above Forty of the latter now in my Eye; several of them in this Town, whose *Learning*, *Manners*, *Temperance*, *Probity*, *Good Nature*, and *Politicks*, are all of a Piece. Others of them in the Country, Oppressing their Tenants, Tyrannizing over the Neighbourhood, Cheating the Vicar, Talking Nonsense, and getting Drunk at the Sessions. It is from such Seminaries as these, that the World is provided with the several Tribes and Denominations of *Free-Thinkers* who, in my Judgment, are not to be reformed by Arguments, offered to prove the Truth of the *Christian Religion;* because Reasoning will never make a Man correct an ill Opinion which by Reasoning he never acquired: For in the Course of Things, Men always grow Vicious before they become Unbelievers; but if you could once convince the Town or Country profligate, by Topicks drawn from the view of their own *Quiet*, *Reputation*, *Health* and *Advantage*, their *Infidelity* would soon drop off: This I confess is no easy Task, because it is almost in a literal Sense, to *fight with Beasts*.[26] Now, to make it clear, that we are to look for no other Original of this *Infidelity* whereof Divines so much complain: It is allowed on all Hands, that the People of *England* are more corrupt in their *Morals* than any other Nation at this Day under the *Sun:* And this Corruption is manifestly owing to other Causes, both *Numerous* and *Obvious*, much more than to the Publication of Irreligious Books, which indeed are but the Consequence of the former. For all the Writers against Christianity since the Revolution have been of the lowest Rank among Men in regard to *Literature*, *Wit*, and good *Sense*, and upon that Account wholly unqualify'd to propagate *Heresies*, unless among People already abandoned.

In an Age where every Thing disliked by those who

---

24. **I do . . . Nature:** With this passage cf. Swift's general argument in his sermon *On the Trinity*, above.

25. **Run:** fixed disposition or persistent attack. 26. **fight . . . Beasts:** "I have fought with beasts at Ephesus" (I Cor. 15:32).

think with the Majority is called *Disaffection*, it may perhaps be ill interpreted, when I venture to tell you that this Universal Depravation of *Manners* is owing to the perpetual Bandying[27] of *Factions* among us for thirty Years past; when without weighing the *Motives* of *Justice*, *Law*, *Conscience* or *Honour*, every Man adjusts his *Principles* to those of the *Party* he hath chosen, and among whom he may best find his own Account:[28] But by reason of our frequent Vicissitudes, Men who were impatient to be out of play,[29] have been forced to recant, or at least to reconcile their former Tenets with every new System of Administration. Add to this, that the old Fundamental Custom of annual Parliaments being wholly laid aside, and Elections growing chargeable,[30] since Gentlemen found that their Country Seats brought them in less than a Seat in the House, the Voters, *that is to say*, the Bulk of the common People have been universally seduced into *Bribery*, *Perjury*, *Drunkeness*, *Malice*, and *Slander*.

Not to be further Tedious, or rather invidious, these are a few among other Causes which have contributed to the Ruin of our *Morals*, and consequently to the contempt of *Religion*: For imagine to your self if you please, a landed Youth whom his Mother would never suffer to look into a Book for fear of spoyling his Eyes, got into Parliament, and observing all Enemies to the Clergy heard with the utmost Applause; what Notions he must imbibe; how readily he will joyn in the Cry; what an Esteem he will conceive of himself; and what a contempt he must entertain, not only for his Vicar at Home, but for the whole Order.

I therefore again conclude, that the Trade of *Infidelity* hath been taken up only for an Expedient to keep in Countenance that universal Corruption of *Morals*, which many other Causes first contributed to introduce and to cultivate. And thus, Mr. *Hobbs*'s saying upon Reason[31] may be much more properly applyed to Religion: That, *if Religion will be against a Man, a Man will be against Religion.* Though after all, I have heard a profligate offer much stronger Arguments against paying his Debts, than ever he was known to do against *Christianity;* indeed the Reason was, because in that Juncture he happened to be closer prest by the *Bayliff* than the *Parson*.

Ignorance may perhaps be the *Mother* of *Superstition;* but *Experience* hath not proved it to be so of *Devotion*: For *Christianity* always made the most easy and quickest Progress in civilized Countries. I mention this because it is affirmed that the Clergy are in most Credit where Ignorance prevails (and surely this Kingdom would be called the *Paradise* of Clergymen if that Opinion were true) for which they instance *England* in the Times of *Popery*. But whoever knoweth any Thing of the three or four Centuries before the Reformation, will find the little Learning then stirring was more equally divided between the *English* Clergy and Laity than it is at present. There were several famous Lawyers in that *Period*, whose Writings are still in the highest Repute, and some *Historians* and *Poets* who were not of the *Church*. Whereas now a-days our Education is so corrupted, that you will hardly find a young Person of Quality with the least Tincture of Knowledge, at the same time that[32] many of the Clergy were never more learned, or so scurvily treated. Here among Us, at least a Man of Letters out of the three Professions, is almost a Prodigy. And those few who have preserved any Rudiments of Learning are (except perhaps one or two Smatterers) the Clergy's Friends to a Man: For, I dare appeal to any Clergyman in this Kingdom whether the greatest Dunce in his Parish be not always the most proud, wicked, fraudulent, and intractable of his Flock.

I think the Clergy have almost given over perplexing themselves and their Hearers with abstruse Points of Predestination, Election and the like; at least it is time they should; and therefore I shall not trouble you further upon this Head.

I have now said all I could think convenient with Relation to your Conduct in the Pulpit: Your Behaviour in the World is another Scene, upon which I shall readily offer you my Thoughts, if you appear to desire them from me by your Approbation of what I have here Written; if not, I have already troubled you too much.

I am Sir | Your Affectionate | Friend and Servant.

January 9th, 1719–20.

---

27. **Bandying:** contention. 28. **find . . . Account:** profit. 29. **out of play:** out of employment or office. 30. **chargeable:** costly. 31. **Mr. . . . . Reason:** "As oft as reason is against a man, so oft will a man be against reason" (Epistle Dedicatory to *The Elements of Law* [1651, 1655]).

32. **the same . . . that:** [Swift's note, 1735 ed.] *N.B. This Discourse was written Fourteen Year ago; since which Time, the Case is extremely altered by Deaths and Successions.*

FROM

[THE DRAPIER'S LETTERS]

👑

In the seven *Drapier's Letters* (1724–25) Swift adopts the *persona* of a Dublin linen draper, thus reversing his usual method of negative identification. Here he speaks directly for the cause of Irish equality, though in the guise of a common, if rather more enlightened, citizen. The immediate occasion for *The Drapier's Letters* was the issuance by the Crown of a patent to one William Wood in July, 1722, for the manufacture of a new copper coinage to be distributed in Ireland. The grievance of the Irish was twofold: neither their Parliament nor their Commissioners of Revenue had been consulted, and both the quantity and the quality of the new money seemed to portend a devaluation of the currency. Protests, official and otherwise, had been loud and frequent, but they met with little satisfaction, and the Irish appeared much in need of a champion when Swift took up the gauntlet. The first of *The Drapier's Letters* was written in February, 1724; the fourth resulted in the prosecution of the printer and a price on the author's head. Unintimidated, Swift kept up the barrage and was preparing a seventh letter for publication in the summer of 1725 when word came that the patent had been revoked. The episode is treated allegorically in *Gulliver's Travels*, Part III, Chapter iii.

The first of the *Letters* was originally titled *A Letter to the Shop-Keepers, Tradesmen, Farmers, and Common-People of Ireland, Concerning the Brass Half-Pence Coined by One William Wood, Hard-Ware-Man, with a Design to Have Them Pass in This Kingdom.* The text is that of the first edition (1724), as discriminated by Herbert Davis in his 1935 edition of *The Drapier's Letters*. Variants (including those in the title) and footnotes have been incorporated from Faulkner's edition of Swift's *Works* (1735).

🏺

[NUMBER 1]

To the Tradesmen, Shop-Keepers, Farmers, and Country-People in General, of the Kingdom of IRELAND.

Brethren, Friends, Countrymen and *Fellow Subjects,* WHAT I intend now to say to you, is, next to your Duty to God, and the Care of your Salvation, of the greatest Concern to your selves, and your Children,

your *Bread* and *Cloathing*, and every common Necessary of Life entirely depend upon it. Therefore I do most earnestly exhort you as *Men*, as *Christians*, as *Parents*, and as *Lovers of your Country*, to read this Paper with the utmost Attention, or get it read to you by others; which that you may do at the less Expence, I have ordered the Printer to sell it at the lowest Rate.

It is a great Fault among you, that when a Person writes with no other Intention than *to do you Good, you will not be at the Pains to Read his Advices:* One Copy of this Paper may serve a Dozen of you, which will be less than a Farthing a-piece. It is your Folly that you have no common or general Interest in your View, not even the Wisest among you, neither do you know or enquire, or care who are your Friends, or who are your Enemies.

About four Years ago, a little Book[1] was written, to advise all People to wear the *Manufactures of this our own Dear Country:* It had no other Design, said nothing against the *King* or *Parliament*, or *any* Person whatsoever, yet the POOR PRINTER[2] was prosecuted two Years, with the utmost Violence, and even some WEAVERS themselves, for whose Sake it was written, being upon the JURY, FOUND HIM GUILTY. This would be enough to discourage any Man from endeavouring to do you Good, when you will either neglect him or fly in his Face for his Pains, and when he must expect only *Danger to himself* and to be fined and imprisoned, perhaps to his Ruin.

However I cannot but warn you once more of the manifest Destruction before your Eyes, if you do not behave your selves as you ought.

I will therefore first tell you the *plain Story of the Fact;* and then I will lay before you how you ought to act in common Prudence, and according to the *Laws of your Country.*

The Fact is thus, It having been many Years since COPPER HALF-PENCE or FARTHINGS were last Coined in this *Kingdom*, they have been for some time very scarce, and many *Counterfeits* passed about under the Name of RAPS,[3] several Applications were made to *England*, that we might have Liberty to *Coin New ones*, as in former times we did; but they did not succeed. At last one Mr. WOOD *a mean ordinary Man,*

THE DRAPIER'S LETTERS: *Number 1.* **1. a little Book:** Swift's own *Proposal for the Universal Use of Irish Manufacture* (1720). **2. the Poor Printer:** Edward Waters. (See *Verses on the Death of Dr. Swift*, above, note to ll. 417–18.) **3. Raps:** counterfeit coins worth about half a farthing.

a *Hard-Ware Dealer*,[4] procured a *Patent* under His MAJESTIES BROAD SEAL to Coin 108000*l.* in *Copper* for this *Kingdom*, which Patent however did not oblige any one here to take them, unless they pleased. Now you must know, that the HALF-PENCE and FARTHINGS in *England* pass for very little more than they are worth. And if you should beat them to Pieces, and sell them to the *Brazier*[5] you would not lose much above a Penny in a Shilling. But Mr. WOOD made his HALF-PENCE of such *Base Metal*,[6] and so much smaller than the *English* ones, that the *Brazier* would hardly give you above a *Penny* of good Money for a *Shilling* of his; so that this Sum of 108000*l.* in good Gold and Silver, must be given for TRASH that will not be worth above *Eight* or *Nine Thousand Pounds* real Value. But this is not the Worst, for Mr. WOOD when he pleases may by Stealth send over *another* 108000*l.* and buy *all our Goods for Eleven Parts in Twelve*, under the Value. For Example, if a *Hatter* sells a Dozen of *Hatts* for *Five Shillings* a-piece, which amounts to *Three Pounds*, and receives the Payment in Mr. WOOD's Coin, he really receives only the Value of *Five Shillings*.

Perhaps you will wonder how such *an ordinary Fellow* as this Mr. WOOD could have so much Interest as to get his MAJESTIES Broad Seal for so great a Sum of bad Money, to be sent to this Poor Country, and that all the *Nobility* and *Gentry* here could not obtain the same Favour, and let us make our own *Half-pence*, as we used to do. Now I will make that Matter very Plain. We are at a great Distance from the *King's Court*, and have no body there to solicite for us, although a great Number of *Lords* and *Squires*, whose Estates are here, and are our Countrymen, spend all their *Lives* and *Fortunes* there. But this same Mr. WOOD was able to attend constantly for his own Interest; he is an ENGLISH MAN and had GREAT FRIENDS,[7] and it seems knew very well *where to give Money*, to those that would speak to OTHERS that could speak to the

KING and would tell A FAIR STORY. And HIS MAJESTY, and perhaps the great Lord[8] or Lords who advised him, might think it was for our *Country's Good;* and so, as the Lawyers express it, the KING was deceived in his Grant, which often happens in *all Reigns.* And I am sure if his MAJESTY knew that such a Patent, if it should take Effect according to the Desire of Mr. WOOD, would utterly Ruin this Kingdom, which hath given such great Proofs of it's *Loyalty*, he would immediately recall it, and perhaps shew his Displeasure to SOME BODY OR OTHER, *But a Word to the Wise is enough.* Most of you must have heard, with what Anger our *Honourable House of Commons* received an Account of this WOOD's PATENT. There were several *Fine Speeches* made upon it, and plain Proofs that it was all A WICKED CHEAT from the *Bottom to the Top*, and several *Smart Votes*[9] were printed, which that same WOOD had the assurance to answer likewise in *Print*, and in so confident a Way, as if he were *A better Man than Our whole Parliament* put together.

This WOOD, as soon as his *Patent* was passed, or soon after, sends over a great many *Barrels of those HALF-PENCE*, to *Cork* and other *Seaport Towns*, and to get them off offered an *Hundred Pounds* in his *Coin* for *Seventy* or *Eighty* in *Silver;* But the *Collectors* of the KING's Customs very honestly refused to take them, and so did almost every body else. And since the *Parliament* hath condemned them, and desired the KING that they might be stopped, all the *Kingdom* do abominate them.

But WOOD is still working *under hand* to force his HALF-PENCE upon us, and if he can by help of his *Friends* in *England* prevail so far as to get an Order that the *Commissioners* and *Collectors* of the KING's Money shall Receive them, and that the ARMY is to be paid with them, then he thinks *his Work shall be done.* And this is the Difficulty you will be under in such a *Case.* For the common Soldier when he goes to the *Market* or *Ale-house* will offer this Money, and if it be refused, perhaps he will SWAGGER and HECTOR, and *Threaten* to *Beat* the BUTCHER or *Ale-Wife*, or take the Goods by Force, and throw them the bad HALF-PENCE. In this and the like Cases, the *Shop-keeper*, or *Victualer*,[10] or *any other Tradesmen* has

---

4. a Hard-Ware Dealer: William Wood (1671–1730) was an ironmaster and mine owner, and not so "mean" or "ordinary" a man as Swift would make out. **5. Brazier:** worker in brass. **6. such . . . Metal:** Sir Isaac Newton, as Comptroller of the Mint, found and reported that Wood's copper was as good as that coined in England and better than that coined for Ireland in previous reigns. But Swift refused to accept the reliability of the sampling upon which the assay was made. **7. Great Friends:** It was rumored that Wood had procured the patent by buying it from the King's mistress, the Duchess of Kendal.

8. the great Lord: Sir Robert Walpole (1676–1745). **9. Smart Votes:** in the form of "Humble Addresses" to the King (September, 1723). **10. Victualer:** retailer of food and drink.

no more to do, than to demand ten times the Price of his Goods, if it is to be paid in WOOD's Money; for Example, Twenty Pence of that Money for A QUART OF ALE, and so in all things else, and not part with his Goods till he gets the *Money*.

For suppose you go to an ALE-HOUSE with that base Money, and the Landlord gives you a Quart for Four of these HALF-PENCE, what must the Victualer do? His BREWER will not be paid in that Coin, or if the BREWER should be such a Fool, the *Farmers* will not take it from them for their *Bere*,[11] because they are bound by their Leases to pay their Rents in Good and Lawful Money of *England*, which this is not, nor of *Ireland* neither, and the 'Squire their Landlord will never be so bewitched to take such *Trash* for his Land, so that it must certainly stop some where or other, and wherever it stops it is the same thing, and we are all undone.

The common weight of these HALF-PENCE is between Four and Five to an *Ounce*, suppose Five, then three Shillings and Four Pence will weigh a Pound, and consequently *Twenty Shillings* will weigh *Six Pounds Butter Weight*.[12] Now there are many Hundred *Farmers* who pay Two Hundred Pounds a Year Rent. Therefore when one of these Farmers comes with his Half Years Rent, which is one Hundred Pound, it will be at least Six Hundred Pound weight, which is Three Horses Load.

If a *'Squire* has a mind to come to Town to buy Cloaths and Wine and Spices for himself and Family, or perhaps to pass the Winter here; he must bring with him Five or Six Horses loaden with *Sacks* as the Farmers bring their Corn; and when his Lady comes in her Coach to our Shops, it must be followed by a Car loaded with Mr. WOOD's Money. And I hope we shall have the Grace to take it for no more than it is worth.

They say 'SQUIRE CONOLLY[13] has *Sixteen Thousand Pounds a Year*, now if he sends for his *Rent* to Town, as *it is likely he does*, he must have Two *Hundred and Fifty Horses* to bring up his *Half Years Rent*, and Two or Three great *Cellars* in his House for Stowage. But what the Bankers will do I cannot tell. For I am assured, that some great Bankers keep by them *Forty Thousand Pounds* in ready Cash to answer all Payments, which Sum, in Mr. WOOD's Money, would require Twelve Hundred Horses to carry it.

For my own Part, I am already resolved what to do; I have a pretty good Shop of *Irish Stuffs* and *Silks*, and instead of taking Mr. WOOD's bad Copper, I intend to Truck[14] with my Neighbours the BUTCHERS, and *Bakers*, and *Brewers*, and the rest, *Goods for Goods*, and the little *Gold* and *Silver* I have, I will keep by me like my *Heart's Blood* till better Times, or until I am just ready to starve, and then I will buy Mr. WOOD's Money as my Father did the Brass Money in K. JAMES's Time, who could buy *Ten Pound* of it with a *Guinea*, and I hope to get as much for a *Pistole*,[15] and so purchase *Bread* from those who will be such Fools as to sell it me.

These HALF-PENCE, if they once pass, will soon be COUNTERFEIT, because it may be cheaply done, the *Stuff* is so *Base*. The DUTCH likewise will probably do the same thing, and send them over to us to pay for our *Goods*. And Mr. WOOD will never be at rest but coin on: So that in some Years we shall have at least five Times 108000*l*. of this *Lumber*.[16] Now the Current Money of this Kingdom is not reckoned to be above *Four Hundred Thousand Pounds in all*, and while there is a *Silver* Six-pence left these BLOOD-SUCKERS will never be quiet.

When once the *Kingdom* is reduced to such a Condition, I will tell you what must be the End: The *Gentlemen of Estates* will all turn off their *Tenants* for want of Payment, because as I told you before, the *Tenants* are obliged by their Leases to pay *Sterling* which is Lawful Current Money of *England*, then they will turn their own *Farmers*, AS TOO MANY OF THEM DO ALREADY, Run *all* into *Sheep* where they can, keeping only such other *Cattle* as are necessary, then they will be their own *Merchants* and send their *Wooll* and *Butter* and *Hydes* and *Linnen* beyond Sea for ready *Money* and *Wine* and *Spices* and *Silks*. They will keep only a few miserable *Cottagers*. The *Farmers* must *Rob* or *Beg*, or leave their *Country*. The *Shop-keepers* in this and every other Town, must *Break* and *Starve*: For it is the *Landed-man* that maintains the *Merchant*, and *Shop-keeper*, and *Handycrafts Man*.

But when the '*Squire* turns *Farmer* and *Merchant* himself, all the good Money he gets from abroad, he will hoard up to send for *England*, and keep some poor

---

11. **Bere:** [Swift's note] *A sort of Barley* in Ireland. 12. **Butter Weight:** eighteen or more ounces to the pound. 13. **'Squire Conolly:** William Conolly (d. 1729), Speaker of the Irish House of Commons from 1715, supported Wood's patent.

14. **Truck:** barter. 15. **Pistole:** a Spanish gold coin worth a little less than an English pound. 16. **Lumber:** worthless or cumbrous material.

Taylor or *Weaver* and the like in his own House, who will be glad to get Bread at any Rate.

I should never have done if I were to tell you all the Miseries that we shall undergo if we be so *Foolish* and *Wicked* as to take this CURSED COYN. It would be very hard if all *Ireland* should be put into *One Scale*, and *this sorry Fellow WOOD into the other*, that Mr. WOOD should weigh down *this whole Kingdom*, by which *England* gets above a Million of good Money every Year clear into their *Pockets*, and that is more than the *English* do by *all the World besides*.

But your *great Comfort is*, that as his *MAJESTIES Patent* does not oblige you to take this *Money*, so the *Laws* have not given the *Crown* a Power of forcing the *Subjects* to take what *Money* the KING pleases: For then by the same Reason we might be bound to take PEBBLE-STONES or *Cockle-shells* or *Stamped Leather*[17] for *Current Coin*, if ever we should happen to live under an ill PRINCE, who might likewise by the same Power make a *Guinea* pass for Ten Pounds, a *Shilling* for Twenty Shillings, and so on, by which he would in a short Time get all the *Silver* and *Gold* of the *Kingdom* into his own Hands, and leave us nothing but *Brass* or *Leather* or what he pleased. Neither is any Thing reckoned more *Cruel* or *Oppressive* in the *French Government* than their common Practice of calling in all their Money after they have sunk it very low, and then coining it a New at a much higher Value, which however is not the Thousandth Part so wicked as this *abominable Project* of Mr. WOOD. For the *French* give their Subjects *Silver* for *Silver* and *Gold* for *Gold*, but *this Fellow* will not so much as give us good *Brass* or *Copper* for our *Gold* and *Silver*, not even a Twelfth Part of their Worth.

Having said thus much, I will now go on to tell you the Judgments of some great *Lawyers* in this Matter, whom I fee'd on purpose for your Sakes, and got their *Opinions* under their *Hands*,[18] that I might be sure I went upon good Grounds.

A Famous Law-Book, *call'd the* Mirrour of Justice,[19] *discoursing of the Charters (or Laws) ordained by our* Antient Kings *declares the* Law *to be as follows: It was ordained that no* King *of this Realm should* Change, *or* Impair *the* Money *or make any other* Money *than of*

Gold *or* Silver *without the Assent of all the Counties, that is, as my Lord* Coke *says,*[20] *without the Assent of* Parliament.

This Book is very Antient, and of great Authority for the Time in which it was wrote, and with that Character is often quoted by that great Lawyer my Lord *Coke*.[21] By the Laws of England, several Metals are divided into *Lawful* or *true Metal* and *unlawful* or *false Metal*, the Former comprehends *Silver* or *Gold*; the Latter all *Baser Metals*: That the Former is only to pass in Payments appears by an Act of *Parliament*[22] made the Twentieth Year of *Edward* the First, called the *Statute concerning the Passing of Pence*, which I give you here as I got it translated into English, for some of our *Laws* at that Time, were, as I am told writ in *Latin: Whoever in Buying or Selling presumeth to refuse an Half-penny or Farthing of Lawful Money, bearing the Stamp which it ought to have, let him be seized on as a Contemner of the King's Majesty, and cast into Prison.*

By this *Statute*, no Person is to be reckoned a *Contemner* of the KING'S *Majesty*, and for that Crime to be *committed to Prison;* but he who refuses to accept the KING's *Coin* made of *Lawful Metal*, by which, as I observed before, *Silver* and *Gold* only are intended.

That this is the true *Construction* of the *Act*, appears not only from the plain Meaning of the Words, but from my Lord *Coke's* Observation upon it.[23] By this Act (say he) it appears, that no Subject can be forc'd to take in *Buying* or *Selling* or other *Payments*, any Money made but of Lawful Metal; that is, of *Silver* or *Gold*.

The Law of *England* gives the KING all Mines of *Gold* and *Silver*, but not the Mines of other *Metals*, the Reason of which *Prerogative* or *Power*, as it is given by my Lord *Coke*[24] is, because Money can be made of *Gold* and *Silver*, but not of other Metals.

Pursuant to this Opinion *Half-pence* and *Farthings* were antiently made of *Silver*, which is evident from the Act of *Parliament* of *Henry* the 4th. Chap. 4. whereby it is enacted as follows: *Item, for the great Scarcity that is at present within the Realm of England of Half-pence and Farthings of Silver, it is ordained and established that the Third Part of all the Money of Silver Plate which shall be brought to the Bullion, shall be made*

---

17. **Stamped Leather:** an ornamental wall-hanging made of leather covered with silver leaf. 18. **under . . . Hands:** with their signatures. 19. **Mirrour of Justice:** a compilation in Old French by Andrew Horn (d. 1328), Chamberlain (i.e., receiver of revenues) of London. It was translated into English in the seventeenth century.

20. **Lord . . . says:** [Swift's note] 2 *Inst.* 576. [Sir Edward Coke (1552–1634) is the eminent English jurist and author of the *Institutes of the Laws of England* (1628 ff.).] 21. **quoted . . . Coke:** [Swift's note] 2 *Inst.* 576.7. 22. **an Act . . . Parliament:** [Swift's note] 2 *Inst.* 577. 23. **my . . . it:** [Swift's note] 2 *Inst.* 577. 24. **given . . . Coke:** [Swift's note] 2 *Inst.* 577.

in Half-pence *and* Farthings. *This shews that by the Word* Half-penny *and* Farthing *of Lawful Money in that Statute concerning the Passing of* Pence, *is meant a small Coin in* Half-pence *and* Farthings *of* Silver.

This is further manifest from the Statute of the Ninth Year of *Edward* the 3d. Chap. 3. which Enacts, *That no Sterling* HALF-PENNY *or* FARTHING *be Molten for to make Vessels, or any other thing by the Gold-smiths, nor others, upon Forfeiture of the* Money *so molten (or melted)*.

By another Act in this *King's* Reign *Black Money*[25] was not to be current in *England,* and by an Act made in the Eleventh Year of his Reign Chap. 5. *Galley Half-pence*[26] were not to pass, what kind of *Coin* these were I do not know, but I presume they were made of *Base Metal,* and that these Acts were no New *Laws,* but further Declarations of the old *Laws* relating to the *Coin.*

Thus the *Law* stands in Relation to *Coin,* nor is there any Example to the contrary, except one in *Davis's Reports,*[27] who tells us that in the time of *Tyrone's* Rebellion[28] QUEEN ELIZABETH ordered *Money of Mixt Metal* to be Coined in the Tower of *London,* and sent over hither for Payment of the ARMY, obliging all People to receive it and Commanding that all Silver Money should be taken only as *Bullion,* that is, for as much as it weighed. *Davis* tells us several Particulars in this Matter too long here to trouble you with, and that the *Privy-Council* of this *Kingdom* obliged a *Merchant* in *England* to receive this mixt Money for Goods transmitted hither.

But this Proceeding is rejected by all the best Lawyers as contrary to Law, the *Privy-Council* here having no such legal Power. And besides it is to be considered, that the *Queen* was then under great Difficulties by a Rebellion in this *Kingdom* assisted from *Spain,* and whatever is done in great Exigences and Dangerous Times should never be an Example to proceed by in Seasons of *Peace* and *Quietness.*

I will now, my Dear Friends to save you the

Trouble, set before you in short, what the *Law* obliges you *to do,* and what it does *not* oblige you to.

First, you are oblig'd to take all Money in Payments which is coin'd by the KING and is of the *English* Standard or Weight, provided it be of *Gold* or *Silver.*

Secondly, you are not obliged to take any Money which is not of *Gold* or *Silver,* not only the HALF-PENCE, or FARTHINGS of *England,* but of any other Country, and it is meerly for Convenience, or Ease, that you are content to take them, because the Custom of Coining *Silver* HALF-PENCE & FAR-THINGS hath long been left off, I suppose on Account of their being subject to be lost.

Thirdly, much less are we obliged to take those *Vile Half-Pence* of that same WOOD, by which you must lose almost Eleven-Pence in every Shilling.

Therefore my *Friends,* stand to it One and All, refuse this *Filthy Trash;* It is no Treason to Rebel against Mr. WOOD, His MAJESTY in his Patent obliges no body to take these Half-Pence, our GRACIOUS PRINCE hath no such ill Advisers about him; or if he had, yet you see the Laws have not left it in the KING's Power, to force us to take any Coin but what is Lawful, of right Standard *Gold* and *Silver,* therefore you have nothing to fear.

And let me in the next Place apply my self particularly to you who are the poorer Sort of *Tradesmen,* perhaps you may think you will not be so great Losers as the Rich, if these *Half-Pence* should pass, because you seldom see any *Silver,* and your *Customers* come to your *Shops* or *Stalls* with nothing but Brass, which you likewise find hard to be got, but you may take my Word, whenever this Money gains Footing among you you will be utterly undone; if you carry these *Half-Pence* to a Shop for *Tobacco* or *Brandy,* or *any other Thing* you want, the *Shop-keeper* will advance his Goods accordingly, or else he must break, and leave the *Key under the Door.*[29] Do you think I will sell you a Yard of ten-penny Stuff for Twenty of Mr. WOOD's *Half-Pence,* no, not under Two hundred at least, neither will I be at the Trouble of counting, but weigh them in a Lump; I will tell you one Thing further, that if Mr. WOOD's Project should take, it will ruin even our Beggars, For when I give a Beggar an half-penny, it will quench his Thirst, or go a good way to fill his Belly, but the Twelfth Part of a Half-penny will do him no more Service than if I should give him three Pins out of my Sleeve.

25. Black Money: money made of base metal. **26. Galley Half-pence:** silver coins believed to have been brought into England by the sailors on trading galleys. **27. Davis's Reports:** Sir John Davies (1569-1626), Attorney General for Ireland and poet (*Orchestra* [1594]), published his *Le Primer Report,* a compilation in French of legal cases decided in the royal courts in Ireland, in 1615. **28. Tyrone's Rebellion:** the rebellion against English authority led by the Earl of Tyrone and supported by Spain; it began in 1598 and ended in 1603, when Tyrone surrendered his tribal authority.

29. leave . . . Door: go bankrupt.

In short these HALF-PENCE are like the accursed Thing,[30] *which as the* Scripture *tells us, the* Children of Israel *were forbidden to touch, they will run about like the* Plague *and destroy every one who lays his Hands upon them. I have heard* Scholars *talk of a Man who told the* King[31] *that he had invented a Way to torment People by putting them into a* Bull of Brass *with Fire under it, but the* Prince *put the* Projector *first into his own* Brazen Bull *to make the Experiment; this very much resembles the Project of Mr.* WOOD, *and the like of this may possibly be Mr.* WOOD's *Fate, that the Brass he contrived to torment this Kingdom with, may prove his own Torment, and his Destruction at last.*

N. B. The AUTHOR of this Paper is informed by Persons who have made it their Business to be exact in their Observations on the true Value of these HALF-PENCE that any Person may expect to get a Quart of Two Penny Ale for Thirty-six of them.

I desire that all Families may keep this Paper carefully by them to Refresh their Memories whenever they shall have farther Notice of Mr. WOOD's Half-Pence, or any other the like Imposture.

FROM

THE INTELLIGENCER

Writing to Pope on June 12, 1732, Swift recalls:

Two or three of us had a fancy three years ago to write a Weekly paper, and call it an Intelligencer: But, it continued not long; for the whole volume (it was re-printed in London, and I find you have seen it) was the work only of two, my self and Dr. [Thomas] Sheridan. If we could have got some ingenious young man to have been the manager, who should have published all that might be sent to him, it might have continued longer, for there were hints enough. But the Printer here could not afford such a young man one farthing for his trouble, the Sale being so small, and the price one half-penny; and so it dropt.

In the first number Swift announces that an "Office of Intelligence" has been established in Dublin to collect "the truest Information" from all walks of Irish life, and declares the purpose of the new periodical "to Inform, or Divert, or Correct, or Vex the Town." *Intelligencer* Number III not only diverts with its lively ironic defense of *The Beggar's Opera* (1728) but also informs with its reflections on comedy and satire.

The text is that of the first edition (Dublin, 1728), with variants incorporated from Faulkner's edition of Swift's *Works* (1735).

✠

NO. III

THE *Players* having now almost done with the Comedy, called the *Beggars Opera*, for the Season,[1] it may be no unpleasant Speculation, to reflect a little upon this *Dramatick Piece*, so singular in the Subject, and manner, so much an Original, and which hath frequently given so very agreeable an Entertainment.

Although an evil *Taste* be very apt to prevail, both here, and in *London*, yet there is a point which whoever can rightly Touch, will never fail of pleasing a very great Majority; so great, that the Dislikers, out of Dulness or Affectation will be silent, and forced to fall in with the Herd; the point I mean, is what we call *Humour*, which in its Perfection is allowed to be much preferable to *Wit*, if it be not rather the most useful, and agreeable Species of it.

I agree with Sir *William Temple*,[2] that the Word is peculiar to our *English Tongue*, but I differ from him in the Opinion, that the thing it self is peculiar to the *English Nation*, because the contrary may be found in many *Spanish*, *Italian*, and *French* Productions, and particularly, whoever hath a *Taste* for *True Humour*, will find a Hundred Instances of it in those Volumes Printed in *France*, under the Name of *Le Theatre Italien*, to say nothing of *Rabelais*, *Cervantes*, and many others.

Now I take the *Comedy* or *Farce*, (or whatever Name the *Criticks* will allow it) called the *Beggars Opera*, to excel in this Article of *Humour*. And, upon that Merit, to have met with such prodigious success both here, and in *England*.

---

30. the accursed Thing: See Josh. 6:18. The "accursed thing" denotes primarily whatever is consecrated to the deity and therefore alienated from common use but also that which is doomed to destruction. 31. the King: Phalarius (c. 570–c. 554 B.C.), tyrant of Sicily, notorious for his cruel pleasures.

THE INTELLIGENCER: *Number III.* 1. for the Season: The play ran a record sixty-two performances in its first season. (See *The Beggar's Opera* later in Part Two.) 2. I . . . Temple: Swift appears indebted to Temple's essay *Of Poetry* for a number of his views in the present piece, most notably his alleged preference for good-humored over scathing satire.

As to *Poetry*, *Eloquence*, and *Musick*, which are said to have most Power over the minds of Men, it is certain that very few have a *Taste* or *Judgment* of the Excellencies of the two former, and if a Man succeed in either, it is upon the Authority of those *few Judges*, that lend their *Taste* to the bulk of Readers, who have none of their own. I am told there are as few good Judges in *Musick*, and that among those who Crowd the Operas, Nine in Ten go thither meerly out of *Curiosity*, *Fashion*, or *Affectation*.

But a Taste for *Humour* is in some manner fixed to the very Nature of Man, and generally Obvious to the Vulgar, except upon Subjects too refined, and Superior to their Understanding.

And as this *Taste* of *Humour* is purely Natural, so is *Humour* it self, neither is it a *Talent* confined to Men of *Wit*, or *Learning;* for we observe it sometimes among common Servants, and the meanest of the People, while the very Owners are often Ignorant of the Gift they possess.

I know very well, that this happy *Talent* is contemptibly Treated by *Criticks*, under the Name of *low Humour*, or *low Comedy;* but I know likewise, that the *Spaniards* and *Italians*, who are allowed to have the most Wit of any *Nation* in *Europe*, do most excell in it, and do most esteem it.

By what Disposition of the mind, what Influence of the Stars, or what Situation of the *Clymate* this endowment is bestowed upon Mankind, may be a Question fit for *Philosophers* to Discuss. It is certainly the best Ingredient towards that kind of Satyr, which is most useful, and gives the least Offence; which instead of lashing, Laughs Men out of their Follies, and Vices, and is the Character that gives *Horace* the Preference to *Juvenal*.

And although some things are too Serious, Solemn, or Sacred to be turned into Ridicule, yet the Abuses of them are certainly not, since it is allowed that Corruptions in *Religion*, *Politicks*, and *Law*, may be proper *Topicks* for this kind of Satyr.

There are two ends that Men propose in Writing Satyr, one of them less Noble than the other, as regarding nothing further than the private Satisfaction, and pleasure of the Writer; but without any View towards *Personal Malice;* The other is a *Publick Spirit*, prompting Men of *Genius* and Virtue, to mend the World as far as they are able. And as both these ends are innocent, so the latter is highly commendable. With Regard to the former, I demand whether I have not as good a Title to Laugh, as Men have to be

Ridiculous, and to expose Vice, as another hath to be Vicious. If I Ridicule the Follies and Corruptions of a *Court*, a *Ministry*, or a *Senate;* are they not amply payed by *Pensions*, *Titles*, and *Power*, while I expect and desire no other Reward, than that of Laughing with a few Friends in a Corner. Yet, if those, who take Offence, think me in the Wrong, I am ready to Change the Scene with them, whenever they please.

But if my Design be to make Mankind better, then I think it is my Duty, at least I am sure it is the Interest of those very *Courts* and *Ministers*, whose Follies or Vices I Ridicule, to reward me for my good Intentions; For, if it be reckoned a high point of Wisdom to get the Laughers on our side, it is much more easy, as well as Wise to get those on our side, who can make Millions Laugh when they please.

My Reason for mentioning *Courts*, and *Ministers*, (*whom I never think on, but with the most profound Veneration*) is because an Opinion obtains, that in the *Beggars Opera* there appears to be some Reflection upon *Courtiers* and *States-Men*, whereof I am by no means a Judge.

It is true indeed that Mr. *GAY*, the Author of this Piece, hath been somewhat singular in the Course of his Fortunes, for it hath happened, that after Fourteen Years attending the *Court*, with a large Stock of real Merit, a Modest, and Agreeable Conversation, a *Hundred Promises*, and five *Hundred Friends* he hath failed of Preferment, and upon a very Weighty Reason. He lay under the Suspicion of having Written a Libel, or Lampoon against a great Minister.[3] It is true that great Minister was demonstratively convinced, and publickly owned his Conviction, that Mr. *Gay* was not the Author; but having lain under the Suspicion, it seemed very just, that he should suffer the Punishment; because in this most reformed Age, the Virtues of a Prime Minister are no more to be suspected, than the Chastity of *Cæsar's* Wife.

It must be allowed, That the *Beggars-Opera* is not the first of Mr. *Gay's* Works, wherein he hath been faulty, with regard to *Courtiers* and *States-Men*. For, to omit his other Pieces, even in his *Fables*, published within two Years past, and Dedicated to the *Duke of Cumberland*, for which he was PROMISED a Reward;[4] he hath been thought somewhat too bold upon *Courtiers*. And although it be highly probable, he meant only the *Courtiers* of former times, yet he

---

3. a great Minister: [Swift's note] Sir *Robert Walpole*. 4. a Reward: See the headnote to Gay's *Fables* later in Part Two.

acted unwarily, by not considering, that the Malignity of some People might misinterpret what he said to the disadvantage of present *Persons*, and Affairs.

But I have now done with Mr. *Gay* as a Politician, and shall consider him henceforward only as Author of the *Beggars-Opera*, wherein he hath by a turn of *Humor*, entirely New, placed Vices of all Kinds in the strongest and most odious Light; and thereby done eminent Service, both to *Religion* and *Morality*. This appears from the unparallel'd Success he hath met with. All *Ranks*, *Parties* and *Denominations* of Men, either crowding to see his *Opera*, or reading it with delight in their Closets,⁵ even *Ministers* of State, whom he is thought to have most offended (next to those whom the Actors more immediately⁶ represent) appearing frequently at the *Theatre*, from a consciousness of their own Innocence, and to convince the World how unjust a Parallel, *Malice*, *Envy*, and *Disaffection to the Government have made*.

I am assured that several worthy *Clergy-Men* in this City, went privately to see the *Beggars-Opera* represented; and that the *fleering*⁷ *Coxcombs* in the *Pit*, amused themselves with making Discoveries, and spreading the Names of those Gentlemen round the Audience.

I shall not pretend to vindicate a *Clergy-Man*, who would appear openly in his Habit at a *Theatre*, with such a vicious Crew, as might probably stand round him, at such *Comedies*, and prophane *Tragedies*, as are often represented. Besides I know very well, that Persons of their Function are bound to avoid the appearance of Evil, or of giving cause of Offence. But when the *Lords Chancellors*, who are Keepers of the King's Conscience, when the *Judges* of the Land, whose Title is *Reverend*, when *Ladies*, who are bound by the Rules of their Sex, to the strictest Decency, appear in the *Theatre* without Censure, I cannot understand, why a young Clergy man who comes concealed out of Curiosity to see an innocent and moral Play, should be so highly condemned; nor do I much approve the Rigor of a great Prelate who said, *he hoped none of his Clergy were there*. I am glad to hear there are no weightier Objections against that Reverend Body, planted in this City, and I wish there never may. But I should be very sorry that any of them should be so weak, as to imitate a COURT-

CHAPLAIN in *England*, who preached against the *Beggars-Opera*,⁸ which will probably do more good than a thousand Sermons of so stupid, so injudicious, and so prostitute a Divine.

In this happy Performance of Mr. *Gay*'s, all the Characters are just, and none of them carried beyond Nature, or hardly beyond Practice. It discovers the whole System of that Common-Wealth, or that *Imperium in Imperio*⁹ of Iniquity, established among us, by which neither our Lives, nor our Properties are secure, either in the High-ways, or in publick Assemblies, or even in our own Houses. It shews the miserable Lives, and the constant Fate of those abandoned Wretches; for how little they sell their Lives and Souls; betrayed by their *Whores;* their *Comrades;* and the *Receivers* and *Purchasers* of those Thefts and Robberies. This *Comedy* contains likewise a *Satyr*, which, without enquiring whether it affects the present Age, may possibly be useful in Times to come. I mean where the Author takes the occasion of comparing those *common Robbers to Robbers of the Publick;* and their several Stratagems of betraying, undermining, and hanging each other, to the several Arts of *Politicians* in times of Corruption.

This *Comedy* likewise exposeth with great Justice, that unnatural Taste for *Italian* Musick among us, which is wholly unsuitable to our Northern *Climat*, and the *genius* of the People, whereby we are over-run with *Italian-Effeminacy*, and *Italian* Nonsense. An old Gentleman said to me, that many Years ago, when the practice of an unnatural Vice grew frequent in *London*, and many were Prosecuted for it, he was sure it would be a Fore-runner of *Italian-Opera*'s, and Singers; and then we should want¹⁰ nothing but Stabbing or Poysoning, to make us perfect *Italians*.

Upon the Whole, I deliver my Judgment, That nothing but servile Attachment to a Party, affectation of Singularity, lamentable Dullness, mistaken Zeal, or studied Hypocrisy, can have the least reasonable Objection against this excellent Moral-performance of the CELEBRATED MR. GAY.

---

8. a Court-Chaplain . . . Beggars-Opera: [Swift's note] *Dr.* Herring, *Chaplain to the Society at* Lincoln's-Inn. [The sermon of Thomas Herring (1693-1757), later Archbishop of Canterbury, has not been recovered, and perhaps was never printed; but contemporary references to it convey its drift.] **9. Imperium in Imperio:** a government within a government. **10. want:** lack.

---

5. Closets: private chambers. **6. more immediately:** This phrase was omitted in the 1735 edition but is here restored for clarity. **7. fleering:** gibing, sneering.

A MODEST PROPOSAL . . .

Swift wrote to Pope on August 11, 1729:

> As to this country, there have been three terrible years dearth of corn, and every place strowed with beggars, but dearths are common in better climates, and our evils here lie much deeper. Imagine a nation the two-thirds of whose revenues are spent out of it, and who are not permitted to trade with the other third, and where the pride of the women will not suffer them to wear their own manufactures even where they excel what come from abroad: This is the true state of Ireland in a very few words.

A Modest Proposal appeared in October. In this, the most devastating of Swift's satires, the author assumes the persona of a political arithmetician (forerunner of the modern socioeconomic planner) whose attitudes reflect the very evils he proposes to remedy by his "project."

The title continues: *for Preventing the Children of Poor People in Ireland from Being a Burthen to Their Parents, or the Country, and for Making Them Beneficial to the Publick.* The text is that of the first edition (1729), from a copy in The Chapin Library at Williams College. Variants have been introduced from Faulkner's edition of Swift's *Works* (1735).

IT is a melancholly Object to those, who walk through this great Town,[1] or travel in the Country, when they see the *Streets,* the *Roads,* and *Cabbin-Doors,* crowded with *Beggars* of the female Sex, followed by three, four, or six Children, *all in Rags,* and importuning every Passenger for an Alms. These *Mothers* instead of being able to work for their honest livelyhood, are forced to employ all their time in Stroling, to beg Sustenance for their *helpless Infants,* who, as they grow up either turn *Thieves* for want of work, or leave their *dear native Country to fight for the Pretender in Spain,*[2] or sell themselves to the *Barbadoes.*[3]

A MODEST PROPOSAL. **1. this . . . Town:** Dublin. **2. fight . . . Spain:** Ireland was long a natural recruiting ground for France and Spain in their wars against England. **3. sell . . . Barbadoes:** The West Indies attracted the impoverished Irish in alarming numbers. They sold themselves by agreeing to work for a period of time in return for their transportation.

I think it is agreed by all Parties, that this prodigious number of Children, in the Arms, or on the Backs, or at the *heels* of their *Mothers,* and frequently of their *Fathers,* is *in the present deplorable state of the Kingdom,* a very great additional grievance; and therefore whoever could find out a fair, cheap and easy method of making these Children sound and useful Members of the common-wealth would deserve so well of the publick, as to have his Statue set up for a preserver of the Nation.

But my Intention is very far from being confined to provide only for the Children of *professed Beggars,* it is of a much greater extent, and shall take in the whole number of Infants at a certain Age, who are born of Parents in effect as little able to support them, as those who demand our Charity in the Streets.

As to my own part, having turned my thoughts, for many Years, upon this important Subject, and maturely weighed the several *Schemes of other Projectors,*[4] I have always found them grossly mistaken in their computation. It is true a Child, *just dropt from it's Dam,* may be supported by her Milk, for a Solar year[5] with little other Nourishment, at most not above the Value of two Shillings, which the Mother may certainly get, or the Value in *Scraps,* by her lawful Occupation of begging, and it is exactly at one year Old that I propose to provide for them, in such a manner, as, instead of being a Charge upon their *Parents,* or the *Parish,* or *wanting Food and Raiment* for the rest of their Lives, they shall, on the Contrary, contribute to the Feeding, and partly to the Cloathing of many Thousands.

There is likewise another great Advantage in my Scheme, that it will prevent those *voluntary Abortions,* and that horrid practice of *Women murdering their Bastard Children,* alas! too frequent among us, Sacrificing the *poor innocent Babes,* I doubt,[6] more to avoid the Expence, than the Shame, which would move Tears and Pity in the most Savage and inhuman breast.

The number of Souls in *Ireland* being usually reckoned one Million and a half, Of these I calculate there may be about two hundred thousand Couple whose Wives are Breeders, from which number I Substract[7] thirty Thousand Couples, who are able to maintain their own Children, although I apprehend

4. Projectors: a term commonly used invidiously to mean speculators or cheats. **5. a Solar year:** the period measured by the passage of the sun through two successive vernal equinoxes. Swift's *persona* is nothing if not precise. **6. doubt:** suspect. **7. Substract:** a former alternative to *subtract.*

there cannot be so many under *the present distresses of the Kingdom*, but this being granted, there will remain an hundred and seventy thousand Breeders. I again Subtract fifty Thousand for those Women who miscarry, or whose Children dye by accident, or disease within the Year. There only remain an hundred and twenty thousand Children of poor Parents annually born. The question therefore is, how this number shall be reared, and provided for, which, as I have already said, under the present Situation of Affairs, is utterly impossible by all the methods hitherto proposed, for we can *neither employ them in Handicraft,* or *Agriculture;* we neither build Houses, (I mean in the Country) nor cultivate Land:[8] They can very seldom pick up a Livelihood *by Stealing* until they arrive at six years Old, except where they are of towardly parts,[9] although, I confess they learn the Rudiments much earlier, during which time, they can however be properly looked upon only as *Probationers,* as I have been informed by a principal Gentleman in the County of *Cavan,* who protested to me, that he never knew above one or two Instances under the Age of six, even in a part of the Kingdom *so renowned for the quickest proficiency in that Art.*

[margin note: UNLESS OF READY ABILITIES]

I am assured by our Merchants, that a Boy or Girl, before twelve years Old, is no saleable Commodity, and even when they come to this Age, they will not yield above three Pounds, or three Pounds and half a Crown at most on the Exchange, which cannot turn to Account[10] either to the Parents or the Kingdom, the Charge of Nutriment and Rags having been at least four times that Value.

I shall now therefore humbly propose my own thoughts, which I hope will not be lyable to the least Objection.

I have been assured by a very knowing *American*[11] *[margin note: BARBARIAN]* of my acquaintance in *London,* that a young healthy Child well Nursed is at a year Old a most delicious, nourishing, and wholesome Food, whether *Stewed, Roasted, Baked,* or *Boyled,* and I make no doubt that it will equally serve in a *Fricasie,* or *Ragoust.*[12]

I do therefore humbly offer it to *publick consideration,* that of the hundred and twenty thousand Children, already computed, twenty thousand may be reserved

[top margin note: INHUMANESS BEGINS TO AROUSE READER]

for Breed, whereof only one fourth part to be Males, which is more than we allow to *Sheep, black Cattle,* or *Swine,* and my reason is that these Children are seldom the Fruits of Marriage, *a Circumstance not much regarded by our Savages,* therefore *one Male* will be sufficient to serve *four Females.* That the remaining hundred thousand may at a year Old be offered in Sale to the *persons of Quality,* and *Fortune,* through the Kingdom, always advising the Mother to let them Suck plentifully in the last Month, so as to render them Plump, and Fat for a good Table. A Child will make two Dishes at an Entertainment for Friends, and when the Family dines alone, the fore or hind Quarter will make a reasonable Dish, and seasoned with a little Pepper or Salt will be very good Boiled on the fourth Day, especially in *Winter.*

I have reckoned upon a Medium, that a Child just born will weigh 12 pounds, and in a solar Year if tollerably nursed encreaseth to 28 Pounds.

I grant this food will be somewhat dear,[13] and therefore very *proper for Landlords,* who, as they have already devoured most of the Parents, seem to have the best Title to the Children. *[margin note: DROPS "MASK," DIRECT ATTACK]*

Infant's flesh will be in Season throughout the Year, but more plentiful in *March,* and a little before and after, for we are told by a grave Author[14] an eminent *French* Physitian, that *Fish being a prolifick Dyet,* there are more Children born in *Roman Catholick Countries* about nine Months after *Lent,* than at any other Season, therefore reckoning a Year after *Lent,* the Markets will be more glutted than usual, because the Number of *Popish Infants,* is at least three to one in this Kingdom, and therefore it will have one other Collateral advantage by lessening the Number of *Papists* among us.

I have already computed the Charge of nursing a Beggars Child (in which list I reckon all *Cottagers,*[15] *Labourers,* and four fifths of the *Farmers*) to be about two Shillings *per Annum,* Rags included, and I believe no Gentleman would repine to give Ten Shillings for the *Carcass of a good fat Child,* which, as I have said will make four Dishes of excellent Nutritive Meat, when he hath only some particular friend, or his own Family to Dine with him. Thus the Squire will learn to be a good Landlord, and grow popular among his

---

8. nor . . . Land: Irish agriculture was severely restricted by England's promotion of the woollen industry, which required extensive pasturage for sheep. **9. towardly parts:** ready abilities. **10. turn to Account:** be of profit. **11. American:** a prototype of barbarism to many British at this time. **12. Ragoust:** (ragout) a highly seasoned meat stew.

13. dear: a play on the two meanings "expensive" and "precious." **14. a grave Author:** [Swift's note] Rabelais. [The reference is to *Gargantua and Pantagruel,* V. 29.] **15. Cottagers:** tenant farmers; usually called cottiers in Ireland.

Tenants, the Mother will have Eight Shillings net profit, and be fit for Work until she produceth another Child.

Those who are more thrifty (*as I must confess the Times require*) may flay the Carcass; the Skin of which, Artificially[16] dressed, will make admirable *Gloves for Ladies*, and *Summer Boots for fine Gentlemen.* MEAT MARKETS

As to our City of *Dublin*, Shambles[17] may be appointed for this purpose, in the most convenient parts of it, and Butchers we may be assured will not be wanting, although I rather recommend buying the Children alive, and dressing them hot from the Knife, as we do *roasting Pigs*.

A very worthy Person, *a true Lover of his Country*, and whose Virtues I highly esteem, was lately pleased, in discoursing on this matter, to offer a refinement upon my Scheme. He said, that many Gentlemen of this Kingdom, having of late destroyed their Deer, he conceived that the want of Venison might be well supplied by the Bodies of young Lads and Maidens, not exceeding fourteen Years of Age, nor under twelve, so great a Number of both Sexes in every County being now ready to Starve, for want of Work and Service: And these to be disposed of by their Parents if alive, or otherwise by their nearest Relations. But with due deference to so excellent a friend, and so deserving a Patriot, I cannot be altogether in his Sentiments, for as to the Males, my *American* acquaintance assured me from frequent Experience, that their flesh was generally Tough and Lean, like that of our School-boys, by continual exercise, and their Taste disagreeable, and to Fatten them would not answer the Charge. Then as to the Females, it would, I think with humble Submission,[18] *be a loss to the Publick*, because they soon would become Breeders themselves: And besides it is not improbable that some scrupulous People might be apt to Censure such a Practice, (although indeed very unjustly) as a little bordering upon Cruelty, which, I confess, hath always been with me the strongest objection against any Project, how well soever intended.

But in order to justify my friend, he confessed, that this expedient was put into his head by the famous *Sallmanaazor*,[19] a Native of the Island *Formosa*, who came from thence to *London*, above twenty Years ago,

and in Conversation told my friend, that in his Country when any young Person happened to be put to Death, the Executioner sold the Carcass to *Persons of Quality*, as a prime Dainty, and that, in his Time, the Body of a plump Girl of fifteen, who was crucifyed for an attempt to Poison the Emperor, was sold to his Imperial *Majesty's prime Minister of State*, and other great *Mandarins* of the Court, *in Joints from the Gibbet*, at four hundred Crowns. Neither indeed can I deny, that if the same use were made of several plump young Girls in this Town, who, without one single Groat to their Fortunes, cannot stir abroad without a Chair,[20] and appear at the *Play-House*, and *Assemblies* in Foreign fineries, which they never will Pay for; the Kingdom would not be the worse. DIRECT ATTACK

Some Persons of a desponding Spirit are in great concern about that vast Number of poor People, who are aged, diseased, or maimed, and I have been desired to imploy my thoughts what Course may be taken, to ease the Nation of so grievous an Incumbrance. But I am not in the least pain upon that matter, because it is very well known, that they are every Day *dying*, and *rotting*, by *cold*, and *famine*, and *filth*, and *vermin*, as fast as can be reasonably expected. And as to the younger Labourers they are now in almost as hopeful a Condition. They cannot get Work, and consequently pine away for want of Nourishment, to a degree, that if at any time they are accidentally hired to common Labour, they have not strength to perform it, and thus the Country and themselves are in a fair Way[21] of being soon delivered from the Evils to come.

I have too long degressed, and therefore shall return to my subject. I think the advantages by the Proposal which I have made are obvious and many as well as of the highest importance.

For first, as I have already observed, it would greatly lessen *the Number of Papists*, with whom we are Yearly over-run, being the principal Breeders of the Nation, as well as our most dangerous Enemies, and who stay at home on purpose with a design *to deliver the Kingdom to the Pretender*, hoping to take their Advantage by the absence *of so many good Protestants*,[22] who have chosen rather to leave their Country, than stay at home, and pay Tythes against their *Conscience*, to an idolatrous *Episcopal Curate*. (EPISCOPAL) DISSENTERS FROM ANGLICAN CHURCH - REALLY MEANS BAD PROTESTANTS

---

16. **Artificially:** skillfully. 17. **Shambles:** meat markets, slaughterhouses. 18. **with . . . Submission:** respectfully. 19. **Sallmanaazor:** George Psalmanazar (c. 1679–1763), a Frenchman who traveled in Europe and England posing as a Formosan. His *Historical and Geographical Description of Formosa* (1704) was exposed not long after its publication.

20. **Chair:** sedan chair. 21. **are . . . Way:** have a good chance. 22. **good Protestants:** Nonconformists, or, in Swift's view, *bad* Protestants.

450   JONATHAN SWIFT

Secondly, the poorer Tenants will have something valuable of their own, which by Law may be made lyable to Distress,[23] and help to pay their Landlord's Rent, their Corn and Cattle being already seazed, and *Money a thing unknown.*

Thirdly, Whereas the Maintenance of an hundred thousand Children, from two Years old, and upwards, cannot be computed at less than Ten Shillings a piece *per Annum*, the Nation's Stock will be thereby encreased fifty thousand pounds *per Annum*, besides the profit of a new Dish, introduced to the Tables of all *Gentlemen of Fortune* in the Kingdom, who have any refinement in Taste, and the Money will circulate among our selves, the Goods being entirely of our own Growth and Manufacture.

Fourthly, The constant Breeders, besides the gain of Eight Shillings *Sterling per Annum*, by the Sale of their Children, will be rid of the Charge of maintaining them after the first Year.

Fifthly, this food would likewise bring great *Custom to Taverns*, where the Vintners will certainly be so prudent as to procure the best receipts[24] for dressing it to perfection, and consequently have their Houses frequented by all the *fine Gentlemen*, who justly value themselves upon their knowledge in good Eating, and a skillful Cook, who understands how to oblige his Guests will contrive to make it as expensive as they please.

Sixthly, This would be a great Inducement to Marriage, which all wise Nations have either encouraged by Rewards, or enforced by Laws and Penalties. It would encrease the care and tenderness of Mothers towards their Children, when they were sure of a Settlement for Life, to the poor Babes, provided in some sort by the Publick to their Annual profit instead of Expence, we should soon see an honest Emulation among the married Women, *which of them could bring the fattest Child to the Market,* Men would become as fond of their *Wives,* during the Time of their Pregnancy, as they are now of their *Mares* in Foal, their *Cows* in Calf, or *Sows* when they are ready to Farrow, nor offer to Beat or Kick them (as it is too frequent a practice) for fear of a Miscarriage.

Many other advantages might be enumerated: For Instance, the addition of some thousand Carcases in our exportation of Barreled Beef. The Propagation of *Swines Flesh*, and Improvement in the Art of making good *Bacon*, so much wanted among us by the great destruction of *Pigs,* too frequent at our Tables, which are no way comparable in Taste, or Magnificence to a well grown, fat Yearling Child, which Roasted whole will make a considerable Figure at a *Lord Mayor's Feast,* or any other Publick Entertainment. But this, and many others I omit being studious of Brevity.

Supposing that one thousand Families in this City, would be constant Customers for Infants Flesh, besides others who might have it at *Merry-meetings,* particularly *Weddings* and *Christenings,* I compute that *Dublin* would take off Annually about twenty thousand Carcases, and the rest of the Kingdom (where probably they will be Sold somewhat Cheaper) the remaining eighty thousand.

I can think of no one Objection, that will possibly be raised against this Proposal, unless it should be urged that the Number of People will be thereby much lessened in the Kingdom. This I freely own, and it was indeed one Principal design in offering it to the World. I desire the Reader will observe, that I Calculate my Remedy *for this one individual Kingdom of IRELAND, and for no other that ever was, is, or, I think, ever can be upon Earth.* Therefore let no Man talk to me of other Expedients:[25] *Of taxing our Absentees at five Shillings a pound: Of using neither Cloaths, nor household Furniture, except what is of our own Growth and Manufacture: Of utterly rejecting the Materials and Instruments that promote Foreign Luxury: Of curing the Expenciveness of Pride, Vanity, Idleness, and Gaming in our Women: Of introducing a Vein of Parcimony, Prudence and Temperance: Of learning to Love our Country, wherein we differ even from LAPLANDERS, and the Inhabitants of TOPINAMBOO:[26] Of quitting our Animosities, and Factions, nor Act any longer like the Jews, who were Murdering one another at the very moment their City was taken:[27] Of being a little Cautious not to Sell our Country and Consciences for nothing: Of teaching Landlords to have at least one degree of Mercy towards their Tenants. Lastly of putting a Spirit of Honesty, Industry and Skill into our Shop-keepers, who, if a Resolution could now be taken to Buy only our Native Goods, would immediatly unite to Cheat and Exact[28] upon us in the Price, the Measure, and the Goodness, nor could ever yet be brought to make one*

ALTERNATIVES TO EATING CHILDREN

23. **Distress:** seizure for debt. 24. **receipts:** recipes.

25. **other Expedients:** Swift's positive proposals, to be found set forth among his nonironic tracts. 26. **Topinamboo:** a district of Brazil. 27. **taken:** Jerusalem was besieged, taken, and destroyed by the Emperor Titus in 70 A.D. 28. **Exact:** impose.

fair *Proposal of just dealing, though often and earnestly invited to it.*

Therefore I repeat, let no Man talk to me of these and the like Expedients, till he hath at least a Glimpse of Hope, that there will ever be some hearty and sincere Attempt to put them in Practice.

But as to my self, having been wearied out for many Years with offering vain, idle, visionary thoughts, and at length utterly despairing of Success, I fortunately fell upon this Proposal, which as it is wholly new, so it hath something Solid and Real, of no Expence and little Trouble, full in our own Power, and whereby we can incur no Danger in *disobliging England.* For this kind of Commodity will not bear Exportation, the Flesh being of too tender a Consistance, to admit a long continuance in Salt, *although perhaps I could name a Country,*[29] *which would be glad to Eat up our whole Nation without it.*

After all I am not so violently bent upon my own Opinion, as to reject any Offer, proposed by wise Men, which shall be found equally Innocent, Cheap, Easy and Effectual. But before something of that kind shall be advanced in Contradiction to my Scheme, and offering a better, I desire the Author, or Authors will be pleased maturely to consider two points. *First,* as things now stand, how they will be able to find Food and Raiment for a hundred thousand useless Mouths and Backs. And *Secondly,* there being a round Million of Creatures in human Figure, throughout this Kingdom, whose whole Subsistance put into a common Stock, would leave them in Debt two Millions of Pounds *Sterling* adding those, who are Beggars by Profession, to the Bulk of Farmers, Cottagers and Labourers with their Wives and Children, who are Beggars in Effect; I desire those *Politicians,* who dislike my Overture, and may perhaps be so bold to attempt an Answer, that they will first ask the Parents of these Mortals, whether they would not at this Day think it a great Happiness to have been sold for Food at a year Old, in the manner I prescribe, and thereby have avoided such a perpetual Scene of Misfortunes, as they have since gone through, by the *oppression of Landlords,* the Impossibility of paying Rent without Money or Trade, the want of common Sustenance, with neither House nor Cloaths to cover them from Inclemencies of Weather, and the most inevitable Prospect of intailing the like, or greater Miseries upon their Breed for ever.

29. a **Country:** England.

I Profess in the sincerity of my Heart that I have not the least personal Interest in endeavouring to promote this necessary Works having no other Motive than the *publick Good of my Country,* by *advancing our Trade, providing for Infants, relieving the Poor, and giving some Pleasure to the Rich.* I have no Children, by which I can propose to get a single Penny; the youngest being nine Years old, and my Wife past Child-bearing.

[handwritten margin note: TESTIMONY TO HIS SINCERITY]

FROM

DIRECTIONS TO SERVANTS

The *Directions to Servants* is an unfinished work, composed over a long period of time and never subjected to any careful organization or polishing. Of the "about twenty several stations, from the steward and waiting-woman down to the scullion and pantry-boy" mentioned by Swift in a letter to Gay, only fifteen "directions" were actually written, and more than half of these are the merest fragments. The "Directions to the Footman" perhaps approaches most closely the final form Swift intended for the work as a whole and is conceived and executed in his best mock-sympathetic vein.

The text is that of the first edition, posthumously published by Faulkner in 1745, with variants incorporated from Faulkner's edition of 1751 (which appears to have been based on Swift's corrected manuscript) and from other contemporary manuscripts (collated in *Jonathan Swift: Directions to Servants and Miscellaneous Pieces,* ed. Herbert Davis [1959]).

CHAP. III

Directions to the FOOTMAN.

YOUR Employment being of a mixt Nature, extends to a great Variety of Business, and you stand in a fair way[1] of being the Favourite of your Master or Mistress, or of the young Masters and Misses; you are the fine Gentleman of the Family, with whom all the Maids are in Love. You are sometimes a Pattern of Dress to

DIRECTIONS TO SERVANTS: *Chapter III.* **1. in . . . way:** a good chance.

your Master, and sometimes he is so to you. You wait at Table in all Companies, and consequently have the Opportunity to see and know the World, and to understand Men and Manners; I confess your Vails[2] are but few, unless you are sent with a Present, or attend the Tea in the Country; but you are called Mr. in the Neighbourhood, and sometimes pick up a Fortune, perhaps your Master's Daughter; and I have known many of your Tribe to have good Commands in the Army. In Town you have a Seat reserved for you in the Play-House, where you have an Opportunity of becoming Wits and Criticks: You have no profest Enemy except the Rabble, and my Lady's Waiting-woman, who are sometimes apt to call you Skip-kennels.[3] I have a true Veneration for your Office, because I had once the Honour[4] to be one of your Order, which I foolishly left by demeaning myself with accepting an Employment in the Custom-house. —But that you, my Brethren, may come to better Fortunes, I shall here deliver my Instructions, which have been the Fruits of much Thought and Observation, as well as of seven Years Experience.

In order to learn the Secrets of other Families, tell your Brethren those of your Master's; thus you will grow a Favourite both at home and abroad, and be regarded as a Person of Importance.

Never be seen in the Streets with a Basket or Bundle in your Hands, and carry nothing but what you can hide in your Pocket, otherwise you will disgrace your Calling: to prevent which, always retain a Black-guard[5] Boy to carry your Loads; and if you want[6] Farthings, pay him with a good Slice of Bread or Scrap of Meat.

Let a Shoe-boy clean your own Shoes first, for fear of fouling the Chambers, and then let him clean your Master's; keep him on Purpose for that Use and to run of Errands, and pay him with Scraps. When you are sent on an Errand, be sure to hedge in[7] some Business of your own, either to see your Sweetheart, or drink a Pot of Ale with some Brother Servant, which is so much Time clear gained.

There is a great Controversy about the most convenient and genteel Way of holding your Plate, when you wait on your Master, and his Company, at Meals; some Butlers stick it between the Frame and the Back of the Chair, which is an excellent Expedient, where the make of the Chair will allow it: Others, for Fear the Plate should fall, grasp it so firmly, that their Thumb reacheth to the Middle of the Hollow; which however, if your Thumb be dry, is no secure Method; and therefore in that Case, I advise your wetting the Bowl of it with your Tongue: As to that absurd Practice of letting the Back of the Plate lye leaning on the Hollow of your Hand, which some Ladies recommend, it is universally exploded, being liable to so many Accidents. Others again, are so refined, that they hold their Plate directly under the Left Arm-pit, which is the best Situation for keeping it warm; but this may be dangerous in the Article of taking away a Dish, where your Plate may happen to fall upon some of the Company's Heads. I confess myself to have objected against all these Ways, which I have frequently tryed; and therefore I recommend a Fourth, which is to stick your Plate up to the Rim inclusive, in the left Side between your Waistcoat and your Shirt: This will keep it at least as warm as under your Arm-pit, or Ockster,[8] (as the *Scots* call it) this will hide it so, as Strangers may take you for a better Servant, too good to hold a Plate; this will secure it from falling, and thus disposed, it lies ready for you to whip it out in a Moment, ready warmed, to any Guest within your Reach, who may want it. And lastly, there is another Convenience in this Method, that if, any Time during your waiting, you find yourselves going to cough or sneeze, you can immediately snatch out your Plate, and hold the hollow Part close to your Nose or Mouth, and, thus prevent spirting[9] any Moisture from either, upon the Dishes or the Ladies Head-dress: You see Gentlemen and Ladies observe a like Practice on such an Occasion, with a Hat or a Handkerchief: yet a Plate is less fouled and sooner cleaned than either of these; for, when your Cough or Sneese is over, it is but returning your Plate to the same Position, and your Shirt will clean it in the Passage.

Take off the largest Dishes, and set them on with one Hand, to shew the Ladies your Vigour and Strength of Back; but always do it between two Ladies, that if the Dish happens to slip, the Soup or Sauce may fall on their Cloaths and not daub the Floor: By this Practice two of our Brethren, my worthy Friends, got considerable Fortunes.

---

2. Vails: tips, especially those given by guests. **3. Skip-kennels:** a contemptuous term for a footboy or footman, descriptive of one of their offices. **4. the Honour:** Swift characteristically assumes the profession and point of view of his satiric butt. **5. Black-guard:** vagrant. **6. want:** lack. **7. hedge in:** intrude.

8. Ockster: (oxter) the armpit or the underside of the upper arm; the armhole of a coat. **9. spirting:** spurting, squirting.

Learn all the new-fashion Words, and Oaths, and Songs, and Scraps of Plays that your Memory can hold. Thus, you will become the Delight of nine Ladies in ten, and the Envy of ninety nine Beaux in a hundred.

Take Care, that at certain Periods, during Dinner especially, when Persons of Quality are there, you and your Brethren be all out of the Room together, by which you will give yourselves some Ease from the Fatigue of waiting, and at the same Time leave the Company to converse more freely, without being constrained by your Presence.

When you are sent on a Message, deliver it in your own Words, altho' it be to a Duke or a Duchess, and not in the Words of your Master or Lady; for how can they understand what belongs to a Message as well as you, who have been bred to the Employment? But never deliver the Answer till it is called for, and then adorn it with your own Style.

When Dinner is done, carry down a great Heap of Plates to the Kitchen, and as you come to the Head of the Stairs, trundle them[10] all before you: There is not a more agreeable Sight or Sound, especially if they be Silver, besides the Trouble they save you, and there they will lie ready near the Kitchen Door, for the Scullion to wash them.

If you are bringing up a Joint of Meat in a Dish, and it falls out of your Hands, before you get into the Dining Room, with the Meat on the Ground, and the Sauce spilled, take up the Meat gently, wipe it with the Lap[11] of your Coat, then put it again into the Dish, and serve it up; and when your Lady misses the Sauce, tell her, it is to be sent up in a Plate by itself.

When you carry up a Dish of Meat, dip your Fingers in the Sauce, or lick it with your Tongue, to try whether it be good, and fit for your Master's Table.

You are the best Judge of what Acquaintance your Lady ought to have, and therefore, if she sends you on a Message of Compliment or Business to a Family you do not like, deliver the Answer in such a Manner, as may breed a Quarrel between them, not to be reconciled: Or, if a Footman comes from the same Family on the like Errand, turn the Answer she orders you to deliver, in such a Manner, as the other Family may take it for an Affront.

When you are in Lodgings, and no Shoe-boy to be got, clean your Master's Shoes with the Bottom of the Curtains, a clean Napkin, or your Landlady's Apron.

Ever wear your Hat in the House, but when your Master calls; and as soon as you come into his Presence, pull it off to shew your Manners.

Never clean your Shoes on the Scraper, but in the Entry, or at the Foot of the Stairs, by which you will have the Credit of being at home, almost a Minute sooner, and the Scraper will last the longer.

Never ask Leave to go abroad, for then it will be always known that you are absent, and you will be thought an idle rambling Fellow; whereas, if you go out, and no body observes, you have a Chance of coming home without being missed, and you need not tell your Fellow-servants when you are gone, for they will be sure to say, you were in the House but two Minutes ago, which is the Duty of all Servants.

Snuff the Candles with your Fingers, and throw the Snuff on the Floor, then tread it out to prevent stinking: This Method will very much save the Snuffers from wearing out. You ought also to snuff them close to the Tallow, which will make them run, and so increase the Perquisite of the Cook's Kitchen-Stuff;[12] for she is the Person you ought in Prudence to be well with.

While Grace is saying after Meat,[13] do you and your Brethren take the Chairs from behind the Company, so that when they go to sit again, they may fall backwards, which will make them all merry; but be you so discreet as to hold your Laughter till you get to the Kitchen, and then divert your Fellow-servants.

When you know your Master is most busy in Company, come in and pretend to settle about the Room,[14] and if he chides, say, you thought he rung the Bell. This will divert him from plodding on Business too much, or spending himself in Talk, or racking his Thoughts, all which are hurtful to his Constitution.

If you are ordered to break the Claw of a Crab or a Lobster, clap it between the Sides of the Dining Room Door between the Hinges: Thus you can do it gradually without mashing the Meat, which is often the Case by using the Street-Door-Key, or the Pestle.

When you take a foul[15] Plate from any of the Guests, and observe the foul Knife and Fork lying on the Plate, shew your Dexterity, take up the Plate, and throw off the Knife and Fork on the Table without

10. **trundle them:** let them roll. 11. **Lap:** skirt, flap.

12. **the Perquisite . . . Kitchen-Stuff:** *Perquisite* here means the leftovers acquired by servants; *Kitchen-Stuff,* the waste products of the kitchen. 13. **after Meat:** after the meal. 14. **settle . . . Room:** put the room in order. 15. **foul:** used.

shaking off the Bones or broken Meat that are left: Then the Guest, who hath more Time than you, will wipe the Fork and Knife already used.

When you carry a Glass of Liquor to any Person who hath called for it, do not bob[16] him on the Shoulder, or cry, Sir, or Madam, here's the Glass; that would be unmannerly, as if you had a Mind to force it down one's Throat; but stand at the Person's Right Shoulder and wait his Time; and if he strikes it down with his Elbow by Forgetfulness, that was his Fault and not yours.

When your Mistress sends you for a Hackney Coach in a wet Day, come back in the Coach to save your Cloaths and the Trouble of walking; it is better the Bottom of her Pettycoats should be daggled[17] with your dirty Shoes, than your Livery be spoiled, and yourself get a Cold.

There is no Indignity so great to one of your Station, as that of lighting your Master in the Streets with a Lanthorn; and therefore, it is very honest Policy to try all Arts how to evade it: Besides, it shews your Master to be either poor or covetous, which are the two worst Qualities you can meet with in any Service. When I was under these Circumstances, I made use of several wise Expedients, which I here recommend to you: Sometimes I took a Candle so long, that it reached to the very Top of the Lanthorn and burnt it: But, my Master after a good Beating, ordered me to paste the Top with Paper. I then used a middling Candle, but stuck it so loose in the Socket that it leaned towards one Side, and burned a whole Quarter of the Horn. Then I used a Bit of Candle of half an Inch, which sunk in the Socket, and melted the Solder, and forced my Master to walk half the Way in the Dark. Then he made me stick two Inches of Candle in the Place where the Socket was; after which, I pretended to stumble, put out the Candle, and broke all the Tin Part to Pieces: At last, he was forced to make use of a Lanthorn-boy out of perfect good Husbandry.[18]

It is much to be lamented, that Gentlemen of our Employment have but two Hands to carry Plates, Dishes, Bottles, and the like out of the Room at Meals; and the Misfortune is still the greater, because one of those Hands is required to open the Door, while you are encumbered with your Load: Therefore, I advise, that the Door may be always left a-jarr, so as to open it with your Foot, and then you may carry out Plates and Dishes from your Belly up to your Chin, besides a good Quantity of Things under your Arms, which will save you many a weary Step; but take Care that none of your Burthen falls until you are out of the Room, and, if possible, out of Hearing.

If you are sent to the Post-Office with a Letter in a cold rainy Night, step to the Ale-house, and drink a Pot of Ale, until it is supposed you have done your Errand, but take the next fair Opportunity to put the Letter in carefully, as becomes an honest Servant.

If you are ordered to make Coffee for the Ladies after Dinner, and the Pot happens to boil over, while you are running up for a Spoon to stir it, or are thinking of something else, or struggling with the Chamber-maid for a Kiss, wipe the Sides of the Pot clean with a Dishclout,[19] carry up your Coffee boldly, and when your Lady finds it too weak, and examines you whether it hath not run over, deny the Fact[20] absolutely, swear you put in more Coffee than ordinary, that you never stirred an Inch from it, that you strove to make it better than usual, because your Mistress had Ladies with her, that the Servants in the Kitchen will justify what you say: Upon this, you will find that the other Ladies will pronounce your Coffee to be very good, and your Mistress will confess that her Mouth is out of Taste, and she will for the future suspect herself, and be more cautious in finding Fault. This I would have you do from a Principle of Conscience, for Coffee is very unwholsome; and out of Affection to your Lady, you ought to give it her as weak as possible: And upon this Argument, when you have a Mind to treat any of the Maids with a Dish of fresh Coffee, you may, and ought to subtract a third Part of the Powder, on account of your Lady's Health and getting her Maids Good-will.

If your Master sends you with a small trifling Present to one of his Friends, be as careful of it as you would of a Diamond Ring: Therefore, if the Present be only half a Dozen Pippins,[21] send up the Servant who received your Message to say, that you were ordered to deliver them with your own Hands. This will shew your Exactness and Care to prevent Accidents or Mistakes; and the Gentleman or Lady cannot do less than give you a Shilling: So when your Master

---

16. **bob:** rap. 17. **daggled:** (or draggled) soiled with mud. 18. **out . . . Husbandry:** for the sake of economy.

19. **Dishclout:** dishcloth. 20. **Fact:** crime, charge. 21. **Pippins:** pippin apples.

receives the like Present, teach the Messenger who brings it to do the same, and give your Master Hints that may stir up his Generosity; for Brother Servants should assist one another, since it is all for their Master's Honour, which is the chief Point to be consulted by every good Servant, and of which he is the best Judge.

When you step but a few Doors off to tattle[22] with a Wench, or take a running[23] Pot of Ale, or to see a Brother Footman going to be hanged, leave the Street Door open, that you may not be forced to knock, and your Master discover you are gone out; for a Quarter of an Hour's Time can do his Honor no Injury.

When you take away the remaining Pieces of Bread after Dinner, put them on foul Plates, and press them down with other Plates over them, so as nobody can touch them; and so, they will be a good Perquisite to your Blackguard Boy in ordinary.[24]

When you are forced to clean your Master's Shoes with your own Hands, use the Edge of the sharpest Case Knife,[25] and dry them with the Toes an Inch from the Fire, because wet Shoes are dangerous; and besides, by these Arts you will get them the sooner for yourself.

In some Families the Master often sends to the Tavern for a Bottle of Wine, and you are the Messenger: I advise you, therefore, to take the smallest Bottle you can find; but however, make the Drawer[26] give you a full Quart, then you will get a good Sup[27] for yourself, and your Bottle will be filled. As for a Cork to stop it, you need be at no Trouble, for the Thumb will do as well, or a Bit of dirty chewed Paper.

In all Disputes with Chairmen and Coachmen, for demanding too much, when your Master sends you down to chaffer[28] with them, take Pity of the poor Fellows, and tell your Master that they will not take a Farthing less: It is more for your Interest to get a Share of a Pot of Ale, than to save a Shilling for your Master, to whom it is a Trifle.

When you attend your Lady in a dark Night, if she useth her Coach, do not walk by the Coach Side, so as to tire and dirty yourself, but get up into your proper Place, behind it, and so hold the Flambeau[29]

sloping forward over the Coach Roof; and when it wants snuffing, dash it against the Corners.

When you leave your Lady at Church on *Sundays*, you have two Hours safe[30] to spend with your Companions at the Ale-house, or over a Beef Stake and a Pot of Beer at home with the Cook and the Maids; and indeed poor Servants have so few Opportunities to be happy, that they ought not to lose any.

Never wear Socks when you wait at Meals, on the Account of your own Health, as well as of them who sit at Table; because as most Ladies like the Smell of young Mens Toes, so it is a sovereign[31] Remedy against Vapours.

Chuse a Service, if you can, where your Livery Colours are least tawdry and distinguishing: Green and Yellow, immediately betray your Office, and so do all Kinds of Lace, except Silver which will hardly fall to your Share, unless with a Duke, or some Prodigal just come to his Estate. The Colours you ought to wish for, are Blue, or Filemot,[32] turn'd up with Red; which with a borrowed Sword, a borrowed Air, your Master's Linen, and a natural and improved[33] Confidence, will give you what Title you please, where you are not known.

When you carry Dishes or other Things out of the Room at Meals, fill both your Hands as full as possible; for although you may sometimes spill, and sometimes let fall, yet you will find at the Year's End, you have made great Dispatch and saved abundance of Time.

If your Master or Mistress happens to walk the Streets, keep on one Side, and as much on the Level[34] with them as you can, which People observing, will either think you do not belong to them, or that you are one of their Companions; but, if either of them happen to turn back and speak to you, so that you are under the Necessity to take off your Hat, use but your Thumb and one Finger, and scratch your Head with the rest.

In Winter time light the Dining-Room Fire but two Minutes before Dinner is served up, that your Mistress may see, how saving you are of her Coals.

When you are ordered to stir up the Fire, clean away the Ashes from between the Bars with the Fire-Brush.

When you are ordered to call a Coach, although it be Midnight, go no further than the Door, for fear of

---

22. tattle: chat, gossip; here, probably, to talk intimately. **23. running:** on the run, quick. **24. in ordinary:** belonging to the regular staff of servants. **25. Case Knife:** variously a hunting knife or a kitchen knife, so called from being fitted in a sheath. **26. Drawer:** tapster, bartender. **27. a good Sup:** a considerable amount. **28. chaffer:** haggle, bargain. **29. Flambeau:** torch.

30. safe: free, secure. **31. sovereign:** most efficacious. **32. Filemot:** (from *feuillemorte*) the color of a dead leaf. **33. improved:** cultivated. **34. on the Level:** abreast.

being out of the Way when you are wanted; and there stand bawling, Coach, Coach, for half an Hour.

Although you Gentlemen in Livery have the Misfortune to be treated scurvily by all Mankind, yet you make a Shift to keep up your Spirits, and sometimes arrive at considerable Fortunes. I was an intimate Friend to one of our Brethren, who was Footman to a Court Lady: She had an honourable Employment, was Sister to an Earl, and the Widow of a Man of Quality. She observed something so polite in my Friend, the Gracefulness with which he tript before her Chair, and put his Hair under his Hat, that she made him many Advances; and one Day taking the Air in her Coach with *Tom* behind it, the Coachman mistook the Way, and stopt at a privileged Chapel,[35] where the Couple were marry'd, and *Tom* came home in the Chariot by his Lady's Side: But he unfortunately taught her to drink Brandy, of which she dy'd, after having pawned all her Plate to purchase it, and *Tom* is now a Journeyman Malster.[36]

Boucher,[37] the famous Gamester, was another of our Fraternity, and when he was worth 50,000*l.* he dunned the Duke of *B——m* for an Arrear of Wages in his Service; and I could instance many more, particularly another, whose Son had one of the chief Employments at Court; and is sufficient to give you the following Advice, which is to be pert and sawcy to all Mankind, especially to the Chaplain, the Waiting-woman, and the better Sort of Servants in a Person of Quality's Family, and value not now and then a Kicking, or a Caning; for your Insolence will at last turn to good Account; and from wearing a Livery, you may probably soon carry a Pair of Colours.[38]

When you wait behind a Chair at Meals, keep constantly wriggling the Back of the Chair, that the Person behind whom you stand, may know you are ready to attend him.

When you carry a Parcel of *China* Plates, if they chance to fall, as it is a frequent Misfortune, your Excuse must be, that a Dog ran across you in the Hall; that the Chamber-maid accidentally pushed the Door against you; that a Mop stood across the Entry, and tript you up; that your Sleeve stuck against the Key, or Button[39] of the Lock.

When your Master and Lady are talking together in their Bed-chamber, and you have some Suspicion that you or your Fellow-servants are concerned in what they say, listen at the Door for the publick Good of all the Servants, and join all to take proper Measures for preventing any Innovation that may hurt the Community.

Be not proud in Prosperity: You have heard that Fortune turns on a Wheel; if you have a good Place, you are at the Top of the Wheel. Remember how often you have been stripped, and kick'd out of Doors, your Wages all taken up[40] beforehand, and spent in translated red-heel'd Shoes,[41] second-hand Toupees, and repair'd Lace Ruffles, besides a swinging[42] Debt to the Ale-wife and the Brandy-shop. The neighbouring Tapster, who before would beckon you over to a savoury Bit of Ox-cheek in the Morning, give it you *gratis*, and only score you up for the Liquor, immediately after you were packt off in Disgrace, carried a Petition to your Master, to be paid out of your Wages, whereof not a Farthing was due, and then pursued you with Bailiffs into every blind Cellar.[43] Remember how soon you grew shabby, thread-bare and out-at-heels, was forced to borrow an old Livery Coat, to make your Appearance while you were looking for a Place; and sneak to every House where you have an old Acquaintance to steal you a Scrap, to keep Life and Soul together; and upon the whole, were in the lowest Station of human Life, which, as the old Ballad says,[44] is that of a Skipkennel turn'd out of Place: I say, remember all this now in your flourishing Condition. Pay your Contributions

---

35. **a privileged Chapel**: a Nonconformist chapel tolerated by the Established Church or government. 36. **Malster**: (maltster) one who makes malt from barley or grain. 37. **Boucher**: Richard Bourchier (d. 1702) was a footman to the Earl of Mulgrave (later Duke of Buckingham) before becoming a successful gambler. The anecdote Swift tells seems to be a variant of that in Theophilus Lucas's *Memoirs of the Lives, Intrigues, and Comical Adventures of the Most Famous Gamesters* (1714), according to which Bourchier won a bet of five hundred pounds from Buckingham, who, when he discovered the identity of his opponent, refused to pay on the grounds that Bourchier could not have paid had he lost. Being assured of his former footman's present affluence, he yielded the point and the sum. 38. **a Pair . . . Colours**: the emblem of an ensign.

39. **Button**: catch. 40. **taken up**: consumed. 41. **translated . . . Shoes**: "Translated" shoes are new shoes made from old ones. 42. **swinging**: (swingeing) whopping. 43. **blind Cellar**: a cellar having only one opening and therefore no escape outlet. 44. **as . . . says**: *A True Character of Sundry Trades and Callings*, st. 7:

> A Mountebank without his fools,
> and a Skip-kennel turn'd out of place,
> A Tinker without any tools,
> they are all in sorrowful case.
>
> (*Roxburghe Ballads*, VII. 18)

duly to your late Brothers the Cadets,[45] who are left to the wide World: Take one of them as your Dependant, to send on your Lady's Messages when you have a Mind to go to the Ale-house; slip him out privately now and then a Slice of Bread, and a Bit of cold Meat, your Master can afford it; and if he be not yet put upon the Establishment[46] for a Lodging, let him lie in the Stable, or the Coach-house, or under the Back-stairs, and recommend him to all the Gentlemen who frequent your House, as an excellent Servant.

To grow old in the Office of a Footman, is the highest of all Indignities: Therefore when you find Years coming on, without Hopes of a Place at Court, a Command in the Army, a Succession to the Steward-ship, an Employment in the Revenue (which two last you cannot obtain without Reading and Writing) or running away with your Master's Niece or Daughter; I directly advise you to go upon the Road, which is the only Post of Honour left you: There you will meet many of your old Comrades, and live a short Life and a merry one, and make a Figure at your Exit, wherein I will give you some Instructions.

The last Advice I shall give you, relates to your Behaviour when you are going to be hanged; which, either for robbing your Master, for House-breaking, or going upon the High-way,[47] or in a drunken Quarrel, by killing the first Man you meet, may very probably be your Lot, and is owing to one of these three Qualities; either a Love of good Fellowship, a Generosity of Mind, or too much Vivacity of Spirits. Your good Behaviour on this Article, will concern your whole Community:[48] At your Tryal deny the Fact[49] with all Solemnity of Imprecations: A hundred of your Brethren, if they can be admitted, will attend about the Bar, and be ready upon Demand to give you a good Character before the Court: Let nothing prevail on you to confess, but the Promise of a Pardon for discovering[50] your Comrades: But, I suppose all this to be in vain, for if you escape now, your Fate will be the same another Day. Get a Speech to be written by the best Author of Newgate:[51] Some of your kind

Wenches will provide you with a *Holland*[52] Shirt, and white Cap crowned with a crimson or black Ribbon: Take Leave chearfully of all your Friends in *Newgate*: Mount the Cart with Courage: Fall on your Knees: Lift up your Eyes: Hold a Book in your Hands although you cannot read a Word: Deny the Fact at the Gallows: Kiss and forgive the Hangman, and so Farewel: You shall be buried in Pomp, at the Charge of the Fraternity: The Surgeon shall not touch a Limb of you;[53] and your Fame shall continue until a Successor of equal Renown succeeds in your Place.

FROM

[LETTERS]

The text is from *The Correspondence of Alexander Pope*, ed. George Sherburn (1956), where the Harleian transcript is followed. One scribal error, *fearing* for *fear* (noted by Sherburn but, unlike others, left standing), is here corrected.

[*To Alexander Pope*]

Sep. 29. 1725

Sir,—I cannot guess the Reason of Mr Stopfords[1] management but impute it at a venture either to hast or bashfullness, in the latter of which he is excessive to a fault, although he had already gone the Tour of Italy and France, to harden him: perhaps this second Journey and for a longer time may amend him. He treated you just as he did Lord Carteret,[2] to whom I

---

45. **Cadets:** gentlemen seeking a career in the army from the bottom up. 46. **put . . . Establishment:** imposed upon the household. 47. **going . . . High-way:** highway robbery. 48. **Community:** professional class; cf. *Fraternity* below. 49. **Fact:** crime, charge. 50. **discovering:** revealing. 51. **the best . . . Newgate:** Swift in this passage describes the kind of theatrical production with which condemned prisoners often glorified their exits. Cf. Polly's speech in *The Beggar's Opera*, I. xii, later in Part Two.

52. **Holland:** a linen fabric that comes from the Netherlands. 53. **The Surgeon . . . you:** The bodies of criminals were given to medical students for use as cadavers. Cf. Matt's first speech in *The Beggar's Opera*, II. i, later in Part Two. LETTER TO POPE. 1. **Mr Stopfords:** the Reverend James Stopford (d. 1759), a close friend of Swift's who later became Bishop of Cloyne. He had delivered to Pope Swift's letter of July 19, but did not allow himself the benefit of Pope's attentions as Swift had requested. 2. **Lord Carteret:** John Carteret (1690–1763), Baron Carteret; later Earl Granville and Viscount Carteret. He was Lord Lieutenant of Ireland from 1724 to 1730.

recommended him. My letter you saw to Lord Bolingb[3] has shewn you the Situation I am in, and the Company I keep: If I do not forget some of the Contents. But I am now returning to the noble Scene of Dublin in to the Grande Monde, for fear of burying my parts to Signalise my self among Curates and Vicars, and correct all Corruption crept in relating to the weight of Bread and Butter through those Dominions where I govern.[4] I have employd my time (besides ditching[5]) in finishing correcting, amending, and Transcribing my Travells,[6] in four parts Compleat newly Augmented, and intended for the press when the world shall deserve them, or rather when a Printer shall be found brave enough to venture his Eares,[7] I like your Schemes of our meeting after Distresses and dispertions[8] but the chief end I propose to my self in all my labors is to vex the world rather then divert it, and if I could compass that designe without hurting my own person or Fortune I would be the most Indefatigable writer you have ever seen without reading[9] I am exceedingly pleased that you have done with Translations[10] Lord Treasurer Oxford often lamented that a rascaly World should lay you under a Necessity of Misemploying your Genius for so long a time. But since you will now be so much better employd when you think of the World give it one lash the more at

my Request. I have ever hated all Nations professions and Communityes and all my love is towards individualls for instance I hate the tribe of Lawyers, but I love Councellor such a one, Judge such a one for so with Physicians (I will not Speak of my own Trade[11]) Soldiers, English, Scotch, French; and the rest but principally I hate and detest that animal called man, although I hartily love John, Peter, Thomas and so forth. this is the system upon which I have governed my self many years (but do not tell) and so I shall go on till I have done with them I have got Materials Towards a Treatis proving the falsity of that Definition *animal rationale;* and to show it should be only *rationis capax.*[12] Upon this great foundation of Misanthropy (though not Timons manner[13]) The whole building of my Travells is erected: And I never will have peace of mind till all honest men are of my Opinion: by Consequence you are to embrace it immediatly and procure that all who deserve my Esteem may do so too The matter is so clear that it will admit little dispute. nay I will hold a hundred pounds that you and I agree in the Point.

I did not know your Odyssey was finished being yet in the Country, which I shall leave in three days I shall thank you kindly for the Present but shall like it three fourths the less from the mixture you mention of another hand,[14] however I am glad you saved yourself so much drudgery—I have been long told by Mr Ford[15] of your great Atchivements in building and planting and especially of your Subterranean Passage to your Garden[16] whereby you turned a blunder into a beauty which is a Piece of Ars Poetica

I have almost done with Harridans[17] and shall soon become old enough to fall in love with Girls of

---

3. Lord Bolingb: Henry St. John (1678–1751), Viscount Bolingbroke; Tory statesman and friend of both Swift and Pope. Pope dedicated to him his *Essay on Man* (see later in Part Two). **4. those . . . govern:** The Dean of St. Patrick's Cathedral had civil jurisdiction over the adjoining area, known as the "liberty" or "liberties." **5. ditching:** digging ditches. Swift was at this time living in the country house of his friend, the Reverend Thomas Sheridan, in the village of Quilca, county Cavan. The house was in bad repair and was undergoing improvements. **6. Transcribing my Travells:** *Gulliver's Travels* was published in London on October 28, 1726. **7. brave . . . Eares:** It was not uncommon for printers to be prosecuted for incendiary publications. (See the headnote to the first of *The Drapier's Letters,* above.) The printer of the *Travels,* Benjamin Motte, tried to protect himself by tampering with Swift's manuscript. **8. after . . . dispertions:** Pope had written: "After so many dispersions, and so many divisions, two or three of us may yet be gather'd together; not to plot, not to contrive silly schemes of ambition, or to vex our own or others hearts with busy vanities (such as perhaps at one time of life or other take their Tour in every man) but to divert ourselves, and the world too if it pleases; or at worst, to laugh at others as innocently and as unhurtfully as at ourselves." **9. without reading:** without being well read; doubtless a stroke of self-irony facetiously delivered. **10. done . . . Translations:** Pope's translation of the *Iliad* was published between 1715 and 1720, the *Odyssey* between 1725 and 1726.

11. my own Trade: The clergy is meant, not writers, though Swift would not have excepted them either. **12. rationis capax:** not a rational animal, but only an animal capable of reason. **13. Timons manner:** the manner of Shakespeare's Timon of Athens, or invective. **14. another hand:** William Broome and Elijah Fenton assisted Pope with his translation of the *Odyssey.* **15. Mr Ford:** Charles Ford (1682–1741), one of Swift's closest friends and principal correspondents. **16. your Garden:** the elaborate grotto Pope had built at Twickenham. **17. Harridans:** Swift had written Pope on July 12 that he would visit him if he would "get me two or three Harridan Ladys that will be content to nurse and talk loud to me while I am deaf," and Pope had replied on September 14, "I'll find you elderly Ladies enough that can hallow, and two that can nurse, and they are too old and feeble to make too much noise; as you will guess when I tell you they are my own mother, and my own nurse."

Fourteen, The Lady whom you describe to live at Court, to be deaf and no party Woman,[18] I take to be Mythology but know not how to moralize it. She cannot be Mercy, for mercy is neither deaf nor lives at Court Justice is blind and perhaps deaf but neither is she a Court Lady. Fortune is both blind and deaf and a Court Lady, but then she is a most Damnable party Woman, and will never make me easy as you promise. It must be riches which Answers all your description; I am glad she visites you but my voice is so weak that I doubt she will never hear me.

Mr Lewis[19] sent me an Account of Dr Arbuthnett's Illness[20] which is a very sensible Affliction to me, who by living so long out of the World have lost that hardness of Heart contracted by years and generall Conversation. I am daily loosing Friends, and neither seeking nor getting others. O, if the World had but a dozen Arbuthnetts in it I would burn my Travells but however he is not without Fault. There is a passage in Bede highly commending the Piety and learning of the Irish in that Age, where after abundance of praises he overthrows them all by lamenting that, Alas, they kept Easter at a wrong time of the Year.[21] So our Doctor has every Quality and virtue that can make a man amiable or usefull, but alas he hath a sort of Slouch in his Walk. I pray god protect him for he is an excellant Christian tho not a Catholick and as fit a man either to dy or Live as ever I knew.

I hear nothing of our Friend Gay, but I find the Court keeps him at hard Meat[22] I advised him to come over here with a Lord Lieutenant.[23] Mr Tickell is in a very good Office[24] I have not seen Philips,[25] tho' formerly we were so intimate He has got nothing, and by what I can find will get nothing though he writes little Flams[26] (as Lord Leicester[27] call'd those sort of Verses) on Miss Carteret[28] and others, it is remarkable and deserves recording that a Dublin Blacksmith[29] a great poet hath imitated his manner in a Poem to the same Miss. Philips is a Complainer, and on this Occasion I told Lord Carteret that Complainers never Succeed at Court though Railers do.

Are you altogether a Country Gentleman that I must Address to you out of London to the Hazard of your losing this pretious Letter, which I will now Conclude although so much Paper is left. I have an ill name and therefore shall not Subscribe it. but you will guess it comes from one who esteems and loves you about half as much as you deserve. I mean as much as he can

I am in great concern at which I am just told is in some News Paper that Lord Bolingbroke is much hurt by a fall in Hunting I am glad he has so much youth and Viger left of which he hath not been thrifty but I wonder he has no more Discretion.

---

18. no . . . Woman: Pope wrote, "I can also help you to a Lady who is as deaf, tho' not so old as your self; you'll be pleas'd with one another, I'll engage, tho' you don't hear one another: you'll converse like spirits by intuition. What you'll most wonder at is, she is considerable at Court, yet no Party-woman, and lives in Court, yet wou'd be easy and make you easy." The lady was Mrs. Henrietta Howard (1681–1767), mistress of the Prince of Wales who was to become George II two years later. In 1731 when her husband succeeded to the earldom, Mrs. Howard became Countess of Suffolk. **19. Mr Lewis:** Erasmus Lewis (1670–1754), friend of Swift and Pope and a henchman of Lord Oxford. **20. Dr . . . Illness:** Pope wrote that Arbuthnot, Queen Anne's physician and friend of both Pope and Swift, had "an imposthume in the bowels; which is broke, but the event is very uncertain." Arbuthnot lived on to 1735. (See Pope's *Epistle to Dr. Arbuthnot* later in Part Two.) **21. a passage . . . Year:** *Ecclesiastical History*, III. 3. The Roman usage for the celebration of Easter was adopted in England in 664.

22. at . . . Meat: under restraint; "hard meat" is an old term for fodder consisting of grain and hay, as opposed to grass. **23. with . . . Lieutenant:** as secretary to the Lord Lieutenant. **24. good Office:** The poet Thomas Tickell (1686–1740) was appointed in 1724 secretary to the Lords Justices in Ireland. **25. Philips:** Ambrose Philips (c. 1675–1749). He came to Ireland in November, 1724, as secretary to the Lord Lieutenant. Gay's *Shepherd's Week* (see later in Part Two) is a parody of Philips's *Pastorals*, published in 1709. (See the selections from Philips in Part Three.) **26. little Flams:** Philips won the nickname Namby-Pamby (suggested by his unusual Christian name, Ambrose) for his prattling verses for children. **27. Lord Leicester:** Robert Sydney (1649–1702), Fourth Earl of Leicester. **28. on . . . Carteret:** *To the Honorable Miss Carteret* (1725). She was the daughter of the Lord Lieutenant. **29. a Dublin Blacksmith:** perhaps Swift himself; at least the anonymous *A Poem upon R——r, a Lady's Spaniel*, which followed hard upon Philips's ode to Miss Carteret, has been attributed to him.

John Dennis

1657–1734

Dennis's reputation for quarrelsomeness has tended to obscure the importance of his critical writings. Brilliantly mocked by Pope, Swift, Gay, and Fielding, he lapsed finally into an ineffectual surliness; but in his heyday—the first decade of the century—he appeared to stand almost alone as a formidable defender of some very consequential literary values. His offense was one of manners rather than of intellect. He deviated from the ideal of the critical gentleman, an ideal considered by Pope in the *Essay on Criticism* (1711) to be especially important when a critic is dealing with a new work.

He was born in London, the son of a saddler; except for his years at school and university and except for a trip to the Continent and occasional rural vacations, he lived in London all his life. After five years at Harrow School, he entered Caius College, Cambridge, at the age of eighteen. When he was expelled from Caius on a charge of assault with a sword—a misadventure typical of the man later nicknamed Critic Furius—he moved to Trinity Hall, where he became Master of Arts in 1683. He remained at Cambridge three more years, probably serving as a tutor. Cambridge was close enough to London for him to go in frequently to see the plays and to enjoy literary argument at the taverns and coffee houses.

In 1688 he took the Grand Tour of the Continent in the company of Lord Francis Seymour, a friend from Harrow days. Always impetuous and passionate, Dennis early found himself fond of being "transported" by both the scenic and the literary sublime. The sight of the Alps, he reported, filled him with "a delightful Horrour, a terrible Joy"; and in one of his early Pindaric odes he inquires,

> What divine Rapture shakes my Soul?
> What Fury rages in my Blood,
> And drives about the stormy Flood,
> What makes my sparkling Eye-balls rowl?

He was back in London in the early 1690's, burning with literary excitement; he frequented the famous Will's Coffee House in Covent Garden, where he established himself as a disciple of Dryden's. Literature was the thing at Will's, and disputes about style and technique were the rule. Under this stimulus Dennis soon became a rapid and virile writer. Beginning with translations and patriotic poems, he moved on to try his hand at plays, of which he eventually wrote nine; he turned out political pamphlets and began to write his important works of criticism.

His first critical performance was *The Impartial Critic* (1693), a reply in a series of five dialogues to Thomas Rymer's *A Short View of Tragedy* (1692). Here Dennis engages in a close examination of the particulars of Greek tragedy and concludes by launching a defense of Shakespeare against Rymer's strictures. He jumped to the defense again in 1698 with *The Usefulness of the Stage*, an answer to Jeremy Collier's *A Short View of the Immorality and Profaneness of the English Stage* (1698). Turning to the question of the role of the passions in poetry, he published *The Advancement and Reformation of Modern Poetry* in 1701, and in 1704 *The Grounds of Criticism in Poetry*, in which he explores wonder and terror as elements of the poetic experience. Conspicuous in these four critical works is the seriousness with which Dennis regards literature. Convinced of the supreme importance of literature to church, state, and the individual, he is distressed that others appear to consider it either as entertainment or as a commercial commodity.

In 1705 he received a government sinecure that enabled him to begin withdrawing from a literary culture in which, since the death of Dryden in 1700, he no longer felt at home. From about 1710 to the end of his long life he was embroiled in the unedifying literary and personal quarrels with Addison, Steele, Swift, and Pope for which he is notorious. Dennis, who was in his sixties when most of the new writers were in their thirties, accused them of frivolity and venality; they responded by taxing him with pedantry and envy. His squat figure, his unlovely dress, his habitual scowl, his boastfulness, and his ready profanity when enraged became familiar targets for satire. Pope was perhaps the most adept at baiting him; his *Narrative of Dr. Robert Norris, Concerning the Strange and Deplorable Frenzy of Mr. John Denn—s* (1713) contains this scene: "Mr. John Dennis . . . finding on . . . Mr. Lintot's counter a book called An Essay on Criticism . . . read a page or two with much frowning, till coming to these two lines,

> Some have at first for wits, then poets past,
> Turn'd critics next, and prov'd plain fools at last,

he flung down the book in a terrible fury, and cried, By G—d he means me."

He declined into poverty and blindness. In the early years of the century many had considered him England's foremost critic, the rightful inheritor of the mantle of Dryden, but he lived into a new age to hear himself mocked as "Rinaldo Furioso, Critick of the Woeful Countenance"; apocryphal anecdotes about his rages were even enshrined in *Joe Miller's Jests* (1739). When he died at seventy-seven he was described by a writer in *The Gentleman's Magazine* as "the last classick wit of King Charles's Reign." William Cowper later thought Dennis "a very sensible fellow," and his criticism was admired by Wordsworth and Coleridge, Landor and Swinburne. His critical principles underlie Samuel Johnson's, and it is his distinction that he not only applied them but was always ready to examine and defend them.

Bibliography will be found in Bonamy Dobrée's *English Literature in the Early Eighteenth Century* (1959); in *The Cambridge Bibliography of English Literature*, ed. F. W. Bateson (4 vols., 1941) and its *Supplement*, ed. George Watson (1957); and in H. G. Paul's *John Dennis: His Life and Criticism* (1911). The critical writings are edited by E. N. Hooker, *The Critical Works of John Dennis* (2 vols., 1939–43); Hooker's biographical and critical introduction at the beginning of Volume II is indispensable. J. W. H. Atkins's *English Literary Criticism: 17th and 18th Centuries* (1952) contains a useful brief account of Dennis's criticism. S. H. Monk's *The Sublime: A Study of Critical Theories in XVIII-Century England* (1935) places Dennis against his aesthetic and psychological background.

FROM

THE ADVANCEMENT AND REFORMATION OF MODERN POETRY . . .

❧

This work, which runs to seventeen chapters, is Dennis's most ambitious and significant piece of criticism; it is the only one of his critical writings to attain even the modest popularity of three editions. He appears to be indebted to Milton's treatise *Of Education* (1644), where Milton expresses his famous conviction that poetry is "simple, sensuous, and passionate"; and where he writes that a study of poetical decorum in each of the primary genres ("which is the grand masterpiece to observe") would show readers "what religious, what glorious and magnificent use might be made of poetry, both in divine and human things." But even more important is Dennis's debt to Longinus, whose name is traditionally associated with the first-century A.D. treatise *Peri Hupsous* (*On the Sublime*). This document is one of the earliest discussions of the importance of the emotional response to poetry. As early as 1717 Dennis had earned the comic sobriquet Sir Tremendous Longinus, and in the twentieth century W. K. Wimsatt has called him the "English counterpart" of Longinus. S. H. Monk writes: "Dennis establishes the sublime beyond the sphere of that moderate urbanity which was the ideal of Augustan literature. But it is important to remember that he did so without apparently disrupting the system." An authentic—if perhaps surprising—"neo-classical" critic, Dennis pleads for emotion, passion, and warmth in poetry, and finds his sanction in the classics.

The text is that of the first edition, *The Advancement and Reformation of Modern Poetry. A Critical Discourse. In Two Parts. The First, Shewing That the Principal Reason Why the Ancients Excel'd the Moderns in the Greater Poetry, Was Because They Mix'd Religion with Poetry. The Second, Proving That by Joyning Poetry with the Religion Reveal'd to Us in Sacred Writ, the Modern Poets Might Come to Equal the Ancient* (1701). The Epistle Dedicatory was originally printed in italics.

❧

[EPISTLE DEDICATORY]

To the Most Noble
JOHN,°
Lord Marquess of *Normanby*,
Earl of *Mulgrave*, &c.
AND
Knight of the Most Noble Order of the Garter.

MY LORD,

I make no question, but that all those Gentlemen, who shall happen to be offended at the Newness and Boldness of the Positions, which are the Subject of the following Treatise, will accuse me of want of Judgment, not only for advancing 'em, but for daring to bring 'em under the protection of so discerning a Judge as your Lordship.

But I desire those Gentlemen to believe, that if I had had a Mind that my faults should have lain conceal'd, or would have consulted my own more than the publick advantage, your Lordship is the person to whom of all mankind I would last have chosen to have address'd them. That tho you had never writ your admirable Essay, I should have been convinc'd by your other Poems, and particularly by your *Temple of Death;* a Temple that is consecrated at the same time to Death and to Immortality, of your perfect knowledge in Criticism, because I have experience enough

---

THE ADVANCEMENT AND REFORMATION OF MODERN POETRY: *Epistle Dedicatory.* **John:** John Sheffield (1648–1721), Third Earl of Mulgrave and later (1703) First Duke of Buckingham and Normanby; a court wit, Sheffield was a military and naval officer, a politician, a duelist, a rake, and a poet. Samuel Johnson, who said of Sheffield that "his character is not to be proposed as worthy of imitation," declared of his stylish *Essay on Poetry* (1682), a heroic-couplet poem of 350 lines, "the precepts are judicious, sometimes new, and often happily expressed; but there are . . . many weak lines, and some strange appearances of negligence . . . ." Sheffield's poem *The Temple of Death* (1695) is a translation from the French of Philippe Habert (c. 1605–37). The works of Sheffield were edited in 1723 by Alexander Pope.

to be satisfied, that there never was a great Poet in the world, who was not an accomplish'd Critick. *Horace*, who was one of the Greatest of the *Roman* Poets, was in the first Rank of Judges,[1] and *Virgil* has taken care to transmit to posterity, one of the exactest pieces of Criticism that ever was writ in the world; tho indeed it is a Criticism by Examples only, of which *Bossu* vouchsaf'd to write the Rules[2] above sixteen hundred years afterwards.

Thus, my Lord, I am sufficiently acquainted with your Character to approach you with awe; but at the same time I am convinc'd that they are mistaken, who believe that the most Discerning are the most Rigid Judges. I am satisfied that a Writer has a great deal of reason to be more apprehensive of half Criticks, who are govern'd by opinion, and guided by prejudice, or sway'd by partial affection; and who see faults but in some places, and at some particular times; for such Censors are inexorable to the least of our Errors. But your Lordship, whose unclouded Understanding sees all our faults, where-ever they are, and who knows how difficult, if not impossible, it is for us not to err, will make large allowances for the Imperfections of Humane Nature, or our particular frailties, if you discover in us the appearance of any good quality, which may bespeak your Indulgence. Imperfect, partial, prejudic'd Criticks have Judgment enough to Discover Faults, but want Discernment to find out Beauties; or if at any time by chance they Discover them, they are perhaps too interested, or too envious, or too fearful to own them. But as Nature, that has given you so many extraordinary qualities, has conspir'd with Fortune, in setting your Lordship infinitely above so mean a Passion as Envy; so she has plac'd you as far above the Imperious sway of opinion, that madly tyrannizes over the multitude. Your Lordship never approves of our actions because they have met with success, but because they deserve to succeed. And here I humbly desire of your Lordship, that in behalf of all the Lovers of Poetry, I may return you thanks for the Protection and Patronage of a great man deceas'd.[3] 'Tis known to all the observing world,

that you generously began to espouse him, when he was more than half opprest by a very formidable party in the Court of King *Charles II.* a faction that wanted neither Power nor Authority to crush him; who, besides that they held the foremost Rank in the State, had got possession of the minds of the people, with whom they had acquir'd a great Reputation, for their Knowledge and Capacity in matters of Wit and Criticism. If that great man had faults, your Lordship wanted no Discernment to find them; but you wanted malice, partiality, prejudice, and the rest of those ungenerous obstacles, that hindred others from discovering or confessing his Beauties. Your Lordship easily found that he had Beauties which over-weigh'd all faults; and it was that consideration that engag'd you to support him against his powerful adversaries. They, upon an unaccountable pique which they had taken to his person, would have opprest his growing merit; your Lordship, in consideration of that rising merit, cherish'd his person, notwithstanding his pretended frailties; and while others, to express their malice to the man, would have hindred the advancement even of that Art which they pretended to esteem so much; your Lordship, on the contrary, by a wise, a good natur'd, and a noble proceeding, cherish'd the man on purpose to make him instrumental in advancing the Art. And as it was after you took him into your protection, that he writ several of his most valuable pieces, 'tis to your Lordship that the world is in some measure indebted for the greater number of his excellencies.

And with the same greatness of mind, with which to advance a noble Art, you rais'd and supported a man oppress'd by very powerful adversaries; so in order to the same design, you pull'd down the Tyranny of publick prejudice, and of a Triumphant opinion. For 'tis known to all the world, that your Lordship declar'd against the Obscenity which was shamefully crept into our *English* Poetry;[4] at a time when not only that way of writing, but the Verses which you particularly hinted at, were in the very height of their Reputation. But the success was answerable to the nobleness of your Lordship's attempt; those Verses have gradually declin'd ever since in their Reputation, and nothing of that nature will now be suffer'd by any but the Rabble. So that your Lordship has done a very signal kindness not only to a noble

1. the first . . . Judges: Dennis is undoubtedly thinking of the *Ars Poetica* (*c.* 19 B.C.), Horace's famous verse essay. **2. the Rules:** René Le Bossu (1631–80), a French priest, helped establish the theory of the epic in his *Traité du poème épique* (1675). **3. a great . . . deceas'd:** John Dryden, who after 1676 was defended by Sheffield against a court faction led by the Duke of Buckingham and the Earl of Rochester.

4. your . . . Poetry: In his *Essay on Poetry* Sheffield had attacked Rochester's "nauseous Songs."

Art, but to Vertue itself, and have highly oblig'd all vertuous men, as well as lovers of Poetry.

My Lord, I have mentioned this the more willingly, because it fairly gives me an opportunity of confirming by your Lordship's Authority, the assertion which is the foundation of the following Treatise; which is, that Religion gives a very great advantage for the exciting of Passion in Poetry. Your Lordship has inform'd us, that Obscenity and Poetry are things that are inconsistent. The assertion must be granted by all to be unquestionably true; for nothing can be possibly consistent with an Art, which runs counter to the very end and design of that Art. Now the end of Poetry is to Instruct and Reform, and Obscenity in writing corrupts the manners. But this on the other side is not to be doubted, that Verses may be produc'd from the ancient Poets, which are at once Obscene and Poetical; tho at the same Time it must be confest, that they would have been more fine, if they had been more chaste. But if any one demands why Ribaldry should be entertaining in the Ancient Poetry, when it is so plainly insufferable in the Modern; to him I answer, that it can be nothing but the Religion of the Ancients which makes the difference; for theirs was very consistent with Obscenity, whereas ours entirely abhors it. A way of writing that was authoriz'd by their Religion, could never be said to be utterly inconsistent with instruction. Besides, Passion is the principal thing in Poetry, and tho Obscenity has something too gross and fulsom in it, to consist with the Delicacy of a tender Passion, yet by mingling with their Obscene Verses, their *Cupid*, their *Venus*, and the rest of their Amorous Divinities, they had the advantage of that other sort of Passion which we call Enthusiasm; whereas the Divinity of our Religion being utterly abhorrent of any thing which is impure, such Ribaldry inserted in our Poetry can never possibly either instruct or move.

The consideration of what your Lordship has done to advance Poetry, has oblig'd me to lay the following Treatise at your feet; a Present, I confess, that is altogether unworthy of you, but it is by much the most valuable that either I have, or ever have had to make; and your Lordship has accepted it with the same goodness, that the *Persian* King did the Apple: He saw that it was all that his Subject could do to testifie his acknowledgment; and for that very reason it was more agreeable to him, than the vain pompous Presents of those who believ'd they could add to his Treasure. I believ'd that the very Design to improve

an Art, which your Lordship has actually so much advanc'd, would prevail upon your goodness to excuse a great many faults, which you may find in the following Treatise.

But upon mentioning the Design of the ensuing Discourse, I find my self sufficiently perplex'd. There are several things of the last importance that ought to be preliminary to the Discourse itself: And I find that I have strong temptations upon me of following Mr *Dryden's* Example, and of saying to your Lordship, what is usually directed to the Reader in general. But then I consider that I have neither Mr *Dryden's* great qualities, nor like him a Reputation long establish'd, nor, what ought chiefly to be considered, the Honour of having often approach'd your Lordship, to authorize such a Liberty. But yet on the other side, the things that I have to say are of important consequence to the good of the Cause which I have undertaken; and I find that I should be wanting to that noble Cause, if I should address my self to the Reader in general; and I should be thought by all discerning persons to proceed as absurdly, as would a Lawyer, who upon a solemn pleading, should apply himself to the Multitude, who have little knowledge of his affair, and no Authority to determine it; instead of speaking to his Awful Judge, who has a perfect knowledge of his Cause, and a Sovereign Authority to decide it.

The Design of all Poetical Criticism, must be, if it is just and good, to advance so useful and so noble an Art as Poetry. And the design of the following Treatise is no less than to set the Moderns upon an equal foot with even admir'd Antiquity. In order to the doing which, I humbly desire leave of your Lordship, that I may make an enquiry in what the preheminence of the Ancient Poets consists; and why I prefer one of the *Grecian* Tragedies, as for example, the *Oedipus* of *Sophocles*, to one of our celebrated *English* Tragedies; as for instance, the *Julius Cæsar* of *Shakespear*. Upon reflection I find that the reason is, because I am more delighted and more instructed by the former; and that for this very reason, because I am more mov'd by it: For I find by experience that I am no further pleas'd nor instructed by any Tragedy, than as it excites Passion in me. But in order to the discovering why I am more mov'd by the former than the latter of those Tragedies, I desire leave to make an enquiry into the principal differences between them, and that in all probability will determine the matter. I find then, my Lord, that there are two very signal differences between the *Oedipus* and the *Julius Cæsar*. First, The *Oedipus* is exactly Just and Regular, and the *Julius Cæsar* is very Extravagant and Irregular. Secondly, the *Oedipus* is very Religious, and the *Julius Cæsar* is Irreligious. For, with submission to your Lordship's Judgment, I conceive that every Tragedy ought to be a very solemn Lecture, inculcating a particular Providence, and showing it plainly protecting the good, and chastizing the bad, or at least the violent; and that if it is otherwise, it is either an empty amusement, or a scandalous and pernicious Libel upon the government of the world. The killing of *Julius Cæsar* in *Shakespear*, is either a Murder or a Lawful Action; if the killing *Cæsar* is a Lawful Action, then the killing of *Brutus* and *Cassius* is downright Murder; and the Poet has been guilty of polluting the Scene with the blood of the very best and last of the *Romans*. But if the killing of *Cæsar* is Murder, and *Brutus* and *Cassius* are very justly punish'd for it; then *Shakespear* is on the other side answerable for introducing so many Noble *Romans*, committing in the open face of an Audience, a very horrible Murder, and only punishing two of them; which proceeding gives an occasion to the people to draw a dangerous inference from it, which may be Destructive to Government, and to Human Society.

Thus, my Lord, I have a great deal of reason to suspect that the *Oedipus* derives its advantage from its Regularity, and its Religion; and the presumption grows still more strong, when upon enquiry I find, that the fore-mention'd Regularity is nothing but the bringing some Rules into practice, which Observation and Philosophy have found requisite for the surer exciting of Passion. For as this, I think, cannot be contested, that of two Combatants, who have equal Strength and equal Courage, he is most likely to have the better who has the most address;[5] so in a contention and prize of Poetry, between persons who have equal force of mind, he will be certain to have the advantage, who is the best instructed to use his strength.

If any of the enemies to Regularity will give themselves the trouble to peruse the *Oedipus* of *Sophocles*, with an impartial eye, he will easily discern how instrumental the Poetical Art is in leading him from Surprize to Surprize, from Compassion to Terror, and from Terror to Compassion again, without giving him so much as a time to breathe; and he will as easily discover, how the Religion that is every where intermix'd with the Play, shews all the Surprizes, even when he least expects this, as so many immediate successive effects of a particular Dreadful Providence, which make them come like so many Thunder-claps from a serene Heaven to confound and astonish him.

A Poet is capacitated by that which is commonly call'd Regularity, to excite the ordinary Passions more powerfully by the constitution of the Fable, and the influence which that must necessarily have both upon the words and thoughts; and Religion, besides the Influence it will have upon the ordinary Passions, will be to a Poet, who has force and skill enough to make his advantage of it, a perpetual source of extraordinary Passion, which is commonly call'd Enthusiasm, for the sentiments and the expressions.

For what concerns Regularity, or the exciting of ordinary Passion, enough has been said already. Your Lordship has particularly made the Publick a Present,[6] which is, I confess, but little in Volume, but is magnificent in Value and Ornament; 'tis a Present in Jewels, which casts a further lustre than Treasures that take up a larger space, and is more solid to those who are near it. Our Writers have been sufficiently told, that writing Regularly is writing Morally, Decently, Justly, Naturally, Reasonably. The Design, my Lord, of the following Treatise is to shew of what use Religion may be to the advancement of Poetry. But because all that has been said concerning Regularity is so necessary a preparative to this Design, that it would be wholly useless without it, I hope your Lordship will not think it to be foreign to my purpose, if at a time when the Rules are neglected by some, and slighted by others, I bestow a little time in proving the necessity of observing those; without the strict observance of which, the following Treatise will be an empty amusement, and we must absolutely despair of making any advancement in Poetry.

The necessity of observing Rules to the attaining a perfection in Poetry is so very apparent, that he who will give himself the trouble of Reflecting, cannot easily doubt of it. Rules are necessary even in all the inferiour Arts, as in Painting and Musick. If any one should pretend to draw a Picture without having ever been taught, or without knowing or practising any thing of Perspective or Proportion, but should pretend to succeed alone by the natural force of his Fancy, that man would certainly be esteem'd a very Impudent and Impertinent person.

5. address: dexterity.

6. a Present: his *Essay on Poetry*.

Your Lordship knows that it is the very same thing in Musick that it is in Painting. If any one should pretend to compose in parts, without understanding the grounds,[7] that person would infallibly render himself very contemptible. Now if they please by Rules in a less noble Art, can they reasonably expect to please without them in one that is more noble? If they please not by Rules in Poetry, how must they please? By Chance! For this is certain, that they must do it by one or the other, for there is no third way.

There is nothing in Nature that is great and beautiful, without Rule and Order; and the more Rule and Order and Harmony we find in the objects that strike our sences, the more worthy and noble we esteem them. I humbly conceive that it is the same in Art, and particularly in Poetry, which ought to be an exact imitation of Nature. Now Nature, taken in a stricter sense, is nothing but that Rule and Order and Harmony which we find in the visible Creation. The Universe owes its admirable beauty to the Proportion, Situation and Dependance of its parts. And the little World, which we call Man, owes not only its Health and Ease and Pleasure, nay, the continuance of its very Being to the Regularity of Mechanical motion, but even the strength too of its boasted Reason, and the piercing force of those aspiring thoughts, which are able to pass the bounds that circumscribe the Universe. As Nature is Order and Rule and Harmony in the visible World, so Reason is the very same throughout the invisible Creation. For Reason is Order, and the Result of Order. And nothing that is Irregular, as far as it is Irregular, ever was or ever can be either Natural or Reasonable. Whatever God Created he designed it Regular, and as the rest of the Creatures cannot swerve in the least from the Eternal Laws pre-ordain'd for them, without becoming fearful or odious to us; so Man, whose mind is a Law to itself, can never in the least transgress that Law, without less'ning his Reason, and debasing his Nature. In fine, whatever is Irregular, either in the Visible or Invisible World, is to the person who thinks right, except in some very extraordinary cases, either Hateful or Contemptible.

But as both Nature and Reason, which two in a larger acceptation is Nature, owe their Greatness, their Beauty, their Majesty, to their perpetual Order; for Order at first made the face of things so beautiful, and the cessation of that Order would once more bring in Chaos; so Poetry, which is an imitation of Nature,

must do the same thing. It can neither have Greatness or Real Beauty, if it swerves from the Laws which Reason severely prescribes it, and the more Irregular any Poetical Composition is, the nearer it comes to extravagance and confusion, and to nonsense, which is nothing.

But, as in some of the numberless parts which constitute this beauteous all, there are some appearing irregularities, which parts notwithstanding contribute with the rest to compleat the Harmony of universal Nature; and as there are some seeming Irregularities even in the wonderful Dispensations of the Supream and Soveraign Reason, as the oppression of the good, and flourishing of the bad, which yet at the bottom are rightly adjusted, and wisely compensated, and are purposely appointed by Divine Fore-knowledge for the carrying on the profound Designs of Providence; so, if we may compare great things with small, in the Creation of an accomplish'd Poem, some things may at first sight be seemingly against Reason, which yet at the bottom are perfectly Regular, because they are indispensably necessary to the admirable conduct of a great and a just Design.

No man knows better than your Lordship, that the Renown'd Masters among the Ancients, *Homer* and *Virgil*, &c. had too much Capacity, and too much Discernment, not to see the necessity of knowing and practising the Rules which Reason and Philosophy have prescrib'd to Poets. They wrote not with a little narrow Design to please a Tumultuous transitory assembly, or a handful of men who were call'd their Countrymen; They wrote to their fellow Citizens of the Universe, to all Countries and to all Ages; and they were perfectly convinc'd that tho Caprice and Extravagance may please the multitude, who are always fluctuating, and always uncertain; yet that nothing but what is great in Reason and Nature, could be able to delight and instruct Mankind. They were clearly convinc'd that nothing could transmit their Immortal works to posterity, but something like that harmonious Order which maintains the Universe; that it was partly to that, they were to owe that wondrous merit, which could be able to render their Fame eternal, to extend and perpetuate the very languages in which they writ, and to illustrate the glory of their Countries by their own.

Your Lordship knows that it was towards the beginning of the last Century, that the *French*, a subtle and discerning Nation, began to be sensible of this, and upon it several of their extraordinary men, both Poets

---

7. the grounds: the technique of simple melodic writing.

and Philosophers, began to cultivate Criticism.[8] Upon which there follow'd two very remarkable things. For first, the cultivating of the Poetical Art advanc'd their Genius's to such a height, as was unknown to *France* before; and secondly, the appearing of those great Genius's, was very instrumental in spreading their language thro all the Christian World; and in raising the esteem of their Nation to that degree, that it naturally prepar'd the way for their Intrigues of State, and facilitated the execution of their vast Designs.

My Lord, these alterations happen'd in *France*, while the *French* reform'd the structure of their Poems, by the noble models of ancient Architects; and your Lordship knows very well, that the very contrary fell out among us; while, notwithstanding your generous attempt to reform us, we resolv'd, with an injudicious obstinacy to adhere to our *Gothick* and Barbarous manner. For in the first place, our Stage has degenerated not only from the taste of Nature, but from the greatness it had in the time of *Shakespear*, in whose *Coriolanus* and *Cassius* we see something of the Invincible Spirit of the *Romans;* but in most of our Heroes which have lately appear'd on the Stage, Love has been still the predominant passion, whether they have been *Grecian* or *Roman* Heroes; which is false in Morality, and of scandalous instruction, and as false and absurd in Physicks. For Ambition makes a man a Tyrant to himself, as well as it does to others; and where it once prevails, enslaves the Reason, and subdues all other Passions. And it was for this very cause, if your Lordship will allow me to make this digression, that in the two Tragedies that I writ my self,[9] I made Love a subordinate Passion, and subjected it in the one to Glory, and in the other to Friendship; that so I might make them fit to entertain the wisest of our Sex, and the best and most virtuous of the other. And it is impossible to tell you with what extream satisfaction I heard that the last of them was not displeasing to you.

But secondly, At the same time that the *French* has been growing almost an universal Language, the *English* has been so far from diffusing itself in so vast a manner, that I know by experience that a man may travel o'er most of these Western Parts of *Europe*, without meeting with three Foreigners, who have any tolerable knowledge of it. And yet the *English* is more strong, more full, more sounding, more significant, and more harmonious than the *French*. I know very well, that a great many will be unwilling to allow the last; but I appeal to your Lordship if this is not a convincing proof of it, that we have Blank Verse which is not inharmonious, and the *French* pretend to no Poetical Numbers, without the assistance of Rhime.[10]

But it may perhaps be alledg'd, that the reason why the *French* has got the advantage of our language, is partly from their situation on the Continent, partly from the intrigues and affairs which they have with their Neighbours, and partly because their Language has more affinity with one of the learned Languages. But to this I answer, that the *Germans* are as advantageously seated as the *French* for diffusing their Language; and the *Spanish* Tongue is rather nearer related to the *Latin* than is the *French;* and all the World knows, that towards the beginning of the last Century, the House of *Austria*, was full as busie with their Neighbours, as the House of *Bourbon* is now; and yet then neither the *German* nor the *Spanish* Tongue made any considerable progress. I will not deny, but that the situation and affairs of the *French* may have been of advantage to them in the diffusing their Language; but 'tis certainly the Learning of any Nation that is most instrumental in it. I make no doubt, but that in Learning, which is useful and necessary, and barely solid, without ornament, we far surpass the *French*. Our practical Physicians have more Reputation than theirs even in *France* itself; and our practical Divines have acquir'd more Fame, throughout the Northern Countries of *Europe*, than either the natives of those places, or any of the Modern *French* Divines, whether they are Reform'd or Papistical. And this last is therefore the more considerable, because they writ in our mother Tongue, whereas the Physicians have employed a learned Language. But I am very much inclin'd to believe, that 'tis the polite Learning of any Nation, that contributes most

8. **several . . . Criticism:** Dennis perhaps has in mind such writers as François de Malherbe (1555–1628) and Jean Chapelain (1595–1674), both partisans of a new poetic sobriety and regularity. 9. **the two . . . my self:** *Rinaldo and Armida* (1698) and *Iphigenia* (1699).

10. **the assistance . . . Rhime:** Because contemporary French versification was based primarily on the number of syllables in the line, rather than, as in most English poetry, the number of stresses (and, in the eighteenth century, the number of syllables as well), French poetic practice generally required rhyme to emphasize the prosodic unity of each line. *Harmonious* means rhythmical. *Numbers* means versification.

to the extending its Language, and Poetry is the branch of polite Learning, which is the most efficacious in it. In order to the proving this, I desire your Lordships leave, to examine who they are who are most Instrumental in making a Language pass the bounds which confine the original speakers of it. And they seem to me to be the Gentlemen of neighbouring Nations, who have time and opportunity to visit foreign Countries, and are capacitated by their Fortunes and their Educations, to cultivate Languages, which they were not born to speak. For, besides that these are the persons who are the most capacitated to learn them, they have by the variety and multiplicity of their conversation most opportunities to spread them. Now the motives that for the most part incite Gentlemen to study are two, Pleasure and Vanity. But Pleasure and Vanity will find their account abundantly more in polite Learning, than in Literature, which is barely solid. For, polite Learning is more easie, and has more of Imagination in it, and instructs them much better how to varnish their defects, and render them agreeable to one another. 'Tis chiefly then the polite Learning of any Nation that engages the Gentlemen of foreign Countries to apply themselves to study the Language of that Nation. But even of polite Learning, Poetry appears to be the most agreeable, and most attractive branch, because it is the most moving. And we find by experience, that in the Learning of those Languages which have been most generally known, Poetry has made a very considerable figure. Gentlemen then in all likelihood will apply themselves most eagerly to the study of that Language, whose Poetry is very agreeable to them. But that Poetry must be most agreeable to the generality of Gentlemen which is most moving and most instructive. For, tho Gentlemen study to please themselves, yet if they are men of sense, they will not be for empty pleasure, but will endeavour to be instructed and delighted together. Besides, when Gentlemen begin to study the Poetry of any language, the first thing they understand is the reasonable part of it. For the fineness of the Imaginative part, which depends in great measure upon force of words, and upon the beauty of expression, must lie conceal'd from them in a good degree till they are perfect in the Language. Thus the Poetry of that Language which is most reasonable and most instructive, must in all likelihood have most attraction for the Gentlemen of neighbouring Nations; and we have shewn above, that that is the most reasonable and most instructive Poetry, which is the most Regular.

My Lord, upon this foot it is easie to determine whether our Poetry or the *French* has most attractions for the rest of *Europe*. This is plain, that *Moliere*, *Corneille* and *Racine* and *Boileau* are known in a manner to all the Christian World; whereas *Spencer* and *Milton*, *Ben Johnson* and *Shakespear* are strangers as it were to all the world, excepting the Subjects of *Great Britain*. I believe that our Language, by reason of the dependance that it has upon the *Saxon*, is not very difficult to be learnt by the people of the Northern Countries; and in short, many of their Clergy have learnt enough of it, to make their advantage of our Ecclesiastical Writings. But both they and their Gentlemen are almost wholly strangers to our Poetry, whereas the *French* Poets are extremely well known to them. But here some angry people will immediately ask if I affirm that our own is inferiour to the *French* Poetry. To satisfie both them and the Truth, I am oblig'd to declare; at the same time submitting this matter to be decided by your Lordship in the last Appeal, that I believe we have naturally more force, and more elevation than the *French;* that several Things in *Shakespear* are superiour to any which the *French* Theatre has produc'd; and that in some little Poems, which either requir'd no symetry, or were writ by those who very well knew how to practise it, we are absolutely superiour to them; that at last I am not so much delivering my own thoughts, as the opinions of others; that the very Design I have even in affirming what I do, is to do what lies in my little capacity to put our Writers in a way to make our Neighbours, and with them all *Europe*, sensible of the advantage which we have by Nature; that even our natural force must receive accession from Art, and augment in proportion as the *French* has done; that both our Force and our Spirit will in all likelihood be augmented by Skill, as address in the use of our Weapons very often adds both to our Force and Courage. That a Poem with a Fable is like a Human Body, and that the weakness of any one part, influences and disables in some degree those which in themselves are strong; that if we are not shock'd at our own Irregularity, 'tis because it has the advantage of long Habitude, for we have been us'd to it from our Infancy; but that to our Neighbours, who have constantly been us'd to Art and Conduct, it must seem as awkward and as disagreeable, as our *Gothick* Cathedrals would to those *Italians* who have always frequented St *Peter's*;[11] and

11. **St Peter's:** The main architectural style of St. Peter's, built from 1450 to 1626, is Baroque.

that what I barely call Irregular here, would be term'd by them Indecent, Immoral, Unjust, Unreasonable, Unnatural. In fine, I appeal to your Lordship, whether the *French* Dramatick Writers, are not believ'd superiour to the *English* by all the rest of *Europe;* tho at the same time I am convinc'd, that our Writers having naturally more elevation, and our Language more Harmony than theirs, and both our Writers and Language more force; we want only Art to make ourselves as superiour to them in Poetry as we formerly were in Empire.

And here, my Lord, I fancy that I see the enemies to Regularity in a little confusion; they are too well satisfied of your Lordships Ability and Impartiality, to decline your Jurisdiction; and they cannot but remember to their sorrow that you have formerly given the Cause against them.

Upon supposition then that for the future they will instruct themselves in the Poetical Art; I must leave it to your Lordship to determine whether the following Treatise may be of any service to them, and give them still another advantage over the *French*, by directing them to choose, or to manage their subjects, in such a manner, as may make them most susceptible of Poetry; and that is to find, or make them Religious; a piece of Criticism, which has I know not how escap'd all the *French* Criticks.

Your Lordship knows very well that some of them, as for instance, *Boileau*, discerning the actual preheminence of the Ancients, have fondly believ'd that they were superiour to us by Nature; and that others, as *Perrault*,[12] very justly disdaining to own such a natural superiority, have very unjustly deny'd their actual preheminence. The first part of the following Treatise was intended to shew, that the Ancient Poets had that actual preheminence, but that they deriv'd it from joyning their Religion with their Poetry; upon which I believe they were thrown at first by chance. The Design of the second part is to shew, that the Moderns, by incorporating Poetry with the Religion reveal'd to us in Sacred Writ, may come to equal the Ancients. But two things must be always suppos'd:

the one, That the Poets have force and skill equal to the subjects they treat of; and a sacred subject requires ten times more of both than a prophane one. The other is, That this is not to be extended to those sorts of Poetry, in which the Moderns cannot possibly make use of their Religion, with the same advantage that the *Grecians* and *Romans* employ'd theirs, as Epic, Pastoral and Amorous Poetry.

My Lord, The ultimate end of the ensuing discourse is to shew that the intention of Poetry and the Christian Religion being alike to move the affections, they may very well be made instrumental to the advancing each other. I have reason to believe that this Design will not be unacceptable to your Lordship, not only upon the account of Religion it self, but as you are an Encourager of Arts, and a great States-man, who knows that the bare endeavour to advance an Art among us, is an effort to augment the Learning, and consequently the Reputation, and consequently the Power of a great people; that the flourishing of the establish'd Religion must have a necessary influence upon the publick Prosperity; that he who does any thing to recommend Christianity to the minds of others, endeavours to promote the common good; as on the other side, He who breaks in upon the Revelation makes a dangerous attempt not only upon the Constitution, but upon Government in general; that there never was, nor ever can be any flourishing Government without a Reveal'd Religion; that several *English-men* have lost, together with the Religion of their Ancestors, their Honour, their Integrity, and their Publick Spirit; and that open and avowed Deism has grown up among us, together with Abominable Corruptions, not only in the manners of private men, but in the administration of publick affairs.

But now, my Lord, I have been so intent upon my Cause, that it has almost made me forget, that for my having detain'd you so long, I ought to beg pardon not only of your Lordship, but of your Friends and the Publick. That by writing this I am guilty of diverting you from writing or speaking your self something which is much more Important, either at Home, or in that Illustrious Assembly, of which you are so solid and shining an Ornament. I humbly desire of your Lordship to excuse the Liberty I have taken, and to believe that I am, with the profoundest Respect, | *My Lord,* | *Your Lordship's most Oblig'd,* | *Most Humble, and* | *Most Obedient Servant,*

JOHN DENNIS.

---

12. Boileau, Perrault: Charles Perrault (1628–1703), French poet, espoused the cause of the Moderns in his poem *Siècle de Louis le Grand* (1687) and in his dialogues *Parallèles des Anciens et des Modernes* (1688–97); on the other hand, Nicolas Boileau-Despréaux (1636–1711), French critic and poet, argued for the preeminence of the Ancients in his *Art poétique* (1674), *Discours sur l'ode* (1693), and *Réflexions sur Longin* (1694).

FROM

PART I

CHAP. IV.

*That the Ancient Poets deriv'd their greatness
from the Nature of their Subjects.*

If the Ancient Poets excell'd the Moderns in the greatness of Poetry; that is, in Epick Poetry, in Tragedy, and in the greater Ode;[1] they must necessarily derive their preheminence from the Subjects of which they treated, since it has been plainly made to appear, that they could not Derive it from any External or Internal advantage. And it follows, that the Subjects which were handled by the Ancients, must be different from those which have been treated of by the Moderns. And if the Poems which have been writ by the Ancients of the forementioned kinds were very much greater than those which have been produced by the Moderns, why then it follows, that the subjects were very different. But here the Favourers of the Moderns assert, that the advantage which is to be drawn from the Subject, is purely on the side of the Moderns. For who, for Example, will compare the atchievements of *Achilles* and *Æneas*, the event of which was only the reducing two pitiful paltry Bourgs,[2] with the glorious actions of some of our Modern Captains. But then the Partizans of the Ancients reply, that there is a difference between one subject and another, which their adversaries seem not to have thought of. For, say they, humane Subjects, can never differ so much among themselves, as Sacred Subjects differ from Humane; for the difference between the Two last is as great as that between God and Man; which we know is infinite. Now, say they, sacred Subjects are infinitely more susceptible of the greatness of Poetry, than prophane ones can be. And the Subjects of the Ancients in the forementioned Poems were sacred. Now that we may engage the Lovers of the Ancients in their turns by supporting their just pretensions, let us endeavour to show in the following Chapters, that Sacred Poems must be greater than Prophane ones can be, supposing equality of Genius, and equal art in the

---

Part I. **1. the greater Ode:** the Pindaric or passionate ode, as distinguished from the more sober and restrained Horatian ode. The difference can be seen by contrasting the procedure in Dryden's *Alexander's Feast* with that in Pope's *Ode on Solitude*. (See both poems in this part.) **2. two . . . Bourgs:** Troy in the *Iliad* and Latinus's city in the *Aeneid*.

Writers, and that the Poems of the Ancients in the forementioned kinds were sacred. But in order to the doing that, we must declare what Poetry is, and what is its chief Excellence.

CHAP. V.

*That Passion is the chief thing in Poetry,
and that all Passion is either
ordinary Passion, or Enthusiasm.*

But before we proceed let us define Poetry; which is the first time that a Definition has been given of that noble Art: For neither Ancient nor Modern Cricks have defin'd Poetry in general.

Poetry then is an imitation of Nature by a pathetick and numerous[3] Speech. Let us explain it.

As Poetry is an Art, it must be an Imitation of Nature. That the instrument with which it makes its Imitation is Speech need not be disputed. That that Speech, must be Musical, no one can doubt: For Numbers distinguish the parts of Poetick Diction from the periods of Prose. Now Numbers are nothing but articulate sounds, and their pauses measur'd by their proper proportions of time. And the periods of Prosaick Diction are articulate sounds, and their pauses unmeasur'd by such proportions. That the Speech, by which Poetry makes its Imitation, must be pathetick is evident; for Passion is still more necessary to it than Harmony. For Harmony only distinguishes its Instrument from that of Prose, but Passion distinguishes its very nature and character. For therefore Poetry is Poetry, because it is more passionate and sensual than Prose. A Discourse that is writ in very good Numbers, if it wants Passion can be but measur'd Prose. But a Discourse that is every where extremely pathetick, and consequently every where bold and figurative, is certainly Poetry without Numbers.

Passion then is the Characteristical mark of Poetry, and consequently must be every where. For whereever a Discourse is not Pathetick, there it is Prosaick. As Passion in a Poem must be every where, so Harmony is usually diffus'd throughout it. But Passion answers the two ends of Poetry better than Harmony can do, and upon that account is preferable to it: For first it pleases more, which is evident: For Passion can please without Harmony, but Harmony tires without Passion. And in Tragedy and in Epick Poetry, a man may instruct without Harmony, but never

---

3. numerous: measured, rhythmical.

without Passion: For the one instructs by Admiration, and the other by Compassion and Terror. And as for the greater Ode, if it wants Passion, it becomes Hateful and Intolerable, and its Sentences grow Contemptible.

Passion is the Characteristical mark of Poetry, and therefore it must be every where; for without Passion there can be no Poetry, no more than there can be Painting. And tho the Poet and the Painter describe action, they must describe it with Passion. Let any one who beholds a piece of Painting, where the Figures are shewn in action, conclude that if the Figures are without Passion the Painting is contemptible. There must be Passion every where in Poetry and Painting, and the more Passion there is, the better the Poetry and the Painting, unless the Passion is too much for the subject; and the Painter and the Poet arrive at the height of their Art, when they describe a great deal of Action with a great deal of Passion. It is plain then from what has been said, that Passion in Poetry must be every where, for where there is no Passion there can be no Poetry, but that which we commonly call Passion, cannot be every where in any Poem. There must be Passion then, that must be distinct from ordinary Passion, and that must be Enthusiasm. I call that ordinary Passion, whose cause is clearly comprehended by him who feels it, whether it be Admiration, Terror or Joy; and I call the very same Passions Enthusiasms, when their cause is not clearly comprehended by him who feels them. And those Enthusiastick Passions are sometimes simple, and sometimes complicated, of all which we shall shew examples lower. And thus I have shewn that the chief thing in Poetry is Passion; but here the Reader is desir'd to observe, that by Poetry we mean Poetry in general, and the Body of Poetry; for as for the form or soul of particular Poems, that is allow'd by all to be a Fable. But Passion is the chief thing in the Body of Poetry, as Spirit is in the Human Body. For without Spirit the Body languishes, and the Soul is impotent: Now every thing that they call Spirit or Genius in Poetry, in short, every thing that pleases, and consequently moves in the Poetick Diction, is Passion, whether it be ordinary or Enthusiastick.

And thus we have shewn what the chief excellence in the Body of Poetry is, which we have prov'd to be Passion. Let us now proceed to the proofs of what we propounded, that sacred subjects are more susceptible of Passion than prophane ones, and that the subjects of the Ancients were sacred in their greater Poetry, I mean either sacred in their own natures, or by their manner of handling them.

CHAP. VI.

That Passion is more to be deriv'd from a Sacred Subject than from a Prophane one.

We have proved that Passion is the chief thing in Poetry, and that Spirit or Genius, and in short every thing that moves is Passion. Now if the chief thing in Poetry be Passion, why then the chief thing in great Poetry must be great Passion. We have shewn too, that Passion in Poetry, is of two sorts, ordinary Passion or Enthusiasm. Let us now proceed to convince the Reader, that a sacred Poem is more susceptible of Passion than a prophane one can be; which to effect, let us shew two things, that a sacred subject is as susceptible of ordinary passions as a prophane one can be, and more susceptible of the Enthusiastick.

The first is evident from experience: For the Poetry among the Ancients, which shall be hereafter prov'd to be sacred, had in it greater ordinary Passions, than their Human Poetry either had or could possibly have.

'Tis now our business to shew that Religious subjects are capable of supplying us with more frequent and stronger Enthusiasms than the prophane. And in order to the clearing this, let us enquire what Poetical Enthusiasm is. Poetical Enthusiasm is a Passion guided by Judgment, whose cause is not comprehended by us. That it is a Passion is plain, because it moves. That the cause is not comprehended is self-evident. That it ought to be guided by Judgment is indubitable. For otherwise it would be Madness, and not Poetical Passion. But now let us enquire what the cause of Poetical Enthusiasm is, that has been hitherto not comprehended by us. That Enthusiasm moves, is plain to sence; why then it mov'd the Writer: But if it mov'd the Writer, it mov'd him while he was thinking. Now what can move a man while he is thinking, but the thoughts that are in his Mind. In short, Enthusiasm as well as ordinary Passions, must proceed from the thoughts, as the Passions of all reasonable creatures must certainly do; but the reason why we know not the causes of Enthusiastick as well as of ordinary Passions, is because we are not so us'd to them, and because they proceed from thoughts, that latently and unobserv'd by us, carry Passion along with them. Here it would be no hard matter to prove that most of our thoughts are naturally attended with some sort and some degree of Passion. And 'tis the expression of this Passion, which gives us so much pleasure, both in Conversation and in Human Authors. For I appeal to any man who is not altogether a Philosopher, whether he is not most pleas'd with Conversation and Books that are Spirited. Now how can this Spirit please him, but because it moves him, or what can move him but Passion? We never speak for so much as a minute together without different inflexions of voice. Now any one will find upon reflection, that these variations and those inflexions mark our different passions. But all this passes unregarded by us, by reason of long use, and the incredible celerity of our thoughts, whose motion is so swift, that it is even to our selves imperceptible; unless we come to reflect, and every one will not be at the trouble of that. Now these passions, when they grow strong I call Enthusiastic motions, and the stronger they are the greater the Enthusiasm must be. If any one asks what sort of passions these are, that thus unknown to us flow from these thoughts; to him I answer, that the same sort of passions flow from the thoughts, that would do from the things of which those thoughts are Ideas. As for example, if the thing that we think of is great, why then admiration attends the Idea of it; and if it is very great, amazement. If the thing is pleasing and delightful, why then Joy and Gayety flow from the Idea of it; if it is sad, melancholy; if 'tis mischievous and powerful, then the Imagination of it is attended with Terror; And if 'tis both great and likely to do hurt and powerful, why then the thought of it is at once accompanied with Wonder, Terror and Astonishment. Add to all this, that the mind producing these thoughts, conceives by reflection a certain Pride, and Joy and Admiration, as at the conscious view of its own excellence. Now he who strictly examines the Enthusiasm that is to be met with in the greater Poetry, will find that it is nothing but the fore-mention'd passions, either simple or complicated, proceeding from the thoughts from which they naturally flow, as being the thoughts or Images of things that carry those passions along with them, as we shall shew by examples in the following Chapter.

But these passions that attend upon our thoughts are seldom so strong, as they are in those kind of thoughts which we call Images. For they being the very lively pictures of the things which they represent, set them, as it were, before our very eyes. But Images are never so admirably drawn, as when they are drawn in motion; especially if the motion is violent. For the mind can never imagine violent motion, without being in a violent agitation it self; and the Imagination being fir'd with that Agitation, sets the very things before our eyes; and consequently makes us have the same passions that we should have from the things themselves. For the warmer the Imagination is, the more present the things are to us, of which we draw the Images, and therefore when once the Imagination is so inflam'd as to get the better of the understanding, there is no difference between the Images and the things themselves; as we see, for example, in Fevers and Mad men.

Thus have we shewn that Enthusiasm flows from the thoughts, and consequently from the subject from which the thoughts proceed. For, as the Spirit in Poetry is to be proportion'd to the Thought, for otherwise it does not naturally flow from it, and consequently is not guided by Judgment; so the Thought is to be proportion'd to the Subject. Now no Subject is so capable of supplying us with thoughts, that necessarily produce these great and strong Enthusiasms, as a Religious Subject: For all which is great in Religion is most exalted and amazing, all that is joyful is transporting, all that is sad is dismal, and all that is terrible is astonishing.

Joseph Butler

1692–1752

Joseph Butler was born on May 29, 1692, at Wantage, Berkshire, the son of a well-to-do retired draper. He was sent to a dissenting academy conducted by Samuel Jones at Gloucester and later at Tewkesbury with the object of preparing him for the Presbyterian ministry. While there he made friends with Thomas Secker, a school-mate, who was to become Archbishop of Canterbury, and precociously began a correspondence with the eminent philosopher-theologian Samuel Clarke. In 1715, having abandoned Presbyterianism in favor of the Anglican Establishment, Butler entered Oriel College, Oxford, where, though he was disgusted with the intellectual bill of fare and meditated a transfer to Cambridge, he nevertheless remained to take his bachelor's degree in 1718. That year he was ordained deacon and priest and appointed preacher at Rolls Chapel, where he delivered the sermons for which, along with his later *Analogy of Religion* (1736), he is best known. *Fifteen Sermons Preached at the Rolls Chapel* was first published in 1726 and was followed by a second edition in 1729, with a substantial preface summarizing his philosophy.

At Oxford, Butler became a close friend of Edward Talbot, a fellow undergraduate, whose father was William Talbot, Bishop of Salisbury, and whose elder brother Charles was to rise to be Lord Chancellor. Through these connections Butler was assisted in his clerical progress, becoming Prebendary of Salisbury in 1721, Rector of Haughton le Skerne in 1722, Rector of Stanhope in 1725, Chaplain to Lord Chancellor Talbot in 1733, and Clerk of the Closet to Queen Caroline and Prebendary of Rochester in 1736. Butler became a particular favorite of the Queen, who welcomed his leadership in the philosophical "discussion groups" to which she was devoted, and his preferment is said to have been her main concern as she lay dying.

In the year following her death, 1738, Butler was raised to the bishopric of Bristol, an eminence that lacked the revenues necessary to support its attendant expenditures, but the situation was eased two years later when the new bishop was also made Dean of St. Paul's. Butler's conception of the use of riches appears wholly in keeping with the character of a moralist: he used his wealth to repair the decays of architecture and the fortunes of the poor.

In 1747 Butler reportedly declined the office of Archbishop of Canterbury, saying that "it was too late for him to try to support a falling Church." While probably not true, the story at least reflects the disillusionment that was part of his character and a strain in his writings. In 1750, however, after clearing the advancement of simoniacal strings, he was translated to the bishopric of Durham. But he did not have long to live. On June 27, 1752, at Bath, where he had gone to restore his failing health, he died. He was buried in Bristol Cathedral.

Butler's theological and moral writings were aimed at saving God from the atheists and even deists, and man from the skeptical philosophers. He did not overlook the forcible evidences of natural and moral evil in the world but sought to accommodate them to a firm belief in God's love and man's virtue. To Butler, human nature was analogous to a constitutional government of separate but related branches, the whole regulated by a hierarchical order of authorities. "Every work both of nature and art is a system," he writes in the Preface to his *Fifteen Sermons*—and human nature is no exception. It is made up of "appetites, passions, affections," none of which is without benefit, and all of which tend either to the good of the individual or to the good of the community. In addition, there are regulative principles—self-love, benevolence, and conscience—that balance the rival claims of the appetites, passions, and affections, and, indeed, of each other, for the most harmonious functioning of the system. Butler's self-love is not the radical selfishness propounded by the skeptics, but a calm, cool, calculating regard for one's true interests and what will be one's greatest happiness in the long run. Self-love regulates that group of passions that tend to the private good. In the same way, benevolence directs those passions that tend to the public good (though Butler commonly treats benevolence as itself one of the elemental passions). Self-love and benevolence are not diametrically opposed, as we might be led to think. They seem so because we commonly tend to identify selfishness or interestedness only with self-oriented thoughts and actions and to judge them immoral. According to Butler, "Every action of every creature must, from the nature of the thing," be selfish or interested, and this is no less true of benevolent than of self-regarding actions. In addition, the proper basis of moral evaluation is what is becoming to the agent or fitting to the circumstances. To make his point, Butler appeals to our experience: Do we not in fact "judge and determine that an action is morally good or evil before we so much as consider whether it be interested or disinterested"?

Occupying the place of supreme authority in the system of human nature is conscience, which by virtue of its capacity to approve, disapprove, and direct the passions is "manifestly superior" to them. Butler is careful, however, to distinguish between power and authority; he recognizes that the strength of a passion may overcome that conscientious reflection which would restrain it. But his concern is to define what is natural to man not in terms of any and every natural impulse, or of any strong or ruling passion, but of the whole constitution, in which conscience enjoys a *de jure*—Butler insists on calling it "natural"—if not *de facto* supremacy. A human being cannot ultimately "be said to act conformably to his constitution of nature unless he allows to that superior principle the absolute authority which is due to it."

That superior principle, interestingly enough, turns up elsewhere, sharing authority. Just as Butler tends to subordinate benevolence to self-love as a regulating principle, so he tends to elevate self-love to equal status with conscience. The end of Sermon iii asserts that

reasonable Self-love and Conscience are the chief or superiour Principles in the Nature of Man: Because an Action may be suitable to this Nature, though all other Principles be violated; but becomes unsuitable, if either of those are. Conscience and Self-love, if we understand our true Happiness, always lead us the same Way. Duty and Interest are perfectly coincident; for the most Part in this World, but intirely and in every Instance if we take in the future, and the whole; this being implied in the Notion of a good and perfect Administration of things.

In short, the system that is human nature cannot, in Butler's view, be considered apart from the system that is God's providence; and as the conception of self-love is enlarged to encompass man's ultimate happiness, it inevitably takes its place alongside the divine principle of conscience.

The unquestioned religious assumptions that so transparently guide Butler's moral philosophy make him vulnerable to rigorous philosophical analysis; yet he manages to speak powerfully even to his critics. Leslie Stephen, a notable case in point, gives Butler little respite from the tests of logic, but is still able to conclude that

> with all his faults, Butler remains, in a practical sense, the deepest moralist of the century. He alone refuses to shut his eyes with the optimistic theists to the dark side of the world, and yet does not, with their opponents, implicitly deny the existence of virtue. . . . Butler's language, regarded as the utterance of a deep conviction of the unspeakable importance of our moral instincts, conveyed a profound rebuke to his age. . . . Theology, in him, seems to utter an expiring protest against the meanness and the flimsiness of the rival theories by which men attempted to replace it.

Butler's writings have been collected and edited by J. H. Bernard, *The Works of Joseph Butler* (2 vols., 1900). An edition by S. M. Brown, Jr., of *Five Sermons Preached at the Rolls Chapel and a Dissertation upon the Nature of Virtue* (1950) is available in the Library of Liberal Arts Series. Butler appears of course in numerous books on ethics, notably in C. D. Broad's *Five Types of Ethical Theory* (1930; often reprinted). A full-scale philosophical analysis is Austin Duncan-Jones's *Butler's Moral Philosophy* (1952). *The Analogy of Religion* and the *Sermons* are discussed at some length (but separately) in Leslie Stephen's *History of English Thought in the Eighteenth Century* (1876). There is also a general study, *Bishop Butler and the Age of Reason* (1936), by E. C. Mossner.

SERMON V

Upon Compassion.

❧❧❧

The text is that of the first edition (1726), with substantive revisions from the second edition (1729).

❧❧❧

ROM. xii. 15.

Rejoyce with them that do rejoyce, and weep with them that weep.

EVERY Man is to be considered in two Capacities, the Private and Publick; as designed to pursue his own Interest, and likewise to contribute to the Good of others. Whoever will consider, may see, that in general there is no Contrariety[1] between these; but that from the original Constitution of Man, and the Circumstances he is placed in, they perfectly coincide, and mutually carry on each other. But amongst the great Variety of Affections[2] or Principles of Action in our Nature, some in their primary Intention and Design seem to belong to the single or private, others to the publick or social Capacity. The Affections required in the Text are of the latter Sort. When we rejoyce in the Prosperity of others, and compassionate their Distresses, we, as it were, substitute them for ourselves, their Interest for our own; and have the same Kind of Pleasure in their Prosperity and Sorrow in their Distress, as we have from Reflection upon our own. Now there is nothing strange or unaccountable in our being thus carried out, and affected towards the Interests of others. For if there be any Appetite, or any inward Principle besides Self-love; why may there not be an Affection to the Good of our Fellow-creatures, and Delight from that Affection's being gratified, and Uneasiness from things going contrary to it[3]?

SERMON V. **1 Contrariety:** opposition, inconsistency. **2. Affections:** passions. **3. why . . . it:** [Butler's note] There being manifestly this Appearance of Men's substituting others for themselves, and being carried out and affected towards them as towards themselves; some Persons, who have a System which excludes every Affection of this Sort, have taken a pleasant Method to solve it; and tell you it is *not another* you are at all concerned about, but your *self only*, when you feel the Affection called Compassion. *i.e.* Here is a

Of these two, Delight in the Prosperity of others and Compassion for their Distresses, the last is felt much more generally than the former. Though Men do not universally rejoyce with all whom they see rejoyce, yet accidental Obstacles removed, they naturally compassionate all in some Degree whom

plain Matter of Fact, which Men cannot reconcile with the general Account they think fit to give of things: They therefore, instead of *that* manifest Fact, substitute *another*, which is reconcileable to their own Scheme. For does not every Body by Compassion mean, an Affection the Object of which is Another in Distress? Instead of this, but designing to have it mistaken for this, they speak of an Affection or Passion, the Object of which is our selves, or Danger to ourselves. *Hobbs* defines *Pity, Imagination, or Fiction of future Calamity to ourselves, proceeding from the Sense* (he means Sight or Knowledge) *of another Man's Calamity.* Thus Fear and Compassion would be the same Idea, and a fearful and a compassionate Man the same Character, which every one immediately sees are totally different. Further, to those who give any Scope to their Affections, there is no Perception or inward Feeling more universal than this; that one who has been merciful and compassionate throughout the Course of his Behaviour, should himself be treated with Kindness, if he happens to fall into Circumstances of Distress. Is Fear then or Cowardice so great a Recommendation to the Favour of the Bulk of Mankind? Or is it not plain, that meer Fearlessness (and therefore not the contrary) is one of the most popular Qualifications? This shews that Mankind are not affected towards Compassion as Fear, but as somewhat totally different.

Nothing would more expose such Accounts as these of the Affections which are favourable and friendly to our Fellow-creatures, than to substitute the Definitions which this Author, and others who follow his Steps, give of such Affections, instead of the Words by which they are commonly expressed. *Hobbs*, after having laid down that Pity or Compassion is only Fear for ourselves, goes on to explain the Reason, why we pity our Friends in Distress more than others. Now substitute the *Definition* instead of the Word *Pity* in this Place, and the Inquiry will be, why we fear our Friends, *&c.* which Words (since he really does not mean why we are afraid of them) make no Question or Sentence at all. So that common Language, the Words *to Compassionate, to Pity*, cannot be accommodated to his Account of Compassion. The very joining of the Words *to Pity our Friends*, is a direct Contradiction to his Definition of Pity: Because those Words so joined, necessarily express that our Friends are the Objects of the Passion; whereas his Definition of it asserts, that ourselves, or Danger to ourselves are the only Objects of it. He might indeed have avoided this Absurdity by plainly saying what he is going to account for; namely, why the Sight of the Innocent, or of our Friends in Distress, raises greater Fear for ourselves than the Sight of other Persons in Distress. But had he put the thing thus plainly, the Fact itself would have been doubted; that *the Sight of our Friends in Distress raises in us greater Fear for ourselves, than the Sight of others in Distress.* And in the next Place it would immediately have occurred to

they see in Distress, so far as they have any real Perception or Sense of that Distress: Insomuch that Words expressing this latter, Pity, Compassion, frequently occur; whereas we have scarce any single one by which the former is distinctly express'd.

every one, that the Fact now mentioned, which at least is *doubtful*, whether true or false, was not the same with this Fact, which no-body ever doubted, that *the Sight of our Friends in Distress raises in us greater Compassion than the Sight of others in Distress*: Every one, I say, would have seen that these are not the *same*, but *two different* Inquiries; and consequently, that Fear and Compassion are not the same. Suppose a Person to be in real Danger, and by some Means or other to have forgot it; any trifling Accident, any Sound might alarm him, recall the Danger to his Remembrance, and renew his Fear: But it is almost too grossly ridiculous (though it is to show an Absurdity) to speak of that Sound or Accident as an Object of Compassion; and yet according to Mr. *Hobbs*, our greatest Friend in Distress is no more to us, no more the Object of Compassion or of any Affection in our Heart. Neither the one nor the other raises any Emotion in our Mind, but only the Thoughts of our liableness to Calamity, and the Fear of it; and both equally do this. It is fit such sort of Accounts of Humane Nature should be shown to be what they really are, because there is raised upon them a general Scheme which undermines the whole Foundation of common Justice and Honesty. See *Hobbs of Hum. Nat. c.9. §10.*

There are often three distinct Perceptions or inward Feelings upon Sight of Persons in Distress: Real Sorrow and Concern for the Misery of our Fellow-creatures; some Degree of Satisfaction from a Consciousness of our Freedom from that Misery; and as the Mind passes on from one thing to another, it is not unnatural from such an Occasion to reflect upon our own Liableness to the same or other Calamities. The two last frequently accompany the first, but it is the first *only* which is properly Compassion, of which the Distressed are the Objects, and which directly carries us with Calmness and Thought to their Assistance. Any one of these, from various and complicated Reasons, may in particular Cases prevail over the other two; and there are, I suppose, Instances where the bare *Sight* of Distress, without our feeling any Compassion for it, may be the Occasion of either or both of the two latter Perceptions. One might add, that if there be really any such thing as the Fiction or Imagination of Danger to ourselves from Sight of the Miseries of others, which *Hobbs* speaks of, and which he has absurdly mistaken for the whole of Compassion; if there be any thing of this Sort common to Mankind, distinct from the Reflection of Reason, it would be a most remarkable Instance of what was furthest from his Thoughts, namely, of a mutual Sympathy between each Particular of the Species, a Fellow-feeling common to Mankind. It would not indeed be an Example of our substituting others for ourselves, but it would be an Example of our substituting ourselves for others. And as it would not be an Instance of Benevolence, so neither would it be any Instance of Self-love; for this Phantom of Danger to ourselves naturally rising to View upon Sight of the Distresses of others, would be no more an Instance of Love to ourselves, than the Pain of Hunger is.

Congratulation indeed answers[4] Condoleance; but both these Words are intended to signify certain Forms of Civility, rather than any inward Sensation or Feeling. This Difference or Inequality is so remarkable, that we plainly consider Compassion as itself an original, distinct, particular Affection in Humane Nature; whereas to rejoyce in the Good of others, is only a Consequence of the general Affection of Love and Good-will to them. The Reason and Account of which Matter is this. When a Man has obtained any particular Advantage or Felicity, his End is gained, and he does not in that particular want[5] the Assistance of another; there was therefore no need of a distinct Affection towards that Felicity of another already obtained, neither would such Affection directly carry him on to do Good to that Person: Whereas Men in Distress want Assistance, and Compassion leads us directly to assist them. The Object of the former is the present Felicity of another; the Object of the latter is the present Misery of another: It is easy to see that the latter wants a particular Affection for its Relief, and that the former does not want one, because it does not want Assistance. And upon Supposition of a distinct Affection in both Cases, the one must rest in the Exercise of itself, having nothing further to gain; the other does not rest in itself, but carries us on to assist the Distressed.

But supposing these Affections natural to the Mind, particularly the last; Has not each Man Troubles enough of his own? Must he indulge an Affection which appropriates to himself those of others? Which leads him to contract the least desirable of all Friendships, Friendships with the Unfortunate? Must we invert the known Rule of Prudence, and choose to associate ourselves with the Distressed? Or allowing that we ought, so far as it is in our Power, to relieve Them; yet is it not better to do this from Reason and Duty? Does not Passion and Affection of every Kind perpetually mislead us? Nay, is not Passion and Affection itself a Weakness, and what a perfect Being must be entirely free from? Perhaps so: But it is Mankind I am speaking of; imperfect Creatures, and who naturally and, from the Condition we are placed in, necessarily depend upon each other. With respect to such Creatures, it would be found of as bad Consequence to eradicate all natural Affections, as to be intirely governed by them. This would almost sink us to the Condition of Brutes, and That would leave us

---

4. answers: corresponds to. **5. want:** need.

without a sufficient Principle of Action. Reason alone, whatever any one may wish, is not in Reality a sufficient Motive of Virtue in such a Creature as Man; but this Reason joined with those Affections which God has impress'd upon his Heart: And when these are allowed Scope to exercise themselves, but under strict Government and Direction of Reason, then it is we act suitably to our Nature, and to the Circumstances God has placed us in. Neither is Affection itself at all a Weakness, nor does it argue Defect, any otherwise than as our Senses and Appetites do: They belong to our Condition of Nature, and are what we cannot be without. God Almighty is to be sure unmoved by Passion or Appetite, unchanged by Affection; but then it is to be added, that he neither sees, nor hears, nor perceives things by any Senses like ours, but in a Manner infinitely more perfect. Now as it is an Absurdity almost too gross to be mentioned, for a Man to endeavour to get rid of his Senses, because the supream Being discerns things more perfectly without them; it is as real, though not so obvious an Absurdity, to endeavour to eradicate the Passions he has given us, because He is without them. For since our Passions are as really a Part of our Constitution as our Senses; since the former as really belong to our Condition of Nature as the latter; to get rid of either, is equally a Violation of and breaking in upon that Nature and Constitution he has given us. Both our Senses and our Passions are a Supply[6] to the Imperfection of our Nature: Thus they shew that we are such sort of Creatures, as to stand in need of those Helps which higher Orders of Creatures do not. But it is not the Supply, but the Deficiency; as it is not a Remedy, but a Disease, which is the Imperfection. However, our Appetites, Passions, Senses, no way imply Disease; nor indeed do they imply Deficiency or Imperfection of any sort, but only this, that the Constitution of Nature according to which God has made us is such as to require them. And it is so far from being true, that a wise Man must intirely suppress Compassion, and all Fellow-feeling for others, as a Weakness; and trust to Reason alone, to teach and enforce upon him the Practice of the several Charities we owe to our Kind; that on the contrary, even the bare Exercise of such Affections would itself be for the Good and Happiness of the World; and the Imperfection of the higher Principles of Reason and Religion in Man, the little Influence they have upon our Practice, and the Strength and Prevalency of contrary ones, plainly require these Affections to be a Restraint upon these latter, and a Supply to the Deficiencies of the former.

First, The very Exercise itself of these Affections, in a just and reasonable Manner and Degree, would upon the whole increase the Satisfactions, and lessen the Miseries of Life. It is the Tendency and Business of Virtue and Religion to procure, as much as may be, universal Good-will, Trust and Friendship amongst Mankind. If this could be brought to obtain,[7] and each Man enjoyed the Happiness of others, as every one does that of a Friend, and looked upon the Success and Prosperity of his Neighbour as every one does upon that of his Children and Family; it is too manifest to be insisted upon how much the Enjoyments of Life would be increased. There would be so much Happiness introduced into the World, without any Deduction or Inconvenience from it, in proportion as the Precept of *rejoycing with those who rejoyce* was universally obeyed. Our Saviour has owned this good Affection as belonging to our Nature, in the Parable of the *lost Sheep;*[8] and does not think it to the Disadvantage of a perfect State, to represent its Happiness as capable of Increase from Reflection upon that of others.

But since in such a Creature as Man, Compassion or Sorrow for the Distress of others, seems necessarily connected with Joy in their Prosperity, as that whoever rejoyces in one must unavoidably compassionate the other; there cannot be that Delight or Satisfaction which appears to be so considerable, without the Inconveniencies, whatever they are, of Compassion.

However, without considering this Connection, there is no doubt but that more Good than Evil, more Delight than Sorrow, arises from Compassion itself; there being so many things which ballance the Sorrow of it. There is first the Relief which the distressed feel from this Affection in others towards them. There is likewise the Additional Misery which they would feel from the Reflection that no one commiserated their Case. It is indeed true, that any Disposition,[9] prevailing beyond a certain Degree, becomes somewhat wrong; and we have ways of speaking, which though they do not directly express that Excess, yet always lead our Thoughts to it, and give us the Notion of it. Thus when mention is made of Delight in being pitied, this always

---

6. **Supply:** support.   7. **obtain:** prevail. 8. **the Parable . . . Sheep:** See Matt. 18:11-14. 9. **Disposition:** emotional tendency.

conveys to our Mind the Notion of somewhat[10] which is really a Weakness: The Manner of speaking, I say, implies a certain Weakness and Feebleness of Mind, which is and ought to be disapproved. But Men of the greatest Fortitude would in Distress feel Uneasiness, from knowing that no Person in the World had any sort of Compassion or real Concern for them; and in some Cases, especially when the Temper is enfeebled by Sickness or any long and great Distress, doubtless would feel a kind of Relief even from the helpless Good-will and ineffectual Assistances of those about them. Over against the Sorrow of Compassion is likewise to be set a peculiar calm Kind of Satisfaction, which accompanies it, unless in Cases where the Distress of Another is by some means so brought home to Ourselves, as to become in a manner our own; or when from Weakness of Mind the Affection rises too high, which ought to be corrected. This Tranquillity or calm Satisfaction proceeds, partly from Consciousness of a right Affection and Temper of Mind, and partly from a Sense of our own Freedom from the Misery we compassionate. This last may possibly appear to some at first sight faulty, but it really is not so. It is the same with that positive Enjoyment, which sudden Ease from Pain for the present affords, arising from a real Sense of Misery, joined with a Sense of our Freedom from it; which in all cases must afford some Degree of Satisfaction.

To these things must be added, the Observation, which respects both the Affections we are considering; that they who have got over all Fellow-feeling for others, have withal[11] contracted a certain Callousness of Heart, which renders them insensible to most other Satisfactions, but those of the grossest kind.

Secondly, Without the Exercise of these Affections, Men would certainly be much more wanting in the Offices of Charity they owe to each other, and likewise more cruel and injurious, than they are at present. The private Interest of the Individual would not be sufficiently provided for by reasonable and cool Self-Love alone; therefore the Appetites and Passions, are placed within as a Guard and further Security, without which it would not be taken due Care of. It is manifest our Life would be neglected, were it not for the Calls of Hunger, and Thirst, and Weariness; notwithstanding that without them Reason would assure us, that the Recruits[12] of Food and Sleep are the necessary

means of our Preservation. It is therefore absurd to imagine, that without Affection, the same Reason alone would be more effectual to engage us to perform the Duties we owe to our Fellow-Creatures. One of this Make would be as defective, as much wanting, considered with respect to Society; as one of the former Make would be defective, or wanting, considered as an Individual, or in his private Capacity. Is it possible any can in earnest think, that a Publick Spirit, *i.e.* a settled reasonable Principle of Benevolence to Mankind, is so prevalent and strong in the Species, as that we may venture to throw off the under Affections, which are its Assistants, carry it forward and mark out particular Courses for it; Family, Friends, Neighbourhood, the Distressed, our Country? The common Joys and the common Sorrows, which belong to these Relations and Circumstances, are as plainly useful to Society; as the Pain and Pleasure belonging to Hunger, Thirst, and Weariness, are of Service to the Individual. In Defect of that higher Principle of Reason, Compassion is often the only Way by which the Indigent can have access to us: And therefore to eradicate this, though it is not indeed formally to deny them that Assistance which is their Due, yet it is to cut them off from that which is too frequently their only way of obtaining it. And as for those who have shut up this Door against the Complaints of the Miserable, and conquered this Affection in themselves; even these Persons will be under great Restraints from the same Affection in others. Thus a Man who has himself no Sense of Injustice, Cruelty, Oppression, will be kept from running the utmost Lengths of Wickedness, by fear of that Detestation, and even Resentment of Inhumanity, in many particular Instances of it, which Compassion for the Object, towards whom such Inhumanity is exercised, excites in the Bulk of Mankind. And this is frequently the chief Danger, and the chief Restraint which Tyrants and the great Oppressours of the World feel.

In general, Experience will shew, that as want of natural Appetite to Food supposes and proceeds from some bodily Disease; so the Apathy[13] the Stoicks talk of as much supposes or is accompanied with somewhat amiss in the Moral Character, in that which is the

---

10. **somewhat:** something. 11. **withal:** at the same time. 12. **Recruits:** replenishments.

13. **Apathy:** freedom from the influence of emotion. The ancient Stoic Zeno and his followers held that a man's best hope of making sound moral judgments lay in his achieving this calm indifference to the claims of personal feeling. Cf. Pope's *Essay on Man*, ii. 91–94, later in Part Two.

Health of the Mind. Those who formerly aimed at this, upon the Foot[14] of Philosophy, appear to have had better Success in eradicating the Affections of Tenderness and Compassion, than they had with the Passions of Envy, Pride, and Resentment; these latter at best were but concealed, and that imperfectly too. How far this Observation may be extended to such as endeavour to suppress the natural Impulses of their Affections, in order to form themselves for Business and the World, I shall not determine. But there does not appear any Capacity or Relation to be named, in which Men ought to be entirely deaf to the Calls of Affection, unless the judicial one is to be excepted.

And as to those who are commonly called the Men of Pleasure, it is manifest that the Reason they set up for[15] Hardness of Heart, is to avoid being interrupted in their Course, by the Ruin and Misery they are the Authors of: Neither are Persons of this Character always the most free from the Impotencies of Envy and Resentment. What may Men at last bring themselves to, by suppressing their Passions and Affections of one Kind, and leaving those of the other in their full Strength? But surely it might be expected, that Persons who make Pleasure their Study and their Business, if they understood what they profess, would reflect, how many of the Entertainments of Life, how many of those Kind of Amusements which seem peculiarly to belong to Men of Leisure and Education, they become insensible to by this acquired Hardness of Heart.

I shall close these Reflections with barely mentioning the Behaviour of that Divine Person, who was the Example of all Perfection in Human Nature, as represented in the Gospels mourning, and even, in a litteral Sense, weeping[16] over the Distresses of his Creatures.

The Observation already made, that of the two Affections mentioned in the Text, the latter exerts itself much more than the former; that from the Original Constitution of Human Nature we much more generally and sensibly[17] compassionate the Distressed, than rejoice with the Prosperous, requires to be particularly considered: This Observation therefore, with the Reflections which arise out of it, and which it leads our Thoughts to, shall be the Subject of another Discourse.[18]

For the Conclusion of This, let me just take Notice of the Danger of over-great Refinements, of going besides or beyond the plain obvious first Appearances of Things, upon the Subject of Morals and Religion. The least Observation will show, how little the Generality of Men are capable of Speculations. Therefore Morality and Religion must be somewhat plain and easy to be understood; it must appeal to what we call plain common Sense, as distinguished from superiour Capacity and Improvement; because it appeals to Mankind. Persons of superior Capacity and Improvement have often fallen into Errors, which no one of meer common Understanding could. Is it possible that one of this latter Character could ever of himself have thought, that there was absolutely no such thing in Mankind as Affection to the Good of others; suppose of Parents to their Children, or that what he felt upon seeing a Friend in Distress, was only Fear for himself; or upon Supposition of the Affections of Kindness and Compassion, that it was the Business of Wisdom and Virtue to set him about extirpating them as fast as he could? And yet each of these manifest Contradictions to Nature has been laid down by Men of Speculation,[19] as a Discovery in Moral Philosophy, which they, it seems, have found out through all the specious Appearances to the contrary. This Reflection may be extended further. The Extravagancies of Enthusiasm[20] and Superstition do not at all lie in the Road of common Sense; and therefore, so far as they are *original Mistakes*, must be owing to going beside or beyond it. Now since Inquiry and Examination can relate only to Things so obscure and uncertain as to stand in need of it, and to Persons who are capable of it; the proper Advice to be given to plain honest Men, to secure them from the Extreams both of Superstition and Irreligion, is that of the Son of *Sirach: In every good Work trust thy own Soul; for this is the keeping of the Commandment.*[21]

---

14. **Foot:** basis. 15. **set up for:** lay claim to. 16. **weeping:** John 11:33–38. 17. **sensibly:** with keen feeling.

18. **another Discourse:** Sermon vi of the *Fifteen Sermons* (1726). 19. **Men of Speculation:** the ancient Stoics and Thomas Hobbes, for example. 20. **Enthusiasm:** religious delusion; specifically, the conviction that one's insights are communicated directly from God. (See the chapter on enthusiasm from Locke's *Essay Concerning Humane Understanding* in Part One.) 21. **In . . . Commandment:** See Ecclus. 32:23.

William Law

⁂⁂⁂⁂⁂⁂⁂⁂⁂⁂⁂⁂⁂⁂⁂⁂

1686–1761

William Law was born in 1686 at King's Cliffe, a village in Northamptonshire, the son of a grocer and chandler. In 1705 he entered Emmanuel College, Cambridge, where he took his bachelor's degree in 1708, was ordained, and became a Fellow in 1711. With the accession of George I, oaths of allegiance to the new monarch and abjuration of the Pretender were imposed; Law refused to take them and resigned his fellowship in 1716. The following year he launched his career as a religious and moral controversialist. His *Three Letters* to Benjamin Hoadly, Bishop of Bangor (1717–19), were a major rebuttal to Hoadly's sermon denying that the Church had received the authority of Christ. *Remarks upon the Fable of the Bees* (1724) was perhaps the ablest answer to Mandeville's thesis of "private vices" and "public benefits." And *The Absolute Unlawfulness of the Stage-Entertainment Fully Demonstrated* (1726) can claim the distinction of having out-Colliered Collier.

If these works helped make a name for this Nonjuring High-Churchman and High-flying Tory, they did not make him a living. Disqualified from an official place in Church or state, he took shelter in a domestic establishment. In 1723 Law joined the Gibbon household at Putney as tutor to the father of the historian, becoming, as Gibbon states in his *Autobiography*, "the much-honored friend and spiritual director of the whole family." He accompanied the apparently undistinguished young man to his old college, Emmanuel, but not, for some reason, on his Grand Tour. Law remained with the family at Putney, where he was visited by the poet John Byrom, whose journal preserves some valuable Lawiana, and by the Wesleys, whose religious development he greatly influenced. John Wesley wrote in his journal:

> But meeting now with Mr. Law's "Christian Perfection" [1726] and "Serious Call" [1729], (although I was much offended at many parts of both, yet) they convinced me more than ever of the exceeding height, and breadth, and depth of the law of God. The light flowed in so mightily upon my soul, that every thing appeared in a new view.

Wesley first visited the oracle at Putney in 1732; six years later he abandoned Law for a newer light.

Some time around his fiftieth year Law himself fell under the influence of a new spiritual mentor, Jakob Böhme, and thereafter his religious thinking took a decidedly mystical direction, leaving behind the claims of institutional orthodoxy. The following passages from *The Spirit of Love* (1752, 1754) will perhaps give some idea of Law's highly developed other-worldliness:

> There is and can be but *one true* Religion for the fallen Soul, and that is, the Dying to *Self*, to *Nature* and *Creature;* and a turning with all the *Will*, the *Desire*, and *Delight* of the Soul to God. . . . religious Practices are then only parts of true Religion, when they mean nothing, seek nothing, but to keep up a continual Dying to Self, and all worldly things, and turn all the Will, Desire, and Delight of the Soul to God alone. . . . the Regeneration, or new Birth of his first angelic Life, is the one only Salvation of the fallen Soul. Ask not therefore, whether we are saved by Faith, or by Works? for we are saved by neither of them. Faith and Works are at first only *preparatory* to the new Birth; afterwards they are the true *genuine Fruits* and Effects of it. But the new Birth, a Life from Heaven, the new Creature, called *Christ in us*, is the one only Salvation of the fallen Soul. Nothing can enter into Heaven, but this life which is born of and comes from Heaven.

By 1737 the Gibbon family had scattered; in 1740 Law retired to King's Cliffe, where he was joined by a well-to-do widow, Mrs. Hutcheson, and Gibbon's maiden aunt, Hester Gibbon (whom tradition has identified with the Miranda of the *Serious Call*), the three of them dedicated to practicing what he preached: religious devotions and charitable dispensations. In 1729 Law had founded a school for girls at King's Cliffe; in 1745 Mrs. Hutcheson returned the compliment by founding one for boys. The two women, said to have been imperfectly devoted to each other, were united in their allegiance to their master. They remained with him until his death in 1761, and Miss Gibbon served as executrix of his will and trustee of his estate.

There is no scholarly edition of Law's writings. G. B. Moreton's edition of the *Works* (privately printed in 9 vols., 1892–93) is a reprint of the edition brought out just after Law's death by J. Richardson (9 vols., 1762). A selection of Law's works has been edited by Stephen Hobhouse under the title *Selected Mystical Writings of William Law* (2nd ed., 1948). The main biographical and critical studies are: J. H. Overton's *William Law, Nonjuror and Mystic* (1881), Stephen Hobhouse's *William Law and Eighteenth-Century Quakerism* (1927), A. W. Hopkinson's *About William Law* (1948), and Henri Talon's *William Law: A Study in Literary Craftsmanship* (1948).

FROM

A SERIOUS CALL TO
A DEVOUT AND HOLY LIFE

William Law was what philosophers call an ethical rigorist. Although he allowed that man is obligated to do no more than his best, that best was generally conceived as no less than perfection. For Law moral relativism was the beginning of complacency and the downward path. His was a doctrine for saints, and even Wesley turned against it, writing to his mentor in 1738: "For two years I have been preaching after the model of your two practical treatises, and all that heard have allowed, that the law is great, wonderful, and holy. But no longer did they attempt to fulfill it, but they found that it is too high for man." If Law's law was too high for the followers of Wesley, and perhaps Wesley himself, it is not surprising that it rubbed Boswell the wrong way:

I began today [December 8, 1793] to read what it is strange I should not have read before, Law's *Serious Call to a devout and holy life*, the book which I have mentioned as having made Dr. Johnson first think earnestly of Religion after his childhood. I wondered at his approbation of it; for though there is not a little vivacity in it, and many characters very well imagined, the scope of it is to make a Religious Life inconsistent with all the feelings and views which animate this state of being, and in short to make us Asceticks upon the Monastick plan. It had a dreary influence on my mind, at present disposed to be gloomy. My son James, to whom I read some of it, very sensibly observed, "Such books do a great deal of harm." I resolved however to read it through.

Johnson, however, heartily approved Law's work. In his *Life of Johnson* Boswell recalls Johnson's saying that he first took up the *Serious Call* at Oxford, "expecting to find it a dull book, (as such books generally are,) and perhaps to laugh at it. But I found Law quite an overmatch for me; and this was the first occasion of my thinking in earnest of religion, after I became capable of rational inquiry."

Gibbon too, of course, knew the *Serious Call;* in the paragraph allotted to it in the *Autobiography*, he swallows its "enthusiasm" for the sake of its satiric efficacy. About the former he cannot help but be sardonic: "Hell-fire and eternal damnation are darted from every page of the book, and it is indeed somewhat whimsical that the fanatics who most vehemently inculcate the love of God should be those who despoil Him of every amiable attribute." Yet, Gibbon saw in Law's work a fundamental truth upon which much of his own ironic interpretation of history was based: "A philosopher must allow that he exposes, with equal severity and truth, the strange contradiction between the faith and the practice of the Christian world."

Both the *Dictionary of National Biography* and the *Cambridge Bibliography of English Literature* date the first edition of the *Serious Call* in 1728, but we have found no edition—or evidence of one—prior to that of 1729 and have chosen that as our text. A few variants from subsequent editions in Law's lifetime have been incorporated.

CHAP. VII

How the imprudent use of an estate corrupts all the tempers of the mind, and fills the heart with poor and ridiculous passions through the whole course of life; represented in the character of Flavia.

IT has already been observ'd, that a prudent and religious care is to be us'd, in the manner of spending our *money* or *estate*, because the manner of spending our estates makes so great a part of our common life, and is so much the business of every day, that according as we are wise, or imprudent, in this respect, the *whole course* of our lives, will be render'd either very wise, or very full of folly.

Persons that are well *affected*[1] to Religion, that receive instructions of piety with *pleasure* and *satisfaction*, often wonder how it comes to pass, that they make no greater *progress* in that Religion which they so much *admire*.

Now the reason of it is this; it is because Religion lives only in their *head*, but something else has possession of their *hearts;* and therefore they continue from *year* to *year* mere *admirers*, and *praisers* of piety, without ever coming up to the reality and perfection of its precepts.

If it be ask'd, why Religion does not get possession of their hearts, the reason is this. It is not because they live in *gross sins*, or *debaucheries*, for their regard to Religion preserves them from such disorders.

But it is because their *hearts* are constantly *employ'd*, *perverted*, and kept in a wrong state, by the *indiscreet use* of such things as are *lawful* to be us'd.

The use and enjoyment of their estates is *lawful*, and therefore it never comes into their heads to imagine any great danger from that quarter. They never reflect, that there is a *vain*, and *imprudent* use of their estates, which, though it does not destroy like *gross sins*, yet so *disorders* the heart, and supports it in such *sensuality* and *dulness*, such *pride* and *vanity*, as makes it incapable of receiving the *life* and *spirit* of Piety.

For our souls may receive an infinite hurt, and be render'd incapable of all virtue, merely by the use of *innocent* and *lawful* things.

What is more innocent than *rest* and *retirement?* And yet what more dangerous, than sloth and idleness? What is more lawful than *eating* and *drinking?* And yet what more destructive of all virtue, what more fruitful of all vice, than *sensuality* and *indulgence?*

How *lawful* and *praise-worthy* is the care of a family? And yet how certainly are many people render'd incapable of all virtue, by a worldly and solicitous temper?

Now it is for want of religious exactness in the use of

A SERIOUS CALL TO A DEVOUT AND HOLY LIFE: *Chapter VII*.
1. affected: disposed.

these *innocent and lawful things*, that Religion cannot get possession of our hearts. And it is in the *right* and *prudent* management of our selves, as to these things, that all the *art* of holy living chiefly consists.

Gross sins are plainly seen, and easily avoided by persons that profess Religion. But the *indiscreet* and *dangerous* use of innocent and lawful things, as it does not *shock* and *offend* our consciences, so it is difficult to make people at all sensible of the danger of it.

A *Gentleman* that expends all his estate in *sports*, and a *woman* that lays out all her fortune upon her self, can hardly be perswaded, that the spirit of Religion cannot subsist in such a way of life.

These persons, as has been observ'd, may live free from debaucheries, they may be friends of Religion, so far as to *praise* and *speak* well of it, and admire it in their imaginations; but it cannot govern their hearts, and be the spirit of their actions, till they change their way of life, and let Religion give laws to the use and spending of their estates.

For a *Woman* that loves *dress*, that thinks no expence too great to bestow upon the *adorning* of her person, cannot stop there. For that temper draws a *thousand* other follies along with it, and will render the whole course of her life, her *business*, her *conversation*, her *hopes*, her *fears*, her *taste*, her *pleasures*, and *diversions*, all suitable to it.

Flavia and *Miranda*[2] are two maiden sisters, that have each of them *two hundred pounds* a year. They buried their parents twenty years ago, and have since that time spent their estate as they pleased.

Flavia has been the *wonder* of all her friends, for her excellent management, in making so surprizing a figure in so moderate a fortune. Several *Ladies* that have twice her fortune, are not able to be always so genteel, and so *constant* at all places of *pleasure* and *expence*. She has every thing that is in the *fashion*, and is in every place where there is any *diversion*. *Flavia* is very *orthodox*, she talks warmly against *hereticks* and

schismaticks, is generally at *Church*, and often at the sacrament. She once commended a *sermon* that was against the *pride* and *vanity* of dress, and thought it very *just* against *Lucinda*, whom she takes to be a great deal finer than she need to be. If any one asks *Flavia* to do something in charity, if she likes the person who makes the proposal, or happens to be in a right *temper*, she will toss him *half* a *crown* or a *crown*, and tell him, if he knew what a *long Milliner's bill* she had just received, he would think it a great deal for her to give. A *quarter* of a year after this, she hears a *sermon* upon the *necessity* of charity; she thinks the man preaches well, that it is a very *proper* subject, that people *want*[3] much to be put in mind of it; but she applies nothing to herself, because she remembers that she gave a *crown* some time ago, when she could so ill spare it.

As for *poor* people themselves, she will admit of no complaints from them; she is very positive they are all *cheats* and *lyars*, and will say any thing to get relief, and therefore it must be a sin to encourage them in their evil ways.

You would think *Flavia* had the tenderest conscience in the world, if you was to see, how *scrupulous* and apprehensive she is of the guilt and danger of *giving* amiss.

She buys all books of *wit* and *humour*, and has made an expensive collection of all our *English Poets*. For she says, one cannot have a *true* taste of any of them, without being very conversant with them all.

She will sometimes read a *book* of *Piety*, if it is a short one, if it is much commended for *stile* and *language*, and she can tell where to *borrow* it.

Flavia is very *idle*, and yet very fond of *fine work*:[4] this makes her often *sit* working in *bed* until *noon*, and be told many a *long story* before she is up; so that I need not tell you, that her morning devotions are not *always* rightly performed.

Flavia would be a *miracle* of Piety, if she was but half so careful of her soul, as she is of her body. The rising of a *pimple* in her face, the sting of a *gnat*, will make her keep her room two or three days, and she thinks they are very *rash* people, that don't take care of things in time. This makes her so over-careful of her *health*, that she never thinks she is well enough; and so *over indulgent*, that she never can be really well. So that it costs her a great deal in *sleeping*-draughts and *waking*-draughts, in *spirits* for the head, in *drops* for the nerves, in *cordials* for the stomach, and in *saffron*[5] for her *tea*.

2. Flavia and Miranda: "In his *Serious Call to a Devout and Holy Life*, my two aunts are described by Mr. Law under the names of Flavia and Miranda, the pagan and Christian sister. The sins of Flavia, which excluded her from the hope of salvation, may not appear to our carnal apprehension of so black a dye. Her temper was gay and lively; she followed the fashion in her dress and indulged her taste for company and public amusements. But her expense was regulated by economy; she practiced the decencies of religion; nor is she accused of neglecting the essential duties of a wife or a mother" (*The Autobiography of Edward Gibbon*, ed. D. A. Saunders [1961]).

3. want: need. **4. work:** needlework. **5. saffron:** a stimulant as well as a coloring and flavoring agent.

If you visit *Flavia* on the *Sunday*, you will always meet *good company*, you will know what is doing in the world, you will hear the last *lampoon*, be told who wrote it, and who is meant by every name that is in it. You will hear what *plays* were acted that week, which is the finest song in the *opera*, who was intolerable at the last assembly, and what games are most in fashion. *Flavia* thinks they are *Atheists* that play at *cards* on the *Sunday*, but she will tell you the *nicety* of all the games, what *cards* she held, how she *play'd* them, and the *history* of all that happened at *play*, as soon as she comes from *Church*. If you would know who is *rude* and *ill-natur'd*, who is *vain* and *foppish*, who lives too *high*, and who is in *debt*. If you would know what is the quarrel at a *certain house*, or who and who are in *love*. If you would know how late *Belinda* comes home at night, what *cloaths* she has bought, how she loves *compliments*, and what a long story she told at such a place. If you would know how cross *Lucius* is to his *wife*, what ill-natur'd things he says to her, when *no body* hears him; if you would know how they hate one another in their *hearts*, tho' they appear so kind in publick; you must visit *Flavia* on the *Sunday*. But still she has so great a regard for the holiness of the *Sunday*, that she has turned a poor old widow out of her house, as a *prophane wretch*, for having been found once *mending her cloaths* on the *Sunday* night.

Thus lives *Flavia;* and if she lives ten years longer, she will have spent about *fifteen hundred and sixty Sundays* after this manner. She will have wore about *two hundred* different suits of cloaths. Out of this *thirty years* of her life, *fifteen* of them will have been disposed of in *bed;* and of the remaining fifteen, about *fourteen* of them will have been consumed in eating, drinking, dressing, visiting, conversation, reading and hearing Plays and Romances, at Opera's, Assemblies, Balls and Diversions. For you may reckon all the time that she is *up*, thus spent, except about an *hour* and half, that is disposed of at Church, most *Sundays* in the year. With great management, and under mighty rules of oeconomy, she will have spent *sixty hundred* pounds upon herself, bating[6] only some *shillings*, *crowns*, or *half-crowns*, that have gone from her in *accidental* charities.

I shall not take upon me to say, that it is impossible for *Flavia* to be saved; but thus much must be said, that she has no grounds from Scripture to think she is in the way of[7] salvation. For her whole life is in direct opposition to all those *tempers*[8] and *practices*, which the Gospel has made necessary to salvation.

If you was to hear her say, that she had lived all her life like *Anna* the Prophetess, who *departed not from the temple, but served God with fastings and prayers night and day,*[9] you would look upon her as very extravagant; and yet this would be no greater an extravagance, than for her to say, that she has been *striving to enter in at the strait gate,*[10] or making any *one doctrine* of the Gospel, a rule of her life.

She may as well say, that she lived with our Saviour when he was upon earth, as that she has lived in imitation of him, or made it any part of her care to live in such tempers, as he required of all those that would be his disciples. She may as truly say, that she has every day *washed the saints feet,*[11] as that she has lived in christian *humility* and *poverty of spirit;* and as reasonably think, that she has taught a *Charity-school*, as that she has lived in *works of charity*. She has as much reason to think, that she has been a *centinel* in an army, as that she has lived in *watching*, and *self-denial*. And it may as fairly be said, that she lived by the labour of her hands, as that she had *given all diligence to make her calling and election sure.*[12]

And here it is to be well observed, that the *poor, vain* turn of mind, the *irreligion*, the *folly* and *vanity* of this whole life of *Flavia*, is all owing to the *manner* of using her estate. It is this that has formed her *spirit*, that has given life to every *idle temper*, that has supported every *trifling passion*, and kept her from all thoughts of a prudent, useful, and devout life.

When her parents dy'd, she had no thought about her two hundred pounds a year, but that she had so much money to do what she would with, to spend upon herself, and purchase the pleasures and gratifications of all her passions.

And it is this setting out, this false judgment, and indiscreet use of her fortune, that has filled her whole life with the same indiscretion, and kept her from thinking of what is *right*, and *wise* and *pious* in every thing else.

If you have seen her delighted in *plays* and *romances*, in *scandal* and *backbiting*, easily *flatter'd*, and soon *affronted*. If you have seen her devoted to *pleasures* and *diversions*, a slave to every *passion* in its turn, nice[13] in

---

6. bating: excepting. **7. in . . . of:** likely to achieve.

8. tempers: habits of mind. **9. Anna . . . day:** See Luke 2:36–37. **10. the strait gate:** See Matt. 7:13. **11. washed . . . feet:** See I Tim. 5:10. **12. given . . . sure:** See II Pet. 1:10. **13. nice:** fastidious.

every thing that concerned her *body* or *dress*, careless of every thing that might benefit her *soul*, always wanting some new entertainment, and ready for every *happy* invention in *shew* or *dress*, it was because she had *purchased* all these tempers with the yearly revenue of her fortune.

She might have been *humble, serious, devout,* a lover of *good books,* an admirer of *prayer* and *retirement,* careful of her *time,* diligent in *good works,* full of *charity* and the *love* of God, but that the imprudent use of her estate forc'd all the contrary tempers upon her.

And it was no wonder, that she shou'd turn her *time,* her *mind,* her *health,* her *strength* to the same uses that she turn'd her fortune. It is owing to her being wrong in so great an *article* of life, that you can see nothing wise, or reasonable, or pious in any other part of it.

Now though the irregular trifling spirit of this *character* belongs, I hope, but to few people, yet many may here learn some instruction from it, and perhaps see something of their own spirit in it.

For as *Flavia* seems to be undone by the unreasonable use of her fortune, so the *lowness* of most peoples virtue, the *imperfections* of their piety, and the disorders of their *passions,* is generally owing to their imprudent use and enjoyment of lawful and innocent things.

More people are kept from a true sense and taste of Religion, by a *regular kind* of sensuality and indulgence, than by *gross drunkenness.* More men live regardless of the great duties of piety, through too *great a concern* for worldly goods, than through *direct injustice.*

This man would perhaps be devout, if he was not so great a *Virtuoso.*[14] Another is deaf to all the motives to piety, by indulging an *idle, slothful* temper.

Could you cure This man of his great *curiosity* and *inquisitive* temper, or That of his *false* satisfaction and *thirst* after *learning,* you need do no more to make them both become men of great piety.

If This *woman* would make *fewer visits,* or That not be *always talking,* they would neither of them find it half so hard to be affected with Religion.

For all these things are only *little,* when they are compared to *great sins;* and though they are little in that respect, yet they are great, as they are *impediments* and *hindrances* of a pious spirit.

For as *consideration* is the only *eye* of the soul, as the truths of Religion can be seen by nothing else, so whatever raises a *levity* of mind, a *trifling* spirit, renders the soul incapable of seeing, apprehending, and relishing the doctrines of piety.

Would we therefore make a real progress in Religion, we must not only abhor *gross* and *notorious* sins, but we must regulate the *innocent* and *lawful* parts of our behaviour, and put the most common and allow'd actions of life under the rules of discretion and piety.

CHAP. VIII

How the wise and pious Use of an Estate naturally carrieth us to great perfection in all the virtues of the Christian Life; represented in the character of Miranda.

ANY one pious regularity of any one part of our life, is of great advantage, not only on its own account, but as it uses[1] us to live by rule, and think of the government of our selves.

A man of business, that has brought one part of his affairs under certain rules, is in a fair way[2] to take the same care of the rest.

So he that has brought any one part of his life under the rules of religion, may thence be taught to extend the same order and regularity into other parts of his life.

If any one is so wise as to think his *time* too precious to be disposed of by chance, and left to be devoured by any thing that happens in his way. If he lays himself under a necessity of observing how every day goes through his hands, and obliges himself to a certain order of time in his *business,* his *retirements,* and *devotions,* it is hardly to be imagined, how soon such a conduct would reform, improve, and perfect the whole course of his life.

He that once thus knows the value, and reaps the advantage of a well–order'd time, will not long be a stranger to the value of any thing else that is of any real concern to him.

A rule that relates even to the smallest part of our life, is of great benefit to us, merely as it is a rule.

For, as the *Proverb* saith, *He that has begun well, has half done:*[3] So he that has begun to live by rule, has gone a great way towards the perfection of his life.

By *rule,* must here be constantly understood, a *religious rule,* observed upon a principle of duty to God.

---

14. Virtuoso: investigator or dabbler in the arts or sciences.

Chapter VIII. **1. uses:** accustoms. **2. in . . . way:** likely. **3. He . . . done:** There are many versions of this proverb, in many languages.

For if a man should oblige himself to be moderate in his *meals*, only in regard to his *stomach;* or abstain from *drinking*, only to avoid the *head-ach;* or be moderate in his *sleep*, through fear of a *lethargy*,[4] he might be exact in these rules, without being at all the better man for them.

But when he is moderate and regular in any of these things, out of a sense of *Christian sobriety* and *self-denial*, that he may offer unto God a more reasonable and holy life, then it is that the *smallest rule* of this kind, is naturally the beginning of great piety.

For the smallest rule in these matters is of great benefit, as it teaches us some part of the government of our selves, as it keeps up a *tenderness*[5] of mind, as it presents God often to our thoughts, and brings a sense of religion into the ordinary actions of our common life.

If a man, whenever he was in company, where any one *swore*, talk'd *lewdly*, or spoke *evil* of his neighbour, should make it a *rule* to himself, either gently to reprove him, or if that was not proper, then to leave the company as decently as he could; he would find that this little rule, like a little *leaven* hid in a great quantity of *meal*, would spread and extend itself through the whole form of his life.

If another should oblige himself to abstain on the *Lords-day* from many *innocent* and *lawful* things, as *travelling*, *visiting*, *common conversation*, and discoursing upon *worldly matters*, as *trade*, *news*, and the like; if he should devote the day, besides the publick worship, to greater retirement, reading, devotion, instruction, and works of Charity: Though it may seem but a small thing, or a needless nicety, to require a man to abstain from such things, as may be done without sin, yet whoever would try the benefit of so little a rule, would perhaps thereby find such a change made in his spirit, and such a taste of piety raised in his mind, as he was an entire stranger to before.

It would be easy to shew in many other instances, how little and small matters are the first steps, and natural beginnings of great perfection.

But the two things which of all others, most want to be under a strict rule, and which are the greatest blessings both to our selves and others, when they are rightly us'd, are our *time*, and our *money*. These talents are continual means and opportunities of doing good.

He that is piously strict, and exact in the wise management of either of these, cannot be long ignorant of the right use of the other. And he that is happy in the religious care and disposal of them both, is already ascended several steps upon the *ladder* of Christian perfection.

Miranda[6] (the sister of *Flavia*) is a sober, reasonable Christian; as soon as she was mistress of her *time* and *fortune*, it was her first thought, how she might *best fulfil* every thing that God requir'd of her in the use of them, and how she might make the best and happiest use of this short life. She depends upon the truth of what our blessed Lord hath said, *that there is but one thing needful*,[7] and therefore makes her whole life but one continual labour after it. She has but one reason for doing or not doing, for liking or not liking any thing, and that is the *will* of God. She is not so weak, as to pretend to add, what is call'd the *fine lady*, to the true Christian; *Miranda* thinks too well, to be taken with the *sound* of such silly words; she has renounc'd the world, to follow Christ in the exercise of humility, charity, devotion, abstinence, and heavenly affections; and that is *Miranda*'s fine breeding.

Whilst she was under her *mother*, she was forced to be *genteel*, to live in *ceremony*, to sit up late at *nights*, to be in the folly of every *fashion*, and always *visiting* on *Sundays*. To go *patch'd*,[8] and loaded with a *burden of finery*, to the holy Sacrament; to be in every polite *conversation*, to hear prophaneness at the *playhouse*, and wanton songs and love intrigues at the *opera*, to dance at publick places, that *fops* and *rakes* might admire the

---

6. **Miranda:** "The sanctity of her sister, the original or the copy of Miranda, was indeed of a higher cast. By austere penance Mrs. Hester Gibbon labored to atone for the faults of her youth, for the profane vanities into which she had been led or driven by authority or example. But no sooner was she mistress of her own actions and plentiful fortune than the pious virgin abandoned forever the house of the brother from whom she was alienated by the interest of this world and of the next. . . . Of the pains and pleasures of a spiritual life I am ill-qualified to speak, yet I am inclined to believe that her lot, even on earth, has not been unhappy. Her penance was voluntary, and in her own eyes, meritorious. Her time was filled by regular occupations, and instead of the insignificance of an old maid, she was surrounded by dependents—poor and abject as they were—who implored her bounty and imbibed her lessons" (*The Autobiography of Edward Gibbon*, ed. D. A. Saunders [1961]). 7. **but . . . needful:** "Martha, Martha, thou art careful and troubled about many things: But one thing is needful: and Mary hath chosen that good part, which shall not be taken away from her" (Luke 10:41–42). The analogy of Martha and Mary and Flavia and Miranda is obvious. 8. **patch'd:** a reference to the fashion of wearing ornamental patches on the face.

---

4. **a lethargy:** a morbidly somnolent state. 5. **tenderness:** sensitivity.

fineness of her *shape*, and the *beauty* of her motions. The remembrance of this way of life, makes her exceeding careful to atone for it, by a contrary behaviour.

Miranda does not divide her duty between God, her neighbour, and her self; but she considers all as due to God, and so does every thing in his name, and for his sake. This makes her consider her *fortune*, as the gift of God, that is to be used as every thing is, that belongs to God, for the wise and reasonable ends of a Christian and holy life. Her *fortune* therefore is divided betwixt her self, and several other *poor People*, and she has only her part of *relief* from it. She thinks it the same folly to indulge her self in needless, vain expences, as to give to other People to spend in the same way. Therefore as she will not give a *poor* man money to go see a *Puppet-shew*, neither will she allow her self any to spend in the same manner; thinking it very proper to be as *wise* her self, as she expects poor men should be. For it is a folly and a crime in a *poor* man, says *Miranda*, to waste what is given him, in foolish trifles, whilst he wants *meat*, *drink*, and *cloaths*.

And is it less folly, or a less crime in me to spend that money in silly diversions, which might be so much better spent in *imitation* of the divine goodness, in works of kindness and charity towards my fellow creatures, and fellow Christians? If a poor man's own *necessities* are a reason why he should not waste any of his money idly, surely the necessities of the *poor*, the *excellency* of Charity, which is receiv'd as done[9] to Christ himself, is a much *greater reason*, why no one should ever waste any of his money. For if he does so, he does not only do like the poor man, only waste that which he wants himself, but he wastes that which is wanted for the most noble use, and which Christ himself is ready to receive at his hands. And if we are angry at a *poor* man, and look upon him as a wretch, when he throws away that which should buy his own bread; how must we appear in the sight of God, if we make a *wanton idle* use of that, which should buy bread and cloaths for the hungry and naked brethren, who are as near and dear to God, as we are, and fellow heirs of the same state of future Glory? This is the spirit of *Miranda*, and thus she uses the gifts of God; she is only one of a certain number of *poor People*, that are *relieved* out of her fortune, and she only differs from them in the *blessedness* of giving.

Excepting her victuals, she never spent ten pound a year upon her self. If you was to see her, you would wonder what poor body it was, that was so surprizingly *neat* and *clean*. She has but one rule that she observes in her dress, to be always *clean*, and in the *cheapest* things. Every thing about her resembles the purity of her soul, and she is always clean without, because she is always pure within.

Every morning sees her *early* at her Prayers, she rejoices in the beginning of every day, because it begins all her pious rules of holy living, and brings the fresh pleasure of repeating them. She seems to be as a *guardian Angel* to those that dwell about her, with her watchings and prayers blessing the place where she dwells, and making intercession with God for those that are asleep.

Her devotions have had some intervals,[10] and God has heard several of her private Prayers, before the light is suffer'd to enter into her sister's room. *Miranda* does not know what it is to have a dull half-day; the returns of her hours of Prayer, and her religious exercises, come too often to let any considerable part of time lye heavy upon her hands.

When you see her at *work*, you see the same wisdom that governs all her other actions, she is either doing something that is necessary for her self, or necessary for others, who want[11] to be assisted. There is scarce a poor family in the neighbourhood, but wears something or other that has had the labour of her hands. Her wise and pious mind neither wants[12] the amusement, nor can bear with the folly of idle and impertinent work. She can admit of no such folly as this in the day, because she is to answer for all her actions at night. When there is no wisdom to be observ'd in the employment of her hands, when there is no *useful* or *charitable* work to be done, *Miranda* will work no more. At her *table* she lives strictly by this rule of holy Scripture, *whether ye eat, or drink, or whatever ye do, do all to the glory of God.*[13] This makes her begin and end every meal, as she begins and ends every day, with acts of devotion: She eats and drinks only for the sake of living, and with so *regular* an abstinence, that every *meal* is an exercise of *self-denial*, and she humbles her body, every time that she is forc'd to *feed* it. If *Miranda* was to run a *race* for her life, she would submit to a *diet* that was proper for it. But as the race which is set

---

9. **as done:** as if done.

10. **intervals:** the intervals between church services. Law imagines Miranda's life as a more or less continuous act of religious worship. 11. **want:** need. 12. **wants:** requires. 13. **whether . . . God:** I Cor. 10:31.

before her, is a race of *holiness, purity,* and *heavenly affection,* which she is to finish in a corrupt, disorder'd body of earthly passions, so her every day diet has only this one end, to make her body fitter for this spiritual race. She does not weigh her meat in a pair of *scales,* but she weighs it in a much better balance; so much as gives a proper strength to her body, and renders it able and willing to obey the soul, to join in Psalms and Prayers, and lift up eyes and hands towards Heaven with greater readiness, so much is *Miranda's meal.* So that *Miranda* will never have her eyes swell with fatness, or pant under a heavy load of flesh, 'till she has *changed* her religion.

The holy Scriptures, especially of the new Testament, are her daily study; these she reads with a watchful attention, constantly casting an eye upon her self, and trying her self, by every doctrine that is there. When she has the new Testament in her hand, she supposes her self at the feet of our Saviour and his Apostles, and makes every thing that she learns of them, so many laws of her life. She receives their sacred words with as much attention, and reverence, as if she saw their persons, and knew that they were just come from Heaven, on purpose to teach her the way that leads to it.

She thinks, that the trying of her self every day by the doctrines of Scripture, is the only possible way to be ready for her trial at the last day. She is sometimes afraid that she lays out too much money in books, because she cannot forbear buying all practical books of any note; especially such as enter into the *heart* of religion, and describe the *inward holiness* of the christian life. But of all human writings, the lives of pious persons, and eminent saints, are her greatest delight. In these she searches as for hidden treasure, hoping to find some secret of holy living, some uncommon degree of piety, which she may make her own. By this means *Miranda* has her head and her heart so stor'd with all the principles of wisdom and holiness, she is so full of the one main business of life, that she finds it difficult to converse upon any other subject; and if you are in her company, when she thinks it proper to talk, you must be made wiser and better, whether you will or no.

To relate her charity, would be to relate the history of every day for twenty years; for so long has all her fortune been spent that way. She has set up near twenty poor tradesmen that had fail'd in their business, and saved as many from failing. She has educated several poor children, that were pick'd up in the streets, and put them in a way of[14] an honest employment. As soon as any labourer is confin'd at home with sickness, she sends him, till he recovers, *twice* the value of his wages, that he may have one part to give to his family, as usual, and the other to provide things convenient for his sickness.

If a family seems too large to be supported by the labour of those that can work in it, she pays their rent, and gives them something yearly towards their cloathing. By this means there are many poor families that live in a comfortable manner, and are from year to year blessing her in their prayers.

If there is any poor man or woman, that is more than ordinarily wicked and reprobate, *Miranda* has her eye upon them, she watches their time of need and adversity; and if she can discover that they are in any great streights or affliction, she gives them speedy relief. She has this care for this sort of people, because she once saved a very profligate person from being carry'd to prison, who immediately became a true penitent.

There is nothing in the character of *Miranda* more to be admir'd, than this temper. For this tenderness of affection towards the most abandon'd sinners, is the highest instance of a divine and godlike soul.

Miranda once passed by a house, where the *man* and his *wife* were cursing and swearing at one another in a most dreadful manner, and three children crying about them; this sight so much affected her compassionate mind, that she went the next day, and bought the three children,[15] that they might not be ruin'd by living with such wicked parents; they now live with *Miranda,* are blessed with her care and prayers, and all the good works which she can do for them. They hear her talk, they see her live, they join with her in Psalms and Prayers. The eldest of them has already converted his parents from their wicked life, and shews a turn of mind so remarkably pious, that *Miranda* intends him for *holy orders;* that being thus sav'd himself, he may be zealous in the salvation of souls, and do to other miserable objects, as she has done to him.

Miranda is a constant relief to poor people in their *misfortunes* and *accidents;* there are sometimes little misfortunes that happen to them, which of themselves

---

14. in . . . of: in a position to gain. **15. bought . . . children:** At this time the head of a family could sell his family members. In Hardy's *Mayor of Casterbridge* (1886), set in mid-nineteenth-century England, Henchard, in a fit of drunkenness, sells his wife.

they could never be able to overcome. The death of a *cow*, or a *horse*, or some little *robbery*, would keep them in distress all their lives. She does not suffer them to grieve under such accidents as these. She immediately gives them the full value of their loss, and makes use of it as a means of raising their minds towards God.

She has a great tenderness for *old people* that are grown past their labour. The parish allowance to such people is very seldom a comfortable maintenance. For this reason, they are the constant objects of her care; she adds so much to their allowance, as somewhat exceeds the wages they got when they were young. This she does to comfort the infirmities of their age, that being free from trouble and distress, they may serve God in peace and tranquility of mind. She has generally a large number of this kind, who by her charities and exhortations to holiness, spend their last days in great piety and devotion.

Miranda never wants[16] compassion, even to common beggars; especially towards those that are *old* or *sick*, or full of *sores*, that want *eyes* or *limbs*. She hears their complaints with tenderness, gives them some proof of her kindness, and never rejects them with hard, or reproachful language, for fear of adding affliction to her fellow creatures.

If a poor old traveller tells her, that he has neither *strength*, nor *food*, nor *money* left, she never bids him go to the place from whence he came, or tells him, that she cannot relieve him, because he may be a *cheat*, or she does not know him; but she relieves him for that reason, because he is a *stranger*, and *unknown* to her. For it is the most noble part of charity, to be kind and tender to those whom we never saw before, and perhaps never may see again in this life. *I was a stranger, and ye took me in*,[17] saith our blessed Saviour; but who can perform this duty, that will not relieve persons that are unknown to him?

Miranda considers, that *Lazarus* was a common beggar, that he was the care of *Angels*, and carry'd into *Abraham's* bosom.[18] She considers, that our blessed Saviour, and his Apostles, were kind to *beggars;* that they spoke comfortably to them, healed their diseases, and restor'd eyes and limbs to the lame and blind. That *Peter* said to the beggar that wanted an alms from him, *silver and gold have I none, but such as I have give I thee; in the name of Jesus Christ of Nazareth, rise up and walk.*[19] *Miranda*, therefore, never treats beggars with

disregard and aversion, but she imitates the kindness of our Saviour and his Apostles towards them; and though she cannot, like them, work miracles for their relief, yet she relieves them with that power that she hath; and may say with the Apostle, *such as I have give I thee, in the name of Jesus Christ.*

It may be, says *Miranda*, that I may often give to those that do not deserve it, or that will make an *ill use* of my alms. But what then? Is not this the very method of divine goodness? Does not God make *his sun to rise on the evil, and on the good?*[20] Is not this the very *goodness* that is recommended to us in Scripture, that by imitating of it, we may be children of our Father which is in Heaven, *who sendeth rain on the just, and on the unjust?*[21] And shall I with-hold a little *money*, or *food*, from my fellow creature, for fear he should not be good enough to receive it of me? Do I beg of God to deal with me, not according to my merit, but according to his own great goodness; and shall I be so absurd, as to with-hold my charity from a poor brother, because he may perhaps not deserve it? shall I use a *measure* towards him, which I pray God never to use towards me?

Besides, where has the Scripture made *merit* the rule or measure of charity? On the contrary, the Scripture saith, *if thy enemy hunger, feed him; if he thirst, give him drink.*[22]

Now this plainly teaches us, that the *merit* of persons is to be no rule of our charity, but that we are to do acts of kindness to those that *least* of all deserve it. For if I am to *love* and do good to my worst enemies; if I am to be charitable to them, notwithstanding all their *spight* and *malice*, surely *merit* is no measure of charity. If I am not to with-hold my charity from such bad people, and who are at the same time my enemies, surely I am not to deny alms to poor beggars, whom I neither know to be bad people, nor any way my enemies.

You will perhaps say, that by this means I encourage people to be *beggars*. But the same thoughtless objection may be made against *all kinds* of charities, for they may encourage people to depend upon them. The same may be said against *forgiving* our enemies, for it may *encourage* people to do us hurt. The same may be said, even against the goodness of God, that by pouring his blessings on the evil and on the good, on the just and on the unjust, evil and unjust men are *encourag'd*

---

16. wants: lacks. **17. I . . . in:** Matt. 25:35. **18. Lazarus . . . bosom:** See Luke 16:19–26. **19. That . . . walk:** See Acts 3:1–11.

20. his . . . good: Matt. 5:45. **21. sendeth . . . unjust:** Ibid. **22. if . . . drink:** See Prov. 25:21.

in their wicked ways. The same may be said against cloathing the naked, or giving medicines to the sick, for that may encourage people to *neglect* themselves, and be *careless* of their health. But when the *love of God dwelleth in you;* when it has enlarged your heart, and filled you with bowels of mercy and compassion, you will make no more such objections as these.[23]

When you are at any time turning away the *poor*, the *old*, the *sick* and *helpless* traveller, the *lame*, or the *blind*, ask your self this question; do I sincerely wish these poor creatures may be as happy as *Lazarus*, that was carry'd by *Angels* into *Abraham's* bosom? Do I sincerely desire that God would make them fellow-heirs with me in eternal Glory? Now if you search into your soul, you will find that there is none of these motions there, that you are wishing nothing of this. For it is impossible for any one heartily to wish a poor creature so *great* a happiness, and yet not have a heart to give him a *small* alms. For this reason, says *Miranda*, as far as I can, I give to *all*, because I pray to God to forgive *all*; and I cannot refuse an *alms* to those whom

I pray God to bless, whom I wish to be partakers of *eternal glory;* but am glad to shew some degree of love to such, as, I hope, will be the objects of the infinite love of God. And if, as our Saviour has assur'd us, *it be more blessed to give than to receive*,[24] we ought to look upon those that ask our alms, as so many *friends* and *benefactors*, that come to do us a greater good than they can receive, that come to *exalt* our virtue, to be *witnesses* of our charity, to be *monuments* of our love, to be our *advocates* with God, to be to us in Christ's stead, to *appear* for us at the day of judgment, and to help us to a blessedness greater than our alms can bestow on them.

This is the spirit, and this is the life of the devout *Miranda;* and if she lives ten years longer, she will have spent *sixty hundred* pounds in charity, for that which she allows her self, may fairly be reckon'd amongst her *alms*.

When she dies, she must shine amongst *Apostles*, and *Saints*, and *Martyrs*, she must stand amongst the *first servants* of God, and be glorious amongst those that have fought the good fight,[25] and finish'd their course with joy.

---

23. **when the . . . these:** "But whoso hath this world's good, and seeth his brother have need, and shutteth up his bowels of compassion from him, how dwelleth the love of God in him?" (I John 3:17).

24. **it . . . receive:** See Acts 20:35. 25. **the good fight:** See II Tim. 4:7.

John Gay

❧❧❧❧❧❧❧❧❧❧❧❧❧❧❧❧❧❧❧❧❧❧❧❧❧❧❧❧

1685–1732

John Gay was born on June 30, 1685, at Barnstaple, Devon, into a family of moderate means and equivalent social pretensions. He had the customary grammar school education, though with the added benefit of a poetical master, the Reverend Robert Luck. When both Gay's parents died in 1694, his upbringing was given over to his uncle, Thomas Gay, whose own death in 1701 left the boy without support or prospects. The next year found him apprenticed to a silk mercer in London, but, according to William Ayre in *Memoirs of Pope* (1745), "he grew so fond of Reading and Study, That he frequently neglected to exert himself in putting off [i.e., selling] Silks and Velvets to the Ladies, and suffer'd them (by reason of his wanting to finish the Sale in too few Words) to go to other Shops." The apprenticeship was terminated in 1706, and the following year Gay became secretary to Aaron Hill, a schoolmate, who was starting up the short-lived journal *The British Apollo*. Hill helped Gay publish his first poem, *Wine* (1708), a comic imitation of Milton evidently suggested by the subject and manner of John Philips's *Cyder*, published three months before. But, as Dr. Johnson remarked of another of Philips's poems, *The Splendid Shilling* (1705):

> The merit of such performances begins and ends with the first author. He that should again adapt Milton's phrase to the gross incidents of common life, and even adapt it with more art, which would not be difficult, must yet expect but a small part of the praise which Philips has obtained; he can only hope to be considered as the repeater of a jest.

In the art of imitation Gay came a long way from this beginning.

By the year 1711 Gay had made friends with Steele, Addison, and especially Pope. The next year he found his first patron in the Duchess of Monmouth, widow of the executed bastard son of Charles II, whom he served as secretary and domestic steward. He had recently published a farce entitled *The Mohocks*, inspired by tales of the midnight escapades of town rakes; it was never produced and is of interest mainly for its anticipations of *The Beggar's Opera* (1728):

> Then a *Mohock*, a *Mohock* I'll be,
> No Laws shall restrain
> Our Libertine Reign,
> We'll riot, drink on, and be free.

He had also contributed to a poetical miscellany by the publisher Lintot. But his first productions of any note appear to be owing to his new-found leisure. In January, 1713, *Rural Sports* was published, "Inscribed to Mr. Pope," and in the same year he wrote the greater part of *The Shepherd's Week*, which appeared in April, 1714. The influence of the Scriblerus Club, to which he was appointed secretary, can be seen particularly in the "learned" annotations to the poem and generally in the burlesque design of the whole.

Through the offices of Swift, Gay was appointed, early in 1714, secretary to Lord Clarendon, Ambassador to the Court of Hanover, whence the Elector was soon to emerge as George I of England. In an effusive welcome-home letter (September 23), Pope speculates on whether Gay has profited materially from his political mission, moralizes on Gay's superiority to party politics, and closes with a practical "word of advice in the Poetical way. Write something on the King, or Prince, or Princess. On whatsoever foot you may be with the Court, this can do no harm—." He wrote something on the Queen—*An Epistle to a Lady. Occasioned by the Arrival of Her Royal Highness* was published in November—or, more precisely, on the subject of writing for preferment. If it did no harm, it did little good.

Toward the end of 1714 Gay composed a burlesque of contemporary tragedy called *The What D' Ye Call It*, performed in February, 1715, with notable success. It was followed by satire in a different vein, the delightful *Trivia: or, the Art of Walking the Streets of London*, published in January, 1716. This "imitation" of a Virgilian georgic, with the town imposing upon the country, is a characteristic Augustan slant, and no one brought it off better than Gay. A year later he collaborated with Pope and Arbuthnot on another satirical comedy, *Three Hours After Marriage*, a piece of Scriblerian character-assassination, with the geologist Dr. John Woodward, Colley Cibber, and the critic John Dennis the chief victims.

In 1720, after a period of impecunious traveling about the Continent and visiting in England with various patrons, Gay came into a large sum of money—a thousand pounds—as a result of a sumptuous subscription edition of his *Poems on Several Occasions* (1720) in two quarto volumes; but, venturing all in South Sea Company stock, he lost all. Not until 1723, when friends arranged an appointment as Commissioner of Lotteries and a residence in Whitehall, did he find anything resembling security. Still, he continued to hunt positions, and to write. *The Captives*, an orthodox Augustan tragedy produced in January, 1724, is the kind of play that Gay ought to have satirized, not written; Fielding later satirized it for him in *Tom Thumb* (1730).

Returning to his *métier*, Gay composed—for the improvement of Princess Caroline's four-year-old son, Prince William—the *Fables;* they were completed in 1726 and published the following year. Upon the death of George I in 1727 and the institution of the new royal household, Gay was appointed Gentleman Usher to the two-year-old Princess Louisa, which post he declined accepting on the grounds of his advanced age, though the official reason ill concealed a sense of injured merit.

Johnson wrote, "All the pain which he suffered from the neglect, or, as he perhaps termed it, the ingratitude of the court, may be supposed to have been driven away by the unexampled success of *The Beggar's Opera*." It might also have been supposed (especially by Johnson) that such happiness would be short-lived. The play opened on January 29, 1728, and with the applause still ringing in his ears Gay went to work on its sequel, the pallid *Polly* (1729), which the Lord Chamberlain banned before it could be produced. Thereupon, Gay's newest patron, the Duchess of Queensberry, led a campaign for a subscription edition, which cost her her place at court. Banished, the Duchess and the Duke took Gay with them from place to place, remaining faithful friends to the end of his life.

Gay's last years were productive mainly of works written for the theater; a notable exception is the second series of *Fables*, posthumously published in 1738. In March, 1731, he brought upon the stage the charming *Acis and Galatea*, an English pastoral opera which he had written to Handel's music ten years before. Two plays, *The Distressed Wife* and *The Rehearsal at Goatham*, and a comic opera, *Achilles*, were left unperformed at his death, though the last was being readied for rehearsal. Gay died on December 4, 1732, in London and was buried in Westminster Abbey with an imposing monument, erected by the Duke and Duchess of Queensberry, on which is inscribed the famous epitaph by Pope:

> OF Manners gentle, of Affections mild;
> In Wit, a Man; Simplicity, a Child;
> With native Humour temp'ring virtuous Rage,
> Form'd to delight at once and lash the age;
> Above Temptation, in a low Estate,
> And uncorrupted, ev'n among the Great;
> A safe Companion, and an easy Friend,
> Unblam'd thro' Life, lamented in thy End.
> These are Thy Honours! not that here thy Bust
> Is mix'd with Heroes, or with Kings thy dust;
> But that the Worthy and the Good shall say,
> Striking their pensive bosoms—*Here* lies GAY.

The standard edition of Gay's poetry is G. C. Faber's *The Poetical Works of John Gay* (1926), which includes the operas and plays that are more or less in verse and the verse extracts from those that are not. The complete plays may be read in The Abbey Classics edition, *The Plays of John Gay* (2 vols., 1923). "*The Present State of Wit*": *Critical Essays and Literary Fragments* is edited by J. C. Collins (1903). W. H. Irving's *John Gay: Favorite of the Wits* (1940) and S. M. Armens's *John Gay: Social Critic* (1954) are the best modern full-length studies.

ON A MISCELLANY
OF POEMS.
TO BERNARD LINTOTT

🏵

Printed anonymously in all four editions of Lintot's *Miscellaneous Poems and Translations* (1712, 1714, 1720, 1722). The text is from the first edition.

Bernard Lintot (1675–1736) published works of many prominent Augustan writers, including Pope, Gay, and Steele. Gay's recipe for a miscellany is not to be read as a table of contents for Lintot's collection; there is a considerable discrepancy between the preferences of the poet and the choices of the publisher.

🏵

Ipsa varietate tentamus efficere us alia aliis;
quædam fortasse omnibus placeant.°

PLIN. EPIST.

As when some skilful Cook, to please each Guest,
Would in one Mixture comprehend a Feast,
With due Proportion and judicious Care
He fills his Dish with diff'rent sorts of Fare,
Fishes and Fowl deliciously unite,
To feast at once the Taste, the Smell, and Sight.

So, *Bernard*, must a Miscellany be
Compounded of all kinds of Poetry;
The Muses *O'lio*,° which all Tastes may fit,
And treat each Reader with his darling Wit.   10

Wouldst thou for Miscellanies raise thy Fame;
And bravely rival *Jacob's*° mighty Name,
Let all the Muses in the Piece conspire,
The Lyrick Bard must strike th' harmonious Lyre;

Heroick Strains must here and there be found,
And nervous° Sense be sung in Lofty Sound;
Let Elegy in moving Numbers° flow,
And fill some Pages with melodious Woe;
Let not your am'rous Songs too num'rous prove,
Nor glut thy Reader with abundant Love;   20
Satyr must interfere, whose pointed Rage
May lash the Madness of a vicious Age;
Satyr, the Muse that never fails to hit,
For if there's Scandal, to be sure there's Wit.
Tire not our Patience with Pindarick Lays,°
Those swell the Piece,° but very rarely please:
Let short-breath'd Epigram its Force confine,
And strike at Follies in a single Line.
Translations should throughout the Work be sown,
And *Homer*'s Godlike Muse be made our own;   30
Horace in useful Numbers should be Sung,
And *Virgil*'s Thoughts adorn the *British* Tongue;
Let *Ovid* tell *Corinna*'s° hard Disdain,
And at her Door in melting Notes complain:
His tender Accents pitying Virgins move,
And charm the list'ning Ear with Tales of Love.
Let every Classick in the Volume shine,
And each contribute to thy great Design:
Through various Subjects let the Reader range,
And raise his Fancy with a grateful° Change;   40
Variety's the Source of Joy below,
From whence still fresh revolving Pleasures flow.
In Books and Love, the Mind one End pursues,
And only Change th' expiring Flame renews.

Where *Buckingham*° will condescend to give,
That honour'd Piece to distant Times must live;
When Noble *Sheffield* strikes the trembling Strings,
The little Loves° rejoyce, and clap their Wings,   48
Anacreon° lives, they cry, th' harmonious Swain
Retunes the Lyre, and tries his wonted Strain, ⎫
'Tis He—our lost *Anacreon* lives again. ⎭
But when th' illustrious Poet soars above
The sportive Revels of the God of Love,
Like *Maro*'s° Muse he takes a loftier flight,
And towres beyond the wond'ring *Cupid*'s Sight.

ON A MISCELLANY OF POEMS. **Ipsa . . . placeant:** "I try by this variety to work it out so that there is something for every taste, and perhaps some things that will please everybody" (Pliny the Younger, *Epistles*, IV. xiv. 3). **9.** O'lio: hodge podge, potpourri; from the Spanish word for a kind of stew. **12. Jacob:** Jacob Tonson. His, or Dryden's (as it is often called) *Miscellany Poems* appeared in successive volumes from 1684. Tonson and Lintot, separately or together, published the bulk of Gay's works.

16. nervous: vigorous. **17. Numbers:** measures, rhythms. **25. Pindarick Lays:** Pindaric odes. **26. the Piece:** the work. **33. Corinna:** the central figure of Ovid's love elegies, *Amores*. **40. grateful:** pleasing. **45. Buckingham:** John Sheffield (1648–1721), Earl of Mulgrave (1658) and Duke of Buckingham and Normanby (1703), politician and poet. **48. Loves:** cupids. **49. Anacreon:** (*c.* 563–478 B.C.), Greek lyric poet. (See Prior's *In Imitation of Anacreon* earlier in Part Two.) **54. Maro:** Virgil.

If thou wouldst have thy Volume stand the Test,
And of all others be reputed Best,
Let *Congreve* teach the list'ning Groves to mourn,
As when he wept o'er fair *Pastora*'s Urn.°

Let *Prior*'s Muse with soft'ning Accents move,   60
Soft as the Strains of constant *Emma*'s Love:°
Or let his Fancy chuse some jovial Theme,
As when he told *Hans Carvel*'s jealous Dream;°
Prior th' admiring Reader entertains,
With *Chaucer*'s Humour, and with *Spencer*'s Strains.

Waller in *Granville* lives;° when *Mira* sings
With *Waller*'s Hand he strikes the sounding Strings,
With sprightly Turns his noble Genius shines,
And manly Sense adorns his easie Lines.

On *Addison*'s sweet Lays Attention waits,   70
And Silence guards the Place while he repeats;°
His Muse alike on ev'ry Subject charms,
Whether she paints the God of Love, or Arms:
In Him, Pathetick° *Ovid* sings again,
And *Homer*'s Iliad shines in his *Campaign*.

Whenever *Garth*° shall raise his sprightly Song,
Sense flows in easie Numbers from his Tongue;
Great *Phœbus*° in his learned Son we see,
Alike in Physick, as in Poetry.

When *Pope*'s harmonious Muse° with pleasure
    roves,   80
Amidst the Plains, the murm'ring Streams, and
    Groves,
Attentive Eccho pleas'd to hear his Songs,
Thro' the glad Shade each warbling Note prolongs;
His various Numbers charm our ravish'd Ears,
His steady Judgment far out-shoots his Years,
And early in the Youth the God appears.

From these successful Bards collect thy Strains,
And Praise with Profit shall reward thy Pains:
Then, while Calves-leather Binding bears the Sway,
And Sheep-skin to its sleeker gloss gives way;   90
While neat old *Elzevir*° is reckon'd better
Than *Pirate Hill*'s° brown Sheets, and scurvy Letter;
While Print Admirers careful *Aldus*° chuse
Before *John Morphew*,° or the weekly News:
So long shall live thy Praise in Books of Fame,
And *Tonson* yield to *Lintott*'s lofty Name.

THE SHEPHERD'S WEEK.
IN SIX PASTORALS

—Libeat mihi sordida rura,
Atque humiles habitare Casas.°
                              VIRG.

✻

The Shepherd's Week is Gay's contribution to the contemporary literary quarrel over the proper style and scope of pastoral poetry. In its immediate inspiration it is a parody of Ambrose Philips's *Pastorals*, which were published in 1709 along with Pope's in *Poetical Miscellanies, The Sixth Part*. The lines of the quarrel are not easily drawn, but we may simplify things by saying that the two opposed schools, which have been called neoclassic and rationalist, were mainly divided over the question of imitating the Ancients (especially Virgil) and thus providing an image of the Golden Age or of adapting the classical mode to the native setting and character in a more or less realistic way. In 1713 five essays by Thomas Tickell in the new periodical *The Guardian* expounded the rationalist position, using Philips for illustration and ignoring Pope entirely. Pope, who had earlier composed *A Discourse on Pastoral Poetry*

---

59. he . . . Urn: *The Mourning Muse of Alexis. A Pastoral Lamenting the Death of Queen Mary* (1695). 61. Emma's Love: *Henry and Emma, a Poem, upon the Model of the Nut-Brown Maid* (1709). 63. Hans . . . Dream: *Hans Carvel* (1701). 66. Waller . . . lives: George Granville (1667–1735), Baron Lansdowne, poet and playwright. Johnson wrote in his *Life of Granville*: "He seems to have no ambition above the imitation of Waller, of whom he has copied the faults, and very little more." "Mira," the object of Granville's amorous verse, was Frances Brudenell, Countess of Newburgh. 71. repeats: recites. 74. Pathetick: arousing pathos. 76. Garth: Sir Samuel Garth (1661–1719), physician and poet; author of the popular mock-heroic poem *The Dispensary* (1699). 78. Great Phœbus: Apollo, god of medicine as well as of the fine arts. 80. Pope's . . . Muse: There are several pieces by Pope in Lintot's miscellany, most notably the first (1712) version of *The Rape of the Lock* (see later in Part Two).

91. neat old Elzevir: Elzevir is the name of a family of Dutch printers, famous for their small editions of the classics. 92. Pirate Hill: Henry Hills (d. 1713) "regularly pirated and printed upon coarse paper every good poem and sermon that was published" (*DNB*). 93. careful Aldus: Aldus Manutius, a Venetian printer of the sixteenth century, also famous for his editions of the classics. 94. John Morphew: bookseller and publisher of political pamphlets, newssheets, and novels; he is known to have been in business from 1706 to 1720. THE SHEPHERD'S WEEK. Libeat . . . Casas: "May it please me to inhabit the squalid country and humble cottages" (Virgil, *Eclogues*, ii. 28–29; for *mihi* read *mecum tibi*: "May it please you to inhabit with me . . . .").

(not published until 1717), retaliated by submitting an anonymous essay (which passed the unwary eye of the editor, Steele), ironically praising Philips and deprecating Pope in such a way as to make clear where the true superiority lay. Actually, Philips's pastorals had been much admired—by Addison, by Swift, and even by Pope, among others—and he was received as a worthy successor to Spenser.

Gay's response to the controversy is a fine example of Augustan satire steering a subtle course between high and low, between romance and realism, between Ancients and Moderns. He "uses" Theocritus, Virgil, Spenser, and Philips—all to his own purpose, which is to mock and to celebrate at the same time. The trick was to mediate between the intentionally sober artifice of Pope's retrospective pastorals and the sometimes ludicrous artifice of Philips's updated ones. We note that in the Proeme Gay promises realistic settings and manners, but also a language "not only such as in the present Times is not uttered, but was never uttered in Times past; and, if I judge aright, will never be uttered in Times future." It is his keen sense of the incongruity of tenor and vehicle—in short his sense of humor—that gives Gay's version of pastoral its unique charm.

During Gay's lifetime *The Shepherd's Week* appeared in four separate editions (two in 1714, 1721, 1728) and also in the two editions of his *Poems on Several Occasions* (1720, 1731). Our text is that of the first edition, with revisions incorporated from the later ones.

❧

THE PROEME°
TO THE COURTEOUS READER

Great Marvell hath it been, (and that not unworthily) to diverse worthy Wits, that in this our Island of Britain, in all rare Sciences so greatly abounding, more especially in all kinds of Poesie highly flourishing, no Poet (though otherways of notable Cunning in Roundelays[1]) hath hit on the right simple Eclogue after the true ancient guise of Theocritus, before this mine Attempt.

Other Poet travailing in this plain High-way of Pastoral know I none. Yet, certes, such it behoveth a Pastoral to be, as Nature in the Country affordeth; and the Manners also meetly copied from the rustical Folk therein. In this also my Love to my native Country Britain much pricketh me forward, to describe aright the Manners of our own honest

and laborious Plough-men, in no wise sure more unworthy a British Poet's imitation, than those of Sicily or Arcadie; albeit, not ignorant I am, what a Rout and Rabblement of Critical Gallimawfry[2] hath been made of late Days by certain young Men of insipid Delicacy, concerning, I wist not what, Golden Age, and other outragious Conceits, to which they would confine Pastoral. Whereof, I avow, I account nought at all, knowing no Age so justly to be instiled Golden, as this of our Soveraign Lady Queen ANNE.[3]

This idle Trumpery (only fit for Schools and Schoolboys) unto that ancient Dorick Shepherd Theocritus, or his Mates, was never known; he rightly, throughout his fifth[4] Idyll, maketh his Louts give foul Language, and behold their Goats at Rut in all Simplicity.

Ὠπόλος ὄκκ' ἐσορῇ τὰς μηκάδας οἷα βατεῦνται
τάκεται ὀφθαλμώς, ὅτι οὐ τράγος αὐτὸς ἐγένετο.[5]
THEOC.

Verily, as little Pleasance receiveth a true homebred Tast, from all the fine finical new-fangled Fooleries of this gay Gothic Garniture, wherewith they so nicely bedeck their Court Clowns,[6] or Clown Courtiers, (for, which to call them rightly, I wot not) as would a prudent Citizen[7] journeying to his Country Farms, should he find them occupied by People of this motley Make, instead of plain downright hearty cleanly Folk; such as be now Tenants to the Burgesses of this Realme.

Furthermore, it is my Purpose, gentle Reader, to set before thee, as it were a Picture, or rather lively Landscape of thy own Country, just as thou mightest see it, didest thou take a Walk in the Fields at the proper Season: even as Maister Milton hath elegantly set forth the same.[8]

As one who long in populous City pent,
Where Houses thick and Sewers annoy the Aire,
Forth issuing on a Summer's Morn to breathe
Among the pleasant Villages and Farms
Adjoin'd, from each thing met conceives Delight;
The Smell of Grain or tedded[9] Grass or Kine
Or Dairie, each rural Sight, each rural Sound.

The Proeme to the Courteous Reader. **Proeme:** Preface.
1. Roundelays: short songs with a refrain.

2. Gallimawfry: hash, jumble. **3. knowing . . . Anne:** a standard compliment; Philips in his *Sixth Pastoral* (1709) has Lanquet say of her: "O ever may she reign! / And bring on Earth a Golden Age again." **4. fifth:** Read *first.* **5.** Ὠπόλος . . . ἐγένετο: "When the goatherd looks upon the she-goats as they are covered, his eyes melt because he was not born a he-goat" (Theocritus, *Idylls*, i. 87–88). **6. Clowns:** rustics. **7. Citizen:** townsman, city dweller. **8. Maister . . . same:** in his description of Satan in the Garden of Eden in *Paradise Lost*, IX. 445–51. **9. tedded:** spread out to dry.

Thou wilt not find my Shepherdesses idly piping on oaten Reeds, but milking the Kine, tying up the Sheaves, or if the Hogs are astray driving them to their Styes. My Shepherd gathereth none other Nosegays but what are the growth of our own Fields, he sleepeth not under Myrtle shades, but under a Hedge, nor doth he vigilantly defend his Flocks from Wolves,[10] *because there are none, as Maister Spencer well observeth.*[11]

> Well is known that since the *Saxon* King
> Never was Wolf seen, many or some
> Nor in all *Kent* nor in Christendom.

For as much, as I have mentioned Maister Spencer, *soothly I must acknowledge him a Bard of sweetest Memorial. Yet hath his Shepherds Boy at some times raised his rustick Reed to Rhimes more rumbling than rural. Diverse grave Points also hath he handled of Churchly Matter and Doubts in Religion daily arising, to great Clerkes only appertaining.*[12] *What liketh me best are his Names, indeed right simple and meet for the Country, such as Lobbin, Cuddy, Hobbinol, Diggon, and others, some of which I have made bold to borrow. Moreover, as he called his Eclogues, the Shepherd's Calendar, and divided the same into the twelve Months, I have chosen (peradventure not overrashly) to name mine by the Days of the Week, omitting* Sunday *or the Sabbath, Ours being supposed to be Christian Shepherds, and to be then at Church worship. Yet further of many of Maister Spencer's Eclogues it may be observed; though Months they be called, of the said Months therein, nothing is specified; wherein I have also esteemed him worthy mine Imitation.*

That principally, courteous Reader, whereof I would have thee to be advised, (seeing I depart from the vulgar Usage) is touching the Language of my Shepherds; which is, soothly to say, such as is neither spoken by the country Maiden nor the courtly Dame; nay, not only such as in the present Times is not uttered, but was never uttered in Times past; and, if I judge aright, will never be uttered in Times future. It having too much of the Country to be fit for the Court; too much of the Court to be fit for the Country, too much of the Language of old Times to be fit for the Present, too much of the Present to have been fit for the Old, and too much of both to be fit for any time to come. Granted also it is, that in this my Language, I seem unto my self, as a London Mason, who calculateth his Work for a Term of Years, when he buildeth with old Materials upon a Ground-rent[13] *that is not his own, which soon turneth to Rubbish and Ruins. For this point, no Reason can I alledge, only deep learned Ensamples*[14] *having led me thereunto.*

But here again, much Comfort ariseth in me, from the Hopes, in that I conceive, when these Words in the course of transitory Things shall decay, it may so hap, in meet time that some Lover of Simplicity shall arise, who shall have the Hardiness to render these mine Eclogues into such more modern Dialect as shall be then understood, to which end, Glosses and Explications of uncouth[15] *Pastoral Terms are annexed.*

Gentle Reader, turn over the Leaf, and entertain thyself with the Prospect of thine own Country, limned[16] *by the painful*[17] *Hand of | thy Loving Countryman*

JOHN GAY.

PROLOGUE

To the Right Honourable the Ld Viscount
Bolingbroke.°

LO, I who erst beneath a Tree
Sung *Bumkinet* and *Bowzybee,*
And *Blouzelind* and *Marian* bright,
In Apron blue or Apron white,
Now write my Sonnets° in a Book,
For my good Lord of *Bolingbroke.*
    As Lads and Lasses stood around
To hear my Boxen Haut-boy° sound,

---

10. nor . . . Wolves: Cf. Pope, *The Guardian*, No. 40: "When I remarked it as a principal Fault to introduce Fruits and Flowers of a Foreign Growth, in Descriptions where the Scene lies in our Country, I did not design that Observation should extend also to Animals, or the Sensitive Life; for *Philips* hath with great Judgement described *Wolves* in *England* in his first Pastoral." Pope refers to the lament of Lobbin: "I only, with the prouling Wolf, constrain'd / All Night to wake." **11. Maister . . . observeth:** in *The Shepheardes Calender*, "September," ll. 151-53. The Saxon King, as Spenser's gloss explains, was Edgar, who reigned in Britain from 957 to 975. He is said to have ordered all the wolves in the land destroyed. **12. Diverse . . . appertaining:** The religious satire, one of the conventions of pastoral (deriving from Virgil), occurs in "July" and in "September."

13. Ground-rent: the rent paid to the owner of land that is built upon, as distinguished from the rent of a house. **14. Ensamples:** examples. **15. uncouth:** unfamiliar. **16. limned:** painted. **17. painful:** painstaking. *Prologue.* **Bolingbroke:** Henry St. John (1678-1751), Viscount Bolingbroke, was Secretary of State and joint leader with Oxford of the Tory administration. **5. Sonnets:** poems. **8. Boxen Haut-boy:** an oboe made of boxwood. In Philips's *Sixth Pastoral* (1709) it is the prize in the singing contest.

Our *Clerk*° came posting o'er the Green
With doleful Tidings of the *Queen;*°   10
That Queen, he said, to whom we owe
Sweet *Peace*° *that maketh Riches flow;*
That *Queen* who eas'd our Tax of late,
Was dead, alas!—and lay in State.

    At this, in Tears was *Cic'ly* seen,
Buxoma tore her Pinners° clean,
In doleful Dumps stood ev'ry Clown,
The Parson rent his Band° and Gown.

    For me, when as I heard that Death
Had snatch'd *Queen ANNE* to *Elzabeth*,   20
I broke my Reed, and sighing swore
I'd weep for *Blouzelind* no more.

    While thus we stood as in a stound,°
And wet with Tears, like Dew, the Ground,
Full soon by Bonefire° and by Bell
We learnt our Liege was passing well.
A skilful Leach, (so God him speed)
They said had wrought this blessed Deed,
This Leach *Arbuthnot*° was yclept
Who many a Night not once had slept;   30
But watch'd our gracious Sov'raign still,
For who cou'd rest when she was ill?
Oh, may'st thou henceforth sweetly sleep.
Sheer, Swains, oh sheer your softest Sheep
To swell his Couch; for well I ween,
He sav'd the Realm who sav'd the Queen.

    Quoth I, please God, I'll hye with Glee
To Court, this *Arbuthnot* to see.
I sold my Sheep and Lambkins too,
For silver Loops and Garment blue;   40
My boxen Haut-boy sweet of sound,
For Lace that edg'd mine Hat around;
For *Lightfoot* and my Scrip° I got
A gorgeous Sword, and eke° a Knot.°

    So forth I far'd to Court with speed,
Of Soldier's Drum withouten Dreed;

For Peace allays the Shepherd's Fear
Of wearing Cap of Granadier.°

    There saw I Ladies all a-row
Before their Queen in seemly Show.   50
No more I'll sing *Buxoma* brown,
Like Goldfinch in her *Sunday* Gown;
Nor *Clumsilis*, nor *Marian* bright,
Nor Damsel that *Hobnelia* hight.
But *Lansdown*° fresh as Flow'r of *May*,
And *Berkely*° Lady blithe and gay,
And *Anglesey*° whose Speech exceeds
The Voice of Pipe, or oaten Reeds;
And blooming *Hide*,° with Eyes so rare,
And *Montague*° beyond compare.   60
Such Ladies fair wou'd I depaint
In Roundelay or Sonnet quaint.

    There many a worthy Wight I've seen
In Ribbon blue and Ribbon green.°
As *Oxford*,° who a Wand doth bear,
Like *Moses*, in our Bibles fair;
Who for our *Traffick*° forms Designs,
And gives to *Britain Indian* Mines.
Now, Shepherds, clip your fleecy Care,
Ye Maids, your Spinning-Wheels prepare,   70
Ye Weavers, all your Shuttles throw,
And bid broad Cloths and Serges grow,

---

48. Of . . . Granadier: of being conscripted. **55. Lansdown:** the wife of George Granville, Baron Lansdowne. She was, as a child, the subject of a poem by Prior. (See Prior's *To a Child of Quality* earlier in Part Two.) **56. Berkely:** Lady Louisa Lennox (1694–1717), daughter of the Duke of Richmond, married James, Third Earl of Berkeley, in 1711, at which time Swift wrote of her, "The chit is but 17 and is ill-natured, covetous, vicious, and proud in extremes." In October, 1714, she was appointed a Lady of the Bedchamber to Princess Caroline. **57. Anglesey:** Mary, daughter of John Thompson, Lord Haversham, married her cousin Arthur, Seventh Earl of Anglesey, in 1702. She died in 1719. **59. Hide:** Lady Jane Hyde, daughter of the Earl of Rochester, married William Capell, Earl of Essex, in 1718 and died in 1734. She was also a Lady of the Bedchamber. Lady Jane and her sister, the Duchess of Queensberry, who was Gay's patron, were considered the reigning beauties of their day. **60. Montague:** Lady Mary Wortley Montagu (1689–1762). She wrote numerous letters and poems and was a friend of Pope's. Pope later satirized her however in his *Moral Essays* (see later in Part Two). (See the selection from Lady Mary in Part Three.) **64. Ribbon . . . green:** Knights of the Garter and of the Thistle (a Scottish order instituted by James II in 1687 and revived by Queen Anne in 1703). **65. Oxford:** Robert Harley (1661–1724) was made Earl of Oxford and Lord High Treasurer in 1712. The "Wand" is his staff of office. **67. Traffick:** trade.

9. Our Clerk: the parish clerk, or lay assistant to the parson. **10. doleful . . . Queen:** Queen Anne suffered an attack of fever on Christmas Eve, 1713, which left her unconscious and supposed dead. **12. Sweet Peace:** the Peace of Utrecht in 1713. **16. Pinners:** pinafores. **18. Band:** strip of collar distinguishing his clerical office. **23. stound:** stupor. **25. Bonefire:** the etymological spelling of *bonfire*. **29. Arbuthnot:** John Arbuthnot (1667–1735), physician to Queen Anne and a writer. He was a friend of both Pope and Swift. (See Pope's *Epistle to Dr. Arbuthnot* later in Part Two.) **43. Lightfoot . . . Scrip:** his dog and his shepherd's satchel. The name Lightfoot is used by Philips in his *Second Pastoral.* **44. eke:** also. **a Knot:** a ribbon or tassel tied to the hilt.

For Trading free shall thrive again,
Nor Leasings leud° affright the Swain.
    There saw I *St. John*,° sweet of Mien,
Full stedfast both to Church and Queen.
With whose fair Name I'll deck my Strain,
St. John, right courteous to the Swain;
    For thus he told me on a Day,
Trim are thy Sonnets, gentle *Gay*,   80
And certes, Mirth it were to see
Thy joyous Madrigals° twice three,
With Preface meet, and Notes profound,
Imprinted fair, and well y-bound.
All suddenly then Home I sped,
And did ev'n as my Lord had said.
    Lo here, thou hast mine Eclogues fair,
But let not these detain thine Ear.
Let not Affairs of States and Kings
Wait, while our *Bowzybeus* sings.   90
Rather than Verse of simple Swain
Should stay the Trade of *France* or *Spain*,
Or for the Plaint of Parson's Maid,
Yon Emp'ror's Packets be delay'd;
In sooth, I swear by holy *Paul*,
I'd burn Book, Preface, Notes and all.

MONDAY;
OR, THE SQUABBLE

Lobbin Clout, Cuddy, Cloddipole.

LOBBIN CLOUT.

THY Younglings, *Cuddy*, are but just awake,
No Thrustles° shrill the Bramble-Bush forsake,
No chirping Lark the Welkin sheen° invokes,
No Damsel yet the swelling Udder strokes;
O'er yonder Hill does scant° the Dawn appear,
Then why does *Cuddy* leave his Cott, so rear°?

CUDDY.

    Ah *Lobbin Clout!* I ween,° my Plight is guest,
For *he that loves, a Stranger is to Rest;*
If Swains belye not, thou hast prov'd the Smart,°
And *Blouzelinda*'s Mistress of thy Heart.   10
This rising rear betokeneth well thy Mind,
Those Arms are folded° for thy *Blouzelind*.
And well, I trow, our piteous Plights agree,
Thee *Blouzelinda* smites, *Buxoma* me.

LOBBIN CLOUT.

    Ah *Blouzelind!* I love thee more by half,
Than Does their Fawns, or Cows the new-fall'n° Calf:
Woe worth° the Tongue! may Blisters sore it gall,
That names *Buxoma, Blouzelind* withal.°

CUDDY.

    Hold, witless *Lobbin Clout*, I thee advise,
Lest Blisters sore on thy own Tongue arise.   20
Lo yonder, *Cloddipole*, the blithsome Swain,
The wisest Lout of all the neighbouring Plain.
From *Cloddipole* we learnt to read the Skies,
To know when Hail will fall, or Winds arise.
He taught us erst° the Heifers tail to view,
When stuck aloft, that Show'rs would strait ensue;
He first that useful Secret did explain,
That pricking Corns foretold the gath'ring Rain.
When Swallows fleet soar high and sport in Air,
He told us that the Welkin wou'd be clear.   30
Let *Cloddipole* then hear us twain rehearse,°
And praise his Sweetheart in alternate Verse.
I'll wager this same *Oaken Staff* with thee,
That *Cloddipole* shall give the Prize to me.

LOBBIN CLOUT.

    See this *Tobacco Pouch* that's lin'd with Hair,
Made of the Skin of sleekest fallow Deer.
This Pouch, that's ty'd with Tape of reddest Hue,
I'll wager, that the Prize shall be my due.

CUDDY.

    Begin thy Carrols then, thou vaunting Slouch,°
Be thine the *Oaken Staff*, or mine the *Pouch*.   40

74. Leasings leud: worthless weavings. **75. St. John:** Bolingbroke. **82. Madrigals:** loosely, songs or poems. According to one etymological theory the original meaning was "pastoral song." *Monday.* **2. Thrustles:** (throstles) thrushes. **3. the Welkin sheen:** [Gay's note] Welkin *the same as* Welken, *an old* Saxon *Word signifying* a Cloud, *by Poetical Licence it is frequently taken for the* Element *or* Sky, *as may appear by this Verse in the* Dream of Chaucer [*The Book of the Duchess*, l. 343]. Ne in all the Welkin was no Cloud. Sheen *or* Shine, *an old Word for* shining *or* bright. **5. scant:** [Gay's note] Scant, *used by ancient* British *Authors for* scarce. **6. rear:** [Gay's note] Rear, *an Expression in several Counties of* England, *for* early in the Morning.

7. ween: [Gay's note] To ween, *derived from the* Saxon, *to think or conceive*. **9. prov'd the Smart:** felt the pain. **12. folded:** a gesture of despair; cf. *Troilus and Criseyde*, IV. 358–60:

> And with his chiere and lokyng al totorn,
> For sorwe of this, and with his armes folden,
> He stood this woful Troilus byforn.

16. new-fall'n: newborn. **17. Woe worth:** may evil befall, a curse upon. **18. withal:** in the same breath. **25. erst:** [Gay's note] Erst, *a Contraction of* ere this, *it signifies* sometime ago *or* formerly. [Gay's etymology is dubious; the *OED* traces the word to Old English *ǽrest*, the superlative of *ǽr*, meaning "the earliest."] **31. rehearse:** recite. **39. Slouch:** lout.

LOBBIN CLOUT.

My *Blouzelinda* is the blithest Lass,
Than Primrose sweeter, or the Clover-Grass.
Fair is the King-Cup that in Meadow blows,
Fair is the Daisie that beside her grows,
Fair is the Gillyflow'r, of Gardens sweet,
Fair is the Mary-Gold, for Pottage meet.°
But *Blouzelind's* than Gillyflow'r more fair,
Than Daisie, Mary-Gold, or King-Cup rare.

CUDDY.

My brown *Buxoma* is the featest° Maid,
That e'er at Wake° delightsome Gambol play'd.   50
Clean as young Lambkins or the Goose's Down,
And like the Goldfinch in her *Sunday* Gown.
The witless lamb may sport upon the Plain,
The frisking Kid delight the gaping Swain,
The wanton Calf may skip with many a Bound,
And my Cur *Tray* play deftest° Feats around:
But neither Lamb nor Kid, nor Calf nor *Tray*,
Dance like *Buxoma* on the first of *May*.

LOBBIN CLOUT.

Sweet is my Toil when *Blouzelind* is near,
Of her bereft 'tis Winter all the Year.   60
With her no sultry Summer's Heat I know;
In Winter, when she's nigh, with Love I glow.
Come *Blouzelinda*, ease thy Swain's Desire,
My Summer's Shadow and my Winter's Fire!

CUDDY.

As with *Buxoma* once I work'd at Hay,
Ev'n Noon-tide Labour seem'd an Holiday;
And Holidays, if haply she were gone,
Like Worky-days I wish'd would soon be done.
Eftsoons,° O Sweet-heart kind, my Love repay,
And all the Year shall then be Holiday.   70

LOBBIN CLOUT.

As *Blouzelinda* in a gamesome Mood,
Behind a Haycock loudly laughing stood,
I slily ran, and snatch'd a hasty Kiss,
She wip'd her Lips, nor took it much amiss.
Believe me, *Cuddy*, while I'm bold to say,
Her Breath was sweeter than the ripen'd Hay.

CUDDY.

As my *Buxoma* in a Morning fair,
With gentle Finger stroak'd her milky Care,°
I queintly° stole a Kiss; at first, 'tis true
She frown'd, yet after granted one or two.   80
Lobbin, I swear, believe who will my Vows,
Her Breath by far excell'd the breathing Cows.

LOBBIN CLOUT.

Leek to the *Welch*, to *Dutchmen Butter's* dear,
Of *Irish* Swains *Potatoe* is the Chear;
Oats for their Feasts the *Scottish* Shepherds grind,
Sweet *Turnips* are the Food of *Blouzelind*.
While she loves *Turnips, Butter* I'll despise,
Nor *Leeks* nor *Oatmeal* nor *Potatoe* prize.°

CUDDY.

In good *Roast Beef* my Landlord sticks his Knife,
The *Capon* fat delights his dainty Wife,   90
Pudding our Parson eats, the Squire loves *Hare*,
But *White-pot*° thick is my *Buxoma's* Fare.
While she loves *White-pot, Capon* ne'er shall be,
Nor *Hare*, nor *Beef*, nor *Pudding*, Food for me.

46. for . . . meet: suitable (as an ingredient) for soup
or porridge. **49. featest:** most graceful. **50. Wake:** a
country festival. **56. deftest:** [Gay's note] Deft, *an old
Word signifying* brisk *or* nimble. [The word was evidently
out of currency during the eighteenth century, though
it returned in the nineteenth. The *OED* misleadingly cites
Gay's use of it without quoting his note.] **69. Eftsoons:**
[Gay's note] Eftsoons, *from* eft *an ancient British Word
signifying* soon. *So that eftsoons is a doubling of the Word*
soon, *which is, as it were to say* twice soon, *or* very soon. [Both
etymology and meaning are here amiss. The *OED* gives as
the original meaning of *eft* "a second time, again; back"
(related to *aft*), and the same primary meaning is assigned to
eftsoon(s). This meaning fits the context of Gay's lines more
easily than his own gloss of "very soon," which sense
("forthwith, immediately") the *OED* recognizes as a modern
archaism.]

78. Care: object of care, charge. **79. queintly:** [Gay's note]
Queint *has various Significations in the ancient* English *Authors.
I have used it in this Place in the same Sense as* Chaucer *hath done
in his* Miller's Tale. *As Clerkes been full subtil and queint,*
(*by which he means* Arch *or* Waggish) *and not in that obscene
Sense wherein he useth it in the Line immediately following*. [To
gloss Gay's gloss, we should say "artful" or "cunning." And
to repair his reticence, "the Line immediately following" is
"And prively he caughte hire by the queynte."]
83–88. Leek . . . prize: [Gay's note]

Populus Alcidæ gratissima, vitis, Iaccho,
Formosæ Myrtus Veneri, sua Laurea Phœbo.
Phillis amat Corylos. Illas dum Phillis amabit,
Nec Myrtus vincet Corylos nec Laurea Phœbi. &c.
                                                  VIRG.

["The poplar is most pleasing to Hercules, the vine to Bacchus,
the myrtle to beautiful Venus, (and) to Phoebus his own
laurel tree. Phyllis loves hazels. As long as Phyllis will love
them, neither the myrtle nor the laurel of Phoebus will surpass
hazels" (Virgil, *Eclogues*, vii. 61–64).] **92. White-pot:** a
custard or milk pudding.

LOBBIN CLOUT.

As once I play'd at *Blindman's-buff*, it hapt
About my Eyes the Towel thick was wrapt.
I miss'd the Swains, and seiz'd on *Blouzelind;*
True speaks that ancient Proverb, *Love is blind.*

CUDDY.

As at *Hot-Cockles°* once I laid me down,
And felt the weighty Hand of many a Clown;   100
Buxoma gave a gentle Tap, and I
Quick rose, and read soft Mischief in her Eye.

LOBBIN CLOUT.

On two near elms, the slacken'd cord I hung,
Now high, now low my *Blouzelinda* swung.
With the rude wind her rumpled garment rose,
And show'd her taper leg, and scarlet hose.

CUDDY.

Across the fallen oak the plank I laid,
And my self pois'd against the tott'ring maid,
High leapt the plank; adown *Buxoma* fell;
I spy'd—but faithful sweethearts never tell.°   110

LOBBIN CLOUT.

This Riddle, *Cuddy,* if thou canst, explain,
This wily Riddle puzzles ev'ry Swain.
What Flower is that which bears the Virgin's *Name,*
The richest Metal joined with the same?°

CUDDY.

Answer, thou Carle,° and judge this Riddle right,
I'll frankly own° thee for a cunning Wight.°
What Flow'r is that which Royal Honour craves,
Adjoin the Virgin, *and 'tis strown on Graves.°*

CLODDIPOLE.

Forbear, contending Louts, give o'er your Strains,
An *Oaken Staff* each merits for his Pains.°   120
But see the Sun-Beams bright to Labour warn,
And gild the Thatch of Goodman° *Hodges'* Barn.
Your Herds for want of Water stand adry,
They're weary of your Songs—and so am I.

99. **Hot-Cockles:** a game in which the person who is "it" lies
or kneels down blindfolded, is hit on the back, and has to
guess who did it. **103–10. On . . . tell:** These two stanzas
were added in *Poems on Several Occasions* (1720) and
preserved in all subsequent editions. **113–14. What . . .
same:** [Gay's note] *Marygold.* **115. Carle:** churl, base fellow.
116. own: acknowledge. **Wight:** creature, person. **117–18.
What . . . Graves:** [Gay's note] *Rosemary. Dic quibus in
terris inscripti nomina Regum / Nascantur Flores.* VIRG. ["Tell
in what lands flowers grow inscribed with the names of
kings" (Virgil, *Eclogues,* iii. 106–07).] **120. An . . . Pains:**
[Gay's note] *Et vitula tu dignus & hic.* VIRG. ["Both you
and he have deserved the heifer" (Virgil, *Eclogues,* iii. 109).]
122. Goodman: a common prefix to the name of a yeoman
or farmer.

TUESDAY; OR, THE DITTY

MARIAN.

YOUNG *Colin Clout,* a Lad of peerless Meed,°
Full well could dance, and deftly tune the Reed;
In ev'ry Wood his Carrols sweet were known,
At ev'ry Wake his nimble Feats were shown.
When in the Ring the Rustick Routs he threw,°
The Damsels pleasure with his Conquests grew;
Or when aslant the Cudgel threats his Head,
His Danger smites the Breast of ev'ry Maid,
But chief of *Marian. Marian* lov'd the Swain,
The Parson's Maid, and neatest of the Plain.   10
Marian who soft could stroak the udder'd Cow,
Or lessen with her sieve the barly mow;°
Marbled° with Sage the hard'ning Cheese she press'd,
And yellow Butter *Marian's* Skill confess'd;
But *Marian* now devoid of Country Cares,
Nor yellow Butter nor Sage Cheese prepares.
For yearning Love the witless Maid employs,
And *Love,* say Swains, *all busie Heed destroys.*
Colin makes mock at all her piteous Smart,°
A Lass who *Cic'ly* hight, had won his Heart,   20
Cic'ly the Western Lass who tends the *Kee,°*
The Rival of the Parson's Maid was she.
In dreary Shade now *Marian* lyes along,
And mixt with Sighs thus wails in plaining Song.

   Ah woful Day! ah woful Noon and Morn!
When first by thee my Younglings white were shorn,
Then first, I ween, I cast a Lover's Eye,
My Sheep were silly,° but more silly I.
Beneath the Shears they felt no lasting Smart,
They lost but Fleeces while I lost a Heart.   30
   Ah *Colin!* canst thou leave thy Sweetheart true!
What I have done for thee will *Cic'ly* do?
Will she thy Linnen wash or Hosen darn,
And knit thee Gloves made of her own-spun Yarn?
Will she with Huswife's Hand provide thy Meat,
And ev'ry *Sunday* Morn thy Neckcloth plait°?
Which o'er thy Kersey Doublet° spreading wide,
In Service-Time drew *Cic'ly's* Eyes aside.

Tuesday. **1. Meed:** See Gay's note to "Wednesday," l. 17.
5. When . . . threw: when he defeated the whole gang of
rustics at wrestling. **12. barly mow:** stack of barley. **13.
Marbled:** colored so as to give the appearance of variegated
marble. **19. Smart:** pain, anguish. **21. Kee:** [Gay's note] Kee,
a West-Country Word fo. Kine or Cow. **28. silly:** pitiable. The
line is borrowed from Philips's *Second Pastoral* (1709): "Ah
silly I! more silly than my Sheep." **36. thy . . . plait:** fold
your neckerchief. **37. Kersey Doublet:** A doublet is a
close-fitting coat or jacket; Kersey a coarse woollen cloth.

Where-e'er I gad° I cannot hide my Care,
My new Disasters in my Look appear.   40
White as the Curd my ruddy Cheek is grown,
So thin my Features that I'm hardly known;
Our Neighbours tell me oft in joking Talk
Of Ashes, Leather, Oatmeal, Bran and Chalk;
Unwittingly of *Marian* they divine,°
And wist not that with thoughtful Love I pine.
Yet *Colin Clout*, untoward° Shepherd Swain,
Walks whistling blithe, while pitiful I plain.

Whilom° with thee 'twas *Marian's* dear Delight
To moil° all Day, and merry make at Night.   50
If in the Soil you guide the crooked Share,
Your early Breakfast is my constant Care.
And when with even Hand you strow° the Grain,
I fright the thievish Rookes from off the Plain.
In misling° Days when I my Thresher heard,
With nappy° Beer I to the Barn repair'd;
Lost in the Musick of the whirling Flail,
To gaze on thee I left the smoaking° Pail;
In Harvest when the Sun was mounted high,
My Leathern Bottle did thy Drought° supply;   60
When-e'er you mow'd I follow'd with the Rake,
And have full oft been Sun-burnt for thy Sake;
When in the Welkin gath'ring Show'rs were seen,
I lagg'd the last with *Colin* on the Green;
And when at Eve returning with thy Carr,°
Awaiting heard the gingling Bells from far;
Strait on the Fire the sooty Pot I plac't,
To warm thy Broth I burnt my Hands for Haste.
When hungry thou stood'st *staring, like an Oaf*,
I slic'd the Luncheon from the Barly Loaf,   70
With crumbled Bread I thicken'd well thy Mess.
Ah, love me more, or love thy Pottage less!

Last *Friday's* Eve, when as the Sun was set,
I, near yon Stile, three sallow Gypsies met.
Upon my Hand they cast a poring Look,
Bid me beware, and thrice their Heads they shook,
They said that many Crosses° I must prove,°
Some in my worldly Gain,° but most in Love.
Next Morn I miss'd three Hens and our old Cock,
And off the Hedge two Pinners and a Smock.   80

I bore these Losses with a Christian Mind,
And no Mishaps could feel, while thou wert kind.
But since, alas! I grew my *Colin's* Scorn,
I've known no Pleasure, Night, or Noon, or Morn.
Help me, ye Gipsies, bring him home again,
And to a constant Lass give back her Swain.

Have I not sate with thee full many a Night,
When dying Embers were our only Light,
When ev'ry Creature did in Slumbers lye,
Besides our Cat, my *Colin Clout*, and I?   90
No troublous Thoughts the Cat or *Colin* move,
While I alone am kept awake by Love.

Remember, *Colin*, when at last Year's Wake,
I bought the costly Present for thy sake,
Couldst thou spell o'er the Posie on thy Knife,°
And with another change thy State of Life?
If thou forget'st, I wot, I can repeat,
My Memory can tell the Verse so sweet.
As this is grav'd upon this Knife of thine,
So is thy Image on this Heart of mine.   100
But Woe is me! Such Presents luckless prove,
For *Knives*, they tell me, *always sever Love*.

Thus *Marian* wail'd, her Eye with Tears brimfull,
When Goody° *Dobbins* brought her Cow to Bull.
With Apron blue to dry her Tears she sought,
Then saw the Cow well serv'd, and took a Groat.°

WEDNESDAY;
OR, THE DUMPS°

SPARABELLA.

THE Wailings of a Maiden I recite,
A Maiden fair, that *Sparabella* hight.
Such Strains ne'er warble in the Linnets Throat,

39. gad: go, wander. **45. Unwittingly . . . divine:** They speculate, unaware of Marian's plight. **47. untoward:** indifferent. **49. Whilom:** once. **50. moil:** toil. **53. strow:** strew. **55. misling:** (mizzling) drizzling. **56. nappy:** foaming. **58. smoaking:** (smoking) steaming (with warm milk). **60. Drought:** thirst. **65. Carr:** cart, wagon. **77. Crosses:** adversities. **prove:** experience. **78. Gain:** The obsolete sense, "source of gain," seems apposite here.

95. Couldst . . . Knife: Could you read the verse engraved on your knife. **104. Goody:** short for *Goodwife*; cf. *Goodman*, "Monday," l. 122. **106. a Groat:** The English groat, originally worth four pence, went out of circulation in 1662. *Wednesday.* **Dumps:** [Gay's note] Dumps, or Dumbs, made use of to express a Fit of the Sullens. *Some have pretended that it is derived from* Dumops *a King of* Egypt, *who built a Pyramid, and dy'd of Melancholy. So* Mopes *after the same Manner is thought to have come from* Merops, *another* Egyptian *King who dy'd of the same Distemper; but our* English *Antiquaries have conjectured that Dumps, which is, a grievous Heaviness of Spirits, comes from the Word* Dumplin, *the heaviest kind of Pudding that is eaten in this Country, much used in* Norfolk, *and other Counties of* England. [The *OED*, which finds the derivation of both *dumps* and *mopes* obscure, takes no account of the etymologies cited by Gay.]

Nor the gay Goldfinch chaunts so sweet a Note,
No Mag-pye chatter'd, nor the painted Jay,
Nor Ox was heard to low, nor Ass to bray.
No rusling Breezes play'd the Leaves among,
While thus her Madrigal the Damsel sung.°

A° while, O D'Urfey,° lend an Ear or twain,
Nor, though in homely Guise, my Verse disdain;   10
Whether thou seek'st new Kingdoms in the Sun,°
Whether thy Muse does at *New-Market* run,
Or does with Gossips° at a Feast regale,
And heighten her Conceits with Sack and Ale,
Or else at Wakes with *Joan* and *Hodge* rejoice,
Where D'Urfey's Lyricks swell in every Voice;
Yet suffer me, thou Bard of wond'rous Meed,°
Amid thy Bays to weave this rural Weed.°

Now the Sun drove adown the western Road,
And Oxen laid at rest forget the Goad,   20
The Clown fatigu'd trudg'd homeward with his Spade,
Across the Meadows stretch'd the lengthen'd Shade;

When *Sparabella* pensive and forlorn,
Alike with yearning Love and Labour worn,
Lean'd on her Rake,° and strait with doleful Guise
Did this sad Plaint in moanful Notes devise.

Come Night as dark as Pitch, surround my Head,
From *Sparabella Bumkinet* is fled;
The Ribbon that his val'rous Cudgel won,
Last *Sunday* happier *Clumsilis* put on.   30
Sure, if he'd Eyes (*but Love*, they say, *has none*)
I whilome° by that Ribbon had been known.
Ah, Well-a-day! I'm shent° with baneful Smart,
For with the Ribbon he bestow'd his Heart.
   My Plaint, ye Lasses, with this Burthen° aid,
   'Tis hard so true a Damsel dies a Maid.

Shall heavy *Clumsilis* with me compare?
View this, ye Lovers, and like me despair.°
Her blubber'd Lip by smutty Pipes is worn,
And in her Breath Tobacco Whiffs are born;   40
The cleanly Cheese-press she could never turn,
Her awkward Fist did ne'er employ the Churn;
If e'er she brew'd, the Drink wou'd strait go sour,
Before it ever felt the Thunder's Pow'r:°
No Huswifry the dowdy Creature knew;
To sum up all, her Tongue confess'd° the Shrew.
   My Plaint, ye Lasses, with this Burthen aid,
   'Tis hard so true a Damsel dies a Maid.

I've often seen my Visage in yon Lake,
Nor are my Features of the homeliest Make.°   50
Though *Clumsilis* may boast a whiter Dye,°
Yet the black Sloe turns in my rolling Eye;°
And fairest Blossoms drop with ev'ry Blast,
But the brown Beauty will like Hollies last.°
Her wan Complexion's like the wither'd Leek,
While *Katherine* Pears° adorn my ruddy Cheek.

5–8. No Mag-pye . . . sung: [Gay's note]

Immemor Herbarum quos est mirata juvenca
Certantes quorum stupefactæ carmine Lynces;
Et mutata suos requierunt flumina cursus.
                                        VIRG.

["At whose contest between the shepherds Damon and Alphesiboeus the heifer marveled, forgetful of grass; by whose song the lynxes were stunned; and the rivers, having changed their course, reposed" (Virgil, *Eclogues*, viii. 2–4).] **9–16. A . . . Voice:** [Gay's note] *Tu mihi seu magni superas jam saxa Timavi, | Sive oram Illyrici legis æquoris—.* ["You, my friend, whether you now pass by the rocks of great Timavus [a river between Trieste and Aquileia], or skirt the shore of the Illyrian sea—" (Virgil, *Eclogues*, viii. 6–7).] **9. D'Urfey:** Thomas D'Urfey (1653–1723), poet and dramatist. His songs were set to music by leading composers, including Purcell. (See the selection from D'Urfey in Part Three.) **11. Kingdoms . . . Sun:** [Gay's note] *An Opera written by this Author, called the* World in the Sun, *or the Kingdom of Birds; he is also famous for his Song on the* Newmarket Horse Race, *and several others that are sung by the British Swains.* [The correct title of the opera is The Wonders in the Sun; or, the Kingdom of the Birds. It was first performed on April 5, 1706, at the Queen's Theatre, and advertised as "a new Dialogue made to the famous Sebel of Signior Baptist Lully." The song is entitled The Horse-Race; a Song Made and Sung to the King at Newmarket; Set to an Excellent Scotch Tune, Called, Cock Up Thy Beaver, in Four Strains. It was first printed in D'Urfey's Choice New Songs (1684).] **13. Gossips:** familiar acquaintances. **17. Meed:** [Gay's note] *Meed, an old Word for* Fame *or* Renown. [The OED cites this occurrence in Gay under the meanings "merit, excellence, worth."] **18. Amid . . . Weed:** [Gay's note]—*Hanc sine tempora circum | Inter Victrices ederam tibi serpere lauros.* ["Let this ivy amid victorious laurel coil around your temples" (Virgil, *Eclogues*, viii. 12–13).]

25. Lean'd . . . Rake: [Gay's note] *Incumbens tereti Damon sic cæpit Olivæ.* ["Leaning on his smooth olive-staff, Damon thus began" (Virgil, *Eclogues*, viii. 16).] **32. whilome:** one day. **33. shent:** [Gay's note] Shent, *an old Word signifying* Hurt *or* harmed. **35. Burthen:** (burden) refrain. **37–38. Shall . . . despair:** [Gay's note] *Mopso Nisa datur. quid non speremus Amantes?* VIRG. ["Nysa is wedded to Mopsus. What may we lovers not expect?" (Virgil, *Eclogues*, viii. 26).] **44. the Thunder's Pow'r:** Thunder was popularly supposed to turn milk and other liquids sour. **46. confess'd:** revealed. **49–50. I've . . . Make:** [Gay's note] *Nec sum adeo informis, nuper me in Littore vidi.* VIRG. ["Nor am I so ugly; lately I saw my reflection by the shore" (Virgil, *Eclogues*, ii. 25).] **51. Dye:** hue. **52. the black . . . Eye:** I am sloe-eyed (black-eyed). **53–54. And . . . last:** [Gay's note] *Alba ligustra cadunt, vaccinia nigra leguntur.* VIRG. ["White privets fall, dark hyacinths are gathered" (Virgil, *Eclogues*, ii. 18).] **56. Katherine Pears:** a variety of pear with red streaks.

Yet she, alas! the witless Lout hath won,
And by her Gain, poor *Sparabell*'s undone!
Let° Hares and Hounds in coupling Straps° unite,
The clocking° Hen make Friendship with the Kite,   60
Let the Fox simply wear the Nuptial Noose,
And join in Wedlock with the wadling Goose;
For Love hath brought a stranger thing to pass,
The fairest Shepherd weds the foulest Lass.

   My Plaint, ye Lasses, with this Burthen aid,
'Tis hard so true a Damsel dies a Maid.

   Sooner° shall Cats disport in Waters clear,
And speckled mackrels graze the Meadows fair,
Sooner shall scriech Owls bask in Sunny Day,
And the slow Ass on Trees, like Squirrels, play,   70
Sooner shall Snails on insect Pinions rove,
Than I forget my Shepherd's wonted Love°!

   My Plaint, ye Lasses, with this Burthen aid,
'Tis hard so true a Damsel dies a Maid.

   Ah! didst thou know what Proffers° I withstood,
When late I met the *Squire* in yonder Wood!
To me he sped, regardless of his Game,
While all my Cheek was glowing red with Shame;
My Lip he kiss'd, and prais'd my healthful Look,
Then from his Purse of Silk a *Guinea* took,   80
Into my Hand he forc'd the tempting Gold,
While I with modest struggling broke his Hold.
He swore that *Dick* in Liv'ry strip'd with Lace,
Should wed me soon to keep me from Disgrace;
But I nor° Footman priz'd nor golden Fee,
For what is Lace or Gold compar'd to thee?

   My Plaint, ye Lasses, with this Burthen aid,
'Tis hard so true a Damsel dies a Maid.

Now° plain I ken° whence *Love* his Rise begun.
Sure he was born some bloody *Butcher*'s Son,   90
Bred up in Shambles,° where our Younglings slain,
Erst taught him Mischief and to sport with Pain.
The *Father* only silly Sheep annoys,
The *Son*, the sillier Shepherdess destroys.
Does *Son* or *Father* greater Mischief do?
The *Sire* is cruel, so the *Son* is too.

   My Plaint, ye Lasses, with this Burthen aid,
'Tis hard so true a Damsel dies a Maid.

   Farewell,° ye Woods, ye Meads, ye Streams that
      flow;
A sudden Death shall rid me of my Woe.   100
This Penknife keen my Windpipe shall divide.—
What, shall I fall as squeaking Pigs have dy'd!
No—To some Tree this Carcass I'll suspend.—
But worrying Curs° find such untimely End!
I'll speed me to the Pond, where the high Stool°
On the long Plank hangs o'er the muddy Pool,
That Stool, the dread of ev'ry scolding Quean.°—
Yet, sure a Lover should not dye so mean!
There plac'd aloft, I'll rave and rail by Fits,
Though all the Parish say I've lost my Wits;   110
And thence, if Courage holds, my self I'll throw,
And quench my Passion in the Lake below.

   Ye Lasses, cease your Burthen, cease to moan,
And, by my Case forewarn'd, go mind your own.

89–96. Now . . . too: [Gay's note]

   Nunc scio quid sit Amor, &c.
   Crudelis mater magis an puer improbus ille?
   Improbus ille puer, crudelis tu quoque mater.
                                          VIRG.

["Now I know what Cupid is. . . . Is the mother more cruel
or that boy more wicked? Wicked the boy, cruel you too,
mother" (Virgil, *Eclogues*, viii. 43 and 49–50).] **89. ken:**
[Gay's note] To ken. *Scire*. Chaucero, *to Ken; and Kende
notus. A.S. cunnan. Goth. Kunnan. Germanis Kennen. Danis
Kiende. Islandis Kunna. Belgis Kennen. This Word is of general
use, but not very common, though not unknown to the Vulgar.
Ken for prospicere is well known and used to discover by the
Eye. Ray. F.R.S.* [John Ray's *A Collection of English Words
Not Generally Used, with Their Significations and Original* was
first published in 1674.] **91. Shambles:** slaughterhouses.
99–112. Farewell . . . below: [Gay's note]

   —vivite Sylvæ
   Præceps aerii specula de montis in undas
   Deferar.
                                          VIRG.

["Farewell, o woods, from the watchtower of the lofty
mountain I shall plunge headlong into the waves" (Virgil,
Eclogues, viii. 58–60).] **104. worrying Curs:** biting dogs.
105. the high Stool: the ducking stool. **107. Quean:**
impudent or ill-behaved woman.

59–64. Let . . . Lass: [Gay's note] *Jungentur jam Gryphes
equis; ævoque sequenti / Cum canibus timidi venient ad pocula
Damæ.* VIRG. ["Now griffins will mate with horses, and in
time to come the timid deer will come to the water with the
dogs" (Virgil, *Eclogues*, viii. 27–28; for *Damæ* read *dammae*).]
59. coupling Straps: used to link animals together. **60.
clocking:** (clucking) sitting on eggs. **67–72. Sooner . . .
Love:** [Gay's note]

   Ante leves ergo pascentur in æthere Cervi
   Et freta destituent nudos in littore Pisces

             . . .

   Quam nostro illius labatur pectore vultus.
                                          VIRG.

["Therefore the light stags shall sooner graze in the sky and
the seas shall leave the fishes naked on the shore . . . than his
countenance shall slip from my heart" (Virgil, *Eclogues*, i.
59–60 and 63; for *littore* read *litore*).] **72. wonted Love:** love
to which I was accustomed. **75. Proffers:** offers. **85. nor:**
neither.

The Sun was set; the Night came on a-pace,
And falling Dews bewet around the Place,
The Bat takes airy Rounds on leathern Wings,
And the hoarse Owl his woeful Dirges sings;
The prudent Maiden deems it now too late,
And 'till to Morrow comes, defers her Fate.   120

THURSDAY; OR, THE SPELL

HOBNELIA.

HOBNELIA seated in a dreary Vale,
In pensive Mood rehears'd her piteous Tale,
Her piteous Tale the Winds in Sighs bemoan,
And pining Eccho answers Groan for Groan.

I rue the Day, a rueful Day I trow,°
The woful Day, a Day indeed of Woe!
When *Lubberkin* to Town his Cattle drove,
A Maiden fine bedight° he hapt to love;
The Maiden fine bedight his Love retains,
And for the Village he forsakes the Plains.   10
Return, my *Lubberkin*, these Ditties hear;
Spells will I try, and Spells shall ease my Care.
  With my sharp Heel I three times mark the Ground,
  And turn me thrice around, around, around.

When first the Year, I heard the Cuckow sing,
And call with welcome Note the budding Spring,
I straitway set a running with such Haste,
Deb'rah who won the Smock scarce ran so fast.
'Till spent for lack of Breath, quite weary grown,
Upon a rising Bank I sat adown,   20
Then doff'd° my Shoe, and by my Troth, I swear,
Therein I spy'd this yellow frizled Hair,
As like to *Lubberkin's* in Curl and Hue,
As if upon his comely Pate it grew.
  With my sharp Heel I three times mark the Ground,
  And turn me thrice around, around, around.

At Eve last *Midsummer* no Sleep I sought,
But to the Field a Bag of Hemp-seed brought,
I scatter'd round the Seed on ev'ry side,
And three times in a trembling Accent cry'd.   30
This Hempseed with my Virgin hand I sow,
Who shall my True-love be, the Crop shall mow.

I strait look'd back, and if my Eyes speak Truth,
With his keen Scythe behind me came the Youth.
  With my sharp Heel I three times mark the Ground,
  And turn me thrice around, around, around.

Last *Valentine*, the Day when Birds of Kind
Their Paramours with mutual Chirpings find;
I rearly° rose, just at the break of Day,
Before the Sun had chas'd the Stars away;   40
A-field I went, amid the Morning Dew
To milk my Kine (for so should Huswives do)
Thee first I spy'd, and the first Swain we see,
In spite of Fortune shall our True-love be;
See, *Lubberkin*, each Bird his Partner take,
And can'st thou then thy Sweetheart dear forsake?
  With my sharp Heel I three times mark the Ground,
  And turn me thrice around, around, around.

Last *May-day* fair I search'd to find a Snail
That might my secret Lover's Name reveal;   50
Upon a Gooseberry Bush a Snail I found,
For always Snails near sweetest Fruit abound.
I seiz'd the Vermine, home I quickly sped,
And on the Hearth the milk-white Embers spread.
Slow crawl'd the Snail, and if I right can spell,
In the soft Ashes mark'd a curious *L*:°
Oh, may this wondrous Omen lucky prove!
For *L* is found in *Lubberkin* and *Love*.
  With my sharp Heel I three times mark the Ground,
  And turn me thrice around, around, around.   60

Two Hazel-Nuts I threw into the Flame,
And to each Nut I gave a Sweet-heart's Name.
This with the loudest Bounce me sore° amaz'd,
That in a Flame of brightest Colour blaz'd.
As blaz'd the Nut so may thy Passion grow,°
For 'twas *thy Nut* that did so brightly glow.°
  With my sharp Heel I three times mark the Ground,
  And turn me thrice around, around, around.

As Peascods° once I pluck'd, I chanc'd to see
One that was closely fill'd with three times three,   70

---

39. **rearly:** early; see Gay's note to "Monday," l. 6.
56. **In . . . L:** The chance formation of an initial or name in the ashes on the hearth was thought to reveal the identity of one's lover. 63. **sore:** extremely. 64–65. **That . . . grow:** [Gay's note] ἐγὼ δ'ἐπὶ Δέλφιδι δάφναν Αἴθω. Χ'ὡς αὐτὰ λακέει μέγα καππυρίσασα. Theoc. ["I burn a laurel against Delphis. And just as having caught fire it crackles loudly . . ." (Theocritus, *Idylls*, ii. 23–24).] 66. **For . . . glow:** [Gay's note] *Daphnis me malus urit, ego hanc in Daphnide [laurum].* ["Wicked Daphnis burns me [with love], I [burn] this [laurel] on Daphnis [i.e., in her image]" (Virgil, *Eclogues*, viii. 83).] 69. **Peascods:** pea pods.

Thursday. 5. **trow:** trust, believe. 8. **bedight:** [Gay's note] Dight *or* bedight, *from the* Saxon *Word* Dihtan, *which signifies* to set in order. [Gay gives but one of several meanings of *dight;* that called for by the present context would appear to be "dressed, arrayed."] 21. **doff'd:** [Gay's note] Doff *and* Don, *contracted from the Words* do off *and* do on.

Which when I crop'd I safely home convey'd,
And o'er my Door the Spell in secret laid.
My Wheel I turn'd, and sung a Ballad new,
While from the Spindle I the Fleeces drew;
The Latch mov'd up, when who should first come
    in,
But in his proper Person,—*Lubberkin.*
I broke my Yarn surpriz'd the Sight to see,
Sure Sign that he would break his Word with me.
Eftsoons° I join'd it with my wonted Slight,°
So may again his Love with mine unite !   80

With my sharp Heel I three times mark the Ground,
And turn me thrice around, around, around.

This *Lady-fly* I take from off the Grass,
Whose spotted Back might scarlet Red surpass:
Fly, Lady-Bird, North, South, or East or West,
Fly where the Man is found that I love best.°
He leaves my Hand, see to the *West* he's flown,
To call my True-love from the faithless Town.

With my sharp Heel I three times mark the Ground,
And turn me thrice around, around, around.   90

I pare this pippin round and round again,
My shepherd's name to flourish on the plain.
I fling th' unbroken Paring o'er my Head,°
Upon the Grass a perfect L is read;
Yet on my Heart a fairer L is seen
Than what the Paring marks upon the Green.

With my sharp Heel I three times mark the Ground,
And turn me thrice around, around, around.

This Pippin shall another Tryal make,
See from the Core two Kernels brown I take;   100
This on my Cheek for *Lubberkin* is worn,
And *Boobyclod* on t' other side is born.
But *Boobyclod* soon drops upon the Ground,
A certain Token that his Love's unsound,
While *Lubberkin* sticks firmly to the last;
Oh were his Lips to mine but join'd so fast !

With my sharp Heel I three times mark the Ground,
And turn me thrice around, around, around.

As *Lubberkin* once slept beneath a Tree,

I twitch'd his dangling Garter from his Knee;   110
He wist not when the hempen String I drew,
Now mine I quickly doff of Inkle Blue;
Together fast I tye the Garters twain,
And while I knit the Knot repeat this Strain.
Three times a True-love's Knot I tye secure,
Firm be the Knot, firm may his Love endure.°

With my sharp Heel I three times mark the Ground,
And turn me thrice around, around, around.

As I was wont, I trudg'd last Market-Day
To Town, with New-laid Eggs preserv'd in Hay.   120
I made my Market long before 'twas Night,
My Purse grew heavy and my Basket light.
Strait to the Pothecary's Shop I went,
And in Love-Powder all my Mony spent;°
Behap what will, next Sunday after Prayers,
When to the Ale-house *Lubberkin* repairs,
These *Golden Flies* into his Mug I'll throw,°
And soon the Swain with fervent Love shall glow.

With my sharp Heel I three times mark the Ground,
And turn me thrice around, around, around.   130

But hold—our *Light-Foot* barks, and cocks his Ears,°
O'er yonder Stile see *Lubberkin* appears.
He comes, he comes, *Hobnelia's* not bewray'd,°
Nor shall she crown'd with Willow° die a Maid.
He vows, he swears, he'll give me a green Gown,
Oh dear ! I fall *adown, adown, adown!*

---

79. Eftsoons: See Gay's note to "Monday," l. 69. The meaning "soon after" or "forthwith" fits here. **Slight:** (sleight) skill, dexterity. **85–86. Fly . . . best:** a charm used for divining one's true love. **93. I . . . Head:** [Gay's note] *Transque Caput jace; ne respexeris.* VIRG. ["Throw it over your head; do not look back" (Virgil, *Eclogues,* viii. 102).]

110–16. I . . . endure: [Gay's note] *Necte tribus nodis ternos, Amarylli, Colores / Necte, Amarylli modo; & Veneris dic vincula necto.* VIRG. ["Tie three colors in three knots, Amaryllis, just tie [them], Amaryllis; and say, 'I tie the bonds of Venus' " (Virgil, *Eclogues,* viii. 77–78).]
123–24. Strait . . . spent: [Gay's note] *Has Herbas, atque hæc Ponto mihi lecta venena, / Ipse dedit Mæris.* VIRG. ["Moeris himself gave me these herbs and these poisons gathered in Pontus" (Virgil, *Eclogues,* viii. 95–96 ; for *Mæris* read *Moeris*).]
127. These . . . throw: [Gay's note] ποτòν κακòν [words transposed] αὔριον οἴσω. THEOC. ["An evil drink I shall bring tomorrow" (Theocritus, *Idylls,* ii. 58).] **131. But . . . Ears:** [Gay's note] *Nescio quid certe est: & Hylax in limine latrat.* ["There surely is something, and Hylax is barking at the threshold" (Virgil, *Eclogues,* viii. 107).] **133. bewray'd:** betrayed. **134. Willow:** the symbol of grief for unrequited love.

FRIDAY; OR, THE DIRGE°

BUMKINET, GRUBBINOL.

BUMKINET.

WHY, *Grubbinol*, dost thou so wistful seem?
There's Sorrow in the Look, if right I deem.
'Tis true, yon Oaks with yellow Tops appear,
And chilly Blasts begin to nip the Year;
From the tall Elm a Show'r of Leaves is born,
And their lost Beauty riven° Beeches mourn.
Yet ev'n this Season Pleasance blithe affords,
Now the squeez'd Press foams with our Apple Hoards.
Come, let us hye, and quaff a cheery Bowl,
Let Cyder New *wash Sorrow from thy Soul.*   10

GRUBBINOL.

Ah *Bumkinet!* since thou from hence wert gone,
From these sad Plains all Merriment is flown;
Should I reveal my Grief 'twould spoil thy Chear,
And make thine Eye o'erflow with many a Tear.

BUMKINET.

Hang Sorrow! Let's to yonder Hutt repair,
And with trim Sonnets *cast away our Care.*°
Gillian of Croydon° well thy Pipe can play,
Thou sing'st most sweet, *o'er Hills and far away.*°
Of *Patient Grissel*° I devise to sing,
And Catches° quaint shall make the Vallies ring.   20
Come, *Grubbinol*, beneath this Shelter, come,
From hence we view our Flocks securely roam.

GRUBBINOL.

Yes, blithesome Lad, a Tale I mean to sing,
But with my Woe shall distant Valleys ring.
The Tale shall make our Kidlings droop their Head,
For Woe is me!—our *Blouzelind* is dead.

BUMKINET.

Is *Blouzelinda* dead? farewel my Glee°!
No Happiness is now reserv'd for me.
As the Wood Pidgeon cooes without his Mate,
So shall my doleful Dirge bewail her Fate.   30
Of *Blouzelinda* fair I mean to tell,
The peerless Maid that did all Maids excell.

Henceforth the Morn shall dewy Sorrow shed,
And Ev'ning Tears upon the Grass be spread;
The rolling Streams with watry Grief shall flow,
And Winds shall moan aloud—when loud they blow.
Henceforth, as oft as *Autumn* shall return,
The dropping Trees, whene'er it rains, shall mourn;
This Season quite shall strip the Country's Pride,
For 'twas in *Autumn Blouzelinda* dy'd.   40

Where-e'er I gad, I *Blouzelind* shall view,
Woods, Dairy, Barn and Mows our Passion knew.
When I direct my Eyes to yonder Wood,
Fresh rising Sorrow curdles in my Blood.
Thither I've often been the Damsel's Guide,
When rotten Sticks our Fuel have supply'd;
There, I remember how her Faggots large,
Were frequently these happy Shoulders charge.
Sometimes this Crook drew Hazel Boughs adown,
And stuff'd her Apron wide with Nuts so brown;   50
Or when her feeding Hogs had miss'd their Way,
Or wallowing 'mid a Feast of Acorns lay;
Th' untoward° Creatures to the Stye I drove,
And whistled all the Way—or told my Love.

If by the Dairy's Hatch° I chance to hie,
I shall her goodly Countenance espie,
For there her goodly Countenance I've seen,
Set off with Kerchief starch'd and Pinners clean.
Sometimes, like Wax, she rolls the Butter round,
Or with the wooden Lilly prints° the Pound.   60
Whilome I've seen her skim the clouted Cream,°
And press from spongy Curds the milky Stream.
But now, alas! these Ears shall hear no more
The whining Swine surround the Dairy Door,

Friday. Dirge: [Gay's note] *Dirge, or Dyrge, a mournful Ditty, or Song of Lamentation over the dead, not a Contraction of the Latin Dirige in the Popish Hymn* Dirige Gressus meos, *as some pretend. But from the Teutonick* Dyrke, Laudare, *to praise and extol. Whence it is possible their* Dyrke *and our* Dirge, *was a laudatory Song to commemorate and applaud the Dead.* Cowell's Interpreter. [John Cowell's *Interpreter*, primarily a dictionary of legal terms, was first published in 1607. It was re-edited by Thomas Manley and appeared in several editions with varying titles into the early part of the eighteenth century.] **6. riven:** split. **15-16. Hang . . . Care:** [Gay's note] *Incipe Mopse prior si quos aut Phyllidis ignes / Aut Alconis habes Laudes, aut jurgia Codri.* ["Begin, Mopsus, first, if you have any passions [songs of love] for Phyllis or praises of Alcon or abuse of Codrus" (Virgil, *Eclogues*, v. 10-11).] **17. Gillian of Croydon:** *Gillian of Croyden, a New Ballad: The Words Made to the Tune of a Country Dance, Called Mall Peatley,* published in D'Urfey's *Pills to Purge Melancholy* (1706). **18. o'er . . . away:** the refrain of an old air, first collected in *Pills to Purge Melancholy;* used by Gay himself as the last line of his song *Were I Laid on Greenland's Coast* in *The Beggar's Opera,* below. **19. Patient Grissel:** an Elizabethan broadside ballad that tells the same story as Chaucer's *Clerk's Tale.* **20. Catches:** rounds.

27. Glee: [Gay's note] Glee, *Joy. from the* Dutch, Glooren, *to recreate.* **53. untoward:** unruly. **55. Hatch:** gate. **60. with . . . prints:** makes an imprint in the figure of the lily of the valley. **61. clouted Cream:** (clotted) cream obtained by heating the milk.

No more her Care shall fill the hollow Tray,
To fat the guzzling Hogs with Floods of Whey.
Lament, ye Swine, in Gruntings spend your Grief,
For you, like me, have lost your sole Relief.

When in the Barn the sounding Flail I ply,
Where from her Sieve the Chaff was wont to fly,   70
The Poultry there will seem around to stand,
Waiting upon her charitable Hand.
No Succour meet° the Poultry now can find,
For they, like me, have lost their *Blouzelind*.

Whenever by yon Barley Mow I pass,
Before my Eyes will trip the tidy Lass.
I pitch'd the Sheaves (oh could I do so now)
Which she in Rows pil'd on the growing Mow.
There ev'ry deale° my Heart by Love was gain'd,
There the sweet Kiss my Courtship has explain'd.°   80
Ah *Blouzelind!* that Mow I ne'er shall see,
But thy Memorial will revive in me.

Lament, ye Fields, and rueful Symptoms show,
Henceforth let not the smelling Primrose grow;
Let Weeds instead of Butter-flow'rs appear,
And Meads, instead of Daisies, Hemlock bear;
For Cowslips sweet let Dandelions spread,°
For *Blouzelinda*, blithesome Maid, is dead!
Lament ye Swains, and o'er her Grave bemoan,
And spell ye right this Verse upon her Stone.°   90
Here Blouzelinda *lyes—Alas, alas!*
Weep Shepherds,—and remember Flesh is Grass.°
GRUBBINOL.
Albeit thy Songs are sweeter to mine Ear,
Than to the thirsty Cattle Rivers clear;°

Or Winter Porridge to the lab'ring Youth,
Or Bunns and Sugar to the Damsel's Tooth;°
Yet *Blouzelinda*'s Name shall tune my Lay,
Of her I'll sing for ever and for aye.

When *Blouzelind* expir'd, the Weather's Bell
Before the drooping Flock toll'd forth her Knell;   100
The solemn Death-watch° click'd the Hour she dy'd,
And shrilling Crickets in the Chimney cry'd;
The boding Raven on her Cottage sate,
And with hoarse Croaking warn'd us of her Fate;
The Lambkin, which her wonted Tendance bred,
Drop'd on the Plains that fatal Instant dead;
Swarm'd on a rotten Stick the Bees I spy'd,
Which erst I saw when Goody *Dobson* dy'd.

How shall I, void of Tears, her Death relate,
While on her Dearling's° Bed her Mother sate!   110
These Words the dying *Blouzelinda* spoke,
And *of the Dead let none the Will revoke.*

Mother, quoth she, let not the Poultry need,
And give the Goose wherewith to raise her Breed,
Be these my Sister's Care—and ev'ry Morn
Amid the Ducklings let her scatter Corn;
The sickly Calf that's hous'd, be sure to tend,
Feed him with Milk, and from bleak Colds defend.
Yet e'er I die—see, Mother, yonder Shelf,
There secretly I've hid my worldly Pelf.   120
Twenty good Shillings in a Rag I laid,
Be ten the Parson's, for my Sermon paid.
The rest is yours—My Spinning-Wheel and Rake,
Let *Susan* keep for her dear Sister's sake;
My new Straw Hat that's trimly lin'd with Green,
Let *Peggy* wear, for she's a Damsel clean.
My leathern Bottle, long in Harvests try'd,
Be *Grubbinol*'s—this Silver Ring beside:
Three silver Pennies, and a Ninepence bent,
A Token kind, to *Bumkinet* is sent.   130

---

73. **meet:** meeting their needs. 79. **ev'ry deale:** in every respect, wholly. 80. **explain'd:** made plainly visible. 84–87. **Henceforth . . . spread:** [Gay's note] *Pro molli violâ, pro purpureo Narcisso | Carduus, & spinis surgit Paliurus acutis.* VIRG. ["Instead of the soft violet and the gleaming narcissus rises the thistle and the thorn with its sharp spines" (Virgil, *Eclogues*, v. 38–39).] 90. **And . . . Stone:** [Gay's note] *Et Tumulum facite, & tumulo superaddite Carmen.* ["And make a tomb, and over the tomb add a song [verse]" (Virgil, *Eclogues*, v. 42).] 92. **Flesh is Grass:** "For all flesh is as grass, and all the glory of man as the flower of grass. The grass withereth, and the flower thereof falleth away" (I Pet. 1:24). 93–94. **Albeit . . . clear:** [Gay's note]

> *Tale tuum Carmen nobis, Divine Poeta,*
> *Quale sopor fessis in gramine: quale per æstum*
> *Dulcis aquæ saliente sitim restinguere rivo.*
>
> · · ·
>
> *Nos tamen hæc quocumque modo tibi nostra vicissim*
> *Dicemus, Daphnique tuum tollemus ad astra.*
>
> VIRG.

["Such is your song to us, o divine poet, as sleep in the grass to the weary, as in the heat to quench the thirst with a dancing stream of sweet water. . . . Yet we in turn shall somehow sing to you these [songs] of ours and shall raise your Daphnis to the stars" (Virgil, *Eclogues*, v. 45–47 and 50–51).] 96. **Or . . . Tooth:** [Gay's note] κρέσσον μελπομένω τεῦ ἀκουέμεν ἠμὲλι λείχειν. THEOC. ["It is better to listen to your song than to lick honey" (Theocritus, *Idylls*, viii. 83).] 101. **Death-watch:** the name given to various insects which, because they make a noise like the ticking of a clock, were supposed to portend death. 110. **Dearling:** darling.

Thus spoke the Maiden, while her Mother cry'd,
And peaceful, like the harmless Lamb, she dy'd.

To show their Love, the Neighbours far and near,
Follow'd with wistful Look the Damsel's Bier.
Sprigg'd Rosemary the Lads and Lasses bore,
While dismally the Parson walk'd before.
Upon her Grave their Rosemary they threw,
The Daisie, Butter-flow'r and Endive Blue.

After the good Man warn'd us from his Text,
That None could tell whose Turn would be the
    next;   140
He said, that Heav'n would take her Soul no doubt.
And spoke the Hour-glass in her Praise—quite out.

To her sweet Mem'ry flow'ry Garlands strung,
O'er her now empty Seat aloft were hung.
With wicker Rods we fenc'd her Tomb around,
To ward from Man and Beast the hallow'd Ground,
Lest her new Grave the Parson's Cattle raze,
For both his Horse and Cow the Church-yard graze.

Now we trudg'd homeward to her Mother's Farm,
To drink new Cyder mull'd, with Ginger warm. 150
For Gaffer° Tread-well told us by the by,
Excessive Sorrow is exceeding dry.

While Bulls bear Horns upon their curled Brow,
Or Lasses with soft Stroakings milk the Cow;
While padling Ducks the standing Lake desire,
Or batt'ning Hogs roll in the sinking Mire;
While Moles the crumbled Earth in Hillocks raise,
So long shall Swains tell *Blouzelinda's* Praise.°

Thus wail'd the Louts, in melancholy Strain,
'Till bonny *Susan* sped a-cross the Plain;   160
They seiz'd the Lass in Apron clean array'd,
And to the Ale-house forc'd the willing Maid;
In Ale and Kisses they forget their Cares,
And *Susan Blouzelinda's* Loss repairs.

---

151. **Gaffer:** a term applied to an elderly man. **153–58.**
While . . . Praise: [Gay's note]

Dum juga montis Aper, fluvios dum Piscis amabit
Dumque Thymo pascentur apes, Dum rore cicadæ,
Semper honos nomenque tuum, laudesque manebunt.
                                                      VIRG.

["As long as the boar shall love the mountain ridges and the
fish the rivers, as long as the bees shall feed on thyme and the
crickets on dew, your honor, name, and praise shall always
endure" (Virgil, *Eclogues,* v. 76–78).]

SATURDAY;
OR, THE FLIGHTS

BOWZYBEUS.

SUBLIMER Strains, O rustick Muse, prepare;
Forget a-while the Barn and Dairy's Care;
Thy homely Voice to loftier Numbers raise,
The Drunkard's Flights require sonorous Lays,
With *Bowzybeus'* Songs exalt thy Verse,
While Rocks and Woods the various Notes rehearse.

'Twas in the Season when the Reaper's Toil
Of the ripe Harvest 'gan to rid the Soil;
Wide through the Field was seen a goodly Rout,°
Clean Damsels bound the gather'd Sheaves about,   10
The Lads with sharpen'd Hook and sweating Brow
Cut down the Labours of the Winter Plow.
To the near Hedge young *Susan* steps aside,
She feign'd her Coat or Garter was unty'd,
What-e'er she did, she stoop'd adown unseen,
And merry Reapers, what they list, will ween.°
Soon she rose up, and cry'd with Voice so shrill
That Eccho answer'd from the distant Hill;
The Youths and Damsels ran to *Susan's* Aid,
Who thought some Adder had the Lass dismay'd.   20
There fast asleep they *Bowzybeus* spy'd,
His Hat and oaken Staff lay close beside.°
That *Bowzybeus* who could sweetly sing,
Or with the rozin'd Bow torment the String;
That *Bowzybeus* who with Finger's speed
Could call soft Warblings from the breathing Reed;
That *Bowzybeus* who with jocond Tongue,
Ballads and Roundelays and Catches sung.
They loudly laugh to see the Damsel's Fright,
And in disport° surround the drunken Wight.   30
Ah *Bowzybeé,* why didst thou stay so long,
The Mugs were large, the Drink was wondrous strong!
Thou should'st have left the Fair before 'twas Night,
But thou sat'st toping 'till the Morning Light.
Cic'ly, brisk Maid, steps forth before the Rout,
And kiss'd with smacking Lip the snoring Lout.

Saturday. 9. Rout: assemblage. **16. what . . . ween:** will
believe what they like. **22. His . . . beside:** [Gay's note]
Serta procul tantum capiti delapsa jacebant. VIRG. ["The garland,
having just slipped from his head, lay close by" (Virgil,
Eclogues, vi. 16).] **30. disport:** merriment.

For Custom says, *Who-e'er this Venture proves,*°
For such a Kiss demands a pair of Gloves.
By her Example *Dorcas* bolder grows,
And plays a tickling Straw within his Nose.°   40
He rubs his Nostril, and in wonted Joke
The sneering Swains with hamm'ring° Speech
    bespoke.
To you, my Lads, I'll sing my Carrols o'er,
As for the Maids,—I've something else in store.°
    No sooner 'gan he raise his tuneful Song,
But Lads and Lasses round about him throng.
Not Ballad-singer plac'd above the Croud
Sings with a Note so shrilling sweet and loud,
Nor Parish Clerk who calls the Psalm so clear,°
Like *Bowzybeus* sooths th' attentive Ear.   50
    Of° Nature's Laws his Carrols first begun,
Why the grave Owl can never face the Sun.
For Owles, as Swains observe, detest the Light,
And only sing and seek their Prey by Night.
How Turnips hide their swelling Heads below,
And how the closing Colworts° upwards grow;
How *Will-a-Wisp*° mis-leads Night-faring Clowns,
O'er Hills, and sinking Bogs, and pathless Downs.

Of Stars he told that shoot with shining Trail,
And of the Glow-worms Light that gilds his Tail.   60
He sung where Wood-cocks in the Summer feed,
And in what Climates they renew their Breed;
Some think to Northern Coasts their Flight they tend,
Or to the Moon in Midnight Hours ascend.
Where Swallows in the Winter's Season keep,
And how the drowsie Bat and Dormouse sleep.
How Nature does the Puppy's Eyelid close,
'Till the bright Sun has nine times set and rose.
For Huntsmen by their long Experience find,
That Puppys still nine rolling Suns are blind.   70
    Now he goes on, and sings of Fairs and Shows,
For still new Fairs before his Eyes arose.
How Pedlars Stalls with glitt'ring Toys are laid,
The various Fairings° of the Country Maid.
Long silken Laces hang upon the Twine,
And Rows of Pins and amber Bracelets shine;
How the tight° Lass, knives, Combs and Scissars spys,
And looks on Thimbles with desiring Eyes.
Of Lott'ries next with tuneful Note he told,
Where silver Spoons are won and Rings of Gold.   80
The Lads and Lasses trudge the Street along,
And all the Fair is crouded in his Song.
The Mountebank now treads the Stage, and sells
His Pills, his Balsoms, and his Ague spells;
Now o'er and o'er the nimble Tumbler springs,
And on the Rope the vent'rous Maiden swings;
Jack-pudding° in his parti-coloured Jacket
Tosses the Glove and jokes at ev'ry Packet.°
Of *Raree-Shows*° he sung, and *Punch's* Feats,
Of Pockets pick'd in Crowds, and various Cheats.   90
    Then sad he sung *the Children in the Wood.*°
Ah barb'rous Uncle, stain'd with Infant Blood!
How Blackberrys they pluck'd in Desarts wild,
And fearless at the glittering Fauchion° smil'd;
Their little Corps° the Robin-red-breasts found,
And strow'd with pious Bill the Leaves around.
Ah gentle Birds! if this Verse lasts so long,
Your Names shall live for ever in my Song.°

---

37. **proves:** tries. 40. **And . . . Nose:** [Gay's note] *Sanguineis frontem Moris & Tempora pingit.* VIRG. ["She paints his forehead and temples with blood-red mulberries" (Virgil, *Eclogues*, vi. 22).] 42. **hamm'ring:** We adopt this reading from the fourth edition; it means "hesitant" or "stammering"; *stamm'ring* occurs in the other editions. 43–44. **To . . . store:** [Gay's note] *Carmina quæ vultis, cognoscite; carmina vobis. | Huic aliud Mercedis erit.* VIRG. ["Hear the songs which you desire; songs for you, for her there shall be another reward" (Virgil, *Eclogues*, vi. 25–26).] 47–49. **Not . . . clear:** [Gay's note] *Nec tantum Phœbo gaudet Parnasia rupes | Nec tantum Rhodope mirantur & Ismarus Orphea.* VIRG. ["Neither does the Parnassian crag take as much joy in Phoebus, nor do Rhodope and Ismarus so marvel at Orpheus" (Virgil, *Eclogues*, vi. 29–30).] 51–70. **Of . . . blind:** [Gay's note] *Our Swain had possibly read* Tusser, *from whence he might have collected these Philosophical Observations.* [*Tusser Redivivus: Being Part of Mr. Thomas Tusser's Five Hundred Points of Husbandry*, an updated edition of the Elizabethan versified manual, was published with a commentary in 1710. Sir Walter Scott described Tusser's object as "a sort of homely, pointed and quaint expression, like that of the old English proverb, which the rhyme and the alliteration tend to fix on the memory of the reader."] *Namque canebat uti magnum per inane coacta, &c.* [*semina terrarumque animaeque marisque fuissent*]. VIRG. ["For he sang how through the vast void there had been gathered [the seeds of the earth, air, and sea]" (Virgil, *Eclogues*, vi. 31–32).] 56. **Colworts:** (coleworts) cabbage plants. 57. **Will-a-Wisp:** a light that sometimes appears in the night, usually over marshland; also called *ignis fatuus* (foolish fire).

74. **Fairings:** presents. 77. **tight:** trim or shapely. 87. **Jack-pudding:** a clown, especially one assisting a mountebank. 88. **Packet:** packet of lies (told by the mountebank). 89. **Raree-Shows:** peep shows. 91. **the Children . . . Wood:** the most popular English broadside ballad—about two orphans left to die by their wicked uncle. 94. **Fauchion:** (falchion) broadsword. 95. **Corps:** corpses. 97–98. **Ah . . . Song:** [Gay's note] *Fortunati ambo, si quid mea Carmina possunt, | Nulla Dies unquam memori vos eximet ævo.* VIRG. ["O happy pair, if my songs have any power, no day shall ever remove you from the memory of time" (*Aeneid*, IX. 446–47).]

For Buxom *Joan* he sung the doubtful Strife,°
How the sly Sailor made the Maid a Wife.   100

To louder Strains he rais'd his Voice, to tell
What woeful Wars in *Chevy-Chace*° befell,
When *Piercy* drove the Deer with Hound and Horn,
Wars to be wept by Children yet unborn!
Ah *With'rington*,° more Years thy Life had crown'd,
If thou had'st never heard the Horn or Hound!
Yet shall the Squire, who fought on bloody Stumps,
By future Bards be wail'd in doleful Dumps.

All in the Land of Essex° next he chaunts,
How to sleek Mares starch Quakers turn Gallants; 110
How the grave Brother stood on Bank so green.
Happy for him if Mares had never been!°

Then he was seiz'd with a religious Qualm,
And on a sudden, sung the hundredth Psalm.

He sung of *Taffey-Welch*,° and *Sawney Scot*,°
Lilly-bullero° and the *Irish Trot*.°
Why° should I tell of *Bateman* or of *Shore*,°

Or *Wantley's Dragon*° slain by valiant *Moore*,
The Bow'r of Rosamond,° or *Robin Hood*,°
And how the *Grass now grows where* Troy Town
    stood°?   120

His Carrols ceas'd: The list'ning Maids and Swains
Seem still to hear some soft imperfect Strains.
Sudden he rose; and as he reels along
Swears Kisses sweet should well reward his Song.
The Damsels laughing fly: the giddy Clown
Again upon a Wheat-Sheaf drops adown;
The Pow'r that Guards the Drunk, his Sleep attends,
'Till, ruddy, like his Face, the Sun descends.

THE BIRTH OF THE SQUIRE.
AN ECLOGUE. IN IMITATION
OF THE *POLLIO*
OF VIRGIL

❧

One of five "eclogues" appearing in Gay's *Poems on Several Occasions* (1720, 1731). The text is from the first edition.

❧

YE sylvan Muses, loftier strains recite,
Not all in shades, and humble cotts° delight.
Hark! the bells ring; along the distant grounds
The driving gales convey the swelling sounds;
Th' attentive swain, forgetful of his work,
With gaping wonder, leans upon his fork.
What sudden news alarms the waking morn?
To the glad Squire a hopeful heir is born.
Mourn, mourn, ye stags; and all ye beasts of chase,
This hour destruction brings on all your race: 10
See the pleas'd tenants duteous off'rings bear,
Turkeys and geese and grocer's sweetest ware;
With the new health° the pond'rous tankard flows,

99. **the doubtful Strife:** [Gay's note] *A Song in the Comedy of* Love for Love, *beginning* A Soldier and a Sailor, &c. [The song, written by Congreve, was set by John Eccles.] 102. **Chevy-Chace:** a venerable minstrel ballad, describing the border encounter between the Scots under Douglas and the English under Percy. 105. **Ah With'rington:** The common broadside version of *Chevy Chace* goes as follows:

> For Witherington needs must I wayle
>   As one in dolefull dumpes,
> For when his leggs were smitte of,
>   He fought upon his stumpes.

109. **All . . . Essex:** [Gay's note] *A Song of Sir J. Denham's. See his Poems.* [Denham's *Poems and Translations* appeared in 1668. The song there is entitled *News from Colchester: or, a Proper New Ballad of Certain Carnal Passages Betwixt a Quaker and a Colt, at Horsly near Colchester in Essex.* See the selection from Denham in Part Three.] 112. **Happy . . . been:** [Gay's note] *Et fortunatam si nunquam Armenta fuissent / Pasiphaen.* VIRG. ["And Pasiphaë, happy if flocks [cattle] had never existed" (Virgil, *Eclogues*, vi. 45–46).] 115. **Taffey-Welch:** a mocking name for a Welshman used in numerous songs and nursery rhymes. **Sawney Scot:** the same for a Scotsman, e.g., D'Urfey's *Sawney Was Tall and of Noble Race.* 116. **Lilly-bullero:** This propaganda song, composed by the Marquis of Wharton, was credited with having driven James II into exile. **the Irish Trot:** a dance form. 117–20. **Why . . . stood:** [Gay's note] *Quid loquar aut Scyllam Nisi, &c.* VIRG. ["Or why should I speak of Scylla the daughter of Nisus . . . ." (Virgil, *Eclogues*, vi. 74).] 117. **Bateman, Shore:** [Gay's note] *Old English Ballads.* [Lord Bateman (Young Beichan in Scottish) was said to be the father of Thomas Becket. Jane Shore was the mistress of Edward IV.]

118. **Wantley's Dragon:** *The Dragon of Wantley* is a broadside ballad that tells the story of the slaying of the dragon by Moore of Moore Hall. 119. **The Bow'r . . . Rosamond:** *Fair Rosamond,* a broadside ballad by Thomas Deloney, tells of the poisoning of Rosamond Clifford, mistress of Henry II, by his queen, Eleanor of Aquitaine. Her bower was at Woodstock, near Oxford. **Robin Hood:** hero of numerous English minstrel ballads. 120. **the Grass . . . stood:** from the seventeenth-century broadside ballad of *Troy Town.* THE BIRTH OF THE SQUIRE. 2. **cotts:** cottages. 13. **the new health:** toasts to the newborn heir.

And old *October*° reddens ev'ry nose.
Beagles and spaniels round his cradle stand,
Kiss his moist lip and gently lick his hand;
He joys to hear the shrill horn's ecchoing sounds,
And learns to lisp the names of all the hounds.
With frothy ale to make his cup o'er-flow,
Barley shall in paternal acres grow;   20
The bee shall sip the fragrant dew from flow'rs,
To give metheglin° for his morning hours;
For him the clustring hop° shall climb the poles,
And his own orchard sparkle in his bowles.

His Sire's exploits he now with wonder hears,
The monstrous tales indulge his greedy ears;
How when youth strung his nerves and warm'd his
        veins,
He rode the mighty *Nimrod*° of the plains:
He leads the staring infant through the hall,
Points out the horny spoils that grace the wall;   30
Tells, how this stag thro' three whole Countys fled,
What rivers swam, where bay'd, and where he bled.
Now he the wonders of the fox repeats,
Describes the desp'rate chase, and all his cheats;°
How in one day beneath his furious speed,
He tir'd sev'n coursers° of the fleetest breed;
How high the pale he leapt, how wide the ditch,
When the hound tore the haunches of the witch°!
These storys which descend from son to son,
The forward° boy shall one day make his own.   40

Ah, too fond mother, think the time draws nigh,
That calls the darling from thy tender eye;
How shall his spirit brook the rigid rules,
And the long tyranny of grammar schools?
Let younger brothers o'er dull authors plod,
Lash'd into *Latin* by the tingling rod;
No, let him never feel that smart disgrace:
Why should he wiser prove than all his race°?
    When rip'ning youth with down o'ershades his
        chin,
And ev'ry female eye incites to sin;   50
The milk-maid (thoughtless of her future shame)
With smacking lip shall raise his guilty flame;

The dairy, barn, the hay-loft and the grove
Shall oft' be conscious of their stolen love.
But think, *Priscilla*, on that dreadful time,
When pangs and watry qualms° shall own° thy crime;
How wilt thou tremble when thy nipple's prest,
To see the white drops bathe thy swelling breast!
Nine moons shall publickly divulge thy shame,
And the young Squire forestall° a father's name.   60
    When twice twelve times the reaper's sweeping
        hand
With levell'd harvests has bestrown the land,
On fam'd *St. Hubert*'s feast,° his winding horn
Shall cheer the joyful hound and wake the morn:
This memorable day his eager speed
Shall urge with bloody heel the rising steed.
O check the foamy bit, nor tempt thy fate,
Think on the murders of a five-bar gate°!
Yet prodigal of life, the leap he tries,
Low in the dust his groveling honour lies,   70
Headlong he falls, and on the rugged stone
Distorts° his neck, and cracks the collar bone;
O vent'rous youth, thy thirst of game allay,
Mayst thou survive the perils of this day!
He shall survive; and in late years be sent
To snore away Debates in *Parliament*.

    The time shall come, when his more solid sense
With nod° important shall the laws dispense;
A Justice with grave Justices shall sit,°
He praise their wisdom, they admire his wit.   80
No greyhound shall attend° the tenant's pace,
No rusty gun the farmer's chimney grace;
Salmons shall leave their covers void of fear,
Nor dread the thievish net or triple spear;°
Poachers shall tremble at his awful name,
Whom vengeance now o'ertakes for murder'd game.

    Assist me, *Bacchus*, and ye drunken Pow'rs,
To sing his friendships and his midnight hours!
    Why dost thou glory in thy strength of beer,
Firm-cork'd, and mellow'd till the twentieth year;   90
Brew'd or° when *Phœbus* warms the fleecy sign,
Or when his languid rays in *Scorpio* shine.°

---

14. **old October:** October ale. 22. **metheglin:** a spiced
mead. 23. **hop:** a climbing plant, the female of which
produces cones used in flavoring malt liquors. 28. **Nimrod:**
"He was a mighty hunter before the Lord" (Gen. 10:9).
34. **cheats:** stratagems. 36. **coursers:** racehorses. 38. **the
witch:** [Gay's note] *The most common accident to Sportsmen;
to hunt a witch in the shape of a hare.* 40. **forward:** eager. 48.
all his race: the "race" of squires.

56. **watry qualms:** nausea. **own:** confess, reveal. 60.
forestall: anticipate; i.e., he will be a father before the proper
time. 63. **St. . . . feast:** November 3. St. Hubert is the patron
saint of hunters. 68. **a five-bar gate:** a high fence or hurdle.
72. **Distorts:** wrenches. 78. **nod:** a nod of the head expressive
of power or authority. 79. **with . . . sit:** The squire sits with
the circuit court. 81. **attend:** lie in wait for. 84. **triple spear:**
the trident. 91. **or:** either. 91–92. **when . . . shine:** in the
spring (Aries) or fall (Scorpio).

Think on the mischiefs which from hence have sprung!
It arms with curses dire the wrathful tongue;
Foul scandal to the lying lip affords,
And prompts the mem'ry with injurious words.
O where is wisdom, when by this o'erpower'd?
The State is censur'd, and the maid deflower'd!
And wilt thou still, O Squire, brew ale so strong?
Hear then the dictates of prophetic song.   100
    Methinks I see him in his hall appear,
Where the long table floats in clammy beer,
'Midst mugs and glasses shatter'd o'er the floor,
Dead-drunk his servile crew supinely snore;
Triumphant, o'er the prostrate brutes he stands,
The mighty bumper trembles in his hands;
Boldly he drinks, and like his glorious Sires,
In copious gulps of potent ale expires.

FROM

ACIS AND GALATEA

❦

This English pastoral opera was written about 1718,
with some incidental aid from Pope and John Hughes,
and set to music by Handel. It first appeared in print in
1732. The singer of the following recitativo and air
from Act II is the villain of the piece, the monster
Polyphemus, who has been distracted from his usual
pursuits—eating infants and drinking blood—by an
amorous passion for the shepherd maid Galatea.
    The text is that of the first edition.

❦

RECITATIVO

Polyph.   I rage, I melt, I burn,
The feeble God° has stab'd me to the Heart.
Thou trusty Pine, Prop of my Godlike Steps,
I lay thee by.
Bring me an hundred Reeds of decent growth,
To make a Pipe for my capacious Mouth.
In soft enchanting Accents let me breathe,
Sweet *Galatea*'s Beauty, and my Love.

ACIS AND GALATEA: *Recitativo.* **2. The feeble God:** Cupid.

AIR

O ruddier than the Cherry,
O sweeter than the Berry,
    O Nymph more bright
    Than Moonshine Night,
Like Kidlings blith and merry.
Ripe as the melting Cluster,
No Lilly has such Lustre,
    Yet hard to tame,
    As raging Flame,
And fierce as Storms that bluster.   10
O Ruddier, &c.°

MY OWN EPITAPH

❦

Early in the year 1729 Gay wrote to Pope despondent-
ly:

I begin to look upon myself as one already dead;
and desire, my dear Mr. *Pope*, (whom I love as my
own Soul) if you survive me, (as you certainly will)
that you will, if a Stone should mark the Place of
my Grave, see these Words put on it:

Life is a Jest, and all Things show it;
I thought so once, but now I know it.

With what more you may think proper.
    If any Body should ask, how I could communi-
cate this after Death? Let it be known, it is not
meant so, but my present Sentiment in Life.

The epitaph had already been printed in Gay's *Poems
on Several Occasions* (1720), from which we take our
text.

❦

LIFE is a jest; and all things show it,
I thought so once; but now I know it.

Air. **11. O . . . &c.:** The musical design of an *aria da capo*
requires that the whole first section be repeated.

FROM

FABLES

The first series of Gay's *Fables* was composed for and dedicated to William, Duke of Cumberland, the four-year-old son of Princess Caroline; it was published in March, 1727. In his letter to Pope quoted in the preceding headnote, Gay laments: "Why did I not take your Advice before my writing Fables for the Duke, not to write them? Or rather, to write them for some young Nobleman? It is my very hard Fate, I must get nothing, write for them or against them." Nevertheless, the *Fables* went into a second and third edition in successive years, and in 1731 Gay began a second series, which was posthumously published in 1738. The text is that of the first edition (1727).

INTRODUCTION TO THE *FABLES*

The SHEPHERD *and the* PHILOSOPHER.

REmote from citys liv'd a Swain,
Unvex'd with all the cares of gain,
His head was silver'd o'er with age,
And long experience made him sage;
In summer's heat and winter's cold
He fed his flock and pen'd the fold,
His hours in cheerful labour flew,
Nor envy nor ambition knew;
His wisdom and his honest fame
Through all the country rais'd his name.   10
  A deep Philosopher (whose rules
Of moral life were drawn from schools)
The Shepherd's homely cottage sought,
And thus explor'd his reach of thought.
  Whence is thy learning? Hath thy toil
O'er books consum'd the midnight oil?
Hast thou old *Greece* and *Rome* survey'd,
And the vast sense of *Plato* weigh'd?
Hath *Socrates* thy soul refin'd,
And hast thou fathom'd *Tully*'s° mind?   20
Or, like the wise *Ulysses* thrown

By various fates on realms unknown,
Hast thou through many citys stray'd,
Their customs, laws and manners weigh'd?
  The Shepherd modestly reply'd.
I ne'er the paths of learning try'd,
Nor have I roam'd in foreign parts
To read mankind, their laws and arts;
For man is practis'd in disguise,
He cheats the most discerning eyes: 30
Who by that search shall wiser grow,
When we ourselves can never know?
The little knowledge, I have gain'd,
Was all from simple nature drain'd;
Hence my life's maxims took their rise,
Hence grew my settled hate to vice.
  The daily labours of the bee
Awake my soul to industry.
Who can observe the careful ant,
And not provide for future want?   40
My dog (the trustiest of his kind)
With gratitude inflames my mind;
I mark his true, his faithful way,
And in my service copy *Tray*.
In constancy, and nuptial love
I learn my duty from the dove.
The hen, who from the chilly air
With pious wing protects her care,
And ev'ry fowl that flies at large
Instructs me in a parent's charge.   50
  From nature too I take my rule
To shun contempt and ridicule.
I never with important air
In conversation overbear;
Can grave and formal pass for wise,
When men the solemn owl despise?
My tongue within my lips I rein,
For who talks much must talk in vain;
We from the wordy torrent fly:
Who listens to the chatt'ring pye°?   60
Nor would I with felonious slight
By stealth invade my neighbour's right;
Rapacious animals we hate:
Kites, hawks and wolves deserve their fate.
Do not we just abhorrence find
Against the toad and serpent kind?
But envy, calumny and spite
Bear stronger venom in their bite.

FABLES: *Introduction.* **20. Tully:** Cicero.

60. pye: magpie.

Thus ev'ry object of creation
Can furnish hints to contemplation,   70
And from the most minute and mean
A virtuous mind can morals glean.
   Thy fame is just, the Sage replys,
Thy virtue proves thee truly wise;
Pride often guides the author's pen,
Books as affected are as men,
But he who studys nature's laws
From certain truth his maxims draws,
And those, without° our schools, suffice
To make men moral, good and wise.   80

FABLE XXXIX

The FATHER and JUPITER.

THE Man to *Jove* his suit preferr'd;°
He begg'd a wife; his prayer was heard.
Jove wonder'd at his bold addressing.
For how precarious is the blessing!
   A wife he takes. And now for heirs
Again he worries heav'n with prayers.
Jove nods assent. Two hopeful boys
And a fine girle reward his joys.
   Now more solicitous he grew,
And set their future lives in view;   10
He saw that all respect and duty
Were paid to wealth, to power, and beauty.
   Once more, he cries, accept my prayer,
Make my lov'd progeny thy care:
Let my first hope, my fav'rite boy,
All fortune's richest gifts enjoy.
My next with strong ambition fire,
May favour teach him to aspire,
'Till he the step of power ascend,
And courtiers to their idol bend.   20
With ev'ry grace, with ev'ry charm
My daughter's perfect features arm.
If Heav'n approve, a father's blest.
Jove smiles, and grants his full request.
   The first, a miser at the heart,
Studious of ev'ry griping° art,
Heaps hoards on hoards with anxious pain,
And all his life devotes to gain.

He feels no joy, his cares encrease,
He neither wakes nor sleeps in peace,   30
In fancy'd want, (a wretch compleat)
He starves, and yet he dares not eat.
   The next to sudden honours grew,
The thriving art of courts he knew;
He reach'd the height of power and place,
Then fell, the victim of disgrace.
   Beauty with early bloom supplies
His daughter's cheek, and points° her eyes:
The vain coquette each suit disdains,
And glories in her lovers pains.   40
With age she fades, each lover flies,
Contemn'd, forlorn, she pines and dies.
   When *Jove* the father's grief survey'd,
And heard him Heav'n and Fate upbraid,
Thus spoke the God. By outward show
Men judge of happiness and woe:
Shall ignorance of good and ill
Dare to direct th' eternal will?
Seek virtue; and of that possest,
To Providence resign the rest.   50

FABLE XLIX

The MAN and the FLEA.

WHether on earth, in air, or main,
Sure ev'ry thing alive is vain!
Does not the hawk all fowls survey,
As destin'd only for his prey?
And do not tyrants, prouder things,
Think men were born for slaves to kings?
   When the crab views the pearly strands,
Or *Tagus,*° bright with golden sands,
Or crawles beside the coral grove,
And hears the ocean roll above;   10
Nature is too profuse, says he,
Who gave all these to pleasure me!
   When bord'ring pinks and roses bloom,
And ev'ry garden breaths perfume,
When peaches glow with sunny dyes,
Like *Laura*'s cheek, when blushes rise;
When with huge figs the branches bend;
When clusters from the vine depend;°

---

79. **without:** outside. *Fable XXXIX.* **1. preferr'd:** proffered, presented. **26. griping:** grasping, avaricious.

38. points: makes prominent. *Fable XLIX.* **8. Tagus:** the river Tagus in Spain (Tajo) and Portugal (Tejo). **18. depend:** hang.

The snail looks round on flow'r and tree,
And cries, all these were made for me!   20

What dignity's in human nature,
Says Man, the most conceited creature,
As from a cliff he cast his eye,
And view'd the sea and arched sky!
The sun was sunk beneath the main,
The moon, and all the starry train
Hung the vast vault of heav'n. The Man
His contemplation thus began.

When I behold this glorious show,
And the wide watry world below,   30
The scaly people° of the main,
The beasts that range the wood or plain,
The wing'd inhabitants of air,
The day, the night, the various year,
And know all these by heav'n design'd
As gifts to pleasure human kind,
I cannot raise my worth too high;
Of what vast consequence am I!

Not of th' importance you suppose,
Replies a Flea upon his nose: 40
Be humble, learn thyself to scan;
Know, pride was never made for man.
'Tis vanity that swells thy mind.
What, heav'n and earth for thee design'd!
For thee! made only for our need;
That more important Fleas might feed.

FABLE L

The HARE and many FRIENDS.

FRiendship, like love, is but a name,
Unless to one you stint° the flame.
The child, whom many fathers share,
Hath seldom known a father's care;
'Tis thus in friendships; who depend
On many, rarely find a friend.

A Hare, who, in a civil way,
Comply'd with ev'ry thing, like *Gay*,
Was known by all the bestial train,
Who haunt the wood, or graze the plain: 10
Her care was, never to offend,
And ev'ry creature was her friend.

As forth she went at early dawn
To taste the dew-besprinkled lawn,
Behind she hears the hunter's cries,
And from the deep-mouth'd thunder flies;
She starts, she stops, she pants for breath,
She hears the near advance of death,
She doubles,° to mis-lead the hound,
And measures back her mazy round;   20
'Till, fainting in the publick way,°
Half dead with fear she gasping lay.

What transport in her bosom grew,
When first the horse appear'd in view!

Let me, says she, your back ascend,
And owe my safety to a friend,
You know my feet betray my flight,
To friendship ev'ry burthen's light.

The horse reply'd, poor honest puss,
It grieves my heart to see thee thus;   30
Be comforted, relief is near;
For all your friends are in the rear.

She next the stately bull implor'd;
And thus reply'd the mighty lord.
Since ev'ry beast alike can tell
That I sincerely wish you well,
I may, without offence, pretend
To take the freedom of a friend;
Love calls me hence; a fav'rite cow
Expects me near yon barley mow:°   40
And when a lady's in the case,
You know, all other things give place.
To leave you thus might seem unkind;
But see, the goat is just behind.

The goat remark'd° her pulse was high,
Her languid head, her heavy eye;
My back, says he, may do you harm;
The sheep's at hand, and wool is warm.

The sheep was feeble, and complain'd,
His sides a load of wool sustain'd,   50
Said he was slow, confest his fears;
For hounds eat sheep as well as hares.

She now the trotting calf addrest,
To save from death a friend distrest.

Shall I, says he, of tender age,
In this important care engage?
Older and abler pass you by;
How strong are those! how weak am I!
Should I presume to bear you hence,

---

31. scaly people: fish; a typical neoclassical circumlocution, like "wing'd inhabitants" of line 33. *Fable L.* **2. stint:**
confine.

19. doubles: turns sharply, or back, on her course. **21. way:**
road. **40. mow:** stack. **45. remark'd:** observed.

Those friends of mine may take offence.   60
Excuse me then. You know my heart.
But dearest friends, alas, must part!
How shall we all lament! Adieu.
For see the hounds are just in view.

THE BEGGAR'S OPERA

The Beggar's Opera opened at the Theatre Royal in Lincoln's Inn Fields on the night of January 29, 1728, and proceeded to run through a record sixty-two performances its first season. The work had been refused by Colley Cibber, manager of Drury Lane, and was accepted by John Rich, manager of Lincoln's Inn Fields, only when Gay's patron, the Duchess of Queensberry, offered to underwrite any loss. Doubts of the play's prospects persisted through rehearsals and into the first night's performance. Pope reported (according to Joseph Spence in *Observations, Anecdotes, and Characters of Books and Men* [1820]):

> We were all at the first night of it, in great uncertainty of the event, till we were very much encouraged by overhearing the Duke of Argyle, who sat in the next box to us, say, "It will do—it must do! I see it in the eyes of them." This was a good while before the first act was over, and so gave us ease soon, for that Duke, besides his own good taste, has as particular a knack as any one now living in discovering the taste of the public. He was quite right in this, as usual. The good nature of the audience appeared stronger and stronger every act, and ended in a clamour of applause.

The play took the town by storm: the papers were full of it; it was preached against from the pulpit; pamphleteers and versifiers found a new subject in it; its songs and scenes made their way onto ladies' fans, playing cards, decorative screens, and other household objects. Lavinia Fenton, who played Polly, won the hearts of the people and the hand of the infatuated Duke of Bolton. The *bon mot* for the occasion was that the play had made Rich gay and Gay rich.

The idea for a beggar's opera seems to have come from Swift, who wrote to Pope—with "friend Gay" in mind—"what think you of a Newgate pastoral, among the thieves and whores there?" Gay, who had already in *The Shepherd's Week* (1714) satisfied one Scriblerian impulse to mock the pastoral, sought an entirely new realm to conquer and landed on the current vogue of Italian opera. According to Robert Hitchcock, writing at the end of the century,

That exotic species of entertainment called Italian Operas, had for several years been rising into fashion, and at that time entirely engrossed the attention of the higher and more fashionable ranks of people. The seduction of foreign music, the novelty of those unnatural warblers then imported, the charms of dancing, with the glare of decorations, had bewitched the fancy, and diverted the tide of encouragement, and applause, from the more rational, though less gaudy representations of the English theatre. This corruption of public taste, and perversion of judgment, it was Mr. Gay's intention, by humorously satirizing, to correct.

In place of "foreign music" Gay offered familiar British songs; in place of elaborate business, simple scenes and characters; in place of lofty language and sentiment, the same in a mock-heroic version.

The political satire of *The Beggar's Opera* is conducted in this mock-heroic vein. As the Beggar-Author says in the moral at the end of the play, "through the whole Piece you may observe such a similitude of Manners in high and low Life, that it is difficult to determine whether (in the fashionable Vices) the fine Gentlemen imitate the Gentlemen of the Road, or the Gentlemen of the Road the fine Gentlemen." But it was not at all difficult to determine that the object of Gay's satire was the government in general and Walpole's administration in particular. The Prime Minister is represented by both Peachum the thief-taker (suggested by the notorious Jonathan Wild, hanged at Tyburn in 1725) and Macheath the thief (suggested by the popular highwayman-hero Jack Sheppard, executed in 1724), as well as, incidentally, by Robin of Bagshot, *alias* Bob Booty. Although Walpole endeared himself—at least to the audience—by his good-natured (not to say shrewd) acceptance of the application to himself, it is noteworthy that Gay's sequel, *Polly* (1729), though comparatively inoffensive politically, was forbidden the stage by the Lord Chamberlain.

If the play was thought by some to be politically seditious, it was also held by others to be morally pernicious. In attacking corruption, it was alleged, the opera made corruption glamorous. This is of course an ancient argument against imaginative literature in general; but the mock-heroic method, as it works by discovering affinities which the "high" forms of life have for the "low," is peculiarly liable to suggest the reverse as well. The denunciation of *The Beggar's Opera* for its encouragement of vice was widespread, and though the moral tendency of the play had its contemporary defenders, it remained for Hazlitt in the next century to put his finger on the subtlety of its import:

> It has been said by a great moralist, "There is some soul of goodness in things evil"; and The Beggar's Opera is a good-natured, but severe comment on

this text. The poet has thrown all the gaiety and sunshine of the imagination, the intoxication of pleasure, and the vanity of despair, round the short-lived existence of his heroes . . . . With the happiest wit, the author has brought out the good qualities and interesting emotions almost inseparable from humanity in the lowest situations, and with the same penetrating glance, has detected the disguises which rank and circumstance lend to exalted vice. It may be said that the moral of the piece (which some respectable critics have been at a loss to discover) *is to shew the vulgarity of vice* . . . .

Or, if one looks to criticism for more complex meanings than that, he will find them in William Empson's essay in *English Pastoral Poetry* (1938; reprinted in 1950 as *Some Versions of Pastoral*).

Our text is that of the first edition (1728), the earliest of its many issues that we have been able to locate, with a few revisions incorporated from the second (1728) and third (1729) editions.

DRAMATIS PERSONÆ.°

MEN.

Peachum.[1]		Mr. *Hippesley.*
Lockit.		Mr. *Hall.*
Macheath.[2]		Mr. *Walker.*
Filch.		Mr. *Clark.*
Jemmy Twitcher.[3]		Mr. *H. Bullock.*
Crook-finger'd Jack.		Mr. *Houghton.*
Wat Dreary.		Mr. *Smith.*
Robin *of* Bagshot.[4]	*Macheath's* Gang.	Mr. *Lacy.*
Nimming[5] Ned.		Mr. *Pit.*
Harry Padington.[6]		Mr. *Eaton.*
Mat *of the* Mint.[7]		Mr. *Spiller.*
Ben Budge.[8]		Mr. *Morgan.*
Beggar.		Mr. *Chapman.*
Player.		Mr. *Milward.*

Constables, *Drawer,*[9] *Turnkey,*[10] &c.

WOMEN.

Mrs. Peachum.		Mrs. *Martin.*
Polly Peachum.		Miss *Fenton.*
Lucy Lockit.		Mrs. *Egleton.*
Diana Trapes.[11]		Mrs. *Martin.*
Mrs. Coaxer.		Mrs. *Holiday.*
Dolly Trull.[12]		Mrs. *Lacy.*
Mrs. Vixen.		Mrs. *Rice.*
Betty Doxy.[13]	*Women of the Town.*	Mrs. *Rogers.*
Jenny Diver.[14]		Mrs. *Clarke.*
Mrs. Shammekin.		Mrs. *Morgan.*
Suky Tawdry.		Mrs. *Palin.*
Molly Brazen.		Mrs. *Sallee.*

THE BEGGAR'S OPERA. *Dramatis Personæ:* The descriptive names of Gay's characters reflect the aliases and nicknames actually found among the denizens of the London underworld. **1. Peachum:** To "peach" is to inform against, or to indict, bring to trial. Peachum is what was known then as a "thief-taker" (and also what is known now as a "fence"). **2. Macheath:** "son of the heath." The heaths around London were the principal places worked by highwaymen.

3. Twitcher: snatcher. **4. Bagshot:** the name of a heath west of London. **5. Nimming:** stealing. **6. Padington:** (Paddington) a village in Middlesex, on the north side of Hyde Park. **7. the Mint:** in Southwark; a sanctuary for debtors and a haunt of thieves and prostitutes. **8. Budge:** sneak thief. **9. Drawer:** tapster. **10. Turnkey:** the jailer in charge of the keys. **11. Trapes:** slattern. **12. Trull:** prostitute. **13. Doxy:** paramour, prostitute. **14. Diver:** pickpocket.

INTRODUCTION

BEGGAR. PLAYER.

Beggar. If Poverty be a Title to Poetry, I am sure No-body can dispute mine. I own myself of the Company of Beggars; and I make one[1] at their Weekly Festivals at St. *Giles*'s.[2] I have a small Yearly Salary for my Catches,[3] and am welcome to a Dinner there whenever I please, which is more than most Poets can say.

Player. As we live by the Muses, 'tis but Gratitude in us to encourage Poetical Merit where-ever we find it. The Muses, contrary to all other Ladies, pay no Distinction to Dress, and never partially[4] mistake the Pertness of Embroidery for Wit, nor the Modesty of Want for Dulness. Be the Author who he will, we push his Play as far as it will go. So (though you are in Want) I wish you Success heartily.

Beggar. This Piece I own was originally writ for the celebrating the Marriage of *James Chanter* and *Moll Lay*, two most excellent Ballad-Singers. I have introduc'd the Similes that are in all your celebrated *Operas*: The *Swallow*, the *Moth*, the *Bee*, the *Ship*, the *Flower*, &c. Besides, I have a Prison Scene which the Ladies always reckon charmingly pathetick. As to the Parts, I have observ'd such a nice Impartiality to our two Ladies,[5] that it is impossible for either of them to take Offence. I hope I may be forgiven, that I have not made my Opera throughout unnatural, like those in vogue; for I have no Recitative:[6] Excepting this, as I have consented to have neither Prologue nor Epilogue, it must be allow'd an Opera in all its forms. The Piece indeed hath been heretofore frequently represented by ourselves in our great Room at St. *Giles*'s, so that I cannot too often acknowledge your Charity in bringing it now on the Stage.

Player. But I see 'tis time for us to withdraw; the Actors are preparing to begin. Play away the Overture.   [*Exeunt.*

Introduction. 1. **make one:** am with them. 2. **St. Giles's:** an almshouse near the parish church of St. Giles-in-the-Fields. 3. **Catches:** rounds. 4. **partially:** with bias. 5. **our two Ladies:** Polly and Lucy, with a side glance at the contemporary rival Italian *prime donne* Cuzzoni and Faustina. 6. **Recitative:** the declamatory parts of the opera, conveyed in a manner intermediate between singing and talking.

ACT I

SCENE I.

SCENE *Peachum's House.*

Peachum *sitting at a Table with a large Book of Accounts before him.*

AIR I. An old Woman cloathed in Gray,[1] &c.

> *THROUGH all the Employments of Life*
> *Each Neighbour abuses his Brother;*
> *Whore and Rogue they call Husband and Wife:*
> *All Professions be-rogue one another.*
> *The Priest calls the Lawyer a Cheat,*
> *The Lawyer be-knaves[2] the Divine;*
> *And the Statesman, because he's so great,*
> *Thinks his Trade as honest as mine.*

A Lawyer is an honest Employment, so is mine. Like me too he acts in a double Capacity, both against Rogues and for 'em; for 'tis but fitting that we should protect and encourage Cheats, since we live by them.

SCENE II.

Peachum, Filch.

Filch. Sir, Black *Moll* hath sent word her Tryal comes on in the Afternoon, and she hopes you will order Matters so as to bring her off.

Peach. Why, she may plead her Belly[1] at worst; to my Knowledge she hath taken care of that Security. But as the Wench is very active and industrious, you may satisfy her that I'll soften the Evidence.

Filch. Tom *Gagg*, Sir, is found guilty.

Peach. A lazy Dog! When I took him the time before, I told him what he would come to if he did not mend his Hand.[2] This is Death without Reprieve. I may venture to Book him. [*writes*] For Tom *Gagg*, forty Pounds.[3] Let *Betty Sly* know that I'll save her

---

Act I, scene i. 1. **An old . . . Gray:** The originals of Gay's airs are traced in W. E. Schultz's *Gay's Beggar's Opera: Its Content, History & Influence* (1923), Appendix II. 2. **be-knaves:** accuses of being a knave. *Act I, scene ii.* 1. **plead her Belly:** Pregnant women were protected by the law against execution; either their trials were postponed or they were disposed of with light sentences. 2. **mend his Hand:** improve his work. 3. **forty Pounds:** the reward money; cf. sc. iv.

from Transportation,[4] for I can get more by her staying in *England*.

Filch. *Betty* hath brought more Goods into our Lock[5] to-year[6] than any five of the Gang; and in truth, 'tis a pity to lose so good a Customer.[7]

Peach. If none of the Gang take her off,[8] she may, in the common course of Business, live a Twelvemonth longer. I love to let Women scape. A good Sportsman always lets the Hen Partridges fly, because the breed of the Game depends upon them. Besides, here the Law allows us no Reward; there is nothing to be got by the Death of Women—except our Wives.[9]

Filch. Without dispute, she is a fine Woman! 'Twas to her I was oblig'd for my Education, and (to say a bold Word)[10] she hath train'd up more young Fellows to the Business than the Gaming-table.

Peach. Truly, *Filch*, thy Observation is right. We and the Surgeons are more beholden to Women[11] than all the Professions besides.

AIR II. The bonny grey-ey'd Morn, &c.

Filch. *'Tis Woman that seduces all Mankind,*
By her we first were taught the wheedling Arts:
Her very Eyes can cheat; when most she's kind,
She tricks us of our Money with our Hearts.
For her, like Wolves by night we roam for Prey,
And practise ev'ry Fraud to bribe her Charms;
For Suits of Love, like Law, are won by Pay,
And Beauty must be fee'd[12] into our Arms.

Peach. But make haste to *Newgate*,[13] Boy, and let my Friends know what I intend; for I love to make them easy one way or other.

Filch. When a Gentleman is long kept in suspence, Penitence may break his Spirit ever after. Besides, Certainty gives a Man a good Air upon his Tryal, and makes him risque another without Fear or Scruple. But I'll away, for 'tis a Pleasure to be the Messenger of Comfort to Friends in Affliction.

SCENE III.

Peachum.

But 'tis now high time to look about me for a decent Execution[1] against next Sessions.[2] I hate a lazy Rogue, by whom one can get nothing 'till he is hang'd. A register of the Gang. [*reading*] Crookfinger'd *Jack*. A Year and a half in the Service; Let me see how much the Stock owes to his Industry; one, two, three, four, five Gold Watches, and seven Silver ones. A mighty clean-handed[3] Fellow! Sixteen Snuff boxes, five of them of true Gold. Six dozen of Handkerchiefs, four silver-hilted Swords, half a dozen of Shirts, three Tye-Perriwigs, and a Piece of Broad Cloth. Considering these are only the Fruits of his leisure Hours, I don't know a prettier Fellow, for no Man alive hath a more engaging Presence of Mind upon the Road. *Wat Dreary*, alias *Brown Will*, an irregular Dog, who hath an underhand way of disposing of his Goods. I'll try him only for a Sessions or two longer upon his good Behaviour. *Harry Padington*, a poor petty-larceny Rascal, without the least Genius; that Fellow, though he were to live these six Months, will never come to the Gallows with any Credit. Slippery *Sam*; he goes off the next Sessions, for the Villain hath the Impudence to have views of following his Trade as a Taylor, which he calls an honest Employment. *Mat* of the *Mint*; listed[4] not above a Month ago, a promising sturdy Fellow, and diligent in his way; somewhat too bold and hasty, and may raise good Contributions on[5] the Publick, if he does not cut himself short by Murder. *Tom. Tipple*, a guzzling soaking Sot, who is always too drunk to stand himself, or to make others stand.[6] A Cart[7] is absolutely necessary for him. *Robin* of *Bagshot*, alias *Gorgon*, alias *Bluff Bob*, alias *Carbuncle*, alias *Bob Booty*.[8]

---

4. **Transportation:** to the colonies. This was a common punishment. 5. **our Lock:** See III. iii. n. 5. 6. **to-year:** this year. 7. **Customer:** in the sense of the person with whom one has business dealings; here, a seller rather than a buyer. But *customer* also meant prostitute. 8. **take her off:** kill her. 9. **except our Wives:** whose property their husbands would inherit. 10. **to . . . Word:** I say confidently. 11. **beholden to Women:** the surgeons because such women spread venereal disease. 12. **fee'd:** paid for. 13. **Newgate:** the principal prison of London.

Act I, scene iii. 1. **Execution:** (1) a seizure of goods in default of payment; (2) capital punishment. Peachum's mind runs in both directions. 2. **against . . . Sessions:** for the next session of the criminal court. 3. **clean-handed:** dexterous; with the additional ironic meaning "innocent." 4. **listed:** enlisted. 5. **on:** from. 6. **make . . . stand:** hold them up. The highwayman's command to his victim was "Stand" or "Stand and deliver." 7. **A Cart:** the hangman's cart. 8. **Robin . . . Booty:** These names were all taken as referring to Walpole.

SCENE IV.

Peachum, *Mrs.* Peachum.

Mrs. Peach.   What of *Bob Booty*, Husband? I hope nothing bad hath betided him. You know, my Dear, he's a favourite Customer of mine. 'Twas he made me a Present of this Ring.

Peach.   I have set his Name down in the Black-List, that's all, my Dear; he spends his Life among Women, and as soon as his Money is gone, one or other of the Ladies will hang him for the Reward, and there's forty Pound lost to us for-ever.

Mrs. Peach.   You know, my Dear, I never meddle in matters of Death; I always leave those Affairs to you. Women indeed are bitter bad Judges in these cases, for they are so partial to the Brave that they think every Man handsome who is going to the Camp or the Gallows.

AIR III. *Cold and Raw, &c.*

If any Wench Venus's Girdle wear,
　　Though she be never so ugly;
Lillys and Roses will quickly appear,
　　And her Face look wond'rous smuggly.[1]
Beneath the left Ear so fit but a Cord,
　　(A Rope so charming a Zone[2] *is!)*
The Youth in his Cart hath the Air of a Lord,
　　And we cry, There dies an Adonis!

But really, Husband, you should not be too hard-hearted, for you never had a finer, braver set of Men than at present. We have not had a Murder among them all, these seven Months. And truly, my Dear, that is a great Blessing.

Peach.   What a dickens is the Woman always a whimpring about Murder for? No Gentleman is ever look'd upon the worse for killing a Man in his own Defence; and if Business cannot be carried on without it, what would you have a Gentleman do?

Mrs. Peach.   If I am in the wrong, my Dear, you must excuse me, for No-body can help the Frailty of an over-scrupulous Conscience.

Peach.   Murder is as fashionable a Crime as a Man can be guilty of. How many fine Gentlemen have we in *Newgate* every Year, purely upon that Article! If they have wherewithal to persuade the Jury to bring it in Manslaughter, what are they the worse for it? So, my Dear, have done upon this Subject. Was

Captain *Macheath* here this Morning, for the Bank-notes[3] he left with you last Week?

Mrs. Peach.   Yes, my Dear; and though the Bank hath stopt Payment, he was so cheerful and so agreeable! Sure there is not a finer Gentleman upon the Road than the Captain! If he comes from *Bagshot*[4] at any reasonable Hour he hath promis'd to make one this Evening with *Polly* and me, and *Bob Booty*, at a Party of Quadrille.[5] Pray, my Dear, is the Captain rich?

Peach.   The Captain keeps too good Company ever to grow rich. *Mary-bone*[6] and the Chocolate-houses[7] are his undoing. The Man that proposes to get Money by Play should have the Education of a fine Gentleman, and be train'd up to it from his Youth.

Mrs. Peach.   Really, I am sorry upon *Polly*'s Account the Captain hath not more Discretion. What business hath he to keep Company with Lords and Gentlemen? he should leave them to prey upon one another.

Peach.   Upon *Polly*'s Account! What, a Plague, does the Woman mean?—Upon *Polly*'s Account!

Mrs. Peach.   Captain *Macheath* is very fond of the Girl.

Peach.   And what then?

Mrs. Peach.   If I have any Skill in the Ways of Women, I am sure *Polly* thinks him a very pretty Man.

Peach.   And what then? You would not be so mad to have the Wench marry him! Gamesters and High-waymen are generally very good to their Whores, but they are very Devils to their Wives.

Mrs. Peach.   But if *Polly* should be in love, how should we help her, or how can she help herself? Poor Girl, I am in the utmost Concern about her.

AIR IV. *Why is your faithful Slave disdain'd? &c.*

If Love the Virgin's Heart invade,
How, like a Moth, the simple Maid
　　Still plays about the Flame!
If soon she be not made a Wife,
Her Honour's sing'd, and then for Life,
　　She's—what I dare not name.

Act I, scene iv. **1. smuggly:** (smugly) smart or trim. **2. Zone:** band.

3. Bank-notes: promissory notes given by a banker, payable to a specified person at a fixed date. The robbery was reported and the payment stopped before Macheath could cash them. **4. Bagshot:** Bagshot Heath. **5. Quadrille:** a four-handed card game. **6. Mary-bone:** Marylebone Gardens, a pleasure resort where gambling at the game of bowling was a main attraction. See III. iv. **7. the Chocolate-houses:** where gambling at cards and dice was a favorite pastime.

Peach. Look ye, Wife. A handsome Wench in our way of Business is as profitable as at the Bar of a *Temple*[8] Coffee-House, who looks upon it as her livelihood to grant every Liberty but one. You see I would indulge the Girl as far as prudently we can. In any thing, but Marriage! After that, my Dear, how shall we be safe? Are we not then in her Husband's Power? For a Husband hath the absolute Power over all a Wife's Secrets but her own. If the Girl had the Discretion of a Court Lady, who can have a dozen young Fellows at her Ear without complying with one, I should not matter it;[9] but *Polly* is Tinder, and a Spark will at once set her on a Flame. Married! If the Wench does not know her own Profit, sure she knows her own Pleasure better than to make herself a Property! My Daughter to me should be, like a Court Lady to a Minister of State, a Key to the whole Gang. Married! If the Affair is not already done, I'll terrify her from it, by the Example of our Neighbours.

Mrs. Peach. May-hap, my Dear, you may injure[10] the Girl. She loves to imitate the fine Ladies, and she may only allow the Captain Liberties in the View of Interest.

Peach. But 'tis your Duty, my Dear, to warn the Girl against her Ruin, and to instruct her how to make the most of her Beauty. I'll go to her this moment, and sift her.[11] In the mean time, Wife, rip out the Coronets and Marks[12] of these dozen of Cambric[13] Handkerchiefs, for I can dispose of them this Afternoon to a Chap[14] in the City.[15]

SCENE V.

Mrs. Peachum.

Never was a Man more out of the way in an Argument than my Husband! Why must our *Polly*, forsooth, differ from her Sex, and love only her Husband? And why must *Polly*'s Marriage, contrary to all Observation, make her the less followed by other Men? All Men are Thieves in Love, and like a Woman the better for being another's Property.

---

8. **Temple:** The Temple is the section of London where the Inns of Court are located. 9. **matter it:** mind it. 10. **injure:** wrong. 11. **sift her:** question her closely. 12. **Coronets and Marks:** insignia of the nobility and other identifying marks. 13. **Cambric:** a fine white linen, originally made at Cambray in Flanders. 14. **Chap:** customer; short for *chapman*. 15. **the City:** the old part of London.

AIR V. Of all the simple Things we do, &c.

> *A Maid is like the golden Oar,*[1]
> *Which hath Guineas intrinsical*[2] *in 't,*
> *Whose Worth is never known, before*
> *It is try'd and imprest*[3] *in the Mint.*
> *A Wife's like a Guinea in Gold,*
> *Stampt with the Name of her Spouse;*
> *Now here, now there; is bought, or is sold;*
> *And is current in every House.*

SCENE VI.

Mrs. Peachum, Filch.

Mrs. Peach. Come hither *Filch.* I am as fond of this Child, as though my Mind misgave me[1] he were my own. He hath as fine a Hand at picking a Pocket as a Woman, and is as nimble-finger'd as a Juggler. If an unlucky Session does not cut the Rope of thy Life, I pronounce, Boy, thou wilt be a great Man in History. Where was your Post last Night, my Boy?

Filch. I ply'd[2] at the Opera, Madam; and considering 'twas neither dark nor rainy, so that there was no great Hurry in getting Chairs and Coaches, made a tolerable hand on 't.[3] These seven Handkerchiefs, Madam.

Mrs. Peach. Colour'd ones, I see. They are of sure Sale from our Ware-house at *Redriff* among the Seamen.[4]

Filch. And this Snuff-box.

Mrs. Peach. Set in Gold! A pretty Encouragement this to a young Beginner.

Filch. I had a fair tug at a charming Gold Watch. Pox take the Taylors for making the Fobs so deep and narrow! It stuck by the way, and I was forc'd to make my Escape under a Coach. Really, Madam, I fear I shall be cut off in the Flower of my Youth, so that every now and then (since I was pumpt[5]) I have thoughts of taking up[6] and going to Sea.

Act I, scene v. **1. Oar:** ore. **2. intrinsical:** of its own kind. **3. try'd and imprest:** refined and stamped (coined). *Act I, scene vi.* **1. misgave me:** inclined me to think. **2. ply'd:** exerted myself. **3. made . . . 't:** made a fair profit (or success) of it. **4. They . . . Seamen:** They are sure to be bought at our warehouse at Redriff by the seamen. Redriff (Rotherhithe) is the dock section of London. **5. pumpt:** ducked under a public pump—a common punishment of young pickpockets, described by Gay in *Trivia*, III. 71–74:

> Ill-fated boy!
> Why did not honest work thy youth employ?
> Seiz'd by rough hands, he's dragg'd amid the rout,
> And stretch'd beneath the pump's incessant spout.

6. taking up: checking myself, mending my ways.

Mrs. Peach.   You should go to *Hockley in the Hole*,[7] and to *Mary-bone*, Child, to learn Valour. These are the School that have bred so many brave Men. I thought, Boy, by this time, thou hadst lost Fear as well as Shame. Poor Lad! how little does he know as yet of the *Old-Baily*![8] For the first Fact[9] I'll insure thee from being hang'd; and going to Sea, *Filch*, will come time enough upon a Sentence of Transportation. But now, since you have nothing better to do, ev'n go to your Book, and learn your Catechism; for really a Man makes but an ill Figure in the Ordinary's Paper,[10] who cannot give a satisfactory Answer to his Questions. But, hark you, my Lad. Don't tell me a Lye; for you know I hate a Lyar. Do you know of any thing that hath past between Captain *Macheath* and our *Polly?*

Filch.   I beg you, Madam, don't ask me; for I must either tell a Lye to you or to Miss *Polly;* for I promis'd her I would not tell.

Mrs. Peach.   But when the Honour of our Family is concern'd—

Filch.   I shall lead a sad Life with Miss *Polly*, if ever she come to know that I told you. Besides, I would not willingly forfeit my own Honour by betraying any body.

Mrs. Peach.   Yonder comes my Husband and *Polly.* Come, *Filch*, you shall go with me into my own Room, and tell me the whole Story. I'll give thee a Glass of a most delicious Cordial that I keep for my own drinking.

SCENE VII.

Peachum, Polly.

Polly.   I know as well as any of the fine Ladies how to make the most of my self and of my Man too. A Woman knows how to be mercenary, though she hath never been in a Court or at an Assembly.[1] We have it in our Natures, Papa. If I allow Captain *Macheath* some trifling Liberties, I have this Watch and other visible Marks of his Favour to show for it.

A Girl who cannot grant some Things, and refuse what is most material, will make but a poor hand of[2] her Beauty, and soon be thrown upon the Common.[3]

AIR VI. What shall I do to show how much I love her, &c.

> *Virgins are like the fair Flower in its Lustre,*
> *Which in the Garden enamels the Ground;*
> *Near it the Bees in Play flutter and cluster,*
> *And gaudy Butterflies frolick around.*
> *But, when once pluck'd, 'tis no longer alluring,*
> *To Covent-Garden[4] 'tis sent, (as yet sweet,)*
> *There fades, and shrinks, and grows past all enduring,*
> *Rots, stinks, and dies, and is trod under feet.*

Peach.   You know, Polly, I am not against your toying and trifling with a Customer in the way of Business, or to get out a Secret, or so. But if I find out that you have play'd the fool and are married, you Jade you, I'll cut your Throat, Hussy. Now you know my Mind.

SCENE VIII.

Peachum, Polly, Mrs. Peachum.

AIR VII. Oh *London* is a fine Town.

Mrs. Peachum, *in a very great Passion.*

> *Our Polly is a sad Slut! nor heeds what we have taught her.*
> *I wonder any Man alive will ever rear a Daughter!*
> *For she must have both Hoods and Gowns, and Hoops to swell her Pride,*
> *With Scarfs and Stays, and Gloves and Lace; and she will have Men beside;*
> *And when she's drest with Care and Cost, all-tempting, fine and gay,*
> *As Men should serve a Cowcumber,[1] she flings herself away.*
> *Our Polly is a sad Slut, &c.*

You Baggage! you Hussy! you inconsiderate Jade! had you been hang'd, it would not have vex'd me, for that might have been your Misfortune; but to do such

---

7. Hockley . . . Hole: a place of public diversion north of London, where bull- and bear-baiting, dogfights, and boxing were the bill of fare. In Jonson's *Every Man out of His Humor* (1599) Hockley-in-the-Hole is mentioned among places notorious for highway robberies. **8. Old-Baily:** (Old Bailey) the criminal courthouse attached to Newgate Prison. **9. Fact:** crime. **10. the Ordinary's Paper:** the prison chaplain's report of confession. *Act I, scene vii.* **1. an Assembly:** a regular gathering of fashionable people for social pastime.

2. will . . . of: will not profit from. **3. the Common:** the wasteland, the heath. **4. Covent Garden:** the market at Covent Garden, where fruit, vegetables, and flowers were sold. Covent ("Convent") Garden was originally the garden of the Abbey of Westminster. Once a fashionable residence, it became a haven for prostitutes and other disreputable characters. *Act I, scene viii.* **1. Cowcumber:** cucumber, i.e., a trifling thing.

a mad thing by Choice! The Wench is married, Husband.

Peach. Married! The Captain is a bold Man, and will risque any thing for Money; to be sure he believes her a Fortune. Do you think your Mother and I should have liv'd comfortably so long together, if ever we had been married? Baggage!

Mrs. Peach. I knew she was always a proud Slut; and now the Wench hath play'd the Fool and married, because forsooth[2] she would do like the Gentry. Can you support the Expence of a Husband, Hussy, in gaming, drinking and whoring? have you Money enough to carry on the daily Quarrels of Man and Wife about who shall squander most? There are not many Husbands and Wives, who can bear the Charges of plaguing one another in a handsome way. If you must be married, could you introduce no-body into our Family but a Highwayman? Why, thou foolish Jade, thou wilt be as ill-us'd, and as much neglected, as if thou hadst married a Lord!

Peach. Let not your Anger, my Dear, break through the Rules of Decency, for the Captain looks upon himself in the Military Capacity, as a Gentleman by his Profession. Besides what he hath already, I know he is in a fair way of getting,[3] or of dying; and both these ways, let me tell you, are most excellent Chances for a Wife. Tell me Hussy, are you ruin'd or no?

Mrs. Peach. With *Polly*'s Fortune, she might very well have gone off to a Person of Distinction. Yes, that you might, you pouting Slut!

Peach. What, is the Wench dumb? Speak, or I'll make you plead by squeezing out an Answer from you.[4] Are you really bound Wife to him, or are you only upon liking?   [*Pinches her.*

Polly. Oh!   [*Screaming.*

Mrs. Peach. How the Mother is to be pitied who hath handsome Daughters! Locks, Bolts, Bars, and Lectures of Morality are nothing to them: They break through them all. They have as much Pleasure in cheating a Father and Mother, as in cheating at Cards.

Peach. Why, *Polly*, I shall soon know if you are married, by *Macheath*'s keeping from our House.

2. **forsooth:** in truth (said derisively). 3. **he . . . getting:** he has a good chance of getting (a fortune). 4. **I'll . . . you:** Accused criminals who defied the legal requirement of pleading either guilty or not guilty were sometimes subjected to pressing by weights until the plea was "squeezed out."

AIR VIII. Grim King of the Ghosts, &c.

Polly.   *Can Love be controul'd by Advice?*
          Will Cupid *our Mothers obey?*
          Though my Heart were as frozen as Ice,
          At his Flame 'twould have melted away.

          When he kist me so closely he prest,
          'Twas so sweet that I must have comply'd:
          So I thought it both safest and best
          To marry, for fear you should chide.

Mrs. Peach. Then all the Hopes of our Family are gone for ever and ever!

Peach. And *Macheath* may hang his Father and Mother-in-Law, in hope to get into their Daughter's Fortune.

Polly. I did not marry him (as 'tis the Fashion) cooly and deliberately for Honour or Money. But, I love him.

Mrs. Peach. Love him! worse and worse! I thought the Girl had been better bred. Oh Husband, Husband! her Folly makes me mad! my Head swims! I'm distracted! I can't support myself—Oh!   [*Faints.*

Peach. See, Wench, to what a Condition you have reduc'd your poor Mother! a Glass of Cordial, this instant. How the poor Woman takes it to Heart!

              [*Polly goes out, and returns with it.*

Ah, Hussy, now this is the only Comfort your Mother has left!

Polly. Give her another Glass, Sir; my Mama drinks double the Quantity whenever she is out of Order. This, you see, fetches[5] her.

Mrs. Peach. The Girl shows such a Readiness, and so much Concern, that I could almost find in my Heart to forgive her.

AIR IX. O Jenny, O Jenny, where hast thou been.

          O Polly, you might have toy'd and kist.
          By keeping Men off, you keep them on.
Polly.   *But he so teaz'd me,*
                    And he so pleas'd me,
          What I did, you must have done.

Mrs. Peach. Not with a Highwayman.—You sorry Slut!

Peach. A Word with you, Wife. 'Tis no new thing for a Wench to take Men without consent of Parents. You know 'tis the Frailty of Woman, my Dear.

5. **fetches:** revives.

Mrs. *Peach.* Yes, indeed, the Sex is frail. But the first time a Woman is frail, she should be somewhat nice[6] methinks, for then or never is the time to make her Fortune. After that, she hath nothing to do but to guard herself from being found out, and she may do what she pleases.

Peach. Make your self a little easy; I have a Thought shall soon set all Matters again to rights. Why so melancholy, *Polly?* since what is done cannot be undone, we must all endeavour to make the best of it.

Mrs. *Peach.* Well, *Polly;* as far as one Woman can forgive another, I forgive thee.—Your Father is too fond of you, Hussy.

Polly. Then all my Sorrows are at an end.

Mrs. *Peach.* A mighty likely Speech in troth, for a Wench who is just married!

AIR X. *Thomas, I cannot, &c.*

Polly. I, like a Ship in Storms, was tost;
　　　　Yet afraid to put in to Land;
　　　　For seiz'd in the Port the Vessel's lost,
　　　　Whose Treasure is contreband.
　　　　The Waves are laid,[7]
　　　　My Duty's paid.
　　　　O Joy beyond Expression!
　　　　Thus, safe a-shore,
　　　　I ask no more,
　　　　My All is in my Possession.

Peach. I hear Customers in t' other Room; Go, talk with 'em, *Polly;* but come to us again, as soon as they are gone.—But, heark ye, Child, if 'tis the Gentleman who was here Yesterday about the Repeating-Watch;[8] say, you believe we can't get Intelligence of it, till to-morrow. For I lent it to *Suky Straddle,* to make a Figure with it to-night at a Tavern in *Drury-Lane.*[9] If t' other Gentleman calls for the Silver-hilted Sword; you know Beetle-brow'd *Jemmy* hath it on, and he doth not come from *Tunbridge*[10] till *Tuesday* Night; so that it cannot be had till then.

SCENE IX.

Peachum, *Mrs.* Peachum.

Peach. Dear Wife, be a little pacified. Don't let your Passion run away with your Senses. *Polly,* I grant you, hath done a rash thing.

Mrs. *Peach.* If she had had only an Intrigue with the Fellow, why the very best Families have excus'd and huddled up a Frailty of that sort: 'Tis Marriage, Husband, that makes it a Blemish.

Peach. But Money, Wife, is the true Fuller's Earth[1] for Reputations, there is not a Spot or a Stain but what it can take out. A rich Rogue now-a-days is fit Company for any Gentleman; and the World, my Dear, hath not such a Contempt for Roguery as you imagine. I tell you, Wife, I can make this Match turn to our Advantage.

Mrs. *Peach.* I am very sensible, Husband, that Captain *Macheath* is worth Money, but I am in doubt whether he hath not two or three Wives already, and then if he should dye in a Session or two, *Polly's* Dower[2] would come into Dispute.

Peach. That, indeed, is a Point which ought to be consider'd.

AIR XI. *A Soldier and a Sailor.*

　　　A Fox may steal your Hens, Sir,
　　　A Whore your Health and Pence, Sir,
　　　Your Daughter rob your Chest, Sir,
　　　Your Wife may steal your Rest, Sir,
　　　　A Thief your Goods and Plate.
　　　But this is all but picking;
　　　With Rest, Pence, Chest and Chicken,
　　　It ever was decreed, Sir,
　　　If Lawyer's Hand is fee'd, Sir,
　　　　He steals your whole Estate.

The Lawyers are bitter Enemies to those in our Way.[3] They don't care that any Body should get a Clandestine Livelihood but themselves.

---

6. **nice**: particular (about whom she gives herself to). 7. **are laid**: have subsided. 8. **Repeating-Watch**: otherwise known as a repeater, a watch that struck the hour (and quarter hour or minute); it was useful for telling the time in the dark. 9. **Drury-Lane**: a hive of prostitution; see II, iii. 10. **Tunbridge**: a town southeast of London.

Act I, scene ix. 1. **Fuller's Earth**: a mineral used in cleaning cloth. 2. **Dower**: that portion of a widow's inheritance from her husband which the law allows to her for her life. 3. **those . . . Way**: such as we.

SCENE X.

Mrs. Peachum, Peachum, Polly.

Polly. 'Twas only Nimming *Ned.* He brought in a Damask Window-Curtain, a Hoop-Petticoat, a Pair of Silver Candlesticks, a Perriwig, and one Silk Stocking, from the Fire that happen'd last Night.

Peach. There is not a Fellow that is cleverer in his way, and saves more Goods out of the Fire than *Ned.* But now, *Polly,* to your Affair; for Matters must not be left as they are. You are married then, it seems?

Polly. Yes, Sir.

Peach. And how do you propose to live, Child?

Polly. Like other Women, Sir, upon the Industry of my Husband.

Mrs. Peach. What, is the Wench turn'd Fool? A Highway-man's Wife, like a Soldier's, hath as little of his Pay, as of his Company.

Peach. And had not you the common Views of a Gentlewoman in your Marriage, *Polly?*

Polly. I don't know what you mean, Sir.

Peach. Of a Jointure,[1] and of being a Widow.

Polly. But I love him, Sir: how then could I have Thoughts of parting with him?

Peach. Parting with him! Why, that is the whole Scheme and Intention of all Marriage Articles. The comfortable Estate of Widow-hood, is the only hope that keeps up a Wife's Spirits. Where is the Woman who would scruple to be a Wife, if she had it in her Power to be a Widow whenever she pleas'd? If you have any Views of this sort, *Polly,* I shall think the Match not so very unreasonable.

Polly. How I dread to hear your Advice! Yet I must beg you to explain yourself.

Peach. Secure what he hath got, have him peach'd[2] the next Sessions, and then at once you are made a rich Widow.

Polly. What, murder the Man I love! The Blood runs cold at my Heart with the very Thought of it.

Peach. Fye, *Polly!* What hath Murder to do in the Affair? Since the thing sooner or later must happen, I dare say, the Captain himself would like that we should get the Reward for his Death sooner than a Stranger. Why, *Polly,* the Captain knows, that as 'tis his Employment to rob, so 'tis ours to take Robbers;

every Man in his Business. So that there is no Malice in the Case.

Mrs. Peach. Ay, Husband, now you have nick'd the Matter.[3] To have him peach'd is the only thing could ever make me forgive her.

AIR XII. Now ponder well, ye Parents dear.

Polly.   *Oh, ponder well! be not severe;*
    So save a wretched Wife!
    For on the Rope that hangs my Dear
    Depends[4] poor Polly's Life.

Mrs. Peach. But your Duty to your Parents, Hussy, obliges you to hang him. What would many a Wife give for such an Opportunity!

Polly. What is a Jointure, what is Widow-hood to me? I know my Heart. I cannot survive him.

AIR XIII. Le printemps rappelle aux armes.[5]

    The Turtle[6] thus with plaintive crying,
    Her Lover dying,
    The Turtle thus with plaintive crying,
    Laments her Dove.
    Down she drops quite spent with sighing,
    Pair'd in Death, as pair'd in Love.

Thus, Sir, it will happen to your poor *Polly.*

Mrs. Peach. What, is the Fool in love in earnest then? I hate thee for being particular:[7] Why, Wench, thou art a Shame to thy very Sex.

Polly. But hear me, Mother.—If you ever lov'd—

Mrs. Peach. Those cursed Play-books she reads have been her Ruin. One Word more, Hussy, and I shall knock your Brains out, if you have any.

Peach. Keep out of the way, *Polly,* for fear of Mischief, and consider of what is propos'd to you.

Mrs. Peach. Away, Hussy. Hang your Husband, and be dutiful.

SCENE XI.

Mrs. Peachum, Peachum.

[Polly *listning.*

Mrs. Peach. The Thing, Husband, must and shall be done. For the sake of Intelligence[1] we must take

---

Act I, scene x. **1. Jointure:** joint ownership of property, undertaken as a provision for the wife in the event of her widowhood. **2. peach'd:** informed against, or indicted.

3. nick'd the Matter: hit the mark. **4. Depends:** punningly —the etymological sense of "hang down" was still current in Gay's time. Cf. *Fables,* above, xlix. 18. **5. Le . . . armes:** Spring calls to arms. **6. Turtle:** turtledove. **7. particular:** in the sense of singling one person out, not playing the field. *Act I, scene xi.* **1. Intelligence:** secret communication.

other Measures, and have him peach'd the next Session without her Consent. If she will not know her Duty, we know ours.

Peach. But really, my Dear, it grieves one's Heart to take off² a great Man. When I consider his Personal Bravery, his fine Stratagem,³ how much we have already got by him, and how much more we may get, methinks I can't find in my Heart to have a Hand in his Death. I wish you could have made *Polly* undertake it.

Mrs. *Peach.* But in a Case of Necessity—our own Lives are in danger.

Peach. Then, indeed, we must comply with the Customs of the World, and make Gratitude give way to Interest.⁴—He shall be taken off.

Mrs. *Peach.* I'll undertake to manage *Polly*.

Peach. And I'll prepare Matters for the *Old-Baily*.

SCENE XII.

Polly.

Now I'm a Wretch, indeed.—Methinks I see him already in the Cart,¹ sweeter and more lovely than the Nosegay² in his Hand!—I hear the Crowd extolling his Resolution and Intrepidity!—What Vollies of Sighs are sent from the Windows of *Holborn*,³ that so comely a Youth should be brought to disgrace!—I see him at the Tree!⁴ The whole Circle are in Tears! —even Butchers weep!—*Jack Ketch*⁵ himself hesitates to perform his Duty, and would be glad to lose his Fee, by a Reprieve. What then will become of *Polly*! —As yet I may inform him of their Design, and aid him in his Escape.—It shall be so.—But then he flies, absents himself, and I bar my self from his dear dear Conversation!⁶ That too will distract me.—If he keep out of the way, my Papa and Mama may in time relent, and we may be happy.—If he stays, he is hang'd, and then he is lost for ever!—He intended to lye conceal'd in my Room, 'till the Dusk of the Evening: If they are abroad, I'll this Instant let him out, lest some Accident should prevent⁷ him.

[*Exit, and returns.*

2. **take off**: kill. 3. **Stratagem**: cunning. 4. **Interest**: self-interest. *Act I, scene xii.* 1. **the Cart**: the hangman's cart. 2. **Nosegay**: the customary ornament on this occasion. 3. **Holborn**: the section (and road) between Newgate and the gallows at Tyburn. 4. **the Tree**: the common euphemism for gallows. 5. **Jack Ketch**: the traditional name for the hangman; from the name of the historic executioner of the seventeenth century. 6. **Conversation**: company; with a sly glance at the meaning "sexual intercourse." 7. **prevent**: hinder.

SCENE XIII.

Polly, Macheath.

AIR XIV. Pretty Parrot, say—

Mach.   *Pretty Polly, say,*
When I was away,
Did your Fancy never stray
To some newer Lover?

Polly.   *Without Disguise,*
Heaving Sighs,
Doating Eyes,
My constant Heart discover.
Fondly let me loll!

Mach.   *O pretty, pretty Poll.*

Polly. And are you as fond as ever, my Dear?

Mach. Suspect my Honour, my Courage, suspect any thing but my Love.—May my Pistols miss Fire, and my Mare slip her Shoulder while I am pursu'd, if I ever forsake thee!

Polly. Nay, my Dear, I have no Reason to doubt you, for I find in the Romance you lent me, none of the great Heroes were ever false in Love.

AIR XV. Pray, Fair One, be kind—

Mach.   *My Heart was so free,*
It rov'd like the Bee,
'Till Polly my Passion requited;
I sipt each Flower,
I chang'd ev'ry Hour,
But here ev'ry Flower is united.

Polly. Were you sentenc'd to Transportation, sure, my Dear, you could not leave me behind you—could you?

Mach. Is there any Power, any Force that could tear me from thee? You might sooner tear a Pension out of the Hands of a Courtier, a Fee from a Lawyer, a pretty Woman from a Looking-glass, or any Woman from *Quadrille*.—But to tear me from thee is impossible!

AIR XVI. Over the Hills and far away.

Were I laid on Greenland's Coast,
And in my Arms embrac'd my Lass;
Warm amidst eternal Frost,
Too soon the Half Year's Night would pass.

Polly. *Were I sold on* Indian *Soil,*
     Soon as the burning Day was clos'd,
     I could mock the sultry Toil,
     When on my Charmer's Breast repos'd.
Mach. *And I would love you all the Day,*
Polly. *Every Night would kiss and play,*
Mach. *If with me you'd fondly stray*
Polly. *Over the Hills and far away.*

Polly. Yes, I would go with thee. But oh!—how shall I speak it? I must be torn from thee. We must part.

Mach. How! Part!

Polly. We must, we must.—My Papa and Mama are set against thy Life. They now, even now are in Search after thee. They are preparing Evidence against thee. Thy Life depends upon a Moment.

AIR XVII. Gin[1] thou wert mine awn thing—

     O what Pain it is to part!
     Can I leave thee, can I leave thee?
     O what Pain it is to part!
     Can thy Polly *ever leave thee?*
     But lest Death my Love should thwart,
     And bring thee to the fatal Cart,
     Thus I tear thee from my bleeding Heart!
     Fly hence, and let me leave thee.

One Kiss and then—one Kiss—begone—farewell.

Mach. My Hand, my Heart, my Dear, is so rivited to thine, that I cannot unloose my Hold.

Polly. But my Papa may intercept thee, and then I should lose the very glimmering of Hope. A few Weeks, perhaps, may reconcile us all. Shall thy *Polly* hear from thee?

Mach. Must I then go?

Polly. And will not Absence change your Love?

Mach. If you doubt it, let me stay—and be hang'd.

Polly. O how I fear! how I tremble!—Go—but when Safety will give you leave, you will be sure to see me again; for 'till then *Polly* is wretched.

AIR XVIII. O the Broom, &c.

Mach. *The Miser thus a Shil-*   [Parting, and
          ling sees,   looking back at
     Which he's oblig'd to   each other with
          pay,   fondness; he at
     With Sighs resigns it by   one Door, she
          degrees,   at the other.
     And fears 'tis gone for
          aye.

Act I, scene xiii. **1. Gin:** if.

Polly. *The Boy, thus, when his Sparrow's flown,*
     The Bird in Silence eyes;
     But soon as out of Sight 'tis gone,
     Whines, whimpers, sobs and cries.

ACT II

SCENE I.

A Tavern near Newgate.

Jemmy Twitcher, *Crook-finger'd* Jack, Wat Dreary, Robin *of* Bagshot, Nimming Ned, Henry Padington, Matt *of the* Mint, Ben Budge, *and the rest of the Gang, at the Table, with Wine, Brandy and Tobacco.*

Ben. But pr'ythee, *Matt*, what is become of thy Brother *Tom*? I have not seen him since my Return from Transportation.

Matt. Poor Brother *Tom* had an Accident this time Twelvemonth, and so clever a made[1] Fellow he was, that I could not save him from those fleaing[2] Rascals the Surgeons; and now, poor Man, he is among the Otamys[3] at *Surgeon's Hall.*[4]

Ben. So it seems, his Time was come.

Jem. But the present Time is ours, and no Body alive hath more. Why are the Laws levell'd at us? are we more dishonest than the rest of Mankind? What we win, Gentlemen, is our own by the Law of Arms, and the Right of Conquest.

Crook. Where shall we find such another Set of practical Philosophers, who to a Man are above the Fear of Death?

Wat. Sound Men, and true!

Robin. Of try'd Courage, and indefatigable Industry!

Ned. Who is there here that would not dye for his Friend?

Harry. Who is there here that would betray him for his Interest?

Mat. Show me a Gang of Courtiers that can say as much.

Ben. We are for a just Partition of the World, for every Man hath a Right to enjoy Life.

Act II, scene i. **1. clever a made:** well-built. Matt observes ironically that the surgeons killed his brother as a particularly good anatomical specimen. **2. fleaing:** (flaying) skin-stripping, torturing. **3. Otamys:** (atomies, a contraction of *anatomies*) skeletons. **4. Surgeon's Hall:** Barber-Surgeons' Hall, in Monkwell Street, City. The cadavers of prisoners were turned over to medical students.

Mat. We retrench[5] the Superfluities of Mankind. The World is avaritious, and I hate Avarice. A covetous fellow, like a Jack-daw,[6] steals what he was never made to enjoy, for the sake of hiding it. These are the Robbers of Mankind, for Money was made for the Free-hearted and Generous, and where is the injury of taking from another, what he hath not the Heart to make use of?

Jem. Our several Stations for the Day are fixt. Good luck attend us all. Fill the Glasses.

AIR XIX. Fill ev'ry Glass, &c.

Matt.   *Fill ev'ry Glass, for Wine inspires us,*
            And fires us
With Courage, Love and Joy.
Women and Wine should Life employ.
Is there ought else on Earth desirous?

Chorus.   *Fill ev'ry Glass, &c.*

SCENE II.

To them enter Macheath.

Mach. Gentlemen, well met. My Heart hath been with you this Hour; but an unexpected Affair hath detain'd me. No Ceremony, I beg you.

Matt. We were just breaking up to go upon Duty. Am I to have the Honour of taking the Air with you, Sir, this Evening upon the Heath? I drink a Dram now and then with the Stage-Coachmen in the way of Friendship and Intelligence; and I know that about this Time there will be Passengers upon the Western Road,[1] who are worth speaking with.

Mach. I was to have been of that Party—but—

Matt. But what, Sir?

Mach. Is there any man who suspects my Courage?

Matt. We have all been witnesses of it.

Mach. My Honour and Truth to the Gang?

Matt. I'll be answerable for it.

Mach. In the Division of our Booty, have I ever shown the least Marks of Avarice or Injustice?

Matt. By these Questions something seems to have ruffled you. Are any of us suspected?

Mach. I have a fixt Confidence, Gentlemen, in you all, as Men of Honour, and as such I value and respect you. *Peachum* is a Man that is useful to us.

Matt. Is he about to play us any foul Play? I'll shoot him through the Head.

Mach. I beg you, Gentlemen, act with Conduct and Discretion. A Pistol is your last resort.

Matt. He knows nothing of this Meeting.

Mach. Business cannot go on without him. He is a Man who knows the World, and is a necessary Agent to us. We have had a slight Difference, and till it is accommodated I shall be oblig'd to keep out of his way. Any private Dispute of mine shall be of no ill consequence to my Friends. You must continue to act under his Direction, for the moment we break loose from him, our Gang is ruin'd.

Matt. As a Bawd[2] to a Whore, I grant you, he is to us of great Convenience.

Mach. Make him believe I have quitted the Gang, which I can never do but with Life. At our private Quarters I will continue to meet you. A Week or so will probably reconcile us.

Matt. Your Instructions shall be observ'd. 'Tis now high time for us to repair to our several Duties; so till the Evening at our Quarters in *Moor-fields*[3] we bid you farewell.

Mach. I shall wish my self with you. Success attend you.   [*Sits down melancholy at the Table.*

AIR XX. March in *Rinaldo*,[4] with Drums and Trumpets.

Matt.   *Let us take the Road.*
Hark! I hear the sound of Coaches!
The hour of Attack approaches,
To your Arms, brave Boys, and load.
See the Ball I hold!
Let the Chymists toil like Asses,
Our fire their fire surpasses,
And turns all our Lead to Gold.[5]

[*The Gang, rang'd in the Front of the Stage, load their Pistols, and stick them under their Girdles;*[6] *then go off singing the first Part in Chorus.*

SCENE III.

Macheath, Drawer.

Mach. What a Fool is a fond Wench! *Polly* is most confoundedly bit.—I love the Sex. And a Man who loves Money, might as well be contented with one

---

5. retrench: cut down, reduce. **6. Jack-daw:** bird of the crow family, notorious for its thieving. *Act II, scene ii.* **1. the Western Road:** the road through Bagshot Heath.

2. Bawd: pimp. **3. Moor-fields:** a district (originally a marshland) outside the walls of the City to the north, popular as a promenade. **4. Rinaldo:** Handel's first London opera (1711). **5. Let . . . Gold:** The thieves outdo the alchemists in turning lead (bullets) into gold (money). **6. Girdles:** belts.

Guinea, as I with one Woman. The Town perhaps hath been as much oblig'd to me, for recruiting it with free-hearted Ladies, as to any Recruiting Officer in the Army. If it were not for us and the other Gentlemen of the Sword, *Drury-Lane* would be uninhabited.

AIR XXI. Would you have a Young Virgin, *&c.*

If the Heart of a Man is deprest with Cares,
The Mist is dispell'd when a Woman appears;
Like the Notes of a Fiddle, she sweetly, sweetly
Raises the Spirits, and charms our Ears,
Roses and Lillies her Cheeks disclose,
But her ripe Lips are more sweet than those.
    Press her,
    Caress her
    With Blisses,
    Her Kisses
Dissolve us in Pleasure, and soft Repose.

I must have Women. There is nothing unbends the Mind like them. Money is not so strong a Cordial for the Time. Drawer.—[*Enter Drawer.*] Is the Porter gone for all the Ladies, according to my directions?

Draw. I expect him back every Minute. But you know, Sir, you sent him as far as *Hockley in the Hole,* for three of the Ladies, for one in *Vinegar Yard,*[1] and for the rest of them somewhere about *Lewkner's Lane.*[2] Sure some of them are below, for I hear the Barr Bell. As they come I will show them up. Coming, Coming.

SCENE IV.

Macheath, *Mrs.* Coaxer, Dolly Trull, *Mrs.* Vixen, Betty Doxy, Jenny Diver, *Mrs.* Slammekin, Suky Tawdry, *and* Molly Brazen.

Mach. Dear Mrs. *Coaxer,* you are welcome. You look charmingly to-day. I hope you don't want the Repairs of Quality, and lay on Paint.[1]—*Dolly Trull!* kiss me, you Slut; are you as amorous as ever, Hussy? You are always so taken up with stealing Hearts, that you don't allow your self Time to steal any thing else. —Ah *Dolly,* thou wilt ever be a Coquette!—Mrs. *Vixen,* I'm yours, I always lov'd a Woman of Wit and Spirit; they make charming Mistresses, but plaguy[2]

Wives.—*Betty Doxy!* Come hither, Hussy. Do you drink as hard as ever? You had better stick to good wholesome Beer; for in troth, *Betty,* Strong-Waters will in time ruin your Constitution. You should leave those to your Betters.—What! and my pretty *Jenny Diver* too! As prim and demure as ever! There is not any Prude, though ever so high bred, hath a more sanctify'd Look, with a more mischievous Heart. Ah! thou art a dear artful Hypocrite.—Mrs. *Slammekin!* as careless and genteel as ever! all you fine Ladies, who know your own Beauty, affect an Undress.[3]—But see, here's *Suky Tawdry* come to contradict what I was saying. Every thing she gets one way she lays out upon her Back. Why, *Suky,* you must keep at least a dozen Tally-men.[4] *Molly Brazen!* [*She kisses him.*] That's well done. I love a free-hearted Wench. Thou hast a most agreeable Assurance, Girl, and art as willing as a Turtle.[5]—But hark! I hear musick. The Harper is at the Door. *If Musick be the Food of Love, play on.*[6] E'er[7] you seat your selves, Ladies, what think you of a Dance? Come in. [*Enter Harper.*] Play the *French* Tune, that Mrs. *Slammekin* was so fond of.

[*A Dance* a la ronde[8] *in the* French *Manner;*
    near the End of it this Song and Chorus.

AIR XXII. Cotillon.

Youth's the Season made for Joys,
    Love is then our Duty,
She alone who that employs,
    Well deserves her Beauty.
        Let's be gay,
        While we may,
Beauty's a Flower, despis'd in decay.
Youth's the Season &c.

Let us drink and sport to-day,
    Ours is not to-morrow.
Love with Youth flies swift away,
    Age is nought but Sorrow.
        Dance and sing,
        Time's on the Wing,
Life never knows the return of Spring.
Chorus. *Let us drink &c.*

Act II, scene iii. **1. Vinegar Yard:** in Drury Lane. **2. Lewkner's Lane:** (Lewknor's) also in Drury Lane. Jonathan Wild kept a house of prostitution here. *Act II, scene iv.* **1. 1 . . . Paint:** I hope you don't indulge in the use of cosmetics the way gentlewomen do. **2. plaguy:** vexatious, troublesome.

3. Undress: casual dress. **4. Tally-men:** merchants who sold on credit. **5. Turtle:** turtledove. **6. If . . . on:** the opening line of *Twelfth Night.* **7. E'er:** ere. **8. A Dance . . . ronde:** a circle dance.

Mach.   Now, pray Ladies, take your Places. Here Fellow. [*Pays the Harper.*] Bid the Drawer bring us more Wine. [*Ex. Harper.*] If any of the Ladies chuse Ginn, I hope they will be so free to call for it.

Jenny.   You look as if you meant me. Wine is strong enough for me. Indeed, Sir, I never drink Strong-Waters, but when I have the Cholic.

Mach.   Just the Excuse of the fine Ladies! Why, a Lady of Quality is never without the Cholic. I hope, Mrs. *Coaxer*, you have had good Success of late in your Visits among the Mercers.[9]

Coax.   We have so many Interlopers—Yet with Industry, one may still have a little Picking. I carried a silver flower'd Lutestring,[10] and a Piece of black Padesoy[11] to Mr. *Peachum*'s Lock but last Week.

Vix.   There's *Molly Brazen* hath the Ogle[12] of a Rattle-Snake. She rivetted a Linnen-draper's Eye so fast upon her, that he was nick'd of[13] three Pieces of Cambric before he could look off.

Braz.   Oh dear Madam!—But sure nothing can come up to your handling of Laces! And then you have such a sweet deluding Tongue! To cheat a Man is nothing; but the Woman must have fine Parts indeed who cheats a Woman!

Vix.   Lace, Madam, lyes in a small Compass, and is of easy Conveyance. But you are apt, Madam, to think too well of your Friends.

Coax.   If any Woman hath more Art than another, to be sure, 'tis *Jenny Diver.* Though her Fellow be never so agreeable,[14] she can pick his Pocket as cooly, as if Money were her only Pleasure. Now that is a Command of the Passions uncommon in a Woman!

Jenny.   I never go to the Tavern with a Man, but in the View of Business. I have other Hours, and other sort of Men for my Pleasure. But had I your Address,[15] Madam—

Mach.   Have done with your Compliments, Ladies; and drink about: You are not so fond of me, *Jenny*, as you use to be.

Jenny.   'Tis not convenient, Sir, to show my Fondness among so many Rivals. 'Tis your own Choice, and not the warmth of my Inclination that will determine you.[16]

AIR XXIII. All in a misty Morning, &c.

Before the Barn-door crowing,
    The Cock by Hens attended,
His Eyes around him throwing,
    Stands for a while suspended.
Then One he singles from the Crew,
    And cheers the happy Hen;
With how do you do, and how do you do,
    And how do you do again.

Mach.   Ah *Jenny!* thou art a dear Slut.

Trull.   Pray, Madam, were you ever in keeping?[17]

Tawd.   I hope, Madam, I ha'nt been so long upon the Town, but I have met with some good Fortune as well as my Neighbours.

Trull.   Pardon me, Madam, I meant no harm by the Question; 'twas only in the way of Conversation.

Tawd.   Indeed, Madam, if I had not been a Fool, I might have liv'd very handsomely with my last Friend. But upon his missing five Guineas, he turn'd me off. Now I never suspected he had counted them.

Slam.   Who do you look upon, Madam, as your best sort of Keepers?

Trull.   That, Madam, is thereafter as they be.[18]

Slam.   I, Madam, was once kept by a *Jew*; and bating[19] their Religion, to Women they are a good sort of People.

Tawd.   Now for my part, I own I like an old Fellow: for we always make them pay for what they can't do.

Vix.   A spruce[20] Prentice, let me tell you, Ladies, is no ill thing, they bleed freely.[21] I have sent at least two or three dozen of them in my time to the Plantations.

Jen.   But to be sure, Sir, with so much good Fortune as you have had upon the Road, you must be grown immensely rich.

Mach.   The Road, indeed, hath done me justice, but the Gaming-Table hath been my ruin.

AIR XXIV. When once I lay with another
Man's Wife, &c.

Jen.   *The Gamesters and Lawyers are Jugglers alike,*
    If they meddle your All is in danger.
Like Gypsies, if once they can finger a Souse,[22]
Your Pockets they pick, and they pilfer your House,
    And give your Estate to a Stranger.

---

9. **Mercers:** textile merchants. 10. **Lutestring:** (lustring) a glossy silk fabric. 11. **Padesoy:** (paduasoy) a corded silk fabric. 12. **Ogle:** eye, alluring glance. 13. **nick'd of:** done out of. 14. **Though . . . agreeable:** no matter how attractive he might be. 15. **Address:** adroitness. 16. **determine you:** decide the event for you.

17. **in keeping:** "kept." 18. **thereafter . . . be:** according to the way they (actually) are. 19. **bating:** except for. 20. **spruce:** lively. 21. **bleed freely:** spend lavishly (money stolen from their masters). 22. **finger a Souse:** lay their hands on a sou.

A Man of Courage should never put any Thing to the Risque, but his Life. These are the Tools of a Man of Honour. Cards and Dice are only fit for cowardly Cheats, who prey upon their Friends.

[*She takes up his Pistol.* Tawdry *takes up the other.*

Tawd. This, Sir, is fitter for your Hand. Besides your Loss of Money, 'tis a Loss to the Ladies. Gaming takes you off from Women. How fond could I be of you! but before Company, 'tis ill bred.

Mach. Wanton Hussies!

Jen. I must and will have a Kiss to give my Wine a zest.

[*They take him about the Neck, and make Signs to* Peachum *and Constables, who rush in upon him.*

SCENE V.

To them, Peachum *and Constables.*

Peach. I seize you, Sir, as my Prisoner.

Mach. Was this well done, *Jenny?*—Women are Decoy Ducks; who can trust them! Beasts, Jades, Jilts, Harpies, Furies, Whores!

Peach. Your Case, Mr. *Macheath*, is not particular.[1] The greatest Heroes have been ruin'd by Women. But, to do them justice, I must own they are a pretty sort of Creatures, if we could trust them. You must now, Sir, take your leave of the Ladies, and if they have a Mind to make you a Visit, they will be sure to find you at home. The Gentleman, Ladies, lodges in *Newgate*. Constables, wait upon the Captain to his Lodgings.

AIR XXV. When first I laid Siege to my *Chloris,* &c.

Mac. At the Tree I shall suffer with pleasure,
    At the Tree I shall suffer with pleasure,
      Let me go where I will,
      In all kinds of Ill,
    I shall find no such Furies as these are.

Peach. Ladies, I'll take care the Reckoning shall be discharg'd.

[*Ex.* Macheath, *guarded with* Peachum *and* Constables.

SCENE VI.

The Women remain.

Vix. Look ye, Mrs. *Jenny*, though Mr. *Peachum* may have made a private Bargain with you and *Suky Tawdry* for betraying the Captain, as we were all assisting, we ought all to share alike.

Coax. I think Mr. *Peachum*, after so long an acquaintance, might have trusted me as well as *Jenny Diver*.

Slam. I am sure at least three Men of his hanging, and in a Year's time too, (if he did me justice) should be set down to my account.

Trull. Mrs. *Slammekin*, that is not fair. For you know one of them was taken in Bed with me.

Jenny. As far as a Bowl of Punch or a Treat, I believe Mrs. *Suky* will join with me.—As for any thing else, Ladies, you cannot in conscience expect it.

Slam. Dear Madam—

Trull. I would not for the World—

Slam. 'Tis impossible for me—

Trull. As I hope to be sav'd, Madam—

Slam. Nay, then I must stay here all Night—

Trull. Since you command me.

[*Exeunt with great Ceremony.*

SCENE VII. *Newgate.*

Lockit, *Turnkeys,* Macheath, *Constables.*

Lock. Noble Captain, you are welcome. You have not been a Lodger of mine this Year and half. You know the custom, Sir. Garnish,[1] Captain, Garnish. Hand me down those Fetters there.

Mach. Those, Mr. *Lockit*, seem to be the heaviest of the whole sett. With your leave, I should like the further pair better.

Lock. Look ye, Captain, we know what is fittest for our Prisoners. When a Gentleman uses me with Civility, I always do the best I can to please him. —Hand them down I say.—We have them of all Prices, from one Guinea to ten, and 'tis fitting every Gentleman should please himself.

Mach. I understand you, Sir. [*Gives Money.*] The Fees here are so many, and so exorbitant, that few Fortunes can bear the Expence of getting off handsomly, or of dying like a Gentleman.

Act II, scene v. **1. particular:** individual, i.e., it is not unusual.

Act II, scene vii. **1. Garnish:** The prisoner was required to pay fees for "services."

Lock. Those, I see, will fit the Captain better.
—Take down the further Pair. Do but examine them,
Sir.—Never was better work.—How genteely they
are made!—They will fit as easy as a Glove, and the
nicest[2] Man in *England* might not be asham'd to wear
them. [*He puts on the Chains.*] If I had the best Gentleman in the Land in my Custody I could not equip him
more handsomly. And so, Sir—I now leave you to
your private Meditations.

SCENE VIII.

Macheath.

AIR XXVI. *Courtiers, Courtiers think it no harm, &c.*

> *Man may escape from Rope and Gun;*
> *Nay, some have out-liv'd the Doctor's Pill;*
> *Who takes a Woman must be undone,*
>   *That Basilisk[1] is sure to kill.*
> *The Fly that sips Treacle is lost in the Sweets,*
> *So he that tastes Woman, Woman, Woman,*
> *He that tastes Woman, Ruin meets.*

To what a woful plight have I brought my self! Here
must I (all day long, 'till I am hang'd) be confin'd to
hear the Reproaches of a Wench who lays her Ruin
at my Door.—I am in the Custody of her Father, and
to be sure if he knows of the matter, I shall have a fine
time on 't betwixt this[2] and my Execution.—But I
promis'd the Wench Marriage.—What signifies a
Promise to a Woman? Does not Man in Marriage
itself promise a hundred things that he never means
to perform? Do all we can, Women will believe us;
for they look upon a Promise as an Excuse for following their own Inclinations.—But here comes *Lucy*,
and I cannot get from her—Wou'd I were deaf!

SCENE IX.

Macheath, Lucy.

Lucy. You base Man you,—how can you look me
in the Face after what hath past between us?—See
here, perfidious Wretch, how I am forc'd to bear
about the load of Infamy you have laid upon me—O
Macheath! thou hast robb'd me of my Quiet—to see
thee tortur'd would give me pleasure.

AIR XXVII. *A lovely Lass to a Friar came, &c.*

> *Thus when a good Huswife sees a Rat*
> *In her Trap in the Morning taken,*
> *With pleasure her Heart goes pit a pat,*
>   *In Revenge for her loss of Bacon.*
>   *Then she throws him*
>   *To the Dog or Cat,*
> *To be worried, crush'd and shaken.*

Mac. Have you no Bowels,[1] no Tenderness, my
dear *Lucy*, to see a Husband in these Circumstances?
Lucy. A Husband!
Mac. In ev'ry respect but the Form, and that, my
Dear, may be said over us at any time.—Friends
should not insist upon Ceremonies. From a Man of
honour, his Word is as good as his Bond.
Lucy. 'Tis the pleasure of all you fine Men to insult
the Women you have ruin'd.

AIR XXVIII. *'Twas when the Sea was roaring,[2] &c.*

> *How cruel are the Traytors,*
>   *Who lye and swear in jest,*
> *To cheat unguarded Creatures*
>   *Of Virtue, Fame, and Rest!*
> *Whoever steals a Shilling,*
>   *Through shame the Guilt conceals:*
> *In Love the perjur'd Villain*
>   *With Boasts the Theft reveals.*

Mac. The very first opportunity, my Dear, (have
but patience) you shall be my Wife in whatever
manner you please.
Lucy. Insinuating[3] Monster! And so you think I
know nothing of the Affair of Miss *Polly Peachum*.
—I could tear thy Eyes out!
Mac. Sure *Lucy*, you can't be such a Fool as to be
jealous of *Polly!*
Lucy. Are you not married to her, you Brute, you?
Mac. Married! Very good. The Wench gives it
out[4] only to vex thee, and to ruin me in thy good
Opinion. 'Tis true, I go to the House; I chat with the
Girl, I kiss her, I say a thousand things to her (as all
Gentlemen do) that mean nothing, to divert my self;
and now the silly Jade hath set it about that I am
married to her, to let me know what she would be at.

---

2. **nicest:** most fastidious. *Act II, scene viii.* 1. **Basilisk:**
the fabulous serpent whose very look was fatal. 2. **this:**
now.

Act II, scene ix. 1. **Bowels:** pity. 2. **'Twas . . . roaring:**
Gay's own song, from his farce *The What D' Ye Call It*, II. viii.
The music is by Handel. 3. **Insinuating:** ingratiating by
devious means. 4. **gives it out:** reports, publishes, circulates
it; the same as is meant by "set it about" in the next sentence.

Indeed, my dear *Lucy*, these violent Passions may be of ill consequence to a Woman in your condition.[5]

Lucy. Come, come, Captain, for all your Assurance, you know that Miss *Polly* hath put it out of your power to do me the Justice you promis'd me.

Mac. A jealous Woman believes ev'ry thing her Passion suggests. To convince you of my Sincerity, if we can find the Ordinary,[6] I shall have no scruples of making you my Wife; and I know the consequence of having two at a time.

Lucy. That you are only to be hang'd, and so get rid of them both.

Mac. I am ready, my dear *Lucy*, to give you satisfaction—if you think there is any in Marriage.—What can a Man of Honour say more?

Lucy. So then it seems, you are not married to Miss *Polly*.

Mac. You know, *Lucy*, the Girl is prodigiously conceited. No Man can say a civil thing to her, but (like other fine Ladies) her Vanity makes her think he's her own for ever and ever.

AIR XXIX. The Sun had loos'd his weary Teams, &c.

> The first time at the Looking-glass
> The Mother sets her Daughter,
> The Image strikes the smiling Lass
> With Self-love ever after.
> Each time she looks, she, fonder grown,
> Thinks ev'ry Charm grows stronger.
> But alas, vain Maid, all Eyes but your own
> Can see you are not younger.

When Women consider their own Beauties, they are all alike unreasonable in their demands; for they expect their Lovers should like them as long as they like themselves.

Lucy. Yonder is my Father—perhaps this way we may light upon[7] the Ordinary, who shall try if[8] you will be as good as your Word.—For I long to be made an honest Woman.

SCENE X.

Peachum, Lockit *with an Account-Book.*

Lock. In this last Affair, Brother *Peachum*, we are agreed. You have consented to go halves in *Macheath*.

Peach. We shall never fall out about an Execution.

—But as to that Article, pray how stands our last Year's account?

Lock. If you will run your Eye over it, you'll find 'tis fair and clearly stated.

Peach. This long Arrear[1] of the Government is very hard upon us! Can it be expected that we should hang our Acquaintance for nothing, when our Betters will hardly save theirs without being paid for it. Unless the People in employment[2] pay better, I promise them for the future, I shall let other Rogues live besides their own.

Lock. Perhaps, Brother, they are afraid these matters may be carried too far. We are treated too by them with Contempt, as if our Profession were not reputable.

Peach. In one respect indeed, our Employment may be reckon'd dishonest, because, like Great Statesmen, we encourage those who betray their Friends.

Lock. Such Language, Brother, any where else, might turn to your prejudice.[3] Learn to be more guarded, I beg you.

AIR XXX. How happy are we, &c.

> When you censure the Age,
> Be cautious and sage,
> Lest the Courtiers offended should be:
> If you mention Vice or Bribe,
> 'Tis so pat[4] to all the Tribe;
> Each crys—That was levell'd at me.

Peach. Here's poor *Ned Clincher's*[5] Name, I see. Sure, Brother *Lockit*, there was a little unfair proceeding in *Ned*'s case: for he told me in the Condemn'd Hold, that for Value receiv'd, you had promis'd him a Session or two longer without Molestation.

Lock. Mr. *Peachum*,—This is the first time my Honour was ever call'd in Question.

Peach. Business is at an end—if once we act dishonourably.

Lock. Who accuses me?

Peach. You are warm,[6] Brother.

Lock. He that attacks my Honour, attacks my Livelyhood.—And this Usage—Sir—is not to be born.

---

5. your condition: pregnancy. Lucy's lament in scene xiii ("Hadst thou been hang'd") reveals that she is five months pregnant. 6. the Ordinary: the prison chaplain. 7. this . . . upon: he will lead us to. 8. try if: test whether.

Act II, scene x. 1. Arrear: delinquency in paying debts; here, the rewards promised for the arrest of criminals. 2. in employment: officially placed. 3. turn . . . prejudice: be used against you (in a court of law). 4. pat: apposite. 5. Clincher: *Clinch* is thieves' slang for a prison cell, especially the "Condemn'd Hold" mentioned in the next sentence. 6. warm: passionate.

Peach. Since you provoke me to speak—I must tell you too, that Mrs. *Coaxer* charges you with defrauding her of her Information-Money, for the apprehending of curl-pated *Hugh.* Indeed, indeed, Brother, we must punctually pay our Spies, or we shall have no Information.

Lock. Is this Language to me, Sirrah—who have sav'd you from the Gallows, Sirrah!

[*Collaring each other.*

Peach. If I am hang'd, it shall be for ridding the World of an arrant Rascal.

Lock. This Hand shall do the office of the Halter[7] you deserve, and throttle you—you Dog!—

Peach. Brother, Brother,—We are both in the Wrong—We shall be both Losers in the Dispute—for you know we have it in our Power to hang each other. You should not be so passionate.

Lock. Nor you so provoking.

Peach. 'Tis our mutual Interest; 'tis for the Interest of the World we should agree. If I said any thing, Brother, to the Prejudice of your Character, I ask pardon.

Lock. Brother *Peachum*—I can forgive as well as resent.—Give me your Hand. Suspicion does not become a Friend.

Peach. I only meant to give you occasion to justifie yourself: But I must now step home, for I expect the Gentleman about this Snuff-box, that *Filch* nimm'd two Nights ago in the Park. I appointed him at this hour.

SCENE XI.

Lockit, Lucy.

Lock. Whence come you, Hussy?

Lucy. My Tears might answer that Question.

Lock. You have then been whimpering and fondling, like a Spaniel, over the Fellow that hath abus'd you.

Lucy. One can't help Love; one can't cure it. 'Tis not in my Power to obey you, and hate him.

Lock. Learn to bear your Husband's Death like a reasonable Woman. 'Tis not the fashion, now-a-days, so much as to affect Sorrow upon these Occasions. No Woman would ever marry, if she had not the Chance of Mortality for a Release. Act like a Woman of Spirit, Hussy, and thank your Father for what he is doing.

7. **Halter:** hangman's noose.

AIR XXXI. *Of a noble Race was* Shenkin.

Lucy.   *Is then his Fate decreed, Sir?*
       Such a Man can I think of quitting?
       When first we met, so moves me yet,
       O see how my Heart is splitting!

Lock. Look ye, *Lucy*—There is no saving him. —So, I think, you must ev'n do like other Widows—Buy your self Weeds, and be cheerful.

AIR XXXII.

You'll think e'er many Days ensue
This Sentence not severe;
I hang your Husband, Child, 'tis true,
But with him hang your Care.
Twang dang dillo dee.

Like a good Wife, go moan over your dying Husband. That, Child, is your Duty—Consider, Girl, you can't have the Man and the Money too—so make yourself as easy as you can, by getting all you can from him.

SCENE XII.

Lucy, Macheath.

Lucy. Though the Ordinary was out of the way to-day, I hope, my Dear, you will, upon the first opportunity, quiet my Scruples—Oh Sir!—my Father's hard Heart is not to be soften'd, and I am in the utmost Despair.

Mac. But if I could raise a small Sum—Would not twenty Guineas, think you, move him?—Of all the Arguments in the way[1] of Business, the Perquisite[2] is the most prevailing.—Your Father's Perquisites for the Escape of Prisoners must amount to a considerable Sum in the Year. Money well tim'd, and properly apply'd, will do any thing.

AIR XXXIII. *London Ladies.*

If you at an Office solicit your Due,
   And would not have Matters neglected;
You must quicken the Clerk with the Perquisite too,
   To do what his Duty directed.
Or would you the Frowns of a Lady prevent,
   She too has this palpable Failing,
The Perquisite softens her into Consent;
   That Reason with all is prevailing.

Lucy. What Love or Money can do shall be done: for all my Comfort depends upon your Safety.

Act II, scene xii. 1. **way:** conduct. 2. **Perquisite:** an emolument beyond salary or wages, a tip.

SCENE XIII.

Lucy, Macheath, Polly.

Polly. Where is my dear Husband?—Was a Rope ever intended for this Neck!—O let me throw my Arms about it, and throttle thee with Love!—Why dost thou turn away from me?—'Tis thy *Polly*— 'Tis thy Wife.

Mac. Was ever such an unfortunate Rascal as I am!

Lucy. Was there ever such another Villain!

Polly. O *Macheath!* was it for this we parted? Taken! Imprison'd! Try'd! Hang'd!—cruel Reflection! I'll stay with thee 'till Death—no Force shall tear thy dear Wife from thee now.—What means my Love?—Not one kind Word! not one kind Look! think what thy *Polly* suffers to see thee in this Condition.

AIR XXXIV. All in the Downs, &c.

Thus when the Swallow, seeking Prey,
Within the Sash is closely pent,
His Consort, with bemoaning Lay,
Without sits pining for th' Event.
Her chatt'ring Lovers all around her skim;
She heeds them not (poor Bird!) her Soul's with him.

Mac. I must disown her. [*Aside.*] The Wench is distracted.

Lucy. Am I then bilk'd[1] of my Virtue? Can I have no Reparation? Sure Men were born to lye, and Women to believe them! O Villain! Villain!

Polly. Am I not thy Wife?—The Neglect of me, thy Aversion to me too severely proves it.—Look on me.—Tell me, am I not thy Wife?

Lucy. Perfidious Wretch!

Polly. Barbarous Husband!

Lucy. Hadst thou been hang'd five Months ago, I had been happy.

Polly. And I too—If you had been kind to me 'till Death, it would not have vex'd me—And that's no very unreasonable Request, (though from a Wife) to a Man who hath not above seven or eight Days to live.

Lucy. Art thou then married to another? Hast thou two Wives, Monster?

Mac. If Women's Tongues can cease for an Answer —hear me.

Lucy. I won't.—Flesh and Blood can't bear my Usage.

Polly. Shall I not claim my own? Justice bids me speak.

AIR XXXV. Have you heard of a frolicksome Ditty, &c.

Mac. *How happy could I be with either,*
Were t' other dear Charmer away!
But while you thus teaze me together,
To neither a Word will I say;
But tol de rol, &c.

Polly. Sure, my Dear, there ought to be some Preference shown to a Wife! At least she may claim the Appearance of it. He must be distracted with his Misfortunes, or he could not use me thus!

Lucy. O Villain, Villain! thou hast deceiv'd me—I could even inform against thee with Pleasure. Not a Prude wishes more heartily to have Facts against her intimate Acquaintance, than I now wish to have Facts against thee. I would have her Satisfaction, and they should all out.[2]

AIR XXXVI. Irish Trot.

Polly. I'm bubbled.[3]

Lucy. ————— I'm bubbled.

Polly. Oh how I am troubled!

Lucy. Bambouzled, and bit!

Polly. ————————— My Distresses are
doubled.

Lucy. When you come to the Tree, should the Hangman refuse,
These Fingers, with Pleasure, could fasten the Noose.

Polly. I'm bubbled, &c.

Mac. Be pacified, my dear *Lucy*—This is all a Fetch[4] of *Polly*'s, to make me desperate with[5] you in case I get off. If I am hang'd, she would fain[6] have the Credit of being thought my Widow—Really, *Polly,* this is no time for a Dispute of this sort; for whenever you are talking of Marriage, I am thinking of Hanging.

Polly. And hast thou the Heart to persist in disowning me?

Mac. And hast thou the Heart to persist in persuading me that I am married? Why, *Polly,* dost thou seek to aggravate my Misfortunes?

Act II, scene xiii. **1. bilk'd:** cheated.

2. out: be exposed. **3. bubbled:** cheated. **4. Fetch:** trick. **5. desperate with:** despairing of. **6. fain:** be pleased to.

Lucy.   Really, Miss *Peachum*, you but expose your-self. Besides, 'tis barbarous in you to worry a Gentle-man in his Circumstances.

AIR XXXVII.

Polly.   *Cease your Funning;*[7]
Force or Cunning
Never shall my Heart trapan.[8]
All these Sallies
Are but Malice
To seduce my constant Man.
'Tis most certain,
By their flirting
Women oft' have Envy shown;
Pleas'd, to ruin
Others wooing;
Never happy in their own!

Polly.   Decency, Madam, methinks might teach you to behave yourself with some Reserve with the Husband, while his Wife is present.

Mac.   But seriously, *Polly*, this is carrying the Joke a little too far.

Lucy.   If you are determin'd, Madam, to raise a Disturbance in the Prison, I shall be oblig'd to send for the Turnkey to show you the Door. I am sorry, Madam, you force me to be so ill-bred.

Polly.   Give me leave to tell you, Madam; These forward Airs don't become you in the least, Madam. And my Duty, Madam, obliges me to stay with my Husband, Madam.

AIR XXXVIII. Good-morrow, Gossip[9] *Joan.*

Lucy.   *Why how now, Madam Flirt?*
If you thus must chatter;
And are for flinging Dirt,
Let's try who best can spatter;
*   Madam Flirt!*
Polly.   *Why how now, saucy Jade;*
Sure the Wench is Tipsy!
How can you see me made   [To him.
The Scoff of such a Gipsy?
*   Saucy Jade!*   [To her.

7. **Funning:** fooling, joking. 8. **trapan:** (trepan) beguile, cheat. 9. **Gossip:** friend.

SCENE XIV.

Lucy, Macheath, Polly, Peachum.

Peach.   Where's my Wench? Ah Hussy! Hussy! —Come you home, you Slut; and when your Fellow is hang'd, hang yourself, to make your Family some amends.

Polly.   Dear, dear Father, do not tear me from him —I must speak; I have more to say to him—Oh! twist thy Fetters about me, that he may not haul me from thee!

Peach.   Sure all Women are alike! If ever they commit the Folly, they are sure to commit another by exposing themselves—Away—Not a Word more —You are my Prisoner now, Hussy.

AIR XXXIX. Irish Howl.

Polly.   *No Power on Earth can e'er divide,*
The Knot that Sacred Love hath ty'd.
When Parents draw against our Mind,
The True-love's Knot they faster bind.
Oh, oh ray, oh Amborah—oh, oh, &c.
[Holding *Macheath*, *Peachum* pulling her.

SCENE XV.

Lucy, Macheath.

Mac.   I am naturally compassionate, Wife; so that I could not use the Wench as she deserv'd; which made you at first suspect there was something in what she said.

Lucy.   Indeed, my Dear, I was strangely puzzled.

Mac.   If that had been the Case, her Father would never have brought me into this Circumstance—No, *Lucy*,—I had rather dye than be false to thee.

Lucy.   How happy am I, if you say this from your Heart! For I love thee so, that I could sooner bear to see thee hang'd than in the Arms of another.

Mac.   But couldst thou bear to see me hang'd?

Lucy.   O *Macheath*, I can never live to see that Day.

Mac.   You see, *Lucy*; in the Account of Love you are in my debt, and you must now be convinc'd, that I rather chuse to die than be another's.—Make me, if possible, love thee more, and let me owe my Life to thee—If you refuse to assist me, *Peachum* and your Father will immediately put me beyond all means of Escape.

Lucy.   My Father, I know, hath been drinking hard with the Prisoners: and I fancy he is now taking his

Nap in his own Room—If I can procure the Keys, shall I go off with thee, my Dear?

Mac. If we are together, 'twill be impossible to lye conceal'd. As soon as the Search begins to be a little cool, I will send to thee—'Till then my Heart is thy Prisoner.

Lucy. Come then, my dear Husband—owe thy Life to me—and though you love me not—be grateful —But that *Polly* runs in my Head strangely.

Mac. A Moment of time [1] may make us unhappy for-ever.

AIR XL. The Lass of *Patie's* Mill, &c.

Lucy. *I like the Fox shall grieve,*
  Whose Mate hath left her side,
  Whom Hounds, from Morn to Eve,
   Chase o'er the Country wide.
  Where can my Lover hide?
  Where cheat the wary Pack?
  If Love be not his Guide,
   He never will come back!

ACT III

SCENE I.

SCENE *Newgate.*

Lockit, Lucy.

Lock. To be sure, Wench, you must have been aiding and abetting to help him to this Escape.

Lucy. Sir, there hath been *Peachum* and his Daughter *Polly*, and to be sure they know the Ways of *Newgate* as well as if they had been born and bred in the Place all their Lives. Why must all your Suspicion light upon me?

Lock. Lucy, Lucy, I will have none of these shuffling[1] Answers.

Lucy. Well then—If I know any Thing of him I wish I may be burnt!

Lock. Keep your Temper, *Lucy*, or I shall pronounce you guilty.

Lucy. Keep yours, Sir,—I do wish I may be burnt. I do—And what can I say more to convince you?

Lock. Did he tip handsomely?—How much did he come down[2] with? Come Hussy, don't cheat your

Father; and I shall not be angry with you—Perhaps, you have made a better Bargain with him than I could have done—How much, my good Girl?

Lucy. You know, Sir, I am fond of him, and would have given Money to have kept him with me.

Lock. Ah *Lucy!* thy Education might have put thee more upon thy Guard; for a Girl in the Bar of an Ale-house is always besieg'd.

Lucy. Dear Sir, mention not my Education—for 'twas to that I owe my Ruin.

AIR XLI. If Love's a sweet Passion, &c.

When young at the Bar you first taught me to score,[3]
And bid me be free of my Lips, and no more;
I was kiss'd by the Parson, the Squire, and the Sot.
When the Guest was departed, the Kiss was forgot.
But his Kiss was so sweet, and so closely he prest,
That I languish'd and pin'd 'till I granted the rest.

If you can forgive me, Sir, I will make a fair[4] Confession, for to be sure he hath been a most barbarous Villain to me.

Lock. And so you have let him escape, Hussy—Have you?

Lucy. When a Woman loves; a kind Look, a tender Word can persuade her to any thing—And I could ask no other Bribe.

Lock. Thou wilt always be a vulgar Slut, *Lucy.* —If you would not be look'd upon as a Fool, you should never do any thing but upon the Foot of Interest. Those that act otherwise are their own Bubbles.[5]

Lucy. But Love, Sir, is a Misfortune that may happen to the most discreet Woman, and in Love we are all Fools alike.—Notwithstanding all he swore, I am now fully convinc'd that *Polly Peachum* is actually his Wife.—Did I let him escape, (Fool that I was!) to go to her?—*Polly* will wheedle herself into his Money, and then *Peachum* will hang him, and cheat us both.

Lock. So I am to be ruin'd, because, forsooth, you must be in Love!—a very pretty Excuse!

Lucy. I could murder that impudent happy Strumpet:—I gave him his Life, and that Creature enjoys the Sweets of it.—Ungrateful *Macheath!*

Act II, scene xv. **1. time:** delay. *Act III, scene i.* **1. shuffling:** evasive. **2. down:** i.e., up.

3. score: reckon the bill. **4. fair:** free, open. **5. Bubbles:** dupes.

AIR XLII. South-Sea Ballad.

My Love is all Madness and Folly,
  Alone I lye,
  Toss, tumble, and cry,
What a happy Creature is Polly!
Was e'er such a Wretch as I!
With Rage I redden like Scarlet,
That my dear inconstant Varlet,[6]
  Stark blind to my Charms,
  Is lost in the Arms
Of that Jilt, that inveigling Harlot!
  Stark blind to my Charms,
  Is lost in the Arms
Of that Jilt, that inveigling Harlot!
This, this my Resentment alarms.

Lock. And so, after all this Mischief, I must stay here to be entertain'd with your catterwauling, Mistress Puss!—Out of my Sight, wanton Strumpet! you shall fast and mortify yourself into Reason, with now and then a little handsome Discipline[7] to bring you to your Senses.—Go.

SCENE II.

Lockit.

Peachum then intends to outwit me in this Affair; but I'll be even with him.—The Dog is leaky[1] in his Liquor, so I'll ply him that way, get the Secret from him, and turn this Affair to my own Advantage. —Lions, Wolves, and Vulturs don't live together in Herds, Droves or Flocks.—Of all Animals of Prey, Man is the only sociable one. Every one of us preys upon his Neighbour, and yet we herd together. —*Peachum* is my Companion, my Friend—According to the Custom of the World, indeed, he may quote thousands of Precedents for cheating me—And shall not I make use of the Privilege of Friendship to make him a Return?

AIR XLIII. *Packington's* Pound.

Thus Gamesters united in Friendship are found,
Though they know that their Industry all is a Cheat;
They flock to their Prey at the Dice-Box's Sound,
And join to promote one another's Deceit.

But if by mishap
  They fail of a Chap,[2]
To keep in their Hands,[3] they each other entrap.
Like Pikes, lank with Hunger, who miss of their Ends,[4]
They bite their Companions, and prey on their Friends.

Now, *Peachum,* you and I, like honest Tradesmen, are to have a fair Tryal which of us two can over-reach the other.—*Lucy.*—[*Enter* Lucy.] Are there any of *Peachum's* People now in the House?

Lucy. Filch, Sir, is drinking a Quartern[5] of Strong-Waters in the next Room with Black *Moll.*

Lock. Bid him come to me.

SCENE III.

Lockit, Filch.

Lock. Why, Boy, thou lookest as if thou wert half starv'd; like a shotten Herring.[1]

Filch. One had need have the Constitution of a Horse to go thorough[2] the Business.—Since the favourite Child-getter[3] was disabled by a Mis-hap, I have pick'd up a little Money by helping the Ladies to a Pregnancy against their being call'd down to Sentence.—But if a Man cannot get an honest Livelyhood any easier way, I am sure, 'tis what I can't undertake for another Session.

Lock. Truly, if that great Man should tip off,[4] 'twoud be an irreparable Loss. The Vigor and Prowess of a Knight Errant never sav'd half the Ladies in Distress that he hath done.—But, Boy, can'st thou tell me where thy Master is to be found?

Filch. At his Lock,[5] Sir, at the *Crooked Billet.[6]*

Lock. Very well.—I have nothing more with you. [*Ex.* Filch.] I'll go to him there, for I have many important Affairs to settle with him; and in the way of those Transactions, I'll artfully get into his Secret. —So that *Macheath* shall not remain a Day longer out of my Clutches.

6. Varlet: knave, rascal. **7. Discipline:** whipping. *Act III, scene ii.* **1. leaky:** talkative.

2. fail . . . Chap: lack a customer (victim). **3. To . . . Hands:** to keep in practice. **4. miss . . . Ends:** fail to secure their objects. **5. Quartern:** quarter of a pint, a gill. *Act III, scene iii.* **1. a shotten Herring:** a herring that has spawned; here, the meaning is "worn out." **2. thorough:** through with. **3. the favourite Child-getter:** Macheath. **4. tip off:** die. **5. Lock:** [Gay's note] A Cant Word, signifying, a Warehouse where stolen Goods are deposited. **6. the Crooked Billet:** Crooked Billet Court, in Moorfields.

SCENE IV. *A Gaming-House.*

Macheath *in a fine tarnish'd*[1] *Coat*, Ben Budge,
Matt *of the Mint.*

Mac. I am sorry, Gentlemen, the Road was so
barren of Money. When my Friends are in Difficulties,
I am always glad that my Fortune can be serviceable
to them. [*Gives them Money.*] You see, Gentlemen, I
am not a meer Court Friend, who professes every
thing and will do nothing.

AIR XLIV. Lillibullero.

The Modes of the Court so common are grown,
  That a true Friend can hardly be met;
Friendship for Interest[2] *is but a Loan,*
  Which they let out for what they can get.
    'Tis true, you find
    Some Friends so kind,
Who will give you good Counsel themselves to defend.
    In sorrowful Ditty,
    They promise, they pity,
But shift you for Money, from Friend to Friend.

But we, Gentlemen, have still Honour enough to
break through the Corruptions of the World.—And
while I can serve you, you may command me.

Ben. It grieves my Heart that so generous a Man
should be involv'd in such Difficulties, as oblige him
to live with such ill Company, and herd with Gamesters.

Matt. See the Partiality of Mankind!—One Man
may steal a Horse, better than another look over a
Hedge[3]—Of all Mechanics,[4] of all servile Handycrafts-
men, a Gamester is the vilest. But yet, as many of
Quality are of the Profession, he is admitted amongst
the politest Company. I wonder we[5] are not more
respected.

Mach. There will be deep Play to-night at *Mary-
bone*, and consequently Money may be pick'd up upon
the Road. Meet me there, and I'll give you the Hint
who is worth Setting.[6]

Matt. The Fellow with a brown Coat with a
narrow Gold Binding, I am told, is never without
Money.

Mach. What do you mean, *Matt?*—Sure you will
not think of meddling with him!—He's a good honest
kind of Fellow, and one of us.[7]

Ben. To be sure, Sir, we will put our selves under
your Direction.

Mach. Have an Eye upon the Money-Lenders.[8]
—A *Rouleau,*[9] or two, would prove a pretty sort of
an Expedition.[10] I hate Extortion.[11]

Matt. Those *Rouleaus* are very pretty Things.—I
hate your Bank Bills.—There is such a Hazard in
putting them off.[12]

Mach. There is a certain Man of Distinction, who
in his Time hath nick'd me out of a great deal of the
Ready.[13] He is in my Cash,[14] *Ben;*—I'll point him out
to you this Evening, and you shall draw upon him for
the Debt.—The Company are met; I hear the Dice-
box in the other Room. So, Gentlemen, your Servant.
You'll meet me at *Marybone.*

SCENE V. Peachum's *Lock.*

A Table with Wine, Brandy, Pipes and Tobacco.

Peachum, Lockit.

Lock. The Coronation Account,[1] Brother *Peachum*,
is of so intricate a Nature, that I believe it will never
be settled.

Peach. It consists indeed of a great Variety of
Articles.—It was worth to our People, in Fees of
different Kinds, above ten Instalments.[2]—This is part
of the Account, Brother, that lies open before us.

Lock. A Lady's Tail[3] of rich Brocade—that, I see,
is dispos'd of.

Peach. To Mrs. *Diana Trapes*, the Tally-woman,[4]
and she will make a good Hand on 't[5] in Shoes and

Act III, scene iv. **1. tarnish'd:** faded. **2. Interest:** self-interest.
3. One . . . Hedge: One man may steal a horse with
impunity while another may not even be caught looking at
one. John Ray (*English Proverbs* [1670]) interprets: "If we
once conceive a good opinion of a man, we will not be
perswaded he doth any thing amiss; but him whom we have
a prejudice against, we are ready to suspect on the sleightest
occasion." **4. Mechanics:** trades, occupations. **5. we:** we
thieves. **6. Setting:** setting upon, robbing.

7. one of us: i.e., a thief. **8. the Money-Lenders:**
apparently, those in attendance at the gambling houses. **9.
Rouleau:** roll of gold coins. **10. an Expedition:**
apparently, in the sense of an execution of justice—part
of the general ironic rationalization of thievery. **11. Extortion:** the illicit exaction of money. **12. putting . . . off:**
disposing of them. See I. iv. n. 3. **13. the Ready:** money.
14. in my Cash: in my debt. *Act III, scene v.* **1. The
Coronation Account:** the account of goods stolen at the
coronation of George II on October 11, 1727. **2. Instalments:** the annual installations of the Lord Mayor. **3. Tail:**
train. **4. Tally-woman:** a merchant who sold on credit. **5.
make . . . 't:** make a profit.

Slippers, to trick out young Ladies, upon their going into Keeping.—

Lock. But I don't see any Article of the Jewels.

Peach. Those are so well known, that they must be sent abroad—You'll find them enter'd under the Article of Exportation.—As for the Snuff-Boxes, Watches, Swords, &c.—I thought it best to enter them under their several Heads.

Lock. Seven and twenty Women's Pockets[6] compleat; with the several things therein contain'd; all Seal'd, Number'd, and enter'd.

Peach. But, Brother, it is impossible for us now to enter upon this Affair.—We should have the whole Day before us.—Besides, the Account of the last Half Year's Plate[7] is in a Book by it self, which lies at the other Office.

Lock. Bring us then more Liquor.—To-day shall be for Pleasure—To-morrow for Business.—Ah Brother, those Daughters of ours are two slippery Hussies—Keep a watchful Eye upon *Polly,* and *Macheath* in a Day or two shall be our own again.

AIR XLV. Down in the North Country, &c.

Lock.   *What Gudgeons*[8] *are we Men!*
        Ev'ry Woman's easy Prey.
        Though we have felt the Hook, agen
            We bite and they betray.
        The Bird that hath been trapt,
            When he hears his calling Mate,
        To her he flies, again he's clapt
            Within the wiry Grate.

Peach. But what signifies catching the Bird, if your Daughter *Lucy* will set open the Door of the Cage?

Lock. If Men were answerable for the Follies and Frailties of their Wives and Daughters, no Friends could keep a good Correspondence[9] together for two Days.—This is unkind of you, Brother; for among good Friends, what they say or do goes for nothing.

Enter a Servant.

Serv. Sir, here's Mrs. *Diana Trapes* wants to speak with you.

Peach. Shall we admit her, Brother *Lockit?*

Lock. By all means—She's a good Customer,[10] and a fine-spoken Woman—And a Woman who drinks and talks so freely, will enliven the Conversation.

Peach. Desire her to walk in.   [*Exit Servant.*

SCENE VI.

Peachum, Lockit, *Mrs.* Trapes.

Peach. Dear Mrs. *Dye,* your Servant—One may know by your Kiss, that your Ginn is excellent.

Trapes. I was always very curious[1] in my Liquors.

Lock. There is no perfum'd Breath like it—I have been long acquainted with the Flavour of those Lips —Han't I, Mrs. *Dye?*

Trapes. Fill it up.—I take as large Draughts of Liquor, as I did of Love.—I hate a Flincher[2] in either.

AIR XLVI. A Shepherd kept Sheep, &c.

In the Days of my Youth I could bill like a Dove, fa, la, la, &c.
Like a Sparrow at all times was ready for Love, fa, la, la, &c.
The Life of all Mortals in Kissing should pass,
Lip to Lip while we're young—then the Lip to the Glass, fa, &c.

But now, Mr. *Peachum,* to our Business.—If you have Blacks[3] of any kind, brought in of late; Mantoes[4]— Velvet Scarfs—Petticoats—Let it be what it will—I am your Chap[5]—for all my Ladies are very fond of Mourning.

Peach. Why, look ye, Mrs. *Dye*—you deal so hard with us, that we can afford to give the Gentlemen, who venture their Lives for the Goods, little or nothing.

Trapes. The hard Times oblige me to go very near[6] in my Dealing.—To be sure, of late Years I have been a great Sufferer by the Parliament.—Three thousand Pounds would hardly make me amends.—The Act

---

6. **Pockets:** purses. 7. **Plate:** domestic utensils and ornaments; the term originally denoted gold and silver but was extended to include other metals. 8. **Gudgeons:** persons, like the fish of the name, easily caught, gulls. 9. **Correspondence:** relationship.

10. **Customer:** See I. ii. n. 7. *Act* III, *scene* vi. 1. **curious:** particular. 2. **a Flincher:** one who shrinks from a dangerous undertaking; a nondrinker. 3. **Blacks:** black clothing, especially mourning wear. 4. **Mantoes:** (manteaus) loose robes, negligees. 5. **Chap:** dealer. 6. **go . . . near:** drive a hard bargain.

for destroying the Mint,[7] was a severe Cut upon our Business—'Till then, if a Customer[8] stept out of the way[9]—we knew where to have her—No doubt you know Mrs. *Coaxer*—there's a Wench now ('till to-day) with a good Suit of Cloaths of mine upon her Back, and I could never set Eyes upon her for three Months together.—Since the Act too against Imprisonment for small Sums,[10] my Loss there too hath been very considerable, and it must be so, when a Lady can borrow a handsome Petticoat, or a clean Gown, and I not have the least Hank[11] upon her! And, o' my Conscience, now-a-days most Ladies take a Delight in cheating, when they can do it with Safety.

Peach. Madam, you had a handsome Gold Watch of us t' other Day for seven Guineas.—Considering we must have our Profit—To a Gentleman upon the Road, a Gold Watch will be scarce worth the taking.

Trap. Consider, Mr. *Peachum*, that Watch was remarkable, and not of very safe Sale.—If you have any black Velvet Scarfs—they are a handsome Winter-wear; and take[12] with most Gentlemen who deal with my Customers.—'Tis I that put the Ladies upon a good Foot.[13] 'Tis not Youth or Beauty that fixes their Price. The Gentlemen always pay according to their Dress, from half a Crown to two Guineas; and yet those Hussies make nothing of bilking of me.—Then too, allowing for Accidents.—I have eleven fine Customers now down under the Surgeon's Hands,[14] —what with Fees and other Expences, there are great Goings-out, and no Comings-in, and not a Farthing to pay for at least a Month's cloathing.—We run great Risques—great Risques indeed.

Peach. As I remember, you said something just now of Mrs. *Coaxer*.

Trap. Yes, Sir.—To be sure I stript her of a Suit of my own Cloaths about two hours ago; and have left her as she should be, in her Shift, with a Lover of hers at my House. She call'd him up Stairs, as he was going to *Marybone* in a Hackney Coach.—And I hope, for her own sake and mine, she will perswade the Captain to redeem her,[15] for the Captain is very generous to the Ladies.

Lock. What Captain?

Trap. He thought I did not know him—An intimate Acquaintance of yours, Mr. *Peachum*—Only Captain *Macheath*—as fine as a Lord.

Peach. To-morrow, dear Mrs. *Dye*, you shall set your own Price upon any of the Goods you like—We have at least half a dozen Velvet Scarfs, and all at your service. Will you give me leave to make you a Present of this Suit of Night-cloaths for your own wearing? —But are you sure it is Captain *Macheath*?

Trap. Though he thinks I have forgot him; no Body knows him better. I have taken a great deal of the Captain's Money in my Time at second-hand, for he always lov'd to have his Ladies well drest.

Peach. Mr. *Lockit* and I have a little business with the Captain;—You understand me—and we will satisfye you for Mrs. *Coaxer*'s Debt.

Lock. Depend upon it—we will deal like Men of Honour.

Trap. I don't enquire after your Affairs—so whatever happens, I wash my Hands on 't.—It hath always

---

7. The Act . . . Mint: "Whereas it is Notorious, that many evil-disposed and wicked Persons have, in Defiance of the known Laws of this Realm, and to the great Dishonour thereof, unlawfully assembled and associated themselves in and about a certain Place in the Parish of St. George in the County of Surrey, commonly called or known by the Name of Suffolk-Place, or the Mint, and have assumed to themselves (by unlawful Combinations and Confederacies) pretended Privileges, altogether Scandalous and Unwarrantable, and have committed great Frauds and Abuses upon many of His Majesty's good Subjects, and by Force and Violence protected themselves, and their wicked Accomplices, against Law and Justice: . . . it is absolutely necessary, that further Provision should be made for more effectually abolishing the pretended Privileges aforesaid, and for bringing all Offenders in the Premisses to more speedy and exemplary Justice . . . ." The Act, effective October 10, 1723, provided for the protection of honest bankrupts but deprived evaders of the same protection where the debt exceeded fifty pounds. It also stipulated a reward of forty pounds for the apprehension of felons, as therein defined. **8. Customer:** prostitute. **9. stept . . . way:** went where she would not be looked for. **10. Since . . . Sums:** "An Act to prevent Frivolous and Vexatious Arrests" provided that after June 24, 1726, "no Person shall be held to Special Bail upon any Process issuing out of any Superior Court, where the Cause of Action shall not amount to the Sum of Ten Pounds or upwards; nor out of any Inferior Court, where the Cause of Action shall not amount to the Sum of Forty Shillings or upwards; and that in all [such] Cases . . . the Plaintiff or Plaintiffs . . . shall not arrest, or cause to be arrested, the Body of the Defendant or Defendants, but shall serve him, her, or them personally, within the Jurisdiction of the Court with a Copy of the Process . . . ." **11. Hank:** restraining hold.

12. take: take effect. **13. upon . . . Foot:** on a good (commercial) standing. **14. under . . . Hands:** for the treatment of venereal disease or (less likely) for obstetrical ministrations. **15. redeem her:** enable her to buy back the clothes.

been my Maxim, that one Friend should assist another
—But if you please—I'll take one of the Scarfs home
with me, 'Tis always good to have something in Hand.

SCENE VII. *Newgate.*

Lucy.

Jealousy, Rage, Love and Fear are at once tearing
me to pieces. How I am weather-beaten and shatter'd
with distresses!

AIR XLVII. One Evening, having lost my Way, &c.

I'm like a Skiff on the Ocean tost,
Now high, now low, with each Billow born,
With her Rudder broke, and her Anchor lost,
Deserted and all forlorn.
While thus I lye rolling and tossing all Night,
That Polly lyes sporting on Seas of Delight!
Revenge, Revenge, Revenge,
Shall appease my restless Sprite.

I have the Rats-bane ready.—I run no Risque; for I
can lay her Death upon the Ginn, and so many dye of
that naturally that I shall never be call'd in Question.
—But say, I were to be hang'd—I never could be
hang'd for any thing that would give me greater
Comfort, than the poysoning that Slut.

Enter Filch.

Filch. Madam, here's our Miss *Polly* come to wait
upon you.
Lucy. Show her in.

SCENE VIII.

Lucy, Polly.

Lucy. Dear Madam, your Servant.—I hope you
will pardon my Passion, when I was so happy[1] to see
you last.—I was so over-run with the Spleen,[2] that I
was perfectly out of my self. And really when one
hath the Spleen, every thing is to be excus'd by a
Friend.

Act III, scene viii. **1. happy:** fortunate (as). **2. the Spleen:**
melancholy, the fashionable affliction of eighteenth-century
society (the same as the "Vapours" in the following
song).

AIR XLVIII. Now *Roger*, I'll tell thee, because thou'rt
my Son.

When a Wife's in her Pout,
(As she's sometimes, no doubt;)
The good Husband as meek as a Lamb,
Her Vapours to still,
First grants her her Will,
And the quieting Draught is a Dram.
Poor Man! And the quieting Draught is a Dram.

—I wish all our Quarrels might have so comfortable
a Reconciliation.
Polly. I have no Excuse for my own Behaviour,
Madam, but my Misfortunes.—And really, Madam,
I suffer too upon your Account.
Lucy. But, Miss *Polly*—in the way of Friendship,
will you give me leave to propose a Glass of Cordial
to you?
Polly. Strong-Waters are apt to give me the Headache—I hope, Madam, you will excuse me.
Lucy. Not the greatest Lady in the Land could have
better in her Closet,[3] for her own private drinking.
—You seem mighty low in Spirits, my Dear.
Polly. I am sorry, Madam, my Health will not
allow me to accept of your Offer.—I should not have
left you in the rude Manner I did when we met last,
Madam, had not my Papa haul'd me away so unexpectedly—I was indeed somewhat provok'd, and perhaps might use some Expressions that were disrespectful.—But really, Madam, the Captain treated me with
so much Contempt and Cruelty, that I deserv'd your
Pity, rather than your Resentment.
Lucy. But since his Escape, no doubt all Matters
are made up again.—Ah *Polly! Polly!* 'tis I am the
unhappy Wife; and he loves you as if you were only
his Mistress.
Polly. Sure, Madam, you cannot think me so
happy as to be the Object of your Jealousy.—A Man
is always afraid of a Woman who loves him too well
—so that I must expect to be neglected and avoided.
Lucy. Then our Cases, my dear *Polly*, are exactly
alike. Both of us indeed have been too fond.

AIR XLIX. O Bessy Bell.

Polly.   *A Curse attends that Woman's Love,*
         Who always would be pleasing.
Lucy.   *The Pertness of the billing Dove,*
         Like tickling, is but teazing.

---

3. Closet: private chamber.

Polly. *What then in Love can Woman do?*
Lucy.   *If we grow fond they shun us.*
Polly.   *And when we fly them, they pursue.*
Lucy.   *But leave us when they've won us.*

Lucy.   Love is so very whimsical in both Sexes, that it is impossible to be lasting.—But my Heart is particular,[4] and contradicts my own Observation.
Polly.   But really, Mistress *Lucy*, by his last Behaviour, I think I ought to envy you.—When I was forc'd from him, he did not shew the least Tenderness. —But perhaps, he hath a Heart not capable of it.

AIR L. Would Fate to me *Belinda* give—

> *Among the Men, Coquets we find,*
> *Who Court by turns all Woman-kind;*
> *And we grant all their Hearts desir'd,*
> *When they are flatter'd, and admir'd.*

The Coquets of both Sexes are Self-lovers, and that is a Love no other whatever can dispossess. I fear, my dear *Lucy*, our Husband is one of those.
Lucy.   Away with these melancholy Reflections, —indeed, my dear *Polly*, we are both of us a Cup too low.—Let me prevail upon you, to accept of my Offer.

AIR LI. Come, sweet Lass, &c.

> *Come, sweet Lass,*
> *Let's banish Sorrow*
> *'Till To-morrow;*
> *Come, sweet Lass,*
> *Let's take a chirping[5] Glass.*
> *Wine can clear*
> *The Vapours of Despair;*
> *And make us light as Air;*
> *Then drink, and banish Care.*

I can't bear, Child, to see you in such low Spirits. —And I must persuade you to what I know will do you good.—I shall now soon be even with the hypocritical Strumpet.   [*Aside.*

SCENE IX.

Polly.

Polly.   All this wheedling of *Lucy* cannot be for nothing.—At this time too! when I know she hates

4. **particular:** biased. 5. **chirping:** cheering.

me!—The Dissembling of a Woman is always the Fore-runner of Mischief.—By pouring Strong-Waters down my Throat, she thinks to pump some Secrets out of me.—I'll be upon my Guard, and won't taste a Drop of her Liquor, I'm resolv'd.

SCENE X.

Lucy, *with Strong-Waters.* Polly.

Lucy.   Come, Miss *Polly.*
Polly.   Indeed, Child, you have given yourself trouble to no purpose.—You must, my Dear, excuse me.
Lucy.   Really, Miss *Polly*, you are so squeamishly affected about taking a Cup of Strong-Waters as a Lady before Company. I vow, *Polly*, I shall take it monstrously ill if you refuse me.—Brandy and Men (though Women love them never so well)[1] are always taken by us with some Reluctance—unless 'tis in private.
Polly.   I protest, Madam, it goes against me. —What do I see! *Macheath* again in Custody!—Now every glimm'ring of Happiness is lost.
          [*Drops the Glass of Liquor on the Ground.*
Lucy.   Since things are thus, I'm glad the Wench hath escap'd: for by this Event, 'tis plain, she was not happy enough to deserve to be poison'd.   [*Aside.*

SCENE XI.

Lockit, Macheath, Peachum, Lucy, Polly.

Lock.   Set your Heart to rest, Captain.—You have neither the Chance of Love or Money for another Escape,—for you are order'd to be call'd down upon your Tryal immediately.
Peach.   Away, Hussies!—This is not a time for a Man to be hamper'd with his Wives.—You see, the Gentleman is in Chains already.
Lucy.   O Husband, Husband, my heart long'd to see thee; but to see thee thus distracts me!
Polly.   Will not my dear Husband look upon his *Polly*? Why hadst thou not flown to me for Protection? with me thou hadst been safe.

Act III, scene x. **1. though . . . well:** no matter how much women love them.

AIR LII. *The last time I went o'er the Moor.*

Polly.   *Hither, dear Husband, turn your Eyes.*
Lucy.   *Bestow one Glance to cheer me.*
Polly.   *Think with that Look, thy Polly dyes.*
Lucy.   *O shun me not—but hear me.*
Polly.   *'Tis Polly sues.*
Lucy.   ——————— *'Tis Lucy speaks.*
Polly.   *Is this true Love requited?*
Lucy.   *My Heart is bursting.*
Polly.   ——————— *Mine too breaks.*
Lucy.   *Must I*
Polly.   ——————— *Must I be slighted?*

Mach.   What would you have me say, Ladies?
—You see, this Affair will soon be at an end, without
my disobliging either of you.

Peach.   But the settling this Point, Captain, might
prevent a Law-suit between your two Widows.

AIR LIII. *Tom Tinker's my true Love.*

Mach.   *Which way shall I turn me?—How can I*
             decide?
          Wives, the Day of our Death, are as fond as a
             Bride.
          One Wife is too much for most Husbands to hear,
          But two at a time there's no Mortal can bear.
          This way, and that way, and which way I will,
          What would comfort the one, t' other Wife
             would take ill.

Polly.   But if his own Misfortunes have made him
insensible to mine—A Father sure will be more compassionate.—Dear, dear Sir, sink[1] the material
Evidence, and bring him off at his Tryal—*Polly* upon
her Knees begs it of you.

AIR LIV. *I am a poor Shepherd undone.*

When my Hero in Court appears,
   And stands arraign'd for his Life;
Then think of poor Polly's Tears;
   For Ah! Poor Polly's his Wife.
Like the Sailor he holds up his Hand,
   Distrest on the dashing Wave.
To die a dry Death at Land,
   Is as bad as a watry Grave.
And alas, poor Polly!
   Alack, and well-a-day!
Before I was in Love,
   Oh! every Month was May.

Act III, scene xi. **1.** **sink:** suppress.

Lucy.   If *Peachum's* Heart is harden'd; sure you, Sir,
will have more Compassion on a Daughter.—I know
the Evidence is in your Power.—How then can you
be a Tyrant to me?   [*Kneeling.*

AIR LV. *Ianthe the lovely, &c.*

When he holds up his Hand arraign'd for his Life,
O think of your Daughter, and think I'm his Wife!
What are Cannons, or Bombs, or clashing of Swords?
For Death is more certain by Witnesses Words.
Then nail up their Lips; that dread Thunder allay;
And each Month of my Life will hereafter be May.

Lock.   *Macheath's* time is come, *Lucy.*—We know
our own Affairs, therefore let us have no more
Whimpering or Whining.

AIR LVI. *A Cobler there was, &c.*

Our selves, like the Great, to secure a Retreat,
   When Matters require it, must give up our Gang;
      And good reason why,
      Or, instead of the Fry,[2]
      Ev'n Peachum and I,
   Like poor petty Rascals, might hang, hang;
   Like poor petty Rascals, might hang.

Peach.   Set your Heart at rest, *Polly.*—Your Husband is to dye to-day.—Therefore, if you are not
already provided, 'tis high time to look about for
another. There's Comfort for you, you Slut.

Lock.   We are ready, Sir, to conduct you to the
Old-Baily.

AIR LVII. *Bonny Dundee.*

Mach.   *The Charge is prepar'd; The Lawyers are met,*
          The Judges all rang'd (a terrible Show!)
          I go, undismay'd.—For Death is a Debt,[3]
          A Debt on demand.—So, take what I owe.
          Then farewell, my Love—Dear Charmers,
             adieu.
          Contented I die—'Tis the better for you.
          Here ends all Dispute the rest of our Lives.
          For this way at once I please all my Wives.[4]

Now, Gentlemen, I am ready to attend you.

2. **Fry:** small fry. **3.** **Death . . . Debt:** This would have
made a jingle in Shakespeare's time, but perhaps no longer.
Cf. *I Henry IV*, I. iii. 185–86 and V. i. 127–28. **4.** **all my**
Wives: anticipating the disclosure of scene xv.

SCENE XII.

Lucy, Polly, Filch.

Polly. Follow then, *Filch*, to the Court. And when the Tryal is over, bring me a particular Account of his Behaviour, and of every thing that happen'd. —You'll find me here with Miss *Lucy*. [*Ex.* Filch.] But why is all this Musick?

Lucy. The Prisoners, whose Tryals are put off till next Session, are diverting themselves.

Polly. Sure there is nothing so charming as Musick! I'm fond of it to distraction!—But alas!— now, all Mirth seems an Insult upon my Affliction. —Let us retire, my dear *Lucy*, and indulge our Sorrows.—The noisy Crew, you see, are coming upon us. [*Exeunt.*

A Dance of Prisoners in Chains, &c.

SCENE XIII.

The Condemn'd Hold.

Macheath, *in a melancholy Posture.*

AIR LVIII. Happy Groves

O cruel, cruel, cruel Case!
Must I suffer this Disgrace?

AIR LIX. Of all the Girls that are so smart.

Of all the Friends in time of Grief,
When threatning Death looks grimmer,
Not one so sure can bring Relief,
As this best Friend, a Brimmer.[1] [*Drinks.*

AIR LX. *Britons* strike home.

Since I must swing,—I scorn, I scorn to wince or whine.
[*Rises.*

AIR LXI. Chevy Chase.

But now again my Spirits sink;
I'll raise them high with Wine.
[*Drinks a Glass of Wine.*

AIR LXII. To old Sir *Simon* the King.

But Valour the stronger grows,
The stronger Liquor we're drinking,
And how can we feel our Woes,
When we've lost the Trouble of Thinking?
[*Drinks.*

AIR LXIII. Joy to great *Cæsar.*

If thus—A man can die
Much bolder with Brandy.
[*Pours out a Bumper of Brandy.*

AIR LXIV. There was an old Woman.

So I drink off this Bumper.—And now I can stand the Test.
And my Comrades shall see, that I die as brave as the Best.
[*Drinks.*

AIR LXV. Did you ever hear of a gallant Sailor.

But can I leave my pretty Hussies,
Without one Tear, or tender Sigh?

AIR LXVI. Why are mine Eyes still flowing.

Their Eyes, their Lips, their Busses[2]
Recall my Love.—Ah must I die!

AIR LXVII. Green Sleeves.

Since Laws were made for ev'ry Degree,[3]
To curb Vice in others, as well as me,
I wonder we han't better Company,
Upon Tyburn Tree!
But Gold from Law can take out the Sting;
And if rich Men like us were to swing,
'Twou'd thin the Land, such Numbers to string
Upon Tyburn Tree!

Jailor. Some Friends of yours, Captain, desire to be admitted.—I leave you together.

SCENE XIV.

Macheath, Ben Budge, Mat *of the Mint.*

Mach. For my having broke Prison, you see, Gentlemen, I am order'd immediate Execution.—The Sheriffs Officers, I believe, are now at the Door. —That *Jemmy Twitcher* should peach me, I own surpriz'd me!—'Tis a plain Proof that the World is all alike, and that even our Gang can no more trust

Act III, scene xiii. **1. a Brimmer:** a brimming cup.

2. Busses: kisses. **3. Degree:** rank.

one another than other People. Therefore, I beg you, Gentlemen, look well to yourselves, for in all probability you may live some Months longer.

Matt. We are heartily sorry, Captain, for your Misfortune.—But 'tis what we must all come to.

Mach. *Peachum* and *Lockit*, you know, are infamous Scoundrels. Their Lives are as much in your Power, as yours are in theirs.—Remember your dying Friend!—'Tis my last Request.—Bring those Villains to the Gallows before you, and I am satisfied.

Matt. We'll do 't.

Jailor. Miss *Polly* and Miss *Lucy* intreat a Word with you.

Mach. Gentlemen, Adieu.

SCENE XV.

Lucy, Macheath, Polly.

Mach. My dear *Lucy*—My dear *Polly*—Whatsoever hath past between us is now at an end.—If you are fond of marrying again, the best Advice I can give you, is to Ship yourselves off for the *West-Indies*, where you'll have a fair chance of getting a Husband a-piece; or by good Luck, two or three, as you like best.

Polly. How can I support this Sight!

Lucy. There is nothing moves one so much as a great Man in Distress.

AIR LXVIII. *All you that must take a Leap, &c.*

Lucy. *Would I might be hang'd!*
Polly. ———————— *And I would so too!*
Lucy. To be hang'd with you.
Polly. ———————— *My Dear, with you.*
Mach. *O Leave me to Thought! I fear! I doubt!*
    I tremble! I droop!—See, my Courage is out.
            [*Turns up the empty Bottle.*
Polly. No token of Love?
Mach. ———————— *See, my Courage is out.*
            [*Turns up the empty Pot.*
Lucy. *No token of Love?*
Polly. ———————— *Adieu.*
Lucy. ———————— *Farewell.*
Mach. *But hark! I hear the Toll of the Bell.*
Chorus. *Tol de rol lol, &c.*

Jailor. Four Women more, Captain, with a Child a-peice! See, here they come.

            Enter Women and Children.

Mach. What—four Wives more!—This is too much.—Here—tell the Sheriffs Officers I am ready.
            [*Exit Macheath guarded.*

SCENE XVI.

To them, Enter Player and Beggar.

Play. But, honest Friend, I hope you don't intend that *Macheath* shall be really executed.

Beg. Most certainly, Sir.—To make the Piece perfect, I was for doing strict poetical Justice.[1]—*Macheath* is to be hang'd; and for the other Personages of the Drama, the Audience must have suppos'd they were all either hang'd or transported.

Play. Why then, Friend, this is a down-right deep Tragedy. The Catastrophe is manifestly wrong, for an Opera must end happily.

Beg. Your Objection, Sir, is very just; and is easily remov'd. For you must allow, that in this kind of Drama, 'tis no matter how absurdly things are brought about.—So—you Rabble there—run and cry a Reprieve—let the Prisoner be brought back to his Wives in Triumph.

Play. All this we must do, to comply with the Taste of the Town.

Beg. Through the whole Piece you may observe such a similitude of Manners in high and low Life, that it is difficult to determine whether (in the fashionable Vices) the fine Gentlemen imitate the Gentlemen of the Road, or the Gentlemen of the Road the fine Gentlemen.—Had the Play remain'd, as I at first intended, it would have carried a most excellent Moral. 'Twould have shown that the lower Sort of People have their Vices in a degree as well as the Rich: And that they are punish'd for them.

SCENE XVII.

To them, Macheath with Rabble, &c.

Mach. So, it seems, I am not left to my Choice, but must have a Wife at last.—Look ye, my Dears, we will have no Controversie now. Let us give this Day to Mirth, and I am sure she who thinks herself my Wife will testifie her Joy by a Dance.

All. Come, a Dance—a Dance.

Act III, scene xvi. **1. strict . . . Justice:** distributing rewards and punishments exactly according to merit. The term "poetical justice" was coined by the critic Thomas Rymer (1641–1713) and became a standard gambit of drama criticism.

Mach. Ladies, I hope you will give me leave to present a Partner to each of you. And (if I may without Offence) for this time, I take *Polly* for mine.—And for Life, you Slut,—for we were really marry'd.—As for the rest.—But at present keep your own Secret.

[*To Polly*.

A DANCE.

AIR LXIX. Lumps of Pudding, &c.

Thus I stand like the Turk, *with his Doxies around;*
From all Sides their Glances his Passion confound;

For black, brown, and fair, his Inconstancy burns,
And the different Beauties subdue him by turns:
Each calls forth her Charms, to provoke his Desires:
Though willing to all; with but one he retires.
But think of this Maxim, and put off your Sorrow,
The Wretch of To-day, may be happy To-morrow.

Chorus. *But think of this Maxim, &c.*

Alexander Pope

1688–1744

Alexander Pope was born in the City of London, where his father was a tradesman in the linen business. His early years are obscure, but his dwarfishness, ill health, and curvature of the spine are believed to be the result of excessive study—he came to speak with some accuracy of "this long Disease, my Life," and the miracle is that it lasted as long as fifty-six years. When he was twelve his parents left London for Binfield in Windsor Forest, perhaps in compliance with the law prohibiting Catholics from living within ten miles of London. It was also because of the family religion that his schooling was mainly private and rather irregular. He taught himself Greek, picked up French and Italian, and eagerly read Latin and English poetry. By the time he was sixteen he had tried his hand at several genres; a year later, after making the acquaintance of the now aging Restoration dramatist William Wycherley and of the poet and critic William Walsh (Pope's early letters to both remain), he was welcomed into the society of wits as a prodigy. His *Pastorals*, written when he was a boy, were submitted to Congreve and others before their publication in 1709. Pope soon formed friendships too with Swift, Gay, Atterbury, and Arbuthnot, and in 1714 they established the Scriblerus Club, a league against the Dunces and abuses of wit. The members met for less than a year, but Pope forgot neither his friends nor the spirit of the association, which in the next decade inspired *The Dunciad* (1728).

How seriously he took himself as a poet is clear from the classical forms in which he began his public career. He produced in turn Virgilian pastorals; the Horatian *Essay on Criticism* (1711); *The Rape of the Lock* (1712, 1714), an epic in miniature; the translation of Homer—both the *Iliad* (1715–20) and the *Odyssey* (1725–26); the Ovidian epistle *Eloisa to Abelard* (1717); and the Ovidian *Elegy to the Memory of an Unfortunate Lady* (1717). In the teens of the century he was acclaimed as the great poet of the age, and soon not only of England but of Europe.

His first poetry to appear before the public was mature, but the poetry he produced after his edition of Shakespeare in 1725, at the end of ten years of criticism and translation, fulfills his genius. It has the kind of rich maturity that one associates for example with Shakespeare's late comedies. *The Dunciad* is a splendid invention for all its debt to the epic form—a debt that enhances its brilliance. The same is true of the *Imitations of Horace* (1733–38); they follow the line of the originals among Horace's satires and epistles but decorate that line with the colors of Pope's own day. And the greatest of the Horatian poems, *An Epistle to Dr. Arbuthnot* (1735), forgoes the advantage (counted so at the time) of recalling Horace pointedly, as do the two fine dialogues that figure in the later editions as the *Epilogue to the Satires*. Nor is Pope at all tied to models in his *Essay on Man* (1733–34) or in the *Moral Essays* (1731–35). In all these, and in his scores of minor occasional poems, he abjures the learned pleasures of adapting an ancient poem; he writes instead an independent, new one, but still he has the Latin poets in mind. He considers himself a reincarnation of Horace or Virgil (perhaps realizing the potential satirist in Virgil) or Lucretius, surveying the human condition and the nature of things.

In 1718, after his father's death, Pope moved with his mother to Twickenham on the Thames, one of the loveliest spots in England and often referred to in his *Imitations of Horace* and in other poems. In his later years he built here what he amusingly called his "works," an elaborate geological grotto, of which some traces still remain. It was at Twickenham that he entertained many of the great literary and political figures of the time, and in the 1730's he became increasingly the laureate of the opposition to Walpole, led by Bolingbroke.

Among the principal delights of Pope's life were his friendships—especially those with women (among whom Martha Blount was his favorite), if we may judge by the number of letters he wrote them. Many of these letters he probably would not have minded seeing in print, for they reflect the same literary genius as his published works in other genres. An example, though written for publication, is the Dedicatory Epistle to Arabella Fermor, which precedes *The Rape of the Lock*.

Pope spent the rest of his life at Twickenham, receiving established friends and admiring young poets. Shortly before his death in 1744, he said to the priest attending him, "There is nothing that is meritorious but virtue and friendship, and indeed friendship itself is only part of virtue."

The greatness of any poet lies in the nature of his subject and its expression. In deciding what to write about, Pope bore in mind, as Chaucer and Shakespeare had done, those whom he called "common readers," and even in *The Dunciad* there was much to interest people who were indifferent to an author's quarrels. His basic concern is one of close interest to all: human beings among their fellows, rich people and poor—and especially rich, for to common readers the rich are so much more interesting than the poor. His expression is concise and forceful. So much is said, or rather sung, in so short a compass, sometimes straightforwardly and sometimes with generous but intense elaboration. Some lines are like blows on the chest; others give us the pleasant sense that they enfold a rich complexity which we can enjoy even before we begin to analyze it. Most of the poems are written in couplets, but if the reader examines any run of a dozen lines he will see how varied are the six two-line stanzas they comprise; this becomes overwhelmingly apparent when, after mastering their meaning, he declaims them with their sense as guide. And yet these little stanzas are not separate beads on a string. They cohere into paragraphs, often of a splendid integrity.

Thomas De Quincey said Pope thought "in jets." No doubt that is the way most of us think. But whatever the initial process, Pope went further, and combined thoughts in a series of cohesive paragraphs. The final effect is not of jets but of flow. His final concern was always to arrange the perfected paragraphs of a poem in as orderly a sequence as possible. At the same time, whether engaged in describing the course of his thoughts or in creating visual impressions or in conveying feelings, Pope always provided a sensuousness that for all his prosaic themes and arrangements makes him truly a poet.

A bibliography of Pope's writings has been compiled by R. H. Griffith (1922). The Twickenham edition, ed. John Butt (1939–67), which is now complete (including the translations of Homer), is the best for the poems. A handy and inexpensive edition of the poems, based on the Twickenham edition, is *The Poems of Alexander Pope*, ed. John Butt (1963). The prose is collected by Norman Ault (Vol. I, 1936; the second and last volume is expected). There is not yet a good complete biography of Pope, but a substitute exists in the headnotes to each year's letters in *The Correspondence of Alexander Pope*, ed. George Sherburn (5 vols., 1956). Sherburn's *Early Career of Alexander Pope* (1934), which traces Pope's work to about 1726, is excellent. Johnson wrote on Pope's poetry in his *Life of Pope;* modern criticism may be represented by the following: Austin Warren's *Alexander Pope as Critic and Humanist* (1929); F. R. Leavis's *Revaluation: Tradition and Development in English Poetry* (1936); Geoffrey Tillotson's *On the Poetry of Pope* (1938) and *Pope and Human Nature* (1958); Reuben Brower's *Alexander Pope: The Poetry of Allusion* (1959); and Maynard Mack's "Wit and Poetry and Pope," now reprinted in *Eighteenth-Century English Literature*, ed. J. L. Clifford (1959). A copious collection of critical materials is *Essential Articles for the Study of Alexander Pope*, ed. Maynard Mack (1964).

WINTER. THE FOURTH PASTORAL, OR DAPHNE

To the MEMORY of a Fair Young LADY.°

❧

Pope came to see that the main interest of his *Pastorals* (1709), of which *Winter* was his favorite, was technical; we are invited to appreciate the run of the lines, of the consonants and vowels—usually varied, sometimes chiming—whose stresses yield the appropriate onomatopoetic effect. The manuscript of the *Pastorals* survives, and the sort of improvement Pope made may be gauged by comparing lines 29 and 30 of our text with the same

WINTER. **Lady:** [Pope's note] This Lady [Mrs. Tempest] was of an ancient family in Yorkshire, and particularly admired by the Author's friend, Mr. *Walsh*, who having celebrated her in a Pastoral Elegy, desired his friend to do the same, as appears from one of his Letters . . . . Her death having happened on the night of the great storm in 1703, gave a propriety to this eclogue, which in its general turn [drift] alludes to it. The Scene of the Pastoral lies in a grove, the Time at midnight.

lines in an earlier version of *Winter:* "'Tis done, and Nature's chang'd, since you are gone, / Behold, the Clouds have put their Mourning on." The change reflects partly a desire for smoothness and partly a new style of thinking. Pope is moving away from the Metaphysical conceit. With the second of the canceled lines, compare Richard Crashaw's *Upon Mr. Staninough's Death* (1652): "Deare reliques of a dislodg'd soule, whose lack / Makes many a mourning Paper put on blacke."

The text is that of the first edition, changed in accordance with Pope's very few revisions.

🐝

LYCIDAS.

T*Hyrsis*, the Musick of that murm'ring Spring
Is not so mournful as the Strains you sing,
Nor Rivers winding thro' the Vales below,
So sweetly warble, or so smoothly flow.
Now sleeping Flocks on their soft Fleeces lye,
The Moon, serene in Glory, mounts the Sky,
While silent Birds forget their tuneful Lays,
Oh sing of *Daphne*'s Fate, and *Daphne*'s Praise !

THYRSIS.

Behold the *Groves* that shine with silver Frost,
Their Beauty wither'd, and their Verdure lost.   10
Here shall I try the sweet *Alexis'* Strain,
That call'd the list'ning *Dryads* to the Plain?°
Thames heard the Numbers as he flow'd along,
And bade his Willows learn the moving Song.

LYCIDAS.

So may kind Rains their vital Moisture yield,
And swell the future Harvest of the Field!
Begin; this Charge the dying *Daphne* gave,
And said; "Ye Shepherds, sing around my Grave."
Sing, while beside the shaded Tomb I mourn,
And with fresh Bays her Rural Shrine adorn.   20

THYRSIS.

Ye gentle *Muses* leave your Crystal Spring,
Let *Nymphs* and *Sylvans* Cypress Garlands bring;
Ye weeping *Loves*, the Stream with Myrtles hide,
And break your Bows, as when *Adonis* dy'd;
And with your Golden Darts, now useless grown,
Inscribe a Verse on this relenting Stone:
"Let Nature change, let Heav'n and Earth deplore,
Fair *Daphne*'s dead, and Love is now no more!"

'Tis done, and Nature's various Charms decay;
See gloomy Clouds obscure the chearful Day!   30
Now hung with Pearls the dropping Trees appear,
Their faded Honours° scatter'd on her Bier.
See, where on Earth the flow'ry Glories lye,
With her they flourish'd, and with her they dye.
Ah what avail the Beauties Nature wore?
Fair *Daphne*'s dead, and Beauty is no more!

For her, the Flocks refuse their verdant Food,
The thirsty Heifers shun the gliding Flood.
The silver Swans her hapless Fate bemoan,
In Notes more sad than when they sing their own.   40
In hollow Caves sweet *Echo* silent lies,
Silent, or only to her Name replies,
Her Name with Pleasure once she taught the Shore,
Now *Daphne*'s dead, and Pleasure is no more!

No grateful° Dews descend from Ev'ning Skies,
Nor Morning Odours from the Flow'rs arise.
No rich Perfumes refresh the fruitful Field,
Nor fragrant Herbs their native Incense yield.
The balmy *Zephyrs*, silent since her Death,
Lament the Ceasing of a sweeter Breath.   50
Th' industrious Bees neglect their Golden Store;
Fair *Daphne*'s dead, and Sweetness is no more!

No more the mounting Larks, while *Daphne* sings,
Shall list'ning in mid Air suspend their Wings;
No more the Birds shall imitate her Lays,
Or hush'd with Wonder, hearken from the Sprays:
No more the Streams their Murmurs shall forbear,
A sweeter Musick than their own to hear,
But tell the Reeds, and tell the vocal Shore,
Fair *Daphne*'s dead, and Musick is no more!   60

Her Fate is whisper'd by the gentle Breeze,
And told in Sighs to all the trembling Trees;
The trembling Trees, in ev'ry Plain and Wood,
Her Fate remurmur to the silver Flood;
The silver Flood, so lately calm, appears
Swell'd with new Passion, and o'erflows with Tears;
The Winds and Trees and Floods her Death deplore,
Daphne, our Grief! our Glory now no more!

But see! where *Daphne* wondring mounts on high,
Above the Clouds, above the Starry Sky.   70
Eternal Beauties grace the shining Scene,
Fields ever fresh, and Groves for ever green!
There, while You rest in *Amaranthine* Bow'rs,
Or from those Meads select unfading Flow'rs,
Behold us kindly who your Name implore,
Daphne, our Goddess, and our Grief no more!

LYCIDAS.

How all things listen, while thy Muse complains!
Such Silence waits on *Philomela*'s Strains,
In some still Ev'ning, when the whisp'ring Breeze
Pants on the Leaves, and dies upon the Trees.°   80
To thee, bright Goddess, oft a Lamb shall bleed,
If teeming Ewes encrease my fleecy Breed.
While Plants their Shade, or Flow'rs their Odours give,
Thy Name, thy Honour, and thy Praise shall live!°

But see *Orion* sheds unwholsome Dews,
Arise, the Pines a noxious Shade diffuse;
Sharp *Boreas* blows, and Nature feels Decay,
Time conquers All, and We must Time obey.
Adieu ye *Vales*, ye *Mountains*, *Streams* and *Groves*,
Adieu ye Shepherd's rural *Lays* and *Loves*,   90
Adieu my Flocks, farewell ye *Sylvan* Crew,
Daphne farewell, and all the World adieu!

11–12. Here . . . Plain: an allusion to the "Summer" eclogue. **32. Honours:** foliage. **45. grateful:** pleasant.

79–80. In . . . Trees: caught in the satire of *An Essay on Criticism*, below, ll. 350–51. **83–84. While . . . live:** Cf. *The Rape of the Lock*, below, iii. 161–70.

ODE ON SOLITUDE

The text is that of the first edition (1717), corrected in accordance with Pope's revisions. He wrote the poem when a boy and last revised it in 1736.

Happy the man, whose wish and care
A few paternal acres bound,
Content to breathe his native air,
    In his own ground.

Whose herds with milk, whose fields with bread,
Whose flocks supply him with attire,
Whose trees in summer yield him shade,
    In winter fire.

Blest! who can unconcern'dly find
Hours, days, and years slide soft away,   10
In health of body, peace of mind,
    Quiet by day,

Sound sleep by night; study and ease
Together mix'd; sweet recreation,
And innocence, which most does please
    With meditation.

Thus let me live, unseen, unknown;
Thus unlamented let me dye;
Steal from the world, and not a stone
    Tell where I lye.   20

AN ESSAY ON CRITICISM

The pattern for delivering literary advice in meter had been set as early as the first century B.C. by Horace in his Ars Poetica. The Italian poet Girolamo Vida, whom Pope praises enthusiastically in this poem, followed the pattern for his De Arte Poetica, published in 1527 (and translated into neat heroic couplets by Pope's young friend Christopher Pitt in 1725). After Vida came the Frenchman Boileau with his Art poétique (1674), which Dryden helped Sir William Soame put into good heroic couplets in 1683. Up to this time English authors had been content with verse translations of such critical

poems; Ben Jonson's translation of Horace's poems stands out as an example. But now original poems began to appear, all in would-be "correct" heroic couplets—the Essay on Poetry (1682) by John Sheffield, First Duke of Buckingham and Normanby, the Earl of Roscommon's Essay on Translated Verse (1684), and Lord Lansdowne's Essay upon Unnatural Flights in Poetry (1701). The year 1711 brought Pope's Essay on Criticism. Acting according to one of the guiding "principles" of his literary career, Pope added his own, and as usual the culminating, composition to a genre already well established and respected. The Essay is indeed a culmination. Johnson described it as "one of his greatest though of his earliest works," adding that "if he had written nothing else [it] would have placed him among the first criticks and the first poets, as it exhibits every mode of excellence that can embellish or dignify didactick composition, selection of matter, novelty of arrangement, justness of precept, splendour of illustration, and propriety of digression."

Johnson also praised its erudition: it "displays . . . such knowledge both of ancient and modern learning as are not often attained by the maturest age." In the notes to the poem (omitted here) Pope quotes from classical writers in order to establish relationships between his own views and theirs. In doing so he is not rifling their brains, but testifying, in the light of his own intense experience of literature, to the permanent truth available to the Moderns just as it was to the Ancients.

In later editions of the Essay, Pope provided a table of contents and divided the poem into three parts—the second beginning at line 201 and the third at line 560. William Warburton, Pope's friend and literary executor, entitled the parts (1) "the Rules for perfecting the Art of Criticism," (2) "the Impediments to it," and (3) "the Morals of the Critic," treated first by precept, then by example. Warburton also noted that though the Essay is directly concerned with "the true judging of a poem," much of it applies indirectly, and sometimes directly, to "the good writing" of one. It is important to realize that Pope is thinking first of the true judging of a new poem: like most poets he fears for the reception of poems of his own.

Johnson praised Pope's "nicety of distinction" in the Essay. His subject matter, intellectual and psychological, is sometimes complex, and no one can justly claim to use diction that is really precise when dealing with such a topic. He tackles the problem bravely, sometimes relying on his illustrations to make the concepts clearer. His illustrations are familiar: husbands and wives and domestic quarrels, horses and asses, and so on. Though he is writing of critics and poets, Pope has made ample provision for the common reader. The Essay, as Johnson saw, is remarkable for its evidence of acquaintance not simply with literary men but with mankind. Even the common reader must assent to the justness of Pope's precepts as well as laugh at his comic satire.

The text is that of the first edition (1711), as later corrected by Pope. Where Pope left dashes in a proper noun, the missing letters have been supplied where identification is straightforward.

✸

> ——— ———*Si quid novisti rectius istis,*
> *Candidus imperti; si non, his utere mecum.*°
>   HORAT.

'TIS hard to say, if greater Want of Skill
Appear in *Writing* or in *Judging* ill;
But, of the two, less dang'rous is th' Offence
To tire our *Patience,* than mis-lead our *Sense:*°
Some few in *that,* but Numbers err in *this,*
Ten Censure wrong for one who Writes amiss;
A *Fool* might once *himself* alone expose,
Now *One* in *Verse* makes many more in *Prose.*
'Tis with our *Judgments* as our *Watches,* none
Go just *alike,* yet each believes his own.   10
In *Poets* as true *Genius* is but rare,
True *Taste* as seldom is the *Critick's* Share;
Both must alike from Heav'n derive their Light,
These *born* to Judge, as well as those to Write.
Let such teach others who themselves excell,
And *censure freely* who have *written well.*
Authors are partial to their *Wit,*° 'tis true,
But are not *Criticks* to their *Judgment* too?
Yet if we look more closely, we shall find
Most have the *Seeds* of Judgment in their Mind;   20
Nature affords at least a *glimm'ring Light;*
The *Lines,* tho' touch'd but faintly, are drawn right.
But as the slightest Sketch, if justly trac'd, ⎫
Is by ill *Colouring* but the more disgrac'd,   ⎬
So by *false Learning* is *good Sense* defac'd; ⎭
Some are bewilder'd in the Maze of Schools,
And some made *Coxcombs*° Nature meant but *Fools.*
In search of *Wit* these lose their *common Sense,*
And then turn Criticks in their own Defence.
Each burns alike, who *can,* or *cannot* write,   30
Or with a *Rival's,* or an *Eunoch's* Spite.
All *Fools* have still° an Itching to deride,

And fain *wou'd* be upon the *Laughing Side:*
If *Mævius*° Scribble in *Apollo's* spight,
There are, who *judge* still *worse* than he can *write.*
Some have at first for *Wits,*° then *Poets* past,
Turn'd *Criticks* next, and prov'd plain *Fools* at last;
Some neither can for *Wits* nor *Criticks* pass,
As heavy Mules are neither *Horse* nor *Ass.*
Those half-learn'd Witlings, num'rous in our Isle,   40
As half-form'd Insects on the Banks of *Nile;*
Unfinish'd Things, one knows not what to call,
Their Generation's so *equivocal:*°
To tell° 'em, wou'd a *hundred Tongues* require,
Or *one vain Wit's,*° that wou'd a hundred tire.
But *you* who seek to *give* and *merit* Fame,
And justly bear a Critick's noble Name,
Be sure *your self* and your own *Reach* to know,
How far your *Genius, Taste,* and *Learning* go;
Launch not beyond your Depth, but be discreet,   50
And mark *that Point* where Sense and Dulness *meet.*
Nature to all things fix'd the Limits fit,
And wisely curb'd proud Man's pretending° Wit:
As on the *Land* while *here* the *Ocean* gains,
In *other Parts* it leaves wide sandy Plains;
Thus in the *Soul* while *Memory*° prevails,
The solid Pow'r of *Understanding* fails;
Where Beams of warm *Imagination* play,
The *Memory's* soft Figures melt away.
One *Science*° only will one *Genius* fit;   60
So *vast* is Art, so *narrow* Human Wit:°
Not only bounded to *peculiar*° Arts,
But oft in *those,* confin'd to *single Parts.*
Like Kings we lose the Conquests gain'd before,
By vain Ambition still to make them more:
Each might his *sev'ral Province* well command,
Wou'd all but *stoop* to what they *understand.*
First follow NATURE, and your Judgment frame
By her just Standard, which is still the same:
Unerring Nature, still divinely bright,   70
One *clear, unchang'd,* and *Universal* Light,
Life, Force, and Beauty, must to all impart,
At once the *Source,* and *End,* and *Test of Art.*

---

34. **Mævius:** a wretched poet, contemporary with Horace and Virgil. 36. **Wits:** geniuses. 41–43. **half-form'd . . . equivocal:** Insects were believed to be formed by the action of the sun on the slimy banks of the Nile, but because this was not known for certain it was equivocal, or doubtful. 44. **tell:** count. 45. **Wit:** writer. 53. **pretending:** aspiring. 56. **Memory:** an aid to learning, so learning itself. 60. **Science:** object of knowledge, subject matter. 61. **Wit:** intellect. 62. **peculiar:** particular.

AN ESSAY ON CRITICISM. **Si . . . mecum:** the ending of Horace's *Epistles,* I. vi: "If you know any maxims better than these, be so good as to let me know them; if not, make use of these as I do." 4. **Sense:** judgment. 17. **Wit:** writings, products of their genius. 27. **Coxcombs:** pretenders to learning and taste. 32. **still:** always.

Art from that *Fund* each just *Supply* provides;
Works without *Show*,° and without *Pomp presides:*
In some fair *Body* thus th' informing *Soul*
With *Spirits* feeds, with *Vigour* fills the whole,
Each *Motion* guides, and ev'ry *Nerve* sustains;
It self unseen, but in th' *Effects*, remains.
Some, to whom Heav'n in *Wit*° has been profuse, 80
Want as much *more*° to turn it to its *Use*;
For *Wit* and *Judgment* often are at strife,
Tho' meant each other's *Aid*, like *Man* and *Wife*.
'Tis more to *guide* than *spur* the Muse's Steed;
Restrain his *Fury*, than provoke his *Speed*;
The winged Courser, like a gen'rous Horse,
Shows most true *Mettle*° when you *check* his Course.
    Those RULES of old *discover'd*, not *devis'd*,
Are *Nature* still, but *Nature Methodiz'd*;
Nature, like *Liberty*, is but restrain'd   90
By the same Laws which first *herself* ordain'd.
    Hear how learned *Greece* her useful *Rules* indites,
When to repress, and when indulge our *Flights*:
High on *Parnassus'* Top her Sons she show'd,
And pointed out those arduous Paths they trod,
Held from afar, aloft, th' Immortal Prize,
And urg'd the rest by equal Steps to rise;
Just *Precepts* thus from great *Examples* giv'n;
She drew from *them* what they deriv'd from *Heav'n*,
The gen'rous Critick *fann'd* the *Poet's Fire*,   100
And taught the World, *with Reason to Admire*.
Then Criticism the Muses Handmaid prov'd,
To dress her Charms, and make her more belov'd;
But following Wits from that Intention stray'd;
Who cou'd not win the Mistress, woo'd the Maid;
Against the Poets *their own Arms* they turn'd,
Sure to hate most the Men from whom they *learn'd*.
So modern 'Pothecaries,° taught the Art
By *Doctor's Bills*° to play the *Doctor's Part*,
Bold in the Practice of *mistaken Rules*,   110
Prescribe, apply, and call their *Masters Fools*.
Some on the Leaves of ancient Authors prey,
Nor Time nor Moths e'er spoil'd so much as they:
Some dryly plain, without Invention's Aid,
Write dull *Receits*° how Poems may be made:
These leave the Sense, their Learning to display,
And those explain the Meaning quite away.

You then whose Judgment the right Course wou'd
    steer,
Know well each ANCIENT's proper *Character*,
His *Fable*,° *Subject*, *Scope* in ev'ry *Page*,   120
Religion, *Country*, *Genius* of his *Age*:
Without all these at once before your Eyes,
Cavil you may, but never *Criticize*.
Be *Homer's* Works your *Study*, and *Delight*,
Read them by Day, and meditate by Night,
Thence form your Judgment, thence your Maxims
    bring,
And trace the Muses *upward* to their *Spring*;
Still with *It self compar'd*, his *Text* peruse;
And let your *Comment* be the *Mantuan Muse*.°
    When first young *Maro*° in his boundless Mind 130
A *Work*, t' outlast Immortal *Rome* design'd,
Perhaps he seem'd *above* the Critick's Law,
And but from *Nature's Fountains* scorn'd to draw:
But when t' examine ev'ry Part he came,
Nature and *Homer* were, he found, the *same*:
Convinc'd, amaz'd, he checks the bold *Design*,°
And Rules as strict his labour'd Work confine,   }
As if the *Stagyrite*° o'erlook'd each Line.
Learn hence for Ancient *Rules* a just Esteem;
To copy *Nature* is to copy *Them*.   140
    Some° Beauties yet, no Precepts can declare,
For there's a *Happiness* as well as *Care*.
Musick resembles *Poetry*, in each
Are *nameless Graces* which no Methods teach,   }
And which a *Master-Hand* alone can reach.
If, where the *Rules* not far enough extend,
(Since Rules were made but to promote their *End*)
Some Lucky LICENCE answer to the full
Th' Intent propos'd, *that Licence is a Rule*.
Thus *Pegasus*, a nearer way to take,   150
May boldly deviate from the common Track;
From *vulgar Bounds* with *brave Disorder* part,
And *snatch* a *Grace* beyond the Reach of Art,
Which, without passing thro' the *Judgment*, gains
The *Heart*, and all its End *at once* attains.

120. **Fable:** the matter he takes for his subject. 129. **Mantuan Muse:** Virgil. 130. **Maro:** Virgil. 136. **the bold Design:** the bold design as first drawn up. 138. **Stagyrite:** Aristotle, who was born at Stagyra, a town in Thrace. 141–60. **Some . . . mend:** Cf. Dryden's Preface to his translation of Du Fresnoy, where he praises Virgil for his luck with words: "These hits of Words a true *Poet* often finds, as I may say, without seeking: but he knows their Value when he finds them, and is infinitely pleas'd."

75. **without Show:** Horace had counseled that art should conceal its presence. 80. **Wit:** genius. 81. **more:** more intelligence. 87. **Mettle:** "spirit; spriteliness; courage" (Johnson's *Dictionary*). 108. **'Pothecaries:** druggists. 109. **Bills:** medical prescriptions. 115. **Receits:** prescriptions.

In *Prospects*, thus, some *Objects* please our Eyes, ⎫
Which *out of* Nature's *common Order* rise,   ⎬
The shapeless *Rock*, or hanging *Precipice*.   ⎭
Great Wits sometimes may *gloriously offend*,
And *rise to Faults*° true *Criticks dare not mend;*   160
But tho' the *Ancients* thus their *Rules* invade,
(As *Kings* dispense with *Laws* Themselves have made)
Moderns, beware! Or if you must offend
Against the *Precept*, ne'er transgress its *End*,
Let it be *seldom*, and *compell'd by Need*,
And have, at least, *Their Precedent* to plead.
The Critick else proceeds without Remorse,
Seizes your Fame, and puts his Laws in force.
    I know there are, to whose presumptuous Thoughts
Those *Freer Beauties*, ev'n in *Them*, seem Faults: 170
Some Figures *monstrous* and *mis-shap'd* appear,
Consider'd *singly*, or beheld too *near*,
Which, but *proportion'd* to their *Light*, or *Place*,
Due Distance *reconciles* to Form and Grace.
A prudent Chief not always must display
His Powr's in *equal Ranks*, and *fair Array*,
But with th' *Occasion* and the *Place* comply,
Conceal his Force, nay seem sometimes to *Fly*.
Those oft are but *Stratagems* which *Errors* seem,
Nor is it *Homer Nods*, but *We* that *Dream*.°   180
    Still green with Bays° each *ancient* Altar stands,
Above the reach of *Sacrilegious* Hands,
Secure from *Flames*, from *Envy's* fiercer Rage,
Destructive *War*, and all-involving *Age*.
See, from *each Clime* the Learn'd their Incense bring!
Hear, in *all Tongues* consenting *Pæans* ring!
In Praise so just, let ev'ry Voice be join'd,
And fill the *Gen'ral Chorus of Mankind!*
Hail *Bards Triumphant!* born in *happier Days;*
Immortal Heirs of *Universal* Praise!   190
Whose Honours with Increase of Ages *grow*,
As Streams roll down, *enlarging* as they flow!
Nations *unborn* your mighty Names shall sound,
And Worlds applaud that must not yet be *found!*
Oh may some Spark of *your* Cœlestial Fire
The last, the meanest of your Sons inspire,
(That on weak Wings, from far, pursues your Flights;
Glows while he *reads*, but *trembles* as he *writes*)

To teach vain Wits that Science *little known*,
T' admire Superior Sense, and *doubt* their own!   200
    Of all the Causes which conspire to blind
Man's erring Judgment, and misguide the Mind,
What the weak Head with strongest Byass rules,
Is *Pride*, the *never-failing Vice of Fools.*
Whatever Nature has in *Worth* deny'd,
She gives in large Recruits° of *needful Pride;*
For as in *Bodies*, thus in *Souls*, we find
What wants in *Blood* and *Spirits*, swell'd with *Wind;*
Pride, where Wit fails, steps in to our Defence,
And fills up all the *mighty Void of Sense!*   210
If once right Reason drives *that Cloud* away,
Truth breaks upon us with *resistless Day;*
Trust not your self; but your Defects to know,
Make use of ev'ry *Friend*—and ev'ry *Foe*.
    A *little Learning* is a dang'rous Thing;
Drink deep, or taste not the *Pierian Spring:*°
There *shallow Draughts* intoxicate the Brain,
And drinking *largely* sobers us again.
Fir'd at first Sight with what the *Muse* imparts,
In *fearless Youth* we tempt the Heights of Arts;   220
While from the bounded *Level* of our Mind,
Short Views we take, nor see the *Lengths behind*,
But *more advanc'd*, behold with strange Surprize
New, distant Scenes of *endless* Science° rise!
So pleas'd at first, the towring *Alps* we try,
Mount o'er the Vales, and seem to tread the Sky;
Th' Eternal Snows appear already past,
And the first *Clouds* and *Mountains* seem the last:
But *those attain'd*, we tremble to survey
The growing Labours of the lengthen'd Way,   230
Th' *increasing* Prospect *tires* our wandring Eyes,
Hills peep o'er Hills, and *Alps* on *Alps* arise!
    A perfect Judge will *read* each Work of Wit
With the same Spirit that its Author *writ*,
Survey the *Whole*, nor seek slight Faults to find,
Where *Nature* moves, and *Rapture warms* the Mind;
Nor lose, for that malignant dull Delight,
The *gen'rous Pleasure* to be charm'd with Wit.
But in such Lays as neither *ebb*, nor *flow*,
Correctly cold, and *regularly low*,   240
That shunning Faults, one quiet *Tenour*° keep;
We cannot *blame* indeed—but we may *sleep*.
In Wit, as Nature, what affects our Hearts
Is not th' Exactness of peculiar Parts;

---

160. Faults: practices that deviate from the "rules." **163–80.
Or . . . Dream:** Develop so intelligent an understanding of
the ancient poems that you can confound the critics who find
fault with yours by pointing to something in those poems
which, though a fault when judged by rule-of-thumb
criticism, is in fact a "glorious" fault, that is, no fault at all
but a new and precious creation. **181. Bays:** laurels.

206. Recruits: supplies. **216. the Pierian Spring:** Hippocrene, the stream associated with the Pierides, the Muses. **224.
Science:** matter inviting the intellect. **241. Tenour:**
continuity.

'Tis not a *Lip*, or *Eye*, we *Beauty* call,
But the joint *Force* and full *Result* of all.
Thus when we view some well-proportion'd *Dome*,°
(The *World*'s just *Wonder*, and ev'n *thine* O *Rome!*)
No single *Parts* unequally surprize;
All comes *united* to th' admiring Eyes;   250
No monstrous *Height*, or *Breadth*, or *Length* appear;
The *Whole* at once is *Bold*, and *Regular*.

Whoever thinks a faultless *Piece* to see,
Thinks what ne'er was, nor is, nor e'er shall be.
In ev'ry *Work* regard the *Writer's End*,
Since none can compass more than they *Intend;*
And if the *Means* be just, the *Conduct* true,
Applause, in spite of trivial *Faults*, is due.
As Men of *Breeding*, sometimes *Men of Wit*,
T' avoid *great Errors*, must the *less* commit,   260
Neglect the Rules each *Verbal Critick* lays,°
For *not* to know some *Trifles*, is a Praise.
Most *Criticks* fond of some subservient *Art*,
Still make the *Whole* depend upon a *Part*,
They talk of *Principles*, but *Notions* prize,
And All to one lov'd *Folly* Sacrifice.

Once on a time, *La Mancha*'s *Knight*,° they say,
A certain *Bard* encountring on the Way,
Discours'd in *Terms* as just, with Looks as Sage,
As e'er cou'd *Dennis*,° of the *Grecian Stage*;   270
Concluding all were desp'rate *Sots* and *Fools*,
That durst depart from *Aristotle*'s Rules.
Our Author, happy in a *Judge* so nice,
Produc'd his Play, and beg'd the *Knight*'s Advice,
Made him observe the *Subject* and the *Plot*,
The *Manners*, *Passions*,° *Unities*,° what not?
All which, exact to *Rule* were brought about,
Were but a *Combate in the Lists*° left out.
What! Leave the Combate out? Exclaims the Knight;
Yes, or we must renounce the Stagyrite.   280
Not so by Heav'n (he answers in a Rage)
Knights, Squires, and Steeds, must enter on the Stage.
So vast a *Throng* the *Stage* can ne'er contain.

---

247. Dome: (fine) dwelling, or cathedral. **261. lays:** lays down. **267. La . . . Knight:** Don Quixote, in a continuation of Cervantes' work (1605, 1615). **270. Dennis:** John Dennis (1657–1734), a critic, some thirty years older than Pope, who had a deep insight into the nature of the more emotional kinds of poetry and whose manners Pope thought too loud (see ll. 584–87). (See the selection from Dennis earlier in Part Two.) **276. Passions:** emotions. **Unities:** It was believed that the Greek poets integrated their plays by confining them to one story, one place, and one day (24 hours) and that Aristotle recommended this practice. **278. Lists:** the field of ceremonial combat.

Then build a New, or act it in a Plain.

Thus *Criticks*, of less *Judgment* than *Caprice*,
Curious,° not *Knowing*, not *exact*,° but *nice*,°
Form *short Ideas;* and offend in *Arts*
(As most in *Manners*) by a Love to *Parts*.
Some to *Conceit*° alone their *Taste* confine,
And glitt'ring *Thoughts* struck out at ev'ry Line;   290
Pleas'd with a *Work* where nothing's just or fit;
One *glaring Chaos* and *wild Heap of Wit:*
Poets like Painters, thus, unskill'd to trace
The *naked Nature* and the *living Grace*,
With *Gold* and *Jewels* cover ev'ry Part,
And hide with *Ornaments* their *Want of Art*.
True Wit° is *Nature* to Advantage drest,
What oft was *Thought*, but ne'er so well *Exprest*,
Something, whose *Truth* convinc'd at Sight we find,
That gives us back the *Image* of our *Mind:*   300
As *Shades* more sweetly recommend the *Light*,
So modest *Plainness* sets off sprightly *Wit:*
For *Works* may have more *Wit* than does 'em good,
As *Bodies* perish through Excess of *Blood*.

Others for *Language* all their *Care* express,
And value *Books*, as *Women Men*, for *Dress:*
Their Praise is still—*The Stile is excellent:*
The *Sense*, they humbly take upon *Content*.°
Words are like *Leaves;* and where they most abound,
Much *Fruit* of *Sense* beneath is rarely found.   310
False Eloquence, like the *Prismatic Glass*,
Its gawdy *Colours* spreads on *ev'ry place;*
The *Face of Nature* we no more *Survey*,
All glares *alike*, without *Distinction* gay:
But true *Expression*, like th' unchanging *Sun*, ⎞
Clears, and *improves* whate'er it shines upon, ⎬
It *gilds* all Objects, but it *alters* none.   ⎠
Expression is the *Dress*° of *Thought*, and still
Appears more *decent*° as more *suitable;*
A vile *Conceit* in pompous *Words* exprest,   320
Is like a *Clown*° in regal *Purple* drest;
For diff'rent *Styles* with diff'rent *Subjects* sort,
As several° *Garbs* with *Country*, *Town*, and *Court*.
Some by *Old Words* to Fame have made Pretence;°
Ancients in *Phrase*, meer *Moderns* in their *Sense!*
Such *labour'd Nothings*, in so *strange* a Style,
Amaze th' unlearn'd, and make the Learned *Smile*.

---

286. Curious: finicky. **exact:** sound. **nice:** fastidious, hard to please. **289. Conceit:** metaphors and similes. **297. True Wit:** great literature. **308. Content:** trust. **318. Dress:** Pope accepts the old belief that dress was the materialization of the wearer's inner self. **319. decent:** becoming, appropriate. **321. Clown:** rustic. **323. several:** various. **324. made Pretence:** laid claim.

Unlucky, as *Fungoso*° in the Play,
These Sparks with aukward Vanity display
What the Fine Gentlemen wore *Yesterday!*
And but so mimick ancient Wits at best,   331
As Apes our Grandsires in their *Doublets drest.*
In *Words,* as *Fashions,* the same Rule will hold;
Alike Fantastick, if *too New,* or *Old;*
Be not the *first* by whom the *New* are try'd,
Nor yet the *last* to lay the *Old* aside.

But most by *Numbers*° judge a Poet's Song,
And *smooth* or *rough,* with them, is *right* or *wrong;*
In the bright *Muse* tho' thousand *Charms* conspire,°
Her *Voice* is all these tuneful Fools admire,   340
Who haunt *Parnassus* but to please their Ear,
Not mend their Minds; as some to *Church* repair,
Not for the *Doctrine,* but the *Musick* there.
These *Equal Syllables* alone require,
Tho'° oft the Ear the *open Vowels* tire,
While *Expletives* their feeble Aid *do* join,
And ten low° Words oft creep in one dull Line,
While they ring round the same *unvary'd Chimes,*
With sure *Returns* of still *expected Rhymes.*
Where-e'er you find *the cooling Western Breeze,*   350
In the next Line, it *whispers thro' the Trees;*
If *Chrystal Streams with pleasing Murmurs creep,*
The *Reader's* threaten'd (not in vain) with *Sleep.*
Then, at the *last,* and *only* Couplet fraught
With some *unmeaning* Thing they call a *Thought,*
A *needless Alexandrine* ends the Song,
That like a wounded Snake, drags its slow Length
     along.
Leave such to tune their own dull Rhimes, and know
What's *roundly smooth,* or *languishingly slow;*
And praise the *Easie Vigor* of a Line,   360
Where *Denham's* Strength, and *Waller's*° Sweetness
     join.
True *Ease in writing* comes from *Art,* not *Chance,*
As those move easiest who have learn'd to dance.
'Tis not enough no Harshness gives Offence,
The *Sound* must seem an *Eccho* to the *Sense.*
Soft is the Strain when *Zephyr* gently blows,
And the *smooth Stream* in *smoother Numbers* flows;

But when loud Surges lash the sounding Shore,
The *hoarse, rough Verse* shou'd like the *Torrent* roar.
When *Ajax*° strives, some Rock's vast Weight to
     throw,   370
The Line too *labours,* and the Words move *slow;*
Not so, when swift *Camilla*° scours the Plain,
Flies o'er th' unbending Corn, and skims along the
     Main.°
Hear how *Timotheus'*° vary'd Lays surprize,
And bid Alternate Passions fall and rise!
While, at each Change, the Son of *Lybian Jove*°
Now *burns* with Glory, and then *melts* with Love;
Now his *fierce Eyes* with *sparkling Fury* glow;
Now *Sighs* steal out, and *Tears begin to flow:*
Persians and *Greeks* like *Turns of Nature*° found,   380
And the *World's Victor* stood subdu'd by *Sound!*
The Pow'r of Musick all our Hearts allow;
And what *Timotheus* was, is *Dryden* now.

Avoid *Extreams;* and shun the Fault of such,
Who still are pleas'd *too little,* or *too much.*
At ev'ry Trifle scorn to take Offence,
That always shows *Great Pride,* or *Little Sense;*
Those *Heads* as *Stomachs* are not sure the best
Which nauseate all, and nothing can digest.
Yet let not each gay *Turn*° thy Rapture move,   390
For Fools *Admire,* but Men of Sense *Approve;*
As things seem *large* which we thro' *Mist* descry,
Dulness is ever apt to *Magnify.*

Some the *French* Writers, some our *own* despise;
The *Ancients* only, or the *Moderns* prize:
Thus *Wit,* like *Faith,* by each Man is apply'd
To *one small Sect,* and All are *damn'd* beside.
Meanly they seek the Blessing to confine,
And force *that Sun* but on a *Part* to Shine;
Which not alone the *Southern Wit* sublimes,°   400
But ripens Spirits in cold *Northern Climes;*
Which from the first has shone on *Ages* past,
Enlights the *present,* and shall warm the *last:*
(Tho' *each* may feel *Increases* and *Decays,*
And see now *clearer* and now *darker Days*)
Regard not then if Wit be *Old* or *New,*
But blame the *False,* and value still the *True.*
Some ne'er advance a Judgment of their own,
But *catch* the *spreading Notion* of the Town;

---

328. **Fungoso:** a poor student in Jonson's *Every Man out of His Humor* (1599), who followed fashion at a distance. 337. **Numbers:** meter, sound. 339. **conspire:** unite. 345-47. **Tho' . . . Line:** These couplets, and several soon to follow, exemplify what they enunciate. 347. **low:** commonplace. 361. **Denham, Waller:** John Denham (1615-69) and Edmund Waller (1606-87); these poets were respected as the most gifted improvers of the heroic couplet. (See the selections from both in Part Three.)

370. **Ajax:** a Greek hero in the *Iliad,* noted for his strength. 372. **Camilla:** an Amazon in the *Aeneid.* 373. **Main:** a broad stretch, here of land. 374. **Timotheus:** Alexander the Great's court musician. 376. **the Son . . . Jove:** Alexander the Great. 380. **like . . . Nature:** similar human feelings. 390. **Turn:** graceful phrase. 400. **sublimes:** exalts.

They reason and conclude by *Precedent,*   410
And own *stale Nonsense* which they ne'er invent.
Some judge of Author's *Names,* not *Works,* and then
Nor praise nor blame the *Writings,* but the *Men.*
Of all this *Servile Herd* the worst is He
That in *proud Dulness* joins with *Quality,°*
A constant Critick at the Great-man's Board,
To *fetch and carry°* Nonsense for my Lord.
What *woful stuff* this Madrigal wou'd be,
In some starv'd Hackny Sonneteer, or me!
But let a *Lord* once own the *happy Lines,*   420
How the *Wit* brightens! How the *Style refines!*
Before *his* sacred Name flies ev'ry Fault,
And each *exalted* Stanza *teems* with *Thought!*

The *Vulgar* thus through *Imitation* err;
As oft the *Learn'd* by being *Singular;*
So much they scorn the Crowd, that if the Throng
By *Chance* go right, they *purposely* go wrong;
So *Schismaticks°* the *plain Believers* quit,
And are but damn'd for having *too much Wit.*
Some praise at Morning what they blame at
    Night;   430
But always think the *last* Opinion *right.*
A Muse by these is like a Mistress us'd,
This hour she's *idoliz'd,* the next *abus'd,*
While their weak Heads, like Towns unfortify'd,
'Twixt Sense and Nonsense daily change their Side.
Ask them the Cause; *They're wiser still,* they say;
And still° to Morrow's wiser than to Day.
We think our *Fathers* Fools, so *wise* we grow;
Our *wiser Sons,* no doubt, will think *us* so.
Once *School-Divines°* our zealous Isle o'erspread;   440
Who knew most *Sentences°* was *deepest read;*
Faith, Gospel, All, seem'd made to be *disputed,*
And none had *Sense* enough to be *Confuted.*
Scotists and *Thomists,°* now, in Peace remain,
Amidst their *kindred Cobwebs* in *Duck-Lane.°*
If *Faith* it self has *diff'rent Dresses* worn,
What wonder *Modes* in *Wit* shou'd take their Turn?
Oft, leaving what is Natural and fit,
The *current Folly* proves the *ready Wit,°*

And Authors think their Reputation safe,   450
Which lives as long as *Fools* are pleas'd to *Laugh.*
Some valuing those of their own *Side,* or *Mind,*
Still make themselves the measure of Mankind;
Fondly we think we honour Merit then,
When we but praise *Our selves* in *Other Men.*
Parties in *Wit* attend on those of *State,*
And publick Faction doubles private Hate.
Pride, Malice, Folly, against *Dryden* rose,
In various Shapes of *Parsons, Criticks, Beaus;°*
But *Sense* surviv'd, when *merry Jests* were past;   460
For rising Merit will *buoy up* at last.
Might he return, and bless once more our Eyes,
New *Blackmores°* and new *Milbourns°* must arise;
Nay shou'd great *Homer* lift his awful Head,
Zoilus° again would start up from the Dead.
Envy will *Merit* as its *Shade* pursue,
But like a Shadow, proves the *Substance* too;
For envy'd Wit, like *Sol* Eclips'd, makes known
Th' *opposing Body's* Grossness, not its *own.*
When first that Sun too powerful Beams displays,   470
It draws up Vapours which obscure its Rays;
But ev'n those Clouds at last adorn its Way,
Reflect new Glories, and augment the Day.

Be thou the *first* true Merit to befriend;
His Praise is lost, who stays till *All* commend;
Short is the Date, alas, of *Modern Rhymes;*
And 'tis but just to let 'em live *betimes.°*
No longer now that Golden Age appears,
When *Patriarch-Wits* surviv'd a *thousand Years;*
Now Length of *Fame* (our *second* Life) is lost,   480
And bare Threescore is all ev'n That can boast:
Our Sons their Father's *failing Language* see,
And such as *Chaucer* is, shall *Dryden* be.
So when the faithful *Pencil* has design'd
Some *bright Idea* of the Master's Mind,
Where a *new World* leaps out at his command,
And ready Nature waits upon his Hand;
When the ripe Colours *soften* and *unite,*
And sweetly *melt* into just Shade and Light,

---

459. Parsons . . . Beaus: Jeremy Collier (1650–1726),
clergyman and author of *Short View of the Immorality and
Profaneness of the English Stage* (1698); George Villiers (1628–87),
Second Duke of Buckingham, who attacked Dryden with
The Rehearsal (1671); John Wilmot (1647–80), Second Earl of
Rochester. (See the selections from Rochester in Part One.)
463. Blackmore: Sir Richard Blackmore (1654–1729),
physician and poet; a favorite target of the Augustan wits.
Milbourn: the contemporary clergyman Luke Milbourne.
465. Zoilus: a fourth-century B.C. critic who attacked Homer.
477. betimes: as long as they can.

---

415. Quality: people of rank. **417. fetch and carry:**
normally used of sporting dogs. **428. Schismaticks:** sectarians
in religion. **437. still:** always. **440. School-Divines:** theologians. **441. Sentences:** sayings, opinions. **444. Scotists
and Thomists:** Followers of Duns Scotus and Thomas
Aquinas formed the two schools of medieval philosophy.
445. Duck-Lane: a street in the City of London where old
books were sold. **449. proves . . . Wit:** gives occasion for
the ready wit to prove itself.

When mellowing Years their full Perfection give, 490
And each Bold Figure just begins to *Live;*
The *treach'rous Colours* the *fair Art* betray,
And all the bright Creation fades away!

Unhappy *Wit,* like most mistaken Things,°
Atones not for that *Envy* which it brings:
In *Youth* alone its empty Praise we boast,
But soon the Short-liv'd Vanity is lost!
Like some fair *Flow'r* the early *Spring* supplies,
And gaily Blooms, but ev'n in blooming *Dies.*
What is this *Wit,* which must our Cares employ? 500
The *Owner's Wife,* that *other Men* enjoy,
Then most our *Trouble* still when most *admir'd;*
And still the more we *give,* the more *requir'd;*
Whose *Fame* with *Pains* we guard, but lose with *Ease;*
Sure *some* to *vex,* but never *all* to *please;*
'Tis what the *Vicious fear,* the *Virtuous shun;*
By *Fools* 'tis *hated,* and by *Knaves undone!*

If *Wit* so much from *Ign'rance* undergo,
Ah let not *Learning* too commence° its Foe!
Of old, those met *Rewards* who cou'd *excel,* 510
And such were *Prais'd* who but *endeavour'd well:*
Tho' *Triumphs* were to *Gen'rals* only due,
Crowns were reserv'd to grace the *Soldiers* too.
Now they who reach *Parnassus'* lofty Crown,
Employ their Pains to spurn some others down;
And while Self-Love each jealous Writer rules,
Contending Wits become the *Sport of Fools:*
But still the *Worst* with most Regret commend,
And each *Ill Author* is as bad a *Friend.*
To what base Ends, and by what abject Ways, 520
Are Mortals urg'd thro' *Sacred° Lust of Praise?*
Ah ne'er so *dire a Thirst of Glory* boast,
Nor in the *Critick* let the *Man* be lost!
Good-Nature and *Good-Sense* must ever join;
To Err is *Human;* to Forgive, *Divine.*

But if in Noble Minds some Dregs remain,
Not yet purg'd off, of Spleen° and sow'r Disdain,
Discharge that Rage on more Provoking° Crimes,
Nor fear a Dearth in these Flagitious Times.
No Pardon vile *Obscenity* should find, 530
Tho' *Wit* and *Art* conspire to move your Mind;
But *Dulness* with *Obscenity* must prove
As Shameful sure as *Impotence* in *Love.*
In the fat Age of Pleasure, Wealth, and Ease,
Sprung the rank Weed, and thriv'd with large Increase;

When *Love* was all an easie Monarch's° Care;
Seldom at *Council,* never in a *War:*
Jilts° rul'd the State, and Statesmen° *Farces* writ;
Nay *Wits* had *Pensions,* and *young Lords°* had *Wit:*
The Fair sate panting at a *Courtier's Play,* 540
And not a *Mask°* went *un-improv'd* away:
The modest Fan was lifted up no more,
And Virgins *smil'd* at what they *blush'd* before—
The following Licence of a Foreign Reign°
Did all the Dregs of bold *Socinus°* drain;
Then Unbelieving Priests reform'd the Nation,
And taught more *Pleasant* Methods of Salvation;
Where Heav'ns Free Subjects might their *Rights*
    dispute,
Lest God himself shou'd seem too *Absolute.*
Pulpits their *Sacred Satire* learn'd to spare, 550
And Vice *admir'd°* to find a *Flatt'rer* there!
Encourag'd thus, Witt's *Titans°* brav'd the Skies,
And the Press groan'd with Licenc'd *Blasphemies*—
These Monsters, Cricks! with your Darts engage,
Here point your Thunder, and exhaust your Rage!
Yet shun their Fault, who, *Scandalously nice,*
Will needs *mistake* an Author *into Vice;*
All seems Infected that th' Infected spy,
As all looks yellow to the Jaundic'd Eye.

Learn then what MORALS Criticks ought to
    show, 560
For 'tis but *half* a *Judge's Task,* to *Know.*
'Tis not enough, Taste, Judgment, Learning, join;
In all you speak, let Truth and Candor° shine:
That not alone what to your *Sense* is due,
All may allow; but seek your *Friendship* too.

Be *silent* always when you *doubt* your Sense;
And *speak,* tho' *sure,* with seeming *Diffidence;*

536. easie Monarch: Charles II (1630–85). Ease was a social grace much admired in his day, and in Pope's. **538. Jilts:** a new term for harlots; hence, an allusion to Charles's many mistresses. **Statesmen:** The Duke of Buckingham wrote *The Rehearsal;* Sir Charles Sedley (*c.* 1639–1701), *The Mulberry Garden* (1668); and Sir George Etherege (1634–91), several lively plays. **539. young Lords:** The most gifted were the Duke of Buckingham, the Earl of Dorset (1638–1706), and the Earl of Rochester. **541. Mask:** Women often wore masks in public. **544. a Foreign Reign:** that of William III (1650–1702), who came from the Netherlands. **545. Socinus:** Faustus Socinus (1539–1604), Italian theologian, who advocated various heresies, including denying divinity to Jesus. **551. admir'd:** wondered, marveled. **552. Titans:** grotesque giant sons of earth and heaven, who were hurled into Tartary for attempting to conquer heaven. **563. Candor:** kindliness.

494. mistaken Things: things on which people set a mistaken value. **509. commence:** begin to be. **521. Sacred:** accursed. **527. Spleen:** See *The Rape of the Lock,* below, iv. 16–88. **528. Provoking:** challenging.

Some positive persisting Fops we know,
That, if *once wrong*, will needs be *always so;*
But you, with Pleasure own your Errors past,   570
And make each Day a *Critique* on the last.
   'Tis not enough your Counsel still be *true,*
Blunt Truths more Mischief than *nice Falshoods* do;
Men must be *taught* as if you taught them *not;*
And Things *unknown* propos'd as Things *forgot:*
Without *Good Breeding*, *Truth* is disapprov'd,
That only makes *Superior* Sense *belov'd.*
   Be Niggards of Advice on no Pretence;°
For the *worst Avarice* is that of *Sense:*
With mean Complacence ne'er betray your
    Trust,°   580
Nor be so *Civil* as to prove *Unjust;*
Fear not the Anger of the Wise to raise;
Those best can *bear Reproof*, who *merit Praise.*
   'Twere well, might Criticks still this Freedom take;
But *Appius°* reddens at each Word you speak,
And *stares, Tremendous!°* with a *threatning Eye;*
Like some *fierce Tyrant* in *Old Tapestry!*
Fear most to tax° an *Honourable°* Fool,
Whose Right it is, *uncensur'd* to be dull;
Such without *Wit* are Poets when they please,   590
As without *Learning* they can take *Degrees.°*
Leave dang'rous *Truths* to unsuccessful *Satyrs,*
And *Flattery* to fulsome *Dedicators,°*
Whom, when they *Praise*, the World believes no
    more,
Than when they promise to give *Scribling* o'er.
'Tis best sometimes your Censure to restrain,
And *charitably* let the dull be *vain:*
Your Silence there is better than your *Spite,*
For who can *rail* so long as they can *write?*
Still humming on, their drowsy Course they keep,   600
And *lash'd* so long, like *Tops*, are lash'd *asleep.*
False Steps but help them to renew the Race,
As after *Stumbling*, Jades will *mend* their Pace.
What Crouds of these, impenitently bold,
In *Sounds* and jingling *Syllables* grown old,

Still *run on°* Poets in a raging Vein,
Ev'n to the Dregs and *Squeezings* of the Brain;
Strain out the last, dull droppings of their Sense,
And Rhyme with all the *Rage* of *Impotence!*
   Such shameless *Bards* we have; and yet 'tis true,   610
There are as mad, abandon'd *Criticks* too.
The Bookful Blockhead, ignorantly read,
With *Loads* of *Learned Lumber* in his Head,
With his own Tongue still edifies his Ears,
And always *List'ning to Himself* appears.
All Books he reads, and all he reads assails,
From *Dryden's Fables°* down to *Durfey's Tales.°*
With *him*, most Authors steal their Works, or buy;
Garth did not write his own *Dispensary.°*
Name a new *Play*, and *he's* the Poet's *Friend,*   620
Nay show'd his Faults—but when wou'd Poets mend?
No Place so Sacred from such Fops is barr'd,
Nor is *Paul's Church* more safe than *Paul's Church-yard:°*
Nay, fly to *Altars; there* they'll talk you dead;
For *Fools* rush in where *Angels* fear to tread.
Distrustful *Sense* with modest Caution speaks; ⎫
It still *looks home*, and *short Excursions* makes; ⎬
But *ratling Nonsense* in full *Vollies* breaks; ⎭
And never shock'd, and never turn'd aside,
Bursts out, resistless, with a thundring *Tyde!*   630
   But where's the Man, who Counsel *can* bestow,
Still *pleas'd to teach*, and yet not *proud to know°?*
Unbiass'd, or by *Favour* or by *Spite;*
Not *dully prepossest*, nor *blindly right;*
Tho' *Learn'd*, well-bred; and tho' well-bred, sincere;
Modestly bold, and *Humanly* severe?
Who to a *Friend* his Faults can freely show,
And gladly praise the Merit of a *Foe?*
Blest with a *Taste* exact, yet unconfin'd;
A *Knowledge* both of *Books* and *Humankind;*   640
Gen'rous Converse;° a *Soul* exempt from *Pride;*
And *Love to Praise*, with *Reason* on his Side?
   Such once were *Criticks*, such the Happy *Few,*
Athens and *Rome* in better Ages knew.

---

578. on no Pretence: however good your reasons for being so. **580. With . . . Trust:** Do not betray your trust, your duty to give a just judgment, by being too polite, too humbly deferential. **585. Appius:** Dennis. He was the author of a tragedy, *Appius and Virginia*, written in 1705. **586. Tremendous:** a favorite adjective of Dennis's. **588. tax:** censure. **Honourable:** the title given to children of certain ranks of the nobility. **591. without . . . Degrees:** Noblemen and their sons were allowed special privileges at the university. **592–93. Satyrs, Dedicators:** a perfect rhyme in Pope's day.

606. run on: continue writing as. **617. Dryden's Fables:** *Fables Ancient and Modern* (1700). (See the Preface to the *Fables* in Part One.) **Durfey's Tales:** *Tales Tragical and Comical* (1704) by Thomas D'Urfey (1653–1723), a prolific popular writer. (See the selection from D'Urfey in Part Three.) **619. Garth . . . Dispensary:** according to William Warburton, "a common slander at that time in prejudice of that deserving author." Sir Samuel Garth (1661–1719), who became a friend of Pope's, first published his mock-heroic *Dispensary* in 1699. **623. Paul's Church-yard:** that of St. Paul's, where booksellers had stalls. **632. to know:** of knowing. **641. Converse:** social intercourse.

The mighty *Stagyrite* first left the Shore,
Spread all his Sails, and durst the Deeps explore;
He steer'd securely, and discover'd far,
Led by the Light of the *Mæonian Star.*°
Poets, a *Race* long unconfin'd and free,
Still fond and proud of *Savage Liberty,*   650
Receiv'd his Laws,° and stood convinc'd 'twas fit
Who conquer'd *Nature,*° shou'd preside o'er *Wit.*

Horace still charms with graceful Negligence,
And without Method *talks* us into Sense,
Will like a *Friend* familiarly convey
The *truest Notions* in the *easiest way.*
He, who Supream in Judgment, as in Wit,
Might boldly censure, as he boldly writ,
Yet *judg'd* with *Coolness* tho' he sung with *Fire;*
His *Precepts* teach but what his *Works* inspire.   660
Our *Criticks* take a contrary Extream,
They *judge* with *Fury,* but they *write* with *Fle'me:*°
Nor suffers *Horace* more in wrong *Translations*
By *Wits,* than *Criticks* in as wrong *Quotations.*

See *Dionysius*° *Homer's Thoughts* refine,
And call new *Beauties* forth from ev'ry *Line!*

Fancy and Art in gay *Petronius*° please,
The *Scholar's Learning,* and the *Courtier's Ease.*

In grave *Quintilian's*° copious Work we find
The justest *Rules,* and clearest *Method* join'd;   670
Thus *useful Arms* in Magazines we place,
All rang'd in *Order,* and dispos'd with *Grace,*
But less to please the Eye, than arm the Hand,
Still fit for *Use,* and ready at *Command.*

Thee, bold *Longinus*°! all the Nine *inspire,*
And blest *their Critick* with a *Poet's Fire.*
An ardent *Judge,* that Zealous in his Trust,
With *Warmth* gives Sentence, yet is always *Just;*
Whose *own Example* strengthens all his Laws,
And *Is himself* that great *Sublime* he draws.   680

Thus long succeeding *Criticks* justly reign'd,
Licence repress'd, and *useful Laws* ordain'd;
Learning and *Rome* alike in Empire grew,
And *Arts* still *follow'd* where her *Eagles flew;*
From the same Foes, at last, both felt their Doom,
And the same Age saw *Learning* fall, and *Rome.*
With *Tyranny,* then *Superstition* join'd,
As that the *Body,* this enslav'd the *Mind;*
Much was *Believ'd,* but little *understood,*
And to be *dull* was constru'd to be *good;*   690
A *second* Deluge Learning thus o'er-run,
And the *Monks* finish'd what the *Goths* begun.

At length, *Erasmus,*° that *great, injur'd* Name,
(The *Glory*° of the Priesthood, and the *Shame*°!)
Stemm'd the *wild Torrent* of a *barb'rous Age,*
And drove those *Holy Vandals*° off the Stage.

But see! each *Muse,* in *Leo's*° Golden Days,
Starts from her *Trance,* and trims her wither'd *Bays!*
Rome's ancient *Genius,*° o'er its *Ruins* spread,
Shakes off the *Dust,* and rears his rev'rend Head!   700
Then *Sculpture* and her *Sister-Arts* revive;
Stones leap'd to *Form,* and *Rocks* began to *live;*
With *sweeter Notes* each *rising Temple* rung;
A *Raphael*° painted, and a *Vida*° sung!
Immortal *Vida!* on whose honour'd Brow
The *Poet's Bays* and *Critick's Ivy*° grow:
Cremona now shall ever boast thy Name,
As next in Place to *Mantua,*° next in Fame!

But soon by Impious Arms from *Latium*° chas'd,
Their *ancient Bounds* the banish'd Muses past;   710
Thence Arts o'er all the *Northern World* advance;
But *Critic Learning* flourish'd most in *France.*

---

648. **the Mæonian Star:** Homer. 651. **Receiv'd his Laws:**
It had long been supposed that Aristotle's *Poetics* contained
rules for dramatic and other compositions. 652. **conquer'd Nature:** Aristotle investigated many aspects of
the physical world. 662. **Fle'me:** Phlegm (fire, heat)
produced disease and so came to mean dullness, apathy.
665. **Dionysius:** of Halicarnassus, a Roman critic of Horace's
time. 667. **Petronius:** Petronius Arbiter (d. A.D. 66) acted as
arbiter elegantiae (judge on questions of taste) in Nero's court.
669. **Quintilian:** (c. A.D. 35–c. 99), Latin rhetorician. His
Institutio Oratoria, in twelve books, is extant, and Pope knew
it well. 675. **Longinus:** (c. 220–73), Greek rhetorician. The
fine treatise *On the Sublime,* much valued in Pope's time, was
formerly attributed to him, but it is now thought to have been
written during the first half of the first century A.D.

693. **Erasmus:** (c. 1466–1536), the spirited Dutch humanist.
His ironic *Praise of Folly* satirizes the abuses of learning,
among other things. 694. **Glory:** because he was a priest.
Shame: because he attacked priests. 696. **Vandals:** Goths,
Germanic barbarians. 697. **Leo:** Pope Leo X (1475–1521), a
great patron of art and letters. 699. **Genius:** tutelary deity.
704. **Raphael:** (1483–1520), long considered the greatest
of painters. **Vida:** Girolamo Vida (c. 1485–1566), Italian poet.
706. **Ivy:** commonly associated with Bacchus, and also with
poets; ivy also symbolized learning. Reserving the more
customary laurel crowns for poets, Pope transfers the ivy
crowns to critics. 707–08. **Cremona, Mantua:** the birth-
places of Vida and Virgil respectively. Pope refers brilliantly
to a famous line of Virgil's: "Mantua, alas! too near to the
unfortunate Cremona" (*Eclogues,* ix. 28). Cremona had been
parceled out to reward veteran soldiers. 709. **Latium:** Italy.
Rome was sacked by the troops of the Holy Roman Empire
in 1527, and Pope suggests that learning fled to other parts of
Europe.

The *Rules*, a Nation born to serve, obeys,
And *Boileau*° still in Right of *Horace* sways.
But *we*, brave *Britains*, *Foreign Laws* despis'd,
And kept *unconquer'd*, and *unciviliz'd*,
Fierce for the *Liberties of Wit*, and bold,
We still defy'd the *Romans*, as *of old*.
Yet *some* there were, among the *sounder Few*
Of those who *less presum'd*, and *better knew*,   720
Who durst assert the *juster Ancient Cause*,
And here *restor'd* Wit's *Fundamental Laws*.
Such was the Muse, whose Rules and Practice tell,
Nature's chief Master-piece is writing well.°
Such was *Roscomon*°—not more *learn'd* than *good*,
With Manners gen'rous as his Noble Blood;
To him the Wit of *Greece* and *Rome* was known,
And ev'ry Author's *Merit*, but his own.
Such late was *Walsh*,°—the Muses Judge and
      Friend,
Who justly knew° to blame or to commend;   730
To Failings *mild*, but *zealous* for Desert;
The *clearest Head*, and the *sincerest Heart*.
This humble Praise, lamented *Shade!* receive,
This Praise at least a grateful Muse may give!
The Muse, whose early Voice you taught to Sing,
Prescrib'd her Heights, and prun'd° her tender
      Wing,
(Her Guide now lost) no more attempts to *rise*,
But in low Numbers° short Excursions tries:
Content, if hence th' Unlearn'd their Wants° may
      view,
The Learn'd reflect on what before they knew: 740
Careless of *Censure*, nor too fond of *Fame*,
Still pleas'd to *praise*, yet not afraid to *blame*,
Averse alike to *Flatter*, or *Offend*,
Not *free* from Faults, nor yet too vain to *mend*.

---

714. Boileau: Nicolas Boileau-Despréaux (1636–1711) wrote satires, epistles, *L'Art poétique* (1674), and the mock-heroic *Lutrin* (1674, 1683)—all of them were much admired in England. **724. Nature's . . . well:** The line is quoted from the *Essay on Poetry* (1682) by John Sheffield (1648–1721), Third Earl of Mulgrave and later First Duke of Buckingham and Normanby, a work of some deserved reputation in its time. **725. Roscomon:** Wentworth Dillon (c. 1630–85), Fourth Earl of Roscommon; poet, didactic writer, and critic. **729. Walsh:** William Walsh (1663–1708), friend of the young Pope and his poetic mentor. (See the selection from Walsh in Part Three.) **730. knew:** knew when. **736. prun'd:** preened. **738. low Numbers:** humble verses. **739. their Wants:** what they lack.

TO A YOUNG LADY, WITH THE WORKS OF VOITURE°

The text is that of the first edition (1712).

IN these gay Thoughts the Loves and Graces shine,
And all the Writer lives in ev'ry Line;
His easie Art may happy Nature seem,
Trifles themselves are Elegant in him.
Sure to charm all was his peculiar Fate,
Who without Flatt'ry pleas'd the Fair and Great;
Still with Esteem no less convers'd° than read;
With Wit well-natur'd, and with Books well-bred;
His Heart, his Mistress and his Friend did share;
His Time, the Muse, the Witty, and the Fair.   10
Thus wisely careless, innocently gay,
Chearful, he play'd the Trifle,° Life, away,
'Till Fate scarce felt his gentle Breath supprest,
As smiling Infants sport themselves to Rest:
Ev'n Rival Wits did *Voiture*'s Fate deplore,
And the Gay mourn'd who never mourn'd before;
The truest Hearts for *Voiture* heav'd with Sighs;
Voiture was wept by all the brightest Eyes;
The *Smiles* and *Loves* had dy'd in *Voiture*'s Death,
But that for ever in his Lines they breath.   20
   Let the strict Life of graver Mortals be
A long, exact, and serious Comedy,
In ev'ry Scene some Moral let it teach,
And, if it can, at once both Please and Preach:
Let mine, an innocent gay Farce appear,
And more Diverting still than Regular,
Have Humour, Wit, a native Ease and Grace;
Tho' not too strictly bound to Time and Place.
Criticks in Wit, or Life, are hard to please,
Few write to those, and none can live to these.   30
   Too much *your Sex* is by their° Forms° confin'd,
Severe to all, but most to Womankind;

TO A YOUNG LADY, WITH THE WORKS OF VOITURE. **Voiture:** Vincent Voiture (1598–1648), French writer of elegant verse. **7. convers'd:** conversed with. *Converse* at this time meant move about with, live with. **12. Trifle:** a reference to line 4. **31. their:** the moral critics'. **Forms:** rules.

Custom, grown blind with Age, must be your Guide;
Your Pleasure is a Vice, but not your Pride;
By nature yielding, stubborn but for Fame;
Made Slaves by Honour, and made Fools by Shame.
Marriage may all those petty Tyrants chace,
But sets up One, a greater, in their Place;
Well might you wish for Change, by those accurst,
But the last Tyrant ever proves the worst.   40
Still in Constraint your suff'ring Sex remains,
Or bound in formal, or in real Chains;
Whole Years neglected for some Months ador'd,
The fawning Servant turns a haughty Lord;
Ah quit not the free Innocence of Life!
For the dull Glory of a virtuous Wife!
Nor let false Shows, or empty Titles please;
Aim not at Joy, but rest content with Ease.

　　The Gods, to curse *Pamela*° with her Pray'rs,
Gave the gilt Coach and dappled *Flanders* Mares,   50
The shining Robes, rich Jewels, Beds of State,
And to compleat her Bliss, a Fool for Mate.
She glares in *Balls*, *Front-boxes*, and the *Ring*,°
A vain, unquiet, glitt'ring, wretched Thing!
Pride, Pomp, and State but reach her outward Part,
She sighs, and is no *Dutchess* at her Heart.

　　But, Madam, if the Fates withstand, and you
Are destin'd *Hymen*'s willing Victim too,
Trust not too much your now resistless Charms,
Those, Age or Sickness, soon or late, disarms;   60
Good Humour only teaches Charms to last,
Still makes new Conquests, and maintains the past:
Love, rais'd on Beauty, will like That decay,
Our Hearts may bear its slender Chain a Day,
As flow'ry Bands in Wantonness are worn;
A Morning's Pleasure, and at Evening torn:
This binds in Ties more easie, yet more strong,
The willing Heart, and only holds it long.

　　Thus *Voiture*'s early Care° still shone the same,
And *Monthausier*° was only chang'd in Name;   70
By this, ev'n now they live, ev'n now they charm,
Their Wit still sparkling and their Flames still warm.

　　Now crown'd with Myrtle, on th' *Elysian* Coast,
Amid those Lovers, joys his gentle Ghost,
Pleas'd while with Smiles his happy Lines you view,
And finds a fairer *Rambouïllet*° in you.

---

49. **Pamela:** accented on the second syllable. 53. **the Ring:** a fashionable drive in Hyde Park. 69. **early Care:** Mlle. Paulet. 70. **Monthausier:** the Duchesse de Monthausier, to whom Voiture was especially devoted. 76. **Rambouïllet:** the paternal name of the Duchesse de Monthausier.

The brightest Eyes of *France* inspir'd his Muse,
The brightest Eyes of *Britain* now peruse,
And dead as living, 'tis our Author's Pride,
Still to charm those who charm the World beside. 80

MESSIAH

A Sacred Eclogue
In Imitation of VIRGIL'S POLLIO

Pastoral poems, as written by Renaissance poets, freely mingled the classical and the biblical, the pagan and the Christian; and Pope, characteristically, saw and took the opportunity to crown this procedure by imitating at once Virgil's "Pollio" eclogue and the "inspired" chapters of Isaiah. In that fourth eclogue Virgil had turned from the usual pastoral themes to hymn the age just beginning, in which it seemed that a child, soon to be born, might become a god and inaugurate a second Golden Age, not only for man but for all creatures; Isaiah similarly had prophesied the coming of Christ, the Messiah, and an ensuing universal brotherhood.

Pope's treatment is characteristic. Whereas Richard Blackmore, "paraphrasing" Isaiah, expanded his source, Pope worked by concentration. His numerous echoes—to have found words wholly his own would have been to slight the august originals—are of phrases rather than passages, which he weaves together rather than dealing with them according to their order in his sources. The eighteenth century has been called an age of divine songs: *Messiah* takes its place beside Christopher Smart's *Song to David* (1763) and the hymns of the Wesleys.

The poem was first printed in *The Spectator*, No. 378 (May 14, 1712). We reproduce the *Spectator* text, incorporating Pope's later revisions.

Ye Nymphs of *Solyma*°! begin the Song:
To heav'nly Themes sublimer Strains belong.
The Mossie Fountains and the Sylvan Shades,
The Dreams of *Pindus*° and th' *Aonian* Maids,

MESSIAH. **1. Solyma:** the second half of the Greek form of *Jerusalem*. **4. Pindus:** the mountain of Thessaly, sacred to the Muses ("*Aonian* Maids").

Delight no more—O Thou my Voice inspire
Who touch'd *Isaiah's* hallow'd Lips with Fire!
  Rapt into future Times, the Bard begun;
A *Virgin* shall conceive, a *Virgin* bear a Son!
From *Jesse's* Root behold a Branch arise,
Whose sacred Flow'r with Fragrance fills the Skies. 10
Th' Æthereal Spirit o'er its Leaves shall move,
And on its Top descends the Mystic Dove.
Ye Heav'ns! from high the dewy Nectar pour,
And in soft Silence shed the kindly Show'r!
The Sick and Weak the healing Plant shall aid;
From Storms a Shelter, and from Heat a Shade.
All Crimes shall cease, and ancient Fraud shall fail;
Returning Justice lift aloft her Scale;
Peace o'er the World her Olive-Wand extend,
And white-roab'd Innocence from Heav'n descend. 20
Swift fly the Years, and rise th' expected Morn!
Oh spring to Light, Auspicious Babe, be born!
See Nature hasts her earliest Wreaths to bring,
With all the Incence of the breathing Spring:
See lofty *Lebanon* his Head advance,
See nodding Forests on the Mountains dance,
See spicy Clouds from lowly *Saron* rise,
And *Carmel's* flow'ry Top perfumes the Skies!
Hark! a glad Voice the lonely Desert chears:
Prepare the Way! a God, a God appears. 30
A God, a God! the vocal Hills reply,
The Rocks proclaim th' approaching Deity.
Lo Earth receives him from the bending Skies!
Sink down ye Mountains and ye Vallies rise:
With Heads declin'd, ye Cedars, Homage pay;
Be smooth ye Rocks, ye rapid Floods give way!
The SAVIOR comes! by ancient Bards foretold:
Hear him ye Deaf, and all ye Blind behold!
He from thick Films shall purge the visual Ray,
And on the sightless Eye-ball pour the Day. 40
'Tis he th' obstructed Paths of Sound shall clear,
And bid new Musick charm th' unfolding Ear.
The Dumb shall sing, the Lame his Crutch foregoe,
And leap exulting like the bounding Roe.
No Sigh, no Murmur the wide World shall hear,
From ev'ry Face he wipes off ev'ry Tear.
In adamantine Chains shall Death be bound,
And Hell's grim Tyrant feel th' eternal Wound.
As the good Shepherd tends his fleecy Care,
Seeks freshest Pasture and the purest Air, 50
Explores° the lost, the wand'ring Sheep directs,
By Day o'ersees them, and by Night protects;

The tender Lambs he raises in his Arms,
Feeds from his Hand, and in his Bosom warms:
Thus shall Mankind his Guardian Care ingage,
The promis'd Father of the future Age.
No more shall Nation against Nation rise,
Nor ardent Warriors meet with hateful Eyes,
Nor Fields with gleaming Steel be cover'd o'er;
The Brazen Trumpets kindle Rage no more: 60
But useless Lances into Scythes shall bend,
And the broad Faulchion in a Plow-share end.
Then Palaces shall rise; the joyful Son
Shall finish what his short-liv'd Sire begun;
Their Vines a Shadow to their Race shall yield;
And the same Hand that sow'd, shall reap the Field.
The Swain in barren Desarts with surprize
See Lillies spring, and sudden Verdure rise;
And Starts, amidst the thirsty Wilds, to hear
New Falls of Water murm'ring in his Ear: 70
On rifted Rocks, the Dragon's late Abodes,
The green Reed trembles, and the Bulrush nods.
Waste sandy Vallies, once perplex'd with Thorn,
The spiry Firr and shapely Box adorn;
To leaf-less Shrubs the flow'ring Palms succeed,
And od'rous Myrtle to the noisome Weed.
The Lambs with Wolves shall graze the verdant Mead,
And Boys in flow'ry Bands the Tyger lead;
The Steer and Lion at one Crib shall meet;
And harmless Serpents lick the Pilgrim's Feet. 80
The smiling Infant in his Hand shall take
The crested Basilisk and speckled Snake;
Pleas'd, the green Lustre of the Scales survey,
And with their forky Tongue shall innocently play.
Rise, crown'd with Light, Imperial *Salem* rise!
Exalt thy Tow'ry Head, and lift thy Eyes!
See, a long Race thy spatious Courts adorn;
See future Sons, and Daughters yet unborn
In crowding Ranks on ev'ry Side arise,
Demanding Life, impatient for the Skies! 90
See barb'rous Nations at thy Gates attend,
Walk in thy Light, and in thy Temple bend.
See thy bright Altars throng'd with prostrate Kings,
And heap'd with Products of *Sabæan*° Springs!
For thee, *Idume's*° spicy Forests blow;
And Seeds of Gold in *Ophyr's*° Mountains glow.
See Heav'n its sparkling Portals wide display,
And break upon thee in a Flood of Day!

94. Sabæan: of Sheba. **95. Idume:** the Greek version of *Edom*, a part of Palestine. **96. Ophyr:** a place famous in antiquity for its gold; for the process alluded to, see *Moral Essays, Of the Characters of Women,* below, ll. 289–90 and note.

51. Explores: finds by searching for.

No more the rising *Sun* shall gild the Morn,
Nor Evening *Cynthia*° fill her silver Horn,   100
But lost, dissolv'd in thy superior Rays;
One Tyde of Glory, one unclouded Blaze,
O'erflow thy Courts: The LIGHT HIMSELF shall shine
Reveal'd; and *God's* eternal Day be thine!
The Seas shall waste; the Skies in Smoke decay;
Rocks fall to Dust, and Mountains melt away;
But fix'd *His* Word, *His* saving Pow'r remains:
Thy *Realm* for ever lasts! thy own *Messiah* reigns!

THE RAPE OF THE LOCK

AN HEROI-COMICAL° POEM.
IN FIVE CANTO'S.

In 1711 Pope's friend and benefactor John Caryll invited
him to write a humorous poem to heal the breach that
had developed between two fashionable families, the
Petres and the Fermors, after Robert Lord Petre cut off
a lock of Arabella Fermor's hair. Pope alone perhaps
could see in Caryll's request the opportunity not for a
mere epistle but for a mock epic in miniature. By the
time the poem was finished—the sylphs were added two
years after the poem was first published; the moralizing
speech of Clarissa, three years after that—it had become
the most perfect of the several European attempts to
keep alive, by the most hopeful means, those of diminution and laughter, the moribund epic form. Pope
developed the theme given him by Caryll according to
the traditions of the genre. The rape of Helen became
that of a lock of hair; the gods became minute sylphs;
Aeneas' voyage up the Tiber became Belinda's up the
Thames; the long description of Achilles' shield became
a brief one of Belinda's petticoat. There are sacrifices,
prayers, laments, harangues, feasts, and so on. But in
addition to this mockery of the main "ingredients,"
there is mockery of the epic style—its invocations,
exclamations, and use of similes—and some of the
speeches follow the framework of actual speeches in
Homer and Virgil, thus adding parody to imitation.
Sometimes, with significant difference, the very words
of epic are drawn on, as when Pope takes from Dryden's
translation of Virgil this description of the afterlife of
heroes:

> The love of Horses which they had, alive,
> And care of Chariots, after Death survive,

100. Cynthia: the moon. THE RAPE OF THE LOCK. **Heroi-
Comical:** mock-heroic.

and uses it to describe a fashionable woman after her
transformation into a sylph:

> Her Joy in gilded Chariots, when alive,
> And Love of *Ombre*, after Death survive.

When the poem was finished, there was little in it that
did not have some sort of parallel in the epics.

Pope, however, made his poem more than a course of
mockery. He enriched it with at least as many kinds of
poetry as Eliot used in *The Waste Land*, which resembles
Pope's poem in length, comprehensiveness, concentration, learning, brilliance, and, especially, sensuous
beauty. As much charmed with his subject as he was
critical of it, Pope sensed that the loss of a lock of hair
touches a girl's soul deeply, that beauty is painfully
fragile.

The poem was first published in 1712; its two cantos
became five in 1714. It was then virtually complete
down to the last syllable except that in the *Works* of
1717 Pope inserted the speech of Clarissa in Canto v.
The text here is that of 1714, corrected in accordance
with Pope's revisions.

Nolueram, Belinda, tuos violare capillos,
  Sed juvat hoc precibus me tribuisse tuis.°
                                          MARTIAL.

TO
Mrs. *ARABELLA FERMOR*.°

Madam,
IT will be in vain to deny that I have some Regard for
this Piece, since I Dedicate it to You. Yet You may
bear me Witness, it was intended only to divert a few
young Ladies, who have good Sense and good Humour
enough, to laugh not only at their Sex's little unguarded Follies, but at their own. But as it was
communicated with the Air of a Secret, it soon found
its Way into the World. An imperfect Copy having
been offer'd to a Bookseller, You had the Good-
Nature for my Sake to consent to the Publication of
one more correct: This I was forc'd to before I had

Nolueram . . . tuis: "I was loathe, Belinda, to violate your
locks; but I am pleased to have granted that much to your
prayers" (*Epigrams*, XII. 84). Martial's Polytimus becomes
Pope's Belinda. **Arabella Fermor:** the daughter of a
Catholic family, probably known to Pope through Caryll.
She was about twenty-three when the poem was first published in 1712, and since 1708 had been celebrated as a beauty.

executed half my Design, for the *Machinery* was entirely wanting to compleat it.

The *Machinery*, Madam, is a Term invented by the Criticks, to signify that Part which the Deities, Angels, or Dæmons, are made to act in a Poem: For the ancient Poets are in one respect like many modern Ladies; Let an Action be never so trivial in it self, they always make it appear of the utmost Importance. These Machines I determin'd to raise on a very new and odd Foundation, the *Rosicrucian* Doctrine of Spirits.

I know how disagreeable it is to make use of hard Words before a Lady; but 'tis so much the Concern of a Poet to have his Works understood, and particularly by your Sex, that You must give me leave to explain two or three difficult Terms.

The *Rosicrucians* are a People I must bring You acquainted with. The best Account I know of them is in a French Book call'd *Le Comte de Gabalis*,[1] which both in its Title and Size is so like a *Novel*, that many of the Fair Sex have read it for one by Mistake. According to these Gentlemen, the four Elements are inhabited by Spirits, which they call *Sylphs, Gnomes, Nymphs,* and *Salamanders.* The *Gnomes,* or *Dæmons* of Earth, delight in Mischief; but the *Sylphs,* whose Habitation is in the Air, are the best-condition'd Creatures imaginable. For they say, any Mortals may enjoy the most intimate Familiarities with these gentle Spirits, upon a Condition very easie to all true *Adepts,* an inviolate Preservation of Chastity.

As to the following Canto's, all the Passages of them are as Fabulous, as the Vision at the Beginning, or the Transformation at the End; (except the Loss of your Hair, which I always mention with Reverence). The Human Persons are as Fictitious as the Airy ones; and the Character of *Belinda,* as it is now manag'd, resembles You in nothing but in Beauty.

If this Poem had as many Graces as there are in Your Person, or in Your Mind, yet I could never hope it should pass thro' the World half so Uncensured as You have done. But let its Fortune be what it will, mine is happy enough, to have given me this Occasion of assuring You that I am, with the truest Esteem, | *Madam,* | *Your Most Obedient Humble Servant.*

A. POPE.

1. Le . . . Gabalis: a "novel" (1670) by the Abbé de Monfaucon de Villars, which had twice been translated into English. It is a skit on the Rosicrucian philosophy, which originated in Germany a hundred years earlier.

CANTO I

WHAT° dire Offence from am'rous Causes springs,
What mighty Contests rise from trivial Things,
I sing—This Verse to *Caryll,*° Muse! is due;
This, ev'n *Belinda* may vouchsafe to view:
Slight is the Subject, but not so the Praise,
If She inspire, and He approve my Lays.

　Say what strange Motive, Goddess! cou'd compel
A well-bred *Lord* t' assault a gentle *Belle?*
Oh say what stranger Cause, yet unexplor'd,
Cou'd make a gentle *Belle* reject a *Lord?*　　　10
In Tasks so bold, can Little Men engage,
And in soft Bosoms dwells such mighty Rage?

　Sol thro' white Curtains° shot a tim'rous Ray,
And op'd those Eyes that must eclipse the Day;
Now Lapdogs give themselves the rowzing Shake,
And sleepless Lovers, just at Twelve, awake:
Thrice rung the Bell, the Slipper knock'd the Ground,
And the press'd Watch° return'd a silver Sound.
Belinda still her downy Pillow prest,
Her Guardian *Sylph* prolong'd the balmy Rest.　　20
'Twas he had summon'd to her silent Bed
The Morning-Dream that hover'd o'er her Head.
A Youth more glitt'ring than a *Birth-night*° Beau,
(That ev'n in Slumber caus'd her Cheek to glow)
Seem'd to her Ear his winning Lips to lay,
And thus in Whispers said, or seem'd to say.

　Fairest of Mortals, thou distinguish'd Care
Of thousand bright Inhabitants of Air!
If e'er one Vision touch'd thy infant Thought,
Of all the Nurse and all the Priest have taught,　　30
Of airy Elves by Moonlight Shadows seen,
The silver Token, and the circled Green,

Canto I. **1–12.** In a note to his epic *Davideis* (1656) Cowley wrote, "The custom of beginning all *Poems* with a *Proposition* of the whole work, and an *Invocation* of some God for his assistance to go through with it, is . . . solemnly and religiously observed by all the ancient *Poets.*" **3. Caryll:** John Caryll (*c.* 1666–1736), a generous Catholic friend of Pope's who owned land in Sussex. **13. Curtains:** those of the four-poster bed. **18. press'd Watch:** Striking a light to see the time was an inconvenience in the days before matches; consequently there was a great demand for "repeater" watches. England manufactured the best of them. When the stem was pressed, a minute bell sounded the hour and then two, four, or six for the quarter just passed. **23. Birth-night:** a reference to celebrations at court on a royal birthday, when the courtiers' clothes were particularly splendid.

Or Virgins visited by Angel-Pow'rs,
With Golden Crowns and Wreaths of heav'nly
    Flow'rs,
Hear and believe! thy own Importance know,
Nor bound thy narrow Views to Things below.
Some secret Truths from Learned Pride conceal'd,
To Maids alone and Children are reveal'd:
What tho' no Credit doubting Wits° may give?
The Fair and Innocent shall still believe.   40
Know then, unnumber'd Spirits round thee fly,
The light *Militia* of the lower Sky;
These, tho' unseen, are ever on the Wing,
Hang o'er the *Box*, and hover round the *Ring*.°
Think what an Equipage thou hast in Air,
And view with scorn *Two Pages* and a *Chair*.°
As now your own, our Beings were of old,
And once inclos'd in Woman's beauteous Mold;
Thence, by a soft Transition, we repair
From earthly Vehicles to these of Air.   50
Think not, when Woman's transient Breath is fled,
That all her Vanities at once are dead:
Succeeding Vanities she still regards,
And tho' she plays no more, o'erlooks the Cards.
Her Joy in gilded Chariots, when alive,
And Love of *Ombre*,° after Death survive.
For when the Fair in all their Pride expire,
To their first Elements their Souls retire:
The Sprights of fiery Termagants° in Flame
Mount up, and take a *Salamander's*° Name.   60
Soft yielding Minds to Water glide away,
And sip with *Nymphs*, their Elemental Tea.
The graver Prude sinks downward to a *Gnome*,
In search of Mischief still on Earth to roam.
The light Coquettes in *Sylphs* aloft repair,
And sport and flutter in the Fields of Air.
    Know farther yet; Whoever fair and chaste
Rejects Mankind, is by some *Sylph* embrac'd:
For Spirits, freed from mortal Laws, with ease
Assume what Sexes and what Shapes they please.   70
What guards the Purity of melting Maids,
In Courtly Balls, and Midnight Masquerades,°

Safe from the treach'rous Friend, the daring Spark,°
The Glance by Day, the Whisper in the Dark;
When kind Occasion prompts their warm Desires,
When Musick softens, and when Dancing fires?
'Tis but their *Sylph*, the wise Celestials know,
Tho' *Honour* is the Word with Men below.
    Some Nymphs there are, too conscious of their
    Face,
For Life predestin'd to the *Gnomes'* Embrace.   80
These swell their Prospects and exalt their Pride,
When Offers are disdain'd, and Love deny'd.
Then gay Ideas crowd the vacant Brain;
While Peers and Dukes, and all their sweeping Train,
And Garters, Stars, and Coronets° appear,
And in soft Sounds, *Your Grace*° salutes their Ear.
'Tis these that early taint the Female Soul,
Instruct the Eyes of young *Coquettes* to roll,
Teach Infant-Cheeks a bidden Blush to know,
And little Hearts to flutter at a *Beau*.   90
    Oft when the World imagine Women stray,
The *Sylphs* thro' mystick Mazes guide their Way,
Thro' all the giddy Circle they pursue,
And old Impertinence expel by new.
What tender Maid but must a Victim fall
To one Man's Treat, but for another's Ball?
When *Florio* speaks, what Virgin could withstand,
If gentle *Damon* did not squeeze her Hand?
With varying Vanities, from ev'ry Part,
They shift the moving Toyshop of their Heart;   100
Where Wigs with Wigs, with Sword-knots Sword-
    knots strive,
Beaus banish Beaus, and Coaches Coaches drive.°
This erring Mortals Levity may call,
Oh blind to Truth! the *Sylphs* contrive it all.
    Of these am I, who thy Protection claim,
A watchful Sprite, and *Ariel* is my Name.
Late, as I rang'd the Crystal Wilds of Air,
In the clear Mirror of thy ruling *Star*
I saw, alas! some dread Event impend,
Ere to the Main this Morning Sun descend.   110
But Heav'n reveals not what, or how, or where:
Warn'd by thy *Sylph*, oh Pious Maid beware!
This to disclose is all thy Guardian can.
Beware of all, but most beware of Man!

---

39. doubting Wits: The skeptic was a rapidly multiplying figure during the late seventeenth century and later. **44. the Ring:** a fashionable drive in Hyde Park. **46. Chair:** a sedan chair. **56. Ombre:** a popular card game of the time, played with only forty cards—the pack minus the eights, nines, and tens. **59. Termagants:** shrews. **60. Salamander:** This lizardlike animal was supposed to live in fire. **72. Masquerades:** masked balls.

73. Spark: a contemptuous term for a showy man about town. **85. Garters . . . Coronets:** insignia of noble rank. **86. Your Grace:** a courtesy title given to a duke or duchess. **101–02. Where . . . drive:** The versification and word order mimic Ovid's when he describes heroic conflict.

He said; when *Shock*,° who thought she slept too
    long,
Leapt up, and wak'd his Mistress with his Tongue.
'Twas then *Belinda!* if Report say true,
Thy Eyes first open'd on a *Billet-doux;*
Wounds, Charms, and *Ardors*, were no sooner read,
But all the Vision vanish'd from thy Head.   120
    And now, unveil'd, the *Toilet°* stands display'd,
Each Silver Vase in mystic Order laid.
First, rob'd in White, the Nymph intent adores
With Head uncover'd, the *Cosmetic* Pow'rs.
A heav'nly Image in the Glass appears,
To that she bends, to that her Eyes she rears;
Th' inferior Priestess, at her Altar's side,
Trembling, begins the sacred Rites of Pride.
Unnumber'd Treasures ope at once, and here
The various Off'rings of the World appear;   130
From each she nicely culls with curious Toil,
And decks the Goddess with the glitt'ring Spoil.
This Casket *India*'s glowing Gems unlocks,
And all *Arabia* breathes from yonder Box.
The Tortoise here and Elephant unite,
Transform'd to *Combs*, the speckled and the white.
Here Files of Pins extend their shining Rows,
Puffs, Powders, Patches, Bibles,° Billet-doux.
Now awful Beauty puts on all its Arms;
The Fair each moment rises in her Charms,   140
Repairs her Smiles, awakens ev'ry Grace,
And calls forth all the Wonders of her Face;
Sees by Degrees a purer Blush arise,
And keener Lightnings quicken in her Eyes.
The busy *Sylphs* surround their darling Care;
These set the Head, and those divide the Hair,
Some fold the Sleeve, while others plait° the Gown;
And *Betty*'s° prais'd for Labours not her own.

CANTO II

Not with more Glories, in th' Etherial Plain,
The Sun first rises o'er the purpled Main,
Than issuing forth, the Rival of his Beams
Lanch'd on the Bosom of the Silver *Thames*.
Fair Nymphs, and well-drest Youths around her shone,
But ev'ry Eye was fix'd on her alone.

115. **Shock:** (or shough) an Icelandic breed of dog, fashionable as a lap dog. 121. **Toilet:** dressing table. 138. **Bibles:**
Booksellers supplied Bibles in very small format; they
were considered fashionable. 147. **plait:** arrange in folds.
148. **Betty:** a stock name for a lady's maid.

On her white Breast a sparkling *Cross* she wore,
Which *Jews* might kiss, and Infidels adore.
Her lively Looks a sprightly Mind disclose,
Quick as her Eyes, and as unfix'd as those: 10
Favours to none, to all she Smiles extends,
Oft she rejects, but never once offends.
Bright as the Sun, her Eyes the Gazers strike,
And, like the Sun, they shine on all alike.
Yet graceful Ease, and Sweetness void of Pride,
Might hide her Faults, if *Belles* had Faults to hide:
If to her share some Female Errors fall,
Look on her Face, and you'll forget 'em all.
    This Nymph, to the Destruction of Mankind,
Nourish'd two Locks, which graceful hung behind 20
In equal Curls, and well conspir'd to deck
With shining Ringlets her smooth Iv'ry Neck.
Love in these Labyrinths his Slaves detains,
And mighty Hearts are held in slender Chains.
With hairy Sprindges° we the Birds betray,
Slight Lines of Hair surprize the Finny Prey,
Fair Tresses Man's Imperial Race insnare,
And Beauty draws us with a single Hair.
    Th' Adventurous *Baron* the bright Locks admir'd,
He saw, he wish'd, and to the Prize aspir'd: 30
Resolv'd to win, he meditates the way,
By Force to ravish, or by Fraud betray;
For when Success a Lover's Toil attends,
Few ask, if Fraud or Force attain'd his Ends.
    For this, ere *Phœbus* rose, he had implor'd
Propitious Heav'n, and ev'ry Pow'r ador'd,
But chiefly *Love*—to *Love* an Altar built,
Of twelve vast *French* Romances, neatly gilt.
There lay three Garters, half a Pair of Gloves;
And all the Trophies of his former Loves.   40
With tender *Billet-doux* he lights the Pyre,
And breathes three am'rous Sighs to raise the Fire.
Then prostrate falls, and begs with ardent Eyes
Soon to obtain, and long possess the Prize:
The Pow'rs gave Ear, and granted half his Pray'r,
The rest, the Winds dispers'd in empty Air.
    But now secure° the painted Vessel glides,
The Sun-beams trembling on the floating Tydes,
While melting Musick steals upon the Sky,
And soften'd Sounds along the Waters die.   50
Smooth flow the Waves, the Zephyrs gently play,
Belinda smil'd, and all the World was gay.
All but the *Sylph*—With careful Thoughts opprest,
Th' impending Woe sate heavy on his Breast.

Canto II. 25. **Sprindges:** (springes) traps. 47. **secure:** free
from care.

He summons strait his Denizens° of Air;
The lucid Squadrons round the Sails repair:
Soft o'er the Shrouds Aerial Whispers breathe,
That seem'd but *Zephyrs* to the Train beneath.
Some to the Sun their Insect-Wings unfold,
Waft on the Breeze, or sink in Clouds of Gold.   60
Transparent Forms, too fine for mortal Sight,
Their fluid Bodies half dissolv'd in Light.
Loose to the Wind their airy Garments flew,
Thin glitt'ring Textures of the filmy Dew;
Dipt in the richest Tincture of the Skies,
Where Light disports in ever-mingling Dies,
While ev'ry Beam new transient Colours flings,
Colours that change whene'er they wave their Wings.
Amid the Circle, on the gilded Mast,
Superior by the Head,° was *Ariel* plac'd;   70
His Purple Pinions opening to the Sun,
He rais'd his Azure Wand, and thus begun.

    Ye *Sylphs* and *Sylphids*,° to your Chief give Ear,
Fays, Fairies, Genii, Elves, and *Dæmons* hear!
Ye know the Spheres and various Tasks assign'd,
By Laws Eternal, to th' Aerial Kind.
Some in the Fields of purest *Æther* play,
And bask and whiten in the Blaze of Day.
Some guide the Course of wandring Orbs on high,
Or roll the Planets thro' the boundless Sky.   80
Some less refin'd, beneath the Moon's pale Light
Pursue the Stars that shoot athwart the Night,
Or suck the Mists in grosser Air below,
Or dip their Pinions in the painted Bow,
Or brew fierce Tempests on the wintry Main,
Or o'er the Glebe distill the kindly Rain.
Others on Earth o'er human Race preside,
Watch all their Ways, and all their Actions guide:
Of these the Chief the Care of Nations own,
And guard with Arms Divine the *British Throne*.   90

    Our humbler Province is to tend the Fair,
Not a less pleasing, tho' less glorious Care.
To save the Powder from too rude a Gale,
Nor let th' imprison'd Essences exhale,
To draw fresh Colours from the vernal Flow'rs,
To steal from Rainbows ere they drop in Show'rs
A brighter Wash;° to curl their waving Hairs,
Assist their Blushes, and inspire their Airs;
Nay oft, in Dreams, Invention we bestow,
To change a *Flounce*, or add a *Furbelo*.   100

This Day, black Omens threat the brightest Fair
That e'er deserv'd a watchful Spirit's Care;
Some dire Disaster, or by Force, or Slight,°
But what, or where, the Fates have wrapt in Night.
Whether the Nymph shall break *Diana's* Law,
Or some frail *China* Jar receive a Flaw,
Or stain her Honour, or her new Brocade,
Forget her Pray'rs, or miss a Masquerade,
Or lose her Heart, or Necklace, at a Ball;
Or whether Heav'n has doom'd that *Shock* must
    fall.   110
Haste then ye Spirits! to your Charge repair;
The flutt'ring Fan be *Zephyretta's* Care;
The Drops° to thee, *Brillante*, we consign;
And, *Momentilla*, let the Watch be thine;
Do thou, *Crispissa*,° tend her fav'rite Lock;
Ariel himself shall be the Guard of *Shock*.

    To Fifty chosen *Sylphs*, of special Note,
We trust th' important Charge, the *Petticoat*:
Oft have we known that sev'nfold Fence to fail,
Tho' stiff with Hoops, and arm'd with Ribs of
    Whale.   120
Form a strong Line about the Silver Bound,
And guard the wide Circumference around.

    Whatever Spirit, careless of his Charge,
His Post neglects, or leaves the Fair at large,
Shall feel sharp Vengeance soon o'ertake his Sins,
Be stopt in *Vials*, or transfixt with *Pins;*
Or plung'd in Lakes of bitter *Washes* lie,
Or wedg'd whole Ages in a *Bodkin's* Eye:
Gums and *Pomatums*° shall his Flight restrain,
While clog'd he beats his silken Wings in vain;   130
Or Alom-*Stypticks*° with contracting Power
Shrink his thin Essence like a rivell'd° Flower.
Or as *Ixion*° fix'd, the Wretch shall feel
The giddy Motion of the whirling Mill,
In Fumes of burning Chocolate shall glow,
And tremble at the Sea that froaths below!

    He spoke; the Spirits from the Sails descend;
Some, Orb in Orb, around the Nymph extend,
Some thrid the mazy Ringlets of her Hair,
Some hang upon the Pendants of her Ear;   140
With beating Hearts the dire Event they wait,
Anxious, and trembling for the Birth of Fate.

---

55. Denizens: The meaning here is, properly, "naturalized
aliens." **70. Superior . . . Head:** The hero of the epics
was taller than his men. **73. Sylphids:** female sylphs.
97. Wash: a cosmetic lotion.

103. Slight: sleight, trick. **113. Drops:** earrings. **115.
Crispissa:** derived from Latin *crispere*, meaning to curl. **129.
Pomatums:** ointments. **131. Stypticks:** astringents that stop
bleeding. **132. rivell'd:** shriveled. **133. Ixion:** in Greek
mythology, a king punished for his love of Hera by being
bound to a perpetually revolving wheel.

CANTO III

CLOSE by those Meads for ever crown'd with Flow'rs,
Where *Thames* with Pride surveys his rising Tow'rs,
There stands a Structure of Majestick Frame,
Which from the neighb'ring *Hampton*° takes its Name.
Here *Britain*'s Statesmen oft the Fall foredoom
Of Foreign Tyrants, and of Nymphs at home;
Here Thou, Great *Anna!* whom three Realms obey,
Dost sometimes Counsel take—and sometimes *Tea.*

Hither the Heroes and the Nymphs resort,
To taste awhile the Pleasures of a Court;   10
In various Talk th' instructive hours they past,
Who gave the *Ball*, or paid the *Visit*° last:
One speaks the Glory of the *British Queen*,
And one describes a charming *Indian Screen;*
A third interprets Motions, Looks, and Eyes;
At ev'ry Word a Reputation dies.
Snuff, or the *Fan*, supply each Pause of Chat,
With singing, laughing, ogling, and all that.

Mean while declining from the Noon of Day,
The Sun obliquely shoots his burning Ray;   20
The hungry Judges soon the Sentence sign,
And Wretches hang that Jury-men may Dine;
The Merchant from th' *Exchange* returns in Peace,
And the long Labours of the *Toilette* cease—
Belinda now, whom Thirst of Fame invites,
Burns to encounter two adventrous Knights,
At *Ombre* singly to decide their Doom;
And swells her Breast with Conquests yet to come.
Strait the three Bands prepare in Arms to join,
Each Band the number of the Sacred Nine.°   30
Soon as she spreads her Hand, th' Aerial Guard
Descend, and sit on each important Card:
First *Ariel* perch'd upon a *Matadore*,°
Then each, according to the Rank they bore;
For *Sylphs*, yet mindful of their ancient Race,
Are, as when Women, wondrous fond of Place.

Behold, four *Kings* in Majesty rever'd,
With hoary Whiskers° and a forky Beard;
And four fair *Queens* whose hands sustain a Flow'r,
Th' expressive Emblem of their softer Pow'r;   40

Four *Knaves* in Garbs succinct,° a trusty Band,
Caps on their heads, and Halberds° in their hand;
And Particolour'd Troops, a shining Train,
Draw forth to Combat on the Velvet Plain.

The skilful Nymph reviews her Force with Care;
Let Spades be Trumps! she said, and Trumps they were.

Now move to War her Sable *Matadores*,
In Show like Leaders of the swarthy *Moors.*
Spadillio° first, unconquerable Lord!
Let off two captive Trumps, and swept the Board.   50
As many more *Manillio*° forc'd to yield,
And march'd a Victor from the verdant Field.
Him *Basto*° follow'd, but his Fate more hard
Gain'd but one Trump and one *Plebeian* Card.
With his broad Sabre next, a Chief in Years,
The hoary Majesty of *Spades* appears;
Puts forth one manly Leg, to sight reveal'd;
The rest his many-colour'd Robe conceal'd.
The Rebel-*Knave*, who dares his Prince engage,
Proves the just Victim of his Royal Rage.   60
Ev'n mighty *Pam*° that Kings and Queens o'erthrew,
And mow'd down Armies in the Fights of *Lu*,
Sad Chance of War! now, destitute of Aid,
Falls undistinguish'd by the Victor *Spade!*

Thus far both Armies to *Belinda* yield;
Now to the *Baron* Fate inclines the Field.
His warlike *Amazon* her Host invades,
Th' Imperial Consort of the Crown of *Spades.*
The *Club*'s black Tyrant first her Victim dy'd,
Spite of his haughty Mien, and barb'rous Pride: 70
What boots the Regal Circle on his Head,
His Giant Limbs in State unwieldy spread?
That long behind he trails his pompous Robe,
And of all Monarchs only grasps the Globe?

The *Baron* now his *Diamonds* pours apace;
Th' embroider'd *King* who shows but half his Face,
And his refulgent *Queen*, with Pow'rs combin'd,
Of broken Troops an easie Conquest find.
Clubs, Diamonds, Hearts, in wild Disorder seen,
With Throngs promiscuous strow the level Green.   80
Thus when dispers'd a routed Army runs,
Of *Asia*'s Troops, and *Africk*'s Sable Sons,
With like Confusion different Nations fly,
Of various Habit and of various Dye,

Canto III. **4. Hampton:** Hampton Court was a royal residence which in Queen Anne's time was associated as much with wits as with statesmen. **12. paid the Visit:** part of the daily routine of a fashionable lady. **30. the Sacred Nine:** the Muses; Pope is suggesting that the number of cards used in ombre has some significance. **33. Matadore:** In ombre the three cards of highest value are called matadores. **38. Whiskers:** mustache.

41. succinct: girded up. **42. Halberds:** weapons combining spear and battleaxe. **49. Spadillio:** the ace of spades. **51. Manillio:** the deuce of spades, which, when trumps are black, is the card second highest in value. **53. Basto:** the ace of clubs, the third highest card. **61. Pam:** the knave of clubs, which in the game of Loo, or Lu, took precedence even of the ace of trumps.

The pierc'd Battalions dis-united fall,
In Heaps on Heaps; one Fate o'erwhelms them all.

　The *Knave* of *Diamonds* tries his wily Arts,
And wins (oh shameful Chance!) the *Queen* of *Hearts*.
At this, the Blood the Virgin's Cheek forsook,
A livid Paleness spreads o'er all her Look;   90
She sees, and trembles at th' approaching Ill,
Just in the Jaws of Ruin, and *Codille*.°
And now, (as oft in some distemper'd State)
On one nice *Trick* depends the gen'ral Fate.
An *Ace* of Hearts steps forth: The *King* unseen
Lurk'd in her Hand, and mourn'd his captive *Queen*.
He springs to Vengeance with an eager pace,
And falls like Thunder on the prostrate *Ace*.
The Nymph exulting fills with Shouts the Sky,
The Walls, the Woods, and long Canals reply.   100

　Oh thoughtless Mortals! ever blind to Fate,
Too soon dejected, and too soon elate!
Sudden these Honours shall be snatch'd away,
And curs'd for ever this Victorious Day.

　For lo! the Board with Cups and Spoons is crown'd,
The Berries crackle, and the Mill turns round.°
On shining Altars of *Japan*° they raise
The silver Lamp; the fiery Spirits blaze.
From silver Spouts the grateful Liquors glide,
While *China*'s Earth receives the smoking Tyde.   110
At once they gratify their Scent and Taste,
And frequent Cups prolong the rich Repast.
Strait hover round the Fair her Airy Band;
Some, as she sip'd, the fuming Liquor fann'd,
Some o'er her Lap their careful Plumes display'd,
Trembling, and conscious of the rich Brocade.
Coffee, (which makes the Politician wise,
And see thro' all things with his half-shut Eyes)
Sent up in Vapours to the *Baron*'s Brain
New Stratagems, the radiant Lock to gain.   120
Ah cease rash Youth! desist ere 'tis too late,
Fear the just Gods, and think of *Scylla*'s Fate°!

Chang'd to a Bird, and sent to flit in Air,
She dearly pays for *Nisus*' injur'd Hair!

　But when to Mischief Mortals bend their Will,
How soon they find fit Instruments of Ill!
Just then, *Clarissa* drew with tempting Grace
A two-edg'd Weapon from her shining Case;
So Ladies in Romance assist their Knight,
Present the Spear, and arm him for the Fight.   130
He takes the Gift with rev'rence, and extends
The little Engine on his Fingers' Ends,
This just behind *Belinda*'s Neck he spread,
As o'er the fragrant Steams she bends her Head:
Swift to the Lock a thousand Sprights repair,
A thousand Wings, by turns, blow back the Hair,
And thrice they twitch'd the Diamond in her Ear,
Thrice she look'd back, and thrice the Foe drew near.
Just in that instant, anxious *Ariel* sought
The close Recesses of the Virgin's Thought;   140
As on the Nosegay in her Breast reclin'd,
He watch'd th' Ideas rising in her Mind,
Sudden he view'd, in spite of all her Art,
An Earthly Lover° lurking at her Heart.
Amaz'd, confus'd, he found his Pow'r expir'd,
Resign'd to Fate, and with a Sigh retir'd.

　The Peer now spreads the glitt'ring *Forfex* wide,
T' inclose the Lock; now joins it, to divide.
Ev'n then, before the fatal Engine clos'd,
A wretched *Sylph* too fondly interpos'd;   150
Fate urg'd the Sheers, and cut the *Sylph* in twain,
(But Airy Substance soon unites again)°
The meeting Points the sacred Hair dissever
From the fair Head, for ever and for ever!

　Then flash'd the living Lightning from her Eyes,
And Screams of Horror rend th' affrighted Skies.
Not louder Shrieks to pitying Heav'n are cast,
When Husbands or when Lap-dogs breathe their last,
Or when rich *China* Vessels, fal'n from high,
In glittring Dust and painted Fragments lie!   160

　Let Wreaths of Triumph now my Temples twine,
(The Victor cry'd) the glorious Prize is mine!
While Fish in Streams, or Birds delight in Air,
Or in a Coach and Six the *British* Fair,
As long as *Atalantis*° shall be read,
Or the small Pillow grace a Lady's Bed,

---

92. Codille: Whoever won more tricks than the principal player was said to have given him *codille*. **106. Berries . . . round:** Coffee beans ("Berries") crackle as they are ground. **107. Altars of Japan:** lacquered tables. **122. Scylla's Fate:** Scylla fell in love with Minos, who was besieging Megara, her father's kingdom. The safety of the kingdom depended on the preservation of a purple hair that grew on her father's head. Scylla plucked it out, but when she offered it to Minos, he was horrified at her impiety. After his victory, Minos sailed away. Scylla clung to his ship until her father, who had become a bird, beat her off. Then she too became a bird.

144. Earthly Lover: See the Dedicatory Epistle, p. 568. **152. But . . . again:** [Pope's note] *See* Milton, *lib. 6: of* Satan *cut asunder by the Angel* Michael. **165. Atalantis:** a libelous novel (1709) by Mary de la Rivière Manley (1672–1724), playwright and political pamphleteer.

While *Visits* shall be paid on solemn Days,
When numerous Wax-lights in bright Order blaze,
While Nymphs take Treats, or Assignations give,
So long my Honour, Name, and Praise shall live!   170
    What Time wou'd spare, from Steel receives its
        date,°
And Monuments, like Men, submit to Fate!
Steel cou'd the Labour of the Gods° destroy,
And strike to Dust th' Imperial Tow'rs of *Troy;*
Steel cou'd the Works of mortal Pride confound,
And hew Triumphal Arches to the Ground.
What Wonder then, fair Nymph! thy Hairs shou'd
    feel
The conqu'ring Force of unresisted Steel?

CANTO IV

BUT anxious Cares the pensive Nymph opprest,
And secret Passions labour'd in her Breast.
Not youthful Kings in Battel seiz'd alive,
Not scornful Virgins who their Charms survive,
Not ardent Lovers robb'd of all their Bliss,
Not ancient Ladies when refus'd a Kiss,
Not Tyrants fierce that unrepenting die,
Not *Cynthia* when her *Manteau's*° pinn'd awry,
E'er felt such Rage, Resentment and Despair,
As Thou, sad Virgin! for thy ravish'd Hair.   10
    For, that sad moment, when the *Sylphs* withdrew,
And *Ariel* weeping from *Belinda* flew,
Umbriel, a dusky melancholy Spright,
As ever sully'd the fair face of Light,
Down to the Central Earth, his proper Scene,
Repair'd to search the gloomy Cave of *Spleen.*°
    Swift on his sooty Pinions flitts the *Gnome,*
And in a Vapour° reach'd the dismal Dome.
No cheerful Breeze this sullen Region knows,
The dreaded *East* is all the Wind that blows.   20
Here, in a Grotto, sheltred close from Air,
And screen'd in Shades from Day's detested Glare,
She sighs for ever on her pensive Bed,
Pain at her Side, and *Megrim*° at her Head.

Two Handmaids wait the Throne: Alike in Place,
But diff'ring far in Figure and in Face.
Here stood *Ill-nature* like an *ancient Maid,*
Her wrinkled Form in *Black* and *White* array'd;
With store of Pray'rs, for Mornings, Nights, and
    Noons,
Her Hand is fill'd; her Bosom with Lampoons.   30
    There *Affectation* with a sickly Mien
Shows in her Cheek the Roses of Eighteen,
Practis'd to Lisp, and hang the Head aside,
Faints into Airs, and languishes with Pride;
On the rich Quilt sinks with becoming Woe,
Wrapt in a Gown, for Sickness, and for Show.
The Fair-ones feel such Maladies as these,
When each new Night-Dress gives a new Disease.
    A constant *Vapour* o'er the Palace flies;
Strange Phantoms rising as the Mists arise;   40
Dreadful, as Hermit's Dreams in haunted Shades,
Or bright as Visions of expiring Maids.
Now glaring Fiends, and Snakes on rolling Spires,°
Pale Spectres, gaping Tombs, and Purple Fires:
Now Lakes of liquid Gold, *Elysian* Scenes,
And Crystal Domes, and Angels in Machines.
    Unnumber'd Throngs on ev'ry side are seen
Of Bodies chang'd to various Forms° by *Spleen.*
Here living *Teapots* stand, one Arm held out,
One bent; the Handle this, and that the Spout: 50
A *Pipkin*° there like *Homer's Tripod* walks;
Here sighs a Jar, and there a Goose-pye° talks;
Men prove with Child, as pow'rful Fancy works,
And Maids turn'd Bottels, call aloud for Corks.
    Safe past the *Gnome* thro' this fantastick Band,
A Branch of healing *Spleenwort* in his hand.°
Then thus addrest the Pow'r—Hail wayward Queen!
Who rule the Sex to Fifty from Fifteen,
Parent of Vapors and of Female Wit,
Who give th' *Hysteric* or *Poetic* Fit,   60
On various Tempers act by various ways,
Make some take Physick, others scribble Plays;
Who cause the Proud their Visits to delay,
And send the Godly in a Pett, to pray.

---

171. date: end. 173. the Labour . . . Gods: The walls of
Troy were thought to have been built by the two gods
Apollo and Poseidon. *Canto IV.* 8. Manteau: a loose upper
garment. 16. Spleen: a new name for an old malady, the
melancholy or ill humor that befell rich people. 18. Vapour:
appropriately, because the spleen was also called the vapors.
24. Megrim: (migraine) a severe headache.

43. Spires: spirals. 48. chang'd . . . Forms: The medical
books of the time testify to splenetic patients' suffering
hallucinations such as those mentioned in lines 48–54. 51.
Pipkin: a small earthenware boiler. 52. Goose-pye: [Pope's
note] *Alludes to a real fact, a Lady of distinction imagin'd herself
in this condition.* 56. A Branch . . . hand: Aeneas passed
into Hades guarded by the golden bough he carried. Pope
changes it to the herb that was supposed to be good for
the spleen.

A Nymph there is, that all thy Pow'r disdains,
And thousands more in equal Mirth maintains.
But oh! if e'er thy *Gnome* could spoil a Grace,
Or raise a Pimple on a beauteous Face,
Like Citron-Waters° Matrons' Cheeks inflame,
Or change Complexions at a losing Game;   70
If e'er with airy Horns I planted Heads,
Or rumpled Petticoats, or tumbled Beds,
Or caus'd Suspicion when no Soul was rude,
Or discompos'd the Head-dress of a Prude,
Or e'er to costive Lap-Dog gave Disease,
Which not the Tears of brightest Eyes could ease:
Hear me, and touch *Belinda* with Chagrin;
That single Act gives half the World the Spleen.

   The Goddess with a discontented Air
Seems to reject him, tho' she grants his Pray'r.   80
A wondrous Bag with both her Hands she binds,
Like that where once *Ulysses* held the Winds;
There she collects the Force of Female Lungs,
Sighs, Sobs, and Passions, and the War of Tongues.
A Vial next she fills with fainting Fears,
Soft Sorrows, melting Griefs, and flowing Tears.
The *Gnome* rejoicing bears her Gifts away.
Spreads his black Wings, and slowly mounts to Day.

   Sunk in *Thalestris'* Arms the Nymph he found,
Her Eyes dejected and her Hair unbound.   90
Full o'er their Heads the swelling Bag he rent,
And all the Furies issued at the Vent.
Belinda burns with more than mortal Ire,
And fierce *Thalestris* fans the rising Fire.
O wretched Maid! she spread her Hands, and cry'd,
(While *Hampton's* Ecchos, wretched Maid! reply'd)
Was it for this you took such constant Care
The *Bodkin*,° *Comb*, and *Essence* to prepare;
For this your Locks in Paper-Durance bound,
For this with tort'ring Irons wreath'd around?   100
For this with Fillets strain'd your tender Head,
And bravely bore the double Loads of Lead?
Gods! shall the Ravisher display your Hair,
While the Fops envy, and the Ladies stare!
Honour forbid! at whose unrival'd Shrine
Ease, Pleasure, Virtue, All, our Sex resign.
Methinks already I your Tears survey,
Already hear the horrid things they say,
Already see you a degraded Toast,
And all your Honour in a Whisper lost!   110

How shall I, then, your helpless Fame defend?
'Twill then be Infamy to seem your Friend!
And shall this Prize, th' inestimable Prize,
Expos'd thro' Crystal to the gazing Eyes,
And heighten'd by the Diamond's circling Rays,°
On that Rapacious Hand for ever blaze?
Sooner shall Grass in *Hide*-Park *Circus* grow,
And Wits take Lodgings in the Sound of *Bow;*°
Sooner let Earth, Air, Sea, to *Chaos* fall,
Men, Monkies, Lap-dogs, Parrots, perish all!   120
   She said; then raging to *Sir Plume*° repairs,
And bids her *Beau* demand the precious Hairs:
(*Sir Plume*, of *Amber Snuff-box* justly vain,
And the nice Conduct° of a *clouded Cane*°)
With earnest Eyes, and round unthinking Face,
He first the Snuff-box open'd, then the Case,
And thus broke out—"My Lord, why, what the
      Devil?
"Z——ds!° damn the Lock! 'fore Gad, you must be
      civil!
"Plague on 't! 'tis past a Jest—nay prithee, Pox!
"Give her the Hair"—he spoke, and rapp'd his
      Box.   130
   It grieves me much (reply'd the Peer again)
Who speaks so well shou'd ever speak in vain.
But by this Lock, this sacred Lock I swear,
(Which never more shall join its parted Hair,
Which never more its Honours shall renew,
Clipt from the lovely Head where late it grew)
That while my Nostrils draw the vital Air,
This Hand, which won it, shall for ever wear.
He spoke, and speaking, in proud Triumph spread
The long-contended Honours of her Head.   140
   But *Umbriel*, hateful *Gnome!* forbears not so;
He breaks the Vial whence the Sorrows flow.
Then see! the *Nymph* in beauteous Grief appears,
Her Eyes half-languishing, half-drown'd in Tears;
On her heav'd Bosom hung her drooping Head,
Which, with a Sigh, she rais'd; and thus she said.
   For ever curs'd be this detested Day.
Which snatch'd my best, my fav'rite Curl away!
Happy! ah ten times happy, had I been,
If *Hampton-Court* these Eyes had never seen!   150

---

69. Citron-Waters: brandy distilled from lemon rind.
98. Bodkin: "an instrument to dress the hair" (Johnson's *Dictionary*).

114–15. Expos'd . . . Rays: She thinks that the Baron will have some of the hair mounted in a ring. **118. Bow:** a locality in the City; it was now wholly occupied by merchants. **121. Sir Plume:** Sir George Browne, a cousin of Arabella's mother. **124. nice Conduct:** skilled management. **a clouded Cane:** a cane fashionably veined with dark color. **128. Z——ds:** *zounds*, a corruption of *God's wounds*.

Yet am not I the first mistaken Maid,
By Love of *Courts* to num'rous Ills betray'd.
Oh had I rather un-admir'd remain'd
In some lone Isle, or distant *Northern* Land;
Where the gilt *Chariot* never marks the Way,
Where none learn *Ombre*, none e'er taste *Bohea*°!
There kept my Charms conceal'd from mortal Eye,
Like Roses that in Desarts bloom and die.
What mov'd my Mind with youthful Lords to rome?
O had I stay'd, and said my Pray'rs at home!   160
'Twas this, the Morning *Omens* seem'd to tell;
Thrice from my trembling hand the *Patch-box* fell;
The tott'ring *China* shook without a Wind,
Nay, *Poll*° sate mute, and *Shock* was most Unkind!
A *Sylph* too warn'd me of the Threats of Fate,
In mystic Visions, now believ'd too late!
See the poor Remnants of these slighted Hairs!
My hands shall rend what ev'n thy Rapine spares:
These, in two sable Ringlets taught to break,
Once gave new Beauties to the snowie Neck.   170
The Sister-Lock now sits uncouth, alone,
And in its Fellow's Fate foresees its own;
Uncurl'd it hangs, the fatal Sheers demands;
And tempts once more thy sacrilegious Hands.
Oh hadst thou, Cruel! been content to seize
Hairs less in sight, or any Hairs but these!

CANTO V

SHE said: the pitying Audience melt in Tears,
But *Fate* and *Jove* had stopp'd the *Baron's* Ears.
In vain *Thalestris* with Reproach assails,
For who can move when fair *Belinda* fails?
Not half so fixt the *Trojan* cou'd remain,
While *Anna* begg'd and *Dido* rag'd in vain.°
Then grave *Clarissa* graceful wav'd her Fan;
Silence ensu'd, and thus the Nymph began.
    Say,° why are Beauties prais'd and honour'd most,
The wise Man's Passion, and the vain Man's
        Toast?   10
Why deck'd with all that Land and Sea afford,
Why Angels call'd, and Angel-like ador'd?

Why round our Coaches crowd the white-glov'd
        Beaus,
Why bows the Side-box from its inmost Rows?
How vain are all these Glories, all our Pains,
Unless good Sense preserve what Beauty gains:
That Men may say, when we the Front-box grace,°
Behold the first in Virtue, as in Face!
Oh! if to dance all Night, and dress all Day,
Charm'd the Small-pox, or chas'd old Age away;   20
Who would not scorn what Huswife's Cares produce,
Or who would learn one earthly Thing of Use?
To patch, nay ogle, might become a Saint,
Nor could it sure be such a Sin to paint.
But since, alas! frail Beauty must decay,
Curl'd or uncurl'd, since Locks will turn to grey,
Since painted, or not painted, all shall fade,
And she who scorns a Man, must die a Maid;
What then remains, but well our Pow'r to use,
And keep good Humour still whate'er we lose?   30
And trust me, Dear! good Humour can prevail,
When Airs, and Flights, and Screams, and Scolding
        fail.
Beauties in vain their pretty Eyes may roll;
Charms strike the Sight, but Merit wins the Soul.
    So spoke the Dame, but no Applause ensu'd;
Belinda frown'd, *Thalestris* call'd her Prude.
To Arms, to Arms! the fierce Virago° cries,
And swift as Lightning to the Combate flies.
All side in Parties, and begin th' Attack;
Fans clap, Silks russle, and tough Whalebones crack;   40
Heroes' and Heroins' Shouts confus'dly rise,
And base, and treble Voices strike the Skies.
No common Weapons in their Hands are found,
Like Gods they fight, nor dread a mortal Wound.
    So when bold *Homer* makes the Gods engage,
And heav'nly Breasts with human Passions rage;
'Gainst *Pallas, Mars; Latona, Hermes* Arms;
And all *Olympus* rings with loud Alarms.
Jove's Thunder roars, Heav'n trembles all around;
Blue *Neptune* storms, the bellowing Deeps resound;   50
Earth shakes her nodding Tow'rs, the Ground gives
        way;
And the pale Ghosts start at the Flash of Day!
    Triumphant *Umbriel* on a Sconce's° Height
Clapt his glad Wings, and sate to view the Fight:

---

156. Bohea: a sort of tea. **164. Poll:** the parrot. *Canto V.*
5–6. Not . . . vain: See *Aeneid,* IV. 296–449. **9–34. Say**
. . . Soul: Pope introduced this speech in the edition of
1717 in order to "*open more clearly the* MORAL *of the Poem.*"
It is, he said, "*a parody of the speech of Sarpedon to Glaucus
in Homer* [*Iliad,* Book XII]."

14–17. Why . . . grace: Ladies preferred the front boxes
(those facing the stage) at the theater, and gentlemen the side
boxes; common citizens occupied the pit. **37. Virago:** "a
woman with the qualities of a man" (Johnson's *Dictionary*).
53. Sconce: "a pensile candlestick" (Johnson's *Dictionary*).

Propt on their Bodkin Spears, the Sprights survey
The growing Combat, or assist the Fray.
     While thro' the Press enrag'd *Thalestris* flies,
And scatters Death around from both her Eyes,
A *Beau* and *Witling* perish'd in the Throng,
One dy'd in *Metaphor*, and one in *Song*.   60
O cruel Nymph! a living Death I bear,
Cry'd *Dapperwit*, and sunk beside his Chair.
A mournful Glance Sir *Fopling* upwards cast,
Those Eyes are made so killing°—was his last:
Thus on *Meander's°* flow'ry Margin lies
Th' expiring Swan, and as he sings he dies.
     When bold Sir *Plume* had drawn *Clarissa* down,
Chloe stept in, and kill'd him with a Frown;
She smil'd to see the doughty Hero slain,
But at her Smile, the Beau reviv'd again.   70
     Now *Jove* suspends his golden Scales in Air,
Weighs the Men's Wits against the Lady's Hair;
The doubtful Beam long nods from side to side;
At length the Wits mount up, the Hairs subside.
     See fierce *Belinda* on the *Baron* flies,
With more than usual Lightning in her Eyes;
Nor fear'd the Chief th' unequal Fight to try,
Who sought no more than on his Foe to die.
But this bold Lord, with manly Strength indu'd,
She with one Finger and a Thumb subdu'd: 80
Just where the Breath of Life his Nostrils drew,
A Charge of *Snuff* the wily Virgin threw;
The *Gnomes* direct, to ev'ry Atome just,
The pungent Grains of titillating Dust.
Sudden, with starting Tears each Eye o'erflows,
And the high Dome re-ecchoes to his Nose.°
     Now meet thy Fate, incens'd *Belinda* cry'd,
And drew a deadly *Bodkin* from her Side.
(The same, his ancient Personage to deck,
Her great great Grandsire wore about his Neck   90
In three *Seal-Rings;* which after, melted down,
Form'd a vast *Buckle* for his Widow's Gown:
Her infant Grandame's *Whistle* next it grew,
The *Bells* she gingled, and the *Whistle* blew;
Then in a *Bodkin* grac'd her Mother's Hairs,
Which long she wore, and now *Belinda* wears.)
     Boast not my Fall (he cry'd) insulting Foe!
Thou by some other shalt be laid as low.

Nor think, to die dejects my lofty Mind;
All that I dread, is leaving you behind!   100
Rather than so, ah let me still survive,
And burn in *Cupid*'s Flames,—but burn alive.
     Restore the Lock! she cries; and all around
Restore the Lock! the vaulted Roofs rebound.
Not fierce *Othello* in so loud a Strain
Roar'd for the Handkerchief that caus'd his Pain.
But see how oft Ambitious Aims are cross'd,
And Chiefs contend 'till all the Prize is lost!
The Lock, obtain'd with Guilt, and kept with Pain,
In ev'ry place is sought, but sought in vain: 110
With such a Prize no Mortal must be blest,
So Heav'n decrees! with Heav'n who can contest?
     Some° thought it mounted to the Lunar Sphere,
Since all things lost on Earth, are treasur'd there.
There Heroes' Wits are kept in pondrous Vases,
And Beaus' in *Snuff-boxes* and *Tweezer-Cases.°*
There broken Vows, and Death-bed Alms are found,
And Lovers' Hearts with Ends of Riband bound;
The Courtier's Promises, and Sick Man's Pray'rs,
The Smiles of Harlots, and the Tears of Heirs,   120
Cages for Gnats, and Chains to Yoak a Flea;
Dry'd Butterflies, and Tomes of Casuistry.
     But trust the Muse—she saw it upward rise,
Tho' mark'd by none but quick Poetic Eyes:
(So *Rome*'s great Founder to the Heav'ns withdrew,
To *Proculus* alone confess'd in view.)°
A sudden Star, it shot thro' liquid Air,
And drew behind a radiant *Trail of Hair*.
Not *Berenice*'s Locks° first rose so bright,
The Heav'ns bespangling with dishevel'd Light.   130
The *Sylphs* behold it kindling as it flies,
And pleas'd pursue its Progress thro' the Skies.
     This the *Beau-monde* shall from the *Mall°* survey,
And hail with Musick its propitious Ray.
This, the blest Lover shall for *Venus* take,
And send up Vows from *Rosamonda*'s Lake.°

113–22. **Some . . . Casuistry:** Pope directs us to consult Ariosto's *Orlando Furioso* (1516–32), where Orlando's lost wits are sought for on the moon. He modernizes Ariosto's instances of lost wits. **116. Tweezer-Cases:** neatly made receptacles for holding miniature knives and so on. **125–26. So . . . view:** It was said that Romulus, who disappeared mysteriously, had been caught up into heaven. **129. Berenice's Locks:** Jupiter was supposed to have made a constellation of her hair which was stolen from the temple where she hung it as a votive offering after her husband returned victorious from the wars. **133. Mall:** a fashionable walk in St. James's Park. **136. Rosamonda's Lake:** an oblong pond in the same park.

64. Those . . . killing: an echo of a song from the opera *Camilla* by Marc Antonio Buononcini. **65. Meander:** a celebrated winding river in Asia Minor. **85–86. Sudden . . . Nose:** The Baron's sneeze cancels the boast he made at iv. 133–38.

This *Partridge*° soon shall view in cloudless Skies,
When next he looks thro' *Galilæo's*° Eyes;
And hence th' Egregious Wizard shall foredoom
The Fate of *Louis*, and the Fall of *Rome*.   140
    Then cease, bright Nymph! to mourn thy ravish'd
        Hair
Which adds new Glory to the shining Sphere!
Not all the Tresses that fair Head can boast
Shall draw such Envy as the Lock you lost.
For, after all the Murders of your Eye,
When, after Millions slain, your self shall die;
When those fair Suns shall sett, as sett they must,
And all those Tresses shall be laid in Dust;
This Lock, the Muse shall consecrate to Fame,
And mid'st the Stars inscribe *Belinda*'s Name!   150

FROM

THE GUARDIAN

NO. 173

The text is that of the first printing (1713) and includes
Pope's translation of Homer's account of the gardens of
Alcinoüs, which was dropped when the piece was
reprinted in *Prose Works* (1741).

Tuesday, 29th September, 1713.

    ———Nec sera comantem
Narcissum, aut flexi tacuissem Vimen Acanthi,
Pallentesque hæderas, et amantes littora myrtos.[1]
                      VIRG.

---

137. Partridge: [Pope's note] *John Partridge was a ridiculous
Star-gazer, who in his Almanacks every year, never fail'd to
predict the downfall of the Pope, and the King of* France, *then at
war with the* English. **138. Galilæo:** His improvement of
the telescope inaugurated a new phase in astronomy.
THE GUARDIAN: *Number 173.* **1. Nec . . . myrtos:** "The late
Narcissus, and the winding Trail / Of Bears-foot, Myrtles
green, and Ivy pale" (Virgil, *Georgics*, IV. 122–24 [Dryden's
translation, IV. 184–85]). These lines occur just before the
description of the old Corycian's garden, which Pope
mentions below.

I lately took a particular Friend of mine to my
House in the Country, not without some Apprehension that it could afford little Entertainment to a Man
of his Polite Taste, particularly in Architecture and
Gardening, who had so long been conversant with all
that is beautiful and great in either. But it was a
pleasant Surprize to me, to hear him often declare, he
had found in my little Retirement that Beauty which
he always thought wanting in the most celebrated
Seats, or if you will Villa's, of the Nation. This he
described to me in those Verses with which *Martial*
begins one of his Epigrams:

> *Baiana nostri Villa, Basse, Faustini,*
> *Non otiosis ordinata myrtetis,*
> *Viduaque platano, tonsilique buxeto,*
> *Ingrata lati spatia detinet campi,*
> *Sed rure vero, barbaroque lætatur.*[2]

    There is certainly something in the amiable Simpli-
city of unadorned Nature, that spreads over the Mind
a more noble Sort of Tranquility, and a loftier Sensation of Pleasure, than can be raised from the nicer
Scenes of Art.

    This was the Taste of the Ancients in their Gardens,
as we may discover from the Descriptions [that] are
extant of them. The two most celebrated Wits[3] of the
World have each of them left us a particular Picture
of a Garden; wherein those great Masters, being
wholly unconfined, and Painting at Pleasure, may be
thought to have given a full Idea of what they esteemed
most excellent in this way. These (one may observe)
consist intirely of the useful Part of Horticulture, Fruit
Trees, Herbs, Water, &c. The Pieces I am speaking of
are *Virgil*'s Account of the Garden of the old *Corycian*,
and *Homer*'s of that of *Alcinous*. The first of these is
already known to the *English* Reader, by the excellent
Versions of Mr. *Dryden* and Mr. *Addison*. The other
having never been attempted in our Language with
any Elegance, and being the most beautiful Plan of
this sort that can be imagined, I shall here present the
Reader with a Translation of it.

---

2. Baiana . . . lætatur: Martial, *Epigrams*, III. lviii. In his
Epigrams of Martial, Englished (1695), Henry Killigrew
translated these lines under the title *To Bassus, on Faustinus
Farm:*

> Faustinus Farm, O Bassus! is not fraught
> With Idle Myrtles, into Order brought;
> There no trim'd Box, or barren Plane Tree's found,
> To fill a vast unprofitable Ground:
> But happy 'tis in rude and fertile Fields.

3. Wits: intellectuals, writers.

The Gardens of *Alcinous*, from *Homer's Odyss. 7.*

Close to the Gates a spacious Garden lies,
From Storms defended and inclement Skies:
Four Acres was th' allotted Space of Ground,
Fenc'd with a green Enclosure all around.
Tall thriving Trees confest the fruitful Mold;
The red'ning Apple ripens here to Gold,
Here the blue Figg with luscious Juice o'erflows,
With deeper Red the full Pomegranate glows,
The Branch here bends beneath the weighty Pear,
And verdant Olives flourish round the Year.
The balmy Spirit of the Western Gale
Eternal breathes on Fruits untaught to fail:
Each dropping Pear a following Pear supplies,
On Apples Apples, Figs on Figs arise:
The same mild Season gives the Blooms to blow,
The Buds to harden, and the Fruits to grow.

Here order'd Vines in equal Ranks appear
With all th' United Labours of the Year,
Some to unload the fertile Branches run,
Some dry the black'ning Clusters in the Sun,
Others to tread the liquid Harvest join,
The groaning Presses foam with Floods of Wine.
Here are the Vines in early Flow'r descry'd,)
Here Grapes discolour'd on the sunny Side,   }
And there in Autumn's richest Purple dy'd.   )

Beds of all various Herbs, for ever green,
In beauteous Order terminate the Scene.

Two plenteous Fountains the whole Prospect crowned;
This thro' the Gardens leads its Streams around,
Visits each Plant, and waters all the Ground:
While that in Pipes beneath the Palace flows,
And thence its Current on the Town bestows;
To various Use their various Streams they bring,
The People one, and one supplies the King.

Sir *William Temple* has remark'd,[4] that this Description contains all the justest Rules and Provisions which can go toward composing the best Gardens. Its Extent was four *Acres*, which, in those times of Simplicity, was look'd upon as a large one, even for a Prince: It was inclos'd all round for Defence; and for Conveniency join'd close to the Gates of the Palace.

He mentions next the Trees, which were Standards,[5] and suffered to grow to their full height. The fine Description of the Fruits that never failed, and the eternal Zephyrs, is only a more noble and poetical way of expressing the continual Succession of one Fruit after another throughout the Year.

The *Vineyard* seems to have been a Plantation distinct from the Garden; as also the *Beds of Greens* mentioned afterwards at the Extremity of the Inclosure, in the Nature and usual Place of our *Kitchen Gardens.*

The two Fountains are disposed very remarkably. They rose within the Inclosure, and were brought by Conduits or Ducts, one of them to water all Parts of the Gardens, and the other underneath the Palace into the Town, for the Service of the Publick.

How contrary to this Simplicity is the modern Practice of Gardening; we seem to make it our Study to recede from Nature, not only in the various Tonsure of Greens into the most regular and formal Shapes, but even in monstrous Attempts beyond the reach of the Art it self: We run into Sculpture, and are yet better pleas'd to have our Trees in the most awkward Figures of Men and Animals, than in the most regular of their own.

Hinc & nexilibus videas e frondibus hortos,
Implexos late muros, & Mœnia circum
Porrigere, & latas e ramis surgere turres;
Deflexam & Myrtum in Puppes, atque ærea rostra:
In buxisque undare fretum, atque e rore rudentes.
Parte alia frondere suis tentoria Castris;
Scutaque spiculaque & jaculantia citria Vallos.[6]

I believe it is no wrong Observation[7] that Persons of Genius, and those who are most capable of Art, are always most fond of Nature, as such are chiefly sensible, that all Art consists in the Imitation and Study of Nature. On the contrary, People of the common Level of Understanding are principally delighted with the little Niceties and Fantastical Operations of Art, and constantly think that *finest* which is least Natural. A citizen is no sooner Proprieter of a couple of Yews, but he entertains Thoughts of erecting them into

---

4. remark'd: in his *Essay upon the Gardens of Epicurus.* **5. Standards:** trees sprung from a stump left standing when a copse is cut down.

6. Hinc . . . Vallos: The source of this quotation is unknown; it is probably from a Renaissance poem. A translation would read: "Hence you can see gardens of intertwined boughs stretching far and wide their plaited walls and ramparts all around, and wide towers of branches rising aloft, and myrtle bushes bent into ships with copper prows, and box hedges that form a billowing sea with cables of rosemary; in another part [you can see] tents making their own leafy camp, with shields and spear points and gourds shooting forth a palisade." **7. no . . . Observation:** the answer to those benighted critics who thought Milton—and Pope—blind to the external world.

Giants,[8] like those of *Guild-hall*.[9] I know an eminent Cook, who beautified his Country Seat with a Coronation Dinner in Greens, where you see the Champion[10] flourishing on Horseback at one end of the Table, and the Queen in perpetual Youth at the other.

For the benefit of all my loving Countrymen of this curious Taste, I shall here publish a Catalogue of Greens to be disposed of by an eminent Town-Gardiner, who has lately applied to me upon this Head. He represents, that for the Advancement of a politer sort of Ornament in the Villa's and Gardens adjacent to this great City, and in order to distinguish those Places from the meer barbarous Countries of gross Nature, the World stands much in need of a Virtuoso[11] Gardiner who has a Turn to Sculpture, and is thereby capable of improving upon the Ancients of his Profession in the Imagery of Evergreens. My Correspondent is arrived to such Perfection, that he cuts Family Pieces of Men, Women or Children. Any Ladies that please may have their own Effigies in Myrtle, or their Husbands in Hornbeam. He is a Puritan[12] Wag, and never fails, when he shows his Garden, to repeat that Passage in the Psalms, *Thy Wife shall be as the fruitful Vine, and thy Children as Olive Branches round thy Table.* I shall proceed to his Catalogue, as he sent it for my Recommendation.

Adam and *Eve* in Yew; *Adam* a little shatter'd by the fall of the Tree of Knowledge in the great Storm; *Eve* and the Serpent very flourishing.

The tower of *Babel*, not yet finished.

St. *George* in Box; his Arm scarce long enough, but will be in a Condition to stick[13] the Dragon by next *April.*

A *green Dragon* of the same, with a Tail of Ground Ivy for the present.

N.B. *These two not to be Sold separately.*

Edward the *Black Prince* in Cypress.

A *Laurustine*[14] Bear in Blossom, with a Juniper Hunter in Berries.

A Pair of Giants, *stunted*, to be sold cheap.

A Queen *Elizabeth* in Phylyræa, a little inclining to the Green Sickness, but of full growth.

Another Queen *Elizabeth* in Myrtle, which was very forward, but Miscarried by being too near a Savine.[15]

An old Maid of Honour in Wormwood.

A topping[16] *Ben Johnson* in Lawrel.

Divers eminent Modern Poets in Bays, somewhat blighted, to be disposed of a Pennyworth.

A Quick-set[17] Hog shot up into a Porcupine, by its being forgot a Week in rainy Weather.

A Lavender Pigg with Sage growing in his Belly.

Noah's Ark in Holly, standing on the Mount; the Ribs a little damaged for want of Water.

A Pair of *Maidenheads*[18] in Firr, in great forwardness.[19]

WINDSOR-FOREST

To the Right Honourable
GEORGE Lord *LANSDOWN.*°

Pope chose as an epigraph for *Windsor-Forest* (1713) a quotation from Virgil's sixth eclogue, in which the poet apologizes for turning to pastoral poetry instead of celebrating his friend Varus, a soldier, in appropriately martial verse. After this graceful bow however, Virgil proceeded to write not a mere pretty pastoral but a poem on lofty themes: the formation of the world from the four elements, the separation of land from water (to which Pope alludes in line 12) and sky from earth, and the dawn of life. In the nineteenth century such a subject for a country poem would seem strange indeed, but in Pope's day the tradition of Roman country poetry, in which nature provided a context for a discussion of human, and often historic and noble, themes, was still very much alive. In keeping with this tradition, Pope transforms Windsor Forest into a microcosm. There he sees men pursuing both the active life—

---

8. **Giants:** "Facing the entrance are two tremendous figures, by some named *Gog* and *Magog;* by Stow [the Elizabethan historian], an antient *Briton* and *Saxon.* I leave to others the important decision" (Thomas Pennant, *Some Account of London* [1791]). 9. **Guild-hall:** the town hall of the City of London. 10. **the Champion:** The champion of the king, or queen, of England used to ride armed into Westminster Hall on the occasion of a coronation, challenging anyone who disputed the sovereign's title. 11. **Virtuoso:** learned, skilled as a collector of natural curiosities; here, as often, used in the depreciatory sense of dilettantish. 12. **Puritan:** and therefore devoted to the Scriptures. 13. **stick:** stab with a sword (but a sword of "stick," i.e., wood).

14. **Laurustine:** a European shrub widely cultivated for its evergreen leaves and fragrant flowers. 15. **Savine:** a small, bushy evergreen shrub. 16. **topping:** very high. 17. **Quick-set:** formed out of living plants. 18. **Maidenheads:** probably in the sense of a bust of the Virgin Mary, but punningly. 19. **forwardness:** advancement toward maturity. WINDSOR-FOREST. **Lansdown:** George Granville (1667–1735), Baron Lansdowne, poet and playwright.

Windsor Forest was the hunting ground of monarchs —and the contemplative—it was considered a haven of the Muses. For him the land bears witness to England's history, to times of peace and times of conflict. Pope concludes the poem with a bright picture of peace and prosperity for England.

Windsor-Forest was written in parts, over a period of perhaps ten years. It was first published in 1713, at Lansdowne's request, to celebrate the Peace of Utrecht. The text is that of the first edition, corrected in accordance with Pope's revisions.

❦❦

Non inussa cano: Te nostræ, Vare, Myricæ
Te Nemus omne canet; nec Phœbo gratior ulla est
Quam sibi quæ Vari præscripsit Pagina nomen?
                                          VIRG.

THY Forests, *Windsor!* and thy green Retreats,
At once the Monarch's and the Muse's Seats,°
Invite my Lays. Be present, Sylvan Maids°!
Unlock your Springs, and open all your Shades.
Granville commands: Your Aid O Muses bring!
What Muse for *Granville* can refuse to sing?

The Groves of *Eden*, vanish'd now so long,
Live in Description,° and look green in Song:°
These, were my Breast inspir'd with equal Flame,
Like them in Beauty, should be like in Fame.   10
Here Hills and Vales, the Woodland and the Plain,
Here Earth and Water seem to strive again,
Not *Chaos*-like together crush'd and bruis'd,
But as the World, harmoniously confus'd:
Where Order in Variety we see,
And where, tho' all things differ, all agree.
Here waving Groves a checquer'd Scene display,
And part admit and part exclude the Day;
As some coy Nymph her Lover's warm Address
Nor quite indulges, nor can quite repress.   20

There, interspers'd in Lawns and opening Glades,
Thin Trees arise that shun each others Shades.
Here in full Light the russet Plains extend;
There wrapt in Clouds the blueish Hills ascend:
Ev'n the wild Heath displays her Purple Dies,
And 'midst the Desart fruitful Fields arise,
That crown'd with tufted Trees° and springing Corn,
Like verdant Isles the sable Waste adorn.
Let *India* boast her Plants, nor envy we
The weeping Amber or the balmy Tree,   30
While by our Oaks° the precious Loads are born,°
And Realms commanded which those Trees adorn.
Not proud *Olympus* yields a nobler Sight,
Tho' Gods assembled grace his tow'ring Height,
Than what more humble Mountains offer here,
Where, in their Blessings, all those Gods appear.
See *Pan* with Flocks, with Fruits *Pomona* crown'd,
Here blushing *Flora* paints th' enamel'd° Ground,
Here *Ceres*' Gifts in waving Prospect stand,
And nodding tempt the joyful Reaper's Hand,   40
Rich Industry sits smiling on the Plains,
And Peace and Plenty tell, a STUART° reigns.

Not° thus the Land appear'd in Ages past,
A dreary Desart and a gloomy Waste,
To Savage Beasts and Savage Laws° a Prey,
And Kings more furious and severe than they:
Who claim'd the Skies, dispeopled° Air and Floods,
The lonely Lords of empty Wilds and Woods.
Cities laid waste, they storm'd the Dens and Caves
(For wiser Brutes were backward to be Slaves)   50
What could be free, when lawless Beasts obey'd,
And ev'n the Elements° a Tyrant sway'd?
In vain kind Seasons swell'd the teeming Grain,
Soft Show'rs distill'd, and Suns grew warm in vain;
The Swain with Tears his frustrate Labour yields,
And famish'd dies amidst his ripen'd Fields.

Non . . . nomen: "I was venturing from my pastoral into epic poetry when Apollo, god of poesy, warned me back. It will be a rural poem, then, that I shall present to you, Varus, my soldier friend. But even a rural poem can bestow a lasting fame" (Virgil, *Eclogues*, vi. 9–12). **2. the Monarch's . . . Seats:** Windsor Forest had long been the seat of monarchs, at least from Norman and perhaps from earlier times. Arthur is supposed to have founded his court of the Round Table here. It was also considered home of the Muses, for Denham and Cowley had lived nearby (see ll. 261 ff.). **3. Sylvan Maids:** nymphs—dryads and naiads. **8. Description:** in Genesis and elsewhere. **Song:** *Paradise Lost.*

27. tufted Trees: trees in a clump. Milton had used the phrase in *L'Allegro* (1632). **31. Oaks:** "hearts of oaks," ships of the merchant navy. **born:** borne. **38. enamel'd:** This complimentary metaphor, derived from exquisite enamel work on metal, had been used of external nature since the mid-seventeenth century. **42. a Stuart:** Queen Anne (1702–14). **43–86. Not . . . rise:** Lines 43–86 refer to the use of the New Forest (not Windsor Forest) as a game preserve by the Norman kings and, especially, by William I. **45. Savage Laws:** [Pope's note] The Forest Laws. [These prescribed savage punishment for the killing of game.] **47. dispeopled:** The nonhuman inhabitants of earth, air, and water were often called people, e.g., "the feathered people." **52. Elements:** See l. 47. Pope's exaggeration shows his anger.

What wonder then, a Beast or Subject slain
Were equal Crimes in a Despotick Reign;
Both doom'd alike for sportive Tyrants bled,
But while the Subject starv'd the Beast was fed.   60
Proud *Nimrod*° first the bloody Chace began,
A mighty Hunter, and his Prey was Man.
Our haughty *Norman* boasts that barb'rous Name,
And makes his trembling Slaves the Royal Game.
The Fields are ravish'd from th' industrious Swains,
From Men their Cities, and from Gods their Fanes:°
The levell'd Towns with Weeds lie cover'd o'er,
The hollow Winds thro' naked Temples roar;
Round broken Columns clasping Ivy twin'd;
O'er Heaps of Ruins stalk'd the stately Hind;   70
The Fox obscene to gaping Tombs retires,
And savage Howlings fill the sacred Quires.°
Aw'd by his Nobles, by his Commons curst,
Th' Oppressor rul'd Tyrannick where he *durst*,
Stretch'd o'er the Poor, and Church, his Iron Rod,
And serv'd alike his Vassals and his God.
Whom ev'n the *Saxon* spar'd, and bloody *Dane*,
The wanton Victims of his *Sport* remain.
But see the Man who spacious Regions gave
A Waste for Beasts, himself deny'd a Grave°!   80
Stretch'd on the Lawn his second Hope° survey,
At once the Chaser and at once the Prey.
Lo *Rufus*, tugging at the deadly Dart,
Bleeds in the Forest, like a wounded Hart.°
Succeeding Monarchs heard the Subjects Cries,
Nor saw displeas'd the peaceful Cottage rise.
Then gath'ring Flocks on unknown° Mountains fed,
O'er sandy Wilds were yellow Harvests spread,
The Forests wonder'd at th' unusual Grain,
And secret Transport touch'd the conscious°
            Swain.   90
Fair *Liberty*, *Britannia's* Goddess, rears
Her chearful Head, and leads the golden Years.

Ye vig'rous Swains! while Youth ferments your
            Blood,
And purer Spirits° swell the sprightly Flood,
Now range the Hills, the gameful Woods beset,
Wind the shrill Horn, or spread the waving Net.
When milder Autumn Summer's Heat succeeds,
And in the new-shorn Field the Partridge feeds,
Before his Lord the ready Spaniel bounds,
Panting with Hope, he tries the furrow'd Grounds,   100
But when the tainted° Gales the Game betray,
Couch'd close he lyes, and meditates the Prey;
Secure they trust th' unfaithful Field, beset,
Till hov'ring o'er 'em sweeps the swelling Net.
Thus (if small Things we may with great compare)
When *Albion* sends her eager Sons to War,
Some thoughtless Town, with Ease and Plenty blest,
Near, and more near, the closing Lines invest;
Sudden they seize th' amaz'd, defenceless Prize
And high in Air *Britannia's* Standard flies.   110

See! from the Brake° the whirring Pheasant springs,
And mounts exulting on triumphant Wings;
Short is his Joy! he feels the fiery Wound,
Flutters in Blood, and panting beats the Ground.
Ah! what avail his glossie, varying Dyes,
His Purple Crest, and Scarlet-circled Eyes,
The vivid Green his shining Plumes unfold;
His painted Wings, and Breast that flames with Gold?

Nor yet, when moist *Arcturus*° clouds the Sky,
The Woods and Fields their pleasing Toils deny.   120
To Plains with well-breath'd Beagles we repair,
And trace the Mazes of the circling Hare.
(Beasts, urg'd by us, their Fellow Beasts pursue,
And learn of Man each other to undo.)°
With slaught'ring Guns th' unwery'd Fowler roves,
When Frosts have whiten'd all the naked Groves;
Where Doves in Flocks the leafless Trees o'ershade,
And lonely Woodcocks haunt the watry Glade.
He lifts the Tube, and levels with his Eye;
Strait a short Thunder breaks the frozen Sky.   130
Oft, as in Airy Rings they skim the Heath,
The clam'rous Lapwings feel the Leaden Death:

---

61. Nimrod: "A mighty one in the earth" and "a mighty hunter before the Lord" (Gen. 10:8–9), he is traditionally thought of also as a tyrant. **66. Fanes:** temples. **72. Quires:** choirs. **80. deny'd a Grave:** According to William of Malmesbury, a certain knight, at the funeral of William I, claimed that the land belonged to him and disputed the King's right of burial in it. **81. second Hope:** [Pope's note] *Richard*, second Son of *William* the Conqueror. [Pope later thought he meant rather William Rufus.] **83–84. Rufus . . . Hart:** William Rufus (William II) was shot accidentally with an arrow while hunting in the New Forest. **87. unknown:** because hitherto forbidden to them. **90. conscious:** in a slightly new sense, "well aware."

94. Spirits: animal spirits. **101. tainted:** carrying the scent of an animal. **111. Brake:** thicket. **119. Arcturus:** one of the stars of the Great Bear, or sometimes the constellation itself. The Ancients thought the weather was stormy during the few days in September when Arcturus rose at the same time as the sun. **123–24. Beasts . . . undo:** Swift knew better: "Big fleas have little fleas . . . ."

Oft as the mounting Larks their Notes prepare,
They fall, and leave their little Lives in Air.

In genial Spring, beneath the quiv'ring Shade
Where cooling Vapours breathe along the Mead,
The patient Fisher takes his silent Stand
Intent, his Angle trembling in his Hand;
With Looks unmov'd, he hopes the Scaly Breed,
And eyes the dancing Cork and bending Reed.   140
Our plenteous Streams a various Race supply;
The bright-ey'd Perch with Fins of *Tyrian* Dye,
The silver Eel, in shining Volumes roll'd,
The yellow Carp, in Scales bedrop'd with Gold,
Swift Trouts, diversify'd with Crimson Stains,
And Pykes, the Tyrants of the watry Plains.

Now *Cancer* glows with *Phœbus'* fiery Car;°
The Youth rush eager to the Sylvan War;
Swarm o'er the Lawns, the Forest Walks surround,
Rowze the fleet Hart, and chear the opening°
     Hound.   150
Th' impatient Courser pants in ev'ry Vein,
And pawing, seems to beat the distant Plain,
Hills, Vales, and Floods appear already crost,
And ere he starts, a thousand Steps are lost.
See! the bold Youth strain up the threatning Steep,
Rush thro' the Thickets, down the Vallies sweep,
Hang o'er their Coursers Heads with eager Speed,
And Earth rolls back beneath the flying Steed.
Let old *Arcadia* boast her ample Plain,
Th' Immortal Huntress, and her Virgin Train;   160
Nor envy *Windsor!* since thy Shades have seen
As bright a Goddess, and as chast a Queen;°
Whose Care, like hers, protects the Sylvan Reign,°
The Earth's fair Light, and Empress of the Main.°

Here, too, 'tis sung, of old *Diana* stray'd,
And *Cynthus'*° Top forsook for *Windsor* Shade;
Here was she seen o'er Airy Wastes to rove,
Seek the clear Spring, or haunt the pathless Grove;
Here arm'd with Silver Bows, in early Dawn,
Her buskin'd Virgins trac'd the Dewy Lawn.   170

Above the rest a rural Nymph was fam'd,
Thy Offspring, *Thames!* the fair *Lodona* nam'd,
(*Lodona's* Fate, in long Oblivion cast,
The Muse shall sing, and what she sings shall last)
Scarce could the Goddess from her Nymph be
     known,
But by the Crescent° and the golden Zone,°
She scorn'd the Praise of Beauty, and the Care;
A Belt her Waste, a Fillet binds her Hair,
A painted Quiver on her Shoulder sounds,
And with her Dart the flying Deer she wounds.   180
It chanc'd, as eager of the Chace the Maid
Beyond the Forest's verdant Limits stray'd,
Pan saw and lov'd, and burning with Desire
Pursu'd her Flight; her Flight increas'd his Fire.
Not half so swift the trembling Doves can fly,
When the fierce Eagle cleaves the liquid° Sky;
Not half so swiftly the fierce Eagle moves,
When thro' the Clouds he drives the trembling Doves;
As from the God she flew with furious Pace,
Or as the God more furious urg'd the Chace.   190
Now fainting, sinking, pale, the Nymph appears;
Now close behind his sounding Steps she hears;
And now his Shadow reach'd her as she run,
(His Shadow lengthen'd by the setting Sun)
And now his shorter Breath with sultry Air
Pants on her Neck, and fans her parting Hair.
In vain on Father *Thames* she calls for Aid,
Nor could *Diana* help her injur'd Maid.
Faint, breathless, thus she pray'd, nor pray'd in vain;
"Ah *Cynthia!* ah—tho' banish'd from thy Train,   200
Let me, O let me, to the Shades repair,
My native Shades—there weep, and murmur there."
She said, and melting as in Tears she lay,
In a soft, silver Stream dissolv'd away.
The silver Stream her Virgin Coldness keeps,
For ever murmurs, and for ever weeps;
Still bears the Name the hapless Virgin bore,
And bathes the Forest where she rang'd before.
In her chast Current oft the Goddess laves,
And with Celestial Tears augments the Waves.   210
Oft in her Glass the musing Shepherd spies
The headlong Mountains and the downward Skies,
The watry Landskip of the pendant Woods,
And absent Trees that tremble in the Floods;
In the clear azure Gleam the Flocks are seen,

---

147. Now . . . Car: The sun enters the sign of the Crab (June 22). **150. opening:** beginning to cry in pursuit of a scent. **162. Queen:** Queen Anne. **163. Whose . . . Reign:** Queen Anne used to follow the hounds in a chaise which she drove herself. **164. Empress . . . Main:** Queen Anne bears another resemblance to Diana: Britannia ruled the seas, and Diana, goddess of the moon, controlled the tides. **166. Cynthus:** Diana is supposed to have been born on Mount Cynthus.

176. the Crescent: the crescent moon, her emblem. **Zone:** girdle. **186. liquid:** clear as liquid.

And floating Forests paint the Waves with Green.
Thro' the fair Scene rowl slow the lingring Streams,
Then foaming pour along, and rush into the *Thames*.

Thou too, great Father° of the *British* Floods!
With joyful Pride survey'st our lofty Woods,   220
Where tow'ring Oaks° their growing Honours rear,
And future Navies on thy Shores appear.
Not *Neptune*'s self from all his Streams receives
A wealthier Tribute, than to thine he gives.
No Seas so rich, so gay no Banks appear,
No Lake so gentle, and no Spring so clear.
Nor *Po* so swells the fabling Poet's Lays,
While led along the Skies his Current strays,°
Than thine, which visits *Windsor*'s fam'd Abodes,
To grace the Mansion of our earthly Gods.   230
Nor all his Stars above a Lustre show,
Like the bright Beauties on thy Banks below:
Where *Jove*, subdu'd by mortal Passion still,
Might change *Olympus* for a nobler Hill.

Happy the Man whom this bright Court approves,
His Sov'reign favours, and his Country loves;
Happy next him who to these Shades retires,
Whom Nature charms, and whom the Muse inspires,
Whom humbler Joys of home-felt Quiet please,
Successive Study, Exercise and Ease.   240
He gathers Health from Herbs the Forest yields,
And of their fragrant Physick spoils° the Fields:
With Chymic Art° exalts° the Min'ral Pow'rs,
And draws° the Aromatick Souls of Flow'rs.
Now marks the Course of rolling Orbs on high;
O'er figur'd Worlds° now travels with his Eye.
Of ancient Writ unlocks the learned Store,
Consults the Dead, and lives past Ages o'er.
Or wandring thoughtful in the silent Wood,
Attends the Duties of the Wise and Good,   250
T' observe a Mean, be to himself a Friend,
To follow Nature, and regard his End.
Or looks on Heav'n with more than mortal Eyes,
Bids his free Soul expatiate in the Skies,
Amid her Kindred Stars familiar roam,
Survey the Region, and confess her Home!

Such was the Life great *Scipio*° once admir'd,
Thus *Atticus*,° and *Trumbal*° thus retir'd.

Ye sacred Nine! that all my Soul possess,
Whose Raptures fire me, and whose Visions bless,   260
Bear me, oh bear me to sequester'd Scenes,
The Bow'ry Mazes and surrounding Greens;
To *Thames*'s Banks which fragrant Breezes fill,
Or where ye Muses sport on *Cooper*'s Hill.
(On *Cooper*'s Hill eternal Wreaths shall grow,°
While lasts the Mountain, or while *Thames* shall flow)
I seem thro' consecrated Walks to rove,
And hear soft Musick dye along the Grove;
Led by the Sound I roam from Shade to Shade,
By God-like Poets Venerable made: 270
Here his first Lays° Majestick° *Denham* sung;
There the last Numbers flow'd from *Cowley*'s
          Tongue.°
O early lost!° what Tears the River shed
When the sad Pomp along his Banks was led?
His drooping Swans on ev'ry Note expire,
And on his Willows hung each Muse's Lyre.

Since Fate relentless stop'd their Heav'nly Voice,
No more the Forests ring, or Groves rejoice;
Who now shall charm the Shades where *Cowley* strung
His living Harp, and lofty *Denham* sung?   280
But hark! the Groves rejoice, the Forest rings!
Are these reviv'd? or is it *Granville* sings?

'Tis yours, my Lord, to bless our soft Retreats,
And call the Muses to their ancient Seats,
To paint anew the flow'ry Sylvan Scenes,
To crown the Forests with Immortal Greens,
Make *Windsor* Hills in lofty Numbers rise,
And lift her Turrets nearer to the Skies;

---

219. **great Father:** the Thames. **221. Oaks:** Cf. l. 31 and
note. **227–28. Nor . . . strays:** The constellation Eridanus
has the shape of a winding river; both Virgil and Ovid gave
this name to the Po River in Italy. **242. spoils:** despoils.
243. Chymic Art: the art of the chemist. **exalts:** refines,
intensifies. **244. draws:** draws up, as in a distillery. **246.
figur'd Worlds:** a globe on which the earth is represented.

257. **Scipio:** Scipio Africanus (*c.* 236–*c.* 183 B.C.), the Roman
general who defeated Hannibal in 202 B.C. After his victory
he lived quietly in Rome before again becoming involved in
public affairs. Ultimately he retired to his country estate.
258. **Atticus:** Titus Pomponius (109–32 B.C.), friend and
correspondent of Cicero; known as Atticus because of his
long and studious sojourn in Athens. **Trumbal:** Sir William
Trumbull, Pope's aged friend. **265. eternal . . . grow:**
because of Denham's poem *Cooper's Hill* (see Part Three).
271. **his . . . Lays:** Before the outbreak of the Civil War,
Denham lived at Egham near Windsor. **Majestick:** describing the then novel style of the couplets of *Cooper's Hill.* 272.
the last . . . Tongue: [Pope's note] *Mr. Cowley died at
Chertsey on the Borders of the Forest, and was from thence
convey'd to* Westminster. **273. O . . . lost:** Cf. Dryden's
poem *To the Memory of Mr. Oldham* in Part One. Cowley
died at the age of forty-eight.

To sing those Honours you deserve to wear,
And add new Lustre to her Silver *Star*.° 290

Here noble *Surrey*° felt the sacred Rage,
Surrey, the *Granville* of a former Age:
Matchless his Pen, victorious was his Lance;
Bold in the Lists, and graceful in the Dance:
In the same Shades the *Cupids* tun'd his Lyre,
To the same Notes, of Love, and soft Desire:
Fair *Geraldine*, bright Object of his Vow,
Then fill'd the Groves, as heav'nly *Myra*° now.

Oh wou'dst thou sing what Heroes *Windsor* bore,
What Kings first breath'd upon her winding
      Shore, 300
Or raise old Warriors whose ador'd Remains
In weeping Vaults her hallow'd Earth contains!
With° *Edward*'s° Acts adorn the shining Page,
Stretch his long Triumphs down thro' ev'ry Age,
Draw Monarchs chain'd; and *Cressi*'s° glorious Field,
The *Lillies*° blazing on the Regal Shield.
Then, from her Roofs when *Verrio*'s Colours fall,
And leave inanimate the naked Wall;
Still in thy Song shou'd vanquish'd *France* appear,
And bleed for ever under *Britain*'s Spear. 310

Let softer Strains Ill-fated *Henry*° mourn,
And Palms Eternal flourish round his Urn.
Here o'er the Martyr-King the Marble weeps,
And fast beside him, once-fear'd *Edward*° sleeps:
Whom not th' extended *Albion* could contain,
From old *Belerium*° to the *Northern* Main,
The Grave unites; where ev'n the Great find Rest,
And blended lie th' Oppressor and th' Opprest!

Make sacred *Charles*'s Tomb for ever known,°
(Obscure the Place, and uninscrib'd the Stone) 320
Oh Fact° accurst! What Tears has *Albion* shed,
Heav'ns! what new Wounds, and how her old have
      bled?
She saw her Sons with purple Deaths° expire,
Her sacred Domes° involv'd in rolling Fire,
A dreadful Series of Intestine Wars,°
Inglorious Triumphs, and dishonest° Scars.
At length great *ANNA*° said—Let Discord cease!
She said, the World obey'd, and all was *Peace*!

In that blest Moment, from his Oozy Bed
Old Father *Thames* advanc'd his rev'rend Head. 330
His Tresses dropt with Dews, and o'er the Stream
His shining Horns° diffus'd a golden Gleam:
Grav'd on his Urn appear'd the Moon, that guides
His swelling Waters, and alternate Tydes;
The figur'd Streams in Waves of Silver roll'd,
And on their Banks *Augusta*° rose in Gold.°
Around his Throne the Sea-born Brothers stood,
Who swell with Tributary Urns his Flood.
First the fam'd Authors of his ancient Name,
The winding *Isis*, and the fruitful *Tame*: 340
The *Kennet* swift, for silver Eels renown'd;
The *Loddon* slow, with verdant Alders crown'd:
Cole, whose dark Streams his flow'ry Islands lave;
And chalky *Wey*, that rolls a milky Wave:

---

319. Make . . . known: Charles I, executed in 1649, was buried in St. George's Chapel, Windsor. Permission to read the burial service was refused by the Puritans, and the site of the coffin was unknown for a long time. **321. Fact:** evil deed. **323. purple Deaths:** deaths from the Great Plague in 1665. **324. Domes:** splendid buildings. **325. Intestine Wars:** the civil wars during the reigns of Charles I, Cromwell (in Ireland), James II, and William III (in Ireland). **326. dishonest:** ignoble. **327. Anna:** Queen Anne. **332. Horns:** River gods were represented as horned, supposedly because they made their way butting and bellowing. **336. Augusta:** a Roman name for London. **Gold:** the new architecture after the Great Fire of 1666 was of brick and white Portland stone with gilded metal decorations. In *Annus Mirabilis* (1667) Dryden described the city rebuilt after the fire:

> Me-thinks already, from this Chymick flame,
>   I see a City of more precious mold:
> Rich as the Town [Mexico] which gives the *Indies* name,
>   With Silver pav'd, and all divine with Gold.

Throughout this last section of *Windsor-Forest*, Pope's debt to the ending of *Annus Mirabilis* is both general and particular.

---

290. Silver Star: the star of the Order of the Garter. Members of this order still gather at Windsor, where the order was founded. **291. Surrey:** [Pope's note] Henry Howard *E. of Surrey, one of the first Refiners of the* English *Poetry; famous in the time of* Henry *the* VIIIth. **298. Myra:** the poetical name for the lady, or ladies, addressed by Granville. **303–10. With . . . Spear:** Lines 303–10 refer to the decorations at Windsor by the Italian painter Verrio (1639–1707). **303. Edward:** [Pope's note] Edward III. *born here.* **305. Cressi:** (Crécy) a village in northern France where, against great odds, Edward III defeated the French, mainly by the use of a new weapon, the longbow. **306. Lillies:** the emblem of France, introduced into the English coat of arms. **311. Ill-fated Henry:** Henry VI, murdered in 1471, was revered as a martyr. **314. Edward:** Edward IV. **316. old Belerium:** Land's End in Cornwall.

The blue, transparent *Vandalis*° appears;
The gulphy *Lee* his sedgy Tresses rears:
And sullen *Mole*, that hides his diving Flood;
And silent *Darent*, stain'd with *Danish* Blood.°

High in the midst, upon his Urn reclin'd,
(His Sea-green Mantle waving with the Wind)   350
The God appear'd; he turn'd his azure Eyes
Where *Windsor*-Domes and pompous Turrets rise,
Then bow'd and spoke; the Winds forget to roar,
And the hush'd Waves glide softly to the Shore.

Hail Sacred *Peace!* hail long-expected Days,
That *Thames*'s Glory to the Stars shall raise!
Tho' *Tyber*'s Streams immortal *Rome* behold,
Tho' foaming *Hermus*° swells with Tydes of Gold,
From Heav'n it self tho' sev'nfold° *Nilus* flows,
And Harvests on a hundred Realms bestows;   360
These now no more shall be the Muse's Themes,
Lost in my Fame, as in the Sea their Streams.
Let *Volga*'s° Banks with Iron Squadrons° shine,
And Groves of Lances glitter on the *Rhine*,
Let barb'rous *Ganges*° arm a servile Train;
Be mine the Blessings of a peaceful Reign.
No more my Sons shall dye with *British* Blood
Red *Iber*'s° Sands, or *Ister*'s° foaming Flood;
Safe on my Shore each unmolested Swain
Shall tend the Flocks, or reap the bearded Grain;   370
The shady Empire shall retain no Trace
Of War or Blood, but in the Sylvan Chace,
The Trumpets sleep, while chearful Horns are
        blown,
And Arms employ'd on Birds and Beasts alone.
Behold! th' ascending *Villa's* on my Side
Project long Shadows o'er the Chrystal Tyde.
Behold! *Augusta*'s glitt'ring Spires increase,
And Temples° rise, the beauteous Works of Peace.

I see, I see where two fair Cities° bend
Their ample Bow,° a new *White-Hall*° ascend!   380
There mighty Nations shall inquire their Doom,
The World's great Oracle in Times to come;
There Kings shall sue, and suppliant States be seen
Once more to bend before a *British* QUEEN.

Thy Trees, fair *Windsor!* now shall leave their
        Woods,
And half thy Forests rush into my Floods,
Bear *Britain*'s Thunder, and her Cross° display,
To the bright Regions of the rising Day;
Tempt Icy Seas, where scarce the Waters roll,
Where clearer Flames glow round the frozen Pole;   390
Or under Southern Skies exalt their Sails,
Led by new Stars, and born by spicy Gales!
For me the Balm° shall bleed, and Amber flow,
The Coral redden, and the Ruby glow,
The Pearly Shell its lucid Globe infold,
And *Phœbus* warm the ripening Ore to Gold.°
The Time shall come, when free as Seas or Wind
Unbounded *Thames* shall flow for all Mankind,
Whole Nations enter with each swelling Tyde,
And Seas but join the Regions they divide;   400
Earth's distant Ends our Glory shall behold,
And the new World launch forth to seek the Old.
Then Ships of uncouth Form shall stem the Tyde,
And Feather'd People crowd my wealthy Side.
And naked Youths and painted Chiefs admire,
Our Speech, our Colour, and our strange Attire!
Oh stretch thy Reign, fair *Peace!* from Shore to Shore,
Till Conquest cease, and Slav'ry be no more:
Till the freed *Indians* in their native Groves
Reap their own Fruits, and woo their Sable Loves, 410
Peru once more a Race of Kings behold,
And other *Mexico's* be roof'd with Gold.
Exil'd by Thee from Earth to deepest Hell,
In Brazen Bonds shall barb'rous *Discord* dwell:

---

345. Vandalis: the Wandle. **348. Danish Blood:** The Danes defeated by Edmund Ironside, King of Wessex, at Otford on the Darent in 1016. **355–422.** The speech of Father Thames. **358. Hermus:** Virgil celebrated this Italian river. **359. sev'nfold:** Alluding to its delta, Ovid called the Nile *septemfluus*. **363. Volga:** an allusion to Charles XII's war against Russia, in which he was defeated in 1709. **Iron Squadrons:** cavalry. **365. Ganges:** an allusion to Aurangzeb's recent wars in India. **368. Iber:** the Ebro in Spain, where Britain had recently been fighting. **Ister:** the Danube. The reference is to the area where Marlborough achieved the victory of Blenheim in 1704. **378. Temples:** [Pope's or Warburton's note] The fifty new Churches.

379. two . . . Cities: London and Westminster. **380. Bow:** the great curve in the river between the two cities. **a new White-Hall:** an allusion to the projected rebuilding of the whole palace of Whitehall, which, apart from Inigo Jones's banqueting hall, had burned down in the fires of 1691 and 1697. **387. Cross:** an allusion to the red cross of St. George which, joined with that of St. Andrew, made at this time the Union flag of Great Britain; also perhaps an allusion to the Anglican missions recently started overseas. **393. Balm:** the sap of incised trees. **396. Phœbus . . . Gold:** Cf. *Moral Essays, Of the Characters of Women*, below, ll. 289–90 and note.

Gigantick *Pride*, pale *Terror*, gloomy *Care*,
And mad *Ambition*, shall attend her there.
There purple *Vengeance* bath'd in Gore retires,
Her Weapons blunted, and extinct her Fires:
There hateful *Envy* her own Snakes shall feel,
And *Persecution* mourn her broken Wheel: 420
There *Faction* roar, *Rebellion* bite her Chain,
And gasping Furies thirst for Blood in vain.

Here cease thy Flight, nor with unhallow'd Lays
Touch the fair Fame of *Albion*'s Golden Days.
The Thoughts of Gods let *Granville*'s Verse recite,
And bring the Scenes of opening Fate to Light.
My humble Muse, in unambitious Strains,
Paints the green Forests and the flow'ry Plains,
Where Peace descending bids her Olives spring,
And scatters Blessings from her Dove-like Wing. 430
Ev'n I more sweetly pass my careless Days,
Pleas'd in the silent Shade with empty Praise;
Enough for me, that to the listning Swains
First in these Fields I sung the Sylvan Strains.

PROLOGUE TO
MR. ADDISON'S TRAGEDY
OF CATO

Addison's play, first performed in 1713, became popular immediately because of its ambiguous political slant: both Whigs and Tories claimed they were glorified in it.
    The text is that of the first edition (1713).

To wake the soul by tender strokes of art,
To raise the genius, and to mend the heart;
To make mankind, in conscious virtue bold,
Live o'er each scene, and be what they behold:
For this the Tragic Muse first trod the stage,
Commanding tears to stream thro' ev'ry age;
Tyrants no more their savage nature kept,
And foes to virtue wonder'd how they wept.
Our author shuns by vulgar springs to move,
The hero's glory, or the virgin's love;   10
In pitying love we but our weakness show,
And wild ambition well deserves its woe.
Here tears shall flow from a more gen'rous cause,
Such tears, as Patriots shed for dying Laws:

He bids your breasts with ancient ardour rise,
And calls forth *Roman* drops from *British* eyes.
Virtue confess'd in human shape he draws,
What *Plato* thought, and godlike *Cato* was:
No common object to your sight displays,
But what with pleasure heav'n itself surveys;   20
A brave man struggling in the storms of fate,
And greatly falling with a falling state!
While *Cato* gives his little senate laws,°
What bosom beats not in his Country's cause?
Who sees him act, but envies ev'ry deed?
Who hears him groan, and does not wish to bleed?
Ev'n when proud *Cæsar* 'midst triumphal cars,
The spoils of nations, and the pomp of wars,
Ignobly vain and impotently great,
Show'd *Rome* her *Cato*'s figure drawn in state;   30
As her dead Father's rev'rend image past,
The pomp was darken'd and the day o'ercast,
The triumph ceas'd—Tears gush'd from ev'ry eye;
The World's great Victor pass'd unheeded by;
Her last good man dejected *Rome* ador'd,
And honour'd *Cæsar*'s less than *Cato*'s sword.
    Britons attend: Be worth like this approv'd,
And show, you have the virtue to be mov'd.
With honest scorn the first fam'd *Cato* view'd
Rome learning arts from *Greece*, whom she subdu'd; 40
Our scene precariously subsists too long
On *French* translation, and *Italian* song.°
Dare to have sense your selves; assert the stage,
Be justly warm'd with your own native rage.
Such Plays alone should please a *British* ear,
As *Cato*'s self had not disdain'd to hear.

PREFACE
[TO THE *ILIAD* (1715)]

The temper and intelligence that distinguished *An Essay on Criticism* (1711) also distinguish this Preface. Written in the prose advocated—and occasionally achieved—in the seventeenth century, it has both grace and firmness of sense. In his comparison of the two great epic poets of antiquity, Pope contrasts the impetuosity of Homer and the equability of Virgil. His own genius seems to share something of both qualities; led by his own "fire" to recognize poetic genius, he weighs its particular

PROLOGUE TO MR. ADDISON'S TRAGEDY OF CATO. **23. While . . . laws:** Cf. *An Epistle to Dr. Arbuthnot*, below, l. 209. **42. Italian song:** opera.

instances with cool judiciousness. He is above taking sides in the Battle of the Books; whether poetry is ancient or modern is immaterial to him. In a few golden words he characterizes the genius not only of Homer and Virgil but of Shakespeare and Milton, and later he pays filial homage to the greatness of his immediate predecessor, Dryden, in a passage which, when taken along with the scattered tributes in the poems, amounts to something like a full-scale elegy. His power to recognize genius enables him to be fair to a poet so unlike himself as George Chapman, in whose headstrong translations of Homer he discerns the animation of a "daring fiery Spirit." Though both frenzy and frigidity are extremes of style, Pope considers frenzy nearer genius. Frigidity, or what some may call simplicity, is really dullness, the worst sin against light.

As a translator discussing the practicalities of his occupation, Pope shows the same qualities of sensitivity and judgment. He discerns the difficulties and selects the soundest course for solving them. Homer, he points out, is an ancient, not a contemporary, and his poetry was addressed to the people of his time. It is only fair to him therefore that a translator should also act as an interpreter. In modernizing the original he should strive to evoke the same response as that of the poet's first audience. Pope's plea for the acquisition and improvement of the historic sense is the first extended one in English. To translate literally, he realized, would sometimes have the effect of burlesque. Yet the modernizing translator must proceed with caution in order to avoid weakening the images of the original. Finally, the translator is at the mercy of his own language in its contemporary state. Pope remarks that to satisfy those who seek separately "a Taste of Poetry" or "competent Learning" is "not in the Nature of this Undertaking, since a meer Modern Wit can like nothing that is not *Modern*, and a Pedant, nothing that is not *Greek*." This answer he might have made when Bentley, acknowledging that his translation was "a pretty poem," warned him, "You must not call it Homer."

The text is that of the first edition (1715), amended in accordance with Pope's revisions. Some of the earlier readings are referred to in the notes.

❀

HOMER is universally allow'd to have had the greatest Invention[1] of any Writer whatever. The

Praise of Judgment *Virgil* has justly contested with him, and others may have their Pretensions as to particular Excellencies; but his Invention remains yet unrival'd. Nor is it a Wonder if he has ever been acknowledg'd the greatest of Poets, who most excell'd in That which is the very Foundation of Poetry. It is the Invention that in different degrees distinguishes all great Genius's: The utmost Stretch of human Study, Learning, and Industry, which masters every thing besides, can never attain to this. It furnishes Art with all her Materials, and without it Judgment itself can at best but *steal wisely:* For Art is only like a prudent Steward that lives on managing the Riches of Nature. Whatever Praises may be given to Works of Judgment, there is not even a single Beauty in them to which the Invention must not contribute: As in the most regular Gardens,[2] Art can only reduce the Beauties of Nature to more Regularity and such a Figure, which the common Eye may better take in, and is therefore more entertain'd with. And perhaps the reason why common Criticks are inclin'd to prefer a judicious and methodical Genius to a great and fruitful one, is, because they find it easier for themselves to pursue their Observations through an uniform and bounded Walk of Art, than to comprehend the vast and various Extent of Nature.

Our Author's Work is a wild Paradise, where if we cannot see all the Beauties so distinctly as in an order'd Garden, it is only because the Number of them is infinitely greater. 'Tis like a copious Nursery which contains the Seeds and first Productions of every kind, out of which those who follow'd him have but selected some particular Plants, each according to his Fancy, to cultivate and beautify. If some things are too luxuriant, it is owing to the Richness of the Soil; and if others are not arriv'd to Perfection or Maturity, it is only because they are over-run and opprest by those of a stronger Nature.

It is to the Strength of this amazing Invention we are to attribute that unequal'd Fire and Rapture, which is so forcible in *Homer*, that no Man of a true Poetical Spirit is Master of himself while he reads him. What he writes is of the most animated Nature imaginable; every thing moves, every thing lives, and is put in Action. If a Council be call'd, or a Battel fought, you

---

PREFACE TO THE *Iliad* (1715). **1. Invention:** Aristotle gave paramountcy to plot among the constituents of a work of literature; Dryden to invention, i.e., the power of finding and making the matter of a poem, of achieving plot in all its fullness. In his *Life of Milton* (1779) Johnson agreed with Dryden: "The highest praise of genius is original invention."

2. regular Gardens: Cf. with this and the next paragraph Addison's *Spectator*, No. 417 (earlier in Part Two), in which he likens the *Iliad* to wild and rugged country and the *Aeneid* to a well-ordered and beautiful garden. Cf. also Johnson's Preface to Shakespeare, p. 1066.

are not coldly inform'd of what was said or done as from a third Person; the Reader is hurry'd out of himself by the Force of the Poet's Imagination, and turns in one place to a Hearer, in another to a Spectator. The Course of his Verses resembles that of the Army he describes,

Οἱ δ' ἄρ' ἴσαν, ὡσέι τε πυρὶ χθὼν πᾶσα νέμοιτο.

They pour along like a Fire that sweeps the whole Earth before it. 'Tis however remarkable that his Fancy, which is every where vigorous, is not discover'd immediately at the beginning of his Poem in its fullest Splendor: It grows in the Progress both upon himself and others, and becomes on Fire like a Chariot-Wheel, by its own Rapidity.[3] Exact Disposition, just Thought, correct Elocution, polish'd Numbers, may have been found in a thousand; but this Poetical *Fire*, this *Vivida vis animi*,[4] in a very few. Even in Works where all those are imperfect or neglected, this can over-power Criticism, and make us admire even while we disapprove. Nay, where this appears, tho' attended with Absurdities, it brightens all the Rubbish about it, 'till we see nothing but its own Splendor. This *Fire* is discern'd in *Virgil*, but discern'd as through a Glass, reflected from *Homer*, more shining than fierce, but every where equal and constant: In *Lucan* and *Statius*, it bursts out in sudden, short, and interrupted Flashes: In *Milton*, it glows like a Furnace kept up to an uncommon Ardor by the Force of Art: In *Shakespear*, it strikes before we are aware, like an accidental Fire from Heaven: But in *Homer*, and in him only, it burns every where clearly, and every where irresistibly.

I shall here endeavour to show, how this vast *Invention* exerts itself in a manner superior to that of any Poet, thro' all the main constituent Parts of his Work, as it is the great and peculiar Characteristick which distinguishes him from all other Authors.

This strong and ruling Faculty was like a powerful Star, which in the Violence of its Course, drew all things within its *Vortex*.[5] It seem'd not enough to have taken in the whole Circle of Arts, and the whole Compass of Nature to supply his Maxims and Reflections; all the inward Passions and Affections of Mankind to furnish his Characters, and all the outward Forms and Images of Things for his Descriptions;

but wanting yet an ampler Sphere to expatiate in, he open'd a new and boundless Walk for his Imagination, and created a World for himself in the Invention of *Fable*.[6] That which *Aristotle* calls the *Soul of Poetry*, was first breath'd into it by *Homer*. I shall begin with considering him in this Part, as it is naturally the first, and I speak of it both as it means the Design of a Poem, and as it is taken for Fiction.

Fable may be divided into the *Probable*,[7] the *Allegorical*,[8] and the *Marvelous*.[9] The *Probable Fable* is the Recital of such Actions as tho' they did not happen, yet might, in the common course of Nature: Or of such as tho' they did, become Fables by the additional Episodes and manner of telling them. Of this sort is the main Story of an Epic Poem, *the Return of Ulysses, the Settlement of the* Trojans *in Italy*, or the like. That of the *Iliad* is *the Anger of* Achilles, the most short and single Subject that ever was chosen by any Poet. Yet this he has supplied with a vaster Variety of Incidents and Events, and crouded with a greater Number of Councils, Speeches, Battles, and Episodes of all kinds, than are to be found even in those Poems whose Schemes are of the utmost Latitude and Irregularity. The Action is hurry'd on with the most vehement Spirit, and its whole Duration employs not so much as fifty Days. *Virgil*, for want of so warm a Genius, aided himself by taking in a more extensive Subject, as well as a greater Length of Time, and contracting the Design of both *Homer*'s Poems into one, which is yet but a fourth part as large as his. The other Epic Poets have us'd the same Practice, but generally carry'd it so far as to superinduce a Multiplicity of Fables, destroy the Unity of Action, and lose their Readers in an unreasonable Length of Time. Nor

---

3. becomes . . . Rapidity: Coleridge was to apply this image to Dryden. **4. Vivida vis animi:** "living power of mind" (Lucretius, *De Rerum Natura*, I. 72). Lucretius used the phrase to describe Epicurus. **5. Vortex:** Descartes's theory of the universe is based on the whirl of matter around a center.

6. Fable: plot. **7. Probable:** Aristotle emphasized the importance of the probability of incidents making up the plot. **8. Allegorical:** From the earliest times the epics of Homer were held to be allegorical. René Le Bossu (1631–80), in his famous treatise on the epic (1675), went so far as to declare that Homer first thought of a moral subject—the great moral of the *Iliad* was the need for amity among leaders of federated states—and "did not undertake to rehearse any particular action of *Achilles* or *Ulysses*. He made his *Fable*, and laid the design of his Poems, without so much as thinking on these Princes; and afterwards, he did them the Honour to bestow their Names on the *Heroes* he had feign'd." **9. Marvelous:** The plot of the ancient epic is, according to Le Bossu, "mix'd with Divinities." They and their acts make up most of the "marvelous." In addition there are omens, talking horses, the "miraculous river" Styx, "immediate healing of wounds." Pope lists them all in the Poetical Index at the end of his translation.

is it only in the main Design that they have been unable to add to his Invention, but they have follow'd him in every Episode and Part of Story. If he has given a regular *Catalogue* of an *Army*, they all draw up their Forces in the same Order. If he has funeral Games for *Patroclus*, *Virgil* has the same for *Anchises*, and *Statius* (rather than omit them) destroys the Unity of his Action for those of *Archemorus*. If *Ulysses* visit the Shades, the *Æneas* of *Virgil* and *Scipio* of *Silius*[10] are sent after him. If he be detain'd from his Return by the Allurements of *Calypso*, so is *Æneas* by *Dido*, and *Rinaldo* by *Armida*.[11] If *Achilles* be absent from the Army on the Score of a Quarrel thro' half the Poem, *Rinaldo* must absent himself just as long, on the like account. If he gives his Heroe a Suit of celestial Armour, *Virgil* and *Tasso* make the same Present to theirs. *Virgil* has not only observ'd this close Imitation of *Homer*, but where he had not led the way, supply'd the Want from other *Greek* Authors. Thus the Story of *Sinon* and the *Taking of Troy*[12] was copied (says *Macrobius*[13]) almost word for word from *Pisander*,[14] as the Loves of *Dido* and *Æneas* are taken from those of *Medæa* and *Jason* in *Apollonius*,[15] and several others in the same manner.

To proceed to the *Allegorical Fable:* If we reflect upon those innumerable Knowledges, those Secrets of Nature[16] and Physical Philosophy[17] which *Homer* is generally suppos'd to have wrapt up in his *Allegories*,[18]

what a new and ample Scene of Wonder may this Consideration afford us? How fertile will that Imagination appear, which was able to cloath all the Properties of Elements, the Qualifications of the Mind, the Virtues and Vices, in Forms and Persons; and to introduce them into Actions agreeable to the Nature of the Things they shadow'd? This is a Field in which no succeeding Poets could dispute with *Homer;* and whatever Commendations have been allow'd them on this Head, are by no means for their Invention in having enlarg'd his Circle, but for their Judgment in having contracted it. For when the Mode of Learning chang'd in following Ages, and Science was deliver'd in a plainer manner, it then became as reasonable in the more modern Poets to lay it aside, as it was in *Homer* to make use of it. And perhaps it was no unhappy Circumstance for *Virgil*, that there was not in his Time that Demand upon him of so great an Invention, as might be capable of furnishing all those Allegorical Parts of a Poem.

The *Marvelous Fable* includes whatever is supernatural, and especially the Machines of the Gods. [Homer][19] seems the first who brought them into a System of *Machinery* for Poetry, and such an one as makes its greatest Importance and Dignity. For we find those Authors who have been offended at the literal Notion of the Gods, constantly laying their Accusation against *Homer* as the chief Support of it. But whatever cause there might be to blame his *Machines* in a Philosophical or Religious View, they are so perfect in the Poetick, that Mankind have been ever since contented to follow them: None have been able to enlarge the Sphere of Poetry beyond the

---

10. **Silius:** Silius Italicus (*c.* A.D. 25–101) wrote *Punica*, an epic about Hannibal. 11. **Rinaldo by Armida:** in Tasso's *Jerusalem Delivered* (1581). 12. **Sinon . . . Troy:** in the *Aeneid*, Book II. 13. **Macrobius:** a Latin writer (nationality uncertain) of about A.D. 400; his Virgilian criticism is contained in his *Saturnalia.* 14. **Pisander:** Greek epic poet of the seventh or sixth century B.C.; it has been suggested that Macrobius confused him with another Pisander who lived after Virgil. 15. **Apollonius:** Alexandrian poet of the third or second century B.C., author of *Argonautica.* 16. **Nature:** human nature. 17. **Physical Philosophy:** natural science. 18. **Allegories:** Critics tried to claim that allegory exists even in the detail of the plot. For example, after Achilles has cursed the body of Hector, the poem continues in Book XXIII:

So spake he, threat'ning: But the Gods made vain
His Threat, and guard inviolate the Slain:
Celestial *Venus* hover'd o'er his Head,
And roseate Unguents, heav'nly Fragrance! shed:
She watch'd him all the Night, and all the Day,
And drove the Bloodhounds from their destin'd Prey.
Nor sacred *Phœbus* less employ'd his Care;
He pour'd around a Veil of gather'd Air,
And kept the Nerves undry'd, the Flesh entire,
Against the Solar Beam and *Sirian* Fire.

On this passage Pope wrote the note: "*Homer* has here introduc'd a Series of Allegories in the Compass of a few Lines: The Body of *Hector* may be suppos'd to have continued beautiful even after he was slain; and *Venus* being the President of Beauty, the Poet by a natural Fiction tells us it was preserv'd by that Goddess. *Apollo's* covering the Body with a Cloud is a very natural Allegory: For the Sun . . . has a double Quality which produces contrary Effects; the Heat of it causes a Dryness, but at the same time it exhales the Vapours of the Earth, from whence the Clouds of Heaven are form'd. This Allegory may be founded upon Truth; there might happen to be a cool season while *Hector* lay unburied, and *Apollo*, or the Sun, raising Clouds which intercept the Heat of his Beams, by a very easy Fiction in Poetry may be introduc'd in Person to preserve the Body of *Hector*." 19. **Homer:** *He* in the text; the alteration to *Homer* was required, but not made, when a passage appearing in earlier editions was omitted (perhaps accidentally).

Limits he has set: Every Attempt of this Nature has prov'd unsuccessful; and after all the various Changes of Times and Religions, his Gods continue to this Day the Gods of Poetry.

We come now to the *Characters* of his Persons, and here we shall find no Author has ever drawn so many with so visible and surprizing a Variety, or given us such lively and affecting Impressions of them. Every one has something so singularly his own, that no Painter could have distinguish'd them more by their Features, than the Poet has by their Manners.[20] Nothing can be more exact than the Distinctions he has observ'd in the different degrees of Virtues and Vices. The single Quality of *Courage* is wonderfully diversify'd in the several Characters of the *Iliad*. That of *Achilles* is furious and intractable; that of *Diomede* forward, yet listening to Advice and subject to Command: That of *Ajax* is heavy, and self-confiding; of *Hector* active and vigilant: The Courage of *Agamemnon* is inspirited by Love of Empire and Ambition, that of *Menelaus* mix'd with Softness and Tenderness for his People: We find in *Idomeneus* a plain direct Soldier, in *Sarpedon* a gallant and generous one. Nor is this judicious and astonishing Diversity to be found only in the principal Quality which constitutes the Main of each Character, but even in the Under-parts of it, to which he takes care to give a Tincture of that principal one. For Example, the main Characters of *Ulysses* and *Nestor* consist in *Wisdom*, and they are distinct in this; that the Wisdom of one is *artificial*[21] and *various*, of the other *natural*, *open*, and *regular*. But they have, besides, Characters of *Courage;* and this Quality also takes a different Turn in each from the difference of his Prudence: For one in the War depends still upon *Caution*, the other upon *Experience*. It would be endless to produce Instances of these Kinds. The Characters of *Virgil* are far from striking us in this open manner; they lie in a great degree hidden and undistinguish'd, and where they are mark'd most evidently, affect us not in proportion

to those of *Homer*. His Characters of Valour are much alike; even that of *Turnus* seems no way peculiar but as it is in a superior degree; and we see nothing that differences the Courage of *Mnestheus* from that of *Sergesthus*, *Cloanthus*, or the rest. In like manner it may be remark'd of *Statius*'s Heroes, that an Air of Impetuosity runs thro' them all; the same horrid and savage Courage appears in his *Capaneus*, *Tydeus*, *Hippomedon*, &c. They have a Parity of Character which makes them seem Brothers of one Family. I believe when the Reader is led into this Track of Reflection, if he will pursue it through the *Epic* and *Tragic* Writers, he will be convinced how infinitely superior in this Point the Invention of *Homer* was to that of all others.

The *Speeches* are to be consider'd as they flow from the Characters, being perfect or defective as they agree or disagree with the Manners of those who utter them.[22] As there is more variety of Characters in the *Iliad*, so there is of Speeches, than in any other Poem. *Every thing in it has Manners* (as *Aristotle* expresses it)[23] that is, every thing is acted or spoken. It is hardly credible in a Work of such length, how small a Number of Lines are employ'd in Narration. In *Virgil* the Dramatic Part is less in proportion to the Narrative; and the Speeches often consist of general Reflections or Thoughts, which might be equally just in any Person's Mouth upon the same Occasion. As many of his Persons have no apparent Characters, so many of his Speeches escape being apply'd and judg'd by the Rule of Propriety. We oftner think of the Author himself when we read *Virgil*, than when we are engag'd in *Homer*: All which are the Effects of a colder Invention, that interests us less in the Action describ'd: *Homer* makes us Hearers, and *Virgil* leaves us Readers.

If in the next place we take a View of the *Sentiments*, the same presiding Faculty is eminent in the Sublimity and Spirit of his Thoughts. *Longinus*[24] has given his Opinion, that it was in this Part *Homer* principally

---

20. **Characters, Manners:** The manners are the moral qualities that make up a person's character. Cf. Le Bossu: "Under the Name of *Manners* we comprehend all the natural or acquired Inclinations, which carry us on to good, bad, or indifferent actions." In the title to the relevant section in Pope's Poetical Index, "characters" and "manners" figure as alternative terms; here Pope provides a catalogue for each of the several heroes. There are five entries under "Achilles"; first "Furious, passionate, disdainful, and reproachful"; secondly "Revengeful and implacable in the highest degree"; and so on. 21. **artificial:** made by art.

22. **The Speeches . . . them:** In the section of the Poetical Index mentioned in note 20, Pope gives a distinguishing mark to those speeches "which depend upon, and flow from these several Characters." 23. **as . . . it:** in *Poetics*, Ch. xxiv. Aristotle praises Homer for not "perpetually coming forward in person"; instead, "after a brief preface [he] brings in forthwith a man, a woman, or some other Character— no one of them characterless, but each with distinctive characteristics." 24. **Longinus:** (c. 220–73), Greek rhetorician and philosopher, long thought—incorrectly—to have written the treatise *On the Sublime*, which Pope was to parody in his *Peri Bathous*, below.

excell'd. What were alone sufficient to prove the Grandeur and Excellence of his Sentiments[25] in general, is that they have so remarkable a Parity with those of the Scripture: Duport,[26] in his Gnomologia Homerica, has collected innumerable Instances of this sort. And it is with Justice an excellent modern Writer allows, that if Virgil has not so many Thoughts that are low and vulgar, he has not so many that are sublime and noble; and that the Roman Author seldom rises into very astonishing Sentiments where he is not fired by the Iliad.

If we observe his Descriptions, Images, and Similes, we shall find the Invention still predominant. To what else can we ascribe that vast Comprehension of Images of every sort, where we see each Circumstance of Art, and Individual of Nature summon'd together by the Extent and Fecundity of his Imagination; to which all things, in their various Views, presented themselves in an Instant, and had their Impressions taken off to Perfection at a Heat? Nay, he not only gives us the full Prospects of Things, but several unexpected Peculiarities and Side-Views, unobserv'd by any Painter but Homer. Nothing is so surprizing as the Descriptions of his Battels, which take up no less than half the Iliad, and are supply'd with so vast a Variety of Incidents, that no one bears a Likeness to another; such different Kinds of Deaths, that no two Heroes are wounded in the same manner; and such a Profusion of noble Ideas, that every Battel rises above the last in Greatness, Horror, and Confusion. It is certain there is not near that Number of Images and Descriptions in any Epic Poet; tho' every one has assisted himself with a great Quantity out of him: And it is evident of Virgil especially, that he has scarce any Comparisons which are not drawn from his Master.

If we descend from hence to the Expression, we see the bright Imagination of Homer shining out in the most enliven'd Forms of it. We acknowledge him the Father of Poetical Diction,[27] the first who taught that Language of the Gods to Men. His Expression is like the colouring of some great Masters, which discovers itself to be laid on boldly, and executed with Rapidity. It is indeed the strongest and most glowing imaginable, and touch'd with the greatest Spirit. Aristotle had

reason to say, He was the only Poet who had found out Living Words; there are in him more daring Figures and Metaphors than in any good Author whatever. An Arrow is impatient to be on the Wing, a Weapon thirsts to drink the Blood of an Enemy, and the like. Yet his Expression is never too big for the Sense, but justly great in proportion to it: 'Tis the Sentiment that swells and fills out the Diction, which rises with it, and forms itself about it: And in the same degree that a Thought is warmer, an Expression will be brighter; and as That is more strong, This will become more perspicuous: Like Glass in the Furnace which grows to a greater Magnitude, and refines to a greater Clearness, only as the Breath within is more powerful, and the Heat more intense.

To throw his Language more out of Prose, Homer seems to have affected the Compound-Epithets. This was a sort of Composition peculiarly proper to Poetry, not only as it heighten'd the Diction, but as it assisted and fill'd the Numbers[28] with greater Sound and Pomp, and likewise conduced in some measure to thicken the Images. On this last Consideration I cannot but attribute these also to the Fruitfulness of his Invention, since (as he has manag'd them) they are a sort of supernumerary Pictures of the Persons or Things to which they are join'd.[29] We see the Motion of Hector's Plumes in the Epithet Κορυθαίολος,[30] the Landscape of Mount Neritus in that of Εἰνοσίφυλλος,[31] and so of others; which particular Images could not have been insisted upon so long as to express them in a Description (tho' but of a single Line) without diverting the Reader too much from the principal Action or Figure. As a Metaphor is a short Simile, one of these Epithets is a short Description.

Lastly, if we consider his Versification, we shall be sensible what a Share of Praise is due to his Invention in that. He was not satisfy'd with his Language as he found it settled in any one Part of Greece, but search'd thro' its differing Dialects with this particular View,

---

25. Sentiments: comments on human affairs. **26. Duport:** James Duport (1606–79), Cambridge classical scholar; author of Homeri Gnomologia (1660), a collection of Homeric aphorisms illustrated by quotations from the Bible and from classical writers. **27. Poetical Diction:** figurative diction unsuitable for prose.

28. Numbers: meter. **29. to . . . join'd:** "they are join'd to" in the first edition; "corrected," along with two similar constructions, in 1720, according to a mistaken theory held by Dryden and others that it is inelegant to end an English sentence with a preposition. **30. Κορυθαίολος:** "moving the helmet quickly," "with glancing helm." In his translation Pope has various equivalents for the clauses that include this recurrent epithet: "nods his Plumy Crest," "his dreadful Plumage nodded." **31. Εἰνοσίφυλλος:** "with quivering foliage." Pope translates: "[Where high Neritos] shakes his waving Woods." See his further comment on this epithet on p. 597.

to beautify and perfect his Numbers: He consider'd these as they had a greater Mixture of Vowels or Consonants, and accordingly employ'd them as the Verse requir'd either a greater Smoothness or Strength. What he most affected was the *Ionic*, which has a peculiar Sweetness from its never using Contractions, and from its Custom of resolving the Diphthongs into two Syllables; so as to make the Words open themselves with a more spreading and sonorous Fluency. With this he mingled the *Attic* Contractions, the broader *Doric*, and the feebler *Æolic*, which often rejects its Aspirate, or takes off its Accent; and compleated this Variety by altering some Letters with the License of Poetry. Thus his Measures, instead of being Fetters to his Sense, were always in readiness to run along with the Warmth of his Rapture; and even to give a farther Representation of his Notions, in the Correspondence of their Sounds to what they signify'd. Out of all these he has deriv'd that Harmony, which makes us confess he had not only the richest Head, but the finest Ear in the World. This is so great a Truth, that whoever will but consult the Tune of his Verses even without understanding them (with the same sort of Diligence as we daily see practis'd in the Case of *Italian Opera's*) will find more Sweetness, Variety, and Majesty of Sound, than in any other Language or Poetry. The Beauty of his Numbers is allow'd by the Criticks to be copied but faintly by *Virgil* himself, tho' they are so just to ascribe it to the Nature of the *Latine* Tongue. Indeed the *Greek* has some Advantages both from the natural *Sound* of its *Words*, and the Turn and *Cadence* of its *Verse*, which agree with the Genius of no other Language. *Virgil* was very sensible of this, and used the utmost Diligence in working up a more intractable Language to whatsoever Graces it was capable of, and in particular never fail'd to bring the Sound of his Line to a beautiful Agreement with its Sense. If the *Grecian* Poet has not been so frequently celebrated on this Account as the *Roman*, the only reason is, that fewer Criticks have understood one Language than the other. *Dionysius* of *Halicarnassus*[32] has pointed out many of our Author's Beauties in this kind, in his Treatise of the *Composition*[33] *of Words*, and others will be taken notice of in the Course of my Notes.[34] It suffices at present to observe of his Numbers, that they flow with so much ease, as to make one imagine *Homer* had no other care than to transcribe as fast as the *Muses* dictated;[35] and at the same time with so much Force and inspiriting Vigour, that they awaken and raise us like the Sound of a Trumpet.[36] They roll along as a plentiful River, always in motion, and always full; while we are born away by a Tide of Verse, the most rapid, and yet the most smooth imaginable.

Thus on whatever side we contemplate *Homer*, what principally strikes us is his *Invention*. It is that which forms the Character of each Part of his Work; and accordingly we find it to have made his Fable more *extensive* and *copious* than any other, his Manners more *lively* and *strongly marked*, his Speeches more *affecting* and *transported*, his Sentiments more *warm* and *sublime*, his Images and Descriptions more *full* and *animated*, his Expression more *rais'd* and *daring*, and his Numbers more *rapid* and *various*. I hope in what has been said of *Virgil* with regard to any of these Heads, I have no way derogated from his Character.[37] Nothing is more absurd or endless, than the common Method of comparing eminent Writers by an Opposition of particular Passages in them, and forming a Judgment from thence of their Merit upon the whole. We ought to have a certain Knowledge of the principal Character and distinguishing Excellence of each: It is in *that* we are to consider him, and in proportion to his Degree in *that* we are to admire him. No Author or Man ever excell'd all the World in more than one Faculty, and as *Homer* has done this in Invention, *Virgil* has in Judgment. Not that we are to think *Homer* wanted Judgment, because *Virgil* had it in a more eminent degree; or that *Virgil* wanted Invention, because *Homer* possest a larger share of it: Each of these great Authors had more of both than perhaps any Man besides, and are only said to have less in Comparison with one another. *Homer* was the greater Genius, *Virgil* the better Artist. In one we most admire the *Man*, in the other the *Work*. *Homer* hurries and transports us with a commanding Impetuosity, *Virgil* leads us with an attractive Majesty: *Homer* scatters with a generous Profusion, *Virgil* bestows with a careful Magnificence: *Homer*, like the *Nile*, pours out his Riches with a boundless Overflow; *Virgil* like a River in its Banks, with a gentle and constant Stream. When we behold

---

32. Dionysius of Halicarnassus: a Roman critic of Horace's time. **33. Composition:** artistic arrangement. **34. Notes:** They are placed after the book of the *Iliad* to which they refer.

35. the Muses dictated: The idea is Milton's. See *Paradise Lost*, IX. 21 ff. **36. Trumpet:** Cf. Sidney's *Defense of Poesy* (1595): "I never heard the olde song of Percy and Duglas, that I found not my heart mooved more than with a Trumpet . . . ." **37. Character:** high standing.

their Battels, methinks the two Poets resemble the Heroes they celebrate: *Homer*, boundless and irresistible as *Achilles*, bears all before him, and shines more and more as the Tumult increases; *Virgil*, calmly daring like *Æneas*, appears undisturb'd in the midst of the Action, disposes all about him, and conquers with Tranquillity: And when we look upon their Machines, *Homer* seems like his own *Jupiter* in his Terrors, shaking *Olympus*, scattering the Lightnings, and firing the Heavens; *Virgil*, like the same Power in his Benevolence, counselling with the Gods, laying Plans for Empires, and regularly ordering his whole Creation.

But after all, it is with great Parts as with great Virtues, they naturally border on some Imperfection; and it is often hard to distinguish exactly where the Virtue ends, or the Fault begins. As Prudence may sometimes sink to Suspicion, so may a great Judgment decline to Coldness; and as Magnanimity may run up to Profusion or Extravagance, so may a great Invention to Redundancy or Wildness. If we look upon *Homer* in this View, we shall perceive the chief *Objections* against him to proceed from so noble a Cause as the Excess of this Faculty.

Among these we may reckon some of his *Marvellous Fictions*, upon which so much Criticism has been spent as surpassing all the Bounds of Probability. Perhaps it may be with great and superior Souls as with gigantick Bodies, which exerting themselves with unusual Strength, exceed what is commonly thought the due Proportion of Parts, to become Miracles in the whole; and like the old Heroes of that Make, commit something near Extravagance amidst a Series of glorious and inimitable Performances. Thus *Homer* has his *speaking Horses*, and *Virgil* his *Myrtles distilling Blood*, where the latter has not so much as contriv'd the easy Intervention of a Deity to save the Probability.

It is owing to the same vast Invention that his *Similes* have been thought too exuberant and full of Circumstances. The Force of this Faculty is seen in nothing more, than its Inability to confine itself to that single Circumstance upon which the Comparison is grounded: It runs out into Embellishments of additional Images, which however are so manag'd as not to overpower the main one. His Similes are like Pictures, where the principal Figure has not only its proportion given agreeable to the Original, but is also set off with occasional Ornaments and Prospects.[38] The same will account for his manner of heaping a Number of

Comparisons together in one Breath, when his Fancy suggested to him at once so many various and correspondent Images. The Reader will easily extend this Observation to more Objections of the same kind.

If there are others which seem rather to charge him with a Defect or Narrowness of Genius, than an Excess of it; those seeming Defects will be found upon Examination to proceed wholly from the Nature of the Times he liv'd in. Such are his *grosser Representations* of the *Gods*, and the vicious and *imperfect Manners* of his *Heroes*, which will be treated of in the following *Essay*:[39] But I must here speak a word of the latter, as it is a Point generally carry'd into Extreams both by the Censurers and Defenders of *Homer*. It must be a strange Partiality to Antiquity to think with Madam *Dacier*,[40] "that those Times and Manners are so much the more excellent, as they are more contrary to ours." Who can be so prejudiced in their Favour as to magnify the Felicity of those Ages, when a Spirit of Revenge and Cruelty join'd with the Practice of Rapine and Robbery reign'd thro' the World, when no Mercy was shown but for the sake of Lucre, when the greatest Princes were put to the Sword, and their Wives and Daughters made Slaves and Concubines? On the other side I would not be so delicate as those modern Criticks, who are shock'd at the *servile Offices* and *mean Employments* in which we sometimes see the Heroes of *Homer* engag'd. There is a Pleasure in taking a view of that Simplicity in Opposition to the Luxury of succeeding Ages; in beholding Monarchs without their Guards, Princes tending their Flocks, and Princesses drawing Water from the Springs. When we read *Homer*, we ought to reflect that we are reading the most ancient Author in the Heathen World; and those who consider him in this Light, will double their Pleasure in the Perusal of him. Let them think they are growing acquainted with Nations and People that are now no more; that they are stepping almost three

---

38. **Prospects:** views opened up into landscape.

39. **Essay:** An *Essay on the Life, Writings, and Learning of Homer* followed this Preface, and Pope's note directs readers especially to its "Articles of *Theology* and *Morality*." Of "manners" he says, "We see a boasting Temper and unmanag'd Roughness in the Spirit of his Heroes, which ran out in Pride, Anger or Cruelty . . . we see his People with the turn of his Age, insatiably thirsting after Glory and Plunder; for which however he has found them a lawful Cause, and taken Care to retard their success by those very Faults." 40. **Madam Dacier:** Anne Dacier (1654–1720), French scholar; her prose translation of the *Iliad* appeared in 1699.

thousand Years back into the remotest Antiquity,[41] and entertaining themselves with a clear and surprizing Vision of Things no where else to be found, and the only true Mirrour of that ancient World. By this means alone their greatest Obstacles will vanish; and what usually creates their Dislike, will become a Satisfaction.[42]

This Consideration may farther serve to answer for the constant Use of the same *Epithets* to his Gods and Heroes, such as the *far-darting Phœbus*, the *blue-ey'd Pallas*, the *swift-footed Achilles*, &c. which some have censured as impertinent and tediously repeated. Those of the Gods depended upon the Powers and Offices then believ'd to belong to them, and had contracted a Weight and Veneration from the Rites and solemn Devotions in which they were us'd: They were a sort of Attributes with which it was a Matter of Religion to salute them on all Occasions, and an Irreverence to omit. As for the Epithets of great Men, Mons. *Boileau*[43] is of Opinion; that they were in the Nature of *Surnames*, and repeated as such; for the *Greeks* having no Names deriv'd from their Fathers, were oblig'd to add some other Distinction of each Person; either naming his Parents expressly, or his Place of Birth, Profession, or the like: As *Alexander* Son of *Philip*, *Herodotus* of *Halicarnassus*, *Diogenes* the *Cynic*, &c. *Homer* therefore complying with the Custom of his Countrey, us'd such distinctive Additions as better agreed with Poetry. And indeed we have something parallel to these in modern Times, such as the Names of *Harold Harefoot*,[44] *Edmund Ironside*,[45] *Edward Long-shanks*,[46] *Edward* the *black Prince*, &c. If yet this be thought to account better for the Propriety than for the Repetition, I shall add a farther Conjecture. *Hesiod* dividing the World into its different Ages, has plac'd a fourth Age between the Brazen and the Iron one,[47] of *Heroes distinct from other Men, a divine Race, who fought at Thebes and Troy, are called Demi-Gods, and live by the Care of Jupiter in the Islands of the Blessed.* Now

among the divine Honours which were paid them, they might have this also in common with the Gods, not to be mention'd without the Solemnity of an Epithet, and such as might be acceptable to them by its celebrating their Families, Actions, or Qualities.

What other Cavils have been rais'd against *Homer* are such as hardly deserve a Reply, but will yet be taken notice of as they occur in the Course of the Work. Many have been occasion'd by an injudicious Endeavour to exalt *Virgil;* which is much the same, as if one should think to raise[48] the Superstructure by undermining the Foundation: One would imagine by the whole Course of their Parallels, that these Criticks never so much as heard of *Homer's* having written first;[49] a Consideration which whoever compares these two Poets ought to have always in his Eye. Some accuse him for the same things which they overlook or praise in the other; as when they prefer the Fable and Moral of the *Æneis* to those of the *Iliad*, for the same Reasons which might set the *Odyssey* above the *Æneis*: as that the Heroe is a wiser Man; and the Action of the one more beneficial to his Countrey than that of the other: Or else they blame him for not doing what he never design'd; as because *Achilles* is not as good and perfect a Prince as *Æneas*, when the very Moral of his Poem requir'd a contrary Character. It is thus that *Rapin* judges in his Comparison of *Homer* and *Virgil*. Others select those particular Passages of *Homer* which are not so labour'd[50] as some that *Virgil* drew out of them: This is the whole Management of *Scaliger*[51] in his *Poetice*. Others quarrel with what they take for low and mean Expressions, sometimes thro' a false Delicacy and Refinement, oftner from an Ignorance of the Graces of the Original; and then triumph in the Aukwardness of their own Translations. This is the Conduct of *Perault* in his *Parallels*.[52] Lastly, there are others, who pretending to a fairer Proceeding, distinguish between the personal Merit of *Homer*, and that of his *Work;* but when they come to assign the Causes of the great Reputation of the *Iliad*, they found

---

41. the remotest Antiquity: According to Archbishop Ussher's calculation in the preceding century the earth was created in 4004 B.C. **42. what . . . Satisfaction:** a classic recommendation, remarkable at this date, of the usefulness of historical knowledge. **43. Mons. Boileau:** Nicolas Boileau-Despréaux (1636–1711), French poet and critic; *L'Art poétique* (1674) contains the body of literary principles respected throughout the eighteenth century. **44. Harold Harefoot:** Harold I (d. 1040). **45. Edmund Ironside:** Edmund (c. 980–1016), King of the English. **46. Edward Long-shanks:** Edward I (1239–1307). **47. a fourth . . . one:** See Hesiod's *Works and Days*, ll. 156 ff.

48. raise: The first edition reads: "praise." **49. Homer's . . . first:** Since paramountcy was given to invention, it followed that priority in inventing came second. Johnson ends his *Life of Milton* with the words: *Paradise Lost* "is not the greatest of heroick poems, only because it is not the first." **50. labour'd:** worked over by art. **51. Scaliger:** Julius Caesar Scaliger (1484–1558), Italian literary and scientific writer, whose *Poetics* was published posthumously in 1561. **52. Perault . . . Parallels:** *Parallèles des Anciens et des Modernes* (4 vols., 1688–97) by Charles Perrault (1628–1703), an advocate for the Moderns.

it upon the Ignorance of his Times, and the Prejudice of those that followed. And in pursuance of this Principle, they make those Accidents (such as the Contention of the Cities,[53] &c.) to be the Causes of his Fame, which were in Reality the Consequences of his Merit. The same might as well be said of *Virgil*, or any great Author, whose general Character[54] will infallibly raise many casual Additions to their Reputation. This is the Method of Mons. *de la Motte;*[55] who yet confesses upon the whole, that in whatever Age *Homer* had liv'd he must have been the greatest Poet of his Nation, and that he may be said in this Sense to be the Master even of those who surpass'd him.

In all these Objections we see nothing that contradicts his Title to the Honour of the chief *Invention;* and as long as this (which is indeed the Characteristic of Poetry itself) remains unequal'd by his Followers, he still continues superior to them. A cooler Judgment may commit fewer Faults, and be more approv'd in the Eyes of *One Sort* of Criticks: but that Warmth of Fancy will carry the loudest and most universal Applauses which holds the Heart of a Reader under the strongest Enchantment.[56] *Homer* not only appears the Inventor of Poetry, but excells all the Inventors of other Arts in this, that he has swallow'd up the Honour of those who succeeded him. What he has done admitted no Encrease, it only left room for Contraction or Regulation. He shew'd all the Stretch of Fancy at once; and if he has fail'd in some of his Flights, it was but because he attempted every thing. A Work of this kind seems like a mighty Tree which rises from the most vigorous Seed, is improv'd with Industry, flourishes, and produces the finest Fruit; Nature and Art conspire to raise it; Pleasure and Profit join to make it valuable: and they who find the justest Faults, have only said, that a few Branches (which run luxuriant thro' a Richness of Nature) might be lopp'd into Form to give it a more regular Appearance.[57]

Having now spoken of the Beauties and Defects of the Original, it remains to treat of the Translation, with the same View to the chief Characteristic. As far as that is seen in the main Parts of the Poem, such as the *Fable, Manners,* and *Sentiments,* no Translator can prejudice it but by wilful Omissions or Contractions. As it also breaks out in every particular *Image, Description,* and *Simile;* whoever lessens or too much softens those, takes off from this chief Character. It is the first grand Duty of an Interpreter to give his Author entire and unmaim'd; and for the rest, the *Diction* and *Versification* only are his proper Province; since these must be his own, but the others he is to take as he finds them.

It should then be consider'd what Methods may afford some Equivalent in our Language for the Graces of these in the *Greek.* It is certain no literal Translation can be just to an excellent Original in a superior Language: but it is a great Mistake to imagine (as many have done) that a rash Paraphrase can make amends for this general Defect; which is no less in danger to lose the Spirit of an Ancient, by deviating into the modern Manners of Expression. If there be sometimes a *Darkness,* there is often a *Light* in Antiquity, which nothing better preserves than a Version almost literal. I know no Liberties one ought to take, but those which are necessary for transfusing the Spirit of the Original, and supporting the Poetical Style of the Translation: and I will venture to say, there have not been more Men missed in former times by a servile dull Adherence to the Letter, than have been deluded in ours by a chimerical[58] insolent Hope of raising and improving their Author. It is not to be doubted that the *Fire* of the Poem is what a Translator should principally regard, as it is most likely to expire in his managing: However it is his safest way to be content with preserving this to his utmost in the Whole, without endeavouring to be more than he finds his Author is, in any particular Place. 'Tis a great Secret in Writing to know when to be plain, and when poetical and figurative; and it is what *Homer* will teach us if we will but follow modestly in his Footsteps. Where his Diction is bold and lofty, let us raise ours as high as we can; but where his is plain and humble, we ought not to be deterr'd from imitating him by the fear of incurring the Censure of a meer *English* Critick. Nothing that belongs to *Homer* seems to have been more commonly mistaken than the just Pitch of his Style: Some of his Translators having swell'd into

---

53. the Contention . . . Cities: Greek cities soon made rival claims of being Homer's birthplace. **54. general Character:** high standing, universally acknowledged. **55. Mons. . . . Motte:** Antoine de la Motte (1672–1731), another champion of the Moderns, made a verse translation of the *Iliad* (1714) based on Mme. Dacier's translation. **56. Enchantment:** A test of great literature was its power of ravishment. **57. A Work . . . Appearance:** Cf. *An Essay on Criticism,* above, ll. 233–52.

58. chimerical: fantastic.

Fustian[59] in a proud Confidence of the *Sublime; others* sunk into Flatness in a cold and timorous Notion of *Simplicity.* Methinks I see these different Followers of *Homer,* some sweating and straining after him by violent Leaps and Bounds, (the certain Signs of false Mettle[60]) others slowly and servilely creeping in his Train, while the Poet himself is all the time proceeding with an unaffected and equal Majesty before them. However of the two Extreams one could sooner pardon Frenzy than Frigidity: No Author is to be envy'd for such Commendations as he may gain by that Character of Style, which his Friends must agree together to call *Simplicity,* and the rest of the World will call *Dulness.* There is a *graceful* and *dignify'd* Simplicity, as well as a *bald* and *sordid* one, which differ as much from each other as the Air of a *plain* Man from that of a *Sloven:* 'Tis one thing to be tricked up, and another not to be dress'd at all. Simplicity is the Mean between Ostentation and Rusticity.

This pure and noble Simplicity is no where in such Perfection as in the *Scripture* and our Author. One may affirm with all respect to the inspired Writings, that the *Divine Spirit* made use of no other Words but what were intelligible and common to Men at that Time, and in that Part of the World; and as *Homer* is the Author nearest to those, his Style must of course bear a greater Resemblance to the sacred Books than that of any other Writer. This Consideration (together with what has been observ'd of the Parity of some of his Thoughts) may methinks induce a Translator on the one hand to give into[61] several of those general Phrases and Manners of Expression, which have attain'd a Veneration even in our Language from being used in the *Old Testament;* as on the other, to avoid those which have been appropriated to the Divinity, and in a manner consign'd to Mystery and Religion.

For a farther Preservation of this Air of Simplicity, a particular Care should be taken to express with all Plainness those *Moral Sentences* and *Proverbial Speeches* which are so numerous in this Poet. They have something Venerable, and as I may say *Oracular,* in that unadorn'd Gravity and Shortness with which they are deliver'd: a Grace which would be utterly lost by endeavouring to give them what we call a more ingenious (that is a more modern) Turn in the Paraphrase.

Perhaps the Mixture of some *Græcisms* and old Words after the manner of *Milton,* if done without too much Affectation,[62] might not have an ill Effect in a Version of this particular Work, which most of any other seems to require a venerable *Antique* Cast. But certainly the use of *modern Terms* of *War* and *Government,* such as *Platoon, Campagne, Junto,* or the like (into which some of his Translators have fallen) cannot be allowable; those only excepted, without which it is impossible to treat the Subjects in any living Language.

There are two Peculiarities in *Homer*'s Diction that are a sort of *Marks* or *Moles,* by which every common Eye distinguishes him at first sight: Those who are not his greatest Admirers look upon them as Defects, and those who are seem pleased with them as Beauties. I speak of his *Compound-Epithets* and of his *Repetitions.* Many of the former cannot be done literally into *English* without destroying the Purity of our Language. I believe such should be retain'd as slide easily of themselves into an *English-Compound,* without Violence to the Ear or to the receiv'd Rules of Composition; as well as those which have receiv'd a Sanction from the Authority of our best Poets, and are become familiar thro' their use of them; such as the *Cloud-compelling Jove, &c.* As for the rest, whenever any can be as fully and significantly exprest in a single word as in a compounded one, the Course to be taken is obvious. Some that cannot be so turn'd as to preserve their full Image by one or two Words, may have Justice done them by Circumlocution; as the Epithet εἰνοσίφυλλος to a Mountain would appear little or ridiculous translated literally *Leaf-shaking,* but affords a majestic Idea in the *Periphrasis: The lofty Mountain shakes his waving Woods.* Others that admit of differing Significations, may receive an Advantage by a judicious Variation according to the Occasions on which they are introduc'd. For Example, the Epithet of *Apollo,* ἑκηβόλος, or *far-shooting,* is capable of two Explications; one literal in respect of the Darts and Bow, the Ensigns of that God; the other allegorical with regard to the Rays of the Sun: Therefore in such Places where *Apollo* is represented as a God in Person, I would use the former Interpretation, and where the Effects of the Sun are describ'd, I would make choice

---

59. Fustian: shoddy; cloth made of cotton and linen, and so "a high swelling kind of writing made up of heterogeneous parts, or of words and ideas ill associated; bombast" (Johnson's *Dictionary*). **60. Mettle:** physical "spirit; spriteliness; courage" (Johnson's *Dictionary*). **61. give into:** "acknowledge the claims of," a new sense at this time.

62. after . . . Affectation: Pope deprecates overdoing the Miltonics in *Peri Bathous,* below, p. 620.

of the latter. Upon the whole, it will be necessary to avoid that perpetual Repetition of the same Epithets which we find in *Homer*, and which, tho' it might be accommodated (as has been already shewn) to the Ear of those Times, is by no means so to ours: But one may wait for Opportunities of placing them, where they derive an additional Beauty from the Occasions on which they are employed; and in doing this properly, a Translator may at once shew his Fancy and his Judgment.

As for *Homer's Repetitions;* we may divide them into three sorts; of whole Narrations and Speeches, of single Sentences, and of one Verse or Hemistich.[63] I hope it is not impossible to have such a Regard to these, as neither to lose so known a Mark of the Author on the one hand, nor to offend the Reader too much on the other. The Repetition is not ungraceful in those Speeches where the Dignity of the Speaker renders it a sort of Insolence to alter his Words; as in the Messages from Gods to Men, or from higher Powers to Inferiors in Concerns of State, or where the Ceremonial of Religion seems to require it, in the solemn Forms of Prayers, Oaths, or the like. In other Cases, I believe the best Rule is to be guided by the Nearness, or Distance, at which the Repetitions are plac'd in the Original: When they follow too close one may vary the Expression, but it is a Question whether a profess'd Translator be authorized to omit any: If they be tedious, the Author is to answer for it.

It only remains to speak of the *Versification*. *Homer* (as has been said) is perpetually applying the Sound to the Sense, and varying it on every new Subject. This is indeed one of the most exquisite Beauties of Poetry, and attainable. by very few: I know only of *Homer* eminent for it in the *Greek*, and *Virgil* in *Latine*. I am sensible it is what may sometimes happen by Chance, when a Writer is warm, and fully possest of his Image: however it may be reasonably believed they design'd this, in whose Verse it so manifestly appears in a superior degree to all others. Few Readers have the Ear to be Judges of it, but those who have will see I have endeavour'd at this Beauty.

Upon the whole, I must confess my self utterly incapable of doing Justice to *Homer*. I attempt him in no other Hope but that which one may entertain without much Vanity, of giving a more tolerable Copy of him than any entire Translation in Verse has yet done. We have only those of *Chapman, Hobbes,*

and *Ogilby. Chapman* has taken the Advantage of an immeasurable Length of Verse, notwithstanding which there is scarce any Paraphrase more loose and rambling than his. He has frequent Interpolations of four or six Lines, and I remember one in the thirteenth Book of the *Odyssey, ver.* 312. where he has spun twenty Verses out of two.[64] He is often mistaken in so bold a manner, that one might think he deviated on purpose, if he did not in other Places of his Notes insist so much upon Verbal Trifles. He appears to have had a strong Affectation of extracting new Meanings out of his Author, insomuch as to promise in his Rhyming Preface, a Poem of the Mysteries he had revealed in *Homer;* and perhaps he endeavoured to strain the obvious Sense to this End. His Expression is involved in Fustian, a Fault for which he was remarkable in his Original Writings, as in the Tragedy of *Bussy d' Amboise,* &c. In a word, the Nature of the Man may account for his whole Performance; for he appears from his Preface and Remarks to have been of an arrogant Turn, and an Enthusiast[65] in Poetry. His own Boast of having finish'd half the *Iliad* in less than fifteen Weeks, shews with what Negligence his Version was performed. But that which is to be allowed him, and which very much contributed to cover his Defects, is a daring fiery Spirit that animates his Translation, which is something like what one might imagine *Homer* himself would have writ before he arriv'd at Years of Discretion. *Hobbes* has given us a correct Explanation of the Sense in general, but for Particulars and Circumstances he continually lopps them, and often omits the most beautiful. As for its being esteem'd a close Translation, I doubt not many have been led into that Error by the Shortness of it, which proceeds not from his following the Original Line by Line,[66] but from the Contractions above-mentioned. He sometimes omits whole Similes and Sentences, and is now and then guilty of Mistakes into which no Writer of his Learning could have fallen, but thro' Carelesness. His Poetry, as well as *Ogilby's*, is too mean for Criticism.

It is a great Loss to the Poetical World that Mr. *Dryden* did not live to translate the *Iliad*. He has left us

---

63. Hemistich: half line.

64. He . . . two: Chapman's *Iliad* (1611) has considerably fewer lines than Pope's (and not as many as Homer's) but they are lines of seven feet. His *Odyssey* (1615), in heroic couplets, is longer than Pope's and both are longer than their original. **65. Enthusiast:** fanatic. **66. Line by Line:** George Sandys (1578-1644) had attempted this line-to-line correspondence in his translation of Ovid.

only the first Book and a small Part of the sixth; in which if he has in some Places not truly interpreted the Sense, or preserved the Antiquities, it ought to be excused on account of the Haste he was obliged to write in. He seems to have had too much Regard to *Chapman*, whose Words he sometimes copies, and has unhappily follow'd him in Passages where he wanders from the Original. However had he translated the whole Work, I would no more have attempted *Homer* after him than *Virgil*, his Version of whom (notwithstanding some human Errors) is the most noble and spirited Translation I know in any Language. But the Fate of great Genius's is like that of great Ministers, tho' they are confessedly the first in the Commonwealth of Letters, they must be envy'd and calumniated only for being at the Head of it.

That which in my Opinion ought to be the Endeavour of any one who translates *Homer*, is above all things to keep alive that Spirit and Fire which makes his chief Character. In particular Places, where the Sense can bear any Doubt, to follow the strongest and most Poetical, as most agreeing with that Character. To copy him in all the Variations of his Style, and the different Modulations of his Numbers. To preserve in the more active or descriptive Parts, a Warmth and Elevation; in the more sedate or narrative, a Plainness and Solemnity; in the Speeches a Fulness and Perspicuity; in the Sentences a Shortness and Gravity. Not to neglect even the little Figures and Turns on the Words, nor sometimes the very Cast of the Periods. Neither to omit nor confound any Rites or Customs of Antiquity. Perhaps too he ought to include the whole in a shorter Compass, than has hitherto been done by any Translator who has tolerably preserved either the Sense or Poetry. What I would farther recommend to him, is to study his Author rather from his own Text than from any Commentaries, how learned soever, or whatever Figure they make in the Estimation of the World. To consider him attentively in Comparison with *Virgil* above all the Ancients, and with *Milton* above all the Moderns. Next these the Archbishop of *Cambray*'s *Telemachus*[67] may give him the truest Idea of the Spirit and Turn of our Author, and *Bossu*'s admirable Treatise of the Epic Poem[68] the

justest Notion of his Design and Conduct. But after all, with whatever Judgment and Study a Man may proceed, or with whatever Happiness he may perform such a Work; he must hope to please but a few, those only who have at once a Taste of Poetry, and competent Learning. For to satisfy such as want either, is not in the Nature of this Undertaking; since a meer Modern Wit can like nothing that is not *Modern*, and a Pedant nothing that is not *Greek*.

What I have done is submitted to the Publick, from whose Opinions I am prepared to learn; tho' I fear no Judges so little as our best Poets, who are most sensible of the Weight of this Task. As for the worst, whatever they shall please to say, they may give me some Concern as they are unhappy Men, but none as they are malignant Writers. I was guided in this Translation by Judgments very different from theirs, and by Persons for whom they can have no Kindness, if an old Observation be true, that the strongest Antipathy in the World is that of Fools to Men of Wit. Mr. *Addison* was the first whose Advice determin'd me to undertake this Task, who was pleas'd to write to me upon that Occasion in such Terms as I cannot repeat without Vanity. I was obliged to Sir *Richard Steele* for a very early Recommendation of my Undertaking to the Publick. Dr. *Swift* promoted my Interest with that Warmth with which he always serves his Friend. The Humanity and Frankness of Sir *Samuel Garth*[69] are what I never knew wanting on any Occasion. I must also acknowledge with infinite Pleasure the many friendly Offices as well as sincere Criticisms of Mr. *Congreve*, who had led me the way in translating some Parts of *Homer*. I must add the Names of Mr. *Rowe*[70] and Dr. *Parnell*,[71] tho' I shall take a farther Opportunity of doing Justice to the last, whose Goodnature (to give it a great Panegyrick) is no less extensive than his Learning. The Favour of these Gentlemen is not entirely undeserved by one who bears them so true an Affection. But what can I say of the Honour so many of the *Great* have done me, while the *First Names* of the Age appear as my Subscribers, and the most distinguish'd Patrons and Ornaments of Learning

---

67. Telemachus: Fénelon's *Télémaque*, a prose epic, was published in 1699. **68. Treatise . . . Poem:** An English translation by "W. J." (not identified) of *Traité du poème épique* was published in 1695; a second edition in 1719.

69. Sir . . . Garth: (1661–1719), eminent physician and author of the mock-heroic poem *The Dispensary* (1699). **70. Mr. Rowe:** Nicholas Rowe (1674–1718), writer of she-tragedies and translator of Lucan (1718). **71. Dr. Parnell:** Thomas Parnell (1679–1718), an Irish clergyman and poet, was a member of the Scriblerus Club; he contributed a fine commendatory poem to Pope's *Works* in 1717. (See the selection from Parnell in Part Three.)

as my chief Encouragers.[72] Among these it is a particular Pleasure to me to find, that my highest Obligations are to such who have done most Honour to the
Name of Poet: That his Grace the *Duke* of *Buckingham*[73]
was not displeas'd I should undertake the Author to
whom he has given (in his excellent *Essay*[74]) so
complete a Praise.

> *Read* Homer *once, and you can read no more;*
> *For all books else appear so mean, so poor,*
> *Verse will seem Prose: yet still persist to read,*
> *And* Homer *will be all the books you need.*[75]

That the Earl of *Halifax*[76] was one of the first to
favour me, of whom it is hard to say whether the
Advancement of the Polite Arts is more owing to his
Generosity or his Example. That such a Genius as my
Lord *Bolingbroke*,[77] not more distinguished in the great
Scenes of Business than in all the useful and enter-
taining Parts of Learning, has not refus'd to be the
Critick of these Sheets, and the Patron of their Writer.
And that the noble Author of the Tragedy of *Heroic
Love*,[78] has continu'd his Partiality to me from my
writing Pastorals to my attempting the *Iliad*. I cannot
deny my self the Pride of confessing, that I have had
the Advantage not only of their Advice for the
Conduct in general, but their Correction of several
Particulars of this Translation.

I could say a great deal of the Pleasure of being
distinguish'd by the *Earl* of *Carnarvon*,[79] but it is

almost absurd to particularize any one generous
Action in a Person whose whole Life is a continued
Series of them. The Right Honourable Mr. *Stanhope*,[80]
the present Secretary of State, will pardon my Desire
of having it known that he was pleas'd to promote this
Affair. The particular Zeal of Mr. *Harcourt*[81] (the Son
of the late Lord Chancellor[82]) gave me a Proof how
much I am honour'd in a Share of his Friendship. I
must attribute to the same Motive that of several others
of my Friends, to whom all Acknowledgments are
render'd unnecessary by the Privileges of a familiar
Correspondence: And I am satisfy'd I can no way
better oblige Men of their Turn, than by my Silence.

In short, I have found more Patrons than ever *Homer*
wanted. He would have thought himself happy to
have met the same Favour at *Athens*, that has been
shewn me by its learned Rival, the University of
Oxford.[83] And I can hardly envy him those pompous
Honours he receiv'd after Death, when I reflect on the
Enjoyment of so many agreeable Obligations, and
easy Friendships which make the Satisfaction of Life.
This Distinction is the more to be acknowledg'd, as it
is shewn to one whose Pen has never gratify'd the
Prejudices of particular *Parties*, or the Vanities of
particular *Men*. Whatever the Success may prove, I
shall never repent of an Undertaking in which I have
experienc'd the Candour[84] and Friendship of so many
Persons of Merit; and in which I hope to pass some of
those Years of Youth that are generally lost in a Circle
of Follies, after a manner neither wholly unuseful to
others, nor disagreeable to my self.

72. the First . . . Encouragers: The first pages of the first
volume of Pope's translation are taken up with a long,
dazzling list of his subscribers. **73. the Duke . . .
Buckingham:** John Sheffield (1648–1721), Third Earl of
Mulgrave and later First Duke of Buckingham and
Normanby. **74. Essay:** the *Essay on Poetry* (1682). **75.
Read . . . need:** The reading here is that of the 1723
(posthumous) edition of Buckingham's *Works*, edited and
revised by Pope; before Pope introduced the revised reading
into the Preface in 1732, he had virtually quoted from editions
of the *Essay* that preceded the one he himself edited.
76. the Earl . . . Halifax: Charles Montagu, First Earl of
Halifax (1661–1715), poet, patron, and distinguished politician.
In 1714 he offered Pope a pension which was refused. Pope
refers to him again appreciatively in the *Epilogue to the Satires*,
ii. 77. He was however partly indebted to him for his satirical
portrait of Bufo in *An Epistle to Dr. Arbuthnot* (see below).
He thought his claims to taste a bit pretentious. **77. Bolingbroke:** Henry St. John (1678–1751), First Viscount Bolingbroke, Tory leader and man of letters; Pope dedicated to him
his *Essay on Man* (see below). **78. the noble . . . Love:**
George Granville (1667–1735), Baron Lansdowne, poet and
playwright. Pope dedicated *Windsor-Forest* (see above) to
him. **79. the Earl . . . Carnarvon:** James Brydges,
Earl of Carnarvon in 1714 and First Duke of Chandos in 1719.

80. Mr. Stanhope: James Stanhope, created First Earl
Stanhope in 1718. **81. Mr. Harcourt:** Pope's friend the
Honorable Simon Harcourt; his commendatory verses were
prefixed to Pope's *Works* (1717). On Harcourt's death in
1720 Pope wrote his epitaph. **82. the late . . . Chancellor:**
Simon Harcourt (c. 1661–1727), First Viscount Harcourt.
83. Oxford: After this, a number of earlier editions go on
to praise the women who encouraged him: "If my Author
had the *Wits* of After-Ages for his Defenders, his Translator
has had the *Beauties* of the present for his Advocates; a
Pleasure too great to be changed for any Fame in Reversion."
84. Candour: kindness, indulgence.

UPON CLEORA'S MARRIAGE AND RETIREMENT

❧

This poem was not acknowledged by Pope but is almost certainly his. It was first printed in *Poems on Several Occasions* (1717), a collection for which Pope seems to have been responsible and to which he banished such pieces, all short, as he did not wish to honor with a place in the *Works* of that year.

The text is that of the first printing.

❧

I.

Happy, *Cleora*, was the time,
E're courts and musick were a crime,
When maidens cou'd uncensur'd go,
With a she-friend from show to show.

II.

When bright *Cleora* cou'd appear
Drest to the season of the year;
And gayly ramble up and down,
The toast and envy of the town.

III.

When in a scarf (our sins forgiven,
No matter how we dress for heaven)   10
She drove to church, display'd her fan,
Took orange chips,° and thought on man.

IV.

Such was the life *Cleora* led,
Who then like blest *Cleora* sped?
Yet for the thing that pleases best,
Cleora gave up all the rest.

V.

And now confin'd to homely cares,
Domestick drudgery and prayers,
Coop't in a lonely fenny house,
One dog, the parson, and her spouse!   20

VI.

No basset° now, no midnight chat,
Of who said this, or who did that:
For scandal too (the joy of life)
No creature but the doctor's wife.

VII.

All this for sins of flesh and blood?
'Tis hard: but yet 'tis for her good.
For now there's time, and some pretence
Why she may think on providence.

VIII.

Beside, whate'er her future fate,
The matter is not now so great;   30
Half of her hell she suffers here,
And has but t' other half to fear.

ELOISA TO ABELARD

❧

When toward 1717 Pope was contemplating a collected edition of his poems, he may have regretted that certain kinds of Roman poems were not represented among them—or not at least by originals as distinct from translations. Like Virgil he had produced pastorals and a (mock) epic; his *Essay on Criticism* (1711) matched Horace's *Ars Poetica*. But the Ovidian element was lacking. Pope filled the gap with the *Elegy to the Memory of an Unfortunate Lady* (1717) and this heroic epistle.

There was much in the story of Eloisa and Abelard to tempt Pope to indulge those powers which, though never entirely absent from any of his poems, he had not always had occasion to develop fully. Material lay ready, almost as if it were waiting for him, in the Latin letters of the two lovers, and especially in the heightened and modernized account available in French and, since 1713, in English. Pope capitalized on this opportunity. His poem glows with a sensuousness that reflects the passion of the lovers. His conception of Eloisa shows him in possession of a kind of Shakespearean dramatic power, which he sustains as most playwrights cannot do because of the necessary give-and-take of stage writing. Eloisa expresses her successive bursts of feeling and argument with abandon; indeed, one of the triumphs of the poem is that everything it concerns—even the lamps in the sanctuary—is seen through her eyes. Pope explores a problem that only time, we feel, can solve. By the end

---

UPON CLEORA'S MARRIAGE AND RETIREMENT. **12. orange chips:** small, irregular slices of orange, presumably candied. No earlier use of the word is recorded.

21. basset: an Italian card game introduced into England in the seventeenth century.

of the poem though, Eloisa has achieved the temporary ease of exhaustion. She is an intellectual woman, completely in love with one who not only is absent but lacks the physical power to respond to her love (at the instigation of Eloisa's uncle, Abelard was cruelly mutilated); moreover she is a nun, pledged to forget the world. This is the person Pope takes in hand, subjecting her "plunging soul" to such consummate art that the poem has been suggestively described as uniting fire and ice.

The text is that of the first printing, in the *Works* of 1717, revised at those very few points where Pope came to feel that revision was called for.

❦

THE ARGUMENT

ABelard and Eloisa *flourish'd in the twelfth Century; they were two of the most distinguish'd persons of their age in learning and beauty, but for nothing more famous than for their unfortunate passion. After a long course of Calamities, they retired each to a several¹ Convent, and consecrated the remainder of their days to religion. It was many years after this separation, that a letter of* Abelard's *to a Friend which contain'd the history of his misfortunes, fell into the hands of* Eloisa. *This awakening all her tenderness, occasion'd those celebrated letters (out of which the following is partly extracted) which give so lively a picture of the struggles of grace and nature, virtue and passion.*

IN these deep solitudes and awful cells,
Where heav'nly-pensive, contemplation dwells,
And ever-musing melancholy reigns;
What means this tumult in a Vestal's veins?
Why rove my thoughts beyond this last retreat?
Why feels my heart its long-forgotten heat?
Yet, yet I love!—From *Abelard* it came,
And *Eloisa* yet must kiss the name.
  Dear fatal name! rest ever unreveal'd,
Nor pass these lips in holy silence seal'd.   10
Hide it, my heart, within that close disguise,
Where, mix'd with God's, his lov'd Idea° lies.
Oh write it not, my hand—The name appears
Already written—wash it out, my tears!
In vain lost *Eloisa* weeps and prays,
Her heart still dictates, and her hand obeys.
  Relentless walls! whose darksom round contains

Repentant sighs, and voluntary pains:
Ye rugged rocks! which holy knees have worn;
Ye grots and caverns shagg'd with horrid thorn!   20
Shrines! where their vigils pale-ey'd virgins keep,
And pitying saints, whose statues learn to weep°!
Tho' cold like you, unmov'd, and silent grown,
I have not yet forgot my self to stone.
All is not Heav'n's while *Abelard* has part,
Still rebel nature holds out half my heart;
Nor pray'rs nor fasts its stubborn pulse restrain,
Nor tears, for ages, taught to flow in vain.
  Soon as thy letters trembling I unclose,
That well-known name awakens all my woes.   30
Oh name for ever sad! for ever dear!
Still breath'd in sighs, still usher'd with a tear.
I tremble too where-e'er my own I find,
Some dire misfortune follows close behind.
Line after line my gushing eyes o'erflow,
Led thro' a sad variety of woe:
Now warm in love, now with'ring in thy bloom,
Lost in a convent's° solitary gloom!
There stern religion quench'd th' unwilling flame,
There dy'd the best of passions, Love and Fame.   40
  Yet write, oh write me all, that I may join
Griefs to thy griefs, and eccho sighs to thine.
Nor foes nor fortune take this pow'r away.
And is my *Abelard* less kind than they?
Tears still are mine, and those I need not spare,
Love but demands what else were shed in pray'r;
No happier task these faded eyes pursue,
To read and weep is all they now can do.
  Then share thy pain, allow that sad relief;
Ah more than share it! give me all thy grief.   50
Heav'n first taught letters for some wretches aid,
Some banish'd lover, or some captive maid;
They live, they speak, they breathe what love inspires,
Warm from the soul, and faithful to its fires,
The virgins wish without her fears impart,
Excuse° the blush, and pour out all the heart,
Speed the soft intercourse from soul to soul,
And waft a sigh from *Indus* to the *Pole.*
  Thou know'st how guiltless first I met thy flame,
When Love approach'd me under Friendship's
      name;   60
My fancy form'd thee of Angelick kind,
Some emanation of th' all-beauteous Mind.
Those smiling eyes, attemp'ring ev'ry ray,

ELOISA TO ABELARD: *The Argument.* **1. several:** different. **12. Idea:** image.

22. statues . . . weep: a reference to the condensed moisture that runs down statues. **38. convent's:** monastery's. **56. Excuse:** exempt from the need of.

Shone sweetly lambent with celestial day:
Guiltless I gaz'd; heav'n listen'd while you sung;
And truths divine came mended from that tongue.°
From lips like those what precept fail'd to move?
Too soon they taught me 'twas no sin to love.
Back thro' the paths of pleasing sense I ran,
Nor wish'd an Angel whom I lov'd a Man.°   70
Dim and remote the joys of saints I see,
Nor envy them, that heav'n I lose for thee.

How oft', when press'd to marriage, have I said,
Curse on all laws but those which love has made!
Love, free as air, at sight of human ties,
Spreads his light wings, and in a moment flies.
Let wealth, let honour, wait the wedded dame,
August her deed, and sacred be her fame;
Before true passion all those views remove,
Fame, wealth, and honour! what are you to Love?   80
The jealous God, when we profane his fires,
Those restless passions in revenge inspires;
And bids them make mistaken mortals groan,
Who seek in love for ought but love alone.
Should at my feet the world's great master fall,
Himself, his throne, his world, I'd scorn 'em all:
Not *Cæsar*'s empress wou'd I deign to prove;
No, make me mistress to the man I love;
If there be yet another name more free,
More fond° than mistress, make me that to thee!   90
Oh happy state! when souls each other draw,
When love is liberty, and nature, law:
All then is full, possessing, and possest,
No craving Void left aking in the breast:
Ev'n thought meets thought e'er from the lips it part,
And each warm wish springs mutual from the heart.
This sure is bliss (if bliss on earth there be)
And once the lot of *Abelard* and me.

Alas how chang'd! what sudden horrors rise!
A naked Lover bound and bleeding lies!   100
Where, where was *Eloise*? her voice, her hand,
Her ponyard, had oppos'd the dire command.
Barbarian stay! that bloody stroke restrain;
The crime was common, common be the pain.°
I can no more; by shame, by rage supprest,
Let tears, and burning blushes speak the rest.

Canst thou forget that sad, that solemn day,

When victims at yon' altar's foot we lay?
Canst thou forget what tears that moment fell,
When, warm in youth, I bade the world farewell? 110
As with cold lips I kiss'd the sacred veil,
The shrines all trembled, and the lamps grew pale:
Heav'n scarce believ'd the conquest it survey'd,
And Saints with wonder heard the vows I made.
Yet then, to those dread altars as I drew,
Not on the Cross my eyes were fix'd, but you;
Not grace, or zeal, love only was my call,
And if I lose thy love, I lose my all.
Come! with thy looks, thy words, relieve my woe;
Those still at least are left thee to bestow.   120
Still on that breast enamour'd let me lie,
Still drink delicious poison from thy eye,
Pant on thy lip, and to thy heart be prest;
Give all thou canst—and let me dream the rest.
Ah no! instruct me other joys to prize,
With other beauties charm my partial eyes,
Full in my view set all the bright abode,
And make my soul quit *Abelard* for God.

Ah think at least thy flock deserves thy care,
Plants of thy hand, and children of thy pray'r.   130
From the false world in early youth they fled,
By thee to mountains, wilds, and deserts led.
You rais'd these hallow'd walls;° the desert smil'd,
And Paradise was open'd in the Wild.
No° weeping orphan saw his father's stores
Our shrines irradiate, or emblaze° the floors;
No silver saints, by dying misers giv'n,
Here brib'd the rage of ill-requited heav'n:
But such plain roofs as piety could raise,
And only vocal with the Maker's praise.   140
In these lone walls (their day's eternal bound)
These moss-grown domes° with spiry turrets
          crown'd,
Where awful arches make a noon-day night,
And the dim windows shed a solemn light;
Thy eyes diffus'd a reconciling ray,
And gleams of glory brighten'd all the day.
But now no face divine contentment wears,
'Tis all blank sadness, or continual tears.
See how the force of others' pray'rs I try,
(Oh pious fraud of am'rous charity!)   150

---

66. And . . . tongue: [Pope's note] *He was her Preceptor in Philosophy and Divinity.* **69–70. Back . . . Man:** Having thought you an angel, I now became a normal human being again and accepted you as human. **90. fond:** Note the contribution of *fond*, meaning doting, to the idea. **104. pain:** penalty.

133. You . . . walls: [Pope's note] *He founded the Monastery.* **135–40. No . . . praise:** Satire was a welcome ingredient in any poem in this period. Dryden had said, "Satire will have place whate'er I write." **136. irradiate, emblaze:** Both verbs, which come from Milton, mean something like "adorn with splendor." **142. domes:** dwellings.

But why should I on others' pray'rs depend?
Come thou, my father,° brother,° husband, friend!
Ah let thy handmaid, sister, daughter move,
And, all those tender names in one, thy love!
The darksom pines that o'er yon' rocks reclin'd
Wave high, and murmur to the hollow wind,
The wandring streams that shine between the hills,
The grots that eccho to the trinkling rills,
The dying gales that pant upon the trees,
The lakes that quiver to the curling breeze;   160
No more these scenes my meditation aid,
Or lull to rest the visionary° maid:
But o'er the twilight groves, and dusky caves,
Long-sounding isles, and intermingled graves,
Black Melancholy sits, and round her throws
A death-like silence, and a dread repose:
Her gloomy presence saddens all the scene,
Shades ev'ry flow'r, and darkens ev'ry green,
Deepens the murmur of the falling floods,
And breathes a browner horror on the woods.   170
    Yet here for ever, ever must I stay;
Sad proof how well a lover can obey!
Death, only death, can break the lasting chain;
And here ev'n then, shall my cold dust remain,
Here all its frailties, all its flames resign,
And wait, till 'tis no sin to mix with thine.
    Ah wretch! believ'd the spouse of God in vain,
Confess'd within the slave of love and man.
Assist me heav'n! but whence arose that pray'r?
Sprung it from piety, or from despair?   180
Ev'n here, where frozen chastity retires,
Love finds an altar for forbidden fires.
I ought to grieve, but cannot what I ought;
I mourn the lover, not lament the fault;
I view my crime, but kindle at the view,
Repent old pleasures, and sollicit new:
Now turn'd to heav'n, I weep my past offence,
Now think of thee, and curse my innocence.
Of all affliction taught a lover yet,
'Tis sure the hardest science° to forget!   190
How shall I lose the sin, yet keep the sense,
And love th' offender, yet detest th' offence?
How the dear object from the crime remove,
Or how distinguish penitence from love?
Unequal task! a passion to resign,
For hearts so touch'd, so pierc'd, so lost as mine.

E'er such a soul regains its peaceful state,
How often must it love, how often hate!
How often, hope, despair, resent, regret,
Conceal, disdain—do all things but forget.   200
But let heav'n seize it, all at once 'tis fir'd,
Not touch'd, but rapt; not waken'd, but inspir'd!
Oh come! oh teach me nature to subdue,
Renounce my love, my life, my self—and you.
Fill my fond heart with God alone, for he
Alone can rival, can succeed to thee.
    How happy is the blameless Vestal's lot!
The world forgetting, by the world forgot.
Eternal sun-shine of the spotless mind!
Each pray'r accepted, and each wish resign'd;   210
Labour and rest, that equal periods keep;
'Obedient slumbers that can wake and weep';°
Desires compos'd, affections ever ev'n,
Tears that delight, and sighs that waft to heav'n.
Grace shines around her with serenest beams,
And whisp'ring Angels prompt her golden dreams.
For her th' unfading rose of *Eden* blooms,
And wings of Seraphs shed divine perfumes;
For her the Spouse° prepares the bridal ring,
For her white virgins *Hymenæals*° sing;   220
To sounds of heav'nly harps, she dies away,
And melts in visions of eternal day.
    Far other dreams my erring soul employ,
Far other raptures, of unholy joy:
When at the close of each sad, sorrowing day,
Fancy restores what vengeance snatch'd away,
Then conscience sleeps, and leaving nature free,
All my loose soul unbounded springs to thee.
O curst, dear horrors of all-conscious° night!
How glowing guilt exalts the keen delight!   230
Provoking Dæmons all restraint remove,
And stir within me ev'ry source of love.
I hear thee, view thee, gaze o'er all thy charms,
And round thy phantom glue my clasping arms.
I wake—no more I hear, no more I view,
The phantom flies me, as unkind as you.
I call aloud; it hears not what I say;
I stretch my empty arms; it glides away:
To dream once more I close my willing eyes;
Ye soft illusions, dear deceits, arise!   240

---

152. father: priest. **brother:** like *sister* in the following line,
a member of a religious community. **162. visionary:**
seeing visions. **190. science:** knowledge.

212. Obedient . . . weep: Pope quotes line 16 from
Description of a Religious House, a poem on a similar subject
by Richard Crashaw (1612–49). **219. Spouse:** Christ. **220.**
Hymenæals: wedding songs. **229. all-conscious:** wholly
conscious.

Alas no more!—methinks we wandring go
Thro' dreary wastes, and weep each other's woe;
Where round some mould'ring tow'r pale ivy creeps,
And low-brow'd rocks hang nodding o'er the deeps.
Sudden you mount! you becken from the skies;
Clouds interpose, waves roar, and winds arise.
I shriek, start up, the same sad prospect find,
And wake to all the griefs I left behind.

    For thee the fates, severely kind, ordain
A cool suspense from pleasure and from pain;   250
Thy life a long, dead calm of fix'd repose;
No pulse that riots, and no blood that glows.
Still as the sea, e'er winds were taught to blow,
Or moving spirit bade the waters flow;
Soft as the slumbers of a saint forgiv'n,
And mild as opening gleams of promis'd heav'n.

    Come *Abelard!* for what hast thou to dread?
The torch of *Venus* burns not for the dead;
Nature stands check'd; Religion disapproves;
Ev'n thou art cold—yet *Eloisa* loves.   260
Ah hopeless, lasting flames! like those that burn
To light the dead, and warm th' unfruitful urn.°

    What scenes appear where-e'er I turn my view!
The dear Ideas, where I fly, pursue,
Rise in the grove, before the altar rise,
Stain all my soul, and wanton in my eyes!
I waste the Matin lamp in sighs for thee,
Thy image steals between my God and me,
Thy voice I seem in ev'ry hymn to hear;
With ev'ry bead I drop too soft a tear.   270
When from the Censer clouds of fragrance roll,
And swelling organs lift the rising soul;
One thought of thee puts all the pomp to flight,
Priests, Tapers, Temples, swim before my sight:
In seas of flame my plunging soul is drown'd,
While Altars blaze, and Angels tremble round.

    While prostrate here in humble grief I lie,
Kind, virtuous drops just gath'ring in my eye,
While praying, trembling, in the dust I roll,
And dawning grace is opening on my soul: 280
Come, if thou dar'st, all charming as thou art!
Oppose thy self to heav'n; dispute° my heart;
Come, with one glance of those deluding eyes,
Blot out each bright Idea of the skies.
Take back that grace, those sorrows, and those tears,
Take back my fruitless penitence and pray'rs,

Snatch me, just mounting, from the blest abode,
Assist the Fiends and tear me from my God!

    No, fly me, fly me! far as Pole from Pole;
Rise *Alps* between us! and whole oceans roll!   290
Ah come not, write not, think not once of me,
Nor share one pang of all I felt for thee.
Thy oaths I quit, thy memory resign,
Forget, renounce me, hate whate'er was mine.
Fair eyes, and tempting looks (which yet I view!)
Long lov'd, ador'd ideas! all adieu!
O grace serene! oh virtue heav'nly fair!
Divine oblivion of low-thoughted care!
Fresh blooming hope, gay daughter of the sky!
And faith, our early immortality°!   300
Enter each mild, each amicable guest;
Receive, and wrap me in eternal rest!

    See in her Cell sad *Eloisa* spread,
Propt on some tomb, a neighbour of the dead!
In each low wind methinks a Spirit calls,
And more than Echoes talk along the walls.
Here, as I watch'd the dying lamps around,
From yonder shrine I heard a hollow sound.
Come, sister come! (it said, or seem'd to say)
Thy place is here, sad sister come away!   310
Once like thy self, I trembled, wept, and pray'd,
Love's victim then, tho' now a sainted maid:
But all is calm in this eternal sleep;
Here grief forgets to groan, and love to weep,
Ev'n superstition loses ev'ry fear:
For God, not man, absolves our frailties here.

    I come, I come! prepare your roseate bow'rs,
Celestial palms, and ever blooming flow'rs.
Thither, where sinners may have rest, I go,
Where flames refin'd in breasts seraphic glow.   320
Thou, *Abelard!* the last sad office pay,
And smooth my passage to the realms of day:
See my lips tremble, and my eye-balls roll,
Suck my last breath, and catch my flying soul!
Ah no—in sacred vestments may'st thou stand,
The hallow'd taper trembling in thy hand,
Present the Cross before my lifted eye,
Teach me at once, and learn of me to die.
Ah then, thy once-lov'd *Eloisa* see!
It will be then no crime to gaze on me.   330
See from my cheek the transient roses fly!
See the last sparkle languish in my eye!

261–62. Ah . . . urn: The Romans believed that they could supply tombs with unextinguishable lamps. **282. dispute:** contend for.

300. faith . . . immortality: The Christian, whose faith remains unchanged through death, may be held to be already in possession of eternity.

Till ev'ry motion, pulse, and breath, be o'er;
And ev'n my *Abelard* be lov'd no more.
O death all-eloquent! you only prove
What dust we doat on, when 'tis man we love.
    Then too, when fate shall thy fair frame destroy,
(That cause of all my guilt, and all my joy)
In trance extatic may thy pangs be drown'd,
Bright clouds descend, and Angels watch thee
        round,   340
From opening skies may streaming glories shine,
And Saints embrace thee with a love like mine.
    May one kind grave° unite each hapless name,°
And graft my love immortal on thy fame.
Then, ages hence, when all my woes are o'er,
When this rebellious heart shall beat no more;
If ever chance two wandring lovers brings
To *Paraclete*'s white walls, and silver springs,
O'er the pale marble shall they join their heads,
And drink the falling tears each other sheds,   350
Then sadly say, with mutual pity mov'd,
Oh may we never love as these have lov'd!
From the full quire° when loud *Hosanna*'s rise,
And swell the pomp of dreadful sacrifice,°
Amid that scene, if some relenting eye
Glance on the stone where our cold reliques lie,
Devotion's self shall steal a thought from heav'n,
One human tear shall drop, and be forgiv'n.
And sure if fate some future Bard° shall join
In sad similitude of griefs to mine,   360
Condemn'd whole years in absence to deplore,
And image charms he must behold no more,
Such if there be, who loves so long, so well;
Let him our sad, our tender story tell;
The well-sung woes will sooth my pensive ghost;
He best can paint 'em, who shall feel 'em most.

---

343. one . . . grave: [Pope's note] Abelard *and* Eloisa *were interr'd in the same grave, or in monuments adjoining, in the Monastery of the* Paraclete. **name:** person, as often in the Bible. **353. quire:** choir. **354. dreadful sacrifice:** the mass. **359. Bard:** Pope himself; he is alluding to his friend Lady Mary Wortley Montagu (1689–1762), who was traveling in the Middle East. (See the selection from Lady Mary in Part Three.)

PREFACE
[TO THE *WORKS* (1717)]

Pope affixed this essay to the first collection of his poems, a substantial and handsome volume, published simultaneously in both folio and quarto forms. In the Preface he pleads both for himself and for writers in general, whether good or bad. To champion bad authors was for him a unique undertaking, and he embarks on it only to serve his real purpose, the denunciation of those incompetent and malicious critics from whom all authors suffer alike. While defending bad writers he does admit, however, that "their obstinacy in persisting to write" is a grave offense. (This is the main charge against them in *The Dunciad* [1728], whereas in *An Epistle to Dr. Arbuthnot* [1735] Pope contends that persistent bad writers are bad men.)

Pope's defense of himself is beautifully subtle as well as forthright; it includes as its climax the claim that a good poet is a good man, a belief that had been held by Renaissance critics, including Milton. In much of the Preface Pope is bent on showing himself as an *honnête homme*, intelligent and well balanced, benevolent and well mannered. But we note how much in earnest, and how autocratic, is the poet in him. In *An Essay on Criticism* (1711) we were told that he "Glows while he reads" and "trembles as he writes," and the conclusion of that poem, as of the *Temple of Fame* (1715), had been a prayer to be worthy of his genius. The tone of this apologia is no less noble and vibrant, and at the same time modest.

Again, as in the *Essay*, he seeks to define that prime problem for writers of his day—their relation to the Ancients. For Pope, the Modern committed to his art "imitates" the Ancients by employing his gifts as they did theirs, by doing his best to build soundly. Taking them for his practical ideal, he will find that the discoveries he himself makes, both as a man and a writer, corroborate truths discovered long ago. To find that the seeming novelties of one's own experience repeat the novelties of thousands of years ago was to feel powerfully that one had the whole human race for witness, and so to be more confident of one's own judgment and hopes.

Joseph Warton held the Preface to be "one of the best pieces of prose in our language." A fair number of revisions were introduced into the text of 1717, some in the 1736 collected edition, and others later, for the sake of clarity and amplification and at one point to remove a small discrepancy. The present text is that of

1717, corrected in accordance with all Pope's revisions except for one passage added in 1736. This is quoted instead in a footnote, since it is not so appropriate in a Preface to which Pope added the date "Nov. 10, 1716."

☙❧

I Am inclined to think that both the writers of books, and the readers of them, are generally not a little unreasonable in their expectations. The first seem to fancy that the world must approve whatever they produce, and the latter to imagine that authors are obliged to please them at any rate. Methinks as on the one hand, no single man is born with a right of controuling the opinions of all the rest; so on the other, the world has no title to demand, that the whole care and time of any particular person should be sacrificed to its entertainment. Therefore I cannot but believe that writers and readers are under equal obligations, for as much fame, or pleasure, as each affords the other.

Every one acknowledges, it would be a wild notion to expect perfection in any work of man: and yet one would think the contrary was taken for granted, by the judgment commonly past upon Poems. A Critic supposes he has done his part, if he proves a writer to have fail'd in an expression, or err'd in any particular point: and can it then be wonder'd at, if the Poets in general seem resolv'd not to own themselves in any error? For as long as one side will make no allowances, the other will be brought to no acknowledgments.

I am afraid this extreme zeal on both sides is ill-plac'd; Poetry and Criticism being by no means the universal concern of the world, but only the affair of idle men who write in their closets, and of idle men who read there. Yet sure upon the whole, a bad Author deserves better usage than a bad Critic; for a Writer's endeavour, for the most part, is to please his Readers, and he fails merely thro' the misfortune of an ill judgment; but such a Critic's is to put them out of humour; a design he could never go upon without both that and an ill temper.

I think a good deal may be said to extenuate the fault of bad Poets. What we call a Genius, is hard to be distinguish'd by a man himself, from a strong inclination: and if his Genius be never so great, he can not at first discover it any other way, than by giving way to that prevalent propensity which renders him the more liable to be mistaken. The only method he has, is to

make the experiment by writing, and appealing to the judgment of others: Now if he happens to write ill (which is certainly no sin in itself) he is immediately made an object of ridicule. I wish we had the humanity to reflect that even the worst authors might, in their endeavour to please us, deserve something at our hands. We have no cause to quarrel with them but for their obstinacy in persisting to write, and this too may admit of alleviating circumstances. Their particular friends may be either ignorant, or insincere; and the rest of the world in general is too well bred to shock them with a truth, which generally their Booksellers[1] are the first that inform them of. This happens not till they have spent too much of their time, to apply to any profession which might better fit their talents; and till such talents as they have are so far discredited, as to be but of small service to them. For (what is the hardest case imaginable) the reputation of a man generally depends upon the first steps he makes in the world, and people will establish their opinion of us, from what we do at that season when we have least judgment to direct us.

On the other hand, a good Poet no sooner communicates his works with the same desire of information, but it is imagin'd he is a vain young creature given up to the ambition of fame; when perhaps the poor man is all the while trembling with the fear of being ridiculous. If he is made to hope he may please the world, he falls under very unlucky circumstances; for from the moment he prints, he must expect to hear no more truth, than if he were a Prince, or a Beauty. If he has not very good sense (and indeed there are twenty men of wit, for one man of sense), his living thus in a course of flattery may put him in no small danger of becoming a Coxcomb:[2] If he has, he will consequently have so much diffidence, as not to reap any great satisfaction from his praise; since if it be given to his face, it can scarce be distinguish'd from flattery, and if in his absence, it is hard to be certain of it. Were he sure to be commended by the best and most knowing, he is as sure of being envy'd by the worst and most ignorant, which are the majority; for it is with a fine Genius as with a fine fashion, all those are displeas'd at it who are not able to follow it: And 'tis to be fear'd that esteem will seldom do any man so

PREFACE TO THE *Works* (1717). **1. Booksellers:** At this time they also fulfilled the function of publishers, and their importance was increasing now that the patron's was decreasing. **2. Coxcomb:** pretender to talent or taste.

much good, as ill-will does him harm. Then there is a third class of people who make the largest part of mankind, those of ordinary or indifferent capacities; and these (to a man) will hate, or suspect him: a hundred honest gentlemen will dread him as a wit,[3] and a hundred innocent[4] women as a satyrist. In a word, whatever be his fate in Poetry, it is ten to one but he must give up all the reasonable aims of life for it. There are indeed some advantages accruing from a Genius to Poetry, and they are all I can think of: the agreeable power of self-amusement[5] when a man is idle or alone; the privilege of being admitted into the best company; and the freedom of saying as many careless things as other people, without being so severely remark'd upon.

I believe, if any one, early in his life should contemplate the dangerous fate of authors, he would scarce be of their number on any consideration. The life of a Wit is a warfare upon earth; and the present spirit of the learned world is such, that to attempt to serve it (any way) one must have the constancy of a martyr, and a resolution to suffer for its sake.[6] I confess it was want of consideration that made me an author; I writ because it amused me; I corrected[7] because it was as pleasant to me to correct as to write; and I publish'd because I was told I might please such as it was a credit to please. To what degree I have done this, I am really ignorant; I had too much fondness for my productions to judge of them at first, and too much judgment to be pleas'd with them at last. But I have reason to think they can have no reputation which will continue long, or which deserves to do so: for they have always fallen

short not only of what I read of others, but even of my own Ideas of Poetry.[8]

If any one should imagine I am not in earnest, I desire him to reflect, that the Ancients (to say the least of them) had as much Genius as we; and that to take more pains, and employ more time, cannot fail to produce more complete pieces. They constantly apply'd themselves not only to that art, but to that single branch[9] of an art, to which their talent was most powerfully bent; and it was the business of their lives to correct and finish their works for posterity. If we can pretend to have used the same industry, let us expect the same immortality: Tho' if we took the same care, we should still lie under a farther misfortune: they writ in languages that became universal and everlasting, while ours are extremely limited both in extent, and in duration. A mighty foundation for our pride! when the utmost we can hope, is but to be read in one Island, and to be thrown aside at the end of one Age.

All that is left us is to recommend our productions by the imitation of the Ancients: and it will be found true, that in every age, the highest character for sense[10] and learning has been obtain'd by those who have been most indebted to them. For to say truth, whatever is very good sense must have been common sense in all times; and what we call Learning, is but the knowledge of the sense of our predecessors. Therefore they who say our thoughts are not our own because they resemble the Ancients, may as well say our faces are not our own, because they are like our Fathers: And indeed it is very unreasonable, that people should expect us to be Scholars, and yet be angry to find us so.

I fairly confess that I have serv'd my self all I could by reading; that I made use of the judgment of authors dead and living; that I omitted no means in my power to be inform'd of my errors, both by my friends and enemies: But the true reason these pieces are not more correct, is owing to the consideration how short a time they, and I, have to live: One may be ashamed to consume half one's days in bringing sense and rhyme

---

3. wit: a genius, a person superior in intellect. **4. innocent:** ironic: they would have no cause for dread if they *were* innocent. **5. self-amusement:** *Amusement* bore a more intellectual meaning in the eighteenth century: keeping the whole mind happily employed. **6. sake:** Here the collected edition of 1736 continues with the following passage: "I could wish people would believe, what I am pretty certain they will not, that I have been much less concerned about Fame than I durst declare till this occasion, when methinks I should find more credit than I could heretofore: since my writings have had their fate already, and it is too late to think of prepossessing the reader in their favour. I would plead it as some merit in me, that the world has never been prepared for these trifles by Prefaces, byassed by recommendations, dazzled with the names of great Patrons, wheedled with fine reasons and pretences, or troubled with excuses." **7. corrected:** This word had a broader sense in the eighteenth century than it has today; it pertained to matter as well as manner.

8. they have . . . Poetry: Cf. the famous speech of Marlowe's Tamburlaine, V. ii. 98 ff.: "If all the pens that ever poets held . . . ." **9. single branch:** a hard and much discussed question, whether a genius can succeed at many things or only at one narrow occupation. Pope seems to be forgetting Virgil and Horace, unless he means that they confined themselves to meter. **10. sense:** the possession of a true knowledge of human nature.

together; and what Critic can be so unreasonable as not to leave a man time enough for any more serious employment, or more agreeable amusement?

The only plea I shall use for the favour of the publick, is, that I have as great a respect for it, as most authors have for themselves; and that I have sacrificed much of my own self-love for its sake, in preventing not only many mean things from seeing the light, but many which I thought tolerable. I would not be like those Authors, who forgive themselves some particular lines for the sake of a whole Poem; and vice versa a whole Poem for the sake of some particular lines. I believe no one qualification is so likely to make a good writer, as the power of rejecting his own thoughts; and it must be this (if any thing) that can give me a chance to be one. For what I have publish'd, I can only hope to be pardon'd; but for what I have burn'd,[11] I deserve to be prais'd. On this account the world is under some obligation to me, and owes me the justice in return, to look upon no verses as mine that are not inserted in this collection. And perhaps nothing could make it worth my while to own what are really so, but to avoid the imputation of so many dull and immoral things, as partly by malice, and partly by ignorance, have been ascribed to me. I must farther acquit my self of the presumption of having lent my name to recommend any Miscellanies,[12] or works of other men, a thing I never thought becoming a person who has hardly credit enough to answer for his own.

In this office of collecting my pieces, I am altogether uncertain, whether to look upon my self as a man building a monument, or burying the dead?

If time shall make it the former, may these Poems (as long as they last) remain as a testimony, that their Author never made his talents subservient to the mean and unworthy ends of Party or self-interest; the gratification of publick prejudices, or private passions; the flattery of the undeserving, or the insult of the unfortunate. If I have written well, let it be consider'd that 'tis what no man can do without good sense, a quality that not only renders one capable of being a good writer, but a good man. And if I have made any acquisition in the opinion of any one under the notion of the former, let it be continued to me under no other title than that of the latter.

But if this publication be only a more solemn funeral of my Remains, I desire it may be known that I die in charity, and in my senses; without any murmurs against the justice of this age, or any mad appeals to posterity. I declare I shall think the world in the right, and quietly submit to every truth which time shall discover to the prejudice of these writings; not so much as wishing so irrational a thing, as that every body should be deceiv'd, meerly for my credit. However, I desire it may then be consider'd, that there are very few things in this collection which were not written under the age of five and twenty; so that my youth may be made (as it never fails to be in Executions) a case of compassion. That I was never so concern'd about my works as to vindicate them in print, believing if any thing was good it would defend itself, and what was bad could never be defended. That I used no artifice to raise or continue a reputation, depreciated no dead author I was obliged to, brib'd no living one with unjust praise, insulted no adversary with ill language, or when I could not attack a Rival's works, encourag'd reports against his Morals. To conclude, if this volume perish, let is serve as a warning to the Critics, not to take too much pains for the future to destroy such things as will die of themselves; and a *Memento mori* to some of my vain cotemporaries the Poets, to teach them that when real merit is wanting, it avails nothing to have been encourag'd by the great, commended by the eminent, and favour'd by the publick in general.[13]

[COUPLET ON NEWTON]

This couplet was first published as Article xlii of *The Present State of the Republic of Letters*, V (June, 1730), where the first line read: "All Nature and her Laws . . . ."

Nature and Nature's Laws lay hid in Night:
God said, *Let* NEWTON *be:* And all was Light!

---

11. burn'd: Pope did burn some of his inferior poetry, but, fortunately, he kept what was almost up to standard and printed it anonymously. He drew a sensible distinction between what he wanted to be known as his, and what not; having drawn it, he had to pretend that he had published no poems not included in this collection. **12. I . . . Miscellanies:** This passage reads differently now that we know that Pope edited in this year what Ault called "Pope's own Miscellany," and possibly one sometime earlier.

13. encourag'd . . . general: All this Pope had enjoyed.

PERI BATHOUS:
OR, MARTINUS SCRIBLERUS,°
HIS TREATISE
OF THE ART OF SINKING
IN POETRY

In March, 1728, the *Peri Bathous* inaugurated what Pope meant to make the fiercest phase of his long campaign against the Dunces, a campaign that was to culminate with *The Dunciad* itself (which followed in its first form two months later). For Pope this campaign was not wholly personal; he considered himself to be acting on behalf of the Scriblerus Club, and with the detail of his attack he may well have had help from its members.

Purporting to be the serious imitation by the German scholar Martinus Scriblerus of a recently discovered first-century A.D. treatise, the *Peri Hupsous* (*On the Sublime*), Pope's *Peri Bathous* is a work of irony. The Moderns whom Martinus is advising and championing are held up as writers who "infinitely excel the . . . Ancients." Here and at the beginning of Chapters v and x Pope's irony is absolute and obvious. At times though the irony is more complicated, and Pope's position does not appear so clear-cut. Finally, Pope dispenses with irony altogether in such passages as the description of the Moderns in terms of birds, beasts, and fish. Here the voice of Martinus is clearly Pope's own, and Martinus's Moderns are Pope's Dunces.

Pope's object was not so simple as he pretends. Indeed he sometimes has difficulty in persuading us that he has made his case. The Dunces were not wholly bad as poets, although they often wrote in a style Pope himself had outgrown in his youth. If Pope the satirist had been disinterested, he would have admitted as much. We can readily find outstanding examples to the contrary. Ambrose Philips is now prominent among Pope's victims, but when his *Pastorals* were first published in 1709—the same year as Pope's—Pope gave them their due praise in a private letter, only changing his tune when he found that they were being preferred to his own. Then he pillories Sir Richard Blackmore. But consider what Johnson had to say of Blackmore's *Creation* (1712).

Its two constituent parts are ratiocination and description. To reason in verse is allowed to be difficult; but Blackmore not only reasons in verse,

but very often reasons poetically; and finds the art of uniting ornament with strength, and ease with closeness. This is a skill that Pope might have condescended to learn from him, when he needed it so much in his *Moral Essays*.

Pope blames Laurence Eusden for effects which, as a translator, Eusden had skillfully imitated from his original, Claudian:

> Ruunt in venerem frondes; omnisque vicissim
> Felix arbor amat; mutant ad mutua palmæ
> Fœdera; popules suspirat populus ictu
> Et platani platanus, alnoque ad sibilat alnus.

We have only to compare this with Eusden's translation (p. 627) to remove his lines from their place in the *Peri Bathous*. Even Shakespeare is held up to ridicule for making Prospero "invite" Miranda to "advance" the "fringed curtains" of her eyes. Pope fails to recognize to what extent this unusual phrase captures the uniqueness and the tender mood of the moment when Prospero invites Miranda to lift her eyes—the process must be very gentle and slow—and look for the first time on the young prince he has magically arranged for her to marry.

By contributing many anonymous examples of poetry from his own pen, whether early or late, Pope is virtually confessing that his case is shaky. The interesting thing about these contributions of Pope's is that they are good of their kind, and we can prove this by filling out for ourselves the context they suggest. Consider such fragments as "*The woodden Guardian of our Privacy | Quick on its Axle turn*" or "*Ye Gods! annihilate but* Space and Time, | *And make two Lovers happy.*" These scraps immediately suggest detailed contexts in which they are appropriate. Pope unfairly strips his quotations of their justifying surroundings in the various kinds of literature in which their authors placed them; as criticism consequently his case is weak.

Several points made in the course of the work enable us to understand Pope's own work better. For example, he criticizes "an ingenious Artist" who "painting the *Spring*, talks of a *Snow* of Blossoms, and thereby raises an unexpected Picture of *Winter*." Readers today would think the artist ingenious, and well within his rights as a poet. Like the Elizabethans we do not mind mixing images if they shed a light on one another that can only so be shed. But Pope was more keenly aware of categories; he was so conscious of snow as snow, with its cold temperature in addition to its whiteness, smoothness, lightness, and flakiness, that the comparison did not help him imagine spring blossoms.

The *Peri Bathous* is to be read mainly as a *jeu d'esprit*, so brilliant that it is hard to believe its victims did not

---

PERI BATHOUS. **Martinus Scriblerus:** [Pope's note] tho' of *German* [and so barbarous] Extraction, was born in *England*.

join in the laugh. Of course they had to be angry, if only to show that they were alive, and this was just what Pope wanted. His quotations were so many stings rousing the inhabitants of Grub Street to reply in kind— and they did. Pope wanted them to retaliate in print for the sake of *The Dunciad* which, ripening over the years, was now nearly ready. By stirring up a general interest in contemporary literature, he guaranteed that when his great poem appeared it would be considered topical and so be read more eagerly by more people.

The text is that of the first printing, in the so-called last volume (1728) of the *Miscellanies*. We have incorporated corrections from later editions for which Pope and Warburton were responsible.

✠

CHAP. I

IT hath been long (my dear Countrymen) the Subject of my Concern and Surprize, that whereas numberless Poets, Criticks and Orators have compiled and digested[1] the Art of *Ancient Poesie*, there hath not arisen among us one Person so publick spirited, as to perform the like for the *Modern*. Altho' it is universally known, that our every-way-industrious Moderns, both in the Weight[2] of their *Writings*, and in the Velocity[3] of their *Judgments*, do so infinitely excel the said Ancients.

NEVERTHELESS, too true it is, that while a plain and direct Road is pav'd to their ὕψος, or *sublime;* no Track has been yet chalk'd out, to arrive at our βάθος, or *profund*. The *Latins*, as they came between the *Greeks* and Us, make use of the Word *Altitudo*, which implies equally *Height* and *Depth*. Wherefore considering with no small Grief, how many promising Genius's of this Age are wandering (as I may say) in the dark without a Guide, I have undertaken this arduous but necessary Task, to lead them as it were by the hand, and step by step, the gentle downhill way to the *Bathos;* the Bottom, the End, the Central Point, the *non plus ultra*[4] of true Modern Poesie!

WHEN I consider (my dear Countrymen) the Extent, Fertility, and Populousness of our *Lowlands* of

Parnassus,[5] the flourishing State of our Trade, and the Plenty of our Manufacture;[6] there are two Reflections which administer great Occasion of Surprize; the one, that all Dignities and Honours should be bestow'd upon the exceeding few meager Inhabitants[7] of the Top of the Mountain; the other, that our own Nation[8] should have arriv'd to that Pitch of Greatness it now possesses, without any regular *System of Laws*. As to the first, it is with great Pleasure I have observ'd of late the gradual Decay of Delicacy and Refinement among Mankind, who are become too reasonable to require that we should labour with infinite Pains to come up to the Taste of these Mountaineers,[9] when they without any, may condescend to ours. But as we have now an *unquestionable Majority* on our side, I doubt not but we shall shortly be able to level the *Highlanders*, and procure a farther Vent[10] for our own Product, which is already so much relish'd, encourag'd, and rewarded, by the Nobility and Gentry of *Great Britain*.

THEREFORE to supply our former Defect, I purpose to collect the scatter'd Rules of our Art into regular Institutes,[11] from the Example and Practice of the deep Genius's of our Nation; imitating herein my Predecessors, the Master of *Alexander*, and the Secretary of the renown'd *Zenobia:*[12] And in this my Undertaking I am the more animated, as I expect more Success than has attended even those great Criticks, since their Laws (tho' they might be good) have ever been slackly executed, and their Precepts (however strict) obey'd only by Fits, and by a very small Number.

AT the same time I intend to do justice upon our Neighbours, Inhabitants of the *upper Parnassus;* who taking advantage of the rising Ground, are perpetually throwing down Rubbish, Dirt, and Stones upon us, never suffering us to live in Peace:[13] These Men, while

---

1. **digested:** arranged methodically. 2. **Weight:** Pope takes advantage, as he does later with *depth*, of the ambiguity of *weight* when used as a critical term. 3. **Velocity:** Martinus shows himself to be an up-to-date Modern, i.e., one versed in the new terms of science. 4. **non . . . ultra:** the farthest point.

5. **Parnassus:** the mountain of Phocis in Greece, sacred to Apollo and the Muses. 6. **the flourishing . . . Manufacture:** Englishmen were justly proud of their commercial prosperity. Again Martinus is up to date, but in his enthusiasm he lumps the works of his Moderns among the practical products of Sheffield and Birmingham. 7. **Inhabitants:** contemporaries such as Swift and Pope as opposed to their inferiors, the Moderns. 8. **Nation:** tribe, i.e., the Moderns. 9. **Mountaineers:** mountain dwellers. 10. **Vent:** outlet, market. 11. **Institutes:** sets of instructions. 12. **Master . . . Zenobia:** Aristotle, whose lectures on the art of poetry survive, and Longinus, supposed author of the treatise *On the Sublime*, which Pope is imitating to some extent in the present work. 13. **throwing . . . Peace:** a reference to the literary satires of Swift and of Pope, who was at this time preparing *The Dunciad* (see below).

they enjoy the Chrystal Stream of *Helicon*,[14] envy us our common Water, which (thank our Stars) tho it is somewhat muddy, flows in much greater abundance. Nor is this the greatest injustice we have to complain of; for tho' it is evident that we never made the least *Attempt* or *Inrode* into *their* Territories, but lived contented in our Native Fens; they have often, not only committed *Petty Larcenys* upon our Borders, but driven the Country, and carried off at once *whole Cart-loads* of our *Manufacture;* to reclaim some of which stolen Goods is part of the Design of this Treatise.

FOR we shall see in the course of this Work, that our greatest Adversaries have sometimes descended towards us; and doubtless might now and then have arrived at the *Bathos* itself, had it not been for that mistaken Opinion they all entertained, that the *Rules* of the *Antients* were *equally necessary* to the *Moderns,* than which there cannot be a more grievous Error, as will be amply proved in the following Discourse.

AND indeed when any of these have gone so far, as by the light of their own Genius to attempt upon *new Models,* it is wonderful to observe, how nearly they have approach'd Us in those particular Pieces; tho' in all their others they differ'd *toto cælo*[15] from us.

CHAP. II

That the Bathos, *or Profund, is the natural Taste of Man, and in particular, of the present Age.*

THE Taste of the *Bathos* is implanted by Nature itself in the Soul of Man; 'till perverted by Custom or Example he is taught, or rather compell'd, to relish the *Sublime.* Accordingly, we see the unprejudiced Minds of Children delight only in such Productions, and in such Images, as our true modern Writers set before them. I have observ'd how fast the general Taste is returning to this first Simplicity and Innocence; and if the Intent of all Poetry be to divert and instruct,[1] certainly that Kind which diverts and instructs the

greatest Number, is to be preferr'd. Let us look round among the Admirers of Poetry, we shall find those who have a Taste of the *Sublime* to be very few, but the *Profund* strikes universally, and is adapted to every Capacity. 'Tis a fruitless Undertaking to write for Men of a nice and foppish *Gusto,*[2] whom, after all, it is almost impossible to please; and 'tis still more Chimerical[3] to write for *Posterity,* of whose Taste we cannot make any Judgment, and whose Applause we can never enjoy.[4] It must be confess'd, our wiser Authors have a present End,

Et prodesse volunt, & delectare Poetæ.[5]

Their true Design is *Profit* or *Gain;*[6] in order to acquire which, 'tis necessary to procure Applause, by administring *Pleasure* to the Reader: From whence it follows demonstrably, that their Productions must be suited to the *present Taste;* and I cannot but congratulate our Age on this peculiar Felicity, that tho' we have made indeed great Progress in all other Branches of Luxury, we are not yet debauch'd with any *high relish*[7] in Poetry, but are in this one Taste, less *nice* than our Ancestors. If an Art is to be estimated by its Success, I appeal to Experience,[8] whether there have not been, in proportion to their Number, as many starving good Poets, as bad ones?

NEVERTHELESS, in making *Gain* the principal End of our Art, far be it from me to exclude any great *Genius's* of *Rank* or *Fortune* from diverting themselves this way. They ought to be praised no less than those Princes, who pass their vacant Hours in some ingenious Mechanical or Manual Art:[9] And to such as these, it would be Ingratitude not to own, that our Art has been often infinitely indebted.

---

14. **Helicon:** a mountain of Boetia on the borders of Phocis, which was sacred to the Muses; its "Chrystal Stream" was Hippocrene. 15. **toto cælo:** by a whole heaven, i.e., completely. *Chapter II.* 1. **divert and instruct:** Horace's view in the famous line which is quoted in convenient but not distorted form below—and then is misinterpreted!

2. **nice . . . Gusto:** fastidious and highly cultivated taste. *Foppish,* a derogatory word, is misapplied; *gusto,* an Italian term, came into use in English around 1650. 3. **Chimerical:** fantastic. 4. **whose Applause . . . enjoy:** Unsuccessful authors sometimes comfort themselves by hoping for a better reception of their work after death. 5. **Et . . . Poetæ:** "The poet's design is both to profit and to please" (adapted from Horace, *Ars Poetica,* l. 333). 6. **Profit or Gain:** Horace intended *prodesse* to mean benefit mentally not materially; again Pope takes advantage of such ambiguity. 7. **high relish:** Pope anglicizes the Italian *gran gusto.* 8. **I . . . Experience:** Martinus invokes the method of the Baconian empiricist. 9. **those . . . Art:** The English nobility and gentry participated in the researches encouraged by the Royal Society, which had been founded in 1660.

CHAP. III

The Necessity of the Bathos, *Physically°* consider'd.

FArthermore, it were great Cruelty and Injustice, if all such Authors as cannot write in the other Way, were prohibited from writing at all. Against this, I draw an Argument from what seems to me an undoubted Physical Maxim, That Poetry is a *natural or morbid Secretion from the Brain.* As I would not suddenly stop a Cold in the Head, or dry up my Neighbour's Issue, I would as little hinder him from necessary Writing. It may be affirm'd with great truth, that there is hardly any human Creature past Childhood, but at one time or other has had some Poetical Evacuation, and no question was much the better for it in his Health; so true is the Saying, *Nascimur Poetæ:*[1] Therefore is the Desire of Writing properly term'd *Pruritus,*[2] the *Titillation of the Generative Faculty of the Brain;* and the Person is said to *conceive;* Now such as conceive must *bring forth.* I have known a Man thoughtful, melancholy, and raving for divers days, but forthwith grow wonderfully easy, lightsome and cheerful, upon a Discharge of the peccant Humour,[3] in exceeding purulent[4] Metre.[5] Nor can I question, but abundance of untimely Deaths are occasion'd by want of this laudable Vent of unruly Passions; yea, perhaps, in poor Wretches, (which is very lamentable) for meer Want of Pen, Ink, and Paper! From hence it follows, that a Suppression of the very worst Poetry is of dangerous consequence to the State: We find by Experience, that the same Humours which vent themselves in Summer in *Ballads* and *Sonnets,*[6] are condens'd by the Winter's Cold into *Pamphlets* and *Speeches* for and against the *Minister:* Nay I know not, but many times a Piece of Poetry may be the most innocent Composition of a *Minister himself.*

It is therefore manifest that *Mediocrity* ought to be allow'd, yea indulg'd, to the good Subjects of *England.* Nor can I conceive how the World has swallow'd the contrary as a Maxim,[7] upon the single Authority of that *Horace?* Why should the *Golden Mean,* and Quintessence of all Virtues, be deem'd so offensive in this Art? Or *Coolness* or *Mediocrity* be so amiable a Quality in a Man, and so detestable in a Poet?

HOWEVER, far be it from me to compare these Writers with those *Great Spirits,* who are born with a *Vivacité de pesanteur,*[8] or (as an *English* Author calls it) an *Alacrity of sinking;*[9] and who by *Strength of Nature* alone can excell. All I mean is to evince the *Necessity* of Rules to these lesser Genius's, as well as the *Usefulness* of them to the Greater.

CHAP. IV

That there is an Art of the Bathos, *or* Profund.

WE come now to prove, that there is an *Art of Sinking* in Poetry. Is there not an Architecture of Vaults and Cellars, as well as of lofty Domes and Pyramids? Is there not as much Skill and Labour in making *Dykes,* as in raising *Mounts?* Is there not an Art of *Diving* as well as of *Flying?* And will any sober Practitioner affirm, That a diving Engine is not of singular Use in making him long-winded, assisting his Sight, and furnishing him with other ingenious means of keeping under Water?

IF we search the Authors of Antiquity, we shall find as few to have been distinguish'd in the *true Profund,* as in the *true Sublime.* And the very same thing (as it appears from *Longinus*) had been imagin'd of that, as now of this; namely, that it was entirely the Gift of Nature. I grant, that to excel in the *Bathos* a Genius is requisite; yet the Rules of Art must be allow'd so far useful, as to add Weight, or as I may say, hang on Lead, to facilitate and enforce our Descent, to guide us to the most advantageous Declivities, and habituate our Imagination to a Depth of thinking. Many there are that can fall, but few can arrive at the Felicity of falling gracefully; much more for a Man who is amongst the lowest of the Creation at the very bottom of the Atmosphere, to descend *beneath himself,* is not so easy a Task unless he calls in Art to his Assistance.

Chapter III. **Physically:** Swift, in particular, was fond of claiming (for his own devastating purposes) that mind was no more than matter. **1. Nascimur Poetæ:** We are born poets. **2. Pruritus:** itching. **3. peccant Humour:** disordered bodily constituent. **4. purulent:** consisting of pus, corrupt matter. **5. Metre:** an echo of *matter* (pus). **6. Sonnets:** love songs.

7. Maxim: [Pope's note] *Mediocribus esse poetis* | *Non dii, non homines,* &c. Hor. ["For poets to be second-rate is a privilege that neither gods nor men [ever allowed]" (Horace, *Ars Poetica,* ll. 372–73).] **8. Vivacité de pesanteur:** quickness in sinking. **9. Alacrity of sinking:** See *The Merry Wives of Windsor,* III. v. 12.

It is with the *Bathos* as with small Beer, which is indeed vapid and insipid, if left at large and let abroad; but being by our Rules confin'd, and well stopt, nothing grows so frothy, pert and bouncing.

THE *Sublime* of Nature is the Sky, the Sun, Moon, Stars, &c. The *Profund* of Nature is Gold, Pearls, precious Stones, and the Treasures of the Deep, which are inestimable as unknown. But all that lies between these, as Corn, Flowers, Fruits, Animals, and Things for the meer Use of Man, are of mean price, and so common as not to be greatly esteem'd by the Curious: It being certain, that any thing, of which we know the true Use, cannot be Invaluable:[1] Which affords a Solution, why *common Sense* hath either been totally despis'd, or held in small Repute, by the greatest modern Criticks and Authors.

CHAP. V

Of the true Genius of the Profund,
and by what it is constituted.

AND I will venture to lay it down, as the first Maxim and Corner-Stone of this our Art, That whoever would excell therein must studiously avoid, detest, and turn his Head from all the Ideas, Ways, and Workings of that pestilent Foe to Wit and Destroyer of fine Figures, which is known by the Name of *Common Sense*. His Business must be to contract the true *Gout de travers;*[1] and to acquire a most *happy, uncommon, unaccountable Way of Thinking.*

HE is to consider himself as a *Grotesque* Painter, whose Works would be spoil'd by an Imitation of Nature, or Uniformity of Design. He is to mingle Bits of the most various, or discordant kinds, Landscape, History, Portraits, Animals, and connect them with a great deal of *Flourishing*, by *Heads* or *Tails*, as it shall please his Imagination, and contribute to his principal End, which is to glare by strong Oppositions of Colours, and surprize by Contrariety of Images.

Serpentes avibus geminentur, tigribus agni.[2]

His Design ought to be like a Labyrinth, out of which no body can get clear but himself. And since the great Art of all Poetry is to mix Truth and Fiction, in order to join the Credible with the Surprizing;[3] our Author shall produce the *Credible*, by painting Nature in her *lowest Simplicity;* and the *Surprizing*, by contradicting *Common Opinion*. In the very *Manners*[4] he will affect the Marvellous; he will draw *Achilles* with the Patience of *Job;* a Prince talking like a Jack-pudding;[5] a Maid of Honour selling *Bargains;*[6] a Footman speaking like a Philosopher; and a fine Gentleman like a Scholar. Whoever is conversant in *modern Plays*, may make a most noble Collection of this kind, and at the same time, form a compleat Body of *Modern Ethicks and Morality*.

NOTHING seem'd more plain to our great Authors, than that the World had long been weary of natural Things. How much the contrary are form'd to please, is evident from the universal Applause daily given to the admirable Entertainments of *Harlequins* and *Magicians* on our Stage. When an Audience behold a Coach turn'd into a Wheel-barrow, a Conjurer into an Old Woman, or a Man's Head where his Heels should be; how are they struck with Transport and Delight? Which can only be imputed to this Cause, that each Object is chang'd into That which hath been suggested to them by their own low Ideas before.

HE ought therefore to render himself Master of this happy and antinatural way of thinking to such a degree, as to be able, on the appearance of any Object, to furnish his Imagination with Ideas infinitely below it. And his Eyes should be like unto the wrong end of a Perspective Glass,[7] by which all the Objects of Nature are lessen'd.

FOR example, when a true Genius looks upon the *Sky*, he immediately catches the Idea of a Piece of *Blue Lutestring*, or a *Child's Mantle*.

The Skies, whose spreading Volumes scarce have room,
Spun thin, and wove in Nature's finest Loom,
The new-born World in their soft Lap embrac'd,
And all around their starry Mantle cast.[8]

---

3. the great . . . Surprizing: suggested by Horace, *Ars Poetica*, l. 151. 4. Manners: the moral qualities that make up a person's character. 5. Jack-pudding: buffoon, clown. 6. selling Bargains: See Swift, *Directions for a Birth-Day Song*, above, note to l. 274. 7. Perspective Glass: telescope. 8. The Skies . . . cast: Sir Richard Blackmore, *Prince Arthur*, pp. 41-42. Pope adds the footnote: "N.B. In order to do justice to these great Poets, our Citations are taken from the best, the last, and most correct Editions of their Works. That which we use of Prince *Arthur*, is in *duodecimo*, 1714. the fourth Edition, revised." The page numbers in this and subsequent references to *Prince Arthur* (1695) are for this edition; they were originally supplied by Pope as marginal notes. Blackmore (1654-1729), physician and poetaster, is one of Pope's chief victims in the *Peri Bathous*.

Chapter IV. 1. all . . . Invaluable: without value; Pope and Swift both valued very highly the usefulness of things to man. Chapter V. 1. Gout de travers: taste for error. 2. Serpentes . . . agni: "[but not so far that] serpents couple with birds, lambs with tigers" (Horace, *Ars Poetica*, l. 13).

IF he looks upon a *Tempest*, he shall have an Image of a tumbled Bed, and describe a succeeding Calm in this manner,

> The Ocean *joy'd to see the* Tempest *fled,*
> New lays *his* Waves *and* smooths his ruffled Bed.[9]

THE *Triumphs* and *Acclamations* of the *Angels*, at the Creation of the Universe, present to his Imagination the *Rejoicings of the Lord Mayor's Day;* and he beholds those glorious Beings celebrating the Creator, by Huzzaing, making Illuminations, and flinging Squibbs, Crackers and Sky-rockets.

> Glorious *Illuminations, made on high*
> By all the Stars and Planets of the Sky,
> In just Degrees, *and* shining Order *plac'd,*
> Spectators charm'd, *and the* blest Dwelling *grac'd.*
> Thro' all th' *enlighten'd Air swift* Fireworks *flew,*
> Which with *repeated* Shouts *glad* Cherubs threw.
> Comets *ascended with their sweeping Train,*
> Then fell *in* starry Showers *and* glittering Rain.
> In Air ten thousand Meteors *blazing hung,*
> Which from *th'* Eternal Battlements *were* flung.[10]

IF a Man who is violently fond of *Wit*, will sacrifice to that Passion his Friend or his God; would it not be a shame, if he who is smit with the Love of the *Bathos* should not sacrifice to it all other transitory Regards? You shall hear a zealous Protestant Deacon invoke a Saint, and modestly beseech her to do more for us than Providence:

> Look down, blest Saint, with Pity then look down,
> Shed on this Land thy kinder Influence,
> And guide us through the Mists of Providence,
> In which we stray.[11]———

Neither will he, if a goodly Simile come in his way, scruple to affirm himself an Eye-witness of things never yet beheld by Man, or never in Existence; as thus,

> Thus have *I* seen, *in* Araby *the blest,*
> A Phœnix *couch'd upon her Fun'ral Nest.*[12]

BUT to convince you, that nothing is so great which a marvellous Genius, prompted by this laudable Zeal, is not able to lessen; hear how the most Sublime of all Beings is represented in the following Images.

9. **The Ocean** . . . **Bed:** *Ibid.,* p. 14. 10. **Glorious** . . . **flung:** *Ibid.,* p. 50. 11. **Look** . . . **stray:** Ambrose Philips, *Lament for Queen Mary,* ll. 87, 91–93. (See the selections from Philips in Part Three.) 12. **Thus** . . . **Nest:** [Pope's note] Anon. [probably by Pope].

First he is a PAINTER.

> Sometimes the Lord of Nature in the Air,
> Spreads forth *his* Clouds, *his* sable Canvass, *where*
> His Pencil, dipt *in heavenly* Colour *bright,*
> Paints *his fair* Rain-bow, *charming to the Sight.*[13]

Now he is a CHYMIST.

> Th' *Almighty* Chymist *does his Work prepare,*
> Pours down his Waters *on the thirsty Plain,*
> Digests *his* Lightning, *and* distills *his Rain.*[14]

Now he is a WRESTLER.

> Me in his *griping Arms* th' *Eternal took,*
> And with such *mighty Force* my *Body shook,*
> That the *strong Grasp* my Members *sorely bruis'd,*
> Broke *all my* Bones, *and all my* Sinews loos'd.[15]

Now a RECRUITING OFFICER.

> For Clouds the Sun-Beams *levy fresh Supplies,*
> And raise Recruits *of Vapours, which arise,*
> Drawn *from the Seas, to* muster *in the Skies.*[16]

Now a peaceable GUARANTEE.

> In Leagues *of* Peace *the* Neighbours *did agree,*
> And to maintain them, *God was Guarantee.*[17]

Then he is an ATTORNEY.

> Job, *as a vile Offender, God* indites,
> And terrible Decrees against me *writes.—*
> God will not be my *Advocate,*
> My Cause *to manage, or debate.*[18]

In the following Lines he is a GOLD-BEATER.

> Who the *rich Metal beats, and then, with Care,*
> Unfolds the Golden Leaves, *to* gild *the Fields of Air.*[19]

Then a FULLER.[20]

> ———th' *exhaling* Reeks *that secret rise,*
> Born on rebounding *Sun-beams thro' the Skies;*
> Are thicken'd, wrought, *and* whiten'd, *'till they grow*
> A Heavenly Fleece.[21]———

13. **Sometimes** . . . **Sight:** Blackmore, *Sometimes the Lord. A Paraphrase on the Book of Job: as likewise on the Songs of Moses, Deborah, David, on Six Select Psalms, Some Chapters of Isaiah, and the Third Chapter of Habakkuk,* p. 172. The page numbers in this and subsequent references to *Job,* as the work is commonly known, are for the second edition, revised, of 1716; they were originally supplied by Pope as marginal notes. 14. **Th' Almighty** . . . **Rain:** *Ibid.,* p. 263. 15. **Me** . . . **loos'd:** *Ibid.,* p. 75. 16. **For** . . . **Skies:** *Ibid.,* p. 170. 17. **In** . . . **Guarantee:** *Ibid.,* p. 70. 18. **Job** . . . **debate:** *Ibid.,* p. 61. 19. **Who** . . . **Air:** *Ibid.,* p. 181. 20. **Fuller:** one who beats cloth to clean or thicken it. 21. **th' exhaling** . . . **Fleece:** Blackmore, *Job,* p. 18.

A MERCER, or PACKER.

Didst thou one End of Air's wide Curtain hold,
And help the Bales of Æther to unfold;
Say, which cerulian Pile was by thy Hand unroll'd?[22]

A BUTLER.

He measures all the Drops with wondrous Skill,
Which the black Clouds, his floating Bottles, fill.[23]

And a BAKER.

God in the Wilderness his Table spread,
And in his Airy Ovens bak'd their Bread.[24]

CHAP. VI

Of the several Kinds of Genius's in
the Profund, and the Marks and
Characters of each.

I DOUBT not but the Reader, by this *Cloud* of Examples, begins to be convinc'd of the Truth of our Assertion, that the *Bathos* is an *Art;* and that the Genius of no Mortal whatever, following the meer Ideas of Nature, and unassisted with an habitual, nay laborious Peculiarity of thinking, could arrive at Images so wonderfully low and unaccountable. The great Author, from whose Treasury we have drawn all these Instances (the Father of the *Bathos*, and indeed the *Homer* of it) has like that immortal *Greek*, confin'd his Labours to the greater Poetry,[1] and thereby left room for others to acquire a due share of Praise in inferiour kinds. Many Painters who could never hit a Nose or an Eye, have with Felicity copied a Small-Pox, or been admirable at a Toad or a Red-Herring. And seldom are we without *Genius's* for *Still Life*, which they can work up and stiffen[2] with incredible Accuracy.

AN universal Genius rises not in an Age; but when he rises, Armies rise in him! he pours forth five or six Epick Poems with greater Facility, than five or six Pages can be produc'd by an elaborate and servile

Copyer after Nature or the Ancients. It is affirm'd by *Quintilian*, that the same Genius which made *Germanicus* so great a General, would with equal Application have made him an excellent Heroic Poet.[3] In like manner, reasoning from the Affinity there appears between Arts and Sciences, I doubt not but an active Catcher of Butterflies, a careful and fanciful Pattern-drawer, an industrious Collector of Shells, a laborious and tuneful Bagpiper, or a diligent Breeder of tame Rabbits, might severally excel in their respective parts of the *Bathos*.

I SHALL range these confin'd and less copious Genius's under proper Classes, and (the better to give their Pictures to the Reader) under the Names of Animals of some sort or other; whereby he will be enabled, at the first sight of such as shall daily come forth, to know to what *Kind* to refer, and with what *Authors* to compare them.

1. THE *Flying Fishes;* these are Writers who now and then *rise* upon their *Fins*, and fly out of the *Profund;* but their Wings are soon *dry*, and they drop down to the *Bottom*. G.S.[4] A.H.[5] C.G.[6]

2. THE *Swallows* are Authors that are eternally *skimming* and *fluttering* up and down, but all their Agility is employ'd to *catch Flies*. LT.[7] WP.[8] Lord H.[9]

3. THE *Ostridges* are such whose Heaviness rarely permits them to raise themselves from the Ground; their Wings are of no use to lift them up, and their Motion is between *flying* and *walking;* but then they *run* very fast. D.F.[10] L.E.[11] The Hon. E.H.[12]

4. THE *Parrots* are they that repeat *another's Words*,

---

22. Didst . . . unroll'd: *Ibid.,* p. 174. 23. He . . . fill: *Ibid.,* p. 131. 24. God . . . Bread: *Ibid.,* p. 218. *Chapter VI.* 1. the Father . . . Poetry: Most of Blackmore's poems were epics or long poems on divine subjects. 2. work . . . stiffen: paint and repaint till it is labored and so looks lifeless.

3. the same . . . Poet: This idea of the "convertibility" of genius became of great interest to nineteenth-century writers. 4. G.S.: George Sewell (1673–1726), with George Stepney and George Stanhope as possible alternates. 5. A.H.: Aaron Hill (1685–1750), a victim again in *The Dunciad* (see below). (See the selections from Hill in Part Three.) 6. C.G.: Charles Gildon (1665–1724). 7. LT.: Lewis Theobald (1688–1744), playwright and critic; Pope again attacked him in *The Dunciad*. 8. WP.: William Pattison (1706–27), and possibly William Philips. 9. Lord H.: John Hervey (1696–1743), Baron Hervey of Ickworth, politician and Lord Privy Seal from 1740 to 1742. The H replaced in later editions the R (of doubtful significance) in the first edition. Here Pope contributes to a long quarrel with Hervey, whom he satirizes as Sporus in *An Epistle to Dr. Arbuthnot* (see below). 10. D.F.: Daniel Defoe (1660–1731). (See the selections from Defoe earlier in Part Two.) 11. L.E.: Laurence Eusden (1688–1730); among those also satirized in *The Dunciad*. Eusden was appointed Poet Laureate in 1718. 12. E.H.: Edward Howard (d. 1732).

in such a *hoarse, odd* Voice, that makes them seem *their own. W.B.*[13] *W.H.*[14] *C.C.*[15] The Reverend *D.D.*[16]

5. THE *Didappers*[17] are Authors that keep themselves long *out of sight*, under water, and *come up* now and then where you *least expected* them. *L.W.*[18] *G.D.*[19] Esq; The Hon. Sir *W.Y.*[20]

6. THE *Porpoises* are unweildly and big; they put all their Numbers[21] into a great *Turmoil* and *Tempest*, but whenever they appear in *plain Light*, (which is seldom) they are only *shapeless* and *ugly Monsters. I.D.*[22] *C.G.*[23] *I.O.*[24]

7. THE *Frogs* are such as can neither *walk* nor *fly*, but can *leap* and *bound* to admiration: They live generally in the *Bottom of a Ditch*, and make a *great Noise* whenever they thrust their *Heads above Water. E.W.*[25] *I.M.*[26] Esq; *T.D.*[27] Gent.

8. THE *Eels* are obscure Authors, that wrap themselves up in their *own Mud*, but are mighty *nimble* and *pert. L.W.*[28] *L.T.*[29] *P.M.*[30] General *C.*[31]

9. THE *Tortoises* are *slow* and *chill*, and like *Pastoral Writers* delight much in *Gardens*: they have for the most part a *fine embroider'd*[32] *Shell*, and underneath it, a *heavy Lump. A.P.*[33] *W.B.*[34] *L.E.*[35] The Rt. Hon. E. of S.[36]

THESE are the chief Characteristicks of the *Bathos*,

---

13. W.B.: William Broome (1689–1745). Pope never fully acknowledged Broome's considerable assistance with the translation of the *Odyssey* (1725–26). Broome too was attacked in *The Dunciad.* **14. W.H.:** William Harrison (1685–1713), or less likely Walter Harte. **15. C.C.:** Colley Cibber (1671–1757), Poet Laureate from 1730 until his death. **16. D.D.:** Richard "Dick" Daniel (1681–1739), Dean of Armagh; also one of Swift's enemies. **17. Didappers:** dabchicks, helldivers. **18. L.W.:** Leonard Welsted (1688–1747). **19. G.D.:** George Duckett (1684–1732), or George Bubb Doddington. **20. W.Y.:** William Yonge (d. 1755). **21. all . . . Numbers:** the number of them in a school. **22. I.D.:** John Dennis (1657–1734), playwright and critic. (See the selection from Dennis earlier in Part Two.) Here and elsewhere Pope uses *I* for *J*; to the Romans these were a single letter. **23. C.G.:** Charles Gildon. **24. I.O.:** John Oldmixon (1673–1742), a historian. **25. E.W.:** Edward "Ned" Ward (1667–1731), pamphleteer and pubkeeper. **26. I.M.:** James Moore (later Moore-Smythe) (1702–34). **27. T.D.:** Thomas "Tom" D'Urfey (1653–1723), dramatist and song writer. (See the selection from D'Urfey in Part Three.) **28. L.W.:** Leonard Welsted. **29. L.T.:** Lewis Theobald. **30. P.M.:** Pierre Antoine Motteux (1660–1718), translator and dramatist. **31. General C.:** not identified. **32. embroider'd:** decorated; often applied to elaborate description. **33. A.P.:** Ambrose Philips (*c.* 1675–1749). (See the selections from Philips in Part Three.) **34. W.B.:** William Broome. **35. L.E.:** Laurence Eusden. **36. E. of S.:** not identified.

and in each of these kinds we have the comfort to be bless'd with sundry and manifold choice Spirits in this our Island.

CHAP. VII

Of the Profund, *when it consists in the Thought.*

WE have already laid down the Principles upon which our Author is to proceed, and the Manner of forming his Thoughts by familiarizing his Mind to the lowest Objects; to which it may be added, that *vulgar Conversation* will greatly contribute. There is no Question but the *Garret*[1] or the *Printer's Boy* may often be discern'd in the Compositions made in such Scenes, and Company; and much of Mr. *Curl*[2] himself has been insensibly infused into the Works of his learned Writers.

THE Physician, by the Study and Inspection of Urine and Ordure, approves himself in the Science; and in like sort should our Author accustom and exercise his Imagination upon the Dregs of Nature.

THIS will render his Thoughts truly and fundamentally Low, and carry him many fathoms beyond Mediocrity. For, certain it is, (tho' some lukewarm Heads imagine they may be safe by temporizing[3] between the Extreams) that where there is not a Triticalness[4] or Mediocrity in the *Thought*, it can never be sunk into the genuine and perfect *Bathos*, by the most elaborate low *Expression*: It can, at most, be only carefully obscured, or metaphorically debased. But 'tis the *Thought* alone that strikes, and gives the whole that Spirit, which we admire and stare at. For instance, in that ingenious Piece on a Lady's drinking the *Bath*-Waters.

> *She drinks! She drinks! Behold the matchless Dame!*
> *To her 'tis Water, but to us 'tis Flame:*
> *Thus Fire is Water, Water Fire, by turns,*
> *And the same Stream at once both cools and burns.*[5]

Chapter VII. **1. Garret:** needy writer; from the fact that poor writers often lived in garrets. **2. Mr. Curl:** Edmund Curll (1675–1747), a notorious London publisher with whom Pope had a long feud. Curll is one of the chief victims of *The Dunciad* (see below). **3. temporizing:** compromising. **4. Triticalness:** triteness. Swift coined the derogatory *tritical* on the basis of *critical*. **5. She . . . burns:** [Pope's note] Anon. [probably by Pope].

WHAT can be more easy and unaffected than the *Diction* of these Verses? 'Tis the Turn of *Thought* alone, and the Variety of Imagination, that charm and surprize us. And when the same Lady goes into the Bath, the Thought (as in justness it ought) goes still deeper.

> *Venus beheld her, 'midst her Crowd of Slaves,*
> *And thought Herself just risen from the Waves.*[6]

How much out of the way of common Sense is this Reflection of *Venus*, not knowing herself from the Lady?

OF the same nature is that noble Mistake of a frighted Stag in full Chace, who (saith the Poet)

> *Hears his own Feet, and thinks they sound like more;*
> *And fears the hind Feet will o'ertake the fore.*[7]

So astonishing as these are, they yield to the following, which is *Profundity* itself,

> *None but* Himself *can be his* Parallel.[8]

unless it may seem borrow'd from the Thought of that *Master of a Show* in *Smithfield*,[9] who writ in large Letters, over the Picture of his Elephant,

This is the greatest Elephant in the World, except Himself.

HOWEVER our next Instance is certainly an Original: Speaking of a beautiful Infant,

> *So fair thou art, that if great* Cupid *be*
> *A Child, as Poets say, sure thou art He.*
> *Fair* Venus *would mistake thee for her own,*
> *Did not thy Eyes proclaim thee not her Son.*
> *There all the Lightnings of thy* Mother's *shine,*
> *And with a fatal Brightness kill in thine.*[10]

FIRST he is *Cupid*, then he is not *Cupid*; first *Venus* would mistake him, then she would not mistake him; next his Eyes are his Mother's; and lastly they are not his Mother's, but his own.

ANOTHER Author, describing a Poet that shines forth amidst a Circle of Criticks,

> *Thus* Phœbus *thro' the Zodiack takes his way,*
> *And amid* Monsters *rises into Day.*[11]

WHAT a Peculiarity is here of Invention? The Author's Pencil, like the Wand of *Circe*, turns all into *Monsters* at a Stroke. A great Genius takes things in the Lump, without stopping at minute Considerations: In vain might the Ram, the Bull, the Goat, the Lion, the Crab, the Scorpion, the Fishes, all stand in his way, as mere natural Animals: much more might it be pleaded that a pair of Scales, an old Man, and two innocent Children, were no Monsters: There were only the Centaur and the Maid that could be esteem'd out of Nature. But what of that? with a Boldness peculiar to these daring Genius's, what he found not Monsters, he made so.

CHAP. VIII

Of the Profound *consisting in the Circumstances, and of Amplification and Periphrase in general.*

WHAT in a great measure distinguishes other Writers from ours, is their chusing and separating such Circumstances in a Description as ennoble or elevate the Subject.

THE Circumstances which are most natural are obvious, therefore not astonishing or peculiar. But those that are far-fetch'd, or unexpected, or hardly compatible, will surprize prodigiously. These therefore we must principally hunt out; but above all, preserve a laudable *Prolixity;* presenting the Whole and every Side at once of the Image to view. For Choice and Distinction are not only a Curb to the Spirit, and limit the Descriptive Faculty, but also lessen the Book, which is frequently of the worst consequence of all to our Author.

WHEN *Job* says in short, *He wash'd his Feet in Butter,* (a Circumstance some Poets would have soften'd, or past over) now hear how this butter is spread out by the Great Genius.

---

6. **Venus . . . Waves:** also marked anonymous in the text; probably by Pope. 7. **Hears . . . fore:** not identified; probably by Pope. 8. **None . . . Parallel:** Lewis Theobald, *Double Falsehood,* III. i. This line is not so silly as Pope makes out. Plutarch inaugurated the practice of bracketing two great men of different countries and times—say, Alexander the Great and Julius Caesar—for contrast and comparison; he called the method a parallel. 9. **Smithfield:** See *The Dunciad,* below, I. 2 and note. 10. **So . . . thine:** William Broome, *On the Birthday of Mr. Robert Trefusis* (1712). Here and in subsequent references to works that have not achieved standard editions we have felt it necessary only to identify each work by title and to give the year of first publication.

11. **Thus . . . Day:** Broome, *Epistle to My Friend Mr. Elijah Fenton* (1726).

With Teats distended with their milky Store,
Such num'rous lowing Herds, before my Door,
Their painful Burden to unload did meet,
That we with Butter might have wash'd our Feet.[1]

How cautious! and particular! He had (says our Author) so many Herds, which Herds thriv'd so well, and thriving so well, gave so much Milk, and that Milk produc'd so much Butter, that if he *did not*, he *might* have wash'd his Feet in it.

THE ensuing Description of Hell is no less remarkable in the Circumstances.

In flaming Heaps the raging Ocean rolls,
Whose livid Waves involve despairing Souls;
The liquid Burnings dreadful Colours shew,
Some deeply red, and others faintly blue.[2]

COULD the most minute *Dutch* Painter have been more exact? How inimitably circumstantial is this also of a War-Horse!

His Eye-Balls burn, he wounds the smoaking Plain,
And knots of scarlet Ribbond deck his Mane.[3]

Of certain Cudgel-Players:

They brandish high in Air their threatning Staves,
Their Hands a woven Guard of Ozier saves,
In which, they fix their hazel weapon's end.[4]

WHO would not think the Poet had past his whole Life at Wakes in such laudable Diversions? since he teaches us how to hold, nay how to make, a Cudgel!

Periphrase is another great Aid to *Prolixity;* being a diffus'd circumlocutory Manner of expressing a known Idea, which should be so misteriously couch'd, as to give the Reader the Pleasure of guessing what it is that the Author can possibly mean; and a strange Surprize when he finds it.

THE Poet I last mention'd is incomparable in this Figure.

A waving Sea of Heads was round me spread,
And still fresh Streams the gazing Deluge fed.[5]

HERE is a waving Sea of Heads, which by a fresh Stream of Heads, grows to be a gazing Deluge of Heads. You come at last to find it means a *great Crowd.*

How pretty and how genteel is the following.

Natures[6] *Confectioner,——*
Whose Suckets[7] *are moist Alchimy:*
The Still of his refining Mold,
Minting the Garden into Gold.

What is this, but a *Bee* gathering Honey?

Little Syren of the Stage
Empty warbler, breathing Lyre,
Wanton Gale of fond desire,
Tuneful mischief, vocal Spell[8]*—.*

Who would think this was only a poor Gentlewoman that sung finely?

WE may define *Amplification* to be making the most of a *Thought;* it is the spinning Wheel of the *Bathos,* which draws out and spreads it in the finest Thread. There are Amplifiers who can extend half a dozen thin Thoughts over a whole Folio; but for which, the Tale of many a vast Romance, and the Substance of many a fair Volume might be reduced into the size of a *Primmer.*

IN the Book of *Job,* are these Words, *Hast thou commanded the Morning, and caused the Day Spring to know his Place?*[9] How is this extended by the most celebrated Amplifier of our Age?

Canst thou set forth th' etherial Mines on high,
Which the refulgent Ore of Light supply?
Is the Celestial Furnace to thee known,
In which I melt the golden Metal down?
Treasures, from whence I deal out Light as fast,
As all my Stars and lavish Suns can waste.[10]

THE same Author hath amplified a Passage in the 104th Psalm; *He looks on the Earth, and it trembles. He touches the Hills, and they smoke.*

The Hills forget they're fix'd, and in their Fright,
Cast off their Weight, and ease themselves for flight:
The Woods, with Terror wing'd, out-fly the Wind,
And leave the heavy, panting Hills behind.[11]

YOU here see the Hills not only trembling, but shaking off the Woods from their Backs, to run the

---

Chapter VIII. **1. With . . . Feet:** Sir Richard Blackmore, *Job,* p. 133. **2. In . . . blue:** Blackmore, *Prince Arthur,* p. 89. **3. His . . . Mane:** [Pope's note] Anon. [probably by Pope]. **4. They . . . end:** Blackmore, *Prince Arthur,* p. 197. **5. A waving . . . fed:** Blackmore, *Job,* p. 78.

6. Natures . . . Gold: John Cleveland, *Fuscara,* ll. 1–4, in *Poems* (8th ed., 1651). **7. Suckets:** sweetmeats. **8. Little . . . Spell:** Ambrose Philips, *To Seignora Cuzzoni,* ll. 1, 3, 4, 9. (See Part Three.) **9. Hast . . . Place:** quoted incompletely from Job 38:12. Pope follows the Authorized Version, not the Douay Version as we should have expected of a Roman Catholic. **10. Canst . . . waste:** Blackmore, *Job,* p. 180. **11. The Hills . . . behind:** *Ibid.,* p. 267.

faster: After this you are presented with a Foot Race of Mountains and Woods, where the Woods distance the Mountains, that like corpulent pursy Fellows, come puffing and panting a vast way behind them.

CHAP. IX

Of Imitation, and the manner of Imitating.

THAT the true Authors of the *Profund* are to imitate diligently the Examples in their own Way, is not to be question'd, and that divers have by this Means attain'd to a Depth whereunto their own Weight could not have carried them, is evident by sundry Instances. Who sees not that *DeFoe* was the Poetical Son of *Withers*, *Tate* of *Ogilby*, *E. Ward* of *John Taylor*, and *Eusden* of *Blackmore*? Therefore when we sit down to write, let us bring some great Author to our Mind, and ask our selves this Question; How would Sir *Richard* have said this? Do I express myself as simply as *Ambrose Philips*? or flow my Numbers with the quiet thoughtlessness of Mr. *Welsted*?

BUT it may seem somewhat strange to assert, that our Proficient[1] should also read the Works of those famous Poets who have excell'd in the Sublime: Yet is not this a Paradox. As *Virgil* is said to have read *Ennius*,[2] out of his Dunghil to draw Gold; so may our Author read *Shakespear*, *Milton*, and *Dryden*, for the contrary End, to bury their Gold in his own Dunghil. A true Genius, when he finds any thing lofty or shining in them, will have the Skill to bring it down, take off the Gloss, or quite discharge the Colour, by some ingenious Circumstance, or Periphrase, some Addition, or Diminution, or by some of those Figures the use of which we shall shew in our next Chapter.

THE Book of *Job* is acknowledg'd to be infinitely sublime, and yet has not the Father of the *Bathos* reduc'd it in every Page? Is there a Passage in all *Virgil* more painted up and labour'd[3] than the Description of *Ætna* in the Third *Æneid*.

————*Horrificis juxta tonat Ætna ruinis,*
Interdumque atram prorumpit ad æthera nubem,
Turbine fumantem piceo, & candente favilla,
Attollitque globos flammarum, & sidera lambit.

Interdum scopulos avulsaque viscera montis
Erigit eructans, liquefactaque saxa sub auras
Cum gemitu glomerat, fundoque exastuat imo.[4]

(I beg Pardon of the gentle *English* Reader, and such of our Writers as understand not *Latin*) Lo! how this is taken down by our *British* Poet, by the single happy Thought of throwing the Mountain into a Fit of the Cholic.

> *Ætna, and all the burning Mountains, find*
> *Their kindled Stores with* inbred *Storms of* Wind
> Blown up *to Rage, and* roaring out, *complain,*
> As torn *with* inward Gripes, *and* torturing Pain:
> Lab'ring, *they* cast *their dreadful* Vomit round,
> *And with their* melted Bowels, *spread* the Ground.[5]

HORACE, in search of the *Sublime*, struck his Head against the Stars;[6] but *Empedocles*, to fathom the *Profund*, threw himself into *Ætna*: And who but would imagine our excellent Modern had also been there, from this Description?

IMITATION is of two Sorts; the First is when we force to our own Purposes the Thoughts of others; The Second consists in copying the Imperfections, or Blemishes of celebrated Authors. I have seen a Play professedly writ in the Stile of *Shakespear*, wherein the Resemblance lay in one single Line,

> *And so good Morrow t'ye, good Master Lieutenant.*[7]

And sundry Poems in Imitation of *Milton*, where with the utmost Exactness, and not so much as one Exception, nevertheless was constantly *nathless*, embroider'd was *broider'd*, Hermits were *Eremites*, disdain'd was *'sdeign'd*, shady *umbrageous*, Enterprize *Emprize*, Pagan *Paynim*, Pinions *Pennons*, sweet *dulcet*, Orchards *Orchats*, Bridge-work *Pontifical;* nay, her was *hir*, and

---

4. Horrificis . . . imo:
The Port capacious, and secure from Wind,
Is to the foot of thundring Etna joyn'd,
By turns a pitchy Cloud she rowls on high;
By turns hot Embers from her entrails fly;
And flakes of mounting Flames, that lick the Skie.
Oft from her Bowels massy Rocks are thrown,
And shiver'd by the force come piece-meal down.
Oft liquid lakes of burning Sulphur flow,
Fed from the fiery Springs that boil below.
    (*Aeneid*, III. 571–74 [Dryden's translation, III. 746–54])

5. Ætna . . . Ground: Blackmore, *Prince Arthur*, p. 75. **6. in . . . Stars:** [Pope's note] *Sublime feriam sidera vertice* [from Horace's *Ode to Maecenas*, l. 36, from *Odes*, I. i]. **7. And . . . Lieutenant:** quoted, accurately, from *Lady Jane Grey*, V. i., by Nicholas Rowe (1674–1718), poet and dramatist.

Chapter IX. **1. Proficient:** student in the process of learning. **2. Ennius:** Roman poet of the second century B.C. **3. painted . . . labour'd:** made splendid and polished.

their was *thir* thro' the whole Poem.[8] And in very Deed, there is no other Way by which the true modern Poet could read to any purpose the Works of such Men as *Milton* and *Shakespear.*

It may be expected, that like other Criticks, I should next speak of the PASSIONS:[9] But as the main End and principal Effect of the *Bathos* is to produce *Tranquillity of Mind,* (and sure it is a better Design to promote Sleep than Madness) we have little to say on this Subject. Nor will the short Bounds of this Discourse allow us to treat at large of the *Emollients* and *Opiats* of *Poesy,* of the *Cool,* and the Manner of producing it, or of the *Methods* us'd by our Authors in *managing* the *Passions.* I shall but transiently remark, that nothing contributes so much to the *Cool,* as the Use of *Wit* in expressing Passion: The true Genius rarely fails of *Points,*[10] *Conceits,* and proper *Similies* on such Occasions: This we may term the *Pathetic epigrammatical,* in which even Puns are made use of with good Success. Hereby our best Authors have avoided throwing themselves or their Readers into any indecent Transports.

But as it is sometimes needful to excite the Passions of our Antagonist in the Polemic way, the true Students in the *Low* have constantly taken their Methods from *Low*-Life, where they observ'd, that to move *Anger,* use is made of *scolding* and *railing;* to move *Love,* of *Bawdry;* to beget *Favour* and Friendship, of gross *Flattery;* and to produce *Fear,* of calumniating an Adversary with *Crimes* obnoxious to the *State.* As for *Shame,* it is a silly Passion, of which as our Authors are incapable themselves, so they would not produce it in others.

CHAP. X

Of Tropes *and* Figures: *and first of the variegating, confounding, and reversing* Figures.

BUT we proceed to the *Figures.* We cannot too earnestly recommend to our Authors the Study of the *Abuse of Speech.* They ought to lay it down as a Principle, to say nothing in the usual way, but (if possible) in the direct contrary. Therefore the Figures must be so turn'd, as to manifest that intricate and wonderful *Cast of Head,* which distinguishes all

Writers of this Kind; or (as I may say) to refer exactly the *Mold* in which they were form'd, in all its *Inequalities, Cavities, Obliquities,* odd *Crannies,* and *Distortions.*

It would be endless, nay impossible to enumerate all *such Figures;* but we shall content ourselves to range the Principal which most powerfully contribute to the *Bathos,* under three Classes.

I. THE Variegating, Confounding, or Reversing *Tropes* and *Figures.*

II. THE Magnifying, and

III. THE Diminishing.

WE cannot avoid giving to these the *Greek* or *Roman* Names; but in Tenderness to our Countrymen and fellow Writers, many of whom, however exquisite, are wholly ignorant of those Languages, we have also explain'd them in our Mother Tongue.

1. OF the First Sort, nothing so much conduces to the *Bathos,* as the

CATACHRESIS.[1]

A Master of this will say,

> *Mow* the Beard,
> *Shave* the Grass,
> *Pin* the Plank,
> *Nail* my Sleeve.

From whence results the same kind of Pleasure to the Mind, as to the Eye when we behold *Harlequin* trimming himself with a Hatchet, hewing down a Tree with a Rasor, making his Tea in a Cauldron, and brewing his Ale in a Tea-pot, to the incredible Satisfaction of the *British* Spectator. Another Source of the *Bathos* is

The METONYMY,

the Inversion of Causes for Effects, of Inventors for Inventions, *&c.*

> *Lac'd in her* Cosins *new appear'd the Bride,*
> *A* Bubble-boy *and* Tompion *at her Side,*
> *And with an Air divine her* Colmar *ply'd.*
> *Then oh! she cries, what Slaves I round me see?*
> *Here a bright* Redcoat, *there a smart* Toupee.[2]

Chapter X. **1. Catachresis:** misuse of words. **2. Lac'd . . . Toupee:** Pope, who probably invented the lines, included a note glossing the words printed in roman type (except *Redcoat*) as follows: stays, tweezer case, watch, fan, and "a sort of Perriwig." He added: "All Words in use this present Year 1727." "Cosins," "Tompion," and "Colmar" were articles named after their manufacturers. *Smart* was a new word in the sense it has here.

---

8. Poem: Pope had John Philips's *Cyder* (1708) in mind. (See the selection from Philips in Part Three.) **9. Passions:** emotions. **10. Points:** witticisms.

The SYNECHDOCHE

Which consists, in the Use of a *Part* for the *Whole;*
you may call a young Woman sometimes Pretty-*face*
and Pigs-*eyes*, and sometimes Snotty-*nose* and Draggle-
tail. Or of *Accidents* for *Persons;* as a Lawyer is call'd
Split-cause, a Taylor *Prick-louse*, &c. Or of things
belonging to a Man, for the Man himself; as a *Sword*-
Man, a *Gown*-man, a *Tom Turd-man;*[3] a *White-Staff*,[4]
a *Turn-key*,[5] &c.

The APOSIOPÈSIS.[6]

An excellent Figure for the Ignorant, as, *What shall I
say?* when one has nothing to say; or *I can no more*,
when one really can no more: Expressions which the
gentle Reader is so good, as never to take in earnest.

The METAPHOR.

The first Rule is to draw it from the lowest things,
which is a certain way to sink the highest; as when
you speak of the Thunder of Heaven, say,

> *The* Lords above *are* angry *and* talk big.[7]

IF you would describe a rich Man refunding his
Treasures, express it thus,

> *Tho' he* (as said) *may Riches gorge, the Spoil
> Painful in* massy Vomit *shall recoil.
> Soon shall he perish with a swift Decay,
> Like his own* Ordure, *cast with Scorn away.*[8]

THE Second, that whenever you *start* a Metaphor,
you must be sure to *Run it down*, and pursue it as far
as it can go. If you get the Scent of a State Negotiation,
follow it in this manner.

> *The Stones and all the Elements with thee
> Shall ratify a strict Confederacy;
> Wild Beasts their savage Temper shall forget,
> And for a firm Alliance with thee treat;
> The finny Tyrant of the spacious Seas
> Shall send a scaly Embassy for Peace:
> His plighted Faith the Crocodile shall keep,
> And seeing thee, for Joy sincerely weep.*[9]

OR if you represent the Creator denouncing War
against the Wicked, be sure not to omit one Circumstance usual in proclaiming and levying War.

> *Envoys and Agents, who by my Command
> Reside in Palestina's Land,
> To whom Commissions I have given,
> To manage there the Interests of Heaven.
> Ye holy Heralds who proclaim
> Or War or Peace, in mine your Master's Name.—
> Ye Pioneers of Heaven, prepare a Road,
> Make it plain, direct and broad;—
> For I in person will my People head;
> —For the divine Deliverer
> Will on his March in Majesty appear,
> And needs the Aid of no Confederate Pow'r.*[10]

UNDER the Article of the *Confounding*, we rank

1. The MIXTURE OF FIGURES,

which raises so many Images, as to give you no Image
at all. But its principal Beauty is when it gives an Idea
just opposite to what it seem'd meant to describe.
Thus an ingenious Artist painting the *Spring*, talks of
a *Snow* of Blossoms, and thereby raises an unexpected
Picture of *Winter*. Of this Sort is the following:

> *The gaping Clouds pour Lakes of Sulphur down,
> Whose livid flashes sickning Sunbeams drown.*[11]

WHAT a noble Confusion? Clouds, Lakes, Brimstone, Flames, Sun-beams, gaping, pouring, sickning,
drowning! all in two Lines.

2. The JARGON,[12]

> *Thy Head shall rise, tho' buried in the Dust,
> And 'midst the Clouds his glittering Turrets thrust.*[13]

Quære, what are the glittering Turrets of a Man's
Head?

> *Upon the Shore, as frequent as the Sand,
> To meet the Prince, the glad Dimetians stand.*[14]

Quære, where these *Dimetians* stood? and of what
Size they were? Add also to the *Jargon* such as the
following.

---

3. Tom Turd-man: one who carted off by night the contents
of privies. **4. White-Staff:** a high official whose sign of
office was a white wand. **5. Turn-key:** jailor. **6. Aposio-
pèsis:** sudden breaking off of speech. **7. The Lords . . . big:**
Nathaniel Lee, *The Rival Queens*, I. i. **8. Tho' . . . away:**
Sir Richard Blackmore, *Job*, pp. 91, 93. **9. The Stones . . .
weep:** *Ibid.*, p. 22.

10. Envoys . . . Pow'r: *Ibid.*, pp. 289, 291–92. **11. The
gaping . . . drown:** Blackmore, *Prince Arthur*, p. 73. **12.
Jargon:** nonsense, gibberish. **13. Thy . . . thrust:** Blackmore, *Job*, p. 107. **14. Upon . . . stand:** Blackmore,
Prince Arthur, p. 157.

Destruction's *Empire shall no longer* last,
And Desolation *lye for ever* waste.[15]

Here Niobe, *sad mother, makes her moan,*
And seems converted to a stone in stone.[16]

But for Variegation, nothing is more useful than

3. The PARANOMASIA, or PUN,

where a Word, like the Tongue of a Jackdaw, speaks twice as much by being split: As this of Mr. *Dennis,*

Bullets that wound, like Parthians *as they fly;*[17]

or this excellent one of Mr. *Welsted,*

Behold the Virgin lye
Naked, and only cover'd *by the* Sky.[18]

To which thou may'st add,

To see her Beauties no Man needs to stoop,
She has the whole Horizon for her Hoop.[19]

4. The ANTITHESIS, or SEE-SAW,

Whereby Contraries and Oppositions are ballanc'd in such a way, as to cause a Reader to remain suspended between them, to his exceeding Delight and Recreation. Such are these, on a Lady who made herself appear out of size,[20] by hiding a young Princess under her Cloaths.

While the kind Nymph changing her faultless Shape
Becomes unhandsome, handsomely *to scape.*[21]

On the Maids of Honour in Mourning:

Sadly they charm, and dismally they please.[22]

———— ————*His Eyes so bright*
Let in *the Object; and let out the Light.*[23]

The Gods look pale *to see us look so* red.[24]

————————*The Fairies and their Queen*
In Mantles blue *came tripping o'er the* Green.[25]

All Nature felt a reverential Shock,
The Sea stood still *to see the Mountains* rock.[26]

CHAP. XI

The Figures continued: Of the
Magnifying and diminishing
Figures.

A GENUINE Writer of the Profound will take Care never to *magnify* any Object without *clouding* it at the same time; His Thought will appear in a true *Mist,* and very unlike what is in Nature. It must always be remember'd that *Darkness* is an essential Quality of the *Profund,* or if there chance to be a Glimmering, it must be as *Milton* expresses it,

No Light, but rather Darkness visible.[1]

The chief Figure of this sort is,

1. The HYPERBOLE, or *Impossible,*

For Instance, of a Lion;

He roar'd so loud, and look'd so wondrous grim,
His very Shadow durst not follow him.[2]

Of a Lady at Dinner.

The silver Whiteness that adorns thy Neck,
Sullies the Plate, and makes the Napkin black.[3]

Of the same.

—*Th' obscureness of her Birth*
Cannot eclipse the Lustre of her Eyes,
Which make her all one Light.[4]

---

15. Destruction's . . . waste: Blackmore, *Job,* p. 89. **16. Here . . . stone:** Thomas Cooke, *An Epistle to the Right Honorable The Earl of Pembroke, at Wilton,* in *Tales, Epistles, Odes, Fables, Etc. With Translations from Homer and Other Ancient Authors* (1729). **17. Bullets . . . fly:** John Dennis, *Upon Our Victory at Sea,* in *Miscellanies in Verse and Prose* (1693). (See the selection from Dennis in Part Two.) **18. Behold . . . Sky:** Leonard Welsted, *Acon and Lavin,* in *The Freethinker* (February 27 and March 2, 1718–19). **19. To . . . Hoop:** not identified; probably by Pope. **20. size:** normal dimensions. **21. While . . . scape:** Edmund Waller, *To My Lady Morton on New Yearsday,* 1650, ll. 29–30. (See the selections from Waller in Part Three.) **22. Sadly . . . please:** Sir Richard Steele, *The Procession. A Poem on Her Majesty's Funeral* (1695). By the time Pope quoted the line, it had been dropped from the second edition (1714). **23. His . . . Light:** Francis Quarles, *On the Body of Man,* in his *Divine Fancies* (1632).

24. The Gods . . . red: Pope refers this line to Lee's *Rival Queens,* but it is actually an inflation of three lines from his *Sophonisba* (I. i. 56–58):

Each God look'd down and shook his awful head,
Mourning to see so many thousands fall,
And then look'd pale, to see us look so red.

25. The Fairies . . . Green: Ambrose Philips, *Sixth Pastoral,* ll. 107–08. **26. All . . . rock:** Blackmore, *Job,* p. 176. Chapter XI. **1. No . . . visible:** *Paradise Lost,* I. 10. **2. He . . . him:** [Pope's note] Vet. Aut. [old author, and so probably by Pope]. **3. The silver . . . black:** not identified; probably by Pope. **4. Th' obscureness . . . Light:** Lewis Theobald, *Double Falsehood,* I. iii.

Of a Bull-baiting.

Up to the Stars the sprawling Mastives fly,
And add new Monsters to the frighted Sky.[5]

Of a Scene of Misery.

Behold a Scene of Misery and Woe!
Here Argus' soon might weep himself quite blind,
Ev'n tho' he had Briareus' hundred Hands
To wipe those hundred Eyes[6]—

And that modest Request of two absent Lovers,

Ye Gods! annihilate but Space *and* Time,
And make two Lovers happy.[7]———

2. The PERIPHRASIS, which the Moderns call the *Circumbendibus*,[8] whereof we have given Examples in the ninth Chapter, and shall again in the twelfth.

To the same Class of the *Magnifying* may be referr'd the following, which are so excellently Modern, that we have yet no Name for them. In describing a Country Prospect

I'd call them Mountains, but can't call them so,
For fear to wrong them with a Name too low;
While the fair Vales beneath so humbly lie,
That even humble seems a Term too high.[9]

3. THE third Class remains, of the *Diminishing* Figures: And, 1. The ANTICLIMAX, where the second Line drops quite short of the first, than which nothing creates greater Surprize.

On the Extent of the *British* Arms.

Under the Tropicks is our Language spoke,
And Part of Flanders *hath received our Yoke.*[10]

On a Warrior.

And thou Dalhoussy the great God of War,
Lieutenant Colonel to the Earl of Mar.[11]

On the Valour of the *English*.

Nor Art nor Nature has the Force
To stop its steddy Course,
Nor Alps nor Pyrenæans *keep it out*
Nor fortify'd Redoubt.[12]

AT other times this Figure operates in a larger Extent; and when the gentle Reader is in Expectation of some great Image, he either finds it surprizingly *imperfect*, or is presented with something *low*, or quite *ridiculous*. A Surprize resembling that of a curious Person in a Cabinet[13] of antique Statues, who beholds on the Pedestal the Names of *Homer*, or *Cato;* but looking up, finds *Homer* without a Head, and nothing to be seen of *Cato* but his privy Member. Such are these Lines of a *Leviathan* at Sea.

His Motion works, and beats the oozy Mud,
And with its Slime incorporates the Flood,
'Till all th' encumber'd, thick, fermenting Stream
Does like one Pot of boiling Ointment seem.
Where'er he swims, he leaves along the Lake
Such frothy Furrows, such a foamy Track,
That all the Waters of the Deep appear
Hoary—with Age, *or grey with sudden Fear.*[14]

BUT perhaps even these are excell'd by the ensuing.

Now the resisted Flames and fiery Store,
By Winds assaulted, in wide Forges roar,)
And raging Seas flow down of melted Oar.)
Sometimes they hear long Iron Bars remov'd,
And to and fro huge Heaps of Cynders shov'd.[15]

2. The VULGAR

Is also a Species of the *Diminishing;* By this a Spear flying into the Air is compar'd to a Boy whistling as he goes on an Errand.

The mighty Stuffa *threw a massy Spear,*
Which, with its Errand *pleas'd, sung thro' the Air.*[16]

A Man raging with Grief to a Mastiff Dog.

I cannot stifle this gigantic Woe,
Nor on my raging Grief a Muzzle throw.[17]

And Clouds big with Water to a Woman in great Necessity.

5. Up . . . Sky: from the first edition (1695) of Sir Richard Blackmore's *Prince Arthur*, p. 232. 6. Behold . . . Eyes: [Pope's note] Anon. [probably by Pope]. 7. Ye . . . happy: not identified; probably by Pope. 8. Circumbendibus: a dog-Latin term, apparently invented by Dryden, meaning a round-about method. If Martinus is right in describing this as a fault, Dryden himself was sometimes guilty of it. 9. I'd . . . high: [Pope's note] Anon. [probably by Pope]. 10. Under . . . Yoke: Edmund Waller, *Upon the Late Storm and the Death of His Highness Ensuing the Same*, ll. 21-22. (See the selections from Waller in Part Three.) 11. And . . . Mar: [Pope's note] Anon. [probably by Pope].

12. Nor Art . . . Redoubt: John Dennis, *Pindaric Ode on the King*, in *Miscellanies in Verse and Prose* (1693). (See the selection from Dennis earlier in Part Two.) 13. Cabinet: museum. 14. His . . . Fear: Blackmore, *Job*, p. 197. 15. Now . . . shov'd: Blackmore, *Prince Arthur*, p. 157. 16. The mighty . . . Air: Pope mistakenly ascribed these lines to Blackmore's *Prince Arthur* instead of to his *King Arthur* (1697). 17. I . . . throw: Blackmore, *Job*, p. 41.

Distended *with the* Waters *in 'em pent,*
The Clouds hang deep *in Air, but* hang unrent.[18]

3. The INFANTINE.

THIS is when a Poet grows so very simple, as to think and talk like a Child. I shall take my Examples from the greatest Master in this way. Hear how he fondles, like a meer Stammerer.

> Little Charm *of placid Mien,*
> Miniature *of Beauty's Queen,*
> *Hither* British *Muse of mine,*
> *Hither, all ye* Græcian Nine,
> *With the lovely Graces* Three,
> *And your* pretty Nurseling *see.*[19]

> *When the Meadows next are seen,*
> *Sweet Enamel, white and green.*
> *When again the Lambkins play,*
> Pretty Sportlings *full of* May.
> *Then the* Neck *so white and round,*
> (*Little Neck with Brilliants bound.*)
> *And thy* Gentleness *of Mind,*
> (*Gentle from a gentle Kind*) &c.
> Happy *thrice, and* thrice agen,
> Happiest *he of* happy Men,[20] &c.

and the rest of those excellent *Lullabies* of his Composition.

How prettily he asks the Sheep to teach him to bleat?

> *Teach me to grieve with bleating Moan, my Sheep.*[21]

Hear how a Babe would reason on his Nurse's Death:

> *That ever she could dye! Oh most* unkind!
> *To die, and leave poor* Colinet *behind?*
> *And yet,—Why blame I her?*[22]———

WITH no less Simplicity does he suppose that Shepherdesses tear their Hair and beat their Breasts, at their own Deaths:

> *Ye brighter Maids, faint Emblems of my Fair,*
> *With Looks cast down, and with dishevel'd Hair,*
> *In bitter Anguish beat your Breasts, and moan*
> *Her Death untimely,* as it were your own.[23]

4. The INANITY, or NOTHINGNESS.

OF this the same Author furnishes us with most beautiful Instances:

> *Ah silly I, more silly than my Sheep,*
> (*Which on the flow'ry Plain I once did keep.*)[24]

> *To the grave Senate she could Counsel give,*
> (*Which with Astonishment they did receive.*)[25]

> *He whom loud Cannon could not terrify,*
> *Falls (from the Grandeur of his Majesty.*)[26]

> *Happy, merry as a King,*
> *Sipping dew, you sip, and sing.*[27]

> *The* Noise *returning with returning* Light,

What did it?

> —*Dispers'd the* Silence, *and dispell'd the* Night.[28]

You easily perceive the Nothingness of every *second* Verse.

> *The Glories of proud* London *to survey,*
> *The Sun himself shall rise—by break of Day.*[29]

5. The EXPLETIVE,

admirably exemplified in the Epithets of many Authors.

> *Th' umbrageous Shadow, and the verdant Green,*
> *The running Current, and odorous Fragrance,*
> *Chear my lone Solitude with joyous Gladness.*[30]

Or in pretty drawling Words like these,

> *All men his tomb, all men his sons adore,*
> *And his sons' sons, till there shall be no more.*[31]

---

18. **Distended . . . unrent:** from the first edition (1700) of Blackmore's *Job*, p. 115. 19. **Little . . . see:** Ambrose Philips, *To Miss Georgianna, Youngest Daughter to Lord Carteret*, ll. 1–2, 13–16. (See the selections from Philips in Part Three.) 20. **When the Meadows . . . Men:** Ambrose Philips, *To the Honorable Miss Carteret*, ll. 21–22, 19–20, 45–46, 75–76, 55–56. 21. **Teach . . . Sheep:** Ambrose Philips, *Sixth Pastoral*, l. 55. 22. **That . . . her:** *Ibid.*, ll. 49–51. In the first edition a further sample from Philips's *Pastorals* (vi. 45–57) followed: "His Shepherd reasons as much like an Innocent, in Love:

> *I love in Secret all a beauteous Maid,*
> *And have my Love in Secret all repay'd:*
> *This coming* Night *she does reserve for me.*

The Love of this Maiden to him appears by her allowing him the Reserve of one Night from her other Lovers; which you see he takes extreamly kindly."

23. **Ye . . . own:** *Ibid.*, ll. 63–66. 24. **Ah . . . keep:** *Ibid.*, ll. 61–62. 25. **To . . . receive:** Ambrose Philips, *Lament for Queen Mary*, ll. 36–37. 26. **He . . . Majesty:** *Ibid.*, ll. 52–53. 27. **Happy . . . sing:** [Pope's note] T. Cook [or Cooke], *To a Grasshopper* [in *Tales, Epistles, Odes, Fables* (1729)]. 28. **The Noise . . . Night:** [Pope's note] Anon. [probably by Pope]. 29. **The Glories . . . Day:** [Pope's note] Autor Vet. [old author, and so probably Pope]. 30. **Th' umbrageous . . . Gladness:** not identified; probably by Pope. 31. **All . . . more:** Thomas Cooke, *Tyrtaeus, on Martial Virtue. To the Duke of Marlborough*, in *Tales, Epistles, Odes, Fables*.

The rising sun our grief did see,
The setting sun did see the same,
While wretched we remembred thee,
O Sion, Sion, lovely name.[32]

6. The MACROLOGY and PLEONASM,

are as generally coupled, as a lean Rabbit with a fat one; nor is it a wonder, the Superfluity of Words and Vacuity of Sense, being just the same thing.[33] I am pleas'd to see one of our greatest Adversaries employ this Figure.

The Growth of Meadows, and the Pride of Fields.
The Food of Armies and Support of Wars.
Refuse of Swords, and Gleanings of a Fight.
Lessen his Numbers, and contract his Host.
Where'er his Friends retire, or Foes succeed.
Cover'd with Tempests, and in Oceans drown'd.[34]

Of all which the Perfection is

7. The TAUTOLOGY.

Break thro' the Billows, and—divide the Main.[35]
In smoother Numbers, and—in softer Verse.[36]

Divide—and part—the sever'd World—in two.[37]

WITH ten thousand others equally musical, and plentifully flowing thro' most of our celebrated modern Poems.

CHAP. XII

Of Expression, *and the several*
Sorts of Style *of the present Age.*

THE *Expression* is adequate, when it is proportionably low to the Profundity of the Thought. It must not be always *Grammatical*, lest it appear pedantic and un-gentlemanly; nor too *clear*, for fear it become vulgar; for Obscurity bestows a Cast of the Wonderful, and throws an oracular Dignity upon a Piece which hath no meaning.

FOR example,[1] sometimes use the wrong Number; *The Sword and Pestilence at once* devours, instead of *devour*. Sometimes the wrong Case; *And who more fit to sooth the God than* thee, instead of *thou*: And rather than say, *Thetis saw Achilles* weep, she *heard* him weep.

WE must be exceeding careful in two things; first, in the *Choice* of *low Words*; secondly, in the *sober* and *orderly* way of *ranging* them. Many of our Poets are naturally bless'd with this Talent, insomuch that they are in the Circumstance of that honest Citizen, who had made *Prose* all his Life without knowing it.[2] Let Verses run in this manner, just to be a Vehicle to the Words. (I take them from my last cited Author, who tho' otherwise by no means of our Rank, seem'd once in his Life to have a mind to be simple.)

If not, a Prize I will my self decree,
From him, or him, or else perhaps from thee.[3]

—— ——full of Days was he;
Two Ages past, he liv'd the third to see.[4]

The King of forty Kings, and honour'd more
By mighty Jove than e'er was King before.[5]

That I may know, if thou my Prayer deny,
The most despis'd of all the Gods am I.[6]

Then let my Mother once be rul'd by me,
Tho' much more wise than I pretend to be.[7]

Or these of the same hand.

I leave the Arts of Poetry and Verse
To them that practice them with more success:
Of greater Truths I now prepare to tell,
And so at once, dear Friend and Muse, farewel.[8]

Sometimes a single *Word* will vulgarize a poetical Idea; as where a Ship set on fire owes all the Spirit of the *Bathos* to one choice Word that ends the Line.

And his scorch'd Ribs the hot Contagion fry'd.[9]

And in that Description of a World in Ruins.

Should the whole Frame of Nature round him break,
He unconcern'd would hear the mighty Crack.[10]

---

32. **The rising . . . name:** Cooke, *Paraphrase of Psalm 137,* in *Tales, Epistles, Odes, Fables.* 33. **Superfluity . . . thing:** Cf. *Essay on Criticism,* above, ll. 309–10. 34. **The Growth . . . drown'd:** Cf. Johnson's *Vanity of Human Wishes,* ll. 31–36, in Part Six. 35. **Break . . . Main:** Thomas Tickell, *The Royal Progress,* l. 61. 36. **In . . . Verse:** Joseph Addison, *An Account of the Greatest English Poets,* l. 105. 37. **Divide . . . two:** Addison's translation of Horace, *Odes,* III. iii. 89.

Chapter XII. 1. **For example:** The three examples in this paragraph come from Book I of Thomas Tickell's translation of the *Iliad,* which appeared in 1715, the same year as Pope's. 2. **that . . . it:** M. Jourdain in Molière's *Le Bourgeois Gentilhomme,* II. iv. 3. **If . . . thee:** *Ibid.* 4. **full . . . see:** *Ibid.* 5. **The King . . . before:** *Ibid.* 6. **That . . . I:** *Ibid.* 7. **Then . . . be:** *Ibid.* 8. **I . . . farewel:** Joseph Addison, *An Account of the Greatest English Poets,* ll. 152–55. 9. **And . . . fry'd:** Sir Richard Blackmore, *Prince Arthur,* p. 151. 10. **Should . . . Crack:** Addison's translation of Horace, *Odes,* III. iii. 14, 16.

So also in these:

Beasts tame and savage to the River's Brink
Come from the Fields and wild Abodes—to drink.[11]

FREQUENTLY two or three Words will do it effectually.

He from the Clouds does the sweet Liquor squeeze,
That chears the Forest and the Garden Trees.[12]

IT is also useful to employ *Technical Terms*, which estrange your Stile from the great and general Ideas of Nature: And the higher your Subject is, the lower should you search into Mechanicks for your Expression. If you describe the Garment of an Angel, say that his *Linnen* was *finely spun*, and *bleach'd on the happy Plains*.[13] Call an Army of Angels, *Angelic Cuirassiers*,[14] and if you have Occasion to mention a Number of Misfortunes, stile them

Fresh Troops of Pains, and regimented Woes.[15]

STILE is divided by the Rhetoricians into the Proper[16] and the Figured. Of the Figur'd we have already treated, and the Proper[17] is what our Authors have nothing to do with. Of Stiles we shall mention only the Principal, which owe to the *Moderns* either their *chief Improvement*, or entire *Invention*.

1. The FLORID *Stile,*

Than which none is more proper to the *Bathos*, as Flowers which are the *Lowest* of Vegetables are the most *Gaudy*, and do many times grow in great Plenty at the bottom of *Ponds* and *Ditches*.

A fine Writer in this kind presents you with the following Posie:

The Groves appear all drest with Wreaths of Flowers,
And from their Leaves drop aromatic Showers,
Whose fragrant Heads in mystic Twines above,
Exchang'd their Sweets, and mix'd with thousand Kisses,
As if the willing Branches strove
To beautify and shade the Grove.[18]—

(Which indeed most Branches do) But this is still excell'd by our Laureat.[19]

Branches in Branches twin'd compose the Grove,
And shoot and spread, and blossom into Love.
The trembling Palms their mutual Vows repeat,
And bending Poplars bending Poplars meet.
The distant Platanes seems to press more nigh,
And to the sighing Alders, Alders sigh.[20]

Hear also our *Homer*.[21]

His Robe of State *is form'd of Light refin'd,*
An endless Train *of Lustre spreads behind.*
His Throne's *of bright* compacted Glory *made,*
With Pearl *celestial, and with* Gems *inlaid:*
Whence Floods *of Joy, and Seas of Splendor flow,*
On all th' Angelic gazing Throng below.[22]

2. The PERT *Stile.*

This does in as peculiar a manner become the low in Wit, as a Pert Air does the low in Stature. Mr. *Thomas Brown*, the Author of the *London Spy*, and all the *Spies* and *Trips*[23] in general, are herein to be diligently study'd: In Verse, Mr. *Cibber's Prologues.*

BUT the Beauty and Energy[24] of it is never so conspicuous, as when it is employ'd in *Modernizing* and *Adapting* to the *Taste of the Times* the Works of the Antients. This we rightly phrase *Doing them into English,* and *making them English;* two Expressions of great Propriety, the one denoting our *Neglect* of the *Manner how,* the other the *Force* and *Compulsion* with which, it is brought about. It is by Virtue of this Stile that *Tacitus* talks like a *Coffee-House Politician,*[25] *Josephus* like the *British Gazeteer,*[26] *Tully* is as short and smart as *Seneca* or Mr. *Asgill,*[27] *Marcus Aurelius* is

19. **our Laureat:** Laurence Eusden (1688–1730); appointed Poet Laureate in 1718. **20. Branches . . . sigh:** Laurence Eusden, translation of Claudian's *Court of Venus,* in *The Guardian,* No. 127 (August 6, 1713). Cf. the fourth of the *Moral Essays, Of the Use of Riches,* below, ll. 117–20. **21. our Homer:** Blackmore. **22. His Robe . . . below:** Blackmore, *Job,* p. 260. **23. Trips:** in the new sense of short voyages or journeys; Pope is laughing at the fashion of calling periodicals by such names as *Mercury, Rambler, Courier,* and *Courant.* **24. Energy:** a term that Aristotle used in his *Rhetoric.* **25. Tacitus . . . Politician:** Thomas Gordon (who appears as Silenus in *The Dunciad,* below, IV. 492) had just published his translation for coffee-house schemers. **26. Josephus . . . Gazeteer:** Sir Roger L'Estrange (1616–1704) translated Josephus, the Jewish historian of the first century A.D. *The British Gazeteer: The Weekly Journal, or, British Gazeteer, Being the Freshest Advices Foreign and Domestic* ran from 1715 on. **27. Tully . . . Asgill:** L'Estrange, who had translated Cicero's *De Officiis,* seems intended. Joseph Asgill was an eccentric, hard-hitting writer who came to be much admired by Coleridge and Southey.

11. **Beasts . . . drink:** Blackmore, *Job,* p. 263. **12. He . . . Trees:** *Ibid.,* p. 264. **13. Linnen . . . Plains:** Blackmore, *Prince Arthur,* p. 19. **14. Angelic Cuirassiers:** *Ibid.,* p. 239. **15. Fresh . . . Woes:** Blackmore, *Job,* p. 86. **16. Proper:** literal, not metaphorical. **17. Proper:** a pun on the meanings "decent," "respectable," "correct"—a sense Swift may have been the first to give the word. **18. The Groves . . . Grove:** Aphra Behn, *The Golden Age,* ll. 9–14, in *Poems upon Several Occasions* (1684).

excellent at *Snipsnap*,²⁸ and honest *Thomas a Kempis* as *Prim* and *Polite* as any Preacher at Court.²⁹

3. THE ALAMODE Stile,

Which is fine by being *new*, and has this Happiness attending it, that it is as durable and extensive as the Poem itself. Take some Examples of it, in the Description of the Sun in a Mourning Coach upon the Death of Q. *Mary*.

See Phœbus now, as once for Phaeton,
Has mask'd *his Face; and put* deep Mourning *on;*
Dark Clouds his sable³⁰ *Chariot do surround,*
And the dull Steeds stalk o'er *the* melancholy Round.³¹

Of Prince *Arthur*'s Soldiers drinking.

While rich Burgundian *Wine, and bright* Champaign,
*Chase from their Minds the Terrors of the Main.*³²

(Whence we also learn, that *Burgundy* and *Champaign* make a Man on Shore despise a Storm at Sea.)

Of the Almighty encamping his Regiments.

———*He sunk a vast capacious deep,*
Where he his liquid Regiments *does keep:*
Thither the Waves file off, *and make their way,*
To form the mighty Body *of the Sea;*
Where they incamp, and in their Station stand,
Entrench'd *in Works of Rock, and* Lines *of Sand.*³³

Of two Armies on the Point of engaging.

Yon' Armies are the Cards which both must play;
At least come off a Saver³⁴ *if you may:*
Throw boldly *at the Sum the Gods have* set;
These on your Side will all their Fortunes bet.³⁵

All perfectly agreeable to the present Customs and best Fashions of our Metropolis.

BUT the principal Branch of the *Alamode* is the PRURIENT, a Stile greatly advanc'd and honour'd of late by the practise of Persons of the *first Quality*, and

by the encouragement of the *Ladies* not unsuccessfully introduc'd even into the *Drawing-Room*. Indeed its *incredible Progress* and *Conquests* may be compar'd to those of the great *Sesostris*,³⁶ and are every where known by the *same Marks*, the Images of the Genital Parts of Men or Women. It consists wholly of Metaphors drawn from two most fruitful Sources or Springs, the very *Bathos* of the human Body, that is to say * * * and * * * * * * * * * * * * * * * *Hiatus Magnus lachrymabilis.*³⁷ *. And *selling of Bargains*,³⁸ and *double Entendre*, and Κιββέρισμος, and Ὀλδφιέλδισμος,³⁹ all derived from the said Sources.

4. The FINICAL *Stile*,

Which consists of the most curious, affected, mincing Metaphors, and partakes of the *alamode*.

As this, of a Brook dry'd by the Sun.

Won by the Summer's importuning Ray.
Th' eloping Stream did from her Channel stray,
*And with enticing Sun-beams stole away.*⁴⁰

Of an easy Death.

When watchful Death shall on his Harvest look,
And see thee ripe with Age, invite *the Hook;*
He'll gently *cut thy bending Stalk, and thee*
Lay kindly *in the Grave, his Granary.*⁴¹

Of Trees in a Storm.

Oaks whose extended Arms the Winds defy,
The Tempest sees their Strength, and sighs, and passes by.⁴²

Of Water simmering over the Fire.

The sparkling Flames raise Water to a Smile,
*Yet the pleas'd Liquor pines, and lessens all the while.*⁴³

36. **Sesostris**: the name given by the Greeks to Rameses II (1292–1225 B.C.), the Egyptian king who overran Syria. 37. **Hiatus . . . lachrymabilis**: a great and lamentable gap. Asterisks made the sort of typographical display with which an editor indicated a missing piece of his text. 38. **selling of Bargains**: fooling someone. See Swift's *Directions for a Birth-Day Song*, above, note to l. 274. 39. Κιββέρισμος, **and** Ὀλδφιέλδισμος: dog-Greek adjectives derived from the names of the dramatist Colley Cibber (1671–1757) and the actress Anne Oldfield, who was associated with him. 40. **Won . . . away**: Blackmore, *Job*, p. 26. 41. **When . . . Granary**: *Ibid.*, p. 23. 42. **Oaks . . . by**: John Dennis, *Upon Our Victory at Sea*, in *Miscellanies in Verse and Prose* (1693). (See the selection from Dennis earlier in Part Two.) 43. **The sparkling . . . while**: from an anonymous poem in one of the miscellanies published by Jacob Tonson.

28. **Marcus . . . Snipsnap**: Jeremy Collier (1650–1726), a clergyman, published his translation as *The Emperor Marcus Antoninus, His Conversation with Himself* in 1701. 29. **honest . . . Court**: George Stanhope (1660–1728) translated the *Imitatio Christi* (1698), attempting to express the Latin in modern English idiom. 30. **sable**: black. 31. **See . . . Round**: Ambrose Philips, *Lament for Queen Mary*, ll. 66–69. (See the selections from Philips in Part Three.) 32. **While . . . Main**: Blackmore, *Prince Arthur*, p. 16. 33. **He . . . Sand**: Blackmore, *Job*, p. 261. 34. **Saver**: a gambling term meaning "one who escapes loss, though without gain" (Johnson's *Dictionary*). 35. **Yon' . . . bet**: Nathaniel Lee, *Sophonisba*, IV. i.158–59 and II. ii.51, 53.

5. LASTLY, I shall place the CUMBROUS, which moves heavily under a Load of Metaphors, and draws after it a long Train of Words.

AND the BUSKIN, or *Stately*, frequently and with great Felicity mix'd with the Former. For as the first is the proper Engine to depress what is High, so is the second to raise what is Base and Low to a ridiculous Visibility: When both these can be done at once, then is the *Bathos* in Perfection; as when a Man is set with his Head downward, and his Breech upright, his Degradation is compleat: One End of him is as high as ever, only that End is the wrong one. Will not every true Lover of the *Profund* be delighted to behold the most vulgar and low Actions of Life exalted in the following Manner?

Who knocks at the Door?

For whom thus rudely pleads my loud-tongu'd Gate,
That he may enter?[44]———

See who is there?

Advance the fringed Curtains of thy Eyes,
And tell me who comes yonder.[45]———

Shut the Door.

The woodden Guardian of our Privacy
Quick on its Axle turn.———

Bring my Cloaths.

Bring me what Nature, Taylor to the Bear,
To Man himself deny'd: She gave me Cold,
But would not give me Cloaths.———

Light the Fire.

Bring forth some Remnant of Promethean Theft,
Quick to expand th' inclement Air congeal'd
By Boreas's rude Breath.———

Snuff the Candle.

Yon Luminary Amputation needs,
Thus shall you save its half-extinguish'd Life.

Open the Letter.

Wax! render up thy Trust.[46]———

44. For . . . enter: This quotation and all but two of the following Pope leaves unidentified. Presumably they are his own; they are certainly witty enough to be his. **45. Advance . . . yonder:** *The Tempest*, I. ii. 409-10. **46. Wax . . . Trust:** Lewis Theobald, *Double Falsehood*, II. ii.

Uncork the Bottle, and chip the Bread.

Apply thine Engine to the spungy Door,
Set Bacchus from his glassy Prison free,
And strip white Ceres of her nut-brown Coat.

APPENDIX

CHAP. XIII

A Project for the Advancement
of the Bathos.

THUS have I (my dear Countrymen) with incredible Pains and Diligence, discover'd the hidden Sources of the *Bathos*, or as I may say broke open the Abysses of this *Great Deep*. And having now establish'd good and wholesome *Laws*, what remains but that all true Moderns with their utmost Might do proceed to put the same in execution? In order whereto, I think I shall in the second place highly deserve of my Country, by proposing such a *Scheme*, as may facilitate this great End.

As our Number is confessedly far superior to that of the Enemy, there seems nothing wanting but Unanimity among our selves. It is therefore humbly offer'd, that all and every Individual of the *Bathos* do enter into a firm *Association*, and incorporate into *one Regular Body*, whereof every Member, even the meanest, will some way contribute to the Support of the whole; in like manner as the weakest Reeds when join'd in one Bundle, become infrangible. To which end our Art ought to be put upon the same foot with other Arts of this Age. The vast Improvement of modern Manufactures ariseth from their being divided into several Branches, and parcel'd out to several *Trades:* For instance, in *Clock-making*, one Artist makes the Balance, another the Spring, another the Crown-Wheels, a fourth the Case, and the principal Workman puts all together; To this Œconomy we owe the Perfection of our modern Watches; and doubtless we also might that of our modern Poetry and Rhetoric, were the several Parts branched out in the like manner.

NOTHING is more evident than that divers Persons, no other way remarkable, have each a strong Disposition to the Formation of some particular Trope or Figure. *Aristotle* saith, that the *Hyperbole* is an

Ornament fit for *young Men of Quality;*[1] accordingly we find in those Gentlemen a wonderful Propensity toward it, which is marvellously improv'd by *travelling. Soldiers* also and *Seamen* are very happy in the same Figure. The *Periphrasis* or *Circumlocution* is the peculiar Talent of *Country Farmers,* the Proverb and Apologue[2] of *old Men* at their Clubs, the *Ellipsis* or Speech by half-words of *Ministers* and *Politicians,* the *Aposiopesis*[3] of *Courtiers,* the *Litotes*[4] or Diminution of *Ladies, Whisperers* and *Backbiters;*[5] and the *Anady-plosis*[6] of Common *Cryers* and *Hawkers,* who by redoubling the same Words, persuade People to buy their Oysters, green Hastings,[7] or new Ballads. *Epithets* may be found in great plenty at *Billinsgate,*[8] *Sarcasm* and *Irony* learn'd upon the *Water,*[9] and the *Epiphonema* or *Exclamation* frequently from the *Beargarden,*[10] and as frequently from the *Hear him* of the House of Commons.

Now each man applying his whole Time and Genius upon his particular Figure, would doubtless attain to Perfection; and when each became incorporated and sworn into the Society, (as hath been propos'd;) a Poet or Orator would have no more to do, but to send to the particular Traders in each Kind; to the *Metaphorist* for his *Allegories,* to the *Simile-maker* for his *Comparisons,* to the *Ironist* for his *Sarcasmes,* to the *Apothegmatist* for his *Sentences, &c.* whereby a *Dedication* or *Speech* would be compos'd in a Moment, the superior Artist having nothing to do but to put together all the Materials.

I THEREFORE propose that there be contrived with all convenient Dispatch, at the publick Expence, a *Rhetorical Chest of Drawers,* consisting of three Stories, the highest for the *Deliberative,* the middle for the *Demonstrative,* and the lowest for the *Judicial.*[11] These shall be divided into *Loci* or *Places,* being Repositories for Matter and Argument in the several Kinds of Oration or Writing; and every Drawer shall again be sub-divided into Cells, resembling those of Cabinets for Rarities. The Apartment for *Peace* or *War,* and that of the *Liberty* of the *Press,* may in a very few Days be fill'd with several Arguments *perfectly new;* and the *Vituperative Partition* will as easily be replenish'd with a most choice Collection, entirely of the Growth and Manufacture of the present Age. Every Composer will soon be taught the Use of this Cabinet, and how to manage all the Registers of it, which will be drawn out much in the Manner of those in an Organ.

THE Keys of it must be kept in honest Hands, by some *Reverend Prelate,* or *Valiant Officer,* of unquestion'd Loyalty and Affection to every present Establishment in *Church* and *State;* which will sufficiently guard against any Mischief which might otherwise be apprehended from it.

AND being lodg'd in such Hands, it may be at discretion *let out* by the *Day,* to several great Orators in both Houses; from whence it is to be hop'd much *Profit* or *Gain* will also accrue to our Society.

CHAP. XIV

How to make Dedications,
Panegyricks *or* Satyrs, *and of the*
Colours° *of Honourable and*
Dishonourable.

NOW of what Necessity the foregoing Project may prove, will appear from this single Consideration, that nothing is of equal consequence to the Success of our Works, as *Speed* and *Dispatch.* Great pity it is, that solid Brains are not, like other solid Bodies, constantly endow'd with a *Velocity* in sinking, proportion'd to their *Heaviness:* For it is with the *Flowers* of the *Bathos* as with those of Nature, which if the careful Gardener brings not hastily to Market in the *Morning,* must unprofitably perish and wither before *Night.*[1] And of all our Productions none is so short-liv'd as the *Dedication* and *Panegyric,* which are often but the

---

Chapter XIII. **1. Aristotle . . . Quality:** Pope, in Swift's manner, twists Aristotle's remark in the *Rhetoric* that the animated mind of youth runs to the use of imagery. **2. Apologue:** moral fable. **3. Aposiopesis:** sudden breaking off of speech. **4. Litotes:** expression of an idea by the negative of its opposite. **5. Backbiters:** slanderers. **6. Anadyplosis:** duplication, i.e., beginning a clause or phrase with a word taken from what precedes. **7. green Hastings:** early-ripened vegetables. **8. Billinsgate:** Billingsgate is the fish market in central London. **9. upon the Water:** The bargemen and rowers of public transport on the Thames were notoriously free-spoken and witty. **10. Beargarden:** a place set aside for bearbaiting and other rough sports. **11. Deliberative, Demonstrative, Judicial:** Aristotle analyzes rhetoric into (1) the deliberative and advisory for the use of politicians, (2) the demonstrative, or ceremonial, for the use of orators, and (3) the legal for the use of lawyers. Pope's terms are from Hobbes's translation of the *Rhetoric.*

Chapter XIV. **Colours:** a rhetorical term pertaining to the various styles of speech and writing; it is used here to convey Bacon's meaning in his essays *Colours of Good and Evil* (1597), i.e., cunningly specious presentation. **1. if . . . Night:** Pope often used gardens, one of his interests, for illustrations; see above, pp. 588 and 596.

Praise of a Day, and become by the next, utterly useless, improper, indecent and false. This is the more to be lamented, inasmuch as these two are the Sorts whereon in a manner depends that *Profit*, which must still be remember'd to be the main end of *our Writers* and *Speakers*.

WE shall therefore employ this Chapter in shewing the *quickest* Method of composing them; after which we will teach a *short Way* to Epick Poetry. And these being confessedly the Works of most Importance and Difficulty, it is presum'd we may leave the rest to each Author's own Learning or Practice.

FIRST of *Panegyrick:*[2] Every Man is *honourable*, who is so by *Law, Custom* or *Title;* The Publick are better Judges of what is honourable, than private Men. The Virtues of great Men, like those of Plants, are *inherent* in them whether they are *exerted* or not; and the more strongly inherent the less they are exerted; as a Man is the more rich the less he spends.

ALL great Ministers, without either private or œconomical Virtue, are virtuous by their *Posts;* liberal and generous upon the *Publick Money*, provident upon *Publick Supplies*, just by paying *Publick Interest*, couragious and magnanimous by the *Fleets* and *Armies*, magnificent upon the *Publick Expences*, and prudent by *Publick Success*. They have by their *Office*, a Right to a share of the *Publick Stock* of Virtues; besides they are by *Prescription immemorial* invested in all the celebrated Virtues of their *Predecessors* in the same *Stations*, especially those of their own *Ancestors*.

As to what are commonly call'd the *Colours* of *Honourable* and *Dishonourable*, they are various in different Countries: In this they are *Blue, Green* and *Red*.[3] But forasmuch as the Duty we owe to the Publick doth often require that we should put some things in a strong Light, and throw a Shade over others, I shall explain the Method of turning a vicious Man into a Hero.

THE first and chief Rule is *the Golden Rule of Transformation*, which consists in converting Vices into their *bordering* Virtues. A man who is a Spendthrift

and will not pay a just Debt, may have his Injustice *transform'd* into Liberality; Cowardice may be metamorphosed into Prudence; Intemperance into good Nature and good Fellowship, Corruption into Patriotism, and Lewdness into Tenderness and Facility.

The Second is the *Rule of Contraries:* It is certain the less a Man is endu'd with any Virtue, the more need he has to have it plentifully bestow'd, especially those good Qualities of which the World generally believes he hath none at all: For who will thank a Man for giving him that which he *has?*

The Reverse of these Precepts will serve for Satire, wherein we are ever to remark, that whoso loseth his Place, or becomes out of Favour with the Government, hath forfeited his Share in *Publick Praise* and *Honour*. Therefore the truly-publick-spirited Writer ought in Duty to strip him whom the Government has stripp'd: Which is the real *poetical Justice* of this Age. For a full Collection of Topics and Epithets to be used in the Praise and Dispraise of Ministerial and Unministerial Persons, I refer to our *Rhetorical Cabinet;* concluding with an earnest Exhortation to all my Brethren, to observe the Precepts here laid down; the Neglect of which hath cost some of them their *Ears* in a *Pillory*.

CHAP. XV°

A Receipt to make an Epic Poem.

AN Epic Poem, the Criticks agree, is the greatest Work Human Nature is capable of.[1] They have already laid down many mechanical Rules for Compositions of this Sort, but at the same time they cut off almost all Undertakers from the Possibility of ever performing them; for the first Qualification they unanimously require in a Poet, is a *Genius*. I shall here endeavour (for the Benefit of my Countrymen) to make it manifest, that Epick Poems may be made *without a Genius*, nay without Learning or much Reading. This must necessarily be of great Use to all those who confess they never *Read*, and of whom the World is convinc'd they never *Learn*. *Moliere* observes of making a Dinner, that any Man can do it *with*

---

2. **Panegyrick:** a speech of commendation, usually flowery.
3. **Blue . . . Red:** In 1725 Robert Walpole persuaded the King to establish (supposedly to revive) the Order of the Bath (its ribbon was red), and he was himself invested with it. The following year he was admitted to the Order of the Garter and acquired the nickname Sir Bluestring. The satirists made the most of his pleasure in his new distinction. The Order of the Thistle (its ribbon was green) had been revived in 1703.

Chapter XV. This in revised form reproduces Pope's paper in *The Guardian*, No. 78 (June 10, 1713). I. **An Epic . . . of:** The characteristic structure of epic had been set down by René Le Bossu (1631–89) in his *Traité du poème épique* (1675), which had been translated into English.

632   ALEXANDER POPE

Money,[2] and if a profess'd Cook cannot do it *without*
he has his Art for nothing; the same may be said of
making a Poem, 'tis easily brought about by him that
has a Genius, but the Skill lies in doing it without one.
In pursuance of this End, I shall present the Reader
with a plain and certain *Recipe*, by which any Author
in the *Bathos* may be qualified for this grand Performance.

For the *Fable*.[3]

TAKE out of an old Poem, History-book, Romance,
or Legend, (for Instance *Geffry of Monmouth* or *Don
Belianis of Greece*) those Parts of Story which afford
most Scope for *long Descriptions:* Put these Pieces
together, and throw all the Adventures you fancy into
one Tale. Then take a Hero, whom you may chuse
for the Sound of his Name, and put him into the
midst of these Adventures: There let him *work*, for
twelve Books; at the end of which you may take him
out, ready prepared to *conquer* or to *marry;* it being
necessary that the Conclusion of an Epick Poem be
fortunate.

To make an Episode.

TAKE any remaining Adventure of your former
Collection, in which you could no way involve your
Hero; or any unfortunate Accident that was too good
to be thrown away; and it will be of Use, apply'd to
any other Person; who may be lost and *evaporate* in the
Course of the Work, without the least Damage to the
Composition.

For the Moral and Allegory.

THESE you may extract out of the Fable afterwards,
at your leisure: Be sure you *strain* them sufficiently.

For the Manners.

FOR those of the *Hero*, take all the best Qualities you
can find in the most celebrated Heroes of Antiquity;
if they will not be reduced to a *Consistency*, lay 'em
all on a Heap upon him. But be sure they are Qualities
which your *Patron* would be thought to have; and to
prevent any Mistake which the World may be subject
to, select from the Alphabet those Capital Letters that
compose his Name, and set them at the Head of a
Dedication before your Poem. However, do not

absolutely observe the exact Quantity of these Virtues,
it not being determin'd[4] whether or no it be necessary
for the Hero of a Poem to be an *honest Man*. For the
Under-Characters, gather them from *Homer* and *Virgil*,
and change the Names as occasion serves.

For the Machines.

TAKE of *Deities*, Male and Female, as many as you
can use. Separate them into two equal Parts, and keep
Jupiter in the middle. Let *Juno* put him in a Ferment,
and *Venus* mollify him. Remember on all occasions to
make use of Volatile *Mercury*. If you have need of
Devils, draw them out of *Milton's Paradise*, and extract
your *Spirits* from *Tasso*. The Use of these Machines
is evident; since no Epick Poem can possibly subsist
without them, the wisest way is to reserve them for
your greatest Necessities. When you cannot extricate
your Hero by any human means, or your self by your
own Wit, seek Relief from Heaven, and the Gods will
do your business very readily. This is according to the
direct Prescription of *Horace* in his Art of Poetry.

> *Nec Deus intersit, nisi dignus vindice Nodus
> Inciderit.*[5]———

That is to say, *A Poet should never call upon the Gods for
their Assistance, but when he is in great Perplexity.*

For the Descriptions.

FOR a *Tempest*. Take *Eurus, Zephyr, Auster* and
Boreas,[6] and cast them together in one Verse: Add to
these of Rain, Lightning and Thunder (the loudest you
can) *quantum sufficit*.[7] Mix your Clouds and Billows
well together 'till they foam, and thicken your
Description here and there with a Quicksand. Brew
your Tempest well in your Head, before you set it a
blowing.

FOR a *Battle*. Pick a large Quantity of Images and
Descriptions from *Homer's Iliads*, with a Spice or two
of *Virgil*, and if there remain any Overplus, you may
lay them by for a *Skirmish*. Season it well with *Similes*,
and it will make an *Excellent Battle*.

FOR a *Burning Town*. If such a Description be
necessary, (because it is certain there is one in *Virgil*,)

---

2. **Moliere . . . Money:** in *L'Avare*, III. i. 3. **Fable:**
story, plot.

4. **determin'd:** decided. 5. **Nec . . . Inciderit:** "And let no
god intervene, unless the knot is worthy of such a deliverer"
(*Ars Poetica*, ll. 191–92). 6. **Eurus . . . Boreas:** the Greek
and Latin names for winds from the east, west, south, and
north. 7. **quantum sufficit:** as much as suffices. This phrase
is a convenient tag in recipes and prescriptions.

Old *Troy* is ready burnt to your Hands. But if you fear that would be thought borrow'd, A Chapter or two of the Theory of the *Conflagration*,[8] well circumstanced, and done into Verse, will be a good *Succedaneum*.[9]

As for *Similes* and *Metaphors*, they may be found all over the Creation; the most ignorant may *gather* them, but the Difficulty is in *applying* them. For this advise with your *Bookseller*.

CHAP. XVI

A Project for the Advancement of the Stage.

IT may be thought that we should not wholly omit the *Drama*, which makes so great and so lucrative[1] a Part of Poetry. But this Province is so well taken care of, by the present *Managers* of the Theatre, that it is perfectly needless to suggest to them any other Methods than they have already practis'd for the Advancement of the *Bathos*.

HERE therefore, in the name of all our Brethren, let me return our sincere and humble Thanks to the Most August Mr. *Barton Booth*, the Most Serene Mr. *Robert Wilks*, and the Most Undaunted Mr. *Colley Cibber*; of whom, let it be known *when the People of this Age shall be Ancestors*, and to all *the Succession of our Successors*, that to this present day they continue to *Out-do* even their *own Out-doings*:[2] And when the inevitable Hand of sweeping *Time* shall have brush'd off all the Works of *To-day*, may this Testimony of a *Co-temporary Critick* to their Fame, be extended as far as *To-morrow!*

YET, if to so wise an Administration it be possible any thing can be added, it is that more ample and comprehensive Scheme[3] which Mr. *Dennis* and Mr.

Gildon, (the two greatest Criticks and Reformers then living) made publick in the Year 1720. in a Project sign'd with their Names, and dated the 2d of *February*. I cannot better conclude than by presenting the Reader with the Substance of it.

1. IT is propos'd that the two *Theatres*[4] be incorporated into one Company; that the *Royal Academy* of *Musick*[5] be added to them as an *Orchestra;* and that Mr. *Figg*[6] with his Prize-fighters, and *Violante*[7] with the Rope-dancers, be admitted in Partnership.

2. THAT a spacious Building be erected at the Publick Expence, capable of containing at least ten thousand Spectators, which is become absolutely necessary by the great addition of Children and Nurses to the Audience,[8] since the new Entertainments. That there be a Stage as large as the *Athenian*, which was near ninety thousand Geometrical Paces square, and separate Divisions for the two *Houses* of *Parliament*, my *Lords* the *Judges*, the honourable the *Directors* of the *Academy*, and the *Court of Aldermen*, who shall all have their Places frank.[9]

3. IF *Westminster Hall* be not allotted to this Service, (which by reason of its Proximity to the two Chambers of Parliament above mention'd, seems not altogether improper;) it is left to the Wisdom of the Nation whether *Somerset House*[10] may not be demolish'd, and a *Theatre* built upon that Scite, which lies convenient to receive Spectators from the County of *Surrey*, who may be wafted thither by Water-Carriage, esteem'd by all Projectors the cheapest whatsoever. To this may be added, that the River *Thames* may in the readiest manner convey those eminent Personages from Courts beyond the Seas, who may be drawn either by Curiosity to behold some of our most celebrated Pieces, or by Affection to see their Countrymen the Harlequins and Eunuchs;[11] Of which convenient notice may be given for two or three Months before, in the Publick Prints.

---

8. **the Theory . . . Conflagration:** Thomas Burnet's *Telluris Theoria Sacra* (1681). 9. **Succedaneum:** a recent borrowing from Latin, meaning a substitute; often used of food. *Chapter XVI.* 1. **lucrative:** The actor-managers at the Drury Lane Theatre, who are saluted below, received salaries that writers thought ridiculously high. 2. **Out-do . . . Out-doings:** Pope adapts a much ridiculed expression used by Cibber in the Preface to his recent play *The Provoked Husband* (1728) in praise of the acting of Mrs. Oldfield, who played the leading female role. 3. **Scheme:** Theater scholars continue to mention this scheme in all good faith, but since they have never been able to find a copy, it seems that Pope has played a trick on them.

4. **the two Theatres:** Drury Lane and the Haymarket. 5. **the Royal . . . Musick:** a new institution. 6. **Mr. Figg:** James Figg, the pugilist, who died in 1734. 7. **Violante:** a Turkish ropedancer; he and his wife had assumed the stage names of Signor and Signora Violante. 8. **the great . . . Audience:** attracted by the spectacular entertainments, which Pope deplored. See *The Rape of the Lock*, above, iv. 43–46, and *The Dunciad*, II. 221–34. 9. **frank:** free. 10. **Somerset House:** the imposing Tudor predecessor of the present building by this name. 11. **Eunuchs:** the Italian *castrati*, who sang female parts in the opera.

4. THAT the *Theatre* abovesaid be environ'd with a fair Quadrangle of Buildings, fitted for the Accommodation of decay'd *Criticks* and *Poets;* out of whom *Six* of the most Aged (their Age to be computed from the Year wherein their first Work was publish'd) shall be elected to manage the Affairs of the Society, provided nevertheless that the *Laureat* for the time being, may be always one. The Head or President over all, (to prevent Disputes, but too frequent among the Learned) shall be the *most ancient Poet* and *Critick* to be found in the whole Island.

5. THE *Male-Players* are to be lodg'd in the Garrets of the said Quadrangle, and to attend the Persons of the *Poets,* dwelling under them, by brushing their Apparel, drawing on their Shoes, and the like. The *Actresses* are to make their Beds, and wash their Linnen.

6. A LARGE Room shall be set apart for a *Library,* to consist of all the modern Dramatick Poems, and all the Criticisms extant. In the midst of this Room shall be a round Table for the *Council of* SIX to sit and deliberate on the Merits of *Plays.* The *Majority* shall determine the Dispute; and if it should happen that *three* and *three* should be of each Side, the President shall have a *casting Voice,* unless where the Contention may run so high as to require a Decision by *Single Combat.*

7. IT may be convenient to place the *Council of* SIX in some conspicuous Situation in the Theatre, where after the manner usually practised by Composers in Musick, they may give *Signs* (before settled and agreed upon) of Dislike or Approbation. In consequence of these Signs the whole Audience shall be requir'd to *clap* or *hiss,* that the Town may learn certainly when and how far they ought to be pleas'd.

8. IT is submitted whether it would not be proper to distinguish the *Council of* SIX by some particular Habit or Gown of an honourable Shape and Colour, to which may be added a square Cap and a white Wand.

9. THAT to prevent unmarried Actresses making away with their Infants, a competent Provision be allow'd for the Nurture of them, who shall for that reason be deem'd the *Children of the Society;* and that they may be educated according to the Genius of their Parents, the said Actresses shall declare upon Oath (as far as their Memory will allow) the true Names and Qualities of their several Fathers. A private Gentleman's Son shall at the Publick Expence be brought up a Page to attend the *Council of* SIX. A more ample Provision shall be made for the Son of a *Poet;* and a greater still for the Son of a *Critick.*

10. IF it be discover'd that any Actress is got with Child, during the Interludes of any Play, wherein she hath a part, it shall be reckon'd neglect of her Business, and she shall *forfeit* accordingly. If any Actor for the future shall commit *Murder,* except upon the Stage, he shall be left to the Laws of the Land; the like is to be understood of *Robbery* and *Theft.* In all other Cases, particularly in those for *Debt,* it is propos'd that this, like the other Courts of *Whitehall* and *St. James's,* may be held a *Place of Priviledge.* And whereas it has been found, that an Obligation to satisfy *paultry Creditors* has been a Discouragement to *Men of Letters,* if any Person of Quality or others shall send for any *Poet* or *Critick* of this Society to any remote Quarter of the Town, the said *Poet* or *Critick* shall freely pass and repass without being liable to an *Arrest.*

11. THE fore-mention'd Scheme in its several Regulations may be supported by Profits arising from every third Night[12] throughout the Year. And as it would be hard to suppose that so many Persons could live without any Food (tho' from the former Course of their Lives, a *very little* will be deemed sufficient) the Masters of Calculation will, we believe, agree, that out of those Profits, the said Persons might be subsisted in a sober and decent manner. We will venture to affirm farther, that not only the proper Magazines of Thunder and Lightning, but *Paint, Diet-Drinks, Spitting-Pots,* and all other *Necessaries* of Life, may in like manner fairly be provided for.

12. IF some of the Articles may at first view seem liable to Objections, particularly those that give so vast a Power to the *Council of* SIX (which is indeed larger than any intrusted to the Great Officers of State) this may be obviated, by swearing those *Six* Persons of his Majesty's Privy Council, and obliging them to pass every thing of Moment *previously* at that most honourable Board.

Vale & Fruere.[13]

MAR. SCRIB.

---

12. **third Night:** the author's benefit night. See *The Dunciad,* below, I. 57. 13. **Vale & Fruere:** Farewell and be happy— Martinus's customary valediction.

AN ESSAY ON MAN

IN FOUR EPISTLES TO
H. St. John, Lord *Bolingbroke*

As Pope's poems grew in number he came to see that there was one topic that solicited him powerfully—the topic of Man in the abstract. In most of his poems he had already said on this subject what the particular occasion required, but this was piecemeal treatment, a very different matter from addressing himself wholly to this one theme. To write sustainedly on Man in poetry is to run the certain risk of being prosy—a risk that Milton had to bear in writing of God in *Paradise Lost*. Pope saw this clearly. However, to write sustainedly on Man in prose (and Pope did first make a draft in that "other harmony") calls for powers that few poets possess, and from the start Pope had to face his deficiencies as an exact philosopher. The poem, then, could never be more than a partial success. Nonetheless it was well worth attempting, for the simple reason that no other topic afforded an opportunity for such grandeur as Pope achieved in those couplets, so very numerous, in which the grand sense is unassailable. The poem obliged Pope to speak of man's pride, his worship of happiness, his contemptible insignificance, and also his glory—on these matters he could speak powerfully and with a finality of ringing phrase. *An Essay on Man* (1733–34) is not a museum piece—out of it breaks a great deal of human truth. It is the Everest of eighteenth-century poetry, as *Paradise Lost* (one line of which Pope consciously quotes) was the Everest of seventeenth-century poetry.

The "thinking" in the poem has been much discussed, ever since it was published, and students who are interested in this aspect could not do better than read Professor Mack's masterly Introduction in the Twickenham edition of the poem. The philosophy and the way it is propounded have had many opponents, but its arousing controversy may be counted a proof that it has much to say that is permanently provocative. The poem obliges the reader to raise his voice (if only in fancy) and read it aloud, as if to an audience. The very fact that any chance audience would feel compelled to listen (as they might not listen if we started reading them a great poem by Keats, for example) proves that the poem has something to say of interest about man—and if today then in any conceivable century, for we have inherited the discoveries of Darwin, Freud, Malinowski, and Rutherford. Still, Man is, as Pope asserted in one of the most splendid lines of the poem, "the Glory [however much damaged], Jest, and Riddle of the World!"

Aesthetically the poem is a triumph, as a whole and in most of its parts. And it is a novel triumph, for Pope writes in a new style—a style new in syntax, diction, tone, and pace. There is a new aesthetic quality in the phrasing of the couplets—"the rash Dexterity of Wit," "the Soul's calm sun-shine," "the pompous Shade," "the Mercury of Man," "argent fields"—that places them on the heights of English poetry. This quality might be described by saying that it mixes the Miltonic and the Johnsonian. And even the few prosy couplets are so tightly braced, so economical in their phrasing, that they too provide a sort of aesthetic pleasure, the kind of grace that Pope says in the Design conciseness of expression can confer.

The text of the Design is that of Warburton's 1753 edition. We have omitted the charts. The text of each epistle is typographically that of the first edition (1733–34) except where Pope made his sometimes exclusive verbal revisions, except for a few places where the punctuation has been regularized, and except for the paragraphing here and there, which with one exception is that of Warburton's edition. The use of the question mark has been retained, whether or not it coincides with modern usage; in Pope it sometimes has almost the value of the modern exclamation point.

⚜

THE DESIGN

Having proposed to write some pieces on Human Life and Manners, such as (to use my lord Bacon's expression) *come home to Men's Business and Bosoms,*[1] I thought it more satisfactory to begin with considering *Man* in the abstract, his *Nature* and his *State; since,* to prove any moral *Duty,* to enforce any moral precept, or to examine the perfection or imperfection of any creature whatsoever, it is necessary first to know what *condition* and *relation* it is placed in, and what is the proper *end* and *purpose* of its *being.*

The science of Human Nature is, like all other sciences, reduced to a *few clear points:* There are not *many certain truths* in this world. It is therefore in the Anatomy of the mind as in that of the Body; more good will accrue to mankind by attending to the

---

AN ESSAY ON MAN: *The Design.* 1. come . . . Bosoms: quoted from Bacon's Dedicatory Epistle in the collected edition of the *Essays* (1625).

large, open, and perceptible parts, than by studying too much such finer nerves and vessels,[2] the conformations and uses of which will for ever escape our observation. The *disputes* are all upon these last, and, I will venture to say, they have less sharpened the *wits* than the *hearts* of men against each other, and have diminished the practice, more than advanced the theory, of Morality. If I could flatter myself that this Essay has any merit, it is in steering betwixt the extremes of doctrines seemingly opposite, in passing over terms utterly unintelligible, and in forming a *temperate* yet not *inconsistent*, and a *short* yet not *imperfect*, system of Ethics.

This I might have done in prose; but I chose verse, and even rhyme, for two reasons. The one will appear obvious; that principles, maxims, or precepts so written, both strike the reader more strongly at first, and are more easily retained by him afterwards: The other may seem odd, but is true, I found I could express them more *shortly* this way than in prose itself; and nothing is more certain, than that much of the *force* as well as *grace* of arguments or instructions, depends on their *conciseness*. I was unable to treat this part of my subject more in *detail*, without becoming dry and tedious; or more *poetically*, without sacrificing perspicuity to ornament, without wandring from the precision, or breaking the chain of reasoning: If any man can unite all these without diminution of any of them, I freely confess he will compass a thing above my capacity.

What is now published, is only to be considered as a *general Map* of MAN, marking out no more than the *greater parts*, their *extent*, their *limits*, and their *connection*, but leaving the particular to be more fully delineated in the charts which are to follow. Consequently, these Epistles in their progress (if I have health and leisure to make any progress) will be less dry, and more susceptible of poetical ornament. I am here only opening the *fountains*, and clearing the passage. To deduce the *rivers*, to follow them in their course, and to observe their effects, may be a task more agreeable.

(Handwritten margin notes: RHYME FOR 2 REASONS: PRINCIPLES STRIKE THE READER MORE STRONGLY — EXPRESS PRINCIPLES MORE SHORTLY)

[EPISTLE I]

AWAKE; my ST. JOHN! leave all meaner Things
To low Ambition and the Pride of Kings.
Let Us (since Life can little more supply
Than just to look about us, and to die)
Expatiate free, o'er all this *Scene of Man;*
A mighty Maze! but not without a Plan;
Or Wild, where weeds and flow'rs promiscuous shoot;
Or Garden, tempting with forbidden fruit.
Together let us beat this ample *Field,*
Try what the open, what the covert,° yield;   10
The latent tracts, the giddy heights explore,
Of all who blindly creep, or sightless soar.°
Eye Nature's walks;° shoot Folly as it flie's,
And catch the Manners, living as they rise;
Laugh where we *must;* be candid° where we *can;*
But vindicate the Ways of *God* to Man.
    1. Say first, of *God* above, or *Man* below,
What can we *reason*, but from what we *know?*
Of Man, what see we but his Station here,
From which to reason, or to which refer?   20
Thro' Worlds unnumber'd tho' the God be known;
'Tis ours to trace him, only in our own.
He° who thro' vast Immensity can pierce,
See Worlds on Worlds compose one Universe,
Observe how System into System runs,
What other Planets circle other Suns?
What vary'd Being peoples ev'ry Star?
May tell, why Heav'n has made us as we are.
But of this Frame the Bearings, and the Ties,
The strong Connections, nice Dependencies,   30
Gradations just, has thy° pervading Soul
Look'd thro? Or can a part contain the Whole?
    Is the great Chain° that draws all to agree,
And drawn supports, upheld by God, or thee?

---

2. **finer . . . vessels:** Pope finds a place for dealing with these in his more individual portraits such as the second of the *Moral Essays, Of the Characters of Women.*

Epistle I. **9–10. beat, open, covert:** hunting terms; go backward and forward over the ground to see what game are to be hunted in the open and in parts that give natural shelter. **12. blindly . . . soar:** The blind creepers are the low-minded and ignorant; the sightless soarers presumptuously try to transcend the limits beyond which man cannot go. **13. walks:** "the region within which something moves" (*OED*). **15. candid:** generous, kindly, indulgent. **23. He:** only he, i.e., no one. **31. thy:** the reader as a representative of mankind in all its limitations. **33. Chain:** It was held that all created things were arranged as links in a chain that reached up to God; angels were the highest links.

II. Presumptuous Man! the Reason wouldst thou
    find,
Why form'd so weak, so little, and so blind?
First, if thou can'st, the harder reason guess,
Why form'd no weaker, blinder, and no less?
Ask of thy Mother Earth, why Oaks are made
Taller or stronger than the Weeds they shade?   40
Or ask of yonder argent fields above,
Why JOVE's Satellites° are less than JOVE?
  Of Systems possible, if 'tis confest
That Wisdom infinite must form the *Best*,
Where all must *full* or not *coherent*° be,
And all that rises rise in due degree;
Then, in the Scale of reas'ning Life, 'tis plain
There must be, *some where*, such a Rank as *Man;*
And all the question (wrangle 'ere so long)
Is only this, if God has *plac'd him wrong?*   50
  Respecting *Man* whatever wrong we call,
May, must be right, as relative to *All.*
In human works, tho' labour'd on with pain,
A thousand movements scarce one purpose gain;
In God's, one single can *its End* produce,
Yet serves to second too some *other Use.*
So Man, who here seems principal alone,
Perhaps acts second to some Sphere unknown,
Touches some Wheel, or verges to some Gole;
'Tis but a Part we see, and not a Whole.   60
  When the proud Steed shall know, why Man
    restrains
His fiery course, or drives him o'er the plains;
When the dull Ox, why now he breaks the clod,
Is now a Victim, and now Ægypt's God;°
Then shall Man's Pride and Dulness comprehend
His Actions', Passions', Being's, Use and End;
Why doing, suff'ring, check'd, impell'd; and why
This Hour a Slave, the next a Deity?
  Then say not Man's imperfect, Heav'n in fault;
Say rather, Man's as perfect as he ought;   70
His Knowledge measur'd to his State, and Place,
His time a Moment, and a Point his space.
If to be perfect in a certain Sphere,
What matter, soon or late, or here or there?
The blesst to day, is as completely so,
As who began a thousand years ago.

III. Heav'n from all creatures hides the book of Fate,
All but the page prescrib'd, their *present state;*
From Brutes what Men, from Men what Spirits know;
Or who could suffer Being here below?   80
The Lamb thy riot° dooms to bleed to day
Had he thy *Reason*, would he skip and play?
Pleas'd to the last, he crops the flow'ry food,
And licks the hand just rais'd to shed his blood.
Oh blindness to the future! kindly giv'n,
That each may fill the Circle mark'd by Heav'n,
Who sees with equal eye, as God of All,
A Hero perish, or a Sparrow fall,
Atoms, or Systems, into ruin hurl'd,
And now a Bubble burst, and now a World!   90
  Hope humbly then; with trembling pinions soar;
Wait the great teacher, Death, and God adore!
What future bliss, he gives not thee to know,
But gives that *Hope* to be thy blessing now.
Hope springs eternal in the human breast;
Man never *is*, but always *to be* blest:
The soul uneasy, and confin'd from home,°
Rests, and expatiates, in a life to come.
  Lo! the poor INDIAN, whose untutor'd mind
Sees God in clouds, or hears him in the wind;   100
His soul, proud Science never taught to stray
Far as the Solar walk, or Milky way,
Yet simple Nature to his hope has giv'n
Behind the cloud-topt hill an humbler Heav'n,
Some safer world in depth of woods embrac'd,
Some happier island in the watry waste;
Where Slaves once more their native land behold,
No Fiends torment, no Christians thirst for Gold.°
To *be*, contents his natural desire,
He asks no Angel's Wing no Seraph's Fire,°   110
But thinks, admitted to that equal sky
His faithful Dog shall bear him company.

81. riot: wasteful living. 97. from home: away from
heaven, its original home. 108. no . . . Gold: John Phillips's
Tears of the Indians (1656), a translation from the Spanish, tells
the following story of a native Cuban prince: "While he was
tyed to the stake, there came to him a Monk of the Order of
St. *Francis*, who began to talk to him of God and of the
Articles of our Faith, telling him, that the small respite which
the Executioner gave him was sufficient for him to make sure
his salvation if he believed. Upon which words after Hathvey
had a little while paus'd, he asked the Monk if the door of
heaven was open to the Spaniards, who answering *Yes, to the
good Spaniards.* Then replyed the other, Let me go to Hell that
I may not come where they are." 110. Seraph's Fire:
According to the supposed derivation of the word, a seraph
was traditionally thought of as fiery.

42. **Satellites:** In Latin a *satelles* is an attendant. Seventeenth-
century astronomers used the word to denote a smaller star
that attended a larger. 45. **full . . . coherent:** Each link in
the chain must be present and complete or there will be a
gap. 64. **Ægypt's God:** Apis, the sacred Memphian bull.

IV. Go, wiser Thou! and in thy scale of sence
Weigh thy *Opinion* against *Providence:*
Call Imperfection what thou fancy'st such,
Say, here he gives too little, there too much;   APPETITE
Destroy all Creatures for thy sport or gust,°
Yet cry, If Man's unhappy, God's unjust;
If Man alone ingross not Heav'n's high care,
Alone made perfect here, immortal there: 120
Snatch from his hand the Balance and the Rod;
Re-judge his Justice, Be the GOD of GOD!
In *Pride* in reas'ning *Pride,* our error lies;
All quit their sphere, and rush into the Skies.
Pride still is aiming at the blest abodes,
Men would be Angels, Angels would be Gods.
Aspiring to be Gods, if Angels fell,
Aspiring to be Angels, Men rebell:
And who but wishes to invert the Laws
Of ORDER, sins against th' Eternal Cause.   130
    V. Ask for what end the heav'nly bodies shine?
Earth for whose use? *Pride* answers, "'Tis for mine:
For me kind Nature wakes her genial power,°
Suckles each herb, and spreads out ev'ry flow'r;
Annual for me, the grape, the rose renew
The juice nectareous, and the balmy dew;
For me, the mine a thousand treasures brings,
For me, health gushes from a thousand springs;
Seas roll to waft me, suns to light me rise;
My footstool Earth, my canopy the Skies!   140
    But errs not Nature from this gracious end,
From burning suns when livid deaths descend,
When Earthquakes swallow, or when tempests sweep
Towns to one grave, whole Nations to the deep?
"No ('tis reply'd) the first Almighty Cause°
Acts not by partial, but by *gen'ral Laws;*
Th' exceptions few; some change since all began;
And what created, perfect?"—Why then *Man?*
If the great end be human Happiness,
Then Nature deviates; and can Man do less?   150
As much that end a constant course requires
Of show'rs and sunshine, as of man's desires,
As much eternal springs and cloudless skies,
As men for ever temp'rate, calm, and wise.
If Plagues or Earthquakes break not Heav'n's design,
Why then a Borgia° or a Catiline°?

Who knows but he, whose hand the Light'ning forms,
Who heaves old Ocean, and who wings the Storms;
Pours fierce Ambition in a Cæsar's mind,   159
Or turns young Ammon° loose to scourge Mankind?
From Pride, from Pride, our very reas'ning springs;
IMPERATIVE→ Account for moral, as for nat'ral things:
Why charge we Heav'n in those, in these acquit?
In both, to reason right is to submit.
    Better for Us, perhaps, it might appear,
Were there all Harmony, all Virtue here;
That never Air or Ocean felt the wind;
That never Passion discompos'd the mind:
But all subsists by Elemental strife;
And Passions are the Elements of Life.   170
The gen'ral ORDER, since the whole began,
Is kept in *Nature,* and is kept in *Man.*
    VI. What would this Man? now upward will he soar,
And little less than Angel would be more;
Now looking downwards, just as griev'd appears
To want the strength of Bulls, the Fur of Bears.
Made for his use all Creatures if he call,
Say what their use, had he the pow'rs of all?
Nature to these, without profusion kind,
The proper organs, proper pow'rs assign'd,   180
Each seeming want compensated° of course,°
Here, with degrees of Swiftness; there, of Force;
All in exact proportion to the state,
Nothing to add, and nothing to abate:
Each Beast, each Insect, happy in its own;
Is Heav'n unkind to Man, and Man alone?
Shall he alone, whom rational we call,
Be pleas'd with nothing, if not bless'd with all?
    The bliss of Man (could Pride that blessing find)
Is, not to act, or think, *beyond* Mankind;   190
No pow'rs of Body or of Soul to share;
But what his Nature and his State can bear.
Why has not Man a microscopic eye?
For this plain reason, Man is not a Fly:
Say what the use, were finer optics giv'n,
T' inspect a Mite, not comprehend the Heav'n?
Or Touch, if tremblingly alive all o'er,
To smart, and agonize at ev'ry pore?
Or quick Effluvia° darting thro' the brain,
Dye of a Rose, in Aromatic pain?   200

---

117. **gust:** appetite. 133. **genial power:** power of generation.
145. **the first . . . Cause:** God, as the Creator. 156. **Borgia:**
Caesar Borgia (1476–1507), an Italian duke notorious for his
career of crime and warfare. **Catiline:** (d. 62 B.C.) the dissolute
Roman who unsuccessfully plotted against the state.

160. **Ammon:** Alexander the Great. 181. **compensated:**
The contemporary pronunciation stressed the second syllable.
of course: in the natural course of things. 199. **Effluvia:**
Epicurus (*c.* 340–*c.* 270 B.C.) held that smells reached the brain
in a stream of invisible particles.

If Nature thunder'd in his opening ears,
And stunn'd him with the music of the Spheres,
How would he wish, that Heav'n had left him still
The whisp'ring Zephyr, and the purling Rill?
Who finds not Providence all good and wise,
Alike in what it gives, and what denies?
   VII. Far as Creation's ample Range extends
The scale of *sensual, mental* Pow'rs ascends:
Mark how it mounts, to Man's imperial race,
From the green Myriads in the peopled Grass!   210
What modes of sight, betwixt each wide extreme,
The Mole's dim curtain, and the Lynx's beam:
Of smell, the headlong Lioness° between,
And Hound, sagacious on the tainted green!
Of hearing, from the Life that fills the flood,
To that which warbles thro' the vernal wood.
The Spider's touch, how exquisitely fine,
Feels at each thread, and lives along the line:
In the nice Bee, what sense so subtly true
From pois'nous herbs extracts the healing dew.   220
How *Instinct* varies in the grov'ling Swine,
Compar'd, half-reas'ning Elephant° with thine!
Twixt that, and *Reason*, what a nice Barrier,°
For ever sep'rate, yet for ever near.
Remembrance, and Reflection, how ally'd!
What thin partitions Sense from Thought divide
And middle Natures, how they long to join,
Yet never pass th' insuperable Line!
Without this just *Gradation*, could they be
Subjected these to those, or all to thee?   230
The Pow'rs of all subdu'd by thee alone,
Is not thy Reason all these pow'rs in one?
   VIII. See, thro' this Air, this Ocean, and this Earth,
All Matter quick, and bursting into birth.
Above, how high progressive life may go?
Around how wide? how deep extend below?
Vast Chain of Being! which from God began,
Natures ethereal, human, Angel, Man,
Beast, Bird, Fish, Insect! what no Eye can see,
No Glass can reach! from Infinite to Thee!   240
From Thee to Nothing!—On superior Pow'rs
Were we to press inferior might on ours;
Or in the full Creation leave a Void,
Where one step broken, the great Scale's destroy'd:

---

213. **the headlong Lioness:** The lion and lioness hunted, according to Pope, "by the Ear, and not by the Nostril." **222. half-reas'ning Elephant:** Of the elephant's "sagacity . . . and even understanding many surprising relations are given" (Johnson's *Dictionary*). **223. Barrier:** pronounced *bareer.*

From Nature's Chain whatever Link you strike,
Tenth, or ten thousandth, breaks the chain alike.
   And if each System in Gradation roll,
Alike essential to th' amazing Whole;
The least confusion but in one, not all
That System only, but the whole must fall.   250
Let Earth unbalanc'd from her Orbit fly,
Planets and Suns run lawless thro' the Sky;
Let ruling Angels from their Spheres be hurl'd,
Being on Being wreck'd, and World on World;
Heav'ns whole Foundations to their Centre nod,
And Nature trembles to the Throne of God.
All this dread Order break—For whom? For thee?
Vile Worm!—O Madness! Pride! Impiety!
   IX. What if the Foot, ordain'd the dust to tread,
Or Hand to toil, aspir'd to be the Head?   260
What if the Head, the eye or ear, repin'd
To serve mere Engines to the ruling Mind?
Just as absurd, for any Part to claim
To be another, in this gen'ral Frame:
Just as absurd, to mourn the tasks or pains,
The great directing MIND of ALL ordains.
   All are but parts of one stupendous Whole:
Whose Body *Nature* is, and *God* the Soul.
That, chang'd thro' all and yet in all the same,
Great in the Earth as in th' Ætherial frame,   270
Warms in the Sun, refreshes in the Breeze,
Glows in the Stars, and blossoms in the Trees,
Lives thro' all Life, extends thro' all extent,
Spreads undivided, operates unspent,
Breathes in our soul, informs our mortal part,
As full, as perfect, in a hair, as heart,
As full, as perfect, in vile Man that mourns,
As the rapt Seraph that adores and burns;
To Him no high, no low, no great, no small;
He fills, he bounds, connects, and equals all.   280
   X. Cease then, nor ORDER *Imperfection* name:
Our proper bliss depends on what we blame.
Know thy own *Point.* This kind, this due degree
Of blindness, weakness, Heav'n bestows on thee.
Submit—in this, or any other Sphere,
Secure to be as blest as thou canst bear.
Safe in the hand of one disposing Pow'r,
Or in the natal, or the mortal Hour.
All Nature is but Art, unknown to thee;
All Chance, Direction which thou canst not see;   290
All Discord, Harmony not understood;
All partial Evil, universal Good:
And spight of Pride, in erring Reason's spight,
One truth is clear; "Whatever Is, is RIGHT."

EPISTLE II

KNOW then Thy-self, presume not God to scan;
The proper Study of Mankind is *Man*.
    Plac'd on this Isthmus of a Middle State,
A Being darkly wise, and rudely great:
With too much Knowledge for the Sceptic° Side,
With too much Weakness for the Stoic's° Pride,
He hangs between; in doubt to act, or rest,
In doubt to deem himself a God, or Beast;
In doubt, his Mind or Body to prefer,
Born but to die, and reas'ning but to err;   10
Alike in Ignorance, his Reason such,
Whether he thinks too little, or too much.
Chaos of Thought and Passion, all confus'd;
Still by himself abus'd, or dis-abus'd;
Created half to rise, and half to fall;
Great Lord of all things, yet a Prey to all;
Sole Judge of Truth, in endless Error hurl'd:°
The Glory, Jest, and Riddle, of the World!
    Go wondrous Creature! mount where Science guides,
Go measure Earth, weigh Air,° and state the Tides,° 20
Instruct the Planets in what Orbs to run,
Correct old Time, and regulate the Sun.°
Go soar with *Plato* to th' empyreal Sphere,°
To the first Good, first Perfect, and first Fair;
Or tread the mazy round his Follow'rs trod,
And quitting Sense° call *Imitating God*,
As Eastern Priests in giddy Circles run,
And turn their heads to imitate the *Sun*.°

Go, teach Eternal Wisdom how to rule;
Then drop into Thy-self, and be a Fool!   30
    Superior Beings, when of late they saw
A mortal Man unfold all Nature's Law,
Admir'd such Wisdom in an earthly Shape,
And show'd a NEWTON as we show an *Ape*.
    Could He whose rules the rapid Comet bind,
Describe, or fix, one Movement of his Mind?
Who saw its Fires here rise, and there descend,
Explain his own Beginning, or his End?
Alas what wonder! Man's superior Part
Uncheck'd may rise, and climb from Art to Art;   40
But when his own great Work is but begun,
What Reason weaves, by Passion is undone.
    Trace Science° then, with Modesty thy Guide;
First strip off all her Equipage of Pride;
Deduct what is but Vanity, or Dress,
Or Learning's Luxury, or Idleness;
Or Tricks to shew the stretch of human Brain,
Mere curious Pleasure, or ingenious Pain;
Expunge the Whole, or lop th' excrescent Parts
Of all our Vices have created Arts;   50
Then see how little the remaining sum,
Which serv'd the past, and must the times to come!
    II. Two Principles in Human Nature reign;
Self-Love,° to urge; and *Reason*, to restrain;
Nor this a good, nor that a bad we call,
Each works its end, to move, or govern all:
And to their proper Operation still
Ascribe all Good; to their improper, Ill.
    Self-Love, the Spring of Motion, acts the Soul;
Reason's comparing Balance rules the whole;   60
Man, but for that, no *Action* could attend,
And but for this, were active to no *End*.
Fix'd like a Plant on his peculiar Spot,
To draw nutrition, propagate, and rot;
Or Meteor-like flame lawless through the Void,
Destroying others, by himself destroy'd.
    Most *Strength* the moving Principle requires,
Active its Task, it prompts, impels, inspires:
Sedate and quiet the comparing lies,
Form'd but to check, delib'rate, and advise.   70
Self-Love still stronger, as its Objects nigh;
Reason's at distance and in prospect lye;
That sees immediate Good, by present Sense,
Reason, the future, and the consequence;

Epistle II. **5. Sceptic:** The Skeptic philosophers, like the Greek Pyrrho and his followers, doubted man's ability to gain any knowledge that was real. **6. Stoic:** The Greek Stoics practiced severe restraints on the will and sought to exclude from the mind feelings of pleasure or pain. **17. in . . . hurl'd:** an incorrect use of *in*, according to Johnson in his *Plan of an English Dictionary.* **20. weigh Air:** an allusion to the experiments of scientists like Torricelli and Boyle. **state the Tides:** Newton and others had sought to understand the operation of the tides. **22. Correct . . . Sun:** This line refers to Newton's astronomical measurements of time and to discussions on the reform of the calendar prior to its introduction in 1752. **23. th' empyreal Sphere:** the outermost sphere of the universe, where God was thought to abide and where Plato may be supposed to have located his ideal types. **26. quitting Sense:** Some later followers of Plato sought to achieve a vision of the divine by suppressing the bodily sensations during induced trances. **27–28. Eastern . . . Sun:** In a letter of September 13, 1719, Pope mentions "the Self-taught [Arabic] Philosopher [Hai Ebn Yocktan] who gave himself up to a devout exercise of making his head giddy with various circumrotations, to imitate the motions of the cælestial bodies." Pope puns in "turn their heads."

43. Science: knowledge. **54. Self-Love:** "Each natural being strives to keep going with its own particular go" (J. Laird, *Philosophical Incursion into English Literature* [1946]).

Thicker than Arguments, Temptations throng,
At best more *watchful* this, but that more *strong*.
The Action of the stronger to suspend,
Reason still *use*, to Reason still *attend*:
Attention, Habit and Experience gains,
Each strengthens Reason and Self-Love restrains.   80
Let subtile Schoolmen teach these Friends to fight,
More studious to divide, than to unite,
And Grace and Virtue, Sense and Reason split,
With all the rash Dexterity of Wit.
Wits, just like Fools, at War about a *Name*,
Have full as oft, *no* Meaning, or *the same*.
Self-Love and Reason to one End aspire,
Pain their Aversion, Pleasure their Desire;
But greedy that its Object would devour,
This taste the Honey, and not wound the Flower.   90
Pleasure, or wrong or rightly understood,
Our greatest Evil, or our greatest Good.

III. Modes of Self-Love, the PASSIONS we may call;
'Tis real Good, or seeming, moves them all:
But since not every Good we can *divide*,
And Reason bids us for *our own* provide;
Passions tho' *selfish*, if their Means be fair,
List° under *Reason*, and deserve her Care:
Those that *imparted*,° court a nobler Aim,
Exalt their Kind, and take some *Virtue*'s Name.   100

In lazy Apathy let Stoics boast
Their Virtue fix'd, 'tis fix'd as in a Frost,
Contracted all, retiring to the Breast;
But Strength of Mind is *Exercise*, not *Rest*:
The rising Tempest puts in act the Soul,
Parts it may ravage, but preserves the whole.
On Life's vast Ocean diversely we sail,
Reason the Card,° but Passion is the Gale:
Nor GOD alone in the still Calm we find;
He mounts the Storm, and *walks upon the Wind*.   110

Passions, like Elements, tho' born to fight,
Yet mix'd and soften'd, in His Work unite:
These, 'tis enough to *temper* and *employ*,
But what composes Man, can Man *destroy*?
Suffice that Reason keep to Nature's Road,
Subject, compound them, follow her, and God.
Love, Hope, and Joy, fair Pleasure's smiling Train,
Hate, Fear, and Grief, the Family of Pain;
These mix'd with Art, and to due Bounds confin'd,
Make, and maintain, the Balance of the Mind:°   120

The Lights and Shades, whose well-accorded Strife
Gives all the *Strength* and *Colour* of our Life.

Pleasures are ever in our Hands or Eyes,
And when in Act they cease, in Prospect rise;
Present to grasp, and future still to find,
The whole Employ of Body and of Mind.
All spread their Charms, but charm not all *alike*;
On diff'rent Senses diff'rent Objects strike:
Hence diff'rent Passions more or less inflame,
As strong, or weak, the Organs of the Frame;   130
And hence one *Master Passion*, in the Breast,
Like *Aaron*'s Serpent,° swallows up the rest.

As Man perhaps, the moment of his Breath,
Receives the lurking Principle of Death,
The young Disease that must subdue at length,
Grows with his growth and strengthens with his
          strength:
So, cast and mingled with his very Frame,
The Mind's Disease, its *ruling Passion* came:
Each vital Humour which should feed the *whole*,
Soon flows to *this*, in Body and in Soul;   140
Whatever warms the Heart, or fills the Head,
As the Mind opens, and its Functions spread,
Imagination plies her dang'rous Art,
And pours it all upon the peccant Part.

Nature its Mother, *Habit* is its Nurse;
Wit, Spirit, Faculties, but make it worse;
Reason itself but gives it Edge and Pow'r,
As Heav'ns blest Beam turns Vinegar more sow'r.

We, wretched Subjects, tho' to lawful Sway,
In this weak *Queen*, some Fav'rite still obey.   150
Ah! if she lend not Arms, as well as Rules
What can she more than *tell us* we are Fools?
Teach us to mourn our Nature, not to mend,
A sharp *Accuser*, but a helpless *Friend*!
Or from a *Judge* turn *Pleader*, to persuade
The Choice we make, or justify it made;
Proud of an easy Conquest all along,
She but removes weak Passions for the strong;
So, when small Humours gather to a Gout,
The Doctor fancies he has driv'n them out.   160

Yes: Nature's Road must ever be prefer'd;
Reason is here no *Guide*, but still a *Guard*;
'Tis her's to *rectify*, not *overthrow*,
And treat this Passion more as Friend than Foe:
A mightier Pow'r the strong direction sends,
And sev'ral° Men impels to sev'ral ends:

---

98. List: enlist. **99. Those . . . imparted**: the passions,
when reason is imparted to them. **108. Card**: the dial of a
mariner's compass. **120. the Balance . . . Mind**: a key to
Pope's conception.

132. Like . . . Serpent: See Ex. 7:10-12. **166. sev'ral**:
different.

Like varying Winds, by *other* Passions tost,
This drives them constant to a certain Coast.
Let Pow'r or Knowledge, Gold, or Glory, please,
Or (oft more strong than all) the Love of Ease: 170
Thro' Life 'tis follow'd, ev'n at Life's Expence;
The Merchant's Toil, the Sage's Indolence,
The Monk's Humility, the Hero's Pride,
All, all alike, find Reason on their side.

Th' Eternal° Art, educing Good from Ill,
Grafts on this Passion our *best Principle:*
'Tis thus, the Mercury of Man is fix'd,
Strong grows the Virtue with his Nature mix'd;
The Dross cements what else were too refin'd,
And in one Int'rest *Body* acts with *Mind.*   180

As Fruits ungrateful to the Planter's care
On *savage Stocks* inserted, learn to bear;
The surest Virtues thus from Passions shoot,
Wild Nature's Vigour working at the Root.
What Crops of Wit and Honesty appear,
From Spleen, from Obstinacy, Hate or Fear!
See Anger,° Zeal and Fortitude supply;
Ev'n Av'rice, Prudence; Sloth, Philosophy;
Lust, thro' some certain Strainers well refin'd,
Is gentle Love, and charms all Womankind;   190
Envy, to which th' ignoble Mind's a slave,
Is Emulation in the Learn'd or Brave:
Nor Virtue, Male or Female, can we name,
But what will grow on *Pride,* or grow on *Shame.*

Thus *Nature* gives us (let it check our Pride)
The Virtue nearest to our Vice ally'd;
Reason the Byas turns to Good from Ill,
And *Nero* reigns a *Titus,*° if he will.
The fiery Soul abhorr'd in *Catiline,*
In *Decius*° charms, in *Curtius*° is divine.   200
The same Ambition can destroy or save,
And makes a Patriot, as it makes a Knave.

175–202. Th' Eternal . . . Knave: [Pope's note] [The] *providential Use* [of this Passion] in fixing our PRINCIPLE, and ascertaining [confirming] our VIRTUE. **187. Anger:** It was generally held that anger was useful when not excessive. **198. Titus:** (A.D. 40 or 41–81), a cruel and profligate Roman who, on becoming emperor in A.D. 79, grew generous and peaceable. **200. Decius:** a Roman general who dreamed before the Battle of Vesuvius around 340 B.C. that the general on one side was doomed and the army on the other; he rushed into battle to guarantee the victory of his men. **Curtius:** Marcus Curtius, a legendary Roman hero of the fourth century B.C. When a wide gap suddenly opened in the Forum and the oracle declared that it would close only when Rome threw into it its most precious possession, the young soldier, armed and on horseback, threw himself into the chasm.

This *Light* and *Darkness* in our Chaos join'd,
What shall divide? The *God* within the *Mind.*
Extremes in Nature equal ends produce,
In Man they join to some mysterious use;
Tho' each by turns the other's bound invade,
As in some well-wrought Picture Light and Shade,
And oft so mix, the diff'rence is too nice
Where ends the Virtue, or begins the Vice.   210

Fools! who from hence into the Notion fall,
That *Vice* or *Virtue* there is none at all.
If white and black, blend, soften, and unite
A thousand ways, is there no Black or White?
Ask your *own Heart,* and nothing is so plain;
'Tis to *mistake* them, costs the *Time* and *Pain.*

Vice is a Monster of so frightful mien,
As, to be hated, needs but to be seen;
Yet seen too *oft,* familiar with her Face,
We first endure, then pity, then embrace.   220
But where th' *Extreme of Vice,* was ne'er agreed:
Ask where's the *North?* at *York* 'tis on the *Tweed,*
In *Scotland* at the *Orcades,* and there
At *Greenland, Zembla,* or the Lord knows where.
No Creature owns it, in the first degree,
But thinks his Neighbour farther gone than he.
Ev'n those who dwell beneath its very Zone,
Or never feel the Rage, or never own;
What happier Natures shrink at with Affright,
The hard Inhabitant contends is right.   230

Virtuous and vicious ev'ry Man must be,
Few in th' Extreme, but all in the Degree:
The Rogue and Fool by fits is fair and wise,
And ev'n the best by fits what they despise.
'Tis but by *Parts* we follow Good or Ill,
For, Vice or Virtue, *Self* directs it still;
Each Individual seeks a sev'ral Goal:
But HEAV'N's great View is *One,* and that the WHOLE:
That counter-works each Folly and Caprice;
That disappoints th' Effect of ev'ry Vice.   240
That happy Frailties to all *Ranks* apply'd,
Shame to the Virgin, to the Matron *Pride,*
Fear to the Statesman, *Rashness* to the Chief,
To Kings *Presumption,* and to Crowds *Belief.*
That Virtue's Ends from *Vanity* can raise,
Which seeks no Int'rest, no Reward but Praise.
And build on *Wants,* and on *Defects* of Mind,
The *Joy,* the *Peace,* the *Glory* of Mankind.

Heav'n forming each on other to depend,
A Master, or a Servant, or a Friend,   250
Bids each on other for Assistance call,
'Till one man's Weakness grows the Strength of all.

Wants, Frailties, Passions, closer still allye
The common Int'rest, or endear the Tye:
To *these* we owe true Friendship, Love sincere,
Each home-felt Joy that Life inherits here!
Yet from the same we learn, in its decline,
Those Joys, those Loves, those Int'rests to resign;
Taught half by Reason, half by mere Decay,
To welcome Death, and calmly pass away.   260
   Whate'er the *Passion*, Knowledge, Fame, or Pelf,
Not one will change his Neighbour with himself.
The Learn'd is happy, Nature to explore;
The Fool is happy, that he knows no more;
The Rich is happy in the Plenty given;
The Poor contents him with the Care of Heaven.
See the blind Beggar dance, the Cripple sing,
The Sot a Hero, Lunatic a King,
The starving Chymist° in his golden Views
Supreamly blest, the Poet in his Muse.   270
   See! some strange *Comfort* ev'ry *State* attend,
And *Pride* bestow'd on all, a common Friend;
See! some fit *Passion* ev'ry *Age* supply,
Hope travels thro', nor quits us when we die.
   Behold the Child, by Nature's kindly Law,
Pleas'd with a Rattle, tickled with a Straw:
Some livelier Play-thing gives his Youth Delight,
A little louder, but as empty quite:
Scarfs,° Garters, Gold, amuse his riper Stage,
And Beads and Pray'r-books are the Toys of Age: 280
Pleas'd with this Bauble still, as that before;
'Till tir'd he sleeps, and Life's poor Play is o'er.
Mean-while *Opinion* gilds with varying rays
Those painted Clouds that beautify our Days;
Each want of Happiness by Hope supply'd,
And each Vacuity of Sense by Pride.
These build as fast as Knowledge can destroy;
In Folly's Cup still laughs the Bubble, *Joy;*
One Prospect lost, another still we gain,
And not a Vanity is giv'n in vain;   290
Even mean *Self-Love* becomes, by Force divine,
The Scale to measure others Wants by thine.
See! and confess, one Comfort still must rise,
'Tis this, tho' *Man's a Fool*, yet GOD IS WISE.

EPISTLE III

HERE then we rest: "The *Universal Cause*
Acts to *one End*, but acts by various Laws.
In all the Madness of superfluous Health,
The Trim of Pride, and Impudence of Wealth,
Let this great Truth be present Night and Day;
But most be present, if we *preach*, or *pray*.
   Look round our World: Behold the Chain of Love
Combining all below, and all above.
See plastic Nature working to this End,
The single Atoms each to other tend,   10
Attract, attracted to, the next in place,
Form'd and impell'd its *Neighbour* to embrace.
See Matter next, with various Life endu'd,
Press to one Centre still, the *Gen'ral Good*.
See dying Vegetables Life sustain,
See Life dissolving vegetate again.
All Forms that perish other Forms supply,
(By turns we catch the vital Breath, and die)
Like Bubbles on the Sea of Matter born,
They rise, they break, and to that Sea return.   20
Nothing is foreign: Parts relate to Whole:
One All-extending, All-preserving Soul
Connects each Being, greatest with the least;
Made Beast in Aid of Man, and Man of Beast:
All serv'd, all serving; nothing stands alone;
The Chain holds on, and *where* it ends, unknown!
   Has God, thou Fool! work'd solely for thy Good,
Thy Joy, thy Pastime, thy Attire, thy Food?
Who for thy Table feeds the wanton Fawn,
For him, as kindly, spread the flow'ry Lawn.   30
Is it for thee the Lark ascends and sings?
Joy tunes his Voice, Joy elevates his Wings:
Is it for thee the Linnet pours his Throat?
Loves of his own, and Raptures, swell the Note.
The bounding Steed you pompously bestride,
Shares with his Lord the Pleasure and the Pride.
Is thine alone the Seed that strews the Plain?
The Birds of Heav'n shall vindicate their Grain.
Thine the full Harvest of the Golden Year?
Part pays, and justly, the deserving Steer.   40
The Hog that plows not, nor obeys thy Call,
Lives on the Labours of this Lord of All.
   Know, Nature's Children all divide her Care;
The Furr that warms a Monarch, warm'd a Bear.
While Man exclaims, see all Things for my Use!
See Man for mine, replies a pamper'd Goose:

---

269. Chymist: alchemist. **279. Scarfs:** badges of office for soldiers and certain officials.

And just as short of Reason, He must fall,
Who thinks *All* made for *One*, not *One* for *All*.

Grant, that the Pow'rful still the Weak controul,
Be Man the *Wit* and *Tyrant* of the Whole.   50
NATURE that Tyrant checks; He only knows
And helps, another Creature's Wants and Woes.
Say, will the Falcon stooping from above,
Smit with her varying Plumage, spare the Dove?
Admires the Jay the Insect's gilded Wings,
Or hears the Hawk, when *Philomela°* sings?
Man cares for All: To Birds he gives his Woods,
To Beasts his Pastures, and to Fish his Floods,
For some, his Int'rest prompts him to provide,
For more, his Pleasure, yet for more his Pride: 60
All feed on one vain Patron, and enjoy
Th' extensive Blessing of his Luxury.
That very Life his learned Hunger craves
He saves from Famine, from the Savage saves:
Nay, feasts the Animal he dooms his Feast,
And 'till he ends the Being, makes it blest.
Which sees no more the Stroke, or feels the Pain,
Than favour'd Man, by Touch Ætherial° slain.
The Creature had his Feast of Life before;
Thou too must perish, when thy Feast is o'er!   70

To each unthinking Being Heav'n a Friend,
Gives not the useless Knowledge of its End;
To Man imparts it; but with such a View,
As while he dreads it, makes him hope it too.
The Hour conceal'd, and so remote the Fear,
Death still draws nearer, never seeming near.
Great standing Miracle! that Heav'n assign'd
Its only Thinking Thing, this Turn of Mind.

II. Whether with *Reason*, or with *Instinct* blest,
Know, all enjoy that Pow'r which *suits them best*,   80
To Bliss, alike, by that Direction tend,
And find the Means proportion'd to their End.
Say, where full *Instinct* is th' unerring Guide,
What *Pope* or *Council* can they need beside?
Reason, however able, cool at best,
Cares not for Service, or but serves when prest;
Stays till we call, and then not often near;
But honest Instinct comes a Volunteer.
Sure never to o'er-shoot, but just to hit;
While still too wide or short is human Wit;   90
Sure by quick Nature Happiness to gain,
Which heavier Reason labours at in vain.

This too serves *always*, Reason never *long*;
One *must* go right, the other *may* go wrong.
See then the *acting* and *comparing* Pow'rs,
One in their Nature, which are two in ours;
And Reason raise o'er Instinct, as you can;
In this, 'tis *God* directs, in that, 'tis *Man*.

Who taught the Nations of the Field and Wood,
To shun their Poison, and to chuse their Food?   100
Prescient, the Tydes or Tempests to withstand,
Build on the Wave, or Arch beneath the Sand?
Who made the Spider Parallels design,
Sure as *De-Moivre,°* without Rule or Line?
Who bid the Stork, *Columbus*-like, explore
Heav'ns not his own, and Worlds unknown before?
Who calls the Council, states the certain Day,
Who forms the Phalanx, and who points the Way?

III. GOD, in the Nature of each Being, founds
Its proper Bliss, and sets its proper Bounds: 110
But as he fram'd a *Whole*, the Whole to bless
On mutual *Wants* built mutual *Happiness*:
So from the first, Eternal ORDER ran,
And Creature link'd to Creature, Man to Man.
What'ere of Life all-quickening *Æther* keeps,
Or breathes thro' Air, or shoots beneath the Deeps,
Or pours profuse on Earth; one Nature feeds
The *vital Flame*, and swells the *genial Seeds*.
Not Man alone, but all that roam the Wood,
Or wing the Sky, or roll along the Flood,   120
Each loves *Itself*, but not itself *alone*,
Each Sex desires alike, till *two* are *one*:
Nor ends the Pleasure with the fierce Embrace;
They love themselves, a third time, in their *Race*.
Thus Beast and Bird their common Charge attend,
The Mothers nurse it, and the Sires defend;
The young dismiss'd to wander Earth or Air,
There stops the Instinct, and there ends the Care,
The Link dissolves, each seeks a fresh Embrace,
Another Love succeeds, another Race.   130
A *longer Care* Man's helpless Kind demands;
That longer Care contracts more lasting Bands:
Reflection, Reason, still the Ties improve,
At once° extend the Int'rest, and the Love:
With *Choice* we fix, with *Sympathy* we burn,
Each *Virtue* in each *Passion* takes its Turn;
And still new *Needs*, new *Helps*, new *Habits* rise,
That graft Benevolence on Charities,

Epistle III. **56. Philomela:** nightingale. **68. Touch Ætherial:**
[Pope's note] Several of the Ancients, and many Orientals at
this day, esteem'd those who were struck by Lightning as
sacred Persons, and the particular Favourites of Heaven.

104. De-Moivre: Abraham de Moivre (1667–1754), a famous
mathematician, member of the Royal Society, and close
friend of Isaac Newton. **134. At once:** at one and the same
time.

Still as one Brood, and as another rose,
These nat'ral Love maintain'd, habitual those;   140
The last, scarce ripen'd into perfect Man,
Saw helpless Him from whom their Life began:
Mem'ry and Forecast just Returns engage,
That pointed back to Youth, this on to Age;
While Pleasure, Gratitude and Hope, combin'd,
Still spread the Int'rest, and preserv'd the Kind.°
    IV. Nor think in Nature's State they blindly trod;
The State of NATURE was the Reign of GOD:
Self-Love and Social at her Birth began,
UNION, the Bond of all Things, and of Man.   150
Pride then was not; nor Arts, that Pride to aid;
Man walk'd with Beast, joint Tenant of the Shade;
The same his Table, and the same his Bed,
No Murder cloath'd him, and no Murder fed.
In the same Temple, the resounding Wood,
All Vocal Beings hymn'd their equal God:
The Shrine with Gore unstain'd, with Gold undrest,
Unbrib'd, unbloody, stood the blameless Priest:
Heav'ns Attribute was Universal Care,
And Man's Prerogative to rule, but spare.   160
Ah how unlike the Man of Times to come!
Of half that live, the Butcher, and the Tomb;°
Who, Foe to Nature, hears the gen'ral Groan,
Murders their Species, and betrays his own.
But just Disease to Luxury succeeds,
And ev'ry Death its own Avenger breeds;
The Fury-Passions from that Blood began,
And turn'd on Man a fiercer Savage, Man.
    See him from Nature rising slow to Art!
To copy Instinct, then, was Reason's Part;   170
Thus then to Man the Voice of Nature spake—
"Go! from the Creatures thy Instructions take;
Learn from the Birds what Food the Thickets yeild;
Learn from the Beasts the Physick of the Field:
Thy Arts of Building from the Bee receive;
Learn of the Mole to plow, the Worm to weave;
Learn of the little Nautilus to sail,
Spread the thin Oar, and catch the driving Gale.
Here too all Forms of social Union find,
And hence let Reason, late, instruct Mankind: 180
Here Subterranean Works and Cities see,
There Towns Aerial on the waving Tree.
Learn each small People's Genius, Policies;

The Ants Republic, and the Realm of Bees;
How those in common all their Wealth bestow,
And Anarchy without Confusion know,
And these for ever, tho' a Monarch reign,
Their sep'rate Cells and Properties maintain.
Mark what unvary'd Laws preserve each State;
Laws wise as Nature, and as fix'd as Fate.   190
In vain thy Reason finer Webs shall draw,
Entangle Justice in her Net of Law,
And Right too rigid harden into Wrong,
Still for the Strong too weak, the Weak too strong.
Yet Go! and thus o'er all the Creatures sway,
Thus let the Wiser make the rest obey,
And for those Arts mere Instinct could afford,
Be crown'd as Monarchs, or as Gods ador'd."
    V. Great Nature spoke; observant Men obey'd;
Cities were built, Societies were made: 200
Here rose one little State; Another near
Grew by like means, and join'd, thro' Love or Fear.
Did here the Trees with ruddier Burdens bend,
And there the Streams in purer Rills descend?
What War could ravish, Commerce could bestow,
And he return'd a Friend, who came a Foe.
Converse and Love Mankind might strongly draw,
When Love was Liberty, and Nature Law.
Thus States were form'd; the Name of King unknown,
'Till common Int'rest plac'd the Sway in One.   210
'Twas VIRTUE ONLY (or in Arts, or Arms,
Diffusing Blessings, or averting Harms)
The same which in a Sire the Sons obey'd,
A Prince the Father of a People made.
    VI. 'Till then, by Nature crown'd, each Patriarch
        sate,
King, Priest, and Parent of his growing State:
On him, their second Providence, they hung,
Their Law, his Eye; their Oracle, his Tongue.
He, from the wondring Furrow call'd the Food,
Taught to command the Fire, controul the Flood,   220
Draw forth the Monsters of th' Abyss profound,
Or fetch th' Aerial Eagle to the Ground.
Till drooping, sick'ning, dying, they began
Whom they rever'd as God, to mourn as Man.
Then, looking up from Sire to Sire, explor'd
One Great, First Father, and that first Ador'd.
Or plain Tradition that this All begun,
Convey'd unbroken Faith from Sire to Son,
The Worker from the Work distinct was known,
And simple Reason never sought but One: 230
E're Wit oblique had broke that steady Light,
Man, like his Maker, saw, that all was right,

135–46. With . . . Kind: Pope sees sexual love in the family spreading its benefits over the rest of the affections. 162. the Tomb: By eating flesh man entombs it within his body.

To Virtue in the Paths of Pleasure trod,
And own'd a *Father* when he own'd a *God.*
LOVE all the *Faith,* and all th' *Allegiance* then;
For Nature knew no *Right Divine* in *Men,*
No *Ill* could fear in *God;* and understood
A *Sovereign Being* but° a *Sovereign Good.*
True Faith, true Policy, united ran,
That was but *Love of God,* and this of *Man.*   240
    Who first taught Souls enslav'd, and Realms
        undone
Th' enormous° Faith of *Many made for one?*
That proud Exception to all Nature's Laws,
T' invert the World, and counter-work its *Cause?*
Force first made *Conquest,* and that Conquest *Law;*
Till *Superstition* taught the Tyrant Awe,
Then shar'd the Tyranny, then lent it Aid,
And Gods of Conqu'rors, Slaves of Subjects made:
She, midst the Light'ning's Blaze and Thunder's
        Sound,
When rock'd the Mountains, and when groan'd the
        Ground,   250
She taught the Weak to bend, the Proud to pray,
To Pow'r unseen, and mightier far than they.
She, from the rending Earth and bursting Skies,
Saw *Gods* descend, and *Fiends* infernal rise,
Here fix'd the dreadful, there the blest Abodes;
Fear made her Devils, and weak *Hope* her Gods:
Gods partial, changeful, passionate, unjust,
Whose Attributes were Rage, Revenge, or Lust:
Such as the Souls of *Cowards* might *conceive,*
And form'd *like Tyrants,* Tyrants would *believe.*   260
Zeal then, not Charity, became the Guide,
And *Hell* was built on *Spite,* and *Heav'n* on *Pride.*
Then sacred seem'd th' Ætherial Vault no more;
Altars grew Marble then, and reek'd with Gore:
Then first the *Flamen*° tasted living Food;
Next his grim Idol smear'd with human Blood;
With Heav'ns own Thunders shook the World below,
And play'd the God an Engine on his Foe.
    So drives *Self-Love,* thro' Just, and thro' Unjust,
To *One* man's Pow'r, Ambition, Lucre, Lust: 270
The same Self-Love, in *All,* becomes the Cause
Of what restrains him, Government and Laws.
For what one likes, if others like as well,
What serves one Will when many Wills rebel?
How shall he keep, what sleeping or awake
A weaker may surprize, a stronger take?

His *Safety* must his *Liberty* restrain;
All join to *guard* what *each* desires to *gain.*
Forc'd into Virtue thus by Self-Defence,
Ev'n Kings learn'd Justice and Benevolence: 280
Self-Love forsook the Path it first pursu'd,
And found the *private* in the *publick* Good.
    'Twas then, the studious Head or gen'rous Mind,
Follow'r of God, or Friend of Humankind,
Poet or Patriot, rose, but to restore
The Faith and Moral, *Nature* gave before;
Re-lum'd her ancient Light, not *kindled new;*
If not God's *Image,* yet his *Shadow* drew;
Taught Pow'rs due Use to *People* and to *Kings,*
Taught, nor to slack, nor strain, its tender strings;   290
The *Less,* or *Greater,* set so justly true,
That touching *one,* must strike the *other* too,
Till jarring Int'rests of themselves create
The according Musick of a *well-mix'd State.*
Such is the WORLD'S *great Harmony,* that springs
From *Order, Union,* full *Consent* of Things!
Where Small and Great, where Weak and Mighty,
        made
To serve, not suffer, strengthen, not invade,
More *pow'rful* each, as *needful* to the rest,
And in Proportion as it blesses, blest,   300
Draw to one Point, and to one Centre bring
Beast, Man, or Angel, Servant, Lord, or King.
    For *Forms* of *Government* let Fools contest;
What'ere is best administred, is best:
For *Modes* of *Faith* let graceless Zealots fight;
His can't be wrong whose *Life* is in the right.
In Faith and Hope the World will disagree,
But all Mankind's concern is Charity:
All must be false, that thwart this *One Great End,*
And all of God, that *bless* Mankind, or *mend.*   310
    Man, like the gen'rous Vine, supported lives,
The *Strength* he gains is from th' *Embrace* he gives.
On their *own Axis* as the Planets run,
Yet make at once their Circle round the *Sun:*
So two consistent Motions act the Soul,
And one regards *Itself,* and one the *Whole.*
    Thus God and Nature link'd the gen'ral Frame,
And bade *Self-Love* and *Social* be the same.

EPISTLE IV

O HAPPINESS! our Being's End and Aim!
Good, Pleasure, Ease, Content! whate'er thy name:
That Something still, which prompts th' eternal sigh,

---

238. but: meaning "could only be." **242. enormous:**
monstrous. **265. Flamen:** a priest appointed to serve a
particular deity.

For which we bear to live, or dare to die;
Which still so near us, yet beyond us lies,
O'erlook'd, seen double, by the fool—and wise.
Plant of Cælestial seed! if dropt below,
Say, in what mortal soil thou deign'st to grow?
Fair-opening to some Court's propitious Shine,
Or deep with diamonds in the flaming Mine,   10
Twin'd with the wreaths Parnassian Laurels yield,
Or reap'd in Iron Harvests of the Field?
Where grows—where grows it not?—If vain our toil,
We ought to blame the Culture, not the Soil:
Fix'd to no spot is Happiness sincere;°
'Tis no where to be found, or ev'ry where;
'Tis never to be bought, but always free,
And fled from Monarchs, St. John! dwells with thee.

    Ask of the Learn'd the way, the Learn'd are blind,
This bids to serve, and that to shun mankind: 20
Some place the bliss in Action, some in Ease,
Those call it Pleasure, and Contentment these:
Some sunk to Beasts, find Pleasure end in Pain;
Some swell'd to Gods, confess ev'n Virtue vain;
Or indolent, to each extreme they fall,
To trust in ev'ry thing or doubt of All.

    Who thus define it, say they more or less
Than this, that Happiness is Happiness?

    Take *Nature*'s path, and mad Opinion's leave,
All States can reach it, and all Heads conceive;   30
Obvious her goods, in no Extreme they dwell,
There needs but thinking right, and meaning well;
And mourn our various portions as we please,
Equal is *common Sense*, and *common Ease*.

    Remember Man! "the Universal Cause
Acts not by partial, but by gen'ral Laws";
And makes what Happiness we justly call,
Subsist not in the Good of one, but all.
There's not a blessing Individuals find,
But some way leans and hearkens° to the Kind.   40
No Bandit fierce, no Tyrant mad with pride,
No cavern'd Hermit, rests self-satisfy'd;
Who most to shun or hate mankind pretend,
Seek an Admirer, or wou'd fix a Friend.
Abstract what others feel, what others think,
All Pleasures sicken, and all Glories sink;

Epistle IV. **15. sincere:** "pure, unmingled" (Johnson's Dictionary). **40. leans and hearkens:** a vivid phrase borrowed from Donne's *Valediction Forbidding Mourning* (1633); Gilbert Wakefield in his *Observations on Pope* (1796) happily paraphrases "Man waits, as it were, all ear! for the approbation of another's feelings, before he can decide upon the reality of his own happiness from a present enjoyment."

Each has his share, and who wou'd more obtain
Shall find, the pleasure pays not half the pain.
    Order is Heav'n's first Law; and this confest,
Some are, and must be, greater than the rest,   50
More rich, more wise: but who infers from hence
That such are *happier*, shocks all common sense.
Heav'n to mankind impartial we confess
If all are equal in their happiness:
But mutual wants this happiness increase,
All Nature's diff'rence keeps all Nature's peace.
Condition, Circumstance is not the thing:
Bliss is the same, in Subject or in King;
In who obtain defence, or who defend;
In him who is, or him who finds, a friend.   60
Heav'n breathes thro' ev'ry member of the whole
One common Blessing, as one common Soul:
But Fortune's gifts if each alike possest,
And each were equal, must not all contest?
If then to all men Happiness was meant,
God in Externals could not place Content.

    Fortune her gifts may variously dispose,
And these be happy call'd, unhappy those;
But Heav'n's just balance equal will appear,
While those are plac'd in Hope, and these in Fear: 70
Not present Good or Ill, the joy or curse,
But future views, of Better, or of Worse.

    Oh Sons of Earth! attempt ye still to rise
By mountains pil'd on mountains, to the Skies?
Heav'n still with laughter the vain toil surveys,
And buries Madmen in the Heaps they raise.

    Know, all the Good that Individuals find,
Or God and Nature meant to meer mankind,
Reason's whole pleasure, all the joys of Sense,
Lie in three words, *Health, Peace,* and *Competence.* 80
But Health consists with Temperance alone,
And Peace, O Virtue! Peace is all thy own;
The good or bad the gifts of Fortune gain;
But these less taste them, as they worse obtain.
Say, in pursuit of Profit or Delight,
Who risque the most, that take wrong means, or
    right?
Of Vice or Virtue, whether blest or curst,
Which meets Contempt, or which Compassion first?
Count all th' advantage prosp'rous Vice attains,
'Tis but what Virtue flies from, and disdains;   90
And grant the bad what happiness they wou'd,
One they must want, which is, to pass for good.

    Oh blind to Truth, and God's whole Scheme
    below!
Who fancy Bliss to Vice, to Virtue Woe:

Who sees and follows that great Scheme the best,
Best knows the blessing, and will most be blest.
But Fools the *Good* alone unhappy call,
For Ills or Accidents that chance to *All*.
See FALKLAND° dies, the virtuous and the just!
See godlike TURENNE° prostrate on the dust!   100
See SIDNEY° bleeds amid the martial strife!
Was this their *Virtue*, or Contempt of life?
Say was it Virtue, more tho' Heav'n ne'er gave,
Lamented DIGBY°! sunk thee to the Grave?
Tell me, if Virtue made the Son expire,
Why, full of Days and Honour, lives the Sire?
Why drew *Marseilles* good Bishop purer breath,
When Nature sicken'd, and each gale was death?°
Or why so long (in Life if long can be)
Lent Heav'n a *Parent* to the Poor and Me?°   110
    What makes all Physical or Moral Ill?
There deviates Nature, and here wanders Will.
God sends not Ill, if rightly understood,
Or partial Ill is universal Good,
Or Change admits, or Nature lets it fall;
Short, and but rare, till Man improv'd° it all.
We just as wisely might of Heav'n complain,
That righteous Abel was destroy'd by Cain,
As that the virtuous Son is ill at ease,
When his lewd Father gave the dire disease.   120
Think we like some weak Prince th' Eternal Cause,
Prone for his Fav'rites to reverse his Laws?
    Shall burning Ætna, if a Sage requires,
Forget to thunder, and recall her fires?°
On Air or Sea new motions be imprest,
O blameless Bethel! to relieve thy breast?°

When the loose Mountain trembles from on high,
Shall Gravitation cease, if you go by?
Or some old Temple nodding to its fall,
For Chartres° head reserve the hanging Wall?   130
    But still this World (so fitted for the Knave)
Contents us not. A better shall we have?
A Kingdom of the Just then let it be:
But first consider how those Just agree?
The Good must merit God's peculiar care;
But who but God can tell us, who they are?
One thinks on Calvin Heav'n's own spirit fell,
Another deems him Instrument of Hell;
If Calvin feel Heav'n's Blessing, or its Rod,
This cries there is, and that, there is no God.   140
What shocks one part will edify the rest,
Nor with one System can they all be blest.
The very best will variously incline,
And what rewards your Virtue, punish mine.
"Whatever *is*, is *right*."—This world, 'tis true,
Was made for Cæsar—but for Titus° too:
And which more *blest?* who chain'd his Country, say,
Or he, whose Virtue sigh'd to lose a day?
    "But sometimes Virtue starves while Vice is fed."
What then? is the reward of Virtue, Bread?   150
That, Vice may merit; 'tis the price of Toil:
The Knave deserves it when he tills the Soil,
The Knave deserves it when he tempts the Main,
Where Folly fights, for Kings, or dives for Gain.
The good man may be weak, be indolent,
Nor is his claim to Plenty, but Content.
But grant him Riches, your demand is o'er?
"No—shall the good want health, the good want
        Pow'r?"
Add health and pow'r, and ev'ry earthly thing:
"Why bounded pow'r? why private? why no
        King?"   160
Nay, why external for internal giv'n,
Why is not Man a God, and Earth a Heav'n?
Who ask and reason thus, will scarce conceive
God gives enough while he has more to give:
Immense the Pow'r, immense were the demand;
Say, at what part of Nature will they stand?
    What nothing earthly gives, or can destroy,
The Soul's calm sun-shine, and the heart-felt joy,
Is Virtue's Prize: A better would you fix?
Then give Humility a Coach and six,   170

---

99. Falkland: Lucius Cary (c. 1610–43), Second Viscount Falkland. At the request of Charles I he became Secretary of State in 1642. Opposed to violent and extremist policies and despairing of his country's happiness after the outbreak of civil war, he welcomed death at the Battle of Newbury. **100. Turenne:** (1611–75), Marshal of France, killed in battle at Sassbach in Baden. **101. Sidney:** Sir Philip Sidney (1554–86), poet and soldier who was fatally wounded at Zutphen. **104. Digby:** The Honorable Robert Digby died in 1726; Pope wrote an epitaph for him. **107–08. Why . . . death:** Belsunce, Bishop of Marseilles, ministered to the sick and dying during a plague in 1721 without succumbing to the disease. **109–10. Or . . . Me:** Pope's mother died in 1733 at the age of ninety-one. **116. improv'd:** in an ironic sense. **123–24. Shall . . . fires:** a reference to Empedocles, Greek philosopher of the fifth century B.C. who, according to one story, was killed by a volcanic eruption of Mount Etna that he was trying to investigate. **125–26. On . . . breast:** Hugh Bethel, a friend of Pope's, suffered from asthma; the reference is probably to his discomfort during a trip to Italy.

130. Chartres: Francis Charteris (1675–1732), the notorious debauchee. **146. Titus:** The Emperor Titus is said to have exclaimed, when he had let a day go by without bestowing a present, "I have lost a day."

Justice a Conqu'ror's sword, or Truth a Gown,
Or Publick Spirit, its great cure, a Crown.
Weak, foolish Man! will Heav'n reward us there
With the same Trash mad Mortals wish for here?
The Boy and Man an individual makes,
Yet sigh'st thou now for Apples and for Cakes?
Go, like the Indian, in another Life
Expect thy Dog, thy Bottle, and thy Wife:
As well as dream such Trifles are assign'd,
As Toys and Empires, for a god-like Mind.   180
Rewards that either would to Virtue bring
No joy, or be destructive of the thing.
How oft by these at sixty are undone
The Virtues of a Saint at twenty-one!
To whom can Riches give Repute, or Trust,
Content, or Pleasure, but the Good and Just?
Judges and Senates have been bought for gold,
Esteem and Love were never to be sold.
O Fool! to think, God hates the worthy Mind,
The Lover, and the Love, of Human kind,   190
Whose Life is healthful, and whose Conscience clear;
Because he wants a thousand pounds a year!
   Honour and *Shame* from no Condition rise;
Act well your part, there all the Honour lies.
Fortune in men has some small diff'rence made,
One flaunts in Rags, one flutters in Brocade,
The Cobler apron'd, and the Parson gown'd,
The Fryar hooded, and the Monarch crown'd.
"What differ more (you cry) than Crown and Cowl?"
I'll tell you, friend: a Wise man and a Fool.   200
You'll find, if once the Monarch acts the Monk,
Or Cobler-like, the Parson will be drunk,
Worth makes the Man, and want of it the Fellow;
The rest, is all but Leather or Prunella.°
   Stuck o'er with *Titles*, and hung round with
          Strings,°
That thou may'st be, by Kings, or Whores of Kings.
Boast the pure Blood of an illustrious Race,
In quiet flow from Lucrece° to Lucrece;
But by your Father's worth if yours you rate,
Count me those only who were good and great.   210
Go! if your ancient but ignoble blood
Has crept thro' Scoundrels ever since the Flood,

Go! and pretend your Family is young;
Nor own your Fathers have been fools so long.
What can ennoble Sots, or Slaves, or Cowards?
Alas! not all the blood of all the HOWARDS.°
   Look next on *Greatness*, say where Greatness lies?
"Where, but among the Heroes, and the Wise?"
Heroes are much the same, the point's agreed,
From Macedonia's Madman° to the Suede;°   220
The whole strange purpose of their lives, to find
Or make, an Enemy of all Mankind:
Not one looks backward, onward still he goes,
Yet ne'er looks foreward, further than his nose.
No less alike the Politick and wise,
All sly slow things, with circumspective eyes;
Men in their loose, unguarded hours they take,
Not that themselves are wise, but others weak.
But grant that those can *conquer*, these can *cheat*,
'Tis phrase absurd to call a Villain *great*.   230
Who wickedly is wise, or madly brave,
Is but *the more* a fool, *the more* a knave.
Who noble ends by noble means obtains,
Or failing, smiles in Exile or in Chains,
Like good Aurelius° let him reign, or bleed
Like Socrates, that Man is great indeed.
   What's *Fame?* a fancy'd Life in others breath!
A thing beyond us ev'n before our death.
Just what you *hear* you have, and what's unknown
The same (my Lord) if Tully's,° or your own.   240
All that we feel of it begins and ends
In the small circle of our foes or friends;
To all beside, as much an empty Shade
An Eugene° living, as a Cæsar dead,
Alike, or when or where, they shone or shine,
Or on the Rubicon, or on the Rhine.
A Wit's a *Feather*, and a Chief a *Rod*;
An honest° man's the noblest Work of God:
Fame but from death a Villain's name can save,
As Justice tears his body from the grave;   250
When what t' Oblivion better were resign'd,
Is hung on high, to poison half mankind.

---

204. **Leather or Prunella:** The cobbler's apron is made of leather; the parson's gown, of prunella. 205. **Strings:** the ribbons of the orders of chivalry. 208. **Lucrece:** After being raped by Sextus Tarquinius, the Roman Lucretia (*c.* 500 B.C.) secured a promise of vengeance from her husband and her father and then stabbed herself.

216. **Howards:** the Howard family ranks first among the English nobility. 220. **Macedonia's Madman:** Alexander the Great (356–323 B.C.). **the Suede:** Charles XII (1682–1718), an inveterate wager of wars. 235. **Aurelius:** Marcus Aurelius (121–180), Roman emperor and Stoic philosopher. 240. **Tully:** Cicero. 244. **Eugene:** Prince Eugene of Savoy (1663–1736), commander of the armies of the Austrian Empire; he was joint victor with Marlborough at Blenheim and Malplaquet. 248. **honest:** virtuous, upright.

All Fame is foreign, but of true Desert,
Plays round the head, but comes not to the heart.
One self-approving Hour whole years out-weighs
Of stupid Starers, and of loud huzza's;
And more true joy Marcellus° exil'd feels
Than Cæsar with a Senate at his heels.

In *Parts*° superior what advantage lies!
Tell (for *You*° can) what is it to be wise?   260
'Tis but to know, how little can be known,
To see all others faults, and feel our own;
Condemn'd in Business or in Arts to drudge
Without a Second, or without a Judge:
Truths would you teach, or save a sinking Land?
All fear, none aid you, and few understand.
Painful Preheminence! yourself to view
Above Life's Weakness, and its Comforts too.

Bring then these Blessings to a strict account,
Make fair deductions, see to what they mount?   270
How much of other each is sure to cost?
How each for other oft is wholly lost?
How inconsistent greater Goods with these?
How sometimes Life is risqu'd, and always Ease?
Think, and if still the *Things* thy envy call,
Say, would'st thou be the *Man* to whom they fall?
To sigh for Ribbands if thou art so silly,
Mark how they grace Lord Umbra,° or Sir Billy.°
Is yellow Dirt° the passion of thy life?
Look but on Gripus, or on Gripus' wife.   280
If Parts allure thee, think how Bacon shin'd,
The wisest, brightest, meanest of Mankind:
Or ravish'd with the whistling of a Name,
See Cromwell, damn'd to everlasting Fame!
If all, united, thy ambition call,
From ancient Story learn to scorn them all.
There, in the rich, the honour'd, fam'd, and great,
See the false Scale of Happiness compleat!
In hearts of Kings or arms of Queens who lay,
(How happy!) those to ruin, these betray,   290
Mark by what wretched steps their Glory grows,
From dirt and sea-weed as proud Venice rose;
In each, how Guilt and Greatness equal ran,
And all that rais'd the Hero sunk the Man.

Now Europe's Lawrels on their brows behold,
But stain'd with Blood, or ill exchang'd for Gold:
Then see them broke with Toils, or sunk in Ease,
Or infamous for plunder'd Provinces.
Oh Wealth ill-fated! which no Act of fame
E'er taught to shine, or sanctify'd from shame!   300
What greater bliss attends their close of life?
Some greedy Minion, or imperious Wife,
The trophy'd Arches, story'd Halls invade,
And haunt their slumbers in the pompous Shade.
Alas! not dazled with their Noontide ray,
Compute the Morn and Evening to the Day:
The whole amount of that enormous Fame
A Tale! that blends their Glory with their Shame!

Know then this Truth (enough for man to know)
VIRTUE alone is Happiness below: 310
The only point where human bliss stands still,
And tastes the good without the fall to ill;
Where only, Merit constant pay receives,
Is bless'd in what it takes, and what it gives:
The joy unequal'd, if its end it gain,
And if it lose, attended with no pain:
Without satiety, tho' e'er so bless'd,
And but more relish'd as the more distress'd:
The broadest mirth unfeeling Folly wears,
Less pleasing far than Virtue's very Tears.   320
Good, from each object, from each place acquir'd,
For ever exercis'd, yet never tir'd;
Never elated, while one man's oppress'd,
Never dejected, while another's bless'd;
And where no wants, no wishes can remain,
Since but to wish more Virtue, is to gain.

See! the sole Bliss Heav'n could on *all* bestow,
Which who but feels, can taste, but thinks, can know:
Yet poor with Fortune, and with Learning blind,
The Bad must miss, the Good untaught will find,   330
Slave to no Sect, who takes no private road,
But looks thro' *Nature* up to *Nature's* GOD,
Pursues that *Chain* which links th' immense Design,
Joyns Heav'n, and Earth, and mortal, and divine;
Sees, that no Being any Bliss can know
But touches some above, and some below;
Learns, from this Union of the rising *Whole*,
The first, last Purpose of the human Soul;
And knows, where Faith, Law, Morals all began,
All end, in LOVE *of* GOD, and LOVE *of* MAN.   340
For him alone, *Hope* leads from gole to gole,
And opens still, and opens, on his soul,
Till lengthen'd on to *Faith*, and unconfin'd,
It pours the bliss that fills up all the mind.

---

257. Marcellus: Marcus Marcellus sided with Pompey against
Caesar and withdrew to Mytilene after the Battle of Pharsalia
in 48 B.C. **259. Parts:** intellectual talents. **260. You:** not the
"you" of line 128, i.e., the reader. Here the word is given a
capital and means Bolingbroke. **278. Lord Umbra:** a *shady*
(i.e., disreputable) lord. **Sir Billy:** perhaps an allusion to Sir
William Yonge (d. 1755), notorious as a despicable Whig
politician. **279. yellow Dirt:** gold.

He sees, why Nature plants in Man alone
Hope of known bliss, and Faith in bliss unknown?
(Nature, whose dictates to no other Kind
Are giv'n in vain, but what they seek they find)
Wise is her Present: she connects in this
His greatest *Virtue* with his greatest *Bliss*,   350
At once his own bright Prospect to be blest,
And strongest Motive to assist the rest.
    Self-Love thus push'd to Social, to Divine,
Gives thee to make thy Neighbour's blessing thine:
Is this too little for the boundless heart?
Extend it, let thy Enemies have part:
Grasp the whole Worlds, of Reason, Life, and Sense,
In one close System of Benevolence.
Happier, as kinder! in whate'er degree,
And height of *Bliss* but height of CHARITY.   360
    GOD loves from Whole to Parts: but human Soul
Must rise from Individual to the Whole.
Self-love but serves the virtuous mind to wake,
As the small pebble stirs the peaceful Lake,
The Centre mov'd, a Circle strait succeeds,
Another still, and still another spreads;
Friend, Parent, Neighbour, first it will embrace,
His Country next, and next all Human-race,
Wide, and more wide, th' O'erflowings of the mind
Take ev'ry Creature in, of ev'ry kind;   370
Earth smiles around, with boundless bounty blest,
And Heav'n beholds its Image in his Breast.
    Come then, my Friend! my Genius come along,
Oh Master of the Poet, and the Song!
And while the Muse now stoops, or now ascends,
To Man's low Passions, or their glorious Ends,
Teach me like thee, in various Nature wise,
To fall with Dignity, with Temper° rise;
Form'd by thy Converse, happily to steer
From grave to gay, from lively to severe,   380
Correct with spirit, eloquent with ease,
Intent to reason, or polite to please.
O! while along the stream of Time, thy Name
Expanded flies, and gathers all its fame,
Say, shall my little Bark attendant sail,
Pursue the Triumph, and partake the Gale?
When Statesmen, Heroes, Kings, in dust repose,
Whose Sons shall blush their Fathers were thy Foes,
Shall then this Verse to future age pretend
Thou wert my Guide, Philosopher, and Friend?   390
That urg'd by thee, I turn'd the tuneful Art
From Sounds to Things, from Fancy to the Heart;

378. Temper: equanimity.

For Wit's false Mirror held up Nature's Light;
Shew'd erring Pride *Whatever Is*, is *Right;*
That *Reason, Passion,* answer *one great Aim;*
That true *Self-love* and *Social* are the *same;*
That *Virtue* only makes our *Bliss below;*
And all our *Knowledge* is, *Ourselves to know.*

ON A CERTAIN LADY AT COURT

The lady was Mrs. Howard, later Countess of Suffolk.
    The text is that of the first edition (1732). There were no later revisions.

    I know the thing that's most uncommon;
      (Envy be silent and attend!)
    I know a Reasonable Woman,
      Handsome and witty, yet a Friend.

    Not warp'd by Passion, aw'd by Rumour,
      Not grave thro' Pride, or gay thro' Folly,
    An equal Mixture of good Humour,
      And sensible soft Melancholy.

    "Has she no Faults then (Envy says) Sir?"
      Yes she has one, I must aver: 10
    When all the World conspires to praise her,
      The Woman's deaf, and does not hear.

FROM

MORAL ESSAYS

Pope considered the four *Moral Essays* (1731–35) his best work and thought of them as related to *An Essay on Man* (1733–34) and to two other similarly composite works. He hoped to collect all of these in a "System of Ethics in the Horatian way." The *Moral Essays* would have formed the second section.

OF THE CHARACTERS
OF WOMEN

AN EPISTLE *To a LADY*.

Pope addressed the second of the *Moral Essays* to Martha Blount, one of his favorites, because she least resembled Silia, Flavia, Chloe, and the rest. He greatly disapproves of such women, but he paints their portraits with the delicacy of Gainsborough. To the first edition he added these words as a preface:

> The Author being very sensible how particular a Tenderness is due to the FEMALE SEX, and at the same time how little they generally show to each other; declares upon his Honour, that *no one Character* is drawn from the Life, in this Epistle. It would otherwise be most improperly inscribed to a *Lady*, who, of all the Women he knows, is the last that would be entertain'd at the Expence of Another.

In fairness to Pope we should note that the character of Atossa, apparently modeled on that of Katherine, Duchess of Buckinghamshire, and also probably on that of Sarah, Duchess of Marlborough, was added to the poem after Pope's death, by which time the Argument had replaced this prefatory note.

The text is that of the first edition (1735), revised according to Warburton's edition of 1751, which represents the text in its complete form. The Argument first appeared in a later edition of 1735.

ARGUMENT

Of the Characters of *Women* (consider'd only as contradistinguished from the other sex.[1]) That these are yet more inconsistent and incomprehensible than those of Men, of which Instances are given even from such Characters as are plainest, and most strongly mark'd; as in the *Affected*, Ver. 7, &c. The *Soft-natur'd*. 29. the *Cunning*, 45. the *Whimsical*, 53. the *Wits and Refiners*, 87. the *Stupid and Silly*, 101. How Contrarieties run thro' them all.

MORAL ESSAYS: *Of the Characters of Women*. **I. the other sex:** The first of the *Moral Essays* is entitled *Of the Characters of Men.*

But tho' the *Particular Characters* of this Sex are more various than those of Men, the *General Characteristick*, as to the *Ruling Passion*,[2] is more uniform and confin'd. In what That lies, and whence it *proceeds*, 207, &c. Men are best known in publick Life, Women in private, 199. What are the *Aims*, and the *Fate* of the Sex, both as to *Power and Pleasure?* 219, 231. &c. Advice for their true Interest, 249. The Picture of an esteemable Woman, made up of the best kind of Contrarieties, 269, &c.

NOTHING so true as what you once let fall,
Most Women have no Characters at all.
Matter too soft a lasting mark to bear,
And best distinguish'd by black, brown, or fair.
How many Pictures of one Nymph we view,
All how unlike each other, all how true!
Arcadia's Countess,° here, in ermin'd pride,°
Is there, *Pastora*° by a Fountain side:
Here *Fannia*° leering on her own good man,
And there a naked *Leda* with a Swan.   10
Let then the Fair-one beautifully cry
In *Magdalen*'s loose hair and lifted eye,
Or drest in smiles of sweet *Cecilia*° shine,
With simp'ring Angels, Palms, and Harps divine;
Whether the Charmer sinner it, or saint it,
If Folly grow romantic,° I must paint it.
Come then, the Colours and the ground prepare!
Dip in the Rainbow, trick her off in Air,
Chuse a firm Cloud before it fall, and in it
Catch, e're she change, the *Cynthia*° of this minute. 20
Rufa,° whose eye quick-glancing o'er the *Park*,
Attracts each light gay Meteor of a Spark,

2. the Ruling Passion: Like others before him, Pope saw man as ultimately governed by that characteristic of his nature which, though often latent, is always ready to take command when an important decision has to be made. **7. Arcadia's Countess:** sister of the soldier and poet Sir Philip Sidney (1554–86), to whom Sidney dedicated his *Arcadia* (1590). **ermin'd pride:** As a countess, she would wear on state occasions robes trimmed with ermine. **8. Pastora:** a fictitious name suggesting a character from pastoral poetry; it had been used by Congreve in *The Mourning Muse of Alexis* (1695), a pastoral elegy on Queen Mary. It was common for ladies to be painted posing as literary, legendary, or biblical figures. **9. Fannia:** The original Fannia was a Roman lady convicted of adultery. **13. Cecilia:** the patron saint of music. **16. romantic:** exuberant. **20. Cynthia:** the goddess of the moon, the changeable one. **21–28. Rufa . . . setting-sun:** [Pope's note] Instances of contrarieties, given even from such Characters as are most strongly mark'd, and seemingly therefore most consistent: As . . . In the *Affected*, [l.] 21, &c. **21. Rufa:** the feminine form of *Rufus*, meaning the red-headed.

Agrees as ill with *Rufa* studying *Locke*,
As *Sappho*'s diamonds with her dirty smock,°
Or *Sappho* at her toilet's greasy task
With *Sappho* fragrant at an evening Mask:
So morning Insects that in Muck begun,
Shine, buzz, and fly-blow, in the setting-sun.

 How° soft is *Silia*! fearful to offend, *SOFT-NATURED*
The frail one's Advocate, the weak one's Friend: 30
To her, *Calista*° prov'd her Conduct nice,
And good *Simplicius*° asks of her Advice.
Sudden, she storms! she raves! You tip the wink,
But spare your censure; *Silia* does not drink.
All eyes may see from what the change arose,
All eyes may see—a Pimple on her nose.

 Papillia,° wedded to her am'rous Spark,
Sighs for the Shades—"How charming is a *Park*!
A *Park* is purchas'd, but the Fair he sees
All bath'd in tears—"Oh odious, odious *Trees*! 40

 Ladies like variegated Tulips show,
'Tis to their Changes half their Charms we owe;
Fine by defect, and delicately weak,
Their happy Spots the nice Admirer take. *CUNNINGE ARTFUL*
'Twas° thus *Calypso*° once our hearts alarm'd,
Aw'd without Virtue, without Beauty charm'd;
Her Tongue bewitch'd as odly as her Eyes,
Less Wit than Mimic, more a Wit than wise:
Strange Graces still, and stranger Flights she had,
Was just not ugly, and was just not mad; 50
Yet ne'er so sure our passion to create,
As when she touch'd the brink of all we hate.

 Narcissa's° nature, tolerably mild,
To make a *Wash*° would hardly stew a Child;
Has ev'n been prov'd to grant a Lover's pray'r,
And paid a Tradesman once to make him stare;
Gave alms at *Easter*, in a christian trim,
And made a Widow happy, for a whim.

Why then declare Good-nature is her scorn,
When 'tis by that alone she can be born? 60
Why pique all mortals, yet affect a name?
A Fool to Pleasure, yet a Slave to Fame!
Now deep in *Taylor*° and the Book of *Martyrs*,°
Now drinking Citron with his Grace and *Chartres*:°
Now Conscience chills her, and now Passion burns,
And Atheism and Religion take their turns;
A very Heathen in the carnal part,
Yet still a sad, good Christian at her heart. *LEWD & VICIOUS*

 See° Sin in State, majestically drunk;
Proud as a Peeress, prouder as a Punk;° 70
Chaste to her Husband, frank to all beside,
A teeming Mistress, but a barren Bride.
What then? let Blood and Body bear the fault,
Her Head's untouch'd, that noble Seat of Thought:
Such this day's doctrine—in another fit
She sins with Poets thro' pure Love of Wit.
What has not fir'd her bosom or her brain?
Cæsar and *Tall-boy*,° *Charles*° and *Charlema'ne*.
As *Helluo*,° late Dictator of the Feast,
The Nose of Hautgout° and the Tip of Taste, 80
Critiqu'd your wine, and analyz'd your meat,
Yet on plain Pudding deign'd at-home to eat:
So *Philomedé*,° lect'ring all mankind
On the soft Passion, and the Taste refin'd,
Th' Address, the Delicacy—stoops at once,
And makes her hearty meal upon a Dunce.

 Flavia's° a Wit, has too much sense to *pray*, *WITTY & REFINED*
To *toast* our wants and wishes, is her way;
Nor asks of *God* but of her *Stars* to give
The mighty blessing, "while we live, to live." 90
Then all for Death, that Opiate of the Soul!
Lucretia's Dagger,° *Rosamonda*'s Bowl.°

---

24. dirty smock: a dig at the writer Lady Mary Wortley Montagu (1689–1762), who was careless of her dress. (See the selection from Lady Mary in Part Three.) **29–36. How . . . nose:** [Pope's note] Contrarieties in the *Soft-natur'd*. **31. Calista:** the guilty heroine of the tragedy *The Fair Penitent* (1703) by Nicholas Rowe (1674–1718). **32. Simplicius:** a simpleton. **37. Papillia:** suggested by the Latin *papilio*, meaning butterfly. **45–52. 'Twas . . . hate:** [Pope's note] Contrarieties in the *Cunning* and *Artful*. **45. Calypso:** a nymph in the *Odyssey* who detains the shipwrecked Ulysses on her island for seven years. **53–68. Narcissa's . . . heart:** [Pope's note] [Contrarieties] in the *Whimsical*. **53. Narcissa:** a feminine form of *Narcissus*. He was a beautiful youth in Greek mythology who fell in love with his reflection. **54. Wash:** a cosmetic preparation.

63. Taylor: Jeremy Taylor (1613–67), the divine. **the Book . . . Martyrs:** by John Foxe (1517–87), a martyrologist. This book was published in English in 1563 under the title *Acts and Monuments of These Latter Perilous Days*. **64. Chartres:** Francis Charteris (1675–1732), the notorious debauchee. **69–86. See . . . Dunce:** [Pope's note] [Contrarieties] In the *Lewd* and *Vicious*. **70. Punk:** harlot. **78. Tall-boy:** an awkward young lover in a comedy by Richard Brome (d. 1652). **Charles:** a stock name for a footman. **79. Helluo:** the Latin for *glutton*. **80. Hautgout:** food at the delicious point of near over-ripeness. **83. Philomedé:** perhaps derived from Homer's epithet for Aphrodite, "laughter-loving." **87–100. Flavia's . . . live:** [Pope's note] Contrarieties in the *Witty* and *Refin'd*. **92. Lucretia's Dagger:** After being raped by the son of Tarquin, King of Rome, Lucretia took her life. **Rosamonda's Bowl:** Rosamond Clifford, mistress of Henry II, died by taking poison.

Say, what can cause such impotence of mind?
A Spark too fickle, or a Spouse too kind.
Wise Wretch! with Pleasures too refin'd to please,
With too much Spirit to be e'er at Ease,
With too much Quickness ever to be taught,
With too much Thinking to have common Thought:
You purchase Pain with all that Joy can give,
And die of nothing but a Rage to live.   100
   Turn° then from Wits; and look on *Simo's*° Mate,
No Ass so meek, no Ass so obstinate:
Or her, that owns her Faults, but never mends
Because she's honest, and the best of Friends:
Or her, whose Life the Church and Scandal share,
For ever in a Passion, or a Pray'r:
Or her, who laughs at Hell, but (like her Grace)
Cries, "Ah! how charming, if there's no such place!"
Or who in sweet Vicissitude appears
Of Mirth and Opium, Ratafie° and Tears,   110
The daily Anodyne, and nightly Draught,
To kill those Foes to Fair ones, Time and Thought.
Woman and Fool are *two* hard Things to hit,
For true No-meaning puzzles more than Wit.
   But what are these to great *Atossa's*° mind?
Scarce once herself, by turns all Womankind!
Who, with herself, or others, from her birth
Finds all her life one warfare upon earth:
Shines, in exposing Knaves, and painting° Fools,
Yet is, whate'er she hates and ridicules.   120
No Thought advances, but her Eddy Brain
Whisks it about, and down it goes again.
Full sixty years the World has been her Trade,
The wisest Fool much Time has ever made.
From loveless youth to unrespected age,
No Passion gratify'd except her Rage.
So much the Fury still out-ran the Wit,
The Pleasure miss'd her, and the Scandal hit.
Who breaks with her, provokes Revenge from Hell,
But he's a bolder man who dares be well:°   130
Her ev'ry turn with Violence pursu'd,
Nor more a storm her Hate than Gratitude:
To that each Passion turns, or soon or late;
Love, if it makes her yield, must make her hate:

101–14. Turn . . . Wit: [Pope's note] the *Stupid* and *Silly*.
101. Simo: a shrewd old man in Terence's comedy *Andrea*.
110. Ratafie: a kind of cherry brandy. 115. Atossa:
originally the name of the daughter of Cyrus the Great, King
of Persia, and here probably intended for Katherine, Duchess
of Buckinghamshire. 119. painting: representing in strong
colors. 130. well: well with her, on good terms.

Superiors? death! and Equals? what a curse!
But an Inferior not dependant? worse.
Offend her, and she knows not to forgive;
Oblige her, and she'll hate you while you live:
But die, and she'll adore you—Then the Bust
And Temple rise—then fall again to dust.   140
Last night, her Lord was all that's good and great;
A Knave this morning, and his Will a Cheat.
Strange! by the Means defeated of the Ends,
By Spirit robb'd of Pow'r, by Warmth of Friends,
By Wealth of Follow'rs! without one distress
Sick of herself thro' very selfishness!
Atossa, curs'd with ev'ry granted pray'r,
Childless with all her Children, wants an Heir.
To Heirs unknown descends th' unguarded store,
Or wanders, Heav'n-directed, to the Poor.°   150
   Pictures like these, (dear Madam) to design,
Asks no firm hand, and no unerring line;
Some wandring Touches, some reflected Light,
Some flying Stroke, alone can hit 'em right:
For how should equal Colours do the knack,°
Camelions who can paint in White and Black?°
   "Yet *Cloe* sure was form'd without a spot."—
Nature in her then err'd not, but forgot.
"With ev'ry pleasing, ev'ry prudent part,
Say, what can *Cloe* want?"—She wants a Heart.   160
She speaks, behaves, and acts just as she ought;
But never, never, reach'd one gen'rous Thought.
Virtue she finds too painful an endeavour,
Content to dwell in Decencies for ever.
So very reasonable, so unmov'd,
As never yet to love, or to be lov'd.
She, while her Lover pants upon her breast,
Can mark the figures on an Indian chest;
And when she sees her Friend in deep despair,
Observes how much a Chintz exceeds Mohair.°   170

149–50. To . . . Poor: Warburton says that in these lines
Pope is "alluding . . . to the great principle of his Philosophy,
which he never loses sight of, and which teaches, that
Providence is incessantly turning the evils arising from the
follies and vices of men to general good." 155. knack: trick.
156. Camelions . . . Black: Warburton adds this note:
"Tho' [the chameleon] instantaneously assumes much of the
colour of every subject on which it chances to be placed, yet,
as the most accurate *Virtuosi* [naturalists] have observed, it has
two native colours of its own, which, (like the *two* ruling
passions of the Sex) amidst all these changes are never totally
discharged, but, tho' often discoloured by the neighbourhood
of adventitious ones, still make the foundation, and give a
tincture to all those which, from thence, it occasionally
assumes." 170. Mohair: "stuff made of camels' or other hair"
(Johnson's *Dictionary*).

Forbid it Heav'n, a Favour or a Debt
She e'er should cancel—but she may forget.
Safe is your Secret still in *Cloe's* ear;
But none of *Cloe's* shall you ever hear.
Of all her Dears she never slander'd one,
But cares not if a thousand are undone.
Would *Cloe* know if you're alive or dead?
She bids her Footman put it in her head.
Cloe is prudent—Would you too be wise?
Then never break your heart when *Cloe* dies.   180

   One certain Portrait may (I grant) be seen,
Which Heav'n has varnish'd out,° and made a *Queen:*
THE SAME FOR EVER!° and describ'd by all
With Truth and Goodness, as with Crown and Ball;
Poets heap Virtues, Painters Gems at will,
And show their zeal, and hide their want of skill.
'Tis well—but, Artists! who can paint or write,
To draw the Naked is your true delight:
That Robe of Quality so struts and swells,
None see what Parts of Nature it conceals.   190
Th' exactest traits of Body or of Mind,
We owe to models of an humble kind.
If QUEENSBERRY° to strip there's no compelling,
'Tis from a Handmaid we must take a Helen.
From Peer or Bishop 'tis no easy thing
To draw the man who loves his God, or King:
Alas! I copy (or my draught would fail)
From honest Mah'met,° or plain Parson Hale.°

   But grant, in publick Men sometimes are shown,
A Woman's seen in Private life alone: 200
Our bolder Talents in full light display'd,
Your Virtues open fairest in the Shade.
Bred to disguise, in Publick 'tis you hide;
There, none distinguish 'twixt your *Shame* or *Pride,*
Weakness or *Delicacy;* all so nice,
That each may seem a *Virtue,* or a *Vice.*

   In Men we various Ruling Passions find,
In Women, two almost divide the Kind,
Those only fix'd, they first or last obey;
The Love of Pleasure, and the Love of Sway.   210

That, Nature gives; and where the Lesson taught
Is but to please, can Pleasure seem a fault?
Experience, This; by Man's Oppression curst,
They seek the second not to lose the first.

   Men, some to Business, some to Pleasure take,
But every Woman is, at heart, a Rake:
Men, some to Quiet, some to publick Strife,
But every Lady would be Queen for life.

   Yet° mark the fate of a whole Sex of Queens!
Pow'r all their end, but Beauty all the means.   220
In Youth they conquer with so wild a rage,
As leaves them scarce a Subject in their Age:
For foreign Glory, foreign Joy, they roam;
No thought of Peace or Happiness at home.
But Wisdom's Triumph is well-tim'd Retreat,
As hard a Science to the Fair as Great° !
Beauties like Tyrants, old and friendless grown,
Yet hate Repose, and dread to be Alone,
Worn out in publick, weary ev'ry eye,
Nor leave one sigh behind them when they die.   230

   Pleasures° the Sex, as Children birds, pursue,
Still out of reach, yet never out of view,
Sure, if they catch, to spoil the Toy at most,
To covet flying, and regret when lost:
At last, to Follies Youth could scarce defend
It grows their Age's prudence to pretend;
Asham'd to own they gave delight before,
Reduc'd to feign it, when they give no more.
As Hags hold *Sabbaths,*° less for joy than spight,
So these their merry, miserable Night;   240
Still round and round the Ghosts of Beauty glide,
And haunt the Places where their Honour dy'd.

   See how the World its Veterans rewards!
A Youth of Frolicks, an old Age of Cards,
Fair to no purpose, artful to no end,
Young without Lovers, old without a Friend,
A Fop their Passion, but their Prize a Sot,
Alive, ridiculous, and dead, forgot!

   Ah° Friend! to dazzle let the Vain design,   249
To raise the Thought and touch the Heart, be thine!
That Charm shall grow, while what fatigues the Ring°
Flaunts and goes down, an unregarded thing.

---

182. varnish'd out: made to shine. **183. The Same . . . Ever:** "The Same [Woman] Forever"; from Queen Elizabeth's motto, *semper eadem.* **193. Queensberry:** Catherine Hyde (1700–77), Duchess of Queensberry, renowned for her beauty. **198. Mah'met:** [Pope's note] servant to the late King, said to be the son of a Turkish Bassa, whom he took at the siege of Buda, and constantly kept about his person. **Parson Hale:** Stephen Hales, a neighbor of Pope's. According to Warburton he was "not more estimable for his useful discoveries as a natural Philosopher [scientist], than for his exemplary Life and Pastoral Charity as a Parish Priest."

219–30. Yet . . . die: [Pope's note] What are the *Aims* and *Fate* of this Sex.—I. As to *Power.* **226. Great:** men highly placed in the state. **231–42. Pleasures . . . dy'd:** [Pope's note] II. As to *Pleasure.* **239. Sabbaths:** midnight meetings of witches and demons at which the Devil supposedly presides. In the Middle Ages they were thought to be held once a year as a kind of festival. **249–92. Ah . . . Poet:** [Pope's note] Advice for [women's] true Interest. **251. Ring:** a fashionable drive in Hyde Park.

So when the Sun's broad beam has tir'd the sight,
All mild ascends the Moon's more sober light,
Serene in Virgin Modesty she shines,
And unobserv'd the glaring Orb declines.

Oh blest with *Temper!* whose unclouded ray
Can make to morrow chearful as to day;
She, who can love a Sister's charms, or hear
Sighs for a Daughter with unwounded ear;
She who ne'er answers till a Husband cools,
Or, if she rules him, never shows she rules;
Charms by accepting, by submitting sways,
Yet has her humour most, when she obeys;
Let Fops or Fortune fly which way they will;
Disdains all loss of Tickets° or Codille;°
Spleen, Vapors, or Small-pox, above them all,
And Mistress of herself, tho' China fall.

And yet believe me, good as well as ill,
Woman's at best a Contradiction still.   270
Heav'n, when it strives to polish all it can
Its last, best work,° but forms a *softer Man;*
Picks from each Sex, to make the Fav'rite blest,
Your love of Pleasure, our desire of Rest,
Blends, in exception to all gen'ral rules,
Your Taste of Follies, with our Scorn of Fools,
Reserve with Frankness, Art with Truth ally'd,
Courage with Softness, Modesty with Pride,
Fix'd Principles, with Fancy ever new;
Shakes all together, and produces—*You.*   280

Be this a Woman's Fame: With this un-blest,
Toasts live a scorn, and Queens may die a jest.
This *Phœbus* promis'd, I forget the Year,°
When those blue eyes first open'd on the Sphere;°
Ascendant *Phœbus* watch'd that hour with care,
Averted half your Parents simple Pray'r,
And gave you *Beauty,* but deny'd the *Pelf*
That buys° your Sex a Tyrant o'er itself:
The gen'rous God, who Wit and Gold refines,
And ripens Spirits as he ripens Mines,°   290
Kept Dross for Duchesses, the world shall know it,
To you gave Sense, Good-humour,° and a Poet.

---

266. Tickets: lottery tickets. **Codille:** a term applied to the loser in the popular card game ombre. **272. Its . . . work:** Eve was created after Adam. **283. forget the Year:** The gallant do not particularize about a woman's age. **284. open'd . . . Sphere:** "saw the light" of Phoebus (the sun). **288. buys:** Brides were expected to bring a dowry to their grooms. **289–90. The gen'rous . . . Mines:** Phoebus, who was the god of wit as well as of the sun, was thought to transform metal into gold with his rays. **292. Good-humour:** See *The Rape of the Lock,* above, v. 29 ff.

OF THE USE OF RICHES

AN

EPISTLE

TO THE

Right Honourable
RICHARD Earl of *BURLINGTON.*
Occasion'd by his Publishing PALLADIO's
Designs of the BATHS, ARCHES, THEATRES,
&c. of Ancient ROME.

In dedicating his poem to Burlington, who favored the Palladian style, Pope was honoring the contemporary arbiter of architectural taste—indeed of taste in all the arts, although Burlington's preference for Italian opera was beginning to seem extravagant. The main interest of the essay, however—the work of a poet who took every opportunity for satire—lies in the discussion of how *not* to build a great house or make a great garden. This interest in good sense reaches its prolonged climax in the brilliant account of Timon's villa and the dinners served there. Pope would have agreed with the judgment made by Anthony Trollope 140 years later in *Sir Harry Hotspur of Humblethwaite:* "a great man goes to work with great means on a great pile, and makes a great failure. The world perceives that grace and beauty have escaped him."

The text is that of the first edition (1731), corrected in accordance with Pope's revisions. The poem was titled *Of the Use of Riches* when it appeared in Pope's *Works* (1735).

ARGUMENT

The Vanity of Expence in People of Wealth and Quality. The abuse of the word *Taste, v.* 13. That the first principle and foundation, in this as in every thing else, is *Good Sense, v.* 40. The chief proof of it is to *follow Nature,* even in works of mere Luxury and Elegance. Instanced in *Architecture* and *Gardening,* where all must be adapted to the *Genius* and *Use* of the Place, and the Beauties not forced into it, but resulting from it, *v.* 50. How men are disappointed in their most expensive undertakings, for want of this true Foundation, without which nothing can please *long,* if *at all;* and the best *Examples* and *Rules* will but be perverted into something *burdensome* or *ridiculous,*

v. 65, &c. to 98. A description of the false *Taste* of
Magnificence; the first grand Error of which is to
imagine that *Greatness* consists in the *Size* and *Dimension*, instead of the *Proportion* and *Harmony* of the
whole, v. 99, and the second, either in joining together
Parts incoherent, or too *minutely resembling*, or in the
Repetition of the *same* too frequently, *v.* 115, &c. A
word or two of false Taste in *Books*, in *Music*, in
Painting, even in *Preaching* and *Prayer*, and lastly in
Entertainments, v. 133, &c. Yet PROVIDENCE is justified
in giving Wealth to be squandered in this manner,
since it is dispersed to the Poor and Laborious part of
mankind, *v.* 169. [Recurring to what is laid down in
the first book, Ep. ii.[1] and in the Epistle preceding
this, *v.* 161, &c.[2]] What are the *proper Objects* of
Magnificence, and a proper field for the Expence of
Great Men, v. 177, &c., and finally, the Great and
Public Works which become a *Prince, v.* 191, *to the
end.*

'Tis strange, the Miser should his Cares employ
To *gain* those riches he can ne'er *enjoy:*
Is it less strange, the Prodigal should *waste*
His Wealth, to purchase what he ne'er can *taste?*
Not for himself he sees, or hears, or eats;
Artists must chuse his Pictures, Music, Meats:
He buys for *Topham*° Drawings and Designs,
For *Pembroke*° Statues, dirty Gods, and Coins;
Rare Monkish Manuscripts for *Hearne*° alone,
And Books for *Mead*, and Butterflies for *Sloane.*°   10
Think we all these are for himself? no more
Than his fine Wife, alas! or finer Whore.
    For what has *Virro*° painted, built, and planted?
Only to shew, *how many* Tastes he wanted.
What brought Sir *Visto's*° ill got Wealth to waste?
Some Dæmon whisper'd, "*Visto! have a Taste.*"

Heav'n visits with a *Taste* the wealthy Fool,
And needs no Rod but *Ripley*° with a Rule.
See! sportive Fate, to punish aukward Pride,
Bids *Bubo*° build, and sends him such a Guide: 20
A standing Sermon! at each Year's expence,
That never Coxcomb reach'd Magnificence.
    You show us, *Rome* was glorious, not profuse,
And pompous Buildings once were things of use.
Yet shall (my Lord) your just, your noble Rules
Fill half the Land with *Imitating Fools,*
Who random Drawings from your Sheets shall take,
And of one Beauty many Blunders make;
Load some vain Church with old Theatric State,
Turn Arcs of Triumph to a Garden-gate;   30
Reverse your Ornaments, and hang them all
On some patch'd Doghole ek'd with Ends of Wall;
Then clap four slices of Pilaster° on 't,
That, lac'd with bits of Rustic,° makes a Front.
Shall call the Winds thro' long Arcades to roar,
Proud to catch cold at a *Venetian* door;°
Conscious they act a true *Palladian* part,
And if they starve,° they starve by Rules of Art.
    Oft have you hinted to your Brother Peer,
A certain Truth, which many buy too dear: 40
Something there is, more needful than Expence,
And something previous ev'n to Taste—'Tis *Sense;*
Good Sense, which only is the Gift of Heav'n,
And tho' no Science,° fairly worth the Seven:°
A Light, which in *yourself* you must perceive;
Jones and *Le Nôtre*° have it not to give.
    To build, to plant, whatever you intend,
To rear the Column, or the Arch to bend,
To swell the Terras, or to sink the Grot;
In all, let *Nature* never be forgot.   50
But treat the Goddess like a modest Fair,
Nor over-dress, nor leave her wholly bare;

Of the Use of Riches. **1. Ep. ii.:** i.e., of *An Essay on Man* (see
above). **2. 161, &c.:** in the third of the *Moral Essays.* **7.
Topham:** [Pope's note] A Gentleman famous for a judicious
collection of Drawings. **8. Pembroke:** Thomas Herbert
(*c.* 1656–1733), Eighth Earl of Pembroke. **9. Hearne:** Thomas
Hearne (1678–1735), the famous medieval scholar. **10. Mead,
Sloane:** [Pope's note] Two eminent Physicians; the one had
an excellent Library, the other the finest collection in Europe
of natural curiosities; both men of great learning and
humanity. [It was largely on the strength of Sloane's collection
that the British Museum was founded in 1753.] **13. Virro:**
borrowed from Juvenal's fifth satire. **15. Visto:** amusingly
adopted from the current gardening terminology; a vista was,
as now, a view stretching into the distance.

18. Ripley: [Pope's note] This man was a carpenter, employ'd
by [Sir Robert Walpole], who rais'd him to an Architect, without any genius in the art; and after some wretched proofs of his
insufficiency in public Buildings, made him Comptroller of
the Board of Works. **20. Bubo:** Bubb Dodington, a Whig
politician and prominent literary patron of the day. **33.
Pilaster:** rectangular column. **34. Rustic:** stone either left
with rough surface or made to appear so. **36. Venetian door:**
[Pope's note] A door or window, so called, from being much
practised at Venice, by Palladio and others. **38. starve:** suffer
extreme cold. **44. Science:** acquired knowledge. **the Seven:**
the seven liberal arts taught in the medieval university. **46.
Jones, Le Nôtre:** [Pope's note] *Inigo Jones* the celebrated
Architect, and M. *Le Nôtre*, the designer of the best Gardens of
France.

Let not each Beauty ev'ry where be spy'd,
Where half the Skill is decently to hide.
He gains all Points, who *pleasingly confounds*,
Surprizes, *varies*, and *conceals the Bounds*.

Consult the *Genius* of the *Place* in all,
That tells the Waters or to rise, or fall,
Or helps th' ambitious Hill the Heav'ns to scale,
Or scoops in circling Theatres° the Vale,   60
Calls in the Country, catches op'ning Glades,
Joins willing Woods, and varies Shades from Shades,
Now breaks, or now directs, th' intending Lines;°
Paints as you plant, and, as you work, *Designs*.

Still follow *Sense*, of ev'ry Art the Soul,
Parts answ'ring Parts shall slide into a Whole,
Spontaneous Beauties all around advance,
Start ev'n from *Difficulty*, strike, from *Chance*;
Nature shall join you; *Time* shall make it grow
A Work to wonder at—perhaps a STOW.°   70

Without it, proud *Versailles*°! thy Glory falls,
And *Nero's* Terrasses° desert their Walls:
The vast *Parterres*° a thousand hands shall make,
Lo! *Cobham* comes, and floats them with a *Lake:*
Or cut wide *Views* thro' Mountains to the Plain,
You'll wish your Hill or shelter'd Seat again.
Ev'n in an Ornament its Place remark,
Nor in an Hermitage set Dr. Clarke.°

Behold *Villario's*° ten years Toil compleat,
His *Quincunx*° darkens, his Espaliers° meet,   80
The Wood supports the Plain, the Parts unite,
And strength of Shade contends with strength of
        Light;
A waving Glow the bloomy Beds display,
Blushing in bright Diversities of Day,°
With silver-quiv'ring Rills mæander'd o'er—

Enjoy them, you! *Villario*, can no more;
Tir'd of the Scene Parterres and Fountains yield,
He finds at last he better likes a Field.

Thro' his young Woods how pleas'd *Sabinus*°
        stray'd,
Or sate delighted in the thick'ning Shade,   90
With annual Joy the red'ning Shoots to greet,
Or see the stretching Branches long to meet!
His Son's fine Taste an op'ner *Vista* loves,
Foe to the *Dryads* of his Father's Groves;
One *boundless Green*, or *flourish'd Carpet* views,
With all the mournful Family of *Yews;*
The thriving Plants, ignoble Broomsticks made,
Now sweep those Allies they were born to shade.

At° *Timon's Villa* let us pass a Day,   99
Where all cry out, "What Sums are thrown away!"
So proud, so grand, of that stupendous Air,
Soft and *Agreeable* come never there.
Greatness, with *Timon*, dwells in such a Draught°
As brings all *Brobdi[n]gnag*° before your Thought.
To compass this, his Building is a Town,
His Pond an Ocean, his Parterre a Down;
Who but must laugh the Master when he sees?
A puny Insect, shiv'ring at a Breeze!
Lo, what huge Heaps of Littleness° around!
The Whole, a labour'd Quarry above ground!"   110
Two *Cupids* squirt before: a Lake behind
Improves° the keenness of the Northern Wind.
His *Gardens* next your Admiration call,
On ev'ry side you look, behold the Wall!
No pleasing Intricacies intervene,
No artful Wildeness to perplex the Scene:
Grove nods at Grove, each Ally has a Brother,
And half the Platform just reflects the other.
The suff'ring Eye inverted Nature sees,
Trees cut to Statues, Statues thick as trees,   120

---

60. Theatres: tiers. **63. th' intending Lines:** the lines
you have designed. **70. Stow:** [Pope's note] The seat and
gardens of the Lord Viscount Cobham in Buckinghamshire.
71. Versailles: the palace of the French kings; the gardens
there were Le Nôtre's masterpiece. **72. Nero's Terrasses:**
The Emperor Nero built himself a celebrated palace, which he
called his golden house. It was profusely adorned with gold
and precious stones, and its spacious grounds contained artificial lakes, woods, and gardens. **73. Parterres:** lawns with
flower beds. **78. Dr. Clarke:** Samuel Clarke (1675–1729), the
philosopher and divine whose bust Queen Caroline had placed
along with others in the mock hermitage she built in Richmond
Park. **79. Villario:** a name made up from *villa*, a (Roman)
country house. **80. Quincunx:** four trees planted in a square
around a fifth. **Espaliers:** either fruit trees trained on lattice,
or the lattices themselves. **84. Blushing . . . Day:** A line
Pope had already used in an early poem, *The Garden* (1736),
written in imitation of Cowley.

89. Sabinus: adapted from the name of the countryside
around Rome, where Horace had a farm. **99–168. At . . .
ill:** [Pope's note] This description is intended to comprize
the principles of a false Taste of Magnificence, and to
exemplify what was said before, that nothing but Good Sense
can obtain it. [It was thought to be aimed at James Brydges,
Duke of Chandos, who had built a great house, Cannons,
near Edgware.] **103. Draught:** design. **104. Brobdi[n]gnag:**
In referring to the land of giants in *Gulliver's Travels* (1726),
Pope may have had particularly in mind the king's palace.
109. huge . . . Littleness: Pope remembered Isaac Watts's
line in *Horae Lyricae* (1706): "Huge Heaps of Shining
Oar." (See the selections from Watts in Part Three.) **112.
Improves:** a verb popular among the garden enthusiasts,
here turned against them.

With here a Fountain, never to be play'd,
And there a Summer-house, that knows no Shade;
Here *Amphitrite*° sails thro' Myrtle bow'rs;
There *Gladiators*° fight, or die, in flow'rs;
Un-water'd see the drooping Sea-horse mourn,
And Swallows roost in *Nilus*'° dusty Urn.

My Lord advances with majestic mien,
Smit with the mighty pleasure, to be seen:
But soft—by regular approach—not yet—
First thro' the length of yon hot Terras sweat;   130
And when up ten steep Slopes you've dragg'd your
    thighs,
Just at his Study-door he'll bless your Eyes.

His *Study?* with what Authors is it stor'd?
In Books, not Authors, curious is my Lord;
To all their *dated Backs* he turns you round;
These *Aldus*° printed, those *Du Suëil*° has *bound*.
Lo some are *Vellom*, and the rest as good
For all his Lordship knows, but they are *Wood*.
For *Locke* or *Milton* 'tis in vain to look,
These Shelves admit not any Modern book.   140

And now the Chappel's silver bell you hear,
That summons you to all the Pride of Pray'r:
Light Quirks of Musick, broken° and uneven,
Make the Soul dance upon a Jig to Heav'n.°
On painted Cielings you devoutly stare,
Where sprawl the Saints of *Verrio*, or *Laguerre*,°
On gilded Clouds in fair expansion lie,
And bring all Paradise before your Eye.
To Rest, the Cushion, and soft *Dean* invite,
Who never mentions Hell to Ears polite.°   150
But hark! the chiming Clocks to Dinner call;
A hundred Footsteps scrape the marble Hall:
The rich Buffet° well-colour'd° *Serpents* grace,
And gaping *Tritons* spew to wash your Face.

Is this a Dinner? this a Genial Room?
No, 'tis a Temple, and a Hecatomb;°
A solemn Sacrifice, perform'd in State,
You drink by Measure, and to Minutes eat.
So quick retires each flying Course, you'd swear
Sancho's dread Doctor and his *Wand*° were there: 160
Between each Act the trembling Salvers ring,
From Soup to Sweetwine, and *God bless the King.*°
In Plenty starving, tantaliz'd in State,
And complaisantly° help'd to all I hate,
Treated, caress'd, and tir'd, I take my leave,
Sick of his civil Pride from Morn to Eve;
I curse such lavish Cost, and little Skill,
And swear, no Day was ever past so ill.

Yet° hence the *Poor* are cloth'd, the *Hungry* fed;
Health to himself, and to his Infants *Bread*   170
The Lab'rer bears: What his hard Heart denies,
His charitable Vanity supplies.

Another Age shall see the golden Ear
Imbrown° the Slope, and nod on the Parterre,
Deep Harvests bury all his Pride has plann'd,
And laughing *Ceres*° re-assume the Land.

Who then shall grace, or who improve, the Soil?
Who plants like BATHURST,° or who builds like BOYLE.°
'Tis *Use* alone that sanctifies Expence,
And Splendor borrows all her Rays from *Sense*.   180

His Father's Acres who enjoys in peace,
Or makes his Neighbours glad, if he encrease;
Whose chearful Tenants bless their yearly toil,
Yet to their Lord owe more than to the soil;
Whose ample Lawns are not asham'd to feed
The milky Heifer and deserving Steed;
Whose rising Forests, not for pride or show,
But future Buildings, future Navies, grow;

123. Amphitrite: the goddess of the sea. **124. Gladiators:** [Pope's note] [copies of the] two famous Statues of the *Gladiator pugnans* and the *Gladiator moriens.* **126. Nilus:** a statue of the river god. **136. Aldus:** the famous late fifteenth-century printer who introduced italic type. **Du Suëil:** a well-known eighteenth-century binder who lived in Paris. **143. broken:** Pope may have in mind the technical sense of "played on stringed instruments." **144. Make . . . Heav'n:** Note the jig rhythm of this line. **146. Verrio, Laguerre:** [Pope's note] Verrio painted many cielings, &c. at Windsor, Hampton-court, &c., and Laguerre at Blenheim-castle, and other Places. **150. Who . . . polite:** [Pope's note] This is a fact; a reverend Dean preaching at Court, threatned the sinner with punishment in "a place which he thought it not decent to name in so polite an assembly." **153. Buffet:** sideboard. **well-colour'd:** colored realistically.

156. Hecatomb: public sacrifice. **160. Sancho's . . . Wand:** [Pope's note] See Don Quixote, chap. xlvii. **162. God . . . King:** the salutation on drinking the royal health. **164. complaisantly:** politely. **169-204. Yet . . . Kings:** [Pope's note] The *Moral* of the whole, where Providence is justified in giving Wealth to those who squander it in this manner. A bad Taste employs more hands, and diffuses Expence more than a good one. [Cf. *An Essay on Man*, above, ii. 230-48.] **174. Imbrown:** a word Milton invented. **176. Ceres:** the goddess of fertility. **178. Bathurst:** To Allen, Lord Bathurst, Pope was later to address a further essay on the use of riches, now the third of the *Moral Essays.* **Boyle:** the family name of the Earl of Burlington to whom this essay is dedicated. By 1731 Burlington was regarded as the arbiter of architectural taste in England. He had designed several great buildings, and the latest, the Assembly Rooms at York, were to be opened to the public in the following year.

Let *His* Plantations stretch from Down to Down,
First shade a Country, and then raise a Town.   190
    You too proceed! make falling Arts your care,
Erect new Wonders, and the Old repair;
Jones and *Palladio* to themselves restore,
And be whate'er *Vitruvius*° was before:
Till Kings call forth th' Ideas of your Mind,
(Proud to accomplish what such hands design'd)
Bid Harbors open, publick Ways extend,
Bid Temples, worthier of the God, ascend;
Bid the broad Arch the dang'rous Flood contain,
The Mole projected break the roaring Main;   200
Back to his bounds their subject Sea command,
And roll obedient Rivers° thro' the Land:
These Honours, Peace to happy *Britain* brings,
These are Imperial Works, and worthy *Kings*.

AN EPISTLE
FROM MR. POPE,
TO DR. ARBUTHNOT

Neque sermonibus Vulgi *dederis te, nec in* Præmiis *humanis
spem posueris rerum tuarum: suis te oportet illecebris ipsa
Virtus trahat ad verum decus. Quid de te alii loquantur,
ipsi videant, sed loquentur tamen.*°

TULLY.

※

This poem, written between 1731 and 1734, was
designed to pay off some old scores against writers Pope
had quarreled with, but that is only the dull part of the
story. It would be fairer to say that Pope felt the need
to clarify and defend his position as a writer and as a
satirist. For this epistle is one of the masterpieces of our
literature. It is that because its subject matter—even
though partly commonplace or unpleasant—is recalled
by a mind as intense as it is magisterial, as quivering as
it is serene, as delicate as it is strong. And not only that,
but by a mind gifted with the power to achieve the sort
of utterance we call classic—utterance which, to put it
negatively, leaves nothing to be desired. Pope's expression here is like that achieved by Shakespeare in *Hamlet*
where every phrase hits a bull's-eye, and usually by
means of language used as nobody has used it before.
Illustration is invidious when the claim is for something
so widespread. Yet not all readers have seen that the
poem has this merit—for the simple reason that a line
like: "Just hint a fault, and hesitate dislike" is so well
known that its linguistic adventurousness is overlooked.
It was this poem that caused Charles Lamb to ask, "Do
you think I would not wish to have been friends with
such a man as this?" Lamb, who knew that Pope had
been charged with cruelty, was a man who thought it a
privilege to associate with men of genius; he could glory
in the beauty of the tiger even if part of the beauty was
its teeth.

Pope was wise to address his poem to such a man as
Arbuthnot, who was well respected, not only as an
author himself, but as a medical doctor; as the poem
recalls, he had been Physician in Ordinary to Queen
Anne. His kindly presence is implied in the poem, and
he breaks in with remarks of his own, all of which help
to lift the argument above the pettily personal. So does
the use of the name Atticus (that of a Roman knight,
who was a friend of Cicero) for Addison. The inspiration
for the character sketch (ll. 193–214), which Pope had
written earlier, came from his dislike of Addison the
man—a dislike he regretted because of his admiration
for Addison the writer.

The text is that of the first edition (1735, dated 1734),
incorporating Pope's few revisions.

※

ADVERTISEMENT

THIS *Paper is a Sort of Bill of Complaint, begun many
years since, and drawn up by snatches, as the several
Occasions offer'd. I had no thoughts of publishing it, till
it pleas'd some Persons of Rank and Fortune* [the Authors
of Verses to the Imitator of Horace, *and of an* Epistle
to a Doctor of Divinity from a Nobleman at Hampton
Court,]¹ *to attack in a very extraordinary manner, not
only my Writings (of which being publick the Publick
is judge) but my Person, Morals, and Family, whereof
to those who know me not, a truer Information may be*

---

194. Vitruvius: (b. 88 B.C.), Roman architect and engineer
and author of *De Architectura.* **202. obedient Rivers:** the
canals which were then being made and which were greatly
used for trade even after the railways had been built a century
later. AN EPISTLE TO DR. ARBUTHNOT. **Neque . . . tamen:**
"You will not give yourself up to the flattery of the vulgar,
nor hope for success in your affairs from mortal hands; virtue
herself will lead to true honour; see that you follow her
guidance. What others see fit to say of you, let them say"
(Cicero, *De Re Publica*, VI. xxiii).

Advertisement. **1. some . . . Court:** Lady Mary Wortley
Montagu (1689–1762) and John Hervey (1696–1743), Baron
Hervey of Ickworth. (See the selection from Lady Mary
in Part Three.)

requisite. Being divided between the Necessity to say something of Myself, and my own Laziness to undertake so awkward a Task, I thought it the shortest way to put the last hand to this Epistle. If it have any thing pleasing, it will be That by which I am most desirous to please, the Truth *and the* Sentiment; *and if any thing offensive, it will be only to those I am least sorry to offend, the* Vicious *or the* Ungenerous.

Many will know their own Pictures in it, there being not a Circumstance but what is true; but I have, for the most part spar'd their Names, and they may escape being laugh'd at, if they please.

I would have some of them know, it was owing to the Request of the learned and candid Friend to whom it is inscribed, that I make not as free use of theirs as they have done of mine. However I shall have this Advantage, and Honour, on my side, that whereas by their proceeding, any Abuse may be directed at any man, no Injury can possibly be done by mine, since a Nameless Character can never be found out, but by its Truth *and* Likeness.

SHUT, shut the door, good *John*°! fatigu'd I said,
Tye up the knocker,° say I'm sick, I'm dead,
The Dog-star rages!° nay 'tis past a doubt,
All *Bedlam*,° or *Parnassus*, is let out:
Fire in each eye, and Papers in each hand,
They rave, recite, and madden° round the land.
    What Walls can guard me, or what Shades can
        hide?
They pierce my Thickets, thro' my Grot° they glide,
By land, by water, they renew the charge,
They stop the Chariot, and they board the Barge.   10
No place is sacred, not the Church is free,
Ev'n *Sunday* shines no *Sabbath-day* to me:
Then from the *Mint*° walks forth the Man of Ryme,
Happy! to catch me, just at Dinner-time.
    Is there a Parson, much be-mus'd in Beer,
A maudlin Poetess, a ryming Peer,
A Clerk, foredoom'd his Father's soul to cross,
Who pens a Stanza° when he should *engross*°?
Is there, who lock'd from Ink and Paper, scrawls
With desp'rate Charcoal round his darken'd walls? 20

1. **John:** his servant. 2. **Tye . . . knocker:** The doorknocker was muffled when someone in the house was sick. 3. **The Dog-star rages:** It was August (1734) when Pope put the poem into final shape. In ancient Rome poetry was rehearsed in late summer. 4. **Bedlam:** the name of a London lunatic asylum. 6. **madden:** a word Pope invented. 8. **Grot:** Pope's grotto at Twickenham. 13. **the Mint:** a sanctuary for debtors in Southwark. 18. **Stanza:** here, a love poem. **engross:** copy in a large hand.

All fly to *Twit'nam*, and in humble strain
Apply to me, to keep them mad or vain.
Arthur,° whose giddy Son neglects the Laws,
Imputes to me and my damn'd works the cause:
Poor *Cornus*° sees his frantic Wife elope,
And curses Wit, and Poetry, and *Pope*.
    Friend to my Life, (which did not you prolong,
The World had wanted many an idle Song)
What *Drop* or *Nostrum*° can this Plague remove?
Or which must end me, a Fool's Wrath or Love? 30
A dire Dilemma! either way I'm sped,°
If Foes, they write, if Friends, they read me dead.
Seiz'd and ty'd down to judge, how wretched I!
Who can't be silent, and who will not lye;
To laugh, were want of Goodness and of Grace,
And to be grave, exceeds all Pow'r of Face.
I sit with sad Civility, I read
With honest anguish, and an aking head;
And drop at last, but in unwilling ears,
This saving counsel, "Keep your Piece nine years."° 40
    Nine years!° cries he, who high in *Drury-lane*°
Lull'd by soft Zephyrs thro' the broken Pane,
Rymes e're he wakes, and prints before *Term*° ends,
Oblig'd by hunger and Request of friends:
"The Piece you think is incorrect? why take it,
I'm all submission, what you'd have it, make it."
    Three things another's modest wishes bound,
My Friendship, and a Prologue,° and ten Pound.
    Pitholeon° sends to me: "You know his Grace,
I want a Patron; ask him for a Place." 50
Pitholeon libell'd me—"but here's a Letter
Informs you Sir, 'twas when he knew no better.
Dare you refuse him? *Curl*° invites to dine,
He'll write a *Journal*,° or he'll turn *Divine*.°"
    Bless me! a Packet.—"'Tis a stranger sues,
A Virgin Tragedy, an Orphan Muse."

23. **Arthur:** Arthur Moore, a politician, and his son James Moore-Smythe. 25. **Cornus:** Latin for *cuckold*. 29. **Drop or Nostrum:** medicines. 31. **sped:** despatched, killed. 40. **Keep . . . years:** This was Horace's counsel to the poet too eager for print. 41. **Nine years:** Note the transition, indeed the overlap, from paragraph to paragraph. **Drury-lane:** then a disreputable neighborhood. 43. **Term:** the legal term, the period preferred for publishing. 48. **a Prologue:** to a play; Dryden got as much as six pounds for one. 49. **Pitholeon:** [Pope's note] The name taken from a foolish Poet at *Rhodes*, who pretended much to Greek. 53. **Curl:** Edmund Curl, or Curll (1675–1747), a notorious London publisher. 54. **Journal:** a periodical that, according to Pope, mixed "news and scandal." **Divine:** Pope seems to have had in mind the poet Leonard Welsted (1688–1747), who at this time was contemplating a religious work.

If I dislike it, "Furies, death and rage!"
If I approve, "Commend it to the Stage."
There (thank my Stars) my whole Commission ends,
The Play'rs and I are, luckily, no friends.   60
Fir'd that the House reject him, "'Sdeath I'll print it
And shame the Fools—your Int'rest, Sir, with *Lintot.*°"
Lintot, dull rogue! will think your price too much.
"Not Sir, if you revise it, and retouch."
All my demurrs but double his attacks,
At last he whispers "Do, and we go snacks.°"
Glad of a quarrel, strait I clap the door,
Sir, let me see your works and you no more.°

    'Tis sung, when *Midas'* Ears° began to spring,
(*Midas,* a sacred Person and a King)   70
His very Minister who spy'd them first,
(Some say his Queen) was forc'd to speak, or burst.
And is not mine, my Friend, a sorer case,
When ev'ry Coxcomb perks° them in my face?
A[rbuthnot]. "Good friend forbear! you deal in
        dang'rous things,
I'd never name Queens, Ministers, or Kings;
Keep close to Ears,° and those let Asses prick,
'Tis nothing"—P[ope]. Nothing? if they bite and kick?
Out with it, *Dunciad!* let the secret pass,
That Secret to each Fool, that he's an Ass: 80
The truth once told, (and wherefore shou'd we lie?)
The Queen of *Midas* slept, and so may I.
    You think this cruel? take it for a rule,
No creature smarts so little as a Fool.
Let Peals of Laughter, *Codrus°!* round thee break,
Thou unconcern'd canst hear the mighty Crack.
Pit, Box and Gall'ry in convulsions hurl'd,
Thou stand'st unshook amidst a bursting World.
Who shames a Scribler? break one cobweb thro',
He spins the slight, self-pleasing thread anew;   90
Destroy his Fib, or Sophistry; in vain,
The Creature's at his dirty work again;
Thron'd in the Centre of his thin designs;
Proud of a vast Extent of flimzy lines.°
Whom have I hurt? has Poet yet, or Peer,

Lost the arch'd eye-brow, or *Parnassian* sneer°?
And has not *Colly*° still his Lord, and Whore?
His Butchers *Henley,*° his Free-masons *Moor°?*
Does not one Table *Bavius*° still admit?
Still to one Bishop *Philips*° seem a Wit?   100
Still *Sapho*°—A. Hold! for God-sake—you'll offend:
No Names—be calm—learn Prudence of a Friend:
I too could write, and I am twice as tall,°
But Foes like these!—P. One Flatt'rer's worse than all;
Of all mad Creatures, if the Learn'd are right,
It is the Slaver kills, and not the Bite.
A Fool quite angry is quite innocent;
Alas! 'tis ten times worse when they *repent.*°

    One dedicates, in high Heroic prose,
And ridicules beyond a hundred foes;   110
One from all *Grubstreet*° will my fame defend,
And, more abusive, calls himself my friend.
This prints my Letters, that expects a Bribe,
And others roar aloud, "Subscribe,° subscribe."

    There are, who to my Person pay their court,
I cough like *Horace,*° and tho' lean, am short,
Ammon's great Son° one shoulder had too high,
Such *Ovid's* nose,° and "Sir! you have an *Eye*—
Go on, obliging Creatures, make me see
All that disgrac'd my Betters, met in me: 120
Say for my comfort, languishing in bed,
"Just so immortal *Maro°* held his head:"

---

62. **Lintot:** Bernard Lintot (1675–1736), publisher of many of Pope's works. 66. **go snacks:** divide profits. Dryden had used this colloquial expression. 68. **Sir . . . more:** a line of powerful monosyllables, with many stresses. 69. **Midas' Ears:** The King of Phrygia's ears were turned into ass's ears after he awarded Pan the prize in his musical contest with Apollo. 74. **perks:** thrusts forward in an impudent manner. 77. **Keep . . . Ears:** Whisper your satire, and into the ears of humble people. 85. **Codrus:** the name, perhaps fictitious, of a poet ridiculed by Virgil and Juvenal. 93–94. **designs, lines:** words applicable to poems.

96. **Parnassian sneer:** quoted from *The Dunciad,* II. 5. 97. **Colly:** Colley Cibber (1671–1757), actor, playwright, and Poet Laureate from 1730; he succeeded Lewis Theobald as hero of a revised version of *The Dunciad* published in 1743. 98. **Henley:** John Henley (1692–1759), the popular preacher, had delivered a "butchers' lecture," i.e., a sermon for butchers, five years before. **Moor:** James Moore-Smythe, who was a prominent member of this organization. 99. **Bavius:** a minor poet who attacked Virgil and Horace. 100. **Philips:** The poet Ambrose Philips (*c.* 1675–1749), Pope's old enemy, was now secretary to the Bishop of Armagh. (See the selections from Philips in Part Three.) 101. **Sapho:** Under the name of the Greek poetess Pope repeatedly scored the writer Lady Mary Wortley Montagu after their quarrel. 103. **twice as tall:** Pope was less than five feet tall. 108. **Alas . . . repent:** Pope is probably referring to Aaron Hill (1685–1750) and Thomas Cooke (*c.* 1703–56). (See the selections from Hill in Part Three.) 111. **Grubstreet:** now Milton Street; then the home of literary hacks. 114. **Subscribe:** Books were often published by subscription. 116. **cough . . . Horace:** Horace had referred in his writings to his cough and to his small plump body. 117. **Ammon's . . . Son:** Alexander the Great. 118. **Ovid's nose:** Ovid's full name was Ovidius Naso. 122. **Maro:** Virgil.

And when I die, be sure you let me know
Great *Homer* dy'd three thousand years ago.

Why did I write? what sin to me unknown
Dipt me in Ink, my Parents', or my own?
As yet a Child, nor yet a Fool to Fame,
I lisp'd in Numbers, for the Numbers came.
I left no Calling for this idle trade,
No Duty broke, no Father dis-obey'd.   130
The Muse but serv'd to ease some Friend, not Wife,
To help me thro' this long Disease, my Life,
To second, Arburthnot! thy Art and Care,
And teach, the Being you preserv'd, to bear.

But why then publish? *Granville* the polite,
And knowing *Walsh*, would tell me I could write;
Well-natur'd *Garth* inflam'd with early praise,
And *Congreve* lov'd, and *Swift* endur'd my Lays;
The Courtly *Talbot, Somers, Sheffield* read,
Ev'n mitred *Rochester* would nod the head,   140
And *St. John*'s° self (great *Dryden*'s friends before)
With open arms receiv'd one Poet more.
Happy my Studies, when by these approv'd!
Happier their Author, when by these belov'd!
From these the world will judge of Men and Books,
Not from the *Burnets, Oldmixons,* and *Cooks.*°

Soft were my Numbers, who could take offence
While pure Description held the place of Sense?
Like gentle *Fanny*'s° was my flow'ry Theme,
A painted Mistress, or a purling Stream.°   150
Yet then did *Gildon*° draw his venal quill;
I wish'd the man a dinner, and sate still:
Yet then did *Dennis*° rave in furious fret;
I never answer'd, I was not in debt:
If want provok'd, or madness made them print,
I wag'd no war with *Bedlam* or the *Mint.*

Did some more sober Critic come abroad?
If wrong, I smil'd; if right, I kiss'd the rod.
Pains, reading, study, are their just pretence,
And all they want is spirit, taste, and sense.   160
Comma's and points they set exactly right,
And 'twere a sin to rob them of their Mite.
Yet ne'r one sprig of Laurel grac'd these ribalds,
From slashing *Bentley*° down to pidling *Tibalds.*°
Each Wight who reads not, and but scans and spells,
Each Word-catcher that lives on syllables,
E'en such small Critics some regard may claim,
Preserv'd in *Milton*'s or in *Shakespear*'s name.
Pretty! in Amber to observe the forms
Of hairs, or straws, or dirt, or grubs, or worms;   170
The things, we know, are neither rich nor rare,
But wonder how the Devil they got there?

Were others angry? I excus'd them too;
Well might they rage; I gave them but their due.
A man's true merit 'tis not hard to find,
But each man's secret standard in his mind,
That Casting-weight Pride adds to Emptiness,
This, who can gratify? for who can *guess?*
The Bard° whom pilf'red Pastorals renown,
Who turns a *Persian* Tale for half a crown,°   180
Just writes to make his barrenness appear,
And strains from hard-bound brains eight lines
    a-year:
He, who still wanting tho' he lives on theft,
Steals much, spends little, yet has nothing left:
And he, who now to sense, now nonsense leaning,
Means not, but blunders round about a meaning:
And he, whose Fustian's so sublimely bad,
It is not Poetry, but Prose run mad:
All these, my modest Satire bad *translate,*
And own'd, that nine such Poets made a *Tate.*°   190
How did they fume, and stamp, and roar, and chafe?
And swear, not *Addison* himself was safe.

Peace to all such! but were there One whose fires
True Genius kindles, and fair Fame inspires,

135–41. Granville . . . St. John: Pope's early friends and patrons. **146. Burnets . . . Cooks:** [Pope's note] Authors of secret and scandalous History. **149. Fanny:** Pope's name for Lord Hervey (1696–1743), court Vice Chamberlain and confidant of Queen Caroline; he had recently attacked Pope, who considered him an "effeminate courtier-poet." Pope later refers to him as Sporus (see ll. 305 ff.). **150. A painted . . . Stream:** Pope had already used this line, almost verbatim from Addison, for similar effect in his imitation of Chaucer, *January and May*, l. 455. **151. Gildon:** Charles Gildon (1665–1724), a miscellaneous writer who had attacked *The Rape of the Lock* (see above). **153. Dennis:** The playwright and critic John Dennis (1657–1734) had also attacked this poem on its appearance in letters not printed till 1728. (See the selection from Dennis earlier in Part Two.)

164. Bentley: Richard Bentley (1662–1742), a classical scholar and the only great name Pope attacks; though a master of textual criticism when dealing with ancient works, Bentley made himself ridiculous by applying his principles to *Paradise Lost* as if it were an ancient work. **Tibalds:** Lewis Theobald (1688–1744), the hero of the first version of *The Dunciad* (see below). **179. The Bard:** Ambrose Philips. **180. half a crown:** the price of a common harlot. **190. Tate:** Nahum Tate (1652–1715), playwright and poet. He succeeded Dryden as Poet Laureate in 1692. In 1696 he and Nicholas Brady published a humdrum translation of the Psalms.

Blest with each Talent and each Art to please,
And born to write, converse, and live with ease:°
Shou'd such a man, too fond to rule° alone,
Bear, like the *Turk*, no brother near the throne,°
View him with scornful, yet with jealous eyes,
And hate for Arts that caus'd himself to rise;   200
Damn with faint praise,° assent with civil leer,
And without sneering, teach the rest to sneer;
Willing to wound, and yet afraid to strike,°
Just hint a fault, and hesitate dislike;
Alike reserv'd to blame, or to commend,
A tim'rous foe, and a suspicious friend,
Dreading ev'n fools, by Flatterers besieg'd,
And so obliging that he ne'er oblig'd;
Like *Cato*,° give his little Senate laws,
And sit attentive to his own applause;   210
While Wits and Templers° ev'ry sentence raise,
And wonder with a foolish face of praise.
Who but must laugh, if such a man there be?
Who would not weep, if *Atticus* were he!
    What tho' my Name stood rubric on the walls?
Or plaister'd posts, with Claps in capitals?°
Or smoking forth, a hundred Hawkers load,
On Wings of Winds came flying all abroad?
I sought no homage from the Race that write;
I kept, like *Asian* Monarchs, from their sight: 220
Poems I heeded (now be-rym'd so long)
No more than Thou, great GEORGE! a Birth-day Song.
I ne'r with Wits or Witlings past my days,
To spread about the Itch of Verse and Praise;

Nor like a Puppy daggled° thro' the Town,
To fetch and carry° Sing-song up and down;
Nor at Rehearsals sweat, and mouth'd, and cry'd,
With Handkerchief and Orange° at my side:
But sick of Fops, and Poetry, and Prate,
To *Bufo*° left the whole *Castalian* State.   230
    Proud, as *Apollo* on his forked hill,°
Sate full-blown *Bufo*, puff'd by ev'ry quill;
Fed with soft Dedication all day long,
Horace and he went hand in hand in song.°
His Library, (where Busts of Poets dead
And a true *Pindar* stood without a head)
Receiv'd of Wits an undistinguish'd race,
Who first his Judgment ask'd, and then a Place:
Much they extoll'd his Pictures, much his Seat,
And flatter'd ev'ry day, and some days eat: 240
Till grown more frugal in his riper days,
He pay'd some Bards with Port, and some with Praise,
To some a dry Rehearsal was assign'd,
And others (harder still) he pay'd in kind.
Dryden alone (what wonder?) came not nigh,
Dryden alone escap'd this judging eye:
But still the Great have kindness in reserve,
He help'd to bury whom he help'd to starve.°
    May some choice Patron bless each gray goose
        quill°!
May ev'ry *Bavius* have his *Bufo* still!   250
So, when a Statesman wants a Day's defence,
Or Envy holds a whole Week's war with Sense,
Or simple Pride for Flatt'ry makes demands;
May Dunce by Dunce be whistled off my hands!
Blest be the *Great!* for those they take away,
And those they left me—For they left me GAY,
Left me to see neglected Genius bloom,
Neglected die! and tell it on his Tomb;
Of all thy blameless Life the sole Return   259
My Verse, and QUEENSB'RY° weeping o'er thy Urn!

---

196. write . . . ease: Pope has in mind Boileau's humanistic
ideal for the poet, outlined in *L'Art poétique* (1674):

> *Que les vers ne soient pas votre éternel emploi.*
> *Cultivez vos amis, soyez homme de foi:*
> *C'est peu d'être agréable et charmant dans un livre;*
> *Il faut savoir encore et converser et vivre.*

197. fond to rule: fond of ruling. **198. Bear . . . throne:**
Cf. the following passage from Samuel Garth's Preface to
Claremont (1715): "Experience shows us every Day that there
are Writers who cannot bear a Brother shou'd succeed."
201. Damn . . . praise: Cf. Aulus Gellius, *Noctes Atticae*,
XIX. 3: "It is more disgraceful to be praised coldly than to be
accused bitterly." In coining this famous phrase, Pope recalled
a line from William Wycherley's Prologue to *The Plain
Dealer*. **203. Willing . . . strike:** Cf. *Essay on Criticism*,
above, l. 742. **209. Cato:** a brilliant stroke, for Addison's play
(1713) had taken him for its hero. Pope's famous Prologue
to that play (see above) included the line: "While *Cato* gives
his little Senate laws." **211. Templers:** young barristers who
occupied rooms in the Inner or Middle Temple. **215–16.**
What . . . capitals: Booksellers advertised their wares by
pasting up title pages like placards ("Claps"). Lintot's title
pages often mixed red letters with the black.

225. daggled: traipsed. **226. fetch and carry:** used mainly of
dogs. **228. Orange:** used as smelling salts and as a disinfectant
in the company of the unwashed. **230. Bufo:** the Latin word
for *toad;* appropriately used here (and by Mallet two years
earlier) for a literary patron, since a prominent recent patron
happened to have the name Bubb Dodington. **231. forked
hill:** Mount Parnassus. **234. Horace . . . song:** a reference
to Dodington's being given the place of Maecenas in a recent
paraphrase from Ovid. **248. He . . . starve:** [Pope's note]
Mr. Dryden, after having liv'd in Exigencies, had a magnificent Funeral bestow'd upon him by the contributions of
several Persons of Quality. **249. gray . . . quill:** The graylag
is the common European goose; pens were made from its
feathers. **260. Queensb'ry:** Both Charles Douglas, Third
Duke of Queensberry, and the Duchess had befriended Gay.

Oh let me live my own, and die so too!
To live and die is all I have to do:°
Maintain a Poet's Dignity and Ease,
And see what Friends, and read what Books I please.
Above a Patron, tho' I condescend
Sometimes to call a Minister my Friend:
I was not born for Courts or great Affairs,
I pay my Debts, believe, and say my Pray'rs,
Can sleep without a Poem in my head,
Nor know, if *Dennis* be alive or dead.   270

Why am I ask'd, what next shall see the light?
Heav'ns! was I born for nothing but to write?
Has Life no Joys for me? or (to be grave)
Have I no Friend to serve, no Soul to save?
"I found him close with *Swift*—Indeed? no doubt
(Cries prating *Balbus*°) "something will come out."
'Tis all in vain, deny it as I will.
"No, such a Genius never can lye still,"
And then for mine obligingly mistakes
The first Lampoon Sir *Will.*° or *Bubo* makes.   280
Poor guiltless I! and can I chuse but smile,
When ev'ry Coxcomb knows me by my *Style?*

Curst be the Verse, how well soe'er it flow,
That tends to make one worthy Man my foe,
Give Virtue scandal, Innocence a fear,
Or from the soft-ey'd Virgin steal a tear!
But he, who hurts a harmless neighbour's peace,
Insults fal'n Worth, or Beauty in distress,
Who loves a Lye, lame slander helps about,
Who writes a Libel, or who copies out: 290
That Fop whose pride affects a Patron's name,
Yet absent, wounds an Author's honest fame;
Who can your Merit selfishly approve,
And show the Sense of it, without the Love;
Who has the Vanity to call you Friend,
Yet wants the Honour injur'd to defend;°
Who tells whate'er you think, whate'er you say,
And, if he lye not, must at least betray:
Who to the *Dean* and *silver Bell* can swear,
And sees at *Cannons* what was never there:°   300
Who reads but with a Lust to mis-apply,
Make Satire a Lampoon, and Fiction, Lye.

A Lash like mine no honest man shall dread,
But all such babling blockheads in his stead.
    Let *Sporus*° tremble—A. What? that Thing of
        silk,
Sporus, that mere white Curd of Ass's milk?
Satire or Sense alas! can *Sporus* feel?
Who breaks a Butterfly upon a Wheel?
P. Yet let me flap this Bug with gilded wings,
This painted Child of Dirt that stinks and stings;   310
Whose Buzz the Witty and the Fair annoys,
Yet Wit ne'er tastes, and Beauty ne'er enjoys,
So well-bred Spaniels civilly delight
In mumbling of the Game they dare not bite.
Eternal Smiles his Emptiness betray,
As shallow streams run dimpling all the way.
Whether in florid Impotence he speaks,
And, as the Prompter breathes, the Puppet squeaks;
Or at the Ear of *Eve*, familiar Toad,
Half Froth, half Venom, spits himself abroad,   320
In Puns, or Politicks, or Tales, or Lyes,
Or Spite, or Smut, or Rymes, or Blasphemies.
His Wit all see-saw, between *that* and *this*,
Now high, now low, now Master up, now Miss,
And he himself one vile Antithesis.
Amphibious Thing! that acting either Part,
The trifling Head, or the corrupted Heart!
Fop at the Toilet, Flatt'rer at the Board,
Now trips a Lady, and now struts a Lord.
Eve's Tempter thus the Rabbins have exprest,   330
A Cherub's face, a Reptile all the rest;
Beauty that shocks you, Parts that none will trust,
Wit that can creep, and Pride that licks the dust.

    Not Fortune's Worshipper, nor Fashion's Fool,
Not Lucre's Madman, nor Ambition's Tool,
Not proud, nor servile, be one Poet's praise
That, if he pleas'd, he pleas'd by manly ways;
That Flatt'ry, ev'n to Kings, he held a shame,
And thought a Lye in Verse or Prose the same:
That not in Fancy's Maze he wander'd long,   340
But stoop'd to Truth, and moraliz'd his song:
That not for Fame, but Virtue's better end,
He stood the furious Foe, the timid Friend,
The damning Critic, half-approving Wit,
The Coxcomb hit, or fearing to be hit;
Laugh'd at the loss of Friends he never had,
The dull, the proud, the wicked, and the mad;
The distant Threats of Vengeance on his head,
The Blow unfelt, the Tear he never shed;

262. To . . . do: Pope is virtually quoting from the poem *Of Prudence* (1668) by Sir John Denham (1615–69). (See the selection from Denham in Part Three.) **276. Balbus:** a Roman lawyer. **280. Sir Will.:** Sir William Yonge (d. 1755), a notorious Whig politician. **296. Yet . . . defend:** an example of Pope's compression: "yet wants the honor to defend you when you are injured." **299–300. Who . . . there:** a reference to details given in the fourth of the *Moral Essays, Of the Use of Riches* (see above).

305. Sporus: Lord Hervey.

The Tale reviv'd, the Lye so oft o'erthrown;   350
Th' imputed Trash, and Dulness not his own;
The Morals blacken'd when the Writings scape;
The libel'd Person, and the pictur'd Shape;
Abuse on all he lov'd, or lov'd him, spread,
A Friend in Exile, or a Father, dead;
The Whisper that to Greatness still too near,
Perhaps, yet vibrates on his SOVEREIGN'S Ear—
Welcome for thee, fair Virtue! all the past:
For thee, fair Virtue! welcome ev'n the *last!*

   A. But why insult the Poor, affront the Great?   360
P. A Knave's a Knave, to me, in ev'ry State,
Alike my scorn, if he succeed or fail,
Sporus at Court, or *Japhet*° in a Jayl,
A hireling Scribler, or a hireling Peer,
Knight of the Post° corrupt, or of the Shire,
If on a Pillory, or near a Throne,
He gain his Prince's Ear, or lose his own.

   Yet soft by Nature, more a Dupe than Wit,
Sapho can tell you how this Man was bit:°
This dreaded Sat'rist *Dennis* will confess   370
Foe to his Pride, but Friend to his Distress:°
So humble, he has knock'd at *Tibald*'s door,
Has drunk with *Cibber*, nay has rym'd for *Moor.*
Full ten years slander'd, did he once reply?
Three thousand Suns went down on *Welsted*'s Lye:°
To please a *Mistress*, One aspers'd his life;
He lash'd him not, but let her be his *Wife:*
Let *Budgel*° charge low *Grubstreet* on his quill,
And write whate'er he pleas'd, except his *Will;*
Let the *Two Curls*° of Town and Court, abuse   380
His Father, Mother, Body, Soul, and Muse.
Yet why? that Father held it for a rule
It was a Sin to call our Neighbour Fool,
That harmless Mother thought no Wife a Whore,—
Hear this! and spare his Family, *James More*
Unspotted Names! and memorable long,
If there be Force in Virtue, or in Song.

   Of gentle Blood (part shed in Honour's Cause,
While yet in *Britain* Honour had Applause)

Each Parent sprung—A. "What Fortune, pray?—P.
   Their own,   390
And better got than *Bestia*'s° from the Throne.
Born to no Pride, inheriting no Strife,
Nor marrying Discord° in a Noble Wife,
Stranger to Civil and Religious Rage,
The good Man walk'd innoxious thro' his Age.
No Courts he saw, no Suits would ever try,
Nor dar'd an Oath, nor hazarded a Lye:
Un-learn'd, he knew no Schoolman's subtle Art,
No Language, but the Language of the Heart.
By Nature honest, by Experience wise,   400
Healthy by Temp'rance and by Exercise:
His Life, tho' long, to sickness past unknown,
His Death was instant, and without a groan.°
Oh grant me thus to live, and thus to die!°
Who sprung from Kings shall know less joy than I.

   O Friend! may each Domestick Bliss be thine!
Be no unpleasing Melancholy mine:
Me, let the tender Office long engage
To rock the Cradle of reposing Age,
With lenient Arts extend a Mother's breath,°   410
Make Languor smile, and smooth the Bed of Death,
Explore° the Thought, explain° the asking Eye,
And keep a while one Parent from the Sky!
On Cares like these if Length of days attend,
May Heav'n, to bless those days, preserve my Friend,
Preserve him social, chearful, and serene,
And just as rich as when he serv'd a QUEEN°!
A.° Whether that Blessing be deny'd, or giv'n,
Thus far was right, the rest belongs to Heav'n.

---

363. Japhet: Japhet Crook, a forger. **365. Knight . . . Post:** one who earned his living by giving false evidence. **369. bit:** deceived, taken in. **371. Friend . . . Distress:** Pope had attempted to launch an edition of Dennis's works by subscription in 1731. **375. Three . . . Lye:** Cf. Eph. 4:26: "Let not the sun go down upon your wrath." **378. Budgel:** Eustace Budgell (1686–1737), the author, apparently forged the will of Dr. Matthew Tindal and thereby wrongfully inherited money. **380. the Two Curls:** Edmund Curll's name is used as a term of abuse—the Curl of the town is Edmund, and of the court, Lord Hervey.

391. Bestia: the name of a Roman consul who accepted bribes; the word also suggests debauchery to an English ear. **393. Discord:** Pope is thinking of Discordia, a malevolent goddess of the Greeks and Romans. **403. without a groan:** Pope took this phrase from Isaac Watts's *Horae Lyricae* (1706). (See the selections from Watts in Part Three.) **404. Oh . . . die:** Cf. ll. 261–62. **408–10. Me . . . breath:** Pope's mother had died two years before the poem was published. Pope is using lines he had written in 1731. **412. Explore:** find by searching for. **explain:** interpret, make intelligible. **417. when . . . Queen:** Arbuthnot had been Queen Anne's physician. **418–19. A. Whether . . . Heav'n:** These two lines were first assigned to Arbuthnot in Warburton's edition (1751).

FROM

IMITATIONS OF HORACE

Pope owed to his friend Bolingbroke the inspiration for the *Imitations of Horace*. "When I had a fever," he told Spence,

> one winter in town, that confined me to my room for five or six days, Lord Bolingbroke, who came to see me, happened to take up a Horace that lay on the table; and in turning it over, dipped on the first satire of the second book, which begins *Sunt quibus in satirâ, &c.* He observed how well it would hit my case, if I were to imitate it in English. After he was gone, I read it over; translated it in a morning or two, and sent it to the press in a week or fortnight after. And this was the occasion of my imitating some other of the satires and epistles afterwards.

By "hitting his case" Bolingbroke meant that Horace's discussion of the ethics of satire was the sort that would help to rehabilitate Pope's moral status after the damage done to it by the counterattacks of the Dunces and by those who felt they had been ill treated in the *Moral Essays* (1731–35).

As a literary form the imitation has to be kept distinct from what may be called copying, or general imitation of style, subject matter, or both. Pope was scornful, as was Johnson after him, of earlier imitations that amounted to little more than writing *nathless* for *nevertheless* and *eremite* for *hermit*. Literary imitation is quite different from copying of this sort. According to Johnson, it is "a method of translating looser than paraphrase" and so "a kind of middle composition between translation and original design." But though it is a *loose* translation and midway between strict translation and original design, it was not independent enough of earlier writing for either Johnson or Edward Young to see just how original it could be. Their disaffection resulted from a failure to keep distinct two meanings of *originality*. For Johnson and Young a writer's originality meant mainly his power to invent a story, an argument, or a literary form. There is, however, a nobler sense, which we invoke when we speak of the Miltonic, for example. An imitation written by Milton will be original because it will be Miltonic. Even Milton's *translation* of a little ode of Horace is completely Miltonic. The nineteenth-century minor critic George Gilfillan expressed his understanding of this second sense of *originality* when he said, "A true original is often most so when he is imitating or even translating others."

Pope's imitations are original because they are Popean. And they are especially valuable because they show the Popean at its most mature (his only later work was the fourth book of *The Dunciad* [1742]). In *A Dialogue Something like Horace* [1738] Pope's friend says, "You grow *correct* that once with Rapture writ." No longer would Pope describe an Eloisa or the huntsmen in *Windsor-Forest* (1713) with so bold an excitement, nor would he sport and flutter in the fields of air with the sylphs of *The Rape of the Lock* (1712–14). But there is no diminution of rapture in his later poems; rapture glows instead through a fuller intellectual sense. In reading these imitations, we should enjoy them best if our knowledge and memory of Horace were as complete as Pope's was; then we should appreciate what Johnson called the "thoughts" that are "unexpectedly applicable" and the "parallels" that are "lucky." But even without a grasp of these learned parallels, we derive pleasure from the originality of the poems. Here we see English verse executed in perfect familiar style. And when Pope lays the text of Horace aside for *An Epistle to Dr. Arbuthnot* (1735) and *A Dialogue Something like Horace*, he achieves perfection in what could be called the "sublime public style." Only some such term will do justice to the characters of the first poem and the towering final paragraph of the second.

The texts printed are those of the first editions (1733 and 1737), revised in accordance with Pope's revisions; we assume that the few changes in Warburton's edition of 1751 and its notes have Pope's authority.

ADVERTISEMENT°

THE Occasion of publishing these *Imitations* was the Clamour raised on some of my *Epistles.*[1] An Answer from *Horace* was both more full, and of more Dignity, than any I could have made in my own person; and the Example of so much greater Freedom in so eminent a Divine as Dr. *Donne*, seem'd a proof with what indignation and contempt a Christian may treat Vice or Folly, in ever so low, or ever so high a Station. Both these Authors were acceptable to the *Princes* and *Ministers* under whom they lived. The

IMITATIONS OF HORACE: *Advertisement.* The Advertisement appeared for the first time in the *Works* of 1735, which brought together such imitations of Horace and Donne as Pope had then published. **1. some . . . Epistles:** notably that addressed to Burlington, published as the fourth of the *Moral Essays, Of the Use of Riches* (see above).

Satires of Dr. *Donne* I versifyed at the desire of the Earl of *Oxford* while he was Lord Treasurer, and of the Duke of *Shrewsbury* who had been Secretary of State; neither of whom look'd upon a Satire on Vicious Courts as any Reflection on those they serv'd in. And indeed there is not in the world a greater error, than that which Fools are so apt to fall into and Knaves with good reason to incourage, the mistaking a *Satyrist* for a *Libeller;* whereas to a *true Satyrist* nothing is so odious as a *Libeller,* for the same reason as to a man *truly virtuous* nothing is so hateful as a *Hypocrite.*

Uni aequus Virtuti atque ejus Amicis.[2]

THE FIRST SATIRE OF THE SECOND BOOK OF HORACE

Imitated in a DIALOGUE between

ALEXANDER POPE, of Twickenham in Com. Midd.° Esq; on the one Part, and his LEARNED COUNCIL° on the other.

P[*ope*]. THERE are (I scarce can think it, but am told)
There are to whom my Satire seems too bold,
Scarce to wise *Peter*° complaisant enough,
And something said of *Chartres*° much too rough.
The Lines are weak, another's pleas'd to say,
Lord *Fanny*° spins a thousand such a Day.
Tim'rous by Nature, of the Rich in awe,
I come to Council learned in the Law.
You'll give me, like a Friend both sage and free,
Advice; and (as you use) without a Fee.   10
  F[*ortescue*]. I'd write no more. *P.* Not write? but then I *think,*

And for my Soul I cannot sleep a Wink.
I nod in Company, I wake at Night,
Fools rush into my Head, and so I write.
  F. You could not do a worse Thing for your Life.°
Why, if the Nights seem tedious—take a Wife;
Or rather truly, if your Point be Rest,
Lettuce and Cowslip Wine; *Probatum est.*°
But talk with *Celsus,*° *Celsus* will advise
Hartshorn, or something that shall close your Eyes.   20
Or if you needs must write, write CÆSAR'S° Praise:
You'll gain at least a *Knighthood,* or the *Bays.*°
  P. What? like Sir *Richard,*° rumbling, rough and fierce,°
With ARMS, and GEORGE, and BRUNSWICK crowd the Verse?
Rend with tremendous Sound your ears asunder,
With Gun, Drum, Trumpet, Blunderbuss & Thunder?
Or nobly wild, with *Budgell's*° Fire and Force,
Paint Angels trembling round his *falling Horse?*
  F. Then all your Muse's softer Art display,
Let *Carolina* smooth the tuneful Lay,   30
Lull with *Amelia's*° liquid Name the Nine,°
And sweetly flow through all the Royal Line.
  P. Alas! few Verses touch their nicer° Ear;
They scarce can bear their *Laureat* twice a Year:°
And justly CÆSAR scorns the Poet's Lays,
It is to *History*° he trusts for Praise.
  F. Better be *Cibber,*° I'll maintain it still,

---

2. **Uni . . . Amicis:** "He was a friend to Virtue only, and to her friends" (Horace, *Satires,* II. i. 70). *To Fortescue.* **Com. Midd.:** county of Middlesex. **Learned Council:** Pope's friend William Fortescue (1687–1749), a barrister who later became a judge and Master of the Rolls. In Warburton's edition of 1751, which gives a briefer form of the title, the inscription "To Mr. Fortescue" is added. **3. Peter:** Peter Walter, or Walters (*c.* 1664–1746), a self-aggrandizing and, in Pope's words, "dextrous" attorney. **4. Chartres:** Francis Charteris (1675–1732), according to Pope "a man infamous for all manner of vices"; he is attacked in the third of the *Moral Essays* (1731–35). **6. Lord Fanny:** Lord Hervey (1696–1743), court Vice Chamberlain and confidant of Queen Caroline.

15. **for your Life:** so as to save your life. **18. Probatum est:** It has been proved, or tested; a phrase used in cookbooks. **19. Celsus:** first-century A.D. Roman writer on medicine. **21. Cæsar's:** the King's, George II's. **22. Bays:** the laurels, and so the office of Poet Laureate. **23. Sir Richard:** Blackmore (1654–1729). Knighted for his eminence as a physician, he was also a poet whom Pope pilloried in the *Peri Bathous* (see above). **rumbling . . . fierce:** Swift had already joked about the rough names that the Hanoverians now obliged poets to work into their lines, allowing that "Caroline" made amends by its smoothness. See Swift's *Directions for a Birth-Day Song,* ll. 209–32, earlier in Part Two. **27. Budgell:** Eustace Budgell (1686–1737), the writer whose *Poem upon His Majesty's Late Journey to Cambridge and Newmarket* (1728) tells of the death of George II's horse in battle. **30–31. Carolina, Amelia:** George II's queen and daughter. **31. the Nine:** the Muses. **33. nicer:** more discriminating. **34. twice a Year:** The Poet Laureate's duties included producing a poem for the New Year and for the king's birthday. **36. History:** The office of Historiographer Royal had been instituted some seventy years earlier. **37. Cibber:** Colley Cibber (1671–1757) was Poet Laureate at this date.

Than ridicule all *Taste*, blaspheme *Quadrille*,
Abuse the City's best good Men in Metre,
And laugh at Peers that put their Trust in *Peter*.   40
Even those you touch not, hate you.

                    P. What should ail 'em?

   F. A hundred smart in *Timon* and in *Balaam:*
The fewer still you name, you wound the more;
Bond is but one, but *Harpax* is a Score.°

   P. Each Mortal has his Pleasure: None deny
Scarsdale° his Bottle, *Darty*° his Ham-Pye;
Ridotta° sips and dances, till she see
The doubling Lustres° dance as well as she;
Fox loves the *Senate*,° *Hockley-Hole*° his Brother°
Like in all else, as one Egg to another.   50
I love to pour out all myself, as plain
As downright *Shippen*,° or as old *Montagne*.°
In them, as certain to be lov'd as seen,
The Soul stood forth, nor kept a Thought within;
In me what Spots (for Spots I have) appear,
Will prove at least the Medium must be clear.
In this impartial Glass,° my Muse intends
Fair to expose myself, my Foes, my Friends;
Publish the present Age, but where my Text
Is Vice too high, reserve it for the next: 60
My Foes shall wish my Life a longer Date,
And ev'ry Friend the less lament my Fate.

   My Head and Heart thus flowing thro' my Quill,
Verse-man or Prose-man, term me which you will,
Papist or Protestant, or both between,
Like good *Erasmus*° in an honest Mean,
In Moderation placing all my Glory,
While Tories call me Whig, and Whigs a Tory.

   Satire's my Weapon, but I'm too discreet

To run a Muck, and tilt at all I meet;   70
I only wear it in a Land of Hectors,°
Thieves, Supercargoes,° Sharpers, and Directors.°
Save but our *Army!*° and let *Jove* incrust
Swords, Pikes, and Guns, with everlasting Rust°!
Peace is my dear Delight—not *Fleury*'s° more:
But touch me, and no Minister so sore.
Who-e'er offends, at some unlucky Time
Slides into Verse, and hitches in a Rhyme,
Sacred to Ridicule! his whole Life long,
And the sad Burthen of some merry Song.   80

   Slander or Poyson, dread from *Delia*'s° Rage,
Hard Words or Hanging, if your Judge be *Page:*°
From furious *Sappho*° scarce a milder Fate,
P—x'd by her Love, or libell'd by her Hate:
Its proper Power to hurt, each Creature feels,
Bulls aim their Horns, and Asses lift their Heels,
'Tis a Bear's Talent not to kick, but hug,
And no Man wonders he's not stung by Pug:°
So drink with *Walters*,° or with *Chartres* eat,
They'll never poison you, they'll only cheat.   90

   Then learned Sir! (to cut the Matter short)
What-e'er my Fate, or well or ill at Court,
Whether old Age, with faint, but chearful Ray,
Attends to gild the Evening of my Day,
Or Death's black Wing already be display'd
To wrap me in the Universal Shade;
Whether the darken'd Room to muse invite,
Or whiten'd Wall provoke the Skew'r to write,
In Durance, Exile, Bedlam, or the Mint,°
Like *Lee*° or *Budgell*,° I will Rhyme and Print.   100

   F. Alas young Man! your Days can ne'r be long,
In Flow'r of Age you perish for a Song!

38–44. **ridicule . . . Score:** Pope is mentioning objects of satire in the third and fourth *Moral Essays* (see above). **46. Scarsdale:** Nicholas Lake (1682–1736), Fourth Earl of Scarsdale. **Darty:** Charles Dartineuf (1664–1737), a notorious gourmet. **47. Ridotta:** "a name for a type of Society woman: from the Italian *ridotto*, a social assembly consisting of music and dancing, introduced into England in 1722" (*OED*). **48. Lustres:** glass balls placed among artificial lights to improve illumination. **49. Senate:** Parliament. **Hockley-Hole:** a bear garden. **Fox, his Brother:** apparently Stephen and Henry Fox. **52. Shippen:** William Shippen (1673–1743), the Tory leader. **Montagne:** the French essayist Michel de Montaigne (1533–92). **57. this . . . Glass:** Cf. Richard Crashaw's *Upon Mr. Staninough's Death*, l. 21: "this unpartiall glasse." **66. Erasmus:** (1466–1536), the celebrated humanist philosopher. His moderation was uncomfortable in his own time: Roman Catholics considered him the renegade instigator of the Reformation, while the reformers thought he was too conservative.

71. Hectors: the name given in the seventeenth century to swaggering bullies who were the terror of London. **72. Supercargoes:** officers on board ship who, as a class, did very well out of their job of supervising cargo. **Directors:** of the South Sea Company. **73. Save . . . Army:** The retention of a standing army was much debated at this time. **74. everlasting Rust:** an amusing variation of *everlasting rest*. **75. Fleury:** André Hercule de Fleury (1653–1743), the much respected adviser of Louis XV of France. **81. Delia:** Mary Howard (1700–44), George II's mistress. **82. Page:** Sir Francis Page (*c.* 1661–1741), who was known as "the hanging judge." **83. Sappho:** Lady Mary Wortley Montagu (1689–1762), with whom Pope had quarreled. (See the selection from Lady Mary in Part Three.) **88. Pug:** a pet name for a dog. **89. Walters:** Peter Walter, pronounced as *Water*. The pronunciation enforces the pun. **99. Mint:** a sanctuary for debtors. **100. Lee:** Nathaniel Lee (*c.* 1653–92), the dramatist, wrote a tragedy after being immured in Bedlam. **Budgell:** Eustace Budgell also went mad.

Plums,° and Directors, *Shylock*° and his Wife,
Will club their Testers,° now, to take your Life!
    P. What? arm'd for *Virtue* when I point the Pen,
Brand the bold Front of shameless, guilty Men,
Dash the proud Gamester in his gilded Car,
Bare the mean Heart that lurks beneath a Star;°
Can there be wanting to defend Her Cause,
Lights of the Church, or Guardians of the Laws?   110
Could pension'd *Boileau* lash in honest Strain
Flatt'rers and Bigots ev'n in *Louis'* Reign?
Could Laureate *Dryden* Pimp and Fry'r engage,
Yet neither *Charles* nor *James* be in a Rage?°
And I not strip the Gilding off a Knave,
Un-plac'd, unpension'd, no Man's Heir, or Slave?
I will, or perish in the gen'rous Cause,
Hear this, and tremble! you, who 'scape the Laws.
Yes, while I live, no rich or noble knave
Shall walk the World, in credit, to his grave.   120
To virtue only and her friends, a friend,°
The World beside may murmur, or commend.
Know, all the distant Din that World can keep
Rolls o'er my *Grotto*,° and but sooths my Sleep.
There, my Retreat the best Companions grace,
Chiefs out of War, and Statesmen, out of Place.
There *St. John*° mingles with my friendly Bowl,
The Feast of Reason, and the Flow of Soul:
And He,° whose Lightning pierc'd th' *Iberian* Lines,
Now forms my Quincunx,° and now ranks my Vines,
Or tames the Genius of the stubborn Plain,   131
Almost as quickly, as he conquer'd *Spain*.
    Envy must own, I live among the Great,
No Pimp of Pleasure, and no Spy of State,
With Eyes that pry not, Tongue that ne'er repeats,
Fond to spread Friendships, but to cover Heats,

To help who want, to forward who excel;
This, all who know me, know; who love me tell;
And who unknown defame me, let them be
Scriblers or Peers, alike are *Mob*° to me.   140
This is my Plea, on this I rest my Cause—
What saith my Council learned in the Laws?
    F. Your Plea is good. But still I say, beware!
Laws are explain'd by Men—so have a care.
It stands on Record, that in *Richard*'s Times
A Man was hang'd for very honest Rhymes.°
Consult the Statute: *quart*.° I think it is,
Edwardi Sext. or *prim. & quint. Eliz:*
See *Libels, Satires*—there you have it—read.
    P. Libels and *Satires!* lawless Things indeed!   150
But grave *Epistles*, bringing Vice to light,
Such as a *King* might read, a *Bishop* write,
Such as Sir *Robert*° would approve—
                                    F. Indeed?
The Case is alter'd°—you may then proceed,
In such a Cause the Plaintiff will be hiss'd,
My Lords the Judges laugh, and you're dismiss'd.

THE FIRST EPISTLE OF THE SECOND BOOK OF HORACE

IMITATED.

To Augustus

Ne Rubeam, pingui donatus Munere!°
                                    Hor.

ADVERTISEMENT.

THE Reflections of Horace, *and the Judgments past in his Epistle to* Augustus, *seem'd so seasonable to the present Times, that I could not help applying them to the use of*

---

103. Plums: men worth a hundred thousand pounds. **Shylock:** a man as close-fisted as the villain of *The Merchant of Venice*. **104. Testers:** sixpences. **108. Star:** the star-shaped decoration worn by members of an order of knighthood. **113–14. Could . . . Rage:** Dryden's *The Spanish Friar* (1680), which satirized the morals of the Catholic clergy, was banned by James II in 1686. **121. To . . . friend:** See n. 2 to the Advertisement. **124. Grotto:** the tunnel connecting Pope's villa at Twickenham with his garden; it ran underneath the intervening highway. Pope found great pleasure in adorning it with pretty stones, pieces of glass, and so on. **127. St. John:** Henry St. John (1678–1751), Viscount Bolingbroke. During Queen Anne's reign he was leader of the Tory party. Pope dedicated to him his *Essay on Man* (see above). **129. He:** [Pope's note] *Charles Mordaunt Earl of Peterborough, who in the Year* 1705 *took Barcelona, and in the Winter following with only* 280 *Horse and* 900 *foot enterprized, and accomplished the capture of Valentia.* **130. Quincunx:** four trees placed in a square around a fifth.

140. Mob: a new slang term shortened from the term for the common people, (*vulgus*) *mobile*. **145–46. It . . . Rhymes:** In the time of Richard III one Collingbourne wrote the fatal couplet: "The Cat, the Rat, and Lovel our Dog / Do rule al England, under a Hog." **147. quart.:** To be exact Pope would have had to write "*tert.* and *quart.*," but he pretends to have forgotten in order to find a rhyme for *Eliz.* and so accommodate this recalcitrant line and the next into his meter. The dexterity is Ovidian. The statutes named were against writing, printing, and singing seditious words. **153. Sir Robert:** Walpole (1676–1745), Whig leader. **154. The Case . . . alter'd:** a proverb usually applied to lawyers who on receipt of a larger fee change their side with this brusque apology. *To Augustus.* **Ne . . . Munere:** "Do not make me blush by presenting me with a gross offering, a bribe" (Horace, *Epistles*, II. i. 267).

my own Country. The Author thought them considerable enough to address them to His Prince; whom he paints with all the great and good Qualities of a Monarch, upon whom the Romans depended for the Encrease of an Absolute Empire.[1] But to make the Poem entirely English, I was willing to add one or two of those which contribute to the Happiness of a Free People, and are more consistent with the Welfare of our Neighbours.

This Epistle will show the learned World to have fallen into two mistakes; one, that Augustus *was a Patron of Poets in general; whereas he not only prohibited all but the Best Writers to name him, but recommended that Care even to the Civil Magistrate:* Admonebat Prætores, ne paterentur Nomen suum obsolefieri,[2] &c. *The other, that this Piece was only a general Discourse of Poetry; whereas it was an Apology for the Poets, in order to render* Augustus *more their Patron.* Horace *here pleads the Cause of his Cotemporaries, first against the Taste of the Town, whose humour[3] it was to magnify the Authors of the preceding Age; secondly against the Court and Nobility, who encouraged only the Writers for the Theatre; and lastly against the Emperor himself, who had conceived them of little use to the Government. He shews (by a view of the Progress of Learning, and the Change of Taste among the* Romans*) that the Introduction of the Polite Arts of* Greece *had given the Writers of his Time great advantages over their Predecessors, that their Morals were much improved, and the Licence of those ancient Poets restrained: that Satire and Comedy were become more just and useful; that whatever extravagancies were left on the Stage, were owing to the Ill Taste of the Nobility; that Poets, under due Regulations, were in many respects useful to the* State; *and concludes, that it was upon them the Emperor himself must depend, for his Fame with Posterity.*

We may farther learn from this Epistle, that Horace *made his Court to this Great Prince, by writing with a decent Freedom toward him, with a just Contempt of his low Flatterers, and with a manly Regard to his own Character.*

WHile You, great Patron of Mankind, sustain
The balanc'd World, and open all the Main;
Your Country, chief,° in Arms abroad defend,
At home, with Morals, Arts, and Laws amend;

1. whom he . . . Empire: Pope, however, inverts Horace's respect, and his praise of George II is ironical. 2. Admonebat . . . obsolefieri: "He often charged the praetors not to let his name be cheapened in prize declamations" (Suetonius, *Life of Augustus*, sec. 89). 3. humour: whim. 3. chief: primarily.

How shall the Muse, from such a Monarch, steal
An hour, and not defraud the Publick Weal?

Edward° and Henry,° now the Boast of Fame,
And virtuous Alfred,° a more sacred Name,
After a Life of gen'rous Toils endur'd,
The Gaul subdu'd, or Property secur'd,   10
Ambition humbled, mighty Cities storm'd,
Or Laws establish'd, and the World reform'd;
Clos'd their long Glories with a sigh, to find
Th' unwilling Gratitude of base mankind!
All human Virtue to its latest breath
Finds Envy never conquer'd, but by Death.
The great Alcides,° ev'ry Labour past,
Had still this Monster to subdue at last.
Sure fate of all, beneath whose rising ray
Each Star of meaner merit fades away;   20
Oppress'd we feel the Beam directly beat,
Those Suns of Glory please not till they set.

To Thee, the World its present homage pays,
The Harvest early, but mature the Praise:
Great Friend of LIBERTY! in *Kings* a Name
Above all Greek, above all Roman Fame:
Whose Word is Truth, as sacred and rever'd,
As Heav'n's own Oracles from Altars heard.
Wonder of Kings! like whom, to mortal eyes
None e'er has risen, and none e'er shall rise.   30

Just in one instance,° be it yet confest
Your People, Sir, are partial in the rest.
Foes to all living worth except your own,
And Advocates for Folly dead and gone.
Authors, like Coins, grow dear as they grow old;
It is the rust we value, not the gold.
Chaucer's worst ribaldry is learn'd by rote,
And beastly Skelton° Heads of Houses quote:

7–16. Edward . . . Death: Cf. Edmund Waller's *A Panegyric to My Lord Protector*, ll. 145–48:

> Had you, some ages past, this race of glory
> Run, with amazement we should read your story;
> But living virtue, all achievement past,
> Meets envy still, to grapple with at last.

(See the selections from Waller in Part Three.) **7. Edward and Henry:** Edward III (1312–77) and Henry V (1387–1422). **8. Alfred:** Alfred the Great (849–99), champion of Christianity and learning as well as leader of his people against the Danish invaders. **17. Alcides:** Hercules. **31. Just . . . instance:** right in ranking you above all former kings. **38. beastly Skelton:** [Pope's note] Poet Laureat to Hen. 8 a Volume of Whose Verses has been lately reprinted consisting almost wholly of Ribaldry, Obscenity, and [scurrilous] Language.

One likes no language but the Faery Queen;
A Scot will fight for Christ's Kirk o' the Green;°   40
And each true Briton is to Ben° so civil,
He swears the Muses met him at the Devil.°

    Tho' justly Greece her eldest sons admires,
Why should not we be wiser than our Sires?
In ev'ry publick Virtue we excell,
We build, we paint, we sing, we dance as well,
And learned Athens to our Art must stoop,
Could she behold us tumbling thro' a hoop.°

    If Time improve our Wit as well as Wine,
Say at what age a Poet grows divine?   50
Shall we, or shall we not, account him so,
Who dy'd, perhaps, an hundred years° ago?
End all dispute; and fix the year precise
When British bards begin t' Immortalize°?
    "Who lasts a Century can have no flaw,
I hold that Wit a Classick, good in law."

    Suppose he wants a year, will you compound?
And shall we deem him Ancient, right and sound,
Or damn to all Eternity at once,
At ninety-nine, a Modern, and a Dunce?   60
    "We shall not quarrel for a year or two;
By Courtesy of England,° he may do."

    Then, by the rule that made the Horse-tail bare;
I pluck out year by year, as hair by hair,
And melt down Ancients like a heap of snow:
While you to measure merits, look in Stowe,°
And estimating Authors by the year,
Bestow a Garland only on a Bier.

    Shakespear, (whom you and ev'ry Play-house bill
Style the divine, the matchless, what you will)   70
For gain, not glory, wing'd his roving flight,
And grew Immortal in his own despight.
Ben, old and poor, as little seem'd to heed

The Life to come, in ev'ry Poet's Creed.°
Who° now reads Cowley? if he pleases yet,
His moral pleases, not his pointed wit;
Forgot his Epic, nay Pindaric° Art,
But still I love the language of his Heart.

    "Yet surely, surely, these were famous men!
What Boy but hears the sayings of old Ben?   80
In all debates where Criticks bear a part,
Not one but nods, and talks of Johnson's Art,
Of Shakespear's Nature, and of Cowley's Wit;
How Beaumont's Judgment check'd what Fletcher
    writ;
How Shadwell hasty, Wycherly was slow;°
But, for the Passions,° Southern sure and Rowe.°

These,° only these, support the crouded stage,°
From eldest Heywood down to Cibber's age."
   All this may be; the People's Voice is odd,
It is, and it is not, the voice of God.   90
To Gammer Gurton° if it give the bays,
And yet deny the Careless Husband° praise,
Or say our fathers never broke a rule;
Why then I say, the Publick is a fool.
But let them own, that greater faults than we
They had, and greater Virtues, I'll agree.°
Spenser himself affects the obsolete,
And Sydney's° verse halts ill on Roman feet:
Milton's strong pinion now not Heav'n can bound,
Now serpent-like, in prose he sweeps the ground,   100
In Quibbles, Angel and Archangel join,°
And God the Father turns a School-Divine.°
Not that I'd lop the Beauties from his book,
Like slashing Bentley with his desp'rate Hook;°
Or damn all Shakespear, like th' affected fool
At Court, who hates whate'er he read at School.°
   But for the Wits of either Charles's days,
The Mob of Gentlemen° who wrote with Ease;
Sprat,° Carew,° Sedley,° and a hundred more,

87–88. These . . . age: Cf. Waller, Prologue to *The Maid's Tragedy*, ll. 35–38:

> In other things the knowing artist may
> Judge better than the people; but a play,
> (Made for delight, and for no other use)
> If you [the audience] approve it not, has no excuse.

87. the crouded stage: the popular stage. 91. Gammer Gurton: [Pope's note] a piece of very low humour, one of the first printed Plays in English, and therefore much valued by some Antiquaries. 92. the Careless Husband: Cibber's comedy (1704). 95–96. greater . . . agree: a handsome compliment to what Dryden called "the giant race." 98. Sydney: Sir Philip Sidney (1554–86) in whose *Arcadia* (1590), which was still widely read, there were poems in meters imitating the quantitative meters of Greece and Rome. 101. In . . . join: See *Paradise Lost*, VI. 609 ff., where Satan and Belial harangue "in . . . gamesom mood." 102. School-Divine: a lecturer on divinity, as in *Paradise Lost*, Books VI and VII. 104. Bentley . . . Hook: Hook was a contemporary word for parenthesis in printing or handwriting. Richard Bentley had used the mark and the term in his edition of Milton (1732). Pope represents him as using an actual metal hook such as that used by farmers to lop boughs, for such is his savage treatment of Milton's exquisite text. 106. whate'er . . . School: perhaps evidence that English literature was taught in schools at this time. 108. Mob of Gentlemen: a contradiction in terms. 109. Sprat: Thomas Sprat (1635–1713), Bishop of Rochester. (See the selection from Sprat in Part One.) Carew: Thomas Carew (*c.* 1595–*c.* 1639), some of whose poems had been reprinted in Dryden's *Miscellanies* (1716). Sedley: Sir Charles Sedley (1639–1701).

(Like twinkling Stars the Miscellanies o'er)   110
One Simile, that solitary shines
In the dry Desert of a thousand lines,
Or lengthen'd Thought that gleams° thro' many a
      page,
Has sanctify'd whole Poems for an age.
   I lose my patience, and I own it too,
When works are censur'd, not as bad, but new;
While if our Elders break all Reason's laws,
These fools demand not Pardon, but Applause.
   On Avon's bank, where flow'rs eternal blow,
If I but ask, if any weed can grow?   120
One Tragic sentence if I dare deride
Which Betterton's° grave Action dignify'd,
Or well-mouth'd Booth° with emphasis proclaims,
(Tho' but, perhaps, a muster-roll of Names)
How will our Fathers rise up in a rage,
And swear, all shame is lost in George's Age!
You'd think no Fools disgrac'd the former Reign,
Did not some grave Examples yet remain,
Who scorn a Lad should teach his Father skill,
And, having once been wrong, will be so still.   130
He, who to seem more deep than you or I,
Extols old Bards, or Merlin's Prophecy,°
Mistake him not; he envies, not admires,
And to debase the Sons, exalts the Sires.
Had ancient Times conspir'd to dis-allow
What then was new, what had been ancient now?
Or what remain'd, so worthy to be read
By learned Criticks of the mighty Dead?
   In Days of Ease, when now the weary Sword
Was sheath'd, and *Luxury* with *Charles*° restor'd; 140
In every Taste of foreign Courts improv'd,
"All, by the King's Example, liv'd and lov'd."
Then Peers grew proud in Horsemanship, t' excell,
New-market's Glory rose, as Britain's fell;
The Soldier breath'd the Gallantries of France,
And ev'ry flow'ry Courtier writ Romance.
Then Marble soften'd into life grew warm,
And yielding Metal flow'd to human form:
Lely° on animated Canvas stole
The sleepy Eye,° that spoke the melting soul.   150

113. gleams: fitfully; a simile ought to shine. 122. Betterton: Thomas Betterton (*c.* 1635–1710), the great actor of his age. 123. Booth: Barton Booth (1681–1733), a tragic actor. 132. Merlin's Prophecy: recently translated as part of Geoffrey of Monmouth's history (1137). 140. Charles: Charles II (1630–85). 149. Lely: Sir Peter Lely (1618–80), portrait painter. 150. sleepy Eye: Dryden was said to have this physical characteristic.

No wonder then, when all was Love and Sport,
The willing Muses were debauch'd at Court;
On each enervate string they taught the Note
To pant, or tremble thro' an Eunuch's throat.°
But Britain, changeful as a Child at play,
Now calls in Princes, and now turns away.°
Now Whig, now Tory, what we lov'd we hate;
Now all for Pleasure, now for Church and State;
Now for Prerogative, and now for Laws;
Effects unhappy! from a Noble Cause.   160
    Time was, a sober Englishman wou'd knock
His servants up, and rise by five a clock,
Instruct his Family in ev'ry rule,
And send his Wife to Church, his Son to school.
To worship like his Fathers was his care;
To teach their frugal Virtues to his Heir;
To prove, that Luxury could never hold;
And place, on good Security, his Gold.
Now Times are chang'd, and one Poetick Itch
Has seiz'd the Court and City, Poor and Rich: 170
Sons, Sires, and Grandsires, all will wear the Bays,
Our Wives read Milton, and our Daughters Plays,
To Theatres, and to Rehearsals throng,
And all our Grace at Table is a Song.
I, who so oft renounce the Muses, lye,
Not ———'s self e'er tells more *Fibs*° than I;
When, sick of Muse, our follies we deplore,
And promise our best Friends to ryme no more;
We wake next morning in a raging Fit,
And call for Pen and Ink to show our Wit.   180
    He serv'd a 'Prenticeship, who sets up shop;
Ward° try'd on Puppies, and the Poor, his Drop;
Ev'n Radcliff's Doctors° travel first to France,
Nor dare to practise till they've learn'd to dance.
Who builds a Bridge that never drove a pyle?
(Should Ripley° venture, all the World would smile)

But those who cannot write, and those who can,
All ryme, and scrawl, and scribble, to a man.
    Yet Sir, reflect, the mischief is not great;
These Madmen never hurt the Church or State: 190
Sometimes the Folly benefits mankind;
And rarely Av'rice taints the tuneful mind.
Allow him but his Play-thing of a Pen,
He ne'er rebels, or plots, like other men:
Flight of Cashiers, or Mobs, he'll never mind;
And knows no losses while the Muse is kind.
To cheat a Friend, or Ward, he leaves to Peter;°
The good man heaps up nothing but mere metre,
Enjoys his Garden and his Book in quiet;
And then—a perfect Hermit in his Diet.   200
Of little use the Man you may suppose,
Who says in verse what others say in prose;
Yet let me show, a Poet's of some weight,
And (tho' no Soldier) useful to the State.
What will a Child learn sooner than a song?
What better teach a Foreigner the tongue?
What's long or short, each accent where to place,
And speak in publick with some sort of grace.
I scarce can think him such a worthless thing,
Unless he praise some monster of a King,   210
Or Virtue, or Religion turn to sport,
To please a lewd, or un-believing Court.
Unhappy Dryden!—In all Charles's days,
Roscommon° only boasts unspotted Bays;
And in our own (excuse some Courtly stains)
No whiter page than Addison remains.
He, from the taste obscene reclaims our Youth,
And sets the Passions on the side of Truth;
Forms the soft bosom with the gentlest art,
And pours each human Virtue in the heart.   220
Let Ireland tell, how Wit upheld her cause,
Her Trade supported, and supply'd her Laws;
And leave on SWIFT this grateful verse ingrav'd,
The Rights a Court attack'd, a Poet sav'd.°
Behold the hand that wrought a Nation's cure,
Stretch'd to relieve the Idiot and the Poor,
Proud Vice to brand, or injur'd Worth adorn,
And stretch the Ray to Ages yet unborn.
Not but there are, who merit other palms;   229
Hopkins and Sternhold° glad the heart with Psalms;

153–54. On . . . throat: a reference to the importation of
singers and the home production of opera. 156. Now . . .
away: Prince Charles (later Charles II) and James II had been
turned away, and William of Orange called in to become
William III. 176. Fibs: This slang word, meaning trivial
lies, was well established by this time. 182. Ward: [Pope's
note] A famous Empyrick, whose Pill and Drop had several
surprising effects, and were one of the principal subjects of
Writing and Conversation at this time. 183. Radcliff's
Doctors: John Radcliffe (1653–1714), a celebrated physician
who bequeathed his fortune to Oxford University for the
advancement of medicine and natural science partly by
sending medical students to study abroad. 186. Ripley:
Thomas Ripley (d. 1758), a famous architect.

197. Peter: Walter (c. 1664–1746), an attorney. 214.
Roscommon: Wentworth Dillon (c. 1633–85), Fourth Earl
of Roscommon, a minor poet. 221–24. Let . . . sav'd:
a reference to Swift's *Drapier's Letters* (see earlier in Part Two).
230. Hopkins and Sternhold: who put the Psalms into
meter in the sixteenth century.

The Boys and Girls whom Charity maintains,
Implore your help in these pathetic strains:
How could Devotion touch the country pews,
Unless the Gods bestow'd a proper Muse?
Verse chears their leisure, Verse assists their work,
Verse prays for Peace, or sings down Pope and Turk.
The silenc'd Preacher yields to potent strain,
And feels that grace his pray'r besought in vain,
The blessing thrills thro' all the lab'ring throng,
And Heav'n is won by violence of Song.°   240
    Our rural Ancestors, with little blest,
Patient of labour when the end was rest,
Indulg'd the day that hous'd their annual grain,
With feasts, and off'rings, and a thankful strain:
The joy their wives, their sons, and servants share,
Ease of their toil, and part'ners of their care:
The laugh, the jest, attendants on the bowl,
Smooth'd ev'ry brow, and open'd ev'ry soul:
With growing years the pleasing Licence grew,
And Taunts alternate innocently flew.   250
But Times corrupt, and Nature ill-inclin'd,
Produc'd the point that left a sting behind;
Till friend with friend, and families at strife,
Triumphant Malice rag'd thro' private life.
Who felt the wrong, or fear'd it, took th' alarm,
Appeal'd to Law, and Justice lent her arm.
At length, by wholesom dread of statutes bound,
The Poets learn'd to please, and not to wound:
Most warp'd to Flatt'ry's side; but some, more nice,
Preserv'd the freedom, and forbore the vice.   260
Hence Satire rose, that just the medium hit,
And heals with Morals what it hurts with Wit.
    We conquer'd France, but felt our captive's charms;
Her Arts victorious triumph'd o'er our Arms;
Britain to soft refinements less a foe,
Wit grew polite, and Numbers learn'd to flow.
Waller° was smooth; but Dryden taught to join ⎫
The varying verse, the full resounding line,   ⎬
The long majestic march, and energy divine.   ⎭
Tho' still some traces of our rustic vein   270
And splay-foot verse,° remain'd, and will remain.

Late, very late, correctness grew our care,
When the tir'd nation breath'd from civil war.
Exact Racine, and Corneille's noble fire
Show'd us that France had something to admire.
Not but the Tragic spirit was our own,
And full in Shakespear, fair in Otway° shone:
But Otway fail'd to polish or refine,
And fluent Shakespear scarce effac'd a line.
Ev'n copious Dryden, wanted, or forgot,   280
The last and greatest Art, the Art to blot.
    Some doubt, if equal pains or equal fire
The humbler Muse of Comedy require?
But in known Images of life I guess
The labour greater, as th' Indulgence less.
Observe how seldom ev'n the best succeed:
Tell me if Congreve's Fools are Fools indeed?
What pert low Dialogue has Farqu'ar° writ!
How Van° wants grace, who never wanted wit!
The stage how loosely does Astræa° tread,   290
Who fairly puts all Characters to bed:
And idle Cibber, how he breaks the laws,
To make poor Pinky° eat with vast applause!
But fill their purse, our Poet's work is done,
Alike to them, by Pathos or by Pun.
    O you! whom Vanity's light bark conveys
On Fame's mad voyage by the wind of Praise;
With what a shifting gale your course you ply;
For ever sunk too low, or born too high!
Who pants for glory finds but short repose,   300
A breath revives him, or a breath o'erthrows!
Farewel the stage! if just as thrives the Play,
The silly bard grows fat, or falls away.
    There still remains to mortify a Wit,
The many-headed Monster of the Pit:
A sense-less, worth-less, and unhonour'd crowd;
Who to disturb their betters mighty proud,
Clatt'ring their sticks, before ten lines are spoke,
Call for the Farce, the Bear, or the Black-joke.°
What dear delight to Britons Farce affords!   310
Ever the taste of Mobs, but now of Lords;
(Taste, that eternal wanderer, which flies
From heads to ears, and now from ears to eyes.)

237–40. **The silenc'd . . . Song:** a reference to the hymn-singing Wesleyans. Cf. Dryden's *Astrea Redux*, l. 144: "As Heav'n it self is took by violence"; Pope's addition gives the phrase prominence, which is reinforced by the rhyme. 267. **Waller:** [Pope's note] Mr. Waller about this time, with the E. of Dorset, Mr. Godolphin, and others, translated the Pompey of Corneille; and the more correct French Poets began to be in reputation. 271. **splay-foot verse:** Pope goes one better than Samuel Butler, who in *Hudibras*, I. iii. 192, had "splay-foot rhymes," i.e., verse with "feet."

277. **Otway:** Thomas Otway (1652–85), writer of verse tragedies. 288. **Farqu'ar:** George Farquhar (1677–1707), comic dramatist. 289. **Van:** Sir John Vanbrugh (1664–1726), another comic dramatist. 290. **Astræa:** [Pope's note] A Name taken by Afra Behn, Authoress of several obscene Plays. 293. **Pinky:** the comic actor Penkethman, who, as *The Tatler*, No. 188, put it, "devours a cold Chick with great Applause." 309. **Black-joke:** popular song.

The Play stands still; damn action and discourse,
Back fly the scenes,° and enter foot and horse;
Pageants on pageants, in long order drawn,
Peers, Heralds, Bishops, Ermin, Gold, and Lawn;
The Champion too! and, to complete the jest,
Old Edward's Armour beams on Cibber's breast!°
With laughter sure Democritus° had dy'd,   320
Had he beheld an Audience gape so wide.
Let Bear or Elephant be e'er so white,
The people, sure, the people are the sight!
Ah luckless Poet! stretch thy lungs and roar,
That Bear or Elephant shall heed thee more;
While all its throats the Gallery extends,
And all the Thunder of the Pit ascends!
Loud as the Wolves on Orcas'° stormy steep,
Howl to the roarings of the Northern deep.
Such is the shout, the long-applauding note,   330
At Quin's° high plume, or Oldfield's° petticoat,°
Or when from Court a birth-day suit° bestow'd
Sinks the lost Actor in the tawdry load.
Booth enters—hark! the Universal Peal!
"But has he spoken?" Not a syllable.
"What shook the stage, and made the people stare?"
Cato's° long Wig, flowr'd gown, and lacquer'd chair.
    Yet lest you think I railly° more than teach,
Or praise malignly Arts I cannot reach,
Let me for once presume t' instruct the times,   340
To know the Poet from the Man of Rymes:
'Tis He, who gives my breast a thousand pains,
Can make me feel each Passion that he feigns,
Inrage, compose, with more than magic Art,
With Pity, and with Terror, tear my heart;
And snatch me, o'er the earth, or thro' the air,
To Thebes, to Athens, when he will, and where.

But not this part of the poetic state
Alone, deserves the favour of the Great:
Think of those Authors, Sir, who would rely   350
More on a Reader's sense, than Gazer's eye.
Or who shall wander where the Muses sing?°
Who climb their Mountain, or who taste their
    spring?
How shall we fill a Library with Wit,
When Merlin's Cave° is half unfurnish'd yet?
    My Liege! why Writers little claim your thought,
I guess; and, with their leave, will tell the fault:
We Poets are (upon a Poet's word)
Of all mankind, the creatures most absurd:
The season, when to come, and when to go,   360
To sing, or cease to sing, we never know;
And if we will recite nine hours in ten,
You lose your patience, just like other men.
Then too we hurt our selves, when to defend
A single verse, we quarrel with a friend;
Repeat unask'd; lament, the Wit's too fine
For vulgar eyes, and point out ev'ry line.
But most, when straining with too weak a wing,
We needs will write Epistles to the King;
And from the moment we oblige the town,   370
Expect a Place, or Pension from the Crown;
Or dubb'd Historians by express command,
T' enroll your triumphs o'er the seas and land;
Be call'd to Court, to plan some work divine,
As once for Loüis, Boileau and Racine.
    Yet think, great Sir! (so many Virtues shown)
Ah think, what Poet best may make them known?
Or chuse at least some Minister of Grace,
Fit to bestow the Laureat's weighty place.
    Charles, to late times to be transmitted fair,   380
Assign'd his figure to Bernini's° care;
And great Nassau° to Kneller's hand decreed
To fix him graceful on the bounding Steed:
So well in paint and stone they judg'd of merit:
But Kings in Wit may want discerning spirit.

---

315. scenes: the wings; they were first shown joined in the middle of the stage and then were parted to reveal the inner setting. **319. Old . . . breast:** [Pope's note] The Coronation of Henry the Eighth and Queen Anne Boleyn, in which the Playhouses vied with each other to represent all the pomp of a Coronation. In this noble contention, the Armour of one of the Kings of England, was borrowed from the Tower, to dress the Champion. **320. Democritus:** Greek philosopher of the fifth century B.C., popularly called the "laughing philosopher." **328. Orcas:** [Pope's note] the farthest Northern Promontory of Scotland, opposite to the Orcades. **331. Quin:** James Quin (1693–1766), an actor. **Oldfield:** the famous actress Anne Oldfield (1683–1730). **high plume, petticoat:** See Addison and Steele, *The Spectator,* No. 42, earlier in Part Two. **332. a birth-day suit:** Suits for royal birthday celebrations were unusually splendid. **337. Cato:** the hero of Addison's play (1713) of that name. **338. railly:** rally, jest.

352. Or . . . sing: Cf. *Paradise Lost,* III. 26–28:
> Yet not the more
> Cease I to wander where the Muses haunt
> Cleer spring.

355. Merlin's Cave: [Pope's note] A Building in the Royal Gardens of Richmond, where is a small, but choice Collection of Books. **381. Bernini:** The Italian architect (1598–1680) made a bust of Charles I that was destroyed by fire at Whitehall in 1696. **382. Nassau:** William III.

The Hero William, and the Martyr Charles,
One knighted Blackmore,° and one pension'd
    Quarles;°
Which made old Ben,° and surly Dennis° swear,
"No Lord's anointed, but a Russian Bear."
    Not with such Majesty, such bold relief,   390
The Forms august of King, or conqu'ring Chief,
E'er swell'd on Marble; as in Verse have shin'd
(In polish'd Verse) the Manners and the Mind.
Oh! could I mount on the Mæonian° wing,
Your Arms, your Actions, your Repose to sing!
What seas you travers'd! and what fields you fought!
Your Country's Peace, how oft, how dearly bought!
How barb'rous rage subsided at your word,
And Nations wonder'd while they dropp'd the sword!
How, when you nodded, o'er the land and deep,   400
Peace stole her wing, and wrapt the world in sleep;
Till Earth's extremes your mediation own,
And Asia's Tyrants tremble at your Throne—
But Verse alas! your Majesty disdains;
And I'm not us'd to Panegyric strains:
The Zeal of Fools offends at any time,
But most of all, the Zeal of Fools in ryme.
Besides, a fate attends on all I write,
That when I aim at praise, they say I bite.
A vile Encomium doubly ridicules;   410
There's nothing blackens like the ink of fools;
If true, a woful likeness, and if lyes,
"Praise undeserv'd is scandal in disguise:"
Well may he blush, who gives it, or receives;
And when I flatter, let my dirty leaves
(Like Journals, Odes, and such forgotten things
As Eusden,° Philips,° Settle,° writ of Kings)
Cloath spice, line trunks, or flutt'ring in a row,
Befringe the rails of Bedlam and Sohoe.°

---

387. **Blackmore:** Sir Richard Blackmore (1654–1729), physician and poetaster; Pope's target in the *Peri Bathous* (see above). **Quarles:** Francis Quarles (1592–1644), Metaphysical poet. 388. **Ben:** Jonson. **Dennis:** John Dennis (1657–1734), playwright and critic. (See the selection from Dennis earlier in Part Two.) 394. **Mæonian:** Homer supposedly lived in Maeonia. 417. **Eusden:** Laurence Eusden (1688–1730); he became Poet Laureate in 1718. **Philips:** Ambrose Philips (c. 1675–1749). (See the selections from Philips in Part Three.) **Settle:** Elkanah Settle (1648–1724), poet and dramatist. 418–19. **flutt'ring . . . Sohoe:** Pamphlets for sale were displayed hanging on railings.

[EPISTLE]

TO *ROBERT* Earl of *OXFORD*,
and Earl MORTIMER

This dedicatory epistle opens Pope's edition of the poems of his deceased friend Thomas Parnell, a member with Pope, Swift, Harley, and others, of the Scriblerus Club.
    The text is from *Poems on Several Occasions* (1722), incorporating Pope's very few revisions.

Such were the Notes, thy once-lov'd Poet sung,
'Till Death untimely stop'd his tuneful Tongue.
Oh just beheld, and lost! admir'd, and mourn'd!
With softest Manners, gentlest Arts adorn'd!
Blest in each Science,° blest in ev'ry Strain°!
Dear to the Muse, to HARLEY dear—in vain!
    For him, thou oft hast bid the World attend,°
Fond to forget the Statesman in the Friend;
For *Swift* and him, despis'd the Farce of State,
The sober Follies of the Wise and Great;   10
Dextrous, the craving, fawning Crowd to quit,
And pleas'd to 'scape from Flattery to Wit.
    Absent or dead, still let a Friend be dear,
(A Sigh the Absent claims, the Dead a Tear)
Recall those Nights that clos'd thy toilsom Days,
Still hear thy *Parnell* in his living Lays:
Who careless, now, of Int'rest, Fame, or Fate,
Perhaps forgets that OXFORD e'er was Great;
Or deeming meanest what we greatest call,
Beholds thee glorious only in thy Fall.°   20
    And sure if ought below the Seats Divine
Can touch Immortals, 'tis a Soul like thine:
A Soul supreme, in each hard Instance try'd,
Above all Pain, all Passion, and all Pride,
The Rage of Pow'r, the Blast of publick Breath,
The Lust of Lucre, and the Dread of Death.°

EPISTLE TO OXFORD. 5. **each Science:** every branch of knowledge. **ev'ry Strain:** Parnell's poems employed various meters. (See the selection from Parnell in Part Three.) 7. **attend:** wait. 20. **Fall:** Oxford, the Tory statesman, was impeached for favoring James Edward, the Old Pretender, at the expense of the Hanoverians. 26. **Dread of Death:** Oxford had been attacked with a knife in Parliament.

In vain to Desarts thy Retreat° is made;
The Muse attends thee to the silent Shade:
'Tis hers, the brave Man's latest Steps to trace,
Re-judge his Acts, and dignify Disgrace.   30
When Int'rest calls off all her sneaking Train.
And all th' Oblig'd desert, and all the Vain;
She waits, or to the Scaffold, or the Cell,
When the last ling'ring Friend has bid farewel.
Ev'n now she shades thy Evening Walk with Bays,
(No Hireling she, no Prostitute to Praise)
Ev'n now, observant of the parting Ray,
Eyes the calm Sun-set of thy Various Day,
Thro' Fortune's Cloud One truly Great can see,
Nor fears to tell, that MORTIMER is He.   40

ONE THOUSAND SEVEN HUNDRED AND THIRTY EIGHT. A DIALOGUE SOMETHING LIKE HORACE

The text is that of the first edition (1738), incorporating
Pope's few revisions. This work is better known as the
first dialogue of the *Epilogue to the Satires.*

Fr[iend]. NOT twice a twelvemonth you appear in
    Print,
And when it comes, the Court see nothing in 't.
You grow *correct* that once with Rapture writ,
And are, besides, too *Moral* for a Wit.
Decay of Parts, alas! we all must feel—
Why now, this moment, don't I see you steal?
'Tis all from *Horace: Horace* long before ye
Said, "Tories call'd him Whig, and Whigs a Tory;"°
And taught his Romans, in much better metre,
"To laugh at Fools who put their trust in *Peter*.°" 10
    But *Horace*, Sir, was delicate, was nice;°
Bubo° observes, he lash'd no sort of *Vice*:

27. **Retreat:** Forbidden the Court, Oxford had retired to
his estates on the Welsh border. A DIALOGUE SOMETHING
LIKE HORACE. **8. Tories . . . Tory:** Cf. *The First Satire of
the Second Book of Horace*, above, l. 68. **10. To . . . Peter:**
Cf. *The First Satire of the Second Book of Horace*, l. 40. **Peter:**
Peter Walter, or Walters (*c.* 1664–1746), an attorney. **11.
nice:** discriminating. **12. Bubo:** [Pope's note] Some guilty
person very fond of making such an observation [probably
Bubb Dodington, a Whig politician and prominent literary
patron of the day].

Horace would say, *Sir Billy*° *serv'd the Crown*,
Blunt° *could do Bus'ness*, *Huggins*° *knew the Town*,
In *Sappho*° touch the *Failing of the Sex*,
In rev'rend Bishops note some *small Neglects*,
And own, the *Spaniard* did a *waggish thing*,
Who cropt our Ears,° and sent them to the King.
His sly, polite, insinuating stile°
Could please at Court, and make AUGUSTUS° smile: 20
An artful Manager,° that crept between
His Friend and Shame, and was a kind of *Screen*.°
But 'faith your very Friends will soon be sore;
Patriots there are, who wish you'd jest no more—
And where's the Glory? 'twill be only thought
The Great man° never offer'd you a Groat.°
Go see Sir ROBERT—

                    P. See Sir ROBERT!—hum—
And never laugh—for all my life to come?
Seen him I have, but in his happier hour
Of Social Pleasure, ill-exchang'd for Pow'r;   30
Seen° him, uncumber'd with the Venal tribe,
Smile without Art, and win without a Bribe.
Would he oblige me? let me only find,
He does not think me what he thinks mankind.
Come, come, at all I laugh He laughs, no doubt,
The only diff'rence is, I dare laugh out.°

    F. Why yes: with *Scripture* still you may be free;
A Horse-laugh, if you please, at *Honesty;*

13. **Sir Billy:** Sir William Yonge (d. 1755), notorious Whig
and a profligate. **14. Blunt:** Sir John Blunt (1665–1733),
projector and director of the South Sea Company. **Huggins:**
[Pope's note] Formerly Jaylor of the Fleet prison, enriched
himself by many exactions, for which he was tried and
expelled. **15. Sappho:** Lady Mary Wortley Montagu
(1689–1762). (See the selection from Lady Mary in Part
Three.) **18. cropt our Ears:** [Pope's note] Said to be executed
by the Captain of a Spanish ship on one Jenkins a Captain of
an English one. He cut off his ears, and bid him carry them
to the King his master. **19. His . . . stile:** Persius described
Horace's satiric method as *vafer* and *callidus;* both of these
epithets mean sly, cunning. Pope quoted Persius' description
in a note. Dryden had translated the words "sly," "insinuating"; he borrowed the happy phrase from Milton's
description of Satan in *Paradise Lost*, IV. 348 ff. **20. Augustus:**
George II. **21. Manager:** This word was by Pope's time
coming to be used in its modern technical sense. **22. Screen:**
Walpole opposed allowing Parliament to investigate public
frauds. **26. The Great man:** [Pope's note] A phrase, by
common use, appropriated to the first minister. **Groat:** This
four-penny piece was not issued after 1662. **31–36. Seen . . .
out:** Note the stabs in the rhyme at the end of each couplet.
36. The only . . . out: a reference to Walpole's boast: "All
men have their price."

A Joke on JEKYL,° or some odd *Old Whig*,
Who never chang'd his Principle, or Wig: 40
A Patriot is a Fool in ev'ry age,
Whom all Lord Chamberlains° allow the Stage:
These nothing hurts; they keep their Fashion still,
And wear their strange old Virtue as they will.

    If any ask you, "Who's the Man, so near
His Prince, that writes in Verse, and has his Ear?
Why answer LYTTELTON,° and I'll engage
The worthy Youth shall ne'er be in a rage:
But were his Verses vile, his Whisper base,
You'd quickly find him in Lord *Fanny*'s° case.   50
Sejanus, Wolsey,° hurt not honest FLEURY,°
But well may put some Statesmen in a fury.

    Laugh then at any, but at Fools or Foes;
These you but anger, and you mend not those:
Laugh at your Friends, and if your Friends are sore,
So much the better, you may laugh the more.
To Vice and Folly to confine the jest,
Sets half the World, God knows, against the rest;
Did not the Sneer of more impartial men
At Sense and Virtue, balance all agen.   60
Judicious Wits spread wide the Ridicule,
And charitably comfort Knave and Fool.

    P. Dear Sir, forgive the Prejudice of Youth:
Adieu Distinction, Satire, Warmth, and Truth!
Come harmless *Characters* that no one hit,
Come *Henley*'s° Oratory, *Osborn*'s° Wit!
The Honey dropping from *Favonio*'s° tongue,

The Flow'rs of *Bubo*, and the Flow of *Young*°!
The gracious Dew of Pulpit Eloquence;°
And all the well-whipt Cream° of Courtly Sense,   70
That first was *Hervey*'s, *Fox*'s° next, and then
The *Senate*'s, and then *Hervey*'s once agen.
O come, that easy *Ciceronian* stile,
So *Latin*, yet so *English* all the while,
As, tho' the Pride of *Middleton*° and *Bland*,°
All Boys may read, and Girls may understand!
Then might I sing without the least Offence,
And all I sung should be the *Nation*'s *Sense*:
Or teach the melancholy Muse to mourn,
Hang the sad Verse on CAROLINA's° Urn,   80
And hail her passage to the Realms of Rest,
All Parts perform'd, and *all* her Children blest!°
So—Satire is no more—I feel it die—
No *Gazeteer*° more innocent than I!
And let, a God's-name, ev'ry Fool and Knave
Be grac'd thro' Life, and flatter'd in his Grave.

    F. Why so? if Satire knows its Time and Place,
You still may lash the Greatest—in Disgrace:
For Merit will by turns forsake them all;
Would you know when? exactly when they fall.   90
But let all Satire in all Changes spare
Immortal *Selkirk*, and grave *Delaware*°!

39. Jekyl: [Pope's note] Sir Joseph Jekyl, Master of the Rolls, a true Whig in his principles, and a man of the utmost probity. He sometimes voted against the Court, which drew upon him the laugh here described of ONE who bestowed it equally upon Religion and Honesty. He died a few months after the publication of this poem [in 1751]. **42. Lord Chamberlains:** They acted as licensers of plays. **47. Lyttelton:** [Pope's note] George Lyttelton, Secretary to the Prince of Wales, distinguished both for his writings and speeches in the spirit of Liberty. **50. Lord Fanny:** Lord Hervey (1696–1743), court Vice Chamberlain and confidant of Queen Caroline. **51. Sejanus, Wolsey:** [Pope's note] The one the wicked minister of Tiberius; the other, of Henry VIII. The writers against the Court usually bestowed these and other odious names on the Minister, without distinction, and in the most injurious manner. **Fleury:** André Hercule de Fleury (1653–1743), Louis XV's adviser. **66. Henley:** John Henley (1692–1756), a flamboyant preacher. **Osborn:** James Pitt, a journalist who wrote under the pseudonym of Francis Osborne. **67. Favonio:** Favonius is the West Wind, gentle and warm.

68. Young: either Sir William Yonge or Edward Young (1683–1765), the poet; in this context more likely the former. **69. The gracious . . . Eloquence:** [Pope's note] Alludes to some court sermons, and florid panegyrical speeches; particularly one very full of puerilities and flatteries; which afterwards got into an address in the same pretty style; and was lastly served up in an Epitaph, between Latin and English, published by its author. **70. well-whipt Cream:** Cf. Swift's *Tale of a Tub*, The Preface of the Author, where "Wit, without Knowledge" is compared to "a Sort of Cream." **71. Fox's:** Henry Fox (1705–74), First Baron Holland. Pope thought that his speech on the death of Queen Caroline in 1737 was written by Lord Hervey. **75. Middleton:** Conyers Middleton (1683–1750), theologian and student of Cicero. **Bland:** Henry Bland (d. 1764), provost of Eton College. **80. Carolina:** [Pope's note] Queen Consort to King George II. She died in 1737. Her death gave occasion, as is observed above, to many indiscreet and mean performances unworthy of her memory, whose last moments manifested the utmost courage and resolution. **82. All . . . blest:** Pope takes the Queen's side in the gossip over her death. There was a doubt whether she had received the sacraments and had been reconciled with the Prince of Wales, with whom she had quarreled. **84. Gazeteer:** journalist. **92. Selkirk, Delaware:** [Pope's note] A title given *that* Lord [Selkirk] by King James II. He was of the Bedchamber to King William: he was so to King George I. He was so to King George II. *This* Lord [De La Warr] was very skilful in all the forms of the House, in which he discharged himself with great gravity.

Silent and soft, as Saints remove to Heav'n,
All Tyes dissolv'd, and ev'ry Sin forgiv'n,
These, may some gentle, ministerial Wing
Receive, and place for ever near a King!
There, where no Passion, Pride, or Shame transport,
Lull'd with the sweet *Nepenthe*° of a Court;
There, where no Father's, Brother's, Friend's
       Disgrace
Once break their Rest, or stir them from their
       Place;   100
But past the Sense of human Miseries,
All Tears are wip'd for ever from all Eyes;°
No Cheek is known to blush, no Heart to throb,
Save when they lose a Question,° or a Job.°

P. Good Heav'n forbid, that I shou'd blast their
       Glory,
Who know how like Whig-Ministers to Tory,
And when three Sov'reigns dy'd, could scarce be
       vext,
Consid'ring what a Gracious Prince was next.
Have I in silent wonder seen such things
As Pride in Slaves, and Avarice in Kings,   110
And at a Peer, or Peeress shall I fret,
Who starves a Sister, or forswears a Debt?
Virtue, I grant you, is an empty boast;
But shall the Dignity of *Vice* be lost?
Ye Gods! shall *Cibber's* Son,° without rebuke
Swear like a Lord? or *Rich*° out-whore a Duke?
A Fav'rite's *Porter* with his Master vie,
Be brib'd as often, and as often lie?
Shall *Ward*° draw Contracts with a Statesman's skill?
Or *Japhet*° pocket, like his Grace,° a Will?   120
Is it for *Bond*° or *Peter* (paltry Things!)
To pay their Debts or keep their Faith like Kings?

If *Blount*° dispatch'd himself, he play'd the man,
And so may'st Thou, Illustrious *Passeran*°!
But shall a *Printer*, weary of his life,
Learn from their Books to hang himself and Wife°?
This, this, my friend, I cannot, must not bear;
Vice thus abus'd, demands a Nation's care;
This calls the Church to deprecate our Sin,
And hurls the Thunder of the Laws on *Gin*.°   130

Let modest *Foster*,° if he will, excell
Ten *Metropolitans*° in preaching well;
A simple Quaker, or a Quaker's Wife,°
Out-do *Landaffe*,° in Doctrine—yea, in Life;
Let humble ALLEN,° with an aukward Shame,
Do good by stealth, and blush to find it Fame.
Virtue may chuse the high or low Degree,
'Tis just alike to Virtue, and to me;
Dwell in a Monk, or light upon a King,
She's still the same, belov'd, contented thing.   140
Vice is undone, if she forgets her Birth,
And stoops from Angels to the Dregs of Earth:
But 'tis the *Fall* degrades her to a Whore;
Let *Greatness* own her, and she's mean no more:
Her Birth, her Beauty, Crowds and Courts confess,
Chaste Matrons praise her, and grave Bishops bless:
In golden Chains the willing World she draws,
And hers the Gospel is, and hers the Laws:
Mounts the Tribunal, lifts her scarlet head,
And sees pale Virtue carted° in her stead!   150
Lo! at the Wheels of her Triumphal Car,
Old *England's* Genius, rough with many a Scar,

---

98. Nepenthe: a drink or drug supposed to bring forget-fulness. **102. All . . . Eyes:** See Isa. 25:8. **104. lose a Question:** have their proposal vetoed by Parliament. **Job:** Originally meaning "a piece of work," this word came to mean in the later seventeenth century "a public service turned to private advantage." **115. Cibber's Son:** Theophilus Cibber (1703–58), an actor. **116. Rich:** John Rich (c. 1682–1761) introduced pantomime into England. **119. Ward:** perhaps John Ward (d. 1755), a Member of Parliament who was convicted of forgery. **120. Japhet:** Japhet Crook (1662–1734) was convicted of obtaining a will fraudulently. **his Grace:** Archbishop Wake handed the will of George I—a political document of dangerous tendency—to George II, who, it is now believed wisely, suppressed it. **121. Bond:** Denis Bond (d. 1747) was expelled from Parliament for fraud and embezzlement.

123. Blount: [Pope's note] Author of an impious and foolish Book called, The Oracles of Reason, who being in love with a near kinswoman of his, and rejected, gave himself a stab in the arm, as pretending to kill himself, of the consequence of which he really died. **124. Passeran:** [Pope's note] Author of another, called a Philosophical Discourse on Death. **126. hang . . . Wife:** [Pope's note] A Fact that happened in London a few years past. The unhappy man left behind him a paper justifying his action by the reasonings of some of these authors. **130. Gin:** [Pope's note] A spirituous liquor, the exorbitant use of which had almost destroyed the lowest rank of the People till it was restrained by an act of Parliament in 1736. **131. Foster:** James Foster (1697–1753), an Anabaptist minister who gave popular Sunday evening lectures. **132. Metropolitans:** bishops in charge of the bishops of an ecclesiastical province. **133. a Quaker's Wife:** probably the (unmarried) sister of the Lord Provost of Edinburgh, Mary Drummond, who preached to crowded audiences. **134. Landaffe:** [Pope's note] A poor Bishoprick in Wales, as poorly supplied. **135. Allen:** Pope's friend, the philanthropist Ralph Allen (1694–1764). **150. carted:** exposed in a cart, the punishment of whores.

Dragg'd in the Dust! his Arms hang idly round,
His Flag inverted trails along the ground!
Our Youth, all liv'ry'd o'er with foreign Gold,
Before her dance; behind her crawl the Old!
See thronging Millions to the Pagod° run,
And offer Country, Parent, Wife, or Son!
Hear her black Trumpet thro' the Land proclaim,
That "Not to be corrupted is the Shame."   160
In Soldier, Churchman, Patriot, Man in Pow'r,
'Tis Av'rice all, Ambition is no more!
See, all our Nobles begging to be Slaves!
See, all our Fools aspiring to be Knaves!
The Wit of Cheats, the Courage of a Whore,
Are what ten thousand envy and adore.
All, all look up, with reverential Awe,
On Crimes that scape, or triumph o'er the Law:
While Truth, Worth, Wisdom, daily they decry—
"Nothing is Sacred now but Villany."   170

Yet may this Verse (if such a Verse remain)
Show there was one who held it in disdain.

[EPIGRAM]

Engraved on the Collar of a
Dog which I gave to his
Royal Highness.

In 1736 Pope presented Frederick, Prince of Wales, whose party in politics he favored, with a puppy of his "rare Bounce"; he had this couplet inscribed on its collar.

I AM his Highness Dog at Kew;
Pray tell me Sir, whose Dog are you?

157. Pagod: heathen idol.

THE UNIVERSAL PRAYER

DEO OPT. MAX.

Published separately in 1738, and perhaps intended to be added to *An Essay on Man* (1733–34), the poem is a prayer suitable for all men, regardless of creed. For this very reason it was not acceptable to those whose religion was dogmatically Christian; in *Loss and Gain* (1848) Newman calls it "a pattern specimen of shallow philosophism." But this is to treat it unfairly. George Sherburn, who ascribes to it an "admirable tolerance," commends its "attempt to express an abstracted essence of all religions, to formulate a petition that all the world could raise to various gods but in one voice." He goes on, however, to disapprove of Pope's technical performance: "the idea of the poem is nobler than the poetry itself." Sherburn perhaps fails to see that Pope is writing in a form that rules out the grandeur displayed, for example, at the close of *The Dunciad* (1728–43) in favor of a grandeur of simplicity. Pope is writing a hymn, as his meter reveals—the same meter Isaac Watts used for such poems as *A Song to Creative Wisdom* (1706). Plainness, conciseness, solidity, a humble solemnity—these are the qualities Pope sought and achieved.

The text is that of the first edition (1738), except at one point where Pope later revised.

I.
FATHER of All! in every Age,
    In every Clime ador'd,
By Saint, by Savage, and by Sage,
    Jehovah, Jove, or Lord!

II.
Thou Great First Cause, least understood!
    Who all my Sense confin'd
To know but this,—that Thou art Good,
    And that my self am blind:

III.
Yet gave me, in this dark Estate,
    To see the Good from Ill;   10
And binding Nature fast in Fate,
    Left free the Human Will.

IV.

What Conscience dictates to be done,
  Or warns me not to doe,
This, teach me more than Hell to shun,
  That, more than Heav'n pursue.

V.

What Blessings thy free Bounty gives,
  Let me not cast away;
For God is pay'd when Man receives,
  T' enjoy, is to obey.   20

VI.

Yet not to Earth's contracted Span,
  Thy Goodness let me bound;
Or think thee Lord alone of Man,
  When thousand Worlds are round.

VII.

Let not this weak, unknowing hand
  Presume Thy Bolts to throw,
And deal Damnation round the land,
  On each I judge thy Foe.

VIII.

If I am right, thy Grace impart
  Still in the right to stay;   30
If I am wrong, oh teach my heart
  To find that better Way.

IX.

Save me alike from foolish Pride,
  Or impious Discontent,
At ought thy Wisdom has deny'd,
  Or ought thy Goodness lent.

X.

Teach me to feel another's Woe;
  To hide the Fault I see;
That Mercy I to others show,
  That Mercy show to me.   40

XI.

Mean tho' I am, not wholly so
  Since quicken'd by thy Breath,
Oh lead me wheresoe'er I go,
  Thro' this day's Life, or Death:

XII.

This day, be Bread and Peace my Lot;
  All else beneath the Sun,
Thou know'st if best bestow'd, or not;
  And let Thy Will be done.

XIII.

To Thee, whose Temple is all Space,
  Whose Altar, Earth, Sea, Skies;   50
One Chorus let all Being raise!
  All Nature's Incence rise!

FROM

THE DUNCIAD

With his *Peri Bathous* (1728) Pope stirred up the Dunces
to play his game, and while they were still fussing about
that, down came *The Dunciad* on them like the Flying
Island in Gulliver's third voyage—"*Volat Irrevocabile
Dunciad*" Pope remarked in a letter to Lord Oxford
on March 13, 1729, when the full-scale version of the
poem appeared.

The Dunciad has not had its due from critics because
its particular difficulties have been allowed to get in the
way. The subject Pope chose had always interested him.
The first poem he published, as far as we know, was a
satire on a Dunce, a writer whose dullness proclaims
that he has chosen the wrong profession; and *An Essay
on Criticism* (1711) was partly an attack on dullness and
pointed at individual offenders. Such a subject when
treated with personal detail is one that in a later age only
scholars can hope to enter into fully. The contemporary
references in the poem were felt to be obscure even
from the start. Swift told Pope that only Londoners,
and indeed only Londoners who were closely interested
in Grub Street, would be able to follow them. "The
notes," he wrote Pope, "I could wish to be very large,
in what relates to the persons concern'd; for I have long
observ'd that twenty miles from London no body
understands hints, initial letters, or town-facts and
passages; and in a few years not even those who live in
London." We suffer the increased disadvantage of the
lapse of two centuries.

Plainly, the better equipped we are with relevant
knowledge, the more *The Dunciad* will mean to us.
But it is equally true that ignorance of contemporary
Grub Street is not fatal to our seeing the poem as one
of the great comic—and also solemn—poems, for it
contains much of universal interest. Take as a small
instance this couplet from Book III: "Silence, ye Wolves!
while Ralph to Cynthia howls, / And makes Night
hideous—Answer him ye Owls!" Scholars know that
the American James Ralph wrote a blank verse poem
called *Night*, published in London in 1727, that the first
half of the second line is a quotation from Hamlet's
address to the Ghost, and that the second half mimics a
line in *Paradise Lost* (V. 197): "Joyn voices all ye living

souls, ye Birds." But even if we do not know all this, it is obvious that the scene suggested is superb—an operalike scene, complete with a solo singer, grotesque choruses right and left, darkened lights, and a conductor gesticulating in silhouette. This effect does not depend on our knowing about Ralph. And is it not also true that the brilliant context of this attack diminishes the pain that Ralph must have suffered? As in the *Peri Bathous* there was some pleasure even for the victims.

The main victim in the first version of the poem was Lewis Theobald, who had challenged Pope as editor of Shakespeare. The very title of his book was a challenge: *Shakespeare Restored: or a Specimen of the Many Errors, as Well Committed, as Unamended, by Mr. Pope in His Late Edition of This Poet* (1726). But again our lack of special knowledge is not fatal. As we read this first version there is little lost if our knowledge of Theobald is scanty, for what Pope gives us is that comic and universal figure—the writer trying to produce immortal works without the necessary inspiration.

The framework of the poem, apart from its details, has recently been related closely to epic. Aubrey L. Williams reminds us that just as Aeneas moves a kingdom from Troy to Latium, so the Goddess of Dulness moves hers from the City of London to the West End, from Lord Mayor's pageants to the theaters, where pantomime and opera were ousting drama. If we miss this scheme in the poem, we miss something important. Even so, its being overlooked for so long suggests that despite the emphasis Pope gave it in a note he did not think it of first importance. Much of the poem, including all of Book IV, exists quite apart from epic. Once Pope had hit on the framework, his powers were exercised on the hundred patches and the thousand details rather than on the outline. Joseph Warton called the poem "one of the most motley compositions that, perhaps, is anywhere to be found in the works of so exact a writer as Pope." Epic is never motley, but always bold and simple in its design; nevertheless, the more thoroughly we know the poem, the more clearly we see the epic nature of its framework.

Bibliographers disagree on which of two 1728 editions is the first. The text printed here—we have reproduced it without the later revisions—is that of the octavo (British Museum, Ashley 1303), which differs only at one or two unimportant points from the other, a duodecimo. We have corrected the octavo reading of *Book* for *Books* in the opening line. Further editions followed in 1728, and in 1729 Pope brought out a revised version of the poem in magnificent style, formidably complete with extensive notes, some purportedly by Martinus Scriblerus, author of the *Peri Bathous*. We have reproduced some of the notes of 1729, in whole or in part. The original text gave most of the proper names in the form of initial or outside letters;

omitted letters were marked by a dash. We have given them complete.

❧

BOOK THE FIRST

BOOKS and the man I sing,° the first° who brings
The *Smithfield*° muses to the ears of kings.
Say great *Patricians!* (since yourselves inspire
These wond'rous works; so *Jove* and fate require°!)
Say from what cause,° in vain decry'd and curst,
Still *Dunce the second reigns like Dunce the first*°?

In eldest time, e'er mortals writ or read,
E'er *Pallas* issued from the Thund'rer's head,°
Dulness o'er all possess'd her antient right,
Daughter of *Chaos* and eternal *Night:*°   10
Fate in their dotage this fair idiot gave,
Gross as her sire, and as her mother grave,
Laborious, heavy, busy, bold, and blind,
She rul'd, in native anarchy, the mind.

Still her old empire to confirm, she tries,
For born a Goddess, *Dulness* never dies.

Where wave the tatter'd ensigns of *Rag-Fair,*°
A yawning ruin hangs and nods in air;

THE DUNCIAD: *Book the First.* **1. Books . . . sing:** a translation, with a significant change, of *Arma virumque cano*, the opening words of the *Aeneid*. **the first:** Ancient poets were pleased to claim this sort of priority whenever possible. **2. Smithfield:** [Pope's note] the place where Bartholomew Fair was kept, whose Shews, Machines, and Dramatical Entertainments, formerly agreeable only to the Taste of the Rabble, were, by the Hero of this Poem and others of equal Genius, brought to the Theatres of Covent-Garden, Lincolns-inn-Fields, and the Hay-Market, to be the reigning Pleasures of the Court and Town. This happened in the Year 1725, and continued to the Year 1728. **4. so . . . require:** You are ruled in this by Jove and Fate, as were the heroes of the ancient epics. **5. Say . . . cause:** customary in the epics. Cf. *The Rape of the Lock*, above, i. 7. **6. Dunce the second . . . first:** This line, which is built on one of Dryden's, is directed primarily at the Dunces, but also at the Hanoverians (George II succeeded his father the year before). **8. Pallas . . . head:** Pallas Athene, the goddess of wisdom, was supposed to have been born full-grown from the head of Jove. **10. Chaos . . . Night:** The most recent reference to such cosmological theories had been Milton's in *Paradise Lost*, II. 894 ff., where he made Chaos and Night the "Ancestors of Nature." **17. Rag-Fair:** a market for secondhand goods near the Tower of London.

Keen, hollow winds howl thro' the bleak recess,
Emblem of music caus'd by emptiness:°   20
Here in one bed two shiv'ring sisters lye,
The cave of *Poverty* and *Poetry*.°
This, the *Great Mother*° dearer held than all
The clubs of *Quidnunc's*,° or her own *Guild-hall*:°
Here stood her Opium, here she nurs'd her Owls,
And destin'd here th' imperial seat of fools.
Hence springs each weekly° muse, the living boast
Of *Curl*'s chaste press,° and *Lintot*'s rubric post;°
Hence hymning *Tyburn*'s elegiac lay,°
Hence the soft sing-song on *Cecilia*'s day,°   30
Sepulchral lyes° our holy walls to grace,
And *New-year-Odes*, and all the *Grubstreet*° race.

'Twas here in clouded majesty she shone;
Four guardian *Virtues*, round, support her throne;
Fierce champion *Fortitude*, that knows no fears
Of hisses, blows, or want, or loss of ears:°
Calm *Temperance*, whose blessings those partake
Who hunger, and who thirst for scribling sake:°
Prudence, whose glass° presents th' approaching jayl;
Poetic *Justice*, with her lifted scale;   40
Where in nice balance, truth with gold she weighs,
And solid pudding against empty praise.

Here she beholds the Chaos dark and deep,
Where nameless *somethings* in their causes° sleep,

'Till genial *Jacob*,° or a warm *third-day*°
Calls forth each mass, a poem or a play.
How hints, like spawn, scarce quick in embryo lie;
How new-born nonesense first is taught to cry;
Maggots° half-form'd, in rhyme exactly meet,
And learn to crawl upon poetic feet.   50
Here one poor *Word* a hundred clenches° makes,
And ductile dulness new meanders takes;
There motley *Images* her fancy strike,
Figures ill-pair'd, and *Similes* unlike.
She sees a mob of *Metaphors* advance,
Pleas'd with the madness of the mazy dance:
How *Tragedy* and *Comedy* embrace;
How *Farce* and *Epic* get a jumbled race;°
How *Time* himself stands still at her command,
Realms shift their place, and Ocean turns to land.   60
Here gay *Description Ægypt* glads with showers,
Or gives to *Zembla* fruits, to *Barca* flowers;
Glitt'ring with ice here hoary hills are seen,
Fast by, fair vallies of eternal green,
On cold *December* fragrant chaplets blow,
And heavy harvests nod beneath the snow.°

All these and more, the cloud-compelling° Queen
Beholds thro' fogs, that magnify the scene;
She, tinsel'd o'er in robes of varying hues,
With self-applause her wild creation views,   70
Sees momentary monsters rise and fall,
And with her own fools-colours gilds them all.

'Twas on the day, when *Thorold*,° rich and grave,
Like *Cimon*° triumph'd both on land and wave,

20. **emptiness:** an empty stomach. **22. The cave . . .
Poetry:** Theobald's poem *The Cave of Poverty, Written
in Imitation of Shakespeare* was published in 1714. **23.
Great Mother:** Dullness. **24. Quidnunc:** [Pope's note] a
name given to the ancient Members of certain political
Clubs, who were constantly enquiring, *Quid nunc?* what news?
Guild-hall: the hall in which a trade guild met. **27. weekly:**
a pun on *weakly*. **28. Curl's . . . press:** Pope takes the
London publisher Edmund Curll (1675–1747) as typical of
publishers of scandal. **Lintot's . . . post:** Pope had quarreled
with Bernard Lintot (1675–1736), publisher of much of his
earlier work. According to Pope, Lintot "usually adorn'd his
shop with Titles in red letters." **29. hymning . . . lay:** [Pope's
note] It is an ancient English custom for the Malefactors
to sing a Psalm at their Execution at Tyburn; and no less
customary to print Elegies on their deaths, at the same time,
or before. **30. on . . . day:** Poets, including Pope, wrote
poems to be set to music and sung on the day honoring the
patron saint of music. **31. Sepulchral lyes:** flattering epitaphs.
32. Grubstreet: favored as lodging by hack writers. **36.
want . . . ears:** Some poets have no ears because they have
had them cut off as a legal punishment; others lack them
because they have no sense of meter. **37–38. Calm . . . sake:**
an echo of Matt. 5:6. **39. glass:** Painters sometimes depicted
Prudence with a perspective glass, i.e., a telescope. **44.
causes:** origins.

45. **genial Jacob:** Jacob Tonson (*c.* 1656–1736), the publisher, is called genial because he is represented as the sun.
warm third-day: The proceeds of the third performance
of a play were handed over to the author. *Warm* means
both hot and rich, or affluent. **49. Maggots:** (1) grubs;
(2) quirks of fancy. **51. clenches:** puns. Pope himself used
puns: he does so brilliantly in the present passage, where the
double meaning improves the sense. He deplored them when
they were used incongruously simply for their own sake.
57–58. How . . . race: Pope's examples of the jumbling of
literary kinds in a work of poor quality would include Lewis
Theobald's *Dramatic Entertainment, Called Harlequin a Sorcerer*
(1725). **59–66. How . . . snow:** examples of ridiculous
factual inaccuracy. **67. cloud-compelling:** [Pope's note]
From *Homer*'s Epithet of *Jupiter*. **73. Thorold:** [Pope's note]
Sir George Thorold Lord Mayor of *London*, in the year 1720.
The Procession of a Lord Mayor is made partly by land, and
partly by water. **74. Cimon:** [Pope's note] famous *Athenian*
General obtained a Victory by sea, and another by land, on
the same day, over the *Persians* and *Barbarians*.

(Pomps without guilt, of bloodless swords and maces,
Glad° chains, warm furs, broad banners, and broad
    faces)
Now night descending, the proud scene was o'er,
Yet liv'd, in *Settle's*° numbers, one day more.
Now *May'rs* and *Shrieves*° in pleasing slumbers lay,
And eat in dreams the custard of the day: 80
But pensive poets painful vigils keep;
Sleepless themselves, to give their readers sleep.
Much to her mind the solemn feast recalls,
What city-*Swans* once sung within the walls,
Much she revolves their arts, their antient praise,
And sure succession down from *Heywood's*° days.
She saw with joy the line immortal run,
Each sire imprest and glaring in his son;°
So watchful *Bruin* forms with plastic care
Each growing lump, and brings it to a Bear.   90
She saw in *Norton*° all his father shine,
And *Eusden*° eke out *Blackmore's*° endless line;
She saw slow *Philips*° creep like *Tate's*° poor page,
And furious *Dunton*° foam in *Wh*——'s° rage.

In each, she marks her image full exprest,
But chief, in *Tibbald's*° monster-breeding breast,
Sees Gods with Dæmons in strange league ingage,
And earth, and heav'n, and hell, her battels wage!

She ey'd the Bard where supperless he sate,
And pin'd, unconscious of his rising fate;   100
Studious he sate, with all his books around,
Sinking from thought to thought, a vast profound°!
Plung'd for his sense, but found no bottom there:
Then writ, and flounder'd on, in mere despair.
He roll'd his eyes that witness'd huge dismay,°
Where yet unpawn'd, much learned lumber lay,
Volumes, whose size the space exactly fill'd;
Or which fond authors were so good to gild;
Or where, by Sculpture made for ever known,
The page admires new beauties, not its own.   110
Here swells the shelf with *Ogleby*° the *great*,
There, stamp'd with arms, *Newcastle*° shines compleat,
Here all his suff'ring brotherhood retire,
And 'scape the martyrdom of jakes and fire;
A° *Gothic* Vatican! of *Greece* and *Rome*
Well-purg'd, and worthy *Wesley, Watts,* and *Blome.*°

But high above, more solid Learning shone,
The *Classicks* of an age that heard of none;°
There *Caxton* slept, with *Wynkin*° at his side,   119
One clasp'd in wood, and one in strong cow-hide:°

---

76. Glad: full of brightness, suggesting cheerfulness in contrast to the usual epithets applied to chains. **78. Settle:** Elkanah Settle (1648–1724), poet and dramatist. **79. Shrieves:** Two sheriffs were elected annually by the City of London to serve as sheriffs of Middlesex; they presided over the county court. **86. Heywood:** Thomas Heywood (d. 1641), playwright and miscellaneous writer. **88. Each . . . son:** James R. Sutherland suggests that "Pope may be alluding here obliquely to the new coinage stamped on the accession of George II. Two hundred gold and eight hundred silver medals had been struck for the new King." **91. Norton:** Benjamin Norton Defoe, apparently a natural son of Daniel Defoe. **92. Eusden:** Laurence Eusden (1688–1730); he became Poet Laureate in 1718. **Blackmore:** Sir Richard Blackmore (1654–1729), physician and poetaster; a favorite target of the Augustan wits. **93. Philips:** either Ambrose (c. 1675–1749) or John (1676–1709). (See selections from both in Part Three.) **Tate:** Nahum Tate (1652–1715), playwright and poet of Dryden's day. **94. Dunton:** the critic John Dunton (1659–1733). **Wh——:** possibly Stephen Whatley (fl. 1720) or Philip Wharton (1698–1731), Duke of Wharton and a rake. **96. Tibbald:** [Pope's note] Author of many forgotten Plays, Poems, and other pieces [including] Farces [of such extravagance that] he alone could properly be represented as successor to *Settle*, who had written . . . pieces for *Bartlemew-Fair.*

102. Sinking . . . profound: Cf. the theme of the *Peri Bathous* (see above) and also the account of Satan's journey through Chaos in *Paradise Lost*, II. 927–50. **105. He . . . dismay:** [Pope's note] Milt. [*Paradise Lost*, I. 56 ff.] *Round he throws his eyes That witness'd huge affliction and dismay.* The progress of a bad Poet in his thoughts being (like the progress of the Devil in *Milton*) thro' a Chaos, might probably suggest this imitation. **111. Ogleby:** [Pope's note] *John Ogilby was one, who from a late initiation into literature, made such a progress as might well stile him the Prodigy of his time! sending into the world so many large Volumes!* . . . WINSTANLY, *Lives of Poets.* **112. Newcastle:** [Pope's note] The *Duchess of Newcastle* was one who busied herself in the ravishing delights of Poetry; leaving to posterity in print three *ample Volumes* of her studious endeavours. WINSTANLY, ibid. *Langbaine* reckons up eight Folio's of her Grace's; which were usually adorn'd with gilded Covers, and had her Coat of Arms upon them. **115–16. A Gothic . . . Blome:** Theobald is represented as taking the modern side in the Battle of the Books. **116. Wesley . . . Blome:** Samuel Wesley (d. 1735) (the father of John Wesley, the Methodist leader), Isaac Watts (1674–1748), and Richard Blome (1600–1705). Pope ought to have spared Watts, if only because he borrowed phrases from him for some of his best poems. (See the selections from Watts in Part Three.) **118. none:** none of the classics of Greece and Rome, that is. **119. Caxton, Wynkin:** Pope saw William Caxton (c. 1422–91), who published a prose translation of the *Aeneid*, and Wynkin de Worde (d. 1534), who published a revised edition of Caxton's *Recueil of the Histories of Troy*, as oases in a desert of ignorance. **120. One . . . cow-hide:** Medieval books were often bound so.

There sav'd by spice, like mummies, many a year,
Old Bodies of Philosophy appear:
De Lyra° there a dreadful front extends,
And there, the groaning Shelves Philemon° bends.

Of these twelve volumes, twelve of amplest size,
Redeem'd from tapers and defrauded pyes,
Inspir'd he seizes: These an altar raise:
An hecatomb° of pure, unsully'd° lays
That altar crowns; a folio Common-place°
Founds the whole pyle, of all his works the base: 130
Quarto's, octavo's, shape the lessening pyre,
And last, a *little Ajax*° tips the spire.

Then he. Great Tamer of all human art!
First in my care, and nearest at my heart!
Dulness! whose good old cause I yet defend,
With whom my muse began, with whom shall end°!
Oh thou! of business the directing soul,
To human heads like byass to the bowl,°
Which as more pond'rous makes their aim more true,
Obliquely wadling to the mark in view.   140
O ever gracious to perplex'd mankind!
Who spread a healing mist before the mind,
And, lest we err by wit's wild, dancing light,
Secure us kindly in our native *night*.
Ah! still o'er *Britain* stretch that peaceful wand,
Which lulls th' *Helvetian* and *Batavian* land,°
Where 'gainst thy throne if rebel Science rise,
She does but show her coward face and dies:
There, thy good *scholiasts*° with unweary'd pains
Make *Horace* flat, and humble *Maro's* strains;   150
Here studious I unlucky Moderns save,

Nor° sleeps one error in its father's grave,
Old puns restore, lost blunders nicely° seek,
And crucify poor *Shakespear* once a week.°
For thee I dim these eyes, and stuff this head,
With all such reading as was never read;°
For thee supplying, in the worst of days,
Notes to dull books, and Prologues to dull plays;
For thee explain a thing 'till all men doubt it,
And write about it, Goddess, and about it;   160
So spins the silkworm small its slender store,
And labours, 'till it clouds itself all o'er.
Not that my pen to criticks was confin'd,
My verse gave ampler lessons to mankind;
So written precepts may successless prove,
But sad examples never fail to move.
As forc'd from wind-guns, lead itself can fly,
And pond'rous slugs cut swiftly thro' the sky;
As clocks to weight their nimble motion owe,
The wheels above urg'd by the load below;   170
Me, Emptiness and Dulness could inspire,
And were my Elasticity, and Fire.
Had heav'n decreed such works a longer date,
Heav'n had decreed to spare the *Grubstreet*-state.°
But see great *Settle* to the dust descend,
And all thy cause and empire at an end!
Cou'd° *Troy* be sav'd by any single hand,
His gray-goose-weapon° must have made her stand.
But what can I! *my Flaccus*° cast aside,

123. De Lyra: Nicholas de Lyra (d. 1340) wrote what when printed later made, in Pope's words, "five vast Folio's." **124. Philemon:** [Pope's note] [Philemon Holland (1552–1637)] translated *so many books*, that a man would think he had done *nothing else*, insomuch that he might be call'd *Translator General of his age* . . . WINSTANLY. **128. hecatomb:** sacrifice. **unsully'd:** In the epics beasts to be sacrificed are purified. The lays have not been "sullied" by any reader's hands. **129. a folio Common-place:** a notebook into which Theobald copied passages for his own use. See l. 130. **132. a little Ajax:** Pope alleged, perhaps wrongly, that Theobald was the translator of Sophocles' *Ajax*, which had appeared in 1714. **136. With . . . end:** This degree of devotion had been claimed by several classic poets. **138. byass . . . bowl:** In the game of bowls, the ball has a "bias"—a weight on one side—that causes it to curve. **146. th' Helvetian . . . land:** Basel in Switzerland (Helvetia) had been famous for its editions of classical texts, and the Netherlands (Batavia) was still; no particular editions of Horace and Virgil seem relevant. **149. scholiasts:** commentators.

152–54. Nor . . . week: [Pope's note, signed Scriblerus] As where [Theobald] laboured to prove *Shakespear* guilty of terrible *Anacronisms*, or low *Conundrums*, which Time had cover'd; and conversant in such authors as *Caxton* and *Wynkin*, rather than in *Homer* or *Chaucer*. Nay so far had he lost his reverence to this incomparable author, as to say in print, *He deserved to be whipt.* An insolence which nothing sure can parallel! but that of *Dennis*, who can be proved to have declared before Company, that *Shakespear was a Rascal. O tempora! O mores!* **153. nicely:** carefully. **154. once a week:** Sutherland says that Theobald's letters to *Mists' Journal* in which he discussed Shakespearean minutiae numbered to date two only. **156. With . . . read:** Pope misses the sense in Theobald's editorial method. **173–74. Had . . . Grubstreet-state:** a reference to the *Aeneid*, II. 641–42, which Dryden had translated (II. 866–67): "Had Heav'n decreed that I shou'd Life enjoy, / Heav'n had decreed to save unhappy *Troy*." **177–78. Cou'd . . . stand:** a reference to the *Aeneid*, II. 291–92, which Dryden had translated (II. 387–88): "If by a Mortal Hand my Father's Throne / Cou'd be defended, 'twas by mine alone." **178. gray-goose-weapon:** the common quill pen. **179. my Flaccus:** [Pope's note] A familiar manner of speaking used by modern Criticks of a favourite Author. [This phrase means "my Horace." Pope forgot that Milton had written "my Shakespeare."]

Take up th' *Attorney's*° (once my better) *guide?*   180
Or rob the *Roman* geese of all their glories,
And save the state by cackling to the Tories?°
Yes, to my country I my pen consign,
Yes, from this moment, mighty *Mist*°! am thine,
And rival, *Curtius*°! of thy fame and zeal,
O'er head and ears plunge for the public weal.
Adieu my children! better thus expire
Un-stall'd,° unsold; thus glorious mount in fire
Fair without spot; than greas'd by grocer's hands,
Or shipp'd with *Ward*° to ape and monkey lands,   190
Or wafting ginger, round the streets to go,
And visit alehouse° where ye first did grow.

With that, he lifted thrice the sparkling brand,
And thrice he dropt it from his quiv'ring hand:
Then lights the structure, with averted eyes;
The rowling smokes involve the sacrifice.
The opening clouds disclose each work by turns,
Now flames old *Memnon*,° now *Rodrigo*° burns,
In one quick flash see *Proserpine* expire,
And last, his own° cold *Æschylus* took fire.   200
Then gush'd the tears, as from the *Trojan's*° eyes
When the last blaze sent *Ilion* to the skies.

Rowz'd by the light, old *Dulness* heav'd the head,
Then snatch'd a sheet of *Thulè*° from her Bed,
Sudden she flies, and whelms it o'er the pyre;
Down sink the flames, and with a hiss expire.

Her ample presence fills up all the place;
A veil of fogs dilates her awful face,
Great in her charms! as when on Shrieves and
     May'rs
She looks, and breathes herself into their airs.°   210
She bids him wait her to the sacred Dome;°
Well-pleas'd he enter'd, and confess'd his home:
So spirits, ending their terrestrial race,
Ascend, and recognize their native place:
Raptur'd, he gazes round the dear retreat,
And in sweet numbers celebrates the seat.°

Here to her Chosen all her works she shows;
Prose swell'd to verse, Verse loitring into prose:
How random thoughts now meaning chance to find,
Now leave all memory of sense behind;   220
How Prologues into Prefaces decay,
And those to Notes are fritter'd quite away:
How Index-learning° turns no student pale,
Yet holds the eel of science° by the Tail:
How, with less reading than makes felons 'scape,°
Less human genius than God gives an ape,
Small thanks to *France*, and none to *Rome* or *Greece*,
A past, vamp'd, future, old, reviv'd, new piece,

---

180. Attorney: Theobald had started his career as an attorney. **181–82. Or . . . Tories:** [Pope's note] Relates to the well-known story of the geese that saved the Capitol. **184. Mist:** Theobald contributed to Nathaniel Mist's Tory newspaper, *The Weekly Journal.* Pope puns on *mist.* **185. Curtius:** See *Essay on Man,* ii., note to l. 200. The oracle had declared that a wide gap in the Forum would close only when Rome threw into it its most precious possession; the young Marcus Curtius, armed and on horseback, threw himself into the chasm, which then closed. **188. Un-stall'd:** not set out for sale on the bookstalls. **190. Ward:** Edward Ward (1667–1731) wrote Hudibrastic rhymes that were sold, Pope alleged, in colonies in or near the tropics, where much of the labor was done by transported criminals. **192. visit alehouse:** The seemingly awkward omission of *the* before *alehouse* occurs because Pope is amusingly echoing a line by Waller: "And visit Mountains where they once did grow." **198. Memnon . . . Rodrigo:** the heroes of two of Theobald's tragedies, *The Persian Princess* (1717) and *The Perfidious Brother* (1715), respectively. **200. his own:** Pope is still laughing at the use of *my* in line 179. **201. Trojan:** Aeneas. **204. Thulè:** [Pope's note] An unfinished Poem of that name, of which one sheet was printed fifteen Years ago by A. Ph[ilips] a Northern Author. It is an usual method of putting out a fire, to cast wet sheets upon it.

209–10. Great . . . airs: Pope recalls Dryden's translation (II. 804–05) of the *Aeneid,* II. 591–92: "Great in her Charms, as when on Gods above / She looks, and breaths her self into their Love." **211. the sacred Dome:** [Pope's note] The *Cave of Poverty* above-mentioned; where he no sooner enters, but he Reconnoitres the place of his original [origin]; as *Plato* says the Spirits shall do, at their entrance into the celestial Regions. His Dialogue of the Immortality of the Soul was translated by *T.* in the familiar modern stile of *Prithee Phædo,* and *For God's sake Socrates:* printed for *B. Lintot,* 1713. **216. in . . . seat:** [Pope's note] He writ a Poem call'd the *Cave of Poverty,* which concludes with a very extraordinary Wish, "That some great Genius, or man of distinguished merit may be *starved,* in order to celebrate her power, and describe her Cave." It was printed in octavo, 1715. **223. Index-learning:** Cf. Swift, *A Tale of a Tub,* sec. viii: "The most accomplisht Way of using Books at present, is twofold: Either first, to serve them as some Men do *Lords,* learn their *Titles* exactly, and then brag of their Acquaintance. Or Secondly, which is indeed the choicer, the profounder, and politer Method, to get a thorough Insight into the *Index,* by which the whole Book is governed and turned, like *Fishes* by the *Tail.*" **224. science:** knowledge. **225. less . . . 'scape:** Until 1827, clergymen who had committed felonies were exempt from trial by a secular court if they proved they could read.

'Twixt *Plautus, Fletcher,*° *Congreve,* and *Corneille,*
Can make a *Cibber,*° *Johnson,*° or *Ozell.*°   230

The Goddess then, o'er his anointed head,
With mystic words the sacred Opium shed;
And lo! her *Bird* (a monster of a fowl!
Something betwixt a *Heidegger*° and Owl)
Perch'd on his crown. All hail! and hail again
My son! the promis'd land expects thy reign.
Know *Settle,* cloy'd with custard and with praise,
Is gather'd to the Dull of antient days,
Safe, where no criticks damn, no duns molest,
Where *Gildon,*° *Banks,*° and high-born *Howard*°
rest!   240
I see a King! who leads my chosen sons
To lands that flow with clenches and with puns:
Till each fam'd theatre my empire own,
Till *Albion,* as *Hibernia,*° bless my throne.
I see! I see!—Then rapt, she spoke no more.
God save King Tibbald! *Grubstreet* alleys roar.

So when *Jove's* block descended from on high,
(As sings thy great fore-father, *Ogilby,*)
Hoarse thunder to its bottom shook the bog,
And the loud nation croak'd, *God save King* Log!°   250

---

229. **Fletcher:** John Fletcher (1579–1625), writer of
comedies and collaborator with Francis Beaumont (c. 1584–
1616) on a number of tragicomedies. 230. **Cibber:** Colley
Cibber (1671–1757), dramatist and poet; he became the
hero of *The Dunciad* in its revised form (1743). **Johnson:**
Charles Johnson (1679–1748), a prolific playwright, most
of whose works were based on earlier famous plays.
Ozell: John Ozell (d. 1743), translator of French plays into
English. 234. **Heidegger:** John James Heidegger (c. 1659–
1749), a Swiss, became prominent in the theater world. 240.
Gildon: Charles Gildon (1665–1724), according to Pope,
"a writer of criticisms and libels of the last age." **Banks:** John
Banks (fl. 1696), a playwright. **Howard:** Edward Howard
(d. 1732), one of the playwriting wits of the Restoration; he
was nicknamed Foolish Ned. 244. **Hibernia:** Ireland.
247–50. **So . . . Log:** Cf. Ogilby's translation of Aesop
(1651), in which, when the frogs ask for a king, Jove drops a
block of wood into the pool, whereupon ". . . all the bog /
Proclaime their King, and cry *Jove* save King Log." The
frogs grew impatient at the block's inactivity, so Jove sent a
stork which devoured them "with a greedie maw."

THE NEW DUNCIAD

As it was Found
In the Year 1741.

✥

In *The New Dunciad* (1742), Pope took a subject much
broader than second-rate authors, and presented a
variety of people—fanatics, pretenders, and perverts—all
claiming intellectual and cultural status. He virtually
abandoned the epic framework, which had been barely
visible in the version of the poem in three books, and
adopted instead the pattern he had given us in his early
poem *The Temple of Fame* (1715), where wise and foolish
aspirants present their petitions to the goddess. This
pattern was familiar in several seventeenth-century
poems collected under the title *The Session of the Poets,*
as well as in some plays by Fielding. In *Studies in English,*
published by the University of Texas, George Sherburn
has accurately described the action of this fourth book:

> The structural pattern of Book IV seems at first
> sight more original, less in the heroic tradition,
> than were the devices of the earlier Books. Book I
> derived from *MacFlecknoe* and other sources; Book
> II, echoing the funeral games for Anchises (*Aeneid
> V*), and Book III, drawing from the prophetic
> visions of *Aeneid VI* and *Paradise Lost* XI and XII,
> seem perhaps more normal for a mock epic. Book
> IV presents a grand drawing-room, appropriate for
> a royal birthday, at which titles or orders of merit
> are bestowed by the Queen of Dulness. The scene
> is chiefly that of such a drawing-room, but it
> unfolds in a slightly confusing dreamlike fashion
> into an academic meeting for the conferring of
> degrees. This latter aspect of the scene intrigued
> both Pope and Warburton, not merely because the
> *Dunciad* was a satire on pedantry, but because in
> 1741 both Pope and Warburton had been proposed
> for the LL.D. at Oxford, and since the grace was
> not voted for Warburton, Pope declined it for
> himself. They were both unusually "degree-
> conscious" at the time the poem was finished.

That the larger subject was well matured in Pope's mind
we gather from his remark to Spence that he had
inserted in this fourth book part of "an Essay on
Education," which he had first intended to use in an
expansion of *An Essay on Man* (1733–34) and the *Moral
Essays* (1731–35). (This is another indication that the
epic had been forgotten.)

The text given here is, up to line 626, that of *The New*

Dunciad, corrected in accordance with Pope's revisions. After that line, *The New Dunciad* concluded as follows:

> While the Great Mother bids Britannia sleep,
> And pours her Spirit o'er the Land and Deep.
> * * * * * * *
> * * * * * *
> De-est FINIS.

In 1743 Pope issued the *Dunciad in Four Books*, which is *The Dunciad* as it has been read ever since; *The New Dunciad* became Book IV of this poem. From the start it had borne the subtitle "Book the Fourth" in the body of the book if not on the title page. Pope transferred what was originally the conclusion of the old poem in three books to the end of the fourth. After line 626, where the tacking took place, we print from the text of 1743. The conclusion deals with a vast subject, the collapse of civilization itself, and is therefore more fitting for a poem including Book IV than it was for the poem when it ended with Book III.

Dates in the footnotes indicate their provenance. Pope was responsible for those in *The New Dunciad* (1742) and in *The Dunciad in Four Books* (1743), though Warburton may have helped him with them. For those of 1751 the responsibility was Warburton's; Pope died in 1744, but Warburton may, at least in part, have been following Pope's wishes. Two of the notes that we have given in their 1751 form had in fact appeared in at least one earlier edition, that of 1750 (dated 1749). The quoted footnotes are not necessarily given in full, and one or two minor corrections have been made.

⚜

TO THE READER

WE *apprehend it can be deemed no Injury to the Author of* the *Three first Books of the* Dunciad, *that we publish this* Fourth. *It was found merely by Accident, in taking a Survey of the* Library *of a late eminent Nobleman; but in so blotted a condition, and in so many detached pieces, as plainly shewed it to be not only* incorrect *but* unfinished: *That the Author of the three first Books had a design to extend and complete his Poem in this manner, appears from the Dissertation prefixt to it, where it is said, that the Design is more extensive, and that we may expect other Episodes to complete it: And from the Declaration in the Argument to the third Book, that the Accomplishment of the Prophecies therein, would be the Theme hereafter of a Greater Dunciad. But whether or no he be the Author of this, we declare ourselves ignorant. If he be, we are no more to be blamed for the Publication of it, than*

Tucca *and* Varius *for that of the last six books of the* Æneid, *tho' perhaps inferior to the former.*

If any person be possessed of a more perfect Copy of this Work, or of any other Fragments of it, and will communicate them to the Publisher, we shall make the next Edition more complete: In which, we also promise to insert any Criticisms that shall be published, if at all to the purpose, with the Names of the Authors; or any Letters sent us (tho' not to the purpose) shall yet be printed under the Title of Epistolæ Obscurorum Virorum; *which, together with some others of the same kind (formerly laid by for that purpose) may make no unpleasant Addition to the future Impressions of this Poem.*

THE ARGUMENT

BOOK the FOURTH.

THE Poet being, in this Book, to declare the *Completion* of the *Prophecies* mention'd at the end of the former, makes a new *Invocation*, (as the greater Poets are wont, when some high and worthy matter is to be sung.) He shows the Goddess coming in her Majesty to destroy *Order* and *Science*, and to substitute the *Kingdom of the Dull* upon earth. How she leads captive the *Sciences*, and silenceth the *Muses;* and what they be who succeed in their stead. All her children, by a wonderful attraction, are drawn about her; and bear along with them also divers others, who promote her Empire by connivance, weak resistance, or discouragement of Arts; such as Half wits, tasteless Admirers, vain Pretenders, the Flatterers of dunces, or the Patrons of them. All these crowd round her: one of them offering to approach her, is driven back by a Rival, but she commends and encourages both. The first who speak in form are the *Genius's* of the *Schools*, who assure her of their care to advance her Cause, by confining Youth to *words*, and keeping them out of the way of real Knowledge. Their Address, and her gracious Answer; with her Charge to them and the Universities. The *Universities* appear by their proper Deputies, and assure her that the same method is observ'd in the progress of Education: The speech of *Aristarchus*[1] on this subject. They are driven off by a band of young Gentlemen, return'd from *Travel* with

---

THE NEW DUNCIAD: *The Argument.* **1. Aristarchus:** [1742] A famous Commentator, and Corrector of Homer, whose name has been frequently used to signify a severe Critic.

their *Tutors;* one of whom delivers to the Goddess, in a polite oration, an account of the whole Conduct and Fruits of their *Travels:* presenting to her at the same time a young Nobleman perfectly accomplished. She receives him graciously and indues him with the happy quality of *Want of Shame.* She sees loitering about her a number of *Indolent Persons* abandoning all business and duty, and dying with laziness; to whom approaches the Antiquary *Annius,* intreating her to make them *Virtuosos*[2] and assign them over to him: But *Mummius,* another Antiquary, complaining of his fraudulent proceeding, she finds a method to reconcile their difference. Then enter a troop of people fantastically adorn'd, offering her strange and exotic presents: Amongst them, one stands forth and demands justice on another, who had deprived him of one of the greatest Curiosities in nature: but he justifies himself so well, that the Goddess gives them both her approbation. She recommends to them to find proper employment for the *Indolents* before-mention'd, in the study of Butterflies, Shells, Birds-nests, Moss, &c. but with particular caution, not to proceed beyond *Trifles,* to any useful or extensive views of Nature, or of the Author of Nature. Against the last of these apprehensions, she is secur'd by a hearty Address from the *Minute Philosophers*[3] and *Free-thinkers,* one of whom speaks in the name of the rest. The Youth thus instructed and principled, are delivered to her in a body by the hands of *Silenus;* and then admitted to taste the Cup of the *Magus* her High Priest, which causes a total oblivion of all Obligations, divine, civil, moral or rational. To these her Adepts she sends *Priests, Attendants,* and *Comforters,* of various kinds; then confers on them *Orders* and *Degrees;* and finally dismissing them with a speech, confirms to each his *Privileges,* warns *One* in particular not to exceed them, and concludes with a *Yawn* of extraordinary virtue,[4] the effects of which are not unfelt at this day.

Book the Fourth.

YET, yet a moment, one dim Ray of Light
Indulge, dread Chaos and eternal Night!
Of Darkness visible° so much be lent,

As half° to show, half veil the deep Intent.
Ye Pow'rs! whose Mysteries restor'd I sing,
To whom Time bears me on his rapid wing,
Suspend a while your Force inertly strong,°
Then take at once the Poet and the Song.
Now flam'd the Dog-star's° unpropitious ray   10
Smote ev'ry Brain, and wither'd ev'ry Bay;
Sick was the Sun, the Owl forsook his bow'r,
The moon-struck Prophet felt the madding hour:
Then rose the Seed of Chaos, and of Night,
To blot out Order, and extinguish Light,°
Of dull and venal a new World to mold,°
And bring Saturnian° days of Lead and Gold.°
  She mounts the Throne: her head a Cloud
    conceal'd,
In broad Effulgence all below° reveal'd,
('Tis thus aspiring Dulness ever shines,)
Soft on her lap her Laureat son reclines.   20
  Beneath her footstool, Science groans in Chains,
And Wit dreads Exile, Penalties and Pains.
There foam'd rebellious Logic, gagg'd and bound,
There stript, fair Rhet'ric languish'd on the ground,
His blunted Arms by Sophistry are born,
And shameless Billingsgate° her Robes adorn.

4. half: [1742] This is a great propriety, for a dull Poet can never express himself otherwise than by *halves* or imperfectly. **7. inertly strong:** [1742] Alluding to the *Vis inertiæ* of *Matter,* which tho' it really has [1743: be] no Power, is yet the Foundation of all its Qualities and Attributes. **9. the Dog-star:** [1743] The Poet introduceth this, (as all great events are supposed by sage Historians to be preceded) by an *Eclipse of the Sun;* but with a peculiar propriety, as the Sun is the *Emblem* of that intellectual light which dies before the face of Dulness. Very apposite likewise is it to make this *Eclipse,* which is occasion'd by the *Moon's predominancy,* the very time when *Dulness* and *Madness* are in *Conjunction.*[Cf. *An Epistle to Dr. Arbuthnot,* above, l. 3 and note.] **14. To . . . Light:** [1742] The two great Ends of her Mission; the one in quality of Daughter of *Chaos,* the other as Daughter of *Night. Order* here is to be understood extensively, both as Civil and Moral, the distinctions between high and low in Society, and true and false in Individuals: *Light* as Intellectual only, Wit, Science [knowledge], Arts. **15. Of . . . mold:** [1742] In allusion to the Epicurean opinion, that from the Dissolution of the present World into Night and Chaos, a new one should arise, which the Poet makes to partake of its original Principles. **16. Saturnian:** Saturn ruled the cosmos before being supplanted by Jupiter. **Lead and Gold:** [1742] dull and venal. **18. all below:** [1742, Scriblerus] the [ancient] Divinities manifested themselves to Men by their Backparts. **26. Billingsgate:** the slang, or "rhetoric" (as it was called), of the fish vendors in Billingsgate.

2. Virtuosos: savants. **3. Minute Philosophers:** trifling thinkers; the term translates one of Cicero's. **4. virtue:** power. *Book the Fourth.* **3. Darkness visible:** See *Paradise Lost,* I. 63.

Morality,° by her false Guardians drawn,
Chicane in Furs, and Casuistry in Lawn,°
Gasps, as they straiten at each end the Cord,
And dies, when Dulness gives her Page° the word.   30
Mad *Mathesis* alone was unconfin'd,°
Too mad for mere material chains to bind,
Now to pure° Space lifts her extatic Stare,
Now running round the Circle, finds it square.°
But held in tenfold bonds the Muses lye,
Watch'd both by Envy's and by Flatt'ry's eye:°
There to her heart sad Tragedy addrest
The Dagger wont to pierce the Tyrant's breast;
But sober History restrain'd her rage,
And promis'd Vengeance on a barb'rous age.   40
There sunk Thalia,° nerveless, cold, and dead.
Had not her Sister Satyr held her head:
Nor cou'd'st thou, Chesterfield°! a tear refuse,
Thou wept'st, and with thee wept each gentle Muse!

When° lo! a Harlot form soft-sliding by,
With mincing step, small voice, and languid eye;
Foreign her air, her robe's discordant pride
In patch-work flutt'ring, and her head aside:
By singing Peers up-held on either hand,
She tripp'd and laugh'd, too pretty much to stand,   50
Cast on the prostrate Nine° a scornful look,
Then thus in quaint Recitativo spoke.
O *Cara!° Cara!* silence all that Train:
Joy to great Chaos! let Division° reign.
Chromatic Tortures soon shall drive them hence,
Break all their nerves, and fritter all their sense.
One Trill shall harmonize joy, grief and rage,
Wake the dull church, and lull the ranting stage;°
To the same notes thy sons shall hum or snore,
And all thy yawning daughters cry *Encore.*   60
Another Phœbus, thy own Phœbus° reigns,
Joys in my jiggs, and dances in my chains.
But soon, ah soon Rebellion will commence,
If Musick meanly borrows aid from Sense:
Strong in new Arms lo Giant Handel stands,
Like bold Briareus,° with a hundred hands;
To stir, to rowze, to shake the soul he comes,
And Jove's own Thunders follow Mars's Drums.

27. Morality: [1743, Scriblerus] *Morality* is the Daughter of *Astræa*. This alludes to the Mythology of the ancient Poets; who tell us that in the *Gold* and *Silver* ages, or in the *State of Nature*, the Gods cohabited with Men here on Earth; but when by reason of human degeneracy men were forced to have recourse to a *Magistrate*, and that the Ages of *Brass* and *Iron* came on, (that is, when Laws were wrote on brazen tablets and inforced by the Sword of Justice) the Celestials soon retired from Earth, and Astræa last of all; and then it was she left this her Orphan Daughter in the hands of the *Guardians* aforesaid. **28. Chicane . . . Lawn:** Chicane ("crafty and litigious pleading") wears furs because the gowns of judges were trimmed with ermine, and Casuistry wears lawn because the sleeves of bishops were made of this fine linen. **30. her Page:** [1742, Scriblerus] Her *Page*, to wit her *Mute; alluding* to the custom of strangling State-Criminals in *Turkey* by Mutes or Pages. A practice more decent than that of *our Pages*, who before they hang any Person, load him with reproachful language. [The allusion is to Sir Francis Page, a "hanging judge."] **31. Mad . . . unconfin'd:** [1742] Alluding to the strange Conclusions some Mathematicians have deduced, from their principles of the *real Quantity of Matter*, the *Reality of Space*, &c. **33. pure:** [1742] defæcated from Matter. **34. running . . . square:** [1742] Regards the wild and fruitless attempts of *squaring the Circle.* **36. by Envy's . . . eye:** [1742] One of the Misfortunes falling on Authors, from the *Act* for subjecting *Plays* to the power of a Licenser [1737], being the false representations to which they were expos'd, from such as either gratify'd their Envy to Merit, or made their Court to Greatness, by perverting general Reflections against Vice into Libels on particular Persons. **41. Thalia:** the Muse of comedy. **43. Chesterfield:** Lord Chesterfield had opposed the Act in question.

45–53. When . . . Cara: [1742] The Attitude given to this phantom represents the nature and genius of the *Italian* Opera: its affected airs, its luxurious and effeminating sounds, and the practise of patching up these Opera's with favourite tunes, incoherently put together. These things were supported by the subscriptions of the Nobility. **51. Nine:** the Muses. **53. O Cara:** O beloved lady! *Caro* and *cara* occur frequently in the operas and sometimes in reiteration—so frequently that by Jane Austen's time they had become thoroughly vulgar; she makes Mrs. Elton in *Emma* (1816) apply *caro sposo*, *cara sposo*, and *cara sposa* to her husband, regardless of grammar. **54. Division:** a pun on the word for the practice of extemporizing florid passages where the composer wrote a long single note. **58. Wake . . . stage:** [1751] i.e. Dissipate the *devotion* of the one by light and wanton airs; and subdue the *Pathos* of the other by recitative and sing-song. **61. thy own Phœbus:** [1742, Scriblerus] *Tuus jam regnat Apollo.* VIRG. Not the ancient *Phœbus*, the God of Harmony, but a modern *Phœbus* of French extraction, married to the Princess *Galimathia* [nonsense], one of the handmaids of Dulness, and an assistant to Opera. [The French term "Phœbus" denoted, according to the Twickenham edition (V. 347), "a Semblance of Meaning without any real Sense; whereas in *Galimatias*, the Obscurity is compleat."] **66. Briareus:** [1742] [Briareus is the mythological giant with fifty heads and a hundred hands.] Mr. *Handel* had introduced a greater number of Hands, and more variety of Instruments into the Orchestra, and employed even Drums and Cannon to make a fuller Chorus.

Arrest him, Empress! or you sleep no more—
She heard, and drove him to th' Hibernian shore.°   70

And now had Fame's posterior° Trumpet blown,
And all the Nations summon'd to the Throne.
The young,° the old, who feel her inward sway,
One Instinct seizes, and transports away.
None need a guide, by sure Attraction led,
And strong, impulsive gravity of head.
None want a place, for all their centre found,
Hung to the Goddess, and coher'd around.°
Not closer, orb in orb conglob'd are seen
The buzzing Bees about their dusky Queen.   80

The gath'ring number, as it moves along,
Involves a vast involuntary throng,
Who gently drawn, and strugling less and less,
Roll in her Vortex,° and her pow'r confess.
Not those alone, who passive own her laws,
But who, weak rebels more advance her cause.
Whate'er of Dunce in College or in Town
Sneers at another, in Toupee° or Gown;
Whate'er of mungril no one class admits,
A Wit with dunces and a Dunce with wits.   90
Nor absent they, no members of her state,
Who pay her homage in her sons the Great;

Who false to Phœbus, bow the knee to Baal,°
Or impious, preach his word without a call.
Patrons, who sneak from living worth to dead,
With-hold the pension, and set up the head:
Or vest dull Flatt'ry in the sacred gown,
Or give from fool to fool the laurel crown.
And (last and worst) with all the cant of wit,
Without the soul, the Muse's Hypocrit.°   100

There march'd the bard and blockhead, side by
            side,
Who rym'd for hire, and patroniz'd for pride.
Narcissus,° prais'd with all a Parson's pow'r,
Look'd a white lilly sunk beneath a show'r.
There mov'd Montalto° with superior air,
His stretch'd-out arm display'd a Volume fair;
Courtiers and Patriots° in two ranks divide,
Thro' both he pass'd, and bow'd from side to side:
But as in graceful act, with awful eye
Compos'd he stood, bold Benson° thrust him by: 110
On two unequal Crutches prop'd he came,
Milton's on this, on that one Jonston's name.
The decent Knight retir'd with sober rage,
Withdrew his hand, and clos'd the pompous page.
[But (happy for him as the times went then)
Appear'd Apollo's May'r and Aldermen,
On whom three hundred gold-capt youths await,
To lug the pond'rous volume off in state.]

70. **drove . . . shore:** Handel retired to Ireland when his London popularity temporarily declined. **71. posterior:** [1742] *Posterior,* viz. her *second* or *more certain* Report: unless we imagine this word *posterior* to relate to the position of one of her Trumpets, according to *Hudibras.*

> She blows not both with the same Wind,
> But one before and one behind,
> And therefore modern Authors name
> One good, and t' other evil Fame.

73–100. The young . . . Hypocrit: [1742] It ought to be observed that here are three classes in this assembly. The first of men absolutely and avowedly dull, who naturally adhere to the Goddess, and are imaged in the simile of the Bees about their Queen. The second involuntarily drawn to her, tho' not caring to own her influence, from Verse 81 to 90. The third of such, as tho' not members of her state, yet advance her service by flattering Dulness, cultivating mistaken talents, patronizing vile scriblers, discouraging living merit, or setting up for wits, and men of taste in Arts they understand not: from Verse 91 to 100. **75–78. None . . . around:** [1742] *None need a* Guide,—*none want a* Place—The sons of Dulness are αὐτοδίδακτος and can introduce themselves into all places, they want no instructors in study, nor guides in life. **84. Vortex:** a term prominent in Descartes's theory of the universe, signifying a rotatory movement about a center. **88. Toupee:** a fashionable artificial lock of hair placed on top of the wig.

93. **Baal:** the chief god of the enemies of the "children of light," the Israelites, and so in general a false god. **99–100. And . . . Hypocrit:** [1743] In this division are reckoned up 1. The Idolizers of Dulness in the Great—2. Ill Judges,—3. Ill Writers,—4. Ill Patrons. But the *last and worst* [is] the Epitome of them all. He who thinks the only end of poetry is to amuse, and the only business of the poet to be witty [full of genius]; and consequently who cultivates only such trifling talents in himself, and encourages only such in others. **103. Narcissus:** Lord Hervey (1696–1743), court Vice Chamberlain and confidant of Queen Caroline. He is Sporus in *An Epistle to Dr. Arbuthnot,* above, ll. 305 ff. He had recently been praised at length by Dr. Conyers Middleton in the Dedication of his *Life of Cicero.* **105. Montalto:** [1742] An eminent person of Quality who was about to publish a very pompous Edition of a great Author, very much at his own expence indeed. [Pope is alluding to Sir Thomas Hanmer and his edition of Shakespeare (1743–44). Hanmer's manners are accurately suggested by the description that follows.] **107. Patriots:** *Patriots* probably applies to all who do not support Walpole's administration, whether Whig or Tory. **110. Benson:** [1742] [William Benson] endeavoured to raise himself to Fame by erecting monuments, striking coins . . . and procuring translations, of *Milton;* and afterwards by a great passion for *Arthur Johnston,* a *Scotch* physician's Version of the Psalms, of which he printed many fine Editions.

When° Dulness, smiling—"Thus revive the Wits;
But murder first, and mince them all to bits;   120
As erst Medæa (cruel, so to save!)
A new Edition of old Æson gave.°
Let Standard°-Authors thus like Trophies born,
Appear more glorious as more hack'd and torn,
And you my Critics in the chequer'd shade,°
Admire new light thro' holes yourselves have made.°
Leave not a foot of Verse, a foot of Stone,
A Page, a Grave,° that they can call their own;
But spread, my sons, your glory thin or thick,
On passive paper, or on solid brick: 130
So by each Bard an Alderman shall sit,°
A heavy Lord shall hang at ev'ry Wit,
And while on Fame's triumphal Car they ride,
Some Slave of mine be pinion'd to their side.°
　Now Crowds on Crowds around the Goddess press,
Each eager to present the first Address.°
Dunce scorning Dunce beholds the next advance;
But Fop shews Fop superior complaisance.
When lo! a Spectre° rose, whose index-hand
Held forth the Virtue of the dreadful Wand;°   140

His beaver'd° brow a birchen° garland wears,
Dropping with Infant's blood, and Mother's tears.°
O'er ev'ry vein a shudd'ring horror runs;
Eton and Winton shake thro' all their Sons.
All flesh is humbled, Westminster's bold race
Shrink, and confess the Genius of the place:
The pale Boy-Senator° yet tingling stands,
And holds his breeches close° with both his hands.
　Then thus. Since Man from beast by Words is
　　known,
Words are Man's province, words we teach alone. 150
When Reason doubtful, like the Samian letter,°
Points him two ways, the narrower is the better.
Plac'd at the door of Learning,° youth to guide,
We never suffer it to stand too wide.
To ask, to guess, to know, as they commence,
As Fancy opens the quick springs of Sense,
We ply the memory, we load the brain,
Bind rebel wit, and double chain on chain;
Confine the thought to exercise the breath;°
And keep them in the pale of Words till death.   160
Whate'er the Talents, or howe'er design'd,
We hang one jingling Padlock on the mind:°
A Poet the first day, he dips his quill;
And what the last? a very Poet still.
Pity! the charm works only in our wall,°
Lost, lost too soon in yonder House or Hall.°

119–34. When . . . side: [1742] The Goddess applauds the practice of tacking the obscure names of Persons not eminent in any branch of Learning to those of the most distinguished Writers; by printing *Editions* of their works with impertinent alterations of their Text, or by setting up *Monuments* disgraced with their own names and inscriptions. 121–22. Medæa . . . gave: Pope refers to the story of the enchantress Medea, the wife of Jason, who rejuvenated Jason's father, Aeson. She did not, however, accept Jason's offer of some of his own youthfulness, and Aeson was provided with a body that was completely unlike Jason's, owing nothing to him. 123. Standard: (1) a military flag; (2) having authority or excellence. 125. chequer'd shade: quoted, with a different meaning, from Milton's *L'Allegro*, l. 96. 126. Admire . . . made: This verse recalls the famous lines 13 and 14 in Waller's *On the Last Verses in the Book*: "The soul's dark cottage, batter'd and decay'd, / Lets in new light through chinks that time has made." 128. Page, Grave: [1742] For what less than a Grave can be granted to a dead author? or what less than a Page can be allow'd a living one? 131. by . . . sit: The 1751 edition explains that Alderman Barber had erected a monument to Samuel Butler. 133–34. while . . . side: In ancient Rome a chained slave was placed beside a victorious general in the triumphal procession. 136. Address: a written discourse of congratulation. 139–42. a Spectre . . . tears: Dr. Busby, the headmaster of Westminster School, was famous for his pedagogy and infamous for his use of the cane. 140. Wand: [1742] A thin cane is usually born by Schoolmasters, which drives the poor Souls about like the wand of Mercury.

141. beaver'd: provided with "a hat of the best kind, so called from being made of the fur of beaver" (Johnson's *Dictionary*). birchen: The instrument of flogging was a bundle of birch twigs. 142. Dropping . . . tears: Cf. *Paradise Lost*, I. 392–93: "First Moloch, horrid King besmear'd with blood / Of human sacrifice, and parents tears." 147. Boy-Senator: a young member of the Houses of Parliament. 148. holds . . . close: [1742] An effect of Fear, somewhat like this, is described in the 7th Æneid [where mothers clasp their children to their breast], nothing being so natural in any apprehension, as to lay close hold on whatever is suppos'd to be most in danger. 151. the Samian letter: [1742] The letter Y, used by Pythagoras as an emblem of the different roads of Virtue and Vice. 153. Plac'd . . . Learning: [1742] This circumstance of the *Genius Loci* (with that of the Index-hand before) seems to be an allusion to the *Table of Cebes*, where the Genius of human Nature points out the road to be pursued by those entering into life. [Cebes was a follower of Socrates.] 159. Confine . . . breath: [1742] By obliging them to get the classick poets by heart, which furnishes them with endless matter for Conversation, and Verbal amusement for their whole lives. 162. We . . . mind: [1743] For youth being used like Pack-horses and beaten on under a heavy load of Words, lest they should tire, their instructors contrive to make the Words jingle in rhyme or metre. 165. wall: limits. 166. House, Hall: the House of Commons and Westminster Hall, where important law cases were tried.

There truant Wyndham every Muse gave o'er,
There Talbot sunk, and was a Wit no more!
How sweet an Ovid, Murray, was our boast,
How many Martials were in Pult'ney lost!   170
Else sure some Bard, to our eternal praise,
In twice ten thousand ryming nights and days,
Had reach'd the Work, the All that mortal can;
And South° beheld that Master-piece of Man°!
   Oh° (cry'd the Goddess) for some pedant Reign,
Some gentle James° to bless the land again!
To stick the Doctor's Chair into the Throne,
Give law to Words, or war with Words alone,
Senates and Courts with Greek and Latin rule,
And turn the Council to a Grammar School.   180
For sure, if Dulness sees a grateful° Day,
'Tis in the shade of Arbitrary Sway,
O! if my sons may learn one earthly thing,
Teach but that one, sufficient for a King;
That which my Priests, and mine alone, maintain,
Which as it dies, or lives, we fall, or reign:
May you, may Cam, and Isis° preach it long!
"The RIGHT DIVINE of KINGS to govern wrong."

   Prompt at the Call, around the Goddess roll
Broad hats, and hoods, and caps,° a sable shoal:°   190
Thick and more thick the black blockade extends,
A hundred head of Aristotle's friends.
Nor wert thou, Isis! wanting to the day,

[Tho' Christ-church long kept prudishly away.]°
Each staunch Polemic stubborn as a rock,
Each fierce Logician still expelling Lock,°
Came whip and spur, and dash'd thro' thin and thick,
On German Crouzaz, and Dutch Burgersdyck.°
As many quit the streams that murm'ring fall
To lull the sons of Marg'ret and Clare-hall,°   200
Where Bentley late tempestuous wont to sport
In troubled waters, but now sleeps in Port.°
Before them march'd that awful Aristarch,°
Plow'd was his front with many a deep Remark.°
His Hat,° which never vail'd° to human pride,
Walker° with rev'rence took, and lay'd aside.
Low bow'd the rest: He kingly, did but nod;
So upright Quakers please both Man and God.
Mistress! dismiss that rabble from your throne.
Avaunt—is Aristarchus yet unknown?   210
Thy mighty Scholiast, whose unweary'd pains
Made Horace dull, and humbled Milton's strains.
Turn what they will to Verse, their toil is vain,
Critics like me shall make it prose again.
Roman and Greek Grammarians! know your Better:°

167–74. Wyndham, Talbot, Murray, Pult'ney, South:
These men, eminent in public life, were "old boys" of the
school. They all had literary gifts. 174. that . . . Man:
[1743] viz. an *Epigram*. The famous Dr. *South* declared
a perfect Epigram to be as difficult a performance as an
Epic Poem. And the Critics say "an Epic Poem is the
greatest work human nature is capable of." 175–88. Oh
. . . wrong: [1743] The matter under debate is how to
confine men to Words for life. The instructors of youth
shew how well they do their parts; but complain that
when men come into the world they are apt to forget their
Learning and turn themselves to useful Knowledge. This was
an evil that wanted to be redressed. And this the Goddess
assures them will need a more extensive Tyranny than that
of Grammar schools . . . and to make all sure, she wishes for
another *Pedant Monarch*. 176. James: [1742] *James* the first
took upon himself to teach the Latin tongue to Car, Earl of
Somerset; and that Gondomar the Spanish Ambassador
wou'd speak false Latin to him, on purpose to give him the
pleasure of correcting it, whereby he wrought himself into
his good graces. 181. grateful: pleasing. 187. Cam, and
Isis: The University of Cambridge is on the river Cam, and
Oxford on the Isis. 190. Broad . . . caps: University dress
allotted hats to doctors, caps to masters, and hoods to both.
shoal: school.

194. Tho' . . . away: The 1742 edition adds a note
signed "Bentley": "This line is doubtless spurious, and
foisted in by the impertinence of the Editor; and accordingly
we have put it between *Hooks*." Christ Church, the largest
college at Oxford, is complimented by Pope because certain
of its men engaged in controversy with Richard Bentley
(1662–1742), famous classical scholar. 196. Lock: [1742] In
the year 1703 there was a meeting of the heads of the University of Oxford to censure Mr. Lock's Essay on Human
Understanding, and to forbid the reading it. [See the selection
from Locke's *Essay* in Part One.] 198. On . . . Burgersdyck: [1742, Scriblerus] There seems to be an improbability
that the Doctors and Heads of houses should ride on horseback, who of late days being gouty or unwieldy, have kept
their coaches. But these are horses of great strength, and fit
to carry any weight, as their German and Dutch extraction
may manifest; and very famous we may conclude, being
honour'd with Names, as were the horses Pegasus and
Bucephalus. [Jean Pierre de Crousaz (1663–1748), the Swiss
philosopher, was noted for his controversial writings;
Burgersdyck (1590–1629) was a famous Dutch logician.]
200. Marg'ret and Clare-hall: Lady Margaret Beaufort
founded St. John's College, Cambridge, in 1511; Clare-hall
is now Clare College, Cambridge. 202. Port: Bentley's
favorite drink was port wine. 203. Aristarch: Aristarchus.
204. Remark: Bentley liked titles beginning *Remarks* . . . .
205. Hat: a characteristic feature of Bentley's dress. vail'd:
removed in a gesture of respect. 206. Walker: Dr. Richard
Walker was a Cambridge friend of Bentley's. 215. Roman
. . . Better: [1742] Imitated from Propertius speaking of the
Æneid. "Cedite, *Romani* scriptores, cedite *Graii*! | *Nescio quid
majus* nascitur Iliade." ["Yield, you writers of Rome and of
Greece! Somethng greater than the *Iliad* is born."]

Author of something° yet more great than letter;
While tow'ring o'er your Alphabet, like Saul,°
Stands our Digamma, and o'er-tops them all.
'Tis true, on Words is still our whole debate,
Disputes° of *Me* or *Te*, of *aut* or *at*,   220
To sound or sink in *cano*,° O or A,
Or give up Cicero to C or K.°
Let Freind affect to speak as Terence spoke,
And Alsop° never but like Horace joke;
For me, what Virgil, Pliny may deny,
Manilius or Solinus° shall supply:
For Attic phrase in Plato let them seek,
I poach in Suidas° for unlicens'd Greek.
In ancient Sense if any needs will deal,
Be sure I give them Fragments,° not a Meal;   230
What Gellius or Stobæus hash'd before,
Or chew'd by blind old Scholiasts o'er and o'er.°
The Critic Eye, that microscope of wit,
Sees hairs and pores, examines bit by bit:
How parts relate to parts, or they to whole,
The body's harmony, the beaming soul,
Are things which Kuster, Burman, Wasse,° shall see,
When Man's whole frame is obvious to a *Flea*.

Ah think not, Mistress! more true Dulness lies
In Folly's Cap, than Wisdom's grave disguise.   240
Like buoys, that never sink into the flood,
On Learning's surface we but lye and nod.
Thine is the genuine° Head of many a house,°
And much Divinity without a *Νοῦς*.°
Nor could a Barrow° work on ev'ry block,°
Nor has one Atterbury spoil'd the flock;
See! still thy own, the heavy Canon roll,
And Metaphysic smokes involve the Pole.°
For thee we dim the eyes, and stuff the head
With all such reading as was never read: 250
For thee explain a thing till all men doubt it,
And write about it, Goddess, and about it:
So spins the silk-worm small its slender store
And labours till it clouds itself all o'er.°
  What° tho' we let some better sort of fool
Thrid ev'ry science, run thro' ev'ry school?

216–18. something . . . all: [1742] Alludes to the boasted restoration of the Eolic Digamma, in his long-projected edition of Homer. He calls it *something more than Letter*, from the enormous figure it would make among the other letters, being one Gamma set upon the shoulders of another. 217. like Saul: See I Sam. 9:2. 220. Disputes: [1742] It was a serious dispute, about which the learned were much divided, and some treatises written, whether at the end of the first Ode of Horace to read, *Me doctarum . . .* , or, *Te doctarum . . . Me gelidum . . .* or, *Te gelidum . . . .* 221. To . . . cano: whether to accent *cano* on the first or second syllable. 222. give . . . K: [1742] Grammatical disputes about the manner of pronouncing Cicero's name. 223–24. Freind, Alsop: [1743] Dr Robert Freind [was] master of Westminster-school, and canon of Christ-church—Dr. Anthony Alsop [was] a happy imitator of the Horatian style. 226. Manilius or Solinus: [1742] Some Critics having had it in their choice, to comment either on Virgil or Manilius, Pliny or Solinus, have chosen the worse author, the more freely to display their critical capacity. [Bentley had edited Manilius. Solinus had based his encyclopedic compilation on Pliny.] 228–31. Suidas, Gellius, Stobæus: [1742] [The first] a Dictionary-writer, a collector of impertinent facts and barbarous words; [the second] a minute Critic; [the third] an author who gave his Common-place-book to the publick, where we happen to find much Mince-meat of old books. 230. Fragments: Bentley had made much use of texts that existed only in part. 232. chew'd . . . o'er: [1742] These taking the same things eternally from the mouth of one another. 237. Kuster . . . Wasse: contemporary scholars associated with Bentley.

243. genuine: an allusion to the dispute whether Bentley was or was not Master of Trinity College. house: college. 244. *Νοῦς*: [1742] A word much affected by the learned Aristarchus in common conversation, to signify *Genius* or natural *acumen*. 245–46. Barrow, Atterbury: [1742] Isaac Barrow Master of Trinity [College], Francis Atterbury Dean of Christ-church, both great Genius's and eloquent Preachers; one more conversant in the sublime Geometry, the other in classical Learning, but who equally made it their care to advance the polite Arts in their several Societies. [See the selection from Atterbury in Part One.] 245. block: (1) a heavy piece of timber, inviting the sculptor; (2) a blockhead. 247–48. the heavy . . . Pole: a good example of Pope's puns. The prime meaning is "the obese cleric rolls in his walk (or sways in his chair), and his obscure ideas about philosophy circle round his head (poll)." But, apart from the one word *metaphysic*, the meaning could concern artillery: "the heavy guns roll along, and their smoke fills the sky up to the zenith (pole)." 249–54. For . . . o'er: Pope has remodeled *The Dunciad*, I. 155–62. 255–70. What . . . Man: [1743] Hitherto Aristarchus hath displayed the art of teaching his Pupils words, without things. He shews greater skill in what follows, which is to teach things, without profit. For with the *better sort of fool* the first expedient is, [ll.] 255 to 258, to run him so swiftly through the circle of the Sciences that he shall stick at nothing, nor nothing stick with him; and though some little, both of words and things, should by chance be gathered up in his passage, yet he shews, [ll.] 259 to 260, that it is never more of the one than just to enable him to *persecute with Rhyme*, or of the other than to *plague with Dispute*. But, if after all, the Pupil will needs *learn* a Science, it is then provided by his careful directors, [ll.] 261, 262, that it shall either be such as he can never *enjoy* when he comes out into life, or such as he will be obliged to *divorce*. And to make all sure, [ll.] 263 to 268, the useless or pernicious Sciences, thus taught, are still applied perversely; the man of Wit *petrified* in Euclid, or *trammelled* in Metaphysics; and the man of Judgment *married*, without his parents consent, to a *Muse*. Thus far the particular

Never by Tumbler thro' the hoops was shown
Such skill in passing all, and touching none.
He may indeed (if sober all this time)
Plague with Dispute, or persecute with Ryme: 260
We only furnish what he cannot use,
Or wed to what he must divorce, a Muse:
Full in the midst of Euclid, dip at once,
And petrify a Genius to a Dunce;
Or set on Metaphysic ground to prance,
Show all his paces, not a step advance.
With the same Cement,° ever sure to bind,
We bring to one dead level ev'ry mind;
Then take him to devellop, if you can,
And hew the Block off, and get out the Man.°   270
But wherefore waste I words? I see advance
Whore, Pupil, and lac'd° Governor from France.
Walker! our hat—nor more he deign'd to say,
But stern as Ajax spectre,° strode away.

In flow'd at once a gay embroider'd race,
And titt'ring push'd the Pedants off the place:
Some would have spoken, but the voice was drown'd
By the French horn, or by the opening° hound.
The first came forwards, with as easy mien
As if he saw St. James's° and the Queen: 280

When thus th' Attendant Orator° begun:
Receive, great Empress! thy accomplish'd son:
Thine from the birth, and sacred from the rod,
A dauntless Infant never scar'd with God!
The Sire saw, one by one, his Virtues wake;
The Mother begg'd the blessing of a Rake:°
Thou gav'st that Ripeness, which so soon began,
And ceas'd so soon, he ne'er was boy nor man.
Thro' School and College, thy kind cloud o'ercast,
Safe and unseen the young Æneas past.   290
Thence bursting glorious,° all at once let down,
Stunn'd with his giddy Larum° half the town;
Intrepid then o'er seas and lands he flew,
Europe he saw, and Europe saw him too.
There all thy gifts and graces we display,
Thou, only thou, directing all our way!
To where the Seine, obsequious as she runs,
Pours at great Bourbon's feet her silken sons,
Or Tyber now no longer Roman rolls,
Vain of Italian Arts, Italian Souls;   300
To happy Convents, bosom'd deep in Vines,
Where slumber Abbots, purple as their Wines;
To Isles of Fragrance, Lilly-silver'd Vales,
Diffusing languor in the panting gales:
To lands of singing, or of dancing slaves,
Love-whisp'ring woods, and Lute-resounding waves.
But chief her shrine where naked Venus keeps,
And Cupids ride the Lyon of the deeps;°
Where, eas'd of Fleets, the Adriatic Main
Wafts the smooth Eunuch and enamour'd swain. 310
Led by my hand, he saunter'd° Europe round,
And gather'd ev'ry Vice on Christian ground;
Saw ev'ry Court, heard ev'ry King declare
His royal sense of Op'ra's or the Fair;°
The Stews and Palace equally explor'd,
Intrigu'd with glory, and with spirit whor'd;
Try'd all hors-d'oeuvres, all Liqueurs defin'd,
Judicious drank, and greatly-daring din'd;
Dropt the dull lumber of the Latin store,
Spoil'd his own Language, and acquir'd no more; 320

arts of modern Education, used partially, and diversified according to the Subject and the Occasion: But there is one general Method, with the encomium of which the great Aristarchus ends his speech, [ll.] 267 to 268, and that is AUTHORITY, the universal *Cement*, which fills all the cracks and chasms of *lifeless* matter, shuts up all the pores of *living* substance, and brings all human minds to *one dead level*. For if Nature should chance to struggle through all the entanglements of the foregoing ingenious expedients to *bind rebel wit*, this claps upon her one sure and entire cover. So that well may Aristarchus defy all human power to *get the Man out* again from under so impenetrable a crust. The Poet alludes to this Master-piece of the Schools in [l.] 501, where he speaks of *Vassals to a name*. **267. Cement:** accented on the first syllable. **270. hew . . . Man:** [1742] A notion of Aristotle, that there was originally in every block of marble a Statue, which would appear on the removal of the superfluous parts. [Pope is mistaken in naming the source of this notion.] **272. lac'd** [1742, Scriblerus] Why *laced?* Because Gold and Silver are necessary trimming to denote the dress of a person of rank, and the Governor must be supposed so in foreign countries, to be admitted into Courts and other places of fair reception. But how comes Aristarchus to know by sight that this Governor comes from France? Why, by the laced coat. At this date *laced* had also come to mean "laced with spirits." **274. Ajax spectre:** [1742] See Homer, Odyss. 11 when the Ghost of Ajax turns sullenly from Ulysses. **278. opening:** beginning to cry in pursuit of a scent. **280. St. James's:** the palace.

281.   th' Attendant Orator: [1742, Scriblerus] The Governor abovesaid. **286. The Mother . . . Rake:** an allusion to the common maternal wish to give birth to a male. **290–91. the young . . . glorious:** [1742] See Virg. Æn. 1 [411–14]. **292. Larum:** hubbub. **308. the Lyon . . . deeps:** [1742] The winged Lyon the Arms of Venice. This Republic heretofore the most considerable in Europe, for her Naval Force and the extent of her Commerce; now illustrious for her Carnivals. **311. saunter'd:** strolled, a fairly new sense at this date. **313–14. heard . . . Fair:** an allusion to the taste of George II.

All Classic learning lost on Classic ground;
And last turn'd Air, the *Eccho* of a *Sound*°!
See now, half cur'd,° and perfectly well-bred,
With nothing but a Solo in his head,
As much Estate, and Principle, and Wit,
As Jansen, Fleetwood, Cibber,° shall think fit,
Stol'n from a Duel, follow'd by a Nun,
And, if a Borough chuse him, not undone;°
See! to my country happy I restore
This glorious Youth, and add one Venus more.   330
Her too receive, (for her my soul adores)
So may the sons of sons of sons of whores,°
Prop thine, O Empress! like each neighbour Throne,
And make a long Posterity thy own.

Pleas'd, she accepts the Hero, and the Dame,
Wraps in her Veil, and frees from sense of shame.

Then look'd, and saw a lazy, lolling sort,
Unseen at Church, at Senate, or at Court,
Of ever-listless loit'rers, that attend
No cause, no trust, no duty, and no friend,   340
Thee too my Paridel°! she mark'd thee there,
Stretch'd on the rack of a too-easy Chair;
And heard thy everlasting yawn confess
The Pains and penalties of Idleness.°
She pity'd! but her pity only shed
Benigner influence on thy nodding head.

But Annius,° crafty Seer, with Ebon wand,

And well-dissembl'd Em'rald on his hand,
False as his Gems and canker'd as his Coins,
Came cramm'd with Capon,° from where Pollio°
    dines.   350
Soft, as the wily Fox is seen to creep
Where bask on sunny banks the simple sheep,
Walk round and round, now prying here, now there;
So he; but pious, whisper'd first his prayer.
Grant, gracious Goddess! grant me still to cheat,
O may thy cloud still cover the deceit!
Thy choicer mists on this assembly shed,
But pour them thickest on the noble head!
So shall each youth, assisted by our eyes,
See other Cæsars, other Homers rise,   360
Thro' twilight ages hunt th' Athenian fowle
Which Chalcis Gods, and mortals call an Owle,°
Now see an Attys, now a Cecrops° clear,
Nay Mahomet! the Pigeon at thine ear;°
Be rich in ancient brass, tho' not in gold,
And keep his Lares,° tho' his house be sold;
To head-less Phæbe his fair bride postpone,
Honour a Syrian Prince above his own;
Lord of an Otho, if I vouch it true;
Blest in one Niger, till he knows of two.   370

Mummius° o'erheard him; Mummius, Fool-
    renown'd,°
Who like his Cheops,° stinks above the ground,
Fierce as a startled Adder, swell'd and said;
Ratling an ancient Sistrum° at his head.

---

322. And . . . Sound: a modern metamorphosis. 323.
cur'd: prepared as meat is by salting. 326. Jansen . . .
Cibber: [1742] very eminent persons, all Managers of *Plays;*
who tho' not Governors by profession, had each in his way
concern'd themselves in the Education of youth, and regulated
their Wits, their Morals, or their Finances, at that period of
their age which is the most important, their entrance into the
polite world. [The Twickenham edition points out that the
play Sir Henry Jansen managed was that of the card table.]
328. if . . . undone: Members of Parliament could not be
arrested for debt. 332. So . . . whores: [1742] Virg. *Et nati
natorum, & qui nascentur ab illis.* ["And the sons of sons, and
those who shall be born from them."] Æn. 3. 341. my Paridel:
[1742] The Poet seems to speak of this young gentleman with
great affection. The name is taken from Spenser, who gives
it to a *wandering Courtly Squire,* that travell'd about for the
same reason, for which many young Squires are now fond of
travelling, and especially to *Paris.* Faery Queen. Lib [III.]
Can. 9. 342-44. Stretch'd . . . Idleness: [1742] Virg. Æn.
6. Sedet, æternumque sedebit. [The "easy chair" was a recent
invention.] 347. Annius: [1742] The name taken from Annius
the Monk of Viterbo, famous for many Impositions and
Forgeries of ancient manuscripts and inscriptions, which he
was prompted to from mere vanity; but our Annius had a
more substantial motive.

350. Capon: chicken. Pollio: a Roman consul of the
first century B.C. who collected books and statues. 361-62.
th' Athenian . . . Owle: [1742] The Owle stamp'd on the
reverse of the ancient mony of Athens. [Line 362 is the verse
by which Hobbes renders that of Homer (*Iliad,* XIV. 291).]
363. Attys, Cecrops: [1742] The first Kings of Athens,
of whom it is hard to suppose any Coins are extant; but
not so improbable as what follows, that there should be
any of Mahomet, who forbad all Images. Nevertheless one of
these Annius's made a counterfeit one, now in the collection
of a learned Nobleman. 364. Mahomet . . . ear: Mahomet
considered a white pigeon which he fed with grains of corn
in his ear to be an angel. 366. Lares: household gods. 371.
Mummius: [1743] is not merely an allusion to the Mummies
he was so fond of, but probably referred to the Roman
General of that name, who burn'd Corinth, and committed
the curious Statues to the Captain of a Ship, assuring him,
"that if any were lost or broken, he should procure others to
be made in their stead:" by which it should seem (whatever
may be pretended) that Mummius was no Virtuoso. Fool-
renown'd: [1751] A compound epithet in the Greek manner,
renown'd by fools, or *renown'd for making Fools.* 372. Cheops:
the mummy of the Egyptian king of that name. 374.
Sistrum: a metal musical instrument, originating in Egypt.

Speak'st thou of Syrian Princes°? Traitor base!
Mine, Goddess! mine is all the horned° race.
True, he had wit, to make their value rise;
From foolish Greeks to steal them was as wise;
More glorious yet, from barb'rous hands to keep,
When Sallee Rovers chac'd him on the deep: 380
Then taught by Hermes, and divinely bold,
Down his own throat he risqu'd the Grecian gold,
Receiv'd each Demi-God with pious care,
Deep in his Entrails—I rever'd them there;
I bought them, shrouded in that living shrine,
And, at their second birth, they issue mine.

Witness great Ammon! by whose horns I swore,°
(Reply'd soft Annius) this our Paunch before
Still bears them faithful; and that thus I eat,
Is to refund the Medals with the meat.   390
To prove me, Goddess! clear of all design,
Bid me with Pollio sup as well as dine:
There all the Learn'd shall at the labour stand,
And Douglas° lend his soft, obstetric hand.

The Goddess smiling seem'd to give consent;
So back to Pollio, hand in hand, they went.

Then thick as locusts black'ning all the ground,
A Tribe, with weeds and shells fantastick crown'd,
Each with some wondrous gift approach'd the pow'r,
A Nest, a Toad, a Fungus, or a Flow'r.   400
But far the foremost, two, with earnest zeal
And aspect ardent to the Throne appeal.
The first thus open'd. Hear thy suppliant's call,
Great Queen, and common Mother of us all!
Fair from its humble bed I rear'd this flow'r,
Suckled, and chear'd, with air, and sun, and show'r;
Soft on the paper ruff its leaves I spread,
Bright with the gilded button tipt its head;
Then thron'd in glass, and nam'd it CAROLINE:°

Each Maid cry'd, charming! and each Youth,
        divine!   410
Did Nature's pencil ever blend such rays,
Such vary'd light in one promiscuous blaze?
Now prostrate! dead! behold that Caroline:
No Maid cries, charming, and no Youth, divine.°
And lo the wretch! whose vile, whose insect lust
Lay'd this gay daughter of the spring in dust.
Oh punish him! or to th' Elysian shades
Dismiss my soul, where no Carnation fades!

He ceas'd, and wept. With innocence of mien,
Th' accus'd stood forth, and thus address'd the
        Queen.   420

Of all th' enamel'd race, whose silv'ry wing
Waves to the tepid Zephyrs of the spring,°
Or swims along the fluid atmosphere,
Once brightest shin'd this child of Heat and Air.
I saw, and started from its vernal bow'r
The rising game, and chac'd from flow'r to flow'r:
It fled, I follow'd; now in hope, now pain;
It stopt, I stopt; it mov'd, I mov'd again.°
At last it fix'd ('twas on what plant it pleas'd)
And where it fix'd, the beauteous bird° I seiz'd: 430
Rose or Carnation, was below my care;
I meddle, Goddess! only in my sphere.
I tell the naked fact without disguise,
And, to excuse it, need but show the prize;
Whose spoils this paper offers to your eye,
Fair ev'n in death! this peerless *Butterfly*.

My sons! (she answer'd) both have done your parts:
Live happy both, and long promote our arts.
But hear a Mother, when she recommends
To your fraternal care, our sleeping friends.°   440
The common Soul, of Heav'ns more frugal make,
Serves but to keep fools pert, and knaves awake;
A drowzy Watchman, that just gives a knock,
And breaks our rest, to tell us what's a clock.

375. of . . . Princes: The 1742 edition cites the source of
this "strange story." 376. horned: See l. 387 and note. 387.
Witness . . . swore: [1742] Jupiter Ammon is call'd to
witness as the father of Alexander, to whom those Kings
succeeded in the division of the Macedonian Empire, and
whose *Horns* they wore on their Medals. 394. Douglas:
[1742] A Physician [Dr. James Douglas, a famous obstetri-
cian] of great Learning and no less Taste. [Pope is the
first recorded user of *obstetric* (OED).] 409. nam'd it Caroline: [1742] It is a compliment which the Florists usually
pay to Princes and great persons, to give their names to the
most curious Flowers of their raising. Some have been very
jealous of vindicating this honour, but none more than that
ambitious Gardner at Hammersmith, who caused his favourite
to be painted on his Sign, with this inscription, *This is My
Queen Caroline*.

410–14. Each . . . divine: The 1742 edition shows that
Pope is translating a poem by Catullus. 421–22. Of . . .
spring: [1742] The Poet seems to have had an eye to Spenser,
Muiopotmos. *Of all the race of silver-winged Flies | Which do
possess the Empire of the Air.* 427–28. It . . . again: [1742]
Milt. [*Paradise Lost*, IV. 462–64]

> ——I started back,
> It started back; but pleas'd I soon return'd,
> Pleas'd it return'd as soon——

430. bird: insect, a seventeenth-century usage. 440. our
. . . friends: [1742] Of whom see V. 345 above.

Yet by some object ev'ry brain is stirr'd;
The dull may waken to a Humming-bird;
The most recluse, discreetly open'd, find
Congenial matter in the Cockle-kind;
The mind in Metaphysics at a loss,
May wander in a wilderness of Moss;°   450
The head that turns at super-lunar things
Poiz'd with a tail, may steer on Wilkins'° wings.

O! would the Sons of men once think their Eyes
And Reason giv'n them, but to study *Flies!*
See Nature in some partial narrow shape,
And let the Author of the Whole escape:
Learn but to trifle; or, who most observe,
To wonder at their Maker, not to serve.

Be that my task (replies a gloomy Clerk,
Sworn foe to Myst'ry,° yet divinely dark,   460
Whose pious hope aspires to see the day
When Moral Evidence° shall quite decay,
And damns implicit faith, and holy lies,
Prompt to impose, and fond to dogmatize.)
Let others creep by timid steps, and slow,
On plain Experience lay foundations low,
By common sense to common knowledge bred,
And last, to Nature's Cause thro' Nature led.
All-seeing in thy mists, we want no guide,
Mother of Arrogance, and Source of Pride!   470
We nobly take the high Priori Road,°
And reason downward, till we doubt of God:
Make Nature still incroach upon his plan;
And shove him off as far as e'er we can:
Thrust some Mechanic Cause into his place;
Or bind in Matter, or diffuse in Space.
Or, at one bound o'erleaping all his laws,
Make God Man's Image, Man the final Cause,°
Find Virtue local, all Relation scorn,
See all in *Self*, and but for self be born: 480
Of nought so certain as our *Reason* still,
Of nought so doubtful as of *Soul* and *Will*.

Oh hide the God still more! and make us see
Such as Lucretius drew, a God like Thee:
Wrapt up in Self, a God without a Thought,
Regardless of our Merit or Default.°
Or that bright Image to our fancy draw,
Which Theocles° in raptur'd Vision saw,
While thro' Poetic scenes the *Genius*° roves,
Or wanders wild in Academic Groves;   490
That NATURE, our Society adores,
Where Tindal° dictates, and Silenus° snores.

Rous'd at his name, up rose the bowzy Sire,
And shook from out his Pipe the seeds of Fire:°
Then snapt his box, and strok'd his belly down,
Rosie and rev'rend, tho' without a Gown.
Bland and familiar to the throne he came,
Led up the Youth, and call'd the Goddess *Dame:*
Then thus. From Priest-craft happily set free,
Lo! ev'ry finish'd Son returns to thee: 500
First Slave to Words, then Vassal to a Name,
Then Dupe to Party; child and man the same;
Bounded by Nature, narrow'd still by Art,
A trifling head, and a contracted heart.
Thus bred, thus taught, how many have I seen,
Smiling on all, and smil'd on by a Queen;
Mark'd out for Honours, honour'd for their Birth;
To thee the most rebellious things on earth:
Now to thy gentle shadow are shrunk;
All melted down, in Pension, or in Punk°!   510
So K* so B** sneak'd into the Grave,
A Monarch's half and half a Harlot's slave.
Poor W**, nipt in Folly's broadest bloom,
Who praises now? his Chaplain on his Tomb.
Then take them all, oh take them to thy breast;
Thy *Magus*,° Goddess! shall perform the rest.

With that, a WIZARD OLD his *Cup* extends,
Which whoso tastes, forgets his former friends,°

---

450. **Moss:** [1742] Of which the Naturalists count above three hundred species. 452. **Wilkins:** [1742] One of the first Projectors of the Royal Society, who among many enlarged and useful notions, entertain'd the extravagant hope of a possibility to fly to the Moon; which has put some volatile Genius's upon making wings for that purpose. 460. **Myst'ry:** the supernatural. 462. **Moral Evidence:** evidence acceptable to the reason. 471. **the high . . . Road:** To argue a priori is to assume truth, e.g., that the universe is the work of a "Mechanic Cause," and then set about proving it. 478. **final Cause:** the end for which a thing is made.

485–86. **Wrapt . . . Default:** adapted from Lucretius, *De Rerum Natura*, II. 646 ff. 488. **Theocles:** a philosopher who figures in Shaftesbury's *Moralists* (1710). (See the selection from Shaftesbury earlier in Part Two.) 489. **Genius:** Shaftesbury's term. 492. **Tindal:** Matthew Tindal (d. 1733), famous Deist and author on Deism. **Silenus:** [1742] an Epicurean Philosopher [who] sings the Principles of that Philosophy in his drink. 494. **the seeds . . . Fire:** [1742] The Epicurean language, *Semina rerum*, or Atoms. Virg. Eclog. 6. *Semina Ignis.* 510. **Punk:** prostitute. 516. **Magus:** priest. 518. **Which . . . friends:** [1742] Homer of the Potion of the Nepenthe. Odyss. 4.

Sire, Ancestors, Himself. One casts his eyes
Up to a *Star,*° and like Endymion° dies: 520
A *Feather* shooting from another's head,
Extracts his brain, and Principle is fled;
Lost is his God, his Country, ev'ry thing,
And nothing left but Homage to a King.
The vulgar herd turn off to roll with Hogs,
To run with Horses, or to hunt with Dogs:
But, sad example! never to escape
Their Infamy, still keep the human shape.

But she, good Goddess, sent to ev'ry child
Firm Impudence, or Stupefaction mild;   530
And strait succeeded, leaving Shame no room,
Cibberian forehead, or Cimmerian° gloom.

Kind Self-conceit to some her Glass applies,
Which no one looks in with another's eyes,
But as the Flatt'rer or Dependant paint,
Beholds himself a Patriot, Chief, or Saint.

On others, Int'rest her gay Liv'ry flings,
Int'rest that waves on Party-colour'd° wings;
Turn'd to the Sun, she casts a thousand dyes,
And as she turns, the Colours fall or rise.   540

Others, the Syren Sisters warble round,
And empty heads console with empty sound.°
No more alas! the voice of Fame they hear,
The balm of Dulness trickling in their ear.
Great C**, H**, P**, R**, K*,
Why all your Toils? your Sons have learn'd to sing;
How quick Ambition hasts to ridicule!
The Sire is made a Peer, the Son a Fool.

On some, a Priest succinct in Amice° white
Attends; all flesh is nothing in his sight!   550
Beeves at his touch at once to jelly turn,
And the huge Boar is shrunk into an Urn.
The board with specious miracles he loads,
Turns Hares to Larks, and Pigeons into Toads.

Another (for in all what one can shine?)
Explains the *Seve* and *Verdeur*° of the Vine.
What cannot copious Sacrifice attone?
Thy Treufles, Perigord! thy Hams, Bayone!
With French libation and Italian strain,°
Wash Bladen white, and expiate Hays's stain.   560
Knight° lifts the head, for what are crowds undone
To three essential Partriges in one°?
Gone ev'ry blush, and silent all reproach,
Contending Princes mount them in their Coach.

Next, bidding all draw near on bended knees,
The Queen confers her *Titles* and *Degrees.*
Her Children first of more distinguish'd sort,
Who study Shakespear at the Inns of Court,
Impale a Glow-worm, or Vertù° profess,
Shine in the dignity of F. R. S.°   570
Some, deep Free-Masons, join the silent race°
Worthy to fill Pythagoras's place:
Some Botanists, or Florists at the least;
Or issue Members of an Annual feast.
Nor past the meanest unregarded, one
Rose a Gregorian, one a Gormogon.°
The last, not least in honour or applause,
Isis and Cam made Doctors of her Laws.

Then, blessing all, Go Children of my care!
To Practise now from Theory repair.   580
All my Commands are easy, short, and full:
My Sons! be proud, be selfish, and be dull.

520–21. Star, Feather: The star and feather refer to decorations worn by certain knights. Pope suggests that the plume worn in the hat of Knights of the Garter takes away from members of that order all principles except paying homage to their king. **520. Endymion:** a shepherd who died for love of the moon goddess, Selene. **532. Cimmerian:** The Cimmerians lived in a part of western Italy so gloomy as to give rise to the expression "Cimmerian darkness." Pope invents *Cibber-ian;* its similarity to *Cimmerian* in sound suggests a similarity in sense. **538. Party-colour'd:** an obvious pun **541–42. the Syren . . . sound:** an allusion to opera. **549. Amice:** a white vestment of a priest; here, it is applied to a cook.

556. Seve and Verdeur: [1742] French Terms relating to Wines. **559. French . . . strain:** signifying wine and music. **560–61. Bladen, Hays, Knight:** [1742] Names of Gamesters [who] lived with the utmost magnificence at Paris, and kept open Tables, frequented by persons of the first Quality of England, and even by Princes of the Blood of France. **562. three . . . one:** [1742] Two dissolved into Quintessence to make sauce for the third. The honour of this invention belongs to France, yet has it been excell'd by our native luxury, an hundred squab [fat] Turkeys being not unfrequently deposited in one Pye in the Bishopric of Durham. [This is an obvious allusion to the doctrine of the Trinity.] **569. Vertù:** a taste for works of art or curios. **570. F. R. S.:** Fellows of the Royal Society (founded 1660) were often the subject of mockery. **571. the silent race:** [1742] The Poet all along expresses a very particular concern for this silent Race: He has here provided, that in case they will not waken or open (as was before proposed) to a *Humming Bird* or *Cockle,* yet at worst they may be made Free-Masons; where *Taciturnity* is the only essential Qualification, as it was one of the chief of the disciples of Pythagoras. **576. Gregorian, Gormogon:** [1742] A sort of Lay-brothers, *Slips* from the root of the Free-Masons. [These bodies were founded in the early eighteenth century on Freemason lines.]

Guard my Prerogative, assert my Throne:
This Nod confirms each Privilege your own.
The Cap and Switch be sacred to his Grace:
With Staff and Pumps° the Marquiss lead the Race:
From Stage to Stage the licens'd° Earl may run,
Pair'd with his Fellow-Charioteer, the Sun:
The learned Baron Butterflies design,
Or draw to silk Arachne's subtile line:°   590
The Judge to dance his brother Sergeant call;
The Senator at Cricket urge the Ball:
The Bishop stowe (Pontific Luxury!)
An hundred Souls of Turkeys in a pye:°
The sturdy Squire to Gallick masters stoop,
And drown his Lands and Manors in a Soupe.
Others import yet nobler Arts from France,
Teach Kings to fiddle, and make Senates dance.
Perhaps more high some daring son may soar,
Proud to my List to add one Monarch more;   600
And nobly conscious, Princes are but things
Born for First Ministers, as Slaves for Kings,
Tyrant supreme! shall three Estates command,
And MAKE ONE MIGHTY DUNCIAD OF THE LAND!

    More she had spoke, but yawn'd—All Nature nods:
What Mortal can resist the Yawn of Gods?°
Churches and Chappels instantly it reach'd,
(St. James's first, for leaden Gilbert° preach'd)
Then catch'd the Schools; the Hall scarce kept awake;
The Convocation° gap'd, but could not speak: 610
Lost was the Nation's Sense,° nor could be found,
While the long solemn Unison went round;
Wide, and more wide, it spread o'er all the realm;
Ev'n Palinurus° nodded at the Helm;
The Vapour mild o'er each Committee crept;
Unfinish'd Treaties in each Office slept;

And Chief-less Armies doz'd out the Campaign;
And Navies yawn'd for Orders on the Main.°

    O Muse! relate (for you can tell alone,
Wits have short Memories, and Dunces none)°   620
Relate, who first, who last resign'd to rest?
Whose Heads she partly, whose compleatly blest?
What Charms could Faction, what Ambition lull,
The Venal quiet, and intrance the Dull;
'Till drown'd was Sense, and Shame, and Right, and
    Wrong—
O sing, and hush the Nations with thy Song!

* * * * * *

    In vain, in vain,—the all-composing Hour
Resistless falls: The Muse obeys the Pow'r.
She comes! she comes! the sable Throne behold
Of Night Primæval, and of Chaos old!   630
Before her, Fancy's gilded clouds decay,
And all its varying Rain-bows die away.
Wit shoots in vain its momentary fires,
The meteor drops, and in a flash expires.
As one by one, at dread Medea's strain,
The sick'ning stars fade off th' ethereal plain;°
As Argus' eyes by Hermes' wand opprest,
Clos'd one by one to everlasting rest;°
Thus at her felt approach, and secret might,
Art after Art goes out, and all is Night.   640

---

586. Staff and Pumps: Like "Cap and Switch" in line 585, an allusion to the rig of jockeys and running footmen. 587. licens'd: A license was necessary before a stagecoach could be run. 590. draw . . . line: Attempts had been made to weave stockings of spider webs. 594. An hundred . . . pye: See l. 562 and note. 606. What . . . Gods: [1742] This verse is truly Homerical, as is the conclusion of the Action, where the great Mother composes all, in the same manner as Minerva at the period [end] of the Odyssey. 608. Gilbert: Dr. John Gilbert was Dean of Exeter. 610. Convocation: an assembly of the clergy that discussed ecclesiastical matters. It had been prorogued in 1717. 611. Nation's Sense: a contemporary phrase denoting the Houses of Parliament. 614. Palinurus: Aeneas' helmsman; here he stands for Prime Minister Walpole.

615–18. The Vapour . . . Main: Here, adapting lines from an anonymous poem of 1704, Pope refers to the Government's delays in fitting out an expedition to South America in 1740 during the war with Spain. 619–20. for . . . none: [1742] This seems to be the reason why the Poets, whenever they give us a Catalogue, constantly call for help on the Muses, who, as the Daughters of Memory, are obliged not to forget any thing. 635–36. As . . . plain: Medea, the daughter of the King of Colchis, fell in love with Jason, who proved false. In Seneca's play Medea she calls on the powers of heaven and hell to avenge her; as a result of her plea, and also because she is a magician, the stars slide from the sky. Line 636—a splendid line—was inspired by earlier poetry: sick'ning had been applied to stars in Nahum Tate's Leander to Hero in Ovid's Epistles Translated by Several Hands (1680) and to the sun in Isaac Watts's Horae Lyricae (1706); Pope's translation of the Iliad, X. 296, reads: "The Stars shine fainter on th' Æthereal Plains," and his Odyssey, XI. 465: "The evening stars still mount th' ethereal plains." 637–38. As . . . rest: Argus, King of Argos, had a hundred eyes, of which only two slept at one time. Juno suspected that Jupiter was in love with Io, whom he had changed into a heifer, and appointed Argus to watch her. Jupiter defeated the plan by employing Mercury (Hermes) to charm Argus wholly asleep with his lyre (Pope says wand), whereupon Juno transferred the eyes to the peacock's tail.

See skulking *Truth* to her old Cavern fled,°
Mountains of Casuistry heap'd o'er her head!
Philosophy,° that lean'd on Heav'n before,
Shrinks to her second cause, and is no more.
Physic° of *Metaphysic* begs defence,
And *Metaphysic* calls for aid on *Sense!*
See *Mystery*° to *Mathematics* fly!
In vain! they gaze, turn giddy, rave, and die.

Religion blushing veils her sacred fires,
And unawares *Morality* expires.°
Nor *public* Flame, nor *private*, dares to shine;
Nor *human* Spark is left, nor Glimpse *divine!*
Lo! thy dread Empire, CHAOS! is restor'd;
Light dies before thy uncreating word:°
Thy hand, great Anarch! lets the curtain fall;
And Universal Darkness buries All.°

650

641. skulking . . . fled: [1729, annotating what was then the conclusion of Book III] Alluding to the saying of Democritus, That Truth lay at the bottom of a deep well. **643–52. Philosophy . . . divine:** Aristotle distinguished four causes when accounting for a thing, of which the first was God, the Creator (Pope's "Heav'n"), and the second the physical substance of which the thing is made. Pope laments the absorption of the "natural philosophers," the scientists, in their rapidly expanding knowledge of the external world; he sees them neglecting the Creator for His creation and stopping in their explanation of things when they have accounted for them in material terms. **645. Physic:** [1743] [natural philosophy, science] Certain writers as Malbranch, Norris, and others, have thought it of importance, in order to secure the existence of the *soul*, to bring in question the reality of *body;* which they have attempted to do by a very refined *metaphysical* reasoning: While others of the same party, in order to persuade us of the necessity of a Revelation which promises immortality, have been as anxious to prove that those qualities which are commonly supposed to belong only to an immaterial Being, are but the result from the sensations of matter, and the soul naturally mortal. Thus between these different reasonings, they have left us neither Soul nor Body: nor the Sciences of Physics and Metaphysics the least support, by making them depend upon and go a begging to one another. **647. Mystery:** [1751] [divine revelation] A sort of men (who make human Reason the adequate measure of all Truth) having pretended that whatsoever is not fully comprehended by it, is contrary to it; certain defenders of Religion, who would not be outdone in a paradox, have gone as far in the opposite folly, and attempted to shew that the mysteries of Religion may be mathematically demonstrated; as the authors of Philosophic, or Astronomic Principles, natural and reveal'd [1743]; who have much prided themselves on reflecting a fantastic light upon religion from the frigid subtilty of school moonshine.

649–50. Religion . . . expires: [1743] It appears from hence that our Poet was of very different sentiments from the Author of the Characteristics, who has written a formal treatise on Virtue, to prove it not only real but durable, without the support of Religion. The word *unawares* alludes to the confidence of those men who suppose that Morality would flourish best without it, and consequently to the surprize such would be in (if any such there are) who indeed love Virtue, and yet do all they can to root out the Religion of their Country. **654. Light . . . word:** This reverses "Let there be light" in the account of the creation of the world in the first chapter of Genesis. **656. And . . . All:** As usual, a great line of poetry stands at the end of a long process: "And universal ruin swallows all" (Dryden, *Amboyna*, V); "And one promiscuous Ruin cover all" (Addison, *Remarks on Italy*); "And one prodigious Ruin swallow All" (Pope's *Iliad*, IV. 199); and the earlier versions of the line when the poem closed at Book III. In the note on his *Iliad*, XVI. 122, Pope quotes Shakespeare's curse in *II Henry IV*, I. i, which may have helped inspire the final paragraph of his poem: "Let Order die / . . . And Darkness be the Burier of the Dead!" It is instructive to compare this last paragraph in the final version in Book IV with its form when it closed Book III in 1728:

And Alma Mater all dissolv'd in *Port!*

Then, when these signs declare the mighty Year,
When the dull Stars roll round, and reappear;
Let there be darkness! (the dread pow'r shall say)
All shall be darkness, as it ne'er were Day;
To their first Chaos Wit's vain works shall fall,
And universal Dulness cover all!

No more the Monarch could such raptures bear;
He wak'd, and all the Vision mix'd with air.

James Thomson

(1700–1748)

James Thomson was born on September 11, 1700, the son of the pastor of the Scottish border village Ednam. As a boy he was a rather backward student, though he began writing poetry at an early age. Each New Year's Day he would burn the previous year's work, ending the little ceremony with a poem in which were stated the grounds for condemnation.

At the age of fifteen he entered the College of Edinburgh, where he remained for ten years. As a member of the Grotesque Club, one of the many literary groups then flourishing in Edinburgh, Thomson continued to write, though his efforts were ridiculed and he was considered the jest of the group. Edinburgh literary culture was at this time wholly directed toward English literature, and it is not strange that Thomson, who spoke broad Scots and who was acquainted with English only through books, did not fare well in such an atmosphere. Enrolled in the divinity class since 1719, he was called on in 1723 to lecture on a Psalm. His performance was so extravagant as to cause the professor to take him aside and remind him that "he must keep a stricter rein upon his imagination, and express himself in language more intelligible to an ordinary congregation." But this was a precept that Thomson could not observe without being false to himself, and, having no compelling interest in the ministry anyway, he decided to make his way as a man of letters.

In 1725 he sailed for London, and by the summer of that year he was employed as a tutor and was writing the detached verses that later grew into *Winter*. Unable to find a publisher himself, Thomson was aided by his Scottish friend and *littérateur* David Mallet (*alias* Malloch), who arranged for the poem's publication in April, 1726. Although it at first gathered dust in the bookseller's stall, Thomson's friends awakened enough interest through letters and personal canvassing to warrant a second edition in July. With this promise of success Thomson began work on *Summer*, writing to Mallet that he was including "a Panegyric on Britain, which may perhaps contribute to make my Poem popular." *Summer* was published, with much advance advertising, in February, 1727, and was dedicated to the ludicrous but openhanded George Bubb Dodington. On March 20 Sir Isaac Newton died, and Thomson's poem on his death, which appeared in late April, went through four editions within the year.

Always alert to new ways of capitalizing on his growing popularity, Thomson undertook a subscription scheme for all four of the *Seasons*, including *Spring*, which he had written during the summer of 1727 while a guest of Lady Hertford at Marlborough Castle, and the as-yet-unwritten *Autumn*. The scheme failed to arouse much interest, and *Spring* was published separately in 1728, though Thomson continued to canvass for a subscription edition as he worked on *Autumn*. Finally, in June, 1730, *The Seasons* appeared in a sumptuous illustrated quarto edition (there was also an octavo edition the same year), with the three previously published poems revised and enlarged. Among the impressive list of subscribers was Pope, who took three copies.

Shortly before the publication of the collected *Seasons*, Thomson's first tragedy, *Sophonisba*, was successfully produced at Drury Lane Theatre. According to Johnson the play "raised such expectation, that every rehearsal was dignified with a splendid audience, collected to anticipate the delight that was preparing for the publick. It was observed, however, that nobody was much affected, and that the company rose as from a moral lecture." Still, Thomson had arrived. Since coming to London only five years before, he had produced a very successful poem and a well-received play and had become the friend of every important man of letters in England.

Thomson was always the sturdy Britisher, for better or for worse, and on the Grand Tour he undertook in 1730 (as companion to the Solicitor General's son) he found much to deplore. Especially, Johnson remarks, he "found or fancied so many evils arising from the tyranny of other governments, that he resolved to write a very long poem, in five parts, upon liberty." The first book of *Liberty* was published in January, 1735; the fifth exactly one year later. The poem was not successful, but it is noteworthy because, fulsomely dedicated to Frederick, Prince of Wales, the leader of the Opposition, and filled with gibes at the Walpole administration, it marks Thomson's entrance into politics. His next two plays, *Agamemnon* and *Edward and Eleanora*, are both thinly disguised attacks on the administration and were great successes. He also collaborated with Mallet on a masque, *Alfred* (1740), for the Prince of Wales. The masque includes the famous ode *Rule, Britannia!*, which is thought to be solely Thomson's.

Sometime during the early 1740's Thomson fell in love and waged a long but unsuccessful courtship. This adversity, however, had its uses. "When seduced," he wrote the young woman, "by that most fatal Syren Indolence and false Pleasure, to the very Brink of Ruin, the Angel of Love came in your form and saved me." Salvation found its fruit in a further revision of *The Seasons*, which was published in July, 1744. Two years later the text was again revised for publication, bringing *The Seasons* to their final form.

Thomson died on August 27, 1748, a few months after the publication of *The Castle of Indolence*, a Spenserian imitation originally intended for the amusement of his friends and markedly different, particularly in its use of wit, from his other verse. The obituary notices in the newspapers give us a picture (even after we make allowances for the occasion) of a rather unusual specimen of a man of letters in the Age of Pope. One paper called him "an honest Man, who has not left one Enemy behind him," while another described him as a "gen'rous, sincere, sublimely simple man!" Thomson was buried in the Church of St. Mary, in suburban Richmond, where he had lived since 1736, and a monument was erected to his memory in Westminster Abbey in 1762.

Thomson's *Seasons* have enjoyed an extraordinary popularity among English-speaking people. Coleridge, on a walk with William Hazlitt, discovered a battered copy of the poem lying in the window seat of an obscure country alehouse and remarked, "*That* is true fame!" At the same time the critic in him delivered the dictum: "Thomson was a great poet, rather than a good one; his style was as meretricious as his thoughts were natural." This estimate was shared by three other poet-critics of note. Wordsworth observed that "notwithstanding his high powers, he wrote a vicious style; and his false ornaments are exactly of that kind which would be most likely to strike the undiscerning." Previously, Johnson had remarked:

His diction is in the highest degree florid and luxuriant, such as may be said to be to his images and thoughts "both their lustre and their shade" [quoting *Hudibras*]; such as invests them with splendour, through which perhaps they are not always easily discerned. It is too exuberant, and sometimes may be charged with filling the ear more than the mind.

And still earlier, Joseph Warton, in a digressive panegyric on Thomson in his *Essay on the Writings and Genius of Pope* (1756), conceded that "the diction of the *Seasons* is sometimes harsh and inharmonious, and sometimes turgid and obscure" and "the numbers are not sufficiently diversified by different pauses."

But on the score of Thomson's distinctive achievement, this critical trio may be heard in even more impressive unison. Warton wrote:

Thomson was blessed with a strong and copious fancy; he hath enriched poetry with a variety of new and original images, which he painted from nature itself, and from his own actual observations: his descriptions have therefore a distinctness and truth, which are utterly wanting to those, of poets who have only copied from each other, and have never looked abroad on the objects themselves.

Johnson discovered the same originality and insight in Thomson's poetry:

As a writer he is entitled to one praise of the highest kind: his mode of thinking and of expressing his thoughts is original. . . . His numbers, his pauses, his diction, are of his own growth, without transcription, without imitation. He thinks in a peculiar train, and he thinks always as a man of genius; he looks round on Nature and on Life with the eye which Nature bestows only on a poet, the eye that distinguishes in every thing presented to its view whatever there is on which imagination can delight to be detained, and with a mind that at once comprehends the vast, and attends to the minute. The reader of *The Seasons* wonders that he never saw before what Thomson shews him, and that he never yet has felt what Thomson impresses.

Finally, Wordsworth too agreed, calling *The Seasons* "a work of inspiration; much of it is written from himself, and nobly from himself." Thomson especially deserved praise, he thought, because "excepting the nocturnal *Reverie of Lady Winchilsea*, and a passage or two in the *Windsor-Forest* of Pope, the poetry of the period intervening between the publication of the *Paradise Lost* and the *Seasons* does not contain a single new image of external nature." For him, Thomson restored to English poetry the kind of familiar image "from which it can be inferred that the eye of the Poet had been steadily fixed upon his object" and "that his feelings had urged him to work upon it in the spirit of genuine imagination."

Thomson's bibliography is a complicated affair owing to both his popularity and his penchant for revision. The best single source is the bibliography in A. D. McKillop's *The Background of Thomson's Seasons* (1942), which provides beginning orientation. The most convenient and reliable modern edition of Thomson's works is that of J. L. Robertson (1908, reprinted 1951) in the Oxford Standard Authors Series. Critical texts are *Thomson's Seasons, Critical Edition*, ed. Otto Zippel (1908), which reproduces all states of Thomson's revisions, and *The Castle of Indolence and Other Poems*, ed. A. D. McKillop (1961), a critical edition of the minor poems with annotation and introductions. McKillop prints seventy-four Thomson letters as well as other material in his *James Thomson: Letters and Documents* (1958). A modern biography is Douglas Grant's *James Thomson, Poet of "The Seasons"* (1951), which also includes some letters. In addition to A. D. McKillop's study of *The Seasons*, critical works include P. M. Spacks's *The Varied God* (1959) and Ralph Cohen's *The Art of Discrimination* (1964).

FROM

THE SEASONS

❧

Although superficially pastoral, *The Seasons* (1746) should be sharply distinguished from the well-established tradition of English pastoral poetry. Thomson describes nature for its own sake, including human incidents as a background, and thus inverts the traditional pattern in which nature is a background for moral dramas or a model of human conditions. If one compares, for example, Pope's *Winter* (1709) with Thomson's, he will readily appreciate the new approach of *The Seasons*.

In the course of the many revisions of *The Seasons*, *Winter* underwent the greatest number of changes simply because it was written first. Beginning in April, 1726, as a poem of 405 lines, it grew through four successive stages (one in July, 1726, two in 1730, one in 1744) into the work of 1096 lines published in 1746. Johnson perceptively remarked of Thomson's "subsequent revisals" that "they are, I think, improved in general; yet I know not whether they have not lost part of what [Sir William] Temple calls their 'race;' a word which, applied to wines, in its primitive sense, means the flavour of the soil."

We print here, as an example of what happens in the revision and maturation of verse, the first version, from the folio *Winter* of April, 1726, and the final text, from the collected *Seasons* of 1746.

❦

WINTER. A POEM

SEE! WINTER comes, to rule the varied Year,
Sullen, and sad;° with all his rising Train,
Vapours, and *Clouds*, and *Storms:* Be these my Theme,
These, that exalt the Soul to solemn Thought,
And heavenly musing. Welcome kindred Glooms!
Wish'd, wint'ry, Horrors, hail!—With frequent
    Foot,
Pleas'd, have I, in my cheerful Morn of Life,
When, nurs'd by careless *Solitude*, I liv'd,
And sung of Nature with unceasing Joy,
Pleas'd, have I wander'd thro' your rough
    Domains;   10
Trod the pure, virgin, Snows, my self as pure:
Heard the Winds roar, and the big Torrent burst:

THE SEASONS: *Winter. A Poem.* **2. sad:** somber.

Or seen the deep, fermenting, Tempest brew'd,
In the red, evening, Sky.—Thus pass'd the Time,
Till, thro' the opening Chambers of the South,
Look'd out the joyous *Spring*, look'd out, and smil'd.

THEE too, Inspirer of the toiling Swain!
Fair AUTUMN, yellow rob'd! I'll sing of thee,
Of thy last, temper'd, Days, and sunny Calms;
When all the golden *Hours* are on the Wing,   20
Attending thy Retreat, and round thy Wain,°
Slow-rolling, onward to the Southern Sky.

BEHOLD! the well-pois'd *Hornet*, hovering, hangs,
With quivering Pinions, in the genial° Blaze;
Flys off, in airy Circles: then returns,
And hums, and dances to the beating Ray.
Nor shall the Man, that, musing, walks alone,
And, heedless, strays within his radiant Lists,°
Go unchastis'd away.—Sometimes, a Fleece
Of Clouds, wide-scattering, with a lucid Veil,   30
Soft, shadow o'er th' unruffled Face of Heaven;
And, thro' their dewy Sluices, shed the Sun,
With temper'd Influence down. Then is the Time,
For those, whom *Wisdom*, and whom *Nature* charm,
To steal themselves from the degenerate Croud,
And soar above this *little* Scene of Things:
To tread low-thoughted *Vice* beneath their Feet:
To lay their Passions in a gentle Calm,
And woo lone *Quiet*, in her silent *Walks*.

Now, solitary, and in pensive Guise,   40
Oft, let me wander o'er the russet Mead,°
Or thro' the pining Grove; where scarce is heard
One dying Strain, to chear the *Woodman's* Toil:
Sad *Philomel*,° perchance, pours forth her Plaint,
Far, thro' the withering Copse. Mean while, the
   Leaves,
That, late, the Forest clad with lively Green,
Nipt by the drizzly Night, and Sallow-hu'd,
Fall, wavering, thro' the Air; or shower amain,°
Urg'd by the Breeze, that sobs amid the Boughs.
Then list'ning *Hares* forsake the rusling Woods,   50
And, starting at the frequent Noise, escape
To the rough Stubble, and the rushy Fen.

Then *Woodcocks*, o'er the fluctuating Main,
That glimmers to the Glimpses of the Moon,
Stretch° their long Voyage to the woodland Glade:
Where, wheeling with uncertain Flight, they mock
The nimble *Fowler's* Aim.—Now *Nature* droops;
Languish the living Herbs, with pale Decay:
And all the *various Family* of Flowers
Their sunny Robes resign. The falling Fruits,   60
Thro' the still Night, forsake the Parent-Bough,
That, in the first, grey, Glances of the Dawn,
Looks wild, and wonders at the wintry Waste.

THE *Year*, yet pleasing, but declining fast,
Soft, o'er the secret Soul, in gentle Gales,
A Philosophic Melancholly breathes,
And bears the swelling Thought aloft to Heaven.
Then forming *Fancy* rouses to conceive,
What never mingled with the Vulgar's° Dream:
Then wake the tender *Pang*, the pitying *Tear*,   70
The *Sigh* for suffering Worth, the *Wish* prefer'd°
For Humankind, the *Joy* to see them bless'd,
And all the *Social Off-spring* of the Heart!

OH! bear me then to high, embowering, Shades;
To twilight Groves, and visionary Vales;
To weeping Grottos, and to hoary Caves;
Where Angel-Forms are seen, and Voices heard,
Sigh'd in low Whispers, that abstract the Soul,
From outward Sense, far into Worlds remote.

Now, when the Western Sun withdraws the
   Day,   80
And humid *Evening*, gliding o'er the Sky,
In her chill Progress, checks the straggling Beams,
And robs them of their gather'd, vapoury, Prey,
Where Marshes stagnate, and where Rivers wind,
Cluster the rolling *Fogs*, and swim along
The dusky-mantled Lawn: then slow descend,
Once more to mingle with their *Watry Friends*.
The vivid Stars shine out, in radiant Files;
And boundless *Ether*° glows, till the fair Moon
Shows her broad Visage, in the crimson'd East;   90
Now, stooping, seems to kiss the passing Cloud:
Now, o'er the pure *Cerulean*,° rides sublime.
Wide the pale Deluge floats, with silver Waves,
O'er the sky'd Mountain, to the low-laid Vale;

---

21. Wain: chariot (of the sun). **24. genial:** pleasantly warm;
cf. l. 331. **28. Lists:** boundaries. **41. Mead:** meadow. **44.
Sad Philomel:** the nightingale; sad because (according to
the myth) she was raped by her brother-in-law Tereus, King
of Thrace; as she was transformed into a nightingale, her
no less aggrieved sister, Procne, was transformed into a
swallow. **48. amain:** with full force.

55. Stretch: here, in the sense of making one's way rapidly
or with effort. **69. Vulgar:** common people. **71. prefer'd:**
held out. **89. Ether:** the medium filling the upper regions
of space. **92. Cerulean:** deep blue; i.e., the cloudless sky.

From the white Rocks, with dim Reflexion, gleams,
And faintly glitters thro' the waving Shades.

ALL Night, abundant Dews, unnoted, fall,
And, at Return of Morning, silver o'er
The Face of Mother-Earth; from every Branch
Depending,° tremble the translucent Gems,   100
And, quivering, seem to fall away, yet cling,
And sparkle in the Sun, whose rising Eye,
With Fogs bedim'd, portends a beauteous Day.

Now, giddy Youth, whom headlong Passions fire,
Rouse the wild Game, and stain the guiltless Grove,
With Violence, and Death; yet call it Sport,
To scatter Ruin thro' the Realms of *Love*,
And *Peace*, that thinks no Ill: But These, the *Muse*,
Whose Charity, unlimited, extends
As wide as *Nature* works, disdains to sing,   110
Returning to her nobler Theme in view—

FOR, see! where *Winter* comes, himself, confest,°
Striding the gloomy Blast. First Rains obscure
Drive thro' the mingling Skies, with Tempest foul;
Beat on the Mountain's Brow, and shake the Woods,
That, sounding, wave below. The dreary Plain
Lies overwhelm'd, and lost. The bellying° Clouds
Combine, and deepening into Night, shut up
The Day's fair Face. The Wanderers of Heaven,°
Each to his Home, retire; save those that love   120
To take their Pastime in the troubled Air,
And, skimming, flutter round the dimply Flood.
The Cattle, from th' untasted Fields, return,
And ask, with Meaning low, their wonted° Stalls;
Or ruminate° in the contiguous Shade:
Thither, the houshold, feathery, People° croud,
The crested Cock, with all his female Train,
Pensive, and wet. Mean while, the Cottage-Swain
Hangs o'er th' enlivening Blaze, and, taleful, there,
Recounts his simple Frolic: Much he talks,   130
And much he laughs, nor recks° the Storm that blows
Without, and rattles on his humble Roof.

AT last, the muddy Deluge pours along,
Resistless, roaring; dreadful down it comes

From the chapt° Mountain, and the mossy Wild,
Tumbling thro' Rocks abrupt, and sounding far:
Then o'er the sanded Valley, floating, spreads,
Calm, sluggish, silent; till again constrain'd,
Betwixt two meeting Hills, it bursts a Way,
Where Rocks, and Woods o'erhang the turbid
     Stream.   140
There gathering triple Force, rapid, and deep,
It boils, and wheels, and foams, and thunders thro'.

NATURE! great Parent! whose directing Hand
Rolls round the Seasons of the changeful Year,
How mighty! how majestick are thy Works!
With what a pleasing Dread° they swell the Soul,
That sees, astonish'd! and, astonish'd sings!
You too, ye *Winds!* that now begin to blow,
With boisterous Sweep, I raise my Voice to you.
Where are your Stores, ye viewless *Beings!* say?   150
Where your aerial Magazines reserv'd,
Against the Day of Tempest perilous?
In what untravel'd Country of the Air,
Hush'd in still Silence, sleep you, when 'tis calm?

LATE, in the louring° Sky, red, fiery, Streaks
Begin to flush about; the reeling Clouds
Stagger with dizzy Aim, as doubting yet
Which Master to obey: while rising, slow,
Sad, in the Leaden-colour'd East, the Moon
Wears a bleak Circle° round her sully'd Orb.   160
Then issues forth the Storm, with loud Control,°
And the thin Fabrick of the pillar'd Air°
O'erturns, at once. Prone, on th' uncertain Main,
Descends th' Etherial Force, and plows its Waves,
With dreadful Rift: from the mid-Deep, appears,
Surge after Surge, the rising, wat'ry, War.
Whitening, the angry Billows rowl immense,
And roar their Terrors, thro' the shuddering Soul
Of feeble Man, amidst their Fury caught,
And, dash'd upon his Fate: Then, o'er the Cliff,   170
Where dwells the *Sea-Mew*,° unconfin'd, they fly,
And, hurrying, swallow up the steril Shore.

---

100. **Depending:** hanging. 112. **confest:** made manifest.
117. **bellying:** swelling. 119. **Wanderers of Heaven:** birds;
cf. l. 230. 124. **wonted:** accustomed. 125. **ruminate:** chew
their cud. The whole line is a memorable example of
Thomson's Latinate style. 126. **houshold . . . People:**
"Feathery people" and the like are "scientific" terms. Until
the nineteenth century, scientists distinguished natural
species according to their habitat or covering. See Geoffrey
Tillotson, *Augustan Poetic Diction* (1964). 131. **recks:** heeds.

135. **chapt:** fissured. 146. **pleasing Dread:** This oxymoron
epitomizes the chief emotion cultivated by the sublime style.
155. **louring:** gloomy, threatening. For this picture of the
gathering storm Thomson is indebted to Virgil's *Georgics*,
I. 351–92. 160. **a bleak Circle:** In folk meteorology, a circle
around the moon is a portent of bad weather. 161. **Control:**
command, domination. 162. **pillar'd Air:** Air is imagined
in the form of an upright column or pillar; the dominant
meaning of *Fabrick* here is thus structure rather than
material. 171. **Sea-Mew:** seagull.

THE Mountain growls; and all its sturdy *Sons*°
Stoop to the Bottom of the Rocks they shade:
Lone, on its Midnight-Side,° and all aghast,
The dark, way-faring, *Stranger*, breathless, toils,
And climbs against the Blast—
Low, waves the rooted Forest, vex'd, and sheds
What of its leafy Honours yet remains.
Thus, struggling thro' the dissipated° Grove,   180
The whirling Tempest raves along the Plain;
And, on the Cottage thacht, or lordly Dome,°
Keen-fastening, shakes 'em to the solid Base.
Sleep, frighted, flies; the hollow Chimney howls,
The Windows rattle, and the Hinges creak.

THEN, too, they say, thro' all the burthen'd Air,
Long Groans are heard, shrill Sounds, and distant
   Sighs,
That, murmur'd by the *Demon* of the Night,
Warn the devoted° *Wretch* of Woe, and Death!
Wild Uproar lords it wide: the Clouds commixt, 190
With Stars, swift-gliding, sweep along the Sky.
All Nature reels.—But hark! the *Almighty* speaks:
Instant, the chidden Storm begins to pant,
And dies, at once, into a noiseless Calm.

As yet, 'tis Midnight's Reign; the weary Clouds,
Slow-meeting, mingle into solid Gloom:
Now, while the drousy World lies lost in Sleep,
Let me associate with the low-brow'd° *Night*,
And *Contemplation*, her sedate Compeer;
Let me shake off th' intrusive Cares of Day,   200
And lay the medling Senses all aside.

AND now, ye lying *Vanities* of Life!
You ever-tempting, ever-cheating Train!
Where are you now? and what is your Amount?
Vexation, Disappointment, and Remorse.
Sad, sickening, Thought! and yet, deluded Man,
A Scene of wild, disjointed, Visions past,
And broken Slumbers, rises, still resolv'd,
With new-flush'd Hopes, to run your giddy Round.

FATHER of Light, and Life! Thou *Good Supreme!* 210
O! teach me what is Good! teach me thy self!
Save me from Folly, Vanity and Vice,
From every low Pursuit! and feed my Soul,
With Knowledge, conscious Peace, and Vertue pure,
Sacred, substantial, never-fading Bliss!

173. sturdy Sons: trees. 175. Midnight-Side: the side of
intense darkness. 180. dissipated: scattered, wasted. 182.
Dome: house, building (from the Latin *domus*). 189.
devoted: doomed. 198. low-brow'd: gloomy.

Lo! from the livid East, or piercing North,
Thick Clouds ascend, in whose capacious Womb,
A vapoury Deluge lies, to Snow congeal'd:
Heavy, they roll their fleecy World along;
And the Sky saddens with th' impending Storm.   220
Thro' the hush'd Air, the whitening Shower descends,
At first, thin-wavering; till, at last, the Flakes
Fall broad, and wide, and fast, dimming the Day,
With a continual Flow. See! sudden, hoar'd,
The Woods beneath the stainless Burden bow,
Blackning,° along the mazy Stream it melts;
Earth's universal Face, deep-hid, and chill,
Is all one, dazzling, Waste. The Labourer-Ox
Stands cover'd o'er with Snow, and then demands
The Fruit of all his Toil. The Fowls of Heaven,   230
Tam'd by the cruel Season, croud around
The winnowing Store,° and claim the little Boon,
That *Providence* allows. The foodless Wilds
Pour forth their brown *Inhabitants;* the Hare,
Tho' timorous of Heart, and hard beset
By Death, in various Forms, dark Snares, and Dogs,
And more unpitying Men, the Garden seeks,
Urg'd on by *fearless* Want. The bleating Kind
Eye the bleak Heavens, and next, the glistening Earth,
With Looks of dumb Despair; then sad, dispers'd, 240
Dig, for the wither'd Herb, thro' Heaps of Snow.

Now, *Shepherds*, to your helpless Charge be kind;
Baffle the raging Year, and fill their Penns
With Food, at will: lodge them below the Blast,
And watch them strict; for from the bellowing East,
In this dire Season, oft the Whirlwind's Wing
Sweeps up the Burthen° of whole wintry Plains,
In one fierce Blast, and o'er th' unhappy Flocks,
Lodg'd in the Hollow of two neighbouring Hills,
The billowy Tempest whelms; till, upwards
   urg'd,   250
The Valley to a shining Mountain swells,
That curls its Wreaths amid the freezing Sky.°

Now, all amid the Rigours of the Year,
In the wild Depth of Winter, while without

226. Blackning: In contrast to the surrounding whiteness,
the flowing stream appears black. 232. winnowing Store:
newly harvested grain set aside in the barn for winnowing
during the winter. 247. Burthen: (burden) load. 251–52.
The Valley . . . Sky: *Wreaths* is a Scotticism for *snowdrifts*.
The picture of an entire herd of sheep buried beneath a
mountain of snow is not fanciful; cf. Smollett's *Humphry
Clinker* (1771), where the sheep in Scotland are said to "run
wild night and day, and thousands are lost under the huge
wreaths of snow."

The ceaseless Winds blow keen, be my Retreat
A rural, shelter'd, solitary, Scene;
Where ruddy Fire, and beaming Tapers join
To chase the chearless Gloom: there let me sit,
And hold high Converse with the mighty Dead,
Sages of ancient Time, as Gods rever'd,   260
As Gods beneficent, who blest Mankind,
With Arts, and Arms, and humaniz'd a World.
Rous'd at th' inspiring Thought—I throw aside
The long-liv'd Volume,° and, deep-musing, hail
The sacred Shades, that, slowly-rising, pass
Before my wondering Eyes—First, Socrates,
Truth's early Champion, Martyr for his God:
Solon,° the next, who built his Commonweal,
On Equity's firm Base: Lycurgus,° then,
Severely good, and him of rugged Rome,   270
Numa,° who soften'd her rapacious Sons.
Cimon° sweet-soul'd, and Aristides° just.
Unconquer'd Cato,° virtuous in Extreme;
With that attemper'd Heroe,° mild, and firm,
Who wept the Brother, while the Tyrant bled.
Scipio,° the humane Warriour, gently brave,
Fair Learning's Friend; who early sought the Shade,
To dwell, with Innocence, and Truth, retir'd.
And, equal to the best, the Theban,° He
Who, single, rais'd his Country into Fame.   280

Thousands behind, the Boast of Greece and Rome,
Whom Vertue owns, the Tribute of a Verse
Demand, but who can count the Stars of Heaven?
Who sing their Influence on this lower World?
But see who yonder comes! nor comes alone,
With sober State, and of majestic Mien,
The Sister-Muses in his Train—'Tis He!
Maro!° the best of Poets, and of Men!
Great Homer too appears, of daring Wing!
Parent of Song! and, equal, by his Side,   290
The British Muse,° join'd Hand in Hand, they walk,
Darkling,° nor miss their Way to Fame's Ascent.

Society divine! Immortal Minds!
Still visit thus my Nights, for you reserv'd,
And mount my soaring Soul to Deeds like yours.
Silence! thou lonely Power! the Door be thine:
See, on the hallow'd Hour, that none intrude,
Save Lycidas,° the Friend, with Sense refin'd,
Learning digested well, exalted Faith,
Unstudy'd Wit, and Humour ever gay.   300

CLEAR Frost succeeds, and thro' the blew Serene,
For Sight too fine, th' Ætherial Nitre° flies,
To bake the Glebe,° and bind the slip'ry Flood.
This of the wintry Season is the Prime;
Pure are the Days, and lustrous are the Nights,
Brighten'd with starry Worlds, till then unseen.
Mean while, the Orient, darkly red, breathes forth
An Icy Gale, that, in its mid Career,
Arrests the bickering° Stream. The nightly Sky,
And all her glowing Constellations pour   310
Their rigid Influence° down: It freezes on
Till Morn, late-rising, o'er the drooping World,
Lifts her pale Eye, unjoyous: then appears
The various Labour of the silent Night,
The pendant Isicle, the Frost-Work fair,
Where thousand Figures rise, the crusted Snow,
Tho' white, made whiter, by the fining° North.
On blithsome Frolics bent, the youthful Swains,
While every Work of Man is laid at Rest,
Rush o'er the watry Plains, and, shuddering,
            view   320

264. The long-liv'd Volume: Plutarch's Lives. 268.
Solon: (c. 640–560 B.C.), poet and statesman who
democratized the constitution and laws of Athens. 269.
Lycurgus: the traditional and perhaps legendary founder of
Spartan laws and institutions. 271. Numa: Numa Pompilius
(715–673 B.C.), the second king of Rome, who is credited by
legend with the founding of many Roman religious institutions and rituals. He was famous above all for keeping the
peace. 272. Cimon: (c. 512–449 B.C.), Athenian statesman and
general, follower of Aristides: (c. 530–c. 468 B.C.), Athenian
statesman and general, known as Aristides the Just. 273. Cato:
Marcus Porcius Cato (95–46 B.C.), surnamed Uticensis, known
as Cato the Younger; Roman patriot and Stoic philosopher
who committed suicide rather than give himself up to
Caesar. Addison's tragedy Cato (1713) was one of the most
popular plays of the eighteenth century. 274. attemper'd
Heroe: [Thomson's note] Timoleon [(d. c. 337 B.C.), Greek
general and statesman who, despite—or because of—his
temperate character, had his brother killed when he sought
to become tyrant of Corinth. He is said to have covered his
head and wept while his companions carried out the assassination.]. 276. Scipio: Scipio Africanus Major (236–184 B.C.),
Roman general and conqueror of Hannibal. 279. the Theban:
either Pelopidas (c. 410–364 B.C.) or Epaminondas (d. 362 B.C.),
both of whom led important campaigns against Sparta. In
his revision (see l. 476 of the 1746 version) Thomson gave up
the notion of an individual for that of a joint achievement.

288. Maro: Virgil (Publius Virgilius Maro). 291. The British
Muse: Milton. 292. Darkling: blind. 298. Lycidas: The
name, from Milton's elegy (1638), became synonymous with
the cultured friend. 302. Nitre: a supposed element in the air
thought to cause freezing. 303. Glebe: field. 309. bickering:
a metaphor expressive of the noisy action of the water. 311.
Influence: the supposed emanation from the stars, conceived
as flowing like water; here, frozen. 317. fining: refining.

The fearful Deeps below: or with the Gun,
And faithful Spaniel, range the ravag'd Fields,
And, adding to the Ruins of the Year,
Distress the Feathery, or the Footed *Game*.

But hark! the nightly Winds, with hollow Voice,
Blow, blustering, from the South—the Frost subdu'd,
Gradual, resolves into a weeping Thaw.
Spotted, the Mountains shine: loose Sleet descends,
And floods the Country round: the Rivers swell,
Impatient for the Day.—Those sullen Seas,   330
That wash th' ungenial Pole,° will rest no more,
Beneath the Shackles of the mighty North;
But, rousing all their Waves, resistless heave,—
And hark!—the length'ning Roar, continuous, runs
Athwart the rifted Main; at once, it bursts,
And piles a thousand Mountains to the Clouds!
Ill fares the Bark, the Wretches' last Resort,
That, lost amid the floating Fragments, moors
Beneath the Shelter of an Icy Isle;
While Night o'erwhelms the Sea, and Horror
     looks   340
More horrible. Can human Hearts endure
Th' assembled *Mischiefs*, that besiege them round:
Unlist'ning *Hunger*, fainting *Weariness*,
The *Roar* of Winds, and Waves, the *Crush* of Ice,
Now, ceasing, now, renew'd, with louder Rage,
And bellowing round the Main: Nations remote,
Shook from their Midnight-Slumbers, deem they hear
Portentous Thunder, in the troubled Sky.
More to embroil the Deep, Leviathan,°
And his unweildy Train, in horrid Sport,   350
Tempest the loosen'd Brine; while, thro' the Gloom,
Far, from the dire, unhospitable Shore,
The Lyon's Rage, the Wolf's sad Howl is heard,
And all the fell° Society of Night.
Yet, *Providence*, that ever-waking *Eye*
Looks down, with Pity, on the fruitless Toil
Of Mortals, lost to Hope, and *lights* them safe,
Thro' all this dreary Labyrinth of Fate.

'Tis done!—Dread WINTER has subdu'd the Year,
And reigns, tremenduous, o'er the desart Plains!   360
How dead the Vegetable Kingdom lies!
How dumb the Tuneful! *Horror* wide extends
His solitary Empire.—Now, fond° *Man!*
Behold thy pictur'd Life: pass some few Years,

Thy flow'ring SPRING, thy short-liv'd SUMMER's
     Strength,
Thy sober AUTUMN, fading into Age,
And pale, concluding, WINTER shuts thy Scene,
And shrouds *Thee* in the Grave—where now, are fled
Those Dreams of Greatness? those unsolid Hopes
Of Happiness? those Longings after Fame?   370
Those restless Cares? those busy, bustling Days?
Those Nights of secret Guilt? those veering°
     Thoughts,
Flutt'ring 'twixt Good, and Ill, that shar'd thy Life?
All, now, are vanish'd! *Vertue*, sole, survives,
Immortal, Mankind's never-failing Friend,
His Guide to Happiness on high—and see!
'Tis come, the Glorious *Morn!* the second Birth
Of Heaven, and Earth!—awakening *Nature* hears
Th' Almighty Trumpet's Voice, and starts to Life,
Renew'd, unfading. Now, th' Eternal *Scheme*,   380
That Dark Perplexity, that Mystic Maze,
Which Sight cou'd never trace, nor Heart conceive,
To *Reason*'s Eye, refin'd, clears up apace.
Angels, and Men, astonish'd, pause—and dread
To travel thro' the Depths of Providence,
Untry'd, unbounded. Ye vain *Learned!* see,
And, prostrate in the Dust, adore that *Power*,
And *Goodness*, oft arraign'd. See now the Cause,
Why conscious° *Worth*, oppress'd, in secret long
Mourn'd, unregarded: Why the *Good Man*'s Share 390
In Life, was Gall, and Bitterness of Soul:
Why the lone *Widow*, and her *Orphans*, pin'd,
In starving Solitude; while *Luxury*,
In Palaces, lay prompting her low Thought,
To form unreal Wants: why Heaven-born *Faith*,
And *Charity*, prime Grace! wore the *red* Marks
Of *Persecution*'s Scourge: why licens'd *Pain*,
That cruel *Spoiler*, that embosom'd *Foe*,
Imbitter'd all our Bliss. Ye Good *Distrest!*
Ye Noble *Few!* that, here, unbending, stand   400
Beneath Life's Pressures—yet a little while,
And all your Woes are past. *Time* swiftly fleets,
And wish'd *Eternity*, approaching, brings
Life undecaying, Love without Allay,
Pure flowing Joy, and Happiness sincere.

---

331. Pole: North Pole. **349. Leviathan:** the whale. **354. fell:** savage. **363. fond:** foolish.

372. veering: vacillating. **389. conscious:** having the witness within oneself.

WINTER

The ARGUMENT.

The Subject proposed. Address to the Earl of WILMINGTON.
*First Approach of Winter. According to the natural Course
of the Season, various Storms described. Rain. Wind.
Snow. The driving of the Snows: A Man perishing among
them; whence Reflections on the Wants and Miseries of
Human Life. The Wolves descending from the* Alps *and*
Apennines. *A Winter-Evening described: as spent by
Philosophers; by the Country People; in the City. Frost.
A View of Winter within the* polar *Circle. A Thaw.
The whole concluding with moral Reflections on a future
State.*

SEE, WINTER comes, to rule the vary'd Year,
Sullen, and sad, with all his rising Train;
Vapours, and *Clouds,* and *Storms.* Be these my Theme,
These, that exalt the Soul to solemn Thought,
And heavenly Musing. Welcome, kindred Glooms!
Cogenial° Horrors, hail! with frequent Foot,
Pleas'd have I, in my chearful Morn of Life,
When nurs'd by careless Solitude I liv'd,
And sung of Nature with unceasing Joy,
Pleas'd have I wander'd thro' your rough Domain; 10
Trod the pure Virgin-Snows, myself as pure;
Heard the Winds roar, and the big Torrent burst;
Or seen the deep fermenting Tempest brew'd,
In the grim Evening-Sky. Thus pass'd the Time,
Till thro' the lucid Chambers of the South
Look'd out the joyous SPRING, look'd out and smil'd.

To Thee, the Patron of *this first* Essay,
The Muse, O WILMINGTON°! renews her Song.
Since has she rounded the revolving Year:°

Skim'd the gay Spring; on Eagle-Pinions borne,   20
Attempted thro the Summer-Blaze to rise;
Then swept o'er Autumn with the shadowy Gale;
And now among the Wintry Clouds again,
Roll'd in the doubling Storm, she tries to soar;
To swell her Note with all the rushing Winds;
To suit her sounding Cadence to the Floods;
As is her Theme, her Numbers° wildly great:
Thrice happy! could she fill thy judging Ear
With bold Description, and with manly Thought.
Nor art thou skill'd in awful Schemes alone,   30
And how to make a mighty People thrive:
But equal Goodness, sound Integrity,
A firm unshaken uncorrupted Soul
Amid a sliding Age, and burning strong,
Not vainly blazing for thy Country's Weal,
A steady Spirit regularly free;
These, each exalting each, the Statesman light
Into the Patriot; These, the publick Hope
And Eye to thee converting,° bid the Muse
Record what Envy dares not Flattery call.   40

Now when the chearless Empire of the Sky
To *Capricorn* the *Centaur-Archer* yields,°
And fierce *Aquarius,* stains th' inverted Year;°
Hung o'er the farthest Verge of Heaven, the Sun
Scarce spreads o'er Ether the dejected Day.
Faint are his Gleams, and ineffectual shoot
His struggling Rays, in horizontal Lines,
Thro the thick Air; as cloath'd in cloudy Storm,
Weak, wan, and broad, he skirts the Southern Sky;
And, soon-descending, to the long dark Night,   50
Wide-shading All, the prostrate World resigns.
Nor is the Night unwish'd; while vital Heat,
Light, Life, and Joy, the dubious Day forsake.
Mean-time, in sable Cincture, Shadows vast,
Deep-ting'd and damp, and congregated Clouds,
And all the vapoury Turbulence of Heaven
Involve° the Face of Things. Thus Winter falls,
A heavy Gloom oppressive o'er the World,
Thro Nature shedding Influence malign,
And rouses up the Seeds of dark Disease.   60
The Soul of Man dies in him, loathing Life,
And black with more than melancholy Views.

Winter. **6. Cogenial:** congenial, of the same temperament. **18.
Wilmington:** Sir Spencer Compton (*c.* 1673–1743), Speaker
of the House of Commons, was appointed Lord Privy Seal
in the Walpole administration and was created Earl of
Wilmington, both in 1730. Four years earlier he had been
addressed in the Dedication (written by Mallet) to the first
publication of *Winter.* Johnson, in his *Life of Thomson* (1781),
states that the Dedication "attracted no regard from him to
the author; till Aaron Hill awakened his attention by some
verses addressed to Thomson, and published in one of the
newspapers, which censured the great for their neglect of
ingenious men. Thomson then received a present of twenty
guineas." **19. the revolving Year:** Although the first of
The Seasons to be written and published, *Winter* was placed
last in the collected edition.

27. Numbers: verses. **39. converting:** turning. **42. To
. . . yields:** The sun passes from Sagittarius to Capricorn
on December 21. **43. And . . . Year:** The sun passes
into Aquarius on January 21. Cf. Horace, *Satires,* I. i.
36: "Soon as Aquarius saddens the inverted year." **57.
Involve:** envelop so as to obscure.

The Cattle droop; and o'er the furrow'd Land,
Fresh from the Plow, the dun discolour'd Flocks,
Untended spreading, crop the wholesome Root.°
Along the Woods, along the moorish Fens,
Sighs the sad *Genius*° of the coming Storm;
And up among the loose disjointed Cliffs,
And fractur'd Mountains wild, the brawling Brook
And Cave, presageful, send a hollow Moan,   70
Resounding long in listening Fancy's Ear.

THEN comes the Father of the Tempest forth,
Wrapt in black Glooms. First joyless Rains obscure
Drive thro the mingling Skies with Vapour foul;
Dash on the Mountain's Brow, and shake the Woods,
That grumbling wave below. Th' unsightly Plain
Lies a brown Deluge; as the low-bent Clouds
Pour Flood on Flood, yet unexhausted still
Combine, and deepening into Night shut up
The Day's fair Face. The Wanderers of Heaven,   80
Each to his Home, retire; save Those that love
To take their Pastime in the troubled Air,
Or skimming flutter round the dimply Pool.
The Cattle from th' untasted Fields return,
And ask, with meaning Lowe,° their wonted Stalls,
Or ruminate in the contiguous Shade.
Thither the houshold feathery People croud,
The crested Cock, with all his female Train,
Pensive, and dripping; while the Cottage-Hind°
Hangs o'er th' enlivening Blaze, and taleful there   90
Recounts his simple Frolick: much he talks,
And much he laughs, nor recks the Storm that blows
Without, and rattles on his humble Roof.

WIDE o'er the Brim, with many a Torrent swell'd,
And the mix'd Ruin of its Banks o'erspread,
At last the rous'd-up River pours along:
Resistless, roaring, dreadful, down it comes,
From the rude Mountain, and the mossy Wild,
Tumbling thro Rocks abrupt, and sounding far;
Then o'er the sanded Valley floating spreads,   100
Calm, sluggish, silent; till again constrain'd,
Between two meeting Hills it bursts a Way,
Where Rocks and Woods o'erhang the turbid Stream;
There gathering triple Force, rapid, and deep,
It boils, and wheels, and foams, and thunders thro.

NATURE! great Parent! whose unceasing Hand
Rolls round the Seasons of the changeful Year,

How mighty, how majestic, are thy Works!
With what a pleasing Dread they swell the Soul!
That sees astonish'd! and astonish'd sings!   110
Ye too, ye Winds! that now begin to blow,
With boisterous Sweep, I raise my Voice to you.
Where are your Stores, ye powerful Beings! say,
Where your aërial Magazines reserv'd,
To swell the brooding Terrors of the Storm?
In what far-distant Region of the Sky,
Hush'd in deep Silence, sleep you when 'tis calm?

WHEN from the palid Sky the Sun descends,
With many a Spot, that o'er his glaring Orb
Uncertain wanders, stain'd; red fiery Streaks   120
Begin to flush around. The reeling Clouds
Stagger with dizzy Poise, as doubting yet
Which Master to obey: while rising slow,
Blank, in the leaden-colour'd East, the Moon
Wears a wan Circle round her blunted Horns.
Seen thro the turbid fluctuating Air,
The Stars obtuse° emit a shivering Ray;
Or frequent seem to shoot athwart the Gloom,
And long behind them trail the whitening Blaze.
Snatch'd in short Eddies, plays the wither'd Leaf; 130
And on the Flood the dancing Feather floats.
With broaden'd Nostrils to the Sky upturn'd,
The conscious° Heifer snuffs the stormy Gale.
Even as the Matron, at her nightly Task,
With pensive Labour draws the Flaxen Thread,
The wasted° Taper and the crackling Flame
Foretel the Blast. But chief the plumy Race,
The Tenants of the Sky, its Changes speak.
Retiring from the Downs,° where all Day long
They pick'd their scanty Fare, a blackening Train 140
Of clamorous Rooks thick-urge their weary Flight,
And seek the closing Shelter of the Grove.°
Assiduous,° in his Bower, the wailing Owl
Plies his sad Song. The Cormorant on high
Wheels from the Deep, and screams along the Land.
Loud shrieks the soaring Hern;° and with wild Wing
The circling Sea-Fowl cleave the flaky Clouds.
Ocean, unequal press'd, with broken Tide
And blind Commotion heaves; while from the Shore,
Eat° into Caverns by the restless Wave,   150

---

65. **the wholesome Root:** turnips. 67. **Genius:** tutelary spirit.
85. **meaning Lowe:** meaningful cry. 89. **Cottage-Hind:**
farm hand.

127. **obtuse:** dulled. 133. **conscious:** sensitive. 136.
wasted: guttering. 139. **Downs:** hilly pastures. 140–42.
a blackening . . . Grove: Cf. *Macbeth*, III. ii. 50–51:
"Light thickens, and the crow / Makes wing to th' rooky
wood." 143. **Assiduous:** unremitting, but with a suggestion
(as so often in Thomson) of the Latin derivation, "sitting
down to." 146. **Hern:** heron. 150. **Eat:** eaten, eroded.

And Forest-rustling Mountain, comes a Voice,
That solemn-sounding bids the World prepare.
Then issues forth the Storm with sudden Burst,
And hurls the whole precipitated Air,
Down, in a Torrent. On the passive Main
Descends th' etherial Force, and with strong Gust
Turns from its Bottom the discolour'd Deep.
Thro' the black Night that sits immense around,
Lash'd into Foam, the fierce conflicting Brine
Seems o'er a thousand raging Waves to burn;   160
Meantime the Mountain-Billows, to the Clouds
In dreadful Tumult swell'd, Surge above Surge,
Burst into Chaos with tremendous Roar,
And anchor'd Navies from their Stations drive,
Wild as the Winds across the howling Waste
Of mighty Waters: now th' inflated Wave
Straining they scale, and now impetuous shoot
Into the secret Chambers of the Deep,
The wintry *Baltick* thundering o'er their Head.
Emerging thence again, before the Breath   170
Of full-exerted Heaven they wing their Course,
And dart on distant Coasts; if some sharp Rock,
Or Shoal insidious break not their Career,
And in loose Fragments fling them floating round.

NOR less at Land the loosen'd Tempest reigns.
The Mountain thunders; and its sturdy Sons
Stoop to the Bottom of the Rocks they shade.
Lone on the midnight Steep, and all aghast,
The dark way-faring Stranger breathless toils,
And, often falling, climbs against the Blast.   180
Low waves the rooted Forest, vex'd, and sheds
What of its tarnish'd Honours yet remain;
Dash'd down, and scatter'd, by the tearing Wind's
Assiduous Fury, its gigantic Limbs.
Thus struggling thro' the dissipated Grove,
The whirling Tempest raves along the Plain;
And on the Cottage thatch'd, or lordly Roof,
Keen-fastening, shakes them to the solid Base.
Sleep frighted flies; and round the rocking Dome,
For Entrance eager, howls the savage Blast.   190
Then too, they say, thro all the burthen'd Air,
Long Groans are heard, shrill Sounds, and distant
    Sighs,
That, utter'd by the Demon of the Night,
Warn the devoted Wretch of Woe and Death.

HUGE Uproar lords it wide. The Clouds commix'd
With Stars swift-gliding sweep along the Sky.
All Nature reels. Till Nature's KING, who oft

Amid tempestuous Darkness dwells alone,
And on the Wings of the careering Wind
Walks dreadfully serene, commands a Calm;°   200
Then straight Air Sea and Earth are hush'd at once.

As yet 'tis Midnight deep. The weary Clouds,
Slow-meeting, mingle into solid Gloom.
Now, while the drowsy World lies lost in Sleep,
Let me associate with the serious *Night*,
And *Contemplation* her sedate Compeer;
Let me shake off th' intrusive Cares of Day,
And lay the meddling Senses all aside.

WHERE now, ye lying Vanities of Life!
Ye ever-tempting ever-cheating Train!   210
Where are you now? and what is your Amount?
Vexation, Disappointment, and Remorse.
Sad, sickening Thought! and yet deluded Man,
A Scene of crude disjointed Visions past,
And broken Slumbers, rises still resolv'd,
With new-flush'd Hopes, to run the giddy Round.

FATHER of Light and Life! thou GOOD SUPREME!
O teach me what is good! teach me THYSELF!
Save me from Folly, Vanity, and Vice,
From every low Pursuit! and feed my Soul   220
With Knowledge, conscious Peace, and Virtue pure,
Sacred, substantial, never-fading Bliss!

THE keener Tempests come: and fuming dun
From all the livid East, or piercing North,
Thick Clouds ascend; in whose capacious Womb
A vapoury Deluge lies, to Snow congeal'd.
Heavy they roll their fleecy World along;
And the Sky saddens with the gather'd Storm.
Thro the hush'd Air the whitening Shower descends,
At first thin-wavering; till at last the Flakes   230
Fall broad, and wide, and fast, dimming the Day,
With a continual Flow. The cherish'd Fields
Put on their Winter-Robe, of purest White.
'Tis Brightness all; save where the new Snow melts,
Along the mazy Current. Low, the Woods
Bow their hoar Head; and, ere the languid Sun
Faint from the West emits his Evening-Ray,
Earth's universal Face, deep-hid, and chill,
Is one wild dazzling Waste, that buries wide

199–200. And . . . Calm: a double reminiscence: Ps.
104:3 ("who walketh upon the wings of the wind") and
Matt. 8:26 ("Then he arose, and rebuked the winds and the
sea; and there was a great calm").

The Works of Man. Drooping, the Labourer-Ox 240
Stands cover'd o'er with Snow, and then demands
The Fruit of all his Toil. The Fowls of Heaven,
Tam'd by the cruel Season, croud around
The winnowing Store, and claim the little Boon
Which PROVIDENCE assigns them. One alone,
The Red-Breast, sacred to the houshold Gods,
Wisely regardful of th' embroiling Sky,
In joyless Fields, and thorny Thickets, leaves
His shivering Mates, and pays to trusted Man
His annual Visit. Half-afraid, he first   250
Against the Window beats; then, brisk, alights
On the warm Hearth; then, hopping o'er the Floor,
Eyes all the smiling Family askance,
And pecks, and starts, and wonders where he is:
Till more familiar grown, the Table-Crumbs
Attract his slender Feet. The foodless Wilds
Pour forth their brown Inhabitants. The Hare,
Tho timorous of Heart, and hard beset
By Death in various Forms, dark Snares, and Dogs,
And more unpitying Men, the Garden seeks,   260
Urg'd on by fearless Want. The bleating Kind
Eye the bleak Heaven, and next the glistening Earth,
With Looks of dumb Despair; then, sad-dispers'd,°
Dig for the wither'd Herb thro Heaps of Snow.

   Now, Shepherds, to your helpless Charge be kind,
Baffle the raging Year, and fill their Pens
With Food at Will; lodge them below the Storm,
And watch them strict: for from the bellowing East,
In this dire Season, oft the Whirlwind's Wing
Sweeps up the Burthen of whole wintry Plains   270
In one wide Waft, and o'er the hapless Flocks,
Hid in the Hollow of two neighbouring Hills,
The billowy Tempest whelms; till, upward urg'd,
The Valley to a shining Mountain swells,
Tipt with a Wreath, high-curling in the Sky.

   As thus the Snows arise; and foul, and fierce,
All Winter drives along the darken'd Air;
In his own loose-revolving Fields,° the Swain
Disaster'd stands; sees other Hills ascend,
Of unknown joyless Brow; and other Scenes,   280
Of horrid Prospect, shag° the trackless Plain:
Nor finds the River, nor the Forest, hid
Beneath the formless Wild; but wanders on
From Hill to Dale, still more and more astray;

Impatient flouncing thro the drifted Heaps,
Stung with the Thoughts of Home; the Thoughts of
   Home
Rush on his Nerves, and call their Vigour forth
In many a vain Attempt. How sinks his Soul!
What black Despair, what Horror fills his Heart!
When for the dusky Spot, which Fancy feign'd   290
His tufted Cottage rising thro the Snow,
He meets the Roughness of the middle Waste,
Far from the Track, and blest Abode of Man;
While round him Night resistless closes fast,
And every Tempest, howling o'er his Head,
Renders the savage Wilderness more wild.
Then throng the busy Shapes into his Mind,
Of cover'd Pits, unfathomably deep,
A dire Descent! beyond the Power of Frost,
Of faithless Bogs; of Precipices huge,   300
Smooth'd up with Snow; and, what is Land unknown,
What Water, of the still unfrozen Spring,
In the loose Marsh or solitary Lake,
Where the fresh Fountain from the Bottom boils.
These check his fearful Steps; and down he sinks
Beneath the Shelter of the shapeless Drift,
Thinking o'er all the Bitterness of Death,
Mix'd with the tender Anguish Nature shoots
Thro the wrung Bosom of the dying Man,
His Wife, his Children, and his Friends unseen.   310
In vain for him th' officious° Wife prepares
The Fire fair-blazing, and the Vestment warm;
In vain his little Children, peeping out
Into the mingling Storm, demand their Sire,
With Tears of artless Innocence. Alas!
Nor Wife, nor Children, more shall he behold,
Nor Friends, nor sacred Home. On every Nerve
The deadly Winter seizes; shuts up Sense;
And, o'er his inmost Vitals creeping cold,
Lays him along the Snows, a stiffen'd Corse,   320
Stretch'd out, and bleaching in the northern Blast.

   AH little think the gay licentious Proud,
Whom Pleasure, Power, and Affluence surround;
They, who their thoughtless Hours in giddy Mirth,
And wanton, often cruel, Riot waste;
Ah little think they, while they dance along,
How many feel, this very Moment, Death
And all the sad Variety of Pain.
How many sink in the devouring Flood,
Or more devouring Flame. How many bleed,   330

263. **sad-dispers'd:** badly scattered. **278. loose-revolving
Fields:** The fields appear to move with the drifting snow.
281. shag: roughen.

311. **officious:** dutiful (performing her offices).

By shameful Variance° betwixt Man and Man.
How many pine in Want, and Dungeon Glooms;
Shut from the common Air, and common Use
Of their own Limbs. How many drink the Cup
Of baleful Grief, or eat the bitter Bread
Of Misery. Sore pierc'd by wintry Winds,
How many shrink into the sordid Hut
Of chearless Poverty. How many shake
With all the fiercer Tortures of the Mind,
Unbounded Passion, Madness, Guilt, Remorse;   340
Whence tumbled headlong from the Height of Life,
They furnish Matter for the Tragic Muse.
Even in the Vale, where Wisdom loves to dwell,
With Friendship, Peace, and Contemplation join'd,
How many, rack'd with honest Passions, droop
In deep retir'd Distress. How many stand
Around the Death-bed of their dearest Friends,
And point° the parting Anguish. Thought fond Man
Of These, and all the thousand nameless Ills,
That one incessant Struggle render Life,   350
One Scene of Toil, of Suffering, and of Fate,
Vice in his high Career would stand appall'd,
And heedless rambling Impulse learn to think;
The conscious° Heart of Charity would warm,
And her wide Wish Benevolence dilate;
The social Tear would rise, the social Sigh;
And into clear Perfection, gradual Bliss,
Refining still, the social Passions work.

AND here can I forget the generous Band,°
Who, touch'd with human Woe, redressive°
    search'd   360
Into the Horrors of the gloomy Jail?
Unpity'd, and unheard, where Misery moans;
Where Sickness pines; where Thirst and Hunger burn,
And poor Misfortune feels the Lash of Vice.
While in the Land of Liberty, the Land
Whose every Street and public Meeting glow
With open Freedom, little Tyrants° rag'd:
Snatch'd the lean Morsel from the starving Mouth;
Tore from cold wintry Limbs the tatter'd Weed;
Even robb'd them of the last of Comforts, Sleep;   370
The free-born BRITON to the Dungeon chain'd,

Or, as the Lust of Cruelty prevail'd,
At pleasure mark'd him with inglorious Stripes;
And crush'd out Lives, by secret barbarous Ways,
That for their Country would have toil'd, or bled.
O great Design! if executed well,
With patient Care, and Wisdom-temper'd Zeal.
Ye Sons of Mercy! yet resume the Search;
Drag forth the legal Monsters into Light,
Wrench from their Hands Oppression's iron Rod,   380
And bid the Cruel feel the Pains they give.
Much still untouch'd remains; in this rank Age,
Much is the Patriot's weeding Hand requir'd.
The Toils° of Law, (what dark insidious Men
Have cumbrous added to perplex the Truth,
And lengthen simple Justice into Trade)
How glorious were the Day! that saw These broke,
And every Man within the Reach of Right.

By wintry Famine rous'd, from all the Tract
Of horrid Mountains which the shining *Alps*,   390
And wavy *Appenines*, and *Pyrenees*,
Branch out stupendous into distant Lands;
Cruel as Death, and hungry as the Grave!
Burning for Blood! bony, and ghaunt, and grim!
Assembling Wolves in raging Troops descend;
And, pouring o'er the Country, bear along,
Keen as the North-Wind sweeps the glossy Snow.
All is their Prize. They fasten on the Steed,
Press him to Earth, and pierce his mighty Heart.
Nor can the Bull his awful Front defend,   400
Or shake the murdering Savages away.
Rapacious, at the Mother's Throat they fly,
And tear the screaming Infant from her Breast.
The godlike Face of Man avails him nought.
Even Beauty, Force divine! at whose bright Glance
The generous Lion stands in soften'd Gaze,°
Here bleeds, a hapless undistinguish'd Prey.
But if, appriz'd of the severe Attack,
The Country be shut up, lur'd by the Scent,
On Church-Yards drear (inhuman to relate!)   410
The disappointed Prowlers fall, and dig
The shrouded Body from the Grave; o'er which,
Mix'd with foul Shades, and frighted Ghosts, they
    howl.

AMONG those hilly Regions, where embrac'd
In peaceful Vales the happy *Grisons*° dwell;

---

331. **Variance:** discord. 348. **point:** give point to, as in "to point a moral." 354. **conscious:** sensitive. 359. **the generous Band:** [Thomson's note] The Jail-Committee, in the Year 1729. [This was a Parliamentary committee headed by James Oglethorpe, which exposed the evil conditions of British prisons.] 360. **redressive:** seeking to redress. 367. **little Tyrants:** prison keepers.

384. **Toils:** snares. 405–06. **Even . . . Gaze:** The lion was traditionally imagined as conquering his appetite in the presence of beauty. Cf. Spenser, *Faerie Queene*, I. ii. 415. **Grisons:** inhabitants of Grisons, a canton of Switzerland.

Oft, rushing sudden from the loaded Cliffs,
Mountains of Snow their gathering Terrors roll.
From Steep to Steep, loud-thundering, down they
     come,
A wintry Waste in dire Commotion all;
And Herds, and Flocks, and Travellers, and
     Swains,   420
And sometimes whole Brigades of marching Troops,
Or Hamlets sleeping in the Dead of Night,
Are deep beneath the smothering Ruin whelm'd.

Now, all amid the Rigours of the Year,
In the wild Depth of Winter, while without
The ceaseless Winds blow Ice, be my Retreat,
Between the groaning Forest and the Shore,
Beat by the boundless Multitude of Waves,
A rural, shelter'd, solitary, Scene;
Where ruddy Fire and beaming Tapers join,   430
To chear the Gloom. There studious let me sit,
And hold high Converse with the MIGHTY DEAD;
Sages of antient Time, as Gods rever'd,
As Gods beneficent, who blest Mankind
With Arts, and Arms, and humaniz'd a World.
Rous'd at th' inspiring Thought, I throw aside
The long-liv'd Volume; and, deep-musing, hail
The sacred Shades, that slowly-rising pass
Before my wondering Eyes. First SOCRATES,
Who firmly good in a corrupted State,   440
Against the Rage of Tyrants *single* stood,
Invincible! calm Reason's holy Law,
That *Voice* of GOD within th' attentive Mind,
Obeying, fearless, or in Life, or Death:
Great Moral Teacher! *Wisest of Mankind!*
SOLON the next, who built his Common-Weal
On Equity's wide Base; by *tender* Laws
A lively People curbing, yet undamp'd
Preserving still that quick peculiar Fire,
Whence in the laurel'd Field of finer Arts,   450
And of bold Freedom, they unequal'd shone,
The Pride of smiling GREECE, and Human-kind.
LYCURGUS then, who bow'd beneath the Force
Of strictest Discipline, *severely wise,*
All human Passions. Following Him, I see,
As at *Thermopylæ* he glorious fell,
The firm DEVOTED CHIEF,° who prov'd by Deeds
The hardest Lesson which the *other* taught.
Then ARISTIDES lifts his honest Front;

Spotless of Heart, to whom th' unflattering Voice 460
Of Freedom gave the noblest Name of *Just;*
In pure majestic Poverty rever'd;
Who, even his Glory to his Country's Weal
Submitting, swell'd a haughty *Rival's*° Fame.
Rear'd by his Care, of softer Ray, appears
CIMON sweet-soul'd; whose Genius, rising strong,
Shook off the Load of young Debauch; abroad
The Scourge of *Persian* Pride, at home the Friend
Of every Worth and every splendid Art;
Modest, and simple, in the Pomp of Wealth.   470
Then the last Worthies of declining GREECE,
Late-call'd to Glory, in *unequal* Times,
Pensive, appear. The fair *Corinthian* Boast,
TIMOLEON, temper'd happy, mild, and firm,
Who wept the *Brother* while the *Tyrant* bled.
And, equal to the best, the THEBAN PAIR,°
Whose Virtues, in *heroic Concord* join'd,
Their Country rais'd to Freedom, Empire, Fame.
He too, with whom *Athenian* Honour sunk,
And left a Mass of sordid Lees behind,   480
PHOCION° the *Good;* in public Life severe,
To Virtue still inexorably firm;
But when, beneath his low illustrious Roof,
Sweet Peace and happy Wisdom smooth'd his Brow,
Not Friendship softer was, nor Love more kind.
And He, the *last* of old LYCURGUS' Sons,
The generous Victim to that vain Attempt,
To save a rotten State, AGIS,° who saw
Even SPARTA's self to servile Avarice sunk.
The two *Achaian* Heroes close the Train.   490
ARATUS,° who a while relum'd° the Soul
Of fondly-lingering Liberty in GREECE:
And He her Darling as her latest Hope,
The *gallant* PHILOPEMON;° who to Arms
Turn'd the luxurious Pomp he could not cure;

---

457. The firm . . . Chief: [Thomson's note] Leonidas [the
Spartan hero of Thermopylae (480 B.C.)].

464. haughty Rival: [Thomson's note] Themistocles.
[Although Aristides had been ostracized by political intrigue
in 483 B.C., he returned to aid Themistocles (c. 528–c.
462 B.C.) in winning the Battle of Salamis.] 476. the Theban
Pair: [Thomson's note] Pelopidas, and Epaminondas. [See
l. 279 and note of the 1726 version.] 481. Phocion: (c. 402–
318 B.C.), Athenian statesman and general. 488. Agis: Agis
IV, King of Sparta from 244 to 240 B.C.; his reforming
measures led to his being put to death. 491. Aratus: Aratus
of Sicyon (271–213 B.C.), Greek general and leader of the
second Achaean League. relum'd: relighted. 494. Philopemon: Philopoemen (c. 252–183 B.C.), a later leader of the
Achaean League, which he restored to a high level of military
efficiency; he was called in tribute to his general talents and
achievements "the Last of the Greeks."

Or toiling in his Farm, a simple Swain;
Or, bold and skilful, thundering in the Field.

OF rougher Front, a mighty People come!
A Race of Heroes! in those virtuous Times
Which knew no Stain, save that with partial
    Flame   500
Their *dearest* Country they *too fondly* lov'd.
Her *better Founder* first, the Light of ROME,
NUMA, who soften'd her rapacious Sons.
SERVIUS° the *King*, who laid the solid Base
On which o'er Earth the *vast Republic* spread.
Then the great Consuls venerable rise.
The PUBLIC FATHER° who the *Private* quell'd,
As on the dread Tribunal sternly sad.
He, whom his thankless Country *could not* lose,
CAMILLUS,° only vengeful to her Foes.   510
FABRICIUS,° Scorner of all-conquering Gold;
And CINCINNATUS,° awful from the Plow.
Thy WILLING VICTIM, *Carthage*,° bursting loose
From all that pleading Nature could oppose,
From a whole City's Tears, by rigid Faith
Imperious call'd, and Honour's dire Command.
SCIPIO, the *gentle Chief*, humanely brave,
Who soon the Race of spotless Glory ran,
And, warm in Youth, to the *Poetic Shade*
With *Friendship* and *Philosophy* retir'd.   520
TULLY,° whose powerful Eloquence a while
Restrain'd the *rapid* Fate of rushing ROME.
Unconquer'd CATO, virtuous in *Extreme*.

504. Servius: Servius Tullius, according to legend the sixth king of Rome (578–534 B.C.), was noted for his democratic constitutional reforms. **507. Public Father:** [Thomson's note] Marcus Junius Brutus [but it was Lucius Junius Brutus, the consul (509 B.C.), who had his two sons executed in his sight because they were implicated in a plot against Rome.] **510. Camillus:** Marcus Furius Camillus (d. 365 B.C.), Roman statesman and general. Accused of unfairly distributing spoils, he went into voluntary exile, from which he was recalled by the Romans when they were besieged by the Gauls. Created dictator, he completely defeated the enemy. **511. Fabricius:** Caius Fabricius Luscinus (d. *c.* 250 B.C.), Roman consul, general, and diplomat. He refused a bribe offered during ransom negotiations with Pyrrhus, King of Epirus. **512. Cincinnatus:** Lucius Quinctius Cincinnatus (b. *c.* 519 B.C.) was summoned from his farm to become dictator; he quickly defeated the besieging Aequi. **513. Thy . . . Carthage:** [Thomson's note] Regulus. [According to tradition, the Roman general Marcus Atilius Regulus (d. *c.* 250 B.C.) was sent home by his Carthaginian captors to negotiate a peace. Instead, he advocated continuing the war, and despite the pleas of his compatriots, he kept his promise to return to Carthage, where he was killed.] **521. Tully:** Cicero.

And Thou, unhappy BRUTUS,° kind of Heart,
Whose steady Arm, by awful Virtue urg'd,
Lifted the *Roman Steel* against thy *Friend*.
Thousands, besides, the Tribute of a Verse
Demand; but who can count the Stars of Heaven?
Who sing their Influence on this lower World?

BEHOLD, who yonder comes! in sober State,   530
Fair, mild, and strong, as is a vernal Sun:
'Tis *Phœbus'* self,° or else the *Mantuan Swain*°!
Great HOMER too appears, of daring Wing,
Parent of Song! and *equal* by his Side,
The BRITISH MUSE; join'd Hand in Hand they walk,
Darkling, full up the middle Steep to Fame.
Nor absent are those Shades,° whose skilful Touch
Pathetic drew th' impassion'd Heart, and charm'd
Transported *Athens* with the MORAL SCENE:
Nor Those who, tuneful, wak'd th' enchanting
    LYRE.°   540

FIRST of your Kind! Society divine!
Still visit thus my Nights, for you reserv'd,
And mount my soaring Soul to Thoughts like yours.
Silence, thou lonely Power! the Door be thine;
See on the hallow'd Hour that none intrude,
Save a few chosen Friends, who sometimes deign
To bless my humble Roof, with Sense refin'd,
Learning digested well, exalted Faith,
Unstudy'd Wit, and Humour ever gay.
Or from the Muses' Hill will POPE° descend,   550
To raise the sacred Hour, to bid it smile,
And with the social Spirit warm the Heart:
For tho not sweeter his own HOMER sings,
Yet is his Life the more endearing Song.

WHERE art Thou, HAMMOND°? Thou the darling
    Pride,
The Friend and Lover of the tuneful Throng!
Ah why, dear Youth, in all the blooming Prime

524. Brutus: Marcus Junius Brutus (*c.* 85–42 B.C.), friend and enemy of Julius Caesar. **532. Phœbus' self:** Apollo, god of poetry. **Mantuan Swain:** Virgil. *Swain* glances at his pastoral *Eclogues* and *Georgics*. **537. those Shades:** the Greek dramatists. **540. Those . . . Lyre:** the lyric poets. **550. Pope:** Twickenham, where Pope lived, was a short walk from Thomson's home at Richmond. **555. Hammond:** James Hammond (1710–42), a minor poet, was with Thomson a member of the opposition to Walpole (ll. 563–65) which had formed around Frederick, Prince of Wales. He was elected to Parliament a year before his death. Johnson, in his *Life of Hammond* (1781), abruptly dismisses his poetic pretensions: "It would be hard to find in all his productions three stanzas that deserve to be remembered."

Of vernal Genius, where disclosing fast
Each active Worth each manly Virtue lay,
Why wert thou ravish'd from our Hope so soon? 560
What now avails that noble Thirst of Fame,
Which stung thy fervent Breast? That treasur'd Store
Of Knowledge, early gain'd? That eager Zeal
To serve thy Country, glowing in the Band
Of YOUTHFUL PATRIOTS, who sustain her Name?
What now, alas! that Life-diffusing Charm
Of sprightly Wit? That Rapture for the Muse,
That Heart of Friendship, and that Soul of Joy,
Which bade with softest Light thy Virtues smile?
Ah! only shew'd, to check our fond Pursuits, 570
And teach our humbled Hopes that Life is vain!

THUS in some deep Retirement would I pass,
The Winter-Glooms, with Friends of pliant Soul,
Or blithe, or solemn, as the Theme inspir'd:
With them would search,° if Nature's boundless
    Frame
Was call'd, late-rising from the Void of Night,
Or sprung *eternal* from th' ETERNAL MIND;
Its Life, its Laws, its Progress, and its End.
Hence larger Prospects of the beauteous Whole
Would, gradual, open on our opening Minds; 580
And each diffusive° Harmony unite,
In full Perfection, to th' astonish'd Eye.
Then would we try to scan the *moral World*,
Which, tho' to us it seems embroil'd, moves on
In higher Order; fitted, and impell'd,
By WISDOM's finest Hand, and issuing all
In *general Good*. The sage Historic Muse
Should next conduct us thro the Deeps of Time:
Shew us how Empire grew, declin'd, and fell,
In scatter'd States; what makes the Nations smile, 590
Improves their Soil, and gives them double Suns;°
And why they pine beneath the brightest Skies,
In Nature's richest Lap. As thus we talk'd,
Our Hearts would burn within us, would inhale
That Portion of Divinity, that Ray
Of purest Heaven, which lights the public Soul
Of Patriots, and of Heroes. But if doom'd,
In powerless humble Fortune, to repress
These ardent Risings of the kindling Soul;
Then, even superior to Ambition, we 600

Would learn the private Virtues; how to glide
Thro Shades and Plains, along the smoothest Stream
Of rural Life: or snatch'd away by Hope,
Thro the dim Spaces of Futurity,
With earnest Eye anticipate those Scenes
Of Happiness, and Wonder; where the Mind,
In endless Growth and infinite Ascent,
Rises from State to State, and World to World.
But when with These the serious Thought is foil'd,
We, shifting for Relief, would play° the Shapes 610
Of frolic Fancy; and incessant form
Those rapid Pictures, that assembled Train
Of fleet Ideas, never join'd before,
Whence lively *Wit* excites to gay Surprize;
Or Folly-painting *Humour*, grave himself,
Calls Laughter forth, deep-shaking every Nerve.

MEAN-TIME the Village rouzes up the Fire;
While well attested, and as well believ'd,
Heard solemn, goes the Goblin-Story round;
Till superstitious Horror creeps o'er all. 620
Or, frequent in the sounding° Hall, they wake
The rural Gambol. Rustic Mirth goes round;
The simple Joke that takes the Shepherd's Heart,
Easily pleas'd; the long loud Laugh, sincere;
The Kiss, snatch'd hasty from the sidelong° Maid,
On purpose guardless, or pretending Sleep:
The Leap, the Slap, the Haul;° and, shook to Notes
Of native Music, the respondent Dance.
Thus jocund fleets with them the Winter-Night.

THE City swarms intense. The public Haunt, 630
Full of each Theme, and warm with mixt Discourse,
Hums indistinct. The Sons of Riot flow
Down the loose Stream of false inchanted Joy,
To swift Destruction. On the rankled Soul
The gaming Fury falls; and in one Gulph
Of total Ruin, Honour, Virtue, Peace,
Friends, Families, and Fortune, headlong sink.
Up-springs the Dance° along the lighted Dome,
Mix'd, and evolv'd,° a thousand sprightly ways.
The glittering Court effuses every Pomp; 640
The Circle deepens: beam'd from gaudy Robes,
Tapers, and sparkling Gems, and radiant Eyes,
A soft Effulgence o'er the Palace waves:

---

575. **search**: speculate. 581. **diffusive**: individual. Thomson makes figurative use of a political term describing a body of people as consisting of its members in their individual capacities. 591. **double Suns**: doubled fertility; with an obvious, if uncharacteristic, pun.

610. **play**: give play to. 621. **sounding**: resounding. 625. **sidelong**: devious, coy. 627. **Haul**: quick turnabout. 638. **the Dance**: The description is of an outdoor dance, such as those for which Vauxhall Gardens was famous. The circle of light is enlarged and brightened as the number of dancers increases. 639. **evolv'd**: opening out.

While, a gay Insect in *his* Summer-shine,
The Fop, light-fluttering, spreads his mealy° Wings.

DREAD o'er the Scene, the Ghost of HAMLET stalks;
OTHELLO rages; poor MONIMIA° mourns;
And BELVIDERA° pours her Soul in Love.
Terror alarms the Breast; the comely Tear
Steels o'er the Cheek: or else the COMIC MUSE   650
Holds to the World a Picture of itself,
And raises sly the fair impartial Laugh.
Sometimes she lifts her Strain, and paints the Scenes
Of beauteous Life; whate'er can deck° Mankind,
Or charm the Heart, in generous BEVIL° shew'd.

O THOU, whose Wisdom, solid yet refin'd,
Whose Patriot-Virtues, and consummate Skill
To touch the finer Springs that move the World,
Join'd to whate'er the *Graces* can bestow,
And all *Apollo*'s animating Fire,   660
Give Thee, with pleasing Dignity, to shine
At once the Guardian, Ornament, and Joy,
Of polish'd Life; permit the *Rural Muse*,
O CHESTERFIELD,° to grace with Thee her Song!
Ere to the Shades again she humbly flies,
Indulge her fond Ambition, in thy Train,
(For every Muse has in thy Train a Place)
To mark thy various full-accomplish'd Mind:
To mark that Spirit, which, with *British Scorn*,
Rejects th' Allurements of corrupted Power;   670
That elegant Politeness, which excels,
Even in the Judgment of presumptuous *France*,
The boasted Manners of her shining Court;
That Wit, the vivid Energy of Sense,
The Truth of Nature, which, with *Attic* Point,°
And kind well-temper'd Satire, smoothly keen,
Steals through the Soul, and without Pain corrects.
Or, rising thence with yet a brighter Flame,
O let me hail thee on some glorious Day,
When to the listening Senate, ardent, croud   680
BRITANNIA's Sons to hear her pleaded Cause.

Then drest by Thee, more amiably fair,
Truth the soft Robe of mild Persuasion wears:
Thou to assenting Reason giv'st again
Her own enlighten'd Thoughts; call'd from the
    Heart,
Th' obedient Passions on thy Voice attend;
And even reluctant Party feels a while
Thy gracious Power: as thro the vary'd Maze
Of Eloquence, now smooth, now quick, now strong,
Profound and clear, you roll the copious Flood.   690

To thy lov'd Haunt return, my happy Muse:
For now, behold, the joyous Winter-Days,
Frosty, succeed; and thro the blue Serene,
For Sight too fine, th' etherial Nitre flies;
Killing infectious Damps, and the spent Air
Storing afresh with elemental Life.°
Close crouds the shining Atmosphere; and binds
Our strengthen'd Bodies in its cold Embrace,
Constringent;° feeds, and animates our Blood;
Refines our Spirits,° thro the new-strung Nerves,   700
In swifter Sallies darting to the Brain;
Where sits the Soul, intense, collected, cool,
Bright as the Skies, and as the Season keen.
All Nature feels the renovating Force
Of Winter, only to the thoughtless Eye
In Ruin seen. The Frost-concocted Glebe°
Draws in abundant vegetable Soul,°
And gathers Vigour for the coming Year.
A stronger Glow sits on the lively Cheek
Of ruddy Fire:° and luculent° along   710
The purer Rivers flow; their sullen Deeps,
Transparent, open to the Shepherd's Gaze,
And murmur hoarser at the fixing Frost.

WHAT art thou, Frost? and whence are thy keen
    Stores
Deriv'd, thou secret all-invading Power,
Whom even th' illusive Fluid° cannot fly?
Is not thy potent Energy, unseen,

---

645. **mealy:** as if covered with a fine powder. Cf. *Troilus and Cressida*, III. iii. 78–79: "for men, like butterflies, / Show not their mealy wings but to the summer." 647. **Monimia:** the heroine of Thomas Otway's *The Orphan* (1680). 648. **Belvidera:** the heroine of Otway's *Venice Preserved* (1682). 654. **deck:** bedeck, adorn. 655. **Bevil:** [Thomson's note] A Character in the *Conscious Lovers*, written by Sir Richard Steele. [Bevil Jr. is the play's hero.] 664. **Chesterfield:** Philip Dormer Stanhope (1694–1773), Fourth Earl of Chesterfield; politician, wit, and patron of letters. He is best known for his *Letters to His Son* (see Part Five). 675. **Attic Point:** the sharpness of the Greek satirists.

694–96. **th' etherial . . . Life:** The nitrous salts believed to cause freezing (see l. 302 of the 1726 version) were also held to have restorative qualities. 699. **Constringent:** causing contraction. 700. **Spirits:** animal spirits, the supposed agency of sensation and voluntary motion, a fluid thought to be carried through the nerves. 706. **Frost-concocted Glebe:** soil mixed with frost. 707. **vegetable Soul:** fertility. 709–10. **A stronger . . . Fire:** Fire burns brighter at the edge (because of the salts in the air). 710. **luculent:** full of light, clear. 716. **th' illusive Fluid:** mercury, which freezes at −38° F.

Myriads of little Salts, or hook'd, or shap'd
Like double Wedges, and diffus'd immense
Thro Water, Earth, and Ether?° Hence at Eve,   720
Steam'd eager° from the red Horizon round,
With the fierce Rage of Winter deep suffus'd,
An icy Gale, oft shifting, o'er the Pool
Breathes a blue Film, and in its mid Career
Arrests the bickering Stream. The loosen'd Ice,
Let down the Flood, and half dissolv'd by Day,
Rustles no more; but to the sedgy Bank
Fast grows, or gathers round the pointed Stone,
A crystal Pavement, by the Breath of Heaven
Cemented firm; till, seiz'd from Shore to Shore,   730
The whole imprison'd River growls below.
Loud rings the frozen Earth, and hard reflects
A double Noise;° while, at his evening Watch,
The village Dog deters the nightly Thief;
The Heifer lows; the distant Water-fall
Swells in the Breeze; and, with the hasty Tread
Of Traveller, the hollow-sounding Plain
Shakes from afar. The full ethereal Round,
Infinite Worlds disclosing to the View,
Shines out intensely keen; and, all one Cope°   740
Of starry Glitter, glows from Pole to Pole.
From Pole to Pole the rigid Influence falls,
Thro the still Night, incessant, heavy, strong,
And seizes Nature fast. It freezes on;
Till Morn, late-rising o'er the drooping World,
Lifts her pale Eye unjoyous. Then appears
The various Labour of the silent Night:
Prone° from the dripping Eave, and dumb Cascade,
Whose idle Torrents only seem to roar,
The pendant Icicle; the Frost-Work fair,   750
Where transient Hues, and fancy'd Figures rise;
Wide-spouted o'er the Hill, the frozen Brook,
A livid Tract, cold-gleaming on the Morn;
The Forest bent beneath the plumy Wave;
And by the Frost refin'd the whiter Snow,
Incrusted hard, and sounding to the Tread
Of early Shepherd, as he pensive seeks
His pining Flock, or from the Mountain-top,
Pleas'd with the slippery Surface, swift descends.

On blithsome Frolicks bent, the youthful
    Swains,   760
While every Work of Man is laid at rest,

Fond o'er the River croud, in various Sport
And Revelry dissolv'd; where mixing glad,°
Happiest of all the Train! the raptur'd Boy
Lashes° the whirling Top. Or, where the *Rhine*
Branch'd out in many a long Canal extends,
From every Province swarming, void of Care,
Batavia° rushes forth; and as they sweep,
On sounding Skates, a thousand different Ways,
In circling Poise, swift as the Winds, along,   770
The *then gay* Land is madden'd all to Joy.
Nor less the northern Courts, wide o'er the Snow,
Pour a new Pomp. Eager, on rapid Sleds,
Their vigorous Youth in bold Contention wheel
The long-resounding Course. Mean-time, to raise
The manly Strife, with highly-blooming Charms,
Flush'd by the Season, *Scandinavia*'s Dames,
Or *Russia*'s buxom Daughters glow around.

PURE, quick, and sportful, is the wholesome Day;
But soon elaps'd. The horizontal Sun,   780
Broad o'er the South, hangs at his utmost Noon;
And, ineffectual, strikes the gelid Cliff.
His azure Gloss the Mountain still maintains,
Nor feels the feeble Touch. Perhaps the Vale
Relents a while to the reflected Ray;
Or from the Forest falls the cluster'd Snow,
Myriads of Gems, that in the waving Gleam
Gay-twinkle as they scatter. Thick around
Thunders the Sport of Those, who with the Gun,
And Dog impatient bounding at the Shot,   790
Worse than the Season, desolate the Fields;
And, adding to the Ruins of the Year,
Distress the footed or the feather'd Game.

BUT what is This? Our infant Winter sinks,
Divested of his Grandeur, should our Eye
Astonish'd shoot into the *Frigid Zone;*
Where, for relentless Months, continual Night,
Holds o'er the glittering Waste her starry Reign.

THERE,° thro the Prison of unbounded Wilds,
Barr'd by the Hand of Nature from Escape,   800
Wide-roams the *Russian* Exile. Nought around
Strikes his sad Eye, but Desarts lost in Snow;
And heavy-loaded Groves; and solid Floods,
That stretch, athwart the solitary Vast,
Their icy Horrors to the frozen Main;
And chearless Towns far-distant, never bless'd,

717–20. Is . . . Ether: a widely held theory of freezing. **721. Steam'd eager:** rising sharply. **733. A double Noise:** an echo. **740. Cope:** cloak, canopy; hence, figuratively, the firmament. **748. Prone:** directed downward.

763. mixing glad: joining (the others) gladly or taking part in gladness. **765. Lashes:** spins (with a string). **768. Batavia:** Holland. **799. There:** in Siberia.

Save when its annual Course the Caravan
Bends to the golden Coast of rich *Cathay,*°
With News of Human-kind. Yet there Life glows;
Yet cherish'd there, beneath the shining Waste,   810
The furry Nations harbour: tipt with Jet,
Fair Ermines, spotless as the Snows they press;
Sables, of glossy Black; and dark-embrown'd,
Or beauteous freakt° with many a mingled Hue,
Thousands besides, the costly Pride of Courts.
There, warm together press'd, the trooping Deer
Sleep on the new-fallen Snows; and, scarce his Head
Rais'd o'er the heapy Wreath, the branching Elk
Lies slumbering sullen in the white Abyss.
The ruthless Hunter wants nor Dogs nor Toils,   820
Nor with the Dread of sounding Bows he drives
The fearful flying Race; with ponderous Clubs,
As weak against the Mountain-Heaps they push
Their beating Breast in vain, and piteous bray,
He lays them quivering on th' ensanguin'd Snows,
And with loud Shouts rejoicing bears them home.°
There thro the piny Forest half-absorpt,°
Rough Tenant of these Shades, the shapeless Bear,
With dangling Ice all horrid, stalks forlorn;
Slow-pac'd, and sourer as the Storms increase,   830
He makes his Bed beneath th' inclement Drift,
And, with stern Patience, scorning weak Complaint,
Hardens his Heart against assailing Want.

WIDE o'er the spacious Regions of the North,
That see *Boötes*° urge his tardy Wain,
A boisterous Race, by frosty *Caurus*° pierc'd,
Who little Pleasure know and fear no Pain,
Prolific swarm. They once relum'd the Flame
Of lost Mankind in polish'd Slavery sunk,
Drove martial Horde on Horde,° with dreadful
    Sweep   840
Resistless rushing o'er th' enfeebled South,
And gave the vanquish'd World another Form.
Not such the Sons of *Lapland:* wisely They
Despise th' insensate barbarous Trade of War;

They ask no more than simple Nature gives,
They love their Mountains and enjoy their Storms.
No false Desires, no Pride-created Wants,
Disturb the peaceful Current of their Time;
And thro the restless ever-tortur'd Maze
Of Pleasure, or Ambition, bid it rage.   850
Their Rain-Deer form their Riches. Those their
    Tents,
Their Robes, their Beds, and all their homely Wealth
Supply, their wholesome Fare, and chearful Cups.
Obsequious at their Call, the docile Tribe
Yield to the Sled their Necks, and whirl them swift
O'er Hill and Dale, heap'd into one Expanse
Of marbled Snow, or far as Eye can sweep
With a blue Crust of Ice unbounded glaz'd.
By dancing Meteors then, that ceaseless shake
A waving Blaze° refracted o'er the Heavens;   860
And vivid Moons, and Stars that keener play
With doubled Lustre from the radiant Waste,
Even in the Depth of *Polar Night*, they find
A wondrous Day: enough to light the Chace,
Or guide their daring Steps to *Finland*-Fairs.
Wish'd Spring returns; and from the hazy South,
While dim Aurora° slowly moves before,
The welcome Sun, just verging up at first,
By small Degrees extends the swelling Curve;
Till seen at last for gay rejoicing Months,   870
Still round and round, his spiral Course he winds,
And as he nearly dips his flaming Orb,
Wheels up again, and reascends the Sky.
In that glad Season, from the Lakes and Floods,
Where pure *Niemi*'s fairy Mountains° rise,
And fring'd with Roses *Tenglio*° rolls his Stream,
They draw the copious Fry. With These, at Eve,
They chearful-loaded to their Tents repair;
Where, all Day long in useful Cares employ'd,

---

808. **Cathay:** [Thomson's note] The old Name for China.
814. **freakt:** flecked. 820–26. **The ruthless . . . home:**
The deer-hunting episode is based on Virgil's *Georgics*,
III. 371–75. 827. **half-absorpt:** half-filled with snow. 835.
Boötes: the constellation called The Ox Driver, situated near
Ursa Major or The Wagon ("Wain"), which moves slowly
around the North Star. 836. **Caurus:** [Thomson's note] The
North-West Wind. 840. **Horde on Horde:** [Thomson's
note] The wandering Scythian-Clans. [These Gothic invaders
were thought to have revived the virtues of the declining
Roman Empire.]

860. **A waving Blaze:** the Aurora Borealis, or Northern
Lights. 867. **Aurora:** the goddess of dawn, leading the
chariot of the sun. 875. **Niemi's . . . Mountains:** [Thom-
son's note] M. de Maupertuis, in his Book on *the Figure
of the Earth* [1738], after having described the beautiful
Lake and Mountain of Niemi in Lapland, says—"From this
height we had Occasion several times to see those Vapours
rise from the Lake which the People of the Country call
Haltios, and which they deem to be the guardian Spirits of the
Mountains. We had been frighted with Stories of Bears that
haunted this Place, but saw none. It seem'd rather a Place of
Resort for *Fairies* and *Genii* than Bears." 876. **Tenglio:**
[Thomson's note] The same Author observes—"I was sur-
prized to see upon the Banks of this River, (the Tenglio)
Roses of as lively a Red as any that are in our Gardens."

Their kind unblemish'd Wives the Fire prepare.   880
Thrice happy Race! by Poverty secur'd
From legal Plunder and rapacious Power:
In whom fell Interest never yet has sown
The Seeds of Vice; whose spotless Swains ne'er knew
Injurious Deed, nor, blasted by the Breath
Of faithless Love, their blooming Daughters Woe.

STILL pressing on, beyond *Tornéa*'s Lake,°
And *Hecla*° flaming thro a Waste of Snow,
And farthest *Greenland*, to the Pole itself,
Where failing gradual Life at length goes out,   890
The Muse expands her solitary Flight;
And, hovering o'er the wild stupendous Scene,
Beholds new Seas beneath another Sky.°
Thron'd in his Palace of cerulean Ice,
Here WINTER holds his unrejoicing Court;
And thro his airy Hall the loud Misrule
Of driving Tempest is for ever heard:
Here the grim Tyrant meditates his Wrath;
Here arms his Winds with all-subduing Frost;
Moulds his fierce Hail, and treasures up his Snows, 900
With which he now oppresses half the Globe.

THENCE winding eastward to the *Tartar*'s Coast,°
She sweeps the howling Margin of the Main;
Where undissolving, from the First of Time,
Snows swell on Snows amazing to the Sky;
And icy Mountains high on Mountains pil'd,
Seem to the shivering Sailor from afar,
Shapeless and white, an Atmosphere of Clouds.
Projected huge, and horrid, o'er the Surge,
Alps frown on Alps; or rushing hideous down,   910
As if old Chaos was again return'd,
Wide-rend the Deep, and shake the solid Pole.
Ocean itself no longer can resist
The binding Fury; but, in all its Rage
Of Tempest taken by the boundless Frost,
Is many a Fathom to the Bottom chain'd,
And bid to roar no more: a bleak Expanse,
Shagg'd o'er with wavy Rocks, chearless, and void
Of every Life, that from the dreary Months
Flies conscious southward. Miserable they!   920
Who, here entangled in the gathering Ice,
Take their last Look of the descending Sun;
While, full of Death, and fierce with tenfold Frost,
The long long Night, incumbent° o'er their Heads,

Falls horrible. Such was the BRITON's° Fate,
As with *first* Prow, (What have not BRITONS dar'd!)
He for the Passage sought, attempted since
So much in vain, and seeming to be shut
By jealous Nature with eternal Bars.
In these fell Regions, in *Arzina* caught,   930
And to the stony Deep his idle Ship
Immediate seal'd, he with his hapless Crew,
Each full exerted at his several Task,
Froze into Statues; to the Cordage glued
The Sailor, and the Pilot to the Helm.

HARD by these Shores, where scarce his freezing
    Stream
Rolls the wild *Oby*,° live the Last of Men;
And, half-enliven'd by the distant Sun,
That rears and ripens Man, as well as Plants,
Here Human Nature wears its rudest Form.   940
Deep from the piercing Season sunk in Caves,
Here by dull Fires, and with unjoyous Chear,
They waste the tedious Gloom. Immers'd in Furs,
Doze the gross Race. Nor sprightly Jest, nor Song,
Nor Tenderness they know; nor aught of Life,
Beyond the kindred Bears that stalk without.
Till Morn at length, her Roses drooping all,
Sheds a long Twilight brightening o'er their Fields,
And calls the quiver'd Savage to the Chace.

WHAT cannot active Government perform,   950
New-moulding Man? Wide-stretching from these
    Shores,
A People savage from remotest Time,
A huge neglected Empire ONE VAST MIND,
By HEAVEN inspir'd, from Gothic Darkness call'd.
Immortal PETER!° First of Monarchs! He
His stubborn Country tam'd, her Rocks, her Fens,
Her Floods, her Seas, her ill-submitting Sons;
And while the fierce *Barbarian* he subdu'd,
To more exalted Soul he raised the *Man*.
Ye Shades of antient Heroes, ye who toil'd   960

887. **Tornéa's Lake:** in northern Sweden. 888. **Hecla:** a
volcano in Iceland. 893. **another Sky:** [Thomson's note]
The other Hemisphere. 902. **Tartar's Coast:** Siberia. 924.
incumbent: hanging over, threatening.

925. **the Briton:** [Thomson's note] Sir Hugh Willoughby,
sent by Queen Elizabeth to discover the North-East Passage.
[Of the three vessels that set out in 1553, one reached
Archangel, while the other two were driven into the mouth
of the Arzina (l. 930), where all aboard were frozen to death.]
937. **Oby:** the Oby River in Siberia. 955. **Immortal
Peter:** Peter the Great of Russia (1672–1725). After becoming tsar, he traveled, sometimes incognito, through Western
Europe, learning contemporary arts and sciences. So far did
he throw himself into his studies that he worked as a ship's
carpenter in Holland (l. 969).

Thro long successive Ages to build up
A lab'ring Plan of State, behold at once
The Wonder done! behold the matchless Prince!
Who left his native Throne, where reign'd till then
A mighty Shadow of unreal Power;
Who greatly spurn'd the slothful Pomp of Courts;
And roaming every Land, in every Port,
His Scepter laid aside, with glorious Hand
Unweary'd plying the mechanic Tool,
Gather'd the Seeds of Trade, of useful Arts,   970
Of Civil Wisdom, and of Martial Skill.
Charg'd with the Stores of *Europe* home he goes!
Then Cities rise amid th' illumin'd Waste;
O'er joyless Desarts smiles the rural Reign;
Far-distant Flood to Flood is social join'd;
Th' astonish'd *Euxine* hears the *Baltic* roar;°
Proud Navies ride on Seas that never foam'd
With daring Keel before; and Armies stretch
Each Way their dazzling Files, repressing here
The frantic *Alexander* of the North,°   980
And awing there stern *Othman*'s shrinking Sons.°
Sloth flies the Land, and *Ignorance*, and *Vice*,
Of old Dishonour proud: it glows around,
Taught by the ROYAL HAND that rous'd the Whole,
One Scene of Arts, of Arms, of rising Trade:
For what his Wisdom plann'd, and Power enforc'd,
More potent still, his great *Example* shew'd.

MUTTERING, the Winds at Eve, with blunted Point,
Blow hollow-blustering from the South. Subdu'd,
The Frost resolves into a trickling Thaw.   990
Spotted the Mountains shine; loose Sleet descends,
And floods the Country round. The Rivers swell,
Of Bonds impatient. Sudden from the Hills,
O'er Rocks and Woods, in broad brown Cataracts,
A thousand snow-fed Torrents shoot at once;
And, where they rush, the wide-resounding Plain
Is left one slimy Waste. Those sullen Seas,
That wash th' ungenial Pole, will rest no more
Beneath the Shackles of the mighty North;
But, rousing all their Waves, resistless heave—   1000
And hark! the lengthening Roar continuous runs
Athwart the rifted Deep: at once it bursts,

And piles a thousand Mountains to the Clouds.
Ill fares the Bark with trembling Wretches charg'd,
That, tost amid the floating Fragments, moors
Beneath the Shelter of an icy Isle,
While Night o'erwhelms the Sea, and Horror looks
More horrible. Can human Force endure
Th' assembled Mischiefs that besiege them round?
Heart-gnawing Hunger, fainting Weariness,   1010
The Roar of Winds and Waves, the Crush of Ice,
Now ceasing, now renew'd with louder Rage,
And in dire Echoes bellowing round the Main.
More to embroil the Deep, Leviathan
And his unwieldy Train, in dreadful Sport,
Tempest the loosen'd Brine, while thro the Gloom,
Far, from the bleak inhospitable Shore,
Loading the Winds, is heard the hungry Howl
Of famish'd Monsters, there awaiting Wrecks.
Yet PROVIDENCE, that *ever-waking Eye*,   1020
Looks down with Pity on the feeble Toil
Of Mortals lost to Hope, and lights them safe,
Thro all this dreary Labyrinth of Fate.

'TIS done!—Dread WINTER spreads his latest
      Glooms,
And reigns tremendous o'er the conquer'd Year.
How dead the vegetable Kingdom lies!
How dumb the tuneful! Horror wide extends
His desolate Domain. Behold, fond Man!
See here thy pictur'd Life; pass some few Years,
Thy flowering Spring, thy Summer's ardent
      Strength,   1030
Thy sober Autumn fading into Age,
And pale concluding Winter comes at last,
And shuts the Scene. Ah! whither now are fled,
Those Dreams of Greatness? those unsolid Hopes
Of Happiness? those Longings after Fame?
Those restless Cares? those busy bustling Days?
Those gay-spent, festive Nights? those veering
      Thoughts,
Lost between Good and Ill, that shar'd thy Life?
All now are vanish'd! VIRTUE sole survives,
Immortal, never-failing Friend of Man,   1040
His Guide to Happiness on high.—And see!
'Tis come, the glorious Morn! the second Birth
Of Heaven, and Earth! Awakening Nature hears
The *new-creating Word*, and starts to Life,
In every heighten'd Form, from Pain and Death
For ever free. *The great eternal Scheme*
Involving All, and in a *perfect Whole*
Uniting, as the Prospect wider Spreads,

976. Th' astonish'd . . . roar: The Euxine (Black) Sea is connected with the Baltic by a series of canals originally projected by Peter, who died while inspecting a partially completed section of the system at Lake Ladoga, near the Gulf of Finland. 980. Alexander . . . North: Charles XII of Sweden, defeated by the Russians at Poltava in 1709. Cf. Johnson's *Vanity of Human Wishes*, ll. 191–222, in Part Six. 981. Othman's . . . Sons: the Turks.

To Reason's Eye refin'd clears up apace.
Ye vainly wise! ye blind Presumptuous! now,   1050
Confounded in the Dust,° adore that POWER,
And WISDOM oft arraign'd: see now the Cause,
Why unassuming Worth in secret liv'd,
And dy'd, neglected: why the good Man's Share
In Life was Gall and Bitterness of Soul:
Why the lone Widow, and her Orphans pin'd,
In starving Solitude; while Luxury,

In Palaces, lay straining her low Thought,
To form unreal Wants: why Heaven-born Truth,
And Moderation fair, wore the red Marks   1060
Of Superstition's Scourge: why licens'd Pain,
That cruel Spoiler, that embosom'd Foe,
Imbitter'd all our Bliss. Ye good Distrest!
Ye noble Few! who here unbending stand
Beneath Life's Pressure, yet bear up a While,
And what your bounded View, which only saw
A little Part, deem'd *Evil* is no more:
The Storms of WINTRY TIME will quickly pass,
And one unbounded SPRING encircle All.

1051. Confounded . . . Dust: utterly crushed.

Henry Fielding

1707–1754

Best known today as a novelist, Fielding also pursued a busy literary career as a comic playwright, a satirist, and a journalist. But whatever his choice of expressive means, his prevailing business was reform: as a critic and writer always concerned with the identity and integrity of the various literary kinds, he sought to reform stage tragedy, the novel, and even the travel book; as a journalist and as a practicing London police magistrate he labored to amend manners, morals, and the administration of criminal jurisprudence.

He was born in Somerset, the grandson of a judge and the eldest son of a lieutenant general who had fought the French under the Duke of Marlborough. Lady Mary Wortley Montagu was a distant cousin. He attended Eton, where he was given a thorough grounding in the Greek and Latin classics. It is said that when he left at the age of eighteen he knew Horace by heart. He next went to Leyden, in Holland, where he studied law and literature at the university for two years, returning to England only when his money ran out. For the rest of his life he struggled against poverty.

Tall, robust, sanguine, and handsome, he established himself in London and, at the age of twenty, began writing for the stage. Between 1728 and 1737 he wrote twenty-four plays and became the most conspicuous comic dramatist of the day. His copiousness and speed of composition—together with his bohemian habits—became proverbial: the actor Arthur Murphy recalled that "when he had contracted to bring on a play, or a farce . . . he would go home rather late from a tavern, and would, the next morning, deliver a scene to the players, written upon the papers which had wrapped the tobacco, in which he so much delighted." He managed his own theater, the New Theatre in the Haymarket, where he produced his Congrevian comedies of intrigue, his farces, his ballad operas, and, most successfully, his dramatic burlesques, of which *Tom Thumb* (1730; revised as *The Tragedy of Tragedies* in 1731) is the best known. The political satire in *Pasquin* (1736) and *The Historical Register for the Year 1736* (1737) enraged the Walpole administration, which retaliated by passing the Licensing Act of 1737. This Act, which reduced the number of London theaters to two—Drury Lane and Covent Garden—and which subjected new plays to the censorship of the Lord Chamberlain, effectively put Fielding out of business as a writer for the stage.

Even his success as a comic dramatist had not brought him a sufficient living, and he turned next to the law for a livelihood. Resuming his legal studies, this time at the

Middle Temple, he emerged as a barrister in 1740. To help support himself while he read law, he conducted a thrice-weekly anti-Jacobite periodical, *The Champion* (1739–41), most of whose essays he wrote himself.

He had always had a flair for parody, as *The Tragedy of Tragedies* reveals. The appearance of Samuel Richardson's highly regarded *Pamela, or Virtue Rewarded* (1740), the prudential morality of which heartily disgusted him, tempted him to satire. The next year he published *An Apology for the Life of Mrs. Shamela Andrews, by Mr. Conny Keyber*, a riotous, indecent parody not only of Richardson's epistolary technique and of his heroine's pseudo-virtuous self-regard, but also of Colley Cibber's naive self-satisfaction and the Reverend Conyers Middleton's sycophancy in dedications. Fielding never acknowledged the authorship of *Shamela*. He made a second assault on Richardson in *Joseph Andrews* (1742), a novel that begins as a parody of the action of *Pamela* but soon assumes a picaresque shape of its own. Thus it was Fielding's moral outrage at the work of Richardson—who responded by calling *Joseph Andrews* "a lewd and ungenerous engraftment" on *Pamela*—that turned him into a novelist.

In 1743 he collected much of his work in three volumes of *Miscellanies*, which included poems (chiefly Horatian epistles), essays, translations, farces, and prose satires. Here appeared for the first time his ironic *Life of Mr. Jonathan Wild the Great*, a corrosive satire on the ideal of "the great man" which Sir Robert Walpole's faction had done its best to foster. Fielding's grim narrative presents a notorious criminal—hanged in 1725—as an admirable exemplar of an unscrupulous, a powerful, and therefore a "great" man. The implication is that of Peachum's song in Gay's *Beggar's Opera* (1728): "The Statesman, because he's so great, / Thinks his trade as honest as mine." Sir Robert and his friends were not amused.

Appointed Justice of the Peace for Westminster in 1748, Fielding was soon presiding over London's busiest police court. He was an energetic and conscientious magistrate, as the swarm of thieves, highwaymen, and murderers who infested London soon learned. During the next few years he wrote tirelessly on judicial, criminal, and social topics, producing such reformist works as *An Enquiry into the Causes of the Late Increase of Robbers* (1751) and *A Proposal for Making an Effectual Provision for the Poor, for Amending Their Morals, and for Rendering Them Useful Members of the Society* (1753).

His masterpiece, the huge but lively and highly plotted *History of Tom Jones, a Foundling*, appeared in six volumes in 1749. Unlike most of his earlier work, it bore its author's name. One of the innovations in *Tom Jones* is Fielding's frequent regular interruption of the narrative to theorize in brief essays about his genre ("our labours have sufficient title to the name of history"); about his theory of character ("it is often the same person who represents the villain and the heroe"); and about the talents required for novel-writing (genius, learning—a hit at Richardson—and "a good heart"). Richardson, to no one's surprise, found *Tom Jones* coarse and thought its author "indelicate." It was perhaps Fielding's exuberant, carefree attitude towards sexual enjoyment in *Tom Jones* that prompted Samuel Johnson to call Fielding "a blockhead" and "a barren rascal." Others complained that the work was reprehensibly "low." But Edward Gibbon was one of the many who were profoundly impressed: he wrote with characteristic rotundity, "The romance of *Tom Jones*, that exquisite picture of human manners, will outlive the palace of the Escorial, and the imperial eagle of the house of Austria."

Despite the gusto he obviously lavished on *Tom Jones*, Fielding was fondest of his final novel, *Amelia* (1751), a narrative of the domestic distresses of a beautiful and virtuous married woman. More somber than the earlier novels, *Amelia* outsold them, although it did not match their critical success. Samuel Johnson read it through at a sitting.

Although his health had been failing since his mid-thirties, Fielding somehow found the energy to conduct during 1752 *The Covent-Garden Journal*, his last journalistic venture. But his body was wearing out. Emaciated from years of gout, asthma, and dropsy, he set off for Portugal in 1754 in search of a healthier climate. His experiences on the trip are recorded in his posthumously published *Journal of a Voyage to Lisbon* (1755). He was buried in the English cemetery at Lisbon.

Fielding was learned in the ancient classics and loyal to their vision of human nature: in his illness he consoled himself with Cicero, and a copy of Plato accompanied him to Portugal. But at the same time he was a vigorous practical Christian moralist, emphasizing the preeminence of works over faith. His attitude towards knavery in all its forms is that which might be expected of a police-court magistrate; Thackeray observed, "His wit is wonderfully wise and detective; it flashes upon a rogue and lightens up a rascal like a policeman's lantern." And, like a good magistrate, "His sense of values," as George Sherburn has said, "is just and sure." Yet even in his most fervent exposures of human stupidity, perversity, and malignity, he never abandoned his charity; his sympathy remained quick and uncalculating to the very end.

A good bibliography is included in the standard life of Fielding, W. L. Cross's *The History of Henry Fielding* (3 vols., 1918); some modern biographical and critical contributions are listed by Francesco Cordasco in *Fielding: A List of Critical Studies, 1895–1946* (1948). F. H. Dudden's *Henry Fielding: His Life, Works, and Times* (2 vols., 1952) is especially valuable for social background. The standard edition of the *Works*, including most of the plays, is edited by W. E. Henley and others (16 vols., 1903). *The Tragedy of Tragedies* is edited by J. T. Hillhouse (1918); *Shamela* is perhaps best read in the facsimile published by the Augustan Reprint Society (1956), with an introduction by Ian Watt; *Joseph Andrews* has been edited by M. C. Battestin (1967) in the definitive Wesleyan edition, in progress; *Jonathan Wild* is available in the World's Classics; *Tom Jones* is frequently reprinted in inexpensive editions. A perceptive critical interpretation is John Butt's brief *Fielding* (1954). W. L. Renwick's "The Comic Epic in Prose," in *Essays and Studies by Members of the English Association*, XXXII (1946), illuminates Fielding's intentions in the Preface to *Joseph Andrews*.

THE TRAGEDY
OF TRAGEDIES . . .

With the public's appetite for theatrical burlesque whetted by the clamorous success of Gay's *Beggar's Opera* in 1728, Fielding produced *Tom Thumb: A Tragedy*, a two-act afterpiece, on April 24, 1730; he published it a few days later. In its earliest version *Tom Thumb* had a highly successful run. Jonathan Swift once told a friend that he had laughed out loud only twice in his life—once at the antics of a clown and once at a scene in *Tom Thumb*. In 1731 Fielding brought out an expanded, three-act version, retitled *The Tragedy of Tragedies*. This final version contained a mock-pedantic preface and ironical footnotes in the tradition of Pope and the other Scriblerians. Much of this apparatus is devoted to mocking the critic John Dennis for fatuity, prudery, and a taste for the inflated. For his "sources" Fielding drew upon some forty-two tragedies and heroic plays of the seventeenth and eighteenth centuries. And the satire goes beyond the literary and the theatrical, for the play constitutes an implicit satire on current notions of human "greatness" and thus glances disrespectfully in the direction of Sir Robert Walpole. *The Tragedy of Tragedies* held the stage until displaced by Sheridan's *The Critic* (1781).

The text is that of the first "Scriblerian" edition, *The Tragedy of Tragedies; or the Life and Death of Tom Thumb the Great. As It Is Acted at the Theatre in the Hay-Market. With the Annotations of H. Scriblerus Secundus* (1731).

H. Scriblerus Secundus;°

HIS PREFACE

THE Town hath seldom been more divided in its Opinion, than concerning the Merit of the following Scenes. Whilst some publickly affirmed, That no Author could produce so fine a Piece but Mr. *P*——,[1] others have with as much Vehemence insisted, That no one could write any thing so bad, but Mr. *F*——.[2]

THE TRAGEDY OF TRAGEDIES: *Preface.* **H. Scriblerus Secundus:** to be distinguished from the first Scriblerus, Martinus, the pedantic "author" of Pope's *Peri Bathous* (see earlier in Part Two). **1. Mr. P**——: Pope. **2. Mr. F**——: Fielding.

Nor can we wonder at this Dissention about its Merit, when the learned World have not unanimously decided even the very Nature of this Tragedy. For tho' most of the Universities in *Europe* have honoured it with the Name of *Egregium & maximi pretii opus, Tragœdiis tam antiquis quam novis longe anteponendum;*[3] nay, Dr. *B*——[4] hath pronounced, *Citiùs Mœvii Æneadem quam Scribleri istius Tragœdiam hanc crediderim, cujus Autorem Senecam ipsum tradidisse haud dubitârim;*[5] and the great Professor *Burman,*[6] hath stiled *Tom Thumb, Heroum omnium Tragicorum facilè Principem.*[7] Nay, tho' it hath, among other Languages, been translated into *Dutch,* and celebrated with great Applause at *Amsterdam* (where Burlesque never came) by the Title of *Mynheer Vander Thumb,* the Burgomasters receiving it with that reverent and silent Attention, which becometh an Audience at a deep Tragedy: Notwithstanding all this, there have not been wanting some who have represented these Scenes in a ludicrous Light; and Mr. *D*——[8] hath been heard to say, with some Concern, That he wondered a Tragical and Christian Nation would permit a Representation on its Theatre, so visibly designed to ridicule and extirpate every thing that is Great and Solemn among us.

This learned Critick, and his Followers, were led into so great an Error, by that surreptitious and piratical Copy which stole last Year into the World;[9] with what Injustice and Prejudice to our Author, I hope will be acknowledged by every one who shall happily peruse this genuine and original Copy. Nor can I help remarking, to the great Praise of our Author, that, however imperfect the former was, still did even that faint Resemblance of the true *Tom*

3. **Egregium . . . anteponendum:** a distinguished and extremely valuable work, greatly to be preferred to other tragedies, whether ancient or modern. 4. **Dr. B**——: Richard Bentley (1662–1742), the famous classical scholar of the University of Cambridge; he was known for his annotated editions of Horace, Manilius, and Milton. 5. **Citiùs . . . dubitârim:** I should more easily believe that [the poetaster] Maevius wrote the *Aeneid* than that this so-called Scriblerus wrote this tragedy, the author of which Seneca himself doubtless recorded [in a historical work that has never been found]. 6. **Professor Burman:** Pieter Burman the Elder, a contemporary Dutch classical scholar. 7. **Heroum . . . Principem:** easily the first of all tragic heroes. 8. **Mr. D**——: John Dennis (1657–1734), critic and playwright; he had the reputation of espousing the literary sublime with an excessive single-mindedness and solemnity. (See the selection from Dennis earlier in Part Two.) 9. **that . . . World:** the two-act version of *Tom Thumb* (1730).

Thumb, contain sufficient Beauties to give it a Run of upwards of Forty Nights, to the politest Audiences. But, notwithstanding that Applause which it receiv'd from all the best Judges, it was as severely censured by some few bad ones, and I believe, rather maliciously than ignorantly, reported to have been intended a Burlesque on the loftiest Parts of Tragedy, and designed to banish what we generally call Fine Things, from the Stage.

Now, if I can set my Country right in an Affair of this Importance, I shall lightly esteem any Labour which it may cost. And this I the rather undertake, First, as it is indeed in some measure incumbent on me to vindicate myself from that surreptitious Copy beforementioned, published by some ill-meaning People, under my Name: Secondly, as knowing my self more capable of doing Justice to our Author, than any other Man, as I have given my self more Pains to arrive at a thorough Understanding of this little Piece, having for ten Years together read nothing else; in which time, I think I may modestly presume, with the help of my *English* Dictionary, to comprehend all the Meanings of every Word in it.

But should any Error of my Pen awaken *Clariss. Bentleium*[10] to enlighten the World with his Annotations on our Author, I shall not think that the least Reward or Happiness arising to me from these my Endeavours.

I shall wave at present, what hath caused such Feuds in the learned World, Whether this Piece was originally written by *Shakespear*, tho' certainly That, were it true, must add a considerable Share to its Merit; especially, with such who are so generous as to buy and to commend what they never read, from an implicit Faith in the Author only: A Faith! which our Age abounds in as much, as it can be called deficient in any other.

Let it suffice, that the *Tragedy of Tragedies*, or, *The Life and Death of Tom Thumb*, was written in the Reign of Queen *Elizabeth*. Nor can the Objection made by Mr. *D——*, That the Tragedy must then have been antecedent to the History,[11] have any Weight, when we consider, That tho' the *History of Tom Thumb*, printed by and for *Edward M——r*,[12] at

the Looking-Glass on *London-Bridge*, be of a later Date; still must we suppose this History to have been transcribed from some other, unless we suppose the Writer thereof to be inspired: A Gift very faintly contended for by the Writers of our Age. As to this History's not bearing the Stamp of Second, Third, or Fourth Edition, I see but little in that Objection; Editions being very uncertain Lights to judge of Books by: And perhaps Mr. *M——r* may have joined twenty Editions in one, as Mr. *C——l*[13] hath ere now divided one into twenty.

Nor doth the other Argument, drawn from the little Care our Author hath taken to keep up to the Letter of the History, carry any greater Force. Are there not Instances of Plays, wherein the History is so perverted, that we can know the Heroes whom they celebrate by no other Marks than their Names? Nay, do we not find the same Character placed by different Poets in such different Lights, that we can discover not the least Sameness, or even Likeness in the Features. The *Sophonisba* of *Mairet*,[14] and of *Lee*,[15] is a tender, passionate, amorous Mistress of *Massinissa*;[16] *Corneille*,[17] and Mr. *Thomson*[18] give her no other Passion but the Love of her Country, and make her as cool in her Affection to *Massinissa*, as to *Syphax*.[19] In the two latter, she resembles the Character of Queen *Elizabeth*; in the two former, she is the Picture of *Mary* Queen of *Scotland*. In short, the one *Sophonisba* is as different from the other, as the *Brutus* of *Voltaire*,[20] is from the *Marius* Jun.[21] of *Otway*; or as the *Minerva*[22] is from the *Venus* of the Ancients.

Let us now proceed to a regular Examination of the Tragedy before us. In which I shall treat separately of the Fable, the Moral, the Characters, the Sentiments, and the Diction. And first of the

---

10. **Clariss. Bentleium**: the most illustrious Bentley. 11. **the History**: a ballad-stanza narration of the folktale of Tom Thumb, published in 1630 as a crude chapbook. 12. **Edward M——r**: Midwinter, a publisher.

13. **Mr. C——l**: Edmund Curll (1675–1747), a London publisher with a reputation for rascality. 14. **Mairet**: Jean Mairet, seventeenth-century French playwright, whose tragedy *Sophonisbe* appeared in 1634. 15. **Lee**: Nathaniel Lee (c. 1653–92), whose *Sophonisba* was acted in 1675. 16. **Massinissa**: (Masinissa), King of Numidia in the second century B.C. 17. **Corneille**: The *Sophonisbe* of this great French dramatist was produced in 1663. 18. **Thomson**: James Thomson's *The Tragedy of Sophonisba* was produced in 1730. (See the selections from Thomson earlier in Part Two.) 19. **Syphax**: Sophonisba's husband, rival to Masinissa. 20. **Voltaire**: Voltaire's tragedy *Brutus* was produced in 1730. 21. **Marius Jun.**: Marius Junior, the Romeo-like hero of Thomas Otway's tragedy *The History and Fall of Caius Marius* (1680). 22. **Minerva**: the Roman goddess of wisdom and of war.

Fable; which I take to be the most simple imaginable; and, to use the Words of an eminent Author,[23] "One, regular, and uniform, not charged with a Multiplicity of Incidents, and yet affording several Revolutions of Fortune; by which the Passions may be excited, varied, and driven to their full Tumult of Emotion."—Nor is the *Action* of this Tragedy less great than uniform. The Spring of all, is the love of *Tom Thumb* for *Huncamunca;* which causeth the Quarrel between their Majesties in the first Act; the Passion of Lord *Grizzle* in the Second; the Rebellion, Fall of Lord *Grizzle,* and *Glumdalca,* Devouring of *Tom Thumb* by the Cow, and that bloody Catastrophe, in the Third.

Nor is the *Moral* of this excellent Tragedy less noble than the *Fable;* it teaches these two instructive Lessons, *viz.* That Human Happiness is exceeding transient, and, That Death is the certain End of all Men; the former whereof is inculcated by the fatal End of *Tom Thumb;* the latter, by that of all the other Personages.

The *Characters* are, I think, sufficiently described in the *Dramatis Personæ;* and I believe we shall find few Plays, where greater Care is taken to maintain them throughout, and to preserve in every Speech that Characteristical Mark which distinguishes them from each other. "But (says Mr. *D——*) how well doth the Character of *Tom Thumb,* whom we must call the Hero of this Tragedy, if it hath any Hero, agree with the Precepts of *Aristotle,* who defineth *Tragedy to be the Imitation of a short, but perfect Action, containing a just Greatness in it self,*[24] &c. What Greatness can be in a Fellow, whom History relateth to have been no higher than a Span?"[25] This Gentleman seemeth to think, with Serjeant *Kite,*[26] that the Greatness of a Man's Soul is in proportion to that of his Body, the contrary of which is affirmed by our *English* Physiognominical Writers. Besides, if I understand *Aristotle* right, he speaketh only of the Greatness of the Action, and not of the Person.

As for the *Sentiments* and the *Diction,* which now only remain to be spoken to; I thought I could afford

them no stronger Justification, than by producing parallel Passages out of the best of our *English* Writers. Whether this Sameness of Thought and Expression which I have quoted from them, proceeded from an Agreement in their Way of Thinking; or whether they have borrowed from our Author, I leave the Reader to determine. I shall adventure to affirm this of the Sentiments of our Author; That they are generally the most familiar which I have ever met with, and at the same time delivered with the highest Dignity of Phrase; which brings me to speak of his *Diction.*—Here I shall only beg one Postulatum, *viz.* That the greatest Perfection of the Language of a Tragedy is, that it is not to be understood; which granted (as I think it must be) it will necessarily follow, that the only ways to avoid this, is by being too high or too low for the Understanding, which will comprehend every thing within its Reach. Those two Extremities of Stile Mr. *Dryden* illustrates[27] by the familiar Image of two Inns, which I shall term the Aerial and the Subterrestrial.

Horace goeth farther, and sheweth when it is proper to call at one of these Inns, and when at the other;

Telephus & Peleus, cùm pauper & exul uterque,
Projicit Ampullas & Sesquipedelia Verba.[28]

That he approveth of the *Sesquipedelia Verba,* is plain; for had not *Telephus & Peleus* used this sort of Diction in Prosperity, they could not have dropt it in Adversity. The Aerial Inn, therefore (says *Horace*) is proper only to be frequented by Princes and other great Men, in the highest Affluence of Fortune; the Subterrestrial is appointed for the Entertainment of the poorer sort of People only, whom *Horace* advises,

—dolere Sermone pedestri.[29]

The true Meaning of both which Citations is, That Bombast is the proper Language for Joy, and Doggrel for Grief, the latter of which is literally imply'd in the *Sermo pedestris,* as the former is in the *Sesquipedelia Verba.*

Cicero recommendeth the former of these. *Quid est tam furiosum vel tragicum quàm verborum sonitus inanis,*

---

23. **an eminent Author:** Thomson, in his Preface to *The Tragedy of Sophonisba.* 24. **the Imitation . . . self:** See *Poetics,* vi. 2. 25. **Span:** the distance from the tip of the outstretched thumb to the tip of the outstretched little finger. 26. **Serjeant Kite:** In George Farquhar's comedy *The Recruiting Officer* (1706), Sergeant Kite, a recruiting sergeant, tells a group of villagers that "he that has the good fortune to be born six foot high, was born to be a great man."

27. **illustrates:** in his essay *Of Heroic Plays,* prefaced to *The Conquest of Granada* (1672). 28. **Telephus . . . Verba:** "Telephus and Peleus, when reduced to poverty and exile, reject fustian and long, pretentious words" (*Ars Poetica,* ll. 96–97). 29. **dolere . . . pedestri:** "Express grief in plain prose" (*Ars Poetica,* l. 95).

nullâ subjectâ Sententiâ neque Scientiâ.[30] What can be so proper for Tragedy as a Set of big sounding Words, so contrived together, as to convey no Meaning; which I shall one Day or other prove to be the Sublime of *Longinus.*[31] Ovid declareth absolutely for the latter Inn:

> *Omne genus scripti Gravitate Tragœdia vincit.*[32]

Tragedy hath of all Writings the greatest Share in the *Bathos,* which is the Profound of *Scriblerus.*[33]

I shall not presume to determine which of these two Stiles be properer for Tragedy.—It sufficeth, that our Author excelleth in both. He is very rarely within sight through the whole Play, either rising higher than the Eye of your Understanding can soar, or sinking lower than it careth to stoop. But here it may perhaps be observed, that I have given more frequent Instances of Authors who have imitated him in the Sublime, than in the contrary. To which I answer, First, Bombast being properly a Redundancy of Genius, Instances of this Nature occur in Poets whose names do more Honour to our Author, than the Writers in the Doggrel, which proceeds from a cool, calm, weighty Way of Thinking. Instances whereof are most frequently to be found in Authors of a lower Class. Secondly, That the Works of such Authors are difficultly found at all. Thirdly, That it is a very hard Task to read them, in order to extract these Flowers from them. And Lastly, It is very often difficult to transplant them at all; they being like some Flowers of a very nice Nature, which will flourish in no Soil but their own: For it is easy to transcribe a Thought, but not the Want of one. The *Earl of Essex,*[34] for Instance, is a little Garden of choice Rarities, whence you can scarce transplant one Line so as to preserve its original Beauty. This must account to the Reader for his missing the Names of several of his Acquaintance, which he had certainly found here, had I ever read their Works; for which, if I have not a just Esteem, I can at least say with *Cicero, Quæ non contemno, quippè quæ nunquam legerim.*[35] However, that the Reader may meet with due Satisfaction in this Point, I have a young Commentator from the University, who is reading over all the modern Tragedies, at Five Shillings a Dozen, and collecting all that they have stole from our Author, which shall shortly be added as an Appendix to this Work.

DRAMATIS PERSONÆ.

King *Arthur,* A passionate sort of King, Husband to Queen *Dollallolla,* of whom he stands a little in Fear; Father to *Huncamunca,* whom he is very fond of; and in Love with *Glumdalca.*	Mr. *Mullart.*
Tom *Thumb the Great,* A little Hero with a great Soul, something violent in his Temper, which is a little abated by his Love for *Huncamunca.*	Young *Verhuyck.*
Ghost of *Gaffer*[1] *Thumb,* A whimsical sort of Ghost.	Mr. *Lacy.*
Lord *Grizzle,* Extremely zealous for the Liberty of the Subject, very cholerick in his Temper, and in Love with *Huncamunca.*	Mr. *Jones.*
Merlin, A Conjurer, and in some sort Father to *Tom Thumb.*	Mr. *Hallam.*
Noodle, *Doodle,* Courtiers in Place, and consequently of that Party that is uppermost.	Mr. *Reynolds.* Mr. *Wathan.*
Foodle, A Courtier that is out of Place, and consequently of that Party that is undermost.	Mr. *Ayres.*
Bailiff, and *Follower,* Of the Party of the Plaintiff.	Mr. *Peterson.* Mr. *Hicks.*
Parson, Of the Side of the Church.	Mr. *Watson.*

30. Quid . . . Scientiâ: Fielding translates freely in the next sentence. **31. Longinus:** the presumed Greek author of the first-century rhetorical treatise *On the Sublime.* **32. Omne . . . vincit:** "Tragedy surpasses all other kinds of writing in seriousness." **33. the Profound . . . Scriblerus:** as set forth in Pope's *Peri Bathous.*

34. Earl of Essex: a tragedy (1681) by John Banks (*c.* 1650–1706). **35. Quæ . . . legerim:** "I do not despise them, for I have not read them." *Dramatis Personæ.* **1. Gaffer:** grandfather; godfather; a title denoting a respectable elderly rustic.

WOMEN.

Queen *Dollallolla*, Wife to King *Arthur*, and Mother to *Huncamunca*, a Woman entirely faultless, saving that she is a little given to Drink; a little too much a *Virago* towards her Husband, and in Love with *Tom Thumb*. } Mrs. *Mullart*.

The Princess *Huncamunca*, Daughter to their Majesties King *Arthur* and Queen *Dollallolla*, of a very sweet, gentle, and amorous Disposition, equally in Love with Lord *Grizzle* and *Tom Thumb*, and desirous to be married to them both. } Mrs. *Jones*.

Glumdalca, of the Giants, a Captive Queen, belov'd by the King, but in Love with *Tom Thumb*. } Mrs. *Dove*.

Cleora, *Mustacha*, } Maids of Honour, in Love with { *Noodle*. *Doodle*. }

Courtiers, Guards, Rebels, Drums, Trumpets, Thunder and Lightning.

SCENE *the Court of King* Arthur, *and a Plain thereabouts.*

ACT I

SCENE I.

SCENE, *The Palace.*

Doodle, Noodle.

Dood. Sure, such a Day° as this was never seen!
The Sun himself, on this auspicious Day,
Shines, like a Beau in a new Birth-Day Suit:°
This down the Seams embroider'd, that the Beams.
All Nature wears one universal Grin.

Act I, scene i. **1. Day:** [Fielding's note] Corneille recommends some very remarkable Day, wherein to fix the Action of a Tragedy. This the best of our Tragical Writers have understood to mean a Day remarkable for the Serenity of the Sky, or what we generally call a fine Summer's Day: So that according to this their Exposition, the same Months are proper for Tragedy, which are proper for Pastoral. Most of our celebrated *English* Tragedies, as [Addison's] *Cato*, [Elijah Fenton's] *Mariamne*, [Nicholas Rowe's] *Tamerlane*, &c. begin with their Observations on the Morning. *Lee* seems to have come the nearest to this beautiful Description of our Author's:

> The Morning dawns with an unwonted Crimson,
> The Flowers all odorous seem, the Garden Birds
> Sing louder, and the laughing Sun ascends,
> The gaudy Earth with an unusual brightness,
> All Nature smiles.
>
> Cæs[ar]. Borg[ia].

Massinissa in the new *Sophonisba* [by James Thomson] is also a Favourite of the Sun;

Nood. This Day, O Mr. *Doodle*, is a Day Indeed,° a Day we never saw before.
The mighty *Thomas Thumb*° victorious comes;
Millions of Giants crowd his Chariot Wheels,

> —The Sun too seems
> As conscious of my Joy with broader Eye
> To look abroad the World, and all things smile
> Like Sophonisba.

Memnon in the *Persian Princess* [by Lewis Theobald], makes the Sun decline rising, that he may not peep on Objects, which would prophane his Brightness.

> ————The Morning rises slow,
> And all those ruddy Streaks that us'd to paint
> The Days approach, are lost in Clouds as if
> The Horrors of the Night had sent 'em back,
> To warn the Sun, he should not leave the Sea,
> To Peep, &c.

3. Birth-Day Suit: a new suit of clothes, customarily worn on the monarch's birthday. **6–7. This . . . Indeed:** [Fielding's note] This Line is highly conformable to the beautiful Simplicity of the Antients. It hath been copied by almost every Modern,

> Not to be is not to be in Woe.
> [Dryden's] State of Innocence.
> Love is not Sin but where 'tis sinful Love.
> [Dryden's] Don Sebastian.
> Nature is Nature, Lælius.
> [Thomson's] Sophonisba.
> Men are but Men, we did not make our selves.
> [Edward Young's] Revenge.

8. Thomas Thumb: [Fielding's note] Dr. *B——y* [Bentley] reads the mighty Tall-mast Thumb. Mr. *D——s* [Dennis] the mighty Thumping Thumb. Mr. *T——d* [Theobald] reads Thundering. I think *Thomas* more agreeable to the great Simplicity so apparent in our Author.

Giants°! to whom the Giants in *Guild-Hall*°   10
Are Infant Dwarfs. They frown, and foam, and roar,
While *Thumb* regardless of their Noise rides on.
So some Cock-Sparrow in a Farmer's Yard,
Hops at the Head of an huge Flock of Turkeys.
    Dood.   When Goody° *Thumb* first brought this
        Thomas forth,
The *Genius* of our Land triumphant reign'd;
Then, then, Oh *Arthur!* did thy *Genius* reign.
    Nood.   They tell me it is whisper'd in the Books°
Of all our Sages, that this mighty Hero

10. Giants: [Fielding's note] That learned Historian Mr. *S——n* [Nathaniel Salmon] in the third Number of his *Criticism* on our Author, takes great Pains to explode this Passage. It is, says he, difficult to guess what Giants are here meant, unless the Giant *Despair* in the *Pilgrim's Progress*, or the Giant *Greatness* in the *Royal Villain* [the subtitle of Theobald's *Persian Princess*]; for I have heard of no other sort of Giants in the Reign of King *Arthur. Petrus Burmanus* [Pieter Burman] makes three *Tom Thumbs*, one whereof he supposes to have been the same Person whom the *Greeks* called *Hercules*, and that by these Giants are to be understood the *Centaurs* slain by that Heroe. Another *Tom Thumb* he contends to have been no other than the *Hermes Trismegistus* [the mystical Egyptian deity Thoth] of the Antients. The third *Tom Thumb* he places under the Reign of King *Arthur*, to which third *Tom Thumb*, says he, the Actions of the other two were attributed. Now tho' I know that this Opinion is supported by an Assertion of [the sixteenth-century Dutch scholar] *Justus Lipsius, Thomam illum Thumbum non alium quam Herculem fuisse satis constat* ["It remains clear that this Tom Thumb was none other than Hercules"]; yet shall I venture to oppose one Line of Mr. *Midwinter*, against them all,

    In Arthur's *Court* Tom Thumb *did live.*

But then, says Dr. *B——y*, if we place *Tom Thumb* in the Court of King *Arthur*, it will be proper to place that Court out of *Britain*, where no Giants were ever heard of. *Spencer*, in his *Fairy Queen*, is of another Opinion, where describing *Albion* he says,

    ——*Far within a salvage Nation dwelt*
    Of hideous Giants.

And in the same Canto,

    Then Elfar, who two Brethren Giants had,
    The one of which had two Heads—
        The other three.

Risum teneatis, Amici [Restrain your laughter, friends]. **10. the Giants . . . Guild-Hall:** two tall wooden figures installed in 1708. **15. Goody:** goodwife. **18. whisper'd . . . Books:** [Fielding's note] To Whisper in Books says Mr. *D——s* is arrant Nonsense. I am afraid this learned Man does not sufficiently understand the extensive meaning of the Word Whisper. If he had rightly understood what is meant by the *Senses Whisp'ring the Soul* in the *Persian Princess*, or what *Whisp'ring like Winds* is in [Dryden's] *Aurengzebe*, or

By *Merlin's* Art begot, hath not a Bone   20
Within his Skin, but is a Lump of Gristle.
    Dood.   Then 'tis a Gristle of no mortal kind,
Some God, my *Noodle*, stept into the Place
Of Gaffer *Thumb*, and more than half begot,°
This mighty *Tom.*
    Nood.——Sure he was sent Express
From Heav'n,° to be the Pillar of our State.
Tho' small his Body be, so very small,
A Chairman's° Leg is more than twice as large;
Yet is his Soul like any Mountain big,
And as a Mountain once brought forth a Mouse,   30
So doth this Mouse contain a mighty Mountain.°
    Dood.   Mountain indeed! So terrible his Name,
The Giant Nurses frighten Children with it;°

———

like Thunder in another Author, he would have understood this. *Emmeline* in *Dryden*['s *King Arthur*] sees a Voice, but she was born blind, which is an Excuse *Panthea* cannot claim in [John Banks's] *Cyrus*, who hears a sight.

    ——*Your Description will surpass,*
    All Fiction, Painting, or dumb Shew of Horror,
    That ever Ears yet heard, or Eyes beheld.

When Mr. *D——s* understands these he will understand Whisp'ring in Books. **24. more . . . begot:** [Fielding's note]

    ——*Some Ruffian stept into his Father's Place,*
    And more than half begot him.
        [Banks's] *Mary Q. of Scots.*

25-26. sent . . . Heav'n: [Fielding's note]

    ——*For Ulamar seems sent Express from Heaven,*
    To civilize this rugged Indian Clime.
        [Dennis's] *Liberty Asserted.*

28. Chairman: one who carries a sedan chair. **31. So . . . Mountain:** [Fielding's note] *Omne majus continet in se minus, sed minus non in se majus continere potest* ["The greater always contains the less, but the less cannot contain the greater"], says [the sixteenth-century Italian scholar] *Scaliger* in *Thumbo*. —I suppose he would have cavilled at these beautiful Lines in the Earl of *Essex;*

    ——*Thy most inveterate Soul,*
    That looks through the foul Prison of thy Body.

And at those of *Dryden*,

    The Palace is without too well design'd,
    Conduct me in, for I will view thy Mind.
        Aurengzebe.

33. The Giant . . . it: [Fielding's note] Mr. *Banks* hath copied this almost Verbatim,

    It was enough to say, here's Essex *come,*
    And Nurses still'd their Children with the fright.
        E. of Essex.

And cry *Tom Thumb* is come, and if you are
Naughty, will surely take the Child away.

   Nood. But hark! these Trumpets speak the King's
      Approach.°

   Dood. He comes most luckily for my Petition.

                Flourish.

SCENE II.

King, Queen, Grizzle, Noodle, Doodle, Foodle.

   King. Let nothing but a Face of Joy appear;°
The Man who frowns this Day shall lose his Head,
That he may have no Face to frown withal.°
Smile, *Dollalolla*—Ha! what wrinkled Sorrow,
Hangs, sits, lies, frowns upon thy knitted Brow°?
Whence flow those Tears fast down thy blubber'd
    Cheeks,
Like a swoln Gutter, gushing through the Streets?

   Queen. Excess of Joy, my Lord, I've heard Folks
    say,
Gives Tears as certain as Excess of Grief.°

   King. If it be so, let all Men cry for Joy,   10
'Till my whole Court be drowned with their Tears;°
Nay, till they overflow my utmost Land,

36. these . . . Approach: [Fielding's note] The Trumpet in
a Tragedy is generally as much as to say enter King: Which
makes Mr. *Banks* in one of his Plays call it the Trumpet's
formal Sound. *Act I, scene ii.* **1. Let . . . appear:** [Fielding's
note] Phraortes in the *Captives* [by John Gay] seems to have
been acquainted with King *Arthur*.

> *Proclaim a Festival for seven Days space,*
> *Let the Court shine in all its Pomp and Lustre,*
> *Let all our Streets resound with Shouts of Joy;*
> *Let Musick's Care-dispelling Voice be heard,*
> *The sumptuous Banquet, and the flowing Goblet*
> *Shall warm the Cheek, and fill the Heart with Gladness.*
> *Astarbe shall sit Mistress of the Feast.*

3. withal: with. **5. frowns . . . Brow:** [Fielding's note]

> *Repentance frowns on thy contracted Brow.*
>   [Thomson's] *Sophonisba.*
> *Hung on his clouded Brow, I mark'd Despair.*
>   Ibid.
>   —*A sullen Gloom,*
> *Scowls on his Brow.*
>   [Edward Young's] *Busiris.*

8–9. Excess . . . Grief: [Fielding's note] *Plato* is of this
Opinion, and so is Mr. *Banks;*

> *Behold these Tears sprung from fresh Pain and Joy.*
>   E. of *Essex.*

11. drowned . . . Tears: [Fielding's note] These Floods are
very frequent in the Tragick Authors.

And leave me Nothing but the Sea to rule.

   Dood. My Liege, I a Petition have here got.

   King. Petition me no Petitions, Sir, to-day;
Let other Hours be set apart for Business.
To-day it is our Pleasure to be drunk,°

———————

> *Near to some murmuring Brook I'll lay me down,*
> *Whose Waters if they should too shallow flow,*
> *My Tears shall swell them up till I will drown.*
>   Lee's *Sophonisba.*
> *Pouring forth Tears at such a lavish Rate,*
> *That were the World on Fire, they might have drown'd*
> *The Wrath of Heav'n, and quench'd the mighty Ruin.*
>   [Lee's] *Mithridates.*

One Author changes the Waters of Grief to those of Joy,

> —*These Tears that sprung from Tides of Grief,*
> *Are now augmented to a Flood of Joy.*
>   *Cyrus the Great.*

Another,

> *Turns all the Streams of Hate, and makes them flow*
> *In Pity's Channel.*
>   [Theobald's] *Royal Villain.*

One drowns himself,

> —*Pity like a Torrent pours me down;*
> *Now I am drowning all within a Deluge.*
>   [Banks's] *Anna Bullen.*

Cyrus drowns the whole World,

> *Our swelling Grief*
> *Shall melt into a Deluge, and the World*
> *Shall drown in Tears.*
>   *Cyrus the Great.*

17. drunk: [Fielding's note] An Expression vastly beneath the
Dignity of Tragedy, says Mr. *D*——*s,* yet we find the Word
he cavils at in the Mouth of *Mithridates* less properly used and
applied to a more terrible Idea;

> *I would be drunk with Death.*
>   Mithrid.

The Author of the New *Sophonisba* [i.e., Thomson] taketh
hold of this Monosyllable, and uses it pretty much to the
same purpose,

> *The Carthaginian Sword with Roman Blood*
> *Was drunk.*

I would ask Mr. *D*——*s* which gives him the best Idea, a
drunken King, or a drunken Sword?
Mr. [Nahum] *Tate* dresses up King *Arthur's* Resolution in
Heroicks,

> *Merry, my Lord, o' th' Captain's Humour right,*
> *I am resolv'd to be dead drunk to Night.*

Lee also uses this charming Word;

> *Love's the Drunkenness of the Mind.*
>   Gloriana.

And this our Queen shall be as drunk as We.
    Queen.   (Tho' I already half Seas over am°)
If the capacious Goblet overflow   20
With *Arrack-Punch*—'fore *George!* I'll see it out;
Of *Rum,* and *Brandy*, I'll not taste a Drop.
    King.   Tho' *Rack*, in *Punch*, Eight Shillings be a
    Quart,
And *Rum* and *Brandy* be no more than Six,
Rather than quarrel, you shall have your Will.
                      [*Trumpets.*
But, ha! the Warrior comes; the Great *Tom Thumb;*
The little Hero, Giant-killing Boy,
Preserver of my Kingdom, is arrived.

SCENE III.

Tom Thumb, *to them with Officers, Prisoners,
and Attendants.*

    King.   Oh! welcome most, most welcome° to my
    Arms,
What Gratitude can thank away the Debt,
Your Valour lays upon me.
    Queen. ——————Oh! ye Gods!°   [*Aside.*
    Thumb.   When I'm not thank'd at all, I'm thank'd
    enough,
I've done my Duty, and I've done no more.°
    Queen.   Was ever such a Godlike Creature seen!
                      [*Aside.*
    King.   Thy Modesty's a Candle° to thy Merit,
It shines itself, and shews thy Merit too.

---

19. half . . . am: [Fielding's note] *Dryden* hath borrowed
this, and applied it improperly,

    I'm half Seas o'er in Death.
    Cleom[enes].

Act I, scene iii. **1. welcome most . . . welcome:** [Fielding's
note] This Figure is in great use among the Tragedians;

    'Tis therefore, therefore 'tis.
    [Charles Johnson's] Victim.
    I long repent, repent and long again.
    Busiris.

3. Oh! ye Gods: [Fielding's note] A Tragical Exclamation.
5. I've done my . . . more: [Fielding's note] This Line is
copied verbatim in the *Captives.* **7. Candle:** [Fielding's note]
We find a Candlestick for this Candle in two celebrated
Authors;

    —Each Star withdraws
    His golden Head and burns within the Socket.
    [Lee's] Nero.
    A Soul grown old and sunk into the Socket.
    Sebastian.

But say, my Boy, where did'st thou leave the Giants?
    Thumb.   My Liege, without the Castle Gates they
    stand,   10
The Castle Gates too low for their Admittance.
    King.   What look they like?
    Thumb.   Like Nothing but Themselves.
    Queen.   And sure thou art like nothing but thy
    Self.°   [*Aside.*
    King.   Enough! the vast Idea fills my Soul.
I see them, yes, I see them now before me.
The monst'rous, ugly, barb'rous Sons of Whores.
But, Ha! what Form Majestick strikes our Eyes?
So perfect, that it seems to have been drawn
By all the Gods in Council: So fair she is,
That surely at her Birth the Council paus'd,   20
And then at length cry'd out, This is a Woman°!
    Thumb.   Then were the Gods mistaken.—She is not
A Woman, but a Giantess—whom we
With much ado, have made a shift to hawl°
Within the Town: for she is by a Foot,
Shorter than all her Subject Giants were.°

---

13. thou . . . Self: [Fielding's note] This Simile occurs very
frequently among the Dramatick Writers of both Kinds.
21. This . . . Woman: [Fielding's note] Mr. *Lee* hath stolen
this Thought from our Author;

    ——This perfect Face, drawn by the Gods in Council,
    Which they were long a making.
              Lu[cius]. Jun[ius]. Brut[us].
    ——At his Birth, the heavenly Council paus'd,
    And then at last cry'd out, This is a Man!

Dryden hath improved this Hint to the utmost Perfection:

    So perfect, that the very Gods who form'd you, wonder'd
    At their own Skill, and cry'd, A lucky Hit
    Has mended our Design! Their Envy hindred,
    Or you had been Immortal, and a Pattern,
    When Heaven would work for Ostentation sake,
    To copy out again.

                    All for Love.

Banks prefers the Works of *Michael Angelo* to that of the Gods;

    A Pattern for the Gods to make a Man by,
    Or Michael Angelo to form a Statue.

24. With . . . hawl: [Fielding's note] It is impossible says
Mr. *W*——[perhaps the critic and poet Leonard Welsted]
sufficiently to admire this natural easy Line. **26. Shorter . . .**
were: [Fielding's note] This Tragedy which in most Points
resembles the Antients differs from them in this, that it
assigns the same Honour to Lowness of Stature, which they
did to Height. The Gods and Heroes in *Homer* and *Virgil* are
continually described higher by the Head than their Followers,
the contrary of which is observ'd by our Author: In short, to
exceed on either side is equally admirable, and a Man of three
Foot is as wonderful a sight as a Man of nine.

Glum. We yesterday were both a Queen and
　Wife,
One hundred thousand Giants own'd our Sway,
Twenty whereof were married to our self.
　Queen. Oh! happy State of Giantism—where
　　Husbands 30
Like Mushrooms grow, whilst hapless we are forc'd
To be content, nay, happy thought with one.
　Glum. But then to lose them all in one black Day,
That the same Sun, which rising, saw me wife
To Twenty Giants, setting, should behold
Me widow'd of them all.—My worn out Heart,
That Ship, leaks fast, and the great heavy Lading,
My Soul, will quickly sink.°
　Queen.————————Madam, believe,
I view your Sorrows with a Woman's Eye;
But learn to bear them with what Strength you
　　may, 40
To-morrow we will have our Grenadiers
Drawn out before you, and you then shall choose
What Husbands you think fit.
　Glum.————————Madam, I am
Your most obedient, and most humble Servant.°
　King. Think, mighty Princess, think this Court
　　your own,
Nor think the Landlord me, this House my Inn;
Call for whate'er you will, you'll Nothing pay.
I feel a sudden Pain within my Breast,
Nor know I whether it arise from Love,
Or only the Wind-Cholick. Time must shew.° 50
Oh *Thumb!* What do we to thy Valour owe?
Ask some Reward, great as we can bestow.
　Thumb. I ask not Kingdoms, I can conquer those,

I ask not Money, Money I've enough;°
For what I've done, and what I mean to do,
For Giants slain, and Giants yet unborn,
Which I will slay—if this be call'd a Debt,
Take my Receipt in full—I ask but this,
To Sun my self in *Huncamunca's* Eyes.° 59
　King. Prodigious bold Request. ⎱
　Queen.—Be still my Soul.° ⎰　　[*Aside.*
　Thumb. My Heart is at the Threshold of your
　　Mouth,
And waits its answer there—Oh! do not frown,
I've try'd, to Reason's Tune, to tune my Soul,
But Love did overwind and crack the String.
Tho' *Jove* in Thunder had cry'd out, You SHAN'T,
I should have lov'd her still—for oh strange fate,
Then when I lov'd her least, I lov'd her most.°
　King. It is resolv'd—the Princess is your own.
　Thumb. Oh! happy, happy, happy, happy *Thumb!*°
　Queen. Consider, Sir, reward your Soldiers
　　Merit, 70
But give not *Huncamunca* to *Tom Thumb.*
　King. *Tom Thumb!* Odzooks, my wide extended
　　Realm
Knows not a Name so glorious as *Tom Thumb.*

---

54. Money I've enough: [Fielding's note] Mr. *Dryden* seems
to have had this Passage in his Eye in the first Page of *Love
Triumphant.* **59. Sun . . . Eyes:** [Fielding's note] Don Carlos
in the Revenge suns himself in the Charms of his Mistress,

> *While in the Lustre of her Charms I lay.*

60. Be . . . Soul: [Fielding's note] A Tragical Phrase much
in use. **61–67. My . . . most:** [Fielding's note] This Speech
hath been taken to pieces by several Tragical Authors who
seem to have rifled it and shared its Beauties among them.

> *My Soul waits at the Portal of thy Breast,*
> *To ravish from thy Lips the welcome News.*
> 　Anna Bullen.
> *My Soul stands listning at my Ears.*
> 　Cyrus the Great.
> *Love to his Tune my jarring Heart would bring,*
> *But Reason overwinds and cracks the String.*
> 　[Dryden and Lee's] D[uke]. of Guise.
> 　　　　　—I *should have lov'd*
> *Tho' Jove in muttering Thunder had forbid it.*
> 　New Sophonisba.
> *And when it* (my Heart) *wild resolves to love no more,*
> *Then is the Triumph of excessive Love.*
> 　Ibidem.

69. Oh . . . Thumb: [Fielding's note] *Massinissa* is one
fourth less happy than *Tom Thumb.*

> *Oh! happy, happy, happy.*
> 　New Sophonisba.

---

38. My . . . sink: [Fielding's note]

> *My Blood leaks fast, and the great heavy lading*
> *My Soul will quickly sink.*
> 　Mithrid.
> *My Soul is like a Ship.*
> 　[Nahum Tate's] Injur'd Love.

44. Your . . . Servant: [Fielding's note] This well-bred
Line seems to be copied in the *Persian Princess;*

> *To be your humblest, and most faithful Slave.*

49–50. Nor . . . shew: [Fielding's note] This Doubt of the
King puts me in mind of a Passage in the *Captives,* where the
Noise of Feet is mistaken for the Rustling of Leaves,

> ————*Methinks I hear*
> *The sound of Feet*
> *No, 'twas the Wind that shook yon Cyprus Boughs.*

Let *Macedonia*, *Alexander* boast,
Let Rome her *Cæsar's* and her *Scipio's* show,
Her Messieurs *France*, let *Holland* boast *Mynheers*,
Ireland her *O's*, her *Mac's* let *Scotland* boast,
Let *England* boast no other than *Tom Thumb*.
   Queen.   Tho' greater yet his boasted Merit was,
He shall not have my Daughter, that is Pos'.°   80
   King.   Ha! sayst thou *Dollalolla?*
   Queen.   —I say he shan't.
   King.   Then by our Royal Self° we swear you lye.
   Queen.   Who but a Dog, who but a Dog,°
Would use me as thou dost. Me, who have lain
These twenty Years so loving by thy Side.°
But I will be reveng'd. I'll hang my self,
Then tremble all who did this Match persuade,
For riding on a Cat, from high I'll fall,
And squirt down Royal Vengeance on you all.°
   Food.   Her Majesty the Queen is in a Passion.°   90
   King.   Be she, or be she not°—I'll to the Girl
And pave thy Way, oh *Thumb*—Now, by our self,
We were indeed a pretty King of Clouts,°
To truckle to her Will—For when by Force
Or Art the Wife her Husband over-reaches,

---

80. Pos': positive. **82. by . . . Self:** [Fielding's note]

> *No by my self.*
>   Anna Bullen.

83. who . . . Dog: [Fielding's note]

> ———*Who caus'd,*
> *This dreadful Revolution in my Fate,*
> Ulamar.   *Who but a Dog, who but a Dog.*
>   Liberty Asserted.

85. twenty . . . Side: [Fielding's note]

> ———*A Bride,*
> *Who twenty Years lay* loving *by your Side.*
>   Banks. [*Anna Bullen*]

89. squirt . . . all: [Fielding's note]

> *For born upon a Cloud, from high I'll fall,*
> *And rain down Royal Vengeance on you all.*
>   [Banks's] Albion Queen[s].

90. in a Passion: [Fielding's note] An Information very like this we have in the *Tragedy of Love* [by Banks], where *Cyrus* having stormed in the most violent manner, *Cyaxares* observes very calmly,

> *Why, Nephew Cyrus—you are mov'd.*

91. Be . . . not: [Fielding's note]

>   *'Tis in your Choice,*
> *Love me, or love me not.*
>   Conquest of Granada.

93. Clouts: rags.

Give him the Peticoat, and her the Breeches.
   Thumb.   Whisper, ye Winds, that *Huncamunca's*
     mine;
Echoes repeat, that *Huncamunca's* mine!
The dreadful Bus'ness of the War is o'er,
And Beauty, heav'nly Beauty! crowns my Toils,   100
I've thrown the bloody Garment now aside,
And *Hymeneal* Sweets invite my Bride.
   So when some Chimney-Sweeper, all the Day,
Hath through dark Paths pursu'd the sooty Way,
At Night, to wash his Hands and Face he flies,
And in his t' other Shirt with his *Brickdusta* lies.°

SCENE IV.

Grizzle *solus.*

Where art thou *Grizzle?* where are now thy
     Glories?
Where are the Drums that waken'd thee to Honour?°
Greatness is a lac'd Coat from *Monmouth-Street,*°
Which Fortune lends us for a Day to wear,
To-morrow puts it on another's Back.
The spiteful Sun but yesterday survey'd
His Rival, high as Saint *Paul's* Cupola;
Now may he see me as *Fleet-Ditch* laid low.

SCENE V.

Queen, Grizzle.

   Queen.   Teach me to scold, prodigious-minded
     Grizzle.
Mountain of Treason, ugly as the Devil,°
Teach this confounded hateful Mouth of mine,
To spout forth Words malicious as thy self,
Words, which might shame all *Billingsgate*° to speak.
   Griz.   Far be it from my Pride, to think my
     Tongue
Your Royal Lips can in that Art instruct,
Wherein you so excel. But may I ask,

97–106. Whisper . . . lies: [Fielding's note] There is not one Beauty in this Charming Speech, but hath been borrowed by almost every Tragick Writer. *Act I, scene iv.* **1–2. Where . . . Honour:** [Fielding's note] Mr. *Banks* has (I wish I could not say too servilely) imitated this of *Grizzle* in his *Earl of Essex.*

> *Where art thou* Essex, &c.

3. Monmouth-Street: the haunt of dealers in used clothing. *Act I, scene v.* **2. Mountain . . . Devil:** [Fielding's note] The Countess of *Nottingham* in the *Earl of Essex* is apparently acquainted with *Dollalolla.* **5. Billingsgate:** a rowdy fish market in London.

Without Offence, wherefore my Queen would scold?
  Queen. Wherefore, Oh! Blood and Thunder!
    han't you heard   10
(What ev'ry Corner of the Court resounds)
That little *Thumb* will be a great Man made.
  Griz. I heard it, I confess—for who, alas!
Can always stop his Ears°—but wou'd my Teeth,
By grinding Knives, had first been set on Edge.
  Queen. Would I had heard at the still Noon of
    Night,
The Hallaloo of Fire in every Street!
Odsbobs! I have a mind to hang my self,
To think I shou'd a Grandmother be made
By such a Raskal.—Sure the King forgets,   20
When in a Pudding, by his Mother put,
The Bastard, by a Tinker, on a Stile
Was drop'd.—O, good Lord *Grizzle!* can I bear
To see him from a Pudding, mount the Throne?
Or can, Oh can! my *Huncamunca* bear,
To take a Pudding's Offspring to her Arms?
  Griz. Oh Horror! Horror! Horror! cease my
    Queen,
Thy Voice like twenty Screech-Owls,° wracks my
    Brain.
  Queen. Then rouse thy Spirit—we may yet prevent
This hated Match.—
  Griz.   —We will not Fate it self,   30
Should it conspire with *Thomas Thumb*, should cause it.
I'll swim through Seas; I'll ride upon the Clouds;
I'll dig the Earth; I'll blow out ev'ry Fire;
I'll rave; I'll rant; I'll rise; I'll rush; I'll roar;
Fierce° as the Man whom smiling Dolphins° bore,
From the Prosaick to Poetick Shore.

I'll tear the Scoundrel into twenty Pieces.
  Queen. Oh, no! prevent the Match, but hurt him
    not;
For, tho' I would not have him have my Daughter,
Yet can we kill the Man that kill'd the Giants?   40
  Griz. I tell you, Madam, it was all a Trick,
He made the Giants first, and then he kill'd them;
As Fox-hunters bring Foxes to the Wood,
And then with Hounds they drive them out again.
  Queen. How! have you seen no Giants? Are there
    not
Now, in the Yard, ten thousand proper Giants?
  Griz. Indeed, I cannot positively tell,
But firmly do believe there is not One.°
  Queen. Hence! from my Sight! thou Traitor, hie
    away;
By all my Stars! thou enviest *Tom Thumb.*   50
Go, Sirrah! go, hie° away! hie!—thou art
A setting Dog be gone.
  Griz.   Madam, I go.
Tom Thumb shall feel the Vengeance you have rais'd:
So, when two Dogs are fighting in the Streets,
With a third Dog, one of the two Dogs meets,
With angry Teeth, he bites him to the Bone,
And this Dog smarts for what that Dog had done.

14. stop his Ears: [Fielding's note] *Grizzle* was not
probably possessed of that Glew, of which Mr. *Banks* speaks
in his *Cyrus.*

    I'll glew my Ears to ev'ry word.

28. Thy . . . Screech-Owls: [Fielding's note]

    Screech-Owls, dark Ravens and amphibious Monsters,
    Are screaming in that Voice.
                        Mary Q. of Scots.

35-36. Fierce . . . Shore: [Fielding's note] The Reader may
see all the Beauties of this Speech in a late Ode called the
Naval Lyrick [by Edward Young (1730)]. **35. smiling
Dolphins:** [Fielding's note] This Epithet to a Dolphin doth
not give one so clear an Idea as were to be wished, a smiling
Fish seeming a little more difficult to be imagined than a
flying Fish. Mr. *Dryden* is of Opinion, that smiling is the
Property of Reason, and that no irrational Creature can smile.

    Smiles not allowed to Beasts from Reason move.
                State of Innocence.

47-48. Indeed . . . One: [Fielding's note] These Lines are
written in the same Key with those in the *Earl of Essex;*

    Why sayst thou so, I love thee well, indeed
    I do, and thou shalt find by this, 'tis true.

Or with this in *Cyrus;*

    The most heroick Mind that ever was.

And with above half of the modern Tragedies. **51. hie:**
[Fielding's note] *Aristotle* in that excellent Work of his which
is very justly stiled his Master-piece, earnestly recommends
using the Terms of Art, however coarse or even indecent
they may be [see *Poetics*, xxi–xxii]. Mr. *Tate* is of the same
Opinion.

  Bru. *Do not, like young Hawks, fetch a Course about,*
         Your Game flies fair.
  Fra.   *Do not fear it.*
         He answers you in your own Hawking Phrase.
                      Injur'd Love.

I think these two great Authorities are sufficient to justify
Dollalolla in the use of the Phrase—*Hie away hie;* when in the
same Line she says she is speaking to a setting Dog.

SCENE VI.

Queen *sola.*

And whither shall I go?—Alack-a-day!
I love *Tom Thumb*—but must not tell him so;
For what's a Woman, when her Virtue's gone?
A Coat without its Lace; Wig out of Buckle;
A Stocking with a Hole in 't—I can't live
Without my Virtue, or without *Tom Thumb.*
Then let me weigh them in two equal Scales,°
In this Scale put my Virtue, that, *Tom Thumb.*
Alas! *Tom Thumb* is heavier than my Virtue.
But hold!—perhaps I may be left a Widow: 10
This Match prevented, then *Tom Thumb* is mine:
In that dear Hope, I will forget my Pain.
   So, when some Wench to *Tothill-Bridewell*'s° sent,
With beating Hemp, and Flogging she's content:
She hopes in time to ease her present Pain,
At length is free, and walks the Streets again.

The End of the First ACT.

ACT II

SCENE I.

SCENE *The Street.*

Bailiff, Follower.

Bail.   Come on, my trusty Follower, come on,
This Day discharge thy Duty, and at Night
A Double Mug of Beer and Beer shall glad thee.
Stand here by me, this Way must *Noodle* pass.
   Follow.   No more, no more, Oh Bailiff! every
      Word
Inspires my Soul with Virtue.—Oh! I long
To meet the Enemy in the Street—and nab him;
To lay arresting Hands upon his Back,

And drag him trembling to the Spunging-House.°
   Bail.   There, when I have him, I will spunge° upon
      him.   10
Oh! glorious Thought! by the Sun, Moon, and Stars,
I will enjoy it, tho it be in Thought!
Yes, yes, my Follower, I will enjoy it.°
   Follow.   Enjoy it then some other time, for now
Our Prey approaches.
   Bail.   Let us retire.

SCENE II.

Tom Thumb, Noodle, Bailiff, Follower.

Thumb.   Trust me my *Noodle*, I am wondrous sick;
For tho' I love the gentle *Huncamunca,*
Yet at the Thought of Marriage, I grow pale;
For Oh!—but swear thou'lt keep it ever secret,°
I will unfold a Tale will make thee stare.
   Nood.   I swear by lovely *Huncamunca*'s Charms.
   Thumb.   Then know—my Grand-mamma hath
      often said,
Tom Thumb, beware of Marriage.°
   Nood.   Sir, I blush
To think a Warrior great in Arms as you,
Should be affrighted by his Grand-mamma;   10
Can an old Woman's empty Dreams deter
The blooming Hero from the Virgin's Arms?
Think of the Joy that will your Soul alarm,
When in her fond Embraces clasp'd you lie,
While on her panting Breast dissolv'd in Bliss,
You pour out all *Tom Thumb* in every Kiss.
   Thumb.   Oh! *Noodle,* thou hast fir'd my eager
      Soul;

Act I, scene vi. **7. two . . . Scales:** [Fielding's note] We meet with such another Pair of Scales in *Dryden*'s *King Arthur.*

> *Arthur and Oswald and their different Fates,*
> *Are weighing now within the Scales of Heav'n.*

Also in *Sebastian.*

> *This Hour my Lot is weighing in the Scales.*

13. Tothill-Bridewell: a London jail for women and apprentices.

Act II, scene i. **9. Spunging-House:** a house used as a place of preliminary confinement for debtors. **10. spunge:** press for money. **11–13. Oh . . . it:** [Fielding's note] Mr. *Rowe* is generally imagin'd to have taken some Hints from this Scene in his Character of *Bajazet* [in *Tamerlane*]; but as he, of all the Tragick Writers, bears the least Resemblance to our Author in his Diction, I am unwilling to imagine he would condescend to copy him in this Particular. *Act II, scene ii.* **4. keep . . . secret:** [Fielding's note] This Method of surprizing an Audience by raising their Expectation to the highest Pitch, and then baulking it, hath been practis'd with great Success by most of our Tragical Authors. **8. beware of Marriage:** [Fielding's note] *Almeyda* in *Sebastian* is in the same Distress;

> *Sometimes methinks I hear the Groan of Ghosts,*
> *Thin hollow Sounds and lamentable Screams;*
> *Then, like a dying Echo from afar,*
> *My Mother's Voice that cries, wed not Almeyda*
> *Forewarn'd, Almeyda, Marriage is thy Crime.*

Spight of my Grandmother, she shall be mine;
I'll hug, caress, I'll eat her up with Love.
Whole Days, and Nights, and Years shall be too
    short   20
For our Enjoyment, every Sun shall rise
Blushing, to see us in our Bed together.°
   Nood. Oh Sir! this Purpose of your Soul pursue.
   Bail. Oh, Sir! I have an Action against you.
   Nood. At whose Suit is it?
   Bail.   At your *Taylor's*, Sir.
Your *Taylor* put this Warrant in my Hands,
And I arrest you, Sir, at his Commands.
   Thumb. Ha! Dogs! Arrest my Friend before my
      Face!
Think you *Tom Thumb* will suffer this Disgrace!
But let vain Cowards threaten by their Word,   30
Tom Thumb shall shew his Anger by his Sword.
               [*Kills the Bailiff and his Follower.*
   Bail. Oh, I am slain!
   Follow.   I am murthered also,
And to the Shades, the dismal Shades below,
My Bailiff's faithful Follower I go.
   Nood. Go then to Hell, like Rascals as you are,
And give our Service to the Bailiffs there.°
   Thumb. Thus perish all the Bailiffs in the Land,
Till Debtors at Noon-Day shall walk the Streets,
And no one fear a Bailiff or his Writ.

22. Blushing . . . together: [Fielding's note] As very well
he may if he hath any Modesty in him, says Mr. *D——s.* The
Author of *Busiris,* is extremely zealous to prevent the Sun's
blushing at any indecent Object; and therefore on all such
Occasions he addresses himself to the Sun, and desires him
to keep out of the way.

    Rise never more, O Sun! let Night prevail,
    Eternal Darkness close the World's wide Scene.
      Busiris.
    Sun hide thy Face and put the World in Mourning.
      Ibid.

Mr. *Banks* makes the Sun perform the Office of *Hymen;* and
therefore not likely to be disgusted at such a Sight;

    The Sun sets forth like a gay Brideman with you.
      Mary Q. of Scots.

35–36. Go . . . there: [Fielding's note] *Nourmahal* sends the
same Message to Heaven;

    For I would have you, when you upwards move,
    Speak kindly of us, to our Friends above.
      Aurengzebe.

We find another to Hell, in the *Persian* Princess;

    Villain, get thee down
    To Hell, and tell them that the Fray's begun.

SCENE III.

The Princess Huncamunca's *Apartment.*
Huncamunca, Cleora, Mustacha.

   Hunc. Give me some Musick—see that it be sad.°

        Cleora *sings.*
    Cupid, *ease a Love-sick Maid,*
    Bring thy Quiver to her Aid;
    With equal Ardor wound the Swain:
    Beauty should never sigh in vain.

         II.
    Let him feel the pleasing Smart,
    Drive thy Arrow thro' his Heart;
    When One you wound, you then destroy;
    When Both you kill, you kill with Joy.

   Hunc. O, *Tom Thumb! Tom Thumb!* wherefore
    art thou *Tom Thumb?*°   10
Why had'st thou not been born of Royal Race?
Why had not mighty *Bantam* been thy Father?
Or else the King of *Brentford,*° Old or *New?*
   Must. I am surpriz'd that your Highness can give
your self a Moment's Uneasiness about that little
insignificant Fellow, *Tom Thumb the Great*°—One
properer for a Play-thing, than a Husband.—Were he
my Husband, his Horns should be as long as his
Body.—If you had fallen in Love with a Grenadier,
I should not have wonder'd at it—If you had fallen in
love with Something; but to fall in Love with
Nothing!
   Hunc. Cease, my *Mustacha,* on thy Duty cease.
The *Zephyr,* when in flowry Vales it plays,
Is not so soft, so sweet as *Thummy's* Breath.
The Dove is not so gentle to its Mate.

Act II, scene iii. **1. see . . . sad:** [Fielding's note] *Anthony* [in
Dryden's *All for Love*] gives the same Command in the same
Words. **10. O . . . Thumb:** [Fielding's note]

    Oh! *Marius, Marius;* wherefore art thou *Marius?*
      Otway's Marius.

12–13. Bantam, Brentford: The kings of Bantam and of
Brentford are characters referred to in Fielding's *Author's
Farce* (1730); the two kings of Brentford are burlesqued in
The Rehearsal (1671) by the Duke of Buckingham and others.
Tom . . . Great: [Fielding's note] Nothing is more common
than these seeming Contradictions; such as,

    Haughty Weakness.
      Victim.
    Great small World.
      [Edward Ecclestone's] Noah's Flood.

Must. The Dove is every bit as proper for a Husband—Alas! Madam, there's not a Beau about the Court looks so little like a Man—He is a perfect Butterfly, a Thing without Substance, and almost without Shadow too.

Hunc. This Rudeness is unseasonable, desist; Or, I shall think this Railing comes from Love. *Tom Thumb*'s a Creature of that charming Form,   20 That no one can abuse, unless they love him.

Must. Madam, the King.

SCENE IV.

King, Huncamunca.

King. Let all but *Huncamunca* leave the Room.
                    [*Ex.* Cleora, *and* Mustacha.
Daughter, I have observ'd of late some Grief,
Unusual in your Countenance—your Eyes,
That, like two open Windows, us'd to shew
The lovely Beauty of the Rooms within,
Have now two Blinds before them°—What is the
    Cause?
Say, have you not enough of Meat and Drink?
We've giv'n strict Orders not to have you stinted.

Hunc. Alas! my Lord, I value not my self,
That once I eat two Fowls and half a Pig;   10
Small is that Praise; but oh! a Maid may want,
What she can neither eat nor drink.°

King.   What's that?
Hunc. O spare my Blushes; but I mean a Husband.°
King. If that be all, I have provided one,
A Husband great in Arms, whose warlike Sword
Streams with the yellow Blood of slaughter'd Giants.
Whose Name in *Terrâ Incognitâ*° is known,
Whose Valour, Wisdom, Virtue make a Noise,
Great as the Kettle-Drums of twenty Armies.
Hunc. Whom does my Royal Father mean?
King.   Tom Thumb.   20
Hunc. Is it possible?
King.   Ha! the Window-Blinds are gone,
A Country Dance of Joy is in your Face,°
Your Eyes spit Fire, your Cheeks grow red as Beef.
Hunc. O, there's a Magick-musick in that Sound,
Enough to turn me into Beef indeed.
Yes, I will own, since licens'd by your Word,
I'll own *Tom Thumb* the Cause of all my Grief.
For him I've sigh'd, I've wept, I've gnaw'd my
    Sheets.
King. Oh! thou shalt gnaw thy tender Sheets no
    more,
A Husband thou shalt have to mumble now.   30
Hunc. Oh! happy Sound! henceforth, let no one
    tell,
That *Huncamunca* shall lead Apes in Hell.°
Oh! I am over-joy'd!
King.   I see thou art.

Act II, scene iv. **3–6. your . . . them:** [Fielding's note] *Lee* hath improv'd this Metaphor.

> *Dost thou not view Joy peeping from my Eyes,*
> *The Casements open'd wide to gaze on thee;*
> *So Rome's glad Citizens to Windows rise,*
> *When they some young Triumpher fain would see.*
>   Gloriana.

12. neither . . . drink: [Fielding's note] *Almahide* hath the same Contempt for these Appetites;

> *To eat and drink can no Perfection be.*
>   Conquest of Granada.

The Earl of *Essex* is of a different Opinion, and seems to place the chief Happiness of a General therein.

> *Were but Commanders half so well rewarded,*
> *Then they might eat.*
>   Banks's Earl of Essex.

But if we may believe one, who knows more than either, the Devil himself; we shall find Eating to be an Affair of more moment than is generally imagined.

> *Gods are immortal only by their Food.*
>   Lucifer in the State of Innocence.

13. a Husband: [Fielding's note] This Expression is enough of it self (says Mr. *D——s*) utterly to destroy the Character of *Huncamunca;* yet we find a Woman of no abandon'd Character [Cassandra] in *Dryden,* adventuring farther and thus excusing her self;

> *To speak our Wishes first, forbid it Pride,*
> *Forbid it Modesty: True, they forbid it,*
> *But Nature does not, when we are athirst,*
> *Or hungry, will imperious Nature stay,*
> *Nor eat, nor drink, before 'tis bid fall on.*
>   Cleomenes.

Cassandra speaks before she is asked. *Huncamunca* afterwards. *Cassandra* speaks her Wishes to her Lover. *Huncamunca only* to her Father. **17. Terrâ Incognitâ:** unexplored regions. **22. A Country . . . Face:** [Fielding's note]

> *Her Eyes resistless Magick bear,*
> *Angels I see, and Gods are dancing there.*
>   Lee's Sophonisba.

32. lead . . . Hell: an occupation ascribed to old maids.

Joy lightens in thy Eyes, and thunders from thy
    Brows;
Transports, like Lightning, dart along thy Soul,
As Small-shot thro' a Hedge.°
    Hunc.   Oh! say not small.
    King. This happy News shall on our Tongue ride
    Post,
Our self will bear the happy News to *Thumb.*
Yet think not, Daughter, that your powerful Charms
Must still detain the Hero from his Arms;   40
Various his Duty, various his Delight;
Now is his Turn to kiss, and now to fight;
And now to kiss again. So, mighty *Jove,*
When with excessive thund'ring tir'd above,
Comes down to Earth, and takes a Bit—and then,
Flies to his Trade of Thund'ring, back again.°

SCENE V.

Grizzle, Huncamunca.

  Griz. Oh! *Huncamunca, Huncamunca,* oh,°
Thy pouting Breasts, like Kettle-Drums of Brass,
Beat everlasting loud Alarms of Joy;

34–36. Joy . . . Hedge: [Fielding's note] Mr. *Dennis* in that
excellent Tragedy, call'd *Liberty Asserted,* which is thought to
have given so great a Stroke to the late *French* King, hath
frequent Imitations of this beautiful Speech of King *Arthur;*

> *Conquest light'ning in his Eyes, and thund'ring in his Arm.*
> *Joy lighten'd in her Eyes.*
> *Joys like Light'ning dart along my Soul.*

43–46. mighty . . . again: [Fielding's note]

> *Jove with excessive Thund'ring tir'd above,*
> *Comes down for Ease, enjoys a Nymph, and then*
> *Mounts dreadful, and to Thund'ring goes again.*
>   Gloriana.

Act II, scene v. **1. Oh . . . oh:** [Fielding's note] This beautiful
Line, which ought, says Mr. *W——* [possibly Welsted] to be
written in Gold, is imitated in the New *Sophonisba;*

> Oh! *Sophonisba, Sophonisba,* oh!
> Oh! *Narva, Narva,* oh!

The Author of a Song call'd *Duke upon Duke,* hath
improv'd it.

> *Alas! O Nick, O Nick, alas!*

Where, by the help of a little false Spelling, you have two
Meanings in the repeated Words. [It is said that after the
production of his *Sophonisba* (1730) certain wits greeted James
Thomson as follows: "Oh, Jemmy Thomson! Jemmy
Thomson, oh!"]

As bright as Brass they are, and oh, as hard;
Oh *Huncamunca, Huncamunca!* oh!
    Hunc. Ha! do'st thou know me, Princess as I am,
That thus of me you dare to make your Game.°
    Griz. Oh *Huncamunca,* well I know that you
A Princess are, and a King's Daughter too.   9
But Love no Meanness scorns, no Grandeur fears,
Love often Lords into the Cellar bears,
And bids the sturdy Porter come up Stairs.
For what's too high for Love, or what's too low?
Oh *Huncamunca, Huncamunca,* oh!
    Hunc. But granting all you say of Love were true,
My Love, alas! is to another due!
In vain to me, a Suitoring you come;
For I'm already promis'd to *Tom Thumb.*
    Griz. And can my Princess such a Durgen° wed,
One fitter for your Pocket than your Bed!   20
Advis'd by me, the worthless Baby shun,
Or you will ne'er be brought to bed of one.
Oh take me to thy Arms and never flinch,
Who am a Man by *Jupiter* ev'ry Inch.
Then while in Joys together lost we lie
I'll press thy Soul while Gods stand wishing by.°
    Hunc. If, Sir, what you insinuate you prove
All Obstacles of Promise you remove;
For all Engagements to a Man must fall,
Whene'er that Man is prov'd no Man at all.   30
    Griz. Oh let him seek some Dwarf, some fairy
    Miss,
Where no Joint-stool must lift him to the Kiss.
But by the Stars and Glory, you appear
Much fitter for a *Prussian* Grenadier;
One Globe alone, on *Atlas* Shoulders rests,
Two Globes are less than *Huncamunca's* Breasts:
The Milky-way is not so white, that's flat,°
And sure thy Breasts are full as large as that.
    Hunc. Oh, Sir, so strong your Eloquence I find,
It is impossible to be unkind.   40

---

7. your Game: [Fielding's note] *Edith,* in [John Fletcher's]
the *Bloody Brother,* speaks to her Lover in the same familiar
Language.

> *Your Grace is full of Game.*

19. Durgen: dwarf. **26. press . . . by:** [Fielding's note]

> *Traverse the glitt'ring Chambers of the Sky,*
> *Born on a Cloud in view of Fate I'll lie,*
> *And press her Soul while Gods stand wishing by.*
>   [Lee's] Hannibal.

37. that's flat: That's the absolute truth.

Griz.   Ah! speak that o'er again, and let° the
   Sound
From one Pole to another Pole rebound;
The Earth and Sky, each be a Battledoor°
And keep the Sound, that Shuttlecock, up an Hour;
To *Doctors Commons*, for a License I,
Swift as an Arrow from a Bow will fly.
   Hunc.   Oh no! lest some Disaster we should meet,
'Twere better to be marry'd at the Fleet.°
   Griz.   Forbid it, all ye Powers, a Princess should
By that vile Place, contaminate her Blood;   50
My quick Return shall to my Charmer prove,
I travel on the Post-Horses of Love.
   Hunc.   Those Post-Horses to me will seem too
      slow,
Tho' they should fly swift as the Gods, when they
Ride on behind that Post-Boy, Opportunity.°

SCENE VI.

Tom Thumb, Huncamunca.

Thumb.   Where is my Princess, where's my
      Huncamunca?
Where are those Eyes, those Cardmatches of Love,
That Light up all with Love° my waxen Soul?
Where is that Face which artful Nature made

41–44. let . . . Hour: [Fielding's note]

> *Let the four Winds from distant Corners meet,*
> *And on their Wings first bear it into* France;
> *Then back again to* Edina's *proud Walls,*
> *Till Victim to the Sound th' aspiring City falls.*
>   Albion Queen[s].

43. Battledoor: badminton racquet. **48. the Fleet:** a prison, whose resident parson performed secret marriages. **55. that . . . Opportunity:** [Fielding's note] I do not remember any Metaphors so frequent in the Tragick Poets as those borrow'd from Riding Post;

> *The Gods and Opportunity ride Post.*
>   Hannibal.
> ——*Let's rush together,*
> *For Death rides Post.*
>   Duke of Guise.
> *Destruction gallops to thy murther Post.*
>   Gloriana.

Act II, scene vi. **3. Light . . . Love:** [Fielding's note] This Image too very often occurs;

> ——*Bright as when thy Eye*
> *First lighted up our Loves.*
>   Aurengzebe.
> '*Tis not a Crown alone lights up my Name.*
>   Busiris.

In the same Moulds where *Venus* self was cast°?
   Hunc.   Oh! What is Musick to the Ear that's deaf,°
Or a Goose-Pye to him that has no taste?
What are these Praises now to me, since I
Am promis'd to another?
   Thumb.   Ha! promis'd.
   Hunc.   Too sure; it's written in the Book of
      Fate.   10
   Thumb.   Then I will tear away the Leaf.

5. In . . . cast: [Fielding's note] There is great Dissension among the Poets concerning the Method of making Man. One tells his Mistress that the Mold she was made in being lost, Heaven cannot form such another. *Lucifer,* in *Dryden,* gives a merry Description of his own Formation;

> *Whom Heaven neglecting, made and scarce design'd,*
> *But threw me in for Number to the rest.*
>   State of Innocence.

In one Place, the same Poet supposes Man to be made of Metal;

> *I was form'd*
> *Of that coarse Metal, which when she was made,*
> *The Gods threw by for Rubbish.*
>   All for Love.

In another, of Dough;

> *When the Gods moulded up the Paste of Man,*
> *Some of their Clay was left upon their Hands,*
> *And so they made* Egyptians.
>   Cleomenes.

In another of Clay;

> ——*Rubbish of remaining Clay.*
>   Sebastian.

One makes the Soul of Wax;

> *Her waxen Soul begins to melt apace.*
>   Anna Bullen.

Another of Flint;

> *Sure our two Souls have somewhere been acquainted*
> *In former Beings, or struck out together,*
> *One Spark to* Africk *flew, and one to* Portugal.
>   Sebastian.

To omit the great Quantities of Iron, Brazen and Leaden Souls which are so plenty in modern Authors—I cannot omit the Dress of a Soul as we find it in *Dryden;*

> *Souls shirted but with Air.*
>   King Arthur.

Nor can I pass by a particular sort of Soul in a particular sort of Description, in the New *Sophonisba.*

> *Ye mysterious Powers,*
> ——*Whether thro' your gloomy Depths I wander,*
> *Or on the Mountains walk; give me the calm,*
> *The steady smiling Soul, where Wisdom sheds*
> *Eternal Sun-shine, and eternal Joy.*

6. Oh . . . deaf: [Fielding's note] This Line Mr. *Banks* has plunder'd entire in his *Anna Bullen.*

Wherein it's writ, or if Fate won't allow
So large a Gap within its Journal-Book,
I'll blot it out at least.°

SCENE VII.°

Glumdalca, Tom Thumb, Huncamunca.

Glum.   I need not ask if you are *Huncamunca*,
Your Brandy Nose proclaims—
   Hunc.   I am a Princess;
Nor need I ask who you are.
   Glum.   A Giantess;
The Queen of those who made and unmade Queens.
   Hunc.   The Man, whose chief Ambition is to be
My Sweetheart, hath destroy'd these mighty Giants.
   Glum.   Your Sweetheart? do'st thou think the
      Man, who once
Hath worn my easy Chains, will e'er wear thine?
   Hunc.   Well may your Chains be easy, since if
      Fame
Says true, they have been try'd on twenty
      Husbands.   10
The Glove or Boot, so many times pull'd on,
May well sit easy on the Hand or Foot.°
   Glum.   I glory in the Number, and when I
Sit poorly down, like thee, content with one,
Heaven change this Face for one as bad as thine.
   Hunc.   Let me see nearer what this Beauty is,
That captivates the Heart of Men by Scores.
                        [*Holds a Candle to her Face.*

11–14. Then . . . least: [Fielding's note]

> *Good Heaven, the Book of Fate before me lay,*
> *But to tear out the Journal of that Day.*
> *Or if the Order of the World below,*
> *Will not the Gap of one whole Day allow,*
> *Give me that Minute when she made her Vow.*
>   Conquest of Granada.

Act II, scene vii. **scene vii:** [Fielding's note] I know some of
the Commentators have imagined, that Mr. *Dryden*, in the
Altercative Scene between *Cleopatra* and *Octavia* [in *All for
Love*], a Scene which Mr. *Addison* inveighs against with great
Bitterness [*The Guardian*, No. 110], is much beholden to our
Author. How just this their Observation is, I will not presume
to determine. **11–12. The Glove . . . Foot:** [Fielding's note]
A cobling Poet indeed, says Mr. *D*[ennis]. and yet I believe
we may find as monstrous Images in the Tragick-Authors:
I'll put down one;

> *Untie your folded Thoughts, and let them dangle loose as a*
> *Bride's Hair.*
>   Injur'd Love.

Which Lines seem to have as much Title to a Milliner's
Shop, as our Author's to a Shoemaker's.

Oh! Heaven, thou art as ugly as the Devil.
   Glum.   You'd give the best of Shoes within your
      Shop,
To be but half so handsome.
   Hunc.   —Since you come   20
To that, I'll put my Beauty to the Test;°
Tom Thumb, I'm yours, if you with me will go.
   Glum.   Oh! stay, *Tom Thumb*, and you alone shall
      fill
That Bed where twenty Giants us'd to lie.
   Thumb.   In the Balcony that o'er-hangs the Stage,
I've seen a Whore two 'Prentices engage;
One half a Crown does in his Fingers hold,
The other shews a little Piece of Gold;
She the Half Guinea wisely does purloin,
And leaves the larger and the baser Coin.   30
   Glum.   Left, scorn'd, and loath'd for such a Chit as
      this;
I feel the Storm that's rising in my Mind,
Tempests, and Whirlwinds rise, and rowl and roar.°
I'm all within a Hurricane, as if
The World's four Winds were pent within my
      Carcass.°
Confusion, Horror, Murder, Guts and Death.°

19–21. To . . . Test: [Fielding's note] Mr. *L*—— [possibly
Lee] takes occasion in this Place to commend the great
Care of our Author to preserve the Metre of Blank Verse, in
which *Shakespear*, [Ben] *Johnson* and [John] *Fletcher* were so
notoriously negligent; and the Moderns, in Imitation
of our Author, so laudably observant;

> ——*Then does*
> *Your Majesty believe that he can be*
> *A Traitor!*
>   Earl of Essex.

Every page of *Sophonisba* gives us Instances of this Excellence. **33. Tempests . . . roar:** [Fielding's note]

> *Love mounts and rowls about my stormy Mind.*
>   Aurengzebe.
> *Tempests and Whirlwinds thro' my Bosom move.*
>   Cleom.

35. The World's . . . Carcass: [Fielding's note]

> *With such a furious Tempest on his Brow,*
> *As if the World's four Winds were pent within*
> *His blustring Carcase.*
>   Anna Bullen.

36. Confusion . . . Death: [Fielding's note] Verba Tragica
[tragic language].

SCENE VIII.

King, Glumdalca.

King.   Sure never was so sad a King as I,°
My Life is worn as ragged as a Coat
A Beggar wears; a Prince should put it off,°
To love a Captive and a Giantess.
Oh Love! Oh Love! how great a King art thou!
My Tongue's thy Trumpet, and thou Trumpetest,
Unknown to me, within me.° Oh *Glumdalca!*
Heaven thee design'd a Giantess to make,
But an Angelick Soul was shuffled in.°
I am a Multitude of Walking Griefs,°   10
And only on her Lips the Balm is found,
To spread a Plaister that might cure them all.°
    Glum.   What do I hear?
    King.   What do I see?
    Glum.   Oh!
    King.   Ah!

    Glum.   Ah Wretched Queen°!
    King.   Oh! Wretched King!
    Glum.   Ah!
    King.   Oh!°

SCENE IX.

Tom Thumb, Huncamunca, Parson.

Parson.   Happy's the Wooing, that's not long
    adoing;
For if I guess aright, *Tom Thumb* this Night
Shall give a Being to a New *Tom Thumb.*
    Thumb.   It shall be my Endeavour so to do.
    Hunc.   Oh! fie upon you, Sir, you make me blush.
    Thumb.   It is the Virgin's Sign, and suits you well:
I know not where, nor how, nor what I am,°

---

14. Wretched Queen: [Fielding's note] Our Author, who every where shews his great Penetration into human Nature, here outdoes himself: Where a less judicious Poet would have raised a long Scene of whining Love. He who understood the Passions better, and that so violent an Affection as this must be too big for Utterance, chooses rather to send his Characters off in this sullen and doleful manner: In which admirable Conduct he is imitated by the Author [David Mallet] of the justly celebrated *Eurydice.* Dr. *Young* seems to point at this Violence of Passion;

    ———*Passion choaks*
    Their Words, and they're the Statues of Despair,

And *Seneca* tells us, *Curae leves loquuntur, ingentes stupent* ["Light troubles speak out; heavy ones are silent"]. The Story of the *Egyptian* King in *Herodotus* is too well known to need to be inserted [Psammenitus, King of Egypt, watched silently while his own daughter was led into slavery, but wept and beat his head when one of his friends suffered the same fate]; I refer the more curious Reader to the excellent *Monta[i]gne,* who hath written an Essay [I. 2] on this Subject. **Ah! Oh:** [Fielding's note]

    To part is Death.———
    ———*'Tis Death to part.*
    ———*Ah.*
    ———*Oh.*
    [Otway's] *Don Carlos.*

[The passage is actually from Gay's *What D' Ye Call It.*]
Act II, scene ix. **7. I know . . . am:** [Fielding's note]

    Nor know I whether.
    What am I, who or where.
    Busiris.
    I was I know not what, and am I know not how.
    Gloriana.

Act II, scene viii. **1. so . . . I:** [Fielding's note] This Speech hath been terribly maul'd by the Poets. **2–3. My . . . off:** [Fielding's note]

    —*My Life is worn to Rags,*
    Not worth a Prince's wearing.
    [Dryden's] *Love Triumph[ant].*

5–7. Oh . . . me: [Fielding's note]

    Must I beg the Pity of my Slave?
    Must a King beg! But Love's a greater King,
    A Tyrant, nay a Devil that possesses me.
    He tunes the Organ of my Voice and speaks,
    Unknown to me, within me.
    Sebastian.

9. But . . . in: [Fielding's note]

    When thou wer't form'd, Heaven did a Man begin;
    But a Brute Soul by chance was shuffled in.
    Aurengzebe.

10. I . . . Griefs: [Fielding's note]

    ———*I am a Multitude*
    of walking Griefs.
    New Sophonisba.

12. a Plaister . . . all: [Fielding's note]

    I will take thy Scorpion Blood,
    And lay it to my Grief till I have Ease.
    Anna Bullen.

I'm so transported, I have lost my self.°

Hunc. Forbid it, all ye Stars, for you're so small,
That were you lost, you'd find your self no more. 10
So the unhappy Sempstress once, they say,
Her Needle in a Pottle,° lost, of Hay;
In vain she look'd, and look'd, and made her Moan,
For ah, the Needle was for ever gone.
Parson. Long may they live, and love, and
  propagate,
Till the whole Land be peopled with *Tom Thumbs.*

---

8. I . . . self: [Fielding's note] To understand sufficiently the Beauty of this Passage, it will be necessary that we comprehend every Man to contain two Selfs. I shall not attempt to prove this from Philosophy, which the Poets make so plainly evident.

One runs away from the other;

> *Let me demand your Majesty,*
> *Why fly you from your self?*
> Duke of Guise.

In a 2d. One Self is a Guardian to the other;

> *Leave me the Care of me.*
> Conquest of Granada.

Again,

> *My self am to my self less near.*
> Ibid.

In the same, the first Self is proud of the second;

> *I my self am proud of me.*
> State of Innocence.

In a 3d. Distrustful of him;

> *Fain I would tell, but whisper it in mine Ear,*
> *That none besides might hear, nay not my self.*
> Earl of Essex.

In a 4th. Honours him;

> *I honour* Rome,
> *But honour too my self.*
> Sophonisba.

In a 5th. At Variance with him;

> *Leave me not thus at Variance with my self.*
> Busiris.

Again, in a 6th.

> *I find my self divided from my self.*
> [Charles Johnson's] Medea.
> *She seemed the sad Effigies of her self.*
> Banks. [*Albion Queens*]
> *Assist me, Zulema, if thou would'st be*
> *The Friend thou seemest, assist me against me.*
> Albion Queens.

From which it appears, that there are two Selfs; and therefore *Tom Thumb's* losing himself is no such Solecism as it hath been represented by Men, rather ambitious of Criticizing, than qualify'd to Criticize. **12. Pottle:** bundle.

So when the *Cheshire* Cheese a Maggot breeds,
Another and another still succeeds.
By thousands, and ten thousands they increase,
Till one continued Maggot fills the rotten Cheese.° 20

SCENE X.

Noodle, *and then* Grizzle.

Nood. Sure Nature means to break her solid
  Chain,
Or else unfix the World, and in a Rage,
To hurl it from its Axle-tree and Hinges;°
All things are so confus'd, the King's in Love,
The Queen is drunk, the Princess married is.
Griz. Oh! *Noodle,* hast thou *Huncamunca* seen?
Nood. I've seen a Thousand Sights this day, where
  none
Are by the wonderful Bitch° herself outdone,
The King, the Queen, and all the Court are Sights.
Griz. D——n your Delay, you Trifler, are you
  drunk, ha? 10
I will not hear one Word but *Huncamunca.*°
Nood. By this time she is married to *Tom Thumb.*
Griz. My *Huncamunca.*
Nood. Your *Huncamunca.*
Tom Thumb's Huncamunca, every Man's *Huncamunca.*°
Griz. If this be true all Womankind are damn'd.
Nood. If it be not, may I be so my self.

17–20. So . . . Cheese: [Fielding's note] Mr. *F——* [Fielding] imagines this Parson to have been a *Welsh* one from his Simile. [The Welsh were proverbially fond of cheese.] *Act II, scene x.* **1–3. Sure . . . Hinges:** [Fielding's note] Our Author hath been plunder'd here according to Custom;

> *Great Nature* break thy Chain *that links together,*
> *The Fabrick of the World and make a* Chaos,
> *Like that within my Soul.*
> Love Triumphant.
> ——*Startle Nature, unfix the Globe,*
> *And hurl it from its* Axle-tree *and Hinges.*
> Albion Queens.
> *The tott'ring Earth seems sliding off its Props.*
> [Persian Princess]

8. the wonderful Bitch: a card-playing French dog, one of the current London sights. **10–11. D——n . . . Huncamunca:** [Fielding's note]

> D——*n your Delay, ye Torturers proceed,*
> *I will not hear one Word but* Almahide.
> Conq. of Granada.

14. every . . . Huncamunca: [Fielding's note] Mr. *Dryden* hath imitated this in *All for Love.*

Griz.   See where she comes! I'll not believe a
    Word
Against that Face, upon whose ample Brow,
Sits Innocence with Majesty Enthron'd.°

              Grizzle, Huncamunca.

Griz.   Where has my *Huncamunca* been? See
    here   20
The Licence in my Hand!
    Hunc.   Alas! *Tom Thumb.*
    Griz.   Why dost thou mention him?
    Hunc.   Ah me! *Tom Thumb.*
    Griz.   What means my lovely *Huncamunca?*
    Hunc.   Hum!
    Griz.   Oh! Speak.
    Hunc.   Hum!
    Griz.   Ha! your every Word is Hum.
You force me still to answer you *Tom Thumb.*°
Tom Thumb, I'm on the Rack, I'm in a Flame,
Tom Thumb, Tom Thumb, Tom Thumb, you love the
    Name;°
So pleasing is that Sound, that were you dumb
You still would find a Voice to cry *Tom Thumb.*
    Hunc.   Oh! Be not hasty to proclaim my Doom, 30
My ample Heart for more than one has Room,
A Maid like me, Heaven form'd at least for two,
I married him, and now I'll marry you.°

18-19. upon . . . Enthron'd: [Fielding's note] This
Miltonick Stile abounds in the New *Sophonisba.*

    ————*And on her ample Brow*
    Sat Majesty.

25. You . . . Thumb: [Fielding's note]

    Your ev'ry Answer, still so ends in that,
    You force me still to answer you Morat.
                     Aurengzebe.

27. Tom . . . Name: [Fielding's note]

    Morat, Morat, Morat, *you love the Name.*
                     Aurengzebe.

32-33. A Maid . . . you: [Fielding's note] Here is a Sentiment for the Virtuous *Huncamunca* (says Mr. *D——s*) and yet
with the leave of this great Man, the Virtuous *Panthea* in *Cyrus,*
hath an Heart every whit as Ample;

    For two I must confess are Gods to me,
    Which is my Abradatus *first, and thee.*
                   Cyrus the Great.

Nor is the Lady in *Love Triumphant* more reserv'd, tho' not so
intelligible;

    ————*I am so divided,*
    That I grieve most for both, and love both most.

Griz.   Ha! dost thou own thy Falshood to my
    Face?
Think'st thou that I will share thy Husband's place,
Since to that Office one cannot suffice,
And since you scorn to dine one single Dish on,
Go, get your Husband put into Commission,
Commissioners to discharge, (ye Gods) it fine is,
The Duty of a Husband to your Highness;   40
Yet think not long, I will my Rival bear,
Or unreveng'd the slighted Willow wear;
The gloomy, brooding Tempest now confin'd,
Within the hollow Caverns of my Mind,
In dreadful Whirl, shall rowl along the Coasts,   ⎞
Shall thin the Land of all the Men it boasts,   ⎟
And cram up ev'ry Chink of Hell with Ghosts.° ⎠
So have I seen, in some dark Winter's Day,
A sudden Storm rush down the Sky's High-Way,
Sweep thro' the Streets with terrible ding dong,   50
Gush thro' the Spouts, and wash whole Crowds
    along.
The crowded Shops, the thronging Vermin skreen, ⎞
Together cram the Dirty and the Clean,   ⎟
And not one Shoe-Boy in the Street is seen.°   ⎠
    Hunc.   Oh! fatal Rashness should his Fury slay,
My hapless Bridegroom on his Wedding Day;
I, who this Morn, of two chose which to wed,
May go again this Night alone to Bed;
    So have I seen some wild unsettled Fool,
Who had her Choice of this, and that Joint Stool; 60

47. cram . . . Ghosts: [Fielding's note] A ridiculous Supposition to any one, who considers the great and extensive
Largeness of Hell, says a Commentator: But not so to those
who consider the great Expansion of immaterial Substance.
Mr. *Banks* makes one Soul to be so expanded that Heaven
could not contain it;

    The Heavens are all too narrow for her Soul.
                   Virtue Betray'd.

The *Persian Princess* hath a Passage not unlike the Author of
this;

    We will send such Shoals of murther'd Slaves,
    Shall glut Hell's empty Regions.

This threatens to fill Hell even tho' it were empty; Lord
Grizzle only to fill up the Chinks, supposing the rest already
full. **48-54. So . . . seen:** [Fielding's note] Mr. *Addison* is
generally thought to have had this Simile in his Eye, when he
wrote that beautiful one at the end of the third Act of his
Cato.

To give the Preference to either, loath
And fondly coveting to sit on both:
While the two Stools her Sitting Part confound,
Between 'em both fall Squat upon the Ground.°

The End of the Second ACT.

ACT III

SCENE I.

SCENE *King* Arthur's *Palace.*

Ghost *solus.*°

Hail! ye black Horrors of Midnight's Midnoon!
Ye Fairies, Goblins, Bats and Screech-Owls, Hail!
And Oh! ye mortal Watchmen, whose hoarse
      Throats

Th' Immortal Ghosts dread Croakings counterfeit,
All Hail!—Ye dancing Fantoms, who by Day,
And some condemn'd to fast, some feast in Fire;
Now play in Church-yards, skipping o'er the Graves,
To the loud Musick of the silent Bell,°
All Hail!

SCENE II.

King, *and* Ghost.

King. What Noise is this?—What Villain dares,
At this dread Hour, with Feet and Voice Prophane,
Disturb our Royal Walls?
  Ghost.   One who defies
Thy empty Power to hurt him; one who dares
Walk in thy Bed-Chamber.°
  King.   Presumptuous Slave!
Thou diest:
  Ghost.   Threaten others with that Word,

59–64. So . . . Ground: [Fielding's note] This beautiful Simile is founded on a Proverb, which does Honour to the *English* Language;

  Between two Stools the Breech falls to the Ground.

I am not so pleased with any written Remains of the Ancients, as with those little Aphorisms, which verbal Tradition hath delivered down to us, under the Title of Proverbs. It were to be wished that instead of filling their Pages with the fabulous Theology of the Pagans, our modern Poets would think it worth their while to enrich their Works with the Proverbial Sayings of their Ancestors. Mr. *Dryden* hath chronicl'd one in Heroick;

  Two ifs scarce make one Possibility.
    Conquest of *Granada.*

My Lord *Bacon* is of Opinion, that whatever is known of Arts and Sciences might be proved to have lurked in the Proverbs of *Solomon.* I am of the same Opinion in relation to those abovemention'd: At least I am confident that a more perfect System of Ethicks, as well as Oeconomy, might be compiled out of them, than is at present extant, either in the Works of the Antient Philosophers, or those more valuable, as more voluminous, ones of the modern Divines. *Act III, scene i.* **Ghost solus:** Of all the Particulars in which the modern Stage falls short of the ancient, there is none so much to be lamented, as the great Scarcity of Ghosts in the latter. Whence this proceeds, I will not presume to determine. Some are of opinion, that the Moderns are unequal to that sublime Language which a Ghost ought to speak. One says ludicrously, That Ghosts are out of Fashion; another, That they are properer for Comedy; forgetting, I suppose, that *Aristotle* hath told us, That a Ghost is the Soul of Tragedy; for so I render the ψυχή ὁ μῦθος τῆς τραγωδίας ["The fable (or plot) is

---

the soul of tragedy"], which [the French critic] M. *Dacier,* amongst others, hath mistaken; I suppose mis-led, by not understanding the *Fabula* of the *Latins,* which signifies a *Ghost* as well as a *Fable.*

  ———*Te premet nox, fabulæque Manes.*
  ["Night presses down on thee, and the fabled spirits"
  (Horace, *Odes,* I. iv. 16).]

Of all the Ghosts that have ever appeared on the Stage, a very learned and judicious foreign Critick, gives the Preference to this of our Author. These are his Words, speaking of this Tragedy;

  —*Nec quidquam in illâ admirabilius quam*
  Phasma quoddam horrendum, quod omnibus aliis Spectris,
  quibuscum scatet Anglorum Tragœdia, longè (pace
  D——isii V. Doctiss. dixerim) prætulerim.
  ["—Nor is there anything in it more admirable than that horrid ghost, which I greatly prefer to all other ghosts with which English tragedy abounds— with due respect to that most learned man, Dionysius."]

8. the silent Bell: [Fielding's note] We have already given Instances of this Figure. *Act III, scene ii.* **5. thy Bed-Chamber:** [Fielding's note] *Almanzor* reasons in the same manner;

  ———*A Ghost I'll be*
  And from a Ghost, you know, no Place is free.
    Conq. of *Granada.*

I am a Ghost, and am already dead.°

   King. Ye Stars! 'tis well; were thy last Hour to
     come,
This Moment had been it; yet by thy Shrowd
I'll pull thee backward, squeeze thee to a Bladder,   10
'Till thou dost groan thy Nothingness away.°

                          [*Ghost retires.*

Thou fly'st! 'Tis well.
I thought what was the Courage of a Ghost!°
Yet, dare not, on thy Life—Why say I that,
Since Life thou hast not?—Dare not walk again,
Within these Walls, on pain of the *Red-Sea.*°
For, if henceforth I ever find thee here,
As sure, sure as a Gun, I'll have thee laid—

7. already dead: [Fielding's note] *The Man who writ this
wretched Pun* (says Mr. *D*[ennis].) *would have picked your
Pocket:* Which he proceeds to shew, not only bad in it self,
but doubly so on so solemn an Occasion. And yet in that
excellent Play of *Liberty Asserted,* we find something very
much resembling a Pun in the Mouth of a Mistress, who is
parting with the Lover she is fond of;

> Ul.   *Oh, mortal Woe! one Kiss, and then farewel.*
> Irene.   *The Gods have given to others to farewel.*
> *O miserably must Irene fare.*

Agamemnon, in the *Victim,* is full as facetious on the most
solemn Occasion, that of Sacrificing his Daughter;

> *Yes, Daughter, yes; you will assist the Priest;*
> *Yes, you must offer up your—Vows for Greece.*

9–11. yet . . . away: [Fielding's note]

> *I'll pull thee backwards by thy Shrowd to Light,*
> *Or else, I'll squeeze thee, like a Bladder, there,*
> *And make thee groan thy self away to Air.*
>   Conquest of Granada.
> *Snatch me, ye Gods, this Moment into Nothing.*
>   Cyrus the Great.

13. I . . . Ghost: [Fielding's note]

> *So, art thou gone? Thou canst no Conquest boast,*
> *I thought what was the Courage of a Ghost.*
>   Conquest of *Granada.*

King *Arthur* seems to be as brave a Fellow as *Almanzor,* who
says most heroically,

>   —*In spight of Ghosts, I'll on.*

16. on . . . Red-Sea: a current superstition held that ghosts
liked least of all to be "laid" in the Red Sea. **33. I . . . me:**
[Fielding's note] The Ghost of *Lausaria* in *Cyrus* is a plain
Copy of this, and is therefore worth reading.

> *Ah,* Cyrus!
> *Thou may'st as well grasp Water, or fleet Air,*
> *As think of touching my immortal Shade.*
>   Cyrus the Great.

   Ghost. Were the *Red-Sea,* a Sea of *Holland*'s
     Gin,
The Liquor (when alive) whose very Smell   20
I did detest, did loath—yet for the Sake
Of *Thomas Thumb,* I would be laid therein.

   King. Ha! said you?

   Ghost.   Yes, my Liege, I said *Tom Thumb,*
Whose Father's Ghost I am—once not unknown
To mighty *Arthur.* But, I see, 'tis true,
The dearest Friend, when dead, we all forget.

   King. 'Tis he, it is the honest Gaffer *Thumb.*
Oh! let me press thee in my eager Arms,
Thou best of Ghosts! Thou something more than
     Ghost!

   Ghost. Would I were Something more, that we
     again   30
Might feel each other in the warm Embrace.
But now I have th' Advantage of my King,
For I feel thee, whilst thou dost not feel me.°

   King. But say, thou dearest Air,° Oh! say, what
     Dread,
Important Business sends thee back to Earth?

   Ghost. Oh! then prepare to hear—which, but to
     hear,
Is full enough to send thy Spirit hence.
Thy Subjects up in Arms, by *Grizzle* led,
Will, ere the rosy finger'd Morn shall ope
The Shutters of the Sky, before the Gate   40
Of this thy Royal Palace, swarming spread:
So have I seen the Bees in Clusters swarm,
So have I seen the Stars in frosty Nights,
So have I seen the Sand in windy Days,
So have I seen the Ghosts on *Pluto*'s Shore,
So have I seen the Flowers in Spring arise,
So have I seen the Leaves in *Autumn* fall,
So have I seen the Fruits in Summer smile,
So have I seen the Snow in Winter frown.°

   King. D——n all thou'st seen!—Dost thou,
     beneath the Shape   50
Of Gaffer *Thumb,* come hither to abuse me,
With Similes to keep me on the Rack?
Hence—or by all the Torments of thy Hell,

34. thou . . . Air: [Fielding's note]

> *Thou better Part of heavenly Air.*
>   Conquest of *Granada.*

42–49. So . . . frown: [Fielding's note] *A String of Similies*
(says one) *proper to be hung up in the Cabinet of a Prince.*

I'll run thee thro' the Body, tho' thou'st none.°

Ghost.   *Arthur*, beware; I must this Moment hence,
Not frighted by your Voice, but by the Cocks;
Arthur beware, beware, beware, beware!
Strive to avert thy yet impending Fate;
For if thou'rt kill'd To-day,
To-morrow all thy Care will come too late.   60

SCENE III.

King *solus*.

King.   Oh! stay, and leave me not uncertain thus!
And whilst thou tellest me what's like my Fate,
Oh, teach me how I may avert it too!
Curst be the Man who first a Simile made!
Curst, ev'ry Bard who writes!—So have I seen
Those whose Comparisons are just and true,
And those who liken things not like at all.
The Devil is happy, that the whole Creation
Can furnish out no Simile to his Fortune.

SCENE IV.

King, Queen.

Queen.   What is the Cause, my *Arthur*, that you
      steal
Thus silently from *Dollallolla*'s Breast?
Why dost thou leave me in the Dark alone,
When well thou know'st I am afraid of Sprites?°
King.   Oh *Dollallolla*! do not blame my Love;
I hop'd the Fumes of last Night's Punch had laid
Thy lovely Eye-lids fast.—But, Oh! I find
There is no Power in Drams, to quiet Wives;
Each Morn, as the returning Sun, they wake,
And shine upon their Husbands.
Queen.   Think, Oh think!   10

What a Surprize it must be to the Sun,
Rising, to find the vanish'd World away.
What less can be the wretched Wife's Surprize,
When, stretching out her Arms to fold thee fast,
She folds her useless Bolster in her Arms.
Think, think on that—Oh! think, think well on
      that.°
I do remember also to have read
In *Dryden's Ovid's Metamorphosis*,°
That *Jove* in Form inanimate did lie
With beauteous *Danae*; and trust me, Love,   20
I fear'd the Bolster might have been a *Jove*.°
King.   Come to my Arms, most virtuous of thy
      Sex;
Oh *Dollallolla*! were all Wives like thee,
So many Husbands never had worn Horns.
Should *Huncamunca* of thy Worth partake,
Tom Thumb indeed were blest.—Oh fatal Name!
For didst thou know one Quarter what I know,
Then would'st thou know—Alas! what thou would'st
      know!
Queen.   What can I gather hence? Why dost thou
      speak
Like Men who carry *Raree-Shows* about,   30
Now you shall see, Gentlemen, what you shall see?
O tell me more, or thou hast told too much.

SCENE V.

King, Queen, Noodle.

Noodle.   Long Life attend your Majesties serene,
Great *Arthur*, King, and *Dollallolla*, Queen!
Lord *Grizzle*, with a bold, rebellious Crowd,
Advances to the Palace, threat'ning loud,
Unless the Princess be deliver'd straight,
And the victorious *Thumb*, without his Pate,
They are resolv'd to batter down the Gate.

---

54. I'll . . . none: [Fielding's note] This Passage hath been understood several different Ways by the Commentators. For my Part, I find it difficult to understand it at all. Mr. *Dryden* says,

> *I have heard something how two Bodies meet,*
> *But how two Souls join, I know not.*
>   [*King Arthur*]

So that 'till the Body of a Spirit be better understood, it will be difficult to understand how it is possible to run him through it. *Act III, scene iv.* **3–4. Why . . . Sprites:** [Fielding's note] Cydaria is of the same fearful Temper with *Dollallolla;*

> *I never durst in Darkness be alone.*
>   [Dryden's] Ind[ian]. Emp[eror].

16. Think . . . that: [Fielding's note]

> *Think well of this, think that, think every way.*
>   Sophonisba.

18. Dryden's . . . Metamorphosis: [Fielding's note] These Quotations are more usual in the Comick, than in the Tragick Writers. **21. I . . . Jove:** [Fielding's note] *This Distress* (says Mr. D——) *I must allow to be extremely beautiful, and tends to heighten the virtuous Character of* Dollallolla, *who is so exceeding delicate, that she is in the highest Apprehension from the inanimate Embrace of a Bolster. An Example worthy of Imitation from all our Writers of Tragedy.*

SCENE VI.

King, Queen, Huncamunca, Noodle.

King. See where the Princess comes! Where is
Tom Thumb?

Hunc. Oh! Sir, about an Hour and half ago
He sallied out to encounter with the Foe,
And swore, unless his Fate had him mis-led,
From *Grizzle*'s Shoulders to cut off his Head, ⎫
And serve 't up with your Chocolate in Bed.   ⎭

King. 'Tis well, I find one Devil told us both.
Come *Dollallolla, Huncamunca,* come,
Within we'll wait for the victorious *Thumb;*
In Peace and Safety we secure may stay,   10
While to his Arm we trust the bloody Fray;
Tho' Men and Giants should conspire with Gods,
He is alone equal to all these Odds.°

Queen. He is indeed, a Helmet to us all,
While he supports, we need not fear to fall;°
His Arm dispatches all things to our Wish,
And serves up every Foe's Head in a Dish.

Act III, scene vi. 13. He . . . Odds:

> *Credat Judæus Appelles*
> *Non ego*
> ["Apella the Jew may believe it,
> but I don't" (Horace, *Satires*, I. v. 100–101).]

—(says Mr. *D.*)—*For, passing over the Absurdity of being equal
to Odds, can we possibly suppose a little insignificant Fellow—I
say again, a little insignificant Fellow able to vie with a Strength
which all the Sampsons and Hercules's of Antiquity would be
unable to encounter.*

I shall refer this incredulous Critick to Mr. *Dryden's*
Defence of his *Almanzor* [as set forth in *Of Heroic Plays*]; and
lest that should not satisfy him, I shall quote a few Lines from
the Speech of a much braver Fellow than *Almanzor,* Mr.
[Charles] *Johnson's Achilles;*

> *Tho' Human Race rise in embattel'd Hosts,*
> *To force her from my Arms—Oh! Son of* Atreus!
> *By that immortal Pow'r, whose deathless Spirit*
> *Informs this Earth, I will oppose them all.*
> > Victim.

14–15. He . . . fall: [Fielding's note] *I have heard of being
supported by a Staff (says Mr. D.) but never of being supported
by an Helmet. I believe he never heard of Sailing with Wings,
which he may read in no less a Poet than Mr. Dryden;*

> *Unless we borrow Wings, and sail thro' Air.*
> > Love Triumphant.

What will he say to a kneeling Valley?

> ———*I'll stand*
> *Like a safe Valley, that low bends the Knee,*
> *To some aspiring Mountain.*
> > Injur'd Love.

Void is the Mistress of the House of Care,
While the good Cook presents the Bill of Fare;
Whether the Cod, that Northern King of Fish, 20
Or Duck, or Goose, or Pig, adorn the Dish;
No Fears the Number of her Guests afford,
But at her Hour she sees the Dinner on the Board.

SCENE VII. *a Plain.*

Lord Grizzle, Foodle, *and* Rebels.

Grizzle. Thus far our Arms with Victory are
crown'd;
For tho' we have not fought, yet we have found
No Enemy to fight withal.°

Foodle.   Yet I,
Methinks, would willingly avoid this Day,
The First of *April,* to engage our Foes.°

Griz. This Day, of all the Days of th' Year, I'd
choose,
For on this Day my Grandmother was born.
Gods! I will make *Tom Thumb* an *April* Fool;
Will teach his Wit an Errand it ne'er knew,
And sent it Post to the *Elysian* Shades.°   10

Food. I'm glad to find our Army is so stout,
Nor does it move my Wonder less than Joy.

Griz. What Friends we have, and how we came
so strong,
I'll softly tell you as we march along.°

I am asham'd of so ignorant a Carper, who doth not know
that an Epithet in Tragedy is very often no other than an
Expletive. Do not we read in the New *Sophonisba* of *grinding
Chains, blue Plagues, white Occasions,* and *blue Serenity?* Nay,
'tis not the Adjective only, but sometimes half a Sentence is
put by way of Expletive, as *Beauty pointed high with Spirit,*
in the same Play—and, *In the Lap of Blessing, to be most curst.*
In the *Revenge. Act III, scene vii.* **3. No . . . withal:**
[Fielding's note] *A Victory like that of Almanzor.*

> Almanzor *is victorious without Fight.*
> > Conq. of Granada.

4–5. avoid . . . Foes: [Fielding's note]

> *Well have we chose an happy Day for Fight,*
> *For every Man in course of Time has found,*
> *Some Days are lucky, some unfortunate.*
> > K. Arthur.

9–10. teach . . . Shades: [Fielding's note] We read of such
another in *Lee;*

> *Teach his rude Wit a Flight she never made,*
> *And send her Post to the Elysian Shade.*
> > Gloriana.

13–14. What . . . along: [Fielding's note] These Lines are
copied *verbatim* in the *Indian Emperor.*

SCENE VIII.

Thunder and Lightning.

Tom Thumb, Glumdalca *cum suis.*°

Thumb. Oh, *Noodle!* hast thou seen a Day like
    this?
The unborn Thunder rumbles o'er our Heads,°
As if the Gods meant to unhinge the World;
And Heaven and Earth in wild Confusion hurl;
Yet will I boldly tread the tott'ring Ball.°
Merl. Tom Thumb!
Thumb.   What Voice is this I hear?
Merl.   Tom Thumb!
Thumb. Again it calls.
Merl.   Tom Thumb!
Glum.   It calls again.
Thumb. Appear, whoe'er thou art, I fear thee not.
Merl. Thou hast no Cause to fear, I am thy
    Friend,
Merlin by Name, a Conjuror by Trade,   10
And to my Art thou dost thy Being owe.
Thumb. How!
Merl. Hear then the mystick Getting of *Tom
Thumb.*

    His Father was a Ploughman plain,
      His Mother milk'd the Cow;
    And yet the Way to get a Son,
      This Couple knew not how.
    Until such time the good old Man
      To learned Merlin goes,
    And there to him, in great Distress,   20
      In secret manner shows;
    How in his Heart he wish'd to have
      A Child, in time to come,
    To be his Heir, tho' it might be
      No bigger than his Thumb:

Act III, *scene viii.* **cum suis:** with their attendants. **2. The
unborn . . . Heads:** [Fielding's note]

    Unborn Thunder rolling in a Cloud.
                Conq. of *Gran.*

3–5. As . . . Ball: [Fielding's note]

Were Heaven and Earth in wild Confusion hurl'd,
Should the rash Gods unhinge the rolling World,
Undaunted, would I tread the tott'ring Ball,
Crush'd, but unconquer'd, in the dreadful Fall.
      [Charles Hopkins's] *Female Warrior.*

    Of which old Merlin *was foretold,*
      That he his Wish should have;
    And so a Son of Stature small,
      The Charmer to him gave.°

Thou'st heard the past, look up and see the future.   30
    Thumb. Lost in Amazement's Gulph, my Senses
    sink;°
See there, *Glumdalca,* see another Me°!
    Glum. O Sight of Horror! see, you are devour'd
By the expanded Jaws of a red Cow.
    Merl. Let not these Sights deter thy noble Mind,
For lo! a Sight more glorious courts thy Eyes;
See from a far a Theatre arise;
There, Ages yet unborn, shall Tribute pay
To the Heroick Actions of this Day:
Then Buskin° Tragedy at length shall choose   40
Thy Name the best Supporter of her Muse.°
    Thumb. Enough, let every warlike Musick sound,
We fall contented, if we fall renown'd.

SCENE IX.

Lord Grizzle, Foodle, *Rebels, on one Side.*
  Tom Thumb, Glumdalca, *on the other.*

Food. At length the Enemy advances nigh,
I hear them with my Ear, and see them with my Eye.°

14–29. His . . . gave: [Fielding's note] See the History of
Tom Thumb, pag. 2. **31. Lost . . . sink:** [Fielding's note]

    —*Amazement swallows up my Sense,*
    And in th' impetuous Whirl of circling Fate,
    Drinks down my Reason.
                    Pers. Princess.

32. another Me: [Fielding's note]

    ————*I have outfaced my self,*
    What! am I two? Is there another Me?
                    K. Arthur.

40. Buskin: tragic; the buskin was an elevated boot worn
by an ancient tragic actor to increase his stature. **41. Thy . . .
Muse:** [Fielding's note] The Character of *Merlin* is wonderful
throughout, but most so in this Prophetick Part. We find
several of these Prophecies in the Tragick Authors, who
frequently take this Opportunity to pay a Compliment to
their Country, and sometimes to their Prince. None but our
Author (who seems to have detested the least Appearance of
Flattery) would have past by such an Opportunity of being a
Political Prophet. Act III, *scene ix.* **2. see . . . Eye:** [Fielding's
note]

    I saw the Villain, Myron, *with these Eyes I saw him.*
                    Busiris.

In both which Places it is intimated, that it is sometimes
possible to see with other Eyes than your own.

Griz.   Draw all your Swords, for Liberty we fight,
And Liberty the Mustard is of Life.°

Thumb.   Are you the Man whom Men fam'd
Grizzle name?

Griz.   Are you the much more fam'd *Tom Thumb?*°

Thumb.   The same.

Griz.   Come on, our Worth upon our selves we'll
prove,
For Liberty I fight.

Thumb.   And I for Love.

[*A bloody Engagement between the two Armies
here, Drums beating, Trumpets sounding,
Thunder and Lightning.—They fight off and
on several times. Some fall. Grizzle and
Glumdalca remain.*

Glum.   Turn, Coward, turn, nor from a Woman fly.

Griz.   Away—thou art too ignoble for my Arm.

Glum.   Have at thy Heart.

Griz.   Nay then, I thrust at thine.   11

Glum.   You push too well, you've run me thro'
the Guts,
And I am dead.

Griz.   Then there's an End of One.

Thumb.   When thou art dead, then there's an End
of Two,
Villain.

Griz.   Tom Thumb!

Thumb.   Rebel!

Griz.   Tom Thumb!

Thumb.   Hell!

Griz.   Huncamunca!°

4. Liberty . . . Life: [Fielding's note] *This Mustard (says
Mr. D.) is enough to turn one's Stomach: I would be glad to
know what Idea the Author had in his Head when he wrote it.
This will be, I believe, best explained by a Line of Mr.
Dennis;*

> *And gave him Liberty, the Salt of Life.*
>   Liberty Asserted.

The Understanding that can digest the one, will not rise at the
other. **5–6. Are . . . Thumb:** [Fielding's note]

> *Han.   Are you the Chief, whom Men fam'd Scipio call?*
> *Scip.   Are you the much more famous Hannibal?*
>   Hannib.

15. Villain . . . Huncamunca: [Fielding's note] Dr. *Young*
seems to have copied this Engagement in his *Busiris*:

> *Myr.   Villain!*
> *Mem.   Myron!*
> *Myr.   Rebel!*
> *Mem.   Myron!*
> *Myr.   Hell!*
> *Mem.   Mandane.*

Thumb.   Thou hast it there.

Griz.   Too sure I feel it.

Thumb.   To Hell then, like a Rebel as you are,
And give my Service to the Rebels there.

Griz.   Triumph not, *Thumb*, nor think thou shalt
enjoy
Thy *Huncamunca* undisturb'd, I'll send   20
My Ghost to fetch her to the other World;°
It shall but bait at Heaven, and then return.°
But, ha! I feel Death rumbling in my Brains,°
Some kinder Spright knocks softly at my Soul,
And gently whispers it to haste away:°
I come, I come, most willingly I come.
So; when some City Wife, for Country Air,
To *Hampstead*, or to *Highgate* does repair;
Her, to make haste, her Husband does implore,
And cries, My Dear, *the Coach is at the Door.*   30
With equal Wish, desirous to be gone,
She gets into the Coach, and then she cries—*Drive on!*°

Thumb.   With those last Words he vomited his
Soul,°

20–21. I'll . . . World: [Fielding's note] This last Speech of
my Lord *Grizzle*, hath been of great Service to our Poets;

> *—I'll hold it fast*
> *As Life, and when Life's gone, I'll hold this last;*
> *And if thou tak'st it from me when I'm slain,*
> *I'll send my Ghost, and fetch it back again.*
>   Conquest of *Granada.*

22. It . . . return: [Fielding's note]

> *My Soul should with such Speed obey,*
> *It should not bait at Heaven to stop its way.*
>   [*Conquest of Granada*]

Lee seems to have had this last in his Eye;

> *'Twas not my Purpose, Sir, to tarry there,*
> *I would but go to Heaven to take the Air.*
>   Gloriana.

23. Death . . . Brains: [Fielding's note]

> *A rising Vapour rumbling in my Brains.*
>   Cleomenes.

24–25. Some . . . away: [Fielding's note]

> *Some kind Spright knocks softly at my Soul,*
> *To tell me Fate's at Hand.*
>
>   [*Don Sebastian*]

27–32. So . . . on: [Fielding's note] Mr. *Dryden* seems to
have had this Simile in his Eye, when he says,

> *My Soul is packing up, and just on Wing.*
>   Conquest of *Granada.*

33. he . . . Soul: [Fielding's note]

> *And in a purple Vomit pour'd his Soul.*
>   Cleomenes.

Which, like whipt Cream, the Devil will swallow
  down.°
Bear off the Body, and cut off the Head,
Which I will to the King in Triumph lug;
Rebellion's dead, and now I'll go to Breakfast.

SCENE X.

King, Queen, Huncamunca, and Courtiers.

King.   Open the Prisons, set the Wretched free,
And bid our Treasurer disburse six Pounds
To pay their Debts.—Let no one weep To-day.
Come, *Dollallolla;* Curse that odious Name!
It is so long, it asks an Hour to speak it.
By Heavens! I'll change it into *Doll,* or *Loll,*
Or any other civil Monosyllable
That will not tire my Tongue.°—Come, sit thee down,
Here seated, let us view the Dancer's Sports;
Bid 'em advance. This is the Wedding-Day   10
Of Princess *Huncamunca* and *Tom Thumb;*
Tom Thumb! who wins two Victories To-day,°
And this way marches, bearing *Grizzle's* Head.

A Dance here.

Nood.   Oh! monstrous, dreadful, terrible, Oh! Oh!
Deaf be my Ears, for ever blind, my Eyes!
Dumb be my Tongue! Feet lame! All Senses lost!

---

34. like . . . down: [Fielding's note]

> *The Devil swallows vulgar Souls*
> *Like whipp'd Cream.*
>   Sebastian.

Act III, scene x. **6–8. I'll . . . Tongue:** [Fielding's note]

> *How I could curse my Name of* Ptolemy!
> *It is so long, it asks an Hour to write it.*
> *By Heav'n! I'll change it into* Jove, *or* Mars,
> *Or any other civil Monosyllable,*
> *That will not tire my Hand.*
>   Cleomenes.

12. two . . . To-day: [Fielding's note] Here is a visible
Conjunction of two Days in one, by which our Author may
have either intended an Emblem of a Wedding; or to insinuate, that Men in the Honey-Moon are apt to imagine
Time shorter than it is. It brings into my Mind a Passage in
the Comedy [by Henry Fielding (1730)] call'd the *Coffee-
House Politician;*

> *We will celebrate this Day at my House To-morrow.*

Howl Wolves, grunt Bears, hiss Snakes, shriek all ye
  Ghosts!°
  King.   What does the Blockhead mean?
  Nood.   I mean, my Liege
Only to grace my Tale with decent Horror;°
Whilst from my Garret, twice two Stories high,   20
I look'd abroad into the Streets below;
I saw *Tom Thumb* attended by the Mob,
Twice Twenty Shoe-Boys, twice two Dozen
  Links,°
Chairmen and Porters, Hackney-Coachmen,
  Whores;
Aloft he bore the grizly Head of *Grizzle;*
When of a sudden thro' the Streets there came
A Cow, of larger than the usual Size,
And in a Moment—guess, Oh! guess the rest!
And in a Moment swallow'd up *Tom Thumb.*
  King.   Shut up again the Prisons, bid my
  Treasurer   30
Not give three Farthings out—hang all the *Culprits,*
Guilty or not—no matter—Ravish Virgins,
Go bid the Schoolmasters whip all their Boys;
Let Lawyers, Parsons, and Physicians loose,
To rob, impose on, and to kill the World.
  Nood.   Her Majesty the Queen is in a Swoon.
  Queen.   Not so much in a Swoon, but I have still
Strength to reward the Messenger of ill News.
                        [*Kills* Noodle.

  Nood.   Oh! I am slain.
  Cle.   My Lover's kill'd, I will revenge him so. 40
                      [*Kills the* Queen.
  Hunc.   My Mamma kill'd! vile Murtheress,
  beware.   [*Kills* Cleora.
  Dood.   This for an old Grudge, to thy Heart.
                    [*Kills Huncamunca.*
  Must.   And this
I drive to thine, Oh *Doodle!* for a new one.
                      [*Kills* Doodle.

14–17. Oh . . . Ghosts: [Fielding's note] These beautiful
Phrases are all to be found in one single Speech of *King
Arthur,* or *The British Worthy.* **19. grace . . . Horror:**

> *I was but teaching him to grace his Tale*
> *With decent Horror.*
>   Cleomenes.

23. Links: link-boys, hired by pedestrians to light the way
with torches.

King.   Ha! Murtheress vile, take that   [*Kills* Must.
                                   And take thou this.
                          [*Kills himself, and falls.*°
So when the Child whom Nurse from Danger
     guards,
Sends *Jack* for Mustard° with a Pack of Cards;
Kings, Queens and Knaves throw one another
     down,
'Till the whole Pack lies scatter'd and o'erthrown;
So all our Pack upon the Floor is cast,
And all I boast is—that I fall the last.   50
                                               [*Dies.*

---

44. Kills . . . falls: [Fielding's note] We may say with *Dryden,*

> *Death did at length so many Slain forget,*
> *And left the Tale* [count]*, and took them by the Great.*
>   [*Conquest of Granada*]

I know of no Tragedy which comes nearer to this charming and bloody Catastrophe, than *Cleomenes,* where the Curtain covers five principal Characters dead on the Stage. These Lines too,

> *I ask no Questions then, of Who kill'd Who?*
> *The Bodies tell the Story as they lie.*

seem to have belonged more properly to this Scene of our Author.—Nor can I help imagining they were originally his. [Dryden's] The Rival Ladies too seem beholden to this Scene;

> *We're now a Chain of Lovers link'd in Death,*
> Julia *goes first,* Gonsalvo *hangs on her,*
> *And* Angelina *hangs upon* Gonsalvo,
> *As I on* Angelina.

No Scene, I believe, ever received greater Honours than this. It was applauded by several *Encores,* a Word very unusual in Tragedy—And it was very difficult for the Actors to escape without a second Slaughter. This I take to be a lively Assurance of that fierce Spirit of Liberty which remains among us, and which Mr. *Dryden* in his *Essay on Dramatick Poetry* hath observed—*Whether Custom* (says he) *hath so insinuated it self into our Countrymen, or Nature hath so formed them to Fierceness, I know not, but they will scarcely suffer Combats, and other Objects of Horror, to be taken from them.*—And indeed I am for having them encouraged in this Martial Disposition: Nor do I believe our Victories over the *French* have been owing to any thing more than to those bloody Spectacles daily exhibited in our Tragedies, of which the *French* Stage is so entirely clear. **46. Sends . . . Mustard:** To "send Jack for mustard" was to throw a deck of cards into the air and then pick them all up again.

PREFACE
TO . . . *JOSEPH ANDREWS* . . .

𝕬𝕸𝕬

Fielding began his novel *Joseph Andrews* (published anonymously in 1742) as a spicy burlesque of Samuel Richardson's *Pamela, or Virtue Rewarded* (1740). He maintained the parody only until the eleventh chapter, where Pamela's "brother" Joseph, footman to the lustful Lady Booby, against whose addresses he has stoutly defended his virtue, sets off—like an idealized Sancho Panza—on a farcical turnpike odyssey with the quixotic Abraham Adams, a benign, absent-minded, poverty-stricken country curate. At this point Fielding largely forgoes parody and pursues instead the methods of the picaresque romance, as his subtitle promises. Mock-heroic, sardonic, and comical episodes follow digressively until Joseph's genteel background finally comes to light, and he marries his rural fiancée, the buxom Fanny Goodwill.

Persuaded that the English comic novel was, as he reiterated in *Tom Jones* (1749), "a new province of writing," Fielding took pains in the Preface to *Joseph Andrews* to provide the genre with an ancient sanction. His conception of the "comic Epic-Poem in Prose" seems indebted not only to the practice of Cervantes but also to that of the French burlesque writer Paul Scarron, with whose *Roman comique* (1651–57) Fielding was familiar.

The text (originally set in italics) is that of the first edition, *The History of the Adventures of Joseph Andrews, and of His Friend, Mr. Abraham Adams. Written in Imitation of the Manner of Cervantes, Author of Don Quixote* (2 vols., 1742); we have incorporated the substantive variants of the second edition (1742).

𝕬𝕸𝕬

AS it is possible the mere *English* Reader may have a different Idea of Romance with the Author of these little Volumes; and may consequently expect a kind of Entertainment, not to be found, nor which was even intended, in the following Pages; it may not be improper to premise a few Words concerning this kind of Writing, which I do not remember to have seen hitherto attempted in our Language.

The EPIC, as well as the DRAMA, is divided into Tragedy and Comedy. *Homer,* who was the Father of this Species of Poetry, gave us a Pattern of both these, tho' that of the latter kind[1] is entirely lost; which *Aristotle* tells us,[2] bore the same Relation to Comedy which his *Iliad* bears to Tragedy. And perhaps, that we have no more Instances of it among the Writers of Antiquity, is owing to the Loss of this great Pattern, which, had it survived, would have found its Imitators equally with the other Poems of this great Original.

And farther, as this Poetry may be Tragic or Comic, I will not scruple to say it may be likewise either in Verse or Prose: for tho' it wants one particular, which the Critic enumerates in the constituent Parts of an Epic Poem, namely Metre; yet, when any kind of Writing contains all its other Parts, such as Fable, Action, Characters, Sentiments, and Diction, and is deficient in Metre only; it seems, I think, reasonable to refer it to the Epic; at least, as no Critic hath thought proper to range it under any other Head, nor to assign it a particular Name to itself.

Thus the *Telemachus* of the Archbishop of *Cambray*[3] appears to me of the Epic Kind, as well as the *Odyssey* of *Homer;* indeed, it is much fairer and more reasonable to give it a Name common with that Species from which it differs only in a single Instance, than to confound it with those which it resembles in no other. Such are those voluminous Works commonly called *Romances*, namely, *Clelia, Cleopatra, Astræa, Cassandra*, the *Grand Cyrus*,[4] and innumerable others which contain, as I apprehend, very little Instruction or Entertainment.

Now a comic Romance is a comic Epic-Poem in Prose; differing from Comedy, as the serious Epic from Tragedy: its Action being more extended and comprehensive; containing a much larger Circle of Incidents, and introducing a greater Variety of Characters. It differs from the serious Romance in its Fable and Action, in this; that as in the one these are grave and solemn, so in the other they are light and ridiculous: it differs in its Characters, by introducing Persons of inferiour Rank, and consequently of inferiour Manners, whereas the grave Romance, sets the highest before us; lastly in its Sentiments and Diction; by preserving the Ludicrous instead of the Sublime. In the Diction I think, Burlesque itself may be sometimes admitted; of which many Instances will occur in this Work, as in the Description of the Battles,[5] and some other Places, not necessary to be pointed out to the Classical Reader; for whose Entertainment those Parodies or Burlesque Imitations are chiefly calculated.

But tho' we have sometimes admitted this in our Diction, we have carefully excluded it from our Sentiments and Characters: for there it is never properly introduced, unless in Writings of the Burlesque kind, which this is not intended to be. Indeed, no two Species of Writing can differ more widely than the Comic and the Burlesque: for as the latter is ever the Exhibition of what is monstrous and unnatural, and where our Delight, if we examine it, arises from the surprizing Absurdity, as in appropriating the Manners of the highest to the lowest, or *è converso;*[6] so in the former, we should ever confine ourselves strictly to Nature from the just Imitation of which, will flow all the Pleasure we can this way convey to a sensible Reader. And perhaps, there is one Reason, why a Comic Writer should of all others be the least excused for deviating from Nature, since it may not be always so easy for a serious Poet to meet with the Great and the Admirable; but Life every where furnishes an accurate Observer with the Ridiculous.

I have hinted this little, concerning Burlesque; because, I have often heard that Name given to Performances, which have been truly of the Comic kind, from the Author's having sometimes admitted it in his Diction only; which as it is the Dress of Poetry, doth like the Dress of Men establish Characters, (the one of the whole Poem, and the other of the whole Man,) in vulgar Opinion, beyond any of their greater Excellencies: But surely, a certain Drollery in Style, where the Characters and Sentiments are perfectly natural, no more constitutes the Burlesque, than an empty Pomp and Dignity of Words, where every thing else is mean and low, can entitle any Performance to the Appellation of the true Sublime.

PREFACE TO *Joseph Andrews*. **1. that . . . kind:** the *Margites*, a lost ancient poem; it is referred to as a satirical epic with a fool (*margos*) for a hero. It is doubtful that Homer had anything to do with it. **2. tells us:** in *Poetics*, iv. 9. **3. Archbishop of Cambray:** Fénelon (1651–1715), French theologian and writer, author of *Télémaque* (1699), a didactic romance in prose. **4. Clelia . . . Grand Cyrus:** popular seventeenth-century French prose romances, heroic and pastoral.

5. the Description . . . Battles: e.g., in Book III, Ch. ix, where a brawl at an inn is described in epic terms. **6. è converso:** vice versa.

And I apprehend, my Lord *Shaftesbury's* Opinion of mere Burlesque agrees with mine, when he asserts,[7] "There is no such Thing to be found in the Writings of the Antients." But perhaps, I have less Abhorrence than he professes for it: and that not because I have had some little Success on the Stage this way; but rather, as it contributes more to exquisite Mirth and Laughter than any other; and these are probably more wholesome Physic for the Mind, and conduce better to purge away Spleen, Melancholy and ill Affections, than is generally imagined. Nay, I will appeal to common Observation, whether the same Companies are not found more full of Good-Humour and Benevolence, after they have been sweeten'd for two or three Hours with Entertainments of this kind, than when soured by a Tragedy or a grave Lecture.

But to illustrate all this by another Science, in which, perhaps, we shall see the Distinction more clearly and plainly: Let us examine the Works of a Comic History-Painter, with those Performances which the *Italians* call *Caricatura;* where we shall find the true Excellence of the former, to consist in the exactest copying of Nature; insomuch, that a judicious Eye instantly rejects any thing *outré;*[8] any Liberty which the Painter hath taken with the Features of that *Alma Mater.*[9]—Whereas in the *Caricatura* we allow all Licence. Its Aim is to exhibit Monsters, not Men; and all Distortions and Exaggerations whatever are within its proper Province.

Now what *Caricatura* is in Painting, Burlesque is in Writing; and in the same manner the Comic Writer and Painter correlate to each other. And here I shall observe, that as in the former, the Painter seems to have the Advantage; so it is in the latter infinitely on the side of the Writer: for the *Monstrous* is much easier to paint than describe, and the *ridiculous* to describe than paint.

And tho' perhaps this latter Species doth not in either Science so strongly affect and agitate the Muscles as the other; yet it will be owned, I believe, that a more rational and useful Pleasure arises to us

from it. He who should call the Ingenious *Hogarth*[10] a Burlesque Painter, would, in my Opinion, do him very little Honour: for sure it is much easier, much less the Subject of Admiration, to paint a Man with a Nose, or an other Feature of a preposterous Size, or to expose him in some absurd or monstrous Attitude, than to express the Affections of Men on Canvas. It hath been thought a vast Commendation of a Painter, to say his Figures *seem to breathe;* but surely, it is a much greater and nobler Applause, *that they appear to think.*

But to return—The Ridiculous only, as I have before said, falls within my Province in the present Work.— Nor will some Explanation of this Word be thought impertinent by the Reader, if he considers how wonderfully it hath been mistaken, even by Writers who have profess'd it: for to what but such a Mistake, can we attribute the many Attempts to ridicule the blackest Villanies; and what is yet worse, the most dreadful Calamities? What could exceed the Absurdity of an Author, who should write *the Comedy of Nero, with the merry Incident of ripping up his Mother's Belly;*[11] or what would give a greater Shock to Humanity, than an Attempt to expose the Miseries of Poverty and Distress to Ridicule? And yet, the Reader will not want much Learning to suggest such Instances to himself.

Besides, it may seem remarkable, that *Aristotle,* who is so fond and free of Definitions, hath not thought proper to define the Ridiculous. Indeed, where he tells us it is proper to Comedy, he hath remarked that Villany is not its Object: but he hath not, as I remember, positively asserted what is. Nor doth the *Abbé Bellegarde,* who hath writ a Treatise[12] on this Subject, tho' he shews us many Species of it, once trace it to its Fountain.

The only Source of the true Ridiculous (as it

---

7. **when he asserts:** in *Sensus Communis: An Essay on the Freedom of Wit and Humour* (1709), by Anthony Ashley Cooper (1671–1713), Third Earl of Shaftesbury. (See the selection from Shaftesbury earlier in Part Two.) **8. outré:** exaggerated. **9. Alma Mater:** fostering mother, i.e., Nature.

10. **the Ingenious Hogarth:** the painter, draftsman, and engraver William Hogarth (1697–1764) was well known for his painted and engraved series *A Harlot's Progress* (1731–32) and *A Rake's Progress* (1735). A friend of Fielding's, he not only provided a comic frontispiece for *The Tragedy of Tragedies* (1731) but also produced in 1743 an engraving of over one hundred faces illustrating the difference between Characters and *Caricaturas.* At the bottom of the plate he wrote: "*For a farthar Explanation of the Difference Betwixt* Character & Caricatura *See ỹ Preface to* Joᵇ *Andrews.*" **11. ripping . . . Belly:** The Emperor Nero (A.D. 37–68) had his mother, Agrippina, murdered because she criticized his behavior. **12. a Treatise:** *Réflexions sur le ridicule* (1723) by Jean-Baptiste Morvan de Bellegarde (1648–1734).

appears to me) is Affectation. But tho' it arises from one Spring only, when we consider the infinite Streams into which this one branches, we shall presently cease to admire at the copious Field it affords to an Observer. Now Affectation proceeds from one of these two Causes, Vanity, or Hypocrisy: for as Vanity puts us on affecting false Characters, in order to purchase Applause; so Hypocrisy sets us on an Endeavour to avoid Censure by concealing our Vices under an Appearance of their opposite Virtues. And tho' these two Causes are often confounded, (for there is some Difficulty in distinguishing them) yet, as they proceed from very different Motives, so they are as clearly distinct in their Operations: for indeed, the Affectation which arises from Vanity is nearer to Truth than the other; as it hath not that violent Repugnancy of Nature to struggle with, which that of the Hypocrite hath. It may be likewise noted, that Affectation doth not imply an absolute Negation of those Qualities which are affected: and therefore, tho', when it proceeds from Hypocrisy, it be nearly allied to Deceit; yet when it comes from Vanity only, it partakes of the Nature of Ostentation: for instance, the Affectation of Liberality in a vain Man, differs visibly from the same Affectation in the Avaricious; for tho' the vain Man is not what he would appear, or hath not the Virtue he affects, to the degree he would be thought to have it; yet it sits less awkwardly on him than on the avaricious Man, who is the very Reverse of what he would *seem* to be.

From the Discovery of this Affectation arises the Ridiculous—which always strikes the Reader with Surprize and Pleasure; and that in a higher and stronger Degree when the Affectation arises from Hypocrisy, than when from Vanity: for to discover any one to be the exact Reverse of what he affects, is more surprizing, and consequently more ridiculous, than to find him a little deficient in the Quality he desires the Reputation of. I might observe that our *Ben Johnson*, who of all Men understood the *Ridiculous* the best, hath chiefly used the hypocritical Affectation.[13]

Now from Affectation only, the Misfortunes and Calamities of Life, or the Imperfections of Nature, may become the Objects of Ridicule. Surely he hath a very ill-framed Mind, who can look on Ugliness, Infirmity, or Poverty, as ridiculous in themselves: nor do I believe any Man living who meets a dirty Fellow riding through the Streets in a Cart, is struck with an Idea of the Ridiculous from it; but if he should see the same Figure descend from his Coach and Six, or bolt from his Chair[14] with his Hat under his Arm, he would then begin to laugh, and with justice. In the same manner, were we to enter a poor House, and behold a wretched Family shivering with Cold and languishing with Hunger, it would not incline us to Laughter, (at least we must have very diabolical Natures, if it would:) but should we discover there a Grate, instead of Coals, adorned with Flowers, empty Plate or China Dishes on the Sideboard, or any other Affectation of Riches and Finery either on their Persons or in their Furniture; we might then indeed be excused, for ridiculing so fantastical an Appearance. Much less are natural Imperfections the Object of Derision: but when Ugliness aims at the Applause of Beauty, or Lameness endeavours to display Agility; it is then that these unfortunate Circumstances, which at first moved our Compassion, tend only to raise our Mirth.

The Poet carries this very far;

> *None are for being what they are in Fault,*
> *But for not being what they would be thought.*[15]

Where if the Metre would suffer the Word *Ridiculous* to close the first Line, the Thought would be rather more proper. Great Vices are the proper Objects of our Detestation, smaller Faults of our Pity: but Affectation appears to me the only true Source of the Ridiculous.

But perhaps it may be objected to me, that I have against my own Rules introduced Vices, and of a very black Kind into this Work. To which I shall answer: First, that it is very difficult to pursue a Series of human Actions and keep clear from them. Secondly, That the Vices to be found here, are rather the accidental Consequences of some human Frailty, or Foible, than Causes habitually existing in the Mind. Thirdly, That they are never set forth as the Objects of Ridicule but Detestation. Fourthly, That they are never the principal Figure at that Time on the Scene; and lastly, they never produce the intended Evil.

---

13. Ben . . . Affectation: In Fielding's day the satirical comedies of Ben Jonson (1572–1637), especially *Volpone, The Alchemist,* and *Every Man in His Humor,* were very popular. The plays teem with eccentrics and hypocrites.

14. chair: sedan chair. **15. None . . . thought:** *Of Pleasing* (ll. 63–64), by the playwright William Congreve (1670–1729).

Having thus distinguished *Joseph Andrews* from the Productions of Romance Writers on the one hand, and Burlesque Writers on the other, and given some few very short Hints (for I intended no more) of this Species of writing, which I have affirmed to be hitherto unattempted in our Language; I shall leave to my good-natur'd Reader to apply my Piece to my Observations, and will detain him no longer than with a Word concerning the Characters in this Work.

And here I solemnly protest, I have no Intention to vilify or asperse any one: for tho' every thing is copied from the Book of Nature, and scarce a Character or Action produced which I have not taken from my own Observations and Experience, yet I have used the utmost Care to obscure the Persons by such different Circumstances, Degrees, and Colours, that it will be impossible to guess at them with any degree of Certainty; and if it ever happens otherwise, it is only where the Failure characterized is so minute, that it is a Foible only which the Party himself may laugh at as well as any other.

As to the Character of *Adams*, as it is the most glaring in the whole, so I conceive it is not to be found in any Book now extant. It is designed a Character of perfect Simplicity; and as the Goodness of his Heart will recommend him to the Good-natur'd; so I hope it will excuse me to the Gentlemen of his Cloth; for whom, while they are worthy of their sacred Order, no Man can possibly have a greater Respect. They will therefore excuse me, notwithstanding the low Adventures in which he is engaged, that I have made him a Clergyman; since no other Office could have given him so many Opportunities of displaying his worthy Inclinations.

FROM

THE COVENT-GARDEN JOURNAL

In January, 1752, Fielding started *The Covent-Garden Journal*, a four-page newspaper which appeared initially twice a week and, after the first six months, weekly. He produced seventy-two numbers before abandoning it in November, 1752. Just as Addison had assumed the role of Mr. Spectator for his efforts at reform, so Fielding adopted the role of Sir Alexander Drawcansir, Knight, "Censor [i.e., overseer of conduct] of Great Britain." A typical issue contained an essay on a social or literary topic by Fielding or others (most of Fielding's are signed "A," for "Alexander"); a few columns of foreign and domestic news borrowed from other newspapers; a listing of current stock prices; and sections of legal notices, news from the police courts, and advertisements, mainly of books. In his essays on social topics Fielding's intent was avowedly reformist: largely through ridicule, he sought to amend the morals of contemporary Londoners, to expose the dangers of gin and gaming, dueling and prostitution, profanity, "gallantry," and freethinking, and especially to assail that crime of crimes, hypocrisy. His literary essays discuss the practice of criticism, the nature of taste, the state of the contemporary theater, the silly excesses of textual emendators, the question of the dramatic unities, and—a subject of which he never tired—the moral implications of the comic and the "humorous."

The text is that of the first edition (1752), as edited by G. E. Jensen (2 vols., 1915).

NUMB. 55

Saturday, July 18, 1752.

> —*Juvat integros accedere Fontes*
> *Atque haurire.*—
> LUCRETIUS.
> —*It is pleasant to handle*
> *An untouched Subject.*

IT hath been observed, that Characters of Humour do abound more in this our Island, than in any other Country; and this hath been commonly supposed to arise from that pure and perfect State of Liberty which we enjoy in a degree greatly superior to every foreign Nation.

This Opinion, I know, hath great Sanction, and yet I am inclined to suspect the Truth of it, unless we will extend the Meaning of the Word Liberty, farther than I think it hath been yet carried, and will include in it not only an Exemption from all Restraint of municipal Laws, but likewise from all Restraint of those Rules of Behaviour which are expressed in the general Term of good Breeding. Laws which, tho' not written, are perhaps better understood, and tho' established by no coercive Power, much better obeyed within the Circle where they are received, than any of those Laws which are recorded in Books, or enforced by public Authority.

A perfect Freedom from these Laws, if I am not greatly mistaken, is absolutely necessary to form the true Character of Humour; a Character which is therefore not to be met with among those People who conduct themselves by the Rules of good Breeding.

For indeed good Breeding is little more than the Art of rooting out all those Seeds of Humour which Nature had originally implanted in our Minds.

To make this evident it seems necessary only to explain the Terms, a Matter in which I do not see the great Difficulty which hath appeared to other Writers. Some of these have spoken of the Word Humour, as if it contained in it some Mystery impossible to be revealed, and no one, as I know of, hath undertaken to shew us expresly what it is, tho' I scarce doubt but it was amply done by Aristotle in his Treatise on Comedy, which is unhappily lost.

But what is more surprizing, is, that we find it pretty well explained in Authors who at the same Time tell us, they know not what it is. Mr. Congreve, in a Letter to Mr. Dennis,[1] hath these Words. *We cannot certainly tell what Wit is, or what Humour is*, and within a few Lines afterwards he says, *There is great Difference between a Comedy wherein there are many things humorously, as they call it, which is pleasantly spoken; and one where there are several Characters of Humour, distinguished by the particular and different Humours appropriated to the several Persons represented, and which naturally arise from the different Constitutions, Complexions, and Dispositions of Men. And again I take Humour to be a singular and unavoidable Manner of saying or doing any thing peculiar and natural to one Man only; by which his Speech and Actions are distinguished from those of other Men. Our Humour hath Relation to us, and to what proceeds from us, as the Accidents have to a Substance; it is a Colour, Taste, and Smell diffused through all; tho' our Actions are ever so many, and different in Form, they are all Splinters of the same Wood, and have naturally one Complexion, &c.*

If my Reader hath any doubt whether this is a just Description of Humour, let him compare it with those Examples of humorous Characters which the greatest Masters have given us, and which have been universally acknowledged as such, and he will be perhaps convinced.

Ben Johnson, after complaining of the Abuse of the Word, proceeds thus,

> Why Humour (as 'tis Ens)[2] we thus define it,
> To be a Quality of Air, or Water,
> And in itself holds these two Properties,
> Moisture and Fluxure;[3] as for Demonstration,
> Pour Water on this Floor, 'twill wet and run;
> Likewise the Air forc'd thro' a Horn or Trumpet
> Flows instantly away, and leaves behind
> A kind of Dew; and hence we do conclude,
> That whatsoe'er hath Fluxure and Humidity,
> As wanting Power to contain itself,
> Is Humour. So in every human Body,
> The Choler, Melancholy, Phlegm and Blood,[4]
> By Reason that they flow continually
> In some one Part, and are not continent,
> Receive the Name of *Humours*. Now thus far
> It may, by Metaphor, apply itself
> Unto the general Disposition:
> As when some one peculiar Quality
> Doth so possess a Man, that it doth draw
> All his Effects, his Spirits, and his Powers,
> In their Confluxions[5] all to run one Way,
> *This may be truly said to be a Humour.*
> But that a Rook[6] by wearing a py'd Feather,
> The Cable Hatband, or the three piled Ruff,
> A Yard of Shoe-tie, or the Switzer's Knot
> On his French Garters should affect a Humour!
> O! it is more than most ridiculous.

This Passage is in the first Act of *Every Man out of his Humour;* and I question not but to some Readers, the Author will appear to have been *out of his Wits* when he wrote it; but others I am positive will discern much excellent Ore shining among the Rubbish. In Truth his Sentiment when let loose from that stiff Boddice in which it is laced, will amount to this that as the Term Humour contains in it the Ideas of Moisture and Fluxure, it was applied to certain moist and flux Habits of the Body, and afterwards metaphorically to peculiar Qualities of the Mind, which when they are extremely prevalent, do, like the predominant Humours of the Body, flow all to one Part, and as the latter are known to absorb and drain off all the corporeal Juices and Strength to themselves, so the former are no less certain of engaging the Affections, Spirits, and Powers of the Mind, and of enlisting

---

THE COVENT-GARDEN JOURNAL: *Number 55*. **1. Mr. Congreve . . . Dennis:** an essay *Concerning Humor in Comedy,* sent by Congreve in 1695 to the critic John Dennis (1657–1734). (See the selection from Dennis earlier in Part Two.)

2. as 'tis Ens: considered in its material aspect. **3. Fluxure:** the property of being fluid. **4. Choler . . . Blood:** the four fluids ("humors") which in medieval and Renaissance medical theory constituted the liquids of the human body. **5. Confluxions:** flowing together. **6. Rook:** simpleton.

them as it were, into their own Service, and under their own absolute Command.

Here then we have another pretty adequate Notion of Humour, which is indeed nothing more than a violent Bent or Disposition of the Mind to some particular Point. To enumerate indeed these several Dispositions would be, as Mr. Congreve observes, as endless as to sum up the several Opinions of Men; nay, as he well says, the *Quot homines tot sententiæ*[7] may be more properly interpreted of their Humours, than their Opinions.

Hitherto there is no Mention of the Ridiculous, the Idea of which, tho' not essential to Humour, is always included in our Notions of it. The Ridiculous is annexed to it these two ways, either by the Manner or the Degree in which it is exerted.

By either of these the very best and worthiest Disposition of the Human Mind may become ridiculous. Excess, says Horace, even in the Pursuit of Virtue, will lead a wise and good Man into Folly and Vice—So will it subject him to Ridicule; for into this, says the judicious Abbé Bellegarde, a Man may tumble headlong with an excellent Understanding, and with the most laudable Qualities. Piety, Patriotism, Loyalty, Parental Affection, &c. have all afforded Characters of Humour for the Stage.

By the Manner of exerting itself likewise a Humour becomes ridiculous. By this Means chiefly the Tragic Humour differs from the Comic; it is the same Ambition which raises our Horror in Macbeth, and our Laughter at the drunken Sailors in the Tempest; the same Avarice which causes the dreadful Incidents in the Fatal Curiosity of Lillo,[8] and in the Miser of Moliere;[9] the same Jealousy which forms an Othello, or a Suspicious Husband.[10] No Passion or Humour of the Mind is absolutely either Tragic or Comic in itself. Nero had the Art of making Vanity the Object of Horror,[11] and Domitian, in one Instance, at least, made Cruelty ridiculous.[12]

As these Tragic Modes however never enter into our Notion of Humour, I will venture to make a small Addition to the Sentiments of the two great Masters I have mentioned, by which I apprehend my Description of Humour will pretty well coincide with the general Opinion. By Humour, then I suppose, is generally intended a violent Impulse of the Mind, determining it to some one peculiar Point, by which a Man becomes ridiculously distinguished from all other Men.

If there be any Truth in what I have now said, nothing can more clearly follow than the manifest Repugnancy between Humour and good Breeding. The latter being the Art of conducting yourself by certain common and general Rules, by which Means, if they were universally observed, the whole World would appear (as all Courtiers actually do) to be, in their external Behaviour at least, but one and the same Person.

I have not room at present, if I were able, to enumerate the Rules of good Breeding: I shall only mention one, which is a Summary of them all. This is the most golden of all Rules, no less than that *of doing to all Men as you would they should do unto you.*

In the Deviation from this Law, as I hope to evince in my next, all that we call Humour principally consists. I shall at the same Time, I think, be able to shew, that it is to this Deviation we owe the general Character mentioned in the Beginning of this Paper, as well as to assign the Reasons why we of this Nation have been capable of attracting to ourselves such Merit in Preference to others.

A.

NUMB. 56

Saturday, July 25, 1752.

> *Hoc Fonte derivata.*
> HOR.
> *These are the Sources.*

AT the Conclusion of my last Paper, I asserted that the Summary of Good Breeding was no other than that comprehensive and exalted Rule, which the greatest Authority hath told us is the Sum Total of all Religion and all Morality.

Here, however, my Readers will be pleased to observe that the subject Matter of good Breeding being only what is called Behaviour, it is this only to which we are to apply it on the present Occasion.

---

7. **Quot . . . sententiæ:** as many opinions as men. 8. **Lillo:** George Lillo (1693–1739), whose play *Fatal Curiosity* appeared in 1736. 9. **Moliere:** pen name of the great French dramatist (1622–73), whose *L'Avare* appeared in 1668. 10. **Suspicious Husband:** the title character in a comedy (1747) by Dr. Benjamin Hoadly (1706–57). 11. **Nero . . . Horror:** when he set fire to Rome to provide an appropriate background for his public recitation of the Homeric hymns. 12. **Domitian . . . ridiculous:** The Roman Emperor Domitian (A.D. 51–96) is reputed to have been fond of catching and torturing flies.

Perhaps therefore we shall be better understood if we vary the Word, and read it thus: *Behave unto all Men, as you would they should behave unto you.*

This will most certainly oblige us to treat all Mankind with the utmost Civility and Respect, there being nothing which we desire more than to be treated so by them. This will most effectually restrain the Indulgence of all those violent and inordinate Desires, which, as we have endeavoured to shew, are the true Seeds of Humour in the Human Mind: the Growth of which Good Breeding will be sure to obstruct; or will at least so overtop and shadow, that they shall not appear. The Ambitious, the Covetous, the Proud, the Vain, the Angry, the Debauchee, the Glutton, are all lost in the Character of the Well-Bred Man; or if Nature should now and then venture to peep forth, she withdraws in an Instant, and doth not shew enough of herself to become ridiculous.

Now Humour arises from the very opposite Behaviour, from throwing the Reins on the Neck of our favorite Passion, and giving it a full Scope and Indulgence. The ingenious Abbé, whom I quoted in my former Paper, paints this admirably in the Characters of Ill-Breeding, which he mentions as the very first Scene of the Ridiculous. "Ill-Breeding (L'Impolitesse) says he, is not a single Defect, it is the Result of many. It is sometimes a gross Ignorance of Decorum, or a stupid Indolence, which prevents us from *giving to others what is due to them.* It is a peevish Malignity which inclines us to oppose the Inclinations of those with whom we converse. It is the Consequence of a foolish Vanity, which hath no Complaisance for any other Person: *The Effect of a proud and whimsical Humour, which soars above all the Rules of Civility;* or, lastly, it is produced by a melancholly Turn of Mind, which pampers itself (*qui trouve du Ragoût*) with a rude and disobliging Behaviour."

Having thus shewn, I think very clearly, that Good Breeding is, and must be, the very Bane of the Ridiculous, that is to say, of all humorous Characters; it will perhaps be no difficult Task to discover why this Character hath been in a singular Manner attributed to this Nation.

For this I shall assign two Reasons only, as these seem to me abundantly satisfactory, and adequate to the Purpose.

The first is that Method so general in this Kingdom of giving no Education to the Youth of both Sexes; I say general only, for it is not without some few Exceptions.

Much the greater Part of our Lads of Fashion return from School at fifteen or sixteen, very little wiser, and not at all the better for having been sent thither. Part of these return to the Place from whence they came, their Fathers' Country Seats; where Racing, Cock fighting, Hunting, and other rural Sports, with Smoaking, Drinking, and Party become their Pursuit, and form the whole Business and Amusement of their future Lives. The other Part escape to Town in the Diversions, Fashion, Follies and Vices of which they are immediately initiated. In this Academy some finish their Studies, while others by their wiser Parents are sent abroad to add the Knowledge of the Diversions, Fashions, Follies, and Vices of all Europe, to that of those of their own Country.

Hence then we are to derive two great general Characters of Humour, which are the Clown and the Coxcomb, and both of these will be almost infinitely diversified according to the different Passions and natural Dispositions of each Individual; and according to their different Walks in Life. Great will be the Difference; for Instance, whether the Country Gentleman be a Whig or a Tory, whether he prefers Women, Drink, or Dogs; so will it be whether the Town Spark be allotted to serve his Country as a Politician, a Courtier, a Soldier, a Sailor, or possibly a Churchman, (for by Draughts from this Academy, all these Offices are supplied); or lastly whether his Ambition shall be contented with no other Appellation than merely that of a Beau.

Some of our Lads however, are destined to a further Progress in Learning; these are not only confined longer to the Labours of a School, but are sent thence to the University. Here if they please, they may read on, and if they please they may (as most of them do) let it alone, and betake themselves as their Fancy leads, to the Imitation of their elder Brothers either in Town or Country.

This is a Matter which I shall handle very tenderly, as I am clearly of an Opinion that an University Education is much the best we have; for here at least there is some Restraint laid on the Inclinations of our Youth. The Sportsman, the Gamester, and the Sot, cannot give such a Loose to their Extravagance, as if they were at home and under no manner of Government; nor can our Spark who is disposed to the Town Pleasures, find either Gaming-houses or Play-houses, nor half the Taverns or Bawdy-houses which are ready to receive him in Covent-Garden.

So far however I hope I may say without Offence,

that among all the Schools at the Universities, there is none where the Science of Good-Breeding is taught; no Lectures like the excellent Lessons on the Ridiculous, which I have quoted above, and which I do most earnestly recommend to all my young Readers. Hence the learned Professions produce such excellent Characters of Humour; and the Rudeness of Physicians, Lawyers, and Parsons, however dignified or distinguished, affords such pleasant Stories to divert private Companies, and sometimes the Public.

I come now to the beautiful Part of the Creation, who, in the Sense I here use the Word, I am assured can hardly (for the most Part) be said to have any Education.

As to the Counterpart of my Country Squire, the Country Gentlewoman, I apprehend, that except in the Article of the Dancing-Master, and perhaps in that of being barely able to read and write, there is very little Difference between the Education of many a Squire's Daughter, and that of his Dairy Maid, who is most likely her principal Companion; nay the little Difference which there is, is, I am afraid, not in the Favour of the Former; who, by being constantly flattered with her Beauty and her Wealth, is made the vainest and most selfconceited Thing alive, at the same Time that such Care is taken to instil into her the Principles of Bashfulness and Timidity, that she becomes ashamed and afraid of she knows not what.

If by any Chance this poor Creature drops afterwards, as it were, into the World, how absurd must be her Behaviour! If a Man looks at her, she is confounded, and if he speaks to her, she is frightened out of her Wits. She acts, in short, as if she thought the whole Sex was engaged in a Conspiracy to possess themselves of her Person and Fortune.

This poor Girl, it is true, however she may appear to her own Sex, especially if she is handsome, is rather an Object of Compassion, than of just Ridicule; but what shall we say when Time or Marriage have carried off all this Bashfulness and Fear, and when Ignorance, Aukwardness, and Rusticity, are embellished with the same Degree, tho' perhaps not the same kind of Affectation, which are to be found in a Court. Here sure is a plentiful Source of all that various Humour which we find in the Character of a Country Gentlewoman.

All this, I apprehend, will be readily allowed; but to deny Good-Breeding to the Town-Lady, may be the more Dangerous Attempt. Here, besides the Professors of Reading, Writing, and Dancing, the French and Italian Masters, the Music Master, and of Modern Times, the Whist Master, all concur in forming this Character. The Manners Master alone I am afraid is omitted. And what is the Consequence? not only Bashfulness and Fear are intirely subdued, but Modesty and Discretion are taken off at the same Time. So far from running away from, she runs after the Men; and instead of blushing when a modest Man looks at her, or speaks to her, she can bear, without any such Emotion to stare an impudent Fellow in the Face, and sometimes to utter what, if he be not very impudent indeed, may put him to the Blush.—Hence all those agreable Ingredients which form the Humour of a Rampant Woman of—the Town.

I cannot quit this Part of my Subject, in which I have been obliged to deal a little more freely than I am inclined with the loveliest Part of the Creation, without preserving my own Character of Good-Breeding, by saying that this last Excess, is by much the most rare; and that every Individual among my Female Readers, either is already, or may be, when she pleases, an Example of a contrary Behaviour.

The second general Reason why Humour so much abounds in this Nation, seems to me to arise from the great Number of People, who are daily raised by Trade to the Rank of Gentry, without having had any Education at all; or, to use no improper Phrase, Without having served an Apprenticeship to this Calling. But I have dwelt so long on the other Branch, that I have no Room at present to animadvert on this; nor is it indeed necessary I should, since most Readers with the Hints I have already given them, will easily suggest to themselves, a great Number of humorous Characters with which the Public have been furnished this Way. I shall conclude by wishing, that this excellent Source of Humour may still continue to flow among us, since tho' it may make us a little laughed at, it will be sure to make us the Envy of all the Nations of Europe.

A.

Samuel Richardson

1689–1761

That the main facts about the life of the master of the epistolary novel should be known to us from his correspondence is a happy instance of historical logic. Richardson's first editor and biographer, Anna Laetitia Barbauld, made ample use of his letters to unfold his life, and at this date there is still no good reason not to. One letter in particular—to the Reverend Johannes Stinstra of Harlingen, dated June 2, 1753, and written expressly to gratify a literary admirer's biographical curiosity—is a rich repository and offers a concise and candid introduction.

> My Father was a very honest Man, descended of a Family of middling Note, in yᵉ County of Surry; but which having for several Generations a large Number of Children, the *not* large Possessions were split & divided; so that he & his Brothers were put to Trades; & the Sisters were married to Tradesmen. . . . [His father, a joiner, is represented as a favorite of the Duke of Monmouth and the Earl of Shaftesbury, forced by the failure of the rebellion into retirement to Derbyshire, where Samuel was born.]
>
> He designed me for the Cloth. I was fond of this Choice: But while I was very young, some heavy Losses having disabled him from supporting me as genteelly as he wished in an Education proper for the Function, he left me to choose at the Age of 15 or 16, a Business; having been able to give me only common School-Learning: I chose that of a Printer, tho' a Stranger to it, as what I thought would gratify my Thirst after Reading. I served a diligent Seven Years to it, to a Master who grudged every Hour to me . . . . I stole from the Hours of Rest & Relaxation, my Reading Times for Improvement of my Mind; & being engaged in a Correspondence with a Gentleman greatly my superior in Degree, & of ample Fortunes, who, had he lived, intended high things for me; those were all the Opportunities I had in my Apprenticeship to carry it on. But this little Incident I may mention; I took Care, that even my Candle was of my own purchasing, that I might not in the most trifling Instance make my Master a Sufferer (& who used to call me the Pillar of his House) & not to disable myself by Watching or Sitting-up, to perform my Duty to him in the Day-time.
>
>   . . . . .
>
> Multitudes of Letters passed between this Gentleman & me. He wrote well, was a Master of yᵉ Epistolary Style: Our Subjects were various: But his Letters were mostly narrative, giving me an Account of his Proceedings, and what befell him in

yᵉ different Nations thro' which he travelled. I could from them, had I been at Liberty, & had I at that time thought of writing as I have since done, have drawn great Helps: But many Years ago, all yᵉ Letters that passed between us, by a particular Desire of his (lest they should ever be published) were committed to the Flames.

I continued 5 or 6 years after yᵉ Expiration of my Apprenticeship (Part of yᵉ Time, as an Overseer of a Printing-House) working as a Compositor, & correcting yᵉ Press: As I hinted, in a better Expectation. But *that* failing, I began for myself, married, & pursued Business with an Assiduity that, perhaps, has few Examples; & with yᵉ more Alacrity, as I improved a Branch of it, that interfered not with any other Person; & made me more independent of Booksellers (tho' I did much Business for them) than any other Printer. Some of them even thought fit to seek me, rather than I them, because of the Readiness I shewed to oblige them, with writing Indexes, Prefaces, & sometimes, for their minor Authors, *honest* Dedications; abstracting, abridging, compiling, and giving my Opinion of Pieces offered them. I have been twice married; to good Women both times. My Business, Sir, has ever been my chief Concern. My Writing-time has been at such times of Leisure as have not interfered with that. . . .

You complement me, Sir, in your next Question, with a Knowledge of the Manners of Mankind, & ask, Whence I attained this kindly-imputed Knowledge? I had greater Opportunities than I made use of, from the Correspondence I mentioned above. From my earliest Youth, I had a Love of Letter-writing. I was not Eleven Years old, when I wrote, spontaneously, a Letter to a Widow of near Fifty, who, pretending to a Zeal for Religion, & who was a constant Frequenter of Church Ordinances, was continually fomenting Quarrels & Disturbances, by Backbiting & Scandal, among all her Acquaintance. I collected from yᵉ Scripture Texts that made against her. Assuming the Stile and Address of a Person in Years, I exhorted her; I expostulated with her. But my Hand-writing was known: I was challenged with it, & owned yᵉ Boldness; for she complained of it to my Mother with Tears. My Mother chid me for the Freedom taken by such a Boy with a Woman of her Years: But knowing that her Son was not of a pert or forward Nature, but, on yᵉ contrary, shy & bashful, she commended my Principles, tho' she censured the Liberty taken.

As a bashful and not forward Boy, I was an early Favourite with all the young Women of Taste and Reading in the Neighbourhood. Half a Dozen of them when met to Work with their Needles, used, when they got a Book they liked, & thought I should, to borrow me to read to them; their Mothers sometimes with them; & both Mothers & Daughters used to be pleased with the Observations they put me upon making.

I was not more than Thirteen when three of these young Women, unknown to each other, having an high Opinion of my Taciturnity, revealed to me their Love Secrets, in order to induce me to give them Copies to write after, or correct, for Answers to their Lovers Letters: Nor did any one of them ever know, that I was the Secretary to the others. . . .

I recollect, that I was early noted for having Invention. I was not fond of Play, as other Boys: My Schoolfellows used to call me *Serious* and *Gravity*: And five of them particularly delighted to single me out, either for a Walk, or at their Fathers' Houses or at mine, to tell them Stories, as they phrased it. Some I told them from my Reading as true; others from my Head, as mere Invention; of which they would be most fond; & often were affected by them. One of them, particularly, I remember, was for putting me to write a History, as he called it, on the Model of Tommy Potts; I now forget what it was; only, that it was of a Servant-Man preferred by a fine young Lady (for his Goodness) to a Lord, who was a Libertine. All my Stories carried with them, I am bold to say, an useful Moral.

Though originally conceived more in the spirit of the trade than anything else, the *Familiar Letters*, as the *Letters Written to and for Particular Friends* (1741) came to be known, are equally instructive. The letter to Stinstra relates how the project developed.

Two Booksellers, my particular Friends, entreated me to write for them a little Volume of Letters, in a common Style, on such Subjects as might be of Use to those Country Readers who were unable to indite for themselves. Will it be any Harm, said I, in a Piece you want to be written so low, if we should instruct them how they should think & act in common Cases, as well as indite? They were the more urgent with me to begin the little Volume, for this Hint. I set about it, & in the Progress of it, writing two or three Letters [cxxxviii and cxxxix, below] to instruct handsome Girls, who were obliged to go out to Service, as we phrase it, how to avoid the Snares that might be laid against their Virtue; the above Story recurred to my Thought: And hence sprung Pamela. This Volume of Letters is not worthy your Perusal. I laid aside several Letters after I had written them as too high for the View of my two Friends.

The "above Story"—the truelife Pamela—Richardson had from a gentleman, he wrote, "Fifteen Years before I sat down to write it." In November, 1739, he put aside the *Familiar Letters* and started *Pamela, or Virtue Rewarded*. The two works were published in close succession: the novel in November, 1740, and the handbook the following January. His second major novel, *Clarissa Harlowe*, like *Pamela* epistolary in form, appeared in 1747–48. In 1754 Richardson ended his career as a novelist with the publication of *Sir Charles Grandison*. He remained busy as a printer though until his death in 1761.

The standard bibliography of Richardson is W. M. Sale Jr.'s *Samuel Richardson: A Bibliographical Record* (1936). By the same author is *Samuel Richardson: Master Printer* (1950). The literary career is fully treated in A. D. McKillop's *Samuel Richardson: Printer and Novelist* (1936). A. L. Barbauld's edition of *The Correspondence of Samuel Richardson* (6 vols., 1804) has not yet been superseded; her observations on the novels contained in the introductory biographical account remain remarkably fresh and pertinent. John Carroll's edition of *Selected Letters of Samuel Richardson* (1964) is a useful collection of letters of primarily literary interest. K. G. Hornbeak's *The Complete Letter-Writer in English, 1568–1800* (1934) is the best introduction to the *Familiar Letters*. The only modern reprint of the *Familiar Letters* is by B. W. Downs (1928).

LETTERS WRITTEN
TO AND FOR
PARTICULAR FRIENDS°...

Letter writing as a literary (or in most cases a subliterary) genre may be considered a development of the rise of the bourgeoisie and their attempts at self-education. The two main strands woven into the design of the formulary are the practical and the rhetorical—the assumptions are that something needs to be said and that there is a particularly effective way of saying it. It follows that in the reading of model letters the possibilities of delight are equal to those of instruction; indeed the conditions of fiction are not far removed. In her scholarly survey of the letter writer, Katherine Hornbeak has shown how far Richardson advanced beyond his predecessors in this direction. Against the background of a remote and complex ancestry, Richardson's collection may be placed in a native English tradition, to which, if we are to judge from the extent of his borrowings from such late seventeenth- and early eighteenth-century specimens as *The Young Secretary's Guide*, *The Experienced Secretary*, and *The Secretary's Guide*, he seems cheerfully to have submitted. But while the *Familiar Letters* have to be regarded in large part as models modeled after models, Richardson put his own stamp on them, and in ways characteristic of the novelist-to-be. The work as a whole, like the average letter, runs to a considerably greater length than those of his predecessors; in running longer, the letters tend to fall into groups (with embryonic plot and character development); the affairs of women and the subjects of love, courtship, and marriage, while central to the tradition, now loom even larger; and the rhetorical or technical aims appear more decidedly subordinated to ethical concerns. On this last point Miss Hornbeak remarks, "No other letter-writer had pretended to give a working philosophy of life. *Familiar Letters*, however, does so; its foundation is Prudence or Caution; its keystone, Reputation."

To the sophisticated reader the very idea of recommending reply formulas appears naive, if not disingenuous. In all but the most routine communications, and especially where personal emotions are involved, it is impossible to tell someone what to write, for to tell him that is to tell him what to think. Richardson glances at this problem in his letter of June 2, 1753, to the Reverend Johannes Stinstra, in which he tells of writing model love letters for young women.

I have been directed to chide, & even repulse, when an Offence was either taken or given, at the very time that the Heart of the Chider or Repulser was open before me, overflowing with Esteem and Affection; & the fair Repulser dreading to be taken at her Word; directing *this* Word, or *that* Expression, to be softened or changed. One, highly gratified with her Lover's Fervor, & Vows of everlasting Love, has said, when I have asked her Direction: "I cannot tell you what to write; But (her Heart on her Lips) you cannot write too kindly."

Nevertheless, it was Richardson's ambition to "instruct them how they should think & act." Happily, however, the bludgeon of the moralist was cushioned by the imagination of the novelist, and occasionally in the *Familiar Letters* (as pervasively in the novels) models of exemplary behavior are colored by his strong sense of individual psychology. Richardson's accomplishment finally is not in prescribing what people should write or how they should think and act but in showing by what they do write how they do think and act. For this reason the *Familiar Letters* may be considered literature.

The text is that of the sixth edition (1755), the last in Richardson's lifetime. This departure from our general policy may be justified by the fact that Richardson subjected his text to stylistic revision from the first edition to the sixth, and of course was his own printer. It is also a fact, however, that along with improvements and corrections some degeneration of the punctuation and spelling was allowed to take place, and we have accordingly restored a few earlier readings. The full title reads: *Letters Written to and for Particular Friends, on the Most Important Occasions. Directing Not Only the Requisite Style and Forms to Be Observed in Writing Familiar Letters; but How to Think and Act Justly and Prudently, in the Common Concerns of Human Life. Containing One Hundred and Seventy-three Letters. None of Which Were Ever Before Published.*

PREFACE

THE following Letters are published at the Solicitation of particular Friends, who are of Opinion, that they will answer several good Ends, as they may not only direct the *Forms* requisite to be observed on the most important Occasions; but, what is more to the Purpose, by the Rules and Instructions contained in them, contribute to *mend the Heart*, and *improve the Understanding*.

LETTERS WRITTEN TO AND FOR PARTICULAR FRIENDS. **Friends:** Our copy text lacks a title page, but according to the advertisements of the sixth edition this word was changed to *Persons*.

NATURE, PROPRIETY of CHARACTER, PLAIN SENSE, and GENERAL USE, have been the chief Objects of the Author's Attention in the Penning of these Letters; and as he every-where aimed to write to the *Judgment*, rather than to the *Imagination*, he would choose, that they should generally be found more *useful* than *diverting:* Tho' where the Subjects require *Strokes of Humour*, and *innocent Raillery*, it will be seen, perhaps, that the Method he has taken, was the Effect of *Choice*, and not merely of *Necessity*.

The Writer is no Friend to long Prefaces; but it may be necessary, however, to say, what he has *aimed at* in this Performance; and to leave his *Merit* in the *Execution* of it, to proper Judges.

He has endeavour'd then, in general, throughout the great Variety of his Subjects, to inculcate the Principles of *Virtue* and *Benevolence;* to describe *properly*, and recommend *strongly*, the SOCIAL and RELATIVE DUTIES; and to place them in such *practical* Lights, that the Letters may serve for Rules to THINK and ACT by, as well as Forms to WRITE after.

Particularly, he has endeavoured to point out the Duty of a *Servant*, not a *Slave;* the Duty of a *Master*, not a *Tyrant;* that of the *Parent*, not as a Person morose and sour, and hard to be pleased; but mild, indulgent, kind, and such an one as would rather govern by *Persuasion*, than *Force*.

He has endeavour'd to direct the young Man in the Choice of his *Friends* and *Companions;* to excite him to *Diligence;* to discourage *Extravagance*, *Sottishness*, and *Vice* of all Kinds.

He has aimed to set forth, in a Variety of Cases, to *both Sexes*, the Inconveniencies attending *unsuitable Marriages;* to expose the Folly of a *litigious Spirit;* to console the *Unhappy;* to comfort the *Mourner:* And many of these by Arguments, though *easy* and *familiar*, yet *new* and *uncommon*.

With regard to the Letters of *Courtship*, the Author has aimed to point out such Methods of Address to a young Man, as may stand the Test of the *Parents Judgment*, as well as the *Daughter's Opinion;* and, at the same time, that they should not want the proper Warmth of Expression, which Complaisance, and Passion for the beloved Object, inspire (and is so much expected in Addresses of this Nature), they should have their Foundation laid in *common Sense*, and a *manly Sincerity;* and, in a Word, be such as a *prudent Woman* need not blush to receive, nor a *discreet Man* be ashamed to look back upon, when the *doubtful Courtship* is changed into *matrimonial Certainty*.

With this View he has also attempted to expose the *empty Flourishes*, and *incoherent Rhapsodies*, by which *shallow Heads*, and *designing Hearts*, endeavour to exalt their Mistresses into *Goddesses*, in hopes of having it in their Power to sink them into the Characters of the *most Credulous* and *Foolish* of their Sex.

Orphans, and *Ladies* of *independent Fortunes*, he has particularly endeavour'd to guard against the insidious Arts of their *flattering* and selfish *Dependents*, and the *clandestine* Addresses of *Fortune-hunters*, those Beasts of Prey, as they may well be called, who spread their Snares for the *innocent* and *thoughtless* Heart.

These, among other no less material Objects, have been the Author's principal *Aim:* How well he has *succeeded*, must, as has been hinted, be left to the Judgment of the candid Reader.

Letter XV

From a young Lady to her Father, acquainting him with a Proposal of Marriage made to her.

Honoured Sir,   Nottingham, April 4.

I THINK it my Duty to acquaint you, that a Gentleman of this Town, by Name *Derham*, and by Business a Linen-draper, has made some Overtures to my Cousin *Morgan*, in the way of Courtship to me. My Cousin has brought him once or twice into my Company, which he could not well decline doing, because he has Dealings with him, and has an high Opinion of him and his Circumstances. He has been set up Three Years, and has very good Business, and lives in Credit and Fashion. He is about Twenty-seven Years old, and a likely Man enough: He seems not to want Sense or Manners; and is come of a good Family. He has broken his Mind to me, and boasts how well he can maintain me: But, I assure you, Sir, I have given him no Encouragement; and told him, that I had no Thoughts of changing my Condition, yet-a-while; and should never think of it but in Obedience to my Parents; and I desired him to talk no more on that Subject to me. Yet he resolves to persevere, and pretends[1] extraordinary Affection and Esteem. I would not, Sir, by any means, omit to acquaint you with the *Beginnings* of an Affair that would be want of Duty in me to conceal from you, and shew a Guilt and Disobedience unworthy of the kind Indulgence and Affection you have always shewn to, Sir, | *Your most dutiful Daughter*.

1. pretends: professes.

My humble Duty to my honour'd Mother; Love to my Brother and Sister; and Respects to all Friends. Cousin *Morgan*, and his Wife and Sister, desire their kind Respects. I cannot speak enough of their Civility to me.

Letter XVI

The Father's Answer, on a Supposition that he approves not of the young Man's Addresses.

Dear Polly,   *Northampton, Apr.* 10.
I HAVE received your Letter dated the 4th Instant, wherein you acquaint me of the Proposals made to you, thro' your Cousin *Morgan's* Recommendation, by one Mr. *Derham*. I hope, as you assure me, that you have given no Encouragement to him: For I by no means approve of him for your Husband. I have inquired of one of his Townsmen, who knows him and his Circumstances very well; and I am neither pleased with them, nor with his Character; and wonder my Cousin would so inconsiderately recommend him to you. Indeed, I doubt not Mr. *Morgan's* good Intentions; but I insist upon it, that you think nothing of the Matter, if you would oblige | *Your indulgent Father.*

Your Mother gives her Blessing to you, and joins with me in the above Advice. Your Brother and Sister, and all Friends, send their Love and Respects to you.

Letter XVII

The Father's Answer, on a Supposition that he does not disapprove of the young Man's Addresses.

My dear Daughter,   *Northampt. Apr.* 10.
IN Answer to yours of the 4th Instant, relating to the Addresses of Mr. *Derham*, I would have you neither wholly encourage nor discourage his Suit; for if, on Inquiry into his Character and Circumstances, I shall find, that they are answerable to your Cousin's good Opinion of them, and his own Assurances, I know not but his Suit may be worthy of Attention. But, my Dear, consider, that Men are deceitful, and always put the best Side outwards; and it may possibly, on the strict Inquiry, which the Nature and Importance of the Case demands, come out far otherwise than it at present appears. Let me advise you, therefore, to act in this Matter with great Prudence, and that you make not yourself too cheap; for Men are apt to slight what is too easily obtained. Your

Cousin will give him Hope enough, while you don't absolutely deny him; and, in the mean time, he may be told, that you are not at your own Disposal, but intirely resolved to abide by my Determination and Direction, in an Affair of this great Importance: And this will put him upon applying to me, who, you need not doubt, will in this Case, as in all others, study your Good; as becomes | *Your indulgent Father.*

Your Mother gives her Blessing to you, and joins with me in the above Advice. Your Brother and Sister, and all Friends, send their Love and Respects to you.

Letter XVIII

The young Gentleman's Letter to the Father, apprising him of his Affection for his Daughter.

SIR,   *Nottingham, Apr.* 12.
I TAKE the Liberty, tho' personally unknown to you, to declare the great Value and Affection I have for your worthy Daughter, whom I have had the Honour to see at my good Friend Mr. *Morgan's*. I should think myself intirely unworthy of *her* Favour, and of *your* Approbation, if I could have a Thought of influencing her Resolution but in Obedience to your Pleasure; as I should, on such a Supposition, offer an Injury likewise to that Prudence in *herself*, which, I flatter myself, is not the least of her amiable Perfections. If I might have the Honour of your Countenance,[2] Sir, on this Occasion, I would open myself and Circumstances to you, in that frank and honest manner which should convince you of the Sincerity of my Affection for your Daughter, and at the same time of the Honourableness of my Intentions. In the mean time I will in general say, That I have been set up in my Business in the Linen-drapery Way, upwards of three Years; that I have a very good Trade for the Time: That I had 1000*l.* to begin with, which I have improved to 1500*l.* as I am ready to make appear to your Satisfaction: That I am descended of a creditable Family; have done nothing to stain my Character; and that my Trade is still farther improveable, as I shall, I hope, inlarge my Bottom.[3] This, Sir, I thought but honest and fair to acquaint you with, that you might know something of a Person, who sues to you for your Countenance, and that of your good Lady, in an Affair that I hope may prove one Day the greatest Happiness of my Life; as it *must* be, if I can be

2. Countenance: encouragement, show of favor. **3. inlarge my Bottom:** increase my capital.

blessed with that, and your Daughter's Approbation. In Hope of which, and the Favour of a Line, I take the Liberty to subscribe myself, good Sir, | *Your most obedient humble Servant.*

Letter XIX

From the Cousin to the Father and Mother, in Commendation of the young Gentleman.

Dear Cousins,   Nottingham, *April* 12.

I GIVE you both Thanks for so long continuing with us the Pleasure of Cousin *Polly*'s Company. She has intirely captivated a worthy Friend of mine, Mr. *Derham*, a Linen-draper of this Town. And I would have acquainted you with it myself, but that I knew and advised Cousin *Polly* to write to you about it; for I would not for the World any thing of this sort should be carried on unknown to you, at my House, especially. Mr. *Derham* has shewn me his Letter to you; and I believe every Tittle of it to be true; and really, if you and my Cousin approve it, as also Cousin *Polly*, I don't know where she can do better. I am sure I should think so, if I had a Daughter he could love.

Thus much I thought myself obliged to say; and, with my kind Love to your other Self, and all my Cousins, as also my *Wife's*, and *Sister's*, I remain | *Your affectionate Cousin.*

Letter XX

From the Father, in Answer to the young Gentleman.

SIR,   Northampton, *April* 16.

I HAVE received yours of the 12th, and am obliged to you for the good Opinion you express of my Daughter: But I think she is yet full young to alter her Condition, and embark in the Cares of a Family. I cannot but say, that the Account you give of yourself, and your Application to *me*, rather than first to try to engage the Affections of my Daughter, carry a very honourable Appearance, and such as must be to the Advantage of your Character. As to your Beginning, Sir, that is not to be so much looked upon, as the *Improvement;* and I doubt not that you can make good Proof of what you assert on this Occasion. But still I must needs say, that I think, and so does her Mother, that it is too early to incumber her with the Cares of the World; and as I am sure she will do nothing in so

important an Affair without our Advice, so I would not, for the World, in a Case so nearly concerning her, and her future Welfare, constrain her in the least. I intend shortly to send for her home, for she has been longer absent from us than we intended; and then I shall consult her Inclinations; and you will excuse me to say (for she is my Daughter, and a very good Child, tho' I say it), that I shall then determine myself by that, and by what shall appear to offer most for her Good. In the mean time, Sir, I thank you for the Civility and commendable Openness of yours; and am | *Your humble Servant.*

The Father in this Letter referring pretty much to the Daughter's Choice, the young Gentleman cannot but construe it as an Encouragement to him to prosecute his Addresses to *her;* in which he doubles his Diligence (on the Hint that she will soon return to *Northampton*), in order to gain a Footing in her good Will; and she, finding her Father and Mother not averse to the Affair, ventures to give him some room to think his Addresses not indifferent to her; but still altogether on Condition of her Parents Consent and Approbation. By the Time then that she is recall'd home (nothing disagreeable having appeared in the young Gentleman's Behaviour, and his general Character being consistent with his Pretensions), there may be supposed some Degree of Familiarity and Confidence to have pass'd between them; and she gives him Hope, that she will receive a Letter from him, tho' she shall not promise an Answer; intirely referring to her Duty to her Parents, and their good Pleasure. He attends her on her Journey a good Part of the Way, as far as she will permit; and when her Cousin, his Friend, informs him of her safe Arrival at *Northampton*, he sends the following Letter.

Letter XXI

From the young Gentleman to his Mistress, on her Arrival at her Father's.

Dear Madam,   *May* 25.

I HAVE understood, with great Pleasure, your safe Arrival at your Father's House; of which I take the Liberty to congratulate your good Parents, as well as your dear Self. I will not, Madam, fill this Letter with the Regret I had to part with you, because I have no Reason nor Merit, at present, to expect that you should be concerned for me on this Score. Yet,

Madam, I am not without Hope, from the Sincerity of my Affection for you, and the Honesty of my Intentions, to deserve, in time, those Regards which I cannot at present flatter myself with. As your good Father, in his kind Letter to me, assured me, that he should consult your Inclinations, and determine by them, and by what should offer most for your Good; how happy should I be, if I could find my humble Suit not quite indifferent to your dear Self, and not rejected by Him! If what I have already opened to him, as to my Circumstances, be not unacceptable, I should humbly hope for Leave to pay you and him a Visit at *Northampton;* or, if this be too great a Favour, till he has made further Inquiry, that he would be pleased to give himself that Trouble, and put it in my Power, as soon as possible, to convince him of the Truth of my Allegations, upon which I desire to stand or fall in my Hopes of your Favour and his. For I think, far different from many in the World, that a Deception in an Affair of this weighty Nature should be less forgiven than in any other. Since then, dearest Madam, I build my Hopes more on the Truth of my Affection for you, and the Honour of my Intentions, than any other Merit, or Pretensions, I hope you will condescend, if not to become an Advocate for me, which would be too great a Presumption to expect, yet to let your good Parents know, that you have no Aversion to the Person or Address of, dearest Madam, | *Your for ever obliged, and affectionate humble Servant.*

My best Respects attend your good Father and Mother, and whole Family.

As this puts the Matter into such a Train, as may render more Writing unnecessary; the next Steps to be taken being the Inquiry into the Truth of the young Man's Assertions, and a Confirmation of his Character; and then the Proposals on the Father's Part of what he will give with his Daughter; all which may be done best by Word of Mouth, or Interposition of Friends; so shall we have no Occasion to pursue this Instance of Courtship farther.

Letter XXVIII

From a Maid-servant in Town, acquainting her Father and Mother in the Country with a Proposal of Marriage, and asking their Consents.

Honoured Father and Mother,

I Think it my Duty to acquaint you, that I am addressed to for Change of Condition, by one Mr.

John Tanner, who is a Glazier,[4] and lives in the Neighbourhood by us. He is a young Man of a sober Character, and has been set up about two Years, has good Business for his Time, and is well beloved and spoken of by every one. My Friends here think well of it, particularly my Master and Mistress; and he says, he doubts not, by God's Blessing on his Industry, to maintain a Family very prettily: And I have fairly told him, how little he has to expect with me. But I would not conclude on any thing, however, till I had acquainted you with his Proposals, and asked your Blessings and Consents. For I am, and ever will be, | *Your dutiful Daughter.*

Letter XXIX

From the Parents, in Answer to the preceding.

Dear Nanny,

WE have received your dutiful Letter. We can only pray to God to bless and direct you in all your Engagements. Our Distance from you must make us leave every thing to your own Discretion; and as you are so well satisfied in Mr. *Tanner's* Character, as well as all Friends, and your Master and Mistress, we give our Blessings and Consents with all our Hearts: We are only sorry we can do no more for you. But let us know when it is done, and we will do some little Matters, as far as we are able, towards House-keeping. Our Respects to Mr. *Tanner.* Every body joins with us in Wishes for your Happiness; and may God bless you, is all that can be said by | *Your truly loving Father and Mother.*

Letter XLVII

From a Son reduced by his own Extravagance, requesting his Father's Advice, on his Intention to turn Player.

Honoured Sir,

AFTER the many Occasions I have given for your Displeasure, permit me to ask your Advice in an Affair which may render my whole Life comfortable or miserable. You know, Sir, to what a low Ebb my Folly and Extravagance have reduced me. Your generous Indulgence has made you stretch your Power, to my Shame I speak it, even beyond the Bounds which Wisdom, and a necessary Regard to

---

4. **Glazier:** window maker.

the rest of your Family, would permit; therefore I cannot hope for further Assistance from you. Something, however, I must resolve upon to gain a Maintenance: And an Accident fell out Yesterday, which offers me, at least, present Bread.

Mr. *Rich*,[5] Master of one of the Theatres, happened to dine at my Uncle's when I was there: After Dinner, the Subject of Discourse was, the Art of a Comedian: On which my Uncle took Occasion to mention the little Flights in that way with which I have diverted myself in my gayer Moments; and partly compelled me to give an Instance of my Abilities. Mr. *Rich* was pleased to declare his Approbation of my Manner and Voice; and, on being told my Circumstances, offer'd at once to take me into his Company, with an Allowance sufficient for present Subsistence, and additional Encouragement, as I should be found to deserve it. Half a Benefit[6] he promised me the first Season; which, by my (otherwise too) numerous Acquaintance, might, I believe, be turned to pretty good Account. I am not fond of this Life; but see no other Means of supporting myself like a Gentleman. Your speedy Answer will be ever gratefully acknowledged by, honoured Sir, | *Your dutiful, tho' unhappy Son.*

Letter XLVIII

The Father's Answer, setting forth the Inconveniencies and Disgrace attending the Profession of a Player.

Dear Gilbert,

I SHOULD be glad to have you in any Situation which would afford you a comfortable and reputable Subsistence: But cannot think the Life of a Stage-player proper for that End. You must consider, that tho' in the gay Trappings of that Employment a Man may represent a Gentleman, yet none can be farther from that Character, if a perpetual Dependence be the worst Kind of Servility. In the first Place, the Company you will be in a manner obliged to keep, will be

such as will tend little to the Improvement of your Mind, or Amendment of your Morals: To the Master of the Company you list[7] in, you must be obsequious to a Degree of Slavery. Not one of an Audience that is able to *hiss*, but you must *fear;* and each single Man you come to know personally, you must oblige, on every Occasion that offers, to engage their Interest at your Benefit. A Thought the most shocking to a free and generous Mind! And if to this you add the little Profit that will attend making a low Figure on the Stage, and, besides the Qualifications necessary, the incredible Fatigue attending the Support of a good Figure upon it; you will easily see, that more Credit, more Satisfaction, more Ease, and more Profit, may be got in many other Stations, without the mortifying Sense of being deemed a Vagrant by the Laws of your Country.[8] I hope this will be enough to dissuade you from farther Thoughts of the Stage: And in any other Employment, you may yet expect some small Assistance from | *Your loving Father.*

Letter LXV

Against too great a Love of Singing and Music.

Dear Cousin,

I AM sure you have the good Sense to take kindly what I am going to mention to you, in which I can have no possible View but your Benefit. When you were last with me at *Hertford*, you much obliged us all with the Instances you gave us of your Skill in Music, and your good Voice. But as you are so young a Man, and seem to be so very much pleased *yourself* with these Acquirements, I must enter a Caution or two on this score, because of the Consequences that may follow from too much Delight in these Amusements, which, while they are pursued as Amusements *only*, may be safe and innocent; but when they take up too much of a Man's Time, may be not a little pernicious.

In the first place, my dear Cousin, these Pleasures of *Sound* may take you off from the more desirable ones of *Sense*, and make your Delights stop at the *Ear*,

---

5. Mr. Rich: John Rich (*c.* 1682–1761), son of Christopher Rich, the proprietor-manager of Drury Lane Theatre, himself became a manager—first of the theater in Lincoln's Inn Fields (which opened in 1714) and then of the one in Covent Garden (1732). He was famous also for his creation and acting of pantomimes. **6. Half a Benefit:** Benefits for actors (as well as for other theater personnel) originated as a means of making up arrears in pay but came to be granted as bonuses. "Half a Benefit" in this instance means that the young man would share a benefit jointly with another actor.

7. list: enlist. **8. deemed . . . Country:** "Early in the century, when Jeremy Collier's attack upon the stage made everyone conscious of his claims of immorality in the theatres, actors occasionally were hailed into court, sometimes fined, for their part in acting presumably licentious roles, and their legal status as actors was perilously close to the standing of a vagabond" (*The London Stage 1660–1800*, Part 2: 1700–1729, ed. Emmett L. Avery [1960]).

which should go deeper, and be placed in the *Understanding*. For whenever a chearful Singer is in Company, adieu to all Conversation of an improving or intellectual Nature!

In the second place, it may expose you to *Company*, and that not the *best* and *most* eligible neither; and by which your *Business*, and your other *more useful* Studies, may be greatly, if not wholly, neglected, and very possibly your *Health* itself much impaired.

In the third place, it may tend (for so it naturally does) to *enervate the Mind*, and make you haunt musical Societies, Operas, and Concerts; and what Glory is it to a Gentleman, if he were even a fine Performer, that he can strike a String, touch a Key, or sing a Song, with the Grace and Command of an *hired Musician?*

Fourthly, Music, to arrive at any tolerable Proficiency in it, takes up *much Time*, and requires so much Application, as leaves but little *Room*, and, what is worse, when delighted in, little *Inclination*, for other Improvements: And as Life is a *short Stage*, where *longest*, surely the most precious Moments of it ought to be better employed, than in so light and airy an Amusement. The Time of *Youth* will be soon over, and that is the Time of laying the Foundation of more solid Studies. The *Mind*, as well as the *Body*, will become stiff by Years, and unsusceptible of those Improvements, that cannot be attained, but in particular Periods of it: And, when once an airy Delight engages the Faculties, an Habit is formed; and nothing but great Struggle, and absolute Necessity, if *that* will do it, can shake it off. One Part of Life is for *Improvement*, that is, *Youth;* another Part is for turning that Improvement to solid Benefits to one's Self, one's Family, or Acquaintance; that is, the *middle Part;* another Part carries a Retrospect[9] to a *future State:* And shall we lose the Time of *Improvement*, which can never come again; forfeit all the Benefits of it, in our *Middle-life;* and imbitter our *future Prospects*, as well *mundane* as *eternal*, with Reflections on our past Neglect of Opportunities that can never be recalled? And all for what? Why only to be deemed, for eight or ten empty Years of Life, *a good Companion*, as the Phrase is:—Tho', perhaps, a bad *Husband*, a bad *Father*, a bad *Friend*, and, of course, a bad *Man!*

Some there are, who divide Life into four Stages or Opportunities. He, they say, who is not handsome by Twenty, strong by Thirty, wise by Forty, rich by

Fifty, will never be either *handsome, strong, wise,* or *rich.* And this, generally speaking, is a good and improving Observation; which should teach us, as we go along, to make a right Use of those Periods of Life, which may be proper Entrances for us into a still more important one than that behind it.

I have but lightly touch'd on these weighty Points, because I know you have good Sense enough to improve as much from Hints, as others can from tedious Lectures. And when I have repeated, that I am far from dissuading you from these Amusements, while they are restrained to due Bounds, and are regarded as Amusements *only;* I know you will think me, what I always desire to be thought, and what I truly am, | *Your affectionate Uncle, and sincere Friend.*

Letter XCV[10]

Mrs. Pratt,

I INCLOSE the Letter you put into my Hands, and hope it will be the last I shall ever receive from you, or any body else, on the like Occasion. I am intirely satisfied in the Care and Kindness of my Guardian, and shall encourage no Proposal of this sort, but what comes recommended to me by *his* Approbation. He knows the World. I do not; and that which is not fit for *him* to *know*, is not fit for *me* to *receive;* and I am sorry either you or the Writer looks upon me in so weak a Light, as to imagine I would wish to take myself out of the Hands of so *experienced* a *Friend*, to throw myself into those of a *Stranger*. Yet I would not, as this is the first Attempt of the kind from you, and that it may rather be the Effect of Inconsideration than Design, shew it my Guardian; because he would not perhaps impute it to so favourable a Motive in you, as I am willing to do, being | *Your Friend and Servant.*

If there be no Go-between, but that a young Fellow takes upon himself to send Letters to teaze a young Lady to encourage his Address, by his romantic Professions of his Affection and Regard for her, and attributing such Perfections to her, as no one Woman ever had; and if she is desirous, but knows not how, to get rid of his troublesome Importunity; and that even a contemptuous Silence, which it is prudent for a young Lady to

---

9. Retrospect: reference.

10. Letter XCV: This letter comes under the rubric "Instructions to young Orphan Ladies, as well as others, how to judge of Proposals of Marriage made to them without their Guardians or Friends Consent, by their Milaners, Manteaumakers, or other Go-betweens."

shew on such an Occasion, has no Effect upon him;
nor yet that he will desist, tho' she returns his
Letters *unopened*, or in a *blank Cover*,[11] after she
happens to have read them; then let the Lady get
some Friend to write to him, looking upon him as
beneath her own Notice: For even a *Denial*, if
given in *Writing* under *her own Hand*, will encourage
some presumptuous Men; or at least they may make
some Use of it to the Lady's Disadvantage; and
ought not to have it to boast, that they have
received a Letter from her, tho' ever so much to
their own Discredit, if it were shewn. And the
following may be the Form:

Letter XCVI

SIR,
YOU have thought fit to write to Miss *Knollys*
twice or thrice in a very troublesome manner. She
cannot possibly so far forget what belongs to Herself
and Character, as to answer you any other way than
by the Contempt of Silence. Yet since she cannot, it
seems, be free from your Impertinence, she wishes you
may be told, That you must have as mean an Opinion
of *her* Judgment, as all who read your Epistles, must
have of *yours*, if you can expect Success from such
inconsistent Rhapsodies.

I will from myself venture to give you one Piece of
Advice: That the next Person you pretend to address
with your bright Compositions, you don't in them
forget one Ingredient, which is *Common Sense;* though
you should be forced to borrow it. I am | *Yours,
unknown.*

Or, if this be thought too affronting, the following:

Letter XCVII

SIR,
YOU are desired to send no more of your elaborate
Epistles to Miss *Knollys.* You are quite mistaken in the
Lady. She knows *herself*, and by your Letter she knows
you, so well, that she sends it back, that you may find
some other Person to send it to, whose Sentiments and
Understanding are better proportioned to your own.
I am, Sir, *&c.*

If the Letters of the young Fellow deserve less
Severity, and are such as have not their Foundation

11. in . . . Cover: not addressed, and therefore not recognizing him. A cover was the wrapper of a letter.

in Romance and Bombast, but yet the Lady thinks
not proper to encourage his Address, this Form
may serve:

Letter XCVIII

SIR,
I AM desired to acquaint you, that Miss *Knollys*
thinks herself obliged to every one who has a good
Opinion of her; but begs, that you will not give
yourself, or her, the Trouble of any more Letters.
For things are so circumstanced, that she has neither
Inclination nor Power to encourage your Address. I
am, Sir, | *Your humble Servant, unknown.*

If the Lady has a mind to rebuke the Attempt of
a clandestine Address to her, and yet thinks the
Proposal not absolutely unworthy of Attention,
did it come *regularly* to her, by means of her
Father, Mother, Guardian, &c. this Form may be
observed:

Letter XCIX

SIR,
MISS *Knollys* desires you should be informed, which
she presumes you did not know, That she never can
think herself at her own Disposal, while she has so
near and so good a Friend to advise with as Mr. *Archer*,
whose Wisdom she much prefers to her own, as his
Experience in the World, and Kindness to her, make
him deserve to be consulted, in all her Affairs of
Moment. Whatever shall appear fit to him, will have
great Weight with her; and there is but that one
possible Way to engage her Attention. I am, Sir, |
Yours, &c.

Or, if the Lady has not a Guardian, or Father, or
Mother, but some Friend in whom she can confide,
the following may be a proper Form:

Letter C

SIR,
IT may not be amiss to acquaint you, that Miss
Knollys is so happy as to have a Friend of Experience
and Probity, without whose Advice she undertakes
nothing of Consequence. It is Mr. *Salter*, of *Grace-
church-street.* And she will not care to admit of any
Proposal of Moment to her that has not passed his

Approbation. This, she hopes, will save her and your-self the Trouble of any further Application. I am | *Your humble Servant.*

Or this:

Letter CI

SIR,

MR. *Salter*, of *Grace-church-street*, being a Gentleman that Miss *Knollys* consults in all her Affairs, she refers to him all Proposals that are or may be of Importance to her; and desires to receive no more Letters or Messages from you, by any other Hand. I am | *Your humble Servant, unknown.*

Letter CII

From a Town-Tenant to his Landlord, excusing Delay of Payment.

Honoured Sir,

I AM under a great Concern, that I cannot at present answer your just Expectations. I have sustained such heavy Losses, and met with such great Disappointments of late, that I must intrude another Quarter on your Goodness. Then, whatever Shifts I am put to, you shall hear to more Satisfaction than at present, from, Sir, | *Your most humble Servant.*

Letter CIII

From a Country Tenant to the same Purpose.

Honoured Sir,

The Season has been so bad, and I have had such unhappy Accidents to encounter with in a sick Family, Loss of Cattle, &c. that I am obliged to trespass upon your Patience a Month or two longer. The Wheat-harvest, I hope, will furnish me the Means to answer your just Expectations: which will be a great Contentment to | *Your honest Tenant, and humble Servant.*

Letter CIV

The Landlord's Answer.

Mr. Jacobs,

I HAVE yours: I hope you'll be as good as your Word at the Expiration of the Time you have men-tioned. I am unwilling to distress any *honest* Man; and

I hope, that I shall not meet with the *worse* Usage for my Forbearance: For *Lenity* abused, even in generous Tempers, provokes Returns, that some People would call *severe;* but should not be deemed such, if *just.* I am | *Yours,* &c.

Letter CV

A threatening Letter from a Steward on Delay of Payment.

Mr. Atkins,

I HAVE mentioned your Case to Sir *John,* as you requested. He is exceedingly provoked at your Usage, and swears bloodily he'll seize, and throw you into Gaol, if he has not 20*l.* at least paid him by Quarter-day, which is now at hand. So you know what you have to trust to; and I would have you avoid the Consequences at any rate; for he is resolved otherwise to do as he says. Of this I assure you, who am | *Yours,* &c.

Letter CVI

The poor Tenant's moving Answer.

Good Mr. Taverner,

I AM at my Wit's End almost on what you write. But if I *am* to be ruined, with my numerous Family, and a poor, industrious, but *ailing* Wife, how can I help it? For I cannot possibly raise 20*l.* any manner of way by the Time you mention. I hope Sir *John* won't be hard-hearted. For if God Almighty, our common Landlord, should be *equally* hard upon us, what would become of us *all?* Forgive my Boldness to talk of God Almighty to his *Honour,* in this free manner.

I would do it, if it was to be done; but you know, Sir, what a *Season* we have had. And an honester Tenant his Honour will never have, that I am sure of. But if Money *won't* rise,[12] what can I *do?* Should I sell my Team, and my Utensils for Labour, there is an End of *all.* I shall have no Means left me then where-with to pay his *Honour,* or *any body* else. If his Honour will not be moved, but *will* seize, pray, good Mr. *Taverner,* prevail on him not to throw me into Gaol; for a Prison pays no Debts; but let my poor Wife and Six small Children lie in the Barn, till I can get a little Day-labour; for that must be all I can have to trust to,

---

12. **rise:** turn up.

if his Honour seizes. I hear my Man *William*, that was,[13] has just taken a Farm; may be, he will employ his poor ruin'd Master, if I am not *'prison'd*. But if I be, why then the Parish must do something for my poor Children, tho' I hoped they would never trouble it. Lay these things before his Honour, good Sir, and forgive this Trouble from | *His Honour's honest, tho' unfortunate Tenant.*

Letter CVII

The Steward's Reply, giving more Time.

Mr. Atkins,

I HAVE laid your Letter and your Case before Sir *John:* He is moved with it, and says he will have Patience another Quarter, to see what you'll do. Consider, Man, however, that Gentlemen live at a great Expence; are obliged to keep up their Port; and if their Tenants fail *them*, why then they must fail their *Tradesmen*, and suffer in their *Credit*. You have good Crops of all Kinds on the Ground; and surely may, by next *Quarter*, raise 40 or 50l. tho' you could not raise 20l. in a *Fortnight*. This Sir *John* will expect at least, I can tell you. And you may comply with it from the Produce of so good a Farm, surely. I am | *Yours*, &c.

Letter CVIII

The poor Man's thankful Letter in Return.

GOD bless his Honour, and God bless you, Mr. *Taverner*, that's all I can say. We will now set our Hands to the Plough, as the Saying is, with chearful Hearts, and try what can be done. I am sure, I, and my Wife and Children too, tho' three of them can but lisp their Prayers, shall, Morning, Noon, and Night, pray to God for his Honour's Health and Prosperity, as well as for you and yours; and to enable me to be just to his Expectations. I'm sure it would be the Pride of my Heart to pay every body, his Honour especially. I have not run behind-hand for want of Industry; that all my Neighbours know; but Losses and Sickness I could not help; and nobody could live more frugal and sparing than both my Wife and I. Indeed we have hardly allowed ourselves Cloaths to our Backs, nor for our Children neither, tight,[14] and clean, and wholsome as they may appear to those who see them: And

we will continue to live so low as may only keep us in Heart to do our Labour, until we are got before-hand;[15] which God grant. But all this I told you before, Mr. *Taverner;* and so will say no more, but I will do all I can, and God give a Blessing to my Labours, as I mean honestly. So no more, but that I am, Sir, | *Your ever-obliged Servant.*

Letter CXXIV

To one who, upon a very short Acquaintance, and without any visible Merit but Assurance, wants to borrow a Sum of Money.

SIR,

YOU did me the Favour of inquiring for me two or three times while I was out of Town. And among my Letters I find one from you, desiring the Loan of 50 Guineas. You must certainly have mistaken *yourself* or *me* very much, to think we were enough known to each other for such a Transaction. I was twice in your Company; I was delighted with your Conversation: You seemed as much pleased with mine: And if we both acted with Honour, the Obligation is mutual, and there can be no room to suppose me your Debtor. I have no churlish nor avaritious Heart, I will venture to say; but there must be Bounds to every thing; and Discretion is as necessary in conferring as in receiving a Kindness. To a Friend my helping Hand ought to be lent, when his Necessities require it: You cannot think our Intimacy enough to commence that Relation; and should I answer the Demands of every *new* Acquaintance, I should soon want Power to oblige my *old* Friends, and even to serve *myself*. Surely, Sir, a Gentleman of your Merit cannot be so little beloved, as to be forced to seek to a new Acquaintance, and to have no better Friend than one of *Yesterday*. I will not do you the Injury to suppose, that you have not *many*, who have the *best* Reasons, from long Knowledge, to oblige you: And, by your Application to *me*, I cannot think *Bashfulness* should stand in your way to *them*. Be this as it may, it does not at all suit my Conveniency to comply with your Request; and so I must beg you to excuse | *Yours*, &c.

---

13. **my . . . was:** my former man(-servant) William.
14. **tight:** neat.

15. **got before-hand:** back on our feet (to change the metaphor).

Letter CXXXVIII

A Father to a Daughter in Service, on hearing of her Master's attempting her Virtue.

My dear Daughter,

I Understand, with great Grief of Heart, that your Master has made some Attempts on your Virtue, and yet that you stay with him. God grant that you have not already yielded to his base Desires! For when once a Person has so far forgotten what belongs to himself, or his Character, as to make such an Attempt, the very Continuance with him, and in his Power, and under the same Roof, is an Encouragement to him to prosecute his Designs. And if he carries it better, and more civil, at present, it is only the more certainly to undo you when he attacks you next. Consider, my dear Child, your Reputation is all you have to trust to. And if you have not already, which God forbid! yielded to him, leave it not to the Hazard of another Temptation; but come away directly (as you ought to have done on your own Motion) at the Command of | *Your grieved and indulgent Father.*

Letter CXXXIX

The Daughter's Answer.

Honoured Sir,

I Received your Letter Yesterday, and am sorry I stay'd a Moment in my Master's House after his vile Attempt. But he was so full of his Promises of never offering the like again, that I hop'd I might believe him; nor have I yet seen any thing to the contrary: But am so much convinced, that I ought to have done as you say, that I have this Day left the House; and hope to be with you soon after you will have receiv'd this Letter. I am | *Your dutiful Daughter.*

Letter CLIII

From the same.[16]
V. Describing Bethlehem Hospital.

Honoured Madam,

YOU tell me, in your last, that my Descriptions and Observations are very superficial, and that both my Uncle and yourself expect from me much better

---

16. **From the same:** "*From a young Lady in Town to her Aunt in the Country.*" There are eleven letters in this series.

Accounts than I have yet given you: For I must deliver my *Opinion,* it seems, on what I see, as well as tell you what I have been shewn. 'Tis well I left my bettermost Subjects to the last; such, I mean, as will best bear Reflection; and I must try what I can do, to regain that Reputation which your Indulgence, rather than my Merit, had form'd for me in your kind Thoughts —Yet, I doubt[17] I shan't please you, after all. But 'tis my Duty to try for it, and it will be yours, I had almost said, to forgive Imperfections, which I should have conceal'd, but for your undeserv'd good Opinions of me, which draw them into Light.

I have this Afternoon been with my Cousins, to gratify the odd Curiosity most People have to see *Bethlehem* or *Bedlam* Hospital.

A more affecting Scene my Eyes never beheld; and surely, Madam, any one inclined to be proud of human Nature, and to value themselves above others, cannot go to a Place that will more effectually convince them of their Folly: For there we see Man destitute of every Mark of Reason and Wisdom, and levell'd to the Brute Creation, if not beneath it; and all the Remains of good Sense or Education serve only to make the unhappy Person appear more deplorable!

I had the Shock of seeing the late polite and ingenious Mr. —— in one of these woful Chambers: We had heard, you know, of his being somewhat disorder'd; but I did not expect to find him here: No sooner did I put my Face to the Grate, but he leap'd from his Bed, and call'd me, with frightful Fervency, to come into his Room. The Surprise affected me pretty much; and my Confusion being observ'd by a Croud of Strangers, I heard it presently whisper'd, That I was his Sweetheart, and the Cause of his Misfortune. My Cousin assured me, such Fancies were frequent upon these Occasions: But this Accident drew so many Eyes upon me, as oblig'd me soon to quit the Place.

I was much at a Loss to account for the Behaviour of the Generality of People, who were looking at these melancholy Objects. Instead of the Concern I think unavoidable at such a Sight, a sort of Mirth appeared on their Countenances; and the distemper'd Fancies of the miserable Patients most unaccountably provoked Mirth, and loud Laughter, in the unthinking Auditors; and the many hideous Roarings, and wild Motions of others, seemed equally entertaining to them. Nay, so shamefully inhuman were some, among whom (I am

---

17. **doubt:** suspect.

sorry to say it!) were several of my own Sex, as to endeavour to provoke the Patients into Rage to make them Sport.

I have been told, this dreadful Place is often used for the Resort of lewd Persons to meet and make Assignments: But that I cannot credit; since the Heart must be abandon'd indeed, that could be vicious amidst so many Examples of Misery, and of such Misery, as, being wholly involuntary, may overtake the most secure.

I am no great Admirer of public Charities, as they are too often managed; but if we consider the Impossibility of poor Peoples bearing this Misfortune, or providing suitably for the Distempered at their own Beings,[18] no Praise can, surely, be too great for the Founders and Supporters of an Hospital, which none can visit, without receiving the most melancholy *Proof* of its being needful. I am, with Respects where due, honoured Madam, | *Your most dutiful Niece.*

Letter CLXVIII

From a Gentleman who in a small Fortune experiences the Slights of his Friends; but being suddenly reputed to be rich, is oppressed with the fawning Caresses and Adulation of those who had before neglected him.

Dear Sir,

I MUST, for once, postpone every thing I would say to you, in order to make room for an Account you little expect.

What will you say, when I tell you, that a current Report of my being *immensely rich* is the greatest *Misfortune* I at present labour under? Nor do I find it so supportable as you may be apt to imagine. The Occasion was owing to the frequent Slights I had received from the Gentlewoman with whom I lodge, and from others of my Friends, who, believing that I lived up to my scanty Fortune, as in Truth I do (tho' I take care to be beholden to nobody, and pay ready Money for every thing), could not treat me negligently enough. I complain'd of this to that Arch Wag *Tony Richards*, who told me he would change every one's Behaviour to me in a few Days. And he has done it effectually: For what does he do, but, as a kind of Secret, acquaints my Landlady, that beside my poor little Estate (which you know to be my All) he had lately discovered, that I had twenty thousand Pounds Stock in one of our great Companies!

Such was the Force of this whimsical Delusion, that, the very next Morning, I had a clean Towel hung over my Water-bottle, tho' I never before had more than one a Week during the twenty Years I have lodg'd here.

About a Week after this, my Cousin *Tom*, who, for the two Years he has been in the *Temple*,[19] has let me see him but three times, came, in a most complaisant manner, plainer dressed than I ever had before seen him; and begg'd, if the Length of the Evening was in any Degree burthensome, I would permit him to wait upon me with such Peices of Wit, Humour, or Entertainment, as the Town afforded; the reading of which under *my Ear*,[20] he was sure would be a great Advantage to *him;* and assured me, that, for a Beginning, he had presumed to bring the last new Tragedy in his Pocket: I thank'd my young Spark. Upon which he is so much in earnest in his Observances, that three Nights in a Week he thus entertains me: Which will, at least, be of so much Service, as to keep him out of more expensive Company. And you cannot think what Pains the Rogue takes to read with the Cadence he knows I admire, and sits till his Teeth chatter before he offers to look towards the Fire.

What you will still more wonder at, Sir *John Hookhim* called upon me before *Christmas;* and tho' I have not had a Visit from him these Five Years, was so obliging as to run away with me in his Chariot into *Hertfordshire,* to keep the Holidays in his Family; where his Lady treated me with the utmost Respect, and her Daughters paid me their Morning Devoirs, with the same Deference as if I had been their Grand Papa. No Dinner was concluded upon without consulting my Palate; and the young Gentlemen, his Sons, are as ambitious of my hearing their Exercises, as if their Fortunes depended upon my Approbation.

Sir *John* acquainted me with every Improvement he had made in his Estate; and assured me, that his second Son *Will.* my Namesake, has a Genius singularly turned for managing Country Business, had he not the Misfortune of having a Brother born before him; and gave me several Reasons to believe, that a fine Estate which lay in the Neighbourhood, and was then to be sold, would be a great Penyworth.[21] I took the

---

18. at . . . Beings: on their own means of support.

19. the Temple: The Inner Temple, the Middle Temple, Lincoln's Inn, and Gray's Inn were the four Inns of Court —the combined law schools and bar associations of London. **20. under my Ear:** under my discriminating attention. **21. Penyworth:** bargain.

Hint; but said, I had no Inclination to purchase: He shook his Head at my Thousands, and told me, that, in his Opinion, a Land Estate was preferable to the best Stock in the Kingdom.

When I came to Town the 4th of *January*, I was no sooner out of Sir *John*'s Chariot, but my Landlady, in Person, informed me, that since I had been absent, I had had so many Presents sent me, that she had been in an hundred Fears for their spoiling: I ask'd her the Particulars, and found Five Turkeys, Three Chines,²² Three Hampers of *Madeira* for the Gout,²³ Two Collars of Brawn,²⁴ Geese, Chickens, Hares, and Wild-Fowl, to a large Amount.

At Night I was welcom'd to Town by all my *old* Acquaintance, and about Twenty almost new ones: I was a little tired with my Journey; and had a slight Cold besides; which being observed, one was running for a Physician, another for a Surgeon, to bleed me: One thought an Emetic not improper: Another recommended a gentle Sweat, or composing Draught; and, amidst the general Officiousness, I could hear it whisper'd, that, if my Will was not made, Delays might prove dangerous: And, in the Morning, five Messengers after my Welfare arrived before Day.

Thus, Sir, you see my Peace is gone; my Tongue is of no Use; for no one believes me when I declare my real Circumstances: And, under the Happiness of a very small Fortune, I suffer all the Afflictions attending a Man immoderately rich; and if *you* keep not your usual Behaviour, I shall not know myself, nor any Man else; since all my Companions are become Flatterers, and all around me are so obsequious, that it is impossible for me to know when I do right or wrong. I am, dear Sir, tho' thus whimsically situated, | *Your real Friend.*

Letter CLXXII

To a Father, on the Loss of an hopeful Son, who died at Man's Estate.

SIR,

I AM truly sorry for your Loss. So hopeful a Son, just arriv'd at Man's Estate, and who was so great a Comfort and Assistance to you, to be snatched away,

is what must administer to you the greatest Grief of any thing that could possibly befal you.

But, alas! yours is no *new* Case. The greatest Families have been thus afflicted, and with the Aggravation to some of them, that perhaps they have been deprived of their *Heirs*, and have not a *Son left* to continue their Name and Honours. The late Queen *Anne*, when Princess of *Denmark*, lost her beloved Duke of *Gloucester*, not only *her* Hopes, but the Hopes of the *Nation;* and the Crown, to which he seemed not only *born*, but *fashioned*, was obliged to be settled, on that Occasion, upon a distant Branch of the Royal Line.²⁵

The great Duke of MARLBOROUGH, who by his Merit, and his Victories, had raised a princely Estate, as well as Titles, had but one Son, the Marquis of *Blandford*, on whom he and his Duchess built all their Hopes, for the perpetuating of those new Honours in their Family; and he was snatched away by Death, when he was at the University, training up to become the Dignities, to which he was intitled.²⁶

Still more recent was the unhappy Fate of a Lady of the first Quality in *England*. Her Lord had a Son lent to his advanced Years. This Son was the last of that noble Family, and on his Life depended all his Father's and his Mother's Hopes; and on his living till of Age, a valuable Part of the Estate itself, which otherwise was to fall to an illegitimate Offspring. What Care was not used to preserve the noble Youth! An eminent Physician was taken into the Family, to be made a constant Watchman, as it were, over his Health and Exercises. The young Nobleman himself was hopeful, dutiful, and as distinguished in the Graces of his Mind, as by his Birth. He travelled; his indulgent Mother travelled with him: He made a Campaign under his Uncle, the greatest General then surviving in an Age of Generals. He again travell'd to restore and confirm his Health, and all the noble Mother's Hopes and Views were employ'd on the finding for

---

22. **Chines:** A chine is the backbone and adjoining parts of an animal. 23. **for the Gout:** The moderate use of wines such as madeira and sherry, which were least apt to produce acid, was regularly prescribed as a tonic for the gout-affected stomach. 24. **Collars of Brawn:** rolls of boar meat.

25. **the Crown . . . Line:** William, Duke of Gloucester, was born to Princess Anne and Prince George of Denmark on July 24, 1689; he died on July 29, 1700. The following year the Act of Settlement placed Sophia, Electress of Hanover, next to Anne in the succession to the English throne. Sophia was the granddaughter of James I, and her son became George I upon the death of Queen Anne in 1714. 26. **he was . . . intitled:** John, Marquis of Blandford, Marlborough's only surviving son, died of smallpox at King's College, Cambridge, on February 20, 1703, at the age of seventeen. The honors and dignities fell to his sister, Henrietta, Countess of Godolphin.

her beloved Son, on his Return, a Wife suitable to his Quality, and who might be a Means to preserve one of the first Families in the Kingdom from utter Extinction.

What was the Event of all her Cares, her Hopes, her Vows, her Prospects?—Why, just as the young Nobleman had (within a few Months) arrived at Age, and could have made those Family Settlements which were most desirable should be made, and the want of which involved his noble Mother in perplexing Law-suits, which, too, turned against her; it pleased God to deprive her of him, and he died in a foreign Land, far distant from his fond Mother, who (still more grievous, if true!) for Reasons of State, as was said, had been deny'd to accompany and attend him: And so ended all her Hopes of above twenty Years standing, and in him his Family likewise.

A still more recent Calamity to a great Family I might mention, in the Death of two hopeful Children, the only Sons of their Father, and the only Heirs Male of one of the first Families in the Kingdom, both snatched away, in the Space of a few Hours of one another, from healthy Constitutions, and no Ailments previous to the sudden one that carried them off, which was only believed to be a sore Throat. In vain were the Consultations of the most eminent Physicians and Surgeons, who gave Attendance all Night, minutely to watch every Change of the Distemper; in vain proved the Assurance of the Skilful to the fond Parents, that there was no Danger. Death mocked all their Hopes; and when the first died, in vain was he open'd, in order to find out, if possible, the Cause of the fatal Malady, in order to administer, with greater Hopes of Success, Remedies against it, to preserve the other. That other hopeful Youth followed his Brother, and their Fate deeply wounded the Hearts of half a dozen noble Families, whose intimate Relationship gave them a very near Interest in the awful Event.

Like Instances of the Loss of hopeful Sons, and of the only Male Heirs, might be produced in other Families of prime Distinction in the List of the *British* Nobility;

but I need not enumerate more to a Mind considerate as yours, which will reflect, that Death is a common Lot, from which no Rank or Degree is exempted. And I hope these Reflections, and such as you will be able to add to them by your own Reason and Piety, will serve to rebuke the Overflowings of your Grief, and confine it to the natural Chanels, into which both God and Nature will *indulge* it to flow.

I mention not to your enlightened Mind, you see, the Motives, that, nevertheless, might be insisted on with great Propriety, on so grievous an Occasion; such as, The Uncertainty of Life: The Gratitude you ought to shew for having had your Son *so long* continued to you, as he was: The great Probability of his being happy in God's Mercies, by reason of his Hopefulness and Duty: The *early* Release he has met with from the Troubles and Chances of a changeable and transitory Life: His Escape from the Danger of the Temptations which his Virtue might have been tried with, had he lived to *maturer* Years: That this your Deprivation is God's Work: That he died not in a distant Land, and by an untimely Death:[27] But that you had the Satisfaction of knowing, that every thing was done for him that could be done: That his Morals were still untainted, and he was not cut off in the Pursuit of some capital Sin, as has too often been the Case with bold and daring Spirits in the Heat of their youthful Passions: And that he escaped the Snares usually laid for young Men by idle Companions, and vicious Women, which too often entangle and catch the unthinking Mind. These will be all suggested to you from your own better Reason; and to that *secondarily*, as to a due Resignation to the Divine Will *primarily*, let me refer you, on this trying Occasion: Who am, with a sympathizing Affection, dear Sir, |
Your sincere Friend, and humble Servant.

---

27. **an untimely Death:** death that does not allow time to meet it as a religious person should.

Part Three

A MISCELLANY
OF
POEMS

Sir John Denham
1615–1669

COOPER'S HILL

Sure there are Poets which did never dreame
Upon Parnassus, nor did tast the streame
Of Helicon,° we therefore may suppose,
Those made not Poets, but the Poets those.
And as Courts make not Kings, but Kings the Court,
So where the Muses and their traine resort,
Parnassus stands; if I can be to thee°
A Poet, thou Parnassus art to me.
Nor wonder, if (advantag'd in my flight,
By taking wing from thy auspicious height)   10
Through untrac't waies, and ayrie paths I flye,
More boundlesse in my Fancy than my eye:
My eye, which swift as thought contracts the space
That lyes between, and first salutes the place
Crown'd with that sacred pile, so vast, so high,
That whether 'tis a part of Earth, or sky,
Uncertaine seems, and may be thought a proud
Aspiring mountain, or descending cloud,
Pauls, the late theme of such a Muse° whose flight
Has bravely reach't and soar'd above thy height: 20

Now shalt thou stand, though sword, or time, or fire,
Or zeale more fierce than they, thy fall conspire,
Secure, whilst thee the best of Poets sings,
Preserv'd from ruine by the best of Kings.°
Vnder his proud survay the Citty lyes,
And like a mist beneath a hill doth rise;
Whose state and wealth, the business and the crowd,
Seems at this distance but a darker cloud:
And is to him, who rightly things esteems,
No other in effect than what it seems: 30
Where with like hast, though several waies, they run,
Some to undo, and some to be undone;
While luxury, and wealth, like war and peace,
Are each the others ruine, and increase;
As Rivers lost in Seas some secret veine
Thence reconveighs, there to be lost again.
Oh happinesse of sweet retir'd content!
To be at once secure, and innocent.
  Windsor the next (where *Mars* with *Venus* dwells,
Beauty with strength) above the valley swells   40
Into my eye, and doth it self present
With such an easie and unforc't ascent,
That no stupendous precipice denyes
Accesse, no horror turnes away our eyes:
But such a Rise, as doth at once invite
A pleasure, and a reverence from the sight.
Thy mighty Masters Embleme, in whose face
Sate meeknesse, heightned with Majestick Grace.
Such seems thy gentle height, made onely proud
To be the basis of that pompous load,   50
Than which, a Nobler weight no Mountain Bears,
But *Atlas* only that supports the Sphears.
When Natures hand this ground did thus advance,
'Twas guided by a wiser power than Chance;
Mark't out for such a use, as if 'twere meant
T' invite the builder, and his choice prevent.°
Nor can we call it choice, when what we chuse,
Folly, or blindnes only could refuse.
A Crown of such Majestick towrs doth Grace
The Gods great Mother,° when her heavenly race   60
Doe homage to her, yet she cannot boast
Amongst that numerous, and Celestiall hoast,
More *Hero's* than can *Windsor*, nor doth Fames
Immortall booke record more noble names.
Not to look back so far, to whom this Ile
Owes the first Glory of so brave a pile,

COOPER'S HILL. The text is that of the first authorized edition (1655); we have incorporated the variants of the version in Denham's *Poems and Translations* (1668). Cooper's Hill is about eighteen miles from London; from its top one sees Windsor Castle to the left and London to the right. Samuel Johnson has said of *Cooper's Hill* that it is "the work that confers upon [Denham] the rank and dignity of an original author. He seems to have been, at least among us, the author of a species of composition that may be denominated *local poetry*, of which the fundamental subject is some particular landscape, to be poetically described, with the addition of such embellishments as may be supplied by historical retrospection, or incidental meditation." **3. Helicon:** a mountain sacred to the Muses; on it were the springs of Hippocrene and Aganippe, whose waters were held to stimulate poetic inspiration. **7. thee:** Cooper's Hill. **19. a Muse:** Edmund Waller, whose poem *Upon His Majesty's Repairing of Paul's* appeared in 1645. (See the selections from Waller later in Part Three.)

24. the best . . . Kings: Charles I. **56. prevent:** anticipate. **60. The Gods . . . Mother:** Cybele.

Whether to *Cæsar*, *Albanact*, or *Brute*,°
The Brittish *Arthur*, or the Danish *Knute*,°
(Though this of old no lesse contest did move,
Than when for *Homers* birth seven Cities strove)   70
(Like him in birth, thou should'st be like in Fame,
As thine his fate, if mine had been his Flame)
But whosoere it was, Nature design'd
First a brave place, and then as brave a minde.
Not to recount those severall Kings, to whom
It gave a Cradle, or to whom a Tombe,
But thee (great *Edward*) and thy greater sonne,
(The lillies which his Father wore, he wonne)°
And thy *Bellona*,° who the Consort came
Not onely to thy bed, but to thy Fame,   80
She to thy Triumph led one Captive King,
And brought that sonne, which did the second° bring.
Then didst thou found that Order° (whither° love
Or victory thy Royall thoughts did move)
Each was a noble cause, and nothing lesse,
Than the designe, had been the great successe:
Which forraigne Kings, and Emperors esteeme
The second Honour to their Diadem.
Had thy great destiny but given thee skill,
To know as well, as power to act her will,   90
That from those Kings, who then thy captives were,
In after-times should spring a Royall paire,°
Who should possesse all that thy mighty power,
Or thy desires more mighty, did devoure;
To whom their better Fate reserves what ere
The Victor hopes for, or the Vanquisht feare;
That blood, which thou and thy great Grandsire shed,
And all that since these sister Nations bled,
Had bin unspilt, had happy *Edward* known
That all the blood he spilt, had been his own.   100
When he that Patron° chose, in whom are joyn'd
Souldier and Martyr, and his arms confin'd

Within the Azure Circle,° he did seem
But to foretel, and prophecie of him,°
Who to his Realms that Azure round hath joyn'd,
Which Nature for their bound at first design'd.
That bound, which to the Worlds extreamest ends,
Endlesse it selfe, its liquid arms extends;
Nor doth he need those Emblemes which we paint,
But is himself the Souldier and the Saint.   110
Here should my wonder dwell, and here my praise,
But my fixt thoughts my wandring eye betrays,
Viewing a neighboring hill, whose top of late
A Chappel crown'd, till in the Common Fate,
The adjoyning Abby fell:° (may no such storme
Fall on our times, where ruine must reform.)
Tell me (my Muse) what monstrous dire Offence,
What crime could any Christian King incense
To such a rage? was 't Luxury, or lust?
Was he so temperate, so chast, so just?   120
Were these their crimes? they were his own much
     more:
But wealth is Crime enough to him that's poor,
Who having spent the Treasures of his Crown,
Condemns their Luxury to feed his own.
And yet this Act, to varnish o're the shame
Of sacriledge, must bear devotions name.
No Crime so bold, but would be understood
A reall, or at least a seeming good.
Who fears not to do ill, yet fears the Name,
And free from Conscience, is a slave to Fame.   130
Thus he the Church at once protects, and spoyles:
But Princes swords are sharper than their styles.°
And thus to th' ages past he makes amends,
Their Charity destroyes, their Faith defends.
Then did Religion in a lazie Cell,
In empty, airie contemplations dwell;
And like the block, unmoved lay: but ours,
As much too active, like the storke devours.°
Is there no temperate Region can be knowne,
Betwixt their Frigid, and our Torrid Zone?   140
Could we not wake from that Lethargicke Dreame,

---

67. **Brute:** Brutus, the grandson of Aeneas; he was the traditional founder of London. Albanact was one of Brutus's sons.
68. **Knute:** (Canute) King of England during the eleventh
century. 78. **The lillies . . . wonne:** The Black Prince, son
of Edward III, defeated the French and became Prince of
Aquitaine and Gascony. 79. **Bellona:** the Roman goddess of
war. Edward III's wife, Queen Philippa, was famous for
having exhorted the troops before the Battle of Neville's
Cross, which resulted in the capture of King David II of
Scotland. 82. **the second:** King John II of France, captured
by the Black Prince at the Battle of Poitiers. 83. **that Order:**
the Order of the Garter, founded by Edward III about 1344;
the seat of the order is the chapel at Windsor Castle.
whither: possibly *whether*. 92. **a Royall paire:** Charles I and
Henrietta Maria. 101. **that Patron:** St. George.

103. **the Azure Circle:** the blue garter surrounding the
red cross of St. George on the insignia of the order. 104.
him: Charles I. 115. **The adjoyning . . . fell:** Chertsey
Abbey, on St. Anne's hill; abbey and chapel were destroyed
by Henry VIII. 132. **their styles:** a reference to King
Henry's book *Assertio Septem Sacramentorum Adversus
Martinum Lutherum* (1521), for which the Pope granted Henry
the title Defender of the Faith. 138. **like . . . devours:** In a
traditional fable, Jove sends a kingless nation of frogs a log to
serve as ruler; when the frogs complain that the log does
nothing, Jove sends a stork, which devours them.

But to be restlesse in a worse extreame?
And for that Lethargy was there no cure,
But to be cast into a Calenture°?
Can knowledge have no bound, but must advance
So farre, to make us wish for ignorance?
And rather in the darke to grope our way,
Than led by a false guide to erre by day?
Who sees these dismall heaps, but would demand,
What barbarous Invader sackt the land?   150
But when he heares, no Goth, no Turk did bring
This desolation, but a Christian King;
When nothing, but the Name of Zeale, appears
'Twixt our best actions and the worst of theirs,
What does he think our Sacriledge would spare,
When such th' effects of our devotions are?
Parting from thence 'twixt anger, shame, and feare,
Those for what's past, and this for what's too neare:
My eye descending from the Hill, survaies
Where *Thames* amongst the wanton vallies
   strayes.   160
Thames, the most lov'd of all the Oceans sonnes,
By his old Sire, to his imbraces runnes,
Hasting to pay his tribute to the Sea,
Like mortall life to meet Eternity.
Though with those streames he no resemblance hold,
Whose foame is Amber, and their Gravell Gold;°
His genuine, and lesse guilty wealth t' explore,
Search not his bottom, but survey his shore;
Ore which he kindly spreads his spacious wing,
And hatches plenty for th' ensuing Spring.   170
Nor then destroyes it with too fond a stay,
Like Mothers which their Infants overlay.
Nor with a suddain and impetuous wave,
Like profuse Kings, resumes the wealth he gave.
No unexpected inundations spoyle
The mowers hopes, nor mock the plowmans toyle:
For Godlike his unwearied Bounty flows;
First loves to do, then loves the Good he does.
Nor are his Blessings to his banks confin'd,
But free, and common, as the Sea or Wind;   180
When he to boast, or to disperse his stores
Full of the tributes of his gratefull shores,
Visits the World, and in his flying towers
Brings home to us, and makes both Indies ours;
Finds wealth where 'tis, bestows it where it wants,

Cities in deserts, woods in Cities plants.
So that to us no thing, no place is strange,
While his fayre bosome is the worlds exchange.
O could I flow like thee, and make thy streame
My great example, as it is my theme!   190
Though deep, yet cleare, though Gentle, yet not dull,
Strong without rage, without ore-flowing full.
Heaven her *Eridanus*° no more shall boast,
Whose Fame in thine, like lesser Currents lost,
Thy Nobler streams shall visit *Jove's* aboads,
To shine amongst the Stars, and bath the Gods.
Here Nature, whether more intent to please
Us, or her selfe, with strange varieties,
(For things of wonder give no lesse delight
To the wise Maker's, than beholder's sight.   200
Though these delights from severall causes move,
For so our children, thus our friends we love)
Wisely she knew, the harmony of things,
As well as that of sounds, from discords springs.
Such was the discord, which did first disperse
Forme, order, beauty through the Universe;
While drynesse moysture, coldnesse heat resists,
All that we have, and that we are, subsists.
While the steepe horrid roughnesse of the Wood
Strives with the gentle calmnesse of the flood. 210
Such huge extreames when Nature doth unite,
Wonder from thence results, from thence delight.
The streame is so transparent, pure, and cleare,
That had the selfe-enamour'd youth° gaz'd here,
So fatally deceiv'd he had not been,
While he the bottome, not his face had seene.
But his proud head the ayery Mountaine hides
Among the Clouds; his shoulders, and his sides
A shady mantle cloaths; his curled brows
Frowne on the Gentle streame, which calmly
   flows,   220
While winds and stormes his lofty forhead beat:
The common fate of all that's high, or great.
Low at his foot a spacious plaine is plac't,
Between the mountaine and the streame imbrac't:
Which shade and shelter from the Hill derives,
While the kind river wealth and beauty gives;
And in the mixture of all these appeares
Variety, which all the rest indears.
This scene had some bold Greek, or Brittish Bard

---

144. Calenture: a violent fever and delirium that afflicts travelers in the tropics. **166. Whose . . . Gold:** The trees along the Po River were held to exude amber; since the days of Midas, the Pactolus River was reputed to be full of gold.

193. Eridanus: Phaethon, who is associated variously with a stream running through ancient Athens and with the Po River in Italy. **214. the selfe-enamour'd youth:** Narcissus, who fell in love with his own image reflected from a fountain.

Beheld of old, what stories had we heard,   230
Of Fairies, Satyrs, and the Nymphs their Dames,
Their feasts, their revells, & their amorous flames!
'Tis still the same, although their ayery shape
All but a quick Poetick sight escape.
There Faunus and Sylvanus° keep their Courts,
And thither all the horned hoast resorts,
To graze the rancker mead, that noble heard
On whose sublime and shady fronts is reard
Natures great Masterpeece; to shew how soone
Great things are made, but sooner are undone.   240
Here have I seene the King, when great affaires
Give leave to slacken, and unbend his cares,
Attended to the Chase by all the flower
Of youth, whose hopes a Nobler prey devoure:
Pleasure with Praise, and danger, they would buy,
And wish a foe that would not only fly.
The stagg now conscious of his fatall Growth,
At once indulgent to his feare and sloth,
To some darke covert his retreat had made,
Where nor mans eye, nor heavens should invade   250
His soft repose; when th' unexpected sound
Of doggs, and men, his wakefull ear doth wound.
Rouz'd with the noyse, he scarce believes his eare,
Willing to think th' illusions of his feare
Had given this false Alarm, but straight his view
Confirmes, that more than all he feares is true.
Betray'd in all his strengths, the wood beset,
All instruments, all Arts of ruine met;
He calls to mind his strength, and then his speed,
His winged heeles, and then his armed head;   260
With these t' avoyd, with that his Fate to meet:
But feare prevails, and bids him trust his feet.
So fast he flyes, that his reviewing eye
Has lost the chasers, and his eare the cry;
Exulting, till he finds, their Nobler sense
Their disproportion'd speed does recompense.
Then curses his conspiring feet, whose scent
Betrayes that safety which their swiftnesse lent.
Then tryes his friends, among the baser heard,
Where he so lately was obey'd, and fear'd,   270
His safety seeks: the heard, unkindly wise,
Or chases him from thence, or from him flyes.
Like a declining Statesman, left forlorne
To his friends pitty, and pursuers scorne,
With shame remembers, while himselfe was one
Of the same heard, himselfe the same had done.
Thence to the coverts, and the conscious° Groves,

The scenes of his past triumphs, and his loves;
Sadly surveying where he rang'd alone
Prince of the soyle, and all the heard his owne;   280
And like a bold Knight Errant did proclaime
Combat to all, and bore away the Dame;
And taught the woods to eccho to the streame
His dreadfull challenge, and his clashing beame.°
Yet faintly now declines the fatall strife;
So much his love was dearer than his life.
Now every leafe, and every moving breath
Presents a foe, and every foe a death.
Wearied, forsaken, and pursu'd, at last
All safety in despaire of safety plac'd,   290
Courage he thence resumes, resolv'd to beare
All their assaults, since 'tis in vaine to feare.
And now too late he wishes for the fight
That strength he wasted in Ignoble flight:
But when he sees the eager chase renew'd,
Himself by doggs, the doggs by men pursu'd:
He straight revokes his bold resolve, and more
Repents his courage, than his feare before;
Finds that uncertaine waies unsafest are,
And Doubt a greater mischiefe than Despaire.   300
Then to the streame, when neither friends, nor force,
Nor speed, nor Art availe, he shapes his course;
Thinks not their rage so desperate t' assay,
An Element more mercilesse than they.
But feareless they pursue, nor can the flood
Quench their dire thirst; alas, they thirst for blood.
So towards a Ship the oarefin'd° Gallyes ply,
Which wanting Sea to ride, or wind to fly,
Stands but to fall reveng'd on those that dare
Tempt the last fury of extreame despayre.   310
So fares the Stagg among th' inraged hounds,
Repells their force, and wounds returns for wounds.
And as a Hero, whom his baser foes
In troops surround, now these assailes, now those,
Though prodigall of life, disdaines to dy
By common hands; but if he can descry
Some nobler foes approach, to him he calls,
And beggs his Fate, and then contented falls.
So when the King a mortall shaft lets fly
From his unerring hand, then glad to dy,   320
Proud of the wound, to it resigns his blood,
And staines the Chrystall with a Purple flood.
This a more Innocent, and happy chase,
Than when of old, but in the selfe-same place,°

235. **Faunus and Sylvanus:** ancient woodland deities. 277.
conscious: sympathetic.

284. **beame:** the main trunk of a stag's horn bearing the
antlers. 307. **oarefin'd:** supplied with oars. 324. **the selfe-
same place:** Runnymede.

Faire liberty pursu'd, and meant a Prey
To lawless power, here turn'd, and stood at bay.
When in that remedy all hope was plac't
Which was, or should have been at least, the last.
Here was that Charter° seal'd, wherein the Crowne
All markes of Arbitrary power layes downe: 330
Tyrant and slave, those names of hate and feare,
The happier stile of King and Subject beare:
Happy, when both to the same Center move,
When Kings give liberty, and Subjects love.
Therefore not long in force this Charter stood;
Wanting that seale, it must be seal'd in blood.
The Subjects arm'd, the more their Princes gave,
Th' advantage only took the more to crave:
Till Kings by giving, give themselves away,
And even that power, that should deny, betray.   340
"Who gives constrain'd, but his owne feare reviles,
Not thank't, but scorn'd; nor are they gifts but
     spoyles."
Thus Kings, by grasping more than they could hold,
First made their Subjects by oppression bold:
And popular sway, by forcing Kings to give
More than was fit for Subjects to receive,
Ran to the same extreames; and one excesse,
Made both, by striving to be greater, lesse.
When a calme River rais'd with sudden raines,
Or Snowes dissolv'd, o'reflowes th' adjoyning
     Plaines,   350
The Husbandmen with high-rais'd banks secure
Their greedy hopes, and this he can endure.
But if with bayes and Dammes they strive to force
His channell to a new, or narrow course;
No longer then within his banks he dwels,
First to a Torrent, then a Deluge swels:
Stronger, and fiercer by restraint he roares,
And knows no bound, but makes his power his
     shores.

329. that Charter: Magna Carta.

Edmund Waller

1606–1687

TO THE KING ON HIS NAVY

Where ere thy Navy spreads her canvas wings
Homage to thee, and peace to all she brings:
The French and Spaniard when thy flags appear
Forget their hatred, and consent to fear.
So *Iove* from *Ida* did both hoasts° survey,
And when he pleas'd to thunder part the fray:
Ships heretofore in seas like fishes sped,
The mightiest still upon the smallest fed.
Thou on the deep imposest nobler laws;
And by that justice hast remov'd the cause   10
Of those rude tempests which for rapine sent,
Too oft alas, involv'd the innocent.
Now shall the Ocean as thy Thames be free
From both those fates of stormes and piracie:
But we most happy, who can fear no force
But winged troops, or Pegasean horse.
'Tis not so hard for greedy foes to spoyle
Another Nation as to touch our soyle.
Should natures selfe invade the world againe,
And ore the center spread the liquid maine: 20
Thy power were safe and her distructive hand,
Would but enlarge the bounds of thy command.
Thy dreadfull fleet would style thee Lord of all,
And ride in triumph ore the drowned ball.
Those towers of oake ore fertile plaines might goe
And visit mountains where they once did grow.
     The worlds restorer° once could not endure
That finish'd Babell should those men secure:

TO THE KING ON HIS NAVY. The text is that of the first printing,
in Waller's *Poems* (1645); we have incorporated the variants
from the version in *Poems Written upon Several Occasions*
(1686). The king to whom the poem is addressed is Charles I.
5. both hoasts: Greeks and Trojans, whom Jove observed
from Mount Ida, which overlooked the plain of Troy. **27.
The worlds restorer:** the God of Gen. 9:11, who restored
the world after the Flood only to be faced with the impious
ambition of the builders of the Tower of Babel (Gen. 11:1–9).

Whose pride design'd that fabric to have stood
Above the reach of any second floud.   30
To thee his chosen more indulgent he
Dares trust such power with so much piety.

OF ENGLISH VERSE

Poets may boast, [as safely-Vain,]°
Their work shall with the world remain:
Both bound together, live, or die,
The Verses and the Prophecy.

But who can hope his Lines should long
Last in a daily-changing Tongue?
While they are new, Envy prevails,
And as that dies, our Language fails.

When Architects have done their part,
The Matter may betray their Art: 10
Time, if we use ill-chosen Stone,
Soon brings a well-built Palace down.

Poets that lasting Marble seek,
Must carve in *Latine*, or in *Greek*;
We write in Sand, our Language grows,
And like the Tide our work o'reflows.

Chaucer his Sense can only boast,
The glory of his Numbers° lost,
Years have defac'd his matchless strain;
And yet he did not sing in vain;   20

The Beauties which adorn'd that Age,
The shining Subjects of his Rage,°
Hoping they should Immortal prove,
Rewarded with success his Love.

This was the generous Poet's scope,
And all an *English* Pen can hope
To make the Fair approve his Flame,
That can so far extend their Fame.

Verse thus design'd has no ill Fate,
If it arrive but at the Date°   30
Of fading Beauty, if it prove
But as long-liv'd as present Love.

OF ENGLISH VERSE. The text is from *Poems Written upon
Several Occasions* (1686). **1. as safely-Vain:** The brackets
appear in the original text. **18. Numbers:** versification. **22.
Rage:** poetic inspiration. **30. Date:** term of life.

♔

Thomas D'Urfey

1653–1723

[I'LE SAIL
UPON THE DOG-STAR]

I'le sail upon the Dog-Star,°
and then persue the Morning;
I'le chase the Moon 'till it be Noon,
but I'le make her leave her Horning.°

I'le climb the frosty Mountain,
and there I'le coyn° the Weather;
I'le tear the Rainbow from the Sky,
and tye both ends together.

The Stars pluck from their Orbs too,
and crowd them in my Budget;°   10
and whether I'm a roaring Boy,°
let all the Nation judge it.

♔

John Pomfret

1667–1702

THE CHOICE

IF Heav'n the grateful° Liberty wou'd give,
That I might chuse my Method how to live:
And all those Hours propitious Fate shou'd lend,
In blissful Ease and Satisfaction spend.

I'LE SAIL UPON THE DOG STAR. The text is from *New Songs
Sung in the Fool's Preferment* (1688). The music is by Henry
Purcell. In its original context the poem constitutes a "mad
song." **1. Dog-Star:** Sirius. **4. Horning:** becoming a
crescent, with puns glancing at both hunting and cuckoldry.
6. coyn: create, influence. **10. Budget:** wallet. **11. a
roaring Boy:** a riotous bully. THE CHOICE. According to
Samuel Johnson, "Perhaps no composition in our language
has been oftener perused than Pomfret's *Choice.*" The text
is that of the first edition (1700); we have incorporated the
variants of the final version in Pomfret's *Miscellany Poems
on Several Occasions* (1702). **1. grateful:** pleasing.

Near some fair Town I'd have a private Seat,
Built Uniform, not little, nor too great:
Better, if on a rising Ground it stood,
Fields on this side, on that a Neighb'ring Wood.
It shou'd within no other Things contain,
But what were Useful, Necessary, Plain: 10
Methinks, 'tis Nauseous, and I'd ne'er endure
The needless Pomp of gawdy Furniture:
A little Garden, grateful to the Eye,
And a cool Rivulet run Murmuring by:
On whose delicious Banks a stately Row
Of shady Lymes, or Sycamores, shou'd grow.
At th' End of which a silent Study plac'd,
Shou'd be with all the Noblest Authors grac'd.
Horace and *Virgil*, in whose Mighty Lines,
Immortal Wit, and solid Learning shines.   20
Sharp *Juvenal*, and am'rous *Ovid* too,
Who all the turns of Loves soft Passion knew:
He, that with Judgment reads his Charming Lines,
In which strong Art, with stronger Nature joyns,
Must grant, his Fancy does the best Excel:
His Thoughts so tender, and exprest so well;
With all those Moderns, Men of steady Sense,
Esteem'd for Learning, and for Eloquence:
In some of These, as Fancy shou'd advise,
I'd always take my Morning Exercise.   30
For sure, no Minutes bring us more Content,
Than those in pleasing useful Studies spent.

I'd have a Clear and Competent Estate,
That I might Live Genteelly, but not Great.
As much as I cou'd moderately spend,
A little more sometimes t' Oblige a Friend.
Nor shou'd the Sons of Poverty Repine
Too much at Fortune, they shou'd taste of Mine;
And all that Objects of true Pity were,
Shou'd be reliev'd with what my Wants cou'd
        spare;   40
For that, our Maker has too largely giv'n,
Shou'd be return'd in gratitude to Heav'n.
A frugal Plenty shou'd my Table spread,
With healthy, not luxurious Dishes, fed:
Enough to satisfy, and something more
To feed the Stranger, and the Neighb'ring Poor.
Strong Meat indulges Vice, and Pampering Food
Creates Diseases, and inflames the Blood.
But what's sufficient to make Nature Strong,
And the bright Lamp of Life continue long,   50
I'd freely take, and as I did possess
The bounteous Author of my Plenty bless.

I'd have a little Vault, but always stor'd
With the Best Wines, each Vintage cou'd afford.
Wine whets the Wit, improves its Native Force,
And gives a pleasant Flavour to Discourse;
By making all our Spirits Debonair,
Throws off the Lees, the Sediment of Care.
But as the greatest Blessing Heaven lends
May be debauch'd, and serve ignoble Ends;   60
So, but too oft, the Grapes refreshing Juice,
Does many mischievous Effects produce.
My House, shou'd no such rude Disorders know,
As from high Drinking consequently flow.
Nor wou'd I use what was so kindly giv'n,
To the dishonour of Indulgent Heav'n.
If any Neighbour came he shou'd be free, ⎫
Us'd with respect, and not Uneasy be,   ⎬
In my Retreat, or to himself, or me.   ⎭
What Freedom, Prudence, and Right Reason
        give,   70
All Men, may with Impunity receive;
But the least swerving from their Rule's too much;
For, what's forbidden Us, 'tis Death to touch.

That Life might be more comfortable yet,
And all my Joys refin'd, sincere and great,
I'd chuse two Friends, whose Company wou'd be
A great Advance to my Felicity.
Well born, of Humours suited to my own;
Discreet, and Men as well as Books have known.
Brave, Gen'rous, Witty, and exactly° free   80
From loose Behaviour, or Formality.
Airy, and Prudent, Merry, but not Light,
Quick in discerning, and in Judging Right.
Secret° they shou'd be, faithful to their Trust,
In Reasoning Cool, Strong, Temperate and Just.
Obliging, Open, without huffing, Brave;
Brisk in gay Talking, and in sober Grave.
Close° in Dispute, but not tenacious, try'd
By solid Reason, and let that decide;
Not prone to Lust, Revenge, or envious Hate;   90
Nor busy Medlers with Intrigues of State.
Strangers to Slander, and sworn Foes to spight,
Not Quarrelsom, but Stout enough to Fight:
Loyal and Pious, Friends to *Cæsar* true
As dying Martyrs to their Maker too.
In their Society I cou'd not miss,
A permanent, sincere, substantial Bliss.

80. exactly: perfectly. **84. Secret**: discreet. **88. Close**: rigorous.

Wou'd° bounteous Heav'n once more indulge, I'd
   chuse,
(For, who wou'd so much Satisfaction lose,
As Witty Nymphs in Conversation give)   100
Near some obliging Modest-Fair to live;
For there's that sweetness in a Female Mind,
Which in a Man's we cannot hope to find:
That by a secret, but a pow'rful Art,
Winds up the Springs of Life, and does impart }
Fresh Vital Heat to the transported Heart.

   I'd have her Reason all her Passions sway,
Easy in Company, in private Gay.
Coy° to a Fop, to the Deserving free,
Still constant to her self, and just to me.   110
A Soul she shou'd have for great Actions fit,
Prudence, and Wisdom to direct her Wit.
Courage to look bold danger in the Face,
No Fear, but only to be proud, or base:
Quick to advise by an Emergence° prest,
To give good Counsel, or to take the best.
I'd have th' Expression of her Thoughts be such,
She might not seem Reserv'd, nor talk too much;
That shows a want of Judgment, and of Sense:
More than enough, is but Impertinence.   120
Her Conduct Regular, her Mirth refin'd,
Civil to Strangers, to her Neighbours kind.
Averse to Vanity, Revenge, and Pride,
In all the Methods of Deceit untry'd:
So faithful to her Friend, and good to all,
No Censure might upon her Actions fall.
Then wou'd e'en Envy be compell'd to say,
She goes the least of Womankind astray.

   To this fair Creature I'd sometimes retire,
Her Conversation° wou'd new Joys inspire,   130
Give Life an Edge so keen, no surly Care
Wou'd venture to assault my Soul, or dare }
Near my Retreat to hide one secret Snare.
But so Divine, so Noble a Repast
I'd seldom, and with Moderation taste.
For highest Cordials all their Virtue lose,

By a too frequent, and too bold an use;
And what would cheer the Spirits in distress,
Ruins our Health when taken to Excess.

   I'd be concern'd in no litigious Jarr,°   140
Belov'd by all, not vainly popular:
What e'er Assistance I had power to bring
T' oblige my Country, or to serve my King,
When e'er they call'd, I'd readily afford,
My Tongue, my Pen, my Counsel, or my Sword.
Law Suits I'd shun with as much Studious Care,
As I wou'd Dens, where hungry Lyons are;
And rather put up° Injuries, than be
A Plague to him, who'd be a Plague to me.
I value Quiet, at a Price too great,   150
To give for my Revenge so dear a Rate:
For what do we by all our Bustle gain,
But counterfeit Delight for real Pain.

   If Heav'n a date of many years wou'd give,
Thus I'd in Pleasure, Ease, and Plenty live.
And as I near approach'd the Verge of Life,
Some kind Relation (for I'd have no Wife)
Shou'd take upon him all my Worldly Care,
While I did for a better State prepare.
Then I'd not be with any trouble vex't,   160
Nor have the Evening of my Days perplext.
But by a silent, and a peaceful Death,
Without a Sigh, Resign my Aged Breath:
And when committed to the Dust, I'd have
Few Tears, but Friendly, dropt into my Grave.
Then wou'd my Exit so propitious be,
All Men wou'd wish to live and dye like me.

♛

William Walsh

1663–1708

THE DESPAIRING LOVER

DIstracted with Care,
  For *Phillis* the Fair;
Since nothing cou'd move her,
  Poor *Damon*, her Lover,

98–139. Wou'd . . . Excess: The warmth of lines 98–139, especially in the light of the assertion (l. 157) that "I'd have no Wife," seems to have prevented Pomfret, who was in orders, from rising in the church. As Johnson points out, "He found a troublesome obstruction [to his clerical ambitions] raised by a malicious interpretation of [this] passage in his *Choice,* from which it was inferred that he considered happiness as more likely to be found in the company of a mistress than of a wife." **109. Coy:** reserved, disdainful. **115. Emergence:** emergency. **130. Conversation:** intimate company.

140. Jarr: dispute. **148. put up:** suffer quietly. THE DESPAIRING LOVER. Our text is from Tonson's *Miscellany* (Vol. V, 1704).

Resolves in Despair
No longer to languish,
Nor bear so much Anguish;
But, mad with his Love,
To a Precipice goes;
Where, a Leap from above   10
Wou'd soon finish his Woes.

When in Rage he came there,
Beholding how steep
The Sides did appear,
And the Bottom how deep;
His Torments projecting,°
And sadly reflecting,
That a Lover forsaken
A new Love may get;
But a Neck, when once broken,   20
Can never be set:
And, that he cou'd die
Whenever he wou'd;
But, that he cou'd live
But as long as he cou'd:
How grievous soever
The Torment might grow,
He scorn'd to endeavour
To finish it so.
But Bold, Unconcern'd   30
At Thoughts of the Pain,
He calmly return'd
To his Cottage again.

John Philips
1676–1709

THE SPLENDID SHILLING

AN IMITATION OF MILTON.

HAPPY the Man, who void of Cares and Strife,
In Silken, or in Leathern Purse retains
A *Splendid Shilling:* He nor hears with Pain
New Oysters cry'd, nor sighs for chearful Ale;
But with his Friends, when nightly Mists arise,

To *Juniper's, Magpye,* or *Town-Hall*° repairs:
Where, mindful of the Nymph, whose wanton Eye
Transfix'd his Soul, and kindled Amorous Flames,
Chloe, or *Phillis;* he each Circling Glass
Wisheth her Health, and Joy, and equal Love.   10
Mean while he smoaks, and laughs at merry Tale,
Or *Pun* ambiguous, or *Conundrum* quaint.
But I, whom griping Penury surrounds,
And Hunger, sure Attendant upon Want,
With scanty Offals, and small acid Tiff°
(Wretched Repast!) my meagre Corps sustain:
Then Solitary walk, or doze at home
In Garret vile, and with a warming puff
Regale chill'd Fingers; or from Tube as black
As Winter-Chimney, or well-polish'd Jet,   20
Exhale *Mundungus,*° ill-perfuming Scent:
Not blacker Tube, nor of a shorter Size
Smoaks *Cambro-Britain*° (vers'd in Pedigree,
Sprung from *Cadwalader* and *Arthur,* Kings,
Full famous in Romantic tale) when he
O'er many a craggy Hill, and barren Cliff,
Upon a Cargo of fam'd *Cestrian*° Cheese,
High over-shadowing rides, with a design
To vend his Wares, or at th' *Arvonian* Mart,
Or *Maridunum,* or the ancient Town   30
Eclips'd *Brechinia,* or where *Vaga's* Stream
Encircles *Ariconium,* fruitful Soil,
Whence flow Nectareous Wines, that well may vye
With *Massic, Setin,* or renown'd *Falern.*

Thus while my joyless Minutes tedious flow
With Looks demure, and silent Pace, a *Dunn,*°
Horrible Monster! hated by Gods and Men,
To my aerial Citadel ascends;
With Vocal Heel thrice thund'ring at my Gates,
With hideous Accent thrice he calls; I know   40
The Voice ill-boding, and the solemn Sound.
What shou'd I do? or whither turn? amaz'd,
Confounded, to the dark Recess I fly
Of Woodhole;° strait my bristling Hairs erect
Thrô sudden Fear; a chilly Sweat bedews
My shud'ring Limbs, and (wonderful to tell!)
My Tongue forgets her Faculty of Speech;

---

16. **projecting:** considering. THE SPLENDID SHILLING. The poem was first published in 1701; our text is that of the first authorized edition (1705).

6. **Juniper's . . . Town-Hall:** names of actual coffee houses and alehouses. 15. **Tiff:** bad, weak liquor. 21. **Mundungus:** a "mean" tobacco. 23. **Cambro-Britain:** mock-pompous for *Welshman.* 27. **Cestrian:** mock-Latinate diction for *Cheshire;* the similar names following refer likewise to places in Southern Wales. 36. **Dunn:** importunate creditor. 44. **Woodhole:** low closed cupboard beside the fireplace.

So horrible he seems! his faded Brow
Entrench'd with many a Frown, and *Conic* Beard,
And spreading Band,° admir'd by Modern Saints,   50
Disastrous Acts forebode; in his Right Hand
Long Scrolls of Paper solemnly he waves,
With Characters, and Figures dire inscrib'd
Grievous to mortal Eyes; (ye Gods avert
Such Plagues from righteous Men!) behind him stalks
Another Monster, not unlike himself,
Sullen of Aspect, by the Vulgar call'd
A *Catchpole,*° whose polluted Hands the Gods
With Force incredible, and Magick Charms
Erst° have indu'd, if he his ample Palm   60
Should haply on ill-fated Shoulder lay
Of Debtor, strait his Body, to the Touch
Obsequious, (as whilom Knights were wont)
To some enchanted Castle is convey'd,
Where Gates impregnable, and coercive Chains
In Durance strict detain him, 'till in form
Of Mony, *Pallas*° sets the Captive free.

Beware, ye Debtors, when ye walk beware,
Be circumspect; oft with insidious Ken°
This Caitif° eyes your Steps aloof, and oft   70
Lies perdue° in a Nook or gloomy Cave,
Prompt to enchant some inadvertent° wretch
With his unhallow'd Touch. So (Poets sing)
Grimalkin° to Domestick Vermin sworn
An everlasting Foe, with watchful Eye,
Lyes nightly brooding o'er a chinky gap,
Protending° her fell° Claws, to thoughtless Mice
Sure Ruin. So her disembowell'd Web
Arachne° in a Hall, or Kitchin spreads,
Obvious° to vagrant Flies: She secret stands   80
Within her woven Cell; the Humming Prey,
Regardless of their Fate, rush on the toils
Inextricable, nor will aught avail
Their Arts, nor Arms, nor Shapes of lovely Hue;
The Wasp insidious, and the buzzing Drone,
And Butterfly proud of expanded wings
Distinct° with Gold, entangled in her Snares,
Useless Resistance make: With eager strides,

She tow'ring flies to her expected Spoils;
Then with envenom'd Jaws the vital Blood   90
Drinks of reluctant Foes, and to her Cave
Their bulky Carcasses triumphant drags.

So pass my Days. But when Nocturnal Shades
This World invelop, and th' inclement Air
Persuades Men to repel benumming Frosts,
With pleasant Wines, and crackling blaze of Wood;
Me Lonely sitting, nor the glimmering Light
Of Make-weight Candle,° nor the joyous Talk
Of loving Friend delights; distress'd, forlorn,
Amidst the horrors of the tedious Night,   100
Darkling° I sigh, and feed with dismal Thoughts
My anxious Mind; or sometimes mournful Verse
Indite,° and sing of Groves and Myrtle Shades,
Or desperate Lady near a purling Stream,
Or Lover pendent on a Willow-Tree:
Mean while I Labour with eternal Drought,
And restless Wish, and Rave; my parched Throat
Finds no Relief, nor heavy Eyes Repose:
But if a Slumber haply does Invade
My weary Limbs, my Fancy's still awake,   110
Thoughtful of Drink, and Eager in a Dream,
Tipples Imaginary Pots of Ale;
In Vain; awake, I find the settled Thirst
Still gnawing, and the pleasant Phantom curse.

Thus do I live from Pleasure quite debarr'd,
Nor taste the Fruits that the Sun's genial Rays
Mature, *John-Apple,*° nor the downy *Peach,*
Nor *Walnut* in rough-furrow'd Coat secure,
Nor *Medlar,*° Fruit delicious in decay;
Afflictions Great! yet Greater still remain: 120
My *Galligaskins*° that have long withstood
The Winter's Fury, and Encroaching Frosts,
By Time subdu'd, (what will not Time subdue!)
An horrid Chasm disclose, with Orifice
Wide, Discontinuous;° at which the Winds
Eurus and *Auster,* and the dreadful Force
Of *Boreas,*° that congeals the *Cronian*° Waves,
Tumultuous enter with dire chilling Blasts,

---

50. spreading Band: broad collar such as those affected by some Dissenters. **58. Catchpole:** sheriff's officer. **60. Erst:** of old. **67. Pallas:** Pallas Athene, goddess of wisdom and skill. **69. Ken:** awareness. **70. Caitif:** villain. **71. perdue:** hidden. **72. inadvertent:** heedless. **74. Grimalkin:** traditional name for an aged female cat. **77. Protending:** stretching. **fell:** fierce. **79. Arachne:** an elegant term for a spider ever since Pallas Athene changed a Lydian girl of that name into one. **80. Obvious:** lying in the way of. **87. Distinct:** adorned.

98. Make-weight Candle: a small candle of little value added to a purchase to make the whole reach a certain weight. **101. Darkling:** in the dark. **103. Indite:** compose. **117. John-Apple:** a preserved apple, wrinkled like a prune. **119. Medlar:** a small fruit such as a loquat. **121. Galligaskins:** trousers, especially loose "Dutch" ones. **125. Discontinuous:** gaping. **126-27: Eurus, Auster, Boreas:** east, south, and north winds. **127. Cronian:** pertaining to the north polar sea.

Portending Agues. Thus a well-fraught Ship
Long sail'd secure, or thrô th' *Ægean* Deep,   130
Or the *Ionian*, 'till Cruising near
The *Lilybean*° Shoar, with hideous Crush
On *Scylla*, or *Charybdis* (dang'rous Rocks)
She strikes rebounding, whence the shatter'd Oak,
So fierce a Shock unable to withstand,
Admits the Sea; in at the gaping Side
The crouding Waves Gush with impetuous Rage,
Resistless, Overwhelming; Horrors seize
The Mariners, Death in their Eyes appears,
They stare, they lave,° they pump, they swear, they
    pray: 140
(Vain Efforts!) still the battering Waves rush in
Implacable, 'till delug'd by the Foam,
The Ship sinks found'ring in the vast Abyss.

♛

Anne Finch, Countess of Winchilsea
1661–1720

ADAM POS'D°

COu'd our first Father, at his toilsome Plough,
Thorns in his Path, and Labour on his Brow,
Cloath'd only in a rude, unpolish'd Skin;
Cou'd he, a vain, fantastick Nymph have seen,
In all her Airs, in all her Antick Graces;
Her various Fashions, and more various Faces;
How had it pos'd that Skill, which late Assign'd
Just Appellations to each sev'ral Kind,°   8
A right Idea of the Sight to frame,
T' have guest from what new Element she came,
T' have hit the wavering Form, or giv'n this Thing
    a Name.

THE ATHEIST AND THE ACORN

MEthinks this World is oddly made,
And ev'ry thing's amiss,
A dull presuming Atheist said,
As stretch'd he lay beneath a Shade;
    And instanced in this:

Behold, quoth he, that mighty thing,
    A *Pumpkin*, large and round,
Is held but by a little String,
Which upwards cannot make it spring,
    Or bear it from the Ground.   10

Whilst on this *Oak*, a Fruit so small,
    So disproportion'd, grows;
That, who with Sence surveys this *All*,
This universal Casual° Ball,
    Its ill Contrivance knows.

My better Judgment wou'd have hung
    That Weight upon a Tree,
And left this Mast,° thus slightly strung,
'Mongst things which on the Surface sprung,
    And small and feeble be.   20

No more the Caviller cou'd say,
    Nor farther Faults descry;
For, as he upwards gazing lay,
An *Acorn*, loosen'd from the Stay,°
    Fell down upon his Eye.

Th' offended Part with Tears ran o'er,
    As° punish'd for the Sin:
Fool! had that Bough a *Pumpkin* bore,
Thy Whimseys must have work'd no more,
    Nor Scull had kept them in.   30

A NOCTURNAL REVERIE

IN such a *Night*,° when every louder Wind
Is to its distant Cavern safe confin'd;
And only gentle *Zephyr* fans his Wings,
And lonely *Philomel*, still waking, sings;

132. Lilybean: Sicilian. **140. lave:** bail. ADAM POS'D. The
text is from Tonson's *Miscellany* (1709); we have incorporated
the variants from Finch's *Miscellany Poems on Several Occasions,
Written by a Lady* (1713). **Pos'd:** perplexed. **8. Just . . .
Kind:** See Gen. 2:19–20. THE ATHEIST AND THE ACORN. The text is from Finch's
Miscellany Poems (1713). **14. Casual:** created by chance. **18.
Mast:** acorn. **24. Stay:** support; i.e., bough. **27. As:** as if.
A NOCTURNAL REVERIE. The text is from *Miscellany Poems*
(1713). **1. In . . . Night:** Cf. *The Merchant of Venice*, V. i.
1–22.

Or from some Tree, fam'd for the *Owl*'s delight,
She, hollowing clear, directs the Wand'rer right:
In such a *Night*, when passing Clouds give place,
Or thinly vail the Heav'ns mysterious Face;
When in some River, overhung with Green,
The waving Moon and trembling Leaves are seen;   10
When freshen'd Grass now bears it self upright,
And makes cool Banks to pleasing Rest invite,
Whence springs the *Woodbind*, and the *Bramble*-Rose,
And where the sleepy *Cowslip* shelter'd grows;
Whilst now a paler Hue the *Foxglove* takes,
Yet checquers still with Red the dusky brakes:
When scatter'd *Glow-worms*, but in Twilight fine,
Shew trivial Beauties watch their Hour to shine;
Whilst *Salisb'ry*° stands the Test of every Light,
In perfect Charms, and perfect Virtue bright: 20
When Odours, which declin'd repelling Day,
Thro' temp'rate Air uninterrupted stray;
When darken'd Groves their softest Shadows wear,
And falling Waters we distinctly hear;
When thro' the Gloom more venerable shows
Some ancient Fabrick,° awful in Repose,
While Sunburnt Hills their swarthy Looks conceal,
And swelling Haycocks thicken up the Vale:
When the loos'd *Horse* now, as his Pasture leads,
Comes slowly grazing thro' th' adjoining Meads,   30
Whose stealing Pace, and lengthen'd Shade we fear,
Till torn up Forage in his Teeth we hear:
When nibbling *Sheep* at large pursue their Food,
And unmolested Kine rechew the Cud;
When *Curlews* cry beneath the Village-walls,
And to her straggling Brood the *Partridge* calls;
Their shortliv'd Jubilee the Creatures keep,
Which but endures, whilst Tyrant-*Man* do's sleep:
When a sedate Content the Spirit feels,
And no fierce Light disturbs, whilst it reveals;   40
But silent Musings urge the Mind to seek
Something, too high for Syllables to speak;
Till the free Soul to a compos'dness charm'd,
Finding the Elements of Rage disarm'd,
O'er all below a solemn Quiet grown,
Joys in th' inferiour° World, and thinks it like her
    Own:
In such a *Night* let Me abroad remain,
Till Morning breaks, and All's confus'd again;
Our Cares, our Toils, our Clamours are renew'd,
Or Pleasures, seldom reach'd, again pursu'd.   50

19. Salisb'ry: Lady Salisbury, the daughter of one of Finch's best friends. **26. Fabrick:** building. **46. inferiour:** lower.

Henry Carey

c. 1687–1743

SALLY IN OUR ALLEY

OF all the Girls that are so smart,
There's none like pretty *Sally;*
She is the darling of my Heart,
& She lives in our alley;
There is no Lady in the Land
Is half so sweet as *Sally;*
She is the darling of my Heart,
& She lives in our alley.

2

Her Father he makes Cabbage nets
And through the street does cry 'em.   10
Her mother She sells Laces long,
To such as please to buy 'em.
But sure such Folks cou'd neer Beget,
So sweet a Girl as *Sally.*
She is the darling of my Heart,
& She lives in our alley.

3

When she is by I leave my work,
(I love her so sincerely)
My master comes like any *Turk*,
And he bangs me most severely.   20

SALLY IN OUR ALLEY. The text is that of the engraved broadsheet which appeared about 1715. In an introduction to the poem written later (for *Poems on Several Occasions* [1729]) Carey observes of the occasion of the piece: "A Shoemaker's 'Prentice making Holiday with his Sweet-heart, treated her with a sight of Bedlam, the Puppet-shews, the Flying-chairs, and all the Elegancies of Moor-fields: From whence proceeding to the Farthing Pye-house, he gave her a Collation of Buns, Cheesecakes, Gammon of Bacon, Stuff'd-beef, and Bottled-ale; through all which Scenes the Author dodged Them (charm'd with the Simplicity of their Courtship), from whence he drew this little Sketch of Nature; but being then young and obscure, he was very much ridicul'd by some of his Acquaintance for this Performance; which nevertheless made its way into the Polite World, and amply recompenced him by the Applause of the divine *Addison*, who was pleased (more than once) to mention it with Approbation."

But let him bang his belly full,
I'd bear it all for *Sally*.
She is the darling of my Heart,
& She lives in our alley.

4

Of all the days that's in the week,
I dearly love but one day,
And thats the day that comes betwixt
A saturday & munday.
For then I'm drest all in my best,
To walk abroad with *Sally*.   30
She is the darling of my Heart,
And She lives in our alley.

5

My master carries me to *Church*,
And often am I blamed,
Because I leave him in the lurch,
As soon as Text is named.
I leave the *Church* in sermon time,
And slink away to *Sally*.
She is the darling of my Heart,
& She lives in our alley.   40

6

When *Christmass* comes about again,
O then I shall have money.
I'll hoard it up & Box & all,
I'll give it to my Honey.
I wou'd it were Ten Thousand Pound,
I'd give it all to *Sally*.
She is the darling of my Heart,
& She lives in our alley.

7

My master & the neighbours all,
Make game of me & *Sally*,   50
And (but for her) I'd better be,
A slave & row a *Galley*.
But when my 7 long Years° are out,
O then I'll marry *Sally*.
O then we'll wed & then we'll Bed,
But not in our alley.

53. 7 . . . **Years:** the period of an apprenticeship to a trade, during which the apprentice was not allowed to marry.

Ambrose Philips

c. 1675–1749

THE FIRST PASTORAL

LOBBIN.

If we, O *Dorset*,° quit the City Throng
To meditate in Shades the Rural Song
By your Commands; be present: And, O, bring
The Muse along! The Muse to you shall sing.

Begin.—A Shepherd Boy, one Ev'ning fair,
As Western Winds had cool'd the sultry Air,
When as his Sheep within their Fold were pent,
Thus plain'd him of his dreary Discontent;
So pitiful, that all the starry Throng
Attentive seem'd to hear his mournful Song.   10

Ah well a Day! How long must I endure
This pining Pain? Or who shall work my Cure?
Fond Love no Cure will have; seeks no Repose;
Delights in Grief; nor any Measure knows.
And now the Moon begins in Clouds to rise;
The twinkling Stars are lighted in the Skies;
The Winds are hush'd; the Dews distil; and Sleep
With soft Embrace has seiz'd my weary Sheep.
I only, with the prouling Wolf, constrain'd
All Night to wake. With Hunger is he pain'd,   20
And I with Love. His Hunger he may tame:
But who in Love can stop the growing Flame?

Whilome° did I, all as° this Pop'lar fair,
Up-raise my heedless Head, devoid of Care,
'Mong rustic Routs the chief for wanton Game;
Nor could they merry make 'till *Lobbin* came.

THE FIRST PASTORAL. The text is from Tonson's *Miscellany* (1709). Philips published six pastorals in all, and his apparent devotion to the realistic manner of Theocritus instead of the more idealized mode of Virgil generated a small literary controversy; John Gay's *Shepherd's Week* (see Part Two) reflects the reaction of the Scriblerus Club to Philips's work. **1. Dorset:** Philips's patron Lionel Cranfield Sackville (1688–1765), Seventh Earl of Dorset. **23. Whilome:** once upon a time. **all as:** just like.

Who better seen, than I, in Shepherds Arts,
To please the Lads and win the Lasses Hearts?
How deffly° to mine oaten Reed, so sweet,
Wont they,° upon the Green, to shift their Feet?   30
And, when the Dance was done, how would they
    yearn
Some well devised Tale from me to learn?
For, many Songs and Tales of Mirth had I,
To chase the lingring Sun adown the Sky.
But, ah! since *Lucy* coy has wrought her Spite
Within my Heart; unmindful of Delight,
The jolly Grooms° I fly; and all alone
To Rocks and Woods pour forth my fruitless Moan.

Oh quit thy wonted Scorn, relentless Fair!
E'er, lingring long, I perish thro' Despair.   40
Had *Rosalind* been Mistress of my Mind,
Tho' not so fair, she would have been more kind.
O think, unwitting Maid, while yet is Time,
How flying Years impair our youthful Prime!
Thy Virgin Bloom will not for ever stay;
And Flow'rs, tho' left ungather'd, will decay.
The Flow'rs anew returning Seasons bring;
But Beauty faded has no second Spring.

My Words are Wind! She, deaf to all my Cries,
Takes Pleasure in the Mischief of her Eyes.   50
Like frisking Heifers, loose in flow'ry Meads,
She gads where-e'er her roving Fancy leads;
Yet still from me. Ah me, the tiresome Chase!
While, wing'd with Scorn, she flies my fond
    Embrace.
She flies indeed: But ever leaves behind,
Fly where she will, her Likeness in my Mind.
Ah turn thee then! unthinking Damsel! Why,
Thus from the Youth, who loves thee, should'st thou
    fly?
No cruel Purpose in my Speed I bear:
'Tis all but Love; and Love why should'st thou
    fear?   60
What idle Fears a Maiden Breast alarm!
Stay, simple Girl! a Lover cannot harm.

Two Kidlins, sportive as thy self, I rear;
Like tender Buds their shooting Horns appear.
A Lambkin too, pure white, I breed, as tame,
As my fond Heart could wish my scornful Dame.
A Garland, deck'd with all the Pride of *May*,

Sweet as thy Breath, and as thy Beauty gay,
I'll weave. But why these unavailing Pains?
The Gifts alike and Giver she disdains.   70
Oh would my Gifts but win her wanton Heart!
Oh could I half the Warmth I feel impart!
How would I wander ev'ry Day to find
The ruddy Wildings°! Were but *Lucy* kind,
For glossy Plumbs I'd climb the knotty Tree,
And of fresh Hony rob the thrifty Bee.
Or, if thou deign to live a Shepherdess,
Thou *Lobbin's* Flock, and *Lobbin*, shalt possess.
Fair is my Flock; nor yet uncomely I,
If liquid Fountains flatter not: And why   80
Should liquid Fountains flatter us? yet show
The bord'ring Flow'rs less beauteous than they grow.

O come, my Love! Nor think th' Employment
    mean,
The Dams to milk, and little Lambkins wean;
To drive a-Field by Morn the fat'ning Ewes,
E'er the warm Sun drinks up the cooly Dews.
How would the Crook beseem thy beauteous Hand!
How would my Younglins round thee gazing stand!
Ah witless Younglins! gaze not on her Eye:
Such heedless Glances are the Cause I die.   90
Nor trow I when this bitter Blast will end;
Or if Kind Love will ever me befriend.
Sleep, sleep, my Flock: For, happy you may take
Your Rest, tho' nightly thus your Master wake.

Now, to the waining Moon, the Nightingale
In doleful Ditties told her piteous Tale.
The Love-sick Shepherd list'ning found Relief,
Pleas'd with so sweet a Partner in his Grief:
'Till by degrees her Notes and silent Night
To Slumbers soft his heavy Heart invite.   100

ANACREON, ODE 34

WHY so Coy, my lovely Maid?
Why of Age so much afraid?
Your Cheeks, like Roses, to the Sight;
And my Hair, as Lillies white;
In Love's Garland, we'll suppose
Me the Lilly, you the Rose.

---

29. **deffly:** deftly. 30. **Wont they:** Weren't they accustomed. 37. **Grooms:** pastoral term for young men.

74. **Wildings:** crabapples. ANACREON, ODE 34. The text is from the sixth part of Tonson's *Miscellany* (1709).

TO SEIGNORA CUZZONI

Little *Syren* of the Stage,
Charmer of an idle Age,
Empty Warbler, breathing Lyre,
Wanton Gale of fond Desire,
Bane of ev'ry manly Art,
Sweet Enfeebler of the Heart;
Oh, too pleasing is thy Strain!
Hence, to Southern Climes again;
Tuneful Mischief, Vocal Spell,
To this Island bid farewel.   10
Leave us as we ought to be,
Leave the *Britons* rough and free.

TO MISS MARGARET PULTENEY, DAUGHTER OF DANIEL PULTENEY ESQ; IN THE NURSERY

April 27, 1727

DImply Damsel, sweetly Smiling,
All caressing, none beguiling,
Bud of Beauty fairly blowing,
Every Charm to Nature owing;
This and that, new thing admiring,
Much of this, and that, enquiring;
Knowledge by degrees attaining,
Day by day, some Virtue gaining:
Ten Years hence when I leave Chiming,
Beardless Poets, fondly Rhiming,   10

TO SEIGNORA CUZZONI. The text is from *The Musical Miscellany* (1731). The addressee of the poem is Francesca Cuzzoni, a famous Italian singer. TO MISS MARGARET PULTENEY. The text is from the Dublin broadside of 1725; we have incorporated the variant in the last line which appears in Philips's *Pastorals, Epistles, Odes, and Other Original Poems* (1748). This poem is typical of a number addressed to children—especially the children of the rich and politically powerful—which won Philips the sobriquet of Namby-Pamby from Jonathan Swift and Henry Carey. Carey observed:

Now the venal poet sings
Baby clouts and baby things
. . . .
That her father's Gracey-Grace
Might give him a placey-place.

(Fescued° now, perhaps in spelling)
On thy riper Beauties dwelling,
Shall accuse each killing Feature
Of the cruel charming Creature,
Whom I knew complying willing,
Tender and averse to killing.

Allan Ramsay

1686–1758

POLWART ON THE GREEN

AT Polwart *on the Green*°
If you'll meet me the Morn,
Where Lasses do conveen
To dance about the Thorn;
A kindly welcome you shall meet
    Frae her wha likes to view
A Lover and a Lad complete,
    The Lad and Lover you.

Let dorty° Dames say *Na,*
As lang as e'er they please,   10
Seem caulder than the Sna',
While inwardly they bleez;
But I will frankly shaw my Mind,
    And yield my Heart to thee;
Be ever to the Captive kind,
    That langs na to be free.

At *Polwart* on the Green,
Amang the new mawn Hay,
With Sangs and dancing keen
We'll pass the heartsome Day,   20
At Night if Beds be o'er thrang laid,°
    And thou be twin'd of° thine,
Thou shalt be welcome, my dear Lad,
    To take a Part of mine.

11. Fescued: equipped with a fescue, a small pointer used in teaching children the alphabet. POLWART ON THE GREEN. The text is from Ramsay's *Poems* (dated 1720; issued 1722). **1. Polwart . . . Green:** the town of Polwarth, in Berwickshire. **9. dorty:** haughty. **21. o'er . . . laid:** overcrowded. **22. twin'd of:** excluded from.

[MY PEGGY IS
A YOUNG THING]

MY Peggy is a young thing,
  Just enter'd in her Teens,
Fair as the Day, and sweet as May,
Fair as the Day, and always gay.
My Peggy is a young thing,
  And I'm not very auld,
Yet well I like to meet her at
  The Wawking of the Fauld.°

My Peggy speaks sae sweetly,
  When'er we meet alane,   10
I wish nae mair to lay my Care,
I wish nae mair of a' that's rare.
My Peggy speaks sae sweetly,
  To a' the lave° I'm cauld;
But she gars° a' my Spirits glow
  At Wawking of the Fauld.

My Peggy smiles sae kindly,
  Whene'er I whisper Love,
That I look down on a' the Town,
That I look down upon a Crown.   20
My Peggy smiles sae kindly,
  It makes me blythe and bauld,
And naithing gi'es me sic Delight,
  As Wawking of the Fauld.

My Peggy sings sae saftly,
  When on my Pipe I play;
By a' the rest it is confest,
By a' the rest, that she sings best.
My Peggy sings sae saftly,
  And in her Sangs are tald,   30
With Innocence the Wale° of Sense,
  At Wawking of the Fauld.

☙☙☙

Walter Titley
1700–1768

THE SECOND ODE IN THE
THIRD BOOK OF HORACE,
IMITATED

I.

HE who would great in Science° grow,
  By whom bright Virtue is ador'd,
First must be content to know
  An humble Roof, and homely Board.

II.

With Want, and rigid College Laws,
  Let him inur'd betimes° comply;
Firm to Religion's sacred Cause,
  The learned Combat let him try.

III.

Let him her envy'd Praises tell,
  And all his Eloquence disclose;   10
The fierce Endeavours to repell,
  And still the Tumults of her Foes.

IV.

Him early form'd, and season'd Young,
  Subtle Opposers soon will fear;
And tremble at his artful Tongue,
  Like *Parthians*° at a *Roman* Spear.

V.

Grim Death, th' inevitable Lot
  Which Fools and Cowards strive to fly,
Is with a noble Pleasure sought
  By him who bravely dares to die.   20

MY PEGGY IS A YOUNG THING. This song is sung in the first
act of Ramsay's pastoral ballad-opera *The Gentle Shepherd:
A Scots Pastoral-Comedy* by the young hero Patie, "The
Gentle Shepherd, in Love with Peggy." The text is that
of the edition of 1730. **8. The Wawking . . . Fauld**: the
watching of the sheep. **14. the lave**: the rest. **15. gars**: makes.
31. Wale: best.

THE SECOND ODE IN THE THIRD BOOK OF HORACE, IMITATED.
The texts of this and the following poem are from *The
Grove; or, a Collection of Original Poems, Translations, &c.*
(1721). **1. Science**: knowledge. **6. betimes**: early. **16.
Parthians**: said to have perfected the military art of shoot-
ing arrows accurately while in rapid retreat.

VI.

With brightest Lustre of her own,
  Pure, and exalted Vertue shines:
Nor, as the Vulgar smile and frown,
  Advances now, and now declines.

VII.

A glorious and immortal Prize
  She on her hardy Son bestows;
She shows him Heav'n, and bids him rise,
  Tho' Toil, and Pain, and Death, oppose;
With labouring Flight he wings th' obstructed Way,
Leaving both *common Souls*, and *common Clay*.   30

A REPLY, IN THE SAME MEASURE AND NUMBER OF LINES

BY DR. B——Y.

I.

WHO strives to mount *Parnassus* Hill,
  And thence Poetick Laurels bring,
Must first acquire due Force and Skill,
  Must fly with Swan's, or Eagle's, Wing.

II.

Who Nature's Treasures wou'd explore,
  Her Mysteries and Arcana know,
Must high, as lofty *Newton*, soar,
  Must stoop, as searching *Woodward*,° low.

III.

Who studies ancient Laws and Rites,
  Tongues, Arts and Arms, all History,   10
Must drudge like *Selden*,° Days and Nights,
  And in the endless Labour dye.

IV.

Who travels in Religious Jars,°
  (Truth mixt with Errors, Shade with Rays,)
Like *Whiston*,° wanting *Pyx*° and Stars,
  In Ocean wide or sinks, or strays.

A REPLY. Titley's *persona* here, Dr. Richard Bentley (1662–1742), was the famous Master of Trinity College, Cambridge, and a noted classical scholar. He is caricatured by Pope in *The Dunciad* (see Part Two) for pedantry and bad manners. **8. Woodward:** Dr. John Woodward's (1665–1728) focus on fossils was as intent as Sir Isaac Newton's on galaxies. **11. Selden:** John Selden (1584–1654), antiquarian and orientalist. **13. travels . . . Jars:** toils in religious disputes. **15. Whiston:** William Whiston (1667–1752), a divine known for his prophetic lectures. **Pyx:** [Titley's note] The Compass.

V.

But grant, our Heroe's Hopes long Toil,
  And comprehensive Genius, crown;
All Sciences, all Arts, his Spoil,
  Yet what Reward, or what Renown?   20

VI.

Envy innate in vulgar Souls,
  Envy steps in, and stops his Rise;
Envy with poison'd Tarnish fouls
  His Lustre, and his Worth decrys.

VII.

Inglorious, or by Wants inthrall'd,
  To Colledge, and old Books, confin'd,
A Pedant from his Learning call'd,
  Dunces advanc'd, he's left behind;
Yet left *Content*, a Genuine *Stoick* He,
Great without *Patron*, *rich* without *South-Sea*°!   30

Thomas Parnell

1679–1718

SONG

WHEN thy Beauty appears
  In its Graces and Airs,
All bright as an Angel new dropt from the Sky;
  At distance I gaze, and am aw'd by my Fears,
  So strangely you dazzle my Eye!

But when without Art,
  Your kind Thoughts you impart,
When your Love runs in Blushes thro' ev'ry Vein;
  When it darts from your Eyes, when it pants in your
      Heart,
  Then I know you're a Woman again.   10

There's a Passion and Pride
  In our Sex, (she reply'd,)
And thus (might I gratify both) I wou'd do:
  Still an Angel appear to each Lover beside,
  But still be a Woman to you.

30. South-Sea: a reference to the fever of speculative investment in the South Sea Company, founded in 1711 to advance trade with Spanish America. SONG. The text is from Parnell's posthumous *Poems on Several Occasions*, published in 1722 under the aegis of Alexander Pope.

♕♕♕

William Hamilton of Bangour

1704–1754

THE BRAES OF YARROW

BUsk° ye, busk ye, my bonny bonny bride,
Busk ye, busk ye, my winsom marrow,°
Busk ye, busk ye, my bonny bonny bride,
And let us leave the braes of *Yarrow*.°

Where got ye that bonny bonny bride,
Where got ye that winsom marrow?
I got her where I durst not well be seen,
Puing the birks° on the braes of *Yarrow*.

Weep not, weep not, my bonny bonny bride,
Weep not, weep not, my winsom marrow,   10
Nor let thy heart lament to leave
Puing the birks on the braes of *Yarrow*.

Why does she weep, thy bonny bonny bride?
Why does she weep, thy winsome marrow?
And why dare ye nae mair well be seen,
Puing the birks on the braes of *Yarrow?*

Lang must she weep, lang must she, must she weep,
Lang must she weep with dole and sorrow,
And lang must I nae mair well be seen
Puing the birks on the braes of *Yarrow*.   20

For she has tint° her lover, lover dear,
Her lover dear, the cause of sorrow,
And I have slain the comliest swain,
That ever pued birks on the braes of *Yarrow*.

Why runs thy stream, O *Yarrow*, *Yarrow*, reid°?
Why on thy braes heard the voice of sorrow?
And why yon melancholious weeds,
Hung on the bony birks of *Yarrow?*

What's yonder floats on the rueful, rueful flood?
What's yonder floats? O dole and sorrow,   30
O 'tis the comely swain I slew
Upon the doleful braes of *Yarrow*.

Wash, O wash his wounds his wounds in tears,
His wounds in tears of dole and sorrow,
And wrap his limbs in murning weeds,
And lay him on the braes of *Yarrow*.

Then build, then build, ye sisters sisters sad,
Ye sisters sad, his tomb with sorrow,
And weep around in woful wise,
His helpless fate on the braes of *Yarrow*.   40

Curse ye, curse ye, his useless useless shield,
My arm that wrought the deed of sorrow,
The fatal spear that pierc'd his breast
His comly breast on the braes of *Yarrow*.

Did I not warn thee not to, not to love,
And warn from fight? but to my sorrow,
Too rashly bold, a stronger arm
Thou met'st, and fell on the braes of *Yarrow*.

Sweet smells the birk, green grows, green grows the
        Grass,
Yellow on *Yarrow*'s braes the gowan,°   50
Fair hangs the apple frae the rock,
Sweet the wave of *Yarrow* flowan.

Flows *Yarrow* sweet, as sweet, as sweet flows *Tweed*,
As green its grass, its gowan as yellow,
As sweet smells on its braes the birk,
The apple from its rocks as mellow.

Fair was thy love, fair, fair indeed thy love,
In flow'ry bands thou him didst fetter;
Tho' he was fair, and well belov'd again,°
Than me he never lov'd thee better.   60

Busk ye, then busk, my bony bony bride,
Busk ye, then busk, my winsom marrow,
Busk ye, and loe° me on the banks of *Tweed*,
And think nae mare on the braes of *Yarrow*.

How can I busk a bony bony bride?
How can I busk a winsom marrow?
How loe him on the banks of *Tweed*,
That slew my love on the braes of *Yarrow?*

THE BRAES OF YARROW. The text is from the ninth edition
of Allan Ramsay's *The Tea-Table Miscellany: or, a Collection
of Scots Sangs* (1733). **1. Busk:** dress, adorn, make ready. **2.
marrow:** mate. **4. braes of Yarrow:** the hills adjoining the
Yarrow River. **8. Puing the birks:** pulling the birches. **21.
tint:** lost. **25. reid:** red.

50. gowan: daisy. **59. again:** in return. **63. loe:** love.

O *Yarrow* fields, may never, never rain,
No dew thy tender blossoms cover,   70
For there was vilely kill'd my love,
My love as he had not been a lover.

The boy put on his robes, his robes of green,
His purple vest, 'twas my awn sewing,
Ah! wretched me, I little, little knew,
He was in these to meet his ruin.

The boy took out his milk white, milk white steed,
Unheedful of my dole and sorrow,
But e'er the toofal° of the night,
He lay a corps on the braes of *Yarrow*.   80

Much I rejoyc'd that woeful, woeful day,
I sung, my voice the woods returning,
But lang e'er night, the spear was flown
That slew my love, and left me mourning.

What can my barbarous, barbarous father do,
But with his cruel rage pursue me?
My lover's blood is on thy spear;
How can'st thou, barbarous man, then woo me?

My happy sisters may be, may be proud,
With cruel and ungentle scoffing,   90
May bid me seek on *Yarrow*'s braes
My lover nailed in his coffin.

My brother *Douglas* may upbraid,
And strive with threatning words to move me.
My lover's blood is on thy spear,
How can'st thou ever bid me love thee?

Yes, yes, prepare the bed, the bed of love,
With bridal sheets my body cover,
Unbar, ye bridal maids, the door,
Let in the expected husband lover.   100

But who the expected husband husband is?
His hands, methink, are bath'd in slaughter.
Ah me! what ghastly spectre's yon,
Comes, in his pale shroud, bleeding after?

Pale as he is, here lay him, lay him down,
O lay his cold head on my pillow;
Take aff, take aff these bridal weeds,°
And crown my careful head with yellow.

Pale tho' thou art, yet best, yet best belov'd,
O could my warmth to life restore thee;   110
Yet lye all night between my breasts;
No youth lay ever there before thee.

Pale, pale indeed, O lovely, lovely youth!
Forgive, forgive so foul a slaughter,
And ly all night between my breasts,
No youth shall ever lye there after.

Return, return, O mournful, mournful bride,
Return and dry thy useless sorrow,
Thy lover heeds nought of thy sighs,
He lies a corps in the braes of *Yarrow*.   120

Edward Young

1683–1765

FROM

LOVE OF FAME,
THE UNIVERSAL PASSION.
IN SEVEN
CHARACTERISTICAL SATIRES

SATIRE I

TO HIS GRACE THE DUKE OF DORSET.

—Tanto major Famae sitis est, quam Virtutis.°
Juv. Sat. 10

My Verse is Satire; DORSET,° lend your ear,
And Patronize a Muse You cannot Fear.
To Poets sacred is a DORSET's name,
Their wonted Passport thro' the Gates of Fame;
It Bribes the partial Reader into Praise,
And throws a Glory round the shelter'd lays;

79. toofal: oncoming. **107. weeds:** garments.

LOVE OF FAME, THE UNIVERSAL PASSION: *Satire I*. The text is
that of the first edition (1725); we have incorporated the
variants from the edition of 1762. (See also the selection from
Young in Part Five.) **Tanto . . . Virtutis:** "So much
greater is the thirst for fame than for virtue." **1. Dorset:**
Lionel Cranfield Sackville (1688–1765), Seventh Earl of
Dorset; Young's patron as well as Ambrose Philips's.

The dazzled Judgment fewer Faults can see,
And gives applause to *B——e*,° or to Me.
But You decline the Mistress we pursue;
Others are fond of *Fame*, but *Fame* of You.   10
  INSTRUCTIVE Satire, true to Virtue's cause!
Thou shining Supplement of publick Laws!
When *Flatter'd Crimes* of a licentious age
Reproach our Silence, and demand our Rage;
When *Purchas'd Follies* from each distant land,
Like Arts, Improve in *Britain's* skilful hand;
When the *Law* shews her teeth, but dares not Bite,
And *South-Sea* Treasures° are not brought to light;
When *Churchmen* Scripture for the Classics quit,
Polite Apostates from God's Grace to Wit;   20
When men grow Great from their Revenue spent,
And fly from Bayliffs into Parliament;
When dying Sinners, to blot out their Score,
Bequeath the Church the Leavings of a Whore;
To chase our Spleen when Themes like these increase,
Shall Panegyrick reign, and Censure cease?
  Shall Poesy, like Law, turn wrong to right,
And Dedications wash an *Æthiop* white,
Set up each senseless wretch for Nature's boast,
On whom Praise shines as Trophies on a Post?   30
Shall Funeral Eloquence her Colours spread,
And scatter Roses on the Wealthy Dead?
Shall Authors smile on such Illustrious days,
And Satyrise with nothing—but their Praise?
  Why slumbers *Pope*, who leads the tuneful Train,
Nor hears that Virtue, which He loves, complain?
Donne, Dorset,° *Dryden, Rochester* are dead,
And Guilt's chief Foe in *Addison* is fled;
Congreve, who crown'd with Lawrels fairly won,
Sits smiling at the Goal while Others run,   40
He will not Write; and (more provoking still!)
Ye Gods! He will not write, and *Mævius*° will.
  Doubly distrest, what Author shall we find
Discreetly Daring, and Severely Kind,
The courtly *Roman's*° shining path to tread,
And sharply Smile prevailing Folly dead?
Will no superior Genius snatch the quill,
And save me, on the Brink, from Writing Ill?
Tho' vain the Strife, I'll strive my voice to raise.

What will not men attempt for sacred Praise?   50
  The *Love of Praise*, howe'er conceal'd by art,
Reigns more, or less, and glows in every heart:
The Proud to gain it toils on toils endure,
The Modest shun it, but to make it sure.
O'er Globes, and scepters, now, on Thrones it swells,
Now, trims the midnight Lamp in College-cells.
'Tis Tory, Whig; it Plots, Prays, Preaches, Pleads,
Harangues in Senates, Squeaks in Masquerades.
Here, to *S——e's*° Humour makes a bold pretence,
There, bolder aims at *P——y's*° Eloquence.   60
It aids the Dancer's heel, the Writer's head,
And heaps the plain with mountains of the dead;
Nor ends with Life; but nods in sable Plumes,
Adorns our Herse, and Flatters on our Tombs.
  What is not *Proud?* The *Pimp* is Proud to see
So many like himself in high degree:
The *Whore* is proud her beauties are the dread
Of peevish Virtue, and the Marriage-bed;
And the brib'd *Cuckold*, like crown'd Victims born
To slaughter, glories in his Gilded Horn.   70
  Some go to Church, *Proud* humbly to repent,
And come back much more guilty than they went:
One way they Look, another way they Steer,
Pray to the Gods; but would have Mortals hear;
And when their Sins they set sincerely down,
They'll find that their Religion has been One.
  Others with wishful eyes on *Glory* look,
When they have got their *Picture* tow'rds a book,
Or pompous *Title*, like a gawdy Sign
Meant to betray dull Sots to wretched Wine.   80
If at his Title *T——*° had dropt his quill,
T—— might have past for a great Genius still;
But *T——* alas! (excuse him, if you can)
Is now a Scribbler, who was once a Man.
  Imperious Some a Classic *Fame* demand,
For heaping up with a laborious hand
A Waggon-load of meanings for One word,
While *A's* Depos'd, and *B* with pomp restor'd.
  Some for *Renown* on scraps of Learning doat,
And think they grow Immortal as they *Quote*.   90
To Patch-work learn'd Quotations are ally'd,
Both strive to make our Poverty our Pride.
  On *Glass*° how witty is a noble Peer?

8. B——e: Sir Richard Blackmore (1654–1729), notorious as
the author of bad epic poems. 18. South-Sea Treasures: a
reference to the fortunes made in the South-Sea speculation.
37. Dorset: Charles Sackville (1638–1706), Sixth Earl of
Dorset, author of songs and satires; he was the father of
the dedicatee of this poem. 42. Mævius: a poetaster who
attacked the work of Virgil and Horace. 45. The courtly
Roman: [Young's note] Horace.

59. S——e: Sir Hans Sloane (1660–1753), physician,
botanist, and traveler. 60. P——y: Sir William Pulteney
(1684–1764), Earl of Bath; Whig parliamentarian and orator.
81. T——: not identified. 93. On Glass: a reference to the
practice of writing brief verses on window glass with
diamonds.

Did ever Diamond cost a man so Dear?
   Polite Diseases make some Ideots *vain*,
Which, if unfortunately well, they Feign.
   Of Folly, Vice, Disease, men proud we see;
And (stranger still!) of Blockhead's Flattery,
Whose Praise Defames; as if a Fool shoud mean
By spitting on your face to make it Clean.   100
   Nor is 't enough all hearts are swoln with *Pride*,
Her Power is mighty, as her Realm is wide.
What can she not perform? The Love of Fame
Made bold *Alphonsus*° his Creator blame,
Empedocles° hurl'd down the burning Steep,
And (stronger still!) made *Alexander* weep.°
Nay, it holds *Delia* from a second Bed,
Tho' her lov'd Lord has four half months been
    dead.
   This Passion with a Pimple have I seen
Retard a Cause,° and give a Judge the spleen.   110
By *this* inspir'd (O! ne'er to be forgot)
Some Lords have learnt to spell, and some to Knot.°
It makes *Globose* a Speaker in the House;
He Hems, and is Deliver'd of his Mouse;°
It makes *Dear Self* on well-bred tongues prevail,
And *I* the *Little Hero* of each Tale.
   Sick with the *Love of Fame* what throngs pour in,
Unpeople Court, and leave the Senate thin?
My growing Subject seems but just begun,
And, Chariot-like, I kindle as I run.°   120
Aid me, great *Homer!* with thy *Epic* rules
To take a Catalogue of *British* Fools.
Satire, had I thy *Dorset's* force divine,
A Knave, or Fool shou'd perish in each line;
Tho' for the First all *Westminster*° should plead,
And for the Last all *Gresham*° intercede.
   Begin. Who first the *Catalogue* shall grace?
To *Quality* belongs the highest place.
My Lord comes forward; forward let him come!
Ye Vulgar! at your peril give him room: 130
He stands for *Fame* on his Forefather's feet,

By Heraldry prov'd Valiant, or Discreet.
With what a decent pride he throws his eyes
Above the man by Three Descents less Wise?
If Virtues at his noble hands you crave,
You bid him raise his Fathers from the grave.
Men should press forward in Fame's glorious chace,
Nobles look *backward*, and so lose the Race.
   Let high Birth triumph! What can be more great?
Nothing—but Merit in a low estate.   140
To Virtue's humblest Son let none prefer
Vice, tho' descended from the Conqueror.°
Shall Men, like *Figures*,° pass for high, or base,
Slight, or important, only by their Place?
Titles are marks of Honest men, and Wise;
The Fool, or Knave that wears a Title, Lies.
   They that on glorious Ancestors inlarge,
Produce their Debt instead of their Discharge.
Dorset, let those who proudly boast their Line,
Like Thee, in worth Hereditary shine.   150
   Vain as false Greatness is, the Muse must own
We want not fools to buy that *Bristol* Stone.°
Mean Sons of Earth, who on a *South-sea* tyde
Of full success swam into Wealth, and Pride,
Knock with a purse of Gold at *Anstis*'° gate,
And beg to be Descended from the Great.
   When Men of Infamy to Grandeur soar,
They light a Torch to shew their shame the more.
Those Governments which curb not Evils, cause;
And a rich Knave's a Libel on our Laws.   160
   Belus with solid *Glory* will be crown'd;
He buys no Phantome, no vain empty sound,
But *Builds* himself a name; and to be great,
Sinks in a Quarry an immense estate;
In cost and grandeur *Ch—dos*° he'll out-do,
And, *B—l—ton*,° thy Taste is not so true.
The Pile is finisht, every toil is past,
And full Perfection is arriv'd at last;
When lo! my Lord to some small Corner runs,
And leaves State-rooms to Strangers, and to Duns. 170

---

104. bold Alphonsus: Alfonso the Wise (1221–84), scholar and patron of learning. **105. Empedocles:** (d. *c.* 430 B.C.), Greek philosopher who committed suicide by jumping into the crater of Mount Etna. **106. made . . . weep:** traditionally, because he had no more worlds to conquer. **110. a Cause:** a law case. **112. Knot:** knit. **114. He . . . Mouse:** a reference to a fable of Aesop's, in which, when a huge hole appears in the side of a mountain, a little mouse finally pokes its head out. **120. Chariot-like . . . run:** Coach axles tended to heat up at high speeds. **125. Westminster:** the seat of government. **126. Gresham:** Gresham College, the seat of the Royal Society for scientific knowledge.

142. the Conqueror: William the Conqueror (1027–87), to whose period many British families trace their pedigrees and honors. **143. Figures:** statues. **152. Bristol Stone:** mock diamonds found near Bristol. **155. Anstis:** John Anstis (1669–1744), Garter King-of-Arms during Young's time; his duty was the award of heraldic arms to those entitled to them. **165. Ch—dos:** James Brydges (1673–1744), First Baron Chandos, whose estate named Canons, near Edgware, became a byword for ostentation. **166. B—l—ton:** Richard Boyle (1695–1753), Third Earl of Burlington, well known as a connoisseur of architecture. (See Pope's *Moral Essays, Of the Use of Riches*, in Part Two.)

The man who Builds, and wants wherewith to pay,
Provides a Home from which to run away.
In *Britain* what is many a lordly Seat
But a Discharge in full for an estate?

In smaller compass lyes *Pygmalion's* Fame;
Not Domes, but Antique Statues are his Flame.
Not *F—t—n's*° self more *Parian*° charms has known;
Nor is good *P—b—ke,*° more in love with Stone.
The Bayliffs come (rude men, prophanely bold!)
And bid him turn his *Venus* into gold.   180
"No, Sirs, he crys, I'll sooner rot in Jayl.
Shall *Grecian* Arts be truckt° for *English* Bayl?"
Such Heads might make their very *Busto's*° laugh.
His Daughter starves, but *Cleopatra's*° safe.

Men overloaded with a large estate
May spill their treasure in a nice Conceit;
The Rich may be Polite, but Oh! 'tis sad
To say you're Curious, when we swear you're Mad.
By your Revenue measure your expence,
And to your Funds and Acres joyn your Sense: 190
No man is blest by Accident, or Guess,
True Wisdom is the price of Happiness;
Yet few without long Discipline are sage,
And our Youth only lays up sighs for Age.

But how, my Muse, canst thou resist so long
The bright temptation of the Courtly throng,
Thy most inviting Theme? the *Court* affords
Much food for Satire, it abounds in Lords.
"What Lords are those saluting with a grin?"
One is just *out*, and One as lately *in*.   200
"How comes it then to pass we see preside
On both their Brows an equal share of Pride?"
Pride, that impartial passion, reigns thro' all,
Attends our Glory, nor deserts our Fall.
As in its Home, it triumphs in High-place,
And frowns a haughty Exile in Disgrace.
Some Lords it bids admire their Wands° so white,
Which bloom, like *Aaron's*,° to their ravisht sight;
Some Lords it bids Resign, and turns their Wands,
Like *Moses'*,° into Serpents in their hands.   210
These sink, as Divers, for Renown; and boast
With pride Inverted of their Honours lost.

---

177. **F—t—n**: Sir Andrew Fountaine (1676–1753), a famous antiquary. **Parian**: Paros, an island of the Cyclades, is noted for the whiteness of its marble. 178. **P—b—ke**: Henry Herbert (1693–1751), Ninth Earl of Pembroke, known as an architect and collector of sculpture. 182. **truckt**: traded. 183. **Busto's**: sculpture busts. 184. **Cleopatra**: [Young's note] A famous statue. 207. **Wands**: the emblems of court office. 208. **like Aaron's**: See Num. 17:8. 210. **like Moses'**: See Ex. 7:9 and 17:6.

But against Reason sure 'tis equal sin
To boast of meerly being *out*, or *in*.

What numbers, *Here*, thro' odd Ambition strive
To seem the most transported Things alive?
As if by Joy Desert was understood,
And all the fortunate were Wise, and Good.
Hence aching bosoms wear a visage gay,
And stifled Groans frequent the Ball, and Play.   220
Compleatly drest by *Monteuil*° and Grimace,
They take their Birth-day suit,° and Publick Face;
Their smiles are only part of what they *wear*,
Put off at night with lady *B——*'s Hair.
What bodily fatigue is half so bad?
With anxious Care they labour to be Glad.

What numbers, *Here*, would into Fame advance,
Conscious of merit in the Coxcomb's Dance?
The Tavern! Park! Assembly! Mask, and Play!
Those dear Destroyers of the Tedious day!   230
That Wheel of Fops! that Saunter of the Town!
Call it Diversion, and the Pill goes down;
Fools grin on Fools, and, *Stoic*-like, support
Without one sigh the Pleasures of a Court.
Courts can give nothing to the Wise, and Good,
But scorn of Pomp, and love of Solitude.
High stations Tumult, but not Bliss create,
None think the Great unhappy but the Great;
Fools gaze, and envy; Envy darts a sting,
Which makes a Swain as wretched as a King.   240

I envy none their Pageantry, and Show,
I envy none the Gilding of their woe.
Give me, indulgent Gods! with mind serene,
And guiltless heart to range the sylvan scene.
No splendid Poverty, no smiling Care,
No well-bred Hate, or servile Grandeur There;
There pleasing Objects useful thoughts suggest,
The Sense is ravisht, and the Soul is blest;
On every Thorn delightful Wisdom grows,
In every Rill a sweet Instruction flows: 250
But some, untaught, o'erhear the whisp'ring Rill,
In spight of sacred Leisure Blockheads still;
Nor shoots up Folly to a nobler bloom
In her own native soil the Drawing-room.

The *Squire* is *Proud* to see his Coursers strain,
Or well-breath'd Beagles sweep along the plain.
Say, dear *Hippolitus* (whose drink is Ale,
Whose Erudition is a *Christmas*-tale,

---

221. **Monteuil**: [Young's note] A famous taylor. 222. **Birth-day suit**: It was the custom for the genteel to wear new suits of clothes on the monarch's birthday.

Whose Mistress is saluted with a Smack,
And Friend receiv'd with Thumps upon the back) 260
When thy sleek Gelding nimbly leaps the Mound,
And *Ringwood* Opens on the tainted ground,°
Is That *thy* Praise? Let *Ringwood*'s Fame alone,
Just *Ringwood* leaves each Animal his own,
Nor envies when a Gypsy You Commit,
And shake the clumsy Bench with Country wit;
When you the dullest of dull Things have said,
And then ask pardon for the Jest you made.
　　Here breathe, my Muse! and then thy task renew.
Ten thousand Fools unsung are still in view.　　270
Fewer Lay-atheists made by Church-debates;
Fewer Great Beggars fam'd for large estates;
Ladies, whose Love is constant as the Wind;
Cits,° who prefer a Guinea to Mankind;
Fewer grave lords to *Scr—pe*° discreetly bend;
And fewer Shocks a Statesman gives his Friend.
　　Is there a man of an eternal Vein,
Who lulls the Town in Winter with his strain,
At *Bath* in Summer chants the reigning Lass,
And sweetly Whistles as the Waters pass?　　280
Is there a Tongue, like *Delia*'s o'er her cup,
That runs for ages without Winding up?
Is there, whom his Tenth *Epic* mounts to Fame?°
Such, and such only might exhaust my Theme;
Nor would These Heroes of the task be glad;
For who can Write so fast as men run Mad.

Anonymous

SONG

I.

FOrgive, fair Creature, form'd to please,
　　Forgive a wond'ring Youth's Desire:
Those Charms, those Virtues when he sees,
　　How can he see, and not admire?

262. And . . . ground: And the hunting dog named Ringwood barks to indicate that he scents game lying before him. **274. Cits:** citizens, London tradesmen. **275. Scr——pe:** John Scrope (*c.* 1662–1752), parliamentarian and a strong supporter of Sir Robert Walpole. **283. Is . . . Fame:** The allusion here is to Blackmore. SONG. The text is from David Lewis's *Miscellaneous Poems, by Several Hands* (1726).

II.

While each the other still improves,
　　The fairest Face, the fairest Mind;
Not, with the Proverb, he that loves,
　　But he that loves You not, is blind.

John Dyer

c. 1699–1758

GRONGAR HILL

[Pindaric Version]

I

Fancy! Nymph, that loves to lye
　　On the lonely Eminence;
Darting Notice thro' the Eye,
　　Forming Thought, and feasting Sense:
Thou! that must lend Imagination Wings,
And stamp Distinction, on all worldly Things!
　　Come, and with thy various *Hues*,
　　Paint and adorn thy *Sister* Muse.
Now, while the Sun's hot Coursers, bounding high;
Shake Lustre on the Earth, and burn, along the
　　Sky.　　10

II

More than *Olympus* animates my Lays,
Aid me, o'erlabour'd, in its wide surveys;
And crown its Summit with immortal Praise:
Thou, aweful *Grongar!* in whose mossy Cells,
　　Sweetly musing *Quiet* dwells:
　　Thou! deep, beneath whose shado'wy Side,
Oft, my sick Mind serene Refreshment took,
Near the cool winding of some bubbling Brook:

GRONGAR HILL [Pindaric Version]: The text is from Richard Savage's *Miscellaneous Poems and Translations by Several Hands* (1726). Samuel Johnson says that as a young man "having always amused himself with drawing, [Dyer] resolved to turn painter, and became pupil to Mr. [Jonathan] Richardson, an artist then of high reputation . . . . Having studied a while under his master, he became . . . an itinerant painter, and wandered about South Wales and the parts adjacent; but he mingled poetry with painting, and [in 1726] printed *Grongar Hill*." Grongar Hill is in Southern Wales; the river Towy runs by it. The top of the hill is notable for the remains of ruined earthworks and fortifications.

There have I, pensive, press'd the grassy Bed,
And, while my bending Arm sustain'd my Head,   20
Stray'd my Charm'd Eyes o'er *Towy*'s wand'ring
    Tide,
Swift as a Start of Thought, from Wood to Mead,
Glancing, from dark to bright, from Vale to Hill,
Till tir'd Reflection had no *Void* to fill.

III

Widening, beneath the Mountain's bushy Brow,
Th' unbounded Landskip softens off below;
    No skreeny Vapours intervene;
    But the gay, the splendid Scene,
Does Nature's smiling Face all *open* show,
In the mix'd Glowings of the tinctur'd *Bow*.   30
And, gently changing, into soft and light,
Expands immensely wide, and leads the *journeying*
    Sight.

IV

White, on the rugged Cliffs, Old *Castles* rise,
    And shelter'd Villages lie warm and low,
    Close by the Streams that at their *Bases* flow.
Each watry Face bears pictur'd Woods, and Skies,
Where, as the Surface curls, when Breezes rise,
Faint fairy Earthquakes tremble to the Eyes.
Up thro' the Forest's Gloom, distinguish'd, bright,
    Tops of high Buildings catch the Light: 40
The quick'ning Sun a show'ry Radiance sheds,
And lights up all the Mountain's russet Heads.
Gilds the fair Fleeces of the distant Flocks;
And, glittering, plays betwixt the broken Rocks.
Light, as the Lustre of the rising Dawn,
Spreads the gay Carpet of yon level Lawn:
Till a steep Hill starts horrid, wild, and high,
Whose Form uncommon holds the wond'ring Eye;
Deep is its Base, in *Towy*'s bord'ring Flood,
Its bristly Sides are shagg'd with sullen Wood: 50
Towers, ancient as the Mountain, crown its Brow,
Aweful in Ruin, to the Plains below.
Thick round the ragged Walls pale Ivy creeps,
Whose circling Arms the nodding Fabrick keeps;
While both combine to check th' insulting Wind,
As Friends, in Danger, mutual Comfort find.

V

Once a proud Palace, This,—a Seat of Kings!
Alas! th' o'erturning Sweep of Time's broad Wings!
    Now, 'tis the Raven's bleak Abode,
And shells, in marbly Damps, the inbred Toad.   60
There the safe Fox, unfearing Huntsmen, feeds;

And climbs o'er Heaps of Stone to pendant Weeds.
The Prince's Tenure in his Roofs of Gold,
    Ends like the Peasant's homelier Hold;
Life's but a Road, and he who travels right,
Treats Fortune as an Inn, and rests his Night.

VI

    Ever changing, ever new,
Thy Scenes, O *Grongar*.! cannot tire the View:
    Lowly Vallies, waving Woods,
    Windy Summits, wildly high,   70
    Rough, and rustling in the Sky!
    The pleasant Seat, the ruin'd Tower;
    The naked Rock, the rosy Bower;
The Village and the Town, the Palace and the Farm,
Each does, on each, reflect a doubled Charm;
As Pearls look brighter on a *Æthiop*'s Arm.°

VII

Southward, along the Mountain's waving Side,
The Vale grows liberal, and the Prospect wide.
Glowing, beneath a kind and purply Sky,
Broad flower-dress'd Meadows and rich Pastures
    lie.   80
Green Hedges, in long Parallels, are seen;
And silv'ry Lawns draw Streaks of Light between:
Distant, those *Thorns* diminish'd scarce appear;
As Dangers scape, unseen, that are not *near*.
Smiling, like this fair Prospect, soft and gay,
The flatt'ring Glass of Hope our *Future* shows;
But Ills, *at hand*, their Face, unmask'd display,
And Fortune *rougher* still when *nearer*, grows:
Still we tread, tir'd, along the same deep Way;
And still the *present* proves a *cloudy* Day.   90
O, may I ever with my self agree,
Nor hope the unpossess'd Delights I see!
Nobly content, within some silent Shade,
My Passions calm, and my proud Wishes laid:
Ne'er may Desire's rough *Sea* beneath me roll,
Drown my wish'd Peace, and *tempest* all my Soul!
While, idly busy, I but beat the Air,
And, lab'ring after Bliss, embosom Care!

VIII

Here, while on humble Earth, unmark'd I lie,
I subject *Heav'n* and *Nature* to my Eye;   100
Solid, my Joys, and my free Thoughts run high.
For me, this soft'ning Wind in *Zephyrs* sings,
And in yon flow'ry Vale perfumes his Wings.

76. Æthiop's Arm: Cf. *Romeo and Juliet*, I. v. 47–48.

To sooth my Ear, those Waters murmur deep;
To shade my Eye, these bow'ry Woodbines creep.
Wanton, to yield me Sport, these Birds fly low;
And a sweet *Chase* of Harmony bestow.
Like me too yon sweet Stream serenely glides;
Just *views* and *quits* the Charms which tempt its Sides:
Calmly regardless, hast'ning to the Sea,   110
As I, thro' *Life*, shall reach *Eternity*.

GRONGAR HILL

[Octosyllabic Version]

SILENT Nymph, with curious Eye!
Who, the purple Ev'ning, lye
On the Mountain's lonely Van,°
Beyond the Noise of busy Man,
Painting fair the form of Things,
While the yellow Linnet sings;
Or the tuneful Nightingale
Charms the Forest with her Tale;
Come with all thy various Hues,
Come, and aid thy Sister Muse;   10
Now while *Phœbus*° riding high
Gives Lustre to the Land and Sky!
Grongar Hill invites my Song,
Draw the Landskip bright and strong;
Grongar, in whose Mossie Cells
Sweetly-musing Quiet dwells:
Grongar, in whose silent Shade,
For the modest Muses made,
So oft I have, the Even still,
At the Fountain of a Rill,   20
Sate upon a flow'ry Bed,
With my Hand beneath my Head;
And stray'd my Eyes o'er *Towy*'s Flood,
Over Mead, and over Wood,
From House to House, from Hill to Hill,
'Till Contemplation had her fill.
   About his chequer'd Sides I wind,
And leave his Brooks and Meads behind,
And Groves, and Grottoes where I lay,
And Vistoes° shooting Beams of Day: 30

Wider and wider spreads the Vale;
As Circles on a smooth Canal:
The Mountains round, unhappy Fate,
Sooner or later, of all Height!
Withdraw their Summits from the Skies,
And lessen as the others rise:
Still the Prospect wider spreads,
Adds a thousand Woods and Meads,
Still it widens, widens still,
And sinks the newly-risen Hill.   40
   Now, I gain the Mountain's Brow,
What a Landskip lies below!
No Clouds, no Vapours intervene,
But the gay, the open Scene
Does the Face of Nature show,
In all the Hues of Heaven's Bow!
And, swelling to embrace the Light,
Spreads around beyond the Sight.
   Old Castles on the Cliffs arise,
Proudly tow'ring in the Skies!   50
Rushing from the Woods, the Spires
Seem from hence ascending Fires!
Half his Beams *Apollo* sheds,
On the yellow Mountain-Heads!
Gilds the Fleeces of the Flocks;
And glitters on the broken Rocks!
   Below me Trees unnumber'd rise,
Beautiful in various Dies:
The gloomy Pine, the Poplar blue,
The yellow Beech, the sable Yew,   60
The slender Firr, that taper grows,
The sturdy Oak with broad-spread Boughs.
And beyond the purple Grove,
Haunt of *Phillis*,° Queen of Love!
Gawdy as the op'ning Dawn,
Lies a long and level Lawn,
On which a dark Hill, steep and high,
Holds and charms the wand'ring Eye!
Deep are his Feet in *Towy*'s Flood,
His Sides are cloath'd with waving Wood,   70
And antient Towers crown his Brow,
That cast an awful Look below;
Whose ragged Walls the Ivy creeps,
And with her Arms from falling keeps;
So both a Safety from the Wind
On mutual Dependance find.
   'Tis now the Raven's bleak Abode;
'Tis now th' Apartment of the Toad;   78

GRONGAR HILL [Octosyllabic Version]: The text is from
David Lewis's *Miscellaneous Poems, by Several Hands* (1726),
corrected by the text of *Poems* (1761). **3. Van:** summit. **11.
Phœbus:** Apollo, the classical god of light, poetry, and music;
his abode is the sun. **30. Vistoes:** a painterly term for *vistas*.

64. Phillis: conventional name for a pastoral sweetheart.

And there the Fox securely feeds;
And there the pois'nous Adder breeds,
Conceal'd in Ruins, Moss and Weeds:
While, ever and anon, there falls,
Huge heaps of hoary moulder'd Walls.
Yet Time has seen, that lifts the low,
And level lays the lofty Brow,
Has seen this broken Pile compleat,
Big with the Vanity of State;
But transient is the Smile of Fate!
A little Rule, a little Sway,
A Sun-beam in a Winter's Day   90
Is all the Proud and Mighty have,
Between the Cradle and the Grave.

   And see the Rivers how they run,
Thro' Woods and Meads, in Shade and Sun,
Sometimes swift, and sometimes slow,
Wave succeeding Wave they go
A various Journey to the Deep,
Like human Life to endless Sleep!
Thus is Nature's Vesture wrought,
To instruct our wand'ring Thought;   100
Thus she dresses green and gay,
To disperse our Cares away.

   Ever charming, ever new,
When will the Landskip tire the View!
The Fountain's Fall, the River's Flow,
The woody Vallies, warm and low;
The windy Summit, wild and high,
Roughly rushing on the Sky!
The pleasent Seat, the ruin'd Tow'r,
The naked Rock, the shady Bow'r;   110
The Town and Village, Dome and Farm,
Each give each a double Charm,
As Pearls upon an *Æthiop*'s Arm.

   See on the Mountain's southern side,
Where the Prospect opens wide,
Where the Ev'ning gilds the Tide;
How close and small the Hedges lie!
What streaks of Meadows cross the Eye!
A Step methinks may pass the Stream,
So little distant Dangers seem;   120
So we mistake the Future's face,
Ey'd thro' Hope's deluding Glass;
As yon Summits soft and fair,
Clad in Colours of the Air,
Which, to those who journey near,
Barren, and brown, and rough appear;
Still we tread tir'd the same coarse Way.
The Present's still a cloudy Day.

O may I with my self agree,
And never covet what I see: 130
Content me with an humble Shade,
My Passions tam'd, my Wishes laid;
For while our Wishes wildy roll,
We banish Quiet from the Soul:
'Tis thus the Busy beat the Air;
And Misers gather Wealth and Care.

   Now, ev'n now, my Joy runs high,
As on the Mountain-turf I lie;
While the wanton *Zephir* sings,
And in the Vale perfumes his Wings;   140
While the Waters murmur deep;
While the Shepherd charms his Sheep;
While the Birds unbounded fly,
And with Musick fill the Sky.
Now, ev'n now, my Joy runs high.

   Be full, ye Courts, be great who will;
Search for Peace with all your skill:
Open wide the lofty Door,
Seek her on the marble Floor,
In vain ye search, she is not there;   150
In vain ye search the Domes° of Care!
Grass and Flowers Quiet treads,
On the Meads, and Mountain-heads,
Along with Pleasure, close ally'd,
Ever by each other's Side:
And often, by the murm'ring Rill,
Hears the Thrush, while all is still,
Within the Groves of *Grongar Hill*.

THE ENQUIRY

YE poor little Sheep, ah well may ye stray,
While sad is your Shepherd, and *Clio* away!
Tell where have you been, have you met with my
   Love,
On the Mountain, or Valley, or Meadow, or Grove?
Alas-aday, No—Ye are starv'd and half dead,
Ye saw not my Love, or ye all had been fed.

   Oh, Sun, did you see her?—Ay surely you did:
Mong what Willows, or Woodbines, or Reeds, is she
   hid?
Ye tall, whistling Pines, that on yonder Hill grow,
And o'erlook the beautiful Valley below,   10
Did you see her a roving in Wood or in Brake?
Or bathing her fair Limbs in some silent Lake?

151. Domes: houses. THE ENQUIRY. The text is from Richard
Savage's *Miscellaneous Poems and Translations by Several Hands*
(1726).

Ye Mountains, that look on the vigorous East,
And the North, and the South, and the wearisom West,
Pray tell where she hides her, you surely do know,
And let not her Lover pine after her so.

Oh, had I the Wings of an Eagle, I'd fly,
Along with bright *Phœbus* all over the Sky.
Like an Eagle, look down, with my Wings wide
    display'd,
And dart in my Eyes at each whisp'ring Shade: 20
I'd search ev'ry Tuft in my diligent Tour,
I'd unravel the Woodbines, and look in each Bow'r,
Till I found out my *Clio*, and ended my Pain,
And made my self quiet, and happy again.

Mrs. B—ll M—rt—n (?)

THE HUMBLE WISH

I Ask not wit, nor beauty do I crave,
Nor wealth, nor pompous titles wish to have;
But since 'tis doom'd, in all degrees of life,
(Whether a daughter, sister, or a wife,)
That females shall the stronger males obey,
And yield per force to their tyrannic sway;
Since this, I say, is ev'ry woman's fate,
Give me a mind to suit my slavish state.

Walter Harte

1709–1774

TO MR. POPE

To move the springs of nature as we please,
To think with spirit, but to write with ease:
With living words to warm the conscious heart,
Or please the soul with nicer charms of art,

For this the *Grecian*° soar'd in *Epic* strains,
And softer *Maro* left the *Mantuan*° plains:
Melodious *Spenser* felt the lover's fire,
And awful *Milton* strung his heav'nly lyre.

'Tis yours, like these, with curious toil to trace
The pow'rs of language, harmony, and grace,   10
How nature's self with living lustre shines;
How judgment strengthens, and how art refines;
How to grow bold with conscious sense of fame,
And force a pleasure which we dare not blame:
To charm us more thro' negligence than pains,
And give ev'n life and action to the strains:
Led by some law, whose pow'rful impulse guides
Each happy stroke, and in the soul presides:
Some fairer image of perfection, giv'n
T' inspire mankind, itself deriv'd from heav'n.   20

O ever worthy, ever crown'd with praise;
Blest in thy life, and blest in all thy lays!
Add that the *Sisters*° ev'ry thought refine:
Or ev'n thy life be faultless as thy line;
Yet envy still with fiercer rage pursues,
Obscures the virtue, and defames the muse.
A soul like thine, in pains, in grief resign'd,
Views with vain scorn the malice of mankind:
Not critics, but their planets prove unjust:
And are they blam'd who sin because they must?   30

Yet sure not so must all peruse thy lays;
I cannot rival—and yet dare to praise.
A thousand charms at once my thoughts engage,
Sappho's soft sweetness, *Pindar*'s warmer rage,
Statius' free vigour, *Virgil*'s studious care,
And *Homer*'s force, and *Ovid*'s° easier air.

So seems some Picture, where exact design,
And curious pains, and strength and sweetness join:
Where the free thought its pleasing grace bestows,
And each warm stroke with living colour glows: 40

5. **the Grecian:** Homer. 6. **Mantuan:** Virgil (Publius Virgilius Maro) is said to have been born near Mantua. 23. **the Sisters:** the Muses. **34–36. Sappho, Pindar, Statius, Ovid:** Sappho and Pindar were Greek lyric poets of the sixth and fifth centuries B.C., respectively, whose influence is visible in Pope's *Ode on St. Cecilia's Day* and *The Dying Christian to His Soul* (1730); as a boy Pope was fond of translating and imitating Statius, the minor Roman epic poet of the first century A.D.; and Pope's *Eloisa to Abelard* (see Part Two) is written in the mode of the heroic epistles of Ovid, the first-century B.C. Roman poet famous for his warmth.

THE HUMBLE WISH. The text is from *A New Miscellany* (Bath, 1726). TO MR. POPE. The text is from Harte's *Poems on Several Occasions* (1727).

Soft without weakness, without labour fair;
Wrought up at once with happiness and care!

How blest the man that from the world removes
To joys that MORDAUNT,° or his POPE approves;
Whose taste exact each author can explore,
And live the present and past ages o'er:
Who free from pride, from penitence, or strife,
Moves calmly forward to the verge of life:
Such be my days, and such my fortunes be,
To live by reason, and to write by thee!   50

Nor deem this verse, tho' humble, thy disgrace;
All are not born the glory of their race:
Yet all are born t' adore the great man's name,
And trace his footsteps in the paths to fame.
The Muse who now this early homage pays,
First learn'd from thee to animate her lays:
A Muse as yet unhonour'd, but unstain'd,
Who prais'd no vices, no preferment gain'd:
Unbyass'd or to censure or commend,
Who knows no envy, and who grieves no friend;   60
Perhaps too fond to make those virtues known,
And fix her fame immortal on thy own.

Anonymous

MR. J. M. S——E CATECHIZED ON HIS ONE EPISTLE TO MR. POPE

WHAT makes you write at this odd Rate?
Why, Sir, it is to imitate.
What makes you steal and trifle so?
Why 'tis to do, as others do.
But there's no Meaning to be seen!
Why, that's the very thing I mean.

44. **Mordaunt:** Charles Mordaunt (1658–1735), Third Earl of Peterborough, one of Pope's friends in the peerage. MR. J. M. S——E CATECHIZED. The texts of this epigram and the two following are from *Certain Epigrams in Laud and Praise of the Gentlemen of the Dunciad* (c. 1730). James Moore-Smythe (1702–34) was a minor playwright and wit accused by Pope of plagiarism and satirized in *The Dunciad* (see Part Two). His *One Epistle to Mr. Pope*, which he wrote together with the critic Leonard Welsted (1688–1747), appeared in 1730.

ON THE GENTLEMEN IN *THE DUNCIAD*

THE craven Rook, and pert Jackdaw,
   (Tho' neither Birds of moral kind)
Yet serve, if hang'd, or stuff'd with Straw,
   To show us, which way blows the Wind.
Thus dirty Knaves or chatt'ring Fools,
   Strung up by Dozens in thy Lay,
Teach more by half than *Dennis*'° Rules,
   And point Instruction ev'ry way.
With *Ægypt*'s Art thy Pen may strive,
   One potent Drop let this but shed,   10
And ev'ry Rogue that stunk alive
   Becomes a precious Mummy dead.

THE MOLE

INSCRIBED TO MR. WELSTED, OR MR. TIBBALD,° NO MATTER WHICH.

DEAR *W——d*, mark, in dirty Hole
That painful Animal, a *Mole:*
Above-ground never born to go,
What mighty stir it keeps *below?*
To make a Molehill, all this strife!
It digs, pokes, undermines, for Life;
How proud, a little Dirt to spread!
Conscious of nothing o'er its Head:
Till, lab'ring on for want of Eyes,
It blunders into Light—and dies.   10

ON THE GENTLEMEN IN *The Dunciad*. 7. **Dennis:** John Dennis (1657–1734), the critic. (See the selection from Dennis in Part Two.) THE MOLE. **Mr. Tibbald:** Lewis Theobald (1688–1744), the editor of Shakespeare who served as the hero of the first (1728) version of *The Dunciad* (see Part Two).

♔

Aaron Hill

1685–1750

THE PROGRESS OF WIT: A CAVEAT

FOR THE USE OF AN EMINENT WRITER.

TUNEFUL ALEXIS, on the *Thame*'s fair Side,
The Ladies Play-thing, and the Muses Pride,
With *Merit*, popular, with *Wit*, polite,
Easy, tho' *vain*, and elegant, tho' *light*:
Desiring, and deserving, others Praise,
Poorly *accepts* a Fame, he ne'er *repays;*
Unborn to *cherish*, sneakingly *approves*,
And wants the Soul to *spread* the Worth, he *loves:*
This to the *Juniors* of his Tribe gave Pain,
For mean Minds praise, but to be prais'd again;   10
Henceforth, renouncing an *ungracious* BAAL,°
His Altars smoak not, and their Off'rings fail:
The Heat, his Scorn had rais'd, his Pride inflam'd,
'Till what they worshipp'd first, they next defam'd;

Depos'd, at length, from PINDUS' Top,° he roll'd,
While Insect Witlings, pleas'd, his Fall behold,
And each cold-croaking *Heliconian Frog*
Leaps, scornful, and bestrides th' *unreigning* Log.°

Far-fall'n ALEXIS, who so ill aspir'd,
Sick of successless War, from Wounds retir'd,   20
Where, while, in Sleep, his Sorrows ebb'd away,
And, hush'd in Darkness, Indignation lay;
Fancy, fair Mistress of the Poet's Mind,
For ever changing, yet, for ever kind;
Soft, o'er his Dreams, her formful Radiance shed,
And his rapt Soul thro' Heaven's thin Purlieus led;
Seated beside the Star-invading Dame,
Whose Steeds, Wind-footed, paw'd the lambent Flame,
High, as a Widow'd Lover's Grief can climb,
Her Air-built Chariot rose, and hung sublime.   30

Unveiling, thence, the World's bleak Wastes, below,
They saw the *Stream of Life* beneath 'em flow;
Dim, from the sable Sea of *Birth* it rose,
In a slow, silent, sullen, dread Repose:
For, round th' emerging Source, that glimmer'd pale,
Mountains of Midnight Darkness roll'd a Veil:
But, as the evolving Surge swell'd into Day,
Quick'ning, it mov'd, and roar'd, and rush'd away.

Broad, on the Left, from low *Oblivion*'s Shore,
Quicksands, and Rocks, reach'd half the Current o'er: 40
Lucid, like Truth, the treach'rous Water shone,
And, o'er gay gilded Shoals, ran, tuneful, on;
Pebbles, of Gem-like Hue, with painted Pride,
Glow'd thro' the Wave, and burnt, amid the Tide:
Wantonly kind, the Sun's enliv'ning Beams
Shower'd, in light Spangles, on the dancing Streams:
While Insect Nations, *Gnats*, and *Wasps*, and *Flies*,
Ting'd in the Rainbow's ever-changing Dyes,
Sheathing their Stings, and, smiling, like the *Fair*,
Peopled the Sunshine, and adorn'd the Air.   50

Less lively, on the Right, the Stream's *deep* Flow,
There, no false Colours mix'd their varied Glow;
No gawdy Bottom catch'd the *downcast* Eye:
Above, no flutt'ring Insects wing'd the Sky:

THE PROGRESS OF WIT: A CAVEAT. The text is that of the first edition (1730). The poem is introduced by a prose discourse spoken in the *persona* of one Gamelial Gunson, "Professor of Physick and Astrology," who has first suspected that the poem, found in manuscript on the floor of a coach, is treasonable: he discovered "Popery in it, as well as Jacobitism. Not to mention that the Pope's Name, Itself, in great Letters, stands audaciously written at the end of it." But Gunson's son, a university student, has given the poem a different interpretation: "Nothing is more easily perceived, than, that this Satire is the Consequence of some Pieces, lately publish'd [by Alexander Pope], which savour, to say Truth, of a Sensibility, too like Levity . . . . It is an Art to trifle, importantly; and even to trifle, agreeably, has its Attraction: But to trifle, unseasonably, indecently [i.e., unbecomingly] or improperly, let who will be the Trifler, must be, either, inhumane, or unguarded . . . . What Pity, that the warmest of [Pope's] Admirers, are, lately, forc'd to confess, there are Grossnesses, in some of his Sallies, obscene enough to blot out any Wit, but their Author's! Insults, low enough to become the most vulgar-spirited among his Enemies: And Malice, animated enough to be beautiful, in any of his Friends, but Himself!" **11. Baal:** a heathen deity.

15. Pindus' Top: the summit of a Greek mountain range associated, like Mount Helicon, with the Muses. **18. th' unreigning Log:** See *Cooper's Hill*, note to l. 138, earlier in Part Three.

Serenely solemn, All!—One equal *Whole*
Flash'd not upon the Sense, but touch'd the Soul:
Instead of Rocks, green Islands flourish'd, here,
Silent, and fruitful, as the full-grown Year;
In Place of *Flies*, grave *Swans*, of Snow-like Hue,
Sweetly majestick, in slow Circles, flew: 60
But, tho' these Isles the distant Prospect chear'd,
No Bay, no Port, no Landing-Place appear'd;
Kind Birds, alone, gave Entrance o'er the Mound,
Nor, from the Stream, below, was Inlet found.

Then *Fancy*, thus—FAME's future Regions, These,
Where nothing *surfeits*, yet, where all Things *please*.
Here, Memory stands fix'd, while Time runs on,
And worth blooms fresh, when Life itself is gone;
Danger keeps Distance, soften'd Spleen grows kind,
Ambition temperate, and Love refin'd: 70
Nor Pride, nor Jealousy, can, here, annoy,
Nothing is Ecstacy, tho' all is Joy:
Peace without Languor, Labour, void of Pain,
Glory unenvied, and unslander'd Gain.

Tho' differing, thus, the Stream's unsocial *Sides*,
Yet, *one* broad Gulph absorb'd the double Tides;
From *Birth* devolving, *Death's* blind *Sea*, below,
Boundless, and formless, snatch'd the mingled Flow;
Both rounding Oceans, backward, seem'd to tend,
And vast, *beneath*, their sable Surges *blend:*   80
But far most frightful *This!*—whose dark *Profound*,
A Depth Eternal! Life wants Line to sound:
Unbottom'd Shade roll'd loose o'er swallow'd Light—
Fancy grew giddy, nor sustain'd the Sight:
But, starting into Fear, transpos'd Remark,
And sought the *Source*, less dreadful, tho' as dark.

Thick, on the rising Stream's emitted Tide,
Millions of shapeless Bodies seem'd to glide;
Whose breathing Bulks, to Life, and Motion, blown,
Shot into human Forms, compleatly grown;   90
Mix'd Rank, and Sex, sprung thro' the liquid Jet,
But, pouring outward, clear *Distinction* met;
Some, wading, naked, trod the slipp'ry Plain,
Some cut the fluent Wave—Some, tir'd with Pain,
Failing to float, or wade, neglected fell,
And sunk, unsnatch'd at, in the troubled Swell:
To others, rising happier, and serene,
Fortune, dark, bustling, Power, obscurely seen,
Reach'd, with blind Bounty, and with hasty Hand,
Thin Boats—and buoy'd 'em o'er the shining
  Sand: 100
Of diff'rent Form, these Boats—A *single Oar*

Distinguish'd some:—Some wing'd their Sides with
  more;
Others, with *Oars*, and *Sails*, *conjoin'd*, made Way,
And mow'd the murm'ring Surge, with sweepy
  Sway:
While some, *slow Pole-men*, o'er their Toil reclin'd,
Push'd their check'd Barks, and, labouring, lagg'd
  behind.

While *Some* essay'd to *cross*, and veering wide, ⎫
Would, with strong Stem, the stubborn Stream   ⎬
  divide,   ⎪
And slowly slanting, sought the silent Side;   ⎭
Swift, to the shelvy° Shore *light Gallies* flew,   110
As the fierce Channel's rapid Current drew,
'Twixt Rocks, and Whirlpools, driven, obliquely gay,
And, thro' the shoaly Sunshine, danc'd away.

Caught, by the gulphy *Void*, that gloom'd, below,
These, from the Current's fair-descending Flow,
Indrawn, at once, by Darkness swallow'd o'er,
Sunk, from their Sunny Scene, and rose no more;
Still gap'd th' unclosing Deep; o'er Millions gone,
Yet, still insatiate, hourly swallow'd on!
Titles, Distinctions, Forms, rush mingled down,   120
Not Levity itself wants Weight to drown:
Gamesters, Beaux, Casuists, Jinglers,° Jesters, Drinkers,
Fox-hunters, Politicians, and Free-thinkers,
Prudes, Devotees, Coquets, Grave, Light, Young, Old,
In one mixt Night the covering Waves infold:
Swept from the Noise they sought, to rest they shun'd,
They plunge, for ever, into *Death's Profund:*
While *abler Pilots*, who, resolv'd, *stood o'er*,
And, edging broad, gain'd, slow, the *safer Shore;*
Snatch'd, from their sinking Seats, were born to
  Land,   130
By watchful Swans, whose Wings the Surface fann'd:
There, on green Islands, reign'd, escap'd from Cares,
Lords of a blooming World, for ever, Theirs,

Wide, o'er the Scene, ALEXIS winds his Eye,
Swift, as the Progress of the Gliders by;
A strange Confusion rose!—of all who past,
With earnest Emptyness, and barren Haste,
Few, *cross* the Flood, repugnant, strove to steer,
Fewer had Strength of Oars to *hold* them, *near!*
Tir'd by the Current's ill-resisted Force,   140
Or, bulg'd° by envious Prows, which cross'd their
  Course,

110. **shelvy:** having shelves or dangerous sand-banks. **122.**
Jinglers: poetasters. **141. bulg'd:** struck.

The boldest Keels, pursuing, or pursu'd,
Entangling, and perplex'd, were lost in Feud:
While others, heedless of their sleeping Oars,
Drove, in light Negligence, nor shun'd the Shores;
But, pendent o'er the Helm, each Shoal explor'd,
And snatch'd, in Transport, Shells, and Stones, on
    board:
Or, leaping wanton, catch'd the glittering Prey,
That buzz'd, and gambol'd, in their sportive Way.

Mean-while, most mournful, of the motley
    Scene!   150
Cherish'd Effect of Pride, and Food of Spleen!
Boat, over Boat, destructive Passage made,
And weeping Pity mourn'd defective Aid:
Sailing Presumers, pressing, proudly, on,
Bore down each envied *Rower*, who, nearest, shone;
The *Oar-wing'd* Vessel ey'd, with dumb Disdain,
The creeping *Pole-man*'s slow-availing Pain;
And, *lordly wanton*, with invasive Beak,°
Sunk the faint Struggler, *criminally*, *weak!*
He, too, in Concert with superior Hate,   160
Loth to exert less Guilt, than match'd his State,
Triumphant, in his Turn, sought equal Prey,
And, o'er the *naked Wader*, forc'd his Way:

ALEXIS, pondering in suspended Thought,
What Meaning all these mazy Mixtures taught,
Sudden, a Shout, from every distant Side,
Eddied the Air, and broke the back'ning Tide;
Acclamatory Thousands rose, alarm'd,
All Eyes attracted, and each Hearing charm'd;
Pointing in Transport, All their Helms forsook,   170
And, on one Object, hung their length'ning Look.

Down, from the gloomy Source, in sidelong Float,
Proudly descending, mov'd a glittering Boat;
Her silken Sails a colour'd Radiance threw,
And ting'd the Sunny Beams, thro' which they flew;
While Oars, of Silver, dash'd the watry Spray,
That rain'd in gemmy Showers, and dazled Day:
High, on the painted Stern, a Youth appear'd,
Who, rather *happily*, than *strongly*, steer'd;
Faint and unstriking was his anguish'd Mien,   180
Sadden'd by Sickness, and o'ercast with Spleen;
Yet, from his Eyes, there beam'd a living Light,
Keen, and intent, as a fir'd Eagle's Sight:
And, from his Voice, (for, as he sail'd, he *sung*)
Such magick Sounds of melting Musick sprung,

That the hush'd Heaven all downward seem'd to
    bend,
And, against Nature, the charm'd Earth ascend.

Careless, he look'd, yet, heedful of his Way,⎫
Broke the kind Current's unobstructing Sway,⎬
That kiss'd his Oars, and hasten'd to obey:⎭
Scarce was his Course *oblique*, for each glad Boat,   191
That, envious, stem'd all other's rival Float,
Fix'd, and enchanted, when this Youth drew nigh,
Hung on his passing Notes, and help'd him by:
The *Muses* row'd him, and the *Graces'* Care
Trim'd his light Sails, and spread them to the Air;
In his Boat's Bottom green-ey'd *Envy* lay,
And serv'd, as *Ballast*, while she clog'd his way:
Down from her Chariot light-wing'd *Fancy* flew,
And o'er him, loose, her Starry Mantle threw;   200
Pleasure, *Praise*, *Beauty*, 'twixt his Shrouds trod gay,
And danc'd the measur'd Moments soft away:
Sportful as ZEPHYRS, in his Smiles, they strove,
And the Young *Loves* forsook their Mother's Grove.

Thus fortunate, thus favour'd, and thus bright,
Luckily negligent, and aptly light,
He touch'd no Shoal, safe rounded every Rock,
Despis'd all Danger, and sustain'd no Shock;
'Till to that calmer Coast approaching nigh,
And gliding, 'twixt green Islands, safely high,   210
Circles of hovering Swans, with joyful Note,
Clapp'd their broad Wings, in Triumph, o'er his Boat,
Charm'd, that, so soon, he reach'd their solemn Side,
Ere yet one Third of the Stream's Length was try'd.

Steering, from Isle to Isle, with joyless Awe,
Thin, o'er each Height, their white-rob'd Lords he
    saw,
Pleas'd, without Transport, bow the Palms, they bore,
To hail his Passage near their silent Shore;
Cold, and *uncharm'd*, he sought his favourite Croud,
Immensely distant, now, tho', late, so loud: 220
All was serene, the Air was hush'd around,
The Waters calm!—Lost even *His* Musick's Sound!
Back to the Left impatient Looks he cast
And long'd for every shining Insect past;
Distant he saw them, Wings o'er Wings, display,
And, in light Chases, thread the colour'd Ray:
Eager, for these, contending Pilots strove,
And catch'd them, careless how their Vessels drove;
Then, with their Trophies, dress'd each gaudy Sail,
While humming *Drones*, in Swarms, their Fortune
    hail: 230

158. Beak: prow.

Record past Leaps, foretel their next Essays,
And buzz, melodious, in the *Fly-men's* Praise.

Warm'd, and misled, by this false Fire of Fame,
His beaming Eyes with Emulation flame;
And have I, Recreant, thus, renounc'd a Field,
Where baffled Danger can such Glory yield?
Lives there a *Catch-Fly*, of yon venturous Press,
More brave than I am?—Or, who fears them less?
Shew me the warring Wasp, whose threatning Wing
I dare not strike at, and provoke his Sting !   240
Swans ! give me Way—your shoreless Islands keep,
Too safe your Clime is, and too calm your Deep;
I chuse a rapid Glory, not a slow,
Shoals are *sought Harbours*, where these *Jewels* grow:

He said, and rising, push'd, with liquid Sweep,
Th' inverted Helm, and goar'd the groaning Deep:
Flaming erect, resought the surgy Side,
And bounded, threatning, o'er the foaming Tide:
Sailing athwart the Swarms, and skipping high,
He snatch'd, triumphant, every tempting *Fly:*   250
Gave his loos'd Rudder to the Current's Claim,
And drove, disdainful, thro' his Rival's Game;
Press'd by *invaded Wasp's* excited Stings,
He warr'd, revengeful, on their falling Wings:
Thro' Dust of slaughter'd *Gnats* he fought, in Shade,
And squeez'd them, deathful, on the Wounds, they
        made;
Fleets of cold Opposites, from all Sides, join,
And, wedg'd, against this general Foe, combine:
Vainly indignant, they resist his Sway,
Yet block his Passage, and obstruct his Way: 260
Still, tho' he stagnates, he the Fight maintains,
While Drones, applausive, with their ductile Strains,
Homage the rising Hero's new Renown,
And *Prince of Fly-Catchers* the Champion crown.

The *Swans*, mean-while, which, from the calmer
        Side,
Forsaken, saw him trust the fatal Tide;
Mournful, with pendent Wing, his Triumph griev'd,
And wish'd his wasted Vigour less deceiv'd:
Trembling, they mark'd his Vessel, downward bent,
Hang o'er th' engulphing Ocean's dark Descent,   270
While he, regardless, still, new Trophies won,
And, bent to *conquer*, saw not what to *shun*.

Fancy, still busied, still enamour'd, staid,
And, still concurring, lent his Rashness Aid;
To *Her*, far distant, touch'd ALEXIS cry'd,
And, with strain'd Voice, to reach her Notice, try'd:

"O ! save him, warn him, bid him *turn*, and *think*,—
Let not his Bark in yon black Ocean sink !
Teach me to call him, by his powerful Name,
Point out his Danger, quench his devious Flame;   280
Rash Spleen of Heart, that could such War advise !
Blind Rage ! to lose *Himself*, and catch but *Flies!*
Oh teach my Tongue his Name"—Then *Fancy* heard
And, smiling, at her Chariot's Side appear'd:
"Why dost thou ask, she cry'd, what *Nations* know,
Even *All*, whom Wit, or Worth, inspire, below?
His is a Name, that dwells on every Mind,
Tunes every Tongue, and sails with every Wind !
Not surer is that River *Life's Extent*,
Or, by those Oceans, *Birth*, and *Death*, are meant;   290
Not surer *Fortune* is That dark Power's Name,
That Left, *Oblivion*, and That Right Side, *Fame*,
Than, that no Son of Wit dares, *justly*, hope,
Fame dwells in *Folly's Paths*, but thou, O POPE !"

ALEXIS, starting, heard his own lov'd Name,
Felt his Pride shrink, and blush'd with conscious
        Shame !
Pitch'd from the Chariot, lost to *Fancy's* Call;
And, had not waiting *Judgment* broke his Fall,
Contempt's cold Vale had caught him, wak'd, and
        stunn'd,
And deep intomb'd him, in his *own* PROFUND.   300

ALONE, IN AN INN, (AT SOUTHAMPTON)

APRIL THE 25th, 1737.

TWENTY *lost* years have stoln their hours away,
Since, in *this inn*, ev'n in this *room*, I lay:
How chang'd ! what, *then*, was *rapture, fire*, and *air*,
Seems, *now*, sad *silence*, all, and blanc *despair!*
Is it, that youth paints every view too bright,
And, *life* advancing, *fancy* fades her light?
Ah ! no—nor, yet, is day so far declin'd,
Nor can *time's* creeping coldness reach the *mind*.

'TIS—that I miss th' *inspirer* of that youth;
Her, whose soft *smile* was *love*, whose soul was *truth*. 10
Her, from whose pain, I never wish'd *relief*,
And, for whose *pleasure*, I could smile at *grief*.
Prospects, that (view'd with her) *inspir'd*, before,
Now, seen without her, can delight no more.

ALONE, IN AN INN, (AT SOUTHAMPTON). The text is that of the first printing, in Hill's posthumous *Works* (4 vols., 1753).

Death snatch'd my *joys*, by cutting off *her* share,
But left her *griefs*, to multiply my *care*.

PENSIVE, and cold, this room, in each chang'd part,
I *view*, and, shock'd, from ev'ry object, start:
There hung the *watch*, that beating hours, from day,
Told its sweet *owner's* lessening life away.   20
There, her dear *diamond* taught the sash my name;°
'Tis gone! frail *image* of *love*, *life*, and *fame*.
That glass, she dress'd at, keeps her form no more;
Not one dear foot-step *tunes* th' unconscious *floor*,
There sat she—yet, those *chairs* no sense retain,
And busy *recollection* smarts, in vain.
Sullen, and dim, what faded scenes are here!
I wonder, and retract a starting tear.
Gaze, in attentive doubt—with anguish, swell,
And o'er, and o'er, on each weigh'd object, dwell.   30
Then, to the window, rush, gay views invite,
And tempt *idea*, to permit *delight*.
But unimpressive, all in sorrow, drown'd,
One void forgetful desert glooms, around.

OH life!—deceitful lure of lost desires!
How *short* thy *period*, yet, how *fierce* thy *fires*!
Scarce can a passion start, (we *change* so fast)
E're *new* lights strike us, and the *old* are past.
Schemes following schemes, so long life's taste
     explore,
That, e'er we learn to live, we live no more.   40
Who, then, can think—yet sigh, to part with *breath*?
Or shun the healing hand of friendly *death*?
Guilt, penitence, and wrongs; and pain, and strife,
Form thy whole heap'd *amount*, thou flatterer, *life*!
Is it for *this*, that toss'd, 'twixt hope, and fear,
Peace, by new shipwrecks, numbers each *new year*?
Oh, take me, *death!* indulge desir'd *repose*,
And draw thy silent *curtain* round my woes.

YET, hold—*one* tender pang revokes that *pray'r*,
Still, there remains *one claim*, to tax my *care*.   50
Gone, tho' she is, she left her *soul* behind,
In four dear *transcripts* of her copy'd *mind*.
They chain me down to life, new task supply,
And leave me not, at leisure, yet, to *die!*
Busied, for them, I, yet, forego release;
And teach my wearied *heart*, to wait for *peace*.
But, when their day breaks broad, I welcome *night*,
Smile at discharge from *care*, and shut out *light*.

21. her . . . name: Eighteenth-century lovers were fond of
cutting their names on inn windowpanes with diamonds.

♛

Lady Mary Wortley Montagu

1689–1762

LADY M. M——'S FAREWEL
TO BATH

TO all you ladies now at *Bath*,
     And eke,° ye beaus, to you,
With aking heart, and wat'ry eyes,
     I bid my last adieu.

Farewel ye nymphs, who waters sip
     Hot reeking from the pumps,
While music lends her friendly aid,
     To cheer you from the dumps.

Farewel ye wits, who prating stand,
     And criticise the fair;   10
Yourselves the joke of men of sense,
     Who hate a coxcomb's air.

Farewel to *Deard's*,° and all her toys,
     Which glitter in her shop,
Deluding traps to girls and boys,
     The warehouse of the fop.

Lindsay's and *Hayes's*° both farewel,
     Where in the spacious hall,
With bounding steps, and sprightly air,
     I've led up many a ball.   20

Where *Somerville* of courteous mein,
     Was partner in the dance,
With swimming *Haws*, and *Brownlow* blithe,
     And *Britton*° pink° of *France*.

LADY M. M——'S FAREWEL TO BATH. The text is that of the
first printing, in *The Gentleman's Magazine* (July, 1731). **2.
eke:** also. **13. Deard's:** a clothing and novelty shop. **17.
Lindsay's and Hayes's:** famous assembly and gaming
rooms. **21–24. Somerville, Haws, Brownlow, Britton:**
Bath friends and dancing partners of Lady Mary's. **24. pink:**
Pink clothes were a passing fashion among the macaronis
of the 1730's.

Poor *Nash,*° farewel! may fortune smile,
  Thy drooping soul revive,
My heart is full I can no more—
  John,° bid the coachman drive.

✦✦✦

William Oldys

1696–1761

AN ANACREONTICK

Busy, curious, thirsty Fly,
Gently drink, and drink as I;
Freely welcome to my Cup,
Could'st thou sip, and sip it up;
Make the most of Life you may,
Life is short and wears away.

Just alike, both mine and thine,
Hasten quick to their Decline;
Thine's a Summer, mine's no more,
Though repeated to threescore;   10
Threescore Summers when they're gone,
Will appear as short as one.

✦✦✦

Anonymous

THE VICAR OF BRAY

In good King Charles's golden days,
  When Loyalty no harm meant;
A Furious High-Church Man I was,
  And so I gain'd Preferment:

Unto my Flock, I daily Preach'd,
  Kings are by God appointed,
And Damn'd are those who dare resist,
  Or touch the Lord's Anointed.
And this is Law, I will maintain
  Unto my Dying Day Sir,   10
That whatsoever King shall Reign,
  I will be Vicar of Bray Sir.

When Royal James, possest the Crown,
  And Popery grew in fashion;
The Penal Law I Houted down,
  And read the Declaration:°
The Church of Rome, I found would fit,
  Full well my Constitution,
And I had been a Jesuit,
  But for the Revolution.   20
And this is Law, &c.

When William, our Deliverer came,
  To heal the Nations Greivance,
I turn'd the Cat in Pan° again,
  And swore to him Allegiance:
Old Principles I did revoke,
  Set Conscience at a distance,
Passive obedience is a Joke,
  A Jest is non resistance.
And this is Law, &c.   30

When Glorious Ann, became our Queen,
  The Church of Englands Glory,
Another face of things was seen,
  And I became a Tory:
Occasional Conformists° base,
  I Damn'd, and Moderation,
And thought the Church in danger was,
  From such Prevarication.
And this is Law, &c.

When George in Pudding time° came o'er,   40
  And Moderate Men look'd big Sir,
My Principles I chang'd once more,
  And so became a Whigg Sir:

---

25. **Nash:** Richard Nash (1674–1762), often called Beau Nash; the celebrated Bath entrepreneur and master of ceremonies. 28. **John:** a servant.   AN ANACREONTICK. The text is that of the first printing, in *The Scarborough Miscellany. An Original Collection of Poems* (1732). An Anacreontic (from the Greek lyric poet Anacreon [*c.* 563–478 B.C.]) is traditionally a song about either love or drinking.   THE VICAR OF BRAY. The text is from Volume I of *The British Musical Miscellany* (1734). Opinions differ about his name, but it is generally accepted that he was the Vicar of Bray, in Berkshire, during the reigns of the last four Tudors.

15–16. **Penal Law, Declaration:** acts passed during the reign of Charles II first persecuting and then suspending persecution of Roman Catholics. 24. **turn'd . . . Pan:** altered principles (cf. *tourner côte en peine,* to change sides when in trouble). 35. **Occasional Conformists:** Dissenters who managed to qualify for public office by participating in the Anglican communion only once or a very few times. 40. **Pudding time:** a time of good fortune and prosperity.

And thus Preferment I procur'd,
 From our Faiths Great Defender,
And almost every day abjur'd,
 The Pope, and the Pretender.
And this is Law, &c.

The Illustrious House of Hannover,
 And Protestant Succession,   50
To these I lustily will swear,
 Whilst they can keep possession:
For in my Faith, and Loyalty,
 I never once will faulter,
But George, my Lawful King shall be,
 Except the Times shou'd alter.
And this is Law, &c.

Stephen Duck

1705–1756

[handwritten: MITES ≠ MEN MADE ‖ IN MANY ATTRIBUTES]

ON MITES

[handwritten: FAVORABLE OR UNFAVORABLE VIEW OF MAN – WHY?]

To a Lady.

[handwritten: ADJECTIVES MAKE REPUGNANT PICTURES]

'Tis but by way of (Simile). *[handwritten: WHY TO A LADY?]*
       PRIOR.

[handwritten: 8 SYLABLE LINE IAMBIC]

DEAR Madam, did you never gaze, *[handwritten: 3 COUPLETS]*
Thro' Optic-glass, on rotten Cheese? *[handwritten: VISUAL RHYMES]*
There, Madam, did you ne'er perceive
A Crowd of dwarfish Creatures live?
The little Things, elate with Pride,
Strut to and fro, from Side to Side:
In tiny Pomp, and pertly vain,
Lords of their pleasing Orb, they reign; *[handwritten: WHY ITALICS]*
And, fill'd with harden'd Curds and Cream,
Think the whole Dairy made for *them.* 10
So Men, conceited Lords of all, *[handwritten: WHY DID HE ¶ – SIGNAL TO READER; MEN ARE LIKE THIS]*
Walk proudly o'er this pendent° Ball, *[handwritten: EARTH]*
Fond of their little Spot below,
Nor greater Beings care to know;
But think, those *Worlds,* which deck the Skies,
Were only form'd to please *their* Eyes.

ON MITES. The text is that of the first printing, in *Poems on Several Occasions* (1736). **12. pendent:** floating unsupported in space.

[handwritten: GOOD ARGUMENT? ARE ALL MEN LIKE THESE MITES? DO MITES HAVE CONSCIENCE?]

John Hoadly

1711–1776

CHLOE RESOLVED

A BALLAD

As Cloe on Flowers reclin'd o'er the Stream
She sigh'd to the Breeze and made Colin her Theme
Tho' Pleasant the Stream, & tho' cooling the Breeze
And the Flowers tho' fragrant she panted for Ease.

2

The Stream it was fickle and hasted away,
It kiss'd the Sweet Banks but no longer cou'd stay,
Tho' Beauteous Inconstant and Faithless tho' Fair,
Ah! Colin look in and behold thyself there.

3

The Breeze that so Sweet on its Bosom did play,
Now rose to a Tempest and darkned the Day, 10
As soft as the Breeze and as loud as the wind,
Such Colin when Angry and Colin when kind.

4

The Flowers when gather'd so Beauteous and sweet,
Now fade on her Bosom and Dye at her Feet,
So fair in their Bloom and so foul in Decay,
Such Colin when Present and Colin away.

5

In Rage and dispair from the Ground she arose,
And from her the Flowers so faded she throws,
She weeps in the Stream and she sighs to the wind,
And resolves to Drive Colin quite out of her mind. 20

6

But what her resolves when her Colin appear'd,
The Stream it stood still and no Tempest was heard,
The Flowers recover'd their beautiful Hue,
She found he was kind and believ'd he was True.

CHLOE RESOLVED. The text is that of a broadside of about 1743; we have incorporated the substantive variants in Dodsley's *Collection* (Vol. V, 1758). In the broadside the title appears as *Chloe's Resolves.*

Edward Moore

1712–1757

FROM

FABLES
FOR THE FEMALE SEX

FABLE V

The POET, *and his* PATRON.

WHY, Celia, is your spreading waist
So loose, so negligently lac'd?
Why must the wrapping bed-gown hide
Your snowy bosom's swelling pride?
How ill that dress adorns your head,
Distain'd, and rumpled from the bed!
Those clouds, that shade your blooming face,
A little water might displace,
As nature ev'ry morn bestows
The crystal dew, to cleanse the rose.   10
Those tresses, as the raven black,
That wav'd in ringlets down your back,
Uncomb'd, and injur'd by neglect,
Destroy the face, which once they deck'd.
  Whence this forgetfulness of dress?
Pray, madam, are you marry'd? Yes.
Nay, then indeed the wonder ceases,
No matter now how loose your dress is;
The end is won, your fortune's made,
Your sister now may take the trade.°   20
  Alas! what pity 'tis to find
This fault in half the female kind!
From hence proceed aversion, strife,
And all that sours the wedded life.
Beauty can only point the dart,
'Tis neatness guides it to the heart;
Let neatness then, and beauty strive
To keep a wav'ring flame alive.

'Tis harder far (you'll find it true)
To keep the conquest, than subdue;   30
Admit us once behind the screen,
What is there farther to be seen?
A newer face may raise the flame,
But ev'ry woman is the same.
  Then study chiefly to improve
The charm, that fix'd your husband's love;
Weigh well his humour. Was it dress,
That gave your beauty pow'r to bless?
Pursue it still; be neater seen,
'Tis always frugal to be clean;   40
So shall you keep alive desire,
And time's swift wing shall fan the fire.

  In garret high (as stories say)
A Poet sung his tuneful lay;
So soft, so smooth his verse, you'd swear
Apollo,° and the muses there;
Thro' all the town his praises rung,
His sonnets at the playhouse sung;
High waving o'er his lab'ring head,
The goddess Want her pinions spread,   50
And with poetic fury fir'd,
What Phœbus faintly had inspir'd.
  A noble Youth, of taste, and wit,
Approv'd the sprightly things he writ,
And sought him in his cobweb dome,
Discharg'd his rent, and brought him home.
  Behold him at the stately board,
Who, but the Poet, and my Lord!
Each day, deliciously he dines,
And greedy quaffs the gen'rous wines;   60
His sides were plump, his skin was sleek,
And plenty wanton'd on his cheek;
Astonish'd at the change so new,
Away th' inspiring goddess flew.
  Now, dropt for politics, and news,
Neglected lay the drooping muse,
Unmindful whence his fortune came,
He stifled the poetic flame;
Nor tale, nor sonnet, for my lady,
Lampoon, nor epigram was ready.   70
  With just contempt his Patron saw,
(Resolv'd his bounty to withdraw)
And thus, with anger in his look,
The late-repenting fool bespoke.

FABLES FOR THE FEMALE SEX: *Fable V*. The text is that of the
first edition (May, 1744). **20. take . . . trade:** take up the
work that you have laid aside.

46. Apollo: Phoebus, the classical god of light, health, and
poetry.

Blind to the good that courts thee grown,
Whence has the sun of favour shone?
Delighted with thy tuneful art,
Esteem was growing in my heart,
But idly thou reject'st the charm,
That gave it birth, and kept it warm.   80
  Unthinking fools, alone despise
The arts, that taught them first to rise.

Sneyd Davies

1709–1769

AT SEEING ARCHBISHOP WILLIAMS'S MONUMENT AT CARNARVONSHIRE

IN that remote and solitary Place,
Which the Seas wash, and circling Hills embrace,
Where those lone Walls amid the Groves arise,
All that remains of thee, fam'd *Williams*, lies.
Thither, sequester'd Shade, Creation's Nook,
The wand'ring Muse her pensive Journey took,
Curious to trace the Statesman° to his Home,
And moralize at Leisure o'er his Tomb:
She came not, with the Pilgrim, Tears to shed,
Mutter a Vow, or trifle with a Bead,   10
But such a Sadness did her Thoughts employ,
As lives within the Neighbourhood of Joy.
Reflecting much upon the mighty Shade,
His Glories, and his Miseries,° she said:

  "How poor the Lot of the once honour'd Dead!
Perhaps the Dust is *Williams*', that we tread.

The learn'd, ambitious, politick, and great,
Statesman, and Prelate, this alas! thy Fate.
Cou'd not thy *Lincoln* yield her Pastor room,
Cou'd not thy *York* supply thee with a Tomb?   20
Was it for this thy lofty Genius soar'd,
Caress'd by Monarchs and by Crouds ador'd?
For this, thy Hand o'er Rivals cou'd prevail,
Grasping by Turns the Crosier and the Seal°?
Who dar'd on *Laud's*° meridian Pow'r to frown,
And on aspiring *Buckingham*° look down.
This thy gay Morn,—but e'er the Day decline
Clouds gather, and Adversity is thine:
Doom'd to behold thy Country's fierce Alarms,
What had thy trembling Age to do with Arms?   30
Thy Lands dragoon'd, thy Palaces in Dust,
Why was thy Life protracted to be curst?
Thy King° in Chains,—thyself by lawless Might
Strip't of all Pow'r, and exil'd from thy Right.

  A while the venerable Hero stood,
And stemm'd with quiv'ring Limbs the boist'rous
    Flood;
At length, o'er-match'd by Injuries and Time,
Stole from the World, and sought his native Clime."

  Cambria° for him with Moans her Region fills;
She wept his Downfal from a thousand Hills: 40
Tender embrac'd her Prelate tho' undone,
Stretch'd out the Mother Rocks to hide her Son:
Search'd, while alive, each Vale for his Repast,
And, when he died, receiv'd him in her Breast.
Envied Ambition! What are all thy Schemes,
But waking Misery, or pleasing Dreams,
Sliding and tottering on the Heights of State!
The Subject of this Verse declares thy Fate.
Great as he was, you see how small the Gain,
A Burial so obscure, a Muse so mean.   50

AT SEEING ARCHBISHOP WILLIAMS'S MONUMENT. The text is from John Whaley's *A Collection of Original Poems and Translations* (1745). A note on the title in the original text reads: "*John Williams* [b. 1582] was consecrated Bishop of *Lincoln* November 11. 1621. was translated to *York* December 4. 1641. and died *March* 25. 1649 and was buried at *Landegay* near *Bangor* [in the Welsh county of Carnarvonshire, which could be held to be 'obscure' (l. 50)]." **7. the Statesman:** Williams had been active in Royalist politics during the civil wars. **14. his Miseries:** Williams spent the years 1637–40 imprisoned in the Tower of London.

24. the Crosier . . . Seal: The crosier is a staff symbolic of a bishop's authority; the seal is the official seal of English state documents, formally in the charge of the Lord High Chancellor. A note in the original text reads: "He was made Lord Keeper of the great Seal *July* 20, 1621." **25. Laud:** Archbishop William Laud (b. 1573), beheaded in 1645 by the Parliamentarians. **26. Buckingham:** George Villiers (1592–1628), First Duke of Buckingham. **33. Thy King:** Charles I. **39. Cambria:** the medieval Latin name for Wales.

Thomas Edwards

1699–1757

SONNET V.
ON A FAMILY-PICTURE

DETERIORATION OF A FINE FAMILY [handwritten]

DEPRESSING VIEW OF LIFE [handwritten]

When pensive on that Portraiture I gaze,
  Where my four Brothers round about me stand,
  And four fair Sisters smile with graces bland,°
The goodly monument of happier days;

And think how soon insatiate Death, who preys
  On all, has cropp'd the rest with ruthless hand;
  While only I survive of all that band,
Which one chaste bed did to my Father raise;

It seems that like a Column left alone,
  The tottering remnant of some splendid Fane,°   10
  Scape'd from the fury of the barbarous Gaul,
And wasting Time, which has the rest o'erthrown;
  Amidst our House's ruins I remain
  Single, unpropp'd, and nodding° to my fall.

Paul Whitehead

1710–1774

A HUNTING SONG

The Sun from the East tips the Mountains with Gold,
And the Meadows all spangled with Dew drops
    behold,
Hear the Larks early Mattin proclaims the new Day,
And the Horns cheerfull Summons rebukes our delay.
With the Sports of the Field there's no Pleasure can
    vie,
While jocund we follow the Hounds in full Cry.

2

Let the Drudge of the Town make Riches his Sport,
And the Slave of the State hunt the smiles of the
    Court.
No care nor Ambition our Patience annoy,
But Innocence still gives it rest° to our Joy.   10
  Cho: With the Sports &c:

3

Mankind are all Hunters in various degree,
The Preist hunts a Living the Lawyer a Fee:
The Doctor a Patient, the Courtier a Place,
Tho often like us they're flung out with Disgrace.°
  Cho: With the Sports &c:

4

The Cit° hunts a Plumb,° while the Soldier hunts
    Fame,
The Poet a Dinner, the Patriot a Name:
And the artfull° Coquet tho she seems to refuse,
Yet in spite of her Airs, she her Lover pursues.   20
  Cho: With the Sports &c:

5

Let the Bold and the Busy hunt Glory and wealth,
All the Blessings we ask, is the Blessing of Health,
With Hounds & with Horns, thro the Woodlands to
    roam
And when tired abroad, find contentment at home.
  Cho: With the Sports &c:

SONNET V. The text is from *The Canons of Criticism* (6th ed.,
1758). **3. bland:** gentle. **10. Fane:** temple. **14. nodding:**
swaying, tottering. A HUNTING SONG. The text is from the
earliest version, a folio music sheet published around 1765;
because the text is obviously corrupt we indicate below
some unauthoritative variants from Whitehead's posthumous
Collected Poems of 1777.

10. it rest: The 1777 edition reads: "a zest." **15. they're
. . . Disgrace:** The 1777 edition reads: "he's flung-out
in the chace." **17. Cit:** citizen, i.e., a London small business-
man. **Plumb:** the slang term for a hundred thousand pounds.
19. artfull: The 1777 edition reads: "practis'd."

Hymns and Divine Songs

Joseph Addison

1672–1719

ODE

The Spacious Firmament on high,
With all the blue Etherial Sky,
And spangled Heav'ns, a Shining Frame,
Their great Original proclaim:
Th' unwearied Sun, from Day to Day,
Does his Creator's Power display,
And publishes to every Land
The Work of an Almighty Hand.

Soon as the Evening Shades prevail,
The Moon takes up the wondrous Tale,   10
And nightly to the listning Earth
Repeats the Story of her Birth:
Whilst all the Stars that round her burn,
And all the Planets, in their turn,
Confirm the Tidings as they rowl,
And spread the Truth from Pole to Pole.

ODE. The text is from *The Spectator*, No. 465 (August 23, 1712), where Addison introduces the poem as follows: "The Supream Being has made the best Arguments for his own Existence, in the Formation of the Heavens and the Earth, and these are Arguments which a Man of Sense cannot forbear attending to, who is out of the Noise and Hurry of human Affairs. *Aristotle* says, that should a Man live under Ground, and there converse with Works of Art and Mechanism, and should afterwards be brought up into the open Day, and see the several Glories of the Heav'n and Earth, he would immediately pronounce them the Works of such a Being as we define God to be."

What though, in solemn Silence, all
Move round the dark terrestrial Ball?
What tho' nor real Voice nor Sound
Amid their radiant Orbs be found?
In Reason's Ear they all rejoice,   20
And utter forth a glorious Voice,
For ever singing, as they shine,
"The Hand that made us is Divine."

Isaac Watts

1674–1748

A PROSPECT OF HEAVEN MAKES DEATH EASY

1   There is a Land of pure Delight
    Where Saints Immortal reign,
Infinite Day excludes the Night,
    And Pleasures banish Pain.

2   There everlasting Spring abides,
    And never-withering Flowers:
Death like a narrow Sea divides
    This Heav'nly Land from ours.

3   Sweet Fields beyond the swelling Flood
    Stand drest in living Green:
So to the *Jews* Old *Canaan* stood,
    While *Jordan* roll'd between.

A PROSPECT OF HEAVEN MAKES DEATH EASY. The text is from Watts's *Hymns and Spiritual Songs* (1707).

4   But timorous Mortals start and shrink   *[COMPARES GOD & MAN]*
    To cross this narrow Sea,
  And linger shivering on the Brink,
    And fear to lanch° away.

5   O could we make our Doubts remove,
    These gloomy Doubts that rise,
  And see the *Canaan* that we love,
    With unbeclouded Eyes: 20

6   Could we but climb where *Moses* stood,   *[LOOK BEYOND DEATH TO PARADISE BEYOND]*
    And view the Landskip o're,
  Not *Jordan*'s Stream, nor Death's cold Flood
    Should fright us from the Shore.

CRUCIFIXION TO THE WORLD
BY THE CROSS
OF CHRIST

Gal. 6. 14.

1   When I survey the wondrous Cross
  On which the Prince of Glory dy'd,   *[HUMBLENESS]*
  My richest Gain I count but Loss
  And pour Contempt on all my Pride.

2   Forbid it, Lord, that I should boast
  Save in the Death of Christ my God;   *[ELABORATION ON 1ST STANZA]*
  All the vain things that charm me most,
  I sacrifice them to his Blood.

3   See from his Head, his Hands, his Feet,
  Sorrow and Love flow mingled down;   *[SURPRISE]*
  Did e're such Love and Sorrow meet?   *[10 PUNCH]* *[MAIN ARGUMENT]*
  Or Thorns compose so rich a Crown?

4   His dying Crimson like a Robe
  Spreads o'er his Body on the Tree,   *[NOTHING ELSE IN WORLD MATTERS BESIDES CRUCIFIXION]*
  Then am I dead to all the Globe,
  And all the Globe is dead to me.

5   Were the whole Realm of Nature mine,
  That were a Present far too small;   *[ATTEMPTS TO TAKE READER THERE]*
  Love so amazing, so divine
  Demands my Soul, my Life, my All.   20

MAN FRAIL
AND GOD ETERNAL

Our God, our Help in Ages past,
  Our Hope for Years to come,
Our Shelter from the Stormy Blast,
  And our eternal Home.

Under the Shadow of thy Throne,
  Thy Saints have dwelt secure;
Sufficient is thine Arm alone,
  And our Defence is sure.

Before the Hills in order stood,
  Or Earth receiv'd her Frame,   10
From everlasting Thou art Good,
  To endless Years the same.

Thy Word commands our Flesh to Dust,
  Return, ye Sons of Men.
All Nations rose from Earth at first,
  And turn to Earth again.

A thousand Ages in thy Sight
  Are like an Evening gone;
Short as the Watch that ends the Night
  Before the rising Sun.   20

The busy Tribes of Flesh and Blood
  With all their Lives and Cares
Are carried downwards by thy Flood,
  And lost in following Years.

Time like an ever-rolling Stream
  Bears all its Sons away;
They fly forgotten as a Dream
  Dies at the opening Day.

Like flow'ry Fields the Nations stand
  Pleas'd with the Morning-light;   30
The Flowers beneath the Mower's Hand
  Ly withering e'er 'tis Night.

Our God, our Help in Ages past,
  Our Hope for Years to come,
Be thou our Guard while Troubles last
  And our eternal Home.

---

16. lanch: launch. CRUCIFIXION TO THE WORLD BY THE CROSS OF CHRIST. The text is from *Hymns and Spiritual Songs* (1707); we have incorporated the variants appearing in the fourteenth edition (1740). The passage in Galatians reads: "But God forbid that I should glory, save in the cross of our Lord Jesus Christ, by whom the world is crucified unto me, and I unto the world."

MAN FRAIL AND GOD ETERNAL. The text is from *The Psalms of David Imitated* (1719).

AGAINST QUARRELING AND FIGHTING

Let Dogs delight to bark and bite,
  For GOD hath made them so;
Let Bears and Lions growl and fight,
  For 'tis their Nature too.

But, Children, you should never let
  Such angry Passions rise;
Your little Hands were never made
  To tear each other's Eyes.

Let Love thro' all your Actions run,
  And all your Words be mild;   10
Live like the blessed Virgin's Son,
  That sweet and lovely Child.

His Soul was gentle as a Lamb;
  And as his Stature grew,
He grew in Favour both with Man,
  And God his Father too.

Now, LORD of all, he reigns above,
  And from his heav'nly Throne
He sees what Children dwell in Love,
  And marks them for his own.   20

THE SLUGGARD

'Tis the Voice of the Sluggard; I heard him complain,
"You have wak'd me too soon, I must slumber again."
As the Door on its Hinges, so he on his Bed,
Turns his Sides and his Shoulders and his heavy Head.

"A little more Sleep, and a little more Slumber;"
Thus he wastes half his Days and his Hours without
    Number;
And when he gets up, he sits folding his Hands,
Or walks about sauntring, or trifling he stands.

I pass'd by his Garden, and saw the wild Brier,
The Thorn and the Thistle grow broader and
    higher;   10
The Clothes that hang on him are turning to Rags;
And his Money still wastes, till he starves or he begs.

I made him a Visit, still hoping to find
He had took better Care for improving his Mind:
He told me his Dreams, talk'd of Eating and Drinking;
But he scarce reads his Bible, and never loves
    Thinking.

Said I then to my Heart, "Here's a Lesson for me,"
That Man's but a Picture of what I might be:
But Thanks to my Friends for their Care in my
    Breeding,
Who taught me betimes° to love Working and
    Reading.   20

AGAINST QUARRELING AND FIGHTING. The texts of this and the following poem are from *Divine Songs for the Use of Children* (1720).

THE SLUGGARD. See Prov. 24:30–34. **20. betimes:** early.

Part Four

FACSIMILES FROM
THE GENTLEMAN'S
MAGAZINE

The Gentleman's Magazine

Nowhere in eighteenth-century literature is the influence of the new, educated middle-class audience more evident than in the proliferation of newspapers and magazines. The journals and miscellanies of the previous age, mainly aristocratic and learned, had not addressed themselves specifically to these highly practical readers. What they wanted was news, both foreign and domestic, with commentary and useful information of a scientific and political sort. They wanted to be both amused and edified. Their needs were amply supplied by the first magazine—in the modern sense of the term—*The Gentleman's Magazine*, begun in 1731 by Edward Cave. Indeed, Cave's use of *magazine* in his title gave the word a new meaning in English, and his publication defined the word's most common use today. *The Gentleman's Magazine* became *the* periodical of the century; it continued, in fact, until 1922.

Edward Cave, the son of a cobbler, was born in 1691 in the village of Newtown, Warwickshire. As a local boy he was eligible to attend Rugby School, and, although his schooling was cut short, he came away with the rudiments of a literary education. While in his teens he was apprenticed to a London printer, and at twenty-two he was sent by him to found a newspaper in Norwich. This experience as a provincial editor probably suggested to him his next occupation. Soon after 1725 he set himself up to supply London news to a number of papers outside the city and apparently continued in this work for the next five or six years. When exactly he decided to publish a digest of other periodicals and newspapers is not known, but he is said to have discussed the idea with several printers and booksellers before he set up a print shop of his own at St. John's Gate where, in 1731, the first number of *The Gentleman's Magazine* was published.

Cave's original advertisement suggests the variety and types of material he undertook to provide. Of particular interest is the promise of controversy—something other miscellanies had carefully avoided. Cave maintained he would be impartial; but by this he meant he would display both sides of a controversy, thereby capitalizing on the interest controversy could arouse and gaining the readership of both factions. Even his pseudonym, Sylvanus Urban, was chosen to appeal to both the country and the town.

In a few Days will be Publish'd, Number 1
for January, 1731.
The Gentleman's Magazine; or Traders Monthly
Intelligencer: Being a Collection of all
Matters of Information and Amusement: Com-
priz'd under the following Heads, viz.

Publick Affairs, Foreign and Domestick,
Births, Marriages, and Deaths of Eminent Persons,
Preferments, Ecclesiastical and Civil.
Prices of Goods, Grain and Stocks.
Bankrupts declar'd and Books Publish'd
Pieces of Humour and Poetry
Disputes in Politicks and Learning.
Remarkable Advertisements and Occurrences.
Lists of the Civil and Military Establishment.
And whatever is worth quoting from the
Numerous Papers of News and Entertainment, British
and Foreign; or shall be Communicated
proper for Publication.
With Instructions in Gardening, and the Fairs for
February.

By Sylvanus Urban of Aldermanbury, Gent.
Prodesse et Delectare.

Printed for A. Dodd without Temple-Bar.   Price 6d.

The magazine was an immediate success. It began as a digest of other publications, but Cave soon had numerous correspondents supplying him with original articles, and he employed a number of writers in London to do piecework. (The misery of some of these hacks is illustrated by a contemporary description of one of them, Samuel Boise, shivering naked in bed writing verses with a pen stuck through a hole in his blanket in order to earn enough to redeem the clothes he had pawned.) Young Samuel Johnson, who was later to be Cave's most distinguished contributor, wrote to him from Lichfield as early as 1734 offering to supply "poems, inscriptions, etc., never published before," as well as "short literary dissertations in Latin or English, critical remarks on authors ancient and modern, forgotten poems that deserve revival, etc." Nothing came of this suggestion at the time, but the letter indicates the kind of influence Cave's magazine was beginning to have, as well as Johnson's awareness of the possibility of a career in writing. When Johnson first saw St. John's Gate, he later told Boswell, he "beheld it with reverence."

No enterprise so successful as Cave's could go unchallenged for long. The most formidable competition came from *The London Magazine*, established in 1732. Printed and distributed by a powerful group of London booksellers, it had certain advantages over Cave's magazine; it could compete not only on editorial grounds but also in distribution. The competition was rough and tumble. In 1738 a correspondent from Bristol informed Cave that his magazines there were being mutilated and anti-Cave advertisements from *The London Magazine* were being pasted into them. Charges and countercharges followed in the two periodicals.

Though it continued until 1785, *The London Magazine* seems to have presented little competition after the early 1740's. In 1741, at the beginning of *The Gentleman's* second decade of publication, Cave was able to boast that his magazine was read "as far as the English language extends," and in his Preface for that year he remarks on the frequency with which articles from *The Gentleman's* were reprinted "from several presses in Great Britain, Ireland and the Plantations." He observes, "Our Debates and Poetical pieces are copied by some, our Foreign History by others, and the Lives which we have inserted of eminent men, have been taken into works of a larger size, and with other parts of our Book have been translated into foreign languages." Forty years later, when Johnson revised his *Life of Cave* (originally written when Cave died in 1754), he took note of the fiftieth anniversary of the magazine's first publication and acknowledged its singular success: "*The Gentleman's Magazine*, which has now subsisted fifty years, and still continues to enjoy the favor of the world is one of the most successful and lucrative pamphlets which literary history has upon record."

Johnson's own contribution to this success was not small: the idea for the lives of eminent men (the best of which he wrote himself) was his, and the Parliamentary debates, for which he was solely responsible from November, 1740, until February, 1743, were not only masterly but popular. After his first proposal from Lichfield, Johnson next addressed Cave in 1737, offering to translate Paolo Sarpi's *History of the Council of Trent* (1619). Nothing came of this proposal either, although his life of the so-called Father Paul appeared elsewhere a year later. Johnson's first piece to be published in *The Gentleman's* was an unsolicited Latin poem, *Ad Urbanum* (1738), praising Cave and defending him against both competitors and critics. For the next decade Johnson was a regular contributor of essays, biographies, and verse, and Boswell speculates that Cave employed Johnson as a "regular coadjutor in his magazine."

The fictitious Parliamentary debates, published under the title *Debates in the Senate of Magna Lilliputia*, first came out in 1738 in response to a similar serial appearing in *The London Magazine*. Parliamentary news had been published in *The Gentleman's* from the beginning as an addition to the "Monthly Intelligencer," and the King's addresses to the combined Houses were frequently reprinted. But this news was mainly hearsay, for to quote actual speeches from Parliament was regarded as a breach of privilege. (Cave had once been called before the bar and charged with supplying Parliamentary news to several provincial newspapers. He was released after begging pardon on his knees and being reprimanded and fined.) As a protection it was necessary to indulge in an elaborate pretense: the debates were said to have been sent back to London by Gulliver's grandson from the parliament of Lilliput. This subterfuge, in which Walpole became Walelop and Halifax became Haxilaf, was patent, but, because public opinion sufficiently favored freedom of the press, Parliament seemed unwilling to prosecute. Years after they appeared, the speeches were generally considered genuine; in his *History of England* (1757–58) Smollett quoted them as if they were. The first speeches and debates were actually put together by Cave and William Guthrie either from memory or from a few penciled notes taken during a session of Parliament. Guthrie worked up the speeches and, at least at the beginning, Johnson revised them. Later Johnson took complete control of composing the speeches from "scanty notes furnished by persons employed to attend both Houses of Parliament." He told Boswell that "sometimes he had nothing more communicated to him than the names of the several speakers and the part which they had taken in the debate." The extent to which the speeches were truly his is indicated by his remark made years later when he was praised for his impartiality: "I saved appearances tolerably well; but I took care that the WHIG DOGS should not have the best of it." Few people at the time, however, knew of Johnson's connection with the debates. Johnson himself was surprised to discover this; when he realized that the public had been deceived and believed the speeches to be authentic, he decided to give them up. As he told Boswell, "he would not be an accessory to the propagation of a falsehood." Still, nothing did more to promote sales and gain publicity for the magazine than the debates. According to Sir John Hawkins, they increased sales of the magazine from 10,000 copies to 15,000 in one month.

In 1749, after ten years during which, Boswell says, Johnson made a tolerable living through *The Gentleman's,* he gave up his active role with the magazine in order to follow his announced plan for a dictionary and to embark on *The Rambler* (1750–52). What the magazine meant to him during those years he attested to often during the rest of his life. It had given him a livelihood without forcing him to resort to patronage, and he always spoke of its founder with affection. In his *Life of Cave,* where he describes one of Cave's last acts of reason as "fondly to press the hand that is now writing this little narrative," he says:

> He was a friend rather easy and constant, than zealous and active; yet many instances might be given, where both his money and his diligence were employed liberally for others. His enmity was, in like manner, cool and deliberate; but though cool, it was not insidious, and though deliberate, not pertinacious.
>
> His mental faculties were slow. He saw little at a time, but that little he saw with great exactness. He was long in finding the right, but seldom failed to find it at last. His affections were not easily gained, and his opinions not quickly discovered. His reserve, as it might hide his faults, concealed his virtues; but such he was, as they who best knew him have most lamented.

Although Johnson is quoted as having called Cave "a penurious pay-master" who would "contract for lines by the hundred and expect the long hundred," magazines such as *The Gentleman's* made a journalistic career tolerable and offered the first regular outlet for the miscellaneous writer. Johnson, who often regarded writing as an item of commerce to be supplied on demand and who was willing to allow the customer the final judgment of a writer's worth, was undoubtedly grateful for this opportunity.

The debates and biographies and essays, for which Johnson was largely responsible, were admirable as well as successful, but the same cannot be said for the magazine's original poetical pieces. These seldom were better than second- or third-rate. In the early issues original poems were rare; most were reprinted from journals and poetical miscellanies and generally included poems by Pope and Swift, the two most frequently reprinted poets, who would hardly have considered submitting original work to Cave. Much of the poetry was occasional or humorous, and it was frequently coarse. The tone of controversy that characterized much of the rest of the magazine often dominated the poetry section too. The issue of January, 1732, for example, contains the Poet Laureate Colley Cibber's ode for New Year's Day, followed by an anonymous burlesque of it, an English translation of it prepared by *The Grub Street*

Journal, a poem in which the Laureate is preferred to Pope, and finally a poem that purports to be the Laureate's reply. Though Cave is said to have loved poetry, his taste was not impeccable, and he was unwilling to sacrifice space to poetry at the expense of a full discussion of political issues. Nevertheless Cave fancied himself a patron of the arts, and in 1733 he began a series of yearly poetry contests in an attempt to attract original poetry from (as Johnson says) "the first authors of the Kingdom." None of these entered the contest, but scores of nameless poets did. Cave himself acted as judge for the first competition, the subject of which was the group of portrait busts of Newton, Locke, Wollaston, Clarke, and Boyle that Queen Caroline had recently placed near her grotto at Richmond. The first two prizes were awarded to Moses Browne and his kinsman John Duick, both hitherto unknown, who became frequent contributors to *The Gentleman's Magazine*. The second competition, on the subject of astronomy, was judged by a panel that included Isaac Watts and was also won by Browne and Duick. The competition for 1735, which boasted Pope as one of the judges, was on the subject "Life, Death, Judgement, Heaven and Hell"—"all the said subjects jointly, and not any single one independent of the rest." Despite its weighty theme, the contest once more failed to attract the "men of wit and genius" Cave so ardently wished for, and the first and second prizes were again awarded to Browne and Duick. If annual competitions failed to turn up poets of wit and genius, they did give the magazine valuable publicity and a new readership. They were followed with great interest, and every would-be poet bought the magazine.

The true popularity of *The Gentleman's Magazine* came, however, from its miscellaneous political, scientific, and practical items. The subjects most frequently treated in the magazine indicate the wide range of intellectual interests of the average middle-class Englishman of the period—interests of the dilettante, it is true, rather than those of the specialist. The curious mixture of fact and fancy in the articles reflects the state of science at the time. Among the earliest scientific articles were short medical notes such as cures for worms and whooping cough; the merits of cold baths and inoculations to prevent disease received equally serious consideration. One popular remedy was Joanna Stephens's cure for stones, which she offered to reveal "on Consideration of a Sum of £5000, to be rais'd by Contribution." *The Gentleman's* helped this cause by publishing testimonials from the Lord Bishop of Bath, the Honorable Mr. Carteret, Postmaster General, and the Reverend Dr. Shippen, principal of Brasenose College. When the subscription failed, Parliament, in a breathtaking spirit of philanthropy, voted a special appropriation to supplement it. Similarly, the magazine noted the properties of Bishop Berkeley's cure-all tar-water and the antidotes for poison and snakebite made public by a Negro in South Carolina in return for his freedom and one hundred pounds from the General Assembly. At the same time it included discussions of quinine as a cure for tropical distempers and of Pringle's revolutionary "Experiments and Observations on Septic and Antiseptic Substances." Accounts of voyages and travels satisfied a natural curiosity about unknown places, as well as a scientific curiosity, and, one suspects, political and commercial interests too. The colonies in America were frequent subjects of articles. The founding of a colony in Georgia received considerable notice; and in this case at least, the humanitarian and Christian motives of its founders seem to have elicited as much interest as the possibility of commercial ventures there.

The early history of *The Gentleman's Magazine* reflects not only the concerns and influence of the middle class in eighteenth-century England but also the development of a free press. The middle-class audience was not a self-critical one, nor was it one given to social reform. But the coming of reform was to depend finally on the existence of a popular press with an influential, broadly based readership.

The fifteen facsimile pages here are reproduced from the copy of Number XIII (January, 1732) in the Princeton University Library.

The Gentleman's Magazine:

St. John's Gate.

Lond Gazette
Lond. Jour.
Fog's Journ.
Applebee's ::
Head's : : : :
Craftsman ::
L. Spectator
Grubstreet J.
Wkly Register
Free-Briton
Fly - Doctor
Saint Courãt
Daily - Post.:
Dai. Journal
Dai. Post-boy
D. Advertiser
Evening Post
St James's Eb.
Whitehall Eb.
London Evening
Flying - Post.

York Journals
Dublin ditto:
Edinburgh 2
Norwich two
Exeter two :
Worcester 2.:
Northamptõ
Gloucester ::
Stamford: :
Nottingham
Bristol News
Bury Journ.
Ipswich do.
Chester ditto
Leeds Merc.
Newcastle C.
Derby Journ.
Reading ditto
Canterbury
Boston : : : b
Jamaica, &c.

Or, Monthly Intelligencer.

Numb. XIII. for JANUARY, 1732.

CONTAINING,

(more in Quantity, and greater Variety, than any Book of the Kind and Price)

I. A View of the *Weekly Essays*, viz. *A* Vindication of Mankind ; *the* Religion *of* Philosophers ; Deist's Creed ; Coffee-house Savages ; *Sr* Wm Paget's New-year's-Gift ; Conjugal Love ; *Mr* Pope's Epistle *on* Taste censur'd *and* defended ; Foolish Fondness ; Love *and* Grandeur : *the* Laureat's pretentions canvass'd ; Female Heroism ; Lessons of Morality ; *of the* Stage ; Love *of* Fame ; Remarks *on Dr.* Bentley's Edition *of* Milton ; *on* Authors ; Rules *for* Courtship ; *of* Immortality.

II. POLITICAL POINTS ; viz. On *the* Jury Act ; Severities *in* B—ke's Administration ; *the* Craftsman's Hague Letter *with* Remarks ; *the* King's Speech ; *of* Publick Credit, Monopolies, &c. Affidavits *about* S. Sea private Trade ; Charitable Corporation Accounts ; *on the* Pragmatick Sanction ; Sheriff's Act eluded ; *a* Scheme *to* pay *the* publick Debts ; political Charity : *K.* Charles II. vindicated.

III. POETRY : viz. Ode *for* new year's Day, burlesqu'd ; translated *into* English ; *the* Laureat's *Answer* ; Keyberian *manner* ; C—r preferr'd *to* P—pe.

IV. DOMESTIC Occurrences, &c.

V. Prices of Goods, Grain, Stocks.

VI. FOREIGN Affairs.

VII. Books and Pamphlets.

VIII. A Table of Contents.

By *SYLVANUS URBAN* Gent.

Prodesse & Delectare.

LONDON: Printed, and sold at St *John's Gate*; by F *Jefferies* in *Ludgatestreet*, and *T. Dormer* at the *Star* and *Garter*, against the *Castle Tavern* in *Fleetstreet*. Where may had the former Numbers.

(PRICE SIXPENCE.)

CONTENTS.

THE
Gentleman's Magazine :
JANUARY, 1732.

A View of the Weekly DISPUTES *and* ESSAYS *in this Month.*

𝕷𝖔𝖓𝖉𝖔𝖓 Journal, Sat. *January* 1, No. 653.
A Vindication of Mankind.

Hilofophers, Wits andDivines, have maintained, that Men in all Ages Countries, Religions and Governments, have been generally wicked; they all fay, they are *bad*, altho' they know they are *good*. But, if Men are *bad by Nature*, and *wicked by Practice*, it is the ftrongeft Argument againft all that has been advanced concerning the *Attributes of God, and the Faculties of Men*; for neither God nor Man can be good, but by their Works. The prefent Argument is, to prove that Men are as generally *good*, as they are reputed *bad*.

Goodnefs is a Difpofition and Endeavour to make others Happy. That Men have this Goodnefs, may be proved by their *well fubfifting* in all Ages and Countries, under all Religions and Governments. *Savages* joyfully affift each other in Diftrefs. And if we confider Mankind as reduced into Communities, we fhall find them honeftly employ'd in getting Bread for themfelves and Families, and *denying* themfelves a thoufand Pleafures, to make the better Provifion for their Pofterity; and they *die with Pleafure*, that thofe whom they love, fhall, *by their Means*, live Happily when themfelves are no more. Can we conceive *more abfolute Difinterefdnefs!*

Our Goodnefs is more apparent *by Comparifon*; for we are *more Happy by living in Society*, than *Singly*; which could not be, unlefs we were *well difpofed* to do good Offices. He who faid, *Never lefs alone, than when alone*, was a proud, vain Pretender to Philofophy. The *Pleafures of Solitude*, are all with a *View to Society.* So good a Creature is Man, that he can't be happy without *giving and receiving Happinefs!*

But if Man is fo good, how fhall we account for *the Evils* which infeft us? The anfwer is, that the Good we do, is *unobferved, or leffen'd*; and the Evil we do, *taken Notice of and aggravated.* We *receive* a thoufand good Things without thinking much about them; but *one Ill*, we never forget. Good Actions are often *concealed*, both by the Doer and Receiver; Men would owe Nothing to *Benevolence or Fortune*, but attribute all to their *own Induftry and Wifdom.*

Another falfe Way of judging is, We ceafe to call a Man *good*, if he does *one ill Action*, tho' he has done a *thoufand good Ones.*

There is not fo much Wickednefs in the World as we imagined. We have, *fince forgiving Sins has been*
           A   *made*

made a Trade, been taught to call a great many Actions *Sins or Vices*, which are not so. There is *one plain Rule* to judge of an Action, that is, by its *Tendency to produce Evil or Good.*

Again, when we consider, that all the *national or general Evils* in the World, are raised by the Ambition, Lust, or Vices of *Great Men*, we shall not attribute those Evils to the *Wickedness of Mankind. Tyannical Princes and wicked Priests* have done more Hurt in the World, in one Age, than all Mankind, not thus animated, would do thro' an Eternity of Ages.

Men seldom do Ill to others, till by *Intemperance and Imprudence*, they have first done *Ill to themselves.* The very *Ill they do* often proceeds from an *human Motive*, to *relieve from Misery* those about them. Upon the Whole, there are few Men, who have not vastly more Good than Ill in them ; and none *who are absolutely Ill.*

Applebee's Journal, Sat. January 1.
A Free Thinker's Religion.

MR. *Sidney* agrees with our *Free Thinkers*, that the Reasonings of the ancient Philosophers were acute, and their Precepts excellent. The Discourses of *Plato* are sublimely wrote, the Arguments of *Aristotle* wonderfully strong and conclusive, and the Behaviour of *Socrates*, admirable and heroick: But did these great Men ever turn their Thoughts on the Principles of Religion ? Are not the Speculations of *Plato* confused and unintelligible, when they relate to the Deity ? *Aristotle* sacrificed to his Patron, and wrote Hymns to his Mistress, as to a Deity ; and *Socrates*, at his Death, commanded that a *Cock* should be immolated to *Æsculapius.* The Philosophers only believed any thing relating to the Unity of the Almigh-

ty Being, the common People, both *Greeks* and *Romans*, adored a Multitude of Gods. These Things must be owned inconsistent with a *Deist's* Creed, who, while they combate all *Revelation*, confess the Almighty Being *One, Infinite in all Perfections, Eternal, Immutable, and Beneficent to his Creatures.* Whence then did they borrow these Sentiments, but from the *Jews*, who derived them from *Moses* their Law-giver ; nor could *Moses* receive his System of Divinity from the *Egyptian* Priests, who worshipped *Cattle, Pot-herbs* and *Onions.* It was *revealed* to him by that God whom he teaches us to Obey. This was pretended to by *Numa Pompilius* and others ; but they never demonstrated the Truth of such Pretences, nor taught the People to Worship only One God. How should a Nation shut up in the narrow Territory of *Palestine*, contrive so rational a System of Religion and Government, if it had not been promulgated by the immediate Revelation of *Jehovah* ? Nothing is asserted in it but what is agreeable to our Idea of an infinite Being ; one plain, uniform and undisguised Narration is given us of the sacred History, from whence our *Free Thinkers* have derived all the rational Principles of their Opinions.

Universal Spectator, Sat. Jan. 1, No. 169.
Coffee-House Savages.

A Society of Sober Citizens, who frequent a *Coffee-House* to read the News, and smoke their Pipes peaceably, complain to Mr. *Stonecastle*, that they are often pester'd with a Company of *young Rakes*, with Toupee Wigs, swinging oaken Clubs, and shallow Understandings, who make such intolerable Noise with their filthy Ribaldry and Horse-laughs, singing, swearing, and damning themselves, and

and curfing the Waiters, and blaf-
pheming all that's facred, that they
difturb every Body about 'em; and
for no other Reafon but what *Draw-
canfir* in the *Rehearfal* gives, *All this
I do, becaufe I dare.*

Thefe *Delinquents* Mr. *Stonecaftle*
ftigmatifes with the Name of *Savages,*
as having neither *Senfe* nor *Manners*; and authorizes the Mafters of
fuch Houfes where they are thus
troublefome, with the affiftance of a
Conftable, to fhew them out of Doors.

Fog's Journal, *Jan.* 1. No. 165,

A new years Gift.

IN a Tract of Hiftory *Fog* met
with a New Year's Gift prefent-
ed to the Duke of *Somerfet,* by Sir
Wm Paget, afterwards Ld *Paget,* in
the Reign of *Henry* VIII. The
Token was inclofed in a Letter to
his Grace, and writ as follows;

*Deliberate maturelye in all things—
Execute quyckelye the Determynati-
ons— Do Juftice without Refpecte—
Make affured and ftayed wife Men
Mynifters under you. Maynetayne the
Mynifters in their Offices— Punnyfbe
the difobedient according to their De-
ferts — In the Kings Caufes give
Comyffion in the Kings Name— Rewarde the Kings worthye Servants li-
berallye and quicklye — Give your
owne to your owne, and the Kings
to the Kings frankelye.— Difpatche
fuyters fhortlye— Be affable to the
Good, and fterne to the Evill——Fol-
lowe advife in Counfaill——Take Fee
or Rewarde of the King onlye——
Keepe your Mynifters about you uncor-
rupte——Thus God will profper youe,
the Kinge favour youe, and all Men
love you.*——Such a New Years Gift
now adays is feldom given to Minifters; and this was of fuch a Nature,
as it well deferves we fhou'd enquire
into the Character of the Donor,
who was fo highly efteem'd abroad
for his many excellent Qualificati-

ons that the Emperor *Charles* V. faid
of him *He as well deferv'd to be a
King as to reprefent a King*; and fee-
ing him once coming into the Court,
Yonder, fays he, *is the Man to whom
I can deny nothing.*

Fog has heard of an Ambaffador,
of whom it was faid, he was *as fit
to be a King as reprefent a King*;
whofe Carriage never gain'd him
Efteem, and whofe Stile was fit for
the Mob to hear, and a Jack-pudding
to fpeak; upon whofe entring the
Court one Day, *Here comes the Man,*
faid the Prince, *to whom we can never
find in our Hearts to grant any thing.*

The Northampton Mercury, Jan. 5.

On Conjugal Love.

THere is as much Unhappinefs
caus'd by the Indulgence of a
paffionate Fondnefs, as any other
Paffion human Nature is fubject to.
Marriage is a State which moft per-
fons one time or other are defirous
of entering into; and thofe who
exclaim againft it are generally fuch
as have been difappointed in their
Amours. When good Nature, Re-
fpect, and Equality of Tempers
meet, this State is an inexhauftible
fource of Felicity, as on the contrary, where there is neither of
thefe, it is a Fund of innumerable Inquietudes and Difturbances. Thefe
Domeftick Calamities are frequently the Confequents of a fecond Contract. The Children, who are the
Fruits of the firft Marriage, are
commonly ufed with feverity and
negligence in the fecond; while
their natural Parents with Grief fee
themfelves reduc'd to the neceffity
of fubmitting to thofe Evils which
they have foolifhly put out of their
power to redrefs. Gives an Inftance
in *TomPenitent,* a neighbouring *Gentleman*; who is obliged to dif-regard
his firft Wife's Children in complai-
fance to his fecond.

The

The Merits of the JURY Act controverted.

Craftsman, *Sat, Jan.* 1. No. 287.   ☞ The **Free Briton,** Thur. *Jan.* 5, No. 110

'NEVER, says Mr. *Walsingham* in a former *Free Briton*, was a better Sign of an happy People, or a more certain Proof of an *upright Administration*, than the late Act for the better Regulation of *Juries*. It is a more national Act A than the *Habeas Corpus Act*, and most properly a *Court Law*".

Mr. *D'anvers* then concurred with Mr. *Walsingham*, except where he stiles it a *Court Law*; but perhaps B he call'd it so with a View to *special Juries*; which, he confesses, he was not then aware of, that is, he did not apprehend it was design'd to extend to criminal Prosecutions, C where the Crown is immediately concern'd. Asks *W.* whether the Design and Consequences of the Clause relating to *Special Juries*, did not also escape his penetration? And whether it may not weaken the Act? D Or want further Explanation?

Mr. *Walsingham's* many Encomiums on this Act are founded on the following Provisions of it; *That none but Men of fit Qualifications* E *shall be returned on the Panels; these Returns made publick at proper Places before Trial; that all Freeholders serve in their natural Turns; and that those that are sworn be drawn by Lots.*

But none of these Provisions have F any Effect in the Case of *Special Juries*, which are no more exempt from Corruption, than if this Bill had never passed; nor has the Court put it out of their Power, to *practice* G *upon Juries.* In *civil Cases*, where great Points of Property are concern'd, it seems reasonable that the *Jury* consist of the most *considerable* Gentlemen in the Country for *Fortune, Integrity and Understanding.*

Expects that Mr. *W.* will abide by H his former Remarks on Trials by *Information;* and insists that he will
give

MR. *Walsingham owns he has formerly express'd his approbation of the* Jury Act, *and still believes it a great Benefit to the* People of England, *yet is not such a Bigot as to i imagine that it may not be improved. But if there was any Deficiency, why should these Gentlemen sneer at his Penetration, in not discerning it immediately, when* their own marvellous Sagacity *could not discover it till now; tho' they boast that the Bill had its Rise, Progress and Perfection from themselves?*

As to the Clause relating to Special Juries, *conceives the* Jury Act *cannot be reasonably censur'd. Before this Act was obtained, the Judges had a discretionary Power of granting* Special Juries; *which by this Act are made a Right of the Subject.*

The seven Bishops were tried by a Special Jury, and did not complain of hard Usage; why then should the Craftsman *make any Difference between the Case of those Prelates, and that of his own Publisher, except that they were acquitted, and he convicted?*

If great Points of Property deserve this manner of Trial, how have we forfeited this Advantage in Favour of our Liberties *and* Reputation? *Or why should these important Interests be Subject to Jurors of less Integrity and Understanding, than we have a Right to in Favour of our Estates? Against* Franklin, *there was no Suspicion of extraordinary Practice. But 'twas said that his Patron took out One of the Gentlemen on the Pannel, and talk'd with him in the Exchequer Coffee-house.* (See *Crafts. Jan.* 22.)

He still adheres to his former Paper, wherein he observed, how the Practice of Informations, *grounded on the common* Law, *and granted by the Court of* King's-Bench, *might one Day be liable to great Abuse.*

As

give his Opinion, as a Lawyer, concerning the Power of *Secretaries of State* to grant Warrants, seize Persons, break open Locks, commit to Custody, and hold to good Behaviour. And whether Precedents from the *Star-Chamber*, or any other Court in *arbitrary Reigns*, ought to be esteem'd authoritative now, since our Liberties are secured by the Abolition of all such Laws.

As to the Power of Secretaries of State W. answers, that a *Justice of Peace has near as great*. If D'anvers *thinks himself aggriev'd, let him try it in* Westminster-Hall. *And if he wants Advice, let him ask his Friend* B—ke, *whence he had his Power to apprehend, commit, enlarge and discharge, when he was Secretary of State? Or by what Authority he apprehended and bound over* 14 *Booksellers, Printers*

and Publishers in one Vacation; And by *what Power he sent* Popping, Hurt, Ridpath, &c. *to* Newgate *for Papers commonly call'd Libels?*

Mr. POPE's EPISTLE *on* TASTE *censur'd and defended.*

The *Daily Courant, December 23.*

To J. Gay, *Esq;*

SIR,

HAD the Author (of the *Epistle on Taste*) attack'd Vice at a time when it is not only tolerated but triumphant, and proclaim'd with Ostentation as a Merit, I should have been under some Apprehensions for the Consequence.

'Tis said, the Satire is *personal*. I thought it could not be so, because all its Reflections are on *Things*, and not *on Persons*; not on the Man, but on his House and Gardens, Pictures, Statues, trim'd Trees, and Violins.

Some fancy, that to say a Thing is *personal*, is the same as to say, it is *unjust*, not considering, that nothing can be *just*, but what is *personal*. I am afraid such Writings as touch no Man, will mend no Man.

The Application of *Timon's* Character to the D. of *Ch*— is monstrous; as it is imputed to the Person the most different in the World from a *Man-hater*, and the Person whose *Taste* and Encouragement of *Wit* have been ever shewn in the *rightest Place*. This Author has always been distinguished and favour'd by this very Person. Besides, Is his Garden crowded with *Walls*? Are his Trees cut into *Figures of Men*? Do his Basons want *Water*? I am Sick of such Fool-applications.

The *White-Hall Evening Post, Jan.* 4.

To A—— P—pe, *Esq;*

SIR,

YOU *insinuate*, as if Vice was authorized by Law, and so triumphant *as not to be opposed without ill* Consequences, ——*at a Time when the Laws against Immorality were never so strictly executed since the Reformation.*

Are not the following Strokes personal?
Who but must laugh, the Master when he sees
A puny Insect, shivering at a Breeze?
Behold, my Lord advances o'er the Green,
Smit with the mighty Pleasure to be seen.

By the Word just *you must mean* like; *and by unjust injurious: For the more just* (like) *a personal Reflection is, so much the more unjust* (injurious) *it must be. So that these inconsidering Men seem to reason very Right.*

If you had consulted your Scotch Retailer of Bayle *and* Moreri, *he could tell you that* Timon *was first eminent for his extraordinary Generosity, the Abuse of which drew him into a hatred of Mankind. Is not the Character you have drawn of* Timon *wholly different from a Manhater? viz.*

Treated, caress'd, and tir'd, I take my Leave,
Sick of his Civil Pride, from Morn to Eve.

It is a known Trick amongst Lampooners, when a Man of Distinction is to be ridiculed, to draw the remarkable Lines of his Picture beyond the Life, yet with such a Resemblance, that all the World may cry 'Tis He.
Universal

ODE *for New-Years-Day* 1732.
By *C. Cibber,* Efq; Poet Laureat.

Recit.

AWAKE with *joyous fongs the day*
That leads *the op'ning year* ;
The year advancing to prolong,
Augustus' fway demands our fong,
And cills for univerfal cheer.

Air.

Your antient Annals, Britain, read,
And mark the Reign you moft admire ;
The prefent fhall the paft exceed,
And yield enjoyment to defire.
Or *if you find the coming year*
In bleffings fhould tranfcend the laft,
The diff'rence only will declare
The prefent fweeter than the paft.

Recit.

But, ah ! the *fweets his fway beftows,*
Are greater far than Grea nefs knows.
With various penfive cares oppref'd,
Unfeen, alas, the Royal Breaft
Endures *his many a weight,*
Unfek by fwains of humble ftate.

Air.

Thus *brooding* on her *lonely* neft,
Aloft the Eagle wakes,
Her due delights forfakes,
The *Monarch of the air confefs'd,*
Her drooping eyes refufe to clofe ;
While fearlefs of annoy,
Her young belov'd enjoy
Protection, food, and fweet repofe.

Recit.

What thanks, ye *Britons,* can repay
So mild, fo juft, fo tender fway ?

Air.

Your annual aid when he defires,
Lefs the King than land requires ;
All the dues to him that flow
Are ftill but Royal wants to you :
So the feafons lend the earth
Their kindly rains to raife her birth,
And well the mutual labours fuit,
His the glory, yours the fruit.

Recit.

Affift, affift, ye fplendid throng,
Who now the Royal circle form ;
With duteous wifhes blend the fong.
And every grateful wifh be warm.

CHORUS.

May *Cæfar's* health his reign fupply,
'Till faction fhall be pleas'd, or die ;
'Till loyal hearts defire his fate :
'Till happier fubjects know,
Or foreign realms can fhow
A land fo blefs'd, a King fo great !

N 'B. *The Words and Expreffions in this Character*
being chiefly carp'd at, are defended by way of
Irony in the Grub-ftreet Journal No: 105.]

The Poet Laureat's *Ode for New-Years-Day* burlefqu'd.

Recit.

AWake, with *Grub-ftreet* Odes, the Day
That leads the op'ning Year ;
The Year advancing to prolong
Great *C..bb—r's* Fame, demands a Song,
Infpir'd by *Gin,* or by *Small Beer.*

Air.

Your Ancient *Ballad-Makers* read,
And mark the *Fool* you moft admire ;
The *prefent* fhall the *paft* exceed,
And yield *Enjoyment* to Defire :
Or, if you find the coming Ode,
In *Nonfenfe* fhould tranfcend the laft,
The Diff'rence only will make good
The prefent *duller* than the paft !

Recit.

But ah ! the *Staff* his *Strain* beftows
Is duller far than Dulnefs knows ;
With various *lumpifh Loads* opprefs
Unfeen, alas! the Laureat's Breaft
Endures his many a Weight,
Unfelt by all but *Bards of State.*

Air.

Thus brooding o'er her lovely Neft,
The *watchful Owl* awakes,
Her due Delight forfakes,
Reftlefs to give all others Reft ;
Her drooping Eyes refufe to clofe,
Whilft, fearlefs of Numbers
To threaten their Slumbers,
All around her enjoy much Sleep and Repofe.

Recit.

What Praifes can repay an *Owl*
So flat, fo heavy, and fo *dull* ?
His *annual Odes* which he admires,
Lefs the *Dunce* than *Fool* infpires !
All the *Strains* which from him flow,
Are ftill of *noble Ufe* to you ;
Whilft his kindly Sheets enrich
Every Bard *to wipe his B——*
And well the *mutual Labours* fuit,
His the *Glory,* yours the *Fruit.*

Recit.

Affift, affift, ye warbling Throng,
Who now the *Grub-ftreet Chorus* form ;
With gen'rous Wifhes blend the Song,
And ev'ry grateful Wifh be warm.

CHORUS.

May *C..bb—r's Mufe* his *Odes* fupply,
Till *Nonfenfe* fhall be pleas'd to die ;
Till *ftupid Fools* defire his *Place,*
Till happier *Courts* fhall know,
Or Foreign Realms can fhow,
A *Dunce* fo *dull,* an *Ode* fo *low* ;
What *Thanks* are due to —— *G——* !

The *Ode* for *New-Years-Day* translated into *English* in the *Grub-street Journal*, *Jan.* 13.

Recitativo.

AWake, with Songs, the opening day,
　　That call for general *cheer* :
Since nothing *good* can live too *long*,
Let *Augustus* have a *song* ;
And, *hey*, for gambols, and strong beer !

Air.

Britons, your Chronicles go read ,
See what King's reign you most admire :
The present shall the past exceed,
And *be* whate'er your hearts *desire.*
For it, by chance, the *next* new year
But proves as lucky as the *last,*
Why, *then*——- the *present*, 'is most *clear,*
Is far more happy then the *past.*

Recitativo,

But, ah ! ——- so sweet a Prince as he,
Is greater far then *great can be!*
With cares, which none can *see*, oppress'd,
And *thoughtful too*, the Royal breast
Endures full many a weight,
Unfelt by *Cottagers of state.*

Air.

Thus *brooding, single,* in her rest,
The *she* King Eagle wakes ;
Nor, half her due of pleasure takes,
Tho' Monarch of the air confess'd.
Nay, tho' she *wakes,* her eyes don't *close* ;——
She keeps strict watch and ward,
Her young ones, yet *unhatch'd,* to guard ;
That they may *eat, unborn,* in sweet repose.

Recitativo,

What thanks, ye *Britons !* can repay
So mild, so just, so soft, a sway ?

Air.

When once a year he asks your aid,
The *Land*, and not the *King*, is paid.
Nay, and what's *more,* his *Royal due*
Is but a *Royal want* in *you.*
Air, *moist* or dry, alike sends rain,
To raise up earth, that's *born again :*
Blessings more grateful, uninvok'd :
His fame well *spred,* your land well *soak'd.*

Recitativo

Help me, O help me, shining *crowd,*
　Who now stand round in *Royal form :*
Sing, sing your wishes clear and loud ,
And, *ah !* be grateful, and be *warm.*

Chorus

'The reign of Cæsar let his health *supply*
'Till faction shall be *pleas'd to die ;*
Or they who *love him,* wish him *down :*
Till happier folks than *we,*
In some far country, *see*
　A King so *prais'd,* in so *bee mus'd* a Town.
With *such a Laureat to insure Renown.*

Imitation of the Keyberian *Stile*
and Manner.

IF when at all, suppose it should be so,
　Without regarding either to or for,
Some, not in vain, together, blindly go,
Then only them, however I abhor,

Not that because, which some I know will say,
Indubitable reasons may be giv'n ;
　Yea, if bright Phœbus gilds the golden day,
Our thoughts ascend insensibly to heav'n!

If ought there be, who own, that is, if there
Be any, who will not this truth deny,
None for *Parnassus'* hill e'er bid so fair,
Or easier climb'd the steep ascent than I.

C - B B - R *prefer'd to* P - P E.

WHile *C---y C---r* Lawrel-Crowned
　　　Lyrick
Debases Majesty in Panegyrick,
Fraught Spider-like, with Venom and ill Nature,
P---- dares attack a Noble Peer in Satyre.
But lo ! to Honour see his just Pretence,
Flatters one Lord at t'others Lord's Expence;
And more his honest Soul to recommend,
In the same Page he owns and stabs his Friend.
But ah ! what cursed Dæmon could induce
The Puny Wretch to personal Abuse ?
How could he think to paint the sta v'ling Elf,
Without a sore Reflection on himself ;
Had but his misplac'd Toils conspir'd to raise
The people's Wonder in his Monarch's Praise,
To Such a Task if equal he would seem,
His Numbers might have reach'd the noble
　　Theme.
Or had but *C---y* with malicious Spite,
Invectives on his Grace presum'd to write ;
The gen'rous *Timon's* Soul had then not griev'd.
But scorn'd the Wound his Character receiv'd.
But know, O *P---,* that while thy murd'rous Pen
Assaults thy Country's Friend, the Friend of Men,
And *C---'s* Lyre, howe'er untun'd the Strings
With honest Zeal resounds the best of Kings,
With greater Patience shall his Lays be heard,
And even *C---r* be to *P---e* prefer'd.

The LAUREAT's *Answer to the* POETS

MY Brother Poets all are d——n'd severe,
　Because I've got a Hundred Pounds a
　　　　　　　　　　　　　　Year ; (grace,
They rail, they write, and threaten dire Dis-
And each is angry he has not the Place
But let these worthy Gentlemen consider,
As a Dramatic Poet, I'm best Bidder;
My *Careless Husband* I'll transmit to Fate,
With any Comedy produc'd of late.
O ! but, say they, *He's a sad Wretch at Rhime,*
Why Gentlemen ! Is that so great a Crime ;
If want of Jingle, I supply wi h Sense,
I to the Laurel have a just Pretence,

THIS

THE
Monthly Intelligencer.
JANUARY, 1732.

ABOUT the latter end of laſt Month, the Books and M. S. of Dr. *Tanner*, Bp. of St. *Aſaph*, being on their Removal from *Norwich* to *Chriſt-Church* Colledge in *Oxford*, fell into and lay under Water 20 Hours, and received great Damage. Among them were near 300 Volumes of M. S. purchaſed of Mr. *Bateman*, a Bookſeller, who bought them of A.B. *Sancroft*'s Nephew.   There were in all 7 Cart Loads.

Saturday, *Jan.* 1.

Being New-Year's-Day, it was ſolemnized as uſual at Court. See the Occurrences of the ſame Day, and of the 12th Day. *Vol.* I.

Tueſday, *Jan.* 4.

Was held a Board of Admiralty, when his Majeſty's Ships, *Kingſton*, *Dolphin*, and *Sheerneſs* were put in Commiſſion for the *Weſt India* Service.

The Owners of the *Anne-Galley*, taken *June* 13, 1728, by a *Spaniſh Guard da Coſta*, which carried her into St. *Jago de Cuba*, received from the D. of *Newcaſtle* the Duplicate of an Order, ſigned by his Catholick Majeſty, for the immediate Reſtitution of the Ship and Cargo, and Satisfaction for the Trouble and Expence occaſioned by the ſaid Seizure, or in Lieu thereof 10500l. on Condition however that ſhe carried on no contraband Trade.

Friday, *Jan.* 7.

The *Chriſtmas* Jury's Collection in *Weſtminſter*, for diſcharging poor Debtors from the *Gatehouſe* Priſon, and for other charitable Purpoſes, amount to 269 l.

Monday, *Jan.* 10.

M. *Como*, Agent from the Court of *Parma*, delivered to the D. of *Newcaſtle*, for his Majeſty, a Letter from the Dutcheſs Dowager *Dorothea* of *Parma*, acquainting his Majeſty with the happy Accompliſhment of *Don Carlos's* Succeſſion to the Dominions of *Parma* and *Placencia*, deſiring his Acceptance of a Medal ſtruck upon that Occaſion.

Thurſday, *Jan.* 13.

The Parliament met at *Weſtminſter*, when his Majeſty opened the Seſſions with a Speech, which (ſee p. 560.)

Friday, *Jan.* 14.

Was held a General Court of the *South-Sea* Company, when the Sub-Governor inform'd them that in the Year 1720, the Company ow'd on Bonds above 4,400000 l. and that now they do not owe above Two Millions. That ſince the 25th of *March*, 1721, to *Chriſtmas* laſt, they had receiv'd by the *Aſſiento* Trade 250,000 l. more than ſent out, and very conſiderable Demands they ſtill have; —— and that by the *Greenland* Trade they had loſt above 30,000 l. —— He ſatisfied them alſo of the State of the Trade to *America*; and of the Meaſures they had taken upon an Information of a Breach of Covenants committed by the Captain of their annual Ship, *Prince William*, in her late Voyage to *Carthagena* and *Porto Bello*, having in her Paſſage touch'd at St. *Chriſtopher's*, and taken Goods on Board to the Amount of 150 Tons. (*See the* Affidavit *p* 582.

The Court then agreed, that the Dividend for the Half year ended at *Chriſt*-

B   may

mas laſt, be 2 *per Cent* in Money, and be paid on the 11th of next Month; not to proſecute any more of the Debtors on the Loan of the Year, 1720, ſince the Trial with Col. *Duncomb* went a-gainſt the Company; that the *Greenland* Trade go on this Year, in hopes of the Favour of Parliament to enlarge the Power; which their Sub-Governor intimated was intended to be applied for this Seſſions; and laſtly ordered, that the Court of Directors examine into the Truth of the Account of the Diſburſements and Receipts relating to the Company's Trade to *America*.

The Buſineſs of the Day being ended, a Reſolution was made, that the Thanks of the General Court be given to the Governors and Directors for their juſt and wiſe Adminiſtration of the Company's Affairs.

Monday, *Jan.* 17.

The following Letter was ſent to every Member of the H. of Commons
SIR,

Your Commiſeration *is moſt humbly craved, in behalf of all* aggrieved Suitors *at* Law, *that the* Grand Committee *for* Courts *of* Juſtice, *may fit to chuſe a* Chairman *to do* Buſineſs; *then will the* Oppreſſion *of the* Law *appear, and the* numerous, burthenſome, *and* uſeleſs Offices *thereof, with the* Exorbitances *of their* Fees, *be duly expoſed.*

Wedneſday, *Jan.* 19.

The Seſſions which held 5 Days ended at the *Old Bailey*, 61 Priſoners were tried, 37 of which were acquitted 20 to be tranſported, 2 whipt, and 2 received Sentence of Death, viz. **George Scroggs** for robbing Mr. *Bellinger*, Miniſter of *Tottenham*, on *Sunday* 14th of *Feb.* laſt, as going to preach, of a-bout the Value of 14 s. and **Robert Fallam**, Waterman, for the Murder of his Wife, by beating her, and throwing her out of a Chamber Window, when big with Child. **Peter Noakes**, was tried for the Murder of *William Turner*, by ſhooting him in the Head with a Piſtol, at the *King's Arms* Tavern in the *Strand*. They were by

themſelves in a Room, a Piſtol went off, and the Priſoner ran away. It appeared the Deceas'd had hir'd the Piſtol, and one Mrs. *Falkingham*, with whom they kept Company, and who had been with them juſt before the Accident, ſwearing ſhe ſaw him twice attempt to kill himſelf with a Poker and Sword, the Priſoner was acquitted. **Corbet Weſey** of *Mile-end, Stepney*, was tried for murdering his Wife. A few Days before her Death ſhe made Oath that he had confined her above a Year in a Garret, without Fire, Candle, or ſufficient Food. It appeared ſhe was like a ſtarved Skeleton; but he pleading that he locked her up becauſe ſhe robb'd him, and proving he often ſent her Victuals; he was acquitted.

At a General Court of the Royal *African* Company were choſen,
The King's moſt Excell: Majeſty. Gov.
Sir *Bibye Lake*, Bar. Sub-Gov.
James Oglethorpe, Eſq; Dept. Gov.
    A S S I S T A N T S.
Sir *Thomas Saunderſon*, Kt. of the Bath.
* Sir *Robert Sutton*, Kt. of the Bath.
Solomon Aſhley,   * John Gaſcoyne,
John Baker,   Charles Hayes,
Thomas Bodicoate,   * John Laroche,
John Bodicoate,   Charles Lloyd,
* Francis Boteler,   Henry Parſons,
Thomas Bradſhaw,   Thomas Revell,
* Joſeph Bradſhaw,   John Thompſon,
Chriſtin Cole,   Francis Townley,
Robert Cruikſhank, Thomas Watts,
Joſeph Danvers,   * Philip Wilkinſon
Daniel Finch,   Benj. Periam, *Eſqu.*
Thoſe mark'd with * were not of the late Court of Aſſiſtants.

Thurſday *Jan.* 20.

At a General Court of the Bank of *England*, it was reſolved to build a new Bank in *Threadneedle ſtreet*, and to erect an Equeſtrian Statue of K. *William* before it.

Monday, *Jan.* 24.

Being the firſt Day of Term, Mr *Franklin*, and ſeveral other Printers and Publiſhers, appear'd for the *Craftſman*, *Fog's Journal*, &c. and were continued on their Recognizances.

Dr.

Tuesday, *Jan.* 25.

Dr. *Tanner*, Bp. of St. *Asaph*, and Dr. *Clagget*, Bp of St. *David's*, were introduc'd into the House of Lords.

Orders were given, that Officers in Half-pay shall be provided for as Vacancies shall happen in the Army, in order to reduce that Establishment.

Wednesday *Jan.* 26.

An Account from *Shrivenham* in *Berks* of this Date imported, that the Widow *Haggard* of that Parish, who had been tapp'd for the Dropsy 21 Times, was ready to be tapp'd again, and was likely to be several more, and the following Quantities of Water had been taken from her, *viz*.

1730.	Gall.	Q.	1731.	Gall.	Q.
April 1.	5	1	March 27.	6	3
May 24.	5	3	April 24.	6	2
June 30.	6	1	May 24.	6	3
Aug. 1.	6	2	June 19.	6	2
Sept. 7.	7	0	July 16.	7	0
Octob. 12.	7	2	Aug. 14.	6	3
Nov. 12.	6	2	Sept. 17.	6	3
Dec. 11.	6	3	Octob. 23.	8	0
Jan. 9.	7	1	Nov. 27.	6	1
Feb. 4.	7	3	Jan. 1.	7	$\frac{1}{2}$
27.	6	3			

Monday, *Jan.* 31.

Was observed for the 30th, as the Anniversary of the Martyrdom of K. *Charles* I. Dr. *Hare*, Bp. of *Chichester*, preached before the Lords from *Prov.* xxiv. 21. in which he vindicated that King, and argued for observing the Day. Dr. *Alured Clarke* preached before the Commons, to somewhat different Purport from *Ps.* lxxviii. v. 8.

An Account was given in the Papers of a Society who call themselves *Free Sawyers*, and claim Priority to the *Free Masons*, *Gormogons*, or ancient *Hums*; as dating their Standing before the Tower of *Babel*, alledging they cut the Stones for those mad Builders, the *Free Masons*. At their Meetings they have a Silver-Saw laid on their Table with this Motto, *Let it work.*

That the Revd. Mr. *Doiley* of *Ingarstone*, in *Essex*, had given to the Corporation, for Support of poor Widows and Children of Clergymen, the Sum of 3000 *l.* on Condition that they settle 100 *l. per Ann.* to be paid for ever ; 70 *l.* of it to 7 such Widows with Families as most want it, at 10 *l.* a Year each ; and 30 *l.* to such Clergymens Children as shall be named by Trustees to be appointed by his Will.

Kings Ships put in Commission, The *Scarborough*, a 6th Rate, 20 Guns, and 120 Men ; also the *Otter-Sloop*.

His Majesty's Answer to the House of Commons Address.

Gentlemen,

I Return you my Thanks for this dutiful and loyal Address I make no Doubt of of the Continuance of your Duty, Affection, and Confidence in me ; and you will always find that all my Views tends to the Honour, Interest, and Security of my Crown and People.

——Answer to the Lords Address.

My Lords,

I Thank you for this affectionate and loyal Address. As the Interests of my People, and the securing the Peace and Balance of Power in Europe, has been my chief Care and Concern ; the Satisfaction you shew in the Success of my Endeavours cannot but be extremely acceptable to me. You may depend upon my Favour and Protection ; and I am persuaded I may always rely upon your Duty and Support.

Members of Parliament chose this Month.

The Hon. *John Spencer*, Esq; for *Woodstock*, in *Oxfordshire*.

Philip Lloyd, Esq; for *Christ Church*, in *Hants.*

George Purvis, Esq; for *Aldborough* in *Suffolk.*

Sir *Henry Gough*. Bart for *Totness.*

Nich. Fazakerly, Esq; for *Preston*, in *Lancashire.*

The following Sheriffs were appointed, *viz.*

Lincoln, Thomas A'yson, jun. Esq;

Rutland, Joseph Herrendine, Esq;

Berks, John Watts of Reading, Esq;

Lincoln, Thomas Hurst, of *Gunnerby*, Esq;

DEATHS

MARRIAGES.

Jan. 5. JOhn *Yorke*, Esq; Representative for *Richmond* in *Yorkshire*, married to Miss *Ann D'arcy*, Daughter to the Ld *D'arcy*, of *Sedbury*, in the same County.

6 Mr *Botefeur*, a *Hamburgh* Merchant, ⌒ to Miss *Doreen*, a *Dutch* Lady.

9 *Rowland Mitchell*, Esq; a *Scots* Gentleman, ⌒ to Mrs *Wiseman*.

Davenport, of *Shropshire*, Esq; ⌒ to Miss *Rodd*, of *Lincolns-Inn-Fields*, Niece to Mr Justice *Price*.

Claudius Rondeau, Esq; the *British* Resident at the Court of *Russia*, ⌒ to the Widow of *Thomas Ward*, Esq; late Consul General for that Empire, and to whom Mr *Rondeau* had been Secretary.

The Ld Visc. *Bulkeley*, Member of Parliament for *Beaumaris* in *Anglesea*, ⌒ to the Daughter and Heiress of *Lewis Owen*, of *Penjarth* in *Merionethshire*, Esq; a Fortune of 60,000*l.*

20. Mr *Desbouvrie*, ⌒ to the only Daughter of *James Reynolds*, Esq;

22 The D. of *Cleaveland* and *Southampton*, ⌒ to the Lady *Harriot Finch*, Daughter to the late E. of *Nottingham*.

23 *Morgan Vane*, Esq; Comptroller of the Stamp Office, ⌒ to Miss *Knight*, a Fortune of 8000*l.*

The Revd Mr *Comars*, M. A. to a Daughter of the late *Peter Raneu*, Esq;

Sir *John Glynne*, of *Harwarden* in *Flintshire*, Bart ⌒ to Miss *Conway*, sole Heiress of Sir *John Conway*, Bart a Fortune of 50,000 *l.*

24 The Ld Visc. *Tryconnel*, Representative for *Grantham* in *Lincolnshire*, ⌒ to Miss *Carteret* of *Hampshire*.

29. *George Bill*, of *Hertfordshire*, Esq; ⌒ to the eldest Daughter of *Tyringham Backwel*, of *Buckinghamshire*, Esq;

The Dutchess Dowager of *Ancaster*, brought to bed of a Son.

Ecclesiastical Preferments *conferr'd on the following Reverend Gentlemen.*

DR *Middleton*, chosen Dr *Woodward*'s Philosophical Professor in *Cambr.*

Mr *Thomas*, presented to the Rectory of *Kellen* in *Cardiganshire.*

Mr *John Ell's* presented to a Prebend in the Cathedral Church of St *Davids.*

Mr *James Meredith*, presented to the Vicarage of *Stokely*, in *Somersetshire.*

Mr *Walter Morgan*, A. M. constituted Arch Deacon of St *Davids.*

Mr *Birch*, chosen Minister of St *Davids* at Dover.

Mr *Francis Johnson*, presented to the *Sine Cure* of *Wadleigh* in *Dorsetshire.*

Mr *Capper*, presented to the Rectory of *Thorp* in *Norfolk.*

Mr *George Stephens*, Chaplain to the Ld *Onslow*, appointed Chaplain to *Arthur Onslow* Esq; Speaker of the House of Commons.

Mr *William Ross*, L. L. B. presented to the Rectory of St *Michael*'s near *Stamford* in *Lincolnshire.*

Mr *Samuel Disney*, chosen Lecturer of *Wakefield* in *Yorkshire.*

Mr *Mawly*, presented to the Rectory of *Bawtree* in *Yorkshire.*

BANKRUPTS.

Francis Emilie, of *London*, Merchant.

John Mills, of *Bisley*, *Gloucestershire*, Clothier and Chapman.

John Aldwin, of *Pinner*, *Middlesex*, Chapman.

Thomas Cole, of *Southwark*, *Surry*, Lighterman.

Thomas Haylet, of *West Rainham*, *Norfolk*, Mercer.

William Appley, of St *Clements Danes*, *Middlesex*, Mercer.

James Baynham, of *Newgate-street*, *London*, Hosier.

Jervis Rawson, of *Poplar*, *Middlesex*, Miller.

AT our Entrance upon the New Year it may be proper to refresh the Memories of our Readers with what has happen'd moft remarkable in the Preceding: Efpecially as the Year 1731 has brought about the Execution of a Project which had cut out work for all *Europe* ever fince the Year 1718, that is, the Introduction of *Don Carlos* into *Italy*; in which the *Spaniards* have demonftrated that a well-timed Patience will accomplish any thing defired. How ftrongly did the *Imperialifts* oppofe it at the Time of making the Quadruple Alliance? What Pains were taken to fettle the Article of Neutral Garrifons? An Article, which was the only Caufe of the Non-Execution of the Treaty of Quadruple Alliance, and of the Congreffes of *Cambray*, *Soiffons*, and *Paris*; and gave Birth to the Treaties of *Vienna*, *Hanover*, and *Seville*; and to thofe concluded this Year at *Vienna*; occafion'd the Equipment of feveral Squadrons, and the March of 80,000 Men from *Germany*, *Hungary*, *Bohemia*, to the Heart of *Italy*.

Who wou'd have thought twelve Months ago, that the Year 1731 would ferve for an *Ephocha* from which to date the Eftablifhment of the Publick Tranquillity and of the Ballance of Power in *Europe*? Efpecially confidering the indefatigable Pains *France* was then taking to make her Plan of Operations pafs Mufter, which wou'd have open'd a Scene of War upon the *Rhine*, the *Po*, the *Scheld*, and the *Mediterranean*, yet was the fhe firft that fet the Example of not arming when the Treaty of *Seville* came to be executed in good in earneft.

The Sham Pregnancy of the Dutchefs Dowager of *Parma*, was as diverting as ferious, yet neceffary, as it gave the Emperor Leifure to regulate the fucceffion of that Dutchy, and occafioned feveral Steps, which

all turn'd to the Advantage of the Infante Duke, in whom is united the Blood of *Bourbon*, *Neuburg*, and *Farnefe*. Befides which, the Year pafs'd has furnifh'd us with the following Events. 1. The Guaranty of the *Pragmatick Sanction*. 2. The Perfecution of the Proteftants of *Saltsburg*. 3 The Death of the Duke of *Deuxponts*; whofe Succeffion is yet in Difpute. 4. The Treaty of Alliance between the Electorates of *Saxony* and *Hanover*. 5. The Difgrace and Reconciliation of the Prince Royal of *Pruffia*, and the Marriage of the Princefs Royal his Sifter. 6. The Revolution at *Conftantinople*. 7. The Affairs in *Perfia*. 8. The Boils of the Clergy and Parliament of *France*. 9 The Rebellion in *Corfica*, which has been carried on with that Obftinacy by the Male-contents, who ftand up for for their ancient Rights and Liberties, on one Hand and the *Genoefe*, who as vigoroufly endeavour their Subjection, on the other, that the whole County is almoft defolated by the unhappy Contention.

From *Conftantinople*, 'twas advis'd, That the *Turks* had actually fet up the Horfe-tail (in token of War) againft the Chriftians, and were fitting out a large Squadron in order to attack the *Venetians*.

From *Ratisbon*, That the Affair of the *Pragmatick Sanction* was concluded in the Affembly by a Majority of Voices, according to the Emperor's Intention; but that the Minifters of *Bavaria*, *Saxony*, and *Palatine*, had enter'd Protefts againft all the Proceedings in that Affair.

From the *Hague*, That the States of the Province of *Holland*, had refolved to Accede to the Treaty of *Vienna*; which being reported to the States General, the Deputies of *Utrecht*, *Overyffel*, *Friefland*, and *Gelderland*, declared themfelves Ready to concur in it.

Towards the End of the Month.

STOCKS.

S. *Sea* 102 $\frac{1}{8}$	*Afric.* 49
— *Bonds* 5 l. 17*s.*	*Royal Aff.* 97
— *Annu.* 109 $\frac{1}{2}$	*Lon. ditto* 12 $\frac{1}{4}$
Ban 145 $\frac{3}{4}$	*York Build.* 14 $\frac{1}{4}$ a $\frac{1}{2}$
—*Circulation* 4*l.* 15*s.*	3 *per Ct. An.* 94 $\frac{1}{4}$
— *Mil. Bank* 107 $\frac{1}{2}$	*EngCopper* 2*l.* 18*s.*
India 174 $\frac{3}{4}$ *a* $\frac{1}{4}$	*Welsh ditto* 2*l.* 3*s.*
— *Bonds* 5 l. 15 s.	*Lottery Tick.* 15*l.*

The Course of EXCHANGE.

Amst. 34 10	*Hamb.* 33 5
D. Sight 34 8	*Paris Sight* 31 $\frac{7}{8}$
Rotter. 35 *a* 34 11	*Bourd.* 31 $\frac{1}{2}$
Antwer. 35 8	*Cadiz* 42
Madrid 42	*Venice* 48 $\frac{1}{2}$
Bilboa 41 $\frac{5}{8}$	*Dublin* 11 $\frac{7}{8}$ 12
Leghor. 50 *a* $\frac{3}{4}$	*Lisbon* 5 5 $\frac{3}{4}$
Genoa 53 $\frac{3}{4}$	*Oporto* 5 5 $\frac{3}{4}$

Prices of Goods at *Bear-Key.*

Wheat 26 *to* 28	*Oates* 9 *to* 15
Rye 13 *to* 15 6*d.*	*Tares* 20 *to* 24 0*d.*
Barley 15 *to* 18	*Pease* 20 *to* 22 6*d.*
H. *Beans* 16 *to* 22 6*d.*	H. *Pease* 12 *to* 16
P. *Malt* 20 *to* 24	B. *Malt* 20 *to* 23

Abstract of the *London* WEEKLY BILL from *Jan.* 4. to *Jan.* 25.

Christned	Males	723	1437
	Females	714	
Buried	Males	1104	2189
	Females	1085	

Of which dy'd of Consump. 371, Fevers 252, Small pox 125.

Died under 2 Years old,			—	810
Between	2	and 5	—	131
Between	5	and 10	—	81
Between	10	and 20	—	60
Between	20	and 30	—	144
Between	30	and 40	—	211
Between	40	and 50	—	204
Between	50	and 60	—	192
Between	60	and 70	—	171
Between	70	and 80	—	101
Between	80	and 90	—	67
Between	90	and 100	—	14
		102	—	2
		105	—	1

Prices of Goods, &c. in *London.* Hay 3*l.* 6*s.* a load.

Coals per Chaldron 26 *to* 28
New Hops per Hun. 4*l.* to 5*l.*
Old Hops 1*l.* 19*s.* to 2*l.* 19*s.*
Rape Seed 11 *l.* to 12 *l.* 00*s.*
Lead the Fodder 19 *Hun.* 1 *half* on board, 16 *l.* 10 *s.*
Tin in Blocks 4 *l.* 00 *s.*
Ditto in Bars 4 *l* 00 *s. exclusive of* 3 *s. per Hun. Duty.*
Copper Eng. best 5 *l.* 14 *s. per C.*
Ditto ordinary 4 *l.* 14 *s. per C.*
Ditto Barbary 70*l.* to 80*l.* 00 *s. per C.*
Iron of Bilboa 14 *l.* 10 *s. per Tun*
Dit of Sweden 15 *l.* 10 *s. per Ton*
Tallow 41 *s. per C. or* 5*d.* Far. *p. lb.*
Country Tallow 1 *l.* 19 *s.* 0*d.*
Cochineal 17 *s.* 3*d. per lb.*

Grocery Wares.

Rasins of the Sun 27 *s.* 0*d per C.*
Ditto Malaga Frailes new none
Ditto Smirna new 17 *s.*
Ditto Ascant none
Ditto Lipra new none
Ditto Belvedera none
Currants 37 *s.*
Ditto new none
Prunes French 17 *s.*
Figs none
Sugar Powder best 59 *s. per C.*
Ditto second sort 49 *s. per C.*
Loaf Sugar double refine 09 *d Farthing per lb.*
Ditto single refin. 60 *s.* to 70 *s. per C.*
Cinamon 7 *s.* 9 *d.*
Cloves 9 *s.* 1 *d.*
Mace 17 *s.* 6*d. per lb.*
Nutmegs 8 *s* 7 *d. per lb.*
Sugar Candy white 12 *d.* to 17 *d.*
Ditto brown 6 *d. Halfpenny per lb.*
Pepper for Home consump 14 *d.*
Ditto for exportation 10 *d. H.Pen.*
Tea Bohea fine 10 *s.* to 12 *s. per lb.*
Ditto ordinary 10 *s. per lb.*
Ditto Congo 10 *s.* to 14 *s. per lb.*
ditto Pekoe 14 *s. per lb.*
ditto Green fine 10 *s.* to 13 *s. per lb.*
ditto Imperial 12 *s. per lb.*
ditto Hyson 35 *s.*

Drugs by the lb.

Balsam Peru 16 *s*
Cardamoms 3 *s.* 4 *d.*
Camphire refin'd 16 *s.*
Crabs Eyes 2 *s d.*
Jalop 3 *s.* 9*d.*
Manna 1 *s.* 6 *d a* 2 *s* 6 *d.*
Mastick white 4 *s.* 6 *d.*
Opium 10 *s.* 06 *d.*
Quicksilver 4 *s.* 6 *d.*
Rhubarb 20 *s. a* 22 *s.*
Sarsaparilla 3 *s,* 00 *d.*
Saffron Eng 26 *s.* 00 *d.*
Wormseeds 4 *s.* 6 *d.*
Balsam Capivi 2 *s.* 10 *d,*
Balsam of Gilliad 14 *s.* 00 *d.*
Hypecacuana 6 *s.* 0*d.*
Ambergreece per oz. 14 *s.* 00 *d.*

Wine, Brandy, and Rum.

Oporto red, per T. 32 *l. a* 34 *l.*
ditto white 40 *l.*
Lisbon r.d 35.
ditto white 26 *l.*
Sherry 27 *l.*
Canary new 26 *l.*
ditto old 36 l.
Florence 30 *l.*
French red 36 *l. a* 50*l.*
ditto white 20*l.*
M untain malaga old 30l.
ditto new 24 *l.*
Brandy Fr. per Gal. 6*s.* to 6*s* 6*d.*
Rum of Jam 6 *s,* 6*d. a* 7*s.* 6*d.*
ditto Lew. Islands 6*s.* 4 *d.* to 6*s.* 10*d.*

Part Five

WRITERS
OF THE
MID-CENTURY

Philip Dormer Stanhope, Fourth Earl of Chesterfield

1694–1773

Lord Chesterfield—parliamentarian, diplomat, and wit—has become in the popular mind the symbol of Augustan urbanity, elegance, and cynicism. But Chesterfield the humanist and moralist is less well known. This complicated liberal aristocrat, born in London of a distinguished patrician family, entered Cambridge at the age of eighteen and, ambitious to prepare himself for a life of moral statesmanship, studied assiduously the arts of rhetoric and oratory in the Latin writers of the Augustan Age. After a brief polishing excursion into Dutch and French society, he began his Parliamentary career as Whig member for St. Germans, Cornwall. Despite his family fortune and position, Stanhope found himself with many physical disadvantages to overcome: he was short and not very attractive—his head appeared too big for his body, and he had bad teeth. But on the floor of Parliament, although he was a shy and nervous speaker, his political idealism and independence made him a luminous rarity in an age of corrupt and cynical partisanship. Fond of literature, architecture, and elegant gambling, Stanhope moved in the highest circles of both fashion and intelligence and was considered by many to be the wittiest man of his day. He corresponded and conversed with Montesquieu, Fontenelle, and Voltaire, and among his English friends were Steele, Swift, Arbuthnot, Gay, Bolingbroke, Addison, and Pope. He once wrote his son, "I used to think myself in company as much above me when I was with Mr Addison and Mr Pope, as if I had been with all the Princes of Europe."

Upon his father's death in 1726, Stanhope became Fourth Earl of Chesterfield and inherited a seat in the House of Lords, or, as he was fond of calling it, "the hospital of incurables." From 1728 to 1732, while serving conscientiously as Ambassador to The Hague, he contracted a liaison with Mlle. Elizabeth du Bouchet: an illegitimate son was born in 1732. For this boy, Chesterfield envisaged a distinguished diplomatic career, and he unremittingly tutored him, by means of frequent letters, in the arts of personal diplomacy.

In 1745 Chesterfield served as Lord Lieutenant of Ireland and endeared himself to the Irish by his temperate policies, his humane tolerance, and his devotion to his duties. He was perhaps the most popular Englishman ever to rule in Ireland. After serving as a Secretary of State under George II from 1746 to 1748, Chesterfield entered an early and elegant Ciceronian retirement; although he still attended the House of Lords from time to time (notably in 1751, when he argued on behalf of the successful Calendar Reform Bill), he now devoted himself primarily to his house, his collection of pictures, his garden, and his correspondence. Afflicted with severe deafness (he delighted to observe that he spent his time in his garden conversing with the other vegetables), Chesterfield ripened serenely into a gentle stoicism that was hardly ruffled by Johnson's famous letter of attack in 1755. Much of Chesterfield's later life was spent in attempts to advance the diplomatic career of his disappointingly unprepossessing son, who remained shy and gauche despite all his father's heroic educational efforts in the famous letters.

Although Chesterfield wrote over forty periodical essays and left at his death some formal character sketches and dialogues imitative of the work of La Bruyère and Fontenelle, his reputation as sage and wit rests almost wholly on the *Letters to His Son*, published by Chesterfield's needy daughter-in-law the year after his death. Evangelicals and sentimentalists like John Wesley and William Cowper were shocked by Chesterfield's emphasis on social dissimulation, as well as by his recommendation of a temperate Roman hedonism. Well known is Johnson's observation that the letters "teach the morals of a whore, and the manners of a dancing master." Less often recalled is his later remark, "Lord Chesterfield's Letters to his son, I think, might be made a very pretty book. Take out the immorality, and it should be put into the hands of every young gentleman." But whatever one's attitude toward the suave sexual morality suggested in the letters, it is undeniable that, in Chesterfield's total set of values, charity, learning, and absolute personal integrity occupy a high place. Side by side with Chesterfield's recommendations of "harmless gallantries" and fine manners appear injunctions like these: "Give nobly to indigent merit, and do not refuse your charity even to those who have no merit but their misery"; "the strictest and most scrupulous honour and virtue can alone make you esteemed and valued by mankind"; "Never be proud of your rank or birth, but be as proud as you please of your character." Chesterfield continually emphasizes, however, that these indispensable moral virtues, if unadorned by grace and polish, tend to remain inoperative, passive, and merely theoretical. "The Graces" are thus important not only in themselves but as a means to the triumph of virtue: so important to Chesterfield are manners that "virtue, which is moral beauty, wants some of its charms if unaccompanied by them."

The best modern edition of Chesterfield's correspondence is edited by Bonamy Dobrée (6 vols., 1932); Dobrée's first volume contains a biography, which may be supplemented with the entertaining treatments by Willard Connely (*The True Chesterfield* [1939]) and Samuel Shellabarger (*Lord Chesterfield* [1935]). The edition by Charles Strachey and Annette Calthorp (2 vols., 1901), although superseded in some respects by Dobrée's, contains a judicious introduction. Roger Coxon's *Chesterfield and His Critics* (1925) undertakes to defend Chesterfield as man of letters and moralist. Useful volumes of selections from Chesterfield's writings are R. P. Bond's *Chesterfield's Letters and Other Pieces* (1935) and the editions of the *Letters* in the World's Classics and Everyman's Library.

FROM

[LETTERS . . .
TO HIS SON . . .]

Chesterfield began writing letters on learning and conduct to his natural son Philip in 1738, when the boy (first referred to privately by Chesterfield as Frisky and later, as Philip's learning increased, as Polyglot) was five. The letters poured forth for thirty years, until Philip's early death in 1768.

The letters, more than four hundred in number, carry on the tradition of a complete system of gentlemanly education, and, despite the constant presence of Chesterfield's urgent personal tone, they are highly conventional. They carry on into the mid-eighteenth century the tradition of the courtesy book, which perhaps may be said to have begun with Cicero's *De Officiis*, written in 44 B.C. The function of a courtesy book is to define the ideal gentleman and to suggest the education necessary for his highest development. The Renaissance flowering of the gentlemanly ideal resulted in the most famous of courtesy books, Baldassare Castiglione's *Il Cortegiano*, published in 1528. Other notable performances in the same genre are Sir Thomas Elyot's *Thè Book Named the Governor* (1531), Francis Osborne's *Advice to a Son* (1658), and a courtesy book for young women, *The Lady's New-Year's Gift, or Advice to a Daughter* (1688), by Chesterfield's grandfather, George Savile, Marquis of Halifax. In allying himself with this tradition, Chesterfield is affirming, in a rapidly changing, "progressive," and sentimentalist age, a very Roman and unsentimental version of the Renaissance gentlemanly ideal. The *Letters to His Son* are thus not so much personal communications, like the letters of Samuel Johnson or Horace Walpole, as they are informal essays or even secular (and skeptical) sermons; it is primarily Chesterfield's self-conscious, single-minded concentration on one crucial object, the redemption of his son from the ordinary and the crude, that gives the letters their tone of personal sincerity.

And how did young Philip react to receiving almost every week a new Ciceronian exhortation on deportment? His feelings are perhaps suggested by the words he wrote at the age of seven to his famous father:

MY DEAR PAPA,

It is true that you give me praise; but it is true also that you make me pay for it; for you make me work like a galley-slave to get it. No matter:

one cannot buy glory too dear. So thought Alexander the Great, and so thinks Philip the Little.

The text is that of the first edition, *Letters Written by the Late Right Honourable Philip Dormer Stanhope, Earl of Chesterfield, to His Son, Philip Stanhope, Esq; Late Envoy Extraordinary at the Court of Dresden . . . Published by Mrs. Eugenia Stanhope from the Originals Now in Her Possession* (2 vols., 1774). Diacritical marks have been supplied for French names and expressions.

London, October the 16th, O.S.[1] *1747.*

DEAR BOY,

The art of pleasing is a very necessary one to possess; but a very difficult one to acquire. It can hardly be reduced to rules; and your own good sense and observation will teach you more of it than I can. Do as you would be done by, is the surest method that I know of pleasing. Observe carefully what pleases you in others, and probably the same things in you will please others. If you are pleased with the complaisance and attention of others to your humours, your tastes, or your weaknesses, depend upon it, the same complaisance and attention, on your part, to theirs, will equally please them. Take the tone of the company, that you are in, and do not pretend to give it; be serious, gay, or even trifling, as you find the present humour of the company; this is an attention due from every individual to the majority. Do not tell stories in company; there is nothing more tedious and disagreeable: if by chance you know a very short story, and exceedingly applicable to the present subject of conversation, tell it in as few words as possible; and even then, throw out that you do not love to tell stories; but that the shortness of it tempted you. Of all things, banish the egotism out of your conversation, and never think of entertaining people with your own personal concerns, or private affairs; though they are interesting to you, they are tedious and impertinent to every body else: besides that, one cannot keep one's

LETTERS TO HIS SON. I. O.S.: Old Style, in reference to the Julian calendar, used in England until 1752, when it was replaced by the Gregorian calendar (New Style, the standard on the Continent), largely as a result of Chesterfield's advocacy of the change in the House of Lords. When England finally changed to the New Style, the day following September 2, 1752, became September 14.

own private affairs too secret. Whatever you think your own excellencies may be, do not affectedly display them in company; nor labour, as many people do, to give that turn to the conversation, which may supply you with an opportunity of exhibiting them. If they are real, they will infallibly be discovered, without your pointing them out yourself, and with much more advantage. Never maintain an argument with heat and clamour, though you think or know yourself to be in the right; but give your opinion modestly and cooly, which is the only way to convince; and, if that does not do, try to change the conversation, by saying, with good humour, "We shall hardly convince one another, nor is it necessary that we should, so let us talk of something else."

Remember that there is a local propriety to be observed in all companies; and that what is extremely proper in one company may be, and often is, highly improper in another.

The jokes, the *bons mots*,[2] the little adventures, which may do very well in one company, will seem flat and tedious, when related in another. The particular characters, the habits, the cant of one company may give merit to a word, or a gesture, which would have none at all if divested of those accidental circumstances. Here people very commonly err; and, fond of something that has entertained them in one company, and in certain circumstances, repeat it with emphasis in another, where it is either insipid, or, it may be, offensive, by being ill-timed or misplaced. Nay, they often do it with this silly preamble; "I will tell you an excellent thing;" or, "I will tell you the best thing in the world." This raises expectations, which, when absolutely disappointed, make the relator of this excellent thing look, very deservedly, like a fool.

If you would particularly gain the affection and friendship of particular people, whether men or women, endeavour to find out their predominant excellency, if they have one, and their prevailing weakness, which every body has; and do justice to the one, and something more than justice to the other. Men have various objects in which they may excel, or at least would be thought to excel; and, though they love to hear justice done to them, where they know that they excel, yet they are most and best flattered upon those points where they wish to excel, and yet are doubtful whether they do or not. As, for example;

Cardinal Richelieu,[3] who was undoubtedly the ablest Statesman of his time, or perhaps of any other, had the idle vanity of being thought the best Poet too; he envied the great Corneille his reputation, and ordered a criticism to be written upon the Cid.[4] Those, therefore, who flattered skilfully, said little to him of his abilities in state affairs, or at least but *en passant*,[5] and as it might naturally occur. But the incense which they gave him, the smoke of which, they knew, would turn his head in their favour, was as a *bel esprit*[6] and a Poet. Why? Because he was sure of one excellency, and distrustful as to the other. You will easily discover every man's prevailing vanity, by observing his favourite topic of conversation; for every man talks most of what he has most a mind to be thought to excel in. Touch him but there, and you touch him to the quick. The late Sir Robert Walpole,[7] (who was certainly an able man) was little open to flattery upon that head; for he was in no doubt himself about it; but his prevailing weakness was, to be thought to have a polite and happy turn to gallantry; of which he had undoubtedly less than any man living: it was his favourite and frequent subject of conversation; which proved, to those who had any penetration, that it was his prevailing weakness. And they applied to it with success.

Women have, in general, but one object, which is their beauty; upon which, scarce any flattery is too gross for them to swallow. Nature has hardly formed a woman ugly enough, to be insensible to flattery upon her person; if her face is so shocking, that she must, in some degree, be conscious of it, her figure and air, she trusts, make ample amends for it. If her figure is deformed, her face, she thinks, counterbalances it. If they are both bad, she comforts herself, that she has graces; a certain manner; a *je ne sçais quoi*,[8] still more engaging than beauty. This truth is evident, from the studied and elaborate dress of the ugliest women in the world. An undoubted, uncontested, conscious beauty, is, of all women, the least sensible of flattery upon that head; she knows it is her due, and

2. **bons mots:** witticisms.

3. **Cardinal Richelieu:** (1585–1642), French statesman; powerful chief minister under Louis XIII from 1624 to 1642. 4. **the Cid:** a classical French tragedy (1636) by Pierre Corneille (1606–84). 5. **en passant:** by the way. 6. **bel esprit:** wit, intellectual. 7. **Sir . . . Walpole:** (1676–1745), Whig party leader, and Prime Minister during the reigns of George I and George II; father of Horace Walpole. 8. **a je . . . quoi:** a *je ne sais quoi* (I know not what), an indefinable something.

is therefore obliged to nobody for giving it her. She must be flattered upon her understanding; which, though she may possibly not doubt of herself, yet she suspects that men may distrust.

Do not mistake me, and think that I mean to recommend to you, abject and criminal flattery: no; flatter nobody's vices or crimes: on the contrary, abhor and discourage them. But there is no living in the world without a complaisant indulgence for people's weaknesses, and innocent, though ridiculous vanities. If a man has a mind to be thought wiser, and a woman handsomer, than they really are, their error is a comfortable one to themselves, and an innocent one with regard to other people; and I would rather make them my friends, by indulging them in it, than my enemies, by endeavouring (and that to no purpose) to undeceive them.

There are little attentions, likewise, which are infinitely engaging, and which sensibly affect that degree of pride and self-love, which is inseparable from human nature; as they are unquestionable proofs of the regard and consideration which we have for the persons to whom we pay them. As for example; to observe the little habits, the likings, the antipathies, and the tastes of those whom we would gain; and then take care to provide them with the one, and to secure them from the other; giving them, genteely, to understand, that you had observed they liked such a dish, or such a room; for which reason you had prepared it: or, on the contrary, that having observed they had an aversion to such a dish, a dislike to such a person, etc. you had taken care to avoid presenting them. Such attention, to such trifles, flatters self-love much more than greater things, as it makes people think themselves almost the only objects of your thoughts and care.

These are some of the arcana's[9] necessary for your initiation in the great society of the world. I wish I had known them better, at your age; I have paid the price of three-and-fifty years for them, and shall not grudge it, if you reap the advantage. Adieu.

Bath, March the 9th, O.S. 1748.

DEAR BOY,

I must, from time to time, remind you of what I have often recommended to you, and of what you cannot attend to too much; *sacrifice to the Graces.* The different effects of the same things, said or done, when accompanied or abandoned by them, is almost inconceivable. They prepare the way to the heart; and the heart has such an influence over the understanding, that it is worth while to engage it in our interest. It is the whole of women, who are guided by nothing else; and it has so much to say, even with men, and the ablest men too, that it commonly triumphs in every struggle with the understanding. Monsieur de la Rochefoucault,[10] in his Maxims, says, that *l'esprit est souvent la dupe du coeur.*[11] If he had said, instead of *souvent, presque toujours,*[12] I fear he would have been nearer the truth. This being the case, aim at the heart. Intrinsic merit alone will not do: it will gain you the general esteem of all; but not the particular affection, that is the heart, of any. To engage the affection of any particular person, you must, over and above your general merit, have some particular merit to that person; by services done, or offered; by expressions of regard and esteem; by complaisance, attentions, etc. for him: and the graceful manner of doing all these things opens the way to the heart, and facilitates, or rather insures, their effects. From your own observation, reflect what a disagreeable impression an awkward address, a slovenly figure, an ungraceful manner of speaking, whether stuttering, muttering, monotony, or drawling; an unattentive behaviour, etc. make upon you, at first sight, in a stranger, and how they prejudice you against him, though, for ought you know, he may have great intrinsic sense and merit. And reflect, on the other hand, how much the opposites of all these things prepossess you, at first sight, in favour of those who enjoy them. You wish to find all good qualities in them, and are in some degree disappointed if you do not. A thousand little things, not separately to be defined, conspire to form these Graces, this *je ne sçais quoi*, that always pleases. A pretty person, genteel motions, a proper degree of dress, an harmonious voice, something open and chearful in the countenance, but without laughing; a distinct and properly varied manner of speaking: all these things, and many others, are necessary ingredients in the composition of the pleasing *je ne sçais quoi*, which every body feels,

---

9. **arcana's:** secrets; correctly, *arcana*.

10. **Rochefoucault:** François de Marsillac (1613–80), Duc de la Rochefoucauld, French writer, author of *Réflexions, ou sentences et maximes morales* (1665), a collection of sagacious, if somewhat cynical, aphorisms. 11. **l'esprit . . . coeur:** "The understanding is often the dupe of the heart." 12. **souvent . . . toujours:** often, almost always.

though no body can describe. Observe carefully, then, what displeases or pleases you, in others; and be persuaded, that, in general, the same things will please or displease them, in you. Having mentioned laughing, I must particularly warn you against it: and I could heartily wish, that you may often be seen to smile, but never heard to laugh, while you live. Frequent and loud laughter is the characteristic of folly and ill manners: it is the manner in which the mob express their silly joy, at silly things; and they call it being merry. In my mind, there is nothing so illiberal, and so ill-bred, as audible laughter. True wit, or sense, never yet made any body laugh; they are above it: they please the mind, and give a chearfulness to the countenance. But it is low buffoonery, or silly accidents, that always excite laughter; and that is what people of sense and breeding should show themselves above. A man's going to sit down, in the supposition that he has a chair behind him, and falling down upon his breech for want of one, sets a whole company a laughing, when all the wit in the world would not do it; a plain proof, in my mind, how low and unbecoming a thing laughter is. Not to mention the disagreeable noise that it makes, and the shocking distortion of the face that it occasions. Laughter is easily restrained, by a very little reflection; but, as it is generally connected with the idea of gaiety, people do not enough attend to its absurdity. I am neither of a melancholy, nor a Cynical disposition; and am as willing, and as apt to be pleased as any body; but I am sure that, since I have had the full use of my reason, nobody has ever heard me laugh. Many people, at first from awkwardness and *mauvaise honte*,[13] have got a very disagreeable and silly trick of laughing, whenever they speak: and I know a man of very good parts, Mr. Waller,[14] who cannot say the commonest thing without laughing; which makes those, who do not know him, take him at first for a natural fool.

This and many other very disagreeable habits, are owing to *mauvaise honte* at their first setting out in the world. They are ashamed in company, and so disconcerted that they do not know what they do, and try a thousand tricks to keep themselves in countenance; which tricks afterwards grow habitual to them. Some put their fingers in their nose, others

scratch their head, others twirl their hats; in short, every awkward, ill-bred body has his trick. But the frequency does not justify the thing; and all these vulgar habits and awkwardness, though not criminal indeed, are most carefully to be guarded against, as they are great bars in the way of the art of pleasing. Remember, that to please, is almost to prevail, or at least a necessary previous step to it. You, who have your fortune to make, should more particularly study this art. You had not, I must tell you, when you left England, *les manières prévenantes*;[15] and I must confess they are not very common in England: but I hope that your good sense will make you acquire them abroad. If you desire to make yourself considerable in the world (as, if you have any spirit, you do) it must be intirely your own doing: for I may very possibly be out of the world at the time you come into it. Your own rank and fortune will not assist you; your merit and your manners can, alone, raise you to figure and fortune. I have laid the foundations of them, by the education which I have given you; but you must build the superstructure yourself. . . .

London, *September the 5th, O.S. 1748.*

DEAR BOY,

I have received yours, with the enclosed German letter to Mr. Grevenkop,[16] which he assures me is extremely well written, considering the little time that you have applied yourself to that language. As you have now got over the most difficult part, pray go on diligently, and make yourself absolutely master of the rest. Whoever does not entirely possess a language, will never appear to advantage, or even equal to himself, either in speaking or writing it. His ideas are fettered, and seem imperfect or confused, if he is not master of all the words and phrases necessary to express them. I therefore desire, that you will not fail writing a German letter, once every fortnight, to Mr. Grevenkop; which will make the writing of that language familiar to you: and, moreover, when you shall have left Germany, and be arrived at Turin, I shall require you to write even to me in German; that you may not forget, with ease, what you have with difficulty learned. I likewise desire, that, while you are in Germany, you will take all opportunities of conversing in German, which is the only way of knowing

---

13. **mauvaise honte:** bashfulness. 14. **Mr. Waller:** Edmund Waller, descendant of Edmund Waller the poet; Member of Parliament and coauthor, with Chesterfield, of political pamphlets.

15. **les . . . prévenantes:** prepossessing manners. 16. **Mr. Grevenkop:** Gaspar Grevenkop, a Danish friend of Chesterfield's.

that, or any other language, accurately. You will also desire your German master to teach you the proper titles and superscriptions to be used to people of all ranks; which is a point so material, in Germany, that I have known many a letter returned unopened, because one title in twenty has been omitted in the direction.

St. Thomas's Day now draws near, when you are to leave Saxony and go to Berlin; and I take it for granted, that, if any thing is yet wanting, to complete your knowledge of the state of that Electorate, you will not fail to procure it before you go away. I do not mean, as you will easily believe, the number of churches, parishes, or towns; but I mean the constitution, the revenues, the troops, and the trade of that Electorate. A few questions, sensibly asked, of sensible people, will procure you the necessary informations; which I desire you will enter in your little book. Berlin will be entirely a new scene to you, and I look upon it, in a manner, as your first step into the great world: take care that step be not a false one, and that you do not stumble at the threshold. You will there be in more company than you have yet been; Manners and Attentions will therefore be more necessary. Pleasing in company, is the only way of being pleased in it yourself. Sense and Knowledge are the first and necessary foundations for pleasing in company; but they will by no means do alone, and they will never be perfectly welcome, if they are not accompanied with Manners and Attentions. You will best acquire these by frequenting the companies of people of fashion; but then you must resolve to acquire them, in those companies, by proper care and observation; for I have known people, who, though they have frequented good company all their life-time, have done it in so inattentive and unobserving a manner, as to be never the better for it, and to remain as disagreeable, as awkward, and as vulgar, as if they had never seen any person of fashion. When you go into good company (by good company is meant the people of the first fashion of the place) observe carefully their turn, their manners, their address; and conform your own to them. But this is not all neither: go deeper still; observe their characters, and pry, as far as you can, into both their hearts and their heads. Seek for their particular merit, their predominant passion, or their prevailing weakness; and you will then know what to bait your hook with, to catch them. Man is a composition of so many, and such various ingredients, that it requires both time and care to analyze him: for

though we have, all, the same ingredients in our general composition, as Reason, Will, Passions, and Appetites; yet the different proportions and combinations of them, in each individual, produce that infinite variety of characters, which, in some particular or other, distinguishes every individual from another. Reason ought to direct the whole, but seldom does. And he who addresses himself singly to another man's reason, without endeavouring to engage his heart in his interest also, is no more likely to succeed, than a man who should apply only to a King's nominal Minister, and neglect his Favourite. I will recommend to your attentive perusal, now that you are going into the world, two books, which will let you as much into the characters of men, as books can do. I mean, *Les Réflexions Morales de Monsieur de la Rochefoucault*, and *Les Caractères de la Bruyère:*[17] but remember, at the same time, that I only recommend them to you as the best general maps, to assist you in your journey, and not as marking out every particular turning and winding that you will meet with. There, your own sagacity and observation must come to their aid. La Rochefoucault is, I know, blamed, but I think without reason, for deriving all our actions from the source of self-love. For my own part, I see a great deal of truth, and no harm at all, in that opinion. It is certain, that we seek our own happiness in every thing we do; and it is as certain, that we can only find it in doing well, and in conforming all our actions to the rule of right reason, which is the great law of Nature. It is only a mistaken self-love that is a blameable motive, when we take the immediate and indiscriminate gratification of a passion, or appetite, for real happiness. But am I blameable, if I do a good action, upon account of the happiness which that honest consciousness will give me? Surely not. On the contrary, that pleasing consciousness is a proof of my virtue. The reflection, which is the most censured in Monsieur de la Rochefoucault's book, as a very ill-natured one, is this; *On trouve dans le malheur de son meilleur ami, quelque chose qui ne déplaît pas.*[18] And why not? Why may I not feel a very tender and real concern for the misfortune of my friend, and yet at the same time feel a pleasing consciousness at having

17. **la Bruyère:** Jean de la Bruyère (1645–96), French moralist; author of *Caractères* (1688), a collection of aphorisms, ethical essays, and shrewd character sketches. **18. On . . . pas:** "Everyone finds something not entirely unpleasant in the misfortune of his best friend." See Swift's *Verses on the Death of Dr. Swift* in Part Two.

discharged my duty to him, by comforting and assisting him to the utmost of my power in that misfortune? Give me but virtuous actions, and I will not quibble and chicane about the motives. And I will give any body their choice of these two truths, which amount to the same thing: He, who loves himself best, is the honestest man; or, The honestest man loves himself best.

The characters of La Bruyère are pictures from the life; most of them finely drawn, and highly coloured. Furnish your mind with them first; and when you meet with their likeness, as you will every day, they will strike you the more. You will compare every feature with the original; and both will reciprocally help you to discover the beauties and the blemishes.

As women are a considerable, or at least a pretty numerous part of company; and as their suffrages go a great way towards establishing a man's character, in the fashionable part of the world (which is of great importance to the fortune and figure he proposes to make in it) it is necessary to please them. I will therefore, upon this subject, let you into certain *Arcana's* that will be very useful for you to know, but which you must, with the utmost care, conceal; and never seem to know. Women, then, are only children of a larger growth; they have an entertaining tattle, and sometimes wit; but for solid, reasoning good sense, I never in my life knew one that had it, or who reasoned or acted consequentially for four-and-twenty hours together. Some little passion or humour always breaks in upon their best resolutions. Their beauty neglected, or controverted, their age increased, or their supposed understandings depreciated, instantly kindles their little passions, and overturns any system of consequential conduct, that, in their most reasonable moments, they might have been capable of forming. A man of sense only trifles with them, plays with them, humours and flatters them, as he does with a sprightly, forward child; but he neither consults them about, nor trusts them with, serious matters; though he often makes them believe that he does both; which is the thing in the world that they are proud of; for they love mightily to be dabbling in business (which, by the way, they always spoil;) and being justly distrustful, that men in general look upon them in a trifling light, they almost adore that man, who talks more seriously to them, and who seems to consult and trust them: I say, who seems; for weak men really do, but wise ones only seem to do it. No flattery is either too high or too low for them. They will greedily swallow the highest, and gratefully accept of the lowest; and you may safely flatter any woman, from her understanding, down to the exquisite taste of her fan. Women, who are either indisputably beautiful, or indisputably ugly, are best flattered upon the score of their understandings: but those who are in a state of mediocrity, are best flattered upon their beauty, or at least their graces; for every woman, who is not absolutely ugly, thinks herself handsome; but not hearing often that she is so, is the more grateful, and the more obliged to the few who tell her so whereas a decided and conscious beauty looks upon every tribute, paid to her beauty, only as her due; but wants to shine, and to be considered on the side of her understanding: and a woman, who is ugly enough to know that she is so, knows that she has nothing left for it but her understanding, which is, consequently, (and probably in more senses than one) her weak side. But there are secrets, which you must keep inviolably, if you would not, like Orpheus, be torn to pieces by the whole sex:[19] on the contrary, a man, who thinks of living in the great world, must be gallant, polite, and attentive to please the women. They have, from the weakness of men, more or less influence in all Courts; they absolutely stamp every man's character in the *beau monde*,[20] and make it either current, or cry it down, and stop it in payments.[21] It is, therefore, absolutely necessary to manage, please, and flatter them; and never to discover the least marks of contempt, which is what they never forgive: but in this they are not singular, for it is the same with men; who will much sooner forgive an injustice than an insult. Every man is not ambitious, or covetous, or passionate; but every man has pride enough in his composition to feel and resent the least slight and contempt. Remember, therefore, most carefully to conceal your contempt, however just, wherever you would not make an implacable enemy. Men are much more unwilling to have their weaknesses and their imperfections known, than their crimes; and, if you hint to a man, that you think him silly, ignorant, or even ill-bred, or awkward, he will hate you more, and longer, than if you tell him, plainly, that you think him a rogue. Never yield to that temptation, which, to most young men, is very strong, of exposing other people's weaknesses

19. the whole sex: Orpheus, a legendary pre-Homeric poet and musician, was torn limb from limb by Thracian women. The story is told in Ovid's *Metamorphoses*. 20. beau monde: fashionable world. 21. make it . . . payments: the figure is that of a sound *vs.* a devalued currency.

and infirmities, for the sake either of diverting the company, or of showing your own superiority. You may get the laugh on your side by it, for the present; but you will make enemies by it for ever; and even those who laugh with you then, will, upon reflection, fear, and consequently hate you: besides that, it is ill-natured; and that a good heart desires rather to conceal, than expose, other people's weaknesses or misfortunes. If you have wit, use it to please, and not to hurt: you may shine, like the sun in the temperate Zones, without scorching. Here it is wished for; under the Line[22] it is dreaded.

These are some of the hints, which my long experience in the great world enables me to give you; and which, if you attend to them, may prove useful to you in your journey through it. I wish it may be a prosperous one; at least, I am sure that it must be your own fault if it is not.

Make my compliments to Mr. Harte,[23] who, I am very sorry to hear, is not well. I hope by this time he is recovered. Adieu.

Bath, October the 12th, O.S. 1748.

DEAR BOY,

I came here three days ago, upon account of a disorder in my stomach, which affected my head, and gave me vertigos. I already find myself something better; and consequently do not doubt, but that the course of these waters will set me quite right. But how-ever, and where-ever I am, your welfare, your character, your knowledge, and your morals, employ my thoughts more than any thing that can happen to me, or that I can fear or hope for myself. I am going off of the stage, you are coming upon it: with me, what has been, has been, and reflection now would come too late; with you, every thing is to come, even, in some manner, reflection itself: so that this is the very time when my reflections, the result of experience, may be of use to you, by supplying the want of yours. As soon as you leave Leipsig, you will gradually be going into the great world; where the first impressions that you shall give of yourself will be of great importance to you; but those which you shall receive will be decisive, for they always stick. To keep good company, especially at your first setting out, is

the way to receive good impressions. If you ask me what I mean by good company, I will confess to you, that it is pretty difficult to define; but I will endeavour to make you understand it as well as I can.

Good Company, is not what respective sets of company are pleased either to call or think themselves; but it is that company which all the people of the place call, and acknowledge to be, good company, notwithstanding some objections which they may form to some of the individuals who compose it. It consists chiefly (but by no means without exception) of people of considerable birth, rank, and character: for people of neither birth nor rank, are frequently, and very justly, admitted into it, if distinguished by any peculiar merit, or eminency in any liberal art or science. Nay, so motley a thing is good company, that many people, without birth, rank, or merit, intrude into it by their own forwardness, and others slide into it by the protection of some considerable person; and some even of indifferent characters and morals make part of it. But, in the main, the good part preponderates, and people of infamous and blasted characters are never admitted. In this fashionable good company, the best manners, and the best language, of the place are most unquestionably to be learnt; for they establish, and give the tone to both, which are therefore called the language and manners of good company: there being no legal tribunal to ascertain either.

A company consisting wholly of people of the first quality, cannot, for that reason, be called good company, in the common acceptation of the phrase, unless they are, into the bargain, the fashionable and accredited company of the place; for people of the very first quality can be as silly, as ill-bred, and as worthless, as people of the meanest degree. On the other hand, a company consisting intirely of people of very low condition, whatever their merit or parts may be, can never be called good company; and consequently should not be much frequented, though by no means despised.

A company wholly composed of men of learning, though greatly to be valued and respected, is not meant by the words, *good company:* they cannot have the easy manners and *tournure*[24] of the world, as they do not live in it. If you can bear your part well in such a company, it is extremely right to be in it sometimes, and you will be but more esteemed, in other companies, for having a place in that. But then do not let

---

22. under the Line: on the equator. **23. Mr. Harte:** Walter Harte (1709–74), Oxford scholar, minor poet, friend of Pope's; Chesterfield appointed him Philip's tutor in 1745. (See the selection from Harte in Part Three.)

24. tournure: cultivated address.

it engross you; for if you do, you will be only considered as one of the *litterati* by profession; which is not the way either to shine, or rise in the world.

The company of professed Wits and Poets is extremely inviting to most young men; who, if they have wit themselves, are pleased with it, and if they have none, are sillily proud of being one of it: but it should be frequented with moderation and judgment, and you should by no means give yourself up to it. A Wit is a very unpopular denomination, as it carries terror along with it; and people in general are as much afraid of a live Wit, in company, as a woman is of a gun, which she thinks may go off of itself, and do her a mischief. Their acquaintance is, however, worth seeking, and their company worth frequenting; but not exclusively of others, nor to such a degree as to be considered only as one of that particular set.

But the company, which of all others you should most carefully avoid, is, that low company, which, in every sense of the word, is low indeed; low in rank, low in parts, low in manners, and low in merit. You will, perhaps, be surprized, that I should think it necessary to warn you against such company; but yet I do not think it wholly unnecessary, after the many instances which I have seen, of men of sense and rank, discredited, vilified, and undone, by keeping such company. Vanity, that source of many of our follies, and of some of our crimes, has sunk many a man into company, in every light infinitely below himself, for the sake of being the first man in it. There he dictates, is applauded, admired; and, for the sake of being the *Coryphaeus*[25] of that wretched chorus, disgraces, and disqualifies himself soon for any better company. Depend upon it, you will sink or rise to the level of the company which you commonly keep: people will judge of you, and not unreasonably, by that. There is good sense in the Spanish saying, "Tell me whom you live with, and I will tell you who you are." Make it therefore your business, wherever you are, to get into that company, which every body of the place allows to be the best company, next to their own: which is the best definition that I can give you, of good company. But here, too, one caution is very necessary; for want of which many young men have been ruined, even in good company. Good company (as I have before observed) is composed of a great variety of fashionable people, whose characters and morals are very different, though their manners are pretty much

the same. When a young man, new in the world, first gets into that company, he very rightly determines to conform to, and imitate it. But then he too often, and fatally, mistakes the objects of his imitation. He has often heard that absurd term of genteel and fashionable vices. He there sees some people who shine, and who in general are admired and esteemed; and observes, that these people are whoremasters, drunkards, or gamesters: upon which he adopts their vices, mistaking their defects for their perfections, and thinking that they owe their fashion and their lustre to those genteel vices. Whereas it is exactly the reverse; for these people have acquired their reputation by their parts, their learning, their good-breeding, and other real accomplishments; and are only blemished and lowered, in the opinions of all reasonable people, and of their own, in time, by these genteel and fashionable vices. A whoremaster, in a flux,[26] or without a nose, is a very genteel person indeed, and well worthy of imitation. A drunkard, vomiting up at night the wine of the day, and stupefied by the head-ach all the next, is, doubtless, a fine model to copy from. And a gamester, tearing his hair, and blaspheming, for having lost more than he had in the world, is surely a most amiable character. No; these are allays,[27] and great ones too, which can never adorn any character, but will always debase the best. To prove this; suppose any man, without parts and some other good qualities, to be merely a whoremaster, a drunkard, or a gamester; How will he be looked upon, by all sorts of people? Why, as a most contemptible and vicious animal. Therefore it is plain, that, in these mixed characters, the good part only makes people forgive, but not approve, the bad.

I will hope, and believe, that you will have no vices; but if, unfortunately, you should have any, at least I beg of you to be content with your own, and to adopt no other body's. The adoption of vice has, I am convinced, ruined ten times more young men, than natural inclinations.

As I make no difficulty of confessing my past errors, where I think the confession may be of use to you, I will own, that, when I first went to the university, I drank and smoked, notwithstanding the aversion I had to wine and tobacco, only because I thought it genteel, and that it make me look like a man. When I went

25. **Coryphaeus:** chorus leader in Greek tragedy.

26. **in a flux:** exhibiting the active symptoms of venereal disease. The deterioration of the tissue of the nose was a common sign of advanced venereal disease. 27. **allays:** alien elements, blemishes.

abroad, I first went to the Hague, where gaming was much in fashion; and where I observed that many people, of shining rank and character, gamed too. I was then young enough, and silly enough, to believe, that gaming was one of their accomplishments; and, as I aimed at perfection, I adopted gaming as a necessary step to it. Thus I acquired, by error, the habit of a vice, which, far from adorning my character, has, I am conscious, been a great blemish in it.

Imitate, then, with discernment and judgment, the real perfections of the good company which you may get into; copy their politeness, their carriage, their address, and the easy and well-bred turn of their conversation; but remember, that, let them shine ever so bright, their vices, if they have any, are so many spots, which you would no more imitate, than you would make an artificial wart upon your face, because some very handsome man had the misfortune to have a natural one upon his: but, on the contrary, think how much handsomer he would have been without it.

Having thus confessed some of my *égaremens*,[28] I will now show you a little of my right side. I always endeavoured to get into the best company, wherever I was, and commonly succeeded. There I pleased, to some degree, by showing a desire to please. I took care never to be absent or *distrait*;[29] but, on the contrary, attended to every thing that was said, done, or even looked, in company: I never failed in the minutest attentions, and was never *journalier*.[30] These things, and not my *égaremens*, made me fashionable.

Adieu! this letter is full long enough.

Bath, October the 19th, O.S. 1748.

DEAR BOY,

Having, in my last, pointed out, what sort of company you should keep, I will now give you some rules for your conduct in it; rules which my own experience and observation enable me to lay down, and communicate to you, with some degree of confidence. I have often given you hints of this kind before, but then it has been by snatches; I will now be more regular and methodical. I shall say nothing with regard to your bodily carriage and address, but leave them to the care of your dancing-master, and to your own attention to the best models: remember, however, that they are of consequence.

Talk often, but never long; in that case, if you do not please, at least you are sure not to tire your hearers. Pay your own reckoning, but do not treat the whole company; this being one of the very few cases in which people do not care to be treated, every one being fully convinced that he has wherewithal to pay.

Tell stories very seldom, and, absolutely, never but where they are very apt, and very short. Omit every circumstance that is not material, and beware of digressions. To have frequent recourse to narrative, betrays great want of imagination.

Never hold any body by the button, or the hand, in order to be heared out; if people are not willing to hear you, you had much better hold your tongue than them.

Most long talkers single out some one unfortunate man in company (commonly him whom they observe to be the most silent) or their next neighbour, to whisper, or at least, in a half voice, to convey a continuity of words to. This is excessively ill-bred, and, in some degree, a fraud; conversation-stock being a joint and common property. But, on the other hand, if one of these unmerciful talkers lays hold of you, hear him with patience, (and at least seeming attention) if he is worth obliging; for nothing will oblige him more than a patient hearing, as nothing would hurt him more, than either to leave him in the midst of his discourse, or to discover your impatience under your affliction.

Take, rather than give, the tone of the company you are in. If you have parts you will show them, more or less, upon every subject; and if you have not, you had better talk sillily upon a subject of other people's, than of your own chusing.

Avoid, as much as you can, in mixed companies, argumentative, polemical conversations; which, though they should not, yet certainly do, indispose, for a time, the contending parties towards each other: and, if the controversy grows warm and noisy, endeavour to put an end to it, by some genteel levity or joke. I quieted such a conversation-hubbub once, by representing to them, that, though I was persuaded none there present would repeat, out of company, what passed in it, yet I could not answer for the discretion of the passengers in the street, who must necessarily hear all that was said.

Above all things, and upon all occasions, avoid speaking of yourself, if it be possible. Such is the natural pride and vanity of our hearts, that it perpetually breaks out, even in people of the best parts, in all the various modes and figures of the egotism.

28. **égaremens:** (*égarements*) mistakes. 29. **distrait:** preoccupied. 30. **journalier:** flighty.

Some, abruptly, speak advantageously of themselves, without either pretence or provocation. They are impudent. Others proceed more artfully, as they imagine; and forge accusations against themselves, complain of calumnies which they never heard, in order to justify themselves, by exhibiting a catalogue of their many virtues. *They acknowledge it may, indeed, seem odd, that they should talk in that manner of themselves; it is what they do not like, and what they never would have done; no, no tortures should ever have forced it from them, if they had not been thus unjustly and monstrously accused. But, in these cases, justice is surely due to one's self, as well as to others; and, when our character is attacked, we may say, in our own justification, what otherwise we never would have said.* This thin veil of Modesty, drawn before Vanity, is much too transparent, to conceal it, even from very moderate discernment.

Others go more modestly and more slily still (as they think) to work; but, in my mind, still more ridiculously. They confess themselves (not without some degree of shame and confusion) into all the Cardinal Virtues; by first degrading them into weaknesses, and then owning their misfortune, in being made up of those weaknesses. *They cannot see people suffer, without sympathizing with, and endeavouring to help them. They cannot see people want, without relieving them; though, truly, their own circumstances cannot very well afford it. They cannot help speaking truth, though they know all the imprudence of it. In short, they know that, with all these weaknesses, they are not fit to live in the world, much less to thrive in it. But they are now too old to change, and must rub on as well as they can.* This sounds too ridiculous and *outré*,[31] almost, for the stage; and yet, take my word for it, you will frequently meet with it, upon the common stage of the world. And here I will observe, by the bye, that you will often meet with characters in nature so extravagant, that a discreet Poet would not venture to set them upon the stage, in their true and high colouring.

This principle of vanity and pride is so strong in human nature, that it descends even to the lowest objects; and one often sees people angling for praise, where, admitting all they say to be true, (which, by the way, it seldom is) no just praise is to be caught. One man affirms that he has rode post an hundred miles in six hours: probably it is a lie; but, supposing it to be true, what then? Why he is a very good post-boy, that is all. Another asserts, and probably not

without oaths, that he has drank six or eight bottles of wine at a sitting: out of charity, I will believe him a liar; for, if I do not, I must think him a beast.

Such, and a thousand more, are the follies and extravagancies, which vanity draws people into, and which always defeat their own purpose; and, as Waller[32] says, upon another subject,

> Make the wretch the most despised,
> Where most he wishes to be prized.[33]

The only sure way of avoiding these evils, is, never to speak of yourself at all. But when, historically, you are obliged to mention yourself, take care not to drop one single word, that can, directly or indirectly, be construed as fishing for applause. Be your character what it will, it will be known; and nobody will take it upon your own word. Never imagine that any thing you can say, yourself, will varnish your defects, or add lustre to your perfections; but, on the contrary, it may, and nine times in ten will, make the former more glaring, and the latter obscure. If you are silent upon your own subject, neither envy, indignation, nor ridicule, will obstruct or allay the applause which you may really deserve; but if you publish your own panegyric, upon any occasion, or in any shape whatsoever, and however artfully dressed or disguised, they will all conspire against you, and you will be disappointed at the very end you aim at.

Take care never to seem dark and mysterious; which is not only a very unamiable character, but a very suspicious one too: if you seem mysterious with others, they will be really so with you, and you will know nothing. The height of abilities is, to have *volto sciolto*, and *pensieri stretti;* that is, a frank, open, and ingenuous exterior, with a prudent and reserved interior: to be upon your own guard, and yet, by a seeming natural openness, to put people off of theirs. Depend upon it, nine in ten of every company you are in, will avail themselves of every indiscreet and unguarded expression of yours, if they can turn it to their own advantage. A prudent reserve is therefore as

---

31. outré: exaggerated.

32. Waller: Edmund Waller (1606–87), English poet frequently regarded in the eighteenth century as the most important early developer of the heroic couplet brought to perfection by Dryden and Pope. In contrast to earlier writers in the decasyllabic couplet, Dryden says, "He first made writing easily an art." (See the selections from Waller in Part Three.) **33. Make . . . prized:** Waller actually wrote, in *On Love*, "Postures which render him despised, / Where he endeavours to be prized."

necessary, as a seeming openness is prudent. Always look people in the face when you speak to them; the not doing it is thought to imply conscious guilt; besides, that you lose the advantage of observing, by their countenances, what impression your discourse makes upon them. In order to know people's real sentiments, I trust much more to my eyes than to my ears; for they can say whatever they have a mind I should hear; but they can seldom help looking, what they have no intention that I should know.

Neither retail nor receive scandal, willingly; for though the defamation of others may, for the present, gratify the malignity of the pride of our hearts, cool reflection will draw very disadvantageous conclusions from such a disposition: and in the case of scandal, as in that of robbery, the receiver is always thought as bad as the thief.

Mimickry, which is the common and favourite amusement of little, low minds, is in the utmost contempt with great ones. It is the lowest and most illiberal of all buffoonery. Pray, neither practise it yourself, nor applaud it in others. Besides that, the person mimicked is insulted; and, as I have often observed to you before, an insult is never forgiven.

I need not (I believe) advise you to adapt your conversation to the people you are conversing with: for I suppose you would not, without this caution, have talked upon the same subject, and in the same manner, to a Minister of State, a Bishop, a Philosopher, a Captain, and a Woman. A man of the world must, like the Cameleon, be able to take every different hue; which is by no means a criminal or abject, but a necessary complaisance, for it relates only to Manners, and not to Morals.

One word only, as to swearing; and that, I hope and believe, is more than is necessary. You may sometimes hear some people, in good company, interlard their discourse with oaths by way of embellishment, as they think; but you must observe, too, that those who do so, are never those who contribute, in any degree, to give that company the denomination of good company. They are always subalterns, or people of low education; for that practice, besides that it has no one temptation to plead, is as silly, and as illiberal, as it is wicked.

Loud laughter is the mirth of the mob, who are only pleased with silly things; for true Wit or good Sense never excited a laugh, since the creation of the world. A man of parts and fashion is therefore only seen to smile, but never heard to laugh.

But, to conclude this long letter; all the above-mentioned rules, however carefully you may observe them, will lose half their effect, if unaccompanied by the Graces. Whatever you say, if you say it with a supercilious, Cynical face, or an embarrassed countenance, or a silly, disconcerted grin, will be ill received. If, into the bargain, *you mutter it, or utter it indistinctly, and ungracefully*, it will be still worse received. If your air and address are vulgar, awkward, and *gauche*, you may be esteemed indeed, if you have great intrinsic merit; but you will never please: and, without pleasing, you will rise but heavily. Venus, among the Ancients, was synonimous with the Graces, who were always supposed to accompany her: and Horace tells us, that even Youth, and Mercury, the God of Arts and Eloquence, would not do without her.

Parum comis *sine te Juventas Mercuriusque.*

They are not inexorable Ladies, and may be had, if properly and diligently pursued. Adieu.

London, November the 24th, O.S. 1749.

DEAR BOY,

Every rational Being (I take it for granted) proposes to himself some object more important than mere respiration and obscure animal existence. He desires to distinguish himself among his fellow-creatures; and, *alicui negotio intentus, præclari facinoris, aut artis bonæ, famam quærit.*[34] Cesar, when embarking, in a storm, said, that it was not necessary he should live; but that it was absolutely necessary he should get to the place to which he was going. And Pliny leaves mankind this only alternative; either of doing what deserves to be written, or of writing what deserves to be read. As for those who do neither, *eorum vitam mortemque juxta æstumo; quoniam de utraque siletur.*[35] You have, I am convinced, one or both of these objects in view; but you must know, and use the necessary means, or your pursuit will be vain and frivolous. In either case, *sapere est et principium et fons;*[36] but it is by no means all. That knowledge must be adorned, it must have lustre as well as weight, or it will be oftener taken for

34. alicui . . . quærit: "Whatever he does, he seeks the honor of either a famous deed or a useful invention" (Pliny the Younger). 35. eorum . . . siletur: "I regard their lives and deaths as equally meaningless; neither is worth mentioning" (Ibid.). 36. sapere . . . fons: "Knowledge is both the source and the fountain" (Ibid.).

Lead than for Gold. Knowledge you have, and will have: I am easy upon that article. But my business, as your friend, is not to compliment you upon what you have, but to tell you with freedom what you want; and I must tell you, plainly, that I fear you want every thing but knowledge.

I have written to you so often, of late, upon Good-breeding, Address, *les manières liantes*,[37] the Graces, etc. that I shall confine this letter to another subject, pretty near akin to them, and which, I am sure, you are full as deficient in; I mean, Style.

Style is the dress of thoughts; and let them be ever so just, if your style is homely, coarse, and vulgar, they will appear to as much disadvantage, and be as ill received, as your person, though ever so well proportioned, would, if dressed in rags, dirt, and tatters. It is not every understanding that can judge of matter; but every ear can and does judge, more or less, of style: and were I either to speak or write to the public, I should prefer moderate matter, adorned with all the beauties and elegancies of style, to the strongest matter in the world, ill-worded, and ill-delivered. Your business is, Negotiation abroad, and Oratory in the House of Commons at home. What figure can you make in either case, if your style be inelegant, I do not say bad? Imagine yourself writing an office-letter[38] to a Secretary of State, which letter is to be read by the whole Cabinet Council, and very possibly, afterwards, laid before Parliament; any one barbarism, solecism, or vulgarism in it, would, in a very few days, circulate through the whole kingdom, to your disgrace and ridicule. For instance; I will suppose you had written the following letter from The Hague, to the Secretary of State at London; and leave you to suppose the consequences of it.

My Lord,

I *had*, last night, the honour of your Lordship's letter, of the 24th; and will *set about doing* the orders contained *therein;* and *if so be* that I can get that affair done by the next post, I will not fail *for to* give your Lordship an account of it by *next post.* I have told the French Minister, *as how, that if that* affair be not soon concluded, your Lordship would think it *all long of him;* and that he must have neglected *for to* have wrote to his Court about it. I must beg leave to put your Lordship in mind, *as how*, that I am now full three quarters in arrear;

and if *so be* that I do not very soon receive at least one half year, I shall *cut a very bad figure; for this here* place is very dear. I shall be *vastly beholden* to your Lordship for *that there* mark of your favour; and so I *rest*, or *remain*, Your, etc.

You will tell me, possibly, that this is a *caricatura* of an illiberal and inelegant style; I will admit it: but assure you, at the same time, that a dispatch with less than half these faults would blow you up forever. It is by no means sufficient to be free from faults, in speaking and writing; you must do both correctly and elegantly. In faults of this kind, it is not *ille optimis qui minimis urgetur.*[39] But he is unpardonable who has any at all, because it is his own fault. He need only attend to, observe and imitate the best authors.

It is a very true saying, that a man must be born a Poet, but that he may make himself an Orator; and the very first principle of an Orator is, to speak, his own language, particularly, with the utmost purity and elegancy. A man will be forgiven, even great errors, in a foreign language; but in his own, even the least slips are justly laid hold of and ridiculed.

A person of the House of Commons, speaking two years ago upon naval affairs, asserted, that we had then the finest navy *upon the face of the yearth.* This happy mixture of blunder and vulgarism, you may easily imagine, was matter of immediate ridicule; but, I can assure you, that it continues so still, and will be remembered as long as he lives and speaks. Another, speaking in defence of a gentleman, upon whom a censure was moved, happily said, that he thought that gentleman was more *liable* to be thanked and rewarded, than censured. You know, I presume, that *liable* can never be used in a good sense.

You have with you three or four of the best English Authors, Dryden, Atterbury, and Swift; read them with the utmost care, and with a particular view to their language; and they may possibly correct that *curious infelicity of diction,* which you acquired at Westminster.[40] Mr. Harte excepted, I will admit that you have met with very few English abroad, who could improve your style; and with many, I dare say, who speak as ill as yourself, and it may be worse; but, therefore, you must take the more pains, and consult

---

37. les . . . liantes: affable manners. **38. office-letter:** official letter.

39. ille . . . urgetur: "He is best who commits the fewest blunders." **40. Westminster:** Philip had attended Westminster School from 1743 to 1746. Locke, Dryden, Gibbon, and Cowper were also students at this important public school, founded by Elizabeth I in 1560.

your authors, and Mr. Harte, the more. I need not tell you how attentive the Romans and Greeks, particularly the Athenians, were to this object. It is also a study among the Italians and the French, witness their respective Academies and Dictionaries, for improving and fixing their languages. To our shame be it spoken, it is less attended to here than in any polite country; but that is no reason why you should not attend to it; on the contrary, it will distinguish you the more. Cicero says, very truly, that it is glorious to excel other men in that very article, in which men excel brutes; *speech.*

Constant experience has shown me, that great purity and elegance of style, with a graceful elocution, cover a multitude of faults, in either a speaker or a writer. For my own part, I confess (and I believe most people are of my mind) that if a speaker should ungracefully mutter or stammer out to me the sense of an angel, deformed by barbarisms and solecisms, or larded with vulgarisms, he should never speak to me a second time, if I could help it. Gain the heart, or you gain nothing; the eyes and the ears are the only roads to the heart. Merit and knowledge will not gain hearts, though they will secure them when gained. Pray have that truth ever in your mind. Engage the eyes, by your address, air, and motions; sooth the ears, by the elegancy and harmony of your diction: the heart will certainly follow; and the whole man, or woman, will as certainly follow the heart. I must repeat it to you, over and over again, that, with all the knowledge which you may have at present, or hereafter acquire; and with all the merit that ever man had, if you have not a graceful address, liberal and engaging manners, a prepossessing air, and a good degree of eloquence in speaking and writing, you will be nobody: but will have the daily mortification of seeing people, with not one tenth part of your merit or knowledge, get the start of you, and disgrace you, both in company and in business.

You have read Quintilian; the best book[41] in the world to form an orator: pray read *Cicero de Oratore;* the best book in the world to finish one. Translate and retranslate, from and to Latin, Greek, and English; make yourself a pure and elegant English style: it requires nothing but application. I do not find that God has made you a Poet; and I am very glad that he has not; therefore, for God's sake, make yourself an

Orator, which you may do. Though I still call you boy, I consider you no longer as such; and when I reflect upon the prodigious quantity of manure that has been laid upon you, I expect that you should produce more at eighteen, than uncultivated soils do at eight-and-twenty.

Pray tell Mr. Harte, that I have received his letter of the 13th, N.S. Mr. Smith[42] was much in the right, not to let you go, at this time of the year, by sea; in the summer you may navigate as much as you please: as for example; from Leghorn to Genoa, etc. Adieu.

FROM

[LETTERS . . .
TO HIS GODSON . . .]

In 1755, when Philip Stanhope was twenty-three and already revealing by his apparently permanent awkwardness that his father's tuition had been largely unsuccessful, a son was born to Chesterfield's fourth cousin, Arthur Stanhope, who hopefully named the infant Philip after Chesterfield and asked Chesterfield to become the boy's godfather and to superintend his education. Avidly seizing this second chance to shape, by correspondence, the complete gentleman, Chesterfield began writing weekly letters to his godson, nicknamed Sturdy, when the boy was six; Chesterfield wrote him over two hundred letters, and the correspondence was terminated only by Chesterfield's death. Sturdy, who lived until 1815, inherited the earldom.

The text is that of *Letters of Philip Dormer, Fourth Earl of Chesterfield, to His Godson and Successor,* ed. the Earl of Carnarvon (1890). Diacritical marks have been supplied for French expressions.

[Bath, December 12, 1765]

MY DEAR LITTLE BOY,

If you have not command enough over yourself to conquer your humour, as I hope you will, and as I am sure every rational creature may have, never go into company while the fit of ill humour is upon you.

---

41. **the best book:** *Institutio Oratoria* by Marcus Fabius Quintilianus (A.D. 40–c. 100), Latin rhetorician.

42. **Mr. Smith:** Joseph Smith, British consul at Venice from 1740 to 1760.

Instead of companys diverting you in those moments, you will displease and probably shock them, and you will part worse friends than you met. But whenever you find in yourself a disposition to sullenness, contradiction, or testyness, it will be in vain to seek for a cure abroad; stay at home, let your humour ferment and work itself off. Chearfullness and good humour are of all qualifications the most amiable in company, for though they do not necessarily imply good nature and good breeding, they act them at least very well, and that is all that is required in mixed company. I have indeed known some very ill-natured people who are very good humoured in company, but I never knew any body generally ill humoured in company, who was not essentially ill natured. When there is no malevolence in the heart, there is always a chearfullness and ease in the countenance and the manners. By good humour and chearfullness, I am far from meaning noisy mirth and loud peals of laughter, which are the distinguishing characteristicks of the vulgar and the ill-bred, whose mirth is a kind of a storm. Observe it, the vulgar often laugh, but never smile, whereas well bred people often smile, and seldom or never laugh. A witty thing never excited laughter, it pleases only the mind and never distorts the countenance. A glaring absurdity, a blunder, a silly accident, and those things that are generally called Comical may excite a momentary laugh, though never a loud nor a long one among well bred people. Sudden passion is called a short lived madness; it is a madness indeed, but the fitts of it generally return so often in cholerick people that it may well be called a continuall madness. Should you happen to be of this unfortunate disposition, which God forbid, make it your constant study to subdue, or at least to check it. When you find your choler rising, resolve neither to speak to, nor answer the person who excites it, but stay till you find it subsiding, and then speak deliberately. I have known many people, who by the rapidity of their speech have run away with themselves into a passion. I will mention to you a trifling and perhaps you will think a ridiculous receipt, toward checking the excess of passion, of which I think that I have experienced the utility myself. Do everything in Menuet time, speak, think, and move always in that measure, equally free from the dullness of slow, or the hurry and huddle of quick time. This movement moreover will allow you some moments to think forwards, and the Graces to accompany what you say or do, for they are never represented, as either running, or dozing. Observe a man in a passion, see his eyes glaring, his face inflamed, his limbs trembling, and his tongue stammering and faulting with rage, and then ask yourself calmly whether you would upon any account be that human wild beast. Such creatures are hated and dreaded in all companys where they are let loose, as people do not chuse to be exposed to the disagreeable necessity of either knocking down these brutes or being knocked down by them. Do on the contrary endeavour to be cooll and steddy upon all occasions. The advantages of such a steddy calmness, are innumerable, and would be too tedious to relate. It may be acquired by care and reflexion. If it could not, that reason which distinguishes men from brutes, would be given to us to very little purpose. As a proof of this I never saw, and scarcely ever heard of a quaker in a passion. In truth there is in that sect, a decorum, a decency, and an amiable simplicity, that I know in no other. Having mentioned the *Graces* in this letter, I cannot end it, without recommending to you most earnestly the advice of the wisest of the Antients, to sacrifice to them devoutly and daily. When they are propitious they adorn everything and engage everybody.—But are they to be acquired? Yes to a certain degree they are, by attention, observation, and assiduous worship. Nature, I admitt, must first have made you capable of adopting them, and then observation and imitation will make them in time your own. There are *Graces* of the mind as well as of the body; the former give an easy engaging turn to the thoughts and the expressions, the latter to motions, attitude and address. No man perhaps ever possessed them all; he would be too happy that did, but if you will attentively observe those gracefull and engaging manners, which please you most in other people, you may easily collect what will equally please others in you, and engage the majority of the *Graces* on your side, insure the casting vote, and be returned *Aimable*. There are people whom the *Précieuse* of Molière,[1] very justly, though very affectedly calls *les Antipodes des Grâces*. If these unhappy people are formed by nature invincibly *Maussades*[2] and awkward, they are to be pitied, rather than blamed or ridiculed, but nature has disinherited few people to that degree.

LETTERS TO HIS GODSON. **1. the Précieuse . . . Molière:** an affected and snobbish young lady in Molière's one-act farce *Les Précieuses Ridicules* (1659). **2. Maussades:** disagreeable.

Edward Young

1683–1765

Edward Young was born in the Hampshire village of Upham, where his father was rector. He entered Winchester in 1695 and New College, Oxford, in 1702; within the year he moved to Corpus Christi. The length of his preparation at Winchester suggests that he was not precocious. Law was his subject, and in 1708 he became a fellow of All Souls, where he proceeded Bachelor of Civil Laws in 1714 and Doctor in 1719. Oxford was his headquarters until his mid-forties. As a young university scholar, he belonged to a coterie of minor poets, and he occasionally visited the London coffee houses to hear the literary conversation of Addison and his circle; before long he had met Colley Cibber and Richard Steele, and later he knew Pope, Swift, and the novelist Samuel Richardson.

He was an ambitious young man. As Henry C. Shelley observes, "He began to publish at a time when literary effusions were regarded as the surest passport to preferment in the State and Church; and . . . he was never able to quite disabuse himself of the idea. . . ." His first attempt to recommend himself to those who controlled perquisites and sinecures was *An Epistle to the Right Honorable the Lord Lansdown* (1713), a panegyric in heroic couplets. When this performance failed of its purpose, he brought out *A Poem on the Last Day* (1714), a diffuse couplet treatment of the Day of Judgment; this poem he dedicated to Queen Anne, who, unluckily, died two months after its appearance. His third try was *The Force of Religion, or Vanquished Love* (1714), a couplet poem on the tragedy of Lady Jane Grey; this he dedicated to the Countess of Salisbury, but again he was disappointed. After one more attempt of this kind, *A Paraphrase on Part of the Book of Job* (1719), dedicated to the Earl of Macclesfield, Young, by now a slightly disillusioned man of the town, turned to the writing of blank-verse tragedy.

His *Busiris, King of Egypt*, produced at Drury Lane in 1719, retained many of the mannerisms of Restoration heroic drama and provided Fielding with a ready object of ridicule in *The Tragedy of Tragedies* (1731). Young had better luck with *The Revenge*, produced in 1721, which proved popular throughout the century. His last play, *The Brothers*, although probably finished by 1726, waited until 1753 for production.

Satire engaged him next. In 1728 appeared his *Love of Fame, the Universal Passion, in Seven Characteristical Satires*, a volume that collected the heroic-couplet satires he had been publishing since 1725. These Horation satires, which Johnson pronounced "a very great performance," anticipated by some eight years Pope's triumphs in this genre. And most contemporary critics ranked them just below Pope's.

But by his forty-fourth year, having tried in succession panegyric, religious verse, tragedy, and satire, Young despaired not merely of attaining preferment by his writing but even of earning a steady income. He consequently took holy orders. Because he soon became Royal Chaplain to George II, he easily assumed that richer sinecures were in the offing. But he received only the clerical living at Welwyn, a Hertfordshire village some twenty miles from London. Here he moved in 1730, and here he lived for the rest of his life.

He married in 1731 and for nine years led a quiet, rural family life. When his wife died in 1740, he was profoundly affected; according to his son, he was never cheerful afterward. Two years later he brought out a curiously somber meditative and argumentative poem in blank verse, *The Complaint, or Night Thoughts on Life, Death, and Immortality*. Further copious installments followed until the work was complete in nine "Nights"—and over nine thousand lines—in 1746. Collected and reissued in 1747, it swept into vast popularity both in England and on the Continent, where it was translated even into Portuguese and Hungarian. The poem consists largely of elegiac meditations designed to mitigate the fear of death and of ratiocinative Christian consolations useful to the bereaved; its orthodoxy, enlivened by occasional Gothic tremors and graveyard thrills, found an enthusiastic audience. Almost forty editions appeared before the end of the century, and a favorite gift item until the middle of the next century was a volume that included within one binding *Paradise Lost*, Thomson's *Seasons*, and Young's *Night Thoughts*. John and Charles Wesley used the *Night Thoughts* for public devotional purposes; Boswell sought comfort from it; Burke admired it; Blake illustrated it; Johnson approved its use of blank verse; and even Robespierre kept his copy close at hand. Young became widely famed. Gray's friend William Mason, traveling in Germany in 1755, wrote home describing a woman who "askd me who was the famous Poet that writ the Nitt toats. I replyd Doct^r Yonge. She begd leave to drink his Health in a Glass of sweet wine adding that he was her favrite English Author. We toasted the Doctor."

Despite the fame the *Night Thoughts* brought him, Young remained placidly at Welwyn, where he gardened, drank the local therapeutic waters, and played host to Richardson and "Old Cibber," now in his eighties. He never entirely abandoned his efforts to attain a pension, but he was disappointed again and again. In 1755 his moral disgust at the age boiled over in his anonymous treatise *The Centaur Not Fabulous*, which, in *Five Letters to a Friend*, attacked the infidelity and sensuality of "The Life in Vogue." In the profligate and the licentious, he explained, "as in the fabled Centaur, the brute runs away with the man." His enthusiasm for the idea of the dignity and the power of the human will found expression once more before his death, in his famous *Conjectures on Original Composition* (1759), published when he was seventy-six. Finally, in 1761, he was granted a court place as Clerk of the Closet to the Princess Dowager, but by this time he was feeble and almost blind. His last long poem, published when he was seventy-seven, is titled *Resignation*.

For bibliography consult the list of recent studies in Francesco Cordasco's *Edward Young: A Handlist of Critical Notices and Studies* (1950). Young's *Complete Works* is edited by John Doran (2 vols., 1854). *Conjectures* has been edited by E. J. Morley (1918). A serviceable biography is H. C. Shelley's *The Life and Letters of Edward Young* (1914).

CONJECTURES
ON ORIGINAL
COMPOSITION . . .

Young was at work on the *Conjectures* as early as December, 1756. His friend Richardson, whose *History of Sir Charles Grandison* (1753) had recently appeared, helped him make extensive revisions before the essay was published in 1759. Although no name appeared on the title page, Young's authorship was guessed immediately.

The *Conjectures* may be regarded as one of the last oblique contributions to the late-Renaissance controversy between the Ancients and the Moderns. Young's "Modern" critical position has been traced to his reading of the treatise *On the Sublime*, then attributed to the Greek author Longinus, and "Longinian" influence has been noted in the neo-Euphuistic style as well.

The essay was widely read and generally approved, although some, like Hugh Blair, thought it displayed "too much glitter." Boswell records that Johnson, who had heard Young read it aloud at Richardson's, "was surprised to find the Doctor receive as novelties what Mr. Johnson thought very common thoughts." But Johnson's friend Mrs. Thrale was dazzled: "In the *Conjectures upon Original Composition*," she observed, ". . . we shall perhaps read the wittiest piece of prose our whole language has to boast; yet from its over twinkling, it seems little gazed at and too little admired perhaps."

The text is that of the first edition, *Conjectures on Original Composition. In a Letter to the Author of Sir Charles Grandison* (1759). We have incorporated the substantive variants of the second edition (1759).

DEAR SIR,

We confess the Follies of Youth without a Blush; not so, those of Age. However, keep me a little in countenance by considering, that Age wants Amusements more, tho' it can justify them less, than the preceding periods of life. How you may relish the Pastime here sent you, I know not. It is miscellaneous in its Nature, somewhat licentious in its Conduct; and, perhaps, not over important in its End. However, I have endeavoured to make some amends, by digressing into subjects more important, and more suitable to my season of life. A serious Thought standing single among many of a lighter nature, will sometimes strike the careless Wanderer after Amusement only, with useful Awe: As monumental Marbles scattered in a wide Pleasure-Garden (and such there are) will call to Recollection those who would never have sought it in a Churchyard-walk of mournful Yews.

To One such Monument I may conduct you, in which is a hidden Lustre, like the sepulchral Lamps of old; but not like those will This be extinguished, but shine the brighter for being produced, after so long Concealment, into open Day.

You remember that your worthy Patron, and our common Friend,[1] put some Questions on the *Serious Drama*, at the same time when he desired our Sentiments on *Original*, and on *Moral* Composition. Tho' I despair of breaking thro' the frozen Obstructions of Age, and Care's incumbent[2] Cloud, into that Flow of thought, and Brightness of expression, which Subjects so polite require; yet will I hazard some Conjectures on them.

I begin with *Original* Composition; and the more willingly, as it seems an original subject to me, who have seen nothing hitherto written on it: but, first, a few Thoughts on Composition in general. Some are of Opinion, that its Growth, at present, is too luxuriant and that the Press is overcharged. Overcharged, I think, it could never be, if none were admitted, but such as brought their Imprimatur from *sound Understanding*, and the *Public Good*. Wit, indeed, however brilliant, should not be permitted to gaze self-enamour'd on its useless Charms, in that Fountain of

CONJECTURES ON ORIGINAL COMPOSITION. **1. your . . . Friend:** a fiction: Richardson suggested the topic. (See the selection from Richardson in Part Two.) **2. incumbent:** weighty.

Fame (if so I may call the Press,) if Beauty is all that it has to boast; but, like the first *Brutus*, it should sacrifice its most darling Offspring to the sacred interests of Virtue, and real Service of mankind.[3]

This Restriction allowed, the more Composition the better. To Men of Letters, and Leisure, it is not only a noble Amusement, but a sweet Refuge; it improves their Parts, and promotes their Peace: It opens a back-door out of the Bustle of this busy, and idle world, into a delicious Garden of Moral and Intellectual fruits and flowers; the Key of which is denied to the rest of mankind. When stung with idle Anxieties, or teazed with fruitless Impertinence, or yawning over insipid Diversions, then we perceive the Blessing of a letter'd recess. With what a Gust do we retire to our disinterested, and immortal Friends in our Closet, and find our minds, when applied to some favourite Theme, as naturally, and as easily quieted, and refreshed, as a peevish Child (and peevish Children are we all till we fall asleep) when laid to the breast? Our Happiness no longer lives on Charity; nor bids fair for a fall, by leaning on that most precarious, and thorny Pillow, another's Pleasure, for our repose. How independent of the world is he, who can daily find new Acquaintance, that at once enter-tain, and improve him, in the little World, the minute but fruitful Creation, of his own mind?

These advantages *Composition* affords us, whether we write ourselves, or in more humble amusement peruse the Works of others. While we bustle thro' the thronged walks of public Life, it gives us a respite, at least, from Care; a pleasing Pause of refreshing Recollection. If the Country is our Choice, or Fate, there it rescues us from *Sloth* and *Sensuality*, which, like obscene vermin, are apt gradually to creep un-perceived into the delightful bowers of our retirement, and to poison all its sweets. Conscious guilt robs the Rose of its scent, the Lilly of its lustre; and makes an *Eden* a deflowered, and dismal scene.

Moreover, if we consider life's endless Evils, what can be more prudent, than to provide for consolation under them? A consolation under them the wisest of men have found in the pleasures of the Pen. Witness, among many more, *Thucydides, Xenophon, Tully, Ovid, Seneca, Pliny* the younger, who says, *In uxoris infirmitate, & amicorum periculo, aut morte turbatus, ad studia, unicum doloris levamentum, confugio.*[4] And why not add to these their modern Equals, *Chaucer, Rawleigh, Bacon, Milton, Clarendon,*[5] under the same shield, unwounded by misfortune, and nobly smiling in distress?

Composition was a Cordial to These under the Frowns of Fortune; but Evils there are, which her Smiles cannot prevent, or cure. Among these are the Languors of old Age. If those are held honourable, who in a hand benumbed by Time have grasped the just sword in defence of their Country; shall they be less esteemed, whose unsteady Pen vibrates to the last in the cause of Religion, of Virtue, of Learning? Both These are happy in This, that by fixing their attention on objects most important, they escape numberless little Anxieties, and that *Tedium Vitæ*[6] which often hangs so heavy on its evening hours. May not This insinuate some Apology for my spilling Ink, and spoiling Paper, so late in Life?

But there are, who write with vigor, and success, to the world's Delight, and their own Renown. These are the glorious fruits where Genius prevails. The mind of a man of Genius is a fertile and pleasant field, pleasant as *Elysium*, and fertile as *Tempe;*[7] it enjoys a perpetual Spring. Of that Spring, *Originals* are the fairest Flowers: *Imitations* are of quicker growth, but fainter bloom. *Imitations* are of two kinds; one of Nature, one of Authors: The first we call *Originals*, and confine the term *Imitation* to the second. I shall not enter into the curious enquiry of what is, or is not, strictly speaking, *Original*, content with what all must allow, that some Compositions are more so than others; and the more they are so, I say, the better. *Originals* are, and ought to be, great Favourites, for they are great Benefactors; they extend the Republic of Letters, and add a new province to its dominion: *Imitators* only give us a sort of Duplicates of what we had, possibly much better, before; increasing the mere Drug of books, while all that makes them valuable, *Knowlege* and *Genius*, are at a stand. The pen of an *Original* Writer, like *Armida's* wand,[8] out of a barren

---

4. In . . . confugio: "Distracted by my wife's sickness and by the serious illness or death of my friends, I fly to my studies, the sole comfort of my sorrow" (*Epistles*, VIII. xix). **5. Clarendon:** Edward Hyde (1609–74), Earl of Clarendon, wrote his *History of the Rebellion* (1702–04) while in exile in France. **6. Tedium Vitæ:** weariness of life. **7. pleasant . . . Tempe:** Elysium is the classical paradise; Tempe is a Greek valley sacred to Apollo. **8. Armida's wand:** Armida is a powerful enchantress in Tasso's *Jerusalem Delivered* (1576–93).

3. sacrifice . . . mankind: The Roman Lucius Junius Brutus is said to have executed his own two sons for attempting to restore the reign of the despotic Tarquins.

waste calls a blooming spring: Out of that blooming spring an *Imitator* is a transplanter of Laurels, which sometimes die on removal, always languish in a foreign soil.

But suppose an *Imitator* to be most excellent (and such there are), yet still he but nobly builds on another's foundation; his Debt is, at least, equal to his Glory; which therefore, on the ballance, cannot be very great. On the contrary, an *Original*, tho' but indifferent (its *Originality* being set aside,) yet has something to boast; it is something to say with him in *Horace*,

Meo *sum Pauper in ære;*[9]

and to share ambition with no less than *Cæsar*, who declared he had rather be the First in a Village, than the Second at *Rome*.

Still farther: An *Imitator* shares his crown, if he has one, with the chosen Object of his Imitation; an *Original* enjoys an undivided applause. An *Original* may be said to be of a *vegetable* nature; it rises spontaneously from the vital root of Genius; it *grows*, it is not *made*: Imitations are often a sort of *Manufacture* wrought up by those *Mechanics*, *Art*, and *Labour*, out of pre-existent materials not their own.

Again: We read *Imitation* with somewhat of his languor, who listens to a twice-told tale: Our spirits rouze at an *Original*; that is a perfect stranger, and all throng to learn what news from a foreign land: And tho' it comes, like an *Indian* Prince, adorned with feathers only, having little of weight; yet of our attention it will rob the more Solid, if not equally New: Thus every Telescope is lifted at a new-discovered star; it makes a hundred Astronomers in a moment, and denies equal notice to the sun. But if an *Original*, by being as excellent, as new, adds admiration to surprize, then are we at the Writer's mercy; on the strong wing of his Imagination, we are snatched from *Britain* to *Italy*, from Climate to Climate, from Pleasure to Pleasure; we have no Home, no Thought, of our own; till the Magician drops his Pen: And then falling down into ourselves, we awake to flat Realities, lamenting the change, like the Beggar who dreamt himself a Prince.

It is with Thoughts, as it is with Words; and with both, as with Men; they may grow old, and die. Words tarnished, by passing thro' the mouths of the Vulgar, are laid aside as inelegant, and obsolete. So Thoughts, when become too common, should lose their Currency; and we should send new metal to the Mint, that is, new meaning to the Press. The Division of tongues at *Babel* did not more effectually debar men from *making themselves a name* (as the Scripture speaks,)[10] than the too great Concurrence, or Union of tongues will do for ever. We may as well grow good by another's Virtue, or fat by another's Food, as famous by another's Thought. The world will pay its Debt of Praise but once; and instead of applauding, explode a second Demand, as a Cheat.

If it is said, that most of the *Latin* Classics, and all the *Greek*, except, perhaps, *Homer*, *Pindar*, and *Anacreon*, are in the number of *Imitators*, yet receive our highest applause; our answer is, That They, tho' not *real*, are *accidental Originals;* the works they imitated, few excepted, are lost: They, on their Fathers' Decease, enter, as lawful Heirs, on their Estates in Fame: The Fathers of our Copyists are still in possession; and secured in it, in spite of *Goths*, and Flames, by the perpetuating power of the Press. Very late must a modern *Imitator's* Fame arrive, if it waits for their Decease.

An *Original* enters early upon Reputation: *Fame*, fond of new Glories, sounds her Trumpet in Triumph at its birth; and yet how few are awaken'd by it into the noble ambition of like attempts? Ambition is sometimes no Vice in life; it is always a Virtue in Composition. High in the towering *Alps* is the Fountain of the *Po;* high in Fame, and in Antiquity, is the Fountain of an *Imitator's* Undertaking; but the River, and the Imitation, humbly creep along the Vale. So few are our *Originals*, that, if all other books were to be burnt, the letter'd World would resemble some Metropolis in flames, where a few incombustible buildings, a Fortress, Temple, or Tower, lift their Heads, in melancholy Grandeur, amid the mighty ruin. Compared with this Conflagration, old *Omar*[11] lighted up but a small Bonfire, when he heated the baths of the Barbarians, for eight months together, with the famed *Alexandrian* Library's inestimable spoils, that no prophane book might obstruct the triumphant progress of his holy *Alcoran* round the Globe.

---

9. **Meo . . . ære:** "I am poor but not, at least, in debt" (*Epistles*, II. ii. 12).

10. **The Division . . . speaks:** See Gen. 11:1–9. **11. Omar:** (*c.* 581–644) a Mohammedan caliph; the famed Alexandrian library was actually burned long before Omar captured the city in 641.

But why are *Originals* so few? not because the Writer's harvest is over, the great Reapers of Antiquity having left nothing to be gleaned after them; nor because the human mind's teeming time is past, or because it is incapable of putting forth unprecedented births; but because illustrious Examples *engross*, *prejudice*, and *intimidate*. They *engross* our attention, and so prevent a due inspection of ourselves; they *prejudice* our Judgment in favour of their abilities, and so lessen the sense of our own; and they *intimidate* us with the splendor of their Renown, and thus under Diffidence bury our strength. Nature's Impossibilities, and those of Diffidence, lie wide asunder.

Let it not be suspected, that I would weakly insinuate any thing in favour of the Moderns, as compared with antient Authors; no, I am lamenting their great Inferiority. But I think it is no *necessary* Inferiority; that it is not from divine Destination, but from some cause far beneath the moon:[12] I think that human Souls, thro' all periods, are equal; that due care, and exertion, would set us nearer our immortal Predecessors than we are at present; and he who questions and confutes this, will show abilities not a little tending toward a proof of that Equality, which he denies.

After all, the first Antients had no Merit in being *Originals*: They could *not* be *Imitators*. Modern Writers have a *Choice* to make; and therefore have a Merit in their power. They may soar in the Regions of *Liberty*, or move in the soft Fetters of easy *Imitation;* and *Imitation* has as many plausible Reasons to urge, as *Pleasure* had to offer to *Hercules. Hercules* made the Choice of an Hero,[13] and *so* became immortal.

Yet let not Assertors of Classic Excellence imagine, that I deny the Tribute it so well deserves. He that admires not antient Authors, betrays a secret he would conceal, and tells the world, that he does not understand them. Let us be as far from neglecting, as from copying, their admirable Compositions: Sacred be their Rights, and inviolable their Fame. Let our Understanding feed on theirs; they afford the noblest nourishment: But let them nourish, not annihilate,

our own. When we read, let our Imagination kindle at their Charms; when we write, let our Judgment shut them out of our Thoughts; treat even *Homer* himself, as his royal Admirer[14] was treated by the Cynic; bid him stand aside, nor shade our Composition from the beams of our own Genius; for nothing *Original* can rise, nothing Immortal can ripen, in any other Sun.

Must we then, you say, not imitate antient Authors? Imitate them, by all means; but imitate aright. He that imitates the divine *Iliad*, does not imitate *Homer;* but he who takes the same method, which *Homer* took, for arriving at a capacity of accomplishing a work so great. Tread in his steps to the sole Fountain of Immortality; drink where he drank, at the true *Helicon,*[15] that is, at the breast of Nature: Imitate; but imitate not the *Composition*, but the *Man*. For may not this Paradox pass into a Maxim? *viz.* "The less we copy the renowned Antients, we shall resemble them the more."

But possibly you may reply, that you must either imitate *Homer*, or depart from Nature. Not so: For suppose You was to change place, in time, with *Homer;* then, if you write naturally, you might as well charge *Homer* with an imitation of You. Can you be said to imitate *Homer* for writing *so*, as you would have written, if *Homer* had never been? As far as a regard to Nature, and sound Sense, will permit a Departure from your great Predecessors; so far, ambitiously, depart from them; the farther from them in *Similitude*, the nearer are you to them in *Excellence;* you rise by it into an *Original;* become a noble Collateral, not an humble Descendant from them. Let us build our Compositions with the Spirit, and in the Taste, of the Antients; but not with their Materials: Thus will they resemble the structures of *Pericles* at *Athens*, which *Plutarch* commends for having had an air of Antiquity as soon as they were built. All Eminence, and Distinction, lies out of the beaten road; Excursion, and Deviation, are necessary to find it; and the more remote your Path from the Highway, the more reputable; if, like poor *Gulliver* (of whom anon,) you fall not into a Ditch, in your way to Glory.

What glory to come near, what glory to reach, what

12. **that . . . moon:** [Young's note] Enquiry into the Life of *Homer*, p. 76. [Young's reference is to Thomas Blackwell's *An Enquiry into the Life and Writings of Homer* (1735); the passage alluded to contains a speculation that planetary influence perhaps causes genius and originality.] 13. **the Choice . . . Hero:** It is said that Hercules, confronted with a choice between Pleasure and Virtue (personified as women), chose Virtue.

14. **his . . . Admirer:** Alexander the Great, who, according to legend, once asked the Cynic Diogenes what he could do for him. Diogenes replied, "Just stand aside so you don't keep the sun off me." 15. **Helicon:** a mountain sacred to the Muses; location of the sacred springs.

glory (presumptuous thought!) to surpass, our Predecessors? And is that then in Nature absolutely impossible? Or is it not, rather, contrary to Nature to fail in it? Nature herself sets the Ladder, all wanting is our ambition to climb. For by the bounty of Nature we are as strong as our Predecessors; and by the favour of Time (which is but another Round in Nature's Scale,) we stand on higher ground. As to the *First*, were *they* more than men? Or are *we* less? Are not our minds cast in the same mould with those before the Flood? The flood affected Matter, Mind escaped. As to the *Second;* tho' we are Moderns, the World is an Antient; more antient far, than when they, whom we most admire, filled it with their Fame. Have we not their Beauties, as stars, to guide; their Defects, as rocks, to be shunn'd; the Judgment of Ages on both, as a chart to conduct, and a sure helm to steer us in our passage to greater Perfection than Theirs? And shall we be stopt in our rival pretensions to Fame by this just Reproof?

> *Stat contra, dicitque tibi tua Pagina,*
> *Fur es.*[16]
>   MART.

It is by a sort of noble Contagion, from a general familiarity with their Writings, and not by any particular sordid Theft, that we can be the better for those who went before us. Hope we, from Plagiarism, any Dominion in Literature; as that of *Rome* arose from a nest of Thieves?

Rome was a powerful Ally to many States; antient Authors are our powerful Allies; but we must take heed, that they do not succour, till they enslave, after the manner of *Rome*. Too formidable an Idea of their Superiority, like a Spectre, would fright us out of a proper use of our Wits; and dwarf our Understanding, by making a Giant of theirs. Too great Awe for them lays Genius under restraint, and denies it that free scope, that full elbow-room, which is requisite for striking its most masterly strokes. Genius is a Master-workman, Learning is but an Instrument; and an Instrument, tho' most valuable, yet not always indispensable. Heaven will not admit of a Partner in the accomplishment of some favourite Spirits; but rejecting all human means, assumes the whole glory to itself. Have not some, tho' not famed for Erudition, *so* written, as almost to persuade us, that they shone

brighter, and soared higher, for escaping the boasted aid of that proud Ally?

Nor is it strange; for what, for the most part, mean we by Genius, but the Power of accomplishing great things without the means generally reputed necessary to that end? A *Genius* differs from a *good Understanding*, as a Magician from a good Architect; *That* raises his structure by means invisible; *This* by the skilful use of common tools. Hence Genius has ever been supposed to partake of something Divine. *Nemo unquam vir magnus fuit, sine aliquo afflatu Divino.*[17]

Learning, destitute of this superior Aid, is fond, and proud, of what has cost it much pains; is a great Lover of Rules, and Boaster of famed Examples: As Beauties less perfect, who owe half their Charms to cautious Art, learning inveighs against natural unstudied Graces, and small harmless inaccuracies, and sets rigid Bounds to that Liberty, to which Genius often owes its supreme Glory; but the No-Genius its frequent Ruin. For unprescribed Beauties, and unexampled Excellence, which are Characteristics of *Genius*, lie without the Pale of *Learning's* Authorities, and Laws; which Pale, Genius must leap to come at them: But by that Leap, if Genius is wanting, we break our Necks; we lose that little credit, which possibly we might have enjoyed before. For Rules, like Crutches, are a needful Aid to the Lame, tho' an Impediment to the Strong. A *Homer* casts them away; and, like his *Achilles*,

> *Jura negat sibi nata, nihil non arrogat,*[18]

by native force of mind. There is something in Poetry beyond Prose-reason; there are Mysteries in it not to be explained, but admired; which render mere Prose-men Infidels to their Divinity. And here pardon a second Paradox; *viz.* "*Genius* often then deserves most to be praised, when it is most sure to be condemned; that is, when its Excellence, from mounting high, to weak eyes is quite out of sight."

If I might speak farther of Learning, and Genius, I would compare Genius to Virtue, and Learning to Riches. As Riches are most wanted where there is least Virtue; so Learning where there is least Genius. As Virtue without much Riches can give Happiness,

---

16. **Stat . . . es:** "Your page confronts you and calls you a thief" (Martial, *Epigrams*, I. lv. 12).

17. **Nemo . . . Divino:** "No one was ever a great man without some divine inspiration" (Cicero, *De Natura Deorum*, II. 167). 18. **Jura . . . arrogat:** "He denies that laws apply to him and claims everything for his own" (Horace, *Ars Poetica*, l. 122).

so Genius without much Learning can give Renown. As it is said in *Terence, Pecuniam negligere interdum maximum est Lucrum;*[19] so to neglect of Learning, Genius sometimes owes its greater glory. Genius, therefore, leaves but the second place, among men of letters, to the Learned. It is their Merit, and Ambition, to fling light on the works of Genius, and point out its Charms. We most justly reverence their informing Radius for that favour; but we must much more admire the radiant Stars pointed out by them.

A Star of the first magnitude among the Moderns was *Shakespeare;* among the Antients, *Pindar;* who, (as *Vossius*[20] tells us) boasted of his No-learning, calling himself the Eagle, for his Flight above it. And such Genii as these may, indeed, have much reliance on their own native powers. For Genius may be compared to the natural strength of the body; Learning to the superinduced Accoutrements of Arms: if the First is equal to the proposed exploit, the Latter rather encumbers, than assists; rather retards, than promotes, the Victory. *Sacer nobis inest Deus,*[21] says Seneca. With regard to the Moral world, *Conscience,* with regard to the Intellectual, *Genius,* is that God within. Genius can set us right in Composition, without the Rules of the Learned; as Conscience sets us right in Life, without the Laws of the Land: *This,* singly, can make us Good, as Men; *That,* singly, as Writers, can, sometimes, make us Great.

I say, sometimes, because there is a Genius, which stands in need of Learning to make it shine. Of Genius there are two species, an Earlier, and a Later; or call them *Infantine,* and *Adult.* An Adult Genius comes out of Nature's hand, as *Pallas* out of *Jove's* head, at full growth, and mature: *Shakespeare's* Genius was of this kind: On the contrary, *Swift* stumbled at the threshold, and set out for Distinction on feeble knees:[22] His was an Infantine Genius; a Genius, which, like other Infants, must be nursed, and educated, or it will come to nought: Learning is its Nurse, and Tutor; but this Nurse may overlay with an indigested Load, which smothers common sense; and this Tutor may mislead, with pedantic Prejudice, which vitiates the best understanding: As too great admirers of the Fathers of the Church have sometimes set up their Authority against the true Sense of Scripture; so too great admirers of the Classical Fathers have sometimes set up their Authority, or Example, against Reason.

> *Neve minor, neu sit quinto productior actu*
> *Fabula.*[23]

So says Horace, so says antient Example. But Reason has not subscribed. I know but one book that can justify our implicit acquiescence in it. And (by the way) on that book a noble disdain of undue deference to prior opinion has lately cast, and is still casting, a new and inestimable light.[24]

But superstition for our predecessors set aside, the Classicks are for ever our rightful, and revered Masters in *Composition;* and our understandings bow before them: But when? When a master is wanted; which, sometimes, (as I have shown) is not the case. Some are Pupils of nature only, nor go farther to school: From such we reap often a double advantage; they not only rival the reputation of the great antient authors, but also reduce the number of mean ones among the moderns. For when they enter on subjects which have been in former hands, such is their Superiority, that, like a tenth Wave,[25] they overwhelm, and bury in oblivion all that went before: And thus not only enrich and adorn, but remove a load, and lessen the labour, of the letter'd world.

"But, you say, since *Originals* can arise from Genius only, and since Genius is so very rare, it is scarce worth while to labour a point so much, from which we can reasonably expect so little." To show that Genius is not so very rare as you imagine, I shall point out strong instances of it, in a far distant quarter from that mentioned above. The minds of the Schoolmen were almost as much cloistered as their bodies; they had but little learning, and few books; yet may the most learned be struck with some astonishment at their so singular natural sagacity, and most exquisite edge of thought. Who would expect to find *Pindar* and *Scotus, Shakespear* and *Aquinas,* of the same Party? Both

---

19. Pecuniam . . . Lucrum: "Sometimes the best way to get money is to despise it" (*Adelphoe,* l. 216). **20. Vossius:** Gerhard Johannes Vossius (1618–89), Dutch classical scholar; he discussed the Greek lyric poet Pindar (*c.* 522–443 B.C.) in his *De Artis Poeticae Natura ac Constitutione* (1647). **21. Sacer . . . Deus:** "God is within us." This idea is often repeated by Seneca but not in these exact words. **22. stumbled . . . knees:** Swift began unsuccessfully by writing Pindaric odes.

23. Neve . . . Fabula: "Let the play be neither more nor less than five acts long" (Horace, *Ars Poetica,* ll. 189–90). **24. a new . . . light:** Young perhaps has in mind *De Sacra Poesi Hebraeorum* (1753) by Robert Lowth (1710–87), Bishop of London. Lowth was one of the first to focus on Scriptural poetry as poetry. **25. tenth Wave:** It was once thought that every tenth ocean wave was larger than the nine waves preceding.

equally shew an *original*, unindebted, energy; the *Vigor igneus* and *Cælestis origo*[26] burns in both; and leaves us in doubt whether Genius is more evident in the sublime flights and beauteous flowers of poetry, or in the profound penetrations, and marvelously keen and minute distinctions, called the Thorns of the schools. There might have been more able Consuls called from the plough, than ever arrived at that honour: Many a Genius, probably, there has been, which could neither write, nor read. So that Genius, that supreme Lustre of literature, is less rare than you conceive.

By the praise of Genius we detract not from Learning; we detract not from the value of Gold, by saying that Diamond has greater still. He who disregards Learning, shows that he wants its aid; and he that overvalues it, shows that its aid has done him harm. Overvalued indeed it cannot be, if Genius, as to *Composition*, is valued more. Learning we thank, Genius we revere; That gives us pleasure, This gives us rapture; That informs, This inspires; and is itself inspired; for Genius is from Heaven, Learning from man: *This* sets us above the low, and illiterate; *That*, above the learned, and polite. Learning is borrowed knowlege; Genius is knowlege innate, and quite our own. Therefore, as *Bacon* observes, it may take a nobler name, and be called Wisdom; in which sense of wisdom, some are born wise.

But here a caution is necessary against the most fatal of errors in those Automaths, those self-taught Philosophers of our age, who set up Genius, and often, mere *fancied* Genius, not only above human Learning, but divine Truth. I have called Genius wisdom; but let it be remembered, that in the most renowned ages of the most refined Heathen wisdom (and theirs is not Christian) *"the world by wisdom knew not God, and it pleased God by the foolishness of preaching to save those that believed."*[27] In the Fairyland of Fancy, Genius may wander wild; there it has a creative power, and may reign arbitrarily over its own empire of Chimeras.[28] The wide field of Nature also lies open before it, where it may range unconfined, make what discoveries it can, and sport with its infinite objects uncontrouled, as far as visible nature extends, painting them as wantonly as it will: But what Painter of the most unbounded and exalted Genius can give us the true portrait of a Seraph? He can give us only what by his own, or others eyes, has been seen; though that indeed infinitely compounded, raised, burlesqued, dishonoured, or adorned: In like manner, who can give us divine Truth unrevealed? Much less should any presume to set aside divine Truth when revealed, as incongruous to their own Sagacities.—Is this too serious for my subject? I shall be more so before I close.

Having put in a Caveat against the most fatal of errors, from the too great indulgence of Genius, return we now to that too great suppression of it, which is detrimental to Composition; and endeavour to rescue the writer, as well as the man. I have said, that some are born Wise; but they, like those that are born Rich, by neglecting the cultivation and produce of their own Possessions, and by running in debt, may be beggared at last; and lose their reputations, as younger brothers estates, not by being born with less abilities than the rich heir, but at too late an hour.

Many a great man has been lost to himself, and the Publick, purely because great ones were born before him. *Hermias*[29] in his collections on *Homer*'s blindness, says, that *Homer* requesting the Gods to grant him a sight of *Achilles*, that Hero rose, but in armour so bright, that it struck *Homer* blind with the blaze. Let not the blaze of even *Homer*'s Muse darken us to the discernment of our own Powers; which may possibly set us above the rank of *Imitators;* who, though most excellent, and even immortal (as some of them are) yet are still but *Dii minorum gentium*,[30] nor can expect the largest share of incense, the greatest profusion of praise, on their secondary altars.

But farther still: a spirit of *Imitation* hath many ill effects; I shall confine myself to three. *First,* It deprives the liberal and politer arts of an advantage which the mechanic enjoy: In these, men are ever endeavouring to go beyond their Predecessors; in the former, to follow them. And since copies surpass not their *Originals*, as streams rise not higher than their spring, rarely so high; hence, while arts Mechanic are in perpetual progress, and increase, the Liberal are in retrogradation, and decay. *These* resemble Pyramids, are broad at bottom, but lessen exceedingly as they rise; *Those* resemble Rivers which, from a small fountain-head, are spreading ever wider, and wider,

---

26. **Vigor . . . origo:** "fiery power" and "heavenly origin" (*Aeneid*, VI. 730). 27. **the word . . . believed:** I Cor. 1:21. 28. **Chimeras:** imaginary creatures.

29. **Hermias:** presumably Hermeias, Prince of Atarneus and patron of Aristotle. 30. **Dii . . . gentium:** lesser gods.

as they run. Hence it is evident, that different portions of understanding are not (as some imagine) allotted to different periods of time; for we see, in the same period, understanding rising in one set of artists, and declining in another. Therefore *Nature* stands absolved, and our inferiority in Composition must be charged on ourselves.

Nay, so far are we from complying with a necessity, which Nature lays us under, that, *Secondly*, by a spirit of *Imitation* we counteract Nature, and thwart her design. She brings us into the world all *Originals:* No two faces, no two minds, are just alike; but all bear Nature's evident mark of Separation on them. Born *Originals*, how comes it to pass that we die *Copies?* That medling Ape *Imitation*, as soon as we come to years of *Indiscretion* (so let me speak), snatches the Pen, and blots out nature's mark of Separation, cancels her kind intention, destroys all mental Individuality; the letter'd world no longer consists of Singulars, it is a Medly, a Mass; and a hundred books, at bottom, are but One. Why are Monkies such masters of mimickry? Why receive they such a talent at imitation? Is it not as the *Spartan* slaves received a licence for ebriety; that their Betters might be ashamed of it?

The *Third* fault to be found with a spirit of *Imitation* is, that with great incongruity it makes us Poor, and Proud; makes us think little, and write much; gives us huge folios, which are little better than more reputable cushions to promote our repose. Have not some sevenfold volumes put us in mind of *Ovid*'s sevenfold channels of the *Nile* at the conflagration,

Ostia septem
Pulverulenta vacant septem sine flumine Valles.[31]

Such leaden labours are like *Lycurgus*'s iron money, which was so much less in value, than in bulk, that it required Barns for Strong-boxes, and a yoke of oxen to draw five hundred pounds.[32]

But notwithstanding these disadvantages of *Imitation*, imitation must be the lot, (and often an honourable lot it is) of most writers. If there is a famine of *Invention* in the land, like *Joseph*'s brethren,[33] we must travel far for food; we must visit the remote, and

rich, Antients; but an inventive Genius may safely stay at home; that, like the Widow's cruse,[34] is divinely replenished from within; and affords us a miraculous delight. Whether our own Genius be such, or not, we diligently should inquire; that we may not go a begging with Gold in our purse. For there is a Mine in man, which must be deeply dug ere we can conjecture its contents. Another often sees that in us, which we see not ourselves; and may there not be that in us which is unseen by both? That there may, Chance often discovers, either by a luckily chosen Theme, or a mighty Premium, or an absolute Necessity of exertion, or a noble stroke of Emulation from another's Glory; as that on *Thucydides* from hearing *Herodotus* repeat part of his History at the *Olympic* Games: Had there been no *Herodotus*, there might have been no *Thucydides*, and the world's admiration might have begun at *Livy* for excellence in that province of the pen. *Demosthenes* had the same stimulation on hearing *Callistratus;* or *Tully* might have been the first of consummate renown at the bar.

Quite clear of the dispute concerning *antient and modern Learning*, we speak not of Performance, but Powers. The modern powers are equal to those before them; modern performance in general is deplorably short. How great are the names just mentioned? Yet who will dare affirm, that as great may not rise up in some future, or even in the present age? Reasons there are why talents may not *appear*, none why they may not *exist*, as much in one period as in another. An Evocation of vegetable fruits depends on rain, air, and sun; an Evocation of the fruits of Genius no less depends on Externals. What a marvellous crop bore it in *Greece*, and *Rome?* And what a marvellous sunshine did it there enjoy? What encouragement from the nature of their governments, and the spirit of their people? *Virgil* and *Horace* owed their divine talents to Heaven; their immortal works, to men; thank *Mæcenas*, and *Augustus*[35] for them. Had it not been for these, the Genius of those poets had lain buried in their ashes. *Athens* expended on her Theatre, Painting, Sculpture, and Architecture, a tax levied for the support of a war. *Cæsar* dropt his papers when *Tully* spoke; and *Philip*[36] trembled at the voice of *Demosthenes:* And has there shone but one *Tully*, one

31. Ostia . . . Valles: "seven dry and dusty mouths, seven valleys without a stream" (*Metamorphoses*, II. 255–56). The conflagration of the earth resulted when the frightened Phaethon lost control of the sun. **32. Lycurgus's . . . pounds:** The story of the iron coinage of Lycurgus, a Spartan leader of the ninth century B.C., is told by Plutarch. **33. like . . . brethren:** See Gen. 42 ff.

34. the Widow's cruse: (pot); see I Kings 17:16. **35. Mæcenas, and Augustus:** both renowned for their support of writers. **36. Philip:** Philip of Macedon (*c.* 382–336 B.C.) conducted aggressive war against Greece and was cautioned by the orator Demosthenes in his *Philippics*.

Demosthenes, in so long a course of years? The powerful eloquence of them both in one stream, should never bear me down into the melancholy persuasion, that several have not been born, though they have not emerged. The sun as much exists in a cloudy day, as in a clear; it is outward, accidental circumstances that with regard to Genius either in nation, or age,

> *Collectas fugat nubes, solemque reducit.*[37]
>   VIRG.

As great, perhaps, greater than those mentioned (presumptuous as it may sound) may, possibly, arise; for who hath fathomed the mind of man? Its bounds are as unknown, as those of the creation; since the birth of which, perhaps, not One has so far exerted, as not to leave his Possibilities beyond his Attainments, his Powers beyond his Exploits. Forming our judgments, altogether by what *has* been done, without knowing, or at all inquiring, what possibly *might* have been done, we naturally enough fall into too mean an opinion of the human mind. If a sketch of the divine Iliad before *Homer* wrote, had been given to mankind, by some superior being, or otherwise, its execution would, probably, have appeared beyond the power of man. Now, to surpass it, we think impossible. As the First of these opinions would evidently have been a mistake, why may not the Second be so too? Both are founded on the same bottom; on our ignorance of the possible dimensions of the mind of man.

Nor are we only ignorant of the dimensions of the human mind in general, but even of our own. That a Man may be scarce less ignorant of his own powers, than an Oyster of its pearl, or a Rock of its diamond; that he may possess dormant, unsuspected abilities, till awakened by loud calls, or stung up by striking emergencies; is evident from the sudden eruption of some men, out of perfect obscurity, into publick admiration, on the strong impulse of some animating occasion; not more to the world's great surprize, than their own. Few authors of distinction but have experienced something of this nature, at the first beamings of their yet unsuspected Genius on their hitherto dark Composition: The writer starts at it, as at a lucid Meteor in the night; is much surprized; can scarce believe it true. During his happy confusion, it may be said to him, as to *Eve* at the Lake,

> *What there thou seest, fair creature! is thyself.*
>   MILT.

Genius, in this view, is like a dear Friend in our company under disguise; who, while we are lamenting his absence, drops his mask, striking us, at once, with equal surprize and joy. This sensation, which I speak of in a writer, might favour, and so promote, the fable of poetic Inspiration: A Poet of a strong imagination, and stronger vanity, on feeling it, might naturally enough realize the world's mere compliment, and think himself truly inspired. Which is not improbable; for Enthusiasts of all kinds do no less.

Since it is plain that men may be strangers to their own abilities; and by thinking meanly of them without just cause, may possibly lose a name, perhaps, a name immortal; I would find some means to prevent these Evils. Whatever promotes Virtue, promotes something more, and carries its good influence beyond the *moral* man: To prevent these evils, I borrow two golden rules from *Ethics*, which are no less golden in *composition*, than in life. 1. *Know thyself;* 2dly, *Reverence thyself.* I design to repay Ethics in a future Letter,[38] by two rules from Rhetoric for its service.

1st. *Know thyself.* Of ourselves it may be said, as *Martial* says of a bad neighbour,

> *Nil tam prope, proculque nobis.*[39]

Therefore dive deep into thy bosom; learn the depth, extent, biass, and full fort of thy mind; contract full intimacy with the Stranger within thee; excite, and cherish every spark of Intellectual light and heat, however smothered under former negligence, or scattered through the dull, dark mass of common thoughts; and collecting them into a body, let thy Genius rise (if a Genius thou hast) as the sun from Chaos; and if I should then say, like an *Indian, worship it,* (though too bold) yet should I say little more than my second rule enjoins, (*viz.*) *Reverence thyself.*

That is, let not great Examples, or Authorities, browbeat thy Reason into too great a diffidence of thyself: Thyself so reverence as to prefer the native growth of thy own mind to the richest import from abroad; such borrowed riches make us poor. The man who thus reverences himself, will soon find the world's reverence to follow his own. His works will stand distinguished; his the sole Property of them; which Property alone can confer the noble title of an *Author;* that is, of one who (to speak accurately) *thinks,* and

---

37. Collectas . . . reducit: "drives away the gathered clouds and brings back the sun" (*Aeneid*, I. 143).

38. a future Letter: Young had in mind a sequel, on moral genius; it never appeared. **39. Nil . . . nobis:** "No one is so near and yet so far away from us" (*Epigrams*, I. lxxxvi. 10).

composes; while other invaders of the Press, how voluminous, and learned soever, (with due respect be it spoken) only *read,* and *write.*

This is the difference between those two Luminaries in Literature, the well-accomplished Scholar, and the divinely-inspired Enthusiast; the *First* is, as the bright morning star; the *Second,* as the rising sun. The writer who neglects those two rules above will never stand alone; he makes one of a group, and thinks in wretched unanimity with the throng: Incumbered with the notions of others, and impoverished by their abundance, he conceives not the least embryo of new thought; opens not the least vista thro' the gloom of ordinary writers, into the bright walks of rare Imagination, and singular Design; while the true Genius is crossing all publick roads into fresh untrodden ground; he, up to the knees in Antiquity, is treading the sacred footsteps of great examples, with the blind veneration of a bigot saluting the papal toe; comfortably hoping full absolution for the sins of his own understanding, from the powerful charm of touching his idol's infallibility.

Such meanness of mind, such prostration of our own powers, proceeds from too great admiration of others. Admiration has, generally, a degree of two very bad ingredients in it; of Ignorance, and of Fear; and does mischief in Composition, and in Life. Proud as the world is, there is more superiority in it *given,* than *assumed;* And its Grandees of all kinds owe more of their elevation to the Littleness of others minds, than to the Greatness of their own. Were not prostrate spirits their voluntary pedestals, the figure they make among mankind would not stand so high. *Imitators* and *Translators* are somewhat of the pedestal-kind, and sometimes rather raise their *Original's* reputation, by showing him to be by them inimitable, than their own. *Homer* has been translated into most languages; *Ælian*[40] tells us, that the *Indians,* (hopeful tutors!) have taught him to speak their tongue. What expect we from them? Not *Homer's* Achilles, but something, which, like *Patroclus,* assumes his name, and, at its peril, appears in his stead; nor expect we *Homer's* Ulysses, gloriously bursting out of his cloud into royal grandeur, but an *Ulysses* under disguise, and a beggar to the last. Such is that inimitable Father of poetry, and Oracle of all the wise whom *Lycurgus* transcribed; and for an annual publick recital of whose works *Solon*[41]

enacted a law; that it is much to be feared, that his so numerous translations are but as the publish'd testimonials of so many nations, and ages, that this author so divine is untranslated still.

But here,

> *Cynthius aurem*
> *Vellit.*[42]—
>   VIRG.

and demands justice for his favourite, and ours. Great things he[43] has done; but he might have done greater. What a fall is it from *Homer's* numbers, free as air, lofty, and harmonious as the spheres, into childish shackles, and tinkling sounds! But, in his fall, he is still great—

> *Nor appears*
> *Less than Archangel ruin'd, and the excess*
> *Of glory obscur'd.*—
>   MILT.

Had *Milton* never wrote, *Pope* had been less to blame:[44] But when in *Milton's* Genius, *Homer,* as it were, personally rose to forbid *Britons* doing him that ignoble wrong; it is less pardonable, by that *effeminate* decoration, to put *Achilles* in petticoats a second time: How much nobler had it been, if his numbers had rolled on in full flow, through the various modulations of *masculine* melody, into those grandeurs of solemn sound, which are indispensably demanded by the native dignity of Heroick song? How much nobler, if he had resisted the temptation of that *Gothic Dæmon,*[45] which modern Poesy tasting, became mortal? O how unlike the deathless, divine harmony of three great names (how justly join'd!), of *Milton, Greece,* and *Rome?* His Verse, but for this little speck of mortality, in its extreme parts, as his Hero had in his Heel; like him, had been invulnerable, and immortal. But, unfortunately, *that* was undipt in *Helicon;* as *this,* in *Styx.*[46] Harmony as well as Eloquence is essential to poesy; and a murder of his Musick is putting half *Homer* to death. *Blank* is a term of diminution; what we mean by blank verse, is verse unfallen, uncurst; verse reclaim'd, reinthron'd in the true *language of the Gods;* who never thunder'd, nor

---

40. **Ælian:** Claudius Aelianus, third-century Roman rhetorician. 41. **Solon:** (c. 638–c. 559 B.C.), an Athenian lawgiver.

42. **Cynthius . . . Vellit:** "Apollo twitches my ear [i.e., warns me]" (Virgil, *Eclogues,* vi. 4). 43. **he:** Pope. 44. **Pope . . . blame:** in his Homeric translations (1715–26). (See Pope's Preface to the *Iliad* in Part Two.) 45. **that . . . Dæmon:** rhyme. 46. **Styx:** the main river of Hades; it was thought to possess a deadly property.

suffer'd their *Homer* to thunder, in Rhime; and therefore, I beg you, my Friend, to crown it with some nobler term; nor let the greatness of the thing lie under the defamation of such a name.

But supposing *Pope*'s *Iliad* to have been perfect in its kind; yet it is a *Translation* still; which differs as much from an *Original*, as the moon from the sun.

> —*Phœben alieno jusserat igne*
> *Impleri, solemque suo.*[47]
>   CLAUD.

But, as nothing is more easy than to write originally wrong; Originals are not here recommended, but under the strong guard of my first rule—*Know thyself*. *Lucian*,[48] who was an Original, neglected not this rule, if we may judge by his reply to one who took some freedom with him. He was, at first, an apprentice to a Statuary; and when he was reflected on as such, by being called *Prometheus*,[49] he replied, "I am indeed the Inventor of new work, the model of which I owe to none; and, if I do not execute it well, I deserve to be torne by twelve Vulturs, instead of one."

If so, O *Gulliver!* dost thou not shudder at thy brother *Lucian*'s Vulturs hovering o'er thee? Shudder on! they cannot shock thee more, than Decency has been shock'd by thee. How have thy *Houyhnhunms* thrown thy judgment from its seat, and laid thy imagination in the mire? In what ordure hast thou dipt thy pencil? What a monster hast thou made of the

> —*Human face Divine?*
>   MILT.

This writer has so satirised human nature, as to give a demonstration in himself, that it deserves to be satirised. But, say his wholesale admirers, Few could *so* have written; true, and Fewer *would*. If it required great abilities to commit the fault, greater still would have saved him from it. But whence arise such warm advocates for such a performance? From hence, (*viz.*) before a character is established, Merit makes Fame; afterwards fame makes merit. *Swift* is not commended for this piece, but this piece for *Swift*. He has given us some beauties which deserve all our praise; and our

comfort is, that his faults will not become common; for none can be guilty of them, but who have Wit as well as Reputation to spare. His wit had been less wild, if his Temper had not jostled his Judgment. If his favourite *Houyhnhunms* could write, and *Swift* had been one of them, every Horse with him would have been an Ass, and he would have written a panegyrick on mankind, saddling with much reproach the present heroes of his pen: On the contrary, being born amongst men, and, of consequence, piqued by many, and peevish at more, he has blasphemed a nature little lower than that of Angels, and assumed by far higher than they: But surely the contempt of the world is not a greater virtue, than the contempt of mankind is a vice. Therefore I wonder that, though forborn by others, the laughter-loving *Swift*, was not reproved by the venerable Dean, who could sometimes be very grave.

For I remember, as I and others were taking with him an evening's walk, about a mile out of *Dublin*, he stopt short; we passed on; but perceiving that he did not follow us, I went back; and found him fixed as a statue, and earnestly gazing upward at a noble elm, which in its uppermost branches was much withered, and decayed. Pointing at it, he said, "I shall be like that tree, I shall die at top." As in this he seemed to prophesy like the Sybils; if, like one of them, he had burnt part of his works, especially *this* blasted branch of a noble Genius, like her too, he might have risen in his demand for the rest.[50]

Would not his friend *Pope* have succeeded better in an *original* attempt? Talents untried are talents unknown. All that I know, is, that, contrary to these sentiments, he was not only an avowed professor of Imitation, but a zealous recommender of it also. Nor could he recommend any thing better, except Emulation, to those who write. One of these all writers must call to their aid; but aids they are of unequal repute. Imitation is inferiority confessed; Emulation is superiority contested, or denied; Imitation is servile, Emulation generous; That fetters, This fires; That may give a name; This, a name immortal: This made

---

47. **Phœben . . . suo:** "He decreed that the moon should shine with a light not her own but that the sun should shine with its own light" (Claudian). 48. **Lucian:** (*c.* 115–*c.* 200), Greek satirist and rhetorician. 49. **Prometheus:** a legendary Greek who stole fire from the gods; as a punishment he was sentenced to be bound to a lonely crag, where a vulture perpetually tore out and devoured his liver.

50. **he . . . rest:** It is said that the Cumaean Sibyl (a prophetess) offered Tarquinius Superbus, the last king of Rome, nine volumes of her prophecies at a high price; when he refused to pay so much, she burned three of the volumes and offered the remainder at the same price; when her offer was refused again, she burned three more. Finally, when only three remained, the king bought them and had to pay the original price.

Athens to succeeding ages the rule of taste, and the standard of perfection. Her men of Genius struck fire against each other; and kindled, by conflict, into glories, which no time shall extinguish. We thank *Eschylus* for *Sophocles;* and *Parrhasius* for *Zeuxis;*[51] *Emulation,* for both. That bids us fly the general fault of *Imitators;* bids us not be struck with the loud report of former fame, as with a Knell, which damps the spirits; but, as with a Trumpet, which inspires ardour to rival the renown'd. Emulation exhorts us, instead of learning our discipline for ever, like raw troops, under antient leaders in composition, to put those laurel'd veterans in some hazard of losing their superior posts in glory.

Such is Emulation's high-spirited advice, such her immortalizing call. *Pope* would not hear, pre-engaged with Imitation, which blessed him with all her charms. He chose rather, with his namesake of *Greece,*[52] to triumph in the old world, than to look out for a new. His taste partook the error of his Religion; it denied not worship to Saints and Angels; that is, to writers, who, canonized for ages, have received their apotheosis from established and universal fame. True Poesy, like true Religion, abhors idolatry; and though it honours the memory of the exemplary, and takes them willingly (yet cautiously) as guides in the way to glory; real, though unexampled, excellence is its only aim; nor looks it for any inspiration less than divine.

Though *Pope*'s noble Muse may boast her illustrious descent from *Homer, Virgil, Horace,* yet is an *Original* author more nobly born. As *Tacitus* says of *Curtius Rufus,*[53] an *Original* author is born of himself, is his own progenitor, and will probably propagate a numerous offspring of Imitators, to eternize his glory; while mule-like Imitators, die without issue. Therefore, tho' we stand much obliged for his giving us an *Homer,* yet had he doubled our obligation, by giving us—a *Pope.* Had he a strong Imagination, and the true

Sublime? That granted, we might have had two *Homers* instead of one, if longer had been his life; for I heard the dying swan talk over an Epic plan a few weeks before his decease.

Bacon, under the shadow of whose great name I would shelter my present attempt in favour of *Originals,* says, "Men seem not to know their own stock, and abilities; but fancy their possessions to be greater, and their abilities less, than they really are." Which is, in effect, saying, "That we ought to exert more than we do; and that, on exertion, our probability of success is greater than we conceive."

Nor have I *Bacon*'s opinion only, but his assistance too, on my side. His mighty mind travelled round the intellectual world; and, with a more than eagle's eye, saw, and has pointed out blank spaces, or dark spots in it, on which the human mind never shone: Some of these have been enlightened since; some are benighted still.

Moreover, so boundless are the bold excursions of the human mind, that in the vast void beyond real existence, it can call forth shadowy beings, and unknown worlds, as numerous, as bright, and, perhaps, as lasting, as the stars; such quite-original beauties we may call Paradisaical,

Natos sine semine flores.[54]
OVID.

When such an ample area for renowned adventure in *original* attempts lies before us, shall we be as mere leaden pipes, conveying to the present age small streams of excellence from its grand reservoir in antiquity; and those too, perhaps, mudded in the pass? *Originals* shine, like comets; have no peer in their path; are rival'd by none, and the gaze of all: All other compositions (if they shine at all) shine in clusters; like the stars in the galaxy; where, like bad neighbours, all suffer from all; each particular being diminished, and almost lost in the throng.

If thoughts of this nature prevailed; if Antients and Moderns were no longer considered as masters and pupils, but as hard-match'd rivals for renown; then moderns, by the longevity of their labours, might, one day, become antients themselves: And old Time, that best weigher of merits, to keep his balance even, might have the golden weight of an *Augustan* age in both his scales: Or rather our scale might descend;

---

51. Parrhasius for Zeuxis: The painter Parrhasius of Ephesus is said to have competed with the Greek painter Zeuxis in the fifth century B.C. According to legend, Zeuxis in one picture painted grapes so successfully that the birds flew down to peck at them. After this triumph, he turned to Parrhasius and bid him open the curtain concealing his picture; he then discovered that Parrhasius's picture was a painting of a curtain. **52. with . . . Greece:** Alexander the Great, who conquered Persia, Syria, and Egypt. **53. Curtius Rufus:** first-century A.D. Roman author of a ten-book history of Alexander's campaigns.

54. Natos . . . flores: "flowers produced without seed" (*Metamorphoses,* I. 108).

and that of antiquity (as a modern match for it strongly speaks) might *kick the beam*.[55]

And why not? For, consider, *since* an impartial Providence scatters talents indifferently, as thro' all orders of persons, so thro' all periods of time; *since*, a marvelous light, unenjoy'd of old, is pour'd on us by revelation, with larger prospects extending our Understanding, with brighter objects enriching our Imagination, with an inestimable prize setting our Passions on fire, thus strengthening every power that enables composition to shine; *since*, there has been no fall in man on this side *Adam*, who left no works, and the works of all other antients are our auxiliars against themselves, as being perpetual spurs to our ambition, and shining lamps in our path to fame; *since*, this world is a school, as well for intellectual, as moral, advance; and the longer human nature is at school, the better scholar it should be; *since*, as the moral world expects its glorious Milennium, the world intellectual may hope, by the rules of analogy, for some superior degrees of excellence to crown her latter scenes; nor may it only hope, but must enjoy them too; for *Tully, Quintillian,* and all true critics allow, that virtue assists Genius, and that the writer will be more able, when better is the man—All these particulars, I say, consider'd, why should it seem altogether impossible, that heaven's latest editions of the human mind may be the most correct, and fair; that the day may come, when the moderns may proudly look back on the comparative darkness of former ages, on the children of antiquity; reputing *Homer,* and *Demosthenes,* as the dawn of divine Genius; and *Athens* as the cradle of infant Fame; what a glorious revolution would this make in the rolls of renown?

What a rant, say you, is here?—I partly grant it: Yet, consider, my Friend! knowlege physical, mathematical, moral, and divine, increases; all arts and sciences are making considerable advance; with them, all the accommodations, ornaments, delights, and glories of human life; and these are new food to the Genius of a polite writer; these are as the root, and composition, as the flower; and as the root spreads, and thrives, shall the flower fail? As well may a flower flourish, when the root is dead. It is Prudence to read, Genius to relish, Glory to surpass, antient authors; and Wisdom to try our strength in an attempt in which it would be no great dishonour to fail.

Why condemn'd *Maro* his admirable Epic to the flames?[56] Was it not because his discerning eye saw some length of perfection beyond it? And what he saw, may not others reach? And who bid fairer than our countrymen for that glory? Something new may be expected from *Britons* particularly; who seem not to be more sever'd from the rest of mankind by the surrounding sea, than by the current in their veins; and of whom little more appears to be required, in order to give us *Originals,* than a consistency of character, and making their compositions of a piece with their lives. May our genius shine; and proclaim us in that nobler view!

> . . . *minimâ contentos nocte Britannos.*[57]
> VIRG.

And so it does; for in polite composition, in natural, and mathematical, knowlege, we have great *Originals* already: *Bacon, Boyle,*[58] *Newton, Shakespeare, Milton,* have showed us, that all the winds cannot blow the *British* flag farther, than an Original spirit can convey the *British* fame; their names go round the world; and what foreign Genius strikes not as they pass? Why should not their posterity embark in the same bold bottom of new enterprize, and hope the same success? Hope it they may; or you must assert, that either those *Originals,* which we already enjoy, were written by Angels, or deny that we are Men. As *Simonides* said to *Pausanias,*[59] reason should say to the writer, "Remember thou art a man." And for man not to grasp at all which is laudable within his reach, is a dishonour to human nature, and a disobedience to the divine; for as heaven does nothing in vain, its gift of talents implies an injunction of their use.

A friend of mine[60] has obeyed that injunction; he has relied on himself, and with a Genius, as well moral, as *original* (to speak in bold terms), has cast out evil spirits; has made a convert to virtue of a species of composition, once most its foe. As the first christian Emperors expell'd dæmons, and dedicated their temples to the living God.

55. kick the beam: See *Paradise Lost,* IV. 990–1015.

56. condemn'd . . . flames: Virgil (Publius Virgilius Maro) is said to have asked that the *Aeneid* be burned after his death because he had not finished revising it. **57. minimâ . . . Britannos:** "Britons, satisfied with the shortest night" (from Juvenal, *Satires,* I. ii. 161, rather than Virgil). **58. Boyle:** Sir Robert Boyle (1627–91), chemist and physicist; one of the founders of the Royal Society. **59. Simonides, Pausanias:** Simonides of Ceos, a Greek lyric poet, was the influential friend of many men of action of the fifth century B.C., including the overbearing Spartan general Pausanias. **60. a friend . . . mine:** Richardson.

But you, I know, are sparing in your praise of this author; therefore I will speak of one, which is sure of your applause. *Shakespeare* mingled no water with his wine, lower'd his Genius by no vapid Imitation. *Shakespeare* gave us a *Shakespeare*, nor could the first in antient fame have given us more. *Shakespeare* is not their Son, but Brother; their Equal, and that, in spite of all his faults. Think you this too bold? Consider, in those antients what is it the world admires? Not the fewness of their Faults, but the number and brightness of their Beauties; and if *Shakespeare* is their equal (as he doubtless is) in that, which in them is admired, then is *Shakespeare* as great as they; and not impotence, but some other cause, must be charged with his defects. When we are setting these great men in competition, what but the comparative size of their Genius is the subject of our inquiry? And a giant loses nothing of his size, tho' he should chance to trip in his race. But it is a compliment to those heroes of antiquity to suppose *Shakespeare* their equal only in dramatic powers; therefore, tho' his faults had been greater, the scale would still turn in his favour. There is at least as much Genius on the *British*, as on the Grecian stage, tho' the former is not swept so clean; so clean from violations not only of the *dramatic*, but *moral* rule; for an honest heathen, on reading some of our celebrated scenes, might be seriously concerned to see, that our obligations to the religion of nature were cancel'd by Christianity.

Johnson, in the serious drama, is as much an Imitator, as *Shakespeare* is an Original. He was very learned, as *Sampson* was very strong, to his own hurt: Blind to the nature of Tragedy, he pulled down all antiquity on his head, and buried himself under it; we see nothing of *Johnson*, nor indeed, of his admired (but also murdered) antients; for what shone in the Historian is a cloud on the Poet; and *Cataline*[61] might have been a good play, if *Salust*[62] had never writ.

Who knows whether *Shakespeare* might not have thought less, if he had read more? Who knows if he might not have laboured under the load of *Johnson's* learning, as *Enceladus* under *Ætna?*[63] His mighty Genius, indeed, thro' the most mountainous oppres-sion would have breathed out some of his inextin-guishable fire; yet, possibly, he might not have risen up into that giant, that much more than common man, at which we now gaze with amazement, and delight. Perhaps he was as learned as his dramatic province required; for whatever other learning he wanted, he was master of two books, unknown to many of the profoundly read, tho' books, which, the last conflagration alone can destroy; the book of Nature, and that of Man. These he had by heart, and has transcribed many admirable pages of them, into his immortal works. These are the fountain-head, whence the *Castalian* streams[64] of *original* composition flow; and these are often mudded by other waters, tho' waters in their distinct chanel, most wholesome and pure: As two chymical liquors, separately clear as crystal, grow foul by mixture, and offend the sight. So that he had not only as much learning as his dramatic province required, but, perhaps, as it could safely bear. If *Milton* had spared some of his learning, his muse would have gained more glory, than he would have lost, by it.

Dryden, destitute of *Shakespeare's* Genius, had almost as much learning as *Johnson*, and, for the buskin,[65] quite as little taste. He was a stranger to the Pathos, and, by numbers, expression, sentiment, and every other dramatic cheat, strove to make amends for it; as if a Saint could make amends for the want of conscience; a Soldier, for the want of valour; or a Vestal, of modesty. The noble nature of tragedy disclaims an equivalent; like virtue, it demands the heart; and *Dryden* had none to give. Let Epic poets *think*, the tragedian's point is rather to *feel;* such distant things are a tragedian and a poet, that the latter indulged, destroys the former. Look on *Barnwell*, and *Essex*,[66] and see how as to these distant characters *Dryden* excells, and is excelled. But the strongest demonstration of his no-taste for the buskin, are his tragedies fringed with rhyme; which, in Epic poetry, is a sore disease; in the Tragic, absolute death. To *Dryden's* enormity, *Pope's* was a light offence. As lacemen[67] are foes to mourning, these two authors,

---

61. **Cataline:** Ben Jonson's Roman tragedy *Catiline* was produced in 1611. 62. **Salust:** The Roman historian Gaius Sallustius Crispus (86–34 B.C.) wrote a history of Catiline's conspiracy. 63. **Enceladus . . . Ætna:** Enceladus was a rebellious giant whom the gods imprisoned beneath Mount Etna, in Sicily.

64. **the Castalian streams:** flowing from a fountain on Mount Parnassus, sacred to Apollo and the Muses. 65. **for the buskin:** for tragedy. 66. **Barnwell, and Essex:** George Barnwell is the main character in a domestic tragedy (1731) by George Lillo (1693–1739); the Earl of Essex is the hero in tragedies (1681, 1750) by John Banks (c. 1650–c. 1700) and Henry Brooke (c. 1703–83). 67. **lacemen:** dealers in lace.

rich in rhyme, were no great friends to those solemn ornaments which the nature of their works required.

Must rhyme then, say you, be banished? I wish the nature of our language could bear its intire expulsion; but our lesser poetry stands in need of a toleration for it; it raises That, but sinks the Great; as spangles adorn children, but expose men. Prince *Henry* bespangled all over in his oylet-hole suit,[68] with glittering pins; and an *Achilles*, or an *Almanzor*,[69] in his *Gothic* array; are very much on a level, as to the majesty of the poet, and the prince. *Dryden* had a great, but a general capacity; and as for a general Genius, there is no such thing in nature: A Genius implies the rays of the mind concenter'd, and determined to some particular point; when they are scatter'd widely, they act feebly, and strike not with sufficient force, to fire, or dissolve, the heart. As what comes from the Writer's heart, reaches ours; so what comes from his head, sets our brains at work, and our hearts at ease. It makes a circle of thoughtful Critics, not of distressed Patients; and a passive audience, is what tragedy requires. Applause is not to be given, but extorted; and the silent lapse of a single tear, does the writer more honour, than the rattling thunder of a thousand hands. Applauding hands, and dry eyes (which during *Dryden's* theatrical reign often met), are a satire on the Writer's talent, and the Spectator's taste. When by such judges the laurel is blindly given, and by such a poet proudly received, they resemble an intoxicated hoste, and his tasteless guests, over some sparkling adulteration, commending their Champaign.

But *Dryden* has his glory, tho' not on the stage: What an inimitable *original* is his Ode?[70] A small one, indeed, but of the first lustre, and without a flaw; and, amid the brightest boasts of antiquity, it may find a foil.

Among the brightest of the moderns, Mr. *Addison* must take his place. Who does not approach his character with great respect? They who refuse to close with the public in his praise, refuse at their peril. But, if men will be fond of their own opinions, some hazard must be run. He had, what *Dryden* and *Johnson* wanted, a warm, and feeling heart; but, being of a grave and bashful nature, thro' a philosophic reserve,

and a sort of moral prudery, he conceal'd it, where he should have let loose all his fire, and have show'd the most tender sensibilities of heart. At his celebrated *Cato*,[71] few tears are shed, but *Cato's* own; which, indeed, are truly great, but unaffecting, except to the noble Few, who love their country better than themselves. The bulk of mankind want virtue enough to be touched by them. His strength of Genius has reared up one glorious image, more lofty, and truly golden, than that in the plains of *Dura*,[72] for cool admiration to gaze at, and warm patriotism (how rare!) to worship; while those two throbbing pulses of the drama, by which alone it is shown to live, *terror* and *pity*, neglected thro' the whole, leave our unmolested hearts at perfect peace. Thus the poet, like his hero, thro' mistaken excellence, and virtue overstrain'd, becomes a sort of suicide; and that which is most dramatic in the drama, dies. All his charms of poetry are but as funeral flowers, which adorn; all his noble Sentiments but as rich spices, which embalm, the tragedy deceased.

Of tragedy, Pathos is not only the life and soul, but the soul inextinguishable; it charms us thro' a thousand faults. Decorations, which in this author abound, tho' they might immortalize other poesy, are the *splendida peccata*[73] which damn the drama; while, on the contrary, the murder of all other beauties is a venial sin, nor plucks the Laurel from the tragedian's brow. Was it otherwise, *Shakespeare* himself would run some hazard of losing his crown.

Socrates frequented the plays of *Euripides;* and, what living *Socrates* would decline the theatre, at the representation of *Cato?* *Tully's* assassins found him in his litter, reading the *Medea* of the *Grecian* poet, to prepare himself for death. Part of *Cato* might be read to the same end. In the weight and dignity of moral reflection, *Addison* resembles that poet, who was called the dramatic philosopher; and is himself, as he says of *Cato, ambitiously sententious.* But as to the singular talent so remarkable in *Euripides*, at melting down hearts into the tender streams of grief and pity, there the resemblance fails. His beauties sparkle, but do not warm; they sparkle as stars in a frosty night. There is, indeed, a constellation in his play; there is the

---

68. **oylet-hole suit:** a suit decorated with many small perforations (eyelets). 69. **Almanzor:** the bombastic hero of Dryden's *Conquest of Granada* (see the Epilogue in Part One). 70. **his Ode:** Young probably had in mind Dryden's *Song for St. Cecilia's Day* (see Part One).

71. **his . . . Cato:** Addison's tragedy was first performed at Drury Lane in 1713. 72. **that . . . Dura:** a golden image made by Nebuchadnezzar (Dan. 3:1). 73. **splendida peccata:** magnificent sins.

philosopher, patriot, orator, and poet; but where is the tragedian? And, if that is wanting,

> Cur in theatrum Cato severe venisti?[74]
>> MART.

And, when I recollect what passed between him and *Dryden*, in relation to this drama, I must add the next line,

> An ideo tantum veneras, ut exires?[75]

For, when *Addison* was a student at *Oxford*, he sent up this play to his friend *Dryden*, as a proper person to recommend it to the Theatre, if it deserved it; who returned it, with very great commendation; but with his opinion, that, on the stage, it could not meet with its deserved success. But tho' the performance was denied the theatre, it brought its author on the public stage of life. For persons in power inquiring soon after of the head of his college for a youth of parts, *Addison* was recommended, and readily received, by means of the great reputation which *Dryden* had just then spread of him above.

There is this similitude between the poet and the play; as This is more fit for the closet than the stage; so, That shone brighter in private conversation than on the public scene. They both had a sort of *local* excellency, as the heathen gods a local divinity; beyond such a bound *they*, unadmired; and *these*, unadored. This puts me in mind of *Plato*, who denied *Homer* to the public; that *Homer*, which, when in his closet, was rarely out of his hand. Thus, tho' *Cato* is not calculated to signalize himself in the warm emotions of the theatre, yet we find him a most amiable companion, in our calmer delights of recess.

Notwithstanding what has been offered, This, in many views, is an exquisite piece. But there is so much more of art, than nature in it, that I can scarce forbear calling it, an exquisite piece of statuary,

> *Where the smooth chisel all its skill has shown,*
> *To soften into flesh the rugged stone.*
>> ADDISON.

That is, where art has taken great pains to labour undramatic matter into dramatic life; which is impossible. However, as it is, like *Pygmalion*, we cannot but fall in love with it, and wish it was alive. How would a *Shakespeare*, or an *Otway*,[76] have answered our wishes? They would have outdone *Prometheus*, and, with their heavenly fire, have given him not only life, but immortality. At their dramas (such is the force of nature) the Poet is out of sight, quite hid behind his *Venus*, never thought of, till the curtain falls. Art brings our author forward, he stands before his piece; splendidly indeed, but unfortunately; for the writer must be forgotten by his audience, during the representation, if for ages he would be remembered by posterity. In the theatre, as in life, delusion is the charm; and we are undelighted, the first moment we are undeceived. Such demonstration have we, that the theatre is not yet opened, in which solid happiness can be found by man; because none are more than comparatively good; and folly has a corner in the heart of the wise.

A Genius fond of *ornament* should not be wedded to the tragic muse, which is in *mourning:* We want not to be diverted at an entertainment, where our greatest pleasure arises from the depth of our concern. But whence (by the way) this odd generation of pleasure from pain? The movement of our melancholy passions is pleasant, when we ourselves are safe: We love to be, at once, miserable, and unhurt: So are we made; and so made, perhaps, to show us the divine goodness; to show that none of our passions were designed to give us pain, except when being pain'd is for our advantage on the whole; which is evident from this instance, in which we see, that passions the most painful administer greatly, sometimes, to our delight. Since great names have accounted otherwise for this particular, I wish this solution, though to me probable, may not prove a mistake.

To close our thoughts on *Cato:* He who sees not much beauty in it, has no taste for poetry; he who sees nothing else, has no taste for the stage. While it justifies censure, it extorts applause. It is much to be admired, but little to be felt. Had it not been a tragedy, it had been immortal; as it is a tragedy, its uncommon fate somewhat resembles his, who, for conquering gloriously, was condemn'd to die. Both shone, but shone fatally; because in breach of their respective laws, the laws of the drama, and the laws of arms. But how rich in reputation must that author be, who can spare a *Cato*, without feeling the loss.

---

74. Cur . . . venisti: "Why, severe Cato, did you come to the theater?" (Martial, *Epigrams*, I., Preface). **75. An . . . exires:** "Did you come only so you could go away again?" (*Ibid.*).

76. Otway: Thomas Otway (1652–85), best known for his heroic plays *Don Carlos* (1676) and *Venice Preserved* (1682).

That loss by our author would scarce be felt; it would be but dropping a single feather from a wing, that mounts him above his contemporaries. He has a more refined, decent, judicious, and extensive Genius, than *Pope*, or *Swift*. To distinguish this triumvirate from each other, and, like *Newton*, to discover the different colours in these genuine and meridian rays of literary light, *Swift* is a singular wit, *Pope* a correct poet, *Addison* a great author. *Swift* looked on Wit as the *Jus divinum*[77] to dominion and sway in the world; and considered as usurpation, all power that was lodged in persons of less sparkling understandings. This inclined him to tyranny in wit; *Pope* was somewhat of his opinion, but was for softening tyranny into lawful monarchy; yet were there some acts of severity in his reign. *Addison's* crown was elective, he reigned by the public voice:

————*Volentes*
Per populos dat jura viamque affectat Olympo.[78]
VIRG.

But as good books are the medicine of the mind, if we should dethrone these authors, and consider them, not in their royal, but their medicinal capacity, might it not then be said, that *Addison* prescribed a wholesome and pleasant regimen, which was universally relished, and did much good; that *Pope* preferred a purgative of satire, which, tho' wholesome, was too painful in its operation; and that *Swift* insisted on a large dose of ipecacuanha, which, tho' readily swallowed from the fame of the physician, yet, if the patient had any delicacy of taste, he threw up the remedy, instead of the disease?

Addison wrote little in Verse, much in sweet, elegant, *Virgilian*, Prose; so let me call it, since *Longinus* calls *Herodotus* most *Homeric*, and *Thucydides* is said to have formed his style on *Pindar*. *Addison's* compositions are built with the finest materials, in the taste of the antients, and (to speak his own language) on truly *Classic ground:* And tho' they are the delight of the present age, yet am I persuaded that they will receive more justice from posterity. I never read him, but I am struck with such a disheartening idea of perfection, that I drop my pen. And, indeed, far superior writers should forget his compositions, if they would be greatly pleased with their own.

And yet (perhaps you have not observed it) what is the common language of the world, and even of his admirers, concerning him? They call him an *elegant* writer: That elegance which shines on the surface of his compositions, seems to dazzle their understanding, and render it a little blind to the depth of sentiment, which lies beneath: Thus (hard fate!) he loses reputation with them, by doubling his title to it. On subjects the most interesting, and important, no author of his age has written with greater, I had almost said, with equal weight: And they who commend him for his elegance, pay him such a sort of compliment, by their abstemious praise, as they would pay to *Lucretia*, if they should commend her only for her beauty.[79]

But you say, that you know his value already—You know, indeed, the value of his writings, and close with the world in thinking them immortal; but, I believe, you know not, that his name would have deserved immortality, tho' he had never written; and that, by a better title than the pen can give: You know too, that his life was amiable; but, perhaps, you are still to learn, that his death was triumphant: That is a glory granted to very few: And the paternal hand of Providence, which, sometimes, snatches home its beloved children in a moment, must convince us, that it is a glory of no great consequence to the dying individual; that, when it is granted, it is granted chiefly, for the sake of the surviving world, which may profit by his pious example, to whom is indulged the strength, and opportunity to make his virtue shine out brightest at the point of death: And, here, permit me to take notice, that the world will, probably, profit more by a pious example of lay-extraction, than by one born of the church; the latter being, usually, taxed with an abatement of influence by the bulk of mankind: Therefore, to smother a bright example of this superior good influence, may be reputed a sort of murder injurious to the living, and unjust to the dead.

Such an example have we in *Addison;* which, tho' hitherto suppressed, yet, when once known, is insuppressible, of a nature too rare, too striking to be forgotten. For, after a long, and manly, but vain struggle with his distemper, he dismissed his physicians, and with them all hopes of life: But with his hopes of life he dismissed not his concern for the living, but

---

77. **Jus divinum:** divine right. 78. **Volentes . . . Olympo:** "He gives laws to a willing people and thus makes his way to Olympus" (Virgil, *Georgics*, IV. 561–62).

79. **only . . . beauty:** Lucretia, wife of Lucius Tarquinius Collatinus, was a Roman matron known for her virtue and sense of honor. See Shakespeare's *Rape of Lucrece.*

sent for a youth nearly related,[80] and finely accomplished, but not above being the better for good impressions from a dying friend: He came; but life now glimmering in the socket, the dying friend was silent: After a decent, and proper pause, the youth said, "Dear Sir! you sent for me: I believe, and I hope, that you have some commands; I shall hold them most sacred:" May distant ages not only hear, but feel, the reply! Forcibly grasping the youth's hand, he softly said, "See in what peace a Christian can die." He spoke with difficulty, and soon expired. Thro' Grace divine, how great is man? Thro' divine Mercy, how stingless death? Who would not thus expire?

What an inestimable legacy were those *few dying words* to the youth beloved? What a glorious supplement to his own valuable fragment on the truth of Christianity?[81] What a full demonstration, that his fancy could not feign beyond what his virtue could reach? For when he would strike us most strongly with the grandeur of *Roman* magnanimity, his dying hero is ennobled with this sublime sentiment,

> *While yet I live, let me not live in vain.*
> CATO.

But how much more sublime is that sentiment when realized in life; when dispelling the languors, and appeasing the pains of a last hour; and brightening with illustrious action the dark avenue, and all-awful confines of an Eternity? When his soul scarce animated his body, strong Faith, and ardent Charity, animated his soul into divine ambition of saving more than his own. It is for our honour, and our advantage, to hold him high in our esteem: For the better men are, the more they will admire him; and the more they admire him, the better will they be.

By undrawing the long-closed curtain of his deathbed, have I not showed you a stranger in him whom you knew so well? Is not this of your favourite author,

> —*Notâ major imago?*[82]
> VIRG.

His compositions are but a noble preface; the grand work is his death: That is a work which is read in heaven: How has it join'd the final approbation of angels to the previous applause of men? How gloriously has he opened a splendid path, thro' fame immortal, into eternal peace? How has he given religion to triumph amidst the ruins of his nature? And, stronger than death, risen higher in virtue when breathing his last?

If all our men of Genius had *so* breathed their last; if all our men of Genius, like him, had been men of Genius for *eternals; then*, had we never been pained by the report of a latter end—oh! how unlike to this? But a little to balance our pain, let us consider, that such reports as make us, at once, adore, and tremble, are of use, when too many there are, who must tremble before they will adore; and who convince us, to our shame, that the surest refuge of our endanger'd virtue is in the fears, and terrors of the disingenuous human heart.

"But reports, you say, may be false; and you farther ask me, If all reports were true, how came an anecdote of so much honour to human nature, as mine, to lie so long unknown? What inauspicious planet interposed to lay its lustre under so lasting, and so surprizing an eclipse?"

The fact is indisputably true; nor are you to rely on me for the truth of it: My report is but a second edition: It was published before,[83] tho' obscurely, and with a cloud before it. As clouds before the sun are often beautiful; so, this of which I speak. How finely pathetic are those two lines, which this so solemn, and affecting scene inspired?

> *He taught us how to live; and, oh! too high*
> *A price for knowledge, taught us how to die.*
> TICKELL.

With truth wrapped in darkness, so sung our oracle to the public; but explained himself to me: He was present at his patron's death, and that account of it here given, he gave to me before his eyes were dry: By what means *Addison taught us how to die*, the Poet left to be made known by a late, and less able hand; but one more zealous for his patron's glory: Zealous, and impotent, as the poor *Ægyptian*, who gather'd a few splinters of a broken boat, as a funeral-pile for the great *Pompey*, studious of doing honour to so renown'd a name: Yet had not this poor plank (permit me, here, so to call this imperfect page) been thrown

---

80. **a youth . . . related:** Addison's stepson, Edward Henry Rich, Seventh Earl of Warwick. 81. **fragment . . . Christianity:** Addison's unfinished *Evidences of the Christian Religion*, written a few months before his death and printed in 1721, two years after. 82. **Notâ . . . imago:** "A greater image even than the well-known one" (*Aeneid*, II. 773).

83. **It . . . before:** by the poet Thomas Tickell (1686–1740), Addison's first posthumous editor, in a poem *To the Earl of Warwick on the Death of Mr. Addison* (1721).

out, the chief article of his patron's glory, would probably have been sunk for ever, and late ages have received but a fragment of his fame: A fragment glorious indeed, for his Genius how bright! But to commend him for composition, tho' immortal, is detraction *now;* if there our encomium ends: Let us look farther to that concluding scene, which spoke human nature not unrelated to the divine. To that let us pay the long, and large arrear of our greatly posthumous applause.

This you will think a long digression; and justly; if that may be called a digression, which was my chief inducement for writing at all: I had long wished to deliver up to the public this sacred deposit, which by Providence was lodged in my hands; and I entered on the present undertaking partly as an introduction to that, which is more worthy to see the light; of which I gave an intimation in the beginning of my Letter: For this is the *monumental marble* there mentioned, to which I promised to conduct you; this is the *sepulchral lamp,* the long-hidden lustre of our accomplished countryman, who now rises, as from his tomb, to receive the regard so greatly due to the dignity of his death; a death to be distinguished by tears of joy; a death which angels beheld with delight.

And shall that, which would have shone conspicuous amid the resplendent lights of Christianity's glorious morn, by these dark days be dropped into oblivion? Dropped it is; and dropped by our sacred, august, and ample register of renown, which has entered in its marble-memoirs the dim splendor of far inferior worth: Tho' so lavish of praise, and so talkative of the dead, yet is it silent on a subject, which (if any) might

have taught its unletter'd stones to speak: If powers were not wanting, a monument more durable than those of marble, should proudly rise in this ambitious page, to the new, and far nobler *Addison,* than that which you, and the public have so long, and so much admired; nor this nation only; for it is *Europe's Addison,* as well as ours; tho' *Europe* knows not half his title to her esteem; being as yet unconscious that the *dying Addison* far outshines her *Addison immortal:* Would we resemble him? Let us not limit our ambition to the least illustrious part of his character; heads, indeed, are crowned on earth; but hearts only are crowned in heaven: A truth, which, in such an *age of authors,* should not be forgotten.

It is piously to be hoped, that this narrative may have some effect, since all listen, when a death-bed speaks; and regard the person departing as an Actor of a part, which the great master of the drama has appointed us to perform to-morrow: This was a *Roscius*[84] on the stage of life; his Exit how great? Ye lovers of virtue! *plaudite:*[85] And let us, my Friend! ever "remember his end, as well as our own, that we may never do amiss."[86] I am. | *Dear* SIR, | *Your most obliged,* | *humble Servant.*

P. S. How far *Addison* is an *Original,* you will see in my next;[87] where I descend from this consecrated ground into his sublunary praise: And great is the descent, tho' into noble heights of *intellectual* power.

84. Roscius: famous Roman actor of the first century B.C. **85. plaudite:** applaud. **86. remember . . . amiss:** adapted from the Apocryphal Ecclus. 7:36. **87. in my next:** Young's projected essay on moral genius.

David Hume

1711–1776

In his own day Hume was known as an essayist, a historian, and a clever philosopher who appeared to the sophisticated as a skeptic and to most people as an atheist. During the two centuries following his death it has gradually become apparent that his genius for turning questions of metaphysics into questions of psychology has profoundly influenced Western philosophy. He is now regarded as one of the greatest European philosophers, and, in his empiricism and his appeal to instinct and custom instead of to reason, he is one of the most characteristic British thinkers of his age.

He was born in Edinburgh of a land-owning middle-class family, and after his father's early death he was raised by his mother on the family estate of Ninewells, in Berwickshire. On weekdays he read and did his lessons under a tutor; on Sundays he underwent the grim devotions enjoined by the local Calvinistic kirk. When he entered the University of Edinburgh in 1722, he was an earnest and pious boy. A reading of Locke soon persuaded him to leave behind his Calvinistic Christianity, and, advancing boldly toward philosophic skepticism, he began to develop the fearless and witty anti-Christian bias that, in his later writings, scandalized most of his British contemporaries.

His early ambition was twofold: he wanted to become a famous writer, and he wanted to discover a mode of thinking whereby he could ground philosophy on the foundation of "human nature, upon which every moral conclusion must depend." After three years at the university and nine years of private study in Edinburgh and Berwickshire, he traveled to the French town of La Flèche, where he read and wrote for three years. He returned to England in 1737, bringing with him the manuscript of *A Treatise of Human Nature*. This two-volume work, significantly subtitled *Being an Attempt to Introduce the Experimental Method of Reasoning into Moral Subjects*, appeared anonymously early in 1739, and a third volume was added in 1740. He hoped to burst on the intellectual scene like a new Francis Bacon—instead he found his book ignored. As he wrote later, "Never literary Attempt was more unfortunate than my Treatise of human Nature. It fell *dead-born from the Press;* without reaching such distinction as even to excite a Murmur among the Zealots."

He turned in 1741 to a lighter kind of composition, bringing out fifteen *Essays Moral and Political*, which was a success. But the failure of the *Treatise* troubled him— he was sure that he had said something important in it—and during the late 1740's he rewrote it, aiming this time for elegance and ease. The new version of the first portion appeared in 1748 as *Philosophical Essays Concerning Human Understanding* (in 1758 retitled *An Enquiry Concerning Human Understanding*); the new version of the last portion appeared in 1751 as *An Enquiry Concerning the Principles of Morals*. His work now began to attract attention. In 1754 he published the first volume of his politically conservative *History of England*, completed in six volumes in 1762; this *History* remained a classic for a century. In 1756 appeared his *Four Dissertations*, a book that included *The Natural History of Religion*, in which he explored the psychological motives of religious belief. His reputation as an infidel and a subversive was now such that the Reverend William Warburton observed, "A wickeder mind, and one more obstinately bent on public mischief, I never knew." By 1758 he had become famous enough to attract the celebrity hunter James Boswell, who was both horrified and fascinated by Hume's cheerful infidelity. Boswell once heard him say that "when he heard a man was religious, he concluded he was a rascal; though he had known some instances of very good men being religious."

But if the name of Hume constituted a scandal in England, it was the object of an almost mystical reverence in France. Hume was consequently delighted in 1763 to join the staff of the British embassy in Paris. In the French courts and salons he was received with an adulation bordering on hysteria; as he wrote a friend, "Here I feed on ambrosia, drink nothing but nectar, breathe incense only, and walk on flowers." The contrast between the British and French reception of his works and his person persuaded him that Britain was "relapsing fast into the deepest stupidity, Christianity and ignorance."

Nevertheless, he returned to England in 1766, bringing with him Jean-Jacques Rousseau, whom he hoped to shelter against Continental persecution. Rousseau was difficult, however, and the two became estranged to the noisy accompaniment of published accusations and recriminations.

Hume found himself back in Edinburgh in 1769. Here he lived for the rest of his life, growing obese and enjoying whist, merriment, and elegant cookery. The guests at his famous dinner parties—he was renowned for his claret, and Boswell referred to him as "the Northern Epicurus"—included the Edinburgh intellectuals Adam Smith, William Robertson, Hugh Blair, and Lord Kames. Public curiosity over his undisguised infidelity persisted until the end. Boswell achieved a deathbed interview in which he quizzed him on his final opinions about the immortality of the soul, but Hume remained placid and jolly. As George Sherburn has said, "the calm cheerfulness of his demise . . . greatly annoyed the orthodox." As a further outrage he left behind at his death the manuscript of the skeptical *Dialogues Concerning Natural Religion* (1779), which he had written in the early 1750's.

Those who knew him intimately attest not only to his amiability but to his virtue. Adam Smith remarked after his death, "Upon the whole, I have always considered him . . . as approaching as nearly to the idea of a perfectly wise and virtuous man, as perhaps the nature of human frailty will admit." But as Lord Charlemont pointed out:

Wisdom never before disguised herself in so uncouth a garb. . . . His face was broad and fat, his mouth wide, and without any other expression than that of imbecility. . . . [and] the corpulence of his whole person, was far better fitted to communicate the idea of a turtle-eating alderman, than of a refined philosopher.

Hume's interesting religious writings have tended to distract attention from the philosophy on which they depend. The essence of his philosophy is his skepticism toward rational inductive and analogical procedures, especially those that hitherto had been thought to demonstrate a causal relationship between events. C. W. Hendel summarizes thus the main question posed in Hume's thought: "What reason have we, what logic is there, for presupposing as we always do . . . that the course of nature must be uniform, that the past can be made a rule for the future, or that the future must resemble the past? No reason can be given for such a presupposition." In his suspicion of reason and systems as a guide to life, Hume allies himself with the tradition of Swift and Burke; as J. Y. T. Greig has said, "What he doubted was the power of human reason to pronounce judgement on the highest themes. What he never doubted was the power of human instinct—or imagination, as he often called it—to conduct and regulate our everyday affairs."

For bibliography see T. E. Jessop's *A Bibliography of Hume and of Scottish Philosophy from Hutcheson to Lord Balfour* (1938). The most authoritative biography is the monumental *Life of David Hume* (1954) by E. C. Mossner; Mossner's *The Forgotten Hume* (1943), on Hume's personal relationships, is almost equally interesting. An engaging work is Hume's brief autobiography (1777, and included in most later editions of the writings). The letters are edited by J. Y. T. Greig (2 vols., 1932) and by R. Klibansky and E. C. Mossner (*New Letters of David Hume* [1954]). The philosophical writings are found in the edition by T. H. Green and T. H. Grose (4 vols., 1874–75). The most accurate modern text of the *Enquiry* is edited by L. A. Selby-Bigge (2nd ed., 1902); the inexpensive edition by C. W. Hendel (1955) contains a perspicuous introduction and useful apparatus. N. K. Smith's *Philosophy of David Hume* (1941) is a critical study of origins and doctrines.

FROM

AN ENQUIRY CONCERNING HUMAN UNDERSTANDING

✿

Hume wrote his famous essay *Of Miracles* around 1736 as part of *A Treatise of Human Nature*, but, finally convinced that it was too strong, he withheld it until 1748, when it appeared as one of the twelve sections of *Philosophical Essays Concerning Human Understanding* (later titled *An Enquiry* . . .).

Recalling the circumstances of composition, Hume wrote later, with his accustomed shrewdness:

I was walking in the cloisters of the Jesuits' College of La Flèche . . . , and engaged in conversation with a Jesuit of some parts and learning, who was relating to me, and urging some nonsensical miracle performed in their convent, when I was tempted to dispute against him; and as my head was full of the topics of my *Treatise of Human Nature*, which I was at that time composing, this argument [i.e., the one employed in *Of Miracles*] immediately occurred to me, and I thought it very much gravelled my companion; but at last he observed to me, that it was impossible for the argument to have any solidity, because it operated equally against the Gospel as the Catholic Miracles; —which observation I thought proper to admit as a sufficient answer.

It was perhaps this essay more than any other work of Hume's that earned him the sobriquet The Great Infidel. During the 1750's the *Philosophical Essays* was the target of sixteen published attacks, most of them focusing on *Of Miracles*. In the opinion of Warburton and many others, Hume had written "a rank atheistical book." In 1761 all his writings were placed on the Roman Catholic Index.

The text is that of the first printing, in *Philosophical Essays Concerning Human Understanding* (1748); we have incorporated the substantive revisions appearing in *Essays and Treatises on Several Subjects* (2 vols., 1777).

☙❧

SECTION X. OF MIRACLES

PART I.

THERE is in Dr. *Tillotson's* Writings an Argument against the *real Presence*,[1] which is as concise and elegant, and strong as any Argument can possibly be suppos'd against a Doctrine, so little worthy of a serious Refutation. It is acknowledg'd on all hands, says that learned Prelate, that the Authority, either of the Scripture or of Tradition, is founded merely in the Testimony of the Apostles, who were Eye-witnesses to those Miracles of our Saviour, by which he prov'd his divine Mission. Our Evidence, then, for the Truth of the *Christian* Religion is less than the Evidence for the Truth of our Senses; because, even in the first Authors of our Religion, it was no greater; and it is evident it must diminish in passing from them to their Disciples; nor can any one rest such confidence in their Testimony, as in the immediate Object of his Senses. But a weaker Evidence can never destroy a stronger; and therefore, were the Doctrine of the real Presence ever so clearly reveal'd in Scripture, it were directly contrary to the Rules of just Reasoning to give our Assent to it. It contradicts Sense, tho' both the Scripture and Tradition, on which it is suppos'd to be built, carry not such Evidence with them as Sense; when they are consider'd merely as external Evidences, and are not brought home to every one's Breast, by the immediate Operation of the Holy Spirit.

NOTHING is so convenient as a decisive Argument of this Kind, which must at least *silence* the most arrogant Bigotry and Superstition, and free us from their impertinent Sollicitations. I flatter myself, that I have discover'd an Argument of a like Nature, which, if just, will, with the Wise and Learned, be an everlasting Check to all Kinds of superstitious Delusion, and consequently, will be useful as long as the World endures. For so long, I presume, will the Accounts of Miracles and Prodigies be found in all History, sacred and profane.

THO' Experience be our only guide in reasoning concerning Matters of Fact; it must be acknowledg'd, that this Guide is not altogether infallible, but in some Cases is apt to lead us into Errors. One, who, in our Climate, should expect better Weather in any Week of *June* than in one of *December*, would reason justly, and conformably to Experience; but it is certain, that he may happen, in the Event, to find himself mistaken. However, we may observe, that, in such a Case, he would have no Cause to complain of Experience; because it commonly informs us beforehand of the Uncertainty, by that Contrariety of Events, which we may learn from a diligent Observation. All Effects follow not with like Certainty from their suppos'd Causes. Some Events are found, in all Countries and all Ages, to have been constantly conjoin'd together: Others are found to have been more variable, and sometimes to disappoint our Expectations; so that in our Reasonings concerning Matter of Fact, there are all imaginable Degrees of Assurance, from the highest Certainty to the lowest Species of moral Evidence.

A WISE Man, therefore, proportions his Belief to the Evidence. In such Conclusions as are founded on an infallible Experience, he expects the Event with the last Degree of Assurance, and regards his past Experience as a full *Proof* of the future Existence of that Event. In other Cases, he proceeds with more Caution: He weighs the opposite Experiments: He considers which Side is supported by the greater Number of Experiments: To that Side he inclines, with Doubt and Hesitation; and when at last he fixes his Judgment, the Evidence exceeds not what we properly call *Probability*. All Probability, then, supposes an Opposition of

---

AN ENQUIRY CONCERNING HUMAN UNDERSTANDING: *Section X.*
1. the real Presence: the actual presence of the flesh and blood of Christ (as set forth in Roman Catholic doctrine) at the performance of the ceremony of the Eucharist. The sermons of John Tillotson (1630–94), Archbishop of Canterbury, tend toward the latitudinarian and the practical rather than the metaphysical. (See the selection from Tillotson in Part One.)

Experiments and Observations; where the one Side is found to over-balance the other, and to produce a Degree of Evidence, proportion'd to the Superiority. A hundred Instances or Experiments on one Side, and fifty on another, afford a doubtful Expectation of any Event; tho' a hundred uniform Experiments, with only one that is contradictory, reasonably beget a pretty strong Degree of Assurance. In all Cases, we must balance the opposite Experiments, where they are opposite, and deduct the smaller Number from the greater, in order to know the exact Force of the superior Evidence.

To apply these Principles to a particular Instance; we may observe, that there is no Species of Reasoning more common, more useful, and even necessary to human Life, than that which is deriv'd from the Testimony of Men, and the Reports of Eye-witnesses and Spectators. This Species of Reasoning, perhaps, one may deny to be founded on the Relation of Cause and Effect.[2] I shall not dispute about a Word. It will be sufficient to observe, that our Assurance in any Argument of this Kind is deriv'd from no other Principle than our Observation of the Veracity of human Testimony, and of the usual Conformity of Facts to the Reports of Witnesses. It being a general Maxim, that no Objects have any discoverable Connexion together, and that all the Inferences which we can draw from one to another are founded merely on our Experience of their constant and regular Conjunction; it is evident, that we ought not to make an Exception to this Maxim in Favour of human Testimony, whose Connexion with any Event seems, in itself, as little necessary as any other. Were not the memory tenacious to a certain degree; had not men commonly an Inclination to Truth and a principle of Probity; were they not sensible to Shame, when detected in a Falshood: Were not these, I say, discover'd by *Experience* to be Qualities, inherent in human Nature, we should never repose the least Confidence in human Testimony. A Man delirious, or noted for Falshood and Villany, has no Manner of Authority with us.

AND as the Evidence, deriv'd from Witnesses and human Testimony, is founded on past Experience, so it varies with the Experience, and is regarded either as a *Proof* or a *Probability*, according as the Conjunction between any particular Kind of Report and any Kind of Object has been found to be constant or variable.

There are a Number of Circumstances to be taken into Consideration in all Judgments of this Kind; and the ultimate Standard, by which we determine all Disputes, that may arise concerning them, is always deriv'd from Experience and Observation. Where this Experience is not intirely uniform on any Side, it is attended with an unavoidable Contrariety in our Judgments, and with the same Opposition and mutual Destruction of Argument as in every other Kind of Evidence. We frequently hesitate concerning the Reports of others. We balance the opposite Circumstances, which cause any Doubt or Uncertainty; and when we discover a Superiority on any Side, we incline to it; but still with a Diminution of Assurance, in proportion to the Force of its Antagonist.

THIS Contrariety of Evidence, in the present Case, may be deriv'd from several different Causes; from the Opposition of contrary Testimony; from the Character or Number of the Witnesses; from the Manner of their delivering their Testimony; or from the Union of all these Circumstances. We entertain a Suspicion concerning any Matter of Fact, when the Witnesses contradict each other; when they are but few, or of a doubtful Character; when they have an Interest in what they affirm; when they deliver their Testimony with Hesitation, or on the contrary, with too violent Asseverations. There are many other Particulars of the same Kind, which may diminish or destroy the Force of any Argument, deriv'd from human Testimony.

SUPPOSE, for Instance, that the Fact, which the Testimony endeavours to establish, partakes of the Extraordinary and the Marvellous; in that Case, the Evidence, resulting from the Testimony, admits of a Diminution, greater or less, in proportion as the Fact is more or less unusual. The Reason, why we place any Credit in Witnesses and Historians is not derived from any *Connexion*, which we perceive *a priori*,[3] between Testimony and Reality, but because we are accustom'd to find a Conformity between them. But when the Fact attested is such a one as has seldom fallen under our Observation, here is a Contest of two opposite Experiences; of which the one destroys the other as far as its Force goes, and the Superior can only operate on the Mind by the Force, which remains. The very same Principle of Experience, which gives us a certain Degree of Assurance in the Testimony of Witnesses,

2. the Relation . . . Effect: Hume has devoted much of the preceding portion of his book to arguing that the apparent relation between cause and effect in natural phenomena is not one discoverable by reason or logic.

3. a priori: beforehand, as a result of reasoning rather than experience.

gives us also, in this Case, another Degree of Assurance against the Fact, which they endeavour to establish; from which Contradiction there necessarily arises a Counterpoize, and mutual Destruction of Belief and Authority.

I should not believe such a story were it told me by Cato, was a proverbial saying in Rome, even during the lifetime of that philosophical patriot.[4] The incredibility of a fact, it was allowed, might invalidate so great an authority.

The Indian prince, who refused to believe the first relations concerning the effects of frost, reasoned justly; and it naturally required very strong testimony to engage his assent to facts, that arose from a state of nature, with which he was unacquainted, and which bore so little analogy to those events, of which he had had constant and uniform experience. Though they were not contrary to his experience, they were not conformable to it.[5]

But in order to increase the Probability against the Testimony of Witnesses, let us suppose, that the Fact, which they affirm, instead of being only marvellous, is really miraculous; and suppose also that the Testimony, consider'd apart, and in itself, amounts to an entire Proof; in that Case there is Proof against Proof, of which the strongest must prevail, but still with a Diminution of its Force, in proportion to that of its Antagonist.

A Miracle is a Violation of the Laws of Nature; and as a firm and unalterable Experience has establish'd these Laws, the Proof against a Miracle, from the very Nature of the Fact, is as entire as any Argument from Experience can possibly be imagin'd. Why is it more than probable, that all Men must die; that Lead cannot, of itself, remain suspended in the Air; that Fire consumes Wood, and is extinguish'd by Water; unless it be that these Events are found agreeable to the Laws of Nature, and there is requir'd a Violation of these Laws, or in other Words, a Miracle, to prevent them? Nothing is esteem'd a Miracle if it ever happen in the common Course of Nature. It is no Miracle that a Man, seemingly in good Health, should die on a sudden; because such a Kind of Death, tho' more unusual than any other, has yet been frequently observ'd to happen. But it is a Miracle, that a dead Man should come to Life; because that has never been observ'd, in any Age or Country: There must, therefore, be a uniform Experience against every miraculous Event, otherwise the Event would not merit that Appellation. And as a uniform Experience amounts to a Proof, there is here a direct and full *Proof*, from the Nature of the Fact, against the Existence of any Miracle; nor can such a Proof be destroy'd, or the Miracle render'd credible, but by an opposite Proof, which is superior.[6]

The plain Consequence is (and it is a general Maxim

---

4. that . . . patriot: [Hume's note] Plutarch, in vita Catonis. [Hume refers to *The Life of Marcus Portius Cato* (234–149 B.C.), the Roman statesman, written by Plutarch, the Greek biographer of the first century A.D.]. **5. not . . . it:** [Hume's note] No Indian, it is evident, could have experience that water did not freeze in cold climates. This is placing nature in a situation quite unknown to him; and it is impossible for him to tell *a priori* what will result from it. It is making a new experiment, the consequence of which is always uncertain. One may sometimes conjecture from analogy what will follow; but still this is but conjecture. And it must be confessed, that, in the present case of freezing, the event follows contrary to the rules of analogy, and is such as a rational Indian would not look for. The operations of cold upon water are not gradual, according to the degrees of cold; but whenever it comes to the freezing point, the water passes in a moment, from the utmost liquidity to perfect hardness. Such an event, therefore, may be denominated *extraordinary*, and requires a pretty strong testimony, to render it credible to people in a warm climate: But still it is not *miraculous*, nor contrary to uniform experience of the course of nature in cases where all the circumstances are the same. The inhabitants of Sumatra have always seen water fluid in their own climate, and the freezing of their rivers ought to be deemed a prodigy: But they never saw water in Muscovy during the winter; and therefore they cannot reasonably be positive what would there be the consequence.

6. an opposite . . . superior: [Hume's note] Sometimes an Event may not, *in itself*, seem to be contrary to the Laws of Nature, and yet, if it were real, it might, by reason of some Circumstances, be denominated a Miracle, because, in *Fact*, it is contrary to these Laws. Thus if a Person, claiming a divine Authority, should command a sick Person to be well, a healthful Man to fall down dead, the Clouds to pour Rain, the Winds to blow, in short, should order many natural Events, which immediately follow upon his Command; these might justly be esteem'd Miracles, because they are really, in this Case, contrary to the Laws of Nature. For if any Suspicion remain, that the Event and Command concurr'd by Accident, there is no Miracle and no Transgression of the Laws of Nature. If this Suspicion be remov'd, there is evidently a Miracle, and a Transgression of these Laws; because nothing can be more contrary to Nature than that the Voice or Command of a Man should have such an Influence. A Miracle may be accurately defin'd, *a Transgression of a Law of Nature by a particular Volition of the Deity, or by the interposition of some invisible Agent.* A Miracle may either be discoverable by Men or not. This alters not its Nature and Essence. The raising of a House or Ship into the Air is a visible Miracle. The raising of a Feather, when the Wind wants ever so little of a Force requisite for that Purpose, is as real a Miracle, tho' not so sensible with regard to us.

worthy of our Attention) "That no Testimony is sufficient to establish a Miracle, unless the Testimony be of such a Kind, that its Falshood would be more miraculous, than the Fact, which it endeavours to establish: And even in that Case, there is a mutual Destruction of Arguments, and the Superior only gives us an Assurance suitable to that Degree of Force, which remains, after deducting the Inferior." When any one tells me, that he saw a dead Man restor'd to Life, I immediately consider with myself, whether it be more probable, that this Person should either deceive or be deceiv'd, or that the Fact, which he relates, should really have happen'd. I weigh the one Miracle against the other, and according to the Superiority, which I discover, I pronounce my Decision, and always reject the greater Miracle. If the Falshood of his Testimony would be more miraculous, than the Event, which he relates; then, and not till then, can he pretend to command my Belief or Opinion.

PART II.

IN the foregoing Reasoning we have suppos'd, that the Testimony, upon which a Miracle is founded, may possibly amount to an entire Proof, and that the Falshood of that Testimony would be a real Prodigy. But it is easy to shew, that we have been a great deal too liberal in our Concession, and that there never was a miraculous Event establish'd on so full an Evidence.

FOR first, there is not to be found, in all History, any Miracle attested by a sufficient Number of Men, of such unquestion'd Good-sense, Education, and Learning as to secure us against all Delusion in themselves; of such undoubted Integrity, as to place them beyond all Suspicion of any Design to deceive others; of such Credit and Reputation in the Eyes of Mankind as to have a great deal to lose in case of their being detected in any Falshood; and at the same time attesting Facts perform'd in such a public Manner, and in so celebrated a Part of the World, as to render the Detection unavoidable: All which Circumstances are requisite to give us a full Assurance in the Testimony of Men.

SECONDLY. We may observe in human Nature a Principle, which, if strictly examin'd, will be found to diminish extremely the Assurance, which we might, from human Testimony, have, in any Kind of Prodigy. The Maxim, by which we commonly conduct ourselves in our Reasonings, is, that the Objects, of which we have no Experience, resemble those, of which we have; that what we have found to be most usual is always most probable; and that where there is an Opposition of Arguments we ought to give the Preference to such as are founded on the greatest Number of past Observations. But tho' in proceeding by this Rule, we readily reject any Fact, which is unusual and incredible in an ordinary Degree; yet in advancing farther, the Mind observes not always the same Rule; but when any Thing is affirm'd utterly absurd and miraculous, it rather the more readily admits of such a Fact, upon account of that very Circumstance, which ought to destroy all its Authority. The Passion of *Surprize* and *Wonder*, arising from Miracles, being an agreeable Emotion, gives a sensible Tendency towards the Belief of those Events, from which it is deriv'd. And this goes so far, that even those who cannot enjoy this Pleasure immediately, nor can believe those miraculous Events, of which they are inform'd, yet love to partake of the Satisfaction at Second-hand, or by Rebound, and place a Pride and Delight in exciting the Admiration of others.

WITH what Greediness are the miraculous Accounts of Travellers receiv'd, their descriptions of Sea and Land-Monsters, their Relations of wonderful Adventures, strange Men, and uncouth Manners? But if the Spirit of Religion join itself to the Love of Wonder, there is an End of common Sense; and human Testimony, in these Circumstances, loses all Pretensions to Authority. A Religionist may be an Enthusiast, and imagine he sees what has no Reality: He may know his narrative to be false, and yet persevere in it, with the best Intentions in the World, for the sake of promoting so holy a Cause: Or even where this Delusion has no Place, Vanity, excited by so strong a Temptation, operates on him more powerfully than on the rest of Mankind in any other Circumstances; and Self-Interest with equal Force. His Auditors may not have, and commonly have not sufficient Judgment to canvass his Evidence: What Judgment they have, they renounce by Principle, in these sublime and mysterious Subjects: Or if they were ever so willing to employ it, Passion and a heated Imagination disturb the Regularity of its Operations. Their Credulity increases his Impudence: And his Impudence over-powers their Credulity.

ELOQUENCE, when at its highest Pitch, leaves little room for Reason or Reflection; but addressing itself entirely to the Fancy or the Affections, captivates the willing Hearers, and subdues their Understanding. Happily, this Pitch it seldom attains. But what a Tully or a *Demosthenes*[7] could scarcely effect over a *Roman* or *Athenian* Audience, every *Capuchin*, every itinerant or stationary Teacher can perform over the Generality of Mankind, and in a higher Degree, by touching such gross and vulgar Passions.

The many Instances of forg'd Miracles, and Prophecies and supernatural Events, which, in all Ages, have either been detected by contrary Evidence, or which detect themselves by their Absurdity, prove sufficiently the strong Propensity of Mankind to the Extraordinary and the Marvellous, and ought reasonably to beget a Suspicion against all Relations of this Kind. This is our natural Way of thinking even with regard to the most common and most credible Events. For Instance: There is no Kind of Report, which rises so easily, and spreads so quickly, especially in Country-places and Provincial Towns, as those concerning Marriages; insomuch that two young Persons of equal Condition never see each other twice, but the whole Neighbourhood immediately join them together. The Pleasure of telling a Piece of News so interesting, of propagating it, and of being the first Reporters of it, spreads the Intelligence. And this is so well known, that no Man of Sense gives attention to these Reports, till he find them confirm'd by some greater Evidence. Do not the same Passions, and others still stronger, incline the Generality of Mankind to believe and report, with the greatest Vehemence and Assurance, all religious Miracles?

THIRDLY. It forms a strong Presumption against all supernatural and miraculous Relations, that they are observed chiefly to abound among ignorant and barbarous Nations; or if a civiliz'd People has ever given Admission to any of them, that People will be found to have receiv'd them from ignorant and barbarous Ancestors, who transmitted them with that inviolable Sanction and Authority, which always attend receiv'd Opinions. When we peruse the first Histories of all Nations, we are apt to imagine ourselves transported into some new World, where the whole Frame of Nature is disjointed, and every Element performs its Operations in a different Manner, from what it does at present. Battles, Revolutions, Pestilence, Famine and Death, are never the Effect of those natural Causes, which we experience. Prodigies, Omens, Oracles, Judgments quite obscure the few natural Events, that are intermingled with them. But as the former grow thinner every Page, in proportion as we advance nearer the enlighten'd Ages, we soon learn, that there is nothing mysterious or supernatural in the Case, but that all proceeds from the usual Propensity of Mankind towards the Marvellous, and that tho' this Inclination may at Intervals receive a Check from Sense and Learning, it can never be thoroughly extirpated from human Nature.

It is strange, a judicious Reader is apt to say, upon the Perusal of these wonderful Historians, *that such prodigious Events never happen in our Days*. But it is nothing strange, I hope, that Men should lye in all Ages. You must surely have seen Instances enough of that Frailty. You have yourself heard many such marvellous Relations started, which being treated with Scorn by all the Wise and Judicious, have at last been abandon'd, even by the Vulgar. Be assur'd, that those renown'd Lyes, which have spread and flourish'd to such a monstrous Height, arose from like Beginnings; but being sown in a more proper Soil, shot up at last into Prodigies almost equal to those, which they relate.

It was a wise Policy in that false prophet, *Alexander*,[8] who, tho' now forgotten, was once so famous, to lay the first Scene of his Impostures in *Paphlagonia*, where, as *Lucian* tells us, the People were extremely ignorant and stupid, and ready to swallow even the grossest Delusion. People at a Distance, who are weak enough to think the Matter at all worth Enquiry, have no Opportunity of receiving better Information. The Stories come magnify'd to them by a hundred Circumstances. Fools are industrious in propagating the imposture; while the Wise and Learned are contented, in general, to deride its Absurdity, without informing themselves of the particular Facts, by which it may be distinctly refuted. And thus the Impostor abovementioned was enabled to proceed, from his ignorant *Paphlagonians*, to the inlisting of Votaries, even among

---

7. a Tully . . . Demosthenes: Both the Roman Cicero and the Greek Demosthenes are renowned as orators.

8. that . . . Alexander: a religious mountebank of the second century A.D., whose fraudulent miracles in the backward Roman province of Paphlagonia are exposed by the second-century A.D. Greek satirist Lucian. Alexander's triumph, according to Lucian, was convincing the Paphlagonians that the god Asclepius, in the form of a snake with a human head, was lodging at his house. The head, Lucian says, was actually fashioned of linen, and the mouth, which appeared to utter prophecies, was operated by fine horsehairs.

the *Grecian* Philosophers, and Men of the most eminent Rank and Distinction in *Rome*. Nay could engage the Attention of that sage Emperor, *Marcus Aurelius;* so far as to make him trust the Success of a military Expedition to his delusive Prophecies.

THE Advantages are so great of starting an Imposture among an ignorant People, that even tho' the Delusion should be too gross to impose on the Generality of them (*which, tho' seldom, is sometimes the Case*) it has a much better Chance for succeeding in remote Countries, than if the first Scene had been laid in a City renown'd for Arts and Knowledge. The most ignorant and barbarous of these Barbarians carry the Report abroad. None of their Countrymen have a large Correspondence or sufficient Credit and Authority to contradict and beat down the Delusion. Men's Inclination to the Marvellous has full Opportunity to display itself. And thus a Story, which is universally exploded in the Place where it was first started, shall pass for certain at a thousand Miles Distance. But had *Alexander* fix'd his Residence at *Athens*, the Philosophers of that renown'd Mart of Learning, had immediately spread, throughout the whole *Roman* Empire, their Sense of the Matter, which, being supported by so great Authority, and display'd by all the Force of Reason and Eloquence, had entirely open'd the Eyes of Mankind. It is true; *Lucian* passing by chance thro' *Paphlagonia* had an Opportunity of performing this good Office. But, tho' much to be wish'd, it does not always happen, that every *Alexander* meets with a *Lucian*, ready to expose and detect his Impostures.

I MAY add as a fourth Reason, which diminishes the Authority of Prodigies, that there is no Testimony for any, even those which have not been expressly detected, that is not oppos'd by an infinite Number of Witnesses; so that not only the Miracle destroys the Credit of Testimony, but the Testimony destroys itself. To make this the better understood, let us consider, that, in Matters of Religion, whatever is different is contrary, and that it is impossible the Religions of antient *Rome*, of *Turkey*, of *Siam*, and of *China* should all of them be establish'd on any solid Foundation. Every Miracle, therefore, pretended to have been wrought in any of these Religions (and all of them abound in Miracles) as its direct Scope is to establish the particular System, to which it is attributed; so has it the same Force, tho' more indirectly, to overthrow every other System. In destroying a Rival-System, it likewise destroys the Credit of those Miracles, on which that System was establish'd; so

that all the Prodigies of different Religions are to be regarded as contrary Facts, and the Evidence of these Prodigies, whether weak or strong, as opposite to each other. According to this Method of Reasoning, when we believe any Miracle of *Mahomet* or his Successors, we have for our Warrant the Testimony of a few barbarous *Arabians:* and on the other hand, we are to regard the Authority of *Titus Livius*,[9] *Plutarch*, *Tacitus*,[10] and in short of all the Authors and Witnesses, *Grecian*, *Chinese*, and *Roman Catholic*, who have related any Miracle in their particular Religion; I say, we are to regard their Testimony in the same Light as if they had mention'd that *Mahometan* Miracle, and had in express Terms contradicted it, with the same Certainty as they have for the Miracle they relate. This Argument may appear over-subtile and refin'd; but is not in Reality different from the Reasoning of a Judge, who supposes, that the Credit of two Witnesses, maintaining a Crime against any one, is destroy'd by the Testimony of two others, who affirm him to have been two hundred Leagues distant, at the same Instant when the Crime is said to have been committed.

ONE of the best attested Miracles in all prophane History is that which *Tacitus* reports of *Vespasian*,[11] who cur'd a blind Man in *Alexandria*, by means of his Spittle, and a lame Man by the mere Touch of his Foot; in Obedience to a Vision of the God, *Serapis*,[12] who had enjoin'd them to have recourse to the Emperor, for these miraculous Cures. The Story may be seen in that fine Historian;[13] where every Circumstance seems to add Weight to the Testimony, and might be display'd at large with all the Force of Argument and Eloquence, if any one were now concern'd to enforce the Evidence of that exploded and idolatrous Superstition. The Gravity, Solidity, Age, and Probity of so great an Emperor, who, thro' the whole Course of his Life, convers'd in a familiar manner with his Friends and Courtiers, and never affected those extraordinary Airs of Divinity, assum'd

---

9. **Titus Livius:** a Roman historian of the first century B.C. 10. **Tacitus:** a Roman historian of the first century A.D. 11. **Vespasian:** first-century A.D. Roman emperor, the first of the Flavian family. 12. **Serapis:** an Egyptian deity whose cult was introduced into Greece and Rome. 13. **that . . . Historian:** [Hume's note] Hist. lib. v. cap. 8. Suetonius [the second-century A.D. Roman historian] gives nearly the same account *in vita* Vesp.

by *Alexander* and *Demetrius*.[14] The Historian, a contemporary Writer, noted for Candour and Veracity, and withal, the greatest and most penetrating Genius, perhaps, of all Antiquity; and so free from any Tendency to Credulity, that he even lies under the contrary Imputation, of Atheism and Prophaneness: The Persons, from whose authority he related the Miracle, of establish'd Character for Judgment and Veracity, as we may well presume; Eye-witnesses of the Fact, and confirming their testimony, after the *Flavian* Family was despoil'd of the Empire, and could no longer give any Reward, as the Price of a Lye. *Utrumque, qui interfuere, nunc quoque memorant, postquam nullum mendacio pretium.*[15] To which if we add the public Nature of the facts, as related, it will appear, that no Evidence can well be suppos'd stronger for so gross and so palpable a Falshood.

There is also a memorable Story related by *Cardinal de Retz*,[16] which may well deserve our Consideration. When that intriguing Politician fled into *Spain*, to avoid the Persecution of his Enemies, he pass'd through *Saragossa*, the Capital of *Arragon*, where he was shewn, in the Cathedral, a Man, who had serv'd seven Years as a Door-keeper, and was well known to every Body in town, that had ever paid his Devotions at that church. He had been seen, for so long a Time, wanting a Leg; but recover'd that Limb by the rubbing of holy Oil upon the Stump; and the Cardinal assures us that he saw him with two legs. This Miracle was vouch'd by all the Canons of the Church; and the whole Company in Town were appealed to for a Confirmation of the Fact; whom the Cardinal found, by their zealous Devotion, to be thorough Believers of the Miracle. Here the Relater was also contemporary to the suppos'd Prodigy, of an incredulous and libertine Character as well as of great Genius, the Miracle of so *singular* a Nature as could scarcely admit of a Counterfeit, and the Witnesses very numerous, and all of them, in a Manner, Spectators of the Fact, to which they gave their Testimony. And what adds mightily

to the Force of the Evidence, and may double our Surprise on this Occasion, is, that the Cardinal himself, who relates the Story, seems not to give any Credit to it, and consequently cannot be suspected of any Concurrence in the holy Fraud. He consider'd justly, that it was not requisite, in order to reject a Fact of this Nature, to be able accurately to disprove the Testimony, and to trace its Falshood, thro' all the Circumstances of Knavery and Credulity, which produc'd it. He knew, that as this was commonly altogether impossible, at any small Distance of Time and Place; so was it extremely difficult, even where one was immediately present, by Reason of the Bigotry, Ignorance, Cunning, and Roguery of a great Part of Mankind. He therefore concluded, like a just Reasoner, that such an Evidence carry'd falshood upon the very Face of it, and that a Miracle, supported by any human Testimony, was more properly a Subject of Derision than of Argument.

There surely never was a greater Number of Miracles ascrib'd to one Person, than those, which were lately said to have been wrought in *France* upon the Tomb of *Abbé Paris*,[17] the famous *Jansenist*, with whose Sanctity the People were so long deluded. The curing of the Sick, giving Hearing to the Deaf, and Sight to the Blind were every where talk'd of, as the usual Effects of that holy Sepulchre. But what is more extraordinary; many of the Miracles were immediately prov'd, upon the Spot, before Judges of unquestion'd Integrity, attested by Witnesses of Credit and Distinction, in a learned Age, and on the most eminent Theatre, that is now in the World. Nor is this all: A Relation of them was publish'd, and dispers'd every where; nor were the *Jesuits*, tho' a learned Body, supported by the civil Magistrate, and determin'd Enemies to those Opinions, in whose Favour the Miracles were said to have been wrought, ever able

14. **Alexander and Demetrius:** Alexander the Great (356–323 B.C.) and Demetrius Poliorcetes (*c.* 337–283 B.C.), kings of Macedonia. 15. **Utrumque . . . pretium:** Those who were present mention both incidents still, even now when there is no longer any reward for telling a lie. 16. **Cardinal de Retz:** Paul de Gondi (1614–79), cardinal from 1652 until his death; his *Memoirs* were published in 1717.

17. **Abbé Paris:** François de Paris (1690–1727), an austere and charitable French priest who espoused the quasi-Calvinistic heresy of Jansenism, especially the doctrine of predestination. The faction of Jansenists was opposed by the Molinists, who sought to reconcile the doctrine of free will with the ideas of grace and divine foreknowledge. After the death of the Abbé Paris, so many grotesque and unseemly miracles were reported taking place at his tomb that in 1732 Louis XV ordered the cemetery closed. A wit thereupon erected at the entrance a famous sign that read "By order of the King, God is forbidden to perform any miracles in this place."

distinctly to refute or detect them.[18] Where shall we find such a Number of Circumstances, agreeing to the Corroboration of one Fact? And what have we to oppose to such a Cloud of Witnesses, but the absolute Impossibility or miraculous Nature of the Events,

18. A Relation . . . them: [Hume's note] This book was written by Mons. Montgeron, counsellor or judge of the parliament of Paris, a man of figure and character, who was also a martyr to the cause, and is now said to be somewhere in a dungeon on account of his book.

There is another book in three volumes (called *Recueil des Miracles de l'Abbé* Paris) giving an account of many of these miracles, and accompanied with prefatory discourses, which are very well written. There runs, however, through the whole of these a ridiculous comparison between the miracles of our Saviour and those of the Abbé; wherein it is asserted, that the evidence for the latter is equal to that for the former: As if the testimony of men could ever be put in the balance with that of God himself, who conducted the pen of the inspired writers. If these writers, indeed, were to be considered merely as human testimony, the French author is very moderate in his comparison; since he might, with some appearance of reason, pretend, that the Jansenist miracles much surpass the other in evidence and authority. The following circumstances are drawn from authentic papers, inserted in the above-mentioned book.

Many of the miracles of Abbé Paris were proved immediately by witnesses before the officiality or bishop's court at Paris, under the eye of cardinal Noailles, whose character for integrity and capacity was never contested even by his enemies.

His successor in the archbishopric was an enemy to the Jansenists, and for that reason promoted to the see by the court. Yet 22 rectors or *curés* of Paris, with infinite earnestness, press him to examine those miracles, which they assert to be known to the whole world, and undisputably certain: But he wisely forbore.

The Molinist party had tried to discredit these miracles in one instance, that of Mademoiselle le Franc. But, besides that their proceedings were in many respects the most irregular in the world, particularly in citing only a few of the Jansenist witnesses, whom they tampered with: Besides this, I say, they soon found themselves overwhelmed by a cloud of new witnesses, one hundred and twenty in number, most of them persons of credit and substance in Paris, who gave oath for the miracle. This was accompanied with a solemn and earnest appeal to the parliament. But the parliament were forbidden by authority to meddle in the affair. It was at last observed, that where men are heated by zeal and enthusiasm, there is no degree of human testimony so strong as may not be procured for the greatest absurdity: And those who will be so silly as to examine the affair by that medium, and seek particular flaws in the testimony, are almost sure to be confounded. It must be a miserable imposture, indeed, that does not prevail in that contest.

All who have been in France about that time have heard of the reputation of Mons. Heraut, the *lieutenant de Police*, whose vigilance, penetration, activity, and extensive intelligence have been much talked of. This magistrate, who by the

which they relate? And this surely, in the Eyes of all reasonable People, will alone be regarded as a sufficient Refutation.

Is the Consequence just; because some human Testimony has the utmost Force and Authority in

nature of his office is almost absolute, was vested with full powers, on purpose to suppress or discredit these miracles; and he frequently seized immediately, and examined the witnesses and subjects of them: But never could reach any thing satisfactory against them.

In the case of Mademoiselle Thibaut he sent the famous De Sylva to examine her; whose evidence is very curious. The physician declares, that it was impossible she could have been so ill as was proved by witnesses; because it was impossible she could, in so short a time, have recovered so perfectly as he found her. He reasoned, like a man of sense, from natural causes; but the opposite party told him, that the whole was a miracle, and that his evidence was the very best proof of it.

The Molinists were in a sad dilemma. They durst not assert the absolute insufficiency of human evidence, to prove a miracle. They were obliged to say, that these miracles were wrought by witchcraft and the devil. But they were told, that this was the resource of the Jews of old.

No Jansenist was ever embarrassed to account for the cessation of the miracles, when the church-yard was shut up by the king's edict. It was the touch of the tomb, which produced these extraordinary effects; and when no one could approach the tomb, no effects could be expected. God, indeed, could have thrown down the walls in a moment; but he is master of his own graces and works, and it belongs not to us to account for them. He did not throw down the walls of every city like those of Jericho, on the sounding of the rams horns, nor break up the prison of every apostle, like that of St. Paul.

No less a man, than the Duc de Chatillon, a duke and peer of France, of the highest rank and family, gives evidence of a miraculous cure, performed upon a servant of his, who had lived several years in his house with a visible and palpable infirmity.

I shall conclude with observing, that no clergy are more celebrated for strictness of life and manners than the secular clergy of France, particularly the rectors or curés of Paris, who bear testimony to these impostures.

The learning, genius, and probity of the gentlemen, and the austerity of the nuns of Port-Royal, have been much celebrated all over Europe. Yet they all give evidence for a miracle, wrought on the niece of the famous Pascal, whose sanctity of life, as well as extraordinary capacity, is well known. The famous Racine gives an account of this miracle in his famous history of Port-Royal, and fortifies it with all the proofs, which a multitude of nuns, priests, physicians, and men of the world, all of them of undoubted credit, could bestow upon it. Several men of letters, particularly the bishop of Tournay, thought this miracle so certain, as to employ it in the refutation of atheists and free-thinkers. The queen-regent of France, who was extremely prejudiced against the Port-Royal, sent her own physician to examine the miracle,

some Cases, when it relates the battle of *Philippi* or *Pharsalia*,[19] for Instance; that therefore all Kinds of Testimony must, in all Cases, have equal Force and Authority? Suppose that the *Cæsarean* and *Pompeian* Factions had, each of them, claimed the Victory in these Battles, and that the Historians of each Party had uniformly ascrib'd the Advantage to their own Side; how could Mankind, at this Distance, have been able to determine between them? The Contrariety is equally strong between the Miracles related by *Herodotus*[20] or *Plutarch*, and those delivered by *Marianna, Bede*,[21] or any monkish Historian.

The Wise lend a very academic[22] Faith to every Report, which favours the Passion of the Reporter, whether it magnifies his Country, his Family, or himself, or in any other Way strikes in with his natural Inclinations and Propensities. But what greater Temptation than to appear a Missionary, a Prophet, an Ambassador from Heaven? Who would not encounter many Dangers and Difficulties, in order to attain so sublime a Character? Or if, by the Help of Vanity and a heated Imagination, a Man has first made a Convert of himself, and enter'd seriously into the Delusion; who ever scruples to make use of pious Frauds, in support of so holy and meritorious a Cause?

The smallest Spark may here kindle into the greatest Flame; because the Materials are always

---

prepar'd for it. The *avidum genus auricularum*,[23] the gazing populace, receive greedily, without Examination, whatever sooths Superstition, and promotes Wonder.

How many Stories of this Nature have, in all Ages, been detected and exploded in their Infancy? How many more have been celebrated for a Time, and have afterwards sunk into Neglect and Oblivion? Where such Reports, therefore, fly about, the Solution of the Phaenomenon is obvious; and we judge in Conformity to regular Experience and Observation, when we account for it by the known and natural Principles of Credulity and Delusion. And shall we, rather than have a Recourse to so natural a solution, allow of a miraculous Violation of the most establish'd Laws of Nature?

I need not mention the Difficulty of detecting a Falshood in any private or even public History, at the Place, where it is said to happen; much more when the Scene is remov'd to ever so small a Distance. Even a Court of Judicature, with all the Authority, Accuracy, and Judgment, which they can employ, find themselves often at a loss to distinguish between Truth and Falshood in the most recent Actions. But the Matter never comes to any Issue, if trusted to the common Method of Altercations and Debate and flying Rumours; especially when Men's Passions have taken part on either Side.

In the Infancy of new Religions, the Wise and Learned commonly esteem the Matter too inconsiderable to deserve their Attention or Regard: And when afterwards they would willingly detect the Cheat, in order to undeceive the deluded Multitude, the Season is now past, and the Records and Witnesses, which might clear up the Matter, have perish'd beyond Recovery.

No Means of Detection remain, but those which must be drawn from the very Testimony itself of the Reporters: And these, tho' always sufficient with the Judicious and Knowing, are commonly too fine to fall under the Comprehension of the Vulgar.

Upon the whole, then, it appears, that no Testimony for any Kind of Miracle has ever amounted to a Probability, much less to a Proof; and that even supposing it amounted to a Proof, it would be oppos'd by another Proof, deriv'd from the very Nature of the Fact, which it would endeavour to establish. It is

---

who returned an absolute convert. In short, the supernatural cure was so uncontestable, that it saved, for a time, that famous monastery from the ruin with which it was threatened by the Jesuits. Had it been a cheat, it had certainly been detected by such sagacious and powerful antagonists, and must have hastened the ruin of the contrivers. Our divines, who can build up a formidable castle from such despicable materials; what a prodigious fabric could they have reared from these and many other circumstances, which I have not mentioned! How often would the great names of Pascal, Racine, Arnaud, Nicole, have resounded in our ears? But if they be wise, they had better adopt the miracle, as being more worth, a thousand times, than all the rest of the collection. Besides, it may serve very much to their purpose. For that miracle was really performed by the touch of an authentic holy prickle of the holy thorn, which composed the holy crown, which, &c. **19. Philippi or Pharsalia:** The forces of Brutus and Cassius were defeated at Philippi in 42 B.C.; those of Pompey were defeated by Caesar in Pharsalia in 48 B.C. **20. Herodotus:** Greek historian of the fifth century B.C. **21. Mariana, Bede:** Juan de Mariana was an early seventeenth-century Spanish Jesuit and historian; Bede was an early eighth-century English priest and historian. **22. academic:** skeptical.

23. avidum . . . auricularum: [Hume's note] Lucret[ius, IV. 594].

Experience only, which gives Authority to human Testimony; and it is the same Experience, which assures us of the Laws of Nature. When, therefore, these two Kinds of Experience are contrary, we have nothing to do but subtract the one from the other, and embrace an Opinion, either on one Side or the other, with that Assurance, which arises from the Remainder. But according to the Principle here explain'd, this Subtraction, with regard to all popular Religions, amounts to an entire Annihilation; and therefore we may establish it as a Maxim, that no human Testimony can have such Force as to prove a Miracle, and make it a just Foundation for any such System of Religion.

I beg the Limitations here made may be remark'd, when I say, that a Miracle can never be prov'd, so as to be the Foundation of a System of Religion. For I own, that otherwise, there may possibly be Miracles, or Violations of the usual Course of Nature, of such a Kind as to admit of Proof from human Testimony; tho', perhaps, it will be impossible to find any such in all the Records of History. Thus suppose, all Authors, in all Languages, agree, that from the first of *January* 1600, there was a total Darkness over the whole Earth for eight Days: Suppose that the Tradition of this extraordinary Event, is still strong and lively among the People: That all Travellers, who return from foreign Countries, bring us Accounts of the same Tradition, without the least Variation or Contradiction; it is evident, that our present Philosophers, instead of doubting the Fact, ought to receive it as certain, and ought to search for the Causes, whence it might be deriv'd. The decay, corruption, and dissolution of nature, is an event rendered probable by so many analogies, that any phenomenon, which seems to have a tendency towards that catastrophe, comes within the reach of human testimony, if that testimony be very extensive and uniform.

But suppose, that all the Historians, who treat of *England*, should agree, that on the first of *January* 1600, Queen *Elizabeth* died; that both before and after her Death she was seen by her Physicians and the whole Court, as is usual with Persons of her Rank; that her Successor was acknowledg'd and proclaim'd by the Parliament; and that, after being interr'd a Month, she again appear'd, resumed the Throne, and govern'd *England* for three Years: I must confess that I should be surpriz'd at the Concurrence of so many odd Circumstances, but should not have the least Inclination to believe so miraculous an Event. I should not

doubt of her pretended Death, and of those other public Circumstances, that follow'd it: I should only assert it to have been pretended, and that it neither was, nor possibly could be real. You would in vain object to me the Difficulty, and almost Impossibility of deceiving the World in an Affair of such Consequence; the Wisdom and solid judgement of that renown'd Queen; with the little or no Advantage which she could reap from so poor an Artifice: All this might astonish me; but I would still reply, that the Knavery and Folly of Men are such common Phænomena, that I should rather believe the most extraordinary Events to arise from their Concurrence than admit of so signal a Violation of the Laws of Nature.

But should this Miracle be ascrib'd to any new System of Religion; Men, in all Ages, have been so much impos'd on by ridiculous Stories of that Kind; that this very Circumstance would be a full Proof of a Cheat, and sufficient, with all Men of Sense, not only to make them reject the Fact, but even reject it without farther Examination. Tho' the Being, to whom the Miracle is ascrib'd, be, in this Case, Almighty, it does not, upon that Account, become a whit more probable; since it is impossible for us to know the Attributes or Actions of such a Being, otherwise than from the Experience, which we have, of his Productions, in the usual Course of Nature. This still reduces us to past Observation, and obliges us to compare the Instances of the Violation of Truth in the Testimony of Men with those of the Violation of the Laws of Nature by Miracles, in order to judge which of them is most likely and probable. As the Violations of Truth are more common in the Testimony concerning religious Miracles than in that concerning any other Matter of Fact; this must diminish very much the Authority of the former Testimony, and make us form a general Resolution never to lend any Attention to it, with whatever specious pretence it may be cover'd.

Lord Bacon seems to have embraced the same principles of reasoning. "We ought," says he, "to make a collection or particular history of all monsters and prodigious births or productions, and in a word of every thing new, rare, and extraordinary in nature. But this must be done with the most severe scrutiny, lest we depart from truth. Above all, every relation must be considered as suspicious, which depends in any degree upon religion, as the prodigies of Livy: And no less so, every thing that is to be found in the writers of natural magic or alchemy, or such authors, who seem, all of them, to have an unconquerable appetite for falsehood and fable."[24]

I am the better pleas'd with the Method of Reasoning here delivered, as I think it may serve to confound those dangerous Friends or disguis'd Enemies to the *Christian Religion*, who have undertaken to defend it by the Principles of human Reason. Our most holy Religion is founded on *Faith*, not on Reason; and it is a sure Method of exposing it to put it to such a Trial as it is, by no Means, fitted to endure. To make this more evident, let us examine those Miracles, related in Scripture; and not to lose ourselves in too wide a Field, let us confine ourselves to such as we find in the *Pentateuch*, which we shall examine, according to the principles of these pretended Christians, not as the Word or Testimony of God himself, but as the Production of a mere human Writer and Historian. Here then we are first to consider a Book, presented to us by a barbarous and ignorant People, written in an Age when they were still more barbarous, and in all Probability long after the Facts which it relates; corroborated by no concurring Testimony, and resembling those fabulous Accounts, which every Nation gives of its Origin. Upon reading this Book, we find it full of Prodigies and Miracles. It gives an Account of a State of the World and of human Nature entirely different from the present: Of our Fall from that State: Of the Age of Man, extended to near a thousand Years: Of the Destruction of the World by a Deluge: Of the arbitrary Choice of one People, as the Favourites of Heaven; and that People, the Countrymen of the Author: Of their Deliverance from Bondage by Prodigies the most astonishing imaginable: I desire any one to lay his Hand upon his Heart, and after a serious Consideration declare, whether he thinks, that the Falshood of such a Book, supported by such a Testimony, would be more extraordinary and miraculous than all the Miracles it relates; which is, however, necessary to make it be receiv'd, according to the Measures of Probability above establish'd.

What we have said of Miracles may be apply'd, without any Variation, to Prophecies; and indeed, all Prophecies are real Miracles, and as such only, can be admitted as Proofs of any Revelation. If it did not exceed the Capacity of human Nature to foretell future Events, it would be absurd to employ any Prophecy as an argument for a divine Mission or Authority from Heaven. So that, upon the whole, we may conclude, that the *Christian Religion*, not only was at first attended with Miracles, but even at this Day cannot be believ'd by any reasonable Person without one. Mere Reason is insufficient to convince us of its Veracity: And whoever is mov'd by *Faith* to assent to it, is conscious of a continued Miracle in his own Person, which subverts all the Principles of his Understanding, and gives him a Determination to believe what is most contrary to Custom and Experience.

24. for . . . fable: [Hume's note] Nov. Org. lib. ii. aph. 29 [Hume refers to a passage in the *Novum Organum* (1620) by Francis Bacon (1561–1626)].

William Shenstone

1714–1763

William Shenstone was a rustic, but by no means a primitive—an elegant rustic, on the model of Virgil or Horace. He was born in the town of Halesowen, Worcestershire, of simple parents who owned a farm called The Leasowes. Despite his large, ungainly body, Shenstone was oddly frail, and his weak constitution caused continual ill health as well as a not entirely unpleasing melancholy. A sensitive, solemn, and indolent child, he applied himself to books early. He attended school at Halesowen and Solihull, near Birmingham, and entered Pembroke College, Oxford, in 1732, where he dissipated, wrote satiric verses, and read the classics. After three timid but pleasant years at Oxford, he came into his inheritance—The Leasowes and an annual three hundred pounds. He left Oxford without his degree the next year and soon established himself on his deceased parents' farm, which he now increasingly conceived of as an estate. He lived there for the rest of his life, with the exception of occasional winter visits to Cheltenham, Bath, and London.

His quiet existence he spent largely in the art of landscape gardening. His ambition was to improve and beautify The Leasowes according to the newly fashionable principles of natural gardening. Allying himself with Shaftesbury, Addison, William Mason, and the Pope of *The Guardian*, No. 173, he reacted against the idea—given wide currency by the late seventeenth-century gardens at Hampton Court and Versailles—of the garden as an expression of geometry and symmetry. Shenstone favored variety and an apparently artless asymmetry; as he saw it, art should wait upon nature, not the reverse. At The Leasowes, straight lines gave way to serpentine lines, and elaborately artificial flower beds to seemingly natural groupings. When he had saved enough money—and the whole project was costly—he installed a few Gothic ruins to evoke mildly melancholy associations. He also added waterfalls, statues, urns, and inscriptions (Ovid, Horace, Virgil, and Pope were favorites), and he contrived a dramatic dale known as Virgil's Grove. An illusion of informality without accident, of gentlemanly and literate rusticity, was his ideal. Thus his name belongs to the history of taste as well as to the history of literature, and indeed he was famous as a gardening theorist before he was known as a writer.

Unexpectedly lonely in his rural detachment, he delighted in exhibiting his reformed landscaping to the local gentry. Soon he became famous as a proponent of garden reform, and, although his premises were sometimes spoken of locally as Shenstone's Folly, important people began to arrive to admire his accomplishments in the picturesque. James Thomson was a visitor, and so were Thomas Percy, Joseph Spence, Thomas Warton, William Pitt, the neighboring printer John Baskerville, and the publisher Robert Dodsley. On one Sunday evening in 1749, one hundred and fifty visitors came to approve and also—to Shenstone's horror—to pick the flowers. The streams of visitors were generally well behaved, however, and their comings and goings as well as their praise served to divert him from his own problems of nervousness, constitutional depression, and feelings of social inferiority.

Another diversion was his writing. His first publication was a collection of his college poems, which he issued anonymously in 1737 *"for the Amusement of a few Friends Prejudic'd in his Favour."* The poems were not extraordinary, but the volume did contain the first version of *The Schoolmistress*, a mock-Spenserian performance that later became very popular. *The Judgment of Hercules*, a ruminative didactic piece in heroic couplets, appeared in 1741. Robert Dodsley's *Collection of Poems, by Several Hands* (3 vols., 1748) contained a number of Shenstone's poems, and subsequent volumes contained even more. But most of his writing did not appear until after his death, when Dodsley collected and published not only Shenstone's poems but his witty essays and amiable letters. Many of the poems in this three-volume posthumous collection are elegies and pastorals tinctured with a pretty melancholy and devoted to the praise of country retirement and the simple—but not too simple—life. His facetious poems, *Levities, or Pieces of Humor*, are those of a gentleman of the day.

Although Robert Burns was an enthusiastic admirer of the "sensibility" revealed in Shenstone's serious poems, Samuel Johnson (together with Gray and Walpole, who were fond of saying, "Poor Shenstone!") thought his achievement a modest one. "Whether to plant a walk in undulating curves," says Johnson, "demands any great powers of mind, I will not inquire." And of Shenstone's poems he writes, "The general recommendation of Shenstone is easiness and simplicity; his general defect is want of comprehension and variety. Had his mind been better stored with knowledge, whether he could have been great, I know not; he could certainly have been agreeable."

Bibliography is supplied by I. A. Williams's *Seven XVIIIth-Century Bibliographies* (1924). E. M. Purkis's *William Shenstone: Poet and Landscape Gardener* (1931) and Marjorie Williams's *William Shenstone: A Chapter in Eighteenth Century Taste* (1935) are useful for biography, and both contain interesting photographs of The Leasowes. Samuel Johnson's witty *Life of Shenstone* (1781) is still very worth reading. Duncan Mallam has edited the letters (1939), as has Marjorie Williams (1939). For criticism see Geoffrey Tillotson's essay on Shenstone in *Essays in Criticism and Research* (1942). A. R. Humphreys's *William Shenstone: An Eighteenth-Century Portrait* (1937) is a thoroughly delightful interpretation of Shenstone and of his theory of landscaping.

... TO THE
VIRTUOSOS ...

❦

The text is from Dodsley's *Collection of Poems, by Several Hands* (Vol. V, 1758), where the title reads: *The Beau to the Virtuosos; Alluding to a Proposal for the Publication of a Set of Butterflies.* Substantive variants have been introduced from the edition of 1764.

❦

HAIL curious wights, to whom so fair
   The form of mortal flies is!
Who deem those grubs beyond compare,
   Which *common* sense despises.

Whether o'er hill, morass or mound,
   You make your sportsman sallies;
Or that your prey in gardens found
   Is urg'd thro' walks and allies,

Yet, in the fury of the chace,
   No slope could e'er retard you;   10
Blest, if one fly repay the race,
   Or painted wing reward you.

Fierce as Camilla,° o'er the plain,
   Pursu'd the glittering stranger;
Still ey'd the purple's pleasing stain,
   And knew not fear nor danger.

'Tis you dispense the fav'rite meat
   To nature's filmy people;
Know what conserves they choose to eat,
   And what *liqueurs*, to tipple.   20

And, if her brood of insects dies,
   You sage assistance lend her;
Can stoop to pimp for am'rous flies,
   And help 'em to engender.

'Tis you protect their pregnant hour;
   And when the birth's at hand,
Exerting your obstetric pow'r,
   Prevent a mothless land.

Yet oh! howe'er your tow'ring view
   Above gross objects rises;   30
Whate'er refinements you pursue,
   Hear, what a friend advises.

A friend, who, weigh'd with yours, must prize
   Domitian's idle passion;
That wrought the *death* of teazing flies,
   But ne'er their *propagation*.°

Let FLAVIA's eyes more deeply warm,
   Nor thus your hearts determine,
To slight dame Nature's fairest form,
   And sigh for Nature's vermin.   40

And speak with *some* respect of beaux;
   No more, as triflers, treat 'em:
'Tis better learn to save one's cloaths,
   Than cherish moths that eat 'em.

WRITTEN AT AN INN
[AT HENLEY] ...

❦

Boswell reports that in 1776 Samuel Johnson, after declaring that "there is nothing which has yet been contrived by man, by which so much happiness is produced as by a good tavern or inn," repeated the last stanza of this poem "with great emotion."

The text is from Dodsley's *Collection* (Vol. V, 1758), where the title reads: *Written at an Inn on a Particular Occasion.* Substantive variants have been introduced from the edition of 1764.

❦

To thee, fair Freedom! I retire,
   From flattery, cards, and dice, and din;
Nor art thou found in mansions higher
   Than the low cot, or humble *inn*.

'Tis here with boundless power I reign,
   And every health° which I begin,
Converts dull port to bright champain;
   Such Freedom crowns it, at an *inn*.

TO THE VIRTUOSOS. **13. Camilla:** a legendary Volscian maiden known for her fleetness of foot in pursuing enemies. See *Aeneid*, VII. 803 ff.

34-36. Domitian's ... propagation: According to the second-century A.D. Roman historian Suetonius, the Emperor Domitian (A.D. 51-96) "spent hours alone every day catching flies—if you can believe it!—and stabbing them with a sharp pen-point." WRITTEN AT AN INN AT HENLEY. **6. health:** toast.

I fly from pomp, I fly from plate,
  I fly from Falshood's specious grin;   10
Freedom I love, and form I hate,
  And chuse my lodgings, at an *inn*.

Here, waiter! take my sordid ore,
  Which lacqueys else might hope to win;
It buys what courts have not in store,
  It buys me Freedom, at an *inn*.

Whoe'er has travell'd life's dull round,
  Where'er his stages may have been,
May sigh to think he still has found
  The warmest welcome—at an *inn*.   20

FROM

ESSAYS ON MEN, MANNERS, AND THINGS

In genre most of these essays, which were popular in the latter part of the century, consist of *pensées* or "detached thoughts." Fragmentary and often epigrammatic, the separate utterances glance lightly at a subject without giving the impression of trying to exhaust it. The late seventeenth-century *Pensées* of Blaise Pascal are perhaps the most famous work of this kind, and Denis Diderot's *Pensées philosophiques* (1746) and *Pensées sur l'interprétation de la nature* (1754) were familiar in Shenstone's own time.

The text is that of the first printing, in *The Works in Verse and Prose of William Shenstone* (3 vols., 1764–69).

AN OPINION OF GHOSTS

It is remarkable how much the belief of ghosts and apparitions of persons departed, has lost ground within these fifty years. This may perhaps be explained by the general growth of knowledge; and by the consequent decay of superstition, even in those kingdoms, where it is most essentially interwoven with their religion.

The same credulity which disposed the mind to believe the miracles of a popish saint, set aside at once the interposition of reason; and produced a fondness for the marvellous, which it was the priest's advantage to promote.

It may be natural enough to suppose that a belief of this kind might spread in the days of popish infatuation. A belief, as much supported by ignorance, as the ghosts themselves were indebted to the night.

But whence comes it that narratives of this kind have at any time been given, by persons of veracity, of judgment, and of learning? Men neither liable to be deceived themselves, nor to be suspected of an inclination to deceive others, though it were their interest; nor who could be supposed to have any interest in it, even though it were their inclination.

Here seems a further explanation wanting than what can be drawn from superstition.

I go upon a supposition, that the relations themselves were false. For as to the arguments sometimes used in this case, that had there been no true shilling there had been no counterfeit, it seems wholly a piece of sophistry. The true shilling here, should mean the living person; and the counterfeit resemblance, the posthumous figure of him, that either strikes our senses, or our imagination.

Supposing no ghost then ever appeared, is it a consequence that no man could ever imagine that they saw the figure of a person deceased? Surely those, who say this, little know the force, the caprice, or the defects of the imagination.

Persons after a debauch of liquor, or under the influence of terror, or in the deleria of a fever, or in a fit of lunacy, or even walking in their sleep, have had their brains as deeply impressed with chimerical[1] representations, as they could possibly have been, had these representations struck their senses.

I have mentioned but a few instances, wherein the brain is primarily affected. Others may be given, perhaps not quite so common, where the stronger passions, either acute or chronical, have impressed their object upon the brain; and this in so lively a manner, as to leave the visionary no room to doubt of their real presence.

How difficult then must it be to undeceive a person as to objects thus imprinted? Imprinted absolutely with the same force as their eyes themselves could have pourtrayed them! And how many persons must there needs be, who could never be undeceived at all!

Some of these causes might not improbably have given rise to the notion of apparitions: and when the

ESSAYS: *An Opinion of Ghosts.* **1. chimerical:** grotesquely fanciful; from Chimera, a monster in Greek mythology.

notion had been once promulgated, it had a natural tendency to produce more instances.

THE gloom of night, that was productive of terror, would be naturally productive of apparitions. The event confirmed it.

THE passion of grief for a departed friend, of horror for a murdered enemy, of remorse for a wronged testator, of love for a mistress killed by inconstancy, of gratitude to a wife for long fidelity, of desire to be reconciled to one who died at variance, of impatience to vindicate what was falsely construed, of propensity to consult with an adviser, that is lost.—The more faint as well as the more powerful passions, when bearing relation to a person deceased, have often, I fancy, with concurrent circumstances, been sufficient to exhibit the dead to the living.

BUT, what is more, there seems no other account that is adequate to the case as I have stated it. Allow this, and you have at once a reason, why the most upright may have published a falsehood, and the most judicious, confirmed an absurdity.

SUPPOSING then that apparitions of this kind may have some real use in God's moral government: Is not any moral purpose, for which they may be employed, as effectually answered on my supposition, as the other? for surely it cannot be of any importance, by what means the brain receives these images. The effect, the conviction, and the resolution consequent, may be just the same in either of the cases.

SUCH appears, to me at least, to be the true existence of apparitions.

THE reasons against any external apparition, among others that may be brought, are these that follow.

THEY are, I think, never seen by day; and darkness being the season of terror and uncertainty, and the imagination less restrained, they are never visible to more than one person: which had more probably been the case, were not the vision internal.

THEY have not been reported to have appeared these twenty years. What cause can be assigned, were their existence real, for so great a change as their discontinuance?

THE cause of superstition has lost ground for this last century; the notion of ghosts has been, together, exploded: A reason why the imagination should be less prone to conceive them; but not a reason why they themselves should cease.

MOST of those, who relate that these spectres have appeared to them, have been persons either deeply superstitious in other respects; of enthusiastick imagina-

tions, or strong passions which are the consequence; or else have allowedly felt some perturbation at the time.

SOME few instances may be supposed, where the caprice of imagination, so very remarkable in dreams, may have presented fantasms to those that waked. I believed there are few but can recollect some, wherein it has wrought mistakes at least equal to that of a white-horse for a winding sheet.

To conclude. As my hypothesis supposes the chimera to give terror equal to the reality, our best means of avoiding it, is to keep a strict guard over our passions— To avoid intemperance, as we would a charnel-house; and by making frequent appeals to cool reason and common-sense, secure to ourselves the property of a well regulated imagination.

FROM

UNCONNECTED THOUGHTS ON GARDENING

. . . GROUND should first be considered with an eye to it's peculiar character: whether it be the grand, the savage, the sprightly, the melancholy, the horrid, or the beautiful. As one or other of these characters prevail, one may somewhat strengthen it's effect, by allowing every part some denomination, and then supporting it's title by suitable appendages—For instance, The lover's walk may have assignation seats, with proper mottoes—urns to faithful lovers— trophies, garlands, &c. by means of art.

WHAT an advantage must some Italian seats derive from the circumstance of being situate on ground mentioned in the classicks? And, even in England, wherever a park or garden happens to have been the scene of any event in history, one would surely avail one's self of that circumstance, to make it more interesting to the imagination. Mottoes should allude to it, columns, &c. record it; verses moralize upon it; and curiosity receive it's share of pleasure.

IN designing a house and gardens, it is happy when there is an opportunity of maintaining a subordination of parts; the house so luckily placed as to exhibit a view of the whole design. I have sometimes thought that there was room for it to resemble an epick or dramatick poem. It is rather to be wished than required, that the more striking scenes may succeed those which are less so.

. . .

LANDSKIP should contain variety enough to form a picture upon canvas; and this is no bad test, as I think the landskip painter is the gardiner's best designer. The eye requires a sort of ballance here; but not so as to encroach upon probable nature. A wood, or hill, may ballance a house or obelisk; for exactness would be displeasing. We form our notions from what we have seen; and though, could we comprehend the universe, we might perhaps find it uniformly regular; yet the portions that we see of it, habituate our fancy to the contrary.

. . .

IT is not easy to account for the fondness of former times for strait-lined avenues to their houses; strait-lined walks through their woods; and, in short, every kind of strait-line; where the foot is to travel over, what the eye has done before. This circumstance, is one objection. Another, somewhat of the same kind, is the repetition of the same object, tree after tree, for a length of way together. A third is, that this identity is purchased by the loss of that variety, which the natural country supplies every where; in a greater or less degree. To stand still and survey such avenues, may afford some slender satisfaction, through the change derived from perspective; but to move on continually and find no change of scene in the least attendant on our change of place, must give actual pain to a person of taste. For such an one to be condemned to pass along the famous vista[1] from Moscow to Petersburg, or that other from Agra to Lahor in India, must be as disagreeable a sentence, as to be condemned to labour at the gallies. I conceived some idea of the sensation he must feel, from walking but a few minutes, immured, betwixt Lord D——'s high-shorn yew-hedges; which run exactly parallel, at the distance of about ten feet; and are contrived perfectly to exclude all kind of objects whatsoever.

. . .

RUINATED structures appear to derive their power of pleasing, from the irregularity of surface, which is VARIETY; and the latitude they afford the imagination, to conceive an enlargement of their dimensions, or to recollect any events or circumstances appertaining to

their pristine grandeur, so far as concerns grandeur and solemnity. The breaks in them should be as bold and abrupt as possible.——If mere beauty be aimed at (which however is not their chief excellence) the waving line, with more easy transitions, will become of greater importance.——Events relating to them may be simulated by numberless little artifices; but it is ever to be remembered, that high hills and sudden descents are most suitable to castles; and fertile vales, near wood and water, most imitative of the usual situation for abbeys and religious houses; large oaks, in particular, are essential to these latter.

> Whose branching arms, and reverend height
> Admit a dim religious light.

. . .

URNS are more solemn, if large and plain; more beautiful, if less and ornamented. Solemnity is perhaps their point, and the situation of them should still cooperate with it.

. . .

WHERE some artificial beauties are so dexterously managed that one cannot but conceive them natural, some natural ones [are] so extremely fortunate that one is ready to swear they are artificial.

. . .

ART should never be allowed to set a foot in the province of nature, otherwise than clandestinely and by night. Whenever she is allowed to appear here, and men begin to compromise the difference—Night, gothicism, confusion and absolute chaos are come again.

. . .

IT is always to be remembered in gardening that sublimity or magnificence, and beauty or variety, are very different things. Every scene we see in nature is either tame and insipid; or compounded of those. It often happens that the same ground may receive from art, either certain degrees of sublimity and magnificence, or certain degrees of variety and beauty; or a mixture of each kind. In this case it remains to be considered in which light they can be rendered most remarkable, whether as objects of beauty, or magnificence. Even the temper of the proprietor should not perhaps be wholly disregarded: for certain complexions of soul will prefer an orange tree or a myrtle, to an oak or cedar. However this should not induce a gardiner to parcel out a lawn into knots of shrubbery; or invest a mountain with a garb of roses. This would

---

1. vista: [Shenstone's note] In Montesquieu, on Taste.

be like dressing a giant in a sarsenet[2] gown, or a saracen's head in a Brussels[3] night-cap. Indeed the small and circular clumps of firs, which I see planted upon some fine large swells, put me often in mind of a coronet placed on an elephant or camel's back. I say a gardiner should not do this, any more than a poet should attempt to write of the king of Prussia in the style of Philips.[4] On the other side, what would become of Lesbia's sparrow[5] should it be treated in the same language with the anger of Achilles?

HEDGES, appearing as such, are universally bad. They discover art in nature's province.

ART, indeed, is often requisite to collect and epitomize the beauties of nature; but should never be suffered to set her mark upon them: I mean in regard to those articles that are of nature's province; the shaping of ground, the planting of trees, and the disposition of lakes and rivulets. Many more particulars will soon occur, which, however, she is allowed to regulate, somewhat clandestinely, upon the following account.—Man is not capable of comprehending the universe at one survey. Had he faculties equal to this, he might well be censured for any minute regulations of his own. It were the same, as if, in his present situation, he strove to find amusement in contriving the fabrick of an ant's nest, or the partitions of a bee-hive. But we are placed in the corner of a sphere; endued neither with organs, nor allowed a station, proper to give us an universal view; or to exhibit to us the variety, the orderly proportions, and dispositions of the system. We perceive many breaks and blemishes, several neglected and unvariegated places in the part; which, in the whole would appear either imperceptible, or beautiful. And we might as rationally expect a snail to be satisfied with the beauty of our parterres,[6] slopes, and terrasses—or an ant to prefer our buildings to her own orderly range of granaries, as that man should be satisfied, without a single thought that he can improve the spot that falls to his share. But, though art be necessary for collecting nature's beauties, by what reason is she authorized to thwart

and to oppose her? Why fantastically endeavor to humanize those vegetables, of which nature, discreet nature, thought it proper to make trees? Why endow the vegetable bird with wings, which nature has made momentarily dependent upon the soil? Here art seems very affectedly to make a display of that industry, which it is her glory to conceal. The stone which represents an asterisk, is valued only on account of it's natural production: Nor do we view with pleasure the laboured carvings and futile diligence of Gothic artists. We view with much more satisfaction some plain Grecian fabric, where art, indeed, has been equally, but less visibly, industrious. It is thus we, indeed, admire the shining texture of the silk-worm; but we loath the puny author, when she thinks proper to emerge; and to disgust us with the appearance of so vile a grub.

IN gardening it is no small point to enforce either grandeur or beauty by surprize; for instance, by abrupt transition from their contraries—but to lay a stress upon surprize only; for example, on the surprize occasioned by an aha![7] without including any nobler purpose; is a symptom of bad taste, and a violent fondness for mere concetto.[8]

SMOOTHNESS and easy transitions are no small ingredient in the beautiful; abrupt and rectangular breaks have more of the nature of the sublime. Thus a tapering spire is, perhaps, a more beautiful object than a tower, which is grander.

FROM

EGOTISMS. FROM MY OWN SENSATIONS

I HATE maritime expressions, similes, and allusions; my dislike, I suppose, proceeds from the unnaturalness of shipping, and the great share which art ever claims in that practice.

I BEGIN, too soon in life, to slight the world more than is consistent with making a figure in it. The "non

---

2. **sarsenet:** a delicate silk. 3. **Brussels:** lace. 4. **Philips:** Ambrose Philips (c. 1675–1749), famous for his delicate verses about children. (See the selections from Philips in Part Three.) 5. **Lesbia's sparrow:** the subject of a famous lyric by the Roman poet Catullus (c. 84–c. 54 B.C.). 6. **parterres:** ornamental flower beds.

7. **aha:** a garden boundary (often a fence placed in a deep ditch) designed to be invisible until closely approached. 8. **concetto:** conceit, false wit.

est tanti"[1] of Ovid grows upon me so fast that in a few years I shall have no passion.

. . .

IT is some loss of liberty to resolve on schemes before-hand.

. . .

I CANNOT avoid comparing the ease and freedom I enjoy, to the ease of an old shoe; where a certain degree of shabbiness is joined with the convenience.

. . .

HAD I a fortune of 8 or 10,000 l. a year, I would methinks make myself a neighbourhood. I would first build a village with a church, and people it with inhabitants of some branch of trade that was suitable to the country round. I would then at proper distances erect a number of genteel boxes of about a 1000 l. a piece, and amuse myself with giving them all the advantages they could receive from taste. These would I people with a select number of well-chosen friends, assigning to each annually the sum of 200 l. for life. The salary should be irrevocable, in order to give them independency. The house, of a more precarious tenure, that, in cases of ingratitude, I might introduce another inhabitant.

How plausible soever this may appear in speculation, perhaps a very natural and lively novel might be founded upon the inconvenient consequences of it, when put in execution.

. . .

FROM

ON WRITING AND BOOKS

III.

THE world may be divided into people that read, people that write, people that think, and fox-hunters.

. . .

VII.

THERE is no word in the Latin language, that signifies a female friend. "Amica" means a mistress: and perhaps there is no friendship betwixt the sexes wholly disunited from a degree of love.

VIII.

THE chief advantage that ancient writers can boast over modern ones, seems owing to simplicity. Every noble truth and sentiment was expressed by the

Egotisms. From My Own Sensations. **1. non est tanti:** "It is of no great importance."

former in the natural manner; in word and phrase, simple, perspicuous, and incapable of improvement. What then remained for later writers but affectation, witticism, and conceit?

. . .

XX.

PEOPLE in high or in distinguished life ought to have a greater circumspection in regard to their most trivial actions. For instance, I saw Mr. Pope—and what was he doing when you saw him?—why to the best of my memory, he was picking his nose.

. . .

XXIX.

IT is obvious to discover that imperfections of one kind have a visible tendency to produce perfections of another. Mr. Pope's bodily disadvantages must incline him to a more laborious cultivation of his talent, without which he foresaw that he must have languished in obscurity. The advantages of person are a good deal essential to popularity in the grave world as well as the gay. Mr. Pope, by an unwearied application to poetry, became not only the favourite of the learned, but also of the ladies.

. . .

XXXVII.

POPE has made the utmost advantage of alliteration, regulating it by the pause with the utmost success:

Die and endow a college or a cat, &c. &c.

It is an easy kind of beauty. Dryden seems to have borrowed it from Spenser.

. . .

XLI.

THERE is a vast beauty (to me) in using a word of a particular nature in the eighth and ninth syllables of an English verse. I mean what is virtually a dactyl. For instance

And pikes, the tyrants of the watry plains

Let any person of an ear substitute "liquid" instead of "watry," and he will find the disadvantage. Mr. Pope (who has improved our versification through a judicious disposition of the pause) seems not enough aware of this beauty.

. . .

LI.

EVERY person insensibly fixes upon some degree of refinement in his discourse, some measure of thought which he thinks worth exhibiting. It is wise to fix this pretty high, although it occasions one to talk the less.

LXXVIII.

EVERY good poet includes a critick; the reverse will not hold.

LXXXIII.

IT is idle to be much assiduous in the perusal of inferior poetry. Homer, Virgil, and Horace, give the true taste in composition; and a person's own imagination should be able to supply the rest.

IF one would think with philosophers, one must converse but little with the vulgar. These by their very number will force a person into a fondness for appearance, a love of money, a desire of power; and other plebeian passions: Objects which they admire, because they have no share in; and have not learning to supply the place of experience.

NOTHING tends so much to produce drunkenness, or even madness, as the frequent use of parentheses in conversation.

FROM

OF MEN AND MANNERS

XIV.

ZEALOUS men are ever displaying to you the strength of their belief, while judicious men are shewing you the grounds of it.

XXVII.

PEOPLE frequently use this expression, "I am inclined to think so and so;" not considering that they are then speaking the most literal of all truths.

XLI.

WHAT man of sense, for the benefit of coal-mines, would be plagued with colliers conversation!

LXXV.

I BELIEVE there was never so reserved a solitary, but felt some degree of pleasure at the first glimpse of an human figure. The soul, however unconscious of it's

social bias in a crowd, will in solitude feel some attraction towards the first person that we meet.

LXXXVI.

. . . VIRTUE seems to be nothing more than a motion consonant to the system of things. Were a planet to fly from it's orbit, it would represent a vitious man.

ONE scarce sees how it is possible for a country girl, or a country fellow to preserve their chastity. They have neither the philosophical pleasure of books, nor the luxurious pleasure of a table, nor the refined amusement of building, planting, drawing, or designing, to divert their imagination from an object to which they seem continually to stimulate it by provocative allusions. Add to this the health and vigour that are almost peculiar to them.

THINK when you are enraged at any one, what would probably become your sentiments should he die during the dispute.

TASTE is pursued at a less expence than fashion.

FROM

ON RELIGION

. . . WHEN misfortunes happen to such as dissent from us in matters of religion, we call them judgments: When to those of our own sect, we call them tryals: When to persons neither way distinguished, we are content to impute them to the settled course of things.

IT is not now, "We have seen his star in the east," but "We have seen the star on his breast,[1] and are come to worship him."

How happy may a lord bishop render a peasant at the hour of death by bestowing on him his blessing, and giving him assurance of salvation! It is the same with regard to religious opinions in general. They may be confirmed and established to their hearts content, because they assent implicitly to the opinions of men who, they think, should know. A person of distinguished parts and learning has no such advantages. Friendless, wavering, solitary, and, through his

On Religion. **1. star . . . breast:** Noblemen wore the large badges of their orders on the breasts of their coats.

very situation, incapable of much assistance: If the rustick's tenor of behavior approach nearer to the brutes, he also appears to approach nearer to their happiness.

. . .

PRAYER is not used to inform, for God is omniscient: Not to move compassion, for God is without passions: Not to shew our gratitude, for God knows our hearts. May not a man, that has true notions, be a pious man though he be silent?

. . .

I KNOW not how Mr. Pope's assertion is consistent with the scheme of a particular Providence:

———The Almighty cause
Acts not by partial, but by general laws.

WHAT one understands by a general Providence is that attention of the Almighty to the works of his Creation, by which they pursue their original course, without deviating into such eccentrick motions as must immediately tend to the destruction of it. Thus a philosopher is enabled to foretell eclipses with precision; and a stone thrown upward, drops uniformly to the ground. Thus an injury awakes resentment; and a good office endears to us our benefactor. And it seems no unworthy idea of omnipotence, perhaps, to suppose he at first constituted a system, that stood in no need either of his counter-acting or suspending the first laws of motion.

. . . .

FROM

ON TASTE

. . . DIVIDING the world into an hundred parts, I am apt to believe the calculation might be thus adjusted.

Pedants – – – – – –	15
Persons of common sense – – –	40
Wits – – – – – –	15
Fools – – – – – –	15
Persons of a wild uncultivated taste –	10
Persons of original taste, improved by art –	5

. . .

I KNOW not, if one reason of the different opinions concerning beauty, be not owing to self-love. People are apt to form some criterion, from their own persons, or possessions. A tall person approves the look of a folio or octavo: A square thick-set man is more delighted with a quarto. This instance, at least, may serve to explain what I intend.

. . .

AN obvious connexion may be traced betwixt moral and physical beauty; the love of symmetry, and the love of virtue; an elegant taste, and perfect honesty. We may, we must, rise from the love of natural to that of moral beauty: Such is the conclusion of Plato, and of my Lord Shaftesbury.

WHEREVER there is a want of taste, we generally observe a love of money, and cunning: And whenever taste prevails, a want of prudence, and an utter disregard to money.

TASTE (or a just relish of beauty) seems to distinguish us from the brute creation, as much as intellect, or reason. We do not find that brutes have any sensation of this sort. A bull is goaded by the love of sex in general, without the least appearance of any distinction in favor of the more beautiful individual. Accordingly men, devoid of taste, are in a great measure indifferent as to make, complexion, feature; and find a difference of sex sufficient to excite their passion in all its fervor. It is not thus where there is a taste for beauty, either accurate or erroneous. The person of a good taste, requires real beauty in the object of his passion; and the person of bad taste, requires something which he substitutes in the place of beauty.

. . .

THERE is a kind of counter-taste, founded on surprize and curiosity, which maintains a sort of rivalship with the true; and may be expressed by the name Concetto. Such is the fondness of some persons for a knife-haft made from the royal-oak,[1] or a tobacco-stopper from a mulberry-tree of Shakespear's own planting. It gratifies an empty curiosity. Such is the casual resemblance of Apollo and the nine Muses in a piece of agate; a dog expressed in feathers, or a wood-cock in mohair. They serve to give surprize. But a just fancy will no more esteem a picture, because it proves to be produced by shells, than a writer would prefer a pen, because a person made it with his toes. In all such cases, difficulty should not be allowed to give a casting weight; nor a needle be considered as a painter's instrument, when he is so much better furnished with a pencil.[2]

. . .

On Taste. **1. royal-oak:** a tree at Boscobel, Shropshire, in which Charles II hid briefly after the Battle of Worcester in 1651. **2. pencil:** [Shenstone's note] Cornelius Ketel, born at Gonda in 1548; landed in England 1573; settled at Amsterdam 1581; took it into his head to grow famous by painting with his fingers instead of pencils.—The whim took—His success encreased—His fingers appearing too easy tools, he then undertook to paint with his feet.—See H. Walpole's Book of Painters.

William Collins

1721–1759

The biography of "poor dear Collins" is perhaps best entrusted to his friend Samuel Johnson, who once declared, "I have often been near his state, and therefore have it in great commiseration":

"WILLIAM COLLINS was born at Chichester, on the 25th of December, about 1720. His father was a hatter of good reputation. He was in 1733, as Dr. [Joseph] Warton has kindly informed me, admitted scholar of Winchester College, where he was educated by Dr. [John] Burton. His English exercises were better than his Latin.

"He first courted the notice of the publick by some verses to a 'Lady weeping,' published in 'The Gentleman's Magazine.'

"In 1740, he stood first in the list of the scholars to be received in succession at New College [Oxford], but unhappily there was no vacancy. This was the original misfortune of his life. He became a Commoner of Queen's College, probably with a scanty maintenance; but was, in about half a year, elected a *Demy* [i.e., a scholar on the foundation] of Magdalen College, where he continued till he had taken a Bachelor's degree [1743], and then suddenly left the University; for what reason I know not that he told.

"He now (about 1744) came to London a literary adventurer, with many projects in his head, and very little money in his pocket. He designed many works; but his great fault was irresolution; or the frequent calls of immediate necessity broke his schemes, and suffered him to pursue no settled purpose. A man doubtful of his dinner, or trembling at a creditor, is not much disposed to abstracted meditation, or remote enquiries. He published proposals for a History of the Revival of Learning; and I have heard him speak with great kindness of Leo the Tenth, and with keen resentment of his tasteless successor. But probably not a page of the History was ever written. He planned several tragedies, but he only planned them. He wrote now and then odes and other poems, and did something, however little.

"About this time I fell into his company. His appearance was decent and manly; his knowledge considerable, his views extensive, his conversation elegant, and his disposition cheerful. By degrees I gained his confidence; and one day was admitted to him when he was immured by a bailiff, that was prowling in the street. On this occasion recourse was had to the booksellers, who, on the credit of a translation of Aristotle's Poeticks, which he engaged to write with a large commentary, advanced

914

as much money as enabled him to escape into the country. He shewed me the guineas safe in his hand. Soon afterwards [1749] his uncle, Mr. Martin, a lieutenant-colonel, left him about two thousand pounds; a sum which Collins could scarcely think exhaustible, and which he did not live to exhaust. The guineas were then repaid, and the translation neglected.

"But man is not born for happiness. Collins, who, while he *studied to live*, felt no evil but poverty, no sooner *lived to study* than his life was assailed by more dreadful calamities, disease and insanity.

"Having formerly written his character, while perhaps it was yet more distinctly impressed upon my memory, I shall insert it here.

Mr. Collins was a man of extensive literature, and of vigorous faculties. He was acquainted not only with the learned tongues, but with the Italian, French, and Spanish languages. He had employed his mind chiefly upon works of fiction, and subjects of fancy; and, by indulging some peculiar habits of thought, was eminently delighted with those flights of imagination which pass the bounds of nature, and to which the mind is reconciled only by a passive acquiescence in popular traditions. He loved fairies, genii, giants, and monsters; he delighted to rove through the meanders of inchantment, to gaze on the magnificence of golden palaces, to repose by the water-falls of Elysian gardens.

This was however the character rather of his inclination than his genius; the grandeur of wildness, and the novelty of extravagance, were always desired by him, but not always attained. Yet, as diligence is never wholly lost, if his efforts sometimes caused harshness and obscurity, they likewise produced in happier moments sublimity and splendour. This idea which he had formed of excellence led him to oriental fictions and allegorical imagery, and perhaps, while he was intent upon description, he did not sufficiently cultivate sentiment. His poems are the productions of a mind not deficient in fire, nor unfurnished with knowledge either of books or life, but somewhat obstructed in its progress by deviation in quest of mistaken beauties.

His morals were pure, and his opinions pious; in a long continuance of poverty, and long habits of dissipation, it cannot be expected that any character should be exactly uniform. There is a degree of want by which the freedom of agency is almost destroyed; and long association with fortuitous companions will at last relax the strictness of truth, and abate the fervour of sincerity. That this man, wise and virtuous as he was, passed always unentangled through the snares of life, it would be prejudice and temerity to affirm; but it may be said that at least he preserved the source of action unpolluted, that his principles were never shaken, that his distinctions of right and wrong were never confounded, and that his faults had nothing of malignity or design, but proceeded from some unexpected pressure, or casual temptation.

The latter part of his life cannot be remembered but with pity and sadness. He languished some years under that depression of mind which enchains the faculties without destroying them, and leaves reason the knowledge of right without the power of pursuing it. These clouds which he perceived gathering on his intellects, he endeavoured to disperse by travel, and passed into France [around 1754]; but found himself constrained to yield to his malady, and returned. He was for some time confined in a house of lunaticks, and afterwards retired to the care of his sister in Chichester, where death in 1759 came to his relief.

After his return from France, the writer of this character paid him a visit at Islington, where he was waiting for his sister, whom he had directed to meet him: there was then nothing of disorder discernible in his mind by any but himself; but he had withdrawn from study, and travelled with no other book than an English Testament, such as children carry to the school: when his friend took it into his hand, out of curiosity to see what companion a Man of Letters had chosen, "I have but one book," said Collins, "but that is the best."

"Such was the fate of Collins, with whom I once delighted to converse, and whom I yet remember with tenderness.

"He was visited at Chichester, in his last illness, by his learned friends Dr. Warton and his brother [Thomas]; to whom he spoke with disapprobation of his Oriental Eclogues [1757; originally issued as *Persian Eclogues* (1742)], as not sufficiently expressive of Asiatick manners, and called them his Irish Eclogues. He shewed them, at the same time, an ode inscribed to Mr. John Hume, on the superstitions of the Highlands; which they thought superior to his other works, but which no search has yet found. [The ode appears on p. 924.]

"His disorder was not alienation of mind, but general laxity and feebleness, a deficiency rather of his vital than intellectual powers. What he spoke wanted neither judgment nor spirit; but a few minutes exhausted him, so that he was forced to rest upon the couch, till a short cessation restored his powers, and he was again able to talk with his former vigour.

"The approaches of this dreadful malady he began to feel soon after his uncle's death; and, with the usual weakness of men so diseased, eagerly snatched that temporary relief with which the table and the bottle flatter and seduce. But his health continually declined, and he grew more and more burthensome to himself.

"To what I have formerly said of his writings may be added, that his diction was often harsh, unskilfully laboured, and injudiciously selected. He affected the obsolete when it was not worthy of revival; and he puts his words out of the common order, seeming to think, with some later candidates for fame, that not to write prose is certainly to write poetry. His lines commonly are of slow motion, clogged and impeded with clusters of consonants. As men are often esteemed who cannot be loved, so the poetry of Collins may sometimes extort praise when it gives little pleasure."

Because Collins had only a few years of adulthood before his insanity, his poetic production was small: he published only about twenty poems, most of them in his *Odes on Several Descriptive and Allegoric Subjects* (1746, dated 1747), a book that was hardly noticed. It is said that, disgusted at the neglect of the age, Collins himself burned the many unsold copies.

A bibliography of first editions is included in I. A. Williams's *Seven XVIIIth-Century Bibliographies* (1924); for a listing of modern studies see *The Cambridge Bibliography of English Literature*, ed. F. W. Bateson (4 vols., 1941), with its *Supplement*, ed. George Watson (1957). The sparse biographical data are brought together by

E. G. Ainsworth in *Poor Collins: His Life, His Art, and His Influence* (1937), which also contains good material on Collins's reading and poetic sources. H. W. Garrod's *Collins* (1928) is a critical analysis and assessment. A good discussion of Collins's aesthetic theories is A. S. P. Woodhouse's "Collins and the Creative Imagination: A Study in the Critical Background of His Odes," in *Studies in English by Members of University College, Toronto* (1931). Collins's techniques of personification and allegorical imagery are treated by C. F. Chapin in *Personification in Eighteenth-Century English Poetry* (1955).

A SONG FROM SHAKESPEAR'S *CYMBELYNE*

SUNG BY GUIDERUS AND ARVIRAGUS OVER FIDELE, SUPPOS'D TO BE DEAD.

✿

In *Cymbeline* (c. 1610) the noble and chaste Imogen, forced to disguise herself as the boy Fidele, unwittingly swallows a potion that makes her appear dead. In a pastoral setting she is mourned by Guiderius and Arviragus, sons of King Cymbeline, who are disguised as mountaineers. Shakespeare's song is the famous one that begins "Fear no more the heat o' the sun." This song of Collins's was appended by Johnson to his commentary on *Cymbeline* in his edition of Shakespeare (1765).

The text is that of the first printing, in *An Epistle Addressed to Sir Thomas Hanmer on His Edition of Shakespeare's Works* (2nd ed., 1744); we have incorporated one substantive variant from the text in Robert Dodsley's *A Collection of Poems* (Vol. IV, 1755).

✿

See page 278 of the 7th Vol. of THEOBALD'S *Edition of* SHAKESPEAR.

I.

To fair FIDELE's grassy Tomb
   Soft Maids, and Village Hinds shall bring
Each op'ning Sweet, of earliest Bloom,
   And rifle all the breathing Spring.

II.

No wailing Ghost shall dare appear
   To vex with Shrieks this quiet Grove:
But Shepherd Lads assemble here,
   And melting Virgins own their Love.

III.

No wither'd Witch shall here be seen,
   No Goblins lead their nightly Crew: 10
The Female Fays shall haunt the Green,
   And dress thy Grave with pearly Dew!

IV.

The Redbreast oft at Ev'ning Hours
   Shall kindly lend his little Aid:
With hoary Moss, and gather'd Flow'rs,
   To deck the Ground where thou art laid.

V.

When howling Winds, and beating Rain,
   In Tempests shake the sylvan Cell:
Or midst the Chace on ev'ry Plain,
   The tender Thought on thee shall dwell.   20

VI.

Each lonely Scene shall thee restore,
   For thee the Tear be duly shed:
Belov'd, till Life can charm no more;
   And mourn'd, till Pity's self be dead.

ODE TO FEAR

This poem and its companion piece, *Ode to Pity* (1747) (with its praise of the Greek tragic dramatist Euripedes), were perhaps occasioned by Collins's deep interest in Aristotle's *Poetics*. Aristotle asserts that the function of stage tragedy is to arouse pity and fear in the beholder and thus to purge him of those emotions.

The text is that of the first printing, in *Odes on Several Descriptive and Allegoric Subjects* (1746, dated 1747). We have omitted Collins's notes.

Thou, to whom the World unknown
With all its shadowy Shapes is shown;
Who see'st appall'd th' unreal Scene,
While Fancy° lifts the Veil between:
   Ah *Fear!* Ah frantic *Fear!*
   I see, I see Thee near.
I know thy hurried Step, thy haggard Eye!
Like Thee I start, like Thee disorder'd fly,
For lo what *Monsters* in thy Train appear!
Danger, whose Limbs of Giant Mold   10
What mortal Eye can fix'd behold?
Who stalks his Round, an hideous Form,
Howling amidst the Midnight Storm,
Or throws him on the ridgy Steep
Of some loose hanging Rock to sleep:
And with him thousand Phantoms join'd,
Who prompt to Deeds accurs'd the Mind:
And those, the Fiends, who near allied,°
O'er Nature's Wounds, and Wrecks preside;
Whilst *Vengeance*, in the lurid Air,   20
Lifts her red Arm, expos'd and bare:
On whom that rav'ning Brood of Fate,°
Who lap the Blood of Sorrow, wait;
Who, *Fear*, this ghastly Train can see,
And look not madly wild, like Thee?

EPODE.

In earliest *Greece* to Thee with partial Choice,
   The Grief-full Muse addrest her infant Tongue;
The Maids and Matrons, on her awful Voice,
   Silent and pale in wild Amazement hung.

Yet He,° the Bard who first invok'd thy Name,   30
   Disdain'd in *Marathon* its Pow'r to feel:
For not alone he nurs'd the Poet's flame,
   But reach'd from Virtue's Hand the Patriot's Steel.

But who is He° whom later Garlands grace,
   Who left a-while o'er *Hybla*'s° Dews to rove,
With trembling Eyes thy dreary Steps to trace,
   Where Thou and *Furies*° shar'd the baleful Grove°?

Wrapt in thy cloudy Veil th' *Incestuous Queen*°
   Sigh'd the sad Call her Son and Husband hear'd,
When once alone it broke the silent Scene,   40
   And He the Wretch of *Thebes* no more appear'd.

O *Fear*, I know Thee by my throbbing Heart,
   Thy with'ring Pow'r inspir'd each mournful Line,
Tho' gentle *Pity* claim her mingled Part,
   Yet all the Thunders of the Scene are thine!

ANTISTROPHE.

Thou who such weary Lengths hast past,
Where wilt thou rest, mad Nymph, at last?
Say, wilt thou shroud in haunted Cell,
Where gloomy *Rape* and *Murder* dwell?

Or, in some hollow'd Seat,   50
'Gainst which the big Waves beat,
Hear drowning Sea-men's cries in Tempests brought!
Dark Pow'r, with shudd'ring meek submitted
   Thought
Be mine, to read the Visions old,
Which thy awak'ning Bards have told:

ODE TO FEAR. **4. Fancy:** imagination. **18. near allied:** to "Phantoms" in line 16. **22. that . . . Fate:** In a footnote Collins refers to a passage in Sophocles' *Electra* where the chorus, mentioning various agents of retribution, speaks of "the hounds which none can flee."

30. He: Aeschylus (525–456 B.C.), earliest of the three Greek tragic dramatists; he fought the Persians at Marathon in 490 B.C. **34. He:** Sophocles (495–406 B.C.), the Greek tragic dramatist. **35. Hybla:** an area of Sicily famous for its honey; Sophocles' final tragedy, *Oedipus at Colonus* (produced in 401 B.C.), is the source of his reputation for "sweetness." **37. Furies:** in Greek mythology, the three goddesses of vengeance. **the baleful Grove:** the setting of *Oedipus at Colonus*. **38. th' Incestuous Queen:** Jocasta, mother and wife of Oedipus. See Sophocles' *Oedipus the King* and *Oedipus at Colonus*.

And lest thou meet my blasted View,
Hold each strange Tale devoutly true;
Ne'er be I found, by Thee o'eraw'd,
In that thrice-hallow'd Eve° abroad,
When Ghosts, as Cottage-Maids believe,   60
Their pebbled Beds permitted leave,
And *Gobblins* haunt from Fire, or Fen,
Or Mine, or Flood, the Walks of Men!
   O Thou whose Spirt most possest
The sacred Seat of *Shakespear's* Breast!
By all that from thy Prophet broke,
In thy Divine Emotions spoke:
Hither again thy Fury deal,
Teach me but once like Him to feel:
His *Cypress Wreath*° my Meed decree,   70
And I, O *Fear*, will dwell with *Thee*!

ODE ON THE POETICAL CHARACTER

In 1796 Samuel Taylor Coleridge wrote to a friend:

Now Collins's *Ode on the Poetical Character*—that
part of it, I should say, beginning with "The band
(as fairy legends say) Was wove on that creating
day,"—has . . . whirled *me* along with greater
agitations of enthusiasm than any the most *impassioned* scene in Schiller or Shakespeare, using the
word "impassioned" in its confined sense, for
writing in which the human passions of pity, fear,
anger, revenge, jealousy, or love are brought into
view with their workings.

The text is that of the first printing, in *Odes* . . .
(1747).

As once, if not with light Regard,°
I read aright that gifted Bard,
(Him whose School above the rest
His Loveliest *Elfin* Queen has blest.)

One, only One, unrival'd Fair,°
Might hope the magic Girdle wear,
At solemn Turney hung on high,
The Wish of each love-darting Eye;

Lo! to each other Nymph in turn applied,
   As if, in Air unseen, some hov'ring Hand,   10
Some chaste and Angel-Friend to Virgin-Fame,
   With whisper'd Spell had burst the starting Band,
It left unblest her loath'd dishonour'd Side;
   Happier hopeless Fair, if never
   Her baffled Hand with vain Endeavour
Had touch'd that fatal Zone° to her denied!
Young *Fancy* thus, to me Divinest Name,
   To whom, prepar'd and bath'd in Heav'n,
   The Cest° of amplest Pow'r is giv'n:
   To few the God-like Gift assigns,   20
   To gird their blest prophetic Loins,
And gaze° her Visions wild, and feel unmix'd her
   Flame!

2.

The Band, as Fairy Legends say,
Was wove on that creating Day,
When He, who call'd with Thought to Birth
Yon tented° Sky, this laughing Earth,
And drest with Springs, and Forests tall,
And pour'd the Main engirting all,
Long by the lov'd *Enthusiast* woo'd,
Himself in some Diviner Mood,   30
Retiring, sate with her alone,
And plac'd her on his Saphire Throne,
The whiles, the vaulted Shrine around,
Seraphic Wires were heard to sound,
Now sublimest Triumph swelling,
Now on Love and Mercy dwelling;
And she, from out the veiling Cloud,
Breath'd her magic Notes aloud:
And Thou, Thou rich-hair'd Youth of Morn,°
And all thy subject Life was born!   40
The dang'rous Passions kept aloof,
Far from the sainted growing Woof:°

5. **One . . . Fair:** [Collins's note] *Florimel.* See *Spenser* Leg.
4th. [An error. In *The Faerie Queene*, IV. v, Florimel's magic
belt, which "gaue the vertue of chast loue," fitted only
the virtuous Amoret.] **16. Zone:** belt. **19. Cest:** belt, band.
22. gaze: "to view stedfastly" (Johnson's *Dictionary*). **26.
tented:** the earliest use recorded in the *OED*. **39. Thou
. . . Morn:** Phoebus Apollo, god of poetry and music.
He is often depicted with flaming sunlike hair. **42. Woof:**
threads.

59. thrice-hallow'd Eve: Hallowe'en. **70. Cypress Wreath:**
the emblem of the tragic poet; cypress has funereal connotations. ODE ON THE POETICAL CHARACTER. **1. Regard:** attention.

But near it sate Ecstatic *Wonder*,
List'ning the deep applauding Thunder:
And *Truth*, in sunny Vest array'd,
By whose the Tarsel's Eyes were made;°
All the shad'wy Tribes of *Mind*,
In braided Dance their Murmurs join'd,
And all the bright uncounted *Pow'rs*,
Who feed on Heav'n's ambrosial° Flow'rs.   50
Where is the Bard, whose Soul can now
Its high presuming Hopes avow?
Where He who thinks, with Rapture blind,
This hallow'd Work° for Him design'd?

                              3.
High on some Cliff, to Heav'n up-pil'd,
Of rude Access, of Prospect wild,
Where, tangled round the jealous Steep,
Strange Shades o'erbrow the Valleys deep,
And holy *Genii* guard the Rock,°
Its Gloomes embrown, its Springs unlock,   60
While on its rich ambitious Head,
An *Eden*, like his own, lies spread.
I view that Oak,° the fancied Glades among,
By which as *Milton* lay, His Ev'ning Ear,
From many a Cloud that drop'd Ethereal Dew,
Nigh spher'd in Heav'n its native Strains could hear:
On which that ancient Trump he reach'd was hung;
     Thither oft his Glory greeting,
     From *Waller's*° Myrtle° Shades retreating,
With many a Vow from Hope's aspiring Tongue,   70
My trembling Feet his guiding Steps pursue;
     In vain—Such Bliss to One alone,
     Of all the Sons of Soul was known,
     And Heav'n, and *Fancy*, kindred Pow'rs,
     Have now o'erturned th' inspiring Bow'rs,
Or curtain'd close such Scene from ev'ry future View.

---

46. By . . . made: By reference to whose eyes the eyes of the falcon were made. **50. ambrosial:** from *ambrosia*, the food of the Greek gods. **54. Work:** the belt of poetry. **59. the Rock:** Cf. Mount Parnassus, the Greek mountain sacred to Apollo and the Muses. **63. that Oak:** See Milton's *Il Penseroso*, l. 60. **69. Waller:** Edmund Waller (1606–87), the poet known for the "sweetness" of his verses. (See the selections from Waller in Part Three.) **Myrtle:** Among the ancients myrtle was associated with love and was sacred to Venus.

ODE, WRITTEN
IN THE BEGINNING
OF THE YEAR 1746

In 1745 and early 1746 the British army fought three important battles. It was defeated in each. In May, 1745, it fought the French at Fontenoy, in Belgium; and in September, 1745, and January, 1746, it fought the Jacobites at Prestonpans and Falkirk, in Scotland.

The text is that of the first printing, in *Odes . . .* (1747).

How sleep the Brave, who sink to Rest,
By all their Country's Wishes blest!
When *Spring*, with dewy Fingers cold,
Returns to deck their hallow'd Mold,
She there shall dress a sweeter Sod,
Than *Fancy*'s Feet have ever trod.

                              2.
By Fairy Hands their Knell is rung,
By Forms unseen their Dirge is sung;
There *Honour* comes, a Pilgrim grey,
To bless the Turf that wraps their Clay,   10
And *Freedom* shall a-while repair,
To dwell a weeping Hermit there!

ODE TO EVENING

In genre this poem is a Horatian ode. The unrhymed verse form is imitated from Horace's ode *To Pyrrha* (Book I, Ode v). Although the absence of rhyme troubled some critics who did not see how many substitutes for rhyme Collins makes use of nor that he occasionally inserts a rhyme or half-rhyme, most readers were delighted with the "imagery and enthusiasm" of the performance. Robert Southey observed in 1837, "Everyone who has an ear for metre and a heart for poetry must have felt how perfectly the metre of Collins's *Ode to Evening* [1747] is in accordance with the imagery and the feeling."

The text is that of the first printing, in *Odes . . .* (1747); we have incorporated the substantive variants of the text in Dodsley's *Collection* (Vol. I, 1748).

If ought of Oaten Stop,° or Pastoral Song,
May hope, chaste EVE, to soothe thy modest ear,
  Like thy own solemn Springs,
  Thy Springs, and dying Gales,
O *Nymph* reserv'd, while now the bright-hair'd Sun
Sits in yon western Tent, whose cloudy Skirts,
  With Brede° ethereal wove,
  O'erhang his wavy Bed:
Now Air is hush'd, save where the weak-ey'd Bat,
With short shrill Shriek flits by on leathern Wing, 10
  Or where the Beetle winds
  His small but sullen Horn,
As oft he rises 'midst the twilight Path,
Against the Pilgrim born in heedless Hum:
  Now teach me, *Maid* compos'd,
  To breathe some soften'd Strain,
Whose Numbers° stealing thro' thy darkning Vale,
May not unseemly with its Stillness suit,
  As musing slow, I hail
  Thy genial° lov'd Return!   20
For when thy folding Star° arising shews
His paly Circlet, at his warning Lamp
  The fragrant *Hours*, and *Elves*
  Who slept in flow'rs the day,
And many a *Nymph* who wreaths her Brows with
    Sedge,
And sheds the fresh'ning Dew, and lovelier still,
  The *Pensive Pleasures* sweet
  Prepare thy shadowy Car.°
Then lead, calm Vot'ress, where some sheety lake
Cheers the lone heath, or some time-hallow'd pile, 30
  Or up-land fallows grey
  Reflect its last cool gleam.
But when chill blustring Winds, or driving Rain,
Forbid my willing Feet, be mine the Hut,
  That from the Mountain's Side,
  Views Wilds, and swelling Floods,
And Hamlets brown, and dim-discover'd Spires,
And hears their simple Bell, and marks o'er all
  Thy Dewy Fingers draw
  The gradual dusky Veil.   40
While *Spring* shall pour his Show'rs, as oft he wont,
And bathe thy breathing° Tresses, meekest *Eve!*

While *Summer* loves to sport,
  Beneath thy ling'ring Light:
While sallow *Autumn* fills thy Lap with Leaves,
Or *Winter* yelling thro' the troublous Air,
  Affrights thy shrinking Train,
  And rudely rends thy Robes.
So long, sure-found beneath the Sylvan shed,
Shall FANCY, FRIENDSHIP, SCIENCE,° rose-lip'd
  HEALTH,   50
  Thy gentlest Influence own,
  And hymn thy fav'rite Name!

THE PASSIONS, AN ODE FOR MUSIC

❧

The elevated and passionate "ode for music," as a received kind of poetry, had been popular since Dryden's *Alexander's Feast* (1697) and Pope's *Ode for Music on St. Cecilia's Day* (1713). Collins's *The Passions* (1747) was set to music by Dr. William Hayes and performed at Oxford in 1750. It was greatly admired in its own time, and by the early nineteenth century it had become one of the best-known English poems and a favorite text for expressive dramatic reading and public declamation (see Dickens's *Great Expectations*, Ch. vii). In 1793 a writer in *The Gentleman's Magazine* declared:

> Next . . . to the Alexander's Feast, and in some respects superior, is Collins's noble Ode to the Passions, which, whether we consider the originality and magnificence of the design of the whole, and its parts, or its imagery, its sentiments, its expressions, and its versification, has ever appeared to me one of the happiest efforts of human poetry.

The text is that of the first printing, in *Odes . . .* (1747).

❧

When Music,° Heav'nly Maid, was young,
While yet in early *Greece* she sung,
The Passions oft to hear her Shell,°
Throng'd around her magic Cell,

ODE TO EVENING. **1. Oaten Stop:** shepherd's reed flute. **7. Brede:** embroidery. **17. Numbers:** versification, rhythm. **20. genial:** first use recorded by the *OED* in the sense of "cheering, enlivening." **21. thy . . . Star:** Hesperus, the evening star, whose appearance is a signal to the shepherd to drive his sheep into the fold. Cf. Milton's *Comus*, l. 93. **28. Car:** chariot. **42. breathing:** fragrant.

50. Science: knowledge. THE PASSIONS, AN ODE FOR MUSIC. **1. Music:** Euterpe, Muse of music. **3. Shell:** lyre, made from a tortoise shell.

Exulting, trembling, raging, fainting,
Possest beyond the Muse's Painting;
By turns they felt the glowing Mind,
Disturb'd, delighted, rais'd, refin'd.
Till once, 'tis said, when all were fir'd,
Fill'd with Fury, rapt, inspir'd,   10
From the supporting Myrtles round,
They snatch'd her Instruments of Sound,
And as they oft had heard a-part
Sweet Lessons of her forceful Art,
Each, for Madness rul'd the Hour,
Would prove his own expressive Pow'r.

First *Fear* his Hand, its Skill to try,
    Amid the Chords° bewilder'd laid,
And back recoil'd he knew not why,
    Ev'n at the Sound himself had made.   20

Next *Anger* rush'd, his Eyes on fire,
    In Lightnings own'd his secret Stings,
In one rude Clash he struck the Lyre,
    And swept with hurried Hand the Strings.

With woful Measures wan *Despair*
    Low sullen Sounds his Grief beguil'd,
A solemn, strange, and mingled Air,
    'Twas sad by Fits, by Starts 'twas wild.

But thou, O *Hope*, with Eyes so fair,
    What was thy delightful Measure?   30
Still it whisper'd promis'd Pleasure,
    And bad the lovely Scenes at distance hail!

Still would Her Touch the Strain prolong,
    And from the Rocks, the Woods, the Vale,
She call'd on Echo still thro' all the Song;
    And, where Her sweetest Theme She chose,
A soft responsive Voice was heard at ev'ry Close,°
And *Hope* enchanted smil'd, and wav'd Her golden
    Hair.
And longer had She sung,—but with a Frown,
    Revenge impatient rose,   40
He threw his blood-stain'd Sword in Thunder down,
    And with a with'ring Look,
    The War-denouncing° Trumpet took,
And blew a Blast so loud and dread,
Were ne'er Prophetic Sounds so full of Woe.
    And ever and anon he beat
    The doubling Drum with furious Heat;

And tho' sometimes each dreary Pause between,
    Dejected *Pity* at his Side,
    Her Soul-subduing Voice applied,   50
    Yet still He kept his wild unalter'd Mien,
While each strain'd Ball of Sight seem'd bursting from
    his Head.

Thy Numbers, *Jealousy*, to nought were fix'd,
    Sad Proof of thy distressful State,
Of diff'ring Themes the veering Song was mix'd,
    And now it courted *Love*, now raving call'd on
        Hate.

With Eyes up-rais'd, as one inspir'd,
Pale *Melancholy* sate retir'd,
And from her wild sequester'd Seat,
In Notes by Distance made more sweet,   60
Pour'd thro' the mellow *Horn* her pensive Soul:
    And dashing soft from Rocks around,
    Bubbling Runnels° join'd the Sound;
Thro' Glades and Glooms the mingled Measure stole,
    Or o'er some haunted Stream with fond Delay,
    Round an holy Calm diffusing,
    Love of Peace, and lonely Musing,
In hollow Murmurs died away.
But O how alter'd was its sprightlier Tone!
When *Chearfulness*, a Nymph of healthiest Hue,   70
    Her Bow a-cross her Shoulder flung,
    Her Buskins° gem'd with Morning Dew,
Blew an inspiring Air, that Dale and Thicket rung,
    The Hunter's Call to *Faun* and *Dryad* known!
    The Oak-crown'd *Sisters*, and their chast-eye'd
        Queen,°
    Satyrs and sylvan Boys were seen,
    Peeping from forth their Alleys green;
Brown *Exercise* rejoic'd to hear,
    And *Sport* leapt up, and seiz'd his Beechen Spear.

Last came *Joy*'s Ecstatic Trial,   80
He with viny Crown advancing,
    First to the lively Pipe his Hand addrest,
But soon he saw the brisk awak'ning Viol,
    Whose sweet entrancing Voice he lov'd the best.
    They would have thought who heard the Strain,
    They saw in *Tempe*'s° Vale her native Maids,
    Amidst the festal sounding Shades,

---

18. Chords: strings. **37. ev'ry Close:** the end of every musical theme or strain. **43. War-denouncing:** war-proclaiming.

63. Runnels: brooks. **72. Buskins:** boots. **75. Queen:** Artemis (Diana), virgin goddess of the hunt and protectress of young people. Her "sisters" are the wood nymphs who serve her. **86. Tempe:** a Greek valley sacred to Apollo.

To some unwearied Minstrel dancing,
  While as his flying Fingers kiss'd the Strings,
  LOVE fram'd with *Mirth*, a gay fantastic Round, 90
  Loose were Her Tresses seen, her Zone unbound,
    And HE° amidst his frolic Play,
    As if he would the charming Air repay,
  Shook thousand Odours from his dewy Wings.

O *Music*, Sphere-descended° Maid,
  Friend of Pleasure, *Wisdom*'s Aid,
  Why, Goddess, why to us deny'd?
  Lay'st Thou thy antient Lyre aside?
  As in that lov'd *Athenian* Bow'r,
  You learn'd an all-commanding Pow'r,   100
  Thy mimic Soul, O Nymph endear'd,
  Can well recall what then it heard.
  Where is thy native simple Heart,
  Devote to Virtue, Fancy, Art?
  Arise as in that elder Time,
  Warm, Energic, Chaste, Sublime!
  Thy Wonders in that God-like Age,
  Fill thy recording *Sister*'s° Page—
  'Tis said, and I believe the Tale,
  Thy humblest *Reed* could more prevail,   110
  Had more of Strength, diviner Rage,
  Than all which charms this laggard Age,
  Ev'n all at once together found,
  Cæcilia's° mingled World of Sound—
  O bid our vain Endeavours cease,
  Revive the just Designs of *Greece*,
  Return in all thy simple State!
  Confirm the Tales Her Sons relate!

ODE OCCASION'D
BY THE DEATH
OF MR. THOMSON

For the last twelve years of his life the poet James Thomson lived in retirement at Richmond, a Thames village a few miles from London. Collins saw a great deal of him at Richmond, and the two became close friends. When Thomson died in 1748, he was buried in the Church of St. Mary, Richmond.

In 1791 Robert Burns was asked by a noble patron to try his hand at a poem in memory of Thomson. Burns replied, "Your lordship hints at an Ode for the occasion, but who would write after Collins? I read over his verses to the memory of Thomson and despaired." Wordsworth's *Lines Written near Richmond* (1798) suggests that Wordsworth as well as Burns found the poem impressive.

The text is that of the first edition (1749).

ADVERTISEMENT.

THE Scene of the following STANZAS is suppos'd to lie on the *Thames* near *Richmond*.

I.

IN yonder Grave a DRUID° lies
  Where slowly winds the stealing Wave!
The *Year*'s° best Sweets shall duteous rise
  To deck *it's* POET'*s* sylvan Grave!

II.

In yon deep Bed of whisp'ring Reeds
  His airy Harp° shall now be laid,
That He, whose Heart in Sorrow bleeds
  May love thro' Life the soothing Shade.

III.

Then Maids and Youths shall linger here,
  And while it's Sounds at distance swell,   10
Shall sadly seem in Pity's Ear
  To hear the WOODLAND PILGRIM's Knell.

IV.

REMEMBRANCE oft shall haunt the Shore
  When THAMES in Summer-wreaths is drest,
And oft suspend the dashing Oar
  To bid his gentle Spirit rest!

---

92. He: Love. **95. Sphere-descended:** It was once thought that the motion of the spheres (the planetary orbits conceived as transparent spheres) generated heavenly harmonies. **108. thy . . . Sister:** Clio, Muse of history. **114. Cæcilia:** St. Cecilia, patroness of music and reputed inventor of the organ.

ODE OCCASION'D BY THE DEATH OF MR. THOMSON. **1. a Druid:** Thomson celebrated woods and vales. **3. Year:** an allusion to Thomson's most famous work, *The Seasons* (see Part Two). **6. His . . . Harp:** [Collins's note] The Harp of *Æolus*, of which see a Description in [Thomson's] the *Castle of Indolence* [i. 40].

V.

And oft as EASE and HEALTH retire
　To breezy Lawn, or Forest deep,
The Friend shall view yon whit'ning Spire,°
　And 'mid the varied Landscape weep.　　20

VI.

But Thou, who own'st that Earthy Bed,
　Ah! what will ev'ry Dirge avail?
Or Tears, which LOVE and PITY shed
　That mourn beneath the gliding Sail!

VII.

Yet lives there one, whose heedless Eye
　Shall scorn thy pale Shrine glimm'ring near?
With Him, Sweet Bard, may FANCY die,
　And JOY desert the blooming Year.

VIII.

But thou, lorn STREAM, whose sullen Tide
　No sedge-crown'd SISTERS now attend,　　30
Now waft me from the green Hill's Side
　Whose cold Turf hides the buried FRIEND!

IX.

And see, the Fairy Valleys fade,
　Dun *Night* has veil'd the solemn View!
—Yet once again, Dear parted SHADE
　Meek NATURE's CHILD again adieu!

X.

The genial Meads assign'd to bless
　Thy Life, shall mourn thy early Doom,
Their Hinds, and Shepherd-Girls shall dress
　With simple Hands thy rural Tomb.　　40

XI.

Long, long, thy Stone and pointed Clay
　Shall melt the musing BRITON's Eyes,
O! VALES, and WILD WOODS, shall HE say
　In yonder Grave YOUR DRUID lies!

---

19. yon . . . Spire: [Collins's note] *Richmond*-Church.

AN ODE ON THE POPULAR SUPERSTITIONS OF THE HIGHLANDS OF SCOTLAND, CONSIDERED AS THE SUBJECT OF POETRY

The person addressed in the first line is John Home (1722–1808), a Scottish divine, patriot, and playwright best known for his popular tragedy *Douglas* (1756). In the autumn of 1749 Home came to England, hoping to persuade David Garrick to produce his tragedy *Agis*. Collins met Home at the house of a friend, Thomas Barrow, in Winchester. Here they conversed for two weeks before Home's return to Scotland. He apparently carried with him a draft of this poem, and it was this manuscript that found its way into print in 1788.

The text is that of the first printing, in *Transactions of the Royal Society of Edinburgh* (Vol. I, 1788); we have restored the manuscript readings where necessary, and we have reduced and omitted some of the footnotes.

I.

H——, thou return'st from Thames, whose Naiads
　　long
　Have seen thee ling'ring, with a fond delay,
Mid those soft friends, whose hearts, some future day,
　Shall melt, perhaps, to hear thy tragic song.
Go, not unmindful of that cordial youth,°
　Whom, long endear'd, thou leav'st by Lavant's°
　　side;
Together let us wish him lasting truth,
　And joy untainted with his destin'd bride.
Go! nor regardless, while these numbers boast
　My short-liv'd bliss, forget my social name;　　10
But think far off how, on the southern coast,
　I met thy friendship with an equal flame!
Fresh to that soil° thou turn'st, whose ev'ry vale
　Shall prompt the poet, and his song demand:

ODE ON THE SUPERSTITIONS OF THE HIGHLANDS. 5. that . . . youth: Thomas Barrow. 6. Lavant: the river running through Chichester, where Collins was living. 13. that soil: Scotland.

To thee thy copious subjects ne'er shall fail;
    Thou need'st but take the pencil to thy hand,
And paint what all believe who own° thy genial land.

II.

THERE must thou wake perforce thy Doric° quill,
    'Tis Fancy's land to which thou sett'st thy feet;
Where still, 'tis said, the fairy people meet   20
    Beneath each birken° shade on mead or hill.
There each trim lass that skims the milky store
    To the swart tribes° their creamy bowl allots;
By night they sip it round the cottage-door,
    While airy minstrels warble jocund notes.
There every herd,° by sad experience, knows
    How, wing'd with fate, their elf-shot arrows fly;
When the sick ewe her summer food foregoes,
    Or, stretch'd on earth, the heart-smit heifers lie.
Such airy beings awe th' untutor'd swain: 30
    Nor thou, though learn'd, his homelier thoughts
        neglect;
Let thy sweet muse the rural faith sustain:
    These are the themes of simple, sure effect,
That add new conquests to her boundless reign,
    And fill, with double force, her heart-commanding
        strain.

III.

EV'N yet preserv'd, how often may'st thou hear,
    Where to the pole the Boreal mountains° run,
Taught by the father to his list'ning son
    Strange lays, whose power had charm'd a SPENCER's
        ear.
At ev'ry pause, before thy mind possest,   40
    Old RUNIC bards° shall seem to rise around,
With uncouth lyres, in many-coloured vest,
    Their matted hair with boughs fantastic crown'd:
Whether thou bid'st the well-taught hind repeat
    The choral dirge that mourns some chieftain brave,
When ev'ry shrieking maid her bosom beat,
    And strew'd with choicest herbs his scented grave;
Or whether, sitting in the shepherd's shiel,°
    Thou hear'st some sounding tale of war's alarms;

When, at the bugle's call, with fire and steel,   50
    The sturdy clans pour'd forth their bony° swarms,
And hostile brothers met to prove each other's arms.

IV.

'TIS thine to sing, how framing hideous spells
    In SKY's lone isle° the gifted wizzard seer,
Lodged in the wintry cave with ——,°
    Or in the depth of UIST's° dark forests dwells:
How they, whose sight° such dreary dreams engross,
    With their own visions oft astonish'd droop,
When o'er the wat'ry strath° or quaggy moss
    They see the gliding ghosts unbodied troop.   60
Or if in sports, or on the festive green,
    Their —— glance some fated youth descry,
Who, now perhaps in lusty vigour seen
    And rosy health, shall soon lamented die.
For them the viewless forms of air obey
    Their bidding heed, and at their beck repair.
They know what spirit brews the stormful day,
    And heartless, oft like moody madness stare
To see the phantom train their secret work prepare.°

    . . .

VI.

What though far off, from some dark dell espied
    His glimm'ring mazes cheer th' excursive sight,
Yet turn, ye wand'rers, turn your steps aside,
    Nor trust the guidance of that faithless light;
For watchful, lurking 'mid th' unrustling reed,
    At those mirk° hours the wily monster lies,   100
And listens oft to hear the passing steed,
    And frequent round him rolls his sullen eyes,
If chance his savage wrath may some weak wretch
    surprise.

VII.

AH, luckless swain, o'er all unblest indeed!
    Whom late bewilder'd in the dank, dark fen,
Far from his flocks and smoking hamlet then!
    To that sad spot ——————:

---

17. **own:** acknowledge, appreciate. 18. **Doric:** rustic, simple. 21. **birken:** birch. 23. **swart tribes:** brownies. 26. **herd:** shepherd, herdsman. 37. **the Boreal mountains:** the northern mountains, in the Hebrides. 41. **Runic bards:** ancient Scottish poets writing with the Runic alphabet. 48. **shiel:** [original note, but not by Collins] A kind of hut, built for a summer habitation to the herdsmen, when the cattle are sent to graze in distant pastures.

51. **bony:** probably *bonnie*, meaning handsome. 54. **Sky's . . . isle:** the isle of Skye, off the northwest coast of Scotland, the largest of the Hebridean islands. 55. ——: Here and at other dashes the manuscript was blank. 56. **Uist:** the name of two islands in the Outer Hebrides. 57. **sight:** second sight, a visionary and prophetic talent often ascribed to the Highlanders. 59. **strath:** wide valley. 69. **prepare:** One leaf of the manuscript, containing twenty-five lines (all of stanza 5 and eight lines of stanza 6) was lost before the poem was printed. 100. **mirk:** dark.

On him enrag'd, the fiend, in angry mood,
   Shall never look with pity's kind concern,
But instant, furious, raise the whelming flood   110
   O'er its drown'd bank, forbidding all return.
Or, if he meditate his wish'd escape
   To some dim hill that seems uprising near,
To his faint eye the grim and grisly shape,
   In all its terrors clad, shall wild appear.
Meantime, the wat'ry surge shall round him rise,
   Pour'd sudden forth from ev'ry swelling source.
What now remains but tears and hopeless sighs?
   His fear-shook limbs have lost their youthly force,
And down the waves he floats, a pale and breathless
    corse.   120

VIII.

FOR him, in vain, his anxious wife shall wait,
   Or wander forth to meet him on his way;
For him, in vain, at to-fall of the day,
   His babes shall linger at th' unclosing gate.
Ah, ne'er shall he return! Alone,° if night
   Her travell'd° limbs in broken slumbers steep,
With dropping willows drest, his mournful sprite
   Shall visit sad, perchance, her silent sleep:
Then he, perhaps, with moist and wat'ry hand,
   Shall fondly seem to press her shudd'ring cheek,   130
And with his blue swoln face before her stand,
   And, shiv'ring cold, these piteous accents speak:
Pursue, dear wife, thy daily toils pursue
   At dawn or dusk, industrious as before;
Nor e'er of me one hapless thought renew,
   While I lie welt'ring on the ozier'd shore,°
Drown'd by the KAELPIE's° wrath, nor e'er shall aid
   thee more!

IX.

UNBOUNDED is thy range; with varied stile
   Thy muse may, like those feath'ry tribes which spring
From their rude rocks, extend her skirting wing   140
   Round the moist marge of each cold Hebrid isle,
To that hoar pile° which still its ruin shows:

In whose small vaults a pigmy-folk is found,
   Whose bones the delver with his spade upthrows,
   And culls them, wond'ring, from the hallow'd
     ground!
Or thither where beneath the show'ry west
   The mighty kings of three fair realms are laid:°
Once foes, perhaps, together now they rest.
   No slaves revere them, and no wars invade:
Yet frequent now, at midnight's solemn hour,   150
   The rifted mounds their yawning cells unfold,
And forth the monarch's stalk with sov'reign pow'r
   In pageant robes, and wreath'd with sheeny gold,
And on their twilight tombs aerial council hold.

X.

BUT O! o'er all, forget not KILDA's race,°
   On whose bleak rocks, which brave the wasting
     tides,
Fair Nature's daughter, Virtue, yet abides.
   Go, just, as they, their blameless manners trace!
Then to my ear transmit some gentle song
   Of those whose lives are yet sincere and plain,   160
Their bounded walks the rugged cliff along,
   And all their prospect but the wintry main.
With sparing temp'rance, at the needful time,
   They drain the sainted spring, or, hunger-prest,
Along th' Atlantic rock undreading climb,
   And of its eggs despoil the Solan's° nest.
Thus blest in primal innocence they live,
   Suffic'd and happy with that frugal fare
Which tasteful toil and hourly danger give.
   Hard is their shallow soil, and bleak and bare;   170
Nor ever vernal bee was heard to murmur there!

---

125. Alone: Collins may intend the archaic meaning "only."
126. travell'd: tired. **136. welt'ring . . . shore:** drenched on the willowed shore. **137. Kaelpie:** [original note] A name given in Scotland to a supposed spirit of the waters. **142. that . . . pile:** [original note] ON the largest of the *Flannan islands* (isles of the Hebrides) are the ruins of a chapel dedicated to St FLANNAN. This is reckoned by the inhabitants of the Western Isles a place of uncommon sanctity. One of the Flannan islands is termed the *Isle of Pigmies;* and [Martin] MARTIN [d. 1718] says [in *A Description of the Western Islands of Scotland* (1703)], there have been many small bones dug up there, resembling in miniature those of the human body.

146–47. where . . . laid: [original note] The island of *Iona* or *Icolmkill.* See MARTIN's Description of the Western Islands of Scotland. That author informs us, that forty-eight kings of Scotland, four kings of Ireland, and five of Norway, were interred in the Church of St OURAN in that island. . . . COLLINS has taken all his information respecting the Western Isles from MARTIN; from whom he may likewise have derived his knowledge of the popular superstitions of the Highlanders, with which this ode shows so perfect an acquaintance. **155. Kilda's race:** [original note] The character of the inhabitants of St Kilda, as here described, agrees perfectly with the accounts given by MARTIN [in *A Late Voyage to St. Kilda* (1698)] and by [the Reverend Kenneth] MACAULAY [in his *History of St. Kilda* (1764)], of the people of that island. It is the most westerly of all the Hebrides, and is above 130 miles distant from the main land of Scotland. **166. Solan:** the gannet, a sea bird.

XI.

NOR needs't thou blush, that such false themes engage
    Thy gentle mind, of fairer stores possest;
For not alone they touch the village breast,
    But fill'd in elder time th' historic page.
There SHAKESPEARE's self, with ev'ry garland crown'd,
    In musing hour, his wayward sisters° found,
And with their terrors drest the magic scene.
From them he sung, when mid his bold design,
    Before the Scot° afflicted and aghast,   180
The shadowy kings of BANQUO's fated line,
    Through the dark cave in gleamy pageant past.°
Proceed, nor quit the tales which, simply told,
    Could once so well my answ'ring bosom pierce;
Proceed, in forceful sounds and colours bold
    The native legends of thy land rehearse;
To such adapt thy lyre and suit thy powerful verse.

XII.

IN scenes like these, which, daring to depart
    From sober truth, are still to nature true,
And call forth fresh delight to fancy's view,   190
    Th' heroic muse employ'd her TASSO's° art!
How have I trembled, when at TANCRED's° stroke,
    Its gushing blood the gaping cypress pour'd;
When each live plant with mortal accents spoke,
    And the wild blast up-heav'd the vanish'd sword°!

How have I sat, when pip'd the pensive wind,
    To hear his harp, by British FAIRFAX strung.
Prevailing poet, whose undoubting mind
    Believ'd the magic wonders which he sung!
Hence at each sound imagination glows;   200
Hence his warm lay with softest sweetness flows;
    Melting it flows, pure, num'rous, strong and clear,
And fills th' impassion'd heart, and wins th'
    harmonious ear.

XIII.

ALL hail, ye scenes that o'er my soul prevail,
    Ye ——— friths° and lakes which, far away,
Are by smooth ANNAN fill'd, or past'ral TAY,
    Or DON's° romantic springs, at distance, hail!
The time shall come when I, perhaps, may tread
    Your lowly glens, o'erhung with spreading broom,
Or o'er your stretching heaths by fancy led: 210
    Then will I dress once more the faded bow'r,
Where JOHNSON sat in DRUMMOND's° ——— shade,
    Or crop from Tiviot's dale each ———,
And mourn on Yarrow's° banks ———.
Meantime, ye Pow'rs, that on the plains which bore
    The cordial youth,° on LOTHIAN's plains attend,
Where'er he dwell, on hill, or lowly muir,°
    To him I lose, your kind protection lend,
And, touch'd with love like mine, preserve my absent
    friend.

---

177. wayward sisters: the Weird Sisters in *Macbeth.* **180. the Scot:** Macbeth. **182. pageant past:** See *Macbeth,* IV. i. **191. Tasso:** Torquato Tasso (1544–95), Italian poet, author of the romantic epic *Jerusalem Delivered* (1581–93), which was translated into English (1600) by Edward Fairfax (d. 1635). **192. Tancred:** a Norman knight who participated in the first Crusade; one of the heroes of *Jerusalem Delivered.* **195. the vanish'd sword:** See *Jerusalem Delivered,* Book XIII, sts. 44 ff.

205. friths: long, narrow coastal indentations. **206–07. Annan, Tay, Don:** rivers in Scotland. **212. Drummond:** The Scottish poet William Drummond of Hawthornden (1585–1649) entertained Ben Jonson and recorded his conversation in 1618–19. **213–14. Tiviot, Yarrow:** rivers in Scotland. **216. The cordial youth:** Home, who lived in the county of East Lothian. **217. muir:** moor.

Joseph Warton 1722–1800

Thomas Warton 1728–1790

The scholarly Warton brothers, who both became teachers of literature, were the sons of Thomas Warton the Elder (*c.* 1688–1745), an underrated poet who, after ten years as the not very competent professor of poetry at Oxford, settled in the Hampshire town of Basingstoke as Vicar and as headmaster of the local grammar school.

The elder son, Joseph, was educated at Winchester College, where the poet William Collins was one of his friends. He entered Oriel College, Oxford, in 1740 and, upon graduation, took holy orders and returned to Basingstoke as his father's curate. In 1744 he published *The Enthusiast: or, the Lover of Nature*, a Miltonic blank-verse encomium on the scenic primitive and sublime as opposed to "Art's vain Pomps." This work was followed in 1746 by a volume of *Odes on Various Subjects*, where the author announces in the Advertisement that "the fashion of moralizing in verse has been carried too far." The model of many of these odes is Milton's *Il Penseroso*. In 1753 Joseph published a four-volume edition of Virgil, and during the early 1750's Samuel Johnson accepted a number of his literary essays for *The Adventurer*. The first volume of his *Essay on the Writings and Genius of Pope* (the two terms in the title were later transposed) was published in 1756, just after he had attained an appointment as second master at Winchester. He became headmaster in 1766. His long administration at Winchester was troubled by numerous schoolboy mutinies, and everyone seems to have been relieved when, in 1793, he retired to clerical duties at nearby Wickham. Joseph was friendly with Johnson, whose Literary Club he joined in 1773, as well as with Burke, Reynolds, and Garrick; he enlivened their social gatherings with an excessively energetic and ecstatic manner in conversation that made him on occasion appear comic. His last work was an edition of Pope in nine volumes (1797). When he died he was working on an edition of Dryden, which was finished in 1811 by his son John.

If Joseph was primarily a critic, his younger brother, Thomas, was primarily an antiquarian with a fondness for the Gothic both in architecture and in literature. After graduating from Trinity College, Oxford, he took orders and, in 1751, became a Fellow of Trinity. At Oxford he presented a curious spectacle: he was short, fat, and ruddy, a beer drinker and a frequenter of uncouth company. Among his earliest writings is *The Pleasures of Melancholy* (1747), a Miltonic blank-verse poem full of ruined abbeys, druids, and pensive moods. His *Observations on the Faerie Queene of Spenser* (1754) established his reputation as a scholar and brought him Johnson's friendship. From 1757 to 1767 he served as professor of poetry at Oxford, delivering Latin lectures on classical literature. In 1770 his edition of Theocritus appeared, and in 1774 the first volume of his massive *History of English Poetry from the Close of the Eleventh to the Commencement of the Eighteenth Century*. This work was never finished; the third volume, bringing the history up to only the beginning of the seventeenth century, came out in 1781. Although it is more digressive, the *History of English Poetry* is comparable in magnitude of materials to the achievements in history of Gibbon, Hume, and William Robertson. In 1777 Thomas published a volume of poems, including some sonnets, which revealed his devotion to Spenser and Milton. It was these poems that Johnson once ridiculed in the Wartons' beloved *Il Penseroso* meter:

> Phrase that Time has flung away;
> Uncouth words in disarray,
> Trick'd in antique ruff and bonnet,
> Ode, and elegy, and sonnet.

"But remember," Johnson reminded Mrs. Thrale, "I love the fellow dearly, now— for all I laugh at him." Johnson approved, on the other hand, of Warton's *Enquiry into the Authenticity of the Poems Attributed to Thomas Rowley* (1782), which demonstrated that Chatterton's poems were not medieval. Thomas was accepted into Johnson's Club during the year the *Enquiry* was published. Upon the death of William Whitehead in 1785, he was appointed Poet Laureate. His last important work was a distinguished edition of Milton's early poems (1785).

A convenient selection of the verse of the Wartons, father and sons, is Eric Partridge's *The Three Wartons: A Choice of Their Verse* (1927). W. D. MacClintock's *Joseph Warton's Essay on Pope: A History of the Five Editions* (1933) explores the significance of the interesting textual changes. The standard work on Thomas Warton is Clarissa Rinaker's *Thomas Warton: A Biographical and Critical Study* (1916). René Wellek's *The Rise of English Literary History* (1941) assesses Thomas's achievements as a literary historian. Arthur Johnston's *Enchanted Ground: The Study of Medieval Romance in the Eighteenth Century* (1964) contains a chapter on Thomas Warton.

Joseph Warton

THE DYING INDIAN

❦

The text is from Dodsley's *A Collection of Poems* (Vol. IV, 1755); we have incorporated the substantive variants of the text in Dodsley's second edition (Vol. IV, 1758).

❦

THE dart of Izdabel prevails! 'twas dipt
In double poison—I shall soon arrive
At the blest island, where no tigers spring
On heedless hunters; where anana's° bloom
Thrice in each moon; where rivers smoothly glide,
Nor thundering torrents whirl the light canoe
Down to the sea; where my forefathers feast
Daily on hearts of Spaniards!—O my son,
I feel the venom busy in my breast,
Approach, and bring my crown, deck'd with the teeth   10

THE DYING INDIAN. **4. anana's:** pineapples.

Of that bold christian who first dar'd deflour
The virgins of the sun; and, dire to tell!
Robb'd PACHACAMAC's° altar of its gems!
I mark'd the spot where they interr'd this traitor,
And once at midnight stole I to his tomb,
And tore his carcass from the earth, and left it
A prey to poisonous flies. Preserve this crown
With sacred secrecy: if e'er returns
Thy much-lov'd mother from the desart woods
Where, as I hunted late, I hapless lost her,   20
Cherish her age. Tell her I ne'er have worship'd
With those that eat their God. And when disease
Preys on her languid limbs, then kindly stab her
With thine own hands, nor suffer her to linger,
Like christian cowards, in a life of pain.
I go! great COPAC° beckons me! farewell!

DEDICATION
[TO *AN ESSAY*
ON . . . POPE]

TO THE REV. DR. YOUNG,° *Rector of Welwyn*,
IN HERTFORDSHIRE.

The first volume of Joseph Warton's *Essay on the Genius and Writings of Pope* appeared anonymously in 1756; the second, curiously delayed for twenty-six years, appeared only in 1782. The work as a whole, comprising fourteen sections and almost five hundred pages, is a minute and systematic critical examination of Pope's works in chronological order. Reviewing the first volume in *The Literary Magazine* (1756), Samuel Johnson found it "a work abounding with curious quotations and pleasing disquisitions." He continued:

> He must be much acquainted with literary history, both of remote and late times, who does not find in this essay many things which he did not know before: and if there be any too learned to be instructed in facts or opinions, he may yet properly read this book as a just specimen of literary moderation.

Several years later Boswell wondered why Warton was delaying so long in bringing out the final volume.

---

13. **Pachacamac:** the site of a pre-Inca temple in western Peru, despoiled by the Spanish under Pizarro in the 1530's. 26. **Copac:** (Capac) a deified early Inca chief. DEDICATION TO *An Essay on Pope.* **Young:** Edward Young (1683–1785), poet and critic. (See the selections from Young earlier in Part Five and in Part Three.)

Johnson answered, "Why, Sir, I suppose he finds himself a little disappointed, in not having been able to persuade the world to be of his opinion as to Pope."

Because Warton's final revisions suggest important shifts in taste, we have printed the text of the fifth edition (1806) and supplied in the footnotes all the variant readings of the first edition (1756).

DEAR SIR,

PERMIT me to break into your retirement, the residence of virtue and literature, and to trouble you with a few reflections on the merits and real character of an admired Author, and on other collateral subjects of criticism,[1] that will naturally arise in the course of such an enquiry.[2] No love of singularity, no affectation of paradoxical opinions, gave rise to the following Work. I revere the memory of POPE, I respect and honour his abilities; but I do not think him at the head of his profession. In other words, in that species of poetry wherein POPE excelled, he is superior to all mankind: and I only say, that this species of poetry is not the most excellent one of the art.

We do not, it should seem, sufficiently attend to the difference there is betwixt a MAN OF WIT, a MAN OF SENSE, and a TRUE POET. Donne[3] and Swift were undoubtedly men of wit, and men of sense: but what traces have they left of PURE POETRY? It is remarkable, that Dryden says of Donne, "He was the greatest wit, though not the greatest poet, of this nation."[4] Fontenelle and La Motte[5] are entitled to the former character; but what can they urge to gain the latter? Which of these characters is the most valuable and useful, is entirely out of the question: all I plead for, is, to have their several provinces kept distinct from each other; and to impress on the reader, that a clear head, and acute understanding, are not sufficient, alone, to make a POET; that the most solid observations on human life, expressed with the utmost elegance and brevity, are MORALITY, and not POETRY; that the EPISTLES of Boileau[6] in RHYME, are no more poetical,

---

1. **of criticism:** omitted in 1756. 2. **in . . . enquiry:** omitted in 1756. 3. **Donne:** John Donne (1572–1631), the most conspicuous of the Metaphysical poets. (See the selection from Johnson's *Life of Cowley* in Part Six.) 4. **It . . . nation:** omitted in 1756. 5. **Fontenelle and La Motte:** contemporary French poets. 6. **the Epistles . . . Boileau:** twelve verse letters by Nicolas Boileau-Despréaux (1636–1711), modeled on the *Epistles* of Horace and published during Boileau's lifetime and posthumously.

than the CHARACTERS of La Bruyere[7] in PROSE; and that it is a creative and glowing IMAGINATION, "acer spiritus ac vis,"[8] and that alone, that can stamp a writer with this exalted and very uncommon character, which so few possess, and of which so few can properly judge.

For one person who can adequately relish and enjoy a work of imagination, twenty are to be found who can taste, and judge of, observations on familiar life, and the manners of the age. The Satires of Ariosto are more read than the Orlando Furioso,[9] or even Dante. Are there so many cordial admirers of Spenser and Milton, as of *Hudibras*,[10] if we strike out of the number of these supposed admirers, those who appear such out of fashion, and not of feeling? Swift's Rhapsody on Poetry[11] is far more popular than Akenside's noble Ode to Lord Huntingdon.[12] The EPISTLES on the Characters of Men and Women,[13] and your sprightly Satires,[14] my good friend, are more frequently perused, and quoted, than L'Allegro and Il Penseroso of Milton. Had you written only these Satires, you would, indeed, have gained the title of a man of wit, and a man of sense; but, I am confident, would not insist on being denominated a POET MERELY on their account.

NON SATIS EST PURIS VERSUM PERSCRIBERE VERBIS.[15]

It is amazing this matter should ever have been mistaken, when Horace has taken particular and repeated pains to settle and adjust the opinion in question. He has more than once disclaimed all right and title to the name of POET on the score of his ethic and satiric pieces.

—NEQUE ENIM CONCLUDERE VERSUM
DIXERIS ESSE SATIS[16]—

are lines often repeated, but whose meaning is not extended and weighed as it ought to be. Nothing can be more judicious than the method he prescribes,[17] of trying whether any composition be essentially poetical or not; which is, to drop entirely the measures and numbers, and transpose and invert the order of the words: and in this unadorned manner to peruse the passage. If there be really in it a true poetical spirit, all your inversions and transpositions will not disguise and extinguish it; but it will retain its lustre, like a diamond unset, and thrown back into the rubbish of the mine. Let us make a little experiment on the following well-known lines: "*Yes, you despise the man that is confined to books, who rails at humankind from his study; though what he learns, he speaks; and may, perhaps, advance some general maxims, or may be right by chance. The coxcomb bird, so grave and so talkative, that cries whore, knave, and cuckold, from his cage, though he rightly call many a passenger, you hold him no philosopher. And yet, such is the fate of all extremes, men may be read too much, as well as books. We grow more partial, for the sake of the observer, to observations which we ourselves make; less so to written wisdom, because another's. Maxims are drawn from notions, and those from guess.*"[18] What shall we say of this passage? Why, that it is most excellent sense, but just as poetical as the "Qui fit Mæcenas"[19] of the author who recommends this method of trial. Take ten[20] lines of the Iliad, Paradise Lost, or even of the Georgics of Virgil, and see whether, by any process of critical chemistry, you can lower and reduce them to the tameness of prose. You will find that they will appear like Ulysses in his disguise of rags, still a hero, though lodged in the cottage of the herdsman Eumæus.[21]

The sublime and the pathetic are the two chief nerves of all genuine poesy. What is there transcendently sublime or pathetic in POPE?[22] In his Works there is, indeed, "nihil inane, nihil arcessitum; puro

---

7. the Characters . . . Bruyere: character sketches and ethical comments published in 1688–94 by Jean de la Bruyère (1645–96). 8. acer . . . vis: "the animation and force of inspiration" (Horace, *Satires*, I. iv. 46). 9. Orlando Furioso: a romantic epic (1532) by the Italian poet Ludovico Ariosto (1474–1533), whose seven satires appeared from 1517 to 1525. 10. Hudibras: the rollicking anti-Presbyterian satire (1663–78) by Samuel Butler (1612–80). 11. Swift's . . . Poetry: published in 1733. (See Part Two.) 12. Ode . . . Huntingdon: a panegyric on nobility and virtue published in 1748 by Mark Akenside (1721–70). (See the selection from Akenside in Part Eight.) 13. The Epistles . . . Women: Pope's first two *Moral Essays: The Knowledge and Characters of Men* (1733) and *Of the Characters of Women* (1735). (For the latter, see Part Two.) 14. your . . . Satires: Edward Young published his seven heroic-couplet satires, titled *Love of Fame, the Universal Passion* (see Part Three) from 1725 to 1728. 15. Non . . . verbis: "It is not enough to use the proper words in writing verses" (Horace, *Satires*, I. iv. 54).

16. Neque . . . satis: "Nor would you call it enough to be able to round off a verse" (*Ibid.*, l. 40). 17. the method . . . prescribes: in *Satires*, I. iv. 56 ff. 18. Yes . . . guess: Cf. the first of Pope's *Moral Essays*, ll. 1–14. 19. Qui fit Mæcenas: Horace's *Satires*, I. i. 1. 20. Take ten: The 1756 edition reads: "Take any ten." 21. the herdsman Eumæus: See *Odyssey*, Book XIV. 22. What . . . Pope: The 1756 edition reads: "What is there very sublime or very Pathetic in POPE?"

tamen fonti quam magno flumini proprior;"[23] as the excellent Quintilian[24] remarks of Lysias.[25] And because I am, perhaps, unwilling[26] to speak out in plain English, I will adopt the following passage of Voltaire, which, in my opinion, as exactly characterizes POPE as it does his model Boileau, for whom it was originally designed: "INCAPABLE PEUT-ÊTRE DU SUBLIME QUI ÉLÈVE L'ÂME, ET DU SENTIMENT QUI L'ATTENDRIT, MAIS FAIT POUR ÉCLAIRER CEUX À QUI LA NATURE ACCORDA L'UN ET L'AUTRE, LABORIEUX, SÉVÈRE, PRÉCIS, PUR, HARMONIEUX, IL DEVINT, ENFIN, LE POÈTE DE LA RAISON."[27]

Our English Poets may, I think, be disposed in four different classes and degrees. In the first class I would place[28] our only three sublime and pathetic poets; SPENSER, SHAKESPEARE, MILTON.[29] In the second class should be ranked[30] such as possessed the true poetical genius, in a more moderate degree, but who[31] had noble talents for moral, ethical, and panegyrical poesy.[32] At the head of these are DRYDEN, PRIOR, ADDISON, COWLEY, WALLER, GARTH, FENTON, GAY, DENHAM, PARNELL.[33] In the third class may be placed

men of wit, of elegant taste, and lively fancy[34] in describing familiar life, though not the higher scenes of poetry.[35] Here may be numbered, BUTLER, SWIFT, ROCHESTER, DONNE, DORSET, OLDHAM.[36] In the fourth class, the mere versifiers, however smooth and mellifluous some of them may be thought, should be disposed.[37] Such as PITT, SANDYS, FAIRFAX, BROOME, BUCKINGHAM, LANSDOWN.[38] This enumeration is not intended as a complete catalogue of writers, and in their proper order, but only to mark out briefly the different species of our celebrated authors.[39] In which of these classes POPE deserves to be placed, the following Work is intended to determine.[40]

I am, DEAR SIR, | Your affectionate | And faithful Servant.

1756.[41]

---

23. nihil . . . proprior: "nothing empty, nothing far-fetched; but I would liken him to a clear spring rather than to a great river" (Quintilian, *Institutio Oratoria*, X. i. 78). **24. Quintilian:** the great first-century A.D. Latin rhetorician. **25. Lysias:** Greek orator of the fifth century B.C. **26. unwilling:** The 1756 edition reads: "ashamed or afraid." **27. Incapable . . . raison:** "Incapable, perhaps, of that sublimity which ennobles and of those feelings which soften the soul, but nevertheless made to direct and enlighten those blessed by nature with both qualities; laborious, severe, accurate, pure, harmonious, he might be called, in short, the poet of reason." **28. In . . . place:** The 1756 edition reads: "I would place first." **29. Milton:** The 1756 edition adds: "and then, at proper intervals, OTWAY and LEE." Thomas Otway (1652–85) and Nathaniel Lee (c. 1653–92) were both writers of stage tragedy. **30. ranked:** The 1756 edition reads: "placed." **31. who:** omitted in 1756. **32. moral . . . poesy:** The 1756 edition reads: "moral and ethical poesy." **33. Dryden . . . Parnell:** The 1756 edition reads: "DRYDEN, DONNE, DENHAM, COWLEY, CONGREVE." Matthew Prior (1664–1721) is especially well known for his satires and epigrams (see the selections from Prior in Part Two); Edmund Waller (1606–87) was known for the "sweetness" of his verses (see the selections from Waller in Part Three); Sir Samuel Garth (1661–1719) wrote *The Dispensary* (1699), a mock epic in heroic couplets; Elijah Fenton (1683–1730) helped Pope translate the *Odyssey* and wrote a successful tragedy *Marianne* (1723); John Gay (1685–1732) is most famous for *The Beggar's Opera* (see Part Two); Sir John Denham (1615–69) is chiefly remembered for his topographical poem *Cooper's Hill* (see Part Three); Thomas Parnell (1679–1718), a friend of Pope's, wrote *A Night-Piece on Death* (1721) and other poems (see the selection from Parnell in Part Three).

34. lively fancy: The 1756 edition reads: "some fancy." **35. through . . . poetry:** omitted in 1756. **36. Butler . . . Oldham:** The 1756 edition reads: "PRIOR, WALLER, PARNELL, SWIFT, FENTON." John Wilmot (1648–80), Second Earl of Rochester, wrote *A Satyr Against Mankind* and other witty poems (see Part One); Charles Sackville (1638–1706), Sixth Earl of Dorset, wrote songs and satires; John Oldham (1653–83) wrote satires in the manner of Juvenal. **37. disposed:** The 1756 edition reads: "ranked." **38. Pitt . . . Lansdown:** Christopher Pitt (1699–1748) translated the *Aeneid* in 1740; George Sandys (1578–1644) translated Ovid's *Metamorphoses* between 1621 and 1626; Edward Fairfax (d. 1635) translated Torquato Tasso's *Jerusalem Delivered* in 1600; William Broome (1689–1745) helped Pope translate the *Odyssey;* George Villiers (1628–87), Second Duke of Buckingham, wrote minor plays and poems, as did George Granville (1667–1735), Baron Lansdowne. **39. This . . . authors:** omitted in 1756. **40. In . . . determine:** After his thorough examination of Pope's works, Warton concludes at the end of his second volume, "*Where then . . . shall we with justice be authorized to place our admired* POPE? Not, assuredly, in the same rank with *Spencer, Shakespeare,* and *Milton;* however justly we may applaud the *Eloisa* and *Rape of the Lock;* but, considering the correctness, elegance, and utility of his works, the weight of sentiment, and the knowledge of man they contain, we may venture to assign him a place, *next to Milton,* and *just* above *Dryden.*" **41. 1756:** omitted in 1756.

Thomas Warton

POSTSCRIPT [TO OBSERVATIONS ON THE FAERIE QUEENE OF SPENSER]

❦

Thomas Warton's *Observations on the Faerie Queene* appeared in 1754. It consists of eleven chapters and runs to over three hundred pages. Treated are the structure, diction, and versification of *The Faerie Queene* (1590–96); Spenser's sources in medieval romance, Chaucer, and Ariosto; and Spenser's allegory. Johnson wrote Warton soon after the book was published:

> I . . . pay you a very honest acknowledgement for the advancement of the literature of our native Country. You have shown to all who shall hereafter attempt the study of our ancient authours the way to success, by directing them to the perusal of the books which those authours had read. . . . The Reason why the authours which are yet read of the sixteenth Century are so little understood is that they are read alone, and no help is borrowed from those who lived with them or before them.

The text is that of the second edition, "corrected and enlarged," of 1762; two minor footnotes are omitted.

❦

AT the close of this work, I shall beg leave to subjoin an apology, for the manner in which it has been conducted and executed.

I presume it will be objected, that these remarks would have appeared with greater propriety, connected with Spenser's text, and arranged according to their respective references; at least it may be urged, that such a plan would have prevented much unnecessary transcription. But I was dissuaded from this method by two reasons. The first is, that these OBSERVATIONS, thus reduced to general heads,[1] form a series of distinct essays on Spenser, and exhibit a course of systematical criticism on the FAERIE QUEENE. But my principal argument was, that a formal edition of this poem with notes, would have been at once impertinent and superfluous; as two publications of Spenser, under that form, are at present expected from the hands of two learned and ingenious critics.[2] Besides, it was never my design, to give so complete and perpetual a comment on every part of our author, as such an attempt seemed to require. But while some passages are entirely overlooked, or but superficially touched, others will be found to have been discussed more at large, and investigated with greater research and accuracy, than such an attempt would have permitted.

As to more particular objections, too many, I am sensible, must occur; one of which will probably be, that I have been more diligent in remarking the faults than the beauties of Spenser. That I have been deficient in encomiums on particular passages, did not proceed from a want of perceiving or acknowledging beauties; but from a persuasion, that nothing is more absurd or useless than the panegyrical comments of those, who criticise from the imagination rather than from the judgment, who exert their admiration instead of their reason, and discover more of enthusiasm than discernment. And this will most commonly be the case of those critics, who profess to point out beauties; because, as they naturally approve themselves to the reader's apprehension by their own force, no reason can often be given why they please. The same cannot always be said of faults, which I have frequently displayed without reserve or palliation.

It was my chief aim, to give a clear and comprehensive estimate of the characteristical merits and manner, of this admired, but neglected, poet. For this purpose I have considered the customs and genius of his age; I have searched his cotemporary writers, and examined the books on which the peculiarities of his style, taste, and composition, are confessedly founded.

I fear I shall be censured for quoting too many pieces of this sort. But experience has frequently and fatally proved, that the commentator whose critical enquiries are employed on Spenser, Jonson,[3] and the rest of our elder poets, will in vain give specimens of his classical erudition, unless, at the same time, he

---

POSTSCRIPT TO *Observations on The Faerie Queene*. **1. general heads:** chapters.

2. two . . . critics: John Upton (1707–60) and Ralph Church (d. 1787), whose editions of Spenser appeared in 1758. **3. Jonson:** Ben Jonson (1572–1637).

brings to his work a mind intimately acquainted with those books, which though now forgotten, were yet in common use and high repute about the time in which his authors respectively wrote, and which they consequently must have read. While these are unknown, many allusions and many imitations will either remain obscure, or lose half their beauty and propriety: "as the figures vanish when the canvas is decayed."

Pope laughs at Theobald[4] for giving us, in his edition of Shakespeare, a sample of

—All such READING as was never read.[5]

But these strange and ridiculous books which Theobald quoted, were unluckily the very books which Shakespeare himself had studied; the knowledge of which enabled that useful editor to explain so many difficult allusions and obsolete customs in his poet, which otherwise could never have been understood. For want of this sort of literature, Pope tells us,[6] that the DREADFUL SAGITTARY in Troilus and Cressida, signifies Teucer,[7] so celebrated for his skill in archery. Had he deigned to consult an old history, called the DESTRUCTION of TROY, a book which was the delight of Shakespeare and of his age, he would have found that this formidable archer, was no other than an imaginary beast, which the grecian army brought against Troy. If Shakespeare is worth reading, he is worth explaining; and the researches used for so valuable and elegant a purpose, merit the thanks of genius and candour, not the satire of prejudice and ignorance. That labour, which so essentially contributes to the service of true taste, deserves a more honourable repository than The TEMPLE of DULNESS. In the same strain of false satire, Pope observes with an air of ridicule that Caxton[8] speaks of the Æneid "as a history, as a book hardly known."[9] But the satirist perhaps would have expressed himself with not much more precision or propriety concerning the Æneid, had he been Caxton's cotemporary. Certainly, had he wrote english poetry in so unenlightened a period, the

world would have lost his refined diction and harmonious versification, the fortunate effects of better times. Caxton, rude and uncouth as he is, co-operated in the noblest cause: he was a very considerable instrument in the grand work of introducing literature into his country. In an illiterate and unpolished age he multiplied books, and consequently readers. The books he printed, besides the grossest barbarisms of style and composition, are chiefly written on subjects of little importance and utility; almost all, except the works of Gower[10] and Chaucer, translations from the french: yet, such as they were, we enjoy their happy consequences at this day. Science, the progressive state of which succeeding generations have improved and completed, dates her original from these artless and imperfect efforts.

Mechanical critics will perhaps be disgusted at the liberties I have taken in introducing so many anecdotes of ancient chivalry. But my subject required frequent proofs of this sort. Nor could I be persuaded that such enquiries were, in other respects, either useless or ridiculous; as they tended at least, to illustrate an institution of no frivolous or indifferent nature. Chivalry is commonly looked upon as a barbarous sport, or extravagant amusement, of the dark ages. It had however no small influence on the manners, policies, and constitutions of antient times, and served many public and important purposes. It was the school of fortitude, honour, and affability. Its exercises, like the grecian games, habituated the youth to fatigue and enterprise, and inspired the noblest sentiments of heroism. It taught gallantry and civility to a savage and ignorant people, and humanised the native ferocity of the northern nations. It conduced to refine the manners of the combatants, by exciting an emulation in the devices and accoutrements, the splendour and parade, of their tilts and tournaments: while its magnificent festivals, thronged with noble dames and courteous knights, produced the first efforts of wit and fancy.

I am still further to hope, that, together with other specimens of obsolete literature in general, hinted at before, the many references I have made, in particular to Romances, the necessary appendage of antient Chivalry, will also plead their pardon. For however monstrous and unnatural these compositions may appear to this age of reason and refinement, they merit more attention than the world is willing to bestow.

4. Theobald: Lewis Theobald (1688–1744), whose edition of Shakespeare was published in 1734. He is one of the principal victims of Pope's Dunciad (see Part Two). **5. All . . . read:** The Dunciad, IV. 250. **6. Pope . . . us:** in his edition of Shakespeare (1725). **7. Teucer:** the half brother of Ajax and a noted archer among the besiegers of Troy. **8. Caxton:** William Caxton, fifteenth-century English printer. **9. as a history . . . known:** The quotation comes from a footnote to The Dunciad, I. 149.

10. Gower: John Gower (c. 1330–1408), English poet, best known for his Confessio Amantis (1390).

They preserve many curious historical facts, and throw considerable light on the nature of the feudal system. They are the pictures of antient usages and customs; and represent the manners, genius, and character of our ancestors. Above all, such are their Terrible Graces of magic and enchantment, so magnificently marvellous are their fictions and fablings, that they contribute, in a wonderful degree, to rouse and invigorate all the powers of imagination: to store the fancy with those sublime and alarming images, which true poetry best delights to display.

Lastly, in analysing the Plan and Conduct of this poem, I have so far tried it by epic rules, as to demonstrate the inconveniencies and incongruities, which the poet might have avoided, had he been more studious of design and uniformity. It is true, that his romantic materials claim great liberties; but no materials exclude order and perspicuity. I have endeavoured to account for these defects, partly from the peculiar bent of the poet's genius, which at the same time produced infinite beauties, and partly from the predominant taste of the times in which he wrote.

Let me add, that if I have treated some of the italian poets,[11] on certain occasions, with too little respect, I did not mean to depreciate their various incidental excellencies. I only suggested, that those excellencies, like some of Spenser's, would have appeared to greater advantage, had they been more judiciously disposed. I have blamed, indeed, the vicious excess of their fictions; yet I have found no fault in general, with their use of magical machinery; notwithstanding, I have so far conformed to the reigning maxims of modern criticism, as, in the mean time, to recommend classical propriety.

I cannot take my final leave of the reader, without the satisfaction of acknowledging, that this work has proved a most agreeable task; and I hope this consideration will at least plead my pardon for its length, whatever censure or indulgence the rest of its faults may deserve. The business of criticism is commonly laborious and dry; yet it has here more frequently amused than fatigued my attention, in its excursions upon an author, who makes such perpetual and powerful appeals to the fancy. Much of the pleasure that Spenser experienced in composing the FAIRY QUEEN,

must, in some measure, be shared by his commentator; and the critic, on this occasion, may speak in the words, and with the rapture, of the poet.

> The wayes through which my weary steppes I guyde
> In this DELIGHTFULL LAND OF FAERIE,
> Are so exceeding spacious and wyde,
> And sprinkled with such sweet varietie
> Of all that pleasant is to ear or eye,
> That I nigh ravisht with rare thoughts delight,
> My TEDIOUS TRAVEL do forgett thereby:
> And when I gin to feele decay of might,
> It strength to me supplies, and cheares my dulled spright.
>
> 6.I.I.

VERSES ON SIR JOSHUA REYNOLDS'S PAINTED WINDOW AT NEW-COLLEGE OXFORD

The window at New College, Oxford, was executed by the glass painter Thomas Jervais (d. 1799), who worked from an original painting exhibited by Reynolds at the Royal Academy show in 1779. The window depicts the Nativity, and below pose the Christian virtues of Faith, Hope, and Charity, as well as the classical virtues of Temperance, Fortitude, Justice, and Prudence.

The text is that of the first edition (1782); we have incorporated the substantive variants of the second edition (1783).

AH, stay thy treacherous hand, forbear to trace
Those faultless forms of elegance and grace!
Ah, cease to spread the bright transparent mass,
With Titian's° pencil, o'er the speaking glass!
Nor steal, by strokes of art with truth combin'd,
The fond illusions of my wayward mind!
For long, enamour'd of a barbarous age,
A faithless truant to the classic page;

---

11. **some . . . poets:** especially Ludovico Ariosto (1474–1533), author of *Orlando Furioso* (1532), a romantic epic that Warton compared disadvantageously with *The Faerie Queene*.

VERSES ON SIR JOSHUA REYNOLDS'S PAINTED WINDOW. **4. Titian:** This Italian painter (*c.* 1477–1576) was highly regarded by Reynolds, especially as a colorist.

Long have I lov'd to catch the simple chime
Of minstrel-harps, and spell the fabling rime;   10
To view the festive rites, the knightly play,
That deck'd heroic Albion's° elder day;
To mark the mouldering halls of barons bold,
And the rough castle, cast in giant-mould;
With Gothic manners Gothic arts explore,
And muse on the magnificence of yore.

But chief, enraptur'd have I lov'd to roam,
A lingering votary, the vaulted dome,
Where the tall shafts, that mount in massy pride,
Their mingling branches shoot from side to side;   20
Where elfin sculptors, with fantastic clew,°
Oer the long roof their wild embroidery drew;
Where SUPERSTITION, with capricious hand
In many a maze the wreathed window plann'd,
With hues romantic ting'd the gorgeous pane,
To fill with holy light the wonderous fane;°
To aid the builder's model, richly rude,
By no Vitruvian° symmetry subdued;
To suit the genius of the mystic pile:
Whilst as around the far-retiring ile,°   30
And fretted° shrines with hoary trophies hung,
Her dark illumination wide she flung,
With new solemnity, the nooks profound,
The caves of death, and the dim arches frown'd.
From bliss long felt unwillingly we part:
Ah, spare the weakness of a lover's heart!
Chase not the phantoms of my fairy dream,
Phantoms that shrink at Reason's painful gleam!
That softer touch, insidious artist, stay,
Nor to new joys my struggling breast betray!   40

Such was a pensive bard's mistaken strain.—
But, oh, of ravish'd pleasures why complain?
No more the matchless skill I call unkind
That strives to disenchant my cheated mind.
For when again I view thy chaste Design,
The just proportion, and the genuin line;
Those native pourtraitures of Attic° art,

That from the lucid surface seem to start;
Those tints, that steal no glories from the day,
Nor ask the sun to lend his streaming ray;   50
The doubtful radiance of contending dies,
That faintly mingle, yet distinctly rise;
Twixt light and shade the transitory strife;
The feature blooming with immortal life:
The stole in casual foldings taught to flow,
Not with ambitious ornaments to glow;
The tread majestic, and the beaming eye
That lifted speaks its commerce with the sky:
Heaven's golden emanation, gleaming mild
Oer the mean cradle of the virgin's child: 60
Sudden, the sombrous imagery is fled,
Which late my visionary rapture fed:
Thy powerful hand has broke the Gothic chain,
And brought my bosom back to truth again:
To truth, by no peculiar taste confin'd,
Whose universal pattern strikes mankind;
To truth, whose bold and unresisted aim
Checks frail caprice, and fashion's fickle claim;
To truth, whose Charms deception's magic quell,
And bind coy Fancy in a stronger spell.   70

Ye brawny Prophets, that in robes so rich,
At distance due, possess the crisped° nich;
Ye Rows of Patriarchs, that sublimely rear'd,
Diffuse a proud primeval length of beard:
Ye Saints, who clad in crimson's bright array,
More pride than humble poverty display:
Ye Virgins meek, that wear the palmy crown
Of patient faith, and yet so fiercely frown:
Ye Angels, that from clouds of gold recline,
But boast no semblance to a race divine: 80
Ye tragic Tales of legendary lore,
That draw devotion's ready tear no more:
Ye Martyrdoms of unenlighten'd days,
Ye Miracles, that now no wonder raise:
Shapes, that with one broad glare the gazer strike,
Kings, Bishops, Nuns, Apostles, all alike!
Ye Colours, that th' unwary sight amaze,
And only dazzle in the noontide blaze!
No more the Sacred Window's round disgrace,
But yield to Grecian groupes the shining space.   90
Lo, from the canvas Beauty shifts her throne,
Lo, Picture's powers a new formation own!
Behold, she prints upon the crystal plain,

---

12. Albion: England. **21. clew:** ball of embroidery thread. **26. fane:** temple. **28. Vitruvian:** according to the classical architectural principles of the treatise *De Architectura*, written in the first century B.C. by the famous Roman architect Marcus Vitruvius Pollio. **30. ile:** aisle. **31. fretted:** highly ornamented with relief work. **47. Attic:** from Attica, the region surrounding ancient Athens; elegant simplicity was considered to be the chief characteristic of the Attic style.

72. crisped: undulating, curling.

With her own energy, th' expressive stain!
The mighty Master spreads his mimic toil
More wide, nor only blends the breathing oil;
But calls the lineaments of life compleat
From genial alchymy's creative heat;
Obedient forms to the bright fusion gives,
While in the warm enamel Nature lives.   100

REYNOLDS, tis thine, from the broad window's
    height,
To add new lustre to religious light:
Not of it's pomp to strip this antient shrine,
But bid that pomp with purer radiance shine:
With arts unknown before, to reconcile
The willing Graces to the Gothic pile.

Thomas Gray

1716–1771

Although only thirteen of his poems were published during his lifetime, the shy and melancholy Thomas Gray became the foremost lyric poet of his age. Born of a modest commercial family in London's Cornhill district, he was the only one of twelve children to survive childhood. At the age of nine he entered Eton College, where an uncle was one of the masters. Here he remained for nine idyllic years, reading Virgil, Spenser, Shakespeare, and Milton; daydreaming over the beauty of the pastoral setting and the Gothic and Tudor architecture; avoiding athletics; and making friends with Horace Walpole, Richard West, and Thomas Ashton. This clever but fragile foursome, which called itself the Quadruple Alliance, prided itself on its aestheticism, urbanity, and sense of style, and these qualities manifested themselves in frequent sallies of literate and fantastic humor.

Gray proceeded to Peterhouse, Cambridge, in 1734. He found the curriculum dull and the faculty idle. He wrote Walpole, "The Masters of Colledges are twelve grey-hair'd Gentlefolks, who are all mad with Pride; the Fellows are sleepy, drunken, dull, illiterate Things." For the next five years he led a solitary and studious life reading Latin, English, Italian, and French literature and playing the harpsichord.

Walpole, who had gone to King's College, Cambridge, had not forgotten his boyhood friend. In 1739 he invited Gray to accompany him as his guest on his Grand Tour of France, Switzerland, and Italy. All went well for a while, but it soon became clear that the travelers could not continue together: Walpole wanted sophistication and parties, while the less affluent Gray wanted to contemplate history and take notes on antiquities. At the Italian town of Reggio they quarreled and parted, and Gray returned to England. They did not meet again for five years.

In 1742 Richard West, Gray's frail Eton friend, died of tuberculosis at the age of twenty-five, and it was in the summer of this year that Gray, shocked and horrified by West's death, began seriously writing poems. Later the same year he returned to Cambridge, where, except for occasional rural trips and stays in London and in Stoke Poges (where his mother and aunt maintained a house), he spent the rest of his life in frugal and celibate retirement. He had always been shy and delicate; he now became a trifle fussy and frigid. Some observers thought they detected signs of effeminacy.

Gray once wrote, "To find oneself business is the great art of Life." At his old Cambridge college, Peterhouse, he was ostensibly studying law, but actually he was keeping busy by a self-imposed program of literary, historical, and scientific reading:

classical literature, especially Greek, Old and Middle English poetry, and early Scandinavian literature; medieval history and archeology; and botany and zoology. In his cloistered rooms he read and took notes, becoming one of the most learned men of his time. When he felt the need for diversion, he played Scarlatti and Vivaldi on the harpsichord; sometimes he sang, and sometimes he sketched. He pursued both studies and relaxations methodically and fastidiously.

His elegant bashfulness, his high critical standards, and perhaps his apprehension of possible failure severely limited his poetic output: he once wrote Walpole that he feared his collected works would be "mistaken for the works of a flea, or a pismire." His poems began appearing in 1747, when *An Ode on a Distant Prospect of Eton College* was published. The next year he permitted Robert Dodsley to print *Ode on the Spring* and *Ode on the Death of a Favourite Cat* in his famous *Collection of Poems*. In 1751 he grudgingly allowed the publication of the *Elegy Written in a Country Church-Yard*, which he had begun, apparently, in 1742. Almost overnight the *Elegy* became the sensation of literary England, and Gray found himself, to his profound distress, famous. The periodical *The World* described him as "the sweetest of our elegiac poets"; and James Boswell, impressed by the manly stoicism of the *Elegy*, exhorted himself in his daily memoranda to "Be Gray."

At Cambridge Gray's timidities and eccentricities made him seem to many a disagreeable and even a comical figure. He was nervous about dogs and feared thieves; and in an age when everyone, even Dr. Johnson, rode, he was so frightened of horses that he never got on one. Developing an extravagant fear of fire, he had a conspicuous rope ladder installed in his college rooms. All this proved too much for the rowdy undergraduates to bear. Their drunken mockeries grew so offensive that in 1756 Gray moved across the street to Pembroke College.

Since their reconciliation in 1745, Walpole had been devoted to the cause of Gray and his poems. He prevailed upon Gray in 1757 to let him print on his private press at Strawberry Hill the two Pindaric odes *The Progress of Poesy* and *The Bard*. The same year, upon the death of Colley Cibber, Gray was offered the laureateship. He emphatically declined.

In 1759 he took rooms in London, where he spent almost three years in research at the newly opened British Museum Library. He was projecting a history of English poetry, but he never finished it. His reading, however, took him into early Scandinavian, Gaelic, and Welsh poetry, and in 1760 he wrote two poems adapted from the Icelandic, *The Descent of Odin* and *The Fatal Sisters*.

Poems by Mr. Gray, his slender collected works, appeared in 1768. The same year he was made Regius Professor of Modern History at Cambridge. The professorship required only nominal duties, and, although he took elaborate notes toward some lectures, he never delivered any. In the summer of this year he journeyed to the Lake District in search of the picturesque and the sublime.

Once past his carefree days at Eton, he had given an impression of coldness and reserve. He once wrote Thomas Wharton, "As to Humanity you know my aversion to it; which is barbarous & inhuman, but I can not help it. God forgive me." All the affection that he had apparently repressed burst out in 1769 when he met in Cambridge an exotic Swiss youth of twenty-one, Charles-Victor de Bonstetten. Gray's delight with Bonstetten's discipleship warmed to something like infatuation, and he was heartbroken when, two months after they had met, Bonstetten had to return to Switzerland. Gray lived for only two more lonely years. He was buried beside his mother in the churchyard at Stoke Poges.

Despite Johnson's strictures in his *Life of Gray* (1781), Gray's reputation in his own time was immense. Most contemporary readers tended to agree with William Cowper, who considered Gray "the only poet since Shakespeare entitled to the character of sublime."

Bibliography is supplied by C. S. Northrup's *A Bibliography of Thomas Gray* (1917) and by H. W. Starr's *A Bibliography of Thomas Gray, 1917–1951* (1953). A convenient edition of the poems is that in the Oxford Standard Authors Series, edited by A. L. Poole and revised by Leonard Whibley (1937). The *Elegy* has been edited by F. G. Stokes (1929). R. W. Ketton-Cremer's *Thomas Gray: A Biography* (1955) is standard. W. P. Jones's *Thomas Gray, Scholar* (1937) contains interesting material on Gray's learned projects. The delightful letters are edited by Paget Toynbee and Leonard Whibley (3 vols., 1935). Samuel Johnson's *Life of Gray* (1781), with its famous criticism of the odes, is always refreshing. Some of the complexities of Gray's achievement are explored by Lord David Cecil in *The Poetry of Thomas Gray* (1945) and by Geoffrey Tillotson in *Augustan Studies* (1961). Interpretation and criticism of the *Elegy* are to be found in Cleanth Brooks's *The Well Wrought Urn* (1947) and in a penetrating article by F. H. Ellis, "Gray's *Elegy*: The Biographical Problem in Literary Criticism," *PMLA*, LXVI (1951), 971–1008.

AN ODE ON A DISTANT PROSPECT OF ETON COLLEGE

In genre this poem falls within the tradition of the Horatian (or "lesser") ode, which is distinguished from the passionate and rhapsodic Pindaric (or "greater") ode by its quiet ease and reflective calm. Elements of the pastoral are also apparent. Written in August, 1742, but not published until May, 1747, the poem, which Walpole thought Gray's most perfect, was barely noticed by contemporary readers.

The text is that of the first edition.

Ye distant Spires, ye antique Towers,
That crown the watry Glade,

Where grateful Science° still adores
Her *Henry's*° holy Shade;
And ye that from the stately Brow
Of *Windsor's* Heights th' Expanse below
Of Grove, of Lawn, of Mead survey,
Whose Turf, whose Shade, whose Flowers among
Wanders the hoary *Thames* along
His Silver-winding Way.   10

Ah happy Hills, ah pleasing Shade,
Ah Fields belov'd in vain,
Where once my careless Childhood stray'd,
A Stranger yet to Pain!
I feel the Gales, that from ye blow,
A momentary Bliss bestow,
As waving fresh their gladsome Wing,
My weary Soul they seem to sooth,
And, redolent of Joy and Youth,
To breathe a second Spring.   20

AN ODE ON A DISTANT PROSPECT OF ETON COLLEGE. **3. Science:** knowledge. **4. Henry:** Henry VI (1421–71), founder of Eton in 1440.

Say, Father *Thames*, for thou hast seen
Full many a sprightly Race°
Disporting on thy Margent° green
The Paths of Pleasure trace,
Who foremost now delight to cleave
With pliant Arm thy glassy Wave?
The captive Linnet which enthrall?
What idle Progeny succeed
To chase the rolling Circle's Speed,
Or urge the flying Ball?   30

While some on earnest Business bent
Their murm'ring Labours ply,
'Gainst graver Hours, that bring Constraint
To sweeten Liberty:
Some bold Adventurers disdain
The Limits of their little Reign,
And unknown Regions dare descry:
Still as they run they look behind,
They hear a Voice in every Wind,
And snatch a fearful Joy.   40

Gay Hope is theirs by Fancy fed,
Less pleasing when possest;
The Tear forgot as soon as shed,
The Sunshine of the Breast;
Theirs buxom Health of rosy Hue,
Wild Wit, Invention ever-new,
And lively Chear of Vigour born;
The thoughtless Day, the easy Night,
The Spirits pure, the Slumbers light,
That fly th' Approach of Morn.   50

Alas, regardless of their Doom,
The little Victims play!
No Sense have they of Ills to come,
Nor Care beyond to-day:
Yet see how all around 'em wait
The Ministers of human Fate,
And black Misfortune's baleful Train!
Ah, shew them where in Ambush stand
To seize their Prey the murth'rous Band!
Ah, tell them they are Men!   60

These shall the Fury Passions tear,
The Vulturs of the Mind,
Disdainful Anger, pallid Fear,
And Shame that sculks behind;
Or pineing Love shall waste their Youth,
Or Jealousy with rankling Tooth,

That inly gnaws the secret Heart,
And Envy wan, and faded Care,
Grim-visag'd comfortless Despair,
And Sorrow's piercing Dart.   70

Ambition This shall tempt to rise,
Then whirl the Wretch from high,
To bitter Scorn a Sacrifice,
And grinning Infamy.
The Stings of Falshood Those shall try,
And hard Unkindness' alter'd Eye,
That mocks the Tear it forc'd to flow;
And keen Remorse with Blood defil'd,
And moody Madness laughing wild
Amid severest Woe.   80

Lo, in the Vale of Years beneath
A griesly Troop are seen,
The painful Family of Death,
More hideous than their Queen:
This racks the Joints, this fires the Veins,
That every labouring Sinew strains,
Those in the deeper Vitals rage:
Lo, Poverty, to fill the Band,
That numbs the Soul with icy Hand,
And slow-consuming Age.   90

To each his Suff'rings: all are Men,
Condemn'd alike to groan,
The Tender for another's Pain;
Th' Unfeeling for his own.
Yet ah! Why should they know their Fate?
Since Sorrow never comes too late,
And Happiness too swiftly flies.
Thought would destroy their Paradise.
No more; where Ignorance is Bliss,
'Tis Folly to be wise.   100

SONNET ON THE DEATH
OF MR. RICHARD WEST

✦

Although this poem was written in 1742, Gray did not
publish it during his lifetime.
    The text is that of the first printing, in *The Poems of
Mr. Gray*, ed. William Mason (1775).

22. Race: generation. **23. Margent:** (margin) bank.

In vain to me the smiling Mornings shine,
And redd'ning Phoebus lifts his golden fire:
The birds in vain their amorous descant join;
Or chearful fields resume their green attire:
These ears, alas! for other notes repine,
A different object do these eyes require.
My lonely anguish melts no heart but mine;
And in my breast the imperfect joys expire.
Yet Morning smiles the busy race to chear,
And new-born pleasure brings to happier men: 10
The fields to all their wonted tribute bear:
To warm their little loves the birds complain:
I fruitless mourn to him, that cannot hear,
And weep the more, because I weep in vain.

ODE ON THE DEATH OF A FAVOURITE CAT, DROWNED IN A TUB OF GOLD FISHES

In genre a combination of fable and mock elegy, this poem was written in 1747 to commemorate the death by drowning of Horace Walpole's cat, Selima. Long afterward Walpole exhibited the fatal china vase on a pedestal at Strawberry Hill. According to Walpole, "Humour was Gray's natural and original turn. . . . He never wrote anything easily but things of Humour."

The text is from Dodsley's *A Collection of Poems* (3 vols., 1748), with the substantive variants from *Poems by Mr. Gray* (1768).

I.

'Twas on a lofty vase's side,
Where China's gayest art had dy'd
The azure flowers, that blow;
Demurest of the Tabby kind,
The pensive Selima reclin'd,
Gazed on the lake below.

II.

Her conscious tail her joy declar'd;
The fair round face, the snowy beard,
The velvet of her paws,
Her coat that with the tortoise vies,   10
Her ears of jet, and emerald eyes,
She saw; and purr'd applause.

III.

Still had she gaz'd: but 'midst the tide
Two angel forms were seen to glide,
The Genii of the stream:
Their scaly armour's Tyrian° hue
Thro' richest purple to the view
Betray'd a golden gleam.

IV.

The hapless nymph with wonder saw:
A whisker first and then a claw,   20
With many an ardent wish,
She stretch'd in vain to reach the prize.
What female heart can gold despise?
What Cat's averse to fish?

V.

Presumptuous maid! with looks intent
Again she stretch'd, again she bent,
Nor knew the gulf between;
(Malignant fate sat by and smil'd)
The slipp'ry verge her feet beguil'd,
She tumbled headlong in.   30

VI.

Eight times emerging from the flood
She mew'd to ev'ry watry God,
Some speedy aid to send.
No Dolphin came, no Nereid° stirr'd:
Nor cruel Tom, nor Susan° heard.
A fav'rite has no friend!

VII.

From hence, ye beauties, undeceiv'd,
Know, one false step is ne'er retriev'd,
And be with caution bold.
Not all that tempts your wand'ring eyes   40
And heedless hearts, is lawful prize;
Nor all, that glisters, gold.

ODE ON THE DEATH OF A FAVOURITE CAT. **16. Tyrian:** purple.
34. Nereid: sea nymph. **35. Tom, Susan:** servants.

ELEGY WRITTEN IN A COUNTRY CHURCH-YARD

❧

Probably around 1750 Walpole, who had happily possessed for some years a transcript of the *Elegy*, allowed a copy to be taken. Gray wrote him on February 11, 1751:

As you have brought me into a little sort of Distress, you must assist me, I believe, to get out of it, as well as I can. yesterday I had the Misfortune of receiving a Letter from certain Gentlemen (as their Bookseller expresses it) who have taken the *Magazine of Magazines* [a notoriously low journal] into their Hands. they tell me, that an *ingenious* Poem . . . has been communicated to them, which they are printing forthwith: that they are inform'd, that the *excellent* Author of it is I by name, & that they beg not only his *Indulgence*, but the *Honor of his Correspondence*, &c: as I am not at all disposed to be either so indulgent, or so correspondent, as they desire; I have but one bad Way left to escape the Honour they would inflict upon me. & therefore am obliged to desire you would make Dodsley print it immediately . . . from your Copy, but without my Name. . . . he must . . . print it without any Interval between the Stanza's, because the Sense is in some Places continued beyond them. [In the editions of 1753 and following years the stanzas are separated.]

The poem was instantly popular: it was pirated, imitated, quoted, translated into Latin and Greek, and parodied. The ornaments that Dodsley's printer supplied for the title page, including skulls and crossbones, picks and shovels, and hourglasses, suggest that he thought of it as a graveyard poem. Later readers have considered it a pastoral elegy deeply infused with a Gothic tincture.

The text is that of the first quarto edition (1751); we have incorporated the substantive variants of the version in *Poems by Mr. Gray* (1768).

❧

night-time

The Curfew tolls the Knell of parting Day,
The lowing Herd wind slowly o'er the Lea,
The Plow-man homeward plods his weary Way,
And leaves the World to Darkness, and to me.

1. sets the scene

Now fades the glimmering Landscape on the Sight,
And all the Air a solemn Stillness holds;
Save where the Beetle wheels his droning Flight,
And drowsy Tinklings lull the distant Folds.

Save that from yonder Ivy-mantled Tow'r *church*
The mopeing Owl does to the Moon complain   10
Of such, as wand'ring near her secret Bow'r,
Molest her ancient solitary Reign.

Beneath those rugged Elms, that Yew-Tree's Shade, *2. looks at graves*
Where heaves the Turf in many a mould'ring Heap,
Each in his narrow Cell for ever laid,
The rude Forefathers of the Hamlet sleep.

The breezy Call of Incense-breathing Morn,
The Swallow twitt'ring from the Straw-built Shed,
The Cock's shrill Clarion, or the ecchoing Horn, *3. describing what their lives were like*
No more shall rouse them from their lowly Bed.   20

For them no more the blazing Hearth shall burn,
Or busy Houswife ply her Evening Care:
No Children run to lisp their Sire's Return,
Or climb his Knees the envied Kiss to share.

Oft did the Harvest to their Sickle yield,
Their Furrow oft the stubborn Glebe° has broke;
How jocund did they drive their Team afield!
How bow'd the Woods beneath their sturdy Stroke!

Let not Ambition mock their useful Toil,
Their homely Joys and Destiny obscure;   30
Nor Grandeur hear with a disdainful Smile,
The short and simple Annals of the Poor.

The Boast of Heraldry, the Pomp of Pow'r,
And all that Beauty, all that Wealth e'er gave,
Awaits alike th' inevitable Hour. *WARNING TO GREAT AND MIGHTY THAT DEATH LEVELS ALL MEN*
The Paths of Glory lead but to the Grave.

Nor you, ye Proud, impute to These the fault,
If Mem'ry o'er their Tomb no Trophies raise,
Where thro' the long-drawn Isle° and fretted° Vault
The pealing Anthem swells the Note of Praise.   40

Can storied Urn or animated Bust
Back to its Mansion call the fleeting Breath?
Can Honour's Voice provoke the silent Dust,
Or Flatt'ry sooth the dull cold Ear of Death?

Perhaps in this neglected Spot is laid
Some Heart once pregnant with celestial Fire,
Hands that the rod of Empire might have sway'd,
Or wak'd to Extacy the living Lyre.

But Knowledge to their Eyes her ample Page

ELEGY WRITTEN IN A COUNTRY CHURCH-YARD. **26. Glebe:** soil. **39. Isle:** aisle. **fretted:** highly ornamented with relief work.

speculates who the people were

Rich with the Spoils of Time did ne'er unroll;   50
Chill Penury repress'd their noble Rage,
And froze the genial Current of the Soul.

    Full many a Gem of purest Ray serene,
The dark unfathom'd Caves of Ocean bear:
Full many a Flower is born to blush unseen,
And waste its Sweetness on the desart Air.

    Some Village-*Hampden*° that with dauntless Breast
The little Tyrant of his Fields withstood;
Some mute inglorious *Milton* here may rest,   *a person dieing*
Some *Cromwell* guiltless of his Country's Blood.   60

    Th' Applause of list'ning Senates to command,
The Threats of Pain and Ruin to despise,
To scatter Plenty o'er a smiling Land,
And read their Hist'ry in a Nation's Eyes

    Their Lot forbad: nor circumscrib'd alone
Their growing Virtues, but their Crimes confin'd;
Forbad to wade through Slaughter to a Throne,
And shut the Gates of Mercy on Mankind,

    The struggling Pangs of conscious Truth to hide,
To quench the Blushes of ingenuous Shame,   70
Or heap the Shrine of Luxury and Pride
With Incense, kindled at the Muse's Flame.°

    Far from the madding Crowd's ignoble Strife,
Their sober Wishes never learn'd to stray;
Along the cool sequester'd Vale of Life
They kept the noiseless Tenor of their Way.

death itself

    Yet ev'n these Bones from Insult to protect
Some frail Memorial still erected nigh,
With uncouth Rhimes and shapeless Sculpture deck'd,
Implores the passing Tribute of a Sigh.   80

    Their Name, their Years, spelt by th' unletter'd
      Muse,
The Place of Fame and Elegy supply:
And many a holy Text around she strews,
That teach the rustic Moralist to dye.

    For who to dumb Forgetfulness a Prey,   *none die w/out regret*
This pleasing anxious Being e'er resign'd,
Left the warm Precincts of the chearful Day,
Nor cast one longing ling'ring Look behind?

    On some fond Breast the parting Soul relies,
Some pious Drops the closing Eye requires;   90
Ev'n from the Tomb the Voice of Nature cries,
Ev'n in our Ashes live their wonted Fires.

    For thee, who mindful of th' unhonour'd Dead
Dost in these Lines their artless Tale relate;
If chance, by lonely Contemplation led,
Some kindred Spirit shall inquire thy Fate,°

    Haply some hoary-headed Swain may say,
"Oft have we seen him at the Peep of Dawn
Brushing with hasty Steps the Dews away
To meet the Sun upon the upland Lawn.°   100

    "There at the Foot of yonder nodding Beech
That wreathes its old fantastic Roots so high,
His listless Length at Noontide wou'd he stretch,
And pore upon the Brook that babbles by.

    "Hard by yon Wood, now smiling as in Scorn,
Mutt'ring his wayward Fancies he wou'd rove,
Now drooping, woeful wan, like one forlorn,
Or craz'd with Care, or cross'd in hopeless Love.

    "One Morn I miss'd him on the custom'd Hill,
Along the Heath, and near his fav'rite Tree;   110
Another came; nor yet beside the Rill,
Nor up the Lawn, nor at the Wood was he.

talks about his own death — epitaph at end

57. Hampden: John Hampden (1594–1643), English states-man and patriot known for his resistance to Charles I. **72. Flame:** the following four stanzas, with which, according to William Mason, the poem originally ended, appear in the manuscript preserved at Eton College:

> The thoughtless World to Majesty may bow
> Exalt the brave, & idolize Success
> But more to Innocence their Safety owe
> Than Power & Genius e'er conspired to bless
>
> And thou, who mindful of the unhonour'd Dead
> Dost in these Notes their artless Tale relate
> By Night & lonely Contemplation led
> To linger in the gloomy Walks of Fate
>
> Hark how the sacred Calm, that broods around
> Bids ev'ry fierce tumultuous Passion cease
> In still small Accents whisp'ring from the Ground
> A grateful Earnest of eternal Peace
>
> No more with Reason & thyself at Strife
> Give anxious Cares & endless Wishes room
> But thro' the cool sequester'd Vale of Life
> Pursue the silent Tenor of thy Doom.

96. Fate: The following alternative stanza appears in the Eton manuscript:

> If chance that e'er some pensive Spirit more,
> By sympathetic Musings here delay'd,
> With vain, tho' kind, Enquiry shall explore
> Thy once-loved Haunt, this long-deserted Shade.

100. Lawn: After this stanza the following appears in the Eton manuscript:

> Him have we seen the Green-wood Side along
> While o'er the Heath we hied, our Labours done,
> Oft as the Woodlark piped her farewell Song
> With whistful Eyes pursue the setting Sun.

"The next with Dirges due in sad Array
Slow thro' the Church-way Path we saw him born.
Approach and read (for thou can'st read) the Lay,
Grav'd on the Stone beneath yon aged Thorn.°"

The EPITAPH.

Here rests his Head upon the Lap of Earth
A Youth to Fortune and to Fame unknown:
Fair Science frown'd not on his humble Birth,
And Melancholy mark'd him for her own.   120

Large was his Bounty, and his Soul sincere,
Heav'n did a recompence as largely send:
He gave to Mis'ry all he had, a Tear:
He gain'd from Heav'n ('twas all he wish'd) a Friend.

No farther seek his Merits to disclose,
Or draw his Frailties from their dread Abode,
(There they alike in trembling Hope repose)
The Bosom of his Father and his God.

THE PROGRESS
OF POESY

A PINDARIC ODE

This poem and *The Bard*, which was initially published with it in 1757, constitute Gray's response to the contemporary cult of the Sublime. These two odes in the manner of Pindar (*c.* 522–442 B.C.), the Greek lyricist known for the audacity of his techniques, were considered by Gray to be his masterpieces; he was bitterly disappointed to find them ill understood. He wrote a friend soon after the odes had appeared:

> One very great man [Henry Fox], writing to an acquaintance of his and mine, says that he had read them seven or eight times, and that now, when he next sees him, he shall not have above thirty questions to ask. . . . in short, I have heard of nobody but a player [Garrick] and a doctor of divinity [Dr. John Brown] that profess their esteem

116. Thorn: After this stanza the following appears in the Eton manuscript and in several of the editions published during Gray's lifetime:

> There scatter'd oft the earliest of ye Spring
> By Hands unseen are frequent Vi'lets found
> The Robin loves to build & warble there
> And little Footsteps lightly print the Ground.

for them. Oh yes! a lady of quality [Lady Holdernesse] . . . who is a great reader. She knew there was a compliment to Dryden, but never suspected there was anything said about Shakespeare or Milton, till it was explained to her.

Samuel Johnson commented, "The obscurity in which he has involved himself will not persuade us that he is sublime." Johnson had the two odes in mind when, in answer to Boswell's observation "Surely [Gray] was not dull in poetry," he said, "Sir, he was dull in company, dull in his closet, dull every where. He was dull in a new way, and that made many people think him GREAT. He was a mechanical poet."

The text is that of the first printing, in *Odes by Mr. Gray* (1757). We have taken from *Poems by Mr. Gray* (1768) the present title (it was simply *Ode I* in 1757), Gray's Advertisement, and some of his notes.

ADVERTISEMENT.

When the Author first published this and the following Ode, he was advised, even by his Friends, to subjoin some few explanatory Notes; but had too much respect for the understanding of his Readers to take that liberty.

I. I.°

AWAKE, Æolian lyre,° awake,
And give to rapture all thy trembling strings.
From Helicon's° harmonious springs
A thousand rills their mazy progress take:

THE PROGRESS OF POESY. **I. I:** [Gray's note]

> Awake, my glory: awake, lute and harp.
>   *David's Psalms.*

Pindar styles his own poetry with its musical accompanyments, Αἰοληὶς μολπή, Αἰολίδες χορδαί, Αἰολίδων πνοαὶ αὐλῶν, Æolian song, Æolian strings, the breath of the Æolian flute.

The subject and simile, as usual with Pindar, are united. The various sources of poetry, which gives life and lustre to all it touches, are here described; its quiet majestic progress enriching every subject (otherwise dry and barren) with a pomp of diction and luxuriant harmony of numbers; and its more rapid and irresistible course, when swoln and hurried away by the conflict of tumultuous passions. **1. Æolian lyre:** the spirit of passionate poetry; the Aeolian mode in Greek music was joyous. **3. Helicon:** a mountain sacred to the nine Muses, who live in its springs.

The laughing flowers, that round them blow,
Drink life and fragrance as they flow.
Now the rich stream of music winds along
Deep, majestic, smooth, and strong,
Thro' verdant vales, and Ceres'° golden reign:°
Now rowling down the steep amain,   10
Headlong, impetuous, see it pour:
The rocks, and nodding groves rebellow to the roar.

I. 2.°

Oh! Sovereign° of the willing soul,
Parent of sweet and solemn-breathing airs,
Enchanting shell°! the sullen Cares,
And frantic Passions hear thy soft controul.
On Thracia's° hills the Lord of War,
Has curb'd the fury of his car,
And drop'd his thirsty lance at thy command.
Perching on the scept'red hand   20
Of Jove, thy magic lulls the feather'd king°
With ruffled plumes, and flagging wing:
Quench'd in dark clouds of slumber lie
The terror of his beak, and light'nings of his eye.

I. 3.°

Thee the voice, the dance, obey,
Temper'd to thy warbled lay.
O'er Idalia's° velvet-green
The rosy-crowned Loves are seen
On Cytherea's° day
With antic Sports, and blue-eyed Pleasures,   30
Frisking light in frolic measures;
Now pursuing, now retreating,
Now in circling troops they meet:
To brisk notes in cadence beating
Glance their many-twinkling feet.
Slow melting strains their Queen's approach declare:
Where'er she turns the Graces° homage pay.
With arms sublime, that float upon the air,
In gliding state she wins her easy way:

O'er her warm cheek, and rising bosom, move   40
The bloom of young Desire, and purple light of Love.

II. 1.°

Man's feeble race what Ills await,
Labour, and Penury, the racks of Pain,
Disease, and Sorrow's weeping train,
And Death, sad refuge from the storms of Fate!
The fond complaint, my Song, disprove,
And justify the laws of Jove.
Say, has he giv'n in vain the heav'nly Muse?
Night, and all her sickly dews,
Her Spectres wan, and Birds of boding cry,   50
He gives to range the dreary sky:
Till down the eastern cliffs afar
Hyperion's° march they spy, and glitt'ring shafts of war.

II. 2.°

In climes beyond the solar road,
Where shaggy forms o'er ice-built mountains roam,
The Muse has broke the twilight-gloom
To chear the shiv'ring Native's dull abode.
And oft, beneath the od'rous shade
Of Chili's boundless forests laid,
She deigns to hear the savage Youth repeat   60
In loose numbers wildly sweet
Their feather-cinctured Chiefs, and dusky Loves.
Her track, where'er the Goddess roves,
Glory pursue, and generous Shame,
Th' unconquerable Mind, and Freedom's holy flame.

II. 3.°

Woods, that wave o'er Delphi's steep,°
Isles, that crown th' Egæan deep,

---

9. **Ceres:** goddess of agriculture. **reign:** territory. **I. 2:** [Gray's note] Power of harmony to calm the turbulent sallies of the soul. The thoughts are borrowed from the first Pythian [Ode] of Pindar. **13. Sovereign:** the Aeolian lyre. **15. shell:** The lyre was first made from a tortoise shell. **17. Thracia:** the area north of Greece; birthplace of Orpheus, the great mythical singer to the lyre. **21. the feather'd king:** Jove's eagle. **I. 3:** [Gray's note] Power of harmony to produce all the graces of motion in the body. **27. Idalia:** a town in Cyprus sacred to Aphrodite, goddess of love. **29. Cytherea:** Aphrodite. **37. Graces:** Aphrodite's three handmaidens.

II. 1: [Gray's note] To compensate the real and imaginary ills of life, the Muse was given to Mankind by the same Providence that sends the Day by its chearful presence to dispel the gloom and terrors of the Night. **53. Hyperion:** the sun. **II. 2:** [Gray's note] Extensive influence of poetic Genius over the remotest and most uncivilized nations: its connection with liberty, and the virtues that naturally attend on it. (See the Erse, Norwegian, and Welch Fragments, the Lapland and American songs.) **II. 3:** [Gray's note] Progress of Poetry from Greece to Italy, and from Italy to England. Chaucer was not unacquainted with the writings of Dante or of Petrarch. The Earl of Surrey and Sir Tho. Wyatt had travelled in Italy, and formed their taste there; Spenser imitated the Italian writers; Milton improved on them: but this School expired soon after the Restoration, and a new one arose on the French model, which has subsisted ever since. **66. Delphi's steep:** site of the oracle of Apollo, at the foot of Mount Parnassus, a mountain sacred to the Muses.

Fields, that cool Ilissus° laves,
Or where Mæander's° amber waves
In lingering Lab'rinths creep,   70
How do your tuneful Echos languish,
Mute, but to the voice of Anguish?
Where each old poetic Mountain
Inspiration breath'd around:
Ev'ry shade and hallow'd Fountain
Murmur'd deep a solemn sound:
Till the sad Nine in Greece's evil hour
Left their Parnassus for the Latian° plains.
Alike they scorn the pomp of tyrant-Power,
And coward Vice, that revels in her chains.   80
When Latium had her lofty spirit lost,
They sought, oh Albion°! next thy sea-encircled coast.

III. 1.

Far from the sun and summer-gale,
In thy green lap was Nature's Darling° laid,
What time, where lucid Avon stray'd,
To Him the mighty Mother did unveil
Her aweful face: The dauntless Child
Stretch'd forth his little arms, and smiled.
This pencil take (she said) whose colours clear
Richly paint the vernal year: 90
Thine too these golden keys, immortal Boy!
This can unlock the gates of Joy;
Of Horrour that, and thrilling Fears,
Or ope the sacred source of sympathetic Tears.

III. 2.

Nor second He,° that rode sublime
Upon the seraph-wings of Extasy,
The secrets of th' Abyss to spy.
He pass'd the flaming bounds of Place and Time:
The living Throne, the saphire-blaze,
Where Angels tremble, while they gaze,   100
He saw; but blasted with excess of light,
Closed his eyes in endless night.
Behold, where Dryden's less presumptuous car,
Wide o'er the fields of Glory bear
Two Coursers° of ethereal race,
With necks in thunder cloath'd, and long-resounding
    pace.

III. 3.

Hark, his hands the lyre explore!
Bright-eyed Fancy hovering o'er
Scatters from her pictur'd urn
Thoughts, that breath, and words, that burn.   110
But ah! 'tis heard no more°—
Oh! Lyre divine, what daring Spirit
Wakes thee now? tho' he inherit
Nor the pride, nor ample pinion,
That the Theban Eagle° bear
Sailing with supreme dominion
Thro' the azure deep of air:
Yet oft before his infant eyes would run
Such forms, as glitter in the Muse's ray
With orient hues, unborrow'd of the Sun: 120
Yet shall he mount, and keep his distant way
Beyond the limits of a vulgar fate,
Beneath the Good how far—but far above the Great.°

FROM

[LETTERS]

Gray's letters reveal his genuine capacity for friendship as well as his humor and playfulness. He was fond of whimsy—the minor poet William Mason he addressed as Scroddles—and in letters to members of the Eton Quadruple Alliance he used schoolboy nicknames: Walpole was Celadon, Ashton was Almanzor, West was Favonius or Zephyrus, and Gray himself was Orosmades.

The text is from *The Correspondence of Thomas Gray,* ed. Paget Toynbee and Leonard Whibley (3 vols., 1935). We have silently corrected Gray's minor inadvertences.

---

68. Ilissus: a river near Athens. **69. Mæander:** a river in Asia Minor famous for its windings. **78. Latian:** Roman. **82. Albion:** Britain. **84. Nature's Darling:** [Gray's note] Shakespear. **95. He:** [Gray's note] Milton. **105. Two Coursers:** [Gray's note] Meant to express the stately march and sounding energy of Dryden's rhimes.

111. 'tis . . . more: [Gray's note] We have had in our language no other odes of the sublime kind, than that of Dryden on St. Cecilia's day: for Cowley (who had his merit) yet wanted judgment, style, and harmony, for such a task. That of Pope is not worthy of so great a man. Mr. [William] Mason indeed of late days has touched the true chords, and with a masterly hand, in some of his Choruses—above all in the last of [his play] Caractacus,

    Hark! heard ye not yon footstep dread? &c.

115. the Theban Eagle: Pindar. **123. the Great:** the rich and powerful.

To Horace Walpole

[Cambridge] Jan: 12 [1735]

> How severe is forgetful old Age
> To confine a poor Devil so?
> That I almost despair
> To see even the Air;
> Much more my dear Damon—hey ho!

Thou dear envious Imp, to set me a longing with accounts of Plays & Opera's, & Masquerades after hearing of which, I can no more think of Logick & Stuff, than you could of Divinity at a Ball, or of Caudle[1] and Carraway-Comfits after having been stuffed at a Christening: heaven knows! we have nobody in our Colledge, that has seen London, but one; and he, I believe comes out of Vinegar-yard,[2] & looks like toasted Cheshire cheese, strewed with brown Sugar. I beg you, give me the minutest Circumstances of your Diversions & your Indiversions; tho' if it is as great a trouble to you to write, as it is a pleasure to me to get 'em by heart, I fear I shan't hear from you once in a twelve-month, & dear now, be very punctual and very long: if I had the least particle of pleasure, you should know it; & so you should if I had any thing troublesome; tho' in Cambridge there is nothing so troublesome, as that one has nothing to trouble one. Every thing is so tediously regular, so samish, that I expire for want of a little variety. I am just as I was, & so is every thing about me; I hope you'll forgive my formality, in being just the same | Friend of yours, & just | the same Servant

OROZMADES.

To Horace Walpole

[Cambridge, January 14, 1735]

Tityre, dum patulæ recubo sub tegmine fagi[3]

Though you'll think perhaps it's a little too cold weather for giving oneself languishing airs under a tree; however supposing it's by the fireside, it will be full as well; so as I was going to say—but, I believe, I was going to say nothing, so I must begin over again—

MY DEAREST CELADON

Yesterday morning, (being the morning I set apart for lying abed till one aclock) I was waked about ten with hollowing & the Noise of a Bagpipe at the door; so I got up, & open'd the door, & saw all the court full of strange appearances: at first I concluded 'twas you with a whole Masquerade at your heels, but upon more mature deliberation imagined it might be Amadis de Gaul[4] come to set me free from this enchanted Castle with his train of conquer'd Monsters & Oddities: the first, whom I took for the Knight in person, had his face painted after the manner of ye ancient Britains. He played melodiously on the afore-named Instrument, & had a Plow upon his Back; what it meant, I did not apprehend at first: he said nothing at all, but made many very significant Grimaces: before him & on each side a Number of Folks cover'd over with Tags & Points[5] form'd themselves into a Country Dance: there follow'd something, which I apprehended was the beauteous Oriana,[6] in a white Dimoty Petticoat & Boddice; her head & face were veil'd: she was supported by her two Gentlemen-ushers, & seem'd to be very obstreperous, for she struggled & kicked, & snorted, & fizzled: I concluded she was falling in fits, & was running with my Hungary water[7] Bottle: when she was so violent, that she got loose from her Attendants, & run away upon all fours into the middle of ye Court, & her hood falling off discover'd a large pair of Ears. In short, Oriana was metamorphosed into a very genteel Jack-ass: upon this the whole crowd set up a great Shout of, God speed the Plough. After all I was inform'd by a Negro Gentlewoman with a very long beard, who had a great deal to do in the Ceremony, that it was Plough-Monday,[8] & that all this was the Custom of the Country; they march in this manner thro' all the Colledges in Town. The Term is now begun again, & I have made such a wonderful progress in Philosophy, that I begin to be quite persuaded, that black is white, & that fire will not burn, & that I ought not, either to give credit to my eyes or feeling; they tell me too, that I am nothing in the world, & that I only fancy, I exist: do but come to me quickly & one lesson of thine, my dear Philosopher, will restore me to the use of my Senses, and make me think myself something, as long as I am | your friend & Servant

T : GRAY

LETTERS. **1. Caudle:** warm gruel mixed with spiced wine. **2. Vinegar-yard:** in Drury Lane. **3. Tityre . . . fagi:** "Tityrus, reclining beneath the canopy of the spreading beech tree" (adapted from Virgil's *Eclogues*, i. 1).

4. Amadis de Gaul: the hero of a Hispanic chivalric romance of the Renaissance. **5. Tags & Points:** ribbons and decorative cords. **6. Oriana:** heroine of the romance *Amadis of Gaul*. **7. Hungary water:** brandy flavored with rosemary flowers. **8. Plough-Monday:** the first Monday after Epiphany; ceremonial beginning of the plowing season.

P:S: The inclosed is the oath of Matriculation.[9] I am charmed with Popes Letter[10]—never did any body long for anything, as I do for your Masquerade; pray d'ye design to go, as a Judge, or a Devil; or undisguised: or as an Angel in propriâ Personâ.[11] I wonder how you can dislike the Distressed Mother[12]—

To Richard West

Turin, Nov 16, N.S.[13] 1739.

After eight days journey through Greenland,[14] we arrived at Turin. You approach it by a handsome avenue of nine miles long, and quite strait. The entrance is guarded by certain vigilant dragons, called Douaniers,[15] who mumbled[16] us for some time. The city is not large, as being a place of strength, and consequently confined within its fortifications; it has many beauties and some faults; among the first are streets all laid out by the line, regular uniform buildings, fine walks that surround the whole, and in general a good lively clean appearance: But the houses are of brick plaistered, which is apt to want repairing; the windows of oiled paper, which is apt to be torn; and every thing very slight, which is apt to tumble down. There is an excellent Opera, but it is only in the Carnival: Balls every night, but only in the Carnival: Masquerades, too, but only in the Carnival. This Carnival lasts only from Christmas to Lent; one half of the remaining part of the year is passed in remembering the last, the other in expecting the future Carnival. We cannot well subsist upon such slender diet, no more than upon an execrable Italian Comedy, and a Puppet-Show, called Rapresentazione d'un' anima dannata,[17] which, I think, are all the present diversions of the place; except the Marquise de Cavaillac's Conversazione, where one goes to see people play at Ombre and Taroc, a game with 72 cards all painted with suns, and moons, and devils and monks. Mr. Walpole has been at court; the family[18] are at present at a country palace, called La Venerie.

The palace here in town is the very quintessence of gilding and looking-glass; inlaid floors, carved pannels, and painting, wherever they could stick a brush. I own I have not, as yet, any where met with those grand and simple works of Art, that are to amaze one, and whose sight one is to be the better for: But those of Nature have astonished me beyond expression. In our little journey up to the Grande Chartreuse,[19] I do not remember to have gone ten paces without an exclamation, that there was no restraining: Not a precipice, not a torrent, not a cliff, but is pregnant with religion and poetry. There are certain scenes that would awe an atheist into belief, without the help of other argument. One need not have a very fantastic imagination to see spirits there at noon-day: You have Death perpetually before your eyes, only so far removed, as to compose the mind without frighting it. I am well persuaded St. Bruno was a man of no common genius, to choose such a situation for his retirement; and perhaps should have been a disciple of his, had I been born in his time. You may believe Abelard and Heloïse[20] were not forgot upon this occasion: If I do not mistake, I saw you too every now and then at a distance among the trees; il me semble, que j'ai vu ce chien de visage là quelque part.[21] You seemed to call to me from the other side of the precipice, but the noise of the river below was so great, that I really could not distinguish what you said; it seemed to have a cadence like verse. In your next you will be so good to let me know what it was. The week we have since passed among the Alps, has not equalled the single day upon that mountain, because the winter was rather too far advanced, and the weather a little foggy. However, it did not want its beauties; the savage rudeness of the view is inconceivable without seeing it: I reckoned in one day, thirteen cascades, the least of which was, I dare say, one hundred feet in height. I had Livy in the chaise with me, and beheld his "Nives cœlo propè immistæ, tecta informia imposita rupibus, pecora jumentaque torrida frigore, homines intonsi & inculti, animalia inanimaque omnia rigentia

---

9. **oath of Matriculation:** sworn by the entering scholar at the university. 10. **Popes Letter:** the *Epistle to Dr. Arbuthnot* (see Part Two). 11. **in . . . Personâ:** in your own character. 12. **the Distressed Mother:** title of a she-tragedy (1712) by Ambrose Philips (*c.* 1675–1749). (See the selections from Philips in Part Three.) 13. **N.S:** New Style, in reference to the Gregorian calendar, used on the Continent. 14. **Greenland:** Switzerland. 15. **Douaniers:** customs officers. 16. **mumbled:** maltreated. 17. **Rapresentazione . . . dannata:** *Representation of a Damned Soul.* 18. **the family:** the royal family.

19. **the Grande Chartreuse:** a famous Carthusian monastery on a mountain top near Grenoble, founded by St. Bruno about 1084. 20. **Abelard and Heloïse:** twelfth-century French lovers who retired to convents after a tragic love affair. (See Pope's *Eloisa to Abelard* in Part Two.) 21. **il . . . part:** It seems to me that I saw that beastly face there somewhere.

gelu; omnia confragosa, præruptaque."[22] The creatures that inhabit them are, in all respects, below humanity; and most of them, especially women, have the tumidum guttur,[23] which they call goscia. Mont Cenis, I confess, carries the permission mountains have of being frightful rather too far; and its horrors were accompanied with too much danger to give one time to reflect upon their beauties. There is a family of the Alpine monsters I have mentioned, upon its very top, that in the middle of winter calmly lay in their stock of provisions and firing, and so are buried in their hut for a month or two under the snow. When we were down it, and got a little way into Piedmont, we began to find "Apricos quosdam colles, rivosque prope sylvas, & jam humano cultu digniora loca."[24] I read Silius Italicus[25] too, for the first time; and wished for you according to custom. We set out for Genoa in two days time.

To Richard West

London, [8] April, Thursday [1742].

You are the first who ever made a Muse of a Cough; to me it seems a much more easy task to versify in one's sleep, (that indeed you were of old famous for) than for want of it. Not the wakeful nightingale (when she had a cough) ever sung so sweetly. I give you thanks for your warble, and wish you could sing yourself to rest. These wicked remains of your illness will sure give way to warm weather and gentle exercise; which I hope you will not omit as the season advances. Whatever low spirits and indolence, the effect of them, may advise to the contrary, I pray you add five steps to your walk daily for my sake; by the help of which, in a month's time, I propose to set you on horseback.

I talked of the Dunciad[26] as concluding you had seen it; if you have not, do you choose I should get and send it you? I have myself, upon your recommendation, been reading Joseph Andrews.[27] The incidents are ill laid and without invention; but the characters have a great deal of nature, which always pleases even in her lowest shapes. Parson Adams is perfectly well; so is Mrs. Slipslop, and the story of Wilson; and throughout he shews himself well read in Stage-Coaches, Country Squires, Inns, and Inns of Court. His reflections upon high people and low people, and misses and masters, are very good. However the exaltedness of some minds (or rather as I shrewdly suspect their insipidity and want of feeling or observation) may make them insensible to these light things, (I mean such as characterize and paint nature) yet surely they are as weighty and much more useful than your grave discourses upon the mind, the passions, and what not. Now as the paradisaical pleasures of the Mahometans consist in playing upon the flute and lying with Houris, be mine to read eternal new romances of Marivaux and Crebillon.[28]

You are very good in giving yourself the trouble to read and find fault with my long harangues.[29] Your freedom (as you call it) has so little need of apologies, that I should scarce excuse your treating me any otherwise; which, whatever compliment it might be to my vanity, would be making a very ill one to my understanding. As to matter of stile, I have this to say: The language of the age is never the language of poetry; except among the French, whose verse, where the thought or image does not support it, differs in nothing from prose. Our poetry, on the contrary, has a language peculiar to itself; to which almost every one, that has written, has added something by enriching it with foreign idioms and derivatives: Nay sometimes words of their own composition or invention. Shakespear and Milton have been great creators this way; and no one more licentious than Pope or Dryden, who perpetually borrow expressions from the former. Let me give you some instances from Dryden, whom every body reckons a great master of our poetical tongue.—Full of *museful mopeings*—unlike the *trim* of love—a pleasant *beverage*—a *roundelay* of love—stood silent in his *mood*—with knots and *knares*

---

22. Nives . . . præruptaque: "snows almost merging with the sky; shapeless hovels perched on crags; frost-bitten livestock; shaggy, unkempt men; both animals and things stiff with cold; the whole place rugged and steep" (adapted from Livy, *Ab Urbe Condita*, XXI. 32). **23. tumidum guttur:** goiter. **24. Apricos . . . loca:** "sunny slopes and little streams, with woods nearby and spots that are almost fit for human habitation" (Livy, *Ab Urbe Condita*, XXI. 37). **25. Silius Italicus:** (A.D. 25–101), minor Roman epic poet. **26. the Dunciad:** Book IV of Pope's mock epic (see Part Two) had appeared in March of this year.

27. Joseph Andrews: Fielding's novel (see the Preface in Part Two) had appeared in February of this year. **28. Marivaux and Crebillon:** contemporary French novelists; authors, respectively, of *Marianne* (1731) and *Le Sopha* (1740). **29. harangues:** portions of Gray's unfinished blank-verse tragedy *Agrippina*.

deformed—his *ireful mood*—in proud *array*—his *boon* was granted—and *disarray* and shameful rout—*wayward* but wise—*furbished* for the field—the *foiled doddered* oaks—*disherited*—*smouldring* flames—*retchless* of laws—*crones* old and ugly—the *beldam* at his side—the *grandam-hag*—*villanize* his Father's fame.—But they are infinite: And our language not being a settled thing (like the French) has an undoubted right to words of an hundred years old, provided antiquity have not rendered them unintelligible. In truth, Shakespear's language is one of his principal beauties; and he has no less advantage over your Addisons and Rowes[30] in this, than in those other great excellencies you mention. Every word in him is a picture. Pray put me the following lines into the tongue of our modern Dramatics:

> But I, that am not shaped for sportive tricks,
> Nor made to court an amorous looking-glass:
> I, that am rudely stampt, and want love's majesty
> To strut before a wanton ambling nymph:
> I, that am curtail'd of this fair proportion,
> Cheated of feature by dissembling nature,
> Deform'd, unfinish'd, sent before my time
> Into this breathing world, scarce half made up[31]—

And what follows. To me they appear untranslatable;

and if this be the case, our language is greatly degenerated. However, the affectation of imitating Shakespear may doubtless be carried too far; and is no sort of excuse for sentiments ill-suited, or speeches ill-timed, which I believe is a little the case with me. I guess the most faulty expressions may be these—*silken* son of *dalliance*—*drowsier* pretensions—*wrinkled beldams*—*arched* the hearer's brow and *riveted* his eyes in *fearful extasie*. These are easily altered or omitted: and indeed if the thoughts be wrong or superfluous, there is nothing easier than to leave out the whole. The first ten or twelve lines are, I believe, the best; and as for the rest, I was betrayed into a good deal of it by Tacitus;[32] only what he has said in five words, I imagine I have said in fifty lines: Such is the misfortune of imitating the inimitable. Now, if you are of my opinion, una litura[33] may do the business better than a dozen; and you need not fear unravelling my web. I am a sort of spider; and have little else to do but spin it over again, or creep to some other place and spin there. Alas! for one who has nothing to do but amuse himself, I believe my amusements are as little amusing as most folks. But no matter; it makes the hours pass, and is better than ἐν ἀμαθίᾳ καὶ ἀμουσίᾳ καταβιῶναι.[34] Adieu.

30. **Addisons and Rowes:** The essayist Joseph Addison (1672–1719) was also known for his tragedy *Cato* (1713); Nicholas Rowe (1674–1718) was famous for his tragedies *The Fair Penitent* (1703) and *Jane Shore* (1714). 31. **But . . . up:** *Richard III*, I. i. 14–21.

32. **Tacitus:** Roman historian (c. A.D. 55–c. 117), Gray's source for the story of Agrippina. 33. **una litura:** one (great) erasure. 34. ἐν . . . καταβιῶναι: "to live in a state of ignorance and grossness" (Aelian, *Variae Historiae*, VII. 15).

Tobias Smollett

Tobias George Smollett, novelist and journalist, was born in Dunbartonshire, in western Scotland. After a grammar-school education, he became a Glasgow surgeon's apprentice at the age of fifteen and attended medical lectures at the university, where he acquired a local reputation as a writer of earthy satires. When he was eighteen he set off for London to try his hand at literature: his stock in trade was the manuscript of a tragedy, *The Regicide*, which, he found, did not excite the London theater managers. The outbreak of the naval war with Spain in 1739 created a sudden need for ship's doctors, and Smollett, momentarily discouraged with literature, joined H.M.S. *Chichester* as surgeon's second mate. After participating in the bloody battle at Cartagena in 1741–42, he was released from the Navy in the West Indies, where he married in 1743. He returned to England in 1744 with ambitious plans for a medical career, but although he practiced for several years both in London and in the neighboring village of Chelsea, he was not a great success as a doctor: he was too blunt, satirical, and hot-tempered, or so his female patients thought. Thus he drifted gradually back into literature. In his first novel, *Roderick Random* (1748), he transformed his naval experiences into vigorous picaresque fiction—the novel was intended, he explains, as "a satire upon mankind." *Peregrine Pickle*, another lusty satiric novel, followed in 1751.

A rapid writer with a family to support, Smollett labored for the next twelve years as a journalist and publisher's hack. He supervised a translation of *Don Quixote;* as proprietor and editor of *The Critical Review*, he helped conduct the magazine's elaborate Grub Street quarrels; and he produced a hasty four-volume *History of England*. In addition, he was responsible for a translation of the writings of Voltaire, a geographical reference work, and several digests of travels. But all this frantic production barely kept his bills paid. He wrote to a friend in 1758, "[I] wish to God my Circumstances would allow me to consign my Pen to oblivion." These years of hack work under constant pressure damaged his health, and in 1763, suffering from asthma and tuberculosis, he spent two years abroad in search of a beneficial climate. The literary result of this tour was *Travels Through France and Italy* (1766).

In 1771 his masterpiece appeared, *The Expedition of Humphry Clinker*, a satiric novel in epistolary form, presenting the peripatetic search for health of an irascible Welsh invalid, Matthew Bramble, who is accompanied on his travels by a comical retinue of relatives and servants. It is primarily *Humphry Clinker* that has secured Smollett a permanent place among the other eighteenth-century masters of fiction, Defoe, Richardson, Fielding, and Sterne. He died shortly after its publication and was buried at Leghorn, in northern Italy, where he had gone in a final attempt to save his health.

Smollett's old-fashioned medical training still emphasized the Renaissance theory of the four bodily humors, or fluids, to whose imbalance various eccentricities were ascribed. In his portrayal of human beings, he often puts this simple psychology of humors to work by first simplifying and then exaggerating human singularities. His caricatures are reminiscent of the comic characters of Ben Jonson, and he helps transmit the tradition of grotesque characterization to Fanny Burney, Scott, and Dickens. As a broad satirist, Smollett devotes himself to arousing what he calls "that generous indignation which ought to animate the reader against the sordid and vicious disposition of the world." And like most satirists, the vehemently idealistic Smollett performs his task primarily through revelations of the alarming distance between human possibility and human actuality.

Smollett's novels are collected in the Shakespeare Head Edition (11 vols., 1925–26); *Roderick Random*, *Peregrine Pickle*, and *Humphry Clinker* are frequently reprinted in inexpensive format. The best biography is L. M. Knapp's *Tobias Smollett: Doctor of Men and Manners* (1949). E. S. Noyes has edited most of the *Letters* (1926). G. M. Kahrl's *Tobias Smollett: Traveler-Novelist* (1945) shows the connection between Smollett's lifelong love of traveling and his aptitudes for the picaresque and the satiric. *Travels Through France and Italy* is usefully edited by Thomas Seccombe in the World's Classics (1907); another convenient modern edition is that introduced by Osbert Sitwell (1949). W. E. Mead's *The Grand Tour in the Eighteenth Century* (1914) and Eugène Joliat's *Smollett et la France* (1935) provide interesting backgrounds for the *Travels*.

FROM

TRAVELS THROUGH FRANCE AND ITALY

Exhausted from sickness and overwork, and grieving over the recent death of his daughter, Smollett sailed from Dover to Boulogne in June, 1763, accompanied by his wife, two young ladies, and a portable library of a hundred and fifty volumes. Two years later, after an unremitting series of rascally innkeepers and avaricious porters, he thankfully returned to England ("You cannot imagine what pleasure I feel while I survey the white cliffs of Dover," he wrote as he neared home), where he worked up his accumulated observations into forty-one of the "letters" to fictional acquaintances that had become, in his day, one of the most popular ways of putting together a travel book. When he set out to tell, in *Humphry Clinker*, the story of Matthew Bramble's travels, he exploited the same travel-letter convention.

The book of travels was a serious literary genre in the eighteenth century. The form was sufficiently flexible to attract writers as various as Defoe, Fielding, Addison, Boswell, Johnson, and Laurence Sterne, whose *Sentimental Journey Through France and Italy* (1768) was conceived in part as a soft answer to the wrathful passages of Smollett's *Travels* ("the learned Smelfungus," Sterne calls him). As might be expected, most contemporary English readers were charmed by Smollett's rowdy hyperboles ("All the inns of [France] are execrable"); most Continental readers were appalled.

The text is that of the first edition (1766). Diacritical marks have been corrected.

LETTER VII

To Mrs. M——.

Paris, October 12, 1763.

MADAM,

I shall be much pleased if the remarks I have made on the characters of the French people, can afford you the satisfaction you require. With respect to the ladies, I can only judge from their exteriors: but, indeed, these are so characteristic, that one can hardly judge amiss; unless we suppose that a woman of taste and sentiment may be so overruled by the absurdity of what is called fashion, as to reject reason, and disguise nature, in order to become ridiculous or frightful. That this may be the case with some individuals, is very possible. I have known it happen in our own country, where the follies of the French are adopted, and exhibited in the most aukward imitation: but the general prevalence of those preposterous modes, is a plain proof that there is a general want of taste, and a general depravity of nature. I shall not pretend to describe the particulars of a French lady's dress. These you are much better acquainted with than I can pretend to be: but this I will be bold to affirm, that France is the general reservoir from which all the absurdities of false taste, luxury, and extravagance have overflowed the different kingdoms and states of Europe. The springs that fill this reservoir, are no other than vanity and ignorance. It would be superfluous to attempt proving from the nature of things, from the first principles and use of dress, as well as from the consideration of natural beauty, and the practice of the ancients, who certainly understood it as well as the connoisseurs of these days, that nothing can be more monstrous, inconvenient, and contemptible, than the fashion of modern drapery. You yourself are well aware of all its defects, and have often ridiculed them in my hearing. I shall only mention one particular of dress essential to the fashion in this country, which seems to me to carry human affectation to the very farthest verge of folly and extravagance; that is, the manner in which the faces of the ladies are primed and painted. When the Indian chiefs were in England[1]

every body ridiculed their preposterous method of painting their cheeks and eye-lids; but this ridicule was wrong placed. Those critics ought to have considered, that the Indians do not use paint to make themselves agreeable; but in order to be the more terrible to their enemies. It is generally supposed, I think, that your sex make use of *fard*[2] and vermillion for very different purposes; namely, to help a bad or faded complexion, to heighten the graces, or conceal the defects of nature, as well as the ravages of time. I shall not enquire at present, whether it is just and honest to impose in this manner on mankind: if it is not honest, it may be allowed to be artful and politic, and shews, at least, a desire of being agreeable. But to lay it on as the fashion in France prescribes to all the ladies of condition, who indeed cannot appear without this badge of distinction, is to disguise themselves in such a manner, as to render them odious and detestable to every spectator, who has the least relish left for nature and propriety. As for the *fard*, or *white*, with which their necks and shoulders are plaistered, it may be in some measure excusable, as their skins are naturally brown, or sallow; but the *rouge*, which is daubed on their faces, from the chin up to the eyes, without the least art or dexterity, not only destroys all distinction of features, but renders the aspect really frightful, or at best conveys nothing but ideas of disgust and aversion. You know, that without this horrible masque no married lady is admitted at court, or in any polite assembly; and that it is a mark of distinction which no bourgeoise dare assume. Ladies of fashion only have the privilege of exposing themselves in these ungracious colours. As their faces are concealed under a false complexion, so their heads are covered with a vast load of false hair, which is frizzled on the forehead, so as exactly to resemble the wooly heads of the Guinea negroes. As to the natural hue of it, this is a matter of no consequence, for powder makes every head of hair of the same colour; and no woman appears in this country, from the moment she rises till night, without being compleately whitened. Powder or meal was first used in Europe by the Poles, to conceal their scald[3] heads; but the present fashion of using it, as well as the modish method of dressing

---

TRAVELS THROUGH FRANCE AND ITALY: *Letter VII.* **1. Indian . . . England:** A group of visiting Cherokee Indians was the sensation of London during the summer of 1762. Their

paint was so elaborate that when Oliver Goldsmith called on them, they kept him waiting three hours before they felt themselves prepared to appear. **2. fard:** white paint. **3. scald:** scabby.

the hair, must have been borrowed from the Hottentots, who grease their wooly heads with mutton suet, and then paste it over with the powder called *buchu*.[4] In like manner, the hair of our fine ladies is frizzled into the appearance of negroes wool, and stiffened with an abominable paste of hog's grease, tallow, and white powder. The present fashion, therefore, of painting the face, and adorning the head, adopted by the beau monde[5] in France, is taken from those two polite nations the Chickesaws of America and the Hottentots of Afric. On the whole, when I see one of those fine creatures sailing along, in her taudry robes of silk and gauze, frilled, and flounced, and furbelowed, with her false locks, her false jewels, her paint, her patches, and perfumes; I cannot help looking upon her as the vilest piece of sophistication that art ever produced.

This hideous masque of painting, though destructive of all beauty, is, however, favourable to natural homeliness and deformity. It accustoms the eyes of the other sex, and in time reconciles them to frightful objects; it disables them from perceiving any distinction of features between woman and woman; and, by reducing all faces to a level, gives every female an equal chance for an admirer; being in this particular analogous to the practice of the antient Lacedemonians, who were obliged to chuse their help-mates in the dark. In what manner the insides of their heads are furnished, I would not presume to judge from the conversation of a very few to whom I have had access: but from the nature of their education, which I have heard described, and the natural vivacity of their tempers, I should expect neither sense, sentiment, nor discretion. From the nursery they are allowed, and even encouraged, to say every thing that comes uppermost; by which means they acquire a volubility of tongue, and a set of phrases, which constitutes what is called polite conversation. At the same time they obtain an absolute conquest over all sense of shame, or rather, they avoid acquiring this troublesome sensation; for it is certainly no innate idea. Those who have not governesses at home, are sent, for a few years, to a convent, where they lay in a fund of superstition that serves them for life: but I never heard they had the least opportunity of cultivating the mind, of exercising the powers of reason, or of imbibing a taste for letters, or any rational or useful accomplishment. After being

taught to prattle, to dance and play at cards, they are deemed sufficiently qualified to appear in the *grand monde*,[6] and to perform all the duties of that high rank and station in life. In mentioning cards, I ought to observe, that they learn to play not barely for amusement, but also with a view to advantage; and, indeed, you seldom meet with a native of France, whether male or female, who is not a compleat gamester, well versed in all the subtleties and finesses of the art. This is likewise the case all over Italy. A lady of a great house in Piedmont, having four sons, makes no scruple to declare, that the first shall represent the family, the second enter into the army, the third into the church, and that she will breed the fourth a gamester. These noble adventurers devote themselves in a particular manner to the entertainment of travellers from our country, because the English are supposed to be full of money, rash, incautious, and utterly ignorant of play. But such a sharper is most dangerous, when he hunts in couple with a female. I have known a French count and his wife, who found means to lay the most wary under contribution. He was smooth, supple, officious, and attentive: she was young, handsome, unprincipled, and artful. If the Englishman marked for prey was found upon his guard against the designs of the husband, then madam plied him on the side of gallantry. She displayed all the attractions of her person. She sung, danced, ogled, sighed, complimented, and complained. If he was insensible to all her charms, she flattered his vanity, and piqued his pride, by extolling the wealth and generosity of the English; and if he proved deaf to all these insinuations, she, as her last stake, endeavoured to interest his humanity and compassion. She expatiated, with tears in her eyes, on the cruelty and indifference of her great relations; represented that her husband was no more than the cadet[7] of a noble family; that his provision was by no means suitable, either to the dignity of his rank, or the generosity of his disposition: that he had a law-suit of great consequence depending, which had drained all his finances; and, finally, that they should be both ruined, if they could not find some generous friend, who would accommodate them with a sum of money to bring the cause to a determination. Those who are not actuated by such scandalous motives, become gamesters from meer habit, and, having nothing more solid to engage their thoughts,

---

4. **buchu:** a powder derived from a South African plant. 5. **beau monde:** fashionable world.

6. **grand monde:** fashionable world. 7. **cadet:** youngest son.

or employ their time, consume the best part of their lives, in this worst of all dissipation. I am not ignorant that there are exceptions from this general rule: I know that France has produced a Maintenon, a Sévigné, a Scuderi, a Dacier, and a Chatelet;[8] but I would no more deduce the general character of the French ladies from these examples, than I could call a field of hemp a flower-garden, because there might be in it a few *lillies* or *renunculas* planted by the hand of accident.

Woman has been defined a weaker man; but in this country the men are, in my opinion, more ridiculous and insignificant than the women. They certainly are more disagreeable to a rational enquirer, because they are more troublesome. Of all the coxcombs on the face of the earth, a French *petit maître*[9] is the most impertinent: and they are all *petit maîtres*, from the marquis who glitters in lace and embroidery, to the *garçon barbier* covered with meal,[10] who struts with his hair in a long queue, and his hat under his arm. I have already observed, that vanity is the great and universal mover among all ranks and degrees of people in this nation; and as they take no pains to conceal or controul it, they are hurried by it into the most ridiculous and indeed intolerable extravagance.

When I talk of the French nation, I must again except a great number of individuals, from the general censure. Though I have a hearty contempt for the ignorance, folly, and presumption which characterise the generality, I cannot but respect the talents of many great men, who have eminently distinguished themselves in every art and science: these I shall always revere and esteem as creatures of a superior species, produced, for the wise purposes of providence, among the refuse of mankind. It would be absurd to conclude that the Welch or Highlanders are a gigantic people, because those mountains may have produced a few individuals near seven feet high. It would be equally absurd to suppose the French are a nation of philosophers, because France has given birth to a Des Cartes, a Maupertuis, a Réaumur, and a Buffon.

I shall not even deny, that the French are by no means deficient in natural capacity; but they are at the same time remarkable for a natural levity, which hinders their youth from cultivating that capacity.

This is reinforced by the most preposterous education, and the example of a giddy people, engaged in the most frivolous pursuits. A Frenchman is by some Jesuit, or other monk, taught to read his mother tongue, and to say his prayers in a language he does not understand. He learns to dance and to fence, by the masters of those noble sciences. He becomes a compleat connoisseur in dressing hair, and in adorning his own person, under the hands and instructions of his barber and valet de chambre. If he learns to play upon the flute or the fiddle, he is altogether irresistible. But he piques himself upon being polished above the natives of any other country by his conversation with the fair sex. In the course of this communication, with which he is indulged from his tender years, he learns like a parrot, by rote, the whole circle of French compliments, which you know are a set of phrases, ridiculous even to a proverb; and these he throws out indiscriminately to all women, without distinction, in the exercise of that kind of address, which is here distinguished by the name of gallantry: it is no more than his making love to every woman who will give him the hearing. It is an exercise, by the repetition of which he becomes very pert, very familiar, and very impertinent. Modesty, or diffidence, I have already said, is utterly unknown among them, and therefore I wonder there should be a term to express it in their language.

If I was obliged to define politeness, I should call it, the art of making one's self agreeable. I think it an art that necessarily implies a sense of decorum, and a delicacy of sentiment. These are qualities, of which (as far as I have been able to observe) a Frenchman has no idea; therefore he never can be deemed polite, except by those persons among whom they are as little understood. His first aim is to adorn his own person with what he calls fine cloaths, that is the frippery of the fashion. It is no wonder that the heart of a female, unimproved by reason, and untinctured with natural good sense, should flutter at the sight of such a gaudy thing, among the number of her admirers: this impression is enforced by fustian compliments, which her own vanity interprets in a literal sense, and still more confirmed by the assiduous attention of the gallant, who, indeed, has nothing else to mind. A Frenchman in consequence of his mingling with the females from his infancy, not only becomes acquainted with all their customs and humours; but grows wonderfully alert in performing a thousand little offices, which are overlooked by other men, whose time hath been spent in

---

8. a Maintenon . . . Chatelet: all intelligent or scholarly women of letters. **9. petit maître:** effeminate dandy. **10. garçon . . . meal:** apprentice barber covered with cosmetic powder.

making more valuable acquisitions. He enters, without ceremony, a lady's bed-chamber, while she is in bed, reaches her whatever she wants, airs her shift, and helps to put it on. He attends at her toilette, regulates the distribution of her patches, and advises where to lay on the paint. If he visits her when she is dressed, and perceives the least impropriety in her *coeffure*, he insists upon adjusting it with his own hands: if he sees a curl, or even a single hair amiss, he produces his comb, his scissars, and pomatum, and sets it to rights with the dexterity of a professed *friseur*.[11] He 'squires her to every place she visits, either on business, or pleasure; and, by dedicating his whole time to her, renders himself necessary to her occasions. This I take to be the most agreeable side of his character: let us view him on the quarter of impertinence. A Frenchman pries into all your secrets with the most impudent and importunate curiosity, and then discloses them without remorse. If you are indisposed, he questions you about the symptoms of your disorder, with more freedom than your physician would presume to use; very often in the grossest terms. He then proposes his remedy (for they are all quacks), he prepares it without your knowledge, and worries you with solicitation to take it, without paying the least regard to the opinion of those whom you have chosen to take care of your health. Let you be ever so ill, or averse to company, he forces himself at all times into your bed-chamber, and if it is necessary to give him a peremptory refusal, he is affronted. I have known one of those petit maîtres insist upon paying regular visits twice a day to a poor gentleman who was delirious; and he conversed with him on different subjects, till he was in his last agonies. This attendance is not the effect of attachment, or regard, but of sheer vanity, that he may afterwards boast of his charity and humane disposition: though, of all the people I have ever known, I think the French are the least capable of feeling for the distresses of their fellow creatures. Their hearts are not susceptible of deep impressions; and, such is their levity, that the imagination has not time to brood long over any disagreeable idea, or sensation. As a Frenchman piques himself on his gallantry, he no sooner makes a conquest of a female's heart, than he exposes her character, for the gratification of his vanity. Nay, if he should miscarry in his schemes, he will forge letters and stories, to the ruin of the lady's reputation. This is a species of perfidy which one would think should

render them odious and detestable to the whole sex; but the case is otherwise. I beg your pardon, Madam; but women are never better pleased, than when they see one another exposed; and every individual has such confidence in her own superior charms and discretion, that she thinks she can fix the most volatile, and reform the most treacherous lover.

If a Frenchman is admitted into your family, and distinguished by repeated marks of your friendship and regard, the first return he makes for your civilities is to make love to your wife, if she is handsome; if not, to your sister, or daughter, or niece. If he suffers a repulse from your wife, or attempts in vain to debauch your sister, or your daughter, or your niece, he will, rather than not play the traitor with his gallantry, make his addresses to your grandmother; and ten to one, but in one shape or another, he will find means to ruin the peace of a family, in which he has been so kindly entertained. What he cannot accomplish by dint of compliment, and personal attendance, he will endeavour to effect, by reinforcing these with billets-doux, songs, and verses, of which he always makes a provision for such purposes. If he is detected in these efforts of treachery, and reproached with his ingratitude, he impudently declares, that what he had done was no more than simple gallantry, considered in France as an indispensible duty on every man who pretended to good breeding. Nay, he will even affirm, that his endeavours to corrupt your wife, or deflower your daughter, were the most genuine proofs he could give of his particular regard for your family.

If a Frenchman is capable of real friendship, it must certainly be the most disagreeable present he can possibly make to a man of a true English character. You know, Madam, we are naturally taciturn, soon tired of impertinence, and much subject to fits of disgust. Your French friend intrudes upon you at all hours: he stuns you with his loquacity: he teases you with impertinent questions about your domestic and private affairs: he attempts to meddle in all your concerns; and forces his advice upon you with the most unwearied importunity: he asks the price of every thing you wear, and, so sure as you tell him, undervalues it, without hesitation: he affirms it is in a bad taste, ill-contrived, ill-made; that you have been imposed upon both with respect to the fashion and the price; that the marquise of this, or the countess of that, has one that is perfectly elegant, quite in the *bon ton*,[12]

---

11. **friseur:** hairdresser.

12. **bon ton:** fashionable style.

and yet it cost her little more than you gave for a thing that nobody would wear.

If there were five hundred dishes at table, a Frenchman will eat of all of them, and then complain he has no appetite. This I have several times remarked. A friend of mine gained a considerable wager upon an experiment of this kind: the petit maître ate of fourteen different *plats*, besides the desert; then disparaged the cook, declaring he was no better than a *marmiton*, or turnspit.

The French have the most ridiculous fondness for their hair, and this I believe they inherit from their remote ancestors. The first race of French kings were distinguished by their long hair, and certainly the people of this country consider it as an indispensible ornament. A Frenchman will sooner part with his religion than with his hair, which, indeed, no consideration will induce him to forego. I know a gentleman afflicted with a continual head-ach, and a defluxion on his eyes,[13] who was told by his physician that the best chance he had for being cured, would be to have his head close shaved, and bathed every day in cold water. "How (cried he) cut my hair? Mr. Doctor, your most humble servant!" He dismissed his physician, lost his eye-sight, and almost his senses, and is now led about with his hair in a bag, and a piece of green silk hanging like a screen before his face. Count Saxe,[14] and other military writers, have demonstrated the absurdity of a soldier's wearing a long head of hair; nevertheless, every soldier in this country wears a long queue, which makes a delicate mark on his white cloathing; and this ridiculous foppery has descended even to the lowest class of people. The *decrotteur*, who cleans your shoes at the corner of the Pont Neuf, has a tail of this kind hanging down to his rump, and even the peasant who drives an ass loaded with dung, wears his hair *en queue*, though, perhaps, he has neither shirt nor breeches. This is the ornament upon which he bestows much time and pains, and in the exhibition of which he finds full gratification for his vanity. Considering the harsh features of the common people in this country, their diminutive stature, their grimaces, and that long appendage, they have no small resemblance to large baboons walking upright; and perhaps this similitude has helped to entail upon them the ridicule of their neighbours.

A French friend tires out your patience with long visits; and, far from taking the most palpable hints to withdraw, when he perceives you uneasy, he observes you are low-spirited, and therefore declares he will keep you company. This perseverance shews that he must either be void of all penetration, or that his disposition must be truly diabolical. Rather than be tormented with such a fiend, a man had better turn him out of doors, even though at the hazard of being run thro' the body.

The French are generally counted insincere, and taxed with want of generosity. But I think these reproaches are not well founded. High-flown professions of friendship and attachment constitute the language of common compliment in this country, and are never supposed to be understood in the literal acceptance of the words; and, if their acts of generosity are but very rare, we ought to ascribe that rarity, not so much to a deficiency of generous sentiments, as to their vanity and ostentation, which engrossing all their funds, utterly disable them from exerting the virtues of beneficence. Vanity, indeed, predominates among all ranks, to such a degree, that they are the greatest *egotists* in the world; and the most insignificant individual talks in company with the same conceit and arrogance, as a person of the greatest importance. Neither conscious poverty nor disgrace will restrain him in the least either from assuming his full share of the conversation, or making his addresses to the finest lady, whom he has the smallest opportunity to approach: nor is he restrained by any other consideration whatsoever. It is all one to him whether he himself has a wife of his own, or the lady a husband; whether she is designed for the cloister, or pre-ingaged to his best friend and benefactor. He takes it for granted that his addresses cannot but be acceptable; and, if he meets with a repulse, he condemns her taste; but never doubts his own qualifications.

I have a great many thing to say of their military character, and their punctilios[15] of honour, which last are equally absurd and pernicious; but as this letter has run to an unconscionable length, I shall defer them till another opportunity. Mean-while, I have the honour to be, with very particular esteem, | Madam, | Your most obedient servant.

---

13. **defluxion . . . eyes:** watering of the eyes. 14. **Count Saxe:** Comte Hermann Maurice de Saxe (1696–1750), French general and marshal; author of his memoirs.

15. **punctilios:** A punctilio is the system of formalities governing affairs of honor.

LETTER XV

Nice, January 3, 1764.

MADAM,

In your favour which I received by Mr. M——l, you remind me of my promise, to communicate the remarks I have still to make on the French nation; and at the same time you signify your opinion, that I am too severe in my former observations. You even hint a suspicion, that this severity is owing to some personal cause of resentment; but, I protest, I have no particular cause of animosity against any individual of that country. I have neither obligation to, nor quarrel with, any subject of France; and when I meet with a French-man worthy of my esteem, I can receive him into my friendship with as much cordiality, as I could feel for any fellow citizen of the same merit. I even respect the nation, for the number of great men it has produced in all arts and sciences. I respect the French officers, in particular, for their gallantry and valour; and especially for that generous humanity which they exercise towards their enemies, even amidst the horrors of war. This liberal spirit is the only circumstance of antient chivalry, which I think was worth preserving. It had formerly flourished in England, but was almost extinguished in a succession of civil wars, which are always productive of cruelty and rancour. It was Henry IV. of France, (a real knight errant) who revived it in Europe. He possessed that greatness of mind, which can forgive injuries of the deepest dye: and as he had also the faculty of distinguishing characters, he found his account,[1] in favouring with his friendship and confidence, some of those who had opposed him in the field with the most inveterate perseverance. I know not whether he did more service to mankind in general, by reviving the practice of treating his prisoners with generosity, than he prejudiced his own country by patronizing the absurd and pernicious custom of duelling, and establishing a *punto*,[2] founded in dia-metrical opposition to common sense and humanity.

I have often heard it observed, that a French officer is generally an agreeable companion when he is turned of fifty. Without all doubt, by that time, the fire of his vivacity, which makes him so troublesome in his youth, will be considerably abated, and in other respects, he must be improved by his experience. But

there is a fundamental error in the first principles of his education, which time rather confirms than re-moves. Early prejudices are for the most part converted into habits of thinking; and accordingly you will find the old officers in the French service more bigotted than their juniors, to the punctilios of false honour.

A lad of a good family no sooner enters into the service, than he thinks it incumbent upon him to shew his courage in a rencontre. His natural vivacity prompts him to hazard in company every thing that comes uppermost, without any respect to his seniors or betters; and ten to one but he says something, which he finds it necessary to maintain with his sword. The old officer, instead of checking his petulance, either by rebuke or silent disapprobation, seems to be pleased with his impertinence, and encourages every sally of his presumption. Should a quarrel ensue, and the parties go out, he makes no efforts to compromise the dispute; but sits with a pleasing expectation to learn the issue of the rencontre. If the young man is wounded, he kisses him with transport, extols his bravery, puts him into the hands of the surgeon, and visits him with great tenderness every day, until he is cured. If he is killed on the spot, he shrugs up his shoulders—says, *quelle dommage! c'étoit un aimable enfant! ah, patience!*[3] and in three hours the defunct is forgotten. You know, in France, duels are forbid, on pain of death: but this law is easily evaded. The person insulted walks out; the antagonist understands the hint, and follows him into the street, where they justle as if by accident, draw their swords, and one of them is either killed or disabled, before any effectual means can be used to part them. Whatever may be the issue of the combat, the magistrate takes no cognizance of it; at least, it is interpreted into an accidental rencounter, and no penalty is incurred on either side. Thus the purpose of the law is entirely defeated, by a most ridiculous and cruel connivance. The meerest trifles in conversation, a rash word, a distant hint, even a look or smile of contempt, is sufficient to produce one of these combats; but injuries of a deeper dye, such as terms of reproach, the lie direct, a blow, or even the menace of a blow, must be discussed with more formality. In any of these cases, the parties agree to meet in the dominions of another prince, where they can murder each other, without fear of punish-ment. An officer who is struck, or even threatened with a blow, must not be quiet, until he either kills his

---

Letter XV. **1. found his account:** prospered. **2. punto:** punctilio.

3. quelle . . . patience: What a pity! He was a fine boy! But it can't be helped!

antagonist, or loses his own life. A friend of mine, (a Nissard[4]) who was in the service of France, told me, that some years ago, one of their captains, in the heat of passion, struck his lieutenant. They fought immediately: the lieutenant was wounded and disarmed. As it was an affront that could not be made up, he no sooner recovered of his wounds, than he called out the captain a second time. In a word, they fought five times before the combat proved decisive; at last, the lieutenant was left dead on the spot. This was an event which sufficiently proved the absurdity of the punctilio that gave rise to it. The poor gentleman who was insulted, and outraged by the brutality of the aggressor, found himself under the necessity of giving him a further occasion to take away his life. Another adventure of the same kind happened a few years ago in this place. A French officer having threatened to strike another, a formal challenge ensued; and it being agreed that they should fight until one of them dropped, each provided himself with a couple of pioneers to dig his grave on the spot. They engaged just without one of the gates of Nice, in presence of a great number of spectators, and fought with surprising fury, until the ground was drenched with their blood. At length one of them stumbled, and fell; upon which the other, who found himself mortally wounded, advancing, and dropping his point, said, "*Je te donne ce que tu m'as oté.*" "I give thee that which thou hast taken from me." So saying, he dropped dead upon the field. The other, who had been the person insulted, was so dangerously wounded, that he could not rise. Some of the spectators carried him forthwith to the beach, and putting him into a boat, conveyed him by sea to Antibes. The body of his antagonist was denied Christian burial, as he died without absolution, and every body allowed that his soul went to hell: but the gentlemen of the army declared, that he died like a man of honour. Should a man be never so well inclined to make atonement in a peaceable manner, for an insult given in the heat of passion, or in the fury of intoxication, it cannot be received. Even an involuntary trespass from ignorance, or absence of mind, must be cleansed with blood. A certain noble lord, of our country, when he was yet a commoner, on his travels, involved himself in a dilemma of this sort, at the court of Lorrain. He had been riding out, and strolling along a public walk, in a brown study, with his horse-whip in his hand, perceived a caterpillar crawling on the back of a marquis, who chanced to be before him. He never thought of the *petit maître;* but lifting up his whip, in order to kill the insect, laid it across his shoulders with a crack, that alarmed all the company in the walk. The marquis's sword was produced in a moment, and the agressor in great hazard of his life, as he had no weapon of defence. He was no sooner waked from his reverie, than he begged pardon, and offered to make all proper concessions for what he had done through mere inadvertency. The marquis would have admitted his excuses, had there been any precedent of such an affront washed away without blood. A conclave of honour was immediately assembled; and after long disputes, they agreed, that an involuntary offence, especially from *such a kind of man, d'un tel homme,* might be attoned by concessions. That you may have some idea of the small beginning, from which many gigantic quarrels arise, I shall recount one that lately happened at Lyons, as I had it from the mouth of a person who was an ear and eye-witness of the transaction. Two Frenchmen, at a public ordinary,[5] stunned the rest of the company with their loquacity. At length one of them, with a supercilious air, asked the other's name. "I never tell my name, (said he) but in a whisper." "You may have very good reasons for keeping it secret," replied the first. "I will tell you," (resumed the other): with these words he rose; and going round to him, pronounced, loud enough to be heard by the whole company, "*Je m'appelle Pierre Paysan; et vous êtes un impertinent.*"[6] So saying, he walked out: the interrogator followed him into the street, where they justled, drew their swords, and engaged. He who asked the question was run through the body; but his relations were so powerful, that the victor was obliged to fly his country. He was tried and condemned in his absence; his goods were confiscated; his wife broke her heart; his children were reduced to beggary; and he himself is now starving in exile. In England, we have not yet adopted all the implacability of the punctilio. A gentleman may be insulted even with a blow, and survive, after having once hazarded his life against the aggressor. The laws of honour in our country do not oblige him either to slay the person from whom he received the injury, or even to fight to the last drop of his own blood. One finds no examples of duels among the Romans, who were certainly as brave and

4. **Nissard:** resident of the city of Nice.

5. **ordinary:** restaurant. 6. **Je . . . impertinent:** My name is Peter Peasant, and you are an impertinent fellow.

as delicate in their notions of honour, as the French. Cornelius Nepos[7] tells us, that a famous Athenian general, having a dispute with his colleague, who was of Sparta, a man of a fiery disposition, this last lifted up his cane to strike him. Had this happened to a French *petit maître*, death must have ensued: but mark what followed.—The Athenian, far from resenting the outrage, in what is now called a gentleman-like manner, said, "Do, strike if you please; but hear me." He never dreamed of cutting the Lacedemonian's throat; but bore with his passionate temper, as the infirmity of a friend who had a thousand good qualities to overbalance that defect.

I need not expatiate upon the folly and the mischief which are countenanced and promoted by the modern practice of duelling. I need not give examples of friends who have murdered each other, in obedience to this savage custom, even while their hearts were melting with mutual tenderness; nor will I particularize the instances which I myself know, of whole families ruined, of women and children made widows and orphans, of parents deprived of only sons, and of valuable lives lost to the community, by duels, which had been produced by one unguarded expression, uttered without intention of offence, in the heat of dispute and altercation. I shall not insist upon the hardship of a worthy man's being obliged to devote himself to death, because it is his misfortune to be insulted by a brute, a bully, a drunkard, or a madman: neither will I enlarge upon this side of the absurdity, which indeed amounts to a contradiction in terms; I mean the dilemma to which a gentleman in the army is reduced, when he receives an affront: if he does not challenge and fight his antagonist, he is broke with infamy by a court-martial; if he fights and kills him, he is tried by the civil power, convicted of murder, and, if the royal mercy does not interpose, he is infallibly hanged: all this, exclusive of the risque of his own life in the duel, and his conscience being burthened with the blood of a man, whom perhaps he has sacrificed to a punctilio, even contrary to his own judgment. These are reflections which I know your own good sense will suggest, but I will make bold to propose a remedy for this gigantic evil, which seems to gain ground every day: let a court be instituted for taking cognizance of all breaches of honour, with power to punish by fine, pillory, sentence of infamy,

outlawry, and exile, by virtue of an act of parliament made for this purpose; and all persons insulted, shall have recourse to this tribunal: let every man who seeks personal reparation with sword, pistol, or other instrument of death, be declared infamous, and banished the kingdom: let every man, convicted of having used a sword or pistol, or other mortal weapon, against another, either in duel or rencountre, occasioned by any previous quarrel, be subject to the same penalties: if any man is killed in a duel, let his body be hanged upon a public gibbet, for a certain time, and then given to the surgeons: let his antagonist be hanged as a murderer, and dissected also; and some mark of infamy be set on the memory of both. I apprehend such regulations would put an effectual stop to the practice of duelling, which nothing but the fear of infamy can support; for I am persuaded, that no being, capable of reflection, would prosecute the trade of assassination at the risque of his own life, if this hazard was at the same time reinforced by the certain prospect of infamy and ruin. Every person of sentiment would in that case allow, that an officer, who in a duel robs a deserving woman of her husband, a number of children of their father, a family of its support, and the community of a fellow citizen, has as little merit to plead from exposing his own person, as a highwayman, or housebreaker, who every day risques his life to rob or plunder that which is not of half the importance to society. I think it was from the Buccaneers of America, that the English have learned to abolish one solecism in the practice of duelling: those adventurers decided their personal quarrels with pistols; and this improvement has been adopted in Great Britain with good success; though in France, and other parts of the continent, it is looked upon as a proof of their barbarity. It is, however, the only circumstance of duelling, which savours of common sense, as it puts all mankind upon a level, the old with the young, the weak with the strong, the unwieldy with the nimble, and the man who knows not how to hold a sword with the *spadassin*,[8] who has practised fencing from the cradle. What glory is there in a man's vanquishing an adversary over whom he has a manifest advantage? To abide the issue of a combat in this case, does not even require that moderate share of resolution which nature has indulged to her common children. Accordingly, we have seen many instances of a coward's provoking a man of honour to

---

7. Cornelius Nepos: Roman historian and biographer of the first century B.C.

8. spadassin: bully.

battle. In the reign of our second Charles, when duels flourished in all their absurdity, and the seconds fought while their principals were engaged, Villiers, Duke of Buckingham, not content with having debauched the countess of Shrewsbury, and publishing her shame, took all opportunities of provoking the earl to single combat, hoping he should have an easy conquest, his lordship being a puny little creature, quiet, inoffensive, and every way unfit for such personal contests. He ridiculed him on all occasions; and at last declared in public company, that there was no glory in cuckolding Shrewsbury, who had not spirit to resent the injury. This was an insult which could not be overlooked. The earl sent him a challenge; and they agreed to fight, at Barns-Elms, in presence of two gentlemen, whom they chose for their seconds. All the four engaged at the same time: the first thrust was fatal to the earl of Shrewsbury; and his friend killed the duke's second at the same instant. Buckingham, elated with his exploit, set out immediately for the earl's seat at Cliefden, where he lay with his wife, after having boasted of the murder of her husband, whose blood he shewed her upon his sword, as a trophy of his prowess. But this very duke of Buckingham was little better than a poltroon at bottom. When the gallant earl of Ossory challenged him to fight in Chelsea fields, he crossed the water to Battersea, where he pretended to wait for his lordship; and then complained to the house of lords, that Ossory had given him the rendezvous, and did not keep his appointment. He knew the house would interpose in the quarrel, and he was not disappointed. Their lordships obliged them both to give their word of honour, that their quarrel should have no other consequences.

I ought to make an apology for having troubled a lady with so many observations on a subject so unsuitable to the softness of the fair sex; but I know you cannot be indifferent to any thing that so nearly affects the interests of humanity, which I can safely aver have alone suggested every thing which has been said, by | Madam, | Your very humble servant.

LETTER XXXVI

Nice, March 23, 1765.

DEAR SIR,

You ask whether I think the French people are more taxed than the English; but I apprehend, the question would be more apropos if you asked whether the French taxes are more insupportable than the English; for, in comparing burthens, we ought always to consider the strength of the shoulders that bear them. I know no better way of estimating the strength, than by examining the face of the country, and observing the appearance of the common people, who constitute the bulk of every nation. When I, therefore, see the country of England smiling with cultivation; the grounds exhibiting all the perfection of agriculture, parcelled out into beautiful inclosures, cornfields, hay and pasture, woodland and common; when I see her meadows well stocked with black cattle; her downs covered with sheep; when I view her teams of horses and oxen, large and strong, fat and sleek; when I see her farm-houses the habitations of plenty, cleanliness, and convenience; and her peasants well fed, well lodged, well cloathed, tall and stout, and hale and jolly; I cannot help concluding that the people are well able to bear those impositions which the public necessities have rendered necessary. On the other hand, when I perceive such signs of poverty, misery, and dirt, among the commonalty of France, their unfenced fields dug up in despair, without the intervention of meadow or fallow ground, without cattle to furnish manure, without horses to execute the plans of agriculture; their farm-houses mean, their furniture wretched, their apparel beggarly; themselves and their beasts the images of famine; I cannot help thinking they groan under oppression, either from their landlords, or their government; probably from both.

The principal impositions of the French government are these: first, the taille, payed by all the commons, except those that are privileged: secondly, the capitation, from which no persons, (not even the nobles) are excepted: thirdly, the tenths and twentieths, called Dixiêmes and Vingtiêmes, which every body pays. This tax was originally levied as an occasional aid in times of war, and other emergencies; but by degrees is become a standing revenue even in time of peace. All the money arising from these impositions goes directly to the king's treasury; and must undoubtedly amount to a very great sum. Besides these, he has the revenue of the farms,[1] consisting of the droits d'aydes, or excise on wine, brandy, &c; of the custom-house duties; of the gabelle, comprehending that most

---

Letter XXXVI. **1. revenue . . . farms:** taxes collected by "farmers" (professional tax-contractors), who paid the king in advance for the privilege.

oppressive obligation on individuals to take a certain quantity of salt at the price which the farmers shall please to fix; of the exclusive privilege to sell tobacco; of the droits de controlle, insinuation, centiême denier, franchiefs, aubeine, echange et contre-echange arising from the acts of voluntary jurisdiction, as well as certain law-suits. These farms are said to bring into the king's coffers above one hundred and twenty millions of livres yearly, amounting to near five millions sterling: but the poor people are said to pay about a third more than this sum, which the farmers retain to enrich themselves, and bribe the great for their protection; which protection of the great is the true reason why this most iniquitous, oppressive, and absurd method of levying money is not laid aside. Over and above those articles I have mentioned, the French king draws considerable sums from his clergy, under the denomination of dons gratuits, or free-gifts; as well as from the subsidies given by the pays d'etats, such as Provence, Languedoc, and Bretagne, which are exempted from the taille. The whole revenue of the French king amounts to between twelve and thirteen millions sterling. These are great resources for the king: but they will always keep the people miserable, and effectually prevent them from making such improvements as might turn their lands to the best advantage. But besides being eased in the article of taxes, there is something else required to make them exert themselves for the benefit of their country. They must be free in their persons, secure in their property, indulged with reasonable leases, and effectually protected by law from the insolence and oppression of their superiors.

Great as the French king's resources may appear, they are hardly sufficient to defray the enormous expence of his government. About two millions sterling per annum of his revenue are said to be anticipated for paying the interest of the public debts; and the rest is found inadequate to the charge of a prodigious standing army, a double frontier of fortified towns, and the extravagant appointments of ambassadors, generals, governors, intendants, commandants, and other officers of the crown, all of whom affect a pomp, which is equally ridiculous and prodigal. A French general in the field is always attended by thirty or forty cooks; and thinks it is incumbent upon him, for the glory of France, to give a hundred dishes every day at his table. When don Philip, and the marechal duke de Belleisle, had their quarters at Nice, there were fifty scullions constantly employed in the great square

in plucking poultry. This absurd luxury infects their whole army. Even the commissaries keep open table; and nothing is seen but prodigality and profusion. The king of Sardinia proceeds upon another plan. His troops are better cloathed, better payed, and better fed than those of France. The commandant of Nice[2] has about four hundred a year of appointments, which enable him to live decently, and even to entertain strangers. On the other hand, the commandant of Antibes, which is in all respects more inconsiderable than Nice, has from the French king above five times the sum to support the glory of his monarch, which all the sensible part of mankind treat with ridicule and contempt. But the finances of France are so ill managed, that many of their commandants, and other officers, have not been able to draw their appointments these two years. In vain they complain and remonstrate. When they grow troublesome they are removed. How then must they support the glory of France? how, but by oppressing the poor people. The treasurer makes use of their money for his own benefit. The king knows it; he knows his officers thus defrauded, fleece and oppress his people: but he thinks proper to wink at these abuses. That government may be said to be weak and tottering which finds itself obliged to connive at such proceedings. The king of France, in order to give strength and stability to his administration, ought to have sense to adopt a sage plan of oeconomy, and vigour of mind sufficient to execute it in all its parts, with the most rigorous exactness. He ought to have courage enough to find fault, and even to punish the delinquents, of what quality soever they may be: and the first act of reformation ought to be a total abolition of all the farms. There are, undoubtedly, many marks of relaxation in the reins of the French government, and, in all probability, the subjects of France will be the first to take advantage of it. There is at present a violent fermentation of different principles among them, which under the reign of a very weak prince, or during a long minority, may produce a great change in the constitution. In proportion to the progress of reason and philosophy, which have made great advances in this kingdom, superstition loses ground; antient prejudices give way; a spirit of freedom takes the ascendant. All the learned laity of France detest the hierarchy as a plan of despotism, founded on imposture and usurpation.

2. **Nice:** In Smollett's time the city of Nice was part of the kingdom of Sardinia.

The protestants, who are very numerous in the southern parts, abhor it with all the rancour of religious fanaticism. Many of the commons, enriched by commerce and manufacture, grow impatient of those odious distinctions, which exclude them from the honours and privileges due to their importance in the commonwealth; and all the parliaments, or tribunals of justice in the kingdom, seem bent upon asserting their rights and independence in the face of the king's prerogative, and even at the expence of his power and authority. Should any prince therefore be seduced by evil counsellors, or misled by his own bigotry, to take some arbitrary step, that may be extremely disagreeable to all those communities, without having spirit to exert the violence of his power for the support of his measures, he will become equally detested and despised; and the influence of the commons will insensibly encroach upon the pretensions of the crown. But if in the time of a minority, the power of the government should be divided among different competitors for the regency, the parliaments and people will find it still more easy to acquire and ascertain the liberty at which they aspire, because they will have the balance of power in their hands, and be able to make either scale preponderate. I could say a great deal more upon this subject; and I have some remarks to make relating to the methods which might be taken in case of a fresh rupture with France, for making a vigorous impression on that kingdom. But these I must defer till another occasion, having neither room nor leisure at present to add any thing, but that I am, with great truth, | Dear Sir, | Your very humble Servant.

Part Six

THE AGE
OF
JOHNSON

Samuel Johnson

1709–1784

The later eighteenth century is often called The Age of Johnson, perhaps a sufficient token of Johnson's eminence. His character and conversation have become familiar—indeed, legendary—through Boswell's *Life* (1791). But if Boswell and the many other biographers and anecdotists had remained silent, Johnson's writings—even *The Lives of the Poets* (1779–81) alone—would suffice to guarantee his position as the preeminent literary intelligence of his day.

He was born in the town of Lichfield, in Staffordshire, the son of a serious and respectable bookseller. It was clear from the very beginning that something was physically wrong with the child; as he said later, he was "a poor, diseased infant, almost blind." But despite deafness in one ear, near-blindness in one eye, and the hideous scars of scrofula and smallpox, he developed into a sturdy and precocious child. From infancy he displayed a proud and rebellious temperament: he was independent, passionate, and courageous. He became accustomed early to dominating his fellows. Boswell reports that "in winter . . . he took a pleasure in being drawn upon the ice by a boy barefooted, who pulled him along by a garter fixed round him; no very easy operation, as his size was remarkably large." Although he was lazy, he became an excellent student in the grammar schools at Lichfield and at nearby Stourbridge; he mastered Latin and Greek and learned to write English and Latin poems in a great variety of forms. His approach to his studies was characteristically violent and immoderate. He was either totally idle or passionately engaged. He supplemented his school studies by rummaging the books in his father's stock. He wasted no time on frivolous books; as he recalled to Boswell, he read "not voyages and travels, but all literature, Sir, all ancient writers, all manly." Adam Smith observed, "Johnson knew more books than any man alive."

At the age of eighteen he scraped together enough money for thirteen months at Pembroke College, Oxford. As he later remarked, "I was miserably poor, and I thought to fight my way by my literature and my wit; so I disregarded all power and all authority." While at Oxford a reading of William Law's *Serious Call to a Devout and Holy Life* (1729) profoundly affected him, and the boy who before had been a "lax *talker* against religion" firmly persuaded himself of the truth of Christianity as defined by the Established Church. He remained devout, although he constantly searched for additional rational evidence in support of Christian doctrine. Leaving Oxford when his money ran out, he returned to Lichfield a vigorous, sensual, emotional, and guilt-ridden youth, whose powerful appetites seemed dangerously at war with his desire to restrain them. As Boswell says, "Everything about his character and manners was forcible and violent." He was so melancholic that he sometimes feared he would go mad. He now developed odd compulsive tics and curious gestures and swayings that puzzled onlookers and sometimes amused them. All his life he talked to himself and made strange clucking sounds with his tongue. He was so outlandish and unprepossessing that when, at the age of twenty-six, he married a forty-six-year-old widow, Mrs. Elizabeth Porter, her family was appalled, and her eldest son never spoke to her again.

Johnson was attracted by the idea of a legal career, but he had insufficient money. He tried his hand at schoolteaching instead. But he was not a success. The actor David Garrick, one of his pupils, later entertained parties with his superb mimicry of his old schoolmaster's "tumultuous" gestures and manners. Despairing of making a living at anything but literature, he went to London in 1737, accompanied by Garrick and by three acts of an unfinished tragedy, *Irene*. For London, which was his headquarters ever afterward, he felt unbounded enthusiasm. "When a man is tired of London," he once said, "he is tired of life; for there is in London all that life can afford." He was soon making a meager living writing for Edward Cave, editor of *The Gentleman's Magazine*. One of his early assignments was to write up from reports—illegally—the debates in Parliament. Years later at a dinner party, when a speech of Pitt's was highly praised, Johnson, then an eminent man of letters, burst out, "That speech I wrote in a garret in Exeter-street." In 1738 he published anonymously *London. A Poem*, a redaction in heroic couplets of Juvenal's third satire. Alexander Pope was one of the many who were impressed. In 1744 Johnson brought out *An Account of the Life of Mr. Richard Savage*, an unflinching biography of a poverty-stricken and masochistically impulsive friend. Two years later he embarked on the first of his massive literary projects. He contracted with a group of publishers to write an English dictionary. He hoped to finish, with the aid of six assistants, in three years. But the job proved larger than he had imagined, and the *Dictionary* took almost nine years.

In 1749 Johnson's name appeared on a title page for the first time: his *Vanity of Human Wishes*, based on Juvenal's tenth satire, became his best-known poem. Much of his poetic output is in Latin, which was for him a living language. He generally used Latin for poems about his personal experiences—a recovery from an inflammation of the eyes, for example, or a sentimental visit to Lichfield. English he reserved for more public feelings.

In 1749 he also finally finished his sober blank-verse tragedy *Irene*. Garrick produced it, and although it was not a stunning success, it ran for nine nights. Much later, when someone was reading it aloud at a social gathering, Johnson left the room, explaining afterwards, "I thought it had been better."

"In 1750," Boswell writes, "he came forth in the character for which he was eminently qualified, a majestick teacher of moral and religious wisdom." For the next two years he produced twice a week his dignified essay-periodical *The Rambler*, which then as later found its most appreciative audience among the mature and the discriminating. His wife, Tetty, told him, "I thought very well of you before; but I did not imagine you could have written any thing equal to this." Another group of periodical essays, in *The Adventurer*, appeared in 1753 and 1754. His immense *Dictionary*, which was finally published in two folio volumes in 1755, established his reputation as the foremost authority on the English language. Although the etymologies in the *Dictionary* are frequently faulty, the definitions—including such facetiae as "Lexicographer: a writer of dictionaries, a harmless drudge"—are brilliant. Johnson's was the first English dictionary to use illustrative quotations, and his heavy reliance on prose writers of the English Renaissance suggests one important source of his ideas and attitudes. As Boswell says of the *Dictionary*. "The world contemplated with wonder so stupendous a work atchieved by one man, while other countries had thought such undertakings fit only for whole academies." In 1758 he began another series of periodical essays, this time the more sprightly *Idler*, which he wrote once a week for the next two years. And in 1759 appeared his *History of Rasselas, Prince of Abissinia*, an astringent moral fable thinly disguised as an oriental tale.

The year 1762 marks a turning point in his life. In this year George III granted him a lifetime annual pension of three hundred pounds as a reward for his services to English literature; henceforth he enjoyed a respite from the severe poverty that had nagged him all his life. The next year he met in a London bookshop a twenty-two-year-old Scottish boy of touching naiveté; soon James Boswell was recording Johnson's incomparable conversation and laying it up for posterity. Early in 1764 Johnson and Joshua Reynolds founded the famous Club (later called the Literary Club), which met for conversation every week. Among the original members were Burke, Goldsmith, and Sir John Hawkins; they were later joined by such luminaries as Garrick, Thomas Warton, Adam Smith, Thomas Percy, Sheridan, Gibbon, Charles Burney, and Charles James Fox—even Boswell was finally admitted. After the appearance in 1765 of his eight-volume edition of Shakespeare, with Preface, Notes, and Commentary, Johnson was made Doctor of Laws by Trinity College, Dublin.

Tetty had died in 1752, and Johnson, who always hated to be alone with no one to talk to, was delighted to meet Mr. and Mrs. Henry Thrale in 1765. Thrale was a well-to-do Southwark brewer with a comfortable suburban house at nearby Streatham. The Thrales, and especially Mrs. Hester Thrale, provided Johnson with the domestic comforts—including copious dinners—that he had not fully enjoyed since his wife's death. At Streatham he permitted himself to express his love of children, his gaiety, and his gargantuan delight in nonsense and absurdity. As Mrs. Thrale reported in her *Anecdotes of the Late Samuel Johnson, LL.D.* (1786), "No man loved laughing better, and his vein of humour was rich, and apparently inexhaustible." Persuaded by Boswell in 1773 to undertake a tour of Scotland—a place Johnson affected to despise—he perambulated the primitive Hebrides and returned to publish a travel book, *A Journey to the Western Islands of Scotland* (1775). The same year he was made Doctor of Laws again, this time by Oxford.

His last large literary project was his ten volumes of *Prefaces, Biographical and Critical, to the Works of the English Poets* (1779–81). To Boswell, the appearance of this immense labor of criticism in Johnson's seventieth year was "a luminous proof that the vigour of his mind in all its faculties, whether memory, judgement, or imagination, was not in the least abated." But it was not to be expected that even "that great Cham of Literature," as Tobias Smollett called him, could go on much longer. Because of his lifelong terror of extinction, the story of his last days, when he was suffering from acute dropsy, makes unhappy reading. He hoped that his constant prayers for mercy would be heard, but he was not wholly convinced that he was not going to be "sent to Hell . . . and punished everlastingly." After the end his friend William Hamilton declared, "Johnson is dead. Let us go to the next best: there is nobody; no man can be said to put you in mind of Johnson." He was buried in Westminster Abbey near Chaucer and Spenser.

Although he developed gradually into a greatly admired—and feared—general literary oracle and became finally a sort of national institution, his actual profession was that of a remarkably versatile writer for the booksellers. During his long career he exercised himself, often anonymously, in more literary kinds than perhaps any other writer of his time. He worked in tragedy, biography, the periodical essay, the oriental tale, the travel book, the political article, the critical essay, and the book review; in the oration, the sermon, the letter, the prayer, the dedication, the legal brief, and the royal petition; in the poetic satire, the Horatian ode, the elegy, the theatrical prologue and epilogue, the song, the Anacreontic lyric, the epitaph, and the epigram. The only consequential contemporary genres to which he never turned his hand were the realistic novel, stage comedy, and the Pindaric ode: he had no bent for the first two, and he distrusted the third.

He never presented a pretty spectacle. His dress was coarse, disordered, and dirty; and at table, as Boswell reports, "his appetite . . . was so fierce, and indulged with such intenseness, that . . . the veins of his forehead swelled, and generally a strong perspiration was visible." Much has been made, too, of his prejudices, his super-stition, his dogmatism, and his violence and occasional brutality in conversation. He was not admired by people like Horace Walpole, who wrote, "With a lumber of learning and some strong parts, Johnson was an odious and mean character . . . . His manners were sordid, supercilious and brutal; his style ridiculously bombastic and vicious; and, in one word, with all the pedantry he had all the gigantic littleness of a country schoolmaster." But Boswell should be permitted the last word:

> Exulting in his intellectual strength and dexterity, he could, when he pleased, be the greatest sophist that ever contended in the lists of declamation; and, from a spirit of contradiction and a delight in shewing his powers, he would often maintain the wrong side with equal warmth and ingenuity; so that, when there was an audience, his real opinions could seldom be gathered from his talk; though when he was in company with a single friend, he would discuss a subject with genuine fairness: but he was too conscientious to make errour permanent and pernicious, by deliberately writing it; and, in all his numerous works, he earnestly inculcated what appeared to him to be the truth; his piety being con-stant, and the ruling principle of all his conduct.

"Such was Samuel Johnson," Boswell concludes the *Life*, "a man whose talents, acquirements, and virtues, were so extraordinary, that the more his character is considered, the more he will be regarded by the present age, and by posterity, with admiration and reverence."

The standard bibliographies are W. P. Courtney and D. N. Smith's *A Bibliography of Samuel Johnson* (rev. ed., 1925) and R. W. Chapman and A. T. Hazen's

"Johnsonian Bibliography: A Supplement to Courtney," in *Proceedings of the Oxford Bibliographical Society*, V (1938), 119–66. J. L. Clifford's *Johnsonian Studies, 1887–1950: A Survey and Bibliography* (1951) carefully lists modern studies and includes a valuable brief essay on the course of Johnsonian scholarship. The listing is continued in J. L. Clifford and D. J. Greene's *Johnsonian Studies, 1950–1960* (1962). Boswell's *Life of Johnson* is edited by G. B. Hill and revised by L. F. Powell (6 vols., 1934–1950); a convenient one-volume edition with a good index is that by R. W. Chapman (1953). Chapman has also edited the *Letters* (3 vols., 1952). Joseph Wood Krutch's *Samuel Johnson* (1944) is a full critical biography. J. L. Clifford has illuminated the pre-Boswellian years in *Young Sam Johnson* (1955). Until the Yale edition of Johnson's *Works*, ed. A. T. Hazen and others (1958–   ), is complete, the student must rely on the nine-volume Oxford edition (1825). The *Poems* are edited by D. N. Smith and E. L. McAdam, Jr. (1941). *The Lives of the Poets* is best read in the edition by G. B. Hill (3 vols., 1905). Useful volumes of selections from Johnson's writings are edited by Mona Wilson (1950), C. H. Conley (1940), and B. H. Bronson (rev. ed., 1958). J. H. Hagstrum's *Samuel Johnson's Literary Criticism* (1952) is a good discussion, and J. E. Brown's *The Critical Opinions of Samuel Johnson* (1926) is a valuable indexed collection. Bronson's "Johnson Agonistes," in *Johnson Agonistes and Other Essays* (1946), and W. J. Bate's *The Achievement of Samuel Johnson* (1955) interpret Johnson's character.

AN EPITAPH ON CLAUDY PHILLIPS, A MUSICIAN

Charles Claudius Philips, who died in 1732, was an itinerant fiddler, well known in Wales for his musical wanderings. Boswell reports that once, when Garrick and Johnson were conversing,

Garrick repeated an Epitaph upon this Philips by a Dr. [Richard] Wilkes, in these words:

Exalted soul! whose harmony could please
The love-sick virgin, and the gouty ease;
Could jarring discord, like Amphion, move
To beauteous order and harmonious love;
Rest here in peace, till angels bid thee rise,
And meet thy blessed Saviour in the skies.

Johnson shook his head at these common-place funereal lines, and said to Garrick, "I think, Davy, I can make a better." Then, stirring about his tea for a little while, in a state of meditation, he almost extempore produced the following verses.

The text is that of the first printing, in *The Gentleman's Magazine* (September, 1740); we have incorporated the substantive variants from the version in Anna Williams's *Miscellanies in Prose and Verse* (1766).

Philips, whose touch harmonious could remove
The pangs of guilty pow'r, and hapless love,
Rest here, distress'd by poverty no more,
Find here that calm, thou gav'st so oft before.
Sleep, undisturb'd, within this peaceful shrine,
Till angels wake thee, with a note like thine.

PROLOGUE SPOKEN BY MR. GARRICK, AT THE OPENING OF THE THEATRE IN DRURY-LANE 1747

Boswell writes of Johnson in 1747, "This year his old pupil and friend, David Garrick, having become joint patentee and manager of Drury-lane theatre, Johnson honoured his opening of it with a Prologue, which for just and manly dramatick criticism, on the whole range of the English stage, is unrivalled." Johnson once said that he composed the whole poem in his head before writing any of it down.

The text is that of the first edition (1747).

❦

WHEN Learning's Triumph o'er her barb'rous Foes
First rear'd the Stage, immortal SHAKESPEAR rose;
Each Change of many-colour'd Life he drew,
Exhausted Worlds, and then imagin'd new:
Existence saw him spurn her bounded Reign,
And panting Time toil'd after him in vain:
His pow'rful Strokes presiding Truth impress'd,
And unresisted Passion storm'd the Breast.
    Then JOHNSON° came, instructed from the School,
To please in Method, and invent by Rule;   10
His studious Patience, and laborious Art,
By regular Approach essay'd the Heart;
Cold Approbation gave the ling'ring Bays,°
For those who durst not censure, scarce cou'd praise.
A Mortal born he met the general Doom,
But left, like *Egypt*'s Kings, a lasting Tomb.
    The Wits of *Charles*° found easier Ways to Fame,
Nor wish'd for JOHNSON's Art, or SHAKESPEAR's
    Flame;
Themselves they studied, as they felt, they writ,
Intrigue was Plot, Obscenity was Wit.   20
Vice always found a sympathetick Friend;
They pleas'd their Age, and did not aim to mend.
Yet Bards like these aspir'd to lasting Praise,
And proudly hop'd to pimp in future Days.
Their Cause was gen'ral, their Supports were strong,
Their Slaves were willing, and their Reign was long;
Till Shame regain'd the Post that Sense betray'd,
And Virtue call'd Oblivion to her Aid.
    Then crush'd by Rules, and weaken'd as refin'd,
For Years the Pow'r of Tragedy declin'd;°   30

From Bard, to Bard, the frigid Caution crept,
Till Declamation roar'd, while Passion slept.
Yet still did Virtue deign the Stage to tread,
Philosophy remain'd, though Nature fled.
But forc'd at length her antient Reign to quit,
She saw great *Faustus* lay the Ghost of Wit:°
Exulting Folly hail'd the joyful Day,
And Pantomime, and Song, confirm'd her Sway.
    But who the coming Changes can presage,
And mark the future Periods of the Stage?—   40
Perhaps if Skill could distant Times explore,
New *Behns*, new *Durfeys*,° yet remain in Store.
Perhaps, where *Lear* has rav'd, and *Hamlet* dy'd,
On flying Cars° new Sorcerers may ride.
Perhaps, for who can guess th' Effects of Chance?
Here *Hunt* may box, or *Mahomet*° may dance.
    Hard is his lot, that here by Fortune plac'd,
Must watch the wild Vicissitudes of Taste;
With ev'ry Meteor of Caprice must play,
And chase the new-blown Bubbles of the Day.   50
Ah! let not Censure term our Fate our Choice,
The Stage but echoes back the publick Voice.
The Drama's Laws the Drama's Patrons give,
For we that live to please, must please to live.
    Then prompt no more the Follies you decry,
As Tyrants doom their Tools of Guilt to die;
'Tis yours this Night to bid the Reign commence
Of rescu'd Nature, and reviving Sense;
To chase the Charms of Sound, the Pomp of Show,
For useful Mirth, and salutary Woe;   60
Bid scenic Virtue form the rising Age,
And Truth diffuse her Radiance from the Stage.

PROLOGUE SPOKEN BY MR. GARRICK. **9. Johnson:** Ben Jonson (1572–1637), author of *Volpone* (1606), *Epicene* (1609), *The Alchemist* (1610), and other satirical comedies. **13. Bays:** laurels, praises. **17. The Wits . . . Charles:** William Wycherley (1640–1716), Sir George Etherege (*c.* 1634–*c.* 1691), and others. **30. the Pow'r . . . declin'd:** with such playwrights as Dryden (1631–1700), Nathaniel Lee (*c.* 1653–92), Thomas Otway (1652–85), Nicholas Rowe (1674–1718), and Joseph Addison (1672–1719).

36. great . . . Wit: A popular subject of farces and panto- mimes in the early eighteenth century was the story of Dr. Johannes Faustus, the legendary German Renaissance sorcerer. **42. Behns, Durfeys:** Mrs. Aphra Behn (1640–89) was a playwright with a reputation for indecency; Thomas D'Urfey (1653–1723) was the author of numerous farces and melo- dramas disdained by the sophisticated. (See the selection from D'Urfey in Part Three.) **44. Cars:** chariots. **46. Hunt, Mahomet:** Edward Hunt was a popular pugilist; Mahomet was a "Turkish" rope dancer.

THE VANITY
OF HUMAN WISHES

THE TENTH SATIRE OF JUVENAL IMITATED

Decimus Junius Juvenalis (*c.* A.D. 60–*c.* 130) is the author of sixteen famous satires on the vices and follies of Rome in the time of Emperor Domitian. The tenth satire became especially well known: it was widely used during the Middle Ages by preachers in search of sermon materials, and it was popular during the Renaissance with moralists and humanists. Dryden translated five of the satires, including the tenth. Johnson, who once said that he had all Juvenal's satires in his head, wrote in the *Life of Dryden* (1779), "The peculiarity of Juvenal is a mixture of gaiety and stateliness, of pointed sentences, and declamatory grandeur." But Johnson's poem is something more than a translation. In the *Dictionary* he defines the literary imitation as "a method of translating looser than paraphrase, in which modern examples and illustrations are used for ancient, or domestick for foreign." Thus he replaces Juvenal's Sejanus with Cardinal Wolsey, and Hannibal with Charles XII of Sweden.

As usual, he wrote impulsively and rapidly. Boswell says, "The fervid rapidity with which [*The Vanity of Human Wishes*] was produced, is scarcely credible. I have heard him say, that he composed seventy lines of it in one day, without putting one of them upon paper till they were finished." The poem was published in January, 1749, and although some like David Garrick found it "as hard as Greek" and feared that Johnson's next poem would be "as hard as Hebrew," it was greatly admired. Mrs. Thrale reports that much later, when Johnson was reading it over in company at her house, "he burst into a passion of tears."

The text is that of the first edition (1749); we have incorporated Johnson's manuscript corrections of the first edition together with the substantive variants from Dodsley's *Collection of Poems* (1755).

LET Observation with extensive View,
Survey Mankind, from *China* to *Peru;*
Remark each anxious Toil, each eager Strife,
And watch the busy Scenes of crouded Life;
Then say how Hope and Fear, Desire and Hate,
O'erspread with Snares the clouded Maze of Fate,

Where wav'ring Man, betray'd by vent'rous Pride,
To tread the dreary Paths without a Guide;
As treach'rous Phantoms in the Mist delude,
Shuns fancied Ills, or chases airy Good.   10
How rarely Reason guides the stubborn Choice,
Rules the bold Hand, or prompts the suppliant Voice,
How Nations sink, by darling Schemes oppress'd,
When Vengeance listens to the Fool's Request.
Fate wings° with ev'ry Wish th' afflictive Dart,
Each Gift of Nature, and each Grace of Art,
With fatal Heat impetuous Courage glows,
With fatal Sweetness Elocution flows,
Impeachment stops the Speaker's pow'rful Breath,
And restless Fire precipitates on° Death.   20

But scarce observ'd the Knowing and the Bold,
Fall in the gen'ral Massacre of Gold;
Wide-wasting Pest! that rages unconfin'd,
And crouds with Crimes the Records of Mankind,
For Gold his Sword the Hireling Ruffian draws,
For Gold the hireling Judge distorts the Laws;
Wealth heap'd on Wealth, nor Truth nor Safety buys,
The Dangers gather as the Treasures rise.

Let Hist'ry tell where rival Kings command,
And dubious Title shakes the madded Land,   30
When Statutes glean the Refuse of the Sword,
How much more safe the Vassal than the Lord,
Low sculks the Hind° beneath the Rage of Pow'r,
And leaves the wealthy Traytor° in the *Tow'r,*
Untouch'd his Cottage, and his Slumbers sound,
Tho' Confiscation's Vulturs hover round.

The needy Traveller, serene and gay,
Walks the wild Heath, and sings his Toil away.
Does Envy seize thee? crush th' upbraiding Joy,
Encrease his Riches and his Peace destroy,°   40
Now Fears in dire Vicissitude invade,
The rustling Brake° alarms, and quiv'ring Shade,
Nor Light nor Darkness bring his Pain Relief,
One shews the Plunder, and one hides the Thief.

THE VANITY OF HUMAN WISHES. **15. wings:** throws. **20. precipitates on:** hastens. **33. Hind:** peasant. **34. wealthy Traytor:** The first edition reads: "*bonny Traytor.*" The phrase alludes to the Scottish lords executed in 1746 for their part in the Jacobite Rising of 1745. **40. Encrease . . . destroy:** If you envy his happy lot, you can spoil his joy very easily: just give him money. **42. Brake:** thicket.

Yet still one gen'ral Cry the Skies assails
And Gain and Grandeur° load the tainted Gales;
Few know the toiling Statesman's Fear or Care,
Th' insidious Rival and the gaping Heir.

Once more, *Democritus*,° arise on Earth,
With chearful Wisdom and instructive Mirth,   50
See motley Life in modern Trappings dress'd,
And feed with varied Fools th' eternal Jest:
Thou who couldst laugh where Want enchain'd
    Caprice,
Toil crush'd Conceit, and Man was of a Piece;
Where Wealth unlov'd without a Mourner dy'd;
And scarce a Sycophant was fed by Pride;
Where ne'er was known the Form of mock Debate,
Or seen a new-made Mayor's unwieldy State;
Where change of Fav'rites made no Change of Laws,
And Senates heard before they judg'd a Cause;   60
How wouldst thou shake at *Britain*'s modish Tribe,
Dart the quick Taunt, and edge the piercing Gibe?
Attentive Truth and Nature to descry,
And pierce each Scene with Philosophic Eye.
To thee were solemn Toys or empty Shew,
The Robes of Pleasure and the Veils of Woe:
All aid the Farce, and all thy Mirth maintain,
Whose Joys are causeless, or whose Griefs are vain.

Such was the Scorn that fill'd the Sage's Mind,
Renew'd at ev'ry Glance on Humankind;   70
How just that Scorn ere yet thy° Voice declare,
Search every State, and canvass ev'ry Pray'r.

Unnumber'd Suppliants croud Preferment's Gate,
Athirst for Wealth, and burning to be great;
Delusive Fortune hears th' incessant Call,
They mount, they shine, evaporate, and fall.
On ev'ry Stage the Foes of Peace attend,
Hate dogs their Flight, and Insult mocks their End.
Love ends with Hope, the sinking Statesman's Door
Pours in the Morning Worshiper° no more;   80
For growing Names the weekly Scribbler lies,
To growing Wealth the Dedicator flies,
From every Room descends the painted Face,
That hung the bright *Palladium*° of the Place,

And smoak'd in Kitchens, or in Auctions sold,
To better Features yields the Frame of Gold;
For now no more we trace in ev'ry Line
Heroic Worth, Benevolence Divine:
The Form distorted justifies the Fall,
And Detestation rids th' indignant Wall.   90

But will not *Britain* hear the last Appeal,
Sign her Foes Doom, or guard her Fav'rites Zeal;
Through Freedom's Sons no more Remonstrance°
    rings,
Degrading Nobles and controuling Kings;
Our supple Tribes repress their Patriot Throats,
And ask no Questions but the Price of Votes;
With Weekly Libels and Septennial Ale,°
Their Wish is full to riot and to rail.

In full-blown Dignity, see *Wolsey*° stand,
Law in his Voice, and Fortune in his Hand: 100
To him the Church, the Realm, their Pow'rs consign,
Thro' him the Rays of regal Bounty shine,
Turn'd by his Nod the Stream of Honour flows,
His Smile alone Security bestows:
Still to new Heights his restless Wishes tow'r,
Claim leads to Claim, and Pow'r advances Pow'r;
Till Conquest unresisted ceas'd to please,
And Rights submitted, left him none to seize.
At length his Sov'reign° frowns—the Train of State
Mark the keen Glance, and watch the Sign to
    hate.   110
Where-e'er he turns he meets a Stranger's Eye,
His Suppliants scorn him, and his Followers fly;
At once is lost the Pride of aweful State,
The golden Canopy, the glitt'ring Plate,
The regal Palace, the luxurious Board,
The liv'ried Army, and the menial Lord.
With Age, with Cares, with Maladies oppress'd,
He seeks the Refuge of Monastic Rest.
Grief aids Disease, remember'd Folly stings,
And his last Sighs reproach the Faith of Kings.   120

Speak thou, whose Thoughts at humble Peace
    repine,
Shall *Wolsey*'s Wealth, with *Wolsey*'s End be thine?

---

46. Gain and Grandeur: prayers for gain and grandeur. **49. Democritus:** (*c.* 460–*c.* 362 B.C.), Greek philosopher given to laughing at human follies. Juvenal also refers to him. **71. thy:** the reader's. **80. the Morning Worshiper:** Great men's receptions, at which they heard petitioners, were held in the morning. **84. Palladium:** symbol of protection; the word derives from the statue of Pallas Athene in the city of Troy.

93. Remonstrance: Cf. the Grand Remonstrance presented to Charles I in 1641. **97. Septennial Ale:** the ale used for securing votes in the Parliamentary elections every seven years. **99. Wolsey:** Thomas Wolsey (*c.* 1475–1530), Lord Chancellor and cardinal. **109. his Sov'reign:** Henry VIII, who removed Wolsey from office in 1529 and arrested him for high treason in 1530.

Or liv'st thou now, with safer Pride content,
The wisest justice° on the Banks of *Trent*?
For why did *Wolsey* near the steeps of Fate,
On weak Foundations raise th' enormous Weight?
Why but to sink beneath Misfortune's Blow,
With louder Ruin to the Gulphs below?

What gave great *Villiers*° to th' Assassin's Knife,
And fixed Disease on *Harley's*° closing Life?   130
What murder'd *Wentworth*,° and what exil'd *Hyde*,°
By Kings protected and to Kings ally'd?
What but their Wish indulg'd in Courts to shine,
And Pow'r too great to keep or to resign?

When first the College Rolls receive his Name,
The young Enthusiast quits his Ease for Fame;
Through all his veins the Fever of Renown
Burns from the strong Contagion of the Gown;
O'er *Bodley's* Dome his future Labours spread,°
And *Bacon's* Mansion trembles o'er his Head;°   140
Are these thy Views? proceed, illustrious Youth,
And Virtue guard thee to the Throne of Truth,
Yet should thy Soul indulge the gen'rous Heat,
Till captive Science° yields her last Retreat;
Should Reason guide thee with her brightest Ray,
And pour on misty Doubt resistless Day;
Should no false Kindness lure to loose Delight,
Nor Praise relax, nor Difficulty fright;
Should tempting Novelty thy Cell refrain,
And Sloth effuse her opiate Fumes in vain;   150
Should Beauty blunt on Fops her fatal Dart,°
Nor claim the Triumph of a letter'd Heart;

Should no Disease thy torpid Veins invade,
Nor Melancholy's Phantoms haunt thy Shade;
Yet hope not Life from Grief or Danger free,
Nor think the Doom of Man revers'd for thee:
Deign on the passing World to turn thine Eyes,
And pause awhile from letters, to be wise;
There mark what Ills the Scholar's Life assail,
Toil, Envy, Want, the patron,° and the Jail.   160
See Nations slowly wise, and meanly just,
To buried Merit raise the tardy Bust.
If Dreams yet flatter, once again attend,
Hear *Lydiat's*° Life, and *Galileo's*° End.

Nor deem, when Learning her last Prize bestows
The glitt'ring Eminence exempt from Foes;
See when the Vulgar 'scape, despis'd or aw'd,
Rebellion's vengeful Talons seize on *Laud*.°
From meaner Minds, tho' smaller Fines content
The plunder'd Palace or sequester'd Rent;   170
Mark'd out by dangerous Parts° he meets the Shock,
And fatal Learning leads him to the Block:
Around his Tomb let Art and Genius weep,
But hear his Death, ye Blockheads, hear and sleep.

The festal Blazes, the triumphal Show,
The ravish'd Standard, and the captive Foe,
The Senate's Thanks, the Gazette's° pompous Tale,
With Force resistless o'er the Brave prevail.
Such Bribes the rapid *Greek*° o'er *Asia* whirl'd,
For such the steady *Romans* shook the World;   180
For such in distant Lands the *Britons* shine,
And stain with Blood the *Danube* or the *Rhine;*°
This Pow'r has Praise, that Virtue scarce can warm,
Till Fame supplies the universal Charm.
Yet Reason frowns on War's unequal Game,
Where wasted Nations raise a single Name,
And mortgag'd States their Grandsires Wreaths regret,
From Age to Age in everlasting Debt;

---

124. **wisest justice:** The first edition reads: "richest Landlord." **129. great Villiers:** George Villiers (1592–1628), First Duke of Buckingham; a favorite of James I, he was assassinated by one John Felton, who was jealous of his success. **130. Harley:** Robert Harley (1661–1724), First Earl of Oxford; a Tory leader under Queen Anne, he was impeached in 1717. **131. Wentworth:** Sir Thomas Wentworth (1593–1641), First Earl of Strafford; he was an adviser to Charles I and was executed by the Long Parliament. **Hyde:** Edward Hyde (1609–74), First Earl of Clarendon; a former Lord Chancellor, he was impeached and banished in 1668. **139. O'er . . . spread:** In his imagination his as yet unwritten books rise in stacks higher than the Bodleian Library at Oxford. **140. Bacon's . . . Head:** [Johnson's note] *There is a tradition, that the* [Oxford] *study of friar* [Roger] *Bacon, built on an arch over the bridge, will fall, when a man greater than Bacon shall pass under it.* **144. Science:** learning in general. **151. blunt . . . Dart:** and thus make her weapon useless by the time she assaults the scholar.

160. **the patron:** The first edition reads: "the Garret"; for the reason for the change, see Johnson's letter to Chesterfield, below. **164. Lydiat:** Thomas Lydiat (1572–1646) lived in poverty despite his eminence as a mathematician. **Galileo:** (1564–1642), the great astronomer who was forced by the Inquisition to deny the validity of the Copernican theory; he died blind. **168. Laud:** William Laud (1573–1645), Archbishop of Canterbury, impeached and executed by the Long Parliament. **171. Parts:** talents. **177. Gazette:** the official court newspaper. **179. the rapid Greek:** Alexander the Great. **181–82. in . . . Rhine:** The Duke of Marlborough's campaigns in Austria and Bavaria were climaxed in 1704 by the Battle of Blenheim, in Bavaria.

Wreaths which at last the dear-bought Right convey
To rust on Medals, or on Stones decay.   190

On what Foundation stands the Warrior's Pride,
How just his Hopes let *Swedish Charles*° decide;
A Frame of Adamant, a Soul of Fire,
No Dangers fright him, and no Labours tire;
O'er Love, o'er fear, extends his wide Domain,
Unconquer'd Lord of Pleasure and of Pain;
No Joys to him pacific Scepters yield,
War sounds the Trump, he rushes to the Field;
Behold surrounding Kings their Pow'r combine,
And One capitulate, and One resign;   200
Peace courts his Hand, but spreads her Charms in
          vain;
"Think Nothing gain'd, he cries, till nought remain,
On *Moscow*'s Walls till *Gothic* Standards fly,
And all be Mine beneath the Polar Sky."
The March begins in Military State,
And Nations on his Eye suspended wait;
Stern Famine guards the solitary Coast,
And Winter barricades the Realms of Frost;
He comes, not Want and Cold his Course delay;—
Hide, blushing Glory, hide *Pultowa*'s Day: 210
The vanquish'd Hero leaves his broken Bands,
And shews his Miseries in distant Lands;
Condemn'd a needy Supplicant to wait,
While Ladies interpose, and Slaves debate.°
But did not Chance at length her Error mend?
Did no subverted Empire mark his End?
Did rival Monarchs give the fatal Wound?
Or hostile Millions press him to the Ground?
His Fall was destin'd to a barren Strand,
A petty Fortress, and a dubious Hand;°   220
He left the Name, at which the World grew pale,
To point a Moral, or adorn a Tale.

All Times their Scenes of pompous Woes afford,
From *Persia*'s Tyrant to *Bavaria*'s Lord.
In gay Hostility, and barb'rous Pride,
With half Mankind embattled at his Side,
Great *Xerxes*° comes to seize the certain Prey,

192. Swedish Charles: Charles XII (1682–1718), Emperor of
Sweden, conquered Denmark, Saxony, and Poland, only to
be defeated by the Russians at Pultowa in 1709. **214. Ladies
. . . debate:** After his defeat Charles fled to Turkey, where
he remained while his sister in Sweden and the Swedish parliament discussed the possibility of his return. **220. a dubious
Hand:** Charles died of a mysterious bullet wound at Frederiks-
hald, Norway. **227. Xerxes:** (*c.* 519–465 B.C.) "Persia's
tyrant"; he invaded Greece and was defeated at Salamis in
480 B.C.

And starves exhausted Regions in his Way;
Attendant Flatt'ry counts his Myriads o'er,
Till counted Myriads sooth his Pride no more;   230
Fresh Praise is try'd till Madness fires his Mind,
The Waves he lashes, and enchains the Wind;
New Pow'rs are claim'd, new Pow'rs are still
          bestow'd,
Till rude Resistance lops the spreading God;
The daring *Greeks* deride the Martial Shew,
And heap their Vallies with the gaudy Foe;
Th' insulted Sea with humbler Thoughts he gains,
A single Skiff to speed his Flight remains;
Th' incumber'd Oar scarce leaves the dreaded Coast
Through purple Billows and a floating Host.   240

The bold *Bavarian*,° in a luckless Hour,
Tries the dread Summits of *Cesarean* Pow'r,
With unexpected Legions bursts away,
And sees defenceless Realms receive his Sway;
Short Sway! fair *Austria* spreads her mournful
          Charms,
The Queen, the Beauty,° sets the World in Arms;
From Hill to Hill the Beacons rousing Blaze
Spreads wide the Hope of Plunder and of Praise;
The fierce *Croatian*, and the wild *Hussar*,
And all the Sons of Ravage croud the War;   250
The baffled Prince in Honour's flatt'ring Bloom
Of hasty Greatness finds the fatal Doom,
His Foes Derision, and his Subjects Blame,
And steals to Death from Anguish and from Shame.

Enlarge my Life with Multitude of Days,
In Health, in Sickness, thus the Suppliant prays;
Hides from himself his State, and shuns to know,
That Life protracted is protracted Woe.
Time hovers o'er, impatient to destroy,
And shuts up all the Passages of Joy: 260
In vain their Gifts the bounteous Seasons pour,
The Fruit Autumnal, and the Vernal Flow'r,
With listless Eyes the Dotard views the Store,
He views, and wonders that they please no more;
Now pall the tasteless Meats, and joyless Wines,
And Luxury with Sighs her Slave resigns.
Approach, ye Minstrels, try the soothing Strain,
Diffuse the tuneful Lenitives of Pain:

241. The bold Bavarian: Charles Albert (1697–1745),
Elector of Bavaria; he aspired to the leadership of the Holy
Roman Empire. **246. the Queen . . . Beauty:** Maria
Theresa (1717–80), Archduchess of Austria; she defended her
country during the War of the Austrian Succession (1740–48).

No Sounds alas would touch th' impervious Ear,
Though dancing Mountains witness'd *Orpheus*°
    near;   270
Nor Lute nor Lyre his feeble Pow'rs attend,
Nor sweeter Musick of a virtuous Friend,
But everlasting Dictates croud his Tongue,
Perversely grave, or positively wrong.
The still returning Tale, and ling'ring Jest,
Perplex the fawning Niece and pamper'd Guest,
While growing Hopes scarce awe the gath'ring
    Sneer,
And scarce a Legacy can bribe to hear;
The watchful Guests still hint the last Offence,
The Daughter's Petulance, the Son's Expence,   280
Improve his heady Rage with treach'rous Skill,
And mould his Passions till they make his Will.

Unnumber'd Maladies his Joints invade,
Lay Siege to Life and press the dire Blockade;
But unextinguish'd Av'rice still remains,
And dreaded Losses aggravate his Pains;
He turns, with anxious Heart and cripled Hands,
His Bonds of Debt, and Mortgages of Lands;
Or views his Coffers with suspicious Eyes,
Unlocks his Gold, and counts it till he dies.   290

But grant, the Virtues of a temp'rate Prime
Bless with an Age exempt from Scorn or Crime;
An Age that melts with unperceiv'd Decay,
And glides in modest Innocence away;
Whose peaceful Day Benevolence endears,
Whose Night congratulating Conscience cheers;
The gen'ral Fav'rite as the gen'ral Friend:
Such Age there is, and who shall wish its End?

Yet ev'n on this her Load Misfortune flings,
To press the weary Minutes flagging Wings: 300
New Sorrow rises as the Day returns,
A Sister sickens, or a Daughter mourns.
Now Kindred Merit fills the sable° Bier,
Now lacerated Friendship claims a Tear.
Year chases Year, Decay pursues Decay,
Still drops some Joy from with'ring Life away;
New Forms arise, and diff'rent Views engage,
Superfluous lags the Vet'ran on the Stage,
Till pitying Nature signs the last Release,
And bids afflicted Worth retire to Peace.   310

But few there are whom Hours like these await,
Who set unclouded in the Gulphs of Fate.
From *Lydia*'s Monarch° should the Search descend,
By *Solon* caution'd to regard his End,
In Life's last Scene what Prodigies surprise,
Fears of the Brave, and Follies of the Wise?
From *Marlb'rough*'s° Eyes the Streams of Dotage flow,
And *Swift* expires a Driv'ler and a Show.°

The teeming Mother, anxious for her Race,°
Begs for each Birth the Fortune of a Face: 320
Yet *Vane*° could tell what Ills from Beauty spring;
And *Sedley*° curs'd the Form that pleas'd a King.
Ye Nymphs of rosy Lips and radiant Eyes,
Whom Pleasure keeps too busy to be wise,
Whom Joys with soft Varieties invite
By Day the Frolick, and the Dance by Night,
Who frown with Vanity, who smile with Art,
And ask the latest Fashion of the Heart,
What Care, what Rules your heedless Charms shall
    save,
Each Nymph your Rival, and each Youth your
    Slave?°   330
Against your Fame with Fondness Hate combines,
The Rival batters, and the Lover mines.°
With distant Voice neglected Virtue calls,
Less heard, and less the faint Remonstrance falls;
Tir'd with Contempt, she quits the slipp'ry Reign,
And Pride and Prudence take her Seat in vain.
In croud at once, where none the Pass defend,
The harmless Freedom, and the private Friend.
The Guardians yield, by Force superior ply'd;
By Int'rest, Prudence; and by Flatt'ry, Pride.   340
Now Beauty falls betray'd, despis'd, distress'd,
And hissing Infamy proclaims the rest.

270. Orpheus: a legendary Greek musician whose singing and lyre playing caused trees and mountain tops to move. **303. sable:** black.

313. Lydia's Monarch: Croesus, King of Lydia in the sixth century B.C., was told by the wise Athenian legislator Solon to consider no living man happy. **317. Marlb'rough:** John Churchill (1650–1722), First Duke of Marlborough, the great statesman and military commander in the British wars against France. For the last six years of his life he was paralyzed by strokes. **318. a Show:** When Jonathan Swift died in his seventy-eighth year he was entirely senile. It is said that his servants used to exhibit him to the curious for tips. **319. Race:** progeny. **321. Vane:** Anne Vane (1705–36), mistress of Frederick, Prince of Wales, who finally deserted her. **322. Sedley:** Catherine Sedley (1656–1717), mistress of the Duke of York, who deserted her when he became James II. **330. Slave:** After line 330 the first edition reads: "An envious Breast with certain Mischief glows, / And Slaves, the Maxim tells, are always Foes." **332. mines:** digs tunnels beneath the besieged city and packs them with explosives.

Where then shall Hope and Fear their Objects find?
Must dull Suspence° corrupt the stagnant Mind?
Must helpless Man, in Ignorance sedate,
Roll darkling down the torrent of his Fate?
Must no Dislike alarm, no Wishes rise,
No Cries attempt the Mercies of the Skies?
Enquirer, cease, Petitions yet remain,
Which Heav'n may hear, nor deem Religion vain. 350
Still raise for Good the supplicating Voice,
But leave to Heav'n the Measure and the Choice.
Safe in his Pow'r, whose Eyes discern afar
The secret Ambush of a specious Pray'r.
Implore his Aid, in his Decisions rest,
Secure whate'er he gives, he gives the best.
Yet when the Sense of sacred Presence fires,
And strong Devotion to the skies aspires,
Pour forth thy Fervours for a healthful Mind,
Obedient Passions, and a Will resign'd;   360
For Love, which scarce collective Man can fill;°
For Patience sov'reign o'er transmuted Ill;
For Faith, that panting for a happier Seat,
Counts Death kind Nature's Signal of Retreat:°
These Goods for Man the Laws of Heav'n ordain,
These Goods he grants, who grants the Pow'r to gain;
With these celestial Wisdom calms the Mind,
And makes the Happiness she does not find.

THE ANT

❦

This poem was written around 1766. The biblical
passage (Prov. 6:6–11) that Johnson versifies reads:

Go to the ant, thou sluggard; consider her ways,
and be wise:
Which having no guide, overseer, or ruler,
Provideth her meat in the summer, and gathereth her food in the harvest.
How long wilt thou sleep, O sluggard? when
wilt thou arise out of thy sleep?
Yet a little sleep, a little slumber, a little folding
of the hands to sleep:

344. **Suspence:** mental indetermination leading to inaction.
361. **For . . . fill:** This line is puzzling. B. H. Bronson
has suggested the meaning, "Love so all-embracing that
mankind will hardly suffice it." Cf. Pope's *Essay on Man*, iv.
321–24, in Part Two. 364. **Signal of Retreat:** the trumpet
call signifying the end of a day's battle.

So shall thy poverty come as one that travel-
leth, and thy want as an armed man.

The text is that of the first printing, in Anna
Williams's *Miscellanies in Prose and Verse* (1766).

❦

From PROVERBS, *chap.* vi. *ver.* 6

Turn on the prudent Ant, thy heedful eyes,
Observe her labours, Sluggard, and be wise.
No stern command, no monitory voice
Prescribes her duties, or directs her choice,
Yet timely provident, she hastes away
To snatch the blessings of the plenteous day;
When fruitful summer loads the teeming plain,
She gleans the harvest, and she stores the grain.
   How long shall sloth usurp thy useless hours,
Dissolve thy vigour, and enchain thy powers?   10
While artful shades thy downy couch enclose,
And soft solicitation courts repose,
Amidst the drousy charms of dull delight,
Year chases year, with unremitted flight,
Till want, now following fraudulent and slow,
Shall spring to seize thee like an ambush'd foe.

A SHORT SONG
OF CONGRATULATION

❦

The "Sir John" of this poem was Sir John Lade, Henry
Thrale's nephew. Young Sir John once shouted across
the Thrales' parlor, "Mr. Johnson, would you advise
me to marry?" Johnson answered, "I would advise no
man to marry, Sir, who is not likely to propagate
understanding." On another occasion, speaking to
Bennet Langton, Johnson said of Sir John, "Sir, when I
heard of him last, he was running about town shooting
cats." Johnson wrote to Mrs. Thrale in 1780, "You have
heard in the papers how Sir J. Lade is come to age, I
have enclosed a short song of congratulation, which
You must not show to any body . . . . I hope You will
read it with candour, it is I believe, one of the authors
first essays in that way of writing."
   The text is that of the manuscript, as transcribed by
D. N. Smith and E. L. McAdam, Jr., in *The Poems of
Samuel Johnson* (1941).

❦

Long-expected one and twenty
Ling'ring year at last is flown,
Pomp and Pleasure, Pride and Plenty
Great Sir John, are all your own.

Loosen'd from the Minor's tether,
Free to mortgage or to sell,
Wild as wind, and light as feather
Bid the slaves of thrift farewell.

Call the Bettys, Kates, and Jennys
Ev'ry name that laughs at Care,   10
Lavish of your Grandsire's guineas,
Show the Spirit of an heir.

All that prey on vice and folly
Joy to see their quarry fly,
Here the Gamester light and jolly
There the Lender grave and sly.

Wealth, Sir John, was made to wander,
Let it wander as it will;
See the Jocky, see the Pander,
Bid them come, and take their fill.   20

When the bonny Blade carouses,
Pockets full, and Spirits high,
What are acres? What are houses?
Only dirt, or wet or dry.

If the Guardian or the Mother
Tell the woes of wilful waste,
Scorn their counsel and their pother,
You can hang or drown at last.

ON THE DEATH
OF DR. ROBERT LEVET

"Doctor" Robert Levet (1705–82) was a poor, honest, charitable, and uncouth lay physician who lived in Johnson's house together with other unfortunates; he treated the neighboring poor gratis or for trifling fees. Boswell writes:

Ever since I was acquainted with Dr. Johnson [i.e., since 1763], and many years before . . . Mr. Levet had an apartment in his house, or his chambers, and waited upon him every morning, through the whole course of his late and tedious breakfast. He was of a strange, grotesque appearance, stiff and formal in his manner, and seldom said a word while any company was present.

Sir John Hawkins observed that "Johnson in pity loved Levett, because few others could find anything in him to love." Mary Palmer, Sir Joshua Reynolds's niece, once heard Johnson recite this poem "with the tears falling over his cheek."

The text is that of the first printing, in *The Gentleman's Magazine* (August, 1783).

Condemn'd to hope's delusive mine,
    As on we toil from day to day,
By sudden blasts, or slow decline,
    Our social comforts drop away.

Well tried through many a varying year,
    See LEVET to the grave descend;
Officious,° innocent, sincere,
    Of ev'ry friendless name the friend.

Yet still he fills affection's eye,
    Obscurely wise, and coarsely kind;   10
Nor, letter'd arrogance, deny
    Thy praise to merit unrefin'd.

When fainting nature call'd for aid,
    And hov'ring death prepar'd the blow,
His vig'rous remedy display'd
    The power of art without the show.

In misery's darkest caverns known,
    His useful care was ever nigh,
Where hopeless anguish pour'd his groan,
    And lonely want retir'd to die.   20

No summons mock'd by chill delay,
    No petty gain disdain'd by pride,
The modest wants of ev'ry day
    The toil of ev'ry day supplied.

His virtues walk'd their narrow round,
    Nor made a pause, nor left a void;
And sure th' Eternal Master found
    The single talent° well employ'd.

The busy day, the peaceful night,
    Unfelt, uncounted, glided by;   30
His frame was firm, his powers were bright,
    Tho' now his eightieth year was nigh.

ON THE DEATH OF DR. ROBERT LEVET. 8. **Officious:** "kind; doing good offices" (Johnson's *Dictionary*). 28. **The single talent:** See Matt. 25:14–30.

Then with no throbbing fiery pain,
No cold gradations of decay,
Death broke at once the vital chain,
And free'd his soul the nearest way.

[TRANSLATION OF HORACE, *ODES*, BOOK IV, vii]

Horace addressed this ode to his friend L. Manlius Torquatus, an advocate distinguished for eloquence and virtue. When Johnson was at Pembroke College, according to Boswell, "Horace's Odes were the compositions in which he took most delight." This translation is Johnson's last poem in English; the manuscript is dated November, 1784.

The text is that of the manuscript, as transcribed by D. N. Smith and E. L. McAdam, Jr., in *The Poems of Samuel Johnson* (1941).

The snow dissolv'd no more is seen,
The fields, and woods, behold, are green,
The changing year renews the plain,
The rivers know their banks again,
The spritely Nymph and naked Grace°
The mazy dance together trace.
The changing year's successive plan
Proclaims mortality to Man.
Rough Winter's blasts to Spring give way,
Spring yield[s] to Summer['s] sovereign ray,   10
Then Summer sinks in Autumn's reign,
And Winter chils the World again.
Her losses soon the Moon supplies,
But wretched Man, when once he lies
Where Priam and his sons° are laid,
Is naught but Ashes and a Shade.

Who knows if Jove who counts our Score
Will toss us in a morning more?
What with your friend you nobly share
At least you rescue from your heir.   20
Not you, Torquatus, boast of Rome,
When Minos° once has fix'd your doom,
Or Eloquence, or splendid birth,
Or Virtue shall replace on earth.
Hippolytus° unjustly slain
Diana calls to life in vain,
Nor can the might of Theseus rend
The chains of hell that hold his friend.

FROM

THE RAMBLER

Johnson produced a paper of *The Rambler* every Tuesday and Friday from March 20, 1750, to March 17, 1752. His seriousness of purpose is attested by this prayer, which he wrote as he began his task:

Almighty God, the giver of all good things, without whose help all Labour is ineffectual, and without whose grace all wisdom is folly, grant, I beseech Thee, that in this my undertaking thy Holy Spirit may not be witheld from me, but that I may promote thy glory, and the Salvation both of myself and others,—Grant this O Lord for the sake of Jesus Christ. Amen. Lord bless me. So be it.

Boswell writes, "Johnson was, I think, not very happy in the choice of his title . . . which certainly is not suited to a series of grave and moral discourses; which the Italians have literally, but ludicrously, translated by *Il Vagabondo*." He experienced his customary difficulty in meeting his deadlines, and, as Boswell says, ". . . many of these discourses, which we should suppose had been laboured with all the slow attention of literary leisure, were written in haste as the moment pressed, without even being read over by him before they were printed."

TRANSLATION OF HORACE, *Odes*, BOOK IV, vii. **5. The spritely . . . Grace:** In Greek mythology nymphs are nature spirits in the shape of comely girls; the three Graces, representing mirth, bloom, and splendor, like to dance, and they traditionally refuse to appear to the stupid or ill-tempered. **15. Priam . . . sons:** Priam was the last king of Troy; he and his sons, Hector and Paris, were killed in the Trojan War.

22. Minos: formerly a wise king of Crete, now a judge of the dead in Hades. **25. Hippolytus:** son of the legendary early king of Athens Theseus; Phaedra, wife of Theseus, unjustly accused Hippolytus of an attempt on her virtue, and, at the request of Theseus, the sea god Poseidon brought about the boy's death. After the injustice came to light, even Diana, goddess of chastity, was unable to bring Hippolytus back to life.

In most of the papers—there are 208 in all—Johnson devotes himself to analyzing the moral implications of various states of mind, and in many he treats problems of criticism and of authorship. But *The Rambler* is not entirely "a series of grave and moral discourses": some papers are satirical character sketches of snobs, modish ladies, and naive young men; some are brief oriental tales; some are domestic short stories narrated in letters to The Rambler; one is an ironic panegyric on garrets as the fittest places for composition, and one descants on the flattery to which authors are subject from those in search of dinners and free drinks.

Although the separate numbers were not at first a wild success, their reputation gradually increased, and by the time of Johnson's death ten collected editions had been issued in London. Rereading one of the papers much later, Johnson shook his head and murmured, "Too wordy." But on another occasion he said, "My other works are wine and water; but my *Rambler* is pure wine."

The text is that of the first edition (1751–52); we have incorporated the substantive variants of the fourth edition (1756).

NUMB. 32

Saturday, July 7, 1750.

Ὅσσά τε δαιμονίῃσι τύχαις βροτοὶ ἄγλε᾽ ἐχουσιν,
Ὧν ἂν μοῖραν ἔχῃς, πράως φέρε, μηδ᾽ ἀγανάκτει
Ἰᾶσθαι δὲ πρέπει κάθ᾽ ὅσον δύνῃ.

PYTHAG.[1]

Of all the woes that load the mortal state,
Whate'er thy portion, mildly meet thy fate;
But ease it as thou canst—

ELPHINSTON.[2]

SO large a Part of human Life passes in a State contrary to our natural Desires, that one of the principal Topics of moral Instruction is the Art of bearing Calamities. And such is the Certainty of Evil, that it is the Duty of every Man to furnish his Mind with those

Principles that may enable him to act under it with Decency and Propriety.

THE Sect of ancient Philosophers, that boasted to have carried this necessary Science to the highest Perfection, were the Stoics, or Scholars of *Zeno*;[3] whose wild enthusiastick Virtue pretended to an Exemption from the Sensibilities of unenlightened Mortals, and who proclaimed themselves exalted, by the Doctrines of their Sect, above the Reach of those Miseries, which embitter Life to the rest of the World. They therefore removed Pain, Poverty, Loss of Friends, Exile, and violent Death, from the Catalogue of Evils; and passed, in their haughty Stile, a kind of irreversible Decree, by which they forbad them to be counted any longer among the Objects of Terror or Anxiety, or to give any Disturbance to the Tranquility of a wise Man.

THIS edict was, I think, not universally observed, for though one of the more resolute, when he was tortured by a violent Disease, cried out, that let Pain harass him to its utmost Power, it should never force him to consider it as other than indifferent and neutral; yet all had not stubbornness to hold out against their Senses: for a weaker Pupil of *Zeno* is recorded to have confessed in the Anguish of the Gout, that *he now found Pain to be an Evil.*

IT may however be questioned, whether these Philosophers can be very properly numbered among the Teachers of Patience; for if Pain be not an Evil there seems no Instruction requisite how it may be born; and therefore when they endeavour to arm their Followers with Arguments against it, they may be thought to have given up their first Position. But such Inconsistencies are to be expected from the greatest Understandings, when they endeavour to grow eminent by Singularity, and employ their Strength in establishing Opinions opposite to Nature.

THE Controversy about the Reality of external Evils is now at an End. That Life has many Miseries, and that those Miseries are, sometimes at least, equal to all the Powers of Fortitude, is now universally confessed; and therefore it is useful to consider not only how we may escape them, but by what means those which either the Accidents of Affairs, or the infirmities of Nature must bring upon us, may be mitigated and lightened; and how we may make those

THE RAMBLER: *Number 32*. **1. Pythag.:** The quotation is from the *Golden Verses*, an anonymous work mistakenly attributed to Pythagoras, Greek philosopher of the sixth century B.C. **2. Elphinston:** James Elphinston (1721–1809), a schoolmaster who helped Johnson translate many of the *Rambler* mottoes. The classical mottoes and the quotations in the text were left untranslated in the first edition.

3. Zeno: Greek philosopher of the late fourth and early third centuries B.C.; founder of the Stoic school, he taught for fifty years at Athens.

Hours less wretched, which the Condition of our present Existence will not allow to be very happy.

THE Cure for the greatest part of human Miseries is not radical, but palliative. Infelicity is involved in corporeal Nature, and interwoven with our Being; all attempts therefore to decline it wholly are useless and vain: The Armies of Pain send their Arrows against us on every Side, the Choice is only between those which are more or less sharp, or tinged with Poison of greater or less Malignity; and the strongest Armour which Reason can supply, will only blunt their Points, but cannot repel them.

THE great Remedy which Heaven has put in our Hands is Patience, by which, though we cannot lessen the Torments of the Body, we can in a great Measure preserve the Peace of the Mind, and shall suffer only the natural and genuine Force of an Evil, without heightening its Acrimony, or prolonging its Effects.

THERE is indeed nothing more unsuitable to the Nature of Man in any Calamity than Rage and Turbulence, which, without examining whether they are not sometimes impious, are at least always offensive, and incline others rather to hate and despise than to pity and assist us. If what we suffer has been brought upon us by ourselves, it is observed by an ancient Poet, that Patience is eminently our Duty, since no one should be angry at feeling that which he has deserved.

Leniter ex Merito quicquid patiare ferendum est.[4]

(Let pain deserv'd without complaint be borne.)

And, surely, if we are conscious that we have not contributed to our own Sufferings, if Punishment falls upon Innocence, or Disappointment happens to Industry and Prudence, Patience whether more necessary or not, is much easier, since our Pain is then without Aggravation, and we have not the Bitterness of Remorse to add to the Asperity of Misfortune.

IN those Evils which are allotted to us by Providence, such as Deformity, Privation of any of the Senses, or Old Age, it is always to be remembered that Impatience can have no present Effect but to deprive us of the Consolations which our Condition admits, by driving away from us those by whose Conversation or Advice we might be amused or helped; and that with regard to Futurity it is yet less to be justified, since without lessening the Pain, it cuts off the Hope of that Reward, which he by whom it is inflicted will confer upon them that bear it well.

IN all Evils which admit a Remedy, Impatience is to be avoided, because it wastes that Time and Attention in Complaints, that, if properly applied, might remove the Cause. *Turenne*,[5] among the Acknowledgements which he used to pay in Conversation to the Memory of those by whom he had been instructed in the Art of War, mentioned One with Honour, who taught him not to spend his Time in regretting any Mistake which he had made, but to set himself immediately and vigorously to repair it.

PATIENCE and Submission are very carefully to be distinguished from Cowardice and Indolence. We are not to repine, but we may lawfully struggle; for the Calamities of Life, like the Necessities of Nature, are Calls to Labour, and Exercises of Diligence. When we feel any Pressure of Distress, we are not to conclude that we can only obey the Will of Heaven by languishing under it, any more than when we perceive the Pain of Thirst we are to imagine that Water is prohibited. Of Misfortune it never can be certainly known, whether, as proceeding from the Hand of GOD, it is an Act of Favour, or of Punishment: but since all the ordinary Dispensations of Providence are to be interpreted according to the general Analogy of Things, we may conclude, that we have a Right to remove one Inconvenience as well as another; that we are only to take Care lest we purchase Ease with Guilt; and that our Maker's Purpose, whether of Reward or Severity, will be answered by the Labours which he lays us under the Necessity of Performing.

THIS Duty is not more difficult in any State, than in Diseases intensely painful, which may indeed suffer such Exacerbations as seem to strain the Powers of Life to their utmost Stretch, and leave very little of the attention vacant to Precept or Reproof. In this State the Nature of Man requires some Indulgence, and every Extravagance but Impiety may be easily forgiven him. Yet, lest we should think ourselves too soon entitled to the mournful Privileges of irresistible Misery, it is proper to reflect that the utmost anguish which human Wit can contrive, or human Malice can inflict, has been born with Constancy; and that if the Pains of Disease be, as I believe they are, sometimes greater than those of artificial Torture, they are therefore in their own Nature shorter, the vital Frame is quickly broken, or the Union between Soul and Body is for a Time suspended by insensibility, and we soon

---

4. **Leniter . . . est:** Ovid, *Heroides*, v. 7.

5. **Turenne:** Henri de la Tour d'Auvergne de Turenne, seventeeth-century French general and marshal.

cease to feel our Maladies when they once become too violent to be borne. I think there is some Reason for questioning whether the Body and Mind are not so proportioned that the one can bear all which can be inflicted on the other, whether Virtue cannot stand its Ground as long as Life, and whether a Soul well principled will not be separated sooner than subdued.

In Calamities which operate chiefly on our Passions, such as Diminution of Fortune, Loss of Friends, or Declension of Character, the chief Danger of Impatience is upon the first Attack, and many Expedients have been contrived, by which the Blow may be broken. Of these the most general Precept is, not to take Pleasure in any Thing, of which it is not in our Power to secure the Possession to ourselves. This Counsel, when we consider the Enjoyment of any terrestrial Advantage, as opposite to a constant and habitual Solicitude for future Felicity, is undoubtedly just, and delivered by that Authority which cannot be disputed; but in any other Sense, is it not like Advice, not to walk lest we should stumble, or not to see lest our Eyes should light upon Deformity? It seems to me reasonable to enjoy Blessings with Confidence, as well as to resign them with Submission, and to hope for the Continuance of Good which we possess without Insolence or Voluptuousness, as for the Restitution of that which we lose without Despondency or Murmurs.

The chief Security against the fruitless Anguish of Impatience must arise from frequent Reflection on the Wisdom and Goodness of the God of Nature, in whose Hands are Riches and Poverty, Honour and Disgrace, Pleasure and Pain, and Life and Death. A settled Conviction of the Tendency of every thing to our Good, and of the Possibility of turning Miseries into Happiness, by receiving them rightly, will incline us to bless the Name of the Lord, whether he gives or takes away.

NUMB. 37

Tuesday, July 24, 1750.

Canto quæ solitus, si quando Armenta vocabat,
Amphion Dircæus.
VIRG.[1]

Such strains I sing as once *Amphion* play'd,
When list'ning flocks the pow'rful call obey'd.
ELPHINSTON.

Number 37. **1. Virg.:** Virgil, *Eclogues,* ii. 23–24. Virgil's ten eclogues were widely imitated in Johnson's day.

IN writing or judging of Pastoral Poetry, neither the Authors nor Criticks of latter Times seem to have paid sufficient Regard to the Originals left us by Antiquity; but have entangled themselves with unnecessary Difficulties, by advancing Principles, which, having no Foundation in the Nature of Things, are wholly to be rejected from a Species of Composition in which, above all others, mere Nature is to be regarded.

It is, therefore, necessary, to enquire after some more distinct and exact Idea of this kind of Writing. This may, I think, be easily found in the Pastorals of *Virgil;* from whose Opinion it will not appear very safe to depart, if we consider that every Advantage of Nature, and of Fortune, concurred to complete his Productions, that he was born with great Accuracy, and Severity of Judgment, enlightened with all the Learning of one of the brightest Ages, and embellished with the Elegance of the *Roman* Court; that he employed his Powers rather in improving, than inventing; and therefore must have endeavoured to recompense the want of novelty by exactness; that, taking *Theocritus*[2] for his Original, he found Pastoral far advanced towards Perfection, and that having so great a Rival, he must have proceeded with uncommon Caution.

If we search the Writings of *Virgil,* for the true Definition of a Pastoral, it will be found *a Poem in which any Action or Passion is represented by its Effects upon a Country Life.* Whatsoever, therefore, may, according to the common Course of Things, happen in the Country, may afford a Subject for a Pastoral Poet.

In this Definition, it will immediately occur, to those who are versed in the Writings of the modern Criticks, that there is no Mention of the Golden Age.[3] I cannot indeed easily discover why it is thought necessary to refer Descriptions of a rural State to remote Times, nor can I perceive that any Writer has consistently preserved the *Arcadian* Manners and Sentiments. The only Reason that I have read, on which this Rule has been founded, is, that, according to the Customs of modern Life, it is improbable that Shepherds should be capable of harmonious

2. Theocritus: Greek poet of the third century B.C., considered the inventor of pastoral poetry. **3. the Golden Age:** in Greek mythology, a very early period of history when virtue, justice, and innocent happiness flourished. The Golden Age was often associated with Arcadia, an area in Greece.

Numbers,[4] or delicate Sentiments; and therefore the Reader must exalt his Ideas of the Pastoral Character, by carrying his Thoughts back to the Age in which the Care of Herds and Flocks was the Employment of the wisest and greatest Men.

THESE Reasoners seem to have been led into their Hypothesis, by considering Pastoral, not in general, as a Representation of Rural Nature, and consequently as exhibiting the Ideas and Sentiments of those, whoever they are, to whom the Country affords Pleasure or Employment, but simply as a Dialogue, or Narrative of Men actually tending Sheep, and busied in the lowest and most laborious Offices; from whence they very readily concluded, since Characters must necessarily be preserved, that either the Sentiments must sink to the Level of the Speakers, or the Speakers must be raised to the Height of the Sentiments.

IN consequence of these original Errors, a thousand Precepts have been given, which have only contributed to perplex and to confound. Some have thought it necessary that the imaginary Manners of the golden Age should be universally preserved, and have therefore believed, that nothing more could be admitted in Pastoral, than Lilies and Roses, and Rocks and Streams, among which are heard the gentle Whispers of chaste Fondness, or the soft complaints of amorous Impatience. In Pastoral, as in other Writings, Chastity of Sentiment ought doubtless to be observed, and Purity of Manners to be represented; not because the Poet is confined to the Images of the golden Age, but because, having the Subject in his own Choice, he ought always to consult the Interest of Virtue.

THESE Advocates for the golden Age lay down other Principles, not very consistent with their general Plan; for they tell us, that, to support the Character of the Shepherd, it is proper that all Refinement should be avoided, and that some slight Instances of Ignorance should be interspersed. Thus the Shepherd in *Virgil* is supposed to have forgot the Name of *Anaximander*,[5] and in *Pope*[6] the Term *Zodiack*, is too hard for a Rustick Apprehension. But if we place our Shepherds in their primitive Condition, we may give them Learning among their

other Qualifications; and if we suffer them to allude at all to Things of later Existence, which, perhaps, cannot with any great Propriety be allowed, there can be no Danger of making them speak with too much Accuracy, since they conversed with Divinities, and transmitted to succeeding Ages the Arts of Life.

OTHER Writers, having the mean and despicable Condition of a Shepherd always before them, conceive it necessary to degrade the Language of Pastoral, by obsolete Terms and Rustick Words, which they very learnedly call *Dorick*,[7] without reflecting, that they thus became Authors of a mingled Dialect, which no human Being ever could have spoken, that they may as well refine the Speech, as the Sentiments of their Personages, and that none of the Inconsistencies which they endeavour to avoid, is greater than that of joining Elegance of Thought with Coarseness of Diction. *Spenser* begins one of his Pastorals with studied Barbarity,

> Diggon Davie, *I bid her Good-day:*
> Or, Diggon *her is, or I missay.*
> Dig. *Her was her while it was Day-light,*
> But now her is a most wretched Wight.[8]

What will the Reader imagine to be the Subject on which Speakers like these exercise their Eloquence? Will he not be somewhat disappointed, when he finds them met together to condemn the Corruptions of the Church of *Rome?* Surely, at the same time that a Shepherd learns Theology, he may gain some Acquaintance with his native Language.

PASTORAL admits of all Ranks of Persons, because Persons of all Ranks inhabit the Country. It excludes not, therefore, on account of the Characters necessary to be introduced, any Elevation or Delicacy of Sentiment; those Ideas only are improper, which, not owing their Original to rural Objects, are not pastoral. Such is the exclamation in *Virgil*,

> *Nunc scio quid sit Amor, duris in Cautibus illum,*
> *Ismarus, aut Rhodope, aut extremi Garamantes,*
> *Nec Generis nostri Puerum nec Sanguinis, edunt.*[9]

> I know thee, love, in desarts thou wert bred,
> And at the dugs of savage tygers fed:
> Alien of birth, usurper of the plains.
>   DRYDEN.

---

4. **harmonious Numbers:** regular versification. 5. **the Shepherd . . . Anaximander:** Anaximander was a Greek astronomer and physicist of the sixth century B.C.; Menalcas, a character in Virgil's third eclogue, forgets his name. 6. **Pope:** *First Pastoral,* ll. 39–40.

7. **Dorick:** a Greek dialect associated with the Dorian invasion in the twelfth century B.C. 8. **Diggon Davie . . . Wight:** *The Shepheardes Calender,* "September," ll. 1–4. 9. **Nunc . . . edunt:** *Eclogues,* viii. 43–45.

which *Pope* endeavouring to copy, was carried to still greater Impropriety,

> *I know thee* Love, *wild as the raging Main,*
> *More fierce than* Tygers *on the* Libyan *Plain,*
> *Thou wert from* Etna's *burning Entrails torn,*
> *Begot in Tempests, and in Thunders born!*[10]

Sentiments like these, as they have no ground in Nature, are indeed of little Value in any Poem, but in Pastoral they are particularly liable to Censure, because, it wants that exaltation above common life, which in tragick or heroick Writings often reconciles us to bold flights and daring figures.

PASTORAL being the *Representation of an Action or Passion, by its Effects upon a Country Life*, has nothing peculiar but its Confinement to rural Imagery, without which it ceases to be Pastoral. This is its true Characteristick, and this it cannot lose by any Dignity of Sentiment, or Beauty of Diction. The *Pollio of Virgil,*[11] with all its Elevation, is a Composition truly bucolick, though rejected by the Criticks; for all the Images are either taken from the Country, or from the Religion of the Age common to all Parts of the Empire.

THE *Silenus*[12] is indeed of a more disputable kind, because though the Scene lies in the Country, the Song being religious and historical, had been no less adapted to any other Audience or Place: Neither can it well be defended as a Fiction; for the Introduction of a God seems to imply the golden Age, and yet he alludes to many subsequent Transactions, and mentions *Gallus*[13] the Poet's Contemporary.

IT seems necessary, to the Perfection of this Poem,[14] that the Occasion which is supposed to produce it, be at least not inconsistent with a Country Life, or less likely to interest those who have retired into Places of Solitude and Quiet, than the more busy Part of Mankind. It is therefore improper to give the Title of a Pastoral to Verses, in which the Speakers, after the slight Mention of their Flocks, fall to Complaints of Errors in the Church, and Corruptions in the Government, or to Lamentations of the Death of some illustrious Person, whom when once the Poet has called a Shepherd, he has no longer any Labour upon

his Hands, but can make the Clouds weep, and Lilies wither, and the Sheep hang their Heads, without Art or Learning, Genius or Study.

IT is Part of *Claudian's*[15] Character of his Rustick, that he computes his Time not by the Succession of Consuls, but of Harvests. Those who pass their Days in Retreats distant from the Theatres of Business, are always least likely to hurry their Imagination with publick Affairs.

THE Facility of treating actions or events in the pastoral Stile has incited many Writers, from whom more Judgment might have been expected, to put the Sorrow or the Joy which the Occasion required into the mouth of *Daphne* or of *Thyrsis,*[16] and as one Absurdity must naturally be expected to make way for another, they have written with an utter Disregard both of Life and Nature, and filled their Productions with mythological Allusions, with incredible Fictions, and with Sentiments which neither Passion nor Reason could have dictated, since the Change which Religion has made in the whole System of the World.

NUMB. 60

Saturday, October 13, 1750.

> —*Quid sit pulchrum, quid turpe, quid utile, quid non,*
> *Plenius et melius* Chrysippo *et* Crantore *dicit.*
>
> HOR.[1]

> Whose works the beautiful and base contain;
> Of vice and virtue more instructive rules,
> Than all the sober sages of the schools.
>
> FRANCIS.[2]

ALL Joy or Sorrow for the Happiness or Calamities of others is produced by an Act of the Imagination, that realises the Event however fictitious, or approximates it however remote, by placing us, for a Time, in the Condition of him whose Fortune we contemplate; so that we feel, while the Deception lasts, whatever Motions would be excited by the same Good or Evil happening to ourselves.

OUR Passions are therefore more strongly moved, in proportion as we can more readily adopt the Pains

---

10. I . . . born: *Third Pastoral,* ll. 89–92. 11. The Pollio . . . Virgil: the fourth eclogue. 12. The Silenus: Virgil's sixth eclogue. 13. Gallus: Gaius Cornelius Gallus (69–26 B.C.), soldier and poet; Virgil mentions him in the sixth and tenth eclogues. 14. this Poem: this kind of poem.

15. Claudian: Roman poet of the early fifth century A.D. One of his best-known poems depicts an elderly rustic who has never ventured from his rural home. 16. Daphne, Thyrsis: conventional names for characters in pastoral. *Number 60.* 1. Hor.: Horace, *Epistles,* I. ii. 3–4. 2. Francis: Dr. Philip Francis (c. 1708–73), playwright and translator.

or Pleasures proposed to our Minds, by recognising them as once our own, or considering them as naturally incident to our State of Life. It is not easy for the most artful Writer to give us an Interest in Happiness or Misery, which we think ourselves never likely to feel, and with which we have never yet been made acquainted. Histories of the Downfall of Kingdoms, and Revolutions of Empires are read with great Tranquillity; the imperial Tragedy pleases common Auditors only by its Pomp of Ornament, and Grandeur of Ideas; and the Man whose Faculties have been engrossed by Business, and whose Heart never fluttered but at the Rise or Fall of Stocks, wonders how the Attention can be seized, or the Affections agitated by a Tale of Love.

THOSE parallel Circumstances, and kindred Images to which we readily conform our Minds, are, above all other Writings, to be found in Narratives of the Lives of particular Persons; and therefore no Species of Writing seems more worthy of Cultivation than Biography, since none can be more delightful, or more useful, none can more certainly enchain the Heart by irresistible Interest, or more widely diffuse Instruction to every Diversity of Condition.

THE general and rapid Narratives of History, which involve a thousand Fortunes in the Business of a Day, and complicate innumerable Incidents in one great Transaction, afford few Lessons applicable to private Life, which derives its Comforts and its Wretchedness from the right or wrong Management of Things, which nothing but their Frequency makes considerable, *Parva si non fiunt quotidie,* says *Pliny,*[3] and which can have no Place in those Relations which never descend below the Consultation of Senates, the Motions of Armies, and the Schemes of Conspirators.

I HAVE often thought that there has rarely passed a Life of which a judicious and faithful Narrative would not be useful. For, not only every Man has in the mighty Mass of the World great Numbers in the same Condition with himself, to whom his Mistakes and Miscarriages, Escapes and Expedients would be of immediate and apparent Use; but there is such an Uniformity in the state of Man, considered apart from adventitious and separable Decorations and Disguises, that there is scarce any Possibility of Good or Ill, but is common to Humankind. A great Part

of the Time of those who are placed at the greatest Distance by Fortune, or by Temper, must unavoidably pass in the same Manner; and though, when the Claims of Nature are satisfied, Caprice, and Vanity, and Accident, begin to produce Discriminations, and Peculiarities, yet the Eye is not very heedful, or quick, which cannot discover the same Causes still terminating their Influence in the same Effects, though sometimes accelerated, sometimes retarded, or perplexed by multiplied Combinations. We are all prompted by the same Motives, all deceived by the same Fallacies, all animated by Hope, obstructed by Danger, entangled by Desire, and seduced by Pleasure.

IT is frequently objected to Relations of particular Lives, that they are not distinguished by any striking or wonderful Vicissitudes. The Scholar who passed his Life among his Books, the Merchant who conducted only his own Affairs, the Priest whose Sphere of Action was not extended beyond that of his Duty, are considered as no proper Objects of publick Regard, however they might have excelled in their several Stations, whatever might have been their Learning, Integrity, and Piety. But this Notion arises from false Measures of Excellence and Dignity, and must be eradicated by considering, that, in the esteem of uncorrupted Reason, what is of most Use is of most Value.

IT is, indeed, not improper to take honest Advantages of Prejudice, and to gain Attention by a celebrated Name; but the Business of the Biographer is often to pass slightly over those Performances and Incidents, which produce vulgar Greatness, to lead the Thoughts into domestick Privacies, and display the minute Details of daily Life, where exterior Appendages are cast aside, and Men excel each other only by Prudence, and by Virtue. The account of *Thuanus*[4] is, with great Propriety, said by its Author[5] to have been written, that it might lay open to Posterity the private and familiar Character of that Man, *cujus Ingenium et Candorem ex ipsius Scriptis sunt olim semper miraturi,*[6] whose Candour and Genius will to the End of Time be by his Writings preserved in Admiration.

3. **Pliny:** Pliny the Younger (*c.* 61–*c.* 113), Roman advocate and orator. The quotation from Pliny's *Epistles* is roughly translated in the preceding clause.

4. **Thuanus:** Jacques-Auguste de Thou (1553–1617), historian and royal librarian of France, the author of a Latin *History of His Own Times* (1604–20). 5. **its Author:** Nicolas Rigault, who wrote a biographical preface to an edition of Thou's works. 6. **cujus . . . miraturi:** Johnson translates in the next clause, as is his general practice in *The Rambler.*

THERE are many invisible Circumstances, which whether we read as Enquirers after natural or moral Knowledge, whether we intend to enlarge our Science, or encrease our Virtue, are more important than publick Occurrences. Thus *Salust*,[7] the great Master of nature, has not forgot, in his Account of *Catiline*,[8] to remark that *his Walk was now quick, and again slow*, as an Indication of a Mind revolving something with violent Commotion. Thus the story of *Melancthon*[9] affords a striking Lecture on the Value of Time, by informing us that when he made an Appointment, he expected not only the Hour, but the Minute to be fixed, that the day might not run out in the Idleness of Suspense; and all the Plans and Enterprizes of *De Wit*[10] are now of less Importance to the World, than that Part of his personal Character which represents him as careful of his Health, and negligent of his Life.

BUT Biography has often been allotted to Writers who seem very little acquainted with the Nature of their Task, or very negligent about the Performance. They rarely afford any other Account than might be collected from publick Papers, but imagine themselves writing a Life when they exhibit a chronological Series of Actions or Preferments; and so little regard the Manners or Behaviour of their Heroes, that more Knowledge may be gained of a Man's real Character, by a short Conversation with one of his Servants, than from a formal and studied Narrative, begun with his Pedigree, and ended with his Funeral.

IF now and then they condescend to inform the World of particular Facts, they are not always so happy as to select the most important. I know not well what Advantage Posterity can receive from the only Circumstance by which *Tickell*[11] has distinguished *Addison* from the Rest of Mankind, the Irregularity of his Pulse: nor can I think myself overpaid for the Time spent in reading the Life of *Malherb*,[12] by being enabled to relate, after the learned Biographer,[13] that *Malherb* had two predominant Opinions; one, that the Looseness of a single Woman might destroy all her Boast of ancient Descent; the other, that the *French* Beggars made use very improperly and barbarously of the Phrase *noble Gentleman*, because either Word included the Sense of both.

THERE are, indeed, some natural Reasons why these Narratives are often written by such as were not likely to give much Instruction or Delight, and why most Accounts of particular Persons are barren and useless. If a Life be delayed till Interest and Envy are at an End, we may hope for Impartiality, but must expect little Intelligence; for the Incidents which give Excellence to Biography are of a volatile and evanescent Kind, such as soon escape the Memory, and are rarely transmitted by Tradition. We know how few can portray a living Acquaintance, except by his most prominent and observable Particularities, and the grosser Features of his Mind; and it may be easily imagined how much of this little Knowledge may be lost in imparting it, and how soon a Succession of Copies will lose all Resemblance of the Original.

IF the Biographer writes from personal Knowledge, and makes haste to gratify the publick Curiosity, there is Danger lest his Interest, his Fear, his Gratitude, or his Tenderness, overpower his Fidelity, and tempt him to conceal, if not to invent. There are many who think it an act of Piety to hide the Faults or Failings of their Friends, even when they can no longer suffer by their Detection; we therefore see whole Ranks of Characters adorned with uniform Panegyrick, and not to be known from one another, but by extrinsick and casual Circumstances. "Let me remember, says *Hale*,[14] when I find myself inclined to pity a Criminal, that there is likewise a Pity due to the Country." If we owe Regard to the Memory of the Dead, there is yet more Respect to be paid to Knowledge, to Virtue, and to Truth.

---

7. Salust: Gaius Sallustius Crispus, Roman historian of the first century B.C. **8. Catiline:** Roman politician of the first century B.C. **9. Melancthon:** Philipp Melancthon (1497–1560), German religious reformer; his life was written by Joachim Camerarius, a sixteenth-century German classical scholar. **10. De Wit:** John De Witt (1625–72), Dutch statesman and diplomat; his personal character is discussed by Sir William Temple in his *Essay on the Cure of Gout* (1679). **11. Tickell:** Thomas Tickell (1686–1740), professor of poetry at Oxford; as Addison's literary executor, he published his works in 1721. **12. Malherb:** François de Malherbe (1555–1628), French poet.

13. the learned Biographer: Honorat de Racan (1589–1670), French poet, one of Malherbe's disciples. **14. Hale:** Sir Matthew Hale (1609–76), English judge during the Commonwealth and Restoration; his life was written in 1682 by Gilbert Burnet.

NUMB. 71

Tuesday, November 20, 1750.

Vivere quod propero Pauper, nec inutilis Annis
Da veniam, properat vivere nemo satis.
                              MART.[1]

True, sir, to live I haste, your pardon give,
For tell me, who makes haste enough to live?
                              F. LEWIS.[2]

MANY Words and Sentences are so frequently heard
in the Mouths of Men, that a superficial Observer is
inclined to believe, that they must contain some
primary Principle, some great Rule of Action, which
it is proper always to have present to the Attention,
and by which the Use of every Hour is to be adjusted.
Yet, if we consider the Conduct of those sententious
Philosophers, it will often be found, that they repeat
these Aphorisms, merely because they have somewhere heard them, because they have nothing else to
say, or because they think Veneration gained by such
Appearances of Wisdom, but that no Ideas are annexed
to the Words, and that, according to the old Blunder
of the Followers of *Aristotle*, their Souls are mere
Pipes or Organs, which transmit Sounds, but do not
understand them.

OF this kind is the well known and well attested
Position that *Life is short*, which may be heard among
Mankind by an attentive Auditor, many Times a
Day, but which never yet within my Reach of
Observation left any Impression upon the Mind; and
perhaps if my Readers will turn their thoughts back
upon their old friends, they will find it difficult to
call a single Man to Remembrance, who appeared to
know that Life was short till he was about to lose it.

IT is observable that *Horace*, in his Account of the
Characters of Men, as they are diversified by the
various Influence of Time,[3] remarks, that the Old
Man is *Dilator, spe longus*, given to Procrastination,
and inclined to extend his Hopes to a great Distance.
So far are we, generally, from thinking what we often
say of the Shortness of Life, that at the Time when it is

necessarily shortest, we form Projects which we delay
to execute, indulge such Expectations as nothing but a
long Train of Events can gratify, and suffer those
Passions to gain upon us which are only excusable in
the Prime of Life.

THESE Reflections were lately excited in my Mind,
by an Evening's Conversation with my Friend
Prospero, who at the Age of Fifty-five, has bought an
Estate, and is now contriving to dispose and cultivate
it with uncommon Elegance. His great Pleasure is to
walk among stately Trees, and lye musing in the
Heat of Noon under their Shade; he is therefore
maturely considering how he shall dispose his Walks
and his Groves, and has at last determined to send for
the best Plans from *Italy*, and forbear planting till the
next Season.

THUS is Life trifled away in Preparations to do what
never can be done, if it be left unattempted till all the
Requisites which Imagination can suggest are gathered
together. Where our Design terminates only in our
own Satisfaction, the Mistake is of no great Importance; for the Pleasure of expecting Enjoyment is
often greater than that of obtaining it, and the Completion of almost every Wish is found a Disappointment; but when many others are interested in an
Undertaking, when any Design is formed, in which
the Improvement or Security of Mankind is involved,
nothing is more unworthy either of Wisdom or
Benevolence, than to delay it from Time to Time, or
to forget how much every Day that passes over us
takes away from our Power, and how soon an idle
Purpose to do an Action sinks into a mournful Wish
that it had once been done.

WE are frequently importuned, by the Bacchanalian
Writers, to lay hold on the present Hour, to catch the
Pleasures within our Reach, and remember that
Futurity is not at our command.

Τὸ ῥόδον ἀκμάζει βαιὸν χρόνον. ἢν δὲ παρέλθῃς,
Ζητῶν εὑρήσεις οὐ ῥόδον, ἀλλὰ βάτον.

Soon fades the rose; once past the fragrant hour,
The loiterer finds a bramble for a flow'r.[4]

BUT surely these Exhortations may, with equal
Propriety, be applied to better Purposes, it may be at
least inculcated, that Pleasures are more safely postponed than Virtues, and that greater Loss is suffered

---

Number 71. **1. Mart.:** Martial, *Epigrams*, II. xc. 2. **2. F.**
Lewis: the Reverend Francis Lewis, of whom little more
is known than that, as Johnson once said, "He lived in London,
and hung loose upon society." **3. in . . . Time:** *Ars Poetica*,
ll. 158–76. The passage is imitated by Pope; see *Essay on Man*,
ii. 275–82, in Part Two.

4. Soon . . . flow'r: Johnson is translating from the *Greek
Anthology*, xi. 53.

by missing an Opportunity of doing good, than an Hour of giddy Frolick and noisy Merriment.

WHEN *Baxter*[5] had lost a thousand Pounds, which he had laid up for the Erection of a School, he used frequently to mention the Misfortune as an Incitement to be charitable while God gives the Power of bestowing, and considered himself as culpable in some Degree for having left a good Action in the Hands of Chance, and suffered his Benevolence to be defeated for want of Quickness and Diligence.

IT is lamented by *Hearne*,[6] the learned Antiquary of *Oxford*, that this general Forgetfulness of the Fragility of Life, has remarkably infected the Students of Monuments and Records; as their Employment consists first in collecting, and afterwards in arranging or abstracting what libraries afford them, they ought to amass no more than they can digest; but when they have undertaken a Work, they go on searching and transcribing, call for new Supplies, when they are already overburdened, and at last leave their Work unfinished. *It is*, says he, *the Business of a good Antiquary, as of a good Man, to have Mortality always before him.*

THUS, not only in the Slumber of Sloth, but in the Dissipation of ill directed Industry, is the Shortness of Life generally forgotten. As some Men lose their Hours in Laziness, because they suppose, that there is Time enough for the Reparation of neglect; others busy themselves in providing that no length of Life may want Employment; and it often happens, that Sluggishness and Activity are equally surprised by the last Summons, and perish not more differently from each other, than the Fowl that receives the Shot in her Flight, from her that is killed upon the Bush.

AMONG the many Improvements made by the last Centuries in human Knowledge, may be numbered the exact Calculations of the Value of Life; but whatever may be their Use in Traffick,[7] they seem very little to have advanced Morality. They have hitherto been rather applied to the Acquisition of Money, than of Wisdom; the Computer refers none of his Calculations to his own Tenure, but persists, in Contempt of Probability, to foretel old age to himself, and believes that he is marked out to reach the utmost Verge of human Existence, and see thousands and ten thousands fall into the Grave.

So deeply is this Fallacy rooted in the Heart, and so strongly guarded by Hope and Fear against the Approach of Reason, that neither Science nor Experience can shake it, and we act as if Life were without End, though we see and confess its Uncertainty and Shortness.

DIVINES have, with great Strength and Ardour, shewn the absurdity of delaying Reformation and Repentance; a Degree of Folly indeed, which sets Eternity to hazard. It is the same Weakness, in Proportion to the Importance of the Neglect, to transfer any Care, which now claims our Attention, to a future Time: We subject ourselves to needless Dangers from Accidents which early diligence would have obviated, or perplex our Minds by vain Precautions, and make Provision for the execution of designs, of which the opportunity once missed never will return.

As he that lives longest lives but a little While, every man may be certain that he has no Time to waste. The Duties of Life are commensurate to its Duration, and every Day brings its Task, which if neglected is doubled on the Morrow. But he that has already trifled away those Months and Years, in which he should have laboured, must remember, that he has now only a Part of that of which the whole is little; and that since the few Moments remaining are to be considered as the last Trust of Heaven, not one is to be lost.

NUMB. 82

Saturday, December 29, 1750.

> *Omnia, Castor, emit, sic fiet ut omnia vendat.*
>   MART.[1]

Who buys without discretion, buys to sell.

To The RAMBLER.

SIR,

IT will not be necessary to solicit your good Will by any formal Preface, when I have informed you, that I have long been known as the most laborious and zealous Virtuoso[2] that the present Age has had the

---

5. **Baxter:** Richard Baxter, seventeenth-century Presbyterian divine and scholar. 6. **Hearne:** Thomas Hearne (1678–1735), author of *Reliquiae Bodleianae* (1703). 7. **Traffick:** commerce.

Number 82. 1. **Mart.:** Martial, *Epigrams*, VII. xcvii. 2. **Virtuoso:** "a man skilled in antique or natural curiosities" (Johnson's *Dictionary*).

Honour of producing, and that Inconveniencies have been brought upon me by an unextinguishable Ardour of Curiosity, and an unshaken Perseverance in the Acquisition of the Productions of Art and Nature.

It was observed, from my Entrance into the World, that I had something uncommon in my Disposition, and that there appeared in me very early Tokens of superiour Genius. I was always an Enemy to Trifles; the play-things which my mother bestowed upon me I immediately broke that I might discover the method of their structure, and the causes of their motions; of all the toys with which children are delighted I valued only my coral, and as soon as I could speak, asked, like *Peiresc*,[3] innumerable questions which the maids about me could not resolve. As I grew older I was more thoughtful and serious, and instead of amusing myself with puerile Diversions, made Collections of natural Rarities, and never walked into the Fields without bringing home Stones of remarkable Forms, or Insects of some uncommon Species. I never entered an old House, from which I did not take away the painted Glass, and often lamented that I was not one of that happy Generation[4] who demolished the Convents and Monasteries, and broke Windows by Law.

Being thus early possessed by a Taste for solid Knowledge, I passed my Youth with very little Disturbance from Passions and Appetites, and having no Pleasure in the Company of Boys and Girls, who talked of Plays, Politicks, Fashions, or Love, I carried on my Enquiries with incessant Diligence, and had amassed more Stones, Mosses, and Shells, than are to be found in many celebrated Collections, at an age in which the greatest Part of young Men are studying under Tutors, or endeavouring to recommend themselves to Notice by their Dress, their Air, and their Levities.

When I was two and twenty Years old, I became, by the Death of my Father, possessed of a small Estate in Land, with a very large Sum of Money in the public Funds, and must confess that I did not much lament him; for he was a Man of mean Parts, bent rather upon growing rich than wise. He once fretted at the Expence of only ten Shillings, which he happened to overhear me offering for the Sting of a Hornet, though it was a cold moist Summer, in which very few Hornets had been seen. He often recommended to me the Study of Physick, in which, said he, you may at once gratify your Curiosity after natural History, and encrease your Fortune by benefiting Mankind. I heard him, Mr. Rambler, with Pity, and as there was no Prospect of elevating a Mind formed to grovel, suffered him to please himself with hoping that I should sometime follow his Advice. For you know that there are men, with whom, when they have once settled a Notion in their Heads, it is to very little Purpose to dispute.

Being now left wholly to my own Inclinations, I very soon enlarged the Bounds of my Curiosity, and contented myself no longer with such Rarities as required only Judgment and Industry, and when once found, might be had for nothing. I now turned my Thoughts to *Exoticks* and *Antiques*, and became so well known for my generous Patronage of ingenious Men, that my Levee was crowded with Visitants, some to see my Museum, and others to encrease its Treasures, by selling me whatever they had brought from other Countries.

I had always a Contempt of that Narrowness of Conception, which contents itself with cultivating some single Corner of the Field of Science; I took the whole Region into my View, and wished it of yet greater Extent. But no Man's Power can be equal to his Will. I was forced to proceed by slow Degrees, and to purchase what Chance, or Kindness happened to present. I did not, however, proceed without some Design, or imitate the Indiscretion of those, who begin a thousand Collections, and finish none. Having been always a Lover of Geography, I determined to collect the Maps drawn in the rude and barbarous Times, before any regular Surveys, or just Observations, and have, at a great Expence, brought together a Volume, in which, perhaps, not a single Country is laid down according to its true Situation, and by which, he that desires to know the Errors of the antient Geographers may be amply informed.

But my ruling passion is patriotism: my chief care has been to procure the Products of our own Country; and as *Alfred*[5] received the Tribute of the *Welch* in Wolves' Heads, I allowed my Tenants to pay their Rents in Butterflies, till I had exhausted the papilionaceous Tribe. I then directed them to the Pursuit of other Animals, and obtained, by this easy Method,

---

3. **Peiresc:** Nicolas Claude Fabri de Pieresc (1580–1637), French antiquary. 4. **that . . . Generation:** of the first half of the sixteenth century, the age of the English Reformation.

5. **Alfred:** king of the West Saxons in the ninth century.

most of the Grubs and Insects, which Land, Air, or Water can supply. I have three Species of Earthworms not known to the Naturalists, have discovered a new Ephemera,[6] and can shew four Wasps that were taken torpid in their Winter Quarters. I have, from my own Ground, the longest Blade of Grass upon Record, and once accepted, as a half Year's Rent for a Field of Wheat, an Ear containing more Grains than had been seen before upon a single Stem.

ONE of my Tenants so much neglected his own Interest, as to supply me, in a whole Summer, with only two Horse-flies, and those little more than the common Size, and I was upon the Brink of seizing for Arrears, when his good Fortune threw a white Mole in his Way, for which he was not only forgiven, but rewarded.

THESE, however, were petty Acquisitions, and made at small Expence, nor should I have ventured to rank myself among the Virtuosi without better Claims; I have suffered nothing worthy the Regard of a wise Man to escape my Notice. I have ransacked the old and the new World, and been equally attentive to past Ages and the present. For the Illustration of antient History, I can shew a Marble, of which the Inscription, though it is not now legible, appears from some broken Remains of the Letters, to have been *Tuscan*,[7] and therefore, probably, engraved before the Foundation of *Rome*. I have two Pieces of Porphyry found among the Ruins of *Ephesus*, and three Letters broken off by a learned Traveller from the monuments at *Persepolis*, a Piece of Stone which paved the *Areopagus*[8] of *Athens*, and a Plate without Figures or characters, which was found at *Corinth*, and which I therefore believe to be that Metal, which was once valued before Gold. I have Sand gathered out of the *Granicus*,[9] a Fragment of *Trajan's*[10] Bridge over the *Danube*, some of the Mortar which cemented the Watercourse of *Tarquin*,[11] a Horse-shoe broken on the *Flaminian* Way,[12] and a Turf with five Daisies dug from the Field of *Pharsalia*.[13]

I DO not wish to raise the Envy of unsuccessful Collectors, by too pompous a Display of my scien-

tifick Wealth, but cannot forbear to observe, that there are few Regions of the Globe which are not honoured with some Memorial in my Cabinets. The *Persian* Monarchs are said to have boasted the Greatness of their Empire, by being served at their Tables with drink from the *Ganges* and the *Danube:* I can shew one Vial, of which the Water was formerly an Icicle on the Crags of *Caucasus*, and another that contains what once was Snow on the Top of Atlas; in a third is dew brushed from a banana in the gardens of *Ispahan;*[14] and, in another, brine that has rolled in the pacific ocean. I flatter myself that I am writing to a Man who will rejoice at the Honour which my Labours have procured to my Country, and therefore I shall tell you that *Britain* can by my Care boast of a Snail that has crawled upon the Wall of *China*, a humming Bird which an *American* Princess wore in her Ear, the Tooth of an Elephant who carried the Queen of *Siam*, the Skin of an Ape that was kept in the Palace of the Great Mogul,[15] a Ribbon that adorned one of the Maids of a *Turkish* Sultana, and a Symetar once wielded by a Soldier of *Abas* the Great.[16]

IN collecting Antiquities of every Country, I have been careful to chuse only by intrinsick Worth, and real usefulness, without Regard to Party or Opinions. I have therefore a Lock of *Cromwell's* Hair in a Box turned from a Piece of the Royal Oak,[17] and keep, in the same Drawers, Sand scraped from the Coffin of King *Richard*,[18] and a Commission signed by *Henry* VII. I have equal Veneration for the Ruff of *Elizabeth* and the Shoe of *Mary* of *Scotland*, and should lose, with like Regret, a Tobacco-Pipe of *Raleigh*, and a Stirrup of King *James*. I have paid the same Price for a Glove of *Lewis*,[19] and a Thimble of Queen *Mary;* for a fur Cap of the *Czar*, and a Boot of *Charles* of *Sweden*.

YOU will easily imagine that these Accumulations were not made without some Diminution of my Fortune, for I was so well known to spare no Cost, that at every Sale some bid against me for Hire, some for Sport, and some for Malice; and, if I asked the Price of any Thing, it was sufficient to double the

---

6. **Ephemera:** "an insect that lives only one day" (Johnson's *Dictionary*). 7. **Tuscan:** Etruscan. 8. **Areopagus:** a hilltop where the council of ancient Athens met for its deliberations. 9. **Granicus:** a stream in Asia Minor. 10. **Trajan:** (*c.* 53–117), a Roman emperor. 11. **Tarquin:** a legendary king of early Rome. 12. **the Flaminian Way:** a road leading northwest from Rome. 13. **Pharsalia:** site of the battle in 48 B.C. in which Caesar defeated Pompey.

14. **Ispahan:** Isfahan, a Persian city. 15. **the Great Mogul:** the emperor of Delhi. 16. **Abas the Great:** Abbas I (*c.* 1557–1628), Shah of Persia. 17. **the Royal Oak:** a tree at Boscobel, Shropshire, in which Charles II hid briefly after the Battle of Worcester in 1651. 18. **King Richard:** Richard III, defeated and killed by Henry VII at the Battle of Bosworth in 1485. 19. **Lewis:** Joyce Lewis, Protestant martyr, burned in 1557 at the command of Queen Mary.

Demand. For Curiosity, trafficking thus with Avarice, the Wealth of *India* had not been enough; and I, by little and little, transferred all my Money from the Funds[20] to my Closet: Here I was inclined to stop, and live upon my Estate in literary Leisure, but the Sale of the *Harleian* Collection[21] shook my Resolution; I mortgaged my Land, and purchased thirty Medals, which I could never find before. I have at length bought till I can buy no longer, and the Cruelty of my Creditors has seized my Repository; I am therefore condemned to disperse what the Labour of an Age will not reassemble; I submit to that which cannot be opposed, and shall, in a short Time, declare a Sale. I have, while it is yet in my Power, sent you a Pebble, pick'd up by *Tavernier*[22] on the Banks of the *Ganges;* for which I desire no other Recompence than that you will recommend my Catalogue to the Public.

QUISQUILIUS.[23]

NUMB. 83

Tuesday, January 1, 1751.

Nisi utile est quod facias, Stulta est Gloria.
PHÆDRUS.[1]

All useless science is an empty boast.

THE Publication of the Letter in my last Paper has naturally led me to the Consideration of that Thirst after Curiosities, which often draws Contempt and Ridicule upon itself, but which is perhaps no otherwise blameable, than as it wants those circumstantial Recommendations which add Lustre even to moral Excellencies, and are absolutely necessary to the Grace and Beauty of indifferent Actions.

LEARNING confers so much Superiority on those who possess it, that they might probably have escaped all Censure, had they been able to agree among themselves: But as Envy and Competition have divided the Republick of Letters into Factions, they have neglected the common Interest; each has called

in foreign Aid, and endeavoured to strengthen his own Cause by the Frown of Power, the Hiss of Ignorance, and the Clamour of Popularity. They have all engaged in feuds, till by mutual Hostilities they demolished those Out-works which Veneration had raised for their Security, and exposed themselves to barbarians, by whom every Region of Science is equally laid waste.

BETWEEN men of different Studies and Professions, may be observed a constant Reciprocation of Reproaches. The Collector of Shells and Stones derides the Folly of him who pastes Leaves and Flowers upon Paper, pleases himself with Colours that are perceptibly fading, and amasses with Care what cannot be preserved. The Hunter of Insects stands amazed that any Man can waste his short Time upon lifeless Matter, while many Tribes of Animals yet want their history. Every one is inclin'd not only to promote his own Study, but to exclude all others from Regard and having heated his Imagination with some favourite Pursuit, wonders that the rest of Mankind are not seized with the same Passion.

THERE are, indeed, many Subjects of Study which seem but remotely allied to useful Knowledge, and of little Importance to Happiness or Virtue; nor is it easy to forbear some Sallies of Merriment, or Expressions of Pity, when we see a Man wrinkled with Attention, and emaciated with solicitude, in the Investigation of Questions, of which, without visible inconvenience, the World may expire in Ignorance. Yet it is dangerous to discourage well intended Labours, or innocent Curiosity; for he who is employed in Searches, which by any deduction of consequences tend to the Benefit of Life, is surely laudable, in Comparison of those who spend their Time in counteracting Happiness, and filling the World with Wrong and Danger, Confusion and Remorse. No Man can perform so little, as not to have Reason to congratulate himself on his Merits, when he beholds the Multitudes that live in total Idleness, and have never yet endeavoured to be useful.

IT is impossible to determine the Limits of Enquiry, or to foresee what Consequences a new Discovery may produce. He who suffers not his Faculties to lie torpid, has a Chance, whatever be his Employment, of doing Good to his Fellow-creatures. The man that first ranged the Woods in Search of medicinal Springs, or climbed the Mountains for salutary Plants, has undoubtedly merited the Gratitude of Posterity, how much soever his frequent Miscarriages might excite

---

20. **Funds:** government bonds. 21. **the Sale . . . Collection:** The vast library and art collection of Edward Harley (1689–1741), Second Earl of Oxford, were sold in 1742. Johnson wrote a preface to the sale catalogue. 22. **Tavernier:** Jean-Baptiste Tavernier, seventeenth-century French traveler to the Middle East. 23. **Quisquilius:** from Latin *quisquiliae,* meaning rubbish. *Number 83.* 1. **Phædrus:** *Fables,* III. xvii. 12.

the Scorn of his Contemporaries. If what appears little be universally despised, nothing greater can be attained, for all that is great was at first little, and rose to its present Bulk by gradual Accessions, and accumulated Labours.

THOSE who lay out Time or Money in assembling Matter for Contemplation, are doubtless entitled to some Degree of Respect, though in a Flight of Gaiety it be easy to ridicule their Treasure, or in a Fit of Sullenness to despise it. A man who thinks only on the particular object before him, goes not away much illuminated by having enjoyed the Privilege of handling the Tooth of a Shark, or the Paw of a white Bear; yet there is nothing more worthy of Admiration to a philosophical eye than the Structure of Animals, by which they are qualified to support Life in the Elements or climates to which they are appropriated; and of all natural bodies it must be generally confessed, that they exhibit Evidences of infinite Wisdom, bear their Testimony to the supreme Reason, and excite in the Mind new Raptures of gratitude, and new Incentives to Piety.

To collect the Productions of Art and Examples of mechanical Science or manual Ability is unquestionably useful, even when the Things themselves are of small Importance, because it is always advantageous to know how far the human Powers have proceeded, and how much Experience has found to be within the Reach of Diligence. Idleness and Timidity often despair without being overcome, and forbear Attempts for fear of being defeated; and we may promote the Invigoration of faint Endeavours, by shewing what has been already performed. It may sometimes happen that the greatest efforts of Ingenuity have been exerted in Trifles; yet the same Principles and Expedients may be applied to more valuable Purposes, and the movements which put into Action Machines of no Use but to raise the Wonder of Ignorance, may be employed to drain Fens, or manufacture Metals, to assist the Architect, or preserve the Sailor.

FOR the Utensils, Arms, or Dresses of foreign Nations, which make the greatest Part of many Collections, I have little Regard when they are valued only because they are foreign, and can suggest no Improvement of our own Practice. Yet they are not all equally useless, nor can it be always safely determined which should be rejected or retained, for they may sometimes unexpectedly contribute to the Illustration of History, and to the Knowledge of the natural Commodities of the Country, or of the Genius and Customs of its Inhabitants.

RARITIES there are of yet a lower Rank, which owe their worth merely to Accident, and which can convey no Information, nor satisfy any rational Desire. Such are many Fragments of Antiquity, as Urns and Pieces of Pavement, and Things held in Veneration only for having been once the Property of some eminent Person, as the Armour of King *Henry*;[2] or for having been used on some remarkable Occasion, as the Lanthorn of *Guy Faux*.[3] The Loss or Preservation of these seems to be a Thing indifferent, nor can I perceive why the Possession of them should be coveted. Yet, perhaps, even this Curiosity is implanted by Nature, and when I find *Tully*[4] confessing of himself, that he could not forbear at *Athens* to visit the Walks and Houses which the old Philosophers had frequented or inhabited, and recollect the Reverence which every Nation, civil and barbarous, has paid to the Ground where Merit has been buried, I am afraid to declare against the general Voice of Mankind, and am inclined to believe, that this Regard, which we involuntarily pay to the meanest Relique of a Man great and illustrious, is intended as an Incitement to Labour, and an Encouragement to expect the same Renown, if it be sought by the same Virtues.

THE Virtuoso therefore cannot be said to be wholly useless; but perhaps he may be sometimes culpable for confining himself to Business below his Genius, and losing, in petty Speculations, those Hours by which, if he had spent them in nobler Studies, he might have given new Light to the intellectual World. It is never without Grief, that I find a Man capable of Ratiocination or Invention enlisting himself in this secondary Class of Learning; for when he has once discovered a Method of gratifying his Desire of Eminence by Expence rather than by Labour, and known the Sweets of a Life blest at once with the Ease of Idleness, and the Reputation of Knowledge, he will not easily be brought to undergo again the Toil of thinking, or leave his Toys and Trinkets for Arguments and principles, arguments which require Circumspection and Vigilance, and principles which

---

2. **King Henry:** Henry VIII, whose armor is still exhibited in the Tower of London. 3. **Guy Faux:** (Fawkes) executed in 1606 for his part in the attempt to blow up the Houses of Parliament in 1605. 4. **Tully:** Cicero.

cannot be obtained but by the Drudgery of Meditation. He will gladly shut himself up forever with his Shells and Medals, like the Companions of *Ulysses*, who having tasted the Fruit of *Lotos*, would not even by the Hope of seeing their own Country, be tempted again to the Dangers of the Sea.[5]

'Αλλ' αὐτου βούλοντο μετ' ἄνδρασι Λωτοφάγοισι,
Λωτὸν ἐρεπτόμενοι μένεμεν νοστοῦ τε λάθεσθαι.

—Whoso tastes,
Insatiate riots in the sweet repasts;
Nor other home nor other care intends,
But quits his house, his country, and his friends.
POPE.[6]

COLLECTIONS of this Kind are of Use to the Learned, as Heaps of Stone and Piles of Timber are necessary to the Architect. But to dig the Quarry or to search the Field, requires not much of any Quality beyond stubborn Perseverance; and though Genius must often lie inactive without this humble Assistance, yet this can claim little Praise, because every Man can afford it.

To mean Understandings, it is sufficient Honour to be numbered amongst the lowest Labourers of Learning; but different Abilities must find different Tasks. To hew Stone would have been unworthy of *Palladio*,[7] and to have rambled in search of Shells and Flowers, had but ill suited with the Capacity of *Newton*.

NUMB. 106

Saturday, March 23, 1751.

> *Opinionum commenta delet Dies, Naturæ judicia confirmat.*
>
> CIC.[1]

Time obliterates the fictions of opinion, and confirms the decisions of nature.

IT is necessary to the Success of Flattery that it be accommodated to particular Circumstances or Characters, and enter the Heart on that Side where the Passions stand ready to receive it. A Lady seldom listens with Attention to any Praise but that of her Beauty; a merchant always expects to hear of his

Influence at the Bank, his Importance on the Exchange, the Height of his Credit, and the Extent of his Traffick; and the Author will scarcely be pleased without Lamentations of the Neglect of Learning, the Conspiracies against Genius, and the slow Progress of Merit, or some Praises of the Magnanimity of those who encounter Poverty and Contempt in the Cause of knowledge, and trust for the Reward of their Labours to the Judgment and Gratitude of Posterity.

AN Assurance of unfading Laurels and immortal Reputation is the settled Reciprocation of Civility between amicable Writers; to raise *Monuments more durable than Brass, and more conspicuous than Pyramids*,[2] has been long the common Boast of Literature; but among the innumerable Architects that erect Columns to themselves, far the greater Part, either for Want of durable Materials, or of Art to dispose them, see their Edifices perish as they are towering to Completion, and those few that for a while attract the Eye of Mankind, are generally weak in the Foundation, and soon sink by the Saps[3] of Time.

No Place affords a more striking Conviction of the Vanity of human Hopes, than a publick Library; for who can see the Wall crouded on every Side by mighty Volumes, the Works of laborious Meditation and accurate Enquiry, now scarcely known but by the Catalogue, and preserved only to encrease the Pomp of Learning, without considering how many Hours have been wasted in vain Endeavours, how often Imagination has anticipated the Praises of Futurity, how many Statues have risen to the Eye of Vanity, how many ideal Converts have elevated Zeal, how often Wit has exulted in the eternal Infamy of his Antagonists, and dogmatism has delighted in the gradual Advances of his Authority, the Immutability of his Decrees, and the Perpetuity of his Power.

> —*Non unquam dedit,*
> *Documenta Fors majora, quam fragili loco*
> *Starent Superbi.*[4]———

Insulting chance ne'er call'd with louder voice,
On swelling mortals to be proud no more.

Of the innumerable Authors whose Performances are thus treasured up in magnificent Obscurity, most are forgotten, because they never deserved to be

---

5. like . . . Sea: See *Odyssey*, Book IX. **6. Pope:** translation of the *Odyssey*, IX. 107–10. **7. Palladio:** Andrea Palladio (1518–80), Italian Neoclassical architect. *Number 106.* **1. Cic.:** Cicero, *Ad Atticum*, vi. 1.

2. Monuments . . . Pyramids: Cf. Horace, *Odes*, III. xxx. 1. **3. Saps:** deep trenches or tunnels dug underneath an enemy's fortifications. **4. Non . . . Superbi:** Seneca, *Troades*, ll. 4–6.

remembered, and owed the Honours which they once obtained, not to Judgment or to Genius, to Labour or to Art, but to the Prejudice of Faction, the Stratagem of Intrigue, or the Servility of Adulation.

NOTHING is more common than to find Men whose Works are now totally neglected, mentioned with Praises by their Contemporaries, as the Oracles of their Age, and the Legislators of science. Curiosity is naturally excited, their Volumes after long Enquiry are found, but seldom reward the Labour of the Search; every Period of Time has produced these Bubbles of artificial Fame, which are kept up a while by the Breath of Fashion, and then break at once and are annihilated. The Learned often bewail the Loss of ancient Writers whose Characters have survived their Works; but, perhaps, if we could now retrieve them, we should find them only the *Granvilles*, *Montagues*, *Stepneys*, and *Sheffields*[5] of their Time, and wonder by what Infatuation or Caprice they could be raised to notice.

IT cannot, however, be denied, that many have sunk into Oblivion whom it were unjust to number with this despicable Class. Various Kinds of literary Fame seem destined to various Measures of Duration. Some spread into Exuberance with a very speedy Growth, but soon wither and decay; some rise more slowly, but last long. *Parnassus*[6] has its Flowers of transient Fragrance, as well as its Oaks of towering Height, and its Laurels of eternal Verdure.

AMONG those whose Reputation is exhausted in a short Time by its own Luxuriance, are the Writers who take Advantage of present Incidents or Characters which strongly interest the Passions and engage universal Attention. It is not difficult to obtain Readers when we discuss a Question which every one is desirous to understand, which is debated in every Assembly, and has divided the Nation into Parties; or when we display the Faults or Virtues of him whose publick Conduct has made almost every Man his Enemy or his Friend. To the quick Circulation of such Productions all the Motives of Interest and Vanity concur; the Disputant enlarges his Knowledge, the Zealot animates his Passion, and every Man is desirous to inform himself concerning Affairs so vehemently agitated and variously represented.

5. **Granvilles . . . Sheffields:** all highly regarded aristocratic or upper-class writers whose works have proved, in time, inconsequential. 6. **Parnassus:** The Greek mountain sacred to Apollo, god of poetry.

IT is scarcely to be imagined, through how many Subordinations of Interest, the Ardour of Party is diffused; and what Multitudes fancy themselves affected by every Satire or Panegyrick on a Man of Eminence. Whoever has, at any time, taken Occasion to mention him with Praise or Blame, whoever happens to love or hate any of his Adherents, as he wishes to confirm his Opinion, and to strengthen his Party, will diligently peruse every Paper from which he can hope for Sentiments like his own. An Object, however small in itself, if placed near to the Eye, will engross all the Rays of Light; and a Transaction, however trivial, swells into Importance, when it presses immediately on our attention. He that shall peruse the political Pamphlets of any past Reign, will wonder why they were so eagerly read, or so loudly praised; many of the Performances which had Power to enflame Factions, and fill a Kingdom with Confusion, have now very little Effect upon a frigid Critick, and the Time is coming, when the Compositions of later Hirelings shall lie equally despised. In Proportion, as those who write on temporary Subjects, are exalted above their Merit at first, they are afterwards depressed below it; nor can the brightest Elegance of Diction, or most artful Subtilty of Reasoning, hope for much Esteem from those whose Regard is no longer quickened by curiosity or Pride.

IT is, indeed, the Fate of Controvertists, even when they contend for philosophical or theological Truth, to be soon laid aside and slighted. Either the Question is decided and there is no more Place for Doubt and Opposition; or Mankind despair of understanding it, and grow weary of disturbance, content themselves with quiet Ignorance, and refuse to be harassed with Labours which they have no hopes of recompensing with Knowledge.

THE Authors of new Discoveries may surely expect to be reckoned among those whose Writings are secure of Veneration, yet it often happens that the general Reception of a Doctrine obscures the Books in which it was delivered. When any Tenet is generally received and adopted as an incontrovertible Principle, we seldom look back to the Arguments upon which it was first established, or can bear that Tediousness of Deduction and Multiplicity of Evidence by which its Author was forced to reconcile it to Prejudice, and fortify it in the Weakness of Novelty against Obstinacy and Envy.

IT is well known how much of our Philosophy is

derived from *Boyle's*[7] Discovery of the Qualities of the Air; yet of those who now adopt or enlarge his Theory, very few have read the Detail of his Experiments. His Name is, indeed, reverenced, but his Works are neglected; we are contented to know that he conquered his Opponents, without enquiring what Cavils were produced against him, or by what Proofs they were confuted.

SOME Writers apply themselves to Studies boundless and inexhaustible, as Experiments and natural Philosophy. These are always lost in successive Compilations, as new Advances are made, and former Observations become more familiar. Others spend their Lives in Remarks on Language, or Explanations of Antiquities, and only afford Materials for Lexicographers and Commentators, who are themselves overwhelmed by subsequent Collectors, that equally destroy the Memory of their Predecessors by Amplification, Transposition, or Contraction. Every new System of Nature gives Birth to a Swarm of Expositors, whose Business is to explain and illustrate it, and who can hope to exist no longer than the Founder of their Sect preserves his Reputation.

THERE are, indeed, few Kinds of Composition from which an Author, however learned or ingenious, can hope a long Continuance of Fame. He who has carefully studied human Nature, and can well describe it, may with most Reason flatter his ambition. *Bacon*, among all his Pretensions to the Regard of Posterity, seems to have pleased himself chiefly with his Essays,[8] *which come home to Mens Business and Bosoms*, and of which, therefore, he declares his Expectation, that they *will live as long as Books last.* It may, however, satisfy an honest and benevolent Mind to have been useful, though less conspicuous; nor will he that extends his Hope to higher Rewards, be so much anxious to obtain Praise, as to discharge the Duty which Providence assigns him.

NUMB. 128

Saturday, June 8, 1751.

Αἰὼν δ' ἀσφαλὴς
Οὐκ ἐγένετ', οὔτ' Αἰακίδᾳ παρὰ Πηλεῖ,
Οὔτε πὰρ' ἀντιθέῳ
Κάδμῳ' λέγονταί γε μὰν βρότων
Ὄλβον ὑπέρτατον οἳ
Σχεῖν.

PIND.[1]

For not the brave, or wise, or great,
E'er yet had happiness compleat;
Nor *Peleus*, grandson of the sky,
Nor *Cadmus*, scap'd the shafts of pain,
Though favour'd by the pow'rs on high,
With ev'ry bliss that man can gain.

THE Writers who have undertaken the Task of reconciling Mankind to their present State, and relieving the Discontent produced by the various Distribution of terrestrial Advantages, frequently remind us that we judge too hastily of Good and Evil, that we view only the Superficies of Life, and determine of the whole by a very small Part; and that in the Condition of Men it frequently happens, that Grief and Anxiety lye hid under the golden Robes of Prosperity, and the Gloom of Calamity is cheered by secret Radiations of Hope and Comfort; as in the Works of Nature the Bog is sometimes covered with Flowers, and the Mine concealed in the barren Crags.

NONE but those who have learned the Art of subjecting their Senses as well as Reason to hypothetical Systems can be persuaded by the most specious Rhetorician that the Lots of Life are equal; yet it cannot be denied that every one has his peculiar Pleasures and Vexations, that external Accidents operate variously upon different Minds, and that no Man can exactly judge from his own Sensations, what another would feel in the same Circumstances.

IF the general Disposition of Things be estimated by the Representation which every one makes of his own State, the World must be considered as the Abode of Sorrow and Misery: for how few can forbear to relate their Troubles and Distresses? If we judge by the Account which may be obtained of every Man's Fortune from others, it may be concluded,

---

7. **Boyle:** Robert Boyle (1627–91), chemist, one of the founders of the Royal Society. 8. **Essays:** The *Essays* of Sir Francis Bacon (1561–1626) were published in 1597 and issued in final form in 1625.

Number 128. I. **Pind.:** Pindar, *Pythian Odes*, iii. 153–58.

that we all are placed in an Elysian[2] Region, overspread with the Luxuriance of Plenty, and fanned by the Breezes of Felicity, since scarcely any Complaint is uttered without Censure from those that hear it, and almost all are allowed to have obtained a Provision at least adequate to their Virtue or their Understanding, to possess either more than they deserve, or more than they enjoy.

WE are either born with such Dissimilitude of Temper and Inclinations, or receive so many of our Ideas and Opinions from the State of Life in which we are engaged, that the Griefs and Cares of one Part of Mankind seem to the other Hypocrisy, Folly, and Affectation; every Class of Society has its Cant of Lamentation, which is understood or regarded by none but themselves, and every Part of Life has its Uneasinesses which those who do not feel them will not commiserate. An Event which spreads Distraction over half the Commercial World, assembles the trading Companies in Councils and Committees, and shakes the Nerves of a thousand Stockjobbers, is read by the Landlord and the Farmer with frigid Indifference. An Affair of Love which fills the young Breast with incessant Alternations of Hope and Fear, and steals away the Night and Day from every other Pleasure or Employment, is regarded by them whose Passions Time has extinguished, as an Amusement, which can properly raise neither Joy, nor Sorrow, and, though it may be suffered to fill the Vacuity of an idle Moment, should always give Way to Prudence or Interest.

HE that never had any other Desire than to fill a Chest with Money, or to add another Manour to his Estate, who never grieved but at a bad Mortgage, or entered a Company but to make a Bargain, would be astonished to hear of Beings known among the Polite and Gay, by the denomination of Wits. How would he gape with Curiosity, or grin with Contempt at the mention of beings who have no Wish but to speak what was never spoken before, who if they happen to inherit Wealth, often exhaust their Patrimonies in treating those who will hear them talk, and if they are poor, neglect Opportunities of improving their Fortunes for the Pleasure of making others laugh? How slowly would he believe that there are Men who would rather lose a Legacy than the Reputation of a Distich,[3] who think it less Disgrace to want Money than Repartee, whom the Vexation of having been

foiled in a Contest of Raillery is sometimes sufficient to deprive of Sleep, and who would esteem it a lighter Evil to miss a profitable Bargain by some accidental Delay, than not to have thought of a smart Reply till the Time of producing it was past? How little would he suspect that this Child of Idleness and Frolick enters every Assembly with a beating Bosom, like a litigant on the day of decision, and revolves the Probability of Applause with the Anxiety of a Conspirator, whose fate depends upon the next night; that at the Hour of Retirement he carries home, under a shew of airy Negligence, a Heart lacerated with Envy, or depressed with Disappointment, and immures himself in his Closet, that he may disencumber his Memory at Leisure, review the Progress of the Day, state with Accuracy his Loss or Gain of Reputation, and examine the Causes of his Failure or Success.

YET more remote from common Conceptions are the numerous and restless Anxieties, by which female Happiness is particularly disturbed. A solitary Philosopher would imagine Ladies born with an exemption from Care and Sorrow, lulled in perpetual quiet, and feasted with unmingled Pleasure; for what can interrupt the Content of those, upon whom one Age has laboured after another to confer Honours, and accumulate Immunities; those to whom Rudeness is Infamy, and Insult is Cowardice; whose Eye commands the Brave, and whose Smile softens the Severe; whom the Sailor travels to adorn, the Soldier bleeds to defend, and the Poet wears out Life to celebrate; who claim Tribute from every Art and Science, and for whom all who approach them endeavour to multiply Delights, without requiring from them any Return but Willingness to be pleased.

SURELY, among these Favourites of Nature, thus unacquainted with Toil and Danger, Felicity must have fixed her Residence; they must know only the Changes of more vivid or more gentle Joys; their Life must always move either to the slow or sprightly Melody of the Lyre of Gladness; they can never assemble but to Pleasure, or retire but to Peace.

SUCH would be the Thoughts of every Man who should hover at a Distance round the World, and know it only by Conjecture and Speculation. But Experience will soon discover how easily those are disgusted who have been made nice by plenty, and tender by Indulgence. He will soon see to how many Dangers Power is exposed which has no other Guard than youth and Beauty, and how easily that Tranquillity is molested which can only be soothed with

2. **Elysian:** from Elysium, in Greek mythology the happy abode of the virtuous after death. 3. **Distich:** couplet.

the Songs of flattery. It is impossible to supply Wants as fast as an idle Imagination may be able to form them, or to remove all Inconveniencies by which elegance refined into Impatience may be offended. None are so hard to please as those whom Satiety of Pleasure makes weary of themselves; nor any so readily provoked as those who have been always courted with an Emulation of Civility.

THERE are indeed some Strokes which the Envy of Fate aims immediately at the Fair. The Mistress of *Catullus* wept for her Sparrow many Centuries ago,[4] and Lapdogs will be sometimes sick in the present Age. The most fashionable Brocade is subject to Stains, a Pinner,[5] the Pride of *Brussels*, may be torn by a careless Washer, a Picture may drop from a Watch, or the Triumph of a new Suit may be interrupted on the first Day of its Enjoyment, and all Distinctions of Dress unexpectedly obliterated by a general Mourning.[6]

SUCH is the State of every Age, every Sex, and every Condition, all have their Cares, either from Nature or from Folly, and whoever therefore finds himself inclined to envy another, should remember that he knows not the real Condition which he desires to obtain, but is certain that by indulging a vicious Passion, he must lessen that Happiness which he thinks already too sparingly bestowed.

NUMB. 146

Saturday, August 10, 1751.

Sunt illic duo, tresve, qui revolvant
Nostrarum tineas ineptiarum:
Sed cum sponsio, fabulæque lassæ
De Scorpo fuerint et Incitato.
                              MART.[1]

'Tis possible that one or two
These fooleries of mine may view;
But then the bettings must be o'er,
Nor *Crab* or *Childers*[2] talk'd of more.
                              F. LEWIS.

NONE of the Projects or Designs which exercise the Mind of Man, are equally subject to Obstructions

and Disappointments with the Pursuit of Fame. Riches cannot easily be denied to them who have something of greater Value to offer in Exchange; he whose Fortune is endangered by Litigation, will not refuse to augment the Wealth of the Lawyer; he whose Days are darkened by Languor, or whose Nerves are excruciated by Pain, is compelled to pay Tribute to the Science of Healing. But Praise may be always omitted without Inconvenience; when once a Man has made Celebrity necessary to his Happiness, he has put it in the Power of the weakest and most timorous Malignity if not to take away his Satisfaction, at least to withhold it. His enemies may indulge their Pride by airy Negligence, and gratify their Malice by quiet Neutrality. They that could never have injured a Character by Invectives may combine to annihilate it by Silence, as the Women of *Rome* threatened, to put an End to Conquest and Dominion, by supplying no Children to the Commonwealth.

WHEN a Writer has with long Toil produced a Work intended to burst upon Mankind with unexpected Lustre, and withdraw the Attention of the learned World from every other controversy or enquiry, he is seldom contented to wait long without the Enjoyment of his new Praises. With an Imagination full of his own Importance, he walks out like a Monarch in Disguise, to learn the various Opinions of his Readers. Prepared to feast upon Admiration, composed to encounter Censures without Emotion, and determined not to suffer his Quiet to be injured by a Sensibility too exquisite of Praise or Blame, but to laugh with equal Contempt at vain Objections and injudicious Commendations, he enters the Places of mingled conversation, sits down to his Tea in an obscure Corner, and while he appears to examine a File of antiquated Journals, catches the Conversation of the whole Room. He listens, but hears no Mention of his Book, and therefore supposes that he has disappointed his Curiosity by Delay, and that as Men of Learning would naturally begin their Conversation with such a wonderful Novelty, they had digressed to other Subjects before his Arrival. The Company disperses, and their Places are supplied by others equally ignorant, or equally careless. The same Expectation hurries him to another Place, from which the same Disappointment drives him soon away. His Impatience then grows violent and tumultuous; he ranges over the Town with restless Curiosity, and hears in one Quarter of a Cricket-match, in another of a Pick-pocket; is told by some of an unexpected

---

4. The Mistress . . . ago: in a well-known lyric, *Lugete, O Veneres Cupidinesque*, by the first-century B.C. Roman poet Gaius Valerius Catullus. **5. Pinner:** woman's headdress with long flaps pinned on at the sides. **6. general Mourning:** e.g., upon the death of royalty. *Number 146.* **1. Mart.:** Martial, *Epigrams*, XI. i. 13–16. **2. Crab or Childers:** two famous racehorses.

Bankruptcy, by others of a Turtle Feast; is sometimes provoked by importunate Enquiries after the white Bear, and sometimes with praises of the dancing Dog; he is afterwards entreated to give his Judgment upon a Wager about the Height of the Monument;[3] invited to see a Foot Race in the adjacent Villages, desired to read a ludicrous Advertisement, or consulted about the most effectual Method of making Enquiry after a favourite Cat. The whole World is busied in Affairs, which he thinks below the Notice of reasonable Creatures, and which are nevertheless sufficient to withdraw all Regard from his Labours and his Merits.

He resolves at last to violate his own Modesty, and to recal the Talkers from their Folly by an Enquiry after himself; he finds every one provided with an Answer. One has seen the Work advertised, but never met with any that had read it; another has been so often imposed upon by specious Titles that he never buys a Book till its Character is established; a third wonders what any Man can hope to produce after so many Writers of greater Eminence; the next has enquired after the Author, but can hear no Account of him, and therefore suspects the Name to be fictitious; and another knows him to be a Man condemned by Indigence to write too frequently what he does not understand.

Many are the Consolations with which the unhappy Author endeavours to allay his Vexation, and fortify his Patience. He has written with too little Indulgence to the Understanding of common Readers; he has fallen upon an Age in which solid Knowledge, and delicate Refinement, have given Way to low Merriment and idle Buffoonery, and therefore no Writer can hope for Distinction, who has any higher Purpose than to raise Laughter. He finds that his Enemies, such as Superiority will always raise, have been industrious, while his Performance was in the Press, to vilify and blast it; and that the Bookseller, whom he had resolved to enrich, has Rivals that obstruct the Circulation of his Copies. He at last reposes upon the Consideration, that the noblest Works of Learning and Genius have always made their Way slowly against Ignorance and Prejudice; and that Reputation which is never to be lost must be gradually obtained, as Animals of longest Life are

observed not soon to attain their full Stature and Strength.

By such Arts of voluntary Delusion does every Man endeavour to conceal his own Unimportance from himself. It is long before we are convinced of the small Proportion which every Individual bears to the collective Body of Mankind, or learn how few can be interested in the Fortune of any single Man, how little Vacancy is left in the World for any new Object of Attention, to how small Extent the brightest Blaze of Merit can be spread amidst the Mists of Business and of Folly, and how soon it is clouded by the Intervention of other Novelties. Not only the Writer of books, but the Commander of Armies, and the Deliverer of Nations will easily outlive all noisy and popular Reputation; he may be celebrated for a Time by the publick Voice, but his Actions and his Name will soon be considered as remote and unaffecting, and be rarely mentioned but by those whose Alliance gives them some Vanity to gratify by frequent Commemoration.

It seems not to be sufficiently considered how little Renown can be admitted in the World. Mankind are kept perpetually busy by their Fears or Desires, and have not more Leisure from their own Affairs, than to acquaint themselves with the Accidents of the current Day. Engaged in contriving some Refuge from Calamity, or in shortening the Way to some new Possession, they seldom suffer their Thoughts to wander to the past or future; none but a few solitary Students have Leisure to enquire into the Claims of ancient Heroes or Sages; and names which hoped to range over Kingdoms and Continents, shrink at last into Cloysters or Colleges.

Nor is it certain, that even of these dark and narrow Habitations, these last Retreats of Fame, the Possession will be long kept. Of Men devoted to Literature very few extend their Views beyond some particular science, and the greater Part seldom enquire even in their own Profession for any Authors but those whom the present Mode of Study happens to force upon their Notice; they desire not to fill their Minds with unfashionable Knowledge, but contentedly resign to Oblivion those books which they now find censured or neglected.

The Hope of Fame is necessarily connected with such Considerations as must abate the Ardour of Confidence, and repress the Vigour of Pursuit. Whoever claims Renown from any kind of Excellence, expects to fill the Place which is now possessed

3. the **Monument**: erected in the City of London between 1671 and 1676 to commemorate the Great Fire of 1666. It is 202 feet high.

by another; for there are already Names of every Class sufficient to employ all that will desire to remember them; and surely he that is pushing his Predecessors into the Gulph of Obscurity, cannot but sometimes suspect, that he must himself sink in like Manner, and as he stands upon the same Precipice be swept away with the same Violence.

It sometimes happens, that Fame begins when Life is at an End, but far the greater Number of Candidates for Applause have owed their Reception in the World to some favourable casualties, and have therefore immediately sunk into Neglect, when death stripped them of their casual influence, and neither Fortune nor Patronage operated in their Favour. Among those who have better Claims to Regard, the Honour paid to their Memory is commonly proportionate to the Reputation which they enjoyed in their Lives, tho' still growing fainter, as it is at a greater Distance from the first Emission; and since it is so difficult to obtain the Notice of Contemporaries, how little is to be hoped from future Times? What can Merit effect by its own Force, when the Help of Art or Friendship can scarcely support it?

NO. 154

Saturday, September 7, 1751.

—*Tibi res antiquæ laudis & artis*
Aggredior, sanctos ausus recludere fontes.
VIRG.[1]

For thee my tuneful accents will I raise,
And treat of arts disclos'd in ancient days;
Once more unlock for thee the sacred spring.
DRYDEN.

THE Direction of *Aristotle* to those that study Politicks, is, first to examine and understand what has been written by the Antients upon Government, then to cast their Eyes round upon the World, and consider by what Causes the Prosperity of Communities is visibly influenced, and why some are worse and others better administered.[2]

THE same Method must be pursued by him who hopes to become eminent in any other Part of Knowledge. The first Task is to search Books, the next to contemplate Nature. He must first possess himself of

Number 154. **1.** Virg.: Virgil, *Georgics,* II. 174–75. **2. The Direction . . . administered:** *Politics,* II.

the intellectual Treasures which the Diligence of former Ages has accumulated, and then endeavour to encrease them by his own Collections.

THE mental Disease of the present Generation, is Impatience of Study, Contempt of the great Masters of antient Wisdom, and a Disposition to rely wholly upon unassisted Genius and natural Sagacity. The Wits of these happy Days have discovered a Way to Fame, which the dull Caution of our laborious Ancestors durst never attempt, they cut the Knots of Sophistry which it was formerly the Business of Years to untie, solve Difficulties by sudden Irradiations of Intelligence, and comprehend long Processes of Argument by immediate Intuition.

MEN who have flattered themselves into this Opinion of their own Abilities, look down on all who waste their Lives over Books, as a Race of inferior Beings, condemned by Nature to perpetual Pupillage, and fruitlessly endeavouring to remedy their Barrenness by incessant Cultivation, or succour their Feebleness by subsidiary Strength. They presume that none would be more industrious than they, if they were not more sensible of Deficiencies, and readily conclude, that he who places no Confidence in his own Powers, owes his Modesty only to his Weakness.

IT is however certain that no Estimate is more in Danger of erroneous Calculations than those by which a Man computes the Force of his own Genius. It generally happens at our Entrance into the World, that by the natural Attraction of Similitude, we associate with Men like ourselves, young, sprightly, and ignorant, and rate our Accomplishments by Comparison with theirs; when we have once obtained an acknowledged Superiority over our Acquaintances, Imagination and Desire easily extend it over the rest of Mankind, and if no Accident forces us into new Emulations, we grow old and die in Admiration of ourselves.

VANITY, thus confirmed in her Dominion, readily listens to the Voice of Idleness, and sooths the Slumber of Life with continual Dreams of Excellence and Greatness. A Man elated by confidence in his natural Vigour of Fancy and Sagacity of Conjecture, soon concludes that he already possesses whatever Toil and Enquiry can confer; he then listens with Eagerness to the wild Objections which Folly has raised against the common Means of Improvement, talks of the dark Chaos of indigested Knowledge, describes the mischievous Effects of heterogeneous Sciences fermenting in the Mind, relates the Blunders of lettered Ignorance, expatiates on the heroick Merit of those who deviate from Prescription, or shake off Authority, and gives Vent to the Inflations of his Heart by declaring that he owes nothing to Pedants and Universities.

ALL these Pretensions, however confident, are very often vain. The Laurels which superficial Acuteness gains in Triumphs over Ignorance unsupported by Vivacity, are observed by *Locke* to be lost, whenever real Learning and rational Diligence appear against her;[3] the Sallies of Gaiety are soon repressed by calm confidence; and the Artifices of Subtilty are readily detected by those, who, having carefully studied the Question, are not easily confounded or surprised.

BUT though the Contemner of Books had neither been deceived by others nor himself, and was really born with a Genius surpassing the ordinary Abilities of Mankind; yet surely such Gifts of Providence may be more properly urged as Incitements to Labour, than Encouragements to Negligence. He that neglects the Culture of Ground, naturally fertile, is more shamefully culpable than he whose Field would scarcely recompence his Husbandry.

CICERO remarks, that not to know what has been transacted in former Times is to continue always a Child.[4] If no use is made of the Labours of past ages, the World must remain always in the Infancy of Knowledge. The Discoveries of every Man must terminate in his own Advantage, and the Studies of every Age be employed on Questions, which the past Generation had discussed and determined. We may with as little Reproach borrow Science as Manufactures from our Ancestors, and it is as rational to live in Caves till our own Hands have erected a Palace, as to reject all Knowledge of Architecture, which our Understandings will not supply.

To the strongest and quickest Mind it is far easier to learn than to invent. The Principles of Arithmetick and Geometry may be comprehended by a close Attention in a few Days, yet who can flatter himself, that the Study of a long Life would have enabled him to discover them, when he sees them yet unknown to so many Nations, whom he cannot suppose less liberally endowed with natural Reason, than the *Grecians* or *Egyptians*?

EVERY Science was thus far advanced towards Perfection, by the emulous Diligence of contemporary Students, and the gradual Discoveries of one Age improving on another. Sometimes unexpected Flashes of Instruction were struck out by the fortuitous Collision of happy Incidents, or an involuntary Concurrence of Ideas, in which the Philosopher to whom they happened had no other Merit than that of knowing their Value, and transmitting unclouded to Posterity that Light which had been kindled by Causes out of his Power. The Happiness of these casual Illuminations no Man can promise to himself, because no Endeavours can procure them; and therefore whatever be our Abilities or Application, we must submit to learn from others what perhaps would have lain hid for ever from human Penetration, had not some remote Enquiry brought it to view, as Treasures are thrown up by the Ploughman and the Digger in the rude Exercise of their common Occupations.

THE Man whose Genius qualifies him for great Undertakings must at least be content to learn from Books the present State of human Knowledge, that he may not ascribe to himself the Invention of Arts generally known, weary his Attention with Experiments of which the Event has been long registered, and waste, in Attempts which have already succeeded or miscarried, that Time, which might have been spent, with Usefulness and Honour, upon new Undertakings.

BUT though the Study of Books is necessary, it is not sufficient to constitute literary Eminence. He that wishes to be counted among the Benefactors of Posterity, must add by his own Toil to the Acquisitions of his Ancestors, and secure his Memory from Neglect by some valuable Improvement. This can only be effected by looking out upon the Wastes of the intellectual World, and extending the Power of Learning over Regions yet undisciplined and barbarous; or by surveying more exactly her antient Dominions, and driving Ignorance from the Fortresses and Retreats where she skulks undetected and undisturbed. Every Science has its Difficulties which yet call for Solution before we attempt new Systems of Knowledge, as every Country has its Forests and Marshes, which it would be wise to cultivate and drain, before distant Colonies are projected as a necessary Discharge of the Exuberance of Inhabitants.

No man ever yet became great by Imitation. Whatever hopes for the Veneration of Mankind must have Invention in the Design or the Execution, either the Effect must itself be new, or the Means by which it is produced. Either Truths hitherto unknown must be discovered, or those which are already known

3. **The Laurels . . . her:** *Of the Conduct of the Understanding,* sec. 38. **4. Cicero . . . Child:** *De Oratore,* l. 120.

enforced by stronger Evidence, facilitated by clearer Method, or elucidated by brighter Illustrations.

FAME cannot spread wide or endure long that is not rooted in Nature, and manured by Art. That which hopes to resist the Blast of Malignity, and stand firm against the Attacks of Time, must contain in itself some original Principle of Growth. The Reputation which arises from the Detail or Transposition of borrowed Sentiments may spread for a while, like Ivy on the Rind of Antiquity, but will be torn away by Accident or Contempt, and suffered to rot unheeded on the Ground.

NO. 158

Saturday, September 21, 1751.

Grammatici certant et adhuc sub Judice lis est.
                    HOR.[1]
        —Criticks yet contend,
And of their vain disputings find no end.
                    FRANCIS.

CRITICISM, though dignified from the earliest Ages by the Labours of Men eminent for Knowledge and Sagacity, and since the Revival of polite Literature, the favourite Study of *European* Scholars, has not yet attained the Certainty and Stability of Science. The Rules hitherto received are seldom drawn from any settled Principle or self-evident Postulate, or adapted to the natural and invariable Constitution of Things; but will be found upon Examination the arbitrary Edicts of legislators,[2] authorised only by themselves, who out of various Means by which the same End may be attained, selected such as happened to occur to their own Reflection, and then by a law which Idleness and Timidity were too willing to obey, prohibited new Experiments of Wit, restrained Fancy from the Indulgence of her innate Inclination to hazard and adventure, and condemned all future flights of Genius to pursue the Path of the *Meonian Eagle.*[3]

THIS authority may be more justly opposed, as it is apparently derived from them whom they endeavour to controul; for we owe few of the Rules of Writing to the Acuteness of Criticks, who have generally no other Merit than that, having read the Works of great Authors with Attention, they have observed the Arrangement of their Matter, or the Graces of their Expression, and then expected Honour and Reverence for Precepts which they never could have invented; so that Practice has introduced Rules, rather than Rules have directed Practice.

FOR this Reason the Laws of every Species of Writing have been settled by the Ideas of him who first raised it to Reputation, without Enquiry whether his Performances were not yet susceptible of Improvement. The Excellencies and Faults of celebrated Writers have been equally recommended to Posterity, and so far has blind Reverence prevailed, that even the Number of their Books has been thought worthy of Imitation.

THE Imagination of the first Authors of lyrick Poetry was vehement and rapid, and their Knowledge various and extensive. Living in an Age when Science had been little cultivated, and when the Minds of their Auditors not being accustomed to accurate Inspection, were easily dazzled by glaring Ideas; they applied themselves to instruct, rather by short Sentences and striking Thoughts than by regular Argumentation, and finding Attention more successfully excited by sudden Sallies and unexpected Exclamations, than by the more artful and placid Beauties of methodical Deduction, they loosed their Genius to its own course, passed from one Sentiment to another, without expressing the intermediate Ideas, and roved at large over the ideal World, with such Lightness and Agility that their Footsteps are scarcely to be traced.

FROM this accidental Peculiarity of the antient Writers, the Criticks deduce the Rules of lyrick Poetry, which they have set free from all the Laws by which other Compositions are confined, and allow to neglect the Niceties of Transition, to start into remote Digressions, and to wander without Restraint from one Scene of Imagery to another.

A WRITER of later Times[4] has, by the Vivacity of his Essays, reconciled Mankind to the same Licentiousness in short Dissertations, and he therefore who wants Skill to form a Plan or Diligence to pursue it, needs only entitle his Performance an Essay to acquire the Right of heaping together the Collections of half his Life, without Order, Coherence or Propriety.

Number 158. 1. Hor.: Horace, *Ars Poetica,* l. 78. **2. legislators:** The first edition reads: "Dictators." **3. the Meonian Eagle:** Homer, thought to have been born in Maeonia.

4. A Writer . . . Times: Michel de Montaigne (1533–92), the French humanist, whose *Essais* were published in 1580 and in 1588.

In Writing, as in Life, Faults are endured without Disgust when they are associated with transcendent Merit, and may be sometimes recommended to weak Judgments by the Lustre which they obtain from their Union with Excellence; but it is the Business of those who presume to superintend the Taste or Morals of Mankind, to separate delusive Combinations, and distinguish that which may be praised from that which can only be excused. As Vices never promote Happiness, though, when overpowered by more active and more numerous Virtues they cannot totally destroy it; so Confusion and Irregularity produce no Beauty, though they cannot always obstruct the brightness of Genius and Learning. To proceed from one Truth to another, and connect distant Propositions by regular Consequences is the great Prerogative of Man. Independent and unconnected Sentiments flashing upon the Mind in quick Succession may for a Time delight by their Novelty, but they differ from systematical Reasoning, as single Notes from Harmony, as Glances of Lightning from the Radiance of the Sun.

When Rules are thus drawn, rather from Precedents than Reason, there is Danger not only from the Faults of an Author but from the Errors of those who criticise his Works, since they may often mislead their Pupils by false Representations as the *Ciceronians* of the sixteenth Century[5] were betrayed into Barbarisms by corrupt Copies of their darling Writer.

It is established at present, that the proemial Lines of a Poem, in which the general Subject is proposed, must be void of Glitter and Embellishment. "The first Lines of *Paradise Lost*," says *Addison*, "are perhaps as plain, simple and unadorned as any of the whole Poem, in which Particular the Author has conformed himself to the Example of *Homer* and the Precept of *Horace*."[6]

This Observation seems to have been made by an implicit Adoption of the common Opinion without Consideration either of the Precept or Example. Had *Horace* been consulted, he would have been found to direct only what should be comprised in the Proposition, not how it should be expressed, and to have commended *Homer* in Opposition to a meaner Poet, not for the gradual Elevation of his Diction, but the judicious Expansion of his Plan, for displaying unpromised Events, not for producing unexpected Elegancies.

—*Speciosa dehinc miracula promit*
Antiphaten Scyllamque & cum Cyclope Charybdim.[7]

But from a cloud of smoke he breaks to light,
And pours his specious miracles to sight;
Antiphates his hideous feast devours,
Charybdis barks, and *Polyphemus* roars.
FRANCIS.

If the exordial[8] verses of *Homer* be compared with the rest of the Poem, they will not appear remarkable for Plainness or Simplicity, but rather eminently adorned and illuminated.

Ἄνδρά μοι ἔννεπε, Μοῦσα, πολύτροπον, ὃς μάλα πολλὰ
Πλάγχθη, ἐπεὶ Τροίης ἱερὸν πτολίεθρον ἔπερσε·
Πολλῶν δ' ἀνθρώπων ἴδεν ἄστεα, καὶ νόον ἔγνω·
Πολλὰ δ' ὅγ' ἐν πόντῳ πάθεν ἄλγεα ὃν κατὰ θυμόν,
Ἀρνύμενος ἥν τε ψυχὴν καὶ νόστον ἑταίρων·
Ἀλλ' οὐδ' ὣς ἑτάρους ἐρρύσατο, ἱέμενός περ·
Αὐτῶν γὰρ σφετέρῃσιν ἀτασθαλίῃσιν ὄλοντο·
Νήπιοι, οἳ κατὰ βοῦς ὑπερίονος Ἠελίοιο
Ἤσθιον· αὐτὰρ ὁ τοῖσιν ἀφείλετο νόστιμον ἦμαρ·
Τῶν ἀμόθεν γε, θεά, θύγατερ Διός, εἰπὲ καὶ ἡμῖν.

The man, for wisdom's various arts renown'd,
Long exercis'd in woes, O muse! resound.
Who, when his arms had wrought the destin'd fall
Of sacred *Troy*, and raz'd her heav'n-built wall,
Wand'ring from clime to clime, observant stray'd,
Their manners noted, and their states survey'd.
On stormy seas unnumber'd toils he bore,
Safe with his friends to gain his natal shore:
Vain toils! their impious folly dar'd to prey
On herds devoted to the god of day;
The god vindictive doom'd them never more
(Ah men unbless'd) to touch that natal shore.
O snatch some portion of these acts from fate,
Celestial muse! and to our world relate.
POPE.

The first Verses of the *Iliad* are in like manner particularly splendid, and the Proposition of the *Æneid* closes with Dignity and Magnificence not often to be found even in the Poetry of *Virgil*.

The Intent of the Introduction is to raise Expectation and suspend it, something therefore must be

---

5. the Ciceronians . . . Century: writers like Sir John Cheke and Roger Ascham, who, in writing Latin, tried to eschew words not found in Cicero's writings. 6. The first . . . Horace: *The Spectator*, No. 303.

7. Speciosa . . . Charybdim: Horace, *Ars Poetica*, ll. 144–45. 8. exordial: prefatory.

discovered and something concealed; and the Poet while the Fertility of his Invention is yet unknown, may properly recommend himself by the Grace of his Language.

HE that reveals too much or promises too little, he that never irritates the intellectual Appetite, or that immediately satiates it, equally defeats his own Purpose. It is necessary to the Pleasure of the Reader, that the Events should not be anticipated, and how then can his Attention be invited, but by Grandeur of Expression?

✓NO. 168

Saturday, October 26, 1751.

——Decipit
Frons prima multos, rara mens intelligit
Quod interiore condidit cura angulo.
                    PHÆDRUS.[1]
The tinsel glitter, and the specious mien,
Delude the most; few pry behind the scene.

IT has been observed by *Boileau*, that "a mean or common Thought expressed in pompous Diction, generally pleases more than a new or noble Sentiment delivered in low and vulgar Language; because the Number is greater of those whom Custom has enabled to judge of Words, than whom Study has qualified to examine Things."[2]

THIS Solution might satisfy, if such only were offended with Meanness of Expression as are unable to distinguish Propriety of Thought, and to separate Propositions or Images from the Vehicles by which they are conveyed to the Understanding. But this Kind of Disgust is by no means confined to the ignorant or superficial; it operates uniformly and universally upon Readers of all Classes; every Man, however profound or abstracted, perceives himself irresistibly alienated by low Terms; they who profess the most zealous Adherence to Truth are forced to admit that she owes Part of her Charms to her Ornaments, and loses much of her Power over the Soul, when she appears disgraced by a Dress uncouth or ill-adjusted.

WE are all offended by low Terms, but are not disgusted alike by the same Compositions, because

we do not all agree to censure the same Terms as low. No Word is naturally or intrinsically meaner than another; our opinion therefore of Words, as of other Things arbitrarily and capriciously established, depends wholly upon Accident and Custom. The Cottager thinks those Apartments splendid and spacious, which an Inhabitant of Palaces will despise for their Inelegance; and to him who has passed most of his Hours with the delicate and polite, many Expressions will seem sordid, which another, equally acute, may hear without Offence; but a mean Term never fails to displease him to whom it appears mean, as Poverty is certainly and invariably despised, though he who is poor in the eyes of some, may by others be envied for his Wealth.

WORDS become low by the Occasions to which they are applied, or the general Character of them who use them, and the Disgust which they produce, arises from the Revival of those images with which they are commonly united. Thus if, in the most solemn Discourse, a Phrase happens to occur which has been successfully employed in some ludicrous Narrative, the gravest Auditor finds it difficult to refrain from Laughter, when they who are not prepossessed by the same accidental Association, are utterly unable to guess the Reason of his Merriment. Words which convey Ideas of Dignity in one Age, are banished from elegant Writing or Conversation in another, because they are in time debased by vulgar Mouths, and can be no longer heard without the involuntary Recollection of unpleasing Images.

WHEN *Macbeth* is confirming himself in the horrid Purpose of stabbing his king, he breaks out amidst his Emotions into a Wish natural to a Murderer,

—Come, thick Night!
And pall thee in the dunnest Smoke of Hell,
That my keen Knife see not the Wound it makes;
Nor Heav'n peep through the Blanket of the dark,
To cry, Hold, hold![3]——

In this Passage is exerted all the Force of Poetry, that Force which calls new Powers into Being, which embodies Sentiment and animates Matter; yet perhaps scarce any Man now peruses it without some Disturbance of his Attention from the Counteraction of the Words to the Ideas. What can be more dreadful than to implore the Presence of Night, invested not in

---

Number 168. **1. Phædrus:** *Fables*, IV. ii. 5–7. **2. a mean . . . Things:** *Critical Reflections on Some Passages out of Longinus,* Reflection ix.

3. Come . . . hold: *Macbeth*, I. v. 51–55. The speaker is actually Lady Macbeth.

common Obscurity, but in the Smoke of Hell? Yet the efficacy of this Invocation is destroyed by the Insertion of an Epithet now seldom heard but in the Stable, and *dun* Night may come or go without any other Notice than Contempt.

IF we start into Raptures when some Hero of the Iliad tells us that δόρυ μαίνεται, his Lance rages with Eagerness to destroy; if we are alarmed at the Terror of the Soldiers commanded by *Cæsar* to hew down the sacred Grove, who dreaded, says *Lucan*, lest the Axe aimed at the Oak should fly back upon the striker:

—*Si robora sacra ferirent,*
In sua credebant redituras membra secures,[4]

None dares with impious steel the grove to rend,
Lest on himself the destin'd stroke descend;

we cannot surely but sympathise with the Horrors of a Wretch about to murder his Master, his Friend, his Benefactor, who suspects that the Weapon will refuse its Office, and start back from the Breast which he is preparing to violate. Yet this Sentiment is weakened by the Name of an Instrument used by Butchers and Cooks in the meanest Employments; we do not immediately conceive that any Crime of Importance is to be committed with a *Knife;* or who does not, at last, from the long Habit of connecting a Knife with sordid Offices, feel Aversion rather than Terror?

MACBETH proceeds to wish, in the Madness of Guilt, that the Inspection of Heaven may be intercepted, and that he may in the Involutions of infernal Darkness escape the Eye of Providence. This is the utmost Extravagance of determined Wickedness; yet this is so debased by two unfortunate Words, that while I endeavour to impress on my Reader the Energy of the Sentiment, I can scarce check my Risibility, when the Expression forces itself upon my Mind; for who, without some Relaxation of his Gravity, can hear of the avengers of guilt *peeping thro' a Blanket.*

THESE Imperfections of Diction are less obvious to the Reader, as he is less acquainted with common Usages; they are therefore wholly imperceptible to a Foreigner, who learns our Language from Books, and will strike a solitary Academick less forcibly than a modish Lady.

AMONG the numerous Requisites that must concur

to complete an Author, few are of more Importance than an early Entrance into the living World. The Seeds of Knowledge may be planted in Solitude, but must be cultivated in publick. Argumentation may be taught in Colleges, and Theories formed in Retirement, but the Artifice of Embellishment, and the Powers of attraction, can be gained only by general Converse.

AN Acquaintance with prevailing Customs and fashionable Elegance is necessary likewise for other Purposes. The Injury that grand imagery suffers from unsuitable Language, personal Merit may fear from Rudeness and Indelicacy. When the Success of *Æneas* depended on the Favour of the Queen upon whose Coasts he was driven, his celestial protectress thought him not sufficiently secured against Rejection by his piety or Bravery, but decorated him for the Interview with preternatural Beauty.[5] Whoever desires, for his writings or himself, what none can reasonably contemn, the Favour of Mankind, must add Grace to Strength, and make his thoughts agreeable as well as useful. Many complain of Neglect who never tried to attract Regard. It cannot be expected that the Patrons of Science or Virtue should be solicitous to discover Excellencies, which they who possess them shade and disguise. Few have Abilities so much needed by the rest of the World as to be caressed on their own Terms, and he that will not condescend to recommend himself by external Embellishments, must submit to the Fate of just Sentiments meanly expressed, and be ridiculed and forgotten before he is understood.

✓ NO. 180

Saturday, December 7, 1751.

Ταῶτ εἰδὼς σοφὸς ἰσθι μάτην δ' Επίκουρον ἔασον
Ποῦ τὸ κενὸν ζητεῖν, καὶ τίνες αἱ μονάδες.
　　　　　　　　　　　　AUTOMEDON.[1]

On life, on morals, be thy thoughts employ'd;
Leave to the schools their atoms and their void.

IT is somewhere related by *Le Clerc,*[2] that a wealthy Trader of good Understanding, having the common Ambition to breed his Son a Scholar, carried him to

---

4. Si . . . secures: *Pharsalia,* III. 430–31.

5. When . . . Beauty: *Aeneid,* I. 586–93. *Number 180.* I.
Automedon: *Greek Anthology,* xi. 50. 2. Le Clerc: Jean
Le Clerc (1657–1736), Swiss critic and theologian.

an University, resolving to use his own Judgment in the Choice of a Tutor. He had been taught, by whatever Intelligence, the nearest Way to the Heart of an Academick, and at his Arrival entertained all who came about him with such Profusion, that the Professors were lured by the Smell of his Table from their Books, and flocked round him with all the cringes of aukward Complaisance. This Eagerness answered the Merchant's Purpose; he glutted them with Delicacies, and softened them with Caresses, till he prevailed upon one after another to open his Bosom, and make a Discovery of his Competitions, Jealousies, and Resentments. Having thus learned each Man's Character, partly from himself, and partly from his Acquaintances, he resolved to find some other education for his Son, and went away convinced, that a scholastic Life has no other Tendency than to vitiate the Morals, and contract the Understanding: nor would he afterwards hear with Patience the Praises of the ancient Authors, being persuaded that Scholars of all Ages must have been the same, and that Xenophon[3] and Cicero were Professors of some former University, and therefore mean and selfish, ignorant and servile, like those whom he had lately visited and forsaken.

Envy, Curiosity, and a Sense of the Imperfection of our present State, incline us to estimate the Advantages which are in the Possession of others above their real Value. Every one must have remarked, what Powers and Prerogatives the Vulgar imagine to be conferred by Learning. A Man of Science is expected to excel the unlettered and unenlightened, even on Occasions where Literature is of no Use, and among weak Minds, loses Part of his Reverence by discovering no Superiority in those Parts of Life, in which all are unavoidably equal; as when a Monarch makes a Progress to the remoter Provinces, the Rusticks are said sometimes to wonder that they find him of the same Size with themselves.

These Demands of Prejudice and Folly can never be satisfied; and therefore many of the Imputations which Learning suffers from disappointed Ignorance, are without Reproach. But there are some Failures, to which Men of Study are peculiarly exposed. Every Condition has its Disadvantages. The Circle of Knowledge is too wide for the most active and diligent Intellect, and while Science is pursued, other accomplishments are neglected; as a small Garrison

must leave one Part of an extensive Fortress naked when an Alarm calls them to another.

The Learned, however, might generally support their Dignity with more Success, if they suffered not themselves to be misled by the Desire of superfluous Attainments. Raphael in return to Adam's Enquiries into the Courses of the Stars, and the Revolutions of Heaven, counsels him to withdraw his Mind from idle Speculations, and employ his Faculties upon nearer and more interesting Objects, the Survey of his own Life, the Subjection of his Passions, the Knowledge of Duties which must daily be performed, and the Detection of Dangers which must daily be incurred.[4]

This angelick Counsel every Man of Letters should always have before him. He that devotes himself to retired Study, naturally sinks from omission to forgetfulness of social Duties; he must be therefore sometimes awakened and recalled to the general Condition of Mankind.

I am far from any Intention to limit Curiosity, or confine the Labours of Learning to Arts of immediate and necessary Use. It is only from the various Essays of experimental Industry, and the vague Excursions of Minds, sent out upon Discovery, that any Advancement of Knowledge can be expected; and tho' many must be disappointed in their labours, yet they are not to be charged with having spent their Time in vain; their Example contributed to inspire Emulation, and their Miscarriages taught others the Way to Success.

But the distant Hope of being one Day useful or eminent, ought not to mislead us too far from that study which is equally requisite to the great and mean, to the celebrated and obscure; the Art of moderating the Desires, of repressing the Appetites, and of conciliating or retaining the Favour of Mankind.

No Man can imagine the course of his own Life, or the Conduct of the world around him, unworthy his Attention; yet, among the Sons of Learning, many seem to have Thought of every Thing rather than of themselves, and to have observed every thing but what passes before their Eyes: Many who toil through the Intricacy of complicated Systems, are insuperably embarrassed with the least Perplexity in common Affairs; many who compare the Actions, and ascertain the Characters of ancient Heroes, let their own Days glide away without Examination, and suffer vicious

---

3. Xenophon: (c. 434–c. 355 B.C.), Greek historian.

4. Raphael . . . incurred: See Paradise Lost, VIII. 167–97.

Habits to encroach upon their Minds without Resistance or Detection.

THE most frequent Reproach of the scholastick Race is the Want of Fortitude, not martial but philosophick. Men bred in Shades and Silence, taught to immure themselves at Sunset, and accustomed to no other Weapon than Syllogism, may be allowed to feel terror at personal Danger, and to be disconcerted by Tumult and Alarm. But why should he whose Life is spent in Contemplation, and whose Business is only to discover Truth, be unable to rectify the Fallacies of Imagination, or contend successfully against Prejudice and Passion? To what end has he read and meditated, if he gives up his Understanding to false Appearances, and suffers himself to be enslaved by Fear of Evils to which only Folly or Vanity can expose him, or elated by Advantages to which, as they are equally conferred upon the good and bad, no real Dignity is annexed.

SUCH, however, is the State of the World, that the most obsequious of the Slaves of Pride, the most rapturous of the Gazers upon Wealth, the most officious of the Whisperers of Greatness, are collected from Seminaries appropriated to the Study of Wisdom and of Virtue, where it was intended that Appetite should learn to be content with little, and that hope should aspire only to Honours which no human Power can give or take away.

THE Student, when he comes forth into the world, instead of congratulating himself upon his Exemption from the Errors of those whose Opinions have been formed by accident or custom, and who live without any certain principles of conduct, is commonly in Haste to mingle with the Multitude, and shew his Sprightliness and Ductility by an expeditious Compliance with Fashions or Vices. The first Smile of a Man, whose Fortune gives him Power to reward his Dependents, commonly enchants him beyond Resistance; the Glare of Equipage, the Sweets of Luxury, the Liberality of general Promises, the Softness of habitual Affability, fill his Imagination, and he soon ceases to have any other Wish than to be well received, or any Measure of Right and Wrong but the Opinion of his Patron.

A MAN flattered and obeyed, learns to exact grosser Adulation, and enjoin lower Submission. Neither our Virtues nor Vices are all our own; if there were no Cowardice, there would be little Insolence; pride cannot rise to any great Degree, but by the Concurrence of Blandishment or the Sufferance of Tameness. The Wretch who would shrink and crouch before one that should dart his Eyes upon him with the Spirit of natural Equality, becomes capricious and tyrannical when he sees himself approached with a downcast Look, and hears the soft Address of Awe and Servility. To those who are willing to purchase Favour by Cringes and Compliance, is to be imputed the haughtiness that leaves nothing to be hoped by Firmness and Integrity.

IF instead of wandering after the Meteors of Philosophy which fill the World with Splendor for a while, and then sink and are forgotten, the Candidates of Learning fixed their Eyes upon the permanent Lustre of moral and religious Truth, they would find a more certain Direction to Happiness. A little plausibility of Discourse, and Acquaintance with unnecessary Speculations, is dearly purchased when it excludes those Instructions which fortify the Heart with Resolution and exalt the Spirit to Independence.

NO. 208

Saturday, March 14, 1752.

Ἡράκλειτος ἐγώ· τί με ὦ κάτω ἕλκετ' ἄμουσι;
Οὐχ' ὑμῖν ἐπόνουν, τοῖς δὲ μ' ἐπισταμένοις·
Εἷς ἐμοὶ ἄνθρωπος τρισμύριοι· οἱ δ' ἀνάριθμοι
Οὐδείς· ταῦτ' αὐδῶ καὶ παρὰ Περσεφόνῃ·
                                   DIOG. LAERT.[1]

Begone, ye blockheads, *Heraclitus* cries,
And leave my labours to the learn'd and wise,
By wit, by knowledge, studious to be read,
I scorn the multitude, alive and dead.

TIME, which puts an End to all human Pleasures and Sorrows, has likewise concluded the Labours of the RAMBLER. Having supported for two Years the anxious Employment of a periodical Writer, and multiplied my Essays to four volumes, I have now determined to desist.

THE Reasons of this Resolution it is of little Importance to declare, since Justification is unnecessary when no Objection is made. I am far from supposing, that the Cessation of my Performances will raise any Inquiry; for I have never been much a Favourite of the Publick, nor can boast that, in the Progress of my Undertaking, I have been animated by the Rewards

Number 208. **1. Diog. Laert.:** Diogenes Laertius, *Lives,* IX. i. 16.

of the Liberal, the Caresses of the Great, or the Praises of the Eminent.

But I have no design to gratify Pride by Submission, or Malice by Lamentation; nor think it reasonable to complain of Neglect from those whose regard I never solicited. If I have not been distinguished by the Distributers of literary Honours, I have seldom descended to the Arts by which Favour is obtained. I have seen the Meteors of Fashion rise and fall, without any Attempt to add a Moment to their Duration; I have never complied with temporary Curiosity, nor enabled my Readers to discuss the Topic of the Day; I have rarely exemplified my Assertions by living Characters; in my Papers, no Man could look for Censures of his Enemies, or Praises of himself; and they only were expected to peruse them, whose Passions left them Leisure for abstracted Truth, and whom Virtue could please by its naked Dignity.

To Some, however, I am indebted for Encouragement, and to others for Assistance; the Number of my Friends was never great, but they have been such as would not suffer me to think that I was writing in vain, and I did not feel much dejection from the Want of Popularity.

My Obligations having not been frequent, my Acknowledgements may be soon dispatched. I can restore to all my Correspondents their Productions, with little Diminution of the Bulk of my Volumes, tho' not without the Loss of some Pieces to which particular Honours have been paid.

The Parts, from which I claim no other Praise than that of having given them an Opportunity of appearing, are the four Billets in the tenth Paper, the second Letter in the fifteenth; the thirtieth, the forty-fourth, the ninety-seventh, and the hundredth Papers; and the second Letter in the hundred and seventh.

Having thus deprived myself of many Excuses, which Candor might have admitted for the Inequality of my Compositions, being no longer able to allege the Necessity of gratifying Correspondents, the Importunity with which Publication was solicited, or Obstinacy with which Correction was rejected, I must remain accountable for all my Faults, and submit without Subterfuge to the Censures of Criticism; which, however, I shall not endeavour to soften by a formal Deprecation, or to overbear by the Influence of a Patron. The Supplications of an Author never yet reprieved him a Moment from Oblivion; and, though Greatness has sometimes sheltered Guilt, it

can afford no Protection to Ignorance or Dulness. Having hitherto attempted only the Propagation of Truth, I will not at last violate it by the Confession of Terrors which I do not feel: Having laboured to maintain the Dignity of Virtue, I will not now degrade it by the Meanness of Dedication.

The seeming Vanity with which I have sometimes spoken of myself, would perhaps require an Apology, were it not extenuated by the Example of those who have published Essays before me, and by the Privilege which every nameless Writer has been hitherto allowed. "A Mask, says *Castiglione*, confers a Right of acting and speaking with less Restraint, even when the Wearer happens to be known."[2] He that is discovered without his own Consent, may claim some Indulgence, and cannot be rigorously called to justify those Sallies or Frolicks which his Disguise must prove him desirous to conceal.

But I have been cautious lest this Offence should be frequently or grossly committed; for as one of the Philosophers directs us to live with a Friend, as with one that is sometime to become an Enemy,[3] I have always thought it the Duty of an anonymous Author to write, as if he expected to be hereafter known.

I am willing to flatter my self with Hopes, that, by collecting these Papers, I am not preparing for my future Life either Shame or Repentance. That all are happily imagined, or accurately polished; that the same Sentiments have not sometimes recurred, or the same Expressions been too frequently repeated, I have not Confidence in my Abilities sufficient to warrant. He that condemns himself to compose on a stated Day, will often bring to his Task, an Attention dissipated, a Memory embarrassed, an Imagination overwhelmed, a Mind distracted with Anxieties, a Body languishing with Disease: He will labour on a barren Topic, till it is too late to change it; or, in the Ardour of Invention, diffuse his Thoughts into wild Exuberance, which the pressing Hour of Publication cannot suffer Judgment to examine or reduce.

Whatever shall be the final Sentence of Mankind, I have at least endeavoured to deserve their Kindness; I have laboured to refine our Language to grammatical Purity, and to clear it from colloquial Barbarisms, licentious Idioms, and irregular Combinations.

---

2. **A Mask . . . known:** *The Courtier,* Book II. 3. **live . . . Enemy:** one of the maxims of Publilius Syrus, Roman playwright of the first century B.C.

Something, perhaps, I have added to the Elegance of its Construction, and something to the Harmony of its Cadence. When common Words were less pleasing to the Ear, or less distinct in their Signification, I have familiarized the Terms of Philosophy,[4] by applying them to popular Ideas, but have rarely admitted any Word, not authorized by former Writers; for I believe, that whoever knows the *English* Tongue in its present Extent, will be able to express his Thoughts without further Help from other Nations.

As it has been my principal Design to inculcate Wisdom or Piety, I have allotted few Papers to the idle Sports of Imagination. Some, perhaps, may be found, of which the highest Excellence is harmless Merriment; but scarcely any Man is so steadily serious as not to complain, that the Severity of dictatorial Instruction has been too seldom relieved, and that he is driven by the Sternness of the Rambler's Philosophy to more chearful and airy Companions.

NEXT to the Excursions of Fancy are the Disquisitions of Criticism, which, in my Opinion, is only to be ranked among the subordinate and instrumental Arts. Arbitrary Decision and general Exclamation, I have carefully avoided, by asserting nothing without a Reason, and establishing all my Principles of Judgment on unalterable and evident Truth.

IN the Pictures of Life I have never been so studious of Novelty or Surprize, as to depart wholly from all Resemblance; a Fault which Writers deservedly celebrated frequently commit, that they may raise, as the Occasion requires, either Mirth or Abhorrence. Some Enlargement may be allowed to Declamation, and some Exaggeration to Burlesque; but as they deviate farther from reality, they become less useful, because their Lessons will fail of Application. The Mind of the Reader is carried away from the Contemplation of his own Manners; he finds in himself no Likeness to the Phantom before him; and though he laughs or rages, is not reformed.

THE Essays professedly serious, if I have been able to execute my own Intentions, will be found exactly conformable to the Precepts of Christianity, without any Accommodation to the Licentiousness and Levity of the present Age. I therefore look back on this Part of my Work with Pleasure, which no Blame or Praise of Man shall diminish or augment; I shall never envy the Honours which Wit and Learning obtain in any

4. **Philosophy:** experimental physical science.

other Cause, if I can be numbered among the Writers, who have given Ardour to Virtue, and Confidence to Truth.

Αὐτῶν ἐκ μακάρων ἀντάξιος εἴη ἀμοιβή.

Celestial pow'rs! that piety regard,
From you my labours wait their last reward.[5]

FROM

THE LITERARY MAGAZINE: OR, UNIVERSAL REVIEW

In 1757 Soame Jenyns (1704–87), a Cambridge graduate who became a miscellaneous writer and a member of Parliament, published *A Free Inquiry into the Nature and Origin of Evil*, a book in six "letters" that attempted to palliate the evils inherent in man's mortal condition, in physical nature, in politics, and even in systems of organized religion. Jenyns's conclusion is similar to Pope's in *An Essay on Man* (1733–34):

All Nature is but Art, unknown to thee;
All Chance, Direction which thou canst not see;
All Discord, Harmony not understood;
All partial Evil, universal Good.

Johnson would have none of it. He reviewed the book the same year in *The Literary Magazine*, and before he had had his entire say, his review grew so long that it had to be spread over three numbers (May, June, and July). Boswell thought it "Johnson's most exquisite critical essay."

The text is that of the first printing, in *The Literary Magazine: or, Universal Review* (1757). Our selection comprises slightly less than half the original.

This doctrine of the regular subordination of beings, the scale of existence, and the chain of nature,[1] I have

5. **Celestial . . . reward:** Johnson is translating Dionysius' *Periegesis*, l. 1186. THE LITERARY MAGAZINE. **I. the chain . . . nature:** At the beginning of his second "Letter," Jenyns argues that God's arrangement of His creatures in a hierarchical "scale of beings" presupposes a harmony in the whole "vast and magnificent fabrick"; but this harmony, he goes on, is purchased by limitations on the felicity of individuals.

often considered, but always left the Inquiry in doubt and uncertainty.

That every being not infinite, compared with infinity, must be imperfect, is evident to intuition; that whatever is imperfect must have a certain line which it cannot pass, is equally certain. But the reason which determined this limit, and for which such being was suffered to advance thus far and no further, we shall never be able to discern. Our discoveries tell us, the Creator has made beings of all orders, and that therefore one of them must be such as man. But this system seems to be established on a concession which if it be refused cannot be extorted.

Every reason which can be brought to prove, that there are beings of every possible sort, will prove that there is the greatest number possible of every sort of beings; but this with respect to man we know, if we know any thing, not to be true.

It does not appear even to the imagination, that of three orders of being, the first and the third receive any advantage from the imperfection of the second, or that indeed they may not equally exist, though the second had never been, or should cease to be, and why should that be concluded necessary, which cannot be proved even to be useful?

The scale of existence from infinity to nothing, cannot possibly have being. The highest being not infinite must be, as has been often observed, at an infinite distance below infinity. *Cheyne*,[2] who, with the desire inherent in mathematicians to reduce every thing to mathematical images, considers all existence as a *cone*, allows that the basis[3] is at an infinite distance from the body. And in this distance between finite and infinite, there will be room for ever for an infinite series of indefinable existence.

Between the lowest positive existence and nothing, wherever we suppose positive existence to cease, is another chasm infinitely deep; where there is room again for endless orders of subordinate nature, continued for ever and for ever, and yet infinitely superior to non-existence.

To these meditations humanity is unequal. But yet we may ask, not of our maker, but of each other, since on the one side creation, wherever it stops, must stop infinitely below infinity, and on the other infinitely above nothing, what necessity there is that it

should proceed so far either way, that beings so high or so low should ever have existed. We may ask; but I believe no created wisdom can give an adequate answer.

Nor is this all. In the scale, wherever it begins or ends, are infinite vacuities. At whatever distance we suppose the next order of beings to be above man, there is room for an intermediate order of beings between them; and if for one order then for infinite orders; since every thing that admits of more or less, and consequently all the parts of that which admits them, may be infinitely divided. So that, as far as we can judge, there may be room in the vacuity between any two steps of the scale, or between any two points of the cone of being for infinite exertion of infinite power.

Thus it appears how little reason those who repose their reason upon the scale of being have to triumph over them who recur to any other expedient of solution, and what difficulties arise on every side to repress the rebellions of presumptuous decision. *Qui pauca considerat, facile pronunciat*.[4] In our passage through the boundless ocean of disquisition we often take fogs for land, and after having long toiled to approach them find, instead of repose and harbours, new storms of objection and fluctuations of uncertainty.

We are next entertained with *Pope's* alleviations of those evils which we are doomed to suffer.[5]

"Poverty, or the want of riches, is generally compensated by having more hopes and fewer fears, by a greater share of health, and a more exquisite relish of the smallest enjoyments, than those who possess them are usually bless'd with. The want of taste and genius, with all the pleasures that arise from them, are commonly recompensed by a more useful kind of common sense, together with a wonderful delight, as well as success, in the busy pursuits of a scrambling world. The sufferings of the sick are greatly relieved by many trifling gratifications imperceptible to others, and sometimes almost repaid by the inconceivable transports occasioned by the return of health and vigour. Folly cannot be very grievous, because imperceptible; and I doubt not but there is some truth in that rant of a mad poet, that there is a pleasure in

2. Cheyne: George Cheyne (1671–1743), a Bath physician and mathematician, author of *Philosophical Principles of Natural Theology* (1705–15). **3. basis:** base.

4. Qui . . . pronunciat: He who thinks little judges readily. **5. Pope's . . . suffer:** See *Essay on Man*, ii. 249–94, in Part Two.

being mad, which none but madmen know.[6] Ignorance, or the want of knowledge and literature, the appointed lot of all born to poverty, and the drudgeries of life, is the only opiate capable of infusing that insensibility which can enable them to endure the miseries of the one, and the fatigues of the other. It is a cordial administered by the gracious hand of providence; of which they ought never to be deprived by an ill-judged and improper education. It is the basis of all subordination, the support of society, and the privilege of individuals: and I have ever thought it a most remarkable instance of the divine wisdom, that whereas in all animals, whose individuals rise little above the rest of their species, knowledge is instinctive; in man, whose individuals are so widely different, it is acquired by education; by which means the prince and the labourer, the philosopher and the peasant, are in some measure fitted for their respective situations."

Much of these positions is perhaps true, and the whole paragraph might well pass without censure, were not objections necessary to the establishment of knowledge. *Poverty* is very gently paraphrased by *want of riches*. In that sense almost every man may in his own opinion be poor. But there is another poverty which is *want of competence*, of all that can soften the miseries of life, of all that can diversify attention, or delight imagination. There is yet another poverty which is want *of necessaries*, a species of poverty which no care of the publick, no charity of particulars, can preserve many from feeling openly, and many secretly.

That hope and fear are inseparably or very frequently connected with poverty, and riches, my surveys of life have not informed me. The milder degrees of poverty are sometimes supported by hope, but the more severe often sink down in motionless despondence. Life must be seen before it can be known. This author and *Pope* perhaps never saw the miseries which they imagine thus easy to be born. The poor indeed are insensible of many little vexations which sometimes imbitter the possessions and pollute the enjoyments of the rich. They are not pained by casual incivility, or mortified by the mutilation of a compliment; but this happiness is like that of a malefactor who ceases to feel the cords that bind him when the pincers are tearing his flesh.

That want of taste for one enjoyment is supplied by the pleasures of some other, may be fairly allowed.

But the compensations of sickness I have never found near to equivalence, and the transports of recovery only prove the intenseness of the pain.

With folly no man is willing to confess himself very intimately acquainted, and therefore its pains and pleasures are kept secret. But what the author says of its happiness seems applicable only to fatuity, or gross dulness, for that inferiority of understanding which makes one man without any other reason the slave, or tool, or property of another, which makes him sometimes useless, and sometimes ridiculous, is often felt with very quick sensibility. On the happiness of madmen, as the case is not very frequent, it is not necessary to raise a disquisition, but I cannot forbear to observe, that I never yet knew disorders of mind encrease felicity: every madman is either arrogant and irascible, or gloomy and suspicious, or possessed by some passion or notion destructive to his quiet. He has always discontent in his look, and malignity in his bosom. And, if we had the power of choice, he would soon repent who should resign his reason to secure his peace.

Concerning the portion of ignorance necessary to make the condition of the lower classes of mankind safe to the public and tolerable to themselves, both morals and policy exact a nicer enquiry than will be very soon or very easily made. There is undoubtedly a degree of knowledge which will direct a man to refer all to providence, and to acquiesce in the condition which omniscient goodness has determined to allot him; to consider this world as a phantom that must soon glide from before his eyes, and the distresses and vexations that encompass him, as dust scattered in his path, as a blast that chills him for a moment, and passes off for ever.

Such wisdom, arising from the comparison of a part with the whole of our existence, those that want it most cannot possibly obtain from philosophy, nor unless the method of education, and the general tenour of life are changed, will very easily receive it from religion. The bulk of mankind is not likely to be very wise or very good: and I know not whether there are not many states of life, in which all knowledge less than the highest wisdom, will produce discontent and danger. I believe it may be sometimes found, that a *little learning* is to a poor man a *dangerous thing*.[7] But such is the condition of humanity, that we easily see,

---

6. **that rant . . . know:** Dryden, *The Spanish Friar*, II. i.

7. **a little . . . thing:** See Pope's *Essay on Criticism*, l. 215, in Part Two.

or quickly feel the wrong, but cannot always distinguish the right. Whatever knowledge is superfluous, in irremediable poverty, is hurtful, but the difficulty is to determine when poverty is irremediable, and at what point superfluity begins. Gross ignorance every man has found equally dangerous with perverted knowledge. Men left wholly to their appetites and their instincts, with little sense of moral or religious obligation, and with very faint distinctions of right and wrong, can never be safely employed, or confidently trusted: they can be honest only by obstinacy, and diligent only by compulsion or caprice. Some instruction, therefore, is necessary, and much perhaps may be dangerous.

Though it should be granted that those who are *born to poverty and drudgery* should not be *deprived* by an *improper education* of the *opiate of ignorance;* even this concession will not be of much use to direct our practice, unless it be determined who are those that are *born to poverty.* To entail irreversible poverty upon generation after generation only because the ancestor happened to be poor, is in itself cruel, if not unjust, and is wholly contrary to the maxims of a commercial nation, which always suppose and promote a rotation of property, and offer every individual a chance of mending his condition by his diligence. Those who communicate literature to the son of a poor man, consider him as one not born to poverty, but to the necessity of deriving a better fortune from himself. In this attempt, as in others, many fail, and many succeed. Those that fail will feel their misery more acutely; but since poverty is now confessed to be such a calamity as cannot be born without the opiate of insensibility, I hope the happiness of those whom education enables to escape from it, may turn the ballance against that exacerbation which the others suffer.

I am always afraid of determining on the side of envy or cruelty. The privileges of education may sometimes be improperly bestowed, but I shall always fear to with-hold them, lest I should be yielding to the suggestions of pride, while I persuade myself that I am following the maxims of policy; and under the appearance of salutary restraints, should be indulging the lust of dominion, and that malevolence which delights in seeing others depressed.

Pope's doctrine is at last exhibited in a comparison, which, like other proofs of the same kind, is better adapted to delight the fancy than convince the reason.

"Thus the universe resembles a large and well-regulated family, in which all the officers and servants, and even the domestic animals, are subservient to each other in a proper subordination: each enjoys the privileges and perquisites peculiar to his place, and at the same time contributes by that just subordination to the magnificence and happiness of the whole."

The magnificence of a house is of use or pleasure always to the master, and sometimes to the domestics. But the magnificence of the universe adds nothing to the supreme Being; for any part of its inhabitants with which human knowledge is acquainted, an universe much less spacious or splendid would have been sufficient; and of happiness it does not appear that any is communicated from the Beings of a lower world to those of a higher.

The enquiry after the cause of *natural evil* is continued in the third Letter, in which, as in the former, there is mixture of borrowed truth, and native folly, of some notions just and trite, with others uncommon and ridiculous.

His opinion of the value and importance of happiness is certainly just, and I shall insert it, not that it will give any information to any reader, but it may serve to shew how the most common notion may be swelled in sound, and diffused in bulk, till it shall perhaps astonish the author himself.

"Happiness is the only thing of real value in existence; neither riches, nor power, nor wisdom, nor learning, nor strength, nor beauty, nor virtue, nor religion, nor even life itself, being of any importance, but as they contribute to its production. All these are in themselves neither good nor evil; happiness alone is their great end, and they are desireable only as they tend to promote it."

Success produces confidence. After this discovery of the value of happiness, he proceeds without any distrust of himself to tell us what has been hid from all former enquirers.

"The true solution of this important question, so long and so vainly searched for by the philosophers of all ages and all countries, I take to be at last no more than this, that these real evils proceed from the same source as those imaginary ones of imperfection before treated of, namely, from that subordination, without which no created system can subsist; all subordination implying imperfection, all imperfection evil, and all evil some kind of inconveniency or suffering: so that there must be particular inconveniencies and sufferings annexed to every particular rank of created beings by the circumstances of things, and their modes of existence.

"God indeed might have made us quite other creatures, and placed us in a world quite differently constituted; but then we had been no longer men, and whatever beings had occupied our stations in the universal system, they must have been liable to the same inconveniences."

In all this there is nothing that can silence the enquiries of curiosity, or calm the perturbations of doubt. Whether subordination implies imperfection may be disputed. The means respecting themselves, may be as perfect as the end. The weed as a weed is no less perfect than the oak as an oak. That *imperfection implies evil, and evil suffering*, is by no means evident. Imperfection may imply privative[8] evil, or the absence of some good, but this privation produces no suffering, but by the help of knowledge. An infant at the breast is yet an imperfect man, but there is no reason for belief that he is unhappy by his immaturity, unless some positive pain be superadded.

When this author presumes to speak of the universe, I would advise him a little to distrust his own faculties, however large and comprehensive. Many words easily understood on common occasion, become uncertain and figurative when applied to the works of Omnipotence. Subordination in human affairs is well understood, but when it is attributed to the universal system, its meaning grows less certain, like the petty distinctions of locality, which are of good use upon our own globe, but have no meaning with regard to infinite space, in which nothing is *high* or *low*.

That if man, by exaltation to a higher nature were exempted from the evils which he now suffers, some other being must suffer them; that if man were not man, some other being must be man, is a position arising from his established notion of the scale of being. A notion to which *Pope* has given some importance by adopting it,[9] and of which I have therefore endeavoured to show the uncertainty and inconsistency. This scale of being I have demonstrated to be raised by presumptuous imagination, to rest on nothing at the bottom, to lean on nothing at the top, and to have vacuities from step to step through which any order of being may sink into nihility without any inconvenience, so far as we can judge to the next rank above or below it. We are therefore little enlightened by a writer who tells us that any being in the state of man must suffer what man suffers, when the only question, that requires to be resolved is, Why any being is in this state?

Of poverty and labour he gives just and elegant representations, which yet do not remove the difficulty of the first and fundamental question, though supposing the present state of man necessary, they may supply some motives to content.

"Poverty is what all could not possibly have been exempted from, not only by reason of the fluctuating nature of human possessions, but because the world could not subsist without it; for had all been rich, none could have submitted to the commands of another, or the necessary drudgeries of life; thence all governments must have been dissolved, arts neglected, and lands uncultivated, and so an universal penury have overwhelmed all, instead of now and then pinching a few. Hence, by the by, appears the great excellence of charity, by which men are enabled by a particular distribution of the blessings and enjoyments of life, on proper occasions, to prevent that poverty which by a general one omnipotence itself could never have prevented: so that, by inforcing this duty, God as it were demands our assistance to promote universal happiness, and to shut out misery at every door, where it strives to intrude itself.

"Labour, indeed, God might easily have excused us from, since at his command, the earth would readily have poured forth all her treasures without our inconsiderable assistance: but if the severest labour cannot sufficiently subdue the malignity of human nature, what plots and machinations, what wars, rapine and devastation, what profligacy and licentiousness must have been the consequences of universal idleness! so that labour ought only to be looked upon as a task kindly imposed upon us by our indulgent creator, necessary to preserve our health, our safety, and our innocence."

I am afraid that *the latter end of his commonwealth forgets the beginning.*[10] If God *could easily have excused us from labour*, I do not comprehend why *he could not possibly have exempted all from poverty*. For poverty, in its easier and more tolerable degree, is little more than necessity of labour, and, in its more severe and deplorable state, little more than inability for labour. To be poor is to work for others, or to want the succour of others without work. And the same exuberant fertility which would make work unnecessary might make poverty impossible.

---

8. **privative:** "consisting in the absence of something" (Johnson's *Dictionary*). 9. **by . . . it:** in *An Essay on Man.*

10. **the latter . . . beginning:** *The Tempest,* II. i. 158.

Surely a man who seems not completely master of his own opinion, should have spoken more cautiously of omnipotence, nor have presumed to say what it could perform, or what it could prevent. I am in doubt whether those who stand highest in *the scale of being* speak thus confidently of the dispensations of their maker.

For fools rush in, where angels fear to tread.[11]

Of our inquietudes of mind his account is still less reasonable. "Whilst men are injured, they must be inflamed with anger; and whilst they see cruelties, they must be melted with pity; whilst they perceive danger, they must be sensible of fear." This is to give a reason for all evil, by shewing that one evil produces another. If there is danger there ought to be fear; but if fear is an evil, why should there be danger? His vindication of pain is of the same kind; pain is useful to alarm us, that we may shun greater evils, but those greater evils must be presupposed that the fitness of pain may appear.

Treating on death, he has expressed the known and true doctrine with spriteliness of fancy and neatness of diction. I shall therefore insert it. There are truths which, as they are always necessary, do not grow stale by repetition.

"Death, the last and most dreadful of all evils, is so far from being one, that it is the infallible cure for all others.

> To die, is landing on some silent shore,
> Where billows never beat, nor tempests roar.
> Ere well we feel the friendly stroke, 'tis o'er.
> GARTH[12]

For, abstracted from the sickness and sufferings usually attending it, it is no more than the expiration of that term of life God was pleased to bestow on us, without any claim or merit on our part. But was it an evil ever so great, it could not be remedied but by one much greater, which is by living for ever; by which means our wickedness, unrestrained by the prospect of a future state, would grow so insupportable, our sufferings so intolerable by perseverance, and our pleasures so tiresome by repetition, that no being in the universe could be so compleatly miserable as a species of immortal men. We have no reason, therefore, to look upon death as an evil, or to fear it as a punish-

ment, even without any supposition of a future life: but if we consider it as a passage to a more perfect state, or a remove only in an eternal succession of still improving states (for which we have the strongest reasons) it will then appear a new favour from the divine munificence; and a man must be as absurd to repine at dying, as a traveller would be, who proposed to himself a delightful tour through various unknown countries, to lament that he cannot take up his residence at the first dirty inn which he baits at on the road.

"The instability of human life, or of the changes of its successive periods, of which we so frequently complain, are no more than the necessary progress of it to this necessary conclusion; and are so far from being evils deserving these complaints, that they are the source of our greatest pleasures as they are the source of all novelty, from which our greatest pleasures are ever derived. The continual succession of seasons in the human life, by daily presenting to us new scenes, render it agreeable, and like those of the year, afford us delights by their change, which the choicest of them could not give us by their continuance. In the spring of life, the gilding of the sunshine, the verdure of the fields, and the variegated paintings of the sky, are so exquisite in the eyes of infants at their first looking abroad into a new world, as nothing perhaps afterwards can equal. The heat and vigour of the succeeding summer of youth ripens for us new pleasures, the blooming maid, the nightly revel, and the jovial chace: the serene autumn of complete manhood feasts us with the golden harvests of our worldly pursuits: nor is the hoary winter of old age destitute of its peculiar comforts and enjoyments, of which the recollection and relation of those past are perhaps none of the least; and at last death opens to us a new prospect, from whence we shall probably look back upon the diversions and occupations of this world with the same contempt we do now on our tops and hobby-horses, and with the same surprize, that they could ever so much entertain or engage us."

I would not willingly detract from the beauty of this paragraph, and in gratitude to him who has so well inculcated such important truths, I will venture to admonish him, since the chief comfort of the old is the recollection of the past, so to employ his time and his thoughts, that when the imbecillity of age shall come upon him, he may be able to recreate its languors by the remembrance of hours spent, not in presumptuous decisions, but modest inquiries, not in dogmatical limitations of omnipotence, but in humble

11. For . . . tread: Pope, *Essay on Criticism*, l. 625. 12. To . . . o'er: Sir Samuel Garth, *The Dispensary*, III. 225-27.

acquiescence and fervent adoration. Old age will shew him that much of the book now before us has no other use than to perplex the scrupulous, and to shake the weak, to encourage impious presumption, or stimulate idle curiosity.

Having thus dispatched the consideration of particular evils, he comes at last to a general reason for which *evil* may be said to be *our good.* He is of opinion that there is some inconceivable benefit in pain abstractedly considered; that pain however inflicted, or wherever felt, communicates some good to the general system of being, and that every animal is some way or other the better for the pain of every other animal. This opinion he carries so far as to suppose that there passes some principle of union through all animal life, as attraction is communicated to all corporeal nature, and that the evils suffered on this globe, may by some inconceivable means contribute to the felicity of the inhabitants of the remotest planet.

How the origin of evil is brought nearer to human conception by any *inconceivable* means, I am not able to discover. We believed that the present system of creation was right, though we could not explain the adaptation of one part to the other, or for the whole succession of causes and consequences. Where has this enquirer added to the little knowledge that we had before? He has told us of the benefits of evil, which no man feels, and relations between distant parts of the universe, which he cannot himself conceive. There was enough in this question inconceivable before, and we have little advantage from a new inconceivable solution.

I do not mean to reproach this author for not knowing what is equally hidden from learning and from ignorance. The shame is to impose words for ideas upon ourselves or others. To imagine that we are going forward when we are only turning round. To think that there is any difference between him that gives no reason, and him that gives a reason, which by his own confession cannot be conceived.

But that he may not be thought to conceive nothing but things inconceivable, he has at last thought on a way by which human sufferings may produce good effects. He imagines that as we have not only animals for food, but choose some for our diversion, the same privilege may be allowed to some beings above us, *who may deceive, torment, or destroy us for the ends only of their own pleasure or utility.* This he again finds impossible to be conceived, *but that impossibility lessens not the probability of the conjecture, which by analogy is so strongly confirmed.*

I cannot resist the temptation of contemplating this analogy, which I think he might have carried further very much to the advantage of his argument. He might have shewn that these *hunters whose game is man* have many sports analogous to our own. As we drown whelps and kittens, they amuse themselves now and then with sinking a ship, and stand round the fields of *Blenheim* or the walls of *Prague,*[13] as we encircle a cock-pit. As we shoot a bird flying, they take a man in the midst of his business or pleasure, and knock him down with an apoplexy. Some of them, perhaps, are virtuosi, and delight in the operations of an asthma, as a human philosopher[14] in the effects of the air pump. To swell a man with a tympany[15] is as good sport as to blow a frog. Many a merry bout have these frolic beings at the vicissitudes of an ague, and good sport it is to see a man tumble with an epilepsy, and revive and tumble again, and all this he knows not why. As they are wiser and more powerful than we, they have more exquisite diversions, for we have no way of procuring any sport so brisk and so lasting as the paroxysms of the gout and stone which undoubtedly must make high mirth, especially if the play be a little diversified with the blunders and puzzles of the blind and deaf. We know not how far their sphere of observation may extend. Perhaps now and then a merry being may place himself in such a situation as to enjoy at once all the varieties of an epidemical disease, or amuse his leisure with the tossings and contortions of every possible pain exhibited together.

One sport the merry malice of these beings has found means of enjoying to which we have nothing equal or similar. They now and then catch a mortal proud of his parts, and flattered either by the submission of those who court his kindness, or the notice of those who suffer him to court theirs. A head thus prepared for the reception of false opinions, and the projection of vain designs, they easily fill with idle notions, till in time they make their plaything an author: their first diversion commonly begins with an Ode or an epistle, then rises perhaps to a political irony, and is at last brought to its height, by a treatise of philosophy. Then begins the poor animal to entangle

13. **the fields . . . Prague:** The Battle of Blenheim was fought in 1704; the Battle of Prague in 1757. **14. philosopher:** scientific experimenter. **15. tympany:** "a kind of obstructed flatulence that swells the body like a drum" (Johnson's *Dictionary*).

himself in sophisms, and flounder in absurdity, to talk confidently of the scale of being, and to give solutions which himself confesses impossible to be understood. Sometimes, however, it happens that their pleasure is without much mischief. The author feels no pain, but while they are wondering at the extravagance of his opinion, and pointing him out to one another as a new example of human folly, he is enjoying his own applause, and that of his companions, and perhaps is elevated with the hope of standing at the head of a new sect.

Many of the books which now croud the world, may be justly suspected to be written for the sake of some invisible order of beings, for surely they are of no use to any of the corporeal inhabitants of the world. Of the productions of the last bounteous year, how many can be said to serve any purpose of use or pleasure. The only end of writing is to enable the readers better to enjoy life, or better to endure it: and how will either of those be put more in our power by him who tells us, that we are puppets, of which some creature not much wiser than ourselves manages the wires. That a set of beings unseen and unheard, are hovering about us, trying experiments upon our sensibility, putting us in agonies to see our limbs quiver, torturing us to madness, that they may laugh at our vagaries, sometimes obstructing the bile, that they may see how a man looks when he is yellow: sometimes breaking a traveller's bones to try how he will get home; sometimes wasting a man to a skeleton, and sometimes killing him fat for the greater elegance of his hide.

This is an account of natural evil, which though, like the rest, not quite new is very entertaining, though I know not how much it may contribute to patience. The only reason why we should contemplate evil is, that we may bear it better, and I am afraid nothing is much more placidly endured, for the sake of making others sport.

. . .

FROM

THE IDLER

❧

The papers titled *The Idler* first appeared in the weekly newspaper *The Universal Chronicle* from April 15, 1758,

to April 5, 1760. The series consists of 104 papers in all, of which a few were contributed by friends of Johnson like Thomas Warton and Sir Joshua Reynolds. The collected edition first appeared in 1761. To Boswell *The Idler* seemed to exhibit "less body and more spirit" than *The Rambler* (1750–52). But like *The Rambler*,

Many of these excellent essays were written as hastily as an ordinary letter. Mr. Langton remembers Johnson, when on a visit at Oxford, asking him one evening how long it was till the post went out; and upon being told about half an hour, he exclaimed, "then we shall do very well." He upon this instantly sat down and finished an *Idler*, which it was necessary should be in London the next day. Mr. Langton having signified a wish to read it, "Sir, (said he) you shall not do more than I have done myself." He then folded it up and sent it off.

The text is that of the first printing, in *The Universal Chronicle*.

❧

NO. 61

[*Saturday, June 9, 1759*]
CRITICISM is a study by which men grow important and formidable at very small expence. The power of invention has been conferred by nature upon few, and the labour of learning those sciences which may, by mere labour, be obtained, is too great to be willingly endured; but every man can exert such judgment as he has upon the works of others, and he whom Nature has made weak and Idleness keeps ignorant, may yet support his vanity by the name of a Critick.

I hope it will give comfort to great numbers who are passing thro' the world in obscurity, when I inform them how easily distinction may be obtained. All the other powers of literature are coy and haughty, they must be long courted, and at last are not always gained; but Criticism is a goddess easy of access and forward of advance, who will meet the slow and encourage the timorous; the want of meaning she supplies with words, and the want of spirit with malignity.

This profession has one recommendation peculiar to itself, that it gives vent to malignity without real mischief. No genius was ever blasted by the breath of Criticks. The poison, which, if confined, would have burst the heart, fumes away in empty hisses, and malice is set at ease with very little danger to merit. The Critick is the only man whose triumph is without another's pain, and whose greatness does not rise upon another's ruin.

To a study at once so easy and so reputable, so malicious, and so harmless, it cannot be necessary to invite my readers by a long or laboured exhortation; it is sufficient, since all would be Criticks if they could, to shew by one eminent example that all can be Criticks if they will.

Dick Minim,[1] after the common course of puerile studies, in which he was no great proficient, was put apprentice to a Brewer, with whom he had lived two years, when his uncle died in the city, and left him a large fortune in the Stocks. Dick had for six months before used the company of the lower Players, of whom he had learned to scorn a trade, and being now at liberty to follow his genius, he resolved to be a man of wit and humour. That he might be properly initiated in his new character, he frequented the coffee-houses near the theatres, where he listened very diligently day after day to those who talked of language and sentiments, and unities and catastrophes, till by slow degrees he began to think that he understood something of the Stage, and hoped in time to talk himself.

But he did not trust so much to natural sagacity as wholly to neglect the help of books. When the theatres were shut, he retired to Richmond with a few select writers, whose opinions he impressed upon his memory by unwearied diligence; and when he returned with other wits to the town, was able to tell in very proper phrases that the chief business of art is to copy Nature; that a perfect writer is not to be expected, because genius decays as judgment increases; that the great art is the art of blotting, and that according to the rule of Horace every piece should be kept nine years.[2]

Of the great Authors he now began to display the Characters, laying down as an universal position that all had beauties and defects. His opinion was, that Shakespeare committing himself wholly to the impulse of nature wanted that correctness which learning would have given him; and that Johnson, trusting to learning, did not sufficiently cast his eye on nature. He blamed the Stanza of Spenser, and could

not bear the Hexameters of Sidney.[3] Denham and Waller he held the first reformers of English numbers,[4] and thought that if Waller could have obtained the strength of Denham, or Denham the sweetness of Waller, there had been nothing wanting to compleat a Poet.[5] He often expressed his commiseration of Dryden's poverty, and his indignation at the age which suffered him to write for bread; he repeated with rapture the first lines of *All for Love*,[6] but wondered at the corruption of taste which could bear any thing so unnatural as rhyming Tragedies. In Otway[7] he found uncommon powers of moving the passions, but was disgusted by his general negligence, and blamed him for making a Conspirator his Hero.[8] He never concluded his disquisition without remarking how happily the sound of the clock is made to alarm the audience. Southerne[9] would have been his favourite, but that he mixes comic with tragic scenes, intercepts the natural course of the passions, and fills the mind with a wild confusion of mirth and melancholy. The versification of Rowe[10] he thought too melodious for the stage, and too little varied in different passions. He made it the great fault of Congreve, that all his persons were wits, and that he always wrote with more art than nature. He considered Cato[11] rather as a poem than a play, and allowed Addison to be the complete master of allegory and grave humour, but paid no great deference to him as a Critic. He thought the chief merit of Prior was in his easy tales and lighter poems, though he allowed that his Solomon[12] had many noble sentiments elegantly expressed. In Swift he discovered an inimitable vein of irony, and an easiness which all would

THE IDLER. *Number 61*. **1. Minim:** "a small being; a dwarf" (Johnson's *Dictionary*). **2. every . . . years:** *Ars Poetica*, ll. 386–89.

3. the Stanza . . . Sidney: Edmund Spenser's *Faerie Queene* (1589–96) is written in an intricate nine-line stanza; Sir Philip Sidney's sonnet sequence *Astrophel and Stella* (1591) contains sone sonnets written in hexameter instead of pentameter lines. **4. numbers:** versification. **5. if . . . Poet:** See Pope's *Essay on Criticism*, l. 361, in Part Two. **6. All for Love:** Dryden's redaction (1678) of *Antony and Cleopatra*. **7. Otway:** Thomas Otway (1652–85), author of three famous tragedies: *Don Carlos* (1676), *The Orphan* (1680), and *Venice Preserved* (1682). **8. a Conspirator . . . Hero:** Jaffier, in *Venice Preserved*. **9. Southerne:** Thomas Southerne (1660–1746), best known as the author of the tragedies *The Fatal Marriage* (1694) and *Oroonoko* (1695). **10. Rowe:** Nicholas Rowe (1674–1718), author of *The Fair Penitent* (1703) and other tragedies. **11. Cato:** the famous tragedy (1713) by Joseph Addison. **12. Solomon:** a long heroic-couplet poem by Matthew Prior (1664–1721). (See the selections from Prior in Part Two.)

hope and few would attain. Pope he was inclined to degrade from a Poet to a Versifier, and thought his numbers rather luscious than sweet. He often lamented the neglect of Phædra and Hippolitus,[13] and wished to see the Stage under better regulations.

These assertions passed commonly uncontradicted,[14] and if now and then an opponent started up, he was quickly repressed by the suffrages of the company, and Minim went away from every dispute with elation of heart, and encrease of confidence.

He now grew conscious of his abilities, and began to talk of the present state of dramatic poetry, wondered what was become of the comick genius which supplied our ancestors with wit and pleasantry, and why no writer could be found that durst now venture beyond a Farce. He saw no reason for thinking that the vein of humour was exhausted, since we live in a country where liberty suffers every character to spread itself to its utmost bulk, and which therefore produces more originals than all the rest of the world together. Of Tragedy he concluded business[15] to be the soul, and yet often hinted that love predominates too much upon the modern stage.

He was now an acknowledged Critick, and had his own seat in the Coffee-house, and headed a party in the pit. Minim has more vanity than ill-nature, and seldom desires to do much mischief; he will, perhaps, murmur a little in the ear of him that sits next him, but endeavours to influence the audience to favour, by clapping, when an Actor exclaims ye Gods, or laments the miseries of his country.

By degrees he was admitted to Rehearsals, and many of his friends are of opinion, that our present Poets are indebted to him for their happiest thoughts; by his contrivance the bell was rung twice in Barbarossa,[16] and by his persuasion the Author of Cleone[17] concluded his Play without a couplet; for what can be more absurd, said Minim, than that part of a Play should be rhymed, and part written in blank verse? and by what acquisition of faculties is the Speaker who never could find rhymes before, enabled to rhyme at the conclusion of an Act?

He is the great investigator of hidden beauties, and is particularly delighted when he finds *the Sound an Echo to the Sense*.[18] He has read all our Poets with particular attention to this delicacy of Versification, and wonders at the supineness with which their Works have been hitherto perused, so that no man has found the sound of a Drum in this distich,

> When Pulpit, Drum ecclesiastic,
> Was beat with fist instead of a stick;[19]

and that the wonderful lines upon Honour and a Bubble have hitherto passed without notice.

> Honour is like the glassy Bubble,
> Which costs Philosophers such trouble,
> Where one part crack'd, the whole does fly,
> And Wits are crack'd to find out why.[20]

In these Verses, says Minim, we have two striking accommodations of the Sound to the Sense. It is impossible to utter the two lines[21] emphatically without an act like that which they describe; *Bubble* and *Trouble* causing a momentary inflation of the Cheeks by the retention of the breath which is afterwards forcibly emitted as in the practice of *blowing bubbles*. But the greatest excellence is in the third line which is *cracked* in the middle to express a crack, and then shivers into monosyllables. Yet has [this] diamond lain neglected with common stones, and among the innumerable admirers of Hudibras the observation of this superlative passage has been reserved for the sagacity of Minim.

NO. 62

[Saturday, June 16, 1759]

MR. Minim had now advanced himself to the zenith of critical reputation; when he was in the Pit, every eye in the Boxes was fixed upon him, when he entered his Coffee-house, he was surrounded by circles of candidates who passed their noviciate of literature under his tuition; his opinion was asked by all who had no opinion of their own, and yet loved to debate and decide, and no composition was supposed to pass in safety to posterity, till it had been secured by Minim's approbation.

---

13. **Phædra and Hippolitus:** a tragedy (1707) by Edmund Smith (1672–1710). 14. **These . . . uncontradicted:** They are all clichés from the critical writings of Horace, Dryden, Addison, Pope, Dennis, Johnson, Joseph Warton, and many others. 15. **business:** action, plot. 16. **Barbarossa:** a tragedy (1754) by Dr. John Brown (1715–66). 17. **Cleone:** a tragedy (1758) by the bookseller Robert Dodsley (1703–64).

18. **the Sound . . . Sense:** See Pope's *Essay on Criticism*, l. 365. 19. **When . . . stick:** Samuel Butler, *Hudibras*, I. i. 11–12. 20. **Honour . . . why:** *Ibid.*, II. ii. 385–88. 21. **two lines:** the first two lines.

Minim professes great admiration of the wisdom and munificence, by which the Academies are formed on the Continent, and often wishes for some standard of taste, for some tribunal, to which merit might appeal from caprice, prejudice, and malignity. He has formed a plan for an Academy of Criticism, where every work of Imagination may be read before it is printed, and which shall authoritatively direct the Theatres what pieces to receive or reject, to exclude or to revive.

Such an institution would, in Dick's opinion, spread the fame of English Literature over Europe, and make London the metropolis of elegance and politeness, the place to which the learned and ingenious of all countries would repair for instruction and improvement, and where nothing would any longer be applauded or endured that was not conformed to the nicest rules, and finished with the highest elegance.

'Till some happy conjunction of the planets shall dispose our Princes or Ministers to make themselves immortal by such an Academy, Minim contents himself to preside four nights in a week in a Critical society selected by himself, where he is heard without contradiction, and whence his judgment is disseminated through the great vulgar and the small.

When he is placed in the chair of Criticism, he declares loudly for the noble simplicity of our ancestors, in opposition to the petty refinements, and ornamental luxurance. Sometimes he is sunk in despair, and perceives false delicacy daily gaining ground, and sometimes brightens his countenance with a gleam of hope, and predicts the revival of the true sublime. He then fulminates his loudest censures against the monkish barbarity of Rhime, wonders how beings that pretend to reason can be pleased with one line always ending like another; tells how unjustly and unnaturally sense is sacrificed to sound, how often the best thoughts are mangled by the necessity of confining or extending them to the dimensions of a couplet, and rejoices that genius has in our days shaken off the shackles which had encumbered it so long. Yet he allows that rhyme may sometimes be borne, if the lines be often broken, and the pauses judiciously diversified.

From Blank Verse he makes an easy transition to Milton, whom he produces as an example of the slow advance of lasting reputation. Milton is the only writer whose books Minim can read for ever without weariness. What cause it is that exempts this pleasure from satiety he has long and diligently enquired, and believes it to consist in the perpetual variation of the numbers, by which the ear is gratified, and the attention awakened. The lines that are commonly thought rugged and unmusical he conceives to have been written to temper the melodious luxury of the rest, or to express things by a proper cadence: for he scarcely finds a verse that has not this favourite beauty; he declares that he could shiver in a hot-house when he reads that

> the ground
> Burns frore, and cold performs th' effect of fire.[1]

And that when Milton bewails his Blindness, the verse

> So thick a drop serene has quench'd these orbs,[2]

has, he knows not how, something that strikes him with an obscure sensation like that which he fancies would be felt from the sound of Darkness.

Minim is not so confident of his Rules of Judgment as not very eagerly to catch new light from the name of the Author. He is commonly so prudent as to spare those whom he cannot resist, unless, as will sometimes happen, he finds the Public combined against them. But a new pretender to Fame he is strongly inclined to censure, till his own honour requires that he commend him. 'Till he knows the success of a new production, he intrenches himself in general terms; there are some new thoughts, and beautiful passages, but there is likewise much which he would have advised the Author to expunge. He has several favourite Epithets, of which he has never settled the meaning, but which are very commodiously applied to books which he has not read, or cannot understand. One is *manly*, another is *dry*, another *stiff*, and another *flimzy*; sometimes he discovers delicacy of stile, and sometimes meets with *strange expressions*.

He is never so great, or so happy, as when a youth of promising parts is brought to receive his advice for the prosecution of his studies. He then puts on a very serious air; he advises the pupil to read none but the best Authors, and when he finds one congenial to his own mind, to study his beauties, to avoid his faults, and, when he sits down to write, to consider how his favourite Author would think at the present time on the present occasion. He directs him to catch those moments when he finds his thoughts expanded, and his genius exalted, but to take care lest his imagination hurry him beyond the bounds of Nature. He holds

Number 62. **1. Burns . . . fire:** *Paradise Lost*, II. 595. **2. So . . . orbs:** *Ibid.*, III. 25.

Diligence the Mother of Success, yet enjoins him, with great earnestness, not to read more than he can digest, and not to confuse his mind by pursuing studies of contrary tendencies. He tells him, that every man has his genius, and that Cicero could never be a Poet. The Boy retires illuminated, resolves to follow his genius, and to think how Milton would have thought; and Minim feasts upon his own beneficence till another day brings another Pupil.

. . . RASSELAS . . .

In January, 1759, deeply shocked and grieved by the death of his mother, Johnson set to work writing something "to defray," as Boswell says, "the expense of [her] funeral, and pay some little debts which she had left." Johnson told Reynolds that he wrote *Rasselas* "in the evenings of one week, [and] sent it to the press in portions as it was written." He originally planned to title it *The Choice of Life*. The title pages of the early editions give the title *The Prince of Abissinia*, but the first page of the text is headed *The History of Rasselas, Prince of Abissinia*, and it is that title, or simply *Rasselas*, which has become customary. Both title and setting may owe something to Johnson's memories of his translation (1735) from the French of Father Jerome Lobo's travel book *A Voyage to Abyssinia* (i.e., Ethiopia), in which a man named Rassela Christos is mentioned.

In genre *Rasselas* is an oriental tale, in Johnson's day a literary form associated with noble moral instruction. *Rasselas* is perhaps also related to the narrative dialogue as employed by Plato and to the utopia as developed by Sir Thomas More. The many similarities between *Rasselas* and Voltaire's *Candide*, which was published about two months earlier, have disturbed some readers. But Johnson had not read *Candide*, and the analogies between the two works are entirely fortuitous.

Rasselas was an immediate success. Six English editions appeared during Johnson's lifetime, and it was soon widely translated abroad. Boswell declared himself "not satisfied if a year passes without my having read it through," and added, "To those who look no further than the present life, or who maintain that human nature has not fallen from the state in which it was created, the instruction of this sublime story will be of no avail."

The text is that of the first edition (1759); we have incorporated the substantive variants of the second edition (1759).

CHAP. I

Description of a palace in a valley.

Ye who listen with credulity to the whispers of fancy, and pursue with eagerness the phantoms of hope; who expect that age will perform the promises of youth, and that the deficiencies of the present day will be supplied by the morrow; attend to the history of Rasselas prince of Abissinia.

Rasselas was the fourth son of the mighty emperour, in whose dominions the Father of waters begins his course; whose bounty pours down the streams of plenty, and scatters over half the world the harvests of Egypt.

According to the custom which has descended from age to age among the monarchs of the torrid zone, Rasselas was confined in a private palace, with the other sons and daughters of Abissinian royalty, till the order of succession should call him to the throne.

The place, which the wisdom or policy of antiquity had destined for the residence of the Abissinian princes, was a spacious valley in the kingdom of Amhara, surrounded on every side by mountains, of which the summits overhang the middle part. The only passage, by which it could be entered, was a cavern that passed under a rock, of which it has long been disputed whether it was the work of nature or of human industry. The outlet of the cavern was concealed by a thick wood, and the mouth which opened into the valley was closed with gates of iron, forged by the artificers of ancient days, so massy that no man could, without the help of engines, open or shut them.

From the mountains on every side, rivulets descended that filled all the valley with verdure and fertility, and formed a lake in the middle inhabited by fish of every species, and frequented by every fowl whom nature has taught to dip the wing in water. This lake discharged its superfluities by a stream which entered a dark cleft of the mountain on the northern side, and fell with dreadful noise from precipice to precipice till it was heard no more.

The sides of the mountains were covered with trees, the banks of the brooks were diversified with flowers; every blast shook spices from the rocks, and every month dropped fruits upon the ground. All animals that bite the grass, or brouse the shrub, whether wild or tame, wandered in this extensive circuit, secured from beasts of prey by the mountains which confined them. On one part were flocks and herds feeding in the pastures, on another all the beasts of chase frisking in the lawns; the spritely kid was bounding on the rocks, the subtle monkey frolicking in the trees, and the solemn elephant reposing in the shade. All the diversities of the world were brought together, the blessings of nature were collected, and its evils extracted and excluded.

The valley, wide and fruitful, supplied its inhabitants with the necessaries of life, and all delights and superfluities were added at the annual visit which the emperour paid his children, when the iron gate was opened to the sound of musick; and during eight days every one that resided in the valley was required to propose whatever might contribute to make seclusion pleasant, to fill up the vacancies of attention, and lessen the tediousness of time. Every desire was immediately granted. All the artificers of pleasure were called to gladden the festivity; the musicians exerted the power of harmony, and the dancers shewed their activity before the princes, in hope that they should pass their lives in this blissful captivity, to which these only were admitted whose performance was thought able to add novelty to luxury. Such was the appearance of security and delight which this retirement afforded, that they to whom it was new always desired that it might be perpetual; and as those, on whom the iron gate had once closed, were never suffered to return, the effect of longer experience could not be known. Thus every year produced new schemes of delight, and new competitors for imprisonment.

The palace stood on an eminence raised about thirty paces above the surface of the lake. It was divided into many squares or courts, built with greater or less magnificence according to the rank of those for whom they were designed. The roofs were turned into arches of massy stone joined with a cement that grew harder by time, and the building stood from century to century, deriding the solstitial rains and equinoctial hurricanes, without need of reparation.

This house, which was so large as to be fully known to none but some ancient officers who successively inherited the secrets of the place, was built as if suspicion herself had dictated the plan. To every room there was an open and secret passage, every square had a communication with the rest, either from the upper stories by private galleries, or by subterranean passages from the lower apartments. Many of the columns had

unsuspected cavities, in which a long race of monarchs had reposited their treasures. They then closed up the opening with marble, which was never to be removed but in the utmost exigencies of the kingdom; and recorded their accumulations in a book which was itself concealed in a tower not entered but by the emperour, attended by the prince who stood next in succession.

CHAP. II

The discontent of Rasselas in the happy valley.

Here the sons and daughters of Abissinia lived only to know the soft vicissitudes of pleasure and repose, attended by all that were skilful to delight, and gratified with whatever the senses can enjoy. They wandered in gardens of fragrance, and slept in the fortresses of security. Every art was practised to make them pleased with their own condition. The sages who instructed them, told them of nothing but the miseries of publick life, and described all beyond the mountains as regions of calamity, where discord was always raging, and where man preyed upon man.

To heighten their opinion of their own felicity, they were daily entertained with songs, the subject of which was the *happy valley*. Their appetites were excited by frequent enumerations of different enjoyments, and revelry and merriment was the business of every hour from the dawn of morning to the close of even.

These methods were generally successful; few of the princes had ever wished to enlarge their bounds, but passed their lives in full conviction that they had all within their reach that art or nature could bestow, and pitied those whom fate had excluded from this seat of tranquility, as the sport of chance, and the slaves of misery.

Thus they rose in the morning, and lay down at night, pleased with each other and with themselves, all but Rasselas, who, in the twenty-sixth year of his age, began to withdraw himself from their pastimes and assemblies, and to delight in solitary walks and silent meditation. He often sat before tables covered with luxury, and forgot to taste the dainties that were placed before him: he rose abruptly in the midst of the song, and hastily retired beyond the sound of musick. His attendants observed the change and endeavoured to renew his love of pleasure: he neglected their officiousness, repulsed their invitations, and spent day after day on the banks of rivulets sheltered with trees, where he sometimes listened to the birds in the branches, sometimes observed the fish playing in the stream, and anon cast his eyes upon the pastures and mountains filled with animals, of which some were biting the herbage, and some sleeping among the bushes.

This singularity of his humour made him much observed. One of the Sages, in whose conversation he had formerly delighted, followed him secretly, in hope of discovering the cause of his disquiet. Rasselas, who knew not that any one was near him, having for some time fixed his eyes upon the goats that were brousing among the rocks, began to compare their condition with his own.

"What," said he, "makes the difference between man and all the rest of the animal creation? Every beast that strays beside me has the same corporal necessities with myself; he is hungry and crops the grass, he is thirsty and drinks the stream, his thirst and hunger are appeased, he is satisfied and sleeps; he rises again and is hungry, he is again fed and is at rest. I am hungry and thirsty like him, but when thirst and hunger cease I am not at rest; I am, like him, pained with want, but am not, like him, satisfied with fulness. The intermediate hours are tedious and gloomy; I long again to be hungry that I may again quicken my attention. The birds peck the berries or the corn, and fly away to the groves where they sit in seeming happiness on the branches, and waste their lives in tuning one unvaried series of sounds. I likewise can call the lutanist and the singer, but the sounds that pleased me yesterday weary me to day, and will grow yet more wearisome to morrow. I can discover within me no power of perception which is not glutted with its proper pleasure, yet I do not feel myself delighted. Man has surely some latent sense for which this place affords no gratification, or he has some desires distinct from sense which must be satisfied before he can be happy."

After this he lifted up his head, and seeing the moon rising, walked towards the palace. As he passed through the fields, and saw the animals around him, "Ye, said he, are happy, and need not envy me that walk thus among you, burthened with myself; nor do I, ye gentle beings, envy your felicity; for it is not the felicity of man. I have many distresses from which ye are free; I fear pain when I do not feel it; I sometimes shrink at evils recollected, and sometimes start at evils anticipated: surely the equity of providence has

balanced peculiar sufferings with peculiar enjoyments."

With observations like these the prince amused himself as he returned, uttering them with a plaintive voice, yet with a look that discovered him to feel some complacence in his own perspicacity, and to receive some solace of the miseries of life, from consciousness of the delicacy with which he felt, and the eloquence with which he bewailed them. He mingled cheerfully in the diversions of the evening, and all rejoiced to find that his heart was lightened.

CHAP. III

The wants of him that wants nothing.

On the next day his old instructor, imagining that he had now made himself acquainted with his disease of mind, was in hope of curing it by counsel, and officiously sought an opportunity of conference, which the prince, having long considered him as one whose intellects were exhausted, was not very willing to afford: "Why, said he, does this man thus intrude upon me; shall I be never suffered to forget those lectures which pleased only while they were new, and to become new again must be forgotten?" He then walked into the wood, and composed himself to his usual meditations; when, before his thoughts had taken any settled form, he perceived his persuer at his side, and was at first prompted by his impatience to go hastily away; but, being unwilling to offend a man whom he had once reverenced and still loved, he invited him to sit down with him on the bank.

The old man, thus encouraged, began to lament the change which had been lately observed in the prince, and to enquire why he so often retired from the pleasures of the palace, to loneliness and silence. "I fly from pleasure, said the prince, because pleasure has ceased to please; I am lonely because I am miserable, and am unwilling to cloud with my presence the happiness of others." "You, Sir, said the sage, are the first who has complained of misery in the happy valley. I hope to convince you that your complaints have no real cause. You are here in full possession of all that the emperour of Abissinia can bestow; here is neither labour to be endured nor danger to be dreaded, yet here is all that labour or danger can procure or purchase. Look round and tell me which of your wants is without supply: if you want nothing, how are you unhappy?"

"That I want nothing, said the prince, or that I know not what I want, is the cause of my complaint; if I had any known want, I should have a certain wish; that wish would excite endeavour, and I should not then repine to see the sun move so slowly towards the western mountain, or lament when the day breaks and sleep will no longer hide me from myself. When I see the kids and the lambs chasing one another, I fancy that I should be happy if I had something to persue. But, possessing all that I can want, I find one day and one hour exactly like another, except that the latter is still more tedious than the former. Let your experience inform me how the day may now seem as short as in my childhood, while nature was yet fresh, and every moment shewed me what I never had observed before. I have already enjoyed too much; give me something to desire."

The old man was surprised at this new species of affliction, and knew not what to reply, yet was unwilling to be silent. "Sir, said he, if you had seen the miseries of the world, you would know how to value your present state." "Now, said the prince, you have given me something to desire; I shall long to see the miseries of the world, since the sight of them is necessary to happiness."

CHAP. IV

The prince continues to grieve and muse.

At this time the sound of musick proclaimed the hour of repast, and the conversation was concluded. The old man went away sufficiently discontented to find that his reasonings had produced the only conclusion which they were intended to prevent. But in the decline of life shame and grief are of short duration; whether it be that we bear easily what we have born long, or that, finding ourselves in age less regarded, we less regard others; or, that we look with slight regard upon afflictions, to which we know that the hand of death is about to put an end.

The prince, whose views were extended to a wider space, could not speedily quiet his emotions. He had been before terrified at the length of life which nature promised him, because he considered that in a long time much must be endured; he now rejoiced in his youth, because in many years much might be done.

This first beam of hope, that had been ever darted into his mind, rekindled youth in his cheeks, and doubled the lustre of his eyes. He was fired with the desire of doing something, though he knew not yet with distinctness, either end or means.

He was now no longer gloomy and unsocial; but, considering himself as master of a secret stock of happiness, which he could enjoy only by concealing it, he affected to be busy in all schemes of diversion, and endeavoured to make others pleased with the state of which he himself was weary. But pleasures never can be so multiplied or continued, as not to leave much of life unemployed; there were many hours, both of the night and day, which he could spend without suspicion in solitary thought. The load of life was much lightened: he went eagerly into the assemblies, because he supposed the frequency of his presence necessary to the success of his purposes; he retired gladly to privacy, because he had now a subject of thought.

His chief amusement was to picture to himself that world which he had never seen; to place himself in various conditions; to be entangled in imaginary difficulties, and to be engaged in wild adventures: but his benevolence always terminated his projects in the relief of distress, the detection of fraud, the defeat of oppression, and the diffusion of happiness.

Thus passed twenty months of the life of Rasselas. He busied himself so intensely in visionary bustle, that he forgot his real solitude; and, amidst hourly preparations for the various incidents of human affairs, neglected to consider by what means he should mingle with mankind.

One day, as he was sitting on a bank, he feigned to himself an orphan virgin robbed of her little portion by a treacherous lover, and crying after him for restitution and redress. So strongly was the image impressed upon his mind, that he started up in the maid's defence, and run forward to seize the plunderer with all the eagerness of real persuit. Fear naturally quickens the flight of guilt. Rasselas could not catch the fugitive with his utmost efforts; but, resolving to weary, by perseverance, him whom he could not surpass in speed, he pressed on till the foot of the mountain stopped his course.

Here he recollected himself, and smiled at his own useless impetuosity. Then raising his eyes to the mountain, "This, said he, is the fatal obstacle that hinders at once the enjoyment of pleasure, and the exercise of virtue. How long is it that my hopes and wishes have flown beyond this boundary of my life, which yet I never have attempted to surmount!"

Struck with this reflection, he sat down to muse, and remembered, that since he first resolved to escape from his confinement, the sun had passed twice over him in his annual course. He now felt a degree of regret with which he had never been before acquainted. He considered how much might have been done in the time which had passed, and left nothing real behind it. He compared twenty months with the life of man. "In life, said he, is not to be counted the ignorance of infancy, or imbecility of age. We are long before we are able to think, and we soon cease from the power of acting. The true period of human existence may be reasonably estimated as forty years, of which I have mused away the four and twentieth part. What I have lost was certain, for I have certainly possessed it; but of twenty months to come who can assure me?"

The consciousness of his own folly pierced him deeply, and he was long before he could be reconciled to himself. "The rest of my time, said he, has been lost by the crime or folly of my ancestors, and the absurd institutions of my country; I remember it with disgust, yet without remorse: but the months that have passed since new light darted into my soul, since I formed a scheme of reasonable felicity, have been squandered by my own fault. I have lost that which can never be restored: I have seen the sun rise and set for twenty months, an idle gazer on the light of heaven: In this time the birds have left the nest of their mother, and committed themselves to the woods and to the skies: the kid has forsaken the teat, and learned by degrees to climb the rocks in quest of independant sustenance. I only have made no advances, but am still helpless and ignorant. The moon, by more than twenty changes, admonished me of the flux of life; the stream that rolled before my feet upbraided my inactivity. I sat feasting on intellectual luxury, regardless alike of the examples of the earth, and the instructions of the planets. Twenty months are passed, who shall restore them!"

These sorrowful meditations fastened upon his mind; he past four months in resolving to lose no more time in idle resolves, and was awakened to more vigorous exertion by hearing a maid, who had broken a porcelain cup, remark, that what cannot be repaired is not to be regretted.

This was obvious; and Rasselas reproached himself that he had not discovered it, having not known, or not considered, how many useful hints are obtained by chance, and how often the mind, hurried by her own ardour to distant views, neglects the truths that lie open before her. He, for a few hours, regretted his regret, and from that time bent his whole mind upon the means of escaping from the valley of happiness.

CHAP. V

The prince meditates his escape.

He now found that it would be very difficult to effect that which it was very easy to suppose effected. When he looked round about him, he saw himself confined by the bars of nature which had never yet been broken, and by the gate, through which none that once had passed it were ever able to return. He was now impatient as an eagle in a grate.[1] He passed week after week in clambering the mountains, to see if there was any aperture which the bushes might conceal, but found all the summits inaccessible by their prominence. The iron gate he despaired to open; for it was not only secured with all the power of art, but was always watched by successive sentinels, and was by its position exposed to the perpetual observation of all the inhabitants.

He then examined the cavern through which the waters of the lake were discharged; and, looking down at a time when the sun shone strongly upon its mouth, he discovered it to be full of broken rocks, which, though they permitted the stream to flow through many narrow passages, would stop any body of solid bulk. He returned discouraged and dejected; but, having now known the blessing of hope, resolved never to despair.

In these fruitless searches he spent ten months. The time, however, passed cheerfully away: in the morning he rose with new hope, in the evening applauded his own diligence, and in the night slept sound after his fatigue. He met a thousand amusements which beguiled his labour, and diversified his thoughts. He discerned the various instincts of animals, and properties of plants, and found the place replete with wonders, of which he purposed to solace himself with the contemplation, if he should never be able to accomplish his flight; rejoicing that his endeavours, though yet unsuccessful, had supplied him with a source of inexhaustible enquiry.

But his original curiosity was not yet abated; he resolved to obtain some knowledge of the ways of

RASSELAS: *Chapter V.* **I. grate:** cage.

men. His wish still continued, but his hope grew less. He ceased to survey any longer the walls of his prison, and spared to search by new toils for interstices which he knew could not be found, yet determined to keep his design always in view, and lay hold on any expedient that time should offer.

CHAP. VI

A dissertation of the art of flying.

Among the artists that had been allured into the happy valley, to labour for the accommodation and pleasure of its inhabitants, was a man eminent for his knowledge of the mechanick powers, who had contrived many engines both of use and recreation. By a wheel, which the stream turned, he forced the water into a tower, whence it was distributed to all the apartments of the palace. He erected a pavillion in the garden, around which he kept the air always cool by artificial showers. One of the groves, appropriated to the ladies, was ventilated by fans, to which the rivulet that run through it gave a constant motion; and instruments of soft musick were placed at proper distances, of which some played by the impulse of the wind, and some by the power of the stream.

This artist was sometimes visited by Rasselas, who was pleased with every kind of knowledge, imagining that the time would come when all his acquisitions should be of use to him in the open world. He came one day to amuse himself in his usual manner, and found the master busy in building a sailing chariot: he saw that the design was practicable upon a level surface, and with expressions of great esteem solicited its completion. The workman was pleased to find himself so much regarded by the prince, and resolved to gain yet higher honours. "Sir, said he, you have seen but a small part of what the mechanick sciences can perform. I have been long of opinion, that, instead of the tardy conveyance of ships and chariots, man might use the swifter migration of wings; that the fields of air are open to knowledge, and that only ignorance and idleness need crawl upon the ground."

This hint rekindled the prince's desire of passing the mountains; having seen what the mechanist had already performed, he was willing to fancy that he could do more; yet resolved to enquire further before he suffered hope to afflict him by disappointment. "I am afraid, said he to the artist, that your imagination prevails over your skill, and that you now tell me rather what you wish than what you know. Every animal has his element assigned him; the birds have the air, and man and beasts the earth." "So, replied the mechanist, fishes have the water, in which yet beasts can swim by nature, and men by art. He that can swim needs not despair to fly: to swim is to fly in a grosser fluid, and to fly is to swim in a subtler. We are only to proportion our power of resistance to the different density of the matter through which we are to pass. You will be necessarily upborn by the air, if you can renew any impulse upon it, faster than the air can recede from the pressure."

"But the exercise of swiming, said the prince, is very laborious; the strongest limbs are soon wearied; I am afraid the act of flying will be yet more violent, and wings will be of no great use, unless we can fly further than we can swim."

"The labour of rising from the ground, said the artist, will be great, as we see it in the heavier domestick fowls; but, as we mount higher, the earth's attraction, and the body's gravity, will be gradually diminished, till we shall arrive at a region where the man will float in the air without any tendency to fall: no care will then be necessary, but to move forwards, which the gentlest impulse will effect. You, Sir, whose curiosity is so extensive, will easily conceive with what pleasure a philosopher, furnished with wings, and hovering in the sky, would see the earth, and all its inhabitants, rolling beneath him, and presenting to him successively, by its diurnal motion, all the countries within the same parallel. How must it amuse the pendent spectator to see the moving scene of land and ocean, cities and desarts! To survey with equal security the marts of trade, and the fields of battle; mountains infested by barbarians, and fruitful regions gladdened by plenty, and lulled by peace! How easily shall we then trace the Nile through all his passage; pass over to distant regions, and examine the face of nature from one extremity of the earth to the other!"

"All this, said the prince, is much to be desired, but I am afraid that no man will be able to breathe in these regions of speculation and tranquility. I have been told, that respiration is difficult upon lofty mountains, yet from these precipices, though so high as to produce great tenuity of the air, it is very easy to fall: therefore I suspect, that from any height, where life can be supported, there may be danger of too quick descent."

"Nothing, replied the artist, will ever be attempted,

if all possible objections must be first overcome. If you will favour my project I will try the first flight at my own hazard. I have considered the structure of all volant¹ animals, and find the folding continuity of the bat's wings most easily accommodated to the human form. Upon this model I shall begin my task to morrow, and in a year expect to tower into the air beyond the malice or pursuit of man. But I will work only on this condition, that the art shall not be divulged, and that you shall not require me to make wings for any but ourselves."

"Why, said Rasselas, should you envy others so great an advantage? All skill ought to be exerted for universal good; every man has owed much to others, and ought to repay the kindness that he has received."

"If men were all virtuous, returned the artist, I should with great alacrity teach them all to fly. But what would be the security of the good, if the bad could at pleasure invade them from the sky? Against an army sailing through the clouds neither walls, nor mountains, nor seas, could afford any security. A flight of northern savages might hover in the wind, and light at once with irresistible violence upon the capital of a fruitful region that was rolling under them. Even this valley, the retreat of princes, the abode of happiness, might be violated by the sudden descent of some of the naked nations that swarm on the coast of the southern sea."

The prince promised secrecy, and waited for the performance, not wholly hopeless of success. He visited the work from time to time, observed its progress, and remarked many ingenious contrivances to facilitate motion, and unite levity with strength. The artist was every day more certain that he should leave vultures and eagles behind him, and the contagion of his confidence seized upon the prince.

In a year the wings were finished, and, on a morning appointed, the maker appeared furnished for flight on a little promontory: he waved his pinions a while to gather air, then leaped from his stand, and in an instant dropped into the lake. His wings, which were of no use in the air, sustained him in the water, and the prince drew him to land, half dead with terrour and vexation.

CHAP. VII

The prince finds a man of learning.

The prince was not much afflicted by this disaster, having suffered himself to hope for a happier event, only because he had no other means of escape in view. He still persisted in his design to leave the happy valley by the first opportunity.

His imagination was now at a stand; he had no prospect of entering into the world; and, notwithstanding all his endeavours to support himself, discontent by degrees preyed upon him, and he began again to lose his thoughts in sadness, when the rainy season, which in these countries is periodical, made it inconvenient to wander in the woods.

The rain continued longer and with more violence than had been ever known: the clouds broke on the surrounding mountains, and the torrents streamed into the plain on every side, till the cavern was too narrow to discharge the water. The lake overflowed its banks, and all the level of the valley was covered with the inundation. The eminence, on which the palace was built, and some other spots of rising ground, were all that the eye could now discover. The herds and flocks left the pastures, and both the wild beasts and the tame retreated to the mountains.

This inundation confined all the princes to domestick amusements, and the attention of Rasselas was particularly seized by a poem, which Imlac rehearsed upon the various conditions of humanity. He commanded the poet to attend him in his apartment, and recite his verses a second time; then entering into familiar talk, he thought himself happy in having found a man who knew the world so well, and could so skilfully paint the scenes of life. He asked a thousand questions about things, to which, though common to all other mortals, his confinement from childhood had kept him a stranger. The poet pitied his ignorance, and loved his curiosity, and entertained him from day to day with novelty and instruction, so that the prince regretted the necessity of sleep, and longed till the morning should renew his pleasure.

As they were sitting together, the prince commanded Imlac to relate his history, and to tell by what accident he was forced, or by what motive induced, to close his life in the happy valley. As he was going to begin his narrative, Rasselas was called to a concert, and obliged to restrain his curiosity till the evening.

Chapter VI. **1. volant:** flying.

CHAP. VIII

The history of Imlac.

The close of the day is, in the regions of the torrid zone, the only season of diversion and entertainment, and it was therefore mid-night before the musick ceased, and the princesses retired. Rasselas then called for his companion and required him to begin the story of his life.

"Sir, said Imlac, my history will not be long: the life that is devoted to knowledge passes silently away, and is very little diversified by events. To talk in publick, to think in solitude, to read and to hear, to inquire, and answer inquiries, is the business of a scholar. He wanders about the world without pomp or terrour, and is neither known nor valued but by men like himself.

"I was born in the kingdom of Goiama, at no great distance from the fountain of the Nile. My father was a wealthy merchant, who traded between the inland countries of Africk and the ports of the red sea. He was honest, frugal and diligent, but of mean sentiments, and narrow comprehension: he desired only to be rich, and to conceal his riches, lest he should be spoiled by the governours of the province."

"Surely, said the prince, my father must be negligent of his charge, if any man in his dominions dares take that which belongs to another. Does he not know that kings are accountable for injustice permitted as well as done? If I were emperour, not the meanest of my subjects should be oppressed with impunity. My blood boils when I am told that a merchant durst not enjoy his honest gains for fear of losing them by the rapacity of power. Name the governour who robbed the people, that I may declare his crimes to the emperour."

"Sir, said Imlac, your ardour is the natural effect of virtue animated by youth: the time will come when you will acquit your father, and perhaps hear with less impatience of the governour. Oppression is, in the Abissinian dominions, neither frequent nor tolerated; but no form of government has been yet discovered, by which cruelty can be wholly prevented. Subordination supposes power on one part and subjection on the other; and if power be in the hands of men, it will sometimes be abused. The vigilance of the supreme magistrate may do much, but much will still remain undone. He can never know all the crimes that are committed, and can seldom punish all that he knows."

"This, said the prince, I do not understand, but I had rather hear thee than dispute. Continue thy narration."

"My father, proceeded Imlac, originally intended that I should have no other education, than such as might qualify me for commerce; and discovering in me great strength of memory, and quickness of apprehension, often declared his hope that I should be some time the richest man in Abissinia."

"Why, said the prince, did thy father desire the increase of his wealth, when it was already greater than he durst discover or enjoy? I am unwilling to doubt thy veracity, yet inconsistencies cannot both be true."

"Inconsistencies, answered Imlac, cannot both be right, but, imputed to man, they may both be true. Yet diversity is not inconsistency. My father might expect a time of greater security. However, some desire is necessary to keep life in motion, and he, whose real wants are supplied, must admit those of fancy."

"This, said the prince, I can in some measure conceive. I repent that I interrupted thee."

"With this hope, proceeded Imlac, he sent me to school; but when I had once found the delight of knowledge, and felt the pleasure of intelligence and the pride of invention, I began silently to despise riches, and determined to disappoint the purpose of my father, whose grossness of conception raised my pity. I was twenty years old before his tenderness would expose me to the fatigue of travel, in which time I had been instructed, by successive masters, in all the literature of my native country. As every hour taught me something new, I lived in a continual course of gratifications; but, as I advanced towards manhood, I lost much of the reverence with which I had been used to look on my instructors; because, when the lesson was ended, I did not find them wiser or better than common men.

"At length my father resolved to initiate me in commerce, and, opening one of his subterranean treasuries, counted out ten thousand pieces of gold. This, young man, said he, is the stock with which you must negociate. I began with less than the fifth part, and you see how diligence and parsimony have increased it. This is your own to waste or to improve. If you squander it by negligence or caprice, you must wait for my death before you will be rich: if, in four years, you double your stock, we will thenceforward let subordination cease, and live together as friends and partners; for he shall always be equal with me, who is equally skilled in the art of growing rich.

"We laid our money upon camels, concealed in bales of cheap goods, and travelled to the shore of the red sea. When I cast my eye on the expanse of waters my heart bounded like that of a prisoner escaped. I felt an unextinguishable curiosity kindle in my mind, and resolved to snatch this opportunity of seeing the manners of other nations, and of learning sciences unknown in Abissinia.

"I remembered that my father had obliged me to the improvement of my stock, not by a promise which I ought not to violate, but by a penalty which I was at liberty to incur, and therefore determined to gratify my predominant desire, and by drinking at the fountains of knowledge, to quench the thirst of curiosity.

"As I was supposed to trade without connexion with my father, it was easy for me to become acquainted with the master of a ship, and procure a passage to some other country. I had no motives of choice to regulate my voyage; it was sufficient for me that, wherever I wandered, I should see a country which I had not seen before. I therefore entered a ship bound for Surat, having left a letter for my father declaring my intention.

CHAP. IX

The history of Imlac continued.

"When I first entered upon the world of waters, and lost sight of land, I looked round about me with pleasing terrour, and thinking my soul enlarged by the boundless prospect, imagined that I could gaze round for ever without satiety; but, in a short time, I grew weary of looking on barren uniformity, where I could only see again what I had already seen. I then descended into the ship, and doubted for a while whether all my future pleasures would not end like this in disgust and disappointment. Yet, surely, said I, the ocean and the land are very different; the only variety of water is rest and motion, but the earth has mountains and vallies, desarts and cities: it is inhabited by men of different customs and contrary opinions; and I may hope to find variety in life, though I should miss it in nature.

"With this thought I quieted my mind; and amused myself during the voyage; sometimes by learning from the sailors the art of navigation, which I have never practised, and sometimes by forming schemes for my conduct in different situations, in not one of which I have been ever placed.

"I was almost weary of my naval amusements when we landed safely at Surat. I secured my money, and purchasing some commodities for show, joined myself to a caravan that was passing into the inland country. My companions, for some reason or other, conjecturing that I was rich, and, by my inquiries and admiration, finding that I was ignorant, considered me as a novice whom they had a right to cheat, and who was to learn at the usual expence the art of fraud. They exposed me to the theft of servants, and the exaction of officers, and saw me plundered upon false pretences, without any advantage to themselves, but that of rejoicing in the superiority of their own knowledge."

"Stop a moment, said the prince, is there such depravity in man, as that he should injure another without benefit to himself? I can easily conceive that all are pleased with superiority; but your ignorance was merely accidental, which, being neither your crime nor your folly, could afford them no reason to applaud themselves; and the knowledge which they had, and which you wanted, they might as effectually have shewn by warning, as betraying you."

"Pride, said Imlac, is seldom delicate, it will please itself with very mean advantages; and envy feels not its own happiness, but when it may be compared with the misery of others. They were my enemies because they grieved to think me rich, and my oppressors because they delighted to find me weak."

"Proceed, said the prince: I doubt not of the facts which you relate, but imagine that you impute them to mistaken motives."

"In this company, said Imlac, I arrived at Agra, the capital of Indostan, the city in which the great Mogul commonly resides. I applied myself to the language of the country, and in a few months was able to converse with the learned men; some of whom I found morose and reserved, and others easy and communicative; some were unwilling to teach another what they had with difficulty learned themselves; and some shewed that the end of their studies was to gain the dignity of instructing.

"To the tutor of the young princes I recommended myself so much, that I was presented to the emperour as a man of uncommon knowledge. The emperour asked me many questions concerning my country and my travels; and though I cannot now recollect any thing that he uttered above the power of a common man, he dismissed me astonished at his wisdom, and enamoured of his goodness.

"My credit was now so high, that the merchants, with whom I had travelled, applied to me for recommendations to the ladies of the court. I was surprised at their confidence of solicitation, and gently reproached them with their practices on the road. They heard me with cold indifference, and shewed no tokens of shame or sorrow.

"They then urged their request with the offer of a bribe; but what I would not do for kindness I would not do for money; and refused them, not because they had injured me, but because I would not enable them to injure others; for I knew they would have made use of my credit to cheat those who should buy their wares.

"Having resided at Agra, till there was no more to be learned, I travelled into Persia, where I saw many remains of ancient magnificence, and observed many new accommodations[1] of life. The Persians are a nation eminently social, and their assemblies afforded me daily opportunities of remarking characters and manners, and of tracing human nature through all its variations.

"From Persia I passed into Arabia, where I saw a nation at once pastoral and warlike; who live without any settled habitation; whose only wealth is their flocks and herds; and who have yet carried on, through all ages, an hereditary war with all mankind, though they neither covet nor envy their possessions.

CHAP. X

Imlac's history continued. A dissertation upon poetry.

"Wherever I went, I found that Poetry was considered as the highest learning, and regarded with a veneration somewhat approaching to that which man would pay to the Angelick Nature. And it yet fills me with wonder, that, in almost all countries, the most ancient poets are considered as the best: whether it be that every other kind of knowledge is an acquisition gradually attained, and poetry is a gift conferred at

Chapter IX. **1. accommodations:** "conveniencies, things requisite to ease or refreshment" (Johnson's *Dictionary*).

once; or that the first poetry of every nation surprised them as a novelty, and retained the credit by consent which it received by accident at first: or whether, as the province of poetry is to describe Nature and Passion, which are always the same, the first writers took possession of the most striking objects for description, and the most probable occurrences for fiction, and left nothing to those that followed them, but transcription of the same events, and new combinations of the same images. Whatever be the reason, it is commonly observed that the early writers are in possession of nature, and their followers of art: that the first excel in strength and invention, and the latter in elegance and refinement.

"I was desirous to add my name to this illustrious fraternity. I read all the poets of Persia and Arabia, and was able to repeat by memory the volumes that are suspended in the mosque of Mecca. But I soon found that no man was ever great by imitation. My desire of excellence impelled me to transfer my attention to nature and to life. Nature was to be my subject, and men to be my auditors: I could never describe what I had not seen: I could not hope to move those with delight or terrour, whose interests and opinions I did not understand.

"Being now resolved to be a poet, I saw every thing with a new purpose; my sphere of attention was suddenly magnified: no kind of knowledge was to be overlooked. I ranged mountains and deserts for images and resemblances, and pictured upon my mind every tree of the forest and flower of the valley. I observed with equal care the crags of the rock and the pinnacles of the palace. Sometimes I wandered along the mazes of the rivulet, and sometimes watched the changes of the summer clouds. To a poet nothing can be useless. Whatever is beautiful, and whatever is dreadful, must be familiar to his imagination: he must be conversant with all that is awfully vast or elegantly little. The plants of the garden, the animals of the wood, the minerals of the earth, and meteors of the sky, must all concur to store his mind with inexhaustible variety: for every idea is useful for the inforcement or decoration of moral or religious truth; and he, who knows most, will have most power of diversifying his scenes, and of gratifying his reader with remote allusions and unexpected instruction.

"All the appearances of nature I was therefore careful to study, and every country which I have surveyed has contributed something to my poetical powers."

"In so wide a survey, said the prince, you must

surely have left much unobserved. I have lived, till now, within the circuit of these mountains, and yet cannot walk abroad without the sight of something which I had never beheld before, or never heeded.

"The business of a poet, said Imlac, is to examine, not the individual, but the species; to remark general properties and large appearances: he does not number the streaks of the tulip, or describe the different shades in the verdure of the forest. He is to exhibit in his portraits of nature such prominent and striking features, as recal the original to every mind; and must neglect the minuter discriminations, which one may have remarked, and another have neglected, for those characteristicks which are alike obvious to vigilance and carelessness.

"But the knowledge of nature is only half the task of a poet; he must be acquainted likewise with all the modes of life. His character requires that he estimate the happiness and misery of every condition; observe the power of all the passions in all their combinations, and trace the changes of the human mind as they are modified by various institutions and accidental influences of climate or custom, from the spriteliness of infancy to the despondence of decrepitude. He must divest himself of the prejudices of his age or country; he must consider right and wrong in their abstracted and invariable state; he must disregard present laws and opinions, and rise to general and transcendental truths, which will always be the same: he must therefore content himself with the slow progress of his name; contemn the applause of his own time, and commit his claims to the justice of posterity. He must write as the interpreter of nature, and the legislator of mankind, and consider himself as presiding over the thoughts and manners of future generations; as a being superiour to time and place. His labour is not yet at an end: he must know many languages and many sciences; and, that his stile may be worthy of his thoughts, must, by incessant practice, familiarize to himself every delicacy of speech and grace of harmony."

CHAP. XI

Imlac's narrative continued. A hint on pilgrimage.

Imlac now felt the enthusiastic fit, and was proceeding to aggrandize his own profession, when the prince cried out, "Enough! Thou hast convinced me, that no human being can ever be a poet. Proceed with thy narration."

"To be a poet, said Imlac, is indeed very difficult." "So difficult, returned the prince, that I will at present hear no more of his labours. Tell me whither you went when you had seen Persia."

"From Persia, said the poet, I travelled through Syria, and for three years resided in Palestine, where I conversed with great numbers of the northern and western nations of Europe; the nations which are now in possession of all power and all knowledge; whose armies are irresistible, and whose fleets command the remotest parts of the globe. When I compared these men with the natives of our own kingdom, and those that surround us, they appeared almost another order of beings. In their countries it is difficult to wish for any thing that may not be obtained: a thousand arts, of which we never heard, are continually labouring for their convenience and pleasure; and whatever their own climate has denied them is supplied by their commerce."

"By what means, said the prince, are the Europeans thus powerful? or why, since they can so easily visit Asia and Africa for trade or conquest, cannot the Asiaticks and Africans invade their coasts, plant colonies in their ports, and give laws to their natural princes? The same wind that carries them back would bring us thither."

"They are more powerful, Sir, than we, answered Imlac, because they are wiser; knowledge will always predominate over ignorance, as man governs the other animals. But why their knowledge is more than ours, I know not what reason can be given, but the unsearchable will of the Supreme Being."

"When, said the prince with a sigh, shall I be able to visit Palestine, and mingle with this mighty confluence of nations? Till that happy moment shall arrive, let me fill up the time with such representations as thou canst give me. I am not ignorant of the motive that assembles such numbers in that place, and cannot but consider it as the center of wisdom and piety, to which the best and wisest men of every land must be continually resorting."

"There are some nations, said Imlac, that send few visitants to Palestine; for many numerous and learned sects in Europe, concur to censure pilgrimage as superstitious, or deride it as ridiculous."

"You know, said the prince, how little my life has made me acquainted with diversity of opinions: it will be too long to hear the arguments on both sides; you, that have considered them, tell me the result."

"Pilgrimage, said Imlac, like many other acts of piety, may be reasonable or superstitious, according to the principles upon which it is performed. Long journies in search of truth are not commanded. Truth, such as is necessary to the regulation of life, is always found where it is honestly sought. Change of place is no natural cause of the increase of piety, for it inevitably produces dissipation of mind. Yet, since men go every day to view the fields where great actions have been performed, and return with stronger impressions of the event, curiosity of the same kind may naturally dispose us to view that country whence our religion had its beginning; and I believe no man surveys those awful scenes without some confirmation of holy resolutions. That the Supreme Being may be more easily propitiated in one place than in another, is the dream of idle superstition; but that some places may operate upon our own minds in an uncommon manner, is an opinion which hourly experience will justify. He who supposes that his vices may be more successfully combated in Palestine, will, perhaps, find himself mistaken, yet he may go thither without folly: he who thinks they will be more freely pardoned, dishonours at once his reason and religion."

"These, said the prince, are European distinctions. I will consider them another time. What have you found to be the effect of knowledge? Are those nations happier than we?"

"There is so much infelicity, said the poet, in the world, that scarce any man has leisure from his own distresses to estimate the comparative happiness of others. Knowledge is certainly one of the means of pleasure, as is confessed by the natural desire which every mind feels of increasing its ideas. Ignorance is mere privation, by which nothing can be produced: it is a vacuity in which the soul sits motionless and torpid for want of attraction; and, without knowing why, we always rejoice when we learn, and grieve when we forget. I am therefore inclined to conclude, that, if nothing counteracts the natural consequence of learning, we grow more happy as our minds take a wider range.

"In enumerating the particular comforts of life we shall find many advantages on the side of the Europeans. They cure wounds and diseases with which we languish and perish. We suffer inclemencies of weather which they can obviate. They have engines for the despatch of many laborious works, which we must perform by manual industry. There is such communication between distant places, that one friend can hardly be said to be absent from another. Their policy removes all publick inconveniencies: they have roads cut through their mountains, and bridges laid upon their rivers. And, if we descend to the privacies of life, their habitations are more commodious, and their possessions are more secure."

"They are surely happy, said the prince, who have all these conveniencies, of which I envy none so much as the facility with which separated friends interchange their thoughts."

"The Europeans, answered Imlac, are less unhappy than we, but they are not happy. Human life is every where a state in which much is to be endured, and little to be enjoyed."

CHAP. XII

The story of Imlac continued.

"I am not yet willing, said the prince, to suppose that happiness is so parsimoniously distributed to mortals; nor can believe but that, if I had the choice of life, I should be able to fill every day with pleasure. I would injure no man, and should provoke no resentment: I would relieve every distress, and should enjoy the benedictions of gratitude. I would choose my friends among the wise, and my wife among the virtuous; and therefore should be in no danger from treachery, or unkindness. My children should, by my care, be learned and pious, and would repay to my age what their childhood had received. What would dare to molest him who might call on every side to thousands enriched by his bounty, or assisted by his power? And why should not life glide quietly away in the soft reciprocation of protection and reverence? All this may be done without the help of European refinements, which appear by their effects to be rather specious than useful. Let us leave them and persue our journey."

"From Palestine, said Imlac, I passed through many regions of Asia; in the more civilized kingdoms as a trader, and among the Barbarians of the mountains as a pilgrim. At last I began to long for my native country, that I might repose after my travels, and fatigues, in the places where I had spent my earliest years, and gladden my old companions with the recital of my adventures. Often did I figure to myself those, with whom I had sported away the gay hours of dawning life, sitting round me in its evening, wondering at my tales, and listening to my counsels.

"When this thought had taken possession of my mind, I considered every moment as wasted which did not bring me nearer to Abissinia. I hastened into Egypt, and, notwithstanding my impatience, was detained ten months in the contemplation of its ancient magnificence, and in enquiries after the remains of its ancient learning. I found in Cairo a mixture of all nations; some brought thither by the love of knowledge, some by the hope of gain, and many by the desire of living after their own manner without observation, and of lying hid in the obscurity of multitudes: for, in a city, populous as Cairo, it is possible to obtain at the same time the gratifications of society, and the secrecy of solitude.

"From Cairo I travelled to Suez, and embarked on the red sea, passing along the coast till I arrived at the port from which I had departed twenty years before. Here I joined myself to a caravan and re-entered my native country.

"I now expected the caresses of my kinsmen, and the congratulations of my friends, and was not without hope that my father, whatever value he had set upon riches, would own with gladness and pride a son who was able to add to the felicity and honour of the nation. But I was soon convinced that my thoughts were vain. My father had been dead fourteen years, having divided his wealth among my brothers, who were removed to some other provinces. Of my companions the greater part was in the grave, of the rest some could with difficulty remember me, and some considered me as one corrupted by foreign manners.

"A man used to vicissitudes is not easily dejected. I forgot, after a time, my disappointment, and endeavoured to recommend myself to the nobles of the kingdom: they admitted me to their tables, heard my story, and dismissed me. I opened a school, and was prohibited to teach. I then resolved to sit down in the quiet of domestick life, and addressed a lady that was fond of my conversation, but rejected my suit, because my father was a merchant.

"Wearied at last with solicitation and repulses, I resolved to hide myself for ever from the world, and depend no longer on the opinion or caprice of others. I waited for the time when the gate of the *happy valley* should open, that I might bid farewell to hope and fear: the day came; my performance was distinguished

with favour, and I resigned myself with joy to perpetual confinement."

"Hast thou here found happiness at last? said Rasselas. Tell me without reserve; art thou content with thy condition? or, dost thou wish to be again wandering and inquiring? All the inhabitants of this valley celebrate their lot, and, at the annual visit of the emperour, invite others to partake of their felicity."

"Great prince, said Imlac, I shall speak the truth: I know not one of all your attendants who does not lament the hour when he entered this retreat. I am less unhappy than the rest, because I have a mind replete with images, which I can vary and combine at pleasure. I can amuse my solitude by the renovation of the knowledge which begins to fade from my memory, and by recollection of the accidents of my past life. Yet all this ends in the sorrowful consideration, that my acquirements are now useless, and that none of my pleasures can be again enjoyed. The rest, whose minds have no impression but of the present moment, are either corroded by malignant passions, or sit stupid in the gloom of perpetual vacancy."

"What passions can infest those, said the prince, who have no rivals? We are in a place where impotence precludes malice, and where all envy is repressed by community of enjoyments." *why are men malicious*

"There may be community, said Imlac, of material possessions, but there can never be community of love or of esteem. It must happen that one will please more than another; he that knows himself despised will always be envious; and still more envious and malevolent, if he is condemned to live in the presence of those who despise him. The invitations, by which they allure others to a state which they feel to be wretched, proceed from the natural malignity of hopeless misery. They are weary of themselves, and of each other, and expect to find relief in new companions. They envy the liberty which their folly has forfeited, and would gladly see all mankind imprisoned like themselves.

"From this crime, however, I am wholly free. No man can say that he is wretched by my persuasion. I look with pity on the crowds who are annually soliciting admission to captivity, and wish that it were lawful for me to warn them of their danger."

"My dear Imlac, said the prince, I will open to thee my whole heart. I have long meditated an escape from the happy valley. I have examined the mountains on every side, but find myself insuperably barred: teach me the way to break my prison; thou shalt be the companion of my flight, the guide of my rambles, the partner of my fortune, and my sole director in the *choice of life.*"

"Sir, answered the poet, your escape will be difficult, and, perhaps, you may soon repent your curiosity. The world, which you figure to yourself smooth and quiet as the lake in the valley, you will find a sea foaming with tempests, and boiling with whirlpools: you will be sometimes overwhelmed by the waves of violence, and sometimes dashed against the rocks of treachery. Amidst wrongs and frauds, competitions and anxieties, you will wish a thousand times for these seats of quiet, and willingly quit hope to be free from fear."

"Do not seek to deter me from my purpose, said the prince: I am impatient to see what thou hast seen; and, since thou art thyself weary of the valley, it is evident, that thy former state was better than this. Whatever be the consequence of my experiment, I am resolved to judge with my own eyes of the various conditions of men, and then to make deliberately my *choice of life.*"

"I am afraid, said Imlac, you are hindered by stronger restraints than my persuasions; yet, if your determination is fixed, I do not counsel you to despair. Few things are impossible to diligence and skill."

CHAP. XIII

Rasselas discovers the means of escape.

The prince now dismissed his favourite to rest, but the narrative of wonders and novelties filled his mind with perturbation. He revolved all that he had heard, and prepared innumerable questions for the morning.

Much of his uneasiness was now removed. He had a friend to whom he could impart his thoughts, and whose experience could assist him in his designs. His heart was no longer condemned to swell with silent vexation. He thought that even the *happy valley* might be endured with such a companion, and that, if they could range the world together, he should have nothing further to desire.

In a few days the water was discharged, and the ground dried. The prince and Imlac then walked out together to converse without the notice of the rest. The prince, whose thoughts were always on the wing, as he passed by the gate, said, with a countenance of sorrow, "Why art thou so strong, and why is man so weak?"

"Man is not weak, answered his companion; knowledge is more than equivalent to force. The master of mechanicks laughs at strength. I can burst the gate, but cannot do it secretly. Some other expedient must be tried."

As they were walking on the side of the mountain, they observed that the conies,[1] which the rain had driven from their burrows, had taken shelter among the bushes, and formed holes behind them, tending upwards in an oblique line. "It has been the opinion of antiquity, said Imlac, that human reason borrowed many arts from the instinct of animals; let us, therefore, not think ourselves degraded by learning from the coney. We may escape by piercing the mountain in the same direction. We will begin where the summit hangs over the middle part, and labour upward till we shall issue out beyond the prominence."

The eyes of the prince, when he heard this proposal, sparkled with joy. The execution was easy, and the success certain.

No time was now lost. They hastened early in the morning to chuse a place proper for their mine. They clambered with great fatigue among crags and brambles, and returned without having discovered any part that favoured their design. The second and the third day were spent in the same manner, and with the same frustration. But, on the fourth, they found a small cavern, concealed by a thicket, where they resolved to make their experiment.

Imlac procured instruments proper to hew stone and remove earth, and they fell to their work on the next day with more eagerness than vigour. They were presently exhausted by their efforts, and sat down to pant upon the grass. The prince, for a moment, appeared to be discouraged. "Sir, said his companion, practice will enable us to continue our labour for a longer time; mark, however, how far we have advanced, and you will find that our toil will some time have an end. Great works are performed, not by strength, but perseverance: yonder palace was raised by single stones, yet you see its height and spaciousness. He that shall walk with vigour three hours a day will pass in seven years a space equal to the circumference of the globe."

They returned to their work day after day, and, in a short time, found a fissure in the rock, which enabled them to pass far with very little obstruction. This Rasselas considered as a good omen. "Do not disturb

Chapter XIII. **1. conies:** rabbits.

your mind, said Imlac, with other hopes or fears than reason may suggest: if you are pleased with prognosticks of good, you will be terrified likewise with tokens of evil, and your whole life will be a prey to superstition. Whatever facilitates our work is more than an omen, it is a cause of success. This is one of those pleasing surprises which often happen to active resolution. Many things difficult to design prove easy to performance."

CHAP. XIV

Rasselas and Imlac receive an unexpected visit.

They had now wrought their way to the middle, and solaced their toil with the approach of liberty, when the prince, coming down to refresh himself with air, found his sister Nekayah standing before the mouth of the cavity. He started and stood confused, afraid to tell his design, and yet hopeless to conceal it. A few moments determined him to repose on her fidelity, and secure her secrecy by a declaration without reserve.

"Do not imagine, said the princess, that I came hither as a spy: I had long observed from my window, that you and Imlac directed your walk every day towards the same point, but I did not suppose you had any better reason for the preference than a cooler shade, or more fragrant bank; nor followed you with any other design than to partake of your conversation. Since then not suspicion but fondness has detected you, let me not lose the advantage of my discovery. I am equally weary of confinement with yourself, and not less desirous of knowing what is done or suffered in the world. Permit me to fly with you from this tasteless tranquility, which will yet grow more loathsome when you have left me. You may deny me to accompany you, but cannot hinder me from following."

The prince, who loved Nekayah above his other sisters, had no inclination to refuse her request, and grieved that he had lost an opportunity of shewing his confidence by a voluntary communication. It was therefore agreed that she should leave the valley with them; and that, in the mean time, she should watch, lest any other straggler should, by chance or curiosity, follow them to the mountain.

At length their labour was at an end; they saw light beyond the prominence, and, issuing to the top of the mountain, beheld the Nile, yet a narrow current, wandering beneath them.

The prince looked round with rapture, anticipated all the pleasures of travel, and in thought was already transported beyond his father's dominions. Imlac, though very joyful at his escape, had less expectation of pleasure in the world, which he had before tried, and of which he had been weary.

Rasselas was so much delighted with a wider horizon, that he could not soon be persuaded to return into the valley. He informed his sister that the way was open, and that nothing now remained but to prepare for their departure.

CHAP. XV

The prince and princess leave the valley,
and see many wonders.

The prince and princess had jewels sufficient to make them rich whenever they came into a place of commerce, which, by Imlac's direction, they hid in their cloaths, and, on the night of the next full moon, all left the valley. The princess was followed only by a single favourite, who did not know whither she was going.

They clambered through the cavity, and began to go down on the other side. The princess and her maid turned their eyes towards every part, and, seeing nothing to bound their prospect, considered themselves as in danger of being lost in a dreary vacuity. They stopped and trembled. "I am almost afraid, said the princess, to begin a journey of which I cannot perceive an end, and to venture into this immense plain where I may be approached on every side by men whom I never saw." The prince felt nearly the same emotions, though he thought it more manly to conceal them.

Imlac smiled at their terrours, and encouraged them to proceed; but the princess continued irresolute till she had been imperceptibly drawn forward too far to return.

In the morning they found some shepherds in the field, who set milk and fruits before them. The princess wondered that she did not see a palace ready for her reception, and a table spread with delicacies; but, being faint and hungry, she drank the milk and eat the fruits, and thought them of a higher flavour than the products of the valley.

They travelled forward by easy journeys, being all unaccustomed to toil or difficulty, and knowing, that though they might be missed, they could not be persued. In a few days they came into a more populous region, where Imlac was diverted with the admiration which his companions expressed at the diversity of manners, stations and employments.

Their dress was such as might not bring upon them the suspicion of having any thing to conceal, yet the prince, wherever he came, expected to be obeyed, and the princess was frighted, because those that came into her presence did not prostrate themselves before her. Imlac was forced to observe them with great vigilance, lest they should betray their rank by their unusual behaviour, and detained them several weeks in the first village to accustom them to the sight of common mortals.

By degrees the royal wanderers were taught to understand that they had for a time laid aside their dignity, and were to expect only such regard as liberality and courtesy could procure. And Imlac, having, by many admonitions, prepared them to endure the tumults of a port, and the ruggedness of the commercial race, brought them down to the sea-coast.

The prince and his sister, to whom every thing was new, were gratified equally at all places, and therefore remained for some months at the port without any inclination to pass further. Imlac was content with their stay, because he did not think it safe to expose them, unpractised in the world, to the hazards of a foreign country.

At last he began to fear lest they should be discovered, and proposed to fix a day for their departure. They had no pretensions to judge for themselves, and referred the whole scheme to his direction. He therefore took passage in a ship to Suez; and, when the time came, with great difficulty prevailed on the princess to enter the vessel. They had a quick and prosperous voyage, and from Suez travelled by land to Cairo.

CHAP. XVI

They enter Cairo, and find every man happy.

As they approached the city, which filled the strangers with astonishment, "This, said Imlac to the prince, is the place where travellers and merchants assemble from all the corners of the earth. You will here find men of every character, and every occupation. Commerce is here honourable: I will act as a merchant, and you shall live as strangers, who have no other end of travel than curiosity; it will soon be observed that we are rich; our reputation will procure us access to all whom we shall desire to know; you will see all the conditions of humanity, and enable yourself at leisure to make your *choice of life*."

They now entered the town, stunned by the noise, and offended by the crowds. Instruction had not yet so prevailed over habit, but that they wondered to see themselves pass undistinguished along the street, and met by the lowest of the people without reverence or notice. The princess could not at first bear the thought of being levelled with the vulgar, and, for some days, continued in her chamber, where she was served by her favourite Pekuah as in the palace of the valley.

Imlac, who understood traffick, sold part of the jewels the next day, and hired a house, which he adorned with such magnificence, that he was immediately considered as a merchant of great wealth. His politeness attracted many acquaintance, and his generosity made him courted by many dependants. His table was crowded by men of every nation, who all admired his knowledge, and solicited his favour. His companions, not being able to mix in the conversation, could make no discovery of their ignorance or surprise, and were gradually initiated in the world as they gained knowledge of the language.

The prince had, by frequent lectures, been taught the use and nature of money; but the ladies could not, for a long time, comprehend what the merchants did with small pieces of gold and silver, or why things of so little use should be received as equivalent to the necessaries of life.

They studied the language two years, while Imlac was preparing to set before them the various ranks and conditions of mankind. He grew acquainted with all who had any thing uncommon in their fortune or conduct. He frequented the voluptuous and the frugal, the idle and the busy, the merchants and the men of learning.

The prince, being now able to converse with fluency, and having learned the caution necessary to be observed in his intercourse with strangers, began to accompany Imlac to places of resort, and to enter into all assemblies, that he might make his *choice of life*.

For some time he thought choice needless, because all appeared to him equally happy. Wherever he went he met gayety and kindness, and heard the song of joy, or the laugh of carelessness. He began to believe that the world overflowed with universal plenty, and that nothing was withheld either from want or merit; that every hand showered liberality, and every heart melted with benevolence: "and who then, says he, will be suffered to be wretched?"

Imlac permitted the pleasing delusion, and was unwilling to crush the hope of inexperience, till one day, having sat a while silent, "I know not, said the prince, what can be the reason that I am more unhappy than any of our friends. I see them perpetually and unalterably chearful, but feel my own mind restless and uneasy. I am unsatisfied with those pleasures which I seem most to court; I live in the crowds of jollity, not so much to enjoy company as to shun myself, and am only loud and merry to conceal my sadness."

"Every man, said Imlac, may, by examining his own mind, guess what passes in the minds of others: when you feel that your own gaiety is counterfeit, it may justly lead you to suspect that of your companions not to be sincere. Envy is commonly reciprocal. We are long before we are convinced that happiness is never to be found, and each believes it possessed by others, to keep alive the hope of obtaining it for himself. In the assembly, where you passed the last night, there appeared such spriteliness of air, and volatility of fancy, as might have suited beings of an higher order, formed to inhabit serener regions inaccessible to care or sorrow: yet, believe me, prince, there was not one who did not dread the moment when solitude should deliver him to the tyranny of reflection."

"This, said the prince, may be true of others, since it is true of me; yet, whatever be the general infelicity of man, one condition is more happy than another, and wisdom surely directs us to take the least evil in the *choice of life*."

"The causes of good and evil, answered Imlac, are so various and uncertain, so often entangled with each other, so diversified by various relations, and so much subject to accidents which cannot be foreseen, that he who would fix his condition upon incontestable reasons of preference, must live and die enquiring and deliberating."

"But surely, said Rasselas, the wise men, to whom we listen with reverence and wonder, chose that mode of life for themselves which they thought most likely to make them happy."

"Very few, said the poet, live by choice. Every man is placed in his present condition by causes which acted without his foresight, and with which he did not always willingly co-operate; and therefore you will rarely meet one who does not think the lot of his neighbour better than his own."

"I am pleased to think, said the prince, that my birth has given me at least one advantage over others, by enabling me to determine for myself. I have here the world before me; I will review it at leisure: surely happiness is somewhere to be found."

CHAP. XVII

The prince associates with young men of spirit and gaiety.

Rasselas rose next day, and resolved to begin his experiments upon life. "Youth, cried he, is the time of gladness: I will join myself to the young men, whose only business is to gratify their desires, and whose time is all spent in a succession of enjoyments."

To such societies he was readily admitted, but a few days brought him back weary and disgusted. Their mirth was without images, their laughter without motive: their pleasures were gross and sensual, in which the mind had no part: their conduct was at once wild and mean; they laughed at order and at law, but the frown of power dejected, and the eye of wisdom abashed them.

The prince soon concluded, that he should never be happy in a course of life of which he was ashamed. He thought it unsuitable to a reasonable being to act without a plan, and to be sad or chearful only by chance. "Happiness, said he, must be something solid and permanent, without fear and without uncertainty."

But his young companions had gained so much of his regard by their frankness and courtesy, that he could not leave them without warning and remonstrance. "My friends, said he, I have seriously considered our manners and our prospects, and find that we have mistaken our own interest. The first years of man must make provision for the last. He that never thinks never can be wise. Perpetual levity must end in ignorance; and intemperance, though it may fire the spirits for an hour, will make life short or miserable. Let us consider that youth is of no long duration, and that in maturer age, when the enchantments of fancy shall cease, and phantoms of delight dance no more about us, we shall have no comforts but the esteem of wise men, and the means of doing good. Let us, therefore, stop, while to stop is in our power: let us live as men who are sometime to grow old, and to whom it will be the most dreadful of all evils not to count their past years but by follies, and to be reminded of their former luxuriance of health only by the maladies which riot has produced."

They stared a while in silence one upon another, and, at last, drove him away by a general chorus of continued laughter.

The consciousness that his sentiments were just, and his intentions kind, was scarcely sufficient to support him against the horrour of derision. But he recovered his tranquility, and persued his search.

CHAP. XVIII

The prince finds a wise and happy man.

As he was one day walking in the street, he saw a spacious building which all were, by the open doors, invited to enter: he followed the stream of people, and found it a hall or school of declamation, in which professors read lectures to their auditory. He fixed his eye upon a sage raised above the rest, who discoursed with great energy on the government of the passions. His look was venerable, his action graceful, his pronunciation clear, and his diction elegant. He shewed, with great strength of sentiment, and variety of illustration, that human nature is degraded and debased, when the lower faculties predominate over the higher; that when fancy, the parent of passion, usurps the dominion of the mind, nothing ensues but the natural effect of unlawful government, perturbation and confusion; that she betrays the fortresses of the intellect to rebels, and excites her children to sedition against reason their lawful sovereign. He compared reason to the sun, of which the light is constant, uniform, and lasting; and fancy to a meteor, of bright but transitory lustre, irregular in its motion, and delusive in its direction.

He then communicated the various precepts given from time to time for the conquest of passion, and displayed the happiness of those who had obtained the important victory, after which man is no longer the slave of fear, nor the fool of hope; is no more emaciated by envy, inflamed by anger, emasculated by tenderness, or depressed by grief; but walks on calmly through the tumults or the privacies of life, as the sun persues alike his course through the calm or the stormy sky.

He enumerated many examples of heroes immovable by pain or pleasure, who looked with indifference on those modes or accidents to which the vulgar give the names of good and evil. He exhorted his hearers to lay aside their prejudices, and arm themselves against the shafts of malice or misfortune, by invulnerable patience; concluding, that this state only was happiness, and that this happiness was in every one's power.

Rasselas listened to him with the veneration due to the instructions of a superiour being, and, waiting for him at the door, humbly implored the liberty of visiting so great a master of true wisdom. The lecturer hesitated a moment, when Rasselas put a purse of gold into his hand, which he received with a mixture of joy and wonder.

"I have found, said the prince, at his return to Imlac, a man who can teach all that is necessary to be known, who, from the unshaken throne of rational fortitude, looks down on the scenes of life changing beneath him. He speaks, and attention watches his lips. He reasons, and conviction closes his periods. This man shall be my future guide: I will learn his doctrines, and imitate his life." "Be not too hasty, said Imlac, to trust, or to admire, the teachers of morality: they discourse like angels, but they live like men."

Rasselas, who could not conceive how any man could reason so forcibly without feeling the cogency of his own arguments, paid his visit in a few days, and was denied admission. He had now learned the power of money, and made his way by a piece of gold to the inner apartment, where he found the philosopher in a room half darkened, with his eyes misty, and his face pale. "Sir, said he, you are come at a time when all human friendship is useless; what I suffer cannot be remedied, what I have lost cannot be supplied. My daughter, my only daughter, from whose tenderness I expected all the comforts of my age, died last night of a fever. My views, my purposes, my hopes are at an end: I am now a lonely being disunited from society."

"Sir, said the prince, mortality is an event by which a wise man can never be surprised: we know that death is always near, and it should therefore always be expected." "Young man, answered the philosopher, you speak like one that has never felt the pangs of separation." "Have you then forgot the precepts, said Rasselas, which you so powerfully enforced? Has wisdom no strength to arm the heart against calamity?

Consider, that external things are naturally variable, but truth and reason are always the same." "What comfort, said the mourner, can truth and reason afford me? of what effect are they now, but to tell me, that my daughter will not be restored?"

The prince, whose humanity would not suffer him to insult misery with reproof, went away convinced of the emptiness of rhetorical sound, and the inefficacy of polished periods and studied sentences.

CHAP. XIX

A Glimpse of pastoral life.

He was still eager upon the same enquiry; and, having heard of a hermit, that lived near the lowest cataract of the Nile, and filled the whole country with the fame of his sanctity, resolved to visit his retreat, and enquire whether that felicity, which publick life could not afford, was to be found in solitude; and whether a man, whose age and virtue made him venerable, could teach any peculiar art of shunning evils, or enduring them.

Imlac and the princess agreed to accompany him, and, after the necessary preparations, they began their journey. Their way lay through fields, where shepherds tended their flocks, and the lambs were playing upon the pasture. "This, said the poet, is the life which has been often celebrated for its innocence and quiet: let us pass the heat of the day among the shepherds tents, and know whether all our searches are not to terminate in pastoral simplicity."

The proposal pleased them, and they induced the shepherds, by small presents and familiar questions, to tell their opinion of their own state: they were so rude and ignorant, so little able to compare the good with the evil of the occupation, and so indistinct in their narratives and descriptions, that very little could be learned from them. But it was evident that their hearts were cankered with discontent; that they considered themselves as condemned to labour for the luxury of the rich, and looked up with stupid malevolence toward those that were placed above them.

The princess pronounced with vehemence, that she would never suffer these envious savages to be her companions, and that she should not soon be desirous of seeing any more specimens of rustick happiness; but could not believe that all the accounts of primeval pleasures were fabulous, and was yet in doubt whether life had any thing that could be justly preferred to the placid gratifications of fields and woods. She hoped that the time would come, when, with a few virtuous and elegant companions, she should gather flowers planted by her own hand, fondle the lambs of her own ewe, and listen, without care, among brooks and breezes, to one of her maidens reading in the shade.

CHAP. XX

The danger of prosperity.

On the next day they continued their journey, till the heat compelled them to look round for shelter. At a small distance they saw a thick wood, which they no sooner entered than they perceived that they were approaching the habitations of men. The shrubs were diligently cut away to open walks where the shades were darkest; the boughs of opposite trees were artificially interwoven; seats of flowery turf were raised in vacant spaces, and a rivulet, that wantoned along the side of a winding path, had its banks sometimes opened into small basons, and its stream sometimes obstructed by little mounds of stone heaped together to increase its murmurs.

They passed slowly through the wood, delighted with such unexpected accommodations, and entertained each other with conjecturing what, or who, he could be, that, in those rude and unfrequented regions, had leisure and art for such harmless luxury.

As they advanced, they heard the sound of musick, and saw youths and virgins dancing in the grove; and, going still further, beheld a stately palace built upon a hill surrounded with woods. The laws of eastern hospitality allowed them to enter, and the master welcomed them like a man liberal and wealthy.

He was skilful enough in appearances soon to discern that they were no common guests, and spread his table with magnificence. The eloquence of Imlac caught his attention, and the lofty courtesy of the princess excited his respect. When they offered to depart he entreated their stay, and was the next day still more unwilling to dismiss them than before. They were easily persuaded to stop, and civility grew up in time to freedom and confidence.

The prince now saw all the domesticks chearful, and all the face of nature smiling round the place, and could not forbear to hope that he should find here what he was seeking; but when he was congratulating the master upon his possessions, he answered with a sigh, "My condition has indeed the appearance of happiness, but appearances are delusive. My prosperity puts my life in danger; the Bassa of Egypt is my enemy, incensed only by my wealth and popularity. I have been hitherto protected against him by the princes of the country; but, as the favour of the great is uncertain, I know not how soon my defenders may be persuaded to share the plunder with the Bassa. I have sent my treasures into a distant country, and, upon the first alarm, am prepared to follow them. Then will my enemies riot in my mansion, and enjoy the gardens which I have planted."

They all joined in lamenting his danger, and deprecating his exile; and the princess was so much disturbed with the tumult of grief and indignation, that she retired to her apartment. They continued with their kind inviter a few days longer, and then went forward to find the hermit.

CHAP. XXI

The happiness of solitude. The hermit's history.

They came on the third day, by the direction of the peasants, to the hermit's cell: it was a cavern in the side of a mountain, over-shadowed with palm-trees; at such a distance from the cataract, that nothing more was heard than a gentle uniform murmur, such as composed the mind to pensive meditation, especially when it was assisted by the wind whistling among the branches. The first rude essay of nature had been so much improved by human labour, that the cave contained several apartments, appropriated to different uses, and often afforded lodging to travellers, whom darkness or tempests happened to overtake.

The hermit sat on a bench at the door, to enjoy the coolness of the evening. On one side lay a book with pens and papers, on the other mechanical instruments of various kinds. As they approached him unregarded, the princess observed that he had not the countenance of a man that had found, or could teach, the way to happiness.

They saluted him with great respect, which he repaid like a man not unaccustomed to the forms of courts. "My children, said he, if you have lost your way, you shall be willingly supplied with such conveniencies for the night as this cavern will afford. I have all that nature requires, and you will not expect delicacies in a hermit's cell."

They thanked him, and, entering, were pleased with the neatness and regularity of the place. The hermit set flesh and wine before them, though he fed only upon fruits and water. His discourse was chearful without levity, and pious without enthusiasm.[1] He soon gained the esteem of his guests, and the princess repented of her hasty censure.

At last Imlac began thus: "I do not now wonder that your reputation is so far extended; we have heard at Cairo of your wisdom, and came hither to implore your direction for this young man and maiden in the choice of life."

"To him that lives well, answered the hermit, every form of life is good; nor can I give any other rule for choice, than to remove from all apparent evil."

"He will remove most certainly from evil, said the prince, who shall devote himself to that solitude which you have recommended by your example."

"I have indeed lived fifteen years in solitude, said the hermit, but have no desire that my example should gain any imitators. In my youth I professed arms, and was raised by degrees to the highest military rank. I have traversed wide countries at the head of my troops, and seen many battles and sieges. At last, being disgusted by the preferment of a younger officer, and feeling that my vigour was beginning to decay, I resolved to close my life in peace, having found the world full of snares, discord, and misery. I had once escaped from the persuit of the enemy by the shelter of this cavern, and therefore chose it for my final residence. I employed artificers to form it into chambers, and stored it with all that I was likely to want.

"For some time after my retreat, I rejoiced like a tempest-beaten sailor at his entrance into the harbour, being delighted with the sudden change of the noise and hurry of war, to stillness and repose. When the pleasure of novelty went away, I employed my hours in examining the plants which grow in the valley, and the minerals which I collected from the rocks. But that enquiry is now grown tasteless and irksome. I have been for some time unsettled and distracted: my mind is disturbed with a thousand perplexities of doubt, and vanities of imagination, which hourly prevail upon me, because I have no opportunities of relaxation or diversion. I am sometimes ashamed to think that I could not secure myself from vice, but by

Chapter XXI. 1. enthusiasm: "a vain belief of private revelation" (Johnson's Dictionary).

retiring from the exercise of virtue, and begin to suspect that I was rather impelled by resentment, than led by devotion, into solitude. My fancy riots in scenes of folly, and I lament that I have lost so much, and have gained so little. In solitude, if I escape the example of bad men, I want likewise the counsel and conversation of the good. I have been long comparing the evils with the advantages of society, and resolve to return into the world to morrow. The life of a solitary man will be certainly miserable, but not certainly devout."

They heard his resolution with surprise, but, after a short pause, offered to conduct him to Cairo. He dug up a considerable treasure which he had hid among the rocks, and accompanied them to the city, on which, as he approached it, he gazed with rapture.

CHAP. XXII

The happiness of a life led according to nature.

Rasselas went often to an assembly of learned men, who met at stated times to unbend their minds, and compare their opinions. Their manners were somewhat coarse, but their conversation was instructive, and their disputations acute, though sometimes too violent, and often continued till neither controvertist remembered upon what question they began. Some faults were almost general among them: every one was desirous to dictate to the rest, and every one was pleased to hear the genius or knowledge of another depreciated.

In this assembly Rasselas was relating his interview with the hermit, and the wonder with which he heard him censure a course of life which he had so deliberately chosen, and so laudably followed. The sentiments of the hearers were various. Some were of opinion, that the folly of his choice had been justly punished by condemnation to perpetual perseverance. One of the youngest among them, with great vehemence, pronounced him an hypocrite. Some talked of the right of society to the labour of individuals, and considered retirement as a desertion of duty. Others readily allowed, that there was a time when the claims of the publick were satisfied, and when a man might properly sequester himself, to review his life, and purify his heart.

One, who appeared more affected with the narrative than the rest, thought it likely, that the hermit would, in a few years, go back to his retreat, and, perhaps, if shame did not restrain, or death intercept him, return

once more from his retreat into the world: "For the hope of happiness, said he, is so strongly impressed, that the longest experience is not able to efface it. Of the present state, whatever it be, we feel, and are forced to confess, the misery, yet, when the same state is again at a distance, imagination paints it as desirable. But the time will surely come, when desire will be no longer our torment, and no man shall be wretched but by his own fault."

"This, said a philosopher, who had heard him with tokens of great impatience, is the present condition of a wise man. The time is already come, when none are wretched but by their own fault. Nothing is more idle, than to enquire after happiness, which nature has kindly placed within our reach. The way to be happy is to live according to nature, in obedience to that universal and unalterable law with which every heart is originally impressed; which is not written on it by precept, but engraven by destiny, not instilled by education, but infused at our nativity. He that lives according to nature will suffer nothing from the delusions of hope, or importunities of desire: he will receive and reject with equability of temper; and act or suffer as the reason of things shall alternately prescribe. Other men may amuse themselves with subtle definitions, or intricate raciocination. Let them learn to be wise by easier means: let them observe the hind of the forest, and the linnet of the grove: let them consider the life of animals, whose motions are regulated by instinct; they obey their guide and are happy. Let us therefore, at length, cease to dispute, and learn to live; throw away the incumbrance of precepts, which they who utter them with so much pride and pomp do not understand, and carry with us this simple and intelligible maxim, That deviation from nature is deviation from happiness."

When he had spoken, he looked round him with a placid air, and enjoyed the consciousness of his own beneficence. "Sir, said the prince, with great modesty, as I, like all the rest of mankind, am desirous of felicity, my closest attention has been fixed upon your discourse: I doubt not the truth of a position which a man so learned has so confidently advanced. Let me only know what it is to live according to nature."

"When I find young men so humble and so docile, said the philosopher, I can deny them no information which my studies have enabled me to afford. To live according to nature, is to act always with due regard to the fitness arising from the relations and qualities of causes and effects; to concur with the great and

satire on lofty philosophism

unchangeable scheme of universal felicity; to co-operate with the general disposition and tendency of the present system of things." *unintelligible*

The prince soon found that this was one of the sages whom he should understand less as he heard him longer. He therefore bowed and was silent, and the philosopher, supposing him satisfied, and the rest vanquished, rose up and departed with the air of a man that had co-operated with the present system.

CHAP. XXIII

The prince and his sister divide between them the work of observation.

Rasselas returned home full of reflexions, doubtful how to direct his future steps. Of the way to happiness he found the learned and simple equally ignorant; but, as he was yet young, he flattered himself that he had time remaining for more experiments, and further enquiries. He communicated to Imlac his observations and his doubts, but was answered by him with new doubts, and remarks that gave him no comfort. He therefore discoursed more frequently and freely with his sister, who had yet the same hope with himself, and always assisted him to give some reason why, though he had been hitherto frustrated, he might succeed at last.

"We have hitherto, said she, known but little of the world: we have never yet been either great or mean. In our own country, though we had royalty, we had no power, and in this we have not yet seen the private recesses of domestick peace. Imlac favours not our search, lest we should in time find him mistaken. We will divide the task between us: you shall try what is to be found in the splendour of courts, and I will range the shades of humbler life. Perhaps command and authority may be the supreme blessings, as they afford most opportunities of doing good: or, perhaps, what this world can give may be found in the modest habitations of middle fortune; too low for great designs, and too high for penury and distress."

CHAP. XXIV

The prince examines the happiness of high stations.

Rasselas applauded the design, and appeared next day with a splendid retinue at the court of the Bassa. He

was soon distinguished for his magnificence, and admitted, as a prince whose curiosity had brought him from distant countries, to an intimacy with the great officers, and frequent conversation with the Bassa himself.

He was at first inclined to believe, that the man must be pleased with his own condition, whom all approached with reverence, and heard with obedience, and who had the power to extend his edicts to a whole kingdom. "There can be no pleasure, said he, equal to that of feeling at once the joy of thousands all made happy by wise administration. Yet, since, by the law of subordination, this sublime delight can be in one nation but the lot of one, it is surely reasonable to think that there is some satisfaction more popular and accessible, and that millions can hardly be subjected to the will of a single man, only to fill his particular breast with incommunicable content."

These thoughts were often in his mind, and he found no solution of the difficulty. But as presents and civilities gained him more familiarity, he found that almost every man who stood high in employment hated all the rest, and was hated by them, and that their lives were a continual succession of plots and detections, stratagems and escapes, faction and treachery. Many of those, who surrounded the Bassa, were sent only to watch and report his conduct; every tongue was muttering censure, and every eye was searching for a fault.

At last the letters of revocation arrived, the Bassa was carried in chains to Constantinople, and his name was mentioned no more.

"What are we now to think of the prerogatives of power, said Rasselas to his sister; is it without any efficacy to good? or, is the subordinate degree only dangerous, and the supreme safe and glorious? Is the Sultan the only happy man in his dominions? or, is the Sultan himself subject to the torments of suspicion, and the dread of enemies?"

In a short time the second Bassa was deposed. The Sultan, that had advanced him, was murdered by the Janisaries,[1] and his successor had other views and different favourites.

Chapter XXIV. **1. Janisaries:** guards of the Turkish court.

CHAP. XXV

The princess persues her enquiry with more
diligence than success.

The princess, in the mean time, insinuated herself into
many families; for there are few doors, through which
liberality, joined with good humour, cannot find its
way. The daughters of many houses were airy[1] and
chearful, but Nekayah had been too long accustomed
to the conversation of Imlac and her brother to be
much pleased with childish levity and prattle which
had no meaning. She found their thoughts narrow,
their wishes low, and their merriment often artificial.
Their pleasures, poor as they were, could not be
preserved pure, but were embittered by petty competitions and worthless emulation. They were always
jealous of the beauty of each other; of a quality to
which solicitude can add nothing, and from which
detraction can take nothing away. Many were in love
with triflers like themselves, and many fancied that
they were in love when in truth they were only idle.
Their affection was seldom fixed on sense or virtue,
and therefore seldom ended but in vexation. Their
grief, however, like their joy, was transient; every
thing floated in their mind unconnected with the past
or future, so that one desire easily gave way to another,
as a second stone cast into the water effaces and
confounds the circles of the first.

With these girls she played as with inoffensive
animals, and found them proud of her countenance,
and weary of her company.

But her purpose was to examine more deeply, and
her affability easily persuaded the hearts that were
swelling with sorrow to discharge their secrets in her
ear; and those whom hope flattered, or prosperity
delighted, often courted her to partake their pleasures.

The princess and her brother commonly met in the
evening in a private summer-house on the bank of the
Nile, and related to each other the occurrences of
the day. As they were sitting together, the princess
cast her eyes upon the river that flowed before her.
"Answer, said she, great father of waters, thou that
rollest thy floods through eighty nations, to the
invocations of the daughter of thy native king. Tell
me if thou waterest, through all thy course, a single
habitation from which thou dost not hear the murmurs
of complaint?"

"You are then, said Rasselas, not more successful in
private houses than I have been in courts." "I have,
since the last partition of our provinces,[2] said the
princess, enabled myself to enter familiarly into many
families, where there was the fairest show of prosperity
and peace, and know not one house that is not haunted
by some fury that destroys its quiet.

"I did not seek ease among the poor, because I
concluded that there it could not be found. But I saw
many poor whom I had supposed to live in affluence.
Poverty has, in large cities, very different appearances:
it is often concealed in splendour, and often in extravagance. It is the care of a very great part of mankind
to conceal their indigence from the rest: they support
themselves by temporary expedients, and every day
is lost in contriving for the morrow.

"This, however, was an evil, which, though frequent, I saw with less pain, because I could relieve it.
Yet some have refused my bounties; more offended
with my quickness to detect their wants, than pleased
with my readiness to succour them: and others, whose
exigencies compelled them to admit my kindness,
have never been able to forgive their benefactress.
Many, however, have been sincerely grateful without
the ostentation of gratitude, or the hope of other
favours."

CHAP. XXVI

The princess continues her remarks
upon private life.

Nekayah perceiving her brother's attention fixed,
proceeded in her narrative.

"In families, where there is or is not poverty, there
is commonly discord: if a kingdom be, as Imlac tells
us, a great family, a family likewise is a little kingdom,
torn with factions and exposed to revolutions. An
unpractised observer expects the love of parents and
children to be constant and equal; but this kindness
seldom continues beyond the years of infancy: in a
short time the children become rivals to their parents.
Benefits are allayed[1] by reproaches, and gratitude
debased by envy.

Chapter XXV. **1. airy:** "sprightly; vivacious; lively"
(Johnson's *Dictionary*).

2. provinces: "proper offices or business" (Johnson's
Dictionary). *Chapter XXVI.* **1. allayed:** debased, as in *alloyed*.

"Parents and children seldom act in concert: each child endeavours to appropriate the esteem or fondness of the parents, and the parents, with yet less temptation, betray each other to their children; thus some place their confidence in the father, and some in the mother, and, by degrees, the house is filled with artifices and feuds.

"The opinions of children and parents, of the young and the old, are naturally opposite, by the contrary effects of hope and despondence, of expectation and experience, without crime or folly on either side. The colours of life in youth and age appear different, as the face of nature in spring and winter. And how can children credit the assertions of parents, which their own eyes show them to be false?

"Few parents act in such a manner as much to enforce their maxims by the credit of their lives. The old man trusts wholly to slow contrivance and gradual progression: the youth expects to force his way by genius, vigour, and precipitance. The old man pays regard to riches, and the youth reverences virtue. The old man deifies prudence: the youth commits himself to magnanimity and chance. The young man, who intends no ill, believes that none is intended, and therefore acts with openness and candour: but his father, having suffered the injuries of fraud, is impelled to suspect, and too often allured to practice it. Age looks with anger on the temerity of youth, and youth with contempt on the scrupulosity of age. Thus parents and children, for the greatest part, live on to love less and less: and, if those whom nature has thus closely united are the torments of each other, where shall we look for tenderness and consolation?"

"Surely, said the prince, you must have been unfortunate in your choice of acquaintance: I am unwilling to believe, that the most tender of all relations is thus impeded in its effects by natural necessity."

"Domestick discord, answered she, is not inevitably and fatally necessary; but yet is not easily avoided. We seldom see that a whole family is virtuous: the good and evil cannot well agree; and the evil can yet less agree with one another: even the virtuous fall sometimes to variance, when their virtues are of different kinds, and tending to extremes. In general, those parents have most reverence who most deserve it: for he that lives well cannot be despised.

"Many other evils infest private life. Some are the slaves of servants whom they have trusted with their affairs. Some are kept in continual anxiety to the caprice of rich relations, whom they cannot please,

and dare not offend. Some husbands are imperious, and some wives perverse: and, as it is always more easy to do evil than good, though the wisdom or virtue of one can very rarely make many happy, the folly or vice of one may often make many miserable."

"If such be the general effect of marriage, said the prince, I shall, for the future, think it dangerous to connect my interest with that of another, lest I should be unhappy by my partner's fault."

"I have met, said the princess, with many who live single for that reason; but I never found that their prudence ought to raise envy. They dream away their time without friendship, without fondness, and are driven to rid themselves of the day, for which they have no use, by childish amusements, or vicious delights. They act as beings under the constant sense of some known inferiority, that fills their minds with rancour, and their tongues with censure. They are peevish at home, and malevolent abroad; and, as the out-laws of human nature, make it their business and their pleasure to disturb that society which debars them from its privileges. To live without feeling or exciting sympathy, to be fortunate without adding to the felicity of others, or afflicted without tasting the balm of pity, is a state more gloomy than solitude: it is not retreat but exclusion from mankind. Marriage has many pains, but celibacy has no pleasures."

"What then is to be done? said Rasselas; the more we enquire, the less we can resolve. Surely he is most likely to please himself that has no other inclination to regard."

CHAP. XXVII

Disquisition upon greatness.

The conversation had a short pause. The prince, having considered his sister's observations, told her, that she had surveyed life with prejudice, and supposed misery where she did not find it. "Your narrative, says he, throws yet a darker gloom upon the prospects of futurity: the predictions of Imlac were but faint sketches of the evils painted by Nekayah. I have been lately convinced that quiet is not the daughter of grandeur, or of power: that her presence is not to be bought by wealth, nor enforced by conquest. It is evident, that as any man acts in a wider compass, he must be more exposed to opposition from enmity or miscarriage from chance; whoever has many to please or to govern, must use the ministry of many agents, some of whom will be wicked, and some ignorant; by some he will be misled, and by others betrayed. If he gratifies one he will offend another: those that are not favoured will think themselves injured; and, since favours can be conferred but upon few, the greater number will be always discontented."

"The discontent, said the princess, which is thus unreasonable, I hope that I shall always have spirit to despise, and you, power to repress."

"Discontent, answered Rasselas, will not always be without reason under the most just or vigilant administration of publick affairs. None, however attentive, can always discover that merit which indigence or faction may happen to obscure; and none, however powerful, can always reward it. Yet, he that sees inferiour desert[1] advanced above him, will naturally impute that preference to partiality or caprice; and, indeed, it can scarcely be hoped that any man, however magnanimous by nature, or exalted by condition, will be able to persist for ever in fixed and inexorable justice of distribution: he will sometimes indulge his own affections, and sometimes those of his favourites; he will permit some to please him who can never serve him; he will discover in those whom he loves qualities which in reality they do not possess; and to those, from whom he receives pleasure, he will in his turn endeavour to give it. Thus will recommendations sometimes prevail which were purchased by money, or by the more destructive bribery of flattery and servility.

"He that has much to do will do something wrong, and of that wrong must suffer the consequences; and, if it were possible that he should always act rightly, yet when such numbers are to judge of his conduct, the bad will censure and obstruct him by malevolence, and the good sometimes by mistake.

"The highest stations cannot therefore hope to be the abodes of happiness, which I would willingly believe to have fled from thrones and palaces to seats of humble privacy and placid obscurity. For what can hinder the satisfaction, or intercept the expectations, of him whose abilities are adequate to his employments, who sees with his own eyes the whole circuit of his influence, who chooses by his own knowledge all whom he trusts, and whom none are tempted to deceive by hope or fear? Surely he has nothing to do but to love and to be loved, to be virtuous and to be happy."

Chapter XXVII. **1. desert:** merit.

"Whether perfect happiness would be procured by perfect goodness, said Nekayah, this world will never afford an opportunity of deciding. But this, at least, may be maintained, that we do not always find visible happiness in proportion to visible virtue. All natural and almost all political evils, are incident alike to the bad and good: they are confounded in the misery of a famine, and not much distinguished in the fury of a faction; they sink together in a tempest, and are driven together from their country by invaders. All that virtue can afford is quietness of conscience, a steady prospect of a happier state; this may enable us to endure calamity with patience; but remember that patience must suppose pain."

CHAP. XXVIII

Rasselas and Nekayah continue their conversation.

"Dear princess, said Rasselas, you fall into the common errours of exaggeratory declamation, by producing, in a familiar disquisition, examples of national calamities, and scenes of extensive misery, which are found in books rather than in the world, and which, as they are horrid, are ordained to be rare. Let us not imagine evils which we do not feel, nor injure life by misrepresentations. I cannot bear that querulous eloquence which threatens every city with a siege like that of Jerusalem, that makes famine attend on every flight of locusts, and suspends pestilence on the wing of every blast that issues from the south.

"On necessary and inevitable evils, which overwhelm kingdoms at once, all disputation is vain: when they happen they must be endured. But it is evident, that these bursts of universal distress are more dreaded than felt: thousands and ten thousands flourish in youth, and wither in age, without the knowledge of any other than domestick evils, and share the same pleasures and vexations whether their kings are mild or cruel, whether the armies of their country persue their enemies, or retreat before them. While courts are disturbed with intestine competitions, and ambassadours are negotiating in foreign countries, the smith still plies his anvil, and the husbandman drives his plow forward; the necessaries of life are required and obtained, and the successive business of the seasons continues to make its wonted revolutions.

"Let us cease to consider what, perhaps, may never happen, and what, when it shall happen, will laugh at human speculation. We will not endeavour to modify the motions of the elements, or to fix the destiny of kingdoms. It is our business to consider what beings like us may perform; each labouring for his own happiness, by promoting within his circle, however narrow, the happiness of others.

"Marriage is evidently the dictate of nature; men and women were made to be companions of each other, and therefore I cannot be persuaded but that marriage is one of the means of happiness."

"I know not, said the princess, whether marriage be more than one of the innumerable modes of human misery. When I see and reckon the various forms of connubial infelicity, the unexpected causes of lasting discord, the diversities of temper, the oppositions of opinion, the rude collisions of contrary desire where both are urged by violent impulses, the obstinate contests of disagreeing virtues, where both are supported by consciousness of good intention, I am sometimes disposed to think with the severer casuists[1] of most nations, that marriage is rather permitted than approved, and that none, but by the instigation of a passion too much indulged, entangle themselves with indissoluble compacts."

"You seem to forget, replied Rasselas, that you have, even now, represented celibacy as less happy than marriage. Both conditions may be bad, but they cannot both be worst. Thus it happens when wrong opinions are entertained, that they mutually destroy each other, and leave the mind open to truth."

"I did not expect, answered the princess, to hear that imputed to falshood which is the consequence only of frailty. To the mind, as to the eye, it is difficult to compare with exactness objects vast in their extent, and various in their parts. Where we see or conceive the whole at once we readily note the discriminations and decide the preference: but of two systems, of which neither can be surveyed by any human being in its full compass of magnitude and multiplicity of complication, where is the wonder, that judging of the whole by parts, I am alternately affected by one and the other as either presses on my memory or fancy? We differ from ourselves just as we differ from each other, when we see only part of the question, as in the multifarious relations of politicks and morality: but when we perceive the whole at once, as in numerical computations, all agree in one judgment, and none ever varies his opinion."

"Let us not add, said the prince, to the other evils

of life, the bitterness of controversy, nor endeavour to vie with each other in subtilties of argument. We are employed in a search, of which both are equally to enjoy the success, or suffer by the miscarriage. It is therefore fit that we assist each other. You surely conclude too hastily from the infelicity of marriage against its institution. Will not the misery of life prove equally that life cannot be the gift of heaven? The world must be peopled by marriage, or peopled without it."

"How the world is to be peopled, returned Nekayah, is not my care, and needs not be yours. I see no danger that the present generation should omit to leave successors behind them: we are not now enquiring for the world, but for ourselves."

CHAP. XXIX

The debate on marriage continued.

"The good of the whole, says Rasselas, is the same with the good of all its parts. If marriage be best for mankind it must be evidently best for individuals, or a permanent and necessary duty must be the cause of evil, and some must be inevitably sacrificed to the convenience of others. In the estimate which you have made of the two states, it appears that the incommodities of a single life are, in a great measure, necessary and certain, but those of the conjugal state accidental and avoidable.

"I cannot forbear to flatter myself that prudence and benevolence will make marriage happy. The general folly of mankind is the cause of general complaint. What can be expected but disappointment and repentance from a choice made in the immaturity of youth, in the ardour of desire, without judgment, without foresight, without enquiry after conformity of opinions, similarity of manners, rectitude of judgment, or purity of sentiment.

"Such is the common process of marriage. A youth and maiden meeting by chance, or brought together by artifice, exchange glances, reciprocate civilities, go home, and dream of one another. Having little to divert attention, or diversify thought, they find themselves uneasy when they are apart, and therefore conclude that they shall be happy together. They marry, and discover what nothing but voluntary blindness had before concealed; they wear out life in altercations, and charge nature with cruelty.

Chapter XXVIII. **1. casuists:** moralists.

"From those early marriages proceeds likewise the rivalry of parents and children: the son is eager to enjoy the world before the father is willing to forsake it, and there is hardly room at once for two generations. The daughter begins to bloom before the mother can be content to fade, and neither can forbear to wish for the absence of the other.

"Surely all these evils may be avoided by that deliberation and delay which prudence prescribes to irrevocable choice. In the variety and jollity of youthful pleasures life may be well enough supported without the help of a partner. Longer time will increase experience, and wider views will allow better opportunities of enquiry and selection: one advantage, at least, will be certain; the parents will be visibly older than their children."

"What reason cannot collect, said Nekayah, and what experiment has not yet taught, can be known only from the report of others. I have been told that late marriages are not eminently happy. This is a question too important to be neglected, and I have often proposed it to those, whose accuracy of remark, and comprehensiveness of knowledge, made their suffrages worthy of regard. They have generally determined, that it is dangerous for a man and woman to suspend their fate upon each other, at a time when opinions are fixed, and habits are established; when friendships have been contracted on both sides, when life has been planned into method, and the mind has long enjoyed the contemplation of its own prospects.

"It is scarcely possible that two travelling through the world under the conduct of chance, should have been both directed to the same path, and it will not often happen that either will quit the track which custom has made pleasing. When the desultory levity of youth has settled into regularity, it is soon succeeded by pride ashamed to yield, or obstinacy delighting to contend. And even though mutual esteem produces mutual desire to please, time itself, as it modifies unchangeably the external mien, determines likewise the direction of the passions, and gives an inflexible rigidity to the manners. Long customs are not easily broken: he that attempts to change the course of his own life, very often labours in vain; and how shall we do that for others which we are seldom able to do for ourselves?"

"But surely, interposed the prince, you suppose the chief motive of choice forgotten or neglected. Whenever I shall seek a wife, it shall be my first question, whether she be willing to be led by reason?"

"Thus it is, said Nekayah, that philosophers are deceived. There are a thousand familiar disputes which reason never can decide; questions that elude investigation, and make logick ridiculous; cases where something must be done, and where little can be said. Consider the state of mankind, and enquire how few can be supposed to act upon any occasions, whether small or great, with all the reasons of action present to their minds. Wretched would be the pair above all names of wretchedness, who should be doomed to adjust by reason every morning all the minute detail of a domestick day.

"Those who marry at an advanced age, will probably escape the encroachments of their children; but, in diminution of this advantage, they will be likely to leave them, ignorant and helpless, to a guardian's mercy: or, if that should not happen, they must at least go out of the world before they see those whom they love best either wise or great.

"From their children, if they have less to fear, they have less also to hope, and they lose, without equivalent, the joys of early love, and the convenience of uniting with manners pliant, and minds susceptible of new impressions, which might wear away their dissimilitudes by long cohabitation, as soft bodies, by continual attrition, conform their surfaces to each other.

"I believe it will be found that those who marry late are best pleased with their children, and those who marry early with their partners."

"The union of these two affections, said Rasselas, would produce all that could be wished. Perhaps there is a time when marriage might unite them, a time neither too early for the father, nor too late for the husband."

"Every hour, answered the princess, confirms my prejudice in favour of the position so often uttered by the mouth of Imlac, 'That nature sets her gifts on the right hand and on the left.' Those conditions, which flatter hope and attract desire, are so constituted, that, as we approach one, we recede from another. There are goods so opposed that we cannot seize both, but, by too much prudence, may pass between them at too great a distance to reach either. This is often the fate of long consideration; he does nothing who endeavours to do more than is allowed to humanity. Flatter not yourself with contrarieties of pleasure. Of the blessings set before you make your choice, and be content. No man can taste the fruits of autumn while he is delighting his scent with the flowers of the spring: no man can, at the same time, fill his cup from the source and from the mouth of the Nile."

CHAP. XXX

Imlac enters, and changes the conversation.

Here Imlac entered, and interrupted them. "Imlac, said Rasselas, I have been taking from the princess the dismal history of private life, and am almost discouraged from further search."

"It seems to me, said Imlac, that while you are making the choice of life, you neglect to live. You wander about a single city, which, however large and diversified, can now afford few novelties, and forget that you are in a country, famous among the earliest monarchies for the power and wisdom of its inhabitants; a country where the sciences first dawned that illuminate the world, and beyond which the arts cannot be traced of civil society or domestick life.

"The old Egyptians have left behind them monuments of industry and power before which all European magnificence is confessed to fade away. The ruins of their architecture are the schools of modern builders, and from the wonders which time has spared we may conjecture, though uncertainly, what it has destroyed."

"My curiosity, said Rasselas, does not very strongly lead me to survey piles of stone, or mounds of earth; my business is with man. I came hither not to measure fragments of temples, or trace choaked aqueducts, but to look upon the various scenes of the present world."

"The things that are now before us, said the princess, require attention, and deserve it. What have I to do with the heroes or the monuments of ancient times? with times which never can return, and heroes, whose form of life was different from all that the present condition of mankind requires or allows."

"To know any thing, returned the poet, we must know its effects; to see men we must see their works, that we may learn what reason has dictated, or passion has incited, and find what are the most powerful motives of action. To judge rightly of the present we must oppose it to the past; for all judgment is comparative, and of the future nothing can be known. The truth is, that no mind is much employed upon the present: recollection and anticipation fill up almost all our moments. Our passions are joy and grief, love and hatred, hope and fear. Of joy and grief

the past is the object, and the future of hope and fear; even love and hatred respect the past, for the cause must have been before the effect.

"The present state of things is the consequence of the former, and it is natural to inquire what were the sources of the good that we enjoy, or of the evil that we suffer. If we act only for ourselves, to neglect the study of history is not prudent: if we are entrusted with the care of others, it is not just. Ignorance, when it is voluntary, is criminal; and he may properly be charged with evil who refused to learn how he might prevent it.

"There is no part of history so generally useful as that which relates the progress of the human mind, the gradual improvement of reason, the successive advances of science, the vicissitudes of learning and ignorance, which are the light and darkness of thinking beings, the extinction and resuscitation of arts, and all the revolutions of the intellectual world. If accounts of battles and invasions are peculiarly the business of princes, the useful or elegant arts are not to be neglected; those who have kingdoms to govern have understandings to cultivate.

"Example is always more efficacious than precept. A soldier is formed in war, and a painter must copy pictures. In this, contemplative life has the advantage: great actions are seldom seen, but the labours of art are always at hand for those who desire to know what art has been able to perform.

"When the eye or the imagination is struck with any uncommon work the next transition of an active mind is to the means by which it was performed. Here begins the true use of such contemplation; we enlarge our comprehension by new ideas, and perhaps recover some art lost to mankind, or learn what is less perfectly known in our own country. At least we compare our own with former times, and either rejoice at our improvements, or, what is the first motion towards good, discover our defects."

"I am willing, said the prince, to see all that can deserve my search." "And I, said the princess, shall rejoice to learn something of the manners of antiquity."

"The most pompous monument of Egyptian greatness, and one of the most bulky works of manual industry, said Imlac, are the pyramids; fabricks raised before the time of history, and of which the earliest narratives afford us only uncertain traditions. Of these the greatest is still standing, very little injured by time."

always element of chance which jeopardizes future, but statement is not true

"Let us visit them to-morrow, said Nekayah. I have often heard of the Pyramids, and shall not rest, till I have seen them within and without with my own eyes."

CHAP. XXXI

They visit the Pyramids.

The resolution being thus taken, they set out the next day. They laid tents upon their camels, being resolved to stay among the pyramids till their curiosity was fully satisfied. They travelled gently, turned aside to every thing remarkable, stopped from time to time and conversed with the inhabitants, and observed the various appearances of towns ruined and inhabited, of wild and cultivated nature.

When they came to the great pyramid they were astonished at the extent of the base, and the height of the top. Imlac explained to them the principles upon which the pyramidal form was chosen for a fabrick intended to co-extend its duration with that of the world: he showed that its gradual diminution gave it such stability, as defeated all the common attacks of the elements, and could scarcely be overthrown by earthquakes themselves, the least resistible of natural violence. A concussion that should shatter the pyramid would threaten the dissolution of the continent.

They measured all its dimensions, and pitched their tents at its foot. Next day they prepared to enter its interiour apartments, and having hired the common guides climbed up to the first passage, when the favourite of the princess, looking into the cavity, stepped back and trembled. "Pekuah, said the princess, of what art thou afraid?" "Of the narrow entrance, answered the lady, and of the dreadful gloom. I dare not enter a place which must surely be inhabited by unquiet souls. The original possessors of these dreadful vaults will start up before us, and, perhaps, shut us in for ever." She spoke, and threw her arms round the neck of her mistress.

"If all your fear be of apparitions, said the prince, I will promise you safety: there is no danger from the dead; he that is once buried will be seen no more."

"That the dead are seen no more, said Imlac, I will not undertake to maintain against the concurrent and unvaried testimony of all ages, and of all nations. There is no people, rude or learned, among whom apparitions of the dead are not related and believed.

This opinion, which, perhaps, prevails as far as human nature is diffused, could become universal only by its truth: those, that never heard of one another, would not have agreed in a tale which nothing but experience can make credible. That it is doubted by single cavillers can very little weaken the general evidence, and some who deny it with their tongues confess it by their fears.

"Yet I do not mean to add new terrours to those which have already seized upon Pekuah. There can be no reason why spectres should haunt the pyramid more than other places, or why they should have power or will to hurt innocence and purity. Our entrance is no violation of their privileges; we can take nothing from them, how then can we offend them?"

"My dear Pekuah, said the princess, I will always go before you, and Imlac shall follow you. Remember that you are the companion of the princess of Abissinia."

"If the princess is pleased that her servant should die, returned the lady, let her command some death less dreadful than enclosure in this horrid cavern. You know I dare not disobey you: I must go if you command me; but, if I once enter, I never shall come back."

The princess saw that her fear was too strong for expostulation or reproof, and embracing her, told her that she should stay in the tent till their return. Pekuah was yet not satisfied, but entreated the princess not to persue so dreadful a purpose as that of entering the recesses of the pyramid. "Though I cannot teach courage, said Nekayah, I must not learn cowardise; nor leave at last undone what I came hither only to do."

CHAP. XXXII

They enter the Pyramid.

Pekuah descended to the tents, and the rest entered the pyramid: they passed through the galleries, surveyed the vaults of marble, and examined the chest in which the body of the founder is supposed to have been reposited. They then sat down in one of the most spacious chambers to rest a while before they attempted to return.

"We have now, said Imlac, gratified our minds with an exact view of the greatest work of man, except the wall of China.

"Of the wall it is very easy to assign the motives. It secured a wealthy and timorous nation from the incursions of Barbarians, whose unskilfulness in arts made it easier for them to supply their wants by rapine than by industry, and who from time to time poured in upon the habitations of peaceful commerce, as vultures descend upon domestick fowl. Their celerity and fierceness made the wall necessary, and their ignorance made it efficacious.

"But for the pyramids no reason has ever been given adequate to the cost and labour of the work. The narrowness of the chambers proves that it could afford no retreat from enemies, and treasures might have been reposited at far less expence with equal security. It seems to have been erected only in compliance with that hunger of imagination which preys incessantly upon life, and must be always appeased by some employment. Those who have already all that they can enjoy, must enlarge their desires. He that has built for use, till use is supplied, must begin to build for vanity, and extend his plan to the utmost power of human performance, that he may not be soon reduced to form another wish.

"I consider this mighty structure as a monument of the insufficiency of human enjoyments. A king, whose power is unlimited, and whose treasures surmount all real and imaginary wants, is compelled to solace, by the erection of a pyramid, the satiety of dominion and tastelesness of pleasures, and to amuse the tediousness of declining life, by seeing thousands labouring without end, and one stone, for no purpose, laid upon another. Whoever thou art, that, not content with a moderate condition, imaginest happiness in royal magnificence, and dreamest that command or riches can feed the appetite of novelty with perpetual gratifications, survey the pyramids, and confess thy folly!"

CHAP. XXXIII

The princess meets with an unexpected misfortune.

They rose up, and returned through the cavity at which they had entered, and the princess prepared for her favourite a long narrative of dark labyrinths, and costly rooms, and of the different impressions which the varieties of the way had made upon her. But, when they came to their train, they found every one silent and dejected: the men discovered shame and fear in their countenances, and the women were weeping in the tents.

What had happened they did not try to conjecture, but immediately enquired. "You had scarcely entered into the pyramid, said one of the attendants, when a troop of Arabs rushed upon us: we were too few to resist them, and too slow to escape. They were about to search the tents, set us on our camels, and drive us along before them, when the approach of some Turkish horsemen put them to flight; but they seized the lady Pekuah with her two maids, and carried them away: the Turks are now persuing them by our instigation, but I fear they will not be able to overtake them."

The princess was overpowered with surprise and grief. Rasselas, in the first heat of his resentment, ordered his servants to follow him, and prepared to persue the robbers with his sabre in his hand. "Sir, said Imlac, what can you hope from violence or valour? the Arabs are mounted on horses trained to battle and retreat; we have only beasts of burthen. By leaving our present station we may lose the princess, but cannot hope to regain Pekuah."

In a short time the Turks returned, having not been able to reach the enemy. The princess burst out into new lamentations, and Rasselas could scarcely forbear to reproach them with cowardice; but Imlac was of opinion, that the escape of the Arabs was no addition to their misfortune, for, perhaps, they would have killed their captives rather than have resigned them.

CHAP. XXXIV

They return to Cairo without Pekuah.

There was nothing to be hoped from longer stay. They returned to Cairo repenting of their curiosity, censuring the negligence of the government, lamenting their own rashness which had neglected to procure a guard, imagining many expedients by which the loss of Pekuah might have been prevented, and resolving to do something for her recovery, though none could find any thing proper to be done.

Nekayah retired to her chamber, where her women attempted to comfort her, by telling her that all had their troubles, and that lady Pekuah had enjoyed much happiness in the world for a long time, and might reasonably expect a change of fortune. They hoped that some good would befal her wheresoever she was, and that their mistress would find another friend who might supply her place.

The princess made them no answer, and they continued the form of condolence, not much grieved in their hearts that the favourite was lost.

Next day the prince presented to the Bassa a memorial of the wrong which he had suffered, and a petition for redress. The Bassa threatened to punish the robbers, but did not attempt to catch them, nor, indeed, could any account or description be given by which he might direct the persuit.

It soon appeared that nothing would be done by authority. Governors, being accustomed to hear of more crimes than they can punish, and more wrongs than they can redress, set themselves at ease by indiscriminate negligence, and presently forget the request when they lose sight of the petitioner.

Imlac then endeavoured to gain some intelligence by private agents. He found many who pretended to an exact knowledge of all the haunts of the Arabs, and to regular correspondence with their chiefs, and who readily undertook the recovery of Pekuah. Of these, some were furnished with money for their journey, and came back no more; some were liberally paid for accounts which a few days discovered to be false. But the princess would not suffer any means, however improbable, to be left untried. While she was doing something she kept her hope alive. As one expedient failed, another was suggested; when one messenger returned unsuccessful, another was despatched to a different quarter.

Two months had now passed, and of Pekuah nothing had been heard; the hopes which they had endeavoured to raise in each other grew more languid, and the princess, when she saw nothing more to be tried, sunk down inconsolable in hopeless dejection. A thousand times she reproached herself with the easy compliance by which she permitted her favourite to stay behind her. "Had not my fondness, said she, lessened my authority, Pekuah had not dared to talk of her terrours. She ought to have feared me more than spectres. A severe look would have overpowered her; a peremptory command would have compelled obedience. Why did foolish indulgence prevail upon me? Why did I not speak and refuse to hear?"

"Great princess, said Imlac, do not reproach yourself for your virtue, or consider that as blameable by which evil has accidentally been caused. Your tenderness for the timidity of Pekuah was generous and kind. When we act according to our duty, we commit the event to him by whose laws our actions are governed, and who will suffer none to be finally punished for obedience. When, in prospect of some good, whether natural or moral, we break the rules prescribed us, we withdraw from the direction of superiour wisdom, and take all consequences upon ourselves. Man cannot so far know the connexion of causes and events, as that he may venture to do wrong in order to do right. When we persue our end by lawful means, we may always console our miscarriage by the hope of future recompense. When we consult only our own policy, and attempt to find a nearer way to good, by overleaping the settled boundaries of right and wrong, we cannot be happy even by success, because we cannot escape the consciousness of our fault; but, if we miscarry, the disappointment is irremediably embittered. How comfortless is the sorrow of him, who feels at once the pangs of guilt, and the vexation of calamity which guilt has brought upon him?

"Consider, princess, what would have been your condition, if the lady Pekuah had intreated to accompany you, and, being compelled to stay in the tents, had been carried away; or how would you have born the thought, if you had forced her into the pyramid, and she had died before you in agonies of terrour."

"Had either happened, said Nekayah, I could not have endured life till now: I should have been tortured to madness by the remembrance of such cruelty, or must have pined away in abhorrence of myself."

"This at least, said Imlac, is the present reward of virtuous conduct, that no unlucky consequence can oblige us to repent it."

CHAP. XXXV

The princess languishes for want of Pekuah.

Nekayah, being thus reconciled to herself, found that no evil is insupportable but that which is accompanied with consciousness of wrong. She was, from that time, delivered from the violence of tempestuous sorrow, and sunk into silent pensiveness and gloomy tranquillity. She sat from morning to evening recollecting all that had been done or said by her Pekuah, treasured up with care every trifle on which Pekuah had set an accidental value, and which might recal to mind any little incident or careless conversation. The sentiments of her, whom she now expected to see no more, were treasured in her memory as rules of life, and she deliberated to no other end than to conjecture on any occasion what would have been the opinion and counsel of Pekuah.

The women, by whom she was attended, knew nothing of her real condition, and therefore she could not talk to them but with caution and reserve. She began to remit her curiosity, having no great care to collect notions which she had no convenience of uttering. Rasselas endeavoured first to comfort and afterwards to divert her; he hired musicians, to whom she seemed to listen, but did not hear them, and procured masters to instruct her in various arts, whose lectures, when they visited her again, were again to be repeated. She had lost her taste of pleasure and her ambition of excellence. And her mind, though forced into short excursions, always recurred to the image of her friend.

Imlac was every morning earnestly enjoined to renew his enquiries, and was asked every night whether he had yet heard of Pekuah, till not being able to return the princess the answer that she desired, he was less and less willing to come into her presence. She observed his backwardness, and commanded him to attend her. "You are not, said she, to confound impatience with resentment, or to suppose that I charge you with negligence, because I repine at your unsuccessfulness. I do not much wonder at your absence; I know that the unhappy are never pleasing, and that all naturally avoid the contagion of misery. To hear complaints is wearisome alike to the wretched and the happy; for who would cloud by adventitious grief the short gleams of gaiety which life allows us? or who, that is struggling under his own evils, will add to them the miseries of another?

"The time is at hand, when none shall be disturbed any longer by the sighs of Nekayah: my search after happiness is now at an end. I am resolved to retire from the world with all its flatteries and deceits, and will hide myself in solitude, without any other care than to compose my thoughts, and regulate my hours by a constant succession of innocent occupations, till, with a mind purified from all earthly desires, I shall enter into that state, to which all are hastening, and in which I hope again to enjoy the friendship of Pekuah."

"Do not entangle your mind, said Imlac, by irrevocable determinations, nor increase the burthen of life by a voluntary accumulation of misery: the weariness of retirement will continue or increase when the loss of Pekuah is forgotten. That you have

been deprived of one pleasure is no very good reason for rejection of the rest."

"Since Pekuah was taken from me, said the princess, I have no pleasure to reject or to retain. She that has no one to love or trust has little to hope. She wants the radical[1] principle of happiness. We may, perhaps, allow that what satisfaction this world can afford, must arise from the conjunction of wealth, knowledge and goodness: wealth is nothing but as it is bestowed, and knowledge nothing but as it is communicated: they must therefore be imparted to others, and to whom could I now delight to impart them? Goodness affords the only comfort which can be enjoyed without a partner, and goodness may be practised in retirement."

"How far solitude may admit goodness, or advance it, I shall not, replied Imlac, dispute at present. Remember the confession of the pious hermit. You will wish to return into the world, when the image of your companion has left your thoughts." "That time, said Nekayah, will never come. The generous frankness, the modest obsequiousness, and the faithful secrecy of my dear Pekuah, will always be more missed, as I shall live longer to see vice and folly."

"The state of a mind oppressed with a sudden calamity, said Imlac, is like that of the fabulous inhabitants of the new created earth, who, when the first night came upon them, supposed that day never would return. When the clouds of sorrow gather over us, we see nothing beyond them, nor can imagine how they will be dispelled: yet a new day succeeded to the night, and sorrow is never long without a dawn of ease. But they who restrain themselves from receiving comfort, do as the savages would have done, had they put out their eyes when it was dark. Our minds, like our bodies, are in continual flux; something is hourly lost, and something acquired. To lose much at once is inconvenient to either, but while the vital powers remain uninjured, nature will find the means of reparation. Distance has the same effect on the mind as on the eye, and while we glide along the stream of time, whatever we leave behind us is always lessening, and that which we approach increasing in magnitude. Do not suffer life to stagnate; it will grow muddy for want of motion: commit yourself again to the current of the world; Pekuah will vanish by degrees; you will meet in your way some other

Chapter XXXV. 1. radical: basic, original.

favourite, or learn to diffuse yourself in general conversation."

"At least, said the prince, do not despair before all remedies have been tried: the enquiry after the unfortunate lady is still continued, and shall be carried on with yet greater diligence, on condition that you will promise to wait a year for the event, without any unalterable resolution."

Nekayah thought this a reasonable demand, and made the promise to her brother, who had been advised by Imlac to require it. Imlac had, indeed, no great hope of regaining Pekuah, but he supposed, that if he could secure the interval of a year, the princess would be then in no danger of a cloister.

CHAP. XXXVI

Pekuah is still remembered. The progress of sorrow.

Nekayah, seeing that nothing was omitted for the recovery of her favourite, and having, by her promise, set her intention of retirement at a distance, began imperceptibly to return to common cares and common pleasures. She rejoiced without her own consent at the suspension of her sorrows, and sometimes caught herself with indignation in the act of turning away her mind from the remembrance of her, whom yet she resolved never to forget.

She then appointed a certain hour of the day for meditation on the merits and fondness of Pekuah, and for some weeks retired constantly at the time fixed, and returned with her eyes swollen and her countenance clouded. By degrees she grew less scrupulous, and suffered any important and pressing avocation to delay the tribute of daily tears. She then yielded to less occasions; sometimes forgot what she was indeed afraid to remember, and, at last, wholly released herself from the duty of periodical affliction.

Her real love of Pekuah was yet not diminished. A thousand occurrences brought her back to memory, and a thousand wants, which nothing but the confidence of friendship can supply, made her frequently regretted. She, therefore, solicited Imlac never to desist from enquiry, and to leave no art of intelligence untried, that, at least, she might have the comfort of knowing that she did not suffer by negligence or sluggishness. "Yet what, said she, is to be expected from our persuit of happiness, when we find the state of life to be such, that happiness itself is the cause of misery? Why should we endeavour to attain that, of which the possession cannot be secured? I shall henceforward fear to yield my heart to excellence, however bright, or to fondness, however tender, lest I should lose again what I have lost in Pekuah."

CHAP. XXXVII

The princess hears news of Pekuah.

In seven months, one of the messengers, who had been sent away upon the day when the promise was drawn from the princess, returned, after many unsuccessful rambles, from the borders of Nubia, with an account that Pekuah was in the hands of an Arab chief, who possessed a castle or fortress on the extremity of Egypt. The Arab, whose revenue was plunder, was willing to restore her, with her two attendants, for two hundred ounces of gold.

The price was no subject of debate. The princess was in extasies when she heard that her favourite was alive, and might so cheaply be ransomed. She could not think of delaying for a moment Pekuah's happiness or her own, but entreated her brother to send back the messenger with the sum required. Imlac, being consulted, was not very confident of the veracity of the relator, and was still more doubtful of the Arab's faith, who might, if he were too liberally trusted, detain at once the money and the captives. He thought it dangerous to put themselves in the power of the Arab, by going into his district, and could not expect that the Rover would so much expose himself as to come into the lower country, where he might be seized by the forces of the Bassa.

It is difficult to negotiate where neither will trust. But Imlac, after some deliberation, directed the messenger to propose that Pekuah should be conducted by ten horsemen to the monastry of St. Anthony, which is situated in the deserts of Upper-Egypt, where she should be met by the same number, and her ransome should be paid.

That no time might be lost, as they expected that the proposal would not be refused, they immediately began their journey to the monastry; and, when they arrived, Imlac went forward with the former messenger to the Arab's fortress. Rasselas was desirous to go with them, but neither his sister nor Imlac would consent. The Arab, according to the custom of his nation, observed the laws of hospitality with great exactness to those who put themselves into his power, and, in a few days, brought Pekuah with her maids, by easy journeys, to their place appointed, where receiving the stipulated price, he restored her with great respect to liberty and her friends, and undertook to conduct them back towards Cairo beyond all danger of robbery or violence.

The princess and her favourite embraced each other with transport too violent to be expressed, and went out together to pour the tears of tenderness in secret, and exchange professions of kindness and gratitude. After a few hours they returned into the refectory of the convent, where, in the presence of the prior and his brethren, the prince required of Pekuah the history of her adventures.

CHAP. XXXVIII

The adventures of the lady Pekuah.

"At what time, and in what manner, I was forced away, said Pekuah, your servants have told you. The suddenness of the event struck me with surprise, and I was at first rather stupified than agitated with any passion of either fear or sorrow. My confusion was encreased by the speed and tumult of our flight while we were followed by the Turks, who, as it seemed, soon despaired to overtake us, or were afraid of those whom they made a shew of menacing.

"When the Arabs saw themselves out of danger they slackened their course, and, as I was less harassed by external violence, I began to feel more uneasiness in my mind. After some time we stopped near a spring shaded with trees in a pleasant meadow, where we were set upon the ground, and offered such refreshments as our masters were partaking. I was suffered to sit with my maids apart from the rest, and none attempted to comfort or insult us. Here I first began to feel the full weight of my misery. The girls sat weeping in silence, and from time to time looked on me for succour. I knew not to what condition we were doomed, nor could conjecture where would be the place of our captivity, or whence to draw any hope of deliverance. I was in the hands of robbers and savages, and had no reason to suppose that their pity was more than their justice, or that they would forbear the gratification of any ardour of desire, or caprice of cruelty. I, however, kissed my maids, and endeavoured

to pacify them by remarking, that we were yet treated with decency, and that, since we were now carried beyond pursuit, there was no danger of violence to our lives.

"When we were to be set again on horseback, my maids clung round me, and refused to be parted, but I commanded them not to irritate those who had us in their power. We travelled the remaining part of the day through an unfrequented and pathless country, and came by moonlight to the side of a hill, where the rest of the troop was stationed. Their tents were pitched, and their fires kindled, and our chief was welcomed as a man much beloved by his dependants.

"We were received into a large tent, where we found women who had attended their husbands in the expedition. They set before us the supper which they had provided, and I eat it rather to encourage my maids than to comply with any appetite of my own. When the meat was taken away they spread the carpets for repose. I was weary, and hoped to find in sleep that remission of distress which nature seldom denies. Ordering myself therefore to be undrest, I observed that the women looked very earnestly upon me, not expecting, I suppose, to see me so submissively attended. When my upper vest was taken off, they were apparently struck with the splendour of my cloaths, and one of them timorously laid her hand upon the embroidery. She then went out, and, in a short time, came back with another woman, who seemed to be of higher rank, and greater authority. She did, at her entrance, the usual act of reverence, and, taking me by the hand, placed me in a smaller tent, spread with finer carpets, where I spent the night quietly with my maids.

"In the morning, as I was sitting on the grass, the chief of the troop came towards me: I rose up to receive him, and he bowed with great respect. "Illustrious lady, said he, my fortune is better than I had presumed to hope; I am told by my women, that I have a princess in my camp." Sir, answered I, your women have deceived themselves and you; I am not a princess, but an unhappy stranger who intended soon to have left this country, in which I am now to be imprisoned for ever. "Whoever, or whencesoever, you are, returned the Arab, your dress, and that of your servants, show your rank to be high, and your wealth to be great. Why should you, who can so easily procure your ransome, think yourself in danger of perpetual captivity? The purpose of my incursions is to encrease my riches, or more properly to gather tribute. The sons of Ishmael are the natural and hereditary lords of this part of the continent, which is usurped by late invaders, and low-born tyrants, from whom we are compelled to take by the sword what is denied to justice. The violence of war admits no distinction; the lance that is lifted at guilt and power will sometimes fall on innocence and gentleness."

"How little, said I, did I expect that yesterday it should have fallen upon me."

"Misfortunes, answered the Arab, should always be expected. If the eye of hostility could learn reverence or pity, excellence like yours had been exempt from injury. But the angels of affliction spread their toils alike for the virtuous and the wicked, for the mighty and the mean. Do not be disconsolate; I am not one of the lawless and cruel rovers of the desert; I know the rules of civil life: I will fix your ransome, give a passport to your messenger, and perform my stipulation with nice[1] punctuality."

"You will easily believe that I was pleased with his courtesy; and finding that his predominant passion was desire of money, I began now to think my danger less, for I knew that no sum would be thought too great for the release of Pekuah. I told him that he should have no reason to charge me with ingratitude, if I was used with kindness, and that any ransome, which could be expected for a maid of common rank, would be paid, but that he must not persist to rate me as a princess. He said, he would consider what he should demand, and then, smiling, bowed and retired.

"Soon after the women came about me, each contending to be more officious[2] than the other, and my maids themselves were served with reverence. We travelled onward by short journeys. On the fourth day the chief told me, that my ransome must be two hundred ounces of gold, which I not only promised him, but told him, that I would add fifty more, if I and my maids were honourably treated.

"I never knew the power of gold before. From that time I was the leader of the troop. The march of every day was longer or shorter as I commanded, and the tents were pitched where I chose to rest. We now had camels and other conveniencies for travel, my own women were always at my side, and I amused myself with observing the manners of the vagrant nations, and with viewing remains of ancient edifices with which these deserted countries appear to have been, in some distant age, lavishly embellished.

"The chief of the band was a man far from illiterate: he was able to travel by the stars or the compass, and had marked in his erratick expeditions such places as are most worthy the notice of a passenger. He observed to me, that buildings are always best preserved in places little frequented, and difficult of access: for, when once a country declines from its primitive splendour, the more inhabitants are left, the quicker ruin will be made. Walls supply stones more easily than quarries, and palaces and temples will be demolished to make stables of granate, and cottages of porphyry.

CHAP. XXXIX

The adventures of Pekuah continued.

"We wandered about in this manner for some weeks, whether, as our chief pretended, for my gratification, or, as I rather suspected, for some convenience of his own. I endeavoured to appear contented where sullenness and resentment would have been of no use, and that endeavour conduced much to the calmness of my mind; but my heart was always with Nekayah, and the troubles of the night much overbalanced the amusements of the day. My women, who threw all their cares upon their mistress, set their minds at ease from the time when they saw me treated with respect, and gave themselves up to the incidental alleviations of our fatigue without solicitude or sorrow. I was pleased with their pleasure, and animated with their confidence. My condition had lost much of its terrour, since I found that the Arab ranged the country merely to get riches. Avarice is an uniform and tractable vice: other intellectual distempers are different in different constitutions of mind; that which sooths the pride of one will offend the pride of another; but to the favour of the covetous there is a ready way, bring money and nothing is denied.

"At last we came to the dwelling of our chief, a strong and spacious house built with stone in an island of the Nile, which lies, as I was told, under the tropick.[1] "Lady, said the Arab, you shall rest after your journey a few weeks in this place, where you are

---

Chapter XXXVIII. **1. nice:** scrupulous. **2. officious:** "kind; doing good offices" (Johnson's *Dictionary*); cf. *On the Death of Dr. Robert Levet,* above, l. 7.

Chapter XXXIX. **1. under the tropick:** south of the Tropic of Cancer.

to consider yourself as sovereign. My occupation is war: I have therefore chosen this obscure residence, from which I can issue unexpected, and to which I can retire unpersued. You may now repose in security: here are few pleasures, but here is no danger." He then led me into the inner apartments, and seating me on the richest couch, bowed to the ground. His women, who considered me as a rival, looked on me with malignity; but being soon informed that I was a great lady detained only for my ransome, they began to vie with each other in obsequiousness and reverence.

"Being again comforted with new assurances of speedy liberty, I was for some days diverted from impatience by the novelty of the place. The turrets overlooked the country to a great distance, and afforded a view of many windings of the stream. In the day I wandered from one place to another as the course of the sun varied the splendour of the prospect, and saw many things which I had never seen before. The crocodiles and river-horses[2] are common in this unpeopled region, and I often looked upon them with terrour, though I knew that they could not hurt me. For some time I expected to see mermaids and tritons, which, as Imlac has told me, the European travellers have stationed in the Nile, but no such beings ever appeared, and the Arab, when I enquired after them, laughed at my credulity.

"At night the Arab always attended me to a tower set apart for celestial observations, where he endeavoured to teach me the names and courses of the stars. I had no great inclination to this study, but an appearance of attention was necessary to please my instructor, who valued himself for his skill, and, in a little while, I found some employment requisite to beguile the tediousness of time, which was to be passed always amidst the same objects. I was weary of looking in the morning on things from which I had turned away weary in the evening: I therefore was at last willing to observe the stars rather than do nothing, but could not always compose my thoughts, and was very often thinking on Nekayah when others imagined me contemplating the sky. Soon after the Arab went upon another expedition, and then my only pleasure was to talk with my maids about the accident by which we were carried away, and the happiness that we should all enjoy at the end of our captivity."

"There were women in your Arab's fortress, said the princess, why did you not make them your companions, enjoy their conversation, and partake their diversions? In a place where they found business or amusement, why should you alone sit corroded with idle melancholy? or why could not you bear for a few months that condition to which they were condemned for life?"

"The diversions of the women, answered Pekuah, were only childish play, by which the mind accustomed to stronger operations could not be kept busy. I could do all which they delighted in doing by powers merely sensitive, while my intellectual faculties were flown to Cairo. They ran from room to room as a bird hops from wire to wire in his cage. They danced for the sake of motion, as lambs frisk in a meadow. One sometimes pretended to be hurt that the rest might be alarmed, or hid herself that another might seek her. Part of their time passed in watching the progress of light bodies that floated on the river, and part in marking the various forms into which clouds broke in the sky.

"Their business was only needlework, in which I and my maids sometimes helped them; but you know that the mind will easily straggle from the fingers, nor will you suspect that captivity and absence from Nekayah could receive solace from silken flowers.

"Nor was much satisfaction to be hoped from their conversation: for of what could they be expected to talk? They had seen nothing; for they had lived from early youth in that narrow spot: of what they had not seen they could have no knowledge, for they could not read. They had no ideas but of the few things that were within their view, and had hardly names for any thing but their cloaths and their food. As I bore a superior character, I was often called to terminate their quarrels, which I decided as equitably as I could. If it could have amused me to hear the complaints of each against the rest, I might have been often detained by long stories, but the motives of their animosity were so small that I could not listen without intercepting the tale."

"How, said Rasselas, can the Arab, whom you represented as a man of more than common accomplishments, take any pleasure in his seraglio, when it is filled only with women like these. Are they exquisitely beautiful?"

"They do not, said Pekuah, want that unaffecting and ignoble beauty which may subsist without spriteliness or sublimity, without energy of thought or dignity of virtue. But to a man like the Arab such beauty was only a flower casually plucked and carelessly

2. **river-horses:** hippopotamuses.

thrown away. Whatever pleasures he might find among them, they were not those of friendship or society. When they were playing about him he looked on them with inattentive superiority: when they vied for his regard he sometimes turned away disgusted. As they had no knowledge, their talk could take nothing from the tediousness of life: as they had no choice, their fondness, or appearance of fondness, excited in him neither pride nor gratitude; he was not exalted in his own esteem by the smiles of a woman who saw no other man, nor was much obliged by that regard, of which he could never know the sincerity, and which he might often perceive to be exerted not so much to delight him as to pain a rival. That which he gave, and they received, as love, was only a careless distribution of superfluous time, such love as man can bestow upon that which he despises, such as has neither hope nor fear, neither joy nor sorrow."

"You have reason, lady, to think yourself happy, said Imlac, that you have been thus easily dismissed. How could a mind, hungry for knowledge, be willing, in an intellectual famine, to lose such a banquet as Pekuah's conversation?"

"I am inclined to believe, answered Pekuah, that he was for some time in suspense; for, notwithstanding his promise, whenever I proposed to dispatch a messenger to Cairo, he found some excuse for delay. While I was detained in his house he made many incursions into the neighbouring countries, and, perhaps, he would have refused to discharge me, had his plunder been equal to his wishes. He returned always courteous, related his adventures, delighted to hear my observations, and endeavoured to advance my acquaintance with the stars. When I importuned him to send away my letters, he soothed me with professions of honour and sincerity; and, when I could be no longer decently denied, put his troop again in motion, and left me to govern in his absence. I was much afflicted by this studied procrastination, and was sometimes afraid that I should be forgotten; that you would leave Cairo, and I must end my days in an island of the Nile.

"I grew at last hopeless and dejected, and cared so little to entertain him, that he for a while more frequently talked with my maids. That he should fall in love with them, or with me, might have been equally fatal, and I was not much pleased with the growing friendship. My anxiety was not long; for, as I recovered some degree of chearfulness, he returned to me, and I could not forbear to despise my former uneasiness.

"He still delayed to send for my ransome, and would, perhaps, never have determined, had not your agent found his way to him. The gold, which he would not fetch, he could not reject when it was offered. He hastened to prepare for our journey hither, like a man delivered from the pain of an intestine conflict. I took leave of my companions in the house, who dismissed me with cold indifference."

Nekayah, having heard her favourite's relation, rose and embraced her, and Rasselas gave her an hundred ounces of gold, which she presented to the Arab for the fifty that were promised.

CHAP. XL

The history of a man of learning.

They returned to Cairo, and were so well pleased at finding themselves together, that none of them went much abroad. The prince began to love learning, and one day declared to Imlac, that he intended to devote himself to science, and pass the rest of his days in literary solitude.

"Before you make your final choice, answered Imlac, you ought to examine its hazards, and converse with some of those who are grown old in the company of themselves. I have just left the observatory of one of the most learned astronomers in the world, who has spent forty years in unwearied attention to the motions and appearances of the celestial bodies, and has drawn out his soul in endless calculations. He admits a few friends once a month to hear his deductions and enjoy his discoveries. I was introduced as a man of knowledge worthy of his notice. Men of various ideas and fluent conversation are commonly welcome to those whose thoughts have been long fixed upon a single point, and who find the images of other things stealing away. I delighted him with my remarks, he smiled at the narrative of my travels, and was glad to forget the constellations, and descend for a moment into the lower world.

"On the next day of vacation I renewed my visit, and was so fortunate as to please him again. He relaxed from that time the severity of his rule, and permitted me to enter at my own choice. I found him always busy, and always glad to be relieved. As each knew much which the other was desirous of learning, we exchanged our notions with great delight. I perceived that I had every day more of his confidence, and always found new cause of admiration in the profundity of his mind. His comprehension is vast, his memory capacious and retentive, his discourse is methodical, and his expression clear.

"His integrity and benevolence are equal to his learning. His deepest researches and most favourite studies are willingly interrupted for any opportunity of doing good by his counsel or his riches. To his closest retreat, at his most busy moments, all are admitted that want his assistance: "For though I exclude idleness and pleasure, I will never, says he, bar my doors against charity. To man is permitted the contemplation of the skies, but the practice of virtue is commanded."

"Surely, said the princess, this man is happy."

"I visited him, said Imlac, with more and more frequency, and was every time more enamoured of his conversation: he was sublime without haughtiness, courteous without formality, and communicative without ostentation. I was at first, great princess of your opinion, thought him the happiest of mankind, and often congratulated him on the blessing that he enjoyed. He seemed to hear nothing with indifference but the praises of his condition, to which he always returned a general answer, and diverted the conversation to some other topick.

"Amidst this willingness to be pleased, and labour to please, I had quickly reason to imagine that some painful sentiment pressed upon his mind. He often looked up earnestly towards the sun, and let his voice fall in the midst of his discourse. He would sometimes, when we were alone, gaze upon me in silence with the air of a man who longed to speak what he was yet resolved to suppress. He would often send for me with vehement injunctions of haste, though, when I came to him, he had nothing extraordinary to say. And sometimes, when I was leaving him, would call me back, pause a few moments and then dismiss me.

CHAP. XLI

The astronomer discovers the cause of his uneasiness.

"At last the time came when the secret burst his reserve. We were sitting together last night in the turret of his house, watching the emersion[1] of a satellite of Jupiter. A sudden tempest clouded the sky, and disappointed our observation. We sat a while silent in the dark, and then he addressed himself to me in these words: "Imlac, I have long considered thy friendship as the greatest blessing of my life. Integrity without knowledge is weak and useless, and knowledge without integrity is dangerous and dreadful. I have found in thee all the qualities requisite for trust, benevolence, experience, and fortitude. I have long discharged an office which I must soon quit at the call of nature, and shall rejoice in the hour of imbecility and pain to devolve it upon thee."

"I thought myself honoured by this testimony, and protested that whatever could conduce to his happiness would add likewise to mine."

"Hear, Imlac, what thou wilt not without difficulty credit. I have possessed for five years the regulation of weather, and the distribution of the seasons: the sun has listened to my dictates, and passed from tropick to tropick by my direction; the clouds, at my call, have poured their waters, and the Nile has overflowed at my command; I have restrained the rage of the dog-star, and mitigated the fervours of the crab.[2] The winds alone, of all the elemental powers, have hitherto refused my authority, and multitudes have perished by equinoctial tempests which I found myself unable to prohibit or restrain. I have administered this great office with exact justice, and made to the different nations of the earth an impartial dividend of rain and sunshine. What must have been the misery of half the globe, if I had limited the clouds to particular regions, or confined the sun to either side of the equator?"

CHAP. XLII

The opinion of the astronomer is explained and justified.

"I suppose he discovered in me, through the obscurity of the room, some tokens of amazement and doubt, for, after a short pause, he proceeded thus:"

"Not to be easily credited will neither surprise nor offend me; for I am, probably, the first of human beings to whom this trust has been imparted. Nor do I know whether to deem this distinction a reward or

Chapter XLI. **1. emersion:** reappearance from obscurity. **2. the crab:** a constellation.

punishment; since I have possessed it I have been far less happy than before, and nothing but the consciousness of good intention could have enabled me to support the weariness of unremitted vigilance."

"How long, Sir, said I, has this great office been in your hands?"

"About ten years ago, said he, my daily observations of the changes of the sky led me to consider, whether, if I had the power of the seasons, I could confer greater plenty upon the inhabitants of the earth. This contemplation fastened on my mind, and I sat days and nights in imaginary dominion, pouring upon this country and that the showers of fertility, and seconding every fall of rain with a due proportion of sunshine. I had yet only the will to do good, and did not imagine that I should ever have the power.

"One day as I was looking on the fields withering with heat, I felt in my mind a sudden wish that I could send rain on the southern mountains, and raise the Nile to an inundation. In the hurry of my imagination I commanded rain to fall, and, by comparing the time of my command, with that of the inundation, I found that the clouds had listned to my lips."

"Might not some other cause, said I, produce this concurrence? the Nile does not always rise on the same day."

"Do not believe, said he with impatience, that such objections could escape me: I reasoned long against my own conviction, and laboured against truth with the utmost obstinacy. I sometimes suspected myself of madness, and should not have dared to impart this secret but to a man like you, capable of distinguishing the wonderful from the impossible, and the incredible from the false."

"Why, Sir, said I, do you call that incredible, which you know, or think you know, to be true?"

"Because, said he, I cannot prove it by any external evidence; and I know too well the laws of demonstration to think that my conviction ought to influence another, who cannot, like me, be conscious of its force. I, therefore, shall not attempt to gain credit by disputation. It is sufficient that I feel this power, that I have long possessed, and every day exerted it. But the life of man is short, the infirmities of age increase upon me, and the time will soon come when the regulator of the year must mingle with the dust. The care of appointing a successor has long disturbed me; the night and the day have been spent in comparisons of all the characters which have come to my knowledge, and I have yet found none so worthy as thyself.

CHAP. XLIII

The astronomer leaves Imlac his directions.

"Hear therefore, what I shall impart, with attention, such as the welfare of a world requires. If the task of a king be considered as difficult, who has the care only of a few millions, to whom he cannot do much good or harm, what must be the anxiety of him, on whom depend the action of the elements, and the great gifts of light and heat!—Hear me therefore with attention.

"I have diligently considered the position of the earth and sun, and formed innumerable schemes in which I changed their situation. I have sometimes turned aside the axis of the earth, and sometimes varied the ecliptick of the sun: but I have found it impossible to make a disposition by which the world may be advantaged; what one region gains, another loses by any imaginable alteration, even without considering the distant parts of the solar system with which we are unacquainted. Do not, therefore, in thy administration of the year, indulge thy pride by innovation; do not please thyself with thinking that thou canst make thyself renowned to all future ages, by disordering the seasons. The memory of mischief is no desirable fame. Much less will it become thee to let kindness or interest prevail. Never rob other countries of rain to pour it on thine own. For us the Nile is sufficient."

"I promised that when I possessed the power, I would use it with inflexible integrity, and he dismissed me, pressing my hand." "My heart, said he, will be now at rest, and my benevolence will no more destroy my quiet: I have found a man of wisdom and virtue, to whom I can chearfully bequeath the inheritance of the sun."

The prince heard this narration with very serious regard, but the princess smiled, and Pekuah convulsed herself with laughter. "Ladies, said Imlac, to mock the heaviest of human afflictions is neither charitable nor wise. Few can attain this man's knowledge, and few practise his virtues; but all may suffer his calamity. Of the uncertainties of our present state, the most dreadful and alarming is the uncertain continuance of reason."

The princess was recollected, and the favourite was abashed. Rasselas, more deeply affected, enquired of Imlac, whether he thought such maladies of the mind frequent, and how they were contracted.

CHAP. XLIV

The dangerous prevalence of imagination.

"Disorders of intellect, answered Imlac, happen much more often than superficial observers will easily believe. Perhaps, if we speak with rigorous exactness, no human mind is in its right state. There is no man whose imagination does not sometimes predominate over his reason, who can regulate his attention wholly by his will, and whose ideas will come and go at his command. No man will be found in whose mind airy notions do not sometimes tyrannise, and force him to hope or fear beyond the limits of sober probability. All power of fancy over reason is a degree of insanity; but while this power is such as we can controll and repress, it is not visible to others, nor considered as any depravation of the mental faculties: it is not pronounced madness but when it comes ungovernable, and apparently influences speech or action.

"To indulge the power of fiction, and send imagination out upon the wing, is often the sport of those who delight too much in silent speculation. When we are alone we are not always busy; the labour of excogitation is too violent to last long; the ardour of enquiry will sometimes give way to idleness or satiety. He who has nothing external that can divert him, must find pleasure in his own thoughts, and must conceive himself what he is not; for who is pleased with what he is? He then expatiates in boundless futurity, and culls from all imaginable conditions that which for the present moment he should most desire, amuses his desires with impossible enjoyments, and confers upon his pride unattainable dominion. The mind dances from scene to scene, unites all pleasures in all combinations, and riots in delights which nature and fortune, with all their bounty, cannot bestow.

"In time some particular train of ideas fixes the attention, all other intellectual gratifications are rejected, the mind, in weariness or leisure, recurs constantly to the favourite conception, and feasts on the luscious falsehood whenever she is offended with the bitterness of truth. By degrees the reign of fancy is confirmed; she grows first imperious, and in time despotick. Then fictions begin to operate as realities, false opinions fasten upon the mind, and life passes in dreams of rapture or of anguish.

"This, Sir, is one of the dangers of solitude, which the hermit has confessed not always to promote goodness, and the astronomer's misery has proved to be not always propitious to wisdom."

"I will no more, said the favourite, imagine myself the queen of Abissinia. I have often spent the hours, which the princess gave to my own disposal, in adjusting ceremonies and regulating the court; I have repressed the pride of the powerful, and granted the petitions of the poor; I have built new palaces in more happy situations, planted groves upon the tops of mountains, and have exulted in the beneficence of royalty, till, when the princess entered, I had almost forgotten to bow down before her."

"And I, said the princess, will not allow myself any more to play the shepherdess in my waking dreams. I have often soothed my thoughts with the quiet and innocence of pastoral employments, till I have in my chamber heard the winds whistle, and the sheep bleat; sometimes freed the lamb entangled in the thicket, and sometimes with my crook encountered the wolf. I have a dress like that of the village maids, which I put on to help my imagination, and a pipe on which I play softly, and suppose myself followed by my flocks."

"I will confess, said the prince, an indulgence of fantastick delight more dangerous than yours. I have frequently endeavoured to image the possibility of a perfect government, by which all wrong should be restrained, all vice reformed, and all the subjects preserved in tranquility and innocence. This thought produced innumerable schemes of reformation, and dictated many useful regulations and salutary edicts. This has been the sport and sometimes the labour of my solitude; and I start, when I think with how little anguish I once supposed the death of my father and my brothers."

"Such, says Imlac, are the effects of visionary schemes: when we first form them we know them to be absurd, but familiarise them by degrees, and in time lose sight of their folly."

CHAP. XLV

They discourse with an old man.

The evening was now far past, and they rose to return home. As they walked along the bank of the Nile, delighted with the beams of the moon quivering on the water, they saw at a small distance an old man, whom the prince had often heard in the assembly of the sages. "Yonder, said he, is one whose years have calmed his passions, but not clouded his reason: let us close the disquisitions of the night, by enquiring what are his sentiments of his own state, that we may know whether youth alone is to struggle with vexation, and whether any better hope remains for the latter part of life."

Here the sage approached and saluted them. They invited him to join their walk, and prattled a while as acquaintance that had unexpectedly met one another. The old man was chearful and talkative, and the way seemed short in his company. He was pleased to find himself not disregarded, accompanied them to their house, and, at the prince's request, entered with them. They placed him in the seat of honour, and set wine and conserves before him.

"Sir, said the princess, an evening walk must give to a man of learning, like you, pleasures which ignorance and youth can hardly conceive. You know the qualities and the causes of all that you behold, the laws by which the river flows, the periods in which the planets perform their revolutions. Every thing must supply you with contemplation, and renew the consciousness of your own dignity."

"Lady, answered he, let the gay and the vigorous expect pleasure in their excursions, it is enough that age can obtain ease. To me the world has lost its novelty: I look round, and see what I remember to have seen in happier days. I rest against a tree, and consider, that in the same shade I once disputed upon the annual overflow of the Nile with a friend who is now silent in the grave. I cast my eyes upwards, fix them on the changing moon, and think with pain on the vicissitudes of life. I have ceased to take much delight in physical truth; for what have I to do with those things which I am soon to leave?"

"You may at least recreate yourself, said Imlac, with the recollection of an honourable and useful life, and enjoy the praise which all agree to give you."

"Praise, said the sage, with a sigh, is to an old man an empty sound. I have neither mother to be delighted with the reputation of her son, nor wife to partake the honours of her husband. I have outlived my friends and my rivals. Nothing is now of much importance; for I cannot extend my interest beyond myself. Youth is delighted with applause, because it is considered as the earnest of some future good, and because the prospect of life is far extended: but to me, who am now declining to decrepitude, there is little to be feared

from the malevolence of men, and yet less to be hoped from their affection or esteem. Something they may yet take away, but they can give me nothing. Riches would now be useless, and high employment would be pain. My retrospect of life recalls to my view many opportunities of good neglected, much time squandered upon trifles, and more lost in idleness and vacancy. I leave many great designs unattempted, and many great attempts unfinished. My mind is burthened with no heavy crime, and therefore I compose myself to tranquility; endeavour to abstract my thoughts from hopes and cares, which, though reason knows them to be vain, still try to keep their old possession of the heart; expect, with serene humility, that hour which nature cannot long delay; and hope to possess in a better state that happiness which here I could not find, and that virtue which here I have not attained."

He rose and went away, leaving his audience not much elated with the hope of long life. The prince consoled himself with remarking, that it was not reasonable to be disappointed by this account; for age had never been considered as the season of felicity, and, if it was possible to be easy in decline and weakness, it was likely that the days of vigour and alacrity might be happy; that the noon of life might be bright, if the evening could be calm.

The princess suspected that age was querulous and malignant, and delighted to repress the expectations of those who had newly entered the world. She had seen the possessors of estates look with envy on their heirs, and known many who enjoy pleasure no longer than they can confine it to themselves.

Pekuah conjectured, that the man was older than he appeared, and was willing to impute his complaints to delirious dejection; or else supposed that he had been unfortunate, and was therefore discontented: "For nothing, said she, is more common than to call our own condition, the condition of life."

Imlac, who had no desire to see them depressed, smiled at the comforts which they could so readily procure to themselves, and remembered, that at the same age, he was equally confident of unmingled prosperity, and equally fertile of consolatory expedients. He forbore to force upon them unwelcome knowledge, which time itself would too soon impress. The princess and her lady retired; the madness of the astronomer hung upon their minds, and they desired Imlac to enter upon his office, and delay next morning the rising of the sun.

CHAP. XLVI

The princess and Pekuah visit the astronomer.

The princess and Pekuah having talked in private of Imlac's astronomer, thought his character at once so amiable and so strange, that they could not be satisfied without a nearer knowledge, and Imlac was requested to find the means of bringing them together.

This was somewhat difficult; the philosopher had never received any visits from women, though he lived in a city that had in it many Europeans who followed the manners of their own countries, and many from other parts of the world that lived there with European liberty. The ladies would not be refused, and several schemes were proposed for the accomplishment of their design. It was proposed to introduce them as strangers in distress, to whom the sage was always accessible; but, after some deliberation, it appeared, that by this artifice, no acquaintance could be formed, for their conversation would be short, and they could not decently importune him often. "This, said Rasselas, is true; but I have yet a stronger objection against the misrepresentation of your state. I have always considered it as treason against the great republick of human nature, to make any man's virtues the means of deceiving him, whether on great or little occasions. All imposture weakens confidence and chills benevolence. When the sage finds that you are not what you seemed, he will feel the resentment natural to a man who, conscious of great abilities, discovers that he has been tricked by understandings meaner than his own, and, perhaps, the distrust, which he can never afterwards wholly lay aside, may stop the voice of counsel, and close the hand of charity; and where will you find the power of restoring his benefactions to mankind, or his peace to himself?"

To this no reply was attempted, and Imlac began to hope that their curiosity would subside; but, next day, Pekuah told him, she had now found an honest pretence for a visit to the astronomer, for she would solicit permission to continue under him the studies in which she had been initiated by the Arab, and the princess might go with her either as a fellow-student, or because a woman could not decently come alone. "I am afraid, said Imlac, that he will be soon weary of your company: men advanced far in knowledge do not love to repeat the elements of their art, and I am not

certain, that even of the elements, as he will deliver them connected with inferences, and mingled with reflections, you are a very capable auditress." "That, said Pekuah, must be my care: I ask of you only to take me thither. My knowledge is, perhaps, more than you imagine it, and by concurring always with his opinions I shall make him think it greater than it is."

The astronomer, in pursuance of this resolution, was told, that a foreign lady, travelling in search of knowledge, had heard of his reputation, and was desirous to become his scholar. The uncommonness of the proposal raised at once his surprise and curiosity, and when, after a short deliberation, he consented to admit her, he could not stay without impatience till the next day.

The ladies dressed themselves magnificently, and were attended by Imlac to the astronomer, who was pleased to see himself approached with respect by persons of so splendid an appearance. In the exchange of the first civilities he was timorous and bashful; but, when the talk became regular, he recollected his powers, and justified the character which Imlac had given. Enquiring of Pekuah what could have turned her inclination towards astronomy, he received from her a history of her adventure at the pyramid, and of the time passed in the Arab's island. She told her tale with ease and elegance, and her conversation took possession of his heart. The discourse was then turned to astronomy: Pekuah displayed what she knew: he looked upon her as a prodigy of genius, and intreated her not to desist from a study which she had so happily begun.

They came again and again, and were every time more welcome than before. The sage endeavoured to amuse them, that they might prolong their visits, for he found his thoughts grow brighter in their company; the clouds of solicitude vanished by degrees, as he forced himself to entertain them, and he grieved when he was left at their departure to his old employment of regulating the seasons.

The princess and her favourite had now watched his lips for several months, and could not catch a single word from which they could judge whether he continued, or not, in the opinion of his preternatural commission. They often contrived to bring him to an open declaration, but he easily eluded all their attacks, and on which side soever they pressed him escaped from them to some other topick.

As their familiarity increased they invited him often to the house of Imlac, where they distinguished him by extraordinary respect. He began gradually to delight in sublunary pleasures. He came early and departed late; laboured to recommend himself by assiduity and compliance; excited their curiosity after new arts, that they might still want his assistance; and when they made any excursion of pleasure or enquiry, entreated to attend them.

By long experience of his integrity and wisdom, the prince and his sister were convinced that he might be trusted without danger; and lest he should draw any false hopes from the civilities which he received, discovered to him their condition, with the motives of their journey, and required his opinion on the choice of life.

"Of the various conditions which the world spreads before you, which you shall prefer, said the sage, I am not able to instruct you. I can only tell that I have chosen wrong. I have passed my time in study without experience; in the attainment of sciences which can, for the most part, be but remotely useful to mankind. I have purchased knowledge at the expence of all the common comforts of life: I have missed the endearing elegance of female friendship, and the happy commerce of domestick tenderness. If I have obtained any prerogatives above other students, they have been accompanied with fear, disquiet, and scrupulosity; but even of these prerogatives, whatever they were, I have, since my thoughts have been diversified by more intercourse with the world, begun to question the reality. When I have been for a few days lost in pleasing dissipation, I am always tempted to think that my enquiries have ended in errour, and that I have suffered much, and suffered it in vain."

Imlac was delighted to find that the sage's understanding was breaking through its mists, and resolved to detain him from the planets till he should forget his task of ruling them, and reason should recover its original influence.

From this time the astronomer was received into familiar friendship, and partook of all their projects and pleasures: his respect kept him attentive, and the activity of Rasselas did not leave much time unengaged. Something was always to be done; the day was spent in making observations which furnished talk for the evening, and the evening was closed with a scheme for the morrow.

The sage confessed to Imlac, that since he had mingled in the gay tumults of life, and divided his hours by a succession of amusements, he found the conviction of his authority over the skies fade gradually from his mind, and began to trust less to an opinion which he never could prove to others, and which he

now found subject to variation from causes in which reason had no part. "If I am accidentally left alone for a few hours, said he, my inveterate persuasion rushes upon my soul, and my thoughts are chained down by some irresistible violence, but they are soon disentangled by the prince's conversation, and instantaneously released at the entrance of Pekuah. I am like a man habitually afraid of spectres, who is set at ease by a lamp, and wonders at the dread which harrassed him in the dark, yet, if his lamp be extinguished, feels again the terrours which he knows that when it is light he shall feel no more. But I am sometimes afraid lest I indulge my quiet by criminal negligence, and voluntarily forget the great charge with which I am intrusted. If I favour myself in a known errour, or am determined by my own ease in a doubtful question of this importance, how dreadful is my crime!"

"No disease of the imagination, answered Imlac, so difficult of cure, as that which is complicated with the dread of guilt: fancy and conscience then act interchangeably upon us, and so often shift their places, that the illusions of one are not distinguished from the dictates of the other. If fancy presents images not moral or religious, the mind drives them away when they give it pain, but when melancholick notions take the form of duty, they lay hold on the faculties without opposition, because we are afraid to exclude or banish them. For this reason the superstitious are often melancholy, and the melancholy almost always superstitious.

"But do not let the suggestions of timidity overpower your better reason: the danger of neglect can be but as the probability of the obligation, which when you consider it with freedom, you find very little, and that little growing every day less. Open your heart to the influence of the light, which, from time to time, breaks in upon you: when scruples importune you, which you in your lucid moments know to be vain, do not stand to parley, but fly to business or to Pekuah, and keep this thought always prevalent, that you are only one atom of the mass of humanity, and have neither such virtue nor vice, as that you should be singled out for supernatural favours or afflictions."

CHAP. XLVII

The prince enters and brings a new topick.

"All this, said the astronomer, I have often thought, but my reason has been so long subjugated by an uncontrolable and overwhelming idea, that it durst not confide in its own decisions. I now see how fatally I betrayed my quiet, by suffering chimeras to prey upon me in secret; but melancholy shrinks from communication, and I never found a man before, to whom I could impart my troubles, though I had been certain of relief. I rejoice to find my own sentiments confirmed by yours, who are not easily deceived, and can have no motive or purpose to deceive. I hope that time and variety will dissipate the gloom that has so long surrounded me, and the latter part of my days will be spent in peace."

"Your learning and virtue, said Imlac, may justly give you hopes."

Rasselas then entered with the princess and Pekuah, and enquired whether they had contrived any new diversion for the next day. "Such, said Nekayah, is the state of life, that none are happy but by the anticipation of change: the change itself is nothing; when we have made it, the next wish is to change again. The world is not yet exhausted; let me see something to morrow which I never saw before."

"Variety, said Rasselas, is so necessary to content, that even the happy valley disgusted me by the recurrence of its luxuries; yet I could not forbear to reproach myself with impatience, when I saw the monks of St. Anthony support without complaint, a life, not of uniform delight, but uniform hardship."

"Those men, answered Imlac, are less wretched in their silent convent than the Abissinian princes in their prison of pleasure. Whatever is done by the monks is incited by an adequate and reasonable motive. Their labour supplies them with necessaries; it therefore cannot be omitted, and is certainly rewarded. Their devotion prepares them for another state, and reminds them of its approach, while it fits them for it. Their time is regularly distributed; one duty succeeds another, so that they are not left open to the distraction of unguided choice, nor lost in the shades of listless inactivity. There is a certain task to be performed at an appropriated hour; and their toils are cheerful, because they consider them as acts of piety, by which they are always advancing towards endless felicity."

"Do you think, said Nekayah, that the monastick rule is a more holy and less imperfect state than any other? May not he equally hope for future happiness who converses openly with mankind, who succours the distressed by his charity, instructs the ignorant by his learning, and contributes by his industry to the general system of life; even though he should omit some of the mortifications which are practised in the cloister, and allow himself such harmless delights as his condition may place within his reach?"

"This, said Imlac, is a question which has long divided the wise, and perplexed the good. I am afraid to decide on either part. He that lives well in the world is better than he that lives well in a monastery. But, perhaps, every one is not able to stem the temptations of publick life; and, if he cannot conquer, he may properly retreat. Some have little power to do good, and have likewise little strength to resist evil. Many are weary of their conflicts with adversity, and are willing to eject those passions which have long busied them in vain. And many are dismissed by age and diseases from the more laborious duties of society. In monasteries the weak and timorous may be happily sheltered, the weary may repose, and the penitent may meditate. Those retreats of prayer and contemplation have something so congenial to the mind of man, that, perhaps, there is scarcely one that does not purpose to close his life in pious abstraction with a few associates serious as himself."

"Such, said Pekuah, has often been my wish, and I have heard the princess declare, that she should not willingly die in a croud."

"The liberty of using harmless pleasures, proceeded Imlac, will not be disputed; but it is still to be examined what pleasures are harmless. The evil of any pleasure that Nekayah can image is not in the act itself, but in its consequences. Pleasure, in itself harmless, may become mischievous, by endearing to us a state which we know to be transient and probatory, and withdrawing our thoughts from that, of which every hour brings us nearer to the beginning, and of which no length of time will bring us to the end. Mortification is not virtuous in itself, nor has any other use, but that it disengages us from the allurements of sense. In the state of future perfection, to which we all aspire, there will be pleasure without danger, and security without restraint."

The princess was silent, and Rasselas, turning to the astronomer, asked him, whether he could not delay her retreat, by shewing her something which she had not seen before.

"Your curiosity, said the sage, has been so general, and your pursuit of knowledge so vigorous, that novelties are not now very easily to be found: but what you can no longer procure from the living may be given by the dead. Among the wonders of this country are the catacombs, or the ancient repositories, in which the bodies of the earliest generations were lodged, and where, by the virtue of the gums which embalmed them, they yet remain without corruption."

"I know not, said Rasselas, what pleasure the sight of the catacombs can afford; but, since nothing else is offered, I am resolved to view them, and shall place this with many other things which I have done, because I would do something."

They hired a guard of horsemen, and the next day visited the catacombs. When they were about to descend into the sepulchral caves, "Pekuah, said the princess, we are now again invading the habitations of the dead; I know that you will stay behind; let me find you safe when I return." "No, I will not be left, answered Pekuah; I will go down between you and the prince."

They then all descended, and roved with wonder through the labyrinth of subterraneous passages, where the bodies were laid in rows on either side.

CHAP. XLVIII

Imlac discourses on the nature of the soul.

"What reason, said the prince, can be given, why the Egyptians should thus expensively preserve those carcasses which some nations consume with fire, others lay to mingle with the earth, and all agree to remove from their sight, as soon as decent rites can be performed?"

"The original of ancient customs, said Imlac, is commonly unknown; for the practice often continues when the cause has ceased; and concerning superstitious ceremonies it is vain to conjecture; for what reason did not dictate reason cannot explain. I have long believed that the practice of embalming arose only from tenderness to the remains of relations or friends, and to this opinion I am more inclined, because it seems impossible that this care should have been general: had all the dead been embalmed, their repositories must in time have been more spacious than the dwellings of the living. I suppose only the rich or honourable were secured from corruption, and the rest left to the course of nature.

"But it is commonly supposed that the Egyptians believed the soul to live as long as the body continued undissolved, and therefore tried this method of eluding death."

"Could the wise Egyptians, said Nekayah, think so grosly of the soul? If the soul could once survive its separation, what could it afterwards receive or suffer from the body?"

"The Egyptians would doubtless think erroneously, said the astronomer, in the darkness of heathenism, and the first dawn of philosophy. The nature of the soul is still disputed amidst all our opportunities of clearer knowledge: some yet say, that it may be material, who, nevertheless, believe it to be immortal."

"Some, answered Imlac, have indeed said that the soul is material, but I can scarcely believe that any man has thought it, who knew how to think; for all the conclusions of reason enforce the immateriality of mind, and all the notices of sense and investigations of science concur to prove the unconsciousness of matter.

"It was never supposed that cogitation is inherent in matter, or that every particle is a thinking being. Yet, if any part of matter be devoid of thought, what part can we suppose to think? Matter can differ from matter only in form, density, bulk, motion, and direction of motion: to which of these, however varied or combined, can consciousness be annexed? To be round or square, to be solid or fluid, to be great or little, to be moved slowly or swiftly one way or another, are modes of material existence, all equally alien from the nature of cogitation. If matter be once without thought, it can only be made to think by some new modification, but all the modifications which it can admit are equally unconnected with cogitative powers."

"But the materialists, said the astronomer, urge that matter may have qualities with which we are unacquainted."

"He who will determine, returned Imlac, against that which he knows, because there may be something which he knows not; he that can set hypothetical possibility against acknowledged certainty, is not to be admitted among reasonable beings. All that we know of matter is, that matter is inert, senseless and lifeless; and if this conviction cannot be opposed but by referring us to something that we know not, we have all the evidence that human intellect can admit. If that which is known may be over ruled by that which is unknown, no being, not omniscient, can arrive at certainty."

"Yet let us not, said the astronomer, too arrogantly limit the Creator's power."

"It is no limitation of omnipotence, replied the poet, to suppose that one thing is not consistent with another, that the same proposition cannot be at once true and false, that the same number cannot be even and odd, that cogitation cannot be conferred on that which is created incapable of cogitation."

"I know not, said Nekayah, any great use of this question. Does that immateriality, which, in my opinion, you have sufficiently proved, necessarily include eternal duration?"

"Of immateriality, said Imlac, our ideas are negative, and therefore obscure. Immateriality seems to imply a natural power of perpetual duration as a consequence of exemption from all causes of decay: whatever perishes, is destroyed by the solution[1] of its contexture, and separation of its parts; nor can we conceive how that which has no parts, and therefore admits no solution, can be naturally corrupted or impaired."

"I know not, said Rasselas, how to conceive any thing without extension: what is extended must have parts, and you allow, that whatever has parts may be destroyed."

"Consider your own conceptions, replied Imlac, and the difficulty will be less. You will find substance without extension. An ideal form is no less real than material bulk: yet an ideal form has no extension. It is no less certain, when you think on a pyramid, that your mind possesses the idea of a pyramid, than that the pyramid itself is standing. What space does the idea of a pyramid occupy more than the idea of a grain of corn? or how can either idea suffer laceration? As is the effect such is the cause; as thought is, such is the power that thinks; a power impassive and indiscerpible."[2]

"But the Being, said Nekayah, whom I fear to name, the Being which made the soul, can destroy it."

"He, surely, can destroy it, answered Imlac, since, however unperishable, it receives from a superiour nature its power of duration. That it will not perish by any inherent cause of decay, or principle of corruption, may be shown by philosophy; but philosophy can tell no more. That it will not be annihilated by him that made it, we must humbly learn from higher authority."

The whole assembly stood a while silent and collected. "Let us return, said Rasselas, from this scene of mortality. How gloomy would be these mansions of the dead to him who did not know that he shall never die; that what now acts shall continue its agency, and what now thinks shall think on for ever. Those that lie here stretched before us, the wise and the powerful of antient times, warn us to remember the shortness of our present state: they were, perhaps, snatched away while they were busy, like us, in the choice of life."

"To me, said the princess, the choice of life is become less important; I hope hereafter to think only on the choice of eternity."

They then hastened out of the caverns, and, under the protection of their guard, returned to Cairo.

CHAP. XLIX

The conclusion, in which nothing is concluded.

It was now the time of the inundation of the Nile: a few days after their visit to the catacombs, the river began to rise.

They were confined to their house. The whole region being under water gave them no invitation to any excursions, and, being well supplied with materials for talk, they diverted themselves with comparisons of the different forms of life which they had observed, and with various schemes of happiness which each of them had formed.

Pekuah was never so much charmed with any place as the convent of St. Anthony, where the Arab restored her to the princess, and wished only to fill it with pious maidens, and to be made prioress of the order: she was weary of expectation and disgust, and would gladly be fixed in some unvariable state.

The princess thought, that of all sublunary things, knowledge was the best: She desired first to learn all sciences, and then purposed to found a college of learned women, in which she would preside, that, by conversing with the old, and educating the young, she might divide her time between the acquisition and communication of wisdom, and raise up for the next age models of prudence, and patterns of piety.

The prince desired a little kingdom, in which he might administer justice in his own person, and see all the parts of government with his own eyes; but he could never fix the limits of his dominion, and was always adding to the number of his subjects.

Imlac and the astronomer were contented to be driven along the stream of life without directing their course to any particular port.

Of these wishes that they had formed they well knew that none could be obtained. They deliberated a while what was to be done, and resolved, when the inundation should cease, to return to Abissinia.

Chapter XLVIII. **1. solution:** disruption. **2. indiscerpible:** indestructible.

FROM

PREFACE [TO *THE PLAYS OF WILLIAM SHAKESPEARE*]

Johnson's edition of Shakespeare appeared in eight volumes in October, 1765, although he had issued his proposals some nine years earlier and had long since spent his subscribers' money. Five editors of Shakespeare had preceded him: Nicholas Rowe (1709), Pope (1725), Lewis Theobald (1734), Sir Thomas Hanmer (1744), and William Warburton (1747). Johnson emended the text of the plays more conservatively than most of his predecessors, and in addition to the Preface he wrote footnotes and a brief "General Observation" at the end of each play.

He was convinced that Shakespeare was the greatest English poet, just as he was convinced that Milton was the second greatest. But as Joseph Wood Krutch has pointed out, he also believed that "the first business of criticism was not enthusiastic eulogy or even interpretation. It was evaluation and discrimination." Hence his careful listing of Shakespeare's "faults," a listing which indeed had been customary in critical introductions to Shakespeare since Pope's Preface to his edition. That few have equaled Johnson in acute sensitivity to Shakespeare is suggested by his footnote to *Othello*, Act V, scene ii (the scene in which Desdemona is murdered): "I am glad that I have ended my revisal of this dreadful scene. It is not to be endured."

Edmond Malone, one of Johnson's successors as an editor of Shakespeare, called Johnson's Preface "perhaps the finest composition in our language"; Malone went on to declare that "his vigorous and comprehensive understanding threw more light on his author than all his predecessors had done." And Adam Smith regarded the Preface as "the most manly piece of criticism that was ever published in any country."

The text is that of the first edition (1765); we have incorporated the substantive variants of the fifth edition (1778). Our selection comprises slightly less than half the original.

❦

THAT praises are without reason lavished on the dead, and that the honours due only to excellence are paid to antiquity, is a complaint likely to be always continued by those, who, being able to add nothing to truth, hope for eminence from the heresies of paradox; or those, who, being forced by disappointment upon consolatory expedients, are willing to hope from posterity what the present age refuses, and flatter themselves that the regard which is yet denied by envy, will be at last bestowed by time.

Antiquity, like every other quality that attracts the notice of mankind, has undoubtedly votaries that reverence it, not from reason, but from prejudice. Some seem to admire indiscriminately whatever has been long preserved, without considering that time has sometimes co-operated with chance; all perhaps are more willing to honour past than present excellence; and the mind contemplates genius through the shades of age, as the eye surveys the sun through artificial opacity. The great contention of criticism is to find the faults of the moderns, and the beauties of the ancients. While an authour is yet living we estimate his powers by his worst performance, and when he is dead we rate them by his best.

To works, however, of which the excellence is not absolute and definite, but gradual and comparative; to works not raised upon principles demonstrative and scientifick, but appealing wholly to observation and experience, no other test can be applied than length of duration and continuance of esteem. What mankind have long possessed they have often examined and compared, and if they persist to value the possession, it is because frequent comparisons have confirmed opinion in its favour. As among the works of nature no man can properly call a river deep or a mountain high, without the knowledge of many mountains and many rivers; so in the productions of genius, nothing can be stiled excellent till it has been compared with other works of the same kind. Demonstration immediately displays its power, and has nothing to hope or fear from the flux of years; but works tentative and experimental must be estimated by their proportion to the general and collective ability of man, as it is discovered in a long succession of endeavours. Of the first building that was raised, it might be with certainty determined that it was round or square, but whether it was spacious or lofty must have been referred to time. The Pythagorean scale of numbers[1]

PREFACE TO *The Plays of William Shakespeare*. **1. the Pythagorean . . . numbers:** Pythagoras, Greek philosopher of the sixth century B.C., maintained that numbers have a real existence and that the orderliness of mathematical systems underlies the orderliness of the universe.

was at once discovered to be perfect; but the poems of *Homer* we yet know not to transcend the common limits of human intelligence, but by remarking, that nation after nation, and century after century, has been able to do little more than transpose his incidents, new name his characters, and paraphrase his sentiments.

The reverence due to writings that have long subsisted arises therefore not from any credulous confidence in the superior wisdom of past ages, or gloomy persuasion of the degeneracy of mankind, but is the consequence of acknowledged and indubitable positions, that what has been longest known has been most considered, and what is most considered is best understood.

The Poet, of whose works I have undertaken the revision, may now begin to assume the dignity of an ancient, and claim the privilege of established fame and prescriptive veneration. He has long outlived his century, the term commonly fixed as the test of literary merit.[2] Whatever advantages he might once derive from personal allusions, local customs, or temporary opinions, have for many years been lost; and every topick of merriment or motive of sorrow, which the modes of artificial life afforded him, now only obscure the scenes which they once illuminated. The effects of favour and competition are at an end; the tradition of his friendships and his enmities has perished; his works support no opinion with arguments, nor supply any faction with invectives; they can neither indulge vanity nor gratify malignity, but are read without any other reason than the desire of pleasure, and are therefore praised only as pleasure is obtained; yet, thus unassisted by interest or passion, they have past through variations of taste and changes of manners, and, as they devolved from one generation to another, have received new honours at every transmission.

But because human judgment, though it be gradually gaining upon certainty, never becomes infallible; and approbation, though long continued, may yet be only the approbation of prejudice or fashion; it is proper to inquire, by what peculiarities of excellence *Shakespeare* has gained and kept the favour of his countrymen.

Nothing can please many, and please long, but just representations of general nature. Particular manners can be known to few, and therefore few only can judge how nearly they are copied. The irregular

combinations of fanciful invention may delight awhile, by that novelty of which the common satiety of life sends us all in quest; but the pleasures of sudden wonder are soon exhausted, and the mind can only repose on the stability of truth.

Shakespeare is above all writers, at least above all modern writers, the poet of nature; the poet that holds up to his readers a faithful mirrour of manners and of life. His characters are not modified by the customs of particular places, unpractised by the rest of the world; by the peculiarities of studies or professions, which can operate but upon small numbers; or by the accidents of transient fashions or temporary opinions: they are the genuine progeny of common humanity, such as the world will always supply, and observation will always find. His persons act and speak by the influence of those general passions and principles by which all minds are agitated, and the whole system of life is continued in motion. In the writings of other poets a character is too often an individual; in those of *Shakespeare* it is commonly a species.

It is from this wide extension of design that so much instruction is derived. It is this which fills the plays of *Shakespeare* with practical axioms and domestick wisdom. It was said of *Euripides*, that every verse was a precept;[3] and it may be said of *Shakespeare*, that from his works may be collected a system of civil and œconomical prudence. Yet his real power is not shown in the splendour of particular passages, but by the progress of his fable, and the tenour of his dialogue; and he that tries to recommend him by select quotations, will succeed like the pedant in *Hierocles*,[4] who, when he offered his house to sale, carried a brick in his pocket as a specimen.

It will not easily be imagined how much *Shakespeare* excels in accommodating his sentiments to real life, but by comparing him with other authours. It was observed of the ancient schools of declamation, that the more diligently they were frequented, the more was the student disqualified for the world, because he found nothing there which he should ever meet in any other place. The same remark may be applied to every stage but that of *Shakespeare*. The theatre, when it is under any other direction, is peopled by such characters as were never seen, conversing in a language which was never heard, upon topicks which will never arise in the

---

2. the term . . . merit: by Horace, in *Epistles*, II. i. 39.

3. It . . . precept: See Cicero, *Ad Familiares*, XVI. 8. **4. Hierocles:** Hierocles Alexandrinus, a fifth-century A.D. Greek philosopher.

commerce of mankind. But the dialogue of this authour is often so evidently determined by the incident which produces it, and is pursued with so much ease and simplicity, that it seems scarcely to claim the merit of fiction, but to have been gleaned by diligent selection out of common conversation, and common occurrences.

Upon every other stage the universal agent is love, by whose power all good and evil is distributed, and every action quickened or retarded. To bring a lover, a lady and a rival into the fable; to entangle them in contradictory obligations, perplex them with oppositions of interest, and harrass them with violence of desires inconsistent with each other; to make them meet in rapture and part in agony; to fill their mouths with hyperbolical joy and outrageous sorrow; to distress them as nothing human ever was distressed; to deliver them as nothing human ever was delivered, is the business of a modern dramatist. For this probability is violated, life is misrepresented, and language is depraved. But love is only one of many passions, and as it has no great influence upon the sum of life, it has little operation in the dramas of a poet, who caught his ideas from the living world, and exhibited only what he saw before him. He knew, that any other passion, as it was regular or exorbitant, was a cause of happiness or calamity.

Characters thus ample and general were not easily discriminated and preserved, yet perhaps no poet ever kept his personages more distinct from each other. I will not say with *Pope*,[5] that every speech may be assigned to the proper speaker, because many speeches there are which have nothing characteristical; but, perhaps, though some may be equally adapted to every person, it will be difficult to find any that can be properly transferred from the present possessor to another claimant. The choice is right, when there is reason for choice.

Other dramatists can only gain attention by hyperbolical or aggravated characters, by fabulous and unexampled excellence or depravity, as the writers of barbarous romances invigorated the reader by a giant and a dwarf; and he that should form his expectations of human affairs from the play, or from the tale, would be equally deceived. *Shakespeare* has no heroes; his scenes are occupied only by men, who act and speak as the reader thinks that he should himself have

spoken or acted on the same occasion: Even where the agency is supernatural the dialogue is level with life. Other writers disguise the most natural passions and most frequent incidents; so that he who contemplates them in the book will not know them in the world: *Shakespeare* approximates the remote, and familiarizes the wonderful; the event which he represents will not happen, but if it were possible, its effects would be probably such as he has assigned; and it may be said, that he has not only shewn human nature as it acts in real exigencies, but as it would be found in trials, to which it cannot be exposed.

This therefore is the praise of *Shakespeare*, that his drama is the mirrour of life; that he who has mazed his imagination, in following the phantoms which other writers raise up before him, may here be cured of his delirious extasies, by reading human sentiments in human language; by scenes from which a hermit may estimate the transactions of the world, and a confessor predict the progress of the passions.

His adherence to general nature has exposed him to the censure of criticks, who form their judgments upon narrower principles. *Dennis* and *Rhymer*[6] think his *Romans* not sufficiently Roman; and *Voltaire* censures his kings as not completely royal.[7] *Dennis* is offended, that *Menenius*,[8] a senator of *Rome*, should play the buffoon; and *Voltaire* perhaps thinks decency violated when the *Danish* Usurper[9] is represented as a drunkard. But *Shakespeare* always makes nature predominate over accident; and if he preserves the essential character, is not very careful of distinctions superinduced and adventitious. His story requires Romans or kings, but he thinks only on men. He knew that *Rome*, like every other city, had men of all dispositions; and wanting a buffoon, he went into the senate-house for that which the senate-house would certainly have afforded him. He was inclined to shew an usurper and a murderer not only odious but despicable, he therefore added drunkenness to his other qualities, knowing that kings love wine like other men, and that wine exerts its natural power upon kings. These are the petty cavils of petty minds; a poet overlooks the casual distinction

---

5. with Pope: in the Preface to his edition of Shakespeare (1725).

6. Dennis and Rhymer: John Dennis (1657–1734), a critic, and Thomas Rymer (1641–1713), also a critic and the author of *The Tragedies of the Last Age Considered* (1677) and *A Short View of Tragedy* (1692). (See the selection from Dennis in Part Two.) 7. Voltaire . . . royal: Voltaire makes this observation in his *Du théâtre anglais* (1761). 8. Menenius: in *Coriolanus*. 9. the Danish Usurper: King Claudius, in *Hamlet*.

of country and condition, as a painter, satisfied with the figure, neglects the drapery.

The censure which he has incurred[10] by mixing comick and tragick scenes, as it extends to all his works, deserves more consideration. Let the fact be first stated, and then examined.

Shakespeare's plays are not in the rigorous and critical sense either tragedies or comedies, but compositions of a distinct kind; exhibiting the real state of sublunary nature, which partakes of good and evil, joy and sorrow, mingled with endless variety of proportion and innumerable modes of combination; and expressing the course of the world, in which the loss of one is the gain of another; in which, at the same time, the reveller is hasting to his wine, and the mourner burying his friend; in which the malignity of one is sometimes defeated by the frolick of another; and many mischiefs and many benefits are done and hindered without design.

Out of this chaos of mingled purposes and casualties the ancient poets, according to the laws which custom had prescribed, selected some the crimes of men, and some their absurdities; some the momentous vicissitudes of life, and some the lighter occurrences; some the terrours of distress, and some the gayeties of prosperity. Thus rose the two modes of imitation, known by the names of *tragedy* and *comedy*, compositions intended to promote different ends by contrary means, and considered as so little allied, that I do not recollect among the *Greeks* or *Romans* a single writer who attempted both.

Shakespeare has united the powers of exciting laughter and sorrow not only in one mind but in one composition. Almost all his plays are divided between serious and ludicrous characters, and, in the successive evolutions of the design, sometimes produce seriousness and sorrow, and sometimes levity and laughter.

That this is a practice contrary to the rules of criticism will be readily allowed; but there is always an appeal open from criticism to nature. The end of writing is to instruct; the end of poetry is to instruct by pleasing. That the mingled drama may convey all the instruction of tragedy or comedy cannot be denied, because it includes both in its alterations[11] of exhibition, and approaches nearer than either to the appearance of life, by shewing how great machinations and slender designs may promote or obviate one another,

and the high and the low co-operate in the general system by unavoidable concatenation.

It is objected, that by this change of scenes the passions are interrupted in their progression, and that the principal event, being not advanced by a due gradation of preparatory incidents, wants at last the power to move, which constitutes the perfection of dramatick poetry. This reasoning is so specious, that it is received as true even by those who in daily experience feel it to be false. The interchanges of mingled scenes seldom fail to produce the intended vicissitudes of passion. Fiction cannot move so much, but that the attention may be easily transferred; and though it must be allowed that pleasing melancholy be sometimes interrupted by unwelcome levity, yet let it be considered likewise, that melancholy is often not pleasing, and that the disturbance of one man may be the relief of another; that different auditors have different habitudes; and that, upon the whole, all pleasure consists in variety.

The players,[12] who in their edition divided our authour's works into comedies, histories, and tragedies, seem not to have distinguished the three kinds, by any very exact or definite ideas.

An action which ended happily to the principal persons, however serious or distressful through its intermediate incidents, in their opinion constituted a comedy. This idea of a comedy continued long amongst us, and plays were written, which, by changing the catastrophe, were tragedies to-day and comedies to-morrow.

Tragedy was not in those times a poem of more general dignity or elevation than comedy; it required only a calamitous conclusion, with which the common criticism of that age was satisfied, whatever lighter pleasure it afforded in its progress.

History was a series of actions, with no other than chronological succession, independent of each other, and without any tendency to introduce or regulate the conclusion. It is not always very nicely distinguished from tragedy. There is not much nearer approach to unity of action in the tragedy of *Antony and Cleopatra*, than in the history of *Richard the Second*. But a history might be continued through many plays; as it had no plan, it had no limits.

Through all these denominations of the drama,

10. **The censure . . . incurred:** from Voltaire. 11. **alterations:** changed to *alternations* in the edition of 1785.

12. **The players:** the actors John Heminge and Henry Condell, members of Shakespeare's dramatic company, who published the first folio (1623).

Shakespeare's mode of composition is the same; an interchange of seriousness and merriment, by which the mind is softened at one time, and exhilarated at another. But whatever be his purpose, whether to gladden or depress, or to conduct the story, without vehemence or emotion, through tracts of easy and familiar dialogue, he never fails to attain his purpose; as he commands us, we laugh or mourn, or sit silent with quiet expectation, in tranquillity without indifference.

When *Shakespeare*'s plan is understood, most of the criticisms of *Rhymer* and *Voltaire* vanish away. The play of *Hamlet* is opened, without impropriety, by two sentinels; *Iago* bellows at *Brabantio*'s window, without injury to the scheme of the play, though in terms which a modern audience would not easily endure; the character of *Polonius* is seasonable and useful; and the Grave-diggers themselves may be heard with applause.

Shakespeare engaged in dramatick poetry with the world open before him; the rules of the ancients were yet known to few; the publick judgment was unformed; he had no example of such fame as might force him upon imitation, nor criticks of such authority as might restrain his extravagance: He therefore indulged his natural disposition, and his disposition, as *Rhymer* has remarked, led him to comedy. In tragedy he often writes with great appearance of toil and study, what is written at last with little felicity; but in his comick scenes, he seems to produce without labour, what no labour can improve. In tragedy he is always struggling after some occasion to be comick, but in comedy he seems to repose, or to luxuriate, as in a mode of thinking congenial to his nature. In his tragick scenes there is always something wanting, but his comedy often surpasses expectation or desire. His comedy pleases by the thoughts and the language, and his tragedy for the greater part by incident and action. His tragedy seems to be skill, his comedy to be instinct.

The force of his comick scenes has suffered little diminution from the changes made by a century and a half, in manners or in words. As his personages act upon principles arising from genuine passion, very little modified by particular forms, their pleasures and vexations are communicable to all times and to all places; they are natural, and therefore durable; the adventitious peculiarities of personal habits, are only superficial dies, bright and pleasing for a little while, yet soon fading to a dim tinct, without any remains of former lustre; but the discriminations of true passion are the colours of nature; they pervade the whole mass, and can only perish with the body that exhibits them. The accidental compositions of heterogeneous modes are dissolved by the chance which combined them; but the uniform simplicity of primitive qualities neither admits increase, nor suffers decay. The sand heaped by one flood is scattered by another, but the rock always continues in its place. The stream of time, which is continually washing the dissoluble fabricks of other poets, passes without injury by the adamant of *Shakespeare*.

If there be, what I believe there is, in every nation, a stile which never becomes obsolete, a certain mode of phraseology so consonant and congenial to the analogy and principles of its respective language as to remain settled and unaltered; this stile is probably to be sought in the common intercourse of life, among those who speak only to be understood, without ambition of elegance. The polite are always catching modish innovations, and the learned depart from established forms of speech, in hope of finding or making better; those who wish for distinction forsake the vulgar, when the vulgar is right; but there is a conversation above grossness and below refinement, where propriety resides, and where this poet seems to have gathered his comick dialogue. He is therefore more agreeable to the ears of the present age than any other authour equally remote, and among his other excellencies deserves to be studied as one of the original masters of our language.

These observations are to be considered not as unexceptionably constant, but as containing general and predominant truth. *Shakespeare*'s familiar dialogue is affirmed to be smooth and clear, yet not wholly without ruggedness or difficulty; as a country may be eminently fruitful, though it has spots unfit for cultivation: His characters are praised as natural, though their sentiments are sometimes forced, and their actions improbable; as the earth upon the whole is spherical, though its surface is varied with protuberances and cavities.

Shakespeare with his excellencies has likewise faults, and faults sufficient to obscure and overwhelm any other merit.[13] I shall shew them in the proportion in which they appear to me, without envious malignity or superstitious veneration. No question can be more innocently discussed than a dead poet's pretensions to

13. **faults sufficient . . . merit:** Johnson means "faults sufficient to obscure and overwhelm" any lesser merits than the transcendent ones just treated.

renown; and little regard is due to that bigotry which sets candour higher than truth.

His first defect is that to which may be imputed most of the evil in books or in men. He sacrifices virtue to convenience, and is so much more careful to please than to instruct, that he seems to write without any moral purpose. From his writings indeed a system of social duty may be selected, for he that thinks reasonably must think morally; but his precepts and axioms drop casually from him; he makes no just distribution of good or evil, nor is always careful to shew in the virtuous a disapprobation of the wicked; he carries his persons indifferently through right and wrong, and at the close dismisses them without further care, and leaves their examples to operate by chance. This fault the barbarity of his age cannot extenuate; for it is always a writer's duty to make the world better, and justice is a virtue independant on time or place.

The plots are often so loosely formed, that a very slight consideration may improve them, and so carelessly pursued, that he seems not always fully to comprehend his own design. He omits opportunities of instructing or delighting which the train of his story seems to force upon him, and apparently rejects those exhibitions which would be more affecting, for the sake of those which are more easy.

It may be observed, that in many of his plays the latter part is evidently neglected. When he found himself near the end of his work, and in view of his reward, he shortened the labour, to snatch the profit. He therefore remits his efforts where he should most vigorously exert them, and his catastrophe is improbably produced or imperfectly represented.

He had no regard to distinction of time or place, but gives to one age or nation, without scruple, the customs, institutions, and opinions of another, at the expence not only of likelihood, but of possibility. These faults *Pope* has endeavoured, with more zeal than judgment, to transfer to his imagined interpolators. We need not wonder to find *Hector* quoting *Aristotle*,[14] when we see the loves of *Theseus* and *Hippolyta* combined with the *Gothick* mythology of fairies. *Shakespeare*, indeed, was not the only violator of chronology, for in the same age *Sidney*, who wanted not the advantages of learning, has, in his *Arcadia*,[15] confounded the pastoral with the feudal

times, the days of innocence, quiet and security, with those of turbulence, violence and adventure.

In his comick scenes he is seldom very successful, when he engages his characters in reciprocations of smartness and contests of sarcasm; their jests are commonly gross, and their pleasantry licentious; neither his gentlemen nor his ladies have much delicacy, nor are sufficiently distinguished from his clowns by any appearance of refined manners. Whether he represented the real conversation of his time is not easy to determine; the reign of *Elizabeth* is commonly supposed to have been a time of stateliness, formality and reserve, yet perhaps the relaxations of that severity were not very elegant. There must, however, have been always some modes of gayety preferable to others, and a writer ought to chuse the best.

In tragedy his performance seems constantly to be worse, as his labour is more. The effusions of passion which exigence forces out are for the most part striking and energetick; but whenever he solicits his invention, or strains his faculties, the offspring of his throes is tumour, meanness, tediousness, and obscurity.

In narration he affects a disproportionate pomp of diction and a wearisome train of circumlocution, and tells the incident imperfectly in many words, which might have been more plainly delivered in few. Narration in dramatick poetry is naturally tedious, as it is unanimated and inactive, and obstructs the progress of the action; it should therefore always be rapid, and enlivened by frequent interruption. *Shakespeare* found it an encumbrance, and instead of lightening it by brevity, endeavoured to recommend it by dignity and splendour.

His declamations or set speeches are commonly cold and weak, for his power was the power of nature; when he endeavoured, like other tragick writers, to catch opportunities of amplification, and instead of inquiring what the occasion demanded, to show how much his stores of knowledge could supply, he seldom escapes without the pity or resentment of his reader.

It is incident to him to be now and then entangled with an unwieldy sentiment, which he cannot well express, and will not reject; he struggles with it a while, and if it continues stubborn, comprises it in words such as occur, and leaves it to be disentangled and evolved by those who have more leisure to bestow upon it.

Not that always where the language is intricate the

14. **Hector . . . Aristotle:** in *Troilus and Cressida*, II. ii. 166–67. 15. **Arcadia:** a prose romance (1590).

thought is subtle, or the image always great where the line is bulky; the equality of words to things is very often neglected, and trivial sentiments and vulgar ideas disappoint the attention, to which they are recommended by sonorous epithets and swelling figures.

But the admirers of this great poet have never less reason to indulge their hopes of supreme excellence, than when he seems fully resolved to sink them in dejection, and mollify them with tender emotions by the fall of greatness, the danger of innocence, or the crosses of love. He is not long soft and pathetick without some idle conceit, or contemptible equivocation. He no sooner begins to move, than he counteracts himself; and terrour and pity, as they are rising in the mind, are checked and blasted by sudden frigidity.

"PUN"

A quibble[16] is to *Shakespeare*, what luminous vapours are to the traveller; he follows it at all adventures, it is sure to lead him out of his way, and sure to engulf him in the mire. It has some malignant power over his mind, and its fascinations are irresistible. Whatever be the dignity or profundity of his disquisition, whether he be enlarging knowledge or exalting affection, whether he be amusing attention with incidents, or enchaining it in suspense, let but a quibble spring up before him, and he leaves his work unfinished. A quibble is the golden apple for which he will always turn aside from his career, or stoop from his elevation. A quibble poor and barren as it is, gave him such delight, that he was content to purchase it, by the sacrifice of reason, propriety and truth. A quibble was to him the fatal *Cleopatra* for which he lost the world, and was content to lose it.

It will be thought strange, that, in enumerating the defects of this writer, I have not yet mentioned his neglect of the unities; his violation of those laws which have been instituted and established by the joint authority of poets and of criticks.

For his other deviations from the art of writing, I resign him to critical justice, without making any other demand in his favour, than that which must be indulged to all human excellence; that his virtues be rated with his failings: But, from the censure which this irregularity may bring upon him, I shall, with due reverence to that learning which I must oppose, adventure to try how I can defend him.

His histories, being neither tragedies nor comedies,

are not subject to any of their laws; nothing more is necessary to all the praise which they expect, than that the changes of action be so prepared as to be understood, that the incidents be various and affecting, and the characters consistent, natural and distinct. No other unity is intended, and therefore none is to be sought.

In his other works he has well enough preserved the unity of action. He has not, indeed, an intrigue regularly perplexed and regularly unravelled; he does not endeavour to hide his design only to discover it, for this is seldom the order of real events, and *Shakespeare* is the poet of nature: But his plan has commonly what *Aristotle* requires,[17] a beginning, a middle, and an end; one event is concatenated with another, and the conclusion follows by easy consequence. There are perhaps some incidents that might be spared, as in other poets there is much talk that only fills up time upon the stage; but the general system makes gradual advances, and the end of the play is the end of expectation.

To the unities of time and place he has shewn no regard, and perhaps a nearer view of the principles on which they stand will diminish their value, and withdraw from them the veneration which, from the time of *Corneille*,[18] they have very generally received by discovering that they have given more trouble to the poet, than pleasure to the auditor.

The necessity of observing the unities of time and place arises from the supposed necessity of making the drama credible. The criticks hold it impossible, that an action of months or years can be possibly believed to pass in three hours; or that the spectator can suppose himself to sit in the theatre, while ambassadors go and return between distant kings, while armies are levied and towns besieged, while an exile wanders and returns, or till he whom they saw courting his mistress, shall lament the untimely fall of his son. The mind revolts from evident falsehood, and fiction loses its force when it departs from the resemblance of reality.

From the narrow limitation of time necessarily arises the contraction of place. The spectator, who knows that he saw the first act at *Alexandria*, cannot suppose that he sees the next at *Rome*, at a distance to which not the dragons of *Medea*[19] could, in so short a time, have transported him; he knows with certainty that he has not changed his place; and he knows

16. **quibble:** "a low conceit depending on the sound of words; a pun" (Johnson's *Dictionary*).

17. **what . . . requires:** in *Poetics*, vii. 2–3. 18. **Corneille:** The unities of time and place were espoused by the French playwright Pierre Corneille (1606–84) in his *Discours dramatiques* (1660). 19. **Medea:** an enchantress in Greek mythology.

that place cannot change itself; that what was a house cannot become a plain; that what was *Thebes* can never be *Persepolis.*

Such is the triumphant language with which a critick exults over the misery of an irregular poet, and exults commonly without resistance or reply. It is time therefore to tell him, by the authority of *Shakespeare,* that he assumes, as an unquestionable principle, a position, which, while his breath is forming it into words, his understanding pronounces to be false. It is false, that any representation is mistaken for reality; that any dramatick fable in its materiality was ever credible, or, for a single moment, was ever credited.

The objection arising from the impossibility of passing the first hour at *Alexandria,* and the next at *Rome,* supposes, that when the play opens the spectator really imagines himself at *Alexandria,* and believes that his walk to the theatre has been a voyage to *Egypt,* and that he lives in the days of *Antony* and *Cleopatra.* Surely he that imagines this, may imagine more. He that can take the stage at one time for the palace of the *Ptolemies,* may take it in half an hour for the promontory of *Actium.* Delusion, if delusion be admitted, has no certain limitation; if the spectator can be once persuaded, that his old acquaintance are *Alexander* and *Cæsar,* that a room illuminated with candles is the plain of *Pharsalia,* or the bank of *Granicus,* he is in a state of elevation above the reach of reason, or of truth, and from the heights of empyrean poetry, may despise the circumscriptions of terrestrial nature. There is no reason why a mind thus wandering in extasy should count the clock, or why an hour should not be a century in that calenture[20] of the brains that can make the stage a field.

The truth is, that the spectators are always in their senses, and know, from the first act to the last, that the stage is only a stage, and that the players are only players. They come to hear a certain number of lines recited with just gesture and elegant modulation. The lines relate to some action, and an action must be in some place; but the different actions that compleat a story may be in places very remote from each other; and where is the absurdity of allowing that space to represent first *Athens,* and then *Sicily,* which was always known to be neither *Sicily* nor *Athens,* but a modern theatre.

By supposition, as place is introduced, time may be

20. **calenture:** delirium.

extended; the time required by the fable elapses for the most part between the acts; for, of so much of the action as is represented, the real and poetical duration is the same. If, in the first act, preparations for war against *Mithridates* are represented to be made in *Rome,* the event of the war may, without absurdity, be represented, in the catastrophe, as happening in *Pontus;* we know that there is neither war, nor preparation for war; we know that we are neither in *Rome* nor *Pontus;* that neither *Mithridates* nor *Lucullus* are before us. The drama exhibits successive imitations of successive actions, and why may not the second imitation represent an action that happened years after the first; if it be so connected with it, that nothing but time can be supposed to intervene. Time is, of all modes of existence, most obsequious to the imagination; a lapse of years is as easily conceived as a passage of hours. In contemplation we easily contract the time of real actions, and therefore willingly permit it to be contracted when we only see their imitation.

It will be asked, how the drama moves, if it is not credited. It is credited with all the credit due to a drama. It is credited, whenever it moves, as a just picture of a real original; as representing to the auditor what he would himself feel, if he were to do or suffer what is there feigned to be suffered or to be done. The reflection that strikes the heart is not, that the evils before us are real evils, but that they are evils to which we ourselves may be exposed. If there be any fallacy, it is not that we fancy the players, but that we fancy ourselves unhappy for a moment; but we rather lament the possibility than suppose the presence of misery, as a mother weeps over her babe, when she remembers that death may take it from her. The delight of tragedy proceeds from our consciousness of fiction; if we thought murders and treasons real, they would please no more.

Imitations produce pain or pleasure, not because they are mistaken for realities, but because they bring realities to mind. When the imagination is recreated by a painted landscape, the trees are not supposed capable to give us shade, or the fountains coolness; but we consider, how we should be pleased with such fountains playing beside us, and such woods waving over us. We are agitated in reading the history of *Henry* the Fifth, yet no man takes his book for the field of *Agencourt.* A dramatick exhibition is a book recited with concomitants that encrease or diminish its effect. Familiar comedy is often more powerful on the theatre, than in the page; imperial tragedy is always less. The humour of *Petruchio*[21] may be heightened by grimace; but what voice or what gesture can hope to add dignity or force to the soliloquy of *Cato*.[22]

A play read, affects the mind like a play acted. It is therefore evident, that the action is not supposed to be real, and it follows that between the acts a longer or shorter time may be allowed to pass, and that no more account of space or duration is to be taken by the auditor of a drama, than by the reader of a narrative, before whom may pass in an hour the life of a hero, or the revolutions of an empire.

Whether *Shakespeare* knew the unities, and rejected them by design, or deviated from them by happy ignorance, it is, I think, impossible to decide, and useless to inquire. We may reasonably suppose, that, when he rose to notice, he did not want[23] the counsels and admonitions of scholars and criticks, and that he at last deliberately persisted in a practice, which he might have begun by chance. As nothing is essential to the fable, but unity of action, and as the unities of time and place arise evidently from false assumptions, and, by circumscribing the extent of the drama, lessen its variety, I cannot think it much to be lamented, that they were not known by him, or not observed: Nor, if such another poet could arise, should I very vehemently reproach him, that his first act passed at *Venice*, and his next in *Cyprus*. Such violations of rules merely positive, become the comprehensive genius of *Shakespeare*, and such censures are suitable to the minute and slender criticism of *Voltaire*:

> *Non usque adeo permiscuit imis*
> *Longus summa dies, ut non, si voce Metelli*
> *Serventur leges, malint a Cæsare tolli.*[24]

Yet when I speak thus slightly of dramatick rules, I cannot but recollect how much wit and learning may be produced against me; before such authorities I am afraid to stand, not that I think the present question one of those that are to be decided by mere authority, but because it is to be suspected, that these precepts have not been so easily received but for better reasons

than I have yet been able to find. The result of my enquiries, in which it would be ludicrous to boast of impartiality, is, that the unities of time and place are not essential to a just drama, that though they may sometimes conduce to pleasure, they are always to be sacrificed to the nobler beauties of variety and instruction; and that a play, written with nice observation of critical rules, is to be contemplated as an elaborate curiosity, as the product of superfluous and ostentatious art, by which is shewn, rather what is possible, than what is necessary.

He that, without diminution of any other excellence, shall preserve all the unities unbroken, deserves the like applause with the architect, who shall display all the orders of architecture in a citadel, without any deduction from its strength; but the principal beauty of a citadel is to exclude the enemy; and the greatest graces of a play, are to copy nature and instruct life.

Perhaps, what I have here not dogmatically but deliberately written, may recal the principles of the drama to a new examination. I am almost frighted at my own temerity; and when I estimate the fame and the strength of those that maintain the contrary opinion, am ready to sink down in reverential silence; as *Æneas* withdrew from the defence of *Troy*, when he saw *Neptune* shaking the wall, and *Juno* heading the besiegers.[25]

Those whom my arguments cannot persuade to give their approbation to the judgment of *Shakespeare*, will easily, if they consider the condition of his life, make some allowance for his ignorance.

Every man's performances, to be rightly estimated, must be compared with the state of the age in which he lived, and with his own particular opportunities; and though to the reader a book be not worse or better for the circumstances of the authour, yet as there is always a silent reference of human works to human abilities, and as the enquiry, how far man may extend his designs, or how high he may rate his native force, is of far greater dignity than in what rank we shall place any particular performance, curiosity is always busy to discover the instruments, as well as to survey the workmanship, to know how much is to be ascribed to original powers, and how much to casual and adventitious help. The palaces of *Peru* or *Mexico* were certainly mean and incommodious habitations, if compared to the houses of *European* monarchs; yet who could forbear to view them with astonishment,

21. The humour . . . Petruchio: in *The Taming of the Shrew*. 22. the soliloquy . . . Cato: The soliloquy in Addison's *Cato* (V. i. 1–40) was one of the purple passages of the eighteenth-century theater. It was considered noble. 23. want: lack. 24. Non . . . tolli: "The course of time has not so confused things that it would not be better for Caesar to destroy the laws than for Metellus to save them" (Lucan, *Pharsalia*, III. 138–40).

25. as . . . besiegers: See *Aeneid*, II. 610–14.

who remembered that they were built without the use of iron?

The *English* nation, in the time of *Shakespeare*, was yet struggling to emerge from barbarity. The philology of *Italy* had been transplanted hither in the reign of *Henry* the Eighth; and the learned languages had been successfully cultivated by *Lilly*, *Linacer*, and *More*; by *Pole*, *Cheke*, and *Gardiner*, and afterwards by *Smith*, *Clerk*, *Haddon*, and *Ascham*.[26] Greek was now taught to boys in the principal schools; and those who united elegance with learning, read, with great diligence, the *Italian* and *Spanish* poets. But literature was yet confined to professed scholars, or to men and women of high rank. The publick was gross and dark; and to be able to read and write, was an accomplishment still valued for its rarity.

Nations, like individuals, have their infancy. A people newly awakened to literary curiosity, being yet unacquainted with the true state of things, knows not how to judge of that which is proposed as its resemblance. Whatever is remote from common appearances is always welcome to vulgar, as to childish credulity; and of a country unenlightened by learning, the whole people is the vulgar. The study of those who then aspired to plebeian learning was laid out upon adventures, giants, dragons, and enchantments. *The Death of Arthur*[27] was the favourite volume.

The mind, which has feasted on the luxurious wonders of fiction, has no taste of the insipidity of truth. A play which imitated only the common occurrences of the world, would, upon the admirers of *Palmerin* and *Guy of Warwick*,[28] have made little impression; he that wrote for such an audience was under the necessity of looking round for strange events and fabulous transactions, and that incredibility, by which maturer knowledge is offended, was the chief recommendation of writings, to unskilful curiosity.

Our authour's plots are generally borrowed from novels, and it is reasonable to suppose, that he chose the most popular, such as were read by many, and related by more; for his audience could not have followed him through the intricacies of the drama, had they not held the thread of the story in their hands.

The stories, which we now find only in remoter authours, were in his time accessible and familiar. The fable of *As you like it*, which is supposed to be copied from *Chaucer's* Gamelyn,[29] was a little pamphlet of those times; and old Mr. *Cibber*[30] remembered the tale of *Hamlet* in plain *English* prose, which the criticks have now to seek in *Saxo Grammaticus*.[31]

His *English* histories he took from *English* chronicles and *English* ballads; and as the ancient writers were made known to his countrymen by versions,[32] they supplied him with new subjects; he dilated some of *Plutarch's* lives into plays, when they had been translated by *North*.[33]

His plots, whether historical or fabulous, are always crouded with incidents, by which the attention of a rude people was more easily caught than by sentiment or argumentation; and such is the power of the marvellous even over those who despise it, that every man finds his mind more strongly seized by the tragedies of *Shakespeare* than of any other writer;[34] others please us by particular speeches, but he always makes us anxious for the event, and has perhaps excelled all but *Homer* in securing the first purpose of a writer, by exciting restless and unquenchable curiosity, and compelling him that reads his work to read it through.[35]

The shows and bustle with which his plays abound have the same original. As knowledge advances, pleasure passes from the eye to the ear, but returns, as it declines, from the ear to the eye. Those to whom our authour's labours were exhibited had more skill in

---

26. **Lilly . . . Ascham:** British humanists and classical scholars of the fifteenth and sixteenth centuries. 27. **The Death . . . Arthur:** The English prose epic *Le Morte d'Arthur* (1485) by Sir Thomas Malory (c. 1408–71). 28. **Palmerin . . . Warwick:** two medieval romances full of wonders and exaggeration.

29. **Chaucer's Gamelyn:** Actually it was taken from Thomas Lodge's *Rosalynde* (1590). 30. **old Mr. Cibber:** the actor Colley Cibber (1671–1757); also a poet and dramatist, he was Poet Laureate from 1730 to his death. 31. **Saxo Grammaticus:** a thirteenth-century Danish historian; his *Gesta Danorum* includes the story of Prince Hamlet. 32. **versions:** translations. 33. **North:** Sir Thomas North's translation of the Greek biographer Plutarch's *Lives of the Noble Grecians and Romans* was published in 1579. 34. **every . . . writer:** In her *Anecdotes* (1786), Mrs. Thrale writes of Johnson: "When he was about nine years old, having got the play of Hamlet in his hand, and reading it quietly in his father's kitchen, he kept on steadily through, till coming to the Ghost scene, he suddenly hurried up stairs to the street door that he might see people about him." 35. **to . . . through:** In 1773, according to Boswell, "Mr. Elphinston talked of a new book that was much admired, and asked Dr. Johnson if he had read it. JOHNSON. 'I have looked into it.' 'What (said Elphinston), have you not read it through?' Johnson, offended at being thus pressed, and so obliged to own his cursory mode of reading, answered tartly, 'No, Sir; do *you* read books *through?*' "

pomps or processions than in poetical language, and perhaps wanted some visible and discriminated events, as comments on the dialogue. He knew how he should most please; and whether his practice is more agreeable to nature, or whether his example has prejudiced the nation, we still find that on our stage something must be done as well as said, and inactive declamation is very coldly heard, however musical or elegant, passionate or sublime.

Voltaire expresses his wonder, that our authour's extravagancies are endured by a nation, which has seen the tragedy of *Cato*. Let him be answered, that *Addison* speaks the language of poets, and *Shakespeare*, of men. We find in *Cato* innumerable beauties which enamour us of its authour, but we see nothing that acquaints us with human sentiments or human actions; we place it with the fairest and the noblest progeny which judgment propagates by conjunction with learning, but *Othello* is the vigorous and vivacious offspring of observation impregnated by genius. *Cato* affords a splendid exhibition of artificial and fictitious manners, and delivers just and noble sentiments, in diction easy, elevated and harmonious, but its hopes and fears communicate no vibration to the heart; the composition refers us only to the writer; we pronounce the name of *Cato*, but we think on *Addison*.

The work of a correct and regular writer is a garden accurately formed and diligently planted, varied with shades, and scented with flowers; the composition of *Shakespeare* is a forest, in which oaks extend their branches, and pines tower in the air, interspersed sometimes with weeds and brambles, and sometimes giving shelter to myrtles and to roses; filling the eye with awful pomp, and gratifying the mind with endless diversity. Other poets display cabinets of precious rarities, minutely finished, wrought into shape, and polished unto brightness. *Shakespeare* opens a mine which contains gold and diamonds in unexhaustible plenty, though clouded by incrustations, debased by impurities, and mingled with a mass of meaner minerals.

. . .

FROM

THE LIVES
OF THE . . . POETS

Johnson had long been meditating a series of biographies of post-Restoration poets. During his famous interview with George III in 1767, the King, according to Boswell, "expressed a desire to have the literary biography of this country ably executed, and proposed to Dr. Johnson to undertake it. Johnson signified his readiness to comply with His Majesty's wishes." But the project began in earnest only ten years later, when Johnson contracted with a group of thirty-six London booksellers to furnish prefaces to selections from fifty-two poets, most of them chosen by the booksellers. No living poet was to be included. The series begins with Abraham Cowley, who died in 1667, and ends with Thomas Gray, who died in 1771. The first four volumes of *Prefaces, Biographical and Critical, to the Works of the English Poets* appeared in 1779; the remaining six volumes appeared in 1781. In the second edition (1781) the title became *The Lives of the Most Eminent English Poets*, and the collection has been known as *The Lives of the Poets* ever since.

Johnson addressed himself here, as everywhere, to the general reading public, and among that public the *Lives* had a great success, although Johnson's disinclination to exhaust himself in tiresome research resulted in occasional lapses that annoyed the learned. His remark on Congreve's *Incognita* (1691) is famous: "I would rather praise it than read it." And enthusiasts of the memories of Milton, Lord Lyttelton, and Gray, who were thought to have received less than due veneration, were angry. After reading the *Life of Milton* (1779), William Cowper declared, "Oh! I could thresh his old jacket, till I made his pension jingle in his pocket." Horace Walpole, scandalized at Johnson's disparagement of Gray's odes, wrote, "Prejudice, and bigotry, and pride, and presumption, and arrogance, and pedantry are the hags that brew his ink." But in its review of the first four volumes, *The Monthly Review* enunciated the opinion of the common reader: "In the walk of biography and criticism, Dr. Johnson has long been without a rival. It is barely justice to acknowledge that he still maintains his superiority."

The text is that of the first edition (1779–81); we have incorporated the substantive variants of the third edition (1783). The selection from the *Life of Cowley* (1779) comprises less than one-twentieth of the original; that from the *Life of Dryden* (1779) slightly more than one-third of the original; and that from the *Life of Pope* (1781) slightly less than one-fourth.

FROM

COWLEY

COWLEY,[1] like other poets who have written with narrow views, and instead of tracing intellectual pleasures in the minds of men, paid their court to temporary prejudices, has been at one time too much praised, and too much neglected at another.

Wit, like all other things subject by their nature to the choice of man, has its changes and fashions, and at different times takes different forms. About the beginning of the seventeenth century appeared a race of writers that may be termed the metaphysical poets; of whom, in a criticism on the works of Cowley, it is not improper to give some account.

The metaphysical poets[2] were men of learning, and to shew their learning was their whole endeavour: but, unluckily resolving to shew it in rhyme, instead of writing poetry, they only wrote verses, and very often such verses as stood the trial of the finger better than of the ear; for the modulation was so imperfect, that they were only found to be verses by counting the syllables.

If the father of criticism has rightly denominated poetry τέχνη μιμητική, an imitative art,[3] these writers will, without great wrong, lose their right to the name of poets; for they cannot be said to have imitated any thing; they neither copied nature nor life; neither painted the forms of matter, nor represented the operations of intellect.

Those however who deny them to be poets, allow them to be wits. Dryden confesses of himself and his contemporaries, that they fall below Donne in wit, but maintains that they surpass him in poetry.[4]

If Wit be well described by Pope, as being "that which has been often thought, but was never before so well expressed,"[5] they certainly never attained, nor ever sought it; for they endeavoured to be singular in their thoughts, and were careless of their diction. But Pope's account of wit is undoubtedly erroneous: he depresses it below its natural dignity, and reduces it from strength of thought to happiness of language.

If by a more noble and more adequate conception that be considered as Wit, which is at once natural and new, that which, though not obvious, is, upon its first production, acknowledged to be just; if it be that, which he that never found it wonders how he missed; to wit of this kind the metaphysical poets have seldom risen. Their thoughts are often new, but seldom natural; they are not obvious, but neither are they just; and the reader, far from wondering that he missed them, wonders more frequently by what perverseness of industry they were ever found.

But Wit, abstracted from its effects upon the hearer, may be more rigorously and philosophically considered as a kind of *discordia concors;*[6] a combination of dissimilar images, or discovery of occult resemblances in things apparently unlike. Of wit, thus defined, they have more than enough. The most heterogeneous ideas are yoked by violence together; nature and art are ransacked for illustrations, comparisons, and allusions; their learning instructs, and their subtlety surprises; but the reader commonly thinks his improvement dearly bought, and though he sometimes admires is seldom pleased.

From this account of their compositions it will be readily inferred, that they were not successful in representing or moving the affections. As they were wholly employed on something unexpected and surprising, they had no regard to that uniformity of sentiment which enables us to conceive and to excite the pains and the pleasure of other minds: they never enquired what, on any occasion, they should have said or done; but wrote rather as beholders than partakers of human nature; as Beings looking upon good and evil, impassive and at leisure; as Epicurean deities[7] making remarks on the actions of men, and the vicissitudes of life, without interest and without emotion. Their courtship was void of fondness, and

---

LIFE OF COWLEY. **1. Cowley:** the poet and essayist Abraham Cowley (1618–67), whom Dryden thought "sunk in his reputation because he could never forgive any conceit which came in his way, but swept like a drag-net great and small." **2. metaphysical poets:** This use of the word *metaphysical* derives from Dryden, who once observed that the poet John Donne (1572–1631) "too much affects the metaphysics." Other seventeenth-century Metaphysical poets, who wrote poems of intellectual analysis full of quasi-learned paradoxes and extravagant metaphors (conceits), are George Herbert, Andrew Marvell, Richard Crashaw, and Henry Vaughan. **3. an imitative art:** See Aristotle's *Poetics*, i. 2. **4. Dryden . . . poetry:** in *A Discourse Concerning the Original and Progress of Satire* (1693).

5. that . . . expressed: See *Essay on Criticism*, ll. 297–98, in Part Two. **6. discordia concors:** dissimilar similarity (Manilius, *Astronomica*, I. 142). **7. Epicurean deities:** The Greek philosopher Epicurus (341–270 B.C.) held that the gods do not intervene in human affairs.

their lamentation of sorrow. Their wish was only to say what they hoped had been never said before.

Nor was the sublime more within their reach than the pathetick; for they never attempted that comprehension and expanse of thought which at once fills the whole mind, and of which the first effect is sudden astonishment, and the second rational admiration. Sublimity is produced by aggregation, and littleness by dispersion. Great thoughts are always general, and consist in positions not limited by exceptions, and in descriptions not descending to minuteness. It is with great propriety that Subtlety, which in its original import means exility[8] of particles, is taken in its metaphorical meaning for nicety of distinction. Those writers who lay on the watch for novelty could have little hope of greatness; for great things cannot have escaped former observation. Their attempts were always analytick; they broke every image into fragments; and could no more represent, by their slender conceits and laboured particularities, the prospects of nature, or the scenes of life, than he, who dissects a sun-beam with a prism, can exhibit the wide effulgence of a summer noon.

What they wanted however of the sublime, they endeavoured to supply by hyperbole; their amplification had no limits; they left not only reason but fancy behind them; and produced combinations of confused magnificence, that not only could not be credited, but could not be imagined.

Yet great labour, directed by great abilities, is never wholly lost: if they frequently threw away their wit upon false conceits, they likewise sometimes struck out unexpected truth: if their conceits were far-fetched, they were often worth the carriage. To write on their plan, it was at least necessary to read and think. No man could be born a metaphysical poet, nor assume the dignity of a writer, by descriptions copied from descriptions, by imitations borrowed from imitations, by traditional imagery, and hereditary similies, by readiness of rhyme, and volubility of syllables.

In perusing the works of this race of authours, the mind is exercised either by recollection or inquiry; either something already learned is to be retrieved, or something new is to be examined. If their greatness seldom elevates, their acuteness often surprises; if the imagination is not always gratified, at least the powers of reflection and comparison are employed; and in

the mass of materials which ingenious absurdity has thrown together, genuine wit and useful knowledge may be sometimes found, buried perhaps in grossness of expression, but useful to those who know their value; and such as, when they are expanded to perspicuity, and polished to elegance, may give lustre to works which have more propriety, though less copiousness of sentiment.

. . .

FROM

DRYDEN

DRYDEN may be properly considered as the father of English criticism, as the writer who first taught us to determine upon principles the merit of composition. Of our former poets, the greatest dramatist wrote without rules, conducted through life and nature by a genius that rarely misled, and rarely deserted him. Of the rest, those who knew the laws of propriety had neglected to teach them.

Two *Arts of English Poetry* were written in the days of Elizabeth by Webb and Puttenham,[1] from which something might be learned, and a few hints had been given by Jonson and Cowley; but Dryden's *Essay on Dramatick Poetry*[2] was the first regular and valuable treatise on the art of writing.

He who, having formed his opinions in the present age of English literature, turns back to peruse this dialogue, will not perhaps find much increase of knowledge, or much novelty of instruction; but he is to remember that critical principles were then in the hands of a few, who had gathered them partly from the Ancients, and partly from the Italians and French. The structure of dramatick poems was not then generally understood. Audiences applauded by instinct, and poets perhaps often pleased by chance.

A writer who obtains his full purpose loses himself in his own lustre. Of an opinion which is no longer doubted, the evidence ceases to be examined. Of an art universally practised, the first teacher is forgotten.

---

8. **exility:** smallness.

LIFE OF DRYDEN. **1. Webb and Puttenham:** William Webbe published *A Discourse of English Poetry* in 1586; George Puttenham published *The Art of English Poesy* in 1589. **2. Essay . . . Poetry:** a critical essay (1668) in the form of a dialogue between four speakers (see Part One).

Learning once made popular is no longer learning; it has the appearance of something which we have bestowed upon ourselves, as the dew appears to rise from the field which it refreshes.

To judge rightly of an author, we must transport ourselves to his time, and examine what were the wants of his contemporaries, and what were his means of supplying them. That which is easy at one time was difficult at another. Dryden at least imported his science, and gave his country what it wanted before; or rather, he imported only the materials, and manufactured them by his own skill.

The dialogue on the Drama was one of his first essays of criticism, written when he was yet a timorous candidate for reputation, and therefore laboured with that diligence which he might allow himself somewhat to remit, when his name gave sanction to his positions, and his awe of the public was abated, partly by custom, and partly by success. It will not be easy to find, in all the opulence of our language, a treatise so artfully variegated with successive representations of opposite probabilities, so enlivened with imagery, so brightened with illustrations. His portraits of the English dramatists are wrought with great spirit and diligence. The account of Shakespeare may stand as a perpetual model of encomiastick criticism; exact without minuteness, and lofty without exaggeration. The praise lavished by Longinus,[3] on the attestation of the heroes of Marathon, by Demosthenes,[4] fades away before it. In a few lines is exhibited a character, so extensive in its comprehension, and so curious in its limitations, that nothing can be added, diminished, or reformed; nor can the editors and admirers of Shakespeare, in all their emulation of reverence, boast of much more than of having diffused and paraphrased this epitome of excellence, of having changed Dryden's gold for baser metal, of lower value though of greater bulk.

In this, and in all his other essays on the same subject, the criticism of Dryden is the criticism of a poet; not a dull collection of theorems, nor a rude detection of faults, which perhaps the censor was not able to have committed; but a gay and vigorous dissertation, where delight is mingled with instruction, and where the author proves his right of judgement, by his power of performance.

The different manner and effect with which critical knowledge may be conveyed, was perhaps never more clearly exemplified than in the performances of Rymer and Dryden. It was said of a dispute between two mathematicians, "malim cum Scaligero errare, quam cum Clavio recte sapere;" that *it was more eligible to go wrong with one than right with the other.* A tendency of the same kind every mind must feel at the perusal of Dryden's prefaces and Rymer's discourses. With Dryden we are wandering in quest of Truth; whom we find, if we find her at all, drest in the graces of elegance; and if we miss her, the labour of the pursuit rewards itself; we are led only through fragrance and flowers: Rymer, without taking a nearer, takes a rougher way; every step is to be made through thorns and brambles; and Truth, if we meet her, appears repulsive by her mien, and ungraceful by her habit. Dryden's criticism has the majesty of a queen; Rymer's has the ferocity of a tyrant.

As he had studied with great diligence the art of Poetry, and enlarged or rectified his notions, by experience perpetually increasing, he had his mind stored with principles and observations; he poured out his knowledge with little labour; for of labour, notwithstanding the multiplicity of his productions, there is sufficient reason to suspect that he was not a lover. To write *con amore*, with fondness for the employment, with perpetual touches and retouches, with unwillingness to take leave of his own idea, and an unwearied pursuit of unattainable perfection, was, I think, no part of his character.

His Criticism may be considered as general or occasional. In his general precepts, which depend upon the nature of things and the structure of the human mind, he may doubtless be safely recommended to the confidence of the reader; but his occasional and particular positions were sometimes interested, sometimes negligent, and sometimes capricious. It is not without reason that Trapp,[5] speaking of the praises which he bestows on Palamon and Arcite, says, "Novimus judicium Drydeni de poemate quodam *Chauceri,* pulchro sane illo, et admodum laudando, nimirum quod non modo vere epicum sit, sed Iliada etiam atque Æneada æquet, imo superet. Sed novimus eodem tempore viri illius maximi non semper accuratissimas esse censuras, nec ad severissimam critices normam

---

3. by Longinus: in *On the Sublime,* Ch. xvi, a first-century A.D. treatise mistakenly attributed to him. **4. Demosthenes:** the famous Athenian orator of the fourth century B.C.

5. Trapp: Joseph Trapp (1679–1747), professor of poetry at Oxford, author of *Praelectiones Poeticae* (*Lectures on Poetry*) (1711–36).

exactas: illo judice id plerumque optimum est, quod nunc præ manibus habet, & in quo nunc occupatur."[6]

He is therefore by no means constant to himself. His defence and desertion of dramatick rhyme is generally known. *Spence*,[7] in his remarks on Pope's Odyssey, produces what he thinks an unconquerable quotation from Dryden's preface to the Eneid, in favour of translating an epick poem into blank verse; but he forgets that when his author attempted the Iliad, some years afterwards, he departed from his own decision, and translated into rhyme.

When he has any objection to obviate, or any license to defend, he is not very scrupulous about what he asserts, nor very cautious, if the present purpose be served, not to entangle himself in his own sophistries. But, when all arts are exhausted, like other hunted animals, he sometimes stands at bay; when he cannot disown the grossness of one of his plays, he declares that he knows not any law that prescribes morality to a comick poet.

His remarks on ancient or modern writers are not always to be trusted. His parallel of the versification of Ovid with that of Claudian has been very justly censured by *Sewel*.[8] His comparison of the first line of Virgil with the first of Statius[9] is not happier. Virgil, he says, is soft and gentle, and would have thought Statius mad if he had heard him thundering out

> Quæ superimposito moles geminata colosso.[10]

Statius perhaps heats himself, as he proceeds, to exaggerations somewhat hyperbolical; but undoubtedly Virgil would have been too hasty, if he had condemned him to straw for one sounding line. Dryden wanted an instance, and the first that occurred was imprest into the service.

What he wishes to say, he says at hazard; he cited *Gorbuduc*,[11] which he had never seen; gives a false account of *Chapman's*[12] versification; and discovers, in the preface to his Fables,[13] that he translated the first book of the Iliad, without knowing what was in the second.

It will be difficult to prove that Dryden ever made any great advances in literature. As having distinguished himself at Westminster under the tuition of Busby,[14] who advanced his scholars to a height of knowledge very rarely attained in grammar-schools, he resided afterwards at Cambridge, it is not to be supposed that his skill in the ancient languages was deficient, compared with that of common students; but his scholastick acquisitions seem not proportionate to his opportunities and abilities. He could not, like Milton or Cowley, have made his name illustrious merely by his learning. He mentions but few books, and those such as lie in the beaten track of regular study; from which if ever he departs, he is in danger of losing himself in unknown regions.

In his Dialogue on the Drama, he pronounces with great confidence that the Latin tragedy of Medea is not Ovid's, because it is not sufficiently interesting and pathetick. He might have determined the question upon surer evidence; for it is quoted by Quintilian[15] as the work of Seneca;[16] and the only line which remains of Ovid's play, for one line is left us, is not there to be found. There was therefore no need of the gravity of conjecture, or the discussion of plot or sentiment, to find what was already known upon higher authority than such discussions can ever reach.

His literature, though not always free from ostentation, will be commonly found either obvious, and made his own by the art of dressing it; or superficial, which, by what he gives, shews what he wanted; or erroneous, hastily collected, and negligently scattered.

Yet it cannot be said that his genius is ever unprovided of matter, or that his fancy languishes in penury of ideas. His works abound with knowledge, and sparkle with illustrations. There is scarcely any science or faculty that does not supply him with

---

6. **Novimus . . . occupatur:** "We know our countryman Mr. Dryden's judgment about a poem of Chaucer's [*The Knight's Tale*], truly beautiful indeed and worthy of praise: namely, that it was not only equal, but even superior to the *Iliad* and the *Aeneid*. But we know also that his opinion was not always the most accurate, nor formed upon the severest rules of criticism. What was in hand was generally most in esteem; if it was uppermost in his thoughts it was so in his judgment too." 7. **Spence:** Joseph Spence (1699–1768), tutor and professor of poetry at Oxford, author of *An Essay on Pope's Odyssey* (1727). 8. **Sewel:** [Johnson's note] Preface to Ovid's Metamorphoses [translated in 1717 by George Sewell (c. 1690–1726) and others]. 9. **Status:** Publius Papinius Statius (A.D. 61– c. 96), Roman author of the *Thebiad*, a twelve-book epic, and *Sylvae*, a five-book miscellany of poems. 10. **Quæ . . . colosso:** "What huge mass, doubled by the colossus set upon it" (*Sylvae*, I. i. 1).

11. **Gorbuduc:** an early English tragedy (1561) by Thomas Norton and Thomas Sackville. 12. **Chapman:** George Chapman (c. 1559–c. 1634), playwright and translator of Homer (1611–14). 13. **the preface . . . Fables:** published in 1700. (See Part One.) 14. **Busby:** Richard Busby (1606–95), headmaster of Westminster School. 15. **Quintilian:** first-century A.D. Latin rhetorician. 16. **Seneca:** first-century A.D. Stoic philosopher and author of tragedies.

occasional images and lucky similitudes; every page discovers a mind very widely acquainted both with art and nature, and in full possession of great stores of intellectual wealth. Of him that knows much, it is natural to suppose that he has read with diligence; yet I rather believe that the knowledge of Dryden was gleaned from accidental intelligence and various conversation, by a quick apprehension, a judicious selection, and a happy memory, a keen appetite of knowledge, and a powerful digestion; by vigilance that permitted nothing to pass without notice, and a habit of reflection that suffered nothing useful to be lost. A mind like Dryden's, always curious, always active, to which every understanding was proud to be associated, and of which every one solicited the regard, by an ambitious display of himself, had a more pleasant, perhaps a nearer, way to knowledge than by the silent progress of solitary reading. I do not suppose that he despised books, or intentionally neglected them; but that he was carried out, by the impetuosity of his genius, to more vivid and speedy instructors; and that his studies were rather desultory and fortuitous than constant and systematical.

It must be confessed that he scarcely ever appears to want book-learning but when he mentions books; and to him may be transferred the praise which he gives his master Charles.

His conversation, wit, and parts,
His knowledge in the noblest useful arts,
    Were such, dead authors could not give,
    But habitudes of those that live,
Who, lighting him, did greater lights receive:
    He drain'd from all, and all they knew,
    His apprehension quick, his judgement true:
That the most learn'd with shame confess
His knowledge more, his reading only less.[17]

Of all this, however, if the proof be demanded, I will not undertake to give it; the atoms of probability, of which my opinion has been formed, lie scattered over all his works; and by him who thinks the question worth his notice, his works must be perused with very close attention.

Criticism, either didactick or defensive, occupies almost all his prose, except those pages which he has devoted to his patrons; but none of his prefaces were ever thought tedious. They have not the formality of a settled style, in which the first half of the sentence betrays the other. The clauses are never balanced, nor the periods modelled; every word seems to drop by chance, though it falls into its proper place. Nothing is cold or languid; the whole is airy, animated and vigorous; what is little, is gay; what is great, is splendid. He may be thought to mention himself too frequently; but while he forces himself upon our esteem, we cannot refuse him to stand high in his own. Every thing is excused by the play of images and the spriteliness of expression. Though all is easy, nothing is feeble; though all seems careless, there is nothing harsh; and though, since his earlier works, more than a century has passed, they have nothing yet uncouth or obsolete.

He who writes much, will not easily escape a manner, such a recurrence of particular modes as may be easily noted. Dryden is always *another and the same*,[18] he does not exhibit a second time the same elegancies in the same form, nor appears to have any art other than that of expressing with clearness what he thinks with vigour. His stile could not easily be imitated, either seriously or ludicrously; for being always equable and always varied, it has no prominent or discriminative characters. The beauty who is totally free from disproportion of parts and features cannot be ridiculed by an overcharged resemblance.

From his prose however, Dryden derives only his accidental and secondary praise; the veneration with which his name is pronounced by every cultivator of English Literature, is paid to him as he refined the language, improved the sentiments, and tuned the numbers of English Poetry.

After about half a century of forced thoughts, and rugged metre, some advances towards nature and harmony had been already made by Waller and Denham;[19] they had shewn that long discourses in rhyme grew more pleasing when they were broken into couplets, and that verse consisted not only in the number but the arrangement of syllables.

But though they did much, who can deny that they left much to do? Their works were not many, nor were their minds of very ample comprehension. More examples of more modes of composition were necessary for the establishment of regularity, and the introduction of propriety in word and thought.

---

17. His conversation . . . less: *Threnodia Augustalis: A Funeral-Pindaric Poem Sacred to the Happy Memory of King Charles II*, ll. 337–45.

18. another . . . same: Cf. Horace, *Carmen Saeculare*, l. 10.
19. Waller and Denham: Edmund Waller (1606–87) and Sir John Denham (1615–59). (See selections from both in Part Three.)

Every language of a learned nation necessarily divides itself into diction scholastick and popular, grave and familiar, elegant and gross; and from a nice distinction of these different parts, arises a great part of the beauty of stile. But if we except a few minds, the favourites of nature, to whom their own original rectitude was in the place of rules, this delicacy of selection was little known to our authors; our speech lay before them in a heap of confusion, and every man took for every purpose what chance might offer him.

There was therefore before the time of Dryden no poetical diction, no system of words at once refined from the grossness of domestick use, and free from the harshness of terms appropriated to particular arts. Words too familiar, or too remote, defeat the purpose of a poet. From those sounds which we hear on small or on coarse occasions, we do not easily receive strong impressions, or delightful images, and words to which we are nearly strangers, whenever they occur, draw that attention on themselves which they should transmit to things.

Those happy combinations of words which distinguish poetry from prose, had been rarely attempted; we had few elegancies or flowers of speech, the roses had not yet been plucked from the bramble, or different colours had not been joined to enliven one another.

It may be doubted whether Waller and Denham could have over-born the prejudices which had long prevailed, and which even then were sheltered by the protection of Cowley. The new versification, as it was called, may be considered as owing its establishment to Dryden; from whose time it is apparent that English poetry has had no tendency to relapse to its former savageness.

The affluence and comprehension of our language is very illustriously displayed in our poetical translations of Ancient Writers; a work which the French seem to relinquish in despair, and which we were long unable to perform with dexterity. Ben Jonson thought it necessary to copy Horace almost word by word; Feltham,[20] his contemporary and adversary, considers it as indispensably requisite in a translation to give line for line. It is said that Sandys,[21] whom Dryden calls the best versifier of the last age, has struggled hard to comprise every book of his English Metamorphoses in the same number of verses with the original.

Holyday[22] had nothing in view but to shew that he understood his author, with so little regard to the grandeur of his diction, or the volubility of his numbers, that his metres can hardly be called verses; they cannot be read without reluctance, nor will the labour always be rewarded by understanding them. Cowley saw that such *copyers* were a *servile race;* he asserted his liberty, and spread his wings so boldly that he left his authors. It was reserved for Dryden to fix the limits of poetical liberty, and give us just rules and examples of translation.

When languages are formed upon different principles, it is impossible that the same modes of expression should always be elegant in both. While they run on together, the closest translation may be considered as the best; but when they divaricate, each must take its natural course. Where correspondence cannot be obtained, it is necessary to be content with something equivalent. *Translation therefore*, says Dryden, *is not so loose as paraphrase, nor so close as metaphrase.*

All polished languages have different styles; the concise, the diffuse, the lofty, and the humble. In the proper choice of style consists the resemblance which Dryden principally exacts from the translator. He is to exhibit his author's thoughts in such a dress of diction as the author would have given them, had his language been English: rugged magnificence is not to be softened: hyperbolical ostentation is not to be repressed, nor sententious affectation to have its points blunted. A translator is to be like his author; it is not his business to excel him.

The reasonableness of these rules seems sufficient for their vindication; and the effects produced by observing them were so happy, that I know not whether they were ever opposed but by Sir Edward Sherburne,[23] a man whose learning was greater than his powers of poetry; and who, being better qualified to give the meaning than the spirit of Seneca, has introduced his version of three tragedies by a defence of close translation. The authority of Horace, which the new translators cited in defence of their practice, he has, by a judicious explanation, taken fairly from them; but reason wants not Horace to support it.

It seldom happens that all the necessary causes concur to any great effect: will is wanting to power, or

20. **Feltham:** Owen Felltham (c. 1602–68), poet, essayist, and traveler. 21. **Sandys:** George Sandys (1578–1644), translator of Ovid and author of religious poems.

22. **Holyday:** Barten Holiday (1593–1661), translator of Juvenal, Persius, and Horace. 23. **Sir . . . Sherburne:** (1618–1702), a translator known especially for his versions of Seneca and Manilius.

power to will, or both are impeded by external obstructions. The exigencies in which Dryden was condemned to pass his life, are reasonably supposed to have blasted his genius, to have driven out his works in a state of immaturity, and to have intercepted the full-blown elegance which longer growth would have supplied.

Poverty, like other rigid powers, is sometimes too hastily accused. If the excellence of Dryden's works was lessened by his indigence, their number was increased; and I know not how it will be proved, that if he had written less he would have written better; or that indeed he would have undergone the toil of an author, if he had not been solicited by something more pressing than the love of praise.

But, as is said by his Sebastian,

> What had been, is unknown; what is, appears.[24]

We know that Dryden's several productions were so many successive expedients for his support; his plays were therefore often borrowed, and his poems were almost all occasional.

In an occasional performance no height of excellence can be expected from any mind, however fertile in itself, and however stored with acquisitions. He whose work is general and arbitrary, has the choice of his matter, and takes that which his inclination and his studies have best qualified him to display and decorate. He is at liberty to delay his publication, till he has satisfied his friends and himself; till he has reformed his first thoughts by subsequent examination; and polished away those faults which the precipitance of ardent composition is likely to leave behind it. Virgil is related to have poured out a great number of lines in the morning, and to have passed the day in reducing them to fewer.

The occasional poet is circumscribed by the narrowness of his subject. Whatever can happen to man has happened so often, that little remains for fancy or invention. We have been all born; we have most of us been married; and so many have died before us, that our deaths can supply but few materials for a poet. In the fate of princes the publick has an interest; and what happens to them of good or evil, the poets have always considered as business for the Muse. But after so many inauguratory gratulations, nuptial hymns, and funeral dirges, he must be highly favoured by nature, or by fortune, who says any thing not said

before. Even war and conquest, however splendid, suggest no new images; the triumphal chariot of a victorious monarch can be decked only with those ornaments that have graced his predecessors.

Not only matter but time is wanting. The poem must not be delayed till the occasion is forgotten. The lucky moments of animated imagination cannot be attended; elegancies and illustrations cannot be multiplied by gradual accumulation; the composition must be dispatched while conversation is yet busy, and admiration fresh; and haste is to be made, lest some other event should lay hold upon mankind.

Occasional compositions may however secure to a writer the praise both of learning and facility; for they cannot be the effect of long study, and must be furnished immediately from the treasures of the mind.

The death of Cromwel[25] was the first publick event which called forth Dryden's poetical powers. His heroick stanzas have beauties and defects; the thoughts are vigorous, and though not always proper, shew a mind replete with ideas; the numbers are smooth, and the diction if not altogether correct, is elegant and easy.

Davenant[26] was perhaps at this time his favourite author, though Gondibert never appears to have been popular; and from Davenant he learned to please his ear with the stanza of four lines alternately rhymed.

Dryden very early formed his versification: there are in this early production no traces of Donne's or Jonson's ruggedness; but he did not so soon free his mind from the ambition of forced conceits. In his verses on the Restoration, he says of the King's exile,

> He, toss'd by Fate—
> Could taste no sweets of youth's desired age,
> But found his life too true a pilgrimage.[27]

And afterwards, to shew how virtue and wisdom are increased by adversity, he makes this remark:

> Well might the ancient poets then confer
> On Night the honour'd name of *counsellor*,
> Since, struck with rays of prosperous fortune blind,
> We light alone in dark afflictions find.[28]

25. The death . . . Cromwel: in 1658. Dryden's poem is *A Poem upon the Death of His Late Highness, Oliver* (1659). **26. Davenant:** Sir William D'Avenant (1606–68), poet and dramatist; his romantic epic *Gondibert*, which he abandoned from boredom after some seventeen hundred quatrains, was published in 1651. **27. He . . . pilgrimage:** *Astraea Redux: A Poem on the Happy Restoration and Return of his Sacred Majesty Charles the Second*, ll. 51, 53–54. **28. Well . . . find:** *Ibid.*, ll. 93–96.

24. What . . . appears: *Don Sebastian*, IV. iii.

His praise of Monk's[29] dexterity comprises such a cluster of thoughts unallied to one another, as will not elsewhere be easily found:

> 'Twas Monk, whom Providence design'd to loose
> Those real bonds false freedom did impose.
> The blessed saints that watch'd this turning scene,
> Did from their stars with joyful wonder lean,
> To see small clues[30] draw vastest weights along,
> Not in their bulk but in their order strong.
> Thus pencils can by one slight touch restore
> Smiles to that changed face that wept before.
> With ease such fond chimæras[31] we pursue,
> As fancy frames for fancy to subdue:
> But when ourselves to action we betake,
> It shuns the mint like gold that chymists make:
> How hard was then his task, at once to be
> What in the body natural we see!
> Man's Architect distinctly did ordain
> The charge of muscles, nerves, and of the brain;
> Thro' viewless conduits spirits to dispense
> The springs of motion from the seat of sense.
> 'Twas not the hasty product of a day,
> But the well-ripen'd fruit of wise delay.
> He, like a patient angler, ere he strook,
> Would let them play a-while upon the hook.
> Our healthful food the stomach labours thus,
> At first embracing what it straight doth crush.
> Wise leaches[32] will not vain receipts obtrude,
> While growing pains pronounce the humours
>   crude;
> Deaf to complaints, they wait upon the ill,
> Till some safe crisis authorize their skill.[33]

He had not yet learned, indeed he never learned well, to forbear the improper use of mythology. After having rewarded the heathen deities for their care,

> With *Alga* who the sacred altar strows?
> To all the sea-gods Charles an offering owes;
> A bull to thee, Portunus, shall be slain;
> A ram to you, ye Tempests of the Main.[34]

He tells us, in the language of religion,

> Prayer storm'd the skies, and ravish'd Charles from
>   thence,
> As heav'n itself is took by violence.[35]

And afterwards mentions one of the most awful passages of Sacred History.[36]

Other conceits there are, too curious to be quite omitted; as,

> For by example most we sinn'd before,
> And, glass-like, clearness mix'd with frailty bore.[37]

How far he was yet from thinking it necessary to found his sentiments on Nature, appears from the extravagance of his fictions and hyperboles:

> The winds, that never moderation knew,
> Afraid to blow too much, too faintly blew;
> Or, out of breath with joy, could not enlarge
> Their straiten'd lungs.—
> It is no longer motion cheats your view;
> As you meet it, the land approacheth you;
> The land returns, and in the white it wears
> The marks of penitence and sorrow bears.[38]

I know not whether this fancy, however little be its value, was not borrowed. A French poet read to Malherbe some verses, in which he represents France as moving out of its place to receive the King. "Though this," said Malherbe, "was in my time, I do not remember it."

His poem on the *Coronation* has a more even tenour of thought. Some lines deserve to be quoted:

> You have already quench'd sedition's brand,
> And zeal that burnt it, only warms the land;
> The jealous sects that durst not trust their cause
> So far from their own will as to the laws,
> Him for their umpire and their synod take,
> And their appeal alone to Cæsar make.[39]

Here may be found one particle of that old versification, of which, I believe, in all his works, there is not another:

> Nor is it duty, or our hope alone,
> Creates that joy, but full *fruition*,[40]

In the verses to the lord chancellor Clarendon, two years afterwards, is a conceit so hopeless at the first

---

36. one . . . History: Lines 262–65 of *Astraea Redux* read:

> . . . when th' Almighty would to *Moses* give
> A sight of all he could behold and live;
> A voice before his Entry did proclaim
> *Long-Suffring, Goodness, Mercy* in his Name.

37. For . . . bore: *Astraea Redux*, ll. 207–08. **38. The winds . . . bears:** *Ibid.*, ll. 242–45, 252–55. **39. You . . . make:** *To His Sacred Majesty, A Panegyric on His Coronation*, ll. 79–84. **40. Nor . . . fruition:** *Ibid.*, ll. 69–70.

---

29. Monk: George Monk (1608–70), First Duke of Albemarle; he helped manage the return to England of Charles II. **30. clues:** threads. **31. chimæras:** unreal conceptions. **32. leaches:** physicians. **33. 'Twas . . . skill:** *Astraea Redux*, ll. 150–78. **34. With . . . Main:** *Ibid.*, ll. 119–22. **35. Prayer . . . violence:** *Ibid.*, ll. 142–44.

view, that few would have attempted it; and so success-fully laboured, that though at last it gives the reader more perplexity than pleasure, and seems hardly worth the study that it costs, yet it must be valued as a proof of a mind at once subtle and comprehensive:

> In open prospect nothing bounds our eye,
> Until the earth seems join'd unto the sky:
> So in this hemisphere our outmost view
> Is only bounded by our king and you:
> Our sight is limited where you are join'd,
> And beyond that no farther heav'n can find.
> So well your virtues do with his agree,
> That, tho' your orbs of different greatness be,
> Yet both are for each other's use dispos'd,
> His to enclose, and your's to be enclos'd.
> Nor could another in your room have been,
> Except an emptiness had come between.[41]

The comparison of the Chancellor to the Indies leaves all resemblance too far behind it:

> And as the Indies were not found before
> Those rich perfumes which from the happy shore
> The winds upon their balmy wings convey'd,
> Whose guilty sweetness first their world betray'd;
> So by your counsels we are brought to view
> A new and undiscover'd world in you.[42]

There is another comparison, for there is little else in the poem, of which, though perhaps it cannot be explained into plain prosaick meaning, the mind per-ceives enough to be delighted, and readily forgives its obscurity for its magnificence:

> How strangely active are the arts of peace,
> Whose restless motions less than wars do cease!
> Peace is not freed from labour, but from noise;
> And war more force, but not more pains employs:
> Such is the mighty swiftness of your mind,
> That, like the earth's, it leaves our sense behind,
> While you so smoothly turn and rowl our sphere,
> That rapid motion does but rest appear.
> For as in nature's swiftness, with the throng
> Of flying orbs while our's is born along,
> All seems at rest to the deluded eye,
> Mov'd by the soul of the same harmony:
> So carry'd on by your unwearied care,
> We rest in peace, and yet in motion share.[43]

To this succeed four lines, which perhaps afford Dryden's first attempt at those penetrating remarks on

human nature, for which he seems to have been peculiarly formed:

> Let envy then those crimes within you see,
> From which the happy never must be free;
> Envy that does with misery reside,
> The joy and the revenge of ruin'd pride.[44]

Into this poem he seems to have collected all his powers; and after this he did not often bring upon his anvil such stubborn and unmalleable thoughts; but, as a specimen of his abilities to unite the most unsociable matter, he has concluded with lines, of which I think not myself obliged to tell the meaning:

> Yet unimpair'd with labours, or with time,
> Your age but seems to a new youth to climb.
> Thus heav'nly bodies do our time beget,
> And measure change, but share no part of it:
> And still it shall without a weight increase,
> Like this new year, whose motions never cease.
> For since the glorious course you have begun
> Is led by Charles, as that is by the sun,
> It must both weightless and immortal prove,
> Because the centre of it is above.[45]

In the *Annus Mirabilis*[46] he returned to the quatrain, which from that time he totally quitted, perhaps from this experience of its inconvenience, for he complains of its difficulty. This is one of his greatest attempts. He had subjects equal to his abilities, a great naval war, and the Fire of London. Battles have always been described in heroick poetry; but a sea-fight and artillery had yet something of novelty. New arts are long in the world before poets describe them; for they borrow every thing from their predecessors, and commonly derive very little from nature or from life. Boileau was the first French writer that had ever hazarded in verse the mention of modern war, or the effects of gunpowder. We, who are less afraid of novelty, had already possession of those dreadful images: Waller had described a sea-fight. Milton had not yet transferred the invention of fire-arms to the rebellious angels.[47]

This poem is written with great diligence, yet does not fully answer the expectation raised by such subjects and such a writer. With the stanza of Davenant he has

---

41. In . . . between: *To My Lord Chancellor, Presented on New-Years-Day, 1662*, ll. 31–42. 42. And . . . you: *Ibid.*, ll. 73–78. 43. How . . . share: *Ibid.*, ll. 105–18.

44. Let . . . pride: *Ibid.*, ll. 119–22. 45. Yet . . . above: *Ibid.*, ll. 147–56. 46. Annus Mirabilis: *Annus Mirabilis, The Year of Wonders, 1666. An Historical Poem: Containing the Progress and Various Successes of our Naval War with Holland and Describing the Fire of London* (1667). 47. transferred . . . angels: *Paradise Lost*, VI. 507 ff.

sometimes his vein of parenthesis, and incidental disquisition, and stops his narrative for a wise remark.

The general fault is, that he affords more sentiment than description, and does not so much impress scenes upon the fancy, as deduce consequences and make comparisons.

The initial stanzas have rather too much resemblance to the first lines of Waller's poem on the war with Spain;[48] perhaps such a beginning is natural, and could not be avoided without affectation. Both Waller and Dryden might take their hint from the poem on the civil war of Rome, *Orbem jam totum,*[49] &c.

Of the king collecting his navy, he says,

> It seems as every ship their sovereign knows,
>   His awful summons they so soon obey:
> So hear the scaly herds when Proteus blows,
>   And so to pasture follow through the sea.[50]

It would not be hard to believe that Dryden had written the two first lines seriously, and that some wag had added the two latter in burlesque. Who would expect the lines that immediately follow, which are indeed perhaps indecently hyperbolical, but certainly in a mode totally different?

> To see this fleet upon the ocean move,
>   Angels drew wide the curtains of the skies;
> And heaven, as if there wanted lights above,
>   For tapers made two glaring comets rise.[51]

The description of the attempt at Bergen will afford a very compleat specimen of the descriptions in this poem:

And now approach'd their fleet from India, fraught
  With all the riches of the rising sun:
And precious sand from southern climates brought,
  The fatal regions where the war begun.

Like hunted castors,[52] conscious of their store,
  Their way-laid wealth to Norway's coast they bring:
Then first the North's cold bosom spices bore,
  And winter brooded on the eastern spring.

By the rich scent we found our perfum'd prey,
  Which, flank'd with rocks, did close in covert lie:
And round about their murdering cannon lay,
  At once to threaten and invite the eye.

Fiercer than cannon, and than rocks more hard,
  The English undertake th' unequal war:
Seven ships alone, by which the port is barr'd,
  Besiege the Indies, and all Denmark dare.

These fight like husbands, but like lovers those:
  These fain would keep, and those more fain enjoy:
And to such height their frantic passion grows,
  That what both love, both hazard to destroy.

Amidst whole heaps of spices lights a ball,
  And now their odours arm'd against them fly:
Some preciously by shatter'd porcelain fall,
  And some by aromatic splinters die.

And tho' by tempests of the prize bereft,
  In heaven's inclemency some ease we find:
Our foes we vanquish'd by our valour left,
  And only yielded to the seas and wind.[53]

In this manner is the sublime too often mingled with the ridiculous. The Dutch seek a shelter for a wealthy fleet: this surely needed no illustration, yet they must fly, not like all the rest of mankind on the same occasion, but *like hunted castors;* and they might with strict propriety be hunted; for we winded them by our noses—their *perfumes* betrayed them. The *Husband* and the *Lover,* though of more dignity than the Castor, are images too domestick to mingle properly with the horrors of war. The two quatrains that follow are worthy of the author.

The account of the different sensations with which the two fleets retired, when the night parted them, is one of the fairest flowers of English poetry.

> The night comes on, we eager to pursue
>   The combat still, and they asham'd to leave:
> Till the last streaks of dying day withdrew,
>   And doubtful moon-light did our rage deceive.

> In th' English fleet each ship resounds with joy,
>   And loud applause of their great leader's fame:
> In fiery dreams the Dutch they still destroy,
>   And, slumbering, smile at the imagin'd flame.

> Not so the Holland fleet, who, tir'd and done,
>   Stretch'd on their decks like weary oxen lie;
> Faint sweats all down their mighty members run,
>   (Vast bulks which little souls but ill supply.)

> In dreams they fearful precipices tread,
>   Or, shipwreck'd, labour to some distant shore:
> Or, in dark churches, walk among the dead;
>   They wake with horror, and dare sleep no more.[54]

48. Waller's . . . Spain: *Of a War with Spain, and Fight at Sea* (1661). 49. Orbem . . . totum: "the whole world" (from Petronius' *Satyricon,* l. 119; probably parodying Lucan's ten-book epic *Pharsalia*). 50. It . . . sea: *Annus Mirabilis,* st. 15. 51. To . . . rise: *Ibid.,* st. 16. 52. castors: beavers.

53. And now approach'd . . . wind: *Annus Mirabilis,* sts. 24–30. 54. The night . . . more: *Ibid.,* sts. 68–71.

It is a general rule in poetry, that all appropriated terms of art should be sunk in general expressions, because poetry is to speak an universal language. This rule is still stronger with regard to arts not liberal, or confined to few, and therefore far removed from common knowledge; and of this kind, certainly, is technical navigation. Yet Dryden was of opinion that a sea-fight ought to be described in the nautical language; *and certainly*, says he, *as those, who in a logical disputation keep to general terms would hide a fallacy, so those who do it in any poetical description would veil their ignorance.*[55]

Let us then appeal to experience; for by experience at last we learn as well what will please as what will profit. In the battle, his terms seem to have been blown away; but he deals them liberally in the dock:

So here some pick out bullets from the side,
 Some drive old *okum* thro' each *seam* and rift:
Their left-hand does the *calking iron* guide,
 The rattling mallet with the right they lift.

With boiling pitch another near at hand
 (From friendly Sweden brought) the *seams instops:*
Which, well laid o'er, the salt-sea waves withstand,
 And shake them from the rising beak in drops.

Some the *gall'd* ropes with dawby *marling* bind,
 Or sear-cloth masts with strong *tarpawling* coats:
To try new *shrouds* one mounts into the wind,
 And one below, their ease or stiffness notes.[56]

I suppose there is not one term which every reader does not wish away.

His digression to the original and progress of navigation, with his prospect of the advancement which it shall receive from the Royal Society, then newly instituted, may be considered as an example seldom equalled of seasonable excursion and artful return.

One line, however, leaves me discontented; he says, that, by the help of the philosophers,

Instructed ships shall sail to quick commerce,
By which remotest regions are allied.[57]—

Which he is constrained to explain in a note, *By a more exact measure of longitude.* It had better become Dryden's learning and genius to have laboured science into

poetry, and have shewn, by explaining longitude, that verse did not refuse the ideas of philosophy.

His description of the Fire[58] is painted by resolute meditation, out of a mind better formed to reason than to feel. The conflagration of a city, with all its tumults of concomitant distress, is one of the most dreadful spectacles which this world can offer to human eyes; yet is seems to raise little emotion in the breast of the poet; he watches the flame coolly from street to street, with now a reflection, and now a simile, till at last he meets the king, for whom he makes a speech, rather tedious in a time so busy; and then follows again the progress of the fire.

There are, however, in this part some passages that deserve attention; as in the beginning.

 The diligence of trades and noiseful gain
  And luxury more late asleep were laid;
 All was the night's, and in her silent reign
  No sound the rest of Nature did invade
 In this deep quiet[59]——

The expression *All was the night's* is taken from Seneca, who remarks[60] on Virgil's line,

 Omnia noctis erant placida composta quiete,[61]

that he might have concluded better,

  Omnia noctis erant.

The following quatrain is vigorous and animated.

The ghosts of traytors from the bridge descend
 With bold fanatick spectres to rejoice;
About the fire into a dance they bend
 And sing their sabbath notes with feeble voice.[62]

His prediction of the improvements which shall be made in the new city is elegant and poetical, and, with an event which Poets cannot always boast, has been happily verified. The poem concludes with a simile that might have better been omitted.

Dryden, when he wrote this poem, seems not yet

<hr/>

55. **and . . . ignorance:** in *An Account of the Ensuing Poem, in a Letter to the Honorable Sir Robert Howard.* 56. **So . . . notes:** *Annus Mirabilis,* sts. 146–48. 57. **Instructed . . . allied:** *Ibid.,* st. 163.

58. **the Fire:** In four days (September 2–6, 1666) the Great Fire of London devastated over four hundred acres, destroying thirteen thousand houses and eighty-seven churches, including St. Paul's. 59. **The diligence . . . quiet:** *Annus Mirabilis,* sts. 216–17. 60. **Seneca, who remarks:** in *Controversies,* III. 16. "Seneca" here is Seneca the Elder, father of the author of tragedies. 61. **Omnia . . . quiete:** "It was night, and all the world was lulled to rest." The line is not from Virgil but from the *Argonautica* of Marcus Terentius Varro, Roman poet and scholar of the first century B.C. 62. **The ghosts . . . voice:** *Annus Mirabilis,* st. 223.

fully to have formed his versification, or settled his system of propriety.

From this time, he addicted himself almost wholly to the stage, *to which*, says he, *my genius never much inclined me*, merely as the most profitable market for poetry. By writing tragedies in rhyme he continued to improve his diction and his numbers. According to the opinion of *Harte*,[63] who had studied his works with great attention, he settled his principles of versification in 1676, when he produced the play of *Aureng Zeb;* and according to his own account of the short time in which he wrote *Tyrannick Love*, and the *State of Innocence*, he soon obtained the full effect of diligence, and added facility to exactness.

Rhyme has been so long banished from the theatre, that we know not its effect upon the passions of an audience; but it has this convenience, that sentences stand more independent on each other, and striking passages are therefore easily selected and retained. Thus the description of Night in the *Indian Emperor*, and the rise and fall of empire in the *Conquest of Granada* are more frequently repeated than any lines in *All for Love*, or *Don Sebastian*.

To search his plays for vigorous sallies, and sententious elegancies, or to fix the dates of any little pieces which he wrote by chance, or by solicitation, were labour too tedious and minute.

His dramatic labours did not so wholly absorb his thoughts but that he promulgated the laws of translation in a preface to the English Epistles of Ovid,[64] one of which he translated himself, and another in conjunction with the Earl of Mulgrave.

Absalom and Achitophel[65] is a work so well known, that particular criticism is superfluous. If it be considered as a poem political and controversial, it will be found to comprise all the excellencies of which the subject is susceptible; acrimony of censure, elegance of praise, artful delineation of characters, variety and vigour of sentiment, happy turns of language and pleasing harmony of numbers; and all these raised to such a height as can scarcely be found in any other English composition.

It is not, however, without faults; some lines are inelegant or improper, and too many are irreligiously licentious. The original structure of the poem was defective; allegories drawn to great length will always break; Charles could not run continually parallel with David.

The subject had likewise another inconvenience: it admitted little imagery or description, and a long poem of mere sentiments easily becomes tedious; though all the parts are forcible, and every line kindles new rapture, the reader, if not relieved by the interposition of something that sooths the fancy, grows weary of admiration, and defers the rest.

As an approach to historical truth was necessary, the action and catastrophe were not in the poet's power; there is therefore an unpleasing disproportion between the beginning and the end. We are alarmed by a faction formed out of many sects various in their principles, but agreeing in their purpose of mischief, formidable for their numbers and strong by their supports, while the king's friends are few and weak. The chiefs on either part are set forth to view; but when expectation is at the height, the king makes a speech, and

Henceforth a series of new times began.[66]

Who can forbear to think of an enchanted castle, with a wide moat and lofty battlements, walls of marble, and gates of brass, which vanishes at once into air, when the destined knight blows his horn before it?

In the second part, written by *Tate*,[67] there is a long insertion,[68] which for poignancy of satire, exceeds any part of the former. Personal resentment, though no laudable motive to satire, can add great force to general principles. Self-love is a busy prompter.

The *Medal*,[69] written upon the same principles with *Absalom and Achitophel*, but upon a narrower plan, gives less pleasure, though it discovers equal abilities in the writer. The superstructure cannot extend beyond the foundation; a single character or incident cannot furnish as many ideas, as a series of events, or multiplicity of agents. This poem therefore, since time has left it to itself, is not much read, nor perhaps generally understood, yet it abounds with touches both of humorous and serious satire. The picture of a man whose propensions to mischief are such, that his best actions are but inability of wickedness, is very skilfully delineated and strongly coloured.

63. **Harte:** Walter Harte (1709–74), Pope's friend. (See Harte's poem *To Mr. Pope* in Part Three.) **64. a preface . . . Ovid:** Dedication to *Examen Poeticum* (1693). **65. Absalom and Achitophel:** published in 1681. (See Part One.)

66. **Henceforth . . . began:** *Absalom and Achitophel,* l. 1028. 67. **Tate:** Nahum Tate (1652–1715) wrote most of the second part (1692) of *Absalom and Achitophel*. **68. a long insertion:** ll. 310–509, by Dryden. **69. The Medal:** *The Medal: A Satire Against Sedition* (1682).

Power was his aim: but thrown from that pretence, }
The wretch turn'd loyal in his own defence, }
And malice reconcil'd him to his Prince. }
Him, in the anguish of his soul, he serv'd;
Rewarded faster still than he deserv'd:
Behold him now exalted into trust;
His counsels oft convenient, seldom just.
Ev'n in the most sincere advice he gave,
He had a grudging still to be a knave.
The frauds he learnt in his fanatic years,
Made him uneasy in his lawful gears:
At least as little honest as he cou'd:
And, like white witches, mischievously good.
To this first bias, longingly, he leans;
And rather wou'd be great by wicked means.[70]

The *Threnodia*, which by a term, I am afraid neither authorized nor analogical, he calls *Augustalis*, is not among his happiest productions. Its first and obvious defect is the irregularity of its metre, to which the ears of that age, however, were accustomed. What is worse, it has neither tenderness nor dignity, it is neither magnificent nor pathetick. He seems to look round him for images which he cannot find, and what he has he distorts by endeavouring to enlarge them. He is, he says, *petrified with grief;* but the marble sometimes relents,[71] and trickles in a joke.

　　The sons of art all med'cines try'd,
　And every noble remedy apply'd;
　　With emulation each essay'd
　　His utmost skill; *nay more, they pray'd:*
Was never losing game with better conduct play'd.[72]

He had been a little inclined to merriment before upon the prayers of a nation for their dying sovereign, nor was he serious enough to keep heathen fables out of his religion.

With him th' innumerable croud of armed prayers
　Knock'd at the gates of heav'n and knock'd aloud;
The first well-meaning rude petitioners,
　All for his life assail'd the throne,
All would have brib'd the skies by offering up their own.
So great a throng not heaven itself could bar;
'Twas almost borne by force as in the giants war.[73]
The prayers, at least, for his reprieve were heard;
His death, like Hezekiah's,[74] was deferr'd.[75]

There is throughout the composition a desire of splendor without wealth. In the conclusion, he seems too much pleased with the prospect of the new reign to have lamented his old master with much sincerity.

He did not miscarry in this attempt for want of skill either in lyrick or elegiack poetry. His poem *on the death* of Mrs. *Killigrew*,[76] is undoubtedly the noblest ode that our language ever has produced. The first part flows with a torrent of enthusiasm. *Fervet immensusque ruit.*[77] All the stanzas indeed are not equal. An imperial crown cannot be one continued diamond; the gems must be held together by some less valuable matter.

In his first ode for Cecilia's day, which is lost in the splendor of the second,[78] there are passages which would have dignified any other poet. The first stanza is vigorous and elegant, though the word *diapason*[79] is too technical, and the rhymes are too remote from one another.

From harmony, from heavenly harmony,
　This universal frame began:
When nature underneath a heap of jarring atoms lay,
　And could not heave her head,
The tuneful voice was heard from high,
　Arise ye more than dead.
Then cold and hot, and moist and dry,
In order to their stations leap,
　And music's power obey.
From harmony, from heavenly harmony,
　This universal frame began:
　From harmony to harmony
Through all the compass of the notes it ran,
　The diapason closing full in man.[80]

The conclusion is likewise striking, but it includes an image so awful in itself, that it can owe little to poetry; and I could wish the antithesis of *musick untuning* had found some other place.

　　As from the power of sacred lays
　　　The spheres began to move,
　　And sung the great Creator's praise
　　　To all the bless'd above.

---

70. Power . . . means: *Ibid.,* ll. 50–64; the poem satirizes the Earl of Shaftesbury. **71. relents:** liquefies. **72. The sons . . . play'd:** *Threnodia Augustalis,* ll. 160–64. **73. the giants war:** In Greek mythology, the giants conducted a war against the gods, who finally had to call upon Athene to assist their side. **74. like Hezekiah's:** See II Kings 20: 1–6. **75. With . . . deferr'd:** *Threnodia Augustalis,* ll. 97–106.

76. poem . . . Killigrew: *To the Pious Memory of the Accomplisht Young Lady Mrs. Anne Killigrew, Excellent in the Two Sister-Arts of Poesie, and Painting. An Ode* (see Part One). **77. Fervet . . . ruit:** "It foams and rushes boundlessly" (Horace, *Odes,* IV. ii. 7). **78. the second:** The "first ode" is *A Song for St. Cecilia's Day* (1687); "the second" is *Alexander's Feast; or, the Power of Musique* (1697). (See both poems in Part One.) **79. diapason:** a musical chord comprising all the harmonizing notes within an octave. **80. From . . man:** *A Song for St. Cecilia's Day,* st. 1.

So when the last and dreadful hour
This crumbling pageant shall devour,
The trumpet shall be heard on high,
The dead shall live, the living die,
And music shall untune the sky.[81]

Of his skill in Elegy he has given a specimen in his *Eleonora*,[82] of which the following lines discover their author.

Tho' all these rare endowments of the mind
Were in a narrow space of life confin'd,
The figure was with full perfection crown'd;
Tho' not so large an orb, as truly round.
As when in glory, thro' the public place,
The spoils of conquer'd nations were to pass,
And but one day for triumph was allow'd,
The consul was constrain'd his pomp to crowd;
And so the swift procession hurry'd on,
That all, tho' not distinctly, might be shown:
So in the straiten'd bounds of life confin'd,
She gave but glimpses of her glorious mind;
And multitudes of virtues pass'd along;
Each pressing foremost in the mighty throng,
Ambitious to be seen, and then make room
For greater multitudes, that were to come.
Yet unemploy'd no minute slipp'd away;
Moments were precious in so short a stay.
The haste of heaven to have her was so great,
That some were single acts, tho' each compleat;
And every act stood ready to repeat.[83]

This piece, however, is not without its faults, there is so much likeness in the initial comparison, that there is no illustration. As a king would be lamented, Eleonora was lamented.

As when some great and gracious monarch dies,
Soft whispers, first, and mournful murmurs rise
Among the sad attendants; then the sound
Soon gathers voice, and spreads the news around,
Thro' town and country, till the dreadful blast
Is blown to distant colonies at last;
Who, then, perhaps, were offering vows in vain,
For his long life, and for his happy reign:
So slowly by degrees, unwilling fame
Did matchless Eleonora's fate proclaim,
Till public as the loss the news became.[84]

This is little better than to say in praise of a shrub, that it is as green as a tree, or of a brook, that it waters a garden, as a river waters a country.

Dryden confesses that he did not know the lady whom he celebrates; the praise being therefore inevitably general, fixes no impression upon the reader, nor excites any tendency to love, nor much desire of imitation. Knowledge of the subject is to the poet, what durable materials are to the architect.

The *Religio Laici*,[85] which borrows its title from the *Religio Medici* of Browne,[86] is almost the only work of Dryden which can be considered as a voluntary effusion; in this, therefore, it might be hoped, that the full effulgence of his genius would be found. But unhappily the subject is rather argumentative than poetical: he intended only a specimen of metrical disputation.

And this unpolish'd rugged verse I chose,
As fittest for discourse, and nearest prose.[87]

This, however, is a composition of great excellence in its kind, in which the familiar is very properly diversified with the solemn, and the grave with the humorous; in which metre has neither weakened the force, nor clouded the perspicuity of argument; nor will it be easy to find another example equally happy of this middle kind of writing, which though prosaick in some parts, rises to high poetry in others, and neither towers to the skies, nor creeps along the ground.

Of the same kind or not far distant from it is, the *Hind and Panther*,[88] the longest of all Dryden's original poems; an allegory intended to comprize and to decide the controversy between the Romanists and Protestants. The scheme of the work is injudicious and incommodious; for what can be more absurd than that one beast should counsel another to rest her faith upon a pope and council? He seems well enough skilled in the usual topicks of argument, endeavours to shew the necessity of an infallible judge, and reproaches the Reformers with want of unity; but is weak enough to ask, why since we see without knowing how, we may not have an infallible judge without knowing where.

The *Hind* at one time is afraid to drink at the common brook, because she may be worried; but walking home with the *Panther*, talks by the way of the *Nicene Fathers*,[89] and at last declares herself to be the Catholic church.

---

81. As . . . sky: *Ibid.*, st. 7. 82. Eleonora: *Eleonora, a Panegyrical Poem: Dedicated to the Memory of the Late Countess of Abingdon* (1692). 83. Tho' all . . . repeat: *Ibid.*, ll. 270–90. 84. As . . . became: *Ibid.*, ll. 1–11.

85. Religio Laici: *Religio Laici or a Layman's Faith* (see Part One). 86. Browne: Sir Thomas Browne (1605–82) published *Religio Medici* in 1643. 87. And . . . prose: *Religio Laici*, ll. 453–54. 88. Hind and Panther: a theological allegory published in 1687. 89. Nicene Fathers: the theologians who attended the First Council of Nicaea in 325.

This absurdity was very properly ridiculed in the *City Mouse* and *Country Mouse* of *Montague* and *Prior;*[90] and in the detection and censure of the incongruity of the fiction chiefly consists the value of their performance, which, whatever reputation it might obtain by the help of temporary passions, seems to readers almost a century distant, not very forcible or animated.

Pope, whose judgement was perhaps a little bribed by the subject, used to mention this poem as the most correct specimen of Dryden's versification. It was indeed written when he had completely formed his manner, and may be supposed to exhibit, negligence excepted, his deliberate and ultimate scheme of metre.

We may therefore reasonably infer, that he did not approve the perpetual uniformity which confines the sense to couplets, since he has broken his lines in the initial paragraph.

> A milk-white Hind, immortal and unchang'd,
> Fed on the lawns, and in the forest rang'd;
> Without unspotted, innocent within,
> She fear'd no danger, for she knew no sin.
> Yet had she oft been chac'd with horns and hounds
> And Scythian shafts, and many winged wounds
> Aim'd at her heart; was often forc'd to fly,
> And doom'd to death, though fated not to die.[91]

These lines are lofty, elegant, and musical, notwithstanding the interruption of the pause, of which the effect is rather increase of pleasure by variety than offence by ruggedness.

To the first part it was his intention, he says, *to give the majestick turn of heroick poesy;*[92] and perhaps he might have executed his design not unsuccessfully, had not an opportunity of satire, which he cannot forbear, fallen sometimes in his way. The character of a Presbyterian, whose emblem is the *Wolf*, is not very heroically majestick.

> More haughty than the rest, the wolfish race ⎫
> Appear with belly gaunt and famish'd face: ⎬
> Never was so deform'd a beast of grace. ⎭
> His ragged tail betwixt his legs he wears, ⎫
> Close clapp'd for shame; but his rough creast he rears, ⎬
> And pricks up his predestinating ears.[93] ⎭

His general character of the other sorts of beasts that never go to church, though spritely and keen, has, however, not much of heroick poesy.

> These are the chief; to number o'er the rest,
> And stand, like Adam, naming every beast,
> Were weary work; nor will the muse describe
> A slimy-born, and sun-begotten tribe;
> Who far from steeples and their sacred sound,
> In fields their sullen conventicles[94] found.
> These gross, half animated lumps I leave;
> Nor can I think what thoughts they can conceive;
> But if they think at all, 'tis sure no higher
> Than matter, put in motion, may aspire;
> Souls that can scarce ferment their mass of clay; ⎫
> So drossy, so divisible are they, ⎬
> As would but serve pure bodies for allay:[95] ⎭
> Such souls as shards produce, such beetle things
> As only buz to heaven with evening wings;
> Strike in the dark, offending but by chance;
> Such are the blindfold blows of ignorance.
> They know not beings, and but hate a name;
> To them the Hind and Panther are the same.[96]

One more instance, and that taken from the narrative part, where style was more in his choice, will show how steadily he kept his resolution of heroic dignity.

> For when the herd, suffic'd, did late repair
> To ferny heaths, and to their forest laire,
> She made a mannerly excuse to stay,
> Proferring the Hind to wait her half the way:
> That since the sky was clear, an hour of talk
> Might help her to beguile the tedious walk.
> With much good-will the motion was embrac'd,
> To chat a while on their adventures pass'd:
> Nor had the grateful Hind so soon forgot
> Her friend and fellow-sufferer in the plot.
> Yet wondering how of late she grew estrang'd,
> Her forehead cloudy and her count'nance chang'd,
> She thought this hour th' occasion would present
> To learn her secret cause of discontent,
> Which well she hop'd, might be with ease redress'd, ⎫
> Considering her a well-bred civil beast, ⎬
> And more a gentlewoman than the rest. ⎭
> After some common talk what rumours ran,
> The lady of the spotted muff began.[97]

The second and third parts he professes to have reduced to diction more familiar and more suitable to

90. City . . . **Prior:** *The Hind and the Panther Transversed to the Story of the Country Mouse and the City Mouse; Much Malice Mingled with a Little Wit* (1687), by Charles Montagu (1661–1715), First Earl of Halifax, and Matthew Prior (1664–1721). (See the selections from Prior in Part Two.) **91.** A milk-white . . . die: *The Hind and the Panther,* I. 1–8. **92.** to . . . poesy: *Ibid.,* "To the Reader." **93.** More . . . ears: *Ibid.,* I. 160–65.

94. conventicles: the meeting houses of Dissenters. **95.** allay: alloy. **96.** These are . . . same: *The Hind and the Panther,* I. 308–26. **97.** For . . . began: *Ibid.,* ll. 554–72.

dispute and conversation; the difference is not, however, very easily perceived; the first has familiar and the two others have sonorous lines. The original incongruity runs through the whole; the king is now *Cæsar*, and now the *Lyon;* and the name *Pan* is given to the Supreme Being.

But when this constitutional absurdity is forgiven, the poem must be confessed to be written with great smoothness of metre, a wide extent of knowledge, and an abundant multiplicity of images; the controversy is embellished with pointed sentences, diversified by illustrations, and enlivened by sallies of invective. Some of the facts to which allusions are made are now become obscure, and perhaps there may be many satirical passages little understood.

As it was by its nature a work of defiance, a composition which would naturally be examined with the utmost acrimony of criticism, it was probably laboured with uncommon attention; and there are, indeed, few negligences in the subordinate parts. The original impropriety, and the subsequent unpopularity of the subject, added to the ridiculousness of its first elements, has sunk it into neglect; but it may be usefully studied, as an example of poetical ratiocination, in which the argument suffers little from the metre.

In the poem on *the Birth of the Prince of Wales*,[98] nothing is very remarkable but the exorbitant adulation, and that insensibility of the precipice on which the king was then standing,[99] which the laureate apparently shared with the rest of the courtiers. A few months cured him of controversy, dismissed him from court, and made him again a playwright and translator.

Of Juvenal there had been a translation by Stapylton,[100] and another by Holiday; neither of them is very poetical. Stapylton is more smooth, and Holiday's is more esteemed for the learning of his notes. A new version was proposed to the poets of that time, and undertaken by them in conjunction. The main design was conducted by Dryden, whose reputation was such that no man was unwilling to serve the Muses under him.

The general character of this translation will be given, when it is said to preserve the wit, but to want the dignity of the original. The peculiarity of Juvenal

is a mixture of gaiety and stateliness, of pointed sentences and declamatory grandeur. His points[101] have not been neglected; but his grandeur none of the band seemed to consider as necessary to be imitated, except *Creech*,[102] who undertook the thirteenth satire. It is therefore perhaps possible to give a better representation of that great satirist, even in those parts which Dryden himself has translated, some passages excepted, which will never be excelled.

With Juvenal was published Persius,[103] translated wholly by Dryden. This work, though like all the other productions of Dryden it may have shining parts, seems to have been written merely for wages, in an uniform mediocrity, without any eager endeavour after excellence, or laborious effort of the mind.

There wanders an opinion among the readers of poetry, that one of these satires is an exercise of the school. Dryden says that he once translated it at school; but not that he preserved or published the juvenile performance.

Not long afterwards he undertook, perhaps the most arduous work of its kind, a translation of Virgil,[104] for which he had shewn how well he was qualified by his version of the Pollio, and two episodes, one of Nisus and Euryalus,[105] the other of Mezentius and Lausus.[106]

In the comparison of Homer and Virgil, the discriminative excellence of Homer is elevation and comprehension of thought, and that of Virgil is grace and splendor of diction. The beauties of Homer are therefore difficult to be lost, and those of Virgil difficult to be retained. The massy trunk of sentiment is safe by its solidity, but the blossoms of elocution easily drop away. The author, having the choice of his own images, selects those which he can best adorn: the translator must, at all hazards, follow his original, and express thoughts which perhaps he would not have chosen. When to this primary difficulty is added the inconvenience of a language so much inferior in harmony to the Latin, it cannot be expected that they who read the Georgick and the Eneid should be much delighted with any version.

---

98. **the Birth . . . Wales:** *Britannia Rediviva: A Poem on the Birth of the Prince* (1688). 99. **the precipice . . . standing:** James II fled to France in 1688. 100. **Stapylton:** Sir Robert Stapleton (d. 1669). His translation of Juvenal's *Sixteen Satires* appeared in 1647; Holiday's appeared in 1673.

101. **points:** stinging epigrams. 102. **Creech:** Thomas Creech (1659–1700); he also translated Lucretius, Horace, Theocritus, Manilius, and parts of Plutarch. 103. **Persius:** Aulus Persius Flaccus (A.D. 34–62), Roman poet best known for his six satires. 104. **a translation . . . . Virgil:** Dryden's translation of *The Works of Virgil: Containing His Pastorals, Georgics, and Aeneis* appeared in 1697. 105. **Nisus and Euryalus:** See *Aeneid*, Book IX. 106. **Mezentius and Lausus:** See *Aeneid*, Book X.

All these obstacles Dryden saw, and all these he determined to encounter. The expectation of his work was undoubtedly great; the nation considered its honour as interested in the event. One gave him the different editions of his author, and another helped him in the subordinate parts. The arguments of the several books were given him by Addison.

The hopes of the publick were not disappointed. He produced, says Pope, *the most noble and spirited translation that I know in any language.* It certainly excelled whatever had appeared in English, and appears to have satisfied his friends, and, for the most part, to have silenced his enemies. Milbourne,[107] indeed, a clergyman, attacked it; but his outrages seem to be the ebullitions of a mind agitated by stronger resentment than bad poetry can excite, and previously resolved not to be pleased.

His criticism extends only to the Preface, Pastorals, and Georgicks; and, as he professes, to give his antagonist an opportunity of reprisal, he has added his own version of the first and fourth Pastorals, and the first Georgick. The world has forgotten his book; but since his attempt has given him a place in literary history, I will preserve a specimen of his criticism, by inserting his remarks on the invocation before the first Georgick, and of his poetry, by annexing his own version.[108]

Ver. 1. "*What makes a plenteous harvest, when to turn*
          The fruitful soil, and when to sow the corn—

It's *unlucky,* they say, *to stumble at the threshold,* but what has a *plenteous harvest* to do here? *Virgil* would not pretend to prescribe *rules* for *that* which depends not on the *husbandman's* care, but the *disposition of Heaven* altogether. Indeed, the *plenteous crop* depends somewhat on the *good method of tillage,* and where the *land's* ill-manur'd, the *corn,* without a miracle, can be but *indifferent;* but the *harvest* may be *good,* which is its *properest* epithet, tho' the *husbandman's skill* were never so *indifferent.* The next *sentence* is *too literal,* and *when to plough* had been *Virgil's* meaning, and intelligible to every body; and *when to sow the corn,* is a needless *addition.*"

Ver. 3. "*The care of sheep, of oxen, and of kine,*
          And when to geld the lambs, and shear the swine,[109]

would as well have fallen under the *cura boum, qui cultus habendo sit pecori,*[110] as Mr. *D's* deduction of particulars."

Ver. 5. "*The birth and genius of the frugal bee*
          I sing, Mæcenas, and I sing to thee.

—But where did *experientia*[111] ever signify *birth and genius?* or what ground was there for such a *figure* in this place? How much more manly is Mr. *Ogylby's* version!"[112]

What makes rich grounds, in what celestial signs,
'Tis good to plough, and marry elms with vines.
What best fits cattle, what with sheep agrees,
And several arts improving frugal bees,
I sing, Mæcenas.

Which four lines, tho' faulty enough, are yet much more to the purpose than Mr. *D's* six."

Ver. 22. "*From fields and mountains to my song repair.*

For *patrium linquens nemus, saltusque Lycæi*[113]—Very well explain'd!"

Ver. 23, 24. "*Inventor Pallas, of the fatning oil,*
               Thou founder of the plough, and ploughman's
                                          toil!

Written as if *these* had been *Pallas's* invention. The *ploughman's toil's* impertinent."

Ver. 25. ——"*The shroud-like cypress——*

Why *shroud-like?* Is a *cypress* pull'd up by the *roots,* which the *sculpture* in the *last Eclogue* fills *Sylvanus's* hand with so very like a *shroud?* Or did not Mr. *D.* think of that kind of *cypress* us'd often for *scarves and hatbands* at funerals formerly, or for *widow's vails,* &c. if so, 'twas a *deep good thought.*"

Ver. 26. ——————"*That wear*
           The royal honours, and increase the year—

107. **Milbourne:** the Reverend Luke Milbourne (1649–1720), author of *Notes on Dryden's Virgil* (1698). 108. **his own version:** Johnson quotes Milbourne's translation at the very end of the *Life of Dryden.* We have omitted it.

109. **And . . . swine:** Dryden's line actually reads: "And how to raise on elms the teeming vine." 110. **cura . . . pecori:** what tending the cattle need, what care the herd require in breeding. 111. **experientia:** skill. 112. **Mr. Ogylby's version:** John Ogilby (1600–76) published his translation of *The Works of Publius Virgilius Maro* in 1649. 113. **patrium . . . Lycæi:** leaving thy native woods and the glades of Lycaeus.

What's meant by *increasing the year?* Did the *gods* or *goddesses* add more *months*, or *days*, or *hours* to it? Or how can *arva tueri*[114]—signify to *wear rural honours?* Is this to *translate,* or *abuse an author?* The next *couplet* are borrow'd from *Ogylby,* I suppose, because *less to the purpose* than ordinary."

Ver. 33. "*The patron of the world, and* Rome's *peculiar guard—*

Idle, and none of *Virgil's,* no more than the sense of the *precedent couplet;* so again, he *interpolates Virgil* with that and *the round circle of the year to guide powerful of blessings, which thou strew'st around.* A ridiculous *Latinism,* and an *impertinent addition;* indeed the whole *period* is but one piece of *absurdity* and *nonsense,* as those who lay it with the *original* must find."

Ver. 42, 43. "*And* Neptune *shall resign the fasces of the sea.*

Was he *consul* or *dictator* there?

"*And watry virgins for thy bed shall strive.*

Both absurd *interpolations.*"

Ver. 47, 48. "*Where in the void of heaven a place is free.*
Ah, happy D——*n, were that place for thee!*

But where is *that void?* Or what does our *translator* mean by it? He knows *what* Ovid says, *God* did to prevent such a *void* in heaven; perhaps, this was then forgotten: but *Virgil* talks more sensibly."

Ver. 49. "*The scorpion ready to receive thy laws.*

No, he would not then have *gotten out of his way* so fast."

Ver. 56. "*Tho'* Proserpine *affects her silent seat—*

What made *her* then so *angry* with *Ascalaphus,* for preventing her return? She was now mus'd to *Patience* under the *determinations of Fate,* rather than *fond* of her *residence.*"

Ver. 61, 2, 3. "*Pity the poets, and the ploughmans cares,*
Interest thy greatness in our mean affairs,
And use thyself betimes to hear our prayers.

Which is such a wretched *perversion* of *Virgil's* noble thought, as *Vicars* would have blush'd at; but Mr. *Ogylby* makes us some amends, by his better lines.

---

114. **arva tueri:** fields are cared for.

O whereso'er thou art, from thence incline,
And grant assistance to my bold design!
Pity with me, poor husbandmens affairs,
And now, as if translated, hear our prayers.

This is *sense,* and *to the purpose:* the other, poor *mistaken stuff.*"

Such were the strictures of Milbourne, who found few abettors; and of whom it may be reasonably imagined, that many who favoured his design were ashamed of his insolence.

When admiration had subsided, the translation was more coolly examined, and found, like all others, to be sometimes erroneous, and sometimes licentious. Those who could find faults, thought they could avoid them; and Dr. Brady attempted in blank verse a translation of the Eneid,[115] which, when dragged into the world, did not live long enough to cry. I have never seen it; but that such a version there is, or has been, perhaps some old catalogue informed me.

With not much better success, Trapp, when his Tragedy[116] and his Prelections had given him reputation, attempted another blank version of the Eneid;[117] to which, notwithstanding the slight regard with which it was treated, he had afterwards perseverance enough to add the Eclogues and Georgicks. His book may continue its existence as long as it is the clandestine refuge of schoolboys.

Since the English ear has been accustomed to the mellifluence of Pope's numbers, and the diction of poetry has become more splendid, new attempts have been made to translate Virgil; and all his works have been attempted by men better qualified to contend with Dryden. I will not engage myself in an invidious comparison, by opposing one passage to another; a work of which there would be no end, and which might be often offensive without use.

It is not by comparing line with line that the merit of great works is to be estimated, but by their general effects and ultimate result. It is easy to note a weak line, and write one more vigorous in its place; to find a happiness of expression in the original, and transplant it by force into the version: but what is given to the parts, may be subducted from the whole, and the reader may be weary, though the critick may commend. Works of imagination excel by their allurement

---

115. **Dr. Brady . . . Eneid:** The translation of the *Aeneid* by Nicholas Brady (1659–1726) appeared in 1716–17. 116. **his Tragedy:** *Abra-Mule; or, Love and Empire* (1704). 117. **blank . . . Eneid:** published in 1716–35.

and delight; by their power of attracting and detaining the attention. That book is good in vain, which the reader throws away. He only is the master, who keeps the mind in pleasing captivity; whose pages are perused with eagerness, and in hope of new pleasure are perused again; and whose conclusion is perceived with an eye of sorrow, such as the traveller casts upon departing day.

By his proportion of this predomination I will consent that Dryden should be tried; of this, which, in opposition to reason, makes Ariosto[118] the darling and the pride of Italy; of this, which, in defiance of criticism, continues Shakespeare the sovereign of the drama.

His last work was his *Fables*,[119] in which he gave us the first example of a mode of writing which the Italians call *refaccimento*,[120] a renovation of ancient writers, by modernizing their language. Thus the old poem of *Boiardo*[121] has been new-dressed by *Domenichi* and *Berni*.[122] The works of Chaucer, upon which this kind of rejuvenescence has been bestowed by Dryden, require little criticism. The tale of the Cock[123] seems hardly worth revival; and the story of *Palamon* and *Arcite*,[124] containing an action unsuitable to the times in which it is placed, can hardly be suffered to pass without censure of the hyperbolical commendation which Dryden has given it in the general Preface, and in a poetical Dedication, a piece where his original fondness of remote conceits seems to have revived.

Of the three pieces borrowed from Boccace,[125] *Sigismunda* may be defended by the celebrity of the story. *Theodore* and *Honoria*, though it contains not much moral, yet afforded opportunities of striking description. And *Cymon* was formerly a tale of such repution, that, at the revival of letters, it was translated into Latin by one of the *Beroalds*.[126]

Whatever subjects employed his pen, he was still improving our measures and embellishing our language.

In this volume are interspersed some short original poems, which, with his prologues, epilogues, and songs, may be comprised in Congreve's remark, that even those, if he had written nothing else, would have entitled him to the praise of excellence in his kind.

One composition must however be distinguished. The ode for *St. Cecilia's* Day,[127] perhaps the last effort of his poetry, has been always considered as exhibiting the highest flight of fancy, and the exactest nicety of art. This is allowed to stand without a rival. If indeed there is any excellence beyond it, in some other of Dryden's works that excellence must be found. Compared with the Ode on *Killigrew*, it may be pronounced perhaps superior in the whole; but without any single part, equal to the first stanza of the other.

It is said to have cost Dryden a fortnight's labour; but it does not want its negligences: some of the lines are without correspondent rhymes; a defect, which I never detected but after an acquaintance of many years, and which the enthusiasm of the writer might hinder him from perceiving.

His last stanza has less emotion than the former; but it is not less elegant in the diction. The conclusion is vitious; the musick of *Timotheus*,[128] which *raised a mortal to the skies*, had only a metaphorical power; that of *Cecelia*, which *drew an angel down*,[129] had a real effect: the crown therefore could not reasonably be divided.

IN a general survey of Dryden's labours, he appears to have had a mind very comprehensive by nature, and much enriched with acquired knowledge. His compositions are the effects of a vigorous genius operating upon large materials.

The power that predominated in his intellectual operations was rather strong reason than quick sensibility. Upon all occasions that were presented, he studied rather than felt, and produced sentiments not such as Nature enforces, but meditation supplies. With the simple and elemental passions, as they spring

---

118. **Ariosto:** Ludovico Ariosto (1474–1533), author of the *Orlando Furioso* (1532), a long romantic epic poem. 119. **Fables:** Dryden's *Fables, Ancient and Modern; Translated into Verse, from Homer, Ovid, Boccace, and Chaucer* was published in 1700. 120. **refaccimento:** *rifacimento* (recasting). 121. **the old . . . Boiardo:** *Orlando Inamorato* (1487), an unfinished romantic epic by Matteo Maria Boiardo (c. 1441–94). 122. **Domenichi and Berni:** sixteenth-century Italian poets. 123. **The tale . . . Cock:** See Chaucer's *Nun's Priest's Tale.* 124. **the story . . . Arcite:** See Chaucer's *Knight's Tale.* 125. **Boccace:** Giovanni Boccaccio (c. 1313–75), Italian humanist, author of the *Decameron* (1348–58), a collection of tales. 126. **Beroalds:** Filippo Beroaldo (1453–1505), one of a family of famous Italian humanists.

127. **The ode . . . Day:** *Alexander's Feast.* 128. **Timotheus:** Greek poet and musician of the fourth century B.C. In Dryden's poem he entertains at a triumphal feast of Alexander the Great, whom he affects profoundly by his music. See Pope's *Essay on Criticism*, ll. 374–83, in Part Two. 129. **that . . . down:** St. Cecilia, a Roman Christian martyr of the third century, is the patroness of church music. An angel is said to have appeared to her.

separate in the mind, he seems not much acquainted; and seldom describes them but as they are complicated by the various relations of society, and confused in the tumults and agitations of life.

What he says of Love may contribute to the explanation of his character:

> Love various minds does variously inspire;
> It stirs in gentle bosoms gentle fire,
> Like that of incense on the altar laid;
> But raging flames tempestuous souls invade;
> A fire which every windy passion blows,
> With pride it mounts, or with revenge it glows.[130]

Dryden's was not one of the *gentle bosoms:* Love, as it subsists in itself, with no tendency but to the person loved, and wishing only for correspondent kindness; such love as shuts out all other interest; the love of the Golden Age, was too soft and subtle to put his faculties in motion. He hardly conceived it but in its turbulent effervescence with some other desires; when it was inflamed by rivalry, or obstructed by difficulties; when it invigorated ambition, or exasperated revenge.

He is therefore, with all his variety of excellence, not often pathetick; and had so little sensibility of the power of effusions purely natural, that he did not esteem them in others. Simplicity gave him no pleasure; and for the first part of his life he looked on *Otway* with contempt, though at last, indeed very late, he confessed that in his play *there* was *Nature, which is the chief beauty.*

We do not always know our own motives. I am not certain whether it was not rather the difficulty which he found in exhibiting the genuine operations of the heart, than a servile submission to an injudicious audience, that filled his plays with false magnificence. It was necessary to fix attention; and the mind can be captivated only by recollection, or by curiosity; by reviving natural sentiments, or impressing new appearances of things: sentences[131] were readier at his call than images; he could more easily fill the ear with some splendid novelty, than awaken those ideas that slumber in the heart.

The favourite exercise of his mind was ratiocination; and, that argument might not be too soon at an end, he delighted to talk of liberty and necessity, destiny and contingence; these he discusses in the language of the school with so much profundity, that the terms which he uses are not always understood. It is indeed learning, but learning out of place.

When once he had engaged himself in disputation, thoughts flowed in on either side: he was now no longer at a loss; he had always objections and solutions at command; *verbaque provisam rem*[132]—give him matter for his verse, and he finds without difficulty verse for his matter.

In Comedy, for which he professes himself not naturally qualified, the mirth which he excites will perhaps not be found so much to arise from any original humour, or peculiarity of character nicely distinguished and diligently pursued, as from incidents and circumstances, artifices and surprizes; from jests of action rather than of sentiment. What he had of humorous or passionate, he seems to have had not from nature, but from other poets; if not always as a plagiary, at least as an imitator.

Next to argument, his delight was in wild and daring sallies of sentiment, in the irregular and eccentrick violence of wit. He delighted to tread upon the brink of meaning, where light and darkness begin to mingle; to approach the precipice of absurdity, and hover over the abyss of unideal vacancy. This inclination sometimes produced nonsense, which he knew; as,

> Move swiftly, sun, and fly a lover's pace,
> Leave weeks and months behind thee in thy race.[133]

> Amariel flies
> To guard thee from the demons of the air;
> My flaming sword above them to display,
> All keen, and ground upon the edge of day.[134]

And sometimes it issued in absurdities, of which perhaps he was not conscious:

> Then we upon our orb's last verge shall go,
>   And see the ocean leaning on the sky;
> From thence our rolling neighbours we shall know,
>   And on the lunar world securely pry.[135]

These lines have no meaning; but may we not say, in imitation of Cowley on another book,

> 'Tis so like *sense* 'twill serve the turn as well?[136]

---

130. Love . . . glows: *Tyrannic Love*, II. iii. 131. sentences: witty moral axioms.

132. verbaque . . . rem: Horace, *Ars Poetica*, l. 311. 133. Move . . . race: *Conquest of Granada, Part II*, V. ii. 134. Amariel . . . day: *Tyrannic Love*, IV. i. 135. Then . . . pry: *Annus Mirabilis*, st. 164. 136. 'Tis . . . well: adapted from Cowley's Pindaric ode *To Mr. Hobs*, on Thomas Hobbes's *Leviathan* (1651).

This endeavour after the grand and the new produced many sentiments either great or bulky, and many images either just or splendid:

I am as free as Nature first made man,
Ere the base laws of servitude began,
When wild in woods the noble savage ran.[137]

—'Tis but because the Living death ne'er knew,
They fear to prove it as a thing that's new:
Let me th' experiment before you try,
I'll show you first how easy 'tis to die.[138]

—There with a forest of their darts he strove,
And stood like *Capaneus* defying Jove;
With his broad sword the boldest beating down,
While Fate grew pale lest he should win the town,
And turn'd the iron leaves of his dark book
To make new dooms, or mend what it mistook.[139]

—I beg no pity for this mouldering clay;
For if you give it burial, there it takes
Possession of your earth;
If burnt, and scatter'd in the air, the winds
That strew my dust diffuse my royalty,
And spread me o'er your clime; for where one atom
Of mine shall light, know there Sebastian reigns.[140]

Of these quotations the two first may be allowed to be great, the two latter only tumid.

Of such selection there is no end. I will add only a few more passages; of which the first, though it may perhaps not be quite clear in prose, is not too obscure for poetry, as the meaning that it has is noble:

No, there is a necessity in Fate,
Why still the brave bold man is fortunate;
He keeps his object ever full in sight,
And that assurance holds him firm and right;
True, 'tis a narrow way that leads to bliss,
But right before there is no precipice;
Fear makes men look aside, and so their footing
    miss.[141]

Of the images which the two following citations afford, the first is elegant, the second magnificent; whether either be just, let the reader judge:

What precious drops are these,
Which silently each other's track pursue,
Bright as young diamonds in their infant dew?[142]

——Resign your castle——
—Enter, brave Sir; for when you speak the word,
The gates shall open of their own accord;
The genius of the place its Lord shall meet,
And bow its towery forehead at your feet.[143]

These bursts of extravagance, Dryden calls the *Dalilahs* of the Theatre; and owns that many noisy lines of Maximin and Almanzor[144] call out for vengeance upon him; but *I knew*, says he, *that they were bad enough to please, even when I wrote them*. There is surely reason to suspect that he pleased himself as well as his audience; and that these, like the harlots of other men, had his love, though not his approbation.

He had sometimes faults of a less generous and splendid kind. He makes, like almost all other poets, very frequent use of Mythology, and sometimes connects religion and fable too closely, without distinction.

He descends to display his knowledge with pedantick ostentation; as when, in translating Virgil, he says, *tack to the larboard*,—and *veer starboard;* and talks in another work of *virtue spooming before the wind*.[145] His vanity now and then betrays his ignorance:

They Nature's king thro' Nature's opticks view'd;
Revers'd they view'd him lessen'd to their eyes.[146]

He had heard of reversing a telescope, and unluckily reverses the object.

He is sometimes unexpectedly mean. When he describes the Supreme Being as moved by prayer to stop the Fire of London, what is his expression?

A hollow crystal pyramid he takes,
    In firmamental waters dipp'd above,
Of this a broad *extinguisher* he makes,
    And *hoods* the flames that to their quarry strove.[147]

When he describes the Last Day, and the decisive tribunal, he intermingles this image:

When rattling bones together fly,
From the four quarters of the sky.[148]

137. I . . . ran: *Conquest of Granada*, Part I, I. i. 138. 'Tis . . . die: *Tyrannic Love*, V. i. 139. There . . . mistook: *Tyrannic Love*, I. i. 140. I . . . reigns: *Don Sebastian*, I. i. 141. No . . . miss: *Conquest of Granada*, Part I, IV. ii. 142. What . . . dew: *Ibid.*, Part II, III. i.

143. Resign . . . feet: *Ibid.*, iii. 144. Maximin and Almanzor: the heroes of *Tyrannic Love* and *The Conquest of Granada*. 145. virtue . . . wind: *The Hind and the Panther*, III. 96. 146. They . . . eyes: *Ibid.*, I. 57. 147. A hollow . . . strove: *Annus Mirabilis*, st. 281. 148. When . . . sky: *To the Pious Memory of Mrs. Anne Killigrew*, ll. 184–85.

It was indeed never in his power to resist the temptation of a jest. In his Elegy on Cromwel:

No sooner was the Frenchman's cause embrac'd,
Than the *light Monsieur* the *grave Don* outweigh'd;
His fortune turn'd the scale[149]——

He had a vanity unworthy of his abilities; to shew, as may be suspected, the rank of the company with whom he lived, by the use of French words, which had then crept into conversation; such as *fraicheur* for *coolness*, *fougue* for *turbulence*, and a few more, none of which the language has incorporated or retained. They continue only where they stood first, perpetual warnings to future innovators.

These are his faults of affectation; his faults of negligence are beyond recital. Such is the unevenness of his compositions, that ten lines are seldom found together without something of which the reader is ashamed. Dryden was no rigid judge of his own pages; he seldom struggled after supreme excellence, but snatched in haste what was within his reach, and when he could content others was himself contented. He did not keep present to his mind an idea of pure perfection, nor compare his works, such as they were, with what they might be made. He knew to whom he should be opposed. He had more musick than Waller, more vigour than Denham, and more nature than Cowley; and from his contemporaries he was in no danger. Standing therefore in the highest place, he had no care to rise by contending with himself; but while there was no name above his own, was willing to enjoy fame on the easiest terms.

He was no lover of labour. What he thought sufficient, he did not stop to make better; and allowed himself to leave many parts unfinished, in confidence that the good lines would overbalance the bad. What he had once written, he dismissed from his thoughts; and, I believe, there is no example to be found of any correction or improvement made by him after publication. The hastiness of his productions might be the effect of necessity; but his subsequent neglect could hardly have any other cause than impatience of study.

What can be said of his versification, will be little more than a dilatation of the praise given it by Pope.

Waller was smooth; but Dryden taught to join
The varying verse, the full-resounding line,
The long majestick march, and energy divine.[150]

Some improvements had been already made in English numbers; but the full force of our language was not yet felt; the verse that was smooth was commonly feeble. If Cowley had sometimes a finished line, he had it by chance. Dryden knew how to chuse the flowing and the sonorous words; to vary the pauses, and adjust the accents; to diversify the cadence, and yet preserve the smoothness of his metre.

Of Triplets and Alexandrines, though he did not introduce the use, he established it. The triplet has long subsisted among us. Dryden seems not to have traced it higher than to Chapman's Homer; but it is to be found in Phaer's[151] Virgil, written in the reign of Mary; and in Hall's Satires,[152] published five years before the death of Elizabeth.

The Alexandrine was, I believe, first used by Spenser, for the sake of closing his stanza with a fuller sound. We had a longer measure of fourteen syllables, into which the Eneid was translated by Phaer, and other works of the ancients by other writers; of which Chapman's Iliad was, I believe, the last.

The two first lines of *Phaer*'s third Eneid will exemplify this measure:

When Asia's state was overthrown, and Priam's
    kingdom stout,
All giltless, by the power of gods above was rooted out.

As these lines had their break, or *cæsura*, always at the eighth syllable, it was thought in time commodious to divide them; and quatrains of lines, alternately consisting of eight and six syllables, make the most soft and pleasing of our lyrick measures; as,

Relentless Time, destroying power,
    Which stone and brass obey,
Who giv'st to every flying hour
    To work some new decay.[153]

In the Alexandrine, when its power was once felt, some poems, as *Drayton's Polyolbion*,[154] were wholly written; and sometimes the measures of twelve and fourteen syllables were interchanged with one another.

---

149. No . . . scale: *Heroic Stanzas*, st. 23. **150. Waller . . . divine:** *Epistle to Augustus*, ll. 267–69. (See the *Epistle to Augustus* in Part Two.)

151. Phaer: Thomas Phaer (*c.* 1510–60); his translation in fourteen-syllable lines of nine books of the *Aeneid* appeared in 1555–60. **152. Hall's Satires:** The satires of Joseph Hall (1574–1656), Bishop of Exeter and Norwich, were published in 1597–98. **153. Relentless . . . decay:** *An Imitation of Some French Verses*, ll. 1–4, by Thomas Parnell (1679–1718). (See the selection from Parnell in Part Three.) **154. Drayton's Polyolbion:** a poem (1622) on the topography of Britain by Michael Drayton (1563–1631).

Cowley was the first that inserted the Alexandrine at pleasure among the heroick lines of ten syllables, and from his Dryden professes to have adopted it.

The Triplet and Alexandrine are not universally approved. *Swift* always censured them, and wrote some lines to ridicule them.[155] In examining their propriety, it is to be considered that the essence of verse is regularity, and its ornament is variety. To write verse is to dispose syllables and sounds harmonically by some known and settled rule; a rule however lax enough to substitute similitude for identity, to admit change without breach of order, and to relieve the ear without disappointing it. Thus a Latin hexameter is formed from dactyls and spondees differently combined; the English heroick admits of acute or grave syllables variously disposed. The Latin never deviates into seven feet, or exceeds the number of seventeen syllables; but the English Alexandrine breaks the lawful bounds, and surprises the reader with two syllables more than he expected.

The effect of the Triplet is the same: the ear has been accustomed to expect a new rhyme in every couplet; but is on a sudden surprised with three rhymes together, to which the reader could not accommodate his voice, did he not obtain notice of the change from the braces of the margins. Surely there is something unskilful in the necessity of such mechanical direction.

Considering the metrical art simply as a science, and consequently excluding all casualty, we must allow that Triplets and Alexandrines inserted by caprice are interruptions of that constancy to which science aspires. And though the variety which they produce may very justly be desired, yet to make our poetry exact there ought to be some stated mode of admitting them.

But till some such regulation can be formed, I wish them still to be retained in their present state. They are sometimes grateful to the reader, and sometimes convenient to the poet. *Fenton*[156] was of opinion, that Dryden was too liberal and Pope too sparing in their use.

The rhymes of Dryden are commonly just, and he valued himself for his readiness in finding them; but he is sometimes open to objection.

It is the common practice of our poets to end the second line with a weak or grave syllable:

> Together o'er the Alps methinks we fly,
> Fill'd with ideas of fair *Italy*.[157]

Dryden sometimes puts the weak rhyme in the first:

> Laugh all the powers that favour *tyranny*,
> And all the standing army of the sky.[158]

Sometimes he concludes a period or paragraph with the first line of a couplet, which, though the French seem to do it without irregularity, always displeases in English poetry.

The Alexandrine, though much his favourite, is not always very diligently fabricated by him. It invariably requires a break at the sixth syllable; a rule which the modern French poets never violate, but which Dryden sometimes neglected:

> And with paternal thunder vindicates his throne.[159]

Of Dryden's works is was said by Pope, that *he could select from them better specimens of every mode of poetry than any other English writer could supply*. Perhaps no nation ever produced a writer that enriched his language with such variety of models. To him we owe the improvement, perhaps the completion of our metre, the refinement of our language, and much of the correctness of our sentiments. By him we were taught *sapere & fari*,[160] to think naturally and express forcibly. Though Davies[161] has reasoned in rhyme before him, it may be perhaps maintained that he was the first who joined argument with poetry. He shewed us the true bounds of a translator's liberty. What was said of Rome, adorned by Augustus, may be applied by an easy metaphor to English poetry embellished by Dryden, *lateritiam invenit, marmoream reliquit*.[162] He found it brick, and he left it marble.

. . .

157. **Together . . . Italy:** Pope, *Epistle to Mr. Jervas*, ll. 25–26. **158. Laugh . . . sky:** *Palamon and Arcite*, III. 671–72. **159. And . . . throne:** *The Hind and the Panther*, II. 537. **160. sapere & fari:** Horace, *Epistles*. I. iv. 9. **161. Davies:** Sir John Davies (1569–1626), author of *Nosce Teipsum* (*Know Thyself*), a poem (1599) in quatrains on the immortality of the soul. **162. lateritam . . . reliquit:** Suetonius, *Life of Augustus*, Ch. xxviii.

155. **lines . . . them:** See *A Description of a City Shower*, ll. 61–63, in Part Two. **156. Fenton:** Elijah Fenton (1683–1730), a poet who assisted Pope in the translation of the *Odyssey*.

FROM

POPE

Of his intellectual character, the constituent and fundamental principle was Good Sense, a prompt and intuitive perception of consonance and propriety. He saw immediately, of his own conceptions, what was to be chosen, and what to be rejected; and, in the works of others, what was to be shunned, and what was to be copied.

But good sense alone is a sedate and quiescent quality, which manages its possessions well, but does not increase them; it collects few materials for its own operations, and preserves safety, but never gains supremacy. Pope had likewise genius; a mind active, ambitious, and adventurous, always investigating, always aspiring; in its widest searches still longing to go forward, in its highest flights still wishing to be higher; always imagining something greater than it knows, always endeavouring more than it can do.

To assist these powers, he is said to have had great strength and exactness of memory. That which he had heard or read was not easily lost; and he had before him not only what his own meditation suggested, but what he had found in other writers that might be accommodated to his present purpose.

These benefits of nature he improved by incessant and unwearied diligence; he had recourse to every source of intelligence, and lost no opportunity of information; he consulted the living as well as the dead; he read his compositions to his friends, and was never content with mediocrity when excellence could be attained. He considered poetry as the business of his life, and however he might seem to lament his occupation, he followed it with constancy; to make verses was his first labour, and to mend them was his last.

From his attention to poetry he was never diverted. If conversation offered any thing that could be improved, he committed it to paper; if a thought, or perhaps an expression more happy than was common, rose to his mind, he was careful to write it; an independent distich was preserved for an opportunity of insertion, and some little fragments have been found containing lines, or parts of lines, to be wrought upon at some other time.

He was one of those few whose labour is their pleasure: he was never elevated to negligence, nor wearied to impatience; he never passed a fault unamended by indifference, nor quitted it by despair. He laboured his works first to gain reputation, and afterwards to keep it.

Of composition there are different methods. Some employ at once memory and invention, and, with little intermediate use of the pen, form and polish large masses by continued meditation, and write their productions only when, in their own opinion, they have completed them. It is related of Virgil, that his custom was to pour out a great number of verses in the morning, and pass the day in retrenching exuberances and correcting inaccuracies. The method of Pope, as may be collected from his translation, was to write his first thoughts in his first words, and gradually to amplify, decorate, rectify, and refine them.

With such faculties, and such dispositions, he excelled every other writer in *poetical prudence*: he wrote in such a manner as might expose him to few hazards. He used almost always the same fabrick of verse; and, indeed, by those few essays which he made of any other, he did not enlarge his reputation. Of this uniformity the certain consequence was readiness and dexterity. By perpetual practice, language had in his mind a systematical arrangement; having always the same use for words, he had words so selected and combined as to be ready at his call. This increase of facility he confessed himself to have perceived in the progress of his translation.

But what was yet of more importance, his effusions were always voluntary, and his subjects chosen by himself. His independence secured him from drudging at a task, and labouring upon a barren topick: he never exchanged praise for money, nor opened a shop of condolence or congratulation. His poems, therefore, were scarce ever temporary. He suffered coronations and royal marriages to pass without a song, and derived no opportunities from recent events, nor any popularity from the accidental disposition of his readers. He was never reduced to the necessity of soliciting the sun to shine upon a birth-day, of calling the Graces and Virtues to a wedding, or of saying what multitudes have said before him. When he could produce nothing new, he was at liberty to be silent.

His publications were for the same reason never hasty. He is said to have sent nothing to the press till it had lain two years under his inspection: it is at least certain, that he ventured nothing without nice examination. He suffered the tumult of imagination to subside, and the novelties of invention to grow familiar. He knew that the mind is always enamoured of its own productions, and did not trust his first fondness. He consulted his friends, and listened with great willingness to criticism; and, what was of more importance, he consulted himself, and let nothing pass against his own judgement.

He professed to have learned his poetry from Dryden, whom, whenever an opportunity was presented, he praised through his whole life with unvaried liberality; and perhaps his character may receive some illustration, if he be compared with his master.

Integrity of understanding and nicety of discernment were not allotted in a less proportion to Dryden than to Pope. The rectitude of Dryden's mind was sufficiently shewn by the dismission of his poetical prejudices, and the rejection of unnatural thoughts and rugged numbers. But Dryden never desired to apply all the judgement that he had. He wrote, and professed to write, merely for the people; and when he pleased others, he contented himself. He spent no time in struggles to rouse latent powers; he never attempted to make that better which was already good, nor often to mend what he must have known to be faulty. He wrote, as he tells us, with very little consideration; when occasion or necessity called upon him, he poured out what the present moment happened to supply, and, when once it had passed the press, ejected it from his mind; for when he had no pecuniary interest, he had no further solicitude.

Pope was not content to satisfy; he desired to excel, and therefore always endeavoured to do his best: he did not court the candour, but dared the judgement of his reader, and expecting no indulgence from others, he shewed none to himself. He examined lines and words with minute and punctilious observation, and retouched every part with indefatigable diligence, till he had left nothing to be forgiven.

For this reason he kept his pieces very long in his hands, while he considered and reconsidered them. The only poems which can be supposed to have been written with such regard to the times as might hasten their publication, were the two satires of *Thirty-eight;*[1] of which Dodsley[2] told me, that they were brought to him by the author, that they might be fairly copied. "Almost every line," he said, "was then written twice over; I gave him a clean transcript, which he sent

some time afterwards to me for the press, with almost every line written twice over a second time."

His declaration, that his care for his works ceased at their publication, was not strictly true. His parental attention never abandoned them; what he found amiss in the first edition, he silently corrected in those that followed. He appears to have revised the *Iliad,* and freed it from some of its imperfections; and the *Essay on Criticism* received many improvements after its first appearance. It will seldom be found that he altered without adding clearness, elegance, or vigour. Pope had perhaps the judgement of Dryden; but Dryden certainly wanted the diligence of Pope.

In acquired knowledge, the superiority must be allowed to Dryden, whose education was more scholastick, and who before he became an author had been allowed more time for study, with better means of information. His mind has a larger range, and he collects his images and illustrations from a more extensive circumference of science. Dryden knew more of man in his general nature, and Pope in his local manners. The notions of Dryden were formed by comprehensive speculation, and those of Pope by minute attention. There is more dignity in the knowledge of Dryden, and more certainty in that of Pope.

Poetry was not the sole praise of either; for both excelled likewise in prose; but Pope did not borrow his prose from his predecessor. The style of Dryden is capricious and varied, that of Pope is cautious and uniform; Dryden obeys the motions of his own mind, Pope constrains his mind to his own rules of composition. Dryden is sometimes vehement and rapid; Pope is always smooth, uniform, and gentle. Dryden's page is a natural field, rising into inequalities, and diversified by the varied exuberance of abundant vegetation; Pope's is a velvet lawn, shaven by the scythe, and levelled by the roller.

Of genius, that power which constitutes a poet; that quality without which judgement is cold and knowledge is inert; that energy which collects, combines, amplifies, and animates; the superiority must, with some hesitation, be allowed to Dryden. It is not to be inferred that of this poetical vigour Pope had only a little, because Dryden had more; for every other writer since Milton must give place to Pope; and even of Dryden it must be said, that if he has brighter paragraphs, he has not better poems. Dryden's performances were always hasty, either excited by some external occasion, or extorted by domestick necessity; he composed without consideration, and

LIFE OF POPE. **1. the two . . . Thirty-eight:** *Epilogue to the Satires,* in two dialogues (see Part Two). **2. Dodsley:** Robert Dodsley, the bookseller.

published without correction. What his mind could supply at call, or gather in one excursion, was all that he sought, and all that he gave. The dilatory caution of Pope enabled him to condense his sentiments, to multiply his images, and to accumulate all that study might produce, or chance might supply. If the flights of Dryden therefore are higher, Pope continues longer on the wing. If of Dryden's fire the blaze is brighter, of Pope's the heat is more regular and constant. Dryden often surpasses expectation, and Pope never falls below it. Dryden is read with frequent astonishment, and Pope with perpetual delight.

This parallel will, I hope, when it is well considered, be found just; and if the reader should suspect me, as I suspect myself, of some partial fondness for the memory of Dryden, let him not too hastily condemn me; for meditation and enquiry may, perhaps, shew him the reasonableness of my determination.

THE Works of Pope are now to be distinctly examined, not so much with attention to slight faults or petty beauties, as to the general character and effect of each performance.

It seems natural for a young poet to initiate himself by Pastorals, which, not professing to imitate real life, require no experience, and, exhibiting only the simple operation of unmingled passions, admit no subtle reasoning or deep enquiry. Pope's Pastorals[3] are not however composed but with close thought; they have reference to the times of the day, the seasons of the year, and the periods of human life. The last, that which turns the attention upon age and death, was the author's favourite. To tell of disappointment and misery, to thicken the darkness of futurity, and perplex the labyrinth of uncertainty, has been always a delicious employment of the poets. His preference was probably just. I wish, however, that his fondness had not overlooked a line in which the *Zephyrs* are made *to lament in silence.*

To charge these Pastorals with want of invention, is to require what never was intended. The imitations[4] are so ambitiously frequent, that the writer evidently means rather to shew his literature than his wit. It is surely sufficient for an author of sixteen not only to be able to copy the poems of antiquity with judicious selection, but to have obtained sufficient power of language, and skill in metre, to exhibit a series of

versification, which had in English poetry no precedent, nor has since had an imitation.

The design of *Windsor Forest*[5] is evidently derived from *Cooper's Hill,*[6] with some attention to Waller's poem on *The Park;* but Pope cannot be denied to excel his masters in variety and elegance, and the art of interchanging description, narrative, and morality. The objection made by Dennis[7] is the want of plan, of a regular subordination of parts terminating in the principal and original design. There is this want in most descriptive poems, because as the scenes, which they must exhibit successively, are all subsisting at the same time, the order in which they are shewn must by necessity be arbitrary, and more is not to be expected from the last part than from the first. The attention, therefore, which cannot be detained by suspense, must be excited by diversity, such as his poem offers to its reader.

But the desire of diversity may be too much indulged; the parts of *Windsor Forest* which deserve least praise, are those which were added to enliven the stillness of the scene, the appearance of Father Thames, and the transformation of *Lodona.*[8] Addison had in his *Campaign* derided the *Rivers* that *rise from their oozy beds* to tell stories of heroes,[9] and it is therefore strange that Pope should adopt a fiction not only unnatural but lately censured. The story of *Lodona* is told with sweetness; but a new metamorphosis is a ready and puerile expedient; nothing is easier than to tell how a flower was once a blooming virgin, or a rock an obdurate tyrant.

The *Temple of Fame*[10] has, as Steele warmly declared, *a thousand beauties.* Every part is splendid; there is great luxuriance of ornaments; the original vision of

---

5. Windsor Forest: published in 1713. (See Part Two.) **6. Cooper's Hill:** published in 1642 by Sir John Denham. (See Part Three.) **7. The objection . . . Dennis:** in *Remarks upon Mr. Pope's Translation of Homer, with Two Letters Concerning Windsor Forest, and The Temple of Fame* (1717). **8. the transformation . . . Lodona:** See *Windsor-Forest,* ll. 171–218, in Part Two. **9. Addison . . . heroes:** In *The Campaign* (1705), ll. 467–72, Addison writes:

> When actions, unadorn'd, are faint and weak,
> Cities and Countries must be taught to speak;
> Gods may descend in factions from the skies,
> And Rivers from their oozy beds arise;
> Fiction may deck the truth with spurious rays,
> And round the Hero cast a borrow'd blaze.

10. The Temple . . . Fame: Pope's imitation (1715) of Chaucer's *House of Fame.*

---

3. Pope's Pastorals: published in 1709. (See *Winter. The Fourth Pastoral,* in Part Two.) **4. imitations:** of well-known classical passages.

Chaucer was never denied to be much improved; the allegory is very skilfully continued, the imagery is properly selected, and learnedly displayed: yet, with all this comprehension of excellence, as its scene is laid in remote ages, and its sentiments, if the concluding paragraph be excepted, have little relation to general manners or common life, it never obtained much notice, but is turned silently over, and seldom quoted or mentioned with either praise or blame.

That the *Messiah*[11] excels the *Pollio* is no great praise, if it be considered from what original[12] the improvements are derived.

The *Verses on the unfortunate Lady*[13] have drawn much attention by the illaudable singularity of treating suicide with respect; and they must be allowed to be written in some parts with vigorous animation, and in others with gentle tenderness; nor has Pope produced any poem in which the sense predominates more over the diction. But the tale is not skilfully told; it is not easy to discover the character of either the Lady or her Guardian. History relates that she was about to disparage herself by a marriage with an inferior; Pope praises her for the dignity of ambition, and yet condemns the unkle to detestation for his pride; the ambitious love of a niece may be opposed by the interest, malice, or envy of an unkle, but never by his pride. On such an occasion a poet may be allowed to be obscure, but inconsistency never can be right.

The *Ode for St. Cecilia's Day*[14] was undertaken at the desire of Steele: in this the author is generally confessed to have miscarried, yet he has miscarried only as compared with Dryden; for he has far outgone other competitors. Dryden's plan is better chosen; history will always take stronger hold of the attention than fable: the passions excited by Dryden are the pleasures and pains of real life, the scene of Pope is laid in imaginary existence; Pope is read with calm acquiescence, Dryden with turbulent delight; Pope hangs upon the ear, and Dryden finds the passes of the mind.

Both the odes want the essential constituent of metrical compositions, the stated recurrence of settled numbers. It may be alleged, that Pindar is said by Horace to have written *numeris lege solutis;*[15] but as no such lax performances have been transmitted to us,

the meaning of that expression cannot be fixed; and perhaps the like return might properly be made to a modern Pindarist, as Mr. Cobb received from Bentley,[16] who, when he found his criticisms upon a Greek Exercise, which Cobb had presented, refuted one after another by Pindar's authority, cried out at last, *Pindar was a bold fellow, but thou art an impudent one.*

If Pope's ode be particularly inspected, it will be found that the first stanza consists of sounds well chosen indeed, but only sounds.

The second consists of hyperbolical commonplaces, easily to be found, and perhaps without much difficulty to be as well expressed.

In the third, however, there are numbers, images, harmony, and vigour, not unworthy the antagonist of Dryden. Had all been like this—but every part cannot be the best.

The next stanzas place and detain us in the dark and dismal regions of mythology, where neither hope nor fear, neither joy nor sorrow, can be found: the poet however faithfully attends us; we have all that can be performed by elegance of diction, or sweetness of versification; but what can form avail without better matter?

The last stanza recurs again to common places. The conclusion is too evidently modelled by that of Dryden; and it may be remarked that both end with the same fault, the comparison of each is literal on one side, and metaphorical on the other.

Poets do not always express their own thoughts; Pope, with all this labour in the praise of Musick, was ignorant of its principles, and insensible of its effects.

One of his greatest though of his earliest works is the *Essay on Criticism,*[17] which, if he had written nothing else, would have placed him among the first criticks and the first poets, as it exhibits every mode of excellence that can embellish or dignify didactick composition, selection of matter, novelty of arrangement, justness of precept, splendour of illustration, and propriety of digression. I know not whether it be pleasing to consider that he produced this piece at twenty, and never afterwards excelled it: he that delights himself with observing that such powers may

---

11. the Messiah: published in 1712. (See Part Two.) 12. original: the Book of Isaiah. 13. Verses . . . Lady: *Elegy to the Memory of an Unfortunate Lady* (1717). 14. Ode . . . Day: published in 1713. 15. numeris . . . solutis: "verse unrestrained by laws" (*Odes*, IV. ii. 11–12).

16. Mr. Cobb . . . Bentley: Samuel Cobb, translator and minor poet, studied at Trinity College, Cambridge, under Richard Bentley (1662–1742), the distinguished classical scholar. 17. Essay on Criticism: published in 1711. (See Part Two.)

be so soon attained, cannot but grieve to think that life was ever after at a stand.

To mention the particular beauties of the Essay would be unprofitably tedious; but I cannot forbear to observe, that the comparison of a student's progress in the sciences with the journey of a traveller in the Alps,[18] is perhaps the best that English poetry can shew. A simile, to be perfect, must both illustrate and ennoble the subject; must shew it to the understanding in a clearer view, and display it to the fancy with greater dignity; but either of these qualities may be sufficient to recommend it. In didactick poetry, of which the great purpose is instruction, a simile may be praised which illustrates, though it does not ennoble; in heroicks, that may be admitted which ennobles, though it does not illustrate. That it may be complete, it is required to exhibit, independently of its references, a pleasing image; for a simile is said to be a short episode. To this antiquity was so attentive, that circumstances were sometimes added, which, having no parallels, served only to fill the imagination, and produced what Perrault[19] ludicrously called *comparisons with a long tail*. In their similies the greatest writers have sometimes failed; the ship-race, compared with the chariot-race, is neither illustrated nor aggrandised;[20] land and water make all the difference: when Apollo, running after Daphne, is likened to a greyhound chasing a hare,[21] there is nothing gained; the ideas of pursuit and flight are too plain to be made plainer, and a god and the daughter of a god are not represented much to their advantage by a hare and dog. The simile of the Alps has no useless parts, yet affords a striking picture by itself; it makes the foregoing position better understood, and enables it to take faster hold on the attention; it assists the apprehension, and elevates the fancy.

Let me likewise dwell a little on the celebrated paragraph,[22] in which it is directed that *the sound should seem an echo to the sense;* a precept which Pope is allowed to have observed beyond any other English poet.

This notion of representative metre, and the desire of discovering frequent adaptations of the sound to the sense, have produced, in my opinion, many wild conceits and imaginary beauties. All that can furnish this representation are the sounds of the words considered singly, and the time in which they are pronounced. Every language has some words framed to exhibit the noises which they express, as *thump, rattle, growl, hiss*. These however are but few, and the poet cannot make them more, nor can they be of any use but when sound is to be mentioned. The time of pronunciation was in the dactylick measures of the learned languages capable of considerable variety; but that variety could be accommodated only to motion or duration, and different degrees of motion were perhaps expressed by verses rapid or slow, without much attention of the writer, when the image had full possession of his fancy; but our language having little flexibility, our verses can differ very little in their cadence. The fancied resemblances, I fear, arise sometimes merely from the ambiguity of words; there is supposed to be some relation between a *soft* line and a *soft* couch, or between *hard* syllables and *hard* fortune.

Motion, however, may be in some sort exemplified; and yet it may be suspected that even in such resemblances the mind often governs the ear, and the sounds are estimated by their meaning. One of the most successful attempts has been to describe the labour of Sisyphus:

> With many a weary step, and many a groan,
> Up a high hill he heaves a huge round stone;
> The huge round stone, resulting[23] with a bound,
> Thunders impetuous down, and smoaks along the
>   ground.[24]

Who does not perceive the stone to move slowly upward, and roll violently back? But set the same numbers to another sense;

> While many a merry tale, and many a song,
> Chear'd the rough road, we wish'd the rough road
>   long.
> The rough road then, returning in a round,
> Mock'd our impatient steps, for all was fairy ground.

We have now surely lost much of the delay, and much of the rapidity.

But to shew how little the greatest master of numbers can fix the principles of representative

---

18. the comparison . . . Alps: See *Essay on Criticism*, ll. 219–32, in Part Two. 19. Perrault: Charles Perrault (1628–1703), French poet and critic. 20. the ship-race . . . aggrandised: See *Aeneid*, V. 144–47. 21. Apollo . . . hare: See Ovid, *Metamorphoses*, I. 533–38. 22. the celebrated paragraph: See *Essay on Criticism*, ll. 337–83.

23. resulting: springing back. 24. With . . . ground: Pope's *Odyssey*, XI. 735–38.

harmony, it will be sufficient to remark that the poet, who tells us, that

When Ajax strives some rock's vast weight to throw,
The line too labours, and the words move slow:
Not so when swift Camilla[25] scours the plain,
Flies o'er th' unbending corn, and skims along the
      main;[26]

when he had enjoyed for about thirty years the praise of Camilla's lightness of foot, tried another experiment upon *sound* and *time*, and produced this memorable triplet;

Waller was smooth; but Dryden taught to join
The varying verse, the full resounding line,
The long majestick march, and energy divine.

Here are the swiftness of the rapid race, and the march of slow-paced majesty, exhibited by the same poet in the same sequence of syllables, except that the exact prosodist will find the line of *swiftness* by one time longer than that of *tardiness*.

Beauties of this kind are commonly fancied; and when real, are technical and nugatory, not to be rejected, and not to be solicited.

To the praises which have been accumulated on *The Rape of the Lock*[27] by readers of every class, from the critick to the waiting-maid, it is difficult to make any addition. Of that which is universally allowed to be the most attractive of all ludicrous compositions, let it rather be now enquired from what sources the power of pleasing is derived.

Dr. Warburton, who excelled in critical perspicacity, has remarked that the preternatural agents are very happily adapted to the purposes of the poem.[28] The heathen deities can no longer gain attention: we should have turned away from a contest between Venus and Diana; the employment of allegorical persons always excites conviction of its own absurdity; they may produce effects, but cannot conduct actions; when the phantom is put in motion it dissolves; thus *Discord* may raise a mutiny, but *Discord* cannot conduct a march, nor besiege a town. Pope brought into view a new race of Beings, with powers and passions proportionate to their operation. The sylphs and gnomes act at the toilet and the tea-table, what more terrifick and more powerful phantoms perform on the stormy ocean, or the field of battle, they give their proper help, and do their proper mischief.

Pope is said, by an objector, not to have been the inventor of this petty nation;[29] a charge which might with more justice have been brought against the author of the *Iliad*, who doubtless adopted the religious system of his country; for what is there but the names of his agents which Pope has not invented? Has he not assigned them characters and operations never heard of before? Has he not, at least, given them their first poetical existence? If this is not sufficient to denominate his work original, nothing original ever can be written.

In this work are exhibited, in a very high degree, the two most engaging powers of an author. New things are made familiar, and familiar things are made new. A race of aerial people, never heard of before, is presented to us in a manner so clear and easy, that the reader seeks for no further information, but immediately mingles with his new acquaintance, adopts their interests, and attends their pursuits, loves a sylph, and detests a gnome.

That familiar things are made new, every paragraph will prove. The subject of the poem is an event below the common incidents of common life; nothing real is introduced that is not seen so often as to be no longer regarded, yet the whole detail of a female-day is here brought before us invested with so much art of decoration, that, though nothing is disguised, every thing is striking, and we feel all the appetite of curiosity for that from which we have a thousand times turned fastidiously away.

The purpose of the Poet is, as he tells us, to laugh at *the little unguarded follies of the female sex*. It is therefore without justice that Dennis charges the *Rape of the Lock* with the want of a moral,[30] and for that reason sets it below the *Lutrin*,[31] which exposes the pride and discord of the clergy. Perhaps neither Pope nor Boileau has made the world much better than he found it; but if they had both succeeded, it were easy to tell who would have deserved most from publick

25. Camilla: a fleet-footed maiden mentioned in the *Aeneid*.
26. When . . . main: *Essay on Criticism*, ll. 370–73.
27. The Rape . . . Lock: published 1712–14. (See Part Two.) **28. the preternatural . . . poem:** from the commentary in Pope's *Works* (1751), edited by William Warburton (1698–1779), Bishop of Gloucester.

29. Pope . . . nation: Joseph Warton, *An Essay on the Genius and Writings of Pope* (1756). (See Warton's Dedication to the *Essay* in Part Five.) **30. Dennis . . . moral:** in *Remarks on Mr. Pope's Rape of the Lock* (1728). (See the selection from Dennis in Part Two.) **31. the Lutrin:** a mock-heroic poem (1674–83) by the French poet and critic Nicolas Boileau-Despréaux (1636–1711).

gratitude. The freaks, and humours, and spleen, and vanity of women, as they embroil families in discord, and fill houses with disquiet, do more to obstruct the happiness of life in a year than the ambition of the clergy in many centuries. It has been well observed, that the misery of man proceeds not from any single crush of overwhelming evil, but from small vexations continually repeated.

It is remarked by Dennis likewise, that the machinery is superfluous;[32] that, by all the bustle of preternatural operation, the main event is neither hastened nor retarded. To this charge an efficacious answer is not easily made. The sylphs cannot be said to help or to oppose, and it must be allowed to imply some want of art, that their power has not been sufficiently inter-mingled with the action. Other parts may likewise be charged with want of connection; the game at *ombre* might be spared, but if the Lady had lost her hair while she was intent upon her cards, it might have been inferred that those who are too fond of play will be in danger of neglecting more important interests. Those perhaps are faults; but what are such faults to so much excellence!

The Epistle of *Eloise to Abelard*[33] is one of the most happy productions of human wit: the subject is so judiciously chosen, that it would be difficult, in turning over the annals of the world, to find another which so many circumstances concur to recommend. We regularly interest ourselves most in the fortune of those who most deserve our notice. Abelard and Eloise were conspicuous in their days for eminence of merit. The heart naturally loves truth. The adventures and misfortunes of this illustrious pair are known from undisputed history. Their fate does not leave the mind in hopeless dejection; for they both found quiet and consolation in retirement and piety. So new and so affecting is their story, that it supersedes invention, and imagination ranges at full liberty without straggling into scenes of fable.

The story, thus skilfully adopted, has been diligently improved. Pope has left nothing behind him, which seems more the effect of studious perseverance and laborious revisal. Here is particularly observable the *curiosa felicitas*,[34] a fruitful soil, and careful cultivation. Here is no crudeness of sense, nor asperity of language.

The sources from which sentiments, which have so much vigour and efficacy, have been drawn, are shewn to be the mystick writers by the learned author of the *Essay on the Life and Writings of Pope;*[35] a book which teaches how the brow of Criticism may be smoothed, and how she may be enabled, with all her severity, to attract and to delight.

The train of my disquisition has now conducted me to that poetical wonder, the translation of the *Iliad;*[36] a performance which no age or nation can pretend to equal. To the Greeks translation was almost unknown; it was totally unknown to the inhabitants of Greece. They had no recourse to the Barbarians for poetical beauties, but sought for every thing in Homer, where, indeed, there is but little which they might not find.

The Italians have been very diligent translators; but I can hear of no version, unless perhaps Anguillara's Ovid[37] may be excepted, which is read with eagerness. The *Iliad* of Salvini[38] every reader may discover to be punctiliously exact; but it seems to be the work of a linguist skilfully pedantick, and his countrymen, the proper judges of its power to please, reject it with disgust.

Their predecessors the Romans have left some specimens of translation behind them, and that employ-ment must have had some credit in which Tully and Germanicus[39] engaged; but unless we suppose, what is perhaps true, that the plays of Terence[40] were versions of Menander,[41] nothing translated seems ever to have risen to high reputation. The French, in the meridian hour of their learning, were very laudably industrious to enrich their own language with the wisdom of the ancients; but found themselves reduced, by whatever necessity, to turn the Greek and Roman poetry into prose. Whoever could read an author, could translate him. From such rivals little can be feared.

The chief help of Pope in this arduous undertaking was drawn from the versions of Dryden. Virgil had borrowed much of his imagery from Homer, and part

32. the machinery . . . superfluous: in *Remarks on Mr. Pope's Rape of the Lock.* 33. Eloise to Abelard: published in 1717. (See Part Two.) 34. curiosa felicitas: careful felicity (said of Horace by Petronius, *Satyricon*, l. 118).

35. Essay . . . Pope: by Joseph Warton. 36. the transla-tion . . . Iliad: published 1715–20. (See Pope's Preface to this translation in Part Two.) 37. Anguillara's Ovid: *Le Metamorfosi d'Ovidio* (1584), translated by Giovanni Anguillara (c. 1517–64). 38. The Iliad . . . Salvini: published in 1723 by Anton Maria Salvini (1653–1729). 39. Tully and Germanicus: Marcus Tullius Cicero (106–43 B.C.) and Germanicus Caesar (15 B.C.–A.D. 19) both made translations of Greek philosophical writings. 40. Terence: a Roman comic playwright of the second century B.C. 41. Menander: a Greek comic playwright of the fourth century B.C.

of the debt was now paid by his translator. Pope searched the pages of Dryden for happy combinations of heroic diction; but it will not be denied that he added much to what he found. He cultivated our language with so much diligence and art, that he has left in his *Homer* a treasure of poetical elegancies to posterity. His version may be said to have tuned the English tongue; for since its appearance no writer, however deficient in other powers, has wanted melody. Such a series of lines so elaborately corrected, and so sweetly modulated, took possession of the publick ear, the vulgar was enamoured of the poem, and the learned wondered at the translation.

But in the most general applause discordant voices will always be heard. It has been objected by some, who wish to be numbered among the sons of learning, that Pope's version of Homer is not Homerical; that it exhibits no resemblance of the original and characteristick manner of the Father of Poetry, as it wants his awful simplicity, his artless grandeur, his unaffected majesty. This cannot be totally denied; but it must be remembered that *necessitas quod cogit defendit;*[42] that may be lawfully done which cannot be forborn. Time and place will always enforce regard. In estimating this translation, consideration must be had of the nature of our language, the form of our metre, and, above all, of the change which two thousand years have made in the modes of life and the habits of thought. Virgil wrote in a language of the same general fabrick with that of Homer, in verses of the same measure, and in an age nearer to Homer's time by eighteen hundred years; yet he found, even then, the state of the world so much altered, and the demand for elegance so much increased, that mere nature would be endured no longer; and perhaps, in the multitude of borrowed passages, very few can be shewn which he has not embellished.

There is a time when nations emerging from barbarity, and falling into regular subordination, gain leisure to grow wise, and feel the shame of ignorance and the craving pain of unsatisfied curiosity. To this hunger of the mind plain sense is grateful; that which fills the void removes uneasiness, and to be free from pain for a while is pleasure; but repletion generates fastidiousness; a saturated intellect soon becomes luxurious, and knowledge finds no willing reception till it is recommended by artificial diction. Thus it will be found, in the progress of learning, that in all nations the first writers are simple, and that every age improves in elegance. One refinement always makes way for another, and what was expedient to Virgil was necessary to Pope.

I suppose many readers of the English *Iliad*, when they have been touched with some unexpected beauty of the lighter kind, have tried to enjoy it in the original, where, alas! it was not to be found. Homer doubtless owes to his translator many *Ovidian* graces not exactly suitable to his character; but to have added can be no great crime, if nothing be taken away. Elegance is surely to be desired, if it be not gained at the expence of dignity. A hero would wish to be loved, as well as to be reverenced.

To a thousand cavils one answer is sufficient; the purpose of a writer is to be read, and the criticism which would destroy the power of pleasing must be blown aside. Pope wrote for his own age and his own nation: he knew that it was necessary to colour the images and point the sentiments of his author; he therefore made him graceful, but lost him some of his sublimity.

The copious notes with which the version is accompanied, and by which it is recommended to many readers, though they were undoubtedly written to swell the volumes, ought not to pass without praise: commentaries which attract the reader by the pleasure of perusal have not often appeared; the notes of others are read to clear difficulties, those of Pope to vary entertainment.

It has however been objected, with sufficient reason, that there is in the commentary too much of unseasonable levity and affected gaiety; that too many appeals are made to the Ladies, and the ease which is so carefully preserved is sometimes the ease of a trifler. Every art has its terms, and every kind of instruction its proper style; the gravity of common criticks may be tedious, but is less despicable than childish merriment.

Of the *Odyssey*[43] nothing remains to be observed: the same general praise may be given to both translations, and a particular examination of either would require a large volume. The notes were written by Broome,[44] who endeavoured not unsuccessfully to imitate his master.

Of the *Dunciad*[45] the hint is confessedly taken from Dryden's *Mac Fleckno;*[46] but the plan is so enlarged

---

42. **necessitas . . . defendit:** an ancient proverb.

43. **Odyssey:** published 1725–26. 44. **Broome:** William Broome (1689–1745), one of Pope's assistants in the translation. 45. **the Dunciad:** published 1728–43. (See Part Two.) 46. **Mac Fleckno:** (Mac Flecknoe) See Part One.

and diversified as justly to claim the praise of an original, and affords perhaps the best specimen that has yet appeared of personal satire ludicrously pompous.

That the design was moral, whatever the author might tell either his readers or himself, I am not convinced. The first motive was the desire of revenging the contempt with which Theobald had treated his *Shakespeare*,[47] and regaining the honour which he had lost, by crushing his opponent. Theobald was not of bulk enough to fill a poem, and therefore it was necessary to find other enemies with other names, at whose expence he might divert the publick.

In this design there was petulance and malignity enough; but I cannot think it very criminal. An author places himself uncalled before the tribunal of Criticism, and solicits fame at the hazard of disgrace. Dulness or deformity are not culpable in themselves, but may be very justly reproached when they pretend to the honour of wit or the influence of beauty. If bad writers were to pass without reprehension, what should restrain them? *impune diem consumpserit ingens Telephus;*[48] and upon bad writers only will censure have much effect. The satire which brought Theobald and Moore[49] into contempt, dropped impotent from Bentley, like the javelin of Priam.[50]

All truth is valuable, and satirical criticism may be considered as useful when it rectifies error and improves judgement; he that refines the publick taste is a publick benefactor.

The beauties of this poem are well known; its chief fault is the grossness of its images. Pope and Swift had an unnatural delight in ideas physically impure, such as every other tongue utters with unwillingness, and of which every ear shrinks from the mention.

But even this fault, offensive as it is, may be forgiven for the excellence of other passages; such as the formation and dissolution of Moore, the account of the Traveller, the misfortune of the Florist, and the crouded thoughts and stately numbers which dignify the concluding paragraph.

The alterations which have been made in the *Dunciad*,

not always for the better, require that it should be published, as in the last collection, with all its variations.

The *Essay on Man*[51] was a work of great labour and long consideration, but certainly not the happiest of Pope's performances. The subject is perhaps not very proper for poetry, and the poet was not sufficiently master of his subject; metaphysical morality was to him a new study, he was proud of his acquisitions, and, supposing himself master of great secrets, was in haste to teach what he had not learned. Thus he tells us, in the first Epistle, that from the nature of the Supreme Being may be deduced an order of beings such as mankind, because Infinite Excellence can do only what is best. He finds out that these beings must be "somewhere;" and that *all the question is whether man be in a wrong place*. Surely if, according to the poet's Leibnitian reasoning,[52] we may infer that man ought to be, only because he is, we may allow that his place is the right place, because he has it. Supreme Wisdom is not less infallible in disposing than in creating. But what is meant by *somewhere* and *place*, and *wrong place*, it had been vain to ask Pope, who probably had never asked himself.

Having exalted himself into the chair of wisdom, he tells us much that every man knows, and much that he does not know himself; that we see but little, and that the order of the universe is beyond our comprehension; an opinion not very uncommon; and that there is a chain of subordinate beings *from infinite to nothing*, of which himself and his readers are equally ignorant. But he gives us one comfort, which, without his help, he supposes unattainable, in the position *that though we are fools, yet God is wise*.

This Essay affords an egregious instance of the predominance of genius, the dazzling splendour of imagery, and the seductive powers of eloquence. Never were penury of knowledge and vulgarity of sentiment so happily disguised. The reader feels his mind full, though he learns nothing; and when he meets it in its new array, no longer knows the talk of his mother and his nurse. When these wonder-working sounds sink into sense, and the doctrine of the Essay disrobed of its ornaments, is left to the powers of its naked excellence, what shall we discover? That we are,

47. The contempt . . . Shakespeare: The poet, playwright, and editor Lewis Theobald (1688–1744) disparaged Pope's edition of Shakespeare in *Shakespeare Restored* (1726). **48. impune . . . Telephus:** "Shall a huge *Telephus* [a bad tragedy] occupy a whole day's time without penalty?" (Juvenal, *Satires*, I. i. 5). **49. Moore:** James Moore-Smythe (1702–34), playwright and fop satirized in *The Dunciad*. **50. the javelin . . . Priam:** See *Aeneid*, II. 544.

51. Essay on Man: published 1733–34. (See Part Two.) **52. Leibnitian reasoning:** The name of the German philosopher Gottfried Wilhelm Leibnitz (1646–1716) was popularly associated with mechanical and rationalistic explanations of the nature of the universe.

in comparison with our Creator, very weak and ignorant; that we do not uphold the chain of existence, and that we could not make one another with more skill than we are made. We may learn yet more; that the arts of human life were copied from the instinctive operations of other animals; that if the world be made for man, it may be said that man was made for geese. To these profound principles of natural knowledge are added some moral instructions equally new; that self-interest, well understood, will produce social concord; that men are mutual gainers by mutual benefits; that evil is sometimes balanced by good; that human advantages are unstable and fallacious, of uncertain duration, and doubtful effect; that our true honour is not to have a great part, but to act it well; that virtue only is our own; and that happiness is always in our power.

Surely a man of no very comprehensive search may venture to say that he has heard all this before; but it was never till now recommended by such a blaze of embellishment, or such sweetness of melody. The vigorous contraction of some thoughts, the luxuriant amplification of others, the incidental illustrations, and sometimes the dignity, sometimes the softness of the verses, enchain philosophy, suspend criticism, and oppress judgement by overpowering pleasure.

This is true of many paragraphs; yet if I had undertaken to exemplify Pope's felicity of composition before a rigid critick, I should not select the *Essay on Man;* for it contains more lines unsuccessfully laboured, more harshness of diction, more thoughts imperfectly expressed, more levity without elegance, and more heaviness without strength, than will easily be found in all his other works.

The *Characters of Men and Women*[53] are the product of diligent speculation upon human life; much labour has been bestowed upon them, and Pope very seldom laboured in vain. That his excellence may be properly estimated, I recommend a comparison of his *Characters of Women*[54] with Boileau's Satire;[55] it will then be seen with how much more perspicacity female nature is investigated, and female excellence selected; and he surely is no mean writer to whom Boileau shall be found inferior. The *Characters of Men*,[56] however, are

written with more, if not with deeper, thought, and exhibit many passages exquisitely beautiful. The *Gem and the Flower* will not easily be equalled. In the women's part are some defects; the character of *Attossa* is not so neatly finished as that of *Clodio;* and some of the female characters may be found perhaps more frequently among men; what is said of *Philomede*[57] was true of *Prior*.[58]

In the Epistles to Lord Bathurst and Lord Burlington,[59] Dr. Warburton has endeavoured to find a train of thought which was never in the writer's head, and, to support his hypothesis, has printed that first which was published last. In one, the most valuable passage is perhaps the Elogy[60] on *Good Sense*, and the other the *End of the Duke of Buckingham.*

The Epistle to Arbuthnot,[61] now arbitrarily called the *Prologue to the Satires*, is a performance consisting, as it seems, of many fragments wrought into one design, which by this union of scattered beauties contains more striking paragraphs than could probably have been brought together into an occasional work. As there is no stronger motive to exertion than self-defence, no part has more elegance, spirit, or dignity, than the poet's vindication of his own character. The meanest passage is the satire upon *Sporus*.

Of the two poems which derived their names from the year, and which are called the *Epilogue to the Satires*, it was very justly remarked by Savage, that the second was in the whole more strongly conceived, and more equally supported, but that it had no single passages equal to the contention in the first for the dignity of Vice, and the celebration of the triumph of Corruption.

The Imitations of Horace[62] seem to have been written as relaxations of his genius. This employment became his favourite by its facility; the plan was ready to his hand, and nothing was required but to accommodate as he could the sentiments of an old author to recent facts or familiar images; but what is easy is seldom excellent; such imitations cannot give pleasure to common readers; the man of learning may be sometimes surprised and delighted by an unexpected parallel; but the comparison requires knowledge of the original, which will likewise often detect strained

---

53. Characters . . . Women: the four *Moral Essays*, published 1731–35. (See Part Two for the second and fourth.) **54. Characters of Women:** the second of the *Moral Essays*. **55. Boileau's Satire:** the tenth, modeled on Juvenal's sixth. **56. Characters of Men:** the first of the *Moral Essays*.

57. what . . . Philomede: See the second of the *Moral Essays*, ll. 83–86. **58. Prior:** See Part Two. **59. Epistles . . . Burlington:** the third and fourth *Moral Essays*. **60. Elogy:** panegyric. **61. Epistle to Arbuthnot:** published in 1735. (See Part Two.) **62. Imitations of Horace:** published 1733–38. (See Part Two.)

applications. Between Roman images and English manners there will be an irreconcileable dissimilitude, and the work will be generally uncouth and party-coloured; neither original nor translated, neither ancient nor modern.

Pope had, in proportions very nicely adjusted to each other, all the qualities that constitute genius. He had *Invention*, by which new trains of events are formed, and new scenes of imagery displayed, as in the *Rape of the Lock;* and by which extrinsick and adventitious embellishments and illustrations are connected with a known subject, as in the *Essay on Criticism.* He had *Imagination*, which strongly impresses on the writer's mind, and enables him to convey to the reader the various forms of nature, incidents of life, and energies of passion, as in his *Eloisa, Windsor Forest*, and the *Ethick Epistles.* He had *Judgement*, which selects from life or nature what the present purpose requires, and by separating the essence of things from its concomitants often makes the representation more powerful than the reality: and he had colours of language always before him, ready to decorate his matter with every grace of elegant expression, as when he accommodates his diction to the wonderful multiplicity of Homer's sentiments and descriptions.

Poetical expression includes sound as well as meaning; *Musick*, says Dryden, *is inarticulate poetry;*[63] among the excellencies of Pope, therefore, must be mentioned the melody of his metre. By perusing the works of Dryden, he discovered the most perfect fabrick of English verse, and habituated himself to that only which he found the best; in consequence of which restraint his poetry has been censured as too uniformly musical, and as glutting the ear with unvaried sweetness. I suspect this objection to be the cant of those who judge by principles rather than perception; and who would even themselves have less pleasure in his works, if he had tried to relieve attention by studied discords, or affected to break his lines and vary his pauses.

But though he was thus careful of his versification, he did not oppress his powers with superfluous rigour. He seems to have thought with Boileau, that the practice of writing might be refined till the difficulty should overbalance the advantage. The construction of his language is not always strictly grammatical; with those rhymes which prescription had conjoined he contented himself, without regard to Swift's

remonstrances,[64] though there was no striking consonance; nor was he very careful to vary his terminations, or to refuse admission at a small distance to the same rhymes.

To Swift's edict for the exclusion of Alexandrines and Triplets he paid little regard; he admitted them, but, in the opinion of Fenton, too rarely; he uses them more liberally in his translation than his poems.

He has a few double rhymes; and always, I think, unsuccessfully, except once in the *Rape of the Lock.*

Expletives he very early ejected from his verses; but he now and then admits an epithet rather commodious than important. Each of the six first lines of the *Iliad* might lose two syllables with very little diminution of the meaning; and sometimes, after all his art and labour, one verse seems to be made for the sake of another. In his latter productions the diction is sometimes vitiated by French idioms, with which Bolingbroke had perhaps infected him.

I have been told that the couplet by which he declared his own ear to be most gratified was this:

> Lo, where Mæotis sleeps, and hardly flows
> The freezing Tanais through a waste of snows.[65]

But the reason of this preference I cannot discover.

It is remarked by Watts, that there is scarcely a happy combination of words, or a phrase poetically elegant in the English language, which Pope has not inserted into his version of Homer.[66] How he obtained possession of so many beauties of speech, it were desirable to know. That he gleaned from authors, obscure as well as eminent, what he thought brilliant or useful, and preserved it all in a regular collection, is not unlikely. When, in his last years, Hall's Satires were shewn him, he wished that he had seen them sooner.

New sentiments and new images others may produce; but to attempt any further improvement of versification will be dangerous. Art and diligence have now done their best, and what shall be added will be the effort of tedious toil and needless curiosity.

After all this, it is surely superfluous to answer the question that has once been asked, Whether Pope was a poet? otherwise than by asking in return, If Pope be not a poet, where is poetry to be found? To

---

63. Musick . . . poetry: Preface to *Tyrannic Love* (1669).

64. Swift's remonstrances: in a letter of June 28, 1715. **65. Lo . . . snows:** *The Dunciad*, III. 87–88. **66. It . . . Homer:** in *The Improvement of the Mind* (1741). (See the selections from Watts in Part Three.)

circumscribe poetry by a definition will only shew the narrowness of the definer, though a definition which shall exclude Pope will not easily be made. Let us look round upon the present time, and back upon the past; let us enquire to whom the voice of mankind has decreed the wreath of poetry; let their productions be examined, and their claims stated, and the pretensions of Pope will be no more disputed. Had he given the world only his version,[67] the name of poet must have been allowed him: if the writer of the *Iliad* were to class his successors, he would assign a very high place to his translator, without requiring any other evidence of Genius.

. . .

GRAY

THOMAS GRAY, the son of Mr. Philip Gray, a scrivener[1] of London, was born in Cornhill, November 26, 1716. His grammatical education he received at Eaton under the care of Mr. Antrobus, his mother's brother, then assistant to Dr. George; and when he left school, in 1734, entered a pensioner at Peterhouse in Cambridge.

The transition from the school to the college is, to most young scholars, the time from which they date their years of manhood, liberty, and happiness; but Gray seems to have been very little delighted with academical gratifications; he liked at Cambridge neither the mode of life nor the fashion of study, and lived sullenly on to the time when his attendance on lectures was no longer required. As he intended to profess the Common Law, he took no degree.

When he had been at Cambridge about five years, Mr. Horace Walpole, whose friendship he had gained at Eaton, invited him to travel with him as his companion. They wandered through France into Italy; and Gray's Letters contain a very pleasing account of many parts of their journey. But unequal friendships are easily dissolved: at Florence they quarrelled, and parted; and Mr. Walpole is now content to have it told that it was by his fault. If we look however without prejudice on the world, we shall find that men, whose consciousness of their own merit sets them above the compliances of servility, are apt enough in

their association with superiors to watch their own dignity with troublesome and punctilious jealousy, and in the fervour of independance to exact that attention which they refuse to pay. Part they did, whatever was the quarrel, and the rest of their travels was doubtless more unpleasant to them both. Gray continued his journey in a manner suitable to his own little fortune, with only an occasional servant.

He returned to England in September 1741, and in about two months afterwards buried his father, who had, by an injudicious waste of money upon a new house, so much lessened his fortune, that Gray thought himself too poor to study the law. He therefore retired to Cambridge, where he soon after became Bachelor of Civil Law; and where, without liking the place or its inhabitants, or professing to like them, he passed, except a short residence at London, the rest of his life.

About this time he was deprived of Mr. West,[2] the son of a chancellor of Ireland, a friend on whom he appears to have set a high value, and who deserved his esteem by the powers which he shews in his Letters, and in the Ode to *May*, which Mr. Mason has preserved, as well as by the sincerity with which, when Gray sent him part of *Agrippina*, a tragedy that he had just begun, he gave an opinion which probably intercepted the progress of the work, and which the judgement of every reader will confirm. It was certainly no loss to the English stage that *Agrippina* was never finished.

In this year (1742) Gray seems first to have applied himself seriously to poetry; for in this year were produced the *Ode to Spring*, his *Prospect of Eaton*, and his *Ode to Adversity*. He began likewise a Latin poem, *de Principiis cogitandi*.[3]

It may be collected from the narrative of Mr. Mason,[4] that his first ambition was to have excelled in Latin poetry: perhaps it were reasonable to wish that he had prosecuted his design; for though there is at present some embarrassment in his phrase, and some harshness in his Lyrick numbers, his copiousness of language is such as very few possess; and his lines, even when imperfect, discover a writer whom practice would quickly have made skilful.

---

67. **his version:** his translation (of Homer). LIFE OF GRAY. 1. **scrivener:** money-lender and drawer of contracts.

2. **Mr. West:** Richard West died in 1742. (See Gray's sonnet on the death of West in Part Five.) 3. **de . . . cogitandi:** a long didactic poem in hexameters on the philosophy of John Locke. 4. **the narrative . . . Mason:** *Memoirs of the Life and Writings of Mr. Gray* (1775) by the minor poet William Mason.

He now lived on at Peterhouse, very little solicitous what others did or thought, and cultivated his mind and enlarged his views without any other purpose than of improving and amusing himself; when Mr. Mason, being elected fellow of Pembroke-hall, brought him a companion who was afterwards to be his editor, and whose fondness and fidelity has kindled in him a zeal of admiration, which cannot be reasonably expected from the neutrality of a stranger and the coldness of a critick.

In this retirement he wrote (1747) an ode on the *Death of Mr. Walpole's Cat;* and the year afterwards attempted a poem of more importance, on *Government and Education*, of which the fragments which remain have many excellent lines.

His next production (1750) was his far-famed *Elegy in the Church-yard*, which, finding its way into a Magazine, first, I believe, made him known to the publick.

An invitation from lady Cobham[5] about this time gave occasion to an odd composition called *a Long Story*, which adds little to Gray's character.

Several of his pieces were published (1753), with designs, by Mr. Bentley; and, that they might in some form or other make a book, only one side of each leaf was printed. I believe the poems and the plates recommended each other so well, that the whole impression was soon bought. This year he lost his mother.

Some time afterwards (1756) some young men of the college, whose chambers were near his, diverted themselves with disturbing him by frequent and troublesome noises, and, as is said, by pranks yet more offensive and contemptuous. This insolence, having endured it a while, he represented to the governors of the society, among whom perhaps he had no friends; and, finding his complaint little regarded, removed himself to Pembroke-hall.

In 1757 he published *The Progress of Poetry* and *The Bard*, two compositions at which the readers of poetry were at first content to gaze in mute amazement. Some that tried them confessed their inability to understand them, though Warburton said that they were understood as well as the works of Milton and Shakespeare, which it is the fashion to admire. Garrick wrote a few lines in their praise.[6] Some hardy

champions undertook to rescue them from neglect, and in a short time many were content to be shewn beauties which they could not see.

Gray's reputation was now so high, that, after the death of Cibber, he had the honour of refusing the laurel, which was then bestowed on Mr. Whitehead.[7]

His curiosity, not long after, drew him away from Cambridge to a lodging near the Museum,[8] where he resided near three years, reading and transcribing; and, so far as can be discovered, very little affected by two odes on *Oblivion* and *Obscurity*,[9] in which his Lyrick performances were ridiculed with much contempt and much ingenuity.

When the Professor of Modern History at Cambridge[10] died, he was, as he says, *cockered and spirited up*, till he asked it of lord Bute, who sent him a civil refusal; and the place was given to Mr. Brocket,[11] the tutor of Sir James Lowther.

His constitution was weak, and believing that his health was promoted by exercise and change of place, he undertook (1765) a journey into Scotland, of which his account, so far as it extends, is very curious and elegant; for as his comprehension was ample, his curiosity extended to all the works of art, all the appearances of nature, and all the monuments of past events. He naturally contracted a friendship with Dr. Beattie,[12] whom he found a poet, a philosopher, and a good man. The Mareschal College at Aberdeen offered him the degree of Doctor of Laws, which, having omitted to take it at Cambridge, he thought it decent to refuse.

What he had formerly solicited in vain, was at last given him without solicitation. The Professorship of History became again vacant, and he received (1768) an offer of it from the duke of Grafton. He accepted, and retained it to his death; always designing lectures, but never reading them; uneasy at his neglect of duty, and appeasing his uneasiness with designs of reformation, and with a resolution which he believed himself

---

5. **lady Cobham:** the Dowager Viscountess Cobham, a widow living at Stoke Poges. 6. **Garrick . . . praise:** In a six-stanza poem, Garrick exhorted Gray to "droop not," and implored him to write some more odes in order to "rouse us to *reflect* and *feel*."

7. **Mr. Whitehead:** William Whitehead (1715–85), playwright and poet. (See the selection from Whitehead in Part Eight.) 8. **the Museum:** the British Museum in London, until 1759 the residence of the Montagu family. 9. **two . . . Obscurity:** by George Colman and Robert Lloyd. 10. **Professor . . . Cambridge:** Shallet Turner. 11. **Mr. Brocket:** Laurence Brocket, a drunken, disreputable Fellow of Trinity, had the advantage of being tutor to Lowther, who was son-in-law to Lord Bute. 12. **Dr. Beattie:** James Beattie (1735–1803), professor of moral philosophy at Marischal College, Aberdeen.

to have made of resigning the office, if he found himself unable to discharge it.

Ill health made another journey necessary, and he visited (1769) Westmoreland and Cumberland. He that reads his epistolary narration wishes, that to travel, and to tell his travels, had been more of his employment; but it is by studying at home that we must obtain the ability of travelling with intelligence and improvement.

His travels and his studies were now near their end. The gout, of which he had sustained many weak attacks, fell upon his stomach, and, yielding to no medicines, produced strong convulsions, which (July 30, 1771) terminated in death.

His character I am willing to adopt, as Mr. Mason has done, from a letter written to my friend Mr. Boswell, by the Rev. Mr. Temple, rector of St. Gluvias in Cornwall; and am as willing as his warmest well-wisher to believe it true.

"Perhaps he was the most learned man in Europe. He was equally acquainted with the elegant and profound parts of science, and that not superficially but thoroughly. He knew every branch of history, both natural and civil; had read all the original historians of England, France, and Italy; and was a great antiquarian. Criticism, metaphysics, morals, politics, made a principal part of his study; voyages and travels of all sorts were his favourite amusements; and he had a fine taste in painting, prints, architecture, and gardening. With such a fund of knowledge, his conversation must have been equally instructing and entertaining; but he was also a good man, a man of virtue and humanity. There is no character without some speck, some imperfection; and I think the greatest defect in his was an affectation in delicacy, or rather effeminacy, and a visible fastidiousness, or contempt and disdain of his inferiors in science. He also had, in some degree, that weakness which disgusted Voltaire so much in Mr. Congreve: though he seemed to value others chiefly according to the progress they had made in knowledge, yet he could not bear to be considered himself merely as a man of letters; and though without birth, or fortune, or station, his desire was to be looked upon as a private independent gentleman, who read for his amusement. Perhaps it may be said, What signifies so much knowledge, when it produced so little? Is it worth taking so much pains to leave no memorial but a few poems? But let it be considered that Mr. Gray was, to others, at least innocently employed; to himself, certainly beneficially. His time passed agreeably;

he was every day making some new acquisition in science; his mind was enlarged, his heart softened, his virtue strengthened; the world and mankind were shewn to him without a mask; and he was taught to consider every thing as trifling, and unworthy of the attention of a wise man, except the pursuit of knowledge and practice of virtue, in that state wherein God hath placed us."

To this character Mr. Mason has added a more particular account of Gray's skill in zoology. He has remarked, that Gray's effeminacy was affected most *before those whom he did not wish to please;* and that he is unjustly charged with making knowledge his sole reason of preference, as he paid his esteem to none whom he did not likewise believe to be good.

What has occurred to me, from the slight inspection of his Letters in which my undertaking has engaged me, is, that his mind had a large grasp; that his curiosity was unlimited, and his judgement cultivated; that he was a man likely to love much where he loved at all, but that he was fastidious and hard to please. His contempt however is often employed, where I hope it will be approved, upon scepticism and infidelity. His short account of Shaftesbury[13] I will insert.

You say you cannot conceive how lord Shaftesbury came to be a philosopher in vogue; I will tell you: first, he was a lord; secondly, he was as vain as any of his readers; thirdly, men are very prone to believe what they do not understand; fourthly, they will believe any thing at all, provided they are under no obligation to believe it; fifthly, they love to take a new road, even when that road leads no where; sixthly, he was reckoned a fine writer, and seems always to mean more than he said. Would you have any more reasons? An interval of above forty years has pretty well destroyed the charm. A dead lord ranks with commoners: vanity is no longer interested in the matter; for a new road has become an old one.

Mr. Mason has added, from his own knowledge, that though Gray was poor, he was not eager of money; and that, out of the little that he had, he was very willing to help the necessitous.

As a writer he had this peculiarity, that he did not write his pieces first rudely, and then correct them, but

---

13. **Shaftesbury:** Anthony Ashley Cooper (1671–1713), Third Earl of Shaftesbury; author of *Characteristics of Men, Manners, Opinions, Times* (1711–13). (See the selection from Shaftesbury in Part Two.)

laboured every line as it arose in the train of composition; and he had a notion not very peculiar, that he could not write but at certain times, or at happy moments; a fantastick foppery, to which my kindness for a man of learning and virtue wishes him to have been superior.

GRAY'S Poetry is now to be considered; and I hope not to be looked on as an enemy to his name, if I confess that I contemplate it with less pleasure than his life.

His ode on *Spring* has something poetical, both in the language and the thought; but the language is too luxuriant, and the thoughts have nothing new. There has of late arisen a practice of giving to adjectives, derived from substantives, the termination of participles; such as the *cultured* plain, the *daisied* bank; but I was sorry to see, in the lines of a scholar like Gray, the *honied* Spring. The morality is natural, but too stale; the conclusion is pretty.

The poem on the *Cat* was doubtless by its author considered as a trifle, but it is not a happy trifle. In the first stanza *the azure flowers* that *blow* shew resolutely a rhyme is sometimes made when it cannot easily be found. *Selima*, the *Cat*, is called a nymph, with some violence both to language and sense; but there is good use made of it when it is done; for of the two lines,

> What female heart can gold despise?
> What cat's averse to fish?

the first relates merely to the nymph, and the second only to the cat. The sixth stanza contains a melancholy truth, that *a favourite has no friend;* but the last ends in a pointed sentence of no relation to the purpose; if *what glistered* had been *gold*, the cat would not have gone into the water; and, if she had, would not less have been drowned.

The *Prospect of Eaton College* suggests nothing to Gray, which every beholder does not equally think and feel. His supplication to father *Thames*, to tell him who drives the hoop or tosses the ball, is useless and puerile. Father *Thames* has no better means of knowing than himself. His epithet *buxom health* is not elegant; he seems not to understand the word. Gray thought his language more poetical as it was more remote from common use: finding in Dryden *honey redolent of Spring*, an expression that reaches the utmost limits of our language, Gray drove it a little more beyond common apprehension, by making *gales* to be *redolent of joy and youth.*

Of the *Ode on Adversity*, the hint was at first taken from *O Diva, gratum quæ regis Antium;*[14] but Gray has excelled his original by the variety of his sentiments, and by their moral application. Of this piece, at once poetical and rational, I will not by slight objections violate the dignity.

My process has now brought me to the *wonderful Wonder of Wonders*, the two Sister Odes; by which, though either vulgar ignorance or common sense at first universally rejected them, many have been since persuaded to think themselves delighted. I am one of those that are willing to be pleased, and therefore would gladly find the meaning of the first stanza of the *Progress of Poetry*.

Gray seems in his rapture to confound the images of *spreading sound* and *running water*. A *stream of musick* may be allowed; but where does *Musick*, however *smooth and strong*, after having visited the *verdant vales*, *rowl down the steep amain*, so as that *rocks and nodding groves rebellow to the roar?* If this be said of *Musick*, it is nonsense; if it be said of *Water*, it is nothing to the purpose.

The second stanza, exhibiting Mars's car and Jove's eagle, is unworthy of further notice. Criticism disdains to chase a school-boy to his common places.

To the third it may likewise be objected, that it is drawn from Mythology, though such as may be more easily assimilated to real life. Idalia's *velvet-green* has something of cant. An epithet or metaphor drawn from Nature ennobles Art; an epithet or metaphor drawn from Art degrades Nature. Gray is too fond of words arbitrarily compounded. *Many-twinkling* was formerly censured as not analogical; we may say *many-spotted*, but scarcely *many-spotting*. This stanza, however, has something pleasing.

Of the second ternary of stanzas, the first endeavours to tell something, and would have told it, had it not been crossed by Hyperion: the second describes well enough the universal prevalence of Poetry; but I am afraid that the conclusion will not rise from the premises. The caverns of the North and the plains of Chili are not the residences of *Glory* and *generous Shame*. But that Poetry and Virtue go always together is an opinion so pleasing, that I can forgive him who resolves to think it true.

The third stanza sounds big with *Delphi*, and *Egean*, and *Ilissus*, and *Meander*, and *hallowed fountain* and *solemn sound;* but in all Gray's odes there is a kind of

14. O . . . **Antium:** "O goddess, queen of the beloved Antium" (Horace, *Odes.* I. xxxv. 1).

cumbrous splendour which we wish away. His position is at last false: in the time of Dante and Petrarch, from whom he derives our first school of Poetry, Italy was over-run by *tyrant power* and *coward vice;* nor was our state much better when we first borrowed the Italian arts.

Of the third ternary, the first gives a mythological birth of Shakespeare. What is said of that mighty genius is true; but it is not said happily: the real effects of his poetical power are put out of sight by the pomp of machinery. Where truth is sufficient to fill the mind, fiction is worse than useless; the counterfeit debases the genuine.

His account of Milton's blindness, if we suppose it caused by study in the formation of his poem, a supposition surely allowable, is poetically true, and happily imagined. But the *car* of Dryden, with his *two coursers*, has nothing in it peculiar; it is a car in which any other rider may be placed.

The Bard appears, at the first view, to be, as Algarotti[15] and others have remarked, an imitation of the prophecy of Nereus.[16] Algarotti thinks it superior to its original; and, if preference depends only on the imagery and animation of the two poems, his judgement is right. There is in *The Bard* more force, more thought, and more variety. But to copy is less than to invent, and the copy has been unhappily produced at a wrong time. The fiction of Horace was to the Romans credible; but its revival disgusts us with apparent and unconquerable falsehood. *Incredulus odi.*[17]

To select a singular event, and swell it to a giant's bulk by fabulous appendages of spectres and predictions, has little difficulty, for he that forsakes the probable may always find the marvellous; and it has little use, we are affected only as we believe; we are improved only as we find something to be imitated or declined. I do not see that *The Bard* promotes any truth, moral or political.

His stanzas are too long, especially his epodes; the ode is finished before the ear has learned its measures, and consequently before it can receive pleasure from their consonance and recurrence.

Of the first stanza the abrupt beginning[18] has been celebrated; but technical beauties can give praise only to the inventor. It is in the power of any man to rush abruptly upon his subject, that has read the ballad of *Johnny Armstrong.*

Is there ever a man in all Scotland—

The initial resemblances, or alliterations, *ruin, ruthless, helm nor hauberk*, are below the grandeur of a poem that endeavours at sublimity.

In the second stanza the *Bard* is well described; but in the third we have the puerilities of obsolete mythology. When we are told that *Cadwallo hush'd the stormy main*, and that *Modred* made *huge Plinlimmon*[19] *bow his cloud-top'd head*, attention recoils from the repetition of a tale that, even when it was first heard, was heard with scorn.

The *weaving* of the *winding sheet* he borrowed, as he owns, from the northern Bards; but their texture, however, was very properly the work of female powers, as the art of spinning the thread of life in another mythology. Theft is always dangerous; Gray has made weavers of his slaughtered bards by a fiction outrageous and incongruous. They are then called upon to *Weave the warp, and weave the woof*, perhaps with no great propriety; for it is by crossing the *woof* with the *warp* that men *weave* the *web* or piece; and the first line was dearly bought by the admission of its wretched correspondent, *Give ample room and verge enough.* He has, however, no other line as bad.

The third stanza of the second ternary is commended, I think, beyond its merit. The personification is indistinct. *Thirst* and *Hunger* are not alike; and their features, to make the imagery perfect, should have been discriminated. We are told, in the same stanza, how *towers* are *fed*. But I will no longer look for particular faults; yet let it be observed that the ode might have been concluded with an action of better example;[20] but suicide is always to be had, without expence of thought.

These odes are marked by glittering accumulations of ungraceful ornaments; they strike rather than please; the images are magnified by affectation; the language is laboured into harshness. The mind of the writer seems to work with unnatural violence. *Double, double, toil and trouble.*[21] He has a kind of strutting dignity, and is tall by walking on tiptoe. His art and his struggle are too visible, and there is too little appearance of ease and nature.

---

15. Algarotti: Francesco Algarotti (1712–64), Italian critic and philosopher. **16. the prophecy . . . Nereus:** See Horace, *Odes*, I. xv. **17. Incredulus odi:** "Not believing it, I despise it" (Horace, *Ars Poetica*, l. 188). **18. the abrupt beginning:** "Ruin seize thee, ruthless King!"

19. Plinlimmon: a mountain in Wales. **20. an action . . . example:** At the end of *The Bard* (1757), the ancient poet hurls himself from a mountain top. **21. Double . . . trouble:** *Macbeth*, IV. i. 10.

To say that he has no beauties would be unjust: a man like him, of great learning and great industry, could not but produce something valuable. When he pleases least, it can only be said that a good design was ill directed.

His translations of Northern and Welsh Poetry deserve praise; the imagery is preserved, perhaps often improved; but the language is unlike the language of other poets.

In the character of his Elegy I rejoice to concur with the common reader; for by the common sense of readers uncorrupted with literary prejudices, after all the refinements of subtilty and the dogmatism of learning, must be finally decided all claim to poetical honours. The *Church-yard* abounds with images which find a mirrour in every mind, and with sentiments to which every bosom returns an echo. The four stanzas beginning *Yet even these bones*, are to me original: I have never seen the notions in any other place; yet he that reads them here, persuades himself that he has always felt them. Had Gray written often thus, it had been vain to blame, and useless to praise him.

no critic could attack or praise him

FROM

[PRAYERS AND MEDITATIONS]

Boswell writes:

On Friday, June 11, [1784] we talked at breakfast, of forms of prayer. JOHNSON. "I know of no good prayers but those in the 'Book of Common Prayer.'" DR. [William] ADAMS, (in a very earnest manner): "I wish, Sir, you would compose some family prayers." JOHNSON. "I will not compose prayers for you, Sir, because you can do it for yourself. But I have thought of getting together all the books of prayer which I could, selecting those which should appear to me the best, putting out some, inserting others, adding some prayers of my own, and prefixing a discourse on prayer."

Although Johnson never executed this project, he did leave behind a collection of manuscripts, which were published the year after his death by his friend the Reverend George Strahan. Johnson's *Prayers and Meditations*, says Boswell, "proves with unquestionable authenticity, that amidst all his constitutional infirmities, his earnestness to conform his practice to the precepts of

Christianity was unceasing, and that he habitually endeavoured to refer every transaction of his life to the will of the Supreme Being."

The conventional form of prayer that Johnson used most often is the Collect, the most frequent form in the Book of Common Prayer. A Collect traditionally consists of Salutation, Ascription, Petition, Reason for Petition, and Conclusion.

The text is from Johnson's *Diaries, Prayers, and Annals* (1958), ed. E. L. McAdam, Jr., with Donald and Mary Hyde, who have made new transcriptions of the manuscripts deposited by Strahan in the library of Pembroke College, Oxford.

April 25, 1752.

O Lord, our heavenly Father, almighty and most merciful God, in whose hands are life and death, who givest and takest away, castest down and raisest up, look with mercy on the affliction of thy unworthy servant, turn away thine anger from me, and speak peace to my troubled soul. Grant me the assistance and comfort of thy Holy Spirit, that I may remember with thankfulness the blessings so long enjoyed by me in the society of my departed wife;[1] make me so to think on her precepts and example, that I may imitate whatever was in her life acceptable in thy sight, and avoid all by which she offended Thee. Forgive me, O merciful Lord, all my sins, and enable me to begin and perfect that reformation which I promised her, and to persevere in that resolution, which she implored Thee to continue, in the purposes which I recorded in thy sight, when she lay dead before me, in obedience to thy laws, and faith in thy word. And now, O Lord, release me from my sorrow, fill me with just hopes, true faith, and holy consolations, and enable me to do my duty in that state of life to which Thou hast been pleased to call me, without disturbance from fruitless grief, or tumultuous imaginations; that in all my thoughts, words, and actions, I may glorify thy Holy Name, and finally obtain, what I hope Thou hast granted to thy departed servant, everlasting joy and felicity, through our Lord Jesus Christ. Amen.

Easter Eve. 1757.

Almighty God, heavenly Father, who desirest not the death of a sinner, look down with mercy upon me

PRAYERS AND MEDITATIONS. **1. my . . . wife:** Tetty died on March 28, 1752.

depraved with vain imaginations, and entangled in long habits of Sin. Grant me that grace without which I can neither will nor do what is acceptable to thee. Pardon my sins, remove the impediments that hinder my obedience. Enable me to shake off Sloth, and to redeem the time mispent in idleness and Sin by a diligent application of the days yet remaining to the duties which thy Providence shall allot me. O God grant me thy Holy Spirit that I may repent and amend my life, grant me contrition, grant me resolution for the sake of Jesus Christ, to whose covenant I now implore admission, of the benefits of whose death I implore participation; for his sake have mercy on me O God; for his sake, O God, pardon and receive me. Amen.

Easter Eve. 1761.

Since the Communion of last Easter I have led a life so dissipated and useless, and my terrours and perplexities have so much encreased, that I am under great depression and discouragement, yet I purpose to present myself before God tomorrow with humble hope that he will not break the bruised reed.

Come unto me all ye that travail.[2]

I have resolved, I hope not presumptuously, till I am afraid to resolve again. Yet hoping in God I steadfastly purpose to lead a new life. O God, enable me, for Jesus Christs sake.

My Purpose is

I[3]

2 To avoid Idleness.

To regulate my sleep as to length and choice of hours.

To set down every day what shall be done the day following.

To keep a Journal.

3 To worship God more diligently.

To go to Church every Sunday.

4 To study the Scriptures.

To read a certain portion every week.

Almighty and most merciful Father look down upon my misery with pity, strengthen me that I may overcome all sinfull habits, grant that I may with effectual faith commemorate the death of thy son Jesus Christ, so that all corrupt desires may be extinguished, and all vain thoughts may be dispelled.

Enlighten me with true knowledge, animate me with reasonable hope, comfort me with a just sense of thy love, and assist me to the performance of all holy purposes, that after the sins, errours, and miseries of this world I may obtain everlasting happiness for Jesus Christs sake. To whom &c.[4] Amen.

I hope to attend on God in his ordinances to morrow. Trust in God O my soul. O God let me trust in Thee.

April 21, 1764.—3—M.[5]

My indolence, since my last reception of the Sacrament, has sunk into grosser sluggishness, and my dissipation spread into wilder negligence. My thoughts have been clouded with sensuality, and, except that from the beginning of this year I have in some measure forborn excess of Strong Drink my appetites have predominated over my reason. A kind of strange oblivion has overspread me, so that I know not what has become of the last year, and perceive that incidents and intelligence pass over me without leaving any impression.

This is not the life to which Heaven is promised. I purpose to approach the altar again to morrow. Grant, O Lord, that I may receive the sacrament with such resolutions of a better life as may by thy Grace be effectual, for the sake of Jesus Christ. Amen.

April 21. I read the whole Gospel of St. John. The[n] sat up till the 22d.

My Purpose is from this time

1 To reject or expel sensual images, and idle thoughts.

To provide some useful amusement for leisure time.

2 To avoid Idleness.

To rise early.

To study a proper portion of every day.

3 To worship God diligently.

4 To read the Scriptures.

To let no week pass without reading some part.

To write down my observations.

I will renew my resolutions made at Tetty's death.

I perceive an insensibility and heaviness upon me. I am less than commonly oppressed with the sense of sin, and less affected with the shame of Idleness. Yet I

---

2. Come . . . travail: See Matt. 11:28. **3. I:** Someone, presumably Strahan, obliterated in the manuscript the first of Johnson's resolutions.

4. To . . . &c.: ". . . to whom with thee and the Holy Ghost be all honour and glory, world without end" ("A General Thanksgiving," Book of Common Prayer). **5. —3—M:** three o'clock in the morning.

will not despair. I will pray to God for resolution, and will endeavour to strengthen my faith in Christ by commemorating his Death.

I prayed for Tett.

Sept. 18. 1764. About 6. evening.

This is my fifty sixth birthday, the day on which I have concluded fifty five years.

I have outlived many friends. I have felt many sorrows. I have made few improvements. Since my resolution formed last Easter I have made no advancement in knowledge or in Goodness; nor do I recollect that I have endeavoured it. I am dejected but not hopeless.

O God for Jesus Christs Sake have mercy upon me. 7 in the evening. I went to Church prayed *to be loosed from the chain of my sins.*[6]

I have now spent fifty five years in resolving, having from the earliest time almost that I can remember been forming schemes of a better life. I have done nothing; the need of doing therefore is pressing, since the time of doing is short. O God grant me to resolve aright, and to keep my resolution for Jesus Christs Sake. Amen. . . .

Sept. 18. [1771]. 9. at night.

I am now come to my sixty third year. For the last year I have been slowly recovering both from the violence of my last ilness, and, I think, from the general disease of my life. My Breath is less obstructed, and I am more capable of motion and exercise. My mind is less encumbered, and I am less interrupted in mental employment. Some advances I hope have been made towards regularity. I have missed Church since Easter only two Sundays both which I hope I have endeavoured to supply by attendance on Divine Worship in the following week. Since Easter my Evening devotions have been lengthened. But Indolence and indifference has been neither conquered nor opposed. No plan of study has been persued or formed except that I have commonly read every week, if not on Sunday, a stated portion of the New Testament in greek. But what is most to be considered I have neither attempted nor formed any scheme of Life by which I may do good, and please God.

One great hindrance is want of rest; my nocturnal complaints grow less troublesome towards morning, and I am tempted [to] repair the deficiencies of the night. I think however to try to rise every day by eight, and to combat indolence as I shall obtain strength. Perhaps Providence has yet some use for the remnant of my life.

Almighty and everlasting God, whose mercy is over all thy works, and who hast no pleasure in the Death of a Sinner, look with pity upon me, succour, and preserve me; enable me to conquer evil habits, and surmount temptations. Give me Grace so to use the degree of health which Thou hast restored to my Mind and Body, that I may perform the task thou shalt yet appoint me. Look down, O gracious Lord upon my remaining part of Life, grant if it please thee that the days few or many which thou shalt yet allow me, may pass in reasonable confidence, and holy tranquillity. Withold not thy Holy Spirit from me but strengthen all good purposes till they shall produce a life pleasing to thee. And when thou shalt call me to another state, forgive me my sins, and receive me to Happiness, for the sake of Jesus Christ, our Lord. Amen.

Safely brought us.[7] &c.

[March] 30. [1777] Easter Day. 1ma Mane.[8]

The day is now come again in which, by a custom which since the death of my wife, I have by the Divine assistance always observed, I am to renew the great covenant with my Maker and my Judge. I humbly hope to perform it better. I hope for more efficacy of resolution, and more diligence of endeavour. When I survey my past life, I discover nothing but a barren waste of time with some disorders of body, and disturbances of the mind very near to madness; which I hope he that made me, will suffer to extenuate many faults, and excuse many deficiencies. Yet much remains to be repented and reformed. I hope that I refer more to God than in former times, and consider more what submission is due to his dispensations. But I have very little reformed my practical life, and the time in which I can struggle with habits cannot be now expected to be long. Grant O God that I may no longer resolve in vain, or dream away the life which thy indulgence gives me, in vacancy and uselessness.

---

6. **to . . . sins:** an allusion to one of the "Prayers upon Several Occasions" in the Book of Common Prayer.

7. **Safely . . . us:** a reference to "The Third Collect, for Grace," in "The Order for Morning Prayer," Book of Common Prayer. 8. **1ma Mane:** one o'clock in the morning.

Apr. 6. [1777]

By one strange hindrance or another, I have been witheld from the continuation of my thoughts to this day, the Sunday following Easter day.

On Easter day I was at Church early, and there prayed over my prayer and commended Tetty, and my other Friends. I was for some time much distressed, but at last obtained, I hope from the God of peace more quiet than I have enjoyed for a long time. I had made no resolution, but as my heart grew lighter, my hopes revived and my courage increased, and I wrote with my pencil in my common prayer book.

> Vita ordinanda.
> Biblia legenda.
> Theologiae opera danda.
> Serviendum et laetandum.
> Scrupulis obsistendum.[9]

I then went to the altar having I believe, again read my prayer. I then went to the table and communicated, praying for some time afterwards, but the particular matter of my prayer I do not remember.

I dined by an appointment with Mrs. Gardiner,[10] and passed the afternoon with such calm gladness of Mind as it is very long since I felt before. I came home and began to read the Bible. I passed the night in such sweet uninterrupted sleep, as I have not known since I slept at Fort Augustus.[11]

On Monday I dined with Sheward,[12] on Tuesday with Paradise;[13] the mornings have been devoured by company, and one intrusion has through the whole week succeeded to another.

At the beginning of the year I proposed to myself a scheme of life, and a plan of study, but neither life has been rectified nor study followed. Days and months pass in a dream, and I am afraid that my memory grows less tenacious, and my observation less attentive. If I am decaying it is time to make haste. My nights are restless and tedious, and my days drowsy. The flatulence which torments me, has some times so obstructed my breath, that the act of respiration became not only voluntary but laborious in a decumbent posture. By copious bleeding I was relieved, but not cured.

I have this year omitted church on most Sundays, intending to supply the deficience in the week. So that I owe twelve attendances on worship. I will make no more such superstitious stipulations which entangle the mind with unbid obligations.

My purpose once more, O Thou merciful Creatour, that governest all our hearts and actions, βιοτῆς οἴηκα κυβερνῶν,[14] let not my purpose be vain. My purpose once more is

1 To rise at eight.
   To keep a journal.
2 To read the whole Bible in some language before Easter.
3 To gather the arguments for Christianity.
4 To worship God more frequently in publick.

Good Friday. Apr. 2 [1779]. *11. P.M.*

I am now to review the last year, and find little but dismal vacuity, neither business nor pleasure; much intended and little done. My health is much broken; my nights afford me little rest. I have tried opium, but its help is counter ballanced with great disturbance; it prevents the spasms, but it hinders sleep. O God, have mercy on me.

Last week I published the lives of the poets written I hope in such a manner, as may tend to the promotion of Piety.

In this last year I have made little acquisition, I have scarcely read any thing. I maintain Mrs. Desmoulins and her daughter,[15] other good of myself I know not where to find, except a little Charity.

But I am now in my seventieth year, what can be done ought not to be delayed.

Apr. 13. Good Friday 1781.

I forgot my Prayer and resolutions till two days ago I found this paper.

Sometime in March I finished the lives of the Poets, which I wrote in my usual way, dilatorily and hastily,

---

9. **Vita . . . obsistendum:** Regulate your life; read the Bible; study theology; serve and rejoice; resist religious doubts. 10. **Mrs. Gardiner:** Anne Gardiner, described by Boswell as the "wife of a tallow-chandler on Snow-hill, not in the learned way, but a worthy good woman." 11. **Fort Augustus:** on Loch Ness, near Inverness, Scotland. Johnson had stayed there overnight with Boswell during their tour of the Hebrides in 1773. 12. **Sheward:** probably William Seward (1747–99), a minor author and friend of the Thrales'. Johnson's spelling reveals his Staffordshire pronunciation. 13. **Paradise:** John Paradise (1743–95), an Oxford scholar, was an old friend of Johnson's.

14. βιοτῆς . . . κυβερνῶν: steering the helm of life. 15. **Mrs. Desmoulins . . . daughter:** like Dr. Levet, members of Johnson's household at No. 8, Bolt Court, London, and recipients of his charity.

unwilling to work, and working with vigour, and haste.

On Wednesday, 11, was buried my dear Friend Thrale who died, on Wednesday, 4, and with him were buried many of my hopes and pleasures.

Against Inquisitive and Perplexing Thoughts.

Aug. 12 [17]84

O Lord, my Maker and Protector, who hast graciously sent me into this world, to work out my salvation, enable me to drive from me all such unquiet and perplexing thoughts as may mislead or hinder me in the practice of those duties which thou hast required. When I behold the works of thy hands and consider the course of thy providence, give me Grace always to remember that thy thoughts are not my thoughts, nor thy ways my ways. And while it shall please thee to continue me in this world where much is to be done and little to be known, teach me by thy Holy Spirit to withdraw my Mind from unprofitable and dangerous enquiries, from difficulties vainly curious, and doubts impossible to be solved. Let me rejoice in the light which thou hast imparted, let me serve thee with active zeal, and humble confidence, and wait with patient expectation for the time in which the soul which Thou receivest, shall be satisfied with knowledge. Grant this, O Lord, for Jesus Christs sake. Amen.

FROM

[LETTERS]

The texts of some fifteen hundred letters of Johnson's survive, written from his tenth to his seventy-fifth year. Although he never developed a critical theory of the letter as a literary form, he did devote *The Rambler*, No. 152, to suggesting that it was a definite genre and that one of its artistic conventions was the writer's adapting his length, matter, structure, and style to the sensibility of the recipient. As he says, "Letters are written to the great and to the mean, to the learned and the ignorant . . . . Nothing can be more improper than ease and laxity of expression when the importance of the subject impresses solicitude or the dignity of the person exacts reverence."

The text is from *The Letters of Samuel Johnson, with*

Mrs. Thrale's Genuine Letters to Him, ed. R. W. Chapman (3 vols., 1952). Where Johnson's inadvertences might cause confusion, we have silently amended them.

❦

[*To Lord Chesterfield*]

February 1755

MY LORD

I have been lately informed by the proprietor of The World[1] that two Papers in which my Dictionary is recommended to the Public were written by your Lordship. To be so distinguished is an honour which, being very little accustomed to favours from the Great, I know not well how to receive, or in what terms to acknowledge.

When upon some slight encouragement I first visited your Lordship I was overpowered like the rest of Mankind by the enchantment of your adress, and could not forbear to wish that I might boast myself Le Vainqueur du Vainqueur de la Terre,[2] that I might obtain that regard for which I saw the world contending, but I found my attendance so little incouraged, that neither pride nor modesty would suffer me to continue it. When I had once adressed your Lordship in public, I had exhausted all the art of pleasing which a retired and uncourtly Scholar can possess. I had done all that I could, and no Man is well pleased to have his all neglected, be it ever so little.

Seven years, My Lord, have now past since I waited in your outward Rooms or was repulsed from your Door, during which time I have been pushing on my work through difficulties of which It is useless to complain, and have brought it at last to the verge of Publication without one Act of assistance, one word of encouragement, or one smile of favour. Such treatment I did not expect, for I never had a Patron before.

The Shepherd in Virgil grew at last acquainted with Love, and found him a Native of the Rocks.[3] Is not a

LETTERS. **I. The World:** a periodical in which Philip Dormer Stanhope (1694–1773), Fourth Earl of Chesterfield, had recently published two essays praising Johnson's forthcoming *Dictionary*. Chesterfield had been silent on the subject since 1747, when Johnson addressed to him his *Plan of an English Dictionary*. **2. Le . . . Terre:** The Conqueror of the Conqueror of the World. **3. The Shepherd . . . Rocks:** See *Eclogues*, viii. 43. Dryden translates Virgil's line: "I know thee, Love; in Desarts thou wert bred."

Patron, My Lord, one who looks with unconcern on a Man struggling for Life in the water and when he has reached ground encumbers him with help. The notice which you have been pleased to take of my Labours, had it been early, had been kind; but it has been delayed till I am indifferent and cannot enjoy it, till I am solitary and cannot impart it, till I am known and do not want[4] it.

I hope it is no very cinical asperity not to confess obligation where no benefit has been received, or to be unwilling that the Public should consider me as owing that to a Patron, which Providence has enabled me to do for myself.

Having carried on my work thus far with so little obligation to any Favourer of Learning I shall not be disappointed though I should conclude it, if less be possible, with less, for I have been long wakened from that Dream of hope, in which I once boasted myself with so much exultation, My lord Your Lordship's Most humble Most Obedient Servant,

SAM: JOHNSON

[*To Sarah Johnson*]

Jan. 20, 1759.

DEAR HONOURED MOTHER

Neither your condition[5] nor your character make it fit for me to say much. You have been the best mother, and I believe the best woman in the world. I thank you for your indulgence to me, and beg forgiveness of all that I have done ill, and all that I have omitted to do well. God grant you his Holy Spirit, and receive you to everlasting happiness, for Jesus Christ's sake. Amen. Lord Jesus receive your spirit. Amen.

I am, dear, dear mother, Your dutiful son,

SAM: JOHNSON

[*To a Lady*]

June 8, 1762.

MADAM

I hope you will believe that my delay in answering Your letter could proceed only from my unwillingness to destroy any hope that You had form'd. Hope is itself a species of happiness, & perhaps the chief happiness which this World affords, but like all other pleasures immoderately enjoyed, the excesses of hope

must be expiated by pain, & expectations improperly indulged must end in disappointment. If it be asked, what is the improper expectation which it is dangerous to indulge, experience will quickly answer, that it is such expectation, dictated not by reason but by desire; expectation raised not by the common occurrences of life but by the wants of the Expectant; an Expectation that requires the common course of things to be changed, and the general rules of Action to be broken.

When you made Your request to me, You should have considered, Madam, what You were asking. You ask me to solicit a great Man[6] to whom I never spoke, for a young Person whom I had never seen, upon a supposition which I had no means of knowing to be true. There is no reason why amongst all the great, I should chuse to supplicate the Archbishop, nor why among all the possible objects of his bounty, the Archbishop should chuse your Son. I know, Madam, how unwillingly conviction is admitted, when interest opposes it; but surely, Madam, You must allow that there is no reason why that should be done by me which every other man may do with equal reason, and which indeed no man can do properly without some very particular Relation both to the Archbishop & to You. If I could help You in this exigence by any proper means, it would give me pleasure, but this proposal is so very remote from all usual methods, that I cannot comply with it, but at the risque of such answer & suspicions, as I believe you do not wish me to undergo.

I have seen your Son this morning, he seems a pretty Youth, and will perhaps find some better friend than I can procure him, but though he should at last miss the University he may still be wise, useful, & happy.

I am Madam, Your most humble Servant,

SAM: JOHNSON

[*To James Boswell*]

London, Dec. 8, 1763.

DEAR SIR

You are not to think yourself forgotten, or criminally neglected, that you have had yet no letter from me. I love to see my friends, to hear from them, to talk to them, and to talk of them; but it is not without

---

4. **want:** need. 5. **condition:** Mrs. Johnson, who was almost ninety, was dying.

6. **a great Man:** Thomas Secker, Archbishop of Canterbury from 1758 to 1768.

a considerable effort of resolution that I prevail upon myself to write. I would not, however, gratify my own indolence by the omission of any important duty, or any office of real kindness.

To tell you that I am or am not well, that I have or have not been in the country, that I drank your health in the room in which we sat last together, and that your acquaintance continue to speak of you with their former kindness, topicks with which those letters are commonly filled which are written only for the sake of writing, I seldom shall think worth communicating; but if I can have it in my power to calm any harassing disquiet, to excite any virtuous desire, to rectify any important opinion, or fortify any generous resolution, you need not doubt but I shall at least wish to prefer the pleasure of gratifying a friend much less esteemed than yourself, before the gloomy calm of idle vacancy. Whether I shall easily arrive at an exact punctuality of correspondence, I cannot tell. I shall, at present, expect that you will receive this in return for two which I have had from you. The first, indeed, gave me an account so hopeless of the state of your mind, that it hardly admitted or deserved an answer; by the second I was much better pleased; and the pleasure will still be increased by such a narrative of the progress of your studies, as may evince the continuance of an equal and rational application of your mind to some useful enquiry.

You will, perhaps, wish to ask, what study I would recommend. I shall not speak of theology, because it ought not to be considered as a question whether you shall endeavour to know the will of God.

I shall, therefore, consider only such studies as we are at liberty to pursue or to neglect; and of these I know not how you will make a better choice, than by studying the civil law, as your father advises, and the ancient languages, as you had determined for yourself; at least resolve, while you remain in any settled residence, to spend a certain number of hours every day amongst your books. The dissipation of thought, of which you complain, is nothing more than the vacillation of a mind suspended between different motives, and changing its direction as any motive gains or loses strength. If you can but kindle in your mind any strong desire, if you can but keep predominant any wish for some particular excellence or attainment, the gusts of imagination will break away, without any effect upon your conduct, and commonly without any traces left upon the memory.

There lurks, perhaps, in every human heart a desire of distinction, which inclines every man first to hope, and then to believe, that Nature has given him something peculiar to himself. This vanity makes one mind nurse aversions, and another actuate desires, till they rise by art much above their original state of power; and as affectation, in time, improves to habit, they at last tyrannise over him who at first encouraged them only for show. Every desire is a viper in the bosom, who, while he was chill, was harmless; but when warmth gave him strength, exerted it in poison. You know a gentleman, who, when first he set his foot in the gay world, as he prepared himself to whirl in the vortex of pleasure, imagined a total indifference and universal negligence to be the most agreeable concomitants of youth, and the strongest indication of an airy temper and a quick apprehension. Vacant to every object, and sensible of every impulse, he thought that all appearance of diligence would deduct something from the reputation of genius; and hoped that he should appear to attain, amidst all the ease of carelessness and all the tumult of diversion, that knowledge and those accomplishments which mortals of the common fabrick obtain only by mute abstraction and solitary drudgery. He tried this scheme of life awhile, was made weary of it by his sense and his virtue, he then wished to return to his studies; and finding long habits of idleness and pleasure harder to be cured than he expected, still willing to retain his claim to some extraordinary prerogatives, resolved the common consequences of irregularity into an unalterable decree of destiny, and concluded that Nature had originally formed him incapable of rational employment.

Let all such fancies, illusive and destructive, be banished henceforward from your thoughts for ever. Resolve, and keep your resolution; choose, and pursue your choice. If you spend this day in study, you will find yourself still more able to study to-morrow; not that you are to expect that you shall at once obtain a complete victory. Depravity is not very easily overcome. Resolution will sometimes relax, and diligence will sometimes be interrupted; but let no accidental surprize or deviation, whether short or long, dispose you to despondency. Consider these failings as incident to all mankind. Begin again where you left off, and endeavour to avoid the seducements that prevailed over you before.

This, my dear Boswell, is advice which, perhaps, has been often given you, and given you without effect. But this advice, if you will not take from others, you must take from your own reflections, if you purpose to do the duties of the station to which the bounty of Providence has called you.

Let me have a long letter from you as soon as you can. I hope you continue your journal, and enrich it with many observations upon the country in which you reside. It will be a favour if you can get me any books in the Frisick language,[7] and can enquire how the poor are maintained in the Seven Provinces.[8]

I am, dear Sir, Your most affectionate servant,

SAM: JOHNSON

[*To James Boswell*]

Brighthelmstone,[9] *Sept. 9, 1769.*

DEAR SIR

Why do you charge me with unkindness? I have omitted nothing that could do you good, or give you pleasure, unless it be that I have forborne to tell you my opinion of your account of Corsica.[10] I believe my opinion, if you think well of my judgement, might have given you pleasure; but when it is considered how much vanity is excited by praise, I am not sure that it would have done you good. Your History is like other histories, but your Journal is in a very high degree curious and delightful. There is between the history and the journal that difference which there will always be found between notions borrowed from without, and notions generated within. Your history was copied from books; your journal rose out of your own experience and observation. You express images which operated strongly upon yourself, and you have impressed them with great force upon your readers. I know not whether I could name any narrative by which curiosity is better excited, or better gratified.

I am glad that you are going to be married; and as I wish you well in things of less importance, wish you well with proportionate ardour in this crisis of your life. What I can contribute to your happiness, I should be very unwilling to with-hold; for I have always loved and valued you, and shall love you and value you still more, as you become more regular and useful: effects which a happy marriage will hardly fail to produce.

I do not find that I am likely to come back very soon from this place. I shall, perhaps, stay a fortnight longer; and a fortnight is a long time to a lover absent from his mistress. Would a fortnight ever have an end?

I am, dear Sir, | Your most affectionate humble servant,

SAM. JOHNSON.

[*To Hester Maria Thrale*[11]]

Ashbourn, Nov. 2, 1772

DEAR SWEETING

Your pretty letter was too short. If Lucy[12] is not good, you must try to mend her by good advice, and good example, for all the little girls will try to be like you. I am glad to hear of the improvement and prosperity of my hen. Miss Porter[13] has buried her fine black cat. So things come and go. Generations, as Homer says, are but like leaves; and you now see the faded leaves falling about you.

You are sorry to come to town, and I am sorry for dear Granmamma that will be left in the country, be sure that you make my compliments to her.

I am, Dear Miss, Your most obedient servant

SAM: JOHNSON

[*To Mrs. Thrale*]

Skie.[14] *Sep. 21. 1773*

DEAREST MADAM

I am so vexed at the necessity of sending yesterday so short a Letter that I purpose to get a long letter beforehand by writing something every day, which I may the more easily do, as a cold makes me now too deaf to take the usual pleasure in conversation. Lady Macleod is very kind to me, and the place at which we now are, is equal in strength of situation, in the wildness of the adjacent country, and in the plenty and elegance of the domestick entertainment, to a Castle in Gothick romances. The sea with a little Island is

---

7. **Frisick language:** Frisian, the language of Friesland, a province in northern Holland. 8. **Seven Provinces:** the United Provinces of Holland. 9. **Brighthelmstone:** Brighton, a sea resort on the southern coast. 10. **your . . . Corsica:** Boswell's *An Account of Corsica, the Journal of a Tour to That Island, and Memoirs of Pascal Paoli* was published in 1768.

11. **Hester . . . Thrale:** Eight years old in 1772, Hester was the eldest daughter of Mrs. Hester Lynch Thrale (1741–1821), the lively lady in whose household Johnson was entertained almost as a member of the family from 1766 to 1781. Mr. Thrale died in 1781, and Mrs. Thrale incurred the lonely Johnson's severe displeasure by marrying in 1784 Gabriel Piozzi, an Italian musician. 12. **Lucy:** Hester's younger sister, aged three. 13. **Miss Porter:** Lucy Porter, in Lichfield; Johnson's stepdaughter. 14. **Skie:** a large island in northern Scotland.

before us, cascades play within view. Close to the house is the formidable skeleton of an old Castle probably Danish; and the whole mass of building stands upon a protuberance of rock, inaccessible till of late but by a pair of stairs on the sea side, and secure in ancient times against any Enemy that was likely to invade the kingdom of Skie. Macleod has offered me an Island, if it were not too far off I should hardly refuse it; my Island would be pleasanter than Brighthelmston, if you and Master could come to it, but I cannot think it pleasant to live quite alone. Oblitusque meorum, obliviscendus et illis.[15] That I should be elated by the dominion of an Island to forgetfulness of my friends at Streatham, and I hope never to deserve that they should be willing to forget me.

It has happened that I have been often recognized in my journey where I did not expect it. At Aberdeen I found one of my acquaintance Professor of Physick. Turning aside to dine with a country Gentleman, I was owned at a table by one who had seen me at a Philosophical Lecture. At Macdonald's I was claimed by a Naturalist, who wanders about the Islands to pick up curiosities, and I had once in London attracted the notice of Lady Macleod. I will now go on with my Account.

The Highland Girl made tea, and looked and talked not inelegantly. Her Father was by no means an ignorant or a weak man. There were books in the cottage, among which were some volumes of Prideaux's Connexion.[16] This man's conversation we were glad of while we staid. He had been *out* as they call it, in forty five,[17] and still retained his old opinions. He was going to America, because his rent was raised beyond what he thought himself able to pay.

At night our beds were made, but we had some difficulty in persuading ourselves to lye down in them, though we had put on our own sheets. At last we ventured, and I slept very soundly, in the vale called Glenmorison amidst the rocks and mountains. Next morning our Landlord liked us so well, that he walked some miles with us for our company through a country so wild and barren that the proprietor does not with all his pressure upon his tenants raise more than four hundred a year from near an hundred square miles, or sixty thousand acres. He let us know that he had forty head of black cattle, an hundred Goats, and an hundred sheep upon a farm which he remembred let at five pounds a year, but for which he now paid twenty. He told us some stories of their march into England. At last he left us, and we went forward, winding among mountains sometimes green and sometimes naked, commonly so steep as not easily to be climbed by the greatest vigour and activity. Our way was often crossed by little rivulets, and we were entertained with small streams trickling from the rocks, which after heavy rains must be tremendous torrents.

About noon, we came to a small glen, so they call a valley, which compared with other places appeared rich and fertile. Here our Guides desired us to stop that the horses might graze, for the journey was very laborious, and no more grass would be found. We made no difficulty of compliance, and I sat down to take notes on a green bank, with a small stream running at my feet, in the midst of savage solitude, with Mountains before me, and on either hand covered with heath. I looked round me, and wondered that I was not more affected, but the mind is not at all times equally ready to be put in motion. If my Mistress, and Master, and Queeny[18] had been there we should have produced some reflections among us either poetical or philosophical, for though *Solitude* be *the nurse of woe*,[19] conversation is often the parent of remarks and discoveries.

In about an hour we remounted, and persued our journey. The lake by which we had travelled from some time ended in a river, which we passed by a bridge and came to another Glen with a collection of huts, called Auknashealds, the huts were generally built of clods of earth held together by the intertexture of vegetable fibres, of which earth there are great levels in Scotland which they call mosses. Moss in Scotland, is Bog in Ireland, and Moss trooper is Bog trotter. There was however one hut built of loose

---

15. Oblitusque . . . illis: "My own forgetting, by my own forgot" (Horace, *Epistles*, I. ii. 9). **16. Prideaux's Connexion:** *The Old and New Testament Connected in the History of the Jews* (1716–18) by Humphrey Prideaux (1648–1724). **17. forty five:** In 1745 Charles Edward Stuart, the so-called Young Pretender to the throne of Great Britain, landed in the Scottish Highlands from France and led an insurgent march on England. His forces penetrated as far as Derby but were there forced back to be finally defeated at the Battle of Culloden in 1746. The Jacobite Rising, the intent of which was to restore the Stuart monarchy, was often called simply The Forty-Five.

18. Queeny: Johnson's nickname for Hester Maria Thrale. **19. Solitude . . . woe:** See Thomas Parnell's *Hymn to Contentment*, l. 24. (See the selection from Parnell in Part Three.)

stones piled up with great thickness into a strong though not solid wall. From this house we obtained some great pails of milk, and having brought bread with us, were very liberally regaled. The Inhabitants, a very coarse tribe, ignorant of any language but Earse,[20] gathered so fast about us, that if we had not had Highlanders with us, they might have caused more alarm than pleasure. They are called the clan of Macrae.

We have been told that nothing gratified the Highlanders so much as snuff and tobacco, and had accordingly stored ourselves with both at fort Augustus. Boswel opened his treasure and gave them each a piece of tobacco roll. We had more bread than we could eat for the present, and were more liberal than provident. Boswel cut it in slices and gave each of them an opportunity of tasting wheaten bread for the first time. I then got some halfpence for a shilling and made up the deficiencies of Boswels distribution, who had given some money among the children. We then directed that the mistress of the stone house should be asked what we must pay her, she who perhaps had never sold any thing but cattle before, knew not, I believe, well what to ask, and referred herself to us. We obliged her to make some demand, and our Highlanders settled the account with her at a shilling. One of the men advised her, with the cunning that clowns never can be without, to ask more but she said that a shilling was enough. We gave her half a crown and she offered part of it again. The Macraes were so well pleased with our behaviour, that they declared it the best day they had seen since the time of the old Laird of MacLeod, who I suppose, like us, stopped in their valley, as he was travelling to Skie.

We were mentioning this view of the Highlander's life at Macdonald's, and mentioning the Macraes with some degree of pity, when a Highland Lady informed us, that we might spare our tenderness, for she doubted not, but the Woman who supplied us with milk, was Mistress of thirteen or fourteen milch cows.

I cannot forbear to interrupt my Narrative. Boswel, with some of his troublesome kindness, has informed this family, and reminded me that the eighteenth of September is my birthday. The return of my Birthday, if I remember it, fills me with thoughts which it seems to be the general care of humanity to escape. I can now look back upon threescore and four years, in which

little has been done, and little has been enjoyed, a life diversified by misery, spent part in the sluggishness of penury, and part under the violence of pain, in gloomy discontent, or importunate distress. But perhaps I am better than I should have been, if I had been less afflicted. With this I will try to be content.

In proportion as there is less pleasure in retrospective considerations the mind is more disposed to wander forward into futurity, but at sixty four what promises, however liberal of imaginary good, can Futurity venture to make. Yet something will be always promised, and some promises will always be credited. I am hoping, and I am praying that I may live better in the time to come, whether long or short, than I have yet lived, and in the solace of that hope endeavour to repose. Dear Queeney's day is next, I hope, she at sixty four will have less to regret.

I will now complain no more, but tell my Mistress of my travels.

After we left the Macraes, we travelled on through a country like that which we passed in the morning, the highlands are very uniform, for there is little variety in universal barrenness. The rocks however are not all naked, some have grass on their sides, and Birches and Alders on their tops, and in the vallies are often broad and clear streams which have little depth, and commonly run very quick. The channels are made by the violence of wintry floods, the quickness of the stream is in proportion to the declivity of the descent, and the breadth of the channel makes the water shallow in a dry season.

There are Red Deer and Roebucks in the mountains, but we found only Goats in the road, and had very little entertainment as we travelled either for the eye or ear. There are, I fancy, no singing birds in the Highlands.

Towards Night we came to a very formidable Hill called Rattiken, which we climbed with more difficulty than we had yet experienced, and at last came to Glanelg a place on the Seaside opposite to Skie. We were by this time weary and disgusted, nor was our humour much mended, by an inn, which, though it was built with lime and slate, the highlander's description of a house which he thinks magnificent, had neither wine, bread, eggs, nor any thing that we could eat or drink. When we were taken up stairs, a dirty fellow bounced out of the bed in which one of us was to lie. Boswel blustered, but nothing could be got. At last a Gentleman in the Neighbourhood who heard of our arrival sent us rum and white sugar. Boswel was

---

20. Earse: (Erse) the form of the Gaelic language spoken in the Scottish Highlands.

now provided for in part, and the Landlord prepared some mutton chops, which we could not eat, and killed two Hens, of which Boswel made his servant broil a limb, with what effect I know not. We had a lemon, and a piece of bread, which supplied me with my supper.

When the repast was ended, we began to deliberate upon bed. Mrs Boswel had warned us that we should *catch something*, and had given us Sheets for our security; for Sir Alexander and Lady Macdonald, she said, came back from Skie, so scratching themselves—. I thought sheets a slender defence, against the confederacy with which we were threatned, and by this time our highlanders had found a place where they could get some hay; I ordered hay to be laid thick upon the bed, and slept upon it in my great coat. Boswel laid sheets upon his hay, and reposed in Linen like a Gentleman. The horses were turned out to grass, with a man to watch them. The hill Ratiken, and the inn at Glanelg, are the only things of which we or travellers yet more delicate, could find any pretensions to complain.

Sept. 2. I rose rustling from the hay, and went to tea, which I forget whether we found or brought. We saw the Isle of Skie before us darkening the horizon with its rocky coast. A boat was procured, and we launched into one of the Straits of the Atlantick Ocean. We had a passage of about twelve miles to the point where Sir Alexander resided, having come from his Seat in the midland part, to a small house on the shore, as we believe, that he might with less reproach entertain us meanly. If he aspired to meanness his retrograde ambition was completely gratified, but he did not succeed equally in escaping reproach. He had no cook, nor, I suppose, much provision, nor had the Lady the common decencies of her tea table. We picked up our Sugar with our fingers. Boswel was very angry, and reproached him with his improper parsimony. I did not much reflect upon the conduct of a man with whom I was not likely to converse as long at any other time.

You will now expect that I should give you some account of the Isle of Skie, of which though I have been twelve days upon it, I have little to say. It is an Island perhaps fifty miles long, so much indented by inlets of the Sea, that there is no part of it removed from the water more than six miles. No part that I have seen is plain you are always climbing or descending, and every step is upon rock or mire. A walk upon plowed ground in England is a dance upon carpets, compared to the toilsome drudgery, of wandering in Skie. There is neither town nor village in the Island, nor have I seen any house but Macleod's, that is not much below your habitation at Brighthelmston. In the mountains there are Stags and Roebucks, but no hares and few rabbits, nor have I seen any thing that interested me, as Zoologist, except an Otter, bigger than I thought an otter could have been.

You are perhaps imagining that I am withdrawn from the gay and the busy world into regions of peace and pastoral felicity, and am enjoying the reliques of the golden age; that I am surveying Nature's magnificence from a mountain, or remarking her minuter beauties on the flowery bank of a winding rivulet, that I am invigorating myself in the sunshine, or delighting my imagination with being hidden from the invasion of human evils and human passions, in the darkness of a Thicket, that I am busy in gathering shells and pebbles on the Shore, or contemplative on a rock, from which I look upon the water and consider how many waves are rolling between me and Streatham.

The use of travelling is to regulate imagination by reality, and instead of thinking how things may be, to see them as they are. Here are mountains which I should once have climbed, but to climb steeps is now very laborious, and to descend them dangerous, and I am now content with knowing that by a scrambling up a rock, I shall only see other rocks, and a wider circuit of barren desolation. Of streams we have here a sufficient number, but they murmur not upon pebbles but upon rocks; of flowers, if Chloris[21] herself were here, I could present her only with the bloom of Heath. Of Lawns and Thickets, he must read, that would know them, for here is little sun and no shade. On the sea I look from my window, but am not much tempted to the shore for since I came to this Island, almost every Breath of air has been a storm, and what is worse, a storm with all its severity, but without its magnificence, for the sea is here so broken into channels, that there is not a sufficient volume of water either for lofty surges, or loud roar.

On Sept. 6. We left Macdonald, to visit Raarsa, the Island which I have already mentioned. We were to cross part of Skie on horseback, a mode of travelling very uncomfortable, for the road is so narrow, where any road can be found that only one can go, and so craggy that the attention can never be remitted, it

---

21. **Chloris:** the Greek goddess of spring and flowers.

allows therefore neither the gayety of conversation nor the laxity of solitude, nor has it in itself the amusement of much variety, as it affords only all the possible transpositions of Bog, Rock, and Rivulet. Twelve Miles, by computation, make a reasonable journey for a day.

At night we came to a tenants house of the first rank of tenants where we were entertained better than the Landlords. There were books, both English and Latin. Company gathered about us, and we heard some talk of the Second sight[22] and some talk of the events of forty five, a year which will not soon be forgotten among the Islanders. The next day we were confined by a storm, the company, I think, encreased and our entertainment was not only hospitable but elegant. At night, a Minister's sister in very fine Brocade, sung Earse songs. I wished to know the meaning, but the Highlanders are not much used to scholastick questions, and no translation could be obtained.

Next day, Sept. 8. The weather allowed us to depart, a good boat was provided us, and we went to Raarsa, under the conduct of Mr Malcolm Macleod, a Gentleman who conducted Prince Charles through the mountains in his distresses. The prince, he says, was more active than himself, they were at least one night, without any shelter.

The wind blew enough to give the boat a kind of dancing agitation, and in about three or four hours we arrived at Raarsa, where we were met by the Laird and his friends upon the Shore. Raarsa, for such is his title, is Master of two Islands, upon the smaller of which, called Rona, he has only flocks and herds. Rona gives title to his eldest Son. The money which he raises by rent from all his dominions which contain at least fifty thousand acres, is not believed to exceed two hundred and fifty pounds, but as he keeps a large farm in his own hands, he sells every year great numbers of cattle which he adds to his revenue, and his table is furnished from the Farm and from the sea with little expence, except for those things this country does not produce, and of those he is very liberal. The Wine circulates vigorously, and the tea and Chocolate and Coffee, however they are got are always at hand. I am Madam Your most obedient servant

SAM: JOHNSON

We are this morning trying to get out of Skie.

22. the Second sight: the capacity to see future or distant events, a talent sometimes attributed to the Highlanders.

[*To James Macpherson*[23]]

Jan. 20. 1775

Mr James Macpherson—I received your foolish and impudent note. Whatever insult is offered me I will do my best to repel, and what I cannot do for myself the law will do for me. I will not desist from detecting what I think a cheat, from any fear of the menaces of a Ruffian.

You want me to retract. What shall I retract? I thought your book an imposture from the beginning, I think it upon yet surer reasons an imposture still. For this opinion I give the publick my reasons which I here dare you to refute.

But however I may despise you, I reverence truth and if you can prove the genuineness of the work I will confess it. Your rage I defy, your abilities since your Homer[24] are not so formidable, and what I have heard of your morals disposes me to pay regard not to what you shall say, but to what you can prove.

You may print this if you will.

SAM: JOHNSON

[*To Dr. William Dodd*[25]]

June 26, 1777.

DEAR SIR,

That which is appointed to all men is now coming upon you. Outward circumstances, the eyes and the thoughts of men, are below the notice of an immortal being about to stand the trial for eternity, before the Supreme Judge of heaven and earth. Be comforted: your crime, morally or religiously considered, has no

23. James Macpherson: (1736–96), a Scot who published a number of narrative fragments in "poetic prose" purported to be translations from the Erse of an ancient poet named Ossian. Johnson, who found the material "a mere unconnected rhapsody," expressed his disbelief and his contempt in *A Journey to the Western Islands of Scotland*, which was published in January, 1775. His suggestion that Macpherson exhibit the original Ossianic manuscripts was met by a threatening letter. **24. your Homer:** Macpherson had published a prose translation of the *Iliad* in 1773. **25. Dr. . . . Dodd:** (1729–77), a clergyman who had once been tutor to Lord Chesterfield's godson. Dr. Dodd was convicted of forging Chesterfield's name on a bond for over four thousand pounds. Forgery was a capital crime, and he was hanged the day after Johnson wrote this letter. Johnson, who thought Dodd's punishment likely to damage the Church, intervened on his behalf by writing for him, even to the King, petitioning that the sentence of public hanging be commuted to exile.

very deep dye of turpitude. It corrupted no man's principles; it attacked no man's life. It involved only a temporary and reparable injury. Of this, and of all other sins, you are earnestly to repent; and may God, who knoweth our frailty and desireth not our death, accept your repentance, for the sake of his Son JESUS CHRIST our Lord.

In requital of those well-intended offices which you are pleased so emphatically to acknowledge,[26] let me beg that you make in your devotions one petition for my eternal welfare.

I am, dear Sir, Your affectionate servant,

SAM. JOHNSON.

[*To Mrs. Thrale*]

Lichfield Oct. 27. 1777

DEAR MADAM

You talk of writing and writing as if you had all the writing to yourself. If our Correspondence were printed I am sure Posterity, for Posterity is always the authours favourite, would say that I am a good writer too. Anch' io sonô Pittore.[27] To sit down so often with nothing to say, to say something so often, almost without consciousness of saying, and without any remembrance of having said, is a power of which I will not violate my modesty by boasting, but I do not believe that every body has it.

Some when they write to their friends are all affection, some are wise and sententious, some strain their powers for efforts of gayety, some write news, and some write secrets, but to make a letter without affection, without wisdom, without gayety, without news, and without a secret is, doubtless, the great epistolick art.

In a Man's Letters you know, Madam, his soul lies naked, his letters are only the mirrour of his breast, whatever passes within him is shown undisguised in its natural process. Nothing is inverted, nothing distorted, you see systems in their elements, you discover actions in their motives.

Of this great truth sounded by the knowing to the ignorant, and so echoed by the ignorant to the

knowing, what evidence have you now before you. Is not my soul laid open in these veracious pages? do not you see me reduced to my first principles? This is the pleasure of corresponding with a friend, where doubt and distrust have no place, and everything is said as it is thought. The original Idea is laid down in its simple purity, and all the supervenient conceptions, are spread over it stratum super stratum,[28] as they happen to be formed. These are the letters by which souls are united, and by which Minds naturally in unison move each other as they are moved themselves. I know, dearest Lady, that in the perusal of this such is the consanguinity of our intellects, you will be touched as I am touched. I have indeed concealed nothing from you, nor do I expect ever to repent of having thus opened my heart.

I am, Madam, Your most humble servant,

SAM: JOHNSON

[*To James Boswell*]

March 14, 1781.

DEAR SIR

I hoped you had got rid of all this hypocrisy of misery.[29] What have you to do with Liberty and Necessity? Or what more than to hold your tongue about it? Do not doubt but I shall be most heartily glad to see you here again, for I love every part about you but your affectation of distress.

I have at last finished my Lives, and have laid up for you a load of copy, all out of order, so that it will amuse you a long time to set it right. Come to me, my dear Bozzy, and let us be as happy as we can. We will go again to the Mitre,[30] and talk old times over.

I am, dear Sir, Yours, affectionately,

SAM. JOHNSON

[*To Mrs. Thrale*]

Bolt Court Fleet Street June 19. 1783

DEAR MADAM

I am sitting down in no chearful solitude to write a narrative which would once have affected you with tenderness and sorrow, but which you will perhaps

---

26. **those . . . acknowledge:** Dodd had written from prison the day before: "Accept, thou *great* and *good* heart, my earnest and fervent thanks and prayers for all thy benevolent and kind efforts in my behalf." 27. **Anch' . . . Pittore:** "I too am a painter" (doubtfully attributed to Correggio, who is said to have made this remark upon seeing a painting by Raphael).

28. **stratum . . . stratum:** layer upon layer. 29. **this . . . misery:** Boswell had written in February to complain of melancholy; he said that he was worried about the question of free will *versus* determinism. 30. **the Mitre:** a London tavern.

pass over now with the careless glance of frigid indifference. For this diminution of regard however, I know not whether I ought to blame You, who may have reasons which I cannot know, and I do not blame myself who have for a great part of human life done You what good I could, and have never done you evil.

I had been disordered in the usual way, and had been relieved by the usual methods, by opium and catharticks, but had rather lessened my dose of opium.

On Monday the 16. I sat for my picture, and walked a considerable way with little inconvenience. In the afternoon and evening I felt myself light and easy, and began to plan schemes of life. Thus I went to bed, and in a short time waked and sat up as has been long my custom, when I felt a confusion and indistinctness in my head which lasted, I suppose about half a minute; I was alarmed and prayed God, that however he might afflict my body he would spare my understanding. This prayer, that I might try the integrity of my faculties I made in Latin verse. The lines were not very good, but I knew them not to be very good, I made them easily, and concluded myself to be unimpaired in my faculties.

Soon after I perceived that I had suffered a paralytick stroke, and that my Speech was taken from me. I had no pain, and so little dejection in this dreadful state that I wondered at my own apathy, and considered that perhaps death itself when it should come, would excite less horrour than seems now to attend it.

In order to rouse the vocal organs I took two drams. Wine has been celebrated for the production of eloquence; I put myself into violent motion, and, I think, repeated it. But all was vain; I then went to bed, and, strange as it may seem, I think, slept. When I saw light, it was time to contrive what I should do. Though God stopped my speech he left me my hand, I enjoyed a mercy which was not granted to my Dear Friend Laurence,[31] who now perhaps overlooks me as I am writing and rejoices that I have what he wanted. My first note was necessarily to my servant, who came in talking, and could not immediately comprehend why he should read what I put into his hands.

I then wrote a card to Mr Allen, that I might have a discreet friend at hand to act as occasion should require. In penning this note I had some difficulty, my hand,

I knew not how nor why, made wrong letters. I then wrote to Dr Taylor to come to me, and bring Dr Heberden, and I sent to Dr Brocklesby, who is my neighbour. My Physicians are very friendly and very disinterested,[32] and give me great hopes, but you may imagine my situation. I have so far recovered my vocal powers, as to repeat the Lord's Prayer with no very imperfect articulation. My memory, I hope, yet remains as it was. But such an attack produces solicitude for the safety of every Faculty.

How this will be received by You I know not, I hope You will sympathise with me, but perhaps

> My Mistress gracious, mild, and good,
> Cries, Is he dumb? 'tis time he shou'd.[33]

But can this be possible, I hope it cannot. I hope that what, when I could speak, I spoke of You, and to You, will be in a sober and serious hour remembered by You, and surely it cannot be remembered but with some degree of kindness. I have loved you with virtuous affection, I have honoured You with sincere Esteem. Let not all our endearment be forgotten, but let me have in this great distress your pity and your prayers. You see I yet turn to You with my complaints as a settled and unalienable friend, do not, do not drive me from You, for I have not deserved either neglect or hatred.

To the Girls, who do not write often, for Susy has written only once, and Miss Thrale owes me a letter, I earnestly recommend as their Guardian and Friend, that They remember their Creator in the days of their Youth.

I suppose you may wish to know how my disease is treated by the physitians. They put a blister upon my back, and two from my ear to my throat, one on a side. The blister on the back had done little, and those on the throat have not risen. I bullied, and bounced, (it sticks to our last sand)[34] and compelled the apothecary to make his salve according to the Edinburgh dispensatory, that it might adhere better. I have two on now of my own prescription. They likewise give me salt of hartshorn, which I take with no great

32. **disinterested:** "superior to regard of private advantage; not influenced by private profit" (Johnson's *Dictionary*). 33. **My . . . shou'd:** Cf. Swift, *Verses on the Death of Dr. Swift*, ll. 181–82, in Part Two. 34. **it . . . sand:** an allusion to the first of Pope's *Moral Essays*, l. 225, where Pope, speaking of each man's ruling passion, insists that it remains constant until the last sand of life has run through the hourglass.

31. **Laurence:** Dr. Thomas Lawrence (1711–83) had died on June 6, 1783, following a paralytic stroke.

confidence, but am satisfied that what can be done is done for me.

O God, give me comfort and confidence in Thee, forgive my sins, and if it be thy good pleasure, relieve my diseases for Jesus Christs sake, Amen.

I am almost ashamed of this querulous letter, but now it is written, let it go.

I am, Madam Your most humble servant

SAM: JOHNSON.

[*To Mrs. Thrale*]

July 2. 1784

MADAM

If I interpret your letter right, you are ignominiously married,[35] if it is yet undone, let us once talk together. If you have abandoned your children and your religion, God forgive your wickedness; if you have forfeited your Fame, and your country, may your folly do no further mischief.

If the last act is yet to do, I, who have loved you, esteemed you, reverenced you, and served you, I who long thought you the first of human kind, entreat that before your fate is irrevocable, I may once more see you. I was, I once was, | Madam, most truly yours.

SAM: JOHNSON.

I will come down if you permit it.

[*To Mrs. Thrale*]

London July 8. 1784

DEAR MADAM

What you have done, however I may lament it, I have no pretence to resent, as it has not been injurious

to me. I therefore breathe out one sigh more of tenderness perhaps useless, but at least sincere.

I wish that God may grant you every blessing, that you may be happy in this world for its short continuance, and eternally happy in a better state. and whatever I can contribute to your happiness, I am ready to repay for that kindness which soothed twenty years of a life radically wretched.

Do not think slightly of the advice which I now presume to offer. Prevail upon Mr. Piozzi to settle in England. You may live here with more dignity than in Italy, and with more security. Your rank will be higher, and your fortune more under your own eye. I desire not to detail all my reasons; but every argument of prudence and interest is for England, and only some phantoms of imagination seduce you to Italy.

I am afraid, however, that my counsel is vain, yet I have eased my heart by giving it.

When Queen Mary took the resolution of sheltering herself in England, the Archbishop of St. Andrew's attempting to dissuade her, attended on her journey and when they came to the irremeable[36] stream that separated the two kingdoms, walked by her side into the water, in the middle of which he seized her bridle, and with earnestness proportioned to her danger and his own affection, pressed her to return. The Queen went forward.———If the parallel reaches thus far; may it go no further. The tears stand in my eyes.

I am going into Derbyshire, and hope to be followed by your good wishes, for I am with great affection | Your most humble servant,

SAM: JOHNSON

Any letters that come for me hither, will be sent me.

35. **you . . . married:** She was not married to Piozzi yet; they married on July 23.

36. **irremeable:** "admitting no return" (Johnson's *Dictionary*).

James Boswell

1740–1795

James Boswell was the eldest son of a stern and sober Scottish judge, Alexander Boswell, Laird of Auchinleck, who all his life gazed with chill disapproval on his son's passions for notoriety and for the company of famous men. From 1753 to 1760 Boswell studied classics and law at the universities of Edinburgh and Glasgow, and, although his father wanted him to settle down in Scotland as a lawyer, he himself was determined to pursue the career of a rake in the infinitely more glamorous London. With this object in view, he set off in 1762 to solicit a commission in the Foot Guards, a gaudy London military unit. He failed to secure a commission, but while gallivanting about London in 1763 he attained something better: the friendship of the fifty-four-year-old Samuel Johnson, whose *Rambler* (1750–52) and *Rasselas* (1759) Boswell had often consulted in his search for principles of ethical regularity. Although the young Boswell was capable of alarming erotic and alcoholic excesses and although his naiveté and ambition impelled him to play the fool very frequently, most of his acquaintances found him an extremely attractive young man, and Johnson, who did not give his friendship readily to either fools or bores, saw in this giddy but forthright young person a charming companion. "Give me your hand," said Johnson during their fourth meeting; "I have taken a liking to you." Henceforth Boswell visited Johnson as often as possible, and, delighted by Johnson's vigorous and copious talk, which he soon learned to record very accurately at the end of a day, he refined his skill in asking embarrassing questions productive of pungent Johnsonian responses.

During the year 1763–64 Boswell placated his father by enduring a year of further legal study in Utrecht, where he found himself sometimes reduced to total immobility by melancholy. To cheer himself up, he embarked on the Grand Tour of Europe. In the character of "Baron Boswell" he circulated briskly through the German courts. Although he was disappointed in his plan to introduce himself to Frederick the Great, he did manage interviews with Rousseau and Voltaire, whom he alternately bored and astonished with sprightly exhibitions of his vanity. "What a singular being do I find myself!" he paused to reflect after his visit to Voltaire. Proceeding southward, he toured the island of Corsica and there made the acquaintance of Pasquale di Paoli, a newsworthy revolutionary general. But in 1766 these heady adventures were abruptly terminated. The Laird of Auchinleck insisted that his son return now to a responsible life, and Boswell sadly exchanged the delights of Continental travel for the rigors of the Scottish bar.

But he burned for celebrity. He exploited his visit to Paoli by writing *An Account of Corsica* (1768), which became a sensationally popular book. Widely translated, it had a better sale (10,000 copies) in Boswell's lifetime than either of his Johnsonian works and brought him a welcome notoriety as "Corsica Boswell." "I am really the *Great Man* now," he observed with satisfaction. After such a triumph, he chafed more than ever under the routine of his very undistinguished Edinburgh law practice, and it was with exultation that he escaped momentarily in 1773 to conduct Johnson on an unlikely tour of the primitive Hebridean islands.

Boswell's father died in 1782 and Johnson in 1784. Deprived of these two models of stability, Boswell grew ever more extravagant and pathetic in his dissipations: to Horace Walpole he was known as "that sot." He started now to organize his massive accumulation of Johnsoniana, which consisted primarily of records of Johnson's talk that he had been industriously laying up in his intimate journals for over twenty years. Johnson's death had created a clamor for reminiscences of him, and by revising one of his journals, Boswell produced a novel work, *The Journal of a Tour to the Hebrides with Samuel Johnson, LL.D.* (1785); its dispassionate accuracy delighted and scandalized the public. This success stimulated him to labor at the immense biography of Johnson he had long contemplated; the magnitude of the task, however, frequently reduced him to despair. Faced both with the fantastic volume of his materials and with his own rigid standards of accuracy and order, he sometimes came near to breaking down altogether. "Sorted till I was stupefied," he tells his journal after one especially disheartening day, and on another occasion he notes, "I was so depressed that the tears run down my cheeks." But he persevered somehow, often with the perhaps crucial moral support of his old friend and Johnson's, Edmond Malone, and in 1791, after postponements and delays, his masterpiece, *The Life of Samuel Johnson, LL.D.*, appeared. Boswell lived only four more years—years darkened by compulsive drinking and squalid sexual dissipation.

Writing early in his life to his friend William Temple, Boswell declared, "Sometimes I think myself good for nothing, and sometimes the finest fellow in the world. . . . Good heaven! what is Boswell?" The answer to this perplexing question he sought constantly through painful self-analysis, and he often attempted to identify and fix his erratic character by imitating various respected elders. "Be Father," he exhorts himself in one memorandum; in another, "Be Johnson"; again, he commands, "Be Rock of Gibraltar." Although he undeniably delighted to associate with Johnson because of his fame, he also loved Johnson for trying to teach him, through conversation and letters, a few precious principles of self-restraint.

A conscious egoist as well as a lawyer trained in the value of written evidence, Boswell was a scrupulous accumulator of personal documents. After the age of thirteen he apparently never threw away a scrap of paper even remotely connected with "that favorite subject, Myself." He was convinced that no experience became wholly real unless he wrote it down. "I should live no more than I can record," he observes; "There is a waste of good if it be not preserved." Thousands of Boswell's personal papers, stored in an ebony cabinet, an old croquet box, and a stable loft in the houses of his descendants and his executor, were discovered between 1920 and 1949. This material, now at Yale University, fully records the most private transactions of his life. As a result of the surprising recovery of his personal archives, which for over a century had been regarded as permanently lost, the modern reader is in a position to know James Boswell more intimately than any other literary figure.

F. A. Pottle's *The Literary Career of James Boswell* (1929) provides bibliography together with illuminating commentary. Boswell's Johnsonian works are best read in F. A. Pottle and C. H. Bennett's edition of *The Journal of a Tour to the Hebrides* (1936) and G. B. Hill and L. F. Powell's edition of *The Life of Johnson* (6 vols., 1934–50). *The Life of Johnson* is often reprinted in inexpensive editions; the one-volume edition by R. W. Chapman (1953) contains a very full index. The mass of recently discovered Boswell papers can be studied in *The Private Papers of James Boswell*, ed. Geoffrey Scott and F. A. Pottle (18 vols., 1928–34); a more accessible reading version is provided by The Yale Editions of the Private Papers of James Boswell, of which *Boswell's London Journal, 1762–1763* (1950) and *Boswell on the Grand Tour: Germany and Switzerland, 1764* (1953), both edited by Pottle, are especially interesting. C. B. Tinker has edited Boswell's *Letters* (2 vols., 1924) and has interpreted Boswell sympathetically in *Young Boswell* (1922). The two-volume biography by Pottle and Frank Brady (Vol. I, 1966) is the most authoritative. The essay "Boswell's Boswell," in B. H. Bronson's *Johnson Agonistes and Other Essays* (1946), explores Boswell's character with sensitivity.

FROM

[JOURNAL]

Boswell began keeping a candid and accurate journal at the age of eighteen, and he journalized conscientiously for the rest of his life. His private journal, he came to believe, was his most important activity: his major published works consist largely of pieces carved from his continuous life-record and then arranged and polished. In recording conversations, he did not, as some detractors have imagined, scribble away in public. He wrote nothing down at the time, but he remembered everything. Later (frequently the same night) and in private, he wrote sketchy but precise notes of the day's proceedings, recording not only the exact words he had heard but also important minute particulars of dress, gesture, and tone of voice. He trained himself to observe specific details and to recall them when writing his notes: "With how small a speck," he writes, "does a Painter give life to an eye." Later—sometimes several weeks later—he wrote from his notes the carefully shaped accounts in his journal. Johnson, who encouraged him to keep a journal, pointed out that he could always instruct a friend to burn it after his death. But Boswell was horrified by the prospect of his life disappearing up some chimney. He writes in 1763, "I have at present

such an affection for this my journal that it shocks me to think of burning it. I rather encourage the idea of having it carefully laid up among the archives of Auchinleck." It remained hidden in Boswell's archives until the twentieth century.

Much of the following selection was originally written in very imperfect French. Geoffrey Scott, the original editor of Boswell's private papers, not only translated most of the French but also added in the conversations the names of the speakers (as Boswell does in his Johnsonian works). The text is from *The Private Papers of James Boswell from Malahide Castle in the Collection of Lt.-Colonel Ralph Heyward Isham*, ed. Geoffrey Scott and F. A. Pottle (18 vols., 1928–34). Scott's translation of Boswell's French has been slightly revised.

[Neuchâtel, Switzerland] Monday 3 December [1764].

I let Jacob[1] go for a week to see his Relations, which made him very happy. One great Object which I have ever had in view since I left Britain, has been to obtain the Acquaintance, and if possible the regard, of

---

JOURNAL. **1. Jacob:** Jacob Hänni, Boswell's Swiss servant.

Rousseau.[2] I was informed that he lived in a wild Valley, five leagues from Neufchâtel. I set out early this morning, mounted on a little horse with a *Reysesac*,[3] which held some shirts. I was joined by Abraham François, a merchant here. My horse was lazy; he lent me a spur and a whip, and on we jogged very cordially. He taught me a French Song, "*Sous le nom de l'Amitié, Phillis Je vous adore*"[4] to a Minuet tune. I amused my self with him; and this amusement formed an excellent Contrast to the great object which occupied my mind. We had a fine, hard road amidst Mountains covered with snow. We stopped at Bro, the halfway Inn. M. Sando, the Landlord, had a handsom daughter, very lively and very talkative, or rather chatty, to give the Young Lady a lighter word. She told us, "*Monsieur*[5] *Rousseau vient souvent passer quelques jours ici avec sa Gouvernante, Mademoiselle Vasseur.*[6] *C'est l'homme le plus aimable. Il a une belle Physionomie. Mais il n'aime pas qu'on vienne le regarder comme un Homme à deux têtes. Mon Dieu! la curiosité des Gens est bien grande. Il y a tant tant du monde qui vient pour le voire; et souvent il ne veut pas le recevoir. Il est malade, et il ne veut pas être incommodé. Voilà un Clus où Je suis allé avec lui et Mademoiselle Vasseur. Nous y avons diné. Il se promène dans ces lieux sauvages toute*

une journée. Des Messieurs qui sont venus ici m'ont demandé mille questions. 'Et sa Gouvernante, est elle jeune? est elle jolie?'" All this chat of Mademoiselle helped to frighten me. There was here a Stone-cutter who had wrought for Voltaire.[7] The most stupid of human Beings will remember some Anecdote or other of a Great man whom he has had occasion to see. This Stone cutter told me, "*Monsieur, il y avoit un Cheval à tirer un Char à Fernier, et M. Voltaire disoit toujours, 'Pauvre Cheval! vous êtes maigre, vous êtes comme moi.'*"[8] Any trifle of such a Genius has a value. Abraham François and I drank a glass of good wine, and pursued our journey. We passed one Place exactly like Gillikranky[9] and another where a groupe of broken rocks seemed every moment ready to tumble down upon us. It will most certainly tumble e'er long. M. Rousseau lives in the Village of Môtiers. A league on this side of it, Abraham parted from me after I had returned him his whip and his spur. I advanced with a kind of pleasing trepidation. I wished that I might not see Rousseau till the moment that I had permission to wait upon him. I perceived a white house with green window-boards. He mentions such a one in *Emile*. I imagined it might perhaps be his, and turned away my eyes from it. I rode calmly down the street, and put up at the *Maison de Village*. This Inn is kept by Madame Grande Pierre, a Widow, and her two daughters, fat, motherly Maidens. The eldest received me. I told her, "*J'ai donné permission à mon Domestique d'aller voir ses amis et Parents. Je suis donc seul. Il faut que vous ayez bien soin de moi.*"[10] Said she, "*Nous ferons notre mieux.*"[11] I asked for M. Rousseau. I found he kept himself very quiet here as My Landlady had little or nothing to chatter concerning him. I had heard all that could be said as to his being difficult of access. My Lord Marischal[12] had given me

2. **Rousseau:** Jean-Jacques Rousseau (1712–78), French philosopher and reformer; his antimonarchist and antiecclesiastical writings called into question most of the conservative ideas of his time. He had just attained spectacular public notice by producing during 1761 and 1762 three revolutionary books: *Julie, ou la nouvelle Héloïse*, a sentimental antisocial romance; *Le Contrat social*, a political treatise assuming the ultimate sovereignty of the people; and *Emile*, a treatise on natural education. The anti-Christian tendency of Book IV of *Emile* caused the public condemnation of the work by the Parliament of Paris; to escape arrest Rousseau was obliged to flee from Paris to Switzerland. He had been living in exile at Môtiers for about two years when Boswell sought him out. 3. **Reysesac:** portmanteau. 4. **Sous . . . adore:** "In the name of friendship, Phyllis, I adore you." 5. **Monsieur . . . jolie:** Monsieur Rousseau often comes to spend a few days here with his housekeeper, Mademoiselle Vasseur. He is a very amiable man. He has a handsome face. But he does not like people to come stare at him as if he were a man with two heads. Heavens! some people's curiosity is amazing. Many, many people come to see him; and often he will not receive them. He is ill, and he does not want to be disturbed. Over there is a little valley where I have gone with him and Mademoiselle Vasseur. We have eaten there. He will walk in such wild places for a whole day. Gentlemen who have come here have asked me a thousand questions: "And his housekeeper, is she young? is she pretty?" 6. **Mademoiselle Vasseur:** Thérèse Le Vasseur, Rousseau's mistress of long standing, now forty-three years old.

7. **Voltaire:** François-Marie Arouet (1694–1778), known by his pen name Voltaire; this witty and skeptical philosopher, historian, and poet had been living for four years at nearby Ferney. 8. **Monsieur . . . moi:** Sir, there used to be a horse that pulled a cart at Ferney, and M. Voltaire always said, "Poor horse, you are thin, you are like me." 9. **Gillikranky:** a deep mountain pass in Scotland. 10. **J'ai . . . moi:** I have given permission to my servant to go see his friends and relatives, so I am alone. You must take good care of me. 11. **Nous . . . mieux:** We shall do our best. 12. **Marischal:** George Keith (1693–1778), Tenth Earl Marischal of Scotland, an acquaintance of Boswell's; he had been living in exile since the repression of the Jacobite Rising of 1745 and was now serving the King of Prussia as Governor of Neuchâtel, the principality in which Môtiers was located. Here he had become Rousseau's friend and protector.

a card with compliments to him, which I was sure would procure me admission. Colonel Chaillet[13] had given me a letter to the *Châtelin*,[14] M. Martinet, the principal Justice of the Place, which could introduce me without difficulty. But my romantic Genius, which will never be extinguished, made me eager to put my own merit to the severest tryal. I had therefore prepared a letter to Mr. Rousseau, in which I informed him that an ancient Scots Gentleman of twenty four, was come hither with the hopes of seeing him. I assured him that I deserved his regard, that I was ready to stand the test of his penetration. Towards the end of my letter I shewed him that I had a heart and a soul. I have here given no idea of my letter; It can neither be abridged nor transposed, for it is realy a Master-Piece. I shall ever preserve it as a Proof that my Soul can be sublime.[15] I drest and dined and sent my letter *chez*[16] M. Rousseau, ordering the Maid to leave it, and say she'd return for the Answer; so that I might give him time to consider a little, lest perhaps he might be ill and suddenly refuse to see me. I was filled with anxiety. Is not this romantic madness? Was I not sure of admittance by my Reccommendations? Could I not see him as any other Gentleman would do? No: I am above the Vulgar crowd. I would have my merit fairly tried by this Great Judge of human Nature. I must have things in my own way. If my bold attempt succeeds, the recollection of it will be grand as long as I live. But, perhaps, I may appear to him so vain, or so extraordinary, that he may be shocked by such a character and may not admit me. I shall then be in a pretty situation; for I shall be ashamed to present my recommendations. But why all this doubt and uneasiness? It is the effect of my melancholy timidity. What! can the Authour of *Eloïsa* be offended at the enthusiasm

of an ingenuous mind? But if he does admit me,[17] I shall have a very difficult character to support; for I have written to him with unusual elevation, and given him an idea of me which I shall hardly come up to.

. . .

To prepare myself for the great Interview, I walked out alone. I stroled pensive by the side of the River Ruse in a beautifull Wild Valley surrounded by immense Mountains, some covered with frowning rocks, others with clustering Pines, and others with glittering Snow. The fresh, healthfull air and the romantic Prospect arround me gave me a vigourous and solemn tone. I recalled all my former ideas of J. J. Rousseau, the admiration with which he is regarded over all Europe, his *Héloïse*, his *Emile*, in short, a crowd of great thoughts. This half hour was one of the most remarkable that I ever past.

I returned to my Inn, and the Maid delivered to me a card with the following Answer from M. Rousseau. "*Je suis malade, souffrant, hors d'état de recevoir des visites. Cependant, Je ne puis me refuser à celle de Monsieur Boswell, pourvu que par égard pour mon état, il veuille bien la faire courte.*"[18]

My sensibility dreaded the word *courte*. But I took courage, and went immediately. I found at the street door Mademoiselle Vasseur waiting for me. She was a little, lively, neat french Girl and did not increase my fear. She conducted me up a darkish stair, then opened a door. I expected, "Now I shall see him"—But it was not so. I entered a room which serves for Vestibule and for Kitchen. My Fancy formed many, many a Portrait of the wild Philosopher. At length his door opened and I beheld him, a genteel, black[19] man in the dress of an Armenian. I entered saying, "Many, Many thanks." After the first looks and bows were over, He said, "Will you be seated? Or would you rather take a turn with me in the room?" I chose the last, and happy I was to escape being formally placed upon a chair. I asked him how he was. "Very ill. But I have given up Doctors." "Yes, yes; you have no love for them." As it is impossible for me to relate exactly our conversation, I shall not endeavour at order, but give sentences as I recollect them.

---

13. **Colonel Chaillet:** an acquaintance of Boswell's who lived in Neuchâtel. 14. **Châtelin:** squire. 15. **Proof . . . sublime:** Some idea of Boswell's letter can be gathered from these extracts, as translated by F. A. Pottle: "Your writings, Sir, have melted my heart, have elevated my soul, have fired my imagination. Believe me, you will be glad you have seen me. . . . I have a presentiment that a noble friendship will be born today. . . . I have much to tell you. Though I am only a young man, I have experienced a variety of existence that will amaze you. I find myself in serious and delicate circumstances concerning which I eagerly hope to have the counsel of the author of the Nouvelle Héloïse. . . . Open your door, then, Sir, to a man who dares to tell you that he deserves to enter it. Place your confidence in a stranger who is different. You will not regret it." 16. **chez:** to.

17. **if . . . me:** Boswell wrote this passage after he had been received by Rousseau. 18. **Je . . . courte:** I am ill, in pain, quite incapable of receiving visits. However, I am unable to refuse myself Mr. Boswell's, provided that, out of consideration of my health, he is willing to make it short. 19. **black:** dark-haired.

BOSWELL. "The thought of your books, Sir, is a great source of pleasure to you?" ROUSSEAU. "I am fond of them; but when I think of my books so many misfortunes which they have brought upon me are revived in my memory, that really I cannot answer you. My books have saved my life." He spoke of the Parliament of Paris: "If any Society could be covered with disgrace, that would be. I could bring them into great disgrace simply by printing their edict against me on one side, and the Law of Nations and Equity on the side opposite. But I have reasons against doing so at present." BOSWELL. "We shall have it one day, perhaps?" ROUSSEAU. "Perhaps." I was drest in a coat and Waistcoat, scarlet with Gold lace, Buckskin Breeches and Boots. Above all I wore a Great coat of Green Camlet lined with Fox-skin fur, with the collar and Cuffs of the same fur. I held under my arm a hat with a sollid gold lace, at least with the air of being sollid. I had it last winter at the Hague. I had a free air and spoke well, and when M. Rousseau said what touched me more than ordinary, I seised his hand, I thumped him on the shoulder. I was without restraint. When I found that I realy pleased him, I said, "Are you aware, Sir, that I am recommended to you by a man you hold in high regard?" ROUSSEAU. "Ah! My Lord Marischal?" BOSWELL. "Yes, Sir; My Lord has furnished me with a Note of introduction to you." ROUSSEAU. "And you were unwilling to take advantage of it?" BOSWELL. "Nay, Sir; I wished to have a proof of my own merits." ROUSSEAU. "Sir, there would have been no kind of merit in gaining access to me by a Note of Lord Marischal's. Whatever he sends will always find a welcome from me. He is my Protector, my Father; I would venture to say, my Friend." One circumstance embarrassed me a little: I had forgotten to bring with me from Neufchâtel My Lord's Billet. But a generous consciousness of Innocence and honesty gives a freedom which cannot be counterfeited. I told M. Rousseau, "To speak truly, I have forgotten to bring his letter with me; but you accept my word for it?" ROUSSEAU. "Why, certainly. Numbers of people have shown themselves ready to serve me in their own fashion; My Lord Marischal has served me in mine. He is the only man on earth to whom I owe an obligation." Continuing, "When I speak of Kings, I do not include the King of Prussia. He is a King quite alone and apart. That force of his! Sir, There's the great matter, to have force—Revenge, even;—You can always find stuff to make something out of.

But when force is lacking, when everything is small and split up, there's no hope. The French, for example, are a contemptible nation." BOSWELL. "But the Spaniards, Sir?" ROUSSEAU. "Yes, you will find great souls in Spain." BOSWELL. "And in the Mountains of Scotland. But since our cursed union,[20] Ah . . ." ROUSSEAU. "You undid yourselves." BOSWELL. "Truly, yes. But I must tell you a great satisfaction given me by My Lord. He calls you Jean Jacques out of affection. One day he said to me, 'Jean Jacques is the most grateful man in the world. He wanted to write my brother's life; but I begged him rather to write the Life of Mr. Fletcher[21] of Saultoun, and he promised me he would do so.' " ROUSSEAU. "Yes, Sir; I will write it with the greatest care and pleasure. I shall offend the English, I know. But that is no matter. Will you furnish me with some Anecdotes on the Characters of those who made your Treaty of Union, and details that cannot be found in the Historians?" BOSWELL. "Yes, Sir; but with the warmth of an ancient Scot." ROUSSEAU. "By all means."

He spoke of ecclesiastics; "When one of these Gentlemen provides a new explanation of something incomprehensible, leaving it as incomprehensible as before, everyone cries, 'Here's a great Man.' But, Sir, they will tell you that no single point of Theology may be neglected, that every stone in God's Building, the mystic Jerusalem, must be considered as sacred. But they have added stones to it.—'Here, take off this; take off that! Now you see, the Building is admirably complete, and you have no need to stand there to hold it up.' 'But we want to be necessary!' 'Ah! . . .' "

"Sir, you don't see before you the Bear you have heard tell of. Sir, I have no liking for the world. I live here in a world of fantasies, and I cannot tolerate the world as it is." BOSWELL. "But when you come across fantastical men, are they not to your liking?" ROUSSEAU. "Why, Sir, they have not the same fantasies as myself. Sir, your Country is formed for liberty. I like your habits. You and I feel at liberty to stroll here together without talking. That is more than two Frenchmen can do. Mankind disgusts me. And my Housekeeper tells me that I am in far better humour on the days when I have been alone than on

---

20. union: Scotland and England were brought under a single parliament by the Act of Union in 1707. 21. Mr. Fletcher: Andrew Fletcher (1655–1716), Scottish patriot; Lord Marischal's brother was a famous field marshal.

those when I have been in company." *BOSWELL*. "There has been a great deal written against you, Sir." *ROUSSEAU*. "They have not understood me. As for Monsieur Vernet[22] at Geneva, he is an Arch-Jesuit, that is all I can say of him."

BOSWELL. "Tell me, Sir, do you not find that I answer to the description I gave you of myself?" *ROUSSEAU*. "Sir, it is too early for me to judge. But all Appearances are in your favour." *BOSWELL*. "I fear I have stayed too long. I shall take the honour of returning tomorrow." *ROUSSEAU*. "O, as to that, I can't tell." *BOSWELL*. "Sir, I shall stay quietly here in the Village. If you are able to see me, I shall be enchanted; if not, I shall make no complaint." *ROUSSEAU*. "My Lord Marischal has a perfect understanding of man's feelings, in Solitude no less than in Society. I am overwhelmed with visits from idle people." *BOSWELL*. "And how do they spend their time?" *ROUSSEAU*. "In paying Compliments. Also I get a prodigious quantity of letters. And the writer of each of them believes that he is the only One." *BOSWELL*. "You must be greatly surprised, Sir, that a man who has not the honour of your acquaintance, should take the liberty of writing to you?" *ROUSSEAU*. "No. It gives me no surprise. For I had such a letter yesterday, the day before yesterday and ever so often." *BOSWELL*. "Sir, Your very humble Servant—What, you are coming further?" *ROUSSEAU*. "I am not coming with you. I am going for a walk in the passage. Goodbye."

I had great satisfaction after finding that I could support the character which I had given of myself, after finding that I should most certainly be regarded by the illustrious Rousseau. I had a strange kind of feeling after having at last seen the Authour of whom I had thought so much. I sat down immediatly and wrote to Dempster.[23] I sat up too late.

Tuesday 4 December.

After taking a walk in the Vallon[24] I went to the door of M. Rousseau. Mademoiselle Vasseur was abroad, and I could not get in. I met her on the street, and she said "*M. Rousseau vous fera dire l'apres midi a quelle heure il peut vous voir.*"[25] I dined at the *table d'hôte*[26] with a M. du Rhé, a Parisian, son to a rich Financier, but obliged to fly on account of *lettres de cachet*[27] which were taken out against him by his Sister's influence, who is married to a man in power, and wants to have all the fortune of her father. This same Du Rhé is, however, a sad dog. He has spent a vast deal of money upon women, and upon absurd plans for the young Pretender.[28] He is a kind of Authour, writes you a criticism in the *Journal Encyclopédique*, and even composes you a system of education on a plan entirely new. This last has not yet seen the light. Small will be the light which it will impart— "Not light, but rather darkness visible."[29] M. du Rhé lives snug at Motiers and eats in the Inn, when some good freind does not invite him. My other Companion was M. de Turo who has an estate in the neighbourhood, has travelled a good deal, has a good deal of knowledge, and is a tall, stout young fellow. But with the whim of an English oddity he lives constantly in this Inn. The Inhabitants of the Village have named him their Governour, an office of small Authority but of consequence enough to make M. de Turo hold his head extremely high. I have seen him grant a pass to a Beggar with great dignity. He generally keeps a parcel of dogs, and goes a hunting on the hills. Scandal says that he is intimately connected with my youngest Landlady. Perhaps I have done him an injury in the spelling of his name. Perhaps he writes it Thurot, and possibly may be a near Relation of the gallant Captain Thurot who during the last war awed and dismayed the coasts of Caledonia. After dinner I waited on M. Martinet, the *Châtelin*, a knowing hearty fellow. He engaged me to sup with him. At five I went to M. Rousseau, whom I found more gay than he had been yesterday. We joked on Mademoiselle Vasseur for keeping him under lock and key. She, to defend

22. **Monsieur Vernet:** perhaps Jacob Vernet, a Calvinist minister who had recently criticized Rousseau for pretending to be an orthodox Protestant. 23. **Dempster:** George Dempster, Member of Parliament; a Scottish friend of Boswell's. Boswell wrote to him: "Dempster, I have been with him. I have been most politely received. Would you see easy elegance, see the author of Héloïse. . . . I am supremely happy. I write this partly from a pardonable vanity, partly from a desire to give you pleasure." 24. **Vallon:** small valley.

25. **M. Rousseau . . . voir:** M. Rousseau will tell you this afternoon when he can see you. 26. **table d'hôte:** the general public table, as distinguished from an exclusive table in a private room. 27. **lettres de cachet:** orders given under the king's private seal directing the arrest and confinement without trial of the person named in them. 28. **the young Pretender:** Charles Edward, grandson of the Stuart monarch James II. Charles had commanded the flamboyant but unsuccessful Jacobite Rising of 1745 and since then had tried to interest many Continental monarchs in lending him enough force to obtain the British throne for his exiled father, James III. 29. **Not . . . visible:** *Paradise Lost,* I. 64.

herself, said he had another door to get out at. Said he, "*Ah Mademoiselle vous dites tout.*"[30]

He gave me the character of the Abbé de St. Pierre,[31] "a man who did good, simply because he chose to do good: a man without enthusiasm. One might say that he was passionately reasonable. He was seen agonizing through the writing of his memoirs,[32] and he used to say, 'I shall be sneered at for this,' 'I shall get a hissing for that.' But it was all one to him. He carried his principles into the merest trifles. For example, he used to wear his watch suspended from a button on his coat, because that was more convenient. As he was precluded from marriage, he kept Mistresses, and made no secret of it. He had a number of sons. He would allow them to adopt none but the most strictly useful professions; for example, he would not allow any son of his to be a Wig-maker. 'For,' said he, 'so long as Nature continues to supply us with hair, the profession of Wig-making must always be full of uncertainty.' He was completely indifferent to the opinion of men, saying that they were merely over-grown children. After paying a long visit to a certain Lady, he said to her, 'Madam, I perceive I am weari-some to you; but that is a matter of no moment to me. You amuse me.' One of Louis the XIV's creatures had him turned out of the Academy for a speech he had made there. Yet he perpetually visited this man. 'For,' said he, 'he acted in his own interests; and I bear him no grudge for that. He amuses me. He has no grounds for being offended with me. I have grounds for offence against him; but I am not offended.' In short, he continued to call on this Academician, until the latter put a stop to it because he found it disagreeable to see a man whom he had injured. He had plenty of good sense, but a faulty style: long-winded and diffuse, yet always proving his point. He was a favourite with women; he would go his own way independently, and he won respect. If you become a Member of Parliament, you must resemble the Abbé de St. Pierre. You must stick to your principles." BOSWELL. "But, then, one must be very well instructed." ROUSSEAU. "Ah, sure enough. You must have a well furnished head." BOSWELL. "But, Sir, a Member of Parliament who behaves as a strictly honest man is regarded as a crazy fool." ROUSSEAU. "Well then, you must be a crazy fool of a Member; and believe me, such a man will be respected;—that is, if he holds consistently by his principles. A man who changes round on every occasion, is another affair."

He talked of his "*Plan for perpetual Peace, taken from the Abbé de St. Pierre.*"[33] I frankly owned that I had not read it. "No?" said he—then took one down from his Book-case and gave it me. I asked him smilingly if he would not put his name upon it. He laughed heartily at me. I talked to him of the German *Album* and how I had been forced to take one; but that except what was written by the Person who gave it me, there was nothing in it. Said he "Then your *Album* is *Album.*[34]" There was a Sally for you. A Precious Pearl; a Pun made by Rousseau. He said, "I have seen the Scottish Highlanders in France. I love the Scots; not because My Lord Marischal is one of them but because he praises them. *You* are irksome to me. It's my nature. I cannot help it." BOSWELL. "Do not stand on ceremony with me." ROUSSEAU. "Go away." Mademoiselle allways accompanys me to the door. She said, "I have been twenty-two years with Monsieur Rousseau; I would not give up my place to be Queen of France. I try to profit by the good advice he gives me. If he should die, I shall have to go into a Convent." She is a very good girl, and deserves to be esteemed for her constancy to a man so valuable. His Simplicity is beautifull. He consulted Mademoiselle and her mother on the merits of his *Héloïse* and his *Emile*. I supt with the Squire. He said, "We two are alone, so as to be free to talk of My Lord Marischal and nothing else." We were hearty.

Wednesday 5 December.

When I waited upon Monsieur Rousseau this morning, he said, "My dear Sir, I am sorry not to be able to talk with you as I would wish." I took care to wave such excuses, and immediately set conversa-tion agoing. I told him how I had turned Roman Catholic[35] and had intended to hide myself in a Convent in France. He said, "What madness! I too was Catholic in my youth. I changed, and then

---

30. Ah . . . tout: Ah, Mademoiselle, you can't keep any-thing secret. 31. the Abbé . . . Pierre: Charles Irénée (1658–1743), French economist and reformer, considered a visionary by most of his contemporaries. 32. He . . . memoirs: the translation of this sentence is conjectural; Boswell's French is quite unclear at this point.

33. Plan . . . Pierre: an abstract of St. Pierre's *Projet de paix perpetuelle* (1713), which Rousseau had published in 1761. 34. Album: Latin for *white*. 35. turned . . . Catholic: Boswell had impulsively become a Catholic in 1760, when he was twenty, but, easily convinced that his decision had been too hasty, he was soon persuaded by an acquaintance of his father's to abandon this commitment.

changed back again. I returned to Geneva and was readmitted to Protestantism. I went among Catholics, and would say to them, 'I am no longer one of you'; and I got on with them excellently." I stopped him in the middle of the room and I said to him, "But tell me, sincerely, are you a Christian?" I looked at him with a searching eye. His countenance was no less animated. Each stood steady and watched the other's looks. He struck his breast, and replied, "Yes. I pique myself upon being one." *BOSWELL.* "Sir, the soul can be sustained by nothing save the Gospel." *ROUSSEAU.* "I feel that. I am unaffected by all the objections. I am weak; there may be things beyond my reach; or perhaps he who recorded them made a mistake. I say, God the Father, God the Son and God the Holy Ghost." *BOSWELL.* "But tell me, do you suffer from melancholy?" *ROUSSEAU.* "I was born placid. I have no natural disposition to melancholy. My misfortunes have infected me with it." *BOSWELL.* "I, for my part, suffer from it severely. And how can I be happy, I, who have done so much harm?" *ROUSSEAU.* "Begin your life anew. God is good, for He is just. Do good. You will pay off all the harm you have done. Say to yourself in the morning, 'Come now, I am going to *pay off* so much harm.' Six well spent years will pay off all the harm you have done." *BOSWELL.* "What is your view of Cloisters, Penances, and remedies of that sort?" *ROUSSEAU.* "Mummeries, all of them; invented by men. Do not be guided by men's judgments, or you will find yourself tossed to and fro perpetually. Do not base your life on the judgments of others, first because they are as likely to be mistaken as yourself, and further because you cannot know that they are telling you their true feelings; they may be impelled by motives of interest or convention to talk to you in a way not corresponding to their thoughts." *BOSWELL.* "Will you, Sir, look after me?" *ROUSSEAU.* "I cannot. I can be responsible only for myself." *BOSWELL.* "But I shall come back to you." *ROUSSEAU.* "I don't promise to see you. I am in pain. I need a chamber-pot every minute." *BOSWELL.* "Yes you will see me." *ROUSSEAU.* "Be off; and a good journey to you."[36]

Friday 14 December.

At eight I got on Horseback and had for my Guide a Smith called Dupuis. I said, "Since when (*depuis*

quand) have you had that name?" I past the Mountain Lapidosa which is monstrously steep and in a great measure covered with snow. I was going to Rousseau which consideration levelled the roughest mountains. I arrived at Môtiers before noon. I alighted at Rousseau's door. Up and I went and found Mademoiselle Vasseur who told me, "He is very ill." "But can I see him for a moment?" "I will find out. Step in, Sir." I found him sitting in great pain.[37] *ROUSSEAU.* "I am overcome with ailments, disappointments, and sorrow. I am using a probe. Everyone thinks it my duty to attend to him." *BOSWELL.* "That is most natural; and is it not a source of satisfaction to you to find you can be of so much help to others?" He gave a deprecatory shrug. I had left with him when I was last here what I called a *Sketch of my Life*, in which I gave him the important incidents of my History and my melancholy apprehensions, and begged his advice and friendship. It was an interesting Piece.[38] He said, "I have read your Memoir. You have been gulled. You ought never to see a Priest." *BOSWELL.* "But can I yet hope to make something of myself?" *ROUSSEAU.* "Why, yes. Your great difficulty is that you think it so difficult a matter. Come back in the afternoon. But put your watch on the table." *BOSWELL.* "For how long?" *ROUSSEAU.* "A quarter of an hour, and no longer." *BOSWELL.* "Twenty minutes." *ROUSSEAU.* "Be off with you!—Ha! Ha!" Notwithstanding the pain he was in, he was touched with my singular sally, and laughed most realy. He had a gay look immediately. I dined in my old Room with the two Boarders. After dinner I walked out. There had fallen much rain, and the Vallon was all overflowed. Nature looked somewhat different from the time that I was first here. I was sorry that such a scene was subject to any change. At four I went to Monsieur Rousseau. "I have but a moment allowed me; I must use it well. Is it possible to live amongst other men, and to retain singularity?" *ROUSSEAU.* "Yes, I have done it." *BOSWELL.* "But to remain on good terms with them?"

---

36. **good . . . you:** Boswell spent the next nine days visiting Neuchâtel and Yverdun.

37. **in . . . pain:** Rousseau suffered from a urethral constriction that he now attempted to treat himself by means of a probe or dilator. 38. **an interesting Piece:** In this document, written in fourteen pages of beginner's French, Boswell confesses that before leaving Scotland he had been indulging himself in a passionate affair with a young married woman (probably Jean Home, daughter of Lord Kames). Boswell maintains that he feels guilty about the relationship and solicits Rousseau's advice.

ROUSSEAU. "Oh, if you want to be a Wolf, you must howl. I attach very little importance to books." BOSWELL. "Even to your own Books?" ROUSSEAU. "Oh, they are just Rigmarole." BOSWELL. "Now you are howling." ROUSSEAU. "When I put my trust in books I was tossed about, as you are (though it is rather by talking that you have been tossed). I had nothing stable here" (striking his head) "before I began to meditate." BOSWELL. "But you would not have meditated to such good purpose, if you had not read." ROUSSEAU. "No. I should have meditated to better purpose if I had begun sooner." BOSWELL. "But I, for example, would never have had the agreeable ideas I possess of the Christian religion, had I not read the *Savoyard's Creed*.[39] But to tell the truth, I can find no certain System. Morality appears to me an uncertain thing. For instance, I would like to have thirty women. Could I not satisfy that desire?" ROUSSEAU. "No!" BOSWELL. "Why?" ROUSSEAU. "Ha! Ha! If Mademoiselle were not here, I would give you a most ample reason why." BOSWELL. "But consider; if I am rich, I can take a number of girls: I get them with child; Propagation is thus increased. I give them doweries, and I marry them off to good Peasants who are very happy to have them. Thus they become wives at the same age as would have been the case if they had remained virgins, and I, on my side, have had the benefit of enjoying a great variety of women." ROUSSEAU. "Ah! You will be landed in jealousies, betrayals and treachery." BOSWELL. "But cannot I follow the oriental usage?" ROUSSEAU. "In the Orient, the women are kept shut up; it means keeping slaves; and, mark you, their women do nothing but harm, whereas ours do much good since they do a great deal of work." BOSWELL. "I should like to follow the example of the old Patriarchs, worthy men whose memory I hold in respect." ROUSSEAU. "But are you not a Citizen? You must not pick and choose one law here and another law there; you must take the laws of your own Society. Fulfill your duties as a Citizen, and if you hold fast, you will win respect. I should not talk about what I was doing; I'd simply

do it. And as for your lady,[40] when you go back to Scotland you will say, 'Madam, such conduct is against my conscience, and there shall be no more of it.' She will applaud you; if not, she is to be despised." BOSWELL. "Suppose her passion is still lively, and she threatens to tell her husband what has happened unless I agree to continue our intrigue?" ROUSSEAU. "In the first place, she will not tell him. In the second, you have no right to do harm for the sake of good." BOSWELL. "True. None the less, I can picture some very embarrassing situations. And pray explain how I can expiate the evil I have already done?" ROUSSEAU. "Ah, Sir, there is no expiation for evil, except good." A beautifull thought this. Nevertheless I maintained my doctrine of satisfaction by Punishment. Yes, I must ever think that immutable Justice requires attonement to be made for transgressions, and this attonement is to be made by suffering. This is the universal idea of all nations, and seems to be a leading principle of Christianity. I gave myself full scope; for since I left England I have not had anybody to whom I could lay open entirely my mind till I found Monsieur Rousseau. I asked him, "When I get to France and Italy, may I not indulge in the gallantries, usual to those countries, where the husbands do not resent your making love to their wives? Nay, should I not be happier as the citizen of such a nation?" ROUSSEAU. "They are corpses. Do you want to be a Corpse?" He was right. BOSWELL. "But pray tell me, has a virtuous man any true advantages, is he really better off than a man given up to sensuality?" ROUSSEAU. "We cannot doubt that we are spiritual beings; and when the soul escapes from this prison, from this flesh, the virtuous man will find things to his liking. He will enjoy the contemplation of happy souls, nobly employed. He will say, 'I have already lived a life like that.' Whereas those who experience nothing but the vile Passions which have their origin in the body, will be dissatisfied by the spectacle of pleasures which they have no means of enjoying." BOSWELL. "Upon my word, I am at a loss how to act in this world; I cannot determine whether or not I should adopt some profession." ROUSSEAU. "One must have a great Plan." BOSWELL. "What about those Studies, on which so much stress is laid? Such as History, for instance?" ROUSSEAU. "They are just Amusements." BOS-WELL. "My Father desires me to be called to the

---

39. the Savoyard's Creed: In "The Creed of a Savoyard Vicar," which constitutes most of Book IV of *Emile*, Rousseau expresses a belief in a benevolent deity, the immortality of the soul, and an innate conscience, but he denies the necessity of scriptures, churches, or priests. It was this scheme of natural religion that outraged the Christian authorities in Paris. Boswell had read the "Creed" only a few days before, in preparation for his interviews with Rousseau.

40. your lady: the married woman mentioned in Boswell's *Sketch of My Life*.

Scottish Bar; I am certainly doing right in satisfying my Father; I have no such certainty if I follow my light inclinations. It follows that I must give my mind to the study of the laws of Scotland." ROUSSEAU. "To be sure; they are your tools. If you mean to be a Carpenter, you must have a plane." BOSWELL. "I do not get on well with my Father. I am not at my ease with him." ROUSSEAU. "To be at ease you need to share some amusement." BOSWELL. "We look after the planting together." ROUSSEAU. "That's too serious a business. You should have some amusement that puts you on an equal footing: shooting, for example. A shot is missed and a joke is made of it, without any infringement of respect; you enjoy a freedom which you take for granted. Once you are involved in a Profession, you must keep on with it even though another, and apparently better, should present itself. If you keep changing, you can achieve nothing. (I should have observed that when I pushed the conversation on women, Mademoiselle went out, and M. Rousseau said, "See now, you are driving Mademoiselle out of the room." She was now returned.) He stopped, and looked at me in a singular manner, "Are you greedy?" BOSWELL. "Yes." ROUSSEAU. "I am sorry to hear it." BOSWELL. "Ha! Ha! I was joking; for in your books, you write in favour of greed. I know what you are about to say, and it is just what I was hoping to hear. I wanted you to invite me to dinner. I had a great desire to share a meal with you." ROUSSEAU. "Well, if you are not greedy, will you dine here tomorrow? But I give you fair warning, you will find yourself badly off." BOSWELL. "No, I shall not be badly off; I am above all such considerations." ROUSSEAU. "Come then at noon; it will give us time to talk." BOSWELL. "All my thanks." ROUSSEAU. "Good evening." Mademoiselle carried me to the house of a poor woman with a great many children whom M. Rousseau aids with his charity. I contributed my part. I was not pleased to hear Mademoiselle repeat to the Poor Woman just the common consolatory sayings. She should have said something singular.

Saturday 15 December.

At seven in the morning I got on horseback and rode about a league to St. Sulpice where I saw the source of the *Ruse*, the river which runs thro' the Vall de Travers. It is a prodigious romantic Place. I could not determine whether the water gushes in an immediate spring from the rock, or only issues out here having pierced the mountain upon which is a lake. The water comes forth with great violence. All arround here I saw Mountains and rocks as at Hartfell in Annandale.[41] Some of the rocks were in great courses[42] like huge Stone walls along which grew the towring Pines which we call Pitch firs, and which are much handsomer than the firs of Scotland. I was full of fine spirits. Gods! Am I now then realy the freind of Rousseau? What a rich assemblage of ideas! I relish my felicity truly in such a scene as this. Shall I not truly relish it at Auchinleck? I was quite gay, my fancy was youthfull, and vented it's gladness in sportive sallies. I supposed myself in the rude world. I supposed a parcel of young fellows saying, "Come, Boswell, you'll dine with us today?" "No, Gentlemen, excuse me; I'm engaged. I dine today with Rousseau." My tone, my air, my native Pride when I pronounced this! Temple![43] You would have given half a guinea to see me at that moment. I returned to my Inn where I found the Court of Justice of the Vallon assembled. I entered and was amused to hear a Justice of Peace and honest Farmers and a Country Minister all talking french.

I then went to M. Rousseau. "I hope your health is better today." ROUSSEAU. "Oh don't speak of it." He seemed unusually gay. Before dinner we are all so, if not made to wait too long. A keen appetite gives a vivacity to the whole frame. I said, "You say nothing in regard to a child's duties towards his Parents. You tell us nothing of your Emile's Father." ROUSSEAU. "Oh he hadn't any. He didn't exist." It is, however, a real pity that M. Rousseau has not treated of the duties between Parents and Children. It is an important and a delicate subject and deserves to be illustrated by a Sage of so clear a Judgment and so elegant a Soul. He praised *the Spectator*. He said, "One comes across Allegories in it. I have no taste for Allegories; though your nation shows a great liking for them." I gave him very fully the character of Mr. Johnson. He said with force, "I would like that man. I would respect him. I would refrain from shattering his principles, were I

41. **Hartfell in Annandale:** a mountain in one of the valleys of the Scottish Lowlands. 42. **courses:** strata. 43. **Temple:** William Johnson Temple, lawyer and, later, clergyman; one of Boswell's most intimate Scottish friends, to whom he often sent full accounts of his adventures. Boswell reports that Temple, who had read parts of his journal, once said that "he imagined that my journal did me harm, as it made me hunt about for adventures to adorn it with. . . ."

to find I could do so. I should like to see him; but from far off for fear he might deal me a blow." I told him how averse Mr. Johnson was to write, and how he had his levee. "Ah, (said he,) I understand. He is a man who enjoys holding forth." I told him Mr. Johnson's *Bon Mot* upon the Innovators: That Truth is a Cow which will yeild them no more milk, and so they are gone to milk the Bull.[44] He said, "He would detest me. He would say, 'Here is a Corrupter: a Man who comes here to milk the Bull.'" I had diverted myself by pretending to help Mademoiselle Vasseur to make the Soup. We din'd in the Kitchen which was neat and chearfull. There was something singularly agreable in this scene. Here was Rousseau in all his Simplicity, with his Armenian dress which I have surely mentioned before now. His long coat and Nightcap made him look easy and well. Our dinner was as follows: 1 A dish of excellent Soup. 2 A Bouilli[45] of Beef and Veal. 3 Cabbage, Turnip and Carrot. 4 Cold Pork. 5 Pickled Trout which he jestingly called *Tongue*. 6 Some little dish which I forget. The Desert consisted of stoned Pears and of Chesnuts. We had red and white wines. It was a simple good Repast. We were quite at our ease. I sometimes forgot myself and became ceremonious. "May I help you to some of this dish?" ROUSSEAU. "No, Sir. I can help myself to it." Or, "Might I help myself to some more of that?" ROUSSEAU. "Is your arm long enough? A man does the honours of his house from a motive of vanity. He does not want it forgotten who is the Master. I would like everyone to be his own Master, and that no one should play the part of Host. Let each one ask for what he wants; if it is there to give, let him be given it; otherwise, he must be satisfied without. Here you see true hospitality." BOSWELL. "In England, it is quite another matter. They do not want to be at ease; they are stiff and silent, in order to win respect." ROUSSEAU. "In France, you find no such gloom among folk of distinction. There is even an affectation of the utmost liberty, as though they would have you understand, 'We stand in no fear of losing our dignity.' That is a more refined form of self esteem." BOSWELL. "Well, and do you not share that yourself?" ROUSSEAU. "Yes, I grant that I like to be respected; but only in matters of importance."

BOSWELL. "You are so simple. I expected to find you quite different from this: the great Rousseau. But you do not see yourself in the same light as others see you. I expected to find you enthroned and talking with a grave authority." ROUSSEAU. "I? Uttering Oracles? Ha! Ha! Ha!" BOSWELL. "Yes, and that I should be much in awe of you. And, in truth, your simplicity might be open to criticism; it might be said, 'M. Rousseau does not make himself sufficiently respected.' In Scotland, I can assure you, a very different tone must be taken to escape from the shocking familiarity which is prevalent in that country. Upon my word, I cannot put up with it. Should I not be justified in forestalling it by fighting a duel with the first man who should treat me that way, and thus live at peace for the rest of my life?" ROUSSEAU. "No. That is not allowable. It is not right to stake one's life on such follies. Life is given us for objects of importance. Pay no heed to what such men say. They will get tired of talking to a man who does not answer them." BOSWELL. "If you were in Scotland, they would start right off by calling you 'Rousseau.' 'Jean Jacques,' they would say, with the utmost familiarity, 'how goes it?'" ROUSSEAU. "That is perhaps a good thing." BOSWELL. "But they would say, 'Poh! Jean Jacques, why do you allow yourself all these fantasies? You're a pretty man to put forward such claims. Come, Come, settle down in society like other people'; and this they would say to you with a sourness which, for my part, I am quite unable to imitate for you." ROUSSEAU. "Ah, that's bad." There he felt the thistle, when it was applied to himself on the tender part. It was just as if I had said, "Howt Johnie Rousseau man, what for hae ye sae mony figmagairies[46]? Ye're a bony Man indeed to mauk sicana wark; set ye up. Canna ye just live like ither fowk?" It was the best idea could be given in the polite french language of the rude Scots sarcastical vivacity. BOSWELL. "I have leanings towards despotism, let me tell you. On our estates, I am like an ancient Lord, and I insist on respect from the tenants." ROUSSEAU. "But when you see an Old Man with white hair do you, as a young man, have no feelings at all? Have you no respect for age?" BOSWELL. "Yes. I have even, on many occasions, been very affable. I have talked quite freely with the tenants." ROUSSEAU. "Yes, you forgot yourself, and became a man." BOSWELL. "But I was sorry for it afterwards. I used to think,

44. **Truth . . . Bull:** When he made the remark, Johnson actually had been referring to Rousseau and David Hume. "Rousseau," Johnson told Boswell on another occasion, "is a very bad man." 45. **Bouilli:** boiled meat dish.

46. **figmagairies:** whims.

'I have lowered myself.' " ROUSSEAU. "Ha! Ha! Ha!" BOSWELL. "Yesterday I thought of asking a favour of you, to give me credentials as your ambassador to the Corsicans.[47] Will you make me His Excellency? Are you in need of an Ambassador? I offer you my services: Mr. Boswell, Ambassador Extraordinary of M. Rousseau to the Isle of Corsica." ROUSSEAU. "Would you care to be King of Corsica?" BOSWELL. "By my word! Ha! Ha! Not I. It is beyond my powers (with a low bow); all the same, I can say, 'I have refused to be a King.' " ROUSSEAU. "Do you like Cats?" BOSWELL. "No." ROUSSEAU "I was sure of that. It is my test of character. There you have the despotic instinct of men. They do not like cats because the cat is free, and will never consent to become a slave. He will do nothing to your order, as the other animals do." BOSWELL. "Nor a Chicken, either." ROUSSEAU. "A Chicken would obey your orders if you could make them intelligible to it. But a cat will understand you perfectly, and not obey them." BOSWELL. "But a Cat is ungrateful and treacherous." ROUSSEAU. "No. That's all untrue. A Cat is an animal that can be very attached to you; he will do anything you please out of friendship. I have a Cat here. He has been brought up with my Dog; they play together. The Cat will give the Dog a blow with his tail, and the Dog will offer him his paw." (He described the playing of his dog and cat with exquisite eloquence, as a fine Painter draws a small Piece.) He put some victuals on a trencher, and made his dog dance round it. He sung to him a lively air with a sweet voice and great taste. "You see the Ballet. It is not a gala performance, but a pretty one all the same." I think the Dog's name was Sultan. He stroked him and fed him, and with an arch air said, "He is not much *respected*, but he gets well looked after."

BOSWELL. "Suppose you were to walk in upon a drinking party of young folk, who should treat you with ridicule, would you be above minding it?" ROUSSEAU. "It would put me out of countenance. I am shy by nature. I have often, for example, been overcome by raillery of women. A party such as you describe would be disagreeable to me. I would leave it." I was comforted to find that my sensibility is not despicable weakness.

BOSWELL. "The Anglican Church is the one for me." ROUSSEAU. "Yes. It is no doubt an excellent Religion; but it is not the Gospel, which is all simplicity. It is another kind of religion." BOSWELL. "The Gospel, at the outset, was simple and rigid equally; as when Paul says it is better not to marry, than to marry." ROUSSEAU. "Paul? But that is not the Gospel." BOSWELL. "Then you have no liking for Paul?" ROUSSEAU. "I respect him, but I think he is partly responsible for muddling your head. He would have been an Anglican Clergyman." BOSWELL. "Mr. Johnson is a Jacobite,[48] but he has a Pension of £300 sterling from the King." ROUSSEAU. "He ought not to have accepted a Pension." BOSWELL. "He says that he does not drink the health of King James with the wine given him by King George." ROUSSEAU. "But you should not employ the substance given you by this wine in attacking King George." MLLE. LEVASSEUR. "Shall you, Sir, see M. de Voltaire?" BOSWELL. "Most certainly. (*To Rousseau*) M. de Voltaire has no liking for you. That is natural enough." ROUSSEAU. "Yes. One does not like those whom one has greatly injured. His talk is most enjoyable; it is even better than his books." BOSWELL. "Have you looked at the *Philosophical Dictionary*[49]?" ROUSSEAU. "Yes." BOSWELL. "And what of it?" ROUSSEAU. "I don't like it. I am not intolerant, but he deserves. . . ." (I forget his expression here). "It is very well to argue against men's opinions; but to show contempt, and to say, 'You are idiots to believe this,' is to be personally offensive. Now go away." BOSWELL. "Not yet. I will leave at three o'clock. I have still five and twenty minutes." ROUSSEAU. "But I can't give you five and twenty minutes." BOSWELL. "I will give you even more than that." ROUSSEAU. "What! Of my own time? All the Kings on earth cannot give me my own time." BOSWELL. "But if I had stayed till tomorrow I should have had five and twenty minutes, and next

47. **Corsicans:** The island of Corsica was in rebellion against the Republic of Genoa. Rousseau, in his *Le Contrat social*, had written that Corsica was now ready to become the only European country with a sound, reformed government. A Corsican officer had written Rousseau asking him to contrive a constitution for Corsica, and Pasquale di Paoli, the leader of the revolt, had invited Rousseau to come observe the birth of the new government.

48. **Jacobite:** one loyal to the exiled Stuart family, the family of James (Latin, *Jacobus*) III. 49. **Philosophical Dictionary:** Voltaire's *Dictionnaire philosophique portatif* (1764), a collection of witty, ironic articles attacking contemporary religious and historical superstitions. The book, which gave great offense to the respectable, was proscribed by both the Parliament of Paris and the Church of Rome.

day another twenty-five. I am not taking those minutes. I am making you a present of them." ROUSSEAU. "Ah! Since you don't steal my money, you are giving it to me." He then repeated part of a french satire ending with, *and whatever they leave you, they count as a gift.* BOSWELL. "Pray speak for me, Mademoiselle. (*To Rousseau*) I have an excellent friend here." ROUSSEAU. "Nay, but this is a league." BOSWELL. "No league at all." MLLE. LEVASSEUR. "Gentlemen, I will tell you the moment the clock strikes." ROUSSEAU. "Come; I need to take the air after eating." We walked out to a gallery pendent upon his wall. BOSWELL. "In old days I was a great mimic. I could imitate everyone I saw. But I do it no longer." ROUSSEAU. "It is a bad talent; for it compels one to seize upon all that is small in a character." BOSWELL. "True; but I assure you there was a nobleness about my art; I carried mimicry to such a point of perfection. I was a kind of Virtuoso. When I espied any singular character I would say, 'It must be added to my collection.'" He laughed with all his nerves: "You are an oddity." BOSWELL. "I am a Physiognomist, believe me. I have studied that art very attentively, I assure you, and I can rely on my conclusions." He seemed to agree to this. ROUSSEAU. "Yet I think the features of the Face vary between one nation and another, as do accent and tone of voice; and these signify different feelings among different peoples." This Observation struck me as new and most ingenious. BOSWELL. "But, in time, one learns to understand them." ROUSSEAU. "The Roads are bad. You will be late." BOSWELL. "I take the bad parts on foot; the last league of the way is good. Do you think that I shall make a good Barrister before a Court of Justice?" ROUSSEAU. "Yes. But I regret you have the talents necessary for defending a bad case." BOSWELL. "Have you any commands for Italy?" ROUSSEAU. "I will send a letter to Geneva for you to carry to Parma." BOSWELL. "Can I send you anything back?" ROUSSEAU. "A few pretty tunes from the Opera." BOSWELL. "By all means. Oh, I have had so much to say, that I have neglected to beg you to play me a tune." ROUSSEAU. "It's too late." MLLE. LEVASSEUR. "Sir, your man is calling for you to start." M. Rousseau embraced me. He was quite the tender St. Preux.[50] He kist me several times, and held me in his arms with elegant

cordiality. O! I shall never forget that I have been thus. ROUSSEAU. "Good-bye. You are a fine fellow." BOSWELL. "You have shown me great goodness, but I deserved it." ROUSSEAU. "Yes. You are malicious; but 'tis a pleasant malice, a malice I don't dislike. Write and tell me how you are." BOSWELL. "And you will write to me?" ROUSSEAU. "I know not how to reach you." BOSWELL. "Yes, you shall write to me in Scotland." ROUSSEAU. "Certainly; and even at Paris." BOSWELL. "Bravo! If I live twenty years, you will write to me for twenty years?" ROUSSEAU. "Yes." BOSWELL. "Good-bye. If you live for seven years, I shall return to Switzerland from Scotland to see you." ROUSSEAU. "Do so. We shall be old acquaintances." BOSWELL. "One word more. Can I feel sure that I am held to you by the slenderest thread? By a hair?" (Seising a hair of my head). ROUSSEAU. "Yes. Remember always that there are points where our souls are linked." BOSWELL. "It is enough. I, with my melancholy, I, who often look on myself as a despicable being, as a good for nothing creature who should make his escape from life,—I shall be upheld forever by the thought that I am linked to M. Rousseau. Good-bye. Bravo! I will live to the end of my days." ROUSSEAU. "That is undoubtedly a thing one must do. Good-bye."

Mademoiselle accompanied me to the outer door. Before dinner She told me, "M. Rousseau has a high regard for you. The first time you came, I said to him 'That Gentleman has an honest Face. I am sure you will like him.'" I said, "Mademoiselle is a good judge." "Yes," said She, "I have seen Strangers enough in the twenty-two years that I have lived with M. Rousseau, and believe me, I have sent many away simply because I did not fancy their way of talking." I said, "You have promised to let me have your news from time to time." "Yes, Sir." "And tell me what I can send you from Geneva. Make no ceremony." "Well, if you will, a Garnet Necklace.[51]" We shook hands cordialy, and away I went to my Inn. My eldest Landlady looked at me and said, "Sir, I think you are crying." This I retain as a true Elogium of my Humanity. I replied, "I may well be unhappy to leave M. Rousseau. I will see you again in seven years." I got a-horseback and rode by the house of M. Rousseau. Mademoiselle waited for me at the door,

---

50. **St. Preux:** an idealized, virtuous character in *La Nouvelle Héloïse.*

51. **Garnet Necklace:** Boswell did send Thérèse a garnet necklace from Geneva, sixteen days later.

and cried, "Bon Voyage; write to us." Good Creature. I rode gravely to Yverdun contemplating how this day will appear to my mind some years hence. I was received cordially by my gallant Baron and my amiable Madame de Brackel: Yet did my spirits sink pretty low; No wonder after such a high flow.

THE JOURNAL OF A TOUR TO THE HEBRIDES WITH SAMUEL JOHNSON, LL.D.

As early as 1763 Johnson indicated to Boswell his willingness to take a trip someday through the north of Scotland, but it was not until ten years later that Boswell succeeded in enticing him to Edinburgh to begin the tour. Since Johnson loved neither Scots nor scenery, the trip produced many piquant situations. Despite the absence of the comforts he was used to and despite the physical strains of traveling by foot and horseback in his sixty-fourth year, Johnson enjoyed himself mightily. He wrote to Boswell later, "Shall we ever have another frolick like our journey to the Hebrides?" Johnson's account of the trip, *A Journey to the Western Islands of Scotland* (1775), is a quiet, scholarly, and impersonal book compared to Boswell's. Travel books had long been popular, and so had biographical sketches, but a book like Boswell's, which combined the methods of the two genres and then added an inimitable personal touch, was quite unprecedented. Never before had a great man been exhibited in one stage-managed "scene" after another; never before had a great man's actual words, postures, and even diet been caught with "that authentick Precision," as Boswell describes his goal, "which alone can render Biography valuable."

The following selection is the beginning of the book. We have printed from the first edition (1785), without including the variants of the third (1786)—variants now known to be Edmond Malone's grave corrections of Boswell's happily impulsive style. We have omitted some of Boswell's footnotes.

DR. JOHNSON had for many years given me hopes that we should go together, and visit the Hebrides. Martin's Account of those islands[1] had

THE JOURNAL OF A TOUR TO THE HEBRIDES. 1. Martin's . . . islands: *A Description of the Western Islands of Scotland* (1703) by Martin Martin.

impressed us with a notion that we might there contemplate a system of life almost totally different from what we had been accustomed to see; and, to find simplicity and wildness, and all the circumstances of remote time or place, so near to our native great island, was an object within the reach of reasonable curiosity. Dr. Johnson has said in his Journey, "that he scarcely remembered how the wish to visit the Hebrides was excited;" but he told me, in summer, 1763, that his father put Martin's Account into his hands when he was very young, and that he was much pleased with it. We reckoned there would be some inconveniencies and hardships, and perhaps a little danger; but these we were persuaded were magnified in the imagination of every body. When I was at Ferney, in 1764, I mentioned our design to *Voltaire*. He looked at me, as if I had talked of going to the North Pole, and said, "You do not insist on my accompanying you?"—"No, sir."—"Then I am very willing you should go."[2] I was not afraid that our curious expedition would be prevented by such apprehensions; but I doubted that it would not be possible to prevail on Dr. Johnson to relinquish, for some time, the felicity of a London life, which, to a man who can enjoy it with full intellectual relish, is apt to make existence in any narrower sphere seem insipid or irksome. I doubted that he would not be willing to come down from his elevated state of philosophical dignity; from a superiority of wisdom amongst the wise, and of learning amongst the learned; and from flashing his wit upon minds bright enough to reflect it.

He had disappointed my expectations so long, that I began to despair; but in spring, 1773, he talked of coming to Scotland that year with so much firmness, that I hoped he was at last in earnest. I knew that, if he were once launched from the metropolis, he would go forward very well; and I got our common friends there to assist in setting him afloat. To Mrs. *Thrale*[3] in particular, whose enchantment over him seldom failed, I was much obliged. It was, "*I'll give thee a wind.*"—"*Thou art kind.*"[4]—To *attract* him, we had invitations from the chiefs Macdonald and Macleod;

2. He . . . go: Voltaire, who was bored and irritable during this interview, is sarcastically telling Boswell to get out of his sight. 3. Mrs. Thrale: Hester Lynch Thrale (1741–1821), wife of a wealthy brewer and for twenty years one of Johnson's intimate friends. 4. I'll . . . kind: Boswell quotes speeches of the First and Second Witches in *Macbeth*, I. iii. 11–12.

and, for additional aid, I wrote to Lord *Elibank*, Dr. *William Robertson*, and Dr. *Beattie*.[5]

To Dr. *Robertson*, so far as my letter concerned the present subject, I wrote as follows:

"OUR friend, Mr. *Samuel Johnson*, is in great health and spirits; and, I do think, has a serious resolution to visit Scotland this year. The more attraction, however, the better; and therefore, though I know he will be happy to meet you there, it will forward the scheme, if, in your answer to this, you express yourself concerning it with that power of which you are so happily possessed, and which may be so directed as to operate strongly upon him."

His answer to that part of my letter was quite as I could have wished. It was written with the address and persuasion of the historian of America.

"WHEN I saw you last, you gave us some hopes that you might prevail with Mr. *Johnson* to make out that excursion to Scotland, with the expectation of which we have long flattered ourselves. If he could order matters so, as to pass some time in *Edinburgh*, about the close of the summer session,[6] and then visit some of the Highland scenes, I am confident he would be pleased with the grand features of nature in many parts of this country: he will meet with many persons here who respect him, and some whom I am persuaded he will think not unworthy of his esteem. I wish he would make the experiment. He sometimes cracks his jokes upon us; but he will find that we can distinguish between the stabs of malevolence, and *the rebukes of the righteous, which are like excellent oil,*[7] *and break not the head.* Offer my best compliments to him, and assure him that I shall be happy to have the satisfaction of seeing him under my roof."

To Dr. *Beattie* I wrote, "The chief intention of this letter is to inform you, that I now seriously believe Mr. *Samuel Johnson* will visit *Scotland* this year: but I wish that every power of attraction may be employed to secure our having so valuable an acquisition, and therefore I hope you will, without delay, write to me what I know you think, that I may read it to the mighty sage, with proper emphasis, before I leave London, which I must do soon. He talks of you with the same warmth that he did last year. We are to see as much of *Scotland* as we can, in the months of August and September. We shall not be long of being at *Marischal College.*[8] He is particularly desirous of seeing some of the Western Islands."

Dr. Beattie did better: *ipse venit.*[9] He was, however, so polite as to wave his privilege of *nil mihi rescribas,*[10] and wrote as follows:

"YOUR very kind and agreeable favour of the 20th of April overtook me here yesterday, after having gone to Aberdeen, which place I left about a week ago. I am to set out this day for London, and hope to have the honour of paying my respects to Mr. *Johnson* and you, about a week or ten days hence. I shall then do what I can, to enforce the topick you mention; but at present I cannot enter upon it, as I am in a very great hurry; for I intend to begin my journey within an hour or two."

He was as good as his word, and threw some pleasing motives into the northern scale. But, indeed, Mr. Johnson loved all that he heard, from one whom he tells us, in his Lives of the Poets,[11] *Gray* found "a poet, a philosopher, and a good man."

My Lord *Elibank* did not answer my letter to his lordship for some time. The reason will appear, when we come to the isle of *Sky*. I shall then insert my letter, with letters from his lordship, both to myself and Mr. *Johnson*. I beg to be understood, that I insert my own letters, as I relate my own sayings, rather as keys to what is valuable belonging to others, than for their own sake.

Luckily Mr. Justice (now Sir *Robert*) Chambers,[12] who was about to sail for the East-Indies, was going to take leave of his relations at *Newcastle*, and he conducted Dr. *Johnson* to that town. Mr. *Scott*,[13] of *University College*, Oxford, (now Dr. *Scott*, of the Commons,) accompanied him from thence to

5. **Lord . . . Beattie:** Patrick Murray, Fifth Baron Elibank, was a Scot whose knowledge even Johnson respected; Dr. William Robertson, principal of Edinburgh University, was a famous historian; Dr. James Beattie, professor of moral philosophy at Marischal College, Aberdeen, was the author of *An Essay on the Nature and Immutability of Truth* (1770), which was thought by the orthodox to constitute a sufficient reply to Hume's skeptical queries. 6. **summer session:** one of the two yearly sittings of the Court of Session, Scotland's supreme civil court. 7. **excellent oil:** [Boswell's note] Our friend *Edmund Burke*, who by this time had received some pretty sore rubs from Dr. Johnson, on account of the unhappy difference in their politics, upon my repeating this passage to him, exclaimed, "Oil of Vitriol!"

8. **We . . . College:** [Boswell's note] This I find is a Scotticism. I should have said, "It will not be long before we shall be at *Marischal* College." 9. **ipse venit:** He came himself. 10. **nil . . . rescribas:** not replying to me. 11. **Lives . . . Poets:** published 1779–81. 12. **Chambers:** Chambers served as a judge in India and, since 1768, had been a member of Johnson's Club. 13. **Mr. Scott:** William Scott, later Sir William Scott and Baron Stowell; a lawyer and legal scholar, and member of the Club.

Edinburgh. With such propitious convoys did he proceed to my native city. But, lest metaphor should make it be supposed he actually went by sea, I choose to mention that he travelled in post-chaises, of which the rapid motion was one of his most favourite amusements.

Dr. *Samuel Johnson's* character, religious, moral, political, and literary, nay his figure and manner, are, I believe, more generally known than those of almost any man; yet it may not be superfluous here to attempt a sketch of him. Let my readers then remember that he was a sincere and zealous christian, of high-church of England and monarchical principles, which he would not tamely suffer to be questioned; steady and inflexible in maintaining the obligations of piety and virtue, both from a regard to the order of society, and from a veneration for the Great Source of all order; correct, nay stern in his taste; hard to please, and easily offended; impetuous and irritable in his temper; but of a most humane and benevolent heart; having a mind stored with a vast and various collection of learning and knowledge, which he communicated with peculiar perspicuity and force, in rich and choice expression. He united a most logical head with a most fertile imagination, which gave him an extraordinary advantage in arguing; for he could reason close or wide, as he saw best for the moment. He could, when he chose it, be the greatest sophist that ever wielded a weapon in the schools of declamation; but he indulged this only in conversation, for he owned he sometimes talked for victory. He was too conscientious to make errour permanent and pernicious, by deliberately writing it. He was conscious of his superiority. He loved praise when it was brought to him; but was too proud to seek for it. He was somewhat susceptible of flattery. His mind was so full of imagery, that he might have been perpetually a poet. It has been often remarked, that in his poetical pieces, which it is to be regretted are so few, because so excellent, his style is easier than in his prose. There is deception in this: it is not easier, but better suited to the dignity of verse; as one may dance with grace, whose motions, in ordinary walking—in the common step, are aukward. He had a constitutional melancholy, the clouds of which darkened the brightness of his fancy, and gave a gloomy cast to his whole course of thinking: yet, though grave and aweful in his deportment, when he thought it necessary or proper, he frequently indulged himself in pleasantry and sportive sallies. He was prone to superstition, but not to credulity. Though his imagination might incline him to a belief of the

marvellous, and the mysterious, his vigorous reason examined the evidence with jealousy. He had a loud voice, and a slow deliberate utterance, which no doubt gave some additional weight to the sterling metal of his conversation. Lord *Pembroke*[14] said once to me at *Wilton*, with a happy pleasantry, and some truth, that "Dr. *Johnson's* sayings would not appear so extraordinary were it not for his *bow-wow way;*" but I admit the truth of this only on some occasions. The *Messiah,*[15] played upon the *Canterbury organ*, is more sublime than when played upon an inferior instrument: but very slight music will seem grand, when conveyed to the ear through that majestic medium. *While therefore Doctor Johnson's sayings are read, let his manner be taken along.* Let it however be observed, that the sayings themselves are generally great; that, though he might be an ordinary composer at times, he was for the most part a *Handel*. His person was large, robust, I may say approaching to the gigantic, and grown unwieldy from corpulency. His countenance was naturally of the cast of an ancient statue, but somewhat disfigured by the scars of that *evil*, which, it was formerly imagined, the *royal touch*[16] could cure. He was now in his sixty-fourth year: he was become a little dull of hearing. His sight had always been somewhat weak; yet, so much does mind govern, and even supply the deficiency of organs, that his perceptions were uncommonly quick and accurate. His head, and sometimes also his body, shook with a kind of motion like the effect of a palsy: he was frequently disturbed by cramps, or convulsive contractions,[17] of the nature of

14. **Lord Pembroke:** Henry Herbert, Tenth Earl of Pembroke, a soldier and administrator; his splendor dazzled Boswell but caused Horace Walpole to regard him as "a young profligate." 15. **Messiah:** famous oratorio (1742) by George Frederick Handel (1685–1759), German composer naturalized as a British subject in 1726. 16. **royal touch:** Johnson's mother, following an ancient superstition that the monarch's touch could cure scrofula (often called the king's evil), took Johnson, aged two and a half, to London to be touched by Queen Anne at St. James's Palace. Ever after Johnson wore around his neck the gold token, or touchpiece, given him by the Queen on this occasion. 17. **convulsive contractions:** [Boswell's note, added to the second edition (1785)] Such they appeared to me; but since the former edition, Sir Joshua Reynolds has observed to me, "that Dr. Johnson's extraordinary gestures were only habits, in which he indulged himself at certain times. When in company, where he was not free, or when engaged earnestly in conversation, he never gave way to such habits, which proves that they were not involuntary." I still however think, that these gestures were involuntary; for surely had not that been the case, he would have restrained them in the publick streets.

that distemper called *St. Vitus's* dance. He wore a full suit of plain brown clothes, with twisted hair buttons of the same colour, a large bushy greyish wig, a plain shirt, black worsted stockings, and silver buckles. Upon this tour, when journeying, he wore boots, and a very wide brown cloth great coat, with pockets which might have almost held the two volumes of his folio dictionary; and he carried in his hand a large English oak stick. Let me not be censured for mentioning such minute particulars. Every thing relative to so great a man is worth observing. I remember Dr. *Adam Smith,*[18] in his rhetorical lectures at *Glasgow,* told us he was glad to know that *Milton* wore latchets in his shoes, instead of buckles. When I mention the oak stick, it is but letting *Hercules* have his club; and, by-and-by, my readers will find this stick will bud, and produce a good joke.[19]

This imperfect sketch of "the COMBINATION and the *form*" of that Wonderful Man, whom I venerated and loved while in this world, and after whom I gaze with humble hope, now that it has pleased ALMIGHTY GOD to call him to a better world, will serve to introduce to the fancy of my readers the capital object of the following journal, in the course of which I trust they will attain to a considerable degree of acquaintance with him.

His prejudice against *Scotland* was announced almost as soon as he began to appear in the world of letters. In his *London,* a poem, are the following nervous[20] lines:

> For who would leave, unbrib'd, *Hibernia's* land?
> Or change the rocks of *Scotland* for the Strand?
> There none are swept by sudden fate away;
> But all, whom hunger spares, with age decay.

The truth is, like the ancient *Greeks* and *Romans,* he allowed himself to look upon all nations but his own as barbarians: not only Hibernia, but Spain, Italy, and France, are attacked in the same poem. If he was particularly prejudiced against the *Scots,* it was because they were more in his way; because he thought their success in *England* rather exceeded the due proportion of their real merit; and because he could not but see in them that nationality which I should think no liberal minded Scotsman will deny.[21] He was indeed, if I may be allowed the phrase, at bottom much of a *John Bull;* much of a blunt *true-born Englishman.* There was a stratum of common clay under the rock of marble. He was voraciously fond of good eating; and he had a great deal of that quality called *humour,* which gives an oiliness and a gloss to every other quality.

I am, I flatter myself, compleatly a citizen of the world.—In my travels through Holland, Germany, Switzerland, Italy, Corsica, France, I never felt myself from home; and I sincerely love "every kindred and tongue, and people and nation." I subscribe to what my late truly learned and philosophical friend Crosbie[22] said, that the English are better animals than the Scots; they are nearer the sun; their blood is richer, and more mellow: but when I humour any of them in an outrageous contempt of Scotland, I fairly own I treat them as children. And thus I have, at some moments, found myself obliged to treat even Dr. Johnson.

To *Scotland* however he ventured; and he returned from it in great good humour, with his prejudices much lessened, and with very grateful feelings of the hospitality with which he was treated; as is evident from that admirable work, his "Journey to the Western Islands of Scotland," which to my utter astonishment, has been misapprehended, even to rancour, by many of my countrymen.

To have the company of *Chambers* and *Scott,* he delayed his journey so long, that the court of session, which rises on the eleventh of August, was broke up before he got to Edinburgh.

On Saturday the fourteenth of August, 1773, late in the evening, I received a note from him, that he was arrived at *Boyd's* inn, at the head of the *Canongate.* I went to him directly. He embraced me cordially; and I exulted in the thought, that I now had him actually

---

18. Dr. . . . Smith: (1723–90), professor of logic and, later, of moral philosophy at Glasgow University; author of *An Inquiry into the Nature and Causes of the Wealth of Nations* (1776), a classic of political economy that helped establish the modern study of economics. **19. this . . . joke:** Johnson never tired of amusing himself by reminding Boswell of the scarcity of trees in Scotland. He lost his walking stick on the Isle of Mull in early October, and on October 16 Boswell writes; "I could not persuade him out of a suspicion that it had been stolen. 'No, no, my friend (said he), it is not to be expected that any man in Mull, who has got it, will part with it. Consider, sir, the value of such a *piece of timber* here !' " **20. nervous:** vigorous, forceful.

21. The truth . . . deny: Johnson's lines actually say the opposite of what Boswell imagines. *London. A Poem* (1738), written in imitation of Juvenal's third satire, rejects London, with its atrocious follies and crimes, in favor of the peace and quiet of rural Wales. **22. Crosbie:** Andrew Crosbie, a Scottish lawyer and very distant relation of Boswell's; he had died less than four months before.

in *Caledonia*. Mr. *Scott's* amiable manners, and attachment to our *Socrates*, at once united me to him. He told me that, before I came in, the doctor had unluckily had a bad specimen of *Scottish* cleanliness. He then drank no fermented liquor. He asked to have his lemonade made sweeter; upon which the waiter, with his greasy fingers, lifted a lump of sugar, and put it into it. The doctor, in indignation, threw it out of the window. *Scott* said, he was afraid he would have knocked the waiter down. Mr. *Johnson* told me, that such another trick was played him at the house of a lady in *Paris*. He was to do me the honour to lodge under my roof. I regretted sincerely that I had not also a room for Mr. *Scott*. Mr. *Johnson* and I walked arm-in-arm up the High-street, to my house in *James's court*: it was a dusky night: I could not prevent his being assailed by the evening effluvia of Edinburgh. I heard a late baronet, of some distinction in the political world in the beginning of the present reign, observe, that "walking the streets of Edinburgh at night was pretty perilous, and a good deal odoriferous." The peril is much abated, by the care which the magistrates have taken to enforce the city laws against throwing foul water from the windows; but, from the structure of the houses in the old town, which consist of many stories, in each of which a different family lives, and there being no covered sewers, the odour still continues. A zealous Scotsman would have wished Mr. *Johnson* to be without one of his five senses upon this occasion. As we marched slowly along, he grumbled in my ear, "I smell you in the dark!" But he acknowledged that the breadth of the street, and the loftiness of the buildings on each side, made a noble appearance.

My wife had tea ready for him, which it is well known he delighted to drink at all hours, particularly when sitting up late, and of which his able defence against Mr. *Jonas Hanway*[23] should have obtained him a magnificent reward from the East-India Company. He shewed much complacency, upon finding that the

mistress of the house was so attentive to his singular habit; and as no man could be more polite when he chose to be so, his address to her was most courteous and engaging; and his conversation soon charmed her into a forgetfulness of his external appearance.

I did not begin to keep a regular full journal till some days after we had set out from Edinburgh; but I have luckily preserved a good many fragments of his *Memorabilia* from his very first evening in *Scotland*.

We had, a little before this, had a trial for murder, in which the judges had allowed the lapse of twenty years since its commission as a plea in bar,[24] in conformity with the doctrine of prescription in the *civil* law, which *Scotland* and several other countries in *Europe* have adopted. He at first disapproved of this; but then he thought there was something in it, if there had been for twenty years a neglect to prosecute a crime which was *known*. He would not allow that a murder, by not being *discovered* for twenty years, should escape punishment. We talked of the ancient trial by duel. He did not think it so absurd as is generally supposed; "For (said he) it was only allowed when the question was *in equilibrio*,[25] as when one affirmed and another denied; and they had a notion that Providence would interfere in favour of him who was in the right. But as it was found that in a duel, he who was in the right had not a better chance than he who was in the wrong, therefore society instituted the present mode of trial, and gave the advantage to him who is in the right."

We sat till near two in the morning, having chatted a good while after my wife left us. She had insisted, that to shew all respect to the Sage, she would give up our own bed-chamber to him and take a worse. This I cannot but gratefully mention, as one of a thousand obligations which I owe her, since the great obligation of her being pleased to accept of me as her husband.

Sunday, 15th August.

Mr. Scott came to breakfast, at which I introduced to Dr. Johnson, and him, my friend Sir *William Forbes*, now of *Pitsligo*; a man of whom too much good cannot be said; who, with distinguished abilities, and application in his profession of a Banker, is at once a good companion, and a good christian; which I think is saying enough. Yet it is but justice to record, that

---

23. Mr. . . . Hanway: traveler, philanthropist, and reformer; he published in 1756 what Boswell calls a "violent attack" upon the use of tea. Johnson reviewed Hanway's *An Essay on Tea* in *The Literary Magazine;* in his review he described himself as "a hardened and shameless tea-drinker, who has, for twenty years, diluted his meals with only the infusion of this fascinating plant; whose kettle has scarcely time to cool; who with tea amuses the evening, with tea solaces the midnight, and, with tea, welcomes the morning."

24. a plea . . . bar: a defense plea of sufficient weight to impel the court to dismiss the indictment. 25. in equilibrio: unascertainable.

once, when he was in a dangerous illness, he was watched with the anxious apprehension of a general calamity; day and night his house was beset with affectionate inquiries; and, upon his recovery, *Te Deum*[26] was the universal chorus from the *hearts* of his countrymen.

Mr. Johnson was pleased with my daughter *Veronica*, then a child of about four months old. She had the appearance of listening to him. His motions seemed to her to be intended for her amusement; and when he stopped, she fluttered and made a little infantine noise, and a kind of signal for him to begin again. She would be held close to him; which was a proof, from simple nature, that his figure was not horrid. Her fondness for him endeared her still more to me, and I declared she should have five hundred pounds of additional fortune.

We talked of the practice of the law. Sir William Forbes said, he thought an honest lawyer should never undertake a cause which he was satisfied was not a just one. "Sir (said Mr. Johnson) a lawyer has no business with the justice or injustice of the cause which he undertakes, unless his client asks his opinion, and then he is bound to give it honestly. The justice or injustice of the cause is to be decided by the judge. Consider, Sir; what is the purpose of courts of justice? It is, that every man may have his cause fairly tried, by men appointed to try causes. A lawyer is not to tell what he knows to be a lie: he is not to produce what he knows to be a false deed; but he is not to usurp the province of the jury and of the judge, and determine what shall be the effect of evidence—what shall be the result of legal argument. As it rarely happens that a man is fit to plead his own cause, lawyers are a class of the community, who, by study and experience, have acquired the art and power of arranging evidence, and of applying to the points at issue what the law has settled. A lawyer is to do for his client all that his client might fairly do for himself, if he could. If, by a superiority of attention, of knowledge, of skill, and a better method of communication, he has the advantage of his adversary, it is an advantage to which he is entitled. There must always be some advantage, on one side or other; and it is better that advantage should be had by talents, than by chance. If lawyers were to undertake no causes till they were sure they were just,

a man might be precluded altogether from a trial of his claim, though, were it judicially examined, it might be found a very just claim."—This was sound practical doctrine, and rationally repressed a too refined scrupulosity of conscience.

Emigration was at this time a common topick of discourse. Dr. Johnson regretted it as hurtful to human happiness: "For (said he) it spreads mankind, which weakens the defence of a nation, and lessens the comfort of living. Men, thinly scattered, make a shift, but a bad shift, without many things. A smith is ten miles off: they'll do without a nail or a staple. A taylor is far from them: they'll botch their own clothes. It is being concentrated which produces high convenience."

Sir William Forbes, Mr. Scott, and I, accompanied Mr. Johnson to the chapel, founded by Lord Chief Baron Smith, for the service of the Church of England. The Reverend Mr. Carre, the senior clergyman, preached from these words, "Because the Lord reigneth, let the earth be glad."—I was sorry to think Mr. Johnson did not attend to the sermon, Mr. Carre's low voice not being strong enough to reach his hearing. A selection of Mr. Carre's sermons[27] has, since his death, been published by Sir William Forbes, and the world has acknowledged their uncommon merit. I am well assured Lord Mansfield[28] has pronounced them to be excellent.

Here I obtained a promise from Lord Chief Baron Orde, that he would dine at my house next day. I presented Mr. Johnson to his Lordship, who politely said to him, "I have not the honour of knowing you; but I hope for it, and to see you at my house. I am to wait on you to-morrow." This respectable English judge will be long remembered in Scotland, where he built an elegant house, and lived in it magnificently. His own ample fortune, with the addition of his salary, enabled him to be splendidly hospitable. It may be fortunate for an individual amongst ourselves to be Lord Chief Baron; and a most worthy man now has the office; but, in my opinion, it is better for Scotland in general, that some of our publick employments should be filled by gentlemen of distinction from the south side of the Tweed, as we have the benefit of promotion in England. Such an interchange would make a beneficial mixture of manners, and render our

26. Te Deum: a hymn of praise in the Book of Common Prayer; an English version of the medieval Latin hymn beginning *Te Deum laudamus* (We praise thee, O Lord).

27. Mr. . . . sermons: by the Reverend George Carr; published in 1777. **28. Lord Mansfield:** William Murray, Fifth Earl of Mansfield, regarded as one of the greatest English lawyers and judges of his day.

union more complete. Lord Chief Baron Orde was on good terms with us all, in a narrow country filled with jarring interests and keen parties; and, though I well knew his opinion to be the same with my own, he kept himself aloof at a very critical period indeed, when the *Douglas cause*[29] shook the sacred security of *birthright* in Scotland to its foundation; a cause, which had it happened before the Union, when there was no appeal to a British House of Lords, would have left the great fortress of honours and of property in ruins.

When we got home, Dr. Johnson desired to see my books. He took down Ogden's Sermons on Prayer,[30] on which I set a very high value, having been much edified by them, and he retired with them to his room. He did not stay long, but soon joined us in the drawing room. I presented to him Mr. Robert Arbuthnot, a relation of the celebrated Dr. Arbuthnot,[31] and a man of literature and taste. To him we were obliged for a previous recommendation, which secured us a very agreeable reception at St. Andrews, and which Dr. Johnson, in his Journey, ascribes to "some invisible friend."

Of Dr. Beattie, Mr. Johnson said, "Sir, he has

written[32] like a man conscious of the truth, and feeling his own strength. Treating your adversary with respect, is giving him an advantage to which he is not entitled. The greatest part of men cannot judge of reasoning, and are impressed by character; so that, if you allow your adversary a respectable character, they will think, that though you differ from him, you may be in the wrong. Sir, treating your adversary with respect, is striking soft in a battle. And as to *Hume*[33]—a man who has so much conceit as to tell all mankind that they have been bubbled[34] for ages, and he is the wise man who sees better than they—a man who has so little scrupulosity as to venture to oppose those principles which have been thought necessary to human happiness—is he to be surprised if another man comes and laughs at him? If he is the great man he thinks himself, all this cannot hurt him: it is like throwing peas against a rock." He added *"something much too rough,"* both as to Mr. Hume's head and heart, which I suppress.[35] Violence is, in my opinion, not suitable to the Christian cause. Besides, I always lived on good terms with Mr. Hume, though I have frankly told him, I was not clear that it was right in me to keep company with him. "But (said I) how much better are you than your books!" He was cheerful, obliging, and instructive; he was charitable to the poor; and many an agreeable hour have I passed with him. I have preserved some entertaining and interesting memoirs of him, particularly when he knew himself to be dying, which I may some time or other communicate to the world. I shall not, however, extol him so very highly as Dr. *Adam Smith* does, who says, in a letter to Mr. *Strahan* the Printer (not a confidential letter to his friend, but a letter which is

29. Douglas cause: (case) one of the most sensational civil law cases of Boswell's time, and a case in which he was deeply interested. The question at issue was the legitimacy of the surviving heir of Archibald, Duke of Douglas; the legitimacy was disputed by the Hamilton family, which stood to benefit by inheritance if the Douglas heir was unable to prove his right to the estate. In 1767 the Court of Session declared in favor of the Hamiltons, but two years later the House of Lords, sitting on an appeal, reversed this decision and proclaimed the legitimate continuation of the Douglas inheritance. The conservative Boswell, instinctively enthusiastic for both the prerogatives of noble families and the absolute security of inheritance, busied himself about the Douglas case, writing—among other inflammatory pieces—*Dorando, a Spanish Tale* (1767), which presents the issues, thinly disguised, in an allegory favorable to Douglas. After the case was finally settled, Boswell was rewarded by being retained as counsel by Archibald Douglas, the successful heir. **30. Ogden's . . . Prayer:** *Sermons on the Efficacy of Prayer and Intercession* (1770) by Dr. Samuel Ogden. Boswell, who calls Ogden "my favourite preacher," refers to these sermons so frequently in *The Journal of a Tour* that Thomas Rowlandson, artist and caricaturist, produced a satiric engraving that portrays Boswell setting out on his tour from Edinburgh, his as yet empty journal and his copy of Ogden under his arm. **31. Dr. Arbuthnot:** Dr. John Arbuthnot (1667–1735), personal physician to Queen Anne; he was intimate with Pope, Swift, and Gay and contributed to the satiric projects of the Scriblerus Club. Robert Arbuthnot, an Edinburgh banker, was a distant relative. (See Pope's *Epistle to Dr. Arbuthnot* in Part Two.)

32. written: in his *Essay on Truth*, in opposition to Hume's skepticism. **33. Hume:** the contemporary reputation of David Hume (1711–76), philosopher, historian, and political economist, was largely that of a dangerous religious skeptic and subversive, whose *Philosophical Essays Concerning Human Understanding* (see Part Five) and *The Natural History of Religion* (1757) were considered to threaten the absolutist philosophic basis of traditional Christian knowledge and belief. **34. bubbled:** cheated. **35. I suppress:** The recently discovered Boswell papers contain Johnson's complete remark: to Boswell's question "Why attack [Hume's] heart?" Johnson replied, "Why, sir, because his head has corrupted it. Or perhaps it has perverted his head. I know not indeed whether he has first been a blockhead and that has made him a rogue, or first been a rogue and that has made him a blockhead." Boswell's phrase "something much too rough" alludes to line 4 of Pope's *First Satire of the Second Book of Horace* (see Part Two).

published with all formality): "Upon the whole, I have always considered him, both in his life-time and since his death, as approaching as nearly to the idea of a perfectly wise and virtuous man as perhaps the nature of human frailty will permit." Let Dr. Smith consider: Was not Mr. Hume blest with good health, good spirits, good friends, a competent and increasing fortune? And had he not also a perpetual feast of fame? But, as a learned friend[36] has observed to me, "What trials did he undergo, to prove the perfection of his virtue? Did he ever experience any great instance of adversity?"—When I read this sentence, delivered by my old *Professor of Moral Philosophy*, I could not help exclaiming with the *Psalmist*, "Surely I have now more understanding than my teachers!"

When we were talking, there came a note to me from Dr. William Robertson.

DEAR SIR,

I have been expecting every day to hear from you, of Dr. Johnson's arrival. Pray, what do you know about his motions? I long to take him by the hand. I write this from the college, where I have only this scrap of paper. Ever yours,

Sunday.   W. R.

It pleased me to find Dr. Robertson thus eager to meet Dr. Johnson. I was glad I could answer, that he was come: and I begged Dr. Robertson might be with us as soon as he could.

Sir William Forbes, Mr. Scott, Mr. Arbuthnot, and another gentleman, dined with us. "Come, Dr. Johnson, (said I) it is commonly thought that our veal in Scotland is not good. But here is some which I believe you will like."—There was no catching him.— *Johnson.* "Why, Sir, what is commonly thought, I should take to be true. *Your* veal may be good; but that will only be an exception to the general opinion; not a proof against it."

Dr. Robertson, according to the custom of Edinburgh at that time, dined in the interval between the forenoon and afternoon service, which was then later than now; so we had not the pleasure of his company till dinner was over, when he came and drank wine with us. And then began some animated dialogue, of which here follows a pretty full note.

We talked of Mr. Burke.[37]—Dr. Johnson said, he

had great variety of knowledge, store of imagery, copiousness of language.—*Robertson.* "He has wit too."—*Johnson,* "No, Sir; he never succeeds there. 'Tis low; 'tis conceit.[38] I used to say, Burke never once made a good joke.[39] What I most envy Burke for, is,

---

into the Origin of Our Ideas of the Sublime and Beautiful (1756), and for a few scattered political pamphlets. (See the selections from Burke later in Part Six.) **38. conceit:** verbal cunning; cf. "false wit." **39. Burke . . . joke:** [Boswell's note] This was one of the points upon which Dr. Johnson was strangely heterodox. For, surely, Mr. Burke, with his other remarkable qualities, is also distinguished for his wit, and for wit of all kinds too; not merely that power of language which Pope chuses to denominate wit,

(True wit is Nature to advantage drest;
What oft was thought, but ne'er so well exprest.)

but surprising allusions, brilliant sallies of vivacity, and pleasant conceits. His speeches in parliament are strewed with them. Take, for instance, the variety which he has given in his wide range, yet exact detail, when exhibiting his Reform Bill. And his conversation abounds in wit. Let me put down a specimen.—I told him, I had seen, at a *Blue-stocking* assembly, a number of ladies sitting round a worthy and tall friend of ours [Bennet Langton], listening to his literature. "Aye (said he) like maids round a May-pole."—I told him, I had found out a perfect definition of human nature, as distinguished from the animal. An ancient philosopher [Plato] said, Man was "a two-legged animal without feathers"—upon which his rival Sage [Diogenes] had a Cock plucked bare, and set him down in the school before all the disciples, as a "Philosophic Man." Dr. [Benjamin] Franklin said, Man was "a tool-making animal," which is very well; for, no animal but man makes a thing, by means of which he can make another thing. But this applies to very few of the species. My definition of *Man* is, "a Cooking Animal." The beasts have memory, judgement, and all the faculties and passions of our mind, in a certain degree; but no beast is a cook. The trick of the monkey using the cat's paw to roast a chestnut, is only a piece of shrewd malice in that *turpissima bestia* [most vile animal], which humbles us so sadly by its similarity to us. Man alone can dress a good dish; and every man whatever is more or less a cook, in seasoning what he himself eats—Your definition is good, said Mr. Burke, and I now see the full force of the common proverb, "There is *reason* in roasting of eggs."—When Mr. Wilkes, in his days of tumultuous opposition, was borne upon the shoulders of the mob, Mr. Burke (as Mr. Wilkes told me himself, with classical admiration) applied to him what *Horace* says of *Pindar,*

———*Numeri*sque fertur
LEGE *solutis*

[and he is borne along in numbers unrestrained by laws].

Sir Joshua Reynolds, who agrees with me entirely as to Mr. Burke's fertility of wit, said, that this was "dignifying a pun." He also observed, that he has often heard Burke say, in the course of an evening, ten good things, each of which would have served a noted wit (whom he named) to live upon for a twelvemonth.

---

36. a learned friend: perhaps Edmond Malone. **37. Mr. Burke:** Edmund Burke (1729–97), parliamentarian and political theorist, had not yet published his major political works and was known as a writer mainly for his treatise on psychology and aesthetics, *A Philosophical Enquiry*

his being constantly the same. He is never what we call hum-drum; never unwilling to begin to talk, nor in a haste to leave off."—*Boswell.* "Yet he can listen."—*Johnson.* "No; I cannot say he is good at that. So desirous is he to talk, that, if one is speaking at this end of the table, he'll speak to somebody at the other end. Burke, Sir, is such a man, that if you met him for the first time in a street where you were stopped by a drove of oxen, and you and he stepped aside to take shelter but for five minutes, he'd talk to you in such a manner, that, when you parted, you would say, this is an extraordinary man. Now, you may be long enough with me, without finding any thing extraordinary." He said, he believed Burke was intended for the law; but either had not money enough to follow it, or had not diligence enough. He said, he could not understand how a man could apply to one thing, and not to another. *Robertson* said, one man had more judgement, another more imagination.—*Johnson.* "No, Sir; it is only one man has more mind than another. He may direct it differently; he may, by accident, see the success of one kind of study, and take a desire to excel in it. I am persuaded that, had Sir Isaac Newton[40] applied to poetry, he would have made a very fine epic poem. I could as easily apply to law as to tragick poetry."—*Boswell.* "Yet, Sir, you did apply to tragick poetry, not to law."—*Johnson.* "Because, Sir, I had not money to study law. Sir, the man who has vigour may walk to the east, just as well as to the west, if he happens to turn his head that way."—*Boswell.* "But, Sir, 'tis like walking up and down a hill; one man will naturally do the one better than the other. A hare will run up a hill best, from her legs[41] being short; a dog down."—*Johnson.* "Nay, Sir; that is from mechanical powers. If you make mind mechanical, you may argue in that manner. One mind is a vice, and holds fast; there's a good memory. Another is a file; and he is a disputant, a controversialist. Another is a razor; and he is sarcastical."—We talked of *Whitefield.*[42] He said, he was at the same college with him, and knew him *before he began to be better than other people* (smiling); that he believed he sincerely meant well, but had a mixture of politicks and ostentation: whereas *Wesley*[43] thought of religion only.[44]—*Robertson* said, Whitefield had strong natural eloquence, which, if cultivated, would have done great things.—*Johnson.* "Why, Sir, I take it he was at the height of what his abilities could do, and was sensible of it. He had the ordinary advantages of education; but he chose to pursue that oratory which is for the mob."—*Boswell.* "He had great effect on the passions."—*Johnson.* "Why, Sir, I don't think so. He could not represent a succession of pathetick images. He vociferated, and made an impression. *There*, again, was a mind like a hammer."—Dr. Johnson now said, a certain eminent political friend of our's[45] was wrong, in his maxim of sticking to a certain set of *men* on all occasions. "I can see that a man may do right to stick to a *party* (said he); that is to say, he is a *Whig*, or he is a *Tory*, and he thinks one of those parties upon the whole the best, and that, to make it prevail, it must be generally supported, though, in particulars, it may be wrong. He takes its faggot of principles, in which there are fewer rotten sticks than in the other, though some rotten sticks to be sure; and they cannot well be separated. But, to bind one's self to one man, or one set of men, (who may be right to-day and wrong to-morrow) without any general preference of system, I must disapprove."

He told us of Cooke,[46] who translated Hesiod, and lived twenty years on a translation of Plautus, for which he was always taking subscriptions; and that he presented Foote[47] to a Club, in the following singular

---

40. Sir . . . Newton: (1642–1727), brilliant mathematician, physicist, and philosopher, whose *Principia Mathematica* (1687) provided his age with its version of the laws of motion and the principle of universal gravitation. President of the Royal Society for twenty-five years, Newton was the greatest British scientist of his time. **41. legs:** altered to *fore-legs* in the second edition (1785). **42. Whitefield:** George Whitefield (1714–70), a Methodist preacher of notable oratorical and histrionic powers.

43. Wesley: John Wesley (1703–91), founder of Methodism. **44. religion only:** [Boswell's note] That cannot be said now, after the flagrant part which Mr. *John Wesley* took against our American brethren, when, in his own name, he threw amongst his enthusiastick flock, the very individual combustibles of Dr. *Johnson's* [anti-American pamphlet] "Taxation no Tyranny;" and after the intolerant spirit which he manifested against our fellow christians of the Roman Catholick Communion, for which that able champion, Father *O'Leary*, has given him so hearty a drubbing. But I should think myself very unworthy, if I did not at the same time acknowledge Mr. John Wesley's merit, as a veteran "Soldier of Jesus Christ," who has, I do believe, "turned many from darkness into light, and from the power of *Satan* to the living GOD." **45. friend of our's:** Burke. **46. Cooke:** Thomas Cooke (1703–56), poet, journalist, and pamphleteer, sometimes called Hesiod Cooke for his translations from that Greek poet. Cooke is baited by Pope in *The Dunciad*, II. 138. **47. Foote:** Samuel Foote (1720–77), mimic, comic actor, and playwright; his younger uncle Samuel Goodere was hanged in 1741 for murdering his brother.

manner: "This is the nephew of the gentleman who was lately hung in chains for murdering his brother."

In the evening I introduced to Mr. Johnson[48] two good friends of mine, Mr. William Nairne, Advocate, and Mr. Hamilton of Sundrum, my neighbour in the country, both of whom supped with us. I have preserved nothing of what passed, except that Dr. Johnson displayed another of his heterodox opinions, —a contempt of tragick acting. He said, "the action of all players in tragedy is bad. It should be a man's study to repress those signs of emotion and passion, as they are called." He was of a direct contrary opinion to that of *Fielding,* in his *Tom Jones;* who makes *Partridge* say, of *Garrick,*[49] "why, I could act as well as he himself. I am sure, if I had seen a ghost, I should have looked in the very same manner, and done just as he did." For, when I asked him, "Would not you, Sir, start as Mr. Garrick does, if you saw a ghost?" He answered, "I hope not. If I did, I should frighten the ghost."

Monday, 16th August.

Dr. William Robertson came to breakfast. We talked of *Ogden* on Prayer. Dr. Johnson said, "The same arguments which are used against GOD's hearing prayer, will serve against his rewarding good, and punishing evil. He has resolved, he has declared, in the former case as in the latter." He had last night looked into Lord *Hailes's* "Remarks on the History of Scotland." Dr. Robertson and I said, it was a pity Lord Hailes did not write greater things. His lordship had not then published his "Annals of Scotland."— *Johnson.* "I remember I was once on a visit at the house of a lady for whom I had a high respect. There was a good deal of company in the room. When they were gone, I said to this lady, 'What foolish talking have we had!'—'Yes, (said she) but while they talked, you said nothing.'—I was struck with the reproof. How much better is the man who does any thing that is innocent, than he who does nothing. Besides, I love

anecdotes. I fancy mankind may come, in time, to write all aphoristically, except in narrative; grow weary of preparation, and connection, and illustration, and all those arts by which a big book is made.—If a man is to wait till he weaves anecdotes into a system, we may be long in getting them, and get but few, in comparison of what we might get."

Dr. Robertson said, the notions of *Eupham Macallan,* a fanatick woman, of whom Lord Hailes gives a sketch, were still prevalent among some of the Presbyterians; and therefore it was right in Lord Hailes, a man of known piety, to undeceive them.

We walked out, that Dr. Johnson might see some of the things which we have to shew at Edinburgh. We went to the *Parliament House,* where the Parliament of Scotland sat, and where the *Ordinary Lords* of Session hold their courts; and to the *New Session House* adjoining to it, where our Court of *Fifteen* (the fourteen *Ordinaries,* with the Lord President at their head) sit as a Court of Review. We went to the *Advocates Library,* of which Dr. Johnson took a cursory view, and then to what is called the *Laigh* (or under) Parliament House, where the records of Scotland, which has an universal security by register,[50] are deposited, till the great Register Office be finished. I loved to behold Dr. Samuel Johnson rolling about in this old magazine of antiquities. There was, by this time, a pretty numerous circle of us attending upon him. Somebody talked of happy moments for composition; and how a man can write at one time, and not at another.—"Nay (said Dr. Johnson) a man may write at any time, if he will set himself doggedly to it."

I here began to indulge *old Scottish* sentiments, and to express a warm regret, that, by our Union with *England,* we were no more;—our independent kingdom was lost.—*Johnson.* "Sir, never talk of your independency, who could let your Queen remain twenty years in captivity, and then be put to death,[51] without even a pretence of justice, without your ever attempting to rescue her; and such a Queen too! as every man of any gallantry of spirit would have sacrificed his life for."—*Worthy Mr. James Kerr, Keeper of the Records.* "Half our nation was bribed by *English* money."—*Johnson.* "Sir, that is no defence.

---

48. **Mr. Johnson:** [Boswell's note] It may be observed, that I sometimes call my great friend, *Mr.* Johnson, sometimes *Dr.* Johnson; though he had at this time a doctor's degree from Trinity College, Dublin. The University of Oxford afterwards conferred it upon him by a diploma, in very honourable terms. It was some time before I could bring myself to call him Doctor; but, as he has been long known by that title, I shall give it to him in the rest of this Journal. 49. **Garrick:** David Garrick (1717–79), dramatist, theater manager, and the greatest actor of his time. Johnson and he had been friends since 1736, when Garrick was a pupil at Johnson's short-lived school near Lichfield.

50. **universal . . . register:** the right to copies of all legal documents concerning landed property. 51. **let . . . death:** Johnson refers to Mary Stuart, Queen of Scots, who was taken prisoner by Queen Elizabeth in 1568 and executed in 1587.

That makes you worse."—*Good Mr. Brown, Keeper of the Advocates Library.* "We had better say nothing about it."—*Boswell.* "You would have been glad, however, to have had us last war, Sir, to fight your battles!"—*Johnson.* "We should have had you for the same price, though there had been no union, as we might have had Swiss, or other troops. No, no, I shall agree to a separation. You have only to *go home.*"— Just as he had said this, I, to divert the subject, shewed him the signed assurances of the three successive Kings of the Hanover family, to maintain the Presbyterian establishment in Scotland.—"We'll give you that into the bargain," said he.

We next went to the great church of St. Giles, which has lost its original magnificence in the inside, by being divided into four places of Presbyterian worship. "Come (said Dr. Johnson jocularly to Principal Robertson) let me see what was once a church!" We entered that division which was formerly called the *New Church*, and of late the *High Church*, so well known by the eloquence of Dr. *Hugh Blair.*[52] It is now very elegantly fitted up; but it was then shamefully dirty. Dr. Johnson said nothing at the time; but when we came to the great door of the Royal Infirmary, where, upon a board, was this inscription, *"Clean your feet!"* he turned about slyly, and said, "There is no occasion for putting this at the doors of your churches!"

We then conducted him down the Post-house stairs, Parliament-close, and made him look up from the Cow-gate to the highest building in Edinburgh (from which he had just descended) being thirteen floors or stories from the ground upon the back elevation; the front wall being built upon the edge of the hill, and the back wall rising from the bottom of the hill several stories before it comes to a level with the front wall. We proceeded to the College, with the Principal at our head. Dr. Adam Fergusson, whose "Essay on the History of civil Society" gives him a respectable place in the ranks of literature, was with us. As the College buildings are indeed very mean, the Principal said to Dr. Johnson, that he must give them the same epithet that a Jesuit did when shewing a poor college abroad: *"Hæ miseriæ nostræ."*[53] Dr. Johnson was, however, much pleased with the library, and with the conversation of Dr. James Robertson,

Professor of Oriental Languages, the Librarian. We talked of *Kennicot's* Translation of the Bible,[54] and hoped it would be quite faithful.—*Johnson.* "Sir, I know not any crime so great that a man could contrive to commit, as poisoning the sources of eternal truth."

I pointed out to him where there formerly stood an old wall enclosing part of the college, which I remember bulged out in a threatening manner, and of which there was a common saying, as of *Bacon's* Study at *Oxford*, that it would fall upon the most learned man.[55] It had some time before this been taken down, that the street might be widened, and a more convenient wall built. Mr. Johnson, glad of an opportunity to have a pleasant hit at Scottish learning, said, "they have been afraid it never would fall."

We shewed him the Royal Infirmary, for which, and for every other exertion of generous publick spirit in his power, that noble-minded citizen of Edinburgh, *George Drummond,*[56] will be ever held in honourable remembrance. And we were too proud not to carry him to the Abbey of *Holyrood-house*, that beautiful piece of architecture, but, alas! that deserted mansion of royalty, which *Hamilton* of *Bangour,*[57] in one of his elegant poems, calls

"A virtuous palace, where no monarch dwells."

I was much entertained while Principal Robertson fluently harangued to Dr. Johnson, upon the spot, concerning scenes of his celebrated History of Scotland. We surveyed that part of the palace appropriated to the Duke of Hamilton, as Keeper, in which our beautiful Queen Mary lived, and in which *David Rizzio*[58] was murdered; and also the State Rooms. Dr. Johnson was a great reciter of all sorts of things serious or comical. I over heard him repeating here, in

52. Dr. . . . . Blair: (1718–1800), Presbyterian divine, professor of rhetoric at the University of Edinburgh; author of *Lectures on Rhetoric and Belles Lettres* (1783). **53. Hæ . . . nostræ:** these misfortunes of ours.

54. Kennicot's . . . Bible: Dr. Benjamin Kennicott (1718–83) spent most of his life ascertaining the Hebrew text of the Old Testament; his edition appeared from 1776 to 1780. **55. a common . . . man:** This superstition about the Oxford room thought to have been occupied by Roger Bacon (c. 1214–94) is alluded to by Johnson in line 140 of *The Vanity of Human Wishes* (see earlier in Part Six). **56. George Drummond:** (1687–1766), Lord Provost of Edinburgh and patron of the university; he improved the city by public works. **57. Hamilton of Bangour:** William Hamilton (1704–54), Scottish poet. (See the selection from Hamilton in Part Three.) **58. David Rizzio:** (c. 1533–66), an Italian, Mary Stuart's favorite musician, who became her French secretary and finally a haughty and over-bearing chief minister; he was stabbed to death by Mary's husband, Lord Darnley, and his followers.

a kind of muttering tone, a line of the old ballad, *Johnny Armstrong's Last Good-Night:*

"And ran him through the fair body!"[59]

I suppose his thinking of the stabbing of *Rizzio* had brought this into his mind, by association of ideas.

We returned to my house, where there met him, at dinner, the Duchess of Douglas, Sir Adolphus Oughton, Lord Chief Baron, Sir William Forbes, Principal Robertson, Mr. Cullen, advocate. Before dinner, he told us of a curious conversation between the famous George Faulkner[60] and him. George said that England had drained Ireland of fifty thousand pounds in specie,[61] annually, for fifty years. "How so, Sir! (said Dr. Johnson) you must have a very great trade?" "No trade."—"Very rich mines?" "No mines."—"From whence, then, does all this money come?" "Come! why out of the blood and bowels of the poor people of Ireland!"

He seemed to me to have an unaccountable prejudice against *Swift;* for I once took the liberty to ask him, if Swift had personally offended him, and he told me, he had not. He said to-day, "Swift is clear, but he is shallow. In coarse humour, he is inferiour to Arbuthnot; in delicate humour, he is inferiour to Addison: So he is inferiour to his contemporaries; without putting him against the whole world. I doubt if the "Tale of a Tub" was his; it has so much more thinking, more knowledge, more power, more colour, than any of the works which are indisputably his. If it was his, I shall only say, He was *impar sibi.*"[62]

We gave him as good a dinner as we could. Our Scots muir-fowl, or growse, were then abundant, and quite in season; and, so far as wisdom and wit can be aided by administering agreeable sensations to the palate, my wife took care that our great guest should not be deficient.

Sir Adolphus Oughton, then our Deputy Commander in Chief, who was not only an excellent officer, but one of the most universal scholars I ever knew, had learned the Erse language, and expressed his belief in the authenticity of Ossian's Poetry.[63] Dr. Johnson took the opposite side of that perplexed question; and I was afraid the dispute would have run high between them. But Sir Adolphus, who had a charming sweet temper, changed the discourse, grew playful, laughed at Lord *Monboddo's* notion of men having tails,[64] and called him a Judge *a posteriori*,[65] which amused Dr. Johnson; and thus hostilities were prevented.

At supper we had Dr. Cullen, his son the advocate, Dr. Adam Fergusson, and Mr. Crosbie, advocate. Witchcraft was introduced. *Crosbie* said, he thought it the greatest blasphemy to suppose evil spirits counteracting the Deity, and raising storms, for instance, to destroy his creatures.—*Johnson.* "Why, Sir, if moral evil be consistent with the government of the Deity, why may not physical evil be also consistent with it? It is not more strange that there should be evil spirits, than evil men; evil unembodied spirits, than evil embodied spirits. And as to storms, we know there are such things; and it is no worse that evil spirits raise them, than that they rise."—*Crosbie.* "But it is not credible, that such stories as we are told of witches have happened."—*Johnson.* "Sir, I am not defending their credibility. I am only saying, that your arguments are not good, and will not overturn the belief of witchcraft.—(Dr. Fergusson said to me, aside, 'He is right.')—And then, Sir, you have all mankind, rude and civilized, agreeing in the belief of the agency of preternatural powers. You must take evidence: you must consider, that wise and great men have condemned witches to die."—*Crosbie.* "But an act of Parliament put an end to witchcraft."—*Johnson.* "No, Sir! witchcraft had ceased; and therefore an act of

---

59. And . . . body: [Boswell's note] The stanza from which he took this line is,

"But then rose up all Edinburgh,
    They rose up by thousands three;
A cowardly Scot came John behind,
    And ran him through the fair body!"

60. George Faulkner: (*c.* 1699–1775), Dublin publisher and bookseller called by Swift the Prince of Dublin Printers. **61. specie:** coin. **62. impar sibi:** strangely inconsistent.

63. Ossian's Poetry: The narrative poems *Fingal* (1762) and *Temora* (1763), published, among others, by the Scot James Macpherson (1736–96) as translations of the Erse, or Gaelic, epics of the fictitious ancient poet Ossian. Although Macpherson's Ossianic poems were admired by many (including, later, Napoleon) for their melancholy and simplicity, a few (including Johnson) thought them stupid and justly suspected Macpherson of fraud. (See Johnson's letter to Macpherson earlier in Part Six.) **64. men . . . tails:** James Burnett (1714–99), Lord Monboddo, Scottish judge and anthropologist, in *The Origin and Progress of Language* (1773–92) suggested, among other things, that man was related to the orangutan. Lord Monboddo and his theories were occasional butts of Johnsonian humor: James Beattie reports that whenever Johnson mentioned Monboddo's name, he "grinned horribly a ghastly smile." **65. a posteriori:** reasoning from experience and not from axioms (a priori); the pun implies that Monboddo is a judge of the nature of men's posteriors.

parliament was passed to prevent persecution for what was not witchcraft. Why it ceased, we cannot tell, as we cannot tell the reason of many other things."—Dr. *Cullen*, to keep up the gratification of mysterious disquisition, with the grave address for which he is remarkable in his companionable as in his professional hours, talked, in a very entertaining manner, of people walking and conversing in their sleep. I am very sorry I have no note of this. We talked of the *Ouran-Outang*, and of Lord Monboddo's thinking that he might be taught to speak. Dr. Johnson treated this with ridicule. Mr. *Crosbie* said, that Lord Monboddo believed the existence of every thing possible; in short, that all which is in *posse* might be found in *esse*.[66]—*Johnson.* "But, Sir, it is as possible that the *Ouran-Outang* does not speak, as that he speaks. However, I shall not contest the point. I should have thought it not possible to find a Monboddo; yet *he* exists."—I again mentioned the stage.—*Johnson.* "The appearance of a Player, with whom I have drank tea, counteracts the imagination that he is the character he represents. Nay, you know, nobody imagines that he is the character he represents. They say, 'See *Garrick!* how he looks to-night! See how he'll clutch the dagger!' That is the buz of the theatre."

Tuesday, 17th August.

Sir William Forbes came to breakfast, and brought with him Dr. *Blacklock*,[67] whom he introduced to Dr. Johnson, who received him with a most humane complacency; "Dear Dr. Blacklock, I am glad to see you!"—Blacklock seemed to be much surprized, when Dr. Johnson said, "it was easier to him to write poetry than to compose his Dictionary. His mind was less on the stretch in doing the one than the other. Besides, composing a Dictionary requires books and a desk. You can make a poem walking in the fields, or lying in bed."—Dr. *Blacklock* spoke of scepticism in morals and religion, with apparent uneasiness, as if he wished for more certainty. Dr. *Johnson*, who had thought it all over, and whose vigorous understanding was fortified by much experience, thus encouraged the blind Bard to apply to higher speculations, what

we all willingly submit to in common life. In short, he gave him more familiarly the able and fair reasoning of *Butler's Analogy*:[68] "Why, Sir, the greatest concern we have in this world, the choice of our profession, must be determined without demonstrative reasoning. Human life is not yet so well known, as that we can have it. And take the case of a man who is ill. I call two physicians: they differ in opinion. I am not to lye down, and die between them: I must do something."—The conversation then turned on Atheism; on that horrible book *Système de la Nature*;[69] and on the supposition of an eternal necessity, without design, without a governing mind.—*Johnson.* "If it were so, why has it ceased? Why don't we see men thus produced around us now? Why, at least, does it not keep pace, in some measure, with the progress of time? If it stops because there is now no need of it, then it is plain there is, and ever has been, an all-powerful intelligence. But stay! (said he, with one of his satyrick laughs). Ha! ha! ha! I shall suppose Scotchmen made necessarily, and Englishmen by choice."

At dinner this day, we had Sir Alexander Dick, whose amiable character, and ingenious and cultivated mind, is so generally known (he was then on the verge of seventy, and is now eighty-one, with his faculties entire, his heart warm, and his temper gay); Sir David Dalrymple; Lord Hailes; Mr. Maclaurin, advocate; Dr. Gregory, who now worthily fills his father's medical chair; and my uncle, Dr. Boswell. This was one of Dr. Johnson's best days. He was quite in his element. All was literature and taste, without any interruption. Lord *Hailes*, who is one of the best philologists in Great-Britain, who has written papers in the *World*, and a variety of other works in prose and in verse, both Latin and English, pleased him highly. He told him, he had discovered the Life of *Cheynel*, in the *Student*, to be his.—*Johnson.* "No one else knows it."—Dr. Johnson had, before this, dictated to me a law-paper, upon a question purely in the law of Scotland, concerning *vicious intromission*, that is to say, intermeddling with the effects of a deceased person, without a regular title, which formerly was understood to subject the intermeddler to payment of all the defunct's debts. The principle has of late been relaxed. Dr. Johnson's argument was, for a renewal of its strictness. The paper was printed, with additions by me, and given into the Court of Session. Lord Hailes knew Dr. Johnson's part not to be mine, and pointed out exactly where it began, and where it ended. Dr. Johnson said, "It is much, now, that his lordship can distinguish so."

In Dr. Johnson's *"Vanity of Human Wishes,"* there is the following passage:

"The teeming mother, anxious for her race,
Begs, for each birth, the fortune of a face:
Yet *Vane*[70] could tell, what ills from Beauty spring;
And *Sedley*[71] cursed the charms which pleased a king."

Lord Hailes told him he was mistaken in the instances he had given of unfortunate fair ones; for neither *Vane* nor *Sedley* had a title to that description. His Lordship has since been so obliging as to send me a note of this, for the communication of which I am sure my readers will thank me.

"The lines in the tenth Satire of Juvenal, according to my alteration, should have run thus:

"Yet *Shore*[72] could tell.
And *Valiere*[73] curs'd."

"The first was a penitent by compulsion, the second by sentiment; though the truth is, Mademoiselle de la Valiere threw herself (but still from sentiment) in the King's way.

"Our friend chose *Vane*, who was far from being well-looked; and *Sedley*, who was so ugly, that Charles II. said, his brother had her by way of penance."

Mr. Maclaurin's learning and talents enabled him to do his part very well in Dr. Johnson's company. He produced two epitaphs upon his father, the celebrated mathematician. One was in English, of which Dr. Johnson did not change one word. In the other, which was in Latin, he made several alterations. In place of the very words of *Virgil*, "*Ubi luctus et pavor et plurima mortis imago,*" he wrote "*Ubi luctus regnant et pavor.*" He introduced the word *prorsus* into the line "*Mortalibus prorsus non absit solatium;*" and after "*Hujus enim*

scripta evolve,*" he added, ('*Mentemque tantarum rerum capacem corpori caduco superstitem crede;'*)[74] which is quite applicable to Dr. Johnson himself.

Mr. Murray, advocate, who married a niece of Lord Mansfield's, and is now one of the Judges of Scotland, by the title of Lord *Henderland*, sat with us a part of the evening; but did not venture to say any thing, that I remember, which he certainly might have done, had not an over anxiety prevented him.

At supper we had Dr. Alexander Webster, who, though not learned, had such a knowledge of mankind, such a fund of information and entertainment, so clear a head and such accommodating manners, that Dr. Johnson found him a very agreeable companion.

When Dr. Johnson and I were left by ourselves, I read to him my notes of the Opinions of our Judges upon the Question of Literary Property. He did not like them; and said, "they make me think of your Judges not with that respect which I should wish to do." To the argument of one of them, that there can be no property in blasphemy or nonsense, he answered, "then your rotten sheep are mine!—By that rule, when a man's house falls into decay, he must lose it."— I mentioned an argument of mine, that literary performances are not taxed. As *Churchill*[75] says,

"No statesman yet has thought it worth his pains
To tax our labours, or excise our brains;"

and therefore they are not property.—"Yet, (said he) we hang a man for stealing a horse, and horses are not taxed."—Mr. Pitt has since put an end to that argument.[76]

Wednesday, 18th August.

On this day we set out from Edinburgh. We should gladly have had Mr. Scott to go with us; but he was obliged to return to England.—I have given a sketch of Dr. Johnson. My readers may wish to know a little

---

74. **In . . . crede:** Johnson alters Virgil's "everywhere was grief and fear and every appearance of death" to "where grief and fear prevail"; by adding the intensifier *prorsus* (indeed), he emphasizes the clause "so that human beings shall not be deprived of consolation"; and by adding the final clause, he exhorts readers of the epitaph to "have faith that a soul capable of so much will not cease to exist with the mortal body." 75. **Churchill:** Charles Churchill (1731–64), poetic satirist, author of *The Rosciad* (1761), a satire on contemporary actors, and *The Prophecy of Famine* (1763), a satire on the Scots. 76. **that argument:** In 1784 William Pitt the Younger (1759–1806), Prime Minister from 1783 to 1801, levied a tax of ten shillings per year on each horse used for pleasure.

---

70. **Vane:** Anne Vane (1705–36), mistress of Frederick, Prince of Wales. 71. **Sedley:** Catherine Sedley (1657–1717), mistress of the Duke of York (later King James II). 72. **Shore:** [Boswell's note] Mistress of Edward IV. 73. **Valiere:** [Boswell's note] Mistress of Louis XIV.

of his fellow-traveller. Think, then, of a gentleman of ancient blood, the pride of which was his predominant passion. He was then in his thirty-third year, and had been about four years happily married. His inclination was to be a Soldier; but his father, a respectable Judge, had pressed him into the profession of the law. He had travelled a good deal, and seen many varieties of human life. He had thought more than any body supposed, and had a pretty good stock of general learning and knowledge. He had all Dr. Johnson's principles, with some degree of relaxation. He had rather too little, than too much prudence; and, his imagination being lively, he often said things of which the effect was very different from the intention. He resembled sometimes

"The best good man, with the worst natur'd muse."

He cannot deny himself the vanity of finishing with the encomium of Dr. Johnson, whose friendly partiality to the companion of his Tour represents him as one "whose acuteness would help my inquiry, and whose gaiety of conversation, and civility of manners, are sufficient to counteract the inconveniencies of travel, in countries less hospitable than we have passed."

Dr. Johnson thought it unnecessary to put himself to the additional expence of bringing with him *Francis Barber*, his faithful black servant;[77] so we were attended only by my man, *Joseph Ritter*, a Bohemian; a fine stately fellow above six feet high, who had been over a great part of Europe, and spoke many languages. He was the best servant I ever saw in my life. Let not my readers disdain his introduction! For Dr. Johnson gave him this character: "Sir, he is a civil man, and a wise man."

From an erroneous apprehension of violence, Dr. Johnson had provided a pair of pistols, some gunpowder, and a quantity of bullets. But upon being assured we should run no risk of meeting any robbers, he left his arms and ammunition in an open drawer, of which he gave my wife the charge. He also left in that drawer one volume of a pretty full and curious Diary of his Life, of which I have a few fragments; but the book has been destroyed. I wish female curiosity had been strong enough to have had it all transcribed, which might easily have been done; and I should think the theft, being *pro bono publico*,[78] might have

been forgiven. But I may be wrong. My wife told me she never once looked into it.—She did not seem quite easy when we left her. But away we went!

Mr. Nairne, advocate, was to go with us as far as St. Andrews. It gives me pleasure that, by mentioning his *name*, I connect his title to the just and handsome compliment paid him by Dr. Johnson, in his book, "A gentleman who could stay with us only long enough to make us know how much we lost by his leaving us." When we came to Leith, I talked with perhaps too boasting an air, how pretty the Frith of Forth looked; as indeed, after the prospect from Constantinople, of which I have been told, and that from Naples, which I have seen, I believe the view of that Frith and its environs, from the Castle-hill of Edinburgh, is the finest prospect in Europe. "Aye, (said Mr. Johnson) that is the state of the world. Water is the same every where.

Una est injusti cærula forma maris.[79]

I told him the port here was the mouth of the river or water of *Leith*. "Not *Lethe*,"[80] said Mr. Nairne.— "Why, sir, (said Dr. Johnson,) when a Scotsman sets out from this port for England, he forgets his native country."—*Nairne*. "I hope, sir, you shall forget England here."—*Johnson*. "Then, 'twill be still more *Lethe*."—He observed of the Pier or Quay, "you have no occasion for so large a one: your trade does not require it: but you are like a shopkeeper who takes a shop, not only for what he has to put into it, but that it may be believed he has a great deal to put into it." It is very true, that there is now, comparatively, little trade upon the eastern coast of Scotland. The riches of Glasgow shew how much there is in the west; and perhaps we shall find trade travel westwards, on a great scale, as well as a small.

We talked of a man's drowning himself.—*Johnson*. "I should never think it time to make away with myself."—I put the case of *Eustace Budgell*,[81] who was accused of forging a will, and sunk himself in the Thames, before the trial of its authenticity came on. "Suppose, Sir, (said I) that a man is absolutely sure, that, if he lives a few days longer, he shall be detected

---

77. his . . . servant: Frank Barber was Johnson's servant from about 1752 until Johnson's death. 78. pro . . . publico: on behalf of the public good.

79. Una . . . maris: There is only the deep-blue surface of the oppressive sea. 80. Lethe: "oblivion; a draught of oblivion" (Johnson's *Dictionary*). 81. Eustace Budgell: (1686–1737), miscellaneous writer, cousin of Joseph Addison. He sank into debt, from which he sought to rescue himself by forgery; finally, with his reputation blasted and his mind shaken, he drowned himself in the Thames.

in a fraud, the consequence of which will be utter disgrace and expulsion from society?"—*Johnson*. "Then, Sir, let him go abroad to a distant country; let him go to some place where he is *not* known. Don't let him go to the devil where he *is* known!"

He then said, "I see a number of people bare-footed here: I suppose you all went so before the Union. Boswell, your ancestors went so, when they had as much land as your family has now. Yet *Auchinleck* is the *Field of Stones:* there would be bad going bare footed there. The *Lairds* however did it."—I bought some *speldings*, fish (generally whitings) salted and dried in a particular manner, being dipped in the sea and dried in the sun, and eat by the Scots by way of a relish. He had never seen them, though they are sold in London. I insisted on *scottifying* his palate; But he was very reluctant. With difficulty I prevailed with him to let a bit of one of those *speldings* lye in his mouth. He did not like it.

In crossing the Frith, Dr. Johnson determined that we should land upon Inch Keith. On approaching it, we first observed a high rocky shore. We coasted about, and put into a little bay on the North-west. We clambered up a very steep ascent, on which was very good grass, but rather a profusion of thistles. There were sixteen head of black cattle grazing upon the island. Lord Hailes observed to me, that *Brantôme*[82] calls it *L'isle des Chevaux*,[83] and that it was probably "a *safer* stable" than many others in his time. The fort, with an inscription on it, *Maria Re*[84] 1564, is strongly built. Dr. Johnson examined it with much attention. He stalked like a giant among the luxuriant thistles and nettles. There are three wells in the island; but we could not find one in the fort. There must probably have been one, though now filled up, as a garrison could not subsist without it. But I have dwelt too long on this little spot. Dr. Johnson afterwards bid me try to write a description of our discovering Inch Keith, in the usual style of travellers, describing fully every particular; how we concluded that it must have once been inhabited, and introducing many sage reflections; and we should see how a thing might be covered in words, so as to induce people to come and see it. All that was said might be true, and yet in reality there might be nothing to see. He said, "I'd have this island.

I'd build a house, make a good landing-place, have a garden, and vines, and all sorts of trees. A rich man, of a hospitable turn, here, would have many visitors from Edinburgh." When we had got into our boat again, he called to me, "Come, now, pay a classical compliment to the island on quitting it." I happened luckily, in allusion to the beautiful Queen Mary, whose name is upon the fort, to think of what Virgil makes Æneas say, on leaving the country of his charming *Dido*.

Invitus, regina, tuo de littore cessi.[85]

"Very well hit off!" said he.

We dined at Kinghorn, and then got into a post-chaise. Mr. Nairne and his servant, and Joseph, rode by us. We stopped at Cupar, and drank tea. We talked of parliament; and I said, I supposed very few of the members knew much of what was going on, as indeed very few gentlemen know much of their own private affairs.—*Johnson*. "Why, Sir, if a man is not of a sluggish mind, he may be his own steward. If he will look into his affairs, he will soon learn. So it is as to publick affairs. There must always be a certain number of men of business in parliament."—*Boswell*. "But consider, sir, what is the House of Commons? Is not a great proportion of it chosen by Peers? Do you think, sir, they ought to have such an influence?"—*Johnson*. "Yes, sir. Influence must ever be in proportion to property; and it is right it should."—*Boswell*. "But is there not reason to fear that the common people may be oppressed?"—*Johnson*. "No, sir. Our great fear is from want of power in government. Such a storm of vulgar force has broke in."—*Boswell*. "It has only roared."—*Johnson*. "Sir, it has roared, till the Judges in Westminster-Hall have been afraid to pronounce sentence in opposition to the popular cry. You are frightened by what is no longer dangerous, like Presbyterians by Popery."—He then repeated a passage, I think, in Butler's *Remains*, which ends, "and would cry, Fire! Fire! in Noah's flood."

We had a dreary drive, in a dusky night, to St. Andrews, where we arrived late. We found a good supper at Glass's inn, and Dr. Johnson revived agreeably. He said, the collection called "The Muses' Welcome to King James," (first of England, and sixth of Scotland,) on his return to his native kingdom, shewed that there was then abundance of learning in

82. **Brantôme:** Pierre de Bourdeilles (*c.* 1540–1614), Seigneur de Brantôme, French soldier and author of memoirs, visited Scotland in 1561. 83. **L'isle des Chevaux:** Horse Island. 84. **Maria Re:** Queen Mary.

85. **Invitus . . . cessi:** Unwillingly, O Queen, I left your shore.

Scotland; and that the conceits in that collection, with which people find fault, were mere mode. He said, we could not now entertain a sovereign so; that Buchanan[86] had spread the spirit of learning amongst us, but we had lost it during the civil wars. He did not allow the Latin Poetry of Pitcairne so much merit as has been usually attributed to it; though he owned that one of his pieces, which he mentioned, but which I am sorry is not specified in my notes, was "very well." It is not improbable that it was the poem which Prior has so elegantly translated.[87]

After supper, we made a *procession* to *Saint Leonard's College*, the landlord walking before us with a candle, and the waiter with a lantern. That college had some time before been dissolved; and Dr. Watson, a professor here, (the historian of Philip II.) had purchased the ground, and what buildings remained. When we entered his court, it seemed quite academical; and we found in his house very comfortable and genteel accommodation.[88]

Thursday, 19th August.

We rose much refreshed. I had with me a map of Scotland, a Bible, which was given me by Lord Mountstuart[89] when we were together in Italy, and Ogden's Sermons on Prayer. Mr. Nairne introduced us to Dr. Watson, whom we found a well-informed man, of very amiable manners. Dr. Johnson, after they were acquainted, said, "I take great delight in him."—His daughter, a very pleasing young lady, made breakfast. Dr. Watson observed, that Glasgow University had fewer home students, since trade increased, as learning was rather incompatible with it.—*Johnson.* "Why, sir, as trade is now carried on by subordinate hands, men in trade have as much leisure as others; and now learning itself is a trade. A man goes to a bookseller, and gets what he can. We have done with patronage. In the infancy of learning, we find some great man praised for it. This diffused it among others. When it becomes general, an authour

leaves the great, and applies to the multitude."—*Boswell.* "It is a shame that authours are not now better patronized."—*Johnson.* "No, sir. If learning cannot support a man, if he must sit with his hands across till somebody feeds him, it is as to him a bad thing, and it is better as it is. With patronage, what flattery! what falsehood! While a man is in equilibrio,[90] he throws truth among the multitude, and lets them take it as they please: in patronage, he must say what pleases his patron, and it is an equal chance whether that be truth or falsehood."—*Watson.* "But is not the case now, that, instead of flattering one person, we flatter the age?"—*Johnson.* "No, sir. The world always lets a man tell what he thinks, his own way. I wonder however, that so many people have written, who might have let it alone. That people should endeavour to excel in conversation, I do not wonder; because in conversation praise is instantly reverberated."

We talked of change of manners. Dr. Johnson observed, that our drinking less than our ancestors was owing to the change from ale to wine. "I remember (said he) when all the *decent* people in Lichfield got drunk every night, and were not the worse thought of. Ale was cheap, so you pressed strongly.[91] When a man must bring a bottle of wine, he is not in such haste. Smoaking has gone out. To be sure, it is a shocking thing, blowing smoak out of our mouths into other people's mouths, eyes, and noses, and having the same thing done to us. Yet I cannot account why a thing which requires so little exertion, and yet preserves the mind from total vacuity, should have gone out. Every man has something by which he calms himself: beating with his feet, or so.[92] I remember when people in England changed a shirt only once a week: a Pandour,[93] when he gets a shirt, greases it to make it last. Formerly, good tradesmen had no fire but in the kitchen; never in the parlour, except on Sunday. My father, who was a magistrate of Lichfield, lived thus. They never began to have a fire in the parlour, but on leaving off business, or some great revolution of their life."—Dr. *Watson* said, the hall was as a kitchen, in old squires' houses.—*Johnson.* "No, Sir. The hall was for great occasions, and never was used

86. **Buchanan:** George Buchanan (1506–82), Scottish scholar and author, tutor of James I. 87. **the poem . . . translated:** as the poem *Studious the Busy Moments to Deceive.* Dr. Archibald Pitcairne (1652–1713) was a Scottish physician and a reputed atheist who wrote Latin poems. 88. **accommodation:** [Boswell's note] My Journal, from this day inclusive, was read by Dr. Johnson. 89. **Lord Mountstuart:** John Stuart (1744–1814), Lord Mountstuart, eldest son of Lord Bute; he traveled with Boswell from Rome to Milan in 1765.

90. **in equilibrio:** under no obligation. 91. **pressed strongly:** drank freely. In the *Dictionary*, Johnson defines *press:* "to go forward with violence to any object." 92. **beating . . . so:** [Boswell's note] Dr. Johnson used to practice this himself very much. 93. **Pandour:** Yugoslavian soldier.

for domestick refection."—We talked of the Union, and what money it had brought into Scotland. Dr. Watson observed, that a little money formerly went as far as a great deal now.—*Johnson*. "In speculation, it seems that a smaller quantity of money, equal in value to a larger quantity, if equally divided, should produce the same effect. But it is not so in reality. Many more conveniences and elegancies are enjoyed where money is plenty, than where it is scarce. Perhaps a great familiarity with it, which arises from plenty, makes us more easily part with it."

After what Dr. Johnson has said of St. Andrews, which he had long wished to see, as our ancient university, and the seat of our Primate in the days of episcopacy, I can say little. Since the publication of Dr. Johnson's book, I find that he has been censured for not seeing here the ancient chapel of *St. Rule*, a curious piece of sacred architecture. But this was neither his fault nor mine. We were both of us abundantly desirous of surveying such sort of antiquities: but neither of us knew of this. I am afraid the censure must fall on those who did not tell us of it. In every place, where there is any thing worthy of observation, there should be a short printed directory for strangers, such as we find in all the towns of Italy, and in some of the towns in England. I was told that there is a manuscript account of St. Andrews, by Martin, secretary to Archbishop Sharp; and that one Douglas has published a small account of it. I inquired at a bookseller's, but could not get it. Dr. Johnson's veneration for the Hierarchy is well known. There is no wonder then, that he was affected with a strong indignation, while he beheld the ruins of religious magnificence. I happened to ask where John Knox[94] was buried. Dr. Johnson burst out, "I hope in the high-way. I have been looking at his reformations."

It was a very fine day. Dr. Johnson seemed quite wrapt up in the contemplation of the scenes which were now presented to him. He kept his hat off while he was upon any part of the ground where the Cathedral had stood. He said well, that "Knox had set on a mob, without knowing where it would end; and that differing from a man in doctrine was no reason why you should pull his house about his ears." As we walked in the cloisters, there was a solemn echo, while he talked loud of a proper retirement from the world. Mr. *Nairne* said, he had an inclination to retire. I called Dr. Johnson's attention to this, that I might hear his opinion if it was right.—*Johnson*. "Yes, when he has done his duty to society. In general, as every man is obliged not only to "love GOD, but his neighbour as himself," he must bear his part in active life; yet there are exceptions. Those who are exceedingly scrupulous (which I do not approve, for I am no friend to scruples) and find their scrupulosity invincible, so that they are quite in the dark, and know not what they shall do—or those who cannot resist temptations, and find they make themselves worse by being in the world, without making it better, may retire. I never read of a hermit, but in imagination I kiss his feet; never of a monastery, but I could fall on my knees, and kiss the pavement. But I think putting young people there, who know nothing of life, nothing of retirement, is dangerous and wicked. It is a saying as old as Hesiod,

Ἔργα νεῶν, βουλαίτε μέσων, ἔνχαιτε γερόντων.[95]

That is a very noble line: not that young men should not pray, or old men not give counsel, but that every season of life has its proper duties. I have thought of retiring, and have talked of it to a friend; but I find my vocation is rather to active life." I said *some* young monks might be allowed, to shew that it is not age alone that can retire to pious solitude; but he thought this would only shew they could not resist temptation.

He wanted to mount the steeples, but it could not be done. There are no good inscriptions here. Bad Roman characters he naturally mistook for half Gothick,[96] half Roman. One of the steeples, which he was told was in danger, he wished not to be taken down; "for, said he, it may fall on some of the posterity of John Knox; and no great matter!" Dinner was mentioned.—*Johnson*. "Aye, aye; amidst all these sorrowful scenes, I have no objection to dinner."

We went and looked at the castle, where Cardinal Beaton was murdered,[97] and then visited Principal Murison at his college, where is a good library-room; but the Principal was abundantly vain of it, for he

---

94. John Knox: (1505–72), Scottish religious reformer, founder of Presbyterianism. He preached against Roman Catholicism and introduced into Scotland John Calvin's doctrines of predestination.

95. Ἔργα ... γερόντων: [Boswell's note, added to the second edition (1785)] Let youth in deeds, in counsel men engage; / Prayer is the proper duty of old age. **96. Gothick:** an extinct Germanic language. **97. Cardinal . . . murdered:** David Beaton (1494–1546), Scottish Roman Catholic prelate, was murdered, Johnson writes, "by the ruffians of reformation."

seriously said to Dr. Johnson, "you have not such a one in England."

The professors entertained us with a very good dinner. Present: Murison, Shaw, Cooke, Hill, Haddo, Watson, Flint, Brown. I observed, that I wondered to see him eat so well, after viewing so many sorrowful scenes of ruined religious magnificence. "Why, said he, I am not sorry, after seeing these gentlemen; for they are not sorry."—*Murison* said, all sorrow was bad, as it was murmuring against the dispensations of Providence.—*Johnson*. "Sir, sorrow is inherent in humanity. As you cannot judge two and two to be either five, or three, but certainly four, so, when comparing a worse present state with a better which is past, you cannot but feel sorrow. It is not cured by reason, but by the incursion of present objects, which wear out the past. You need not murmur, though you are sorry."—*Murison*. "But St. Paul says, 'I have learnt, in whatever state I am, therewith to be content.' "—*Johnson*. "Sir, that relates to riches and poverty; for we see St. Paul, when he had a thorn in the flesh, prayed earnestly to have it removed; and then he could not be content."—Murison, thus refuted, tried to be smart, and drank to Dr. Johnson, "Long may you lecture!"—Dr. Johnson afterwards, speaking of his not drinking wine, said, "The Doctor spoke of *lecturing* (looking to him). I give all these lectures on water."[98]

He defended requiring subscription[99] in those admitted to universities, thus: "As all who come into the country must obey the king, so all who come into an university must be of the church."

And here I must do Dr. Johnson the justice to contradict a very absurd and ill-natured story, as to what passed at St. Andrews. It has been circulated, that, after grace was said in English, in the usual manner, he with the greatest marks of contempt, as if he had held it to be no grace in an university, would not sit down till he had said grace aloud in Latin. This would have been an insult indeed to the gentlemen who were entertaining us. But the truth was precisely thus. In the course of conversation at dinner, Dr. Johnson, in very good humour, said, "I should have

expected to have heard a Latin grace, among so many learned men: we had always a Latin grace at Oxford. I believe I can repeat it." Which he did, as giving the learned men in one place a specimen of what was done by the learned men in another place.

We went and saw the church, in which is Archbishop Sharp's monument. I was struck with the same kind of feelings with which the churches of Italy impressed me. I was pleased, curiously pleased to see Dr. Johnson actually in St. Andrews, of which we had talked so long. Professor Haddo was with us this afternoon, along with Dr. Watson. We looked at St. Salvador's College. The rooms for students seemed very commodious, and Dr. Johnson said, the chapel was the neatest place of worship he had seen. The key of the library could not be found; for it seems Professor Hill, who was out of town, had taken it with him. Dr. Johnson told a joke he had heard of a monastery abroad, where the key of the library could never be found.

It was somewhat dispiriting, to see this ancient archiepiscopal city now sadly deserted. We saw in one of its streets a remarkable proof of liberal toleration; a nonjuring clergyman,[100] with a jolly countenance and a round belly, like a well-fed monk, strutting about in his canonicals.

We observed two occupations united in the same person, who had hung out two sign-posts. Upon one was, "James Hood, White Iron Smith" (*i.e.* Tin-plate Worker). Upon another, "The Art of Fencing taught, by James Hood."—Upon this last were painted some trees, and two men fencing, one of whom had hit the other in the eye, to shew his great dexterity; so that the art was well taught.—*Johnson*. "Were I studying here, I should go and take a lesson. I remember *Hope*, in his book on this art, says, 'the Scotch are very good fencers.' "

We returned to the inn, where we had been entertained at dinner, and drank tea in company with some of the Professors, of whose civilities I beg leave to add my humble and very grateful acknowledgement to the honourable testimony of Dr. Johnson, in his "Journey."

We talked of composition, which was a favourite topick of Dr. Watson's, who first distinguished himself by lectures on rhetorick.—*Johnson*. "I advised Chambers, and would advise every young man

---

98. water: Although Johnson drank wine very freely on occasion early in his life, he appears to have drunk little but water and tea from 1765 on. **99. subscription:** to the thirty-nine "Articles of Religion" of the established Church, compiled in 1562 "for the avoiding of diversities of opinions, and for the establishing of consent touching true religion" (Book of Common Prayer).

100. a nonjuring clergyman: one who refused to take the oath of allegiance to the Hanoverian succession, remaining loyal to the House of Stuart.

beginning to compose, to do it as fast as he can, to get a habit of having his mind to start promptly; it is so much more difficult to improve in speed than in accuracy."—*Watson.* "I own I am for much attention to accuracy in composing, lest one should get bad habits of doing it in a slovenly manner."—*Johnson.* "Why, Sir, you are confounding *doing* inaccurately with the *necessity* of doing inaccurately. A man knows when his composition is inaccurate, and when he thinks fit he'll correct it. But, if a man is accustomed to compose slowly, and with difficulty, upon all occasions, there is danger that he may not compose at all, as we do not like to do that which is not done easily; and, at any rate, more time is consumed in a small matter than ought to be."—*Watson* said, "Dr. Hugh Blair took a week to compose a sermon."—*Johnson.* "Then, Sir, that is for want of the habit of composing quickly, which I am insisting one should acquire."—*Watson* said, "Blair was not composing all the week, but only such hours as he found himself disposed for composition."—*Johnson.* "Nay, Sir, unless you tell me the time he took, you tell me nothing. If I say I took a week to walk a mile, and have had the gout five days, and been ill otherwise another day, I have taken but one day. I myself have composed about forty sermons. I have begun a sermon after dinner, and sent it off by the post that night. I wrote forty-eight of the printed octavo pages of the Life of Savage[101] at a sitting; but then I sat up all night. I have

101. **Life of Savage:** published in 1744.

also written six sheets in a day of translation from the French."—*Boswell.* "We have all observed how one man dresses himself slowly, and another fast."—*Johnson.* "Yes, Sir; it is wonderful how much time some people will consume in dressing; taking up a thing and looking at it, and laying it down, and taking it up again. Every one should get the habit of doing it quickly. I would say to a young divine, 'Here is your text; let me see how soon you can make a sermon.' Then I'd say, 'Let me see how much better you can make it.' Thus I should see both his powers and his judgement."

We all went to Dr. Watson's to supper. Miss Sharp, great grandchild of Archbishop Sharp, was there; as was Mr. Craig, the ingenious architect of the new town of Edinburgh, and nephew of Thomson,[102] to whom Dr. Johnson has since done so much justice, in his "Lives of the Poets."

We talked of memory, and its various modes.—*Johnson.* "Memory will play strange tricks. One sometimes loses a single word. I once lost *fugaces* in the Ode *Posthume, Posthume.*"[103] I mentioned to him, that a worthy gentleman of my acquaintance actually forgot his own name.—*Johnson.* "Sir, that was a morbid oblivion."

102. **Thomson:** James Thomson (1700–48), Scottish poet, author of *The Seasons* (see Part Two). 103. **Posthume, Posthume:** Johnson refers to Horace's Ode xiv in Book II, which begins *Eheu fugaces, Postume, Postume, | Labuntur anni* ("Alas, friend Posthumus, the years glide swiftly by").

Christopher Smart

1722–1771

The unfortunate Christopher Smart earned at Kentish schools a reputation as a clever student even before his admission to Pembroke Hall, Cambridge, where he spent ten years in classical literary scholarship as student, tutor, and fellow. At Cambridge he distinguished himself by his poetic ingenuity, his obscure, waggish learning, and his convivial gaiety, which frequently ended in debts and embarrassment. So conspicuous was Smart's merry instability at Cambridge that his colleague Thomas Gray was moved to prophesy, "All this, must come to a Jayl or Bedlam." In 1749 Smart left Cambridge for London, where, after a year of writing songs for the popular entertainments at Vauxhall Gardens, he associated himself as a journalist with John Newbery, a bustling publisher and dealer in patent medicines. From 1750 until 1756 he produced for Newbery a great variety of conventional saleable materials: poems, translations, facetious essays, and labored journalistic jokes. His *Poems on Several Occasions* (1752), which includes much of his college verse, is notable for its variety in the standard genres: Smart here seems equally fertile in epigrams, animal fables, light lyric poems, pastorals, epitaphs, "ballads," and verse epistles. Smart's continued lapses into debt and drunkenness did not prevent his accomplishing also a prose translation of Horace (1756), which was accurate enough to remain a popular schoolboy crib through the nineteenth century.

But in 1756 Smart fell victim to a religious monomania, which took the form of a disconcerting impulse toward public prayer; as he records in *Jubilate Agno*, "I blessed God in St. James's Park till I routed all the company." After a year's confinement for insanity in St. Luke's Hospital, he was discharged uncured in 1758, but, his mental disorder apparently growing worse, he was confined again from 1759 until 1763. While restrained in the asylum, he devoted himself to praying, writing, gardening on the premises, and caring for his cat. He was visited by Garrick, Goldsmith, and Johnson. "I did not think he ought to be shut up," Johnson commented later. "His infirmities were not noxious to society. He insisted on people praying with him; and I'd as lief pray with Kit Smart as any one else. Another charge was, that he did not love clean linen; and I have no passion for it." Dating from Smart's period of confinement are two of his most important experiments in religious verse, *Jubilate Agno* (begun in 1759) and *A Song to David* (1763).

Upon his release in 1763, Smart found himself estranged from his family and embroiled in bitter, self-righteous quarrels with hostile reviewers. But he continued writing poetry, turning now increasingly to religious and ethical themes. His *Translation of the Psalms of David* appeared in 1765, and in 1767 he published a verse translation of Horace. To many of his contemporaries, his peculiar, obscure constructions, his archaisms and startling usages, and his extraordinarily personal poetic tone suggested raving insanity. But Smart himself hinted that he derived his technique of stamping upon words what he called an impression of rarity from no more exotic a source than Horace himself.

In 1769, a final calamity: he was arrested for debt and confined in King's Bench prison. There he wrote *Hymns for the Amusement of Children* (1770). He died in prison.

His outwardly unhappy life seems never to have undermined his optimism. Unlike William Cowper, who, actually blameless, fancied that he was damned, the often vain and quarrelsome Smart never doubted that he was gloriously saved. His important religious poems constitute elaborate celebrations of the goodness of God as witnessed in the Book of Nature—the specific detail of the physical world, which Smart, like George Crabbe, knew intimately. Smart was learned in botany, physics, and zoology; his curious knowledge of rare animals, fish, and insects derives from a lifetime's reading in the lore of natural history.

A bibliography of Smart's writings, by G. J. Gray, appears in *Transactions of the Bibliographical Society*, VI (1900–02), 269–303. Most of Smart's poems are brought together in the editions by Norman Callan, *The Collected Poems of Christopher Smart* (2 vols., 1949), and Robert Brittain, *Poems by Christopher Smart* (1950). The latter contains interesting commentary and a long biographical introduction. *Jubilate Agno* is best read in the edition by W. H. Bond (1954), although W. F. Stead's edition, titled *Rejoice in the Lamb* (1939), is still useful for some of its notes and commentary. Christopher Devlin's *Poor Kit Smart* (1961) is a good brief critical biography, largely superseding E. G. Ainsworth and C. E. Noyes's *Christopher Smart: A Biographical and Critical Study* (1943). Arthur Sherbo's *Christopher Smart: Scholar of the University* (1967) presents the most recent biographical discoveries.

FROM

JUBILATE AGNO

✥

Smart worked on *Jubilate Agno* in the asylum from 1759 until 1763, but the manuscript remained unpublished until 1939. The work consists of over twelve hundred lines: all the lines in some sections begin with the word *Let;* those in other sections begin with *For.* Editing the work in 1950, W. H. Bond discovered that, in general, each *Let* line is completed by a corresponding *For* line. Many of the correspondences between related lines are based upon puns or sound resemblances. For example:

Let Eliada rejoice with the Gier-eagle who is Swift and of great penetration.

For I bless the Lord Jesus for the memory of GAY, POPE and SWIFT.

As Bond has found, "The poem was intended as a responsive reading; and that is why the *Let* and *For* sections [of the manuscript] are physically distinct while corresponding verse for verse." When Smart began the work he was apparently attempting to reform the Anglican liturgy: he was hoping to contrive a long poem to be recited or sung antiphonally by two choirs. But as he went on, the original plan deteriorated, although elements of the antiphonal form remained. The *Let* counterparts of the *For* lines in the following selection have not been found; it is doubtful that any were ever written.

The text is from W. H. Bond's edition (1954), prepared from the manuscript in The Houghton Library, Harvard University.

✥

For I will consider my Cat Jeoffry. *rightfully*

For he is the servant of the Living God duly and daily serving him. *small "h"*

For at the first glance of the glory of God in the East he worships in his way.

For is this done by wreathing his body seven times round with elegant quickness. *his prayer, worship* *SAME: NO METAPHOR*

For then he leaps up to catch the musk, wᶜʰ is the blessing of God upon his prayer. *the catnip-like plant* *his reward for prayer*

For he rolls upon prank to work(it)in. *the blessing*

For having done duty and received blessing he begins to consider himself. *after*

For this he performs in ten degrees. *starts observing & descriptive powers*

For first he looks upon his fore-paws to see if they are clean.

For secondly he kicks up behind to clear away there. 10

For thirdly he works it upon stretch with the fore paws extended.

For fourthly he sharpens his paws by wood.

For fiftly he washes himself.

For Sixthly he rolls upon wash.

For Seventhly he fleas himself, that he may not be interrupted upon the beat. *SUCH AS HUNTING* *HIS ACTIVITIES, WILL NOT BE INTERRUPTED BY SCRATCHING*

For Eighthly he rubs himself against a post.

For Ninthly he looks up for his instructions.

For Tenthly he goes in quest of food.

For having consider'd God and himself he will consider his neighbour.

For if he meets another cat he will kiss her in kindness. *his neighbors* 20

For when he takes his prey he plays with it to give it chance.

For one mouse in seven escapes by his dallying.

For when his day's work is done his business more properly begins.

For keeps the Lord's watch in the night against the adversary.

as god watches over his people, (at night as they sleep), the cat remains awake at Night

For he counteracts the powers of darkness by his electrical skin & glaring eyes. *gaurds by hair, purring, eyes*

For he counteracts the Devil, who is death, by brisking about the life. *where there is life, devil cannot enter*

For in his morning orisons he loves the sun and the sun loves him. *prayers*

For he is of the tribe of Tiger.

For the Cherub Cat is a term of the Angel Tiger. *small & childlike* *immature or diminutive phase of large creature*

For he has the subtlety and hissing of a serpent, which in goodness he suppresses. 30

For he will not do destruction, if he is well-fed, neither will he spit without provocation.

For he purrs in thankfulness, when God tells him he's a good Cat.

For he is an instrument for the children to learn benevolence upon. *humans should, can compare to him*

For every house is incompleat without him & a blessing is lacking in the spirit.

For the Lord commanded Moses concerning the cats at the departure of the Children of Israel from Egypt. *THE CAT DOES NOT APPEAR IN THE BIBLE*

For every family had one cat at least in the bag.

For the English Cats are the best in Europe. *adds cats to what the Israelites took*

For he is the cleanest in the use of his fore-paws of any quadrupede. *most blessed, holiest quadrupede* *mammal w/ 4 ft,*

For the dexterity of his defence is an instance of the love of God to him exceedingly.

For he is the quickest to his mark of any creature. *another instance* 40

For he is tenacious of his point. *another*

For he is a mixture of gravity and waggery. *action of a wag* *another*

For he knows that God is his Saviour. *because he knows*

For there is nothing sweeter than his peace when at rest. *another*

For there is nothing brisker than his life when in motion. *another*

For he is of the Lord's poor and so indeed is he called by benevolence perpetually—Poor Jeoffry! poor Jeoffry! the rat has bit thy throat.

For I bless the name of the Lord Jesus that Jeoffry is better. *[Holy spirit has come to heal him]*

For the divine spirit comes about his body to sustain it in compleat cat.

For his tongue *[voice]* is exceeding pure so that it has in purity what it wants in musick. *[conception of universe — orbiting spheres, create pure music]*

For he is docile and can learn certain things. 50

For he can set up with gravity which is patience upon approbation. *[approval]* *[from God]*

For he can fetch and carry, which is patience in employment.

For he can jump over a stick which is patience upon proof positive.

For he can spraggle upon waggle at the word of command.

For he can jump from an eminence into his master's bosom.

For he can catch the cork and toss it again.

For he is hated by the hypocrite and miser.

For the former is affraid of detection.

For the latter refuses the charge.

For he camels his back to bear the first notion of business. 60

For he is good to think on, if a man would express himself neatly.

For he made a great figure in Egypt for his signal services.

For he killed the Icneumon-rat very pernicious by land. *[confused — killing good in a sense]* *[BENEFICIAL, NOT — KILLS RATS & MICE]*

For his ears are so acute that they sting again.

For from this proceeds the passing quickness of his attention.

For by stroaking of him I have found out electricity.

For I perceived God's light about him both wax and fire. *[as a candle]*

For the Electrical fire is the spiritual substance, which God sends from heaven to sustain the bodies both of man and beast.

For God has blessed him in the variety of his movements. *[by giving him a]*

For, tho he cannot fly, he is an excellent clamberer. 70

For his motions upon the face of the earth are more than any other quadrupede.

For he can tread to all the measures upon the musick.

For he can swim for life.

For he can creep.

A SONG TO DAVID

In 1763 James Boswell wrote his friend Sir David Dalrymple, "I have sent you Smart's *Song to David,* which is a very curious composition, being a strange mixture of *dun obscure* and glowing genius at times." The minor poet William Mason wrote to Thomas Gray with less enthusiasm: the poem, said Mason, reveals that Smart is "as mad as ever." Smart's nephew, Christopher Hunter, was another who thought he detected signs of insanity: he was careful to omit *A Song to David* from his 1791 edition of the poems. But to Wordsworth, Leigh Hunt, and especially Browning, the poem seemed one of the few great lyrics of the eighteenth century.

    Smart was a Freemason, and the biblical presentation of the reformed sinner David as the architect of Solomon's temple, the orderly harmony of which is a central idea in Masonic symbolism, seized his imagination. Smart arranged his poem with a design almost rococo in its intricacy; the stanzas, for example, are generally organized in groups of the mystic numbers three or seven, or their multiples. He likewise delights to sport with the surface of his poem, as he does when he permits the word *Adoration* to slip twice slowly down from line to line through stanzas 51–63 and then to recover itself and remain triumphant through stanzas 64–71. Perhaps this behavior of *Adoration* suggests the action of bowing.

    The text is that of the Pembroke College copy of the first edition (1763). Misprints have been corrected.

DAVID the Son of JESSE said, and the MAN who was RAISED UP ON HIGH, the ANOINTED OF THE GOD of JACOB, and the SWEET PSALMIST OF ISRAEL, said, The SPIRIT OF THE LORD spake by ME, and HIS WORD was in my TONGUE. 2 SAM. xxiii. 1, 2.

CONTENTS

Christopher Smart.[1]

I.

O THOU, that sit'st upon a throne,
With harp of high majestic tone,
   To praise the King of kings;
And voice of heav'n-ascending swell,
Which, while its deeper notes excell,
   Clear, as a clarion, rings:

II.

To bless each valley, grove and coast,
And charm the cherubs to the post
   Of gratitude in throngs;
To *keep* the days on Zion's mount,   10
And send the year to his account,
   With dances and with songs:

III.

O Servant of God's holiest charge,
The minister of praise at large,
   Which thou may'st now receive;
From thy blest mansion hail and hear,
From topmost eminence appear
   To this the wreath I weave.

A SONG TO DAVID. **1. Christopher Smart:** This signature is carefully written in ink. Smart signed all copies of the first edition.

IV.

Great, valiant, pious, good, and clean,
Sublime, contemplative, serene,   20
   Strong, constant, pleasant, wise!
Bright effluence of exceeding grace;
Best man!—the swiftness and the race,
   The peril, and the prize!

V.

Great—from the lustre of his crown,
From Samuel's horn° and God's renown,
   Which is the people's voice;
For all the host, from rear to van,
Applauded and embrac'd the man—
   The man of God's own choice.   30

VI.

Valiant—the word and up he rose—
The fight—he triumph'd o'er the foes,°
   Whom God's just laws abhor;
And arm'd in gallant faith he took
Against the boaster, from the brook,
   The weapons of the war.°

VII.

Pious—magnificent and grand;
'Twas he the famous temple° plan'd:
   (The seraph in his soul)
Foremost to give his Lord his dues,   40
Foremost to bless the welcome news,
   And foremost to condole.

VIII.

Good—from Jehudah's genuine vein,°
From God's best nature good in grain,°
   His aspect and his heart;
To pity, to forgive, to save,
Witness En-gedi's conscious cave,°
   And Shimei's blunted dart.°

26. Samuel's horn: According to I Sam. 16:12–13, Samuel anointed David with a horn of oil, "and the Spirit of the Lord came upon David from that day forward." **32. foes:** Philistines. **36. war:** David's combat with Goliath. See I Sam. 17:40. **38. temple:** According to I Chron. 28, David was the inspired architect of Solomon's temple. **43. from . . . vein:** David was traditionally considered a descendant of the ancient kings of Judah. **44. in grain:** innately. **47. En-gedi's . . . cave:** In a cave in the wilderness of En-gedi, David experienced pangs of conscience after cutting off the skirts of Saul's robe. See I Sam. 24. **48. Shimei's . . . dart:** David refused to proceed against Shimei, who had cursed and stoned him. See II Sam. 16.

IX.

Clean—if perpetual prayer be pure,
And love, which could itself innure   50
  To fasting and to fear—
Clean in his gestures, hands, and feet,
To smite the lyre, the dance compleat,
  To play the sword and spear.

X.

Sublime—invention ever young,
Of vast conception, tow'ring tongue,
  To God th' eternal theme;
Notes from yon exaltations caught,
Unrival'd royalty of thought,
  O'er meaner strains supreme.   60

XI.

Contemplative—on God to fix
His musings, and above the six
  The sabbath-day he blest;
'Twas then his thoughts self-conquest prun'd,
And heavenly melancholy tun'd,
  To bless and bear the rest.

XII.

Serene—to sow the seeds of peace,
Rememb'ring, when he watch'd the fleece,
  How sweetly Kidron° purl'd—
To further knowledge, silence vice,   70
And plant perpetual paradise
  When God had calm'd the world.

XIII.

Strong—in the Lord, who could defy
Satan, and all his powers that lie
  In sempiternal night;
And hell, and horror, and despair
Were as the lion and the bear°
  To his undaunted might.

XIV.

Constant—in love to God THE TRUTH,
Age, manhood, infancy, and youth—   80
  To Jonathan his friend

Constant, beyond the verge of death;
And Ziba, and Mephibosheth,°
  His endless fame attend.

XV.

Pleasant—and various as the year;
Man, soul, and angel, without peer,
  Priest, champion, sage and boy;
In armour, or in ephod° clad,
His pomp, his piety was glad;
  Majestic was his joy.   90

XVI.

Wise—in recovery from his fall,°
Whence rose his eminence o'er all,
  Of all the most revil'd;
The light of Israel in his ways,
Wise are his precepts, prayer and praise,
  And counsel to his child.°

XVII.

His muse, bright angel of his verse,
Gives balm for all the thorns that pierce,
  For all the pangs that rage;
Blest light, still gaining on the gloom,   100
The more than Michal° of his bloom,
  Th' Abishag° of his age.

XVIII.

He sung of God—the mighty source
Of all things—the stupendous force
  On which all strength depends;
From whose right arm, beneath whose eyes,
All period, pow'r, and enterprize
  Commences, reigns, and ends.

83. Ziba, and Mephibosheth: Mephibosheth was the lame son of Jonathan, of the house of Saul. To show his loyalty to the memory of his old friend Jonathan, David restored to Mephibosheth the property and rights of the house of Saul and appointed Ziba, an old servant of Saul's, as Mephibosheth's steward. See II Sam. 9. **88. ephod:** a Hebrew priest's vestment. **91. fall:** David fell from the Lord's favor when he cunningly brought about the death of Uriah, whose wife Bathsheba had become pregnant by David. Aware of his sin, he "recovered" by sincere repentance and confession. See II Sam. 11—12. **96. child:** Solomon. **101. Michal:** David's first wife, daughter of Saul. **102. Abishag:** a beautiful young virgin whose attempt to solace David in his old age was unsuccessful. See I Kings 1:1–4. The point of the last two lines of this stanza is that David's muse was more important to him than any earthly woman.

69. Kidron: (or Kedron) a brook, now a ravine, in central Palestine. **77. the lion . . . bear:** David, like many other folk heroes, was reputed to be a great slayer of wild animals. See I Sam. 17:34–35.

XIX.

Angels—their ministry and meed,
Which to and fro with blessings speed,   110
    Or with their citterns° wait;
Where Michael° with his millions bows,
Where dwells the seraph and his spouse,
    The cherub and her mate.

XX.

Of man—the semblance and effect
Of God and Love—the Saint elect
    For infinite applause—
To rule the land, and briny broad,
To be laborious in his laud,
    And heroes in his cause.   120

XXI.

The world—the clustring spheres he made,
The glorious light, the soothing shade,
    Dale, champaign, grove, and hill;
The multitudinous abyss,
Where secrecy remains in bliss,
    And wisdom hides her skill.

XXII.

Trees, plants, and flow'rs—of virtuous° root;
Gem° yielding blossom, yielding fruit,
    Choice gums and precious balm;
Bless ye the nosegay in the vale,   130
And with the sweetners of the gale
    Enrich the thankful psalm.

XXIII.

Of fowl—e'en ev'ry beak and wing
Which chear the winter, hail the spring,
    That live in peace or prey;
They that make music, or that mock,
The quail, the brave domestic cock,
    The raven, swan, and jay.

XXIV.

Of fishes—ev'ry size and shape,
Which nature frames of light escape,   140
    Devouring man to shun:
The shells are in the wealthy deep,
The shoals upon the surface leap,
    And love the glancing sun.

XXV.

Of beasts—the beaver plods his task;
While the sleek tygers roll and bask,

Nor yet the shades arouse:
Her cave the mining coney° scoops;
Where o'er the mead the mountain stoops,
    The kids exult and brouse.   150

XXVI.

Of gems—their virtue and their price,
Which hid in earth from man's device,
    Their darts of lustre sheathe;
The jasper of the master's stamp,°
The topaz blazing like a lamp
    Among the mines beneath.

XXVII.

Blest was the tenderness he felt
When to his graceful harp he knelt,
    And did for audience call;
When satan with his hand he quell'd,   160
And in serene suspense he held
    The frantic throes of Saul.°

XXVIII.

His furious foes no more malign'd
As he such melody divin'd,
    And sense and soul detain'd;
Now striking strong, now soothing soft,
He sent the godly sounds aloft,
    Or in delight refrain'd.

XXIX.

When up to heav'n his thoughts he pil'd,
From fervent lips fair Michal smil'd,   170
    As blush to blush she stood;
And chose herself the queen, and gave
Her utmost from her heart, "so brave,
    And plays his hymns so good."

XXX.

The pillars of the Lord are seven,°
Which stand from earth to topmost heav'n;
    His wisdom drew the plan;

---

148. coney: rabbit. 154. the master's stamp: Smart may have in mind the jewel, or symbol of authority, of the Grand Master of a Masonic lodge. Or perhaps *master's* means "God's." 161–62. he . . . Saul: David cast an evil spirit out of Saul by playing for him on the harp. See I Sam. 16:23. 175. seven: In this stanza and the following seven, Smart appears to be uniting three ideas: (1) that of the seven pillars of wisdom (Prov. 9:1); (2) that of the seven days of the Creation (Gen. 1—2:3); and (3) that of the numerous decorated pillars of Solomon's temple, planned by David (I Kings 5—8). In addition, the whole passage is obscurely connected with the symbolism of Freemasonry, which largely derives from the biblical account of the building of Solomon's temple.

III. citterns: lutelike instruments. 112. Michael: the commander of God's angelic armies. 127. virtuous: possessing medicinal powers, or "virtues." 128. Gem: bud.

His WORD accomplish'd the design,
From brightest gem to deepest mine,
　　From CHRIST enthron'd to man.　　　180

XXXI.

Alpha,° the cause of causes, first
In station, fountain, whence the burst
　　Of light, and blaze of day;
Whence bold attempt, and brave advance,
Have motion, life, and ordinance,
　　And heav'n itself its stay.

XXXII.

Gamma supports the glorious arch
On which angelic legions march,
　　And is with sapphires pav'd;
Thence the fleet clouds are sent adrift,　　190
And thence the painted folds, that lift
　　The crimson veil, are wav'd.

XXXIII.

Eta with living sculpture breathes,
With verdant carvings, flow'ry wreathes
　　Of never-wasting bloom;
In strong relief his goodly base
All instruments of labour grace,
　　The trowel, spade, and loom.

XXXIV.

Next Theta stands to the Supreme—
Who form'd, in number, sign,° and scheme,　　200
　　Th' illustrious lights that are;
And one° address'd his saffron robe,
And one, clad in a silver globe,°
　　Held rule with ev'ry star.

XXXV.

Iota's tun'd to choral hymns
Of those that fly, while he that swims
　　In thankful safety lurks;
And foot, and chapitre,° and niche,
The various histories enrich
　　Of God's recorded works.°　　　210

XXXVI.

Sigma presents the social droves,
With him that solitary roves,
　　And man of all the chief;
Fair on whose face, and stately frame,
Did God impress his hallow'd name,
　　For ocular belief.

XXXVII.

OMEGA! GREATEST and the BEST,
Stands sacred to the day of rest,
　　For gratitude and thought;
Which bless'd the world upon his pole,°　　220
And gave the universe his goal,
　　And clos'd th' infernal draught.°

XXXVIII.

O DAVID, scholar of the Lord!
Such is thy science, whence reward
　　And infinite degree;°
O strength, O sweetness, lasting ripe!
God's harp thy symbol, and thy type°
　　The lion and the bee!

For the SUN is an intelligence and an angel of the human
form.
For the MOON is an intelligence and an angel in shape
like a woman.
For they are together in the spirit every night like man
and wife.

181. Alpha: The exact significance of the names of the Greek letters in this stanza and the following six has baffled all commentators. Perhaps we can accept the interpretation of an early reviewer of the poem (*The Monthly Review*, April, 1763); Smart, who read the review, did not trouble to correct this interpretation: "These [letters], we conjecture, are made choice of, as consecrated for the following reasons. *Alpha* and *Omega*, from a well-known text in the Revelation [21:6]. *Iota*, *Eta*, and *Sigma* because they are used to signify our Saviour, on altars and pulpits. *Theta*, as being the initial of God [θεός]; and *Gamma*, as denoting the number three, held sacred by some Christians." But even this interpretation fails to account for the order (alternating vowels and consonants) in which the letters appear. Perhaps an anagram is intended. **200. sign:** constellation. **202. one:** the sun. **203. one . . . globe:** the moon. The sun and moon are symbols of male and female in Masonic imagery. Cf. *Jubilate Agno*, sec. B2, 317–19:

208. chapitre: the capital of a pillar. **208–10. And . . . works:** Smart is perhaps thinking of the fantastically decorated pillars of Solomon's temple. See I Kings 7. **220. pole:** perhaps axis. **222. draught:** Smart may be using the word to mean either "wind" or "drain." If "wind," the meaning might be: "The creation of the final day finished God's work of distinguishing the created cosmos from the winds of chaos." If "drain," Smart may mean that the completed Creation assumes the reentry of God into History as the Redeemer, who will make possible the closing of the draught, or drain, into hell. **225. degree:** rank, dignity. Smart perhaps has in mind too a Masonic or academic degree. **227. type:** biblical symbol. The lion (strength) and the bee (sweetness) allude to the riddle of Samson. See Judg. 14:18.

XXXIX.

There is but One who ne'er rebell'd,
But One by passion unimpell'd,   230
　　By pleasures unintic't;
He from himself his semblance sent,
Grand object of his own content,
　　And saw the God in CHRIST.

XL.

Tell them I am, JEHOVA said
To MOSES; while earth heard in dread,
　　And smitten to the heart,
At once above, beneath, around,
All nature, without voice or sound,
　　Replied, O Lord, THOU ART.   240

XLI.

Thou art—to give and to confirm,
For each his talent and his term;
　　All flesh thy bounties share:
Thou shalt not call thy brother fool;
The porches° of the Christian school
　　Are meekness, peace, and pray'r.

XLII.

Open, and naked of offence,
Man's made of mercy, soul, and sense;
　　God arm'd the snail and wilk;°
Be good to him that pulls thy plough;   250
Due food and care, due rest, allow
　　For her that yields thee milk.

XLIII.

Rise up before the hoary head,
And God's benign commandment dread,
　　Which says thou shalt not die:
"Not as I will, but as thou wilt,"
Pray'd He whose conscience knew no guilt;
　　With whose bless'd pattern vie.

XLIV.

Use all thy passions!—love is thine,
And joy, and jealousy divine;   260
　　Thine hope's eternal fort,
And care thy leisure to disturb,
With fear concupiscence to curb,
　　And rapture to transport.

XLV.

Act simply, as occasion asks;
Put mellow wine in season'd casks;
　　Till not with ass and bull:°
Remember thy baptismal bond;
Keep from commixtures foul and fond,
　　Nor work thy flax with wool.°   270

XLVI.

Distribute: pay the Lord his tithe,
And make the widow's heart-strings blithe;
　　Resort with those that weep:
As you from all and each expect,
For all and each thy love direct,
　　And render as you reap.

XLVII.

The slander and its bearer spurn,
And propagating praise sojourn
　　To make thy welcome last;
Turn from old Adam to the New;°   280
By hope futurity pursue;
　　Look upwards to the past.

XLVIII.

Controul thine eye, salute success,
Honour the wiser, happier bless,
　　And for thy neighbour feel;
Grutch not of° mammon and his leaven,
Work emulation up to heaven
　　By knowledge and by zeal.

XLIX.

O DAVID, highest in the list
Of worthies, on God's ways insist,   290
　　The genuine word repeat:°
Vain are the documents of men,
And vain the flourish of the pen
　　That keeps the fool's conceit.

L.

PRAISE above all—for praise prevails;
Heap up the measure, load the scales,
　　And good to goodness add:
The gen'rous soul her saviour aids,
But peevish obloquy degrades;
　　The Lord is great and glad.   300

---

267. **Till . . . bull:** Cf. "Thou shalt not plow with an ox and an ass together" (Deut. 22:10). 270. **Nor . . . wool:** Cf. "Thou shalt not wear a garment of divers sorts, as of woollen and linen together" (Deut. 22:11). 280. **New:** Christ, the New Adam in the sense that he regains for man the paradise lost by the old Adam. 286. **Grutch not of:** envy not. 291. **The genuine . . . repeat:** [Smart's note] Ps. 119.

---

245. **porches:** Smart here uses in a partly Masonic sense the imagery of I Kings 7, which describes Solomon's temple. 249. **wilk:** (whelk) a shellfish.

LI.

For ADORATION all the ranks
Of angels yield eternal thanks,
   And DAVID in the midst;
With God's good poor, which, last and least
In man's esteem, thou to thy feast,
   O blessed bride-groom, bidst.

LII.

For ADORATION seasons change,
And order, truth, and beauty range,
   Adjust, attract, and fill:
The grass the polyanthus cheques;°   310
And polish'd porphyry reflects,
   By the descending rill.

LIII.

Rich almonds colour to the prime
For ADORATION; tendrils climb,
   And fruit-trees pledge their gems;
And Ivis° with her gorgeous vest
Builds for her eggs her cunning nest,
   And bell-flowers bow their stems.

LIV.

With vinous syrup cedars spout;
From rocks pure honey gushing out,   320
   For ADORATION springs:
All scenes of painting croud the map
Of nature; to the mermaid's pap
   The scaled infant clings.

LV.

The spotted ounce° and playsome cubs
Run rustling 'mongst the flow'ring shrubs,
   And lizards feed° the moss;
For ADORATION beasts embark,°
While waves upholding halcyon's ark°
   No longer roar and toss.   330

LVI.

While Israel sits beneath his fig,°
With coral root and amber sprig
   The wean'd advent'rer° sports;

Where to the palm the jasmin cleaves,
For ADORATION 'mongst the leaves
   The gale his peace reports.

LVII.

Increasing days their reign exalt,
Nor in the pink and mottled vault
   Th' opposing spirits tilt;°
And, by the coasting reader° spied,   340
The silverlings and crusions° glide
   For ADORATION gilt.

LVIII.

For ADORATION rip'ning canes
And cocoa's purest milk detains
   The western pilgrim's staff;
Where rain in clasping boughs inclos'd,
And vines with oranges dispos'd,
   Embow'r the social laugh.

LIX.

Now labour his reward receives,
For ADORATION counts his sheaves   350
   To peace, her bounteous prince;
The nectarine his strong tint imbibes,
The apples of ten thousand tribes,
   And quick° peculiar quince.

LX.

The wealthy crops of whit'ning rice,
'Mongst thyine° woods and groves of spice,
   For ADORATION grow;
And, marshall'd in the fenced land,
The peaches and pomegranates stand,
   Where wild carnations blow.   360

LXI.

The laurels with the winter strive;
The crocus burnishes alive
   Upon the snow-clad earth:
For ADORATION myrtles stay
To keep the garden from dismay,
   And bless the sight from dearth.

310. cheques: checkers, decorates; *polyanthus* is the subject of the clause. **316. Ivis:** [Smart's note] Humming-bird. **325. ounce:** leopard. **327. feed:** eat. **328. embark:** [Smart's note, added to the 1765 edition] There is a large quadruped [possibly the beaver] that preys upon fish, and provides himself with a large piece of timber for that purpose, with which he is very handy. **329. ark:** the nest of the kingfisher, or halcyon. The bird, floating in its nest on the waves, was traditionally thought to quiet the seas. **331. Israel . . . fig:** See Mic. 4:4. **333. wean'd advent'rer:** child.

339. tilt: the storm clouds, or winds, cease their conflicting motion in the "vault" of the sky. **340. coasting reader:** a person reading a book while floating ("coasting") slowly down a stream in a canoe or punt. **341. silverlings and crusions:** tarpon and carplike fish. **354. quick:** pungent. **356. thyine:** sweet. See Rev. 18:12.

LXII.

The pheasant shows his pompous neck;
And ermine, jealous of a speck,
  With fear eludes offence:
The sable, with his glossy pride,   370
For ADORATION is descried,
  Where frosts the wave condense.

LXIII.

The chearful holly, pensive yew,
And holy thorn,° their trim renew;
  The squirrel hoards his nuts:
All creatures batten o'er their stores,
And careful nature all her doors
  For ADORATION shuts.

LXIV.

For ADORATION, DAVID's psalms
Lift up the heart to deeds of alms;   380
  And he, who kneels and chants,
Prevails his passions to controul,
Finds meat and med'cine to the soul,
  Which for translation pants.

LXV.

For ADORATION, beyond match,
The scholar bulfinch° aims to catch
  The soft flute's iv'ry touch;
And, careless on the hazle spray,
The daring redbreast keeps at bay
  The damsel's greedy clutch.   390

LXVI.

For ADORATION, in the skies,
The Lord's philosopher° espies
  The Dog, the Ram, and Rose;°
The planets ring, Orion's sword;
Nor is his greatness less ador'd
  In the vile worm that glows.

LXVII.

For ADORATION on the strings°
The western breezes work their wings,
  The captive ear to sooth.—

LXVIII.

Hark! 'tis a voice°—how still, and small—   400
That makes the cataracts to fall,
  Or bids the sea be smooth.

LXVIII.

For ADORATION, incense comes
From bezoar,° and Arabian gums;
  And on the civet's° furr.
But as for prayer, or e're it faints,
Far better is the breath of saints
  Than galbanum° and myrrh.

LXIX.

For ADORATION from the down,
Of dam'sins° to th' anana's crown,°   410
  God sends to tempt the taste;
And while the luscious zest invites,
The sense, that in the scene delights,
  Commands desire be chaste.

LXX.

For ADORATION, all the paths
Of grace are open, all the baths
  Of purity refresh;
And all the rays of glory beam
To deck the man of God's esteem,
  Who triumphs o'er the flesh.   420

LXXI.

For ADORATION, in the dome
Of Christ the sparrows find an home,
  And on his olives perch:
The swallow also dwells with thee,
O man of God's humility,
  Within his Saviour CHURCH.°

LXXII.

Sweet is the dew that falls betimes,
And drops upon the leafy limes;
  Sweet Hermon's° fragrant air:
Sweet is the lilly's silver bell,   430
And sweet the wakeful tapers smell
  That watch for early pray'r.

---

374. thorn: hawthorn, associated with Christ and with St. Joseph of Arimathea. **386. scholar bulfinch:** so called because the bird can learn to imitate a tune. **392. philosopher:** natural scientist; here, astronomer. **393. The Dog . . . Rose:** constellations. **397. strings:** [Smart's note] Æolian harp. [A crude harp hung in a tree and "played" by the wind, a popular "romantic" novelty in Smart's time.]

400. voice: God's. **404. bezoar:** substance found in the stomachs of ruminants. **405. civet's:** civet cat's. **408. galbanum:** a gum resin used in making perfume. **410. dam'sins:** damson plums. **anana's crown:** spiky tuft of the pineapple. **426. Church:** This stanza paraphrases Ps. 84:3. **429. Hermon:** a Syrian mountain.

LXXIII.

Sweet the young nurse with love intense,
Which smiles o'er sleeping innocence;
   Sweet when the lost arrive:
Sweet the musician's ardour beats,
While his vague mind's in quest of sweets,
   The choicest flow'rs to hive.

LXXIV.

Sweeter in all the strains of love,
The language of thy turtle dove,   440
   Pair'd to thy swelling chord;
Sweeter with ev'ry grace endu'd,
The glory of thy gratitude,
   Respir'd unto the Lord.

LXXV.

Strong is the horse upon his speed;
Strong in pursuit the rapid glede,°
   Which makes at once his game:
Strong the tall ostrich on the ground;
Strong thro' the turbulent profound
   Shoots xiphias° to his aim.   450

LXXVI.

Strong is the lion—like a coal
His eye-ball—like a bastion's mole°
   His chest against the foes:
Strong the gier-eagle° on his sail,
Strong against tide, th' enormous whale
   Emerges as he goes.

LXXVII.

But stronger still, in earth and air,
And in the sea, the man of pray'r;
   And far beneath the tide;
And in the seat to faith assign'd,   460
Where ask is have, where seek is find,
   Where knock is open wide.

LXXVIII.

Beauteous the fleet before the gale;
Beauteous the multitudes in mail,
   Rank'd arms and crested heads:
Beauteous the garden's umbrage mild,
Walk, water, meditated wild,°
   And all the bloomy beds.

LXXIX.

Beauteous the moon full on the lawn;
And beauteous, when the veil's withdrawn,   470
   The virgin to her spouse:
Beauteous the temple deck'd and fill'd,
When to the heav'n of heav'n's they build
   Their heart-directed vows.

LXXX.

Beauteous, yea beauteous more than these,
The shepherd king upon his knees,
   For his momentous trust:
With wish of infinite conceit,°
For man, beast, mute,° the small and great,
   And prostrate dust to dust.°   480

LXXXI.

Precious the bounteous widow's mite;
And precious, for extream delight,
   The largess from the churl:°
Precious the ruby's blushing blaze,
And alba's blest imperial rays,°
   And pure cerulean pearl.

LXXXII.

Precious the penitential tear;
And precious is the sigh sincere,
   Acceptable to God:
And precious are the winning flow'rs,   490
In gladsome Israel's feast of bow'rs,
   Bound on the hallow'd sod.°

LXXXIII.

More precious that diviner part
Of David, ev'n the Lord's own heart,
   Great, beautiful, and new:
In all things where it was intent,
In all extreams, in each event,
   Proof—answ'ring true to true.

LXXXIV.

Glorious the sun in mid career;
Glorious th' assembled fires appear;   500
   Glorious the comet's train:

---

446. **glede:** hawk. 450. **xiphias:** [Smart's note] The sword-fish. 452. **mole:** heavy wall; the figure is from the mechanics of fortification. 454. **gier-eagle:** vulture. 467. **meditated wild:** Smart seems to have in mind the planned "wildness" of the English garden, as distinguished from the symmetry of the French style.

478. **conceit:** conception. 479. **mute:** fish, the "mute" creation. 480. **prostrate . . . dust:** Cf. II Sam. 12:16: ". . . David fasted, and went in, and lay all night upon the earth." 483. **The largess . . . churl:** [Smart's note] Sam. 25:18. 485. **alba's . . . rays:** [Smart's note] Rev. 2:17. [Alba here is the white stone mentioned in this verse of the Book of Revelation.] 490–92. **precious are . . . sod:** Cf. Lev. 23:40.

Glorious the trumpet and alarm;
Glorious th' almighty stretch'd-out arm;
    Glorious th' enraptur'd main:

LXXXV.

Glorious the northern lights astream;
Glorious the song, when GOD's the theme;
    Glorious the thunder's roar:
Glorious hosanna from the den;°
Glorious the catholic amen;
    Glorious the martyr's gore: 510

LXXXVI.

Glorious—more glorious is the crown
Of Him that brought salvation down
    By meekness, call'd thy Son;
Thou at stupendous truth believ'd,
And now the matchless deed's atchiev'd,
    DETERMINED, DARED, and DONE.

---

508. **den:** Daniel was delivered safely from a den of lions
because of his faith.

FROM

THE WORKS OF HORACE, TRANSLATED INTO VERSE

Writing to Smart's sister, his friend Hugh Hawkesworth
explained, "He told me his principal motive for translating Horace into verse, was to supersede the prose
translation [1756] which he did for Newbery, which he
said would hurt his memory."
    The text is that of the first edition (4 vols., 1767).

BOOK I, ODE XXXVIII

TO HIS SERVANT.

Persian pomps, boy, ever I renounce them:
Scoff o' the plaited coronet's refulgence;
Seek not in fruitless vigilance the rose-tree's
    Tardier offspring.

Mere honest myrtle that alone is order'd,
Me the mere myrtle decorates, as also
Thee the prompt waiter to a jolly toper
    Hous'd in an arbour.

Horace Walpole, Fourth Earl of Orford

1717–1797

Horace Walpole, letter writer and connoisseur, was born in London, the youngest child of the wealthy Whig Prime Minister Sir Robert Walpole. Although he always admired his father and was sometimes even embarrassingly loyal to his memory, Horace was quite different: the father was coarse and practical; the son was exquisite and fanciful. But the two were similar in their shrewdness and in their boundless enthusiasm for experience.

At the age of nine Walpole entered Eton, where he became an intimate of Thomas Gray, Richard West, and Thomas Ashton. These four, who called themselves the Quadruple Alliance, cultivated a supercilious detachment from their more rugged fellows and enjoyed among themselves hours of literate whimsy. At eighteen Walpole entered King's College, Cambridge, where he was not a brilliant student. For four years he attended the university irregularly—masquerades in London were more amusing—and he left without taking a degree. His father wanted him to study law, but he was not interested; he had plenty of money and decided to travel. In 1739 he set off on the Grand Tour, taking Thomas Gray with him. After indulging in the Alps their taste for thrilling scenery, they settled in Florence, where Walpole spent his time in parties and elegance while the shy and sober Gray stayed home reading. Their friendship ceased abruptly at the town of Reggio on the way back to England, and they were not reconciled until 1745.

Walpole returned to England in 1741 to stand for Parliament on the Whig side. He was elected, and for twenty-seven years he gratified his appetite for complex political intrigue. In 1742 Sir Robert was forced to resign as Prime Minister. He retired to Houghton, his splendid country estate in Norfolk, where Horace lived too for the next few years, browsing among his father's picture collections and attending to his own elaborate, witty correspondence. When his father died in 1745, Horace, who remained a bachelor, found himself with a great deal of money, complete freedom, and little to do.

Although he owned a London house, he felt the need for a summer place as well. He discovered "a little plaything-house" on a hill overlooking the Thames at Twickenham, ten miles from London, which he rented in 1747 and bought two years later. He now discovered his true calling—a devotion to Gothic architecture and medieval antiquities. The house was only a cottage when Walpole began; before he had finished his alterations it was a thirty-room Gothic castle, complete with plaster battlements and towers, fan vaulting and slender arched windows, a great hall, an armory, a cloister, a gallery, and a chapel. It was all slightly ridiculous but at the same time exciting, and visitors came to admire his exquisite version of medieval architecture and stained glass, as well as the thousands of prints, paintings, porcelains, bronzes, and relics with which he filled the house. The relics, which made the place a virtual museum, ranged from Cardinal Wolsey's hat to "an Egyptian pebble, with a *lusus naturae* that represents Voltaire in his nightgown and cap." Soon visitors were being admitted by ticket only. A sort of Gothic-Rococo Sabine Farm, Strawberry Hill satisfied the contemporary craving for the pleasant shudder in an atmosphere of "gloomth" at the same time that it met the calm Horatian ideal of rural retirement. For Walpole it was a refuge from the contemporary; as he wrote his friend George Montagu, "Old castles, old pictures, old histories, and the babble of old people make one live back into centuries that cannot disappoint one."

In 1757 he established his own printing press at Strawberry Hill. Its first production was an edition of Gray's *Odes*, and Walpole later printed many of his own works. Some contemporary readers considered his writings shallow and capricious, but he defended himself by insisting that he did not pretend to be a scholar and that he wrote for his own pleasure. Some light poems of his appeared in Dodsley's *Collection* (1748), and during the 1740's he also published a number of political pamphlets and whimsical essays. In 1758 he brought out one of his major works, *A Catalogue of the Royal and Noble Authors of England*, a sprightly collection of anecdotes that made good reading. From 1762 to 1771 appeared the four volumes of another major work, a digressive history of English graphic art titled *Anecdotes of Painting in England*, which was based upon notebooks of the contemporary engraver George Vertue. The last volume contained an essay titled *History of the Modern Taste in Gardening*, in which Walpole, like Shenstone, argued for natural rather than geometrical effects. In 1764 Walpole turned to fiction, bringing out *The Castle of Otranto, Translated by William Marshal from the Original Italian of Onuphrio Muralto*. Set in medieval Italy, this fantastic Gothic romance placed its quite conventional characters in the midst of inexplicable horrible events—a giant helmet falls from the skies; a statue bleeds; gigantic hands and feet intrude. This romance—reminiscent of the grotesqueries of the Quadruple Alliance—spawned numerous imitations, and Walpole was pleased to reveal his authorship in the second edition (1765). In 1768 he published *Historic Doubts on the Life and Reign of King Richard III*, in which he attempted to vindicate Richard's character. Many found this book amateurish and unconvincing. In the same year he printed at his private press his bold tragedy of incest, *The Mysterious Mother*. His last important publication was *A Description of Strawberry Hill* (1774), a catalog of his collections, executed with loving attention to detail. At his death he left behind many volumes of memoirs of the reigns of George II and III; these were published during the first half of the nineteenth century.

During the last twenty years of his long life he was plagued by public insinuations that his refusal to accept Thomas Chatterton's Rowley poems as genuine had somehow been the cause of Chatterton's early suicide. But despite his uneasiness over these rumors and despite debilitating attacks of gout, he continued gracefully to improve Strawberry Hill and to record in his incomparable letters the antics of a whole gallery of grotesques and eccentrics of his own class. Upon the death of his insane nephew in 1791, he became Fourth Earl of Orford. Growing more abstemious and more elegantly slender yearly, he lived long enough to become a relic himself. When George Selwyn visited Strawberry Hill, he found Walpole "one of the most carefully finished miniatures and best-preserved mummies in the whole collection." But even in his last years he managed to summon new supplies of cheerfulness to enliven his unflagging correspondence. Tranquil and a trifle affected on the outside, he remained underneath warm and affectionate, with an undiminished talent for friendship. He was buried beside his famous father in Houghton Church.

In the age that followed he found both detractors and defenders. Lord Macaulay wrote, "In everything in which Walpole busied himself . . . he was drawn by some strange attraction from the great to the little, and from the useful to the odd." But to Thomas Carlyle he was "one of the clearest sighted men of the Eighteenth Century . . . a determined despiser and merciless dissector of cant." And if Walpole was a gossip, he was at least, as George Sherburn has said, "the best informed gossip of his century."

A. T. Hazen has edited two important bibliographies, *A Bibliography of the Strawberry Hill Press* (1942) and *A Bibliography of Horace Walpole* (1948). Two convenient selections of the letters are edited by W. S. Lewis: *A Selection of the Letters of Horace Walpole* (2 vols., 1926) and *Letters of Horace Walpole* (1951). The important *Yale Edition of Horace Walpole's Correspondence*, ed. W. S. Lewis and others, began appearing in 1937; it will consist of some fifty volumes. Until it is complete, the reader should use Mrs. Paget Toynbee's edition of the letters (16 vols., 1903–05), together with Paget Toynbee's *Supplement* (3 vols., 1918–25). *The Castle of Otranto* has been edited by Oswald Doughty (1929). The standard biography is by R. W. Ketton-Cremer (rev. ed., 1946). Austin Dobson's *Horace Walpole: A Memoir* (rev. by Paget Toynbee, 1927) is graceful. The fascinating *Collector's Progress* (1951), by the great Walpole collector and authority W. S. Lewis, is full of illuminating material about Strawberry Hill. Lewis's *Horace Walpole* (1961) is an elegantly illustrated account.

FROM

[LETTERS]

👑

Walpole wrote more than four thousand letters. He began at the age of eight with "Dear mama I hop you are wall" and ended in his eightieth year by asking Lady Ossory to "accept the resignation of your Ancient Servant, O." He conceived of his letters, which he designed for posthumous publication, as a contribution to the social history of his age. He felt an almost Boswellian obligation to leave records behind him; as he once said, "I have everything in the world to tell posterity." But unlike Boswell what he tells is social, not personal.

The genre he chose for his social history was that of the familiar letter, with its convention of spontaneity and its illusions of negligence and ease. If he had a model, it was the anecdotal letters of Mme. de Sévigné, first published in 1725. But Walpole's letters exhibit something all his own—the sheer delight with which he seeks out and confronts the absurd. Through the technique of light irony he renders his carefully controlled vision of a world far gone in futility and farce.

To help him focus his interests and bring some sort of system into his letter-writing, he specialized his correspondences. Thus he reported on politics and international affairs to Sir Horace Mann; on contemporary literature to Thomas Gray and, after Gray's death, to William Mason; on antiquities and collecting to William Cole and John Chute; on upper-class social life and gossip to George Montagu and, later, to Lady Ossory and to Mary and Agnes Berry. When a correspondent died or lost interest, Walpole quickly found a replacement and carried on. Despite the many competing interests of a remarkably busy life, the letters were his primary occupation.

We have taken our texts from *The Yale Edition of Horace Walpole's Correspondence* (1937–   ), ed. W. S. Lewis and others, except for the letters to Chute, October 10, 1766; to Mann, May 12, 1768; and to Jephson, February, 1775, which we have taken from Mrs. Paget Toynbee's *The Letters of Horace Walpole* (16 vols., 1903–05) and Paget Toynbee's *Supplement* (3 vols., 1918–25); and the letter to the Countess of Upper Ossory, August 11, 1778, which is from W. S. Lewis's *Letters of Horace Walpole* (1951). The texts that follow are not exact transcripts of what Walpole wrote. Texts printed from Lewis's editions retain Walpole's punctuation and his spelling of proper names, but other spellings and Walpole's capitals are normalized. Texts printed from Mr. and Mrs. Toynbee's editions generally retain Walpole's spelling of proper names, but other spellings and Walpole's punctuation are normalized. We have silently corrected two of Walpole's obvious slips of the pen.

❦

[*To Sir Horace Mann*[1]]

Newmarket, Oct. 3d 1743.

I am writing to you in an inn, on the road to London. What a paradise should I have thought this, when I was in the Italian inns! In a wide barn with four ample windows, which had nothing more like glass than shutters and iron bars! No tester to the bed, and the saddles and portmanteaus heaped on me to keep off the cold. What a paradise did I think the inn at Dover when I came back, and what magnificence were twopenny prints, salt-cellars, and boxes to hold the knives: but the *summum bonum*[2] was small beer and the newspaper.

I blessed my stars and call'd it luxury![3]

Who was the Neapolitan ambassadress, that could not live at Paris, because there was no macaroni?— Now am I relapsed into all the dissatisfied repinement of a true English grumbling voluptuary. I could find in my heart to write a *Craftsman*[4] against the government, because I am not quite so much at my ease as on my own sofa. I could persuade myself that it is my Lord Carteret's fault,[5] that I am only sitting in a common arm-chair, when I would be lolling in a *péché-mortel*.[6] How dismal, how solitary, how scrub does this town look, and yet it has actually a street of houses better than Parma or Modena. Nay, the houses of the people of fashion who come hither for the races, are palaces to what houses in London itself were fifteen years ago. People do begin to live again now, and I suppose in a term we shall revert to York Houses, Clarendon Houses etc. But from that grandeur, all the nobility had contracted themselves to live in coops of a dining-room, a dark back room with one eye[7] in a corner, and a closet. Think what London would be, if the chief houses were in it, as in the cities in other countries, and not dispersed like great rarity plums in a vast pudding of country! Well! 'tis a tolerable place as it is! Were I a physician, I would prescribe nothing, but *recipe CCCLXV drachm. Londin.*[8] Would you know why I like London so much? Why, if the world consist of so many fools as it does, I choose to take them in the gross, and not made into separate pills, as they are prepared in the country. Besides, there is no being alone but in a metropolis: the worst place in the world to find solitude is the country: questions grow there, and that unpleasant Christian commodity, neighbours. Oh! they are all good Samaritans, and do so pour balms and nostrums upon one, if one has but the

---

LETTERS. **1. Sir . . . Mann:** (1706–86), British Minister at Florence (1740–86). Walpole became acquainted with Mann, one of the social ornaments of the Florentine British colony, late in 1739, while on the Grand Tour with Gray. Although Walpole and Mann never met again after 1741, they corresponded for forty-five years. Among Mann's official duties were entertaining British visitors to Florence and reporting to London on the activities of the Stuart Pretender and his two sons, who were living in Rome.

2. summum bonum: supreme good. **3. I . . . luxury:** adapted from Joseph Addison, *Cato*, I. iv. 71. **4. Craftsman:** a weekly anti-Administration newspaper. **5. Lord Carteret's fault:** Carteret, Secretary of State, was blamed for everything by the Opposition. **6. péché-mortel:** literally, a mortal sin; the term also refers to a wide chaise longue which holds two people. **7. eye:** small window. **8. recipe . . . Londin:** take 365 drams of London.

toothache or a journey to take, that they break one's head—a journey to take—ay! they talk over the miles to you, and tell you, you will be late in. My Lord Lovel says, *John* always goes two hours in the dark in the morning, to avoid being one hour in the dark in the evening. I was pressed to set out today before seven: I did before nine; and here am I arrived at a quarter past five for the rest of the night! I am more convinced every day that there is not only no knowledge of the world out of a great city, but no decency, no practicable society—I had almost said, not a virtue. I will only instance in modesty, which all *Old Englishmen*[9] are persuaded cannot exist within the atmosphere of Middlesex.[10] Lady Mary[11] has a remarkable taste and knowledge of music and can sing—I don't say, like your sister, but I am sure she would be ready to die if obliged to sing before three people, or before one with whom she is not intimate. T'other day there came to see her a Norfolk heiress: the young gentlewoman had not been three hours in the house, and that for the first time of her life, before she notified her talent for singing, and invited herself upstairs to Lady Mary's harpsichord; where with a voice like thunder, and with as little harmony, she sung to nine or ten people for an hour, "Was ever nymph like Rossymonde?"[12] no, *d'honneur.*[13] We told her, she had a very strong voice—"Lord, Sir, my master says 'tis nothing to what it was."—My dear child, she brags abominably; if it had been a thousandth degree louder, you must have heard it to Florence.

I did not write to you last post, being overwhelmed with this sort of people: I will be more punctual in London. Patapan[14] is in my lap: I had him wormed lately, which he took heinously: I made it up with him by tying a collar of rainbow ribband about his neck, for a token that he is never to be wormed any more; which he received as implicitly, as good folks do the assurance of their never being drowned in a collective body,[15] though all their doctors do not scruple to let them know they are to be burned.

I had your long letter of two sheets of Sept. 17th and wonder at your perseverance in telling me so much as you always do, when I, dull creature, find so little for you. I can only tell you that the more you write, the happier you make me; and I assure you, the more details the better: I so often lay schemes for returning to you, that I am persuaded I shall, and would keep up my stock of Florentine ideas.

I honour Matthews's punctilious observance of his *Holiness's* dignity.[16] How incomprehensible Englishmen are! I should have sworn that he would have piqued himself on calling the Pope the Whore of Babylon, and have begun his remonstrance with you *"old damned bitch."* What extremes of absurdities! To flounder from Pope Joan[17] to his Holiness! I like your reflection "that everybody can bully the Pope." There was a humourist called Sir James of the Peak, who had been beat by a fellow, who afterwards underwent the same operation from a third hand. "Zounds," said Sir James, "that I did not know this fellow would take a beating!"—Nay, my dear child, I don't know that Matthews would!

You know I always thought the Tesi[18] *comique, pendant que ça devrait être tragique.* I am happy that my sovereign lady expressed my opinion so well—by the way, is De Sade still with you? Is he still in pawn by the proxy of his clothes? Has the Princess as constant retirements to her bedchamber with the *colique*[19]—and Antenori? Oh! I was struck t' other day with a resemblance of mine hostess at Brandon to old Sarazin.[20] You must know, the ladies of Norfolk universally wear periwigs and affirm that it is the fashion at London. "Lord, Mrs White, have you been ill, that you have shaved your head?" Mrs White, in all the days of my acquaintance with her, had a professed head of red hair: today she had no hair at all before, and at a distance above her ears, I descried a

---

9. **Old Englishmen:** readers of the periodical *Old England.* 10. **Middlesex:** one of the London counties. 11. **Lady Mary:** Walpole's sister. 12. **Rossymonde:** the title of a song from Addison's opera *Rosamond* (1707); the music is by Thomas Arne (1710–78). 13. **d'honneur:** upon my honor. 14. **Patapan:** Walpole's small white dog, given him by Elisabetta Grifoni, a Florentine beauty thought by some of Walpole's friends to have been his mistress in 1740. 15. **the assurance . . . body:** See Gen. 8:21.

16. **Matthew's . . . dignity:** In his letter to Walpole of September 17, Mann had reported that Admiral Thomas Mathews, commander in chief of the British navy in the Mediterranean, had sent the Pope a formal—if somewhat illiterate—note protesting his interference in the naval warfare against Spain. 17. **Pope Joan:** a mythical female pope, said to have reigned in the ninth century. 18. **the Tesi:** Vittoria Tesi, an operatic contralto. In his letter of September 17, Mann had reported the Princess de Craon as observing, while Tesi was singing and gesturing in "a violent scene," "That is really comic, while it ought to be tragic." 19. **colique:** stomach ache. 20. **old Sarazin:** an eccentric elderly woman in Florence who impoverished herself by immoderate gambling.

smart brown bob, from beneath which had escaped
some long strings of original scarlet—so like old
Sarazin at two in the morning, when she has been
losing at pharaoh, and clawed her wig aside, and her
old trunk is shaded with the venerable white ivy of
her own locks!

I agree with you that it would be too troublesome
to send me the things now the quarantine exists, except
the gun barrels for Lord Conway,[21] the length of
which I know nothing about, being, as you conceive,
no sportsman. I must send you, with the life of
Theodore,[22] a vast pamphlet[23] in defense of the new
administration, which makes the greatest noise. It is
written, as supposed, by Dr Pearse of St Martin's,
whom Lord Bath[24] lately made a Dean; the matter
furnished by him. There is a good deal of useful
knowledge of the famous Change[25] to be found in it,
and much more impudence. Some parts are extremely
fine; in particular, the answer to the Hanoverian
pamphlets, where he has collected the flower of all
that was said in defence of that measure. Had you those
pamphlets? I will make up a parcel: Tell me what other
books you would have: I will send you nothing else,
for if I give you the least bauble, it puts you to infinite
expense, which I can't forgive, and indeed will never
bear again: you would ruin yourself, and there is
nothing I wish so much as the contrary.

Here is a good ode, written on the supposition of
that new book being Lord Bath's; I believe by the same
hand as those charming ones which I sent you last
year: the author is not yet known.[26]

1.

Your sheets I've perused,
  Where the Whigs you've abused,
And on Tories most falsely reflected;
  But, my Lord, I'm afraid,
  From all that's there said,
'Tis you, and not they, are *detected*.

2.

Both parties, I hear,
  Most freely declare,
That 'tis not approved of by either;
  If it's damned then by both,
  It must be the growth
Of Somebody, who is of neither.

3.

'Tis easy to name
  From what quarter it came,
And the thing of itself stands confessed:
  'Tis that pitiful crew
  Of your creatures and you,
Whom both parties scorn and detest.

4.

But stay, let me see,
  Which tool it could be,
That such a huge book could indite?
  For of all you have made,
  If there's one that can read,
I'm sure there's not one that can write.

5.

'Tis above poor Sir John,
  Nor by Sand's could be done,
And Bootle's too stupid and dark;
  Ord hardly reads well,
  Jeff never could spell,
And you know Harry Vane sets his mark.[27]

6.

Then since all your tools
  Are such ignorant fools,
It must be your Lordship's own doing.
  You have taken your ply,
  But you'll soon own with me,
That you've settled yourself in your ruin.

7.

As diff'rent winds blew,
  Like the weathercock, you
Long wavered both parties betwixt:
  But did not you know
  That weathercocks grow
Quite useless the moment they're fixed?

The Duke of Argyle is dead—a death of how little
moment, and of how much it would have been a year
or two ago! It is provoking, if one must die, that one
can't even die *à propos!*[28]

---

21. **Lord Conway:** Francis Seymour-Conway, Earl of
Hertford; Walpole's first cousin. 22. **the life . . .
Theodore:** *The History of Theodore I, King of Corsica* (1743).
23. **a vast pamphlet:** Lord Perceval's 175-page *Faction
Detected*, an attack on Sir Robert Walpole's administration.
24. **Lord Bath:** William Pulteney, Earl of Bath; he had been
Secretary of War under Walpole (1714–17) but had opposed
Walpole's administration since 1721. 25. **the famous
Change:** the change in the ministry after the defeat of Sir
Robert Walpole in 1742. 26. **the author . . . known:** The
author was Sir Charles Hanbury Williams (1708–59),
satirist and diplomat. Samuel Johnson thought him "a
wretched Scribbler."

27. **sets . . . mark:** is unable to write his name. The persons
referred to in this stanza are Sir John Rushout; Samuel,
Baron Sandys; Sir Thomas Bootle; Robert Ord; and
John Jeffries. All were opposed to Sir Robert Walpole.
28. **à propos:** at an appropriate time.

How does your friend Dr Cocchi?[29] You never mention him: do only knaves and fools deserve to be spoken of? Adieu!

[To Sir Horace Mann]

Strawberry Hill, June 12, 1753.

I could not rest any longer with the thought of your having no idea of a place of which you hear so much, and therefore desired Mr Bentley[30] to draw you as much idea of it, as the post would be persuaded to carry from Twickenham to Florence. The enclosed enchanted little landscape then is Strawberry Hill; and I will try to explain so much of it to you as will help to let you know whereabouts we are, when we are talking to you, for it is uncomfortable in so intimate a correspondence as ours, not to be exactly master of every spot where one another is writing or reading or sauntering. This view of the castle is what I have just finished, and is the only side that will be at all regular. Directly before it is an open grove, through which you see a field which is bounded by a serpentine wood of all kind of trees and flowering shrubs and flowers. The lawn before the house is situated on the top of a small hill, from whence to the left you see the town and church of Twickenham encircling a turn of the river, that looks exactly like a seaport in miniature. The opposite shore is a most delicious meadow, bounded by Richmond Hill which loses itself in the noble woods of the park to the end of the prospect on the right, where is another turn of the river and the suburbs of Kingston as luckily placed as Twickenham is on the left; and a natural terrace on the brow of my hill, with meadows of my own down to the river, commands both extremities. Is not this a tolerable prospect? You must figure that all this is perpetually enlivened by a navigation of boats and barges, and by a road below my terrace, with coaches, post-chaises, wagons and horsemen constantly in motion, and the fields speckled with cows, horses and sheep. Now you shall walk into the house. The bow-window below leads into a little parlour hung with a stone-colour Gothic paper and Jackson's[31] Venetian prints, which I could never endure while they pretended, infamous as they are, to be after Titian etc. but when I gave them this air of barbarous bas-reliefs, they succeeded to a miracle: it is impossible at first sight not to conclude that they contain the history of Attila or Tottila,[32] done about the very era. From hence under two gloomy arches, you come to the hall and staircase, which it is impossible to describe to you, as it is the most particular and chief beauty of the castle. Imagine the walls covered with (I call it paper, but it is really paper painted in perspective to represent) Gothic fretwork: the lightest Gothic balustrade to the staircase, adorned with antelopes (our supporters)[33] bearing shields; lean windows fattened with rich saints in painted glass, and a vestibule open with three arches on the landing place, and niches full of trophies of old coats of mail, Indian shields made of rhinoceros's hides, broadswords, quivers, long bows, arrows and spears—all *supposed* to be taken by Sir Terry Robsart[34] in the holy wars. But as none of this regards the enclosed drawing, I will pass to that. The room on the ground floor nearest to you is a bedchamber, hung with yellow paper and prints, framed in a new manner invented by Lord Cardigan, that is, with black and white borders printed. Over this is Mr Chute's[35] bechamber, hung with red in the same manner. The bow-window room one pair of stairs is not yet finished; but in the tower beyond it is the charming closet where I am now writing to you. It is hung with green paper and water-colour pictures; has two windows; the one in the drawing looks to the garden, the other to the beautiful prospect; and the top of each glutted with the richest painted glass of the arms of England, crimson roses, and twenty other pieces of green, purple, and historic bits. I must tell you by the way, that the castle, when finished, will have two and thirty windows enriched with painted glass. In this closet, which is Mr Chute's college of arms, are two presses with books of heraldry and antiquities, Madame Sévigné's letters, and any French books that relate to her and her acquaintance. Out of

---

29. **Dr Cocchi:** Antonio Cocchi, a popular Florentine physician. 30. **Mr Bentley:** Richard Bentley (1708–82), only son of the famous Cambridge classical scholar; an artist and architect, he designed many of the Gothic features of Strawberry Hill. 31. **Jackson:** John Baptist Jackson (1701–80), wood-engraver and painter in chiaroscuro, a pictorial technique producing three-dimensional effects of light and shade.

32. **Attila or Tottila:** Kings of the Huns and Ostrogoths respectively in the fifth and sixth centuries. 33. **our supporters:** On the family coat of arms an antelope holds up the shield on either side. 34. **Sir Terry Robsart:** (d. 1496), one of Walpole's forebears. 35. **Mr Chute:** John Chute (1701–76), an intimate friend of Walpole's since their meeting in Florence in 1740. Walpole, Bentley, and Chute constituted the "Committee of Taste," which, after prolonged and serious discussions, determined questions of policy and detail arising from Walpole's decision to Gothicize Strawberry Hill.

this closet is the room where we always live, hung with a blue and white paper in stripes adorned with festoons, and a thousand plump chairs, couches and luxurious settees covered with linen of the same pattern, and with a bow-window commanding the prospect, and gloomed with limes that shade half each window, already darkened with painted glass in chiaroscuro, set in deep blue glass. Under this room is a cool little hall where we generally dine, hung with paper to imitate Dutch tiles.

I have described so much, that you will begin to think that all the accounts I used to give you of the diminutiveness of our habitation were fabulous; but it is really incredible how small most of the rooms are. The only two good chambers I shall have, are not yet built; they will be an eating-room and a library, each 20 by 30, and the latter 15 feet high. For the rest of the house, I could send it you in this letter as easily as the drawing, only that I should have nowhere to live till the return of the post. The Chinese summer house which you may distinguish in the distant landscape, belongs to my Lord Radnor. We pique ourselves upon nothing but simplicity, and have no carvings, gildings, paintings, inlayings or tawdry businesses.

You will not be sorry I believe by this time to have done with Strawberry Hill, and to hear a little news. The end of a very dreaming session has been extremely enlivened by an accidental bill which has opened great quarrels, and those not unlikely to be attended with interesting circumstances. A bill to prevent clandestine marriages, so drawn by the judges as to clog all matrimony in general, was inadvertently espoused by the Chancellor,[36] and having been strongly attacked in the House of Commons by Nugent, the Speaker, Mr Fox and others, the last went very great lengths of severity on the whole body of the law, and on its chieftain in particular, which however at the last reading, he softened and explained off extremely. This did not appease; but on the return of the bill to the House of Lords, where our amendments were to be read, the Chancellor in the most personal terms harangued against Fox, and concluded with saying that "he despised his scurrility as much as his adulation and recantation." As Christian charity is not one of the oaths taken by privy councillors, and as it is not the most eminent virtue in either of the champions, this

quarrel is not likely to be soon reconciled. There are natures whose disposition it is to patch up political breaches, but whether they will succeed, or try to succeed in healing this, can I tell you?

The match for Lord Granville which I announced to you, is not concluded: his rampant flames are cooled in that quarter as well as in others.

I begin a new sheet to you, which does not match with the other, for I have no more of the same paper here. Dr Cameron[37] is executed, and died with the greatest firmness. His parting with his wife the night before, was heroic, and tender: he let her stay till the last moment, when being aware that the gates of the Tower would be locked, he told her so; she fell at his feet in agonies: he said, "Madam, this was not what you promised me" and embracing her, forced her to retire: then with the same coolness, looked at the window till her coach was out of sight; after which he turned about and wept. His only concern seemed to be at the ignominy of Tyburn: he was not disturbed at the dresser for his body, or at the fire to burn his bowels. The crowd was so great, that a friend who attended him, could not get away, but was forced to stay and behold the execution—but what will you say to the minister or priest who accompanied him? The wretch, after taking leave, went into a landau,[38] where not content with seeing the Doctor hanged, he let down the top of the landau for the better convenience of seeing him embowelled! I cannot tell you positively that what I hinted of this Cameron being commissioned from Prussia was true; but so it is believed. Adieu! my dear child; I think this is a very tolerable letter for summer!

[*To George Montagu*[39]]

Paris, Sept. 22d, 1765.

The concern I felt at not seeing you before I left England, might make me express myself warmly, but I assure you it was nothing but concern, nor was mixed with a grain of pouting. I knew some of your reasons, and guessed others. The latter grieve me heartily; but

---

36. the Chancellor: Lord Hardwicke. The bill, which generally required that marriages be performed under Anglican auspices, became a law that obtained until 1823.

37. Dr Cameron: Dr. Archibald Cameron (1707–53), a Jacobite physician who fled to the Continent after the Rising of 1745; he was executed for having returned to Scotland in 1752, allegedly as a secret agent of the Stuarts and perhaps of Frederick the Great as well. **38. landau:** a light carriage with a collapsible top. **39. George Montagu:** Montague (*c.* 1713–80), a lazy, good-humored rural bachelor, had been a friend of Walpole's since Eton.

I advise you to do as I do: when I meet with ingratitude, I take a short leave both of it and its host. Formerly I used to look out for indemnification somewhere else; but having lived long enough to learn that the reparation generally proved a second evil of the same sort, I am content now to skin over such wounds with amusement, which at least leave no scars. It is true, amusements do not always amuse when we bid them. I find it so here; nothing strikes me; everything I do is indifferent to me. I like the people very well, and their way of life very well; but as neither were my object, I should not much care if they were any other people, or it was any other way of life. I am out of England; and my purpose is answered.

Nothing can be more obliging than the reception I meet with everywhere. It may not be more sincere (and why should it?) than our cold and bare civility, but it is better dressed, and looks natural; one asks no more. I have begun to sup in French houses, and as Lady Hertford[40] has left Paris today, shall increase my intimacies. There are swarms of English here, but most of them are going, to my great satisfaction. As the greatest part are very young, they can no more be entertaining to me, than I to them, and it certainly was not my countrymen that I came to live with. Suppers please me extremely; I love to rise and breakfast late, and to trifle away the day as I like. There are sights enough to answer that end, and shops you know are an endless field for me. The city appears much worse to me than I thought I remembered it. The French music as shocking as I knew it was. The French stage is fallen off, though in the only part I have seen Lequin,[41] I admire him extremely. He is very ugly and ill-made, and yet has an heroic dignity which Garrick[42] wants, and great fire. The Dusmenil[43] I have not seen yet, but shall in a day or two: it is a mortification that I cannot compare her with the Clairon[44] who has left the stage. Grandval[45] I saw through a whole play without suspecting it was he—

alas! four and twenty years make strange havoc with us mortals! You cannot imagine how this struck me! The Italian comedy, now united with their *opéra comique*, is their most perfect diversion—but alas! Harlequin, my dear favourite Harlequin,[46] my passion, makes me more melancholy than cheerful. Instead of laughing, I sit silently reflecting, how everything loses charms, when one's own youth does not lend it gilding. When we are divested of that eagerness and illusion with which our youth presents objects to us, we are but the *caput mortuum*[47] of pleasure.

Grave as these ideas are, they do not unfit me for French company. The present tone is serious enough in conscience. Unluckily the subjects of their conversation are duller to me than my own thoughts, which may be tinged with melancholy reflections, but I doubt from my constitution will never be insipid. The French affect philosophy, literature and freethinking—the first never did and never will possess me; of the two others I have long been tired. Freethinking is for one's self, surely not for society; besides one has settled one's way of thinking, or knows it cannot be settled; and for others, I do not see why there is not as much bigotry in attempting conversions from any religion as to it. I dined today with a dozen *savants*,[48] and though all the servants were waiting, the conversation was much more unrestrained, even on the Old Testament, than I would suffer at my own table in England, if a single footman was present. For literature it is very amusing, when one has nothing else to do. I think it rather pedantic in society; tiresome when displayed professedly—and besides in this country, one is sure it is only the fashion of the day. Their taste in it is worst of all: could one believe that when they read our authors, Richardson and Mr Hume[49] should be their favourites? The latter is treated here with perfect veneration. His *History*, so falsified in many points, so partial in as many, so very unequal in its parts, is thought the standard of writing.

40. Lady Hertford: wife of Walpole's cousin. **41. Lequin:** the stage name of Henry-Louis Cain. **42. Garrick:** the British actor and manager David Garrick (1717–79) was at the height of his fame as a Shakespearean at Drury Lane. Walpole found him as an actor more notable for versatility than for depth. **43. The Dusmenil:** Marie-François Dumenil, a famous Parisian actress. **44. the Clairon:** Claire-Joseph Hippolyte Legris de Latude (called Mlle. Clairon for short), another famous Parisian actress. **45. Grandval:** Walpole had earlier seen the actor François-Charles Racot Grandval in 1741, when, after his quarrel with Gray, he was passing through Paris on his way back to England.

46. Harlequin: a droll character in the classical Italian *commedia dell'arte.* **47. caput mortuum:** worthless residue. **48. savants:** intellectuals. This dinner took place at the house of Baron D'Holbach (1723–89), a notorious infidel and author of numerous works discrediting religion. **49. Richardson . . . Hume:** The novels of Samuel Richardson (1689–1761)—*Pamela* (1740–42), *Clarissa* (1747–48), and *Sir Charles Grandison* (1753)—were greatly admired and imitated on the Continent. The *History of England* by the philosopher and historian David Hume (1711–76) was completed in six volumes in 1762. (See the selection from Richardson in Part Two and from Hume in Part Five.)

In their dress and equipages they are grown very simple. We English are living upon their old gods and goddesses; I roll about in a chariot decorated with Cupids, and look like the grandfather of Adonis.

Of their parliaments and clergy, I hear a good deal and attend very little: I cannot take up any history in the middle, and was too sick of politics at home to enter into them here. In short, I have done with the world, and only live in it, rather than in a desert, like you. Few men can bear absolute retirement, and we English worst of all. We grow so humoursome, so obstinate and capricious, and so prejudiced, that it requires a fund of good nature like yours, not to grow morose. Company keeps our rind from growing too coarse and rough; and though at my return I design not to mix in public, I do not intend to be quite a recluse. My absence will put it in my power to take up or drop as much as I please.

Adieu! I shall inquire about your commission of books; but having been arrived but ten days, have not yet had time. Need I say, no, I need not, that nobody can be more affectionately yours than

H. W.

Chez Monsieur Foley Banquier à Paris.

[To John Chute]

Bath, Oct. 10, 1766.

I am impatient to hear that your charity to me has not ended in the gout to yourself[50]—all my comfort is, if you have it, that you have good Lady Brown to nurse you.

My health advances faster than my amusement. However, I have been at one opera, Mr. Wesley's.[51] They have boys and girls with charming voices, that sing hymns, in parts, to Scotch ballad tunes; but indeed so long, that one would think they were already in eternity, and knew how much time they had before them. The chapel is very neat, with true Gothic windows (yet I am not converted); but I was glad to see that luxury is creeping in upon them before persecution: they have very neat mahogany stands for branches,[52] and brackets[53] of the same in taste. At the upper end is a broad *haut-pas*[54] of four steps, advancing in the middle: at each end of the broadest part are two of *my* eagles,[55] with red cushions for the parson and clerk. Behind them rise three more steps, in the midst of which is a third eagle for pulpit. Scarlet armed-chairs to all three. On either hand, a balcony for elect ladies. The rest of the congregation sit on forms.[56] Behind the pit, in a dark niche, is a plain table within rails; so you see the throne is for the apostle. Wesley is a lean elderly man, fresh-coloured, his hair smoothly combed, but with a *soupçon*[57] of curl at the ends. Wondrous clean, but as evidently an actor as Garrick. He spoke his sermon, but so fast, and with so little accent, that I am sure he has often uttered it, for it was like a lesson. There were parts and eloquence in it; but towards the end he exalted his voice, and acted very ugly enthusiasm; decried learning, and told stories, like Latimer,[58] of the fool of his college, who said, "I *thanks* God for everything." Except a few from curiosity, and *some honourable women*, the congregation was very mean. There was a Scotch Countess of Buchan, who is carrying a pure rosy vulgar face to heaven, and who asked Miss Rich, if that was *the author of the poets*. I believe she meant me and the *Noble Authors*.[59]

The Bedfords came last night. Lord Chatham was with me yesterday two hours; looks and walks well, and is in excellent political spirits.

Yours ever,

HOR. WALPOLE.

[To Sir Horace Mann]

Arlington Street, Thursday, May 12, 1768.

You sit very much at your ease, my dear Sir, demanding ribands[60] and settling the conveyance. We are a little more gravely employed. We are glad if we can keep our windows whole, or pass and repass unmolested. I call it reading history as one goes along

---

50. **your . . . yourself:** Chute, who was abnormally susceptible to gout, had kept Walpole company at Bath.
51. **Mr. Wesley:** John Wesley (1703–91), founder of Methodism. The day Walpole heard Wesley was Sunday, October 5. Wesley wrote in his *Journal* for that date, "At eight I administered the Sacrament at Lady H[untingdon]'s chapel in Bath. At eleven I preached there on those words in the Gospel for the day, 'Thou shalt love thy neighbour as thyself.' The word was quick and powerful, and I trust many even of the rich and great felt themselves sinners before God."

52. **branches:** candelabra. 53. **brackets:** candleholders on the walls. 54. **haut-pas:** platform. 55. **my eagles:** eagles like a Roman one in marble at Strawberry Hill. 56. **forms:** benches. 57. **soupçon:** tiny bit. 58. **Latimer:** Hugh Latimer (c. 1485–1555), Protestant reformer and popular preacher. 59. **Noble Authors:** Walpole's *A Catalogue of the Royal and Noble Authors of England* (1758). 60. **demanding ribands:** Mann was seeking the red ribbon of the Order of the Bath to help him raise his social standing in aristocratic Florence.

the streets. Now we have a chapter of Clodius[61]—now an episode of Prynne,[62] and so on. I do not love to think what the second volume must be of a flourishing nation running riot. You have my text; now for the application.

Wilkes,[63] on the 27th of last month, was committed to the King's Bench.[64] The mob would not suffer him to be carried thither, but took off the horses of his hackney-coach and drew him through the City to Cornhill. He there persuaded them to disperse, and then stole to the prison and surrendered himself. Last Saturday his cause was to be heard, but his counsel pleading against the validity of the outlawry, Lord Mansfield took time to consider, and adjourned the hearing till the beginning of next term, which is in June.

The day before yesterday the Parliament met. There have been constant crowds and mobbing at the prison, but, on Tuesday, they insisted on taking Wilkes out of prison and carrying him to Parliament. The tumult increased so fast, that the Riot Act was read, the soldiers fired, and a young man was shot. The mob bore the body about the streets to excite more rage, and at night it went so far that four or five more persons were killed, and the uproar quashed, though they fired on the soldiers from the windows of houses. The partisans of Wilkes say the young man was running away, was pursued and killed; and the jury have brought it in wilful murder against the officer and men: so they must take their trials; and it makes their case very hard, and lays Government under great difficulties. On the other side, the young man is said to have been very riotous, and marked as such by the Guards. But this is not all. We have independent mobs, that have nothing to do with Wilkes, and who only take advantage of so favourable a season. The dearness of provisions incites, the hope of increase of wages allures, and drink puts them in motion. The coal-heavers began, and it is well it is not a hard frost, for they have stopped all coals coming to town. The sawyers rose too, and at last the sailors, who have committed great outrages on merchant ships, and prevented them from sailing. I just touch the heads, which would make a great figure if dilated in Baker's Chronicle[65] among the calamities at the end of a reign. The last mob, however, took an extraordinary turn; for many thousand sailors came to petition the Parliament yesterday, but in the most respectful and peaceable manner; desired only to have their grievances examined; if reasonable, redressed; if not reasonable, they would be satisfied. Being told that their flags and colours, with which they paraded, were illegal, they cast them away. Nor was this all: they declared for the King and Parliament, and beat and drove away Wilkes's mob.

It is now Friday morning; everything was quiet yesterday. Lord Suffolk moved the Lords to address the King to confer some mark of favour on the Lord Mayor Harley, for his active and spirited behaviour. The Duke of Grafton answered that it was intended; and the House were very zealous. I hope neither the King of Westminster nor the King of London will think of the red riband!

I wish with all my heart I may have no more to tell you of riots; not that I ever think them very serious things, but just to the persons on whom the storm bursts. But I pity poor creatures who are deluded to their fate, and fall by gin or faction, when they have not a real grievance to complain of, but what depends on the elements, or causes past remedy. I cannot bear to have the name of Liberty profaned to the destruction of the cause; for frantic tumults only lead to that terrible corrective, Arbitrary Power, —which cowards call out for as protection, and knaves are so ready to grant.

I believe you will soon hear of the death of Princess Louisa,[66] who is in a deep consumption.

I am much obliged to Lord Stormont for his kind thoughts, and am glad you are together. You will be a comfort to him, and it must be very much so to you at this time, to have a rational man to talk with instead of old fools and young ones, boys and travelling governors.

I say nothing about the riband, because you must

61. Clodius: (Claudius) (10 B.C.–A.D. 54), Roman emperor and historian of the Roman civil wars. **62. Prynne:** William Prynne (1600–69), English Puritan pamphleteer and historian of the English Civil War. **63. Wilkes:** John Wilkes (1727–97), a clever and unscrupulous popular politician. He maligned George III in *The North Briton*, No. 45 (1763), and was expelled from the House of Commons the next year on a charge of having committed a seditious libel. He fled to the Continent to avoid further punishment, but, although formally an outlaw, he returned in 1768 to be reelected to Parliament and simultaneously imprisoned on the libel charge. Wilkes became the idol of the populace, who rioted under the slogan "Wilkes and Liberty!" **64. the King's Bench:** a prison.

65. Baker's Chronicle: the *Chronicle of the Kings of England* (1643), a widely used book of annals by Sir Richard Baker (1568–1645). **66. Princess Louisa:** sister of George III; she died the next day.

be sensible how very unlikely it is to make its appearance just now. Adieu!

[*To Thomas Chatterton*⁶⁷]

Arlington Street, March 28, 1769.

SIR,

I cannot but think myself singularly obliged by a gentleman with whom I have not the pleasure of being acquainted, when I read your very curious and kind letter, which I have this minute received. I give you a thousand thanks for it, and for the very obliging offer you make me of communicating your MSS to me. What you have already sent me is very valuable and full of information; but instead of correcting you, Sir, you are far more able to correct me. I have not the happiness of understanding the Saxon language, and without your learned notes, should not have been able to comprehend Rowley's text.

As a second edition of my *Anecdotes* was published but last year, I must not flatter myself that a third will be wanted soon; but I shall be happy to lay up any notices you will be so good as to extract for me and send me at your leisure; for as it is uncertain when I may use them, I would by no means borrow and detain your MSS.

Give me leave to ask you where Rowley's poems are to be found. I should not be sorry to print them, or at least a specimen of them, if they have never been printed.

The Abbot John's verses,⁶⁸ that you have given me, are wonderful for their harmony and spirit, though there are some words I do not understand. You do not point out exactly the time when he lived, which I wish to know, as I suppose it was long before John ab Eyck's⁶⁹ discovery of oil painting. If so, it confirms what I had guessed, and have hinted in my *Anecdotes*, that oil painting was known here much earlier than that discovery or revival.

I will not trouble you with more questions now, Sir; but flatter myself from the humanity and politeness you have already shown me, that you will sometimes give me leave to consult you. I hope too you will forgive the simplicity of my direction, as you have favoured me with no other. I am, Sir, Your much obliged and obedient humble servant,

HOR. WALPOLE

PS. Be so good as to direct to Mr Walpole in Arlington Street.

[*To Thomas Chatterton*⁷⁰]

[c. July 27–August 4, 1769]

SIR,

I do not see, I must own, how those precious MSS of which you have sent me a few extracts, should be lost to the world by my detaining your letters. Do the originals not exist, from whence you say you copied your extracts, and from which you offered me more extracts? In truth, by your first letter, I understood that the originals themselves were in your possession by the free and voluntary offer you made me of them, and which you know I did not choose to accept. If Mr Barrett⁷¹ (who, give me leave to say, cannot know much of antiquity if he believes in the authenticity of those papers) intends to make use of them, would he not do better to have recourse to the originals, than to the slight fragments you have sent me? You say, Sir, you know them to be genuine; pray let me

67. Thomas Chatterton: (1752–70), a Bristol youth who at the age of twelve began writing poems purporting to be those of one Thomas Rowley, whom he imagined to have been a fifteenth-century priest. Disappointed by the failure of the Rowley poems to bring him the recognition he craved, Chatterton killed himself before his eighteenth birthday. In a letter to Walpole on March 25, 1769, he had "transcribed" a document "bie T. Rowlie" titled "The Ryse of Peyncteynge yn Englāde," which he hoped Walpole would find useful in any future revision of the first two volumes of his *Anecdotes of Painting in England* (1762). (See the selections from Chatterton later in Part Six.)
68. The Abbot . . . verses: Chatterton had included in his manuscript twelve lines about Richard I purporting to be written by "Johne Seconde Abbate of Seyncte Austyns Mynsterre . . . the fyrste Englyshe Paynctere yn Oyles." **69. John ab Eyck:** Jan van Eyck (*c.* 1385–1441), Flemish painter.

70. To . . . Chatterton: When Chatterton demanded the return of his transcripts, Walpole wrote this letter but decided not to send it. Instead, he simply returned Chatterton's papers without enclosing any communication. Chatterton took his revenge in the following lines, which his sister dissuaded him from sending to Walpole:

> Walpole! I thought not I should ever see
> So mean a Heart as thine has proved to be;
> Thou, who in Luxury nurs'd behold'st with Scorn
> The Boy, who Friendless, Penniless, Forlorn,
> Asks thy high Favour,—thou mayst call me Cheat—
> Say, didst thou ne'er indulge in such Deceit?
> Who wrote Otranto? But I will not chide,
> Scorn I'll repay with Scorn, & Pride with Pride.
> Still, Walpole, still, thy Prosy Chapters write,
> And twaddling Letters to some Fair indite . . . .

71. Mr Barrett: a Bristol antiquary and local historian who had regarded Chatterton's medieval writings as genuine.

ask again, of what age are they? and how have they been transmitted? In what book of any age is there mention made either of Rowley or of the poetical monk, his ancient predecessor is such pure poetry? poetry, so resembling both Spenser and the moderns, and written in metre invented long since Rowley, and longer since the monk wrote. I doubt Mr Barrett himself will find it difficult to solve these doubts.

For myself, I undoubtedly will never print those extracts as genuine, which I am far from believing they are. If you want them, Sir, I will have them copied, and will send you the copy. But having a little suspicion that your letters may have been designed to laugh at me, if I had fallen into the snare, you will allow me to preserve your original letters, as an ingenious contrivance, however unsuccessful. This seems the more probable, as any man would understand by your first letter, that you either was possessed of the original MSS or had taken copies of them; whereas now you talk as if you had no copy but those written at the bottom of the very letters I have received from you.

I own I should be better diverted, if it proved that you have chosen to entertain yourself at my expense, than if you really thought these pieces ancient. The former would show you had little opinion of my judgment; the latter, that you ought not to trust too much to your own. I should not at all take the former ill, as I am not vain of it; I should be sorry for the latter, as you say, Sir, that you are very young, and it would be pity an ingenious young man should be too early prejudiced in his own favour.

[*To William Cole*[72]]

Arlington Street, Jan. 28, 1772.

It is long indeed, dear Sir, since we corresponded. I should not have been silent if I had had anything worth telling you in your way—but I grow such an antiquity myself, that I think I am less fond of what remains of our predecessors.

Thank you for Bannerman's proposal,[73] I mean, for

taking the trouble to send it, for I am not at all disposed to subscribe. Thank you more for the notes on King Edward; I mean too for your friendship in thinking of me. Of Dean Milles I cannot trouble myself to think any more. His piece[74] is at Strawberry; perhaps I may look at it for the sake of your note. The bad weather keeps me in town, and a good deal at home, which I find very comfortable, literally practising what so many persons pretend they intend, being quiet and enjoying my fireside in my elderly days.

Mr Mason[75] has shown me the relics of poor Mr Gray. I am sadly disappointed at finding them so very inconsiderable. He always persisted, when I inquired about his writings, that he had nothing by him. I own I doubted. I am grieved he was so very near exact—I speak of my own satisfaction; as to his genius, what he published during his life will establish his fame as long as our language lasts, and there is a man of genius left. There is a silly fellow, I do not know who, that has published a volume of letters on the English nation,[76] with characters of our modern authors. He has talked such nonsense on Mr Gray, that I have no patience with the compliments he had paid me. He must have an excellent taste! and gives me a woeful opinion of my own trifles, when he likes them, and cannot see the beauties of a poet that ought to be ranked in the first line. I am more humbled by any applause in the present age, than by hosts of such critics as Dr Milles. Is not Garrick reckoned a tolerable author, though he has proved how little sense is necessary to form a great actor? His *Cymon*,[77] his prologues and epilogues and forty such pieces of trash are below mediocrity, and yet delight the mob in the boxes as well as in the footman's gallery. I do not mention the things written in his praise, because he writes most of them himself. But you know any one popular merit can confer all merit: two women talking of Wilkes, one said he squinted—t' other replied—"Squints!—Well, if he does, it is not more than a man should squint." For my part, I can see how

---

72. **William Cole:** The Reverend William Cole (1714–82), a Fellow of the Society of Antiquaries, was a conservative country clergyman more interested in medieval British antiquities and biography than in his parochial duties. Walpole and Cole had been close friends at Eton and Cambridge, and they corresponded from 1762 until Cole's death. 73. **Bannerman's proposal:** Alexander Bannerman, an engraver, presumably was soliciting subscriptions for a series of engravings.

74. **His piece:** a learned paper titled *Observations on the Wardrobe Account* (1770) by Jeremiah Milles, Dean of Exeter, an antiquary who had impugned the reasoning in Walpole's *Historic Doubts on the Life and Reign of King Richard III* (1768). 75. **Mr Mason:** The minor poet William Mason (1724–97) was the executor of Thomas Gray, who had died in 1771. (See the selections from Gray in Part Five.) 76. **a volume . . . nation:** *Letters Concerning the Present State of England* (1772). The author has not been identified. 77. **Cymon:** a dramatic romance (1767) with music by Thomas Arne.

extremely well Garrick acts, without thinking him six feet high. It is said Shakespeare was a bad actor; why do not his divine plays make our wise judges conclude that he was a good one? They have not a proof of the contrary, as they have in Garrick's works—but what is it to you or me what he is. We may see him act with pleasure, and nothing obliges us to read his writings. Adieu! Dear Sir, Yours most sincerely,

HOR. WALPOLE

[*To Robert Jephson*[78]]

February 1775

You have drawn more trouble on yourself, Sir, than you expected; and would probably excuse my not performing the rest of my promise: but though I look upon myself as engaged to send you my thoughts, you are neither bound to answer them, nor regard them. They very likely are not new, and it is presumption in me to send hints to a much abler writer than myself. I can only plead in apology, that I interest myself in your fame; and as you are the only man capable of restoring and improving our stage, I really mean no more than to exhort and lead you on to make use of your great talents.

I have told you, as is true, that I am no poet. It is as true that you are a genuine one; and therefore I shall not say one word on that head. For the construction of a drama—it is mechanic, though much depends on it. A bystander may be a good director at least; for mechanism is certainly independent of, though easily possessed by, a genius. Banks[79] never wrote six tolerable lines, yet disposed his fable with so much address, that I think three plays have been constructed on his plot of the Earl of Essex, not one of which is much better than the original. The disposition is the next step to the choice of a subject, on which I have said enough in a former letter. A genius can surmount defects in both. If there is art in *Othello* and *Macbeth*, it seems to have been by chance; for Shakespeare certainly took no pains to adjust a plan, and in his historic

plays seem to have turned Hollinshed and Stowe[80] into verse and scenes as fast as he could write—though every now and then his divine genius flashed upon particular scenes and made them immortal; as in his *King John*, where nature itself has stamped the scenes of Constance, Arthur, and Hubert with her own impression, though the rest is as defective as possible. He seems to recall the Mahometan idea of lunatics, who are sometimes inspired, oftener changelings. Yet what signifies all his rubbish? He has scenes, and even speeches, that are infinitely superior to all the correct elegance of Racine.[81] I had rather have written the two speeches of Lady Percy, in the second part of *Henry IV*, than all Voltaire,[82] though I admire the latter infinitely, especially in *Alzire*, *Mahomet*, and *Semiramis*. Indeed, when I think over all the great authors of the Greeks, Romans, Italians, French, and English (and I know no other languages), I set Shakespeare first and alone, and then begin anew.

Well, Sir, I give up Shakespeare's dramas; and yet prefer him to every man. Why? For his exquisite knowledge of the passions and nature; for his simplicity too, which he possesses too when most natural. Dr. Johnson says[83] he is bombast whenever he attempts to be sublime: but this is never true but when he aims at sublimity in the expression; the glaring fault of Johnson himself.—But as simplicity is the grace of sublime, who possesses it like Shakespeare? Is not the

Him, wondrous Him!

in Lady Percy's speech,[84] exquisitely sublime and pathetic too? He has another kind of sublime which no man ever possessed but he; and this is, his art in dignifying a vulgar or trivial expression. Voltaire is so grossly ignorant and tasteless as to condemn this, as to condemn *the bare bodkin*.—But my enthusiasm for Shakespeare runs away with me.

I was speaking of the negligence of his construction.

80. Hollinshed and Stowe: Raphael Holinshed and John Stow were sixteenth-century chroniclers used by Shakespeare as sources for his history plays. **81. Racine:** Jean Racine (1639–99), the famous French dramatist whose plays on classical themes were known for their unified construction. **82. Voltaire:** François-Marie Arouet (1694–1778) wrote a number of formal plays on classical themes, and in his *Lettres philosophiques* (1734) he denigrated Shakespeare for meanness of expression and for inattention to the formal rules of dramatic writing. **83. Dr. Johnson says:** in the Preface to his edition of Shakespeare (1765). (See the selection from the Preface earlier in Part Six.) **84. Lady Percy's speech:** in *II Henry IV*, II. iii.

78. Robert Jephson: (1736–1803), an Irish playwright whose tragedy *Braganza*, with an epilogue by Walpole, played at Drury Lane in February, 1775. Jephson later wrote a dramatic version of *The Castle of Otranto* (*The Count of Narbonne* [1781]), which played at Covent Garden. **79. Banks:** John Banks (c. 1650–1706), playwright; author of *The Unhappy Favorite; or, the Earl of Essex* (1681).

You have not that fault. I own I do not admire your choice of *Braganza*, because in reality it admits of but two acts, the conspiracy and the revolution. You have not only filled it out with the most beautiful dialogue, but made the interest rise, though the revolution has succeeded. I can never too much admire the appearance of the friar, which disarms Valasquez: and yet you will be shocked to hear, that, notwithstanding all I could say at the rehearsal, I could not prevail to have Velasquez drop the dagger instantly, the only artful way of getting it out of his hand; for as Lady P——[85] observed, if he kept it two moments, we would recollect that it was the only way of preserving himself. But actors are not always judges. They persisted, for show-sake, against my remonstrances, to exhibit the Duke and Duchess on a throne in the second act; which could not but make the audience conclude that the revolution had even then taken place.

If I could find a fault in your tragedy, Sir, it would be a want of more short speeches, of a sort of serious repartee, which gives great spirit. But I think the most of what I have to say may be comprised in a recommendation of keeping the audience in suspense, and of touching the passions by the pathetic familiar. By the latter, I mean the study of Shakespeare's strokes of nature, which, soberly used, are alone superior to poetry, and, with your ear, may easily be made harmonious.

If there is any merit in *my* play,[86] I think it is in interrupting the spectator's fathoming the *whole* story till the last, and in making every scene tend to advance the catastrophe. These arts are mechanic, I confess; but at least they are as meritorious as the scrupulous delicacy of the French in observing, not only the unities, but a fantastic decorum, that does not exist in nature, and which consequently reduce all their tragedies, wherever the scene may lie, to the manners of modern Paris. Corneille[87] could be Roman; Racine never but French, and consequently, though a better poet, less natural and less various. Both indeed have prodigious merit. *Phèdre* is exquisite, *Britannicus* admirable;[88] and both excite pity and terror. Corneille is scarce ever tender, but always grand; yet never equal

in a whole play to Racine. *Rodogune*,[89] which I greatly admire, is very defective; for the two Princes are so equally good, and the two women so very bad, that they divide both our esteem and indignation. Yet I own, Racine, Corneille, and Voltaire ought to rank before all our tragedians, but Shakespeare. *Jane Shore*[90] is perhaps our best play after his. I admire *All for Love*[91] very much; and some scenes in *Don Sebastian*,[92] and Young's *Revenge*.[93] *The Siege of Damascus*[94] is very pure—and *Phaedra and Hippolitus*[95] fine poetry, though wanting all the nature of the original. We have few other tragedies of signal merit, though the first four acts of *The Fair Penitent*[96] are very good. It is strange that Dryden, who showed such a knowledge of nature in *The Cock and the Fox*,[97] should have so very little in his plays—he could rather describe it than put it into action. I have said all this, Sir, only to point out to you what a field is open for you—and though so many subjects, almost all the known, are exhausted, nature is inexhaustible, and genius can achieve anything. We have a language far more energic, and more sonorous too, than the French. Shakespeare could do what he would with it in its unpolished state. Milton gave it pomp from the Greek, and softness from the Italian; Waller now and then, here and there, gave it the elegance of the French. Dryden poured music into it; Prior gave it ease; and Gray used it masterly for either elegy or terror. Examine, Sir, the powers of a language you command, and let me again recommend to you a diction of your own, at least in some one play. The majesty of *Paradise Lost* would have been less imposing, if it had been written in the style of *The Essay on Man*. Pope pleases, but never surprises; and astonishment is one of the springs of tragedy. *Coups de théâtre*,[98] like the sublime one in *Mahomet*,[99]

---

85. P——: Pembroke. 86. my play: Walpole's *The Mysterious Mother* (1768) was printed at Strawberry Hill in an edition of fifty copies. Its theme of incest made performance on the contemporary stage impossible. Byron was later enthusiastic about it, proclaiming it "the last tragedy in our language." 87. Corneille: Pierre Corneille (1606–84), the founder of classical tragedy in France. 88. Phèdre, Britannicus: *Phèdre* (1677) and *Britannicus* (1669) are tragedies by Racine.

89. Rodogune: (1644–45), a tragedy by Corneille. 90. Jane Shore: a tragedy (1714) by Nicholas Rowe (1674–1718). 91. All for Love: Dryden's version (1678) of *Antony and Cleopatra*. 92. Don Sebastian: a tragi-comedy by Dryden. 93. Young's Revenge: a tragedy (1721) by Edward Young (1683–1765). (See the selections from Young in Parts Three and Five.) 94. The Siege . . . Damascus: (1720), by John Hughes (1677–1720). 95. Phaedra and Hippolitus: a tragedy (1707) based on Racine's *Phèdre*, by Edmund Smith (1672–1710). 96. The Fair Penitent: (1703), by Rowe. 97. The Cock . . . Fox: Dryden's paraphrase of Chaucer's *Nun's Priest's Tale*, which appeared in *Fables Ancient and Modern* (1700). (See the Preface to the *Fables* in Part Two.) 98. Coups de théâtre: theatrical surprises. 99. the sublime . . . Mahomet: in this tragedy (1742) by Voltaire, a young man, Séide, discovers after murdering an old man for religious motives that he has murdered his father.

have infinite effect. The incantations in *Macbeth*, that almost border on the burlesque, are still terrible. What French criticism can wound the ghosts of Hamlet or Banquo? Scorn rules, Sir, that cramp genius, and substitute delicacy to imagination in a barren language. Shall we not soar, because the French dare not rise from the ground?

You seem to possess the *tender*. The *terrible* is still more easy, at least I know to me. In all my tragedy, Adeliza contents me the least. Contrasts, though mechanic too, are very striking; and though Molière[100] was a comic writer, he might give lessons to a tragic. But I have passed all bounds; and yet shall be glad if you can cull one useful hint out of my rhapsodies. I here put an end to them; and wish, out of all I have said, that you may remember nothing, Sir, but my motives in writing, obedience to your commands, and a hearty eagerness for fixing on our stage so superior a writer.

I am, Sir, | With great esteem and truth, | Your most obedient humble servant,

HOR. WALPOLE.

P.S.—I must beg you, Sir, not to let these letters go out of your hands; for they are full of indigested thoughts, some perhaps capricious, as those on novel diction—but I wish to tempt genius out of the beaten road; and originality is the most captivating evidence of it.

[*To William Cole*[101]]

Strawberry Hill, June 19, 1777.

I thank you for your notices, dear Sir, and shall remember that on Prince William. I did see the *Monthly Review*, but hope one is not guilty of the death of every man who does not make one the dupe of a forgery. I believe Macpherson's success with Ossian[102] was more the ruin of Chatterton than I. Two years passed between my doubting the authenticity of Rowley's poems and his death. I never knew he had been in London till some time after he had undone and poisoned himself there. The poems he sent me were transcripts in his own hand, and even in that circumstance he told a lie; he said he had them from the very person at Bristol to whom he had given them. If any man was to tell you that monkish rhymes had been dug up in Herculaneum which was destroyed several centuries before there was any such poetry, should you believe it? Just the reverse is the case of Rowley's pretended poems. They have all the elegance of Waller and Prior, and more than Lord Surry[103]—but I have no objection to anybody believing what he pleases. I think poor Chatterton was an astonishing genius—but I cannot think that Rowley foresaw metres that were invented long after he was dead, or that our language was more refined at Bristol in the reign of Henry V than it was at court under Henry VIII. One of the chaplains of the Bishop of Exeter has found a line of Rowley in *Hudibras*[104]—the monk might foresee that too! The prematurity of Chatterton's genius is however full as wonderful, as that such a prodigy as Rowley should never have been heard of till the eighteenth century. The youth and industry of the former are miracles too, yet still more credible. There is not a symptom in the poems but the old words that savours of Rowley's age. Change the old words for modern, and the whole construction is of yesterday.

The other story you tell me, is very credible, and perfectly in character.

Yours ever,

H. W.

---

100. Molière: the comedies of Jean-Baptiste Poquelin (1622–73), who called himself Molière, exhibit broad contrasts in characters. **101. To . . . Cole:** In a letter of June 15, Cole had sent Walpole both a historical note on the fourteenth-century William of Hatfield and a transcription of the following passage from *The Monthly Review* for May: "In 1770, Chatterton went to London, and carried all this treasure [the Rowley manuscripts] with him, in hopes . . . of disposing of it to his advantage; he accordingly applied . . . to that learned antiquary, Mr. Horace Walpole, but met with little or no encouragement from him; soon after which, in a fit of despair . . . he put an end to his unhappy life, having first cut to pieces and destroyed all the MSS he had in his possession." Cole suggested to Walpole that this passage "may by an unobserving reader be construed into an accusation of homicide against you."

102. Macpherson's . . . Ossian: The Scot James Macpherson (1736–96) published in the early 1760's a number of works purporting to be translations of Scottish Gaelic epic materials written by one "Ossian." Although the Ossianic writings met with a great deal of enthusiasm, especially among the Scots, their authenticity was vigorously challenged, notably by Samuel Johnson (see Johnson's letter to Macpherson earlier in Part Six). The poems of Ossian ultimately proved to be largely fabrications by Macpherson, and Ossian proved to be wholly fictitious. **103. Lord Surry:** Henry Howard, Earl of Surrey (c. 1517–47), one of the earliest poets in Modern English. **104. Hudibras:** an octosyllabic-couplet satire (1663–78) on the Puritans by Samuel Butler (1612–80).

[*To the Countess of Upper Ossory*[105]]

Strawberry Hill, Aug. 11, 1778

I had neither room nor time, Madam, to tell you in my last how much I am ashamed to hear the kind things you are so good as to say to me. Very moderate friendship and good nature would incline one to try to amuse such reasonable grief as yours,[106] especially if letters could effect it, and letters from one that is so accustomed to write them, that they cost but the mere half hour. The remnant of an useless life is dedicated to my friends; I have no other employment; and the long and invariable favour your Ladyship has shown me, intitles you to every suit and service I can perform. You cannot lessen yourself in my eyes by disparaging yourself—nay, though I dislike it, it exalts you; it adds to my esteem. Vanity is to me the most ridiculous of all human faults. Humility, if not a virtue, is a love of virtue, and a respect for truth. The Pharisee and the Magdalen is the most beautiful story in the new Testament.[107] Your last has realized what Rousseau's presumption thought nobody but himself could dare to achieve. I have got his preface to his *Mémoires:*[108] It is the superlative of arrogant eloquence; it would be the sublime of madness, were the madness real. As it is not, it is the affectation of singularity pushed to distraction. Not content to be unlike all mankind, he hopes at the day of Judgment to be sent to Bedlam.—It is even shocking! He aims at extorting a confession—it is not right to say how far his vanity goes—that he was the most extraordinary mortal ever created. To glory in confessing our crimes, and to brave mankind to imitate him, has more of Diogenes,[109] than of the penitent Magdalen. I will

send you this frantic piece of meditated extravagance, but beg you not to give a copy. It will get about, but I should not like to be the dispenser.

I told you, Madam, that I had some history of myself for you; consequently very insignificant to anybody; but it will amuse you for a moment. In the first place I have been printing for Lady Craven a translation of her *Somnabule*,[110] and that you shall have too. It is not ill done; but if it were, she is so pretty and good humoured, that I am pleased to please her.

The next chapter is not so agreeable to me. Contrary to my determination, I have been writing again for the public. I have a horror for the stage of authors, which they call their *Senilia*, and which therefore they ought not to write, for what can age produce that is worth showing? My present case is not of choice, but necessity. Somebody[111] has published the poems of Chatterton the Bristol boy, and in the Preface intimates that I was the cause of his despair and poisoning himself, and a little more openly is of opinion that I ought to be stoned. This most groundless accusation has driven me to write the whole story—and yet now I have done it in a pamphlet of near thirty pages of larger paper than this, I think I shall not bring myself to publish it.[112] My story was clear as daylight, I am as innocent as of the death of Julius Caesar, I never saw the lad with my eyes, and he was the victim of his own extravagance two years after all correspondence had ceased between him and me—and yet I hate to be the talk of the town, and am more inclined to bear this aspersion, than to come again upon the stage. I intend to consult every friend I have before I resolve, and of course, Lord Ossory and your Ladyship. It is impossible to have a moment's doubt on the case. The whole foundation of the accusation is reduced to this—If I had been imposed upon, my countenance might have saved the poor lad from poisoning himself for want, which he brought on by his excesses. Those few words are a full acquittal, and would indeed be sufficient—but the story in itself is so marvelous, that I could not

---

105. the Countess . . . Ossory: Anne Liddell (1738–1804), formerly the Duchess of Grafton; she became Countess of Upper Ossory after her marriage in 1769 to John Fitzpatrick, Second Earl of Upper Ossory. When Walpole and George Montagu ceased corresponding in the autumn of 1770—the cause of the breach in their long friendship is not fully known—Walpole lost no time in replacing Montagu as a regular correspondent with Lady Ossory, with whom he had been in desultory correspondence for several years. **106. such . . . yours:** Lady Holland, a relative of Lady Ossory's, was gravely ill; she died on October 6, 1778. **107. The Pharisee . . . Testament:** See Luke 7:36–50. **108. Mémoires:** The *Confessions* of the daring French philosopher and reformer Jean-Jacques Rousseau (1712–78), composed between 1764 and 1770, were published (July, 1778) only after his death. **109. Diogenes:** Greek philosopher of the fourth century B.C., a representative of the school of Cynics, who tended to reject prevailing morality.

110. Somnabule: *The Sleep-Walker, a Comedy* (1778), a translation by Elizabeth, Countess of Craven, of *Le Somnambule* by Antoine Ferriol, Comte de Pont-de-Veyle. **111. Somebody:** John Broughton, the editor of *Miscellanies in Prose and Verse, by Thomas Chatterton* (1778). **112. I shall . . . it:** Walpole printed on his private press two hundred copies of his *A Letter to the Editor of the Miscellanies of Thomas Chatterton* (1779), but he did not publish this essay until 1782, when it was printed in *The Gentleman's Magazine*.

help going into the whole account of such a prodigy as Chatterton was. You will pity him, as I do; it was a deep tragedy, but interests one chiefly from his extreme youth, for it was his youth that made his talents and achievements so miraculous. I doubt, neither his genius nor his heart would have interested one, had he lived twenty years more. You will be amazed at what he was capable of before eighteen, the period of his existence—yet I had rather anybody else were employed to tell the story.

As I have taken such an aversion to the character of Author, I have fallen into a taste that I never had in my life, that of music. The swan, you know, Madam, is drawing towards its end, when it thinks of warbling, but as I have not begun to sing myself, I trust it is but distantly symptomatic. In short, I have only lived with musicians lately and liked them, Mr Jerningham is here at Twickengham and sings in charming taste to his harp. My niece Miss Churchill has been here with her harp, and plays ten times better and sings worse—but I am quite enchanted with Mr Gammon, the Duke of Grafton's brother-in-law. It is the most melodious voice I ever heard; like Mr Meynell's, but more perfect. As I pass a great deal of time at Hampton Court, in a way very much like the remnant of the Court of St Germain's[113] (—and I assure you, where there are some that I believe were at that Court) I was strolling in the gardens in the evening with my nieces, who joined Lady Schaub and Lady Fitzroy, and the former asked Mr Gammon to sing. His taste is equal to his voice, and his deep notes, the part I prefer, are calculated for the solemnity of Purcel's[114] music, and for what I love particularly, his mad songs and the songs of sailors. It was moonlight and late, and very hot, and the lofty façade of the palace, and the trimmed yews and canal, made me fancy myself of a party in Grammont's time[115]—so you don't wonder that by the help of imagination I never passed an evening more deliciously. When by the aid of some historic vision and local circumstance I can romance myself into pleasure, I know nothing transports me so much. Pray, steal from your soldiery,[116] and try this secret at Bevis Mount and Netley Abbey.[117] There are Lord and Lady Peterborough and Pope to people the former scene, and who you please at Netley.—I sometimes dream, that one day or other somebody will stroll about poor Strawberry and talk of Lady Ossory—but alas! I am no poet, and my castle is of paper, and my castle and my attachments and I, shall soon vanish and be forgotten together!

[*To William Mason*]

Berkeley Square, Jan 27, 1781.

We shall certainly have no difference about the Yorkshire address or directions.[118] It would be very idle to enter into an altercation about the mode of wrapping up a medicine, which the patient never intends to swallow. It is true, I think the *disease* cannot dislike the prescription, for it finds more fault with half of the doctors, than with the distemper, but I look on the case as desperate; unless, as has been known to happen, poverty and fasting should root out the scurvy, when neither the College[119] nor quacks could make any impression, and we are likely to experience whether fasting can expel the kind of devils by which we have been visited. Indeed I have many reasons for not disputing with you, I hate disputes. I have much higher opinion too of your abilities than of my own; and I suspect my own prejudices, and I know that persons who dispute, though with their friends, grow more angry with those they are angry with last, than with their enemies; as I see has happened to your York Association, which has wandered from the national cause to a county quarrel; and my last reason is that I despair. I think this country ruined; what may be saved from the general wreck, I do not know, perhaps shall not see. Mr Hartley's system,[120] had it been adopted, was in my eyes the best to have been pursued, I mean, all possible efforts to put an end to the American war. He has proved that the

---

113. **the Court . . . Germain's:** Both Louis XIV and, after his removal to Versailles, James II, the exiled Stuart monarch, held court at St. Germain-en-Laye, near Paris, in the late seventeenth century. 114. **Purcel:** Henry Purcell (*c.* 1658–95), English composer. 115. **Grammont's time:** the late seventeenth century. 116. **your soldiery:** Lord Ossory, Colonel of the Bedfordshire militia, was encamped at Winchester.

117. **Bevis . . . Abbey:** Alexander Pope visited Bevis Mount, seat of the Peterborough family, in 1734 and wrote one of his most vivid letters describing the occasion. Netley Abbey was a medieval ruin. 118. **no . . . directions:** Mason was active in the Yorkshire Association, a Whig group agitating for Parliamentary reform and a reduction of the influence of the Crown. The "address" was a draft of instructions to the London representatives of the association. Walpole and Mason disagreed about the association's policy. 119. **the College:** the Royal College of Physicians. 120. **Mr Hartley's system:** a plan of conciliation for ending the American war, set forth in *Letters on the American War* (1778) by David Hartley (1732–1813).

continuation is positive destruction, any piddling may amuse, or turn attention aside, but in this age of the world to arm a stripling with a sling and a pebble will not fell a giant; but why be metaphoric? ruin comes on with strides. Russia has sent us a thundering monitory:[121] and probably we shall soon be at war with the whole armed neutrality, which, like idiots, we imagined meant no more than neutral armament; well, I shall not be very sorry if all Europe combined compels us to make peace. I long to be able to die in quiet, we shall be but a little brow-beaten island, and as *that* is not the England in which I was born, I must be excused if I do not care about it.

I have been and am still very unhappy about General Conway.[122] With a broken arm he embarked in a storm for Jersey at a moment's warning. He could not mount the ladder of the frigate; a sailor gave him a tug and wrenched that very arm. For two days and nights he was tossed in a furious tempest, could not reach his island, and at last was thrown on Plymouth. He returned quite lame again, with a fever from pain and a violent rheumatism from cold, and has kept his bed almost ever since. His last year's speech[123] has just been published. Woodfall[124] sent him word that he had notes of it and was going to print it, on which Mr Conway thought it better to give him his own notes. I like much of it, though he and I do not agree in his sentiments about the recovery of America: for though I do not love to dispute, especially with my best friends, I cannot give up my opinions, if they are my opinions: but then I do not maintain that I must be in the right, except in judging for myself, and that leave which I take, I should be very absurd, nay, very impertinent, if I did not allow, but alas! he and you and I might as well be disputing about the time of keeping Easter: I most gladly turn away from politics to other matters.

Mr Gilpin has sent me his book and dedication.[125] I thank you for the latter being so moderate, yet he talks

of my researches, which makes me smile; I know as Gray would have said, how little I have *researched*, and what slender pretensions are mine to so pompous a term. Apropos to Gray, Johnson's life, or rather criticism on his odes,[126] is come out; a most wretched, dull, tasteless, *verbal* criticism, yet timid too. But he makes amends, he admires Thompson and Akenside, and Sir Richard Blackmore,[127] and has reprinted Dennis's criticism on *Cato*,[128] to save time and swell his pay. In short as usual, he has proved that he has no more ear than taste. Mrs Montagu[129] and all her Mænades[130] intend to tear him limb from limb for despising their moppet Lord Lyttelton.[131] You will be diverted to hear that Mr Gibbon[132] has quarrelled with me. He lent me his second volume in the middle of November. I returned it with a most civil panegyric. He came for more incense, I gave it, but alas! with too much sincerity, I added, "Mr Gibbon, I am sorry *you* should have pitched on so disgusting a subject as the Constantinopolitan history. There is so much of the Arians and Eunomians, and semi-Pelagians; and there is such a strange contrast between Roman and Gothic manners, and so little harmony between a Consul Sabinus and a Ricimer, Duke of the palace, that though you have written the story as well as it could be written, I fear few will have patience to read it." He coloured; all his round features squeezed themselves into sharp angles; he screwed up his button-mouth and rapping his snuff-box, said, "It had never been put together before"—*so well* he meant to add—

121. **monitory:** a warning against British interference with Russian ships. 122. **General Conway:** Henry Seymour Conway (1721–95), Walpole's first cousin; Governor of the Isle of Jersey (1772–95). 123. **speech:** recommending conciliation with the American colonies. 124. **Woodfall:** Henry Woodfall, a printer. 125. **his . . . dedication:** the third edition of *An Essay on Prints* (1781), dedicated to Walpole by the Reverend William Gilpin (1724–1804), schoolmaster, artist, and popularizer of the picturesque. The dedication reads: "To the Honourable Horace Walpole in deference to his taste in the polite arts; and the valuable researches he has made to improve them."

126. **Apropos . . . odes:** in Samuel Johnson's *Lives of the Poets* (1779–81). (See Johnson's *Life of Gray* earlier in Part Six.) 127. **Thompson . . . Blackmore:** James Thomson (1700–48) wrote *The Seasons;* Mark Akenside (1721–70) wrote *The Pleasures of the Imagination* (1744–57); Blackmore (1654–1729) wrote epics that were generally despised. Johnson however praised his *Creation* (1712), a poem arguing for the existence and providence of God. (See the selections from Thomson in Part Two and the selection from Akenside in Part Three.) 128. **Dennis's . . . Cato:** The dramatist and critic John Dennis (1657–1734) attacked Addison's *Cato* in his *Remarks upon Cato* (1713). (See the selection from Dennis in Part Two.) 129. **Mrs Montagu:** Mrs. Elizabeth Montagu (1720–1800), a literary lady. 130. **Mænades:** the female followers of Dionysus; etymologically, "mad women." 131. **Lord Lyttelton:** (1709–73), minor poet and patron of literature. In the *Life of Lyttelton* (1781) Johnson wrote of Lyttelton's poems, "They have nothing to be despised, and little to be admired." 132. **Mr Gibbon:** *The History of the Decline and Fall of the Roman Empire* (see later in Part Six), the great six-volume work by Edward Gibbon (1737–94), was in the process of being published from 1776 to 1788.

but gulped it. He meant *so well* certainly, for Tillemont,[133] whom he quotes in every page, has done the very thing. Well from that hour to this I have never seen him, though he used to call once or twice a week; nor has sent me the third volume, as he promised. I well knew his vanity, even about his ridiculous face and person, but thought he had too much sense to avow it so palpably. The history is admirably written, especially in the characters of Julian and Athanasius,[134] in both which he has piqued himself on impartiality—but the style is far less sedulously enamelled than the first volume, and there is flattery to the Scots that would choke anything but Scots, who can gobble feathers as readily as thistles. David Hume and Adam Smith[135] are *legislators* and sages, but the homage is intended for his patron, Lord Loughborough[136]—so much for literature and its fops! except what interests me a thousand times more and which I kept for the *bonne bouche*,[137] your Fresnoy and 4th *Garden;*[138] I shall certainly ask for the former the instant I return (for I go tomorrow to Park Place, to see Mr Conway, who cannot yet get to town) but not to interfere a moment with Sir Joshua Reynolds, who will execute his task[139] so well—I long too for the *Garden*—I beg to recommend a note to you; last year a man at Turnham Green fixed up a board with this notice, *Ready made Temples sold here.* I would put over the Convocation,[140] *Ready made Priests sold here.* The Turnhamite now sells only curicles[141] and whiskies.

If my gazette is long, remember you ordered me to amuse Mr Palgrave.[142] I am glad you have him, and will do anything I can to fix him with you, pray assure him how much I am his. I can say no more, for I have not left half room to thank you for your very kind promise of coming to me in the spring. It amply compensates my disappointment of seeing you here; here I only get a snatch of you for an instant, nowhere I have enough of you. And which I lament more, for I am not selfish, the world has not enough of you[143]—you know what I mean.

[*To William Mason*]

Berkeley Square, June 25, 1782.

I find there is a correspondence commenced between you and Mr Hayley[144] by the Parnassus post. I did not know you were acquainted; I suppose you met at Calliope's:[145] if you love incense, he has fumigated you like a flitch of bacon; however, I hope in the Lord Phœbus that you will not take his advice any more than Pope did that of such another sing-song warbler, Lord Lyttelton;[146] nor be persuaded to write an epic poem, that most senseless of all the species of poetic composition and which pedants call the *chef-d'œuvre*[147] of the human mind; well, you may frown, as in duty bound, yet I shall say what I list. Epic poetry is the art of being as long as possible in telling an uninteresting story: and an epic poem is a mixture of history without truth and of romance without imagination. We are well off when from that *mésalliance*[148] there spring some bastards called episodes, that are lucky enough to resemble their romantic mother, more than their solemn father. So far from epic poetry being at the head of composition, I am persuaded that the reason why so exceedingly few have succeeded, is from the absurdity of the species. When nothing has been impossible to genius in every other walk, why has everybody failed in this but the inventor Homer? You will stare, but what are the rest? Virgil with every beauty of expression and harmony that can be conceived has accomplished but

133. Tillemont: Sebastien Tillemont (1637–98), French historian. **134. Julian and Athanasius:** Julian the Apostate was a Roman emperor of the fourth century A.D.; Athanasius was a Christian thinker and administrator who flourished in the late third and early fourth centuries. **135. Adam Smith:** (1723–90), Scottish ethical and economic philosopher. **136. Lord Loughborough:** He had helped Gibbon get a government sinecure in 1779. **137. bonne bouche:** dainty morsel. **138. your . . . Garden:** Mason had just finished translating *The Art of Painting*, originally a Latin poem (1668) by Charles-Alphonse du Fresnoy (1611–65); the fourth book of Mason's poem *The English Garden* was published in 1781. **139. his task:** The painter Sir Joshua Reynolds (1723–92) had agreed to supply notes to Mason's translation of Fresnoy. The book appeared in 1783. (See the selection from Reynolds later in Part Six.) **140. Convocation:** an assembly of the higher Anglican clergy, meeting at Canterbury. It had just issued an address to the King that Walpole found repulsively sycophantic. **141. curicles:** (curricles) carriages. **142. Mr Palgrave:** a companion of Mason's.

143. world . . . you: Oddly convinced that Mason possessed rare satiric powers, Walpole was constantly exhorting him to write satire against the government. **144. Mr Hayley:** William Hayley (1745–1820), a minor poet who published in 1782 a poetical *Essay on Epic Poetry in Five Epistles to the Reverend Mr. Mason.* **145. Calliope:** the Muse of epic poetry. **146. Lord Lyttelton:** In 1730 he wrote *An Epistle to Mr. Pope* exhorting Pope to forgo satire in favor of some of the higher poetic genres. **147. chef-d'œuvre:** masterpiece. **148. mésalliance:** unsuitable marriage.

an insipid imitation. His hero is a nullity, like Melle-font[149] and the virtuous characters of every comedy, and some of his incidents as the harpies and the ships turned to nymphs, as silly as Mother Goose's tales. Milton, all imagination, and a thousand times more sublime and spirited, has produced a monster. Lucan,[150] who often says more in half a line than Virgil in a whole book, was lost in bombast if he talked for thirty lines together. Claudian and Statius[151] had all his fustian with none of his quintessence. Camoens[152] had more true grandeur than they, but with grosser faults. Dante was extravagant, absurd, disgusting, in short a Methodist parson in Bedlam. Ariosto[153] was a more agreeable *Amadis de Gaul*[154] in a bawdy-house, and Spencer, John Bunyan in rhyme. Tasso[155] wearies one with their insuperable crime of stanza[156] and by a thousand puerilities that are the very opposite of that dull dignity which is demanded for epic: and Voltaire who retained his good sense in heroics, lost his spirit and fire in them. In short, epic poetry is like what it first celebrated, the heroes of a world that knew nothing better than courage and conquest. It is not suited to an improved and polished state of things. It has continued to degenerate from the founder of the family, and happily expired in the last bastard of the race, Ossian.

Still as Mr Hayley has allowed such a latitude to heroic poesy as to admit the *Lutrin*, *The Dispensary*, and *The Dunciad*[157] as epic poems, I can forgive a man who recommends to a friend to pen a tragedy, when he will accept *The Way of the World*[158] as one.

For Mr Hayley himself, though he chants in good tune, and has now and then pretty lines amongst several both prosaic and obscure, he has, I think no genius, no fire and not a grain of *originality*, the first of merits (in my eyes) in these latter ages, and a more certain mark of genius than in the infancy of the world, when no ground was broken, nor even, in the sportsman's phrase, *foiled*.[159] It is that originality that I admire in your *Heroic Epistle*[160] and in your genuine style, which I trust you will not quit to satisfy the impartial Mr Hayley (who though a good patriot equally cherishes janizaries[161])

> That to you *do not belong*
> The beauties of envenomed song.[162]

For writing an epic poem, it would be as wise to set about copying Noah's ark, if Mons. de Buffon[163] should beg you to build a menagerie for a couple of every living creatures upon earth, when there is no longer any danger of a general inundation.

I doubt your new friend will write his readers and his own reputation to death; every poem has a train of prose as long as Cheapside, with a vast parade of reading that would be less dear if it had any novelty or vivacity to recommend it. I know as little new as he, except that Lord Rockingham[164] is very ill, I believe not without danger; should he fail, there would be a new scene indeed! Adieu!

PS. I find I have said above, every living *creatures*—is not that bad English? and if it is, is not it better than *a couple of every living creature?*

[*To Mary Berry*[165]]

No. 34.[166]

Berkeley Square, May 26, 1791.

I am rich in letters from you: I received that by Lord Elgin's courier first, as you expected, and its

---

149. Mellefont: in *The Double-Dealer* (1694), a play by William Congreve (1670–1729). **150. Lucan:** (A.D. 39–65), Roman poet; author of *Pharsalia*, a ten-book epic on the war between Caesar and Pompey. **151. Claudian and Statius:** Claudian, who flourished in Rome in the latter part of the fifth century A.D., wrote epics on the wars against the Goths; Statius, a Roman poet of the first century A.D., wrote the twelve-book *Thebiad*. **152. Camoens:** Luis de Camoëns (1524–80), Portuguese author of *The Lusiads* (1572). **153. Ariosto:** Ludovico Ariosto (1474–1533), Italian author of the romantic epic *Orlando Furioso* (1532). **154. Amadis de Gaul:** a Hispanic chivalric romance of the Renaissance. **155. Tasso:** Torquato Tasso (1544–95), Italian author of *Jerusalem Delivered* (1581–93). **156. crime of stanza:** The text is probably corrupt here; the manuscript of the letter is lost. The emendations "insufferable rhyming stanza" and "chime of stanza" have been suggested. **157. the Lutrin . . . Dunciad:** all mock epics, by Boileau, Garth, and Pope respectively. **158. The Way . . . World:** Congreve's comedy (1700).

159. foiled: scented out. **160. Heroic Epistle:** Mason's satire *An Heroic Epistle to Sir William Chambers* (1773). **161. janizaries:** Turkish soldiers; i.e., non-Christians and ironists like Edward Gibbon, to whom Hayley had written *An Essay on History in Three Epistles* in 1780. **162. That . . . song:** an adaptation of a couplet in Epistle v of Hayley's poem. **163. Mons. de Buffon:** George-Louis Leclerc de Buffon (1707–88), French naturalist; author of a thirty-six-volume *Natural History* (1749–88). **164. Lord Rockingham:** the Whig Prime Minister; he died on July 1. **165. Mary Berry:** Walpole first met the beautiful and agreeable Berry sisters in 1787, when they were in their early twenties and he was in his seventieth year. Walpole became infatuated with them, especially with Mary (1763–1852), whom he appointed his literary executrix. She was now traveling with her sister Agnes and her father in Florence. **166. No. 34:** Walpole numbered each of the letters he sent the Berrys while they were touring the Continent. The first was written on October 10, 1790; the fifty-ninth on October 27, 1791.

elder the next day. You tell me mine entertain you; *tant mieux;*[167] it is my wish, but my wonder, for I live so very little in the world, that I do not know the present generation by sight, for though I pass them in the streets, the hats with valances,[168] the folds above the chin of the ladies, and the dirty shirts and shaggy hair of the young men, who have *levelled nobility* almost as much as the *mobility*[169] in France have, have confounded all individuality. Besides, if I did go to public places and assemblies, which my going to roost earlier prevents, the bats and owls do not begin to fly abroad till far in the night, when they begin to see and be seen. However, one of the empresses of fashion, the Duchess of Gordon, uses fifteen or sixteen hours of her four and twenty. I heard her journal of last Monday—She first went to Handel's music in the Abbey; she then clambered over the benches and went to Hastings' trial[170] in the Hall—after dinner to the play, then to Lady Lucan's assembly; after that to Ranelagh, and returned to Mrs Hobart's faro table; gave a ball herself in the evening of that morning into which she must have got a good way, and set out for Scotland the next day. Hercules could not have achieved a quarter of her labours in the same space of time. What will the Great Duke[171] think of our Amazons, if he has letters opened, as the Emperor[172] was wont? One of our Camillas[173]—but in a freer style, I hear he saw (I fancy just before your arrival) and he must have wondered at the familiarity of the dame[174] and the nincompoophood of her Prince.[175] Sir William Hamilton is arrived—his nymph of the attitudes[176] was too prudish to visit the rambling peeress.

Mrs Cholmeley was so very good as to call on me

again yesterday; Mr French was with me, and fell in love with her understanding, and probably with her face too—but with that he did not trust me. He says we shall have Dr Darwin's stupendous poem[177] in a fortnight, of which you saw parts. George Cholmondeley's wife after a dreadful labour is delivered of a dead child.

The rest of my letter must be literary, for we have no news. Boswell's book[178] is gossiping, but having numbers of proper names, would be more readable, at least by me, were it reduced from two volumes to one—but there are woeful *longueurs*,[179] both about his hero, and himself, the *fidus Achates*,[180] about whom one has not the smallest curiosity; but I wrong the original Achates; one is satisfied with his fidelity in keeping his master's secrets and weaknesses, which modern led-captains betray for their patron's glory, and to hurt their own enemies, which Boswell has done shamefully, particularly against Mrs Piozzi and Mrs Montagu, and Bishop Percy.[181] Dr Blagdon says justly, that it is a new kind of libel, by which you may abuse anybody, by saying, some dead person said so and so of somebody alive—Often indeed Johnson made the most brutal speeches to living persons, for though he was good-natured at bottom, he was very ill-natured at top. He loved to dispute to show his superiority. If his opponents were weak, he told them they were fools; if they vanquished him, he was scurrilous—to nobody more than to Boswell himself who was contemptible for flattering him so grossly, and for enduring the coarse things he was continually vomiting on Boswell's own country, Scotland. I expected amongst the excommunicated to find myself, but am very gently treated. I never would be in the least acquainted with Johnson, or as Boswell calls it, had not a just value for him, which the biographer imputes to my resentment for the Doctor's putting bad arguments (purposely out of Jacobitism) into the speeches which he wrote fifty years ago for my father in the *Gentleman's*

167. tant mieux: so much the better. **168. valances:** sun visors. **169. mobility:** the mob. **170. Hasting's trial:** the trial at Westminster Hall of Warren Hastings (1732–1818) for corruption and cruelty in his Governor-Generalship of India was a contemporary oratorical sensation running, with long recesses, from 1788 to 1795. R. B. Sheridan, Edmund Burke, and Charles James Fox spoke for the prosecution. Hastings was finally acquitted. **171. the Great Duke:** Frederick III, Grand Duke of Tuscany. **172. the Emperor:** Leopold II, father of Frederick III. **173. Camilla:** a brave maiden mentioned in Virgil's *Aeneid,* known for her fleetness of foot. **174. the dame:** Lady Elizabeth Craven. **175. her Prince:** the Margrave of Anspach. **176. nymph . . . attitudes:** Emma, Lady Hamilton; later mistress to Lord Nelson. She earned her sobriquet by her fondness for posing in living-pictures and tableaux.

177. Dr Darwin's . . . poem: The Botanic Garden, Part I (1791) by Erasmus Darwin (1731–1802). **178. Boswell's book:** The Life of Samuel Johnson, LL.D., had been out just ten days. **179. longueurs:** tedious passages. **180. fidus Achates:** faithful Achates, the companion of Aeneas. **181. Mrs Piozzi . . . Percy:** In Boswell's Life of Johnson, Mrs. Hester Thrale Piozzi is presented as a highly untrustworthy anecdotist; Mrs. Montagu as a superficial pretender to learning; and Bishop Thomas Percy (on one occasion) as the possessor of a "narrow mind."

Magazine,[182] which I did not read then, or ever knew Johnson wrote till Johnson died, nor have looked at since. Johnson's blind Toryism and known brutality kept me aloof, nor did I ever exchange a syllable with him; nay, I do not think I ever was in a room with him six times in my days. The first time I think was at the Royal Academy. Sir Joshua[183] said, "Let me present Dr Goldsmith[184] to you"; he did. "Now I will present Dr Johnson to you."—"No," said I, "Sir Joshua, for Dr Goldsmith, pass—but you shall *not* present Dr Johnson to me."

Some time after, Boswell came to me, said Dr J. was writing the lives of the poets, and wished I would give him anecdotes of Mr Gray. I said very coldly, I had given what I knew to Mr Mason.[185] B. hummed and hawed and then dropped, "I suppose you know Dr J. does not admire Mr Gray"—Putting as much contempt as I could into my look and tone, I said, "Dr Johnson don't!—humph!"—and with that monosyllable ended our interview—After the Doctor's death, Burke, Sir Joshua Reynolds and Boswell sent an ambling circular letter to me begging subscriptions for a monument for him—the two last, I think impertinently, as they could not but know my opinion, and could not suppose I would contribute to a monument for one who had endeavoured, poor soul! to degrade my friend's superlative poetry—I would not deign to write an answer, but sent down word by my footman, as I would have done to parish officers with a brief, that I would not subscribe. In the two new volumes, Johnson says—and very probably did, or is made to say, that Gray's poetry is *dull*, and that he was a *dull* man! The same oracle dislikes Prior, Swift and Fielding. If an elephant could write a book, perhaps one that had read a great deal would say that an Arabian horse is a very clumsy ungraceful animal—pass to a better chapter—

Burke has published another pamphlet against the French Revolution, in which he attacks it still more grievously. The beginning is very good, but it is not equal, nor quite so injudicious as parts of its predecessor;[186] is far less brilliant, as well as much shorter; but were it ever so long, his mind overflows with such a torrent of images, that he cannot be tedious. His invective against Rousseau is admirable, just and new. Voltaire he passes almost contemptuously. I wish he had dissected Mirabeau[187] too: and I grieve that he has omitted the violation of the consciences of the clergy; nor stigmatized those universal plunderers, the National Assembly, who gorge themselves with eighteen *livres* a day, which to many of them would three years ago have been astonishing opulence.

When you return, I shall lend you three volumes in quarto of another work with which you will be delighted. They are state letters in the reigns of Henry VIII, Mary, Elizabeth and James, being the correspondence of the Talbot and Howard families, given by a Duke of Norfolk to the Herald's Office, where they have lain for a century neglected, buried under dust and unknown, till discovered by a Mr Lodge, a genealogist, who to gratify his passion procured to be made a Pursuivant.[188] Oh! how curious they are! Henry seizes an alderman who refused to contribute to a benevolence, sends him to the army on the borders, orders him to be exposed in the front line, and if that does not do, to be treated with the utmost rigour of military discipline. His daughter Bess is not less a Tudor. The mean unworthy treatment of the Queen of Scots is striking; and you will find how Elizabeth's jealousy of her crown and her avarice were at war, and how the more ignoble passion predominated. But the most amusing passage is one in a private letter, as it paints the awe of children for their parents a *little* differently from modern habitudes. Mr Talbot second son of the Earl of Shrewsbury, was a member of the House of Commons and was married. He writes to the Earl his father, and tells him that a young woman

---

182. the speeches . . . Magazine: During the early 1740's Samuel Johnson earned a living by writing up the Parliamentary debates for *The Gentleman's Magazine*. Since open Parliamentary reporting was unlawful, the custom in *The Gentleman's Magazine* was to disguise the proceedings as *Debates in the Senate of Magna Lilliputia*. In reporting—or sometimes merely contriving—the speeches of Sir Robert Walpole (anagrammatized as "Walelop"), Johnson had Sir Robert abuse the Hanoverian monarchy and argue in favor of the Stuart succession. **183. Sir Joshua:** Reynolds was president of the Royal Academy. **184. Dr Goldsmith:** When Walpole met Oliver Goldsmith (1730–74), Goldsmith was famous as the author of *The Citizen of the World* (1762), *The Vicar of Wakefield* (1766), and the comedy *The Good Natured Man* (1768). (See the selections from Goldsmith later in Part Six.) **185. Mr Mason:** Mason was writing a life of Gray; it appeared in 1775.

186. its predecessor: The new work by Edmund Burke (1729–97), the great parliamentarian, was *A Letter from Mr. Burke to a Member of the National Assembly* (1791); its predecessor was *Reflections on the Revolution in France* (see later in Part Six). **187. Mirabeau:** Honoré-Gabriel de Riquetti (1749–91), Comte de Mirabeau, a great, if venal, orator of the French Revolution. **188. Pursuivant:** the lowest ranking officer in the Herald's Office.

of a very good character has been recommended to him for chambermaid to his wife, and if his Lordship does not disapprove of it, he will hire her. There are many letters of news that are very entertaining too—but it is nine o'clock and I must go to Lady Cecilia's.

Friday.

The Conways, Mrs Damer, the Farrens, and Lord Mt Edgcumbe supped at the Johnstones. Lord Mount Edgcumbe said excellently, that *Mlle D'Éon is her own widow*.[189]

I wish I had seen you both in your court-*plis*[190] at your presentation—but that is only one wish amongst a thousand.

East winds and blights have succeeded our April spring, as you guessed, but though I have been at Strawberry every week, I have caught no cold, I kindly thank you. Adieu!

189. Mlle D'Éon . . . widow: Charles, Chevalier d'Eon (1728–1810), was a French political adventurer and secret agent who dressed as a woman; Louis XVI required him to dress as a woman for the rest of his life to receive his pension.

190. court-plis: court dress that girls wore when being presented to the Tuscan court.

Sir Joshua Reynolds

1723–1792

Born in the town of Plympton, in south Devonshire, Joshua Reynolds was the son of an amiably eccentric schoolmaster, in whose miscellaneous library he browsed as a child to supplement his classical education at the local grammar school. He never attended a university and was largely self-educated; at times he seemed almost fanatically devoted to an ideal of strenuous self-improvement. In boyhood he practiced drawing, and, although he always entertained lively literary ambitions, Raphael early displaced Pope as his idol.

At the age of seventeen he went to London for three years of diligent apprenticeship under Thomas Hudson, a leading portrait painter. Returning to Devonshire, he settled at Plymouth Dock, where he set up as a portrait painter of the naval officers and the local gentry. In 1749, conscious of the defects in his painterly education, he set off for almost three years in Italy. It was first his ambition and finally his achievement to redeem British portraiture from parochialism by infusing it with the "grand style" of the Continental Renaissance masters. At Naples, Rome, Florence, and Venice, he studied and sketched and copied, searching tirelessly for the elements of the noble and the sublime in Raphael, Rubens, Titian, Rembrandt, and above all, Michelangelo.

This devotion to his art soon brought handsome dividends. He returned to London in 1753 and began producing portraits of the lesser nobility. Almost overnight he became a fashionable artist. Business was so brisk that the customary studio assistants were soon needed. Reynolds posed the sitter, sketched the figure, and painted the face; the canvas was then finished by "the drapery man," "the accessory man," and "the furniture man." Within two years he was turning out one hundred and fifty portraits annually. He had become England's leading portrait painter.

His success as a painter carried him into intellectual and literary society. In 1756 he met Samuel Johnson, who, as he wrote later, "may be said to have formed my mind, and to have brushed off from it a deal of rubbish." They became lifetime friends, and through Johnson he became acquainted with Burke, Garrick, Goldsmith, and other Johnsonian devotees. He was soon contributing letters on aesthetics to Johnson's *Idler*.

In 1760, finding himself rich, he settled in a comfortable house and studio in Leicester Fields (later Leicester Square), where he presided over intellectual dinner parties for the rest of his life. Much of the furniture of this house was in the popular

Chinese taste, and one of the conspicuous objects of virtu was a chest, the gift of Garrick, made from Shakespeare's mulberry tree at Stratford. In Leicester Fields he lived in a style that generated envy in his less fortunate colleagues, even equipping himself with a coach so ostentatious that it occasioned giggles. No British painter had ever attained such financial and social success.

In 1764, sensing the need for a forum where Johnson could exercise his powers of mind, Reynolds helped found the Literary Club. It began with nine members, among them Burke and Goldsmith, who met weekly for conversation; the membership was gradually increased to thirty-five, among whom were most of the eminent men of the age. At the Literary Club and elsewhere in London, Reynolds's ear trumpet—he was deaf for most of his life—was a familiar fixture. An eminently social creature, he was sometimes said to love wine better than churchgoing. His energy, politeness, and flair for gentle mischief delighted his friends. But it was his supreme poise that people valued most: Johnson once praised him by saying that he was "the same all the year round."

In 1768 a number of painters organized the Royal Academy under the sponsorship of George III. Reynolds, who had long been interested in just such a school for artists, accepted the presidency. The Royal Academy had forty members, including Thomas Gainsborough, Benjamin West, Angelica Kauffmann, and Johann Zoffany; although all the members were supposed to be producing artists, Reynolds contrived the appointment of Johnson as Honorary Professor of Ancient Literature and of Goldsmith as Honorary Professor of Ancient History. Annual events at the Academy were the exhibitions, where Reynolds usually showed a dozen new pictures, and the prize-award meetings, where, between 1769 and 1790, Reynolds delivered his fifteen famous *Discourses*. The presidency of the Academy brought him a knighthood from the King in 1769, and he was further honored by Oxford, which made him Doctor of Civil Laws in 1773. Upon the death of Allan Ramsay the Younger in 1784, Reynolds was appointed His Majesty's Principal Painter in Ordinary.

Johnson's death in 1784 left Reynolds lonely, and he turned to Boswell, whom he encouraged to press forward with the writing of the *Life of Johnson* (1791). Boswell gratefully dedicated the book to him. By 1789 his painting career was over, for he had lost entirely the sight of one eye. But he was still able to enjoy a bottle of wine—several bottles, his enemies said—in the company of Burke, Sheridan, and the Prince of Wales. His last years were troubled by quarrels with the Academy, during one of which, in 1790, he resigned but subsequently returned. He was buried in St. Paul's after a splendid funeral that required ninety-one coaches.

As both a creator and a critic his proudest accomplishment was to make the art of painting entirely respectable in England. He succeeded in elevating the intellectual tone of British painters, largely by urging them to turn their attention toward the Continent. He had little bent for any of the pictorial kinds but portraiture, although he wanted desperately to succeed in history painting, which was held to be heroic and thus the highest genre. Landscape he eschewed; as a contemporary recalled, "He used to say the human face was *his* landscape." He produced nearly four thousand paintings, among them the authoritative portraits of Sterne, Goldsmith, Garrick, Gibbon, Burke, Boswell, and his beloved Johnson, whom he painted five times.

A bibliography of Reynolds's writings is contained in F. W. Hilles's indispensable *Literary Career of Sir Joshua Reynolds* (1936). A good edition of the *Discourses* is R. R. Wark's (1959). Reynolds's superb character sketches of Johnson, Goldsmith, and Garrick, together with an ironical discourse and other interesting materials, are edited by Hilles in *Portraits by Sir Joshua Reynolds* (1952). Derek Hudson's *Sir Joshua Reynolds: A Personal Study* (1958) is a readable, gossipy biography. Hilles has edited the *Letters* (1929). Reproductions of Reynolds's paintings may be studied conveniently in E. K. Waterhouse's *Reynolds* (1955). W. J. Bate's *From Classic to Romantic: Premises of Taste in Eighteenth-Century England* (1946) is helpful for the interpretation of the *Discourses*.

FROM

DISCOURSES

The first of Reynolds's fifteen *Discourses* was delivered at the official opening of the Royal Academy in 1769. Thereafter Reynolds read a presidential discourse annually through 1772, when he decided to speak only every other year. Each discourse was printed as a pamphlet after delivery. The first seven were collected and published in 1778, with an orotund dedication to the King supplied by Johnson. The complete set of fifteen was collected and published by Edmond Malone in 1797.

Writing did not come easily to Reynolds: he worried and paced and revised and revised. Some people, Horace Walpole among them, suspected that Johnson or Burke had contributed too zealously to the writing, but, although the influence of Johnson's mind is readily apparent and although Johnson occasionally polished the style, the writing is Reynolds's own. He said of the *Discourses*, "Whatever merit they have, must be imputed, in a great measure, to the education which I may be said to have had under Dr. Johnson. I do not mean to say . . . that he contributed even a single sentiment to them; but he qualified my mind to think justly." An old injury to his upper lip made Reynolds an unimpressive speaker, and doubtless there were smiles among his student audience when, in 1790, Edmund Burke stepped to the platform after the final discourse and, taking Reynolds's hand, quoted from *Paradise Lost*:

The angel ended, and in Adam's ear
So charming left his voice, that he awhile
Thought him still speaking, still stood fix'd to hear.

Because he was addressing an audience of young student painters, Reynolds conceived of his rhetorical obligation as partly pedagogical and even disciplinary. The students, he thought, needed to have redressed their breezy confidence in their own unaided powers. If the *Discourses* can be said to have one subject, that subject is the rigorous intellectual and ethical preparation required by the history painter.

Most contemporary readers tended to agree with a group of gentlemen who concluded in 1807, as the painter Joseph Farington reports, "that Sir Joshua Reynolds, in His Lectures, wrote with more purity & simplicity than any other modern writer, & might for the excellence of His style in that respect be compared with Addison;—having clearness, ease, and no affectation." But not everyone was pleased. William Blake, depressed by poverty and burning with outrage, found Reynolds "full of Self-Contradiction & Knavery."

The texts are those of the first editions in quarto; we have incorporated the substantive variants of the *Works* (2 vols., 1797) but have retained only one of Reynolds's footnotes.

DISCOURSE III

*Delivered to the Students of the Royal Academy,
on the Distribution of the Prizes,
December 14, 1770*

GENTLEMEN,

It is not easy to speak with propriety to so many students of different ages and different degrees of advancement. The mind requires nourishment adapted to its growth; and what may have promoted our earlier efforts, might retard us in our nearer approaches to perfection.

The first endeavours of a young Painter, as I have remarked in a former discourse, must be employed in the attainment of mechanical dexterity, and confined to the mere imitation of the object before him. Those who have advanced beyond the rudiments, may, perhaps, find advantage in reflecting on the advice which I have likewise given them, when I recommended the diligent study of the works of our great predecessors; but I at the same time endeavoured to guard them against an implicit submission to the authority of any one master however excellent; or by a strict imitation of his manner, precluding themselves from the abundance and variety of Nature. I will now add, that nature herself is not to be too closely copied. There are excellencies in the Art of Painting beyond what is commonly called the imitation of nature: and these excellencies I wish to point out. The students who, having passed through the initiatory exercises, are more advanced in the art, and who, sure of their hand, have leisure to exert their understanding, must now be told, that a mere copier of nature can never produce any thing great, can never raise and enlarge the conceptions, or warm the heart of the spectator.

The wish of the genuine Painter must be more extensive: instead of endeavouring to amuse mankind with the minute neatness of his imitations, he must endeavour to improve them by the grandeur of his ideas; instead of seeking praise, by deceiving the superficial sense of the spectator, he must strive for fame, by captivating the imagination.

The principle now laid down, that the perfection of this Art does not consist in mere imitation, is far from being new or singular. It is, indeed, supported by the general opinion of the enlightened part of mankind. The Poets, Orators, and Rhetoricians of antiquity, are continually enforcing this position, that all the arts receive their perfection from an ideal beauty, superior to what is to be found in individual nature. They are ever referring to the practice of the Painters and Sculptors of their times, particularly Phidias[1] (the favourite Artist of Antiquity) to illustrate their assertions. As if they could not sufficiently express their admiration of his genius by what they knew, they have recourse to poetical enthusiasm. They call it Inspiration, a Gift from Heaven; the artist is supposed to have ascended the celestial regions, to furnish his mind with this perfect Idea of beauty. "He," says Proclus, "who takes for his model such forms as nature produces, and confines himself to an exact imitation of them, will never attain to what is perfectly beautiful. For the works of nature are full of disproportion, and fall very short of the true standard of beauty. So that Phidias, when he formed his Jupiter, did not copy any object ever presented to his sight; but contemplated only that image which he had conceived in his mind from Homer's description."[2] And thus Cicero, speaking of the same Phidias; "Neither did this artist," says he, "when he carved the image of Jupiter or Minerva, set before him any one human figure, as a pattern, which he was to copy; but having a more perfect Idea of beauty fixed in his mind, this he steadily contemplated, and to the imitation of this all his skill and labour were directed."[3]

The Moderns are not less convinced than the Ancients of this superior power existing in the Art; nor less sensible of its effects. Every language has adopted terms expressive of this excellence; the *Gusto grande* of the Italians; the *Beau ideal* of the French; and the *great style, genius,* and *taste* among the English, are but different appellations of the same thing. It is this intellectual dignity, they say, that ennobles the Painter's art, that lays the line between him and the mere mechanic, and produces those great effects in an instant, which eloquence and poetry, by slow and repeated efforts, are scarcely able to attain.

Such is the warmth with which both the Antients and Moderns speak of this divine principle of the art; but, as I have formerly observed, enthusiastic admiration seldom promotes knowledge. Though a Student by such praise may have his attention roused, and a desire excited, of running in this great career; yet it is possible that what has been said to excite, may only serve to deter him. He examines his own mind, and perceives there nothing of that divine inspiration, with which, he is told, so many others have been favoured. He never travelled to Heaven to gather new ideas; and he finds himself possessed of no other qualifications than what mere common observation and a plain understanding can confer. Thus he becomes gloomy amidst the splendor of figurative declamation, and thinks it hopeless, to pursue an object which he supposes out of the reach of human industry.

DISCOURSE III. **I. Phidias:** Greek sculptor of the fifth century B.C., to whom are attributed gigantic figures of Zeus (Jupiter) in the temple at Olympia, and of Athene (Minerva) in the Parthenon. These statues were the wonder of his time.

2. He . . . description: *On Plato's Dialogue Timaeus* by Proclus, a Greek neo-Platonic philosopher of the fifth century B.C. **3. Neither . . . directed:** *De Oratore,* ii. 9.

But on this, as upon many other occasions, we ought to distinguish how much is to be given to enthusiasm, and how much to reason. We ought to allow for, and we ought to commend, that strength of vivid expression, which is necessary to convey, in its full force, the highest sense of the most complete effect of art; taking care at the same time, not to lose in terms of vague admiration, that solidity and truth of principle, upon which alone we can reason, and may be enabled to practice.

It is not easy to define in what this great style consists; nor to describe, by words, the proper means of acquiring it, if the mind of the Student should be at all capable of such an acquisition. Could we teach taste or genius by rules, they would be no longer taste and genius. But though there neither are, nor can be, any precise invariable rules for the exercise, or the acquisition, of these great qualities; yet we may truly say that they always operate in proportion to our attention in observing the works of nature, to our skill in selecting, and to our care in digesting, methodizing, and comparing our observations. There are many beauties in our art, that seem at first, to lie without the reach of precept, and yet may easily be reduced to practical principles. Experience is all in all; but it is not every one who profits by experience; and most people err, not so much from want of capacity to find their object, as from not knowing what object to pursue. This great ideal perfection and beauty are not to be sought in the heavens, but upon the earth. They are about us, and upon every side of us. But the power of discovering what is deformed in nature, or in other words, what is particular and uncommon, can be acquired only by experience; and the whole beauty and grandeur of the art consists, in my opinion, in being able to get above all singular forms, local customs, particularities, and details of every kind.

All the objects which are exhibited to our view by nature, upon close examination will be found to have their blemishes and defects. The most beautiful forms have something about them like weakness, minuteness, or imperfection. But it is not every eye that perceives these blemishes; it must be an eye long used to the contemplation and comparison of these forms; and which, by a long habit of observing what any set of objects of the same kind have in common, has acquired the power of discerning what each wants in particular. This long laborious comparison should be the first study of the painter, who aims at the greatest style. By this means, he acquires a just Idea of beautiful

forms; he corrects nature by herself, her imperfect state by her more perfect. His eye being enabled to distinguish the accidental deficiencies, excrescences and deformities of things from their general figures, he makes out an abstract idea of their forms more perfect than any one original; and what may seem a paradox, he learns to design naturally by drawing his figures unlike to any one object. This idea of the perfect state of nature, which the artist calls the Ideal Beauty, is the great leading principle, by which works of genius are conducted. By this Phidias acquired his fame. He wrought upon a sober principle, what has so much excited the enthusiasm of the world; and by this method you, who have courage to tread the same path, may acquire equal reputation.

This is the idea which has acquired, and which seems to have a right to the epithet of *Divine;* as it may be said to preside, like a supreme judge, over all the productions of nature; appearing to be possessed of the will and intention of the Creator, as far as they regard the external form of living beings.

When a man once possesses this idea in its perfection, there is no danger, but that he will be sufficiently warmed by it himself, and be able to warm and ravish every one else.

Thus it is from a reiterated experience, and a close comparison of the objects in nature, that an artist becomes possessed of the idea of that central form, if I may so express it, from which every deviation is deformity. But the investigation of this form I grant is painful, and I know but of one method of shortening the road; this is, by a careful study of the works of the antient sculptors; who, being indefatigable in the school of nature, have left models of that perfect form behind them, which an artist would prefer as supremely beautiful, who had spent his whole life in that single contemplation. But if industry carried them thus far, may not you also hope for the same reward from the same labour? We have the same school opened to us, that was opened to them; for nature denies her instructions to none, who desire to become her pupils.

This[4] laborious investigation, I am aware, must appear superfluous to those who think every thing is to be done by felicity, and the powers of native genius. Even the great Bacon treats with ridicule the idea of confining proportion to rules, or of producing beauty

---

4. This . . . sagacity: This paragraph and the one following were added in the edition of 1797.

by selection. "A man cannot tell, says he, whether Apelles[5] or Albert Durer[6] were the more trifler: whereof the one would make a personage by geometrical proportions; the other, by taking the best parts out of divers faces, to make one excellent. . . . The painter," (he adds,) "must do it by a kind of felicity, . . . and not by rule."[7]

It is not safe to question any opinion of so great a writer, and so profound a thinker, as undoubtedly Bacon was. But he studies brevity to excess; and therefore his meaning is sometimes doubtful. If he means that beauty has nothing to do with rule, he is mistaken. There is a rule, obtained out of general nature, to contradict which is to fall into deformity. Whenever any thing is done beyond this rule, it is in virtue of some other rule which is followed along with it, but which does not contradict it. Every thing which is wrought with certainty, is wrought upon some principle. If it is not, it cannot be repeated. If by felicity is meant any thing of chance or hazard, or something born with a man, and not earned, I cannot agree with this great philosopher. Every object which pleases must give us pleasure upon some certain principles; but as the objects of pleasure are almost infinite, so their principles vary without end, and every man finds them out, not by felicity or successful hazard, but by care and sagacity.

To the principle I have laid down, that the idea of beauty in each species of Beings is an invariable one, it may be objected, that in every particular species there are various central forms, which are separate and distinct from each other, and yet are undeniably beautiful; that in the human figure, for instance, the beauty of the Hercules is one, of the Gladiator another, of the Apollo[8] another; which makes so many different ideas of beauty.

It is true, indeed, that these figures are each perfect in their kind, though of different characters and proportions; but still none of them is the representation of an individual, but of a class. And as there is one general form, which, as I have said, belongs to the human kind at large, so in each of these classes there is one common idea and central form, which is the abstract of the various individual forms belonging to that class. Thus, though the forms of childhood and age differ exceedingly; there is a common form in childhood, and a common form in age, which is the more perfect, as it is more remote from all peculiarities. But I must add further, that though the most perfect forms of each of the general divisions of the human figure are ideal, and superior to any individual form of that class; yet the highest perfection of the human figure is not to be found in any one of them; it is not in the Hercules, nor in the Gladiator, nor in the Apollo; but in that form which is taken from them all, and which partakes equally of the activity of the Gladiator, of the delicacy of the Apollo, and of the muscular strength of the Hercules. For perfect beauty in any species must combine all the characters which are beautiful in that species. It cannot consist in any one to the exclusion of the rest: no one, therefore, must be predominant, that no one may be deficient.

The knowledge of these different characters, and the power of separating and distinguishing them, is undoubtedly necessary to the painter, who is to vary his compositions with figures of various forms and proportions, though he is never to lose sight of the general idea of perfection in each kind.

There is, likewise, a kind of symmetry, or proportion, which may properly be said to belong to deformity. A figure lean or corpulent, tall or short, though deviating from beauty, may still have a certain union of the various parts, which may contribute to make them on the whole, not unpleasing.

When the Artist has by diligent attention acquired a clear and distinct idea of beauty and symmetry; when he has reduced the variety of nature to the abstract idea; his next task will be to become acquainted with the genuine habits of nature, as distinguished from those of fashion. For in the same manner, and on the same principles, as he has acquired the knowledge of the real forms of nature, distinct from accidental deformity, he must endeavour to separate simple chaste nature, from those adventitious, those affected and forced airs or actions, with which she is loaded by modern education.

Perhaps I cannot better explain what I mean, than by reminding you of what was taught us, by the Professor of Anatomy,[9] in respect to the natural

---

5. Apelles: Greek painter of the fourth century B.C. **6. Albert Durer:** Albrecht Dürer (1471-1528), Nuremberg painter, engraver, and maker of woodcuts. **7. A man . . . rule:** *Of Beauty,* one of the *Essays* of Sir Francis Bacon (1561-1626), published in 1597 and 1625. **8. Hercules, Gladiator, Apollo:** three famous sculptures: the *Farnese Hercules* (at Naples), the *Borghese Warrior* (in the Louvre), and the *Apollo Belvedere* (in the Vatican).

9. the Professor . . . Anatomy: Dr. William Hunter (1718-83).

position and movement of the feet. He observed that the fashion of turning them outwards was contrary to the intent of nature, as might be seen from the structure of the bones, and from the weakness that proceeded from that manner of standing. To this we may add the erect position of the head, the projection of the chest, the walking with straight knees, and many such actions, which we know to be merely the result of fashion, and what nature never warranted, as we are sure that we have been taught them when children.

I have mentioned but a few of those instances, in which vanity or caprice have contrived to distort and disfigure the human form; your own recollection will add to these a thousand more of ill-understood methods, which have been practised to disguise nature, among our dancing-masters, hair-dressers, and taylors, in their various schools of deformity.[10]

However the mechanic and ornamental arts may sacrifice to fashion, she must be entirely excluded from the Art of Painting; the painter must never mistake this capricious changeling for the genuine offspring of nature; he must divest himself of all prejudices in favour of his age or country; he must disregard all local, and temporary ornaments, and look only on those general habits which are every where and always the same. He addresses his works to the people of every country and every age; he calls upon posterity to be his spectators, and says with Zeuxis, *In æternitatem pingo.*[11]

The neglect of separating modern fashions from the habits of nature, leads to that ridiculous stile which has been practised by some painters, who have given to Græcian Heroes the airs and graces practised in the court of Lewis the Fourteenth;[12] an absurdity almost as great as it would have been to have dressed them after the fashion of that court.

To avoid this error, however, and to retain the true simplicity of nature, is a task more difficult than at first sight it may appear. The prejudices in favour of the fashions and customs that we have been used to, and which are justly called a second nature, make it too often difficult to distinguish that which is natural, from that which is the result of education; they frequently even give a predilection in favour of the artificial mode; and almost every one is apt to be guided by those local prejudices who has not chastised his mind, and regulated the instability of his affections, by the eternal invariable idea of nature.

Here then, as before, we must have recourse to the Ancients as instructors. It is from a careful study of their works that you will be enabled to attain to the real simplicity of nature; they will suggest many observations, which would probably escape you, if your study were confined to nature alone. And, indeed, I cannot help suspecting, that in this instance, the Ancients had an easier task than the moderns. They had, probably, little or nothing to unlearn, as their manners were nearly approaching to this desirable simplicity; while the modern artist, before he can see the truth of things, is obliged to remove a veil, with which the fashion of the times has thought proper to cover her.

Having gone thus far in our investigation of the great stile in painting; if we now should suppose that the artist has formed the true idea of beauty, which enables him to give his works a correct and perfect design; if we should suppose also, that he has acquired a knowledge of the unadulterated habits of nature, which gives him simplicity; the rest of his task is, perhaps, less than is generally imagined. Beauty and simplicity have so great a share in the composition of a great stile, that he who has acquired them has little else to learn. It must not, indeed, be forgotten, that there is a nobleness of conception, which goes beyond any thing in the mere exhibition, even of perfect form; there is an art of animating and dignifying the figures with intellectual grandeur, of impressing the appearance of philosophic wisdom, or heroick virtue. This can only be acquired by him that enlarges the sphere of his understanding by a variety of knowledge, and warms his imagination with the best productions of antient and modern poetry.

A hand thus exercised, and a mind thus instructed, will bring the Art to a higher degree of excellence than, perhaps, it has hitherto attained in this country. Such a student will disdain the humbler walks of painting, which, however profitable, can never assure him a permanent reputation. He will leave the meaner artist servilely to suppose that those are the best pictures, which are most likely to deceive the spectator.

---

10. **those . . . deformity:** [Reynolds's note] "Those," says Quintilian, "who are taken with the outward shew of things, think that there is more beauty in persons, who are trimmed, curled, and painted, than uncorrupt nature can give; as if beauty were merely the effect of the corruption of manners." 11. **In . . . pingo:** "I paint for eternity," a remark attributed to Zeuxis, a Greek painter of the late fifth century B.C. 12. **the court . . . Fourteenth:** Louis XIV reigned in France from 1643 to 1715.

He will permit the lower painter, like the florist or collector of shells, to exhibit the minute discriminations, which distinguish one object of the same species from another; while he like the philosopher will consider nature in the abstract, and represent in every one of his figures the character of its species.

If deceiving the eye were the only business of the Art, there is no doubt, indeed, but the minute painter would be more apt to succeed: but it is not the eye, it is the mind, which the painter of genius desires to address; nor will he waste a moment upon those smaller objects, which only serve to catch the sense, to divide the attention, and to counteract his great design of speaking to the heart.

This is the ambition which I wish to excite in your minds; and the object I have had in my view, throughout this discourse, is that one great idea, which gives to painting its true dignity, which entitles it to the name of a Liberal Art, and ranks it as a sister of poetry.

It may possibly have happened to many young students whose application was sufficient to overcome all difficulties, and whose minds were capable of embracing the most extensive views, that they have, by a wrong direction originally given, spent their lives in the meaner walks of painting, without ever knowing there was a nobler to pursue. Albert Durer, as Vasari[13] has justly remarked, would, probably, have been one of the first painters of his age (and he lived in an æra of great artists) had he been initiated into those great principles of the Art, which were so well understood, and practised, by his contemporaries in Italy. But unluckily having never seen or heard of any other manner, he, without doubt, considered his own as perfect.

As for the various departments of painting, which do not presume to make such high pretensions, they are many; none of them are without their merit, though none enter into competition with this universal presiding idea of the Art. The painters who have applied themselves more particularly to low and vulgar characters, and who express with precision, the various shades of passion, as they are exhibited by vulgar minds (such as we see in the works of Hogarth[14]) deserve great praise; but as their genius has been employed on low and confined subjects, the praise which we give must be as limited as its object. The merry-making, or quarrelling of the Boors of Teniers;[15] the same sort of productions of Brouwer, or Ostade,[16] are excellent in their kind; and the excellence and its praise will be in proportion, as, in those limited subjects, and peculiar forms, they introduce more or less of the expression of those passions, as they appear in general and more enlarged nature. This principle may be applied to the Battle-pieces of Bourgognone,[17] the French Gallantries of Watteau,[18] and even beyond the exhibition of animal life, to the Landscapes of Claude Lorraine,[19] and the Sea-Views of Vandervelde.[20] All these painters have, in general, the same right, in different degrees, to the name of a Painter, which a satirist, an epigrammatist, a sonnetteer, a writer of pastorals, or descriptive poetry, has to that of a poet.

In the same rank, and, perhaps, of not so great merit, is the cold painter of portraits; but his correct and just imitation of his object has its merit. Even the painter of still life, whose highest ambition is to give a minute representation of every part of those low objects, which he sets before him, deserves praise in proportion to his attainment; because no part of this excellent Art, so much the ornament of polished life, is destitute of value and use. These, however, are by no means the views to which the mind of the student ought to be *primarily* directed. Having begun by aiming at better things, if from particular inclination, or from the taste of the time and place he lives in, or from necessity, or from failure in the highest attempts, he is obliged to descend lower; he will bring into the lower sphere of art, a grandeur of composition and character, that will raise and ennoble his works far above their natural rank.

A man is not weak, though he may not be able to wield the club of Hercules; nor does a man always practise that which he esteems the best; but does that which he can best do. In moderate attempts, there are

13. **Vasari:** Giorgio Vasari (1511–74), Italian painter, architect, and art historian; author of *Lives of the Most Excellent Italian Painters, Sculptors, and Architects* (1550). 14. **Hogarth:** William Hogarth (1697-1764), English painter and engraver best known for his realistic and satiric pictorial series such as *The Rake's Progress* and *Marriage à la Mode.*

15. **Teniers:** David Teniers the Younger (1610–90), Flemish painter of low life. 16. **Brouwer, Ostade:** Adriaen Brouwer and Adriaen van Ostade, seventeenth-century Flemish painters of low life. 17. **Bourgognone:** Jacques Courtois (1621–76), called Le Bourguignon (the Burgundian), famous for his paintings of cavalry warfare. 18. **Watteau:** Jean Antoine Watteau (1684–1721), French painter known for his stylish and aristocratic pseudo-pastoral pictures. 19. **Claude Lorraine:** Claude Gellée (1600–82), French painter. 20. **Vandervelde:** Willem van de Velde the Younger (1633–1707), Dutch painter of seascapes and naval battles.

many walks open to the artist. But as the idea of beauty is of necessity but one, so there can be but one great mode of painting; the leading principle of which I have endeavoured to explain.

I should be sorry, if what is here recommended, should be at all understood to countenance a careless or indetermined manner of painting; for though the painter is to overlook the accidental discriminations of nature, he is to exhibit distinctly, and with precision, the general forms of things. A firm and determined outline is one of the characteristics of the great style in painting; and let me add that he who possesses the knowledge of the exact form which every part of nature ought to have, will be fond of expressing that knowledge with correctness and precision in all his works.

To conclude; I have endeavoured to reduce the idea of beauty to general principles. And I had the pleasure to observe that the professor of painting[21] proceeded in the same method, when he shewed you that the artifice of contrast was founded but on one principle. I am convinced that this is the only means of advancing science, of clearing the mind from a confused heap of contradictory observations, that do but perplex and puzzle the student, when he compares them, or mis-guide him if he gives himself up to their authority: bringing them under one general head, can alone give rest and satisfaction to an inquisitive mind.

DISCOURSE VII

Delivered to the Students of the Royal Academy,
on the Distribution of the Prizes,
December 10, 1776

GENTLEMEN,

It has been my uniform endeavour since I first addressed you from this place, to impress you strongly with one ruling idea. I wish you to be persuaded, that success in your Art depends almost entirely on your own in-dustry; but the industry which I principally recom-mended, is not the industry of the *hands*, but of the *mind*.

As our art is not a divine *gift*, so neither is it a mechanical *trade*. Its foundations are laid in solid science. And practice, though essential to perfection, can never attain that to which it aims, unless it works under the direction of principle.

Some writers upon art carry this point too far, and suppose that such a body of universal and profound learning is requisite, that the very enumeration of its kinds is enough to frighten a beginner. Vitruvius, after going through the many accomplishments of nature, and the many acquirements of learning, necessary to an architect, proceeds with great gravity to assert, that he ought to be well skilled in the civil law, that he may not be cheated in the title of the ground he builds on.[1] But without such exaggeration, we may go so far as to assert, that a painter stands in need of more knowledge than is to be picked off his pallet, or collected by looking on his model, whether it be in life or in picture. He can never be a great artist, who is grossly illiterate.

Every man whose business is description ought to be tolerably conversant with the poets, in some language or other; that he may imbibe a poetical spirit, and enlarge his stock of ideas. He ought to acquire an habit of comparing and digesting his notions. He ought not to be wholly unacquainted with that part of philosophy which gives an insight into human nature, and relates to the manners, characters, passions and affections. He ought to know *something* concerning the mind, as well as *a great deal* concerning the body of man.

For this purpose, it is not necessary that he should go into such a compass of reading, as must, by dis-tracting his attention, disqualify him for the practical part of his profession, and make him sink the per-former in the critic. Reading, if it can be made the favourite recreation of his leisure hours, will improve and enlarge his mind, without retarding his actual industry.

What such partial and desultory reading cannot afford, may be supplied by the conversation of learned and ingenious men, which is the best of all substitutes for those who have not the means or opportunities of deep study. There are many such men in this age; and they will be pleased with communicating their ideas to artists, when they see them curious and docile, if they are treated with that respect and deference which is so justly their due. Into such society, young artists, if they make it the point of their ambition, will by degrees be admitted. There without formal teaching,

---

21. **the professor . . . painting:** Edward Penny (1714–91).

DISCOURSE VII. **1. he ought . . . on:** *De Architectura*, I. i. 10, by Marcus Vitruvius Pollio, Roman architect and engineer of the first century B.C.

they will insensibly come to feel and reason like those they live with, and find a rational and systematic taste imperceptibly formed in their minds, which they will know how to reduce to a standard, by applying general truth to their own purposes, better perhaps than those to whom they owed the original sentiment.

Of these studies and this conversation, the desired and legitimate offspring is a power of distinguishing right from wrong, which power applied to works of art, is denominated *taste*. Let me then, without further introduction, enter upon an examination, whether taste be so far beyond our reach, as to be unattainable by care; or be so very vague and capricious, that no care ought to be employed about it.

It has been the fate of arts to be enveloped in mysterious and incomprehensible language, as if it was thought necessary that even the terms should correspond to the idea entertained of the instability and uncertainty of the rules which they expressed.

To speak of genius and taste, as in any way connected with reason or common sense, would be, in the opinion of some towering talkers, to speak like a man who possessed neither, who had never felt that enthusiasm, or, to use their own inflated language, was never warmed by that Promethean fire,[2] which animates the canvas and vivifies the marble.

If, in order to be intelligible, I appear to degrade the art by bringing her down from her visionary situation in the clouds, it is only to give her a more solid mansion upon the earth. It is necessary that at some time or other we should see things as they really are, and not impose on ourselves by that false magnitude with which objects appear when viewed indistinctly as through a mist.

We will allow a poet to express his meaning, when his meaning is not well known to himself, with a certain degree of obscurity, as it is one source of the sublime. But when, in plain prose, we gravely talk of courting the muse in shady bowers; waiting the call and inspiration of Genius, finding out where he inhabits, and where he is to be invoked with the greatest success; of attending to times and seasons when the imagination shoots with the greatest vigour, whether at the summer solstice or the vernal equinox; sagaciously observing how much the wild freedom and liberty of imagination is cramped by attention to established rules; and how this same imagination

begins to grow dim in advanced age, smothered and deadened by too much judgment. When we talk such language, or entertain such sentiments as these, we generally rest contented with mere words, or at best entertain notions not only groundless, but pernicious.

If all this means what it is very possible was originally intended only to be meant, that in order to cultivate an art, a man secludes himself from the commerce of the world, and retires into the country at particular seasons; or that at one time of the year his body is in better health, and consequently his mind fitter for the business of hard thinking than at another time; or that the mind may be fatigued and grow confused by long and unremitted application; this I can understand. I can likewise believe, that a man eminent when young for possessing poetical imagination, may, from having taken another road, so neglect its cultivation, as to show less of its powers in his latter life. But I am persuaded, that scarce a poet is to be found, from Homer down to Dryden, who preserved a sound mind in a sound body, and continued practising his profession to the very last, whose latter works are not as replete with the fire of imagination, as those which were produced in his more youthful days.

To understand literally these metaphors or ideas expressed in poetical language, seems to be equally absurd as to conclude, that because painters sometimes represent poets writing from the dictates of a little winged boy or genius, that this same genius did really inform him in a whisper what he was to write; and that he is himself but a mere machine, unconscious of the operations of his own mind.

Opinions generally received and floating in the world, whether true or false, we naturally adopt and make our own; they may be considered as a kind of inheritance to which we succeed and are tenants for life, and which we leave to our posterity very nearly in the condition in which we received it; it not being much in any one man's power either to impair or improve it.

The greatest part of these opinions, like current coin in its circulation, we are used to take without weighing or examining; but by this inevitable inattention many adulterated pieces are received, which, when we seriously estimate our wealth, we must throw away. So the collector of popular opinions, when he embodies his knowledge, and forms a system, must separate those which are true from those which are only plausible. But it becomes more peculiarly a duty to the professors of art not to let any opinions relating

2. **Promethean fire:** In Greek mythology Prometheus was a Titan who stole fire from the gods and brought it to earth.

to *that* art pass unexamined. The caution and circum-spection required in such examination we shall presently have an opportunity of explaining.

Genius and taste, in their common acceptation, appear to be very nearly related; the difference lies only in this, that genius has superadded to it a habit or power of execution. Or we may say, that taste, when this power is added, changes its name, and is called genius. They both, in the popular opinion, pretend to an entire exemption from the restraint of rules. It is supposed that their powers are intuitive; that under the name of genius great works are produced, and under the name of taste an exact judgment is given, without our knowing why, and without our being under the least obligation to reason, precept, or ex-perience.

One can scarce state these opinions without exposing their absurdity, yet they are constantly in the mouths of men, and particularly of artists. They who have thought seriously on this subject, do not carry the point so far; yet I am persuaded, that even among those few who may be called thinkers, the prevalent opinion allows less than it ought to the powers of reason; and considers the principles of taste, which give all their authority to the rules of art, as more fluctuating, and as having less solid foundations, than we shall find, upon examination, they really have.

The common saying, that *tastes are not to be disputed*, owes its influence, and its general reception, to the same error which leads us to imagine this faculty of too high an original to submit to the authority of an earthly tribunal. It likewise corresponds with the notions of those who consider it as a mere phantom of the imagination, so devoid of substance as to elude all criticism.

We often appear to differ in sentiments from each other, merely from the inaccuracy of terms, as we are not obliged to speak always with critical exactness. Something of this too may arise from want of words in the language in which we speak, to express the more nice discriminations which a deep investigation dis-covers. A great deal however of this difference vanishes, when each opinion is tolerably explained and understood by constancy and precision in the use of terms.

We apply the term *Taste* to that act of the mind by which we like or dislike, whatever be the subject. Our judgment upon an airy nothing, a fancy which has no foundation, is called by the same name which we give to our determination concerning those truths which refer to the most general and most unalterable prin-ciples of human nature; to the works which are only to be produced by the greatest efforts of the human understanding. However inconvenient this may be, we are obliged to take words as we find them; all we can do is to distinguish the *things* to which they are applied.

We may let pass those things which are at once subjects of taste and sense, and which having as much certainty as the senses themselves, give no occasion to enquiry or dispute. The natural appetite or taste of the human mind is for *Truth;* whether that truth results from the real agreement or equality of original ideas among themselves; from the agreement of the repre-sentation of any object with the thing represented; or from the correspondence of the several parts of any arrangement with each other. It is the very same taste which relishes a demonstration in geometry, that is pleased with the resemblance of a picture to an original, and touched with the harmony of music.

All these have unalterable and fixed foundations in nature, and are therefore equally investigated by reason, and known by study; some with more, some with less clearness, but all exactly in the same way. A picture that is unlike, is false. Disproportionate ordonnance[3] of parts is not right, because it cannot be true; until it ceases to be a contradiction to assert, that the parts have no relation to the whole. Colouring is true when it is naturally adapted to the eye, from brightness, from softness, from harmony, from resem-blance; because these agree with their object *nature*, and therefore are true; as true as mathematical demon-stration; but known to be true only to those who study these things.

But besides *real*, there is also *apparent* truth, or opinion, or prejudice. With regard to real truth, when it is known, the taste which conforms to it, is, and must be, uniform. With regard to the second sort of truth, which may be called truth upon sufferance, or truth by courtesy, it is not fixed, but variable. How-ever, whilst these opinions and prejudices, on which it is founded, continue, they operate as truth; and the Art, whose office it is to please the mind, as well as instruct it, must direct itself according to *opinion*, or it will not attain its end.

In proportion as these prejudices are known to be generally diffused, or long received, the taste which conforms to them approaches nearer to certainty, and

---

3. ordonnance: arrangement.

to a sort of resemblance to real science, even where opinions are found to be no better than prejudices. And since they deserve, on account of their duration and extent, to be considered as really true, they become capable of no small degree of stability and determination by their permanent and uniform nature.

As these prejudices become more narrow, more local, more transitory, this secondary taste becomes more and more fantastical; recedes from real science; is less to be approved by reason, and less followed in practice; though in no case perhaps to be wholly neglected, where it does not stand, as it sometimes does, in direct defiance of the most respectable opinions received amongst mankind.

Having laid down these positions, I shall proceed with less method, because less will serve, to explain and apply them.

We will take it for granted, that reason is something invariable and fixed in the nature of things; and without endeavouring to go back to an account of first principles, which for ever will elude our search, we will conclude, that whatever goes under the name of taste, which we can fairly bring under the dominion of reason, must be considered as equally exempt from change. If therefore, in the course of this enquiry, we can shew that there are rules for the conduct of the artist which are fixed and invariable, it follows of course, that the art of the connoisseur, or, in other words, taste, has likewise invariable principles.

Of the judgment which we make on the works of art, and the preference that we give to one class of art over another, if a reason be demanded, the question is perhaps evaded by answering, I judge from my taste; but it does not follow that a better answer cannot be given, though, for common gazers, this may be sufficient. Every man is not obliged to investigate the causes of his approbation or dislike.

The arts would lie open for ever to caprice and casualty, if those who are to judge of their excellencies had no settled principles by which they are to regulate their decisions, and the merit or defect of performances were to be determined by unguided fancy. And indeed we may venture to assert, that whatever speculative knowledge is necessary to the artist, is equally and indispensably necessary to the connoisseur.

The first idea that occurs in the consideration of what is fixed in art, or in taste, is that presiding principle of which I have so frequently spoken in former discourses, the general idea of nature. The beginning, the middle, and the end of every thing that is valuable in taste, is comprized in the knowledge of what is truly nature; for whatever notions are not conformable to those of nature, or universal opinion, must be considered as more or less capricious.

My notion of nature comprehends not only the forms which nature produces, but also the nature and internal fabric and organization, as I may call it, of the human mind and imagination. The terms beauty, or nature, which are general ideas, are but different modes of expressing the same thing, whether we apply these terms to statues, poetry, or picture. Deformity is not nature, but an accidental deviation from her accustomed practice. This general idea therefore ought to be called Nature,[4] and nothing else, correctly speaking, has a right to that name. But we are so far from speaking, in common conversation, with any such accuracy, that, on the contrary, when we criticise Rembrandt[5] and other Dutch painters, who introduced into their historical pictures exact representations of individual objects with all their imperfections, we say, though it is not in a good taste, yet it is nature.

This misapplication of terms must be very often perplexing to the young student. Is not art, he may say, an imitation of nature? Must he not therefore who imitates her with the greatest fidelity, be the best artist? By this mode of reasoning Rembrandt has a higher place than Raffaelle.[6] But a very little reflection will serve to shew us that these particularities cannot be nature: for how can that be the nature of man, in which no two individuals are the same?

It plainly appears, that as a work is conducted under the influence of general ideas, or partial, it is principally to be considered as the effect of a good or a bad taste.

As beauty therefore does not consist in taking what lies immediately before you, so neither, in our pursuit of taste, are those opinions which we first received and adopted, the best choice, or the most natural to the mind and imagination.

In the infancy of our knowledge we seize with greediness the good that is within our reach; it is by after-consideration, and in consequence of discipline, that we refuse the present for a greater good at a distance. The nobility or elevation of all arts, like the excellency of virtue itself, consists in adopting this enlarged and comprehensive idea; and all criticism

4. **Nature:** The first edition (1776) reads: "beauty." 5. **Rembrandt:** Rembrandt Harmensz van Rijn (1606–69). 6. **Raffaelle:** the great Italian painter Raffaello Santi (1483–1520).

built upon the more confined view of what is natural, may properly be called *shallow* criticism, rather than false; its defect is, that the truth is not sufficiently extensive.

It has sometimes happened, that some of the greatest men in our art have been betrayed into errors by this confined mode of reasoning. Poussin,[7] who, upon the whole, may be produced as an artist strictly attentive to the most enlarged and extensive ideas of nature, from not having settled principles on this point, has in one instance at least, I think, deserted truth for prejudice. He is said to have vindicated the conduct of Julio Romano[8] for his inattention to the masses of light and shade, or grouping the figures in the battle of Constantine, as if designedly neglected, the better to correspond with the hurry and confusion of a battle. Poussin's own conduct in many of his pictures, makes us more easily give credit to this report. That it was too much his own practice, THE SACRIFICE TO SILENUS, and THE TRIUMPH OF BACCHUS AND ARIADNE, may be produced as instances; but this principle is still more apparent, and may be said to be even more ostentatiously displayed in his PERSEUS and MEDUSA'S HEAD.

This is undoubtedly a subject of great bustle and tumult, and that the first effect of the picture may correspond to the subject, every principle of composition is violated; there is no principal figure, no principal light, no groups; every thing is dispersed, and in such a state of confusion that the eye finds no repose any where. In consequence of the forbidding appearance, I remember turning from it with disgust, and should not have looked a second time, if I had not been called back to a closer inspection. I then indeed found, what we may expect always to find in the works of Poussin, correct drawing, forcible expression, and just character; in short all the excellencies which so much distinguish the works of this learned painter.

This conduct of Poussin I hold to be entirely improper to imitate. A picture should please at first sight, and appear to invite the spectator's attention: if on the contrary the general effect offends the eye, a second view is not always sought, whatever more substantial and intrinsick merit it may possess.

Perhaps no apology ought to be received for offences committed against the vehicle (whether it be the organ of seeing, or of hearing) by which our pleasures are conveyed to the mind. We must take care that the eye be not perplexed and distracted by a confusion of equal parts, or equal lights, or offended by an unharmonious mixture of colours, as we should guard against offending the ear by unharmonious sounds. We may venture to be more confident of the truth of this observation, since we find that Shakespear, on a parallel occasion, has made Hamlet recommend to the players a precept of the same kind, never to offend the ear by harsh sounds: *In the very torrent, tempest and whirlwind of your passion*, says he, *you must acquire and beget a temperance that may give it smoothness.* And yet, at the same time, he very justly observes, *The end of playing, both at the first, and now, was and is, to hold, as it were, the mirror up to nature.*[9] No one can deny, that violent passions will naturally emit harsh and disagreeable tones; yet this great poet and critic thought that this imitation of nature would cost too much, if purchased at the expence of disagreeable sensations, or, as he expresses it, of splitting the ear. The poet and actor, as well as the painter of genius who is well acquainted with all the variety and sources of pleasure in the mind and imagination, has little regard or attention to common nature, or creeping after common sense. By overleaping those narrow bounds, he more effectually seizes the whole mind, and more powerfully accomplishes his purpose. This success is ignorantly imagined to proceed from inattention to all rules, and a defiance of reason and judgment; whereas it is in truth acting according to the best rules, and the justest reason.

He who thinks nature, in the narrow sense of the word, is alone to be followed, will produce but a scanty entertainment for the imagination: every thing is to be done with which it is natural for the mind to be pleased, whether it proceeds from simplicity or variety, uniformity or irregularity: whether the scenes are familiar or exotic; rude and wild, or enriched and cultivated; for it is natural for the mind to be pleased with all these in their turn. In short, whatever pleases has in it what is analogous to the mind, and is therefore, in the highest and best sense of the word, natural.

It is the sense of nature or truth which ought more particularly to be cultivated by the professors of art; and it may be observed, that many wise and learned men, who have accustomed their minds to admit nothing for truth but what can be proved by mathematical demonstration, have seldom any relish for

---

7. **Poussin:** Nicolas Poussin (1594–1665), French history and landscape painter. 8. **Julio Romano:** Giulio Pippi de' Giannuzzi (1499–1546), Italian painter, whose fresco *The Battle of Constantine* is in the Vatican.

9. **In . . . nature:** See *Hamlet*, III. ii.

those arts which address themselves to the fancy, the rectitude and truth of which is known by another kind of proof: and we may add, that the acquisition of this knowledge requires as much circumspection and sagacity, as is necessary to attain those truths which are more capable of demonstration. Reason must ultimately determine our choice on every occasion; but this reason may still be exerted ineffectually by applying to taste principles which, though right as far as they go, yet do not reach the object. No man, for instance, can deny, that it seems at first view very reasonable, that a statue which is to carry down to posterity the resemblance of an individual, should be dressed in the fashion of the times, in the dress which he himself wore: this would certainly be true, if the dress were part of the man. But after a time, the dress is only an amusement for an antiquarian; and if it obstructs the general design of the piece, it is to be disregarded by the artist. Common sense must here give way to a higher sense.

In the naked form, and in the disposition of the drapery, the difference between one artist and another is principally seen. But if he is compelled to exhibit the modern dress, the naked form is entirely hid, and the drapery is already disposed by the skill of the taylor. Were a Phidias to obey such absurd commands, he would please no more than an ordinary sculptor; since, in the inferior parts of every art, the learned and the ignorant are nearly upon a level.

These were probably among the reasons that induced the sculptor of that wonderful figure of Laocoon[10] to exhibit him naked, notwithstanding he was surprised in the act of sacrificing to Apollo, and consequently ought to have been shewn in his sacerdotal habits, if those greater reasons had not preponderated. Art is not yet in so high estimation with us, as to obtain so great a sacrifice as the antients made, especially the Grecians, who suffered themselves to be represented naked, whether they were generals, lawgivers, or kings.

Under this head of balancing and chusing the greater reason, or of two evils taking the least, we may consider the conduct of Rubens[11] in the Luxembourg gallery, where he has mixed allegorical figures with representations of real personages, which must be acknowledged to be a fault; yet, if the Artist considered himself as engaged to furnish this gallery with a rich, various, and splendid ornament, this could not be done, at least in an equal degree, without peopling the air and water with these allegorical figures: he therefore accomplished all that he purposed. In this case all lesser considerations, which tend to obstruct the great end of the work, must yield and give way.

The variety which portraits and modern dresses, mixed with allegorical figures, produce, is not to be slightly given up upon a punctilio of reason, when that reason deprives the art in a manner of its very existence. It must always be remembered that the business of a great Painter, is to produce a great picture, he must therefore take especial care not to be cajoled by specious arguments out of his materials.

What has been so often said to the disadvantage of allegorical poetry,—that it is tedious, and uninteresting,—cannot with the same propriety be applied to painting, where the interest is of a different kind. If allegorical painting produces a greater variety of ideal beauty, a richer, a more various and delightful composition, and gives to the artist a greater opportunity of exhibiting his skill, all the interest he wishes for is accomplished: such a picture not only attracts, but fixes the attention.

If it be objected that Rubens judged ill at first in thinking it necessary to make his work so very ornamental, this puts the question upon new ground. It was his peculiar stile; he could paint in no other; and he was selected for that work, probably, because it was his stile. Nobody will dispute but some of the best of the Roman or Bolognian schools would have produced a more learned and more noble work.

This leads us to another important province of taste, that of weighing the value of the different classes of the art, and of estimating them accordingly.

All arts have means within them of applying themselves with success both to the intellectual and sensitive part of our natures. It cannot be disputed, supposing both these means put in practice with equal abilities, to which we ought to give the preference; to him who represents the heroic arts and more dignified passions of man, or to him who, by the help of meretricious ornaments, however elegant and graceful, captivates the sensuality, as it may be called, of our taste. Thus the Roman and Bolognian schools are reasonably preferred to the Venetian, Flemish, or Dutch schools

---

10. **Laocoon:** the central figure of a group (now in the Vatican) attributed to three sculptors of Rhodes. Depicted are the Trojan priest Laocoön and his two sons attacked by serpents while sacrificing at an altar. 11. **Rubens:** Peter Paul Rubens (1577–1640), the Flemish painter, executed a number of history and allegorical paintings for the Luxembourg Palace in Paris; they are now in the Louvre.

as they address themselves to our best and noblest faculties.

Well-turned periods in eloquence, or harmony of numbers in poetry, which are in those arts what colouring is in painting, however highly we may esteem them, can never be considered as of equal importance with the art of unfolding truths that are useful to mankind, and which make us better or wiser. Nor can those works which remind us of the poverty and meanness of our nature, be considered as of equal rank with what excites ideas of grandeur, or raises and dignifies humanity; or, in the words of a late poet, which makes the beholder *learn to venerate himself as man.*[12]

It is reason and good sense therefore which ranks and estimates every art, and every part of that art, according to its importance, from the painter of animated, down to inanimated nature. We will not allow a man, who shall prefer the inferior stile, to say it is his taste; taste here has nothing, or at least ought to have nothing to do with the question. He wants not taste, but sense, and soundness of judgment.

Indeed perfection in an inferior stile may be reasonably preferred to mediocrity in the highest walks of art. A landskip of Claude Lorrain may be preferred to a history[13] by Luca Giordano;[14] but hence appears the necessity of the connoisseur's knowing in what consists the excellency of each class, in order to judge how near it approaches to perfection.

Even in works of the same kind, as in history painting, which is composed of various parts, excellence of an inferior species, carried to a very high degree, will make a work very valuable, and in some measure compensate for the absence of the higher kinds of merit. It is the duty of the connoisseur to know and esteem, as much as it may deserve, every part of painting: he will not then think even Bassano[15] unworthy of his notice, who, though totally devoid of expression, sense, grace, or elegance, may be esteemed on account of his admirable taste of colours, which, in his best works, are little inferior to those of Titian.[16]

Since I have mentioned Bassano, we must do him likewise the justice to acknowledge, that though he did not aspire to the dignity of expressing the characters and passions of men, yet, with respect to facility and truth in his manner of touching animals of all kinds, and giving them what painters call *their character,* few have ever excelled him.

To Bassano we may add Paul Veronese and Tintoret,[17] for their entire inattention to what is justly thought the most essential part of our art, the expression of the passions. Notwithstanding these glaring deficiencies, we justly esteem their works; but it must be remembered, that they do not please from those defects, but from their great excellencies of another kind, and in spite of such transgressions. These excellencies too, as far as they go, are founded in the truth of *general* nature. They tell the *truth,* though not *the whole truth.*

By these considerations, which can never be too frequently impressed, may be obviated two errors which I observed to have been, formerly at least, the most prevalent, and to be most injurious to artists; that of thinking taste and genius to have nothing to do with reason, and that of taking particular living objects for nature.

I shall now say something on that part of *taste,* which, as I have hinted to you before, does not belong so much to the external form of things, but is addressed to the mind, and depends on its original frame, or, to use the expression, the organization of the soul, I mean the imagination and the passions. The principles of these are as invariable as the former, and are to be known and reasoned upon in the same manner, by an appeal to common sense deciding upon the common feelings of mankind. This sense, and these feelings, appear to me of equal authority, and equally conclusive.

Now this appeal implies a general uniformity and agreement in the minds of men. It would be else an idle and vain endeavour to establish rules of art; it would be pursuing a phantom to attempt to move affections with which we were entirely unacquainted. We have no reason to suspect there is a greater difference between our minds than between our forms, of which, though there are no two alike, yet there is a general similitude that goes through the whole race of mankind; and those who have cultivated their taste

---

12. learn . . . man: Oliver Goldsmith, *The Traveler,* l. 334. **13. a history:** a painting of a historical subject; generally regarded by critics as a higher genre than landscape. **14. Luca Giordano:** (1632–1705), Neapolitan painter, chiefly of frescoes. **15. Bassano:** Jacopo da Bassano (1510–92), Venetian painter. **16. Titian:** Tiziano Vecelli (1477–1576), the great Venetian painter.

17. Paul Veronese . . . Tintoret: Veronese (1528–88) and Jacopo Robusti, called Il Tintoretto (1518–94), are famous painters of the Venetian school.

can distinguish what is beautiful or deformed, or, in other words, what agrees with or deviates from the general idea of nature, in one case, as well as in the other.

The internal fabrick of our minds, as well as the external form of our bodies, being nearly uniform; it seems then to follow of course, that as the imagination is incapable of producing any thing originally of itself, and can only vary and combine those ideas with which it is furnished by means of the senses, there will be necessarily an agreement in the imaginations as in the senses of men. There being this agreement, it follows, that in all cases, in our lightest amusements, as well as in our most serious actions and engagements of life, we must regulate our affections of every kind by that of others. The well-disciplined mind acknowledges this authority, and submits its own opinion to the public voice.

It is from knowing what are the general feelings and passions of mankind, that we acquire a true idea of what imagination is; though it appears as if we had nothing to do but to consult our own particular sensations, and these were sufficient to ensure us from all error and mistake.

A knowledge of the disposition and character of the human mind can be acquired only by experience: a great deal will be learned, I admit, by a habit of examining what passes in our bosoms, what are our own motives of action, and of what kind of sentiments we are conscious on any occasion. We may suppose an uniformity, and conclude that the same effect will be produced by the same cause in the minds of others. This examination will contribute to suggest to us matters of enquiry; but we can never be sure that our own sensations are true and right, till they are confirmed by more extensive observation.

One man opposing another determines nothing; but a general union of minds, like a general combination of the forces of all mankind, makes a strength that is irresistible. In fact, as he who does not know himself does not know others, so it may be said with equal truth, that he who does not know others, knows himself but very imperfectly.

A man who thinks he is guarding himself against prejudices by resisting the authority of others, leaves open every avenue to singularity, vanity, self-conceit, obstinacy, and many other vices, all tending to warp the judgment, and prevent the natural operation of his faculties.

This submission to others is a deference which we owe, and indeed are forced involuntarily to pay. In fact, we never are satisfied with our opinions, whatever we may pretend, till they are ratified and confirmed by the suffrages of the rest of mankind. We dispute and wrangle for ever; we endeavour to get men to come to us, when we do not go to them.

He therefore who is acquainted with the works which have pleased different ages and different countries, and has formed his opinion on them, has more materials, and more means of knowing what is analogous to the mind of man, than he who is conversant only with the works of his own age or country. What has pleased, and continues to please, is likely to please again: hence are derived the rules of art, and on this immoveable foundation they must ever stand.

This search and study of the history of the mind ought not to be confined to one art only. It is by the analogy that one art bears to another, that many things are ascertained, which either were but faintly seen, or, perhaps, would not have been discovered at all, if the inventor had not received the first hints from the practices of a sister art on a similar occasion. The frequent allusions which every man who treats of any art is obliged to make to others in order to illustrate and confirm his principles, sufficiently shew their near connection and inseparable relation.

All arts having the same general end, which is to please, and addressing themselves to the same faculties through the medium of the senses, it follows that their rules and principles must have as great affinity as the different materials and the different organs or vehicles by which they pass to the mind, will permit them to retain.

We may therefore conclude, that the real substance, as it may be called, of what goes under the name of taste, is fixed and established in the nature of things; that there are certain and regular causes by which the imagination and passions of men are affected; and that the knowledge of these causes is acquired by a laborious and diligent investigation of nature, and by the same slow progress as wisdom or knowledge of every kind, however instantaneous its operations may appear when thus acquired.

It has been often observed that the good and virtuous man alone can acquire this true or just relish even of works of art. This opinion will not appear entirely without foundation, when we consider that the same habit of mind which is acquired by our search after truth in the more serious duties of life, is only transferred to the pursuit of lighter amusements. The same disposition, the same desire to find something steady, substantial and durable, on which the mind can lean as it were, and rest with safety, actuates us in both cases. The subject only is changed.

We pursue the same method in our search after the idea of beauty and perfection in each; of virtue, by looking forwards beyond ourselves to society, and to the whole; of arts, by extending our views in the same manner to all ages and all times.

Every art, like our own, has in its composition fluctuating as well as fixed principles. It is an attentive enquiry into their difference that will enable us to determine how far we are influenced by custom and habit, and what is fixed in the nature of things.

To distinguish how much has solid foundation, we may have recourse to the same proof by which some hold that wit ought to be tried; whether it preserves itself when translated. That wit is false which can subsist only in one language; and that picture which pleases only one age or one nation, owes its reception to some local or accidental association of ideas.

We may apply this to every custom and habit of life. Thus the general principles of urbanity, politeness, or civility, have been ever the same in all nations; but the mode in which they are dressed is continually varying. The general idea of shewing respect is by making yourself less; but the manner, whether by bowing the body, kneeling, prostration, pulling off the upper part of our dress, or taking away the lower, is a matter of custom.

Thus, in regard to ornaments, it would be unjust to conclude that because they were at first arbitrarily contrived, they are therefore undeserving of our attention; on the contrary, he who neglects the cultivation of those ornaments, acts contrary to nature and reason. As life would be imperfect without its highest ornaments the Arts, so these arts themselves would be imperfect without *their* ornaments.

Though we by no means ought to rank these with positive and substantial beauties, yet it must be allowed that a knowledge of both is essentially requisite towards forming a complete, whole and perfect taste. It is in reality from the ornaments, that arts receive their peculiar character and complexion; we may add, that in them we find the characteristical mark of a national taste, as by throwing up a feather in the air, we know which way the wind blows, better than by a more heavy matter.

The striking distinction between the works of the Roman, Bolognian and Venetian schools, consists more in that general effect which is produced by colours, than in the more profound excellencies of the art; at least it is from thence that each is distinguished and known at first sight. Thus it is the ornaments, rather than the proportions of architecture, which at the first glance distinguish the different orders from each other; the Doric is known by its triglyphs,[18] the Ionic by its volutes,[19] and the Corinthian by its acanthus.[20]

What distinguishes oratory from a cold narration, is a more liberal, though chaste use of those ornaments which go under the name of figurative and metaphorical expressions; and poetry distinguishes itself from oratory by words and expressions still more ardent and glowing. What separates and distinguishes poetry, is more particularly the ornament of *verse:*[21] it is this which gives it its character, and is an essential without which it cannot exist. Custom has appropriated different metre to different kinds of composition, in which the world is not perfectly agreed. In England the dispute is not yet settled, which is to be preferred, rhyme or blank verse. But however we disagree about what these metrical ornaments shall be, that some metre is essentially necessary is universally acknowledged.

In poetry or eloquence, to determine how far figurative or metaphorical language may proceed, and when it begins to be affectation or beside the truth, must be determined by taste, though this taste we must never forget is regulated and formed by the presiding feelings of mankind, by those works which have approved themselves to all times and all persons.

Thus, though eloquence has undoubtedly an essential and intrinsic excellence, and immoveable principles common to all languages, founded in the nature of our passions and affections; yet it has its ornaments and modes of address, which are merely arbitrary. What is approved in the eastern nations as grand and majestic, would be considered by the Greeks and Romans as turgid and inflated; and they, in return, would be thought by the Orientals to express themselves in a cold and insipid manner.

We may add likewise to the credit of ornaments, that it is by their means that art itself accomplishes its

---

18. **triglyphs:** on ancient temples in the Doric style, the repeated divisions, consisting of three vertical grooves, between sections of the frieze. 19. **volutes:** the scroll-like spirals at the top of an Ionic column. 20. **acanthus:** the name of the leaves that form the conventional design at the top of a Corinthian column. 21. **verse:** meter.

purpose. Fresnoy[22] calls colouring, which is one of the chief ornaments of painting, *lena sororis*,[23] that which procures lovers and admirers to the more valuable excellencies of the art.

It appears to be the same right turn of mind which enables a man to acquire the *truth*, or the just idea of what is right in the ornaments, as in the more stable principles of art. It has still the same centre of perfection, though it is the centre of a smaller circle.

To illustrate this by the fashion of dress, in which there is allowed to be a good or bad taste. The component parts of dress are continually changing from great to little, from short to long; but the general form still remains; it is still the same general dress which is comparatively fixed, though on a very slender foundation; but it is on this which fashion must rest. He who invents with the most success, or dresses in the best taste, would probably, from the same sagacity employed to greater purposes, have discovered equal skill, or have formed the same correct taste in the highest labours of art.

I have mentioned taste in dress, which is certainly one of the lowest subjects to which this word is applied; yet, as I have before observed, there is a right even here, however narrow its foundation respecting the fashion of any particular nation. But we have still more slender means of determining, to which of the different customs of different ages or countries we ought to give the preference, since they seem to be all equally removed from nature.

If an European, when he has cut off his beard, and put false hair on his head, or bound up his own natural hair in regular hard knots, as unlike nature as he can possibly make it; and after having rendered them immoveable by the help of the fat of hogs, has covered the whole with flour, laid on by a machine with the utmost regularity; if, when thus attired he issues forth, and meets a Cherokee Indian, who has bestowed as much time at his toilet, and laid on with equal care and attention his yellow and red oker on particular parts of his forehead or cheeks, as he judges most becoming; whoever of these two despises the other for this attention to the fashion of his country; which ever first feels himself provoked to laugh, is the barbarian.

All these fashions are very innocent, neither worth disquisition, nor any endeavour to alter them, as the change would, in all probability, be equally distant from nature. The only circumstances against which indignation may reasonably be moved, is where the operation is painful or destructive of health, such as some of the practices at Otaheite,[24] and the strait lacing of the English ladies; of the last of which practices, how destructive it must be to health and long life, the professor of anatomy took an opportunity of proving a few days since in this Academy.

It is in dress as in things of greater consequence. Fashions originate from those only who have the high and powerful advantages of rank, birth, and fortune. Many of the ornaments of art, those at least for which no reason can be given, are transmitted to us, are adopted, and acquire their consequence from the company in which we have been used to see them. As Greece and Rome are the fountains from whence have flowed all kinds of excellence, to that veneration which they have a right to claim for the pleasure and knowledge which they have afforded us, we voluntarily add our approbation of every ornament and every custom that belonged to them, even to the fashion of their dress. For it may be observed that, not satisfied with them in their own place, we make no difficulty of dressing statues of modern heroes or senators in the fashion of the Roman armour or peaceful robe, we go so far as hardly to bear a statue in any other drapery.

The figures of the great men of those nations have come down to us in sculpture. In sculpture remain almost all the excellent specimens of ancient art. We have so far associated personal dignity to the persons thus represented, and the truth of art to their manner of representation, that it is not in our power any longer to separate them. This is not so in painting; because having no excellent antient portraits, that connexion was never formed. Indeed we could no more venture to paint a general officer in a Roman military habit, than we could make a statue in the present uniform. But since we have no antient portraits to shew how ready we are to adopt those kind of prejudices, we make the best authority among the moderns serve the same purpose. The great variety of excellent portraits with which Vandyke[25] has enriched

22. Fresnoy: Charles-Alphonse du Fresnoy (1611–65), French painter and poet, whose Latin poem *De Arte Graphica* (1668) Reynolds annotated for its translator, William Mason, in 1783. **23. lena sororis:** the endearing procuress.

24. Otaheite: Tahiti, made famous by the explorations of Captain James Cook in 1769. **25. Vandyke:** Sir Anthony Van Dyck (1599–1641), Flemish portraitist. A version of the costume worn by his sitters was stylish in English portraits, especially Gainsborough's, during the 1760's and 1770's.

this nation, we are not content to admire for their real excellence, but extend our approbation even to the dress which happened to be the fashion of that age. We all very well remember how common it was a few years ago for portraits to be drawn in this fantastick[26] dress, and this custom is not yet entirely laid aside. By this means it must be acknowledged very ordinary pictures acquired something of the air and effect of the works of Vandyke, and appeared therefore at first sight to be better pictures than they really were; they appeared so, however, to those only who had the means of making this association, and when made, it was irresistible. But this association is nature, and refers to that secondary truth that comes from conformity to general prejudice and opinion; it is therefore not merely fantastical. Besides the prejudice which we have in favour of antient dresses, there may be likewise other reasons for the effect which they produce; among which we may justly rank the simplicity of them, consisting of little more than one single piece of drapery without those whimsical capricious forms by which all other dresses are embarrassed.

Thus, though it is from the prejudice we have in favour of the antients, who have taught us architecture, that we have adopted likewise their ornaments; and though we are satisfied that neither nature nor reason are the foundation of those beauties which we imagine we see in that art, yet if anyone persuaded of this truth should therefore invent new orders of equal beauty, which we will suppose to be possible, they would not please, nor ought he to complain, since the old has that great advantage of having custom and prejudice on its side. In this case we leave what has every prejudice in its favour, to take that which will have no advantage over what we have left, but novelty, which soon destroys itself, and at any rate is but a weak antagonist against custom.

Ancient ornaments, having the right of possession, ought not to be removed, unless to make room for that which not only has higher pretensions, but such pretensions as will balance the evil and confusion which innovation always brings with it.

To this we may add, that even the durability of the materials will often contribute to give a superiority to one object over another. Ornaments in buildings, with which taste is principally concerned, are composed of materials which last longer than those of which dress is composed; the former therefore make higher pretensions to our favour and prejudice.

26. **fantastick:** The first edition (1776) reads: "Gothic."

Some attention is surely due to what we can no more get rid of than we can go out of ourselves. We are creatures of prejudice; we neither can nor ought to eradicate it; we must only regulate it by reason, which kind of regulation is indeed little more than obliging the lesser, the local and temporary prejudices, to give way to those which are more durable and lasting.

He therefore who in his practice of portrait painting wishes to dignify his subject, which we will suppose to be a Lady, will not paint her in the modern dress, the familiarity of which alone is sufficient to destroy all dignity. He takes care that his work shall correspond to those ideas and that imagination which he knows will regulate the judgment of others; and therefore dresses his figure something with the general air of the antique for the sake of dignity, and preserves something of the modern for the sake of likeness. By this conduct his works correspond with those prejudices which we have in favour of what we continually see; and the relish of the antique simplicity corresponds with what we may call the more learned and scientific prejudice.

There was a statue made not long since of Voltaire,[27] which the sculptor, not having that respect for the prejudices of mankind which he ought to have had, made entirely naked, and as meagre and emaciated as the original is said to be. The consequence was what might have been expected; it remained in the sculptor's shop, though it was intended as a public ornament and a public honour to Voltaire, for it was procured at the expence of his cotemporary wits and admirers.

Whoever would reform a nation, supposing a bad taste to prevail in it, will not accomplish his purpose by going directly against the stream of their prejudices. Men's minds must be prepared to receive what is new to them. Reformation is a work of time. A national taste, however wrong it may be, cannot be totally changed at once; we must yield a little to the prepossession which has taken hold on the mind, and we may then bring people to adopt what would offend them, if endeavoured to be introduced by violence. When Battista Franco[28] was employed, in conjunction with Titian, Paul Veronese and Tintoret, to adorn the library of St. Mark,[29] his work, Vasari says, gave less satisfaction than any of the others: the dry manner of

27. **a statue . . . Voltaire:** The statue, which generated some scandal, was made by Jean-Baptise Pigalle (1714–85). 28. **Battista Franco:** (1510–61), Italian painter of the Roman school. 29. **the library . . . Mark:** the Libraria Vecchia near the basilica of St. Mark, in Venice.

the Roman school was very ill calculated to please eyes that had been accustomed to the luxuriancy, splendor and richness of Venetian colouring. Had the Romans been the judges of this work, probably the determination would have been just contrary; for in the more noble parts of the art, Battista Franco was perhaps not inferior to any of his rivals.

GENTLEMEN,

It has been the main scope and principal end of this discourse to demonstrate the reality of a standard in taste, as well as in corporeal beauty; that a false or depraved taste is a thing as well known, as easily discovered as any thing that is deformed, mis-shapen, or wrong in our form or outward make; and that this knowledge is derived from the uniformity of sentiments among mankind, from whence proceeds the knowledge of what are the general habits of nature, the result of which is an idea of perfect beauty.

If what has been advanced be true, that beside this beauty or truth, which is formed on the uniform, eternal and immutable laws of nature, and which of necessity can be but *one;* that beside this one immutable verity there are likewise what we have called apparent or secondary truths, proceeding from local and temporary prejudices, fancies, fashions or accidental connexion of ideas; if it appears that these last have still their foundation, however slender, in the original fabric of our minds; it follows that all these truths or beauties deserve and require the attention of the artist, in proportion to their stability or duration, or as their influence is more or less extensive. And let me add, that as they ought not to pass their just bounds, so neither do they, in a well-regulated taste, at all prevent or weaken the influence of those general principles, which alone can give to art its true and permanent dignity.

To form this just taste is undoubtedly in your own power, but it is to reason and philosophy that you must have recourse; from them you must borrow the balance by which is to be weighed and estimated the value of every pretension that intrudes itself on your notice.

The general objection which is made to the introduction of Philosophy into the regions of taste, is, that it checks and restrains the flights of the imagination, and gives that timidity which an overcarefulness not to err or act contrary to reason is likely to produce.

It is not so. Fear is neither reason nor philosophy. The true spirit of philosophy, by giving knowledge, gives a manly confidence, and substitutes rational firmness in the place of vain presumption. A man of real taste is always a man of judgment in other respects; and those inventions which either disdain or shrink from reason, are generally, I fear, more like the dreams of a distempered brain than the exalted enthusiasm of a sound and true genius. In the midst of the highest flights of fancy or imagination, reason ought to preside from first to last, though I admit her more powerful operation is upon reflexion.

Let me add, that some of the greatest names of antiquity, and those who have most distinguished themselves in works of genius and imagination, were equally eminent for their critical skill. Plato, Aristotle, Cicero and Horace; and among the moderns, Boileau, Corneille,[30] Pope and Dryden, are at least instances of genius not being destroyed by attention or subjection to rules and science. I should hope therefore, that the natural consequence of what has been said, would be to excite in you a desire of knowing the principles and conduct of the great masters of our art, and respect and veneration for them when known.

DISCOURSE XIII

Delivered to the Students of the Royal Academy, on the Distribution of the Prizes, December 11, 1786

GENTLEMEN,

To discover beauties, or to point out faults, in the works of celebrated Masters, and to compare the conduct of one Artist with another, is certainly no mean or inconsiderable part of criticism; but this is still no more than to know the art through the Artist. This test of investigation must have two capital defects, it must be narrow, and it must be uncertain. To enlarge the boundaries of the Art of Painting, as well as to fix its principles, it will be necessary that, *that* art, and *those* principles should be considered in their correspondence with the principles of the other arts, which like this, address themselves primarily and principally to the imagination. When those connected, and kindred principles are brought together to be compared, another comparison will grow out of this,

30. **Boileau, Corneille:** The critic and poet Nicolas Boileau-Despréaux (1636–1711) and the playwright Pierre Corneille (1606–84) are known for their espousal of objective aesthetic principles.

that is, the comparison of them all, with those of human nature, from whence arts derive the materials upon which they are to produce their effects.

When this comparison of art with art, and of all arts, with the nature of man, if once made with success, our guiding lines are as well ascertained and established, as they can be in matters of this description.

This, as it is the highest stile of criticism, is at the same time the soundest; for it refers to the eternal and immutable nature of things.

You are not to imagine that I mean to open to you at large, or to recommend to your research the whole of this vast field of Science. It is certainly much above my faculties to reach it; and though it may not be above yours, to comprehend it fully, if it were fully and properly brought before you, yet, perhaps the most perfect criticism requires habits of speculation and abstraction, not very consistent with the employment which ought to occupy, and the habits of mind which ought to prevail in a practical Artist. I only point out to you these things, that when you do criticise, (as all who work on a plan, will criticise more or less) your criticism may be built on the foundation of true principles; and that though you may not always travel a great way, the way that you do travel, may be the right road.

I observe, as a fundamental ground, common to all the Arts with which we have any concern in this discourse, that they address themselves only to two faculties of the mind, its imagination and its sensibility.

All Theories which attempt to direct, or to control the Art, upon any principles falsely called rational, which we form to ourselves upon a supposition of what ought in reason to be the end or means of Art, independent of the known first effect produced by objects on the imagination, must be false and delusive. For though it may appear bold to say it, the imagination is here the residence of truth. If the imagination be affected, the conclusion is fairly drawn. If it be not affected, the reasoning is erroneous, because the end is not obtained; the effect itself being the test, and the only test of the truth and efficacy of the means.

There is in the commerce of life, as in Art, a sagacity which is far from being contradictory to *right* reason,[1] and is superior to any occasional exercise of that faculty; which supersedes it; and does not wait for the slow progress of deduction, but goes at once, by what

appears a kind of intuition, to the conclusion. A man endowed with this faculty, feels and acknowledges the truth, though it is not always in his power, perhaps, to give a reason for it; because he cannot recollect and bring before him all the materials that gave birth to his opinion; for very many and very intricate considerations, may unite to form the principle, even of small and minute parts, involved in, or dependent on, a great system of things: though these in process of time are forgotten, the right impression still remains fixed in his mind.

This impression, is the result of the accumulated experience of our whole life, and has been collected we do not always know how, or when. But this mass of collective observation, however acquired, ought to prevail over that reason, which however powerfully exerted on any particular occasion, will probably comprehend but a partial view of the subject; and our conduct in life as well as in the Arts, is, or ought to be, generally governed by this habitual reason: it is our happiness that we are enabled to draw on such funds. If we were obliged to enter into a theoretical deliberation on every occasion, before we act, life would be at a stand, and Art would be impracticable.

It appears to me therefore, that our first thoughts, that is, the effect which any thing produces on our minds on its first appearance, is never to be forgotten; and it demands for that reason, because it is the first, to be laid up with care. If this be not done, the Artist may happen to impose on himself by partial reasoning, by a cold consideration of those animated thoughts which proceed, not perhaps from caprice or rashness (as he may afterwards conceit[2]) but from the fullness of his mind, enriched with the copious stores of all the various inventions which he had ever seen, or had ever passed in his mind. These ideas are infused into his design, without any conscious effort; but, if he be not on his guard, he may reconsider and correct them, till the whole matter is reduced to a common-place invention.

This is sometimes the effect of what I mean to caution you against; that is to say, an unfounded distrust of the imagination and feeling, in favour of narrow, partial, confined, argumentative Theories, and of principles that seem to apply to the design in hand, without considering those general impressions on the fancy in which real principles of *sound reason*, and of much more weight and importance, are

---

DISCOURSE XIII. **1. right reason:** instinctive but self-conscious common sense, as distinguished from ratiocination.

2. conceit: imagine.

involved, and, as it were, lye hid, under the appearance of a sort of vulgar sentiment.

Reason, without doubt, must ultimately determine every thing; at this minute it is required to inform us when that very reason is to give way to feeling.

Though I have often spoke of that mean conception of our art which confines it to mere imitation, I must add, that it may be narrowed to such a mere matter of experiment, as to exclude from it the application of science, which alone gives dignity and compass to any art. But to find proper foundations for Science, is neither to narrow or to vulgarise it; and this is sufficiently exemplified in the success of experimental Philosophy. It is the false system of reasoning, grounded on a partial view of things, against which I would most earnestly guard you. And I do it the rather, because those narrow Theories, so coincident with the poorest and most miserable practice, and which are adopted to give it countenance, have *not* had their origin in the poorest minds, but in the mistakes, or possibly in the mistaken interpretations of great and commanding authorities. We are not therefore in this case misled by feeling, but by false speculation.

When such a man as Plato speaks of Painting as only an imitative art, and that our pleasure proceeds from observing and acknowledging the truth of the imitation,[3] I think he misleads us by a partial Theory. It is in this poor, partial, and so far, false view of the art, that Cardinal Bembo[4] has chosen to distinguish even Raffaelle himself, whom our enthusiasm honours with the name of Divine.

The same sentiment is adopted by Pope in his Epitaph on Sir Godfrey Kneller,[5] and he turns the Panegyrick solely on imitation, as it is a sort of deception.

I shall not think my time misemployed, if by any means I may contribute to confirm your opinion of what ought to be the object of your pursuit; because, though the best critics must always have exploded this strange Idea, yet I know that there is a disposition towards a perpetual recurrence to it, on account of its simplicity and superficial plausibility.

For this reason I shall beg leave to lay before you a few thoughts on this subject; to throw out some hints that may lead your minds to an opinion, (which I take to be the truth) that Painting is not only, not to be considered as an imitation, operating by deception, but that it is, and ought to be in many points of view, and strictly speaking, no imitation at all of external nature.

Perhaps it ought to be as far removed from the vulgar Idea of Imitation, as the refined civilized state in which we live, is removed from a gross state of nature; and those who have not cultivated their imaginations, which the majority of mankind certainly have not, may be said, (in regard to arts) to continue in this state of nature. Such men will always prefer imitation, to that excellence which is addressed to another faculty that they do not possess; but these are not the persons to whom a Painter is to look, any more than a judge of morals and manners, ought to refer controverted points upon those subjects, to the opinions of people taken from the banks of the Ohio, or from New Holland.[6]

It is the lowest stile only of arts, whether of Painting, Poetry, or Music, that may be said, in the vulgar sense, to be naturally pleasing.

The higher efforts of those arts, we know by experience do not affect minds wholly uncultivated. This refined taste is the consequence of education and habit; we are born only with a capacity of entertaining this refinement, as we are born with a disposition to receive and obey all the rules and regulations of society; and so far it may be said to be natural to us, and no further.

What has been said, may shew the Artist how necessary it is, when he looks about him for the advice and criticism of his friends, to make some distinction of the character, taste, experience, and observation in this Art, of those, from whom it is received.

An ignorant uneducated man may, like Apelles's critic, be a competent judge of the truth of the representation of a sandal;[7] or to go somewhat higher, like Moliere's old woman, may decide upon what is nature, in regard to comic humour:[8] but a Critic in the higher

3. **Painting . . . imitation:** See Plato, *Republic*, Book X.
4. **Cardinal Bembo:** Pietro Bembo (1470–1547), an Italian author who valued Raphael's portraits for their likeness to their subjects. 5. **his . . . Kneller:** carved on the monument of the painter Kneller (1646–1723) in Westminster Abbey. Pope says: "Living, great Nature fear'd he might outvie / Her works; and dying, fears herself may die."

6. **New Holland:** Australia. 7. **the truth . . . sandal:** It is said that a Greek shoemaker once pointed out to Apelles that he had painted a sandal incorrectly. 8. **like . . . humour:** The great French playwright Molière (Jean-Baptiste Poquelin) (1622–73) is said to have tested his comedies by reading them to his elderly maid.

stile of Art, ought to possess the same refined taste, which directed the Artist in his work.

To illustrate this principle by a comparison with other Arts, I shall now produce some instances to shew that they, as well as our own Art, renounce the narrow idea of nature, and the narrow theories derived from that mistaken principle, and apply to that reason only which informs us, not what imitation is, a natural representation of a given object, but what it is natural for the imagination to be delighted with. And perhaps there is no better way of acquiring this knowledge, than by this kind of analogy: Each art will corroborate and mutually reflect the truth on the other. Such a kind of juxta-position may likewise have this use, that whilst the Artist is amusing himself in the contemplation of other Arts, he may habitually transfer the principles of those Arts to that which he professes, which ought to be always present to his mind, and to which every thing is to be referred.

So far is Art from being derived from, or having any immediate intercourse with particular nature as its model, that there are many Arts that set out with a professed deviation from it.

This is certainly not so exactly true in regard to Painting and Sculpture. Our elements are laid in gross common nature, an exact imitation of what is before us. But when we advance to the higher state, we consider this power of imitation, though first in the order of acquisition, as by no means the highest in the scale of perfection.

Poetry addresses itself to the same faculties and the same dispositions as Painting, though by different means. The object of both is to accommodate itself to all the natural propensities and inclinations of the mind.

The very existence of Poetry depends on the licence it assumes of deviating from actual nature, in order to gratify natural propensities by other means, which are found by experience full as capable of affording such gratification. It sets out with a language in the highest degree artificial, a construction of measured words, such as never is, nor ever was used by man. Let this measure be what it may, whether hexameter or any other metre used in Latin or Greek, or Rhyme, or Blank Verse varied with pauses and accents, in modern languages, they are all equally removed from nature, and equally a violation of common speech. When this artificial mode has been established as the vehicle of sentiment, there is another principle in the human mind, to which the work must be referred, which still renders it more artificial, carries it still further from common nature, and deviates only to render it more perfect. That principle is the sense of congruity, coherence, and consistency, which is a real existing principle in man; and it must be gratified. Therefore having once adopted a stile and a measure not found in common discourse, it is required that the sentiments also should be, in the same proportion, elevated above common nature, from the necessity of there being an agreement of the parts among themselves, that one uniform whole may be produced.

To correspond therefore with this general system of deviation from nature, the manner in which Poetry is offered to the ear, the tone in which it is recited, should be as far removed from the tone of conversation, as the words of which that Poetry is composed.

This naturally suggests the idea of modulating the voice by art, which I suppose may be considered as accomplished to the highest degree of excellence in the recitative of the Italian Opera, as we may conjecture it was in the chorus that attended the antient drama.

And, though the most violent passions, the highest distress, even death itself, are expressed in singing or recitative, I would not admit as sound criticism the condemnation of such exhibitions on account of their being unnatural.

If it is natural for our senses, and our imaginations, to be delighted with singing, with instrumental music, with poetry, and with graceful action taken separately, (none of them being in the vulgar sense natural, even in that separate state,) it is conformable to experience, and therefore agreeable to reason, as connected with, and referred to experience, that we should also be delighted with this union of music, poetry, and graceful action, joined to every circumstance of pomp and magnificence calculated to strike the senses of the spectator.

Shall reason stand in the way and tell us, we ought not to like what we know we do like, and prevent us from feeling the full effect of this complicated exertion of art? This is what I would understand by poets and painters being allowed to dare every thing; for what can be more daring, than accomplishing the purpose and end of art, by a complication of means, none of which have their archetypes in actual nature.

So far therefore is servile imitation from being necessary, that whatever is familiar, or in any way reminds us of what we see and hear every day, perhaps, does not belong to the higher provinces of art, either in poetry or painting.

The mind is to be transported, as Shakspeare expresses it, *beyond the ignorant present*,[9] to ages past. Another, and a higher order of beings is supposed, and to those beings, every thing which is introduced into the work must correspond. Of this conduct, under these circumstances, the Roman and Florentine schools afford sufficient examples. Their style by this means is raised and elevated above all others, and, by the same means, the compass of art itself is enlarged.

We often see grave and great subjects attempted by artists of another school; who, though excellent in the lower class of art, proceeding on the principles which regulate that class, and not recollecting, or not knowing, that they were to address themselves to another faculty of the mind, have become perfectly ridiculous.

The picture which I have at present in my thoughts, is, a sacrifice of Iphigenia, painted by Jean Steen,[10] a painter of whom I have formerly had occasion to speak with the highest approbation; and even in this picture, the subject of which is by no means adapted to his genius, there is nature and expression; but it is such expression, and the countenances are so familiar, and consequently so vulgar, and the whole accompanied with such finery of silks and velvets, that one would be almost tempted to doubt, whether the artist did not purposely intend to burlesque his subject.

Instances of the same kind we frequently see in poetry. Parts of Hobbes's translation of Homer[11] are remembered and repeated merely for the familiarity and meanness of their phraseology, so ill corresponding with the ideas which ought to have been expressed, and, as I conceive, with the style of the original.

We may proceed in the same manner through the comparatively inferior branches of art. There are in works of that class, the same distinction of a higher and a lower style; and they take their rank and degree in proportion as the artist departs more, or less, from common nature, and makes it an object of his attention to strike the imagination of the spectator by ways belonging specially to art,—unobserved and untaught out of the school of its practice.

If our judgements are to be directed by narrow, vulgar, untaught or rather ill-taught reason, we must prefer a portrait by Denner,[12] or any other high

finisher, to those of Titian or Vandyck; and a landskip of Vanderhyde,[13] to those of Titian or Rubens; for they are certainly more exact representations of nature.

If we suppose a view of nature represented with all the truth of the *camera obscura*, and the same scene represented by a great Artist, how little and mean will the one appear in comparison of the other, where no superiority is supposed from the choice of the subject. The scene shall be the same, the difference only will be in the manner in which it is presented to the eye. With what additional superiority then will the same Artist appear when he has the power of selecting his materials as well as elevating his stile.

Like Nicolas Poussin, he transports us to the environs of antient Rome, with all the objects which a literary education makes so precious and interesting to man: or like Sebastian Bourdon,[14] he leads us to the dark antiquity of the Pyramids of Egypt; or, like Claude Lorrain, he conducts us to the tranquillity of Arcadian[15] scenes, and fairy land.

Like the history Painter, a painter of landskips in this stile and with this conduct, sends the imagination back into antiquity; and, like the Poet, he makes the elements sympathise with his subject: Whether the clouds roll in volumes like those of Titian or Salvator Rosa,[16]—or, like those of Claude,[17] are gilded with the setting sun; whether the mountains have sudden and bold projections, or are gently sloped; whether the branches of his trees shoot out abruptly in right angles from their trunks, or follow each other with only a gentle inclination.

All these circumstances contribute to the general character of the work, whether it be of the elegant, or of the more sublime kind.

If we add to this, the powerful materials of lightness and darkness, over which the Artist has complete dominion, to vary and dispose them as he pleases, to diminish, or increase them, as will best suit his purpose, and correspond to the general idea of his work; A landskip thus conducted, under the influence of a Poetical mind, will have the same superiority over the more ordinary and common views, as Milton's *Allegro* and *Penseroso* have over a cold prosaic narration or description; and such a Picture would make a more

---

9. the mind . . . present: See *Macbeth*, I. v. 57. 10. Jean Steen: Jan Steen (1626–79), Dutch painter primarily of low life. 11. Hobbes's . . . Homer: published in 1673–76 by the philosopher Thomas Hobbes (1588–1679). 12. Denner: Balthasar Denner (1685–1749), German painter of portraits and miniatures.

13. Vanderhyde: Jan van der Heyden (1637–1712), Dutch painter of realistic architectural and street scenes. 14. Sebastian Bourdon: (1616–71), French history painter. 15. Arcadian: pastoral. 16. Salvator Rosa: (1615–73), Italian painter known for landscapes and battle scenes. 17. Claude: Claude Gellée (1600–82), also called Claude Lorrain.

forcible impression on the mind than the real scenes, were they presented before us.

If we look abroad to other Arts, we may observe the same distinction, the same division into two classes, each of them acting under the influence of two different principles, in which the one follows nature, the other varies it, and sometimes departs from it.

The Theatre, which is said *to hold the mirror up to nature*, comprehends both those ideas.

The lower kind of Comedy, or Farce, like the inferior style of Painting, the more naturally it is represented, the better; but the higher, appears to me to aim no more at imitation, so far as it belongs to any thing like deception; or to expect that the spectators should think that the events there represented, are really passing before them, than Raffaelle in his Cartoons,[18] or Poussin in his Sacraments,[19] expected it to be believed, even for a moment, that what they exhibited were real figures.

For want of this distinction, the world is filled with false criticism. Raffaelle is praised for naturalness and deception, which he certainly has not accomplished, and as certainly never intended; and our late great actor, Garrick,[20] has been as ignorantly praised by his friend Fielding; who doubtless imagined he had hit upon an ingenious device, by introducing in one of his Novels, (otherwise a work of the highest merit,) an ignorant man, mistaking Garrick's representation of a scene in Hamlet, for reality.[21]

A very little reflection will convince us, that there is not one circumstance in the whole scene that is of the nature of deception. The merit and excellence of Shakespear, and of Garrick, when they were engaged in such scenes, is of a different and much higher kind.

But what adds to the falsity of this intended compliment, is, that the best stage representation, appears even more unnatural to a person of such a character, who is supposed never to have seen a play before, than it does to those who have had a habit of allowing for those necessary deviations from nature which the Art requires.

In Theatric representation, great allowances must always be made for the place in which the exhibition is represented; for the surrounding company, the lighted candles, the scenes visibly shifted in your sight, and the language of blank verse, so different from common English; which merely as English must appear surprising in the mouths of Hamlet, and all the court and natives of Denmark.

These allowances are made, but their being made, puts an end to all manner of deception; and further, we know that the more low, illiterate, and vulgar any person is, the less he will be disposed to make these allowances, and of course to be deceived by any imitation; the things in which the trespass against nature and common probability is made in favour of the Theatre, being quite within the sphere of such uninformed men.

Though I have no intention of entering into all the circumstances of unnaturalness in Theatrical representations, I must observe, that even the expression of violent passion, is not always the most excellent in proportion as it is the most natural, so great terror and such disagreeable sensations may be communicated to the audience, that the balance may be destroyed by which pleasure is preserved, and holds its predominancy in the mind: violent distortion of action, harsh screamings of the voice, however great the occasion, or however natural on such occasion, are therefore not admissible in the Theatric Art. Many of these allowed deviations from nature arise from the necessity which there is, that every thing should be raised and enlarged beyond its natural state, that the full effect may come home to the spectator, which otherwise would be lost in the comparatively extensive space of the Theatre. Hence the deliberate and stately step, the studied grace of action which seems to enlarge the dimensions of the Actor, and alone to fill the stage. All this unnaturalness, though right and proper in its place, would appear affected and ridiculous in a private room; *quid enim deformius, quam scenam in vitam transferre?*[22]

And here I must observe, and I believe it may be considered as a general rule, that no Art can be engrafted with success on another art. For though they all profess the same origin, and to proceed from the same stock, yet each has its own peculiar modes both of imitating nature, and of deviating from it, each for the accomplishment of its own particular purpose.

18. Cartoons: The seven paintings of *The Acts of the Apostles* are all that remain of the original twenty-five made as patterns for the tapestries of the Sistine Chapel, in the Vatican; the figures are life-size. The designs hang in the Victoria and Albert Museum. **19. Sacraments:** a series of seven paintings depicting the origin of the Christian sacraments. **20. Garrick:** the actor David Garrick died in 1779. **21. mistaking . . . reality:** See Fielding's *Tom Jones*, XVI. v.

22. quid . . . transferre: What could be more disgusting than to introduce the theatrical into real life?

These deviations, more especially, will not bear transplantation to another soil.

If a Painter should endeavour to copy the Theatrical pomp and parade of dress and attitude, instead of that simplicity, which is not a greater beauty in life, than it is in Painting, we should condemn such Pictures as painted in the meanest stile.

So also Gardening, as far as Gardening is an Art, or entitled to that appellation, is a deviation from nature; for if the true taste consists, as many hold, in banishing every appearance of Art, or any traces of the footsteps of man, it would then be no longer a Garden.

Even though we define it, "Nature to advantage dress'd,"[23] and in some sense it is such, and much more beautiful and commodious for the recreation of man; it is however, when so dress'd, no longer a subject for the pencil of a Landskip Painter, as all Landskip Painters know, who love to have recourse to Nature herself, and to dress her according to the principles of their own Art, which are far different from those of Gardening, even when conducted according to the most approved principles, and such as a Landskip Painter himself would adopt in the disposition of his own grounds, for his own private satisfaction.

I have brought together as many instances as appear necessary, to make out the several points which I wished to suggest to your consideration in this Discourse; that your own thoughts may lead you further in the use that may be made of the analogy of the Arts, and of the restraint which a full understanding of the diversity of many of their principles ought to impose, on the employment of that analogy.

The great end of all those arts, is, to make an impression on the imagination and the feeling. The imitation of nature frequently does this. Sometimes it fails, and something else succeeds. I think therefore the true test of all the arts, is not solely whether the production is a true copy of nature, but whether it answers the end of art, which is to produce a pleasing effect upon the mind.

It remains only to speak a few words of Architecture, which does not come under the denomination of an imitative art. It applies itself, like Music (and I believe we may add Poetry) directly to the imagination, without the intervention of any kind of imitation.

There is in Architecture, as in Painting, an inferior branch of art, in which the imagination appears to have no concern. It does not however acquire the name of a polite and liberal art, from its usefulness, or administering to our wants or necessities; but, from some higher principle: we are sure that in the hands of a man of genius it is capable of inspiring sentiment, and of filling the mind with great and sublime ideas.

It may be worth the attention of Artists, to consider what materials are in their hands, that may contribute to this end; and whether this art has it not in its power to address itself to the imagination with effect, by more ways than are generally employed by Architects.

To pass over the effect produced by that general symmetry and proportion, by which, the eye is delighted as the ear is with Music, Architecture certainly possesses many principles in common with Poetry and Painting.

Among those which may be reckoned as the first, is, that of affecting the imagination by means of association of ideas. Thus, for instance, as we have naturally a veneration for antiquity, whatever building brings to our remembrance antient customs and manners, such as the Castles of the Barons of antient Chivalry, is sure to give this delight. Hence it is that *Towers and battlements*[24] are so often selected by the Painter and the Poet, to make a part of the composition of their ideal Landskip; and it is from hence in a great degree, that in the buildings of Vanbrugh,[25] who was a Poet as well as an Architect, there is a greater display of imagination, than we shall find perhaps in any other; and this is the ground of the effect which we feel in many of his works, notwithstanding the faults with which many of them are justly charged. For this purpose, Vanbrugh appears to have had recourse to some principles of the Gothic Architecture; which, though not so antient as the Grecian, is more so to our imagination, with which the Artist is more concerned than with absolute truth.

The Barbaric splendor of those Asiatic Buildings, which are now publishing by a member of this Academy,[26] may possibly, in the same manner, furnish an Architect, not with models to copy, but with hints of composition and general effect which would not otherwise have occurred.

23. Nature . . . dress'd: See Pope's *Essay on Criticism*, l. 297, in Part Two.

24. Towers and battlements: See Milton's *L'Allegro*, l. 77. **25. Vanbrugh:** Sir John Vanbrugh (1664–1726), writer of comedies and designer of buildings, many of which resembled castles. Blenheim and Castle Howard are two of his best-known works. **26. a member . . . Academy:** William Hodges (1744–97), who published *Select Views of India* in 1786.

It is, I know, a delicate and hazardous thing, (and as such I have already pointed it out) to carry the principles of one art to another, or even to reconcile in one object, the various modes of the same Art, when they proceed on different principles. The sound rules of the Grecian Architecture are not to be lightly sacrificed. A deviation from them, or even an addition to them, is like a deviation, or addition to, or from the Rules of other Arts, fit only for a great master, who is thoroughly conversant in the nature of man, as well as all combinations in his own Art.

It may not be amiss for the Architect to take advantage *sometimes* of that to which I am sure the Painter ought always to have his Eyes open, I mean the use of accidents; to follow when they lead, and to improve them, rather than always to trust to a regular plan. It often happens that additions have been made to houses, at various times, for use or pleasure. As such buildings depart from regularity, they now and then acquire something of scenery by this accident, which I should think might not unsuccessfully be adopted by an Architect, in an original plan, if it does not too much interfere with convenience. Variety and intricacy is a beauty and excellence in every other of the Arts which address the imagination, and why not in Architecture?

The forms and turnings of the streets of London, and other old Towns, are produced by accident, without any original plan or design, but they are not always the less pleasant to the walker, or spectator, on that account. On the contrary, if the City had been built on the regular plan of Sir Christopher Wren,[27] the effect might have been, as we know it is in some new parts of the Town, rather unpleasing: the uniformity might have produced weariness, and a slight degree of disgust.

I can pretend to no skill in the detail of Architecture. I judge now of the Art, merely as a Painter. When I speak of Vanbrugh, I mean to speak of him in the language of our Art. To speak then of Vanbrugh in the language of a Painter, he had originality of invention, he understood light and shadow, and had great skill in composition. To support his principal object, he produced his second and third groups or masses; he

perfectly understood in *his* Art what is the most difficult in ours; the conduct of the Back-ground, by which the design and invention is set off to the greatest advantage. What the back-ground is, in Painting, in Architecture is the real ground on which the building is erected; and no Architect took greater care than he that his work should not appear crude and hard. That is, it did not abruptly start out of the ground without expectation or preparation.

This is a Tribute, which a Painter owes to an Architect who composed like a Painter; and was defrauded of the due reward of his merit, by the Wits of his time, who did not understand the principles of Composition in Poetry better than he; and who knew little, or nothing, of what he understood perfectly, the general ruling principles of Architecture and Painting.

His fate was that of the great Perrault;[28] both were the objects of the petulant sarcasms of factious men of Letters; and both have left some of the fairest ornaments, which to this day decorate their several countries; the façade of the Louvre, Blenheim, and Castle Howard.

Upon the whole, it seems to me, that the object and intention of all the Arts, is to supply the natural imperfection of things, and often to gratify the mind by realizing, and embodying, what never existed but in the imagination.

It is allowed on all hands, that facts, and events, however they may bind the Historian, have no dominion over the Poet or the Painter. With us, History is made to bend and conform to this great Idea of Art. And why? Because these Arts, in their highest province, are not addressed to the gross senses, but to the desires of the mind, to that spark of divinity which we have within, impatient of being circumscribed and pent up by the world which is about us.

Just so much as our Art has of this, just so much of dignity, I had almost said of divinity, it exhibits; and those of our Artists who possessed this mark of distinction in the highest degree, acquired from thence the glorious appellation of Divine.

---

27. **Sir . . . Wren:** This famous architect (1631–1723) drew up a proposal after the Great Fire of 1666 for rebuilding London on a more orderly pattern; the proposal was not adopted.

28. **the great Perrault:** Claude Perrault (1613–88), French physician and architect who helped design the imposing east façade of the Louvre; his work was criticized for its incongruity with the rest of the structure.

Oliver Goldsmith

c. 1730–1774

Goldsmith was sometimes so vain and ridiculous in company that he is almost as well remembered for his personal follies as for his remarkable literary versatility and ease. Many of his contemporaries found it astonishing that so gauche a creature managed to write anything at all. They would have found it incredible that one novel, one play, and one poem of his have become permanent.

He was born of an Irish rural family locally renowned for improvidence and eccentricity. His father was a crude Anglican curate. Goldsmith attended village schools in the town of Lissoy, which some have been pleased to equate with the "Sweet Auburn" of *The Deserted Village*. He was never a comely child—his upper lip protruded and his chin receded—and an attack of smallpox left him positively ugly. Awkward and stammering, he entered Trinity College, Dublin, in 1745 as a sizar, a poverty-stricken grade of student whose duties included waiting on the more fortunate. At Trinity he became brash, proud, and clever; he was already displaying a talent for disingenuousness—his later plagiarisms are an embarrassment—and he spent almost as much time gambling and rioting as studying. Although his academic career was undistinguished, he obtained his bachelor's degree in 1750 and returned home, where he began reading for holy orders. When he revealed no capacity for divinity, he turned to the study of law and finally to medicine, which he read at the universities of Edinburgh and Leyden from 1752 to 1755. During these years he was almost constantly in debt: he was dressing beyond his means and both gambling and giving away money at every opportunity.

In 1755 he moved from Leyden to Paris, ostensibly to continue his medical studies but actually to embark on a sort of poor man's Grand Tour. For a year he strolled about Europe, supporting himself by playing the flute, "borrowing," and gambling. Returning to England in 1756, he set up as a physician in London, but after a year of struggling in the medical business he abandoned it and started hack writing to redeem himself from poverty. For the rest of his life he scribbled, compiled, reviewed, translated (from French), and edited—and his earnings vanished the moment they were in his hands.

In 1759 he brought out *An Enquiry into the Present State of Polite Learning in Europe,* a survey of national characteristics and of various systems of private and commercial patronage. The same year he published eight numbers of a weekly periodical, *The*

Bee. In 1760 and 1761 *The Public Ledger* carried his *Chinese Letters,* later collected as *The Citizen of the World.* His *Life of Richard Nash, Esq.* (the famous "Beau" Nash of Bath), published in 1762, is a milestone in candid biography. His first work to bear his name was *The Traveler* (1765), a heroic-couplet poem about nationality and happiness. This work brought him fame, and he now circulated—in embarrassingly loud clothes—with Johnson, Reynolds, and Burke, whom he frequently puzzled by his clownishness, impulsiveness, and envy. His idyllic novel *The Vicar of Wakefield* (1766) attained its full popularity only in the next century.

His comedy *The Good Natured Man* (1768) was a failure on its first performance, but after he tinkered with it, it had a successful run. His greatest triumph was his poem *The Deserted Village* (1770), which established his contemporary reputation as a writer second only to Samuel Johnson. He kept up his income if not his reputation for scholarship by compiling a four-volume *History of England* (1771). His best-known play, *She Stoops to Conquer* (1773), was a success at Covent Garden, although it did not drive from the stage, as Goldsmith hoped it would, the sentimental comedies of Hugh Kelly and Richard Cumberland.

He was afflicted by illness during his last years, and even his accustomed lavish expenditure seemed no longer to make him happy. When he died deeply in debt, Johnson, who was always sensitive to Goldsmith's odd charm, commented, "Was ever poet so trusted before?" Some of his debts were liquidated by two works that appeared posthumously in 1774, a two-volume *Grecian History* and an eight-volume *History of the Earth and Animated Nature.*

Goldsmith's appalling blunders in conversation, the result of his frantic desire to be admired, were the wonder of his friends. Reynolds observed:

> No man's company was ever more greedily sought after, for in his company the ignorant and illiterate were not only easy and free from any mortifying restraint, but even their vanity was gratified to find so admirable a writer so much upon a level, or inferior to themselves, in the arts of conversation.

After one humiliating exhibition Mrs. Thrale wrote, "Poor little Dr. how he does disgrace himself!" And although Johnson once said, "He seldom comes where he is not more ignorant than any one else," he also cautioned after Goldsmith's death, "Let not his frailties be remembered; he was a very great man," and in admiration of his happy versatility described him in the Latin epitaph he composed for his monument in Westminster Abbey as poet, physician, and historian, who, working in almost every literary kind, "touched none that he did not adorn." But the tribute that might have delighted Goldsmith most is Reynolds's: "Wherever he was there was no yawning."

Temple Scott's *Oliver Goldsmith Bibliographically and Biographically Considered* (1928) is an interesting discussion; useful bibliographical listings are those by I. A. Williams, in *Seven XVIII-Century Bibliographies* (1924), and R. S. Crane, in *The Cambridge Bibliography of English Literature,* ed. F. W. Bateson (4 vols., 1941). Goldsmith's works are edited by Arthur Friedman (5 vols., 1966); R. S. Crane has edited *New Essays by Oliver Goldsmith* (1927). The disappointing *Letters* are edited by K. C. Balderston (1928). The biography by Austin Dobson (1888) is graceful, and that by R. M. Wardle (1957) is accurate. James Boswell brilliantly displayed Goldsmith's weaknesses in *The Life of Samuel Johnson* (1791); for a more subtle reading of his enigmatic character, see Sir Joshua Reynolds in *Portraits*, ed. F. W. Hilles (1952).

FROM

AN ENQUIRY INTO THE PRESENT STATE OF POLITE LEARNING IN EUROPE

❦

Published anonymously in April, 1759, this work was the fruit of Goldsmith's year of "philosophic vagabondage" in Europe. He was convinced that contemporary literature was in decline and in thirteen chapters surveys the economic and social conditions both favorable and unfavorable to literature in Italy, Germany, Holland, France, and Great Britain. According to Thomas Percy, the book was written "in a wretched dirty room, in which there was but one chair."

The text is that of the first edition (1759), with substantive revisions incorporated from the second edition (1774).

❦

CHAP. IX

Of Learning in Great Britain.

To acquire a character for learning among the English at present, it is necessary to know much more than is either important or useful. It seems the spirit of the times for men here to exhaust their natural sagacity in exploring the intricacies of another man's thought, and thus never to have leisure to think for themselves; others have carried on learning from that stage, where the good sense of our ancestors have thought it too minute or too speculative to instruct or amuse. By the industry of such, the sciences which in themselves are easy of access, affright the learner with the severity of their appearance. He sees them surrounded with speculation and subtilty, placed there by their professors as if with a view of deterring his approach. From hence it happens, that the generality

of readers fly from the scholar to the compiler, who offers them a more safe and speedy conveyance.

FROM this fault also arises that mutual contempt between the scholar and the man of the world, of which every day's experience furnisheth instances.

THE man of taste, however, stands neutral in this controversy; he seems placed in a middle station, between the world and the cell, between learning and common sense. He teaches the vulgar on what part of a character to lay the emphasis of praise, and the scholar where to point his application so as to deserve it. By his means, even the philosopher, acquires popular applause, and all that are truly great the admiration of posterity. By means of polite learning alone, the patriot and the hero, the man who praiseth virtue, and he who practices it, who fights successfully for his country, or who dies in its defence, becomes immortal. But this taste now seems cultivated with less ardour than formerly, and consequently the public must one day expect to see the advantages arising from it, and the exquisite pleasures it affords our leisure entirely annihilated. For if, as it should seem, the rewards of genius are improperly directed; if those who are capable of supporting the honour of the times by their writings, prefer opulence to fame; if the stage should be shut to writers of merit, and open only to interest or intrigue. If such should happen to be the vile complexion of the times, (and that it is nearly so we shall shortly see) the very virtue of the age will be forgotten by posterity; and nothing remembered, except our filling a chasm in the registers of time, or having served to continue the species.

CHAP. X

Of rewarding Genius in England.

THERE is nothing authors are more apt to lament, than want of encouragement from the age. Whatever their differences in other respects, they are all ready to unite in this complaint, and each indirectly offers himself as an instance of the truth of his assertion.

THE beneficed divine, whose wants are only imaginary, expostulates as bitterly as the poorest author. Should interest or good fortune, advance the divine to a bishopric, or the poor son of Parnassus into that place which the other has resign'd; both are authors no longer, one goes to prayers once a day, kneels upon cushions of velvet, and thanks gracious heaven for having made the circumstances of all mankind so extremely happy; the other battens on all the delicacies of life, enjoys his wife and his easy chair, and sometimes, for the sake of conversation, deplores the luxury of these degenerate days.

ALL encouragements to merit are therefore misapplied, which make the author too rich to continue his profession. There can be nothing more just than the old observation, that authors, like running horses, should be fed but not fattened. If we would continue them in our service, we should reward them with a little money and a great deal of praise, still keeping their avarice subservient to their ambition. Not that I think a writer incapable of filling an employment with dignity, I would only insinuate, that when made a bishop or statesman, he will continue to please us as a writer no longer. As to resume a former allusion, the running horse, when fattened, will still be fit for very useful purposes, though unqualified for a courser.

No nation gives greater encouragements to learning than we do; yet, at the same time, none are so injudicious in the application. We seem to confer them with the same view, that statesmen have been known to grant employments at court, rather as bribes to silence, than incentives to emulation.

UPON this principle, all our magnificent endowments of colleges are erroneous, and at best, more frequently enrich the prudent than reward the ingenious. A lad whose passions are not strong enough in youth to mislead him from that path of science, which his tutors, and not his inclinations, have chalked out, by four or five years perseverance, may probably obtain every advantage and honour his college can bestow. I forget whether the simile has been used before, but I would compare the man, whose youth has been thus past in the tranquility of dispassionate prudence, to liquors which never ferment, and consequently, continue always muddy. Passions may raise a commotion in the youthful breast, but they disturb only to refine it. However this be, mean talents are often rewarded in colleges, with an easy subsistence. The candidates for preferments of this kind, often regard their admission as a patent for future indolence;

so that a life begun in studious labour, is often continued in luxurious affluence.

AMONG the universities abroad, I have ever observed their riches and their learning in a reciprocal proportion, their stupidity and pride encreasing with their opulence. Happening once in conversation with Gaubius of Leyden,[1] to mention the college of Edinburgh, he began by complaining, that all the English students, which formerly came to his university, now went intirely there; and the fact surprized him more, as Leyden was now as well as ever furnished with masters excellent in their respective professions. He concluded by asking, if the professors of Edinburgh were rich. I reply'd, that the salary of a professor there seldom amounted to more than thirty pounds a year. Poor men, says he, I heartily wish they were better provided for, until they become rich, we can have no expectation of English students at Leyden.

PREMIUMS also, proposed for literary excellence, when given as encouragements to boys may be useful, but when designed as rewards to men, are certainly misapplied. We have seldom seen a performance of any great merit, in consequence of rewards proposed in this manner. Who has ever observed a writer of any eminence, a candidate in so precarious a contest? The man who knows the real value of his own genius, will no more venture it upon an uncertainty, than he who knows the true use of a guinea, will stake it with a sharper.

EVERY encouragement given to stupidity, when known to be such, is also a negative insult upon genius. This appears in nothing more evident, than the undistinguished success of those who solicit subscriptions. When first brought into fashion, subscriptions were conferred upon the ingenious alone, or those who were reputed such. But at present, we see them made a resource of indigence, and requested not as rewards of merit, but as a relief of distress. If tradesmen happen to want skill in conducting their own business, yet they are able to write a book; if mechanics want money, or ladies shame, they write books and solicit subscriptions. Scarce a morning passes, that proposals of this nature are not thrust into the half-opening doors of the rich, with, perhaps, a paltry petition, shewing the author's wants, but not his merits. I would not willingly prevent that pity which is due to

AN ENQUIRY INTO POLITE LEARNING: *Chapter X.* **1. Gaubius of Leyden:** Jerome-David Gaube (1705–80), professor of botany at the University of Leyden.

indigence, but while the streams of liberality are thus diffused, they must in the end become proportionably shallow.

WHAT then are the proper encouragements of genius? I answer, subsistence and respect, for these are rewards congenial to its nature. Every animal has an aliment peculiarly suited to its constitution. The heavy ox seeks nourishment from earth; the light cameleon has been supposed to exist on air; a sparer diet even than this, will satisfy the man of true genius, for he makes a luxurious banquet upon empty applause. It is this alone, which has inspired all that ever was truly great and noble among us. It is, as Cicero finely calls it the eccho of virtue. Avarice is the passion of inferior natures; money the pay of the common herd. The author who draws his quill merely to take a purse, no more deserves success than he who presents a pistol.

WHEN the link between patronage and learning was entire, then all who deserved fame were in a capacity of attaining it. When the great Somers[2] was at the helm, patronage was fashionable among our nobility. The middle ranks of mankind, who generally imitate the Great, then followed their example; and applauded from fashion, if not from feeling. I have heard an old poet of that glorious age[3] say, that a dinner with his lordship, has procured him invitations for the whole week following: that an airing in his patron's chariot, has supplied him with a citizen's coach on every future occasion. For who would not be proud to entertain a man who kept so much good company?

BUT this link now seems entirely broken. Since the days of a certain prime minister of inglorious memory,[4] the learned have been kept pretty much at a distance. A jockey, or a laced player, supplies the place of the scholar, poet, or the man of virtue. Those conversations, once the result of wisdom, wit, and innocence, are how turned to humbler topics, little more being expected from a companion than a laced coat, a pliant bow, and an immoderate friendship for—a well served table.

WIT, when neglected by the great, is generally despised by the vulgar. Those who are unacquainted with the world, are apt to fancy the man of wit, as leading a very agreeable life. They conclude, perhaps, that he is attended to with silent admiration, and dictates to the rest of mankind, with all the eloquence of conscious superiority. Very different is his present situation. He is called an author, and all know that an author is a thing only to be laughed at. His person, not his jest, becomes the mirth of the company. At his approach, the most fat unthinking face, brightens into malicious meaning. Even aldermen laugh, and revenge on him, the ridicule which was lavish'd on their fore-fathers.

Etiam victis redit in præcordia virtus, Victoresque cadunt.[5]

IT is indeed a reflection somewhat mortifying to the author, who breaks his ranks, and singles out for public favour to think that he must combat contempt, before he can arrive at glory. That he must expect to have all the fools of society united against him, before he can hope for the applause of the judicious. For this, however, he must prepare beforehand; as those who have no idea of the difficulty of his employment, will be apt to regard his inactivity as idleness, and not having a notion of the pangs of uncomplying thought in themselves, it is not to be expected they should have any desire of rewarding it in others.

VOLTAIRE has finely described the hardships a man must encounter, who writes for the public. I need make no apology for the length of the quotation.

"YOUR[6] fate, my dear Le Fevre, is too strongly marked to permit your retiring. The bee must toil in making honey, the silk-worm must spin, the philosopher must dissect them, and you are born to sing of their labours. You must be a poet, and a scholar, even though your inclinations should resist; nature is too strong for inclination. But hope not, my friend, to find tranquillity in the employment you are going to pursue. The rout of genius is not less obstructed with disappointment, than that of ambition.

"IF you have the misfortune not to excel in your profession as a poet, repentence must tincture all your future enjoyments. If you succeed, you make enemies. You tread a narrow path, contempt on one side, and hatred on the other, are ready to seize you upon the slightest deviation.

---

2. **the great Somers:** John, Lord Somers (1651–1716), Lord Chancellor of England and patron of Locke, Newton, Addison, Steele, Congreve, and Swift. 3. **an old . . . age:** probably Edward Young (1683–1765), author of *Love of Fame, the Universal Passion* (see Part Three) and *The Complaint, or Night Thoughts on Life, Death, and Immortality* (1742–45). (See also the selection from Young in Part Five.) 4. **a certain . . . memory:** Sir Robert Walpole (1676–1745), Prime Minister from 1721 to 1742.

5. **Etiam . . . cadunt:** "Courage returns to the hearts of the defeated, and the victors fall" (*Aeneid*, II. 367–68). 6. **Your . . . disappointment:** from Voltaire's *To Mr. Le Fevre, on the Inconveniences Associated with Literature* (1732).

"BUT, why must I be hated, you will, perhaps, reply, why must I be persecuted for having wrote a pleasing poem, for having produced an applauded tragedy, or for otherwise instructing, or amusing mankind, or myself.

"MY dear friend, these very successes shall render you miserable for life. Let me suppose your performance has merit, let me suppose you have surmounted the teazing employments of printing and publishing, how will you be able to lull the critics, who like Cerberus,[7] are posted at all the avenues of literature, and who settle the merits of every new performance. How, I say, will you be able to make them open in your favour? There are always three or four literary journals in France, as many in Holland, each supporting opposite interests. The booksellers, who guide these periodical compilations, find their account in being severe; the authors employed by them, have wretchedness to add to their natural malignity. The majority may be in your favour, but you may depend on being torn by the rest. Loaded with unmerited scurrility, perhaps you reply; they rejoin, both plead at the bar of the public, and both are condemned to ridicule.

"BUT if you write for the stage, your case is still more worthy compassion. You are there to be judged by men, whom the custom of the times has rendered contemptible. Irritated by their own inferiority, they exert all their little tyranny upon you, revenging upon the author, the insults they receive from the public. From such men then you are to expect your sentence. Suppose your piece admitted, acted: one single ill-natured jest from the pit, is sufficient to cancel all your labours. But allowing that it succeeds. There are an hundred squibs flying all abroad to prove, that it should not have succeeded. You shall find your brightest scenes burlesqued by the ignorant; and the learned, who know a little Greek, and nothing of their native language, affect to despise you.

"BUT, perhaps, with a panting heart, you carry your piece before a woman of quality. She gives the labours of your brain to her maid, to be cut into shreds for curling her hair; while the laced footman, who carries the gaudy livery of luxury, insults your appearance, who bear the livery of indigence.

"BUT granting your excellence has at last forced envy to confess, that your works have some merit; this then is all the reward you can expect while living. However, for this tribute of applause, you must expect persecution. You will be reputed the author of scandal which you have never seen, of verses you despise, and of sentiments directly contrary to your own. In short, you must embark in some one party, or all parties will be against you.

"THERE are among us, a number of learned societies, where a lady presides, whose wit begins to twinkle, when the splendour of her beauty begins to decline. One or two men of learning compose her ministers of state. These must be flattered, or made enemies by being neglected. Thus, though you had the merit of all antiquity united in your person, you grow old in misery and disgrace. Every place designed for men of letters, is filled up by men of intrigue. Some nobleman's private tutor, some court flatterer, shall bear away the prize, and leave you to anguish and to disappointment."

YET it were well, if none but the dunces of society, were combined to render the profession of an author ridiculous or unhappy. Men of the first eminence are often found to indulge this illiberal vein of raillery. Two contending writers often by the opposition of their wit, render their profession contemptible in the eyes of ignorants, who should have been taught to admire. And yet, whatever the reader may think of himself, it is at least two to one, but he is a greater blockhead than the most scribling dunce he affects to despise.

THE poet's poverty is a standing topic of contempt. His writing for bread is an unpardonable offence. Perhaps, of all mankind, an author, in these times, is used most hardly. We keep him poor, and yet revile his poverty. Like angry parents, who correct their children till they cry, and then correct them for crying, we reproach him for living by his wit, and yet allow him no other means to live.

HIS taking refuge in garrets and cellars has, of late, been violently objected to him, and that by men, who I dare hope, are more apt to pity than insult his distress. Is poverty the writer's fault? No doubt, he knows how to prefer a bottle of champaign, to the nectar of the neighbouring alehouse, or a venison pasty to a plate of potatoes. Want of delicacy is not in him, but in us, who deny him the opportunity of making an elegant choice.

WIT certainly is the property of these who have it, nor should we be displeased if it is the only property a man sometimes has. We must not under-rate him who

---

7. Cerberus: in Greek mythology, the three-headed dog who guards the entrance to Hades.

uses it for subsistence, and flies from the ingratitude of the age, even to a bookseller for redress. If the profession of an author is to be laughed at by stupids, it is better sure to be contemptibly rich, than contemptibly poor. For all the wit that ever adorned the human mind, will at present no more shield the author's poverty from ridicule, than his high topped gloves conceal the unavoidable omissions of his laundress.

To be more serious, new fashions, follies, and vices, make new monitors necessary in every age. An author may be considered as a merciful substitute to the legislature; he acts not by punishing crimes, but preventing them; however virtuous the present age, there may be still growing employment for ridicule, or reproof, for persuasion, or satire. If the author be, therefore, still so necessary among us, let us treat him with proper consideration, as a child of the public, not a rent-charge on the community. And, indeed, a *child* of the public he is in all respects; for while so well able to direct others, how incapable is he frequently found by guiding himself. His simplicity exposes him to all the insidious approaches of cunning, his sensibility to the slightest invasions of contempt. Though possessed of fortitude to stand unmoved the expected bursts of an earthquake, yet of feelings so exquisitely poignant, as to agonize under the slightest disappointment. Broken rest, tasteless meals, and causeless anxiety, shorten his life, or render it unfit for active employment; prolonged vigils, and intense application still farther contract his span, and make his time glide insensibly away. Let us not then aggravate those natural inconveniencies by neglect; we have had sufficient instances of this kind already. Sale and More[8] will suffice for one age at least. But they are dead, and their sorrows are over. The neglected author of the Persian eclogues,[9] which, however inaccurate, excel any in our language, is still alive. Happy, if *insensible* of our neglect, not *raging* at our

ingratitude. It is enough, that the age has already yielded instances of men pressing foremost in the lists of fame, and worthy of better times, schooled by continued adversity into an hatred of their kind, flying from thought to drunkenness, yielding to the united pressure of labour, penury, and sorrow, sinking unheeded, without one friend to drop a tear on their unattended obsequies, and indebted to charity for a grave.

The author, when unpatronized by the Great, has naturally recourse to the bookseller. There cannot be, perhaps, imagined a combination more prejudicial to taste than this. It is the interest of the one to allow as little for writing, and of the other to write as much as possible; accordingly, tedious compilations, and periodical magazines, are the result of their joint endeavours. In these circumstances, the author bids adieu to fame, writes for bread, and for that only. Imagination is seldom called in; he sits down to address the venal muse with the most phlegmatic apathy; and, as we are told of the Russian, courts his mistress by falling asleep in her lap. His reputation never spreads in a wider circle than that of the trade, who generally value him, not for the fineness of his compositions, but the quantity he works off in a given time.

A long habit of writing for bread, thus turns the ambition of every author at last into avarice. He finds, that he has written many years, that the public are scarcely acquainted even with his name; he despairs of applause, and turns to profit, which invites him. He finds that money procures all those advantages, that respect, and that ease, which he vainly expected from fame. Thus the man, who under the protection of the Great, might have done honour to humanity, when only patronized by the bookseller, becomes a thing little superior to the fellow who works at the press.

---

8. Sale and More: George Sale (*c.* 1697–1736), orientalist and translator of the Koran, was one of the founders of the Society for the Encouragement of Learning; Edward Moore (1712–57), poet and editor, was the author of *Fables for the Female Sex* (see Part Three). In the first edition Goldsmith listed also Nicholas Amhurst, poet and political writer, and the poet Richard Savage, the violent and indigent subject of Samuel Johnson's famous biography. **9. The neglected . . . eclogues:** William Collins (1721–59), best known for his odes; his *Persian Eclogues* appeared in 1742. He died insane about two months after Goldsmith's *Polite Learning* was published. (See the selections from Collins in Part Five.)

CHAP. XI

*Of the Marks of Literary Decay
in* France *and* England.

The faults already mentioned are such, as learning is often found to flourish under; but there is one of a much more dangerous nature, which has begun to fix itself among us, I mean criticism, which may properly be called the natural destroyer of polite learning. We have seen that Critics, or those whose only business is to write books upon other books, are always more numerous as learning is more diffused; and experience has shewn, that, instead of promoting its interest, which they profess to do, they generally injure it. This decay, which criticism produces, may be deplored, but can scarcely be remedied, as the man who writes against the critics, is obliged to add himself to the number. Other depravations in the republic of letters, such as affectation in some popular writer, leading others into vicious imitation; political struggles in the state; a depravity of morals among the people; ill-directed encouragement, or no encouragement from the Great, these have been often found to co-operate in the decline of literature; and it has sometimes declined, as in modern Italy, without them; but an increase of criticism has always portended a decay. Of all misfortunes, therefore, in the commonwealth of letters, this of judging from rule, and not from feeling, is the most severe. At such a tribunal, no work of original merit can please. Sublimity, if carried to an exalted height, approaches burlesque, and humour sinks into vulgarity; the person who cannot feel, may ridicule both as such, and bring rules to corroborate his assertion. There is, in short, no excellence in writing, that such judges may not place among the neighbouring defects. Rules render the reader more difficult to be pleased, and abridge the author's power of pleasing.

IF we turn to either country, we shall perceive evident symptoms of this natural decay beginning to appear. Upon a moderate calculation, there seems to be as many volumes of criticism published in those countries, as of all other kinds of polite erudition united. Paris sends forth not less than four literary journals every month, the Anné-literaire, and the Fuille by Freron, the Journal Etrangere by the Chevalier D'Arc, and Le Mercure by Marmontel. We have two literary reviews in London,[1] with critical news-papers and magazines without number. The compilers of these resemble the commoners of Rome; they are all for levelling property, not by encreasing their own, but by diminishing that of others. The man who has any good nature in his disposition must, however, be somewhat displeased to see distinguished reputations often the sport of ignorance. To see by one false pleasantry, the future peace of a worthy man's life disturbed, and this only because he has unsuccessfully

attempted to instruct or amuse us. Though ill nature is far from being wit, yet it is generally laughed at as such. The critic enjoys the triumph, and ascribes to his parts, what is only due to his effrontery. I fire with indignation when I see persons wholly destitute of education and genius, indent to[2] the press, and thus turn book-makers, adding to the sin of criticism the sin of ignorance also. Whose trade is a bad one, and who are bad workmen in the trade.

WHEN I consider those industrious men as indebted to the works of others for a precarious subsistence, when I see them coming down at stated intervals to rummage the bookseller's compter[3] for materials to work upon; it raises a smile, though mixed with pity. It reminds me on an animal called by naturalists the soldier.[4] This little creature, says the historian, is passionately fond of a shell, but not being supplied with one by nature, has recourse to the deserted shell of some other. I have seen these harmless reptiles, continues he, come down once a-year from the mountains, rank and file, cover the whole shoar and ply busily about, each in quest of a shell to please it. Nothing can be more amusing than their industry upon this occasion. One shell is too big, another too little, they enter and keep possession sometimes for a good while until one is, at last, found entirely to please. When all are thus properly equipped, they march up again to the mountains, and live in their new acquisition, till under a new necessity of changing.

THERE is indeed scarce an error of which our present writers are guilty, that does not arise from their opposing systems, there is scarce an error that criticism cannot be brought to excuse. From this proceeds the affected obscurity of our odes,[5] the tuneless flow of our blank verse, the pompous epithet, laboured diction, and every other deviation from common sense, which procures the poet the applause of the month; he is praised by all, read by a few, and soon forgotten.

THERE never was an unbeaten path trodden by the poet, that the critic did not endeavour to reclaim him, by calling his attempt innovation. This might be

Chapter XI. **1. two . . . London:** *The Monthly Review,* founded in 1749, and *The Critical Review,* founded in 1756.

2. indent to: become servants of. **3. compter:** counter. **4. the soldier:** the hermit crab. **5. the affected . . . odes:** Reviewing Gray's *The Progress of Poesy* and *The Bard* in *The Monthly Review* (1757), Goldsmith wrote, "We cannot . . . without some regret behold those talents so capable of giving pleasure to all, exerted in efforts that, at best, can amuse only the few; we cannot behold this rising poet seeking fame among the learned, without hinting to him the same advice that Isocrates used to give his scholars, *study the people.*"

instanced in Dante, who first followed nature, and was persecuted by the critics as long as he lived. Thus novelty, one of the greatest beauties in poetry, must be avoided, or the connoisseur be displeased. It is one of the chief privileges, however, of genius, to fly from the herd of imitators by some happy singularity; for should he stand still, his heavy pursuers will at length certainly come up, and fairly dispute the victory.

THE ingenious Mr. Hogarth[6] used to assert, that every one, except the connoisseur, was a judge of painting. The same may be asserted of writing; the public in general set the whole piece in the proper point of view; the critic lays his eye close to all its minutenesses, and condemns or approves in detail. And this may be the reason why so many writers at present, are apt to appeal from the tribunal of criticism to that of the people.

FROM a desire in the critic of grafting the spirit of ancient languages upon the English, has proceeded of late several disagreeable instances of pedantry. Among the number, I think we may reckon blank verse. Nothing but the greatest sublimity of subject can render such a measure pleasing; however, we now see it used upon the most trivial occasions; it has particularly found way into our didactic poetry, and is likely to bring that species of composition into disrepute, for which the English are deservedly famous.

THOSE who are acquainted with writing, know that our language runs almost naturally into blank verse. The writers of our novels, romances, and all of this class, who have no notion of stile, naturally hobble into this unharmonious measure. If rhymes, therefore, be more difficult, for that very reason, I would have our poets write in rhyme. Such a restriction upon the thought of a good poet, often lifts and encreases the vehemence of every sentiment; for fancy, like a fountain, plays highest by diminishing the aperture. But rhymes, it will be said, are a remnant of monkish stupidity, an innovation upon the poetry of the ancients. They are but indifferently acquainted with antiquity, who make the assertion. Rhymes are probably of older date than either the Greek or Latin dactyl and sponde. The Celtic, which is allowed to be the first language spoken in Europe, has ever preserved them, as we may find in the Edda of Iceland,[7]

and the Irish carrols still sung among the original inhabitants of that island. Olaus Wormius[8] gives us some of the Teutonic poetry in this way; and Pantoppidan,[9] bishop of Bergen, some of the Norwegian; in short, this jingle of sounds is almost natural to mankind, at least, it is so to our language, if we may judge from many unsuccessful attempts to throw it off.

I SHOULD not have employed so much time in opposing this erroneous innovation, if it were not apt to introduce another in its train: I mean, a disgusting solemnity of manner into our poetry; and as the prose writer has been ever found to follow the poet, it must consequently banish in both, all that agreeable trifling, which, if I may so express it, often deceives us into instruction. The finest sentiment, and the most weighty truth, may put on a pleasant face, and it is even virtuous to jest when serious advice must be disgusting. But instead of this, the most trifling performance among us now, assumes all the didactic stiffness of wisdom. The most diminutive son of fame, or of famine, has his *we* and his *us*, his *firstlys* and his *secondlys* as methodical, as if bound in cow-hide, and closed with clasps of brass. Were these Monthly Reviews and Magazines frothy, pert, or absurd, they might find some pardon; but to be dull and dronish, is an encroachment on the prerogative of a folio. These things should be considered as pills to purge melancholly; they should be made up in our splenetic climate, to be taken as physic, and not so as to be used when we take it.

HOWEVER, by the power of one single monosyllable, our critics have almost got the victory over humour amongst us. Does the poet paint the absurdities of the vulgar; then he is *low*: does he exaggerate the features of folly, to render it more thoroughly ridiculous, he is then very *low*. In short, they have proscribed the comic or satyrical muse from every walk but high life, which, though abounding in fools as well as the humblest station, is by no means so fruitful in absurdity. Among well-bred fools we may despise much, but have little to laugh at; nature seems to present us with an universal blank of silk, ribbands, smiles and whispers; absurdity is the poet's game, and good breeding is the nice concealment of absurdities. The truth is, the critic generally mistakes humour for wit, which is a very

---

6. **Mr. Hogarth:** the painter William Hogarth (1697–1764); although Goldsmith may have heard this opinion from Hogarth himself, it is expressed frequently in his *The Analysis of Beauty* (1753). 7. **the Edda . . . Iceland:** two thirteenth-century collections of Old Norse poems.

8. **Olaus Wormius:** (1588–1654), Danish physician and scholar; his *Runic Literature* was published in 1661. 9. **Pantoppidan:** Erik Pontoppidan (1698–1764), Danish theologian and scholar; his *Natural History of Norway* appeared in 1752–53.

different excellence. Wit raises human nature above its level; humour acts a contrary part, and equally depresses it. To expect exalted humour, is a contradiction in terms; and the critic, by demanding an impossibility from the comic poet, has, in effect, banished new comedy from the stage. But to put the same thought in a different light:

WHEN an unexpected similitude in two objects strikes the imagination; in other words, when a thing is *wittily* expressed, all our pleasure turns into admiration of the artist, who had fancy enough to draw the picture. When a thing is *humourously* described, our burst of laughter proceeds from a very different cause; we compare the absurdity of the character represented with our own, and triumph in our conscious superiority. No natural defect can be a cause of laughter, because it is a misfortune to which ourselves are liable; a defect of this kind, changes the passion into pity or horror; we only laugh at those instances of moral absurdity, to which we are conscious we ourselves are not liable. For instance, should I describe a man as wanting his nose, there is no humour in this, as it is an accident to which human nature is subject, and may be any man's case; but should I represent this man without his nose, as extremely curious in the choice of his snuff-box, we here see him guilty of an absurdity of which we imagine it impossible for ourselves to be guilty, and therefore applaud our own good sense on the comparison. Thus, then, the pleasure we receive from wit, turns on the admiration of another; that which we feel from humour, centers in the admiration of ourselves. The poet, therefore, must place the object he would have the subject of humour in a state of inferiority; in other words, the subject of humour must be low.

THE solemnity worn by many of our modern writers is, I fear, often the mask of dulness; for certain it is, it seems to fit every author who pleases to put it on. By the complexion of many of our late publications, one might be apt to cry out with Cicero, *Civem mehercule non puto esse qui his temporibus ridere possit.* On my conscience, I believe we have all forgot to laugh in these days. Such writers probably make no distinction between what is praised, and what is pleasing; between those commendations which the reader pays his own discernment, and those which are the genuine result of his sensations. It were to be wished therefore that we no longer found pleasure with the inflated stile that has for some years been looked upon as fine writing, and which every young writer is now obliged to adopt, if he chuses to be read. We should now dispense with loaded epithet, and dressing up trifles with dignity. For to use an obvious instance, it is not those who make the greatest noise with their wares in the streets, that have most to sell. Let us, instead of writing finely, try to write naturally. Not hunt after lofty expressions to deliver mean ideas; nor be for ever gaping, when we only mean to deliver a whisper.

FROM

THE BEE

The Bee was a thirty-two-page weekly periodical that Goldsmith began in October, 1759, and abandoned after eight numbers. Each number contained about a half dozen essays, short stories, theatrical anecdotes, translations, and poems. When he occasionally found himself hard pressed as his deadlines drew near, Goldsmith resorted to borrowing without acknowledgment from other works: the essay *Of Eloquence*, for example, was lifted largely from an article supervised by Voltaire in the fifth volume of the twenty-four-volume French *Encyclopédie* (1751–80).

The text is that of the first edition (1759).

A RESVERIE°

SCARCE a day passes in which we do not hear compliments paid to Dryden, Pope, and other writers of the last age, while not a month comes forward that is not loaded with invective against the writers of this. Strange, that our critics should be fond of giving their favours to those who are insensible of the obligation, and their dislike to these who, of all mankind, are most apt to retaliate the injury.

Even though our present writers had not equal merit with their predecessors, it would be politic to use them with ceremony. Every compliment paid them would be more agreeable, in proportion as they least deserved it. Tell a lady with a handsome face that she is pretty, she only thinks it her due; it is what she

THE BEE: *A Resverie.* **Resverie:** a seventeenth-century spelling of *reverie.*

has heard a thousand times before from others, and disregards the compliment: but assure a lady, the cut of whose visage is something more plain, that she looks killing to-day, she instantly bridles up and feels the force of the well-timed flattery the whole day after. Compliments which we think are deserved, we only accept, as debts, with indifference; but those which conscience informs us we do not merit, we receive with the same gratitude that we do favours given away.

Our gentlemen, however, who preside at the distribution of literary fame, seem resolved to part with praise neither from motives of justice, or generosity; one would think, when they take pen in hand, that it was only to blot reputations, and to put their seals to the pacquet which consigns every new-born effort to oblivion.

Yet, notwithstanding the republic of letters hangs at present so feebly together; though those friendships which once promoted literary fame seem now to be discontinued; though every writer who now draws the quill seems to aim at profit, as well as applause, many among them are probably laying in stores for immortality, and are provided with a sufficient stock of reputation to last the whole journey.

As I was indulging these reflections, in order to eke out the present page, I could not avoid pursuing the metaphor, of going a journey, in my imagination, and formed the following Resverie too wild for allegory, and too regular for a dream.

I fancied myself placed in the yard of a large inn, in which there were an infinite number of waggons and stage coaches, attended by fellows who either invited the company to take their places, or were busied in packing their baggage. Each vehicle had its inscription, shewing the place of its destination. On one I could read, *The pleasure stage-coach;* on another, *The waggon of industry;* on a third, *The vanity whim;* and on a fourth, *The landau of riches.* I had some inclination to step into each of these, one after another; but I know not by what means I passed them by, and at last fixed my eye upon a small carriage, Berlin fashion,[1] which seemed the most convenient vehicle at a distance in the world; and, upon my nearer approach, found it to be *The fame machine.*

I instantly made up to the coachman, whom I found to be an affable and seemingly good-natured fellow.

He informed me, that he had but a few days ago returned from the temple of fame, to which he had been carrying Addison, Swift, Pope, Steele, Congreve,[2] and Colley Cibber.[3] That they made but indifferent company by the way, and that he once or twice was going to empty his berlin of the whole cargo: however, says he, I got them all safe home, with no other damage than a black eye, which Colley gave Mr. Pope, and am now returned for another coachful.—"If that be all, friend, said I, and if you are in want of company, I'll make one with all my heart. Open the door; I hope the machine rides easy." "Oh, for that, sir, extremely easy." But still keeping the door shut, and measuring me with his eye, "Pray, sir, have you no luggage? You seem to be a good-natured sort of a gentleman; but I don't find you have got any luggage, and I never permit any to travel with me but such as have something valuable to pay for coach-hire." Examining my pockets, I own I was not a little disconcerted at this unexpected rebuff; but considering that I carried a number of the BEE under my arm, I was resolved to open it in his eyes, and dazzle him with the splendor of the page. He read the title and contents, however, without any emotion, and assured me he had never heard of it before. "In short, friend, said he, now losing all his former respect, you must not come in. I expect better passengers; but, as you seem an harmless creature, perhaps, if there be room left, I may let you ride a while for charity."

I now took my stand by the coachman at the door, and since I could not command a seat, was resolved to be as useful as possible, and earn by my assiduity, what I could not by my merit.

The next that presented for a place, was a most whimsical figure[4] indeed. He was hung round with papers of his own composing, not unlike those who sing ballads in the streets, and came dancing up to the door with all the confidence of instant admittance. The volubility of his motion and address prevented my being able to read more of his cargo than the word

1. **Berlin fashion:** A Berlin was an old-fashioned covered carriage, with an extra covered seat behind.

2. **Congreve:** The playwright William Congreve (1670–1729) is best known for his comedy *The Way of the World* (1700). 3. **Colley Cibber:** (1671–1757), actor, playwright, and Poet Laureate (1730–57); he displaced Theobald as the dull hero of Pope's *Dunciad* (see Part Two) in 1743. 4. **a most . . . figure:** "Sir" John Hill (c. 1716–75), a quack doctor, editor, and writer on the theater, medicine, botany, and horticulture; he was the author of "The Inspector," a daily column in *The London Daily Advertiser* (1751–53), and of such works as *On Exotic Botany* (1759).

Inspector, which was written in great letters at the top of some of the papers. He opened the coach-door himself without any ceremony, and was just slipping in, when the coachman, with as little ceremony, pulled him back. Our figure seemed perfectly angry at this repulse, and demanded gentleman's satisfaction. "Lord, sir! replied the coachman, instead of proper luggage, by your bulk you seem loaded for a West-India voyage. You are big enough, with all your papers, to crack twenty stage-coaches. Excuse me, indeed, sir, for you must not enter." Our figure now began to expostulate; he assured the coachman, that though his baggage seemed so bulky, it was perfectly light, and that he would be contented with the smallest corner of room. But Jehu[5] was inflexible, and the carrier of the inspectors was sent to dance back again, with all his papers fluttering in the wind. We expected to have no more trouble from this quarter, when, in a few minutes, the same figure changed his appearance, like harlequin upon the stage, and with the same confidence again made his approaches, dressed in lace, and carrying nothing but a nosegay. Upon coming near, he thrust the nosegay to the coachman's nose, grasped the brass, and seemed now resolved to enter by violence. I found the struggle soon begin to grow hot, and the coachman, who was a little old, unable to continue the contest, so, in order to ingratiate myself, I stept in to his assistance, and our united efforts sent our literary Proteus,[6] though worsted, unconquered still, clear off, dancing a rigadoon, and smelling to his own nosegay.

The person who after him appeared[7] as candidate for a place in the stage, came up with an air not quite so confident, but somewhat however theatrical; and, instead of entering, made the coachman a very low bow, which the other returned, and desired to see his baggage; upon which he instantly produced some farces, a tragedy, and other miscellany productions. The coachman, casting his eye upon the cargoe, assured him, at present he could not possibly have a place, but hoped in time he might aspire to one, as he seemed to have read in the book of nature, without a careful perusal of which none ever found entrance at the temple of fame. "What, (replied the disappointed

poet) shall my tragedy, in which I have vindicated the cause of liberty and virtue!"—"Follow nature, (returned the other) and never expect to find lasting fame by topics which only please from their popularity. Had you been first in the cause of freedom, or praised in virtue more than an empty name, it is possible you might have gained admittance; but at present I beg, sir, you will stand aside for another gentleman whom I see approaching."

This was a very grave personage,[8] whom at some distance I took for one of the most reserved, and even disagreeable figures I had seen; but as he approached, his appearance improved, and when I could distinguish him thoroughly, I perceived, that, in spite of the severity of his brow, he had one of the most good-natured countenances that could be imagined. Upon coming to open the stage door, he lifted a parcel of folios into the seat before him, but our inquisitorial coachman at once shoved them out again. "What, not take in my dictionary! exclaimed the other in a rage." "Be patient, sir, (replyed the coachman) I have drove a coach, man and boy, these two thousand years; but I do not remember to have carried above one dictionary during the whole time. That little book which I perceive peeping from one of your pockets, may I presume to ask what it contains?" "A mere trifle, (replied the author) it is called the Rambler." "The Rambler! (says the coachman) I beg, sir, you'll take your place; I have heard our ladies in the court of Apollo[9] frequently mention it with rapture; and Clio,[10] who happens to be a little grave, has been heard to prefer it to the Spectator; though others have observed, that the reflections, by being refined, sometimes become minute."

This grave gentleman was scarce seated, when another,[11] whose appearance was something more modern, seemed willing to enter, yet afraid to ask. He carried in his hand a bundle of essays, of which the coachman was curious enough to enquire the contents.

5. **Jehu:** a traditional name for a fast coach driver, from II Kings 9:20. 6. **Proteus:** a Greek sea deity known for his ability to change his shape at will. 7. **The person . . . appeared:** Arthur Murphy (1727–1805), Irish actor and playwright; he was the author of the tragedy *The Orphan of China* (1759).

8. **a very . . . personage:** Samuel Johnson, whose acquaintance Goldsmith had not yet made. Johnson's folio *Dictionary* was published in 1755; his periodical paper *The Rambler* (see earlier in Part Six) appeared from 1750 to 1752. 9. **Apollo:** the Greek deity of light, truth, and poetry. 10. **Clio:** the Muse of history; Joseph Addison signed each of his *Spectator* papers (see Part Two) with one of the letters of the word *Clio*. 11. **another:** David Hume (1711–76), the Scottish philosopher whose early essays had revealed his religious skepticism, published his *History of England* from 1754 to 1762. The "last volume" mentioned in this paragraph appeared in 1759. (See the selection from Hume in Part Five.)

"These, (replied the gentleman) are rhapsodies against the religion of my country." "And how can you expect to come into my coach, after thus chusing the wrong side of the question." "Ay, but I am right (replied the other;) and if you give me leave, I shall in a few minutes state the argument." "Right or wrong, (said the coachman) he who disturbs religion, is a block-head, and he shall never travel in a coach of mine." "If, then, (said the gentleman, mustering up all his courage) if I am not to have admittance as an essayist, I hope I shall not be repulsed as an historian; the last volume of my history met with applause." "Yes, (replied the coachman) but I have heard only the first approved at the temple of fame; and as I see you have it about you, enter without further ceremony." My attention was now diverted to a crowd, who were pushing forward a person[12] that seemed more inclined to the *stage coach of riches*; but by their means he was driven forward to the fame machine, which he, how-ever, seemed heartily to despise. Impelled, however, by their sollicitations, he steps up, flourishing a volu-minous history, and demanding admittance. "Sir, I have formerly heard your name mentioned (says the coachman) but never as an historian. Is there no other work upon which you may claim a place?" "None, replied the other, except a romance; but this is a work of too trifling a nature to claim future attention." "You mistake (says the inquisitor) a well-written romance is no such easy task as is generally imagined. I remember formerly to have carried Cervantes and Segrais;[13] and if you think fit, you may enter." Upon our three literary travellers coming into the same coach, I listened attentively to hear what might be the conversation that passed upon this extraordinary occasion; when, instead of agreeable or entertaining dialogue, I found them grumbling at each other, and each seemed discontented with his companions. Strange! thought I to myself, that they who are thus born to enlighten the world, should still preserve the narrow prejudices of childhood, and, by disagreeing, make even the highest merit ridiculous. Were the

learned and the wise to unite against the dunces of society, instead of sometimes siding into opposite parties with them, they might throw a lustre upon each other's reputation, and teach every rank of subordinate merit, if not to admire, at least not to avow dislike.

In the midst of these reflections, I perceived the coachman, unmindful of me, had now mounted the box. Several were approaching to be taken in, whose pretensions I was sensible were very just, I therefore desired him to stop, and take in more passengers; but he replied, as he had now mounted the box, it would be improper to come down; but that he should take them all, one after the other, when he should return. So he drove away, and, for myself, as I could not get in, I mounted behind, in order to hear the conversation on the way.

[*To be continued.*][14]

OF ELOQUENCE

OF all kinds of success, that of an orator is the most pleasing. Upon other occasions, the applause we deserve is conferred in our absence, and we are insensible of the pleasure we have given; but in eloquence, the victory and the triumph are inseparable. We read our own glory in the face of every spectator, the audience is moved, the antagonist is defeated, and the whole circle bursts into unsolicited applause.

The rewards which attend excellence in this way are so pleasing, that numbers have written professed treatises to teach us the art; schools have been estab-lished with no other intent; rhetoric has taken place among the institutions, and pedants have ranged under proper heads, and distinguished with long learned names, *some* of the strokes of nature, or of passion, which orators have used. I say only *some* for a folio volume could not contain all the figures which have been used by the truly eloquent, and scarce a good speaker or writer, but makes use of some that are peculiar or new.

Eloquence has preceded the rules of rhetoric, as languages have been formed before grammar. Nature renders men eloquent in great interests, or great passions. He that is sensibly touched, sees things with a very different eye from the rest of mankind. All

---

12. a person: Tobias Smollett (1721–71) had published eleven volumes of his *History of England* by 1759; his picaresque novels *Roderick Random, The Adventures of Peregrine Pickle*, and *The Adventures of Ferdinand, Count Fathom*, had appeared from 1748 to 1753. (See the selection from Smollett in Part Five.) **13. Segrais:** Jean Regnault de Segrais (1624–1701), French poet and novelist; he was the author of the novel *Bérénice* (1648–51). Mme. de Lafayette (1634–93) pub-lished two novels under his name.

14. To be continued: It never was. (Brackets are Goldsmith's.)

nature to him becomes an object of comparison and metaphor, without attending to it; he throws life into all, and inspires his audience with a part of his own enthusiasm.

It has been remarked, that the lower parts of mankind generally express themselves most figuratively, and that tropes are found in the most ordinary forms of conversation. Thus, in every language, the heart burns; the courage is rouzed; the eyes sparkle; the spirits are cast down; passion enflames; pride swells, and pity sinks the soul. Nature, every where, speaks in those strong images, which, from their frequency, pass unnoticed.

Nature it is which inspires those rapturous enthusiasms, those irresistible turns; a strong passion, a pressing danger, calls up all the imagination, and gives the orator irresistible force. Thus, a captain of the first caliphs,[1] seeing his soldiers fly, cried out, "Whither do you run? the enemy are not there! You have been told that the caliph is dead; but God is still living. He regards the brave, and will reward the courageous. Advance!"

A man, therefore, may be called eloquent, who transfers the passion or sentiment with which he is moved himself, into the breast of another; and this definition appears the more just, as it comprehends the graces of silence, and of action. An intimate persuasion of the truth to be proved, is the sentiment and passion to be transferred; and he who effects this, is truly possessed of the talent of eloquence.

I have called eloquence a talent, and not an art, as so many rhetoricians have done, as art is acquired by exercise and study, and eloquence is the gift of nature. Rules will never make either a work or a discourse eloquent; they only serve to prevent faults, but not to introduce beauties; to prevent those passages which are truly eloquent, and dictated by nature from being blended with others, which might disgust, or, at least, abate our passion.

What we clearly conceive, (says Boileau) we can clearly express.[2] I may add, that what is felt with

emotion, is expressed also with the same movements; the words arise as readily to paint our emotions, as to express our thoughts with perspicuity. The cool care an orator takes to express passions which he does not feel, only prevents his rising into that passion he would seem to feel. In a word, to feel your subject thoroughly, and to speak without fear, are the only rules of eloquence, properly so called, which I can offer. Examine a writer of genius on the most beautiful parts of his work, and he will always assure you that such passages are generally those which have given him the least trouble, for they came as if by inspiration. To pretend that cold and didactic precepts will make a man eloquent, is only to prove that he is incapable of eloquence.

But, as in being perspicuous, it is necessary to have a full idea of the subject, so in being eloquent, it is not sufficient, if I may so express it, to feel by halves. The orator should be strongly impressed, which is generally the effects of a fine and exquisite sensibility, and not that transient and superficial emotion, which he excites in the greatest part of his audience. It is even impossible to affect the hearers in any great degree, without being affected ourselves. In vain it will be objected, that many writers have had the art to inspire their readers with a passion for virtue, without being virtuous themselves; since it may be answered, that sentiments of virtue filled their minds at the time they were writing. They felt the inspiration strongly, while they praised justice, generosity, or good nature; but, unhappily for them, these passions might have been discontinued, when they laid down the pen. In vain will it be objected again, that we can move without being moved, as we can convince, without being convinced. It is much easier to deceive our reason than ourselves; a trifling defect in reasoning, may be overseen, and lead a man astray; for it requires reason and time to detect the falshood, but our passions are not easily imposed upon, our eyes, our ears, and every sense, is watchful to detect the imposture.

No discourse can be eloquent, that does not elevate the mind. Pathetic eloquence, it is true, has for its only object to affect; but I appeal to men of sensibility, whether their pathetic feelings are not accompanied with some degree of elevation. We may then call eloquence and sublimity the same thing, since it is impossible to be one, without feeling the other. From hence it follows, that we may be eloquent in any language, since no language refuses to paint those sentiments with which we are thoroughly impressed.

Of Eloquence. **1. the first caliphs:** the early Arabian followers of Mohammed. **2. What . . . express:** This sentiment, which appears in Canto i of *L'Art poétique* (1674) by Nicolas Boileau-Despréaux (1636–1711), had been translated by Sir William Soames as follows:

As your Idea's clear, or else obscure,
Th' Expression follows perfect, or impure:
What we conceive, with ease we can express;
Words to the Notions flow with readiness.

What is usually called sublimity of stile, seems to be only an error. Eloquence is not in the words, but in the subject, and in great concerns, the more simply any thing is expressed, it is generally the more sublime. True eloquence does not consist, as the rhetoricians assure us, in saying great things in a sublime style, but in a simple style; for there is, properly speaking, no such thing as a sublime style, the sublimity lies only in the things; and when they are not so, the language may be turgid, affected, metaphorical, but not affecting.

What can be more simply expressed, than the following extract from a celebrated preacher,[3] and yet what was ever more sublime? Speaking of the small number of the elect, he breaks out thus among his audience: "Let me suppose that this was the last hour of us all; that the heavens were opening over our heads; that time was passed, and eternity begun; that Jesus Christ in all his glory, that man of sorrows in all his glory, appeared on the tribunal, and that we were assembled here to receive our final decree of life or death eternal! Let me ask, impressed with terror like you, and not separating my lot from yours, but putting myself in the same situation in which we must all one day appear before God, our judge. Let me ask, if Jesus Christ should now appear to make the terrible separation of the just from the unjust, do you think the greatest number would be saved? Do you think the number of the elect would even be equal to that of the sinners? Do you think, if all our works were examined with justice, would he find ten just persons in this great assembly? Monsters of ingratitude, would he find one?" Such passages as these, are sublime in every language. The expression may be less striking, or more indistinct, but the greatness of the idea still remains. In a word, we may be eloquent in every language and in every style, since elocution is only an assistant, but not a constitutor of eloquence.

Of what use, then, will it be said, are all the precepts given us upon this head, both by the antients and moderns? I answer, that they cannot make us eloquent, but they will certainly prevent us from becoming ridiculous. They can seldom procure a single beauty, but they may banish a thousand faults. The true method of an orator, is not to attempt always to move, always to affect, to be continually sublime, but at proper intervals to give rest both to his own and the passions of his audience. In these periods of relaxation, or of preparation rather, rules may teach him to avoid anything low, trivial, or disgusting. Thus criticism, properly speaking, is intended not to assist those parts which are sublime, but those which are naturally mean and humble, which are composed with coolness and caution, and where the orator rather endeavours not to offend, than attempts to please.

I have hitherto insisted more strenuously on that eloquence which speaks to the passions, as it is a species of oratory almost unknown in England. At the bar it is quite discontinued, and I think with justice. In the senate, it is used but sparingly, as the orator speaks to enlightened judges. But in the pulpit, in which the orator should chiefly address the vulgar, it seems strange, that it should be entirely laid aside.

The vulgar of England are without exception, the most barbarous and the most unknowing of any in Europe. A great part of their ignorance may be chiefly ascribed to their teachers, who, with the most pretty gentleman-like serenity, deliver their cool discourses, and address the reason of men, who have never reasoned in all their lives. They are told of cause and effect, of beings self existent, and the universal scale of beings. They are informed of the excellence of the Bangorian controversy,[4] and the absurdity of an intermediate state.[5] The spruce preacher reads his lucubration without lifting his nose from the text, and never ventures to earn the shame of an enthusiast.

By this means, though his audience feel not one word of all he says, he earns, however, among his acquaintance, the character of a man of sense; among his acquaintance only did I say, nay, even with his bishop.

The polite of every country have several motives to induce them to a rectitude of action; the love of virtue for its own sake, the shame of offending, and the desire of pleasing. The vulgar have but one, the enforcements of religion; and yet those who should push

---

3. **a celebrated preacher:** Jean-Baptiste Massillon (1663–1742), Bishop of Clermont-Ferrand from 1717; his sermons were known for their appeal to psychology rather than to dogma.

4. **the Bangorian controversy:** initiated by a sermon preached in 1717 by Dr. Benjamin Hoadly (1676–1761), Bishop of Bangor and chaplain to George I. Hoadly argued the tolerant, Low-Church position that the deposition of the Stuart monarchy and its replacement by the Hanoverian succession was not of major doctrinal consequence. One of Hoadly's most effective antagonists was William Law. (See the selection from Law in Part Two.) 5. **an intermediate state:** according to Roman Catholic doctrine, a condition of purgatory between death and admission to Heaven when the soul atones for earthly sins.

this motive home to their hearts, are basely found to desert their post. They speak to the squire, the philosopher, and the pedant; but the poor, those who really want instruction, are left uninstructed.

I have attended most of our pulpit orators, who, it must be owned, write extremely well upon the text they assume. To give them their due also, they read their sermons with elegance and propriety, but this goes but a very short way in true eloquence. The speaker must be moved. In this, in this alone, our English divines are deficient. Were they to speak to a few calm dispassionate hearers, they certainly use the properest methods of address; but their audience is chiefly composed of the poor, who must be influenced by motives of reward and punishment, and whose only virtues lie in self-interest or fear.

How then are such to be addressed; not by studied periods, or cold disquisitions; not by the labours of the head, but the honest spontaneous dictates of the heart. Neither writing a sermon with regular periods and all the harmony of elegant expression; neither reading it with emphasis, propriety, and deliberation; neither pleasing with metaphor, simile, or rhetorical fustian; neither arguing coolly, and untying consequences united in *a priori*, nor bundling up inductions *a posteriori;* neither pedantic jargon, nor academical trifling, can persuade the poor; writing a discourse coolly in the closet, then getting it by memory, and delivering it on Sundays, even that will not do. What then is to be done? I know of no expedient to speak; to speak at once intelligibly, and feelingly, except to understand the language. To be convinced of the truth of the object; to be perfectly acquainted with the subject in view, to prepossess yourself with a low opinion of your audience, and to do the rest extempore. By this means strong expressions, new thoughts, rising passions, and the true declamatory style, will naturally ensue.

Fine declamation does not consist in flowery periods, delicate allusions, or musical cadences; but in a plain, open, loose stile, where the periods are long and obvious; where the same thought is often exhibited in several points of view; all this, strong sense, a good memory, and a small share of experience, will furnish to every orator; and without these a clergyman may be called a fine preacher, a judicious preacher, and a man of sound sense; he may make his hearers admire his understanding, but will seldom enlighten theirs.

When I think of the Methodist preachers among us, how seldom they are endued with common sense, and

yet how often and how justly they affect their hearers, I cannot avoid saying within myself, had these been bred gentlemen, and been endued with even the meanest share of understanding, what might they not effect! Did our bishops, who can add dignity to their expostulations, testify the same fervour, and *entreat* their hearers, as well as *argue*, what might not be the consequence! The vulgar, by which I mean the bulk of mankind, would then have a double motive to love religion, first from seeing its professors honoured here, and next from the consequences hereafter. At present, the enthusiasms of the poor are opposed to law; did law conspire with their enthusiasms, we should not only be the happiest nation upon earth, but the wisest also.

Enthusiasm in religion, which prevails only among the vulgar, should be the chief object of politics. A society of enthusiasts, governed by reason among the great, is the most indissoluble, the most virtuous, and the most efficient of its own decrees that can be imagined. Every country that has any degree of strength, have had their enthusiasms, which ever serve as laws among the people. The Greeks had their *Kalokagathia*,[6] the Romans their *Amor Patriæ*,[7] and we the truer and firmer bond of the *Protestant religion*. The principle is the same in all; how much then is it the duty of those whom the law has appointed teachers of this religion to enforce its obligations, and to raise those enthusiasms among people, by which alone political society can subsist.

From eloquence, therefore, the morals of our people are to expect emendation; but how little can they be improved, by men who get into the pulpit rather to shew their parts, than convince us of the truth of what they deliver, who are painfully correct in their stile, musical in their tones, where every sentiment, every expression, seems the result of meditation and deep study.

Tillotson[8] has been commended as the model of pulpit eloquence; thus far he should be imitated, where he generally strives to convince, rather than to please: but to adopt his long, dry, and sometimes tedious discussions, which serve to amuse only divines, and are utterly neglected by the generality of mankind, to

---

6. **Kalokagathia:** the doctrine of the alliance of the good with the beautiful. **7. Amor Patriæ:** love of country. **8. Tillotson:** John Tillotson (1630–94), Archbishop of Canterbury (1691–94). (See the selection from Tillotson in Part One.)

praise the intricacy of his periods, which are too long to be spoken, to continue his cool phlegmatic manner of enforcing every truth, is certainly erroneous. As I said before, the good preacher should adopt no model, write no sermons, study no periods; let him but understand his subject, the language he speaks, and be convinced of the truths he delivers. It is amazing to what heights eloquence of this kind may reach! This is that eloquence the ancients represented as lightning, bearing down every opposer; this the power which has turned whole assemblies into astonishment, admiration, and awe, that is described by the torrent, the flame, and every other instance of irresistible impetuosity.

But to attempt such noble heights, belongs only to the truly great, or the truly good. To discard the lazy manner of reading sermons, or speaking sermons by rote; to set up singly against the opposition of men who are attached to their own errors, and to endeavour to be great, instead of being prudent, are qualities we seldom see united. A minister of the church of England, who may be possessed of good sense, and some hopes of preferment, will seldom give up such substantial advantages for the empty pleasure of improving society. By his present method he is liked by his friends, admired by his dependants, not displeasing to his bishop; he lives as well, eats and sleeps as well, as if a real orator, and an eager asserter of his mission; he will hardly, therefore, venture all this to be called, perhaps, an enthusiast; nor will he depart from customs established by the brotherhood, when, by such a conduct, he only singles himself out for their contempt.

FROM

THE CITIZEN
OF THE WORLD . . .

The 123 letters that make up *The Citizen of the World* first appeared approximately twice a week in *The Public Ledger*, a London daily newspaper conducted by the publisher John Newbery. The first letter was published on January 24, 1760, and the last on August 14, 1761. The device of an oriental observer writing home his naively satiric observations was hardly new when Goldsmith used it: Montesquieu's *Persian Letters* (1721), Lord Lyttelton's *Letters from a Persian in England to His Friend in Ispahan* (1735), and the Marquis d'Argens's *Chinese Letters* (1739) were well known. Goldsmith's Chinese letters were popular partly because of the

Chinese craze of the 1750's and 1760's—a craze that brought forth Chinese furniture, garden ornaments, and porcelains. The letters were praised not for their originality—Goldsmith had borrowed freely from D'Argens and others—but for their agreeableness and ease. Although they appeared without their author's name, everyone knew who had written them.

The text is that of the first edition in *The Public Ledger* (1760–61); substantive variants—as well as the numbers of the letters—have been introduced from the first collected edition, *The Citizen of the World; or Letters from a Chinese Philosopher, Residing in London, to His Friends in the East* (2 vols., 1762).

LETTER IV

To the care of Fipsihi, Tartarean resident in Moscow; to be forwarded by the Russian caravan to Fum Hoam, first president of the ceremonial academy at Pekin in China.

THE English seem as silent as the Japonese, yet vainer than the inhabitants of Siam. Upon my arrival I attributed that reserve to modesty, which I now find has its origin in pride. Condescend to address them first, and you are sure of their acquaintance; stoop to flattery and you conciliate their friendship and esteem. They bear hunger, cold, fatigue, and all the miseries of life without shrinking, danger only calls forth their fortitude; they even exult in calamity, but contempt is what they cannot bear. An Englishman fears contempt more than death; he often flies to death as a refuge from its pressure; and dies when he fancies the world has ceased to esteem him.

Pride seems the source not only of their national vices, but of their national virtues also. An Englishman is taught to love his king as his friend, but to acknowledge no other master than the laws which himself has contributed to enact. He despises those nations, who, that one may be free, are all content to be slaves; who first lift a tyrant into terror, and then shrink under his power as if delegated from heaven. Liberty is ecchoed in all their assemblies, and thousands might be found ready to offer up their lives for the sound, though perhaps not one of all the number understands its meaning. The lowest mechanic however looks upon it as his duty to be a watchful guardian of his country's freedom, and often uses a language that might seem haughty, even in the mouth of the great emperor who traces his ancestry to the moon.

A few days ago, passing by one of their prisons, I could not avoid stopping, in order to listen to a dialogue which I thought might afford me some entertainment. The conversation was carried on between a debtor through the grate of his prison, a porter, who had stopped to rest his burthen, and a soldier at the window. The subject was upon a threatened invasion from France, and each seemed extremely anxious to rescue his country from the impending danger. "For my part, cries the prisoner, the greatest of my apprehensions is for our freedom; if the French should conquer, what would become of English liberty. My dear friends, liberty is the Englishman's prerogative; we must preserve that at the expence of our lives, of that the French shall never deprive us; it is not to be expected that men who are slaves themselves would preserve our freedom should they happen to conquer. Ay, slaves, cries the porter, they are all slaves, fit only to carry burthens every one of them. Before I would stoop to slavery, may this be my poison (and he held the goblet in his hand) may this be my poison—but I would sooner list for a soldier."

The soldier taking the goblet from his friend, with much awe fervently cried out, "It is not so much our liberties as our religion that would suffer by such a change: ay, our religion, my lads. May the Devil sink me into flames (such was the solemnity of his adjuration) if the French should come over, but our religion would be utterly undone." So saying, instead of a libation,[1] he applied the goblet to his lips, and confirmed his sentiments with a ceremony of the most persevering devotion.

In short, every man here pretends to be a politician: even the fair sex are sometimes found to mix the severity of national altercation, with the blandishments of love; and often become conquerors by more weapons of destruction than their eyes.

This universal passion for politics is gratified by Daily Gazettes, as with us at China. But as in ours, the emperor endeavours to instruct his people, in theirs the people endeavour to instruct the administration. You must not, however, imagine, that they who compile these papers have any actual knowledge of the politics, or the government of a state: they only collect their materials from the oracle of some coffee-house, which oracle has himself gathered them the night before from a beau at a gaming table, who has pillaged his knowledge from a great man's porter, who has had his information from the great man's gentleman,[2] who has invented the whole story for his own amusement the night preceding.

The English in general seem fonder of gaining the esteem than the love of those they converse with: this gives a formality to their amusements; their gayest conversations have something too wise for innocent relaxation; though in company you are seldom disgusted with the absurdity of a fool; you are seldom lifted into rapture by those strokes of vivacity which give instant, though not permanent pleasure. What they want, however, in gaiety, thay make up in politeness. You smile at hearing me praise the English for their politeness: you who have heard very different accounts from the missionaries at Pekin, who have seen such a different behaviour in their merchants and seamen at home; but I must still repeat it, the English seem more polite than any of their neighbours: their great art in this respect lies in endeavouring, while they oblige, to lessen the force of the favour. Other countries are fond of obliging a stranger; but seem desirous that he should be sensible of the obligation. The English confer their kindness with an appearance of indifference, and give away benefits with an air as if they despised them. Walking a few days ago between an English and a Frenchman into the suburbs of the city, we were overtaken by a heavy shower of rain. I was unprepared; but they had each large coats, which defended them from what seemed to me a perfect inundation. The Englishman seeing me shrink from the weather, accosted me thus: "Psha, man, what dost shrink at; here, take this coat; I don't want it; I find it no way useful to me; I had as lief be without it." The Frenchman began to shew his politeness in turn. "My dear friend," cries he, "why won't you oblige me by making use of my coat; you see how well it defends me from the rain; I should not chuse to part with it to others, but to such a friend as you, I could even part with my skin to do him service." From such minute instances as these, most reverend Fum Hoam, I am sensible your sagacity will collect instruction. The volume of nature is the book of knowledge; and he becomes most wise who makes the most judicious selection. Farewell.

LIEN CHI ALTANGI.

LETTER XXI

From Lien Chi Altangi, to Fum Hoam, first president of the Ceremonial Academy at Pekin, in China.

THE English are as fond of seeing plays acted as the Chinese; but there is a vast difference in the manner of conducting them. We play our pieces in the open air, the English theirs under cover; we act by daylight, they by the blaze of torches. One of our plays continues eight or ten days successively; an English piece seldom takes up above four hours in the representation.

My companion in black,[1] with whom I am now beginning to contract an intimacy, introduced me a few nights ago to the play-house, where we placed ourselves conveniently at the foot of the stage. As the curtain was not drawn before my arrival, I had an opportunity of observing the behaviour of the spectators, and indulging those reflections which novelty generally inspires.

The richest in general were placed in the lowest seats, and the poor rose above them in degrees proportioned to their poverty. The order of precedence seemed here inverted; those who were undermost all the day now enjoyed a temporary eminence, and became masters of the ceremonies. It was they who called for the music, indulging every noisy freedom, and testifying all the insolence of beggary in exaltation.

They who held the middle region seemed not so riotous as those above them, nor yet so tame as those below; to judge by their looks, many of them seem'd strangers there as well as myself. They were chiefly employed during this period of expectation in eating oranges, reading the story of the play, or making assignations.

Those who sat in the lowest rows, which are called the pit, seemed to consider themselves as judges of the merit of the poet and the performers; they were assembled partly to be amused, and partly to shew their taste; appearing to labour under that restraint which an affectation of superior discernment generally produces. My companion, however, informed me, that not one in an hundred of them knew even the first principles of criticism; that they assumed the right

of being censors because there was none to contradict their pretensions; and that every man who now called himself a connoisseur, became such to all intents and purposes.

Those who sat in the boxes appeared in the most unhappy situation of all. The rest of the audience came merely for their own amusement; these rather to furnish out a part of the entertainment themselves. I could not avoid considering them as acting parts in dumb shew, not a curtesy, or nod, that was not the result of art; not a look nor a smile that was not designed for murder. Gentlemen and ladies ogled each other through spectacles; for my companion observed, that blindness was of late become fashionable; all affected indifference and ease, while their hearts at the same time burned for conquest. Upon the whole, the lights, the music, the ladies in their gayest dresses, the men with chearfulness and expectation in their looks, all conspired to make a most agreeable picture, and to fill a heart that sympathises at human happiness with an expressible serenity. The expected time for the play to begin at last arrived, the curtain was drawn, and the actors came on. A woman, who personated a queen, came in curtesying to the audience, who clapped their hands upon her appearance. Clapping of hands is, it seems, the manner of applauding in England: the manner is absurd; but every country, you know, has its peculiar absurdities. I was equally surprised, however, at the submission of the actress, who should have considered herself as a queen, as at the little discernment of the audience who gave her such marks of applause before she attempted to deserve them. Preliminaries between her and the audience being thus adjusted, the dialogue was supported between her and a most hopeful youth, who acted the part of her confidant. They both appeared in extreme distress, for it seems the queen had lost a child some fifteen years before, and still kept its dear resemblance next her heart, while her kind companion bore a part in her sorrows. Her lamentations grew loud. Comfort is offered, but she detests the very sound. She bids them preach comfort to the winds. Upon this her husband comes in, who, seeing the queen so much afflicted, can himself hardly refrain from tears, or avoid partaking in the soft distress. After thus grieving through three scenes, the curtain dropp'd for the first act.

Truly, said I to my companion, these kings and queens are very much disturbed at no very great misfortune; certain I am were people of humbler

Letter XXI. **1. My . . . black:** In Letter xiii Altangi is guided through Westminster Abbey by a man dressed in black, whose eccentricities and history are the topics of Letters xxvi and xxvii.

stations to act in this manner, they would be thought divested of common sense. I had scarce finish'd this observation, when the curtain rose, and the king came on in a violent passion. His wife had, it seems, refused his proffered tenderness, had spurned his royal embrace; and he seemed resolved not to survive her fierce disdain. After he had thus fretted, and the queen had fretted through the second act, the curtain was let down once more.

Now, says my companion, you perceive the king to be a man of spirit, he feels at every pore; one of your phlegmatic sons of clay would have given the queen her own way, and let her come to herself by degrees; but the king is for immediate tenderness, or instant death: death and tenderness are leading passions of every modern buskin'd heroe;[2] this moment they embrace, and the next stab, mixing daggers and kisses in every period.

I was going to second his remarks, when my attention was engrossed by a new object; a man came in balancing a straw upon his nose, and the audience were clapping their hands in all the raptures of applause. To what purpose, cried I, does this unmeaning figure make his appearance; is he a part of the plot? Unmeaning do you call him, replied my friend in black; this is one of the most important characters of the whole play; nothing pleases the people more than the seeing a straw balanced; there is a great deal of meaning in the straw; there is something suited to every apprehension in the sight; and a fellow possessed of talents like these is sure of making his fortune.

The third act now began with an actor, who came to inform us that he was the villain of the play, and intended to shew strange things before all was over. He was joined by another, who seem'd as much disposed for mischief as he; their intrigues continued through this whole division. If that be a villain, said I, he must be a very stupid one, to tell his secrets without being ask'd; such soliloquies of late are never admitted in China.

The noise of clapping interrupted me once more; a child of six years old was learning to dance on the stage, which gave the ladies and mandarines infinite satisfaction. I am sorry, said I, to see the pretty creature so early learning so very bad a trade. Dancing being, I presume, as contemptible here as it is in China.

Quite the reverse, interrupted my companion; dancing is a very reputable and genteel employment; here men have a greater chance for encouragement from the merit of their heels than their heads. One who jumps up and flourishes his toes three times before he comes to the ground, may have three hundred a year; he who flourishes them four times, gets four hundred; but he who arrives at five is inestimable, and may demand what salary he thinks proper. The female dancers too are valued for this sort of jumping and crossing; and 'tis a cant word among them, that she deserves most who shews highest. But the fourth act is begun, let us be attentive.

In the fourth act the queen finds her long lost child, now grown up into a youth of smart parts and great qualifications; wherefore she wisely considers that the crown will fit his head better than that of her husband, whom she knows to be a driveler. The king discovers her design, and here comes on the deep distress; he loves the queen, and he loves the kingdom; he resolves therefore, in order to possess both, that her son must die. The queen exclaims at his barbarity; is frantic with rage, and at length overcome with sorrow, falls into a fit; upon which the curtain drops, and the act is concluded.

Observe the art of the poet, cries my companion; when the queen can say no more, she falls into a fit. While thus her eyes are shut, while she is supported in the arms of Abigail,[3] what horrors do we not fancy, we feel it in every nerve; take my word for it, that fits are the true aposiopesis[4] of modern tragedy.

The fifth act began, and a busy piece it was. Scenes shifting, trumpets sounding, mobs hallooing, carpets spreading, guards bustling from one door to another; gods, dæmons, daggers, racks and ratsbane. But whether the king was killed, or the queen was drowned, or the son was poisoned, I have absolutely forgotten.

When the play[5] was over, I could not avoid observing, that the persons of the drama appeared in as much distress in the first act as the last: how is it possible, said I, to sympathize with them through five long acts; pity is but a short lived passion; I hate to hear an actor mouthing trifles, neither startings, strainings, nor attitudes affect me unless there be

2. **buskin'd heroe:** hero in a tragedy; players in ancient tragedy wore elevated boots known as buskins to increase their stature.

3. **Abigail:** traditional name for a lady's maid. 4. **aposiopesis:** a term of rhetoric denoting a sudden breaking off in the middle of a sentence. 5. **the play:** It has been thought that Goldsmith perhaps had in mind the tragedy *Douglas* (1757) by John Home (1722–1808), which he reviewed in *The Monthly Review* (May, 1757).

cause: after I have been once or twice deceived by those unmeaning alarms, my heart sleeps in peace, probably unaffected by the principal distress. There should be one great passion aimed at by the actor as well as the poet, all the rest should be subordinate, and only contribute to make that the greater; if the actor therefore exclaims upon every occasion in the tones of despair, he attempts to move us too soon; he anticipates the blow, he ceases to affect though he gains our applause.

I scarce perceived that the audience were almost all departed; wherefore, mixing with the crowd, my companion and I got into the street; where essaying an hundred obstacles from coach wheels and palanquin poles,[6] like birds in their flight through the branches of a forest, after various turnings, we both at length got home in safety. | Adieu.

LETTER XLIX

From Lien Chi Altangi, to Fum Hoam, first president of the Ceremonial Academy at Pekin, in China.

As I was yesterday seated at breakfast over a pensive dish of tea, my meditations were interrupted by my old friend and companion, who introduced a stranger, dressed pretty much like himself. The gentleman made several apologies for his visit, begged of me to impute his intrusion to the sincerity of his respect, and the warmth of his curiosity.

As I am very suspicious of my company, when I find them very civil, without any apparent reason, I answered the stranger's caresses at first with reserve, which my friend perceiving, instantly let me into my visitant's trade and character, asking Mr. Fudge whether he had lately published any thing new? I now conjectured that my guest was no other than a bookseller, and his answer confirmed my suspicions.

Excuse me, Sir, says he, it is not the season, books have their time as well as cucumbers; I would no more bring out a new work in summer, than I would sell pork in the dog days. Nothing in my way goes off in summer, except very light goods indeed. A review, a magazine, or a sessions paper,[1] may amuse a summer reader; but all our stock of value we reserve for a spring and winter trade. *I must confess Sir*, says I, *a curiosity to know what you call a valuable stock, which can only bear a winter perusal.* Sir, reply'd the bookseller, it is not my way to cry up my own goods, but without exaggeration I will venture to shew with any of the trade, my books at least have the peculiar advantage of being always new; and it is my way to clear off my old to the trunkmakers[2] every season. I have ten new title pages now about me, which only want books to be added to make them the finest things in nature. Others may pretend to direct the vulgar, but that is not my way; I always let the vulgar direct me; wherever popular clamour arises, I always eccho the million. For instance, should the people in general say that such a man is a rogue, I instantly give orders to set him down in print a villain; thus every man buys the book, not to learn new sentiments, but to have the pleasure of seeing his own reflected. *But Sir, interrupted I, you speak as if you yourself wrote the books you publish; may I be so bold as to ask a sight of some of those intended publications which are shortly to surprise the world.* As to that, Sir, reply'd the talkative bookseller, I only draw out the plans myself; and though I am very cautious of communicating them to any, yet as in the end I have a favour to ask, you shall see a few of them. Here, Sir, here they are diamonds of the first water, I assure you. Imprimis,[3] A translation of several medical precepts for the use of such physicians as do not understand Latin. Item, the young clergyman's art of placing patches[4] regularly, with a dissertation on the different manner of smiling without distorting the face. Item, the whole art of love made perfectly easy, by a broker of 'Change Alley. Item, the proper manner of cutting black-lead pencils, and making crayons; by the Right Hon. the Earl of * * *. Item, the muster master General, or the review of reviews. *Sir, cry'd I, interrupting him, my curiosity with regard to title pages is satisfied, I should be glad to see some longer manuscript, an history, or an epic poem.*—Bless me, cries the man of industry, now you speak of an epic poem, you shall see an excellent farce. Here it is, dip into it where you will, it will be found replete with true modern humour. Strokes, Sir, it is fill'd with strokes of wit and satire in every line. *Do you call these dashes of the pen strokes, reply'd I, for I must confess I can see no other?* And pray Sir, returned he, what do you call them? Do you see anything good now a-days that is

---

6. **palanquin poles:** poles supporting closed litters, which would be the oriental equivalent of sedan chairs. *Letter XLIX.* 1. **a sessions paper:** a list of law cases, mentioned here for its appeal as light scandal.

2. **clear . . . trunkmakers:** Cf. Pope's *Epistle to Augustus,* ll. 415–19, in Part Two. 3. **Imprimis:** in the first place. 4. **patches:** facial beauty patches.

not filled with strokes—and dashes?—Sir, a well placed dash makes half the wit of our writers of modern humour. I bought last season, a piece that had no other merit upon earth than nine hundred and ninety-five breaks, seventy-two ha-ha's, three good things and a garter. And yet it play'd off, and bounced, and cracked, and made more sport than a fire-work. *I fancy then, Sir, you were a considerable gainer?* It must be owned the piece did pay; but upon the whole I cannot much boast of last winter's success; I gain'd by two murders, but then I lost by an ill timed charity sermon. I was a considerable sufferer by my direct road to an estate, but the infernal guide brought me up again. Ah, Sir, that was a piece touch'd off by the hands of a master, filled with good things from one end to the other. The author had nothing but the jest in view; no dull moral lurking beneath, nor ill-natured satyr to sour the reader's good humour; he wisely considered that moral and humour at the same time were quite overdoing the business. *To what purpose was the book then published,* cried I? Sir, the book was published in order to be sold; and no book sold better, except the criticisms upon it, which came out soon after. Of all kinds of writing that goes off best at present, and I generally fasten a criticism upon every selling book that is published.

I once had an author who never left the least opening for the critics: close was the word, always very right, and very dull, ever on the safe side of an argument; yet, with all his qualifications, incapable of coming into favour. I soon perceived that his bent was for criticism; and, as he was good for nothing else, supplied him with pens and paper, and planted him at the beginning of every month as a censor on the works of others. In short, I found him a treasure, no merit could escape him, but what is most remarkable of all, he ever wrote best and bitterest when drunk. *But are there not some works, interrupted I, that from the very manner of their composition must be exempt from criticism, particularly such as profess to disregard its laws.* There is no work whatsoever but he can criticize, replied the bookseller; even though you wrote in Chinese he would have a pluck at you. Suppose you should take it into your head to publish a book, let it be a volume of Chinese letters, for instance; write how you will, he shall shew the world you could have written better. Should you, with the most local exactness, stick to the manners and customs of the country from whence you come; should you confine yourself to the narrow limits of eastern knowledge,

and be perfectly simple, and perfectly natural, he has then the strongest reason to exclaim; he may with a sneer send you back to China for readers. He may observe, that after the first or second letter the iteration of the same simplicity is insupportably tedious; but the worst of all is, the public in such a case will anticipate his censures, and leave you with all your instructive simplicity to be mauled at discretion.

Yes, cried I, *but in order to avoid his indignation, and what I should fear more, that of the public, I would in such a case write with all the knowledge I was master of. As I am not possessed of much learning, at least I would not suppress what little I had, nor would I appear more stupid than nature made me.* Here then, cries the bookseller, we should have you entirely in our power, unnatural, uneastern, quite out of character; erroneously sensible would be the whole cry; Sir, we should then hunt you down like a rat. *Head of my father!* said I, *sure there are but the two ways; the door must either be shut, or it must be open. I must either be natural or unnatural.* Be what you will, we shall criticize you, returned the bookseller, and prove you a dunce in spite of your teeth. But, Sir, it is time that I should come to business. I have just now in the press an history of China; and if you will but put your name to it as the author, I shall repay the obligation with gratitude. What, Sir, replied I, put my name to a work which I have not written. Never while I retain a proper respect for the public and myself. The bluntness of my reply quite abated the ardour of the bookseller's conversation; and, after about half an hour's disagreeable reserve, he with some ceremony took his leave and withdrew. | Adieu.

LETTER CVIII

From Lien Chi Altangi, to Fum Hoam, first president of the Ceremonial Academy at Pekin, in China.

RELIGIOUS Sects in England are far more numerous than in China. Every man who has interest enough to hire a conventicle[1] here, may set up for himself and sell off a new religion. The sellers of the newest pattern at present give extreme good bargains; and let their disciples have a great deal of *confidence* for very little money.

Their shops are much frequented, and their customers every day encreasing, for people are naturally

---

Letter CVIII. **1. conventicle:** religious meeting house.

fond of going to Paradise at as small expence as possible.

Yet you must not conceive this modern sect as differing in opinion from those of the established religion: Difference of opinion indeed formerly divided their sectaries, and sometimes drew their armies to the field. White gowns and black mantles, flapped hats and cross pocket holes were once the obvious causes of quarrel; men then had some reason for fighting, they knew what they fought about; but at present they are arrived at such refinement in religion making, that they have actually formed a new sect without a new opinion; they quarrel for opinions they both equally defend; they hate each other, and that is all the difference between them.

But though their principles are the same, their practice is somewhat different. Those of the established religion laugh, when they are pleased, and their groans are seldom extorted but by pain or danger. The new sect, on the contrary weep for their amusement, and use little music except a chorus of sighs and groans, or tunes that are made to imitate groaning. Laughter is their aversion; lovers court each other from the lamentations; the bridegroom approaches the nuptial couch in sorrowful solemnity, and the bride looks more dismal than an undertaker's shop. Dancing round the room is with them running in a direct line to the devil; and as for gaming, though but in jest, they would sooner play with a rattle snake's tail, than finger a dice box.

By this time you perceive that I am describing a sect of Enthusiasts, and you have already compared them with the Faquirs, Bramins, and Talapoins[2] of the East. Among these you know are generations that have been never known to smile, and voluntary affliction makes up all the merit they can boast of. Enthusiasms in every country produce the same effects; stick the Faquir with pins, or confine the Bramin to a vermin hospital, spread the Talapoin on the ground, or load the Sectary's brow with contrition; those worshippers who discard the light of reason, are ever gloomy; their fears increase in proportion to their ignorance, as men are continually under apprehensions who walk in darkness.

Yet there is still a stronger reason for the enthusiast's being an enemy to laughter, namely, his being himself so proper an object of ridicule. It is remarkable that the propagators of false doctrines have ever been averse

to mirth, and always begin by recommending gravity, when they intended to disseminate imposture. Fohi, the idol of China is represented as having never laughed; Zoroaster the leader of the Bramins is said to have laughed but twice, upon his coming into the world, and upon his leaving it; and Mahomet himself, though a lover of pleasure, was a professed opposer of gaiety. Upon a certain occasion telling his followers, that they would all appear naked at the resurrection, his favourite wife represented such an assembly as immodest and unbecoming. Foolish woman, cried the grave prophet, though the whole assembly be naked, on that day they shall have forgotten to laugh. Men like him opposed ridicule, because they knew it to be a most formidable antagonist, and preached up gravity, to conceal their own want of importance.

Ridicule has ever been the most powerful enemy of enthusiasm, and properly the only antagonist that can be opposed to it with success. Persecution only serves to propagate new religions; they acquire fresh vigour beneath the executioner and the ax, and like some vivacious insects, multiply by dissection. It is also impossible to combat enthusiasm with reason, for though it makes a shew of resistance, it soon eludes the pressure, refers you to distinctions not to be understood, and feelings which it cannot explain: A man who would endeavour to fix an enthusiast by argument, might as well attempt to spread quicksilver with his fingers. The only way to conquer a visionary is to despise him; the stake, the faggot, and the disputing Doctor,[3] in some measure ennoble the opinions they are brought to oppose; they are harmless against innovating pride; contempt alone is truly dreadful. Hunters generally know the most vulnerable part of the beasts they pursue, by the care which every animal takes to defend the side which is weakest; on what side the enthusiast is most vulnerable, may be known by the care which he takes in the beginning to work his disciples into gravity, and guard them against the power of ridicule.

When Philip the Second was King of Spain[4], there was a contest in Salamanca between two orders of friars for superiority. The legend[5] of one side contained more extraordinary miracles, but the legend of the other was reckoned most authentic. They reviled each

2. **Talapoins:** Buddhist monks.

3. **Doctor:** theologian. 4. **When . . . Spain:** during the latter half of the sixteenth century. 5. **legend:** a book containing biographies of saints, accounts of miracles, and other traditional religious materials.

other, as is usual in disputes of divinity, the people were divided into factions, and a civil war appeared unavoidable. In order to prevent such an imminent calamity, the combatants were prevailed upon to submit their legends to the fiery trial, and that which came forth untouched by the fire, was to have the victory, and to be honoured with a double share of reverence. Whenever the people flock to see a miracle, it is an hundred to one, but that they see a miracle; incredible therefore were the numbers that were gathered round upon this occasion; the friars on each side approached, and confidently threw their respective legends into the flames, when lo to the utter disappointment of all the assembly, instead of a miracle, both legends were consumed. Nothing but thus turning both parties into contempt, could have prevented the effusion of blood. The people now laughed at their former folly, and wondered why they fell out. Adieu.

THE DESERTED VILLAGE

Published on May 26, 1770, "this admirable poem" (as James Boswell called it) attained immediate popularity and went through five editions during the first year. In genre it can be regarded as a pastoral complicated by an admixture of descriptive and didactic elements. Its general mode, the idealization of the past, is one for which Goldsmith, like Chatterton and Walpole, felt a profound instinct. Goldsmith took much more care with this poem than with most of his other work: he polished it slowly and conscientiously for almost two years before he published it, and he had the help of Samuel Johnson, who contributed lines 427–30.

The reasons for the rural depopulation that the poem deplores were, first, the destruction of cottages by the wealthy, anxious to improve their vistas and "prospects"; and second, the private enclosure of lands formerly open to public use and the purchase and consolidation of small landholdings by enterprising and progressive entrepreneurs. The small farmers thus displaced either drifted into industrial work in the cities or emigrated to the colonies.

The text is that of the first quarto edition (1770); we have introduced substantive variants from the fourth quarto edition (1770).

TO SIR JOSHUA REYNOLDS.°

DEAR SIR,

I can have no expectations in an address of this kind, either to add to your reputation, or to establish my own. You can gain nothing from my admiration, as I am ignorant of that art in which you are said to excel; and I may lose much by the severity of your judgment, as few have a juster taste in poetry than you. Setting interest therefore aside, to which I never paid much attention, I must be indulged at present in following my affections. The only dedication I ever made was to my brother,[1] because I loved him better than most other men. He is since dead. Permit me to inscribe this Poem to you.

How far you may be pleased with the versification and mere mechanical parts of this attempt, I don't pretend to enquire; but I know you will object (and indeed several of our best and wisest friends concur in the opinion) that the depopulation it deplores is no where to be seen, and the disorders it laments are only to be found in the poet's own imagination. To this I can scarce make any other answer than that I sincerely believe what I have written; that I have taken all possible pains, in my country excursions, for these four or five years past, to be certain of what I alledge, and that all my views and enquiries have led me to believe those miseries real, which I here attempt to display. But this is not the place to enter into an enquiry, whether the country be depopulating, or not; the discusssion would take up much room, and I should prove myself, at best, an indifferent politician, to tire the reader with a long preface, when I want his unfatigued attention to a long poem.

In regretting the depopulation of the country, I inveigh against the increase of our luxuries; and here also I expect the shout of modern politicians against me. For twenty or thirty years past, it has been the fashion to consider luxury as one of the greatest national advantages; and all the wisdom of antiquity in that particular, as erroneous. Still however, I must remain a professed ancient on that head, and continue to think those luxuries prejudicial to states, by which

THE DESERTED VILLAGE. **Sir . . . Reynolds:** Goldsmith became acquainted with the painter Reynolds, later the president of the Royal Academy, in 1761, and both were among the nine charter members of Johnson's Club. **1. to my brother:** the Reverend Henry Goldsmith, who died in 1768; Goldsmith dedicated *The Traveler* to him in 1764.

so many vices are introduced, and so many kingdoms have been undone. Indeed so much has been poured out of late on the other side of the question, that, merely for the sake of novelty and variety, one would sometimes wish to be in the right.

I am, | Dear Sir, | Your sincere friend, | and ardent admirer,

OLIVER GOLDSMITH.

SWEET AUBURN, loveliest village of the plain,
Where health and plenty cheared the labouring swain,
Where smiling spring its earliest visit paid,
And parting summer's lingering blooms delayed,
Dear lovely bowers of innocence and ease,
Seats of my youth, when every sport could please,
How often have I loitered o'er thy green,
Where humble happiness endeared each scene;
How often have I paused on every charm,
The sheltered cot, the cultivated farm,   10
The never failing brook, the busy mill,
The decent church that topt the neighbouring hill,
The hawthorn bush, with seats beneath the shade,
For talking age and whispering lovers made.
How often have I blest the coming day,
When toil remitting lent its turn to play,
And all the village train from labour free
Led up their sports beneath the spreading tree,
While many a pastime circled in the shade,
The young contending as the old surveyed;   20
And many a gambol frolick'd o'er the ground,
And slights of art and feats of strength went round.
And still as each repeated pleasure tired,
Succeeding sports the mirthful band inspired;
The dancing pair that simply sought renown
By holding out to tire each other down,
The swain mistrustless of his smutted face,
While secret laughter tittered round the place,
The bashful virgin's side-long looks of love,
The matron's glance that would those looks
        reprove.   30
These were thy charms, sweet village; sports like
        these,
With sweet succession, taught even toil to please;
These round thy bowers their chearful influence shed,
These were thy charms—But all these charms are fled.

Sweet smiling village, loveliest of the lawn,
Thy sports are fled, and all thy charms withdrawn;
Amidst thy bowers the tyrant's hand is seen,
And desolation saddens all thy green:

One only master grasps the whole domain,
And half a tillage stints thy smiling plain;   40
No more thy glassy brook reflects the day,
But choaked with sedges, works its weedy way.
Along thy glades, a solitary guest,
The hollow sounding bittern guards its nest;
Amidst thy desert walks the lapwing flies,
And tires their ecchoes with unvaried cries.
Sunk are thy bowers in shapeless ruin all,
And the long grass o'ertops the mouldering wall,
And trembling, shrinking from the spoiler's hand,
Far, far away thy children leave the land.   50

Ill fares the land, to hastening ills a prey,
Where wealth accumulates, and men decay;
Princes and lords may flourish, or may fade;
A breath can make them, as a breath has made.
But a bold peasantry, their country's pride,
When once destroyed, can never be supplied.

A time there was, ere England's griefs began,
When every rood° of ground maintained its man;
For him light labour spread her wholesome store,
Just gave what life required, but gave no more.   60
His best companions, innocence and health;
And his best riches, ignorance of wealth.

But times are altered; trade's unfeeling train
Usurp the land and dispossess the swain;
Along the lawn, where scattered hamlets rose,
Unwieldy wealth, and cumbrous pomp repose;
And every want to oppulence allied,
And every pang that folly pays to pride.
These gentle hours that plenty bade to bloom,
Those calm desires that asked but little room,   70
Those healthful sports that graced the peaceful scene,
Lived in each look, and brightened all the green;
These far departing seek a kinder shore,
And rural mirth and manners are no more.

Sweet AUBURN! parent of the blissful hour,
Thy glades forlorn confess the tyrant's power.
Here as I take my solitary rounds,
Amidst thy tangling walks, and ruined grounds,
And, many a year elapsed, return to view
Where once the cottage stood, the hawthorn grew, 80
Remembrance wakes with all her busy train,
Swells at my breast, and turns the past to pain.

In all my wanderings round this world of care,
In all my griefs—and GOD has given my share—

58. **rood:** about one-fourth of an acre.

I still had hopes my latest hours to crown,
Amidst these humble bowers to lay me down;
To husband out life's taper at the close,
And keep the flame from wasting by repose.
I still had hopes, for pride attends us still,
Amidst the swains to shew my book-learned skill,   90
Around my fire an evening groupe to draw,
And tell of all I felt, and all I saw;
And, as an hare whom hounds and horns pursue,
Pants to the place from whence at first she flew,
I still had hopes, my long vexations past,
Here to return—and die at home at last.

O blest retirement, friend to life's decline,
Retreats from care that never must be mine,
How happy he who crowns in shades like these,
A youth of labour with an age of ease;   100
Who quits a world where strong temptations try,
And, since 'tis hard to combat, learns to fly.
For him no wretches, born to work and weep,
Explore the mine, or tempt the dangerous deep;
No surly porter stands in guilty state
To spurn imploring famine from the gate,
But on he moves to meet his latter end,
Angels around befriending virtue's friend;
Bends to the grave with unperceived decay,
While resignation gently slopes the way;   110
And all his prospects brightening to the last,
His Heaven commences ere the world be past!

Sweet was the sound when oft at evening's close,
Up yonder hill the village murmur rose;
There as I past with careless steps and slow,
The mingling notes came softened from below;
The swain responsive as the milk-maid sung,
The sober herd that lowed to meet their young;
The noisy geese that gabbled o'er the pool,
The playful children just let loose from school;   120
The watch-dog's voice that bayed the whispering wind,
And the loud laugh that spoke the vacant mind,
These all in sweet confusion sought the shade,
And filled each pause the nightingale had made.
But now the sounds of population fail,
No chearful murmurs fluctuate in the gale,
No busy steps the grass-grown foot-way tread,
For all the bloomy flush of life is fled.
All but yon widowed, solitary thing
That feebly bends beside the plashy spring;   130
She, wretched matron, forced, in age, for bread,
To strip the brook with mantling cresses spread,

To pick her wintry faggot from the thorn,
To seek her nightly shed, and weep till morn;
She only left of all the harmless train,
The sad historian of the pensive plain.

Near yonder copse, where once the garden smil'd,
And still where many a garden flower grows wild;
There, where a few torn shrubs the place disclose,
The village preacher's modest mansion rose.   140
A man he was, to all the country dear,
And passing rich with forty pounds a year;
Remote from towns he ran his godly race,
Nor e'er had changed, nor wish'd to change his place;
Unpractised he to fawn, or seek for power,
By doctrines fashioned to the varying hour;
Far other aims his heart had learned to prize,
More skilled to raise the wretched than to rise.
His house was known to all the vagrant train,
He chid their wanderings, but relieved their pain;   150
The long remembered beggar was his guest,
Whose beard descending swept his aged breast;
The ruined spendthrift, now no longer proud,
Claimed kindred there, and had his claims allowed;
The broken soldier, kindly bade to stay,
Sate by his fire, and talked the night away;
Wept o'er his wounds, or tales of sorrow done,
Shouldered his crutch, and shewed how fields were
     won.
Pleased with his guests, the good man learned to glow,
And quite forgot their vices in their woe;   160
Careless their merits, or their faults to scan,
His pity gave ere charity began.

Thus to relieve the wretched was his pride,
And even his failings leaned to Virtue's side;
But in his duty prompt at every call,
He watched and wept, he prayed and felt, for all.
And, as a bird each fond endearment tries,
To tempt its new fledged offspring to the skies;
He tried each art, reproved each dull delay,
Allured to brighter worlds, and led the way.   170

Beside the bed where parting life was layed,
And sorrow, guilt, and pain, by turns dismayed,
The reverend champion stood. At his control,
Despair and anguish fled the struggling soul;
Comfort came down the trembling wretch to raise,
And his last faultering accents whispered praise.

At church, with meek and unaffected grace,
His looks adorned the venerable place;

Truth from his lips prevailed with double sway,
And fools, who came to scoff, remained to pray.   180
The service past, around the pious man,
With steady zeal each honest rustic ran;
Even children followed with endearing wile,
And plucked his gown, to share the good man's smile.
His ready smile a parent's warmth exprest,
Their welfare pleased him, and their cares distrest;
To them his heart, his love, his griefs were given,
But all his serious thoughts had rest in Heaven.
As some tall cliff that lifts its awful form
Swells from the vale, and midway leaves the
   storm,   190
Tho' round its breast the rolling clouds are spread,
Eternal sunshine settles on its head.

Beside yon straggling fence that skirts the way,
With blossomed furze unprofitably gay,
There, in his noisy mansion, skill'd to rule,
The village master taught his little school;
A man severe he was, and stern to view,
I knew him well, and every truant knew;
Well had the boding tremblers learned to trace
The day's disasters in his morning face;   200
Full well they laugh'd with counterfeited glee,
At all his jokes, for many a joke had he;
Full well the busy whisper circling round,
Conveyed the dismal tidings when he frowned;
Yet he was kind, or if severe in aught,
The love he bore to learning was in fault;
The village all declared how much he knew;
'Twas certain he could write, and cypher too;
Lands he could measure, terms and tides° presage,
And even the story ran that he could gauge.°   210
In arguing too, the parson owned his skill,
For e'en tho' vanquished, he could argue still;
While words of learned length, and thundering sound,
Amazed the gazing rustics ranged around,
And still they gazed, and still the wonder grew,
That one small head could carry all he knew.

But past is all his fame. The very spot
Where many a time he triumphed, is forgot.
Near yonder thorn, that lifts its head on high,
Where once the sign-post caught the passing eye,   220

Low lies that house where nut-brown draughts
   inspired,
Where grey-beard mirth and smiling toil retired,
Where village statesmen talked with looks profound,
And news much older than their ale went round.
Imagination fondly stoops to trace
The parlour splendours of that festive place;
The white-washed wall, the nicely sanded floor,
The varnished clock that clicked behind the door;
The chest contrived a double debt to pay,
A bed by night, a chest of drawers by day;   230
The pictures placed for ornament and use,
The twelve good rules,° the royal game of goose;°
The hearth, except when winter chill'd the day,
With aspen boughs, and flowers, and fennel gay,
While broken tea-cups, wisely kept for shew,
Ranged o'er the chimney, glistened in a row.

Vain transitory splendours! Could not all
Reprieve the tottering mansion from its fall!
Obscure it sinks, nor shall it more impart
An hour's importance to the poor man's heart;   240
Thither no more the peasant shall repair
To sweet oblivion of his daily care;
No more the farmer's news, the barber's tale,
No more the wood-man's ballad shall prevail;
No more the smith his dusky brow shall clear,
Relax his ponderous strength, and lean to hear;
The host himself no longer shall be found
Careful to see the mantling bliss go round;
Nor the coy maid, half willing to be prest,
Shall kiss the cup to pass it to the rest.   250

Yes! let the rich deride, the proud disdain,
These simple blessings of the lowly train,
To me more dear, congenial to my heart,
One native charm, than all the gloss of art;
Spontaneous joys, where Nature has its play,
The soul adopts, and owns their first born sway,
Lightly they frolic o'er the vacant mind,
Unenvied, unmolested, unconfined.
But the long pomp, the midnight masquerade,
With all the freaks of wanton wealth arrayed,   260

209. **terms and tides:** *Terms* means days for the payment of rent and other obligations; *tides*, seasons and festivals.
210. **gauge:** calculate the capacity of barrels and similar large vessels.

232. **The twelve . . . rules:** twelve homely maxims (e.g., "Pick no quarrels"; "Lay no wagers") attributed to Charles I; printed beneath his woodcut portrait, they were a common wall decoration in eighteenth-century rural houses and inns. **the royal . . . goose:** a table game in which counters are moved across a board according to throws of the dice.

In these, ere triflers half their wish obtain,
The toiling pleasure sickens into pain;
And, even while fashion's brightest arts decoy,
The heart distrusting asks, if this be joy.

Ye friends to truth, ye statesmen who survey
The rich man's joys encrease, the poor's decay,
'Tis yours to judge, how wide the limits stand
Between a splendid and an happy land.
Proud swells the tide with loads of freighted ore,
And shouting Folly hails them from her shore;   270
Hoards, even beyond the miser's wish abound,
And rich men flock from all the world around.
Yet count our gains. This wealth is but a name
That leaves our useful products still the same.
Not so the loss. The man of wealth and pride,
Takes up a space that many poor supplied;
Space for his lake, his park's extended bounds,
Space for his horses, equipage, and hounds;
The robe that wraps his limbs in silken sloth,
Has robbed the neighbouring fields of half their
         growth;   280
His seat, where solitary sports are seen,
Indignant spurns the cottage from the green;
Around the world each needful product flies,
For all the luxuries the world supplies.
While thus the land adorned for pleasure all
In barren splendour feebly waits the fall.

    As some fair female unadorned and plain,
Secure to please while youth confirms her reign,
Slights every borrowed charm that dress supplies,
Nor shares with art the triumph of her eyes.   290
But when those charms are past, for charms are frail,
When time advances, and when lovers fail,
She then shines forth sollicitous to bless,
In all the glaring impotence of dress.
Thus fares the land, by luxury betrayed,
In nature's simplest charms at first arrayed,
But verging to decline, its splendours rise,
Its vistas strike, its palaces surprize;
While scourged by famine from the smiling land,
The mournful peasant leads his humble band;   300
And while he sinks without one arm to save,
The country blooms—a garden, and a grave.

    Where then, ah, where shall poverty reside,
To scape the pressure of contiguous pride;
If to some common's° fenceless limits strayed,
He drives his flock to pick the scanty blade,

Those fenceless fields the sons of wealth divide,
And even the bare-worn common is denied.

    If to the city sped—What waits him there?
To see profusion that he must not share;   310
To see ten thousand baneful arts combined
To pamper luxury, and thin mankind;
To see those joys the sons of pleasure know,
Extorted from his fellow-creature's woe.
Here, while the courtier glitters in brocade,
There the pale artist° plies the sickly trade;
Here, while the proud their long drawn pomps
         display,
There the black gibbet glooms beside the way.
The dome where pleasure holds her midnight reign,
Here richly deckt admits the gorgeous train,   320
Tumultuous grandeur crowds the blazing square,
The rattling chariots clash, the torches glare;
Sure scenes like these no troubles e'er annoy!
Sure these denote one universal joy!
Are these thy serious thoughts?—Ah, turn thine eyes
Where the poor houseless shivering female lies.
She once, perhaps, in village plenty blest,
Has wept at tales of innocence distrest;
Her modest looks the cottage might adorn,
Sweet as the primrose peeps beneath the thorn;   330
Now lost to all; her friends, her virtue fled,
Near her betrayer's door she lays her head,
And pinch'd with cold, and shrinking from the
         shower,
With heavy heart deplores that luckless hour,
When idly first, ambitious of the town,
She left her wheel and robes of country brown.

    Do thine, sweet AUBURN, thine, the loveliest train,
Do thy fair tribes participate her pain?
Even now, perhaps, by cold and hunger led,
At proud men's doors they ask a little bread!   340

    Ah, no. To distant climes, a dreary scene,
Where half the convex world intrudes between,
Through torrid tracts with fainting steps they go,
Where wild Altama° murmurs to their woe.
Far different there from all that charm'd before,
The various terrors of that horrid shore.
Those blazing suns that dart a downward ray,
And fiercely shed intolerable day;
Those matted woods where birds forget to sing,
But silent bats in drowsy clusters cling,   350

305. common: the village parcel of communal grazing land.

316. artist: artisan, craftsman. 344. Altama: the Altamaha
River, in what was then the colony of Georgia.

Those poisonous fields with rank luxuriance crowned
Where the dark scorpion gathers death around;
Where at each step the stranger fears to wake
The rattling terrors of the vengeful snake;
Where crouching tigers wait their hapless prey,
And savage men more murderous still than they;
While oft in whirls the mad tornado flies,
Mingling the ravaged landscape with the skies.
Far different these from every former scene,
The cooling brook, the grassy vested green,   360
The breezy covert of the warbling grove,
That only sheltered thefts of harmless love.

   Good Heaven! what sorrows gloom'd that parting
     day,
That called them from their native walks away;
When the poor exiles, every pleasure past,
Hung round their bowers, and fondly looked their last,
And took a long farewell, and wished in vain
For seats like these beyond the western main;
And shuddering still to face the distant deep,
Returned and wept, and still returned to weep.   370
The good old sire, the first prepared to go
To new found worlds, and wept for others woe.
But for himself, in conscious virtue brave,
He only wished for worlds beyond the grave.
His lovely daughter, lovelier in her tears,
The fond companion of his helpless years,
Silent went next, neglectful of her charms,
And left a lover's for a father's arms.
With louder plaints the mother spoke her woes,
And blest the cot where every pleasure rose;   380
And kist her thoughtless babes with many a tear,
And claspt them close in sorrow doubly dear;
Whilst her fond husband strove to lend relief
In all the silent manliness of grief.

   O luxury! Thou curst by Heaven's decree,
How ill exchanged are things like these for thee!
How do thy potions with insidious joy,
Diffuse their pleasures only to destroy!
Kingdoms by thee, to sickly greatness grown,
Boast of a florid vigour not their own.   390
At every draught more large and large they grow,
A bloated mass of rank unwieldy woe;
Till sapped their strength, and every part unsound,
Down, down they sink, and spread a ruin round.

   Even now the devastation is begun,
And half the business of destruction done;

Even now, methinks, as pondering here I stand,
I see the rural virtues leave the land.
Down where yon anchoring vessel spreads the sail
That idly waiting flaps with every gale,   400
Downward they move a melancholy band,
Pass from the shore, and darken all the strand.
Contented toil, and hospitable care,
And kind connubial tenderness, are there;
And piety with wishes placed above,
And steady loyalty, and faithful love.
And thou, sweet Poetry, thou loveliest maid,
Still first to fly where sensual joys invade;
Unfit in these degenerate times of shame,
To catch the heart, or strike for honest fame;   410
Dear charming nymph, neglected and decried,
My shame in crowds, my solitary pride.
Thou source of all my bliss, and all my woe,
Thou found'st me poor at first, and keep'st me so;
Thou guide by which the nobler arts excell,
Thou nurse of every virtue, fare thee well.
Farewell, and O where'er thy voice he tried,
On Torno's° cliffs, or Pambamarca's° side,
Whether where equinoctial fervours glow,
Or winter wraps the polar world in snow,   420
Still let thy voice prevailing over time,
Redress the rigours of the inclement clime;
Aid slighted truth, with thy persuasive strain
Teach erring man to spurn the rage of gain;
Teach him that states of native strength possest,
Tho' very poor, may still be very blest;
That trade's proud empire hastes to swift decay,
As ocean sweeps the labour'd mole° away;
While self dependent power can time defy,
As rocks resist the billows and the sky.   430

418. **Torno:** the Tornio River, in northeastern Sweden.
Pambamarca: a mountain near Quito, Equador. **428. mole:**
artificial breakwater.

AN ESSAY
ON THE THEATRE;
OR, A COMPARISON
BETWEEN LAUGHING
AND SENTIMENTAL
COMEDY

❧

This essay was part of Goldsmith's campaign—more fully mounted in *She Stoops to Conquer* (1773)—against the reigning mode of sentimental comedy. It has been thought that he had in mind especially Richard Cumberland's *The Fashionable Lover* (1772), a weepy comedy designed to persuade the audience that the Scots were as good as anyone else.

The text is that of the first printing, in *The Westminster Magazine, or the Pantheon of Taste* (1773).

❧

THE Theatre, like all other amusements, has its Fashions and its Prejudices; and when satiated with its excellence, Mankind begin to mistake Change for Improvement. For some years, Tragedy was the reigning entertainment; but of late it has entirely given way to Comedy, and our best efforts are now exerted in these lighter kinds of composition. The pompous Train, the swelling Phrase, and the unnatural Rant, are displaced for that natural portrait of Human Folly and Frailty, of which all are judges, because all have sat for the picture.

But as in describing Nature it is presented with a double face, either of mirth or sadness, our modern Writers find themselves at a loss which chiefly to copy from; and it is now debated, Whether the Exhibition of Human Distress is likely to afford the mind more Entertainment than that of Human Absurdity?

Comedy is defined by Aristotle[1] to be a picture of the Frailties of the lower part of Mankind, to distinguish it from Tragedy, which is an exhibition of the Misfortunes of the Great. When Comedy therefore ascends to produce the Characters of Princes or Generals upon the Stage, it is out of its walk, since Low Life

and Middle Life are entirely its object. The principal question therefore is, Whether in describing Low or Middle Life, an exhibition of its Follies be not preferable to a detail of its Calamities? Or, in other words, Which deserves the preference? The Weeping Sentimental Comedy, so much in fashion at present, or the Laughing and even Low Comedy, which seems to have been last exhibited by Vanbrugh[2] and Cibber?

If we apply to authorities, all the Great Masters in the Dramatic Art have but one opinion. Their rule is, that as Tragedy displays the Calamities of the Great; so Comedy should excite our laughter by ridiculously exhibiting the Follies of the Lower Part of Mankind. Boileau, one of the best modern Critics, asserts, that Comedy will not admit of Tragic Distress.

Le Comique, ennemi des soupirs et des pleurs,
N'admet point dans ses vers de tragiques doleurs.

Nor is this rule without the strongest foundation in Nature, as the distresses of the Mean by no means affect us so strongly as the Calamities of the Great. When Tragedy exhibits to us some Great Man fallen from his height, and struggling with want and adversity, we feel his situation in the same manner as we suppose he himself must feel, and our pity is increased in proportion to the height from whence he fell. On the contrary, we do not so strongly sympathize with one born in humbler circumstances, and encountering accidental distress: so that while we melt for Belisarius,[3] we scarce give halfpence to the Beggar who accosts us in the street. The one has our pity; the other our contempt. Distress, therefore, is the proper object of Tragedy, since the Great excite our pity by their fall; but not equally so of Comedy, since the Actors employed in it are originally so mean, that they sink but little by their fall.

Since the first origin of the Stage, Tragedy and Comedy have run in distinct channels, and never till of late encroached upon the provinces of each other. Terence,[4] who seems to have made the nearest approaches, yet always judiciously stops short before he comes to the downright pathetic; and yet he is even reproached by Cæsar for wanting the *vis comica*.[5]

AN ESSAY ON THE THEATRE. **1. Comedy . . . Aristotle**: in his *Poetics* (*c.* 330 B.C.).

2. Vanbrugh: the playwright Sir John Vanbrugh (1664–1726), author of *The Relapse* (1697) and *The Provoked Husband*, which he left unfinished and which was completed by Cibber in 1728. **3. Belisarius**: a Roman military commander during the reign (527–565) of the Emperor Justinian; accused of conspiracy, he was blinded and reduced to beggary. **4. Terence**: Publius Terentius Afer (*c.* 190–159 B.C.), Roman comic playwright. **5. vis comica**: comic power.

All the other Comic Writers of antiquity aim only at rendering Folly or Vice ridiculous, but never exalt their characters into buskined pomp, or make what Voltaire humourously calls a *Tradesman's Tragedy*.

Yet, notwithstanding this weight of authority, and the universal practice of former ages, a new species of Dramatic Composition has been introduced under the name of *Sentimental* Comedy, in which the virtues of Private Life are exhibited, rather than the Vices exposed; and the Distresses, rather than the Faults of Mankind, make our interest in the piece. These Comedies have had of late great success, perhaps from their novelty, and also from their flattering every man in his favourite foible. In these Plays almost all the Characters are good, and exceedingly generous; they are lavish enough of their *Tin* Money on the Stage, and though they want Humour, have abundance of Sentiment and Feeling. If they happen to have Faults or Foibles, the Spectator is taught not only to pardon, but to applaud them, in consideration of the goodness of their hearts; so that Folly, instead of being ridiculed, is commended, and the Comedy aims at touching our Passions without the power of being truly pathetic: in this manner we are likely to lose one great source of Entertainment on the Stage; for while the Comic Poet is invading the province of the Tragic Muse, he leaves her lovely Sister quite neglected. Of this, however, he is noway solicitous, as he measures his fame by his profits.

But it will be said, that the Theatre is formed to amuse Mankind, and that it matters little, if this end be answered, by what means it is obtained. If Mankind find delight in weeping at Comedy, it would be cruel to abridge them in that or any other innocent pleasure. If those Pieces are denied the name of Comedies; yet call them by any other name, and if they are delightful, they are good. Their success, it will be said, is a mark of their merit, and it is only abridging our happiness to deny us an inlet to Amusement.

These objections, however, are rather specious than solid. It is true, that Amusement is a great object of the Theatre; and it will be allowed, that these Sentimental Pieces do often amuse us: but the question is, Whether the True Comedy would not amuse us more? The question is, Whether a Character supported throughout a Piece with its Ridicule still attending, would not give us more delight than this species of Bastard Tragedy, which only is applauded because it is new?

A friend of mine who was sitting unmoved at one of these Sentimental Pieces, was asked, how he could be so indifferent. "Why, truly," says he, "as the Hero is but a Tradesman, it is indifferent to me whether he be turned out of his Counting-house on Fish-street Hill, since he will still have enough left to open shop in St. Giles's."

The other objection is as ill-grounded; for though we should give these Pieces another name, it will not mend their efficacy. It will continue a kind of *mulish* production, with all the defects of its opposite parents, and marked with sterility. If we are permitted to make Comedy weep, we have an equal right to make Tragedy laugh, and to set down in Black Verse the Jests and Repartees of all the Attendants in a Funeral Procession.

But there is one Argument in favour of Sentimental Comedy which will keep it on the Stage in spite of all that can be said against it. It is, of all others, the most easily written. Those abilities that can hammer out a Novel, are fully sufficient for the production of a Sentimental Comedy. It is only sufficient to raise the Characters a little, to deck out the Hero with a Ribband, or give the Heroine a Title; then to put an Insipid Dialogue, without Character or Humour, into their mouths, give them mighty good hearts, very fine cloaths, furnish a new sett of Scenes, make a Pathetic Scene or two, with a sprinkling of tender melancholy Conversation through the whole, and there is no doubt but all the Ladies will cry, and all the Gentlemen applaud.

Humour at present seems to be departing from the Stage, and it will soon happen, that our Comic Players will have nothing left for it but a fine Coat and a Song. It depends upon the Audience whether they will actually drive those poor Merry Creatures from the Stage, or sit at a Play as gloomy as at the Tabernacle.[6] It is not easy to recover an art when once lost; and it would be but a just punishment that when, by our being too fastidious, we have banished Humour from the Stage, we should ourselves be deprived of the art of Laughing.

---

6. the Tabernacle: the name of the London chapel of the famous Calvinistic Methodist George Whitefield (1714–70).

Edmund Burke

1729–1797

Born in Dublin of a Protestant father and a Catholic mother, Burke inherited both a vehement Irish articulateness and a hatred of dogma and despotism. During his long and zealous political career he defended against tyranny Catholics and Jews, Americans and Bengalese, French royalty and Negro slaves. His charity and humanity were perhaps fostered by his teacher and friend Abraham Shackleton, a Quaker, who conducted a school in nearby Ballitore. Burke entered Trinity College, Dublin, in 1744 and took his bachelor's degree four years later. His education was primarily a series of unconnected enthusiasms, first for logic, then metaphysics, then history, and finally poetry. In 1750 he entered the Middle Temple (one of London's four legal societies) to read law, but as he haunted the coffee houses and theaters he began to entertain literary ambitions.

He started as a miscellaneous writer, publishing anonymously in 1756 *A Vindication of Natural Society*, a parody of Lord Bolingbroke's simplifications about natural religion. The next year he brought out his famous *Philosophical Enquiry into the Origin of Our Ideas of the Sublime and Beautiful*, a psychological treatment of aesthetics based upon the experienced facts of human nature. Turning to journalism in 1758, he began working on *The Annual Register*, a commentary on current events that he edited (and helped write) for the next thirty years.

He first tasted practical politics in 1759, when he became secretary to the young William "Single Speech" Hamilton, Commissioner of the Board of Trade and Plantations. When Hamilton went to Dublin as secretary to the Viceroy, Burke accompanied him and experienced at first hand some of the *de facto* difficulties of governing a complicated people. But until he was in his mid-thirties he was considered a writer rather than a politician. Horace Walpole, who met him at a dinner party in 1761, observed, "He is a sensible man, but has not worn off his authorism yet, and thinks there is nothing so charming as writers, and to be one. He will know better one of these days." Back in London in 1763—he and Hamilton had quarreled—he became one of the favored charter members of Samuel Johnson's Club. Even Johnson was impressed by Burke's conversation: "He does not talk from a desire of distinction," said Johnson, "but because his mind is full." And Boswell reports: "Once, when Johnson was ill, and unable to exert himself as much as usual without fatigue, Mr. Burke having been mentioned, he said, 'That fellow calls forth all my powers. Were I to see Burke now, it would kill me.'"

Burke's political career began in earnest in 1765, when he became private secretary to the Marquis of Rockingham. His duties were virtually those of manager of the Rockingham Whigs, a group of liberal noblemen faithful to the political principles of the Glorious Revolution of 1688. Elected to Parliament in 1766, he immediately spoke in opposition to the government's American policy, and for the next thirty years—except in 1782, when the Rockingham Whigs rose briefly to power—he was a member of the Opposition. He helped define the position of the Rockingham group in *Thoughts on the Cause of the Present Discontents* (1770), an attack on the excessive influence of the Crown and a defense of the principle of the balance and separation of powers. In 1775 appeared his speech *On Conciliation with the Colonies*, typical of Burke in its acceptance of practical political facts. After the ministry of Lord North collapsed in 1782, the Rockingham Whigs—detested by George III— came momentarily to power, and for eight months Burke occupied his only ministerial post, that of Paymaster General.

While his faction was thus briefly in office, he turned his attention to India. In 1786, after years of detailed research into the management of Indian affairs by the Governor General, Warren Hastings, Burke moved his impeachment on charges of corruption and personal dictatorship. Two years later in Westminster Hall the trial of Hastings before the House of Lords began. It dragged on, with long recesses, for seven years; although Hastings was finally acquitted, the trial provided Burke with a setting for some of his most dramatic oratory. So powerful was the impact of his passionate denunciations of Hastings that women were carried fainting from the hall, and even the celebrated actress Mrs. Siddons expressed envy of Burke's histrionic gifts.

But sensational as it was, the trial was suddenly thrown into the shade by the storming of the Bastille in July, 1789, an event that induced in Burke a state of eloquent antirevolutionary outrage that he maintained at white heat for the rest of his life. With the appearance in 1790 of his *Reflections on the Revolution in France*, he became a political pariah, and most of the Whigs, under the leadership now of Charles James Fox, came to resent what seemed to them the violent apostasy of Burke's speeches. When Boswell informed Johnson that Burke's political enemies represented him as actually mad, Johnson answered, "Sir, if A Man will appear extravagant as he does, and cry, can he wonder that he is represented as mad?" Burke hurled himself into anti-Jacobin activities and turned his estate at Beaconsfield into a virtual asylum for aristocratic French refugees.

Writings on the French Revolution now streamed from his pen. In *A Letter to a Member of the National Assembly* (1791) he denounced Rousseau and the philosophic assumptions behind the Revolution. In *An Appeal from the New to the Old Whigs* (1791) he argued that his own anti-Jacobin position was closer to the sacred Whig principles of 1688 than the position of the Foxites. The execution of Louis XVI and the outbreak of war between England and France in 1793 horrified him; the death of his only son in 1794 left him prostrate: "I am as a man dead," he wrote. Attacked in the House of Lords for accepting a large pension from the Pitt ministry, he responded with his searing *Letter to a Noble Lord* (1796). In his last writings, *Four Letters on the Proposals for Peace with the Regicide Directory of France* (1796–1812), he insisted to the end that traditional Europe could effect no compromise with the doctrines underlying the French Revolution. When he died, his erstwhile colleague Fox, from whom he had been increasingly estranged since 1790, proposed a state funeral in Westminster Abbey, but Burke, who feared that the Jacobins might come to power in England and desecrate his grave, had left instructions for an obscure burial at Beaconsfield.

Persuaded of the dangers of the utopian imagination, he based his political positions on a profound distrust of planners and theoreticians. The great fact to which all political reasoning must adapt itself, he argued repeatedly, is human nature as unfolded in history. If reforms are necessary, he urged, they must be "organic" reforms, changes "grafted" upon long-tried institutions, since these—churches and aristocracies, for example—tend to express a general and permanent human nature. It is his insistence on the examination of actual human nature that gives Burke's utterances—whether their subject is conciliation with America or war with France—their large consistency.

Although he was a master of the plain style as well as the ornate, it was the copious and audacious metaphors of his later works that attracted the most public attention. One political cartoon, in which he is caricatured as usual with a long pointed nose and outsized spectacles, bears as a caption these lines from Samuel Butler's *Hudibras* (1663–78): "For Rhetoric he could not ope / His Mouth but out there flew a Trope." After hearing him speak in 1773, Boswell observed, "It was astonishing how all kinds of figures of speech crowded upon him. He was like a man in an Orchard where boughs loaded with fruit hung around him, and he pulled apples as fast as he pleased and pelted the ministry." But despite this figurative brilliance his speeches were often found intolerably prolix and diffuse. His political enemies nicknamed him the Dinner Bell, pointing out that when he rose to speak the House of Commons went out to dine. Many were offended too by his addiction to theatrical devices: during a debate on French affairs in 1792, for example, he portentously drew a dagger and hurled it to the floor of the house. To Johnson he seemed on occasion "a lion, who lashes himself into a fury with his own tail."

During his lifetime he was the target of immense political abuse. He was accused of being a Papist and a Jesuit in disguise; some thought him a corrupt Irish adventurer turned fanatic, and others, observing that the Burke family had a personal financial interest in discrediting Hastings, assumed that he was some sort of hypocritical stockjobber. In the nineteenth century more than one historian, contemplating Burke's hyperboles on the French Revolution, considered him actually insane during his last years. But Macaulay thought him "the greatest man since Milton," and to Coleridge he was "a seer," gifted with prophecy.

For bibliography, consult the list of modern studies in Francesco Cordasco's *Edmund Burke: A Handlist of Critical Notices and Studies* (1950). A well-annotated selection from Burke is E. J. Payne's (3 vols., 1874–78); the selection by W. J. Bate (1960) has a provocative introduction. The *Sublime and Beautiful* is edited by J. T. Boulton (1958). The biographies by Philip Magnus (1939) and R. H. Murray (1931) are readable. The *Correspondence* is edited by T. W. Copeland and others (6 vols., 1958–   ). John Morley's *Burke* (1879) and Charles Parkin's *The Moral Basis of*

Burke's Political Thought (1956) are good interpretative studies. Copeland's essay "The Little Dogs and All," in his *Our Eminent Friend Edmund Burke* (1949), is an interesting analysis of Burke's perplexing character.

[AN ADDRESS TO THE KING]

In January, 1777, Lord Rockingham and other Whig members of both Houses of Parliament considered seceding completely from Parliament as a dramatic protest against the policy of the North ministry in prosecuting the war with the American colonies and rejecting all appeals for conciliation. Although the proposed total secession never took place, Burke reluctantly prepared this statement and held it ready for transmission to the court. It was found among his papers after his death.

The text is that of the first printing, in Volume V (1812) of *The Works of the Right Honourable Edmund Burke*, ed. French Laurence and Walker King (8 vols., 1792–1827).

WE, your Majesty's most dutiful and loyal Subjects, several of the Peers of the Realm, and several Members of the House of Commons chosen by the people to represent them in Parliament, do in our individual capacity, but with hearts filled with a warm affection to your Majesty, with a strong attachment to your Royal House, and with the most unfeigned devotion to your true interest, beg leave, at this crisis of your affairs, in all humility to approach your Royal presence.

Whilst we lament the measures adopted by the publick Councils of the Kingdom, we do not mean to question the legal validity of their proceedings. We do not desire to appeal from them to any person whatsoever. We do not dispute the conclusive authority of the bodies, in which we have a place, over all their Members. We know, that it is our ordinary duty to submit ourselves to the determinations of the Majority, in every thing, except what regards the just defence of our honour and reputation. But the situation, into which the British Empire has been brought, and the

conduct, to which we are reluctantly driven in that situation, we hold ourselves bound by the relation, in which we stand both to the Crown and the people, clearly to explain to your Majesty and our Country.

We have been called upon in the speech from the Throne at the opening of this Session of Parliament, in a manner peculiarly marked, singularly emphatical, and from a place, from whence any thing implying censure falls with no common weight, to concur in unanimous approbation of those measures, which have produced our present distresses and threaten us in future with others far more grievous. We trust, therefore, that we shall stand justified in offering to our Sovereign and the Publick our reasons for persevering inflexibly in our uniform dissent from every part of those measures. We lament them from an experience of their mischief, as we originally opposed them from a sure foresight of their unhappy and inevitable tendency.

We see nothing in the present events, in the least degree, sufficient to warrant an alteration in our opinion. We were always steadily averse to this civil War—not because we thought it impossible, that it should be attended with victory; but because we were fully persuaded, that in such a contest, victory would only vary the mode of our ruin; and, by making it less immediately sensible, would render it the more lasting and the more irretrievable. Experience had but too fully instructed us in the possibility of the reduction of a free people to slavery by foreign mercenary armies. But we had an horror of becoming the instruments in a design, of which, in our turn, we might become the victims. Knowing the inestimable value of peace, and the contemptible value of what was sought by War, we wished to compose the distractions of our Country, not by the use of foreign arms, but by prudent regulations in our own domestick policy. We deplored, as your Majesty has done in your speech from the Throne, the disorders, which prevail in your Empire: but we are convinced, that the disorders of the people, in the present time and in the present place, are owing to the usual and natural cause of such disorders, at all times and in all places, where such have prevailed,—the misconduct of Government;—that they are owing to plans laid in error, pursued with obstinacy, and conducted without wisdom.

We cannot attribute so much to the power of faction, at the expence of human nature, as to suppose, that, in any part of the world, a combination of men, few in number, not considerable in rank, of no natural hereditary dependencies, should be able, by the efforts of their policy alone, or the mere exertion of any talents, to bring the people of your American Dominions into the disposition, which has produced the present troubles. We cannot conceive, that, without some powerful concurring cause, any management should prevail on some millions of people, dispersed over an whole Continent, in thirteen Provinces, not only unconnected, but in many particulars of religion, manners, government, and local interest totally different and adverse, voluntarily to submit themselves to a suspension of all the profits of industry and all the comforts of civil life, added to all the evils of an unequal War carried on with circumstances of the greatest asperity and rigour. This, Sir, we conceive, could never have happened, but from a general sense of some grievance, so radical in its nature, and so spreading in its effects, as to poison all the ordinary satisfactions of life, to discompose the frame of society, and to convert into fear and hatred, that habitual reverence ever paid by mankind to an antient and venerable Government.

That grievance is as simple in its nature, and as level to the most ordinary understanding, as it is powerful in affecting the most languid passions:—it is

"AN ATTEMPT MADE TO DISPOSE OF THE PROPERTY OF A WHOLE PEOPLE WITHOUT THEIR CONSENT."

Your Majesty's English Subjects in the Colonies, possessing the ordinary faculties of mankind, know, that to live under such a plan of government is not to live in a state of freedom. Your English Subjects in the Colonies, still impressed with the antient feelings of the people from whom they are derived, cannot live under a Government, which does not establish Freedom as its basis.

This scheme being therefore set up in direct opposition to the rooted and confirmed sentiments and habits of thinking of an whole people, has produced the effects, which ever must result from such a collision of power and opinion. For we beg leave, with all duty and humility, to represent to your Majesty, (what we fear has been industriously concealed from you) that

it is not merely the opinion of a very great number or even of the majority, but the universal sense of the whole body of the people in those provinces, that the practice of taxing, in the mode and on the principles, which have been lately contended for and enforced, is subversive of all their rights.

This sense has been declared, as we understand on good information, by the unanimous voice of all their Assemblies; each Assembly also, on this point, is perfectly unanimous within itself. It has been declared as fully by the actual voice of the people without these Assemblies, as by the constructive voice within them; as well by those in that Country, who addressed, as by those, who remonstrated; and it is as much the avowed opinion of those, who have hazarded their all rather than take up arms against your Majesty's forces, as of those, who have run the same risk to oppose them. The difference among them is, not on the grievance, but on the mode of redress; and we are sorry to say, that they, who have conceived hopes from the placability of the Ministers, who influence the publick Councils of this Kingdom, disappear in the multitude of those, who conceive, that passive compliance only confirms and emboldens oppression.

The sense of a whole people, most gracious Sovereign, never ought to be contemned by wise and beneficent rulers; whatever may be the abstract claims, or even rights of *the supreme power*. We have been too early instructed, and too long habituated to believe, that the only firm seat of all authority is in the minds, affections, and interests of the people, to change our opinions on the theoretick reasonings of speculative men, or for the convenience of a mere temporary arrangement of State. It is not consistent with equity or wisdom to set at defiance the general feelings of great communities and of all the orders which compose them. Much power is tolerated and passes unquestioned where much is yielded to opinion. All is disputed where every thing is enforced.

Such are our sentiments on the duty and policy of conforming to the prejudices of a whole people, even where the foundation of such prejudices may be false or disputable. But permit us to lay at your Majesty's feet our deliberate judgment on the real merits of that principle, the violation of which is the known ground and origin of these troubles. We assure your Majesty, that, on our parts, we should think ourselves unjustifiable, as good citizens, and not influenced by the true spirit of Englishmen, if, with any effectual means of prevention in our hands, we were to submit to Taxes, to which we did not consent, either directly, or by a representation of the people securing to us the substantial benefit of an absolutely free disposition of our own property in that important case. And we add, Sir, that if fortune, instead of blessing us with a situation, where we may have daily access to the propitious presence of a gracious Prince, had fixed us in settlements on the remotest part of the globe, we must carry these sentiments with us, as part of our being; persuaded, that the distance of situation would render this privilege in the disposal of property but the more necessary. If no provision had been made for it, such provision ought to be made, or permitted. Abuses of subordinate authority encrease, and all means of redress lessen, as the distance of the Subject removes him from the seat of the supreme power. What, in those circumstances, can save him from the last extremes of indignity and oppression, but something left in his own hands, which may enable him to conciliate the favor and controul the excesses of Government? When no means of power to awe or to oblige, are possessed, the strongest ties, which connect mankind in every relation social and civil, and which teach them mutually to respect each other, are broken.—Independency, from that moment, virtually exists. Its formal declaration will quickly follow. Such must be our feelings for ourselves: we are not in possession of another rule for our brethren.

When the late attempt practically to annihilate that inestimable privilege was made, great disorders and tumults very unhappily and very naturally arose from it. In this state of things, we were of opinion, that satisfaction ought instantly to be given; or that, at least, the punishment of the disorder ought to be attended with the redress of the grievance. We were of opinion, that, if our dependencies had so outgrown the positive institutions made for the preservation of Liberty in this Kingdom, that the operation of their powers was become rather a pressure than a relief to the Subjects in the Colonies, wisdom dictated, that the spirit of the Constitution should rather be applied to their circumstances, than its authority enforced with violence in those very parts, where its reason became wholly inapplicable.

Other methods were then recommended and followed, as infallible means of restoring peace and order. We looked upon them to be, what they have since proved to be, the cause of inflaming discontent into disobedience, and resistance into revolt. The subversion of solemn, fundamental Charters, on a suggestion of abuse, without citation, evidence, or hearing: the total suspension of the commerce of a great maritime city,[1] the capital of a great maritime province, during the pleasure of the Crown: the establishment of a military force, not accountable to the ordinary Tribunals of the Country, in which it was kept up:—these and other proceedings at that time, if no previous cause of dissension had subsisted, were sufficient to produce great troubles: unjust at all times, they were then irrational.

We could not conceive, when disorders had arisen from the complaint of one violated right, that to violate every other was the proper means of quieting an exasperated people. It seemed to us absurd and preposterous, to hold out, as the means of calming a people in a state of extreme inflammation and ready to take up arms, the austere law, which a rigid conqueror would impose, as the sequel of the most decisive victories.

Recourse, indeed, was at the same time had to force; and we saw a force sent out, enough to menace liberty, but not to awe opposition; tending to bring odium on the civil power, and contempt on the military; at once to provoke and encourage resistance. Force was sent out not sufficient to hold one town: Laws were passed to inflame thirteen provinces.

This mode of proceeding, by harsh laws and feeble armies, could not be defended on the principle of mercy and forbearance. For mercy, as we conceive, consists not in the weakness of the means, but in the benignity of the ends. We apprehend that mild measures may be powerfully enforced: and that acts of extreme rigour and injustice may be attended with as much feebleness in the execution, as severity in the formation.

In consequence of these terrors, which, falling upon some, threatened all, the Colonies made a common cause with the sufferers; and proceeded, on their part, to acts of resistance. In that alarming situation, we besought your Majesty's Ministers to entertain some distrust of the operation of coercive measures, and to profit of their experience. Experience had no effect. The modes of legislative rigour were construed, not to have been erroneous in their policy, but too limited in their extent. New severities were adopted. The fisheries of your people in America followed their charters; and their mutual combination to defend

AN ADDRESS TO THE KING. **1. a great . . . city:** Boston, whose port was closed by Act of Parliament in 1774.

what they thought their common rights, brought on a total prohibition of their mutual commercial intercourse. No distinction of persons or merits was observed—the peaceable and the mutinous, friends and foes were alike involved, as if the rigour of the laws had a certain tendency to recommend the authority of the legislator.

Whilst the penal laws encreased in rigour, and extended in application over all the Colonies, the direct force was applied but to one part. Had the great fleet and foreign army since employed, been at that time called for, the greatness of the preparation would have declared the magnitude of the danger. The nation would have been alarmed, and taught the necessity of some means of reconciliation with our countrymen in America, who, whenever they are provoked to resistance, demand a force to reduce them to obedience full as destructive to us as to them. But Parliament and the people, by a premeditated concealment of their real situation, were drawn into perplexities, which furnished excuses for further armaments; and whilst they were taught to believe themselves called to suppress a riot, they found themselves involved in a mighty War.

At length British blood was spilled by British hands —a fatal æra, which we must ever deplore, because your Empire will for ever feel it! Your Majesty was touched with a sense of so great a disaster. Your paternal breast was affected with the sufferings of your English Subjects in America. In your Speech from the Throne, in the beginning of the Session of 1775, you were graciously pleased to declare yourself inclined to relieve their distresses, and to pardon their errors. Your felt their sufferings under the late penal Acts of Parliament. But your Ministry felt differently. Not discouraged by the pernicious effects of all they had hitherto advised, and notwithstanding the gracious declaration of your Majesty, they obtained another Act of Parliament, in which the rigours of all the former were consolidated, and embittered by circumstances of additional severity and outrage. The whole trading property of America (even unoffending shipping in port) was indiscriminately and irrecoverably given, as the plunder of foreign Enemies, to the sailors of your Navy. This property was put out of the reach of your mercy. Your people were despoiled; and your Navy, by a new, dangerous, and prolific example, corrupted with the plunder of their countrymen. Your people in that part of your dominions, were put, in their general and political, as well as their personal capacity, wholly out of the protection of your Government.

Though unwilling to dwell on all the improper modes of carrying on this unnatural and ruinous War, and which have led directly to the present unhappy separation of Great Britain and its Colonies, we must beg leave to represent two particulars, which we are sure must have been entirely contrary to your Majesty's order or approbation. Every course of action in hostility, however that hostility may be just or merited, is not justifiable or excusable. It is the duty of those, who claim to rule over others, not to provoke them beyond the necessity of the case; nor to leave stings in their minds, which must long rankle, even when the appearance of tranquillity is restored.—We therefore assure your Majesty, that it is with shame and sorrow we have seen several acts of hostility, which could have no other tendency than incurably to alienate the minds of your American Subjects. To excite, by a Proclamation issued by your Majesty's Governor, an universal insurrection of Negro Slaves in any of the Colonies, is a measure full of complicated horrors; absolutely illegal; suitable neither to the practice of war, or to the laws of peace. Of the same quality we look upon all attempts to bring down on your Subjects an irruption of those fierce and cruel tribes of Savages and Cannibals, in whom the vestiges of human nature are nearly effaced by ignorance and barbarity. They are not fit Allies for your Majesty, in a war with your people. They are not fit instruments of an English Government. These, and many other acts, we disclaim as having advised, or approved when done; and we clear ourselves to your Majesty and to all civilized nations, from any participation whatever, before or after the fact, in such unjustifiable and horrid proceedings.

But there is one weighty circumstance, which we lament equally with the causes of the War, and with the modes of carrying it on—that no disposition whatsoever towards peace or reconciliation has ever been shewn by those, who have directed the public Councils of this Kingdom, either before the breaking out of these hostilities, or during the unhappy continuance of them. Every proposition, made in your Parliament to remove the original cause of these troubles, by taking off taxes, obnoxious for their principle or their design, has been overruled. Every Bill, brought in for quiet, rejected, even on the first proposition. The Petitions of the Colonies have not been admitted, even to an hearing. The very possibility of public agency, by which such Petitions could authentically arrive at

Parliament, has been evaded and chicaned away. All the public declarations, which indicate any thing resembling a disposition to reconciliation, seem to us loose, general, equivocal, capable of various meanings or of none; and they are accordingly construed differently, at different times, by those, on whose recommendation they have been made; being wholly unlike the precision and stability of public faith; and bearing no mark of that ingenuous simplicity, and native candour and integrity, which formerly characterized the English nation.

Instead of any relaxation of the claim of taxing at the discretion of Parliament, your Ministers have devised a new mode of enforcing that claim, much more effectual, for the oppression of the Colonies, though not for your Majesty's Service, both as to the quantity and application, than any of the former methods; and their mode has been expressly held out by Ministers, as a plan not to be departed from by the House of Commons, and as the very condition, on which the Legislature is to accept the dependence of the Colonies.

At length, when after repeated refusals to hear or to conciliate, an Act, dissolving your Government by putting your people in America out of your protection, was passed, your Ministers suffered several months to elapse, without affording to them, or to any Community or any Individual amongst them, the means of entering into that protection, even on unconditional submission, contrary to your Majesty's gracious Declaration from the Throne, and in direct violation of the public faith.

We cannot, therefore, agree to unite in new severities, against the brethren of our blood, for their asserting an independency, to which, we know in our conscience, they have been necessitated by the conduct of those very persons, who now make use of that argument to provoke us to a continuance and repetition of the acts, which in a regular series have led to this great misfortune.

The reasons, dread Sir, which have been used to justify this perseverance in a refusal to hear or conciliate, have been reduced into a sort of Parliamentary maxims, which we do not approve. The first of these maxims is, "that the Two Houses ought not to receive (as they have hitherto refused to receive) Petitions containing matter derogatory to any part of the authority they claim." We conceive this maxim, and the consequent practice, to be unjustifiable by reason, or the practice of other sovereign powers, and that it must be productive, if adhered to, of a total separation between this kingdom and its dependencies. The supreme power, being in ordinary cases the ultimate judge, can, as we conceive, suffer nothing in having any part of his rights excepted to, or even discussed, before himself. We know, that Sovereigns, in other countries, where the assertion of absolute regal power is as high, as the assertion of absolute power in any politick body can possibly be here, have received many Petitions in direct opposition to many of their claims of prerogative; have listened to them; condescended to discuss, and to give answers to them. This refusal to admit even the discussion of any part of an undefined prerogative, will naturally tend to annihilate any privilege, that can be claimed by every inferior dependent Community and every subordinate order in the State.

The next maxim, which has been put as a bar to any plan of accommodation, is, "that no offer of terms of Peace ought to be made, before Parliament is assured, that these terms will be accepted." On this we beg leave to represent to your Majesty, that if, in all events, the policy of this kingdom is, to govern the people in your Colonies as a free people, no mischief can possibly happen from a declaration, to them and to the world, of the manner and form, in which Parliament proposes that they shall enjoy the freedom it protects. It is an encouragement to the innocent and meritorious, that they, at least, shall enjoy those advantages, which they patiently expected rather from the benignity of Parliament, than their own efforts. Persons more contumacious may also see, that they are resisting terms of, perhaps, greater freedom and happiness, than they are now in arms to obtain. The glory and propriety of offered mercy is neither tarnished or weakened by the folly of those, who refuse to take advantage of it.

We cannot think, that the declaration of Independency makes any natural difference in the reason and policy of the offer. No Prince, out of the possession of his dominions and become a Sovereign *de jure*[2] only, ever thought it derogatory to his rights or his interests, to hold out to his former Subjects a distinct prospect of the advantages to be derived from his readmission, and a security for some of the most fundamental of those popular privileges, in vindication of which he had been deposed. On the contrary, such offers have been almost uniformly made under similar circumstances. Besides, as your Majesty has been graciously pleased,

2. **de jure:** according to law.

in your Speech from the Throne, to declare your intention of restoring your people in the Colonies to a state of Law and Liberty, no objection can possibly lie against defining what that Law and Liberty are; because those, who offer, and those, who are to receive terms, frequently differ most widely and most materially in the signification of these words, and in the objects to which they apply.

To say, that we do not know at this day what the grievances of the Colonies are, (be they real or pretended), would be unworthy of us. But, whilst we are thus waiting to be informed of what we perfectly know, we weaken the powers of the Commissioners; we delay, perhaps we lose, the happy hour of Peace; we are wasting the substance of both countries; we are continuing the effusion of human, of christian, of English blood.

We are sure, that we must have your Majesty's heart along with us, when we declare in favour of mixing something conciliatory with our force. Sir, we abhor the idea of making a conquest of our countrymen. We wish, that they may yield to well ascertained, well authenticated, and well secured terms of reconciliation; not, that your Majesty should owe the recovery of your dominions to their total waste and destruction. Humanity will not permit us to entertain such a desire; nor will the reverence we bear to the civil rights of mankind make us even wish, that questions of great difficulty, of the last importance, and lying deep in the vital principles of the British Constitution, should be solved by the arms of foreign mercenary soldiers.

It is not, Sir, from a want of the most inviolable duty to your Majesty, not from a want of a partial and passionate regard to that part of your Empire, in which we reside, and which we wish to be supreme, that we have hitherto withstood all attempts to render the supremacy of one part of your dominions inconsistent with the liberty and safety of all the rest. The motives of our opposition are found in those very sentiments, which we are supposed to violate. For we are convinced beyond a doubt, that a system of dependence, which leaves no security to the people for any part of their freedom in their own hands, cannot be established in any inferior member of the British Empire, without consequentially destroying the freedom of that very body, in favour of whose boundless pretensions such a scheme is adopted. We know and feel, that arbitrary power over distant regions is not within the competence, nor to be exercised agreeably to the forms or consistently with the spirit of great

popular assemblies. If such assemblies are called to a nominal share in the exercise of such power, in order to screen under general participation the guilt of desperate measures, it tends only the more deeply to corrupt the deliberative character of those assemblies, in training them to blind obedience; in habituating them to proceed upon grounds of fact, with which they can rarely be sufficiently acquainted, and in rendering them executive instruments of designs, the bottom of which they cannot possibly fathom.

To leave any real freedom to Parliament, freedom must be left to the Colonies. A military Government is the only substitute for civil liberty. That the establishment of such a power in America will utterly ruin our finances (though its certain effect) is the smallest part of our concern. It will become an apt, powerful and certain engine for the destruction of our freedom here. Great bodies of armed men, trained to a contempt of popular assemblies representative of an English people; kept up for the purpose of exacting impositions without their consent, and maintained by that exaction; instruments in subverting, without any process of Law, great antient establishments and respected forms of Governments; set free from, and therefore above the ordinary English tribunals of the country where they serve;—these men cannot so transform themselves, merely by crossing the sea, as to behold with love and reverence, and submit with profound obedience, to the very same things in Great Britain, which in America they had been taught to despise, and had been accustomed to awe and humble. All your Majesty's troops, in the rotation of service, will pass through this discipline, and contract these habits. If we could flatter ourselves that this would not happen, we must be the weakest of men: we must be the worst, if we were indifferent whether it happened or not. What, gracious Sovereign, is the Empire of America to us, or the Empire of the world, if we lose our own liberties? We deprecate this last of evils. We deprecate the effect of the doctrines, which must support and countenance the government over conquered Englishmen.

As it will be impossible long to resist the powerful and equitable arguments, in favour of the freedom of these unhappy people, that are to be drawn from the principle of our own liberty; attempts will be made, attempts have been made, to ridicule and to argue away this principle; and to inculcate into the minds of your people, other maxims of government and other grounds of obedience, than those, which have prevailed at and since the glorious Revolution.[3] By degrees, these doctrines, by being convenient, may grow prevalent. The consequence is not certain; but a general change of principles rarely happens among a people, without leading to a change of Government.

Sir, your Throne cannot stand secure upon the principles of unconditional submission and passive obedience; on powers exercised without the concurrence of the people to be governed; on Acts made in defiance of their prejudices and habits; on acquiescence procured by foreign mercenary troops, and secured by standing armies. These may possibly be the foundation of other Thrones; they must be the subversion of yours. It was not to passive principles in our ancestors, that we owe the honour of appearing before a Sovereign, who cannot feel, that he is a Prince, without knowing, that we ought to be free. The Revolution is a departure from the antient course of the descent of this Monarchy. The people, at that time, re-entered into their original rights; and it was not because a positive Law authorized what was then done, but because the freedom and safety of the Subject, the origin and cause of all Laws, required a proceeding paramount and superior to them. At that ever memorable and instructive period, the letter of the Law was superseded in favour of the substance of Liberty. To the free choice, therefore, of the people, without either King or Parliament, we owe that happy Establishment, out of which both King and Parliament were regenerated. From that great principle of Liberty have originated the Statutes, confirming and ratifying the Establishment, from which your Majesty derives your right to rule over us. Those Statutes have not given us our Liberties; our Liberties have produced them. Every hour of your Majesty's reign, your title stands upon the very same foundation, on which it was at first laid; and we do not know a better, on which it can possibly be placed.

Convinced, Sir, that you cannot have different rights, and a different security in different parts of your dominions, we wish to lay an even platform for your Throne; and to give it an unmovable stability, by laying it on the general freedom of your people;

and by securing to your Majesty that confidence and affection, in all parts of your dominions, which makes your best security and dearest title in this, the chief seat of your Empire.

Such, Sir, being, amongst us, the foundation of Monarchy itself, much more clearly and much more peculiarly is it the ground of all Parliamentary power. Parliament is a security, provided for the protection of Freedom, and not a subtile fiction, contrived to amuse the people, in its place. The authority of both Houses can, still less than that of the Crown, be supported upon different principles in different places; so as to be, for one part of your Subjects, a protector of Liberty, and, for another a fund of despotism, through which prerogative is extended by occasional powers, whenever an arbitrary will finds itself straitened by the restrictions of Law. Had it seemed good to Parliament to consider itself as the indulgent guardian and strong protector of the freedom of the subordinate popular Assemblies,[4] instead of exercising its powers to their annihilation, there is no doubt, that it never could have been their inclination, because not their interest, to raise questions on the extent of Parliamentary Rights; or to enfeeble privileges, which were the security of their own. Powers, evident from necessity, and not suspicious from an alarming mode or purpose in the exertion, would, as formerly they were, be cheerfully submitted to; and these would have been fully sufficient for conservation of unity in the Empire, and for directing its wealth to one common centre. Another use has produced other consequences; and a power, which refuses to be limited by moderation, must either be lost, or find other more distinct and satisfactory limitations.

As for us, a supposed, or, if it could be, a real participation in arbitrary power, would never reconcile our minds to its establishment. We should be ashamed to stand before your Majesty, boldly asserting, in our own favour, inherent rights, which bind and regulate the Crown itself, and yet insisting on the exercise, in our own persons, of a more arbitrary sway over our fellow citizens and fellow freemen.

These, gracious Sovereign, are the sentiments, which we consider ourselves as bound, in justification of our present conduct, in the most serious and solemn manner, to lay at your Majesty's feet. We have been called by your Majesty's writs and proclamations, and

---

3. the glorious Revolution: (or Bloodless Revolution) the name given to the series of political and military maneuvers in 1688 and 1689 that resulted in the flight to France of the Roman Catholic James II, the accession of the Protestant William and Mary, the firm establishment of the Whig and Tory parties, and the foundation of the system of limited, constitutional monarchy.

4. the subordinate . . . Assemblies: in the American colonies.

we have been authorized either by hereditary privilege, or the choice of your people, to confer and treat with your Majesty in your highest Councils, upon the arduous affairs of your Kingdom. We are sensible of the whole importance of the duty, which this constitutional summons implies. We know the religious punctuality of attendance, which, in the ordinary course, it demands. It is no light cause, which, even for a time, could persuade us to relax in any part of that attendance. The British Empire is in convulsions, which threaten its dissolution. Those particular proceedings, which cause and inflame this disorder, after many years incessant struggle, we find ourselves wholly unable to oppose, and unwilling to behold. All our endeavours having proved fruitless, we are fearful, at this time, of irritating, by contention, those passions, which we have found it impracticable to compose by reason. We cannot permit ourselves to countenance, by the appearance of a silent assent, proceedings fatal to the Liberty and Unity of the Empire; proceedings, which exhaust the strength of all your Majesty's dominions, destroy all trust and dependence of our Allies, and leave us, both at home and abroad, exposed to the suspicious mercy and uncertain inclinations of our neighbour and rival powers; to whom, by this desperate course, we are driving our Countrymen for protection, and with whom we have forced them into connections, and may bind them by habits and by interests;—an evil, which no victories, that may be obtained, no severities which may be exercised, ever will or can remove.

If but the smallest hope should from any circumstances appear, of a return to the antient maxims and true policy of this Kingdom, we shall with joy and readiness return to our attendance, in order to give our hearty support to whatever means may be left for alleviating the complicated evils, which oppress this Nation.

If this should not happen, we have discharged our consciences by this faithful representation to your Majesty and our Country; and however few in number, or however we may be overborne by practices, whose operation is but too powerful, by the revival of dangerous exploded principles, or by the misguided zeal of such arbitrary factions, as formerly prevailed in this Kingdom, and always to its detriment and disgrace, we have the satisfaction of standing forth and recording our names in assertion of those principles, whose operation hath, in better times, made your Majesty a great Prince, and the British Dominions a mighty Empire.

FROM

REFLECTIONS ON THE REVOLUTION IN FRANCE . . .

The explicit occasion of Burke's renowned *Reflections* was a sermon "On the Love of Our Country" delivered before the Revolutionary Society by Dr. Richard Price, a dissenting divine, on November 4, 1789, the anniversary of the landing in England of William of Orange. Favorably comparing the French Revolution with the British Glorious Revolution of 1688, Dr. Price commended the French on their political wisdom and vigor. After his sermon, which was delivered at a dissenting meeting house in the Old Jewry, Dr. Price conducted many of his congregation to the nearby London Tavern, where a message of congratulation to the French National Assembly was drafted. It was delivered in person by Charles, Lord Stanhope.

Burke immediately began setting down his reactions to Dr. Price's behavior, casting his ideas in the form of a letter to a young Frenchman. Almost a year afterward he was still revising and amending, and by the time the work was ready for the press it had swollen to an immense size. A book of 356 pages, the *Reflections* is surely one of the longest "letters" ever published. In the matter of address as well as in length Burke transcends the conventions of the genre, speaking sometimes only to his young correspondent and sometimes to the whole French people.

Thirty thousand copies were soon in circulation, and although the praise was loud, it was not universal. Thomas Paine was one of the influential voices of the opposition: in his *Rights of Man* (1791–92) he taxed Burke with writing "in a phrenzy of passion," and noting a marked absence in Burke of sympathy with the victims of monarchical and clerical oppression, he declared, "He pities the plumage, but neglects the dying bird." In short, writes Paine, "I cannot consider Mr. Burke's book in any other light than a dramatic performance; and he must, I think, have considered it in the same light himself, by the poetical liberties he has taken of omitting some facts, distorting others, and making the whole machinery bend to produce a stage effect." But admirers of Burke's energetic argument and gorgeous rhetoric were both numerous and influential. George III never tired of saying that the book was one every gentleman should read, and Louis XVI, destined for the guillotine three years later, is said to have translated it himself into French. The historian Edward

Gibbon was moved to a rare moment of enthusiasm; he wrote Lord Sheffield, "I admire his eloquence, I approve his politics, I adore his chivalry, and I can even forgive his superstition."

This selection comprises about one-seventh of the whole. The text is that of the first edition (as discriminated by W. B. Todd), *Reflections on the Revolution in France, and on the Proceedings in Certain Societies in London Relative to That Event. In a Letter Intended to Have Been Sent to a Gentleman in Paris* (London, [November 1,] 1790). We have incorporated the substantive revisions of the "seventh edition" (1790).

⚜

The science of constructing a commonwealth, or renovating it, or reforming it, is, like every other experimental science, not to be taught *à priori*.[1] Nor is it a short experience that can instruct us in that practical science; because the real effects of moral causes are not always immediate; but that which in the first instance is prejudicial may be excellent in its remoter operation; and its excellence may arise even from the ill effects it produces in the beginning. The reverse also happens; and very plausible schemes, with very pleasing commencements, have often shameful and lamentable conclusions. In states there are often some obscure and almost latent causes, things which appear at first view of little moment, on which a very great part of its prosperity or adversity may most essentially depend. The science of government being therefore so practical in itself, and intended for such practical purposes, a matter which requires experience, and even more experience than any person can gain in his whole life, however sagacious and observing he may be, it is with infinite caution that any man ought to venture upon pulling down an edifice which has answered in any tolerable degree for ages the common purposes of society, or on building it up again, without having models and patterns of approved utility before his eyes.

These metaphysic rights entering into common life, like rays of light which pierce into a dense medium, are, by the laws of nature, refracted from their straight line. Indeed in the gross and complicated mass of human passions and concerns, the primitive rights of men[2] undergo such a variety of refractions and reflections, that it becomes absurd to talk of them as if they continued in the simplicity of their original direction. The nature of man is intricate; the objects of society are of the greatest possible complexity; and therefore no simple disposition or direction of power can be suitable either to man's nature, or to the quality of his affairs. When I hear the simplicity of contrivance aimed at and boasted of in any new political constitutions, I am at no loss to decide that the artificers are grossly ignorant of their trade, or totally negligent of their duty. The simple governments are fundamentally defective, to say no worse of them. If you were to contemplate society in but one point of view, all these simple modes of polity are infinitely captivating. In effect each would answer its single end much more perfectly than the more complex is able to attain all its complex purposes. But it is better that the whole should be imperfectly and anomalously answered, than that, while some parts are provided for with great exactness, others might be totally neglected, or perhaps materially injured, by the over-care of a favourite member.

The pretended rights of these theorists are all extremes; and in proportion as they are metaphysically true, they are morally and politically false. The rights of men are in a sort of *middle*, incapable of definition, but not impossible to be discerned. The rights of men in governments are their advantages; and these are often in balances between differences of good; in compromises sometimes between good and evil, and sometimes, between evil and evil. Political reason is a computing principle; adding, subtracting, multiplying, and dividing, morally and not metaphysically or mathematically, true moral denominations.

By these theorists the right of the people is almost always sophistically confounded with their power. The body of the community, whenever it can come to act, can meet with no effectual resistance; but till power and right are the same, the whole body of them has no right inconsistent with virtue, and the first of all

2. rights of men: This phrase, stylish among *philosophes* and radicals of the day, was made especially famous by the Declaration of the Rights of Man and the Citizen, a brief document modeled on the American Declaration of Independence and adopted by the French National Assembly on August 27, 1789. It asserted that among the "natural, inalienable, and sacred rights of man" are liberty, property, security, and resistance to oppression, and that the source of all sovereignty is the will of the people.

virtues, prudence. Men have no right to what is not reasonable, and to what is not for their benefit; for though a pleasant writer said, *Liceat perire poetis*, when one of them, in cold blood, is said to have leaped into the flames of a volcanic revolution, *Ardentem frigidus Ætnam insiluit*,[3] I consider such a frolic rather as an unjustifiable poetic licence, than as one of the franchises of Parnassus; and whether he were poet or divine, or politician that chose to exercise this kind of right, I think that more wise, because more charitable thoughts would urge me rather to save the man, than to preserve his brazen slippers as the monuments of his folly.

The kind of anniversary sermons, to which a great part of what I write refers, if men are not shamed out of their present course, in commemorating the fact, will cheat many out of the principles, and deprive them of the benefits of the Revolution they commemorate. I confess to you, Sir, I never liked this continual talk of resistance and revolution, or the practice of making the extreme medicine of the constitution its daily bread. It renders the habit of society dangerously valetudinary: it is taking periodical doses of mercury sublimate,[4] and swallowing down repeated provocatives of cantharides[5] to our love of liberty.

This distemper of remedy, grown habitual, relaxes and wears out, by a vulgar and prostituted use, the spring of that spirit which is to be exerted on great occasions. It was in the most patient period of Roman servitude that themes of tyrannicide made the ordinary exercise of boys at school—*cum perimit sævos classis numerosa tyrannos*.[6] In the ordinary state of things, it produces in a country like ours the worst effects, even on the cause of that liberty which it abuses with the dissoluteness of an extravagant speculation. Almost all the high-bred republicans of my time have, after a short space, become the most decided, thorough-paced courtiers; they soon left the business of a tedious, moderate, but practical resistance to those of us whom,

in the pride and intoxication of their theories, they have slighted, as not much better than tories. Hypocrisy, of course, delights in the most sublime speculations; for, never intending to go beyond speculation, it costs nothing to have it magnificent. But even in cases where rather levity than fraud was to be suspected in these ranting speculations, the issue has been much the same. These professors, finding their extreme principles not applicable to cases which call only for a qualified, or, as I may say, civil and legal resistance, in such cases employ no resistance at all. It is with them a war or a revolution, or it is nothing. Finding their schemes of politics not adapted to the state of the world in which they live, they often come to think lightly of all public principle; and are ready, on their part, to abandon for a very trivial interest what they find of very trivial value. Some indeed are of more steady and persevering natures; but these are eager politicians out of parliament, who have little to tempt them to abandon their favourite projects. They have some change in the church or state, or both, constantly in their view. When that is the case, they are always bad citizens, and perfectly unsure connexions. For, considering their speculative designs as of infinite value, and the actual arrangement of the state as of no estimation, they are at best indifferent about it. They see no merit in the good, and no fault in the vicious management of public affairs; they rather rejoice in the latter, as more propitious to revolution. They see no merit or demerit in any man, or any action, or any political principle, any further than as they may forward or retard their design of change: they therefore take up, one day, the most violent and stretched prerogative, and another time the wildest democratic ideas of freedom, and pass from the one to the other without any sort of regard to cause, to person, or to party.

In France you are now in the crisis of a revolution, and in the transit from one form of government to another—you cannot see that character of men exactly in the same situation in which we see it in this country. With us it is militant; with you it is triumphant; and you know how it can act when its power is commensurate to its will. I would not be supposed to confine those observations to any description of men, or to comprehend all men of any description within them —No! far from it. I am as incapable of that injustice, as I am of keeping terms with those who profess principles of extremes; and who under the name of religion teach little else than wild and dangerous

---

3. a pleasant . . . insiluit: Line 466 of Horace's *Ars Poetica* reads: "Let poets die in whatever manner they please." He referred to Empedocles, a Greek philosopher, scientist, and poet of the fifth century B.C. who, according to tradition, "coolly leaped into burning Etna." It is said that he wore brass sandals that were later cast up by the volcano. 4. mercury sublimate: a remedy for venereal disease; it is deadly in large quantities. 5. cantharides: a dangerous aphrodisiac. 6. cum . . . tyrannos: "when the class [chanting its school exercises] destroys [in verse] the cruel tyrants" (Juvenal, *Satires*, III. vii. 151).

politics. The worst of these politics of revolution is this; they temper and harden the breast, in order to prepare it for the desperate strokes which are sometimes used in extreme occasions. But as these occasions may never arrive, the mind receives a gratuitous taint; and the moral sentiments suffer not a little, when no political purpose is served by the depravation. This sort of people are so taken up with their theories about the rights of man, that they have totally forgot his nature. Without opening one new avenue to the understanding, they have succeeded in stopping up those that lead to the heart. They have perverted in themselves, and in those that attend to them, all the well-placed sympathies of the human breast.

This famous sermon of the Old Jewry breathes nothing but this spirit through all the political part. Plots, massacres, assassinations, seem to some people a trivial price for obtaining a revolution. A cheap, bloodless reformation, a guiltless liberty, appear flat and vapid to their taste. There must be a great change of scene; there must be a magnificent stage effect; there must be a grand spectacle to rouze the imagination, grown torpid with the lazy enjoyment of sixty years security, and the still unanimating repose of public prosperity. The Preacher found them all in the French revolution. This inspires a juvenile warmth through his whole frame. His enthusiasm kindles as he advances; and when he arrives at his peroration, it is in a full blaze. Then viewing, from the Pisgah[7] of his pulpit, the free, moral, happy, flourishing, and glorious state of France, as in a bird-eye landscape of a promised land, he breaks out into the following rapture:

"What an eventful period is this! I am *thankful* that I have lived to it; I could almost say, *Lord, now lettest thou thy servant depart in peace, for mine eyes have seen thy salvation.*[8]—I have lived to see a *diffusion* of knowledge, which has undermined superstition and error.— I have lived to see *the rights of men* better understood than ever; and nations panting for liberty which seemed to have lost the idea of it.—I have lived to see *Thirty Millions of People*, indignant and resolute, spurning at slavery, and demanding liberty with an irresist-

ible voice. *Their King led in triumph, and an arbitrary monarch surrendering himself to his subjects.*"[9]

Before I proceed further, I have to remark, that Dr. Price seems rather to over-value the great acquisitions of light which he has obtained and diffused in this age. The last century appears to me to have been quite as much enlightened. It had, though in a different place, a triumph as memorable as that of Dr. Price; and some of the great preachers of that period partook of it as eagerly as he has done in the triumph of France. On the trial of the Rev. Hugh Peters[10] for high treason, it was deposed, that when King Charles was brought to London for his trial, the Apostle of Liberty in that day conducted the *triumph.* "I saw," says the witness, "his majesty in the coach with six horses, and Peters riding before the king *triumphing.*" Dr. Price, when he talks as if he had made a discovery, only follows a precedent; for, after the commencement of the king's trial, this precursor, the same Dr. Peters, concluding a long prayer at the royal chapel at Whitehall, (he had very triumphantly chosen his place) said, "I have prayed and preached these twenty years; and now I may say with old Simeon, *Lord, now lettest thou thy servant depart in peace, for mine eyes have seen thy salvation.*"[11] Peters had not the fruits of his prayer; for he neither departed so soon as he wished, nor in peace. He became (what I heartily hope none of his followers may be in this country) himself a sacrifice to the triumph which he led as Pontiff. They dealt at the Restoration, perhaps, too hardly with this poor good man. But we owe it to his memory and his sufferings, that he has as much illumination, and as much zeal, and had as effectually undermined all *the superstition and error* which might impede the great business he was engaged in, as any who follow and repeat after him, in this age, which would assume to itself an exclusive title to the knowledge of the rights of men, and all the glorious consequences of that knowledge.

9. Their . . . subjects: [Burke's note] Another of these reverend gentlemen, who was witness to some of the spectacles which Paris has lately exhibited—expresses himself thus, "*A king dragged in submissive triumph by his conquering subjects* is one of those appearances of grandeur which seldom rise in the prospect of human affairs, and which, during the remainder of my life, I shall think of with wonder and gratification." These gentlemen agree marvellously in their feelings. **10. the Rev. . . . Peters:** (1598–1660), a regular preacher at Whitehall during Cromwell's protectorate; after the Restoration he was put to death for his part in the execution of Charles I. **11. I have . . . salvation:** [Burke's note] State Trials, vol. ii. p. 360, p. 363.

7. Pisgah: the mountain from whose summit Moses viewed the Promised Land (Deut. 34:1–4). **8. Lord . . . salvation:** the words spoken by Simeon upon witnessing the infant Christ in the temple (Luke 2:29–30); these words (known as the *Nunc Dimittis* from the first two words of their form in the Vulgate) are part of the service of Evening Prayer in the Church of England.

After this sally of the preacher of the Old Jewry, which differs only in place and time, but agrees perfectly with the spirit and letter of the rapture of 1648,[12] the Revolution Society, the fabricators of governments, the heroic band of *cashierers* of *monarchs*, electors of sovereigns, and leaders of kings in triumph, strutting with a proud consciousness of the diffusion of knowledge, of which every member had obtained so large a share in the donative, were in haste to make a generous diffusion of the knowledge they had thus gratuitously received. To make this bountiful communication, they adjourned from the church in the Old Jewry, to the London Tavern; where the same Dr. Price, in whom the fumes of his oracular tripod were not entirely evaporated, moved and carried the resolution, or address of congratulation, transmitted by Lord Stanhope to the National Assembly of France.

I find a preacher of the gospel prophaning the beautiful and prophetic ejaculation, commonly called "*nunc dimittis*," made on the first presentation of our Saviour in the Temple, and applying it, with an inhuman and unnatural rapture, to the most horrid, atrocious, and afflicting spectacle, that perhaps ever was exhibited to the pity and indignation of mankind. This "*leading in triumph*," a thing in its best form unmanly and irreligious, which fills our Preacher with such unhallowed transports, must shock, I believe, the moral taste of every well-born mind. Several English were the stupified and indignant spectators of that triumph. It was (unless we have been strangely deceived) a spectacle more resembling a procession of American savages, entering into Onondaga,[13] after some of their murders called victories, and leading into hovels hung round with scalps, their captives, overpowered with the scoffs and buffets of women as ferocious as themselves, much more than it resembled the triumphal pomp of a civilized martial nation;—if a civilized nation, or any men who had a sense of generosity, were capable of a personal triumph over the fallen and afflicted.

This, my dear Sir, was not the triumph of France. I must believe that, as a nation, it overwhelmed you with shame and horror. I must believe that the National Assembly find themselves in a state of the greatest humiliation, in not being able to punish the authors of this triumph, or the actors in it; and that they are in a

situation in which any enquiry they may make upon the subject, must be destitute even of the appearance of liberty or impartiality. The apology of that Assembly is found in their situation; but when we approve what they *must* bear, it is in us the degenerate choice of a vitiated mind.

With a compelled appearance of deliberation, they vote under the dominion of a stern necessity. They sit in the heart, as it were, of a foreign republic: they have their residence in a city whose constitution has emanated neither from the charter of their king, nor from their legislative power. There they are surrounded by an army not raised either by the authority of their crown, or by their command; and which, if they should order to dissolve itself, would instantly dissolve them. There they sit, after a gang of assassins had driven away some hundreds of the members; whilst those who held the same moderate principles, with more patience or better hope, continued every day exposed to outrageous insults and murderous threats. There a majority, sometimes real, sometimes pretended, captive itself, compels a captive king to issue as royal edicts, at third hand, the polluted nonsense of their most licentious and giddy coffee-houses. It is notorious, that all their measures are decided before they are debated. It is beyond doubt, that under the terror of the bayonet, and the lamp-post, and the torch to their houses, they are obliged to adopt all the crude and desperate measures suggested by clubs composed of a monstrous medley of all conditions, tongues, and nations. Among these are found persons, in comparison of whom Catiline would be thought scrupulous, and Cethegus[14] a man of sobriety and moderation. Nor is it in these clubs alone that the publick measures are deformed into monsters. They undergo a previous distortion in academies, intended as so many seminaries for these clubs, which are set up in all the places of publick resort. In these meetings of all sorts, every counsel, in proportion as it is daring, and violent, and perfidious, is taken for the mark of superior genius. Humanity and compassion are ridiculed as the fruits of superstition and ignorance. Tenderness to individuals is considered as treason to the public. Liberty is always to be estimated perfect as property is rendered insecure. Amidst assassination, massacre, and confiscation, perpetrated or meditated, they are forming plans for the

---

12. 1648: the year of the trial and condemnation of Charles I.
13. Onondaga: an Indian village near the present city of Syracuse, N.Y.

14. Catiline, Cethegus: leaders of a Roman rebellion in the first century B.C.; they were characterized by Cicero as moral monsters.

good order of future society. Embracing in their arms the carcases of base criminals, and promoting their relations on the title of their offences, they drive hundreds of virtuous persons to the same end, by forcing them to subsist by beggary or by crime.

The Assembly, their organ, acts before them the farce of deliberation with as little decency as liberty. They act like the comedians of a fair before a riotous audience; they act amidst the tumultuous cries of a mixed mob of ferocious men, and of women lost to shame, who, according to their insolent fancies, direct, control, applaud, explode[15] them; and sometimes mix and take their seats amongst them; domineering over them with a strange mixture of servile petulance and proud presumptuous authority. As they have inverted order in all things, the gallery is in the place of the house. This Assembly, which overthrows kings and kingdoms, has not even the physiognomy and aspect of a grave legislative body—*nec color imperii, nec frons erat ulla senatus.*[16] They have a power given to them, like that of the evil principle, to subvert and destroy; but none to construct, except such machines as may be fitted for further subversion and further destruction.

Who is it that admires, and from the heart is attached to national representative assemblies, but must turn with horror and disgust from such a profane burlesque, and abominable perversion of that sacred institute? Lovers of monarchy, lovers of republicks, must alike abhor it. The members of your Assembly must themselves groan under the tyranny of which they have all the shame, none of the direction, and little of the profit. I am sure many of the members who compose even the majority of that body, must feel as I do, notwithstanding the applauses of the Revolution Society.—Miserable king! miserable Assembly! How must that assembly be silently scandalized with those of their members, who could call a day which seemed to blot the sun out of Heaven, "un beau jour!"[17] How must they be inwardly indignant at hearing others, who thought fit to declare to them, "that the vessel of the state would fly forward in her course towards regeneration with more speed than ever,"[18] from the stiff

gale of treason and murder, which preceded our Preacher's triumph! What must they have felt, whilst with outward patience and inward indignation they heard of the slaughter of innocent gentlemen in their houses, that "the blood spilled was not the most pure?" What must they have felt, when they were besieged by complaints of disorders which shook their country to its foundations, at being compelled coolly to tell the complainants, that they were under the protection of the law, and that they would address the king (the captive king) to cause the laws to be enforced for their protection; when the enslaved ministers of that captive king had formally notified to them, that there were neither law, nor authority, nor power left to protect? What must they have felt at being obliged, as a felicitation on the present new year, to request their captive king to forget the stormy period of the last, on account of the great good which *he* was likely to produce to his people; to the complete attainment of which good they adjourned the practical demonstrations of their loyalty, assuring him of their obedience, when he should no longer possess any authority to command?

This address was made with much good-nature and affection, to be sure. But among the revolutions in France, must be reckoned a considerable revolution in their ideas of politeness. In England we are said to learn manners at second-hand from your side of the water, and that we dress our behaviour in the frippery of France. If so, we are still in the old cut; and have not so far conformed to the new Parisian mode of good-breeding, as to think it quite in the most refined strain of delicate compliment (whether in condolence or congratulation) to say, to the most humiliated creature that crawls upon the earth, that great public benefits are derived from the murder of his servants, the attempted assassination of himself and of his wife, and the mortification, disgrace, and degradation, that he has personally suffered. It is a topic of consolation which our ordinary of Newgate[19] would be too humane to use to a criminal at the foot of the gallows. I should have thought that the hangman of Paris, now that he is liberalized by the vote of the National Assembly, and is allowed his rank and arms in the Herald's College of the rights of men, would be too generous, too gallant a man, too full of the sense of his new dignity, to employ that cutting consolation to

15. **explode:** hoot off the stage. 16. **nec . . . senatus:** neither pretense of authority, nor any appearance of a senate. 17. **un . . . jour:** [Burke's note] 6th of October 1789 [the "beautiful day" on which Louis XVI and Marie-Antoinette were forcibly conducted by the mob from Versailles to the Tuileries]. 18. **that . . . ever:** Burke is translating from a speech by the French revolutionary leader Mirabeau.

19. **ordinary of Newgate:** prison chaplain.

any of the persons whom the *leze nation*[20] might bring under the administration of his *executive powers.*

A man is fallen indeed, when he is thus flattered. The anodyne draught of oblivion, thus drugged, is well calculated to preserve a galling wakefulness, and to feed the living ulcer of a corroding memory. Thus to administer the opiate potion of amnesty, powdered with all the ingredients of scorn and contempt, is to hold to his lips, instead of "the balm of hurt minds,"[21] the cup of human misery full to the brim, and to force him to drink it to the dregs.

Yielding to reasons, at least as forcible as those which were so delicately urged in the compliment on the new year, the king of France will probably endeavour to forget these events, and that compliment. But history, who keeps a durable record of all our acts, and exercises her awful censure over the proceedings of all sorts of sovereigns, will not forget, either those events, or the æra of this liberal refinement in the intercourse of mankind. History will record, that on the morning of the 6th of October 1789, the king and queen of France, after a day of confusion, alarm, dismay, and slaughter, lay down, under the pledged security of public faith, to indulge nature in a few hours of respite, and troubled melancholy repose. From this sleep the queen was first startled by the voice of the centinel at her door, who cried out to her, to save herself by flight—that this was the last proof of fidelity he could give—that they were upon him, and he was dead. Instantly he was cut down. A band of cruel ruffians and assassins, reeking with his blood, rushed into the chamber of the queen, and pierced with an hundred strokes of bayonets and poniards the bed, from whence this persecuted woman had but just time to fly almost naked, and through ways unknown to the murderers had escaped to seek refuge at the feet of a king and husband, not secure of his own life for a moment.

This king, to say no more of him, and this queen, and their infant children (who once would have been the pride and hope of a great and generous people) were then forced to abandon the sanctuary of the most splendid palace in the world, which they left swimming in blood, polluted by massacre, and strewed with scattered limbs and mutilated carcases. Thence they were conducted into the capital of their kingdom. Two had been selected from the unprovoked, unresisted, promiscuous slaughter, which was made of

the gentlemen of birth and family who composed the king's body guard. These two gentlemen, with all the parade of an execution of justice, were cruelly and publickly dragged to the block, and beheaded in the great court of the palace. Their heads were stuck upon spears, and led the procession; whilst the royal captives who followed in the train were slowly moved along, amidst the horrid yells, and shrilling screams, and frantic dances, and infamous contumelies, and all the unutterable abominations of the furies of hell, in the abused shape of the vilest of women. After they had been made to taste, drop by drop, more than the bitterness of death, in the slow torture of a journey of twelve miles, protracted to six hours, they were, under a guard, composed of those very soldiers who had thus conducted them through this famous triumph, lodged in one of the old palaces of Paris, now converted into a Bastile for kings.

Is this a triumph to be consecrated at altars? to be commemorated with grateful thanksgiving? to be offered to the divine humanity with fervent prayer and enthusiastick ejaculation?—These Theban and Thracian Orgies, acted in France, and applauded only in the Old Jewry, I assure you, kindle prophetic enthusiasm in the minds but of very few people in this kingdom; although a saint and apostle, who may have revelations of his own, and who has so completely vanquished all the mean superstitions of the heart, may incline to think it pious and decorous to compare it with the entrance into the world of the Prince of Peace, proclaimed in an holy temple by a venerable sage, and not long before not worse announced by the voice of angels to the quiet innocence of shepherds.

At first I was at a loss to account for this fit of unguarded transport. I knew, indeed, that the sufferings of monarchs make a delicious repast to some sort of palates. There were reflexions which might serve to keep this appetite within some bounds of temperance. But when I took one circumstance into my consideration, I was obliged to confess, that much allowance ought to be made for the Society, and that the temptation was too strong for common discretion; I mean, the circumstance of the Io Pæan[22] of the triumph, the animating cry which called "for *all* the BISHOPS to be hanged on the lamp-posts,"[23] might well have brought forth a burst of enthusiasm on the foreseen consequences of this happy day. I allow to so

---

20. leze nation: (*lèse nation*) treason against the nation. **21. the balm . . . minds:** See *Macbeth*, II. ii. 30.

22. Io Pæan: joyous religious hymn. **23. all . . . lamp-posts:** [Burke's note] Tous les Eveques à la lanterne.

much enthusiasm some little deviation from prudence. I allow this prophet to break forth into hymns of joy and thanksgiving on an event which appears like the precursor of the Millenium, and the projected fifth monarchy,[24] in the destruction of all church establishments. There was, however (as in all human affairs there is) in the midst of this joy something to exercise the patience of these worthy gentlemen, and to try the long-suffering of their faith. The actual murder of the king and queen, and their child, was wanting to the other auspicious circumstances of this *"beautiful day."* The actual murder of the bishops, though called for by so many holy ejaculations, was also wanting. A groupe of regicide and sacrilegious slaughter, was indeed boldly sketched, but it was only sketched. It unhappily was left unfinished, in this great history-piece of the massacre of innocents. What hardy pencil of a great master, from the school of the rights of men, will finish it, is to be seen hereafter. The age has not yet the compleat benefit of that diffusion of knowledge that has undermined superstition and error; and the king of France wants another object or two, to consign to oblivion, in consideration of all the good which is to arise from his own sufferings, and the patriotic crimes of an enlightened age.[25]

Although this work of our new light and knowledge, did not go to the length, that in all probability it was intended it should be carried; yet I must think, that such treatment of any human creatures must be shocking to any but those who are made for accomplishing Revolutions. But I cannot stop here. Influenced by the inborn feelings of my nature, and not being illuminated by a single ray of this new-sprung modern light, I confess to you, Sir, that the exalted rank of the persons suffering, and particularly the sex, the beauty, and the amiable qualities of the descendant of so many kings and emperors, with the tender age of royal infants, insensible only through infancy and innocence of the cruel outrages to which their parents were exposed, instead of being a subject of exultation, adds not a little to my sensibility on that most melancholy occasion.

I hear that the august person, who was the principal object of our preacher's triumph, though he supported himself, felt much on that shameful occasion. As a man, it became him to feel for his wife and his children, and the faithful guards of his person, that were massacred in cold blood about him; as a prince, it became him to feel for the strange and frightful transformation of his civilized subjects, and to be more grieved for them, than sollicitous for himself. It derogates little from his fortitude, while it adds infinitely to the honour of his humanity. I am very sorry to say it, very sorry indeed, that such personages are in a situation in which it is not unbecoming in us to praise the virtues of the great.

I hear, and I rejoice to hear, that the great lady, the other object of the triumph, has borne that day (one is interested that beings made for suffering should suffer well) and that she bears all the succeeding days, that she bears the imprisonment of her husband, and her own captivity, and the exile of her friends, and the insulting adulation of addresses, and the whole weight of her accumulated wrongs, with a serene patience, in a manner suited to her rank and race, and becoming the offspring of a sovereign[26] distinguished for her piety and her courage; that like her she has lofty sentiments; that she feels with the dignity of a Roman matron; that in the last extremity she will save herself from the last disgrace, and that if she must fall, she will fall by no ignoble hand.

It is now sixteen or seventeen years since I saw the queen of France, then the dauphiness, at Versailles; and surely never lighted on this orb, which she hardly seemed to touch, a more delightful vision. I saw her just above the horizon, decorating and cheering the elevated sphere she just began to move in,— glittering like the morning-star, full of life, and splendor, and joy. Oh! what a revolution! and what an heart must I have, to contemplate without emotion that elevation and that fall! Little did I dream when she added titles of veneration to those of enthusiastic, distant, respectful love, that she should ever be obliged to carry the sharp antidote against disgrace concealed in that bosom; little did I dream that I should have lived to see such disasters fallen upon her in a nation of gallant men, in a nation of men of honour and of cavaliers. I thought ten thousand swords must have leaped from their scabbards to avenge even a look that threatened her with insult.—But the age of chivalry

---

24. **fifth monarchy:** See Dan. 2:36–45. In the seventeenth century certain religious fanatics who proclaimed the imminent second coming of Christ were called fifth monarchy men. 25. **age:** Here Burke appends a long footnote quoting a Frenchman's horrified account of the events of the Revolution.

26. **a sovereign:** Maria Theresa (1717–80), Archduchess of Austria and Queen of Hungary and Bohemia.

is gone.—That of sophisters, œconomists, and calculators, has succeeded; and the glory of Europe is extinguished for ever. Never, never more, shall we behold that generous loyalty to rank and sex, that proud submission, that dignified obedience, that subordination of the heart, which kept alive, even in servitude itself, the spirit of an exalted freedom. The unbought grace of life, the cheap defence of nations, the nurse of manly sentiment and heroic enterprize is gone! It is gone, that sensibility of principle, that chastity of honour, which felt a stain like a wound, which inspired courage whilst it mitigated ferocity, which ennobled whatever it touched, and under which vice itself lost half its evil, by losing all its grossness.

This mixed system of opinion and sentiment had its origin in the antient chivalry; and the principle, though varied in its appearance by the varying state of human affairs, subsisted and influenced through a long succession of generations, even to the time we live in. If it should ever be totally extinguished, the loss I fear will be great. It is this which has given its character to modern Europe. It is this which has distinguished it under all its forms of government, and distinguished it to its advantage, from the states of Asia, and possibly from those states which flourished in the most brilliant periods of the antique world. It was this, which, without confounding ranks, had produced a noble equality, and handed it down through all the gradations of social life. It was this opinion which mitigated kings into companions, and raised private men to be fellows with kings. Without force, or opposition, it subdued the fierceness of pride and power; it obliged sovereigns to submit to the soft collar of social esteem, compelled stern authority to submit to elegance, and gave a domination vanquisher of laws, to be subdued by manners.

But now all is to be changed. All the pleasing illusions, which made power gentle, and obedience liberal, which harmonized the different shades of life, and which, by a bland assimilation, incorporated into politics the sentiments which beautify and soften private society, are to be dissolved by this new conquering empire of light and reason. All the decent drapery of life is to be rudely torn off. All the superadded ideas, furnished from the wardrobe of a moral imagination, which the heart owns, and the understanding ratifies, as necessary to cover the defects of our naked shivering nature, and to raise it to dignity in our own estimation, are to be exploded as a ridiculous, absurd, and antiquated fashion.

On this scheme of things, a king is but a man; a queen is but a woman; a woman is but an animal; and an animal not of the highest order. All homage paid to the sex in general as such, and without distinct views, is to be regarded as romance and folly. Regicide, and parricide, and sacrilege, are but fictions of superstition, corrupting jurisprudence by destroying its simplicity. The murder of a king, or a queen, or a bishop, or a father, are only common homicide; and if the people are by any chance, or in any way gainers by it, a sort of homicide much the most pardonable, and into which we ought not to make too severe a scrutiny.

On the scheme of this barbarous philosophy, which is the offspring of cold hearts and muddy understandings, and which is as void of solid wisdom, as it is destitute of all taste and elegance, laws are to be supported only by their own terrors, and by the concern, which each individual may find in them, from his own private speculations, or can spare to them from his own private interests. In the groves of *their* academy, at the end of every visto, you see nothing but the gallows. Nothing is left which engages the affections on the part of the commonwealth. On the principles of this mechanic philosophy, our institutions can never be embodied, if I may use the expression, in persons; so as to create in us love, veneration, admiration, or attachment. But that sort of reason which banishes the affections is incapable of filling their place. These public affections, combined with manners, are required sometimes as supplements, sometimes as correctives, always as aids to law. The precept given by a wise man, as well as a great critic, for the construction of poems, is equally true as to states. *Non satis est pulchra esse poemata, dulcia sunto.*[27] There ought to be a system of manners in every nation which a well-formed mind would be disposed to relish. To make us love our country, our country ought to be lovely.

But power, of some kind or other, will survive the shock in which manners and opinions perish; and it will find other and worse means for its support. The usurpation which, in order to subvert antient institutions, has destroyed antient principles, will hold power by arts similar to those by which it has acquired it. When the old feudal and chivalrous spirit of *Fealty,*

27. Non . . . sunto: "It is not enough that poems be formally beautiful; they must have charm as well" (Horace, *Ars Poetica*, l. 99).

which, by freeing kings from fear, freed both kings and subjects from the precautions of tyranny, shall be extinct in the minds of men, plots and assassinations will be anticipated by preventive murder and preventive confiscation, and that long roll of grim and bloody maxims, which form the political code of all power, not standing on its own honour, and the honour of those who are to obey it. Kings will be tyrants from policy when subjects are rebels from principle.

When antient opinions and rules of life are taken away, the loss cannot possibly be estimated. From that moment we have no compass to govern us; nor can we know distinctly to what port we steer. Europe undoubtedly, taken in a mass, was in a flourishing condition the day on which your Revolution was compleated. How much of that prosperous state was owing to the spirit of our old manners and opinions is not easy to say; but as such causes cannot be indifferent in their operation, we must presume, that, on the whole, their operation was beneficial.

We are but too apt to consider things in the state in which we find them, without sufficiently adverting to the causes by which they have been produced, and possibly may be upheld. Nothing is more certain, than that our manners, our civilization, and all the good things which are connected with manners, and with civilization, have, in this European world of ours, depended for ages upon two principles; and were indeed the result of both combined; I mean the spirit of a gentleman, and the spirit of religion. The nobility and the clergy, the one by profession, the other by patronage, kept learning in existence, even in the midst of arms and confusions, and whilst governments were rather in their causes than formed. Learning paid back what it received to nobility and to priesthood; and paid it with usury, by enlarging their ideas, and by furnishing their minds. Happy if they had all continued to know their indissoluble union, and their proper place! Happy if learning, not debauched by ambition, had been satisfied to continue the instructor, and not aspired to be the master! Along with its natural protectors and guardians, learning will be cast into the mire, and trodden down under the hoofs of a swinish multitude.

If, as I suspect, modern letters owe more than they are always willing to own to ancient manners, so do other interests which we value full as much as they are worth. Even commerce, and trade, and manufacture, the gods of our œconomical politicians, are themselves perhaps but creatures; are themselves but effects, which, as first causes, we choose to worship. They certainly grew under the same shade in which learning flourished. They too may decay with their natural protecting principles. With you, for the present at least, they all threaten to disappear together. Where trade and manufactures are wanting to a people, and the spirit of nobility and religion remains, sentiment supplies, and not always ill supplies their place; but if commerce and the arts should be lost in an experiment to try how well a state may stand without these old fundamental principles, what sort of a thing must be a nation of gross, stupid, ferocious, and at the same time, poor and sordid barbarians, destitute of religion, honour, or manly pride, possessing nothing at present, and hoping for nothing hereafter.

I wish you may not be going fast, and by the shortest cut, to that horrible and disgustful situation. Already there appears a poverty of conception, a coarseness and vulgarity in all the proceedings of the assembly and of all their instructors. Their liberty is not liberal. Their science is presumptuous ignorance. Their humanity is savage and brutal.

It is not clear, whether in England we learned those grand and decorous principles, and manners, of which considerable traces yet remain, from you, or whether you took them from us. But to you, I think, we trace them best. You seem to me to be—*gentis incunabula nostræ.*[28] France has always more or less influenced manners in England; and when your fountain is choaked up and polluted, the stream will not run long, or not run clear with us, or perhaps with any nation. This gives all Europe, in my opinion, but too close and connected a concern in what is done in France. Excuse me, therefore, if I have dwelt too long on the atrocious spectacle of the sixth of October 1789, or have given too much scope to the reflexions which have arisen in my mind on occasion of the most important of all revolutions, which may be dated from that day, I mean a revolution in sentiments, manners, and moral opinions. As things now stand, with every thing respectable destroyed without us, and an attempt to destroy within us, every principle of respect, one is almost forced to apologize for harbouring the common feelings of men.

Why do I feel so differently from the Reverend Dr. Price, and those of his lay flock, who will choose to adopt the sentiments of his discourse?—For this

28. gentis . . . nostræ: the cradle of our race.

plain reason—because it is *natural* I should; because we are so made as to be affected at such spectacles with melancholy sentiments upon the unstable condition of mortal prosperity, and the tremendous uncertainty of human greatness; because in those natural feelings we learn great lessons; because in events like these our passions instruct our reason; because when kings are hurl'd from their thrones by the Supreme Director of this great drama, and become the objects of insult to the base, and of pity to the good, we behold such disasters in the moral, as we should behold a miracle in the physical order of things. We are alarmed into reflexion; our minds (as it has long since been observed) are purified by terror and pity; our weak unthinking pride is humbled, under the dispensations of a mysterious wisdom.—Some tears might be drawn from me, if such a spectacle were exhibited on the stage. I should be truly ashamed of finding in myself that superficial, theatric sense of painted distress, whilst I could exult over it in real life. With such a perverted mind, I could never venture to shew my face at a tragedy. People would think the tears that Garrick formerly, or that Siddons[29] not long since, have extorted from me, were the tears of hypocrisy; I should know them to be the tears of folly.

Indeed the theatre is a better school of moral sentiments than churches, where the feelings of humanity are thus outraged. Poets, who have to deal with an audience not yet graduated in the school of the rights of men, and who must apply themselves to the moral constitution of the heart, would not dare to produce such a triumph as a matter of exultation. There, where men follow their natural impulses, they would not bear the odious maxims of a Machiavelian policy, whether applied to the attainment of monarchical or democratic tyranny. They would reject them on the modern, as they once did on the antient stage, where they could not bear even the hypothetical proposition of such wickedness in the mouth of a personated tyrant, though suitable to the character he sustained. No theatric audience in Athens would bear what has been borne, in the midst of the real tragedy of this triumphal day; a principal actor weighing, as it were in scales hung in a shop of horrors,—so much actual crime against so much contingent advantage,—and

after putting in and out weights, declaring that the balance was on the side of the advantages. They would not bear to see the crimes of new democracy posted as in a ledger against the crimes of old despotism, and the book-keepers of politics finding democracy still in debt, but by no means unable or unwilling to pay the balance. In the theatre, the first intuitive glance, without any elaborate process of reasoning, would shew, that this method of political computation, would justify every extent of crime. They would see, that on these principles, even where the very worst acts were not perpetrated, it was owing rather to the fortune of the conspirators than to their parsimony in the expenditure of treachery and blood. They would soon see, that criminal means once tolerated are soon preferred. They present a shorter cut to the object than through the highway of the moral virtues. Justifying perfidy and murder for public benefit, public benefit would soon become the pretext, and perfidy and murder the end; until rapacity, malice, revenge, and fear more dreadful than revenge, could satiate their insatiable appetites. Such must be the consequences of losing in the splendour of these triumphs of the rights of men, all natural sense of wrong and right.

But the Reverend Pastor exults in this "leading in triumph," because truly Louis XVIth was "an arbitrary monarch;" that is, in other words, neither more nor less, than because he was Louis the XVIth, and because he had the misfortune to be born king of France, with the prerogatives of which, a long line of ancestors, and a long acquiescence of the people, without any act of his, had put him in possession. A misfortune it has indeed turned out to him, that he was born king of France. But misfortune is not crime, nor is indiscretion always the greatest guilt. I shall never think that a prince, the acts of whose whole reign were a series of concessions to his subjects, who was willing to relax his authority, to remit his prerogatives, to call his people to a share of freedom, not known, perhaps not desired by their ancestors; such a prince, though he should be subject to the common frailties attached to men and to princes, though he should have once thought it necessary to provide force against the desperate designs manifestly carrying on against his person, and the remnants of his authority; though all this should be taken into consideration, I shall be led with great difficulty to think he deserves the cruel and insulting triumph of Paris, and of Dr. Price. I tremble for the cause of liberty, from such an example to kings. I tremble for the cause of humanity, in the

---

29. **Garrick, Siddons:** The actor David Garrick died in 1779; Sarah Siddons (1755–1831), the renowned tragic actress, went into temporary retirement in 1789, resuming her career in 1791.

unpunished outrages of the most wicked of mankind. But there are some people of that low and degenerate fashion of mind, that they look up with a sort of complacent awe and admiration to kings, who know to keep firm in their seat, to hold a strict hand over their subjects, to assert their prerogative, and by the awakened vigilance of a severe despotism, to guard against the very first approaches of freedom. Against such as these they never elevate their voice. Deserters from principle, listed with fortune, they never see any good in suffering virtue, nor any crime in prosperous usurpation.

If it could have been made clear to me, that the king and queen of France (those I mean who were such before the triumph) were inexorable and cruel tyrants, that they had formed a deliberate scheme for massacring the National Assembly (I think I have seen something like the latter insinuated in certain publications) I should think their captivity just. If this be true, much more ought to have been done, but done, in my opinion, in another manner. The punishment of real tyrants is a noble and awful act of justice; and it has with truth been said to be consolatory to the human mind. But if I were to punish a wicked king, I should regard the dignity in avenging the crime. Justice is grave and decorous, and in its punishments rather seems to submit to a necessity, than to make a choice. Had Nero, or Agrippina, or Louis the eleventh, or Charles the ninth,[30] been the subject; if Charles the twelfth of Sweden, after the murder of Patkul, or his predecessor Christina, after the murder of Monaldeschi,[31] had fallen into the your hands, Sir, or into mine, I am sure our conduct would have been different.

If the French King, or King of the French, (or by whatever name he is known in the new vocabulary of your constitution) has in his own person, and that of his Queen, really deserved these unavowed but unavenged murderous attempts, and those subsequent indignities more cruel than murder, such a person would ill deserve even that subordinate executory

trust, which I understand is to be placed in him; nor is he fit to be called chief in a nation which he has outraged and oppressed. A worse choice for such an office in a new commonwealth, than that of a deposed tyrant, could not possibly be made. But to degrade and insult a man as the worst of criminals, and afterwards to trust him in your highest concerns, as a faithful, honest, and zealous servant, is not consistent in reasoning, nor prudent in policy, nor safe in practice. Those who could make such an appointment must be guilty of a more flagrant breach of trust than any they have yet committed against the people. As this is the only crime in which your leading politicians could have acted inconsistently, I conclude that there is no sort of ground for these horrid insinuations. I think no better of all the other calumnies.

In England, we give no credit to them. We are generous enemies: We are faithful allies. We spurn from us with disgust and indignation the slanders of those who bring us their anecdotes with the attestation of the flower-de-luce on their shoulder.[32] We have Lord George Gordon fast in Newgate;[33] and neither his being a public proselyte to Judaism, nor his having, in his zeal against Catholick priests and all sort of ecclesiastics, raised a mob (excuse the term, it is still in use here) which pulled down all our prisons, have preserved to him a liberty, of which he did not render himself worthy by a virtuous use of it. We have rebuilt Newgate, and tenanted the mansion. We have prisons almost as strong as the Bastile, for those who dare to libel the queens of France. In this spiritual retreat, let the noble libeller remain. Let him there meditate on his Thalmud, until he learns a conduct more becoming his birth and parts, and not so disgraceful to the ancient religion to which he has become a proselyte; or until some persons from your side of the water, to please your new Hebrew brethren, shall ransom him. He may then be enabled to purchase, with the old hoards of the synagogue, and a very small poundage, on the long compound interest of the thirty pieces of silver (Dr. Price has shewn us what miracles compound interest will perform in 1790

30. Nero . . . ninth: Agrippina (A.D. 15–59), the scandalous mother of the profligate Roman emperor Nero (A.D. 37–68), was finally murdered by him; Louis XI (1423–83) was a treacherous and despotic French monarch; Charles IX (1550–74) was a French monarch who persecuted the Huguenots. **31. Charles . . . Monaldeschi:** The Swedish king Charles XII (1682–1718) cruelly executed the diplomat Johann Reinhold von Patkul in 1707; the Swedish queen Christina (1626–89) first favored and then murdered the Italian nobleman Giovanni Monaldeschi.

32. those . . . shoulder: Certain refugee French courtiers in London had been retailing scandalous anecdotes about the behavior of Marie-Antoinette. **33. Lord . . . Newgate:** Gordon (1751–93) was a naval officer, Member of Parliament, and fanatical anti-Catholic who led the No-Popery Riots in 1780; convicted in 1787 of libeling Marie-Antoinette, he was lodged in Newgate prison, where he finally became a convert to Judaism.

years) the lands which are lately discovered to have been usurped by the Gallican church.[34] Send us your popish Archbishop of Paris, and we will send you our protestant Rabbin. We shall treat the person you send us in exchange like a gentleman and an honest man, as he is; but pray let him bring with him the fund of his hospitality, bounty, and charity; and, depend upon it, we shall never confiscate a shilling of that honourable and pious fund, nor think of enriching the treasury with the spoils of the poor-box.

To tell you the truth, my dear Sir, I think the honour of our nation to be somewhat concerned in the disclaimer of the proceedings of this society of the Old Jewry and the London Tavern. I have no man's proxy. I speak only from myself; when I disclaim, as I do with all possible earnestness, all communion with the actors in that triumph, or with the admirers of it. When I assert any thing else, as concerning the people of England, I speak from observation not from authority; but I speak from the experience I have had in a pretty extensive and mixed communication with the inhabitants of this kingdom, of all descriptions and ranks, and after a course of attentive observation, began early in life, and continued for near forty years. I have often been astonished, considering that we are divided from you but by a slender dyke of about twenty-four miles, and that the mutual intercourse between the two countries has lately been very great, to find how little you seem to know of us. I suspect that this is owing to your forming a judgment of this nation from certain publications, which do, very erroneously, if they do at all, represent the opinions and dispositions generally prevalent in England. The vanity, restlessness, petulance, and spirit of intrigue of several petty cabals, who attempt to hide their total want of consequence in bustle and noise, and puffing, and mutual quotation of each other, makes you imagine that our contemptuous neglect of their abilities is a mark of general acquiescence in their opinions. No such thing, I assure you. Because half a dozen grashoppers under a fern make the field ring with their importunate chink, whilst thousands of great cattle, reposed beneath the shadow of the British oak, chew the cud and are silent, pray do not imagine, that those who make the noise are the only inhabitants of the field; that, of course, they are many in number; or that, after all, they are other than

the little shrivelled, meagre, hopping, though loud and troublesome insects of the hour.

I almost venture to affirm, that not one in a hundred amongst us participates in the "triumph" of the Revolution Society. If the king and queen of France, and their children, were to fall into our hands by the chance of war, in the most acrimonious of all hostilities (I deprecate such an event, I deprecate such hostility) they would be treated with another sort of triumphal entry into London. We formerly have had a king of France in that situation;[35] you have read how he was treated by the victor in the field; and in what manner he was afterwards received in England. Four hundred years have gone over us; but I believe we are not materially changed since that period. Thanks to our sullen resistance to innovation, thanks to the cold sluggishness of our national character, we still bear the stamp of our forefathers. We have not (as I conceive) lost the generosity and dignity of thinking of the fourteenth century; nor as yet have we subtilized ourselves into savages. We are not the converts of Rousseau;[36] we are not the disciples of Voltaire;[37] Helvetius[38] has made no progress amongst us. Atheists are not our preachers; madmen are not our lawgivers. We know that *we* have made no discoveries; and we think that no discoveries are to be made, in morality; nor many in the great principles of government, nor in the ideas of liberty, which were understood long before we were born, altogether as well as they will be after the grave has heaped its mould upon our presumption, and the silent tomb shall have imposed its law on our pert loquacity. In England we have not yet been completely embowelled of our natural entrails; we still feel within us, and we cherish and cultivate, those inbred sentiments which are the faithful guardians, the active monitors of our duty, the true supporters of all liberal and manly morals. We have not been drawn and trussed, in order that we may be filled, like stuffed birds in a museum, with chaff and rags, and paltry, blurred shreds of paper about

---

34. the Gallican church: the Catholic church in France.

35. We . . . situation: John II (1319–64) was captured by Edward the Black Prince at Poitiers in 1356. **36. Rousseau:** Jean-Jacques Rousseau, who died in 1778, was famous for *Le Contrat social* (1762), a radical political treatise proscribed in France until 1789. **37. Voltaire:** (1694–1778), best known as a witty anti-Christian. **38. Helvetius:** Claude-Adrien Helvétius (1715–71) wrote *De l'esprit* (1758), an antireligious ethical treatise that anticipates the theories of the British Utilitarian Jeremy Bentham.

the rights of man. We preserve the whole of our feelings still native and entire, unsophisticated by pedantry and infidelity. We have real hearts of flesh and blood beating in our bosoms. We fear God; we look up with awe to kings; with affection to parliaments; with duty to magistrates; with reverence to priests; and with respect to nobility.[39] Why? Because when such ideas are brought before our minds, it is *natural* to be so affected; because all other feelings are false and spurious, and tend to corrupt our minds, to vitiate our primary morals, to render us unfit for rational liberty; and by teaching us a servile, licentious, and abandoned insolence, to be our low sport for a few holidays, to make us perfectly fit for, and justly deserving of slavery, through the whole course of our lives.

You see, Sir, that in this enlightened age I am bold enough to confess, that we are generally men of untaught feelings; that instead of casting away all our old prejudices, we cherish them to a very considerable degree, and to take more shame to ourselves, we cherish them because they are prejudices; and the longer they have lasted, and the more generally they have prevailed, the more we cherish them. We are afraid to put men to live and trade each on his own private stock of reason; because we suspect that this stock in each man is small, and that the individuals would do better to avail themselves of the general bank and capital of nations, and of ages. Many of our men of speculation, instead of exploding general prejudices, employ their sagacity to discover the latent wisdom which prevails in them. If they find what they seek, and they seldom fail, they think it more wise to continue the prejudice, with the reason involved, than to cast away the coat of prejudice, and to leave nothing but the naked reason; because prejudice, with its reason, has a motive to give action to that reason, and an affection which will give it permanence. Prejudice is of ready application in the emergency; it previously

engages the mind in a steady course of wisdom and virtue, and does not leave the man hesitating in the moment of decision, sceptical, puzzled and unresolved. Prejudice renders a man's virtue his habit; and not a series of unconnected acts. Through just prejudice, his duty becomes a part of his nature.

Your literary men, and your politicians, and so do the whole clan of the enlightened among us, essentially differ in these points. They have no respect for the wisdom of others; but they pay it off by a very full measure of confidence in their own. With them it is a sufficient motive to destroy an old scheme of things, because it is an old one. As to the new, they are in no sort of fear with regard to the duration of a building run up in haste; because duration is no object to those who think little or nothing has been done before their time, and who place all their hopes in discovery. They conceive, very systematically, that all things which give perpetuity are mischievous, and therefore they are at inexpiable war with all establishments. They think that government may vary like modes of dress, and with as little ill effect. That there needs no principle of attachment, except a sense of present conveniency, to any constitution of the state. They always speak as if they were of opinion that there is a singular species of compact between them and their magistrates, which binds the magistrate, but which has nothing reciprocal in it, but that the majesty of the people has a right to dissolve it without any reason, but its will. Their attachment to their country itself, is only so far as it agrees with some of their fleeting projects; it begins and ends with that scheme of polity which falls in with their momentary opinion.

These doctrines, or rather sentiments, seem prevalent with your new statesmen. But they are wholly different from those on which we have always acted in this country.

I hear it is sometimes given out in France, that what is doing among you is after the example of England. I beg leave to affirm, that scarcely any thing done with you has originated from the practice or the prevalent opinions of this people, either in the act or in the spirit of the proceeding. Let me add, that we are as unwilling to learn these lessons from France, as we are sure that we never taught them to that nation. The cabals here who take a sort of share in your transactions as yet consist but of an handful of people. If unfortunately by their intrigues, their sermons, their publications, and by a confidence derived from an expected union with the counsels and forces of the

---

39. We . . . nobility: [Burke's note] The English are, I conceive, misrepresented in a Letter published in one of the papers, by a gentleman thought to be a dissenting minister.—When writing to Dr. Price, of the spirit which prevails at Paris, he says, "The spirit of the people in this place has abolished all the proud *distinctions* which the *king* and *nobles* had usurped in their minds; whether they talk of *the king, the noble, or the priest,* their whole language is that of the most *enlightened and liberal amongst the English*." If this gentleman means to confine the terms *enlightened and liberal* to one set of men in England, it may be true. It is not generally so.

French nation, they should draw considerable numbers into their faction, and in consequence should seriously attempt any thing here in imitation of what has been done with you, the event I dare venture to prophesy, will be, that, with some trouble to their country, they will soon accomplish their own destruction. This people refused to change their law in remote ages,[40] from respect to the infallibility of popes; and they will not now alter it from a pious implicit faith in the dogmatism of philosophers; though the former was armed with the anathema and crusade, and though the latter should act with the libel and the lamp-iron.[41]

Formerly your affairs were your own concern only. We felt for them as men; but we kept aloof from them, because we were not citizens of France. But when we see the model held up to ourselves, we must feel as Englishmen, and feeling, we must provide as Englishmen. Your affairs, in spite of us, are made a part of our interest; so far at least as to keep at a distance your panacea, or your plague. If it be a panacea, we do not want it. We know the consequences of unnecessary physic. If it be a plague; it is such a plague, that the precautions of the most severe quarantine ought to be established against it.

I hear on all hands that a cabal, calling itself philosophic, receives the glory of many of the late proceedings; and that their opinions and systems are the true actuating spirit of the whole of them. I have heard of no party in England, literary or political, at any time, known by such a description. It is not with you composed of those men, is it? whom the vulgar, in their blunt, homely style, commonly call Atheists and Infidels? If it be, I admit that we too have had writers of that description, who made some noise in their day. At present they repose in lasting oblivion. Who, born within the last forty years, has read one word of Collins, and Toland, and Tindal, and Chubb, and Morgan,[42] and that whole race who called themselves Freethinkers? Who now reads Bolingbroke?[43] Who

ever read him through? Ask the booksellers of London what is become of all these lights of the world. In as few years their few successors will go to the family vault of "all the Capulets." But whatever they were, or are, with us, they were and are wholly unconnected individuals. With us they kept the common nature of their kind, and were not gregarious. They never acted in corps, nor were known as a faction in the state, nor presumed to influence, in that name or character, or for the purposes of such a faction, on any of our public concerns. Whether they ought so to exist, and so be permitted to act, is another question. As such cabals have not existed in England, so neither has the spirit of them had any influence in establishing the original frame of our constitution, or in any one of the several reparations and improvements it has undergone. The whole has been done under the auspices, and is confirmed by the sanctions of religion and piety. The whole has emanated from the simplicity of our national character, and from a sort of native plainness and directness of understanding, which for a long time characterized those men who have successively obtained authority amongst us. This disposition still remains, at least in the great body of the people.

We know, and what is better we feel inwardly, that religion is the basis of civil society, and the source of all good and of all comfort.[44] In England we are so convinced of this, that there is no rust of superstition, with which the accumulated absurdity of the human mind might have crusted it over in the course of ages, that ninety-nine in an hundred of the people of England would not prefer to impiety. We shall never be such fools as to call in an enemy to the substance of any system to remove its corruptions, to supply its defects, or to perfect its construction. If our religious tenets should ever want a further elucidation, we shall not call on atheism to explain them. We shall not light up our temple from that unhallowed fire. It will be illuminated with other lights. It will be perfumed with other incense, than the infectious stuff which is

40. in remote ages: during the reign (1199–1216) of King John, signer of the Magna Carta. 41. lamp-iron: lamp-post. 42. Collins . . . Morgan: Anthony Collins wrote *A Discourse of Free-Thinking* (1713); John Toland, *Christianity Not Mysterious* (1696); Matthew Tindal, *Christianity as Old as the Creation* (1730); Thomas Chubb, *The Supremacy of the Father Asserted* (1715); Thomas Morgan, *The Moral Philosopher. In a Dialogue Between Philalethes a Christian Deist, and Theophanes a Christian Jew* (1737). 43. Bolingbroke: Henry St. John (1678–1751), First Viscount Bolingbroke, politician and diplomat; he left at his death some Deistic writings, published as *Philosophical Works* (1752).

44. comfort: Here Burke in a footnote quotes Cicero's *De Legibus*: "Let it be a fundamental principle in all societies that the gods are the supreme lords and governors of everything, that all events are directed by their wisdom, and that they love mankind; and furthermore, that they know what each person really is and does, and that they can distinguish the pious from the hypocritical and the good from the wicked. Once our minds are habituated to this principle, it will not be difficult for them to entertain true and useful sentiments."

imported by the smugglers of adulterated metaphysics. If our ecclesiastical establishment should want a revision, it is not avarice or rapacity, public or private, that we shall employ for the audit, or receipt, or application of its consecrated revenue.—Violently condemning neither the Greek nor the Armenian, nor, since heats are subsided, the Roman system of religion, we prefer the Protestant; not because we think it has less of the Christian religion in it, but because, in our judgment, it has more. We are protestants, not from indifference but from zeal.

We know, and it is our pride to know, that man is by his constitution a religious animal; that atheism is against, not only our reason but our instincts; and that it cannot prevail long. But if, in the moment of riot, and in a drunken delirium from the hot spirit drawn out of the alembick[45] of hell, which in France is now so furiously boiling, we should uncover our nakedness by throwing off that Christian religion which has hitherto been our boast and comfort, and one great source of civilization amongst us, and among many other nations, we are apprehensive (being well aware that the mind will not endure a void) that some uncouth, pernicious, and degrading superstition, might take place of it.

For that reason, before we take from our establishment the natural human means of estimation, and give it up to contempt, as you have done, and in doing it have incurred the penalties you well deserve to suffer, we desire that some other may be presented to us in the place of it. We shall then form our judgment.

On these ideas, instead of quarrelling with establishments, as some do, who have made a philosophy and a religion of their hostility to such institutions, we cleave closely to them. We are resolved to keep an established church, an established monarchy, an established aristocracy, and an established democracy, each in the degree it exists, and in no greater. I shall shew you presently how much of each of these we possess.

It has been the misfortune (not as these gentlemen think it, the glory) of this age, that every thing is to be discussed, as if the constitution of our country were to be always a subject rather of altercation than enjoyment. For this reason, as well as for the satisfaction of those among you (if any such you have among you) who may wish to profit of examples, I venture to trouble you with a few thoughts upon each of these establishments. I do not think they were unwise in

antient Rome, who, when they wished to new-model their laws, sent commissioners to examine the best constituted republics within their reach.

First, I beg leave to speak of our church establishment, which is the first of our prejudices, not a prejudice destitute of reason, but involving in it profound and extensive wisdom. I speak of it first. It is first, and last, and midst in our minds. For, taking ground on that religious system, of which we are now in possession, we continue to act on the early received, and uniformly continued sense of mankind. That sense not only, like a wise architect, hath built up the august fabric of states, but like a provident proprietor, to preserve the structure from prophanation and ruin, as a sacred temple, purged from all the impurities of fraud, and violence, and injustice, and tyranny, hath solemnly and for ever consecrated the commonwealth, and all that officiate in it. This consecration is made, that all who administer in the government of men, in which they stand in the person of God himself, should have high and worthy notions of their function and destination; that their hope should be full of immortality; that they should not look to the paltry pelf of the moment, nor to the temporary and transient praise of the vulgar, but to a solid, permanent existence, in the permanent part of their nature, and to a permanent fame and glory, in the example they leave as a rich inheritance to the world.

Such sublime principles ought to be infused into persons of exalted situations, and religious establishments provided, that may continually revive and enforce them. Every sort of moral, every sort of civil, every sort of politic institution, aiding the rational and natural ties that connect the human understanding and affections to the divine, are not more than necessary, in order to build up that wonderful structure, Man; whose prerogative it is, to be in a great degree a creature of his own making; and who when made as he ought to be made, is destined to hold no trivial place in the creation. But whenever man is put over men, as the better nature ought ever to preside, in that case more particularly, he should as nearly as possible be approximated to his perfection.

The consecration of the state, by a state religious establishment, is necessary also to operate with an wholesome awe upon free citizens; because, in order to secure their freedom, they must enjoy some determinate portion of power. To them therefore a religion connected with the state, and with their duty towards it, becomes even more necessary than in such societies, where the people by the terms of their subjection are confined to private sentiments, and the management of their own family concerns. All persons possessing any portion of power ought to be strongly and awefully impressed with an idea that they act in trust; and that they are to account for their conduct in that trust to the one great master, author and founder of society.

This principle ought even to be more strongly impressed upon the minds of those who compose the collective sovereignty than upon those of single princes. Without instruments, these princes can do nothing. Whoever uses instruments, in finding helps, finds also impediments. Their power is therefore by no means compleat; nor are they safe in extreme abuse. Such persons, however elevated by flattery, arrogance, and self-opinion, must be sensible that, whether covered or not by positive law, in some way or other they are accountable even here for the abuse of their trust. If they are not cut off by a rebellion of their people, they may be strangled by the very Janissaries kept for their security against all other rebellion. Thus we have seen the king of France sold by his soldiers for an encrease of pay. But where popular authority is absolute and unrestrained, the people have an infinitely greater, because a far better founded confidence in their own power. They are themselves, in a great measure, their own instruments. They are nearer to their objects. Besides, they are less under responsibility to one of the greatest controlling powers on earth, the sense of fame and estimation. The share of infamy that is likely to fall to the lot of each individual in public acts, is small indeed; the operation of opinion being in the inverse ratio to the number of those who abuse power. Their own approbation of their own acts has to them the appearance of a public judgment in their favour. A perfect democracy is therefore the most shameless thing in the world. As it is the most shameless, it is also the most fearless. No man apprehends in his person he can be made subject to punishment. Certainly the people at large never ought: for as all punishments are for example towards the conservation of the people at large, the people at large can never become the subject of punishment by any human hand.[46] It is therefore of infinite importance that they should not be suffered to imagine that their will, any more than

that of kings, is the standard of right and wrong. They ought to be persuaded that they are full as little entitled, and far less qualified, with safety to themselves, to use any arbitrary power whatsoever; that therefore they are not, under a false shew of liberty, but, in truth, to exercise an unnatural inverted domination, tyrannically to exact, from those who officiate in the state, not an entire devotion to their interest, which is their right, but an abject submission to their occasional will; extinguishing thereby, in all those who serve them, all moral principle, all sense of dignity, all use of judgment, and all consistency of character, whilst by the very same process they give themselves up a proper, a suitable, but a most contemptible prey to the servile ambition of popular sycophants or courtly flatterers.

When the people have emptied themselves of all the lust of selfish will, which without religion it is utterly impossible they ever should, when they are conscious that they exercise, and exercise perhaps in an higher link of the order of delegation, the power, which to be legitimate must be according to that eternal immutable law, in which will and reason are the same, they will be more careful how they place power in base and incapable hands. In their nomination to office, they will not appoint to the exercise of authority, as to a pitiful job, but as to an holy function; not according to their sordid selfish interest, nor to their wanton caprice, nor to their arbitrary Will; but they will confer that power (which any man may well tremble to give or to receive) on those only, in whom they may discern that predominant proportion of active virtue and wisdom, taken together and fitted to the charge, such, as in the great and inevitable mixed mass of human imperfections and infirmities, is to be found.

When they are habitually convinced that no evil can be acceptable, either in the act or the permission, to him whose essence is good, they will be better able to extirpate out of the minds of all magistrates, civil, ecclesiastical, or military, any thing that bears the least resemblance to a proud and lawless domination.

But one of the first and most leading principles on which the commonwealth and the laws are consecrated, is lest the temporary possessors and life-renters in it, unmindful of what they have received from their ancestors, or of what is due to their posterity, should act as if they were the entire masters; that they should not think it amongst their rights to cut off the entail, or commit waste on the inheritance, by destroying at

---

46. the people at large can . . . hand: [Burke's note] Quicquid multis peccatur inultum ["Wrong committed by the multitude always goes unpunished" (Lucan, *Pharsalia*, V. 260)].

their pleasure the whole original fabric of their society; hazarding to leave to those who come after them, a ruin instead of an habitation—and teaching these successors as little to respect their contrivances, as they had themselves respected the institutions of their forefathers. By this unprincipled facility of changing the state as often, and as much, and in as many ways as there are floating fancies or fashions, the whole chain and continuity of the commonwealth would be broken. No one generation could link with the other. Men would become little better than the flies of a summer.

And first of all the science of jurisprudence, the pride of the human intellect, which, with all its defects, redundancies, and errors, is the collected reason of ages, combining the principles of original justice with the infinite variety of human concerns, as a heap of old exploded errors, would be no longer studied. Personal self-sufficiency and arrogance (the certain attendants upon all those who have never experienced a wisdom greater than their own) would usurp the tribunal. Of course, no certain laws, establishing invariable grounds of hope and fear, would keep the actions of men in a certain course, or direct them to a certain end. Nothing stable in the modes of holding property, or exercising function, could form a solid ground on which any parent could speculate in the education of his offspring, or in a choice for their future establishment in the world. No principles would be early worked into the habits. As soon as the most able instructor had completed his laborious course of institution, instead of sending forth his pupil, accomplished in a virtuous discipline, fitted to procure him attention and respect, in his place in society, he would find every thing altered; and that he had turned out a poor creature to the contempt and derision of the world, ignorant of the true grounds of estimation. Who would insure a tender and delicate sense of honour to beat almost with the first pulses of the heart, when no man could know what would be the test of honour in a nation, continually varying the standard of its coin? No part of life would retain its acquisitions. Barbarism with regard to science and literature, unskilfulness with regard to arts and manufactures, would infallibly succeed to the want of a steady education and settled principle; and thus the commonwealth itself would, in a few generations, crumble away, be disconnected into the dust and powder of individuality, and at length dispersed to all the winds of heaven.

To avoid therefore the evils of inconstancy and versatility, ten thousand times worse than those of obstinacy and the blindest prejudice, we have consecrated the state, that no man should approach to look into its defects or corruptions but with due caution; that he should never dream of beginning its reformation by its subversion; that he should approach to the faults of the state as to the wounds of a father, with pious awe and trembling sollicitude. By this wise prejudice we are taught to look with horror on those children of their country who are prompt rashly to hack that aged parent in pieces, and put him into the kettle of magicians, in hopes that by their poisonous weeds, and wild incantations, they may regenerate the paternal constitution, and renovate their father's life.

Society is indeed a contract. Subordinate contracts for objects of mere occasional interest may be dissolved at pleasure—but the state ought not to be considered as nothing better than a partnership agreement in a trade of pepper and coffee, callico or tobacco, or some other such low concern, to be taken up for a little temporary interest, and to be dissolved by the fancy of the parties. It is to be looked on with other reverence; because it is not a partnership in things subservient only to the gross animal existence of a temporary and perishable nature. It is a partnership in all science; a partnership in all art; a partnership in every virtue, and in all perfection. As the ends of such a partnership cannot be obtained in many generations, it becomes a partnership not only between those who are living, but between those who are living, those who are dead, and those who are to be born. Each contract of each particular state is but a clause in the great primæval contract of eternal society, linking the lower with the higher natures, connecting the visible and invisible world, according to a fixed compact sanctioned by the inviolable oath which holds all physical and all moral natures, each in their appointed place. This law is not subject to the will of those, who by an obligation above them, and infinitely superior, are bound to submit their will to that law. The municipal corporations of that universal kingdom are not morally at liberty at their pleasure, and on their speculations of a contingent improvement, wholly to separate and tear asunder the bands of their subordinate community, and to dissolve it into an unsocial, uncivil, unconnected chaos of elementary principles. It is the first and supreme necessity only, a necessity that is not chosen but chooses, a necessity paramount to deliberation, that admits no discussion, and demands no evidence, which alone can justify a resort to anarchy. This necessity is no exception to the rule; because this necessity itself is a part too of that moral and physical disposition of things to which man must be obedient by consent or force; but if that which is only submission to necessity should be made the object of choice, the law is broken, nature is disobeyed, and the rebellious are outlawed, cast forth, and exiled, from this world of reason, and order, and peace, and virtue, and fruitful penitence, into the antagonist world of madness, discord, vice, confusion, and unavailing sorrow.

These, my dear Sir, are, were, and I think long will be the sentiments of not the least learned and reflecting part of this kingdom. They who are included in this description, form their opinions on such grounds as such persons ought to form them. The less enquiring receive them from an authority which those whom Providence dooms to live on trust need not be ashamed to rely on. These two sorts of men move in the same direction, tho' in a different place. They both move with the order of the universe. They all know or feel this great antient truth: "Quod illi principi et præpotenti Deo qui omnem hunc mundum regit, nihil eorum quæ quidem fiant in terris acceptius quam concilia et cœtus hominum jure sociati quæ civitates appellantur."[47]

. . .

A LETTER . . .
TO A NOBLE LORD . . .

❦

Burke's acceptance of a pension of thirty-seven hundred pounds a year was attacked in the House of Lords late in 1795 by Francis Russell, Fifth Duke of Bedford and Marquis of Tavistock, and by James Maitland, Eighth Earl of Lauderdale. The Duke of Bedford—"an impetuous but aging youth," as W. J. Bate calls him—especially insinuated that Burke's acceptance of so large a pension constituted a cynical betrayal of his earlier principles of government economy and reform. Burke met the Duke's insult with this pamphlet in the form of a letter, addressed not, as is sometimes assumed, to his

luckless attacker, a parlor radical of Fox's party, but to his own friend and younger Whig colleague Lord Fitzwilliam, nephew of Lord Rockingham. The *Letter*, which provided Burke with an occasion for reviewing and vindicating his long career of devotion to constitutional principles, is the closest he ever came to autobiographical utterance. John Morley has called it "the most splendid repartee in the English language." And William Hazlitt recalled that it was his excitement over this performance of Burke's that first interested him in literature.

The text is that of the first edition, *A Letter from the Right Honourable Edmund Burke to a Noble Lord, on the Attacks Made upon Him and His Pension, in the House of Lords, by the Duke of Bedford and the Earl of Lauderdale, Early in the Present Sessions of Parliament* (1796). We have incorporated the substantive variants of the "thirteenth edition" (1796).

❦

MY LORD,

I COULD hardly flatter myself with the hope, that so very early in the season I should have to acknowledge obligations to the Duke of Bedford and to the Earl of Lauderdale. These noble persons have lost no time in conferring upon me, that sort of honour, which it is alone within their competence, and which it is certainly most congenial to their nature and their manners to bestow.

To be ill spoken of, in whatever language they speak, by the zealots of the new sect in philosophy and politicks, of which these noble persons think so charitably, and of which others think so justly, to me, is no matter of uneasiness or surprise. To have incurred the displeasure of the Duke of Orleans[1] or the Duke of Bedford, to fall under the censure of Citizen Brissot[2] or of his friend the Earl of Lauderdale, I ought to consider as proofs, not the least satisfactory, that I have produced some part of the effect I proposed by my endeavours. I have laboured hard to earn, what the noble Lords are generous enough to pay. Personal offence I have given them none. The part they take against me is from zeal to the cause. It is well! It is perfectly well! I have to do homage to their justice. I

---

47. Quod . . . appellantur: "Of all things performed on earth, nothing is more acceptable to that supreme and all-powerful God who rules this whole universe than those assemblies and gatherings of men associated for the purposes of justice, which are called states" (Cicero, *De Republica*, Book VI).

A LETTER TO A NOBLE LORD. **1. the Duke . . . Orleans:** (1747–93), cousin of Louis XVI. Turning reformer and befriending the Revolution, he renounced his title and assumed the name Philippe-Égalité. **2. Citizen Brissot:** Jacques-Pierre Brissot (1754–93), French revolutionary leader, one of the moderates guillotined during the Reign of Terror.

have to thank the Bedfords and the Lauderdales for having so faithfully and so fully acquitted towards me whatever arrear of debt was left undischarged by the Priestleys[3] and the Paines.

Some, perhaps, may think them executors in their own wrong: I at least have nothing to complain of. They have gone beyond the demands of justice. They have been (a little perhaps beyond their intention) favourable to me. They have been the means of bringing out, by their invectives, the handsome things which Lord Grenville has had the goodness and condescension to say in my behalf.[4] Retired as I am from the world, and from all it's affairs and all it's pleasures, I confess it does kindle, in my nearly extinguished feelings, a very vivid satisfaction to be so attacked and so commended. It is soothing to my wounded mind, to be commended by an able, vigorous, and well informed statesman, and at the very moment when he stands forth with a manliness and resolution, worthy of himself and of his cause, for the preservation of the person and government of our Sovereign, and therein for the security of the laws, the liberties, the morals, and the lives of his people. To be in any fair way connected with such things, is indeed a distinction. No philosophy can make me above it: no melancholy can depress me so low, as to make me wholly insensible to such an honour.

Why will they not let me remain in obscurity and inaction? Are they apprehensive, that if an atom of me remains, the sect has something to fear? Must I be annihilated, lest, like old *John Zisca's*,[5] my skin might be made into a drum, to animate Europe to eternal battle, against a tyranny that threatens to overwhelm all Europe, and all the human race?

My Lord, it is a subject of aweful meditation. Before this of France, the annals of all time have not furnished an instance of a *compleat* revolution. That revolution seems to have extended even to the constitution of the mind of man. It has this of wonderful in it, that it resembles what Lord Verulam[6] says of the operations of nature: It was perfect, not only in all its elements and principles, but in all it's members and it's organs from the very beginning. The moral scheme of France furnishes the only pattern ever known, which they who admire will *instantly* resemble. It is indeed an inexhaustible repertory of one kind of examples. In my wretched condition, though hardly to be classed with the living, I am not safe from them. They have tygers to fall upon animated strength. They have hyenas to prey upon carcasses. The national menagerie is collected by the first physiologists of the time; and it is defective in no description of savage nature. They pursue, even such as me, into the obscurest retreats, and haul them before their revolutionary tribunals. Neither sex, nor age—not the sanctuary of the tomb is sacred to them. They have so determined a hatred to all privileged orders, that they deny even to the departed, the sad immunities of the grave. They are not wholly without an object. Their turpitude purveys to their malice; and they unplumb the dead[7] for bullets to assassinate the living. If all revolutionists were not proof against all caution, I should recommend it to their consideration, that no persons were ever known in history, either sacred or profane, to vex the sepulchre, and by their sorceries, to call up the prophetic dead, with any other event, than the prediction of their own disastrous fate.—"Leave, oh leave me to repose!"[8]

In one thing I can excuse the Duke of Bedford for his attack upon me and my mortuary pension. He cannot readily comprehend the transaction he condemns. What I have obtained was the fruit of no bargain; the production of no intrigue; the result of no compromises; the effect of no solicitation. The first suggestion of it never came from me, mediately or immediately, to his Majesty or any of his Ministers. It was long known that the instant my engagements would permit it, and before the heaviest of all calamities[9] had for ever condemned me to obscurity and sorrow, I had resolved on a total retreat. I had executed that design. I was entirely out of the way of serving or of hurting any statesman, or any party, when the Ministers so generously and so nobly carried into effect the spontaneous bounty of the Crown. Both descriptions have acted as became them. When I could no longer serve them, the Ministers have considered my situation. When I could no longer hurt

---

3. Priestleys: Dr. Joseph Priestley (1733–1804), a clergyman and chemist; sympathizing with the French Revolution, he left England and settled in Pennsylvania in 1794. **4. the handsome . . . behalf:** William Wyndham Grenville (1759–1834), Secretary of State for Foreign Affairs, had spoken in the House of Lords in support of Burke's pension. **5. John Zisca:** (*c.* 1360–1424), a Bohemian general who is reputed to have wanted his skin made into drumheads after his death. **6. Lord Verulam:** Francis Bacon (1561–1626).

7. unplumb the dead: Eighteenth-century coffins were often lined with lead. **8. Leave . . . repose:** Cf. Gray's *The Descent of Odin*, ll. 49–50: "Unwilling I my lips unclose: / Leave me, leave me to repose." **9. the heaviest . . . calamities:** the death in 1794 of his son, Richard.

them, the revolutionists have trampled on my infirmity. My gratitude, I trust, is equal to the manner in which the benefit was conferred. It came to me indeed, at a time of life, and in a state of mind and body, in which no circumstance of fortune could afford me any real pleasure. But this was no fault in the Royal Donor, or in his Ministers, who were pleased, in acknowledging the merits of an invalid servant of the publick, to assuage the sorrows of a desolate old man.

It would ill become me to boast of any thing. It would as ill become me, thus called upon, to depreciate the value of a long life, spent with unexampled toil in the service of my country. Since the total body of my services, on account of the industry which was shewn in them, and the fairness of my intentions, have obtained the acceptance of my Sovereign, it would be absurd in me to range myself on the side of the Duke of Bedford and the Corresponding Society,[10] or, as far as in me lies, to permit a dispute on the rate at which the authority appointed by *our* Constitution to estimate such things, has been pleased to set them.

Loose libels ought to be passed by in silence and contempt. By me they have been so always. I knew that as long as I remained in publick, I should live down the calumnies of malice, and the judgments of ignorance. If I happened to be now and then in the wrong, as who is not, like all other men, I must bear the consequence of my faults and my mistakes. The libels of the present day, are just of the same stuff as the libels of the past. But they derive an importance from the rank of the persons they come from, and the gravity of the place where they were uttered. In some way or other I ought to take some notice of them. To assert myself thus traduced is not vanity or arrogance. It is a demand of justice; it is a demonstration of gratitude. If I am unworthy, the Ministers are worse than prodigal. On that hypothesis, I perfectly agree with the Duke of Bedford.

For whatever I have been (I am now no more) I put myself on my country. I ought to be allowed a reasonable freedom, because I stand upon my deliverance; and no culprit ought to plead in irons. Even in the utmost latitude of defensive liberty, I wish to preserve all possible decorum. Whatever it may be in the eyes of these noble persons themselves, to me, their situation calls for the most profound respect. If I

should happen to trespass a little, which I trust I shall not, let it always be supposed, that a confusion of characters may produce mistakes; that in the masquerades of the grand carnival of our age, whimsical adventures happen; odd things are said and pass off. If I should fail a single point in the high respect I owe to those illustrious persons, I cannot be supposed to mean the Duke of Bedford and the Earl of Lauderdale of the House of Peers, but the Duke of Bedford and the Earl of Lauderdale of Palace Yard;—The Dukes and Earls of Brentford.[11] There they are on the pavement; there they seem to come nearer to my humble level; and, virtually at least, to have waved their high privilege.

Making this protestation, I refuse all revolutionary tribunals, where men have been put to death for no other reason, than that they had obtained favours from the Crown. I claim, not the letter, but the spirit of the old English law, that is, to be tried by my peers. I decline his Grace's jurisdiction as a judge. I challenge the Duke of Bedford as a juror to pass upon the value of my services. Whatever his natural parts may be, I cannot recognize in his few and idle years, the competence to judge of my long and laborious life. If I can help it, he shall not be on the inquest of my *quantum meruit.*[12] Poor rich man! He can hardly know any thing of publick industry in it's exertions, or can estimate it's compensations when it's work is done. I have no doubt of his Grace's readiness in all the calculations of vulgar arithmetick; but I shrewdly suspect, that he is very little studied in the theory of moral proportions; and has never learned the Rule of Three in the arithmetick of policy and state.

His Grace thinks I have obtained too much. I answer, that my exertions, whatever they have been, were such as no hopes of pecuniary reward could possible excite; and no pecuniary compensation can possibly reward them. Between money and services of this kind, (I said it long since,[13] when I was not myself concerned) there is no common measurer. Money is made for the comfort and convenience of animal life. It cannot be a reward for what, mere animal life must indeed sustain, but never can inspire. With submission to his Grace, I have not had more

---

10. the **Corresponding Society:** The London Corresponding Society was a radical organization founded in 1792.

11. **The Dukes . . . Brentford:** In *The Rehearsal* (1671), a dramatic burlesque by the Duke of Buckingham and others, appear two ridiculous kings of Brentford (a London suburb); they "enter . . . hand in hand" and always act alike. 12. **quantum meruit:** legal term meaning "How much has he deserved?" 13. **I . . . since:** [Burke's note] Speech on Œconomical Reform, 1780.

than sufficient. As to any noble use, I trust I know how to employ, as well as he, a much greater fortune than he possesses. In a more confined application, I certainly stand in need of every kind of relief and easement much more than he does. When I say I have not received more than I deserve, is this the language I hold to Majesty? No! Far, very far, from it! Before that presence, I claim no merit at all. Every thing towards me is favour, and bounty. One style to a gracious benefactor; another to a proud and insulting foe.

His Grace is pleased to aggravate my guilt, by charging my acceptance of his Majesty's grant as a departure from my ideas, and the spirit of my conduct with regard to œconomy.[14] If it be, my ideas of œconomy were false and ill founded. But they are the Duke of Bedford's ideas of œconomy I have contradicted, and not my own. If he means to allude to certain bills brought in by me on a message from the throne in 1782, I tell him, that there is nothing in my conduct that can contradict either the letter or the spirit of those acts.—Does he mean the pay-office act? I take it for granted he does not. The act to which he alludes, is, I suppose, the establishment act. I greatly doubt whether his Grace has ever read the one or the other. The first of these systems cost me, with every assistance which my then situation gave me, pains incredible. I found an opinion common through all the offices, and general in the publick at large, that it would prove impossible to reform and methodize the office of Paymaster General. I undertook it, however; and I succeeded in my undertaking. Whether the military service, or whether the general œconomy of our finances have profited by that act, I leave to those who are acquainted with the army, and with the treasury, to judge.

An opinion full as general prevailed also at the same time, that nothing could be done for the regulation of the civil-list establishment. The very attempt to introduce method into it, and any limitations to it's services, was held absurd. I had not seen the man, who so much as suggested one œconomical principle, or an œconomical expedient, upon that subject. Nothing but coarse amputation, or coarser taxation, were then talked of, both of them without design, combination, or the

least shadow of principle. Blind and headlong zeal, or factious fury, were the whole contribution brought by the most noisy on that occasion, towards the satisfaction of the publick, or the relief of the Crown.

Let me tell my youthful Censor, that the necessities of that time required something very different from what others then suggested, or what his Grace now conceives. Let me inform him, that it was one of the most critical periods in our annals.

Astronomers have supposed, that if a certain comet, whose path intercepted the ecliptick, had met the earth in some (I forget what) sign, it would have whirled us along with it, in it's excentrick course, into God knows what regions of heat and cold. Had the portentous comet of the rights of man, (which "from it's horrid hair shakes pestilence, and war," and "with fear of change perplexes Monarchs")[15] had that comet crossed upon us in that internal state of England, nothing human could have prevented our being irresistibly hurried, out of the highway of heaven, into all the vices, crimes, horrors and miseries of the French Revolution.

Happily, France was not then jacobinized. Her hostility was at a good distance. We had a limb cut off; but we preserved the body: We lost our Colonies; but we kept our Constitution. There was, indeed, much intestine heat; there was a dreadful fermentation. Wild and savage insurrection quitted the woods, and prowled about our streets in the name of reform. Such was the distemper of the publick mind, that there was no madman, in his maddest ideas, and maddest projects, who might not count upon numbers to support his principles and execute his designs.

Many of the changes, by a great misnomer called parliamentary reforms, went, not in the intention of all the professors and supporters of them, undoubtedly, but went in their certain, and, in my opinion, not very remote effect, home to the utter destruction of the Constitution of this kingdom. Had they taken place, not France, but England, would have had the honour of leading up the death-dance of Democratick Revolution. Other projects, exactly coincident in time with those, struck at the very existence of the kingdom under any constitution. There are who remember the blind fury of some, and the lamentable helplessness of others; here, a torpid confusion, from a panic fear of the danger; there, the same inaction from a stupid insensibility to it; here, well-wishers to the mischief;

14. **my . . . œconomy:** From 1780 to 1782 Burke had called for reforms in the civil list (the royal pension list); his object in large part was to reduce the interference of the Crown in Parliamentary affairs.

15. **from . . . Monarchs:** See *Paradise Lost*, II. 710; I. 598.

there, indifferent lookers-on. At the same time, a sort
of National Convention,[16] dubious in its nature, and
perilous in its example, nosed Parliament in the very
seat of its authority; sat with a sort of superintendance
over it; and little less than dictated to it, not only laws,
but the very form and essence of Legislature itself. In
Ireland things ran in a still more eccentrick course.
Government was unnerved, confounded, and in a
manner suspended. It's equipoise was totally gone. I do
not mean to speak disrespectfully of Lord North. He
was a man of admirable parts; of general knowledge;
of a versatile understanding fitted for every sort of business; of infinite wit and pleasantry; of a delightful
temper; and with a mind most perfectly disinterested.
But it would be only to degrade myself by a weak
adulation, and not to honour the memory of a great
man, to deny that he wanted something of the vigilance, and spirit of command, that the time required.
Indeed, a darkness, next to the fog of this awful day,
loured over the whole region. For a little time the
helm appeared abandoned—

Ipse diem noctemque negat discernere cœlo,
Nec meminisse viæ mediâ Palinurus in undâ.[17]

At that time I was connected with men of high
place in the community. They loved Liberty as much
as the Duke of Bedford can do; and they understood
it at least as well. Perhaps their politicks, as usual, took
a tincture from their character, and they cultivated
what they loved. The Liberty they pursued was a
Liberty inseparable from order, from virtue, from
morals, and from religion, and was neither hypo-
critically nor fanatically followed. They did not wish,
that Liberty, in itself, one of the first of blessings, should
in it's perversion become the greatest curse which
could fall upon mankind. To preserve the Constitution
entire, and practically equal to all the great ends of it's
formation, not in one single part, but in all it's parts,
was to them the first object. Popularity and power they
regarded alike. These were with them only different
means of obtaining that object; and had no preference
over each other in their minds, but as one or the other
might afford a surer or a less certain prospect of arriving

at that end. It is some consolation to me in the chearless gloom, which darkens the evening of my life,
that with them I commenced my political career, and
never for a moment, in reality, nor in appearance, for
any length of time, was separated from their good
wishes and good opinion.

By what accident it matters not, nor upon what
desert, but just then, and in the midst of that hunt of
obloquy, which ever has pursued me with a full cry
through life, I had obtained a very considerable degree
of publick confidence. I know well enough how
equivocal a test this kind of popular opinion forms of
the merit that obtained it. I am no stranger to the
insecurity of it's tenure. I do not boast of it. It is mentioned, to shew, not how highly I prize the thing, but
my right to value the use I made of it. I endeavoured
to turn that short-lived advantage to myself into a
permanent benefit to my Country. Far am I from
detracting from the merit of some Gentlemen, out of
office or in it, on that occasion. No!—It is not my way
to refuse a full and heaped measure of justice to the
aids that I receive. I have, through life, been willing
to give every thing to others; and to reserve nothing
for myself, but the inward conscience, that I had
omitted no pains, to discover, to animate, to discipline,
to direct the abilities of the Country for it's service,
and to place them in the best light to improve their
age, or to adorn it. This conscience I have. I have never
suppressed any man; never checked him for a moment
in his course, by any jealousy, or by any policy. I was
always ready, to the height of my means (and they
were always infinitely below my desires) to forward
those abilities which overpowered my own. He is an
ill-furnished undertaker, who has no machinery but
his own hands to work with. Poor in my own faculties,
I ever thought myself rich in theirs. In that period of
difficulty and danger, more especially, I consulted, and
sincerely cooperated with men of all parties, who
seemed disposed to the same ends, or to any main part
of them. Nothing, to prevent disorder, was omitted:
when it appeared, nothing to subdue it, was left
uncounselled, nor unexecuted, as far as I could prevail.
At the time I speak of, and having a momentary lead,
so aided and so encouraged, and as a feeble instrument
in a mighty hand—I do not say, I saved my Country;
I am sure I did my Country important service. There
were few, indeed, that did not at that time acknowledge
it, and that time was thirteen years ago. It was but one
voice, that no man in the kingdom better deserved an
honourable provision should be made for him.

16. a sort . . . Convention: the mob of the No-Popery
Riots of 1780, which menaced Parliament. 17. Ipse . . .
undâ: "Even Palinurus says that he cannot distinguish day
from night in the sky, nor remember his way amid the waves"
(*Aeneid*, III. 201–02).

So much for my general conduct through the whole of the portentous crisis from 1780 to 1782, and the general sense then entertained of that conduct by my country. But my character, as a reformer, in the particular instances which the Duke of Bedford refers to, is so connected in principle with my opinions on the hideous changes, which have since barbarized France, and spreading thence, threaten the political and moral order of the whole world, that it seems to demand something of a more detailed discussion.

My œconomical reforms were not, as his Grace may think, the suppression of a paltry pension or employment, more or less. Œconomy in my plans was, as it ought to be, secondary, subordinate, instrumental. I acted on state principles. I found a great distemper in the commonwealth; and, according to the nature of the evil and of the object, I treated it. The malady was deep; it was complicated, in the causes and in the symptoms. Throughout it was full of contraindicants. On one hand Government, daily growing more invidious for an apparent increase of the means of strength, was every day growing more contemptible by real weakness. Nor was this dissolution confined to Government commonly so called. It extended to Parliament; which was losing not a little in it's dignity and estimation, by an opinion of it's not acting on worthy motives. On the other hand, the desires of the People, (partly natural and partly infused into them by art) appeared in so wild and inconsiderate a manner, with regard to the œconomical object (for I set aside for a moment the dreadful tampering with the body of the Constitution itself) that if their petitions had literally been complied with, the State would have been convulsed; and a gate would have been opened, through which all property might be sacked and ravaged. Nothing could have saved the Publick from the mischiefs of the false reform but it's absurdity; which would soon have brought itself, and with it all real reform, into discredit. This would have left a rankling wound in the hearts of the People, who would know they had failed in the accomplishment of their wishes, but who, like the rest of mankind in all ages, would impute the blame to any thing rather than to their own proceedings. But there were then persons in the world, who nourished complaint; and would have been thoroughly disappointed if the people were ever satisfied. I was not of that humour. I wished that they *should* be satisfied. It was my aim to give to the People the substance of what I knew they desired, and what I thought was right whether they

desired it or not, before it had been modified for them into senseless petitions. I knew that there is a manifest marked distinction, which ill men, with ill designs, or weak men incapable of any design, will constantly be confounding, that is, a marked distinction between Change and Reformation. The former alters the substance of the objects themselves; and gets rid of all their essential good, as well as of all the accidental evil annexed to them. Change is novelty; and whether it is to operate any one of the effects of reformation at all, or whether it may not contradict the very principle upon which reformation is desired, cannot be certainly known beforehand. Reform is, not a change in the substance, or in the primary modification of the object, but a direct application of a remedy to the grievance complained of. So far as that is removed, all is sure. It stops there; and if it fails, the substance which underwent the operation, at the very worst, is but where it was.

All this, in effect, I think, but am not sure, I have said elsewhere. It cannot at this time be too often repeated; line upon line; precept upon precept; until it comes into the currency of a proverb, *To innovate is not to reform*. The French revolutionists complained of every thing; they refused to reform any thing; and they left nothing, no, nothing at all *unchanged*. The consequences are *before* us,—not in remote history; not in future prognostication: they are about us; they are upon us. They shake the publick security; they menace private enjoyment. They dwarf the growth of the young; they break the quiet of the old. If we travel, they stop our way. They infest us in town; they pursue us to the country. Our business is interrupted; our repose is troubled; our pleasures are saddened; our very studies are poisoned and perverted, and knowledge is rendered worse than ignorance, by the enormous evils of this dreadful innovation. The revolution harpies of France, sprung from night and hell, or from that chaotick anarchy, which generates equivocally "all monstrous, all prodigious things,"[18] cuckoo-like, adulterously lay their eggs, and brood over, and hatch them in the nest of every neighbouring State. These obscene harpies, who deck themselves, in I know not what divine attributes, but who in reality are foul and ravenous birds of prey (both mothers and daughters) flutter over our heads, and souse down upon

---

18. **all monstrous . . . things:** See *Paradise Lost*, II. 625.

our tables, and leave nothing unrent, unrifled, unravaged, or unpolluted with the slime of their filthy offal.[19]

If his Grace can contemplate the result of this compleat innovation, or, as some friends of his will call it, *reform*, in the whole body of it's solidity and compound mass, at which, as Hamlet says,[20] the face of Heaven glows with horror and indignation, and which, in truth, makes every reflecting mind, and every feeling heart, perfectly thought-sick, without a thorough abhorrence of every thing they say, and every thing they do, I am amazed at the morbid strength, or the natural infirmity of his mind.

It was then not my love, but my hatred to innovation, that produced my Plan of Reform. Without troubling myself with the exactness of the logical diagram, I considered them as things substantially opposite. It was to prevent that evil, that I proposed the measures, which his Grace is pleased, and I am not sorry he is pleased, to recall to my recollection. I had (what I hope that Noble Duke will remember in all his operations) a State to preserve, as well as a State to reform. I had a People to gratify, but not to inflame, or to mislead. I do not claim half the credit for what I did, as for what I prevented from being done. In that situation of the publick mind, I did not undertake, as was then proposed, to new model the House of Commons or the House of Lords; or to change the authority under which any officer of the Crown acted, who was suffered at all to exist. Crown, Lords, Commons, judicial system, system of administration,

---

19. These . . . offal: [Burke's note]

Tristius haud illis monstrum, nec sævior ulla
Pestis, & ira Deûm Stygiis sese extulit undis.
Virginei volucrum vultus; fœdissima ventris
Proluvies; uncæque manus; & pallida semper
Ora fame—

["No monster is more pernicious than these harpies; no worse plague or wrath of the gods ever rose from the waves of the river Styx. These birds have the faces of maidens, they drop the foulest filth, they have hands with claws, and their faces are always emaciated with hunger—" (*Aeneid*, III. 214–18).] Here the Poet breaks the line, because he (and that He is Virgil) had not verse or language to describe that monster even as he had conceived her. Had he lived to our time, he would have been more overpowered with the reality than he was with the imagination. Virgil only knew the horror of the times before him. Had he lived to see the Revolutionists and Constitutionalists of France, he would have had more horrid and disgusting features of his harpies to describe, and more frequent failures in the attempt to describe them. **20. as . . . says:** See *Hamlet*, III. iv. 48.

existed as they had existed before; and in the mode and manner in which they had always existed. My measures were, what I then truly stated them to the House to be, in their intent, healing and mediatorial. A complaint was made of too much influence in the House of Commons; I reduced it in both Houses; and I gave my reasons article by article for every reduction, and shewed why I thought it safe for the service of the State. I heaved the lead every inch of way I made. A disposition to expence was complained of; to that I opposed, not mere retrenchment, but a system of œconomy, which would make a random expence without plan or foresight, in future not easily practicable. I proceeded upon principles of research to put me in possession of my matter; on principles of method to regulate it; and on principles in the human mind and in civil affairs to secure and perpetuate the operation. I conceived nothing arbitrarily; nor proposed any thing to be done by the will and pleasure of others, or my own; but by reason, and by reason only. I have ever abhorred, since the first dawn of my understanding to this it's obscure twilight, all the operations of opinion, fancy, inclination, and will, in the affairs of Government, where only a sovereign reason, paramount to all forms of legislation and administration, should dictate. Government is made for the very purpose of opposing that reason to will and to caprice, in the reformers or in the reformed, in the governors or in the governed, in Kings, in Senates, or in People.

On a careful review, therefore, and analysis of all the component parts of the Civil List, and on weighing them each against other, in order to make, as much as possible, all of them a subject of estimate (the foundation and cornerstone of all regular provident œconomy) it appeared to me evident, that this was impracticable, whilst that part, called the Pension List, was totally discretionary in it's amount. For this reason, and for this only, I proposed to reduce it, both in it's gross quantity, and in it's larger individual proportions, to a certainty: lest, if it were left without a *general* limit, it might eat up the Civil List service; if suffered to be granted in portions too great for the fund, it might defeat it's own end; and by unlimited allowances to some, it might disable the Crown in means of providing for others. The Pension List was to be kept as a sacred fund; but it could not be kept as a constant open fund, sufficient for growing demands, if some demands could wholly devour it. The tenour of the Act will shew that it regarded the Civil List *only*, the reduction of which to some sort of estimate was my great object.

No other of the Crown funds did I meddle with, because they had not the same relations. This of the four and a half per cents does his Grace imagine had escaped me, or had escaped all the men of business, who acted with me in those regulations? I knew that such a fund existed, and that pensions had been always granted on it, before his Grace was born. This fund was full in my eye. It was full in the eyes of those who worked with me. It was left on principle. On principle I did what was then done; and on principle what was left undone was omitted. I did not dare to rob the nation of all funds to reward merit. If I pressed this point too close, I acted contrary to the avowed principles on which I went. Gentlemen are very fond of quoting me; but if any one thinks it worth his while to know the rules that guided me in my plan of reform, he will read my printed speech on that subject;[21] at least what is contained from page 230 to page 241 in the second Volume of the collection which a friend[22] has given himself the trouble to make of my publications. Be this as it may, these two Bills (though achieved with the greatest labour, and management of every sort, both within and without the House) were only a part, and but a small part, of a very large system, comprehending all the objects I stated in opening my proposition, and indeed many more, which I just hinted at in my Speech to the Electors of Bristol, when I was put out of that representation. All these, in some state or other of forwardness, I have long had by me.

But do I justify his Majesty's grace on these grounds? I think them the least of my services! The time gave them an occasional value: What I have done in the way of political œconomy was far from confined to this body of measures. I did not come into Parliament to con my lesson. I had earned my pension before I set my foot in St. Stephen's Chapel.[23] I was prepared and disciplined to this political warfare. The first session I sat in Parliament, I found it necessary to analyze the whole commercial, financial, constitutional and foreign interests of Great Britain and it's Empire. A great deal was then done; and more, far more would have been done, if more had been permitted by events. Then in the vigour of my manhood, my constitution sunk under my labour. Had I then died, (and I seemed to myself very near death) I had then earned for those who belonged to me, more than the Duke of Bedford's ideas of service are of power to estimate. But in truth, these services I am called to account for, are not those on which I value myself the most. If I were to call for a reward (which I have never done) it should be for those in which for fourteen years, without intermission, I shewed the most industry, and had the least success; I mean in the affairs of India. They are those on which I value myself the most; most for the importance; most for the labour; most for the judgment; most for constancy and perseverance in the pursuit. Others may value them most for the *intention*. In that, surely, they are not mistaken.

Does his Grace think, that they who advised the Crown to make my retreat easy, consider me only as an œconomist? That, well understood, however, is a good deal. If I had not deemed it of some value, I should not have made political œconomy an object of my humble studies, from my very early youth to near the end of my service in parliament, even before, (at least to any knowledge of mine) it had employed the thoughts of speculative men in other parts of Europe. At that time, it was still in it's infancy in England, where, in the last century, it had it's origin. Great and learned men thought my studies were not wholly thrown away, and deigned to communicate with me now and then on some particulars of their immortal works. Something of these studies may appear incidentally in some of the earliest things I published. The House has been witness to their effect, and has profited of them more or less, for above eight and twenty years.

To their estimate I leave the matter. I was not, like his Grace of Bedford, swaddled, and rocked, and dandled into a Legislator; "*Nitor in adversum*"[24] is the motto for a man like me. I possessed not one of the qualities, nor cultivated one of the arts, that recommend men to the favour and protection of the great. I was not made for a minion or a tool. As little did I follow the trade of winning the hearts, by imposing on the understandings, of the people. At every step of my progress in life (for in every step was I traversed and opposed), and at every turnpike I met, I was obliged to shew my passport, and again and again to prove my sole title to the honour of being useful to my Country, by a proof that I was not wholly unacquainted with

---

21. my . . . subject: *Speech on a Plan for the Better Security of the Independence of Parliament, and the Economical Reformation of the Civil and Other Establishments* (February, 1780). **22. a friend:** French Laurence (1757–1809), lawyer and judge. **23. St. Stephen's Chapel:** the House of Commons.

24. Nitor in adversum: I struggle against opposition.

it's laws, and the whole system of it's interests both abroad and at home. Otherwise no rank, no toleration even, for me. I had no arts, but manly arts. On them I have stood, and, please God, in spite of the Duke of Bedford and the Earl of Lauderdale, to the last gasp will I stand.

Had his Grace condescended to inquire concerning the person, whom he has not thought it below him to reproach, he might have found, that in the whole course of my life, I have never, on any pretence of œconomy, or on any other pretence, so much as in a single instance, stood between any man and his reward of service, or his encouragement in useful talent and pursuit, from the highest of those services and pursuits to the lowest. On the contrary I have, on an hundred occasions, exerted myself with singular zeal to forward every man's even tolerable pretensions. I have more than once had good-natured reprehensions from my friends for carrying the matter to something bordering on abuse. This line of conduct, whatever it's merits might be, was partly owing to natural disposition; but I think full as much to reason and principle. I looked on the consideration of publick service, or public ornament, to be real and very justice: and I ever held, a scanty and penurious justice to partake of the nature of a wrong. I held it to be, in its consequences, the worst œconomy in the world. In saving money, I soon can count up all the good I do; but when by a cold penury, I blast the abilities of a nation, and stunt the growth of it's active energies, the ill I may do is beyond all calculation. Whether it be too much or too little, whatever I have done has been general and systematick. I have never entered into those trifling vexations and oppressive details, that have been falsely, and most ridiculously laid to my charge.

Did I blame the pensions given to Mr. Barré and Mr. Dunning[25] between the proposition and execution of my plan? No! surely, no! Those pensions were within my principles. I assert it, those gentlemen deserved their pensions, their titles,—all they had; and if more they had, I should have been but pleased the more. They were men of talents; they were men of service. I put the profession of the law out of the question in one of them. It is a service that rewards itself. But their *publick service*, though, from their abilities unquestionably of more value than mine, in

it's quantity and in it's duration was not to be mentioned with it. But I never could drive a hard bargain in my life, concerning any matter whatever; and least of all do I know how to haggle and huckster with merit. Pension for myself I obtained none; nor did I solicit any. Yet I was loaded with hatred for every thing that was with-held, and with obloquy for every thing that was given. I was thus left to support the grants of a name ever dear to me,[26] and ever venerable to the world, in favour of those, who were no friends of mine or of his, against the rude attacks of those who were at that time friends to the grantees, and their own zealous partizans. I have never heard the Earl of Lauderdale complain of these pensions. He finds nothing wrong till he comes to me. This is impartiality, in the true modern revolutionary style.

Whatever I did at that time, so far as it regarded order and œconomy, is stable and eternal; as all principles must be. A particular order of things may be altered; order itself cannot lose its value. As to other particulars, they are variable by time and by circumstances. Laws of regulation are not fundamental laws. The publick exigencies are the masters of all such laws. They rule the laws, and are not to be ruled by them. They who exercise the legislative power at the time must judge.

It may be new to his Grace, but I beg leave to tell him, that mere parsimony is not œconomy. It is separable in theory from it; and in fact it may, or it may not, be a *part* of œconomy, according to circumstances. Expence, and great expence, may be an essential part in true œconomy. If parsimony were to be considered as one of the kinds of that virtue, there is however another and an higher œconomy. Œconomy is a distributive virtue, and consists not in saving, but in selection. Parsimony requires no providence, no sagacity, no powers of combination, no comparison, no judgment. Meer instinct, and that not an instinct of the noblest kind, may produce this false œconomy in perfection. The other œconomy has larger views. It demands a discriminating judgment, and a firm sagacious mind. It shuts one door to impudent importunity, only to open another, and a wider, to unpresuming merit. If none but meritorious service or real talent were to be rewarded, this nation has not wanted, and this nation will not want, the means of rewarding all the service it ever will receive, and

25. the pensions . . . Dunning: Isaac Barré, Vice Treasurer of Ireland and Treasurer of the Navy, and John Dunning, Solicitor General, were granted pensions in 1782.

26. a name . . . me: Lord Rockingham.

encouraging all the merit it ever will produce. No state, since the foundation of society, has been impoverished by that species of profusion. Had the œconomy of selection and proportion been at all times observed, we should not now have had an overgrown Duke of Bedford, to oppress the industry of humble men, and to limit by the standard of his own conceptions, the justice, the bounty, or, if he pleases, the charity of the Crown.

His Grace may think as meanly as he will of my deserts in the far greater part of my conduct in life. It is free for him to do so. There will always be some difference of opinion in the value of political services. But there is one merit of mine, which he, of all men living, ought to be the last to call in question. I have supported with very great zeal, and I am told with some degree of success, those opinions, or if his Grace likes another expression better, those old prejudices which buoy up the ponderous mass of his nobility, wealth, and titles. I have omitted no exertion to prevent him and them from sinking to that level, to which the meretricious French faction, his Grace at least coquets with, omit no exertion to reduce both. I have done all I could to discountenance their enquiries into the fortunes of those, who hold large portions of wealth without any apparent merit of their own. I have strained every nerve to keep the Duke of Bedford in that situation, which alone makes him my superiour. Your lordship has been a witness of the use he makes of that pre-eminence.

But be it, that this is virtue! Be it, that there is virtue in this well selected rigour; yet all virtues are not equally becoming to all men and at all times. There are crimes, undoubtedly there are crimes, which in all seasons of our existence, ought to put a generous antipathy in action; crimes that provoke an indignant justice, and call forth a warm and animated pursuit. But all things, that concern, what I may call, the preventive police of morality, all things merely rigid, harsh and censorial, the antiquated moralists, at whose feet I was brought up, would not have thought these the fittest matter to form the favourite virtues of young men of rank. What might have been well enough, and have been received with a veneration mixed with awe and terror, from an old, severe, crabbed Cato, would have wanted something of propriety in the young Scipios, the ornament of the Roman Nobility, in the flower of their life. But the times, the morals, the masters, the scholars have all undergone a thorough revolution. It is a vile illiberal

school, this new French academy of the *sans culottes*.[27] There is nothing in it that is fit for a Gentleman to learn.

Whatever it's vogue may be, I still flatter myself, that the parents of the growing generation will be satisfied with what is to be taught to their children in Westminster, in Eaton, or in Winchester: I still indulge the hope that no *grown* Gentleman or Nobleman of our time will think of finishing at Mr. Thelwall's[28] lecture whatever may have been left incomplete at the old Universities of his country. I would give to Lord Grenville and Mr. Pitt[29] for a motto, what was said of a Roman Censor or Prætor (or what was he?), who in virtue of a Senatûs consultum[30] shut up certain academies,

"Cludere Ludum Impudentiæ jussit."[31]

Every honest father of a family in the kingdom will rejoice at the breaking up for the holidays, and will pray that there may be a very long vacation in all such schools.

The awful state of the time, and not myself or my own justification, is my true object in what I now write; or in what I shall ever write or say. It little signifies to the world what becomes of such things as me, or even as the Duke of Bedford. What I say about either of us is nothing more than a vehicle, as you, my Lord, will easily perceive, to convey my sentiments on matters far more worthy of your attention. It is when I stick to my apparent first subject that I ought to apologize, not when I depart from it. I therefore must beg your Lordship's pardon for again resuming it after this very short digression; assuring you that I shall never altogether lose sight of such matter as persons abler than I am may turn to some profit.

The Duke of Bedford conceives, that he is obliged to call the attention of the House of Peers to his Majesty's grant to me, which he considers as excessive and out of all bounds.

I know not how it has happened, but it really seems,

27. **sans culottes:** literally, without knee breeches; applied to the radicals of the French Revolution who affected slovenly long trousers instead of the aristocratic knee breeches. **28. Mr. Thelwall:** John Thelwall (1764-1834), political radical and lecturer on elocution. **29. Lord . . . Pitt:** Grenville was Foreign Secretary in 1796; William Pitt the Younger was Prime Minister. **30. Senatûs consultum:** decree of the senate. **31. Cludere . . . jussit:** "He ordered closed this school of impudence" (Tacitus, *De Oratoribus*, l. 35).

that, whilst his Grace was meditating his well considered censure upon me, he fell into a sort of sleep. Homer nods; and the Duke of Bedford may dream; and as dreams (even his golden dreams) are apt to be ill-pieced and incongruously put together, his Grace preserved his idea of reproach to *me*, but took the subject-matter from the Crown-grants *to his own family*. This is "the stuff of which his dreams are made."[32] In that way of putting things together his Grace is perfectly in the right. The grants to the House of Russel were so enormous, as not only to outrage œconomy, but even to stagger credibility. The Duke of Bedford is the Leviathan among all the creatures of the Crown. He tumbles about his unwieldly bulk; he plays and frolicks in the ocean of the Royal bounty. Huge as he is, and whilst "he lies floating many a rood,"[33] he is still a creature. His ribs, his fins, his whalebone, his blubber, the very spiracles through which he spouts a torrent of brine against his origin, and covers me all over with the spray—every thing of him and about him is from the Throne. Is it for *him* to question the dispensation of the Royal favour?

I really am at a loss to draw any sort of parallel between the publick merits of his Grace, by which he justifies the grants he holds, and these services of mine, on the favourable construction of which I have obtained what his Grace so much disapproves. In private life, I have not at all the honour of acquaintance with the noble Duke. But I ought to presume, and it costs me nothing to do so, that he abundantly deserves the esteem and love of all who live with him. But as to publick service, why truly it would not be more ridiculous for me to compare myself in rank, in fortune, in splendid descent, in youth, strength, or figure, with the Duke of Bedford, than to make a parallel between his services, and my attempts to be useful to my country. It would not be gross adulation, but uncivil irony, to say, that he has any publick merit of his own to keep alive the idea of the services by which his vast landed Pensions were obtained. My merits, whatever they are, are original and personal; his are derivative. It is his ancestor, the original pensioner, that has laid up this inexhaustible fund of merit, which makes his Grace so very delicate and exceptious about the merit of all other grantees of the Crown. Had he permitted me to remain in quiet, I should have said 'tis his estate; that's enough. It is his by law; what have I to do with it or it's history? He would naturally have said on his side, 'tis this man's fortune.—He is as good now, as my ancestor was two hundred and fifty years ago. I am a young man with very old pensions; he is an old man with very young pensions,—that's all?

Why will his Grace, by attacking me, force me reluctantly to compare my little merit with that which obtained from the Crown those prodigies of profuse donation by which he tramples on the mediocrity of humble and laborious individuals? I would willingly leave him to the Herald's College, which the philosophy of the Sans culottes, (prouder by far than all the Garters, and Norroys and Clarencieux, and Rouge Dragons[34] that ever pranced in a procession of what his friends call aristocrates and despots) will abolish with contumely and scorn. These historians, recorders, and blazoners of virtues and arms, differ wholly from that other description of historians, who never assign any act of politicians to a good motive. These gentle historians, on the contrary, dip their pens in nothing but the milk of human kindness. They seek no further for merit than the preamble of a patent,[35] or the inscription on a tomb. With them every man created a peer is first an hero ready made. They judge of every man's capacity for office by the offices he has filled; and the more offices the more ability. Every General-officer with them is a Marlborough; every Statesman a Burleigh; every Judge a Murray or a Yorke. They, who alive, were laughed at or pitied by all their acquaintance, make as good a figure as the best of them in the pages of Guillim, Edmondson, and Collins.[36]

To these recorders, so full of good nature to the great and prosperous, I would willingly leave the first Baron Russel, and Earl of Bedford, and the merits of his grants. But the aulnager,[37] the weigher, the meter of grants, will not suffer us to acquiesce in the judgment of the Prince reigning at the time when they were made. They are never good to those who earn them. Well then; since the new grantees have war made on them by the old, and that the word of the Sovereign is not to be taken, let us turn our eyes to

---

32. the stuff . . . made: See *The Tempest*, IV. i. 156–57. **33. he . . . rood:** See *Paradise Lost*, I. 196.

34. Garters . . . Dragons: functionaries of the Heralds' College, the corporation in charge of British coats of arms. **35. a patent:** letters patent, a royal document conferring a privilege. **36. Guillim . . . Collins:** authorities on heraldry and the peerage. **37. aulnager:** an officer who determines questions of the quality and size of woolen goods.

history, in which great men have always a pleasure in contemplating the heroic origin of their house.

The first peer of the name, the first purchaser of the grants, was a Mr. Russel, a person of an ancient gentleman's family raised by being a minion of Henry the Eighth. As there generally is some resemblance of character to create these relations, the favourite was in all likelihood much such another as his master. The first of those immoderate grants was not taken from the ancient demesne of the Crown, but from the recent confiscation of the ancient nobility of the land. The lion having sucked the blood of his prey, threw the offal carcase to the jackall in waiting. Having tasted once the food of confiscation, the favourites became fierce and ravenous. This worthy favourite's first grant was from the lay nobility. The second, infinitely improving on the enormity of the first, was from the plunder of the church. In truth his Grace is somewhat excusable for his dislike to a grant like mine, not only in it's quantity, but in it's kind so different from his own.

Mine was from a mild and benevolent sovereign; his from Henry the Eighth.

Mine had not it's fund in the murder of any innocent person of illustrious rank,[38] or in the pillage of any body of unoffending men. His grants were from the aggregate and consolidated funds of judgments iniquitously legal, and from possessions voluntarily surrendered by the lawful proprietors with the gibbet at their door.

The merit of the grantee whom he derives from, was that of being a prompt and greedy instrument of a *levelling* tyrant, who oppressed all descriptions of his people, but who fell with particular fury on every thing that was *great and noble*. Mine has been, in endeavouring to screen every man, in every class, from oppression, and particularly in defending the high and eminent, who in the bad times of confiscating Princes; confiscating chief Governors, or confiscating Demagogues, are the most exposed to jealousy, avarice and envy.

The merit of the original grantee of his Grace's pensions, was in giving his hand to the work, and partaking the spoil with a Prince, who plundered a

part of his national church of his time and country. Mine was in defending the whole of the national church of my own time and my own country, and the whole of the national churches of all countries, from the principles and the examples which lead to ecclesiastical pillage, thence to a contempt of *all* prescriptive titles, thence to the pillage of *all* property, and thence to universal desolation.

The merit of the origin of his Grace's fortune was in being a favourite and chief adviser to a Prince, who left no liberty to their native country. My endeavour was to obtain liberty for the municipal country in which I was born, and for all descriptions and denominations in it.—Mine was to support with unrelaxing vigilance every right, every privilege, every franchise, in this my adopted, my dearer and more comprehensive country; and not only to preserve those rights in this chief seat of empire, but in every nation, in every land, in every climate, language and religion, in the vast domain that still is under the protection, and the larger that was once under the protection, of the British Crown.

His founder's merits were, by arts in which he served his master and made his fortune, to bring poverty, wretchedness and depopulation on his country. Mine were under a benevolent Prince, in promoting the commerce, manufactures and agriculture of his kingdom; in which his Majesty shews an eminent example, who even in his amusements is a patriot, and in hours of leisure an improver of his native soil.

His founder's merit, was the merit of a gentleman raised by the arts of a Court, and the protection of a Wolsey,[39] to the eminence of a great and potent Lord. His merit in that eminence was by instigating a tyrant to injustice, to provoke a people to rebellion.—My merit was, to awaken the sober part of the country, that they might put themselves on their guard against any one potent Lord, or any greater number of potent Lords, or any combination of great leading men of any sort, if ever they should attempt to proceed in the same courses, but in the reverse order, that is, by instigating a corrupted populace to rebellion, and, through that rebellion, introducing a tyranny yet worse than the tyranny which his Grace's ancestor supported, and of which he profited in the manner we behold in the despotism of Henry the Eighth.

38. the murder . . . rank: [Burke's note] See the history of the melancholy catastrophe of the Duke of Buckingham. Temp. [time of] Hen. 8. [Edward Stafford (1478–1521), Third Duke of Buckingham, was accused of treason on flimsy evidence and executed by Henry VIII.]

39. Wolsey: Thomas Wolsey (*c.* 1475–1530), prelate and powerful politician under Henry VIII.

The political merit of the first pensioner of his Grace's house, was that of being concerned as a counsellor of state in advising, and in his person executing the conditions of a dishonourable peace with France; the surrendering the fortress of Boulogne, then our out-guard on the Continent. By that surrender, Calais, the key of France, and the bridle in the mouth of that power, was, not many years afterwards, finally lost. My merit has been in resisting the power and pride of France, under any form of it's rule; but in opposing it with the greatest zeal and earnestness, when that rule appeared in the worst form it could assume; the worst indeed which the prime cause and principle of all evil could possibly give it. It was my endeavour by every means to excite a spirit in the house, where I had the honour of a seat, for carrying on with early vigour and decision, the most clearly just and necessary war,[40] that this or any nation ever carried on; in order to save my country from the iron yoke of it's power, and from the more dreadful contagion of it's principles; to preserve, while they can be preserved pure and untainted, the ancient, inbred integrity, piety, good nature, and good humour of the people of England, from the dreadful pestilence which beginning in France, threatens to lay waste the whole moral, and in a great degree the whole physical world, having done both in the focus of it's most intense malignity.

The labours of his Grace's founder merited the curses, not loud but deep, of the Commons of England, on whom *he* and his master had effected a *compleat Parliamentary Reform*, by making them in their slavery and humiliation, the true and adequate representatives of a debased, degraded, and undone people. My merits were, in having had an active, though not always an ostentatious share, in every one act, without exception, of undisputed constitutional utility in my time, and in having supported on all occasions, the authority, the efficiency, and the privileges of the Commons of Great Britain. I ended my services by a recorded and fully reasoned assertion on their own journals of their constitutional rights, and a vindication of their constitutional conduct. I laboured in all things to merit their inward approbation, and (along with the assistants of the largest, the greatest, and best of my endeavours) I received their free, unbiassed, publick, and solemn thanks.

Thus stands the account of the comparative merits of the Crown grants which compose the Duke of Bedford's fortune as balanced against mine. In the name of common sense, why should the Duke of Bedford think, that none but of the House of Russel are entitled to the favour of the Crown? Why should he imagine that no King of England has been capable of judging of merit but King Henry the Eighth? Indeed, he will pardon me; he is a little mistaken; all virtue did not end in the first Earl of Bedford. All discernment did not lose it's vision when his Creator closed his eyes. Let him remit his rigour on the disproportion between merit and reward in others, and they will make no enquiry into the origin of his fortune. They will regard with much more satisfaction, as he will contemplate with infinitely more advantage, whatever in his pedigree has been dulcified by an exposure to the influence of heaven in a long flow of generations, from the hard, acidulous, metallic tincture of the spring. It is little to be doubted, that several of his forefathers in that long series, have degenerated into honour and virtue. Let the Duke of Bedford (I am sure he will) reject with scorn and horror, the counsels of the lecturers, those wicked panders to avarice and ambition, who would tempt him in the troubles of his country, to seek another enormous fortune from the forfeitures of another nobility, and the plunder of another church. Let him (and I trust that yet he will) employ all the energy of his youth, and all the resources of his wealth, to crush rebellious principles which have no foundation in morals, and rebellious movements, that have no provocation in tyranny.

Then will be forgot the rebellions, which, by a doubtful priority in crime, his ancestor had provoked and extinguished. On such a conduct in the noble Duke, many of his countrymen might, and with some excuse might, give way to the enthusiasm of their gratitude, and in the dashing style of some of the old declaimers, cry out, that if the fates had found no other way in which they could give a Duke of Bedford[41] and his opulence as props to a tottering world, then the butchery of the Duke of Buckingham might be tolerated; it might be regarded even with complacency, whilst in the heir of confiscation they saw the sympathizing comforter of the martyrs, who

---

40. **war:** France declared war on England and Holland on February 1, 1793.

41. **the fates . . . Bedford:** [Burke's note] At si non aliam venturo fata Neroni, &c. ["The Fates could think of no other way to prepare for Nero's coming than the evils of civil war, etc." (Lucan, *Pharsalia*, I. 33)].

suffer under the cruel confiscation of this day; whilst they beheld with admiration his zealous protection of the virtuous and loyal nobility of France, and his manly support of his brethren, the yet standing nobility and gentry of his native land. Then his Grace's merit would be pure and new, and sharp, as fresh from the mint of honour. As he pleased he might reflect honour on his predecessors, or throw it forward on those who were to succeed him. He might be the propagator of the stock of honour, or the root of it, as he thought proper.

Had it pleased God to continue to me the hopes of succession, I should have been, according to my mediocrity, and the mediocrity of the age I live in, a sort of founder of a family; I should have left a son, who, in all the points in which personal merit can be viewed, in science, in erudition, in genius, in taste, in honour, in generosity, in humanity, in every liberal sentiment, and every liberal accomplishment, would not have shewn himself inferior to the Duke of Bedford, or to any of those whom he traces in his line. His Grace very soon would have wanted all plausibility in his attack upon that provision which belonged more to mine than to me. He would soon have supplied every deficiency, and symmetrized every disproportion. It would not have been for that successor to resort to any stagnant wasting reservoir of merit in me, or in any ancestry. He had in himself a salient, living spring, of generous and manly action. Every day he lived he would have re-purchased the bounty of the crown, and ten times more, if ten times more he had received. He was made a public creature; and had no enjoyment whatever, but in the performance of some duty. At this exigent moment, the loss of a finished man is not easily supplied.

But a disposer whose power we are little able to resist, and whose wisdom it behoves us not at all to dispute; has ordained it in another manner, and (whatever my querulous weakness might suggest) a far better. The storm has gone over me; and I lie like one of those old oaks which the late hurricane has scattered about me. I am stripped of all my honours; I am torn up by the roots, and lie prostrate on the earth! There, and prostrate there, I most unfeignedly recognize the divine justice, and in some degree submit to it. But whilst I humble myself before God, I do not know that it is forbidden to repel the attacks of unjust and inconsiderate men. The patience of Job is proverbial. After some of the convulsive struggles of our irritable nature, he submitted himself, and repented in dust and ashes.

But even so, I do not find him blamed for reprehending, and with a considerable degree of verbal asperity, those ill-natured neighbours of his, who visited his dunghill to read moral, political, and œconomical lectures in his misery. I am alone. I have none to meet my enemies in the gate. Indeed, my Lord, I greatly deceive myself, if in this hard season I would give a peck of refuse wheat for all that is called fame and honour in the world. This is the appetite but of a few. It is a luxury; it is a privilege; it is an indulgence for those who are at their ease. But we are all of us made to shun disgrace, as we are made to shrink from pain, and poverty, and disease. It is an instinct; and under the direction of reason, instinct is always in the right. I live in an inverted order. They who ought to have succeeded me are gone before me. They who should have been to me as posterity are in the place of ancestors. I owe to the dearest relation (which ever must subsist in memory) that act of piety, which he would have performed to me; I owe it to him to shew that he was not descended, as the Duke of Bedford would have it, from an unworthy parent.

The Crown has considered me after long service: the Crown has paid the Duke of Bedford by advance. He has had a long credit for any service which he may perform hereafter. He is secure, and long may he be secure, in his advance, whether he performs any services or not. But let him take care how he endangers the safety of that Constitution which secures his own utility or his own insignificance; or how he discourages those, who take up, even puny arms, to defend an order of things, which, like the Sun of Heaven, shines alike on the useful and the worthless. His grants are engrafted on the public law of Europe, covered with the awful hoar of innumerable ages. They are guarded by the sacred rules of prescription, found in that full treasury of jurisprudence from which the jejuneness and penury of our municipal law has, by degrees, been enriched and strengthened. This prescription[42] I had my share (a very full share) in bringing to it's perfection. The Duke of Bedford will stand as long as prescriptive law endures; as long as the great stable laws of property, common to us with all civilized nations, are kept in their integrity, and without the smallest intermixture of laws, maxims, principles, or precedents of the Grand Revolution. They are secure against all changes but one. The whole revolutionary system,

42. **This prescription:** [Burke's note] Sir George Savile's Act, called the *Nullum Tempus* Act.

institutes, digest, code, novels, text, gloss, comment, are, not only not the same, but they are the very reverse, and the reverse fundamentally, of all the laws, on which civil life has hitherto been upheld in all the governments of the world. The learned professors of the Rights of Man regard prescription, not as a title to bar all claim, set up against old possession—but they look on prescription as itself a bar against the possessor and proprietor. They hold an immemorial possession to be no more than a long continued, and therefore an aggravated injustice.

Such are *their* ideas; such *their* religion, and such *their* law. But as to *our* country and *our* race, as long as the well compacted structure of our church and state, the sanctuary, the holy of holies of that ancient law, defended by reverence, defended by power, a fortress at once and a temple,[43] shall stand inviolate on the brow of the British Sion—as long as the British Monarchy, not more limited than fenced by the orders of the State, shall, like the proud Keep of Windsor, rising in the majesty of proportion, and girt with the double belt of it's kindred and coeval towers, as long as this awful structure shall oversee and guard the subjected land—so long the mounds and dykes of the low, fat, Bedford level will have nothing to fear from all the pickaxes of all the levellers of France. As long as our Sovereign Lord the King, and his faithful subjects, the Lords and Commons of this realm,—the triple cord, which no man can break; the solemn, sworn, constitutional frank-pledge of this nation; the firm guarantees of each others being, and each others rights; the joint and several securities, each in it's place and order, for every kind and every quality, of property and of dignity—As long as these endure, so long the Duke of Bedford is safe: and we are all safe together— the high from the blights of envy and the spoliations of rapacity; the low from the iron hand of oppression and the insolent spurn of contempt. Amen! and so be it: and so it will be,

Dum domus Æneæ Capitoli immobile saxum
Accolet; imperiumque pater Romanus habebit.[44]—

43. **a fortress . . . temple:** [Burke's note] Templum in modum arcis ["a temple in the form of a fortress"]. Tacitus of the Temple of Jerusalem. 44. **Dum . . . habebit:** "as long as the race of Aeneas dwells on the immovable rock of the Capitol and the father of Rome maintains sovereignty" (*Aeneid*, IX. 448-49). The paragraph ended by this quotation Burke is said to have regarded as the most successful in all his writings. Thomas De Quincey reports that Burke once said, "A key passage in a rhetorical performance should involve a thought, an image, and a sentiment."

But if the rude inroad of Gallick tumult, with it's sophistical Rights of Man, to falsify the account, and it's sword as a makeweight to throw into the scale, shall be introduced into our city by a misguided populace, set on by proud great men, themselves blinded and intoxicated by a frantick ambition, we shall, all of us, perish and be overwhelmed in a common ruin. If a great storm blow on our coast, it will cast the whales on the strand as well as the periwinkles. His Grace will not survive the poor grantee he despises, no not for a twelvemonth. If the great look for safety in the services they render to this Gallick cause, it is to be foolish, even above the weight of privilege allowed to wealth. If his Grace be one of these whom they endeavour to proselytize, he ought to be aware of the character of the sect, whose doctrines he is invited to embrace. With them, insurrection is the most sacred of revolutionary duties to the state. Ingratitude to benefactors is the first of revolutionary virtues. Ingratitude is indeed their four cardinal virtues compacted and amalgamated into one; and he will find it in every thing that has happened since the commencement of the philosophic revolution to this hour. If he pleads the merit of having performed the duty of insurrection against the order he lives in (God forbid he ever should), the merit of others will be to perform the duty of insurrection against him. If he pleads (again God forbid he should, and I do not suspect he will) his ingratitude to the Crown for it's creation of his family, others will plead their right and duty to pay him in kind. They will laugh, indeed they will laugh, at his parchment and his wax. His deeds will be drawn out with the rest of the lumber of his evidence room, and burnt to the tune of *ça ira*[45] in the courts of Bedford (then Equality) House.

Am I to blame, if I attempt to pay his Grace's hostile reproaches to me with a friendly admonition to himself? Can I be blamed, for pointing out to him in what manner he is like to be affected, if the sect of the cannibal philosophers of France should proselytize any considerable part of this people, and, by their joint proselytizing arms, should conquer that Government, to which his Grace does not seem to me to give all the support his own security demands? Surely it is proper, that he, and that others like him, should know the true genius of this sect, what their opinions are; what they have done: and to whom; and what, (if a

45. **ça ira:** that shall go on; the refrain of a popular song of the French Revolution.

prognostick is to be formed from the dispositions and actions of men) it is certain they will do hereafter. He ought to know, that they have sworn assistance, the only engagement they ever will keep, to all in this country, who bear a resemblance to themselves, and who think as such, that *The whole duty of man*[46] consists in destruction. They are a misallied and disparaged branch of the house of Nimrod.[47] They are the Duke of Bedford's natural hunters; and he is their natural game. Because he is not very profoundly reflecting, he sleeps in profound security: they, on the contrary, are always vigilant, active, enterprizing, and though far removed from any knowledge, which makes men estimable or useful, in all the instruments and resources of evil, their leaders are not meanly instructed, or insufficiently furnished. In the French Revolution every thing is new; and, from want of preparation to meet so unlooked for an evil, every thing is dangerous. Never, before this time, was a set of literary men, converted into a gang of robbers and assassins. Never before, did a den of bravoes and banditti, assume the garb and tone of an academy of philosophers.

Zet me tell his Grace, that an union of such characters, monstrous as it seems, is not made for producing despicable enemies. But if they are formidable as foes, as friends they are dreadful indeed. The men of property in France confiding in a force, which seemed to be irresistible, because it had never been tried, neglected to prepare for a conflict with their enemies at their own weapons. They were found in such a situation as the Mexicans were, when they were attacked by the dogs, the cavalry, the iron, and the gunpowder of an handful of bearded men, whom they did not know to exist in nature. This is a comparison that some, I think, have made; and it is just. In France they had their enemies within their houses. They were even in the bosoms of many of them. But they had not sagacity to discern their savage character. They seemed tame, and even caressing. They had nothing but *douce humanité*[48] in their mouth. They could not bear the punishment of the mildest laws on the greatest criminals. The slightest severity of justice made their flesh creep. The very idea that war existed in the world disturbed their repose. Military glory was no more, with them, than a splendid infamy. Hardly would

they hear of self defence, which they reduced within such bounds, as to leave it no defence at all. All this while they meditated the confiscations and massacres we have seen. Had any one told these unfortunate Noblemen and Gentlemen, how, and by whom, the grand fabrick of the French monarchy under which they flourished would be subverted, they would not have pitied him as a visionary, but would have turned from him as what they call a *mauvais plaisant*.[49] Yet we have seen what has happened. The persons who have suffered from the cannibal philosophy of France, are so like the Duke of Bedford, that nothing but his Grace's probably not speaking quite so good French, could enable us to find out any difference. A great many of them had as pompous titles as he, and were of full as illustrious a race: some few of them had fortunes as ample; several of them, without meaning the least disparagement to the Duke of Bedford, were as wise, and as virtuous, and as valiant, and as well educated, and as compleat in all the lineaments of men of honour as he is: And to all this they had added the powerful outguard of a military profession, which, in it's nature, renders men somewhat more cautious than those, who have nothing to attend to but the lazy enjoyment of undisturbed possessions. But security was their ruin. They are dashed to pieces in the storm, and our shores are covered with the wrecks. If they had been aware that such a thing might happen, such a thing never could have happened.

I assure his Grace, that if I state to him the designs of his enemies, in a manner which may appear to him ludicrous and impossible, I tell him nothing that has not exactly happened, point by point, but twenty-four mile from our own shore. I assure him that the Frenchified faction, more encouraged, than others are warned, by what has happened in France, look at him and his landed possessions, as an object at once of curiosity and rapacity. He is made for them in every part of their double character. As robbers, to them he is a noble booty: as speculatists, he is a glorious subject for their experimental philosophy. He affords matter for an extensive analysis, in all the branches of their science, geometrical, physical, civil and political. These philosophers are fanaticks; independent of any interest, which if it operated alone would make them much more tractable, they are carried with such an headlong rage towards every desperate trial, that they would sacrifice the whole human race to the slightest of their

46. **The whole . . . man:** the title of an anonymous devotional and ethical work published in 1658. **47. Nimrod:** the "mighty hunter" of Gen. 10:8–9. **48. douce humanité:** sweet humanity.

49. **mauvais plaisant:** mischievous jester.

experiments. I am better able to enter into the character of this description of men than the noble Duke can be. I have lived long and variously in the World. Without any considerable pretensions to literature in myself, I have aspired to the love of letters. I have lived for a great many years in habitudes with those who professed them. I can form a tolerable estimate of what is likely to happen from a character, chiefly dependent for fame and fortune, on knowledge and talent, as well in it's morbid and perverted state, as in that which is sound and natural. Naturally men so formed and finished are the first gifts of Providence to the World. But when they have once thrown off the fear of God, which was in all ages too often the case, and the fear of man, which is now the case, and when in that state they come to understand one another, and to act in corps, a more dreadful calamity cannot arise out of Hell to scourge mankind. Nothing can be conceived more hard than the heart of a thorough bred metaphysician. It comes nearer to the cold maligity of a wicked spirit than to the frailty and passion of a man. It is like that of the principle of Evil himself, incorporeal, pure, unmixed, dephlegmated, defecated evil. It is no easy operation to eradicate humanity from the human breast. What Shakespeare calls "the compunctious visitings of nature"[50] will sometimes knock at their hearts, and protest against their murderous speculations. But they have a means of compounding with their nature. Their humanity is not dissolved. They only give it a long prorogation. They are ready to declare, that they do not think two thousand years too long a period for the good that they pursue. It is remarkable, that they never see any way to their projected good but by the road of some evil. Their imagination is not fatigued, with the contemplation of human suffering thro' the wild waste of centuries added to centuries, of misery and desolation. Their humanity is at their horizon—and, like the horizon, it always flies before them. The geometricians, and the chymists bring, the one from the dry bones of their diagrams, and the other from the soot of their furnaces, dispositions that make them worse than indifferent about those feelings and habitudes, which are the supports of the moral world. Ambition is come upon them suddenly; they are intoxicated with it, and it has rendered them fearless of the anger, which may from thence arise to others or to themselves. These philosophers, consider men in their experiments, no more

than they do mice in an air pump, or in a recipient of mephitic[51] gas. Whatever his Grace may think of himself, they look upon him, and every thing that belongs to him, with no more regard than they do upon the whiskers of that little long-tailed animal, that has been long the game of the grave, demure, insidious, spring-nailed, velvet-pawed, green-eyed philosophers, whether going upon two legs, or upon four.

His Grace's landed possessions are irresistibly inviting to an *agrarian* experiment. They are a downright insult upon the Rights of Man. They are more extensive than the territory of many of the Grecian republicks; and they are without comparison more fertile than most of them. There are now republicks in Italy, in Germany and in Switzerland, which do not possess any thing like so fair and ample a domain. There is scope for seven philosophers to proceed in their analytical experiments, upon Harington's seven different forms of republicks,[52] in the acres of this one Duke. Hitherto they have been wholly unproductive to speculation; fitted for nothing but to fatten bullocks, and to produce grain for beer, still more to stupify the dull English understanding. Abbé Sieyes[53] has whole nests of pigeon-holes full of constitutions ready made, ticketed, sorted, and numbered; suited to every season and every fancy; some with the top of the pattern at the bottom, and some with the bottom at the top; some plain, some flowered; some distinguished for their simplicity; others for their complexity; some of blood colour; some of *boue de Paris;*[54] some with directories, others without a direction; some with councils of elders, and councils of youngsters; some without any council at all. Some where the electors choose the representatives; others, where the representatives choose the electors. Some in long coats, and some in short cloaks; some with pantaloons; some without breeches. Some with five shilling qualifications; some totally unqualified. So that no constitution-fancier may go unsuited from his shop, provided he loves a pattern of pillage, oppression, arbitrary imprisonment, confiscation, exile, revolutionary judgment, and legalized premeditated murder, in any shapes into which they can be put. What a pity it is, that the progress of experimental philosophy

50. **the compunctious . . . nature:** See *Macbeth,* I. v. 46.

51. **mephitic:** poisonous. 52. **Harington's . . . republicks:** as set forth in *The Commonwealth of Oceana* (1656), a political romance by James Harrington (1611–77). 53. **Abbé Sieyes:** Emanuel Joseph Sieyès, a churchman and reformer; member of the National Assembly. 54. **boue de Paris:** Parisian mud.

should be checked by his Grace's monopoly! Such are their sentiments, I assure him; such is their language when they dare to speak; and such are their proceedings, when they have the means to act.

Their geographers, and geometricians, have been some time out of practice. It is some time since they have divided their own country into squares. That figure has lost the charms of it's novelty. They want new lands for new trials. It is not only the geometricians of the republick that find him a good subject, the chymists have bespoken him after the geometricians have done with him. As the first set have an eye on his Grace's lands, the chymists are not less taken with his buildings. They consider mortar as a very anti-revolutionary invention in it's present state; but properly employed, an admirable material for overturning all establishments. They have found that the gunpowder of *ruins* is far the fittest for making other *ruins*, and so *ad infinitum*. They have calculated what quantity of matter convertible into nitre is to be found in Bedford House, in Woburn Abbey,[55] and in what his Grace and his trustees have still suffered to stand of that foolish royalist Inigo Jones, in Covent Garden.[56] Churches, play-houses, coffee-houses, all alike are destined to be mingled, and equalized, and blended into one common rubbish; and well sifted and lixiviated,[57] to chrystalize into true democratic explosive insurrectionary nitre. Their Academy del *Cimento* (per antiphrasin)[58] with Morveau and Hassenfrats[59] at it's head, have computed that the brave Sans-culottes may make war on all the aristocracy of Europe for a twelvemonth, out of the rubbish of the Duke of Bedford's buildings.[60]

While the Morveaux and Priestleys are proceeding with these experiments upon the Duke of Bedford's houses, the Seieyes, and the rest of the analytical legislators, and constitution-venders, are quite as busy in their trade of decomposing organization, in forming his Grace's vassals into primary assemblies, national guards, first, second, and third requisitioners, committees of research, conductors of the travelling guillotine, judges of revolutionary tribunals, legislative hangmen, supervisors of domiciliary visitation, exactors of forced loans, and assessors of the maximum.[61]

The din of all this smithery may some time or other possibly wake this noble Duke, and push him to an endeavour to save some little matter from their experimental philosophy. If he pleads his grants from the Crown, he is ruined at the outset. If he pleads he has received them from the pillage of superstitious corporations, this indeed will stagger them a little, because they are enemies to all corporations, and to all religion. However, they will soon recover themselves, and will tell his Grace, or his learned council, that all such property belongs to the *nation;* and that it would be more wise for him, if he wishes to live the natural term of a *citizen*, (that is, according to Condorcet's[62] calculation, six months on an average,) not to pass for an usurper upon the national property. This is what the *Serjeants* at law of the Rights of Man, will say to the puny *apprentices* of the common law of England.

---

55. **Woburn Abbey:** the Bedford country residence. 56. **Covent Garden:** The Dukes of Bedford owned land in and around the London square Covent (formerly "Convent") Garden. Many of the buildings were designed by the famous seventeenth-century architect Inigo Jones; his market piazza was in the eighteenth century a notorious haunt of prostitutes. 57. **lixiviated:** treated with a solvent. 58. **Academy . . . antiphrasin:** Experimental Academy (through expression by opposites). 59. **Morveau and Hassenfrats:** Guyton de Morveau and Jean-Henri Hassenfratz were French chemists who took active parts in the Revolution. 60. **the brave . . . buildings:** [Burke's note] There is nothing, on which the leaders of the Republick, one and indivisible, value themselves, more than on the chymical operations, by which, through science, they convert the pride of Aristocracy, to an instrument of it's own destruction—on the operations by which they reduce the magnificent ancient country seats of the nobility, decorated with the *feudal* titles of Duke, Marquis, or Earl, into magazines of what they call *revolutionary* gunpowder. They tell us, that hitherto things "had not yet been properly and in a *revolutionary* manner explored."—"The strong *chateaus*, those *feudal* fortresses, that *were ordered to be demolished*, attracted next the attention of your Committee. *Nature* there had *secretly* regained her *rights*, and had produced salt-petre for the *purpose*, as it should seem, *of facilitating the execution of your decree by preparing the means of destruction.* From these *ruins*, which *still frown* on the liberties of the Republick, we have extracted the means of producing good; and those piles, which have hitherto glutted the *pride of Despots*, and covered the plots of La Vendée, will soon furnish wherewithal to tame the traitors, and to overwhelm the disaffected."——"The *rebellious cities* also, have afforded a large quantity of salt-petre. *Commune Affranchie*, (that is, the noble city of Lyons reduced in many parts to an heap of ruins) and Toulon will pay a *second* tribute to our artillery." Report 1st. February 1794. 61. **the maximum:** the maximum price for grain. 62. **Condorcet:** the Marquis of Condorcet (1743–94), French mathematician and philosopher; a member of the moderate party of the Revolution.

Is the Genius of Philosophy not yet known? You may as well think the Garden of the Tuilleries was well protected with the cords of ribbon insultingly stretched by the National Assembly to keep the sovereign canaille from intruding on the retirement of the poor King of the French, as that such flimsy cobwebs will stand between the savages of the Revolution and their natural prey. Deep Philosophers are no triflers; brave Sans culottes are no formalists. They will no more regard a Marquis of Tavistock than an Abbot of Tavistock; the Lord of Wooburn will not be more respectable in their eyes than the Prior of Wooburn; they will make no difference between the Superior of a Covent Garden of nuns and of a Covent Garden of another description. They will not care a rush whether his coat is long or short; whether the colour be purple or blue and buff.[63] They will not trouble *their* heads, with what part of *his* head, his hair is cut from; and they will look with equal respect on a tonsure and a crop.[64] Their only question will be that of their *Legendre*,[65] or some other of their legislative butchers, How he cuts up? how he tallows in the cawl[66] or on the kidneys?

Is it not a singular phœnomenon, that whilst the Sans culotte Carcase Butchers, and the philosophers of the shambles, are pricking their dotted lines upon his hide, and like the print of the poor ox that we see in the shop windows at Charing Cross, alive as he is, and thinking no harm in the world, he is divided into rumps, and sirloins, and briskets, and into all sorts of pieces for roasting, boiling, and stewing, that all the while they are measuring *him*, his Grace is measuring *me;* is invidiously comparing the bounty of the Crown with the deserts of the defender of his order, and in the same moment fawning on those who have the knife half out of the sheath—poor innocent!

> Pleas'd to the last, he crops the flow'ry food,
> And licks the hand just rais'd to shed his blood.[67]

No man lives too long, who lives to do with spirit, and suffer with resignation, what Providence pleases to command or inflict: but indeed they are sharp incommodities which beset old age. It was but the other day, that on putting in order some things which had been brought here[68] on my taking leave of London for ever, I looked over a number of fine portraits, most of them of persons now dead, but whose society, in my better days, made this a proud and happy place. Amongst these was the picture of Lord Keppel.[69] It was painted by an artist worthy of the subject,[70] the excellent friend of that excellent man from their earliest youth, and a common friend of us both, with whom we lived for many years without a moment of coldness, of peevishness, of jealousy, or of jar, to the day of our final separation.

I ever looked on Lord Keppel as one of the greatest and best men of his age; and I loved, and cultivated him accordingly. He was much in my heart, and I believe I was in his to the very last beat. It was after his trial at Portsmouth that he gave me this picture. With what zeal and anxious affection I attended him through that his agony of glory, what part my son took in the early flush and enthusiasm of his virtue, and the pious passion with which he attached himself to all my connections, with what prodigality we both squandered ourselves in courting almost every sort of enmity for his sake, I believe he felt, just as I should have felt, such friendship on such an occasion. I partook indeed of this honour, with several of the first, and best, and ablest in the kingdom, but I was behind hand with none of them; and I am sure, that if to the eternal disgrace of this nation, and to the total annihilation of every trace of honour and virtue in it, things had taken a different turn from what they did, I should have attended him to the quarter-deck[71] with no less good will and more pride, though with far other feelings, than I partook of the general flow of national joy that attended the justice that was done to his virtue.

Pardon, my Lord, the feeble garrulity of age, which loves to diffuse itself in discourse of the departed great. At my years we live in retrospect alone: and,

---

63. **purple . . . buff:** In addition to its Roman patrician connotations, purple (together with scarlet) was a color much worn and displayed by the aristocracy; blue and buff, the colors of George Washington's uniform, were often worn by Fox and his followers. 64. **a crop:** a very close haircut to be worn under a wig. 65. **Legendre:** Louis Legendre, the leader of the mob that stormed the Bastille. 66. **cawl:** the fatty membrane enclosing the intestines. 67. **Pleas'd . . . blood:** Pope, *Essay on Man*, i. 83–84.

68. **here:** Beaconsfield. 69. **Lord Keppel:** Augustus, First Viscount Keppel (1725–86), uncle of the Duke of Bedford. After a curiously indecisive naval battle with the French, Keppel, Vice Admiral of the Navy, was tried and acquitted in 1779; he was appointed First Lord of the Admiralty in 1782. 70. **an artist . . . subject:** Sir Joshua Reynolds (1723–92), who painted seven portraits of Keppel between 1749 and 1785. (See the selection from Reynolds earlier in Part Six.) 71. **the quarter-deck:** the place of execution.

wholly unfitted for the society of vigorous life, we enjoy, the best balm to all wounds, the consolation of friendship, in those only whom we have lost for ever. Feeling the loss of Lord Keppel at all times, at no time did I feel it so much as on the first day when I was attacked in the House of Lords.

Had he lived, that reverend form would have risen in its place, and with a mild, parental reprehension to his nephew the Duke of Bedford, he would have told him that the favour of that gracious prince, who had honoured his virtues with the government of the navy of Great Britain, and with a seat in the hereditary great council of his kingdom, was not undeservedly shewn to the friend of the best portion of his life, and his faithful companion and counsellor under his rudest trials. He would have told him, that to whomever else these reproaches might be becoming, they were not decorous in his near kindred. He would have told him that when men in that rank lose decorum, they lose every thing.

On that day I had a loss in Lord Keppel; but the publick loss of him in this awful crisis—! I speak from much knowledge of the person, he never would have listened to any compromise with the rabble rout of this Sans Culotterie of France. His goodness of heart, his reason, his taste, his publick duty, his principles, his prejudices, would have repelled him for ever from all connection with that horrid medley of madness, vice, impiety, and crime.

Lord Keppel had two countries; one of descent, and one of birth. Their interest and their glory are the same; and his mind was capacious of both. His family was noble and it was Dutch. That is, he was of the oldest and purest nobility that Europe can boast, among a people renowned above all others for love of their native land. Though it was never shewn in insult to any human being, Lord Keppel was something high. It was a wild stock of pride, on which the tenderest of all hearts had grafted the milder virtues. He valued ancient nobility; and he was not disinclined to augment it with new honours. He valued the old nobility and the new, not as an excuse for inglorious sloth, but as an incitement to virtuous activity. He considered it as a sort of cure for selfishness and a narrow mind; conceiving that a man born in an elevated place, in himself was nothing, but every thing in what went before, and what was to come after him. Without much speculation, but by the sure instinct of ingenuous feelings, and by the dictates of plain unsophisticated natural understanding, he felt,

that no great Commonwealth could by any possibility long subsist, without a body of some kind or other of nobility, decorated with honour, and fortified by privilege. This nobility forms the chain that connects the ages of a nation, which otherwise (with Mr. Paine) would soon be taught that no one generation can bind another. He felt that no political fabrick could be well made without some such order of things as might, through a series of time, afford a rational hope of securing unity, coherence, consistency, and stability to the state. He felt that nothing else can protect it against the levity of courts, and the greater levity of the multitude. That to talk of hereditary monarchy without any thing else of hereditary reverence in the Commonwealth, was a low-minded absurdity; fit only for those detestable "fools aspiring to be knaves,"[72] who began to forge in 1789, the false money of the French Constitution—That it is one fatal objection to all *new* fancied and *new fabricated* Republicks, (among a people, who, once possessing such an advantage, have wickedly and insolently rejected it,) that the *prejudice* of an old nobility is a thing that *cannot* be made. It may be improved, it may be corrected, it may be replenished: men may be taken from it, or aggregated to it, but the *thing itself* is matter of *inveterate* opinion, and therefore *cannot* be matter of mere positive institution. He felt, that this nobility, in fact does not exist in wrong of other orders of the state, but by them, and for them.

I knew the man I speak of; and, if we can divine the future, out of what we collect from the past, no person living would look with more scorn and horror on the impious parricide committed on all their ancestry, and on the desperate attainder passed on all posterity, by the Orleans, and the Rochefoucaults, and the Fayettes, and the Viscomtes de Noailles, and the false Perigords, and the long *et cætera* of the perfidious Sans Culottes of the court, who act like demoniacs, possessed with a spirit of fallen pride, and inverted ambition, abdicated their dignities, disowned their families, betrayed the most sacred of all trusts, and by breaking to pieces a great link of society, and all the cramps and holdings of the state, brought eternal confusion and desolation in their country. For the fate of the miscreant parricides themselves he would have had no pity. Compassion for the myriads of men, of whom the

---

72. fools . . . knaves: See Pope's *Epilogue to the Satires*, ll. 163–64: "See, all our Nobles begging to be Slaves! / See, all our Fools aspiring to be Knaves!"

world was not worthy, who by their means have perished in prisons, or on scaffolds, or are pining in beggary and exile, would leave no room in his, or in any well-formed mind, for any such sensation. We are not made at once to pity the oppressor and the oppressed.

Looking to his Batavian[73] descent, how could he bear to behold his kindred, the descendants of the brave nobility of Holland, whose blood prodigally poured out, had, more than all the canals, meers, and inundations of their country, protected their independence, to behold them bowed in the basest servitude, to the basest and vilest of the human race; in servitude to those who in no respect, were superior in dignity, or could aspire to a better place than that of hangmen to the tyrants, to whose sceptered pride they had opposed an elevation of soul, that surmounted, and overpowered the loftiness of Castile, the haughtiness of Austria, and the overbearing arrogance of France?[74]

Could he with patience bear, that the children of that nobility, who would have deluged their country and given it to the sea, rather than submit to Louis XIV. who was then in his meridian glory, when his arms were conducted by the Turennes, by the Luxembourgs, by the Boufflers; when his councils were directed by the Colberts, and the Louvois; when his tribunals were filled by the Lamoignons and the Daguessaus[75]—that these should be given up to the cruel sport of the Pichegru's, the Jourdans, the Santerres, under the Rollands, the Brissots, and Gorsas, and Robespierres, the Reubels, the Carnots, and Talliens, and Dantons, and the whole tribe of Regicides, robbers, and revolutionary judges, that, from the rotten carcase of their own murdered country, have poured out innumerable swarms of the lowest, and at once the most destructive of the classes of animated nature, which like columns of locusts, have laid waste the fairest part of the world?

Would Keppel have borne to see the ruin of the virtuous Patricians, that happy union of the noble and the burgher, who with signal prudence and integrity, had long governed the cities of the confederate Republick, the cherishing fathers of their country, who, denying commerce to themselves, made it

flourish in a manner unexampled under their protection? Could Keppel have borne that a vile faction should totally destroy this harmonious construction, in favour of a robbing Democracy, founded on the spurious rights of man?

He was no great clerk, but he was perfectly well versed in the interests of Europe, and he could not have heard with patience, that the country of Grotius,[76] the cradle of the Law of Nations, and one of the richest repositories of all Law, should be taught a new code by the ignorant flippancy of Thomas Paine, the presumptuous foppery of La Fayette, with his stolen rights of man in his hand, the wild profligate intrigue and turbulency of Marat, and the impious sophistry of Condorcet, in his insolent addresses to the Batavian Republick?

Could Keppel, who idolized the house of Nassau, who was himself given to England, along with the blessings of the British and Dutch revolutions; with revolutions of stability; with revolutions which consolidated and married the liberties and the interests of the two nations for ever, could he see the fountain of British liberty itself in servitude to France? Could he see with patience a Prince of Orange expelled as a sort of diminutive despot, with every kind of contumely, from the country, which that family of deliverers had so often rescued from slavery, and obliged to live in exile in another country, which owes it's liberty to his house?

Would Keppel have heard with patience, that the conduct to be held on such occasions was to become short by the knees to the faction of the homicides, to intreat them quietly to retire? or if the fortune of war should drive them from their first wicked and unprovoked invasion, that no security should be taken, no arrangement made, no barrier formed, no alliance entered into for the security of that, which under a foreign name is the most precious part of England? What would he have said, if it was even proposed that the Austrian Netherlands[77] (which ought to be a barrier to Holland, and the tie of an alliance, to protect her against any species of rule that might be erected, or even be restored in France) should be formed into a republick under her influence and dependent upon her power?

---

73. **Batavian:** Dutch. 74. **the overbearing . . . France:** In 1795 the French army invaded the Netherlands, expelled the reigning Prince of Orange, and established a republic. 75. **the Turennes, Luxembourgs, Boufflers, Colberts, Louvois, Lamoignons, Daguessaus:** all noblemen of honor.

76. **Grotius:** Hugo Grotius (1583–1645), famous Dutch jurist and statesman. 77. **the Austrian Netherlands:** now Belgium.

But above all, what would he have said, if he had heard it made a matter of accusation against me, by his nephew the Duke of Bedford, that I was the author of the war? Had I a mind to keep that high distinction to myself, as from pride I might, but from justice I dare not, he would have snatched his share of it from my hand, and held it with the grasp of a dying convulsion to his end.

It would be a most arrogant presumption in me to assume to myself the glory of what belongs to his Majesty, and to his Ministers, and to his Parliament, and to the far greater majority of his faithful people: But had I stood alone to counsel, and that all were determined to be guided by my advice, and to follow it implicitly—then I should have been the sole author of a war. But it should have been a war on my ideas and my principles. However let his Grace think as he may of my demerits with regard to the war with Regicide, he will find my guilt confined to that alone. He never shall, with the smallest colour of reason, accuse me of being the author of a peace with Regicide. But that is high matter; and ought not to be mixed with any thing of so little moment, as what may belong to me, or even to the Duke of Bedford.

I have the honour to be, &c.

EDMUND BURKE.

William Cowper

1731–1800

Son of the rector of Great Berkhamsted, Hertfordshire, William Cowper was a timid and sensitive child. He first experienced despair at the age of six, when his mother died. He was bullied and humiliated at a school in Bedfordshire until, at the age of ten, he entered the distinguished Westminster School, where he spent eight carefree years cultivating friendships and cheerfully laying in a solid store of Latin and Greek learning.

Persuaded by his father to study for the unlikely profession of the law, he entered the Middle Temple in 1753. Here he lived for ten fairly satisfactory years. Because he was too shy and despondent to practice law actively, he diverted himself in London with temperate gaiety and dissipation, and with reading and verse writing. During these years he fell in love with his cousin Theodora Cowper, to whom, as "Delia," he addressed lighthearted poems written in "dear Mat Prior's easy jingle." The reasons for his not marrying at this time are obscure, but it has been thought that some physical deformity lay behind his lifelong celibacy. Up to the age of thirty-two he led a quiet but not wholly unhappy life. In 1763 everything changed.

He was nominated by a cousin to the office of Clerk of the House of Lords, and he approached the day of the oral examination with increasing terror. He wrote later, "They whose spirits are formed like mine, to whom a public exhibition of themselves, on any occasion, is mortal poison, may have some idea of the horrors of my situation." He convinced himself that suicide offered the only escape from his predicament, and he tried to kill himself, first with laudanum, then with a penknife, and finally with his own garter, in which he hanged himself. Although each attempt failed, he did not have to face the examination, for, believing that his attempts at suicide had damned him, he instantly declined into a religious mania that soon terminated in raving insanity.

The remainder of his life was spent largely in a search for recovery. In a private asylum the year after his first attack of madness he took up Bible reading and experienced a conversion to Calvinistic Evangelicalism. The next year, convinced both of his ineradicable guilt and of the iniquity of urban pleasures, he settled in the town of Huntingdon, where he found some comfort with the pious but amiable family of the clergyman Morley Unwin. With the Evangelical Unwins he relished the tame, regular exercises of a devout domesticity, especially prayers and tea, and improving reading by the fireside. Since his conversion he had felt the need for a dominating spiritual adviser: he found one in the Reverend Mr. John Newton, formerly a profane and bibulous sea captain, now a powerful Evangelical divine. Newton was curate in the poverty-stricken town of Olney, and in order to enjoy Newton's ministrations Cowper moved there with Unwin's widow and children in 1767. Always fond of middle-aged women, he also made friends with a local baronet's widow, Lady Anna Austen, a lively creature who interested herself in Cowper, his mental troubles, and his poetry. In Olney, Cowper lived, active in good works, for nineteen years. But in 1773, after another violent, suicidal attack of religious insanity, there grew in him the conviction that he was damned beyond the power of the church to save him, and he began drawing away from Newton and the Evangelical movement to brood and suffer alone in rural retirement. Further attacks of insanity occurred in 1787 and 1794.

For the rest of his life he found gentle therapeutic distraction in his pet hares, dogs, cats, and birds; in quiet tasks of gardening and carpentry; in a large correspondence; and in the composition of poems, which he began writing seriously only when almost fifty. He found that he could write in a great variety of poetic kinds and that he wrote easily and copiously. "When I can find no other occupation," he says, "I think, and when I think, I am very apt to do it in rhyme." His poems he liked to regard as a mere hobby: "I have no more right to the name of a poet," he declares, "than a maker of mouse-traps has to that of an engineer."

The Evangelical *Olney Hymns*, written with Newton "for the use of plain people," appeared in 1779. *Poems by William Cowper of the Inner Temple, Esq.*, was published in 1782. This volume, which contained chiefly delicate satires and didactic poems revealing the influence of Pope, made some stir among Evangelical readers, who, like Benjamin Franklin and Samuel Johnson, admired its high but gentle moral tone. A writer in *The Monthly Review* commented that "his very religion has a smile that is arch, and his sallies of humour an air that is religious." The appearance of *The Task* (1785) established his reputation as a poet. He was considered for the laureateship in 1788, but he declined. He had been a sensitive student of Homer and Homeric translations since his days as a law student, and in 1791 his blank-verse translations of the *Iliad* and the *Odyssey* were published by subscription. This labor had served to distract him for seven years.

Total clarity was his goal in all his poems. As he explains, "In writing, perspicuity is always more than half the battle: the want of it is the ruin of more than half the poetry that is published. A meaning that does not stare you in the face is as bad as no meaning, because nobody will take the pains to poke for it."

His last years were spent ("hermetically sealed," as he says) in rural seclusion and domesticity with Unwin's widow, Mary, with whom he had maintained an affectionate but chaste friendship since her husband's death in 1767. When she died in 1796, he lapsed into terror, apathy, and silence. At the time of his death he was the most famous poet in England, and perhaps the most unhappy man.

A useful checklist is Lodwick Hartley's *William Cowper: A List of Critical and Biographical Studies Published from 1895 to 1949* (1950). Hartley's *William Cowper: The Continuing Revaluation* (1961) lists studies through 1960. See also Norma Russell's splendid bibliography issued by the Oxford Bibliographical Society (1963). A convenient edition of the poems is *Cowper's Poetical Works*, ed. H. S. Milford (4th ed., 1934). Cowper's interesting letters are available in *The Correspondence of William Cowper* (4 vols., 1904) and in *Unpublished and Uncollected Letters* (1925), both edited by Thomas Wright. E. V. Lucas has edited a selection of the letters for the World's Classics. Lord David Cecil's *The Stricken Deer* (1929) is a sympathetic biography, and Charles Ryskamp's excellent *William Cowper of the Inner Temple, Esq.* (1959) contains new biographical material. Kenneth MacLean's essay "William Cowper," in *The Age of Johnson: Essays Presented to Chauncey Brewster Tinker* (1949), is acute.

THE LOVE OF THE WORLD REPROVED; OR, HYPOCRISY DETECTED

Cowper moved freely from one style to another, from the conversational, familiar poetic style of Swift and Prior, on the one hand, to the high style of Milton (or gently humorous imitations of it) on the other. The familiar style in the octosyllabic couplet had been conventional for the genre of the fable since the *Fables* (1727) of John Gay.

The text is that of the first printing, in *The Gentleman's Magazine* (September, 1780), where the poem is titled *The Mahometan Hog: A Tale*. Significant variants have been introduced from the edition of 1782.

THUS says the prophet of the Turk,
"Good Mussulman, abstain from pork:
There is a part in ev'ry swine,
No friend or follower of mine
May taste, whate'er his inclination,
On pain of excommunication."
   Such Mahomet's *mysterious* charge,
And thus he left the point at large.
Had he the sinful part exprest,
They might with safety eat the rest;   10
But for ONE piece—they thought it hard
From the WHOLE Hog to be debarr'd;
And set their wit at work to find
What joint the prophet had in mind.°

THE LOVE OF THE WORLD REPROVED. **9–14. Had . . . mind:** These lines were written by John Newton, an Evangelical divine and close friend of Cowper's.

Much controversy straight arose;
These choose the Back, the Belly *those;*
By *some* 'tis confidently said
He meant not to forbid the Head:
While *others* at that doctrine rail,
And piously prefer the Tail.   20
   Thus, conscience freed from every clog,
Mahometans *eat up* the Hog.—
   You laugh,—'tis well; The tale apply'd,
May make you laugh—on t' other side.
"Renounce the WORLD!" the preacher cries:
"We do," a multitude replies:
While one as innocent regards
A snug and friendly game at *cards;*
And one, whatever you may say,
Can see no evil in a *play:*   30
Some love a *concert*, or a *race;*
And others *shooting*, and the *chace.*
Revil'd and lov'd, renounc'd and follow'd,
Thus bit by bit the *world* is *swallow'd:*
Each thinks his neighbour makes too free,
Yet likes a *slice* as well as he:
With *sophistry* their sauce they sweeten,
Till quite from *tail* to *snout* 'tis eaten.

THE DIVERTING HISTORY OF JOHN GILPIN

Showing how he went farther than he intended, and came safe home again.

The story of John Gilpin was told Cowper by Lady Austen to cheer him in one of his fits of gloom. The poem proved highly popular and was widely pirated after it first appeared, anonymously, in *The Public Advertiser* in 1782. Cowper explained his theory of the genre in a letter to William Unwin: "The ballad is a species of poetry, I believe, peculiar to this country, equally adapted to the drollest and the most tragical subjects. Simplicity and ease are its proper characteristics. Our forefathers excelled in it; but we moderns have lost the art."

The text is that of the first printing, in *The Public Advertiser* (November 14, 1782). Substantive revisions have been incorporated from the edition of 1800.

JOHN GILPIN was a Citizen
  Of Credit and Renown,
A Train-band° Captain eke was he
  Of famous London Town.

John Gilpin's Spouse said to her Dear,
  Though wedded we have been
These twice ten tedious Years, yet we
  No Holiday have seen.

To-morrow is our Wedding-Day,
  And we will then repair   10
Unto the Bell at Edmonton,
  All in a Chaise and Pair.

My Sister and my Sister's Child,
  Myself and Children three,
Will fill the Chaise, so you must ride
  On Horseback after we.

He soon replied, I do admire
  Of Womankind but one
And you are she, my dearest Dear,
  Therefore it shall be done.   20

I am a Linen-draper bold
  As all the World doth know,
And my good Friend, the Callender,°
  Will lend his Horse to go.

Quoth Mrs. Gilpin, that's well said;
  And for that Wine is dear,
We will be furnish'd with our own,
  Which is both bright and clear.

John Gilpin kiss'd his loving Wife,
  O'erjoy'd was he to find,   30
That though on Pleasure she was bent,
  She had a frugal Mind.

The Morning came, the Chaise was brought,
  But yet was not allow'd,
To drive up to the Door, lest all
  Should say that she was proud.

So three Doors off the Chaise was staid,
  Where they did all get in,
Six precious Souls, and all agog
  To dash through Thick and Thin.   40

Smack went the Whip, round went the Wheels,
  Were never Folk so glad;
The Stones did rattle underneath,
  As if Cheapside were mad.

John Gilpin at his Horse's Side
  Seiz'd fast the flowing Mane,
And up he got in haste to ride,
  But soon came down again.

For Saddle-tree scarce reach'd had he,
  His Journey to begin,   50
When turning round his head he saw
  Three Customers come in.

So down he came, for Loss of Time
  Although it griev'd him sore,
Yet Loss of Pence full well he knew
  Would trouble him much more.

'Twas long before the Customers
  Were suited to their Mind,
When Betty° screaming came down stairs,
  —The Wine is left behind.—   60

Good Lack! quoth he, yet bring it me,
  My leathern Belt likewise,
In which I bear my trusty Sword
  When I do exercise.°

Now, Mistress Gilpin, careful Soul!
  Had two Stone Bottles found,
To hold the Liquor that she lov'd,
  And keep it safe and sound.

THE DIVERTING HISTORY OF JOHN GILPIN. **3. Train-band:** trained band, a company of London citizen-soldiers. **23. Callender:** cloth-finisher.

59. Betty: the housemaid. **64. exercise:** drill with the trained band.

Each Bottle had a curling Ear,
   Through which the Belt he drew;   70
And hung a Bottle on each Side,
   To make his Balance true.

Then over all that he might be
   Equipp'd from Top to Toe,
His long red Cloak well brush'd and neat,
   He manfully did throw.

Now see him mounted once again,
   Upon his nimble Steed,
Full slowly pacing o'er the Stones,
   With Caution and good Heed.   80

But finding soon a smoother Road
   Beneath his well-shod Feet,
The snorting Beast began to trot,
   Which gall'd him in his Seat.

So fair and softly, John he cried,
   But John he cry'd in vain,
That Trot became a Gallop soon
   In spite of Curb and Rein.

So stooping down, as needs he must
   Who cannot sit upright,   90
He grasp'd the Mane with both his Hands,
   And eke with all his Might.

His Horse, who never in that sort
   Had handled been before,
What thing upon his back had got
   Did wonder more and more.

Away went Gilpin, Neck or nought,
   Away went Hat and Wig;
He little dreamt when he set out
   Of running such a Rig.   100

The Wind did blow, the Cloak did fly,
   Like Streamer long and gay,
Till Loop and Button failing both,
   At last it flew away.

Then might all People well discern
   The Bottles he had slung,
A Bottle swinging at each Side,
   As hath been said or sung.

The Dogs did bark, the Children screamed,
   Up flew the Windows all,   110
And ev'ry Soul cried out, well done!
   As loud as he could bawl.

Away went Gilpin, who but he!
   His Fame soon spread around,
"He carries Weight,° he rides a Race,
   'Tis for a Thousand Pound."

And still as fast as he drew near,
   'Twas wonderful to view,
How in a Trice, the Turnpike-men,
   Their Gates wide open threw.   120

And now as he went bowing down
   His reeking° Head full low,
The Bottles twain, behind his Back,
   Were shattered at a Blow.

Down ran the Wine into the Road,
   Most piteous to be seen,
Which made his Horse's Flanks to smoke
   As they had basted been.

But still he seemed to carry Weight,
   With leathern Girdle braced,   130
For all might see the bottle-necks
   Still dangling at his Waist.

Thus all through merry Islington
   These Gambols he did play,
And 'till he came unto the Wash°
   Of Edmonton so gay.

And there he threw the Wash about
   On both Sides of the Way,
Just like unto a trundling° Mop
   Or a wild Goose at Play.   140

At Edmonton his loving Wife
   From the Balcony spied
Her tender Husband, wond'ring much
   To see how he did ride.

Stop, Stop, John Gilpin, here's the House,
   They all at once did cry,
The Dinner waits, and we are tired—
   Said Gilpin, so am I.

But yet his Horse was not a Whit
   Inclin'd to tarry there,   150
For why? his Owner had a House
   Full ten Miles off at Ware.

115. He . . . Weight: as a handicapped jockey does. **122. reeking:** steaming. **135. Wash:** a shallow stream running across the road. **139. trundling:** revolving.

So like an Arrow swift he flew
  Shot by an Archer strong,
So did he fly—which brings me to
  The Middle of my Song.

Away went Gilpin, out of Breath,
  And sore against his Will,
Till at his Friend the Callender's
  His Horse at last stood still.   160

The Callender, amaz'd to see
  His neighbour in such Trim,
Laid down his Pipe, flew to the Gate,
  And thus accosted him:

What News, what News, your Tidings tell,
  Tell me you must and shall—
Say, why bare-headed, you are come,
  Or why you come at all.

Now Gilpin had a pleasant Wit,
  And loved a timely Joke,   170
And thus unto the Callender
  In merry guise he spoke.

I came because your Horse would come,
  And if I well forebode,
My Hat and Wig will soon be here,
  They are upon the Road.

The Callender right glad to find
  His Friend in merry Pin,
Return'd him not a single Word,
  But to the House went in.   180

Whence strait he came with Hat and Wig,
  A Wig that flow'd behind,
A Hat not much the worse for Wear,
  Each comely in its Kind.

He held them up, and in his Turn
  Thus show'd his ready Wit—
My Head is twice as big as yours,
  They therefore needs must fit.

But let me scrape the Dirt away
  That hangs upon your Face,   190
And stop and eat—for well you may
  Be in a hungry Case.

Said John, it is my Wedding-day,
  And all the world would stare,
If Wife should dine at Edmonton,
  And I should dine at Ware.

So, turning to his Horse, he said,
  I am in Haste to dine,
'Twas for your Pleasure you came here,
  You shall go back for mine.   200

Ah, luckless speech, and bootless boast!
  For which he paid full dear,
For while he spake, a braying Ass
  Did sing most loud and clear:

Whereat his Horse did snort, as he
  Had heard a Lion roar,
And gallop'd off with all his Might
  As he had done before.

Away went Gilpin,—and away
  Went Gilpin's Hat and Wig;   210
He lost them sooner than at first,
  For why? They were too big.

Now, mistress Gilpin, when she saw
  Her Husband posting down
Into the Country far away,
  She pull'd out Half a Crown.

And thus unto the Youth she said,
  That drove them to the Bell,
This shall be your's, when you bring back
  My Husband safe and well.   220

The Youth did ride, and soon did meet
  John coming back amain;
Whom in a trice he tried to stop,
  By catching at his Rein;

But not performing what he meant
  And gladly would have done,
The frighted steed he frighted more,
  And made him faster run.

Away went Gilpin,—and away
  Went Post-boy at his Heels;   230
The Post-boy's Horse right glad to miss
  The lumb'ring of the Wheels.

Six Gentlemen upon the Road
  Thus seeing Gilpin fly,
With Post-boy scamp'ring in the Rear,
  They rais'd the Hue-and-Cry.

Stop Thief!—Stop Thief!—A Highwayman!
  Not one of them was mute;
And all and each that pass'd that Way
  Did join in the Pursuit.   240

And now the Turnpike-Gates again
  Flew open in short Space,
The toll-men thinking as before,
  That Gilpin rode a Race:

And so he did, and won it too,
  For he got first to Town,
Nor stopp'd till where he had got up
  He did again get down.

Now let us sing—long live the King,
  And Gilpin long live He;   250
And when he next doth ride abroad,
  May I be there to see!

Releas'd him as my story tells,
And found a supper somewhere else.
  Hence jarring sectaries may learn,
Their real int'rest to discern:
That brother should not war with brother,
And worry and devour each other,   30
But sing and shine by sweet consent,
'Till life's poor transient night is spent,
Respecting in each other's case
The gifts of nature and of grace.
  Those christians best deserve the name
Who studiously make peace their aim;
Peace, both the duty and the prize
Of him that creeps and him that flies.

THE NIGHTINGALE
AND GLOW-WORM

The text is that of the first edition (1782).

  A Nightingale that all day long
Had cheer'd the village with his song,
Nor yet at eve his note suspended,
Nor yet when even tide was ended,
Began to feel as well he might
The keen demands of appetite;
When looking eagerly around,
He spied far off upon the ground,
A something shining in the dark,
And knew the glow-worm by his spark,   10
So stooping° down from hawthorn top,
He thought to put him in his crop;
The worm, aware of his intent,
Harangu'd him thus right eloquent.
  Did you admire my lamp, quoth he,
As much as I your minstrelsy,
You would abhor to do me wrong,
As much as I to spoil your song,
For 'twas the self same power divine,
Taught you to sing, and me to shine,   20
That you with music, I with light,
Might beautify and cheer the night.
The songster heard his short oration,
And warbling out his approbation,

FROM

THE TASK

The Task (1785), a poem in six books, originated from a suggestion of Lady Austen's that Cowper, who was casting about for a poetic subject, write about "the sofa." Beginning in the mode of mock epic with "I sing the Sofa," he proceeded for over five thousand lines by the principle of association. As he comments,

  If the work cannot boast a regular plan . . . it may
  yet boast, that the reflections are naturally suggested
  always by the preceding passage, and that the whole
  has one tendency; to discountenance the modern
  enthusiasm after a London life, and to recommend
  rural ease and leisure, as friendly to the cause of
  piety and virtue.

The genre is a subtle combination of the English Georgic (for example, Gay's *Trivia* [1716]) and the mock-Miltonic (for example, John Philips's *The Splendid Shilling* [1705]).

Like most of Cowper's work, the poem was undertaken as a distraction from self-consciousness; he writes, "*In the year when I wrote 'The Task'* (for it occupied me about a year) *I was very often most supremely unhappy*, and am under God indebted in good part to that work for not having been much worse." Cowper's clarity and ease helped make the poem a rousing success. *The Monthly Review* found Cowper's performance "always moral, yet never dull," and Robert Burns voiced the sentiments of most British and American readers of the next half-century: "Is not *The Task* a glorious poem?"

  The text is that of the first edition (1785), with substantive variants introduced from the edition of 1800.

THE NIGHTINGALE AND GLOW-WORM. **11. stooping:** swooping.

BOOK III. THE GARDEN

As one who long in thickets and in brakes
Entangled, winds now this way and now that
His devious course uncertain, seeking home;
Or having long in miry ways been foiled
And sore discomfited, from slough to slough
Plunging, and half despairing of escape,
If chance at length he find a green-sward smooth
And faithful to the foot, his spirits rise,
He chirrups brisk his ear-erecting steed,
And winds his way with pleasure and with ease;   10
So I, designing other themes, and call'd
T' adorn the Sofa with eulogium due,
To tell its slumbers and to paint its dreams,
Have rambled wide. In country, city, seat
Of academic fame (howe'er deserved),
Long held, and scarcely disengaged at last.
But now with pleasant pace, a cleanlier road
I mean to tread. I feel myself at large,
Courageous, and refresh'd for future toil,
If toil await me, or if dangers new.   20

    Since pulpits fail, and sounding-boards reflect
Most part an empty ineffectual sound,
What chance that I, to fame so little known,
Nor conversant with men or manners much,
Should speak to purpose, or with better hope
Crack the satyric thong? 'twere wiser far
For me enamour'd of sequester'd scenes,
And charm'd with rural beauty, to repose,
Where chance may throw me, beneath elm or vine,
My languid limbs when summer sears the plains,   30
Or when rough winter rages, on the soft
And shelter'd Sofa, while the nitrous air°
Feeds a blue flame and makes a chearful hearth;
There undisturb'd by folly, and appriz'd
How great the danger of disturbing her,
To muse in silence, or at least confine
Remarks that gall so many, to the few
My partners in retreat. Disgust conceal'd
Is oft-times proof of wisdom, when the fault
Is obstinate, and cure beyond our reach.   40

    Domestic happiness, thou only bliss
Of Paradise that has survived the fall!
Though few now taste thee unimpair'd and pure,
Or tasting, long enjoy thee, too infirm
Or too incautious to preserve thy sweets
Unmixt with drops of bitter, which neglect
Or temper sheds into thy chrystal cup.
Thou art the nurse of virtue. In thine arms
She smiles, appearing, as in truth she is,
Heav'n born and destined to the skies again.   50
Thou art not known where pleasure is adored,
That reeling goddess with the zoneless° waist
And wand'ring eyes, still leaning on the arm
Of novelty, her fickle frail support;
For thou art meek and constant, hating change,
And finding in the calm of truth-tried love
Joys that her stormy raptures never yield.
Forsaking thee, what shipwreck have we made
Of honor, dignity, and fair renown,
'Till prostitution elbows us aside   60
In all our crowded streets, and senates seem
Convened for purposes of empire less,
Than to release th' adultress from her bond.
Th' adultress! what a theme for angry verse,
What provocation to th' indignant heart
That feels for injured love! but I disdain
The nauseous task to paint her as she is,
Cruel, abandon'd, glorying in her shame!
No. Let her pass, and, chariotted along
In guilty splendor, shake the public ways;   70
The frequency of crimes has wash'd them white.
And verse of mine shall never brand the wretch,
Whom matrons now of character unsmirch'd
And chaste themselves, are not ashamed to own.
Virtue and vice had bound'ries in old time
Not to be pass'd. And she that had renounced
Her sex's honor, was renounced herself
By all that priz'd it; not for prud'ry's sake,
But dignity's, resentful of the wrong.
'Twas hard perhaps on here and there a waif   80
Desirous to return and not received,
But was an wholesome rigor in the main,
And taught th' unblemish'd to preserve with care
That purity, whose loss was loss of all.
Men too were nice in honor in those days,
And judg'd offenders well. Then he that sharp'd,
And pocketted a prize by fraud obtain'd,
Was mark'd and shunn'd as odious. He that sold
His country, or was slack when she required
His ev'ry nerve in action and at stretch,   90

THE TASK: *Book III.* **32. nitrous air:** oxygen.

52. zoneless: unbelted.

Paid with the blood that he had basely spared
The price of his default. But now, yes, now,
We are become so candid and so fair,
So lib'ral in construction, and so rich
In christian charity, good-natured age!
That they are safe, sinners of either sex,
Transgress what laws they may. Well dress'd, well
 bred,
Well equipaged, is ticket good enough
To pass us readily through ev'ry door.
Hypocrisy, detest her as we may,   100
(And no man's hatred ever wrong'd her yet)
May claim this merit still, that she admits
The worth of what she mimics with such care,
And thus gives virtue indirect applause;
But she has burnt her mask not needed here,
Where vice has such allowance, that her shifts
And specious semblances have lost their use.

 I was a stricken deer that left the herd
Long since; with many an arrow deep infixt
My panting side was charged when I withdrew 110
To seek a tranquil death in distant shades.
There was I found by one who had himself
Been hurt by th' archers. In his side he bore
And in his hands and feet the cruel scars.
With gentle force soliciting the darts
He drew them forth, and heal'd and bade me live.
Since then, with few associates, in remote
And silent woods I wander, far from those
My former partners of the peopled scene;
With few associates, and not wishing more. 120
Here much I ruminate, as much I may,
With other views of men and manners now
Than once, and others of a life to come.
I see that all are wand'rers, gone astray
Each in his own delusions; they are lost
In chace of fancied happiness, still wooed
And never won. Dream after dream ensues,
And still they dream that they shall still succeed,
And still are disappointed; rings the world
With the vain stir. I sum up half mankind, 130
And add two-thirds of the remaining half,
And find the total of their hopes and fears
Dreams, empty dreams. The million flit as gay
As if created only like the fly
That spreads his motley wings in th' eye of noon
To sport their season and be seen no more.
The rest are sober dreamers, grave and wise,
And pregnant with discov'ries new and rare.

Some write a narrative of wars and feats
Of heroes little known, and call the rant 140
An history. Describe the man, of whom
His own coevals took but little note,
And paint his person, character and views,
As they had known him from his mother's womb.
They disentangle from the puzzled skein,
In which obscurity has wrapp'd them up,
The threads of politic and shrewd design
That ran through all his purposes, and charge
His mind with meanings that he never had,
Or having, kept conceal'd. Some drill and bore 150
The solid earth, and from the strata there
Extract a register, by which we learn
That he who made it and reveal'd its date
To Moses, was mistaken in its age.
Some more acute and more industrious still
Contrive creation. Travel nature up
To the sharp peak of her sublimest height,
And tell us whence the stars. Why some are fixt,
And planetary some. What gave them first
Rotation, from what fountain flow'd their light. 160
Great contest follows, and much learned dust
Involves the combatants, each claiming truth,
And truth disclaiming both. And thus they spend
The little wick of life's poor shallow lamp,
In playing tricks with nature, giving laws
To distant worlds and trifling in their own.
Is 't not a pity now that tickling rheums
Should ever teaze the lungs and blear the sight
Of oracles like these? Great pity too,
That having wielded th' elements, and built 170
A thousand systems, each in his own way,
They should go out in fume and be forgot?
Ah! what is life thus spent? and what are they
But frantic who thus spend it? all for smoke—
Eternity for bubbles, proves at last
A senseless bargain. When I see such games
Play'd by the creatures of a pow'r who swears
That he will judge the earth, and call the fool
To a sharp reck'ning that has lived in vain,
And when I weigh this seeming wisdom well 180
And prove it in th' infallible result
So hollow and so false—I feel my heart
Dissolve in pity, and account the learn'd,
If this be learning, most of all deceived.
Great crimes alarm the conscience, but it sleeps
While thoughtful man is plausibly amused.
Defend me therefore common sense, say I,
From reveries so airy, from the toil

Of dropping buckets into empty wells,
And growing old in drawing nothing up!   190

'Twere well, says one sage erudite,° profound,
Terribly arch'd and aquiline his nose,
And overbuilt with most impending brows,
'Twere well could you permit the world to live
As the world pleases. What's the world to you?
Much. I was born of woman, and drew milk
As sweet as charity from human breasts.
I think, articulate, I laugh and weep
And exercise all functions of a man.
How then should I and any man that lives   200
Be strangers to each other? Pierce my vein,
Take of the crimson stream meand'ring there
And catechise it well. Apply thy glass,
Search it, and prove now if it be not blood
Congenial with thine own. And if it be,
What edge of subtlety canst thou suppose
Keen enough, wise and skilful as thou art,
To cut the link of brotherhood, by which
One common Maker bound me to the kind.
True; I am no proficient, I confess,   210
In arts like yours. I cannot call the swift
And perilous lightnings from the angry clouds,
And bid them hide themselves in earth beneath,
I cannot analyse the air, nor catch
The parallax of yonder luminous point
That seems half quench'd in the immense abyss;
Such pow'rs I boast not—neither can I rest
A silent witness of the headlong rage
Or heedless folly by which thousands die,
Bone of my bone, and kindred souls to mine.   220

God never meant that man should scale the heav'ns
By strides of human wisdom. In his works
Though wondrous, he commands us in his word
To seek him rather, where his mercy shines.
The mind indeed enlighten'd from above
Views him in all. Ascribes to the grand cause
The grand effect. Acknowledges with joy
His manner, and with rapture tastes his stile.
But never yet did philosophic tube
That brings the planets home into the eye   230
Of observation, and discovers, else
Not visible, his family of worlds,
Discover him that rules them; such a veil

Hangs over mortal eyes, blind from the birth
And dark in things divine. Full often too
Our wayward intellect, the more we learn
Of nature, overlooks her author more,
From instrumental causes proud to draw
Conclusions retrograde and mad mistake.
But if his word once teach us, shoot a ray   240
Through all the heart's dark chambers, and reveal
Truths undiscern'd but by that holy light,
Then all is plain. Philosophy baptized
In the pure fountain of eternal love
Has eyes indeed; and viewing all she sees
As meant to indicate a God to man,
Gives *him* his praise, and forfeits not her own.
Learning has borne such fruit in other days
On all her branches. Piety has found
Friends in the friends of science, and true pray'r   250
Has flow'd from lips wet with Castalian dews,°
Such was thy wisdom, Newton, childlike sage!
Sagacious reader of the works of God,
And in his word sagacious. Such too thine,
Milton, whose genius had angelic wings,
And fed on manna. And such thine, in whom
Our British Themis° gloried with just cause,
Immortal Hale°! for deep discernment praised
And sound integrity not more, than famed
For sanctity of manners undefiled.   260

All flesh is grass, and all its glory fades
Like the fair flow'r dishevell'd in the wind;
Riches have wings, and grandeur is a dream;
The man we celebrate must find a tomb,
And we that worship him, ignoble graves.
Nothing is proof against the gen'ral curse
Of vanity, that seizes all below.
The only amaranthine flow'r° on earth
Is virtue, th' only lasting treasure, truth.
But what is truth? 'twas Pilate's question put   270
To Truth itself, that deign'd him no reply.
And wherefore? will not God impart his light
To them that ask it?—Freely—'tis his joy,
His glory, and his nature to impart.
But to the proud, uncandid, insincere
Or negligent enquirer, not a spark.

---

191. one . . . erudite: perhaps an allusion to Voltaire (1694–1778), who concludes his skeptical romance *Candide* (1759) by suggesting that in a world of violence one does well to cultivate one's own garden in quiet.

251. Castalian dews: poetic inspiration, associated with the Castalian spring, at the foot of Mount Parnassus. **257. Themis:** Greek goddess, personification of justice. **258. Hale:** Sir Matthew Hale (1609–76), author of legal and religious works. **268. amaranthine flow'r:** an imaginary flower that never dies.

What's that which brings contempt upon a book
And him who writes it, though the stile be neat,
The method clear, and argument exact?
That makes a minister in holy things   280
The joy of many and the dread of more,
His name a theme for praise and for reproach?—
That while it gives us worth in God's account,
Depreciates and undoes us in our own?
What pearl is it that rich men cannot buy,
That learning is too proud to gather up;
But which the poor and the despis'd of all
Seek and obtain, and often find unsought?
Tell me, and I will tell thee, what is truth.

Oh friendly to the best pursuits of man,   290
Friendly to thought, to virtue, and to peace,
Domestic life in rural leisure pass'd!
Few know thy value, and few taste thy sweets,
Though many boast thy favours, and affect
To understand and chuse thee for their own.
But foolish man foregoes his proper bliss,
Ev'n as his first progenitor, and quits,
Though placed in paradise (for earth has still
Some traces of her youthful beauty left)
Substantial happiness for transient joy.   300
Scenes form'd for contemplation, and to nurse
The growing seeds of wisdom; that suggest
By ev'ry pleasing image they present
Reflections such as meliorate the heart,
Compose the passions, and exalt the mind;
Scenes such as these, 'tis his supreme delight
To fill with riot and defile with blood.
Should some contagion, kind to the poor brutes
We persecute, annihilate the tribes
That draw the sportsman over hill and dale   310
Fearless, and rapt away from all his cares;
Should never game-fowl hatch her eggs again,
Nor baited hook deceive the fish's eye;
Could pageantry and dance and feast and song
Be quell'd in all our summer-months' retreats;
How many self-deluded nymphs and swains
Who dream they have a taste for fields and groves,
Would find them hideous nurs'ries of the spleen,
And crowd the roads, impatient for the town!
They love the country, and none else, who seek   320
For their own sake its silence and its shade.
Delights which who would leave, that has a heart
Susceptible of pity, or a mind
Cultured and capable of sober thought,
For all the savage din of the swift pack

And clamours of the field? Detested sport,
That owes its pleasures to another's pain,
That feeds upon the sobs and dying shrieks
Of harmless nature, dumb, but yet endued
With eloquence that agonies inspire   330
Of silent tears and heart-distending sighs!
Vain tears alas! and sighs that never find
A corresponding tone in jovial souls.
Well—one at least is safe. One shelter'd hare
Has never heard the sanguinary yell
Of cruel man, exulting in her woes.
Innocent partner of my peaceful home,
Whom ten long years' experience of my care
Has made at last familiar; she has lost
Much of her vigilant instinctive dread,   340
Not needful here, beneath a roof like mine.
Yes—thou may'st eat thy bread, and lick the hand
That feeds thee; thou may'st frolic on the floor
At evening, and at night retire secure
To thy straw-couch, and slumber unalarm'd.
For I have gain'd thy confidence, have pledg'd
All that is human in me, to protect
Thine unsuspecting gratitude and love.
If I survive thee I will dig thy grave,
And when I place thee in it, sighing say,   350
I knew at least one hare that had a friend.

How various his employments, whom the world
Calls idle, and who justly in return
Esteems that busy world an idler too!
Friends, books, a garden, and perhaps his pen,
Delightful industry enjoyed at home,
And nature in her cultivated trim
Dressed to his taste, inviting him abroad—
Can he want occupation who has these?
Will he be idle who has much t' enjoy?   360
Me therefore, studious of laborious ease,
Not slothful; happy to deceive the time,
Not waste it; and aware that human life
Is but a loan to be repaid with use,°
When he shall call his debtors to account,
From whom are all our blessings; bus'ness finds
Ev'n here. While sedulous I seek t' improve,
At least neglect not, or leave unemploy'd
The mind he gave me; driving it, though slack
Too oft, and much impeded in its work   370
By causes not to be divulged in vain,
To its just point—the service of mankind.

364. use: interest; cf. *usury*.

He that attends to his interior self,
That has a heart and keeps it; has a mind
That hungers and supplies it; and who seeks
A social, not a dissipated life,
Has business. Feels himself engaged t' atchieve
No unimportant, though a silent task.
A life all turbulence and noise, may seem
To him that leads it, wise and to be prais'd;   380
But wisdom is a pearl with most success
Sought in still water, and beneath clear skies.
He that is ever occupied in storms,
Or dives not for it, or brings up instead,
Vainly industrious, a disgraceful prize.

The morning finds the self-sequester'd man
Fresh for his task, intend what task he may.
Whether inclement seasons recommend
His warm but simple home, where he enjoys
With her who shares his pleasures and his heart,   390
Sweet converse, sipping calm the fragrant lymph°
Which neatly she prepares; then to his book
Well chosen, and not sullenly perused
In selfish silence, but imparted oft
As aught occurs that she may smile to hear,
Or turn to nourishment digested well.
Or, if the garden with its many cares,
All well repay'd, demand him, he attends
The welcome call, conscious how much the hand
Of lubbard° labour needs his watchful eye,   400
Oft loit'ring lazily if not o'erseen,
Or misapplying his unskilful strength.
Nor does he govern only or direct,
But much performs himself. No works indeed
That ask robust tough sinews bred to toil,
Servile employ—but such as may amuse,
Not tire, demanding rather skill than force.
Proud of his well-spread walls, he views his trees
That meet (no barren interval between)
With pleasure more than ev'n their fruits afford,   410
Which, save himself who trains them, none can feel.
These therefore are his own peculiar charge;
No meaner hand may discipline the shoots,
None but his steel approach them. What is weak,
Distemper'd, or has lost prolific pow'rs,
Impair'd by age, his unrelenting hand
Dooms to the knife. Nor does he spare the soft
And succulent that feeds its giant growth
But barren, at th' expence of neighb'ring twigs
Less ostentatious, and yet studded thick   420

391. fragrant lymph: tea. 400. lubbard: sluggish.

With hopeful gems.° The rest, no portion left
That may disgrace his art, or disappoint
Large expectation, he disposes neat
At measur'd distances, that air and sun
Admitted freely may afford their aid,
And ventilate and warm the swelling buds.
Hence summer has her riches, autumn hence,
And hence ev'n winter fills his wither'd hand
With blushing fruits, and plenty not his own.
Fair recompense of labour well bestow'd,   430
And wise precaution, which a clime so rude
Makes needful still, whose spring is but the child
Of churlish winter, in her froward moods
Discov'ring much the temper of her sire.
For oft, as if in her the stream of mild
Maternal nature had revers'd its course,
She brings her infants forth with many smiles,
But once deliver'd, kills them with a frown.
He therefore, timely warn'd, himself supplies
Her want of care, screening and keeping warm   440
The plenteous bloom, that no rough blast may sweep
His garlands from the boughs. Again, as oft
As the sun peeps and vernal airs breathe mild,
The fence withdrawn, he gives them ev'ry beam,
And spreads his hopes before the blaze of day.

To raise the prickly and green-coated gourd
So grateful to the palate, and when rare
So coveted, else base and disesteem'd—
Food for the vulgar merely—is an art
That toiling ages have but just matured,   450
And at this moment unassay'd in song.
Yet gnats have had, and frogs and mice long since,
Their eulogy; those sang the Mantuan bard,°
And these the Grecian° in ennobling strains,
And in thy numbers, Phillips,° shines for aye
The solitary shilling. Pardon then
Ye sage dispensers of poetic fame!
Th' ambition of one meaner far, whose pow'rs
Presuming an attempt not less sublime,
Pant for the praise of dressing to the taste   460
Of critic appetite, no sordid fare,
A cucumber, while costly yet and scarce.

The stable yields a stercoraceous heap°
Impregnated with quick fermenting salts,

421. gems: buds. 453. the Mantuan bard: Virgil. 454. the
Grecian: Homer. 455. Phillips: John Philips (1676–1709),
poet; author of *The Splendid Shilling* (see Part Three), a
Miltonic burlesque published in 1705. 463. stercoraceous
heap: manure pile.

And potent to resist the freezing blast.
For, ere the beech and elm have cast their leaf
Deciduous, when now November dark
Checks vegetation in the torpid plant
Exposed to his cold breath, the task begins.
Warily therefore, and with prudent heed   470
He seeks a favor'd spot. That where he builds
Th' agglomerated pile, his frame may front
The sun's meridian disk, and at the back
Enjoy close shelter, wall, or reeds, or hedge
Impervious to the wind. First he bids spread
Dry fern or litter'd hay, that may imbibe
Th' ascending damps; then leisurely impose
And lightly, shaking it with agile hand
From the full fork, the saturated straw.
What longest binds the closest, forms secure   480
The shapely side, that as it rises takes
By just degrees an overhanging breadth,
Shelt'ring the base with its projected eaves.
Th' uplifted frame compact at ev'ry joint,
And overlaid with clear translucent glass
He settles next upon the sloping mount,
Whose sharp declivity shoots off secure
From the dash'd pane the deluge as it falls.
He shuts it close, and the first labor ends.
Thrice must the voluble and restless earth   490
Spin round upon her axle, ere the warmth
Slow gathering in the midst, through the square mass
Diffused, attain the surface. When behold!
A pestilent and most corrosive steam,
Like a gross fog Bœotian,° rising fast,
And fast condensed upon the dewy sash,
Asks egress; which obtained, the overcharged
And drench'd conservatory breathes abroad
In volumes wheeling slow, the vapor dank,
And purified, rejoices to have lost   500
Its foul inhabitant. But to assuage
Th' impatient fervor which it first conceives
Within its reeking bosom, threat'ning death
To his young hopes, requires discreet delay.
Experience, slow preceptress, teaching oft
The way to glory by miscarriage foul,
Must prompt him, and admonish how to catch
Th' auspicious moment, when the temper'd heat
Friendly to vital motion, may afford
Soft fomentation, and invite the seed.   510

495. **Bœotian:** Ancient Boeotia, with its moist, foggy atmosphere, was regarded by the neighboring Greeks as the home
of all stupidity and coarseness.

The seed selected wisely, plump and smooth
And glossy, he commits to pots of size
Diminutive, well fill'd with well prepar'd
And fruitful soil, that has been treasur'd long,
And drank no moisture from the dripping clouds.
These on the warm and genial earth that hides
The smoking manure and o'erspreads it all,
He places lightly, and as time subdues
The rage of fermentation, plunges deep
In the soft medium, till they stand immers'd.   520
Then rise the tender germs upstarting quick
And spreading wide their spongy lobes, at first
Pale, wan, and livid, but assuming soon,
If fann'd by balmy and nutritious air
Strain'd through the friendly mats, a vivid green.
Two leaves produced, two rough indented leaves,
Cautious, he pinches from the second stalk
A pimple, that portends a future sprout,
And interdicts its growth. Thence straight succeed
The branches, sturdy to his utmost wish,   530
Prolific all, and harbingers of more.
The crowded roots demand enlargement now
And transplantation in an ampler space.
Indulged in what they wish, they soon supply
Large foliage, overshadowing golden flowers,
Blown on the summit of th' apparent fruit.
These have their sexes, and when summer shines
The bee transports the fertilizing meal
From flow'r to flow'r, and ev'n the breathing air
Wafts the rich prize to its appointed use.   540
Not so when winter scowls. Assistant art
Then acts in nature's office, brings to pass
The glad espousals and insures the crop.

   Grudge not ye rich (since luxury must have
His dainties, and the world's more num'rous half
Lives by contriving delicates for you)
Grudge not the cost. Ye little know the cares,
The vigilance, the labor and the skill
That day and night are exercis'd, and hang
Upon the ticklish balance of suspense,   550
That ye may garnish your profuse regales
With summer fruits brought forth by wintry suns.
Ten thousand dangers lie in wait to thwart
The process. Heat and cold, and wind and steam,
Moisture and drought, mice, worms, and swarming
        flies
Minute as dust and numberless, oft work
Dire disappointment that admits no cure,
And which no care can obviate. It were long,

Too long to tell th' expedients and the shifts
Which he that fights a season so severe   560
Devises, while he guards his tender trust,
And oft, at last, in vain. The learn'd and wise
Sarcastic would exclaim, and judge the song
Cold as its theme, and like its theme, the fruit
Of too much labor, worthless when produced.

   Who loves a garden, loves a green-house too.
Unconscious of a less propitious clime
There blooms exotic beauty, warm and snug,
While the winds whistle and the snows descend.
The spiry myrtle with unwith'ring leaf   570
Shines there and flourishes. The golden boast
Of Portugal and western India there,
The ruddier orange and the paler lime
Peep through their polish'd foliage at the storm,
And seem to smile at what they need not fear.
Th' amomum° there with intermingling flow'rs
And cherries hangs her twigs. Geranium boasts
Her crimson honors, and the spangled beau
Ficoides,° glitters bright the winter long.
All plants of ev'ry leaf that can endure   580
The winter's frown if screen'd from his shrewd bite,
Live there and prosper. Those Ausonia° claims,
Levantine regions these; th' Azores send
Their jessamine, her jessamine remote
Caffraia;° foreigners from many lands
They form one social shade, as if convened
By magic summons of th' Orphean lyre.°
Yet just arrangement, rarely brought to pass
But by a master's hand, disposing well
The gay diversities of leaf and flow'r,   590
Must lend its aid t' illustrate all their charms,
And dress the regular yet various scene.
Plant behind plant aspiring, in the van
The dwarfish, in the rear retired, but still
Sublime above the rest, the statelier stand.
So once were ranged the sons of ancient Rome,
A noble show! while Roscius° trod the stage;
And so, while Garrick as renown'd as he,
The sons of Albion;° fearing each to lose
Some note of Nature's music from his lips,   600

576. **amomum:** an aromatic plant. 579. **Ficoides:** ice-plant.
582. **Ausonia:** Italy. 585. **Caffraia:** South Africa. 587.
Orphean lyre: The playing and singing of the mythological
Orpheus charmed plants and trees. 597. **Roscius:** Quintus
Roscius Gallus (d. 62 B.C.), famous Roman actor. David
Garrick, the great English actor who died in 1779, was some-
times called Roscius Garrick. 599. **Albion:** Britain.

And covetous of Shakespeare's beauty seen
In ev'ry flash of his far-beaming eye.
Nor taste alone and well-contrived display
Suffice to give the marshall'd ranks the grace
Of their complete effect. Much yet remains
Unsung, and many cares are yet behind
And more laborious. Cares on which depends
Their vigor, injured soon, not soon restored.
The soil must be renew'd, which often wash'd
Loses its treasure of salubrious salts,   610
And disappoints the roots; the slender roots
Close interwoven where they meet the vase
Must smooth be shorn away; the sapless branch
Must fly before the knife; the wither'd leaf
Must be detach'd, and where it strews the floor
Swept with a woman's neatness, breeding else
Contagion, and disseminating death.
Discharge but these kind offices, (and who
Would spare, that loves them, offices like these?)
Well they reward the toil. The sight is pleased,   620
The scent regaled, each odorif'rous leaf,
Each opening blossom, freely breathes abroad
Its gratitude, and thanks him with its sweets.

   So manifold, all pleasing in their kind,
All healthful, are th' employs of rural life,
Reiterated as the wheel of time
Runs round, still ending, and beginning still.
Nor are these all. To deck the shapely knoll
That softly swell'd and gaily dress'd, appears
A flow'ry island from the dark green lawn   630
Emerging, must be deem'd a labor due
To no mean hand, and asks the touch of taste.
Here also grateful mixture of well match'd
And sorted hues, (each giving each relief,
And by contrasted beauty shining more)
Is needful. Strength may wield the pond'rous spade,
May turn the clod, and wheel the compost home;
But elegance, chief grace the garden shows
And most attractive, is the fair result
Of thought, the creature of a polish'd mind.   640
Without it, all is Gothic as the scene
To which th' insipid citizen resorts
Near yonder heath; where industry mispent,
But proud of his uncouth ill-chosen task,
Has made a heav'n on earth. With suns and moons
Of close-ramm'd stones has charg'd th' incumber'd
   soil,
And fairly laid the Zodiac in the dust.
He therefore who would see his flow'rs dispos'd

Sightly and in just order, ere he gives
The beds the trusted treasure of their seeds,   650
Forecasts the future whole. That when the scene
Shall break into its preconceived display,
Each for itself, and all as with one voice
Conspiring, may attest his bright design.
Nor even then, dismissing as perform'd
His pleasant work, may he suppose it done.
Few self-supported flow'rs endure the wind
Uninjured, but expect th' upholding aid
Of the smooth-shaven prop, and neatly tied
Are wedded thus like beauty to old age,   660
For int'rest sake, the living to the dead.
Some cloath the soil that feeds them, far diffused
And lowly creeping, modest and yet fair,
Like virtue, thriving most where little seen.
Some more aspiring catch the neighbour shrub
With clasping tendrils, and invest his branch
Else unadorn'd, with many a gay festoon
And fragrant chaplet, recompensing well
The strength they borrow with the grace they lend.
All hate the rank society of weeds   670
Noisome, and ever greedy to exhaust
Th' impov'rish'd earth; an overbearing race,
That like the multitude made faction-mad
Disturb good order, and degrade true worth.

Oh blest seclusion from a jarring world
Which he thus occupied enjoys! Retreat
Cannot indeed to guilty man restore
Lost innocence, or cancel follies past,
But it has peace, and much secures the mind
From all assaults of evil, proving still   680
A faithful barrier, not o'erleap'd with ease
By vicious custom, raging uncontroul'd
Abroad, and desolating public life.
When fierce temptation seconded within
By traitor appetite, and arm'd with darts
Temper'd in hell, invades the throbbing breast,
To combat may be glorious, and success
Perhaps may crown us, but to fly is safe.
Had I the choice of sublunary good,
What could I wish, that I possess not here?   690
Health, leisure, means t' improve it, friendship, peace,
No loose or wanton, though a wand'ring muse,
And constant occupation without care.
Thus blest, I draw a picture of that bliss;
Hopeless indeed that dissipated minds,
And profligate abusers of a world
Created fair so much in vain for them,

Should seek the guiltless joys that I describe
Allur'd by my report. But sure no less
That self-condemn'd they must neglect the prize,   700
And what they will not taste, must yet approve.
What we admire we praise. And when we praise
Advance it into notice, that its worth
Acknowledg'd, others may admire it too.
I therefore recommend, though at the risk
Of popular disgust, yet boldly still,
The cause of piety and sacred truth
And virtue, and those scenes which God ordain'd
Should best secure them and promote them most;
Scenes that I love, and with regret perceive   710
Forsaken, or through folly not enjoyed.
Pure is the nymph, though lib'ral of her smiles,
And chaste, though unconfined, whom I extol.
Not as the prince in Shushan,° when he call'd
Vain-glorious of her charms his Vashti forth
To grace the full pavilion. His design
Was but to boast his own peculiar good,
Which all might view with envy, none partake.
My charmer is not mine alone; my sweets
And she that sweetens all my bitters too,   720
Nature, enchanting Nature, in whose form
And lineaments divine I trace a hand
That errs not, and find raptures still renew'd,
Is free to all men, universal prize.
Strange that so fair a creature should yet want
Admirers, and be destin'd to divide
With meaner objects, ev'n the few she finds.
Stripp'd of her ornaments, her leaves and flow'rs,
She loses all her influence. Cities then
Attract us, and neglected Nature pines   730
Abandon'd, as unworthy of our love.
But are not wholesome airs, though unperfumed
By roses, and clear suns though scarcely felt,
And groves if unharmonious, yet secure
From clamour, and whose very silence charms,
To be preferr'd to smoke, to the eclipse
That Metropolitan volcanos make,
Whose Stygian° throats breathe darkness all day long,
And to the stir of commerce, driving slow,
And thund'ring loud, with his ten thousand
        wheels?   740
They would be, were not madness in the head

714. the prince . . . Shushan: Ahasuerus, a Persian monarch
with a palace at Shushan, rejected his consort Vashti for
refusing to exhibit her beauty to his guests. See Esther 1:
10–19. 738. Stygian: dark and hellish, like the river Styx.

And folly in the heart; were England now
What England was, plain, hospitable, kind,
And undebauch'd. But we have bid farewell
To all the virtues of those better days,
And all their honest pleasures. Mansions once
Knew their own masters, and laborious hinds
Who had surviv'd the father, serv'd the son.
Now the legitimate and rightful Lord
Is but a transient guest, newly arrived   750
And soon to be supplanted. He that saw
His patrimonial timber cast its leaf,
Sells the last scantling, and transfers the price
To some shrewd sharper, ere it buds again.
Estates are landscapes, gazed upon a while,
Then advertised, and auctioneer'd away.
The country starves, and they that feed th' o'ercharg'd
And surfeited lewd town with her fair dues,
By a just judgment strip and starve themselves.
The wings that waft our riches out of sight   760
Grow on the gamester's elbows, and th' alert
And nimble motion of those restless joints
That never tire, soon fans them all away.
Improvement too, the idol of the age,
Is fed with many a victim. Lo, he comes—
The omnipotent magician, Brown,° appears.
Down falls the venerable pile, th' abode
Of our forefathers, a grave whisker'd race,
But tasteless. Springs a palace in its stead,
But in a distant spot; where more expos'd   770
It may enjoy th' advantage of the North,
And aguish East, till time shall have transform'd
Those naked acres to a shelt'ring grove.
He speaks. The lake in front becomes a lawn,
Woods vanish, hills subside, and vallies rise,
And streams, as if created for his use,
Pursue the track of his directing wand
Sinous or straight, now rapid and now slow,
Now murm'ring soft, now roaring in cascades,
Ev'n as he bids. Th' enraptur'd owner smiles.   780
'Tis finish'd. And yet finish'd as it seems,
Still wants a grace, the loveliest it could show,
A mine to satisfy the enormous cost.
Drain'd to the last poor item of his wealth,
He sighs, departs, and leaves the accomplish'd plan
That he has touch'd, retouch'd, many a long day
Labor'd, and many a night pursued in dreams,

Just when it meets his hopes, and proves the heav'n
He wanted, for a wealthier to enjoy.
And now perhaps the glorious hour is come,   790
When having no stake left, no pledge t' indear
Her int'rests, or that gives her sacred cause
A moment's operation on his love,
He burns with most intense and flagrant zeal
To serve his country. Ministerial grace
Deals him out money from the public chest,
Or if that mine be shut, some private purse
Supplies his need with an usurious loan,
To be refunded duly, when his vote,
Well-managed, shall have earn'd its worthy price. 800
Oh innocent compared with arts like these,
Crape° and cock'd pistol and the whistling ball
Sent through the trav'ller's temples! He that finds
One drop of heav'n's sweet mercy in his cup,
Can dig, beg, rot, and perish well-content,
So he may wrap himself in honest rags
At his last gasp; but could not for a world
Fish up his dirty and dependent bread
From pools and ditches of the commonwealth,
Sordid and sick'ning at his own success.   810

   Ambition, av'rice, penury incurr'd
By endless riot; vanity, the lust
Of pleasure and variety, dispatch,
As duly as the swallows disappear,
The world of wand'ring knights and squires to town.
London ingulphs them all. The shark is there
And the shark's prey. The spendthrift and the leech
That sucks him. There the sycophant and he
Who with bare-headed and obsequious bows
Begs a warm office, doom'd to a cold jail   820
And groat° per diem if his patron frown.
The levee swarms, as if in golden pomp
Were character'd on ev'ry statesman's door,
"BATTER'D AND BANKRUPT FORTUNES MENDED HERE."
These are the charms that sully and eclipse
The charms of nature. 'Tis the cruel gripe
That lean hard-handed poverty inflicts,
The hope of better things, the chance to win,
The wish to shine, the thirst to be amused,
That at the sound of Winter's hoary wing,   830
Unpeople all our counties, of such herds
Of flutt'ring, loit'ring, cringing, begging, loose

---

766. Brown: Lancelot "Capability" Brown (1715–83), landscape gardener.

802. Crape: a black cloth used by highwaymen for masks.
821. groat: a four-penny coin.

And wanton vagrants, as make London, vast
And boundless as it is, a crowded coop.

Oh thou resort and mart of all the earth,
Chequer'd with all complexions of mankind,
And spotted with all crimes; in whom I see
Much that I love, and more that I admire,
And all that I abhor; thou freckled fair
That pleasest and yet shock'st me, I can laugh   840
And I can weep, can hope, and can despond,
Feel wrath and pity when I think on thee!
Ten righteous would have saved a city once,
And thou hast many righteous.—Well for thee—
That salt preserves thee; more corrupted else,
And therefore more obnoxious at this hour,
Than Sodom in her day had pow'r to be,
For whom God heard his Abr'am plead in vain.°

ON A SPANIEL,
CALLED BEAU,
KILLING A YOUNG BIRD

This and the following poem were written in July, 1793.
The texts are those of the first printings, in *The Life and
Posthumous Writings of William Cowper, Esqr.*, ed.
William Hayley (1803).

A Spaniel, Beau, that fares like you,
    Well-fed, and at his ease,
Should wiser be, than to pursue
    Each trifle that he sees.

But you have kill'd a tiny Bird,
    Which flew not till to-day,
Against my orders, whom you heard
    Forbidding you the prey.

Nor did you kill, that you might eat,
    And ease a doggish pain,   10
For him, though chas'd with furious heat,
    You left, where he was slain.

Nor was he of the thievish sort,
    Or one, whom blood allures,
But innocent was all his sport,
    Whom you have torn for yours.

My Dog! what remedy remains,
    Since teach you all I can,
I see you, after all my pains,
    So much resemble Man?   20

BEAU'S REPLY

Sir! when I flew to seize the Bird,
    In spite of your command,
A louder voice than yours I heard,
    And harder to withstand:

You cried—"Forbear!"—but in my breast
    A mightier cried—"Proceed!"—
'Twas Nature, Sir, whose strong behest
    Impell'd me to the deed.

Yet much as Nature I respect,
    I ventur'd once to break   10
(As you perhaps may recollect)
    Her precept, for your sake:

And when your Linnet on a day,
    Passing his prison door,
Had flutter'd all his strength away,
    And panting press'd the floor,

Well knowing him a sacred thing,
    Not destin'd to my tooth,
I only kiss'd his ruffled wing,
    And lick'd his feathers smooth.   20

Let my obedience then excuse
    My disobedience now!
Nor some reproof yourself refuse
    From your aggriev'd Bow-wow!

If killing Birds be such a crime,
    (Which I can hardly see)
What think you, Sir, of killing Time
    With verse address'd to me?

THE SNAIL

During the last few months of his life, Cowper diverted himself by translating some Latin poems written by his old Westminster schoolmaster, Vincent Bourne, an untidy but clever fellow. This poem is a translation of Bourne's twelve-line poem *Limax*. Of Bourne, Cowper says:

> It is not common to meet with an author who can make you smile, and yet at nobody's expense; who is always entertaining, and yet always harmless; and who, though always elegant, charms more by the simplicity and playfulness of his ideas, than by the neatness and purity of his verse; yet such was poor Vinny.

The text is that of the first printing, in Hayley (1803).

TO grass, or leaf, or fruit, or wall,
The Snail sticks close, nor fears to fall,
As if he grew there, house and all
        together.

Within that house secure he hides,
When danger imminent betides
Of storm, or other harm besides
        of weather.

Give but his horns the slightest touch,
His self-collecting power is such,   10
He shrinks into his house, with much
        displeasure!

Where'er he dwells, he dwells alone,
Except himself has chattels none,
Well-satisfied to be his own
        whole treasure.

Thus, hermit-like, his life he leads,
Nor partner of his banquet needs,
And if he meets one, only feeds
        the faster.   20

Who seeks him must be worse than blind,
(He and his house are so combin'd)
If finding it, he fails to find
        its master.

THE CAST-AWAY

Written March 20, 1799, this poem may be considered Cowper's valedictory. The prevailing figure is taken from the following account of a sailor's being swept overboard, which Cowper found in Richard Walter's *A Voyage Round the World, by [Lord] George Anson* (1748):

> [In a severe storm] one of our ablest seamen was canted over-board; we perceived that, notwithstanding the prodigious agitation of the waves, he swam very strong, and it was with the utmost concern that we found ourselves incapable of assisting him; indeed we were the more grieved at his unhappy fate, as we lost sight of him struggling with the waves, and conceived from the manner in which he swam, that he might continue sensible, for a considerable time longer, of the horror attending his irretrievable situation.

The text is that of the first printing, in Hayley (1803).

Obscurest night involv'd the sky;
   Th' Atlantic billows roar'd;
When such a destin'd wretch as I,
   Wash'd headlong from on board,
Of friends, of hope, of all bereft,
His floating home for ever left.

No braver chief could Albion boast
   Than he, with whom he went,
Nor ever ship left Albion's coast,
   With warmer wishes sent.   10
He lov'd them both, but both in vain,
Nor him beheld, nor her again.

Not long beneath the 'whelming brine,
   Expert to swim, he lay;
Nor soon he felt his strength decline,
   Or courage die away;
But wag'd with death a lasting strife,
Supported by despair of life.

He shouted: nor his friends had fail'd
   To check the vessel's course,   20
But so the furious blast prevail'd,
   That, pitiless perforce,
They left their out-cast mate behind,
And scudded still before the wind.

Some succour yet they could afford;
　And, such as storms allow,
The cask, the coop, the floated cord
　Delay'd not to bestow.
But he (they knew) nor ship, nor shore,
Whate'er they gave, should visit more.　　30

Nor, cruel as it seem'd, could he
　Their haste himself condemn,
Aware that flight, in such a sea,
　Alone could rescue them;
Yet bitter felt it still to die
Deserted, and his friends so nigh.

He long survives, who lives an hour
　In ocean, self-upheld:
And so long he, with unspent pow'r,
　His destiny repell'd:　　40
And ever, as the minutes flew,
Entreated help, or cry'd—"Adieu!"

At length, his transient respite past,
　His comrades, who before
Had heard his voice in ev'ry blast,
　Could catch the sound no more.

For then, by toil subdued, he drank
The stifling wave, and then he sank.

No poet wept him: but the page
　Of narrative sincere,　　50
That tells his name, his worth, his age,
　Is wet with Anson's tear.
And tears by bards or heroes shed,
Alike immortalize the dead.

I therefore purpose not, or dream,
　Descanting on his fate,
To give the melancholy theme
　A more enduring date.
But misery still delights to trace
Its 'semblance in another's case.　　60

No voice divine the storm allay'd,
　No light propitious shone;
When, snatch'd from all effectual aid,
　We perish'd, each alone;
But I beneath a rougher sea,
And whelm'd in deeper gulphs than he.

Edward Gibbon

1737–1794

The historian Edward Gibbon, who displayed a scholarly turn of mind from his earliest boyhood, had the good fortune to belong to a well-to-do country family with a library. Born in the village of Putney, near London, he proved to be a sickly child. His aunt, Catherine Porten, introduced him to books, and he pored over *The Arabian Nights* and Pope's translations of Homer. He entered Westminster School at the age of eleven, but poor health forced him to leave after two and a half years. Thereafter he was tutored irregularly until, his health suddenly and inexplicably improving, he was able to enter Magdalen College, Oxford, at the age of fifteen.

Oxford he found intellectually torpid. When he discovered that his tutors did not care whether he studied, he devoted himself to genteel dissipation and to his own private program of readings in history. He had always delighted in religious disputation of a completely logical kind, and after a few months at Oxford he discovered that he had read and reasoned himself into a belief in Roman Catholicism. He boldly sought out a London priest and had himself secretly received into the Roman communion. When he confessed his apostasy, his father sent him in disgrace to Lausanne, Switzerland, to lodge with M. Daniel Pavillard, a Calvinist minister whose tutelage he hoped would bring the young man to his senses. The very next year Gibbon was able to gratify his father by announcing that he had reasoned himself back into the Protestant faith. After this episode he became generally more skeptical in religious outlook. In later life his skepticism was so well known that Boswell, recording a conversation at the Literary Club in 1778, quite casually used the initial *J* (that is, *I*) to represent "Infidel" Gibbon.

After his reconversion, Gibbon remained for almost five years in Lausanne, reading in the classics in the intervals between whist games and supper parties. As a result of these years of Continental self-education, the young Gibbon seemed hardly English at all; he spoke and wrote much better French than English, and he delighted to conceive of himself as a citizen of the world. While in Lausanne he fell in love with a country pastor's daughter, Susanne Curchod. She had no dowry, and Gibbon's father disapproved of so unseemly an alliance. Gibbon soberly accommodated himself to his father's wishes; as he observed later, "I sighed as a lover, I obeyed as a son." He never did marry.

His scholarly projects were now interrupted by two and a half years of military service in England. The Seven Years' War had created fear of a French invasion, and the militia was activated. Gibbon and his father, as captain and major, took to the field in 1760 with the Hampshire Grenadiers, and even in the midst of the copious toasts and unrestrained bawdry of the officers' mess, Gibbon calmly pursued his studies. He began several pieces of historical research, and he brushed up on his Greek. Although he regretted the waste of time, he cheerfully accepted his life in the militia and made the most of it. He writes in his *Memoirs* (1796), "The discipline and evolutions of a modern battalion gave me a clearer notion of the phalanx and the legion; and the captain of the Hampshire grenadiers (the reader may smile) has not been useless to the historian of the Roman Empire." He even found time to bring out a book in French, *Essai sur l'étude de la littérature* (1761), a vigorous, if juvenile, defense of classical literary and historical scholarship.

Released from service in 1762, he hastened back to the Continent to undertake the Grand Tour. He began in Paris and then spent almost a year in Lausanne studying ancient history, geography, and numismatics in preparation for his visit to Italy. He had long been casting about in search of a historical topic; in Rome he found it. He records in his *Memoirs:*

> My temper is not very susceptible of enthusiasm, and the enthusiasm which I do not feel I have ever scorned to affect. But, at the distance of twenty-five years, I can neither forget nor express the strong emotions which agitated my mind as I first approached and entered the *eternal city* . . . . It was at Rome, on the 15th of October, 1764, as I sat musing amidst the ruins of the Capitol, while the bare-footed friars were singing vespers in the Temple of Jupiter, that the idea of writing the decline and fall of the city first started to my mind.

Returning to England a year later, Gibbon began working on his great project with an austere self-possession, and as he patiently and single-handedly mastered his materials, his plan broadened to embrace not merely the fall of the city of Rome but the dissolution of the entire Roman Empire during one thousand years of Western history. In 1770 he interrupted his systematic research to publish his first work in English, an anonymous pamphlet titled *Critical Observations on the Sixth Book of the Aeneid.* In the same year his father died; Gibbon rationally "submitted," as he says, "to the order of nature," and pressed forward. He was elected in 1774 both to Parliament and to Johnson's Literary Club, where his precise, ceremonious manner (some people thought him insufferably vain and pompous) and his short, corpulent person ("Mr. Chubby Chubb," one caricaturist called him) made him appear ridiculous to many of the members.

Meanwhile, he was laboring to develop a style worthy of his subject. "Many experiments were made," he reports, "before I could hit the middle tone between a dull chronicle and a rhetorical declamation: three times did I compose the first chapter, and twice the second and third, before I was tolerably satisfied with their effect." He published the first volume of *The History of the Decline and Fall of the Roman Empire* in 1776. It was an immediate success, and the first edition of one thousand copies was exhausted in six weeks; as Gibbon recalls, "My book was on every table, and almost on every toilette [i.e., dressing table]." Volumes II and III appeared in 1781, and they were almost as well received, although the Cambridge scholar and wit Richard Porson was heard to say that there could not be a better exercise for a schoolboy than to turn a page of Gibbon into English. Gibbon had not made as much money as he needed from the first three volumes, and in 1783 he moved permanently back to less expensive Lausanne, where he established an ample and learned bachelor household with his old friend Georges Deyverdun. In the "elegant repose" of his library and garden Gibbon finished *The Decline and Fall:* Volumes IV, V, and VI appeared in 1788. The whole work, consisting of seventy-one chapters, had taken him twenty years. He remained in Switzerland until 1793, when the need for an operation took him once again back to England. Two months later, in his fifty-sixth year, he died of dropsy. He left at his death six separate drafts of his *Memoirs,* on which he had been working for the last four years of his life. These drafts were edited and published in 1796 by a friend, Lord Sheffield. Gibbon had always considered his life a stunning success, and the *Memoirs* radiate an air of dignified self-satisfaction.

Neither Gibbon nor his readers conceived of history as a science, or even as a social science. It was regarded instead as a branch of philosophy and *belles lettres.* Although Gibbon is scrupulously thorough and accurate in his management of facts, he does not aspire to be objective in his interpretations. He writes as an enlightened moralist unremittingly critical of the values and behavior of his historical characters. Assuming the uniformity of human nature, he takes pains to point out to his con-temporaries what he regards as enduring moral principles. For Gibbon the decline and fall of the Roman Empire is a moral and intellectual disaster brought about by religious enthusiasm, narrow patriotism, and pride. He writes, "I am convinced there never, never existed such a nation, and I hope for the happiness of mankind there never will again."

J. E. Norton's *Bibliography of the Works of Edward Gibbon* (1940) is a rich source of biographical and critical information. A full biography is provided by D. M. Low's *Edward Gibbon* (1937); J. C. Morison's briefer *Gibbon* (1878), in the English Men of Letters Series, is still useful. Delightful short biographical treatments are G. M. Young's *Gibbon* (1933) and Peter Quennell's "Edward Gibbon" in *The Profane Virtues* (1945). The *Letters* have been edited by J. E. Norton (3 vols., 1956). The standard edition of *The Decline and Fall* is J. B. Bury's (7 vols., 1896–1900). *The Decline and Fall* is frequently reprinted in inexpensive editions, many of them abridged. *The Memoirs of the Life of Edward Gibbon,* ed. G. B. Hill (1900), contains valuable annotation. The best reading edition of the *Memoirs* is *The Autobiography of Edward Gibbon,* ed. D. A. Saunders (1961). H. L. Bond's *The Literary Art of Edward Gibbon* (1960) is a good critical study.

FROM

THE HISTORY
OF THE DECLINE AND FALL
OF THE ROMAN EMPIRE

FROM

CHAPTER XV

In Chapters xv and xvi, the last two chapters of his first volume, Gibbon examines the contribution of early Christian institutions to the decline of Roman greatness. His serene anti-Christian innuendo in these two chapters, together with his occasional prurient witticisms, offended the devout and the respectable. The famous bluestocking Mrs. Elizabeth Montagu instructed her bookbinder to omit the two offending chapters from her copy, and early in the nineteenth century Thomas Bowdler felt constrained to edit an expurgated edition "For the Use of Families and Young Persons." Richard Porson, who thought Gibbon's *History* (1776–88) the greatest literary production of the eighteenth century, nevertheless had this to say: "[Gibbon] pleads eloquently for the rights of mankind, and the duty of toleration; nor does his humanity ever slumber except when women are ravished, or the Christians persecuted." Commenting on what were thought to be Gibbon's indecencies, Porson adds: "If the history were anonymous, I should guess that these disgraceful obscenities were written by some *débauché*, who, having from age, or accident, or excess, survived the practice of lust, still indulged himself in the luxury of speculation."

Gibbon's treatment of the early church as an essentially secular institution prompted numerous divines to retaliate. Gibbon recalls in his *Memoirs* (1796):

> Had I believed that the majority of English readers were so fondly attached even to the name and shadow of Christianity; had I foreseen that the pious, the timid, and the prudent, would feel, or affect to feel, with such exquisite sensibility, I might perhaps have softened the two invidious chapters, which would create many enemies, and conciliate few friends. But the shaft was shot, the alarm was sounded, and I could only rejoice, that if the voice of our priests was clamorous and bitter, their hands were disarmed from the powers of persecution.

Gibbon read the complaints for three years until finally, exasperated by one particularly shallow pamphlet, which accused him not only of impiety and indecency but, what was far worse, of plagiarism and inaccuracy,

he published in 1779 a triumphant answer titled *A Vindication of Some Passages in the Fifteenth and Sixteenth Chapters of the History of the Decline and Fall of the Roman Empire*. His accuracy and his scholarly honor were vindicated, and the opposition was effectively silenced.

This selection comprises about five-sixths of Chapter xv. The text is that of the first edition (1776); we have incorporated the substantive variants from the third edition (1777). Here, as well as in the selection from Chapter xxiv, we have omitted many of Gibbon's notes, and we have shortened the remaining notes by omitting bibliographical references and classical quotations.

---

*The Progress of the Christian Religion,
and the Sentiments, Manners, Numbers,
and Condition, of the Primitive Christians.*

A candid but rational inquiry into the progress and establishment of Christianity, may be considered as a very essential part of the history of the Roman Empire. While that great body was invaded by open violence, or undermined by slow decay, a pure and humble religion gently insinuated itself into the minds of men, grew up in silence and obscurity, derived new vigour from opposition, and finally erected the triumphant banner of the cross on the ruins of the capitol. Nor was the influence of Christianity confined to the period or to the limits of the Roman empire. After a revolution of thirteen or fourteen centuries, that religion is still professed by the nations of Europe, the most distinguished portion of human kind in arts and learning as well as in arms. By the industry and zeal of the Europeans, it has been widely diffused to the most distant shores of Asia and Africa; and by the means of their colonies has been firmly established from Canada to Chili, in a world unknown to the ancients.

But this inquiry, however useful or entertaining, is attended with two peculiar difficulties. The scanty and suspicious materials of ecclesiastical history seldom enable us to dispel the dark cloud that hangs over the first age of the church. The great law of impartiality too often obliges us to reveal the imperfections of the uninspired teachers and believers of the gospel; and, to a careless observer, *their* faults may seem to cast a shade on the faith which they professed. But the scandal of the pious Christian, and the fallacious triumph of the Infidel, should cease as soon as they recollect not only *by whom*, but likewise *to whom*, the Divine Revelation was given. The theologian may indulge the pleasing task of describing Religion as she descended from Heaven, arrayed in her native purity. A more melancholy duty is imposed on the historian. He must discover the inevitable mixture of error and corruption, which she contracted in a long residence upon earth, among a weak and degenerate race of beings.

Our curiosity is naturally prompted to inquire by what means the Christian faith obtained so remarkable a victory over the established religions of the earth. To this inquiry, an obvious but satisfactory answer may be returned; that it was owing to the convincing evidence of the doctrine itself, and to the ruling providence of its great Author. But as truth and reason seldom find so favourable a reception in the world, and as the wisdom of Providence frequently condescends to use the passions of the human heart, and the general circumstances of mankind, as instruments to execute its purpose; we may still be permitted, though with becoming submission, to ask, not indeed what were the first, but what were the secondary causes of the rapid growth of the Christian church. It will, perhaps, appear that it was most effectually favoured and assisted by the five following causes: I. The inflexible, and, if we may use the expression, the intolerant zeal of the Christians, derived, it is true, from the Jewish religion, but purified from the narrow and unsocial spirit, which, instead of inviting, had deterred the Gentiles from embracing the law of Moses. II. The doctrine of a future life, improved by every additional circumstance which could give weight and efficacy to that important truth. III. The miraculous powers ascribed to the primitive church. IV. The pure and austere morals of the Christians. V. The union and discipline of the Christian republic, which gradually formed an independent and increasing state in the heart of the Roman empire.

I. We have already described the religious harmony of the ancient world, and the facility with which the most different and even hostile nations embraced, or at least respected, each other's superstitions. A single people refused to join in the common intercourse of mankind. The Jews, who, under the Assyrian and Persian monarchies, had languished for many ages the most despised portion of their slaves, emerged from obscurity under the successors of Alexander;[1] and as

they multiplied to a surprising degree in the East, and afterwards in the West, they soon excited the curiosity and wonder of other nations. The sullen obstinacy with which they maintained their peculiar rites and unsocial manners, seemed to mark them out a distinct species of men who boldly professed, or who faintly disguised, their implacable hatred to the rest of human-kind. Neither the violence of Antiochus,[2] nor the arts of Herod,[3] nor the example of the circumjacent nations, could ever persuade the Jews to associate with the institutions of Moses the elegant mythology of the Greeks. According to the maxims of universal toleration, the Romans protected a superstition which they despised. The polite Augustus[4] condescended to give orders, that sacrifices should be offered for his prosperity in the temple of Jerusalem; while the meanest of the posterity of Abraham, who should have paid the same homage to the Jupiter of the capitol, would have been an object of abhorrence to himself and to his brethren. But the moderation of the conquerors was insufficient to appease the jealous prejudices of their subjects, who were alarmed and scandalised at the ensigns of paganism, which necessarily introduced themselves into a Roman province. The mad attempt of Caligula[5] to place his own statue in the temple of Jerusalem, was defeated by the unanimous resolution of a people who dreaded death much less than such an idolatrous profanation.[6] Their attachment to the law of Moses was equal to their detestation of foreign religions. The current of zeal and devotion, as it was contracted into a narrow channel, ran with the strength, and sometimes with the fury, of a torrent.

This inflexible perseverance, which appeared so odious or so ridiculous to the ancient world, assumes a more awful character, since Providence has deigned to reveal to us the mysterious history of the chosen people. But the devout and even scrupulous attachment to the Mosaic religion, so conspicuous among

---

2. Antiochus: Epiphanes Antiochus (*c.* 215–163 B.C.), King of Persia, attempted to force the Jews to adopt Greek polytheism. **3. Herod:** (*c.* 73–4 B.C.), King of Judea, sought to Romanize and Hellenize Jerusalem. **4. Augustus:** (63 B.C.–A.D. 14), first Roman emperor. **5. Caligula:** (A.D. 12–41), Roman emperor. **6. idolatrous profanation:** [Gibbon's note] Philo and Josephus gave a very circumstantial, but a very rhetorical account of this transaction, which exceedingly perplexed the governor of Syria. At the first mention of this idolatrous proposal, king Agrippa fainted away; and did not recover his senses till the third day.

the Jews who lived under the second temple,[7] becomes still more surprising, if it is compared with the stubborn incredulity of their forefathers. When the law was given in thunder from Mount Sinai;[8] when the tides of the ocean, and the course of the planets were suspended for the convenience of the Israelites;[9] and when temporal rewards and punishments were the immediate consequences of their piety or disobedience, they perpetually relapsed into rebellion against the visible majesty of their Divine King, placed the idols of the nations in the sanctuary of Jehovah, and imitated every fantastic ceremony that was practised in the tents of the Arabs, or in the cities of Phœnicia. As the protection of Heaven was deservedly withdrawn from the ungrateful race, their faith acquired a proportionable degree of vigour and purity. The contemporaries of Moses and Joshua had beheld with careless indifference the most amazing miracles. Under the pressure of every calamity, the belief of those miracles has preserved the Jews of a later period from the universal contagion of idolatry; and in contradiction to every known principle of the human mind, that singular people seems to have yielded a stronger and more ready assent to the traditions of their remote ancestors, than to the evidence of their own senses.[10]

The Jewish religion was admirably fitted for defence, but it was never designed for conquest; and it seems probable that the number of proselytes was never much superior to that of apostates. The divine promises were originally made, and the distinguishing rite of circumcision was enjoined to a single family. When the posterity of Abraham had multiplied like the sands of the sea, the Deity, from whose mouth they received a system of laws and ceremonies, declared himself the proper and as it were the national God of Israel; and with the most jealous care, separated his favourite people from the rest of mankind. The conquest of the land of Canaan was accompanied with so many wonderful and with so many bloody circumstances, that the victorious Jews were left in a state of irreconcilable hostility with all their neighbours. They had

been commanded to extirpate some of the most idolatrous tribes, and the execution of the Divine will had seldom been retarded by the weakness of humanity. With the other nations they were forbidden to contract any marriages or alliances, and the prohibition of receiving them into the congregation, which in some cases was perpetual, almost always extended to the third, to the seventh, or even to the tenth generation. The obligation of preaching to the Gentiles the faith of Moses, had never been inculcated as a precept of the law; nor were the Jews inclined to impose it on themselves as a voluntary duty. In the admission of new citizens, that unsocial people was actuated by the selfish vanity of the Greeks, rather than by the generous policy of Rome. The descendants of Abraham were flattered by the opinion, that they alone were the heirs of the covenant,[11] and they were apprehensive of diminishing the value of their inheritance, by sharing it too easily with the strangers of the earth. A larger acquaintance with mankind, extended their knowledge without correcting their prejudices; and whenever the God of Israel acquired any new votaries, he was much more indebted to the inconstant humour of polytheism than to the active zeal of his own missionaries. The religion of Moses seems to be instituted for a particular country, as well as for a single nation; and if a strict obedience had been paid to the order, that every male, three times in the year, should present himself before the Lord Jehovah, it would have been impossible that the Jews could ever have spread themselves beyond the narrow limits of the promised land. That obstacle was indeed removed by the destruction of the temple of Jerusalem;[12] but the most considerable part of the Jewish religion was involved in its destruction; and the pagans, who had long wondered at the strange report of an empty sanctuary, were at a loss to discover what could be the object, or what could be the instruments, of a worship which was destitute of temples and of altars, of priests and of sacrifices. Yet even in their fallen state, the Jews, still asserting their lofty and exclusive privileges, shunned, instead of courting, the society of strangers. They still insisted with inflexible rigour on those parts of the law which it was in their power to practise. Their peculiar[13] distinctions of days, of meats, and a variety of trivial though burdensome observances, were so

---

7. under . . . temple: during the period following the rebuilding of the Temple of Jerusalem in 515 B.C. 8. When . . . Sinai: See Ex. 19–23. 9. when . . . Israelites: See Ex. 14:15–31. 10. that . . . senses: [Gibbon's note] "How long will this people provoke me? and how long will it be ere they *believe* me, for all the *signs* which I have shewn among them?" (Numbers xiv. 11). It would be easy, but it would be unbecoming, to justify the complaint of the Deity from the whole tenor of the Mosaic history.

11. the covenant: God's bond with the people made with Abraham. 12. the destruction . . . Jerusalem: in A.D. 70, by the Romans. 13. peculiar: special.

many objects of disgust and aversion for the other nations, to whose habits and prejudices they were diametrically opposite. The painful and even dangerous rite of circumcision, was alone capable of repelling a willing proselyte from the door of the synagogue.

Under these circumstances, Christianity offered itself to the world, armed with the strength of the Mosaic law, and delivered from the weight of its fetters. An exclusive zeal for the truth of religion, and the unity of God, was as carefully inculcated in the new as in the ancient system: and whatever was now revealed to mankind concerning the nature and designs of the Supreme Being, was fitted to increase their reverence for that mysterious doctrine. The divine authority of Moses and the prophets was admitted, and even established, as the firmest basis of Christianity. From the beginning of the world, an uninterrupted series of predictions had announced and prepared the long expected coming of the Messiah, who, in compliance with the gross apprehensions of the Jews, had been more frequently represented under the character of a King and Conqueror, than under that of a Prophet, a Martyr, and the Son of God. By his expiatory sacrifice, the imperfect sacrifices of the temple were at once consummated and abolished. The ceremonial law, which consisted only of types and figures, was succeeded by a pure and spiritual worship, equally adapted to all climates as well as to every condition of mankind; and to the initiation of blood, was substituted a more harmless initiation of water. The promise of divine favour, instead of being partially confined to the posterity of Abraham, was universally proposed to the freeman and to the slave, to the Greek and to the barbarian, to the Jew and to the Gentile. Every privilege that could raise the proselyte from earth to Heaven, that could exalt his devotion, secure his happiness, or even gratify that secret pride, which, under the semblance of devotion, insinuates itself into the human heart, was still reserved for the members of the Christian church; but at the same time all mankind was permitted, and even solicited, to accept the glorious distinction, which was not only proffered as a favour, but imposed as an obligation. It became the most sacred duty of a new convert to diffuse among his friends and relations the inestimable blessing which he had received, and to warn them against a refusal that would be severely punished as a criminal disobedience to the will of a benevolent but all-powerful deity.

The enfranchisement of the church from the bonds of the synagogue, was a work however of some time and of some difficulty. The Jewish converts, who acknowledged Jesus in the character of the Messiah foretold by their ancient oracles, respected him as a prophetic teacher of virtue and religion; but they obstinately adhered to the ceremonies of their ancestors, and were desirous of imposing them on the Gentiles, who continually augmented the number of believers. These Judaising Christians seem to have argued with some degree of plausibility from the divine origin of the Mosaic law, and from the immutable perfections of its great author. They affirmed, *that* if the Being, who is the same through all eternity, had designed to abolish those sacred rites which had served to distinguish his chosen people, the repeal of them would have been no less clear and solemn than their first promulgation: *that*, instead of those frequent declarations, which either suppose or assert the perpetuity of the Mosaic religion, it would have been represented as a provisionary scheme intended to last only till the coming of the Messiah, who should instruct mankind in a more perfect mode of faith and of worship: *that* the Messiah himself, and his disciples who conversed with him on earth, instead of authorizing by their example the most minute observances of the Mosaic law, would have published to the world the abolition of those useless and obsolete ceremonies, without suffering Christianity to remain during so many years obscurely confounded among the sects of the Jewish church. Arguments like these appear to have been used in the defence of the expiring cause of the Mosaic law; but the industry of our learned divines has abundantly explained the ambiguous language of the Old Testament, and the ambiguous conduct of the apostolic teachers. It was proper gradually to unfold the system of the Gospel, and to pronounce with the utmost caution and tenderness a sentence of condemnation so repugnant to the inclination and prejudices of the believing Jews.

The history of the church of Jerusalem affords a lively proof of the necessity of those precautions, and of the deep impression which the Jewish religion had made on the minds of its sectaries. The first fifteen bishops of Jerusalem were all circumcised Jews; and the congregation over which they presided, united the law of Moses with the doctrine of Christ. It was natural that the primitive tradition of a church which was founded only forty days after the death of Christ, and was governed almost as many years under the immediate inspection of his apostles, should be received as the standard of orthodoxy. The distant churches very frequently appealed to the authority of their venerable Parent, and relieved her distresses by a liberal contribution of alms. But when numerous and opulent societies were established in the great cities of the empire, in Antioch, Alexandria, Ephesus, Corinth, and Rome, the reverence which Jerusalem had inspired to all the Christian colonies insensibly diminished. The Jewish converts, or as they were afterwards called, the Nazarenes, who had laid the foundations of the church, soon found themselves overwhelmed by the increasing multitudes, that from all the various religions of polytheism inlisted under the banner of Christ: and the Gentiles, who, with the approbation of their peculiar apostle, had rejected the intolerable weight of Mosaic ceremonies, at length refused to their more scrupulous brethren the same toleration which at first they had humbly solicited for their own practice. The ruin of the temple, of the city, and of the public religion of the Jews, was severely felt by the Nazarenes, as in their manners, though not in their faith, they maintained so intimate a connexion with their impious countrymen, whose misfortunes were attributed by the Pagans to the contempt, and more justly ascribed by the Christians, to the wrath of the supreme deity. The Nazarenes retired from the ruins of Jerusalem to the little town of Pella beyond the Jordan, where that ancient church languished above sixty years in solitude and obscurity. They still enjoyed the comfort of making frequent and devout visits to the *Holy City*,[14] and the hope of being one day restored to those seats which both nature and religion taught them to love as well as to revere. But at length, under the reign of Hadrian,[15] the desperate fanaticism of the Jews filled up the measure of their calamities; and the Romans, exasperated by their repeated rebellions, exercised the rights of victory with unusual rigour. The emperor founded, under the name of Ælia Capitolina, a new city on Mount Sion, to which he gave the privileges of a colony; and denouncing the severest penalties against any of the Jewish people who should dare to approach its precincts, he fixed a vigilant garrison of a Roman cohort[16] to enforce the execution of his orders. The Nazarenes had only one way left to escape the common proscription, and the force of truth was on this occasion assisted by the

influence of temporal advantages. They elected Marcus for their bishop, a prelate of the race of the Gentiles, and most probably a native either of Italy or of some of the Latin provinces. At his persuasion, the most considerable part of the congregation renounced the Mosaic law, in the practice of which they had persevered above a century. By this sacrifice of their habits and prejudices, they purchased a free admission into the colony of Hadrian, and more firmly cemented their union with the Catholic church.

When the name and honours of the church of Jerusalem had been restored to Mount Sion, the crimes of heresy and schism were imputed to the obscure remnant of the Nazarenes, which refused to accompany their Latin bishop. They still preserved their former habitation of Pella, spread themselves into the villages adjacent to Damascus, and formed an inconsiderable church in the city of Bœrea, or, as it is now called, of Aleppo in Syria. The name of Nazarenes was deemed too honourable for those Christian Jews, and they soon received from the supposed poverty of their understanding, as well as of their condition, the contemptuous epithet of Ebionites.[17] In a few years after the return of the church of Jerusalem, it became a matter of doubt and controversy, whether a man who sincerely acknowledged Jesus as the Messiah, but who still continued to observe the law of Moses, could possibly hope for salvation. The humane temper of Justin Martyr,[18] inclined him to answer this question in the affirmative; and though he expressed himself with the most guarded diffidence, he ventured to determine in favour of such an imperfect Christian, if he were content to practise the Mosaic ceremonies, without pretending to assert their general use or necessity. But when Justin was pressed to declare the sentiment of the church, he confessed that there were very many among the orthodox Christians, who not only excluded their Judaising brethren from the hope of salvation, but who declined any intercourse with them in the common offices of friendship, hospitality, and social life. The more rigorous opinion prevailed, as it was natural to expect, over the milder; and an eternal bar of separation was fixed between the disciples of Moses and those of Christ. The unfortunate Ebionites, rejected from one religion as apostates, and from the other as heretics, found themselves compelled

---

14. **the Holy City:** Jerusalem. **15. Hadrian:** emperor from 117 to 138. **16. cohort:** a body of three hundred to six hundred troops.

17. **Ebionites:** from Hebrew meaning "poor men." **18. Justin Martyr:** (*c.* 100–*c.* 165), Christian scholar and philosopher.

to assume a more decided character; and although some traces of that obsolete sect may be discovered as late as the fourth century, they insensibly melted away either into the church or the synagogue.

While the orthodox church preserved a just medium between excessive veneration and improper contempt for the law of Moses, the various heretics deviated into equal but opposite extremes of error and extravagance. From the acknowledged truth of the Jewish religion, the Ebionites had concluded that it could never be abolished. From its supposed imperfections the Gnostics[19] as hastily inferred that it never was instituted by the wisdom of the Deity. There are some objections against the authority of Moses and the prophets, which too readily present themselves to the sceptical mind; though they can only be derived from our ignorance of remote antiquity, and from our incapacity to form an adequate judgment of the Divine œconomy. These objections were eagerly embraced and as petulantly urged by the vain science of the Gnostics. As those heretics were, for the most part, averse to the pleasures of sense, they morosely arraigned the polygamy of the patriarchs, the gallantries of David, and the seraglio of Solomon. The conquest of the land of Canaan, and the extirpation of the unsuspecting natives,[20] they were at a loss how to reconcile with the common notions of humanity and justice. But when they recollected the sanguinary list of murders, of executions, and of massacres, which stain almost every page of the Jewish annals, they acknowledged that the barbarians of Palestine had exercised as much compassion towards their idolatrous enemies as they had ever shewn to their friends or countrymen. Passing from the sectaries of the law to the law itself, they asserted that it was impossible that a religion which consisted only of bloody sacrifices and trifling ceremonies, and whose rewards as well as punishments were all of a carnal and temporal nature, could inspire the love of virtue, or restrain the impetuosity of passion. The Mosaic account of the creation and fall of man was treated with profane derision by the Gnostics, who would not listen with patience to the repose of the deity after six days labour, to the rib of Adam, the garden of Eden, the trees of life and of knowledge, the speaking serpent, the forbidden fruit, and the condemnation pronounced

against human kind for the venial offence of their first progenitors.[21] The God of Israel was impiously represented by the Gnostics, as a being liable to passion and to error, capricious in his favour, implacable in his resentment, meanly jealous of his superstitious worship, and confining his partial providence to a single people, and to this transitory life. In such a character they could discover none of the features of the wise and omnipotent father of the universe. They allowed that the religion of the Jews was somewhat less criminal than the idolatry of the Gentiles; but it was their fundamental doctrine, that the Christ whom they adored as the first and brightest emanation of the deity, appeared upon earth to rescue mankind from their various errors, and to reveal a *new* system of truth and perfection. The most learned of the fathers,[22] by a very singular condescension, have imprudently admitted the sophistry of the Gnostics. Acknowledging that the literal sense is repugnant to every principle of faith as well as reason, they deem themselves secure and invulnerable behind the ample veil of allegory, which they carefully spread over every tender part of the Mosaic dispensation.

It has been remarked with more ingenuity than truth, that the virgin purity of the church was never violated by schism or heresy before the reign of Trajan[23] or Hadrian, about one hundred years after the death of Christ. We may observe with much more propriety, that, during that period, the disciples of the Messiah were indulged in a freer latitude both of faith and practice, than has ever been allowed in succeeding ages. As the terms of communion were insensibly narrowed, and the spiritual authority of the prevailing party was exercised with increasing severity, many of its most respectable adherents, who were called upon to renounce, were provoked to assert, their private opinions, to pursue the consequences of their mistaken principles, and openly to erect the standard of rebellion against the unity of the church. The Gnostics were distinguished as the most polite, the most learned, and the most wealthy of the Christian name, and that general appellation which expressed a superiority of knowledge,[24] was either assumed by their own pride,

---

19. **Gnostics:** members of a number of second- and third-century heretical sects that claimed esoteric spiritual knowledge. 20. **The conquest . . . natives:** See Judg. 1:1-10.

21. **The Mosaic . . . progenitors:** [Gibbon's note] Dr. Burnet has discussed the first chapters of Genesis with too much wit and freedom. 22. **the fathers:** the Christian writers of the first five centuries. 23. **Trajan:** emperor from A.D. 98 to 117. 24. **knowledge:** The word *gnostic* is derived from the Greek word for knowledge.

or ironically bestowed by the envy of their adversaries. They were almost without exception of the race of the Gentiles, and their principal founders seem to have been natives of Syria or Egypt, where the warmth of the climate disposes both the mind and the body to indolent and contemplative devotion. The Gnostics blended with the faith of Christ many sublime but obscure tenets, which they derived from oriental philosophy, and even from the religion of Zoroaster,[25] concerning the eternity of matter, the existence of two principles, and the mysterious hierarchy of the invisible world.[26] As soon as they launched out into that vast abyss, they delivered themselves to the guidance of a disordered imagination; and as the paths of error are various and infinite, the Gnostics were imperceptibly divided into more than fifty particular sects, of whom the most celebrated appear to have been the Basilidians, the Valentinians, the Marcionites, and, in a still later period, the Manichæans. Each of these sects could boast of its bishops and congregations, of its doctors[27] and martyrs, and, instead of the four gospels adopted by the church, the heretics produced a multitude of histories, in which the actions and discourses of Christ and of his apostles were adapted to their respective tenets. The success of the Gnostics was rapid and extensive. They covered Asia and Egypt, established themselves in Rome, and sometimes penetrated into the provinces of the West. For the most part they arose in the second century, flourished during the third, and were suppressed in the fourth or fifth, by the prevalence of more fashionable controversies, and by the superior ascendant of the reigning power. Though they constantly disturbed the peace, and frequently disgraced the name of religion, they contributed to assist rather than to retard the progress of Christianity. The Gentile converts, whose strongest objections and prejudices were directed against the law of Moses, could find admission into many Christian societies, which required not from their untutored mind any belief of an antecedent revelation. Their faith was insensibly fortified and enlarged, and the church was ultimately benefited by the conquests of its most inveterate enemies.

25. **Zoroaster:** (Zarathustra) Persian religious reformer who flourished around 1000 B.C. 26. **world:** [Gibbon's note] In the account of the Gnostics of the second and third centuries, Mosheim is ingenious and candid; Le Clerc, dull, but exact; Beausobre almost always an apologist; and it is much to be feared, that the primitive fathers are very frequently calumniators. 27. **doctors:** theological scholars.

But whatever difference of opinion might subsist between the Orthodox, the Ebionites, and the Gnostics, concerning the divinity or the obligation of the Mosaic law, they were all equally animated by the same exclusive zeal, and by the same abhorrence for idolatry which had distinguished the Jews from the other nations of the ancient world. The philosopher, who considered the system of polytheism as a composition of human fraud and error, could disguise a smile of contempt under the mask of devotion, without apprehending that either the mockery, or the compliance would expose him to the resentment of any invisible, or as he conceived them, imaginary powers. But the established religions of Paganism were seen by the primitive Christians in a much more odious and formidable light. It was the universal sentiment both of the church and of heretics, that the dæmons were the authors, the patrons, and the objects of idolatry. Those rebellious spirits who had been degraded from the rank of angels, and cast down into the infernal pit, were still permitted to roam upon earth, to torment the bodies, and to seduce the minds of sinful men. The dæmons soon discovered and abused the natural propensity of the human heart towards devotion, and, artfully withdrawing the adoration of mankind from their Creator, they usurped the place and honours of the Supreme Deity. By the success of their malicious contrivances, they at once gratified their own vanity and revenge, and obtained the only comfort of which they were yet susceptible, the hope of involving the human species in the participation of their guilt and misery. It was confessed, or at least it was imagined, that they had distributed among themselves the most important characters of polytheism, one dæmon assuming the name and attributes of Jupiter, another of Æsculapius, a third of Venus, and a fourth perhaps of Apollo; and that by the advantage of their long experience and aërial nature, they were enabled to execute, with sufficient skill and dignity, the parts which they had undertaken. They lurked in the temples, instituted festivals and sacrifices, invented fables, pronounced oracles, and were frequently allowed to perform miracles. The Christians, who, by the interposition of evil spirits, could so readily explain every præternatural appearance, were disposed and even desirous to admit the most extravagant fictions of the Pagan mythology. But the belief of the Christian was accompanied with horror. The most trifling mark of respect to the national worship he considered as a direct homage yielded to the dæmon, and as an act of rebellion against the majesty of God.

In consequence of this opinion, it was the first but arduous duty of a Christian to preserve himself pure and undefiled by the practice of idolatry. The religion of the nations was not merely a speculative doctrine professed in the schools or preached in the temples. The innumerable deities and rites of polytheism were closely interwoven with every circumstance of business or pleasure, of public or of private life; and it seemed impossible to escape the observance of them, without, at the same time, renouncing the commerce of mankind, and all the offices and amusements of society. The important transactions of peace and war were prepared or concluded by solemn sacrifices, in which the magistrate, the senator, and the soldier, were obliged to preside or to participate.[28] The public spectacles were an essential part of the cheerful devotion of the Pagans, and the gods were supposed to accept, as the most grateful offering, the games that the prince and people celebrated in honour of their peculiar festivals.[29] The Christian, who with pious horror avoided the abomination of the circus or the theatre, found himself encompassed with infernal snares in every convivial entertainment, as often as his friends, invoking the hospitable deities, poured out libations to each other's happiness. When the bride, struggling with well-affected reluctance, was forced in hymenæal pomp over the threshold of her new habitation; or when the sad procession of the dead slowly moved towards the funeral pile, the Christian, on these interesting occasions, was compelled to desert the persons who were the dearest to him, rather than contract the guilt inherent to those impious ceremonies. Every art and every trade that was in the least concerned in the framing or adorning of idols was polluted by the stain of idolatry; a severe sentence, since it devoted to eternal misery the far greater part of the community, which is employed in the exercise of liberal or mechanic professions. If we cast our eyes over the numerous remains of antiquity, we shall

perceive, that besides the immediate representations of the Gods, and the holy instruments of their worship, the elegant forms and agreeable fictions consecrated by the imagination of the Greeks, were introduced as the richest ornaments of the houses, the dress, and the furniture, of the Pagans.[30] Even the arts of music and painting, of eloquence and poetry, flowed from the same impure origin. In the style of the fathers, Apollo and the Muses were the organs of the infernal spirit, Homer and Virgil were the most eminent of his servants, and the beautiful mythology which pervades and animates the compositions of their genius, is destined to celebrate the glory of the dæmons. Even the common language of Greece and Rome abounded with familiar but impious expressions, which the imprudent Christian might too carelessly utter, or too patiently hear.[31]

The dangerous temptations, which on every side lurked in ambush to surprise the unguarded believer, assailed him with redoubled violence on the days of solemn festivals. So artfully were they framed and disposed throughout the year, that superstition always wore the appearance of pleasure, and often of virtue. Some of the most sacred festivals in the Roman ritual were destined to salute the new calends of January[32] with vows of public and private felicity, to indulge the pious remembrance of the dead and living, to ascertain the inviolable bounds of property, to hail, on the return of spring, the genial powers of fecundity, to perpetuate the two memorable æras of Rome, the foundation of the city, and that of the republic, and to restore, during the humane license of the Saturnalia,[33] the primitive equality of mankind. Some idea may be conceived of the abhorrence of the Christians for such impious ceremonies, by the scrupulous delicacy which they displayed on a much less alarming occasion. On days of general festivity, it was the custom of the ancients to adorn their doors with lamps and with branches of laurel, and to crown their heads with a garland of flowers. This innocent and elegant practice

28. **solemn . . . participate:** [Gibbon's note] The Roman senate was always held in a temple or consecrated place. Before they entered on business, every senator dropt some wine and frankincense on the altar. 29. **the games . . . festivals:** [Gibbon's note] See Tertullian, De Spectaculis. This severe reformer shews no more indulgence to a tragedy of Euripides, than to a combat of gladiators. The dress of the actors particularly offends him. By the use of the lofty buskin, they impiously strive to add a cubit to their stature.

30. **the elegant . . . Pagans:** [Gibbon's note] Even the reverses of the Greek and Roman coins were frequently of an idolatrous nature. Here indeed the scruples of the Christian were suspended by a stronger passion. 31. **Even . . . hear:** [Gibbon's note] If a Pagan friend (on the occasion perhaps of sneezing) used the familiar expression of "Jupiter bless you," the Christian was obliged to protest against the divinity of Jupiter. 32. **the new . . . January:** the first day of the month. 33. **Saturnalia:** the festival of Saturn, celebrated in December with unlimited merrymaking and freedom from the restraints of social rank.

might perhaps have been tolerated as a mere civil institution. But it most unluckily happened that the doors were under the protection of the household gods, that the laurel was sacred to the lover of Daphne, and that garlands of flowers, though frequently worn as a symbol either of joy or mourning, had been dedicated in their first origin to the service of superstition. The trembling Christians, who were persuaded in this instance to comply with the fashion of their country, and the commands of the magistrate, laboured under the most gloomy apprehensions, from the reproaches of their own conscience, the censures of the church, and the denunciations of divine vengeance.

Such was the anxious diligence which was required to guard the chastity of the gospel from the infectious breath of idolatry. The superstitious observances of public or private rites were carelessly practised, from education and habit, by the followers of the established religion. But as often as they occurred, they afforded the Christians an opportunity of declaring and confirming their zealous opposition. By these frequent protestations their attachment to the faith was continually fortified, and in proportion to the increase of zeal, they combated with the more ardour and success in the holy war, which they had undertaken against the empire of the dæmons.

II. The writings of Cicero[34] represent in the most lively colours the ignorance, the errors, and the uncertainty of the ancient philosophers with regard to the immortality of the soul. When they are desirous of arming their disciples against the fear of death, they inculcate, as an obvious though melancholy position, that the fatal stroke of our dissolution releases us from the calamities of life; and that those can no longer suffer who no longer exist. Yet there were a few sages of Greece and Rome who had conceived a more exalted, and, in some respects, a juster idea of human nature; though it must be confessed, that in the sublime inquiry, their reason had been often guided by their imagination, and that their imagination had been prompted by their vanity. When they viewed with complacency the extent of their own mental powers, when they exercised the various faculties of memory, of fancy, and of judgment, in the most profound speculations, or the most important labours, and when they reflected on the desire of fame, which transported them into future ages, far beyond the bounds of death and of the grave; they were unwilling to confound themselves with the beasts of the field, or to suppose, that a being, for whose dignity they entertained the most sincere admiration, could be limited to a spot of earth, and to a few years of duration. With this favourable prepossession they summoned to their aid the science, or rather the language, of Metaphysics. They soon discovered, that as none of the properties of matter will apply to the operations of the mind, the human soul must consequently be a substance distinct from the body, pure, simple, and spiritual, incapable of dissolution, and susceptible of a much higher degree of virtue and happiness after the release from its corporeal prison. From these specious and noble principles, the philosophers who trod in the footsteps of Plato,[35] deduced a very unjustifiable conclusion, since they asserted, not only the future immortality, but the past eternity of the human soul, which they were too apt to consider as a portion of the infinite and self-existing spirit, which pervades and sustains the universe. A doctrine thus removed beyond the senses and the experience of mankind, might serve to amuse the leisure of a philosophic mind; or, in the silence of solitude, it might sometimes impart a ray of comfort to desponding virtue; but the faint impression which had been received in the schools, was soon obliterated by the commerce and business of active life. We are sufficiently acquainted with the eminent persons who flourished in the age of Cicero, and of the first Cæsars, with their actions, their characters, and their motives, to be assured that their conduct in this life was never regulated by any serious conviction of the rewards or punishments of a future state. At the bar and in the senate of Rome the ablest orators were not apprehensive of giving offence to their hearers, by exposing that doctrine as an idle and extravagant opinion, which was rejected with contempt by every man of a liberal education and understanding.

Since therefore the most sublime efforts of philosophy can extend no farther than feebly to point out the desire, the hope, or, at most, the probability, of a future state, there is nothing, except a divine revelation,

---

34. the writings . . . Cicero: [Gibbon's note] In particular, the first book of the Tusculan Questions, and the treatise De Senectute, and the Somnium Scipionis, contain, in the most beautiful language, everything that Grecian philosophy, or Roman good sense, could possibly suggest on this dark but important subject.

35. Plato: In his dialogues, Plato (c. 427–c. 347 B.C.) expresses his belief in the preexistence of the soul.

that can ascertain the existence, and describe the condition, of the invisible country which is destined to receive the souls of men after their separation from the body. But we may perceive several defects inherent to the popular religions of Greece and Rome, which rendered them very unequal to so arduous a task. I. The general system of their mythology was unsupported by any solid proofs; and the wisest among the Pagans had already disclaimed its usurped authority. 2. The description of the infernal regions had been abandoned to the fancy of painters and of poets, who peopled them with so many phantoms and monsters, who dispensed their rewards and punishments with so little equity, that a solemn truth, the most congenial to the human heart, was oppressed and disgraced by the absurd mixture of the wildest fictions.[36] 3. The doctrine of a future state was scarcely considered among the devout polytheists of Greece and Rome as a fundamental article of faith. The providence of the gods, as it related to public communities rather than to *private individuals*, was principally displayed on the visible theatre of the present world. The *petitions* which were offered on the altars of Jupiter or Apollo, expressed the anxiety of their worshippers for temporal happiness, and their ignorance or indifference concerning a future life. The important truth of the immortality of the soul was inculcated with more diligence as well as success in India, in Assyria, in Egypt, and in Gaul; and since we cannot attribute such a difference to the superior knowledge of the barbarians, we must ascribe it to the influence of an established priesthood, which employed the motives of virtue as the instrument of ambition.

We might naturally expect, that a principle so essential to religion, would have been revealed in the clearest terms to the chosen people of Palestine, and that it might safely have been entrusted to the hereditary priesthood of Aaron.[37] It is incumbent on us to adore the mysterious dispensations of providence, when we discover, that the doctrine of the immortality of the soul is omitted in the law of Moses; it is darkly insinuated by the prophets, and during the long period which elapsed between the Egyptian and the Babylonian servitudes, the hopes as well as fears of the Jews appear to have been confined within the narrow compass of the present life. After Cyrus[38] had permitted the exiled nation to return into the promised land, and after Ezra[39] had restored the ancient records of their religion, two celebrated sects, the Saducees and the Pharisees insensibly arose at Jerusalem. The former selected from the more opulent and distinguished ranks of society, were strictly attached to the literal sense of the Mosaic law, and they piously rejected the immortality of the soul, as an opinion that received no countenance from the divine book, which they revered as the only rule of their faith. To the authority of scripture the Pharisees added that of tradition, and they accepted, under the name of traditions, several speculative tenets from the philosophy or religion of the Eastern nations. The doctrines of fate or predestination, of angels and spirits, and of a future state of rewards and punishments, were in the number of these new articles of belief; and as the Pharisees, by the austerity of their manners, had drawn into their party the body of the Jewish people, the immortality of the soul became the prevailing sentiment of the synagogue, under the reign of the Asmonæan princes and pontiffs.[40] The temper of the Jews was incapable of contenting itself with such a cold and languid assent as might satisfy the mind of a Polytheist; and as soon as they admitted the idea of a future state, they embraced it with the zeal which has always formed the characteristic of the nation. Their zeal, however, added nothing to its evidence, or even probability: and it was still necessary, that the doctrine of life and immortality, which had been dictated by nature, approved by reason, and received by superstition, should obtain the sanction of divine truth from the authority and example of Christ.

When the promise of eternal happiness was proposed to mankind, on condition of adopting the faith and of observing the precepts of the gospel, it is no wonder that so advantageous an offer should have been accepted by great numbers of every religion, of every rank, and of every province in the Roman empire. The ancient Christians were animated by a contempt for their present existence, and by a just confidence of immortality, of which the doubtful and imperfect faith of modern ages cannot give us any adequate

---

36. the wildest fictions: [Gibbon's note] The xith book of the Odyssey gives a very dreary and incoherent account of the infernal shades. Pindar and Virgil have embellished the picture; but even those poets, though more correct than their great model, are guilty of very strange inconsistencies. 37. Aaron: brother of Moses.

38. Cyrus: (*c.* 600–529 B.C.), King of Persia. 39. Ezra: Hebrew priest of the fifth century B.C. 40. the Asmonæan . . . pontiffs: those belonging to the Maccabees, a public-spirited Hebrew family of the second and first centuries B.C.

notion. In the primitive church, the influence of truth was very powerfully strengthened by an opinion, which, however it may deserve respect for its usefulness and antiquity, has not been found agreeable to experience. It was universally believed, that the end of the world, and the kingdom of Heaven, were at hand. The near approach of this wonderful event had been predicted by the apostles; the tradition of it was preserved by their earliest disciples, and those who understood in their literal sense the discourses of Christ himself, were obliged to expect the second and glorious coming of the Son of Man in the clouds, before that generation was totally extinguished, which had beheld his humble condition upon earth, and which might still be witness to the calamities of the Jews under Vespasian[41] or Hadrian. The revolution of seventeen centuries has instructed us not to press too closely the mysterious language of prophecy and revelation; but as long as, for wise purposes, this error was permitted to subsist in the church, it was productive of the most salutary effects on the faith and practice of Christians, who lived in the awful expectation of that moment when the globe itself, and all the various race of mankind, should tremble at the appearance of their divine judge.[42]

The ancient and popular doctrine of the Millennium was intimately connected with the second coming of Christ. As the works of the creation had been finished in six days, their duration in their present state, according to a tradition which was attributed to the prophet Elijah, was fixed to six thousand years. By the same analogy it was inferred, that this long period of labour and contention, which was now almost elapsed, would be succeeded by a joyful Sabbath of a thousand years; and that Christ, with the triumphant band of the saints and the elect who had escaped death, or who had been miraculously revived, would reign upon earth till the time appointed for the last and general resurrection. So pleasing was this hope to the mind of believers, that the *new Jerusalem*, the seat of this blissful kingdom, was quickly adorned with all the gayest colours of the imagination. A felicity consisting only of pure and spiritual pleasure, would

have appeared too refined for its inhabitants, who were still supposed to possess their human nature and senses. A garden of Eden, with the amusements of the pastoral life, was no longer suited to the advanced state of society which prevailed under the Roman empire. A city was therefore erected of gold and precious stones, and a supernatural plenty of corn and wine was bestowed on the adjacent territory; in the free enjoyment of whose spontaneous productions, the happy and benevolent people was never to be restrained by any jealous laws of exclusive property. The assurance of such a Millennium, was carefully inculcated by a succession of fathers from Justin Martyr and Irenæus,[43] who conversed with the immediate disciples of the apostles, down to Lactantius,[44] who was preceptor to the son of Constantine.[45] Though it might not be universally received, it appears to have been the reigning sentiment of the orthodox believers; and it seems so well adapted to the desires and apprehensions of mankind, that it must have contributed in a very considerable degree to the progress of the Christian faith. But when the edifice of the church was almost completed, the temporary support was laid aside. The doctrine of Christ's reign upon earth, was at first treated as a profound allegory, was considered by degrees as a doubtful and useless opinion, and was at length rejected as the absurd invention of heresy and fanaticism. A mysterious prophecy,[46] which still forms a part of the sacred canon, but which was thought to favour the exploded sentiment, has very narrowly escaped the proscription of the church.

Whilst the happiness and glory of a temporal reign were promised to the disciples of Christ, the most dreadful calamities were denounced against an unbelieving world. The edification of the new Jerusalem was to advance by equal steps with the destruction of the mystic Babylon; and as long as the emperors who reigned before Constantine persisted in the profession of idolatry, the epithet of Babylon was applied to the city and to the empire of Rome. A regular series was prepared of all the moral and physical evils which can afflict a flourishing nation; intestine discord, and the invasion of the fiercest barbarians from the unknown regions of the North; pestilence and famine, comets

---

41. **Vespasian:** emperor from A.D. 69 to 79. **42. the appearance . . . judge:** [Gibbon's note] This expectation was countenanced by the twenty-fourth chapter of St. Matthew, and by the first epistle of St. Paul to the Thessalonians. Erasmus removes the difficulty by the help of allegory and metaphor; and the learned Grotius ventures to insinuate, that, for wise purposes, the pious deception was permitted to take place.

43. **Irenæus:** (*c.* 130–*c.* 200), theologian, Bishop of Lyons. **44. Lactantius:** (*c.* 240–*c.* 320), Roman rhetorician converted to Christianity around 300. **45. Constantine:** (*c.* 280–337), first Roman emperor to embrace Christianity. **46. A mysterious prophecy:** the Book of Revelation.

and eclipses, earthquakes and inundations. All these were only so many preparatory and alarming signs of the great catastrophe of Rome, when the country of the Scipios[47] and Cæsars should be consumed by a flame from Heaven, and the city of the seven hills, with her palaces, her temples, and her triumphal arches, should be buried in a vast lake of fire and brimstone. It might, however, afford some consolation to Roman vanity, that the period of their empire would be that of the world itself; which, as it had once perished by the element of water, was destined to experience a second and a speedy destruction from the element of fire. In the opinion of a general conflagration, the faith of the Christian very happily coincided with the tradition of the East, the philosophy of the Stoics, and the analogy of Nature: and even the country, which, from religious motives, had been chosen for the origin and principal scene of the conflagration, was the best adapted for that purpose by natural and physical causes; by its deep caverns, beds of sulphur, and numerous volcanoes, of which those of Ætna, of Vesuvius, and of Lipari, exhibit a very imperfect representation. The calmest and most intrepid sceptic could not refuse to acknowledge, that the destruction of the present system of the world by fire, was in itself extremely probable. The Christian, who founded his belief much less on the fallacious arguments of reason than on the authority of tradition and the interpretation of scripture, expected it with terror and confidence as a certain and approaching event; and as his mind was perpetually filled with the solemn idea, he considered every disaster that happened to the empire as an infallible symptom of an expiring world.[48]

The condemnation of the wisest and most virtuous of the pagans, on account of their ignorance or disbelief of the divine truth, seems to offend the reason and the humanity of the present age. But the primitive church, whose faith was of a much firmer consistence, delivered over, without hesitation, to eternal torture, the far greater part of the human species. A charitable hope might perhaps be indulged in favour of Socrates, or some other sages of antiquity, who had consulted the light of reason before that of the gospel had arisen. But it was unanimously affirmed, that those who, since the birth or the death of Christ, had obstinately persisted in the worship of the dæmons, neither deserved nor could expect a pardon from the irritated justice of the Deity. These rigid sentiments, which had been unknown to the ancient world, appear to have infused a spirit of bitterness into a system of love and harmony. The ties of blood and friendship were frequently torn asunder by the difference of religious faith; and the Christians, who, in this world, found themselves oppressed by the power of the pagans, were sometimes seduced by resentment and spiritual pride to delight in the prospect of their future triumph. "You are fond of spectacles," exclaims the stern Tertullian;[49] "expect the greatest of all spectacles, the last and eternal judgment of the universe. How shall I admire, how laugh, how rejoice, how exult, when I behold so many proud monarchs, and fancied gods, groaning in the lowest abyss of darkness; so many magistrates who persecuted the name of the Lord, liquefying in fiercer fires than they ever kindled against the Christians; so many sage philosophers blushing in red hot flames with their deluded scholars; so many celebrated poets trembling before the tribunal, not of Minos, but of Christ; so many tragedians, more tuneful in the expression of their own sufferings; so many dancers"—But the humanity of the reader will permit me to draw a veil over the rest of this infernal description, which the zealous African pursues in a long variety of affected and unfeeling witticisms.

Doubtless there were many among the primitive Christians of a temper more suitable to the meekness and charity of their profession. There were many who felt a sincere compassion for the danger of their friends and countrymen, and who exerted the most benevolent zeal to save them from the impending destruction. The careless Polytheist, assailed by new and unexpected terrors, against which neither his priests nor his philosophers could afford him any certain protection, was very frequently terrified and subdued by the menace of eternal tortures. His fears might assist the progress of his faith and reason; and if he could once persuade himself to suspect that the Christian religion might possibly be true, it became an easy task to convince him that it was the safest and most prudent party that he could possibly embrace.

47. **Scipios:** a noble Roman family of the second and third centuries, famous for its generals and magistrates. 48. **an expiring world:** [Gibbon's note] On this subject every reader of taste will be entertained with the third part of Burnet's Sacred Theory. He blends philosophy, scripture, and tradition, into one magnificent system; in the description of which, he displays a strength of fancy not inferior to that of Milton himself.

49. **Tertullian:** (*c.* 160–*c.* 220), theologian, member of the Christian church in Africa.

III. The supernatural gifts, which even in this life were ascribed to the Christians above the rest of mankind, must have conduced to their own comfort, and very frequently to the conviction of infidels. Besides the occasional prodigies, which might sometimes be effected by the immediate interposition of the Deity when he suspended the laws of Nature for the service of religion, the Christian church, from the time of the apostles and their first disciples, has claimed an uninterrupted succession of miraculous powers, the gift of tongues, of vision and of prophecy, the power of expelling dæmons, of healing the sick, and of raising the dead. The knowledge of foreign languages was frequently communicated to the contemporaries of Irenæus, though Irenæus himself was left to struggle with the difficulties of a barbarous dialect whilst he preached the gospel to the natives of Gaul. The divine inspiration, whether it was conveyed in the form of a waking or of a sleeping vision, is described as a favour very liberally bestowed on all ranks of the faithful, on women as on elders, on boys as well as upon bishops. When their devout minds were sufficiently prepared by a course of prayer, of fasting, and of vigils, to receive the extraordinary impulse, they were transported out of their senses, and delivered in extasy what was inspired, being mere organs of the holy spirit, just as a pipe or flute is of him who blows into it. We may add, that the design of these visions was, for the most part, either to disclose the future history, or to guide the present administration of the church. The expulsion of the dæmons from the bodies of those unhappy persons whom they had been permitted to torment, was considered as a signal though ordinary triumph of religion, and is repeatedly alleged by the ancient apologists, as the most convincing evidence of the truth of Christianity. The awful ceremony was usually performed in a public manner, and in the presence of a great number of spectators; the patient was relieved by the power or skill of the exorcist, and the vanquished dæmon was heard to confess that he was one of the fabled gods of antiquity, who had impiously usurped the adoration of mankind. But the miraculous cure of diseases of the most inveterate or even preternatural kind, can no longer occasion any surprise, when we recollect, that in the days of Irenæus, about the end of the second century, the resurrection of the dead was very far from being esteemed an uncommon event; that the miracle was frequently performed on necessary occasions, by great fasting and the joint supplication of the church of the place, and that the persons thus restored to their prayers, had lived afterwards among them many years. At such a period, when faith could boast of so many wonderful victories over death, it seems difficult to account for the scepticism of those philosophers, who still rejected and derided the doctrine of the resurrection. A noble Grecian had rested on this important ground the whole controversy, and promised Theophilus, bishop of Antioch, that if he could be gratified with the sight of a single person who had been actually raised from the dead, he would immediately embrace the Christian religion. It is somewhat remarkable, that the prelate of the first eastern church, however anxious for the conversation of his friend, thought proper to decline this fair and reasonable challenge.

The miracles of the primitive church, after obtaining the sanction of ages, have been lately attacked in a very free and ingenious inquiry;[50] which, though it has met with the most favourable reception from the Public, appears to have excited a general scandal among the divines of our own as well as of the other protestant churches of Europe. Our different sentiments on this subject will be much less influenced by any particular arguments, than by our habits of study and reflection; and above all, by the degree of the evidence which we have accustomed ourselves to require for the proof of a miraculous event. The duty of an historian does not call upon him to interpose his private judgment in this nice and important controversy; but he ought not to dissemble the difficulty of adopting such a theory as may reconcile the interest of religion with that of reason, of making a proper application of that theory, and of defining with precision the limits of that happy period exempt from error and from deceit, to which we might be disposed to extend the gift of supernatural powers. From the first of the fathers to the last of the popes, a succession of bishops, of saints, of martyrs, and of miracles, is continued without interruption, and the progress of superstition was so gradual and almost imperceptible, that we know not in what particular link we should break the chain of tradition. Every age bears testimony to the wonderful events by which it was distinguished, and its testimony appears no less weighty and respectable than that of the preceding generation, till we are

50. **a very . . . inquiry:** *A Free Inquiry into the Miraculous Powers Which Are Supposed to Have Subsisted in the Christian Church* (1749) by Conyers Middleton (1683–1750), Fellow of Trinity College, Cambridge.

insensibly led on to accuse our own inconsistency, if in the eighth or in the twelfth century we deny to the venerable Bede,[51] or to the holy Bernard, the same degree of confidence which in the second century we had so liberally granted to Justin or to Irenæus.[52] If the truth of any of those miracles is appreciated by their apparent use and propriety, every age had unbelievers to convince, heretics to confute, and idolatrous nations to convert; and sufficient motives might always be produced to justify the interposition of Heaven. And yet since every friend to revelation is persuaded of the reality, and every reasonable man is convinced of the cessation of miraculous powers, it is evident that there must have been *some period* in which they were either suddenly or gradually withdrawn from the Christian church. Whatever æra is chosen for that purpose, the death of the apostles, the conversion of the Roman empire, or the extinction of the Arian heresy,[53] the insensibility of the Christians who lived at that time will equally afford a just matter of surprise. They still supported their pretensions after they had lost their power. Credulity performed the office of faith; fanaticism was permitted to assume the language of inspiration, and the effects of accident or contrivance were ascribed to supernatural causes. The recent experience of genuine miracles should have instructed the Christian world in the ways of providence, and habituated their eye (if we may use a very inadequate expression) to the style of the divine artist. Should the most skilful painter of modern Italy presume to decorate his feeble imitations with the name of Raphael or of Correggio, the insolent fraud would be soon discovered and indignantly rejected.

Whatever opinion may be entertained of the miracles of the primitive church since the time of the apostles, this unresisting softness of temper, so conspicuous among the believers of the second and third

centuries, proved of some accidental benefit to the cause of truth and religion. In modern times, a latent and even involuntary scepticism adheres to the most pious dispositions. Their admission of supernatural truths, is much less an active consent than a cold and passive acquiescence. Accustomed long since to observe and to respect the invariable order of Nature, our reason, or at least our imagination, is not sufficiently prepared to sustain the visible action of the Deity. But in the first ages of Christianity, the situation of mankind was extremely different. The most curious, or the most credulous, among the pagans, were often persuaded to enter into a society, which asserted an actual claim of miraculous powers. The primitive Christians perpetually trod on mystic ground, and their minds were exercised by the habits of believing the most extraordinary events. They felt, or they fancied, that on every side they were incessantly assaulted by dæmons, comforted by visions, instructed by prophecy, and surprisingly delivered from danger, sickness, and from death itself, by the supplications of the church. The real or imaginary prodigies, of which they so frequently conceived themselves to be the objects, the instruments, or the spectators, very happily disposed them to adopt with the same ease, but with far greater justice, the authentic wonders of the evangelic history; and thus miracles that exceeded not the measure of their own experience, inspired them with the most lively assurance of mysteries which were acknowledged to surpass the limits of their understanding. It is this deep impression of supernatural truths, which has been so much celebrated under the name of faith; a state of mind described as the surest pledge of the divine favour and of future felicity, and recommended as the first or perhaps the only merit of a Christian. According to the more rigid doctors, the moral virtues, which may be equally practised by infidels, are destitute of any value or efficacy in the work of our justification.

IV. But the primitive Christian demonstrated his faith by his virtues; and it was very justly supposed that the divine persuasion which enlightened or subdued the understanding, must, at the same time, purify the heart and direct the actions of the believer. The first apologists of Christianity who justify the innocence of their brethren, and the writers of a later period who celebrate the sanctity of their ancestors, display, in the most lively colours, the reformation of manners which was introduced into the world by the preaching of the gospel. As it is my intention to remark only such

---

51. Bede: (675–735), British scholar and theologian. **52. Irenæus:** [Gibbon's note] It may seem somewhat remarkable, that Bernard of Clairvaux [(1091–1153), French monk and theologian], who records so many miracles of his friend St. Malachi, never takes any notice of his own, which, in their turn, however, are carefully related by his companions and disciples. In the long series of ecclesiastical history, does there exist a single instance of a saint asserting that he himself possessed the gift of miracles? **53. Whatever . . . heresy:** [Gibbon's note] The conversion of Constantine is the æra which is most usually fixed by Protestants. The more rational divines are unwilling to admit the miracles of the ivth, whilst the more credulous are unwilling to reject those of the vth century.

human causes as were permitted to second the influence of revelation, I shall slightly mention two motives which might naturally render the lives of the primitive Christians much purer and more austere than those of their Pagan contemporaries or their degenerate successors; repentance for their past sins, and the laudable desire of supporting the reputation of the society in which they were engaged.

It is a very ancient reproach, suggested by the ignorance or the malice of infidelity, that the Christians allured into their party the most atrocious criminals, who, as soon as they were touched by a sense of remorse, were easily persuaded to wash away, in the water of baptism, the guilt of their past conduct, for which the temples of the gods refused to grant them any expiation. But this reproach, when it is cleared from misrepresentation, contributes as much to the honour as it did to the increase of the church. The friends of Christianity may acknowledge without a blush, that many of the most eminent saints had been before their baptism the most abandoned sinners. Those persons, who in the world had followed, though in an imperfect manner, the dictates of benevolence and propriety, derived such a calm satisfaction from the opinion of their own rectitude, as rendered them much less susceptible of the sudden emotions of shame, of grief, and of terror, which have given birth to so many wonderful conversions. After the example of their Divine Master, the missionaries of the gospel disdained not the society of men, and especially of women, oppressed by the consciousness, and very often by the effects, of their vices. As they emerged from sin and superstition to the glorious hope of immortality, they resolved to devote themselves to a life, not only of virtue, but of penitence. The desire of perfection became the ruling passion of their soul; and it is well known, that while reason embraces a cold mediocrity, our passions hurry us, with rapid violence, over the space which lies between the most opposite extremes.

When the new converts had been enrolled in the number of the faithful, and were admitted to the sacraments of the church, they found themselves restrained from relapsing into their past disorders by another consideration of a less spiritual, but of a very innocent and respectable nature. Any particular society that has departed from the great body of the nation, or the religion to which it belonged, immediately becomes the object of universal as well as invidious observation. In proportion to the smallness of its

numbers, the character of the society may be affected by the virtue and vices of the persons who compose it; and every member is engaged to watch with the most vigilant attention over his own behaviour, and over that of his brethren, since, as he must expect to incur a part of the common disgrace, he may hope to enjoy a share of the common reputation. When the Christians of Bithynia were brought before the tribunal of the younger Pliny,[54] they assured the proconsul, that far from being engaged in any unlawful conspiracy, they were bound by a solemn obligation to abstain from the commission of those crimes which disturb the private or public peace of society, from theft, robbery, adultery, perjury, and fraud. Near a century afterwards, Tertullian, with an honest pride, could boast, that very few Christians had suffered by the hand of the executioner except on account of their religion. Their serious and sequestered life, averse to the gay luxury of the age, inured them to chastity, temperance, œconomy, and all the sober and domestic virtues. As the greater number were of some trade or profession, it was incumbent on them, by the strictest integrity and the fairest dealing, to remove the suspicions which the profane are too apt to conceive against the appearances of sanctity. The contempt of the world exercised them in the habits of humility, meekness, and patience. The more they were persecuted the more closely they adhered to each other. Their mutual charity and unsuspecting confidence has been remarked by infidels, and was too often abused by perfidious friends.

It is a very honourable circumstance for the morals of the primitive Christians, that even their faults, or rather errors, were derived from an excess of virtue. The bishops and doctors of the church, whose evidence attests, and whose authority might influence, the professions, the principles, and even the practice, of their contemporaries, had studied the scriptures with less skill than devotion, and they often received, in the most literal sense, those rigid precepts of Christ and the apostles, to which the prudence of succeeding commentators has applied a looser and more figurative mode of interpretation. Ambitious to exalt the perfection of the gospel above the wisdom of philosophy, the zealous fathers have carried the duties of self-mortification, of purity, and of patience, to a height which it is scarcely possible to attain, and much less to

54. the younger Pliny: (A.D. 63–113), Roman public servant and man of letters, provincial governor (proconsul) of Bithynia around 111.

preserve, in our present state of weakness and corruption. A doctrine so extraordinary and so sublime must inevitably command the veneration of the people; but it was ill calculated to obtain the suffrage of those worldly philosophers, who, in the conduct of this transitory life, consult only the feelings of nature and the interest of society.

There are two very natural propensities which we may distinguish in the most virtuous and liberal dispositions, the love of pleasure and the love of action. If the former is refined by art and learning, improved by the charms of social intercourse, and corrected by a just regard to œconomy, to health, and to reputation, it is productive of the greatest part of the happiness of private life. The love of action is a principle of a much stronger and more doubtful nature. If often leads to anger, to ambition, and to revenge; but when it is guided by the sense of propriety and benevolence, it becomes the parent of every virtue; and if those virtues are accompanied with equal abilities, a family, a state, or an empire, may be indebted for their safety and prosperity to the undaunted courage of a single man. To the love of pleasure we may therefore ascribe most of the agreeable, to the love of action we may attribute most of the useful and respectable, qualifications. The character in which both the one and the other should be united and harmonised, would seem to constitute the most perfect idea of human nature. The insensible and inactive disposition, which should be supposed alike destitute of both, would be rejected by the common consent of mankind, as utterly incapable of procuring any happiness to the individual, or any public benefit to the world. But it was not in *this* world that the primitive Christians were desirous of making themselves either agreeable or useful.

The acquisition of knowledge, the exercise of our reason or fancy, and the cheerful flow of unguarded conversation, may employ the leisure of a liberal mind. Such amusements, however, were rejected with abhorrence, or admitted with the utmost caution, by the severity of the fathers, who despised all knowledge that was not useful to salvation, and who considered all levity of discourse as a criminal abuse of the gift of speech. In our present state of existence, the body is so inseparably connected with the soul, that it seems to be our interest to taste, with innocence and moderation, the enjoyments of which that faithful companion is susceptible. Very different was the reasoning of our devout predecessors; vainly aspiring to imitate the perfection of angels, they disdained, or they affected to disdain, every earthly and corporeal delight. Some of our senses indeed are necessary for our preservation, others for our subsistence, and others again for our information, and thus far it was impossible to reject the use of them. The first sensation of pleasure was marked as the first moment of their abuse. The unfeeling candidate for Heaven was instructed, not only to resist the grosser allurements of the taste or smell, but even to shut his ears against the profane harmony of sounds, and to view with indifference the most finished productions of human art; gay apparel, magnificent houses, and elegant furniture, were supposed to unite the double guilt of pride and of sensuality. A simple and mortified appearance was more suitable to the Christian who was certain of his sins and doubtful of his salvation. In their censures of luxury, the fathers are extremely minute and circumstantial; and among the various articles which excite their pious indignation, we may enumerate false hair, garments of any colour except white, instruments of music, vases of gold or silver, downy pillows (as Jacob reposed his head on a stone),[55] white bread, foreign wines, public salutations, the use of warm baths, and the practice of shaving the beard, which, according to the expression of Tertullian, is a lie against our own faces, and an impious attempt to improve the works of the Creator. When Christianity was introduced among the rich and the polite, the observation of these singular laws was left, as it would be at present, to the few who were ambitious of superior sanctity. But it is always easy as well as agreeable for the inferior ranks of mankind to claim a merit from the contempt of that pomp and pleasure which fortune, has placed beyond their reach. The virtue of the primitive Christians, like that of the first Romans, was very frequently guarded by poverty and ignorance.

The chaste severity of the fathers, in whatever related to the commerce of the two sexes, flowed from the same principle; their abhorrence of every enjoyment, which might gratify the sensual, and degrade the spiritual nature of man. It was their favourite opinion, that if Adam had preserved his obedience to the Creator, he would have lived for ever in a state of virgin purity, and that some harmless mode of vegetation might have peopled paradise with a race of innocent and immortal beings. The use of marriage was permitted only to his fallen posterity, as a necessary expedient to continue the human species,

55. as . . . stone: See Gen. 28:11.

and as a restraint, however imperfect, on the natural licentiousness of desire. The hesitation of the orthodox casuists on this interesting subject, betrays the perplexity of men, unwilling to approve an institution, which they were compelled to tolerate. The enumeration of the very whimsical laws, which they most circumstantially imposed on the marriage-bed, would force a smile from the young and a blush from the fair. It was their unanimous sentiment, that a first marriage was adequate to all the purposes of nature and society. The sensual connexion was refined into a resemblance of the mystic union of Christ with his church, and was pronounced to be indissoluble either by divorce or by death. The practice of second nuptials was branded with the name of a legal adultery; and the persons who were guilty of so scandalous an offence against Christian purity, were soon excluded from the honours, and even from the alms, of the church. Since desire was imputed as a crime, and marriage was tolerated as a defect, it was consistent with the same principles to consider a state of celibacy as the nearest approach to the Divine perfection. It was with the utmost difficulty that ancient Rome could support the institution of six vestals;[56] but the primitive church was filled with a great number of persons of either sex, who had devoted themselves to the profession of perpetual chastity. A few of these, among whom we may reckon the learned Origen, judged it the most prudent to disarm the tempter.[57] Some were insensible and some were invincible against the assaults of the flesh. Disdaining an ignominious flight, the virgins of the warm climate of Africa encountered the enemy in the closest engagement; they permitted priests and deacons to share their bed, and gloried amidst the flames in their unsullied purity. But insulted Nature sometimes vindicated her rights, and this new species of martyrdom served only to introduce a new scandal into the church. Among the Christian ascetics, however, (a name which they soon acquired from their painful exercise[58]) many, as they were less presumptuous, were probably more successful.

The loss of sensual pleasure was supplied and compensated by spiritual pride. Even the multitude of Pagans were inclined to estimate the merit of the sacrifice by its apparent difficulty; and it was in the praise of these chaste spouses of Christ that the fathers have poured forth the troubled stream of their eloquence.[59] Such are the early traces of monastic principles and institutions, which, in a subsequent age, have counterbalanced all the temporal advantages of Christianity.

The Christians were not less adverse to the business than to the pleasures of this world. The defence of our persons and property they knew not how to reconcile with the patient doctrine which enjoined an unlimited forgiveness of past injuries, and commanded them to invite the repetition of fresh insults. Their simplicity was offended by the use of oaths, by the pomp of magistracy, and by the active contention of public life, nor could their humane ignorance be convinced, that it was lawful on any occasion to shed the blood of our fellow-creatures, either by the sword of justice, or by that of war, even though their criminal or hostile attempts should threaten the peace and safety of the whole community. It was acknowledged, that, under a less perfect law, the powers of the Jewish constitution had been exercised, with the approbation of Heaven, by inspired prophets and by anointed kings. The Christians felt and confessed, that such institutions might be necessary for the present system of the world, and they cheerfully submitted to the authority of their Pagan governors. But while they inculcated the maxims of passive obedience, they refused to take any active part in the civil administration or the military defence of the empire. Some indulgence might perhaps be allowed to those persons who, before their conversion, were already engaged in such violent and sanguinary occupations; but it was impossible that the Christians, without renouncing a more sacred duty, could assume the character of soldiers, of magistrates, or of princes. This indolent, or even criminal, disregard to the public welfare, exposed them to the contempt and reproaches of the Pagans, who very frequently asked, what must be the fate of the empire, attacked on every side by the barbarians, if all mankind should adopt the pusillanimous sentiments of the new sect? To this insulting

56. It . . . vestals: [Gibbon's note] Notwithstanding the honours and rewards which were bestowed on those virgins, it was difficult to procure a sufficient number; nor could the dread of the most horrible death always restrain their incontinence. **57. A few . . . tempter:** Origen (c. 185–c. 254), theologian and ascetic of Alexandria, castrated himself under a conviction that he was obliged to interpret literally Matt. 19:12. **58. exercise:** The word *ascetic* is derived from the Greek word for exercise.

59. it . . . eloquence: [Gibbon's note] Dupin gives a particular account of the dialogue of the ten virgins, as it was composed by Methodius, bishop of Tyre. The praises of virginity are excessive.

question the Christian apologists returned obscure and ambiguous answers, as they were unwilling to reveal the secret cause of their security; the expectation that, before the conversion of mankind was accomplished, war, government, the Roman empire, and the world itself, would be no more. It may be observed, that in this instance likewise, the situation of the first Christians coincided very happily with their religious scruples, and that their aversion to an active life contributed rather to excuse them from the service, than to exclude them from the honours, of the state and army.

V. But the human character, however it may be exalted or depressed by a temporary enthusiasm, will return by degrees to its proper and natural level, and will resume those passions that seem the most adapted to its present condition. The primitive Christians were dead to the business and pleasures of the world; but their love of action, which could never be entirely extinguished, soon revived, and found a new occupation in the government of the church. A separate society, which attacked the established religion of the empire, was obliged to adopt some form of internal policy, and to appoint a sufficient number of ministers, intrusted not only with the spiritual functions, but even with the temporal direction of the Christian commonwealth. The safety of that society, its honour, its aggrandisement, were productive, even in the most pious minds, of a spirit of patriotism, such as the first of the Romans had felt for the republic, and sometimes, of a similar indifference, in the use of whatever means might probably conduce to so desirable an end. The ambition of raising themselves or their friends to the honours and offices of the church, was disguised by the laudable intention of devoting to the public benefit, the power and consideration, which, for that purpose only, it became their duty to solicit. In the exercise of their functions, they were frequently called upon to detect the errors of heresy, or the arts of faction, to oppose the designs of perfidious brethren, to stigmatise their characters with deserved infamy, and to expel them from the bosom of a society, whose peace and happiness they had attempted to disturb. The ecclesiastical governors of the Christians were taught to unite the wisdom of the serpent with the innocence of the dove; but as the former was refined, so the latter was insensibly corrupted, by the habits of government. In the church as well as in the world, the persons who were placed in any public station rendered themselves considerable by their eloquence and firmness, by their knowledge of mankind, and by their dexterity in business, and while they concealed from others, and perhaps from themselves, the secret motives of their conduct, they too frequently relapsed into all the turbulent passions of active life, which were tinctured with an additional degree of bitterness and obstinacy from the infusion of spiritual zeal.

The government of the church has often been the subject as well as the prize of religious contention. The hostile disputants of Rome, of Paris, of Oxford, and of Geneva, have alike struggled to reduce the primitive and apostolic model, to the respective standards of their own policy. The few who have pursued this inquiry with more candour and impartiality, are of opinion, that the apostles declined the office of legislation, and rather chose to endure some partial scandals and divisions, than to exclude the Christians of a future age from the liberty of varying their forms of ecclesiastical government according to the changes of times and circumstances. The scheme of policy, which, under their approbation, was adopted for the use of the first century, may be discovered from the practice of Jerusalem, of Ephesus, or of Corinth. The societies which were instituted in the cities of the Roman empire, were united only by the ties of faith and charity. Independence and equality formed the basis of their internal constitution. The want of discipline and human learning was supplied by the occasional assistance of the *prophets*, who were called to that function without distinction of age, of sex, or of natural abilities, and who, as often as they felt the divine impulse, poured forth the effusions of the spirit in the assembly of the faithful. But these extraordinary gifts were frequently abused or misapplied by the prophetic teachers. They displayed them at any improper season, presumptuously disturbed the service of the assembly, and by their pride or mistaken zeal they introduced, particularly into the apostolic church of Corinth, a long and melancholy train of disorders. As the institution of prophets became useless, and even pernicious, their powers were withdrawn, and their office abolished. The public functions of religion were solely intrusted to the established ministers of the church, the *bishops* and the *presbyters;* two appellations which, in their first origin, appear to have distinguished the same office and the same order of persons. The name of Presbyter was expressive of their age, or rather of their gravity and wisdom.[60] The title of

60. The name . . . wisdom: The word *presbyter* is related to the Greek word for old man.

Bishop[61] denoted their inspection over the faith and manners of the christians who were committed to their pastoral care. In proportion to the respective numbers of the faithful, a larger or smaller number of these *episcopal presbyters* guided each infant congregation with equal authority, and with united counsels.

But the most perfect equality of freedom requires the directing hand of a superior magistrate; and the order of public deliberations soon introduces the office of a president invested at least with the authority of collecting the sentiments, and of executing the resolutions, of the assembly. A regard for the public tranquillity, which would so frequently have been interrupted by annual or by occasional elections, induced the primitive christians to constitute an honourable and perpetual magistracy, and to choose one of the wisest and most holy among their presbyters to execute, during his life, the duties of their ecclesiastical governor. It was under these circumstances that the lofty title of Bishop began to raise itself above the humble appellation of Presbyter; and while the latter remained the most natural distinction for the members of every christian senate, the former was appropriated to the dignity of its new president. The advantages of this episcopal form of government, which appears to have been introduced before the end of the first century, were so obvious, and so important for the future greatness, as well as the present peace, of Christianity, that it was adopted without delay by all the societies which were already scattered over the empire, had acquired in a very early period the sanction of antiquity, and is still revered by the most powerful churches, both of the East and of the West, as a primitive and even as a divine establishment. It is needless to observe, that the pious and humble presbyters, who were first dignified with the episcopal title, could not possess, and would probably have rejected, the power and pomp which now encircles the tiara of the Roman pontiff, or the mitre of a German prelate. But we may define, in a few words, the narrow limits of their original jurisdiction, which was chiefly of a spiritual, though in some instances of a temporal, nature. It consisted in the administration of the sacraments and discipline of the church, the superintendency of religious ceremonies, which imperceptibly increased in number and variety, the consecration of ecclesiastical ministers, to whom the bishop assigned their respective functions, the management of the public fund, and the

determination of all such differences as the faithful were unwilling to expose before the tribunal of an idolatrous judge. These powers, during a short period, were exercised according to the advice of the presbyteral college, and with the consent and approbation of the assembly of Christians. The primitive bishops were considered only as the first of their equals, and the honourable servants of a free people. Whenever the episcopal chair became vacant by death, a new president was chosen among the presbyters by the suffrage of the whole congregation, every member of which supposed himself invested with a sacred and sacerdotal character.

Such was the mild and equal constitution by which the Christians were governed more than an hundred years after the death of the apostles. Every society formed within itself a separate and independent republic: and although the most distant of these little states maintained a mutual as well as friendly intercourse of letters and deputations, the christian world was not yet connected by any supreme authority or legislative assembly. As the numbers of the faithful were gradually multiplied, they discovered the advantages that might result from a closer union of their interest and designs. Towards the end of the second century, the churches of Greece and Asia adopted the useful institutions of provincial synods, and they may justly be supposed to have borrowed the model of a representative council from the celebrated examples of their own country, the Amphictyons, the Achæan league, or the assemblies of the Ionian cities. It was soon established as a custom and as a law, that the bishops of the independent churches should meet in the capital of the province at the stated periods of spring and autumn. Their deliberations were assisted by the advice of a few distinguished presbyters, and moderated by the presence of a listening multitude. Their decrees, which were styled Canons, regulated every important controversy of faith and discipline; and it was natural to believe that a liberal effusion of the holy spirit would be poured on the united assembly of the delegates of the christian people. The institution of synods was so well suited to private ambition and to public interest, that in the space of a few years it was received throughout the whole empire. A regular correspondence was established between the provincial councils, which mutually communicated and approved their respective proceedings; and the catholic church soon assumed the form, and acquired the strength, of a great fœderative republic.

61. **Bishop:** derived from the Greek word for overseer.

As the legislative authority of the particular churches was insensibly superseded by the use of councils, the bishops obtained by their alliance a much larger share of executive and arbitrary power; and as soon as they were connected by a sense of their common interest, they were enabled to attack, with united vigour, the original rights of their clergy and people. The prelates of the third century imperceptibly changed the language of exhortation into that of command, scattered the seeds of future usurpations, and supplied by scripture allegories and declamatory rhetoric, their deficiency of force and of reason. They exalted the unity and power of the church, as it was represented in the EPISCOPAL OFFICE, of which every bishop enjoyed an equal and undivided portion. Princes and magistrates, it was often repeated, might boast an earthly claim to a transitory dominion. It was the episcopal authority alone which was derived from the deity, and extended itself over this and over another world. The bishops were the vicegerents[62] of Christ, the successors of the apostles, and the mystic substitutes of the high priest of the Mosaic law. Their exclusive privilege of conferring the sacerdotal character, invaded the freedom both of clerical and of popular elections; and if, in the administration of the church, they still consulted the judgment of the presbyters, or the inclination of the people, they most carefully inculcated the merit of such a voluntary condescension. The bishops acknowledged the supreme authority which resided in the assembly of their brethren; but in the government of his peculiar diocese, each of them exacted from his *flock* the same implicit obedience as if that favourite metaphor had been literally just, and as if the shepherd had been of a more exalted nature than that of his sheep. This obedience, however, was not imposed without some efforts on one side, and some resistance on the other. The democratical part of the constitution was, in many places, very warmly supported by the zealous or interested opposition of the inferior clergy. But their patriotism received the ignominious epithets of faction and schism; and the episcopal cause was indebted for its rapid progress to the labours of many active prelates, who, like Cyprian of Carthage,[63] could reconcile the arts of the most ambitious statesman with the christian virtues which seem adapted to the character of a saint and martyr.

The same causes which at first had destroyed the equality of the presbyters, introduced among the bishops a pre-eminence of rank, and from thence a superiority of jurisdiction. As often as in the spring and autumn they met in provincial synod, the difference of personal merit and reputation was very sensibly felt among the members of the assembly, and the multitude was governed by the wisdom and eloquence of the few. But the order of public proceedings required a more regular and less invidious distinction; the office of perpetual presidents in the councils of each province, was conferred on the bishops of the principal city, and these aspiring prelates, who soon acquired the lofty title of Metropolitans and Primates, secretly prepared themselves to usurp over their episcopal brethren the same authority which the bishops had so lately assumed above the college of presbyters. Nor was it long before an emulation of pre-eminence and power prevailed among the metropolitans themselves, each of them affecting to display, in the most pompous terms, the temporal honours and advantages of the city over which he presided; the numbers and opulence of the Christians, who were subject to their pastoral care; the saints and martyrs who had arisen among them, and the purity with which they preserved the tradition of the faith, as it had been transmitted through a series of orthodox bishops from the apostle or the apostolic disciple, to whom the foundation of their church was ascribed. From every cause either of a civil or of an ecclesiastical nature, it was easy to foresee that Rome must enjoy the respect, and would soon claim the obedience of the provinces. The society of the faithful bore a just proportion to the capital of the empire; and the Roman church was the greatest, the most numerous, and, in regard to the West, the most ancient of all the Christian establishments, many of which had received their religion from the pious labours of her missionaries. Instead of *one* apostolic founder, the utmost boast of Antioch, of Ephesus, or of Corinth, the banks of the Tiber were supposed to have been honoured with the preaching and martyrdom of the *two* most eminent among the apostles;[64] and the bishops of Rome very prudently claimed the inheritance of whatsoever prerogatives were attributed either to the person or to the office of Saint Peter. The bishops of Italy and of the provinces, were disposed to allow them a primacy of order and association (such was their very accurate expression) in the Christian

---

62. **vicegerents:** deputed representatives. 63. **Cyprian of Carthage:** a bishop from 248 until his martyrdom in 258.

64. **the two . . . apostles:** Peter and Paul.

aristocracy. But the power of a monarch was rejected with abhorrence, and the aspiring genius of Rome experienced from the nations of Asia and Africa, a more vigorous resistance to her spiritual than she had formerly done to her temporal dominion. The patriotic Cyprian, who ruled with the most absolute sway the church of Carthage and the provincial synods, opposed with resolution and success the ambition of the Roman pontiff, artfully connected his own cause with that of the eastern bishops, and, like Hannibal,[65] sought out new allies in the heart of Asia. If this Punic war[66] was carried on without any effusion of blood, it was owing much less to the moderation than to the weakness of the contending prelates. Invectives and excommunications were *their* only weapons; and these, during the progress of the whole controversy, they hurled against each other with equal fury and devotion. The hard necessity of censuring either a pope, or a saint and martyr, distresses the modern catholics whenever they are obliged to relate the particulars of a dispute, in which the champions of religion indulged such passions as seem much more adapted to the senate or to the camp.

The progress of the ecclesiastical authority gave birth to the memorable distinction of the laity and of the clergy, which had been unknown to the Greeks and Romans. The former of these appellations comprehend the body of the Christian people; the latter, according to the signification of the word, was appropriated to the chosen portion that had been set apart for the service of religion; a celebrated order of men which has furnished the most important, though not always the most edifying subjects, for modern history. Their mutual hostilities sometimes disturbed the peace of the infant church, but their zeal and activity were united in the common cause, and the love of power, which (under the most artful disguises) could insinuate itself into the breasts of bishops and martyrs, animated them to increase the number of their subjects, and to enlarge the limits of the Christian empire. They were destitute of any temporal force, and they were for a long time discouraged and oppressed, rather than assisted, by the civil magistrate; but they had acquired, and they employed within their own society, the two most efficacious instruments of government, rewards

and punishments; the former derived from the pious liberality, the latter from the devout apprehensions of the faithful.

I. The community of goods,[67] which had so agreeably amused the imagination of Plato, and which subsisted in some degree among the austere sect of the Essenians,[68] was adopted for a short time in the primitive church. The fervour of the first proselytes prompted them to sell those worldly possessions, which they despised, to lay the price of them at the feet of the apostles, and to content themselves with receiving an equal share out of the general distribution. The progress of the Christian religion relaxed, and gradually abolished this generous institution, which, in hands less pure than those of the apostles, would too soon have been corrupted and abused by the returning selfishness of human nature; and the converts who embraced the new religion were permitted to retain the possession of their patrimony, to receive legacies and inheritances, and to increase their separate property by all the lawful means of trade and industry. Instead of an absolute sacrifice, a moderate proportion was accepted by the ministers of the gospel; and in their weekly or monthly assemblies, every believer, according to the exigency of the occasion, and the measure of his wealth and piety, presented his voluntary offering for the use of the common fund. Nothing, however inconsiderable, was refused; but it was diligently inculcated, that in the article of Tythes, the Mosaic law was still of divine obligation, and that since the Jews, under a less perfect discipline, had been commanded to pay a tenth part of all that they possessed, it would become the disciples of Christ to distinguish themselves by a superior degree of liberality, and to acquire some merit by resigning a superfluous treasure, which must so soon be annihilated with the world itself. It is almost unnecessary to observe, that the revenue of each particular church, which was of so uncertain and fluctuating a nature, must have varied with the poverty or the opulence of the faithful, as they were dispersed in obscure villages, or collected in the great cities of the empire. In the time of the emperor Decius,[69] it was the opinion of the magistrates that the Christians of Rome were possessed of very considerable wealth; that vessels of gold and silver

65. Hannibal: (247–183 B.C.), general of Carthage, who, in alliance with the Syrians, warred against Rome. **66. Punic war:** one of a series of wars between Carthage and Rome fought from 264 to 146 B.C.

67. The community . . . goods: public, rather than private, ownership of property. **68. Essenians:** an ascetic Hebrew religious group that flourished in Palestine from the second century B.C. to the second century A.D. **69. Decius:** emperor from 249 to 251.

were used in their religious worship, and that many among their proselytes had sold their lands and houses to increase the public riches of the sect, at the expence, indeed, of their unfortunate children, who found themselves beggars, because their parents had been saints. We should listen with distrust to the suspicions of strangers and enemies; on this occasion, however, they receive a very specious and probable colour from the two following circumstances, the only ones that have reached our knowledge, which define any precise sums, or convey any distinct idea. Almost at the same period, the bishop of Carthage, from a society less opulent than that of Rome, collected an hundred thousand sesterces (above eight hundred and fifty pounds sterling) on a sudden call of charity to redeem the brethren of Numidia, who had been carried away captives by the barbarians of the desert. About an hundred years before the reign of Decius, the Roman church had received, in a single donation, the sum of two hundred thousand sesterces from a stranger of Pontus, who proposed to fix his residence in the capital. These oblations,[70] for the most part, were made in money; nor was the society of Christians either desirous or capable of acquiring to any considerable degree, the incumbrance of landed property. It had been provided by several laws, which were enacted with the same design as our statutes of mortmain,[71] that no real estates should be given or bequeathed to any corporate body, without either a special privilege or a particular dispensation from the emperor or from the senate, who were seldom disposed to grant them in favour of a sect, at first the object of their contempt, and at last of their fears and jealousy. A transaction however is related under the reign of Alexander Severus,[72] which discovers[73] that the restraint was sometimes eluded or suspended, and that the Christians were permitted to claim and to possess lands within the limits of Rome itself.[74] The progress of Christianity, and the civil confusion of the empire, contributed to relax the severity of the laws, and before the close of the third century many considerable estates were bestowed on the opulent churches of Rome, Milan, Carthage, Antioch, Al-

exandria, and the other great cities of Italy and the provinces.

The bishop was the natural steward of the church; the public stock was intrusted to his care without account or control; the presbyters were confined to their spiritual functions, and the more dependent order of deacons was solely employed in the management and distribution of the ecclesiastical revenue. If we may give credit to the vehement declamations of Cyprian, there were too many among his African brethren, who, in the execution of their charge, violated every precept, not only of evangelic perfection, but even of moral virtue. By some of these unfaithful stewards the riches of the church were lavished in sensual pleasures, by others they were perverted to the purposes of private gain, of fraudulent purchases, and of rapacious usury. But as long as the contributions of the Christian people were free and unconstrained, the abuse of their confidence could not be very frequent, and the general uses to which their liberality was applied, reflected honour on the religious society. A decent portion was reserved for the maintenance of the bishop and his clergy; a sufficient sum was allotted for the expences of the public worship, of which the feasts of love, the *agapæ*,[75] as they were called, constituted a very pleasing part. The whole remainder was the sacred patrimony of the poor. According to the discretion of the bishop, it was distributed to support widows and orphans, the lame, the sick, and the aged of the community; to comfort strangers and pilgrims, and to alleviate the misfortunes of prisoners and captives, more especially when their sufferings had been occasioned by their firm attachment to the cause of religion. A generous intercourse of charity united the most distant provinces, and the smaller congregations were cheerfully assisted by the alms of their more opulent brethren. Such an institution, which paid less regard to the merit than to the distress of the object, very materially conduced to the progress of Christianity. The Pagans, who were actuated by a sense of humanity, while they derided the doctrines, acknowledged the benevolence of the new sect. The prospect of immediate relief and of future protection allured into its hospitable bosom many of those unhappy persons whom the neglect of the world would have abandoned to the miseries of want, of sickness, and of old age. There is some reason

---

70. oblations: offerings. 71. statutes of mortmain: laws limiting the amount of property that can be bequeathed to ecclesiastical or other corporations. 72. Alexander Severus: emperor from 222 to 235. 73. discovers: reveals. 74. the Christians . . . itself: [Gibbon's note] The ground had been public; and was now disputed between the society of christians, and that of butchers.

75. agapæ: ritualistic meals presumably imitative of the Last Supper.

likewise to believe, that great numbers of infants, who, according to the inhuman practice of the times, had been exposed[76] by their parents, were frequently rescued from death, baptised, educated, and maintained by the piety of the Christians, and at the expense of the public treasure.

II. It is the undoubted right of every society to exclude from its communion and benefits, such among its members as reject or violate those regulations which have been established by general consent. In the exercise of this power, the censures of the Christian church were chiefly directed against scandalous sinners, and particularly those who were guilty of murder, of fraud, or of incontinence, against the authors, or the followers of any heretical opinions which had been condemned by the judgment of the episcopal order, and against those unhappy persons who, whether from choice or from compulsion, had polluted themselves after their baptism by any act of idolatrous worship. The consequences of excommunication were of a temporal as well as a spiritual nature. The Christian against whom it was pronounced, was deprived of any part in the oblations of the faithful. The ties both of religious and of private friendship were dissolved: he found himself a profane object of abhorrence to the persons whom he the most esteemed, or by whom he had been the most tenderly beloved; and as far as an expulsion from a respectable society could imprint on his character a mark of disgrace, he was shunned or suspected by the generality of mankind. The situation of these unfortunate exiles was in itself very painful and melancholy; but, as it usually happens, their apprehensions far exceeded their sufferings. The benefits of the Christian communion were those of eternal life, nor could they erase from their minds the awful opinion, that to those ecclesiastical governors by whom they were condemned, the Deity had committed the keys of Hell and of Paradise. The heretics indeed, who might be supported by the consciousness of their intentions, and by the flattering hope that they alone had discovered the true path of salvation, endeavoured to regain, in their separate assemblies, those comforts, temporal as well as spiritual, which they no longer derived from the great society of Christians. But almost all those who had reluctantly yielded to the power of vice or idolatry were sensible of their fallen condition, and anxiously desirous of

being restored to the benefits of the Christian communion.

With regard to the treatment of these penitents, two opposite opinions, the one of justice, the other of mercy, divided the primitive church. The more rigid and inflexible casuists[77] refused them for ever, and without exception, the meanest place in the holy community, which they had disgraced or deserted, and leaving them to the remorse of a guilty conscience, indulged them only with a faint ray of hope, that the contrition of their life and death might possibly be accepted by the Supreme Being.[78] A milder sentiment was embraced in practice as well as in theory, by the purest and most respectable of the Christian churches. The gates of reconciliation and of Heaven were seldom shut against the returning penitent; but a severe and solemn form of discipline was instituted, which, while it served to expiate his crime, might powerfully deter the spectators from the imitation of his example. Humbled by a public confession, emaciated by fasting, and clothed in sackcloth, the penitent lay prostrate at the door of the assembly, imploring with tears the pardon of his offences, and soliciting the prayers of the faithful. If the fault was of a very heinous nature, whole years of penance were esteemed an inadequate satisfaction to the Divine Justice; and it was always by slow and painful gradations that the sinner, the heretic, or the apostate, was re-admitted into the bosom of the church. A sentence of perpetual excommunication was, however, reserved for some crimes of an extraordinary magnitude, and particularly for the inexcusable relapses of those penitents who had already experienced and abused the clemency of their ecclesiastical superiors. According to the circumstances or the number of the guilty, the exercise of the Christian discipline was varied by the discretion of the bishops. The councils of Ancyra and Illiberis were held about the same time, the one in Galatia, the other in Spain; but their respective canons, which are still extant, seem to breathe a very different spirit. The Galatian, who after his baptism had repeatedly sacrificed to idols, might obtain his pardon by a penance of seven years, and if he had seduced others to imitate his example, only three years more were added to the term of his

76. **exposed:** abandoned to die in some isolated spot.

77. **casuists:** those who determine specific cases of conscience, often with pedantic nicety. 78. **that . . . Being:** [Gibbon's note] The Montanists and the Novatians, who adhered to this opinion with the greatest rigour and obstinacy, found *themselves* at last in the number of excommunicated heretics.

exile. But the unhappy Spaniard, who had committed the same offence, was deprived of the hope of reconciliation, even in the article of death; and his idolatry was placed at the head of a list of seventeen other crimes, against which a sentence no less terrible was pronounced. Among these we may distinguish the inexpiable guilt of calumniating a bishop, a presbyter, or even a deacon.

The well tempered mixture of liberality and rigour, the judicious dispensation of rewards and punishments, according to the maxims of policy as well as justice, constituted the *human* strength of the church. The bishops, whose paternal care extended itself to the government of both worlds, were sensible of the importance of these prerogatives, and covering their ambition with the fair pretence of the love of order, they were jealous of any rival in the exercise of a discipline so necessary to prevent the desertion of those troops which had inlisted themselves under the banner of the cross, and whose numbers every day became more considerable. From the imperious declamations of Cyprian, we should naturally conclude, that the doctrines of excommunication and penance formed the most essential part of religion; and that it was much less dangerous for the disciples of Christ to neglect the observance of the moral duties, than to despise the censures and authority of their bishops. Sometimes we might imagine that we were listening to the voice of Moses, when he commanded the earth to open, and to swallow up, in consuming flames, the rebellious race which refused obedience to the priesthood of Aaron; and we should sometimes suppose that we heard a Roman consul[79] asserting the majesty of the republic, and declaring his inflexible resolution to enforce the rigour of the laws. "If such irregularities are suffered with impunity (it is thus that the bishop of Carthage chides the lenity of his colleague) if such irregularities are suffered, there is an end of EPISCOPAL VIGOUR; an end of the sublime and divine power of governing the church, an end of Christianity itself." Cyprian had renounced those temporal honours, which it is probable he would never have obtained; but the acquisition of such absolute command over the consciences and understanding of a congregation, however obscure or despised by the world, is more truly grateful to the pride of the human heart, than

the possession of the most despotic power, imposed by arms and conquest on a reluctant people.

In the course of this important, though perhaps tedious, inquiry, I have attempted to display the secondary causes which so efficaciously assisted the truth of the Christian religion. If among these causes we have discovered any artificial ornaments, any accidental circumstances, or any mixture of error and passion, it cannot appear surprising that mankind should be the most sensibly affected by such motives as were suited to their imperfect nature. It was by the aid of these causes, exclusive zeal, the immediate expectation of another world, the claim of miracles, the practice of rigid virtue, and the constitution of the primitive church, that Christianity spread itself with so much success in the Roman empire. To the first of these the Christians were indebted for their invincible valour, which disdained to capitulate with the enemy whom they were resolved to vanquish. The three succeeding causes supplied their valour with the most formidable arms. The last of these causes united their courage, directed their arms, and gave their efforts that irresistible weight which even a small band of well-trained and intrepid volunteers has so often possessed over an undisciplined multitude, ignorant of the subject, and careless of the event of the war. In the various religions of Polytheism, some wandering fanatics of Egypt and Syria, who addressed themselves to the credulous superstition of the populace, were perhaps the only order of priests that derived their whole support and credit from their sacerdotal profession, and were very deeply affected by a personal concern for the safety or prosperity of their tutelar[80] deities. The ministers of polytheism, both in Rome and in the provinces, were, for the most part, men of a noble birth, and of an affluent fortune, who received, as an honourable distinction, the care of a celebrated temple, or of a public sacrifice, exhibited, very frequently at their own expense, the sacred games, and with cold indifference performed the ancient rites, according to the laws and fashion of their country. As they were engaged in the ordinary occupations of life, their zeal and devotion were seldom animated by a sense of interest, or by the habits of an ecclesiastical character. Confined to their respective temples and cities, they remained without any connexion of discipline or government; and whilst they acknowledged the supreme jurisdiction of the senate, of the college

79. consul: the title held by each of the two annually elected chief magistrates of the Roman Republic.

80. tutelar: guardian.

of pontiffs, and of the emperor, those civil magistrates contented themselves with the easy task of maintaining, in peace and dignity, the general worship of mankind. We have already seen how various, how loose, and how uncertain were the religious sentiments of Polytheists. They were abandoned, almost without control, to the natural workings of a superstitious fancy. The accidental circumstances of their life and situation determined the object as well as the degree of their devotion; and as long as their adoration was successively prostituted to a thousand deities, it was scarcely possible that their hearts could be susceptible of a very sincere or lively passion for any of them.

When Christianity appeared in the world, even these faint and imperfect impressions had lost much of their original power. Human reason, which by its unassisted strength is incapable of perceiving the mysteries of faith, had already obtained an easy triumph over the folly of Paganism; and when Tertullian or Lactantius employ their labours in exposing its falsehood and extravagance, they are obliged to transcribe the eloquence of Cicero or the wit of Lucian.[81] The contagion of these sceptical writings had been diffused far beyond the number of their readers. The fashion of incredulity was communicated from the philosopher to the man of pleasure or business, from the noble to the plebeian, and from the master to the menial slave who waited at his table, and who eagerly listened to the freedom of his conversation. On public occasions the philosophic part of mankind affected to treat with respect and decency the religious institutions of their country; but their secret contempt penetrated through the thin and awkward disguise, and even the people, when they discovered that their deities were rejected and derided by those whose rank or understanding they were accustomed to reverence, were filled with doubts and apprehensions concerning the truth of those doctrines, to which they had yielded the most implicit belief. The decline of ancient prejudice exposed a very numerous portion of human kind to the danger of a painful and comfortless situation. A state of scepticism and suspense may amuse a few inquisitive minds. But the practice of superstition is so congenial to the multitude, that if they are forcibly awakened, they still regret the loss of their pleasing vision. Their love of the marvellous and supernatural, their curiosity

with regard to future events, and their strong propensity to extend their hopes and fears beyond the limits of the visible world, were the principal causes which favoured the establishment of Polytheism. So urgent on the vulgar is the necessity of believing, that the fall of any system of mythology will most probably be succeeded by the introduction of some other mode of superstition. Some deities of a more recent and fashionable cast might soon have occupied the deserted temples of Jupiter and Apollo, if, in the decisive moment, the wisdom of Providence had not interposed a genuine revelation, fitted to inspire the most rational esteem and conviction, whilst, at the same time, it was adorned with all that could attract the curiosity, the wonder, and the veneration of the people. In their actual disposition, as many were almost disengaged from their artificial prejudices, but equally susceptible and desirous of a devout attachment; an object much less deserving would have been sufficient to fill the vacant place in their hearts, and to gratify the uncertain eagerness of their passions. Those who are inclined to pursue this reflection, instead of viewing with astonishment the rapid progress of Christianity, will perhaps be surprised that its success was not still more rapid and still more universal.

. . .

FROM

CHAPTER XXIV

Gibbon devotes three chapters of *The Decline and Fall* to the career of the Emperor Julian, "the only character in his history," as G. M. Young says, "for whom Gibbon seems to feel some affection." Son of Julius Constantius and nephew of Constantine, Flavius Claudius Julianus (331–63) discovered early the delights of Greek literature and philosophy. In 355, after the death of his elder half brother, Gallus, the bookish Julian became Caesar, and, to many people's surprise, made a vigorous beginning by conducting a successful campaign against the Germans and the Franks. He became emperor in 361, and shortly after, though he had been raised as a Christian, he proclaimed (among other reforms) an official revival of the service of the ancient gods. Although he generally tolerated Christianity, he worked for the restoration of the old religion through his edicts, his writings, and his conspicuous devotions, winning for himself the appellation Julian the Apostate. He led a

---

81. **Lucian:** Greek satirist of the second century A.D.

punitive expedition against the Persians from March, 362, until his death in January, 363.

Julian's character seems paradoxical: he is at once the retiring scholarly author and the heroic man of action. Gibbon, who calls Julian "the philosophic warrior," concludes his account of him thus:

> The remains of Julian were interred at Tarsus in Cilicia; but his stately tomb, which arose in that city on the banks of the cold and limpid Cydnus, was displeasing to the faithful friends who loved and revered the memory of that extraordinary man. The philosopher expressed a very reasonable wish that the disciple of Plato might have reposed amidst the groves of the Academy, while the soldier exclaimed, in bolder accents, that the ashes of Julian should have been mingled with those of Cæsar, in the field of Mars, and among the ancient monuments of Roman virtue. The history of princes does not very frequently renew the example of a similar competition.

This selection comprises about three-fourths of the chapter. The text is that of the first edition (1781).

ᬀ

*Residence of Julian at Antioch.—His successful
Expedition against the Persians.
—Passage of the Tigris.—The Retreat
and Death of Julian. . . .*

The philosophical fable which Julian composed under the name of the CÆSARS,[1] is one of the most agreeable and instructive productions of ancient wit. During the freedom and equality of the days of the Saturnalia, Romulus[2] prepared a feast for the deities of Olympus, who had adopted him as a worthy associate, and for the Roman princes, who had reigned over his martial people, and the vanquished nations of the earth. The immortals were placed in just order on their thrones of state, and the table of the Cæsars was spread below the Moon, in the upper region of the air. The tyrants, who would have disgraced the society of gods and men, were thrown headlong, by the inexorable Nemesis,[3] into the Tartarean abyss.[4] The rest of the Cæsars successively advanced to their seats; and, as they passed, the vices, the defects, the blemishes of their respective characters, were maliciously noticed by old Silenus, a laughing moralist, who disguised the wisdom of a philosopher under the mask of a Bacchanal. As soon as the feast was ended, the voice of Mercury proclaimed the will of Jupiter, that a celestial crown should be the reward of superior merit. Julius Cæsar, Augustus, Trajan, and Marcus Antoninus,[5] were selected as the most illustrious candidates; the effeminate Constantine was not excluded from this honourable competition, and the great Alexander was invited to dispute the prize of glory with the Roman heroes. Each of the candidates was allowed to display the merit of his own exploits; but, in the judgment of the gods, the modest silence of Marcus pleaded more powerfully than the elaborate orations of his haughty rivals. When the judges of this awful contest proceeded to examine the heart, and to scrutinise the springs of action; the superiority of the Imperial Stoic appeared still more decisive and conspicuous. Alexander and Cæsar, Augustus, Trajan, and Constantine, acknowledged with a blush, that fame, or power, or pleasure, had been the important object of *their* labours: but the gods themselves beheld, with reverence and love, a virtuous mortal, who had practised on the throne the lessons of philosophy; and who, in a state of human imperfection, had aspired to imitate the moral attributes of the Deity. The value of this agreeable composition (the Cæsars of Julian) is enhanced by the rank of the author. A prince, who delineates with freedom the vices and virtues of his predecessors, subscribes, in every line, the censure or approbation of his own conduct.

In the cool moments of reflection, Julian preferred the useful and benevolent virtues of Antoninus: but his ambitious spirit was inflamed by the glory of Alexander; and he solicited, with equal ardour, the esteem of the wise, and the applause of the multitude. In the season of life, when the powers of the mind and body enjoy the most active vigour, the emperor, who was instructed by the experience, and animated by the success, of the German war,[6] resolved to signalise his reign by some more splendid and memorable atchievement. The ambassadors of the East, from the continent

---

Chapter XXIV. **1. Cæsars:** a prose satire in Greek, written at Constantinople in 361. **2. Romulus:** one of the legendary founders of Rome. **3. Nemesis:** a wrathful goddess who punishes the arrogant. **4. the Tartarean abyss:** a deep pit in Hades.

5. Marcus Antoninus: Marcus Aurelius Antoninus (121–80), emperor from 161 and eminent philosopher of the Stoic school, an ascetic system of ethics based upon an attitude of indifference toward accident and misfortune. **6. the German war:** won by Julian.

of India, and the isle of Ceylon, had respectfully saluted the Roman purple. The nations of the West esteemed and dreaded the personal virtues of Julian, both in peace and war. He despised the trophies of a Gothic victory, and was satisfied that the rapacious Barbarians of the Danube would be restrained from any future violation of the faith of treaties, by the terror of his name, and the additional fortifications, with which he strengthened the Thracian and Illyrian frontiers. The successor of Cyrus and Artaxerxes[7] was the only rival whom he deemed worthy of his arms; and he resolved, by the final conquest of Persia, to chastise the haughty nation, which had so long resisted and insulted the majesty of Rome. As soon as the Persian monarch was informed that the throne of Constantius was filled by a prince of a very different character, he condescended to make some artful, or perhaps sincere, overtures, towards a negociation of peace. But the pride of Sapor[8] was astonished by the firmness of Julian; who sternly declared, that he would never consent to hold a peaceful conference among the flames and ruins of the cities of Mesopotamia;[9] and who added, with a smile of contempt, that it was needless to treat by ambassadors, as he himself had determined to visit speedily the court of Persia. The impatience of the emperor urged the diligence of the military preparations. The generals were named; a formidable army was destined for this important service; and Julian, marching from Constantinople through the provinces of Asia Minor, arrived at Antioch about eight months after the death of his predecessor. His ardent desire to march into the heart of Persia, was checked by the indispensable duty of regulating the state of the empire; by his zeal to revive the worship of the gods; and by the advice of his wisest friends; who represented the necessity of allowing the salutary interval of winter-quarters, to restore, the exhausted strength of the legions of Gaul, and the discipline and spirit of the Eastern troops. Julian was persuaded to fix, till the ensuing spring, his residence at Antioch, among a people maliciously disposed to deride the haste, and to censure the delays, of their sovereign.

If Julian had flattered himself, that his personal connection with the capital of the East would be productive of mutual satisfaction to the prince and people, he made a very false estimate of his own character, and of the manners of Antioch. The warmth of the climate disposed the natives to the most intemperate enjoyment of tranquillity and opulence; and the lively licentiousness of the Greeks was blended with the hereditary softness of the Syrians. Fashion was the only law, pleasure the only pursuit, and the splendour of dress and furniture was the only distinction of the citizens of Antioch. The arts of luxury were honoured; the serious and manly virtues were the subject of ridicule; and the contempt for female modesty, and reverent age, announced the universal corruption of the capital of the East. The love of spectacles was the taste, or rather passion, of the Syrians: the most skilful artists were procured from the adjacent cities; a considerable share of the revenue was devoted to the public amusements; and the magnificence of the games of the theatre and circus was considered as the happiness, and as the glory, of Antioch. The rustic manners of a prince who disdained such glory, and was insensible of such happiness, soon disgusted the delicacy of his subjects; and the effeminate Orientals could neither imitate, nor admire, the severe simplicity which Julian always maintained, and sometimes affected. The days of festivity, consecrated, by ancient custom, to the honour of the gods, were the only occasions in which Julian relaxed his philosophic severity; and those festivals were the only days in which the Syrians of Antioch could reject the allurements of pleasure. The majority of the people supported the glory of the Christian name, which had been first invented by their ancestors: they contented themselves with disobeying the moral precepts, but they were scrupulously attached to the speculative doctrines, of their religion. The church of Antioch was distracted by heresy and schism; but the Arians[10] and the Athanasians,[11] the followers of Meletius and those of Paulinus,[12] were actuated by the same pious hatred of their common adversary.

The strongest prejudice was entertained against the character of an apostate, the enemy and successor of a prince who had engaged the affections of a very

---

7. **Cyrus and Artaxerxes:** kings of Persia famous for their conquests. 8. **Sapor:** Shapur II (309–79), King of Persia. 9. **the cities . . . Mesopotamia:** destroyed by Shapur II in 359–60. Mesopotamia had been a Roman province.

10. **Arians:** a sect maintaining the subordination of Christ to God. 11. **Athanasians:** an anti-Arian sect maintaining the equality and paradoxical identity of Christ and God. 12. **the followers . . . Paulinus:** two groups that opposed each other vigorously over the Arian controversy.

numerous sect; and the removal of St. Babylas[13] excited an implacable opposition to the person of Julian. His subjects complained, with superstitious indignation, that famine had pursued the emperor's steps from Constantinople to Antioch: and the discontent of a hungry people was exasperated by the injudicious attempt to relieve their distress. The inclemency of the season had affected the harvests of Syria; and the price of bread, in the markets of Antioch, had naturally risen in proportion to the scarcity of corn. But the fair and reasonable proportion was soon violated by the rapacious arts of monopoly. In this unequal contest, in which the produce of the land is claimed by one party, as his exclusive property; is used by another as a lucrative object of trade; and is required by a third, for the daily and necessary support of life; all the profits of the intermediate agents are accumulated on the head of the defenceless consumers. The hardships of their situation were exaggerated and increased by their own impatience and anxiety; and the apprehension of a scarcity gradually produced the appearances of a famine. When the luxurious citizens of Antioch complained of the high price of poultry and fish, Julian publicly declared, that a frugal city ought to be satisfied with a regular supply of wine, oil, and bread; but he acknowledged that it was the duty of a sovereign to provide for the subsistence of his people. With this salutary view, the emperor ventured on a very dangerous and doubtful step, of fixing, by legal authority, the value of corn. He enacted, that in a time of scarcity, it should be sold at a price which had seldom been known in the most plentiful years; and that his own example might strengthen his laws, he sent into the market four hundred and twenty-two thousand *modii*, or measures, which were drawn, by his order, from the granaries of Hierapolis, of Chalcis, and even of Egypt. The consequences might have been foreseen, and were soon felt. The Imperial wheat was purchased by the rich merchants; the proprietors of land, or of corn, withheld from the city the accustomed supply; and the small quantities that appeared in the market, were secretly sold at an advanced and illegal price. Julian still continued to applaud his own policy, treated the complaints of the people as a vain and ungrateful murmur,

and convinced Antioch, that he had inherited the obstinacy, though not the cruelty, of his brother Gallus. The remonstrances of the municipal senate served only to exasperate his inflexible mind. He was persuaded, perhaps with truth, that the senators of Antioch who possessed lands, or were concerned in trade, had themselves contributed to the calamities of their country; and he imputed the disrespectful boldness which they assumed, to the sense, not of public duty, but of private interest. The whole body, consisting of two hundred of the most noble and wealthy citizens, were sent, under a guard, from the palace to the prison; and though they were permitted, before the close of evening, to return to their respective houses, the emperor himself could not obtain the forgiveness which he had so easily granted. The same grievances were still the subject of the same complaints, which were industriously circulated by the wit and levity of the Syrian Greeks. During the licentious days of the Saturnalia, the streets of the city resounded with insolent songs, which derided the laws, the religion, the personal conduct, and even the *beard* of the emperor; and the spirit of Antioch was manifested by the connivance of the magistrates, and the applause of the multitude. The disciple of Socrates was too deeply affected by these popular insults; but the monarch, endowed with quick sensibility and possessed of absolute power, refused his passions the gratification of revenge. A tyrant might have proscribed, without distinction, the lives and fortunes of the citizens of Antioch; and the unwarlike Syrians must have patiently submitted to the lust, the rapaciousness, and the cruelty of the faithful legions of Gaul. A milder sentence might have deprived the capital of the East of its honours and privileges; and the courtiers, perhaps the subjects, of Julian, would have applauded an act of justice, which asserted the dignity of the supreme magistrate of the republic. But instead of abusing, or exerting, the authority of the state, to revenge his personal injuries, Julian contented himself with an inoffensive mode of retaliation, which it would be in the power of few princes to employ. He had been insulted by satires and libels; in his turn he composed, under the title of the *Enemy of the Beard*, an ironical confession of his own faults, and a severe satire of the licentious and effeminate manners of Antioch. This Imperial reply was publicly exposed before the gates of the palace; and the MISOPOGON still remains a singular monument of the resentment, the wit, the humanity, and the indiscretion of Julian.

13. St. Babylas: Christian Bishop of Antioch, who died around 250. In 362 Julian ordered his remains removed from their resting place in the former Temple of Apollo at Daphne, which had been transformed into a Christian church.

Though he affected to laugh, he could not forgive. His contempt was expressed, and his revenge might be gratified, by the nomination of a governor[14] worthy only of such subjects: and the emperor, for ever renouncing the ungrateful city, proclaimed his resolution to pass the ensuing winter at Tarsus in Cilicia.

Yet Antioch possessed one citizen, whose genius and virtues might atone, in the opinion of Julian, for the vice and folly of his country. The sophist[15] Libanius was born in the capital of the East; he publicly professed the arts of rhetoric and declamation at Nice, Nicomedia, Constantinople, Athens, and, during the remainder of his life, at Antioch. His school was assiduously frequented by the Grecian youth; his disciples, who sometimes exceeded the number of eighty, celebrated their incomparable master; and the jealousy of his rivals, who persecuted him from one city to another, confirmed the favourable opinion which Libanius ostentatiously displayed of his superior merit. The præceptors of Julian had extorted a rash but solemn assurance, that he would never attend the lectures of their adversary: the curiosity of the royal youth was checked and inflamed: he secretly procured the writings of this dangerous sophist, and gradually surpassed, in the perfect imitation of his style, the most laborious of his domestic pupils. When Julian ascended the throne, he declared his impatience to embrace and reward the Syrian sophist, who had preserved, in a degenerate age, the Grecian purity of taste, of manners, and of religion. The emperor's prepossession was encreased and justified by the discreet pride of his favourite. Instead of pressing, with the foremost of the crowd, into the palace of Constantinople, Libanius calmly expected his arrival at Antioch; withdrew from court on the first symptoms of coldness and indifference; required a formal invitation for each visit; and taught his sovereign an important lesson, that he might command the obedience of a subject, but that he must deserve the attachment of a friend. The sophists of every age, despising, or affecting to despise, the accidental distinctions of birth and fortune, reserve their esteem for the superior qualities of the mind, with which they themselves are so plentifully endowed. Julian might disdain the acclamations of a venal court, who adored the Imperial purple; but he was deeply flattered by the praise, the admonition, the freedom,

and the envy of an independent philosopher, who refused his favours, loved his person, celebrated his fame, and protected his memory. The voluminous writings of Libanius still exist; for the most part, they are the vain and idle compositions of an orator, who cultivated the science of words; the productions of a recluse student, whose mind, regardless of his contemporaries, was incessantly fixed on the Trojan war, and the Athenian commonwealth. Yet the sophist of Antioch sometimes descended from this imaginary elevation; he entertained a various and elaborate correspondence; he praised the virtues of his own times; he boldly arraigned the abuses of public and private life; and he eloquently pleaded the cause of Antioch against the just resentment of Julian and Theodosius.[16] It is the common calamity of old age, to lose whatever might have rendered it desirable; but Libanius experienced the peculiar misfortune of surviving the religion and the sciences, to which he had consecrated his genius. The friend of Julian was an indignant spectator of the triumph of Christianity; and his bigotry, which darkened the prospect of the visible world, did not inspire Libanius with any lively hopes of celestial glory and happiness.

The martial impatience of Julian urged him to take the field in the beginning of the spring; and he dismissed, with contempt and reproach, the senate of Antioch, who accompanied the emperor beyond the limits of their own territory, to which he was resolved never to return. After a laborious march of two days, he halted on the third, at Berœa, or Aleppo, where he had the mortification of finding a senate almost entirely Christian; who received with cold and formal demonstrations of respect, the eloquent sermon of the apostle of Paganism. The son of one of the most illustrious citizens of Berœa, who had embraced, either from interest or conscience, the religion of the emperor, was disinherited by his angry parent. The father and the son were invited to the Imperial table. Julian, placing himself between them, attempted, without success, to inculcate the lesson and example of toleration; supported,[17] with affected calmness, the indiscreet zeal of the aged Christian, who seemed to forget the sentiments of nature, and the duty of a subject; and, at length turning towards the afflicted youth, "Since you have lost a father," said he, "for my

---

14. **governor:** Alexander of Heliopolis, known for his cruelty. 15. **sophist:** philosopher and teacher of the arts of oratory.

16. **Theodosius:** (c. 346–95), Roman general, emperor from 379; he punished severely the leaders of an antitaxation uprising (387) in Antioch. 17. **supported:** endured.

sake, it is incumbent on me to supply his place." The emperor was received in a manner much more agreeable to his wishes at Batnæ, a small town pleasantly seated in a grove of cypresses, about twenty miles from the city of Hierapolis. The solemn rites of sacrifice were decently prepared by the inhabitants of Batnæ, who seemed attached to the worship of their tutelar deities, Apollo and Jupiter; but the serious piety of Julian was offended by the tumult of their applause; and he too clearly discerned, that the smoke which arose from their altars was the incense of flattery, rather than of devotion. The ancient and magnificent temple, which had sanctified, for so many ages, the city of Hierapolis, no longer subsisted; and the consecrated wealth, which afforded a liberal maintenance to more than three hundred priests, might hasten its downfall. Yet Julian enjoyed the satisfaction of embracing a philosopher and a friend,[18] whose religious firmness had withstood the pressing and repeated solicitations of Constantius and Gallus, as often as those princes lodged at his house, in their passage through Hierapolis. In the hurry of military preparation, and the careless confidence of a familiar correspondence, the zeal of Julian appears to have been lively and uniform. He had now undertaken an important and difficult war; and the anxiety of the event rendered him still more attentive to observe and register the most trifling presages, from which, according to the rules of divination, any knowledge of futurity could be derived. He informed Libanius of his progress as far as Hierapolis, by an elegant epistle, which displays the facility of his genius, and his tender friendship for the sophist of Antioch.

Hierapolis, situate almost on the banks of the Euphrates, had been appointed for the general rendezvous of the Roman troops, who immediately passed the great river on a bridge of boats, which was previously constructed. If the inclinations of Julian had been similar to those of his predecessor, he might have wasted the active and important season of the year in the circus of Samosata, or in the churches of Edessa. But as the warlike emperor, instead of Constantius, had chosen Alexander for his model, he advanced without delay to Carrhæ, a very ancient city of Mesopotamia, at the distance of fourscore miles from Hierapolis. The temple of the Moon attracted the devotion of Julian; but the halt of a few days was

principally employed in completing the immense preparations of the Persian war. The secret of the expedition had hitherto remained in his own breast; but as Carrhæ is the point of separation of the two great roads, he could no longer conceal, whether it was his design to attack the dominions of Sapor on the side of the Tigris, or on that of the Euphrates. The emperor detached an army of thirty thousand men, under the command of his kinsman Procopius, and of Sebastian, who had been duke of Egypt. They were ordered to direct their march towards Nisibis, and to secure the frontier from the desultory incursions of the enemy, before they attempted the passage of the Tigris. Their subsequent operations were left to the discretion of the generals; but Julian expected, that after wasting with fire and sword the fertile districts of Media and Adiabene, they might arrive under the walls of Ctesiphon about the same time, that he himself, advancing with equal steps along the banks of the Euphrates, should besiege the capital of the Persian monarchy. The success of this well-concerted plan depended, in a great measure, on the powerful and ready assistance of the king of Armenia, who, without exposing the safety of his own dominions, might detach an army of four thousand horse, and twenty thousand foot, to the assistance of the Romans. But the feeble Arsaces Tiranus, king of Armenia, had degenerated still more shamefully than his father Chosroes, from the manly virtues of the great Tiridates;[19] and as the pusillanimous monarch was averse to any enterprize of danger and glory, he could disguise his timid indolence by the more decent excuses of religion and gratitude. He expressed a pious attachment to the memory of Constantius, from whose hands he had received in marriage Olympias, the daughter of the præfect[20] Ablavius; and the alliance of a female, who had been educated as the destined wife of the emperor Constans,[21] exalted the dignity of a Barbarian king. Tiranus professed the Christian religion; he reigned over a nation of Christians; and he was restrained, by every principle of conscience and interest, from contributing to the victory, which would consummate the ruin of the church. The alienated mind of Tiranus was exasperated by the indiscretion of Julian, who treated the king of Armenia

---

18. **a friend:** a man named Sopater, of whom nothing certain is known.

19. **the great Tiridates:** Tiridates III, King of Armenia from 259 to 314. 20. **præfect:** warden of the city of Rome, charged with maintaining order in the city and its environs. 21. **Constans:** emperor from 337 to 350.

as *his* slave, and as the enemy of the gods. The haughty and threatening style of the Imperial mandates awakened the secret indignation of a prince, who, in the humiliating state of dependence, was still conscious of his royal descent from the Arsacides,[22] the lords of the East, and the rivals of the Roman power.

The military dispositions of Julian were skilfully contrived to deceive the spies, and to divert the attention, of Sapor. The legions[23] appeared to direct their march towards Nisibis and the Tigris. On a sudden they wheeled to the right; traversed the level and naked plain of Carrhæ; and reached, on the third day, the banks of the Euphrates, where the strong town of Nicephorium, or Callinicum, had been founded by the Macedonian kings. From thence the emperor pursued his march, above ninety miles, along the winding stream of the Euphrates, till, at length, about one month after his departure from Antioch, he discovered the towers of Circesium, the extreme limit of the Roman dominions. The army of Julian, the most numerous that any of the Cæsars had ever led against Persia, consisted of sixty-five thousand effective and well-disciplined soldiers. The veteran bands of cavalry and infantry, of Romans and Barbarians, had been selected from the different provinces; and a just pre-eminence of loyalty and valour was claimed by the hardy Gauls, who guarded the throne and person of their beloved prince. A formidable body of Scythian auxiliaries had been transported from another climate, and almost from another world, to invade a distant country, of whose name and situation they were ignorant. The love of rapine and war allured to the Imperial standard several tribes of Saracens, or roving Arabs, whose service Julian had commanded, while he sternly refused the payment of the accustomed subsidies. The broad channel of the Euphrates was crowded by a fleet of eleven hundred ships, destined to attend the motions, and to satisfy the wants, of the Roman army. The military strength of the fleet was composed of fifty armed gallies; and these were accompanied by an equal number of flat-bottomed boats, which might occasionally be connected into the form of temporary bridges. The rest of the ships, partly constructed of timber, and partly covered with raw hides, were laden with an almost inexhaustible supply of arms and engines, of utensils and provisions. The

vigilant humanity of Julian had embarked a very large magazine of vinegar and biscuit for the use of the soldiers, but he prohibited the indulgence of wine; and rigorously stopped a long string of superfluous camels that attempted to follow the rear of the army. The river Chaboras falls into the Euphrates at Circesium; and as soon as the trumpet gave the signal of march, the Romans passed the little stream which separated two mighty and hostile empires. The custom of ancient discipline required a military oration; and Julian embraced every opportunity of displaying his eloquence. He animated the impatient and attentive legions by the example of the inflexible courage and glorious triumphs of their ancestors. He excited their resentment by a lively picture of the insolence of the Persians; and he exhorted them to imitate his firm resolution, either to extirpate that perfidious nation, or to devote[24] his life in the cause of the republic. The eloquence of Julian was enforced by a donative of one hundred and thirty pieces of silver to every soldier; and the bridge of the Chaboras was instantly cut away, to convince the troops that they must place their hopes of safety in the success of their arms. Yet the prudence of the emperor induced him to secure a remote frontier perpetually exposed to the inroads of the hostile Arabs. A detachment of four thousand men was left at Circesium, which completed, to the number of ten thousand, the regular garrison of that important fortress.

From the moment that the Romans entered the enemy's country, the country of an active and artful enemy, the order of march was disposed in three columns. The strength of the infantry, and consequently of the whole army, was placed in the centre, under the peculiar command of their master-general Victor. On the right, the brave Nevitta led a column of several legions along the banks of the Euphrates, and almost always in sight of the fleet. The left flank of the army was protected by the column of cavalry. Hormisdas and Arinthæus were appointed generals of the horse; and the singular adventures of Hormisdas are not undeserving of our notice. He was a Persian prince, of the royal race of the Sassanides, who, in the troubles of the minority of Sapor, had escaped from prison to the hospitable court of the great Constantine. Hormisdas, at first, excited the compassion, and, at length acquired the esteem, of his new masters; his valour and fidelity raised him to the military honours

22. the Arsacides: a dynasty of Persian monarchs. 23. legions: a Roman legion, or infantry brigade, consisted of between three thousand and six thousand men.

24. devote: sacrifice.

of the Roman service; and, though a Christian, he might indulge the secret satisfaction of convincing his ungrateful country, that an oppressed subject may prove the most dangerous enemy. Such was the disposition of the three principal columns. The front and flanks of the army were covered by Lucillianus with a flying detachment of fifteen hundred light-armed soldiers, whose active vigilance observed the most distant signs, and conveyed the earliest notice, of any hostile approach. Dagalaiphus, and Secundinus duke of Osrhoene, conducted the troops of the rear-guard; the baggage, securely, proceeded in the intervals of the columns; and the ranks, from a motive either of use or ostentation, were formed in such open order, that the whole line of march extended almost ten miles. The ordinary post of Julian was at the head of the centre column; but as he preferred the duties of a general to the state of a monarch, he rapidly moved, with a small escort of light cavalry, to the front, the rear, the flanks, wherever his presence could animate or protect the march of the Roman army. The country which they traversed from the Chaboras, to the cultivated lands of Assyria, may be considered as a part of the desert of Arabia, a dry and barren waste, which could never be improved by the most powerful arts of human industry. Julian marched over the same ground which had been trod above seven hundred years before by the footsteps of the younger Cyrus,[25] and which is described by one of the companions of his expedition, the sage and heroic Xenophon.[26] "The country was a plain throughout, as even as the sea, and full of wormwood; and if any other kind of shrubs or reeds grew there, they had all an aromatic smell; but no trees could be seen. Bustards and ostriches, antelopes and wild asses, appeared to be the only inhabitants of the desert; and the fatigues of the march were alleviated by the amusements of the chace." The loose sand of the desert was frequently raised by the wind into clouds of dust: and a great number of the soldiers of Julian, with their tents, were suddenly thrown to the ground by the violence of an unexpected hurricane.

The sandy plains of Mesopotamia were abandoned to the antelopes and wild asses of the desert; but a variety of populous towns and villages were pleasantly

situated on the banks of the Euphrates, and in the islands which are occasionally formed by that river. The city of Annah, or Anatho, the actual residence of an Arabian Emir,[27] is composed of two long streets, which inclose within a natural fortification, a small island in the midst, and two fruitful spots on either side, of the Euphrates. The warlike inhabitants of Anatho shewed a disposition to stop the march of a Roman emperor; till they were diverted from such fatal presumption by the mild exhortations of prince Hormisdas, and the approaching terrors of the fleet and army. They implored, and experienced, the clemency of Julian; who transplanted the people to an advantageous settlement, near Chalcis in Syria, and admitted Pusæus, the governor, to an honourable rank in his service and friendship. But the impregnable fortress of Thilutha could scorn the menace of a siege; and the emperor was obliged to content himself with an insulting promise, that when he had subdued the interior provinces of Persia, Thilutha would no longer refuse to grace the triumph of the conqueror. The inhabitants of the open towns, unable to resist, and unwilling to yield, fled with precipitation; and their houses, filled with spoil and provisions, were occupied by the soldiers of Julian, who massacred, without remorse, and without punishment, some defenceless women. During the march, the Surenas, or Persian general, and Malek Rodosaces, the renowned Emir of the tribe of Gassan, incessantly hovered round the army: every straggler was intercepted; every detachment was attacked; and the valiant Hormisdas escaped with some difficulty from their hands. But the Barbarians were finally repulsed: the country became every day less favourable to the operations of cavalry; and when the Romans arrived at Macepracta, they perceived the ruins of the wall, which had been constructed by the ancient kings of Assyria, to secure their dominions from the incursions of the Medes.[28] These preliminaries of the expedition of Julian appear to have employed about fifteen days; and we may compute near three hundred miles from the fortress of Circesium to the wall of Macepracta.

The fertile province of Assyria, which stretched beyond the Tigris, as far as the mountains of Media, extended about four hundred miles from the ancient wall of Macepracta to the territory of Basra, where the

25. **the younger Cyrus**: (*c.* 424–401 B.C.), Persian prince.
26. **Xenophon**: (*c.* 434–*c.* 355 B.C.), Greek historian; author of *Anabasis*, an account of Cyrus's military expedition (401 B.C.) against Artaxerxes II, King of Persia.

27. **Emir**: military commander. 28. **Medes**: the inhabitants, largely nomadic, of Media, a country to the northeast of Persia.

united streams of the Euphrates and Tigris discharge themselves into the Persian Gulf. The whole country might have claimed the peculiar name of Mesopotamia; as the two rivers, which are never more distant than fifty, approach, between Bagdad and Babylon, within twenty-five, miles of each other. A multitude of artificial canals, dug without much labour in a soft and yielding soil, connected the rivers, and intersected the plain, of Assyria. The uses of these artificial canals were various and important. They served to discharge the superfluous waters from one river into the other, at the season of their respective inundations. Subdividing themselves into smaller and smaller branches, they refreshed the dry lands, and supplied the deficiency of rain. They facilitated the intercourse of peace and commerce; and, as the dams could be speedily broke down, they armed the despair of the Assyrians with the means of opposing a sudden deluge to the progress of an invading army. To the soil and climate of Assyria, nature had denied some of her choicest gifts, the vine, the olive, and the fig-tree; but the food which supports the life of man, and particularly wheat and barley, were produced with inexhaustible fertility; and the husbandman, who committed his seed to the earth, was frequently rewarded with an encrease of two, or even of three, hundred. The face of the country was interspersed with groves of innumerable palm-trees;[29] and the diligent natives celebrated, either in verse or prose, the three hundred and sixty uses to which the trunk, the branches, the leaves, the juice, and the fruit, were skilfully applied. Several manufactures, especially those of leather and linen, employed the industry of a numerous people, and afforded valuable materials for foreign trade; which appears, however, to have been conducted by the hands of strangers. Babylon had been converted into a royal park; but near the ruins of the ancient capital, new cities had successively arisen, and the populousness of the country was displayed in the multitude of towns and villages, which were built of bricks, dried in the sun, and strongly cemented with bitumen; the natural and peculiar production of the Babylonian soil. While the successors of Cyrus reigned over Asia, the province of Assyria alone maintained, during a third part of the year, the luxurious plenty of the table and household of the Great King. Four

considerable villages were assigned for the subsistence of his Indian dogs; eight hundred stallions, and sixteen thousand mares, were constantly kept, at the expence of the country, for the royal stables: and as the daily tribute, which was paid to the satrap, amounted to one English bushel of silver, we may compute the annual revenue of Assyria at more than twelve hundred thousand pounds sterling.

The fields of Assyria were devoted by Julian to the calamities of war; and the philosopher retaliated on a guiltless people the acts of rapine and cruelty, which had been committed by their haughty master in the Roman provinces. The trembling Assyrians summoned the rivers to their assistance; and completed, with their own hands, the ruin of their country. The roads were rendered impracticable; a flood of waters was poured into the camp; and, during several days, the troops of Julian were obliged to contend with the most discouraging hardships. But every obstacle was surmounted by the perseverance of the legionaries, who were inured to toil as well as to danger, and who felt themselves animated by the spirit of their leader. The damage was gradually repaired; the waters were restored to their proper channels; whole groves of palm-trees were cut down, and placed along the broken parts of the road; and the army passed over the broad and deeper canals, on bridges of floating rafts which were supported by the help of bladders. Two cities of Assyria presumed to resist the arms of a Roman emperor: and they both paid the severe penalty of their rashness. At the distance of fifty miles from the royal residence of Ctesiphon, Perisabor, or Anbar, held the second rank in the province: a city, large, populous, and well fortified, surrounded with a double wall, almost encompassed by a branch of the Euphrates, and defended by the valour of a numerous garrison. The exhortations of Hormisdas were repulsed with contempt; and the ears of the Persian prince were wounded by a just reproach, that, unmindful of his royal birth, he conducted an army of strangers against his king and country. The Assyrians maintained their loyalty by a skilful, as well as vigorous, defence; till the lucky stroke of a battering-ram, having opened a large breach, by shattering one of the angles of the wall, they hastily retired into the fortifications of the interior citadel. The soldiers of Julian rushed impetuously into the town, and, after the full gratification of every military appetite, Perisabor was reduced to ashes; and the engines which assaulted the citadel were planted on the ruins of the

29. **palm-trees:** [Gibbon's note] The learned Kæmpfer, as a botanist, an antiquary, and a traveller, has exhausted the whole subject of palm-trees.

smoking houses. The contest was continued by an incessant and mutual discharge of missile weapons; and the superiority which the Romans might derive from the mechanical powers of their balistae and catapultae[30] was counterbalanced by the advantage of the ground on the side of the besieged. But as soon as an *Helepolis*[31] had been constructed, which could engage on equal terms with the loftiest ramparts; the tremendous aspect of a moving turret, that would leave no hope of resistance or of mercy, terrified the defenders of the citadel into an humble submission; and the place was surrendered only two days after Julian first appeared under the walls of Perisabor. Two thousand five hundred persons, of both sexes, the feeble remnant of a flourishing people, were permitted to retire: the plentiful magazines of corn, of arms, and of splendid furniture, were partly distributed among the troops, and partly reserved for the public service: the useless stores were destroyed by fire, or thrown into the stream of the Euphrates; and the fate of Amida[32] was revenged by the total ruin of Perisabor.

The city, or rather fortress, of Maogamalcha, which was defended by sixteen large towers, a deep ditch, and two strong and solid walls of brick and bitumen, appears to have been constructed at the distance of eleven miles, as the safeguard of the capital of Persia. The emperor, apprehensive of leaving such an important fortress in his rear, immediately formed the siege of Maogamalcha; and the Roman army was distributed, for that purpose, into three divisions. Victor, at the head of the cavalry, and of a detachment of heavy-armed foot, was ordered to clear the country, as far as the banks of the Tigris, and the suburbs of Ctesiphon. The conduct of the attack was assumed by Julian himself, who seemed to place his whole dependence in the military engines which he erected against the walls; while he secretly contrived a more efficacious method of introducing his troops into the heart of the city. Under the direction of Nevitta and Dagalaiphus, the trenches were opened at a considerable distance, and gradually prolonged as far as the edge of the ditch. The ditch was speedily filled with earth; and, by the incessant labour of the troops, a

mine was carried under the foundations of the walls, and sustained, at sufficient intervals, by props of timber. Three chosen cohorts, advancing in a single file, silently explored the dark and dangerous passage; till their intrepid leader whispered back the intelligence, that he was ready to issue from his confinement into the streets of the hostile city. Julian checked their ardour, that he might ensure their success; and immediately diverted the attention of the garrison, by the tumult and clamour of a general assault. The Persians, who, from their walls, contemptuously beheld the progress of an impotent attack, celebrated, with songs of triumph, the glory of Sapor; and ventured to assure the emperor, that he might ascend the starry mansion of Ormusd,[33] before he could hope to take the impregnable city of Maogamalcha. The city was already taken. History has recorded the name of a private soldier, the first who ascended from the mine into a deserted tower. The passage was widened by his companions, who pressed forwards with impatient valour. Fifteen hundred enemies were already in the midst of the city. The astonished garrison abandoned the walls, and their only hope of safety; the gates were instantly burst open; and the revenge of the soldier, unless it were suspended by lust or avarice, was satiated by an undistinguishing massacre. The governor who had yielded on a promise of mercy, was burnt alive, a few days afterwards, on a charge of having uttered some disrespectful words against the honour of Prince Hormisdas. The fortifications were razed to the ground; and not a vestige was left, that the city of Maogamalcha had ever existed. The neighbourhood of the capital of Persia was adorned with three stately palaces, laboriously enriched with every production that could gratify the luxury and pride of an Eastern monarch. The pleasant situation of the gardens along the banks of the Tigris, was improved, according to the Persian taste, by the symmetry of flowers, fountains, and shady walks: and spacious parks were inclosed for the reception of the bears, lions, and wild boars, which were maintained at a considerable expence for the pleasure of the royal chace. The park-walls were broke down, the savage game was abandoned to the darts of the soldiers, and the palaces of Sapor were reduced to ashes, by the command of the Roman emperor. Julian, on this occasion, shewed himself ignorant, or careless, of the laws of civility,

30. **balistae and catapultae:** military machines for propelling stones, javelins, and other missiles. **31. Helepolis:** (Greek, "taker of cities") a four-wheeled wooden tower used as a siege engine; it was pushed near the city walls, and missiles were discharged from it. **32. Amida:** one of the Mesopotamian cities captured by Shapur II.

33. **Ormusd:** (Ormazd) the primary Persian deity, the lord of goodness and light; his "mansion" was the heavens.

which the prudence and refinement of polished ages have established between hostile princes. Yet these wanton ravages need not excite in our breasts any vehement emotions of pity or resentment. A simple, naked, statue, finished by the hand of a Grecian artist, is of more genuine value than all these rude and costly monuments of Barbaric labour: and, if we are more deeply affected by the ruin of a palace, than by the conflagration of a cottage, our humanity must have formed a very erroneous estimate of the miseries of human life.

Julian was an object of terror and hatred to the Persians: and the painters of that nation represented the invader of their country under the emblem of a furious lion, who vomited from his mouth a consuming fire. To his friends and soldiers, the philosophic hero appeared in a more amiable light; and his virtues were never more conspicuously displayed, than in the last, and most active, period of his life. He practised, without effort, and almost without merit, the habitual qualities of temperance and sobriety. According to the dictates of that artificial wisdom, which assumes an absolute dominion over the mind and body, he sternly refused himself the indulgence of the most natural appetites.[34] In the warm climate of Assyria, which solicited a luxurious people to the gratification of every sensual desire, a youthful conqueror preserved his chastity pure and inviolate: nor was Julian ever tempted, even by a motive of curiosity, to visit his female captives of exquisite beauty, who, instead of resisting his power, would have disputed with each other the honour of his embraces. With the same firmness that he resisted the allurements of love, he sustained the hardships of war. When the Romans marched through the flat and flooded country, their sovereign, on foot, at the head of his legions, shared their fatigues, and animated their diligence. In every useful labour, the hand of Julian was prompt and strenuous; and the Imperial purple was wet and dirty, as the coarse garment of the meanest soldier. The two sieges allowed him some remarkable opportunities of signalising his personal valour, which, in the improved state of the military art, can seldom be exerted by a prudent general. The emperor stood before the citadel of Perisabor, insensible of his extreme danger, and encouraged his troops to burst open the gates of iron,

till he was almost overwhelmed under a cloud of missile weapons, and huge stones, that were directed against his person. As he examined the exterior fortifications of Maogamalcha, two Persians, devoting themselves for their country, suddenly rushed upon him with drawn scimitars: the emperor dexterously received their blows on his uplifted shield; and, with a steady and well-aimed thrust, laid one of his adversaries dead at his feet. The esteem of a prince who possesses the virtues which he approves, is the noblest recompence of a deserving subject; and the authority which Julian derived from his personal merit, enabled him to revive and enforce the rigour of ancient discipline. He punished with death, or ignominy, the misbehaviour of three troops of horse, who, in a skirmish with the Surenas, had lost their honour, and one of their standards: and he distinguished with *obsidional* crowns[35] the valour of the foremost soldiers, who had ascended into the city of Maogamalcha. After the siege of Perisabor, the firmness of the emperor was exercised by the insolent avarice of the army, who loudly complained, that their services were rewarded by a trifling donative of one hundred pieces of silver. His just indignation was expressed in the grave and manly language of a Roman. "Riches are the object of your desires? those riches are in the hands of the Persians; and the spoils of this fruitful country are proposed as the prize of your valour and discipline. Believe me," added Julian, "the Roman republic, which formerly possessed such immense treasures, is now reduced to want and wretchedness; since our princes have been persuaded, by weak and interested ministers, to purchase with gold the tranquillity of the Barbarians. The revenue is exhausted; the cities are ruined; the provinces are dispeopled. For myself, the only inheritance that I have received from my royal ancestors, is a soul incapable of fear; and as long as I am convinced that every real advantage is seated in the mind, I shall not blush to acknowledge an honourable poverty, which, in the days of ancient virtue, was considered as the glory of Fabricius.[36] That glory, and that virtue, may be your own, if you will listen to the voice of Heaven, and of your leader. But if you will rashly persist, if you are determined to renew the

---

34. **he . . . appetites:** [Gibbon's note] The famous examples of Cyrus, Alexander, and Scipio, were acts of justice. Julian's chastity was voluntary, and, in his opinion, meritorious.

35. **obsidional crowns:** the highest Roman military honor; this kind of crown, usually made of grass or flowers, was customarily awarded to the general of an army that had relieved a besieged city. 36. **Fabricius:** Roman general, consul in the third century B.C.; he was traditionally held to be a model of austerity, poverty, and incorruptible virtue.

shameful and mischievous examples of old seditions, proceed—As it becomes an emperor who has filled the first rank among men, I am prepared to die, standing; and to despise a precarious life, which, every hour, may depend on an accidental fever. If I have been found unworthy of the command, there are now among you (I speak it with pride and pleasure), there are many chiefs, whose merit and experience are equal to the conduct of the most important war. Such has been the temper of my reign, that I can retire, without regret, and without apprehension, to the obscurity of a private station." The modest resolution of Julian was answered by the unanimous applause and cheerful obedience of the Romans; who declared their confidence of victory, while they fought under the banners of their heroic prince. Their courage was kindled by his frequent and familiar asseverations (for such wishes were the oaths of Julian), "So may I reduce the Persians under the yoke!" "Thus may I restore the strength and splendour of the republic!" The love of fame was the ardent passion of his soul: but it was not before he trampled on the ruins of Maogamalcha, that he allowed himself to say, "We have now provided some materials for the sophist of Antioch."

The successful valour of Julian had triumphed over all the obstacles that opposed his march to the gates of Ctesiphon. But the reduction, or even the siege, of the capital of Persia, was still at a distance: nor can the military conduct of the emperor be clearly apprehended, without a knowledge of the country which was the theatre of his bold and skilful operations. Twenty miles to the south of Bagdad, and on the eastern bank of the Tigris, the curiosity of travellers has observed some ruins of the palaces of Ctesiphon, which, in the time of Julian, was a great and populous city. The name and glory of the adjacent Seleucia were for ever extinguished; and the only remaining quarter of that Greek colony had resumed, with the Assyrian language and manners, the primitive appellation of Coche. Coche was situate on the western side of the Tigris; but it was naturally considered as a suburb of Ctesiphon, with which we may suppose it to have been connected by a permanent bridge of boats. The united parts contributed to form the common epithet of Al Modain, THE CITIES, which the Orientals have bestowed on the winter residence of the Sassanides; and the whole circumference of the Persian capital was strongly fortified by the waters of the river, by lofty walls, and by impracticable morasses. Near the ruins of Seleucia, the camp of Julian was fixed; and secured,

by a ditch and rampart, against the sallies of the numerous and enterprising garrison of Coche. In this fruitful and pleasant country, the Romans were plentifully supplied with water and forage: and several forts, which might have embarrassed the motions of the army, submitted, after some resistance, to the efforts of their valour. The fleet passed from the Euphrates into an artificial derivation of that river, which pours a copious and navigable stream into the Tigris at a small distance *below* the great city. If they had followed this royal canal, which bore the name of Nahar-Malcha, the intermediate situation of Coche would have separated the fleet and army of Julian; and the rash attempt of steering against the current of the Tigris, and forcing their way through the midst of a hostile capital, must have been attended with the total destruction of the Roman navy. The prudence of the emperor foresaw the danger, and provided the remedy. As he had minutely studied the operations of Trajan in the same country, he soon recollected, that his warlike predecessor had dug a new and navigable canal, which, leaving Coche on the right-hand, conveyed the waters of the Nahar-Malcha into the river Tigris, at some distance *above* the cities. From the information of the peasants, Julian ascertained the vestiges of this ancient work, which were almost obliterated by design or accident. By the indefatigable labour of the soldiers, a broad and deep channel was speedily prepared for the reception of the Euphrates. A strong dike was constructed to interrupt the ordinary current of the Nahar-Malcha: a flood of waters rushed impetuously into their new bed; and the Roman fleet, steering their triumphant course into the Tigris, derided the vain and ineffectual barriers which the Persians of Ctesiphon had erected to oppose their passage.

As it became necessary to transport the Roman army over the Tigris, another labour presented itself, of less toil, but of more danger, than the preceding expedition. The stream was broad and rapid; the ascent steep and difficult; and the intrenchments which had been formed on the ridge of the opposite bank, were lined with a numerous army of heavy cuirassiers,[37] dexterous archers, and huge elephants; who (according to the extravagant hyperbole of Libanius) could trample, with the same ease, a field of corn, or a legion of Romans.[38] In the presence of such an enemy, the

---

37. cuirassiers: armored cavalry. **38. who . . . Romans:** [Gibbon's note] Rien n'est beau que le vrai [Only what is true is beautiful]; a maxim which should be inscribed on the desk of every rhetorician.

construction of a bridge was impracticable; and the intrepid prince, who instantly seized the only possible expedient, concealed his design, till the moment of execution, from the knowledge of the Barbarians, of his own troops, and even of his generals themselves. Under the specious pretence of examining the state of the magazines, fourscore vessels were gradually unladen; and a select detachment, apparently destined for some secret expedition, was ordered to stand to their arms on the first signal. Julian disguised the silent anxiety of his own mind with smiles of confidence and joy; and amused the hostile nations with the spectacle of military games, which he insultingly celebrated under the walls of Coche. The day was consecrated to pleasure; but, as soon as the hour of supper was past, the emperor summoned the generals to his tent; and acquainted them, that he had fixed that night for the passage of the Tigris. They stood in silent and respectful astonishment; but, when the venerable Sallust[39] assumed the privilege of his age and experience, the rest of the chiefs supported with freedom the weight of his prudent remonstrances. Julian contented himself with observing, that conquest and safety depended on the attempt; that, instead of diminishing, the number of their enemies would be increased, by successive reinforcements; and that a longer delay would neither contract the breadth of the stream, nor level the height of the bank. The signal was instantly given, and obeyed: the most impatient of the legionaries leaped into five vessels that lay nearest to the bank; and, as they plied their oars with intrepid diligence, they were lost, after a few moments, in the darkness of the night. A flame arose on the opposite side; and Julian, who too clearly understood that his foremost vessels, in attempting to land, had been fired by the enemy, dexterously converted their extreme danger into a presage of victory. "Our fellow-soldiers," he eagerly exclaimed, "are already masters of the bank; see—they make the appointed signal: let us hasten to emulate and assist their courage." The united and rapid motion of a great fleet broke the violence of the current, and they reached the eastern shore of the Tigris with sufficient speed to extinguish the flames, and rescue their adventurous companions. The difficulties of a steep and lofty ascent were increased by the weight of armour, and the darkness of the night. A shower of stones, darts, and fire, was incessantly discharged on the heads of the assailants; who, after an arduous struggle, climbed the bank, and stood victorious upon the rampart. As soon as they possessed a more equal field, Julian, who, with his light-infantry, had led the attack, darted through the ranks a skilful and experienced eye: his bravest soldiers, according to the precepts of Homer, were distributed in the front and rear; and all the trumpets of the Imperial army sounded to battle. The Romans, after sending up a military shout, advanced in measured steps to the animating notes of martial music; launched their formidable javelins; and rushed forwards with drawn swords, to deprive the Barbarians, by a closer onset, of the advantage of their missile weapons. The whole engagement lasted above twelve hours; till the gradual retreat of the Persians was changed into a disorderly flight, of which the shameful example was given by the principal leaders, and the Surenas himself. They were pursued to the gates of Ctesiphon; and the conquerors might have entered the dismayed city, if their general Victor, who was dangerously wounded with an arrow, had not conjured them to desist from a rash attempt, which must be fatal, if it were not successful. On *their* side, the Romans acknowledged the loss of only seventy-five men; while they affirmed, that the Barbarians had left on the field of battle two thousand five hundred, or even six thousand, of their bravest soldiers. The spoil was such as might be expected from the riches and luxury of an Oriental camp; large quantities of silver and gold, splendid arms and trappings, and beds and tables of massy silver. The victorious emperor distributed, as the rewards of valour, some honourable gifts, civic, and mural, and naval, crowns;[40] which he, and perhaps he alone, esteemed more precious than the wealth of Asia. A solemn sacrifice was offered to the god of war, but the appearances of the victims[41] threatened the most inauspicious events; and Julian soon discovered, by less ambiguous signs, that he had now reached the term of his prosperity.

On the second day after the battle, the domestic guards, the Jovians and Herculians, and the remaining

---

39. **Sallust:** commander (pretorian prefect) of Julian's troop of personal bodyguards.

40. **civic . . . crowns:** Made of flowers, leaves, or metal, these were awarded for specific traditional heroic actions: the civic crown was given to a soldier who, in battle, saved the life of a Roman citizen; the mural crown, to the first soldier to enter the walls of an enemy city; and the naval crown, to the first sailor to board an enemy ship. 41. **victims:** sacrificial birds and animals. The condition of their entrails was thought by the devout to indicate the course of future events.

troops, which composed near two-thirds of the whole army, were securely wafted over the Tigris. While the Persians beheld from the walls of Ctesiphon the desolation of the adjacent country, Julian cast many an anxious look towards the North, in full expectation, that as he himself had victoriously penetrated to the capital of Sapor, the march and junction of his lieutenants, Sebastian and Procopius, would be executed with the same courage and diligence. His expectations were disappointed by the treachery of the Armenian king, who permitted, and most probably directed, the desertion of his auxiliary troops from the camp of the Romans; and by the dissentions of the two generals, who were incapable of forming or executing any plan for the public service. When the emperor had relinquished the hope of this important reinforcement, he condescended to hold a council of war, and approved, after a full debate, the sentiment of those generals, who dissuaded the siege of Ctesiphon, as a fruitless and pernicious undertaking. It is not easy for us to conceive, by what arts of fortification, a city thrice besieged and taken by the predecessors of Julian, could be rendered impregnable against an army of sixty thousand Romans, commanded by a brave and experienced general, and abundantly supplied with ships, provisions, battering engines, and military stores. But we may rest assured, from the love of glory, and contempt of danger, which formed the character of Julian, that he was not discouraged by any trivial or imaginary obstacles. At the very time when he declined the siege of Ctesiphon, he rejected, with obstinacy and disdain, the most flattering offers of a negociation of peace. Sapor, who had been so long accustomed to the tardy ostentation of Constantius, was surprised by the intrepid diligence of his successor. As far as the confines of India and Scythia, the satraps of the distant provinces were ordered to assemble their troops, and to march, without delay, to the assistance of their monarch. But their preparations were dilatory, their motions slow; and before Sapor could lead an army into the field, he received the melancholy intelligence of the devastation of Assyria, the ruin of his palaces, and the slaughter of his bravest troops, who defended the passage of the Tigris. The pride of royalty was humbled in the dust; he took his repasts on the ground; and the disorder of his hair expressed the grief and anxiety of his mind. Perhaps he would not have refused to purchase, with one half of his kingdom, the safety of the remainder; and he would have gladly subscribed himself, in a treaty of peace,

the faithful and dependent ally of the Roman conqueror. Under the pretence of private business, a minister of rank and confidence was secretly despatched to embrace the knees of Hormisdas, and to request, in the language of a suppliant, that he might be introduced into the presence of the emperor. The Sassanian prince, whether he listened to the voice of pride or humanity, whether he consulted the sentiments of his birth, or the duties of his situation, was equally inclined to promote a salutary measure, which would terminate the calamities of Persia, and secure the triumph of Rome. He was astonished by the inflexible firmness of a hero, who remembered, most unfortunately for himself, and for his country, that Alexander had uniformly rejected the propositions of Darius.[42] But as Julian was sensible, that the hope of a safe and honourable peace might cool the ardour of his troops; he earnestly requested, that Hormisdas would privately dismiss the minister of Sapor, and conceal this dangerous temptation from the knowledge of the camp.

The honour, as well as interest, of Julian, forbade him to consume his time under the impregnable walls of Ctesiphon; and as often as he defied the Barbarians, who defended the city, to meet him on the open plain, they prudently replied, that if he desired to exercise his valour, he might seek the army of the Great King. He felt the insult, and he accepted the advice. Instead of confining his servile march to the banks of the Euphrates and Tigris, he resolved to imitate the adventurous spirit of Alexander, and boldly to advance into the inland provinces, till he forced his rival to contend with him, perhaps in the plains of Arbela, for the empire of Asia. The magnanimity of Julian was applauded and betrayed, by the arts of a noble Persian, who, in the cause of his country, had generously submitted to act a part full of danger, of falsehood, and of shame. With a train of faithful followers he deserted to the Imperial camp; exposed, in a specious tale, the injuries which he had sustained; exaggerated the cruelty of Sapor, the discontent of the people, and the weakness of the monarchy, and confidently offered himself as the hostage and guide of the Roman march. The most rational grounds of suspicion were urged, without effect, by the wisdom and experience of Hormisdas; and the credulous Julian, receiving the traitor into his bosom, was persuaded to issue an hasty

---

42. Darius: Darius III (*c.* 380–330 B.C.), King of Persia during the invasion led by Alexander the Great.

order, which, in the opinion of mankind, appeared to arraign his prudence, and to endanger his safety. He destroyed, in a single hour, the whole navy, which had been transported above five hundred miles, at so great an expence of toil, of treasure, and of blood. Twelve, or, at the most, twenty-two, small vessels were saved, to accompany, on carriages, the march of the army, and to form occasional bridges for the passage of the rivers. A supply of twenty days provisions was reserved for the use of the soldiers; and the rest of the magazines, with a fleet of eleven hundred vessels, which rode at anchor in the Tigris, were abandoned to the flames, by the absolute command of the emperor. The Christian bishops, Gregory and Augustin, insult[43] the madness of the apostate, who executed, with his own hands, the sentence of divine justice. Their authority, of less weight, perhaps, in a military question, is confirmed by the cool judgment of an experienced soldier, who was himself spectator of the conflagration, and who could not disapprove the reluctant murmurs of the troops. Yet there are not wanting some specious, and perhaps solid, reasons, which might justify the resolution of Julian. The navigation of the Euphrates never ascended above Babylon, nor that of the Tigris above Opis. The distance of the last-mentioned city from the Roman camp was not very considerable; and Julian must soon have renounced the vain and impracticable attempt of forcing upwards a great fleet against the stream of a rapid river, which in several places was embarrassed[44] by natural or artificial cataracts. The power of sails and oars was insufficient; it became necessary to tow the ships against the current of the river; the strength of twenty thousand soldiers was exhausted in this tedious and servile labour; and if the Romans continued to march along the banks of the Tigris, they could only expect to return home without atchieving any enterprize worthy of the genius or fortune of their leader. If, on the contrary, it was adviseable to advance into the inland country, the destruction of the fleet and magazines was the only measure which could save that valuable prize from the hands of the numerous and active troops which might suddenly be poured from the gates of Ctesiphon. Had the arms of Julian been victorious, we should now admire the conduct, as well as the courage, of a hero, who, by depriving his soldiers of the hopes of a retreat, left them only the alternative of death or conquest.

43. **insult:** attack insolently. 44. **embarrassed:** obstructed.

The cumbersome train of artillery and waggons, which retards the operations of a modern army, were in a great measure unknown in the camps of the Romans. Yet, in every age, the subsistence of sixty thousand men must have been one of the most important cares of a prudent general; and that subsistence could only be drawn from his own or from the enemy's country. Had it been possible for Julian to maintain a bridge of communication on the Tigris, and to preserve the conquered places of Assyria, a desolated province could not afford any large or regular supplies, in a season of the year when the lands were covered by the inundation of the Euphrates, and the unwholesome air was darkened with swarms of innumerable insects. The appearance of the hostile country was far more inviting. The extensive region that lies between the river Tigris and the mountains of Media, was filled with villages and towns; and the fertile soil, for the most part, was in a very improved state of cultivation. Julian might expect, that a conqueror, who possessed the two forcible instruments of persuasion, steel and gold, would easily procure a plentiful subsistence from the fears or avarice of the natives. But, on the approach of the Romans, this rich and smiling prospect was instantly blasted. Wherever they moved, the inhabitants deserted the open villages, and took shelter in the fortified towns; the cattle was driven away; the grass and ripe corn were consumed with fire; and, as soon as the flames had subsided which interrupted the march of Julian, he beheld the melancholy face of a smoking and naked desert. This desperate but effectual method of defence, can only be executed by the enthusiasm of a people who prefer their independence to their property; or by the rigour of an arbitrary government, which consults the public safety without submitting to their inclinations the liberty of choice. On the present occasion, the zeal and obedience of the Persians seconded the commands of Sapor; and the emperor was soon reduced to the scanty stock of provisions, which continually wasted in his hands. Before they were entirely consumed, he might still have reached the wealthy and unwarlike cities of Ecbatana, or Susa, by the effort of a rapid and well-directed march; but he was deprived of this last resource by his ignorance of the roads, and by the perfidy of his guides. The Romans wandered several days in the country to the eastward of Bagdad: the Persian deserter, who had artfully led them into the snare, escaped from their resentment; and his followers, as soon as they were put to the torture, confessed the secret of the conspiracy. The visionary conquests of Hyrcania and India, which had so long amused, now tormented, the mind of Julian. Conscious that his own imprudence was the cause of the public distress, he anxiously balanced the hopes of safety or success, without obtaining a satisfactory answer either from gods or men. At length, as the only practicable measure, he embraced the resolution of directing his steps towards the banks of the Tigris, with the design of saving the army by a hasty march to the confines of Corduene; a fertile and friendly province, which acknowledged the sovereignty of Rome. The desponding troops obeyed the signal of the retreat, only seventy days after they had passed the Chaboras, with the sanguine expectation of subverting the throne of Persia.

As long as the Romans seemed to advance into the country, their march was observed and insulted from a distance, by several bodies of Persian cavalry; who shewing themselves, sometimes in loose, and sometimes in closer, order, faintly skirmished with the advanced guards. These detachments were, however, supported by a much greater force; and the heads of the columns were no sooner pointed towards the Tigris, than a cloud of dust arose on the plain. The Romans, who now aspired only to the permission of a safe and speedy retreat, endeavoured to persuade themselves, that this formidable appearance was occasioned by a troop of wild asses, or perhaps by the approach of some friendly Arabs. They halted, pitched their tents, fortified their camp, passed the whole night in continual alarms; and discovered, at the dawn of day, that they were surrounded by an army of Persians. This army, which might be considered only as the van of the Barbarians, was soon followed by the main body of cuirassiers, archers, and elephants, commanded by Meranes, a general of rank and reputation. He was accompanied by two of the king's sons, and many of the principal satraps; and fame[45] and expectation exaggerated the strength of the remaining powers, which slowly advanced under the conduct of Sapor himself. As the Romans continued their march, their long array, which was forced to bend or divide, according to the varieties of the ground, afforded frequent and favourable opportunities to their vigilant enemies. The Persians repeatedly charged with fury; they were repeatedly repulsed with firmness; and the action at Maronga, which almost deserved the name

of a battle, was marked by a considerable loss of satraps and elephants, perhaps of equal value in the eyes of their monarch. These splendid advantages were not obtained without an adequate[46] slaughter on the side of the Romans: several officers of distinction were either killed or wounded; and the emperor himself, who, on all occasions of danger, inspired and guided the valour of his troops, was obliged to expose his person, and exert his abilities. The weight of offensive and defensive arms, which still constituted the strength and safety of the Romans, disabled them from making any long or effectual pursuit; and as the horsemen of the East were trained to dart their javelins, and shoot their arrows, at full speed, and in every possible direction, the cavalry of Persia was never more formidable than in the moment of a rapid and disorderly flight. But the most certain and irreparable loss of the Romans, was that of time. The hardy veterans, accustomed to the cold climate of Gaul and Germany, fainted under the sultry heat of an Assyrian summer; their vigour was exhausted by the incessant repetition of march and combat; and the progress of the army was suspended by the precautions of a slow and dangerous retreat, in the presence of an active enemy. Every day, every hour, as the supply diminished, the value and price of subsistence increased in the Roman camp. Julian, who always contented himself with such food as a hungry soldier would have disdained, distributed, for the use of the troops, the provisions of the Imperial household, and whatever could be spared from the sumpter-horses[47] of the tribunes and generals. But this feeble relief served only to aggravate the sense of the public distress; and the Romans began to entertain the most gloomy apprehensions, that before they could reach the frontiers of the empire, they should all perish, either by famine, or by the sword of the Barbarians.

While Julian struggled with the almost insuperable difficulties of his situation, the silent hours of the night were still devoted to study and contemplation. Whenever he closed his eyes in short and interrupted slumbers, his mind was agitated with painful anxiety; nor can it be thought surprising, that the Genius of the empire should once more[48] appear before him, covering with a funeral veil, his head, and his horn of abundance, and slowly retiring from the Imperial

45. **fame:** rumor.

46. **adequate:** equal. 47. **sumpter-horses:** pack horses. 48. **once more:** According to Julian, the "Genius," or spirit, of the Empire had appeared before him also in 361, just before his assumption of the office of emperor.

tent. The monarch started from his couch, and stepping forth, to refresh his wearied spirits with the coolness of the midnight air, he beheld a fiery meteor, which shot athwart the sky, and suddenly vanished. Julian was convinced that he had seen the menacing countenance of the god of war; the council which he summoned, of Tuscan Haruspices,[49] unanimously pronounced that he should abstain from action: but on this occasion, necessity and reason were more prevalent than superstition; and the trumpets sounded at the break of day. The army marched through a hilly country; and the hills had been secretly occupied by the Persians. Julian led the van, with the skill and attention of a consummate general; he was alarmed by the intelligence that his rear was suddenly attacked. The heat of the weather had tempted him to lay aside his cuirass;[50] but he snatched a shield from one of his attendants, and hastened, with a sufficient reinforcement, to the relief of the rear-guard. A similar danger recalled the intrepid prince to the defence of the front; and, as he galloped between the columns, the centre of the left was attacked, and almost overpowered, by a furious charge of the Persian cavalry and elephants. This huge body was soon defeated, by the well-timed evolution of the light-infantry, who aimed their weapons, with dexterity and effect, against the backs of the horsemen, and the legs of the elephants. The Barbarians fled; and Julian, who was foremost in every danger, animated the pursuit with his voice and gestures. His trembling guards, scattered and oppressed by the disorderly throng of friends and enemies, reminded their fearless sovereign that he was without armour; and conjured him to decline the fall of the impending ruin. As they exclaimed, a cloud of darts and arrows was discharged from the flying squadrons; and a javelin, after razing the skin of his arm, transpierced the ribs, and fixed in the inferior part of the liver. Julian attempted to draw the deadly weapon from his side; but his fingers were cut by the sharpness of the steel, and he fell senseless from his horse. His guards flew to his relief; and the wounded emperor was gently raised from the ground, and conveyed out of the tumult of the battle into an adjacent tent. The report of the melancholy event passed from rank to rank; but the grief of the Romans inspired them with invincible valour, and the desire of revenge. The bloody and obstinate conflict was

maintained by the two armies till they were separated by the total darkness of the night. The Persians derived some honour from the advantage which they obtained against the left wing, where Anatolius, master of the offices,[51] was slain, and the præfect Sallust very narrowly escaped. But the event of the day was adverse to the Barbarians. They abandoned the field; their two generals, Meranes, and Nohordates,[52] fifty nobles or satraps, and a multitude of their bravest soldiers: and the success of the Romans, if Julian had survived, might have been improved into a decisive and useful victory.

The first words that Julian uttered, after his recovery from the fainting fit, into which he had been thrown by loss of blood, were expressive of his martial spirit. He called for his horse and arms, and was impatient to rush into the battle. His remaining strength was exhausted by the painful effort; and the surgeons, who examined his wound, discovered the symptoms of approaching death. He employed the awful moments with the firm temper of a hero and a sage; the philosophers who had accompanied him in this fatal expedition, compared the tent of Julian with the prison of Socrates;[53] and the spectators, whom duty, or friendship, or curiosity, had assembled round his couch, listened with respectful grief to the funeral oration of their dying emperor. "Friends and fellow-soldiers, the seasonable period of my departure is now arrived, and I discharge, with the cheerfulness of a ready debtor, the demands of nature. I have learned from philosophy, how much the soul is more excellent than the body; and that the separation of the nobler substance, should be the subject of joy, rather than of affliction. I have learned from religion, that an early death has often been the reward of piety; and I accept, as a favour of the gods, the mortal stroke, that secures me from the danger of disgracing a character, which has hitherto been supported by virtue and fortitude. I die without remorse, as I have lived without guilt. I am pleased to reflect on the innocence of my private

49. **Haruspices:** priests who specialized in the prediction of the future through the interpretation of omens. 50. **cuirass:** metal breastplate.

51. **master . . . offices:** chief of court protocol, especially that pertaining to the introduction to the emperor of visitors and petitioners. 52. **Nohordates:** [Gibbon's note] Sapor himself declared to the Romans, that it was his practice, to comfort the families of his deceased satraps, by sending them, as a present, the heads of the guards and officers who had not fallen by their master's side. 53. **the prison . . . Socrates:** According to Plato's *Phaedo*, Socrates spent the moments before his death in prison (399 B.C.) calmly discussing questions of metaphysics with his disciples.

life; and I can affirm with confidence, that the supreme authority, that emanation of the Divine Power, has been preserved in my hands pure and immaculate. Detesting the corrupt and destructive maxims of despotism, I have considered the happiness of the people as the end of government. Submitting my actions to the laws of prudence, of justice, and of moderation, I have trusted the event to the care of Providence. Peace was the object of my counsels, as long as peace was consistent with the public welfare; but when the imperious voice of my country summoned me to arms, I exposed my person to the dangers of war, with the clear fore-knowledge (which I had acquired from the art of divination) that I was destined to fall by the sword. I now offer my tribute of gratitude to the Eternal Being, who has not suffered me to perish by the cruelty of a tyrant, by the secret dagger of conspiracy, or by the slow tortures of lingering disease. He has given me, in the midst of an honourable career, a splendid and glorious departure from this world; and I hold it equally absurd, equally base, to solicit, or to decline, the stroke of fate.—Thus much I have attempted to say; but my strength fails me, and I feel the approach of death.—I shall cautiously refrain from any word that may tend to influence your suffrages in the election of an emperor. My choice might be imprudent, or injudicious; and if it should not be ratified by the consent of the army, it might be fatal to the person whom I should recommend. I shall only, as a good citizen, express my hopes, that the Romans may be blessed with the government of a virtuous sovereign." After this discourse, which Julian pronounced in a firm and gentle tone of voice, he distributed, by a military testament, the remains of his private fortune; and making some enquiry why Anatolius was not present, he understood, from the answer of Sallust, that Anatolius was killed; and bewailed, with amiable inconsistency, the loss of his friend. At the same time he reproved the immoderate grief of the spectators; and conjured them not to disgrace, by unmanly tears, the fate of a prince, who in a few moments would be united with heaven, and with the stars. The spectators were silent; and Julian entered into a metaphysical argument with the philosophers Priscus and Maximus, on the nature of the soul. The efforts which he made, of mind, as well as body, most probably hastened his death. His wound began to bleed with fresh violence; his respiration was embarrassed by the swelling of the veins: he called for a draught of cold water, and, as soon as he had drank

it, expired without pain, about the hour of midnight. Such was the end of that extraordinary man, in the thirty-second year of his age, after a reign of one year and about eight months, from the death of Constantius. In his last moments he displayed, perhaps with some ostentation, the love of virtue and of fame, which had been the ruling passions of his life.[54]

. . .

PREFACE
[TO THE FOURTH VOLUME]

Gibbon brought his *History* to a close by the simultaneous publication, in 1788, of the fourth, fifth, and sixth volumes. In his *Memoirs* (1796) he confesses to mixed emotions upon his completion in Lausanne of the lonely and arduous task to which he had devoted his life:

> It was on the day, or rather night, of the 27th of June, 1787, between the hours of eleven and twelve, that I wrote the last lines of the last page, in a summer-house in my garden. After laying down my pen, I took several turns in a *berceau*, or covered walk of acacias, which commands a prospect of the country, the lake, and the mountains. The air was temperate, the sky was serene, the silver orb of the moon was reflected from the waters, and all nature was silent. I will not dissemble the first emotions of joy on the recovery of my freedom, and, perhaps, the establishment of my fame. But my pride was soon humbled, and a sober melancholy was spread over my mind, by the idea that I had taken an everlasting leave of an old and agreeable companion, and that whatsoever might be the future date of my *History*, the life of the historian must be short and precarious.

The text is that of the first edition (1788).

⚜

I NOW discharge my promise, and complete my design, of writing the History of the Decline and Fall of the Roman Empire, both in the West and the East.

54. **life:** [Gibbon's note] The whole relation of the death of Julian is given by Ammianus, an intelligent spectator. Libanius, who turns with horror from the scene, has supplied some circumstances. The calumnies of Gregory, and the legends of more recent saints, may now be *silently* despised.

The whole period extends from the age of Trajan and the Antonines, to the taking of Constantinople by Mahomet the second;[1] and includes a review of the Crusades and the state of Rome during the middle ages. Since the publication of the first volume, twelve years have elapsed; twelve years, according to my wish, "of health, of leisure, and of perseverance."[2] I may now congratulate my deliverance from a long and laborious service, and my satisfaction will be pure and perfect, if the public favour should be extended to the conclusion of my work.

It was my first intention to have collected under one view, the numerous authors, of every age and language, from whom I have derived the materials of this history; and I am still convinced that the apparent ostentation would be more than compensated by real use. If I have renounced this idea; if I have declined an undertaking which had obtained the approbation of a master-artist,[3] my excuse may be found in the extreme difficulty of assigning a proper measure to such a catalogue. A naked list of names and editions would not be satisfactory either to myself or my readers: the characters of the principal Authors of the Roman and Byzantine History, have been occasionally connected with the events which they describe; a more copious and critical enquiry might indeed deserve, but it would demand, an elaborate volume, which might swell by degrees into a general library of historical writers. For the present I shall content myself with renewing my serious protestation, that I have always endeavoured to draw from the fountain-head; that my curiosity, as well as a sense of duty, has always urged me to study the originals; and that, if they have sometimes eluded my search, I have carefully marked the secondary evidence, on whose faith a passage or a fact were reduced to depend.

I shall soon revisit the banks of the lake of Lausanne, a country which I have known and loved from my early youth. Under a mild government, amidst a beauteous landskip, in a life of leisure and independence, and among a people of easy and elegant manners, I have enjoyed, and may again hope to enjoy, the varied pleasures of retirement and society. But I shall ever glory in the name and character of an Englishman: I am proud of my birth in a free and enlightened country; and the approbation of that country is the best and most honourable reward of my labours. Were I ambitious of any other Patron than the public, I would inscribe this work to a Statesman,[4] who, in a long, a stormy, and at length an unfortunate administration, had many political opponents, almost without a personal enemy: who has retained, in his fall from power, many faithful and disinterested friends; and who, under the pressure of severe infirmity, enjoys the lively vigour of his mind, and the felicity of his incomparable temper. LORD NORTH will permit me to express the feelings of friendship in the language of truth: but even truth and friendship should be silent, if he still dispensed the favours of the crown.

In a remote solitude, vanity may still whisper in my ear, that my readers, perhaps, may enquire, whether, in the conclusion of the present work, I am now taking an everlasting farewell. They shall hear all that I know myself, all that I could reveal to the most intimate friend. The motives of action or silence are now equally balanced; nor can I pronounce in my most secret thoughts, on which side the scale will preponderate. I cannot dissemble that six ample quartos must have tried, and may have exhausted, the indulgence of the Public; that, in the repetition of similar attempts, a successful Author has much more to lose, than he can hope to gain; that I am now descending into the vale of years; and that the most respectable of my countrymen, the men whom I aspire to imitate, have resigned the pen of history about the same period of their lives.[5] Yet I consider that the annals of ancient and modern times may afford many rich and interesting subjects; that I am still possessed of health and leisure; that by the practice of writing, some skill and facility must be acquired; and that in the ardent pursuit of truth and knowledge, I am not conscious of decay. To an active mind, indolence is more painful than labour; and the first months of my liberty will be occupied and amused in the excursions of curiosity and taste. By such temptations, I have been sometimes

Preface to the Fourth Volume. **1. The whole . . . second:** from the second century to the fifteenth. **2. of health . . . perseverance:** Gibbon quotes the last phrase of his Preface to Volume I (1776). **3. the approbation . . . master-artist:** [Gibbon's note] See Dr. Robertson's Preface to his History of America.

4. a Statesman: Lord Frederick North (1732–92), Second Earl of Guilford, was Prime Minister from 1770 to 1782. General Cornwallis capitulated at Yorktown in 1781. **5. the men . . . lives:** Dr. William Robertson and David Hume, the two contemporary historians whom Gibbon valued most, finished their major historical works in their fifties. Gibbon was now fifty-one. (See the selection from Hume in Part Five.)

seduced from the rigid duty even of a pleasing and voluntary task: but my time will now be my own; and in the use or abuse of independence, I shall no longer fear my own reproaches or those of my friends. I am fairly entitled to a year of jubilee: next summer and the following winter will rapidly pass away; and experience only can determine whether I shall still prefer the freedom and variety of study to the design and composition of a regular work, which animates, while it confines, the daily application of the Author. Caprice and accident may influence my choice; but the dexterity of self-love will contrive to applaud either active industry, or philosophic repose.

Downing-Street,
May 1, 1788.

Richard Brinsley Sheridan

1751–1816

The playwright and politician Richard Brinsley Sheridan was one of the fluent, if imprudent, wits that the genius of Dublin seems to delight in bringing forth: he takes his place in a group of brilliant Irish comic writers that includes Swift, Goldsmith, Wilde, Shaw, and Joyce. He was born in Dublin of an articulate and literary family. His grandfather, the Reverend Dr. Thomas Sheridan, was a friend of Swift; his father, Thomas Sheridan, was a well-known actor and teacher of elocution; and his mother, Frances Sheridan, was a novelist and playwright. He entered Harrow School in 1762, where, as he said later, he was "a low-spirited boy, much given to crying when alone." At Harrow he displayed quickness and acuteness and he was inordinately fond of hoaxes, but as the poverty-stricken son of a mere player he had little chance for the social distinction he craved even from an early age.

He left Harrow in his seventeenth year. Instead of proceeding to the university, he went to Bath, where his father was lecturing and reciting. There he fell in love with the stunning young singer Elizabeth Linley, whose voice and demeanor were almost universally described as angelic. In his conduct with Miss Linley, Sheridan acted with the impulsiveness that he manifested all his life. He fought a duel in defense of her honor, and in 1772 the pair eloped to London and then to Calais. They were allegedly married at Calais, and, upon their return to London in 1773, they were married again.

In 1775 Sheridan began his brief and sensational career as a playwright—a career that was virtually over by the time he was twenty-eight. In four years he wrote five plays and two afterpieces. He began with *The Rivals*, a comedy which failed upon its first production at Covent Garden but which he rapidly rewrote and produced again: the second time it was a thundering success. In the same year he brought out a comic opera, *The Duenna;* his talented wife assisted in the choice and arrangement of the music. Samuel Johnson was referring to the success of these two pieces when he said of Sheridan in 1776, on his admission to the Club, "He who has written the two best comedies of his age, is surely a considerable man."

When David Garrick, the actor-manager of the Theatre Royal, Drury Lane, retired in 1776, he sold his interest in the theater to Sheridan and others. Sheridan became manager of Drury Lane, and he kept his hand in the business until 1809. In 1777 he produced there *The School for Scandal*, his best-known comedy and one firmly established in English dramatic repertory. *The Critic*, which followed in

1779, concluded his playwriting career, except for his rewriting of August von Kotzebue's *Die Spanier in Peru* as *Pizarro* (1799).

In 1780 he turned to politics, where he was to score as brilliant a success as he had in the theater. He was elected to Parliament as a Whig member for Staffordshire, and for the next thirty years debate in the House of Commons was enlivened by his imaginative and witty speeches, many of which later appeared as pamphlets. He reached the high point of his career as a political orator in 1787 with his eloquent and theatrical House of Commons speech against Warren Hastings, the former Governor General of India, whom Edmund Burke was working to impeach. Sheridan's political activities carried him—to his intense satisfaction—into upper-class and royal society. He became a friend and confidential adviser of the Prince of Wales and acquired a reputation for prodigal spending, drinking, and stylish flirtations and adulteries. Although he was never given the high political places he sought, he was made Treasurer of the Navy in 1806.

Drury Lane burned down in 1809, and Sheridan was brought to the edge of ruin; when the theater reopened in 1812, it did so without him. In 1813 he lost his seat in Parliament and was arrested for debt. Although he was soon released, creditors at once converged on him from all quarters, and when he died, a bailiff was in attendance at his bedside. He received an almost royal funeral and was buried in Poet's Corner in Westminster Abbey, near Johnson's grave and Goldsmith's monument.

Literary readiness and ease were perhaps his most striking talents. When an assassin shot at George III at Drury Lane Theatre in 1800, the leader of the orchestra struck up "God Save the King," and the actors sang the verses as an expression of loyalty. Sheridan calmly passed a paper to the leader of the singing, who found on it this additional extemporaneous stanza:

> From every latent foe,
> From the assassin's blow,
>   God save the King.
> O'er him thine arm extend,
> For Britain's sake, defend
> Our father, prince, and friend,
>   God save the King.

It was this flair for the theatrical that helped bring Sheridan his astonishing success first in the theater and then in Parliament. When a political enemy called him "this *Harlequin Son* of a *Mountebank Father*," he was speaking with partisan exaggeration, but he was not entirely inaccurate. Sheridan remained somewhat boyish all his life and both his triumphs and his decline are to be ascribed in part to the sanguine effervescence characteristic of the Irish wits.

For bibliography, see I. A. Williams's *Seven XVIII-Century Bibliographies* (1924). The standard text is *The Plays and Poems of Richard Brinsley Sheridan*, ed. R. C. Rhodes (3 vols., 1928). G. H. Nettleton's edition, *The Major Dramas of Richard Brinsley Sheridan* (1906), contains very full notes and commentaries. The standard biography is Rhodes's *Harlequin Sheridan: The Man and the Legends* (1933). W. S. Sichel's *Sheridan* (2 vols., 1909) is also useful.

THE CRITIC . . .

First performed at Drury Lane on October 30, 1779, when its author was twenty-eight, *The Critic* falls into the genre of dramatic burlesque. From the time of Beaumont and Fletcher's *The Knight of the Burning Pestle* (1613), dramatic burlesque had been singularly popular in England; in the Restoration and eighteenth century the form came to maturity with the Duke of Buckingham's *The Rehearsal* (1671), Gay's *Beggar's Opera* (1728), Fielding's *Tragedy of Tragedies* (1731), and Garrick's *A Peep Behind the Curtain; or, the New Rehearsal* (1767). Although contemporaries identified Sheridan's Sir Fretful Plagiary as Richard Cumberland, author of sentimental comedies, Sheridan's deflation of theatrical solemnities (unlike Fielding's) is general rather than particular. As *The Public Advertiser* observed in a review of the first performance, the targets of satire are "the tedious and unartificial Commencements of modern Tragedies, the inflated Diction, the figurative Tautology, the *Jeu de Théâtre* of Embraces and Groans, Vows and Prayers, florid Pathos, whining Heroism, and, above all, the Trick of Stage Situation." These things "are ridiculed with a Burlesque which may be thought rather too refined for the Multitude, but certainly is perfect in its Stile." The expected imminent invasion of southern England by Spanish naval forces lent additional piquancy to the rehearsal of Mr. Puff's *The Spanish Armada*. It is reported that Sheridan valued the first act of *The Critic* above any of his other writings.

The text is that of the first edition, *The Critic, or a Tragedy Rehearsed. A Dramatic Piece in Three Acts as It Is Performed at the Theatre Royal in Drury Lane* (1781). We have added some diacritical marks in the French.

TO Mrs. GREVILLE.°

MADAM,

IN *requesting your permission to address the following pages to you, which as they aim themselves to be critical, require every protection and allowance that approving taste or friendly prejudice can give them, I yet ventured to mention no other motive than the gratification of private friendship and esteem. Had I suggested a hope that your implied approbation would give a sanction to their defects, your particular reserve, and dislike to the reputation of critical taste, as well as of poetical talent, would have made*

THE CRITIC. **Mrs. Greville:** Frances Greville (d. 1789), author of minor poems and an uncompleted novel.

you refuse the protection of your name to such a purpose. However, I am not so ungrateful as now to attempt to combat this disposition in you. I shall not here presume to argue that the present state of poetry claims and expects every assistance that taste and example can afford it: nor endeavour to prove that a fastidious concealment of the most elegant productions of judgment and fancy is an ill return for the possession of those endowments.—Continue to deceive yourself in the idea that you are known only to be eminently admired and regarded for the valuable qualities that attach private friendships, and the graceful talents that adorn conversation. Enough of what you have written, has stolen into full public notice to answer my purpose; and you will, perhaps, be the only person, conversant in elegant literature, who shall read this address and not perceive that by publishing your particular approbation of the following drama, I have a more interested object than to boast the true respect and regard with which | I have the honour to be, | MADAM, | Your very sincere, | And obedient humble servant,

R. B. SHERIDAN.

PROLOGUE

By the Honorable RICHARD FITZPATRICK.°

THE Sister Muses,° whom these realms obey,
Who o'er the Drama hold divided sway,
Sometimes, by evil counsellors, 'tis said
Like earth-born potentates have been misled:
In those gay days of wickedness and wit,
When Villiers criticiz'd what Dryden writ,°
The Tragick Queen, to please a tasteless crow'd,
Had learn'd to bellow, rant, and roar so loud,
That frighten'd Nature, her best friend before,
The blust'ring beldam's company forswore.   10
Her comic Sister, who had wit 'tis true,
With all her merits, had her failings too;
And would sometimes in mirthful moments use
A style too flippant for a well-bred Muse.
Then female modesty abash'd began
To seek the friendly refuge of the fan,
Awhile behind that slight entrenchment stood,

Prologue. **Richard Fitzpatrick:** (1747–1813), Member of Parliament, wit, and soldier; just back from the American war, he was a leader of fashion and a devotee of the theater. **1. The Sister Muses:** Melpomene, Muse of tragedy, and Thalia, Muse of comedy. **6. Villiers . . . writ:** George Villiers (1628–87), Second Duke of Buckingham; he was the author (with others) of the dramatic burlesque *The Rehearsal* (1671), in which Dryden is satirized.

'Till driv'n from thence, she left the stage for good.
In our more pious, and far chaster times!
These sure no longer are the Muse's crimes!   20
But some complain that, former faults to shun,
The reformation to extremes has run.
The frantick hero's wild delirium past,
Now insipidity succeeds bombast;
So slow Melpomene's cold numbers creep,
Here dullness seems her drowsy court to keep,   )
And we, are scarce awake, whilst you are fast asleep.)
Thalia, once so ill behav'd and rude,
Reform'd; is now become an arrant prude,
Retailing nightly to the yawning pit,   30
The purest morals, undefil'd by wit!
Our Author offers in these motley scenes,
A slight remonstrance to the Drama's queens,

Nor let the goddesses be over nice;
Free spoken subjects give the best advice.
Although not quite a novice in his trade,
His cause to night requires no common aid.
To this, a friendly, just, and pow'rful court,
I come Ambassador to beg support.
Can he undaunted, brave the critick's rage?   40
In civil broils, with brother bards engage?
Hold forth their errors to the publick eye,
Nay more, e'en News-papers themselves defy?
Say, must his single arm encounter all?
By numbers vanquish'd, e'en the brave may fall;
And though no leader should success distrust,
Whose troops are willing, and whose cause is just;
To bid such hosts of angry foes defiance,
His chief dependence must be, YOUR ALLIANCE.

DRAMATIS PERSONÆ.

Dangle ————	Mr. DODD.
Sneer ———— ————	Mr. PALMER.
Sir Fretful Plagiary,	Mr. PARSONS.
Signor Pasticcio Ritornello,	Mr. DELPINI.
Interpreter ————	Mr. BADDELEY.
Under Prompter ————	Mr. PHILLIMORE.
AND	
Puff ———— ————	Mr. KING.
Mrs. Dangle ————	Mrs. HOPKINS.
Italian Girls ————	Miss FIELD, and the
	Miss ABRAMS.

Characters of the TRAGEDY.

Lord Burleigh ————	Mr. MOODY.
Governor of Tilbury Fort,	Mr. WRIGHTEN.
Earl of Leicester ————	Mr. FARREN.
Sir Walter Raleigh ————	Mr. BURTON.
Sir Christopher Hatton ————	Mr. WALDRON.
Master of the Horse ————	Mr. KENNY.
Beefeater ———— ————	Mr. WRIGHT.
Justice ———— ————	Mr. PACKER.
Son ———— ————	Mr. LAMASH.
Constable ———— ————	Mr. FAWCETT.
Thames ———— ————	Mr. GAWDRY.
AND	
Don Ferolo Whiskerandos,	Mr. BANNISTER, jun.
1st Niece ————	Miss COLLETT.
2d Niece ———— ————	Miss KIRBY.
Justice's Lady ———— ————	Mrs. JOHNSTON.
Confidant ———— ————	Mrs. BRADSHAW.
AND	
Tilburina ———— ————	Miss POPE.

Guards, Constables, Servants, Chorus, Rivers, Attendants, &c. &c.

ACT I

SCENE I.

MR. *and* MRS. DANGLE *at Breakfast, and reading Newspapers.*

DANGLE *(reading.)*

"BRUTUS TO LORD NORTH."[1]——"Letter of the second, on the STATE OF THE ARMY."——Pshaw! "To the first L—— dash D of the A—— dash Y."[2]—— "Genuine Extract of a Letter from ST. KITT'S."[3]—— "COXHEATH INTELLIGENCE."[4]——"It is now confidently asserted that SIR CHARLES HARDY."[5]——Pshaw! ——Nothing but about the fleet, and the nation!—— and I hate all politics but theatrical politics.—— Where's the MORNING CHRONICLE?

MRS. DANGLE.

Yes, that's your gazette.

DANGLE.

So, here we have it.——
"*Theatrical intelligence extraordinary,*"——"We hear there is a new tragedy in rehearsal at Drury-Lane Theatre, call'd the SPANISH ARMADA, said to be written by Mr. PUFF, a gentleman well known in the theatrical world; if we allow ourselves to give credit to the report of the performers, who, truth to say, are in general but indifferent judges, this piece abounds with the most striking and received beauties of modern composition"——So! I am very glad my friend PUFF's tragedy is in such forwardness.——Mrs. Dangle, my dear, you will be very glad to hear that PUFF's tragedy——

MRS. DANGLE.

Lord, Mr. Dangle, why will you plague me about such nonsense?——Now the plays are begun I shall have no peace.——Isn't it sufficient to make

Act I, scene i. **1. Lord North:** First Lord of the Treasury and virtual Prime Minister; he was carrying out the will of George III in the very discouraging war with America and France. The declaration of war by Spain in June, 1779, had made the situation even more unpromising. **2. the first . . . Y:** Lord Sandwich, First Lord of the Admiralty. **3. St. Kitt's:** St. Christopher, an island in the West Indies, site of French naval actions against the British. **4. Coxheath Intelligence:** In July, 1779, a large body of militia had been assembled at Coxheath Camp, near Maidstone (southeastern England), as security against the anticipated French and Spanish invasion. **5. Sir . . . Hardy:** admiral of the British anti-invasion fleet in the Channel.

yourself ridiculous by your passion for the theatre, without continually teazing me to join you? Why can't you ride your hobby-horse without desiring to place me on a pillion behind you, Mr. Dangle?

DANGLE.

Nay, my dear, I was only going to read——

MRS. DANGLE.

No, no; you never will read any thing that's worth listening to:——you hate to hear about your country; there are letters every day with Roman signatures, demonstrating the certainty of an invasion, and proving that the nation is utterly undone——But you never will read any thing to entertain one.

DANGLE.

What has a woman to do with politics, Mrs. Dangle?

MRS. DANGLE.

And what have you to do with the theatre, Mr. Dangle? Why should you affect the character of a Critic? I have no patience with you!——haven't you made yourself the jest of all your acquaintance by your interference in matters where you have no business? Are not you call'd a theatrical Quidnunc,[6] and a mock Mæcenas[7] to second-hand authors?

DANGLE.

True; my power with the Managers is pretty notorious; but is it no credit to have applications from all quarters for my interest?——From lords to recommend fidlers, from ladies to get boxes, from authors to get answers, and from actors to get engagements.

MRS. DANGLE.

Yes, truly; you have contrived to get a share in all the plague and trouble of theatrical property, without the profit, or even the credit of the abuse that attends it.

DANGLE.

I am sure, Mrs. Dangle, YOU are no loser by it, however; YOU have all the advantages of it:—— mightn't you, last winter, have had the reading of the new Pantomime a fortnight previous to its performance? And doesn't Mr. Fosbrook[8] let you take places for a play before it is advertis'd, and set you down for a Box for every new piece through the season? And didn't my friend, Mr. Smatter, dedicate his last Farce to you at my particular request, Mrs. Dangle?

MRS. DANGLE.

Yes; but wasn't the Farce damn'd, Mr. Dangle? And to be sure it is extremely pleasant to have one's

6. Quidnunc: gossip. **7. Mæcenas:** the literary patron of Virgil and Horace. **8. Mr. Fosbrook:** the treasurer of the Drury Lane Theatre.

house made the motley rendezvous of all the lackeys of literature!——The very high change[9] of trading authors and jobbing critics!——Yes, my drawing-room is an absolute register-office for candidate actors, and poets without character;——then to be continually alarmed with Misses and Ma'ams piping histeric changes on JULIETS and DORINDAS, POLLYS[10] and OPHELIAS; and the very furniture trembling at the probationary starts and unprovok'd rants of would-be RICHARDS and HAMLETS!——And what is worse than all, now that the Manager has monopoliz'd the Opera-House, haven't we the Signors and Signioras calling here, sliding their smooth semibreves, and gargling glib divisions in their outlandish throats——with foreign emissaries and French spies, for ought I know, disguised like fidlers and figure dancers!

DANGLE.

Mercy! Mrs. Dangle!

Mrs. DANGLE.

And to employ yourself so idly at such an alarming crisis as this too——when, if you had the least spirit, you would have been at the head of one of the Westminster associations[11]——or trailing a volunteer pike in the Artillery Ground!——But you——o' my conscience, I believe if the French were landed to-morrow, your first enquiry would be, whether they had brought a theatrical troop with them.

DANGLE.

Mrs. Dangle, it does not signify——I say the stage is "the Mirror of Nature," and the actors are "the Abstract, and brief Chronicles of the Time:"[12]——and pray what can a man of sense study better?——Besides, you will not easily persuade me that there is no credit or importance in being at the head of a band of critics, who take upon them to decide for the whole town, whose opinion and patronage all writers solicit, and whose recommendation no manager dares refuse!

Mrs. DANGLE.

Ridiculous!——Both managers and authors of the least merit, laugh at your pretensions.——The PUBLIC is their CRITIC——without whose fair approbation they know no play can rest on the stage, and with whose applause they welcome such attacks as yours,

and laugh at the malice of them, where they can't at the wit.

DANGLE.

Very well, Madam——very well.

Enter SERVANT.

SERVANT.

Mr. Sneer, Sir, to wait on you.

DANGLE.

O, shew Mr. Sneer up.   [*Exit* Servant.
Plague on 't, now we must appear loving and affectionate, or Sneer will hitch us into a story.

Mrs. DANGLE.

With all my heart; you can't be more ridiculous than you are.

DANGLE.

You are enough to provoke——

Enter Mr. SNEER.

——Hah! my dear Sneer, I am vastly glad to see you. My dear, here's Mr. Sneer.

Mrs. DANGLE.

Good morning to you, Sir.

DANGLE.

Mrs. Dangle and I have been diverting ourselves with the papers.——Pray, Sneer, won't you go to Drury-lane theatre the first night of Puff's tragedy?

SNEER.

Yes; but I suppose one shan't be able to get in, for on the first night of a new piece they always fill the house with orders[13] to support it. But here, Dangle, I have brought you two pieces, one of which you must exert yourself to make the Managers accept, I can tell you that, for 'tis written by a person of consequence.

DANGLE.

So! now my plagues are beginning!

SNEER.

Aye, I am glad of it, for now you'll be happy. Why, my dear Dangle, it is a pleasure to see how you enjoy your volunteer fatigue, and your solicited solicitations.

DANGLE.

It's a great trouble——yet, egad, its pleasant too. ——Why, sometimes of a morning, I have a dozen people call on me at breakfast time, whose faces I never saw before, nor ever desire to see again.

SNEER.

That must be very pleasant indeed!

---

9. **high change:** market place. 10. **Dorindas, Pollys:** Dorinda and Polly are characters in *The Beaux' Stratagem* (1707) by George Farquhar (1678–1707) and John Gay's *Beggar's Opera* (see Part Two) respectively. 11. **Westminster associations:** bodies of militia. 12. **the stage . . . Time:** See *Hamlet*, II. ii. 548; III. ii. 24.

13. **orders:** passes.

DANGLE.

And not a week but I receive fifty letters, and not a line in them about any business of my own.

SNEER.

An amusing correspondence!

DANGLE (reading).

"Bursts into tears, and exit." What, is this a tragedy?

SNEER.

No, that's a genteel comedy, not a translation—— only *taken from the French;* it is written in a stile which they have lately tried to run down; the true senti-mental, and nothing ridiculous in it from the beginning to the end.

Mrs. DANGLE.

Well, if they had kept to that, I should not have been such an enemy to the stage, there was some edification to be got from those pieces, Mr. Sneer!

SNEER.

I am quite of your opinion, Mrs. Dangle; the theatre, in proper hands, might certainly be made the school of morality;[14] but now, I am sorry to say it, people seem to go there principally for their entertainment!

Mrs. DANGLE.

It would have been more to the credit of the Managers to have kept it in the other line.

SNEER.

Undoubtedly, Madam, and hereafter perhaps to have had it recorded, that in the midst of a luxurious and dissipated age, they preserv'd *two* houses[15] in the capital, where the conversation was always moral at least, if not entertaining!

DANGLE.

Now, egad, I think the worst alteration is in the nicety of the audience.——No double entendre, no smart inuendo admitted; even Vanbrugh and Congreve oblig'd to undergo a bungling reformation![16]

SNEER.

Yes, and our prudery in this respect is just on a par with the artificial bashfulness of a courtezan, who

encreases the blush upon her cheek in an exact propor-tion to the diminution of her modesty.

DANGLE.

Sneer can't even give the Public a good word!—— But what have we here?——This seems a very odd——

SNEER.

O, that's a comedy, on a very new plan; replete with wit and mirth, yet of a most serious moral! You see it is call'd "THE REFORMED HOUSEBREAKER;" where, by the mere force of humour, HOUSEBREAKING is put into so ridiculous a light, that if the piece has its proper run, I have no doubt but that bolts and bars will be entirely useless by the end of the season.

DANGLE.

Egad, this is new indeed!

SNEER.

Yes; it is written by a particular friend of mine, who has discovered that the follies and foibles of society, are subjects unworthy the notice of the Comic Muse, who should be taught to stoop only at the greater vices and blacker crimes of humanity——gibbeting capital offences in five acts, and pillorying petty larcenies in two.——In short, his idea is to dramatize the penal laws, and make the Stage a court of ease to the Old Bailey.[17]

DANGLE.

It is truly moral.

Enter SERVANT.

Sir Fretful Plagiary, Sir.

DANGLE.

Beg him to walk up.——[*Exit* Servant.] Now, Mrs. Dangle, Sir Fretful Plagiary is an author to your own taste.

Mrs. DANGLE.

I confess he is a favourite of mine, because every body else abuses him.

SNEER.

——Very much to the credit of your charity, Madam, if not of your judgment.

DANGLE.

But, egad, he allows no merit to any author but himself, that's the truth on 't——tho' he's my friend.

SNEER.

Never.——He is as envious as an old maid verging on the desperation of six-and-thirty: and then the insiduous humility with which he seduces you to give a free opinion on any of his works, can be exceeded

---

14. the theatre . . . morality: an allusion to a solemn pro-nouncement at the end of the sentimental, moralistic comedy *False Delicacy* (1768) by Hugh Kelly (1739–77). **15. two houses:** the two theaters, Covent Garden and Drury Lane. **16. even . . . reformation:** Sheridan had written a "re-formed" version (*A Trip to Scarborough* [1777]) of *The Relapse* (1697) by Sir John Vanbrugh (1664–1726); because the comedies of William Congreve (1670–1729) were some-times thought too risqué for the later eighteenth century, Sheridan, as manager of Drury Lane, cut some of the indeli-cacies from three of Congreve's comedies in 1776 to create more acceptable acting versions.

17. Old Bailey: the main criminal court of London.

only by the petulant arrogance with which he is sure to reject your observations.

DANGLE.

Very true, egad——tho' he's my friend.

SNEER.

Then his affected contempt of all newspaper strictures; tho', at the same time, he is the sorest man alive, and shrinks like scorch'd parchment from the fiery ordeal of true criticism: yet is he so covetous of popularity, that he had rather be abused than not mentioned at all.

DANGLE.

There's no denying it——tho' he is my friend.

SNEER.

You have read the tragedy he has just finished, haven't you?

DANGLE.

O yes; he sent it to me yesterday.

SNEER.

Well, and you think it execrable, don't you?

DANGLE.

Why between ourselves, egad I must own——tho' he's my friend——that it is one of the most——He's here [*Aside*]——finished and most admirable perform——

[*Sir Fretful without.*] Mr. Sneer with him, did you say?

Enter Sir FRETFUL.

Ah, my dear friend!——Egad, we were just speaking of your Tragedy.——Admirable, Sir Fretful, admirable!

SNEER.

You never did any thing beyond it, Sir Fretful—— never in your life.

Sir FRETFUL.

You make me extremely happy;——for without a compliment, my dear Sneer, there isn't a man in the world whose judgment I value as I do yours.——And Mr. Dangle's.

Mrs. DANGLE.

They are only laughing at you, Sir Fretful, for it was but just now that——

DANGLE.

Mrs. Dangle!——Ah, Sir Fretful, you know Mrs. Dangle.——My friend Sneer was rallying just now ——He knows how she admires you, and——

Sir FRETFUL.

O Lord——I am sure Mr. Sneer has more taste and sincerity than to——A damn'd double-faced fellow!   [*Aside*.

DANGLE.

Yes, yes,——Sneer will jest——but a better humour'd——

Sir FRETFUL.

O, I know——

DANGLE.

He has a ready turn for ridicule——his wit costs him nothing.——

Sir FRETFUL.

No, egad——or I should wonder how he came by it.   [*Aside*.

Mrs. DANGLE.

Because his jest is always at the expence of his friend.

DANGLE.

But, Sir Fretful, have you sent your play to the managers yet?——or can I be of any service to you?

Sir FRETFUL.

No, no, I thank you; I believe the piece has sufficient recommendation with it.——I thank you tho'.——I sent it to the manager of COVENT-GARDEN THEATRE this morning.

SNEER.

I should have thought now, that it might have been cast (as the actors call it) better at DRURY-LANE.

Sir FRETFUL.

O lud! no——never send a play there while I live ——harkee!

[*Whispers* Sneer.]

SNEER.

Writes himself!——I know he[18] does——

Sir FRETFUL.

I say nothing——I take away from no man's merit ——am hurt at no man's good fortune——I say nothing.——But this I will say——through all my knowledge of life, I have observ'd——that there is not a passion so strongly rooted in the human heart as envy!

SNEER.

I believe you have reason for what you say, indeed.

Sir FRETFUL.

Besides——I can tell you it is not always so safe to leave a play in the hands of those who write themselves.

SNEER.

What, they may steal from them, hey, my dear Plagiary?

18. **he:** Sheridan.

Sir FRETFUL.

Steal!——to be sure they may; and, egad, serve your best thoughts as gypsies do stolen children, disfigure them to make 'em pass for their own.

SNEER.

But your present work is a sacrifice to Melpomene, and HE, you know, never——

Sir FRETFUL.

That's no security.——A dext'rous plagiarist may do any thing.——Why, Sir, for ought I know, he might take out some of the best things in my tragedy, and put them into his own comedy.

SNEER.

That might be done, I dare be sworn.

Sir FRETFUL.

And then, if such a person gives you the least hint or assistance, he is devilish apt to take the merit of the whole.——

DANGLE.

If it succeeds.

Sir FRETFUL.

Aye——but with regard to this piece, I think I can hit that gentleman, for I can safely swear he never read it.

SNEER.

I'll tell how you may hurt him more——

Sir FRETFUL.

How?——

SNEER.

Swear he wrote it.

Sir FRETFUL.

Plague on 't now, Sneer, I shall take it ill.——I believe you want to take away my character as an author!

SNEER.

Then I am sure you ought to be very much oblig'd to me.

Sir FRETFUL.

Hey!——Sir!——

DANGLE.

O you know, he never means what he says.

Sir FRETFUL.

Sincerely then——how do you like the piece?

SNEER.

Wonderfully!

Sir FRETFUL.

But come now, there must be something that you think might be mended, hey?——Mr. Dangle, has nothing struck you?

DANGLE.

Why faith, it is but an ungracious thing for the most part to——

Sir FRETFUL.

——With most authors it is just so indeed; they are in general strangely tenacious!——But, for my part, I am never so well pleased as when a judicious critic points out any defect to me; for what is the purpose of shewing a work to a friend, if you don't mean to profit by his opinion?

SNEER.

Very true.——Why then, tho' I seriously admire the piece upon the whole, yet there is one small objection; which, if you'll give me leave, I'll mention.

Sir FRETFUL.

SIR, you can't oblige me more.

SNEER.

I think it wants incident.

Sir FRETFUL.

Good God!——you surprize me!——wants incident!——

SNEER.

Yes; I own I think the incidents are too few.

Sir FRETFUL.

Good God!——Believe me, Mr. Sneer, there is no person for whose judgment I have a more implicit deference.——But I protest to you, Mr. Sneer, I am only apprehensive that the incidents are too crowded.——My dear Dangle, how does it strike you?

DANGLE.

Really I can't agree with my friend Sneer.——I think the plot quite sufficient; and the four first acts by many degrees the best I ever read or saw in my life. If I might venture to suggest any thing, it is that the interest rather falls off in the fifth.——

Sir FRETFUL.

——Rises; I believe you mean, Sir.

DANGLE.

No; I don't upon my word.

Sir FRETFUL.

Yes, yes, you do upon my soul——it certainly don't fall off, I assure you——No, no, it don't fall off.

DANGLE.

Now, Mrs. Dangle, didn't you say it struck you in the same light?

Mrs. DANGLE.

No, indeed, I did not——I did not see a fault in any part of the play from the beginning to the end.

Sir FRETFUL.

Upon my soul the women are the best judges after all!

Mrs. DANGLE.

Or if I made any objection, I am sure it was to nothing in the piece; but that I was afraid it was, on the whole, a little too long.

Sir FRETFUL.

Pray, Madam, do you speak as to duration of time; or do you mean that the story is tediously spun out?

Mrs. DANGLE.

O Lud! no.——I speak only with reference to the usual length of acting plays.

Sir FRETFUL.

Then I am very happy——very happy indeed—— because the play is a short play, a remarkably short play:——I should not venture to differ with a lady on a point of taste: but, on these occasions, the watch, you know, is the critic.

Mrs. DANGLE.

Then, I suppose, it must have been Mr. Dangle's drawling manner of reading it to me.

Sir FRETFUL.

O, if Mr. Dangle read it! that's quite another affair!——But I assure you, Mrs. Dangle, the first evening you can spare me three hours and an half, I'll undertake to read you the whole from beginning to end, with the Prologue and Epilogue, and allow time for the music between the acts.

Mrs. DANGLE.

I hope to see it on the stage next.

DANGLE.

Well, Sir Fretful, I wish you may be able to get rid as easily of the news-paper criticisms as you do of ours.——

Sir FRETFUL.

The NEWS-PAPERS!——Sir, they are the most villainous——licentious——abominable——infernal—— Not that I ever read them——No——I make it a rule never to look into a news-paper.

DANGLE.

You are quite right——for it certainly must hurt an author of delicate feelings to see the liberties they take.

Sir FRETFUL.

No!——quite the contrary;——their abuse is, in fact, the best panegyric——I like it of all things.—— An author's reputation is only in danger from their support.

Mr. SNEER.

Why that's true——and that attack now on you the other day——

Sir FRETFUL.

——What? where?

DANGLE.

Aye, you mean in a paper of Thursday; it was compleatly ill-natur'd to be sure.

Sir FRETFUL.

O, so much the better.——Ha! ha! ha!——I wou'dn't have it otherwise.

DANGLE.

Certainly it is only to be laugh'd at; for——

Sir FRETFUL.

——You don't happen to recollect what the fellow said, do you?

SNEER.

Pray, Dangle——Sir Fretful seems a little anxious——

Sir FRETFUL.

——O lud, no!——anxious,——not I,——not the least.——I——But one may as well hear you know.

DANGLE.

Sneer, do *you* recollect?——Make out something.
                                                        [*Aside.*

SNEER.

I will, [*to Dangle.*]——Yes, yes, I remember perfectly.

Sir FRETFUL.

Well, and pray now——Not that it signifies—— what might the gentleman say?

SNEER.

Why, he roundly asserts that you have not the slightest invention, or original genius whatever; tho' you are the greatest traducer of all other authors living.

Sir FRETFUL.

Ha! ha! ha!——very good!

SNEER.

That as to COMEDY, you have not one idea of your own, he believes, even in your common place book ——where stray jokes, and pilfered witticisms are kept with as much method as the ledger of the LOST-and-STOLEN-OFFICE.

Sir FRETFUL.

——Ha! ha! ha!——very pleasant!

SNEER.

Nay, that you are so unlucky as not to have the skill even to *steal* with taste.——But that you gleen from the refuse of obscure volumes, where more judicious plagiarists have been before you; so that the body of your work is a composition of dregs and sediments ——like a bad tavern's worst wine.

Sir FRETFUL.

Ha! ha!

SNEER.

In your more serious efforts, he says, your bombast would be less intolerable, if the thoughts were ever suited to the expression; but the homeliness of the sentiment stares thro' the fantastic encumbrance of it's fine language, like a clown in one of the new uniforms!

Sir FRETFUL.

Ha! ha!

SNEER.

That your occasional tropes and flowers suit the general coarseness of your stile, as tambour sprigs[19] would a ground of linsey-wolsey; while your imitations of Shakespeare resemble the mimicry of Falstaff's Page, and are about as near the standard of the original.

Sir FRETFUL.

Ha!——

SNEER.

——In short, that even the finest passages you steal are of no service to you; for the poverty of your own language prevents their assimilating; so that they lie on the surface like lumps of marl[20] on a barren moor, encumbering what it is not in their power to fertilize!——

Sir FRETFUL. (*after great agitation.*)

——Now another person would be vex'd at this.

SNEER.

Oh! but I wouldn't have told you, only to divert you.

Sir FRETFUL.

I know it——I *am* diverted,——Ha! ha! ha!——not the least invention!——Ha! ha! ha! very good!—— very good!

SNEER.

Yes——no genius! Ha! ha! ha!

DANGLE.

A severe rogue! Ha! ha! ha! But you are quite right, Sir Fretful, never to read such nonsense.

Sir FRETFUL.

To be sure——for if there is any thing to one's praise, it is a foolish vanity to be gratified at it, and if it is abuse,——why one is always sure to hear of it from one damn'd good natur'd friend or another!

Enter SERVANT.

Sir, there is an Italian gentleman, with a French Interpreter, and three young ladies, and a dozen musicians, who say they are sent by LADY RONDEAU and MRS. FUGE.

19. **tambour sprigs:** embroidered ornaments; a tambour is an embroidery frame. 20. **marl:** a clay used as fertilizer.

DANGLE.

Gadso! they come by appointment. Dear Mrs. Dangle do let them know I'll see them directly.

MRS. DANGLE.

You know, Mr. Dangle, I shan't understand a word they say.

DANGLE.

But you hear there's an interpreter.

MRS. DANGLE.

Well, I'll try to endure their complaisance till you come. [*Exit.*

SERVANT.

And Mr. PUFF, Sir, has sent word that the last rehearsal is to be this morning, and that he'll call on you presently.

DANGLE.

That's true——I shall certainly be at home. [*Exit* Servant.] Now, Sir Fretful, if you have a mind to have justice done you in the way of answer——Egad, Mr. PUFF's your man.

Sir FRETFUL.

Pshaw! Sir, why should I wish to have it answered, when I tell you I am pleased at it?

DANGLE.

True, I had forgot that.——But I hope you are not fretted at what Mr. Sneer——

Sir FRETFUL.

——Zounds! no, Mr. Dangle, don't I tell you these things never fret me in the least.

DANGLE.

Nay, I only thought——

Sir FRETFUL.

——And let me tell you, Mr. Dangle, 'tis damn'd affronting in you to suppose that I am hurt, when I tell you I am not.

SNEER.

But why so warm, Sir Fretful?

Sir FRETFUL.

Gadslife! Mr. Sneer, you are as absurd as Dangle; how often must I repeat it to you, that nothing can vex me but your supposing it possible for me to mind the damn'd nonsense you have been repeating to me!——and let me tell you, if you continue to believe this, you must mean to insult me, gentlemen——and then your disrespect will affect me no more than the news-paper criticisms——and I shall treat it——with exactly the same calm indifference and philosophic contempt——and so your servant. [*Exit.*

SNEER.

Ha! ha! ha! Poor Sir Fretful! Now will he go and

vent his philosophy in anonymous abuse of all modern critics and authors——But, Dangle, you must get your friend PUFF to take me to the rehearsal of his tragedy.

DANGLE.

I'll answer for 't, he'll thank you for desiring it. But come and help me to judge of this musical family; they are recommended by people of consequence, I assure you.

SNEER.

I am at your disposal the whole morning——but I thought you had been a decided critic in musick, as well as in literature?

DANGLE.

So I am——but I have a bad ear.——Efaith, Sneer, tho', I am afraid we were a little too severe on Sir Fretful——tho' he is my friend.

SNEER.

Why, 'tis certain, that unnecessarily to mortify the vanity of any writer, is a cruelty which mere dulness never can deserve; but where a base and personal malignity usurps the place of literary emulation, the aggressor deserves neither quarter nor pity.

DANGLE.

That's true egad!——tho' he's my friend!

SCENE II.

*A Drawing Room, Harpsichord, &c. Italian Family,
French Interpreter, Mrs. Dangle
and Servants discovered.*

INTERPRETER.

Je dis madame, ja'i l'honneur to *introduce* & de vous demander votre protection pour le Signor PASTICCIO RITORNELLO & pour sa charmante famille.[1]

Signor PASTICCIO.

Ah! Vosignoria noi vi preghiamo di favoritevi colla vostra protezione.[2]

1st DAUGHTER.

Vosignoria fatevi questi grazzie.[3]

2d DAUGHTER.

Si Signora.

INTERPRETER.

Madame——*me interpret.*——C'est à dire——in English——quils vous prient de leur faire l'honneur——[4]

Mrs. DANGLE.

——I say again, gentlemen, I don't understand a word you say.

Signor PASTICCIO.

Questo Signore spiegheró.[5]

INTERPRETER.

Oui——*me interpret.*——nous avons les lettres de recommendation pour Monsieur Dangle de——[6]

Mrs. DANGLE.

——Upon my word, Sir, I don't understand you.

Signor PASTICCIO.

La CONTESSA RONDEAU e nostra padrona.[7]

3d DAUGHTER.

Si, padre, & mi LADI FUGE.[8]

INTERPRETER.

O!——*me interpret.*——Madame, ils disent——*in* English——Qu'ils ont l'honneur d'être protégés de ces Dames.[9]——*You understand?*

Mrs. DANGLE.

No, Sir,——no understand!

Enter DANGLE *and* SNEER.

INTERPRETER.

Ah voici Monsieur Dangle![10]

All ITALIANS.

A! Signor Dangle!

Mrs. DANGLE.

Mr. Dangle, here are two very civil gentlemen trying to make themselves understood, and I don't know which is the interpreter.

DANGLE

Ebien![11]

Act I, scene ii. **1. Je . . . famille:** I say, Madam, I have the honor to introduce and request your patronage of Signor Pasticcio Ritornello and his charming family. **2. Vosignoria . . . protezione:** Your Ladyship, we beg you to favor us with your patronage. [Sheridan's stage Italian throughout this passage is full of mistakes.] **3. Vosignoria . . . grazzie:** Your Ladyship, grant us this blessing.

4. Madame . . . l'honneur: Madam——I shall interpret.——That is to say——in English——that they beg you to do them the honor——. **5. Questo . . . spiegheró:** This gentleman will interpret. **6. Oui . . . de:** Yes ——I shall interpret——we have letters of recommendation to Mr. Dangle from——. **7. La . . . padrona:** Countess Rondo is our patroness. **8. Si . . . Fuge:** Yes, father, and Lady Fugue. **9. O . . . Dames:** Oh!——I shall interpret—— Madam, they say——in English——that they have the honor to be under the patronage of these ladies. **10. Ah. . . Dangle:** Ah, here is Mr. Dangle! **11. Ebien:** Egad!

INTERPRETER

Monsieur Dangle——le grand bruit de vos talents pour la critique & de votre interest avec Messieurs les Directeurs à tous les Théâtres.[12]

Signor PASTICCIO.

Vosignoria siete si famoso par la vostra conoscensa e vostra interessa colla la Diretore da——[13]

Speaking together.

DANGLE.

Egad I think the Interpreter is the hardest to be understood of the two!

SNEER.

Why I thought, Dangle, you had been an admirable linguist!

DANGLE.

So I am, if they would not talk so damn'd fast.

SNEER.

Well I'll explain that——the less time we lose in hearing them the better,——for that I suppose is what they are brought here for.

[Sneer *speaks to* Sig. Past.——*They sing trios, &c.* Dangle *beating out of time.* Servant *enters and whispers* Dangle.

DANGLE.

Shew him up.   [*Exit* Servant. Bravo! admirable! bravissimo! admirablissimo! ——Ah! Sneer! where will you find such as these voices in England?

SNEER.

Not easily.

DANGLE.

But PUFF is coming.——Signor and little Signora's ——obligatissimo![14] Sposa Signora Danglena—— Mrs. Dangle, shall I beg you to offer them some refreshments, and take their address in the next room.

[*Exit* Mrs. Dangle *with the* Italians *and* Interpreter *ceremoniously.*

Re-enter SERVANT.

Mr. PUFF, Sir!

DANGLE.

My dear PUFF!

Enter PUFF.

My dear Dangle, how is it with you?

DANGLE.

Mr. Sneer, give me leave to introduce Mr. PUFF to you.

PUFF.

Mr. Sneer is this? Sir, he is a gentleman whom I have long panted for the honour of knowing——a gentleman whose critical talents and transcendant judgment——

SNEER.

——Dear Sir——

DANGLE.

Nay, don't be modest, Sneer, my friend PUFF only talks to you in the stile of his profession.

SNEER.

His profession!

PUFF.

Yes, Sir; I make no secret of the trade I follow—— among friends and brother authors, Dangle knows I love to be frank on the subject, and to advertise myself *vivâ voce.*[15]——I am, Sir, a Practitioner in Panegyric, or to speak more plainly——a Professor of the Art of Puffing, at your service——or any body else's.

SNEER.

Sir, you are very obliging!——I believe, Mr. Puff, I have often admired your talents in the daily prints.

PUFF.

Yes, Sir, I flatter myself I do as much business in that way as any six of the fraternity in town—— Devilish hard work all the summer——Friend Dangle,[16] never work'd harder!——But harkee,—— the Winter Managers were a little sore I believe.

DANGLE.

No——I believe they took it all in good part.

PUFF.

Aye!——Then that must have been affectation in them, for egad, there were some of the attacks which there was no laughing at!

SNEER.

Aye, the humourous ones.——But I should think Mr. Puff, that Authors would in general be able to do this sort of work for themselves.

PUFF.

Why yes——but in a clumsy way.——Besides, we look on that as an encroachment, and so take the opposite side.——I dare say now you conceive half the very civil paragraphs and advertisements you see, to be written by the parties concerned, or their friends?——

---

12. Monsieur . . . Théâtres: Mr. Dangle, the great fame of your talents for criticism and of your influence with the managers at all the theatres——. 13. Vosignoria . . . da: Your Lordship, you are so famous for your friendship and influence with the managers that——. 14. obligatissimo: I am most grateful!

15. vivâ voce: by word of mouth. 16. Dangle: The text has a question mark after *Dangle.*

No such thing——Nine out of ten, manufactured by me in the way of business.

SNEER.

Indeed!——

PUFF.

Even the Auctioneers now,——the Auctioneers I say, tho' the rogues have lately got some credit for their language——not an article of the merit their's! ——take them out of their Pulpits, and they are as dull as Catalogues.——No, Sir;——'twas I first enrich'd their style——'twas I first taught them to crowd their advertisements with panegyrical superlatives, each epithet rising above the other——like the Bidders in their own Auction-rooms! From ME they learn'd to enlay their phraseology with variegated chips of exotic metaphor: by ME too their inventive faculties were called forth.——Yes Sir, by ME they were instructed to clothe ideal walls with gratuitous fruits—— to insinuate obsequious rivulets into visionary groves ——to teach courteous shrubs to nod their approbation of the grateful soil! or on emergencies to raise upstart oaks, where there never had been an acorn; to create a delightful vicinage without the assistance of a neighbour; or fix the temple of Hygeia in the fens of Lincolnshire!

DANGLE.

I am sure, you have done them infinite service; for now, when a gentleman is ruined, he parts with his house with some credit.

SNEER.

Service! if they had any gratitude, they would erect a statue to him, they would figure him as a presiding Mercury,[17] the god of traffic and fiction, with a hammer in his hand instead of a caduceus.——But pray, Mr. Puff, what first put you on exercising your talents in this way?

PUFF.

Egad sir,——sheer necessity——the proper parent of an art so nearly allied to invention: you must know Mr. Sneer, that from the first time I tried my hand at an advertisement, my success was such, that for sometime after, I led a most extraordinary life indeed!

SNEER.

How, pray?

PUFF.

Sir, I supported myself two years entirely by my misfortunes.

SNEER.

By your misfortunes!

PUFF.

Yes Sir, assisted by long sickness, and other occasional disorders; and a very comfortable living I had of it.

SNEER.

From sickness and misfortunes!——You practised as a Doctor, and an Attorney at once?

PUFF.

No egad, both maladies and miseries were my own.

SNEER.

Hey!——what the plague!

DANGLE.

'Tis true, efaith.

PUFF.

Harkee!——By advertisements——"To the charitable and humane!" and "to those whom Providence hath blessed with affluence!"

SNEER.

Oh,——I understand you.

PUFF.

And in truth, I deserved what I got, for I suppose never man went thro' such a series of calamities in the same space of time!——Sir, I was five times made a bankrupt, and reduced from a state of affluence, by a train of unavoidable misfortunes! then Sir, tho' a very industrious tradesman, I was twice burnt out, and lost my little all, both times!——I lived upon those fires a month.——I soon after was confined by a most excrutiating disorder, and lost the use of my limbs! ——That told very well, for I had the case strongly attested, and went about to collect the subscriptions myself.

DANGLE.

Egad, I believe that was when you first called on me.——

PUFF.

——In November last?——O no!——I was at that time, a close prisoner in the Marshalsea,[18] for a debt benevolently contracted to serve a friend!——I was afterwards, twice tapped for a dropsy, which declined into a very profitable consumption!——I was then reduced to——O no——then, I became a widow with six helpless children,——after having had eleven husbands pressed,[19] and being left every time eight

17. **Mercury:** patron of the eloquent and of thieves; he is depicted carrying a wand (caduceus) entwined with snakes.

18. **Marshalsea:** debtors' prison. 19. **pressed:** drafted into naval service.

months gone with child, and without money to get me into an hospital!

SNEER.

And you bore all with patience, I make no doubt?

PUFF.

Why, yes,——tho' I made some occasional attempts at felo de se;[20] but as I did not find those *rash actions* answer, I left off killing myself very soon.——Well, Sir,——at last, what with bankruptcies, fires, gouts, dropsies, imprisonments, and other valuable calamities, having got together a pretty handsome sum, I determined to quit a business which had always gone rather against my conscience, and in a more liberal way still to indulge my talents for fiction and embellishment, thro' my favourite channels of diurnal communication ——and so, Sir, you have my history.

SNEER.

Most obligingly communicative indeed; and your confession if published, might certainly serve the cause of true charity, by rescuing the most useful channels of appeal to benevolence from the cant of imposition.——But surely, Mr. PUFF, there is no great *mystery* in your present profession?

PUFF.

Mystery! Sir, I will take upon me to say the matter was never scientifically treated, nor reduced to rule before.

SNEER.

Reduced to rule?

PUFF.

O lud, Sir! you are very ignorant, I am afraid.—— Yes Sir,——PUFFING is of various sorts——the principal are, The PUFF DIRECT——the PUFF PRELIMINARY ——the PUFF COLLATERAL——the PUFF COLLUSIVE, and the PUFF OBLIQUE, or PUFF by IMPLICATION.—— These all assume, as circumstances require, the various forms of LETTER TO THE EDITOR——OCCASIONAL ANECDOTE——IMPARTIAL CRITIQUE——OBSERVATION from CORRESPONDENT——or ADVERTISEMENT FROM THE PARTY.

SNEER.

The puff direct, I can conceive——

PUFF.

O yes, that's simple enough,——for instance——A new Comedy or Farce is to be produced at one of the Theatres (though by the bye they don't bring out half what they ought to do). The author, suppose Mr. Smatter, or Mr. Dapper——or any particular friend

of mine——very well; the day before it is to be performed, I write an account of the manner in which it was received——I have the plot from the author, ——and only add——Characters strongly drawn—— highly coloured——hand of a master——fund of genuine humour——mine of invention——neat dialogue——attic salt! Then for the performance—— Mr. DODD was astonishingly great in the character of SIR HARRY! That universal and judicious actor Mr. PALMER, perhaps never appeared to more advantage than in the COLONEL;——but it is not in the power of language to do justice to Mr. KING![21]——Indeed he more than merited those repeated bursts of applause which he drew from a most brilliant and judicious audience! As to the scenery——The miraculous powers of Mr. DE LOUTHERBOURG's[22] pencil are universally acknowledged!——In short, we are at a loss which to admire most,——the unrivalled genius of the author, the great attention and liberality of the managers——the wonderful abilities of the painter, or the incredible exertions of all the performers!——

SNEER.

That's pretty well indeed, Sir.

PUFF.

O cool——quite cool——to what I sometimes do.

SNEER.

And do you think there are any who are influenced by this?

PUFF.

O, lud! yes, Sir;——the number of those who go thro' the fatigue of judging for themselves is very small indeed!

SNEER.

Well, Sir,——The PUFF PRELIMINARY?

PUFF.

O that, Sir, does well in the form of a *Caution*.—— In a matter of gallantry now——Sir FLIMSY GOSSIMER, wishes to be well with LADY FANNY FETE——He applies to me——I open trenches for him with a paragraph in the Morning Post.——It is recommended to the beautiful and accomplished Lady F four stars F dash E to be on her guard against that dangerous character, Sir F dash G; who, however pleasing and insinuating his manners may be, is certainly not remarkable for the *constancy of his attachments!*——in Italics.——Here you see, Sir FLIMSY GOSSIMER is

20. **felo de se:** the legal term for suicide.

21. **Mr. Dodd, Mr. Palmer, Mr. King:** See Dramatis Personae. 22. **Mr. De Loutherbourg:** the scene designer at Drury Lane.

introduced to the particular notice of Lady FANNY——
who, perhaps never thought of him before——she
finds herself publickly cautioned to avoid him, which
naturally makes her desirous of seeing him;——the
observation of their acquaintance causes a pretty kind
of mutual embarrassment, this produces a sort of
sympathy of interest——which, if Sir Flimsy is unable
to improve effectually, he at least gains the credit of
having their names mentioned together, by a particular
set, and in a particular way,——which nine times out
of ten is the full accomplishment of modern gallantry!

DANGLE.

Egad, Sneer, you will be quite an adept in the
business.

PUFF.

Now, Sir, the PUFF COLLATERAL is much used as an
appendage to advertisements, and may take the form
of anecdote.——Yesterday as the celebrated GEORGE
BON-MOT was sauntering down St. James's-street, he
met the lively Lady MARY MYRTLE, coming out of the
Park,——"Good God, LADY MARY, I'm surprised to
meet you in a white jacket,——for I expected never
to have seen you, but in a full-trimmed uniform, and a
light-horseman's cap!"——"Heavens, GEORGE, where
could you have learned that?"——"Why, replied the
wit, I just saw a print of you, in a new publication called
The CAMP MAGAZINE, which, by the bye, is a devilish
clever thing,——and is sold at No. 3, on the right hand
of the way, two doors from the printing-office, the
corner of Ivy-lane, Paternoster-row, price only one
shilling!"

SNEER.

Very ingenious indeed!

PUFF.

But the PUFF COLLUSIVE is the newest of any; for
it acts in the guise of determined hostility.——It is
much used by bold booksellers and enterprising poets.
——An indignant correspondent observes——that the
new poem called BEELZEBUB'S COTILLION, or PROSER-
PINE'S FETE CHAMPETRE, is one of the most unjustifiable
performances he ever read! The severity with which
certain characters are handled is quite shocking! And
as there are many descriptions in it too warmly
coloured for female delicacy, the shameful avidity with
which this piece is bought by all people of fashion, is a
reproach on the taste of the times, and a disgrace to
the delicacy of the age!——Here you see the two
strongest inducements are held forth;——First, that
nobody ought to read it,——and secondly, that every
body buys it; on the strength of which, the publisher

boldly prints the tenth edition, before he had sold ten
of the first; and then establishes it by threatening
himself with the pillory, or absolutely indicting himself
for SCAN. MAG.![23]

DANGLE.

Ha! ha! ha!——'gad I know it is so.

PUFF.

As to the PUFF OBLIQUE, or PUFF BY IMPLICATION,
it is too various and extensive to be illustrated by an
instance;——it attracts in titles, and presumes in
patents;[24] it lurks in the *limitation* of a subscription,
and invites in the assurance of croud and incommoda-
tion at public places; it delights to draw forth concealed merit, with a most disinterested assiduity; and
sometimes wears a countenance of smiling censure and
tender reproach.——It has a wonderful memory for
Parliamentary Debates, and will often give the whole
speech of a favoured member, with the most flattering
accuracy. But, above all, it is a great dealer in reports
and suppositions.——It has the earliest intelligence of
intended preferments that will reflect *honor* on the
patrons; and embryo promotions of modest gentlemen——who know nothing of the matter themselves.
It can hint a ribband for implied services, in the air of a
common report; and with the carelessness of a casual
paragraph, suggest officers into commands——to
which they have no pretension but their wishes. This,
Sir, is the last principal class in the ART of PUFFING——
An Art which I hope you will now agree with me, is
of the highest dignity——yielding a tablature[25] of
benevolence and public spirit; befriending equally
trade, gallantry, criticism, and politics:——the applause
of genius! the register of charity! the triumph of
heroism! the self defence of contractors! the fame of
orators!——and the gazette of ministers!

SNEER.

Sir, I am compleatly a convert both to the importance and ingenuity of your profession; and now, Sir,
there is but one thing which can possibly encrease my
respect for you, and that is, your permitting me to be
present this morning at the rehearsal of your new
trage——

PUFF.

——Hush, for heaven's sake.——*My* tragedy!——
Egad, Dangle, I take this very ill——you know how
apprehensive I am of being known to be the author.

23. **Scan. Mag:** (*scandalum magnatum*) slander of dignitaries.
24. **patents:** letters patent, the term used for a royal document conferring a privilege or granting a "place" (i.e.,
sinecure). 25. **tablature:** mental image created by description.

DANGLE.

'Efaith I would not have told——but it's in the papers, and your name at length——in the Morning Chronicle.

PUFF.

Ah! those damn'd editors never can keep a secret!——Well, Mr. Sneer,——no doubt you will do me great honour——I shall be infinitely happy——highly flattered——

DANGLE.

I believe it must be near the time——shall we go together.

PUFF.

No; It will not be yet this hour, for they are always late at that theatre: besides, I must meet you there, for I have some little matters here to send to the papers, and a few paragraphs to scribble before I go.

[Looking at memorandums.

——Here is "a CONSCIENTIOUS BAKER, on the Subject of the Army Bread;" and "a DETESTER OF VISIBLE BRICK-WORK, in favor of the new invented Stucco;" both in the style of JUNIUS,[26] and promised for tomorrow.——The Thames navigation too is at a stand.——MISOMUD or ANTI-SHOAL must go to work again directly.——Here too are some political memorandums I see; aye——To take PAUL JONES,[27] and get the INDIAMEN[28] out of the SHANNON——reinforce BYRON[29]——compel the DUTCH to——so!——I must do that in the evening papers, or reserve it for the Morning Herald, for I know that I have undertaken to-morrow; besides, to establish the unanimity of the fleet in the Public Advertiser, and to shoot CHARLES FOX[30] in the Morning Post.——So, egad, I ha'n't a moment to lose!

DANGLE.

Well!——we'll meet in the Green Room.

[Exeunt severally.

END OF ACT I.

26. the style . . . Junius: the style of malignant invective affected by "Junius," the anonymous author of a number of papers (1769–72) in The Public Advertiser attacking the King and the Administration. 27. Paul Jones: (1747–92), the American (formerly Scottish) privateer was conducting raids against the English and Irish coasts. 28. Indiamen: merchant ships from the West Indies that were blockaded in the Shannon River by enemy naval forces. 29. Byron: Vice Admiral John Byron, commander (1778–79) of the West Indies fleet in its actions against the French. 30. Charles Fox: Charles James Fox (1749–1806), Member of Parliament who helped lead the Opposition to the rigid American policy of George III and Lord North.

ACT II

SCENE I.

The Theatre.

Enter DANGLE, PUFF, and SNEER, as before the Curtain.

PUFF.

No, no, Sir; what Shakespeare says of ACTORS may be better applied to the purpose of PLAYS; they ought to be "the abstract and brief Chronicles of the times." Therefore when history, and particularly the history of our own country, furnishes any thing like a case in point, to the time in which an author writes, if he knows his own interest, he will take advantage of it; so, Sir, I call my tragedy The SPANISH ARMADA; and have laid the scene before TILBURY FORT.[1]

SNEER.

A most happy thought certainly!

DANGLE.

Egad it was——I told you so.——But pray now I don't understand how you have contrived to introduce any love into it.

PUFF.

Love!——Oh nothing so easy; for it is a received point among poets, that where history gives you a good heroic out-line for a play, you may fill up with a little love at your own discretion; in doing which, nine times out of ten, you only make up a deficiency in the private history of the times.——Now I rather think I have done this with some success.

SNEER.

No scandal about Queen ELIZABETH, I hope?

PUFF.

O Lud! no, no.——I only suppose the Governor of Tilbury Fort's daughter to be in love with the son of the Spanish Admiral.

SNEER.

Oh, is that all?

DANGLE.

Excellent, Efaith!——I see it at once.——But won't this appear rather improbable?

Act II, scene i. 1. Tilbury Fort: During the threat of invasion posed by the Spanish Armada in 1588, Queen Elizabeth I mustered her troops for the defense at Tilbury Fort, at the mouth of the Thames.

PUFF.

To be sure it will——but what the plague! a play is not to shew occurences that happen every day, but things just so strange, that tho' they never *did*, they *might* happen.

SNEER.

Certainly nothing is unnatural, that is not physically impossible.

PUFF.

Very true——and for that matter DON FEROLO WHISKERANDOS——for that's the lover's name, might have been over here in the train of the Spanish Ambassador; or TILBURINA, for that is the lady's name, might have been in love with him, from having heard his character, or seen his picture; or from knowing that he was the last man in the world she ought to be in love with——or for any other good female reason. ——However, Sir, the fact is, that tho' she is but a Knight's daughter, egad! she is in love like any Princess!

DANGLE.

Poor young lady! I feel for her already! for I can conceive how great the conflict must be between her passion and her duty; her love for her country, and her love for DON FEROLO WHISKERANDOS!

PUFF.

O amazing!——her poor susceptible heart is swayed to and fro, by contending passions like——

Enter UNDER PROMPTER.

UNDER PROMPTER.

Sir, the scene is set, and every thing is ready to begin if you please.——

PUFF.

'Egad; then we'll lose no time.

UNDER PROMPTER.

Tho' I believe, Sir, you will find it very short, for all the performers have profited by the kind permission you granted them.

PUFF.

Hey! what!

UNDER PROMPTER.

You know, Sir, you gave them leave to cut out or omit whatever they found heavy or unnecessary to the plot, and I must own they have taken very liberal advantage of your indulgence.

PUFF.

Well, well.——They are in general very good judges; and I know I am luxuriant.——Now, Mr. HOPKINS, as soon as you please.

UNDER PROMPTER *to the Musick*.

Gentlemen, will you play a few bars of something, just to——

PUFF.

Aye, that's right,——for as we have the scenes, and dresses, egad, we'll go to 't, as if it were the first night's performance;——but you need not mind stopping between the acts.   [*Exit Under Prompter.*

(*Orchestra play. Then the Bell rings.*)

Soh! stand clear gentlemen.——Now you know there will be a cry of down!——down!——hats off! silence!——Then up curtain,——and let us see what our painters have done for us.

SCENE II.

The Curtain rises and discovers TILBURY FORT.

Two Centinels asleep.

DANGLE.

Tilbury Fort!——very fine indeed!

PUFF.

Now, what do you think I open with?

SNEER.

Faith, I can't guess——

PUFF.

A clock.——Hark!——(*clock strikes.*) I open with a clock striking, to beget an aweful attention in the audience——it also marks the time, which is four o'clock in the morning, and saves a description of the rising sun, and a great deal about gilding the eastern hemisphere.

DANGLE.

But pray, are the centinels to be asleep?

PUFF.

Fast as watchmen.

SNEER.

Isn't that odd tho' at such an alarming crisis?

PUFF.

To be sure it is,——but smaller things must give way to a striking scene at the opening; that's a rule. ——And the case is, that two great men are coming to this very spot to begin the piece; now, it is not to be supposed they would open their lips, if these fellows were watching them, so, egad, I must either have sent them off their posts, or set them asleep.

SNEER.

O that accounts for it!——But tell us, who are these coming?——

PUFF.

These are they——SIR WALTER RALEIGH, and SIR CHRISTOPHER HATTON.[1]——You'll know Sir CHRISTOPHER, by his turning out his toes——famous you know for his dancing. I like to preserve all the little traits of character.——Now attend.

Enter Sir WALTER RALEIGH *and* Sir CHRISTOPHER HATTON.

SIR CHRISTOPHER.

"True, gallant Raleigh!"

DANGLE.

What, they had been talking before?

PUFF.

O, yes; all the way as they came along.——I beg pardon gentlemen [*to the Actors*] but these are particular friends of mine, whose remarks may be of great service to us.——Don't mind interrupting them whenever any thing strikes you. [*To Sneer and Dangle.*]

SIR CHRISTOPHER.

"True, gallant Raleigh!
But O, thou champion of thy country's fame,
There *is* a question which I yet must ask;
A question, which I never ask'd before——
What mean these mighty armaments?
This general muster? and this throng of chiefs?"

SNEER.

Pray, Mr. Puff, how came Sir Christopher Hatton never to ask that question before?

PUFF.

What, before the Play began? how the plague could he?

DANGLE.

That's true efaith.

PUFF.

But you will hear what he thinks of the matter.

SIR CHRISTOPHER.

"Alas, my noble friend, when I behold
Yon tented plains in martial symmetry
Array'd.——When I count o'er yon glittering lines
Of crested warriors, where the proud steeds neigh,
And valor-breathing trumpet's shrill appeal,
Responsive vibrate on my listning ear;
When virgin majesty[2] herself I view,
Like her protecting Pallas[3] veil'd in steel,

Act II, scene ii. **1. Sir . . . Hatton:** (1540–91), Lord Chancellor at the time of the Armada. **2. virgin majesty:** Queen Elizabeth I, who in 1588, arrayed in armor and mounted on a horse, reviewed the troops at Tilbury Fort. **3. Pallas:** the Greek goddess Pallas Athene, protectress of cities.

With graceful confidence exhort to arms!
When briefly all I hear or see bears stamp
Of martial vigilance, and stern defence,
I cannot but surmise.——Forgive, my friend,
If the conjecture's rash——I cannot but
Surmise.——The state some danger apprehends!"

SNEER.

A very cautious conjecture that.

PUFF.

Yes, that's his character; not to give an opinion, but on secure grounds——now then.

SIR WALTER.

"O, most accomplished Christopher.——"

PUFF.

He calls him by his christian name, to shew that they are on the most familiar terms.

SIR WALTER.

"O most accomplish'd Christopher, I find
Thy staunch sagacity still tracks the future,
In the fresh print of the o'ertaken past."

PUFF.

Figurative!

SIR WALTER.

"Thy fears are just."

SIR CHRISTOPHER.

"But where? whence? when? and what
The danger is——Methinks I fain would learn."

SIR WALTER.

"You know, my friend, scarce two revolving suns,
And three revolving moons, have closed their course,
Since haughty PHILIP, in despight of peace,
With hostile hand hath struck at ENGLAND's trade."

SIR CHRISTOPHER.

"I know it well."

SIR WALTER.

"PHILIP you know is proud[4] IBERIA's king!"

SIR CHRISTOPHER.

"He is."

SIR WALTER.

"——His subjects in base bigotry
And Catholic oppression held,——while we
You know, the protestant persuasion hold."

SIR CHRISTOPHER.

"We do."

SIR WALTER.

"You know beside,——his boasted armament,
The fam'd Armada,——by the Pope baptized,
With purpose to invade these realms——"

---

4. proud: The text has a comma after *proud*.

SIR CHRISTOPHER.

"———Is sailed,
Our last advices so report."

SIR WALTER.

"While the Iberian Admiral's chief hope,
His darling son———"

SIR CHRISTOPHER.

"———Ferolo Whiskerandoes
hight———"

SIR WALTER.

"The same———by chance a pris'ner hath been ta'en,
And in this fort of Tilbury———"

SIR CHRISTOPHER.

"———Is now
"Confin'd,———'tis true, and oft from yon tall turrets top
I've mark'd the youthful Spaniard's haughty mien
Unconquer'd, tho' in chains!"

SIR WALTER.

"You also know———"

DANGLE.

———Mr. Puff, as he *knows* all this, why does Sir Walter go on telling him?

PUFF.

But the audience are not supposed to know any thing of the matter, are they?

SNEER.

True, but I think you manage ill: for there certainly appears no reason why Sir Walter should be so communicative.

PUFF.

For, egad now, that is one of the most ungrateful observations I ever heard———for the less inducement he has to tell all this, the more I think, you ought to be oblig'd to him; for I am sure you'd know nothing of the matter without it.

DANGLE.

That's very true, upon my word.

PUFF.

But you will find he was *not* going on.

SIR CHRISTOPHER.

"Enough, enough,———'tis plain———and I no more
Am in amazement lost!———"

PUFF.

Here, now you see, Sir Christopher did not in fact ask any one question for his own information.

SNEER.

No indeed:———his has been a most disinterested curiosity!

DANGLE.

Really, I find, we are very much oblig'd to them both.

PUFF.

To be sure you are. Now then for the Commander in Chief, the EARL OF LEICESTER! who, you know, was no favourite but of the Queen's.———We left off———"in amazement lost!"———

SIR CHRISTOPHER.

"Am in amazement lost.———
But, see where noble Leicester comes! supreme
In honours and command."

SIR WALTER.

"And yet methinks,
At such a time, so perilous, so fear'd,
That staff might well become an abler grasp."

SIR CHRISTOPHER.

"And so by heav'n! think I; but soft, he's here!"

PUFF.

Aye, they envy him.

SNEER.

But who are these with him?

PUFF.

O! very valiant knights: one is the Governor of the fort, the other the master of the horse.———And now, I think you shall hear some better language: I was obliged to be plain and intelligible in the first scene, because there was so much matter of fact in it; but now, efaith, you have trope, figure, and metaphor, as plenty as noun-substantives.

Enter Earl of LEICESTER, *the Governor, and others.*

LEICESTER.

"How's this my friends! is 't thus your new fledg'd zeal
And plumed valor moulds in roosted sloth?
Why dimly glimmers that heroic flame,
Whose red'ning blaze by patriot spirit fed,
Should be the beacon of a kindling realm?
Can the quick current of a patriot heart,
Thus stagnate in a cold and weedy converse,
Or freeze in tideless inactivity?
No! rather let the fountain of your valor
Spring thro' each stream of enterprize,
Each petty channel of conducive daring,
Till the full torrent of your foaming wrath
O'erwhelm the flats of sunk hostility!"

PUFF.

There it is,———follow'd up!

SIR WALTER.

"No more! the fresh'ning breath of thy rebuke
Hath fill'd the swelling canvass of our souls!"

And thus, tho' fate should cut the cable of
                                    [*All take hands.*]
Our topmost hopes, in friendship's closing line
We'll grapple with despair, and if we fall,
We'll fall in Glory's wake!"

EARL OF LEICESTER.

"There spoke Old England's genius!
Then, are we all resolv'd?"

ALL.

"We are——all resolv'd."

EARL OF LEICESTER.

"To conquer——or be free?"

ALL.

"To conquer, or be free."

EARL OF LEICESTER.

"All?"

ALL.

"All."

DANGLE.

Nem. con.[5] egad!

PUFF.

O yes, where they *do* agree on the stage, their unanimity is wonderful!

EARL OF LEICESTER.

"Then, let's embrace——and now——"

SNEER.

What the plague, is he going to pray?

PUFF.

Yes, hush!——in great emergencies, there is nothing like a prayer!

EARL OF LEICESTER.

"O mighty Mars!"

DANGLE.

But why should he pray to *Mars?*

PUFF.

Hush!

EARL OF LEICESTER.

                    "If in thy homage bred,
Each point of discipline I've still observ'd;
Nor but by due promotion, and the right
Of service, to the rank of Major-General
Have ris'n; assist thy votary now!"

GOVERNOR.

"Yet do not rise,——hear me!"

MASTER OF HORSE.

"And me!"

KNIGHT.

"And me!"

SIR WALTER.

"And me!"

SIR CHRISTOPHER.

"And me!"

PUFF.

Now, pray all together.

ALL.

"Behold thy votaries submissive beg,
That thou will deign to grant them all they ask;
Assist them to accomplish all their ends,
And sanctify whatever means they use
To gain them!"

SNEER.

A very orthodox quintetto!

PUFF.

Vastly well, gentlemen.——Is that well managed or not? Have you such a prayer as that on the stage?

SNEER.

Not exactly.

(*Earl of Leicester to Puff.*)

But, Sir, you hav'nt settled how we are to get off here.

PUFF.

You could not go off kneeling, could you?

(*Sir Walter to Puff.*)

O no, Sir! impossible!

PUFF.

It would have a good effect efaith, if you could! exeunt praying!——Yes, and would vary the established mode of springing off with a glance at the pit.

SNEER.

O never mind, so as you get them off, I'll answer for it the audience won't care how.

PUFF.

Well then, repeat the last line standing, and go off the old way.

ALL.

"And sanctify whatever means we use to gain them."
                                    [*Exeunt.*

DANGLE.

Bravo! a fine exit.

SNEER.

Well, really Mr. Puff.——

PUFF.

Stay a moment.——

5. **Nem. con:** (*nemine contradicente*) unanimously.

The CENTINELS *get up*.

1ST CENTINEL.

"All this shall to Lord Burleigh's[6] ear."

2d CENTINEL.

"'Tis meet it should."   [*Exeunt Centinels*.

DANGLE.

Hey!——why, I thought those fellows had been asleep?

PUFF.

Only a pretence, there's the art of it; they were spies of Lord Burleigh's.

SNEER.

——But isn't it odd, they were never taken notice of, not even by the commander in chief.

PUFF.

O lud, Sir, if people who want to listen, or over-hear, were not always conniv'd at in a Tragedy, there would be no carrying on any plot in the world.

DANGLE.

That's certain!

PUFF.

But take care, my dear Dangle, the morning gun is going to fire.   [*Cannon fires*.

DANGLE.

Well, that will have a fine effect.

PUFF.

I think so, and helps to realize the scene.——
[*Cannon twice*.
What the plague!——*three* morning guns!——there never is but one!——aye, this is always the way at the Theatre——give these fellows a good thing, and they never know when to have done with it. You have no more cannon to fire?

PROMPTER *from within*.

No Sir.

PUFF.

Now then, for soft musick.

SNEER.

Pray what's that for?

PUFF.

It shews that TILBURNIA is coming; nothing intro-duces you a heroine like soft musick.——Here she comes.

DANGLE.

And her confidant, I suppose?

PUFF.

To be sure: here they are——inconsolable to the minuet in Ariadne![7] (*Soft musick*.)

Enter TILBURINA *and* CONFIDANT.

TILBURINA.

"Now has the whispering breath of gentle morn,
Bad Nature's voice, and Nature's beauty rise;
While orient Phœbus with unborrow'd hues,
Cloaths the wak'd loveliness which all night slept
In heav'nly drapery! Darkness is fled.
Now flowers unfold their beauties to the sun,
And blushing, kiss the beam he sends to wake them.
The strip'd carnation, and the guarded rose,
The vulgar wall flow'r, and smart gillyflower,
The polyanthus mean——the dapper daizy,
Sweet William, and sweet marjoram,——and all
The tribe of single and of double pinks!
Now too, the feather'd warblers tune their notes
Around, and charm the listning grove.——The lark!
The linnet! chafinch! bullfinch! goldfinch! greenfinch!
——but O to me, no joy can they afford!
Nor rose, nor wall flow'r, nor smart gillyflower,
Nor polyanthus mean, nor dapper daizy,
Nor William sweet, nor marjoram——nor lark,
Linnet, nor all the finches of the grove!"

PUFF.

Your white handkerchief madam——

TILBURNIA.

I thought, Sir, I wasn't to use that 'till, "heart rending woe."

PUFF.

O yes madam——at "the finches of the grove," if you please.

TILBURNIA.

                    "Nor lark,
Linnet, nor all the finches of the grove!"   [*Weeps*.

PUFF.

Vastly well madam!

DANGLE.

Vastly well indeed!

TILBURINA.

"For, O too sure, heart rending woe is now
The lot of wretched Tilburina!"

DANGLE.

O!——'tis too much.

6. Lord Burleigh: (1520–98), Lord Treasurer and Queen Elizabeth's chief minister.

7. Ariadne: an opera (1734) by George Frederick Handel (1685–1759).

SNEER.

Oh!——it is indeed.

CONFIDANT.

"Be comforted sweet lady——for who knows,
But Heav'n has yet some milk-white day in store."

TILBURINA.

"Alas, my gentle Nora,
Thy tender youth, as yet hath never mourn'd
Love's fatal dart.——Else wouldst thou know, that when
The soul is sunk in comfortless despair,
It cannot taste of merryment!"

DANGLE.

That's certain.

CONFIDANT.

"But see where your stern father comes;
It is not meet that he should find you thus."

PUFF.

Hey, what the plague!——what a cut is here!——
why, what is become of the description of her first
meeting with Don Whiskerandos? his gallant behaviour in the sea fight, and the simile of the canary
bird?

TILBURINA.

Indeed Sir, you'll find they will not be miss'd.

PUFF.

Very well.——Very well!

TILBURINA.

The cue ma'am if you please.

CONFIDANT.

"It is not meet that he should find you thus."

TILBURINA.

"Thou counsel'st right, but 'tis no easy task
For barefaced grief to wear a mask of joy."

Enter GOVERNOR.

"How's this——in tears?——O Tilburina, shame!
Is this a time for maudling tenderness,
And Cupid's baby woes?——hast thou not heard
That haughty Spain's Pope-consecrated fleet
Advances to our shores, while England's fate,
Like a clipp'd guinea, trembles in the scale!"

TILBURINA.

"Then, is the crisis of *my* fate at hand!
I see the fleets approach——I see——"

PUFF.

Now, pray gentlemen mind.——This is one of the
most useful figures we tragedy writers have, by which
a hero or heroine, in consideration of their being often
obliged to overlook things that *are* on the stage, is
allow'd to hear and see a number of things that are not.

SNEER.

Yes——a kind of poetical second-sight!

PUFF.

Yes——now then madam.

TILBURINA.

"I see their decks
Are clear'd!——I see the signal made!
The line is form'd!——a cable's length asunder!
I see the frigates station'd in the rear;
And now, I hear the thunder of the guns!
I hear the victors shouts——I also hear
The vanquish'd groan!——and now 'tis smoke——and
    now
I see the loose sails shiver in the wind!
I see——I see——what soon you'll see——"

GOVERNOR.

"Hold daughter! peace! this love hath turn'd thy brain:
The Spanish fleet thou *canst* not see——because
——It is not yet in sight!"

DANGLE.

Egad tho', the governor seems to make no allowance
for this poetical figure you talk of.

PUFF.

No, a plain matter-of-fact man——that's his
character.

TILBURINA.

"But will you then refuse his offer?"

GOVERNOR.

"I must——I will——I can——I ought——I do."

TILBURINA.

"Think what a noble price."

GOVERNOR.

"No more——you urge in vain."

TILBURINA.

"His liberty is all he asks."

SNEER.

All *who* asks Mr. Puff? Who is——

PUFF.

Egad Sir, I can't tell.——Here has been such cutting
and slashing, I don't know where they have got to
myself.

TILBURINA.

Indeed Sir, you will find it will connect very well.

"——And your reward secure."

PUFF.

O,——if they had'nt been so devilish free with
their cutting here, you would have found that Don
Whiskerandos has been tampering for his liberty, and
has persuaded Tilburina to make this proposal to her

father——and now pray observe the conciseness with which the argument is conducted. Egad, the *pro & con* goes as smart as hits in a fencing match. It is indeed a sort of small-sword logic, which we have borrowed from the French.

TILBURINA.

"A retreat in Spain!"

GOVERNOR.

"Outlawry here!"

TILBURINA.

"Your daughter's prayer!"

GOVERNOR.

"Your father's oath!"

TILBURINA.

"My lover!"

GOVERNOR.

"My country!"

TILBURINA.

"Tilburina!"

GOVERNOR.

"England!"

TILBURINA.

"A title!"

GOVERNOR.

"Honor!"

TILBURINA.

"A pension!"

GOVERNOR.

"Conscience!"

TILBURINA.

"A thousand pounds!"

GOVERNOR.

"Hah! thou hast touch'd me nearly!"

PUFF.

There you see——she threw in *Tilburina*, Quick, parry cart[8] with *England!*——Hah! thrust in tierce a title!——parried by honor.——Hah! a pension over the arm!——put by by conscience.——Then flanko-nade with a thousand pounds——and a palpable hit egad!

TILBURINA.

"Canst thou——
Reject the *suppliant*, and the *daughter* too?"

GOVERNOR.

"No more; I wou'd not hear thee plead in vain,
The *father* softens——but the *governor* is fix'd!"   [*Exit.*

8. **parry cart**: In this speech Puff uses the technical terms of fencing.

DANGLE.

Aye, that antithesis of persons——is a most estab-lished figure.

TILBURINA.

"'Tis well,——hence then fond hopes,——fond passion hence;
Duty, behold I am all over thine——"

WHISKERANDOS *without.*

"Where is my love——my——"

TILBURINA.

"Ha!"

WHISKERANDOS *entering.*

"My beauteous enemy——"

PUFF.

O dear ma'am, you must start a great deal more than that; consider you had just determined in favour of duty——when in a moment the sound of his voice revives your passion,——overthrows your resolution, destroys your obedience.——If you don't express all that in your start——you do nothing at all.

TILBURINA.

Well, we'll try again!

DANGLE.

Speaking from within, has always a fine effect.

SNEER.

Very.

WHISKERANDOS.

"My conquering Tilburina! How! is't thus
We meet? why are thy looks averse! what means
That falling tear——that frown of boding woe?
Hah! now indeed I am a prisoner!
Yes, now I feel the galling weight of these
Disgraceful chains——which, cruel Tilburina!
Thy doating captive gloried in before.——
But thou art false, and Whiskerandos is undone!"

TILBURINA.

"O no; how little dost thou know thy Tilburina!"

WHISKERANDOS.

"Art thou then true? Begone cares, doubts and fears,
I make you all a present to the winds;
And if the winds reject you——try the waves."

PUFF.

The wind you know, is the established receiver of all stolen sighs, and cast off griefs and apprehensions.

TILBURINA.

"Yet must we part?——stern duty seals our doom:
Though here I call yon conscious clouds to witness,
Could I pursue the bias of my soul,
All friends, all right of parents I'd disclaim,
And thou, my Whiskerandos, should'st be father

And mother, brother, cousin, uncle, aunt,
And friend to me!"

WHISKERANDOS.

"O matchless excellence!——and must we part?
Well, if——we must——we must——and in that case,
The less is said the better."

PUFF.

Hey day! here's a cut!——What, are all the mutual
protestations out?

TILBURINA.

Now, pray Sir, don't interrupt us just here, you
ruin our feelings.

PUFF.

Your feelings!——but zounds, *my* feelings, ma'am!

SNEER.

No; pray don't interrupt them.

WHISKERANDOS.

"One last embrace.——"

TILBURINA.

"Now,——farewell, for ever."

WHISKERANDOS.

"For ever!"

TILBURINA.

"Aye, for ever."   [*Going.*

PUFF.

S' death and fury!——Gadslife! Sir! Madam! if
you go out without the parting look, you might as
well dance out——Here, here!

CONFIDANT.

But pray Sir, how am *I* to get off here?

PUFF.

You, pshaw! what the devil signifies how *you* get
off! edge away at the top,[9] or where you will——
[*Pushes the confidant off.*] Now ma'am you see——

TILBURINA.

We understand you Sir.

"Aye for ever."

BOTH.

"Ohh!——"   [*Turning back and exeunt.*
                                         [*Scene closes.*

DANGLE.

O charming!

PUFF.

Hey!——'tis pretty well I believe——you see I
don't attempt to strike out any thing new——but I
take it I improve on the established modes.

9. **the top:** the rear of the stage, originally higher than the
front (cf. *upstage*).

SNEER.

You do indeed.——But pray is not Queen Elizabeth
to appear?

PUFF.

No not once——but she is to be talked of for ever;
so that egad you'll think a hundred times that she is
on the point of coming in.

SNEER.

Hang it, I think its a pity to keep *her* in the green
room all the night.

PUFF.

O no, that always has a fine effect——it keeps up
expectation.

DANGLE.

But are we not to have a battle?

PUFF.

Yes, yes, you will have a battle at last, but, egad, it's
not to be by land——but by sea——and that is the
only quite new thing in the piece.

DANGLE.

What, Drake at the Armada, hey?

PUFF.

Yes, efaith——fire ships and all——then we shall
end with the procession.——Hey! that will do I think.

SNEER.

No doubt on 't.

PUFF.

Come, we must not lose time——so now for the
UNDER PLOT.

SNEER.

What the plague, have you another plot?

PUFF.

O lord, yes——ever while you live, have two plots
to your tragedy.——The grand point in managing
them, is only to let your under plot have as little connexion with your main plot as possible.——I flatter
myself nothing can be more distinct than mine, for as
in my chief plot, the characters are all great people——
I have laid my under plot in low life——and as the
former is to end in deep distress, I make the other end
as happy as a farce.——Now Mr. Hopkins, as soon
as you please.

Enter UNDER PROMPTER.

UNDER PROMPTER.

Sir, the carpenter says it is impossible you can go
to the Park scene yet.

PUFF.

The Park scene!——No——I mean the description
scene here, in the wood.

UNDER PROMPTER.

Sir, the performers have cut it out.

PUFF.

Cut it out!

UNDER PROMPTER.

Yes Sir.

PUFF.

What! the whole account of Queen Elizabeth?

UNDER PROMPTER.

Yes Sir.

PUFF.

And the description of her horse and side-saddle?

UNDER PROMPTER.

Yes Sir.

PUFF.

So, so, this is very fine indeed! Mr. Hopkins, how the plague could you suffer this?

HOPKINS, *from within.*

Sir, indeed the pruning knife——

PUFF.

The pruning knife——zounds the axe! why, here has been such lopping and topping, I shan't have the bare trunk of my play left presently.——Very well, Sir——the performers must do as they please, but upon my soul, I'll print it every word.

SNEER.

That I would indeed.

PUFF.

Very well——Sir——then we must go on—— zounds! I would not have parted with the description of the horse!——Well, Sir, go on——Sir, it was one of the finest and most laboured things——Very well, Sir, let them go on——there you had him and his accoutrements from the bit to the crupper—very well, Sir, we must go to the Park scene.

UNDER PROMPTER.

Sir, there is the point, the carpenters say, that unless there is some business put in here before the drop, they shan't have time to clear away the fort, or sink Graves-end and the river.

PUFF.

So! this is a pretty dilemma truly!——Gentlemen ——you must excuse me, these fellows will never be ready, unless I go and look after them myself.

SNEER.

O dear Sir——these little things will happen——

PUFF.

To cut out this scene!——but I'll print it——egad, I'll print it every word!   [*Exeunt.*

END OF ACT II.

ACT III

SCENE I.

Before the Curtain.

Enter PUFF, SNEER, *and* DANGLE.

PUFF.

Well, we are ready——now then for the justices.
  [*Curtain rises; Justices, Constables, &c. discovered.*

SNEER.

This, I suppose, is a sort of senate scene.

PUFF.

To be sure——there has not been one yet.

DANGLE.

It is the under plot, isn't it?

PUFF.

Yes. What, gentlemen, do you mean to go at once to the discovery scene?

JUSTICE.

If you please, Sir.

PUFF.

O very well——harkee, I don't chuse to say any thing more, but efaith, they have mangled my play in a most shocking manner!

DANGLE.

It's a great pity!

PUFF.

Now then, Mr. Justice, if you please.

JUSTICE.

"Are all the volunteers without?"

CONSTABLE.

                                "They are.
"Some ten in fetters, and some twenty drunk."

JUSTICE.

"Attends the youth, whose most opprobrious fame
And clear convicted crimes have stampt him soldier?"

CONSTABLE.

"He waits your pleasure; eager to repay
The blest reprieve that sends him to the fields
Of glory, there to raise his branded hand
In honor's cause."

JUSTICE.

        " 'Tis well—'tis Justice arms him!
O! may he now defend his country's laws
With half the spirit he has broke them all!
If 'tis your worship's pleasure, bid him enter."

CONSTABLE.

"I fly, the herald of your will."   [*Exit Constable.*

PUFF.

Quick, Sir!——

SNEER.

But, Mr. Puff, I think not only the Justice, but the clown seems to talk in as high a style as the first hero among them.

PUFF.

Heaven forbid they should not in a free country!
——Sir, I am not for making slavish distinctions, and giving all the fine language to the upper sort of people.

DANGLE.

That's very noble in you indeed.

Enter JUSTICE'S LADY.

PUFF.

Now pray mark this scene.

LADY.

"Forgive this interruption, good my love;
But as I just now past, a pris'ner youth
Whom rude hands hither lead, strange bodings seiz'd
My fluttering heart, and to myself I said,
An if our TOM had liv'd, he'd surely been
This stripling's height!"

JUSTICE.

"Ha! sure some powerful sympathy directs
Us both——"

Enter SON *and* CONSTABLE.

JUSTICE.

"What is thy name?"

SON.

"My name's TOM JENKINS——*alias*, have I none——
Tho' orphan'd, and without a friend!"

JUSTICE.

"Thy parents?"

SON.

"My father dwelt in Rochester——and was,
As I have heard——a fishmonger——no more."

PUFF.

What, Sir, do you leave out the account of your birth, parentage and education?

SON.

They have settled it so, Sir, here.

PUFF.

Oh! oh!

LADY.

"How loudly nature whispers to my heart!
Had he no other name?"

SON.

"I've seen a bill
Of his, sign'd *Tomkins*, creditor."

JUSTICE.

"This does indeed confirm each circumstance
The gypsey told!——Prepare!"

SON.

"I do."

JUSTICE.

"No orphan, nor without a friend art thou——
I am thy father, *here's* thy mother, *there*
Thy uncle——this thy first cousin, and those
Are all your near relations!"

MOTHER.

"O ecstasy of bliss!"

SON.

"O most unlook'd for happiness!"

JUSTICE.

"O wonderful event!"

[*They faint alternately in each others arms.*

PUFF.

There, you see relationship, like murder, will out.

JUSTICE.

"Now let's revive——else were this joy too much!
But come——and we'll unfold the rest within,
And thou my boy must needs want rest and food.
Hence may each orphan hope, as chance directs,
To find a father——where he least expects!"   [*Exeunt.*

PUFF.

What do you think of that?

DANGLE.

One of the finest discovery-scenes I ever saw.——
Why, this under-plot would have made a tragedy itself.

SNEER.

Aye, or a comedy either.

PUFF.

And keeps quite clear you see of the other.

Enter SCENEMEN, *taking away the Seats.*

PUFF.

The scene remains, does it?

SCENEMAN.

Yes, Sir.

PUFF.

You are to leave one chair you know——But it is always awkward in a tragedy, to have you fellows coming in in your playhouse liveries to remove things ——I wish that could be managed better.——So now for my mysterious yeoman.

Enter A BEEFEATER.

BEEFEATER.

"Perdition catch my soul but *I* do love thee."

SNEER.

Haven't I heard that line before?

PUFF.

No, I fancy not——Where pray?

DANGLE.

Yes, I think there is something like it in Othello.[1]

PUFF.

Gad! now you put me in mind on 't, I believe there is——but that's of no consequence——all that can be said is, that two people happened to hit on the same thought——And Shakespeare made use of it first, that's all.

SNEER.

Very true.

PUFF.

Now, Sir, your soliloquy——but speak more to the pit, if you please——the soliloquy always to the pit——that's a rule.

BEEFEATER.

"Tho' hopeless love finds comfort in despair,
It never can endure a rival's bliss!
But soft——I am observ'd."   [*Exit Beefeater.*

DANGLE.

That's a very short soliloquy.

PUFF.

Yes——but it would have been a great deal longer if he had not been observed.

SNEER.

A most sentimental Beefeater that, Mr. Puff.

PUFF.

Hearke—I would not have you be too sure that he *is* a Beefeater.

SNEER.

What! a hero in disguise?

PUFF.

No matter——I only give you a hint——But now for my principal character——Here he comes—— LORD BURLEIGH in person! Pray, gentlemen, step this way——softly——I only hope the Lord High Treasurer is perfect——if he is but perfect!

[*Enter* BURLEIGH, *goes slowly to a chair, and sits.*]

Act III, scene i. **1. something . . . Othello:** See III. iii. 90–91.

SNEER.

Mr. Puff!

PUFF.

Hush!——vastly well, Sir! vastly well! a most interesting gravity!

DANGLE.

What, isn't he to speak at all?

PUFF.

Egad, I thought you'd ask me that——yes it is a very likely thing——that a Minister in his situation, with the whole affairs of the nation on his head, should have time to talk!——but hush! or you'll put him out.

SNEER.

Put him out! how the plague can that be, if he's not going to say any thing?

PUFF.

There's a reason!——why, his part is to *think*, and how the plague! do you imagine he can *think* if you keep talking?

DANGLE.

That's very true upon my word!

[*Burleigh comes forward, shakes his head and exit.*

SNEER.

He is very perfect indeed——Now, pray what did he mean by that?

PUFF.

You don't take it?

SNEER.

No; I don't upon my soul.

PUFF.

Why, by that shake of the head, he gave you to understand that even tho' they had more justice in their cause and wisdom in their measures——yet, if there was not a greater spirit shown on the part of the people——the country would at last fall a sacrifice to the hostile ambition of the Spanish monarchy.

SNEER.

The devil!——did he mean all that by shaking his head?

PUFF.

Every word of it——If he shook his head as I taught him.

DANGLE.

Ah! there certainly is a vast deal to be done on the stage by dumb shew, and expression of face, and a judicious author knows how much he may trust to it.

SNEER.

O, here are some of our old acquaintance.

Enter HATTON *and* RALEIGH.

SIR CHRISTOPHER.

"*My* niece, and *your* niece too!
By heav'n! there's witchcraft in 't——He could not else
Have gain'd their hearts——But see where they
    approach;
Some horrid purpose low'ring on their brows!"

SIR WALTER.

"Let us withdraw and mark them."   [*They withdraw.*

SNEER.

What is all this?

PUFF.

Ah! here has been more pruning!——but the fact
is, these two young ladies are also in love with Don
Whiskerandos.——Now, gentlemen, this scene goes
entirely for what we call SITUATION and STAGE EFFECT,
by which the greatest applause may be obtained, without the assistance of language, sentiment or character:
pray mark!

Enter the TWO NIECES.

1st NIECE.

"Ellena here!
She is his scorn as much as I——that is
Some comfort still."

PUFF.

O dear madam, you are not to say that to her face!
——*aside*, ma'am, *aside*.——The whole scene is to be
aside.

1st NIECE.

"She is his scorn as much as I——that is
Some comfort still!"   [*Aside.*

2d NIECE.

"I know he prizes not Pollina's love,
But Tilburina lords it o'er his heart."   [*Aside.*

1st NIECE.

"But see the proud destroyer of my peace.
Revenge is all the good I've left."   [*Aside.*

2d NIECE.

"He comes, the false disturber of my quiet.
Now vengeance do thy worst——"   [*Aside.*

Enter WHISKERANDOS.

"O hateful liberty——if thus in vain
I seek my Tilburina!"

BOTH NIECES.

"And ever shalt!"

SIR CHRISTOPHER AND SIR WALTER *come forward.*

"Hold! we will avenge you."

WHISKERANDOS

"Hold *you*——or see your nieces bleed!"
    [*The two nieces draw their two daggers to strike
    Whiskerandos, the two Uncles at the instant with
    their two swords drawn, catch their two nieces'
    arms, and turn the points of their swords to
    Whiskerandos, who immediately draws two
    daggers, and holds them to the two nieces'
    bosoms.*]

PUFF.

There's situation for you!——there's an heroic
group!——You see the ladies can't stab Whiskerandos
——he durst not strike them for fear of their uncles
——the uncles durst not kill him, because of their
nieces——I have them all at a dead lock!——for every
one of them is afraid to let go first.

SNEER.

Why, then they must stand there for ever.

PUFF.

So they would, if I hadn't a very fine contrivance
for 't——Now mind——

Enter BEEFEATER *with his Halberd.*

"In the Queen's name I charge you all to drop
Your swords and daggers!"
    [*They drop their swords and daggers.*

SNEER.

That is a contrivance indeed.

PUFF.

Aye——in the Queen's name.

SIR CHRISTOPHER.

"Come niece!"

SIR WALTER.

"Come niece!"   [*Exeunt with the two nieces.*

WHISKERANDOS.

"What's he, who bids us thus renounce our guard?"

BEEFEATER.

"Thou must do more, renounce thy love!"

WHISKERANDOS.

"Thou liest——base Beefeater!"

BEEFEATER.

             "Ha! Hell! the lie!
"By heav'n thou'st rous'd the lion in my heart!
Off yeoman's habit!——base disguise!——off! off!
    [*Discovers himself, by throwing off his upper dress,
          and appearing in a very fine waistcoat.*]
Am I a Beefeater now?
Or beams my crest as terrible as when
In Biscay's Bay I took thy captive sloop."

PUFF.

There, egad! he comes out to be the very Captain
of the privateer who had taken Whiskerandos

prisoner——and was himself an old lover of Tilburina's.

DANGLE.

Admirably manag'd indeed.

PUFF.

Now, stand out of their way.

WHISKERANDOS.

"I thank thee fortune! that hast thus bestow'd
A weapon to chastise this insolent."

[*Takes up one of the swords.*

BEEFEATER.

"I take thy challenge, Spaniard, and I thank
Thee Fortune too!——" [*Takes up the other sword.*

DANGLE.

That's excellently contriv'd!——it seems as if the
two uncles had left their swords on purpose for them.

PUFF.

No, egad, they could not help leaving them.

WHISKERANDOS.

"Vengeance and Tilburina!"

BEEFEATER.

"Exactly so——"
[*They fight—and after the usual number of wounds
given, Whiskerandos falls.*]

WHISKERANDOS.

"O cursed parry!——that last thrust in tierce
Was fatal——Captain, thou hast fenced well!
And Whiskerandos quits this bustling scene
For all eter——"

BEEFEATER.

"——nity——He would have added,
but stern death
Cut short his being, and the noun at once!"

PUFF.

O, my dear Sir, you are too slow, now mind me.
——Sir, shall I trouble you to die again?

WHISKERANDOS.

"And Whiskerandos quits this bustling scene
For all eter——"

BEEFEATER.

"——nity——He would have
added——"

PUFF.

No, Sir——that's not it——once more if you
please——

WHISKERANDOS.

I wish, Sir——you would practise this without me
——I can't stay dying here all night.

PUFF.

Very well, we'll go over it by and bye——I must
humour these gentlemen! [*Exit Whiskerandos.*

BEEFEATER.

"Farewell——brave Spaniard! and when next——"

PUFF.

Dear Sir, you needn't speak that speech as the body
has walked off.

BEEFEATER.

That's true, Sir——then I'll join the fleet.

PUFF.

If you please. [*Exit Beefeater.*
Now, who comes on?

Enter GOVERNOR, *with his hair properly disordered.*

GOVERNOR.

"A hemisphere of evil planets reign!
And every planet sheds contagious phrensy!
My Spanish prisoner is slain! my daughter,
Meeting the dead corse borne along——has gone
Distract! [*A loud flourish of trumpets.*
But hark! I am summon'd to the fort,
Perhaps the fleets have met! amazing crisis!
O Tilburina! from thy aged father's beard
Thou'st pluck'd the few brown hairs which time had
left!" [*Exit Governor.*

SNEER.

Poor gentleman!

PUFF.

Yes——and no one to blame but his daughter!

DANGLE.

And the planets——

PUFF.

True.——Now enter Tilburina!——

SNEER.

Egad, the business comes on quick here.

PUFF.

Yes, Sir——now she comes in stark mad in white
satin.

SNEER.

Why in white satin?

PUFF.

O Lord, Sir——when a heroine goes mad, she
always goes into white satin——don't she, Dangle?

DANGLE.

Always——it's a rule.

PUFF.

Yes——here it is——(*looking at the book.*) "Enter
Tilburina stark mad in white satin, and her confidant
stark mad in white linen."

Enter TILBURINA *and* CONFIDANT *mad, according to custom.*

SNEER.

But what the deuce, is the confidant to be mad too?

PUFF.

To be sure she is, the confidant is always to do whatever her mistress does; weep when she weeps, smile when she smiles, go mad when she goes mad.——Now madam confidant——but——keep your madness in the back ground, if you please.

TILBURINA.

"The wind whistles——the moon rises——see
They have kill'd my squirrel in his cage!
Is this a grasshopper!——Ha! no, it is my
Whiskerandos——you shall not keep him——
I know you have him in your pocket——
An oyster may be cross'd in love!——Who says
A whale's a bird?——Ha! did you call, my love?
——He's here! He's there!——He's every where!
Ah me! He's no where!   [*Exit Tilburina.*

PUFF.

There, do you ever desire to see any body madder than that?

SNEER.

Never while I live!

PUFF.

You observed how she mangled the metre?

DANGLE.

Yes——egad, it was the first thing made me suspect she was out of her senses.

SNEER.

And pray what becomes of her?

PUFF.

She is gone to throw herself into the sea to be sure ——and that brings us at once to the scene of action, and so to my catastrophe——my sea-fight, I mean.

SNEER.

What, you bring that in at last?

PUFF.

Yes——yes——you know my play is *called* the *Spanish Armada*, otherwise, egad, I have no occasion for the battle at all.——Now then for my magnificence!——my battle!——my noise!——and my procession!——You are all ready?

PROMPTER *within.*

Yes, Sir.

PUFF.

Is the Thames drest?

Enter THAMES *with two Attendants.*

THAMES.

Here I am, Sir.

PUFF.

Very well indeed——See, gentlemen, there's a river for you! This is blending a little of the masque with my tragedy——a new fancy you know——and very useful in my case; for as there *must be* a *procession*, I suppose Thames and all his tributary rivers to compliment Britannia with a fete in honor of the victory.

SNEER.

But pray, who are these gentlemen in green with him.

PUFF.

Those?——those are his banks.

SNEER.

His banks?

PUFF.

Yes, one crown'd with alders and the other with a villa!——you take the allusions?——but hey! what the plague! you have got both your banks on one side——Here Sir, come round——Ever while you live, Thames, go between your banks. (*Bell rings.*)—— There, soh! now for 't!——Stand aside my dear friends!——away Thames!

[*Exit Thames between his banks.*
[*Flourish of drums——trumpets——cannon, &c. &c. Scene changes to the sea——the fleets engage——the musick plays "Britons strike home."——Spanish fleet destroyed by fireships, &c.——English fleet advances—— musick plays "Rule Britannia."——The procession of all the English rivers and their tributaries with their emblems, &c. begins with Handels water musick——ends with a chorus, to the march in Judas Maccabæus.[1]—— During this scene, Puff directs and applauds every thing——then*]

PUFF.

Well, pretty well——but not quite perfect——so ladies and gentlemen, if you please, we'll rehearse this piece again to-morrow.

CURTAIN DROPS.

Act III, scene ii. **1. Judas Maccabæus:** Handel's oratorio (1747).

Thomas Chatterton

1752–1770

Thomas Chatterton grew up in the city of Bristol, in the eighteenth century the second largest city in England, a noisy philistine seaport bursting with local pride. For a hundred years Chatterton's forebears had been sextons of the Church of St. Mary Redcliffe, and his father, who died before Thomas was born, was a minor clerk and chorister in Bristol cathedral. Surrounded by medieval buildings and monuments, Chatterton developed an early passion for the Gothic (his infant drawings were of knights and coats of arms); contemptuous even as a child of the raw mercantilism of Bristol, he gradually withdrew to a more heroic medieval world of his own devising, which he fleshed out with characters and events drawn from his precocious reading in medieval history and antiquities. After a dull commercial education, he was apprenticed to a local lawyer, in whose office he seems to have spent much of his time sullenly daydreaming and poeticizing. Although his mother once declared him "an absolute fool," most people thought him not only clever but arrogant. No one remembered him as sweet-natured until considerably after his death.

At the age of eight he was determined to become famous; at twelve he began writing poems. Discovering the name Thomas Rowley in an epitaph at a local church, he embraced it as his pseudonym and, after the fashion of his age, began writing as if he himself were Rowley, whom he conceived as a fifteenth-century Bristol priest of exemplary charity and good sense. To help him write like Rowley, he put together a glossary of medieval terms that he found in Chaucer and in etymological dictionaries; to give the poems an air of authenticity, he copied some of them onto pieces of old parchment. Thomas Percy's *Relics of Ancient English Poetry* (1765) had helped stimulate interest in medieval poetry, and Chatterton found that some Bristol antiquaries, pleased by any intimation that Bristol's past had been illustrious, were not averse to receiving the Rowley parchments and "transcripts" as genuine historical discoveries. Chatterton's original design seems to have been less to deceive than to provide himself with an imaginative medieval identity as a refuge against the hideousness of the contemporary, but as he proceeded he found himself indulging in outright deception.

Observing that many citizens of Bristol accepted Rowley's writings with conviction and enthusiasm, Chatterton sought unsuccessfully to interest James Dodsley, the London publisher of Percy's *Relics*. He then thought of Horace Walpole, who was well known as an antiquary with a special appreciation of the medieval. Walpole was at first charmed with the specimens Chatterton sent him and showed the Rowley materials to Thomas Gray and William Mason. They soon convinced him that the poems were written, as Walpole expresses it, "in the idiom, metres, and ideas of the 18th century."

His pride frustrated by Walpole's return of his manuscripts, Chatterton managed to obtain a release from his apprenticeship in the law office by threatening suicide. He hopefully went to London to try his hand at journalism, and there he wrote satires, political essays, and a comic opera. But his writings in modern English proved to be shallow and imitative: he seemed to become a poet only when he wrote in Rowleyese. Despairing of a rapid triumph in the harsh, competitive world of London journalism, one night he locked the door of his rented room, tore up his manuscripts, and swallowed arsenic. When he killed himself he was seventeen years and nine months old.

Only one of the antique poems (*Elinoure and Juga* [1769]) was published during Chatterton's lifetime. Seven years after his death, Thomas Tyrwhitt, an authority on Chaucer, collected, edited, and published the bulk of the Rowley poems. He thought at first they might be genuine, but before he brought out the third edition in 1778, he was convinced that they were spurious, and he demonstrated in an appendix why he thought so. Tyrwhitt's editions generated a heated "Rowley Controversy," which persisted for years. Certain obscure Bristol antiquaries argued for the authenticity of the poems; they were opposed not only by Tyrwhitt but by Edmond Malone, the Shakespearean scholar, and by Samuel Johnson. Johnson even made a special journey from Bath to Bristol to investigate. Although he saw from the beginning that the poems were modern, he declared of Chatterton, "This is the most extraordinary young man that has encountered my knowledge. It is wonderful how the whelp has written such things." Thomas Warton, who also perceived that the poems were not medieval, was convinced that Chatterton "would have proved the first of English poets, had he reached a maturer age." And to Coleridge, Shelley, Keats, and Wordsworth, Chatterton became a convenient image of instinctive lyric genius exhausting itself in song before a heartless audience.

Bibliography is provided by F. A. Hyett and William Bazeley's *Chattertoniana* (1914). E. H. W. Meyerstein's *A Life of Thomas Chatterton* (1930) is a full and minutely detailed critical biography of great value. The Rowley poems are best read in the facsimile of Tyrwhitt's third edition (1778), edited by M. E. Hare (1911) with interesting introduction and apparatus. B. H. Bronson's essay "Thomas Chatterton," in *The Age of Johnson: Essays Presented to Chauncey Brewster Tinker* (1949), is a sensitive and sympathetic interpretation.

BRISTOWE TRAGEDIE:
OR THE DETHE
OF SYR CHARLES BAWDIN

Chatterton here attempts a ballad to rival those in Percy's *Relics* (1765). Certain details of the story he discovered in John Stow's *Annals* (1615): "I found the argument and versified it," he told his mother. The historical "Syr Charles" was Sir Baldwin Fulford, who was executed at Bristol in 1461 for having attempted to murder the Earl of Warwick, cousin of King Edward IV. Fulford's loyalties remained with Henry VI, the monarch deposed by Edward and Warwick.

When the poem first appeared, two years after Chatterton's death, Horace Walpole wrote to William Mason, "Somebody, I fancy Dr. Percy, has published a dismal, dull poem entitled The Execution of Sir Charles Bawdin, and given it for one of the Bristol poems called Rowley's—but it is a still worse counterfeit than those which were first sent to me." But a writer for *The Monthly Review*, though similarly suspicious, perceived merit in the piece: "We cannot think, on account of the smoothness of the numbers, that the Poem is of so early a date as is suggested. There is, however, a natural pathos, and a beautiful simplicity in it, which cannot but recommend it to the lovers of antique poetry."

The text of the edition of 1772 appears to have been set from an unauthoritative transcript made by the eccentric George Catcott; the heavily antiqued spelling of this version reveals Catcott's textual interference. We have taken the text instead from Tyrwhitt's first edition, *Poems, Supposed to Have Been Written at Bristol, by Thomas Rowley, and Others, in the Fifteenth Century* (1777), where the spelling is closer to Chatterton's own practice.

❧

The featherd songster chaunticleer
  Han wounde hys bugle horne,
And tolde the earlie villager
  The commynge of the morne:°

BRISTOWE TRAGEDIE. **4. morne:** A manuscript note by Chatterton on this first stanza reads: "In my humble opinion, the foregoing lines are far more elegant and poetical than all the Parade of Aurora's whipping away the night, unbarring the gates of the East, etc., etc."

Kynge EDWARDE sawe the ruddie streakes
  Of lyghte eclypse the greie;
And herde the raven's crokynge throte
  Proclayme the fated daie.

"Thou'rt ryght," quod hee, "for, by the Godde
  That syttes enthron'd on hyghe!   10
CHARLES BAWDIN, and hys fellowes twaine,
  To-daie shall surelie die."

Thenne wythe a jugge of nappy° ale
  Hys Knyghtes dydd onne hymm waite;
"Goe tell the traytour, thatt to-daie
  Hee leaves thys mortall state."

Syr CANTERLONE thenne bendedd lowe,
  Wythe harte brymm-fulle of woe;
Hee journey'd to the castle-gate,
  And to Syr CHARLES dydd goe.   20

Butt whenne hee came, hys children twaine,
  And eke hys lovynge wyfe,
Wythe brinie tears dydd wett the floore,
  For goode Syr CHARLESES lyfe.

"O goode Syr CHARLES!" sayd CANTERLONE,
  Badde tydyngs I doe brynge."
"Speke boldlie, manne," sayd brave Syr CHARLES,
  "Whatte says thie traytor kynge?"

"I greeve to telle, before yonne sonne
  Does fromme the welkinn° flye,   30
Hee hath uponne hys honour sworne,
  Thatt thou shalt surelie die."

"Wee all must die," quod brave Syr CHARLES;
  Of thatte I'm not affearde;
Whatte bootes° to lyve a little space?
  Thanke JESU, I'm prepar'd:

"Butt telle thye kynge, for myne hee's not,
  I'de sooner die to-daie
Thanne lyve hys slave, as manie are,
  Tho' I shoulde lyve for aie."   40

Thenne CANTERLONE hee dydd goe out,
  To telle the maior straite
To gett all thynges ynne reddyness
  For goode Syr CHARLESES fate.

---

13. nappy: strong. **30. welkinn:** sky. **35. bootes:** matters.

Thenne Maisterr CANYNGE saughte the kynge,
 And felle down onne hys knee;
'I'm come," quod hee, "unto your grace
 To move your clemencye."

Thenne quod the kynge, "Youre tale speke out,
 You have been much oure friende; 50
Whatever youre request may bee,
 Wee wylle to ytte attende."

"My nobile leige! alle my request
 Ys for a nobile knyghte,
Who, tho' may hap hee has donne wronge,
 Hee thoghte ytte stylle was ryghte:

"Hee has a spouse and children twaine,
 Alle rewyn'd are for aie;
Yff thatt you are resolv'd to lett
 CHARLES BAWDIN die to-daie." 60

"Speke nott of such a traytour vile,"
 The kynge ynne furie sayde;
"Before the evening starre doth sheene,
 BAWDIN shall loose hys hedde:

"Justice does loudlie for hym calle,
 And hee shalle have hys meede:°
Speke, Maister CANYNGE! Whatte thynge else
 Att present doe you neede?"

"My nobile leige!" goode CANYNGE sayde,
 Leave justice to our Godde, 70
And laye the yronne rule asyde;
 Be thyne the olyve rodde.

"Was Godde to serche our hertes and reines,°
 The best were synners grete;
CHRIST'S vycarr only knowes ne synne,
 Ynne alle thys mortall state.

"Lette mercie rule thyne infante reigne,
 'Twylle faste° thye crowne fulle sure;
From race° to race thy familie
 Alle sov'reigns shall endure: 80

"Butt yff wythe bloode and slaughter thou
 Beginne thy infante reigne,
Thy crowne uponne thy childrennes brows
 Wylle never long remayne."

"CANYNGE, awaie! thys traytour vile
 Has scorn'd my power and mee;
Howe canst thou thenne for such a manne
 Intreate my clemencye?"

"My nobile leige! the trulie brave
 Wylle val'rous actions prize, 90
Respect a brave and nobile mynde,
 Altho' ynne enemies."

"CANYNGE, awaie! By Godde ynne Heav'n
 Thatt dydd mee beinge gyve,
I wylle nott taste a bitt of breade
 Whilst thys Syr CHARLES dothe lyve.

"By MARIE, and alle Seinctes ynne Heav'n,
 Thys sunne shall be hys laste."
Thenne CANYNGE dropt a brinie teare,
 And from the presence paste. 100

Wyth herte brymm-fulle of gnawynge grief,
 Hee to Syr CHARLES dydd goe,
And satt hymm downe uponne a stoole,
 And teares beganne to flowe.

"Wee all must die," quod brave Syr CHARLES;
 "Whatte bootes ytte howe or whenne;
Dethe ys the sure, the certaine fate
 Of all wee mortall menne.

"Saye why, my friend, thie honest soul
 Runns overr att thyne eye; 110
Is ytte for my most welcome doome
 Thatt thou dost child-lyke crye?"

Quod godlie CANYNGE, "I doe weepe,
 Thatt thou soe soone must dye,
And leave thy sonnes and helpless wyfe;
 'Tys thys thatt wettes myne eye."

"Thenne drie the tears thatt out thyne eye
 From godlie fountaines sprynge;
Dethe I despise, and alle the power
 Of EDWARDE, traytor kynge. 120

"Whan throgh the tyrant's welcom means
 I shall resigne my lyfe,
The Godde I serve wylle soone provyde
 For bothe mye sonnes and wyfe.

"Before I sawe the lyghtsome sunne,
 Thys was appointed mee;
Shall mortal manne repyne or grudge
 Whatt Godde ordeynes to bee?

66. **meede:** reward. **73. reines:** loins, once thought to be
the seat of the feelings and affections. **78. faste:** secure.
79. race: generation.

"Howe oft ynne battaile have I stoode,
　　Whan thousands dy'd arounde; 130
Whan smokynge streemes of crimson bloode
　　Imbrew'd° the fatten'd grounde:

"Howe dydd I knowe thatt ev'ry darte,
　　Thatt cutte the airie waie,
Myghte nott fynde passage toe my harte,
　　And close myne eyes for aie?

"And shall I nowe, forr feere of dethe,
　　Looke wanne and bee dysmayde?
Ne! fromm my herte flie childyshe feere,
　　Bee alle the manne display'd. 140

"Ah, goddelyke HENRIE! Godde forefende,°
　　And guarde thee and thye sonne,
Yff 'tis hys wylle; but yff 'tis nott,
　　Why thenne hys wylle bee donne.

"My honest friende, my faulte has beene
　　To serve Godde and mye prynce;
And thatt I no tyme-server am,
　　My dethe wylle soone convynce.

"Ynne Londonne citye was I borne,
　　Of parents of grete note; 150
My fadre dydd a nobile armes
　　Emblazon onne hys cote:

"I make ne doubte butt hee ys gone
　　Where soone I hope to goe;
Where wee for ever shall bee blest,
　　From oute the reech of woe:

"Hee taughte mee justice and the laws
　　Wyth pitie to unite;
And eke hee taughte mee howe to knowe
　　The wronge cause fromm the ryghte: 160

"Hee taughte mee wythe a prudent hande
　　To feede the hungrie poore,
Ne lett mye sarvants dryve awaie
　　The hungrie fromme my doore:

"And none can saye, butt alle mye lyfe
　　I have hys wordyes kept;
And summ'd the actyonns of the daie
　　Eche nyghte before I slept.

"I have a spouse, goe aske of her,
　　Yff I defyl'd her bedde? 170
I have a kynge, and none can laie
　　Blacke treason onne my hedde.

"Ynne Lent, and onne the holie eve,
　　Fromm fleshe I dydd refrayne;
Whie should I thenne appeare dismay'd
　　To leave thys worlde of payne?

"Ne! hapless HENRIE! I rejoyce,
　　I shalle ne see thye dethe;
Moste willynglie ynne thye just cause
　　Doe I resign my brethe. 180

"Oh, fickle people! rewyn'd londe!
　　Thou wylt kenne° peace ne moe;
Whyle RICHARD's sonnes exalt themselves,
　　Thye brookes wythe bloude wylle flowe.

"Saie, were ye tyr'd of godlie peace,
　　And godlie HENRIE's reigne,
Thatt you dydd choppe° youre easie daies
　　For those of bloude and peyne?

"Whatte tho' I onne a sledde° bee drawne,
　　And mangled by a hynde,° 190
I doe defye the traytor's pow'r,
　　Hee can ne harm my mynde;

"Whatte tho', uphoisted onne a pole,
　　Mye lymbes shall rotte ynne ayre,
And ne ryche monument of brasse
　　CHARLES BAWDIN's name shall bear;

"Yett ynne the holie booke above,
　　Whyche tyme can't eate awaie,
There wythe the sarvants of the Lorde
　　Mye name shall lyve for aie. 200

"Thenne welcome dethe! for lyfe eterne
　　I leave thys mortall lyfe:
Farewell, vayne worlde, and alle that's deare,
　　Mye sonnes and lovynge wyfe!

"Nowe dethe as welcome to mee comes,
　　As e'er the moneth of Maie;
Nor woulde I even wyshe to lyve,
　　Wyth my dere wyfe to staie."

132. **Imbrew'd:** stained. 141. **forefende:** protect.

182. **kenne:** know. 187. **choppe:** exchange. 189. **sledde:**
sledge. 190. **hynde:** peasant.

Quod CANYNGE, "'Tys a goodlie thynge
  To bee prepar'd to die;
And from thys world of peyne and grefe   210
  To Godde ynne Heav'n to flie."

And nowe the bell beganne to tolle,
  And claryonnes° to sounde;
Syr CHARLES hee herde the horses feete
  A prauncyng onne the grounde:

And just before the officers,
  His lovynge wyfe came ynne,
Weepynge unfeigned teeres of woe,
  Wythe loude and dysmalle dynne.   220

"Sweet FLORENCE! nowe I praie forbere,
  Ynne quiet lett mee die;
Praie Godde, thatt ev'ry Christian soule
  Maye looke onne dethe as I.

"Sweet FLORENCE! why these brinie teeres?
  Theye washe my soule awaie,
And almost make mee wyshe for lyfe,
  Wyth thee, sweete dame, to staie.

"'Tys butt a journie I shalle goe
  Untoe the lande of blysse;   230
Nowe, as a proofe of husbande's love,
  Receive thys holie kysse."

Thenne FLORENCE, fault'ring ynne her saie,°
  Tremblynge these wordyes spoke,
"Ah, cruele EDWARDE! bloudie kynge!
  My herte ys welle nyghe broke:

"Ah, sweete Syr CHARLES! why wylt thou goe,
  Wythoute thye lovynge wyfe?
The cruelle axe thatt cuttes thye necke,
  Ytte eke shall ende mye lyfe."   240

And nowe the officers came ynne
  To brynge Syr CHARLES awaie,
Whoe turnedd toe hys lovynge wyfe,
  And thus toe her dydd saie:

"I goe to lyfe, and nott to dethe;
  Truste thou ynne Godde above,
And teache thye sonnes to feare the Lorde,
  And ynne theyre hertes hym love:

"Teache them to runne the nobile race
  Thatt I theyre fader runne: 250
FLORENCE! shou'd° dethe thee take—adieu!
  Yee officers, leade onne."

Thenne FLORENCE rav'd as anie madde,
  And dydd her tresses tere;
"Oh! staie, mye husbande! lorde! and lyfe!"—
  Syr CHARLES thenne dropt a teare.

'Tyll tyredd oute wythe ravynge loud,
  Shee fellen onne the flore;
Syr CHARLES exerted alle hys myghte,
  And march'd fromm oute the dore.   260

Uponne a sledde hee mounted thenne,
  Wythe lookes fulle brave and swete;
Lookes, thatt enshone ne moe concern
  Thanne anie ynne the strete.

Before hym went the council-menne,
  Ynne scarlett robes and golde,
And tassils spanglynge ynne the sunne,
  Muche glorious to beholde:

The Freers of Seincte AUGUSTYNE next
  Appeared to the syghte,   270
Alle cladd ynne homelie russett weedes,°
  Of godlie monkysh plyghte:°

Ynne diffraunt partes a godlie psaume
  Moste sweetlie theye dydd chaunt;
Behynde theyre backes syx mynstrelles came,
  Who tun'd the strunge bataunt.°

Thenne fyve-and-twentye archers came;
  Echone the bowe dydd bende,
From rescue of kynge HENRIES friends
  Syr CHARLES forr to defend.   280

Bolde as a lyon came Sir CHARLES,
  Drawne onne a clothe-layde sledde,
Bye two blacke stedes ynne trappynges white,
  Wyth plumes uponne theyre hedde:

---

251. shou'd: One manuscript—of doubtful authenticity—
reads: "till." 271. russett weedes: brown garments. 272.
plyghte: fashion. 276. strunge bataunt: Perhaps Chatterton
has in mind some exotic musical instrument, although
bataunt is unknown as a noun. The dubious manuscript—
not, certainly, Chatterton's—reads: "Psaume Bataunt"; John
Kersey's *Dictionarium Anglo-Britannicum* (1708), which
Chatterton used in compiling his "glossary," defines the
obsolete *batauntly* as "boldly."

---

214. claryonnes: trumpets. 233. saie: speech.

Behynde hym fyve-and-twentye moe
  Of archers stronge and stoute,
Wyth bended bowe echone ynne hande,
  Marched ynne goodlie route:

Seincte JAMESES Freers marched next,
  Echone hys parte dydd chaunt;   290
Behynde theyre backs syx mynstrelles came,
  Who tun'd the strunge bataunt:

Thenne came the maior and eldermenne,
  Ynne clothe of scarlett deck't;
And theyre attendyng menne echone,
  Lyke Easterne princes trickt:

And after them, a multitude
  Of citizenns dydd thronge;
The wyndowes were alle fulle of heddes,
  As hee dydd passe alonge.   300

And whenne hee came to the hyghe crosse,
  Syr CHARLES dydd turne and saie,
"O Thou, thatt savest manne fromme synne,
  Washe mye soule clean thys daie!"

Att the grete mynsterr° wyndowe sat
  The kynge ynne myckle° state,
To see CHARLES BAWDIN goe alonge
  To hys most welcom fate.

Soone as the sledde drewe nyghe enowe,
  Thatt EDWARDE hee myghte heare,   310
The brave Syr CHARLES hee dydd stande uppe,
  And thus hys wordes declare:

"Thou seest mee, EDWARDE! traytour vile!
  Expos'd to infamie;
Butt bee assur'd, disloyall manne!
  I'm greaterr nowe thanne thee.

"Bye foule proceedyngs, murdre, bloude,
  Thou wearest nowe a crowne;
And hast appoynted mee to dye,
  By power nott thyne owne.   320

"Thou thynkest I shall dye to-daie;
  I have been dede 'till nowe,
And soone shall lyve to weare a crowne
  For aie uponne my browe:

"Whylst thou, perhapps, for som few yeares,
  Shalt rule thys fickle lande,
To lett them knowe howe wyde the rule
  'Twixt kynge and tyrant hande:

"Thye pow'r unjust, thou traytour slave!
  Shall falle onne thye owne hedde"—   330
Fromm out of hearyng of the kynge
  Departed thenne the sledde.

Kynge EDWARDE's soule rush'd to hys face,
  Hee turn'd hys hedde awaie,
And to hys broder GLOUCESTER
  Hee thus dydd speke and saie:

"To hym that soe-much-dreaded dethe
  Ne ghastlie terrors brynge,
Beholde the manne! hee spake the truthe,
  Hee's greater thanne a kynge!"   340

"Soe lett hym die!" Duke RICHARD sayde;
  "And maye echone oure foes
Bende downe theyre neckes to bloudie axe,
  And feede the carryon crowes."

And nowe the horses gentlie drewe
  Syr CHARLES uppe the hyghe hylle;
The axe dydd glysterr ynne the sunne,
  Hys pretious bloude to spylle.

Syrr CHARLES dydd uppe the scaffold goe,
  As uppe a gilded carre   350
Of victorye, bye val'rous chiefs
  Gayn'd ynne the bloudie warre:

And to the people hee dydd saie,
  "Beholde you see mee dye,
For servynge loyally mye kynge,
  Mye kynge most ryghtfullie.

"As longe as EDWARDE rules thys lande,
  Ne quiet you wylle knowe;
Youre sonnes and husbandes shalle bee slayne,
  And brookes wythe bloude shalle flowe.   360

"You leave youre goode and lawfulle kynge,
  Whenne ynne adversitye;
Lyke mee, untoe the true cause stycke,
  And for the true cause dye."

Thenne hee, wyth preestes, uponne hys knees,
  A pray'r to Godde dydd make,
Beseechynge hym unto hymselfe,
  Hys partynge soule to take.

305. **mynsterr:** cathedral. 306. **myckle:** great.

Thenne, kneelynge downe, hee layd hys hedde
   Most seemlie onne the blocke;   370
Whyche fromme hys bodie fayre at once
   The able heddes-manne stroke:

And oute the bloude beganne to flowe,
   And rounde the scaffolde twyne;
And teares, enow to washe't awaie,
   Dydd flowe fromme each mann's eyne.

The bloudie axe hys bodie fayre
   Ynnto foure parties cutte;
And ev'rye parte, and eke hys hedde,
   Uponne a pole was putte.   380

One parte dydd rotte onne Kynwulph-hylle,
   One onne the mynster-tower,
And one from off the castle-gate
   The crowen dydd devoure:

The other onne Seyncte Powle's goode gate,
   A dreery spectacle;
Hys hedde was plac'd onne the hyghe crosse,
   Ynne hyghe-streete most nobile.

Thus was the ende of BAWDIN's fate:
   Godde prosper longe oure kynge,   390
And grante hee maye, wyth BAWDIN's soule,
   Ynne heav'n Godd's mercie synge!

FROM

ÆLLA, A TRAGYCAL ENTERLUDE

Ælla, a "Discoorseynge Tragedie, wrotenn bie Thomas Rowleie," is Chatterton's most ambitious work. This play of 1248 lines presents the ironic catastrophe that befalls Aella, a Saxon lord occupying Bristol Castle. Aella has just taken a bride, Birtha, but the wedding feast is interrupted by news of a Danish invasion. Torn between love and honor, Aella finally takes leave of his bride and goes off to repel the Danes. He is wounded in the battle and begins to return to Bristol. Meanwhile his friend and rival Celmonde, secretly in love with Birtha, persuades her to accompany him in a search for Aella. Alone in a forest with Celmonde, Birtha is rescued from his amorous designs by a group of chivalrous Danes, who kill Celmonde and conduct Birtha back to the castle. Aella, arriving back at Bristol to discover that his bride has apparently run off with his rival, stabs himself just as Birtha, still faithful, returns. She faints on his dead body.

The first song is sung by minstrels at the wedding celebration. The second is sung to entertain Birtha as she awaits Aella's return from battle and before she departs with Celmonde. The second song is Chatterton's best-known poem. It was quoted and admired by Thomas Warton in his *History of English Poetry* (Vol. II, 1778), even though Warton denied the authenticity of "Rowley." The stanza of the second song beginning "Comme, wythe acorne-coppe & thorne" was one of Keats's favorite passages, and he used to recite it with great delight.

The text is that of Tyrwhitt's first edition (1777).

MYNSTRELLES SONGE [I]

FYRSTE MYNSTRELLE.

The boddynge flourettes bloshes atte the lyghte;
The mees° be sprenged° wyth the yellowe hue;
Ynn daiseyd mantels ys the mountayne dyghte;°
The nesh° yonge coweslepe bendethe wyth the
   dewe;
The trees enlefed,° yntoe Heavenne straughte,°
Whenn gentle wyndes doe blowe, to whestlyng dynne
   ys brought.

The evenynge commes, and brynges the dewe
   alonge;
The roddie welkynne sheeneth° to the eyne;
Arounde the alestake Mynstrells synge the songe;
Yonge ivie rounde the doore poste do entwyne; 10
I laie mee onn the grasse; yette, to mie wylle,
Albeytte alle ys fayre, there lackethe somethynge
   stylle.

SECONDE MYNSTRELLE.

So Adam thoughtenne, whann, ynn Paradyse,
All Heaven and Erthe dyd hommage to hys mynde;
Ynn Womman alleyne° mannes pleasaunce lyes;
As Instrumentes of joie were made the kynde.°
Go, take a wyfe untoe thie armes, and see
Wynter, and brownie hylles, wyll have a charme for
   thee.

ÆLLA: *Mynstrelles Songe* [I]. **2. mees:** meads. **sprenged:** sprinkled. **3. dyghte:** dressed. **4. nesh:** [Chatterton's note] tender. **5. enlefed:** covered with leaves. **straughte:** stretched. **8. roddie . . . sheeneth:** reddish sky glows. **15. alleyne:** only. **16. the kynde:** the (female) sex.

THYRDE MYNSTRELLE.

Whanne Autumpne blake° and sonne-brente doe
    appere,
With hys goulde honde guylteynge° the falleynge
    lefe,   20
Bryngeynge oppe Wynterr to folfylle the yere,
Beerynge uponne hys backe the riped shefe;
Whan al the hyls wythe woddie sede ys whyte;
Whanne levynne-fyres and lemes° do mete from far
    the syghte;

Whann the fayre apple, rudde as even° skie,
Do bende the tree unto the fructyle° grounde;
When joicie peres, and berries of blacke die,
Doe daunce yn ayre, and call the eyne arounde;°
Thenn, bee the even foule, or even fayre,
Meethynckes mie hartys joie ys steynced° wyth somme
    care.   30

SECONDE MYNSTRELLE.

Angelles bee wrogte° to bee of neidher kynde;
Angelles alleyne fromme chafe° desyre bee free;
Dheere ys a somwhatte evere yn the mynde,
Yatte,° wythout wommanne, cannot stylled bee;
Ne seyncte yn celles, botte, havynge blodde and
    tere,°
Do fynde the spryte to joie on syghte of womanne
    fayre:

Wommen bee made, notte for hemselves, botte
    manne,
Bone of hys bone, and chyld of hys desire;
Fromme an ynutyle membere° fyrste beganne,
Ywroghte with moche of water, lyttele fyre;   40
Therefore theie seke the fyre of love, to hete
The milkyness of kynde,° and make hemselfes
    complete.

Albeytte, wythout wommen, menne were pheeres°
To salvage kynde, and wulde botte lyve to slea,
Botte wommenne efte° the spryghte of peace so
    cheres,

Tochelod yn° Angel joie heie° Angeles bee;
  Go, take thee swythyn° to thie bedde a wyfe,
Bee bante° or blessed hie, yn proovynge marryage lyfe.

MYNSTRELLES SONGE [II]

O! synge untoe mie roundelaie,
O! droppe the brynie teare wythe mee,
Daunce ne moe atte hallie daie,°
Lycke a reynynge° ryver bee;
    Mie love ys dedde,
    Gon to hys death-bedde,
    Al under the wyllowe tree.

Blacke hys cryne° as the wyntere nyghte,
Whyte hys rode° as the sommer snowe,°
Rodde hys face as the mornynge lyghte,   10
Cale° he lyes ynne the grave belowe;
    Mie love ys dedde,
    Gon to hys deathe-bedde,
    Al under the wyllowe tree.

Swote hys tyngue as the throstles note,
Quycke ynn daunce as thoughte canne bee,
Defte hys taboure,° codgelle stote,°
O! hee lyes bie the wyllowe tree:
    Mie love ys dedde,
    Gonne to hys deathe-bedde,   20
    Alle underre the wyllowe tree.

Harke! the ravenne flappes hys wynge,
In the briered delle belowe;
Harke! the dethe-owle loude dothe synge,
To the nyghte-mares as heie goe;
    Mie love ys dedde,
    Gonne to hys deathe-bedde,
    Al under the wyllowe tree.

See! the whyte moone sheenes onne hie;
Whyterre ys mie true loves shroude;   30
Whyterre yanne° the mornynge skie,

---

19. blake: [Chatterton's note] Naked. **20. guylteynge:** gilding. **24. levynne-fyres and lemes:** lightning flashes and meteors. **25. even:** evening. **26. fructyle:** fruitful. **28. call . . . arounde:** attract every eye. **30. steynced:** stained. **31. wrogte:** wrought, made. **32. chafe:** [Chatterton's note] Hot. **34. Yatte:** that. **35. tere:** [Chatterton's note] health. **39. an ynutyle membere:** a useless rib. **42. kynde:** their nature. **43. pheeres:** peers, equals. **45. efte:** often.

46. Tochelod yn: This puzzling phrase may mean something like "endowed with." **heie:** they. **47. swythyn:** [Chatterton's note] Quickly. **48. bante:** cursed. *Mynstrelles Songe [II].* **3. hallie daie:** holiday. **4. reynynge:** [Chatterton's note] Running. **8. cryne:** [Chatterton's note] hair. **9. rode:** [Chatterton's note] complexion. **the sommer snowe:** the "summer snowflake," a white flower. **11. Cale:** cold. **17. taboure:** drum: **codgelle stote:** cudgel stout. **31. yanne:** than.

Whyterre yanne the evenynge cloude;
　　Mie love ys dedde,
　　Gon to hys deathe-bedde,
　　Al under the wyllowe tree.

Heere, uponne mie true loves grave,
Schalle the baren fleurs be layde,
Nee one hallie° Seyncte to save
Al the celness° of a mayde.
　　Mie love ys dedde,　　　　　　　　40
　　Gonne to hys death-bedde,
　　Alle under the wyllowe tree.

Wythe mie hondes I'lle dente° the brieres
Rounde his hallie corse to gre,°
Ouphante° fairie, lyghte youre fyres,
Heere mie boddie stylle schalle bee.
　　Mie love ys dedde,
　　Gon to hys death-bedde,
　　Al under the wyllowe tree.

Comme, wythe acorne-coppe & thorne,°　　50
Drayne mie hartys blodde awaie;
Lyfe & all yttes goode I scorne,
Daunce bie nete, or feaste by daie.
　　Mie love ys dedde,
　　Gon to hys death-bedde,
　　Al under the wyllowe tree.

Waterre wytches, crownede wythe reytes,°
Bere mee to yer leathalle tyde.
I die; I comme; mie true love waytes.
Thos the damselle spake, and dyed.　　　60

AN EXCELENTE BALADE
OF CHARITIE

As wroten bie the gode Prieste THOMAS ROWLEY,°
1464.

✦

This is apparently one of Chatterton's last poems. He submitted it to the editor of *The Town and Country Magazine* on July 4, 1770, with this letter:

SIR,

　　If the Glossary annexed to the following piece will make the language intelligible; the Sentiment, Description, and Versification, are highly deserving the attention of the Literati.

　　　　　　　　　　　　　　　　　D. B.

The poem did not appear in the next number of the magazine, but this editorial communication did: "The Pastoral from Bristol . . . has some share of merit: but the author will, doubtless, discover upon another perusal of it, many exceptionable passages." But "the author" had already killed himself.

　　The poem echoes details and phrases from Chaucer's General Prologue to *The Canterbury Tales*, Spenser's *Faerie Queene*, and even Dryden's *The Character of a Good Parson*. The technique and tone are more Spenserian than medieval, and the poem suggests Chatterton's relationship to the Spenserian revival of the century and his odd kinship, thus, with Thomson, Shenstone, and James Beattie.

　　The text is that of Tyrwhitt's first edition (1777). The notes, except for our indicated additions, are Chatterton's.

✦

In Virgyne° the sweltrie sun gan sheene,
And hotte upon the mees did caste his raie;
The apple rodded° from its palie greene,
And the mole° peare did bende the leafy spraie;
The peede chelandri° sunge the livelong daie;

---

38. hallie: holy. **39. celness:** coldness. **43. dente:** fasten. **44. gre:** grow. **45. Ouphante:** elfin. Chatterton perhaps derives this word from *The Merry Wives of Windsor*, V. v. 61: "Strew good luck, ouphs, on every sacred room." The play was performed in Bristol on August 24, 1768. **50. acorne-coppe & thorne:** A cup and a scalpel were the instruments used by the eighteenth-century physician in bleeding a patient. **57. reytes:** [Chatterton's note] Water-flags.

AN EXCELENTE BALADE OF CHARITIE. **Thomas Rowley:** Thomas Rowley, the author, was born at Norton Malreward in Somersetshire, educated at the Convent of St. Kenna in Keynesham, and died at Westbury in Gloucestershire. **1. Virgyne:** [editors' note] Virgo, the sign of the zodiac that the sun enters about August 21. **3. rodded:** reddened, ripened. **4. mole:** soft. **5. peede chelandri:** pied [multicolored] goldfinch.

'Twas nowe the pride, the manhode of the yeare,
And eke° the grounde was dighte° in its mose defte°
    aumere.°

The sun was glemeing in the midde of daie,
Deadde still the aire, and eke the welken° blue,
When from the sea arist° in drear arraie   10
A hepe of cloudes of sable sullen hue,
The which full fast unto the woodlande drewe,
Hiltring° attenes° the sunnis fetive° face,
And the blacke tempeste swolne° and gatherd up
    apace.°

Beneathe an holme,° faste by a pathwaie side,
Which dide unto Seyncte Godwine's covent° lede,
A hapless pilgrim moneynge did abide,
Pore in his viewe,° ungentle° in his weede,°
Longe bretful° of the miseries of neede,
Where from the hail-stone coulde the almer° flie? 20
He had no housen theere, ne anie covent nie.

Look in his glommed° face, his sprighte there scanne,
Howe woe-be-gone, how withered, forwynd,°
    deade!
Haste to thie church-glebe-house,° ashrewed°
    manne!
Haste to thie kiste,° thie onlie dortoure° bedde.
Cale, as the claie whiche will gre on thie hedde,
Is Charitie and Love aminge highe elves;
Knightis and Barons live for pleasure and themselves.

The gathered storme is rype; the bigge drops falle;
The forswat° meadowes smethe,° and drenche° the
    raine;   30
The comyng ghastness do the cattle pall,°
And the full flockes are drivynge ore the plaine;
Dashde from the cloudes the waters flott° againe;
The welkin opes; the yellow levynne° flies;
And the hot fierie smothe° in the wide lowings° dies.

Liste! now the thunder's rattling clymmynge°
    sound
Cheves° slowlie on, and then embollen° clangs,
Shakes the hie spyre, and losst, dispended, drown'd,
Still on the gallard° eare of terroure hanges;
The windes are up; the lofty elmen swanges;° 40
Again the levynne and the thunder poures,
And the full cloudes are braste° attenes in stonen°
    showers.

Spurreynge his palfrie oere the watrie plaine,
The Abbote of Seyncte Godwynes convente came;
His chapournette° was drented° with the reine,
And his pencte° gyrdle met with mickle shame;
He aynewarde tolde his bederoll° at the same;
The storme encreasen, and he drew aside,
With the mist° almes craver neere to the holme to bide.

His cope° was all of Lyncolne clothe so fyne, 50
With a gold button fasten'd neere his chynne;
His autremete° was edged with golden twynne,°
And his shoone pyke° a loverds° mighte have binne;
Full well it shewn he thoughten coste no sinne:
The trammels° of the palfrye pleasde his sighte,
For the horse-millanare° his head with roses dighte.

---

7. **eke:** [editors' note] also. **dighte:** drest, arrayed. **defte,** neat, ornamental. **aumere:** a loose robe or mantle. 9. **welken:** the sky, the atmosphere. 10. **arist:** Arose. 13. **Hiltring:** hiding, shrouding. **attenes:** at once. **fetive:** beauteous. 14. **swolne:** [editors' note] swelled. **apace:** [editors' note] swiftly. 15. **holme:** [editors' note] oak. 16. **covent:** [convent] It would have been *charitable*, if the author had not pointed at personal characters in this Ballad of Charity. The Abbot of St. Godwin's at the time of the writing of this was Ralph de Bellomont, a great stickler for the Lancastrian family. Rowley was a Yorkist. [The families of Lancaster and York opposed each other for the English throne from 1455 until 1485 in the Wars of the Roses.] 18. **viewe:** [editors' note] appearance. **ungentle:** beggarly. **weede** [editors' note] clothing. 19. **bretful:** filled with. 20. **almer:** beggar. 22. **glommed:** clouded, dejected. A person of some note in the literary world [Horace Walpole] is of opinion, that *glum* and *glom* are modern cant words; and from this circumstance doubts the authenticity of Rowley's Manuscripts. Glummong in the Saxon signifies twilight, a dark or dubious light; and the modern word *gloomy* is derived from the Saxon *glum*. 23. **forwynd:** dry, sapless. 24. **church-glebe-house:** The Grave. **ashrewed:** accursed, unfortunate. 25. **kiste:** coffin. **dortoure:** a sleeping room.

30. **forswat:** sun-burnt. **smethe:** smoke. **drenche:** drink. 31. **pall:** a contraction from *appall*, to fright. 33. **flott:** fly. 34. **levynne:** lightning. 35. **smothe:** steam, or vapours. **lowings:** flames. 36. **clymmynge:** noisy. 37. **Cheves:** moves. **embollen:** swelled, strengthened. 39. **gallard:** Frighted. 40. **elmen swanges:** [editors' note] elm tree swings. 42. **braste:** burst. **stonen:** [editors' note] pelting (?). 45. **chapournette:** a small round hat, not unlike the shapournette [symbol for a hood] in heraldry, formerly worn by Ecclesiastics and Lawyers. **drented:** [editors' note] drowned. 46. **pencte:** painted. 47. **He . . . bederoll:** He told his beads backwards; a figurative expression to signify cursing. 49. **mist:** poor, needy. 50. **cope:** a cloke. 52. **autremete:** a loose white robe, worn by Priests. **twynne:** [editors' note] cord. 53. **shoone pyke:** [editors' note] piked (pointed) shoes. King Edward IV passed a law in 1463 limiting the length of the points to two inches. **loverds:** A lord. 55. **trammels:** [editors' note] harness. 56. **horse-millanare:** [horse milliner] I believe this trade is still in being, though but seldom employed.

An almes, sir prieste! the droppynge pilgrim saide,
O! let me waite within your covente dore,
Till the sunne sheneth hie above our heade,
And the loude tempeste of the aire is oer;   60
Helpless and ould am I alas! and poor;
No house, ne friend, ne moneie in my pouche;
All yatte I call my owne is this my silver crouche.°

Varlet, replyd the Abbatte, cease your dinne;
This is no season almes and prayers to give;
Mie porter never lets a faitour° in;
None touch mie rynge who not in honour live.
And now the sonne with the blacke cloudes did
      stryve,
And shettynge on the grounde his glairie raie,
The Abbatte spurrde his steede, and eftsoones° roadde
      awaie.   70

Once moe the skie was blacke, the thounder rolde;
Faste reyneynge oer the plaine a prieste was seen;
Ne dighte full proude, ne buttoned up in golde;
His cope and jape° were graie, and eke were clene;
A Limitoure° he was of order seene;

63. crouche: [editors' note] cross. 66. faitour: a beggar, or
vagabond. 70. eftsoones: [editors' note] quickly. 74. jape:
A short surplice, worn by Friars of an inferior class, and
secular priests. 75. Limitoure: [editors' note] priest licensed
to beg within a limited area.

And from the pathwaie side then turned hee,
Where the poore almer laie binethe the holmen tree.

An almes, sir priest! the droppynge pilgrim sayde,
For sweete Seyncte Marie and your order sake.
The Limitoure then loosen'd his pouche threade,   80
And did thereoute a groate of silver take;
The mister° pilgrim dyd for halline° shake.
Here take this silver, it maie eathe° thie care;
We are Goddes stewards all, nete° of oure owne we
      bare.

But ah! unhailie° pilgrim, lerne of me,
Scathe° anie give a rentrolle° to their Lorde.
Here take my semecope,° thou arte bare I see;
Tis thyne; the Seynctes will give me mie rewarde.
He left the pilgrim, and his waie aborde.°
Virgynne and hallie Seyncte, who sitte yn
      gloure,°   90
Or° give the mittee° will, or give the gode man power.

82. mister: [editors' note] poor. halline: joy. 83. eathe:
ease. 84. nete: nought. 85. unhailie: unhappy. 86. Scathe:
[editors' note] scarcely. rentrolle: [editors' note] a large
portion of one's wealth. 87. semecope: a short under-
cloke. 89. aborde: [editors' note] continued on (?). 90.
gloure: Glory. 91. Or: [editors' note] either. mittee:
mighty, rich.

WRITERS
OF THE END
OF THE CENTURY

Part Seven

WRITERS
OF THE END
OF THE CENTURY

George Crabbe

1754–1832

Raised in the midst of poverty, George Crabbe was further handicapped by uncertainty about his talents and calling: he was at various times a manual laborer, a botanist, an apothecary, a physician, a duke's domestic chaplain, a country clergyman, and a poet. Born to a poor family in Aldborough, a decayed fishing (and smuggling) village on the east coast, he grew up in a setting of rustic lawlessness and misery. His father, a collector of salt taxes, was given to drink and domestic violence. Crabbe bore this harsh environment for twenty-five years; he attended local grammar schools, served apprenticeships with two local surgeons, assisted an apothecary, practiced a little medicine, and earned extra money by moving casks on the wharves; and in his rare hours of freedom he roamed the marshy, cheerless neighborhood, collecting and classifying botanical specimens. But he somehow found time also to read in the English poets, especially Shakespeare and Pope, and to practice writing verse. When he was twenty-one he published *Inebriety*, a Popean satire on drink, the effects of which he had had abundant opportunity to observe in Aldborough and environs. This poem, a derivative discourse in the heroic couplet, went almost unnoticed.

By the age of twenty-six he found that he could endure Aldborough no longer. Abandoning his hopes of a medical career, he went to London to try his hand at literature. His next poem, *The Candidate* (1780), a string of self-conscious couplets on the poet's desire for fame, failed to rescue him from poverty. When he found himself deeply in debt, he sent a letter to the famous parliamentarian Edmund Burke, whom he had never met, entreating assistance and enclosing samples of his poems, including a part of what later was to become *The Village*. Burke was impressed by Crabbe's talent and moved by his hopeless circumstances. He responded with money and encouragement, and even received Crabbe into his house as a guest. Through Burke's good offices Crabbe met Sir Joshua Reynolds and finally Samuel Johnson, who recognized his potential. But although Crabbe's next poem, *The Library* (1781), received some feeble praise from the reviews, it was little more successful than his earlier efforts.

Discouraged by the sluggish beginnings of his literary career, Crabbe turned now to the Church. After a brief period of study, he was ordained in 1781, and the next year he assumed the duties of curate back in Aldborough, where his old acquaintances did not bother to conceal their annoyance at his rapid ascent to respectability. Clearly a different clerical post was required, and through Burke's influence Crabbe attained an appointment as domestic chaplain in the Duke of Rutland's household at Belvoir Castle, in Leicestershire; in this aristocratic setting the rustic Crabbe remained for three uncomfortable and occasionally humiliating years. He had meanwhile been writing (and destroying) vast amounts of poetry. With Johnson's assistance he revised *The Village*, and this poem, published in 1783, established his reputation as a poet.

In 1785 he left the service of the Duke of Rutland, and for the rest of his life he occupied various country clerical livings. As a clergyman Crabbe was conservative and even stubborn; most of his parishioners, although they were grateful for his free medical ministrations, found his sermons cold and dull. Methodism was in the air, and Crabbe never let pass an opportunity to warn his congregations against what he called "that spiritual influenza." While performing the duties of a rural divine, he diversified his days by botanizing and by writing verse, but after the appearance of *The Newspaper* (1785), he published nothing more for twenty-two years. He wrote and then destroyed a treatise on botany. He even produced three novels, all of which he burned, finding them inferior to the dark narrative verse that he was now teaching himself to write. Although he read with interest Wordsworth's and Coleridge's *Lyrical Ballads* (1798), as well as the poems of Burns and Scott, he perceived that his own powers lay in quite a different direction. Finally, in 1807, he published *Poems*, which included *The Parish Register;* in 1810 appeared *The Borough;* in 1812, *Tales*. His reputation was now at its height. Byron proclaimed him "Nature's sternest painter, yet the best," and he appeared triumphantly in London in the company of Thomas Moore, Robert Southey, and Wordsworth. Although heroic-couplet verse now seemed quaint to the avant-garde, Crabbe's poetry was widely admired by conservative readers and critics.

In 1819, in *Tales of the Hall*, Crabbe turned from the miseries of the humble to those of the rich, but most critics found him more at home in his earlier narratives of the poor, based upon his youthful observations of his native place. Until the end of his life he produced regularly his thirty lines a day, and two years after his death his complete poems were published, including a number of posthumous verse tales, which added little to the reputation already soundly established by *The Village*, *The Parish Register*, and *The Borough*.

During his lifetime Crabbe was regarded by some as a mere local pessimist whose discouraging view of human nature resulted entirely from his own early frustrations. The critic William Hazlitt, for example, called Crabbe "a misanthrope in verse" and "a *namby-pamby* Mandeville." Others, who found his subjects and point of view acceptable, deplored his verse technique, which they thought ludicrously pedestrian. The wit James Smith, in *Rejected Addresses* (1812), amused even Crabbe by a parody containing couplets like these:

> John Richard William Alexander Dwyer
> Was footman to Justinian Stubbs, Esquire;

> · · ·

> Emmanuel Jennings brought his youngest boy
> Up as a corn-cutter, a safe employ.

But Francis Jeffrey, editor of the influential *Edinburgh Review*, was among the many who were willing to overlook Crabbe's occasional rusticities of versification and structure for the sake of his originality and honesty. Jeffrey declared him to be "one of the most original, nervous, and pathetic poets of the present century."

The standard biography is René Huchon's *Un Poète réaliste anglais* (1906), translated by F. Clarke as *George Crabbe and His Times* (1907); the book contains a bibliography. *The Life of George Crabbe, by His Son* (1834), edited by E. M. Forster in the World's Classics (1932), is interesting. The *Poems* are edited by A. W. Ward (3 vols., 1905–07). J. H. Evans's *Poems of George Crabbe: A Literary and Historical Study* (1933) is useful. Analysis and criticism of Crabbe's technique are to be found in Lilian Haddakin's *The Poetry of Crabbe* (1955) and in O. F. Sigworth's *Nature's Sternest Painter* (1965).

THE VILLAGE

In 1783 Crabbe gave his friend Sir Joshua Reynolds the manuscript of *The Village* to show to Samuel Johnson. After suggesting some improvements in phrasing, Johnson returned the manuscript and commented in a letter to Reynolds:

> I have sent You back Mr. Crabb's poem which I read with great delight. It is original, vigorous, and elegant. The alterations which I have made, I do not require him to adopt, for my lines are perhaps not often better [than] his own, but he may take mine and his own together, and perhaps between them produce something better than either.

Boswell, in his *Life of Johnson*, offers an explanation of Johnson's high satisfaction with the poem: "Its sentiments as to the false notions of rustick happiness and rustick virtue, were quite congenial with his own."

The text is that of the first edition (1783); we have incorporated substantive variants from the printing in *Poems* (1823). We have omitted Crabbe's notes, which he added to the edition of 1807.

BOOK I

The Subject proposed—Remarks upon Pastoral Poetry—A Tract of Country near the Coast described—An impoverished Borough—Smugglers and their Assistants—Rude Manners of the Inhabitants—Ruinous Effects of a high Tide—The Village Life more generally considered: Evils of it—The youthful Labourer—The old Man: his Soliloquy—The Parish Workhouse: its Inhabitants—The sick Poor: their Apothecary—The dying Pauper—The Village Priest.

The village life, and every care that reigns
O'er youthful peasants and declining swains;
What labour yields, and what, that labour past,
Age, in its hour of languor, finds at last;
What form the real picture of the poor,
Demand a song—The Muse can give no more.

Fled are those times, when, in harmonious strains,
The rustic poet praised his native plains:
No shepherds now in smooth alternate verse,
Their country's beauty or their nymphs' rehearse;   10
Yet still for these we frame the tender strain,
Still in our lays fond Corydons complain,
And shepherds' boys their amorous pains reveal,
The only pains, alas! they never feel.

On° Mincio's° banks, in Caesar's bounteous reign,
If Tityrus° found the golden age again,
Must sleepy bards the flattering dream prolong,

THE VILLAGE: *Book I.* **15–18. On . . . song:** These lines are by Samuel Johnson. **15. Mincio:** a river running through the northern Italian city of Mantua, the traditional birthplace of the Roman poet Virgil (70–19 B.C.); Virgil began his career by writing pastoral poems. **16. Tityrus:** a character through whom Virgil speaks in his first eclogue.

Mechanic echoes of the Mantuan° song?
From Truth and Nature shall we widely stray,
Where VIRGIL, not where fancy leads the way°?   20

Yes, thus the Muses sing of happy swains,
Because the Muses never knew their pains:
They boast their peasants' pipes, but peasants now
Resign their pipes and plod behind the plough;
And few amid the rural-tribe have time
To number syllables and play with rhyme;
Save honest DUCK,° what son of verse could share
The poet's rapture and the peasant's care?
Or the great labours of the field degrade
With the new peril of a poorer trade?   30

From this chief cause these idle praises spring,
That, themes so easy, few forbear to sing;
For no deep thought the trifling subjects ask;
To sing of shepherds is an easy task:
The happy youth assumes the common strain,
A nymph his mistress and himself a swain;
With no sad scenes he clouds his tuneful prayer,
But all, to look like her, is painted fair.

I grant indeed that fields and flocks have charms,
For him that grazes or for him that farms;   40
But when amid such pleasing scenes I trace
The poor laborious natives of the place,
And see the mid-day sun, with fervid ray,
On their bare heads and dewy temples play;
While some, with feebler heads and fainter hearts,
Deplore their fortune, yet sustain their parts,
Then shall I dare these real ills to hide,
In tinsel trappings of poetic pride?

No, cast by Fortune on a frowning coast,
Which neither groves nor happy valleys boast;   50
Where other cares than those the Muse relates,
And other shepherds dwell with other mates;
By such examples taught, I paint the cot,°
As truth will paint it, and as bards will not:
Nor you, ye poor, of letter'd scorn complain,
To you the smoothest song is smooth in vain;
O'ercome by labour and bow'd down by time,
Feel you the barren flattery of a rhyme?

Can poets soothe you, when you pine for bread,
By winding myrtles round your ruin'd shed?   60
Can their light tales your weighty griefs o'erpower,
Or glad with airy mirth the toilsome hour?

Lo! where the heath, with withering brake grown
    o'er,
Lends the light turf that warms the neighbouring poor;
From thence a length of burning sand appears,
Where the thin harvest waves its wither'd ears;
Rank weeds, that every art and care defy,
Reign o'er the land and rob the blighted rye:
There thistles stretch their prickly arms afar,
And to the ragged infant threaten war;   70
There poppies nodding, mock the hope of toil,
There the blue bugloss paints the sterile soil;
Hardy and high, above the slender sheaf,
The slimy mallow waves her silky leaf;
O'er the young shoot the charlock throws a shade,
And clasping tares° cling round the sickly blade;
With mingled tints the rocky coasts abound,
And a sad splendor vainly shines around.

So looks the nymph whom wretched arts adorn,
Betray'd by man, then left for man to scorn;   80
Whose cheek in vain assumes the mimic rose,
While her sad eyes the troubled breast disclose;
Whose outward splendor is but Folly's dress,
Exposing most, when most it gilds distress.

Here joyless roam a wild amphibious race,
With sullen woe display'd in every face;
Who, far from civil arts and social fly,
And scowl at strangers with suspicious eye.

Here too the lawless merchant of the main
Draws from his plough th' intoxicated swain;   90
Want only claim'd the labour of the day,
But vice now steals his nightly rest away.

Where are the swains, who, daily labour done,
With rural games play'd down the setting sun;
Who struck with matchless force the bounding ball,
Or made the pond'rous quoit obliquely fall;
While some huge Ajax, terrible and strong,
Engag'd some artful stripling of the throng,
And fell beneath him, foil'd, while far around
Hoarse triumph rose, and rocks return'd the
    sound?   100

---

18. Mantuan: Virgilian. **20. Where . . . way:** This line is also by Johnson. **27. Duck:** Stephen Duck (1705–56), a self-educated farmer who became stylish as the "Thresher Poet" and was patronized by George II's consort, Queen Caroline. (See the selection from Duck in Part Three.) **53. cot:** cottage.

76. tares: weeds.

Where now are these? Beneath yon cliff they stand,
To show the freighted pinnace where to land;
To load the ready steed with guilty haste,
To fly in terror o'er the pathless waste,
Or when detected in their straggling course,
To foil their foes by cunning or by force;
Or, yielding part (which equal knaves demand),
To gain a lawless passport through the land.

Here wand'ring long amid these frowning fields,
I sought the simple life that Nature yields;　　110
Rapine and Wrong and Fear usurp'd her place,
And a bold, artful, surly, savage race;
Who, only skill'd to take the finny tribe,
The yearly dinner,° or septennial° bribe,
Wait on the shore, and as the waves run high,
On the tost vessel bend their eager eye;
Which to their coast directs its vent'rous way,
Their's, or the ocean's miserable prey.

As on their neighbouring beach yon swallows stand,
And wait for favouring winds to leave the land;　　120
While still for flight the ready wing is spread:
So waited I the favouring hour, and fled;
Fled from these shores where guilt and famine reign,
And cry'd, Ah! hapless they who still remain;
Who still remain to hear the ocean roar,
Whose greedy waves devour the lessening shore;
Till some fierce tide, with more imperious sway,
Sweeps the low hut and all it holds away;
When the sad tenant weeps from door to door,
And begs a poor protection from the poor.　　130

But these are scenes where Nature's niggard hand
Gave a spare portion to the famish'd land;
Her's is the fault if here mankind complain
Of fruitless toil and labour spent in vain;
But yet in other scenes more fair in view,
Where Plenty smiles—alas! she smiles for few,
And those who taste not, yet behold her store,
Are as the slaves that dig the golden ore,
The wealth around them makes them doubly poor:
Or will you deem them amply paid in health,　　140
Labour's fair child, that languishes with Wealth?
Go then! and see them rising with the sun,
Through a long course of daily toil to run;

See them beneath the dog-star's raging heat,°
When the knees tremble and the temples beat;
Behold them leaning on their scythes, look o'er
The labour past, and toils to come explore;
See them alternate suns and showers engage,
And hoard up aches and anguish for their age;
Thro' fens and marshy moors their steps pursue,　　150
When their warm pores imbibe the evening dew;
Then own that labour may as fatal be
To these thy slaves, as thine excess to thee.

Amid this tribe too oft a manly pride
Strives in strong toil the fainting heart to hide;
There may you see the youth of slender frame
Contend with weakness, weariness, and shame;
Yet urged along, and proudly loth to yield,
He strives to join his fellows of the field;
Till long contending nature droops at last,　　160
Declining health rejects his poor repast,
His cheerless spouse the coming danger sees,
And mutual murmurs urge the slow disease.
Yet grant them health, 'tis not for us to tell,
Though the head droops not, that the heart is well;
Or will you praise that homely, healthy fare,
Plenteous and plain, that happy peasants share!
Oh! trifle not with wants you cannot feel,
Nor mock the misery of a stinted meal;
Homely not wholesome, plain not plenteous, such 170
As you who praise would never deign to touch.

Ye gentle souls who dream of rural ease,
Whom the smooth stream and smoother sonnet please;
Go! if the peaceful cot your praises share,
Go look within, and ask if peace be there:
If peace be his—that drooping weary sire,
Or their's, that offspring round their feeble fire,
Or her's, that matron pale, whose trembling hand
Turns on the wretched hearth th' expiring brand!

Nor yet can time itself obtain for these　　180
Life's latest comforts, due respect and ease;
For yonder see that hoary swain, whose age
Can with no cares except his own engage;
Who, propt on that rude staff, looks up to see
The bare arms broken from the withering tree;
On which, a boy, he climb'd the loftiest bough,
Then his first joy, but his sad emblem now.

---

114. yearly dinner: often given to tenants by their landlords at Christmas. **septennial:** Parliamentary elections were held every seven years.

144. the dog-star's . . . heat: The hot weather of July and August was once attributed to the influence of Sirius, the "dog-star."

He once was chief in all the rustic trade;
His steady hand the straightest furrow made;
Full many a prize he won, and still is proud   190
To find the triumphs of his youth allow'd;
A transient pleasure sparkles in his eyes,
He hears and smiles, then thinks again and sighs:
For now he journeys to his grave in pain;
The rich disdain him; nay, the poor disdain;
Alternate masters now their slave command,
Urge the weak efforts of his feeble hand;
And, when his age attempts its task in vain,
With ruthless taunts of lazy poor complain.

Oft may you see him when he tends the sheep,   200
His winter charge, beneath the hillock weep;
Oft hear him murmur to the winds that blow
O'er his white locks, and bury them in snow;
When rouz'd by rage and muttering in the morn,
He mends the broken hedge with icy thorn.

"Why do I live, when I desire to be
At once from life and life's long labour free?
Like leaves in spring, the young are blown away,
Without the sorrows of a slow decay;
I, like yon wither'd leaf, remain behind,   210
Nipt by the frost and shivering in the wind;
There it abides till younger buds come on,
As I, now all my fellow swains are gone;
Then, from the rising generation thrust,
It falls, like me, unnotic'd to the dust.

"These fruitful fields, these numerous flocks I see,
Are others' gain, but killing cares to me;
To me the children of my youth are lords,
Cool in their looks, but hasty in their words:
Wants of their own demand their care, and who   220
Feels his own want and succours others too?
A lonely, wretched man, in pain I go,
None need my help and none relieve my woe;
Then let my bones beneath the turf be laid,
And men forget the wretch they would not aid."

Thus groan the old, till by disease opprest,
They taste a final woe, and then they rest.
Their's is yon house that holds the parish poor,
Whose walls of mud scarce bear the broken door;
There, where the putrid vapours flagging, play,   230
And the dull wheel hums doleful through the day;
There children dwell who know no parents' care,
Parents, who know no children's love, dwell there;
Heart-broken matrons on their joyless bed,
Forsaken wives and mothers never wed;

Dejected widows with unheeded tears,
And crippled age with more than childhood-fears;
The lame, the blind, and, far the happiest they!
The moping idiot and the madman gay.

Here too the sick their final doom receive,   240
Here brought amid the scenes of grief, to grieve,
Where the loud groans from some sad chamber flow,
Mixt with the clamours of the croud below;
Here sorrowing, they each kindred sorrow scan,
And the cold charities of man to man.
Whose laws indeed for ruin'd age provide,
And strong compulsion plucks the scrap from pride;
But still that scrap is bought with many a sigh,
And pride embitters what it can't deny.

Say ye, opprest by some fantastic woes,   250
Some jarring nerve that baffles your repose;
Who press the downy couch, while slaves advance
With timid eye, to read the distant glance;
Who with sad prayers the weary doctor teaze
To name the nameless ever-new disease;
Who with mock patience dire complaints endure,
Which real pain, and that alone can cure;
How would ye bear in real pain to lie,
Despis'd, neglected, left alone to die?
How would ye bear to draw your latest breath,   260
Where all that's wretched paves the way for death?

Such is that room which one rude beam divides,
And naked rafters form the sloping sides;
Where the vile bands that bind the thatch are seen,
And lath and mud are all that lie between;
Save one dull pane, that, coarsely patch'd, gives way
To the rude tempest, yet excludes the day:
Here, on a matted flock,° with dust o'erspread,
The drooping wretch reclines his languid head;
For him no hand the cordial cup applies,   270
Or wipes the tear that stagnates in his eyes;
No friends with soft discourse his pain beguile,
Or promise hope till sickness wears a smile.

But soon a loud and hasty summons calls,
Shakes the thin roof, and echoes round the walls;
Anon, a figure enters, quaintly neat,
All pride and business, bustle and conceit;
With looks unalter'd by these scenes of woe,
With speed that entering, speaks his haste to go;

---

268. matted flock: bed made of small fragments of torn-up cloth.

He bids the gazing throng around him fly,   280
And carries fate and physic in his eye:
A potent quack, long vers'd in human ills,
Who first insults the victim whom he kills;
Whose murd'rous hand a drowsy bench protect,
And whose most tender mercy is neglect.

Paid by the parish for attendance here,
He wears contempt upon his sapient sneer;
In haste he seeks the bed where misery lies,
Impatience mark'd in his averted eyes;
And, some habitual queries hurried o'er,   290
Without reply, he rushes on the door;
His drooping patient, long inur'd to pain,
And long unheeded, knows remonstrance vain;
He ceases now the feeble help to crave
Of man; and silent sinks into the grave.

But ere his death some pious doubts arise,
Some simple fears which "bold bad" men despise;
Fain would he ask the parish priest to prove
His title certain to the joys above;
For this he sends the murmuring nurse, who calls 300
The holy stranger to these dismal walls;
And doth not he, the pious man, appear,
He, "passing rich with forty pounds a year?"°
Ah! no, a shepherd of a different stock,
And far unlike him, feeds this little flock;
A jovial youth, who thinks his Sunday's task
As much as God or man can fairly ask;
The rest he gives to loves and labours light,
To fields the morning and to feasts the night;
None better skill'd, the noisy pack to guide,   310
To urge their chace, to cheer them or to chide;
A sportsman keen, he shoots through half the day,
And, skill'd at whist, devotes the night to play:
Then, while such honours bloom around his head,
Shall he sit sadly by the sick man's bed
To raise the hope he feels not, or with zeal
To combat fears that e'en the pious feel?

Now once again the gloomy scene explore,   ⎫
Less gloomy now; the bitter hour is o'er,   ⎬
The man of many sorrows sighs no more.—   ⎭
Up yonder hill, behold how sadly slow   321
The bier moves winding from the vale below;

---

303. passing . . . year: an allusion to line 142 of Goldsmith's
The Deserted Village (see Part Six), where Goldsmith draws an
idealized portrait of a virtuous village preacher.

There lie the happy dead, from trouble free,
And the glad parish pays the frugal fee;
No more, O Death! thy victim starts to hear
Churchwarden stern, or kingly overseer;
No more the farmer claims his humble bow,
Thou art his lord, the best of tyrants thou!

Now to the church behold the mourners come,
Sedately torpid and devoutly dumb;   330
The village children now their games suspend,
To see the bier that bears their antient friend;
For he was one in all their idle sport,
And like a monarch rul'd their little court;
The pliant bow he form'd, the flying ball,
The bat, the wicket, were his labours all;
Him now they follow to his grave, and stand
Silent and sad, and gazing, hand in hand;
While bending low, their eager eyes explore
The mingled relicks of the parish poor: 340
The bell tolls late, the moping owl flies round,
Fear marks the flight and magnifies the sound;
The busy priest, detain'd by weightier care,
Defers his duty till the day of prayer;
And waiting long, the crowd retire distrest,
To think a poor man's bones should lie unblest.

BOOK II

There are found, amid the Evils of a laborious Life,
some Views of Tranquillity and Happiness—The
Repose and Pleasure of a Summer Sabbath: interrupted by Intoxication and Dispute—Village Detraction—Complaints of the 'Squire—The Evening Riots
—Justice—Reasons for this unpleasant View of Rustic
Life: the Effect it should have upon the Lower Classes;
and the Higher—These last have their peculiar Distresses: Exemplified in the Life and heroic Death of
Lord Robert Manners—Concluding Address to His
Grace the Duke of Rutland.

No longer truth, though shown in verse, disdain,
But own the village life a life of pain;
I too must yield, that oft amid these woes
Are gleams of transient mirth and hours of sweet
          repose.

Such as you find on yonder sportive Green,
The 'Squire's tall gate and churchway-walk between;
Where loitering stray a little tribe of friends,
On a fair Sunday when the sermon ends:

Then rural beaux their best attire put on,
To win their nymphs, as other nymphs are won;   10
While those long wed go plain, and by degrees,
Like other husbands, quit their care to please.
Some of the sermon talk, a sober crowd,
And loudly praise, if it were preach'd aloud;
Some on the labours of the week look round,
Feel their own worth, and think their toil renown'd;
While some, whose hopes to no renown extend,
Are only pleas'd to find their labours end.

Thus, as their hours glide on with pleasure fraught,
Their careful masters brood the painful thought;   20
Much in their mind they murmur and lament,
That one fair day should be so idly spent;
And think that Heaven deals hard, to tythe their store
And tax their time for preachers and the poor.

Yet still, ye humbler friends, enjoy your hour,
This is your portion, yet unclaim'd of power;
This is Heaven's gift to weary men opprest,
And seems the type° of their expected rest:
But yours, alas! are joys that soon decay;
Frail joys, begun and ended with the day;   30
Or yet, while day permits those joys to reign,
The village vices drive them from the plain.

See the stout churl, in drunken fury great,
Strike the bare bosom of his teeming mate!
His naked vices, rude and unrefin'd,
Exert their open empire o'er the mind;
But can we less the senseless rage despise,
Because the savage acts without disguise?

Yet here Disguise, the city's vice, is seen,
And Slander steals along and taints the Green;   40
At her approach domestic peace is gone,
Domestic broils at her approach come on;
She to the wife the husband's crime conveys,
She tells the husband when his consort strays;
Her busy tongue, through all the little state,
Diffuses doubt, suspicion, and debate;
Peace, tim'rous goddess! quits her old domain,
In sentiment and song content to reign.

Nor are the nymphs that breathe the rural air
So fair as Cynthia's,° nor so chaste as fair;   50
These to the town afford each fresher face,

And the clown's trull receives the peer's embrace;
From whom, should chance again convey her down,
The Peer's disease in turn attacks the Clown.

Here too the 'Squire, or 'squire-like farmer, talk,
How round their regions nightly pilferers walk;
How from their ponds the fish are borne, and all
The rip'ning treasures from their lofty wall;
How meaner rivals in their sports delight,
Just rich enough to claim a doubtful right;   60
Who take a licence round their fields to stray,
A mongrel race! the poachers of the day.

And hark! the riots of the Green begin,
That sprang at first from yonder noisy inn;
What time the weekly pay was vanish'd all,
And the slow hostess scored° the threat'ning wall;
What time they ask'd, their friendly feast to close,
A final cup, and that will make them foes;
When blows ensue that break the arm of Toil,
And rustic battle ends the boobies' broil.   70
Save when to yonder hall they bend their way,
Where the grave Justice ends the grievous fray;
He who recites, to keep the poor in awe,
The law's vast volume—for he knows the law.—
To him with anger or with shame repair
The injur'd peasant and deluded fair.

Lo! at his throne the silent nymph appears,
Frail by her shape, but modest in her tears;
And while she stands abash'd, with conscious° eye,
Some favourite female of her judge glides by;   80
Who views with scornful glance the strumpet's fate,
And thanks the stars that made her keeper great:
Near her the swain, about to bear for life
One certain evil, doubts 'twixt war and wife;
But, while the fault'ring damsel takes her oath,
Consents to wed, and so secures them both.

Yet why, you ask, these humble crimes relate,
Why make the poor as guilty as the great?
To show the great, those mightier sons of Pride,
How near in vice the lowest are allied;   90
Such are their natures, and their passions such,
But these disguise too little, those too much:
So shall the man of power and pleasure see
In his own slave as vile a wretch as he;
In his luxurious lord the servant find
His own low pleasures and degenerate mind;

Book II. 28. type: symbol. 50. Cynthia: the Roman
goddess Diana, a virgin and protector of young people; she
required a vow of chastity from nymphs who served her.

66. scored: kept a record of the bill with chalk marks. 79.
conscious: conscience-stricken.

And each in all the kindred vices trace
Of a poor, blind, bewilder'd, erring race;
Who, a short time in varied fortune past,
Die, and are equal in the dust at last.   100

And you, ye poor, who still lament your fate,
Forbear to envy those you call the great;
And know, amid those blessings they possess,
They are, like you, the victims of distress;
While Sloth with many a pang torments her slave,
Fear waits on guilt, and Danger shakes the brave.

Oh! if in life one noble chief appears,
Great in his name, while blooming in his years;
Born to enjoy whate'er delights mankind,
And yet to all you feel or fear resign'd;   110
Who gave up joys and hopes to you unknown,
For pains and dangers greater than your own:
If such there be, then let your murmurs cease,
Think, think of him, and take your lot in peace.

And such there was:—Oh! grief, that checks our pride,
Weeping we say, there was—for MANNERS° died;—
Belov'd of Heaven! these humble lines forgive,
That sing of thee, and thus aspire to live.
As the tall oak, whose vigorous branches form
An ample shade and brave the wildest storm,   120
High o'er the subject wood is seen to grow,
The guard and glory of the trees below;
Till on its head the fiery bolt descends,
And o'er the plain the shatter'd trunk extends;
Yet then it lies, all wond'rous as before,
And still the glory, though the guard no more.

So THOU, when every virtue, every grace,
Rose in thy soul, or shone within thy face;
When, though the Son of GRANBY, thou wert known
Less by thy father's glory than thy own;   130
When Honour lov'd, and gave thee every charm,
Fire to thy eye and vigour to thy arm;
Then from our lofty hopes and longing eyes
Fate and thy virtues call'd thee to the skies;
Yet still we wonder at thy tow'ring frame,
And losing thee, still dwell upon thy name.

Oh! ever honour'd, ever valued! say
What verse can praise thee, or what work repay?

116. **Manners:** Lord Robert Manners, a naval officer of great
skill and gallantry, was killed in action in 1782 at the age of
twenty-four; he was the brother of Crabbe's patron Charles
Manners, Marquis of Granby and Fourth Duke of Rutland.

Yet Verse (in all we can) thy worth repays,
Nor trusts the tardy zeal of future days;—   140
Honours for thee thy Country shall prepare,
Thee in their hearts, the Good, the Brave shall bear;
To deeds like thine shall noblest chiefs aspire,
The Muse shall mourn thee, and the world admire.

In future times, when smit with glory's charms,
The untry'd youth first quits a father's arms;
"Oh be like him," the weeping sire shall say,
"Like MANNERS walk, who walk'd in honour's way;
In danger foremost, yet in death sedate,
Oh! be like him in all things, but his fate!"   150
If for that fate such public tears be shed,
That victory seems to die now THOU art dead;
How shall a friend his nearer hope resign,
That friend a brother, and whose soul was thine?
By what bold lines shall we his grief express,
Or by what soothing numbers make it less?

'Tis not, I know, the chiming of a song,
Nor all the powers that to the Muse belong;
Words aptly cull'd, and meanings well exprest,
Can calm the sorrows of a wounded breast: 160
But Virtue, soother of the fiercest pains,
Shall heal that bosom, RUTLAND, where she reigns.

Yet hard the task to heal the bleeding heart,
To bid the still-recurring thoughts depart;
Tame the fierce grief and stem the rising sigh,
And curb rebellious passion with reply;
Calmly to dwell on all that pleas'd before,
And yet to know that all shall please no more;—
Oh! glorious labour of the soul, to save
Her captive powers, and bravely mourn the brave!   170

To such, these thoughts will lasting comfort give:—
Life is not measured by the time we live:
'Tis not an even course of threescore years,
A life of narrow views and paltry fears,
Gray hairs and wrinkles, and the cares they bring,
That take from death the terrors or the sting;
But 'tis the gen'rous spirit, mounting high
Above the world, that native of the sky;
The noble spirit, that, in dangers brave,
Calmly looks on, or looks beyond the grave.   180
Such MANNERS was, so he resign'd his breath!
If in a glorious, then a timely death.

Cease then that grief, and let those tears subside:
If Passion rule us, be that passion Pride;
If Reason, Reason bids us strive to raise
Our fallen hearts, and be like him we praise;

Or if Affection still the soul subdue,   ⎞
Bring all his virtues, all his worth in view, ⎟
And let Affection find its comfort too;   ⎠
For how can grief so deeply wound the heart,   190
When admiration claims so large a part?

Grief is a foe, expel him then thy soul;
Let nobler thoughts the nearer views controul;
Oh! make the age to come thy better care,
See other RUTLANDS, other GRANBYS there!
And as thy thoughts through streaming ages glide,
See other heroes die as MANNERS died;
And from their fate thy race shall nobler grow,
As trees shoot upward that are prun'd below:
Or, as old Thames, borne down with decent pride, 200
Sees his young streams run warbling at his side;
Though some, by art cut off, no longer run,
And some are lost beneath the summer's sun;
Yet the pure stream moves on, and, as it moves,
Its power increases, and its use improves;
While plenty round its spacious waves bestow,
Still it flows on, and shall for ever flow.

FROM

THE PARISH REGISTER

In the three parts of *The Parish Register* (1807), Crabbe
speaks as a country clergyman reminiscing over the
official records of a year's baptisms, marriages, and
burials in his rural parish. In the Preface, Crabbe argues
that his bleak view of human life is not derived from
any a priori theory; he insists that it is empirically
"natural":

> In the "Parish Register," [the reader] will find an
> endeavour once more to describe the village-
> manners, not by adopting the notion of pastoral
> simplicity or assuming ideas of rustic barbarity, but
> by more natural views of the peasantry, considered
> as a mixed body of persons, sober or profligate, and
> hence, in a great measure, contented or miserable.

Always uncertain about the merits of his work, Crabbe
submitted the manuscript of *The Parish Register* to the
statesman Charles James Fox, just as he had sent *The
Village* to Johnson. "Whatever [Fox] approved,"
Crabbe explains in his Preface, ". . . I have carefully
retained; the parts he disliked are totally expunged, and
others are substituted, which I hope resemble those,
more conformable to the taste of so admirable a judge."

The text is that of the first printing, in *Poems* (1807).
We have introduced substantive variants from the
edition of 1823 and have brought typographical accidentals into conformity with the usage of the first
edition.

PART III. BURIALS

There was, 'tis said, and I believe, a Time,
When humble Christians died with views sublime;
When all were ready for their Faith to bleed,
But few to write or wrangle for their Creed;
When lively Faith upheld the sinking Heart,
And Friends assur'd to meet, prepar'd to part;
When Love felt Hope, when Sorrow grew serene,
And all was Comfort, in the Death-bed Scene.

Alas! when now the gloomy King they wait,
'Tis Weakness yielding to resistless Fate;   10
Like wretched Men upon the Ocean cast,
They labour hard and struggle to the last;
"Hope against Hope," and wildly gaze around,
In search of Help, that never shall be found;
Nor, till the last strong Billow stops the Breath,
Will they believe them in the jaws of Death!

When these my Records, I reflecting read,
And find what Ills, these numerous Births succeed;
What powerful Griefs, these Nuptial Ties attend,
With what regret these painful Journeys end;   20
When from the Cradle to the Grave I look,
Mine I conceive, a melancholy Book.

Where now is perfect Resignation seen?
Alas! it is not on the Village-Green,—
I've seldom known, though I have often read
Of, happy Peasants on their Dying-bed;
Whose Looks proclaim'd that Sunshine of the Breast,
That more than Hope, that Heav'n itself express'd.

What I behold, are feverish fits of Strife,
'Twixt Fears of Dying and Desire of Life;   30
Those earthly Hopes, that to the last indure;
Those Fears, that Hopes superior fail to cure;
At best, a sad submission to the Doom,
Which, turning from the Danger, lets it come.

Sick lies the Man, bewilder'd, lost, afraid,
His Spirits vanquish'd and his Strength decay'd;
No Hope the Friend, the Nurse, the Doctor, lend—
"Call then a Priest, and fit him for his End;"

A priest is call'd, 'tis now, alas! too late,
Death enters with him, at the Cottage Gate;   40
Or Time allow'd—he goes, assur'd to find,
The self-commending, all-confiding mind;
And sighs to hear, what we may justly call,
Death's *Common-Place*, the Train of Thought in all.

"True, I'm a Sinner," feebly he begins—
"But trust in Mercy, to forgive my sins:"
(Such cool Confession no past Crimes excite!
Such Claim on Mercy, seems the Sinner's Right!)
"I know, Mankind are frail, that GOD is just,
And pardons those who in his mercy trust;   50
We're sorely tempted, in a World like this,
All Men have done, and I, like all, amiss;
But now, if spar'd, it is my full Intent,
On all the past to ponder and repent:
Wrongs against me, I pardon, great and small,
And if I die, I die in peace with all."

His Merits thus and not his Sins confest,
He speaks his Hopes and leaves to Heav'n the Rest.
Alas! are these the Prospects, dull and cold,
That dying Christians to their Priests unfold?   60
Or mends the Prospect when th' Enthusiast cries,
"I die assured!" and in a Rapture dies?

Ah, where that humble, self-abasing Mind,
With that confiding Spirit shall we find;
The mind that, feeling what repentance brings,
Dejection's terrors and Contrition's stings,
Feels then the hope, that mounts all care above,
And the pure joy that flows from pardoning love?

Such have I seen in Death, and much deplore,
So many dying—that I see no more: 70
Lo! now my Records, where I grieve to trace,
How Death has triumph'd in so short a Space;
Who are the Dead, how died they, I relate,
And snatch some Portion of their Acts from Fate.

With ANDREW COLLETT we the Year begin,
The blind, fat Landlord of the Old Crown-Inn;
Big as his Butt,° and for the self-same Use,
To take in Stores of strong, fermenting Juice.
On his huge Chair, beside the Fire he sate,
In Revel Chief, and Umpire in Debate;   80
Each Night, his String of vulgar Tales he told;
When Ale was cheap, and Bachelors were bold;
His Heroes all, were famous in their Days,
Cheats were his Boast, and Drunkards had his Praise;

"One, in three Draughts, three Mugs of Ale took
   down,
As Mugs were then—the Champion of the Crown;
For thrice three Days, another liv'd on Ale,
And knew no change, but that of Mild and Stale;°
Two thirsty Soakers watch'd a Vessel's side,
When he the Tap, with dexterous Hand, applied;   90
Nor from their Seats departed, till they found
That Butt was out, and heard the mournful Sound."

He prais'd a Poacher, precious Child of Fun!
Who shot the Keeper, with his own Spring-Gun;°
Nor less the Smuggler who the Exciseman tied,
And left him hanging at the Birch-wood side,
There to expire;—but one who saw him hang
Cut the good Cord—a Traitor of the Gang.

His own Exploits, with boastful Glee, he told,
What Ponds he empty'd and what Pikes° he sold;   100
And how, when blest with Sight alert and gay,
The Night's Amusements kept him through the Day.

He sang the Praises of those Times, when all
"For Cards and Dice, as for their Drink, might call;
When Justice wink'd on every jovial Crew,
And Ten-pins tumbled, in the Parson's View."

He told, when angry Wives, provok'd to rail,
Or drive a third-day Drunkard from his Ale;
What were his Triumphs and how great the Skill
That won the vex'd Virago to his Will;   110
Who raving came; Then talk'd in milder Strain,—
Then wept,—then drank, and pledg'd her Spouse
   again.
Such were his Themes: how Knaves o'er Laws prevail,
Or when made captives, how they fly from Jail;
The Young how brave, how subtle were the Old;
And Oaths attested all that Folly told.

On Death like his, what Name shall we bestow,
So very sudden! yet so very slow?
'Twas slow:—Disease, augmenting year by year,
Show'd the grim King by gradual Steps brought
   near: 120
'Twas not less sudden;—in the Night he died,
He drank, he swore, he jested, and he lied;
Thus aiding Folly, with departing Breath:—
"Beware, *Lorenzo*, the slow-sudden Death."°

---

88. **Mild and Stale:** two kinds of ale: mild and strong. **94.
Spring-Gun:** a concealed gun with a trip wire attached to
the trigger. **100. Pikes:** fish. **124. Beware . . . Death:**
slightly misquoted from line 388 of Edward Young's *The
Complaint, or Night Thoughts on Life, Death, and Immortality,*
"Night the First." (See the selections from Young in Parts
Three and Five.)

THE PARISH REGISTER: *Part III.* **77. Butt:** ale cask.

Next died the Widow GOE, an active Dame,
Fam'd ten Miles round, and worthy all her Fame;
She lost her Husband when their Loves were young,
But kept her Farm, her Credit, and her Tongue;
Full thirty Years she rul'd, with matchless skill,
With guiding Judgment and resistless Will;   130
Advice she scorn'd, Rebellions she suppress'd,
And Sons and Servants bow'd, at her Behest.
Like that great Man's,° who to his SAVIOUR came,
Were the strong Words of this commanding Dame;—
"Come," if she said, they came; if "go," were gone;
And if "do this,"—that instant it was done.
Her Maidens told, she was all Eye and Ear,
In Darkness saw and could at Distance hear;—
No Parish-Business in the Place could stir,
Without Direction or Assent from her;   140
In turn, she took each Office as it fell;
Knew all their Duties, and discharg'd them well;
The lazy Vagrants in her presence shook,
And pregnant Damsels fear'd her stern Rebuke;
She look'd on Want, with Judgment, clear and cool,
And felt with Reason, and bestow'd by Rule:
She match'd both Sons and Daughters to her Mind,
And lent them Eyes; for Love, she heard, was blind;
Yet ceaseless still she throve, alert, alive,
The working Bee, in full or empty Hive;   150
Busy and careful, like that working bee,
No time for love nor tender cares had she;
But when our Farmers made their amorous Vows,
She talk'd of Market-Steeds and patent Ploughs.
Not unemploy'd her Evenings pass'd away,
Amusement clos'd, as Business wak'd the Day;
When to her Toilet's brief Concern she ran,
And Conversation, with her Friends, began;
Who all were welcome, what they saw, to share;
And joyous Neighbours prais'd her Christmas
    Fare,   160
That none around, might, in their Scorn, complain
Of Gossip GOE as greedy in her Gain.
    Thus long she reign'd, admir'd, if not approv'd;
Prais'd, if not honour'd; fear'd, if not belov'd;
When, as the busy Days of Spring drew near,
That call'd for all the Forecast of the Year;
When lively Hope the rising Crops survey'd,
And April promis'd what September pay'd;

When stray'd her Lambs, where Gorse and Greenweed
    grow;
When rose her Grass in richer Vales below;   170
When pleas'd she look'd on all the smiling Land,
And view'd the Hinds, who wrought at her Command;
(Poultry in groups still follow'd where she went;)
Then, Dread o'ercame her,—that her Days were spent.
    "Bless me! I die, and not a warning giv'n,—
With much to do on Earth, and ALL for Heav'n!
No Reparation for my Soul's Affairs,
No Leave petition'd for the Barn's Repairs;
Accounts perplex'd, my Interest yet unpaid,
My Mind unsettled, and my Will unmade;—   180
A Lawyer haste, and, in your way, a Priest;
And let me die in one good Work at least."
She spake, and trembling, dropp'd upon her Knees,
Heaven in her Eye, and in her Hand her Keys:
And still the more she found her life decay,
With greater force she grasp'd those signs of sway:
Then fell and died!—in haste her Sons drew near,
And dropp'd, in haste, the tributary Tear,
Then from th' adhering Clasp the Keys unbound,
And Consolation for their Sorrows, found.—   190

    Death has his Infant-Train; his bony Arm
Strikes from the Baby-Cheek, the rosy Charm;
The brightest Eye, his glazing Film makes dim,
And his cold Touch sets fast the lithest Limb;
He seiz'd the sick'ning Boy, to GERARD° lent,
When three Days' Life, in feeble Cries, were spent;
In Pain brought forth, those painful Hours to stay,
To breathe in Pain, and sigh its Soul away!
    "But why thus lent, if thus recall'd again,
To cause and feel, to live and die, in Pain?"   200
Or rather say, Why grievous these appear,
If all it pays for Heav'n's eternal Year;
If these sad Sobs and piteous Sighs secure
Delights that live, when Worlds no more endure?
    The Sister-Spirit long may lodge below,
And Pains from Nature, Pains from Reason, know;
Through all the common Ills of Life may run,
By Hope perverted, and by Love undone;
A Wife's Distress, a Mother's Pangs, may dread,
And widow-tears, in bitter Anguish, shed;   210
May at Old Age arrive, through numerous Harms,
With children's children in those feeble arms:
Nor, till by Years of Want and Grief oppresst,
Shall the sad Spirit flee and be at rest!

---

133. **that great Man:** the Roman centurion of Luke 7:8,
who said, speaking of his authority over his soldiers, "I say
unto one, Go, and he goeth; and to another, Come, and he
cometh; and to my servant, Do this, and he doeth it."

195. **Gerard:** In Part I ("Baptisms"), Crabbe discusses the
children of Gerard Ablett, a laborer.

Yet happier therefore shall we deem the Boy,
Secur'd from anxious Care and dangerous Joy?
　Not so! for then would Love Divine, in vain
Send all the Burthens weary Men sustain;
All that now curb the Passions, when they rage,
The checks of youth and the regrets of age;　　220
All that now bid us hope, believe, endure,
Our Sorrow's Comfort, and our Vice's Cure;
All that for Heaven's high Joys the Spirits train,
And Charity, the Crown of all, were vain.
　Say, will you call the breathless infant bless'd,
Because no cares the silent grave molest?
So would you deem the nursling from the wing
Untimely thrust and never train'd to sing;
But far more bless'd the bird whose grateful voice
Sings its own Joy, and makes the woods rejoice,　230
Though, while untaught, ere yet he charm'd the ear,
Hard were his trials, and his pains severe!

　Next died the LADY who yon Hall possess'd;
And here they brought her noble Bones to rest.
In Town, she dwelt;—forsaken stood the Hall,
Worms ate the Floors, the Tap'stry fled the Wall;
No Fire the Kitchen's cheerless Grate display'd;
No cheerful Light the long-closed Sash convey'd!
The crawling Worm, that turns a Summer-Fly,
Here spun his Shroud and laid him up to die　　240
The Winter-Death:—upon the Bed of State,
The Bat shrill-shrieking, woo'd his flickering Mate:
To empty Rooms, the curious came no more, ⎤
From empty Cellars turn'd the angry Poor, ⎬
And surly Beggars curs'd the ever-bolted Door. ⎦
To one small Room, the Steward found his way,
Where Tenants follow'd to complain and pay;
Yet no Complaint before the LADY came,
The feeling Servant spar'd the feeble Dame;
Who saw her Farms with his observing Eyes,　　250
And answer'd all Requests with his Replies;
She came not down, her falling Groves to view;
Why should she know, what One so faithful knew?
Why come, from many clamorous Tongues to hear,
What One so just might whisper in her Ear?
Her Oaks or Acres, why with care explore,
Why learn the Wants, the Sufferings of the Poor,
When One so knowing, all their Worth could trace,
And One so piteous, govern'd in her Place?
　Lo! now, what dismal Sons of Darkness° come,　260
To bear this Daughter of Indulgence home!

Tragedians all, and well arranged in Black!
Who Nature, Feeling, Force, Expression lack;—
Who cause no Tear, but gloomily pass by,
And shake their Sables° in the wearied Eye,
That turns disgusted from the pompous Scene,
Proud without Grandeur, with Profusion, mean!
The Tear for Kindness past, Affection owes;
For Worth deceas'd, the Sigh from Reason flows;
E'en well-feign'd Passion, for our Sorrows call,　270
And real Tears for mimic Miseries fall:—
But this poor Farce has neither Truth nor Art,
To please the Fancy, or to touch the Heart;
Unlike the Darkness of the Sky, that pours
On the dry Ground, its fertilizing Showers;
Unlike to that, which strikes the Soul with Dread,
When Thunders roar and forky Fires are shed;
Dark but not aweful, dismal but yet mean,
With anxious Bustle moves the cumbrous Scene;
Presents no Objects, tender or profound,　　280
But spreads its cold, unmeaning Gloom around.
　When Woes are feign'd, how ill such Forms appear,
And oh! how needless, when the Woe's sincere.
　Slow to the Vault they come with heavy tread,
Bending beneath the Lady and her Lead;°
A Case of Elm surrounds that ponderous Chest,
Close on that Case, the Crimson Velvet's press'd;
Ungenerous this, that to the Worm denies,
With niggard-caution, his appointed Prize;
For now, ere yet he works his tedious way,　　290
Through Cloth and Wood and Metal, to his Prey;
That Prey dissolving, shall a Mass remain,
That Fancy loathes and Worms themselves disdain.
　But see! the Master-Mourner makes his way,
To end his Office, for the coffin'd Clay;
Pleas'd that our rustic Men and Maids behold
His Plate,° like Silver, and his Studs, like Gold;
As they approach to spell the Age, the Name,
And all the Titles of th' illustrious Dame.—
This as, (my Duty° done,) some Scholar read,　　300
A Village-Father look'd Disdain, and said:
"Away, my Friends! why take such pains to know,
What some brave° Marble, soon in Church shall show?
Where not alone, her gracious Name shall stand,
But how she liv'd—the Blessing of the Land;

---

265. **Sables:** black mourning garments and accessories. **285.
Lead:** the innermost lining of the coffin. **297. Plate:** nailed
to the top of the coffin just before it is lowered into the
grave. **300. my Duty:** the speaker's duty as a clergyman
of reading the burial service. **303. brave:** splendid.

260. **Sons of Darkness:** professional mourners.

How much we all deplor'd the noble Dead,
What Groans we utter'd and what Tears we shed;—
Tears, true as those, which in the sleepy Eyes
Of weeping Cherubs, on the Stone shall rise;
Tears, true as those, which, ere she found her
    Grave,   310
The noble Lady, to our Sorrows gave."—

    Down by the Church-way Walk, and where the
      Brook
Winds round the Chancel, like a Shepherd's Crook;
In that small House, with those green Pales° before,
Where Jasmine trails on either side the Door;
Where those dark Shrubs that now grow wild at will,
Were clipt in Form and tantaliz'd with Skill;
Where Cockles blanch'd, and Pebbles neatly spread,
Form'd shining Borders for the Larkspurs' Bed;—
There liv'd a LADY, wise, austere, and nice,   320
Who shew'd her Virtue, by her Scorn of Vice;
In the dear Fashions of her Youth she dress'd,
A pea-green *Joseph*° was her favourite Vest;°
Erect she stood, she walk'd with stately Mien,
Tight was her Length of Stays, and she was tall and
    lean.
    There long she liv'd in Maiden-State immur'd,
From Looks of Love and treacherous Man secur'd;
Though Evil-Fame—(but that was long before)
Had blown her dubious Blast at CATHERINE's Door:—
A Captain thither, rich from *India* came,   330
And though a Cousin call'd, it touch'd her Fame;
Her annual Stipend rose from his Behest,
And all the long-priz'd Treasures she possess'd:—
If aught like Joy awhile appear'd to stay
In that stern Face, and chase those Frowns away;
'Twas when her Treasures she dispos'd for View,
And heard the Praises, to their Splendour due:
Silks beyond Price, so rich they'd stand alone,
And Diamonds blazing on the buckled Zone;°
Rows of rare Pearls, by curious Workmen set,   340
And Bracelets fair, in Box of glossy Jet;
Bright polish'd Amber precious from its Size,
Or Forms, the fairest, Fancy could devise:
Her draw'rs of Cedar, shut with secret Springs,
Conceal'd the watch of gold and rubied rings;
Letters, long Proofs of Love, and Verses fine
Round the pink'd Rims of crisped Valentine.

314. **Pales:** fence pickets. 323. **Joseph:** long riding cloak.
Vest: garment. 339. **Zone:** belt.

Her China Closet, cause of daily Care,
For Woman's Wonder, held her pencill'd Ware;
That pictur'd Wealth of *China* and *Japan*,   350
Like its cold Mistress, shunn'd the Eye of Man.
    Her neat small Room, adorn'd with Maiden-Taste,
A clipt French-Puppy, first of Favourites, grac'd.
A Parrot next, but dead, and stuff'd with Art;
(For Poll, when living, lost the Lady's Heart,
And then his Life; for he was heard to speak
Such frightful Words as tinged his Lady's Cheek;)
Unhappy Bird! who had no power to prove,
Save by such Speech, his gratitude, and Love.
A grey old Cat his Whiskers lick'd beside;   360
A Type of Sadness in the House of Pride.
The polish'd Surface of an India-Chest,
A glassy Globe, in Frame of Ivory, prest;
Where swam two finny Creatures; one of Gold,
Of Silver one; both beauteous to behold:
All these were form'd the guiding Taste to suit;
The Beasts well-manner'd, and the Fishes mute:
A widow'd Aunt was there, compell'd by Need
The Nymph to flatter and her Tribe to feed;
Who, veiling well her Scorn, endur'd the Clog,   370
Mute as the Fish and fawning as the Dog.
    As years increas'd, these Treasures, her Delight,
Arose in value, in their Owner's sight:—
A Miser knows that, view it as he will,
A Guinea kept, is but a Guinea still:
And so he puts it to its proper Use,
That something more this Guinea may produce:—
But Silks and Rings in the Possessor's Eyes,
The oft'ner seen, the more in Value rise,
And thus are wisely hoarded, to bestow   380
The kind of pleasure that with years will grow.
    But what avail'd their Worth,—if Worth had they,—
In the sad Summer of her slow Decay?
    Then we beheld her turn an anxious Look
From Trunks and Chests, and fix it on her Book;
A rich-bound Book of Prayer, the Captain gave,
(Some Princess had it, or was said to have,)
And then once more, on all her Stores, look round
And draw a sigh so piteous and profound,
That told, "Alas! how hard from these to part,   390
And for new Hopes and Habits form the Heart!
What shall I do, (she cried) my Peace of Mind
To gain in dying, and to die resign'd?"
    "Hear," we return'd;—"these Bawbles cast aside,
Nor give thy GOD a Rival, in thy Pride;
Thy Closets shut, and ope thy Kitchen's Door;
There own thy Failings, *here* invite the Poor;

A Friend of *Mammon* let thy Bounty make, }
For Widows' Prayers, thy Vanities forsake; }
And let the Hungry, of thy Pride, partake: }
Then shall thy inward Eye with joy survey   401
The Angel *Mercy* tempering *Death*'s Delay!"

Alas! 'twas hard; the Treasures still had Charms,
Hope still its Flattery, Sickness its Alarms;
Still was the same unsettled, clouded View,
And the same plaintive Cry, "What shall I do?"

Nor Change appear'd; for, when her Race was run,
Doubtful we all exclaim'd, "What has been done?"
Apart she liv'd, and still she lies alone;
Yon earthy Heap awaits the flattering Stone,   410
On which Invention shall be long employ'd,
To show the various Worth of CATHERINE LLOYD.

Next to these Ladies, but in nought allied,
A noble Peasant, ISAAC ASHFORD, died.
Noble he was, contemning all Things mean,
His Truth unquestion'd, and his Soul serene:
Of no Man's presence, ISAAC felt afraid;
At no Man's question, ISAAC look'd dismay'd:
Shame knew him not, he dreaded no Disgrace;
Truth, simple Truth was written in his Face: 420
Yet while the serious Thought his Soul approv'd,
Cheerful he seem'd, and Gentleness he lov'd:
To Bliss domestic he his Heart resign'd,
And with the firmest, had the fondest Mind:
Were others joyful, he look'd smiling on,
And gave Allowance where he needed none;
Good he refus'd, with future Ill to buy,
Nor knew a Joy that caus'd Reflection's Sigh;
A Friend to Virtue, his unclouded Breast
No Envy stung, no Jealousy distress'd,   430
(Bane of the Poor! it wounds their weaker Mind,
To miss one Favour which their Neighbours find:)
Yet far was he from Stoic-pride remov'd;
He felt humanely, and he warmly lov'd:
I mark'd his Action, when his Infant died,
And his old Neighbour for Offense was tried;
The still Tears, stealing down that furrow'd Cheek,
Spoke Pity, plainer than the Tongue can speak.
If Pride were his, 'twas not their vulgar Pride,
Who, in their base Contempt, the Great deride;   440
Nor Pride in Learning, though my Clerk agreed,
If Fate should call him, ASHFORD might succeed;
Nor Pride in rustic Skill, although we knew
None his Superior, and his Equals few:—
But if that Spirit, in his Soul, had place,
It was the jealous Pride that shuns Disgrace:

A Pride in honest Fame, by Virtue gain'd,
In sturdy Boys to virtuous Labours train'd;
Pride, in the Power that guards his Country's Coast,
And all that Englishmen enjoy and boast;   450
Pride, in a Life that Slander's Tongue defy'd,—
In fact, a noble Passion, misnamed *Pride*.

He had no Party's Rage, no Sect'ry's° Whim;
Christian and Countryman was *all* with him:
True to his Church he came; no Sunday-Shower
Kept him at Home, in that important Hour;
Nor his firm Feet, could one persuading Sect,
By the strong Glare of their New Light, direct;—
"On Hope, in mine own sober Light, I gaze,
But should be blind and lose it, in your Blaze."   460

In Times severe, when many a sturdy Swain
Felt in his Pride, his Comfort, to complain;
ISAAC their Wants would soothe, his own would hide,
And feel in *that* his Comfort and his Pride.

At length, he found, when Seventy Years were run,
His Strength departed and his Labour done;
When he, save honest Fame, retain'd no more,
But lost his Wife and saw his Children poor:
'Twas then, a Spark of—say not Discontent—
Struck on his Mind, and thus he gave it vent:—   470

"Kind are your Laws, ('tis not to be denied,)
That in yon House, for ruin'd Age, provide,
And they are just;—when young, we give you all,
And for Assistance in our Weakness call.—
Why then this proud Reluctance to be fed,
To join your Poor, and eat the Parish-Bread?
But yet I linger, loth with him to feed,
Who gains his Plenty by the Sons of Need;
He who, by Contract, all your Paupers took,
And gauges Stomachs, with an anxious Look;   480
On some old Master, I could well depend;
See him with Joy, and thank him as a Friend;
But ill on him, who doles the Day's Supply,
And counts our Chances, who at Night may die:
Yet help me, Heav'n! and let me not complain
Of what I suffer, but my Fate sustain."

Such were his Thoughts, and so resign'd he grew;
Daily he plac'd the Workhouse in his View;—
But came not there, for sudden was his Fate,
He dropp'd expiring, at his Cottage-Gate.   490

I feel his Absence in the Hours of Prayer,
And view his Seat, and sigh for ISAAC there;

453. Sect'ry: (sectary) a zealous adherent of a religious
sect.

I see no more, those white Locks thinly spread,
Round the bald polish of that honour'd Head;
No more that aweful Glance, on playful Wight
Compell'd to kneel and tremble at the Sight;
To fold his Fingers all in dread the while,
Till Mister ASHFORD soften'd to a Smile;
No more that meek and suppliant Look in Prayer,
Nor the pure Faith (to give it Force), are there:—   500
But he is blest, and I lament no more
A wise good Man contented to be poor.

Then died a Rambler; not the One° who sails
And trucks,° for female Favours, Beads and Nails;
Not one, who posts from place to place—of Men
And Manners treating, with a flying Pen:°
Not he, who climbs, for Prospects, *Snowden's*° Height,
And chides the Clouds, that intercept the sight;
No curious Shell, rare Plant or brilliant Spar,°
Intic'd our Traveller, from his Home, so far;   510
But all the Reason, by himself assign'd
For so much Rambling, was, a restless Mind;
As on, from place to place, without intent,
Without reflection, ROBIN DINGLEY went.
    Not thus by Nature:—never Man was found
Less prone to wander from his Parish Bound:
Claudian's old Man,° to whom all Scenes were new,
Save those where he, and where his Apples, grew;
Resembled ROBIN, who around would look,
And his Horizon, for the Earth's, mistook.   520
    To this poor Swain a keen Attorney came;—
"I give thee Joy, good Fellow! on thy Name;
The rich old DINGLEY's dead;—no Child has he,
Nor Wife, nor Will; his ALL is left for thee:
To be his Fortune's Heir, thy Claim is good;
Thou hast the Name, and we will prove the blood."
The Claim was made; 'twas tried, it would not stand;
They prov'd the Blood, but were refus'd the Land.
    Assur'd of Wealth, this Man of simple Heart,
To every Friend, had predispos'd a Part;   530
His Wife had Hopes indulg'd of various kind;
The three Miss DINGLEYS had their School assign'd,

Masters were sought for what they each requir'd,
And Books were bought, and Harpsichords were
        hir'd;
So high was Hope:—the Failure touch'd his Brain,
And ROBIN never was himself again:
Yet he no wrath, no angry wish express'd,
But tried, in vain, to labour, or to rest;
Then cast his Bundle on his back, and went
He knew not whither, nor for what Intent.   540
    Years fled;—of ROBIN all remembrance past,
When home he wander'd in his Rags at last:
A Sailor's Jacket, on his limbs was thrown,
A Sailor's Story, he had made his own;
Had suffer'd Battles, Prisons, Tempests, Storms,
Encountering Death in all his ugliest forms;
His Cheeks were haggard, hollow was his Eye,
Where Madness lurk'd, conceal'd in Misery;
Want, and th' ungentle World, had taught a part,
And prompted Cunning, to that simple Heart: 550
"He now bethought him, he would roam no more,
But live at Home, and labour as before."
    Here cloth'd and fed, no sooner he began
To round and redden, than away he ran:
His Wife was dead, their Children past his Aid;
So, unmolested, from his Home he stray'd:
Six Years elaps'd, when, worn with Want and Pain,
Came ROBIN, wrapt in all his Rags, again:—
We chide, we pity;—plac'd among our Poor,
He fed again, and was a Man once more.   560
    As when a gaunt and hungry Fox is found,
Entrapp'd alive, in some rich Hunter's ground;
Fed for the Field, although each Day's a Feast,
Fatten you may, but never *tame* the Beast;
A House protects him, savoury Viands sustain;
But loose his Neck, and off he goes again:
So stole our Vagrant from his warm Retreat,
To rove a Prowler, and be deem'd a Cheat.
    Hard was his Fare: for, him at length we saw,
In Cart convey'd, and laid supine on Straw: 570
His feeble Voice now spoke a sinking Heart;
His Groans now told the Motions of the Cart:
And when it stopp'd, he tried in vain to stand;
Clos'd was his Eye and clench'd his clammy
        Hand;
Life ebb'd apace, and our best Aid no more
Could his weak Sense or dying Heart restore:
But now he fell, a Victim to the Snare,
That vile Attorneys, for the Weak prepare;—
They who, when Profit or Resentment call,
Heed not the groaning Victim they enthrall.   580

---

503. the One: an itinerant peddler. **504. trucks:** exchanges.
505–506. of . . . Pen: Samuel Johnson, from 1750 to 1752
author of the periodical paper *The Rambler* (see Part Six).
507. Snowden: (Snowdon) a group of mountains in
northwestern Wales. **509. Spar:** crystal. **517. Claudian's
old Man:** The Roman poet Claudian (*c.* 370–*c.* 410), in his
poem *Felix, Qui Propriis,* discusses the happiness of an old
man of Verona who has never left his rural home.

Then died lamented, in the Strength of Life,
A valued MOTHER and a faithful WIFE;
Call'd not away, when Time had loos'd each Hold
On the fond Heart, and each Desire grew cold;
But when, to all that knit us to our Kind,
She felt fast-bound, as Charity can bind;—
Not when the Ills of Age, its Pain, its Care,
The drooping Spirit for its Fate prepare;
And, each Affection failing, leaves the Heart
Loos'd from Life's Charm, and willing to
    depart;—   590
But ALL her Ties, the strong Invader broke,
In all their Strength, by one tremendous Stroke!
Sudden and swift the eager Pest came on,
And terror grew, till every Hope was gone;
Still those around appear'd for hope to seek!
But view'd the Sick, and were afraid to speak.—
  Slowly they bore, with solemn Step, the Dead;
When Grief grew loud, and bitter Tears were shed:—
My Part began; a Crowd drew near the Place,
Awe in each Eye, Alarm in every Face: 600
So swift the Ill! and of so fierce a kind,
That Fear, with Pity, mingled in each Mind;
Friends with the Husband came, their Griefs to blend;
For Goodman FRANKFORD was to all a Friend.
The last-born Boy, they held above the Bier,
He knew not Grief, but Cries express'd his Fear;
Each different Age and Sex reveal'd its pain,
In now a louder, now a lower Strain;
While the meek Father, listening to their Tones,
Swell'd the full Cadence of the Grief by Groans.   610
  The elder Sister strove her Pangs to hide,
And soothing Words to younger Minds applied:—
"Be still, be patient," oft she strove to say;
But fail'd as oft, and weeping turn'd away.
  Curious and sad, upon the fresh-dug Hill,
The Village-Lads stood melancholy still;
And idle Children, wandering to-and-fro,
As Nature guided, took the Tone of Woe.
  Arriv'd at Home, how then they gaz'd around,
In every Place, where she—no more, was found;— 620
The Seat at Table, she was wont to fill,
The Fire-side Chair, still set, but vacant still;
The Garden-Walks, a Labour all her own;
The lattic'd Bower with trailing Shrubs o'ergrown;
The Sunday-Pew, she fill'd with all her Race,°
Each Place of hers was now a sacred Place;

625. **Race**: offspring.

That while it call'd up Sorrows in the Eyes,
Pierc'd the full Heart, and forc'd them still to rise.
  Oh sacred Sorrow! by whom Souls are tried,
Sent not to punish Mortals, but to guide;   630
If Thou art mine, (and who shall proudly dare,
To tell his MAKER, he has had his Share?)
Still let me feel, for what thy Pangs are sent,
And be my Guide, and not my Punishment!

  Of LEAH COUSINS, next the Name appears,
With Honours crown'd, and blest with Length of
    Years,
Save, that she liv'd to feel, in Life's Decay,
The Pleasure die, the Honours drop away:
A Matron she, whom every Village-Wife,
View'd as the Help and Guardian of her Life;   640
Fathers and Sons, indebted to her Aid,
Respect to her, and her Profession° pay'd;
Who in the House of Plenty largely fed,
Yet took her station at the Pauper's Bed;
Nor from that Duty could be brib'd again,
While Fear or Danger urg'd her to remain;
In her Experience all her Friends relied,
Heaven was her Help, and Nature was her Guide.
  Thus LEAH liv'd! long trusted, much caress'd,
Till a Town-Dame a youthful Farmer blest;   650
A gay vain Bride, who would Example give,
To that poor Village where she deign'd to live;
Some few Months past, she sent in Hour of Need,
For *Doctor* GLIBB, who came with wondrous speed;
Two days he waited, all his Art applied,
To save the Mother when her Infant died;—
"'Twas well I came," at last he deign'd to say;
"'Twas wondrous well;"—and proudly rode away:
The News ran round;—"How vast the Doctor's
    Pow'r!
He sav'd the Lady in the trying Hour;   660
Sav'd her from Death, when she was dead to Hope,
And her fond Husband had resign'd her up:—
So all, like her, may evil Fate defy,
If Doctor GLIBB, with saving Hand be nigh."
  Fame (now his Friend), Fear, Novelty, and Whim,
And Fashion, sent the varying Sex to Him:
From this, Contention in the Village rose;
And *these*, the Dame espous'd; the Doctor, *those*:
The wealthier Part, to him and Science went;
With Luck and her the Poor remain'd content.   670

642. **Profession**: that of midwife.

The Matron sigh'd; for she was vex'd at heart,
With so much Profit, so much Fame to part;—
    "So long successful in my Art," she cried,
And this proud Man, so young and so untried!"—
    "Nay," said the Doctor, "dare you trust your
        Wives,
The Joy, the Pride, the Solace of your Lives,
To One who acts and knows no Reason why,
But trusts, poor Hag! to Luck for an Ally?—
Who, on Experience, can her Claims advance,
And own the Powers of Accident and Chance?   680
A whining Dame, who prays in Danger's view,
(A Proof she knows not, what beside to do;)
What's her Experience? in the Time that's gone,
Blundering she wrought, and still she blunders on:—
And what is Nature? One who acts in Aid
Of Gossips half asleep, and half afraid;
With such Allies, I scorn my Fame to blend,
Skill is my Luck, and Courage is my Friend:
No Slave to Nature, 'tis my chief Delight,
To win my Way, and act in her despite;—   690
Trust then my Art, that, in itself complete,
Needs no Assistance, and fears no Defeat."
    Warm'd by her well-spic'd Ale and aiding Pipe,
The angry Matron grew for Contest ripe.
    "Can you," she said, "ungrateful and unjust,
Before Experience, Ostentation trust?
What is your Hazard, foolish Daughters, tell?
If safe, you're certain; if secure, you're well:
That I have Luck, must Friend and Foe confess,
And what's good Judgement, but a lucky Guess?   700
He boasts but what he *can* do:—will you run
From me, your Friend! who all *he* boasts, *have* done?
By proud and learned Words, his Powers are known;
By healthy Boys and handsome Girls, my own:
Wives! Fathers! Children! by my Help, you live;
Has this pale Doctor more than Life to give?
No stunted Cripple hops the Village round;
Your Hands are active, and your Heads are sound;
My Lads are all your Fields and Flocks require;
My Lasses all those sturdy Lads admire: 710
Can this proud Leech,° with all his boasted Skill,
Amend the Soul or Body, Wit or Will?
Does he for Courts the Sons of Farmers frame,
Or make the Daughter differ from the Dame?
Or, whom he brings into this World of Woe,
Prepares he them, their Part to undergo?

711. Leech: physician; the eighteenth-century practitioner
sometimes applied leeches as an aid in bleeding a patient.

If not, this Stranger from your Doors repel,
And be content to *be*, and to be *well*."
    She spake: but, ah! with Words too strong and
        plain;
Her Warmth offended, and her Truth was vain: 720
The *many* left her, and the friendly *few*,
If never colder, yet they older grew;
Till, unemploy'd, she felt her Spirits droop,
And took, insidious Aid! th' inspiring Cup;
Grew poor and peevish, as her Powers decay'd,
And propp'd the tottering Frame, with stronger
        Aid;
Then died!—I saw our careful Swains convey,
From this our changeful World, the Matron's Clay,
Who to this World, at least, with equal Care,
Brought them its Changes, Good and Ill to share.   730

    Now to his Grave, was ROGER CUFF convey'd,
And strong Resentment's lingering Spirit laid;
Ship-wreck'd in Youth, he home return'd, and found
His Brethren three,—and thrice they wish'd him
        drown'd.
"Is this a Landman's Love? Be certain then,
We part for ever!"—and they cried, "Amen!"
    His Words were Truth's:—Some forty Summers
        fled,
His Brethren died; his Kin suppos'd him dead:
Three Nephews these, one sprightly Niece, and one,
Less near in Blood; they call'd him *surly John;*   740
He work'd in Woods, apart from all his Kind,
Fierce were his Looks and moody was his Mind.
    For Home, the Sailor now began to sigh;—
"The Dogs are dead, and I'll return and die;
When all I have, my Gains, in Years of Care,
The younger CUFFS with kinder Souls shall share;—
Yet hold!—I'm rich;—with one consent they'll say,
'You're welcome, Uncle, as the Flowers in May.'
No; I'll disguise me, be in Tatters dress'd,
And best befriend the Lads who treat me best."   750
    Now all his Kindred,—neither rich nor poor,
Kept the Wolf Want some distance from the door.
    In piteous plight he knock'd at GEORGE's Gate,
And begg'd for Aid, as he describ'd his State:—
But stern was *George:*—"Let them who had thee
        strong,
Help thee to drag thy weaken'd Frame along:
To us a Stranger, while your Limbs would move,
From us depart, and try a Stranger's Love:—
Ha! dost thou murmur?"—for, in ROGER's Throat,
Was "*Rascal!*" rising with disdainful Note.   760

To pious JAMES he then his Prayer address'd;—
"Good-lack," quoth *James*, "thy Sorrows pierce my
    Breast;
And, had I Wealth, as have my Brethren twain,
One Board should feed us, and one Roof contain:
But plead I will thy Cause, and I will pray:
And so farewell! Heaven help thee on thy Way!"

    "Scoundrel!" said ROGER, (but apart,)—and told
His Case to PETER;—*Peter* too was cold:—
"The Rates° are high; we have a-many Poor;
But I will think,"—he said, and shut the Door.   770

    Then the gay *Niece*, the seeming Pauper press'd;—
"Turn, NANCY, turn, and view this Form distrest;
Akin to thine is this declining Frame,
And this poor Beggar claims an *Uncle*'s Name."

    "Avaunt! begone!" the courteous Maiden said,
"Thou vile impostor! Uncle ROGER's dead;
I hate thee, Beast; thy Look my spirit shocks!
Oh! that I saw thee, starving in the Stocks!"

    "My gentle Niece!" he said;—and sought the
    wood.—
"I hunger, fellow; prithee, give me Food!"   780

    "Give! am I rich? this Hatchet take, and try
Thy proper Strength, nor give those Limbs the Lie;
Work, feed thyself, to thine own Powers appeal,
Nor whine out Woes, thine own Right-Hand can
    heal;
And while that Hand is thine, and thine a Leg,
Scorn, of the Proud or of the Base to beg."

    "Come, surly *John*, thy wealthy Kinsman view;"
Old ROGER said:—"thy Words are brave and true;
Come, live with me; we'll vex those Scoundrel-Boys;
And that prim Shrew shall, envying, hear our
    Joys.—   790
Tobacco's glorious Fume all day we'll share,
With Beef and Brandy kill all kinds of Care,
We'll Beer and Biscuit on our Table heap,
And rail at Rascals, till we fall asleep."

    Such was their Life: but when the Woodman died,
His grieving Kin, for ROGER's Smiles applied;—
In vain; he shut, with stern Rebuke, the Door,
And dying, built a Refuge for the Poor;
With this Restriction, That no CUFF should share
One Meal, or shelter for one Moment there.   800

    My Record ends:—But hark! e'en now I hear
The Bell of Death, and know not whose to fear:
Our Farmers all, and all our Hinds were well;

In no Man's Cottage, Danger seem'd to dwell:—
Yet Death of Man, proclaim these heavy Chimes,
For thrice they sound, with pausing Space, three Times.

    "Go; of my Sexton seek, whose Days are sped?—
    What! he, himself!—and is old DIBBLE dead?"
His eightieth Year he reach'd, still undecay'd,
And Rectors five, to one close Vault convey'd:— 810
But he is gone; his Care and Skill I lose,
And gain a mournful Subject for my Muse:
His Masters lost, he'd oft in turn deplore,
And kindly add,—"Heaven grant, I lose no more!"
Yet while he spake, a sly and pleasant Glance
Appear'd at variance with his Complaisance:
For, as he told their Fate and varying Worth,
He archly look'd,—"I yet may bear thee forth."

    "When first"—(he so began,)—"my Trade I ply'd,
Good master ADDLE was the Parish-Guide;   820
His Clerk and Sexton, I beheld with Fear
His Stride majestic, and his Frown severe;
A noble Pillar of the Church he stood,
Adorn'd with College-Gown and Parish-Hood;
Then, as he pac'd the hallow'd aisles about,
He fill'd the sevenfold Surplice fairly out!
But in his Pulpit, wearied down with Prayer,
He sat, and seem'd as in his Study's Chair;
For while the Anthem swell'd, and when it ceas'd,
Th' expecting People view'd their slumbering
    Priest;—   830
Who, dozing, died.—Our Parson PEELE was next;
'I will not spare you,' was his favourite Text:
Nor did he spare, but rais'd them many a Pound;
Ev'n me he mulct for my poor Rood° of Ground;
Yet car'd he nought, but with a gibing Speech,
'What should I do,' quoth he, 'but what *I* preach?'
His piercing Jokes, (and he'd a plenteous store,)
Were daily offer'd both to Rich and Poor;
His Scorn, his Love, in playful Words he spoke;
His Pity, Praise, and Promise, were a Joke: 840
But though so young, and blest with Spirits high,
He died as grave as any Judge could die:
The strong Attack subdu'd his lively Powers,—
His was the Grave, and Doctor GRANDSPEAR ours.

    "Then were there golden Times, the Village round;
In his Abundance, all appear'd t' abound;
Liberal and rich, a plenteous Board he spread,
E'en cool Dissenters° at his Table fed;

---

834. Rood: a quarter acre. **848. Dissenters:** those worshipping with Protestant sects (e.g., Baptists, Quakers) outside the Established Church.

769. Rates: taxes.

Who wish'd, and hoped,—and thought a Man so kind
A Way to Heaven, though not their own, might
    find;   850
To them, to all, he was polite and free,
Kind to the Poor, and, ah! most kind to me;—
'Ralph,' would he say, 'Ralph Dibble, thou art old;
That Doublet fit, 'twill keep thee from the Cold;
How does my Sexton?—What! the Times are hard;
Drive that stout Pig, and pen him in thy Yard.'
But most, his Rev'rence loved a mirthful Jest:—
'Thy coat is thin; why, Man, thou'rt *barely* drest;
It's worn to th' Thread; but I have nappy° Beer;
Clap that within, and see how they will wear!'   860
    "Gay Days were these: but they were quickly past:
When first he came, we found he cou'dn't last:
A whoreson Cough (and at the Fall of Leaf)
Upset him quite:—but what's the Gain of Grief?
    "Then came the AUTHOR-RECTOR; his Delight
Was all in Books; to read them, or to write:
Women and Men, he strove alike to shun,
And hurried homeward, when his Tasks were done;
Courteous enough, but careless what he said,
For Points of Learning, he reserv'd his Head;   870
And when addressing either Poor or Rich,
He knew no better than his Cassock, which;
He, like an Osier,° was of pliant Kind,
Erect by Nature, but to bend inclin'd;
Not like a Creeper falling to the Ground,
Or meanly catching on the Neighbours round;—
Careless was he, of Surplice, Hood, and Band,—
And kindly took them, as they came to hand;
Nor, like the Doctor, wore a World of Hat,
As if he sought for Dignity in that: 880
He talk'd, he gave, but not with cautious Rules,
Nor turn'd from Gipsies, Vagabonds, or Fools;
It was his Nature, but they thought it Whim,
And so our Beaux and Beauties turn'd from him:
Of Questions, much he wrote, profound and dark,—
How spake the Serpent, and where stopp'd the Ark;
From what far Land the Queen of Sheba came;
Who Salem's° Priest, and what his Father's Name;
He made the Song of Songs its Mysteries yield,
And Revelations, to the World, reveal'd.   890
He sleeps i' the Aisle,—but not a Stone records
His Name or Fame, his Actions or his Words:—
And truth, your Reverence, when I look around,
And mark the Tombs in our sepulchral Ground,

(Though dare I not of one Man's Hope to doubt,)
I'd join the Party who repose without.
    "Next came a Youth from *Cambridge*, and, in truth,
He was a sober and a comely Youth;
He blush'd in Meekness as a modest Man,
And gain'd Attention ere his Task began: 900
When preaching, seldom ventur'd on Reproof,
But touch'd his Neighbours tenderly enough.
Him, in his youth, a clamorous Sect° assail'd,
Advis'd and censur'd, flatter'd,—and prevail'd.—
Then did he much his sober Hearers vex,
Confound the Simple, and the Sad perplex;
To a new Style his Reverence rashly took;
Loud grew his Voice, to Threat'ning swell'd his Look;
Above, below, on either side, he gaz'd,
Amazing all, and most himself amaz'd: 910
No more he read his Preachments pure and plain,
But launch'd outright, and rose and sank again:
At times he smil'd in scorn, at times he wept, ⎫
And such sad Coil with Words of Vengeance kept, ⎬
That our best Sleepers started as they slept.   ⎭
    'Conviction comes like Lightning,' he would cry;
'In vain you seek it, and in vain you fly;
'Tis like the rushing of the mighty Wind,
Unseen its progress, but its power you find;
It strikes the Child ere yet its Reason wakes;   920
His Reason fled, the ancient Sire it shakes;
The proud, learn'd Man, and him who loves to know
How and from whence these Gusts of Grace will blow,
It shuns,—but Sinners in their way impedes,
And Sots and Harlots visits in their Deeds;
Of Faith and Penance it supplies the place;   ⎫
Assures the vilest, that they live by Grace,   ⎬
And, without running, makes them win the Race.' ⎭
    "Such was the Doctrine our young Prophet taught;
And here conviction, there Confusion wrought: 930
When his thin Cheek assum'd a deadly Hue,
And all the Rose to one small Spot withdrew:
They call'd it hectic;° 'twas a fiery Flush,
More fix'd and deeper than the maiden Blush;
His paler Lips the pearly Teeth disclos'd,
And lab'ring Lungs the length'ning Speech oppos'd.
No more his span-girth° Shanks and quiv'ring Thighs
Upheld a Body of the smaller Size;
But down he sank upon his Dying-Bed,   939
And gloomy Crotchets fill'd his wandering Head.—

---

859. **nappy:** strong, with a pun on *nap* meaning fuzz. **873. Osier:** reed. **888. Salem:** Jerusalem.

903. a clamorous Sect: Methodists. **933. hectic:** symptomatic of tuberculosis. **937. span-girth:** capable of being enclosed within a circle formed by the thumb and little finger.

" 'Spite of my Faith, all-saving Faith,' he cried,
'I fear of worldly Works, the wicked Pride;
Poor as I am, degraded, abject, blind,
The Good I've wrought, still rankles in my Mind;
My Alms-deeds all, and every Deed I've done,
My Moral-Rags, defile me every one;
It should not be:—what say'st thou? tell me, Ralph.'—
Quoth I, 'Your Reverence, I believe, you're safe;
Your faith's your Prop, nor have you pass'd such Time
In life's Good-Works, as swell them to a Crime.— 950
If I of Pardon for my Sins were sure,
About my Goodness, I would rest secure.'

"Such was his End; and mine approaches fast;
I've seen my best of Preachers,—and my last."

He bow'd, and archly smil'd at what he said,
Civil but sly:—"And is old DIBBLE dead?"
Yes! he is gone: and WE are going all;
Like Flowers we wither, and like Leaves we fall:—
Here, with an Infant, joyful Sponsors come,
Then bear the new-made Christian to its Home: 960
A few short Years, and we behold him stand
To ask a Blessing, with his Bride in hand:
A few, still seeming shorter, and we hear
His Widow weeping, at her Husband's Bier:—
Thus, as the Months succeed, shall Infants take
Their Names; thus Parents shall the child forsake;
Thus Brides again and Bridegrooms blithe shall kneel,
By Love or Law compell'd their Vows to seal,
Ere I again, or one like me, explore
These simple Annals of the VILLAGE POOR.   970

FROM

THE BOROUGH

The Borough (1810), which Crabbe worked on for five
years, consists of twenty-four verse "letters" to an
imaginary correspondent, who has asked the writer to
describe the institutions and the memorable people in
his rural district. Crabbe begins by focusing on the
Church, the professions of law and medicine, and the
middle-class amusements of clubs and social meetings.
Halfway through he turns to explore once again (but
now in a series of self-contained short stories in verse)
the dark underworld of the indigent, the frustrated, the
criminal, and the insane. Feeling the necessity of
defending his subject matter and point of view, he
reminds readers in his Preface that "it has always been
held as a salutary exercise of the mind, to contemplate
the evils and miseries of our nature."

The text is that of the first edition (1810); substantive
variants have been introduced from the edition of 1823.

FROM

LETTER XII. PLAYERS

DRAWN by the annual Call, we now behold
Our Troop Dramatic, Heroes known of old,
And those, since last they march'd, inlisted and
  enroll'd:
Mounted on Hacks or borne in Waggons some,
The rest on Foot (the humbler Brethren) come.
Three favour'd Places, an unequal Time,
Join to support this Company sublime;
Ours for the longer Period—see how light
Yon Parties move, their former Friends in sight,
Whose Claims are all allow'd, and Friendship glads
  the Night.
Now public Rooms shall sound with Words divine, 11
And private Lodgings hear how Heroes shine;
No talk of Pay shall yet on Pleasure steal,
But kindest Welcome bless the friendly Meal;
While o'er the social Jug and decent Cheer,
Shall be describ'd the Fortunes of the Year.

Peruse these Bills and see what each can do,—
Behold! the Prince, the Slave, the Monk, the Jew;
Change but the Garment, and they'll all engage
To take each Part, and act in every Age: 20
Cull'd from all Houses, what a House are they!
Swept from all Barns, our Borough-Critics say;
But with some Portion of a Critic's Ire,
We all endure them: there are some admire;
They might have Praise, confin'd to Farce alone;
Full well they grin, they should not try to groan;
But then our Servants' and our Seamen's Wives
Love all that Rant and Rapture as their Lives;
He who *Squire Richard*'s° Part could well sustain,
Finds as *King Richard* he must roar amain—   30
"My Horse! my Horse!"—Lo! now to their Abodes,
Come Lords and Lovers, Empresses and Gods.

THE BOROUGH: *Letter XII*. **29. Squire Richard:** a character
in *The Provoked Husband* (1728), a broad comedy by Vanbrugh
and Cibber.

The Master-mover of these Scenes has made
No trifling Gain in this adventurous Trade;
Trade we may term it, for he duly buys
Arms out of use and undirected Eyes;
These he instructs, and guides them as he can,
And vends each Night the manufactur'd Man:
Long as our Custom lasts, they gladly stay,
Then strike their Tents, like Tartars! and away!   40
The Place grows bare where they too long remain,
But Grass will rise ere they return again.

Children of *Thespis*, welcome! Knights and Queens!
Counts! Barons! Beauties! when before your Scenes,
And mighty Monarchs thund'ring from your Throne;
Then step behind, and all your Glory's gone:
Of Crown and Palace, Throne and Guards bereft,
The Pomp is vanish'd, and the Care is left.
Yet strong and lively is the Joy they feel,
When the full House secures the plenteous Meal;   50
Flatt'ring and flatter'd; each attempts to raise
A Brother's Merits for a Brother's Praise:
For never Hero shows a prouder Heart,
Than he who proudly acts a Hero's Part;
Nor without Cause; the Boards, we know, can yield
Place for fierce Contest, like the tented Field.

Graceful to tread the Stage, to be in turn
The Prince we honour and the Knave we spurn;
Bravely to bear the Tumult of the Crowd,
The Hiss tremendous, and the Censure loud;   60
These are their parts,—and he who these sustains
Deserves some Praise and Profit for his Pains.
Heroes at least of gentler kind are they,
Against whose Swords no weeping Widows pray,
No Blood their Fury sheds, nor Havoc marks their
   Way.

Sad happy Race! soon rais'd and soon deprest,
Your Days all past in Jeopardy and Jest;
Poor without Prudence, with Afflictions vain,
Not warn'd by Misery, not enrich'd by Gain;
Whom Justice pitying, chides from Place to Place,   70
A wandering, careless, wretched, merry Race,
Who cheerful Looks assume, and play the Parts
Of happy Rovers with repining Hearts;
Then cast off Care, and in the mimic Pain
Of tragic Woe, feel Spirits light and vain,
Distress and Hope—the Mind's, the Body's Wear,
The Man's Affliction, and the Actor's Tear:
Alternate times of Fasting and Excess
Are yours, ye smiling Children of Distress.   79

Slaves though ye be, your Wandering Freedom
   seems,
And with your varying Views and restless Schemes,
Your Griefs are transient, as your Joys are Dreams.

Yet keen those Griefs—ah! what avail thy Charms,
Fair *Juliet!* what that Infant in thine Arms;
What those heroic Lines thy Patience learns,
What all the Aid thy present *Romeo* earns,
Whilst thou art crowded in that lumbering Wain,°
With all thy plaintive Sisters to complain?

Nor is there lack of Labour—To rehearse,
Day after Day, poor Scraps of Prose and Verse;   90
To bear each other's Spirit, Pride, and Spite;
To hide in Rant the Heart-ache of the Night;
To dress in gaudy Patch-work, and to force
The Mind to think on the appointed Course;—
This is laborious, and may be defin'd
The bootless° Labour of the thriftless Mind.

There is a veteran Dame; I see her stand
Intent and pensive with her Book in hand;
Awhile her Thoughts she forces on her Part,
Then dwells on Objects nearer to the Heart;   100
Across the Room she paces, gets her Tone,
And fits her Features for the Danish Throne;
To-night a Queen—I mark her Motion slow,
I hear her Speech, and *Hamlet's* Mother know.

Methinks 'tis pitiful to see her try
For strength of Arms and energy of Eye;
With Vigour lost, and Spirits worn away,
Her Pomp and Pride she labours to display;
And when awhile she's tried her Part to act,
To find her Thoughts arrested by some Fact;   110
When Struggles more and more severe are seen
In the plain Actress than the Danish Queen,—
At length she feels her Part, she finds Delight,
And fancies all the Plaudits of the Night:
Old as she is, she smiles at every Speech,
And thinks no youthful Part beyond her reach;
But as the Mist of Vanity again
Is blown away, by press of present Pain,
Sad and in doubt she to her Purse applies
For cause of Comfort, where no Comfort lies;   120
Then to her Task she sighing turns again,—
"Oh! *Hamlet*, thou hast cleft my Heart in twain!"

87. Wain: wagon. **96. bootless:** profitless.

And who that poor, consumptive, wither'd thing,
Who strains her slender Throat and strives to sing?
Panting for Breath, and forc'd her Voice to drop,
And far unlike the Inmate of the Shop,
Where she, in Youth and Health, alert and gay,
Laugh'd off at Night the Labours of the Day;
With Novels, Verses, Fancy's fertile Powers,
And Sister-Converse past the Evening-Hours;   130
But *Cynthia's* Soul was soft, her Wishes strong,
Her Judgment weak, and her Conclusions wrong:
The Morning-call and Counter were her Dread,
And her Contempt the Needle and the Thread:
But when she read a gentle Damsel's Part,
Her Woe, her Wish!—she had them all by heart.

At length the Hero of the Boards drew nigh,
Who spake of Love till Sigh re-echo'd Sigh;
He told in honey'd Words his deathless Flame,
And she his own by tender Vows became;   140
Nor Ring nor Licence needed Souls so fond,
Alphonso's Passion was his *Cynthia's* Bond:
And thus the simple Girl, to Shame betray'd,
Sinks to the Grave forsaken and dismay'd.

Sick without Pity, sorrowing without Hope,
See her! the Grief and Scandal of the Troop;
A wretched Martyr to a childish Pride,
Her Woe insulted, and her Praise denied:
Her humble Talents, though derided, us'd,
Her Prospects lost, her Confidence abus'd;   150
All that remains—for she not long can brave
Increase of Evils—is an early Grave.

Ye gentle *Cynthias* of the Shop, take heed
What Dreams ye cherish and what Books ye read.

A decent sum had *Peter Nottage* made,
By joining Bricks—to him a thriving Trade:
Of his Employment Master and his Wife,
This humble Tradesman led a lordly Life;
The House of Kings and Heroes lack'd Repairs,
And *Peter*, though reluctant, serv'd the Players: 160
Connected thus, he heard in way polite,—
"Come, *Master Nottage*, see us play to-night."
At first 'twas Folly, Nonsense, idle Stuff,
But seen for nothing it grew well enough;
And better now—now best, and every Night,
In this Fool's Paradise he drank Delight;
And as he felt the Bliss, he wish'd to know
Whence all this Rapture and these Joys could flow;
For if the seeing could such Pleasure bring,
What must the feeling?—feeling like a King?   170

In vain his Wife, his Uncle, and his Friend
Cried—"*Peter! Peter!* let such Follies end;
'Tis well enough these Vagabonds to see,
But would you Partner with a Showman be?"

"Showman!" said *Peter*, "did not *Quin* and *Clive*,°
And *Roscius-Garrick*° by the Science thrive?
Showman!—'tis Scandal; I'm by Genius led
To join a Class who've *Shakspeare* at their head."

Poor *Peter* thus by easy steps became
A dreaming Candidate for scenic Fame,   180
And, after Years consum'd, infirm and poor,
He sits and takes the Tickets at the Door.

. . .

LETTER XIX. THE POOR OF THE BOROUGH. THE PARISH-CLERK

WITH our late Vicar, and his Age the same,
His Clerk, hight *Jachin*, to his Office came;
The like slow Speech was his, the like tall slender
    Frame.
But *Jachin* was the gravest Man on ground,
And heard his Master's Jokes with look profound;
For worldly Wealth this Man of Letters sigh'd,
And had a sprinkling of the Spirit's Pride:
But he was sober, chaste, devout, and just,
One whom his Neighbours could believe and trust:
Of none suspected, neither Man nor Maid   10
By him were wrong'd, or were of him afraid.

There was indeed a frown, a trick of State
In *Jachin;*—formal was his Air and Gait;
But if he seem'd more solemn and less kind
Than some light Men to light Affairs confin'd,
Still 'twas allow'd that he should so behave
As in high Seat, and be severely grave.

This book-taught Man, to man's first foe profess'd
Defiance stern, and hate that knew not rest;
He held that *Satan*, since the World began,   20
In every act, had Strife with every Man;

175. Quin and Clive: James Quin (1693–1766) and Catherine "Kitty" Clive (1711–85) were famous stage personalities. **176. Roscius-Garrick:** David Garrick (1717–79), the foremost actor of the day, was sometimes called Roscius Garrick after Quintus Roscius Gallus (d. 62 B.C.), an eminent Roman actor.

That never evil Deed on Earth was done,
But of the acting Parties he was one;
The flattering Guide to make ill Prospects clear;
To smooth rough Ways, the constant Pioneer;°
The ever-tempting, soothing, softening Power,
Ready to cheat, seduce, deceive, devour.

"Me has the sly Seducer oft withstood,"
Said pious *Jachin*,—"but he gets no good;
I pass the House where swings the tempting Sign,   30
And pointing, tell him, '*Satan*, that is thine:'
I pass the Damsels pacing down the Street,
And look more grave and solemn when we meet;
Nor doth it irk me to rebuke their Smiles,
Their wanton Ambling and their watchful Wiles:
Nay, like the good *John Bunyan*,° when I view
Those forms, I'm angry at the Ills they do;
That I could pinch and spoil, in Sin's despite,
Beauties! which frail and evil Thoughts excite.

"At Feasts and Banquets seldom am I found,   40
And (save at Church) abhor a tuneful Sound;
To Plays and Shows I run not to and fro,
And where my Master goes, forbear to go."

No wonder *Satan* took the thing amiss,
To be oppos'd by such a Man as this—
A Man so grave, important, cautious, wise,
Who dar'd not trust his Feeling or his Eyes;
No wonder he should lurk and lie in wait,
Should fit his Hooks and ponder on his Bait,
Should on his Movements keep a watchful eye,   50
For he pursued a fish who led the fry.

With his own Peace our Clerk was not content,
He tried, good Man! to make his Friends repent.
"Nay, nay, my Friends, from Inns and Taverns fly,
You may suppress your thirst, but not supply:
A foolish Proverb says, *the Devil's at home*,
But he is there, and tempts in every Room:
Men feel, they know not why, such places please;
His are the Spells—they're Idleness and Ease;
Magic of fatal kind he throws around,   60
Where Care is banish'd but the Heart is bound.

"Think not of Beauty;—when a Maid you meet,
Turn from her view and step across the Street:

Dread all the Sex: their looks create a charm,
A Smile should fright you and a Word alarm:
E'en I myself, with all my watchful care,
Have for an instant felt th' insidious snare,
And caught my sinful eyes at th' endangering stare;
'Till I was forc'd to smite my bounding breast
With forceful blow and bid the bold-one rest.   70

"Go not with Crowds when they to Pleasure run,
But public Joy in private safety shun;
When Bells, diverted from their true intent,
Ring loud for some deluded Mortal sent
To hear or make long Speech in Parliament;
What time the many, that unruly beast,
Roars its rough Joy and shares the final Feast;
Then heed my Counsel, shut thine ears and eyes,
A few will hear me—for the few are wise."

Not *Satan*'s friends, nor *Satan*'s self could bear   80
The cautious Man who took of Souls such care;
An Interloper,—one who, out of place,
Had volunteer'd upon the side of Grace:
There was his Master ready once a week
To give Advice; what further need he seek?
"Amen, so be it"—what had he to do
With more than this?—'twas insolent and new;
And some determin'd on a way to see
How frail he was, that so it might not be.

First they essay'd to tempt our Saint to sin,   90
By points of Doctrine argued at an Inn;
Where he might warmly reason, deeply drink,
Then lose all power to argue and to think.

In vain they try'd; he took the Question up,
Clear'd every Doubt, and barely touch'd the Cup:
By many a Text he prov'd his Doctrine sound,
And look'd in triumph on the Tempters round.

Next 'twas their care an artful Lass to find,
Who might consult him, as perplex'd in Mind;
She they conceived might put her Case with fears,   100
With tender tremblings and seducing tears;
She might such Charms of various kind display,
That he would feel their force and melt away:
For why of Nymphs such caution and such dread,
Unless he felt, and fear'd to be misled.

She came, she spake: he calmly heard her Case,
And plainly told her 'twas a want of Grace;
Bade her "such Fancies and Affections check,
And wear a thicker Muslin on her Neck."

Letter XIX. **25. Pioneer:** a soldier who precedes the main body of troops on a march, building roads and otherwise preparing the way. **36. John Bunyan:** (1628–88), Puritan author of *The Pilgrim's Progress* (1678).

Abased, his human Foes the Combat fled,   110
And the stern Clerk yet higher held his Head.
They were indeed a weak, impatient Set,
But their shrewd Prompter had his Engines yet;
Had various means to make a Mortal trip,
Who shunn'd a flowing Bowl and rosy Lip;
And knew a thousand ways his Heart to move,
Who flies from Banquets and who laughs at Love.

Thus far the playful Muse has lent her aid,
But now departs, of graver theme afraid;
Her may we seek in more appropriate time,—   120
There is no jesting with Distress and Crime.

Our worthy Clerk had now arriv'd at Fame,
Such as but few in his degree might claim;
But he was poor, and wanted not the sense
That lowly rates the Praise without the Pence:
He saw the common Herd with reverence treat
The weakest Burgess° whom they chanc'd to meet;
While few respected his exalted Views,
And all beheld his Doublet and his Shoes:
None, when they meet, would to his Parts allow   130
(Save his poor Boys) a hearing or a bow:
To this false Judgment of the vulgar Mind,
He was not fully, as a Saint, resign'd;
He found it much his jealous Soul affect,
To fear Derision and to find Neglect.

The Year was bad, the Christening-Fees were small,
The Weddings few, the Parties Paupers all:
Desire of Gain with fear of Want combin'd,
Rais'd sad Commotion in his wounded Mind;
Wealth was in all his Thoughts, his Views, his
    Dreams,   140
And prompted base Desires and baseless Schemes.

Alas! how often erring Mortals keep
The strongest Watch against the Foes who sleep;
While the more wakeful, bold and artful Foe
Is suffer'd, guardless and unmark'd, to go.

Once in a month the Sacramental Bread
Our Clerk with Wine upon the Table spread;
The Custom this, that, as the Vicar reads,
He for our Off'rings round the Church proceeds:
Tall spacious Seats the wealthier People hid,   150
And none had view of what his Neighbour did;

127. **Burgess:** a Member of Parliament for a borough.

Laid on the Box and mingled when they fell,
Who should the worth of each Oblation tell?
Now as poor *Jachin* took the usual round,
And saw the Alms and heard the Metal sound,
He had a thought;—at first it was no more
Than "these have Cash and give it to the Poor:"
A second thought from this to work began—
"And can they give it to a poorer Man?"
Proceeding thus,—"My Merit could they know,   160
And knew my Need, how freely they'd bestow;
But though they know not, these remain the same,
And are a strong, although a secret claim:
To me, alas! the Want and Worth are known,
Why then, in fact, 'tis but to take my own."

Thought after thought pour'd in, a tempting train,—
"Suppose it done,—who is it could complain?
How could the Poor? for they such Trifles share,
As add no Comfort, as suppress no Care;
But many a Pittance makes a worthy Heap,—   170
What says the Law? that Silence puts to sleep:—
Nought then forbids, the danger could we shun,
And sure the business may be safely done.

"But am I earnest?—earnest? No.—I say,
If such my Mind, that I could plan a way,
Let me reflect;—I've not allow'd me time
To purse the Pieces, and if dropt they'd chime:"
Fertile is Evil in the soul of Man,—
He paus'd—said *Jachin*, "They may drop on Bran.

"Why then 'tis safe and (all considered) just,   180
The Poor receive it,—'tis no breach of Trust;
The Old and Widows may their Trifles miss,
There must be Evil in a Good like this:
But I'll be kind,—the Sick I'll visit twice,
When now but once, and freely give Advice.
Yet let me think again:"—Again he tried,
For stronger Reasons on his Passion's side,
And quickly these were found, yet slowly he
    complied.

The Morning came: the common Service done,—
Shut every Door,—the solemn Rite begun,—   190
And, as the Priest the sacred Sayings read,
The Clerk went forward, trembling as he tread;
O'er the tall Pew he held the Box, and heard
The offer'd Piece, rejoicing as he fear'd:
Just by the Pillar, as he cautious tript,
And turn'd the Aisle, he then a Portion slipt
From the full Store, and to the Pocket sent,
But held a moment—and then down it went.

The Priest read on, on walk'd the Man afraid,
Till a gold Offering in the Plate was laid;   200
Trembling he took it, for a moment stopt,
Then down it fell, and sounded as it dropt:
Amaz'd he started, for th' affrighted Man,
Lost and bewilder'd, thought not of the Bran;
But all were silent, all on things intent
Of high concern, none ear to Money lent;
So on he walk'd, more cautious than before,
And gain'd the purpos'd Sum and one Piece more.

Practice makes perfect;—when the Month came round,
He dropt the Cash nor listen'd for a Sound;   210
But yet, when last of all th' assembled Flock,
He ate and drank,°—it gave th' electric Shock:
Oft was he forc'd his Reasons to repeat,
Ere he could kneel in quiet at his Seat;
But Custom sooth'd him—ere a single Year
All this was done without Restraint or Fear:
Cool and collected, easy and compos'd,
He was correct 'till all the Service clos'd;
Then to his Home, without a groan or sigh,
Gravely he went, and laid his Treasure by.   220

Want will complain: some Widows had exprest
A doubt if they were favour'd like the rest;
The rest describ'd with like regret their Dole,
And thus from parts they reason'd to the whole;
When all agreed some Evil must be done,
Or rich Men's Hearts grew harder than a Stone.

Our easy Vicar cut the matter short,
He would not listen to such vile Report.   228

All were not thus—there govern'd in that Year ⎫
A stern stout Churl, an angry Overseer;   ⎪
A Tyrant fond of Power, loud, lewd, and most   ⎬
   severe: ⎪
Him the mild Vicar, him the graver Clerk,   ⎭
Advis'd, reprov'd, but nothing would he mark,
Save the Disgrace, "and that, my Friends," said he,
"Will I avenge, whenever time may be."
And now, alas! 'twas time;—from Man to Man
Doubt and Alarm and shrewd Suspicions ran.

With angry spirit and with sly intent,
This Parish Ruler to the Altar went;
A private Mark he fix'd on Shillings three,   240
And but one Mark could in the Money see;
Besides, in peering round, he chanc'd to note

A sprinkling slight on *Jachin*'s Sunday-Coat:
All doubt was over:—when the Flock were blest,
In wrath he rose, and thus his Mind exprest.

"Foul Deeds are here!" and saying this, he took
The Clerk, whose Conscience, in her cold-fit, shook:
His Pocket then was emptied on the place;
All saw his Guilt; all witness'd his Disgrace:
He fell, he fainted, not a groan, a look   250
Escap'd the Culprit; 'twas a final stroke—
A death-wound never to be heal'd—a fall
That all had witness'd, and amazed were all.

As he recover'd, to his Mind it came,
"I owe to *Satan* this Disgrace and Shame:"
All the Seduction now appear'd in view,
"Let me withdraw," he said, and he withdrew;
No one withheld him, all in union cry'd,
E'en the Avenger,—"We are satisfied:"
For what has Death in any form to give,   260
Equal to that Man's Terrors, if he live?

He liv'd in freedom, but he hourly saw
How much more fatal Justice is than Law;
He saw another in his office reign,
And his mild Master treat him with disdain;
He saw that all Men shunn'd him, some revil'd,
The harsh pass'd frowning, and the simple smil'd;
The Town maintain'd him, but with some reproof,
And clerks and scholars proudly kept aloof.

In each lone place, dejected and dismay'd,   270
Shrinking from view, his wasting Form he laid;
Or to the restless Sea and roaring Wind
Gave the strong Yearnings of a ruin'd Mind:
On the broad Beach, the silent Summer-day,
Stretch'd on some Wreck, he wore his Life away;
Or where the River mingles with the Sea,   ⎫
Or on the Mud-bank by the Elder-tree,   ⎬
Or by the bounding Marsh-dyke, there was he: ⎭
And when unable to forsake the Town,
In the blind Courts° he sate desponding down—   280
Always alone; then feebly would he crawl
The Church-way Walk, and lean upon the Wall:
Too ill for this, he lay beside the Door,
Compell'd to hear the Reasoning of the Poor:
He look'd so pale, so weak, the pitying Crowd
Their firm belief of his Repentance vow'd;
They saw him then so ghastly and so thin,
That they exclaim'd, "Is this the work of Sin?"

212. **ate and drank:** took Communion.

280. **blind Courts:** blind alleys.

"Yes," in his better moments, he replied,
"Of sinful Avarice and the Spirit's Pride;—   290
While yet untempted, I was safe and well,
Temptation came; I reason'd and I fell:
To be Man's Guide and Glory I design'd,
A rare Example for our sinful kind;
But now my Weakness and my Guilt I see,
And am a Warning—Man, be warn'd by me!"

He said, and saw no more the human Face;
To a lone Loft he went, his dying place,
And, as the Vicar of his state inquir'd,
Turn'd to the wall and silently expir'd!   300

LETTER XXII. THE POOR OF THE BOROUGH. PETER GRIMES

OLD *Peter Grimes* made Fishing his employ,
His Wife he cabin'd with him and his Boy,
And seem'd that Life laborious to enjoy:
To Town came quiet *Peter* with his Fish,
And had of all a civil word and wish.
He left his Trade upon the Sabbath-Day,
And took young *Peter* in his hand to pray;
But soon the stubborn Boy from care broke loose,
At first refus'd, then added his abuse:
His Father's Love he scorn'd, his Power defied,   10
But being drunk, wept sorely when he died.

Yes! then he wept, and to his Mind there came
Much of his Conduct, and he felt the Shame,—
How he had oft the good old Man revil'd,
And never paid the Duty of a Child;
How, when the Father in his Bible read,
He in contempt and anger left the Shed:
"It is the Word of Life," the Parent cried;
—"This is the Life itself," the Boy replied,
And while old *Peter* in amazement stood,   20
Gave the hot Spirit to his boiling Blood:—
How he, with Oath and furious Speech, began
To prove his Freedom and assert the Man;
And when the Parent check'd his impious Rage,
How he had curs'd the Tyranny of Age,—
Nay, once had dealt the sacrilegious Blow
On his bare Head, and laid his Parent low:
The Father groan'd—"If thou art old," said he,
"And hast a Son—thou wilt remember me:

Thy Mother left me in a happy Time,   30
Thou kill'dst not her—Heav'n spares the double
    Crime."

On an Inn-Settle, in his maudlin Grief,
This he revolv'd, and drank for his Relief.

Now liv'd the Youth in freedom, but debarr'd
From constant Pleasure, and he thought it hard;
Hard that he could not every wish obey,
But must awhile relinquish Ale and Play;
Hard! that he could not to his Cards attend,
But must acquire the Money he would spend.

With greedy eye he look'd on all he saw,   40
He knew not Justice, and he laugh'd at Law;
On all he mark'd he stretch'd his ready Hand,
He fish'd by Water, and he filch'd by Land:
Oft in the Night has *Peter* dropt his Oar,
Fled from his Boat and sought for Prey on shore;
Oft up the Hedge-row glided, on his Back
Bearing the Orchard's Produce in a Sack,
Or Farm-yard Load, tugg'd fiercely from the Stack;
And as these Wrongs to greater numbers rose,
The more he look'd on all Men as his Foes.   50

He built a mud-wall'd Hovel, where he kept
His various Wealth, and there he oft-times slept;
But no Success could please his cruel Soul,
He wish'd for one to trouble and controul;
He wanted some obedient Boy to stand
And bear the blow of his outrageous hand;
And hop'd to find in some propitious hour
A feeling Creature subject to his Power.

Peter had heard there were in London then,—
Still have they being!—Workhouse-clearing Men,   60
Who, undisturb'd by Feelings just or kind,
Would Parish-Boys to needy Tradesmen bind:
They in their want a trifling Sum would take,
And toiling Slaves of piteous Orphans make.

Such *Peter* sought, and when a Lad was found,
The Sum was dealt him, and the Slave was bound.
Some few in Town observ'd in *Peter*'s Trap
A Boy, with Jacket blue and woollen Cap;
But none inquir'd how *Peter* us'd the Rope,
Or what the Bruise, that made the Stripling stoop;   70
None could the Ridges on his Back behold,
None sought him shiv'ring in the Winter's Cold;
None put the question,—"*Peter*, dost thou give
The Boy his Food?—What, Man! the Lad must live:
Consider, *Peter*, let the Child have Bread,

He'll serve thee better if he's stroked and fed."
None reason'd thus—and some, on hearing Cries,
Said calmly, "*Grimes* is at his Exercise."

Pinn'd, beaten, cold, pinch'd, threaten'd, and
    abused,—
His Efforts punish'd and his Food refus'd,—   80
Awake tormented,—soon arous'd from sleep,—
Struck if he wept, and yet compell'd to weep,
The trembling Boy dropt down and strove to pray,
Receiv'd a Blow, and trembling turn'd away,
Or sobb'd and hid his piteous face;—while he,
The savage Master, grinn'd in horrible glee;
He'd now the power he ever loved to show,
A feeling Being subject to his Blow.

Thus liv'd the Lad in Hunger, Peril, Pain,
His Tears despis'd, his Supplications vain: 90
Compell'd by fear to lie, by need to steal,
His Bed uneasy and unblest his Meal,
For three sad Years the Boy his Tortures bore,
And then his Pains and Trials were no more.

"How died he, *Peter?*" when the people said,
He growl'd—"I found him lifeless in his Bed;"
Then try'd for softer tone, and sigh'd, "Poor *Sam*
    is dead."
Yet murmurs were there, and some questions ask'd,—
How he was fed, how punish'd, and how task'd?
Much they suspected, but they little prov'd,   100
And *Peter* past untroubled and unmoved.

Another Boy with equal ease was found,
The Money granted and the Victim bound;
And what his Fate?—One night it chanc'd he fell
From the Boat's Mast and perish'd in her Well,
Where Fish were living kept, and where the Boy
(So reason'd Men) could not himself destroy:—

"Yes! so it was," said *Peter*, "in his play,
(For he was idle both by night and day,)
He climb'd the Main-mast and then fell below;"—   110
Then show'd his Corpse and pointed to the Blow:
"What said the jury?"—they were long in doubt,
But sturdy *Peter* faced the matter out:
So they dismiss'd him, saying at the time,
"Keep fast your Hatchway when you've Boys who
    climb."
This hit the Conscience, and he colour'd more
Than for the closest questions put before.

Thus all his fears the Verdict set aside,
And at the Slave-shop *Peter* still applied.

Then came a Boy, of Manners soft and mild,—   120
Our Seamen's Wives with grief beheld the Child;
All thought (the Poor themselves) that he was one
Of gentle Blood, some noble Sinner's Son,
Who had, belike, deceiv'd some humble Maid,
Whom he had first seduc'd and then betray'd:—
However this, he seem'd a gracious Lad,
In Grief submissive and with Patience sad.

Passive he labour'd, till his slender Frame
Bent with his Loads, and he at length was lame:
Strange that a frame so weak could bear so long   130
The grossest Insult and the foulest Wrong;
But there were causes—in the Town they gave
Fire, Food, and Comfort, to the gentle Slave;
And though stern *Peter*, with a cruel Hand,
And knotted Rope, enforc'd the rude Command,
Yet he consider'd what he'd lately felt,
And his vile Blows with selfish Pity dealt.

One day such Draughts the cruel Fisher made,
He could not vend them in his Borough-Trade,
But sail'd for London-Mart: the Boy was ill,   140
But ever humbled to his Master's will;
And on the River, where they smoothly sail'd,
He strove with terror and awhile prevail'd;
But new to Danger on the angry Sea,
He clung affrighten'd to his Master's knee:
The Boat grew leaky and the Wind was strong,
Rough was the Passage and the Time was long;
His Liquor fail'd, and *Peter's* wrath arose,—
No more is known—the rest we must suppose,   149
Or learn of *Peter;*—*Peter* says, he "spied
The Stripling's danger and for Harbour tried;
Meantime the Fish and then th' Apprentice died."

The pitying Women rais'd a Clamour round,
And weeping said, "Thou hast thy 'Prentice
    drown'd."

Now the stern Man was summon'd to the Hall,
To tell his Tale before the Burghers all:
He gave th' Account, profess'd the Lad he lov'd,
And kept his brazen Features all unmov'd.

The Mayor himself with tone severe replied,
"Henceforth with thee shall never Boy abide;   160
Hire thee a Freeman, whom thou durst not beat,
But who, in thy despite, will sleep and eat:
Free thou art now!—again shouldst thou appear,
Thou'lt find thy Sentence, like thy Soul, severe."

Alas! for *Peter* not a helping Hand,
So was he hated, could he now command;
Alone he row'd his Boat; alone he cast
His Nets beside, or made his Anchor fast;
To hold a Rope or hear a Curse was none,—
He toil'd and rail'd; he groan'd and swore alone.   170

Thus by himself compell'd to live each day,
To wait for certain hours the Tide's delay;
At the same times the same dull views to see,
The bounding Marsh-bank and the blighted Tree;
The Water only, when the Tides were high,
When low, the Mud half-cover'd and half-dry;
The Sun-burn'd Tar that blisters on the Planks,
And Bank-side Stakes in their uneven ranks;
Heaps of entangled Weeds that slowly float,
As the Tide rolls by the impeded Boat.   180

When Tides were neap,° and, in the sultry day,
Through the tall bounding Mud-banks made their
        way,
Which on each side rose swelling, and below
The dark warm Flood ran silently and slow;
There anchoring, *Peter* chose from Man to hide,   ⎫
There hang his Head, and view the lazy Tide   ⎬
In its hot slimy Channel slowly glide;   ⎭
Where the small Eels that left the deeper way
For the warm Shore, within the Shallows play;
Where gaping Muscles, left upon the Mud,   190
Slope their slow passage to the fallen Flood;—
Here dull and hopeless he'd lie down and trace
How side-long Crabs had scrawl'd their crooked race;
Or sadly listen to the tuneless cry
Of fishing *Gull* or clanging *Golden-Eye;*°
What time the Sea-Birds to the Marsh would come,   ⎫
And the loud *Bittern,*° from the Bull-rush home, ⎬
Gave from the Salt-ditch side the bellowing Boom: ⎭
He nurst the Feelings these dull Scenes produce,
And lov'd to stop beside the opening Sluice;   200
Where the small Stream, confin'd in narrow bound,
Ran with a dull, unvaried, sadd'ning sound;
Where all presented to the Eye or Ear
Oppress'd the Soul! with Misery, Grief, and Fear.

Besides these objects, there were places three,
Which *Peter* seem'd with certain dread to see;
When he drew near them he would turn from each,
And loudly whistle till he past the *Reach.*°

A change of Scene to him brought no relief,
In Town, 'twas plain, Men took him for a Thief: 210
The Sailors' Wives would stop him in the Street,
And say, "Now, *Peter,* thou'st no Boy to beat:"
Infants at play, when they perceiv'd him, ran,
Warning each other—"That's the wicked Man:"
He growl'd an oath, and in an angry tone
Curs'd the whole Place and wish'd to be alone.

Alone he was, the same dull Scenes in view,
And still more gloomy in his sight they grew:
Though Man he hated, yet employ'd alone
At bootless labour, he would swear and groan,   220
Cursing the Shoals° that glided by the spot,
And *Gulls* that caught them when his arts could not.

Cold nervous Tremblings shook his sturdy Frame,
And strange Disease—he couldn't say the name;
Wild were his Dreams, and oft he rose in fright,
Wak'd by his view of Horrors in the Night,—
Horrors that would the sternest Minds amaze,
Horrors that Dæmons might be proud to raise: 228
And though he felt forsaken, griev'd at heart,   ⎫
To think he liv'd from all Mankind apart;   ⎬
Yet, if a Man approach'd, in terrors he would start. ⎭

A Winter past since *Peter* saw the Town,
And Summer Lodgers were again come down;
These, idly curious, with their glasses spied
The Ships in Bay as anchor'd for the Tide,—
The River's Craft,—the bustle of the Quay,—
And Sea-port views, which Landmen love to see.

One, up the River, had a Man and Boat
Seen day by day, now anchor'd, now afloat;   239
Fisher he seem'd, yet us'd no Net nor Hook,   ⎫
Of Sea-fowl swimming by, no heed he took,   ⎬
But on the gliding Waves still fix'd his lazy look: ⎭
At certain stations he would view the Stream,
As if he stood bewilder'd in a Dream,
Or that some Power had chain'd him for a time,
To feel a Curse or meditate on Crime.

This known, some curious, some in pity went,
And others question'd—"Wretch, dost thou repent?"
He heard, he trembled, and in fear resign'd
His Boat: new terror fill'd his restless Mind;   250
Furious he grew, and up the Country ran,
And there they seiz'd him—a distemper'd Man:—
Him we received, and to a Parish-bed,
Follow'd and curs'd, the groaning Man was led.

Letter XXII. **181. neap:** lowest. **195. Golden-Eye:** diving
duck. **197. Bittern:** heron. **208. Reach:** promontory.

221. Shoals: schools of fish.

Here when they saw him, whom they us'd to shun,
A lost, lone Man, so harass'd and undone;
Our gentle Females, ever prompt to feel,
Perceiv'd Compassion on their Anger steal;
His Crimes they could not from their Memories blot,
But they were griev'd, and trembled at his Lot.   260

A Priest too came, to whom his words are told,
And all the signs they shudder'd to behold.

"Look! look!" they cried; "his Limbs with horror
        shake,
And as he grinds his Teeth, what noise they make!
How glare his angry Eyes, and yet he's not awake:
See! what cold drops upon his Forehead stand,
And how he clenches that broad bony Hand."

The Priest attending, found he spoke at times
As one alluding to his Fears and Crimes:
"It was the fall," he mutter'd, "I can show   270
The manner how—I never struck a blow:"—
And then aloud—"Unhand me, free my Chain;
On Oath, he fell—it struck him to the Brain:—
Why ask my Father?—that old Man will swear
Against my Life; besides, he wasn't there:—
What, all agreed?—Am I to die to-day?—
My Lord, in Mercy, give me time to pray."

Then, as they watch'd him, calmer he became,
And grew so weak he couldn't move his Frame,
But murmuring spake,—while they could see and
        hear   280
The start of Terror and the groan of Fear;
See the large Dew-beads on his Forehead rise,
And the cold Death-drop glaze his sunken Eyes;
Not yet he died, but with unwonted force
Seem'd with some fancied Being to discourse:
He knew not us, or with accustom'd art
He hid the knowledge, yet exposed his Heart;
'Twas part Confession and the rest Defence,
A Madman's Tale, with gleams of waking Sense.

"I'll tell you all," he said, "the very day   290
When the old Man first plac'd them in my way:
My Father's Spirit—he who always tried
To give me trouble, when he liv'd and died—
When he was gone, he could not be content
To see my Days in painful Labour spent,
But would appoint his Meetings, and he made
Me watch at these, and so neglect my Trade.

"'Twas one hot Noon, all silent, still, serene;
No living Being had I lately seen;

I paddled up and down and dipt my Net,   300
But (such his pleasure) I could nothing get,—
A Father's pleasure! when his Toil was done,
To plague and torture thus an only Son;
And so I sat and look'd upon the Stream,
How it ran on, and felt as in a Dream:
But Dream it was not; No!—I fix'd my Eyes
On the mid Stream and saw the Spirits rise;
I saw my Father on the Water stand,
And hold a thin pale Boy in either hand;
And there they glided ghastly on the top   310
Of the salt Flood, and never touch'd a drop:
I would have struck them, but they knew th' intent,
And smil'd upon the Oar, and down they went.

"Now, from that day, whenever I began
To dip my Net, there stood the hard old Man—
He and those Boys; I humbled me and pray'd
They would be gone;—they heeded not, but stay'd:
Nor could I turn, nor would the Boat go by,
But gazing on the Spirits, there was I;
They bade me leap to death, but I was loth to die:
And every day, as sure as day arose,   321
Would these three Spirits meet me ere the close;
To hear and mark them daily was my doom,
And 'Come,' they said, with weak, sad voices, 'come.'
To row away with all my strength I try'd,
But there were they, hard by me in the Tide,
The three unbodied Forms—and 'Come,' still
        'come,' they cried.

"Fathers should pity—but this old Man shook
His hoary Locks and froze me by a Look:
Thrice, when I struck them, through the water
        came   330
A hollow Groan, that weaken'd all my Frame:
'Father!' said I, 'have Mercy:'—He replied,
I know not what—the angry Spirit lied,—
'Didst thou not draw thy Knife?' said he:—'Twas
        true,
But I had Pity and my Arm withdrew:
He cried for Mercy, which I kindly gave,
But he has no Compassion in his Grave.

"There were three places, where they ever rose,—
The whole long River has not such as those,—
Places accurs'd, where, if a Man remain,   340
He'll see the things which strike him to the Brain;
And there they made me on my Paddle lean,
And look at them for hours;—accursed Scene!

When they would glide to that smooth Eddy-space,
Then bid me leap and join them in the place;
And at my Groans each little villain Sprite
Enjoy'd my Pains and vanish'd in delight.

  "In one fierce Summer-day, when my poor Brain
Was burning-hot and cruel was my Pain,
Then came this Father-foe, and there he stood   350
With his two Boys again upon the Flood;
There was more Mischief in their Eyes, more Glee
In their pale Faces when they glar'd at me:
Still did they force me on the Oar to rest,
And when they saw me fainting and opprest,
He, with his Hand, the old Man, scoop'd the Flood,
And there came Flame about him mix'd with Blood;
He bade me stoop and look upon the place,
Then flung the hot-red Liquor in my Face;
Burning it blaz'd, and then I roar'd for Pain,   360
I thought the Dæmons would have turn'd my Brain.

  "Still there they stood, and forc'd me to behold
A place of Horrors—they cannot be told—
Where the Flood open'd, there I heard the Shriek
Of tortur'd Guilt—no earthly Tongue can speak:
'All Days alike! for ever!' did they say,
'And unremitted Torments every Day'—
Yes, so they said:"—but here he ceas'd and gaz'd
On all around, affrighten'd and amaz'd;
And still he try'd to speak and look'd in dread   370
Of frighten'd Females gathering round his Bed;
Then dropt exhausted and appear'd at rest,
Till the strong Foe the vital Powers possest;
Then with an inward, broken voice he cried,
"Again they come," and mutter'd as he died.

FROM

TALES

Crabbe's *Tales*, published in 1812, contains twenty-one
narratives in verse. In his Preface Crabbe attempts to
defend his kind of poetry against critics who seemed to
assume that a tincture of mystery and even obscurity
was indispensable in a fully successful narrative poem,
such as Coleridge's *Rime of the Ancient Mariner* (1798)
or *Christabel* (1816). Suggesting that he is instead writing
within a tradition of verse narrative originated in
England by Chaucer and reinvigorated by Dryden,
Crabbe argues that those poets "who address their
productions to the plain sense and sober judgment of

their Readers" are just as genuinely poets as those who
appeal to the reader's delight in the unpredictable and
the wonderful. The kind of poetry he is writing, which
he calls "poetry without an atmosphere," necessitates,
he insists, "actuality of relation" and "nudity of
description."

  The tenth tale, titled *The Lover's Journey*, is traditionally thought to represent one of the experiences the
young Crabbe had while he was courting Sarah Elmy,
a pretty girl who lived at Beccles, twenty-five miles
from Aldborough. She later became his wife.

  The text is that of the first edition (1812). We have
omitted a botanical footnote.

THE LOVER'S JOURNEY

I⊤ is the Soul that sees; the outward eyes
Present the object, but the Mind descries;
And thence delight, disgust, or cool indiff'rence rise:
When minds are joyful, then we look around,
And what is seen is all on fairy ground;
Again they sicken, and on every view
Cast their own dull and melancholy hue;
Or, if absorb'd by their peculiar cares,
The vacant eye on viewless matter glares;
Our feelings still upon our views attend,   10
And their own natures to the objects lend;
Sorrow and joy are in their influence sure,
Long as the passion reigns th' effects endure;
But Love in minds his various changes makes,
And clothes each object with the change he takes;
His light and shade on every view he throws,
And on each object, what he feels, bestows.

  Fair was the morning, and the month was June,
When rose a Lover; Love awakens soon;
Brief his repose, yet much he dreamt the while   20
Of that day's meeting, and his *Laura*'s smile;
Fancy and Love that name assign'd to her,
Call'd *Susan* in the parish-register;
And he no more was *John*—his *Laura* gave
The name *Orlando* to her faithful slave.

  Bright shone the glory of the rising day,
When the fond traveller took his favourite way;
He mounted gaily, felt his bosom light,
And all he saw was pleasing in his sight.

  "Ye hours of expectation, quickly fly,   30
And bring on hours of blest reality;
When I shall *Laura* see, beside her stand,
Hear her sweet voice, and press her yielded hand."

First o'er a barren heath beside the coast
Orlando rode, and joy began to boast.

"This neat low gorse," said he, "with golden bloom,
Delights each sense, is beauty, is perfume;
And this gay ling,° with all its purple flowers,
A man at leisure might admire for hours;
This green-fring'd cup-moss has a scarlet tip,   40
That yields to nothing but my *Laura*'s lip;
And then how fine this herbage! men may say
A heath is barren, nothing is so gay;
Barren or bare to call such charming scene,
Argues a mind possess'd by care and spleen."

Onward he went and fiercer grew the heat,
Dust rose in clouds before the horse's feet;
For now he pass'd through lanes of burning sand,
Bounds to thin crops or yet uncultur'd land;
Where the dark poppy flourish'd on the dry   50
And sterile soil, and mock'd the thin-set rye.

"How lovely this!" the rapt *Orlando* said,
"With what delight is labouring man repaid!
The very lane has sweets that all admire,
The rambling suckling and the vigorous brier;
See! wholesome wormwood grows beside the way,
Where, dew-press'd yet, the dog-rose bends the spray;
Fresh herbs the fields, fair shrubs the banks adorn,
And snow-white bloom falls flaky from the thorn;
No fostering hand they need, no sheltering wall,   60
They spring uncultur'd and they bloom for all."

The Lover rode as hasty lovers ride,
And reach'd a common pasture wild and wide;
Small black-legg'd sheep devour with hunger keen
The meager herbage, fleshless, lank, and lean;
Such o'er thy level turf, *Newmarket!*° stray,
And there, with other *Black-legs*,° find their prey:
He saw some scatter'd hovels; turf was pil'd
In square brown stacks; a prospect bleak and wild!
A mill, indeed, was in the centre found,   70
With short sear herbage withering all around;
A smith's black shed oppos'd a wright's long shop,
And join'd an inn where humble travellers stop.

"Aye, this is Nature," said the gentle 'Squire;
This ease, peace, pleasure—who would not admire?
With what delight these sturdy children play,

And joyful rustics at the close of day;
Sport follows labour, on this even space
Will soon commence the wrestling and the race;
Then will the Village-Maidens leave their home   80
And to the dance with buoyant spirits come;
No affectation in their looks is seen,
Nor know they what disguise or flattery mean;
Nor aught to move an envious pang they see,
Easy their service, and their love is free;
Hence early springs that love, it long endures,
And life's first comfort, while they live, ensures:
They the low roof and rustic comforts prize,
Nor cast on prouder mansions envying eyes:
Sometimes the news at yonder town they hear,   90
And learn what busier mortals feel and fear,
Secure themselves, although by tales amaz'd,
Of towns bombarded and of cities raz'd;
As if they doubted, in their still retreat,
The very news that makes their quiet sweet,
And their days happy—happier only knows
He on whom *Laura* her regard bestows."

On rode *Orlando*, counting all the while
The miles he pass'd and every coming mile;
Like all attracted things, he quicker flies,   100
The place approaching where th' attraction lies;
When next appear'd a *dam*,—so call the place,—
Where lies a road confin'd in narrow space;
A work of labour, for on either side
Is level fen, a prospect wild and wide,
With dykes on either hand by Ocean's self supplied:
Far on the right, the distant sea is seen,
And salt the springs that feed the marsh between;
Beneath an ancient bridge, the straiten'd flood
Rolls through its sloping banks of slimy mud;   110
Near it a sunken boat resists the tide,
That frets and hurries to th' opposing side;
The rushes sharp, that on the borders grow,
Bend their brown flowrets to the stream below,
Impure in all its course, in all its progress slow:
Here a grave *Flora* scarcely deigns to bloom,
Nor wears a rosy blush, nor sheds perfume;
The few dull flowers that o'er the place are spread,
Partake the nature of their fenny bed;
Here on its wiry stem, in rigid bloom,   120
Grows the salt lavender that lacks perfume;
Here the dwarf sallows creep, the septfoil° harsh,
And the soft slimy mallow of the marsh;

TALES: *The Lover's Journey.* **38. ling:** heather. **66. Newmarket:** a town near Cambridge famous for horse racing. **67. Black-legs:** racetrack swindlers.

122. septfoil: a low-growing astringent herb.

Low on the ear the distant billows sound,
And just in view appears their stony bound;
No hedge nor tree conceals the glowing sun,
Birds, save a wat'ry tribe, the district shun,
Nor chirp among the reeds where bitter waters run.

"Various as beauteous, Nature, is thy face,"
Exclaim'd *Orlando;* "all that grows has grace;   130
All are appropriate—bog, and marsh, and fen,
Are only poor to undiscerning men;
Here may the nice and curious eye explore,
How Nature's hand adorns the rushy moor;
Here the rare moss in secret shade is found,
Here the sweet myrtle of the shaking ground;
Beauties are these that from the view retire,
But well repay th' attention they require;
For these, my *Laura* will her home forsake,
And all the pleasures they afford partake."   140

Again, the country was enclos'd, a wide
And sandy road has banks on either side;
Where, lo! a hollow on the left appear'd,
And there a Gipsy-tribe their tent had rear'd;
'Twas open spread, to catch the morning sun,
And they had now their early meal begun,
When two brown Boys just left their grassy seat,
The early Trav'ler with their pray'rs to greet:
While yet *Orlando* held his pence in hand,
He saw their Sister on her duty stand;   150
Some twelve years old, demure, affected, sly,
Prepar'd the force of early powers to try;
Sudden a look of languor he descries,
And well-feign'd apprehension in her eyes;
Train'd but yet savage, in her speaking face,
He mark'd the features of her vagrant race;
When a light laugh and roguish leer express'd
The vice implanted in her youthful breast:
Forth from the tent her elder Brother came,
Who seem'd offended yet forbore to blame   160
The young designer, but could only trace
The looks of pity in the Trav'ler's face:
Within, the Father, who from fences nigh
Had brought the fuel for the fire's supply,
Watch'd now the feeble blaze, and stood dejected by:
On ragged rug, just borrow'd from the bed,
And by the hand of coarse indulgence fed,
In dirty patchwork negligently dress'd,
Reclin'd the Wife, an infant at her breast;
In her wild face some touch of grace remain'd,   170
Of vigour palsied and of beauty stain'd;
Her blood-shot eyes on her unheeding mate

Were wrathful turn'd, and seem'd her wants to state,
Cursing his tardy aid—her Mother there
With Gipsy-state engross'd the only chair;
Solemn and dull her look; with such she stands,
And reads the Milk-maid's fortune in her hands,
Tracing the lines of life; assum'd through years,
Each feature now the steady falsehood wears;
With hard and savage eye she views the food,   180
And grudging pinches their intruding brood:
Last in the group, the worn-out Grandsire sits
Neglected, lost, and living but by fits;
Useless, despis'd, his worthless labours done,
And half protected by the vicious Son,
Who half supports him; he with heavy glance,
Views the young ruffians who around him dance;
And, by the sadness in his face, appears
To trace the progress of their future years;
Through what strange course of misery, vice, deceit,
Must wildly wander each unpractis'd cheat;   191
What shame and grief, what punishment and pain,
Sport of fierce passions, must each child sustain—
Ere they like him approach their latter end,
Without a hope, a comfort, or a friend!

But this *Orlando* felt not; "Rogues," said he,
"Doubtless they are, but merry rogues they be;
They wander round the land, and be it true,
They break the laws—then let the laws pursue
The wanton idlers; for the life they live,   200
Acquit I cannot, but I can forgive."
This said, a portion from his purse was thrown,
And every heart seem'd happy like his own.

He hurried forth, for now the town was nigh—
"The happiest man of mortal men am I."
Thou art! but change in every state is near,
(So while the wretched hope, the blest may fear;)
"Say where is *Laura?*"—"That her words must show,"
A lass replied; "read this and thou shalt know!"   209

"What, gone!"—her friend insisted—forc'd to go:—
"Is vex'd, was teiz'd, could not refuse her!—No?"
"But you can follow;" "Yes;" "the miles are few,
The way is pleasant; will you come?—Adieu!
Thy *Laura!*" "No! I feel I must resign
The pleasing hope, thou hadst been here, if mine:
A lady was it?—Was no Brother there?
But why should I afflict me, if there were?"
"The way is pleasant:" "What to me the way?
I cannot reach her till the close of day.
My dumb companion! is it thus we speed?   220

Not I from grief nor thou from toil art freed;
Still art thou doom'd to travel and to pine,
For my vexation—What a fate is mine!"

"Gone to a friend, she tells me; I commend
Her purpose; means she to a female friend?
By Heaven, I wish she suffer'd half the pain
Of hope protracted through the day in vain.
Shall I persist to see th' ungrateful Maid?
Yes, I will see her, slight her and upbraid;
What! in the very hour? She knew the time,   230
And doubtless chose it to increase her crime."

Forth rode *Orlando* by a river's side,
Inland and winding, smooth and full and wide,
That roll'd majestic on, in one soft-flowing tide;
The bottom gravel, flow'ry were the banks,
Tall willows waving in their broken ranks;
The road, now near, now distant, winding led
By lovely meadows which the waters fed;
He pass'd the way-side inn, the village spire,
Nor stopp'd to gaze, to question, or admire;   240
On either side the rural mansions stood,
With hedge-row trees and hills high-crown'd with
     wood,
And many a devious stream that reach'd the nobler
     flood.

"I hate these scenes," *Orlando* angry cried,
"And these proud farmers! yes, I hate their pride:
See! that sleek fellow, how he strides along,
Strong as an ox, and ignorant as strong;
Can yon close crops a single eye detain,
But his who counts the profits of the grain?
And these vile beans with deleterious smell,   250
Where is their beauty? can a mortal tell?
These deep fat meadows I detest; it shocks
One's feelings there to see the grazing ox;—
For slaughter fatted, as a lady's smile
Rejoices man and means his death the while.
Lo! now the sons of labour! every day
Employ'd in toil, and vex'd in every way;
Theirs is but mirth assum'd, and they conceal,
In their affected joys, the ills they feel:
I hate these long green lanes; there's nothing seen 260
In this vile country but eternal green;
Woods! waters! meadows! will they never end?
'Tis a vile prospect:—Gone to see a friend!—"

Still on he rode!—a mansion fair and tall
Rose on his view,—the pride of *Loddon-Hall;*

Spread o'er the park he saw the grazing steer,
The full-fed steed, and herds of bounding deer:
On a clear stream the vivid sun-beams play'd,
Through noble elms, and on the surface made
That moving picture, checker'd light and shade;   270
Th' attended children, there indulg'd to stray,
Enjoy'd and gave new beauty to the day;
Whose happy parents from their room were seen
Pleas'd with the sportive idlers on the green.

"Well!" said *Orlando,* "and for one so blest,
A thousand reasoning wretches are distress'd;
Nay, these so seeming glad, are grieving like the rest:
Man is a cheat—and all but strive to hide
Their inward misery by their outward pride.
What do yon lofty gates and walls contain,   280
But fruitless means to soothe unconquer'd pain?
The parents read each infant daughter's smile,
Form'd to seduce, encourag'd to beguile;
They view the boys unconscious of their fate,
Sure to be tempted, sure to take the bait;
These will be *Lauras,* sad *Orlandos* these—
There's guilt and grief in all one hears and sees."

Our Trav'ler, lab'ring up a hill, look'd down
Upon a lively, busy, pleasant town;
All he beheld were there alert, alive,   290
The busiest bees that ever stock'd a hive:
A pair were married, and the bells aloud
Proclaim'd their joy, and joyful seem'd the crowd;
And now proceeding on his way, he spied,
Bound by strong ties, the Bridegroom and the Bride;
Each by some friends attended, near they drew,
And Spleen beheld them with prophetic view.

"Married! nay, mad!" *Orlando* cried in scorn;
Another wretch on this unlucky morn;
What are this foolish mirth, these idle joys?   300
Attempts to stifle doubt and fear by noise:
To me these robes, expressive of delight,
Foreshow distress and only grief excite;
And for these cheerful friends, will they behold
Their wailing brood in sickness, want, and cold;
And his proud look, and her soft languid air
Will—but I spare you—go, unhappy pair!"

And now approaching to the journey's end,
His anger fails, his thoughts to kindness tend,
He less offended feels! and rather fears t' offend: 310
Now gently rising, Hope contends with Doubt,
And casts a sun-shine on the views without;

And still reviving Joy and lingering Gloom,
Alternate empire o'er his soul assume;
Till, long perplex'd, he now began to find
The softer thoughts engross the settling mind:
He saw the mansion, and should quickly see
His *Laura*'s self—and angry could he be?
No! the resentment melted all away—
"For this my grief a single smile will pay,"   320
Our Trav'ler cried;—"And why should it offend,
That one so good should have a pressing friend?
Grieve not, my heart! to find a favourite guest
Thy pride and boast—ye selfish sorrows, rest;
She will be kind, and I again be blest."

While gentler passions thus his bosom sway'd,
He reach'd the mansion, and he saw the Maid;
"My *Laura!*"—"My *Orlando!*—this is kind;
In truth I came persuaded, not inclin'd;
Our friends' amusement let us now pursue,   330
And I to-morrow will return with you."

Like man entranc'd, the happy Lover stood—
"As *Laura* wills, for she is kind and good;
Ever the truest, gentlest, fairest, best—
As *Laura* wills, I see her and am blest."

Home went the Lovers through that busy place,
By *Loddon-Hall*, the country's pride and grace;
By the rich meadows where the oxen fed,
Through the green vale that form'd the river's bed;
And by unnumber'd cottages and farms,   340
That have for musing minds unnumber'd charms:
And how affected by the view of these
Was then *Orlando*,—did they pain or please?

Nor pain nor pleasure could they yield—and why?
The mind was fill'd, was happy, and the eye
Rov'd o'er the fleeting views, that but appear'd to die.

Alone *Orlando* on the morrow pac'd
The well-known road; the Gipsy-tent he trac'd;
The dam high-rais'd, the reedy dykes between,
The scatter'd hovels on the barren green,   350
The burning sand, the fields of thin-set rye,
Mock'd by the useless *Flora*, blooming by;
And last the heath with all its various bloom,
And the close lanes that led the Trav'ler home.

Then could these scenes the former joys renew?
Or was there now dejection in the view?—
Nor one nor other would they yield—and why?
The mind was absent, and the vacant eye
Wander'd o'er viewless scenes, that but appear'd to die.

Robert Burns

1759–1796

Robert Burns—Scotia's Bard, as he liked to call himself—was born in a rude clay cottage in the village of Alloway, two miles from the county town of Ayr in the western Scottish Lowlands. As a tenant farmer's son he was expected to do a full day's work plowing and threshing—the grim climate and primitive tools made farming a rigorous business—but he found time to study under a local tutor and to soak himself in contemporary literature. He was equally fond of James Thomson and William Shenstone and of the Scots vernacular poets Allan Ramsay and Robert Fergusson. He was not a mere occasional reader; indefatigably literary, he customarily propped a book beside his place at table while he ate. As a youth he was clever, sensitive, and proud, and like his countryman James Boswell he was fascinated by his own character and identity. The commonplace book he began keeping in 1783 bears this title: *Observations, Hints, Songs, Scraps of Poetry &c. by Robt Burness; a Man Who Had Little Art in Making Money, . . . but Was, However, a Man of Some Sense, a Great Deal of Honesty, and Unbounded Good-Will to Every Creature Rational or Irrational*.

At the age of sixteen he had his first taste of what Boswell once referred to as "the irregular connection between the sexes," and from then on lovemaking provided the subject of many of his songs and also of considerable local scandal. As he said later, "My heart was compleatly tinder, and was eternally lighted up by some Goddess or other." During his lifetime he fathered nine illegitimate children. By 1786 his uninhibited enjoyment of what he called "a certain delicious Passion" made his situation in Ayrshire highly uncomfortable—Jean Armour, a local girl, had just borne him twins—and Burns prepared to flee to the West Indies, where he hoped to find in Jamaica a refuge from angry fathers and importunate girls, as well as from the embarrassments of Kirk discipline. To help raise money for his passage he published in the nearby town of Kilmarnock the poems that he had been showing about in manuscript for several years. *Poems, Chiefly in the Scottish Dialect* (1786) contained forty-four poems, a preface at once apologetic and proud, and a glossary of the dialect words. The edition sold out within a month, and it was a sensation not merely with local admirers but with the important Edinburgh literati as well. One reader reported, "On a Saturday evening I opened the volume, by accident, while I was undressing to go to bed. I closed it not, till a late hour on the rising Sunday morn, after I had read over every syllable it contained." *The Edinburgh Magazine* acclaimed

Burns's "native genius" and "untutored fancy," and Henry Mackenzie, author of the stylish sentimental novel *The Man of Feeling* (1771), rhapsodized over the "Heaven-taught ploughman." The book was praised even in London. Eager for fame, Burns abandoned his journey to Jamaica and turned instead toward Edinburgh, where he hoped to arrange for the publication of a second edition. In Edinburgh he was the literary lion of the season: his humble circumstances, his sparkling conversation, and his open and yet proud manner charmed academics, lawyers, and even aristocrats. The sixteen-year-old Walter Scott, who met Burns at this time, recalled that "there was a strong expression of sense and shrewdness in all his lineaments; the eye alone, I think, indicated the poetical character and temperament. It was large, and of a dark cast, and glowed (I say literally *glowed*) when he spoke with feeling or interest."

After the publication in Edinburgh of the enlarged second edition of *Poems* (1787), which sold four times as many copies as the first, he traveled restlessly around Scotland for several months, returning finally to his Ayrshire farm to find himself well known and relatively affluent. Another visit to Edinburgh, in 1788, acquainted him with an engraver, James Johnson, who was bringing out a compilation of Scottish folk songs. To Johnson's six-volume work, and later to George Thomson's similar collection, Burns contributed with enthusiasm until his death. He wrote or rewrote some 250 songs in all.

In 1788 he married Jean Armour and attained an appointment as an officer of His Majesty's Excise in the area of Dumfries. As a customs officer he performed his duty faithfully and enjoyed a successful career, although his outspoken republican opinions caused some trouble. He is said to have shocked loyal ears shortly after the outbreak of the French Revolution with this toast: "Here's to the last verse of the last chapter of the last Book of Kings."

The next eight years he spent in Dumfries, riding out on his weekly customs circuit; reading Fielding, Smollett, Cowper, Molière, and La Fontaine; collecting, rewriting, and composing texts for Scottish songs; and indulging in the wet and bawdy conviviality customary in eighteenth-century Scotland. His death at the age of thirty-seven was caused not, as is sometimes believed, by alcoholism or debauchery, but by rheumatic heart disease aggravated by overwork during his youth.

Burns always liked to gratify his more naive and sentimental admirers by posing as the kind of untaught genius and "Noble Savage" they were looking for. He placed these lines on the title page of the Kilmarnock volume:

> THE Simple Bard, unbroke by rules of Art,
> He pours the wild effusions of the heart:
> And if inspir'd, 'tis Nature's pow'rs inspire:
> Her's all the melting thrill, and her's the kindling fire.

Actually he was entirely aware that he was playing a shrewd role. He once proposed a comical coat of arms for himself with the sardonic motto "Woodnotes wild." And his acquaintance Robert Anderson reported:

> It was . . . a part of the machinery, as he called it, of his poetical character to pass for an illiterate ploughman who wrote from pure inspiration. When I pointed out some evident traces of poetical imitation in his verses, privately, he readily

acknowledged his obligations, and even admitted the advantages he enjoyed in poetic composition from the *copia verborum*, the command of phraseology, which the knowledge and use of [both] the English and Scottish dialects afforded him; but in company he would not suffer his pretensions to pure inspiration to be challenged, and it was seldom done where it might be supposed to affect the success of the subscription for his *Poems*.

Although Burns's literary imagination was suffused at times with an image of pastoral, he was quite satisfied with the literary assumptions of the eighteenth century. His subject was man engaged in ethical action within a social framework. He had no literary interest in scenery or mountains, and he seems hardly to have noticed the nearby sea. He did not respond to the distant or the exotic: when he focused on nature, he was as fond of contemplating the louse as the skylark. Far from striking out in new poetic directions, he brought the eighteenth-century art of literary imitation to one of its fullest flowerings since Pope. Whether in satire or song, his art lies less in his invention than in the tact and decorum with which he exploits a number of literary traditions, with their weight of inherited motifs, rhetorical conventions, and even received phrasings.

Sentimentality and legend as well as critical naiveté abound in the literature on Burns: the student must be on his guard. The bibliographies by W. C. Angus and J. C. Ewing, both published in 1899, are adequate though incomplete. A trustworthy biography is F. B. Snyder's *The Life of Robert Burns* (1932). DeLancey Ferguson's *Pride and Passion: Robert Burns* (1939) is an enlightened biographical treatment in the form of separate essays. Ferguson has edited the complete *Letters* (2 vols., 1931) as well as the interesting selection in the World's Classics (1953). A satisfactory text of the poems is edited by W. E. Henley and T. F. Henderson (4 vols., 1896–97), but James Kinsley's excellent edition (3 vols., 1968) supersedes all others. The rare and famous Kilmarnock first edition is available in facsimile (1911). The *Songs* are edited with the music by J. C. Dick (1903). Two good critical studies are David Daiches's *Robert Burns* (1950) and Thomas Crawford's *Burns: A Study of the Poems and Songs* (1960). Daiches includes a running biographical interpretation, and Crawford is valuable especially on the matter of Burns's literary sources. John Speirs's *The Scots Literary Tradition* (1940) provides the context in which Burns is best read.

THE HOLY FAIR

In a footnote to the title Burns explains, "*Holy Fair* is a common phrase in the West of Scotland for a sacramental occasion." The service of Communion in the Scottish Kirk was generally celebrated only once a year, and every parishioner was expected to attend. The proceedings, which were lively and bibulous, were usually conducted in a tent pitched in an open field convenient to an alehouse.

Burns's poem comes at the end of a long tradition of rowdy, mischievous Scots verse describing popular festivals. It looks back not only to such poems as the anonymous sixteenth-century *Christis Kirk on the Green* and *Peblis to the Play* but also to Robert Fergusson's *Leith Races* and *Hallowfair*, which appeared during the 1770's.

The text is that of the first printing, in *Poems, Chiefly in the Scottish Dialect* (Kilmarnock, 1786); we have incorporated the substantive variants in the Edinburgh edition of 1787.

A robe of seeming truth and trust
    Hid crafty observation;
And secret hung, with poison'd crust,
    The dirk of Defamation:
A mask that like the gorget° show'd,
    Dye-varying, on the pigeon;
And for a mantle large and broad,
    He wrapt him in Religion.
        HYPOCRISY A-LA-MODE

I.

UPON a simmer Sunday morn,
    When Nature's face is fair,
I walked forth to view the corn,
    An' snuff the callor° air.
The rising sun, our° GALSTON Muirs,
    Wi' glorious light was glintan;
The hares were hirplan° down the furrs,°
    The lav'rocks° they were chantan
        Fu' sweet that day.

II.

As lightsomely I glowr'd° abroad,   10
    To see a scene sae gay,
Three *hizzies,*° early at the road,
    Cam skelpan° up the way.
Twa had manteeles o' dolefu' black,
    But ane wi' lyart° lining;
The third, that gaed a wee a-back,°
    Was in the fashion shining
        Fu' gay that day.

III.

The *twa* appear'd like sisters twin,
    In feature, form an' claes;°   20
Their visage wither'd, lang an' thin,
    An' sour as ony slaes:°
The *third* cam up, hap-step-an'-loup,°
    As light as ony lambie,
An' wi' a curchie low did stoop,
    As soon as e'er she saw me,
        Fu' kind that day.

IV.

Wi' bonnet aff, quoth I, "Sweet lass,
    I think ye seem to ken° me;
I'm sure I've seen that bonie face,   30
    But yet I canna name ye."
Quo' she, an' laughan as she spak,
    An' taks me by the han's,
"Ye, for my sake, hae gien the feck°
    Of a' the *ten comman's*
        A screed° some day.

V.

"My name is FUN—your cronie dear,
    The nearest friend ye hae;
An' this is SUPERSTITION here,
    An' that's HYPOCRISY.   40
I'm gaun to *********° holy fair,
    To spend an hour in daffin:°
Gin° ye'll go there, yon runkl'd pair,
    We will get famous laughin
        At them this day."

VI.

Quoth I, "With a' my heart, I'll do 't;
    I'll get my sunday's sark° on,
An' meet you on the holy spot;
    Faith, we'se° hae fine remarkin!"
Then I gaed hame at crowdie-time,°   50
    An' soon I made me ready;
For roads were clad,° frae side to side,
    Wi' monie a wearie body,
        In droves that day.

VII.

Here, farmers gash,° in ridin graith,°
    Gaed hoddan by their cotters;°
There, swankies° young, in braw° braid-claith,
    Are springan owre the gutters.
The lasses, skelpan barefit, thrang,°
    In silks an' scarlets glitter;   60
Wi' *sweet-milk cheese,* in monie a whang,°
    An' *farls,*° bak'd wi' butter,
        Fu' crump° that day.

29. **ken**: know. 34. **feck**: bulk. 36. **screed**: rip. 41. *********: Mauchline, an Ayrshire town. 42. **daffin**: merriment. 43. **Gin**: if. 47. **sark**: shirt. 49. **we'se**: we'll. 50. **crowdie-time**: breakfast time. 52. **clad**: covered. 55. **gash**: self-important. **ridin graith**: riding gear. 56. **hoddan . . . cotters**: jogging past their tenants. 57. **swankies**: strong boys. **braw**: handsome. 59. **thrang**: thronged. 61. **whang**: large slice. 62. **farls**: oatcakes. 63. **crump**: crisp.

THE HOLY FAIR. **gorget**: an area on the throat. 4. **callor**: fresh. 5. **our**: over. 7. **hirplan**: hopping. **furrs**: furrows. 8. **lav'rocks**: larks. 10. **glowr'd**: glanced. 12. **hizzies**: young women. 13. **skelpan**: running. 15. **lyart**: gray. 16. **gaed . . . a-back**: hung back a bit. 20. **claes**: clothes. 22. **slaes**: sloe berries. 23. **loup**: leap.

VIII.

When by the *plate* we set our nose,
　Weel heaped up wi' ha'pence,
A greedy glowr *black-bonnet* throws,
　An' we maun° draw our tippence.
Then in we go to see the show,
　On ev'ry side they're gath'ran;
Some carryan dails,° some chairs an' stools,　70
　An' some are busy bleth'ran°
　　Right loud that day.

IX.

Here stands a shed to fend the show'rs,
　An' screen our countra Gentry;
There, *racer Jess*, an' twathree wh—res,
　Are blinkan° at the entry.
Here sits a raw o' tittlan jads,°
　Wi' heaving breast an' bare neck;
An' there, a batch o' *Wabster*° lads,
　Blackguarding frae K*******ck°　80
　　For *fun* this day.

X.

Here, some are thinkan on their sins,
　An' some upo' their claes;
Ane curses feet that fyl'd° his shins,
　Anither sighs an' prays:
On this hand sits a Chosen swatch,°
　Wi' screw'd-up, grace-proud faces;
On that, a set o' chaps, at watch,
　Thrang° winkan on the lasses
　　To *chairs*° that day.　90

XI.

O happy is that man, an' blest!
　Nae wonder that it pride him!
Whase ain dear lass, that he likes best,
　Comes clinkan° down beside him!
Wi' arm repos'd on the *chair-back*,
　He sweetly does compose him;
Which, by degrees, slips round her *neck*,
　An's loof° upon her *bosom*
　　Unkend° that day.

XII.

Now a' the congregation o'er　100
　In silent expectation;
For ****** speels the holy door,°
　Wi' tidings o' d—mn—t—n.°
Should *Hornie*,° as in ancient days,
　'Mang sons o' G—— present him,
The vera sight o' ******'s face,
　To's ain *het hame*° had sent him
　　Wi' fright that day.

XIII.

Hear how he clears the points o' Faith
　Wi' rattlin an' thumpin!　110
Now meekly calm, now wild in wrath,
　He's stampan, an' he's jumpan!
His lengthen'd chin, his turn'd up snout,
　His eldritch° squeel an' gestures,
O how they fire the heart devout,
　Like *cantharidian*° plaisters
　　On sic a day!

XIV.

But hark! the *tent* has chang'd it's voice;
　There's peace an' rest nae langer;
For a' the *real judges* rise,　120
　They canna sit for anger.
*****° opens out his cauld harangues,
　On *practice* and on *morals;*
An' aff the *godly*° pour in thrangs,
　To gie the jars an' barrels°
　　A lift that day.

XV.

What signifies his barren shine,
　Of *moral pow'rs* an' *reason?*
His English style, an' gesture fine,
　Are a' clean out o' season.　130
Like SOCRATES or ANTONINE,°
　Or some auld pagan heathen,

102. ****** . . . door: (The Reverend Mr. Alexander)
Moodie enters the pulpit. 103. d—mn—t—n: substituted for
the reading "s—lv—t—n" of the first edition; it is said that
Burns's Edinburgh admirer Hugh Blair suggested a revision
here. 104. Hornie: the devil. 107. het hame: hot home. 114.
eldritch: hideous. 116. cantharidian: aphrodisiac. 122.
*****: (the Reverend Mr. George) Smith, a "New Licht,"
or theological liberal. 124. the godly: the "Auld Lichts,"
theological conservatives. 125. jars an' barrels: of liquor.
131. Antonine: Marcus Aurelius Antoninus, Roman Stoic
philosopher.

67. maun: must. 70. dails: planks. 71. bleth'ran: talking
idly. 76. blinkan: smirking. 77. tittlan jads: whispering
and laughing wenches. 79. Wabster: weaver. 80.
K*******ck: Kilmarnock. 84. fyl'd: soiled. 86. swatch:
sample. 89. Thrang: busy. 90. To chairs: to take chairs
next to them. 94. clinkan: sitting. 98. An's loof: and his
palm. 99. Unkend: unperceived.

The *moral man* he does define,
But ne'er a word o' *faith* in
That's right that day.

XVI.

In guid time comes an antidote
Against sic poosion'd nostrum;
For *******,° frae the water-fit,°
Ascends the *holy rostrum:*
See, up he's got the word o' G——,   140
An' meek an' mim° has view'd it,
While COMMON-SENSE has taen the road,
An' aff, an' up the *Cowgate*°
Fast, fast that day.

XVII.

Wee ******° niest,° the Guard relieves,
An' Orthodoxy raibles,°
Tho' in his heart he weel° believes,
An' thinks it auld wives' fables:
But faith! the birkie° wants a *Manse,*°
So, cannilie he hums them;°   150
Altho' his *carnal* Wit an' Sense
Like hafflins-wise° o'ercomes him
At times that day.

XVIII.

Now, butt an' ben,° the Change-house° fills,
Wi' *yill-caup*° Commentators:
Here's crying out for bakes an' gills,°
An' there the pint-stowp° clatters;
While thick an' thrang, an' loud an' lang,
Wi' *Logic,* an' wi' *Scripture,*
They raise a din, that, in the end,   160
Is like to breed a rupture
O' wrath that day.

XIX.

Leeze me on° Drink! it gies us mair
Than either School or Colledge:
It kindles Wit, it waukens Lear,°
It pangs us fou° o' Knowledge.
Be 't *whisky-gill* or *penny-wheep,*°
Or ony stronger potion,
It never fails, on drinkin deep,
To kittle up our *notion,*°   170
By night or day.

XX.

The lads an' lasses, blythely bent
To mind baith *saul* an' *body,*
Sit round the table, weel content,
An' steer° about the *toddy.*
On this ane's dress, an' that ane's leuk,
They're makin observations;
While some are cozie i' the neuk,
An' forming *assignations*
To meet some day.   180

XXI.

But now the L——'s ain trumpet touts,°
Till a' the hills are rairan,°
An' echos back return the shouts;
Black ******° is na spairan:
His piercin words, like Highlan swords,
Divide the joints an' marrow;
His talk o' H—ll, whare devils dwell,
Our vera "Sauls does harrow"°
Wi' fright that day!

XXII.

A vast, unbottom'd, boundless *Pit,*   190
Fill'd fou o' *lowan brunstane,*°
Whase raging flame, an' scorching heat,
Wad melt the hardest whun-stane°!
The *half asleep* start up wi' fear,
An' think they hear it roaran,
When presently it does appear,
'Twas but some neebor *snoran*
Asleep that day.

138. *****:** (the Reverend Mr. William) Peebles; he had his revenge when, after Burns's death, he wrote in his *Burnomania* (1811) that in the poems of Burns "sinfulness, gross immoralities, and irreligion" are "celebrated, extenuated, vindicated: the worst of passions indulged and gratified: the sacred truths of religion treated with levity, and made the song of the drunkard and the abandoned profligate." **water-fit:** river mouth. **141. mim:** prim. **143. Cowgate:** [Burns's note] A street so call'd, which faces the *tent* in ——. **145. ******:** (the Reverend Mr. Alexander) Miller. **niest:** next. **146. raibles:** rattles nonsensically. **147. weel:** only moderately. **149. birkie:** fellow. **Manse:** residence, i.e., a clerical living. **150. cannilie . . . them:** Dextrously he humbugs them. **152. Like hafflins-wise:** almost half. **154. butt an' ben:** kitchen and parlor, i.e., in every space. **Change-house:** tavern. **155. yill-caup:** ale mug. **156. bakes an' gills:** biscuits and half pints of ale. **157. pint-stowp:** pint measure.

163. Leeze me on: lief is to me; i.e., give me above all else. **165. waukens Lear:** awakens learning. **166. pangs us fou:** shoots us full; *fou* also means drunk. **167. penny-wheep:** small beer. **170. kittle . . . notion:** tickle our imagination. **175. steer:** stir. **181. touts:** toots. **182. rairan:** roaring. **184. ******:** (the Reverend Mr. John) Russel. **188. Sauls . . . harrow:** [Burns's note] Shakespeare's *Hamlet* [I. v. 16]. **191. lowan brunstane:** flaming brimstone. **193. whun-stane:** granite.

XXIII.

'Twad be owre lang a tale to tell,
    How monie stories past,   200
An' how they crouded to the yill,
    When they were a' dismist:
How drink gaed round, in cogs an' caups,°
    Amang the furms° an' benches;
An' *cheese* an' *bread*, frae women's laps,
    Was dealt about in lunches,°
        An' dawds° that day.

XXIV.

In comes a gawsie,° gash° *Guidwife*,
    An' sits down by the fire,
Syne draws her *kebbuck*° an' her knife;   210
    The lasses they are shyer.
The auld *Guidmen*, about the *grace*,
    Frae side to side they bother,
Till some ane by his bonnet lays,
    An' gies them 't, like a *tether*,°
        Fu' lang that day.

XXV.

Waesucks!° for him that gets nae lass,
    Or lasses that hae naething!
Sma' need has he to say a grace,
    Or melvie° his braw claithing!   220
O *Wives* be mindfu', ance yoursel,
    How bonie lads ye wanted,
An' dinna, for a *kebbuck-heel*,
    Let lasses be affronted
        On sic a day!

XXVI.

Now *Clinkumbell*,° wi' rattlan tow,°
    Begins to jow an' croon;°
Some swagger hame, the best they dow,°
    Some wait the afternoon.
At slaps° the billies° halt a blink,   230
    Till lasses strip their shoon:
Wi' *faith* an' *hope*, an' *love* an' *drink*,
    They're a' in famous tune
        For crack° that day.

XXVII.

How monie hearts this days converts,
    O' sinners and o' Lasses!
Their hearts o' stane, gin° night are gane,
    As saft as ony flesh is.
There's some are fou o' *love divine;*
    There's some are fou o' *brandy;*   240
An' monie jobs that day begin,
    May end in *Houghmagandie*°
        Some ither day.

THE COTTER'S SATURDAY NIGHT

❦

Burns's model here was Robert Fergusson's *The Farmer's Ingle* (1773), a poem written in a variation of Spenserian stanza. Although Burns had not yet read Spenser himself, he was familiar with the conventions of the stanza from his acquaintance with Shenstone's *The Schoolmistress* (1742) and James Beattie's *The Minstrel* (1771–74). This poem contains phrasal echoes of Shakespeare, Milton, Rochester, Pope, Gay, Thomson, Collins, Gray, Goldsmith, and Sterne. It was extravagantly admired by sentimentalists like Henry Mackenzie. *The English Review* found it the best poem in the whole Kilmarnock volume and observed that Burns's "domestic picture of rustic simplicity . . . must please every reader whose feelings are not perverted."

The text is that of the first printing (Kilmarnock, 1786); we have incorporated the substantive variants in the Edinburgh edition of 1793.

🦋

INSCRIBED TO R. A****,° Esq;

Let not Ambition mock their useful toil,
    Their homely joys, and destiny obscure;
Nor Grandeur hear, with a disdainful smile,
    The short and simple annals of the Poor.
                                        GRAY.

I.

MY lov'd, my honor'd, much respected friend,
    No mercenary Bard his homage pays;
With honest pride, I scorn each selfish end,
    My dearest meed, a friend's esteem and praise:

---

203. cogs an' caups: wooden dishes and bowls. **204. furms:** seats. **206. lunches:** large portions. **207. dawds:** pieces. **208. gawsie:** jolly. **gash:** affable. **210. kebbuck:** whole cheese. **215. tether:** rope. **217. Waesucks:** Alas! **220. melvie:** soil with crumbs. **226. Clinkumbell:** the church bellringer. **rattlan tow:** slender rope. **227. jow an' croon:** swing and sound. **228. dow:** can. **230. slaps:** openings in walls and hedges. **billies:** fellows. **234. crack:** lively conversation.

237. gin: by. **242. Houghmagandie:** fornication. THE COTTER'S SATURDAY NIGHT. **R. A****:** Robert Aiken, an Ayr lawyer.

To you I sing, in simple Scottish lays,
  The *lowly train* in life's sequester'd scene;
The native feelings strong, the guileless ways,
  What A**** in a *Cottage* would have been;
Ah! tho' his worth unknown, far happier there I
  ween°!

II.

November chill blaws loud wi' angry sugh;°   10
  The short'ning winter-day is near a close;
The miry beasts retreating frae the pleugh;
  The black'ning trains o' craws° to their repose:
The toil-worn COTTER frae his labor goes,
  This night his weekly moil° is at an end,
Collects his *spades*, his *mattocks* and his *hoes*,
  Hoping the *morn* in ease and rest to spend,
And weary, o'er the moor, his course does hameward
  bend.

III.

At length his lonely *Cot* appears in view,
  Beneath the shelter of an aged tree;   20
The expectant *wee-things*, toddlan, stacher° through
  To meet their *Dad*, wi' flichterin° noise and glee.
His wee-bit ingle,° blinkan° bonilie,
  His clean hearth-stane, his thrifty *Wifie's* smile,
The *lisping infant*, prattling on his knee,
  Does a' his weary carking° cares beguile,
And makes him quite forget his labor and his toil.

IV.

Belyve,° the *elder bairns* come drapping in,
  At *Service* out, amang the Farmers roun';
Some ca'° the pleugh, some herd, some tentie rin°   30
  A cannie° errand to a neebor town:
Their eldest hope, their *Jenny*, woman-grown,
  In youthfu' bloom, Love sparkling in her e'e,
Comes hame, perhaps, to shew a braw new gown,
  Or deposite her sair-won° penny-fee,
To help her *Parents* dear, if they in hardship be.

V.

With joy unfeign'd, *brothers* and *sisters* meet,
  And each for other's weelfare kindly spiers:°
The social hours, swift-wing'd, unnotic'd fleet;
  Each tells the uncos° that he sees or hears.   40

The Parents partial eye their hopeful years;
  Anticipation forward points the view;
The *Mother*, wi' her needle and her sheers,
  Gars° auld claes look amaist as weel's the new;
The *Father* mixes a' wi' admonition due.

VI.

Their Master's and their Mistress's command,
  The *youngkers* a' are warned to obey;
And mind their labors wi' an eydent° hand,
  And ne'er, tho' out o' sight, to jauk° or play:
"And O! be sure to fear the LORD alway!   50
  And mind your *duty*, duely, morn and night!
Lest in temptation's path ye gang astray,
  Implore his *counsel* and assisting *might*:
They never sought in vain that sought the LORD
  aright."

VII.

But hark! a rap comes gently to the door;
  Jenny, wha kens the meaning o' the same,
Tells how a neebor lad came o'er the moor,
  To do some errands, and convoy her hame.
The wily Mother sees the *conscious flame*
  Sparkle in *Jenny's* e'e, and flush her cheek,   60
With heart-struck, anxious care enquires his name,
  While *Jenny* hafflins° is afraid to speak;
Weel-pleas'd the Mother hears, it's nae wild, worthless
  Rake.

VIII.

With kindly welcome, *Jenny* brings him ben;°
  A *strappan youth;* he takes the Mother's eye;
Blythe *Jenny* sees the *visit's* no ill taen;
  The Father cracks° of horses, pleughs and kye.°
The *Youngster's* artless heart o'erflows wi' joy,
  But blate and laithfu',° scarce can weel behave;
The Mother, wi' a woman's wiles, can spy   70
  What makes the *youth* sae bashfu' and sae grave;
Weel-pleas'd to think her *bairn's* respected like the
  lave.°

IX.

O happy love! where love like this is found!
  O heart-felt raptures! bliss beyond compare!
I've paced much this weary, *mortal round*,
  And sage EXPERIENCE bids me this declare—

9. ween: guess, imagine. **10. sugh:** hum. **13. craws:** crows.
15. moil: drudgery. **21. stacher:** totter. **22. flichterin:**
fluttering. **23. ingle:** hearth fire. **blinkan:** flickering. **26.**
carking: anxious. **28. Belyve:** by and by. **30. ca':** follow.
tentie rin: carefully run. **31. cannie:** quiet. **35. sair-won:**
hard-earned. **38. spiers:** inquires. **40. uncos:** wonders.

44. Gars: makes. **48. eydent:** diligent. **49. jauk:** trifle. **62.**
hafflins: half. **64. ben:** inside. **67. cracks:** chats. **kye:** cattle.
69. blate and laithfu': shy and bashful. **72. lave:** rest.

"If Heaven a draught of heavenly pleasure spare,
   One *cordial* in this melancholy *Vale*,
'Tis when a youthful, loving, *modest* Pair,
   In other's arms, breathe out the tender tale,   80
Beneath the milk-white thorn that scents the ev'ning
    gale."

X.

Is there, in human form, that bears a heart—
   A Wretch! a Villain! lost to love and truth!
That can, with studied, sly, ensnaring art,
   Betray sweet Jenny's unsuspecting youth?
Curse on his perjur'd arts! dissembling smooth!
   Are *Honor, Virtue, Conscience*, all exil'd?
Is there no Pity, no relenting Ruth,
   Points to the Parents fondling o'er their Child?
Then paints the *ruin'd Maid*, and *their* distraction
    wild!   90

XI.

But now the Supper crowns their simple board,
   The healsome° *Porritch*, chief of SCOTIA'S food:
The soupe° their *only Hawkie*° does afford,
   That 'yont the hallan° snugly chows her cood:
The *Dame* brings forth, in complimental mood,
   To grace the lad, her weel-hain'd kebbuck, fell,°
And aft he's prest, and aft he ca's it guid;
   The frugal *Wifie*, garrulous, will tell,
How 'twas a towmond auld, sin' Lint was i' the bell.°

XII.

The chearfu' Supper done, wi' serious face,   100
   They, round the ingle, form a circle wide;
The Sire turns o'er, with patriarchal grace,
   The big *ha'-Bible*,° ance his *Father's* pride:
His bonnet rev'rently is laid aside,
   His *lyart haffets*° wearing thin and bare;
Those strains that once did sweet in ZION glide,
   He wales° a portion with judicious care;
"*And let us worship GOD!*" he says with solemn air.

XIII.

They chant their artless notes in simple guise;
   They tune their *hearts*, by far the noblest aim: 110

Perhaps *Dundee's* wild warbling measures rise,
   Or plaintive *Martyrs*, worthy of the name;
Or noble *Elgin*° beets the heaven-ward flame,
   The sweetest far of SCOTIA's holy lays:
Compar'd with these, *Italian trills* are tame;
   The tickl'd ears no heart-felt raptures raise;
Nae unison hae they, with our CREATOR'S praise.

XIV.

The priest-like Father reads the sacred page,
   How *Abram* was the Friend of GOD on high;
Or, *Moses* bade eternal warfare wage,   120
   With *Amalek's* ungracious progeny;°
Or how the *royal Bard*° did groaning lye,
   Beneath the stroke of Heaven's avenging ire;
Or *Job's* pathetic plaint, and wailing cry;
   Or rapt *Isaiah's* wild, seraphic fire;
Or other *Holy Seers* that tune the *sacred lyre*.

XV.

Perhaps the *Christian Volume*° is the theme,
   How *guiltless blood* for *guilty man* was shed;
How HE, who bore in heaven the second name,°
   Had not on Earth whereon to lay His head: 130
How His first *followers* and *servants* sped;°
   The *Precepts sage* they wrote to many a land:
How *he*,° who lone in *Patmos* banished,
   Saw in the sun a mighty angel stand;
And heard great *Bab'lon's* doom pronounc'd by
    Heaven's command.

XVI.

Then kneeling down to HEAVEN'S ETERNAL
    KING,
   The *Saint*, the *Father*, and the *Husband* prays:
Hope "springs exulting on triumphant wing,"°
   That *thus* they all shall meet in future days:
There, ever bask in *uncreated rays*,   140
   No more to sigh, or shed the bitter tear,
Together hymning their CREATOR'S praise,
   In *such society*, yet still more dear;
While circling Time moves round in an eternal sphere.

---

92. **healsome:** wholesome. 93. **soupe:** milk. **Hawkie:** cow. 94. **'yont the hallan:** beyond the wall. 96. **weel-hain'd . . . fell:** well-saved, pungent cheese. 99. **'twas . . . bell:** 'Twas a twelvemonth old since the flax was in bloom. 103. **ha'-Bible:** hall Bible, used for reading to the family and servants in the hall of a great house. 105. **lyart haffets:** graying temples. 107. **wales:** selects.

111–13. **Dundee, Martyrs, Elgin:** the names of hymn melodies. 120–21. **Moses . . . progeny:** See Ex. 27:8–16. 122. **the royal Bard:** David; see I Chron. 21:16–30. 127. **the Christian Volume:** the New Testament. 129. **the second name:** "the Son." 131. **sped:** flourished. 133. **he:** St. John the Divine, who, according to tradition, experienced the vision recorded in the Book of Revelation while imprisoned on the Greek island of Patmos. 138. **Hope . . . wing:** [Burns's note] Pope's Windsor Forest [see Part Two].

XVII.

Compar'd with *this*, how poor Religion's pride,
    In all the pomp of *method*, and of *art*,
When men display to congregations wide,
    Devotion's ev'ry grace, except the *heart!*
The POWER, incens'd, the Pageant will desert,
    The pompous strain, the sacredotal stole;   150
But haply,° in some *Cottage* far apart,
    May hear, well pleas'd, the language of the *Soul;*
And in His *Book of Life* the Inmates poor enroll.

XVIII.

Then homeward all take off their sev'ral way;
    The youngling *Cottagers* retire to rest:
The Parent-pair their *secret homage* pay,
    And proffer up to Heaven the warm request,
That HE who stills the *raven's* clam'rous nest,
    And decks the *lily* fair in flow'ry pride,
Would, in the way *His Wisdom* sees the best,   160
    For *them* and for their *little ones* provide;
But chiefly, in their hearts with *Grace divine* preside.

XIX.

From scenes like these, old SCOTIA'S grandeur
        springs,
    That makes her lov'd at home, rever'd abroad:
Princes and lords are but the breath of kings,
    "An honest man's the noblest work of GOD:"°
And *certes,*° in fair Virtue's heavenly road,
    The *Cottage* leaves the *Palace* far behind:
What is a lordling's pomp? a cumbrous load,
    Disguising oft the *wretch* of human kind,   170
Studied in arts of Hell, in wickedness refin'd!

XX.

O SCOTIA! my dear, my native soil!
    For whom my warmest wish to heaven is sent!
Long may thy hardy sons of *rustic toil,*
    Be blest with health, and peace, and sweet content!
And O may Heaven their simple lives prevent
    From *Luxury's* contagion, weak and vile!
Then howe'er *crowns* and *coronets* be rent,
    A *virtuous Populace* may rise the while,
And stand a wall of fire around their much-lov'd
        ISLE.   180

XXI.

O THOU! who pour'd the *patriotic tide,*
    That stream'd thro' Wallace's° undaunted heart;
Who dar'd to, nobly, stem tyrannic pride,
    Or *nobly die,* the second glorious part:
(The Patriot's GOD, peculiarly thou art,
    His *friend, inspirer, guardian,* and *reward!*)
O never, never SCOTIA'S realm desert,
    But still the *Patriot,* and the *Patriot-Bard,*
In bright succession raise, her *Ornament* and *Guard!*

TO A MOUSE

On turning her up in her Nest,
with the Plough, November, 1785.

🜸

The stanza of this poem, a traditional form for Scottish
vernacular poetry, is called Standard Habbie after the
stanza of a folk elegy by the seventeenth-century poet
Robert Sempill on the death of Habbie Simson, a
renowned piper of Kilbarchan.

The text is that of the first printing (Kilmarnock,
1786).

🜸

WEE, sleeket,° cowran, tim'rous *beastie,*
    O, what a panic's in thy breastie!
Thou need na start awa sae hasty,
        Wi' bickering brattle°!
I wad be laith° to rin an' chase thee,
        Wi' murd'ring *pattle°!*

I'm truly sorry Man's dominion
Has broken Nature's social union,
An' justifies that ill opinion,
        Which makes thee startle,   10
At me, thy poor, earth-born companion,
        An' *fellow-mortal!*

---

151. **haply:** perhaps. 166. **An . . . God:** Pope, *Essay on Man,*
iv. 248. 167. **certes:** assuredly.

182. **Wallace:** Sir William Wallace, thirteenth-century
Scottish patriot. TO A MOUSE. 1. **sleeket:** sleek. 4. **bickering
brattle:** scampering haste. 5. **laith:** unwilling. 6. **pattle:**
plowstaff.

I doubt na, whyles,° but thou may *thieve;*
What then? poor beastie, thou maun° live!
A *daimen-icker* in a *thrave*°
⠀⠀⠀'S a sma request:
I'll get a blessin wi' the lave,°
⠀⠀⠀An' never miss 't!

Thy wee-bit *housie*, too, in ruin!
It's silly wa's° the win's are strewin!⠀⠀⠀⠀20
An' naething, now, to big° a new ane,
⠀⠀⠀O' foggage° green!
An' bleak *December's winds* ensuin,
⠀⠀⠀Baith snell° an' keen!

Thou saw the fields laid bare an' wast,
An' weary *Winter* comin fast,
An' cozie here, beneath the blast,
⠀⠀⠀Thou thought to dwell,
Till crash! the cruel *coulter*° past
⠀⠀⠀Out thro' thy cell.⠀⠀⠀⠀30

That wee-bit heap o' leaves an' stibble,
Has cost thee monie a weary nibble!
Now thou's turn'd out, for a' thy trouble,
⠀⠀⠀But° house or hald,°
To thole° the *Winter's sleety dribble,*
⠀⠀⠀An' *cranreuch*° cauld!

But Mousie, thou art no thy-lane,°
In proving *foresight* may be vain:
The best laid schemes o' *Mice* an' *Men,*
⠀⠀⠀Gang aft agley,°⠀⠀⠀⠀40
An' lea'e us nought but grief an' pain,
⠀⠀⠀For promis'd joy!

Still, thou art blest, compar'd wi' *me!*
The *present* only toucheth thee:
But Och! I *backward* cast my e'e,
⠀⠀⠀On prospects drear!
An' *forward,* tho' I canna *see,*
⠀⠀⠀I *guess* an' *fear!*

TO A MOUNTAIN-DAISY

On turning one down,
with the Plough, in April—1786.

❧

The text is that of the first printing (Kilmarnock, 1786).

❧

WEE, modest, crimson-tipped flow'r,
Thou's met me in an evil hour;
For I maun crush amang the stoure°
⠀⠀⠀Thy slender stem:
To spare thee now is past my pow'r,
⠀⠀⠀Thou bonie gem.°

Alas! it's no thy neebor sweet,
The bonie *Lark,* companion meet!
Bending thee 'mang the dewy weet!
⠀⠀⠀Wi's spreckl'd breast,⠀⠀⠀⠀10
When upward-springing, blythe, to greet
⠀⠀⠀The purpling East.

Cauld blew the bitter-biting *North*
Upon thy early, humble birth;
Yet chearfully thou glinted forth
⠀⠀⠀Amid the storm,
Scarce rear'd above the *Parent-earth*
⠀⠀⠀Thy tender form.

The flaunting *flow'rs* our Gardens yield,
High-shelt'ring woods and wa's° maun shield,⠀⠀20
But thou, beneath the random bield°
⠀⠀⠀O' clod or stane,
Adorns the histie° *stibble-field,*
⠀⠀⠀Unseen, alane.

There, in thy scanty mantle clad,
Thy snawie bosom sun-ward spread,
Thou lifts thy unassuming head
⠀⠀⠀In humble guise;
But now the *share*° uptears thy bed,
⠀⠀⠀And low thou lies!⠀⠀⠀⠀30

13. **whyles:** sometimes. 14. **maun:** must. 15. **A daimen-icker . . . thrave:** an occasional single ear out of twenty-four sheaves. 17. **lave:** rest. 20. **silly wa's:** puny walls. 21. **big:** build. 22. **foggage:** coarse grass. 24. **snell:** biting. 29. **coulter:** the foremost part of the plow. 34. **But:** without. **hald:** property. 35. **thole:** endure. 36. **cranreuch:** hoarfrost. 37. **no thy-lane:** not alone. 40. **agley:** amiss.

TO A MOUNTAIN-DAISY. 3. **stoure:** dust. 6. **gem:** bud. 20. **wa's:** walls. 21. **bield:** shelter. 23. **histie:** barren. 29. **share:** plowshare.

Such is the fate of artless Maid,
Sweet *flow'ret* of the rural shade!
By Love's simplicity betray'd,
    And guileless trust,
Till she, like thee, all soil'd, is laid
    Low i' the dust.

Such is the fate of simple Bard,
On Life's rough ocean luckless starr'd!
Unskilful he to note the card°
    Of *prudent Lore*,   40
Till billows rage, and gales blow hard,
    And whelm him o'er!

Such fate to *suffering worth* is giv'n,
Who long with wants and woes has striv'n,
By human pride or cunning driv'n
    To Mis'ry's brink,
Till wrench'd of ev'ry stay but HEAV'N,
    He, ruin'd, sink!

Ev'n thou who mourn'st the *Daisy's* fate,
That fate is thine—no distant date;   50
Stern Ruin's *plough-share* drives, elate,
    Full on thy bloom,
Till crush'd beneath the *furrow's* weight,
    Shall be thy doom!

TO A LOUSE

On Seeing one on a Lady's Bonnet at Church.

❧

The text is that of the first printing (Kilmarnock, 1786).

❧

HA! whare ye gaun, ye crowlan ferlie°!
Your impudence protects you sairly:°
I canna say but ye strunt° rarely,
    Owre *gawze* and *lace;*
Tho' faith, I fear ye dine but sparely,
    On sic a place.

Ye ugly, creepan, blastet wonner,
Detested, shunn'd, by saunt an' sinner,
How daur ye set your fit° upon her,
    Sae fine a *Lady!*   10
Gae somewhere else and seek your dinner,
    On some poor body.

Swith,° in some beggar's haffet squattle;°
There ye may creep, and sprawl, and sprattle,°
Wi' ither kindred, jumping cattle,
    In shoals and nations;
Whare *horn* nor *bane*° ne'er daur unsettle,
    Your thick plantations.

Now haud° you there, ye're out o' sight,
Below the fatt'rels,° snug and tight,   20
Na faith ye yet! ye'll no be right,
    Till ye've got on it,
The vera tapmost, towrin height
    O' *Miss's bonnet.*

My sooth! right bauld° ye set your nose out,
As plump an' gray as onie grozet:°
O for some rank, mercurial rozet,°
    Or fell, red smeddum,°
I'd gie you sic a hearty dose o't,
    Wad dress your droddum°!   30

I wad na been surpriz'd to spy
You on an auld wife's *flainen toy;*°
Or aiblins° some bit duddie° boy,
    On's *wylecoat;*°
But Miss's fine *Lunardi,*° fye!
    How daur ye do 't?

O *Jenny* dinna toss your head,
An' set your beauties a' abroad°!
Ye little ken what cursed speed
    The blastie's makin!   40
Thae° *winks* and *finger-ends,* I dread,
    Are notice takin!

9. **fit:** foot. 13. **Swith:** Off! **haffet squattle:** temples
settle. 14. **sprattle:** scramble. 17. **horn nor bane:** (bone)
the materials combs were made of. 19. **haud:** keep. 20.
fatt'rels: ribbon ends. 25. **bauld:** bold. 26. **grozet:** gooseberry. 27. **rozet:** rosin. 28. **fell, red smeddum:** deadly red
powder. 30. **dress . . . droddum:** punish your behind. 32.
flainen toy: flannel cap. 33. **aiblins:** perhaps. **bit duddie:**
small ragged. 34. **wylecoat:** undershirt. 35. **Lunardi:** a kind
of bonnet. 38. **abread:** abroad. 41. **Thae:** those.

39. **card:** compass. TO A LOUSE. 1. **crowlan ferlie:** crawling
phenomenon. 2. **sairly:** sorely. 3. **strunt:** strut.

O wad some Pow'r the giftie gie us
To see oursels as others see us!
It wad frae monie a blunder free us
        An' foolish notion:
What airs in dress an' gait wad lea'e us,
        And ev'n Devotion!

EPISTLE TO J. L*****K,
AN OLD SCOTCH BARD

❧

John Lapraik (1727–1807) was an alehouse keeper, postmaster, and minor poet in the Ayrshire town of
Muirkirk. In 1788, ambitious of a success like Burns's,
he published—also in Kilmarnock—a volume of *Poems
on Several Occasions*, which included a song titled *When I
upon Thy Bosom Lean* that had "thirl'd" Burns's heart-
strings. Burns actually mailed this verse letter about the
song to Lapraik, who replied in kind. The epistle in
"Standard Habbie" had been one of the popular forms
of Scots vernacular poetry since William Hamilton of
Gilbertfield corresponded with Allan Ramsay early in
the century. Robert Fergusson was also fond of the
genre.

The text is that of the first printing (Kilmarnock,
1786).

❧

April 1st, 1785.

WHILE briers an' woodbines budding green,
An' Paitricks scraichan° loud at e'en,
And morning Poossie whiddan° seen,
        Inspire my Muse,
This freedom, in an *unknown* frien',
        I pray excuse.

On Fasteneen° we had a rockin,°
To ca' the crack° and weave our stockin;
And there was muckle° fun and jokin,
        Ye need na doubt;
At length we had a hearty yokin,°   10
        At *sang about.*°

There was ae° *sang*, amang the rest,
Aboon them a' it pleas'd me best,
That some kind husband had addrest,
        To some sweet wife:
It thirl'd° the heart-strings thro' the breast,
        A' to the life.

I've scarce heard ought describ'd sae weel,
What gen'rous, manly bosoms feel;   20
Thought I, "Can this be *Pope*, or *Steele*,
        Or *Beattie's* wark;"
They tald me 'twas an odd kind chiel°
        About *Muirkirk.*

It pat me fidgean-fain° to hear 't,
An' sae about him there I spier't;°
Then a' that kent him round declar'd,
        He had *ingine*,°
That nane excell'd it, few cam near 't,
        It was sae fine.   30

That set him° to a pint of ale,
An' either douse° or merry tale,
Or rhymes an' songs he'd made himsel,
        Or witty catches,
'Tween Inverness and Tiviotdale,
        He had few matches.

Then up I gat, an swoor an aith,
Tho' I should pawn my pleugh an' graith,°
Or die a cadger pownie's° death,
        At some dyke-back,°   40
A *pint* an' *gill* I'd gie them *baith*,
        To hear your crack.°

But first an' foremost, I should tell,
Amaist as soon as I could spell,
I to the *crambo-jingle*° fell,
        Tho' rude an' rough,
Yet crooning° to a body's sel,
        Does weel eneugh.

I am nae *Poet*, in a sense,
But just a *Rhymer* like by chance,   50
An' hae to Learning nae pretence,
        Yet, what the matter?
Whene'er my Muse does on me glance,
        I jingle at her.

EPISTLE TO J. L*****K. **2. Paitricks scraichan:** partridges
calling. **3. Poossie whiddan:** rabbit darting. **7. Fasteneen:**
Shrove Tuesday. **rockin:** sewing party. **8. ca' the crack:**
converse. **9. muckle:** much. **11. yokin:** set-to. **12. sang
about:** a diversion in which each member of the company
sings a song.

13. ae: one. **17. thirl'd:** thrilled. **23. chiel:** fellow. **25. pat me
fidgean-fain:** made me tingle. **26. spier't:** asked. **28. ingine:**
genius. **31. That set him:** that if you treated him. **32. douse:**
serious. **38. graith:** harness. **39. cadger pownie:** peddler's
pony. **40. At . . . dyke-back:** behind some wall. **42. crack:**
talk. **45. crambo-jingle:** doggerel rhyming. **47. crooning:**
humming.

Your Critic-folk may cock their nose,
And say, "How can you e'er propose,
You wha ken hardly *verse* frae *prose*,
    To mak a *sang?*"
But by your leaves, my learned foes,
    Ye're maybe wrang.   60

What's a' your jargon o' your Schools,
Your Latin names for horns an' stools;
If honest Nature made you *fools*,
    What sairs° your Grammars?
Ye'd better taen up *spades* and *shools*,°
    Or *knappin-hammers*.°

A set o' dull, conceited Hashes,°
Confuse their brains in *Colledge-classes!*
They *gang in* Stirks,° and *come out* Asses,
    Plain truth to speak;   70
An' syne° they think to climb Parnassus°
    By dint o' Greek!

Gie me ae° spark o' Nature's fire,
That's a' the learning I desire;
Then tho' I drudge thro' dub° an' mire
    At pleugh or cart,
My Muse, tho' hamely in attire,
    May touch the heart.

O for a spunk° o' ALLAN'S° glee,
Or FERGUSON'S,° the bauld an' slee,°   80
Or bright L*****K'S, my friend to be,
    If I can hit it!
That would be *lear*° eneugh for me,
    If I could get it.

Now, Sir, if ye hae friends enow,
Tho' *real friends* I b'lieve are few,
Yet, if your catalogue be fow,°
    I'se° no insist;
But gif ye want ae friend that's true,
    I'm on your list.   90

I winna blaw about *mysel,*
As ill I like my fauts to tell;
But friends an' folk that wish me well,
    They sometimes roose° me;
Tho' I maun own, as monie still,
    As far abuse me.

There's ae *wee faut* they whiles° lay to me,
I like the lasses—Gude forgie me!
For monie a Plack° they wheedle frae me,
    At dance or fair: 100
Maybe some *ither thing* they gie me
    They weel can spare.

But MAUCHLINE Race or MAUCHLINE Fair,
I should be proud to meet you there;
We'se° gie ae night's discharge to *care,*
    If we forgather,
An' hae a swap o' *rhymin-ware,*
    Wi' ane anither.

The *four-gill chap,*° we'se gar° him clatter,
An' kirs'n° him wi' reekin° water;   110
Syne we'll sit down an' tak our whitter,°
    To chear our heart;
An' faith, we'se be *acquainted* better
    Before we part.

Awa ye selfish, warly° race,
Wha think that havins,° sense an' grace,
Ev'n love an' friendship should give place
    To *catch-the-plack!*
I dinna like to see your face,
    Nor hear your crack.   120

But ye whom social pleasure charms,
Whose hearts the *tide of kindness* warms,
Who hold your *being* on the terms,
    "Each aid the others,"
Come to my bowl, come to my arms,
    My friends, my brothers!

But to conclude my lang epistle,
As my auld pen's worn to the grissle;
Twa lines frae you wad gar me fissle,°
    Who am, most fervent,   130
While I can either sing, or whistle,
    Your friend and servant.

ADDRESS TO THE UNCO GUID, OR THE RIGIDLY RIGHTEOUS

❧

The text is that of the first printing (Edinburgh, 1787).

❧

My Son, these maxims make a rule,
  And lump them ay thegither;
The Rigid Righteous *is a fool,*
  The Rigid Wise *anither:*
The cleanest corn that e'er was dight°
  May hae some pyles o' caff° in;
So ne'er a fellow-creature slight
  For random fits o' daffin.°
          SOLOMON.—Eccles. ch. vii. verse 16.

I.

O YE wha are sae guid yoursel,
  Sae pious and sae holy,
Ye've nought to do but mark and tell
  Your Neebours' fauts and folly!
Whase life is like a weel-gaun° mill,
  Supply'd wi' store o' water,
The heapet happer's° ebbing still,
  And still the clap° plays clatter.

II.

Hear me, ye venerable Core,°
  As counsel for poor mortals,   10
That frequent pass douce° Wisdom's door
  For glaikit° Folly's portals;
I, for their thoughtless, careless sakes,
  Would here propone° defences,
Their donsie° tricks, their black mistakes,
  Their failings and mischances.

III.

Ye see your state wi' their's compar'd,
  And shudder at the niffer,°
But cast a moment's fair regard,
  What maks the mighty differ;   20

IV.

Discount what scant occasion gave,
  That purity ye pride in,
And (what's aft mair than a' the lave°)
  Your better art o' hiding.

Think, when your castigated pulse
  Gies now and then a wallop,
What ragings must his veins convulse,
  That still eternal gallop:
Wi' wind and tide fair i' your tail,
  Right on ye scud your sea-way: 30
But, in the teeth o' baith to sail,
  It maks an unco° leeway.

V.

See Social life and Glee sit down,
  All joyous and unthinking,
Till, quite transmugrify'd,° they're grown
  Debauchery and Drinking:
O would they stay to calculate
  Th' eternal consequences;
Or your more dreaded h—ll to state,
  Damnation of expences!   40

VI.

Ye high, exalted, virtuous Dames,
  Ty'd up in godly laces,
Before ye gie poor *Frailty* names,
  Suppose a change o' cases;
A dear-lov'd lad, convenience snug,
  A treacherous inclination—
But, let me whisper i' your lug,°
  Ye're aiblins° nae temptation.

VII.

Then gently scan your brother Man,
  Still gentler sister woman;   50
Tho' they may gang a-kennin° wrang,
  To step aside is human:
One point must still be greatly dark,
  The moving *Why* they do it;
And just as lamely can ye mark,
  How far perhaps they rue it.

ADDRESS TO THE UNCO GUID. **dight:** sifted. **pyles o' caff:** grains of chaff. **daffin:** merriment. **5. weel-gaun:** well running. **7. heapet happer:** heaped hopper. **8. clap:** clapper. **9. Core:** company. **11. douce:** sober. **12. glaikit:** giddy. **14. propone:** set forth. **15. donsie:** stupid. **18. niffer:** exchange.

23. lave: rest. **32. unco:** extraordinary. **35. transmugrify'd:** transformed. **47. lug:** ear. **48. aiblins:** perhaps. **51. a-kennin:** a little bit.

VIII.

Who made the heart, 'tis *He* alone
    Decidedly can try us,
He knows each chord its various tone,
    Each spring its various bias: 60
Then at the balance let's be mute,
    We never can adjust it;
What's *done* we partly may compute,
    But know not what's *resisted*.

JOHN BARLEYCORN.
A BALLAD

As Burns explains in a footnote to the title, "This is
partly composed on the plan of an old song known by
the same name."
    The text is that of the first printing (Edinburgh, 1787).

I.

THERE was three kings into the east,
    Three kings both great and high,
And they hae sworn a solemn oath
    John Barleycorn should die.

II.

They took a plough and plough'd him down,
    Put clods upon his head,
And they hae sworn a solemn oath
    John Barleycorn was dead.

III.

But the chearful Spring came kindly on,
    And show'rs began to fall;   10
John Barleycorn got up again,
    And sore surpris'd them all.

IV.

The sultry suns of Summer came,
    And he grew thick and strong,
His head weel arm'd wi' pointed spears,
    That no one should him wrong.

V.

The sober Autumn enter'd mild,
    When he grew wan and pale;
His bending joints and drooping head
    Show'd he began to fail.   20

VI.

His colour sicken'd more and more,
    He faded into age;
And then his enemies began
    To show their deadly rage.

VII.

They've taen a weapon, long and sharp,
    And cut him by the knee;
Then ty'd him fast upon a cart,
    Like a rogue for forgerie.

VIII.

They laid him down upon his back,
    And cudgell'd him full sore;   30
They hung him up before the storm,
    And turn'd him o'er and o'er.

IX.

They filled up a darksome pit
    With water to the brim,
They heaved in John Barleycorn,
    There let him sink or swim.

X.

They laid him out upon the floor,
    To work him farther woe,
And still, as signs of life appear'd,
    They toss'd him to and fro.   40

XI.

They wasted, o'er a scorching flame,
    The marrow of his bones;
But a Miller us'd him worst of all,
    For he crush'd him between two stones.

XII.

And they hae taen his very heart's blood,
    And drank it round and round;
And still the more and more they drank,
    Their joy did more abound.

XIII.

John Barleycorn was a hero bold,
    Of noble enterprise,   50
For if you do but taste his blood,
    'Twill make your courage rise.

XIV.

'Twill make a man forget his woe;
    'Twill heighten all his joy:
'Twill make the widow's heart to sing,
    Tho' the tear were in her eye.

XV.
Then let us toast John Barleycorn,
  Each man a glass in hand;
And may his great posterity
  Ne'er fail in old Scotland!   60

TAM O' SHANTER

Burns wrote *Tam o' Shanter* for Captain Francis Grose, a roaming antiquary who found himself interested in the folklore connected with the old church at Alloway. When the second volume of Grose's *Antiquities of Scotland* was published in 1791, *Tam o' Shanter* appeared as a footnote to Grose's account of the church. The basic narrative of Tam's escape from the witch Nannie derives from a widely disseminated folk tale classifiable as "The Comic Wild Ride." Cowper's *John Gilpin* (1782) is perhaps related to the same folk source.

The text is that of the first printing, in *The Edinburgh Magazine* (March, 1791); we have incorporated the substantive variants from the Edinburgh edition of 1793.

Of Brownyis and of Bogillis° full is this buke.
                    GAWIN DOUGLAS.°

When chapman billies° leave the street,
And drouthy° neebors, neebors meet,
As market-days are wearing late,
And folk begin to tak the gate;°
While we sit bowsing at the nappy,°
And getting fou° and unco° happy,
We think na on the lang Scots miles,
The mosses,° waters, slaps° and stiles,
That lie between us and our hame,
Where sits our sulky, sullen dame,   10
Gathering her brows like gathering storm,
Nursing her wrath to keep it warm.—

This truth fand honest TAM O' SHANTER,
As he frae Ayr ae° night did canter;
(Auld Ayr, wham ne'er a town surpasses,
For honest men and bonnie lasses.)

O TAM! hadst thou but been sae wise,
As taen thy ain wife KATE's advice!
She tauld thee weel thou was a skellum,°
A bletherin,° blusterin, drunken blellum;°   20
That frae November till October,
Ae market-day thou was na sober;
That ilka melder,° wi' the Miller,
Thou sat as lang as thou had siller;°
That every naig was ca'd a shoe on,°
The Smith and thee gat roarin fou on;
That at the L——d's house, ev'n on Sunday,
Thou drank wi' Kirkton Jean° till Monday.—
She prophesied that, late or soon,
Thou wad be found deep drown'd in Doon;   30
Or catch'd wi' warlocks in the mirk,
By ALOWAY's auld, haunted kirk.—

Ah, gentle dames! it gars me greet,°
To think how mony counsels sweet,
How mony lengthen'd, sage advices,
The husband frae the wife despises!

But to our Tale: Ae market-night,
TAM had got planted unco right;
Fast by an ingle° bleezin finely,
Wi' reamin swats° that drank divinely;   40
And at his elbow, Souter° Johnie,
His ancient, trusty, drouthy crony,
TAM lo'ed him like a vera brither;
They had been fou for weeks the gither;—
The night drave on wi' sangs and clatter,
And ay the ale was growin better:
The Landlady and TAM grew gracious,
Wi' favors, secret, sweet, and precious;
The Souter tauld his queerest stories,
The Landlord's laugh was ready chorus: 50
The storm without might rair° and rustle,
TAM did na mind the storm a whistle.—

TAM O' SHANTER. **Bogillis:** bogles, bogymen. **Gawin Douglas:** Gavin Douglas (c. 1474–1522), Scottish poet, translator of Virgil's *Aeneid;* the quotation is line 18 of Douglas's Prologue to the sixth book of the *Aeneid.* **1. chapman billies:** peddler fellows. **2. drouthy:** thirsty. **4. gate:** road. **5. nappy:** ale. **6. fou:** full, drunk. **unco:** wonderfully. **8. mosses:** bogs. **slaps:** gaps in walls.

14. ae: one. **19. skellum:** rascal. **20. bletherin:** chattering. **blellum:** babbler. **23. ilka melder:** every meal-grinding time. **24. siller:** money. **25. That . . . on:** that every time a horse was shod. **28. Kirkton Jean:** a woman who kept a tavern in Ayr. **33. gars me greet:** makes me weep. **39. ingle:** fireplace. **40. reamin swats:** foaming new ale. **41. Souter:** cobbler. **51. rair:** roar.

Care, mad to see a man sae happy,
E'en drown'd himsel amang the nappy;
As bees flee hame wi' lades o' treasure,
The minutes wing'd their way wi' pleasure:
Kings may be blest, but TAM was glorious,
O'er a' the ills o' life victorious!

But Pleasures are like poppies spread,
You seize the flower, its bloom is shed;   60
Or like the snow falls in the river,
A moment white—then melts for ever;
Or like the borealis race,
That flit ere you can point their place;
Or like the rainbow's lovely form,
Evanishing amid the storm.—
Nae man can tether Time or Tide,
The hour approaches, TAM maun ride;
That hour, o' night's black arch the key-stane,°
That dreary hour he mounts his beast in,   70
And sic° a night he taks the road in,
As ne'er poor Sinner was abroad in.—

The wind blew as 'twad° blawn its last,
The rattling showers rose on the blast;
The speedy gleams the darkness swallow'd,
Loud, deep, and lang, the thunder bellow'd:
That night, a child might understand
The Deil had business on his hand.—

Weel mounted on his gray meare, Meg,
A better never lifted leg,   80
TAM skelpit° on thro' dub° and mire,
Despising wind, and rain, and fire;
Whiles hadding fast° his gude blue bonnet;
Whiles crooning o'er some auld Scots sonnet;
Whiles glowring round wi' prudent cares,
Lest bogles catch him unawares;
KIRK-ALOWAY was drawing nigh,
Where ghaists and houlets° nightly cry.—

By this time he was cross the ford,
Where in the snaw the chapman smoor'd;°   90
And past the birks and meikle stane,°
Whare drunken Charlie brak's neck-bane;
And thro' the whins° and by the cairn,°
Where hunters fand the murder'd bairn;

And near the thorn, aboon° the well,
Whare Mungo's mither hang'd hersel.—
Before him Doon pours all his floods;
The doubling storm roars thro' the woods;
The lightenings flash from pole to pole;
Near and more near the thunders roll: 100
When, glimmering thro' the groaning trees,
KIRK-ALOWAY seem'd in a bleeze;°
Thro' ilka bore° the gleams were glancing,
And loud resounded mirth and dancing.—

Inspiring, bold John Barleycorn,
What dangers thou canst make us scorn!
Wi' Tippenny,° we fear nae evil;
Wi' Usquabae,° we'll face the Devil!
The swats sae ream'd in TAMMIE's noddle,
Fair-play, he car'd na deils a boddle;°   110
But Maggie stood, right sair astonish'd,
Till by the heel and hand admonish'd,
She ventur'd forward on the light,
And, vow! TAM saw an unco sight!
Warlocks and witches in a dance,
Nae cotillion brent° new frae France,
But hornpipes, jigs, strathspeys and reels,
Put life and mettle in their heels.—
At winnock-bunker° in the east,
There sat auld Nick in shape o' beast;   120
A touzie tyke,° black, grim and large,
To gie them music was his charge:
He screw'd the pipes and gart them skirl,°
Till roof and rafters a' did dirl.°—
Coffins stood round like open presses,°
That shaw'd the Dead in their last dresses,
And (by some devilish cantraip slight°)
Each in its cauld hand held a light.—
By which heroic TAM was able
To note upon the haly table,°   130
A murderer's banes in gibbet-airns;°
Twa span-lang,° wee, unchristen'd bairns;

---

69. **That . . . key-stane**: midnight. **71. sic**: such. **73.
'twad**: it would have. **81. skelpit**: hurried. **dub**: puddles.
83. hadding fast: holding tight. **88. houlets**: owls. **90.
smoor'd**: smothered. **91. birks . . . stane**: birches and large
stone. **93. whins**: furze, gorse. **cairn**: pile of stones.

95. **aboon**: above. 102. **bleeze**: blaze of light. 103. **ilka bore**:
every chink. 107. **Tippenny**: twopenny ale. 108. **Usquabae**:
whisky. 110. **Fair-play . . . boddle**: Given fair play, he
cared not a farthing for devils. 116. **brent**: brand. 119. **At
winnock-bunker**: on a window seat. 121. **touzie tyke**:
shaggy dog. 123. **gart . . . skirl**: made them squeal. 124.
dirl: resound. 125. **presses**: wardrobe cupboards. 127.
cantraip slight: magic trick. 130. **haly table**: altar. 131.
banes in gibbet-airns: bones in gibbet irons. 132. **span-
lang**: as long as the distance from the tip of the thumb to the
tip of the outstretched little finger.

A thief, new cutted frae a rape,°
Wi' his last gasp his gab° did gape;
Five tomahawks wi' blude red-rusted;
Five scimitars wi' murder crusted;
A garter which a babe had strangled;
A knife a father's throat had mangled,
Whom his ain son of life bereft,
The grey hairs yet stack to the heft;   140
With mair o' horrible and awfu',
Which ev'n to name wad be unlawfu'.°

    As TAMMIE glowr'd, amaz'd and curious,
The mirth and fun grew fast and furious:
The Piper loud and louder blew;
The Dancers quick and quicker flew,
They reel'd, they set, they cross'd, they cleekit,°
Till ilka Carlin swat and reekit,°
And coost her dudies to the wark,°
And linket at° it in her sark°!   150

    Now TAM, O TAM! had they been queans°
A' plump and strappin in their teens;
Their sarks, instead o' creeshie flainen,°
Been snaw-white, seventeen-hunder° linen!
Thir breeks° o' mine, my only pair,
That ance were plush o' gude blue hair,
I wad hae gien them aff my hurdies,°
For ae blink o' the bonnie burdies°!

    But wither'd beldams, auld and droll,
Rigwoodie° hags wad spean° a foal,   160
Loupin and flingin on a crummock,°
I wonder didna turn thy stomach.—
But TAM kend° what was what fu' brawly,°
There was ae winsome wench and walie,°
That night enlisted in the core °

133. **rape**: rope. 134. **gab**: mouth. 142. **unlawfu'**: After this line the following passage appeared in the first edition:

    Three Lawyers' tongues, turn'd inside out,
    Wi' lies seam'd like a beggar's clout;
    Three Priests' hearts, rotton, black as muck,
    Lay stinking, vile, in every neuk.—

147. **cleekit**: linked themselves. 148. **ilka . . . reekit**: every old woman sweated and steamed. 149. **coost . . . wark**: threw off her rags in order to dance easier. 150. **linket at**: tripped. **sark**, shift, slip. 151. **queans**: young women. 153. **creeshie flainen**: greasy flannel. 154. **seventeen-hunder**: finely woven. 155. **Thir breeks**: those breeches. 157. **hurdies**: buttocks. 158. **blink . . . burdies**: glimpse of the pretty damsels. 160. **Rigwoodie**: deformed. **spean**: wean. 161. **Loupin . . . crummock**: leaping and kicking with a crooked staff. 163. **kend**: knew. **brawly**: well. 164. **walie**: comely. 165. **core**: company.

(Lang after kend on Carrick shore;
For mony a beast to dead she shot,
And perish'd mony a bonny boat,
And shook baith meikle corn and bear,°
And kept the country-side in fear—)   170
Her cutty sark° o' Paisley harn,°
That while a lassie she had worn,
In longitude tho' sorely scanty,
It was her best, and she was vaunty.°—
Ah! little kenn'd thy reverend Grannie,
That sark she coft° for her wee Nannie,
Wi' twa pund Scots, ('twas a' her riches)
Wad ever grac'd a dance o' witches!

    But here my Muse her wing maun cour,°
Sic flights are far beyond her power;   180
To sing how Nannie lap and flang,
(A souple jad she was and strang)
And how TAM stood like ane bewitch'd,
And thought his vera een° enrich'd;
Even Satan glowr'd, and fidg'd fu' fain,°
And hotch'd,° and blew wi' might and main:
Till first ae caper—syne anither—
TAM tint° his reason a' thegither,
And roars out, "Weel done, Cutty-sark!"
And in an instant all was dark: 190
And scarcely had he Maggie rallied,
When out the hellish legion sallied.—

    As bees biz out wi' angry fyke,°
When plundering herds° assail their byke;°
As open pussie's° mortal foes
When, pop, she starts before their nose;
As eager rins the market-croud,
When "Catch the thief!" resounds aloud;
So Maggie rins, the witches follow,
Wi' monie an eldrich° skreech and hollow.—   200

    Ah TAM! ah TAM! thou'll get thy fairin°!
In hell they'll roast you like a herrin!
In vain thy KATE awaits thy comin!
KATE soon will be a woefu' woman!!!
Now do thy speedy utmost, Meg,
And win the key-stane o' the brig;°

169. **shook . . . bear**: ruined much of both the corn and barley. 171. **cutty sark**: short shift. **harn**: cloth. 174. **vaunty**: proud of it. 176. **coft**: bought. 179. **cour**: curb. 184. **een**: eyes. 185. **glowr'd . . . fain**: stared and fidgeted fondly. 186. **hotch'd**: hitched. 188. **tint**: lost. 193. **fyke**: fuss. 194. **herds**: shepherds. **byke**: hive. 195. **pussie**: rabbit. 200. **eldrich**: ghastly. 201. **fairin**: reward. 206. **brig**: bridge.

There at them thou thy tail may toss,
A running stream they dare na cross;°
But ere the key-stane she could make,
The fient° a tail she had to shake!   210
For Nannie, far before the rest,
Hard upon noble Maggie prest,
And flew at TAM wi' furious ettle,°
But little wist she Maggie's mettle:
Ae spring brought off her Master hale,
But left behind her ain grey tail;
The Carlin claught° her by the rump,
And left poor Maggie scarce a stump.—

Now, wha this tale o' truth shall read,
Ilk man and mother's son tak heed: 220
Whene'er to Drink, you are inclin'd,
Or Cutty Sarks rin in your mind,
Think, ye may buy the joys o'er dear;
Remember TAM O' SHANTER'S Meare.

THE JOLLY BEGGARS.
A CANTATA

This burlesque cantata was not published during
Burns's lifetime. At one point, worried about the
security of his job in the Excise, he even affected to have
forgotten he had written it. As he once wrote in his
commonplace book, "I have often courted the acquaintance of that part of mankind known by the ordinary
phrase of 'blackguards,' sometimes further than was
consistent with the safety of my character." The work
is related to Gay's *Beggar's Opera* (1728) and perhaps
derives more directly from Allan Ramsay's *Merry
Beggars* (1724).

The text is that of the first printing, in Stewart and
Meikle's Poetical Miscellany Series (1799); we have
added lines 92–127, omitted in the first printing, from
the version in Thomas Stewart's *Poems Ascribed to
Robert Burns* (1802).

208. **A running . . . cross:** [Burns's note] It is a well
known fact that witches, or any evil spirits, have no power
to follow a poor wight any farther than the middle of the
next rushing stream.—It may be proper likewise to mention
to the benighted traveller, that when he falls in with *bogles*,
whatever danger may be in his going forward, there is much
more hazard in turning back. **210. fient:** devil. **213. ettle:**
intent. **217. Carlin claught:** old woman seized.

RECITATIVO.

WHEN lyart leaves bestrow the yird,°
Or wavering like the Bauckie bird,°
Bedim cauld Boreas' blast;
When hailstanes drive wi' bitter skyte,°
And infant frosts begin to bite,
In hoary cranreuch° drest;
Ae night at e'en a merry core°
O' randie, gangrel bodies,°
In Poosie-Nansie's° held the splore,°
To drink their orra duddies:°   10
    Wi' quaffing and laughing,
        They ranted and they sang;
    Wi' jumping and thumping,
        The vera girdle° rang.

First, neist° the fire, in auld red rags,°
Ane sat; weel brac'd wi' mealy bags,
And knapsack a' in order;
His doxy° lay within his arm,
Wi' usquebae° an' blankets warm,
She blinket on° her sodger: 20
An' ay° he gies the tozie° drab
The tither skelpin° kiss,
While she held up her greedy gab°
Just like an aumous dish.°
    Ilk° smack still, did crack still,
        Just like a cadger's° whip,
    Then staggering and swaggering
        He roar'd this ditty up—

AIR.
Tune—*Soldier's Joy.*

I.

I am a son of Mars who have been in many wars,
And show my cuts and scars wherever I come;   30
This here was for a wench, and that other in a trench,
When welcoming the French at the sound of the drum.
            Lal de daudle, &c.

THE JOLLY BEGGARS. **1. lyart . . . yird:** withered leaves
bestrew the ground. **2. Bauckie bird:** [Burns's note]
The old Scotch name for the Bat. **4. skyte:** lash. **6.
cranreuch:** hoarfrost. **7. core:** company. **8. randie . . .
bodies:** lawless vagrants. **9. Poosie-Nansie's:** a tavern
in Mauchline. **splore:** spree. **10. drink . . . duddies:** sell
their extra clothes for drink. **14. girdle:** griddle. **15. neist:**
next to. **red rags:** the remains of a soldier's uniform. **18.
doxy:** low girlfriend. **19. usquebae:** whisky. **20. blinket
on:** leered at. **21. ay:** constantly. **tozie:** tipsy. **22. skelpin:**
smacking. **23. gab:** mouth. **24. aumous dish:** alms basin. **25.
Ilk:** each. **26. cadger:** peddler.

II.

My prenticeship I past where my leader breath'd his
  last,
When the bloody die was cast on the heights of
  Abram;°
I served out my trade when the gallant game was
  play'd,
And the Moro° low was laid at the sound of the drum.
                                Lal de daudle, &c.

III.

I lastly was with Curtis,° among the floating batt'ries,
And there I left for witness, an arm and a limb;   40
Yet let my country need me, with Elliot° to head me,
I'd clatter on my stumps at the sound of a drum.
                                Lal de daudle, &c.

IV.

And now tho' I must beg, with a wooden arm and leg,
And many a tatter'd rag hanging over my bum,
I'm as happy with my wallet, my bottle and my
  callet,°
As when I us'd in scarlet to follow a drum.
                                Lal de daudle, &c.

V.

What tho' with hoary locks, I must stand the winter
  shocks,
Beneath the woods and rocks oftentimes for a home, 50
When the tother bag° I sell, and the tother bottle tell,
I could meet a troop of hell, at the sound of the drum.
                                Lal de daudle, &c.

RECITATIVO.

He ended; and the kebars sheuk,°
  Aboon° the chorus roar;
While frighted rattons° backward leuk,
  And seek the benmost bore:°
A fairy° fiddler frae the neuk,°
  He skirl'd° out encore!
But up arose the martial chuck,°   60
  And laid° the loud uproar.

35. **heights of Abram:** The Heights of Abraham, near
Quebec, was the site of a British battle with the French in
1759. 37. **the Moro:** Morro Castle in Havana, captured by
the British in 1762. 39. **Curtis:** Admiral Sir Roger Curtis
(1746–1816), who led the force that destroyed the French floating batteries of artillery at Gibraltar in 1782. 41. **Elliot:**
General George Augustus Eliott (1717–90). 46. **callet:** whore.
51. **tother bag:** of oatmeal. 54. **kebars sheuk:** rafters
shook. 55. **Aboon:** over. 56. **rattons:** rats. 57. **benmost
bore:** farthest hole. 58. **fairy:** tiny. **neuk:** corner. 59. **skirl'd:**
squeaked. 60. **chuck:** darling. 61. **laid:** quieted.

AIR.

Tune—Soldier Laddie.

I.

I once was a maid, tho' I cannot tell when,
And still my delight is in proper° young men;
Some one of a troop of dragoons was my daddie,
No wonder I'm fond of a sodger laddie.
                                Sing, Lal de lal, &c.

II.

The first of my loves was a swaggering blade,
To rattle the thundering drum was his trade;
His leg was so tight, and his cheek was so ruddy,
Transported I was with my sodger laddie.   70
                                Sing, Lal de lal, &c.

III.

But the godly old chaplain left him in the lurch,
The sword I forsook for the sake of the church;
He ventur'd the *soul*, and I risked the *body*,
'Twas then I prov'd false to my sodger laddie.
                                Sing, Lal de lal, &c.

IV.

Full soon I grew sick of my sanctified sot,
The regiment at large for a husband I got;
From the gilded spontoon,° to the fife I was ready,
I asked no more but a sodger laddie.   80
                                Sing, Lal de lal, &c.

V.

But the peace° it reduc'd me to beg in despair,
Till I met my old boy at a Cunningham fair;
His *rags regimental* they flutter'd so gaudy,
My heart it rejoic'd at my sodger laddie.
                                Sing, Lal de lal, &c.

VI.

And now I have lived—I know not how long,
And still I can join in a cup or a song;
But whilst with both hands I can hold the glass steady,
Here's to thee, my hero, my sodger laddie.   90
                                Sing, Lal de lal, &c.

RECITATIVO.

Poor Merry Andrew in the neuk,
  Sat *guzling* wi' a tinkler *hizzie;*°
They mind't na wha the chorus took,
  Between themselves they were sae busy.

63. **proper:** handsome. 79. **spontoon:** pike carried by
infantry officers. 82. **the peace:** of 1783. 93. **tinkler hizzie:**
tinker wench.

At length wi' drink and courting dizzy,
   He stoiter'd° up an' made a face;
Then turn'd an' laid a smack on Grizzy,
   Syne tun'd his pipes wi' grave grimace.

AIR.

Tune—*Auld Sir Symon.*

Sir Wisdom's a fool when he's fou,   100
   Sir Knave is a fool in a session;°
He's there but a prentice I trow,
   But I am a fool by profession.

My Grannie she bought me a beuk,
   An' I held awa° to the school;
I fear I my talent misteuk,
   But what will ye hae of a fool.

For drink I would venture my neck,
   A hizzie's the half of my craft;
But what could ye other expect   110
   Of ane that's avowedly daft.

I ance was ty'd up like a stirk,°
   For civilly swearing an' quaffing;
I ance was abus'd i' the kirk,
   For towzing° a lass i' my daffin.°

Poor Andrew that tumbles for sport,
   Let naebody name wi' a jeer;
There's ev'n, I'm tauld i' the court,
   A *Tumbler* ca'd the *Premier.*

Observ'd ye yon *reverend* lad   120
   Mak faces to tickle the mob;
He rails at our mountebank squad,
   It's *rivalship* just i' the job.

And now my conclusion I'll tell,
   For faith I'm confoundedly dry,
The chiel° that's a fool for himsel,
   Guid L——d, he's far dafter than I.

RECITATIVO.

Then neist outspak a raucle carlin,°
Wha kent fu' weel to cleek the sterling,°
For mony a pursie she had hooked,   130
And had in mony a well been ducked.

Her dove° had been a Highland laddie,
But weary fa' the waefu woodie°!
Wi' sighs and sobs she thus began
To wail her braw° John Highlandman.

AIR.

Tune—*O an ye were dead gudeman.*

I.

A Highland lad my love was born,
The Lalland° laws he held in scorn;
But he still was faithfu' to his clan,
My gallant, braw John Highlandman.

CHORUS.

Sing, hey my braw John Highlandman!   140
Sing, ho my braw John Highlandman!
There's not a lad in a' the lan'
Was match for my John Highlandman.

II.

With his philibeg° an' tartan plaid,
An' gude claymore° down by his side,
The ladies' hearts he did trepan,°
My gallant, braw John Highlandman.

                Sing, hey, &c.

III.

We ranged a' from Tweed to Spey,
An' liv'd like lords and ladies gay;   150
For a Lalland face he feared none,
My gallant, braw John Highlandman.

                Sing, hey, &c.

IV.

They banish'd him beyond the sea,
But ere the bud was on the tree,
Adown my cheeks the pearls ran,
Embracing my John Highlandman.

                Sing, hey, &c.

V.

But, och! they catch'd him at the last,
And bound him in a dungeon fast;   160
My curse upon them every one,
They've hang'd my braw John Highlandman.

                Sing, hey, &c.

---

97. stoiter'd: struggled. **101. session:** law court. **105. held awa:** went off. **112. stirk:** young bullock. **115. towzing:** rumpling. **daffin:** fun. **126. chiel:** fellow. **128. raucle carlin:** sturdy old woman. **129. cleek the sterling:** steal the cash.

132. dove: The manuscripts read: "love." **133. weary . . . woodie:** a plague upon the woeful gallows. **135. braw:** handsome. **137. Lalland:** lowland. **144. philibeg:** kilt. **145. claymore:** sword. **146. trepan:** ensnare.

VI.

And now a widow, I must mourn
The pleasures that will ne'er return;
No comfort but a hearty can,°
When I think on John Highlandman.

Sing, hey, &c.

RECITATIVO.

A pigmy scraper wi' his fiddle,
Wha us'd to trysts° and fairs to driddle,°   170
Her strappan limb and gausy° middle
He reach'd nae higher,
Had hol'd his heartie like a riddle,°
An' blawn 't° on fire.

Wi' hand on haunch,° and upward e'e,
He croon'd his gamut, one, two, three,
Then in an Arioso° key,
The wee Apollo
Set off wi' *Allegretto* glee
His giga° solo.   180

AIR.

Tune—*Whistle owre the lave o't.*

I.

Let me ryke up to dight° that tear,
An' go wi' me to be my dear,
An' then your every care and fear
May whistle owre the lave° o't.

CHORUS.

I am a fiddler to my trade,
An' a' the tunes that e'er I play'd,
The sweetest still to wife or maid,
Was whistle owre the lave o't.

II.

At kirns° and weddings we'se° be there,
An' O! sae nicely's we will fare;   190
We'll bouse about till daddie care,
Sing, whistle owre the lave o't.

I am, &c.

III.

Sae merrily the banes we'll pyke,°
An' sun oursels about the dyke,°
An' at our leisure when ye like,
We'll whistle owre the lave o't.

I am, &c.

IV.

But bless me wi' your heaven o' charms,
And while I kittle hair on thairms,°   200
Hunger, cauld, an' a' sic harms,
May whistle owre the lave o't.

I am, &c.

RECITATIVO.

Her charms had struck a sturdy Caird,°
As weel as poor Gutscraper;
He taks the fiddler by the beard,
And draws a roosty rapier.—
He swoor by a' was swearing worth,
To speet him like a pliver,°
Unless he wou'd from that time forth,   210
Relinquish her for ever.
Wi' ghastly e'e, poor tweedle-dee
Upon his hunkers° bended,
And pray'd for grace wi' ruefu' face,
An' so the quarrel ended.
But tho' his little heart did grieve,
When round the tinker prest her,
He feign'd to snirtle° in his sleeve,
When thus the Caird address'd her.

AIR.

Tune—*Clout the caudron.*

I.

My bonny lass I work in brass,   220
A tinker is my station;
I've travell'd round all Christian ground
In this my occupation.
I've taen the gold, I've been enroll'd
In many a noble squadron;
But vain they search'd, when off I march'd
To go an' clout° the caudron.

I've taen the gold, &c.

---

166. can: of ale. **170. trysts:** markets. **driddle:** toddle.
171. gausy: buxom. **173. hol'd . . . riddle:** pierced his
heart like a sieve. **174. blawn 't:** blown it. **175. haunch:**
hip. **177. Arioso:** like an aria. **180. giga:** Italian for *jig*. **181.
ryke . . . dight:** reach up to wipe. **184. lave:** rest. **189.
kirns:** harvest celebrations. **we'se:** we'll.

194. banes . . . pyke: bones we'll pick. **195. dyke:** fence.
200. kittle . . . thairms: tickle hair on catgut. **204. Caird:**
tinker. **209. speet . . . pliver:** spit him like a plover. **213.
hunkers:** haunches. **218. snirtle:** snigger. **227. clout:** patch.

II.

Despise that shrimp, that wither'd imp,
  Wi' a' his noise an' caprin',   230
An' tak a share wi' those that bear
  The *budget*° an' the *apron*.
An' *by* that stowp°! my faith an' houpe,
  An' *by* that dear Keilbagie,°
If e'er ye want, or meet wi' scant,
  May I ne'er weet my craigie.°

               An' by that stowp, &c.

RECITATIVO.

The Caird prevail'd—the unblushing fair
  In his embraces sunk,
Partly wi' love o'ercome sae sair,   240
  An' partly she was drunk.
Sir Violino with an air,
  That show'd a man of spunk,
Wish'd *unison* between the pair,
  An' made the bottle clunk°
          To their health that night.

But hurchin° Cupid shot a shaft
  That play'd a dame a shavie,°
The fiddler rak'd her fore and aft,
  Behint the chicken cavie.°   250
Her lord, a wight o' Homer's craft,°
  Tho' limping wi' the spavie,°
He hirpl'd° up, an' lap like daft,°
  An' shor'd° them Dainty Davie°
         O' boot° that night.

He was a care-defying blade
  As ever Bacchus listed,°
Tho' Fortune sair upon him laid,
  His heart she ever miss'd it.
He had no wish but—to be glad,   260
  Nor want but—when he thirsted;
He hated nought but—to be sad,
  And thus the muse suggested
         His sang that night.

AIR.

Tune—*For a' that, an' a' that.*

I.

I am a bard of no regard,
  Wi' gentle folks an' a' that;
But *Homer-like*, the glowran byke,°
  Frae town to town I draw that.

CHORUS.

  For a' that, an' a' that,
    An' twice as muckle's° a' that;   270
  I've lost but ane, I've twa behin',
    I've *wife enough* for a' that.

II.

I never drank the Muses' stank,°
  Castalia's burn,° an' a' that;
But there it streams, and richly reams,°
  My *Helicon*° I ca' that.

             For a' that, &c.

III.

Great love I bear to a' the fair,
  Their humble slave an' a' that;
But lordly will, I hold it still   280
  A mortal sin to thraw° that.

             For a' that, &c.

IV.

In raptures sweet, this hour we meet,
  Wi' mutual love an' a' that;
But for how lang the *flie may stang*,°
  Let *inclination* law° that.

             For a' that, &c.

V.

Their tricks and craft have put me daft,
  They've ta'en me in, an' a' that;
But clear the decks, an' here's the *sex*!   290
  I like the jads for a' that.

    For a' that, an' a' that,
      An' twice as muckle's a' that;
    My *dearest bluid*, to do them guid,
      They're welcome till 't° for a' that.

---

232. budget: tool bag. **233. stowp:** ale mug. **234. Keilbagie:** [Burns's note] A peculiar sort of whisky so called: a great favourite with Poosie-Nansie's clubs. **236. weet my craigie:** wet my throat. **245. clunk:** gurgle. **247. hurchin:** urchin. **248. shavie:** trick. **250. cavie:** coop. **251. Homer's craft:** [Burns's note] Homer is allowed to be the oldest ballad singer on record. **252. the spavie:** a sprain. **253. hirpl'd:** hobbled. **lap . . . daft:** leapt like mad. **254. shor'd:** offered. **Dainty Davie:** title of a ballad. **255. O' boot:** without charge, gratis. **257. listed:** enlisted.

267. glowran byke: staring crowd. **270. muckle's:** much as. **273. stank:** pool. **274. burn:** brook. **275. reams:** foams. **276. Helicon:** the classical mountain sacred to the Muses. **281. thraw:** thwart. **285. flie may stang:** fly may sting. **286. law:** decide. **295. till 't:** to it.

RECITATIVO.

So sung the bard—and Nansie's waws°
Shook with a thunder of applause,
  Re-echo'd from each mouth;
They toom'd their pocks, an' pawn'd their duds,°
They scarcely left to coor their fuds,°   300
  To quench their lowan drouth.°

Then owre again, the jovial thrang,
  The poet did request
To lowse his pack an' wale° a sang,
  A ballad o' the best:

    He, rising, rejoicing
      Between his twa *Deborahs*,
    Looks round him, an' found them
      Impatient for the chorus.

AIR.

Tune—*Jolly mortals fill your glasses.*

I.

See! the smoking bowl before us,   310
  Mark our jovial ragged ring!
Round and round take up the chorus,
  And in raptures let us sing.

CHORUS.

  A fig for those by law protected!
    Liberty's a glorious feast!
  Courts for cowards were erected,
    Churches built to please the priest.

II.

What is title? what is treasure?
  What is reputation's care?
If we lead a life of pleasure,   320
  'Tis no matter *how* or *where*!

          A fig, &c.

III.

With the ready trick and fable,
  Round we wander all the day;
And at night, in barn or stable,
  Hug our doxies on the hay.

          A fig, &c.

296. waws: walls. **299. toom'd . . . duds:** emptied their
bags and sold their spare clothes. **300. coor . . . fuds:** cover
their behinds. **301. lowan drouth:** burning thirst. **304.
wale:** choose.

IV.

Does the train-attended *carriage*
  Through the country lighter rove?
Does the sober bed of marriage   330
  Witness brighter scenes of love?

          A fig, &c.

V.

Life is all a *variorum*,
  We regard not how it goes;
Let them cant about *decorum*
  Who have characters to lose.

          A fig, &c.

VI.

Here's to budgets, bags and wallets!
  Here's to all the wandering train!
Here's our ragged *brats* and *callets*!   340
  One and all cry out, Amen!

    A fig for those by law protected!
      Liberty's a glorious feast!
    Courts for cowards were erected,
      Churches built to please the priest.

HOLY WILLIE'S PRAYER: A POEM

"Willie" was William Fisher (1737–1809), one of the
elders of the kirk at Mauchline. As Burns explains:

> Holy Willie . . . was much and justly famed for
> that polemical chattering which ends in tippling
> orthodoxy, and for that spiritualized bawdry which
> refines to liquorish devotion. In a sessional process
> [a case in the church court] with . . . Mr. Gavin
> Hamilton [Burns's landlord, who had responded
> impudently when censured by the kirk session for
> his minor backslidings] . . . *Holy Willie* and his
> priest, Father Auld, after full hearing in the Pres-
> bytery of Ayr, came off but second best, owing
> partly to the oratorical powers of Mr. Robert
> Aiken, Mr. Hamilton's counsel; but chiefly to Mr.
> Hamilton's being one of the most irreproachable
> and truly respectable characters in the country. On
> losing his process, the muse overheard him at his
> devotions, as follows.

Although the poem was never officially published during
Burns's lifetime, it did circulate around Ayrshire in

manuscript and in an unauthorized pamphlet. Burns later recalled that it "alarmed the kirk-Session so much that they held three several meetings to look over their holy artillery, if any of it was pointed against profane Rhymers." Most of the manuscripts have as an epigraph Pope's "And send the godly in a pet to pray" (*The Rape of the Lock*, iv. 64).

The text is that of the first printing, in Stewart and Meikle's Poetical Miscellany Series (1799). The reading of line 94 is that of the manuscripts.

❦

O THOU, wha in the heavens dost dwell,
Wha, as it pleases best thysel',
Sends ane to heaven and ten to hell,
    A' for thy glory,
And no for any guid or ill
    They've done afore thee!

I bless and praise thy matchless might,
Whan thousands thou hast left in night,
That I am here afore thy sight,
    For gifts an' grace,   10
A burnin' an' a shinin' light,
    To a' this place.

What was I, or my generation,°
That I should get such exaltation,
I wha deserve sic° just damnation,
    For broken laws,
Five thousand years 'fore my creation,
    Thro' Adam's cause.

When frae my mither's womb I fell,
Thou might hae plunged me in hell,   20
To gnash my gums, to weep and wail,
    In burnin' lake,
Whar damned devils roar and yell,
    Chain'd to a stake.

Yet I am here a chosen sample,
To show thy grace is great an' ample;
I'm here a pillar in thy temple,
    Strong as a rock,
A guide, a buckler an' example
    To a' thy flock.   30

But yet, O L——d! confess I must,
At times I'm fash'd° wi' fleshly lust;
An' sometimes too, wi' warldly trust
    Vile self gets in;
But thou remembers we are dust,
    Defil'd in sin.

O L——d! yestreen, thou kens,° wi' Meg,
Thy pardon I sincerely beg,
O! may it ne'er be a livin' plague
    To my dishonour,   40
An' I'll ne'er lift a lawless l——g
    Again upon her.

Besides, I farther maun allow,
Wi' Lizie's lass, three times I trow;°
But, L——d, that Friday I was fow,°
    When I came near her,
Or else, thou kens, thy *servant true*,
    Wad ne'er hae steer'd° her.

Maybe thou lets this *fleshly thorn*
Beset thy servant e'en and morn,   50
Lest he owre high and proud shou'd turn,
    'Cause he's sae *gifted;*
If sae, thy han' maun e'en be born,
    Until thou lift it.

L——d bless thy chosen in this place,
For *here* thou hast a *chosen race;*
But G——d confound their stubborn face,
    And blast their name,
Wha bring thy elders to disgrace
    An' public shame.   60

L——d mind G——n H——n's deserts,
He drinks, an' swears, an' plays at carts,
Yet has sae mony takin'° arts,
    Wi' grit an' sma',
Frae G——d's ain priest the people's hearts
    He steals awa'.

An' whan we chasten'd him therefore,
Thou kens how he bred sic a splore,°
As set the warld in a roar
    O' laughin' at us;   70
Curse thou his basket and his store,
    Kail an' potatoes.

HOLY WILLIE'S PRAYER. **13. generation:** begetting. **15. sic:** such.

32. fash'd: troubled. **37. kens:** knows. **44. trow:** believe. **45. fow:** drunk. **48. steer'd:** molested. **63. takin':** persuasive. **68. splore:** revel.

L——d hear my earnest cry an' pray'r,
Against that presbyt'ry o' Ayr;
Thy strong right hand, L——d make it bare,
    Upo' their heads,
L——d weigh it down, and dinna spare,
    For their misdeeds.

O L——d my G——d, that glib-tongu'd A——n,
My very heart an' saul are quakin',   80
To think how we stood sweatin' shakin',
    An' p——d wi' dread,
While he, wi' hingin' lips and snakin'°
    Held up his head.

L——d in the day of vengeance try him,
L——d visit them wha did employ him,
An' pass not in thy mercy by 'em,
    Nor hear their pray'r;
But for thy people's sake destroy 'em,
    And dinna spare.   90

But, L——d remember me and mine
Wi' mercies temp'ral and divine,
That I for gear° and grace may shine,
    Excell'd by nane,°
An' a' the glory shall be thine,
    Amen, Amen!

SKETCH

James Currie, in his Burns edition of 1800, titled this
poem *Poem on Pastoral Poetry*, by which it has been
known. It was found among Burns's papers after his
death and is apparently unfinished.
    The text is that of the manuscript transcription by
Davidson Cook in *The Burns Chronicle* (1927).

Hail, Poesie! thou nymph reserv'd!
In chase o' thee, what crowds hae swerv'd
Frae Common Sense, or sunk ennerv'd
    'Mang heaps o' clavers;°
And Och! o'er aft° thy joes° hae starv'd
    'Mid a' thy favors!

Say, Lassie, why thy train amang,
While loud the trumps heroic clang,
And Sock and buskin skelp° alang
    To death or marriage;   10
Scarce ane has tried the Shepherd-sang
    But wi' miscarriage?

In Homer's craft Jock Milton thrives;
Eschylus' pen Will Shakespeare drives;
Wee Pope, the knurlin,° 'till him rives°
    Horatian fame;
In thy sweet sang, Barbauld,° survives
    E'en Sappho's flame.

But thee, Theocritus,° wha matches?
They're no' Herd's ballats, Maro's catches;°   20
Squire Pope but busks his skinklin° patches
    O' Heathen tatters:
I pass by hunders,° nameless wretches,
    That ape their betters.

In this braw° age o' wit and lear,°
Will nane the Shepherd's whistle mair
Blaw sweetly in his native air
    And rural grace;
And wi' the far-fam'd Grecian share
    A rival place?   30

Yes! there is ane; a Scotish callan°!
There's ane: come forrit, honest Allan°!
Thou need na jouk behint the hallan,°
    A chiel° so clever;
The teeth o' Time may gnaw Tamtallan,°
    But thou's for ever.

Thou paints auld Nature to the nines,
In thy sweet Caledonian lines;

83. hingin' . . . snakin': hanging lips and sneering. **93.
gear:** possessions. **94. Excell'd by nane:** The first edition
reads: "Extoll'd by name." SKETCH. **4. clavers:** nonsense. **5.
o'er aft:** too often. **joes:** sweethearts.

9. Sock . . . skelp: comedy and tragedy hustle. **15. knurlin:**
dwarf. **'till him rives:** tugs to himself. **17. Barbauld:** Mrs.
Anna Laetitia Barbauld (1743–1825), poetess. **19. Theocritus:**
Greek poet of the third century B.C., credited with establishing
the conventions of pastoral poetry. **20. They're . . .
catches:** The eclogues of Publius Virgilius Maro could not
be mistaken for the ballads of the Scottish antiquarian David
Herd (1732–1810). **21. busks his skinklin:** decks out his
glittering. **23. hunders:** hundreds. **25. braw:** fine. **lear:**
learning. **31. callan:** boy. **32. Allan:** Ramsay, who was best
known for his humorous pastorals and for his Scottish
pastoral drama *The Gentle Shepherd* (1725). (See the selections
from Ramsay in Part Three.) **33. jouk . . . hallan:** cower
behind the wall. **34. chiel:** fellow. **35. Tamtallan:** Tantallon
Castle, a rugged fourteenth-century stronghold overlooking
the sea on the east coast of Scotland.

Nae gowden° stream thro' myrtles twines
    Where Philomel,°   40
While midnight gales rustle clustering vines,°
    Her griefs will tell!

Thy rural loves are Nature's sel';
Nae bombast spates° o' nonsense swell;
Nae snap° conceits, but that sweet spell
    O' witchin' loove,
That charm that can the strongest quell,
    The sternest move.

In gowany° glens thy burnie° strays,
Where bonie lasses bleach their claes;   50
Or trots by hazelly shaws and braes°
    Wi' hawthorns gray,
Where blackbirds join the shepherd's lays
    At close o' day.

[SONGS]

Burns's devoted researches for the song collections of
James Johnson and George Thomson made him the
best-informed Scot of his day on the subject. His
scholarly labors in recovering Scottish songs and ballads
are part of the general antiquarian movement of the
second half of the century, and he thus reveals a curious
relationship to men like Horace Walpole, Thomas Gray,
and Thomas Percy. In Scotland, furthermore, antiquarianism took on a highly patriotic coloring. Burns
steadfastly refused payment for his nine years of editorial
work on Scottish song, regarding the work as a pleasant
patriotic obligation.

Although he restored many corrupted texts, his main
job was composing new words to old musical settings.
The music came first: he would find a folk melody and
then contrive words to fit. And the tunes were all-
important. As he wrote in 1785, "There is a certain
irregularity in the old Scotch Songs, a redundancy of
syllables with respect to that exactness of Accent &
measure that the English Poetry requires, but which
glides in, most melodiously with the respective tunes to
which they are set."

Conscious as always of matters of decorum in the
various genres, he once wrote to George Thomson,
"A great critic, [Dr. John] Aikin on songs, says that love
& wine are the exclusive themes for song-writing." And
in his commonplace book he comments (1784):

> Shenstone observes finely that love-verses writ
> without any real passion are the most nauseous of all
> conceits: and I have often thought that no man can
> be a proper critic of Love composition, except he
> himself, in one, or more instances, have been a
> warm votary of this passion.—As I have been all
> along, a miserable dupe to love, and have been led
> into a thousand weaknesses & follies because of it,
> for that reason I put the more confidence in my
> critical skill in distinguishing foppery & conceit,
> from real passion & nature."

The texts are those of the first printings. The first song
is from the Kilmarnock edition of 1786; the second is
from the Edinburgh edition of 1787. The rest are from
James Johnson's *The Scots Musical Museum* (6 vols.,
1787–1803), except *Oh, Open the Door*, *Some Pity to
Shew*, *O Whistle, and I'll Come to You, My Lad*, and
Ye Banks, and Braes, and Streams Around, which are from
George Thomson's *A Select Collection of Original
Scottish Airs* (5 vols., 1793–1818), and *Address to a Lady*,
which is from James Currie's *The Works of Robert Burns*
(4 vols., 1800).

SONG

Tune, Corn rigs are bonie.

I.

IT was upon a Lammas night,°
    When corn rigs° are bonie,
Beneath the moon's unclouded light,
    I held awa° to Annie:
The time flew by, wi' tentless head,°
    Till 'tween the late and early;
Wi' sma' persuasion she agreed,
    To see me thro' the barley.

---

39. gowden: golden. **40. Philomel:** the classical nightingale.
41. vines: In the manuscript the following line is written
above the apparently unfinished line 41: "While nightly
breezes sweep the vines." **44. spates:** floods. **45. snap:** smart.
49. gowany: daisied. **burnie:** little brook. **51. shaws and
braes:** woods and slopes.

SONGS: *It Was upon a Lammas Night*. **1. Lammas night:**
August 1, the date of a traditional British harvest festival. **2.
rigs:** ridges; narrow strip-fields divided by wide ditches. **4.
held awa:** went off. **5. tentless head:** careless heed.

II.

The sky was blue, the wind was still,
    The moon was shining clearly;   10
I set her down, wi' right good will,
    Amang the rigs o' barley:
I ken't her heart was a' my ain;
    I lov'd her most sincerely;
I kiss'd her owre and owre again,
    Amang the rigs o' barley.

III.

I lock'd her in my fond embrace;
    Her heart was beating rarely:
My blessings on that happy place,
    Amang the rigs o' barley!   20
But by the moon and stars so bright,
    That shone that night so clearly!
She ay° shall bless that happy night,
    Amang the rigs o' barley.

IV.

I hae been blythe wi' Comrades dear;
    I hae been merry drinking;
I hae been joyfu' gath'rin gear;°
    I hae been happy thinking:
But a' the pleasures e'er I saw,
    Tho' three times doubl'd fairly,   30
That happy night was worth them a',
    Amang the rigs o' barley.

CHORUS.

Corn rigs, an' barley rigs,
    An' corn rigs are bonie:
I'll ne'er forget that happy night,
    Amang the rigs wi' Annie.

GREEN GROW THE RASHES.
A FRAGMENT

This song Burns "purified" from an indecent original
version.

CHORUS.

Green grow the rashes,° O;
Green grow the rashes, O;
The sweetest hours that e'er I spend,
    Are spent amang the lasses, O.

I.

THERE's nought but care on ev'ry han',
    In ev'ry hour that passes, O:
What signifies the life o' man,
    An'° 'twere na for the lasses, O.
                                    Green grow, &c.

II.

The warly° race may riches chase,   10
    An' riches still may fly them, O;
An' tho' at last they catch them fast,
    Their hearts can ne'er enjoy them, O.
                                    Green grow, &c.

III.

But gie me a canny° hour at e'en,
    My arms about my Dearie, O;
An' warly cares, an' warly men,
    May a' gae tapsalteerie,° O!
                                    Green grow, &c.

IV.

For you sae douse,° ye sneer at this,   20
    Ye're nought but senseless asses, O:
The wisest Man° the warl' saw,
    He dearly lov'd the lasses, O.
                                    Green grow, &c.

V.

Auld Nature swears, the lovely Dears
    Her noblest work she classes, O:
Her prentice han' she try'd on man,
    An' then she made the lasses, O.
                                    Green grow, &c.

* * * * * * * * *

23. ay: always. 27. gath'rin gear: making money.

Green Grow the Rashes. 1. rashes: rushes. 8. An': if. 10.
warly: worldly. 15. canny: quiet. 18. tapsalteerie: topsy-
turvy. 20. douse: grave. 22. The wisest Man: Solomon.

I'M O'ER YOUNG
TO MARRY YET

Burns writes in a manuscript note, "The chorus of this song is old—the rest of it, such as it is, is mine."

I am my mammy's ae bairn,°
  Wi' unco° folk I weary, Sir,
And lying in a man's bed,
  I'm fley'd° it make me irie,° Sir.
    I'm o'er young, I'm o'er young,
      I'm o'er young to marry yet;
    I'm o'er young, 'twad be a sin
      To tak me frae my mammy yet.

Hallowmass° is come and gane,
  The nights are lang in winter, Sir;   10
And you an' I in ae° bed,
  In trowth, I dare na venture, Sir.
              I'm o'er young &c.

Fu' loud and shill° the frosty wind
  Blaws thro' the leafless timmer,° Sir;
But if ye come this gate° again,
  I'll aulder be gin simmer,° Sir.
              I'm o'er young &c.

JOHN ANDERSON MY JO

This song was rewritten from an indecent original version.

John Anderson my jo,° John,
  When we were first Acquent;
Your locks were like the raven,
  Your bony brow was brent;°
But now your brow is beld,° John,
  Your locks are like the snaw;
But blessings on your frosty pow,°
  John Anderson my Jo.

John Anderson my jo, John,
  We clamb the hill the gither;°   10
And mony a canty° day John,
  We've had wi' ane anither:
Now we maun totter down, John,
  And hand in hand we'll go:
And sleep the gither at the foot,
  John Anderson my Jo.

THE RANTIN DOG
THE DADDIE O'T

Burns writes, "I composed this song pretty early in life and sent it to a young girl [Jean Armour], a very particular acquaintance of mine, who was at that time under a cloud."

O wha my babie-clouts° will buy,
O Wha will tent° me when I cry;
Wha will kiss me where I lie.
  The rantin° dog the daddie o't.

O Wha will own he did the faut,
O wha will buy the groanin maut,°
O Wha will tell me how to ca't.
  The rantin dog the daddie o't.

I'm o'er Young to Marry Yet. **1. ae bairn:** only child. **2. unco:** strange. **4. I'm fley'd:** I fear. **irie:** frightened. **9. Hallowmass:** the last day of October. **11. ae:** one. **14. shill:** shrill. **15. timmer:** woods. **16. gate:** way. **17. gin simmer:** by summer.

John Anderson My Jo. **1. jo:** sweetheart. **4. bony . . . brent:** handsome brow was smooth. **5. beld:** bald. **7. pow:** pate. **10. the gither:** together. **11. canty:** happy. *The Rantin Dog the Daddie O't.* **1. babie-clouts:** baby clothes. **2. tent:** care for. **4. rantin:** roistering. **6. groanin maut:** ale for the midwife.

When I mount the Creepie-chair,°
Wha will sit beside me there,   10
Gie me Rob, I'll seek nae mair,
  The rantin dog the Daddie o't.

Wha will crack to me my lane;°
Wha will mak me fidgin fain;°
Wha will kiss me o'er again.
  The rantin dog the Daddie o't.

WILLIE BREW'D
A PECK O' MAUT

This song celebrates a convivial gathering in autumn,
1789, with Burns's cronies William Nicol and Allan
Masterson, in the Dumfriesshire town of Moffat.

O Willie brew'd a peck o' maut,°
  And Rob and Allan cam to see;
Three blyther hearts, that lee lang° night,
  Ye wad na found in Christendie.
      We are na fou,° We're nae that fou,
        But just a drappie° in our e'e;
      The cock may craw the day may daw,
        And ay we'll taste the barley bree.°

Here are we met, three merry boys,
  Three merry boys I trow are we;   10
And mony a night we've merry been,
  And mony mae we hope to be!
              Cho⁵ We are na fou, &c.

It is the moon, I ken her horn,
  That's blinkin in the lift° sae hie;
She shines sae bright to wyle° us hame,
  But by my sooth she'll wait a wee!
              Cho⁵ We are na fou, &c.

Wha first shall rise to gang awa,
  A cuckold, coward loun° is he!   20
Wha first beside his chair shall fa',
  He is the king amang us three.
              Cho⁵ We are na fou, &c.

AE FOND KISS

Ae fond kiss, and then we sever;
  Ae farewell and then for ever!
Deep in heart-wrung tears I'll pledge thee,
  Warring sighs and groans I'll wage thee.
Who shall say that fortune grieves him
  While the star of hope she leaves him?
Me, nae chearfu' twinkle lights me;
  Dark despair around benights me.

I'll ne'er blame my partial fancy,
  Naething could resist my Nancy: 10
But to see her, was to love her;
  Love but her, and love for ever.
Had we never lov'd sae kindly,
  Had we never lov'd sae blindly,
Never met—or never parted,
  We had ne'er been broken-hearted.

Fare thee weel, thou first and fairest!
  Fare thee weel, thou best and dearest!
Thine be ilka° joy and treasure,
  Peace, Enjoyment, Love and Pleasure!   20
Ae fond kiss, and then we sever;
  Ae fareweel, Alas! for ever!
Deep in heart-wrung tears I'll pledge thee,
  Warring sighs and groans I'll wage thee.

I HAE A WIFE O' MY AIN

I hae a wife o' my ain,
  I'll partake wi' naebody
I'll tak Cuckold frae nane,
  I'll gie Cuckold to naebody.

9. **Creepie-chair:** the stool of repentance at the front of the
kirk, which known fornicators were obliged to occupy during
service while awaiting castigation from the pulpit. 13. **crack
. . . lane:** chat with me alone. 14. **fidgin fain:** tingle with
pleasure. *Willie Brew'd a Peck o' Maut.* 1. **maut:** malt, ale. 3.
lee lang: livelong. 5. **fou:** drunk. 6. **drappie:** little drop. 8.
bree: brew. 15. **blinkin . . . lift:** shining in the sky. 16.
wyle: entice.

20. **loun:** rascal. *Ae Fond Kiss.* 19. **ilka:** every.

I hae a penny to spend,
    There, thanks to naebody
I hae naething to lend,
    I'll borrow frae naebody.

I am naebody's lord,
    I'll be slave to naebody;   10
I hae a gude braid sword,
    I'll tak dunts° frae naebody.

I'll be merry and free,
    I'll be sad for naebody;
Naebody cares for me,
    I care for naebody.

THE BANKS O' DOON

Ye Banks and braes° o' bonie Doon,°
    How can ye bloom sae fresh and fair;
How can ye chant, ye little birds,
    And I sae weary fu' o' care!
Thou'll break my heart thou warbling bird,
    That wantons thro' the flowering thorn:
Thou minds me o' departed joys,
    Departed never to return.

Oft hae I rov'd by bonie Doon,
    To see the rose and woodbine twine;   10
And ilka bird sang o' its luve,
    And fondly sae did I o' mine.
Wi' lightsome heart I pu'd° a rose,
    Fu' sweet upon its thorny tree;
And my fause luver staw° my rose,
    But, ah! he left the thorn wi' me.

OH, OPEN THE DOOR,
SOME PITY TO SHEW

Oh, open the door, some pity to shew,
    Oh, open the door to me, Oh;
Tho' thou hast been false, I'll ever prove true,
    Oh, open the door to me, Oh!

Oh, cold is the blast upon my pale cheek,
    But colder thy love for me, Oh!
The frost that freezes the life at my breast,
    Is nought to my pains from thee, Oh!

The wan moon is setting behind the white wave,
    And time is setting with me, Oh!   10
False friends, false Love, farewell! for more
    I'll ne'er trouble them, nor thee, Oh!

She has open'd the door, she has open'd it wide,
    She sees his pale corse on the plain, Oh!
"My true love!" she cried,—and sunk down by
        his side,
    Never to rise again, Oh!

A RED, RED ROSE

James Johnson's *Scots Musical Museum* (6 vols., 1787–1803) provides two settings for this song; in one the song is apparently regarded as complete with the first three stanzas only.

O my Luve's like a red, red rose,
    That's newly sprung in June;
O My Luve's like the melodie
    That's sweetly play'd in tune.

As fair art thou, my bonie lass,
    So deep in luve am I;
And I will luve thee still, my dear,
    Till a' the seas gang dry.

Till a' the seas gang dry, my Dear,
    And the rocks melt wi' the sun: 10
O I will love thee still my dear,
    While the sands o' life shall run.

And fare thee weel, my only Luve!
    And fare thee weel, a while!
And I will come again, my Luve,
    Tho' it ware ten thousand mile!

I Hae a Wife o' My Ain. **12. dunts:** blows. *The Banks o' Doon.*
1. braes: hill slopes. **Doon:** a river in Ayrshire. **13. pu'd:**
pulled. **15. staw:** stole.

COMIN THRO' THE RYE

This song was rewritten from an indecent original version.

Comin thro' the rye, poor body,
  Comin thro' the rye
She draigl't° a' her petticoatie
  Coming thro' the rye.
    Oh Jenny's a' weet° poor body,
      Jenny's seldom dry
    She draigl't a' her petticoatie
      Comin thro' the rye.

Gin° a body meet a body
  Comin thro' the rye,   10
Gin a body kiss a body
  Need a body cry
        Cho? Oh Jenny's a' weet, &c.

Gin a body meet a body
  Comin thro' the glen;
Gin a body kiss a body
  Need the warld ken!
        Cho? Oh Jenny's a' weet, &c.

O WHISTLE, AND I'LL COME TO YOU, MY LAD

The first three lines of the chorus are traditional; all else is original. "Jeany" is Jean Lorimer, one of Burns's many sweethearts.

O whistle, and I'll come to you, my lad,
O whistle, and I'll come to you, my lad;
Tho' father and mother and a' should gae mad,
Thy JEANY will venture wi' ye, my lad.

Comin thro' the Rye. **3. draigl't:** draggled. **5. a' weet:** all wet. **9. Gin:** if.

But warily tent,° when ye come to court me,
And come na unless the back-yett be a-jee;°
Syne° up the back-style, and let naebody see,
And come, as ye were na coming to me,
And come, as ye were na coming to me!

O whistle, and I'll come to you, my lad,   10
O whistle, and I'll come to you, my lad;
Tho' father and mother and a' should gae mad,
Thy JEANY will venture wi' ye, my lad.
At kirk, or at market, whene'er ye meet me,
Gang by me as tho' that ye car'd nae a flie;°
But steal me a blink° o' your bonie black e'e,
Yet look as ye were na looking at me,
Yet look as ye were na looking at me!

O whistle, and I'll come to you, my lad,
O whistle, and I'll come to you, my lad;   20
Tho' father and mother and a' should gae mad,
Thy JEANY will venture wi' ye, my lad.
Ay vow and protest that ye care na for me,
And *whyles* ye may lightly° my beauty a wee;
But court nae anither, tho' joking ye be,
For fear that she wyle° your fancy frae me,
For fear that she wyle your fancy frae me!

YE BANKS, AND BRAES, AND STREAMS AROUND

The "Highland Mary" here is Mary Campbell, who died in 1786. Her precise relationship to Burns and the cause of her death were obscure until her grave at Greenock was opened in 1920. At the foot of her grave were found the remains of an infant's coffin.

Ye banks, and braes, and streams around
  The castle of Montgomery,
Green be your woods, and fair your flowers,
  Your waters never drumlie°!

O Whistle, and I'll Come to You, My Lad. **5. warily tent:** take careful heed. **6. back-yett be a-jee:** back gate be ajar. **7. Syne:** then. **15. flie:** fly. **16. blink:** glance. **24. whyles . . . lightly:** sometimes you may disparage. **26. wyle:** entice. *Ye Banks, and Braes, and Streams Around.* **4. drumlie:** muddy.

There simmer° first unfald her robes,
 And there the langest tarry;
For there I took the last farewel
 Of my sweet Highland MARY.

How sweetly bloom'd the gay, green birk,°
 How rich the hawthorn's blossom;   10
As underneath their fragrant shade,
 I clasp'd her to my bosom?
The golden hours, on angel wings,
 Flew o'er me and my dearie;
For dear to me as light and life
 Was my sweet Highland MARY.

Wi' mony a vow and lock'd embrace,
 Our parting was fu' tender;
And pledging aft to meet again,
 We tore ourselves asunder.   20
But oh! fell° death's untimely frost,
 That nipt my flower sae early!
Now green's the sod, and cauld's the clay,
 That wraps my Highland MARY.

O pale, pale now, those rosy lips
 I aft ha'e kiss'd sae fondly!
And clos'd for ay the sparkling glance
 That dwalt on me sae kindly!
And mouldering now in silent dust,
 The heart that lo'ed me dearly!   30
But still within my bosom's core
 Shall live my Highland MARY.

ADDRESS TO A LADY

✦

This song was written for the eighteen-year-old Jessie
Lewars, Burns's nurse during his last illness.

✦

5. simmer: summer. **9. birk:** birch. **21. fell:** biting, keen.

OH wert thou in the cauld blast,
 On yonder lea, on yonder lea;
My plaidie to the angry airt,°
 I'd shelter thee, I'd shelter thee:
Or did misfortune's bitter storms
 Around thee blaw, around thee blaw,
Thy bield° should be my bosom,
 To share it a' to share it a'.

Or were I in the wildest waste,
 Sae black and bare, sae black and bare,   10
The desart were a paradise,
 If thou wert there, if thou wert there.
Or were I monarch o' the globe,
 Wi' thee to reign, wi' thee to reign;
The brightest jewel in my crown,
 Wad be my queen, wad be my queen.

WEE WILLIE GRAY

Wee Willie Gray, an' his leather wallet;
Peel a willie° wand, to be him boots and jacket.
The rose upon the breer° will be him trouse° an'
 doublet
The rose upon the breer will be him trouse an' doublet.

Wee Willie Gray and his leather wallet;
Twice a lily-flower will be him sark° and cravat;
Feathers of a flee° wad feather up his bonnet,
Feathers of a flee wad feather up his bonnet.

Address to a Lady. **3. airt:** quarter, direction. **7. bield:**
shelter. *Wee Willie Gray.* **2. willie:** willow. **3. breer:** brier.
trouse: breeches. **6. sark:** shirt. **7. flee:** fly.

William Blake

ๆๆๆๆๆๆๆๆๆๆๆๆๆๆๆๆๆๆๆๆๆๆๆๆ

1757–1827

The Christian radical William Blake—engraver, painter, and poet—was born in London of a family of Dissenters who ran a hosiery shop. His lively visual imagination manifested itself almost from the beginning: at the age of four he saw God peering in at his window, and soon afterward he saw angels and the prophet Ezekiel in a nearby field. Although he studied with a drawing master at the age of ten, he never went to school at all, and it was presumably his mother who taught him to read and write. He later observed, "Thank God I never was sent to school / To be flogd into following the Style of a Fool." At fourteen he was apprenticed for a seven-year period to a copper-plate engraver, who set him to drawing the monuments in Westminster Abbey; from this experience he developed, like Chatterton and Walpole, an obsession with the Gothic past. After faithfully serving his apprenticeship, he studied briefly at the Royal Academy, drawing living models; he said later, "Models . . . enslave one—efface from one's mind a conception or reminiscence which was better." He was now making a slender living engraving book illustrations, and in 1782 he married a childlike and illiterate girl, whom he taught to write and to draw. Except for a three-year period on the south coast, the Blakes, childless and poor, lived in and around London.

Blake had not only been drawing and engraving precociously from an early age; he had also been composing poems and songs, and in 1783 some local admirers printed a volume of them for him. The book, *Poetical Sketches* (the title suggests his dual interests), made no impact on contemporary literature. His next work, which he never published, was a farcical and bawdy prose satire, *An Island in the Moon*, which ridicules tepid and self-satisfied intellectuals under such names as Suction the Epicurean, Obtuse Angle, Inflammable Gass the Wind-Finder, and Mrs. Nannicantipot.

Around 1788, after his dead brother had appeared in a vision and outlined the process, Blake devised his famous technique of "illuminated printing." He drew and lettered on paper with an acid-resistant varnish; the paper he then heated and pressed against a copper engraving plate, to which the drawing and lettering were transferred reversed. When the plate was put into an acid bath, those portions unprotected by the varnish were eaten away, and they took no ink during the printing process. After the printing in black, blue-green, or light brown ink, the sheets were individually hand-tinted with water color. From this time on Black produced almost all his works himself by this laborious method of relief etching.

With the outbreak of the French Revolution in 1789 he became an ardent republican, and most of his subsequent works reveal his conviction that a new age had dawned, an age privileged to witness the destruction of organized churches, war, sexual repression, mercantilism, and gentility in the arts. Among the poems, "prophecies," and philosophic tracts of this period are *Songs of Innocence* (1789) and *The Book of Thel* (1789), the earliest of his elaborately symbolical "prophetic books." One book of a projected seven-book poem, *The French Revolution*, was finished and set in type in 1791, but it was never published. In 1793 he engraved and illustrated two more prophetic works: *Visions of the Daughters of Albion* and *America: A Prophecy;* the next year he produced *Europe: A Prophecy*, *The First Book of Urizen*, and *Songs of Experience*. After *The Book of Los* (1795), he brought out nothing important until *Milton* (1804–08) and *Jerusalem: The Emanation of the Giant Albion* (1804–20). Most of these long, turgid poems were seen by very few, and it was not for many years that they were known to more than the small coterie of Blake's friends and admirers, many of them young painters.

His last years were spent largely in book illustration and in unsuccessful attempts to find a clientele, or at least an audience, for his paintings and water colors. But few customers wanted to purchase pictures on such subjects as "The Spiritual Form of Pitt Guiding Behemoth." One memorandum from the year 1807 is eloquent: "Tuesday, Janry. 20 . . . between Two & Seven in the Evening—Despair." When Blake died at the age of seventy he was engraving illustrations to Dante. The painter George Richmond, present at the deathbed, reports that "just before he died his Countenance became fair—His eyes Brighten'd and He burst out in Singing of the things he Saw in Heaven."

Despite his lifelong habit of seeing visions—in addition to God, angels, Ezekiel, and his dead brother, he had visions of the angel Gabriel, Joseph, Shakespeare, Milton, and even Voltaire—and despite the assumption of Wordsworth, Robert Southey, and others that he was mad, Blake was not insane as was Christopher Smart. He was undeniably eccentric and "humorous," reckless and often outrageous in utterance (especially to people he disliked) and extravagant in imagination; but he was quite aware of his relationship to what other people thought of as reality, and he had an acute and saving sense of the comic. Once at a party he was telling a group of children about a vision of sculptured lambs in a field; the children's mother suddenly asked, "I beg pardon, Mr. Blake, but *may* I ask *where* you saw this?" "*Here*, Madam," said Blake, touching his forehead. He was less a mystic than, as Northrop Frye has said, "a Bible-soaked middle-class English Protestant," and his pacifism, his republicanism, his anticlericalism, his pleas for sexual freedom, and his allegiance to the cult of the sublime are those of many other City of London radicals of his time. He once wrote about his painting, "Those who have been told that my Works are but an unscientific and irregular Eccentricity, a Madman's Scrawls, I demand of them to do me the justice to examine before they decide."

The fine bibliography compiled by Geoffrey Keynes (1921) can be supplemented by G. E. Bentley, Jr., and M. K. Nurmi's *Blake Bibliography: Annotated Lists of Works, Studies, and Blakeana* (1964). Modern Blake studies are appraised in Northrop Frye's entertaining essay in *The English Romantic Poets and Essayists: A Review of Research* and Criticism, ed. C. W. and L. H. Houtchens (1957). Two scholarly editions of Blake are *The Poetry and Prose of William Blake*, ed. D. V. Erdman (1965), with a commentary by Harold Bloom, and *The Complete Writings of William Blake, with Variant Readings*, ed. Geoffrey Keynes (1966). *A Concordance to the Writings of William Blake* has been prepared by D. V. Erdman and others (2 vols., 1967). Detaching Blake's poems from their engraved contexts is an offense against art; the interested reader will want to examine the beautiful facsimiles published (1952–65) by the William Blake Trust. The early biography by Alexander Gilchrist (1863) is lively and anecdotal; it has been edited by Ruthven Todd for Everyman's Library (1945). Two modern biographies are Thomas Wright's (2 vols., 1929) and Mona Wilson's (rev. ed., 1948). The letters have been edited by Keynes (1956). Both Mark Schorer's *William Blake: The Politics of Vision* (1946) and Jacob Bronowski's *William Blake: A Man Without a Mask* (1954) examine Blake's response to the political and intellectual situation of his time. D. V. Erdman's *Blake: Prophet Against Empire* (1954) brings to light the specific political sources and backgrounds of many of Blake's works. Northrop Frye's brilliant critical and philosophic study *Fearful Symmetry* (1947) focuses on Blake's achievement as symbolist and mythmaker.

FROM

POETICAL SKETCHES . . .

Poetical Sketches, a seventy-page collection of poems and Ossianic prose pieces, was privately printed and issued in 1783 with an apologetic preface by Blake's early patron the Reverend Henry Mathew, who explained that the poet had been "deprived of the leisure requisite to such a revisal of these sheets, as might have rendered them less unfit to meet the public eye." The poems make clear not only Blake's devotion to Ossian but his enthusiasm for Chatterton's Rowley poems (1777) and Percy's *Relics* (1765), and for Milton, Shakespeare, Thomson, Collins, and Gray. *How Sweet I Roam'd from Field to Field* is said to have been written before Blake was fourteen.

The text is that of the first edition, *Poetical Sketches, by W. B.* (1783).

SONG

HOW sweet I roam'd from field to field,
  And tasted all the summer's pride,
'Till I the prince of love beheld,
  Who in the sunny beams did glide!

He shew'd me lilies for my hair,
  And blushing roses for my brow;
He led me through his gardens fair,
  Where all his golden pleasures grow.

With sweet May dews my wings were wet,
  And Phœbus° fir'd my vocal rage;   10
He caught me in his silken net,
  And shut me in his golden cage.

He loves to sit and hear me sing,
  Then, laughing, sports and plays with me;
Then stretches out my golden wing,
  And mocks my loss of liberty.

SONG

MY silks and fine array,
  My smiles and languish'd air,
By love are driv'n away;
  And mournful lean Despair
Brings me yew to deck my grave:
Such end true lovers have.

POETICAL SKETCHES: *Song*. **10. Phœbus:** Apollo, god of poetry and music.

His face is fair as heav'n,
    When springing buds unfold;
O why to him was 't giv'n,
    Whose heart is wintry cold?   10
His breast is love's all worship'd tomb,
Where all love's pilgrims come.

Bring me an axe and spade,
    Bring me a winding sheet;
When I my grave have made,
    Let winds and tempests beat:
Then down I'll lie, as cold as clay.
True love doth pass away!

TO THE MUSES

WHETHER on Ida's° shady brow,
    Or in the chambers of the East,
The chambers of the sun, that now
    From antient melody have ceas'd;

Whether in Heav'n ye wander fair,
    Or the green corners of the earth,
Or the blue regions of the air,
    Where the melodious winds have birth;

Whether on chrystal rocks ye rove,
    Beneath the bosom of the sea   10
Wand'ring in many a coral grove,
    Fair Nine, forsaking Poetry!

How have you left the antient love
    That bards of old enjoy'd in you!
The languid strings do scarcely move!
    The sound is forc'd, the notes are few!

THERE IS NO NATURAL RELIGION

This tiny book, reminiscent of a Renaissance emblem book, is probably Blake's first engraved and hand-colored work. It was executed around 1788. Each of the propositions appears on a separate page about two by one and a half inches (copper engraving plates were expensive). The designing is cruder than on Blake's later illuminated books.

To the Muses. **1. Ida:** a mountain overlooking the site of Troy.

The texts of this and of all the following engraved works are those of the transcriptions by Geoffrey Keynes in *The Writings of William Blake* (3 vols., 1925), corrected occasionally by Keynes's *Poetry and Prose of William Blake* (1927). Blake's own engraved punctuation, even when decipherable, often seems more decorative than logical, and it constitutes a severe bar to understanding. We have consequently adopted the punctuation by Keynes.

[I]

The *Argument.* Man has no notion of moral fitness but from Education. Naturally he is only a natural organ subject to Sense.

I. Man cannot naturally Percieve but through his natural or bodily organs.

II. Man by his reasoning power can only compare & judge of what he has already perciev'd.

III. From a perception of only 3 senses or 3 elements none could deduce a fourth or fifth.

IV. None could have other than natural or organic thoughts if he had none but organic perceptions.

V. Man's desires are limited by his perceptions, none can desire what he has not perciev'd.

VI. The desires & perceptions of man, untaught by any thing but organs of sense, must be limited to objects of sense.

Conclusion. If it were not for the Poetic or Prophetic character the Philosophic & Experimental would soon be at the ratio[1] of all things, & stand still, unable to do other than repeat the same dull round over again.

[II]

I. Man's perceptions are not bounded by organs of perception; he percieves more than sense (tho' ever so acute) can discover.

II. Reason, or the ratio of all we have already known, is not the same that it shall be when we know more.

III. [*Missing*]

IV. The bounded is loathed by its possessor. The same dull round, even of a universe, would soon become a mill with complicated wheels.

V. If the many become the same as the few when possess'd, More! More! is the cry of a mistaken soul; less than All cannot satisfy Man.

THERE IS NO NATURAL RELIGION. **1. ratio:** rationale; demonstrable material cause, or the sum of the ordinary experience of causality.

VI. If any could desire what he is incapable of possessing, despair must be his eternal lot.

VII. The desire of Man being Infinite, the possession is Infinite & himself Infinite.

Application: He who sees the Infinite in all things, sees God. He who sees the Ratio only, sees himself only.

Therefore God becomes as we are, that we may be as he is.

FROM

SONGS OF INNOCENCE

Produced in 1789, *Songs of Innocence* consists of thirty-one hand-colored pages printed from relief-etched plates; each page contains a single poem together with decorative pastoral figures and borders. The borders are elaborately curvilinear botanical designs of leaves, twigs, tendrils, and flowers. The appearance of the pages suggests both medieval illuminated manuscripts and later emblem books.

Many of the lyrics (e.g., *The Lamb, On Another's Sorrow*) are in the genre of traditional Christian poems for children, such as those by Isaac Watts and Mrs. Anna Letitia Barbauld. But despite appearances the prevailing mode of the poems is perhaps less pastoral than mock-pastoral, for the "contraries" of the innocent states expressed here are close at hand. Some of the poems (e.g., *Nurse's Song, Holy Thursday*) first appeared in *An Island in the Moon*, where they are complacently sung by the fatuous and contemptible characters satirized by Blake. As he later observed, "Innocence dwells with Wisdom, but never with Ignorance."

INTRODUCTION

Piping down the valleys wild,
Piping songs of pleasant glee,
On a cloud I saw a child,
And he laughing said to me:

"Pipe a song about a Lamb!"
So I piped with merry chear.
"Piper, pipe that song again;"
So I piped: he wept to hear.

"Drop thy pipe, thy happy pipe;
Sing thy songs of happy chear:"   10
So I sung the same again,
While he wept with joy to hear.

"Piper, sit thee down and write
In a book, that all may read."
So he vanish'd from my sight,
And I pluck'd a hollow reed,

And I made a rural pen,
And I stain'd the water clear,
And I wrote my happy songs
Every child may joy to hear.   20

THE LAMB

Little Lamb, who made thee?
  Dost thou know who made thee?
Gave thee life, & bid thee feed
By the stream & o'er the mead;
Gave thee clothing of delight,
Softest clothing, wooly, bright;
Gave thee such a tender voice,
Making all the vales rejoice?
  Little Lamb, who made thee?
  Dost thou know who made thee?   10

Little Lamb, I'll tell thee,
  Little Lamb, I'll tell thee:
He is called by thy name,
For he calls himself a Lamb.
He is meek, & he is mild;
He became a little child.
I a child, & thou a lamb,
We are called by his name.
  Little Lamb, God bless thee!
  Little Lamb, God bless thee!   20

THE BLOSSOM

Merry, Merry Sparrow!
Under leaves so green
A happy Blossom
Sees you swift as arrow
Seek your cradle narrow
Near my Bosom.

Pretty, Pretty Robin!
Under leaves so green
A happy Blossom
Hears you sobbing, sobbing,   10
Pretty, Pretty Robin,
Near my Bosom.

THE CHIMNEY SWEEPER

When my mother died I was very young,
And my father sold me while yet my tongue
Could scarcely cry "'weep!° 'weep! 'weep! 'weep!"
So your chimneys I sweep, & in soot I sleep.

There's little Tom Dacre, who cried when his head,
That curl'd like a lamb's back, was shav'd: so I said
"Hush, Tom! never mind it, for when your head's
    bare
You know that the soot cannot spoil your white°
    hair."

And so he was quiet, & that very night,
As Tom was a-sleeping, he had such a sight!   10
That thousands of sweepers, Dick, Joe, Ned, & Jack,
Were all of them lock'd up in coffins of black.

And by came an Angel who had a bright key,
And he open'd the coffins & set them all free;
And down a green plain leaping, laughing, they run,
And wash in a river, and shine in the Sun.

Then naked & white, all their bags° left behind,
They rise upon clouds and sport in the wind;
And the Angel told Tom, if he'd be a good boy,
He'd have God for his father, & never want joy.   20

And so Tom awoke; and we rose in the dark,°
And got with our bags & our brushes to work.
Tho' the morning was cold, Tom was happy & warm;
So if all do their duty they need not fear harm.

NURSE'S SONG

When the voices of children are heard on the green
And laughing is heard on the hill,
My heart is at rest within my breast
    And everything else is still.

"Then come home, my children, the sun is gone down
And the dews of night arise;
Come, come, leave off play, and let us away
Till the morning appears in the skies."

"No, no, let us play, for it is yet day
And we cannot go to sleep;   10
Besides, in the sky the little birds fly
And the hills are all cover'd with sheep."

"Well, well, go & play till the light fades away
And then go home to bed."
The little ones leaped & shouted & laugh'd
    And all the hills ecchoed.

HOLY THURSDAY

'Twas on a Holy Thursday,° their innocent faces clean,
The children walking two & two, in red & blue &
    green,
Grey-headed beadles walk'd before, with wands as
    white as snow,
Till into the high dome of Paul's they like Thames'
    waters flow.

O what a multitude they seem'd, these flowers of
    London town!
Seated in companies they sit with radiance all their
    own.
The hum of multitudes was there, but multitudes of
    lambs,
Thousands of little boys & girls raising their innocent
    hands.

SONGS OF INNOCENCE: *The Chimney Sweeper*. **3. 'weep:**
("Sweep!") the chimney sweeper's street cry. **8. white:**
blond. **17. bags:** used for carrying away chimney soot.
21. in the dark: Sweeps generally began work at five in
the morning in winter, seven in the morning in summer. An
Act of Parliament had been passed in 1788 limiting their
working hours and prohibiting their employment before the
age of eight. It was not enforced.

Holy Thursday. **1. Holy Thursday:** the fortieth day after
Easter, commemorating the Ascension. On this day it was
customary for some six thousand London orphans and charity
children—many of them simply abandoned—to attend a
service at St. Paul's.

Now like a mighty wind they raise to heaven the voice
   of song,
Or like harmonious thunderings the seats of Heaven
   among.   10
Beneath them sit the aged men, wise guardians of the
   poor;
Then cherish pity, lest you drive an angel from your
   door.

ON ANOTHER'S SORROW

Can I see another's woe,
And not be in sorrow too?
Can I see another's grief,
And not seek for kind relief?

Can I see a falling tear,
And not feel my sorrow's share?
Can a father see his child
Weep, nor be with sorrow fill'd?

Can a mother sit and hear
An infant groan an infant fear?   10
No, No! never can it be!
Never, never can it be!

And can he who smiles on all
Hear the wren with sorrows small,
Hear the small bird's grief & care,
Hear the woes that infants bear,

And not sit beside the nest,
Pouring pity in their breast;
And not sit the cradle near,
Weeping tear on infant's tear;   20

And not sit both night & day,
Wiping all our tears away?
O, no! never can it be!
Never, never can it be!

He doth give his joy to all;
He becomes an infant small;
He becomes a man of woe;
He doth feel the sorrow too.

Think not thou canst sigh a sigh
And thy maker is not by;   30
Think not thou canst weep a tear
And thy maker is not near.

O! he gives to us his joy
That our grief he may destroy;
Till our grief is fled & gone
He doth sit by us and moan.

THE MARRIAGE
OF HEAVEN AND HELL

This work, printed from twenty-seven etched plates,
was produced around 1790. The richly colored title page
depicts numerous human couples embracing. The final
Song of Liberty suggests that *The Marriage of Heaven and
Hell* as a whole was written out of Blake's enthusiasm
for the initial stages of the French Revolution. Despite
its serious Ossianic echoes, the genre of the work appears
to be primarily that of parody, operating here in the
service of satire. Specifically parodied are the Book of
Genesis, the Proverbs, the Book of Revelation, the
writings of Emanuel Swedenborg (1688–1772) (especially
his *Treatise Concerning Heaven and Hell*), and—like
Gulliver's Travels (1726)—the travel book in general.
As Northrop Frye has pointed out, "*The Marriage of
Heaven and Hell*, with its blistering ridicule of the
wisdom that dwells with prudence, with its rowdy
guffaws at the doctrines of a torturing hell and a boring
heaven which are taught by cowards to dupes, is
perhaps the epilogue to the golden age of English
satire."

THE ARGUMENT

Rintrah° roars & shakes his fires in the burden'd air;
Hungry clouds swag° on the deep.

Once meek, and in a perilous path,
The just man kept his course along
The vale of death.
Roses are planted where thorns grow,
And on the barren heath
Sing the honey bees.

THE MARRIAGE OF HEAVEN AND HELL: *The Argument.* **1.**
Rintrah: the wrath of righteousness; righteous primitive
energy. **2. swag:** "to sink down by its weight; to hang
heavy" (Johnson's *Dictionary*).

Then the perilous path was planted,
And a river and a spring   10
On every cliff and tomb,
And on the bleached bones
Red clay brought forth;

Till the villain left the paths of ease,
To walk in perilous paths, and drive
The just man into barren climes.

Now the sneaking serpent walks
In mild humility,
And the just man rages in the wilds
Where lions roam.   20

Rintrah roars & shakes his fires in the burden'd air;
Hungry clouds swag on the deep.

[¶]

As a new heaven is begun, and it is now thirty-three
years since its advent, the Eternal Hell revives. And lo!
Swedenborg¹ is the Angel sitting at the tomb: his
writings are the linen clothes folded up. Now is the
dominion of Edom,² & the return of Adam into
Paradise. See Isaiah xxxiv & xxxv Chap.

Without Contraries is no progression. Attraction and
Repulsion, Reason and Energy, Love and Hate, are
necessary to Human existence.

From these contraries spring what the religious call
Good & Evil. Good is the passive that obeys Reason.
Evil is the active springing from Energy.

Good is Heaven. Evil is Hell.

THE VOICE OF THE DEVIL

All Bibles or sacred codes have been the causes of the
following Errors:

1. That Man has two real existing principles: Viz:
a Body & a Soul.

2. That Energy, call'd Evil, is alone from the Body;
& that Reason, call'd Good, is alone from the Soul.

1. **Swedenborg:** Emanuel Swedenborg (1688–1772), Swedish
scientist, philosopher, and religious writer; in his *True
Christian Religion* (1771; English trans., 1781) he asserted that
the spiritual Last Judgment occurred in 1757, the year,
Blake undoubtedly noticed, of his own birth. Blake and his
wife joined a London Swedenborgian society in 1789. **2.**
Edom: Esau, the brother of Jacob; Esau is a biblical type
of the rightful heir dispossessed.

3. That God will torment Man in Eternity for
following his Energies.

But the following Contraries to these are True:

1. Man has no Body distinct from his Soul; for that
call'd Body is a portion of Soul discern'd by the five
Senses, the chief inlets of Soul in this age.

2. Energy is the only life, and is from the Body; and
Reason is the bound or outward circumference of
Energy.

3. Energy is Eternal Delight.

[¶]

Those who restrain desire, do so because theirs is
weak enough to be restrained; and the restrainer or
reason usurps its place & governs the unwilling.

And being restrain'd, it by degrees becomes passive,
till it is only the shadow of desire.

The history of this is written in Paradise Lost, & the
Governor or Reason is call'd Messiah.

And the original Archangel, or possessor of the
command of the heavenly host, is call'd the Devil or
Satan, and his children are call'd Sin & Death.

But in the Book of Job, Milton's Messiah is call'd
Satan.

For this history has been adopted by both parties.

It indeed appear'd to Reason as if Desire was cast
out; but the Devil's account is, that the Messiah fell, &
formed a heaven of what he stole from the Abyss.

This is shewn in the Gospel, where he prays to the
Father to send the comforter, or Desire, that Reason
may have Ideas to build on; the Jehovah of the Bible
being no other than he who dwells in flaming fire.

Know that after Christ's death, he became Jehovah.

But in Milton, the Father is Destiny, the Son a Ratio
of the five senses, & the Holy-ghost Vacuum!

Note: The reason Milton wrote in fetters when he
wrote of Angels & God, and at liberty when of Devils
& Hell, is because he was a true Poet and of the Devil's
party without knowing it.

A MEMORABLE FANCY

As I was walking among the fires of hell, delighted
with the enjoyments of Genius, which to Angels look
like torment and insanity, I collected some of their
Proverbs; thinking that as the sayings used in a nation
mark its character, so the Proverbs of Hell show the

nature of Infernal wisdom better than any description of buildings or garments.

When I came home: on the abyss of the five senses, where a flat sided steep frowns over the present world, I saw a mighty Devil folded in black clouds, hovering on the sides of the rock: with corroding fires he wrote the following sentence now percieved by the minds of men, & read by them on earth:

How do you know but ev'ry Bird that cuts the airy way,[3]

Is an immense world of delight, clos'd by your senses five?

PROVERBS OF HELL

In seed time learn, in harvest teach, in winter enjoy.

Drive your cart and your plow over the bones of the dead.

The road of excess leads to the palace of wisdom.

Prudence is a rich, ugly old maid courted by Incapacity.

He who desires but acts not, breeds pestilence.

The cut worm forgives the plow.

Dip him in the river who loves water.

A fool sees not the same tree that a wise man sees.

He whose face gives no light, shall never become a star.

Eternity is in love with the productions of time.

The busy bee has no time for sorrow.

The hours of folly are measur'd by the clock; but of wisdom, no clock can measure.

All wholesome food is caught without a net or a trap.

Bring out number, weight & measure in a year of dearth.

No bird soars too high, if he soars with his own wings.

A dead body revenges not injuries.

The most sublime act is to set another before you.

If the fool would persist in his folly he would become wise.

Folly is the cloke of knavery.

Shame is Pride's cloke.

Prisons are built with stones of Law, Brothels with bricks of Religion.

The pride of the peacock is the glory of God.

The lust of the goat is the bounty of God.

The wrath of the lion is the wisdom of God.

The nakedness of woman is the work of God.

Excess of sorrow laughs. Excess of joy weeps.

The roaring of lions, the howling of wolves, the raging of the stormy sea, and the destructive sword, are portions of eternity, too great for the eye of man.

The fox condemns the trap, not himself.

Joys impregnate. Sorrows bring forth.

Let man wear the fell[4] of the lion, woman the fleece of the sheep.

The bird a nest, the spider a web, man friendship.

The selfish, smiling fool, & the sullen, frowning fool shall be both thought wise, that they may be a rod.

What is now proved was once only imagin'd.

The rat, the mouse, the fox, the rabbet watch the roots; the lion, the tyger, the horse, the elephant watch the fruits.

The cistern contains: the fountain overflows.

One thought fills immensity.

Always be ready to speak your mind, and a base man will avoid you.

Every thing possible to be believ'd is an image of truth.

The eagle never lost so much time as when he submitted to learn of the crow.

The fox provides for himself, but God provides for the lion.

Think in the morning. Act in the noon. Eat in the evening. Sleep in the night.

He who has suffer'd you to impose on him, knows you.

As the plow follows words, so God rewards prayers.

The tygers of wrath are wiser than the horses of instruction.

Expect poison from the standing water.

You never know what is enough unless you know what is more than enough.

Listen to the fool's reproach! it is a kingly title!

The eyes of fire, the nostrils of air, the mouth of water, the beard of earth.

The weak in courage is strong in cunning.

The apple tree never asks the beech how he shall grow; nor the lion, the horse, how he shall take his prey.

The thankful reciever bears a plentiful harvest.

---

3. How . . . way: Cf. Chatterton, *Bristowe Tragedie*, ll. 133–36, in Part Six.

4. fell: pelt.

If others had not been foolish, we should be so.

The soul of sweet delight can never be defil'd.

When thou seest an Eagle, thou seest a portion of Genius; lift up thy head!

As the caterpiller chooses the fairest leaves to lay her eggs on, so the priest lays his curse on the fairest joys.

To create a little flower is the labour of ages.

Damn braces. Bless relaxes.

The best wine is the oldest, the best water the newest.

Prayers plow not! Praises reap not!

Joys laugh not! Sorrows weep not!

The head Sublime, the heart Pathos, the genitals Beauty, the hands & feet Proportion.

As the air to a bird or the sea to a fish, so is contempt to the contemptible.

The crow wish'd every thing was black, the owl that every thing was white.

Exuberance is Beauty.

If the lion was advised by the fox, he would be cunning.

Improvement makes strait roads; but the crooked roads without Improvement are roads of Genius.

Sooner murder an infant in its cradle than nurse unacted desires.

Where man is not, nature is barren.

Truth can never be told so as to be understood, and not be believ'd.

Enough! or Too much.

[¶]

The ancient Poets animated all sensible objects with Gods or Geniuses, calling them by the names and adorning them with the properties of woods, rivers, mountains, lakes, cities, nations, and whatever their enlarged & numerous senses could percieve.

And particularly they studied the genius of each city & country, placing it under its mental deity;

Till a system was formed, which some took advantage of, & enslav'd the vulgar by attempting to realize or abstract the mental deities from their objects: thus began Priesthood;

Choosing forms of worship from poetic tales.

And at length they pronounc'd that the Gods had order'd such things.

Thus men forgot that All deities reside in the human breast.

A MEMORABLE FANCY

The Prophets Isaiah and Ezekiel dined with me, and I asked them how they dared so roundly to assert that God spoke to them; and whether they did not think at the time that they would be misunderstood, & so be the cause of imposition.

Isaiah answer'd: "I saw no God, nor heard any, in a finite organical perception; but my senses discover'd the infinite in every thing, and as I was then perswaded, & remain confirm'd, that the voice of honest indignation is the voice of God, I cared not for consequences, but wrote."

Then I asked: "does a firm perswasion that a thing is so, make it so?"

He replied: "All poets believe that it does, & in ages of imagination this firm perswasion removed mountains; but many are not capable of a firm perswasion of any thing."

Then Ezekiel said: "The philosophy of the east taught the first principles of human perception: some nations held one principle for the origin, and some another: we of Israel taught that the Poetic Genius (as you now call it) was the first principle and all the others merely derivative, which was the cause of our despising the Priests & Philosophers of other countries, and prophecying that all Gods would at last be proved to originate in ours & to be the tributaries of the Poetic Genius; it was this that our great poet, King David, desired so fervently & invokes so pathetic'ly, saying by this he conquers enemies & governs kingdoms; and we so loved our God, that we cursed in his name all the deities of surrounding nations, and asserted that they had rebelled: from these opinions the vulgar came to think that all nations would at last be subject to the jews."

"This," said he, "like all firm perswasions, is come to pass; for all nations believe the jews' code and worship the jews' god, and what greater subjection can be?"

I heard this with some wonder, & must confess my own conviction. After dinner I ask'd Isaiah to favour the world with his lost works; he said none of equal value was lost. Ezekiel said the same of his.

I also asked Isaiah what made him go naked and barefoot three years? he answer'd: "the same that made our friend Diogenes, the Grecian."

I then asked Ezekiel why he eat dung, & lay so long on his right & left side? he answer'd, "the desire of raising other men into a perception of the infinite: this the North American tribes practise, & is he honest who resists his genius or conscience only for the sake of present ease or gratification?"

[¶]

The ancient tradition that the world will be consumed in fire at the end of six thousand years is true, as I have heard from Hell.

For the cherub with his flaming sword is hereby commanded to leave his guard at tree of life; and when he does, the whole creation will be consumed and appear infinite and holy, whereas it now appears finite & corrupt.

This will come to pass by an improvement of sensual enjoyment.

But first the notion that man has a body distinct from his soul is to be expunged; this I shall do by printing in the infernal method, by corrosives, which in Hell are salutary and medicinal, melting apparent surfaces away, and displaying the infinite which was hid.

If the doors of perception were cleansed every thing would appear to man as it is, infinite.

For man has closed himself up, till he sees all things thro' narrow chinks of his cavern.

A MEMORABLE FANCY

I was in a Printing house in Hell, & saw the method in which knowledge is transmitted from generation to generation.

In the first chamber was a Dragon-Man, clearing away the rubbish from a cave's mouth; within, a number of Dragons were hollowing the cave.

In the second chamber was a Viper folding round the rock & the cave, and others adorning it with gold, silver and precious stones.

In the third chamber was an Eagle with wings and feathers of air: he caused the inside of the cave to be infinite; around were numbers of Eagle-like men who built palaces in the immense cliffs.

In the fourth chamber were Lions of flaming fire, raging around & melting the metals into living fluids.

In the fifth chamber were Unnam'd forms, which cast the metals into the expanse.

There they were reciev'd by Men who occupied the sixth chamber, and took the forms of books & were arranged in libraries.

[¶]

The Giants who formed this world into its sensual existence, and now seem to live in it in chains, are in truth the causes of its life & the sources of all activity; but the chains are the cunning of weak and tame minds which have power to resist energy; according to the proverb, the weak in courage is strong in cunning.

Thus one portion of being is the Prolific, the other the Devouring: to the Devourer it seems as if the producer was in his chains; but it is not so, he only takes portions of existence and fancies that the whole.

But the Prolific would cease to be Prolific unless the Devourer, as a sea, received the excess of his delights.

Some will say: "Is not God alone the Prolific?" I answer: "God only Acts & Is, in existing beings or Men."

These two classes of men are always upon earth, & they should be enemies: whoever tries to reconcile them seeks to destroy existence.

Religion is an endeavour to reconcile the two.

Note: Jesus Christ did not wish to unite, but to seperate them, as in the Parable of sheep and goats![5] & he says: "I came not to send Peace, but a Sword."

Messiah or Satan or Tempter was formerly thought to be one of the Antediluvians who are our Energies.

A MEMORABLE FANCY

An Angel came to me and said: "O pitiable foolish young man! O horrible! O dreadful state! consider the hot burning dungeon thou art preparing for thyself to all eternity, to which thou art going in such career."[6]

I said: "Perhaps you will be willing to shew me my eternal lot, & we will contemplate together upon it, and see whether your lot or mine is most desirable."

So he took me thro' a stable & thro' a church & down into the church vault, at the end of which was a mill: thro' the mill we went, and came to a cave: down the winding cavern we groped our tedious way, till a void boundless as a nether sky appear'd beneath us, & we held by the roots of trees and hung over this immensity; but I said: "if you please, we will commit ourselves to this void, and see whether providence is here also: if you will not, I will:" but he answer'd: "do not presume, O young man, but as we here

5. the Parable . . . goats: See Matt. 25:32. 6. in . . . career: with such speed.

remain, behold thy lot which will soon appear when the darkness passes away."

So I remain'd with him, sitting in the twisted root of an oak; he was suspended in a fungus, which hung with the head downward into the deep.

By degrees we beheld the infinite Abyss, fiery as the smoke of a burning city; beneath us, at an immense distance, was the sun, black but shining; round it were fiery tracks on which revolv'd vast spiders, crawling after their prey, which flew, or rather swum, in the infinite deep, in the most terrific shapes of animals sprung from corruption; & the air was full of them, & seem'd composed of them: these are Devils, and are called Powers of the air. I now asked my companion which was my eternal lot? he said: "between the black & white spiders."

But now, from between the black & white spiders, a cloud and fire burst and rolled thro' the deep, black'ning all beneath, so that the nether deep grew black as a sea, & rolled with a terrible noise; beneath us was nothing now to be seen but a black tempest, till looking east between the clouds & the waves, we saw a cataract of blood mixed with fire, and not many stones' throw from us appear'd and sunk again the scaly fold of a monstrous serpent; at last, to the east, distant about three degrees, appear'd a fiery crest above the waves; slowly it reared like a ridge of golden rocks, till we discover'd two globes of crimson fire, from which the sea fled away in clouds of smoke; and now we saw it was the head of Leviathan; his forehead was divided into streaks of green & purple like those on a tyger's forehead: soon we saw his mouth & red gills hang just above the raging foam, tinging the black deep with beams of blood, advancing toward us with all the fury of a spiritual existence.

My friend the Angel climb'd up from his station into the mill: I remain'd alone; & then this appearance was no more, but I found myself sitting on a pleasant bank beside a river by moonlight, hearing a harper, who sung to the harp; & his theme was: "The man who never alters his opinion is like standing water, & breeds reptiles of the mind."

But I arose and sought for the mill, & there I found my Angel, who, surprised, asked me how I escaped?

I answer'd: "All that we saw was owing to your metaphysics; for when you ran away, I found myself on a bank by moonlight hearing a harper. But now we have seen my eternal lot, shall I shew you yours?" he laugh'd at my proposal; but I by force suddenly caught him in my arms, & flew westerly thro' the night, till we were elevated above the earth's shadow; then I flung myself with him directly into the body of the sun; here I clothed myself in white, & taking in my hand Swedenborg's volumes, sunk from the glorious clime, and passed all the planets till we came to saturn: here I stay'd to rest, & then leap'd into the void between saturn & the fixed stars.

"Here," said I, "is your lot, in this space—if space it may be call'd." Soon we saw the stable and the church, & I took him to the altar and open'd the Bible, and lo! it was a deep pit, into which I descended, driving the Angel before me; soon we saw seven houses of brick; one we enter'd; in it were a number of monkeys, baboons, & all of that species, chain'd by the middle, grinning and snatching at one another, but withheld by the shortness of their chains: however, I saw that they sometimes grew numerous, and then the weak were caught by the strong, and with a grinning aspect, first coupled with, & then devour'd, by plucking off first one limb and then another, till the body was left a helpless trunk; this, after grinning & kissing it with seeming fondness, they devour'd too; and here & there I saw one savourily picking the flesh off his own tail; as the stench terribly annoy'd us both, we went into the mill, & I in my hand brought the skeleton of a body, which in the mill was Aristotle's Analytics.[7]

So the Angel said: "thy phantasy has imposed upon me, & thou oughtest to be ashamed."

I answer'd: "we impose on one another, & it is but lost time to converse with you whose works are only Analytics."

[¶]

Opposition is true Friendship.

[¶]

I have always found that Angels have the vanity to speak of themselves as the only wise; this they do with a confident insolence sprouting from systematic reasoning.

Thus Swedenborg boasts that what he writes is new; tho' it is only the Contents or Index of already publish'd books.

A man carried a monkey about for a shew, &

---

7. **Aristotle's Analytics:** *Prior Analytics* and *Posterior Analytics*, two works on logic, presenting, among other matters, a discussion of the mode of syllogistic reasoning, which was Aristotle's discovery.

because he was a little wiser than the monkey, grew vain, and conciev'd himself as much wiser than seven men. It is so with Swedenborg: he shews the folly of churches, & exposes hypocrites, till he imagines that all are religious, & himself the single one on earth that ever broke a net.

Now hear a plain fact: Swedenborg has not written one new truth. Now hear another: he has written all the old falsehoods.

And now hear the reason. He conversed with Angels who are all religious, & conversed not with Devils who all hate religion, for he was incapable thro' his conceited notions.

Thus Swedenborg's writings are a recapitulation of all superficial opinions, and an analysis of the more sublime—but no further.

Have now another plain fact. Any man of mechanical talents may, from the writings of Paracelsus[8] or Jacob Behmen,[9] produce ten thousand volumes of equal value with Swedenborg's, and from those of Dante or Shakespear an infinite number.

But when he has done this, let him not say that he knows better than his master, for he only holds a candle in sunshine.

A MEMORABLE FANCY

Once I saw a Devil in a flame of fire, who arose before an Angel that sat on a cloud, and the Devil utter'd these words:

"The worship of God is: Honouring his gifts in other men, each according to his genius, and loving the greatest men best: those who envy or calumniate great men hate God; for there is no other God."

The Angel hearing this became almost blue; but mastering himself he grew yellow, & at last white, pink, & smiling, and then replied:

"Thou Idolater! is not God One? & is not he visible in Jesus Christ? and has not Jesus Christ given his sanction to the law of ten commandments? and are not all other men fools, sinners, & nothings?"

The Devil answer'd: "bray a fool in a morter with wheat, yet shall not his folly be beaten out of him; if Jesus Christ is the greatest man, you ought to love him

in the greatest degree; now hear how he has given his sanction to the law of ten commandments: did he not mock at the sabbath, and so mock the sabbath's God? murder those who were murder'd because of him? turn away the law from the woman taken in adultery? steal the labor of others to support him? bear false witness when he omitted making a defence before Pilate? covet when he pray'd for his disciples, and when he bid them shake off the dust of their feet against such as refused to lodge them? I tell you, no virtue can exist without breaking these ten commandments. Jesus was all virtue, and acted from impulse, not from rules."

When he had so spoken, I beheld the Angel, who stretched out his arms, embracing the flame of fire, & he was consumed and arose as Elijah.

Note: This Angel, who is now become a Devil, is my particular friend; we often read the Bible together in its infernal or diabolical sense, which the world shall have if they behave well.

I have also The Bible of Hell, which the world shall have whether they will or no.

[¶]

One Law for the Lion & Ox is Oppression.

A SONG OF LIBERTY

I

The Eternal Female groan'd! it was heard over all the Earth.

2. Albion's[10] coast is sick, silent; the American meadows faint!

3. Shadows of Prophecy shiver along by the lakes and the rivers, and mutter across the ocean: France, rend down thy dungeon!

4. Golden Spain, burst the barriers of old Rome!

5. Cast thy keys, O Rome, into the deep, down falling, even to eternity down falling,

6. And weep.

7. In her trembling hand she took the new born terror, howling.

8. On those infinite mountains of light, now barr'd out by the atlantic sea, the new born fire stood before the starry king!

8. **Paracelsus:** sixteenth-century Swiss alchemist and physician, author of occult writings. **9. Jacob Behmen:** Jakob Böhme, early seventeenth-century German theosophist and mystic.

10. **Albion:** England.

9. Flag'd with grey brow'd snows and thunderous visages, the jealous wings wav'd over the deep.

10. The speary hand burned aloft, unbuckled was the shield; forth went the hand of jealousy among the flaming hair, and hurl'd the new born wonder thro' the starry night.

11. The fire, the fire is falling!

12. Look up! look up! O citizen of London, enlarge thy countenance! O Jew, leave counting gold! return to thy oil and wine. O African! black African! (go, winged thought, widen his forehead.)

13. The fiery limbs, the flaming hair, shot like the sinking sun into the western sea.

14. Wak'd from his eternal sleep, the hoary element roaring fled away.

15. Down rush'd, beating his wings in vain, the jealous king; his grey brow'd councellors, thunderous warriors, curl'd veterans, among helms, and shields, and chariots, horses, elephants, banners, castles, slings, and rocks.

16. Falling, rushing, ruining! buried in the ruins, on Urthona's[11] dens;

17. All night beneath the ruins; then, their sullen flames faded, emerge round the gloomy King.

18. With thunder and fire, leading his starry hosts thro' the waste wilderness, he promulgates his ten commands, glancing his beamy eyelids over the deep in dark dismay.

19. Where the son of fire in his eastern cloud, while the morning plumes her golden breast,

20. Spurning the clouds written with curses, stamps the stony law to dust, loosing the eternal horses from the dens of night, crying:

> EMPIRE IS NO MORE! AND NOW THE LION
> & WOLF SHALL CEASE.

CHORUS

Let the Priests of the Raven of dawn no longer, in deadly black, with hoarse note curse the sons of joy. Nor his accepted brethren—whom, tyrant, he calls free—lay the bound or build the roof. Nor pale religious letchery call that virginity that wishes but acts not!

For every thing that lives is Holy.

11. **Urthona:** a symbolic character representing, in Blake's other works, spirit and creative power.

FROM

SONGS OF EXPERIENCE

This counterpart and "corrective" to the *Songs of Innocence* was etched in 1794, and Blake then issued both parts together under the title *Songs of Innocence and of Experience: Shewing the Two Contrary States of the Human Soul.* The title page of *Songs of Innocence* depicts two pastoral children looking at a book held by a seated woman; that of *Songs of Experience* shows two young people weeping over an elderly couple who lie dead. It would appear that most of the poems in either book are not to be apprehended without their matching "contraries" in the other. Thus *The Lamb* is completed by *The Tyger*, and *The Blossom* by *The Sick Rose*. The poems of experience do not cancel the poems of innocence: they "marry" them instead.

THE CHIMNEY SWEEPER

A little black thing among the snow,
Crying "'weep! 'weep!" in notes of woe!
"Where are thy father & mother? say?"
"They are both gone up to the church to pray."

"Because I was happy upon the heath,
And smil'd among the winter's snow,
They clothed me in the clothes of death,
And taught me to sing the notes of woe.

"And because I am happy & dance & sing,
They think they have done me no injury,   10
And are gone to praise God & his Priest & King,
Who make up a heaven of our misery."

THE SICK ROSE

O Rose, thou art sick!
The invisible worm
That flies in the night,
In the howling storm,

Has found out thy bed
Of crimson joy,
And his dark secret love
Does thy life destroy.

THE TYGER

Tyger! Tyger! burning bright
In the forests of the night,
What immortal hand or eye
Could frame thy fearful symmetry?

In what distant deeps or skies
Burnt the fire of thine eyes?
On what wings dare he aspire?
What the hand dare sieze the fire?

And what shoulder, & what art,
Could twist the sinews of thy heart?   10
And when thy heart began to beat,
What dread hand? & what dread feet?

What the hammer? what the chain?
In what furnace was thy brain?
What the anvil? what dread grasp
Dare its deadly terrors clasp?

When the stars threw down their spears,
And water'd heaven with their tears,
Did he smile his work to see?
Did he who made the Lamb make thee?   20

Tyger! Tyger! burning bright
In the forests of the night,
What immortal hand or eye,
Dare frame thy fearful symmetry?

AH! SUN-FLOWER

Ah, Sun-flower! weary of time,
Who countest the steps of the Sun,
Seeking after that sweet golden clime
Where the traveller's journey is done:

Where the Youth pined away with desire,
And the pale Virgin shrouded in snow
Arise from their graves, and aspire
Where my Sun-flower wishes to go.

THE GARDEN OF LOVE

I went to the Garden of Love,
And saw what I never had seen:
A Chapel was built in the midst,
Where I used to play on the green.

And the gates of this Chapel were shut,
And "Thou shalt not" writ over the door;
So I turn'd to the Garden of Love
That so many sweet flowers bore;

And I saw it was filled with graves,
And tomb-stones where flowers should be;   10
And Priests in black gowns were walking their rounds,
And binding with briars my joys & desires.

LONDON

I wander thro' each charter'd street,
Near where the charter'd Thames does flow,
And mark in every face I meet
Marks of weakness, marks of woe.

In every cry of every Man,
In every Infant's cry of fear,
In every voice, in every ban,°
The mind-forg'd manacles I hear.

How the Chimney-sweeper's cry
Every black'ning Church appalls;   10
And the hapless Soldier's sigh
Runs in blood down Palace walls.

But most thro' midnight streets I hear
How the youthful Harlot's curse
Blasts the new born Infant's tear,
And blights with plagues the Marriage hearse.

INFANT SORROW

My mother groan'd! my father wept.
Into the dangerous world I leapt:
Helpless, naked, piping loud:
Like a fiend hid in a cloud.

Struggling in my father's hands,
Striving against my swadling bands,
Bound and weary I thought best
To sulk upon my mother's breast.

SONGS OF EXPERIENCE: *London*. **7. ban:** curse.

A POISON TREE

I was angry with my friend:
I told my wrath, my wrath did end.
I was angry with my foe:
I told it not, my wrath did grow.

And I water'd it in fears,
Night & morning with my tears;
And I sunned it with smiles,
And with soft deceitful wiles.

And it grew both day and night,
Till it bore an apple bright;   10
And my foe beheld it shine,
And he knew that it was mine,

And into my garden stole
When the night had veil'd the pole:
In the morning glad I see
My foe outstretch'd beneath the tree.

[POEMS
FROM MANUSCRIPT]

The following poems are selected from two Blake
manuscripts. What is now called the Rossetti manuscript Blake used as a rough sketchbook and notebook
for twenty years; the Pickering manuscript is smaller
and contains, in general, fair copies of finished poems.
Although the poems can hardly be dated with accuracy,
it can be said that the first six poems here were written
between 1793 and 1803; the next two around 1803; the
Auguries of Innocence would seem to belong to the years
1800–03; the last four poems were probably written
between 1808 and 1811.

[I LAID ME DOWN
UPON A BANK]

I laid me down upon a bank
Where love lay sleeping.
I heard among the rushes dank
Weeping, Weeping.

Then I went to the heath & the wild
To the thistles & thorns of the waste
And they told me how they were beguil'd,
Driven out, & compel'd to be chaste.

[I SAW A CHAPEL
ALL OF GOLD]

I saw a chapel all of gold
That none did dare to enter in,
And many weeping stood without,
Weeping, mourning, worshipping.

I saw a serpent rise between
The white pillars of the door,
And he forc'd & forc'd & forc'd,
Down the gold hinges tore.

And along the pavement sweet,
Set with pearls & rubies bright,   10
All his slimy length he drew,
Till upon the altar white

Vomiting his poison out
On the bread & on the wine.
So I turn'd into a sty
And laid me down among the swine.

[ARE NOT THE JOYS
OF MORNING SWEETER]

Are not the joys of morning sweeter
Than the joys of night?
And are the vig'rous joys of youth
Ashamed of the light?

Let age & sickness silent rob
The vineyards in the night;
But those who burn with vig'rous youth
Pluck fruits before the light.

[ABSTINENCE SOWS
SAND ALL OVER]

Abstinence sows sand all over
The ruddy limbs & flaming hair,
But Desire Gratified
Plants fruits of life & beauty there.

THE QUESTION ANSWER'D

What is it men in women do require?
The lineaments of Gratified Desire.
What is it women do in men require?
The lineaments of Gratified Desire.

[SOFT DECEIT & IDLENESS]

Soft deceit & Idleness,
These are Beauty's sweetest dress.

[WHEN A MAN HAS MARRIED A WIFE]

When a Man has Married a Wife, he finds out whether
Her knees & elbows are only glewed together.

[MOCK ON, MOCK ON VOLTAIRE, ROUSSEAU]

Mock on, Mock on Voltaire, Rousseau:°
Mock on, Mock on: 'tis all in vain!
You throw the sand against the wind,
And the wind blows it back again.

And every sand becomes a Gem
Reflected in the beams divine;
Blown back they blind the mocking Eye,
But still in Israel's paths they shine.

The Atoms of Democritus
And Newton's Particles of light°   10
Are sands upon the Red sea shore,
Where Israel's tents do shine so bright.

POEMS FROM MANUSCRIPT: *Mock On*. **1. Voltaire, Rousseau:**
Voltaire gained a reputation as a "mocker" not merely from
his witty satirical romances like *Candide* (1759) but also
from his skeptical articles in the *Encyclopédie* (1751–72) and
in his own *Dictionnaire philosophique* (1764); Rousseau had
created a scandal among the orthodox primarily with Book
IV of his *Emile* (1762), where he advances broadly deistic
ideas. **10. Newton's . . . light:** Democritus, the Greek
philosopher of the fifth century B.C., maintained that matter
is made of indestructible and hence eternal atoms; Newton's
theory that light consists of particles was set forth in his
famous *Optics* (1704).

AUGURIES OF INNOCENCE

To see a World in a Grain of Sand
And a Heaven in a Wild Flower,
Hold Infinity in the palm of your hand
And Eternity in an hour.
A Robin Red breast in a Cage
Puts all Heaven in a Rage.
A dove house fill'd with doves & Pigeons
Shudders Hell thro' all its regions.
A dog starv'd at his Master's Gate
Predicts the ruin of the State.   10
A Horse misus'd upon the Road
Calls to Heaven for Human blood.
Each outcry of the hunted Hare
A fibre from the Brain does tear.
A Skylark wounded in the wing,
A Cherubim does cease to sing.
The Game Cock clip'd & arm'd for fight
Does the Rising Sun affright.
Every Wolf's & Lion's howl
Raises from Hell a Human Soul.   20
The wild deer, wand'ring here & there,
Keeps the Human Soul from Care.
The Lamb misus'd breeds Public strife
And yet forgives the Butcher's Knife.
The Bat that flits at close of Eve
Has left the Brain that won't Believe.
The Owl that calls upon the Night
Speaks the Unbeliever's fright.
He who shall hurt the little Wren
Shall never be belov'd by Men.   30
He who the Ox to wrath has mov'd
Shall never be by Woman lov'd.
The wanton Boy that kills the Fly
Shall feel the Spider's enmity.
He who torments the Chafer's° sprite
Weaves a Bower in endless Night.
The Catterpiller on the Leaf
Repeats to thee thy Mother's grief.
Kill not the Moth nor Butterfly,
For the Last Judgment draweth nigh.   40
He who shall train the Horse to War
Shall never pass the Polar Bar.
The Beggar's Dog & Widow's Cat,
Feed them & thou wilt grow fat.

Auguries of Innocence. **35. Chafer:** the cockchafer, or May-
bug, a kind of beetle.

The Gnat that sings his Summer's song
Poison gets from Slander's tongue.
The poison of the Snake & Newt
Is the sweat of Envy's Foot.
The Poison of the Honey Bee
Is the Artist's Jealousy.   50
The Prince's Robes & Beggar's Rags
Are Toadstools on the Miser's Bags.
A truth that's told with bad intent
Beats all the Lies you can invent.
It is right it should be so;
Man was made for Joy & Woe;
And when this we rightly know
Thro' the World we safely go.
Joy & Woe are woven fine,
A Clothing for the Soul divine;   60
Under every grief & pine
Runs a joy with silken twine.
The Babe is more than swadling Bands;
Throughout all these Human Lands
Tools were made, & Born were hands,
Every Farmer Understands.
Every Tear from Every Eye
Becomes a Babe in Eternity;
This is caught by Females bright
And return'd to its own delight.   70
The Bleat, the Bark, Bellow & Roar
Are Waves that Beat on Heaven's Shore.
The Babe that weeps the Rod beneath
Writes Revenge in realms of death.
The Beggar's Rags, fluttering in Air,
Does to Rags the Heavens tear.
The Soldier, arm'd with Sword & Gun,
Palsied strikes the Summer's Sun.
The poor Man's Farthing is worth more
Than all the Gold on Afric's Shore.   80
One Mite wrung from the Labrer's hands
Shall buy & sell the Miser's Lands:
Or, if protected from on high,
Does that whole Nation sell & buy.
He who mocks the Infant's Faith
Shall be mock'd in Age & Death.
He who shall teach the Child to Doubt
The rotting Grave shall ne'er get out.
He who respects the Infant's faith
Triumphs over Hell & Death.   90
The Child's Toys & the Old Man's Reasons
Are the Fruits of the Two seasons.
The Questioner, who sits so sly,
Shall never know how to Reply.

He who replies to words of Doubt
Doth put the Light of Knowledge out.
The Strongest Poison ever known
Came from Caesar's Laurel Crown.
Nought can deform the Human Race
Like to the Armour's iron brace.   100
When Gold & Gems adorn the Plow
To peaceful Arts shall Envy Bow.
A Riddle or the Cricket's Cry
Is to Doubt a fit Reply.
The Emmet's° Inch & Eagle's Mile
Make Lame Philosophy to smile.
He who Doubts from what he sees
Will ne'er Believe, do what you Please.
If the Sun & Moon should doubt,
They'd immediately Go out.   110
To be in a Passion you Good may do
But no Good if a Passion is in you.
The Whore & Gambler, by the State
Licenc'd build that Nation's Fate.
The Harlot's cry from Street to Street
Shall weave Old England's winding Sheet.
The Winner's Shout, the Loser's Curse
Dance before dead England's Hearse.
Every Night & every Morn
Some to Misery are Born.   120
Every Morn & every Night
Some are Born to sweet delight.
Some are Born to sweet delight,
Some are Born to Endless Night.
We are led to Believe a Lie
When we see not Thro' the Eye
Which was Born in a Night to perish in a Night
When the Soul Slept in Beams of Light.
God Appears & God is Light
To those poor Souls who dwell in Night,   130
But does a Human Form Display
To those who Dwell in Realms of day.

[GROWN OLD IN LOVE FROM SEVEN TILL SEVEN TIMES SEVEN]

Grown old in Love from Seven till Seven times Seven,
I oft have wish'd for Hell for Ease from Heaven.

105. Emmet: ant.

[I ASK'D MY DEAR FRIEND, ORATOR PRIG]

I ask'd my dear Friend, Orator Prig:
"What's the first part of Oratory?" he said: "a great
   wig."
"And what is the second?" then dancing a jig
And bowing profoundly he said: "a great wig."
"And what is the third?" then he snor'd like a pig,
And puffing his cheeks he replied: "a Great wig."
So if a Great Painter° with Questions you push,
"What's the first Part of Painting?" he'll say: "a Paint
   Brush."
"And what is the second?" with most modest blush,
He'll smile like a Cherub & say: "a paint Brush."   10
"And what is the third?" he'll bow like a rush,
With a lear in his Eye, he'll reply: "a Paint Brush."
Perhaps this is all a Painter can want;
But look yonder—that house is the house of
   Rembrandt.
                    &c.
               (to come in Barry, a Poem.°)

[SIR JOSHUA PRAISES MICHAEL ANGELO]

Sir Joshua Praises Michael Angelo
'Tis Christian Mildness when Knaves Praise a Foe;
But 'Twould be Madness all the World would say,
Should Michael Angelo praise Sir Joshua—
Christ us'd the Pharisees in a rougher way.°

I Ask'd My Dear Friend, Orator Prig. **7. a Great Painter:**
Sir Joshua Reynolds (1723–92), who, as president of the Royal
Academy, delivered his famous yearly *Discourses* (see Part Six)
from 1769 to 1790. **15. Barry, a Poem:** Blake planned to write
a poem (apparently of some length) on the career and frustrations of the Irish history painter James Barry (1741–1806),
whose work Blake admired. Barry was finally expelled from
the Royal Academy in 1799 for picking quarrels and died in
great poverty. *Sir Joshua Praises Michael Angelo.* **5. Christ
. . . way:** See Matt. 23.

[HE'S A BLOCKHEAD WHO WANTS A PROOF OF WHAT HE CAN'T PERCIEVE]

He's a Blockhead who wants a proof of what he can't
   Percieve,
And he's a Fool who tries to make such a Blockhead
   believe.

FROM

PREFACE [TO *MILTON* . . .]

*Milton, a Poem in Two Books, to Justify the Ways of God to
Men,* was etched from 1804 to 1808. It is an extensive
poem written in long unrhymed accentual lines that
reveal the rhetorical influence of the Old Testament and
Ossian. In it Blake attempts a reinterpretation of Milton
—a poet he loved and one who probably influenced him
more than any other—by purifying him of weaknesses
Blake attributed to his erroneous theology, his repressive
morality, and his excessively Latinate style. The brief
prose Preface to *Milton,* exhorting young authors and
painters to reject "the Stolen and Perverted Writings
of Homer & Ovid, of Plato & Cicero" in favor of "the
Sublime of the Bible," ends with this sentence: "We do
not want either Greek or Roman Models if we are but
just & true to our own Imaginations, those Worlds of
Eternity in which we shall live for ever in JESUS OUR
LORD." This short poem follows immediately as the
conclusion of the Preface.

And did those feet in ancient time
Walk upon England's mountains green?
And was the holy Lamb of God
On England's pleasant pastures seen?

And did the Countenance Divine
Shine forth upon our clouded hills?
And was Jerusalem builded here
Among these dark Satanic Mills?

Bring me my Bow of burning gold:
Bring me my Arrows of Desire: 10
Bring me my Spear: O clouds unfold!
Bring me my Chariot of fire.

I will not cease from Mental Fight,
Nor shall my Sword sleep in my hand
Till we have built Jerusalem
In England's green & pleasant Land.

FROM

[ANNOTATIONS TO REYNOLDS'S *DISCOURSES ON ART*]

Blake was fond of writing pungent observations in the few books he owned. Around 1808 he annotated on the blank leaves and in the margins of his copy of *The Works of Sir Joshua Reynolds, Knight* (2nd ed.; 3 vols., 1798) eight of Reynolds's *Discourses*.

The text is from Keynes, although we have occasionally quoted the Reynolds passages more fully than Keynes does.

This Man was Hired to Depress Art.

This is the Opinion of Will Blake: my Proofs of this Opinion are given in the following Notes.

Advice of the Popes who succeeded the Age of
    Rafael[1]
Degrade first the Arts if you'd Mankind Degrade.
Hire Idiots to Paint with cold light & hot shade:
Give high Price for the worst, leave the best in
    disgrace,
And with Labours of Ignorance fill every place.

Having spent the Vigour of my Youth & Genius under the Opression of Sr Joshua & his Gang of Cunning Hired Knaves Without Employment & as

much as could possibly be Without Bread, The Reader must Expect to Read in all my Remarks on these Books Nothing but Indignation & Resentment. While Sr Joshua was rolling in Riches, Barry was Poor & Unemploy'd except by his own Energy; Mortimer[2] was call'd a Madman, & only Portrait Painting applauded & rewarded by the Rich & Great. Reynolds & Gainsborough[3] Blotted & Blurred one against the other & Divided all the English World between them. Fuseli,[4] Indignant, almost hid himself. I am hid.

The Arts & Sciences are the Destruction of Tyrannies or Bad Governments. Why should A Good Government endeavour to Depress what is its Chief & only Support?

The Foundation of Empire is Art & Science. Remove them or Degrade them, & the Empire is No More. Empire follows Art & Not Vice Versa as Englishmen suppose.

"On peut dire que le Pape Léon Xme en encourageant les Etudes donna Les armes contre lui-même. J'ai oui dire à un Seigneur Anglais qu'il avait vu une Lettre du Seigneur Polus, ou de la Pole, depuis Cardinal, à ce Pape; dans laquelle, en le félicitant sur ce qu'il etendait le progrès de Science en Europe, il l'avertissait *qu'il était dangereux de rendre les hommes trop Savan[t]s.*"[5]
    VOLTAIRE, *Mœurs de Nations*. Tome 4.
O Englishmen! why are you still of this foolish Cardinal's opinion?

Who will Dare to Say that Polite Art is Encouraged or Either Wished or Tolerated in a Nation where The Society for the Encouragement of Art Suffer'd Barry to Give them his Labour for Nothing, A Society Composed of the Flower of the English Nobility & Gentry?—Suffering an Artist to Starve while he Supported Really what They, under Pretence of

---

2. **Mortimer:** John Hamilton Mortimer (1741–79), painter of history and allegory. 3. **Gainsborough:** Thomas Gainsborough (1727–88), like Reynolds, made his living by painting expensive portraits. 4. **Fuseli:** Henry Fuseli (1741–1825), Swiss painter and scholar who came to England in 1763. 5. **On . . . Savants:** "It may be said that Pope Leo X, by the encouragement he gave to learning, furnished arms against himself. I have been told by an English lord that he had seen a letter from Cardinal [Reginald] Pole to this Pope, in which, while congratulating him on having extended the progress of learning in Europe, he warns him *that it was dangerous to make men too well informed*" (Voltaire, *Essays on the Spirit of Nations* [1769]).

ANNOTATIONS TO REYNOLDS'S *Discourses on Art: Introduction.*
1. **the Age . . . Rafael:** It lasted until roughly the middle of the sixteenth century.

Encouraging, were Endeavouring to Depress.—Barry told me that while he Did that Work,[6] he Lived on Bread & Apples.

O Society for Encouragement of Art! O King & Nobility of England! Where have you hid Fuseli's Milton?[7] Is Satan troubled at his Exposure?

[DISCOURSE III]

A work of Genius is a Work "Not to be obtain'd by the Invocation of Memory & her Syren Daughters, but by Devout prayer to that Eternal Spirit, who can enrich with all utterance & knowledge & sends out his Seraphim with the hallowed fire of his Altar to touch & purify the lips of whom he pleases." MILTON.[1]

The following Discourse is particularly Interesting to Block heads, as it endeavours to prove That there is No such thing as Inspiration & that any Man of a plain Understanding may by Thieving from Others become a Mich. Angelo.

[Reynolds:] The wish of the genuine painter must be more extensive [than a desire merely to copy Nature]: instead of endeavouring to amuse man-kind with the minute neatness of his imitations, he must endeavour to improve them by the grandeur of his ideas.

[Blake:] Without Minute Neatness of Execution The Sublime cannot Exist! Grandeur of Ideas is founded on Precision of Ideas.

The Moderns are not less convinced than the Ancients of this superior power [of rising above mere copying of a model] existing in the art; nor less sensible of its effects.

I wish that this was True.

Such is the warmth with which both the Ancients and Moderns speak of this divine principle of the art;

And such is the Coldness with which Reynolds speaks! And such is his Enmity.

but, as I have formerly observed, enthusiastick admiration seldom promotes knowledge.

Enthusiastic Admiration is the first Principle of Knowledge & its last. Now he begins to Degrade, to Deny & to Mock.

Though a student by such praise [of inspiration in art] may have his attention roused, and a desire excited, of running in this great career; yet it is possible that what has been said to excite, may only serve to deter him. He examines his own mind, and perceives there nothing of that divine inspiration, with which, he is told, so many others have been favoured.

The Man who on Examining his own Mind finds nothing of Inspiration ought not to dare to be an Artist, & he is a Fool & a Cunning Knave suited to the Purposes of Evil Demons.

[The student] never travelled to heaven to gather new ideas; and he finds himself possessed of no other qualifications than what mere common observation and a plain understanding can confer.

The Man who never in his Mind & Thoughts travel'd to Heaven Is No Artist.

Artists who are above a plain Understanding are Mock'd & Destroy'd by this President of Fools.

But on this, as upon many other occasions, we ought to distinguish how much is to be given to enthusiasm, and how much to reason. We ought to allow for, and we ought to commend that strength of vivid expression, which is necessary to convey, in its full force, the highest sense of the most complete effect of Art; taking care, at the same time, not to lose in terms of vague admiration, that solidity and truth of principle, upon which alone we can reason, and may be enabled to practise.

It is Evident that Reynolds Wish'd none but Fools to be in the Arts & in order to this, he calls all others Vague Enthusiasts or Madmen.

---

6. that Work: From 1777 to 1783 Barry painted on the walls of the Society of Arts six allegorical pictures titled *The Progress of Human Culture;* he received 250 guineas for the work. 7. Fuseli's Milton: a collection of forty-seven paintings of scenes from Milton's poems, which Fuseli exhibited unsuccessfully in 1779 and 1780. *Discourse III.* 1. Milton: in *The Reason of Church Government Urged Against Prelaty* (1642).

What has Reasoning to do with the Art of Painting?

There are many beauties in our Art that seem, at first, to lie without the reach of precept, and yet may easily be reduced to practical principles. Experience is all in all; but it is not every one who profits from experience; and most people err, not so much from want of capacity to find their object, as from not knowing what object to pursue.

The Man who does not know what Object to Pursue is an Idiot.

This great ideal perfection and beauty are not to be sought in the heavens, but upon the earth.

A Lie!

They are about us, and upon every side of us.

A Lie!

But the power of discovering what is deformed in nature, or in other words, what is particular and uncommon, can be acquired only by experience;

A Lie!

and the whole beauty of the art consists, in my opinion, in being able to get above all singular forms, local customs, particularities, and details of every kind.

A Folly! Singular & Particular Detail is the Foundation of the Sublime.

All the objects which are exhibited to our view by nature, upon close examination will be found to have their blemishes and defects. The most beautiful forms have something about them like weakness, minuteness, or imperfection.

Minuteness is their whole Beauty.

This long laborious comparison [of similar natural forms] should be the first study of the painter, who aims at the greatest style. By this means, he acquires a just idea of beautiful forms; he corrects nature by herself, her imperfect state by her more perfect. His eye being enabled to distinguish the accidental deficiencies, excrescences, and deformities of things, from their general figures, he makes out an abstract idea of their forms more perfect than any one original; and what may seem a paradox, he learns to design naturally by drawing his figures unlike to any one object. This idea of the perfect state of nature, which the Artist calls the Ideal Beauty, is the great leading principle by which works of genius are conducted.

Knowledge of Ideal Beauty is Not to be Acquired. It is Born with us. Innate Ideas are in Every Man, Born with him; they are truly Himself. The Man who says that we have No Innate Ideas must be a Fool & Knave, Having No Con-Science or Innate Science.

Thus it is from a reiterated experience and a close comparison of the objects in nature, that an artist becomes possessed of the idea of that central form, if I may so express it, from which every deviation is deformity.

One Central Form composed of all other Forms being Granted, it does not therefore follow that all other Forms are Deformity.

All Forms are Perfect in the Poet's Mind, but these are not Abstracted nor compounded from Nature, but are from Imagination.

Even the great Bacon treats with ridicule the idea of confining proportion to rules, or of producing beauty by selection.[2]

The Great Bacon—he is Call'd: I call him the Little Bacon—says that Every thing must be done by Experiment; his first principle is Unbelief, and yet here he says that Art must be produc'd Without such Method. He is Like Sr Joshua, full of Self-Contradiction & Knavery.

If [Bacon] means that beauty has nothing to do with rule, he is mistaken. There is a rule, obtained out of general nature, to contradict which is to fall into deformity.

What is General Nature? is there Such a Thing? what is General Knowledge? is there such a Thing? Strictly Speaking All Knowledge is Particular.

To the principle I have laid down, that the idea of beauty in each species of beings is an invariable one, it may be objected, that in every particular species there are various central forms, which are separate and distinct from each other, and yet are each undeniably beautiful.

Here he loses sight of A Central Form & Gets into Many Central Forms.

2. Even . . . selection: See the essay *Of Beauty* (1625) by Francis Bacon (1561-1626).

It is true, indeed, that these figures [i.e., those of Hercules, the Gladiator, the Apollo] are each perfect in their kind, though of different characters and proportions; but still none of them is the representation of an individual, but of a class.

Every Class is Individual.

Thus, though the forms of childhood and age differ exceedingly, there is a common form in childhood, and a common form in age, which is the more perfect, as it is more remote from all peculiarities.

There is no End to the Follies of this Man. Childhood & Age are Equally belonging to Every Class.

But I must add further, that though the most perfect forms of each of the general divisions of the human figure are ideal, and superior to any individual form of that class; yet the highest perfection of the human figure is not to be found in any one of them. It is not in the Hercules, nor in the Gladiator, nor in the Apollo; but in that form which is taken from all . . . .

Here he comes again to his Central Form.

There is, likewise, a kind of symmetry, or proportion, which may properly be said to belong to deformity. A figure lean or corpulent, tall or short, though deviating from beauty, may still have a certain union of the various parts.

The Symmetry of Deformity is a Pretty Foolery. Can any Man who Thinks Talk so? Leanness or Fatness is not Deformity, but Reynolds thought Character Itself Extravagance & Deformity. Age & Youth are not Classes, but Properties of Each Class; so are Leanness & Fatness.

When the Artist has by diligent attention acquired a clear and distinct idea of beauty and symmetry; when he has reduced the variety of nature to the abstract idea . . . .

What Folly!

. . . the painter must never mistake this capricious changeling [i.e., fashion] for the genuine offspring of nature; he must divest himself of all prejudices in favour of his age or country; he must disregard all local and temporary ornaments, and look only on those general habits, which are every where and always the same . . . .

Generalizing in Every thing, the Man would soon be a Fool, but a Cunning Fool.

Albert Durer, as Vasari[3] has justly remarked, would, probably, have been one of the first painters of his age (and he lived in an era of great artists) had he been initiated into those great principles of the art, which were so well understood and practised by his contemporaries in Italy.

What does this mean, *"Would have been"* one of the *first Painters of his Age?* Albert Durer *Is*, Not would have been. Besides, let them look at Gothic Figures & Gothic Buildings & not talk of Dark Ages or of any Age. Ages are all Equal. But Genius is Always Above The Age.

I should be sorry, if what is here recommended, should be at all understood to countenance a careless or indetermined manner of painting. For though the painter is to overlook the accidental discriminations of nature, he is to exhibit distinctly, and with precision, the general forms of things.

Here he is for Determinate & yet for Indeterminate. Distinct General Form Cannot Exist. Distinctness is Particular, Not General.

A firm and determined outline is one of the characteristics of the great style in painting; and let me add, that he who possesses the knowledge of the exact form which every part of nature ought to have, will be fond of expressing that knowledge with correctness and precision in all his works.

A Noble Sentence!
Here is a Sentence, Which overthrows all his Book.

To conclude; I have endeavoured to reduce the idea of beauty to general principles . . . .

[*two words erased*] that Bacon's Philosophy makes both Statesmen & Artists Fools & Knaves.

3. **Vasari:** Giorgio Vasari (1511–74), Italian painter and art historian, comments on the Nuremberg painter and engraver Albrecht Dürer (1471–1528) in his *Lives of the Most Excellent Italian Painters, Sculptors, and Architects* (1550).

[DISCOURSE VII]

The Purpose of the following discourse is to Prove That Taste & Genius are not of Heavenly Origin & that all who have supposed that they Are so, are to be Consider'd as Weak headed Fanatics.

The Obligations Reynolds has laid on Bad Artists of all Classes will at all times make them his Admirers, but most especially for this discourse, in which it is proved that the Stupid are born with Faculties Equal to other Men, Only they have not Cultivated them because they thought it not worth the trouble.

We will allow a poet to express his meaning, when his meaning is not well known to himself, with a certain degree of obscurity, as it is one source of the sublime.

Obscurity is Neither the Source of the Sublime nor of any Thing Else.

But when, in plain prose, we gravely talk of courting the muse in shady bowers; waiting the call and inspiration of Genius, finding out where he inhabits, and where he is to be invoked with the greatest success; of attending to times and seasons when the imagination shoots with greatest vigour, whether at the summer solstice or the vernal equinox; sagaciously observing how much the wild freedom and liberty of imagination is cramped by attention to established rules; and how this same imagination begins to grow dim in advanced age, smothered and deadened by too much judgment; when we talk such language, or entertain such sentiments as these, we generally rest contented with mere words, or at best entertain notions not only groundless but pernicious.

The Ancients & the wisest of the Moderns were of the opinion that Reynolds condemns & laughs at.

. . . I am persuaded, that scarce a poet is to be found, from Homer down to Dryden, who preserved a sound mind in a sound body, and continued practising his profession to the very last, whose latter works are not as replete with the fire of imagination, as those which were produced in his more youthful days.

As Replete, but Not More Replete.

To understand literally these metaphors or ideas expressed in poetical language, seems to be equally absurd as to conclude . . .

The Ancients did not mean to Impose when they affirm'd their belief in Vision & Revelation. Plato was in Earnest: Milton was in Earnest. They believ'd that God did Visit Man Really & Truly & not as Reynolds pretends.

. . . that because painters sometimes represent poets writing from the dictates of a little winged boy or genius, that this same genius did really inform him in a whisper what he was to write; and that he is himself but a mere machine, unconscious of the operations of his own mind.

How very Anxious Reynolds is to Disprove & Contemn Spiritual Perception!

It is supposed that [the powers of Genius and Taste] are intuitive; that under the name of genius great works are produced, and under the name of taste an exact judgement given, without our knowing why, and without our being under the least obligation to reason, precept, or experience.

Who Ever said this?

One can scarce state these opinions without exposing their absurdity . . . .

He states Absurdities in Company with Truths & calls both Absurd.

. . . I am persuaded, that even among those few who may be called thinkers, the prevalent opinion allows less than it ought to the powers of reason . . . .

The Artifice of the Epicurean[1] Philosophers is to Call all other Opinions Unsolid & Unsubstantial than those which are derived from Earth.

We often appear to differ in Sentiments from each other, merely from the inaccuracy of terms.

It is not in Terms that Reynolds & I disagree. Two Contrary Opinions can never by any Language be made alike. I say, Taste & Genius are Not Teachable or Acquirable, but are born with us. Reynolds says the Contrary.

Discourse VII. **1. Epicurean:** empirical, materialist.

We apply the term TASTE to that act of the mind by which we like or dislike, whatever be the subject. Our judgment upon an airy nothing, a fancy which has no foundation, is called by the same name which we give to our determination concerning those truths which refer to the most general and most unalterable principles of human nature: to the works which are only to be produced by the greatest efforts of the human understanding. However inconvenient this may be, we are obliged to take words as we find them; all we can do is to distinguish the THINGS to which they are applied.

This is False; the Fault is not in Words, but in Things. Locke's Opinions of Words & their Fallaciousness[2] are Artful Opinions & Fallacious also.

It is the very same taste which relishes a demonstration in geometry, that is pleased with the resemblance of a picture to an original, and touched with the harmony of musick.

Demonstration, Similitude & Harmony are Objects of Reasoning. Invention, Identity & Melody are Objects of Intuition.

Colouring is true, when it is naturally adapted to the eye, from brightness, from softness, from harmony, from resemblance; because these agree with their object, NATURE, and therefore are true; as true as mathematical demonstration; but known to be true only to those who study these things.

God forbid that Truth should be Confined to Mathematical Demonstration!

But besides real, there is also apparent truth, or opinion, or prejudice. With regard to real truth, when it is known, the taste which conforms to it, is, and must be, uniform.

He who does not Know Truth at Sight is unworthy of Her Notice.

In proportion as these prejudices [which support "variable truth"] are known to be generally diffused, or long received, the taste which conforms to them approaches nearer to certainty . . . .

2. Locke's . . . Fallaciousness: as set forth in Book III of *An Essay Concerning Humane Understanding* (1690). (See selections from Books II and IV in Part One.)

Here is a great deal to do to Prove that All Truth is Prejudice, for All that is Valuable in Knowledge is Superior to Demonstrative Science, such as is Weighed or Measured.

As these prejudices become more narrow, more local, more transitory, this secondary taste becomes more and more fantastical . . . .

And so he thinks he has proved that Genius & Inspiration are All a Hum.

Having laid down these positions, I shall proceed with less method, because less will serve to explain and apply them.

He calls the Above proceeding with Method!

We will take it for granted, that reason is something invariable and fixed in the nature of things . . . .

Reason, or A Ratio of All we have known, is not the Same it shall be when we know More; he therefore takes a Falshood for granted to set out with.

. . . we will conclude, that whatever goes under the name of taste, which we can fairly bring under the dominion of reason, must be considered as equally exempt from change.

Now this is Supreme Fooling.

The arts would lie open for ever to caprice and casualty, if those who are to judge of their excellencies had no settled principles by which they are to regulate their decisions . . . .

He may as well say that if Man does not lay down settled Principles, The Sun will not rise in a Morning.

My notion of nature comprehends not only the forms which nature produces, but also the nature and internal fabrick and organization, as I may call it, of the human mind and imagination.

Here is a Plain Confession that he Thinks Mind & Imagination not to be above the Mortal & Perishing Nature. Such is the End of Epicurean or Newtonian Philosophy; it is Atheism.

This [Nicolas Poussin's painting of Perseus with the head of Medusa] is undoubtedly a subject of great bustle and tumult, and that the first effect of the picture may correspond to the subject, every principle of composition is violated; there is no principal figure, no principal light, no groups; everything is dispersed, and in such a state of confusion, that the eye finds no repose anywhere. In consequence of the forbidding appearance, I remember turning from it with disgust . . . .

Reynolds's Eye could not bear Characteristic Colouring or Light & Shade.

This conduct of Poussin I hold to be entirely improper to imitate. A picture should please at first sight, and appear to invite the spectator's attention . . . .

Please Whom? Some Men cannot see a Picture except in a Dark Corner.

No one can deny, that violent passions will naturally emit harsh and disagreeable tones . . . .

Violent Passions Emit the Real, Good & Perfect Tones.

If it be objected that Rubens judged ill at first in thinking it necessary to make his work so very ornamental, this puts the question upon new ground.

Here it is call'd Ornamental that the Roman & Bolognian Schools may be Insinuated not to be Ornamental.

Nobody will dispute but some of the best of the Roman or Bolognian schools would have produced a more learned and more noble work [than the Rubens paintings in the Luxembourg Palace].

Learned & Noble is Ornamental.

This leads us to another important province of taste, that of weighing the value of the different classes of the art, and of estimating them accordingly.

A Fool's Balance is no Criterion because, tho' it goes down on the heaviest side, we ought to look what he puts into it.

If an European, when he has cut off his beard, and put false hair on his head, or bound up his own natural hair in regular hard knots, as unlike nature as he can possibly make it . . . meets a Cherokee

Indian, who has bestowed as much time at his toilet, and laid on with equal care and attention his yellow and red oker on particular parts of his forehead or cheeks, as he judges most becoming; whoever of these two despises the other for this attention to the fashion of his country, whichever first feels himself provoked to laugh, is the barbarian.

Excellent!

In the midst of the highest flights of fancy or imagination, reason ought to preside from first to last . . . .

If this is True, it is a devilish Foolish Thing to be an Artist.

FROM

[EPILOGUE TO *FOR THE SEXES: THE GATES OF PARADISE*]

Around 1793 Blake engraved a small emblem book of sixteen plates and a frontispiece, with no text except some cryptic captions beneath the little pictures. One picture, for example, shows a figure beginning to ascend a long ladder reaching to the moon, with the caption "I want! I want!" In this first version, titled *For Children: The Gates of Paradise*, the book was apparently intended as a sort of iconographic primer. Around 1818, Blake added a poetic text and this time apparently addressed the book to adults. The following poem, which concludes the 1818 version, is illustrated by a new engraving, which shows a winged black demon hovering just above the figure of a sleeping traveler.

To The Accuser who is
The God of This World

Truly, My Satan, thou art but a Dunce,
And dost not know the Garment from the Man.
Every Harlot was a Virgin once,
Nor can'st thou ever change Kate into Nan.

Tho' thou art Worship'd by the Names Divine
Of Jesus & Jehovah, thou art still
The Son of Morn in weary Night's decline,
The lost Traveller's Dream under the Hill.

FROM

[LETTERS]

❧

The text is from *The Letters of William Blake*, ed. Geoffrey Keynes (1956); the accidentals are those of Blake's manuscripts, except for the punctuation, which Keynes has occasionally supplied.

❧

[To the Reverend Dr. John Trusler[1]]

REV^D SIR,

I really am sorry that you are fall'n out with the Spiritual World, Especially if I should have to answer for it. I feel very sorry that your Ideas & Mine on Moral Painting differ so much as to have made you angry with my method of Study. If I am wrong, I am wrong in good company. I had hoped your plan comprehended All Species of this Art, & Especially that you would not regret that Species which gives Existence to Every other, namely, Visions of Eternity. You say that I want somebody to Elucidate my Ideas. But you ought to know that What is Grand is necessarily obscure to Weak Men. That which can be made Explicit to the Idiot is not worth my care. The wisest of the Ancients consider'd what is not too Explicit as the fittest for Instruction, because it rouzes the faculties to act. I name Moses, Solomon, Esop, Homer, Plato.

LETTERS. **1. the Reverend . . . Trusler:** an eccentric divine who, first having studied medicine, finally turned literary compiler and publisher. He was interested in employing Blake as a book illustrator, and Blake had offered him a water color illustrative of the idea of "Malevolence" that depicted "a Father, taking leave of his Wife & Child, [being] watch'd by Two Fiends incarnate, with intention that when his back is turned they will murder the mother & her infant" (Letter to Trusler, August 16, 1799). Blake explains Trusler's reaction to the picture in a letter to George Cumberland (August 26, 1799): "I have made [Dr. Trusler] a Drawing in my best manner; he has sent it back with a Letter full of Criticisms, in which he says It accords not with his Intentions, which are to Reject all Fancy from his Work. . . . as I cannot paint Dirty rags & old shoes where I ought to place Naked Beauty or simple ornament, I despair of Ever pleasing one Class of Men . . . . Dr Trusler says: '*Your Fancy* . . . seems to be in the other world, or the World of Spirits, which accords not with my Intentions, which, whilst living in This World, Wish to follow *the Nature of it*.' I could not help Smiling at the difference between the doctrines of Dr Trusler & those of Christ." Trusler has written on the manuscript of Blake's letter: "Blake, dim'd with superstition."

But as you have favor'd me with your remarks on my design, permit me in return to defend it against a mistaken one, which is, That I have supposed Malevolence without a Cause. Is not Merit in one a Cause of Envy in another, & Serenity & Happiness & Beauty a Cause of Malevolence? But Want of Money & the Distress of A Thief can never be alledged as the Cause of his Thieving, for many honest people endure greater hardships with Fortitude. We must therefore seek the Cause elsewhere than in want of Money, for that is the Miser's passion, not the Thief's.

I have therefore proved your Reasonings Ill proportion'd, which you can never prove my figures to be; they are those of Michael Angelo, Rafael & the Antique, & of the best living Models. I perceive that your Eye is perverted by Caricature Prints, which ought not to abound so much as they do. Fun I love, but too much Fun is of all things the most loathsom. Mirth is better than Fun, & Happiness is better than Mirth. I feel that a Man may be happy in This World. And I know that This World is a World of imagination & Vision. I see Every thing I paint In This World, but Every body does not see alike. To the Eyes of a Miser a Guinea is more beautiful than the Sun, & a bag worn with the use of Money has more beautiful proportions than a Vine filled with Grapes. The tree which moves some to tears of joy is in the Eyes of others only a Green thing that stands in the way. Some See Nature all Ridicule & Deformity, & by these I shall not regulate my proportions; & Some Scarce see Nature at all. But to the Eyes of the Man of Imagination, Nature is Imagination itself. As a man is, So he Sees. As the Eye is formed, such are its Powers. You certainly Mistake, when you say that the Visions of Fancy are not to be found in This World. To Me This World is all One continued Vision of Fancy or Imagination, & I feel Flatter'd when I am told so. What is it sets Homer, Virgil & Milton in so high a rank of Art? Why is the Bible more Entertaining & Instructive than any other book? Is it not because they are addressed to the Imagination, which is Spiritual Sensation, & but mediately[2] to the Understanding or Reason? Such is True Painting, and such was alone valued by the Greeks & the best modern Artists. Consider what Lord Bacon says: "Sense sends over to Imagination before Reason have judged, & Reason sends over to Imagination before the Decree can be

2. mediately: "by a secondary cause; in such a manner that something acts between the first cause and the last effect" (Johnson's *Dictionary*).

acted." See Advancem^t of Learning, Part 2, P. 47 of first Edition.

But I am happy to find a Great Majority of Fellow Mortals who can Elucidate My Visions, & Particularly they have been Elucidated by Children, who have taken a greater delight in contemplating my Pictures than I even hoped. Neither Youth nor Childhood is Folly or Incapacity. Some Children are Fools & so are some Old Men. But There is a vast Majority on the side of Imagination or Spiritual Sensation.

To Engrave after another Painter is infinitely more laborious than to Engrave one's own Inventions. And of the size you require my price has been Thirty Guineas, & I cannot afford to do it for less. I had Twelve for the Head I sent you as a Specimen; but after my own designs I could do at least Six times the quantity of labour in the same time, which will account for the difference of price as also that Chalk Engraving is at least six times as laborious as Aqua tinta. I have no objection to Engraving after another Artist. Engraving is the profession I was apprenticed to, & should never have attempted to live by any thing else, If orders had not come in for my Designs & Paintings, which I have the pleasure to tell you are Increasing Every Day. Thus If I am a Painter it is not to be attributed to Seeking after. But I am contented whether I live by Painting or Engraving.

I am, Revd Sir, your very obedient servant,

WILLIAM BLAKE

13 Hercules Buildings
Lambeth
August 23. 1799

[*To John Flaxman*³]

DEAR SCULPTOR OF ETERNITY,

We are safe arrived at our Cottage, which is more beautiful than I thought it, & more convenient. It is a perfect Model for Cottages &, I think, for Palaces of Magnificence, only Enlarging, not altering its proportions, & adding ornaments & not principals. Nothing can be more Grand than its Simplicity & Usefulness. Simple without Intricacy, it seems to be the Spon-

taneous Effusion of Humanity, congenial to the wants of Man. No other formed House can ever please me so well; nor shall I ever be perswaded, I believe, that it can be improved either in Beauty or Use.

Mr. Hayley reciev'd us with his usual brotherly affection. I have begun to work. Felpham is a sweet place for Study, because it is more Spiritual than London. Heaven opens here on all sides her golden Gates; her windows are not obstructed by vapours; voices of Celestial inhabitants are more distinctly heard, & their forms more distinctly seen, & my Cottage is also a Shadow of their houses. My Wife & Sister are both well, courting Neptune for an Embrace.

Our Journey was very pleasant; & tho we had a great deal of Luggage, No Grumbling, All was Chearfulness & Good Humour on the Road, & yet we could not arrive at our Cottage before half past Eleven at night, owing to the necessary shifting of our Luggage from one Chaise to another; for we had Seven Different Chaises, & as many different drivers. We set out between Six & Seven in the Morning of Thursday, with Sixteen heavy boxes & portfolios full of prints. And Now Begins a New life, because another covering of Earth is shaken off. I am more famed in Heaven for my works than I could well concieve. In my Brain are studies & Chambers fill'd with books & pictures of old, which I wrote & painted in ages of Eternity before my mortal life; & those works are the delight & Study of Archangels. Why, then, should I be anxious about the riches or fame of mortality. The Lord our father will do for us & with us according to his Divine will for our Good.

You, O Dear Flaxman, are a Sublime Archangel, My Friend & Companion from Eternity; in the Divine bosom is our Dwelling place. I look back into the regions of Reminiscence & behold our ancient days before this Earth appear'd in its vegetated mortality to my mortal vegetated Eyes. I see our houses of Eternity, which can never be separated, tho' our Mortal vehicles should stand at the remotest corners of heaven from each other.

Farewell, My Best Friend. Remember Me & My Wife in Love & Friendship to our Dear Mrs. Flaxman, whom we ardently desire to Entertain beneath our thatched roof of rusted gold, & believe me for ever to remain | Your Grateful & Affectionate,

WILLIAM BLAKE

Felpham
Septr 21, 1800
Sunday Morning

3. **John Flaxman:** (1755–1826), sculptor and draftsman; a master of the style of the classical revival, he illustrated editions of Homer and Aeschylus. Blake was grateful to him for having introduced him to the very minor poet William Hayley. Hayley engaged Blake to execute the engravings for his *Life of Cowper* (1803–04) and had invited Blake and his wife to rent an inexpensive cottage near him at Felpham, a seashore village on the south coast.

Part Eight

A MISCELLANY
OF
POEMS

William Whitehead

1715–1785

THE JE NE SCAI QUOI

A SONG.

I.

YES, I'm in love, I feel it now,
    And CÆLIA has undone me;
And yet I'll swear I can't tell how
    The pleasing plague stole on me.

II.

'Tis not her face that love creates,
    For there no graces revel;
'Tis not her shape, for there the fates
    Have rather been uncivil.

III.

'Tis not her air, for sure in that
    There's nothing more than common;   10
And all her sense is only chat
    Like any other woman.

IV.

Her voice, her touch might give th' alarm—
    'Twas both perhaps, or neither;
In short, 'twas that provoking charm
    Of CÆLIA altogether.

George Berkeley

1685–1753

ON THE PROSPECT
OF PLANTING ARTS
AND LEARNING IN AMERICA

The Muse, disgusted at an Age and Clime,
    Barren of every glorious Theme,
In distant Lands now waits a better Time,
    Producing Subjects worthy Fame:

In happy Climes, where from the genial Sun
    And virgin Earth such Scenes ensue,
The Force of Art by Nature seems outdone,
    And fancied Beauties by the true:

In happy Climes the Seat of Innocence,
    Where Nature guides and Virtue rules,   10
Where Men shall not impose for Truth and Sense,
    The Pedantry of Courts and Schools:

There shall be sung another golden Age,
    The rise of Empire and of Arts,
The Good and Great inspiring epic Rage,
    The wisest Heads and noblest Hearts.

Not such as *Europe* breeds in her decay;
    Such as she bred when fresh and young,
When heav'nly Flame did animate her Clay,
    By future Poets shall be sung.   20

Westward the Course of Empire takes its Way;
    The four first Acts already past,
A fifth shall close the Drama with the Day;
    Time's noblest Offspring is the last.

THE JE NE SCAI QUOI. The title means "the I don't know what." The phrase was often used to denote the "indefinable something" that made an object, often a work of art, significant for the imagination or the emotions. The text is from Dodsley's *A Collection of Poems* (3 vols., 1748).

ON THE PROSPECT OF PLANTING ARTS AND LEARNING IN AMERICA. The text is from *A Miscellany, Containing Several Tracts on Various Subjects* (1752).

ꗈ

Thomas Edwards

1699–1757

SONNET XLIV

To MATTHEW BARNARD.°

MATTHEW, whose skilful hand and well-worn spade
  Shall soon be call'd to make the humble bed,
  Where I at last shall rest my weary head,
And form'd of dust again in dust be laid;

Near, but not in the Church of GOD, be made
  My clay-cold cell, and near the common tread
  Of passing friends; when number'd with the dead,
We're equal all, and vain distinctions fade:

The clowslip, violet, or the pale primrose
  Perhaps may chance to deck the verdant sweard; 10
  Which twisted briar or hasle-bands entwine;
Symbols of life's soon fading glories those—
  Do thou the monumental hillock guard
  From trampling cattle, and the routing swine.

ꗈ

Anonymous

ODE ON A STORM

WITH gallant pomp, and beauteous pride
  The floating pile in harbour rode,
Proud of her freight, the swelling tide
Reluctant left the vessel's side,
  And rais'd it as she flow'd.

The waves with Eastern breezes curl'd,
  Had silver'd half the liquid plain;
The anchors weigh'd, the sails unfurl'd,
Serenely mov'd the wooden world,
  And stretch'd along the main.   10

The scaly natives of the deep,
  Press to admire the vast machine,
In sporting gambols round it leap,
Or swimming low, due distance keep,
  In homage to their queen.

Thus, as life glides in gentle gale
  Pretended friendship waits on pow'r,
But early quits the borrow'd veil
When adverse Fortune shifts the sail,
  And hastens to devour.   20

In vain we fly approaching ill,
  Danger can multiply its form;
Expos'd we fly like Jonas still,
And heaven, when 'tis heaven's will,
  O'ertakes us in a storm.°

The distant surges foamy white
  Foretel the furious blast;
Dreadful, tho' distant was the sight,
Confed'rate winds and waves unite,
  And menace ev'ry mast.   30

Winds whistling thro' the shrouds, proclaim
  A fatal harvest on the deck,
Quick in pursuit as active flame,
Too soon the rolling ruin came,
  And ratify'd the wreck.

Thus, Adam smil'd with new-born grace,
  Life's flame inspir'd by heav'nly breath;°
Thus the same breath sweeps off his race,
Disorders Nature's beauteous face,
  And spreads disease and death.   40

Stripp'd of her pride, the vessel rolls,
  And as by sympathy she knew
The secret anguish of our souls,
With inward deeper groans condoles
  The danger of her crew.

SONNET XLIV. The text is from *The Canons of Criticism* (6th ed., 1758). **Matthew Barnard:** [Edwards's note] The Sexton of the Parish. ODE ON A STORM. The text is from Volume V (1758) of Dodsley's *Collection* (6 vols., 1748–58).

23-25. Expos'd . . . storm: See Jon. 1:1–4. 37. Life's . . . breath: See Gen. 2:7.

Now what avails it to be brave,
    On liquid precipices hung?
Suspended on a breaking wave,
Beneath us yawn'd a sea-green grave,
    And silenc'd ev'ry tongue.   50

The faithless flood forsook her keel,
    And downward launch'd the lab'ring hull,
Stun'd she forgot awhile to reel
And feel almost, or seem'd to feel
    A momentary lull.

Thus in the jaws of death we lay,
    Nor light, nor comfort found us there,
Lost in the gulph and floods of spray
No sun to chear us, nor a ray
    Of hope, but all despair.   60

The nearer shore, the more despair,
    While certain ruin waits on land;
Should we pursue our wishes there,
Soon we recant the fatal pray'r,
    And strive to shun the strand.

At length, the Being whose behest
    Reduc'd this Chaos into form,
His goodness and his pow'r express'd,
He spoke—and, as a God, suppress'd
    Our troubles, and the storm.   70

❦❦❦

Robert Lloyd

1733–1764

SHAKESPEARE: AN EPISTLE TO MR. GARRICK

THANKS to much Industry and Pains,
Much twisting of the Wit and Brains,
Translation has unlock'd the Store,
And spread abroad the *Grecian* Lore,
While *Sophocles* his Scenes are grown,
E'en as familiar as our own.

No more shall Taste presume to speak,
From its Enclosures in the *Greek;*
But, all its Fences broken down,
Lie at the Mercy of the Town.   10

Critic, I hear thy Torrent rage,
"'Tis Blasphemy against that Stage,
Which *Æschylus* his Warmth design'd,
Euripides his Taste refin'd,
And *Sophocles* his last Direction,
Stamp'd with the Signet of Perfection."

Perfection's but a Word ideal,
And bears about it nothing real,
And Excellence was never hit
In the first Essays of Man's Wit.   20
Shall *ancient* Worth, or *ancient* Fame
Preclude the Moderns from their Claim?
Must they be Blockheads, Dolts, and Fools,
Who write not up to *Grecian* Rules?
Who tread in Buskins or in Socks°
Must they be damn'd as Heterodox,
Nor Merit of good Works prevail,
Except within the classic Pale?
'Tis Stuff that bears the Name of Knowledge,
Not current half a Mile from College;   30
Where half their Lectures yield no more
(Be sure I speak of Times of yore)
Than just a niggard Light, to mark
How much we all are in the Dark.
As Rushlights in a spacious Room,
Just burn enough to form a Gloom.

When *Shakespeare* leads the Mind a Dance,
From *France* to *England,* hence to *France,*
Talk not to me of Time and Place;
I own I'm happy in the Chace.   40
Whether the Drama's here or there,
'Tis Nature, *Shakespeare,* every where.
The Poet's Fancy can create,
Contract, enlarge, annihilate,
Bring past and present close together,
In spite of Distance, Seas, or Weather.
And shut up in a single Action,
What cost whole Years in its Transaction.
So, Ladies at a Play, or Rout,°
Can flirt the Universe about,   50

SHAKESPEARE: AN EPISTLE TO MR. GARRICK. The text is from *Shakespeare: An Epistle to Mr. Garrick; with an Ode to Genius* (1760).

25. **Buskins, Socks:** The buskin, an elevated boot worn by ancient tragic actors to increase their stature, is emblematic of tragedy; the sock, of comedy. 49. **Rout:** evening party.

Whose geographical Account
Is drawn and pictur'd on the Mount.°
Yet, when they please, contract the Plan,
And shut the World up in a Fan.

True Genius, like *Armida's*° Wand,
Can raise the Spring from barren Land.
While all the Art of Imitation,
Is pilf'ring from the first Creation;
Transplanting Flowers with useless Toil,
Which wither in a foreign Soil.   60
As Conscience often sets us right,
By its interior active Light,
Without th' Assistance of the Laws
To combat in the moral Cause;
So Genius, of itself discerning,
Without the mystic Rules of Learning,
Can from its present Intuition,
Strike at the truth of Composition.

Yet those who breathe the classic Vein,
Enlisted in the mimic Train,   70
Who ride their Steed with double Bit,
Not run away with by their Wit,
Delighted with the Pomp of Rules,
The specious Pedantry of Schools;
(Which Rules, like Crutches, ne'er became
Of any Use but to the Lame)
Pursue the Method set before 'em,
Talk much of Order and Decorum,
Of Probability of Fiction,
Of Manners, Ornament and Diction,   80
And with a Jargon of hard Names,
(A Privilege which Dulness claims)
And merely us'd by way of Fence,
To keep out plain and common Sense,
Extol the Wit of antient Days,
The simple Fabric of their Plays;
Then from the Fable, all so chaste,
Trick'd up in antient-modern Taste,
So mighty gentle all the While,
In such a sweet descriptive Stile,   90
While Chorus marks the servile Mode
With fine Reflexion, in an Ode,
Present you with a perfect Piece,
Form'd on the Model of old *Greece*.

52. the Mount: the silk or paper that forms the surface of a
fan. 55. Armida: a powerful sorceress in Tasso's *Jerusalem
Delivered* (1576–93).

Come, prithee Critic, set before us,
The Use and Office of a Chorus.
What! Silent! Why then, I'll produce
Its Services from antient Use.

'Tis to be ever on the Stage,
Attendants upon Grief or Rage,   100
To be an arrant Go-between,
Chief-Mourner at each dismal Scene;
Shewing its Sorrow, or Delight,
By shifting Dances, left and right.
Not much unlike our modern Notions,
Adagio or *Allegro* Motions;
To watch upon the deep Distress,
And Plaints of Royal Wretchedness;
And when, with Tears, and Execration,
They've pour'd out all their Lamentation,   110
And wept whole Cataracts from their Eyes,
To call on Rivers for Supplies,
And with their *Hais* and *Hees* and *Hoes*
To make a Symphony of Woes.

Doubtless the Antients want the Art
To strike at once upon the Heart.
Or why their Prologues of a Mile
In simple—call it—humble Stile,
In unimpassion'd Phrase to say
"'Fore the Beginning of this Play,   120
I, hapless *Polydore*, was found
By Fishermen, or others, drown'd!
Or, I, a Gentleman, did wed,
The Lady I wou'd never bed,
Great *Agamemnon's* royal Daughter,
Who's coming hither to draw Water."

Or need the Chorus to reveal
Reflexions, which the Audience feel;
And jog them, least Attention sink,
To tell them how and what to think?   130

Oh, where's the Bard, who at one View,
Cou'd look the whole Creation through,
Who travers'd all the human Heart,
Without Recourse to *Grecian* Art?
He scorn'd the Modes of Imitation,
Of Altering, Pilfering, and Translation,
Nor painted Horror, Grief, or Rage,
From Models of a former Age;
The bright Original he took,
And tore the Leaf from Nature's Book.   140

'Tis *Shakespeare*, thus who stands alone—
Why need I tell what *You* have shown?
How true, how perfect, and how well,
The Feelings of our Hearts must tell.

Anonymous

JOHNNY, I HARDLY KNEW YE

While going the road to sweet Athy,°
   Hurroo! hurroo!
While going the road to sweet Athy,
   Hurroo! hurroo!
While going the road to sweet Athy,
A stick in my hand and a drop in my eye,°
A doleful damsel I heard cry:
   "Och, Johnny, I hardly knew ye!
     With drums and guns, and guns and drums,
     The enemy nearly slew ye;   10
     My darling dear, you look so queer,
     Och, Johnny, I hardly knew ye!

"Where are your eyes that looked so mild?
   Hurroo! hurroo!
Where are your eyes that looked so mild?
   Hurroo! hurroo!
Where are your eyes that looked so mild,
When my poor heart you first beguiled?
Why did you run from me and the child?
   Och, Johnny, I hardly knew ye!   20
    With drums, etc.

"Where are the legs with which you run?
   Hurroo! hurroo!
Where are the legs with which you run?
   Hurroo! hurroo!
Where are the legs with which you run
When first you went to carry a gun?

Indeed, your dancing days are done!
   Och, Johnny, I hardly knew ye!
    With drums, etc.   30

"It grieved my heart to see you sail,
   Hurroo! hurroo!
It grieved my heart to see you sail,
   Hurroo! hurroo!
It grieved my heart to see you sail,
Though from my heart you took leg-bail;°
Like a cod you're doubled up head and tail,
   Och, Johnny, I hardly knew ye!
    With drums, etc.

"You haven't an arm and you haven't a leg,   40
   Hurroo! hurroo!
You haven't an arm and you haven't a leg,
   Hurroo! hurroo!
You haven't an arm and you haven't a leg,
You're an eyeless, noseless, chickenless egg;
You'll have to be put with a bowl to beg:
   Och, Johnny, I hardly knew ye!
    With drums, etc.

"I'm happy for to see you home,
   Hurroo! hurroo!   50
I'm happy for to see you home,
   Hurroo! hurroo!
I'm happy for to see you home,
All from the Island of Sulloon;°
So low in flesh, so high in bone;
   Och, Johnny, I hardly knew ye!
    With drums, etc.

"But sad it is to see you so,
   Hurroo! hurroo!
But sad it is to see you so,   60
   Hurroo! hurroo!
But sad it is to see you so,
And to think of you now as an object of woe,
Your Peggy'll still keep ye on as her beau;
   Och, Johnny, I hardly knew ye!
    With drums and guns, and guns and drums,
    The enemy nearly slew ye;
    My darling dear, you look so queer,
    Och, Johnny, I hardly knew ye!"

JOHNNY, I HARDLY KNEW YE. This Irish street song was probably written in the 1760's; the text is from *Broad-Sheet Ballads*, ed. Padraic Colum (1913). **1. Athy:** a town some forty miles from Dublin on the road to Kilkenny. **6. a drop . . . eye:** slightly drunk.

36. leg-bail: leave without permission. **54. Island of Sulloon:** Sulúan, an island in the Philippines, site of a British victory over the Spanish in 1762.

Michael Bruce

1746–1767

ODE: TO THE CUCKOO

I.

HAIL, beauteous stranger of the wood!
    Attendant on the spring!
Now heav'n repairs thy rural seat,
    And woods thy welcome sing.

II.

Soon as the daisie decks the green,
    Thy certain voice we hear:
Hast thou a star to guide thy path,
    Or mark the rolling year?

III.

Delightful visitant! with thee
    I hail the time of flow'rs,   10
When heav'n is fill'd with music sweet
    Of birds among the bow'rs.

IV.

The schoolboy, wand'ring in the wood
    To pull the flow'rs so gay,
Starts, thy curious voice to hear,
    And imitates thy lay.

V.

Soon as the pea puts on the bloom,
    Thou fly'st thy vocal vale,
An annual guest, in other lands,
    Another spring to hail.   20

ODE: TO THE CUCKOO. Written around 1766, this poem was
first published in *Poems on Several Occasions* (1770), from
which we take our text.

VI.

Sweet bird! thy bow'r is ever green,
    Thy sky is ever clear;
Thou hast no sorrow in thy song,
    No winter in thy year!°

VII.

O could I fly, I'd fly with thee:
    We'd make, with social wing,
Our annual visit o'er the globe,
    Companions of the spring.

Christopher Anstey

1724–1805

FROM

THE NEW BATH GUIDE, OR MEMOIRS OF THE B—R—D FAMILY, IN A SERIES OF POETICAL EPISTLES

*Mr. S——   B—N—R—D, to Lady B—N—R—D,
at ———Hall, North.°*

LETTER X

TASTE *and* SPIRIT.—*Mr. B—N—R—D commences
A BEAU GARÇON.°*

So lively, so gay, my dear Mother, I'm grown,
I long to do something to make myself known;
For Persons of *Taste* and true *Spirit*, I find,
Are fond of attracting the Eyes of Mankind:

24. year: The following stanza is sometimes printed after
stanza 6, but the evidence of Bruce's authorship is not conclusive:

> Alas, sweet bird! not so my fate,
>   Dark scowling skies I see
> Fast gathering round, and fraught with woe
>   And wintry years to me.

THE NEW BATH GUIDE: *Letter X.* The whole work comprises
fifteen verse letters. The text is that of the first edition (1766);
we have incorporated one substantive variant from the third
edition (1766). **Mr. . . . North:** Mr. Simpkin Blunderhead,
to Lady Blunderhead, at ——— Hall, Northumberland. **Beau
Garçon:** fop.

What Numbers one sees, who for that very Reason
Come to make such a Figure at *Bath* ev'ry Season!
'Tis This that provokes Mrs. SHENKIN AP-LEEK
To dine at the Ord'nary° twice in a Week,
Tho' at Home she might eat a good Dinner in
    Comfort,
Nor pay such a cursed extravagant Sum for 't: 10
But then her Acquaintance would never have known
Mrs. SHENKIN AP-LEEK had acquir'd a *Bon Ton;*°
Ne'er shewn how in *Taste* the AP-LEEKS can excel
The Dutchess of TRUFFLES, and Lady MORELL;
Had ne'er been ador'd by Sir PYE MACARONI,
And Count VERMICELLI, his intimate Crony;
Both Men of such *Taste*, their Opinions are taken
From an Ortolan° down to a Rasher of Bacon.

What makes KITTY SPICER, and little Miss SAGO
To Auctions and Milliners Shops ev'ry Day go;   20
What makes them to vie with each other and quarrel
Which spends the most Money for splendid Apparel?
Why *Spirit*—to shew they have much better Sense
Than their Fathers, who rais'd it by Shillings and
    Pence.
What sends PETER TEWKSBURY every Night
To the Play with such infinite Joy and Delight?
Why PETER's a Critic, with true Attic Salt,
Can damn the Performers, can hiss, and find fault,
And tell when we ought to express Approbation,
By thumping, and clapping, and Vociferation;   30
So he gains our Attention, and all must admire
Young TEWKSBURY's Judgment, his *Spirit* and Fire.
But JACK DILETTANTE despises the Play'rs,
To Concerts and musical Parties repairs,
With Benefit-Tickets his Pockets he fills,
Like a Mountebank Doctor distributes his Bills;
And thus his Importance and Interest shews,
By conferring his Favours wherever He goes:
He's extremely polite both to me and my Couzen,
For he often desires us to take off a Dozen: 40
He has Taste, without doubt, and a delicate Ear,
No vile Oratorios ever could bear;
But talks of the Op'ras and his Signiora,
Cries *Bravo, Benissimo, Bravo, Encora!*
And oft is so kind as to thrust in a Note
While old Lady CUCKOW is straining her Throat,
Or little Miss WREN, who's an excellent Singer,
Then he points to the Notes, with a Ring on his Finger,

And shews Her the Crotchet, the Quaver, and Bar,
All the Time that she warbles, and plays the *Guitar:* 50
Yet I think, tho' she's at it from Morning till Noon,
Her queer little Thingumbob's never in Tune.

Thank Heaven of late, my dear Mother, my Face is
Not a little regarded at all public Places;
For I ride in a Chair with my Hands in a Muff,
And have bought a Silk Coat and embroidered the
    Cuff;
But the Weather was cold, and the Coat it was thin,
So the Taylor advis'd me to line it with Skin:
But what with my *Nivernois'* Hat° can compare,
Bag-Wig, and lac'd Ruffles, and black Solitair°?   60
And what can a Man of true Fashion denote,
Like an Ell of good Ribbon ty'd under the Throat?
My Buckles and Box are in exquisite Taste;
The one is of Paper, the other of Paste;
And sure no *Camayeu*° was ever yet seen,
Like that which I purchas'd at WICKSTED's Machine:°
My Stockings of Silk, are just come from the Hosier,
For To-night I'm to dance with the charming Miss
    TOZIER:
So I'd have them to know when I go to the Ball,
I shall shew as much *Taste* as the best of them all: 70
For a Man of great Fashion was heard to declare
He never beheld so engaging an Air,
And swears all the World must my Judgment confess,
My *Solidity, Sense, Understanding* in Dress,
My Manners so form'd, and my Wig so well curl'd,
I look like a Man *of the very first World:*
But my Person and Figure you'll best understand
From the Picture I've sent, by an eminent Hand:
Shew it young Lady BETTY, by Way of Endearance,
And to give her a Spice of my Mien and Appearance:
Excuse any more, I'm in Haste to depart,   81
For a Dance is the Thing that I love at my Heart.
So now my dear Mother, &c. &c. &c.

BATH, 1766.   S—— B—N—R—D.

---

8. Ord'nary: public eating place. **12. Bon Ton:** fine style.
18. Ortolan: a small bird prepared as a delicacy.

59. Nivernois' Hat: a very small three-cornered hat made of delicate material. **60. Solitair:** a loose silk necktie. **65. Camayeu:** cameo. **66. Machine:** coach.

John Hall-Stevenson
1718–1785

FROM

MAKARONY° FABLES

FABLE IV. THE BLACK BIRD

IN concert with the curfew bell,
An Owl was chaunting Vespers in his cell;
Upon the outside of the wall,
A Black Bird, famous in that age;
From a bow window in the hall,
Hung dangling in a wicker cage;
Instead of psalmody and pray'rs,
Like those good children of St. Francis;°
He secularized all his airs,
And took delight in Wanton Fancies.   10
Whilst the bell toll'd, and the Owl chaunted,
Every thing was calm and still;
All nature seem'd rapp'd and enchanted,
Except the querulous, unthankful rill;
Unawed by this imposing scene,
Our Black Bird the enchantment broke;
Flourish'd a sprightly air between,
And whistled the Black Joke.°
This lively unexpected motion,°
Set nature in a gayer light;   20
Quite over-turn'd the Monks devotion,
    And scatter'd all the gloom of night.
I have been taught in early youth,
By an expert Metaphysician;
That ridicule's the test of truth,
And only match for superstition.

Imposing rogues, with looks demure,
At Rome keep all the world in awe;
Wit is profane, learning impure,
And reasoning against the Law;   30
Between two tapers and a book,
Upon a dresser clean and neat,
Behold a sacerdotal Cook,
Cooking a dish of heavenly meat!
How fine he curtsies! Make your bow,
Thump your breast soundly, beat your poll;
Lo! he has toss'd up a Ragout,
To fill the belly of your soul.
Even here there are some holy men,
Would fain lead people by the nose;   40
Did not a Black Bird now and then,
    Benevolently interpose.
My good Lord Bishop, Mr. Dean,
You shall get nothing by your spite;°
Tristram shall whistle at your spleen,
And put Hypocrisy to flight.

Mark Akenside
1721–1770

ODE ON A SERMON
AGAINST GLORY

I.

COME then, tell me, sage divine,
Is it an offence to own
That our bosoms e'er incline
Toward immortal glory's throne?
For with me nor pomp, nor pleasure,
Bourbon's might, Braganza's treasure,°

MAKARONY FABLES: *Fable IV.* **Makarony:** In his *Dictionary* Johnson defines *macaroon:* "a coarse, rude, low fellow; whence *macaronick* poetry, in which the language is purposely corrupted." The word *macaroni* also denotes the extreme type of fop who affects fantastic dress. The text is that of the first edition (1767). **8. children . . . Francis:** Franciscan friars. **18. the Black Joke:** an indecent song. **19. motion:** military march.

43–44. My . . . spite: The irreverencies and indecencies of Laurence Sterne's *Tristram Shandy* (1759–67) gave some offense to Sterne's ecclesiastical superiors. ODE ON A SERMON AGAINST GLORY. Akenside did not publish this poem during his lifetime. The text is from *The Poems of Mark Akenside, M.D.* (1772). **6. Bourbon, Braganza:** Bourbon is the name of the French royal house to which Louis XIV belonged; Braganza is the name of the ruling family of Portugal.

So can fancy's dream rejoice,
So conciliate reason's choice,
As one approving word of her impartial voice.

II.

If to spurn at noble praise   10
Be the pass-port to thy heaven,
Follow thou those gloomy ways;
No such law to me was given,
Nor, i trust, shall i deplore me
Faring like my friends before me;
Nor an holier place desire
Than Timolean's° arms acquire,
And Tully's curule chair,° and Milton's golden lyre.

Anonymous

THE BRITISH GRENADIERS

Some talk of Alexander, and some of Hercules,
Of Conon and Lysander, and some Miltiades;°
But of all the World's brave Heroes, there's none that
    can compare,
With a tow, row, row, row, row, to the British
    Grenadiers.
    Chorus. But of all the World's brave Heroes, &c.

None of those ancient Heroes e'er saw a cannon ball,
Or knew the force of Powder to slay their foes with
    all;°
Bur our brave Boys do know it, and banish all their
    fears,
With a tow, row, row, row, row, the British
    Grenadiers.
    Chorus. But our brave Boys, &c.   10

When e'er we are commanded to storm the Palisades,°
Our Leaders march with Fusees° and we with hand
    Granades;
We throw them from the Glacis° about our Enemies
    Ears,
With a tow, row, row, row, row, the British
    Grenadiers.
    Chorus. We throw them, &c.

The God of War was pleased and great Bellona°
    smiles,
To see these noble Heroes of our British Isles;
And all the Gods celestial, descending from their
    spheres,
Beheld with admiration the British Grenadiers.
    Chorus. And all the Gods celestial, &c.   20

Then let us crown a Bumper,° and drink a health to
    those
Who carry Caps and Pouches, that wear the louped°
    Cloaths;
May they and their Commanders live happy all their
    Years,
With a tow, row, row, row, row, the British
    Grenadiers.
    Chorus. May they and their Commanders, &c.

John Scott

1730–1783

ODE XIII

I HATE that drum's discordant sound,
Parading round, and round, and round:
To thoughtless youth it pleasure yields,
And lures from cities and from fields,

17. Timolean: Greek general and statesman of the fourth century B.C. **18. curule chair:** a curved wooden folding chair restricted to use by the highest Roman magistrates. Marcus Tullius Cicero served as consul in 63 B.C. THE BRITISH GRENADIERS: first sung around 1780; the text is that of D. N. Smith's transcription of an early broadside in his collection, as printed in *The Oxford Book of Eighteenth-Century Verse* (1926). **2. Conon, Lysander, Miltiades:** pre-Christian Athenian and Spartan military commanders. **7. with all:** withal, i.e., with.

11. Palisades: slanting fences of sharpened stakes used in fortification. **12. Fusees:** fusils, light muskets. **13. Glacis:** the earth slope surrounding a fortified area. **16. Bellona:** Roman goddess of war, sister of Mars. **21. crown a Bumper:** fill a large glass to the brim. **22. louped:** adorned with loops. ODE XIII. The text is from Scott's *Poetical Works* (1782).

To sell their liberty for charms
Of tawdry lace, and glittering arms;
And when Ambition's voice commands,
To march, and fight, and fall, in foreign lands.

I hate that drum's discordant sound,
Parading round, and round, and round: 10
To me it talks of ravag'd plains,
And burning towns, and ruin'd swains,
And mangled limbs, and dying groans,
The widows tears, and orphans moans;
And all that Misery's hand bestows,
To fill the catalogue of human woes.

Anonymous

[EPIGRAM]

I have lost my mistress, horse, and wife,
And when I think on human life,
   Cry mercy 'twas no worse.
My mistress sickly, poor and old,
My wife damn'd ugly, and a scold,
   I am sorry for my horse.

James White

1738–1799

WHY THE MOON IS LIKE A FASHIONABLE WIFE

TO A FRIEND.

YOU say, Sir, once a Wit allow'd
A Lady to be like a Cloud;
Then take a simile as soon
Between a Woman and the Moon;

EPIGRAM. The text is from *A New Foundling Hospital for Wit* (6 vols., 1784). WHY THE MOON IS LIKE A FASHIONABLE WIFE. The text is that of the first authorized printing, in *Conway Castle; a Poem* (1789).

For, let mankind say what they will,
The sex are *heav'nly bodies* still.

Grant me (to mimic mortal life)
That Sun and Moon are Man and Wife;
Whate'er kind Sol affords to lend her,
Madame displays in *midnight splendour;*   10
For while to rest he lays him down,
She's up, and gaz'd at thro' the town;
From him her beauties close confining,
And only in his absence shining;
Or else she looks like sullen tapers,
Or else is fairly in the *vapours;*
Or owns at once a wife's ambition,
And fully glares in *opposition.*

Say, is not this a modish pair?
Since each for other feels no care;   20
Whole days in sep'rate coaches driving,
Whole nights to keep asunder striving;
Both in the dumps in gloomy weather,
And lying, once a month, together:
In one sole point unlike the cases,—
On her own head the horns° she places.

William Wordsworth

1770–1850

LINES WRITTEN NEAR RICHMOND, UPON THE THAMES, AT EVENING

How rich the wave, in front, imprest
With evening-twilight's summer hues,
While, facing thus the crimson west,
The boat her silent path pursues!

26. the horns: the traditional emblem of a cuckold. LINES WRITTEN NEAR RICHMOND. This poem was composed in 1789, although it was still being revised as late as 1797. On Coleridge's recommendation Wordsworth later detached the first two stanzas, titled them *Lines Written While Sailing in a Boat at Evening*, and printed them as a separate poem; the remaining stanzas were then titled *Remembrance of Collins, Composed upon the Thames near Richmond*. The text is that of the first published version, in *Lyrical Ballads* (1798).

And see how dark the backward stream!
A little moment past, so smiling!
And still, perhaps, with faithless gleam,
Some other loiterer beguiling.

Such views the youthful bard allure,
But, heedless of the following gloom,   10
He deems their colours shall endure
Till peace go with him to the tomb.
—And let him nurse his fond deceit,
And what if he must die in sorrow!
Who would not cherish dreams so sweet,
Though grief and pain may come to-morrow?

Glide gently, thus for ever glide,
O Thames! that other bards may see,
As lovely visions by thy side
As now, fair river! come to me.   20
Oh glide, fair stream! for ever so;
Thy quiet soul on all bestowing,
'Till all our minds for ever flow,
As thy deep waters now are flowing.

Vain thought! yet be as now thou art,
That in thy waters may be seen
The image of a poet's heart,
How bright, how solemn, how serene!
Such heart did once the poet bless,
Who, pouring here a *later* ditty,°   30
Could find no refuge from distress,
But in the milder grief of pity.

Remembrance! as we glide along,
For him suspend the dashing oar,
And pray that never child of Song
May know his freezing sorrows more.
How calm! how still! the only sound
The dripping of the oar suspended!
—The evening darkness gathers round
By virtue's holiest powers attended.   40

---

30. a later ditty: [Wordsworth's note] Collins's Ode on the death of Thomson [see Part Five], the last written, I believe, of the poems which were published during his life-time. This Ode is also alluded to in the next stanza.

☙☙☙

George Canning,
1770–1827
John Hookham Frere,
1769–1846
William Gifford,
1756–1826
and
George Ellis
1753–1815

FROM

THE ANTI-JACOBIN;
OR, WEEKLY EXAMINER

SAPPHICS

THE FRIEND OF HUMANITY AND THE KNIFE-GRINDER.

FRIEND OF HUMANITY.

"Needy Knife-grinder! whither are you going?
Rough is the road, your Wheel is out of order—
Bleak blows the blast;—your hat has got a hole in 't,
          So have your breeches!

THE ANTI-JACOBIN. Thirty-six numbers of *The Anti-Jacobin* were published during 1797 and 1798. The purpose of the paper was to support Pitt's administration against Whig and republican opposition. Although it contained news and editorial comment, it was notable for employing poetic parodies in the service of Tory politics. Collaboration was the practice among the wits who conducted *The Anti-Jacobin. Sapphics*, a parody of Robert Southey's *The Widow* (1795), is the work of George Canning and John Hookham Frere, Members of Parliament and Under Secretaries for Foreign Affairs in Pitt's administration; *The Progress of Man*, a parody of Richard Payne Knight's *The Progress of Civil Society* (1796), is by Canning and William Gifford, a satirist and translator who served as editor of *The Anti-Jacobin*; the *Song by Rogero*, from *The Rovers*, a travesty of the sentimental German plays of Kotzebue, Schiller, and Goethe, is by Canning and George Ellis, a historian who later edited medieval English romances. The texts are from the original numbers; we have incorporated the substantive variants from the versions in *Poetry of the Anti-Jacobin* (1799), and we have omitted most of the authors' footnotes to *The Progress of Man*.

"Weary Knife-grinder! little think the proud ones,
Who in their coaches roll along the turnpike-
-road, what hard work 'tis crying all day, 'Knives and
                Scissars to grind O!'

"Tell me, Knife-grinder, how came you to grind
    knives?
Did some rich man tyrannically use you?   10
Was it the 'Squire? or Parson of the Parish?
                Or the Attorney?

"Was it the 'Squire for killing of his Game? or
Covetous Parson for his Tythes distraining°?
Or roguish Lawyer made you lose your little
                All in a law-suit?

"(Have you not read the Rights of Man,° by TOM
    PAINE?)
Drops of compassion tremble on my eye-lids,
Ready to fall, as soon as you have told your
                Pitiful story."   20

KNIFE-GRINDER.

"Story! God bless you! I have none to tell, Sir,
Only last night a-drinking at the Chequers,
This poor old hat and breeches, as you see, were
                Torn in a scuffle.

"Constables came for to take me into
Custody; they took me before the Justice;
Justice OLDMIXON put me in the Parish-
              -Stocks for a Vagrant.

"I should be glad to drink your Honour's health in
A Pot of Beer, if you would give me Sixpence;   30
But for my part, I never love to meddle
                With Politics, Sir."

FRIEND OF HUMANITY.

"*I* give thee Sixpence! I will see thee damn'd first—
Wretch! whom no sense of wrongs can rouse to
    vengeance—
Sordid, unfeeling, reprobate, degraded,
                Spiritless outcast!"

(*Kicks the Knife-grinder, overturns his Wheel, and exit
    in a transport of republican enthusiasm
        and universal philanthropy.*)

SAPPHICS. **14. distraining:** suing. **17. the Rights . . . Man:**
Paine's rejoinder to Burke's *Reflections on the Revolution in
France* (see Part Six) appeared in 1791–92.

FROM

THE PROGRESS OF MAN

A DIDACTIC POEM.

IN FORTY CANTOS, WITH NOTES CRITICAL
AND EXPLANATORY: CHIEFLY
OF A PHILOSOPHICAL TENDENCY.

DEDICATED TO R. P. KNIGHT, ESQ.

CANTO FIRST

CONTENTS.

THE *Subject proposed.—Doubts and Waverings.—
Queries not to be answered.—Formation of the stupendous
Whole.—Cosmogony; or the Creation of the World: the
Devil—Man—Various Classes of Being:—Animated
Beings—Birds—Fish—Beasts—the Influence of the Sexual
Appetite—on Tygers—on Whales—on Crimpt° Cod—on
Perch—on Shrimp—on Oysters.—Various Stations as-
signed to different Animals:—Birds—Bears—Mackarel.—
Bears remarkable for their Fur—Mackarel cried on a
Sunday—Birds do not graze—nor Fishes fly—nor Beasts
live in the Water.—*PLANTS *equally contented with their
lot:—Potatoes—Cabbage—Lettuce—Leeks—Cucumbers.
—*MAN *only discontented—born a Savage;—not chusing
to continue so, becomes polished—resigns his Liberty—
Priest-craft—King-craft—Tyranny of Laws and Institutions.—Savage Life—Description thereof:—The Savage
free—roaming Woods—feeds on Hips and Haws—Animal
Food—first notion of it from seeing a Tyger tearing his
prey—wonders if it is good—resolves to try—makes a Bow
and Arrow—kills a Pig—resolves to roast a part of it—
lights a fire—*APOSTROPHE *to Fires—Spits and Jacks
not yet invented.—Digression.—*CORINTH—SHEFFIELD.—
Love the most natural desire after Food.—Savage Courtship.—Concubinage recommended.—Satirical Reflections
on Parents and Children—Husbands and Wives—against
collateral Consanguinity.—*FREEDOM *the only Morality,
&c. &c. &c.*

WHETHER some great, supreme, o'er-ruling
    POW'R
Stretch'd forth its arm at Nature's natal hour,
Compos'd this mighty Whole with plastic skill,
Wielding the jarring Elements at will?

THE PROGRESS OF MAN: *Canto First.* **Crimpt:** sliced.

Or whether, sprung from CHAOS' mingling storm,
The mass of matter started into form?
Or CHANCE o'er Earth's green lap spontaneous fling
The Fruits of Autumn and the Flow'rs of Spring?
Whether MATERIAL SUBSTANCE unrefin'd,
Owns the strong impulse of instinctive MIND,   10
Which to one centre points diverging lines,
Confounds, retracts, invig'rates, and combines?°
Whether the joys of *Earth*, the hopes of *Heav'n*,
By MAN to GOD, or GOD to MAN, were giv'n?
If Virtue leads to Bliss, or Vice to Woe?
Who rules ABOVE? or who reside BELOW?
Vain questions all—shall Man presume to know?
On all these points, and points obscure as these,
Think they who will,—and think whate'er they please!

Let Us a plainer, steadier theme pursue—   20
Mark the grim Savage scoop his light Canoe;—
Mark the dark Rook, on pendant branches hung,
With anxious fondness feed her cawing young;—
Mark the fell Leopard through the Desert prowl,
Fish prey on Fish, and Fowl regale on Fowl;—
How Lybyan Tygers' chawdrons° Love assails,
And warms, midst seas of Ice, the melting Whales;—
Cools the crimpt Cod, fierce pangs to Perch imparts,
Shrinks shrivell'd Shrimps, but opens Oysters' hearts;—
Then say, how all these things together tend   30
To one great truth, prime object, and good end?

First—to each living thing, whate'er its kind,
Some lot, some part, some station is assign'd.
The Feather'd Race with pinions skim the *air*°—
Not so the Mackarel, and still less the Bear:°
This roams the *wood*, carniv'rous, for his prey;
That with soft roe, pursues his *watery* way:—
This slain by Hunters, yields his shaggy hide;
That, caught by Fishers, is on *Sundays* cried.—

But each contented with his humble sphere,   40
Moves unambitious through the circling year;

Nor e'er forgets the fortune of his race,
Nor pines to quit, or strives to change, his place.
Ah! who has seen the mailed Lobster rise,
Clap her broad wings, and soaring claim the skies?
When did the Owl, descending from her bow'r,
Crop, 'midst the fleecy flocks, the tender flow'r;
Or the young Heifer plunge with pliant limb
In the salt wave, and fish-like strive to swim?   49

The same with Plants—Potatoes 'Tatoes breed°—
Uncostly Cabbage springs from Cabbage-seed;
Lettuce to Lettuce, Leeks to Leeks succeed;
Nor e'er did cooling Cucumbers presume
To flow'r like Myrtle, or like Violets bloom.
—MAN, only—rash, refin'd, presumptuous MAN,
Starts from his rank, and mars Creation's plan.
Born the free Heir of Nature's wide Domain,
To Art's strict limits bounds his narrow reign;
Resigns his native Rights for meaner things,
For *Faith* and *Fetters*—LAWS, and PRIESTS, and KINGS. 60

Lo! the rude Savage, free from civil strife,
Keeps the smooth tenour of his guiltless life;
Restrain'd by none, save Nature's lenient Laws,
Quaffs the clear Stream, and feeds on Hips and Haws.
Light to his daily sports behold him rise!
The bloodless Banquet health and strength supplies.
Bloodless not long—one Morn he haps to stray
Through the lone wood—and close beside the way,
Sees the gaunt Tyger tear his trembling prey;
Beneath whose gory fangs a Leveret° bleeds,   70
Or Pig—such Pig as fertile China breeds.

Struck with the sight, the wondering Savage stands,
Rolls his broad eyes, and clasps his lifted hands;
Then restless roams—and loathes his wonted food;
Shuns the salubrious stream, and thirsts for blood.

By thought matur'd, and quicken'd by desire,
New arts, new arms, his wayward wants require.
From the tough yew a slender branch he tears,
With self-taught skill the twisted grass prepares;
Th' unfashion'd Bow with labouring effort bends   80
In circling form, and joins th' unwilling ends.
Next some tall reed he seeks—with sharp-edged stone
Shapes the fell dart, and points with whiten'd bone.

9–12. Whether . . . combines: [authors' note] The influence of Mind upon Matter—comprehending the whole question of the Existence of Mind as independent of Matter, or as co-existent with it, and of Matter considered as an intelligent and self-dependent Essence—will make the subject of a larger Poem, in 127 Books, now preparing under the *same* AUSPICES. **26. chawdrons:** [authors' note] "Add thereto a Tyger's chawdron [entrails]."—MACBETH. **34. The Feather'd . . . air:** [authors' note] Birds fly. **35. Not . . . Bear:** [authors' note] But neither Fish, nor Beasts—particularly as here exemplified.

50. Potatoes . . . breed: [authors' note] Elision for the sake of verse, not meant to imply that the root degenerates. **70. Leveret:** young rabbit.

Then forth he fares—around in careless play,
Kids, Pigs, and Lambkins unsuspecting stray.
With grim delight he views the sportive band,
Intent on blood, and lifts his murderous hand,
Twangs the bent bow—resounds the fateful dart
Swift-wing'd, and trembles in a Porker's heart.

Ah! hapless Porker! what can now avail   90
Thy back's stiff bristles, or thy curly tail?
Ah! what avail those eyes so small and round,
Long pendant ears, and snout that loves the ground?

Not unreveng'd thou diest—in after times
From thy spilt blood shall spring unnumber'd crimes.
Soon shall the slaught'rous arms that wrought thy woe,
Improv'd by malice, deal a deadlier blow;
When *social* Man shall pant for nobler game,
And 'gainst his fellow-man the vengeful weapon aim.

As Love, as Gold, as Jealousy inspires,   100
As wrathful Hate, or wild Ambition fires,
Urged by the Statesman's craft, the Tyrant's rage,
Embattled Nations endless Wars shall wage,
Vast seas of blood the ravaged field shall stain,
And millions perish—that a KING may reign!

For blood once shed, new wants and wishes rise;
Each rising want Invention quick supplies.
To roast his victuals is MAN's next desire,
So, two dry sticks he rubs, and lights a fire,
Hail Fire! &c. &c.   110

FROM

THE ROVERS; OR,
THE DOUBLE ARRANGEMENT

SONG BY ROGERO°

I.

Whene'er with haggard eyes I view
    This Dungeon, that I'm rotting in,
I think of those Companions true

Who studied with me at the U—
    —NIVERSITY of *Gottingen*,—
    —NIVERSITY of *Gottingen*.

(*Weeps, and pulls out a blue kerchief, with which he wipes
his eyes; gazing tenderly at it, he proceeds—*)

II.

Sweet kerchief, check'd with heav'nly blue,
    Which once my love sat knotting in!—
Alas! MATILDA *then* was true!—
    At least I thought so at the U—   10
    —NIVERSITY of *Gottingen*—
    —NIVERSITY of *Gottingen*.

(*At the repetition of this Line* ROGERO *clanks his Chains
in cadence.*)

III.

Barbs!° Barbs! alas! how swift you flew
    Her neat Post-Waggon trotting in!
Ye bore MATILDA from my view.
    Forlorn I languish'd at the U—
    —NIVERSITY of *Gottingen*—
    —NIVERSITY of *Gottingen*.

IV.

This faded form! this pallid hue!
    This blood my veins is clotting in.   20
My years are many—They were few
    When first I entered at the U—
    —NIVERSITY of *Gottingen*—
    —NIVERSITY of *Gottingen*.

V.

There first for thee my passion grew,
    Sweet! sweet MATILDA POTTINGEN!
Thou wast the daughter of my Tu—
    —TOR, *Law Professor* at the U—
    —NIVERSITY of *Gottingen*!—
    —NIVERSITY of *Gottingen*!—   30

VI.

Sun, moon, and thou vain world, adieu,
    That kings and priests are plotting in:
Here doom'd to starve on water-gru—
    —el never shall I see the U—
    —NIVERSITY of *Gottingen*—
    —NIVERSITY of *Gottingen*.

THE ROVERS: *Song by Rogero.* **Rogero:** The character Rogero
is a satire on the Whig Sir Robert Adair, a member of
Charles James Fox's Parliamentary faction. Like Rogero,
Adair had attended the University of Göttingen, where he had
fallen in love with his tutor's daughter.

13. Barbs: the name of a horse.

(During the last Stanza ROGERO *dashes his head repeatedly against the walls of his Prison; and, finally, so hard as to produce a visible contusion. He then throws himself on the floor in an agony. The Curtain drops—the Music still continuing to play, till it is wholly fallen.)*

[EPIGRAM ON AN ACADEMIC VISIT TO THE CONTINENT]

I went to Frankfort and got drunk
  With that most learned professor, Brunck;
I went to Worts° and got more drunken
  With that more learned professor, Ruhnken.°

EPIGRAM ON AN ACADEMIC VISIT TO THE CONTINENT. Although this untitled piece is traditionally attributed to Porson, the renowned witty and bibulous professor of classics at Cambridge, there is no evidence that he wrote it. It is perhaps a characteristic utterance fathered upon him posthumously by a Cambridge undergraduate. The text is from *Facetiae Cantabrigienses* (1825). **3. Worts:** an error for Worms? **4. Ruhnken:** like Professor Brunck, an actual European scholar.

⁂

Richard Porson (?)

1759–1808

Hymns and Divine Songs

⁂

Charles Wesley

1707–1788

IN TEMPTATION

Jesu, Lover of my Soul,
  Let me to thy Bosom fly

While the nearer Waters roll
  While the Tempest still is high.
Hide me, O my Saviour, hide,
  Till the Storm of Life is past:
Safe into the Haven guide;
  O receive my Soul at last.

IN TEMPTATION. The text is that of the first printing, in *Hymns and Sacred Poems* (2nd ed., 1740).

Other Refuge have I none,
    Hangs my helpless Soul on Thee,   10
Leave, ah! leave me not alone,
    Still support, and comfort me.
All my Trust on Thee is stay'd;
    All my Help from Thee I bring;
Cover my defenceless Head,
    With the Shadow of thy Wing.

Wilt thou not regard my Call?
    Wilt thou not accept my Prayer?
Lo! I sink, I faint, I fall—
    Lo! on Thee I cast my Care: 20
Reach me out thy gracious Hand!
    While I of thy Strength receive,
Hoping against Hope I stand,
    Dying, and behold I live!

Thou, O Christ, art all I want,
    More than all in Thee I find:
Raise the Fallen, chear the Faint,
    Heal the Sick, and lead the Blind,
Just, and holy is thy Name,
    I am all Unrighteousness,   30
False, and full of Sin I am,
    Thou art full of Truth and Grace.

Plenteous Grace with Thee is found,
    Grace to cover all my Sin:
Let the healing Streams abound,
    Make, and keep me pure within:
Thou of Life the Fountain art:
    Freely let me take of Thee,
Spring Thou up within my Heart,
    Rise to all Eternity.   40

WRESTLING JACOB

1. Come, O Thou Traveller unknown,
    Whom still I hold, but cannot see,
My Company before is gone,
    And I am left alone with Thee,
With Thee all Night I mean to stay,
And wrestle till the Break of Day.

2. I need not tell Thee who I am,
    My Misery, or Sin declare,
Thyself hast call'd me by my Name,
    Look on Thy Hands, and read it there,   10
But who, I ask Thee, who art Thou,
Tell me Thy Name, and tell me now?

3. In vain Thou strugglest to get free,
    I never will unloose my Hold:
Art Thou the Man that died for me?
    The Secret of Thy Love unfold;
Wrestling I will not let Thee go,
Till I Thy Name, Thy Nature know.

4. Wilt Thou not yet to me reveal
    Thy new, unutterable Name?   20
Tell me, I still beseech Thee, tell,
    To know it Now resolv'd I am;
Wrestling I will not let Thee go,
Till I Thy Name, Thy Nature know.

5. 'Tis all in vain to hold Thy Tongue,
    Or touch the Hollow of my Thigh:
Though every Sinew be unstrung,
    Out of my Arms Thou shalt not fly;
Wrestling I will not let Thee go,
Till I Thy Name, Thy Nature know.   30

6. What tho' my shrinking Flesh complain,
    And murmur to contend so long,
I rise superior to my Pain,
    When I am weak then I am strong,
And when my All of Strength shall fail,
I shall with the GOD-man prevail.

7. My Strength is gone, my Nature dies,
    I sink beneath Thy weighty Hand,
Faint to revive, and fall to rise;
    I fall, and yet by Faith I stand,   40
I stand, and will not let Thee go,
Till I Thy Name, Thy Nature know.

8. Yield to me Now—for I am weak;
    But confident in Self-despair:
Speak to my Heart, in Blessings speak,
    Be conquer'd by my Instant Prayer,
Speak, or Thou never hence shalt move,
And tell me, if Thy Name is LOVE.

9. 'Tis Love, 'tis Love! Thou diedst for Me,
    I hear Thy Whisper in my Heart.   50
The Morning breaks, the Shadows flee:
    Pure UNIVERSAL LOVE Thou art,
To me, to All Thy Bowels move,
Thy Nature, and Thy Name is LOVE.

WRESTLING JACOB. The text is from *Hymns and Sacred Poems*
(1742). Wesley's biblical source is Gen. 32:24–32.

10. My Prayer hath Power with GOD; the Grace
   Unspeakable I now receive,
Thro' Faith I see Thee Face to Face,
   I see Thee Face to Face, and live:
In vain I have not wept, and strove,
Thy Nature, and Thy Name is LOVE.   60

11. I know Thee, Saviour, who Thou art,
   JESUS the feeble Sinner's Friend;
Nor wilt Thou with the Night depart,
   But stay, and love me to the End;
Thy Mercies never shall remove,
Thy Nature, and Thy Name is LOVE.

12. The Sun of Righteousness on Me
   Hath rose with Healing in his Wings,
Wither'd my Nature's Strength; from Thee
   My Soul it's Life and Succour brings,   70
My Help is all laid up above;
Thy Nature, and Thy Name is LOVE.

13. Contented now upon my Thigh
   I halt, till Life's short Journey end;
All Helplessness, all Weakness I,
   On Thee alone for Strength depend,
Nor have I Power, from Thee, to move;
Thy Nature, and Thy Name is LOVE.

14. Lame as I am, I take the Prey,
   Hell, Earth, and Sin with Ease o'ercome;   80
I leap for Joy, pursue my Way,
   And as a bounding Hart fly home,
Thro' all Eternity to prove
Thy Nature, and Thy Name is LOVE.

❦

Augustus Montague Toplady

1740–1778

A PRAYER,
LIVING AND DYING

1.

ROCK of Ages, cleft for me,
Let me hide myself in Thee!

Let the Water and the Blood,
From thy riven Side which flow'd,°
Be of Sin the double Cure,
Cleanse me from it's Guilt and Pow'r.

2.

Not the labors of my hands
Can fullfill thy Law's demands:
Could my zeal no respite know,
Could my tears forever flow,   10
All for Sin could not atone:
Thou must save, and Thou alone!

3.

Nothing in my hand I bring;
Simply to thy Cross I cling;
Naked, come to Thee for Dress;
Helpless, look to Thee for grace;
Foul, I to the fountain fly:
Wash me, SAVIOR, or I die!

4.

While I draw this fleeting breath—
When my eye-strings break in death—
When I soar to worlds unknown—   20
See Thee on thy Judgment-Throne—
ROCK of ages, cleft for me,
Let me hide myself in THEE!

❦

William Cowper

1731–1800

WALKING WITH GOD

Gen. v. 24

OH! for a closer walk with GOD,
   A calm and heav'nly frame;°
A light to shine upon the road
   That leads me to the Lamb!

A PRAYER, LIVING AND DYING. The text is that of the first printing, in *The Gospel Magazine* (March, 1776); we have incorporated the substantive variants in *Psalms and Hymns for Public and Private Worship* (1776).

3–4. the Water . . . flow'd: See John 19:34. WALKING WITH GOD. The texts of this and the following hymn are those of the first printings, in *Olney Hymns* (1779). **2. frame:** state of mind.

Where is the blessedness I knew
  When first I saw the LORD?
Where is the soul-refreshing view
  Of JESUS, and his word?

What peaceful hours I once enjoy'd!
  How sweet their mem'ry still!   10
But they have left an aching void,
  The world can never fill.

Return, O holy Dove, return,
  Sweet messenger of rest;
I hate the sins that made thee mourn,
  And drove thee from my breast.

The dearest idol I have known,
  Whate'er that idol be;
Help me to tear it from thy throne,
  And worship only thee.   20

So shall my walk be close with GOD,
  Calm and serene my frame;
So purer light shall mark the road
  That leads me to the Lamb.

LIGHT SHINING
OUT OF DARKNESS

GOD moves in a mysterious way,
  His wonders to perform;
He plants his footsteps in the sea,
  And rides upon the storm.

Deep in unfathomable mines
  Of never failing skill;
He treasures up his bright designs,
  And works his sovereign will.

Ye fearful saints fresh courage take,
  The clouds ye so much dread   10
Are big with mercy, and shall break
  In blessings on your head.

Judge not the LORD by feeble sense,
  But trust him for his grace;
Behind a frowning providence,
  He hides a smiling face.

His purposes will ripen fast,
  Unfolding ev'ry hour;
The bud may have a bitter taste,
  But sweet will be the flow'r.   20

Blind unbelief is sure to err,
  And scan his work in vain;
GOD is his own interpreter,
  And he will make it plain.°

LIGHT SHINING OUT OF DARKNESS. **23–24. God . . . plain:**
[Cowper's note] John xiii. 7.

Bibliography

A. BIBLIOGRAPHIES AND REVIEWS OF RESEARCH

The standard reference work is *The Cambridge Bibliography of English Literature*, ed. F. W. Bateson (4 vols., 1941), with a *Supplement*, ed. George Watson (1957). *The Concise Cambridge Bibliography of English Literature, 600–1950*, ed. George Watson (1958), is a handy abridgment of the whole.

Modern eighteenth-century studies are listed without annotation in the annual bibliography of *Publications of the Modern Language Association* (since 1922) and in the British *Annual Bibliography of English Language and Literature*, published since 1921 by the Modern Humanities Research Association. A more useful listing appears yearly in *Philological Quarterly* (since 1926), where books (and sometimes even articles) are digested and evaluated. *Philological Quarterly* bibliographies published between 1926 and 1960 are conveniently reprinted under the title *English Literature, 1660–1800: A Bibliography of Modern Studies* (4 vols., 1950–61). An annual discussion of important eighteenth-century scholarship and comment may be found in *The Year's Work in English Studies*, edited since 1922 by the English Association. J. L. Clifford has provided a brief survey of modern eighteenth-century scholarship and criticism in *Contemporary Literary Scholarship: A Critical Review*, ed. Lewis Leary (1958). Each summer number of *Studies in English Literature: 1500–1900*, an issue devoted entirely to essays on Restoration and eighteenth-century literature, contains a review of recent scholarship. Studies of the novel are listed in *The English Novel,*

1578–1956: A Checklist of Twentieth-Century Criticism, ed. I. F. Bell and Donald Baird (1959).

J. E. Tobin's *Eighteenth-Century Literature and Its Cultural Background* (1939) lists eighteenth-century titles in such fields as history, economics, travel, taste, and education. J. W. Draper's *Eighteenth-Century English Aesthetics: A Bibliography* (1931) focuses on general aesthetics and on architecture, gardening, music (including opera), and the pictorial and plastic arts. *Bibliography of British History: The Eighteenth Century (1714–1789)*, ed. Stanley Pargellis and D. J. Medley (1951), describes and appraises works in political, ecclesiastical, economic, military, and social and cultural history. Of interest primarily to collectors of eighteenth-century works are two books by I. A. Williams: *Seven XVIIIth-Century Bibliographies* (1924) (on John Armstrong, Charles Churchill, Shenstone, Akenside, Goldsmith, Collins, and Sheridan) and *Points in Eighteenth-Century Verse* (1934) (on Akenside, Anstey, Collins, Anne Finch, Gray, Walter Harte, Thomson, and others). A listing and description of eighteenth-century works that emphasizes the art of book production is *The Rothschild Library: A Catalogue of the Collection of Eighteenth-Century Printed Books and Manuscripts Formed by Lord Rothschild* (2 vols., 1954). A pleasant adjunct is B. H. Bronson's *Printing as an Index of Taste in Eighteenth-Century England* (1958). Copies of eighteenth-century periodicals in American libraries may be located with *A Census of British Newspapers and Periodicals, 1620–1800*, ed. R. S. Crane and F. B. Kaye (1927), and with W. S. Ward's *Index and Finding List of Serials Published in the British Isles, 1789–1832* (1953).

B. TEXTS AND ANTHOLOGIES

The best single volume of eighteenth-century poems is *A Collection of English Poems, 1660–1800*, ed. R. S. Crane (1932). C. A. Moore, unlike Crane, presents partly modernized texts in his *English Poetry of the Eighteenth Century* (1935). Although K. W. Campbell's collection, *Poems on Several Occasions Written in the Eighteenth Century* (1926), is sparse, it is textually precise. The readily available *Oxford Book of Eighteenth-Century Verse*, ed. D. N. Smith (1926), is convenient, but the reader must beware, for the editor sometimes invents titles and sometimes excerpts, both without sufficient warning. P. M. Spacks's *Eighteenth-Century Poetry* (1964) offers generous selections from Prior, Swift, Gay, Thomson, Collins, Gray, Smart, Johnson, Cowper, and Burns. Other useful anthologies of poetry are *English Poetry of the Mid and Late Eighteenth Century*, ed. Ricardo Quintana and Alvin Whitley (1963) and *The Late Augustans: Longer Poems of the Later Eighteenth Century*, ed. Donald Davie (1958). The volumes in the series of Oxford Standard Authors (Thomson, Collins, Gray, Cowper, Burns, Blake) are handy, but the texts are not entirely trustworthy. Some of the more earthy poems of the period are included in *The Common Muse: An Anthology of Popular British Ballad Poetry, XVth–XXth Centuries*, ed. V. de S. Pinto and A. E. Rodway (1957).

Collections of prose include *Eighteenth-Century Prose*, ed. L. I. Bredvold, R. K. Root, and George Sherburn (1932), and *English Prose of the Eighteenth Century*, ed. C. A. Moore (1933). *Periodical Essays of the Eighteenth Century*, ed. George Carver (1930), offers, in addition to the old standbys, papers by Chesterfield, Walpole, Cowper, Reynolds, and even Soame Jenyns. *Political Writers of Eighteenth-Century England*, ed. Jeffrey Hart (1964), is a useful special collection.

English Prose and Poetry, 1660–1800: A Selection, ed. Frank Brady and Martin Price (1961), which omits by design a number of the major writers of the period, is to be recommended as an auxiliary volume.

The standard collection of critical documents is *Eighteenth-Century Critical Essays*, carefully edited by Scott Elledge (2 vols., 1961). It may be supplemented by H. A. Needham's compact *Taste and Criticism in the Eighteenth Century: A Selection of Texts Illustrating the Evolution of Taste and the Development of Critical Theory* (1952).

The major plays of the period are to be found in *Plays of the Restoration and Eighteenth Century*, ed. Dougald Macmillan and Howard Mumford Jones (1931), and in *British Dramatists from Dryden to Sheridan*, ed. G. H. Nettleton and A. E. Case (1939). Briefer collections are *Eighteenth-Century Plays*, ed. Ricardo Quintana (1952), *Eighteenth-Century Comedy*, ed. W. D. Taylor (1929), and *Eighteenth-Century Tragedy*, ed. M. R. Booth (1965). The Regents Restoration Drama Series, under the general editorship of John Loftis, offers a number of eighteenth-century plays in scrupulously edited texts.

Many rare eighteenth-century texts are now accessible in the reprints (mostly facsimiles) of the Augustan Reprint Society (founded 1946), which has reproduced works by Gray, Johnson, Boswell, and others.

C. LITERARY HISTORY AND CRITICISM

The best concise literary history of the period is George Sherburn's "The Restoration and Eighteenth Century," in *A Literary History of England*, ed. A. C. Baugh and others (1948). Sherburn's section is available separately, in a revision by D. F. Bond (1967). Bonamy Dobrée's *English Literature in the Early Eighteenth Century, 1700–1740* (1959), a volume in the Oxford History of English Literature Series, is now the standard work for this period. (The volume in this series on the mid-eighteenth century is in progress.) A. D. McKillop's handbook, *English Literature from Dryden to Burns* (1948), is a chronologically arranged collection of brief articles on authors and ideas. Two early nineteenth-century works by John Nichols, *Literary Anecdotes of the Eighteenth Century* (9 vols., 1812–15) and *Illustrations of the Literary History of the Eighteenth Century* (8 vols., 1817–58), are a rich if disorderly accumulation of biographical and bibliographical lore. The Scottish contribution is recorded and assessed by J. H. Millar, *A Literary History of Scotland* (1903), and Kurt Wittig, *The Scottish Tradition in Literature* (1958). Sir Paul Harvey's *Oxford Companion to English Literature* (4th ed., 1967) is an indispensable guide.

Among the many comprehensive studies of the literature of the period, the following deserve special mention: W. B. C. Watkins, *Perilous Balance: The Tragic Genius of Swift, Johnson, and Sterne* (1939); Peter Quennell, *The Profane Virtues* (1945) (studies of Boswell, Gibbon, Sterne, and Wilkes); R. W. Chapman, *Johnsonian and Other Essays and Reviews* (1953), which contains civilized discussions of Johnson, Chesterfield, Walpole, and contemporary gardening and printing; Martin Price, *To the Palace of Wisdom: Studies in Order and Energy from Dryden to Blake* (1964); and Paul Fussell, Jr., *The Rhetorical World of Augustan Humanism: Ethics and Imagery from Swift to Burke* (1965).

Several collections of essays contain important interpretations: *Essays on the Eighteenth Century Presented to David Nichol Smith*, ed. J. R. Sutherland and F. P. Wilson (1945); *The Age of Johnson: Essays Presented to Chauncey Brewster Tinker*, ed. F. W. Hilles (1949); *Pope and His Contemporaries: Essays Presented to George Sherburn*, ed. J. L. Clifford and L. A. Landa (1949); *Studies in the Literature of the Augustan Age: Essays Collected in Honor of Arthur Ellicott Case*, ed. R. C. Boys (1952); *Eighteenth-Century English Literature: Modern Essays in Criticism*, ed. J. L. Clifford (1959); *Essential Articles for the Study of English Augustan Backgrounds*, ed. B. N. Schilling (1961); *Aspects of the Eighteenth Century*, ed. E. R. Wasserman (1965); *From Sensibility to Romanticism: Essays Presented to Frederick A. Pottle*, ed. F. W. Hilles and Harold Bloom (1965); and

Studies in Criticism and Aesthetics, 1660–1800: Essays in Honor of Samuel Holt Monk, ed. Howard Anderson and J. S. Shea (1967).

The importance of the ancient classics for eighteenth-century literature is discussed in several books. The appropriate sections of Gilbert Highet's *The Classical Tradition: Greek and Roman Influences on Western Literature* (1949) are a good place to begin. M. L. Clarke's *Classical Education in Britain, 1500–1900*, is illuminating. The main Roman influences are discussed by C. M. Goad, in *Horace in the English Literature of the Eighteenth Century* (1918), and Elizabeth Nitchie, in *Vergil and the English Poets* (1919). D. L. Durling's *Georgic Tradition in English Poetry* (1935) is also useful. The first chapter of Douglas Bush's *Mythology and the Romantic Tradition in English Poetry* (1937) concerns the eighteenth century. Two reference works of great value are *The Oxford Classical Dictionary*, ed. Max Cary and others (1949), and the briefer *Oxford Companion to Classical Literature*, ed. Sir Paul Harvey (rev. ed., 1940).

A good introduction to the premises and conventions of some of the poetry is James Sutherland's *A Preface to Eighteenth-Century Poetry* (1948). Other studies worth consulting are F. R. Leavis, *Revaluations: Tradition and Development in English Poetry* (1936), Ch. iv ("The Augustan Tradition and the Eighteenth Century"); D. N. Smith, *Some Observations on Eighteenth-Century Poetry* (1937); H. N. Fairchild, *Religious Trends in English Poetry*, Vols. I and II (1939, 1942), which cover the period 1700–80; W. C. Brown, *The Triumph of Form: A Study of the Later Masters of the Heroic Couplet* (1948); Paul Fussell, Jr. *Theory of Prosody in Eighteenth-Century England* (1954); Geoffrey Tillotson, *Augustan Poetic Diction* (1964); and Rachel Trickett, *The Honest Muse: A Study in Augustan Verse* (1967). The impact of science on poetry is explored provocatively by Douglas Bush in *Science and English Poetry: A Historical Sketch, 1590–1950* (1950). Kenneth Maclean's *John Locke and English Literature of the Eighteenth Century* (1936) is also relevant.

Discussions of the various poetic genres include J. W. Draper, *The Funeral Elegy and the Rise of English Romanticism* (1929); R. P. Bond, *English Burlesque Poetry, 1700–1750* (1932); G. N. Shuster, *The English Ode from Milton to Keats* (1940); H. T. Swedenberg, *The Theory of the Epic in England, 1650–1800* (1944); and J. E. Congleton, *Theories of Pastoral Poetry in England, 1684–1798* (1952).

Some useful general introductions to satire are David Worcester's *The Art of Satire* (1940), James Sutherland's *English Satire* (1958), and R. C. Elliott's *The Power of Satire: Magic, Ritual, Art* (1960), an anthropological as well as literary study. Ian Jack's *Augustan Satire: 1660–1750* (1952) concentrates on the Restoration and eighteenth century.

Literary criticism in the period has been well treated. R. S. Crane's essay "Neo-Classical Criticism: An Outline Sketch," in *Critics and Criticism Ancient and Modern* (1952), is an excellent brief survey. A fuller discussion is J. W. H. Atkins's *English Literary Criticism: 17th and 18th Centuries* (1951). René Wellek's *The Rise of English Literary History* (1941) chronicles the increasing eighteenth-century awareness of literature as a historical process and interprets the new interest in the medieval. M. H. Abrams's *The Mirror and the Lamp: Romantic Theory and the Critical Tradition* (1953) interprets the relation between theory and expression in late eighteenth- and early nineteenth-century criticism. The first volume (1955) of Wellek's *A History of Modern Criticism, 1750–1950*, a work that explores the interactions of British and Continental literary theory, treats the later eighteenth century. W. K. Wimsatt and Cleanth Brooks's *Literary Criticism: A Short History* (1957) devotes six chapters (v, vi, xii, xiii, xiv, and xv) to issues of criticism important in the eighteenth century.

Two valuable books on the eighteenth-century novel are A. D. McKillop's *The Early Masters of English Fiction* (1956) and Ian Watt's *The Rise of the Novel* (1957). R. D. Mayo's *English Novel in the Magazines, 1740–1815*

(1962) should also be consulted. The contemporary achievement in biographical writing is assessed by J. M. Longaker, in *English Biography in the Eighteenth Century* (1931), and by D. A. Stauffer, in *The Art of Biography in Eighteenth-Century England* (2 vols., 1941). A concise survey of the drama of the later eighteenth-century is the third volume of Allardyce Nicoll's *A History of English Drama, 1660–1900* (6 vols., rev. ed., 1952–59). John Genest's *Some Account of the English Stage from 1660–1830* (10 vols., 1832; reprinted 1964) will be superseded by *The London Stage*, with various editors, in five parts, of which four have been published (1960–63). Two of the most popular dramatic kinds are examined by Arthur Sherbo, in *English Sentimental Drama* (1957), and by Leo Hughes, in *A Century of English Farce* (1956). J. J. Lynch's *Box, Pit, and Gallery: Stage and Society in Johnson's London* (1953) traces the growing influence of the middle-class audience. D. N. Smith's *Shakespeare in the Eighteenth Century* (rev. ed., 1963) and R. W. Babcock's *The Genesis of Shakespeare Idolatry, 1766–1799* (1931) are also of interest. *The Oxford Companion to the Theatre*, ed. Phyllis Hartnoll (3rd ed., 1967), is the standard reference work.

The Johnsonian Newsletter, ed. (since 1940) J. L. Clifford and J. H. Middendorf, appears several times a year with notes, reviews, and bibliographies. *Eighteenth-Century Studies: A Journal of Literature and the Arts* began publication in the fall of 1967.

D. AESTHETIC THEORY AND THE ARTS

B. S. Allen, in *Tides in English Taste: 1619–1800* (2 vols., 1937), considers the connections between the arts and the literature of the period, touching on architecture, gardening, household furnishing, and textiles and discussing the vogues of the Chinese and the Gothic styles. The cult of the sublime is examined exhaustively by S. H. Monk in *The Sublime: A Study of Critical Theories in XVIIIth-Century England* (1935); the primary contemporary document on the subject is Edmund Burke's *A Philosophical Enquiry into the Origin of Our Ideas of the Sublime and Beautiful*, ed. J. T. Boulton (1958). W. J. Hipple, Jr.'s *The Beautiful, the Sublime, and the Picturesque in Eighteenth-Century British Aesthetic Theory* (1957) is a thorough treatment. M. H. Nicolson's *Mountain Gloom and Mountain Glory: The Development of the Aesthetics of the Infinite* (1959) is a valuable contribution. J. H. Hagstrum's *The Sister Arts: The Tradition of Literary Pictorialism and English Poetry from Dryden to Gray* (1958) discusses some relations between painting and poetry.

E. K. Waterhouse's *Painting in Britain, 1530 to 1790* (1953) reproduces many examples of eighteenth-century painting. Illustrated monographs on the foremost painters of the day are Alastair Smart's *The Life and Art of Allan Ramsay* (1952) and Waterhouse's *Reynolds* (1955) and *Gainsborough* (1958).

The fourth volume of Charles Burney's *General History of Music* (4 vols., 1776–79) is a good contemporary account, and P. A. Scholes's *The Great Dr. Burney* (2 vols., 1948) is useful for musical lore. Scholes's *Oxford Companion to Music* (1938) is an informative reference work.

The main forces in contemporary architecture, the classical and the Gothic, are discussed in two important books, Geoffrey Scott's *The Architecture of Humanism: A Study in the History of Taste* (2nd ed., 1924) and Kenneth Clark's *The Gothic Revival: An Essay in the History of Taste* (2nd ed., 1949). John Harvey's *Dublin: A Study in Environment* (1949) contains good architectural photographs, as do John Summerson's *Georgian London* (1946) and Christopher Hussey's *English Country Houses: Mid-Georgian, 1760–1800* (1956). Dress and furniture are treated in C. W. and Phillis Cunnington's *Handbook of English Costume in the Eighteenth Century* (1957) and in Peter Ward-Jackson's *English Furniture Designs of the Eighteenth Century* (1958).

E. INTELLECTUAL HISTORY

Sir Leslie Stephen's *History of English Thought in the Eighteenth Century* (2 vols., 1876; several reprints) is still indispensable. Two works by A. O. Lovejoy are important: *The Great Chain of Being: A Study of the History of an Idea* (1936) examines the sources and significance of this key notion of the period; *Essays in the History of Ideas* (1948) collects a number of interpretative articles, among which " 'Pride' in Eighteenth-Century Thought," " 'Nature' as Aesthetic Norm," "The Parallel of Deism and Classicism," and "The First Gothic Revival and the Return to Nature" are especially useful. A third essential work is J. B. Bury's *The Idea of Progress: An Inquiry into Its Origin and Growth* (1932). Basil Willey's *The Eighteenth-Century Background: Studies in the Idea of Nature in the Thought of the Period* (1940) is a good introduction to some prevailing scientific, religious, and ethical ideas. The philosophic underpinnings of contemporary taste are discussed by W. J. Bate in his *From Classic to Romantic: Premises of Taste in Eighteenth-Century England* (1946).

A History of Science, Technology, and Philosophy in the 18th Century, by Abraham Wolf (2 vols., 1952), is a well-illustrated survey. H. Lyons's *The Royal Society: 1660–1940* (1944) is a good account. The impact of some scientific ideas on the poetry is examined by M. H. Nicolson in *Newton Demands the Muse* (1946) and in *Science and Imagination* (1956). A good introduction to the antiquarian movement is H. B. Walters's *The English Antiquaries of the Sixteenth, Seventeenth, and Eighteenth Centuries* (1934). D. A. Winstanley, in *Unreformed Cambridge* (1935), plumbs the depths of contemporary university life.

The classic study of the Church is C. J. Abbey and J. H. Overton's *The English Church in the Eighteenth Century* (2 vols., 1878). Norman Sykes's *Church and State in England in the XVIIIth Century* (1934) helps clarify the religious controversies. Perhaps the best introduction to the

Methodist movement is John Wesley's *Journal*, ed. Nehemiah Curnock (8 vols., 1909–16). Both J. D. Wade's *John Wesley* (1930) and M. L. Edwards's *John Wesley and the Eighteenth Century* (1933) are good for biography and interpretation. *The Oxford Dictionary of the Christian Church*, ed. F. L. Cross (1957), is helpful on doctrinal matters.

F. POLITICAL HISTORY

The traditional magnum opus is W. E. H. Lecky's *A History of England in the Eighteenth Century* (8 vols., 1878–90); Chapter xxiii (in Vol. VI) is an especially rich essay on the social background. More recent and perhaps more subtle works are William Hunt, *The History of England from the Accession of George III to the Close of Pitt's First Administration (1760–1801)* (1921); L. B. Namier, *The Structure of Politics at the Accession of George III* (2 vols., 1929); and J. S. Watson, *The Reign of George III, 1760–1815* (1960), with a useful bibliography. Sir Charles Petrie's *The Stuart Pretenders: A History of the Jacobite Movement, 1688–1807* (1933) is a pleasant introduction to Jacobitism as far as the early nineteenth century; G. H. Jones's *The Main Stream of Jacobitism* (1954) focuses on the events leading to the Jacobite Rising. A valuable study of contemporary economics is T. S. Ashton's *An Economic History of England: The Eighteenth Century* (1955). An illuminating economic interpretation is R. H. Tawney's classic *Religion and the Rise of Capitalism: A Historical Study* (1926). Dorothy Marshall's *English People of the Eighteenth Century* (1956) traces shifts in the political power of the various classes. Thomas Wright's *Caricature History of the Georges* (2nd ed., 1867) reprints a number of amusing political cartoons.

G. SOCIAL HISTORY

A good starting point is *Johnson's England: An Account of the Life and Manners of the Age*, ed. A. S. Turberville (2 vols., rev. ed., 1952), a collection of twenty-seven authoritative articles, each with bibliography, on such topics as the Army and Navy; travel and communications; poverty, crime, and philanthropy; sports and games; and the law. The work is full of illustrations and facsimiles, as is Turberville's *English Men and Manners in the Eighteenth Century: An Illustrated Narrative* (2nd ed., 1929). The third volume of G. M. Trevelyan's *Illustrated English Social History* (4 vols., 1950–52) concerns the eighteenth century. In *The Augustan World: Life and Letters in Eighteenth-Century England* (1954), A. R. Humphreys gives an account of social life, commerce, politics, religion, and the visual arts, and connects them with the literature.

A number of contemporary letters and diaries make good reading. Fanny Burney's *Diary and Letters*, ed. Charlotte Barrett and Austin Dobson (6 vols., 1904–05), records the *longueurs* of life at court. The serene satisfactions of the country clergyman's life are chronicled in Gilbert White's *The Natural History and Antiquities of Selborne* (1789, and many later printings) and in James Woodforde's *Diary of a Country Parson*, ed. John Beresford (5 vols., 1924–31; one-volume abridgment, 1949). An account of some rural jaunts by a likable traveler is John Byng's *Torrington Diaries*, ed. C. B. Andrews (4 vols., 1934–38; one-volume abridgment, 1954). And the social life of the time is brilliantly recorded in Horace Walpole's *Letters*, ed. W. S. Lewis and others (about 50 vols., 1937–   ), and in James Boswell's journals, especially the *London Journal*, ed. F. A. Pottle (1950), and *The Journal of a Tour to the Hebrides* (1785, and later printings).

Edith Sitwell's *Bath* (1932) is a sprightly account of one of the most popular vacation resorts of the period. G. E. Fussell's brief *Village Life in the Eighteenth Century* (1947), on the other hand, contains more sobering data, as does J. J. Hecht's *The Domestic Servant Class in Eighteenth-Century England* (1956). J. P. Malcolm's *Londinium Redivivum* (4 vols., 1803–07) prints a vast amount of anecdotal material, and his *Anecdotes of the Manners and Customs of London During the Eighteenth Century* (1808) is a delight, especially Chapters ii ("Anecdotes of Depravity, from 1700 to 1800") and vii ("Amusement").

Two modern books by William Kent are useful for reference: *An Encyclopedia of London* (rev. ed., 1951) offers brief articles on such places as Bethlehem Hospital, Fleet Street, the Strand, and Temple Bar, and *London for Everyman* (rev. John Freeman, 1961), an unpretentious guidebook with literary leanings, includes good plans and maps (e.g., Johnson's London).

Index

AUTHORS, TITLES, AND FIRST LINES

Authors' names are in **boldface** type; titles in *italics;* and first lines in roman.

1547